Great Britain & Ireland 2010

Contents

INTRODUCTION

ENGLISH

Commitments

"This volume was created at the turn of the century and will last at least as long".

This foreword to the very first edition of the MICHELIN guide, written in 1900, has become famous over the years and the guide has lived up to the prediction. It is read across the world and the key to its popularity is the consistency of its commitment to its readers, which is based on the following promises.

The Michelin Guide's commitments :

Anonymous inspections: our inspectors make regular and anonymous visits to hotels and restaurants to gauge the quality of products and services offered to an ordinary customer. They settle their own bill and may then introduce themselves and ask for more information about the establishment. Our readers' comments are also a valuable source of information, which we can then follow up with another visit of our own.

Independence: Our choice of establishments is a completely independent one, made for the benefit of our readers alone. The decisions to be taken are discussed around the table by the inspectors and the editor. The most important awards are decided at a European level. Inclusion in the guide is completely free of charge.

Selection and choice: The guide offers a selection of the best hotels and restaurants in every category of comfort and price. This is only possible because all the inspectors rigorously apply the same methods.

Annual updates: All the practical information, the classifications and awards are revised and updated every single year to give the most reliable information possible.

Consistency: The criteria for the classifications are the same in every country covered by the Michelin guide.

... and our aim: to do everything possible to make travel, holidays and eating out a pleasure, as part of Michelin's ongoing commitment to improving travel and mobility.

Dear reader,

We are delighted to introduce the 37th edition of The Michelin guide Great Britain & Ireland.

This selection of the best hotels and restaurants in every price category is chosen by a team of full-time inspectors with a professional background in the industry. They cover every corner of the country, visiting new establishments and testing the quality and consistency of the hotels and restaurants already listed in the Guide.

Every year we pick out the best restaurants by awarding them from ✿ to ✿✿✿. Stars are awarded for cuisine of the highest standards and reflect the quality of the ingredients, the skill in their preparation, the combination of flavours, the levels of creativity and value for money, and the ability to combine all these qualities not just once, but time and time again.
This year again, a number of restaurants have been newly awarded stars for the quality of their cuisine. ´**N**´ highlights the new promotions for this new 2010 edition, announcing their arrival with one, two or three stars.

In addition, we have continued to pick out a selection of « *Rising Stars* ». These establishments, listed in red, are the best in their present category. They have the potential to rise further, and already have an element of superior quality; as soon as they produce this quality consistently, and in all aspects of their cuisine, they will be hot tips for a higher award. We've highlighted these promising restaurants so you can try them for yourselves; we think they offer a foretaste of the gastronomy of the future.
We're very interested to hear what you think of our selection, particularly the " *Rising Stars* ", so please continue to send us your comments. Your opinions and suggestions help to shape your guide, and help us to keep improving it, year after year. Thank you for your support. We hope you enjoy travelling with the Michelin guide 2010.

Consult the Michelin guide at **www.ViaMichelin.com**
and write to us at:
themichelinguide-gbirl@uk.michelin.com

Classification & awards

CATEGORIES OF COMFORT

The Michelin guide selection lists the best hotels and restaurants in each category of comfort and price. The establishments we choose are classified according to their levels of comfort and, within each category, are listed in order of preference.

	Luxury in the traditional style
	Top class comfort
	Very comfortable
	Comfortable
	Quite comfortable
	Pubs serving good food
	Other recommended accommodation (Guesthouses, farmhouses and private homes)
without rest.	This hotel has no restaurant
with rm	This restaurant also offers accommodation

THE AWARDS

To help you make the best choice, some exceptional establishments have been given an award in this year's Guide. They are marked or and **Rest**. For those awarded a Bib Hotel, the mention "**rm**" appears in blue in the description of the establishment.

THE BEST CUISINE

Michelin stars are awarded to establishments serving cuisine, of whatever style, which is of the highest quality. The cuisine is judged on the quality of ingredients, the skill in their preparation, the combination of flavours, the levels of creativity, the value for money and the consistency of culinary standards.

Exceptional cuisine, worth a special journey
One always eats extremely well here, sometimes superbly.

Excellent cooking, worth a detour

Very good cooking in its category

GOOD FOOD AND ACCOMMODATION AT MODERATE PRICES

Bib Gourmand
Establishment offering good quality cuisine for under £28 or €40 in the Republic of Ireland (price of a 3 course meal not including drinks).

Bib Hotel
Establishment offering good levels of comfort and service, with most rooms priced at under £80 or under €105 in the Republic of Ireland (price of a room for 2 people, including breakfast).

PLEASANT HOTELS AND RESTAURANTS

Symbols shown in red indicate particularly pleasant or restful establishments: the character of the building, its décor, the setting, the welcome and services offered may all contribute to this special appeal.

⌂, 🏠 to 🏨	**Pleasant hotels**
🍺, X to XXXXX	**Pleasant restaurants**

OTHER SPECIAL FEATURES

As well as the categories and awards given to the establishment, Michelin inspectors also make special note of other criteria which can be important when choosing an establishment.

LOCATION

If you are looking for a particularly restful establishment, or one with a special view, look out for the following symbols:

🐎	**Quiet hotel**
🐎	**Very quiet hotel**
←	**Interesting view**
←	**Exceptional view**

WINE LIST

If you are looking for an establishment with a particularly interesting wine list, look out for the following symbol:

🍇 **Particularly interesting wine list**

This symbol might cover the list presented by a sommelier in a luxury restaurant or that of a simple pub or restaurant where the owner has a passion for wine. The two lists will offer something exceptional but very different, so beware of comparing them by each other's standards.

SMOKING

In Great Britain and the Republic of Ireland the law prohibits smoking in all pubs, restaurants and hotel public areas.

Facilities & services

30 rm	Number of rooms
	Lift (elevator)
	Air conditioning (in all or part of the establishment)
	Fast Internet access in bedrooms
	Wi-fi Internet access in bedrooms
	Establishment at least partly accessible to those of restricted mobility
	Special facilities for children
	Meals served in garden or on terrace
Spa	An extensive facility for relaxation and well-being
	Sauna – Exercise room
	Swimming pool: outdoor or indoor
	Garden – Park
18	Tennis court – Golf course and number of holes
	Fishing available to hotel guests. A charge may be made
	Equipped conference room
	Private dining rooms
	Hotel garage (additional charge in most cases)
P	Car park for customers only
	No dogs allowed (in all or part of the establishment)
⊖	Nearest Underground station (in London)
May-October	Dates when open, as indicated by the hotelier

Prices

Prices quoted in this guide were supplied in autumn 2009 and apply to low and high seasons. They are subject to alteration if goods and service costs are revised. By supplying the information, hotels and restaurants have undertaken to maintain these rates for our readers.
In some towns, when commercial, cultural or sporting events are taking place the hotel rates are likely to be considerably higher.
Prices are given in £ sterling, except for the Republic of Ireland where euros are quoted.
All accommodation prices include both service and V.A.T. All restaurant prices include V.A.T. Service is also included when an **s** appears after the prices.
Where no **s** is shown, prices may be subject to the addition of a variable service charge which is usually between 10 % - 15 %.
(V.A.T. does not apply in the Channel Islands).
Out of season, certain establishments offer special rates. Ask when booking.

RESERVATION AND DEPOSITS

Some hotels will require a deposit which confirms the commitment of both the customer and the hotelier. Ask the hotelier to provide you with all the terms and conditions applicable to your reservation in their written confirmation.

CREDIT CARDS

	Credit cards accepted by the establishment:
AE ◐ MC VISA	American Express – Diners Club – MasterCard – Visa

ROOMS

rm 🚹 50.00/90.00	Lowest price 50.00 and highest price 90.00 for a comfortable single room
rm 🚹🚹 70.00/120.00	Lowest price 70.00 and highest price 120.00 for a double or twin room for 2 people
rm ☕ 55.00/85.00	Full cooked breakfast (whether taken or not) is included in the price of the room
☕ 6.00	Price of breakfast

SHORT BREAKS

Many hotels offer a special rate for a stay of two or more nights which comprises dinner, room and breakfast usually for a minimum of two people. Please enquire at hotel for rates.

RESTAURANT

Set meals: lowest price £13.00, highest price £28.00, usually for a 3 course meal. The lowest priced set menu is often only available at lunchtimes.
A la carte meals: the prices represent the range of charges from a simple to an elaborate 3 course meal.

s	Service included
🎭	Restaurants offering lower priced pre and/or post theatre menus

⌂: Dinner in this category of establishment will generally be offered from a fixed price menu of limited choice, served at a set time to residents only. Lunch is rarely offered. Many will not be licensed to sell alcohol.

Towns

GENERAL INFORMATION

✉ **York**	Postal address
501 M27, ⑩	Michelin map and co-ordinates or fold
Great Britain	See the Michelin Green Guide Great Britain
pop. 1057	Population Source: 2001 Census (Key Statistics for Urban Areas) Crown copyright 2004
BX **a**	Letters giving the location of a place on a town plan
18	Golf course and number of holes (handicap sometimes required, telephone reservation strongly advised)
	Panoramic view, viewpoint
	Airport
	Shipping line (passengers & cars)
	Passenger transport only
i	Tourist Information Centre

STANDARD TIME

In winter, standard time throughout the British Isles is Greenwich Mean Time (GMT). In summer, British clocks are advanced by one hour to give British Summer Time (BST). The actual dates are announced annually but always occur over weekends in March and October.

TOURIST INFORMATION

STAR-RATING

★★★	Highly recommended
★★	Recommended
★	Interesting
AC	Admission charge

LOCATION

	Sights in town
	On the outskirts
N, S, E, W	The sight lies North, South, East or West of the town
A 22	Take road A 22, indicated by the same symbol on the Guide map
2 mi.	Distance in miles (In the Republic of Ireland kilometres are quoted).

Town plans

Hotels – restaurants

SIGHTS

Place of interest
Interesting place of worship

ROADS

M 1 Motorway
Numbered junctions: complete, limited
Dual carriageway with motorway characteristics
Main traffic artery
A 2 Primary route (GB) and National route (IRL)
One-way street – Unsuitable for traffic or street subject to restrictions
Pedestrian street – Tramway
Piccadilly Shopping street – Car park – Park and Ride
Gateway – Street passing under arch – Tunnel
15'5 Low headroom (16'6" max.) on major through routes
Station and railway
Funicular – Cable-car
B Lever bridge – Car ferry

VARIOUS SIGNS

Tourist Information Centre
Church/Place of worship - Mosque – Synagogue
Communications tower or mast – Ruins
Garden, park, wood – Cemetery
Stadium - Racecourse - Golf course
Golf course (with restrictions for visitors) – Skating rink
Outdoor or indoor swimming pool
View – Panorama
Monument – Fountain – Hospital – Covered market
Pleasure boat harbour – Lighthouse
Airport – Underground station – Coach station
Ferry services: passengers and cars
Main post office
Public buildings located by letter:
C H J County Council Offices – Town Hall – Law Courts
M T U Museum – Theatre – University, College
POL. Police (in large towns police headquarters)

LONDON

BRENT WEMBLEY Borough – Area
Borough boundary
Congestion Zone – Charge applies Monday-Friday 07.00-18.00
Nearest Underground station to the hotel or restaurant

Awards 2010

Starred establishments 2010

The colour corresponds to the establishment with the most stars in this location.

London — This location has at least one 3 star restaurant ✻✻✻

Dublin — This location has at least one 2 star restaurant ✻✻

Belfast — This location has at least one 1 star restaurant ✻

Lochinver
Achiltibuie
Sleat
Fort William
Dalry

Malahide
Dublin
REPUBLIC OF IRELAND
Ardmore
GUERNSEY
JERSEY
La Pulente
St Helier
ISLES OF SCILLY

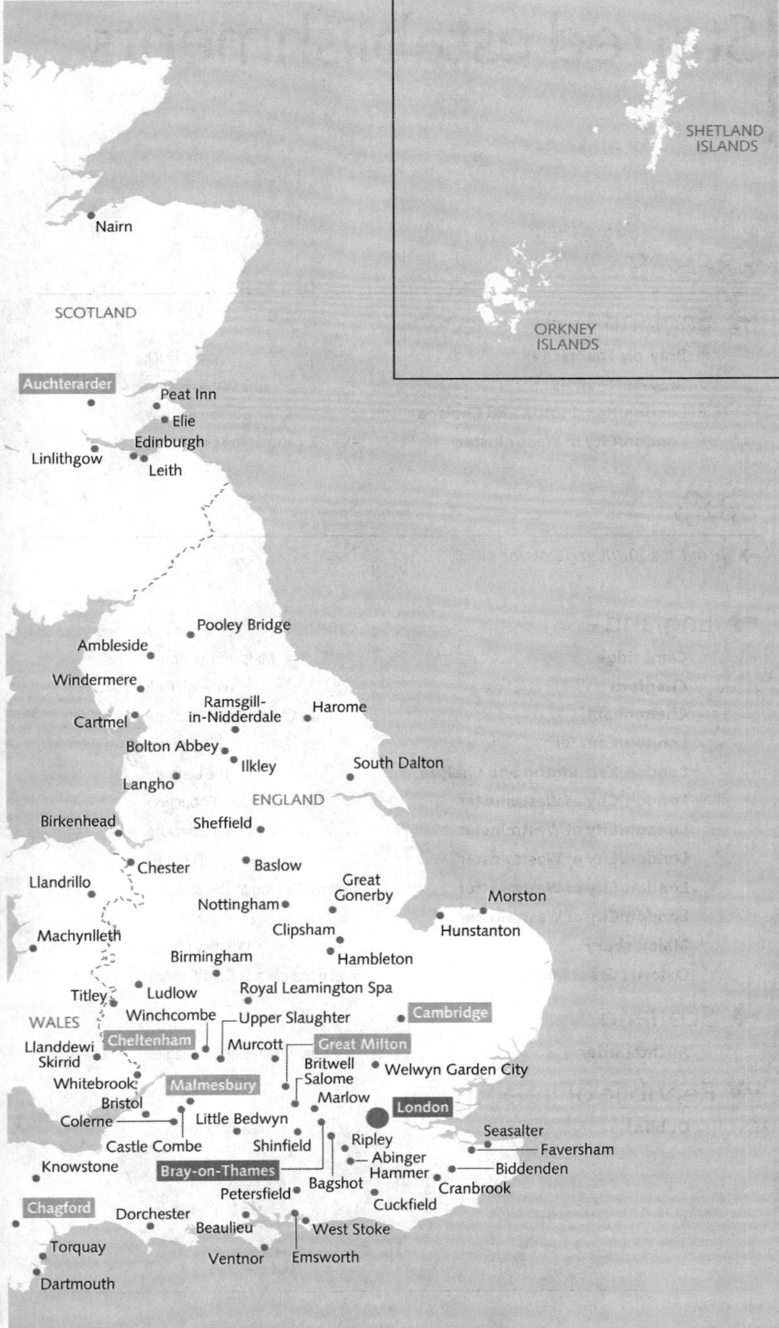

SHETLAND ISLANDS
ORKNEY ISLANDS
Nairn
SCOTLAND
Auchterarder
Peat Inn
Elie
Edinburgh
Linlithgow
Leith
Pooley Bridge
Ambleside
Windermere
Ramsgill-in-Nidderdale
Harome
Cartmel
Bolton Abbey
Ilkley
South Dalton
Langho
ENGLAND
Birkenhead
Sheffield
Chester
Baslow
Llandrillo
Great Gonerby
Morston
Nottingham
Hunstanton
Clipsham
Machynlleth
Birmingham
Hambleton
Titley
Ludlow
Royal Leamington Spa
WALES
Winchcombe
Upper Slaughter
Cambridge
Cheltenham
Murcott
Great Milton
Llanddewi Skirrid
Britwell Salome
Welwyn Garden City
Whitebrook
Malmesbury
Marlow
Bristol
London
Colerne
Little Bedwyn
Seasalter
Castle Combe
Shinfield
Ripley
Faversham
Abinger Hammer
Knowstone
Bray-on-Thames
Biddenden
Bagshot
Cranbrook
Petersfield
Cuckfield
Chagford
Dorchester
Beaulieu
West Stoke
Torquay
Ventnor
Emsworth
Dartmouth

Starred establishments

✿✿✿

→ England

Bray-on-Thames	Fat Duck	
Bray-on-Thames	The Waterside Inn	
London/Kensington and Chelsea	Gordon Ramsay	
London/City of Westminster	Alain Ducasse at The Dorchester	**N**

✿✿

→ *In red the 2010 Rising Stars for* ✿✿✿

→ England

Cambridge	Midsummer House	
Chagford	Gidleigh Park	
Cheltenham	Le Champignon Sauvage	
London/Camden	Pied à Terre	
London/Kensington and Chelsea	The Ledbury	**N**
London/City of Westminster	L'Atelier de Joël Robuchon	
London/City of Westminster	Le Gavroche	
London/City of Westminster	Hibiscus	
London/City of Westminster	Marcus Wareing at The Berkeley	
London/City of Westminster	The Square	
Malmesbury	Whatley Manor	
Oxford / Great Milton	Le Manoir aux Quat' Saisons	

→ Scotland

Auchterarder	Andrew Fairlie at Gleneagles

→ Republic of Ireland

Dublin	Patrick Guilbaud

→ **N** *New*

→ *In red the 2010 Rising Stars for* ✿✿

→ England

Abinger Hammer	Drakes on the Pond	
Ambleside	The Samling	**N**
Bagshot	Michael Wignall at The Latymer (at Pennyhill Park Hotel)	
Baslow	Fischer's at Baslow Hall	
Bath / Colerne	The Park (at Lucknam Park Hotel)	
Beaulieu	The Terrace (at Montagu Arms Hotel)	
Beverley / South Dalton	The Pipe and Glass Inn	**N**
Biddenden	The West House	
Birkenhead	Fraiche	
Birmingham	Purnell's	
Birmingham	Simpsons	
Birmingham	Turners	
Blackburn / Langho	Northcote	
Blakeney / Morston	Morston Hall	
Bolton Abbey	The Burlington (at The Devonshire Arms Country House Hotel)	
Bourton-on-the-Water / Upper Slaughter	Lords of the Manor	
Bray-on-Thames	The Royal Oak	**N**
Bristol	Casamia	
Britwell Salome	The Goose	**N**
Castle Combe	Manor House H. and Golf Club	
Chester	Simon Radley at The Chester Grosvenor	
Chichester / West Stoke	West Stoke House	
Cranbrook	Apicius	
Cuckfield	Ockenden Manor	
Dartmouth	The New Angel	
Dorchester	Sienna	**N**
Emsworth	36 on the Quay	
Faversham	Read's	
Grange-over-Sands / Cartmel	L'Enclume	
Grantham / Great Gonerby	Harry's Place	
Helmsley / Harome	The Star Inn	
Hunstanton	The Neptune	
Ilkley	Box Tree	
Jersey / La Pulente	Atlantic	
Jersey / St Helier	Bohemia (at The Club Hotel and Spa)	
Kington / Titley	The Stagg Inn	
London/Bromley	Chapter One	
London/Camden	Hakkasan	
London/City of London	Club Gascon	
London/City of London	Rhodes Twenty Four	

London/Hammersmith and Fulham	The Harwood Arms	**N**
London/Hammersmith and Fulham	River Café	
London/Hounslow	La Trompette	
London/Islington	St John	
London/Kensington and Chelsea	Rasoi	
London/Kensington and Chelsea	Tom Aikens	
London/Richmond-upon-Thames	Bingham Restaurant (at Bingham Hotel)	**N**
London/Richmond-upon-Thames	The Glasshouse	
London/Wandsworth	Chez Bruce	
London/City of Westminster	Amaya	
London/City of Westminster	Apsleys (at The Lanesborough Hotel)	**N**
London/City of Westminster	Arbutus	
London/City of Westminster	L'Autre Pied	
London/City of Westminster	Benares	
London/City of Westminster	Galvin at Windows	**N**
London/City of Westminster	The Greenhouse	
London/City of Westminster	Hélène Darroze at The Connaught	
London/City of Westminster	Kai	
London/City of Westminster	Locanda Locatelli	
London/City of Westminster	Maze	
London/City of Westminster	Murano	
London/City of Westminster	Nahm (at The Halkin Hotel)	
London/City of Westminster	Nobu (at The Metropolitan Hotel)	
London/City of Westminster	Nobu Berkeley St	
London/City of Westminster	Quilon	
London/City of Westminster	Rhodes W1 (Restaurant) (at The Cumberland Hotel)	
London/City of Westminster	Roussillon	
London/City of Westminster	Semplice	
London/City of Westminster	Sketch (The Lecture Room and Library)	
London/City of Westminster	Tamarind	**N**
London/City of Westminster	Texture	**N**
London/City of Westminster	Umu	
London/City of Westminster	Wild Honey	
London/City of Westminster	Yauatcha	
London/City of Westminster	Zafferano	
Ludlow	La Bécasse	
Ludlow	Mr Underhill's at Dinham Weir	
Marlborough / Little Bedwyn	The Harrow at Little Bedwyn	
Marlow	The Hand and Flowers	
Murcott	The Nut Tree	
Nottingham	Restaurant Sat Bains	
Oakham / Hambleton	Hambleton Hall	
Pateley Bridge / Ramsgill-in-Nidderdale	The Yorke Arms	
Petersfield	JSW	
Reading / Shinfield	L'Ortolan	
Ripley	Drake's	
Royal Leamington Spa	Mallory Court	

Sheffield	Old Vicarage	
South Molton / Knowstone	The Masons Arms	
Stamford / Clipsham	The Olive Branch and Beech House	
Torquay	The Room in the Elephant	
Ullswater / Pooley Bridge	Sharrow Bay Country House	
Welwyn Garden City	Auberge du Lac	
Whitstable / Seasalter	The Sportsman	
Wight (Isle of) / Ventnor	The Hambrough	
Winchcombe	5 North St	
Windermere	Holbeck Ghyll	

➜ Scotland

Achiltibuie	Summer Isles	
Dalry	Braidwoods	
Edinburgh	Number One (at The Balmoral Hotel)	**N**
Edinburgh	21212	**N**
Edinburgh / Leith	The Kitchin	
Edinburgh / Leith	Martin Wishart	
Edinburgh / Leith	Plumed Horse	
Elie	Sangster's	
Fort William	Inverlochy Castle	
Linlithgow	Champany Inn	
Lochinver	The Albannach	
Nairn	Boath House	
Peat Inn	The Peat Inn	**N**
Portpatrick	Knockinaam Lodge	
Skye (Isle of) / Sleat	Kinloch Lodge	**N**

➜ Wales

Abergavenny / Llanddewi Skirrid	The Walnut Tree	**N**
Llandrillo	Tyddyn Llan	**N**
Machynlleth	Ynyshir Hall	**N**
Monmouth / Whitebrook	The Crown at Whitebrook	

➜ Northern Ireland

Belfast	Deanes	

➜ Republic of Ireland

Ardmore	The House (at The Cliff House Hotel)	**N**
Dublin	Chapter One	
Dublin	L'Ecrivain	
Dublin	Thornton's (at The Fitzwilliam Hotel)	
Malahide	Bon Appétit	

➜ *The 2010 Rising Stars for* ✿

Alkham	The Marquis
Helmsley / Oldstead	The Black Swan
Padstow / St Merryn	Rosel and Co.

The 2010 Bib Gourmand

- Places with at least one Bib Gourmand establishment.

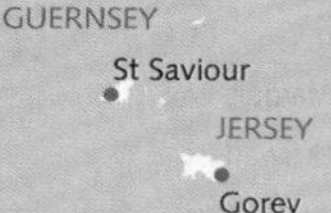

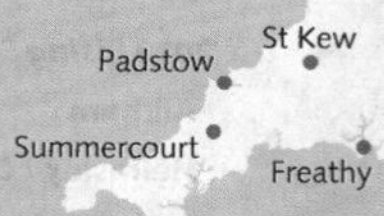

SHETLAND ISLANDS
ORKNEY ISLANDS
SCOTLAND
North Queensferry
Edinburgh
Sorn
Newcastle upon Tyne
Durham
Hutton Magna
Hurworth-on-Tees
Masham
Boroughbridge
Sutton-on-the-Forest
Ferrensby
York
Thornton
Southport
Leeds
Beverley
Bury
Oldham
Sheffield
Alderley Edge
Birchover
Ringstead
Burnham Market
ENGLAND
Stathern
Itteringham
WALES
Stamford
Norwich
Birmingham
Yarpole
Stanton
Stoke Holy Cross
Stratford-upon-Avon
Ullingswick
Stow-on-the-Wold
Little Wilbraham
Aldeburgh
Woolhope
Daylesford
Ross-on-Wye
Chipping Norton
Orford
Abergavenny
Cheltenham
Kelvedon
Haddenham
Kingham
Tetbury
Bray-on-Thames
Bristol
Toot Baldon
London
Chew Magna
East Chisenbury
Hurley
Windlesham
Ramsgate
Wells
Reigate
West Malling
Bruton
Longstock
Lower Hardres
Henfield
Westfield
Rockbeare
Droxford
Hove
Hastings and St Leonards
Brighton
Rushlake Green
Danehill

Bib Gourmand

Good food at moderate prices

➜ England

Aldeburgh	The Lighthouse	
Alderley Edge	The Wizard	
Barnard Castle / Hutton Magna	The Oak Tree Inn	
Beverley	Whites	N
Birmingham	Pascals	
Blackpool / Thornton	Twelve	
Boroughbridge	thediningroom	
Bray-on-Thames	The Hinds Head	
Brighton	Terre à Terre	
Brighton / Hove	The Ginger Pig	
Brighton / Hove	The Meadow	
Bristol	Greens' Dining Room	
Bruton	At The Chapel	N
Burnham Market	The Hoste Arms	
Bury	The Waggon	
Cambridge / Little Wilbraham	The Hole in Wall	
Canterbury / Lower Hardres	The Granville	
Cheltenham	Royal Well Tavern	
Chew Magna	Pony and Trap	N
Chipping Norton	The Masons Arms	
Danehill	Coach and Horses	
Darlington / Hurworth-on-Tees	The Bay Horse	N
Droxford	The Bakers Arms	
Durham	Bistro 21	
East Chisenbury	Red Lion Freehouse	N
Exeter / Rockbeare	Jack in the Green Inn	
Guernsey / St Saviour	The Pavilion	
Haddenham	The Green Dragon	
Hastings and St. Leonards	St Clements	
Henfield	The Ginger Fox	
Hunstanton / Ringstead	The Gin Trap Inn	
Hurley	Black Boys Inn	
Itteringham	The Walpole Arms	
Jersey / Gorey	Village Bistro	
Kelvedon	George and Dragon	N
Kingham	The Kingham Plough	
Knaresborough / Ferrensby	The General Tarleton Inn	
Leeds	Anthony's at Flannels	
Leeds	Piazza by Anthony	N
London/Camden	Bradley's	
London/Camden	Giaconda Dining Room	
London/Camden	Great Queen Street	
London/Camden	Market	
London/Camden	Salt Yard	
London/Ealing	Sushi-Hiro	N
London/Hammersmith and Fulham	The Havelock Tavern	
London/Islington	Comptoir Gascon	
London/Islington	The Drapers Arms	N
London/Islington	500	N
London/Islington	Medcalf	
London/Islington	Metrogusto	
London/Islington	The Modern Pantry	
London/Kensington and Chelsea	Foxtrot Oscar	
London/Kensington and Chelsea	Malabar	
London/Lambeth	Upstairs	
London/Lewisham	Chapters	
London/Richmond-upon-Thames	The Brown Dog	
London/Richmond-upon-Thames	Brula	

➜ **N** *New*

London/Richmond-upon-Thames	Ma Cuisine (Kew)	
London/Richmond-upon-Thames	Ma Cuisine (Twickenham)	
London/Richmond-upon-Thames	Mango and Silk	
London/Richmond-upon-Thames	Le Provence	**N**
London/Southwark	The Anchor and Hope	
London/Tower Hamlets	Cafe Spice Namaste	
London/City of Westminster	Al Duca	
London/City of Westminster	Bar Trattoria Semplice	**N**
London/City of Westminster	Benja	
London/City of Westminster	Bocca di Lupo	**N**
London/City of Westminster	Dehesa	
London/City of Westminster	Galvin Bistrot de Luxe	
London/City of Westminster	Hereford Road	
London/City of Westminster	Terroirs	**N**
London/City of Westminster	Via Condotti	
Masham	Vennell's	
Matlock / Birchover	The Druid Inn	
Melton Mowbray / Stathern	Red Lion Inn	
Millbrook / Freathy	The View	
Newcastle upon Tyne	Grainger Rooms	**N**
Norwich	1 Up at the Mad Moose Arms	
Norwich / Stoke Holy Cross	Wildebeest Arms	
Oldham	The White Hart Inn	
Orford	The Trinity	
Oxford / Toot Baldon	The Mole Inn	
Padstow	Rick Stein's Café	
Ramsgate	Age and Sons	**N**
Reigate	The Westerly	
Ross-on-Wye	The Lough Pool at Sellack	
Rushlake Green	Stone House	
Sheffield	Artisan	
Southport	Warehouse Brasserie	
Stamford	Jim's Yard	
Stanton	The Leaping Hare	
Stockbridge / Longstock	The Peat Spade Inn	
Stow-on-the-Wold	The Old Butchers	
Stow-on-the-Wold / Daylesford	The Cafe at Daylesford Organic	
Stratford-upon-Avon	Malbec Petit Bistro	
Summercourt	Viners	
Sutton-on-the-Forest	Rose and Crown	
Tetbury	The Gumstool Inn	
Ullingswick	Three Crowns Inn	
Wadebridge / St Kew	St Kew Inn	**N**
Wells	The Old Spot	
West Malling	The Swan	
Westfield	The Wild Mushroom	
Windlesham	The Bee	**N**
Woolhope	The Butchers Arms	**N**
Yarpole	The Bell Inn	
York	J. Baker's	

→ Scotland

Edinburgh	The Dogs	
Edinburgh	Tony's Table	**N**
Kintyre (Peninsula) / Kilberry	The Kilberry Inn	
North Queensferry	The Wee Restaurant	
Sorn	The Sorn Inn	

→ Wales

Abergavenny	The Hardwick	

→ Northern Ireland

Ballyclare	Oregano	**N**
Belfast	Cayenne	
Warrenpoint	Restaurant 23	

→ Republic of Ireland

Adare	White Sage	**N**
Cashel (Tipperary)	Cafe Hans	
Clonegall	Sha Roe Bistro	
Dingle	The Chart House	
Dublin	La Maison	**N**
Dublin	Pichet	**N**
Dublin	The Pig's Ear	**N**
Duncannon	Aldridge Lodge	
Dundalk	Rosso	**N**
Durrus	Good Things Cafe	
Kilbrittain	Casino House	
Kinsale	Fishy Fishy Cafe	
Lisdoonvarna	Wild Honey Inn	**N**
Lismore	O'Brien Chop House	**N**

Bib Hotel

Good accommodation at moderate prices

➜ England

Armscote	Willow Corner
Askrigg	The Apothecary's House
Barnard Castle	Greta House
Barnard Castle	Homelands
Bishop's Stortford / Stansted Mountfitchet	Chimneys
Bodmin	Bokiddick Farm
Bourton-on-the-Water	Coombe House
Bovey Tracey	Brookfield House
Bury St Edmunds / Beyton	Manorhouse
Cheddleton	Choir Cottage
Deddington	The Old Post House **N**
Devizes / Potterne	Blounts Court Farm
Eastbourne	Brayscroft
Ely / Little Thetford	Springfields
Harrogate / Kettlesing	Knabbs Ash
Hartland	Golden Park
Henfield / Wineham	Frylands
Hexham	West Close House
Holbeach	Pipwell Manor
Kenilworth	Victoria Lodge **N**
Kirkwhelpington	Shieldhall **N**
Leyburn	Clyde House **N**
Longtown	Bessiestown Farm
Morpeth / Longhorsley	Thistleyhaugh Farm
Oxhill	Oxbourne House
Penrith / Newbiggin	The Old School
Pickering	Bramwood
Ripon	Sharow Cross House
Ross-on-Wye / Kerne Bridge	Lumleys
Salisbury / Little Langford	Little Langford Farmhouse
Scarborough	Alexander
South Molton	Kerscott Farm
Southend-on-Sea	Beaches
Stow-on-the-Wold	Number Nine
Telford	Dovecote Grange
Torquay	Colindale
Tynemouth	Martineau Guest House **N**
Upton-upon-Severn / Hanley Swan	Yew Tree House
Wallingford	North Moreton House
Wareham	Gold Court House
Wells / Easton	Beaconsfield Farm
Whitby / Briggswath	The Lawns
Windermere	Newstead

➜ Scotland

Anstruther	The Spindrift
Auchencairn	Balcary Mews
Aultbea	Mellondale
Ayr	Coila
Ayr	No.26 The Crescent
Ballater	Moorside House
Blairgowrie	Gilmore House

➜ **N** *New*

Carnoustie	The Old Manor	
Crieff	Merlindale	
Dunkeld	Letter Farm	
Edinburgh	The Beverley	
Forres / Dyke	The Old Kirk	
Kingussie	Hermitage	
Montrose	36 The Mall	
Nairn	Bracadale House	
Oban	The Barriemore	
Perth	Taythorpe	
Pitlochry	Dunmurray Lodge	**N**
Skye (Isle of) / Broadford	Tigh an Dochais	
Skye (Isle of) / Dunvegan	Roskhill House	**N**
Stevenston	Ardeer Farm Steading	
Strathpeffer	Craigvar	
Thornhill	Gillbank House	
Ullapool	Point Cottage	

→ Wales

Aberaeron	Llys Aeron	**N**
Betws Garmon	Betws Inn	
Colwyn Bay	Rathlin Country House	**N**
Dolgellau	Tyddyn Mawr	
Llandudno	Abbey Lodge	**N**
Llandudno	Lympley Lodge	**N**
Llanuwchllyn	Eifionydd	
Ruthin	Firgrove	

→ Northern Ireland

Bangor	Cairn Bay Lodge	
Belfast	Ravenhill House	
Crumlin	Caldhame Lodge	

→ Republic of Ireland

Ballynamult	Sliabh gCua Farmhouse	
Ballyvaughan	Drumcreehy House	
Cashel (Tipperary)	Aulber House	
Castlegregory	The Shores Country House	
Donegal	Ardeevin	
Dundalk	Rosemount	
Kinsale / Barrells Cross	Rivermount House	**N**
Oughterard	Railway Lodge	
Oughterard	Waterfall Lodge	
Toormore	Fortview House	
Tramore	Glenorney	

Particularly pleasant hotels

England

Dogmersfield Four Seasons
London/ City of Westminster The Berkeley
London/ City of Westminster Claridge's
London/ City of Westminster The Connaught
London/City of Westminster Dorchester
London/City of Westminster Mandarin Oriental Hyde Park
London/City of Westminster The Ritz
New Milton Chewton Glen
Oxford / Great Milton Le Manoir aux Quat' Saisons
Taplow Cliveden

England

Aylesbury Hartwell House
Bath The Royal Crescent
Bath / Colerne Lucknam Park
Chagford Gidleigh Park
Jersey / St Saviour Longueville Manor
London/City of Westminster The Goring
London/ City of Westminster One Aldwych
London/City of Westminster The Soho
Malmesbury Whatley Manor
Newbury The Vineyard at Stockcross
North Bovey Bovey Castle
Ston Easton Ston Easton Park

Scotland

Ballantrae Glenapp Castle
Bishopton Mar Hall
Eriska Isle of Eriska
Fort William Inverlochy Castle

Republic of Ireland

Dublin The Merrion
Kenmare Park
Killarney Killarney Park

England

Amberley Amberley Castle
Bath Bath Priory
Bolton Abbey The Devonshire Arms Country House
Bourton-on-the-Water / Lower Slaughter Lower Slaughter Manor
Bourton-on-the-Water / Upper Slaughter Lords of the Manor
Broadway / Buckland Buckland Manor
Castle Combe Manor House H. and Golf Club
Dedham Maison Talbooth
East Grinstead Gravetye Manor
Evershot Summer Lodge
Gillingham Stock Hill Country House
Jersey / La Pulente Atlantic
Littlehampton Bailiffscourt and Spa

London/Camden — Covent Garden
London/ Kensington and Chelsea — Blakes
London/ Kensington and Chelsea — The Capital
London/ Kensington and Chelsea — Draycott
London/ Kensington and Chelsea — The Milestone
London/ Kensington and Chelsea — The Pelham
London/ City of Westminster — Charlotte Street
London/City of Westminster — Dukes
London/City of Westminster — The Halkin
London/City of Westminster — Stafford
Newcastle upon Tyne — Jesmond Dene House
Oakham / Hambleton — Hambleton Hall
Royal Leamington Spa — Mallory Court
Scilly (Isles of) — The Island
Scilly (Isles of) — St Martin's on the Isle
Tetbury — Calcot Manor
Ullswater / Pooley Bridge — Sharrow Bay Country House
Winchester / Sparsholt — Lainston House
Windermere / Bowness-on-Windermere — Gilpin Lodge
Yarm — Judges Country House
York — Middlethorpe Hall

→ Scotland

Blairgowrie — Kinloch House
Edinburgh — Prestonfield
Torridon — The Torridon

→ Wales

Llandudno — Bodysgallen Hall
Llangammarch Wells — Lake Country House and Spa

→ Northern Ireland

Belfast — The Merchant

→ Republic of Ireland

Ardmore — Cliff House
Ballyvaughan — Gregans Castle
Dublin — Dylan
Mallow — Longueville House

→ England

Ambleside — The Samling
Bath — Queensberry
Bigbury-on-Sea — Burgh Island
Blakeney / Morston — Morston Hall
Brampton — Farlam Hall
Burnham Market — The Hoste Arms
Cheltenham — Hotel on the Park
Chester — Green Bough
Cirencester / Barnsley — Barnsley House
Cuckfield — Ockenden Manor
Frome — Babington House
Helmsley — Feversham Arms
Horley — Langshott Manor
Kingsbridge / Goveton — Buckland-Tout-Saints
King's Lynn / Grimston — Congham Hall
Lewdown — Lewtrenchard Manor
London/ Kensington and Chelsea — Egerton House
London/ Kensington and Chelsea — Knightsbridge
London/ Kensington and Chelsea — The Levin
London/ Kensington and Chelsea — Number Sixteen
London/ City of Westminster — Dorset Square
North Walsham — Beechwood
Orford — The Crown and Castle
Rushlake Green — Stone House
St Mawes — Tresanton
Southampton / Netley Marsh — Hotel TerraVina
Tavistock / Milton Abbot — Hotel Endsleigh
Torquay / Maidencombe — Orestone Manor
Wareham — The Priory
Windermere — Holbeck Ghyll

→ Scotland

Abriachan	Loch Ness Lodge
Achiltibuie	Summer Isles
Arran (Isle of)	Kilmichael Country House
Killin / Ardeonaig	Ardeonaig
Lochearnhead / Balquhidder	Monachyle Mhor
Nairn	Boath House
Port Appin	Airds
Portpatrick	Knockinaam Lodge
Skye (Isle of) / Sleat	Kinloch Lodge

→ Wales

Llandudno	Osborne House
Machynlleth	Ynyshir Hall
Swansea / Llanrhidian	Fairyhill
Talsarnau	Maes-y-Neuadd

→ Republic of Ireland

Arthurstown	Dunbrody Country House
Ballingarry	Mustard Seed at Echo Lodge
Kinsale	Perryville House

→ England

Ashwater	Blagdon Manor
Bourton-on-the-Water	The Dial House
Burnham Market	Vine House
Chillington	Whitehouse
Coln St Aldwyns	New Inn At Coln
Dartmouth / Kingswear	Nonsuch House
Helmsley / Harome	Cross House Lodge at The Star Inn
Jersey / St Aubin	Cardington House
Keswick / Portinscale	Swinside Lodge
Ludlow	De Grey's Town House
Lynton	Hewitt's - Villa Spaldi
Lynton / Martinhoe	Old Rectory
Porlock	Oaks
Portscatho	Driftwood
St Ives	Blue Hayes
Salisbury / Teffont Magna	Howard's House
Staverton	Kingston House

→ Scotland

Glamis	Castleton House
Kelso / Ednam	Edenwater House
Mull (Isle of) / Tiroran	Tiroran House
Skye (Isle of) / Teangue	Toravaig House
Tain / Cadboll	Glenmorangie House

→ Wales

Betws-y-Coed	Tan-y-Foel Country House
Conwy / Llansanffraid Glan Conwy	Old Rectory Country House
Dolgellau	Ffynnon

→ Republic of Ireland

Bagenalstown	Kilgraney Country House
Castlelyons	Ballyvolane House
Dingle	Emlagh Country House
Lahinch	Moy House

→ England

Arnside	Number 43
Ash	Great Weddington
Austwick	Austwick Hall
Beverley	Burton Mount
Blackpool	Number One St Lukes
Bridport / Burton Bradstock	Norburton Hall
Broad Oak	Fairacres
Cheltenham	Thirty Two
Chipping Campden / Broad Campden	Malt House
Clun	Birches Mill

Crackington Haven Manor Farm
Cranbrook Cloth Hall Oast
East Hoathly Old Whyly
Grange-over-Sands / Cartmel Hill Farm
Hawkshead / Far Sawrey West Vale
Haworth Ashmount Country House
Helmsley / Oldstead Oldstead Grange
Ivychurch Olde Moat House
Kendal Beech House
Lavenham Lavenham Priory
Ledbury / Kynaston Hall End
Lizard Landewednack House
Ludlow Bromley Court
Man (Isle of) / Port St Mary Aaron House
Marazion / Perranuthnoe Ednovean Farm
Moreton-in-Marsh The Old School
North Bovey The Gate House
Padstow Woodlands Country House
Petworth Old Railway Station
Pickering 17 Burgate
Pickering / Levisham The Moorlands Country House
Ripon Sharow Cross House
St Austell / Tregrehan Anchorage House
St Blazey Nanscawen Manor House
Shrewsbury Pinewood House
Stow-on-the-Wold / Lower Swell Rectory Farmhouse
Stratford-upon-Avon Cherry Trees
Stratford-upon-Avon / Pillerton Priors Fulready Manor
Tavistock / Chillaton Tor Cottage
Teignmouth Thomas Luny House
Thursford Green Holly Lodge
Wareham Gold Court House
Warkworth Roxbro House
Willesley Beaufort House
Wold Newton Wold Cottage
York Alexander House

→ Scotland

Ballantrae Cosses Country House
Bute (Isle of) / Ascog Balmory Hall
Connel Ards House
Edinburgh Davenport House
Fortrose Water's Edge
Fort William Crolinnhe
Fort William The Grange
Islay (Isle of) / Ballygrant Kilmeny
Linlithgow Arden House
Lochinver Ruddyglow Park Country House
Orkney Islands/Harray Holland House
Mull (Isle of) / Gruline Gruline Home Farm
Skirling Skirling House
Skye (Isle of) / Bernisdale The Spoons
Strathpeffer Craigvar

→ Wales

Anglesey (Isle of) / Beaumaris Cleifiog
Anglesey (Isle of) / Menai Bridge Neuadd Lwyd
Betws-y-Coed / Penmachno Penmachno Hall
Dolfor Old Vicarage
Dolgellau Tyddyn Mawr
Pwllheli / Boduan The Old Rectory
St Clears Coedllys Country House

→ Northern Ireland

Ballintoy Whitepark House
Dungannon Grange Lodge
Holywood Beech Hill

→ Republic of Ireland

Castlegregory The Shores Country House
Cong Ballywarren House
Fethard Mobarnane House
Kanturk Glenlohane
Kenmare Sallyport House
Kilkenny Blanchville House
Portlaoise Ivyleigh House
Toormore Fortview House

Particularly pleasant restaurants

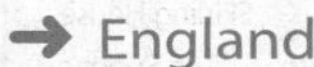

→ England

London/City of Westminster The Ritz Restaurant

→ England

Bath / Colerne The Park (at Lucknam Park)

Bolton Abbey The Burlington (at The Devonshire Arms Country House)

Bray-on-Thames The Waterside Inn

London/City of Westminster Hélène Darroze at The Connaught

London/City of Westminster Marcus Wareing at The Berkeley

Winteringham Winteringham Fields

→ Republic of Ireland

Dublin Patrick Guilbaud

→ England

Baslow Fischer's at Baslow Hall

Birmingham Simpsons

Blackburn / Langho Northcote

Cambridge Midsummer House

Dedham Le Talbooth

Emsworth 36 on the Quay

Grange-over-Sands / Cartmel L'Enclume

Ilkley Box Tree

Lavenham The Great House

London/City of London Coq d'Argent

London/Hackney Boundary

London/ Kensington and Chelsea Bibendum

London/City of Westminster Cecconi's

London/City of Westminster Quo Vadis

London/City of Westminster Scott's

London/ City of Westminster The Wolseley

Newcastle upon Tyne Fisherman's Lodge

Skipton / Hetton Angel Inn and Barn Lodgings

Tavistock / Gulworthy The Horn of Plenty

Welwyn Garden City Auberge du Lac

→ Scotland

Edinburgh 21212

Peat Inn The Peat Inn

→ Wales

Llandrillo Tyddyn Llan

England

- **Alkham** — The Marquis
- **Arlingham** — The Old Passage Inn
- **Derby / Darley Abbey** — Darleys
- **Grantham / Great Gonerby** — Harry's Place
- **Grantham / Hough-on-the-Hill** — Brownlow Arms
- **Jersey / Gorey** — Suma's
- **Kirkby Lonsdale / Cowan Bridge** — Hipping Hall
- **London/Camden** — Mon Plaisir
- **London/ Hammersmith and Fulham** — River Café
- **London/ City of Westminster** — Le Café Anglais
- **London/City of Westminster** — Le Caprice
- **London/City of Westminster** — J. Sheekey
- **London/City of Westminster** — Rules
- **London/City of Westminster** — Wild Honey
- **Ludlow** — Mr Underhill's at Dinham Weir
- **Malmesbury** — Le Mazot
- **Padstow** — The Seafood
- **Pateley Bridge / Ramsgill-in-Nidderdale** — The Yorke Arms
- **Stanton** — The Leaping Hare
- **Windermere** — Miller Howe
- **Yeovil / Barwick** — Little Barwick House

Scotland

- **Kingussie** — The Cross at Kingussie
- **Lochinver** — The Albannach
- **Skye (Isle of) / Dunvegan** — The Three Chimneys and House Over-By

Wales

- **Pwllheli** — Plas Bodegroes

Republic of Ireland

- **Aran Islands / Inishmaan** — Inis Meáin Restaurant and Suites
- **Celbridge** — La Serre
- **Clogheen** — Old Convent
- **Dunfanaghy** — The Mill
- **Dunkineely** — Castle Murray House
- **Kenmare** — The Lime Tree
- **Kilbrittain** — Casino House

England

- **Bray-on-Thames / Bray Marina** — Riverside Brasserie
- **High Ongar** — The Wheatsheaf
- **Jersey / Green Island** — Green Island
- **London/Kensington and Chelsea** — Bibendum Oyster Bar
- **London/Richmond-upon-Thames** — Petersham Nurseries Café
- **London/Southwark** — Oxo Tower Brasserie
- **London/City of Westminster** — L'Atelier de Joël Robuchon
- **London/ City of Westminster** — Bocca di Lupo
- **London/City of Westminster** — Dehesa
- **London/ City of Westminster** — J. Sheekey Oyster Bar
- **Mousehole** — Cornish Range
- **Stow-on-the-Wold / Daylesford** — The Cafe at Daylesford Organic
- **Studland** — Shell Bay

Scotland

- **Thurso / Scrabster** — The Captain's Galley

Republic of Ireland

- **Barna** — O'Grady's on the Pier
- **Dingle** — The Chart House

England

- **Alton / Lower Froyle** — The Anchor Inn
- **Ambleside** — Drunken Duck Inn
- **Barnard Castle / Romaldkirk** — Rose and Crown

Bath / Combe Hay	The Wheatsheaf
Baughurst	The Wellington Arms
Biggleswade / Old Warden	Hare and Hounds
Bildeston	The Bildeston Crown
Bolnhurst	The Plough at Bolnhurst
Broadhembury	The Drewe Arms
Burford / Swinbrook	The Swan Inn
Burnham Market	The Hoste Arms
Chichester / Chilgrove	Fish House
Chichester / East Lavant	The Royal Oak Inn
Cirencester / Sapperton	The Bell
Devizes / Marden	The Millstream
Helmsley / Harome	The Star Inn
Kendal / Crosthwaite	The Punch Bowl Inn
Keyston	The Pheasant
Lydford	The Dartmoor Inn
Milton Keynes / Newton Longville	The Crooked Billet
Mistley	The Mistley Thorn
Shefford	The Black Horse
Skipton / Hetton	Angel Inn
South Molton / Knowstone	The Masons Arms
Stamford / Clipsham	The Olive Branch and Beech House
Stockbridge / Longstock	The Peat Spade Inn
Stokenchurch / Radnage	The Three Horseshoes Inn
Stow-on-the-Wold / Lower Oddington	The Fox Inn
Summercourt	Viners
Sutton-on-the-Forest	Rose and Crown
Tarr Steps	Tarr Farm Inn
Woburn	The Birch
Woolhope	The Butchers Arms

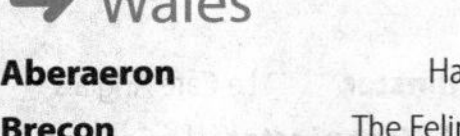

Aberaeron	Harbourmaster
Brecon	The Felin Fach Griffin
Caersws / Pontdolgoch	The Talkhouse
Skenfrith	The Bell at Skenfrith

Further information

Beer...

It's no exaggeration to say that beer and its consumption has pretty much defined popular conception of the British character for hundreds of years. From humble alehouse, via ubiquitous urban tavern, to agreeable coaching inn – all manner of drinking establishments have lined the British highway and byway since medieval times. As an example of the popularity of the properties of ale, by the fourteenth century there were over 350 taverns in London alone, while exactly 400 years ago you could have wandered round the capital's Square Mile and found over a thousand alehouses.

The quality of the beverage proffered to thirsty customers has varied as much as the fixtures and fittings but, generally speaking, the production of beer has followed a time-honoured recipe of four ingredients: barley, hops, yeast and water. The perfect pint begins with barley - the classic beer-making grain - and a clean, plentiful water supply coming together in a maltings, creating sugar for fermentation. The result looks like thin porridge; this boiling sludge is then filtered to a brown, hazy liquid called sweet wort.

Malt imparts sweetness to a beer and so, to give it balance, the addition of hops provides a bitter element to the mix. The hops need to be boiled to release their bitterness; it's at this point the true process of brewing is enacted. Eventually, the 'hopped wort' is cooled and filtered, in preparation for the key operation: fermentation. To ferment the beer, the brewers' little miracle-worker – yeast – is added to the fermentation vessels. Yeast is a living micro-organism, and its great claim to fame (apart from filling jars of Marmite!) is being able to convert the sugars into alcohol, carbon dioxide gas and a host of subtle flavours. With real ale, a secondary fermentation takes place when the finished product is safely ensconced in its barrel or cask, a process known as conditioning which happens before it leaves the brewery, and later, as it lies in the pub cellar. The final link in the chain is the publican, who (hopefully) oversees that decent pint gushing enticingly from the hand pump!

... and Whisky

Translated from the Gaelic term 'water of life', whisky depends for its very existence on the classic qualities of H2O. The local water supply dictates the nature of your glass of whisky; above and beyond that, the characteristics of the drink itself can range from spicy and aromatic to stylish and fruity, from light and fragrant to seaweedy and peaty. The classic Scotch whisky - only produced in the ideal natural environment of Scotland - makes full use of plentiful water supplies: barley is steeped in water for two to three days to turn it into malt, and then dried in a kiln traditionally fuelled by peat, before being ground in a mill.

The milled malt is called grist, and when hot water is added, the mixture is fed into a mash tun. This is where the sugars from malting dissolve, and the resulting solution – wort – oozes through the floor of the tun, to be passed into large wooden or stainless steel vessels. Add yeast, and fermentation occurs, with the sugars turning to alcohol. By now, this looks something like beer, but when it's distilled – a two-pronged process in which condensing vapours are captured - any resemblance to ale is long gone! By the time the different parts of the distillation are gathered together and redistilled, the resultant liquid – the new-make whisky – is ready to spend the next three years (by law) in oak casks maturing: the wood enhances the final aroma and flavour. Whisky makers enjoy a certain pact with the heavens: as the liquid matures, some of it evaporates into the ether, and this is known as the 'Angels' Share'...

Irish whiskey (note the extra 'e') differs slightly from the Scottish version, and not just in the spelling. It's traditionally made from cereals, and peat is hardly ever used in the malting process, so there's a lack of the smoky, earthy characteristics found over the Irish Sea. It's also encouraged to sit around for a much longer time: the maturation period is seven years, more than twice that of Scotch.

The world No.1 in tires with 17.1% of the market

A business presence in over 170 countries

A manufacturing footprint at the heart of markets

In 2008 **68** industrial sites in **19** countries produced:

- **177** million tires
- **16** million maps and guides

Highly international teams

Over **117 500** employees* from all cultures on all continents including **6 000** people employed in R&D centers in Europe, the US and Asia.

*110,252 full-time equivalent staff

The Michelin Group at a glance

Michelin competes

At the end of 2008

- **Le Mans 24-hour race**
  11 consecutive years of victories
- **Endurance 2008**
  - 5 victories on 5 stages in Le Mans Series
  - 10 victories on 10 stages in American Le Mans Series
- **Paris-Dakar**
  Since the beginning of the event, the Michelin group has won in all categories
- **Moto GP**
  26 Drivers' World Champion titles in the premier category
- **Trial**
  Every World Champion title since 1981 (except 1992)

Michelin, established close to its customers

68 plants in 19 countries

- Algeria
- Brazil
- Canada
- China
- Colombia
- France
- Germany
- Hungary
- Italy
- Japan
- Mexico
- Poland
- Romania
- Russia
- Serbia
- Spain
- Thailand
- UK
- USA

A Technology Center spread over 3 continents

- Asia
- Europe
- North America

2 natural rubber plantations

- Brazil

Our mission

To make a sustainable contribution to progress in the mobility of goods and people by enhancing freedom of movement, safety, efficiency and pleasure when on the move.

Michelin committed to environmental-friendliness

Michelin, world leader in low rolling resistance tires, actively reduces fuel consumption and vehicle gas emission.

For its products, Michelin develops state-of-the-art technologies in order to:
- Reduce fuel consumption, while improving overall tire performance.
- Increase life cycle to reduce the number of tires to be processed at the end of their useful lives;
- Use raw materials which have a low impact on the environment.

Furthermore, at the end of 2008, 99.5% of tire production in volume was carried out in ISO 14001* certified plants.

Michelin is committed to implementing recycling channels for end-of-life tires.

*environmental certification

Passenger Car Light Truck

Truck

Michelin a key mobility enabler

Earthmover

Aircraft

Agricultural

Two-wheel **Distribution**

Partnered with vehicle manufacturers, in tune with users, active in competition and in all the distribution channels, Michelinis continually innovating to promote mobility today and to invent that of tomorrow.

Maps and Guides

ViaMichelin, travel assistance services

Michelin Lifestyle, for your travel accessories

MICHELIN
plays on balanced performance

- **Long tire life**
- **Fuel savings**
- **Safety on the road**

... MICHELIN tires provide you with the best performance, without making a single sacrifice.

The MICHELIN tire pure technology

1 Tread
A thick layer of rubber provides contact with the ground. It has to channel water away and last as long as possible.

2 Crown plies
This double or triple reinforced belt has both vertical flexibility and high lateral rigidity. It provides the steering capacity.

3 Sidewalls
These cover and protect the textile casing whose role is to attach the tire tread to the wheel rim.

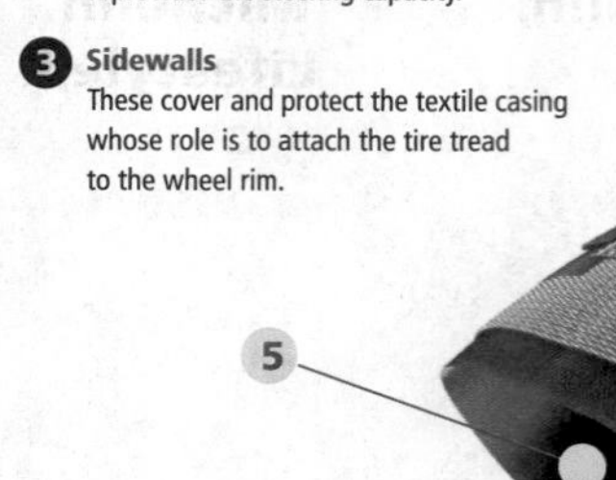

4 Bead area for attachment to the rim
Its internal bead wire clamps the tire firmly against the wheel rim.

5 Inner liner
This makes the tire almost totally impermeable and maintains the correct inflation pressure.

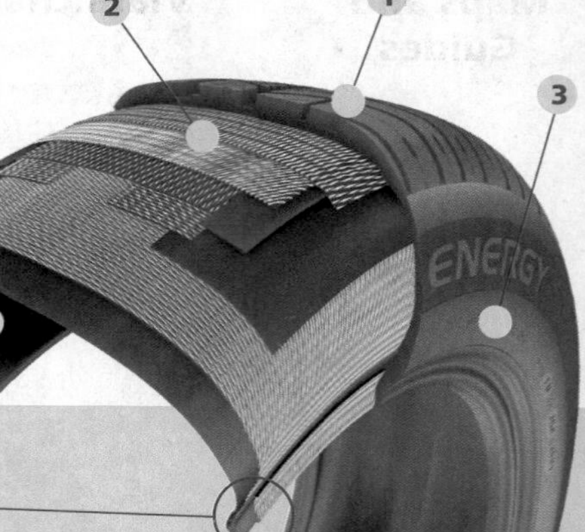

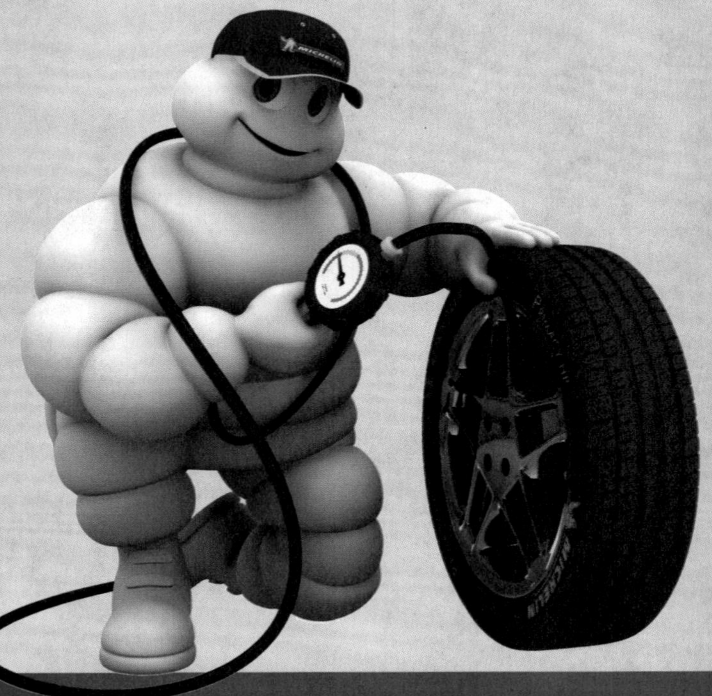

Great Britain

C. Labonne/MICHELIN

England
Channel Islands • Isle of Man

ABBERLEY – Worcestershire – 503 M27 – pop. 654 – ✉ Worcester 18 B2

London 137 mi. – Birmingham 27 mi. – Worcester 13 mi.

The Elms

West : 2 mi. on A 443 ✉ WR6 6AT – ✆ (01299) 896 666 – www.theelmshotel.co.uk – Fax (01299) 896 804

23 rm (dinner included) – £ 200/315 £ 330/510

Rest – Menu £ 21/50 – Carte approx. £ 23

◆ Impressive Queen Anne mansion in well-kept grounds, with countryside views from most bedrooms. Stylishly refurbished interior with contemporary style. Special facilities for children. Restaurant serving classically based dishes with modern touches.

ABBOTSBURY – Dorset – 503 M32 – pop. 422 3 B3

London 146 mi. – Bournemouth 44 mi. – Exeter 50 mi. – Weymouth 10 mi.

Town★★ - Chesil Beach★★ - Swannery★ **AC** – Sub-Tropical Gardens★ **AC**

St Catherine's Chapel★, 0.5 mi. uphill (30 mn rtn on foot). Maiden Castle★★ (★) NE : 7.5 m

Abbey House without rest

Church St ✉ DT3 4JJ – ✆ (01305) 871 330 – www.theabbeyhouse.co.uk – Fax (01305) 871 088

5 rm – £ 70/100 £ 70/100

◆ Historic stone house, part 15C abbey infirmary. Garden holds a unique Benedictine water mill. Breakfast room with low beamed ceiling and fireplace. Cosy bedrooms.

ABINGDON – Oxfordshire – 503 Q28 – pop. 36 010 Great Britain 10 B2

London 64 mi. – Oxford 6 mi. – Reading 25 mi.

from Abingdon Bridge to Oxford (Salter Bros. Ltd) 2 daily (summer only)

Visitor Information Point , Town Council , Abbey Close ✆ (01235) 522711

Drayton Park Drayton Steventon Rd, ✆ (01235) 550 607

Town★ – County Hall★

Upper Reaches

Thames St ✉ OX14 3JA – ✆ (01235) 522 536 – www.upperreaches-abingdon.co.uk – Fax (01235) 555 182

31 rm – £ 120/130 £ 140/160 **Rest** – Menu £ 20 – Carte £ 23/32

◆ Former corn mill, set on an island in the River Thames and accessed via a bridge. Mix of classic and contemporary bedrooms, with junior suites boasting double-aspect windows. Housing a mill wheel and millrace, the restaurant offers an international menu.

at Marcham West : 3 mi. on A 415

Rafters without rest

Abingdon Rd, on A 415 ✉ OX13 6NU – ✆ (01865) 391 298 – www.bnb-rafters.co.uk – Fax (01865) 391 173

4 rm – £ 50/85 £ 120

◆ Modern, well-equipped bedrooms; the superior room, with luxury bathroom and balcony, is best. Friendly owner offers substantial, locally sourced breakfast. Massage chair for relaxation.

ABINGER HAMMER – Surrey – 504 S30 7 C2

London 35 mi. – Brighton 40 mi. – Dover 91 mi. – Portsmouth 50 mi.

Drakes on the Pond (John Morris)

Dorking Rd, on A 25 ✉ RH5 6SA – ✆ (01306) 731 174 – www.drakesonthepond.com – Fax (01306) 731 174 – Closed 2 weeks August, 2 weeks Christmas, Sunday and Monday

Rest – Menu £ 25 (lunch) – Carte dinner £ 44/50

Spec. Ham hock and potato cake with pea panna cotta, celeriac and asparagus. Fillet of beef with cep mushroom barquette and grain mustard sauce. Almond and treacle tart with Earl Grey crème caramel and clotted cream ice cream.

◆ Friendly neighbourhood restaurant in long, simply furnished room; a former cowshed! Selection of simply-presented, classical dishes. Appealing, confident and flavourful cooking.

ACTON BURNELL – Shrops. – 503 L26 – see Shrewsbury

ACTON GREEN – County of Herefordshire – 503 M27 – see Great Malvern

ADDINGHAM – West Yorkshire – 502 O22 – pop. 3 215 Great Britain 22 B2

London 225 mi. – Bradford 16 mi. – Ilkley 4 mi.

Bolton Priory**AC**, N : 3.5 mi. on B 6160

The Fleece

152-154 Main St ✉ LS29 0LY – ✆ (01943) 830 491 – www.thefleeceaddingham.co.uk

Rest – Carte £ 18/26

◆ Personally run pub on village main street. Open fires, solid stone floor, rustic walls filled with country prints. Wide ranging menu with good use of seasonal ingredients.

ALBRIGHTON – Shrops. – 502 L25 – see Shrewsbury

ALDEBURGH – Suffolk – 504 Y27 – pop. 2 654 15 D3

London 97 mi. – Ipswich 24 mi. – Norwich 41 mi.

152 High St ✆ (01728) 453637, atic@suffolkcoastal.gov.uk

ThorpenessHotel and Golf Course Thorpeness, ✆ (01728) 452 176

Wentworth

Wentworth Rd ✉ IP15 5BD – ✆ (01728) 452 312 – www.wentworth-aldeburgh.com – Fax (01728) 454 343

35 rm – £ 86/145 £ 169/236 **Rest** – Menu £ 14/20

◆ Carefully furnished, traditional seaside hotel; coast view bedrooms are equipped with binoculars and all have a copy of 'Orlando the Marmalade Cat', a story set in the area. Formal dining room offers mix of brasserie and classic dishes.

The Lighthouse

77 High St ✉ IP15 5AU – ✆ (01728) 453 377 – www.thelighthouserestaurant.co.uk – Fax (01728) 453 831

Rest – *(booking essential)* Carte £ 21/33

◆ Busy, unpretentious bistro boasts a wealth of Suffolk produce from local meats to Aldeburgh cod and potted shrimps. Good choice of wines; amiable service.

152

152 High St ✉ IP15 5AX – ✆ (01728) 454 594 – www.152aldeburgh.co.uk – Fax (01502) 731 099

Rest – Carte £ 23/31

◆ Choose between the bright, informal restaurant or the courtyard terrace on summer days to enjoy the keenly priced menu that features a wide variety of local produce.

Regatta

171-173 High St ✉ IP15 5AN – ✆ (01728) 452 011 – www.regattaaldeburgh.com – Fax (01728) 453 324 – Closed 24-26 December, 31 December, 1 January and Sunday dinner November-February

Rest – Carte £ 18/31

◆ Long-standing restaurant on main street, with sea-themed mural on one wall. Traditionally prepared, seafood-orientated menus with daily blackboard specials; many dishes available in two sizes.

at Friston Northwest : 4 mi. by A 1094 on B 1121 – ✉ Aldeburgh

The Old School without rest

✉ IP17 1NP – ✆ (01728) 688 173 – www.fristonoldschool.com

3 rm – £ 55 £ 68

◆ Redbrick former school house in pleasant garden. Good breakfast served family style in spacious room. Comfortable modern rooms with good amenities in the house or annexe.

ALDERLEY EDGE – Cheshire – 502 N24 – pop. 5 280 20 B3

London 187 mi. – Chester 34 mi. – Manchester 14 mi. – Stoke-on-Trent 25 mi.

Wilmslow Mobberley Great Warford, ✆ (01565) 872 148

Alderley Edge

Macclesfield Rd ✉ SK9 7BJ – ☎ (01625) 583 033 – www.alderleyedgehotel.com – Fax (01625) 586 343 – Closed 25 December

49 rm – †£ 73/150 ††£ 110/145, ☐ £ 15 – 1 suite

Rest ***The Alderley*** – see restaurant listing

◆ A substantial late Victorian house with an easy-going style. Relaxing lounges furnished with cushion-clad easy chairs. Well-furnished, comfortable bedrooms, some with views.

XXX

The Alderley – at Alderley Edge Hotel

✉ SK9 7BJ – ☎ (01625) 583 033 – www.alderleyedgehotel.com – Fax (01625) 586 343 – Closed 25 December and Sunday dinner

Rest – Menu £ 20/30 – Carte £ 42/44

◆ Conservatory dining room; comfortably spaced tables. The cuisine, served by dinner-suited staff, is modern British. Particularly proud of 500 wine list and 100 Champagnes.

XX

London Road Restaurant and Wine Bar

46 London Rd ✉ SK9 7DZ – ☎ (01625) 584 163 – www.heathcotes.co.uk – Closed 1 January and Monday

Rest – Menu £ 16 (lunch) – Carte £ 27/42

◆ Sleek, modern brasserie with bar, basement, private dining room and terrace. Large menus offer modern European dishes with Northern influences; cooking is clean and unfussy.

X

The Wizard

Macclesfield Rd, Southeast : 1.25 mi. on B 5087 ✉ SK10 4UB – ☎ (01625) 584 000 – www.wizardrestaurant.googlepages.com – Fax (01625) 585 105

Rest – Menu £ 10 – Carte £ 15/40

◆ 200 year old pub displaying immense charm and character, set by a picturesque woodland beauty spot. Crafted from locally sourced produce, dishes are seasonal and generously proportioned.

ENGLAND

ALDERNEY – C.I. – 503 Q33 – see Channel Islands

ALDFIELD – N. Yorks. – 502 P21 – see Ripon

ALDFORD – Cheshire – 502 L24 — 20 A3

London 189 mi. – Chester 6 mi. – Liverpool 25 mi.

The Grosvenor Arms

Chester Rd ✉ CH3 6HJ – ☎ (01244) 620 228 – www.grosvenorarms-aldford.co.uk – Fax (01224) 620 247 – Closed 25 December

Rest – Carte £ 17/30

◆ Spacious 19C red brick pub, with several eating areas indoors and out. Daily changing menu features generous and tasty British pub classics, with a few more sophisticated choices.

ALDRIDGE – West Midlands – 502 O26 – pop. 15 659 – ✉ Walsall — 19 C2

London 130 mi. – Birmingham 12 mi. – Derby 32 mi. – Leicester 40 mi.

Plan : see Birmingham p. 3

Fairlawns

178 Little Aston Rd, East : 1 mi. on A 454 ✉ WS9 0NU – ☎ (01922) 455 122 – www.fairlawns.co.uk – Fax (01922) 743 148 – Restricted opening 24 December-2 January — CT**n**

54 rm ☐ – †£ 80/175 ††£ 110/195 – 6 suites

Rest – *(closed Saturday lunch and Bank Holidays)* Menu £ 20/28 **s** – Carte £ 25/39 **s**

◆ Privately owned hotel with well-equipped leisure facility. A choice range of rooms from budget to superior, all comfy and spacious, some with good views over open countryside. Restaurant gains from its rural ambience.

ALFRISTON – East Sussex – 504 U31 – pop. 1 721 – ✉ Polegate — 8 A3

London 66 mi. – Eastbourne 9 mi. – Lewes 10 mi. – Newhaven 8 mi.

The Star

High St ✉ BN26 5TA – ✆ (01323) 870 495 – www.thestaralfriston.com – Fax (01323) 870 922

37 rm – †£ 70/110 ††£ 110/135

Rest – *(bar lunch Monday-Saturday)* Menu £ 30

◆ 14C coaching inn with original half-timbered façade where smugglers once met. Décor includes flagstone floor and beamed ceilings; bar serves real ale. Well-kept bedrooms. Atmospheric Tudor style restaurant.

Moonrakers

High St. ✉ BN2 5TD – ✆ (01323) 871 199 – www.moonrakersrestaurant.co.uk – Closed 2 weeks January, 1 week Spring, 1 week October, Sunday dinner, Monday and Tuesday

Rest – Menu £ 15 (lunch) – Carte £ 28/43

◆ Attractive 600 year old cottage in pleasant village with low beams, log burner and pretty terrace. Concise modern menu of local, seasonal produce displays precise, flavoursome cooking.

The George Inn with rm

High St ✉ BN26 5SY – ✆ (01323) 870 319 – www.thegeorge-alfriston.com – Closed 25-26 December

6 rm – †£ 60 ††£ 90/130 **Rest** – *(booking advisable)* Carte £ 15/30

◆ Charming stone and timber building in delightful South Downs village, with hanging hops, inglenook fireplaces and large rear garden. Wide range of international dishes. Characterful antique-furnished bedrooms retain oak beams.

ALKHAM – Kent – pop. 607 — 9 D2

London 72 mi. – Bexley 61 mi.

The Marquis with rm

Alkham Valley Rd ✉ CT15 7DF – ✆ (01304) 873 410 – www.themarquisatalkham.co.uk

5 rm – †£ 85/95 ††£ 145/165

Rest – *(in bar Sunday and Monday)* Menu £ 19/39

◆ Delightful former inn in heart of pretty village; well-run and welcoming, with striking, contemporary interior. Precise, seasonal cooking with a few Yorkshire twists. Relaxed, informal atmosphere and keen, friendly service. Modish, understated bedrooms; the best are front facing, with a pleasant view.

ALNWICK – Northumberland – 501 O17 – pop. 7 767 Great Britain — 24 B2

London 320 mi. – Edinburgh 86 mi. – Newcastle upon Tyne 34 mi.

2 The Shambles ✆ (01665) 510 665, alnwicktic@alnwick.gov.uk

Swansfield Park, ✆ (01665) 602 632

Town ★ - Castle★★ **AC**

Dunstanburgh Castle★ **AC**, NE : 8 mi. by B 1340 and Dunstan rd (last 2.5 mi. on foot)

Greycroft without rest

Croft Pl, via Prudhoe St ✉ NE66 1XU – ✆ (01665) 602 127 – www.greycroft.co.uk – Closed 24-26 December

6 rm – †£ 55/80 ††£ 100/120

◆ Quiet 19C house, 5min walk from Alnwick castle. Bedrooms individually decorated to a high standard; breakfast in airy conservatory overlooking walled garden. Hospitable owners.

Aln House without rest

South Rd, Southeast : 0.75 mi. by B 6346 on Newcastle rd ✉ NE66 2NZ – ✆ (01665) 602 265 – www.alnhouse.co.uk

6 rm – †£ 45/80 ††£ 75/90

◆ Semi detached Edwardian house with mature front and rear gardens, an easy walk from castle. Homely lounge enhanced by personal touches. Individually appointed rooms.

Blackmore's with rm

24 Bondgate Without ✉ NE66 1PN – ☎ (01665) 602 395 – www.blackmoresofalnwick.com

13 rm – **†£ 60/105 ††£ 105** **Rest** – Carte £ 18/32

◆ 18C stone building with modern, open-plan interior and central bar. Bistro serves menu of mainly pub classics; first floor restaurant, with interesting display of clocks, offers more ambitious fare. Well-kept, contemporary bedrooms in chocolate tones.

at North Charlton North : 6.75 mi. by A 1 – ✉ Alnwick

North Charlton Farm without rest

✉ NE67 5HP – ☎ (01665) 579 443 – www.northcharltonfarm.co.uk – Fax (01665) 579 407 – Easter-October

3 rm – **†£ 45/80 ††£ 70/80**

◆ Attractive house on working farm with agricultural museum. Offers traditional accommodation. Each bedroom is individually decorated and has countryside views.

at Chathill North : 8.75 mi. by A 1 off B 6347

Doxford Hall H. and Spa

Chathill ✉ NE67 5DN – ☎ (01665) 589 700 – www.doxfordhall.com – Fax (01665) 589 141

23 rm – **†£ 96/160 ††£ 132/220** – 2 suites

Rest *George Runciman* – Menu £ 25 (lunch) **s** – Carte dinner £ 37/42 **s**

◆ 18C house with recent extensions and well-appointed spa. Spacious bedrooms, styled to complement original house; all have mod cons including flat screens, while impressive feature beds add a sense of luxury. Interesting modern cuisine served in formal dining room.

ENGLAND

ALSTON – Cumbria – 501 M19 – pop. 2 065 — 21 B2

London 309 mi. – Carlisle 28 mi. – Newcastle upon Tyne 45 mi.

Alston Moor Tourist Information Centre, Town Hall ☎ (01434) 382244, alston.tic@eden.gov.uk

Alston Moor The Hermitage, ☎ (01434) 381 675

Lovelady Shield Country House

Nenthead Rd, East : 2.5 mi. on A 689 ✉ CA9 3LF – ☎ (01434) 381 203 – www.lovelady.co.uk – Fax (01434) 381 505

12 rm (dinner included) – **†£ 105 ††£ 290/350**

Rest – *(dinner only and Sunday lunch) (booking essential for non-residents)* Menu £ 24/45

◆ Victorian country house in beautiful countryside location with peaceful garden and view to River Nent. Traditional bar and cosy lounge with open fire. Refurbished bedrooms. Ambitious menus served in dining room.

ALTON – Hampshire – 504 R30 – pop. 16 051 — 6 B2

London 53 mi. – Reading 24 mi. – Southampton 29 mi. – Winchester 18 mi.

7 Cross and Pillory Lane ☎ (01420) 88448, petersfieldinfo@btconnect.com

Old Odiham Rd, ☎ (01420) 82 042

Alton Grange

London Rd, Northeast : 1 mi. on B 3004 ✉ GU34 4EG – ☎ (01420) 86 565 – www.altongrange.co.uk – Fax (01420) 541 346 – Closed 24 December-5 January

30 rm – **†£ 80/120 ††£ 99/170**

Rest *Truffles* – Carte £ 22/32

◆ Hotel set in well-kept, oriental inspired gardens. The bar serves bistro-style snacks. Bedrooms are individually decorated, particularly junior suites and Saxon room. Dining room boasts myriad of Tiffany lamps and fusion cuisine.

at Beech Northwest : 2.25 mi. by A 339

Beech Barns without rest
61 Wellhouse Rd ✉ GU34 4AQ – ✆ (01420) 85 575 – www.beechbarns.co.uk
8 rm – †£ 69/85 ††£ 90/130
◆ An early 18C barn conversion in a wooded area. Welcoming young owners. The house has an attractively understated and stylish quality. Breakfast is free range and organic.

at Lower Froyle Northeast : 4.5 mi. by A 31

The Anchor Inn with rm
✉ GU34 4NA – ✆ (01420) 23 261 – www.anchorinnatlowerfroyle.co.uk – Closed 25 December
5 rm – †£ 130 ††£ 130/170 **Rest** – Menu £ 25/32 – Carte £ 22/55
◆ 14C inn boasting cosy, low beamed bar and more formal candlelit drawing room. Traditional British dishes, simply served and precisely crafted from well sourced local ingredients. Well equipped, comfortable bedrooms.

ALTRINCHAM – **Greater Manchester** – **502** N23 – **pop. 40 695** **20** B3

London 191 mi. – Chester 30 mi. – Liverpool 30 mi. – Manchester 8 mi.
20 Stamford New Rd ✆ (0161) 912 5931, tourist.information@trafford.gov.uk
Altrincham Municipal Timperley Stockport Rd, ✆ (0161) 928 0761
Dunham Forest Oldfield Lane, ✆ (0161) 928 2605
Ringway Hale Barns Hale Mount, ✆ (0161) 980 2630

Dilli
60 Stamford New Rd ✉ WA14 1EE – ✆ (0161) 929 7484 – www.dilli.co.uk – Fax (0161) 929 1213 – Closed 25 December
Rest – Indian – Menu £ 15 (lunch) – Carte £ 15/31
◆ Smart restaurant with white walls and intricate fretwork panelling. Originating from Delhi and Pakistan, interesting, well presented dishes range from street food to rich Moghul offerings.

The Fat Loaf
28-32 Greenwood Street – ✆ (0161) 929 67 00 – www.thefatloaf.co.uk – Closed 25-26 December, 1 January and Sunday
Rest – Menu £ 18 (lunch) **s** – Carte £ 22/32 **s**
◆ Stylish, spacious restaurant with open kitchen and relaxed atmosphere. Fresh, interesting cooking offers clear flavours and generous portions; good use of local, seasonal ingredients.

The Victoria
29 Stamford Street ✉ WA14 1EX – ✆ (0161) 613 1855 – Closed 26 December, 1 January and Sunday dinner
Rest – Menu £ 16 (dinner) – Carte £ 22/31
◆ Traditional pub on a quiet town centre side street. Cooking is straightforward, generous and tasty. Original dishes could include battered butties, asparagus scones or ploughman's tart.

at Little Bollington Southwest : 3.25 mi. on A 56 – ✉ Altrincham

Ash Farm without rest
Park Lane ✉ WA14 4TJ – ✆ (0161) 929 9290 – www.ashfarm.co.uk
3 rm – †£ 55 ††£ 82
◆ Attractive 18C farmhouse with light, modern décor and pine-furnished breakfast room, set on quiet country lane close to the airport. Cosy farmhouse-style bedrooms; one with a four-poster.

ALVESTON – **Warks.** – see Stratford-upon-Avon

AMBERLEY – **West Sussex** – **504** S31 – **pop. 525** – ✉ **Arundel** **7** C2
Great Britain

London 56 mi. – Brighton 24 mi. – Portsmouth 31 mi.
Bignor Roman Villa (mosaics★) **AC**, NW : 3.5 mi. by B 2139 via Bury

Amberley Castle

Southwest : 0.5 mi. on B 2139 ✉ BN18 9LT – ✆ (01798) 831 992 – www.amberleycastle.co.uk – Fax (01798) 831 998

13 rm – †£ 190/285 ††£ 405/520 – 6 suites

Rest *Queen's Room* – *(booking essential)* Menu £ 30/60

◆ Enchanting 12C castle with serene gardens, majestic battlements, intimate sitting rooms and sumptuous, characterful bedrooms with luxurious jacuzzi bathrooms. Formal dining, with professional, attentive service. Barrel-vaulted ceiling and mural.

AMBLESIDE – Cumbria – 502 L20 – pop. 3 064 Great Britain 21 A2

London 278 mi. – Carlisle 47 mi. – Kendal 14 mi.

Central Buildings, Market Cross ✆ (015394) 32582 AZ, amblesidetic@southlakeland.gov.ukMain Car Park BY

Lake Windermere★★ – Dove Cottage, Grasmere★ **AC** AY **A** – Brockhole National Park Centre★ **AC**, SE : 3 mi. by A 591 AZ. Wrynose Pass★★, W : 7.5 mi. by A 593 AY – Hard Knott Pass★★, W : 10 mi. by A 593 AY

The Samling

Ambleside Rd, South : 1.5 mi. on A 591 ✉ LA23 1LR – ✆ (015394) 31 922 – www.thesamlinghotel.co.uk – Fax (015394) 30 400

9 rm (dinner included) – †£ 260/305 ††£ 260/305 – 2 suites

Rest – French – *(booking essential for non-residents)* Menu £ 38/55

Spec. Red mullet with Parmesan custard and tomato marmalade. Salt marsh lamb with summer beans and caramelised sweetbreads. Orange caramel flan with ginger parfait and lychee sorbet.

◆ Traditional manor house appearance belies boutique interior; stylish lounge and highly individual bedrooms; two with stunning lake views. Marvellous garden with croquet lawn. Small but very attractively decorated dining room; appealing cooking with a modern edge, with the emphasis on natural flavours.

The Waterhead

Lake Rd ✉ LA22 0ER – ✆ (015394) 32 566 – www.elh.co.uk – Fax (015394) 31 255 BY**x**

41 rm – †£ 212/280 ††£ 280

Rest *The Bay* – *(dinner only)* Carte £ 28/41 **s**

◆ Traditional lakeside house boasting modern interior. Bright, contemporary bedrooms and stylish en suites with heated floors; Luxury rooms have the best lake views. European menu served under purple-hued lighting in The Bay restaurant.

Rothay Manor

Rothay Bridge, South : 0.5 mi. on A 593 ✉ LA22 0EH – ✆ (015394) 33 605 – www.rothaymanor.co.uk – Fax (015394) 33 607 – Closed 3-28 January

16 rm – †£ 90/155 ††£ 130/195 – 3 suites BY**r**

Rest – Menu £ 20/38 – Carte lunch £ 16/21

◆ Elegant Regency house boasting modern, stylish interior. Contemporary drawing room decorated in warm tones. Finely-kept bedrooms; 'Superior' rooms at the front have balconies. Mixture of modern and classic dishes with a distinct French flavour served in formal dining room.

Brathay Lodge without rest

Rothay Rd ✉ LA22 0EE – ✆ (01539) 432 000 – www.brathay-lodge.co.uk – Closed Christmas AZ**e**

19 rm – †£ 67/82 ††£ 89/109

◆ Stylish accommodation in the heart of Ambleside. Unfussy, bright and warm décor. Continental breakfast only. All bedrooms have spa baths and some boast four posters.

Lakes Lodge without rest

Lake Rd ✉ LA22 0DB – ✆ (015394) 33 240 – www.lakeslodge.co.uk – Fax (015394) 33 240 – Closed 19-27 December AZ**s**

12 rm – †£ 80/150 ††£ 100/160

◆ Imposing traditional stone house with relaxed, laid back feel. Contemporary bedrooms in white; 10 has the best view. Continental breakfast plus homemade pastries and muffins.

ENGLAND

AMBLESIDE

Street	Grid	No.
Borrans Rd	BY	2
Cheapside	AZ	4
Church St	AZ	6
Compston St	AZ	8
Kelsick Rd	AZ	12
King St	AZ	13
Lake Rd	AZ	
Market Pl.	AZ	14
North Rd	AZ	17
Old Lake Rd	AZ	20
St Mary's Lane	AZ	22
Smithy Brow	AZ	23

GRASMERE

Street	Grid	No.
Broadgate	BZ	3
Easedale Rd	BZ	10
Swan Lane	AY	24

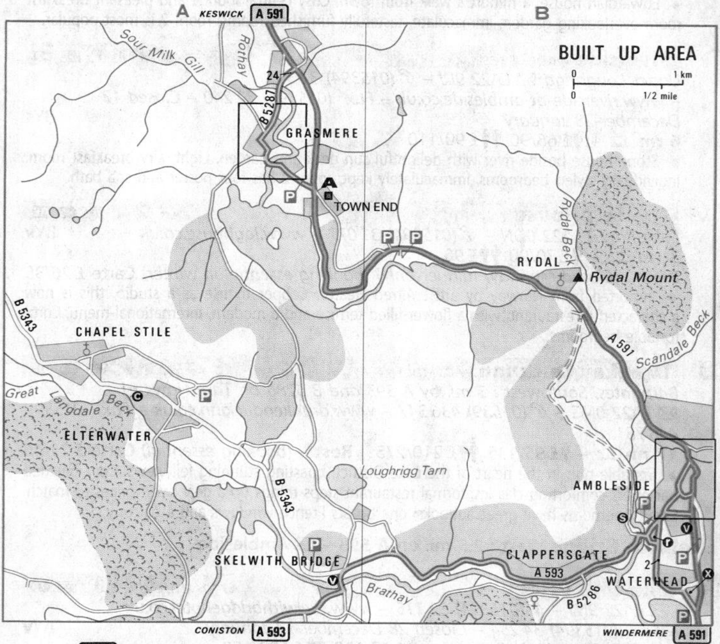

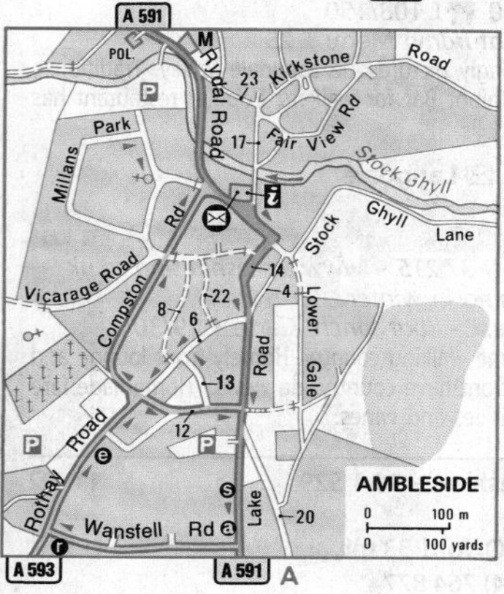

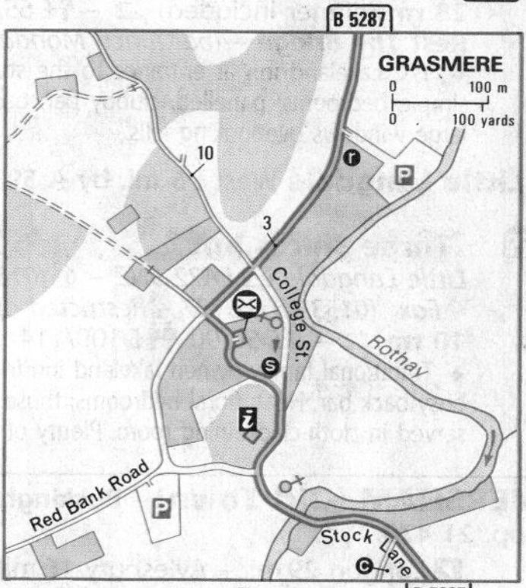

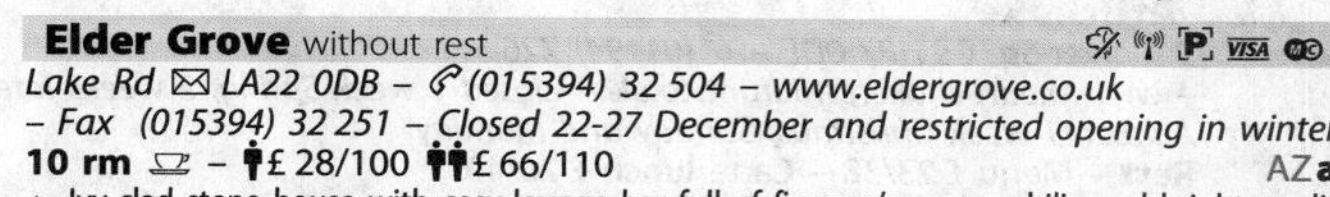

Elder Grove without rest

Lake Rd ✉ LA22 0DB – ✆ (015394) 32 504 – www.eldergrove.co.uk – Fax (015394) 32 251 – Closed 22-27 December and restricted opening in winter

10 rm ☕ – 🚹£ 28/100 🚹🚹£ 66/110 AZ**a**

◆ Ivy-clad stone house with cosy lounge bar full of firemen's memorabilia and bright, traditionally-furnished bedrooms. Locally sourced produce served in neat breakfast room.

Red Bank without rest
Wansfell Rd ✉ LA22 0EG – ✆ (015394) 34 637 – www.red-bank.co.uk
3 rm – £ 60/95 £ 70/95 AZ**r**
◆ Edwardian house, a minute's walk from town. Cosy central lounge and pleasant breakfast room overlooking garden. Immaculate, tastefully furnished rooms; room 2 is most popular.

Riverside without rest
Under Loughrigg ✉ LA22 9LJ – ✆ (015394) 32 395 – www.riverside-at-ambleside.co.uk – Fax (015394) 32 240 – Closed 13 December-28 January BY**s**
6 rm – £ 65/90 £ 90/110
◆ Stone house beside river with delightful sun deck and garden. Light, airy breakfast room. Individually-styled bedrooms, immaculately kept; room 2 has four poster and spa bath.

The Log House with rm
Lake Rd ✉ LA22 0DN – ✆ (015394) 31 077 – www.loghouse.co.uk BY**v**
3 rm – £ 70/90 £ 90
Rest – *(Closed Monday) (dinner only) (booking essential in winter)* Carte £ 26/35
◆ Imported from Norway by artist Alfred Heaton Cooper to use as a studio, this is now a characterful restaurant, with a flower-filled terrace and a modern, international menu. Comfortable bedrooms.

Drunken Duck Inn with rm
Barngates, Southwest : 3 mi. by A 593 and B 5286 on Tarn Hows rd ✉ LA22 0NG – ✆ (01539) 436 347 – www.drunkenduckinn.co.uk – Fax (01539) 436 781
17 rm – £ 95/135 £ 210/275 **Rest** – *(booking essential)* Carte £ 25/45
◆ Sizeable pub in the heart of the Lake District, boasting stunning fell views. Cosy beamed bar offers comforting classics; formal restaurant steps things up a gear, with prices to match. Smart bedrooms have great outlooks; one boasts French windows and a balcony.

ENGLAND

at Skelwith Bridge West : 2.5 mi. on A 593 – ✉ Ambleside

Skelwith Bridge rm, rest,
✉ LA22 9NJ – ✆ (015394) 32 115 – www.skelwithbridgehotel.co.uk – Fax (015394) 34 254 – Closed 28 December-12 January AY**v**
28 rm (dinner included) – £ 65/100 £ 108/150
Rest *The Bridge* – *(bar lunch Monday-Saturday)* Menu £ 25
◆ 17C Lakeland inn at entrance to the stunningly picturesque Langdale Valley. Traditional, simple bedrooms; panelled, clubby bar; busy Talbot Bar for walkers. Popular restaurant has large windows overlooking fells.

at Little Langdale West : 5 mi. by A 593 – ✉ Langdale

Three Shires Inn
Little Langdale ✉ LA22 9NZ – ✆ (015394) 37 215 – www.threeshiresinn.co.uk – Fax (015394) 37 127 – Restricted opening in winter AY**c**
10 rm – £ 50/90 £ 100/114 **Rest** – *(bar lunch)* Carte £ 19/30
◆ Traditional family-owned lakeland inn in prime walking country. Homely front lounge and busy back bar. Neat, floral bedrooms; those at front have countryside views. Homemade fare served in cloth-clad dining room. Plenty of whiskies and wines.

AMERSHAM (Old Town) – Buckinghamshire – 504 S29 – pop. 21 470 **11** D2

London 29 mi. – Aylesbury 16 mi. – Oxford 33 mi.
Little Chalfont Lodge Lane, ✆ (01494) 764 877

Artichoke
9 Market Sq. ✉ HP7 0DF – ✆ (01494) 726 611 – www.theartichokerestaurant.co.uk – Closed 1 week Spring, 2 weeks late August, 1 week Christmas, Sunday and Monday
Rest – Menu £ 23/38 – Carte lunch £ 26/40
◆ 16C brick house with smart façade; an artichoke etched on its window. Narrow room with stylish, modern look but retaining period detail. Accomplished, well-presented cooking.

Gilbey's

1 Market Sq. ✉ HP7 0DF – ☎ (01494) 727 242 – www.gilbeygroup.com – Fax (01494) 431 243 – Closed 24-29 December and 1 January
Rest – *(booking essential)* Menu £ 20 (lunch except Friday and Saturday dinner) – Carte £ 29/33

◆ Part of a former 17C school, this busy neighbourhood restaurant is cosy and informal with modern artwork on walls. Eclectic range of British cooking with global influences.

AMESBURY – Wiltshire – 503 O30 – pop. 8 312 — 4 D2

London 87 mi. – Bristol 52 mi. – Southampton 32 mi. – Taunton 66 mi.

Amesbury Library, Smithfield St ☎ (01980) 622833, amesburytic@wiltshire.gov.uk

Stonehenge★★★ **AC**, W : 2 mi. by A 303. Wilton Village★ Wilton House★★ **AC**, Wilton Carpet Factory★ **AC**), SW : 13 mi. by A 303, B 3083 and A 36

Mandalay without rest

15 Stonehenge Rd, via Church St ✉ SP4 7BA – ☎ (01980) 623 733 – Fax (01980) 626 642
5 rm – †£ 50 ††£ 75

◆ Only two minutes' drive from Stonehenge, this brick-built house boasts a bygone style and pleasant garden. Varied breakfasts. Individual rooms, named after famous authors.

AMPLEFORTH – N. Yorks. – 502 Q21 – see Helmsley

ANSTEY – Hertfordshire — 12 B2

London 38 mi. – Croydon 71 mi. – Barnet 35 mi. – Ealing 47 mi.

Anstey Grove Barn without rest

on Meesden rd. ✉ SG9 0BJ – ☎ (01763) 848 828 – www.ansteygrovebarn.co.uk
6 rm – †£ 65 ††£ 100

◆ Converted barn on what was once a working pig farm. Simply furnished, homely bedrooms named after breeds of pig; the best is Old Yorkshire with its four-poster and roll-top bath.

APPLEBY-IN-WESTMORLAND – Cumbria – 502 M20 – pop. 2 862 — 21 B2

London 285 mi. – Carlisle 33 mi. – Kendal 24 mi. – Middlesbrough 58 mi.

Moot Hall, Boroughgate ☎ (017683) 51177, tic@applebytown.org.uk

Appleby Brackenber Moor, ☎ (017683) 51 432

Appleby Manor Country House

Roman Rd, East : 1 mi. by B 6542 and Station Rd ✉ CA16 6JB – ☎ (017683) 51 571 – www.applebymanor.co.uk – Fax (017683) 52 888 – Closed 24-26 December
31 rm – †£ 130/150 ††£ 150/200
Rest – Menu £ 19 (lunch) **s** – Carte £ 27/37 **s**

◆ Wooded grounds and good views of Appleby Castle at this elevated 19C pink sandstone country manor. Traditional bedrooms in extension; those in main house are more contemporary. Conservatory restaurant serves classic menu.

Tufton Arms

Market Sq ✉ CA16 6XA – ☎ (017683) 51 593 – www.tuftonarmshotel.co.uk – Fax (017683) 52 761 – Closed 25-26 December
20 rm – †£ 75/90 ††£ 125 – 2 suites
Rest – Menu £ 28 (dinner) – Carte £ 19/30

◆ 16C former coaching inn in traditional market town boasts new contemporary interior; chic, comfortable bedrooms in bold colours. Fishing, shooting and stalking can be arranged. Easy-going menu served in modern dining room.

APPLEDORE – Devon – 503 H30 – pop. 2 187 — 2 C1

London 228 mi. – Barnstaple 12 mi. – Exeter 46 mi. – Plymouth 61 mi.

Town★

ENGLAND

West Farm without rest
Irsha St, West : 0.25 mi. ✉ EX39 1RY – ✆ (01237) 425 269
3 rm – £ 67 £ 98
◆ 17C house, boasting particularly pleasant garden at the back, in a charming little coastal village. Delightfully appointed sitting room. Bedrooms feel comfortable and homely.

APPLETREEWICK – North Yorkshire – 502 O21 — 22 B2

London 236 mi. – Harrogate 25 mi. – Skipton 11 mi.

Knowles Lodge without rest
South : 1 mi. on Bolton Abbey rd ✉ BD23 6DQ – ✆ (01756) 720 228 – www.knowleslodge.com – Fax (01756) 720 381
4 rm – £ 55/60 £ 90
◆ Unusual Canadian ranch-house style guesthouse, clad in timber and sited in quiet dales location. Large sitting room with fine outlook. Cosy bedrooms have garden views.

ARLINGHAM – Gloucestershire – 503 M28 – pop. 377 – ✉ Gloucester — 4 C1

London 120 mi. – Birmingham 69 mi. – Bristol 34 mi. – Gloucester 16 mi.

The Old Passage Inn with rm
Passage Rd, West : 0.75 m ✉ GL2 7JR – ✆ (01452) 740 547 – www.theoldpassageinn.com – Fax (01452) 741 871 – Closed Sunday dinner and Monday, restricted opening in winter
3 rm – £ 60/110 £ 80/130, £ 7.50 **Rest** – Seafood – Carte £ 32/59
◆ Eye-catching, former inn with bright yellow interior and colourful local artwork. Appealing seafood menus; unfussy cooking relies on the quality of the produce. Smart rooms with river views.

ARMSCOTE – Warwickshire – 504 P27 — 19 C3

London 91 mi. – Birmingham 36 mi. – Oxford 38 mi.

Willow Corner without rest
✉ CV37 8DE – ✆ (01608) 682 391 – www.willowcorner.co.uk – Closed Christmas-New Year
3 rm – £ 55 £ 80
◆ Lovely thatched property in quaint village with stable door, mullioned windows and low ceilings. Pretty bedrooms with thoughtful extras; homemade biscuits and tea on arrival.

The Fox & Goose Inn with rm
Front St ✉ CV37 8DD – ✆ (01608) 682 293 – www.foxandgoosearmscote.co.uk – Fax (01608) 682 293
4 rm – £ 30/55 £ 55/110 **Rest** – Carte £ 15/50
◆ Creeper-clad red brick inn with modern interior; bright open-plan bar and dining room. Mix of fairly-priced pub and restaurant dishes. Bright, buzzy service. Bedrooms named after Cluedo characters.

ARNSIDE – Cumbria – 502 L21 – pop. 2 301 — 21 3A

London 257 mi. – Liverpool 74 mi. – Manchester 69 mi. – Bradford 97 mi.

Number 43 without rest
43 The Promenade ✉ LA5 0AA – ✆ (01524) 762 761 – www.no43.org.uk
6 rm – £ 100 £ 110/180
◆ Delightfully converted Victorian house with relaxing feel and commanding views of lakes and bay. Immaculately kept, contemporary bedrooms boast quality furnishings. Lovely terrace.

ARUNDEL – West Sussex – 504 S31 – pop. 3 297 Great Britain — 7 C2

London 58 mi. – Brighton 21 mi. – Southampton 41 mi. – Worthing 9 mi.
61 High St ✆ (01903) 882268, arundel.vic@arun.gov.uk
Castle★★ **AC**

ENGLAND

XX **The Town House** with rm

65 High St ✉ BN18 9AJ – ✆ (01903) 883 847 – www.thetownhouse.co.uk – Closed 2 weeks February, 2 weeks October, Sunday and Monday

4 rm – †£ 70/85 ††£ 120 **Rest** – Menu £ 18/28

◆ Grade II listed house at top of town. Beautiful Renaissance ceiling with gilded walnut panels. Cooking is rich, classic, unfussy and skilled, and uses local, seasonal produce. Simple, traditional bedrooms. Best are at front facing castle.

XX **Arundel House** with rm

11 High St ✉ BN18 9AD – ✆ (01903) 882 136 – www.arundelhouseonline.com – Fax (01903) 881 179 – Closed 1 week April,1 week October,24-31 December, Sunday and Monday lunch

5 rm – †£ 140/160 ††£ 140/160, £ 10

Rest – *(residents only Monday dinner)* Menu £ 22/28 (£ 34 dinner Friday-Saturday)

◆ Bow-fronted high street restaurant with pleasant courtyard. Monthly set menus display well-proportioned, highly seasonal dishes, crafted from local and where possible wild, produce. Stylish bedrooms boast Egyptian linen, good mod cons and large writing desks.

at Burpham **Northeast : 3 mi. by A 27 – ✉ Arundel**

Burpham Country House

The Street ✉ BN18 9RJ – ✆ (01903) 882 160 – www.burphamcountryhouse.com – Fax (01903) 884 627 – Closed 2 weeks January and 25 December

10 rm – †£ 60 ††£ 110/135

Rest – *(closed Sunday-Monday) (dinner only)* Menu £ 26 – Carte £ 15/26

◆ Reputedly a hunting lodge for the Duke of Norfolk, this tranquil hotel constitutes the ideal 'stress remedy break'. Calm, pastel-coloured bedrooms overlook exquisite gardens. Seasonal menu of classic dishes served in dining room and conservatory.

George and Dragon

Main St ✉ BN18 9RR – ✆ (01903) 883 131 – www.burphamgeorgeanddragon.com – Fax (01903) 883 341

Rest – Carte £ 18/31

◆ Welcoming pub in picturesque village. Seasonal offerings from local suppliers, including game from the Duke of Norfolk's estate served in bar or more formal dining room.

ENGLAND

ASCOT – Windsor and Maidenhead – 504 R29 – pop. 15 761 11 D3

London 36 mi. – Reading 15 mi.

Mill Ride Ascot, ✆ (01344) 886 777

Berystede

Bagshot Rd, Sunninghill, South : 1.5 mi. on A 330 ✉ SL5 9JH – ✆ (0844) 879 91 04 – www.macdonaldhotels.co.uk/berystede – Fax (01344) 872 301

121 rm – †£ 99/239 ††£ 99/239 – 5 suites

Rest *Hyperion* – *(dinner only and Sunday lunch)* Carte £ 24/36

◆ Turreted red brick Victorian house in mature gardens, boasts classically-styled lounge, panelled bar with terrace and variously-sized bedrooms, with warm, contemporary feel. Formal dining at Hyperion, with classic menus and countryside outlook.

XX **Ascot Oriental**

East : 2.25 mi. on A 329 ✉ SL5 0PU – ✆ (01344) 621 877 – www.ascotoriental.com – Fax (01344) 621 885 – Closed 25-26 December

Rest – Chinese – Menu £ 28/29 – Carte £ 31/45

◆ Stylish modern restaurant with a vibrantly hued interior. Private dining in attractive conservatory. An interesting menu of Chinese dishes prepared with originality and verve.

at Sunninghill **South : 1.5 mi. by A 329 on B 3020 – ✉ Ascot**

XX **Jade Fountain**

38 High St ✉ SL5 9NE – ✆ (01344) 627 070 – www.jadefountain-restaurant.co.uk – Fax (01344) 627 070

Rest – Chinese – Menu £ 21/27 – Carte £ 21/30

◆ Chinese restaurant specialising in sizzling dishes from Sichuan and Beijing - Peking duck, spring rolls and noodles amongst them. Also some Thai specialities.

ASCOTT-UNDER-WYCHWOOD – Oxfordshire – pop. 524 10 A2

London 83 mi. – Birmingham 66 mi. – Bristol 69 mi. – Leicester 73 mi.

The Swan Inn with rm

4 Shipton Rd ✉ OX7 6AY – ☎ (01993) 832 332 – www.swanatascott.com – Closed 25 December, Sunday dinner and Monday

5 rm – ♦£ 71 ♦♦£ 95/125

Rest – *(booking advisable at dinner)* Menu £ 20 (Sunday lunch) – Carte £ 21/29

◆ Traditional community pub with great atmosphere. Classic, quality cooking with dishes like pork belly or sausage and mash – and everything from the bread to the chips home-made. Contemporary bedrooms.

ASENBY – N. Yorks. – see Thirsk

ASH – Kent – 504 X30 9 D2

London 70 mi. – Canterbury 9 mi. – Dover 15 mi.

Great Weddington

Northeast : 0.5 mi. by A 257 on Weddington rd ✉ CT3 2AR – ☎ (01304) 813 407 – www.greatweddington.co.uk – Fax (01304) 812 531 – Closed 21 December-10 January

4 rm – ♦£ 80/90 ♦♦£ 105/120

Rest – *(by arrangement, communal dining)* Menu £ 35

◆ Charming Regency country house, ideally located for Canterbury and Dover. Well appointed drawing room and terrace. Thoughtfully furnished, carefully co-ordinated rooms. Communal dining room; owner an avid cook.

ENGLAND

ASHBOURNE – Derbyshire – 502 O24 – pop. 5 020 Great Britain 16 A2

London 146 mi. – Birmingham 47 mi. – Manchester 48 mi. – Nottingham 33 mi.

13 Market Pl ☎ (01335) 343666, ashbourneinfo@derbyshiredales.gov.uk

Dovedale★★ (Ilam Rock★) NW : 6 mi. by A 515

Callow Hall

Mappleton Rd, West : 0.75 mi. by Union St (off Market Pl) ✉ DE6 2AA – ☎ (01335) 300 900 – www.callowhall.co.uk – Fax (01335) 300 512

15 rm – ♦£ 105/140 ♦♦£ 195 – 1 suite **Rest** – Menu £ 25/45

◆ Victorian country house in 42 acres. Cosy period bar lounge. Spacious bedrooms in main house have views of parkland; those in former servants' wing recently refurbished. Modern European menu; home-smoked salmon.

the dining room

33 St Johns St ✉ DE6 1GP – ☎ (01335) 300 666 – www.thediningroomashbourne.co.uk – Closed 2 weeks Christmas, 1 week Easter, 1 week summer and Sunday-Wednesday

Rest – *(dinner only) (booking essential)* Menu £ 37 (Thursday-Friday) /45 (Saturday)

◆ Modern, stylish décor blends agreeably with period features including exposed beams and cast iron range. Well sourced, seasonal ingredients inform intricate modern dishes.

ASHBURTON – Devon – 503 I32 – pop. 3 309 2 C2

London 220 mi. – Exeter 20 mi. – Plymouth 25 mi.

Dartmoor National Park★★

Agaric with rm

30 and 36 North St ✉ TQ13 7QD – ☎ (01364) 654 478 – www.agaricrestaurant.co.uk – Closed 2 weeks August, 2 weeks Christmas, and Sunday-Tuesday

5 rm – ♦£ 50/65 ♦♦£ 135 **Rest** – *(booking essential)* Carte £ 29/38

◆ 200 year-old house, selling home-made jams, fudge and olives. Relaxed neighbourhood restaurant using a blend of cooking styles. Very stylish, individually themed bedrooms.

ASHFORD – Kent – 504 W30 – pop. 58 936 9 C2

London 56 mi. – Canterbury 14 mi. – Dover 24 mi. – Hastings 30 mi.

Access Channel Tunnel : Eurostar information and reservations (08705) 186186

18 The Churchyard (01233) 629165, tourism@ashford.gov.uk

Eastwell Manor

Eastwell Park, Boughton Lees, North : 3 mi. by A 28 on A 251 ✉ TN25 4HR – (01233) 213 000 – www.eastwellmanor.co.uk – Fax (01233) 635 530

20 rm – £ 110/265 £ 295 – 42 suites – £ 270/445

Rest *Manor* – Menu £ 18/38 – Carte £ 40/61

Rest *Brasserie* – (01233) 213 100 *(Closed Sunday dinner)* Menu £ 20 (dinner) – Carte £ 14/32

◆ Mansion house in formal gardens, replete with interesting detail including carved panelled rooms and stone fireplaces. Smart individual bedrooms. Manor offers seasonal menus. Swish brasserie in luxury spa with marbled entrance hall.

ASHFORD-IN-THE-WATER – Derbs. – 502 O24 – see Bakewell

ASHURST – W. Sussex – 504 T31 – see Steyning

ASHWATER – Devon 2 C2

London 218 mi. – Bude 16 mi. – Virginstow 3 mi.

Blagdon Manor

Beaworthy, Northwest : 2 mi. by Holsworthy rd on Blagdon rd ✉ EX21 5DF – (01409) 211 224 – www.blagdon.com – Fax (01409) 211 634 – Closed January

8 rm – £ 85 £ 180

Rest – *(Closed lunch Monday-Thursday) (booking essential) (residents only Monday and Sunday dinner)* Menu £ 21/35

◆ Proudly run former farmhouse in peaceful, rural location. Modern country house bedrooms, spotlessly kept, named after surrounding villages. Library, lounges and flag-floored bar. Classically-based cooking with a modern touch, served in dining room with conservatory extension.

ASKRIGG – North Yorkshire – 502 N21 – pop. 1 002 – ✉ Leyburn 22 A1

London 251 mi. – Kendal 32 mi. – Leeds 70 mi. – Newcastle upon Tyne 70 mi.

Yorebridge House

Bainbridge, West : 1 mi. ✉ DL8 3EE – (01969) 652 060 – www.yorebridgehouse.com – Fax (01969) 650 258

11 rm – £ 145 £ 240 **Rest** – Menu £ 40

◆ Lovingly restored former school with warm, hospitable owners. Modern, stylish and comfortable interior. Individually designed bedrooms, some with hot tubs. Locally sourced produce in relaxing dining room.

The Apothecary's House without rest

Main St ✉ DL8 3HT – (01969) 650 626 – www.apothecaryhouse.co.uk – Closed 1 January, 25-26 and 31 December

3 rm – £ 45 £ 75

◆ Built in 1756 by the local apothecary in centre of village; overlooks church. Combined lounge and breakfast room has fresh, modern feel. Rear bedroom boasts exposed timbers.

The Kings Arms

Market Place – (01969) 650 817 – Fax (01969) 650 856 – closed 1 week early January

Rest – Carte £ 21/30 **s**

◆ Characterful pub built in mid-18C by racehorse owner; what is now the bar area was once the tack room. Huge open fire, beamed ceilings and games room. Rustic, hearty cooking.

ASTON CANTLOW – Warwickshire – 503 O27 – pop. 1 843 19 C3

Great Britain

London 106 mi. – Birmingham 20 mi. – Stratford-upon-Avon 5 mi.

Mary Arden's House★ **AC**, SE : 2 mi. by Wilmcote Lane and Aston Cantlow Rd

The King's Head

21 Bearley Rd ✉ B95 6HY – ☎ (01789) 488 242 – www.thekh.co.uk – Fax (01789) 488 137 – Closed 25 December

Rest – Menu £ 15 – Carte £ 15/25

◆ Characterful black and white timbered, part 15C inn, set in a picturesque village. Seasonal menus feature traditional pub dishes, with local meats and fish to the fore. Regular duck suppers.

ASTON CLINTON – Buckinghamshire – 504 R28 – pop. 4 038 – ✉ Aylesbury 11 C2

London 42 mi. – Aylesbury 4 mi. – Oxford 26 mi.

West Lodge

45 London Rd ✉ HP22 5HL – ☎ (01296) 630 362 – www.westlodge.co.uk – Fax (01296) 630 151

9 rm – £ 55/72 £ 82/87

Rest – *(Closed Sunday) (dinner only) (residents only)* Menu £ 24 – Carte £ 24/29

◆ 19C former hunting lodge for Rothschild estate with walled Victorian garden. Bedrooms in converted outbuilding are largest/quietest. Balloon theme throughout adds interest. Conservatory dining room serving residents only.

ASTON ROWANT – Oxfordshire – pop. 2 512 – ✉ OX9 11 C2

London 45 mi. – Coventry 69 mi.

The Lambert Arms

London Rd, on A 40 ✉ OX49 5SB – ☎ (01844) 351 496 – www.lambertarms.com – Fax (01844) 351 893

42 rm – £ 79/85 £ 89/95, £ 5.95

Rest – *(Closed Sunday dinner)* Carte £ 20/37 **s**

◆ Traditional timbered inn boasts comfortable, modernised interior, with spacious, well-equipped bedrooms in purpose-built extension. Good French breakfasts. Contemporary dishes served in restaurant or spacious bar.

ASTON TIRROLD – Oxfordshire 10 B3

London 58 mi. – Reading 16 mi. – Streatley 4 mi.

The Sweet Olive at The Chequers Inn

Baker St ✉ OX11 9DD – ☎ (01235) 851 272 – www.sweet-olive.com – Closed February, 1 week July, 25 December, Sunday dinner and Wednesday

Rest – *(booking essential)* Carte £ 24/30

◆ British on the outside, French on the inside; it's cosy, friendly and popular with the locals. Blackboard menus feature interesting French, British and European dishes.

ATCHAM – Shrops. – 503 L25 – see Shrewsbury

AYTHORPE RODING – Essex – see Great Dunmow

AUSTWICK – North Yorkshire – 502 M21 – pop. 467 – ✉ Lancaster (lancs.) 22 A2

London 259 mi. – Kendal 28 mi. – Lancaster 20 mi. – Leeds 46 mi.

ENGLAND

Austwick Traddock

⊠ LA2 8BY – ✆ (015242) 51 224 – *www.thetraddock.co.uk* – *Fax (015242) 51 796*

10 rm – 🛉£ 85/95 🛉🛉£ 175/185

Rest – *(booking essential for non-residents)* Menu £ 17 (lunch) **s** – Carte £ 26/35 **s**

◆ A Georgian country house decorated with both English and Asian antiques. Bedrooms are individually styled to a high standard and overlook the secluded gardens. Dining room split into two rooms and lit by candlelight.

Austwick Hall

Southeast : 0.5 mi. on Townend Lane ⊠ *LA2 8BS* – ✆ *(015242) 51 794* – *www.austwickhall.co.uk* – *Closed January and 25 December*

5 rm – 🛉£ 140 🛉🛉£ 155 **Rest** – Menu £ 30

◆ Spacious and comfortable house with open fires and welcoming atmosphere. Located in a delightful village on the edge of the dales. Very much a family concern. A strong organic base to the cooking.

Wood View without rest

The Green ⊠ *LA2 8BB* – ✆ *(015242) 51 190* – *www.woodviewbandb.com* – *Fax (015242) 51 190*

5 rm – 🛉£ 45/55 🛉🛉£ 76

◆ In a charming spot on the village green, the cottage dates back to 17C with many of the original features still in place including exposed rafters in several bedrooms.

AVONWICK – Devon **2** C2

London 202 mi. – Plymouth 17 mi. – Totnes 8 mi.

The Turtley Corn Mill

Northwest : 1 mi. on Plymouth rd ⊠ *TQ10 9ES* – ✆ *(01364) 646 100* – *www.avonwick.net* – *Fax (01364) 646 101* – *Closed 25 December*

Rest – Carte £ 15/30

◆ Capacious 18C mill with a working water wheel, set in six acres on banks of River Glaze Brook. Light, airy style and buzzing atmosphere. Tasty dishes range from the traditional to the international. Spacious, comfortable bedrooms provide a host of luxuries.

AXBRIDGE – Somerset – **503** L30 – **pop. 2 025** **3** B2

London 142 mi. – Bristol 17 mi. – Taunton 27 mi. – Weston-Super-Mare 11 mi.

The Parsonage without rest

Parsonage Lane, Cheddar Rd, East : 0.75 mi. on A 371 ⊠ *BS26 2DN* – ✆ *(01934) 733 078* – *www.the-parsonage-axbridge.co.uk* – *Fax (01934) 733 078*

3 rm – 🛉£ 50 🛉🛉£ 62

◆ Former Victorian parsonage nestling in the southern slopes of the Mendip Hills overlooking the Somerset Levels. The comfortable bedrooms are tastefully furnished.

AXFORD – Wiltshire – pop. 1 717 – ⊠ Marlborough **4** D2

London 74 mi. – Marlborough 3 mi. – Swindon 15 mi.

The Red Lion Inn

⊠ *SN8 2HA* – ✆ *(01672) 520 271* – *www.redlionaxford.com* – *Closed 2 weeks after Christmas, Sunday dinner and Monday*

Rest – Carte £ 17/30

◆ 16C flint and red-brick pub overlooking the River Kennet and valley beyond; terrace boasts great views. Generous portions of traditional country cooking, with fish and game the specialities.

AXMINSTER – Devon – **503** L31 – **pop. 4 952** **2** D2

London 156 mi. – Exeter 27 mi. – Lyme Regis 5 mi. – Taunton 22 mi.

The Old Courthouse, Church St ✆ (01297) 34386, axminstertic@btopenworld.com

Lyme Regis★ - The Cobb★, SE : 5.5 mi. by A 35 and A 3070

Fairwater Head

Hawkchurch, Northeast : 5.25 mi. by B 3261 and A 35 off B 3165 ✉ EX13 5TX – ✆ (01297) 678 349 – www.fairwaterheadhotel.co.uk – Fax (01297) 678 459 – Closed January

16 rm – ♦£ 85/110 ♦♦£ 95/120

Rest – *(Closed lunch Monday-Tuesday)* Menu £ 30 (dinner) **s** – Carte lunch £ 26/33 **s**

◆ Edwardian hotel in flower-filled gardens. Tea and fresh cakes served in the afternoon. Many rooms have Axe Valley views. Attractive outlook over garden and countryside accompanies diners enjoying locally sourced cooking.

AYLESBURY – Buckinghamshire – 504 R28 – pop. 69 021 — 11 C2

Great Britain

London 46 mi. – Birmingham 72 mi. – Northampton 37 mi. – Oxford 22 mi.

The Kings Head, Kings Head Passage off Market Square ✆ (01296) 330559, tic@aylesburyvaledc.gov.uk

Weston Turville New Rd, ✆ (01296) 424 084

Aylesbury Golf Centre Bierton Hulcott Lane, ✆ (01296) 393 644

Waddesdon Manor★★, NW : 5.5 mi. by A 41 – Chiltern Hills★

Hartwell House

Oxford Rd, Southwest : 2 mi. on A 418 ✉ HP17 8NR – ✆ (01296) 747 444 – www.hartwell-house.com – Fax (01296) 747 450

36 rm – ♦£ 160/200 ♦♦£ 260, £ 7.50 – 10 suites

Rest *The Soane* – Menu £ 20 (lunch)/38 (Sunday-Thursday dinner) – Carte dinner £ 37/47

◆ Where Louis XVIII exiled the King of France. Impressive palatial house in 90 acres of parkland, boasting luxurious lounges, ornate furnishings and magnificent antique-filled bedrooms. Restaurant offers good value lunches and traditional country house cooking.

AYLESFORD – Kent – 504 V30 — 8 B1

London 37 mi. – Maidstone 3 mi. – Rochester 8 mi.

Hengist

7-9 High St ✉ ME20 7AX – ✆ (01622) 719 273 – www.hengistrestaurant.co.uk – Closed 26 December, 1 January, Sunday dinner and Monday

Rest – Menu £ 15 (lunch) – Carte £ 33/37

◆ Converted 16C town house, elegantly appointed throughout, with bonus of exposed rafters and smart private dining room upstairs. Accomplished modern cooking with seasonal base.

AYLESHAM – Kent – 504 X30 – pop. 3 643 — 9 D2

London 69 mi. – Maidstone 37 mi. – Ashford 23 mi. – Margate 18 mi.

at Barfreston Southwest 4 mi. by B2046 and then East following signs for Womenswold, Woolage and Barfreston

The Yew Tree

✉ CT15 7JH – ✆ (01304) 831 000 – www.yewtree.info – Closed 26-27 December and Sunday dinner

Rest – British – *(booking advisable)* Carte £ 23/31

◆ Nestled next to historic village church; tiny bar serves ales from local microbrewery. Precise, unfussy, flavoursome cooking uses locally sourced produce. Good value set lunch menu.

AYLMERTON – Norfolk – 504 X25 — 15 D1

London 138 mi. – Norwich 25 mi. – East Dereham 26 mi. – Taverham 23 mi.

Eiders without rest

Holt Rd ✉ NR11 8QA – ✆ (01263) 837 280 – www.eiders.co.uk – Closed 21 December-10 January

6 rm – ♦£ 60/80 ♦♦£ 80/120

◆ Whitewashed house with large lawned gardens, ornamental pond and swimming pool. Modern, spacious, ground floor bedrooms, 3 with balconies and pond views; excellent bathrooms.

ENGLAND

AYNHO – Northamptonshire – 504 Q28 – pop. 632 16 B3

London 73 mi. – Birmingham 66 mi. – Leicester 62 mi. – Coventry 48 mi.

Cartwright

1-5 Croughton Rd ✉ *OX17 3BE* – ☎ *(01869) 811 885*
– *www.oxfordshire-hotels.co.uk*

21 rm – †£ 90 ††£ 99/130 **Rest** – Menu £ 15/19 – Carte dinner £ 22/39

◆ Modernised 16C inn, ideally placed for Silverstone and Bicester Village. Spacious bedrooms come with complimentary wi-fi and are split between main house and rear conversion. Dining is an informal affair, with a seasonal menu of robust dishes.

AYSGARTH – North Yorkshire – 502 O21 22 A1

London 249 mi. – Ripon 28 mi. – York 56 mi.

George and Dragon Inn with rm

✉ *DL8 3AD* – ☎ *(01969) 663 358* – *www.ganddinn.com* – *Fax (01969) 633 773*

7 rm – †£ 40/55 ††£ 70/90 **Rest** – Menu £ 13/26 – Carte £ 18/30

◆ Laid-back coaching inn, close to the National Park and breathtaking waterfalls. Lunch ranges from snacks and pub classics to a good value three course set menu; dinner is more substantial. Comfy, individually styled bedrooms; one with a whirlpool bath.

BABBACOMBE – Torbay – 503 J32 – see Torquay

BABCARY – Somerset – 503 M30 4 C2

London 128 mi. – Glastonbury 12 mi. – Yeovil 12 mi.

The Red Lion Inn

✉ *TA11 7ED* – ☎ *(01458) 223 230* – *www.redlionbabcary.co.uk*
– *Fax (01458) 224 510* – *Closed Sunday dinner*

Rest – Carte £ 17/28

◆ Attractive stone-built thatched pub; a tasteful blend of the old and the new. Good use of locally sourced produce in satisfying and robust dishes, some with Asian influences.

BADINGHAM Suffolk – Suffolk – 504 Y27 – see Framlingham

BAGSHOT – Surrey – 504 R29 – pop. 5 247 7 C1

London 37 mi. – Reading 17 mi. – Southampton 49 mi.

Windlesham Grove End, ☎ (01276) 452 220

Pennyhill Park

London Rd , Southwest : 1 mi. on A 30 ✉ *GU19 5EU*
– ☎ *(01276) 471 774* – *www.exclusivehotels.co.uk* – *Fax (01276) 473 217*

112 rm – †£ 295 ††£ 295, £ 20 – 11 suites

Rest *Michael Wignall at The Latymer* – see restaurant listing

Rest *Brasserie* – *(buffet lunch)* Carte dinner £ 30/42

◆ Grand drive leads to impressive 19C ivy-clad manor house in 123 acres of parkland. Comfy lounges; traditional country house bedrooms with period furniture and some great views. Strong service. Top-class spa. Smart restaurant displays marble and stained glass.

Michael Wignall at The Latymer – at Pennyhill Park Hotel

London Rd , Southwest : 1 mi. on A30 ✉ *GU19 5EU*
– ☎ *(01276) 486 156* – *www.exclusivehotels.co.uk* – *Fax (01276) 473 217*
– *Closed 1-14 January, Saturday lunch, Sunday and Monday*

Rest – *(booking essential)* Menu £ 32/58

Spec. Tuna with teriyaki mackerel, scallops and carrot jelly. Confit and canon of lamb with haggis wonton and olive jus. Pear and frangipane tart with milk espuma and pear sorbet.

◆ Elegant restaurant with mock-rustic styling, soft lighting and chef's table in smart, glass-walled room. Concise à la carte offers ambitious, detailed and original dishes, carefully crafted from quality produce. Formal service.

BAKEWELL – Derbyshire – 502 O24 – pop. 3 676 Great Britain 16 A1

London 160 mi. – Derby 26 mi. – Manchester 37 mi. – Nottingham 33 mi.

Old Market Hall, Bridge St (01629) 816558, bakewell@peakdistrict.gov.uk

Chatsworth★★★ (Park and Garden★★★) **AC**, NE : 2.5 mi. by A 619 – Haddon Hall★★ **AC**, SE : 2 mi. by A 6

at Ashford-in-the-Water Northwest : 1.75 mi. by A 6 and A 6020 – Bakewell

Riverside House

Fennel St DE45 1QF – (01629) 814 275 – www.riversidehouse.co.uk – Fax (01629) 812 873

14 rm (dinner included) – £ 200 £ 295

Rest *The Riverside Room* – see restaurant listing

◆ Delightful former shooting lodge by River Wye. Comfortable, tastefully decorated rooms boast period features. Ground floor bedrooms in newer wing open onto garden.

The Riverside Room – at Riverside House Hotel

Fennel St DE45 1QF – (01629) 814 275 – www.riversidehouse.co.uk – Fax (01629) 812 873

Rest – Menu £ 15/40

◆ Popular restaurant serving classic French cooking; comprises Regency Room, Garden Room, Range Room and Conservatory.

BALSALL COMMON – W. Mids. – see Coventry

BAMBURGH – Northumberland – 501 O17 – pop. 582 Great Britain 24 B1

London 337 mi. – Edinburgh 77 mi. – Newcastle upon Tyne 51 mi.

Castle★ **AC**

Lord Crewe Arms rest,

Front Street NE69 7BL – (01668) 214 243 – www.lordcrewe.co.uk – Fax (01668) 214 273 – Closed December and January

17 rm – £ 55/110 £ 110/150

Rest *The Olive Tree* – *(bar lunch)* Carte £ 21/33

◆ Privately owned, 17C former coaching inn, in the shadow of the Norman castle. Spacious, comfy lounge and contemporary bedrooms. Characterful, beamed bar is more rustic in style. Italian classics in The Olive Tree.

at Waren Mill West : 2.75 mi. on B 1342 – Belford

Waren House

NE70 7EE – (01668) 214 581 – www.warenhousehotel.co.uk – Fax (01668) 214 484

13 rm – £ 90/123 £ 138/186 – 2 suites

Rest – *(dinner only)* Menu £ 32 s

◆ Personally run country house set in mature, tranquil grounds. Bedrooms, named after the owners' family members, mix classic and modern styles: some have four-posters and coastal views. Formal dining room boasts ornate ceiling; menus showcase local ingredients.

BAMPTON – Devon – 503 J31 – pop. 1 617 2 D1

London 189 mi. – Exeter 18 mi. – Minehead 21 mi. – Taunton 15 mi.

Bark House

Oakfordbridge, West : 3 mi. by B 3227 on A 396 EX16 9HZ – (01398) 351 236 – www.thebarkhouse.co.uk

6 rm – £ 64/74 £ 68/136

Rest – *(Closed Sunday-Tuesday) (dinner only) (booking essential for non-residents)* Menu £ 20

◆ Neat, personally run stone cottages which once stored wood from Exmoor forest. Bright bedrooms of different sizes are decorated in pretty floral fabrics. Terraced rear garden. Home-cooking proudly served in neat dining room.

The Quarrymans Rest with rm
Briton St ✉ EX16 9LN – ☎ (01398) 331 480 – www.thequarrymansrest.co.uk – Closed Sunday dinner
3 rm – †£ 40/50 ††£ 80 **Rest** – Carte £ 20/24
◆ Honest 17C village pub with traditional interior. Appealing, classical menu featuring local produce, regional influences and knowledgeable cooking. Simple, good value bedrooms.

BANBURY – Oxfordshire – 503 P27 – pop. 43 867 Great Britain **10** B1

London 76 mi. – Birmingham 40 mi. – Coventry 25 mi. – Oxford 23 mi.
Spiceball Park Rd ☎ (01295) 259855, banbury.tic@cherwell-dc.gov.uk
Cherwell Edge Chacombe, ☎ (01295) 711 591
Upton House★ **AC**, NW : 7 mi. by A 422

Banbury House rm, rest
Oxford Rd ✉ OX16 9AH – ☎ (01295) 259 361 – www.banburyhouse.co.uk – Fax (01295) 270 954 – Closed 24 December-2 January
64 rm – †£ 54/110 ††£ 92/200
Rest – *(closed Sunday dinner) (bar lunch)* Menu £ 25 **s**
◆ Georgian property combining the traditional with the more modern. Well-maintained bedrooms in contemporary styles. Bar popular for lunchtime snacks. Restaurant offers contemporary British menu.

at Milton South : 5.5 mi. by A 4260 – ✉ Banbury

The Black Boy Inn
✉ OX15 4HH – ☎ (01295) 722 111 – www.blackboyinn.com – Closed Sunday dinner
Rest – Carte £ 27/38
◆ 16C sand-coloured stone pub with traditional bar and spacious garden; popular with the locals. Wide-ranging à la carte displays largely British dishes and the odd international flavour.

at Sibford Gower West : 8 mi. by B 4035 – ✉ Banbury

The Wykham Arms
Temple Mill Rd ✉ OX15 5RX – ☎ (01295) 788 808 – www.wykhamarms.co.uk – Closed 25 December and 1 January
Rest – Carte approx. £ 28
◆ Thatched stone pub set down country lanes in a small village. Featuring local produce, menus range from bar snacks and lights bites to the full 3 courses. Good range of wines by the glass.

BANSTEAD – Surrey **7** D1

London 16 mi.

Tony Tobin @ Post
28 High St ✉ SM7 2LQ – ☎ (01737) 373 839 – www.postrestaurant.co.uk – Fax (01737) 360 742
Rest – *(Closed Bank Holidays) (dinner only Thursday-Saturday)* Menu £ 19 – Carte £ 19/40
Rest *Brasserie* – *(Closed 26 December and 1 January)* Menu £ 14 (lunch) – Carte £ 18/37
◆ Restaurant, brasserie and deli in former post office, owned by celebrity chef Tony Tobin; a piece of London brought to the suburbs. Informal dining upstairs in restaurant. Vast choice on menu in airy brasserie.

BARFRESTON – Kent – 504 X30 – see Aylesham

BARNARD CASTLE – Durham – 502 O20 – pop. 6 714 Great Britain **24** A3

London 258 mi. – Carlisle 63 mi. – Leeds 68 mi. – Middlesbrough 31 mi.
Woodleigh, Flatts Rd ☎ (01833) 690909, tourism@teesdale.gov.uk
Harmire Rd, ☎ (01833) 638 355
Bowes Museum★ **AC**
Raby Castle★ **AC**, NE : 6.5 mi. by A 688

Greta House without rest
89 Galgate ✉ DL12 8ES – ✆ (01833) 631 193 – www.gretahouse.co.uk
– Fax (01833) 631 193
3 rm – £ 50 £ 70
◆ Neat Victorian house with traditional lounge and stylish, individually decorated bedrooms; one with feature bath. Excellent hospitality. Complimentary sherry and homemade biscuits on arrival.

Homelands without rest
85 Galgate ✉ DL12 8ES – ✆ (01833) 638 757
– www.homelandsguesthouse.co.uk
5 rm – £ 40/75 £ 68/75
◆ Immaculately maintained 19C terraced house on main road. Cosy lounge and compact but pleasantly furnished, well-priced rooms, some overlooking the long mature rear garden.

at Whorlton East : 4.75 mi. by A 67

The Bridge Inn
✉ DL12 8XD – ✆ (01833) 627 341 – www.thebridgeinnrestaurant.co.uk
– Fax (01833) 627 995 – Closed 25-26 December, Monday and Tuesday
Rest – Menu £ 14/17 – Carte £ 23/30
◆ Sit in traditional bar or spacious, contemporary restaurant to enjoy precise, accomplished cooking with well-matched flavours. Big city dining in a beautiful countryside location.

at Greta Bridge Southeast : 4.5 mi. off A 66 – ✉ Barnard Castle

The Morritt rm,
✉ DL12 9SE – ✆ (01833) 627 232 – www.themorritt.co.uk
– Fax (01833) 627 392
27 rm – £ 85 £ 175
Rest *The Morritt* – Carte £ 24/34 **s**
Rest *Bistro/Bar* – Carte £ 25/37 **s**
◆ Personally run, 19C former coaching inn displaying a pleasant mix of old and new. Individually designed bedrooms blend contemporary décor with antiques, four-posters and interesting bedsteads. Oak panelled restaurant and cosy bistro offer modern menu. All day snacks available in the bar.

at Hutton Magna Southeast : 7.25 mi. by A 66

The Oak Tree Inn
✉ DL11 7HH – ✆ (01833) 627 371 – Closed 24-27 and 31 December, 1-2 January and Monday
Rest – *(dinner only) (booking essential)* Carte £ 26/33
◆ Small but charming whitewashed pub consisting of a single room. Run by a husband and wife team, he cooks, while she serves. Cooking is hearty and flavoursome with a rustic French feel.

at Romaldkirk Northwest : 6 mi. by A 67 on B 6277 – ✉ Barnard Castle

Rose and Crown with rm
✉ DL12 9EB – ✆ (01833) 650 213 – www.rose-and-crown.co.uk
– Fax (01833) 650 828 – Closed 24-26 December
12 rm – £ 89 £ 140/175
Rest – Menu £ 19/30
Rest *The Restaurant* – *(dinner only and Sunday lunch)* Menu £ 26
◆ Quintessential 18C English inn, set by Saxon church and surrounded by village greens. Choice of atmospheric bar adorned with horse brasses or rear brasserie serving classical fare. More formal restaurant offer seasonally changing four course dinner. Cosy, classical bedrooms boast flat screen TVs and Bose radios.

BARNSLEY – Gloucestershire – **503** O28 – see Cirencester

BARNSTAPLE – Devon – **503** H30 – **pop. 30 765** **2** C1

London 222 mi. – Exeter 40 mi. – Taunton 51 mi.

36 Boutport St ✆ (01271) 375000

Chulmleigh Leigh Rd, ✆ (01769) 580 519

Town★ - Long Bridge★

Arlington Court★★ (Carriage Collection★) **AC**, NE : 6 mi. by A 39

Old Custom House

The Strand ✉ EX31 1EU – ✆ (01271) 370 123 – www.jamesduckett.co.uk – Closed 1-14 January, 26-30 December, Sunday and Monday except Mother's Day and Easter

Rest – Menu £ 15 (lunch) – Carte dinner £ 25/38

◆ Characterful restaurant, with smart first floor dining room. Good value, classical dishes, presented in a modern style; tapas style 'small plates' at lunch; more formal dinner menu.

BARRASFORD – Northumberland **24** A2

London 309 mi. – Newcastle upon Tyne 29 mi. – Sunderland 42 mi. – Middlesbrough 66 mi.

Barrasford Arms with rm

✉ NE48 4AA – ✆ (01434) 681 237 – www.barrasfordarms.co.uk – Closed 25-26 December, Sunday dinner, Monday lunch and Bank Holidays

7 rm – †£ 65 ††£ 85 **Rest** – Menu £ 14/18 – Carte £ 19/27

◆ Close to Kielder Water and Hadrian's Wall, this personally run 19C stone inn has a traditional, homely atmosphere. Pub classics served at lunch; more substantial dishes at dinner. Modern, comfortable bedrooms.

BARROWDEN – Rutland **17** C2

London 94 mi. – Peterborough 17 mi. – Stamford 8 mi.

Exeter Arms with rm

28 Main St ✉ LE15 8EQ – ✆ (01572) 747 247 – www.exeterarms.com – Fax (01572) 747 247 – Closed Sunday dinner and Monday

3 rm – †£ 50 ††£ 79 **Rest** – Carte £ 19/22

◆ Traditional village inn with pleasant views over the green and duck pond. Menus offer well-priced, classical combinations. To the rear is the pub's very own micro-brewery. Simple, cottage-style bedrooms overlook the water.

BARSTON – West Midlands – **504** O26 **19** C2

London 110 mi. – Birmingham 17 mi. – Coventry 11 mi.

The Malt Shovel

Barston Lane, West : 0.75 mi. ✉ B92 0JP – ✆ (01675) 443 223 – www.themaltshovelatbarston.com – Fax (01675) 443 223 – Closed Sunday dinner

Rest – *(lunch bookings not accepted)* Menu £ 25 (dinner) – Carte approx. £ 28

◆ Sizeable ivy-clad pub with large garden. Wide-ranging selection of fresh, seasonal dishes on traditional bar menu; more elaborate set course dinner and fish specials in stylish restaurant.

BARTON-ON-SEA – Hampshire – **503** P31 **6** A3

London 108 mi. – Bournemouth 11 mi. – Southampton 24 mi. – Winchester 35 mi.

Pebble Beach with rm

Marine Drive ✉ BH25 7DZ – ✆ (01425) 627 777 – www.pebblebeach-uk.com – Fax (01425) 610 689

3 rm – †£ 70 ††£ 100, £ 6.50 **Rest** – Seafood – Carte £ 29/49

◆ Cliff-top position: striking terrace views over Solent and The Needles. Bright, modish interior with large windows. Wide range of choice on modern menus. Well-equipped rooms.

BARWICK – Somerset – **503** M31 – see Yeovil

BASHALL EAVES – Lancashire – see Clitheroe

BASILDON – Essex – 504 V29 – pop. 99 876 13 C3

London 30 mi. – Chelmsford 17 mi. – Southend-on-Sea 13 mi.
Clayhill Lane, Kingswood, ✆ (01268) 533 297

Langdon Hills Bulphan Lower Dunton Rd, ✆ (01268) 548 444

at Wickford North : 5.25 mi. by A 132 – ✉ Basildon

Chichester
rm, rest,

Old London Rd, Rawreth, East : 2.75 mi. by A 129 ✉ SS11 8UE – ✆ (01268) 560 555 – www.chichesterhotel.com – Fax (01268) 560 580
35 rm – £ 55/69 £ 55/69, £ 9.50
Rest *Chichester* – *(dinner only and Sunday lunch)* Menu £ 16/19 – Carte dinner £ 18/23
◆ Traditional, family-run hotel surrounded by farmland. Open lounge and immaculately-kept bedrooms set around central courtyard. Simply furnished restaurant serves tried-and-tested dishes.

BASLOW – Derbyshire – 502 P24 – pop. 1 184 – ✉ Bakewell 16 A1

Great Britain

London 161 mi. – Derby 27 mi. – Manchester 35 mi. – Sheffield 13 mi.
Chatsworth★★★ (Park and Garden★★★) **AC**

The Cavendish

Church Lane, on A 619 ✉ DE45 1SP – ✆ (01246) 582 311 – www.cavendish-hotel.net – Fax (01246) 582 312
23 rm – £ 158/171 £ 194/214, £ 17.95 – 1 suite
Rest *The Gallery* – Menu £ 39
Rest *Garden Room* – Carte £ 25/32
◆ Well established, elegant hotel; handsomely decorated, with antiques, oil paintings and log fires. Individually furnished, country house style bedrooms. Classical cooking served in The Gallery, with table in kitchen for watching chefs. Conservatory Garden Room with views of Chatsworth Estate.

Fischer's at Baslow Hall with rm

Calver Rd, on A 623 ✉ DE45 1RR – ✆ (01246) 583 259 – www.fischers-baslowhall.co.uk – Fax (01246) 583 818 – Closed dinner 24 and 31 December and 25-26 December
10 rm – £ 100/140 £ 150/220, £ 6 – 1 suite
Rest – *(closed Sunday dinner to non-residents and Monday lunch) (booking essential)* Menu £ 33/48 – Carte dinner £ 63/68
Spec. Scallops with sweetcorn purée, basil and popcorn crisps. Tasting of pork with apple purée, black pudding and sherry jus. Raspberry soufflé with raspberry sorbet.
◆ Edwardian manor house with impressive formal grounds and walled vegetable garden. Classically based and accomplished cooking, with the occasional modern twist, uses much local produce. Comfortable bedrooms in main house; garden rooms larger.

Rowley's

Church Street ✉ DE45 1RY – ✆ (01246) 583 880 – www.rowleysrestaurant.co.uk – Closed 26 December, 1 January and Sunday dinner
Rest – Carte £ 27/39
◆ Contemporary restaurant and bar set over two floors; downstairs with view of open plan kitchen. Modern menu, with produce sourced from in and around Peak District.

BASSENTHWAITE – Cumbria – 501 K19 – pop. 433 21 A2

London 300 mi. – Carlisle 24 mi. – Keswick 7 mi.

Armathwaite Hall

West : 1.5 mi. on B 5291 ✉ CA12 4RE – ✆ (017687) 76 551 – www.armathwaite-hall.com – Fax (017687) 76 220
42 rm – £ 145/155 £ 240/370 **Rest** – Menu £ 25/45
◆ Lakeside mansion dominates tranquil 400-acre woods and deer park. Rooms, some in rebuilt stables, vary in size and, like the panelled hall, marry modern and period fittings. 'Old-World' restaurant with carved oak ceiling and fireplace.

ENGLAND

The Pheasant

Southwest : 3.25 mi. by B 5291 on Wythop Mill rd, ✉ CA13 9YE – ✆ (017687) 76 234 – www.the-pheasant.co.uk – Fax (017687) 76 002 – Closed 25 December
15 rm ☕ – 🚹£ 83/109 🚹🚹£ 156/200 **Rest** – Menu £ 28/34

◆ Bright bedrooms, sensitively and individually updated, in a rural 16C coaching inn. Firelit bar with oak settles, local prints and game fish trophies serves regional ales. Charmingly simple restaurant decorated with chinaware.

Overwater Hall

Northeast : 0.75 mi. by Uldale rd – ✆ (017687) 76 566 – www.overwaterhall.co.uk – Fax (017687) 76 921 – Closed 29 November-3 December and first 2 weeks January
11 rm (dinner included) ☕ – 🚹£ 150/200 🚹🚹£ 200/260
Rest – *(booking advisable)* Menu £ 45 (dinner) – Carte lunch approx. £ 16

◆ Personally run Georgian house set in 18 acres, with charming country house feel. Open fires, cosy lounge and comfortable, individually styled bedrooms. Formal dining room serves six course dinners using local, seasonal produce.

BATCOMBE – Somerset – 503 M30 – pop. 391 – ✉ Shepton Mallet 4 C2

London 130 mi. – Bournemouth 50 mi. – Bristol 24 mi. – Salisbury 40 mi.

The Three Horseshoes Inn with rm

✉ BA4 6HE – ✆ (01749) 850 359 – www.thethreehorseshoesinn.co.uk – Fax (01749) 850 615 – Closed 25 December dinner, Sunday dinner and Monday
3 rm ☕ – 🚹£ 55/75 🚹🚹£ 75 **Rest** – Carte £ 20/33

◆ Passionately run pub set down a country lane in a peaceful vale. Produce comes from the garden, roaming poultry and local organic suppliers. Honest, classical cooking displays a French bias. Bedrooms are bijou, cosy and neat.

Y. Duhamel/MICHELIN

BATH

County: Bath and North East Somerset
Michelin regional map: 503 M29
London 119 mi. – Bristol 13 mi.
– Southampton 63 mi.
– Taunton 49 mi.

Population: 90 144
Great Britain
Map reference: 4 C2

PRACTICAL INFORMATION

Tourist Information

Abbey Chambers, Abbey Church Yard ✆ (0906) 711 2000, tourism@bathnes.gov.uk

Golf Courses

27 Tracy Park Wick Bath Rd, ✆ (0117) 937 18 00

18 Lansdown, ✆ (01225) 422 138

9 Entry Hill, ✆ (01225) 834 248

SIGHTS

In town

City★★★ - Royal Crescent★★★ AV (No.1 Royal Crescent★★**AC** AV **A**) – The Circus★★★ AV – Museum of Costume★★★ **AC** AV **M7** – Roman Baths★★ **AC** BX **D** – Holburne Museum and Crafts Study Centre★★ **AC** Y **M5** – Pump Room★ BX **B** - Assembly Rooms★ AV – Bath Abbey★ BX – Pulteney Bridge★ BV – Bath Industrial Heritage Centre★ **AC** AV **M1** – Lansdown Crescent★★ (Somerset Place★) Y – Camden Crescent★ Y – Beckford Tower and Museum **AC** (prospect★) Y **M6** – Museum of East Asian Art★ AV **M9** – Orange Grove★ BX

On the outskirts

Claverton (American Museum★★ **AC**, Claverton Pumping Station★ **AC**) E : 3 mi. by A 36 Y

In the surrounding area

Corsham Court★★ **AC**, NE : 8.5 mi. by A 4 – Dyrham Park★ **AC**, N : 6.5 mi. by A 4 and A 46

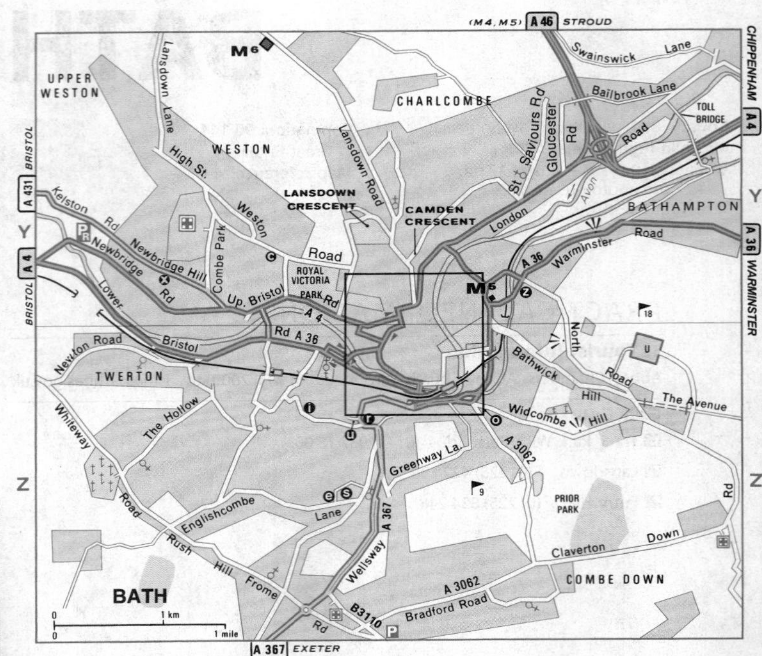

The Royal Crescent

16 Royal Crescent ✉ *BA1 2LS* – ✆ *(01225) 823 333* – *www.royalcrescent.co.uk*
– *Fax (01225) 339 401* AV**a**

35 rm – 🛉 £ 215/310 🛉🛉 £ 460/545 – 10 suites

Rest *The Dower House* – see restaurant listing

◆ Professionally run townhouse in sweeping Georgian crescent, boasting smart fire-lit entrance, period drawing room/library and stylish spa. Elegant Georgian bedrooms display antiques.

Bath Spa

rm, rest,

Sydney Rd ✉ *BA2 6JF* – ✆ *(0870) 400 82 22* – *www.bathspahotel.com*
– *Fax (01225) 444 006* Y**z**

118 rm – 🛉 £ 275 🛉🛉 £ 275, £ 21 – 11 suites

Rest *Vellore* – *(dinner only) (booking essential)* Carte £ 33/48

Rest *Alfresco* – Carte £ 22/41

◆ Impressive 19C mansion in mature gardens; refurbished, with new wing of rooms. Period lounges and contemporary bedrooms; full butler service in Imperial Suites. Superb spa. Vellore is smart with intimate lounge and terrace. Alfresco more informal, with Mediterranean menus.

Bath Priory

Weston Rd ✉ *BA1 2XT* – ✆ *(01225) 331 922* – *www.thebathpriory.co.uk*
– *Fax (01225) 448 276* Y**c**

26 rm – 🛉 £ 185/380 🛉🛉 £ 185/380

Rest – Menu £ 32/70

◆ Impressive Georgian house with mature gardens, classical guest areas, sumptuous sitting room and smart spa. Luxurious bedrooms blend the traditional and the modern. Designer bathrooms. Two dining rooms; the smaller more romantic, the larger more modern. Ambitious cooking uses some unexpected combinations.

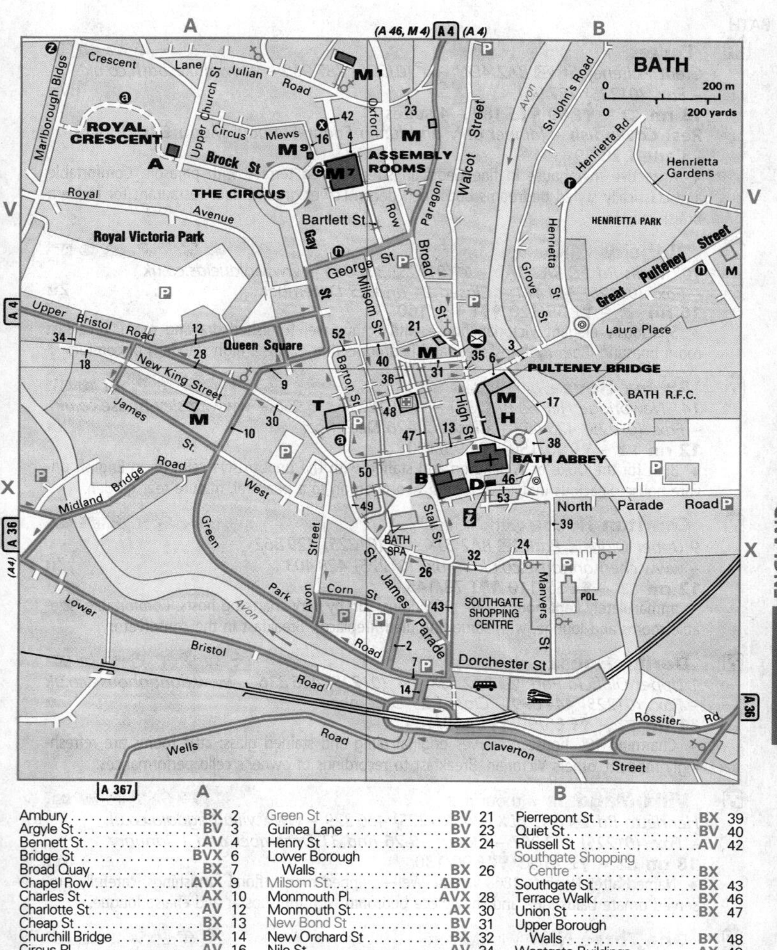

Street		No.
Ambury	BX	2
Argyle St	BV	3
Bennett St	AV	4
Bridge St	BVX	6
Broad Quay	BX	7
Chapel Row	AVX	9
Charles St	AX	10
Charlotte St	AV	12
Cheap St	BX	13
Churchill Bridge	BX	14
Circus Pl.	AV	16
Gay St	AV	
Grand Parade	BX	17
Great Stanhope St	AV	18
Green St	BV	21
Guinea Lane	BV	23
Henry St	BX	24
Lower Borough Walls	BX	26
Milsom St	ABV	
Monmouth Pl.	AVX	28
Monmouth St	AX	30
New Bond St	BV	31
New Orchard St	BX	32
Nile St	AV	34
Northgate St	BVX	35
Old Bond St	BX	36
Orange Grove	BX	38
Pierrepont St	BX	39
Quiet St	BV	40
Russell St	AV	42
Southgate Shopping Centre	BX	
Southgate St	BX	43
Terrace Walk	BX	46
Union St	BX	47
Upper Borough Walls	BX	48
Westgate Buildings	AX	49
Westgate St	ABX	50
Wood St	AV	52
York St	BX	53

Homewood Park

Abbey Lane, Hinton Charterhouse, Southeast : 6.5 mi. on A 36 ✉ BA2 7TB – ✆ (01225) 723 731 – www.homewoodpark.co.uk – Fax (01225) 723 820

19 rm – 🛉£ 205 🛉🛉£ 185/385 **Rest** – Menu £ 18/29 – Carte £ 29/44

◆ Well-proportioned bedrooms, with views of the idyllic wooded gardens and croquet lawn, and cosy country house drawing rooms retain strong elements of the Georgian interior. Ask for dining room window table when garden is in full bloom.

Queensberry

Russel St ✉ BA1 2QF – ✆ (01225) 447 928 – www.thequeensberry.co.uk – Fax (01225) 446 065 AV **x**

29 rm – 🛉£ 120/170 🛉🛉£ 120/425, ☕ £ 15

Rest *Olive Tree* – see restaurant listing

◆ Classy boutique merger of Georgian town house décor with contemporary furnishing, understated style and well-chosen detail. Ample, unfussy rooms; pretty courtyard garden.

Dukes
Great Pulteney St ✉ *BA2 4DN – ☎ (01225) 787 960 – www.dukesbath.co.uk – Fax (01225) 787 961* BV**n**
13 rm ☕ – 🚹£ 99 🚹🚹£ 189 – 4 suites
Rest ***Cavendish*** – *(dinner only and lunch Friday-Sunday)* Menu £ 16 (lunch) – Carte £ 28/39
◆ Attractive townhouse in fine Georgian street. Paved terrace with parasols. Comfortable and classically styled bedrooms boast rich décor. Lower ground floor restaurant for modern British cuisine.

Oldfields without rest
102 Wells Rd ✉ *BA2 3AL – ☎ (01225) 317 984 – www.oldfields.co.uk – Fax (01225) 444 471 – Closed 24 and 25 December* Z**u**
16 rm ☕ – 🚹£ 55/120 🚹🚹£ 120/160
◆ Spaciously elegant Victorian house with comfy, well-furnished drawing room, breakfast room boasting 'Bath rooftops' view and bedrooms that exude a high standard of comfort.

Apsley House without rest
141 Newbridge Hill ✉ *BA1 3PT – ☎ (01225) 336 966 – www.apsley-house.co.uk – Fax (01225) 425 462 – Closed 24-26 December* Y**x**
12 rm ☕ – 🚹£ 90/150 🚹🚹£ 95/180
◆ Built for the Duke of Wellington and staffed with the unobtrusive calm of an English private house. Spacious individual rooms; two open on to a peaceful, mature rear garden.

Cheriton House without rest
9 Upper Oldfield Park ✉ *BA2 3JX – ☎ (01225) 429 862 – www.cheritonhouse.co.uk – Fax (01225) 428 403* Z**u**
12 rm ☕ – 🚹£ 55/110 🚹🚹£ 78/145
◆ Immaculately kept house with 19C origins, run by very charming hosts. Comfortable, sizeable rooms and lounge, with some fine tiled fireplaces. Breakfast in the conservatory.

Dorian House without rest
1 Upper Oldfield Park ✉ *BA2 3JX – ☎ (01225) 426 336 – www.dorianhouse.co.uk – Fax (01225) 444 699 – Closed 25 December* Z**u**
11 rm ☕ – 🚹£ 65/99 🚹🚹£ 110/165
◆ Charming 19C house preserves original tiling and stained glass; attic rooms are refreshingly modern, others Victorian. Breakfast to recordings of owner's cello performances.

Villa Magdala without rest
Henrietta Rd ✉ *BA2 6LX – ☎ (01225) 466 329 – www.villamagdala.co.uk – Fax (01225) 483 207 – Closed 25-26 and 31 December and 1 January* BV**r**
18 rm ☕ – 🚹£ 75/95 🚹🚹£ 90/130
◆ Named after Napier's 1868 victory. Well-equipped rooms, floral furnishings; carefully preserved ornate balustrade and showpiece bedroom with four-poster and chaise longue.

One Three Nine without rest
139 Wells Rd ✉ *BA2 3AL – ☎ (01225) 314 769 – www.139bath.co.uk – Fax (01225) 443 079 – Closed 24-25 December* Z**r**
10 rm ☕ – 🚹£ 65/130 🚹🚹£ 85/185
◆ Unassuming Victorian building conceals the chic, bold décor of a stylish boutique hotel. Individually styled bedrooms may include four-posters or spa baths. Excellent terrace breakfast.

The Town House without rest
7 Bennett St ✉ *BA1 2QJ – ☎ (01225) 422 505 – www.thetownhousebath.co.uk – Fax (01225) 422 505 – Closed Christmas* AV**c**
3 rm ☕ – 🚹£ 125 🚹🚹£ 125
◆ Welcoming 18C house in excellent location, designed by John Wood and rebuilt after war damage. Spacious bedrooms with South African wildlife décor. Communal breakfast.

Lavender House without rest
17 Bloomfield Park, (off Bloomfield Rd) ✉ *BA2 2BY – ☎ (01225) 314 500 – www.lavenderhouse-bath.com* Z**s**
5 rm ☕ – 🚹£ 60/65 🚹🚹£ 90/120
◆ New owners have made a major investment in this Edwardian house. Rooms have plenty of antiques but also boast a modern, clean feel. Breakfast is served family-style.

ENGLAND

Meadowland without rest
36 Bloomfield Park, off Bloomfield Rd ✉ BA2 2BX – ✆ (01225) 311 079
– www.meadowlandbath.co.uk – Fax (01225) 580 055
– Closed Christmas-New Year Ze
3 rm – †£ 55/65 ††£ 105/120
◆ Small suburban guesthouse with a welcoming ambience; comfortably furnished and immaculately maintained accommodation. A neat breakfast room gives onto a lawned garden.

Athole House without rest
33 Upper Oldfield Park ✉ BA2 3JX – ✆ (01225) 320 000
– www.atholehouse.co.uk – Fax (01225) 320 009 – Closed Christmas
4 rm – †£ 60 ††£ 95 Zi
◆ Spacious, bay windowed Victorian guesthouse with large garden, away from city centre. Bright breakfast room; conservatory lounge. Light, airy, contemporary bedrooms.

XXXX **The Dower House** – at The Royal Crescent Hotel
16 Royal Crescent ✉ BA1 2LS – ✆ (01225) 823 333
– www.royalcrescent.co.uk – Fax (01225) 339 401 AVa
Rest – Menu £ 22/60
◆ Plush, contemporary dining room with swish bar, spacious lounge and lovely garden. Creative, seasonal cooking is underpinned by a French base. Attentive, understated service.

XX **Olive Tree** – at Queensberry Hotel
Russel St ✉ BA1 2QF – ✆ (01225) 447 928 – Fax (01225) 446 065 – Closed Monday lunch AVx
Rest – Menu £ 18 (lunch) – Carte £ 31/46
◆ Up-to-date restaurant with a classy, stylish and contemporary ambience. Modern artworks adorn the split-level basement. Modern British cooking. Helpful staff.

X **Hole in the Wall**
16 George St ✉ BA1 2EH – ✆ (01225) 425 242 – www.theholeinthewall.co.uk
– Closed 25 December and 1 January AVn
Rest – Menu £ 14 (lunch) – Carte £ 20/34
◆ Once a starting point of British culinary renaissance; former coal hole mixes whitewashed walls, antique chairs and a relaxed mood. Slightly eclectic cuisine.

X **Bistro La Barrique**
31 Barton Street ✉ BA1 1HG – ✆ (01225) 463 861 – www.bistrolabarrique.co.uk
– Closed 25-26 December and first week January AXa
Rest – French – Carte £ 21/28
◆ Unpretentious bistro-style restaurant, with sheltered courtyard for terrace dining. Small, good value menu of 'petits plats'; classic French dishes with some Mediterranean twists.

The Marlborough Tavern
35 Marlborough Buildings ✉ BA1 2LY – ✆ (01225) 423 731
– www.marlborough-tavern.com – Closed 25 December and Sunday dinner
Rest – *(booking advisable)* Carte £ 20/30 AVz
◆ Spacious, modern pub near the Royal Crescent and Royal Victoria Park. Unfussy, seasonal and local cooking; big on flavour and big of portion. Friendly, attentive service.

White Hart
Widcombe Hill ✉ BA2 6AA – ✆ (01225) 338 053 – www.whitehartbath.co.uk
– Closed 25-26 December, 1 January, Sunday dinner and Bank Holidays
Rest – *(booking essential at dinner)* Carte £ 20/35 Zo
◆ 'Keep it simple', the chef's motto says it all; quality, local produce and unfussy presentation create a concise but hearty British menu. Eat at worn tables or on the attractive terrace.

at Box **Northeast : 4.75 mi. on A 4 - Y – ✉ Bath**

The Northey
Bath Road ✉ SN13 8AE – ✆ (01225) 742 333 – www.ohhcompany.co.uk
Rest – Carte £ 20/35
◆ Traditional exterior belies modern Mediterranean-styled interior, mostly set for dining. Tasty mix of Mediterranean and British cooking on menu. Live jazz every other week.

ENGLAND

at Colerne **Northeast : 6.5 mi. by A 4 - Y - Batheaston rd and Bannerdown Rd – ✉ Chippenham**

Lucknam Park

North : 0.5 mi. on Marshfield rd ✉ SN14 8AZ – ✆ (01225) 742 777 – www.lucknampark.co.uk – Fax (01225) 743 536

36 rm – †£ 280 ††£ 455, ☕ £ 19.50 – 5 suites

Rest ***The Park and The Brasserie*** – see restaurant listing

◆ Grand Palladian mansion with tree-lined drive, rich décor, luxurious furnishings and sumptuous fabrics. Top class facilities include impressive spa complex and renowned equestrian centre. Extremely comfortable bedrooms.

The Park – at Lucknam Park Hotel

North : 0.5 mi. on Marshfield rd ✉ SN14 8AZ – ✆ (01225) 742 777 – www.lucknampark.co.uk – Fax (01225) 743 536 – Closed Sunday dinner and Monday

Rest – *(dinner only and Sunday lunch) (booking essential)* Menu £ 35/65

Spec. Scallops with brandade fritters, tomato and cumin vinaigrette. Trio of lamb, with green olive purée, potato terrine and watercress. Croustillant of pineapple with rum and raisin parfait and coconut sorbet.

◆ Located within an impressive mansion, an opulent dining room with skilled, amiable service and a knowledgeable kitchen team. Classical menus display modern European influences, with dishes expertly crafted from locally sourced farm produce.

The Brasserie – at Lucknam Park Hotel

North : 0.5 mi. on Marshfield rd ✉ SN14 8AZ – ✆ (01225) 742 777 – www.lucknampark.co.uk – Fax (01225) 743 536 – Closed dinner 24 and 31 December, 25-26 December and 1 January

Rest – Menu £ 19/27 – Carte £ 30/33

◆ Set in a state-of-the-art spa complex, this informal all day brasserie follows a 'wellbeing' theme. Wide-ranging menus offer light, healthy dishes; concise set selection available at lunch.

at Monkton Combe **Southeast : 4.5 mi. by A 36 - Y – ✉ Bath**

Wheelwrights Arms with rm

Church Lane ✉ BA2 7HB – ✆ (01225) 722 287 – www.wheelwrightsarms.co.uk – Fax (01225) 722 259

7 rm ☕ – †£ 95 ††£ 145 **Rest** – Menu £ 14 (lunch) – Carte £ 18/26

◆ Intimate 18C pub with regularly-stoked log fire and cosy snug, where honest, hearty cooking comes in portions large enough to revive the most exhausted of walkers. Luxurious bedrooms in converted workshop.

at Combe Hay **Southwest : 5 mi. by A 367 – ✉ Bath**

The Wheatsheaf with rm

✉ BA2 7EG – ✆ (01225) 833 504 – www.wheatsheafcombehay.com – Closed 25 December, Sunday dinner and Monday except Bank Holidays when open for lunch

3 rm ☕ – †£ 140 ††£ 140/150

Rest – Menu £ 19 (lunch) – Carte £ 19/55

◆ Picture perfect pub with a stylish interior. French and British influences inform the concise, contemporary menu, which displays refined, seasonal and flavoursome cooking. Chic bedrooms feature luxury showers; breakfast times are flexible.

BATTLE – East Sussex – 504 V31 – pop. 5 190 Great Britain **8** B3

London 55 mi. – Brighton 34 mi. – Folkestone 43 mi. – Maidstone 30 mi.

Battle and Bexhill TIC, Battle Abbey, High St ✆ (01424) 773721, battletic@rother.gov.uk

Town★ – Abbey and Site of the Battle of Hastings★ **AC**

Powder Mills

Powdermill Lane, South : 1.5 mi. by A 2100 on Catsfield rd ✉ TN33 0SP – ✆ (01424) 775 511 – www.powdermillshotel.com – Fax (01424) 774 540
40 rm – £ 115 ££ 140/350
Rest *Orangery* – Menu £ 20/30
◆ Part Georgian gunpowder mill in 150 acres of woods and lakes. Individually decorated rooms - more sizable in annex and with better views - combine antiques and modern pieces. Dining room terrace overlooks pool.

Nobles

17 High St ✉ TN33 0AE – ✆ (01424) 774 422 – www.noblesrestaurant.co.uk – Closed 1 week Christmas-New Year, Sunday and Bank Holidays
Rest – Menu £ 14/18 (weekday dinner) – Carte £ 23/30
◆ Simple, tasteful eatery with terrace, in heart of historical high street. Regularly changing menus offer unfussy classical dishes of local seasonal produce, with the occasional twist.

BAUGHURST – Hampshire 6 B1

London 61 mi. – Camberley 28 mi. – Farnborough 27 mi.

The Wellington Arms

Baughurst Rd, Southwest : 0.75 mi. ✉ RG26 5LP – ✆ (0118) 982 0110 – www.thewellingtonarms.com – Closed Sunday dinner, Monday and lunch Tuesday
Rest – *(booking essential)* Menu £ 18 (Wednesday-Friday lunch) – Carte £ 18/30
◆ Cosy, characterful former hunting lodge. Blackboard menu features flavoursome, modern British cooking, with pub favourites at lunch. They keep chickens and bees, and grow their own veg.

BEACONSFIELD – Buckinghamshire – 504 S29 – pop. 12 292 11 D3

London 26 mi. – Aylesbury 19 mi. – Oxford 32 mi.
18 Beaconsfield Seer Green, ✆ (01494) 676 545

Crazy Bear

73 Wycombe End ✉ HP9 1LX – ✆ (01494) 673 086 – www.crazybeargroup.co.uk – Fax (01494) 730 183
10 rm – £ 175 ££ 175/430
Rest The Thai – *see restaurant listing*
Rest *English* – *(booking advisable)* Menu £ 19 (lunch) – Carte £ 32/39
◆ Theatrical bedrooms each with their own unique features including leather padded walls and baths which fill from the ceiling. Bars are the ultimate in boutique style, with rich, flamboyant décor. Voluptuous style and European menu in the English restaurant.

The Thai – at Crazy Bear Hotel

73 Wycombe End ✉ HP9 1LX – ✆ (01494) 673 086 – www.crazybeargroup.co.uk – Fax (01494) 730 183
Rest – Thai – *(booking essential)* Menu £ 35 (dinner) – Carte £ 28/46
◆ Dine on authentic, well presented Thai dishes in sumptuous surroundings, with a theatrical design that includes chandeliers, flock wallpaper and studded leather chairs. Personable service.

at Wooburn Common Southwest : 3.5 mi. by A 40 – ✉ Beaconsfield

Chequers Inn

Kiln Lane, Southwest : 1 mi. on Bourne End rd ✉ HP10 0JQ – ✆ (01628) 529 575 – www.chequers-inn.com – Fax (01628) 850 124 – Closed dinner 25 December and 1 January
17 rm – £ 100 ££ 108, £ 9.95
Rest – Menu £ 18 (weekday lunch)/24 – Carte £ 24/36
◆ Attractive 17C red-brick former inn: family-owned and run since 1975. Cosy beamed bar and spacious leather-furnished lounge. Good-sized bedrooms boast flat screen TVs and wi-fi. Choice of bar snacks, or more ambitious dishes in the clothed rear restaurant.

ENGLAND

BEADNELL – Northumberland – 501 P17 — 24 B1

London 341 mi. – Edinburgh 81 mi. – Newcastle upon Tyne 47 mi.

Beach Court without rest

Harbour Rd ✉ NE67 5BJ – ✆ (01665) 720 225 – www.beachcourt.com – Fax (01665) 721 499 – Closed 1 week Christmas

3 rm – †£ 75 ††£ 99/159

◆ Mock-baronial house, superbly set right on the beachfront: ask for the turret room. Traditionally furnished, with bric-a-brac aplenty and doves in the garden. Excellent hospitality.

BEAMHURST – Staffs. – see Uttoxeter

BEAMINSTER – Dorset – 503 L31 – pop. 2 791 — 3 B3

London 154 mi. – Exeter 45 mi. – Taunton 30 mi. – Weymouth 29 mi.

Chedington Court South Perrott, ✆ (01935) 891 413

Bridge House

3 Prout Bridge ✉ DT8 3AY – ✆ (01308) 862 200 – www.bridge-house.co.uk – Fax (01308) 863 700

14 rm – †£ 85/120 ††£ 170/205

Rest – Carte £ 29/35

◆ Priest's house reputed to date back to the 1200s. Large bedrooms, in the new block, with cheerful floral fabrics. Firelit lounge, charming walled garden, informal, rural feel. Oak beamed restaurant with conservatory.

ENGLAND

BEARSTED – Kent – 504 V30 – see Maidstone

BEAULIEU – Hampshire – 503 P31 – pop. 726 – ✉ Brockenhurst — 6 B2

Great Britain

London 102 mi. – Bournemouth 24 mi. – Southampton 13 mi. – Winchester 23 mi.

Town★★ - National Motor Museum★★ **AC**

Buckler's Hard★ (Maritime Museum★ **AC**) SE : 2 m

Montagu Arms

Palace Lane ✉ SO42 7ZL – ✆ (01590) 612 324 – www.montaguarmshotel.co.uk – Fax (01590) 612 188

18 rm – †£ 139 ††£ 180 – 4 suites

Rest *The Terrace* – see restaurant listing

Rest *Monty's Brasserie* – Carte £ 21/27

◆ Ivy-covered inn dating back to 1742, set in beautiful gardens in the heart of the New Forest. Cosy panelled lounge boasts roaring log fire. Bedrooms are comfy and well-kept; some have four-posters. Old favourites served in welcoming Monty's.

The Terrace – at Montagu Arms Hotel

Palace Lane ✉ SO42 7ZL – ✆ (01590) 612 324 – www.montaguarmshotel.co.uk – Fax (01590) 612 188

Rest – Menu £ 23 (lunch) – Carte £ 46/56

Spec. Scallops with glazed pork belly, apple and radish salad. Sea bass with Jersey Royals, crab and samphire. Blackberry sponge with dark chocolate and liquorice ice cream.

◆ Smart dining room with terrace opening onto country garden. Cooking is polished and precise, offering refined dishes that showcase quality local ingredients – including home-smoked meats. Concise set lunch represents particularly good value.

BEAUMONT – C.I. – 503 P33 – see Channel Islands (Jersey)

BEDFORD

Alexandra Rd	X	3
Ampthill Rd	X	4
Ashburnham Rd	Y	6
Castle Rd	XY	7
Church Lane	Y	9
Church Square	X	10
Clapham Rd	Y	12
Commercial Rd	X	13
Eastcotts Rd	Y	15
Embankment (The)	X	16
Ford End Rd	Y	18
Goldington Rd	X	19
Harpur Shopping Centre	X	
Harpur St	X	21
Hassett St	X	22
Haylands Way	Y	24
High St	Y	25
Hillgrounds Rd	Y	26
Horne Lane	X	27
Interchange Retail Park	Y	
Longholme Way	Y	28
Manton Lane	Y	31
Newnham Ave	Y	33
Newnham Rd	X	34
Queen's Drive	Y	36
River St	X	37
Rope Walk	Y	39
St Loyes St	X	30
St Pauls Square	X	40
Shakespeare Rd	Y	42
Silver St	X	43
Thurlow St	X	45
West End Lane	Y	46

A 6
Tavistock St.
Union St.
Foster Hill Rd
De Parys Av.
200 m
200 yards
Kimbolton Rd
A 428
Bromham Rd
ST PETERS
Dame Alice St.
St Peters St.
Greyfriars
High St.
Mill Street
POL.
Midland Rd
HARPUR SHOPPING CENTRE
ST PAUL'S
St. Marys St.
Prebend St.
Great Ouse
River
ST MARYS
Cardington Rd
BOROUGH HALL
Street
Kingsway
St. John's St.
ST JOHN'S
Rope Walk
Cauldwell
ST-JOHNS
(A 428) (A 6)
X

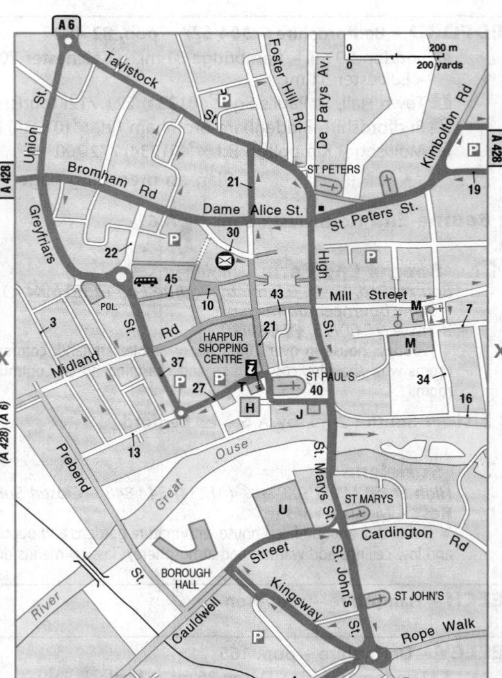

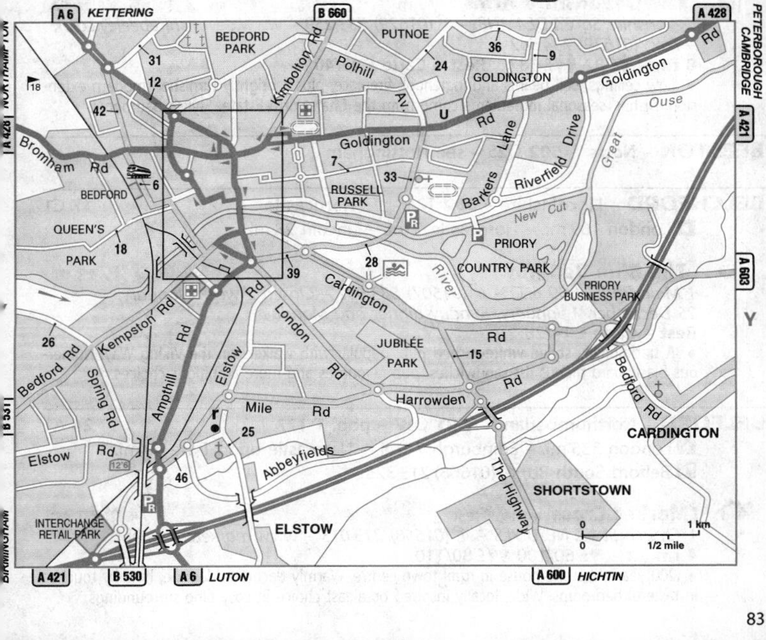

A 6 KETTERING
B 660
A 428
PETERBOROUGH CAMBRIDGE
BEDFORD PARK
PUTNOE
Kimbolton Rd
Polhill Av.
GOLDINGTON
Goldington Rd
Bromham Rd
BEDFORD
RUSSELL PARK
Barkers Lane
Riverfield Drive
Great Ouse
A 421
New Cut
QUEEN'S PARK
PRIORY COUNTRY PARK
A 603
PRIORY BUSINESS PARK
Cardington Rd
River
Kempston Rd
London Rd
Y
Bedford Rd
Spring Rd
Ampthill Rd
Elstow Rd
JUBILEE PARK
Harrowden Rd
Mile Rd
Bedford Rd
CARDINGTON
Abbeyfields
The Highway
SHORTSTOWN
INTERCHANGE RETAIL PARK
ELSTOW
1 km
1/2 mile
A 421
B 530
A 6 LUTON
A 600 HICHTIN

ENGLAND

BEDFORD – Bedfordshire – 504 S27 – pop. 82 488 — 12 A1

London 59 mi. – Cambridge 31 mi. – Colchester 70 mi. – Leicester 51 mi.

Town Hall, St Paul's Sq ✆ (01234) 221 712, touristinfo@bedford.gov.uk

Bedfordshire Biddenham Bromham Rd, ✆ (01234) 261 669

Mowsbury Kimbolton Rd, ✆ (01234) 772 700

Plan on preceding page

at Bourne End Northwest : 8 mi. by A 6

Bourne End Farm without rest

Bourne End, East : 0.5 mi. by Bourne End rd ✉ MK44 1QS – ✆ (01234) 783 184 – www.bourneendfarm.co.uk

3 rm – †£ 60/75 ††£ 80/90

◆ Spotless house in over 100 acres of arable farmland; comfortable, simply furnished bedrooms with showers; cosy lounge and charming hosts. Communal farm breakfast in dining room.

at Elstow South : 2 mi. by A 6 – ✉ Bedford

St Helena

High St ✉ MK42 9XP – ✆ (01234) 344 848 – Closed Sunday and Monday

Rest – Menu £ 28/35 — Yr

◆ Delightful, antique-filled house with mature gardens and popular conservatory. Small rooms and low ceilings add warmth and atmosphere. Classical menus display some Italian influences.

BEECH – Hampshire – see Alton

BEELEY – Derbyshire – pop. 165 — 16 B1

London 160 mi. – Derby 26 mi. – Matlock 5 mi.

The Devonshire Arms with rm

Devonshire Sq ✉ DE4 2NR – ✆ (01629) 733 259 – www.devonshirebeeley.co.uk – Fax (01629) 734 542

8 rm – †£ 82 ††£ 182 **Rest** – Carte £ 22/40

◆ Low ceilings, oak beams and inglenook fireplace, plus a brightly furnished modern extension. Dishes' seasonal ingredients come from the Chatsworth Estate. Stylish bedrooms.

BEESTON – Notts. – 502 Q25 – see Nottingham

BELCHFORD – Lincolnshire – 502 T24 – ✉ Horncastle — 17 C1

London 169 mi. – Horncastle 5 mi. – Lincoln 28 mi.

The Blue Bell Inn

1 Main Rd ✉ LN9 6LQ – ✆ (01507) 533 602 – Closed 2 weeks January, 25 December, 1 January, Sunday dinner and Monday

Rest – Carte £ 14/28

◆ A traditionally styled whitewashed pub, popular with walkers on the Viking Way. Numerous blackboard menus list sandwiches, pub favourites and more ambitious choices.

BELFORD – Northumberland – 501 O17 – pop. 1 177 — 24 A1

London 335 mi. – Edinburgh 71 mi. – Newcastle upon Tyne 49 mi.

Belford South Rd, ✆ (01668) 213 323

Market Cross without rest

1 Church St ✉ NE70 7LS – ✆ (01668) 213 013 – www.marketcross.net

4 rm – †£ 60/100 ††£ 80/110

◆ 200 year-old stone house in rural town centre. Warmly decorated lounge, homely touches in tasteful bedrooms. Wide, locally inspired breakfast choice in cosy pine surroundings.

ENGLAND

BELPER – Derbyshire – 502 P24 – pop. 21 938 16 B2

London 141 mi. – Birmingham 59 mi. – Leicester 40 mi. – Manchester 55 mi.

at Shottle Northwest : 4 mi. by A 517 – ✉ Belper

Dannah Farm Country House without rest

Bowmans Lane, North : 0.25 mi. by Alport rd ✉ DE56 2DR – ✆ (01773) 550 273 – www.dannah.co.uk – Fax (01773) 550 590 – Closed 24-26 December

4 rm – †£ 75/95 ††£ 150/195 – 4 suites – ††£ 180/250

◆ Family-run converted farmhouse - part of a working farm. Spacious, contemporary bedrooms are diverse in style; the two level Studio suite includes hot tub and spiral staircase.

BELTON – Leics. – see Loughborough

BEPTON – W. Sussex – see Midhurst

BERKHAMSTED – Hertfordshire – 504 S28 – pop. 18 800 12 A2

Great Britain

London 34 mi. – Aylesbury 14 mi. – St Albans 11 mi.

Whipsnade Wild Animal Park★ **AC**, N : 9.5 mi. on A 4251, B 4506 and B 4540

Eatfish

163-165 High St ✉ HP4 3HB – ✆ (01442) 879 988 – www.eatfish.co.uk – Closed 25-27 December

Rest – Seafood – Menu £ 15 (lunch) – Carte £ 15/33

◆ Well-run seafood restaurant with characterful, rustic feel; photos of Scottish produce and its suppliers on walls. Flexible menu, with large/smaller portions. Summer terrace.

BERWICK-UPON-TWEED – Northumberland – 501 O16 – pop. 12 870 24 A1

Great Britain

London 349 mi. – Edinburgh 57 mi. – Newcastle upon Tyne 63 mi.

106 Marygate ✆ (01289) 330733, tourism@berwick-upon-tweed.gov.uk

Goswick, ✆ (01289) 387 256

Magdalene Fields, ✆ (01289) 306 130

Town★★ - Walls★

Foulden★, NW : 5 mi. – Paxton House (Chippendale furniture★) **AC**, W : 5 mi. by A 6105, A 1 and B 6461. St Abb's Head★★ (≤★), NW : 12 mi. by A 1, A 1107 and B 6438 - SW : Tweed Valley★★ – Eyemouth Museum★ **AC**, N : 7.5 mi. by A 1 and A 1107 – Holy Island★ (Priory ruins★ **AC**, Lindisfarne Castle★ **AC**), SE : 9 mi. by A 1167 and A 1 – Manderston★ (stables★), W : 13 mi. by A 6105 - Ladykirk (Kirk o'Steil★), SW : 8.5 mi. by A 698 and B 6470

1 Sallyport

1 Sallyport, off Bridge St ✉ TD15 1EZ – ✆ (01289) 308 827 – www.sallyport.co.uk – Fax (01289) 308 827

6 rm – †£ 85/110 ††£ 110/150 **Rest** – *(by arrangement)* Menu £ 40

◆ 17C Grade II listed house on cobbled alley. The bedrooms are a strong point: they boast a boutique style, with a high standard of facilities, and lots of homely extra touches. Characterful farmhouse kitchen style dining room.

West Coates

30 Castle Terrace, North : 0.75 mi. by Castlegate on Kelso rd ✉ TD15 1NZ – ✆ (01289) 309 666 – www.westcoates.co.uk – Fax (01289) 309 666 – Closed 15 December-8 January

3 rm – †£ 70/100 ††£ 100/120

Rest – *(by arrangement, communal dining)* Menu £ 35

◆ Sizeable Victorian house with mature gardens, set in a quiet suburb. Bedrooms are spacious, comfy and well-appointed, with thoughtful touches. Large, open-plan lounge/dining room. Hearty breakfasts and accomplished dinners.

BEVERLEY – East Riding of Yorkshire – **502** S22 – **pop. 29 110** **23** D2
– ✉ **Kingston-Upon-Hull** ▌Great Britain

London 188 mi. – Kingston-upon-Hull 8 mi. – Leeds 52 mi. – York 29 mi.

34 Butcher Row ✆ (01482) 867430, beverley.tic@vhey.co.uk

The Westwood, ✆ (01482) 868 757

Town★ - Minster★★ – St Mary's Church★

Burton Mount

Malton Rd, Cherry Burton ,
Northwest : 2.75 mi. by A164, B1248 on Leconfield rd ✉ HU17 7RA
– ✆ (01964) 550 541 – www.burtonmount.co.uk
3 rm – ♦£ 72 ♦♦£ 91/100
Rest – *(by arrangement)* Menu £ 32

◆ Homely red brick house overlooking large, mature gardens. Dining room boasts French windows opening onto the terrace. Comfy bedrooms display heavy fabrics and dark wood furniture. Good breakfasts; dinners of well sourced local produce cooked on the Aga.

Whites

12a North Bar Without ✉ HU17 7AB
– ✆ (01482) 866 121 – www.whitesrestaurant.co.uk
– Closed 2 weeks December-January, 1 week August, Sunday and Monday
Rest – *(booking advisable)* Menu £ 15 (lunch) – Carte dinner £ 29/37

◆ Restaurant and patisserie in one; its intimate inner hung with vivid ceramics. Good value, classical dishes cooked with skill and care. Freshly baked cakes and a friendly atmosphere.

at Tickton Northeast : 3.5 mi. by A 1035 – ✉ Kingston-Upon-Hull

Tickton Grange

Tickton, on A 1035 ✉ HU17 9SH – ✆ (01964) 543 666
– www.beverleyticktongrange.co.uk
– Fax (01964) 542 556
21 rm – ♦£ 98 ♦♦£ 135/155
Rest ***The Champagne Restaurant*** – Menu £ 23/25 **s**
– Carte dinner £ 27/34 **s**

◆ Carefully renovated bedrooms blend Georgian and contemporary architecture, antique and period-inspired furniture. Richly swagged fabrics and open fires in an inviting lounge. Dine in the Georgian style; large bay windows look out onto the lawn.

at South Dalton Northwest : 5 mi. by A 164 and B 1248 – ✉ Beverley

The Pipe and Glass Inn (James Mackenzie)

West End ✉ HU17 7PN – ✆ (01430) 810 246 – www.pipeandglass.co.uk – Closed 2 weeks January, Sunday dinner and Monday
Rest – Carte £ 18/40
Spec. Wild rabbit rissoles with cockles, capers and sorrel. Venison suet pudding with mushrooms, carrots and smoked bacon. Treacle tart with plums and egg nog ice cream.

◆ Warm, bustling and inviting pub, with experienced and hospitable owners. Roomy bar with roaring log fire; rustic dining room. Seasonally-informed, classic pub dishes and rediscovered English recipes are expertly cooked; local game a highlight.

BEYTON – Suffolk – **504** W27 – see Bury St Edmunds

BIBURY – Gloucestershire – **503** O28 – **pop. 570** – ✉ **Cirencester** **4** D1
▌Great Britain

London 86 mi. – Gloucester 26 mi. – Oxford 30 mi.

Village★

The Swan

✉ GL7 5NW – ✆ (01285) 740 695 – www.cotswold-inns-hotels.co.uk/swan – Fax (01285) 740 473

19 rm – †£ 155/195 ††£ 155/210 – 3 suites

Rest *Gallery* – *(dinner only)* Menu £ 33

Rest *Café Swan* – Carte £ 28/34

◆ Ivy-clad 17C coaching inn with private gardens; idyllic village location by a trout stream. Comfortable rooms with a contemporary edge. Gallery is formally stylish and spacious. Café Swan is a brasserie with stone-flagged courtyard.

Cotteswold House without rest

Arlington, on B 4425 ✉ *GL7 5ND* – ✆ *(01285) 740 609 – www.cotteswoldhouse.net – Fax (01285) 740 609*

3 rm – †£ 48 ††£ 68

◆ Set in a manicured garden outside the picturesque village. Homely, spotless and modestly priced bedrooms, comprehensively remodelled behind a Victorian façade.

The Catherine Wheel

✉ *GL7 5ND* – ✆ *(01285) 740 250 – www.barnsleyhouse.com – Closed Sunday dinner*

Rest – Carte £ 20/25

◆ 15C building in a pretty Cotswold village, with welcoming log fires, wooden beams, exposed stone walls and slate floors. Menu displays pub classics and puddings of the comfort variety.

A red **Rest** mention denotes an establishment with an award for culinary excellence, ✿ (star) or ☺ (Bib Gourmand).

ENGLAND

BICESTER – Oxfordshire – **504** Q28 – **pop. 31 113** **10** B2

▶ London 66 mi. – Birmingham 70 mi. – Leicester 66 mi. – Coventry 51 mi.

Villandry

26 B&C, 50 Pingle Drive, Bicester Village Outlet Shopping, on A 421 at junction of A 41 ✉ *OX26 6WD* – ✆ *(01869) 355 070 – www.villandry.com – Fax (01869) 355 071 – Closed 25 December*

Rest – *(Bookings not accepted at lunch)* Carte £ 21/32

◆ Rest tired shoppers' feet at this bustling bistrot; an outpost of the popular London foodstore. Fresh, tasty modern cooking, from classic French dishes to rotisserie steaks.

BIDDENDEN – Kent – **504** V30 – **pop. 2 205** Great Britain **9** C2

▶ London 52 mi. – Ashford 13 mi. – Maidstone 16 mi.

Bodiam Castle★★, S : 10 mi. by A 262, A 229 and B 2244 – Sissinghurst Garden★, W : 3 mi. by A 262 – Battle Abbey★, S : 20 mi. by A 262, A 229, A 21 and A 2100

Barclay Farmhouse without rest

Woolpack Corner, South : 0.5 mi. by A 262 on Benenden rd ✉ *TN27 8BQ* – ✆ *(01580) 292 626 – www.barclayfarmhouse.co.uk – Fax (01580) 292 288*

3 rm – †£ 60 ††£ 85

◆ Set in an acre of pleasant garden: well-priced, very comfortable accommodation with fine French oak flooring and furniture. Inventive breakfasts in the barn conversion.

Bishopsdale Oast

South : 3 mi. by A 262 and Benenden rd on Tenterden rd ✉ *TN27 8DR* – ✆ *(01580) 291 027 – www.bishopsdaleoast.co.uk – Closed Christmas*

5 rm – †£ 50 ††£ 70/90

Rest – *(by arrangement, communal dining)* Menu £ 28

◆ Extended oast house in four acres of mature grounds with wild flower garden. Comfy lounge with log fire; plenty of trinkets and books in bright, clean, good sized rooms. Family size dining table; interesting meals employ home-grown, organic produce.

The West House (Graham Garrett)

28 High St ✉ TN27 8AH – ✆ (01580) 291 341
– www.thewesthouserestaurant.co.uk – Fax (01580) 291 341
– Closed 2 weeks summer, Christmas and New Year, Saturday lunch, Sunday dinner and Monday
Rest – Menu £ 25/35

Spec. Iberico ham with trotter sausage, beetroot and dandelion. Lamb with pea cream and sea purslane. Strawberry and elderflower jelly with ice cream and fritter.

◆ Pretty part 16C former weavers' cottages in picturesque village. Charming beamed interior with inglenook and modern artwork. Concise seasonal menu; confident and technically skilled cooking allows the ingredients to shine.

The Three Chimneys

Hareplain Road, West : 1.5 mi. off A 262 ✉ TN27 8LW – ✆ (01580) 291 472
– Closed 25 December
Rest – (booking essential) Carte £ 23/35

◆ Hugely characterful, low-ceilinged 15C pub with cask ales, rear restaurant and pleasant garden. Hearty portions of seasonal produce, with nursery puddings like Bakewell tart.

BIDEFORD – Devon – 503 H30 – pop. 16 262 2 C1

London 231 mi. – Exeter 43 mi. – Plymouth 58 mi. – Taunton 60 mi.
to Lundy Island (Lundy Co. Ltd) (1 h 45 mn)
Burton Art Gallery, Kingsley Rd ✆ (01237) 477676, bidefordtic@torridge.gov.uk
18 Royal North Devon Westward Ho Golf Links Rd, ✆ (01237) 473 824
9 Torrington Weare Trees, ✆ (01805) 622 229
Bridge★★ – Burton Art Gallery★ **AC**
Appledore★, N : 2 m. Clovelly★★, W : 11 mi. by A 39 and B 3237 – Lundy Island★★, NW : by ferry - Rosemoor★ – Great Torrington (Dartington Crystal★ **AC**) SE : 7.5 mi. by A 386

Yeoldon House

Durrant Lane, Northam, North : 1.5 mi. by B 3235 off A 386 ✉ EX39 2RL
– ✆ (01237) 474 400 – www.yeoldonhousehotel.co.uk – Fax (01237) 476 618
– Closed Christmas
10 rm – †£ 85 ††£ 135
Rest – (dinner only) (booking essential for non-residents) Menu £ 35 **s**

◆ Privately run 19C house with lovely gardens overlooking the Torridge. Comfortable lounge bar with books, dried flowers and curios. Period-style rooms, some with balconies. Smart restaurant overlooking river.

Memories

8 Fore St, Northam, North : 2 mi. by B 3235 off A 386 ✉ EX39 1AW – ✆ (01237) 473 419 – Fax (01237) 473 419 – Closed 1 week January, 1 week September, 25-26 December, Sunday-Tuesday and Bank Holidays
Rest – (dinner only) Menu £ 25 (Wednesday-Thursday) – Carte Friday-Saturday £ 24/28

◆ Simple, blue and white painted restaurant with vibrant local ambience. Enthusiastic owners serve well-prepared, traditional menus at a reasonable price.

at Instow North : 3 mi. by A 386 on B 3233 – ✉ Bideford

Decks

Marine Par ✉ EX39 4JJ – ✆ (01271) 860 671 – www.decksrestaurant.co.uk
– Closed 25 December, Sunday and Monday
Rest – (dinner only) Carte £ 23/45

◆ Sit on the outside deck and watch the sun go down over Appledore. Enjoy accomplished modern dishes while contemplating the wacky murals. Superb views from all vantage points.

BIGBURY – Devon – 503 I33 2 C3

London 195 mi. – Exeter 41 mi. – Plymouth 22 mi.
Kingsbridge★, E : 13 mi. by B 3392 and A 379

ENGLAND

The Oyster Shack

Milburn Orchard Farm, Stakes Hill, East : 1 mi. on Easton rd ✉ TQ7 4BE – ✆ (01548) 810 876 – www.oystershack.co.uk – Fax (01548) 810 876 – Closed October-December, Monday and Tuesday
Rest – Seafood – *(booking essential)* Carte £ 24/36
◆ Eccentric venue, half a lovely covered terrace, decorated with fishing nets. Seafood, particularly local oyster dishes; classic and modern dishes using the freshest produce.

BIGBURY-ON-SEA – Devon – 503 I33 – pop. 600 – ✉ Kingsbridge 2 C3

London 196 mi. – Exeter 42 mi. – Plymouth 23 mi.

Burgh Island

South : 0.5 mi. by sea tractor ✉ TQ7 4BG – ✆ (01548) 810 514 – www.burghisland.com – Fax (01548) 810 243
14 rm – †£ 280 ††£ 385 – 11 suites – ††£ 440/600
Rest – *(dinner only and Sunday lunch) (booking essential for non-residents)* Menu £ 38/55
◆ Unique Grade II listed 1930s country house in private island setting: stylishly romantic Art Deco interior. Charmingly individual rooms with views: some have fantastic style. Ballroom dining: dress in black tie. Owners pride themselves on accomplished cooking.

Henley

Folly Hill ✉ TQ7 4AR – ✆ (01548) 810 240 – www.thehenleyhotel.co.uk – Fax (01548) 810 240 – March-October
5 rm – †£ 72 ††£ 134
Rest – *(booking essential for non-residents)* Menu £ 34
◆ Personally run cottage of 16C origin. Stunning views of the bay and Bolt Tail from modern conservatory with deep wicker chairs and pleasant, individual rooms in pastel tones. Homely dining room with magnificent sea views.

The sun's out? Then enjoy eating outside on the terrace:

BIGGLESWADE – Bedfordshire – 504 T27 – pop. 15 383 12 B1

London 46 mi. – Bedford 12 mi. – Luton 24 mi.

at Old Warden West : 3.5 mi. by A 6001 off B 658 – ✉ Biggleswade

Hare & Hounds

The Village ✉ SG18 9HQ – ✆ (01767) 627 225 – www.hareandhoundsoldwarden.co.uk – Fax (01767) 627 588 – Closed 26 December, 1 January, Sunday dinner and Monday except Bank Holidays
Rest – Carte £ 20/25
◆ Charming picture postcard pub set in an idyllic village. Monthly changing à la carte offers hearty, flavoursome dishes; blackboard menu presents classic pub fare. Homemade bread and pasta.

BILBROOK – Somerset – 503 J30 3 A2

London 179 mi. – Cardiff 92 mi. – Weston-super-Mare 42 mi. – Taunton 19 mi.

Dragon House

on A39 ✉ TA24 6HQ – ✆ (01984) 640 215 – www.dragonhouse.co.uk
10 rm – †£ 40/65 ††£ 80/120
Rest – Menu £ 13/16 **s** – Carte £ 27/36 **s**
◆ Small hotel with comfortable lounge that boasts leather sofas and central wood burner. Pleasant bar, conservatory and terrace. Clean, modern bedrooms. Smart oak panelled restaurant with modern menu of local, seasonal fare; fresh veg from kitchen garden.

BILDESTON – Suffolk – 504 W27 — 15 C3

London 85 mi. – Bury St Edmunds 18 mi. – Ipswich 15 mi.

The Bildeston Crown with rm

104 High Street ✉ IP7 7EB – ✆ (01449) 740 510 – www.thebildestoncrown.co.uk – Fax (01449) 741 843 – Closed dinner 25-26 December and 1 January

12 rm – †£ 90 ††£ 250

Rest – Menu £ 18 (weekdays) – Carte £ 26/40

♦ Eye-catching 15C pub boasting warm, characterful feel. Two main menus, with emphasis on quality local produce: Crown Classics offers traditional pub meals; Crown Select features more elaborate dishes. Bedrooms are spacious and stylish with up-to-date facilities.

BINGHAM – Nottinghamshire – 502 R25 – pop. 8 685 — 16 B2

London 125 mi. – Leicester 26 mi. – Lincoln 28 mi. – Nottingham 11 mi.

Yeung Sing

Market St ✉ NG13 8AB – ✆ (01949) 831 222 – www.yeung-sing.co.uk – Fax (01949) 838 833 – Closed 25-26 December

Rest – Chinese – *(dinner only and Sunday lunch)* Menu £ 22 – Carte £ 24/32

♦ Long-standing, family-owned restaurant with lounge and bar, serving authentic Cantonese and regional Chinese cuisine. Deep red décor, carved wood and huge 3D dragons on walls.

BINGLEY – West Yorkshire – 502 O22 – pop. 19 884 – ✉ Bradford — 22 B2

London 204 mi. – Bradford 6 mi. – Leeds 15 mi. – Skipton 13 mi.

St Ives Est., ✆ (01274) 562 436

Five Rise Locks

Beck Lane, via Park Rd ✉ BD16 4DD – ✆ (01274) 565 296 – www.five-rise-locks.co.uk – Fax (01274) 568 828

9 rm – †£ 65 ††£ 85/105

Rest – *(dinner only and Sunday lunch) (residents only Sunday and Monday)* Carte £ 18/26

♦ Neat mid-Victorian house named after the locks on the nearby Leeds-Liverpool canal. Cheerful, modern, individuallly styled rooms, some with views of the distant dales. Well-kept dining room employs local produce on menus.

BIRCHOVER – Derbs. – see Matlock

BIRKENHEAD – Merseyside – 502 K23 – pop. 83 729 — 20 A3

London 222 mi. – Liverpool 2 mi.

Access Mersey Tunnels (toll)

to Liverpool and Wallasey (Mersey Ferries) frequent services daily

Arrowe Park Woodchurch, ✆ (0151) 677 1527

Prenton Golf Links Rd, ✆ (0151) 609 3426

Plan : see Liverpool p. 3

River Hill

Talbot Rd, Oxton, Southwest : 2.25 mi. by A 552 on B 5151 ✉ CH43 2HJ – ✆ (0151) 653 3773 – www.theriverhill.co.uk – Fax (0151) 653 7162

15 rm – †£ 78/83 ††£ 106

Rest – *(Closed Bank Holiday Mondays) (dinner only and Sunday lunch)* Menu £ 19 – Carte £ 24/33

♦ Privately owned mock Tudor house with neat garden, set in leafy residential area. Modern bedrooms boast clean, simple colour schemes and up-to-date furnishings; two have four-posters. Restaurant offers plenty of choice.

XXX ✿ **Fraiche** (Marc Wilkinson)

11 Rose Mount, Oxton, Southwest : 2.25 mi. by A 552 and B 5151 ✉ CH43 5SG – ✆ (0151) 652 2914 – www.restaurantfraiche.com – Closed 2 weeks January, 25 December, Monday and Tuesday

Rest – *(dinner only and lunch Friday and Saturday) (booking essential)*
Menu £ 24/40 – Carte £ 50/60

Spec. Scallops with tarragon infused grapes and sweetcorn purée. Fillet of veal with celery heart and pea cream. 'Textures of orange'.

◆ Stylish and sophisticated restaurant with coloured glassware and subtle lighting. Choice of 3 set menus. Creative, modern dishes use fine ingredients from around the globe in unusual combinations. Impressive presentation. Attentive, formal service.

K. Blackwell/MICHELIN

BIRMINGHAM

County: West Midlands
Michelin regional map: 503 O26
London 122 mi. – Bristol 91 mi.
– Liverpool 103 mi.
– Manchester 86 mi.

Population: 970 892
Great Britain
Map reference: 19 C2

PRACTICAL INFORMATION

Tourist Information

The Rotunda, 150 New St ✆ (0121) 202 5000

Airport

Birmingham International Airport : ✆ (0844) 576 6000, E : 6.5 mi. by A 45 DU

Golf Courses

18 Edgbaston Church Rd, ✆(0121) 454 1736

18 Hilltop Handsworth Park Lane, ✆(0121) 554 4463

18 Hatchford Brook Sheldon Coventry Rd, ✆(0121) 743 9821

18 Brandhall Warley Heron Rd, Oldbury, ✆(0121) 552 2195

9 Harborne Church Farm Harborne Vicarage Rd, ✆(0121) 427 1204

SIGHTS

IN TOWN

City★ – Museum and Art Gallery★★ LY **M2** – Barber Institute of Fine Arts★★ (at Birmingham University) EX **U** – Cathedral of St Philip (stained glass portrayals★) LMY – Millennium Point FV

ON THE OUTSKIRTS

Aston Hall★★ FV **M**

IN THE SURROUNDING AREA

Black Country Museum★, Dudley, NW : 10 mi. by A 456 and A 4123 AU – Bournville★, SW : 4 mi. on A 38 and A 441

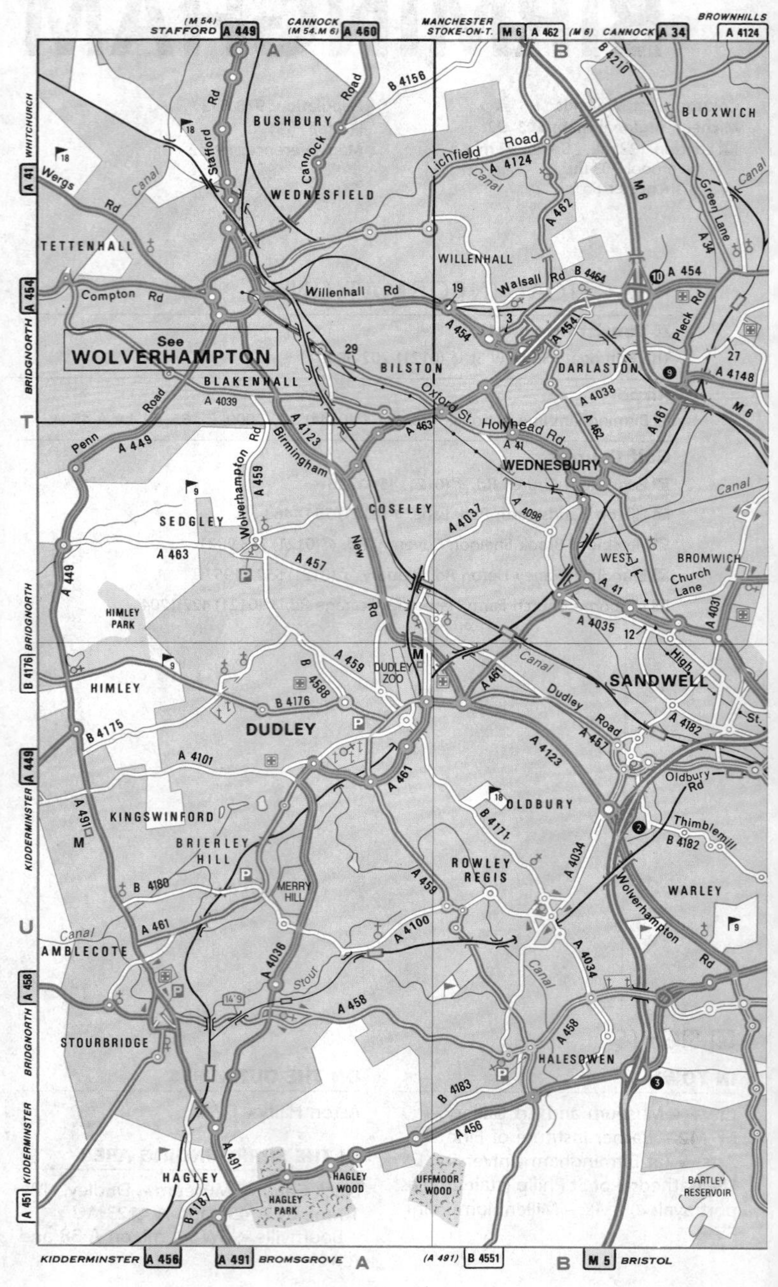

(M 54) STAFFORD A 449
CANNOCK (M 54.M 6) A 460
MANCHESTER STOKE-ON-T. M 6 A 462 (M 6) CANNOCK A 34
BROWNHILLS A 4124
WHITCHURCH A 41
BRIDGNORTH A 454
BRIDGNORTH B 4176
KIDDERMINSTER A 449
BRIDGNORTH A 458
KIDDERMINSTER A 451
KIDDERMINSTER A 456
A 491 BROMSGROVE
(A 491) B 4551
M 5 BRISTOL
BUSHBURY
WEDNESFIELD
TETTENHALL
See WOLVERHAMPTON
BLAKENHALL
BILSTON
WILLENHALL
BLOXWICH
DARLASTON
WEDNESBURY
SEDGLEY
COSELEY
WEST BROMWICH
HIMLEY PARK
HIMLEY
DUDLEY
DUDLEY ZOO
SANDWELL
KINGSWINFORD
BRIERLEY HILL
MERRY HILL
OLDBURY
ROWLEY REGIS
WARLEY
AMBLECOTE
STOURBRIDGE
HALESOWEN
HAGLEY
HAGLEY WOOD
HAGLEY PARK
UFFMOOR WOOD
BARTLEY RESERVOIR
Canal
Stour

BIRMINGHAM AND WOLVERHAMPTON

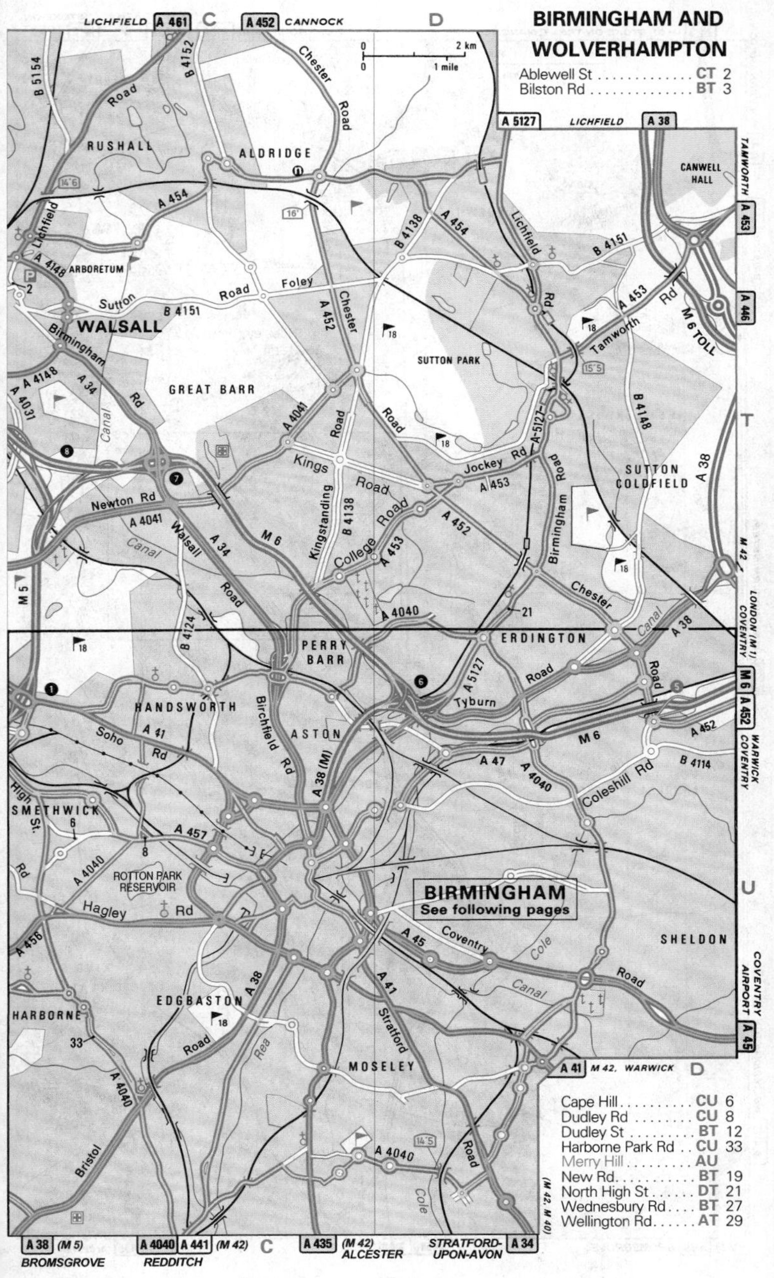

Ablewell St . . . . CT 2
Bilston Rd . . . . BT 3

Cape Hill . . . . CU 6
Dudley Rd . . . . CU 8
Dudley St . . . . BT 12
Harborne Park Rd . . CU 33
Merry Hill . . . . AU
New Rd. . . . . BT 19
North High St . . . . . . DT 21
Wednesbury Rd. . . . . BT 27
Wellington Rd. . . . . . AT 29

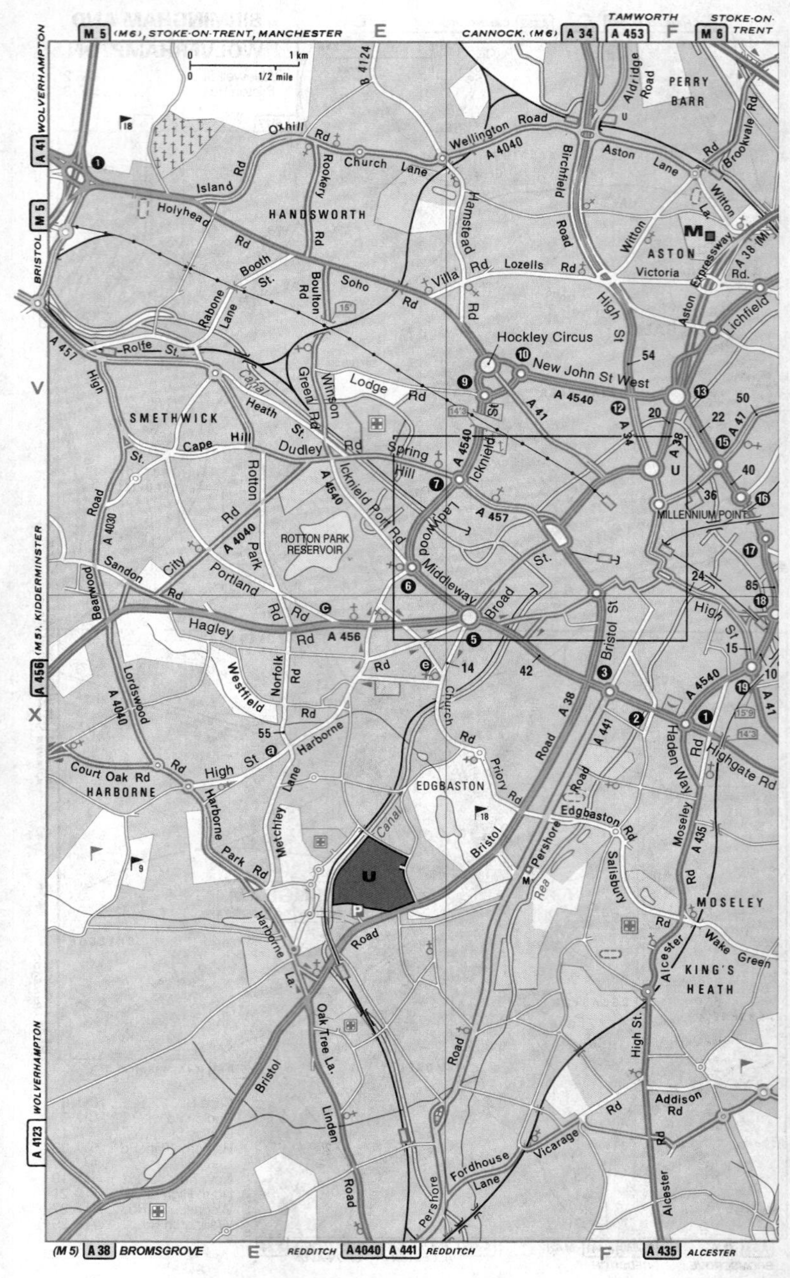
M 5 (M6), STOKE-ON-TRENT, MANCHESTER
CANNOCK, (M6) A 34 A 453
TAMWORTH
M 6 STOKE-ON-TRENT
A 41 WOLVERHAMPTON
M 5 BRISTOL
A 456 (M 5), KIDDERMINSTER
A 4123 WOLVERHAMPTON
(M 5) A 38 BROMSGROVE
REDDITCH A4040 A 441 REDDITCH
A 435 ALCESTER
HANDSWORTH
PERRY BARR
ASTON
SMETHWICK
HARBORNE
EDGBASTON
MOSELEY
KING'S HEATH
Hockley Circus
MILLENNIUM POINT
ROTTON PARK RESERVOIR
Holyhead Rd
Soho Rd
Wellington Road
Aston Lane
Lozells Rd
Hagley Rd
Bristol Road
Pershore Road
Alcester Rd
Broad St.
New John St West
Cape Hill
Dudley Rd
Harborne Park Rd
Edgbaston Rd
Highgate Rd

BIRMINGHAM

Calthorpe Rd . . . . . FX 14
Camp Hill . . . . FX 15
Corporation St . . . . FV 20
Darmouth Middleway . . . . . FV 22
Digbeth. . . . . FV 24
Dudley Park Rd . . . GX 25
High St SALTLEY . GV 31
Jennen's Rd. . . . . . FV 36
Lawley St. . . . . FV 40
Lee Bank Middleway . . . . . FX 42
Nechell's Parkway . FV 50
New Town Row . . . . FV 54
Nursery Rd. . . . . . . EX 55
Saltley Rd . . . . GV 66
Sandy Lane . . . . . . FX 10
Solihull Lane . . . . . GX 74
Watery Lane . . . . . FV 85
Westley Rd . . . . . . GX 87

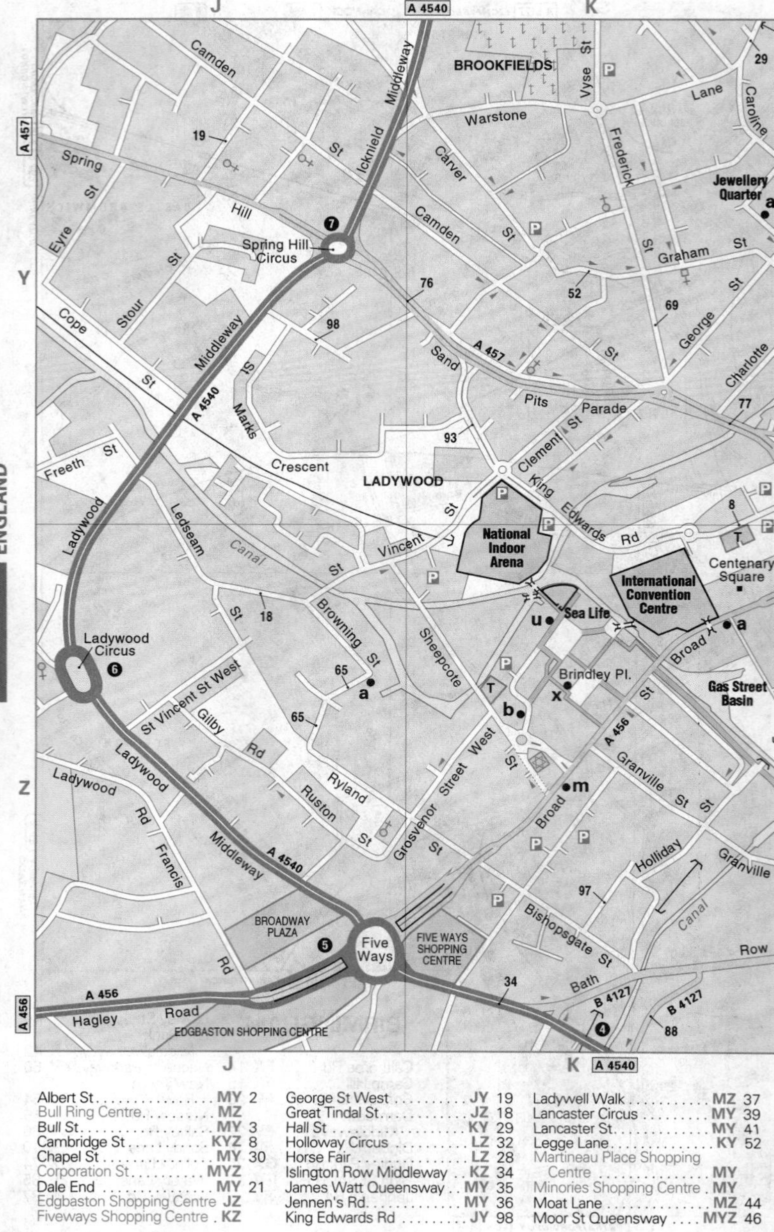

Albert St . . . . MY 2
Bull Ring Centre . . . . MZ
Bull St . . . . MY 3
Cambridge St . . . . KYZ 8
Chapel St . . . . MY 30
Corporation St . . . . MYZ
Dale End . . . . MY 21
Edgbaston Shopping Centre JZ
Fiveways Shopping Centre . KZ

George St West . . . . JY 19
Great Tindal St . . . . JZ 18
Hall St . . . . KY 29
Holloway Circus . . . . LZ 32
Horse Fair . . . . LZ 28
Islington Row Middleway . . KZ 34
James Watt Queensway . . MY 35
Jennen's Rd . . . . MY 36
King Edwards Rd . . . . JY 98

Ladywell Walk . . . . MZ 37
Lancaster Circus . . . . MY 39
Lancaster St . . . . MY 41
Legge Lane . . . . KY 52
Martineau Place Shopping Centre . . . . MY
Minories Shopping Centre . MY
Moat Lane . . . . MZ 44
Moor St Queensway . . . . MYZ 46

BIRMINGHAM

Street	Grid	No.
Morville St	JZ	65
Navigation St	LZ	49
Newhall Hill	KY	69
Newton St	MY	53
New St	LMZ	
Paradise Circus	LYZ	56
Paradise Forum Shopping Centre	LYZ	
Priory Queensway	MY	59
St. Chads Queensway	MY	63
St Chads Circus	LY	62
St Martin's Circus	MZ	64
Shadwell St	LMY	70
Smallbrook Queensway	LMZ	71
Snow Hill Queensway	LMY	73
Summer Hill Rd	JKY	76
Summer Hill St	KY	93
Summer Row	KY	77
Temple Row	MY	80
Waterloo St	LY	84
Wheeley's Lane	KZ	88
William St	KZ	97

INDEX OF STREET NAMES IN BIRMINGHAM

Hyatt Regency

2 Bridge St ✉ B1 2JZ – ✆ (0121) 643 1234 – www.birmingham.regency.hyatt.com – Fax (0121) 616 2323 KZ**a**

315 rm – †£ 209 ††£ 209, ☕ £ 15.75 – 4 suites

Rest *Aria* – Menu £ 15 – Carte £ 27/42

◆ Striking mirrored exterior. Glass enclosed lifts offer panoramic views. Sizeable rooms with floor to ceiling windows. Covered link with International Convention Centre. Contemporary style restaurant in central atrium; modish cooking.

Malmaison

Mailbox, 1 Wharfside St ✉ B1 1RD – ✆ (0121) 246 5000 – www.malmaison.com – Fax (0121) 246 5002 LZ**e**

184 rm – †£ 170 ††£ 170/350, ☕ £ 13.95 – 5 suites

Rest *Brasserie* – Menu £ 16 (dinner) – Carte £ 26/33

◆ Stylish, modern boutique hotel, forms centrepiece of Mailbox development. Stylish bar. Spacious contemporary bedrooms with every modern facility; superb petit spa. Brasserie serving contemporary French influenced cooking at reasonable prices.

Hotel Du Vin

25 Church St ✉ B3 2NR – ✆ (0121) 200 0600 – www.hotelduvin.com – Fax (0121) 236 0889 LY**e**

66 rm – †£ 170 ††£ 170/185, ☕ £ 13.50

Rest *Bistro* – Carte £ 25/35

◆ Former 19C eye hospital in heart of shopping centre; has relaxed, individual, boutique style. Low lighting in rooms of muted tones: Egyptian cotton and superb bathrooms. Champagne in "bubble lounge"; Parisian style brasserie.

City Inn

1 Brunswick Sq, Brindley Pl ✉ B1 2HW – ✆ (0121) 643 1003 – www.cityinn.com – Fax (0121) 643 1005 KZ**b**

238 rm ☕ – †£ 59/225 ††£ 69/245

Rest *City Café* – Menu £ 15/17 **s** – Carte £ 25/34 **s**

◆ In heart of vibrant Brindley Place; the spacious atrium with bright rugs and blond wood sets the tone for equally stylish rooms. Corporate friendly with many meeting rooms. Eat in restaurant, terrace or bar.

Simpsons (Andreas Antona) with rm

20 Highfield Rd, Edgbaston ✉ B15 3DU – ✆ (0121) 454 3434 – www.simpsonsrestaurant.co.uk – Fax (0121) 454 3399 – Closed 24-26 and 31 December and 1 January EX**e**

4 rm – †£ 160/225 ††£ 160/225

Rest – Contemporary – *(closed Sunday dinner and Bank Holiday Mondays)* Menu £ 30/33 – Carte £ 40/51

Spec. Lobster with coconut rice,onions and coriander. Suckling pig with ravioli of trotter and spiced pears. Chocolate and raspberry mousse with cacao streusel and raspberry sorbet.

◆ Smart Georgian mansion with stylish lounges, pleasant garden terrace and summer house. Tables are well-spaced; service is formal and efficient. Classical menu displays Mediterranean influences, contemporary twists and excellent produce. Spacious bedrooms boast French country styling.

Purnell's (Glynn Purnell)

55 Cornwall St ✉ B3 2DH – ✆ (0121) 212 9799 – www.purnellsrestaurant.com – Closed 2 weeks July-August, 1 week Christmas, 1 week Easter, Saturday lunch, Sunday and Monday LY**b**

Rest – Modern – Menu £ 25/40

Spec. Salad of crab with smoked paprika and honeycomb. Lamb with fennel and cos lettuce. Custard egg surprise with strawberries and tarragon.

◆ Passionately run, stylish restaurant in sizeable red-brick property with large lounge. Refined and modern cooking displays plenty of original and individual touches. The tasting menus are particularly innovative in style.

ENGLAND

Pascal's

1 Montague Rd ✉ B16 9HN – ✆ (0121) 455 0999 – www.pascalsrestaurant.co.uk – Fax (0121) 455 0999 – Closed 2 weeks July-August, 1 week Christmas, 1 week Easter, Saturday lunch, Sunday dinner, Monday and Tuesday EX**c**

Rest – French – Menu £ 20/29

◆ Two main rooms; a darker inner hall and lighter, more airy conservatory with views of the small rear garden. Classical, carefully priced cooking with strong French overtones.

Opus

54 Cornwall St ✉ B3 2DE – ✆ (0121) 200 2323 – www.opusrestaurant.co.uk – Fax (0121) 200 2090 – Closed 24 December-4 January, Saturday lunch, Sunday and Bank Holidays LY**z**

Rest – Modern – Menu £ 19 (except Saturday dinner) – Carte £ 29/40

◆ Restaurant of floor-to-ceiling glass in evolving area of city. Seafood and shellfish bar for diners on the move. Assured cooking underpins modern menus with traditional base.

Asha's

12-22 Newhall St – ✆ (0121) 200 27 67 – www.ashasuk.co.uk – Fax (0121) 236 10 62 – Closed 25 December, 1 January and lunch Saturday and Sunday

Rest – Indian – Menu £ 13/25 – Carte £ 25/32 LY**m**

◆ Smart restaurant with delightful décor and vivid artwork. Owned by renowned artiste/-gourmet Asha Bhosle. Authentic North West Indian cuisine cooked by chefs originally from that region.

ENGLAND

Edmunds

6 Central Sq, Brindley Place ✉ B1 2JB – ✆ (0121) 633 4944 – www.edmundsbirmingham.com – Fax (0121) 497 49 74 – Closed 1 week per season, Saturday lunch and Sunday KZ**x**

Rest – Modern European – Menu £ 21/41

◆ Formal restaurant in heart of city. Smart interior with neutral décor and modern lighting. Immaculately laid tables boast fine china and glassware. Smart, attentive staff.

Turners (Richard Turner)

69 High Street, Harborne ✉ B17 9NS – ✆ (0121) 426 4440 – www.turnersofharborne.com – Closed 2 weeks August, 1 week Christmas, 1 week Easter, Saturday lunch, Sunday and Monday EX**a**

Rest – Modern – *(booking essential set menu only Tuesday dinner)*
Menu £ 22/45

Spec. Foie gras three ways with vanilla Sauternes sauce. Lemon sole with truffle and scallop velouté. Apricot soufflé with almond ice cream.

◆ Neat neighbourhood restaurant in suburban parade, with wood panels, etched mirrors and velvet chairs. Concise à la carte and tasting menus offer refined, flavoursome dishes of accomplished, classical cooking with modern touches. Formal, structured service.

Loves

The Glasshouse – ✆ (0121) 454 5151 – www.loves-restaurant.co.uk – Fax (0121) 455 7788 – Closed 2 weeks Christmas, 2 weeks August, Sunday and Monday

Rest – Inventive – Menu £ 20/39 JZ**a**

◆ Situated on the ground floor of an apartment block on the canal basin, with spacious, contemporary interior and smartly laid tables. Cooking uses modern techniques and presentation.

Lasan

3-4 Dakota Buildings, James St, St Pauls Sq ✉ B3 1SD – ✆ (0121) 212 3664 – www.lasangroup.com – Fax (0121) 212 3665 – Closed 25 December and Saturday lunch KY**a**

Rest – Indian – Menu £ 40 (dinner) – Carte £ 26/45

◆ Jewellery quarter restaurant of sophistication and style; good quality ingredients allow the clarity of the spices to shine through in this well-run Indian establishment.

Bank

4 Brindleyplace ✉ B1 2JB – ✆ (0121) 633 4466 – www.bankrestaurants.com – Fax (0121) 633 4465 KZ**u**

Rest – Modern – Menu £ 15 (until 7pm) – Carte £ 21/40

◆ Capacious, modern and busy bar-restaurant where chefs can be watched through a glass wall preparing the tasty modern dishes. Pleasant terrace area.

XX **Metro Bar and Grill**

73 Cornwall St ✉ B3 2DF – ✆ (0121) 200 1911 – www.metrobarandgrill.co.uk – Closed 25 December-2 January and Sunday LY**n**

Rest – Modern – *(booking essential)* Menu £ 18 – Carte £ 21/27

◆ Gleaming chrome and mirrors in a bright, contemporary basement restaurant. Modern cooking with rotisserie specialities. Spacious, ever-lively bar serves lighter meals.

XX **Shimla Pinks**

214 Broad St ✉ B15 1AY – ✆ (0121) 633 0366 – www.shimlapinks.com – Fax (0121) 643 3325 – Closed 25-26 December and 1 January KZ**m**

Rest – Indian – *(dinner only)* Menu £ 30 – Carte £ 20/32

◆ A vast establishment in a street full of restaurants. Buzzy ambience prevails: open-plan kitchen adds to atmosphere. Authentic, modern Indian cuisine; impressive set menus.

at Hall Green Southeast : 5.75 mi. by A 41 on A 34 – ✉ Birmingham

XX **Liaison**

1558 Stratford Rd ✉ B28 9HA – ✆ (0121) 733 7336 – www.liaisonrestaurant.co.uk – Fax (0121) 733 1677 – Closed 10 days January, 1 week September, Saturday lunch, Sunday and Monday GX**i**

Rest – Classic – Menu £ 18/28

◆ Pleasant restaurant with understated décor in residential location. Linen table cloths and friendly service. Classically based modern eclectic cooking.

at Birmingham Airport Southeast : 9 mi. by A 45 - DU – ✉ Birmingham

Novotel Birmingham Airport rm,

Terminal 1 ✉ B26 3QL – ✆ (0121) 782 7000 – www.novotel.com – Fax (0121) 782 0445

195 rm – †£ 139 ††£ 139, ☕ £ 14.50

Rest – *(bar lunch Saturday, Sunday and Bank Holidays)* Menu £ 17 (lunch) – Carte £ 24/38

◆ Opposite main terminal building: modern hotel benefits from sound proofed doors and double glazing. Mini bars and power showers provided in spacious rooms with sofa beds. Open-plan garden brasserie.

at National Exhibition Centre Southeast : 9.5 mi. on A 45 - DU – ✉ Birmingham

Crowne Plaza rm,

Pendigo Way ✉ B40 1PS – ✆ (0870) 400 9160 – www.crowneplaza.co.uk – Fax (0121) 781 4321 – closed 21 December-4 January

242 rm ☕ – †£ 89/269 ††£ 89/269

Rest – *(closed Sunday lunch)* Menu £ 15/25 – Carte £ 22/35

◆ Modern hotel adjacent to NEC. Small terrace area overlooks lake. Extensive conference facilities. State-of-the-art bedrooms with a host of extras. Basement dining room: food with a Yorkshire twist.

BIRMINGHAM AIRPORT – W. Mids. – **503** O26 – see Birmingham

BISHOP'S STORTFORD – Hertfordshire – **504** U28 – pop. 35 325 **12** B2

Great Britain

London 34 mi. – Cambridge 27 mi. – Chelmsford 19 mi. – Colchester 33 mi.

Stansted Airport : ✆ (0844) 3351803, NE : 3.5 m

2 Market Square ✆ (01279) 655831, tic@bishopsstortford.org

Audley End★★ **AC**, N : 11 mi. by B 1383

The Cottage without rest

71 Birchanger Lane, Northeast : 2.25 mi. by B 1383 on Birchanger rd ✉ CM23 5QA – ✆ (01279) 812 349 – www.thecottagebirchanger.co.uk – Fax (01279) 815 045 – Closed Christmas and New Year

14 rm ☕ – †£ 45/60 ††£ 80/85

◆ Rurally-set part 17/18C cottages - yet close to airport. Cosy reception rooms with oak panelling and exposed beams. Conservatory style breakfast room and homely bedrooms.

ENGLAND

The Lemon Tree

14-16 Water Lane ✉ CM23 2LB – ☎ (01279) 757 788 – www.lemontree.co.uk – Fax (01279) 757 766 – Closed 25-26 December, 1 January, Sunday dinner and most Bank Holidays

Rest – Carte £ 22/34

◆ Cosy, vibrant restaurant in centre of town. Light and airy dining rooms, open bar; spacious private dining room on first floor. Wide-ranging menu, locally sourced ingredients.

Host

4 The Corn Exchange, Market Sq ✉ CM23 3UU – ☎ (01279) 657 000 – www.hostrestaurant.co.uk – Fax (01279) 657 826 – Closed 25-26 December and Sunday dinner

Rest – Menu £ 15 – Carte dinner £ 17/27

◆ Grade I listed building with unique roof terrace. Main restaurant has industrial feel, with modern bar and open kitchen. Oft-changing menu incorporates global influences.

at Stansted Mountfitchet Northeast : 3.5 mi. by B 1383 on B 1051 – ✉ Bishop'S Stortford

Chimneys without rest

44 Lower St, on B 1351 ✉ CM24 8LR – ☎ (01279) 813 388 – www.chimneysguesthouse.co.uk – Fax (01376) 310 169

4 rm – †£ 55/60 ††£ 78

◆ Charming 17C house with friendly hosts, beamed ceilings, snug breakfast room and homely lounge. Comfy bedrooms - single has largest bathroom. Usefully located for airport.

at Great Hallingbury East : 3mi. by A 1060 and Great Hallingbury rd.

Great Hallingbury Manor

Great Hallingbury ✉ CM22 7TJ – ☎ (01279) 506 475 – www.greathallingburymanor.com – Fax (01279) 505 523

31 rm – †£ 75/120 ††£ 120/240

Rest Anton's – *see restaurant listing*

◆ Tudor-style hotel, 5min from Stansted airport. Good-sized, stylish bedrooms with excellent beds and flat screen TVs; most have wet room showers; two have roll-top baths.

Anton's – at Great Hallingbury Manor Hotel

✉ CM22 7TJ – ☎ (01279) 506 475 – www.antonsrestaurant.co.uk – Fax (01279) 505 523 – Closed Saturday lunch and Sunday dinner

Rest – *(booking advisable)* Menu £ 18 (lunch) – Carte £ 28/46

◆ Formally laid, modern restaurant behind hotel, with piano, bar and terrace. Classic dishes presented in a modern style, some with a slight Oriental twist. Good breads; hearty puddings.

at Hatfield Heath Southeast : 6 mi. on A 1060 – ✉ Bishop'S Stortford

Down Hall Country House

rest,

South : 1.5 mi. by Matching Lane ✉ CM22 7AS – ☎ (01279) 731 441 – www.downhall.co.uk – Fax (01279) 730 416

99 rm – †£ 120/180 ††£ 180/320, £ 15.95

Rest *Ibbetsons* – *(closed Sunday to Wednesday) (dinner only) (booking essential for non-residents)* Carte £ 39/53

Rest *The Grill Room* – *(closed Saturday lunch)* Carte £ 28/41

◆ Ornate 19C Italianate mansion house in delightful grounds. Period style bedrooms; the most characterful in the old part of the house. Fine dining in traditional Ibbetsons restaurant. The contemporary Grill Room is less formal.

BISHOPSTONE – Swindon – 503 P29 – see Swindon

BISPHAM GREEN – Lancashire 20 A2

Eagle & Child

✉ L40 3SG – ☎ (01257) 462 297 – www.ainscoughs.co.uk – Fax (01257) 464 718 – Closed dinner 1 January

Rest – Carte £ 17/23

◆ Traditional 200 year old pub with a warm, cosy feel. Hearty, tasty cooking includes simple British classics and more ambitious daily specials. Up to 12 real ales available.

ENGLAND

BLACKAWTON – Devon – 503 I32 – see Dartmouth

BLACKBURN – Blackburn with Darwen – 502 M22 – pop. 105 085 — 20 B2

London 228 mi. – Leeds 47 mi. – Liverpool 39 mi. – Manchester 24 mi.
50-54 Church St ✆ (01254) 688040, visit@blackburn.gov.uk
Pleasington, ✆ (01254) 202 177
Wilpshire 72 Whalley Rd, ✆ (01254) 248 260
Great Harwood Harwood Bar, Whalley Rd, ✆ (01254) 884 391

The Clog & Billycock

Billinge End Rd, Pleasington , West : 2 mi. by A 677 ✉ BB2 6QB – ✆ (01254) 201 163 – www.theclogandbillycock.com – Closed 25 December
Rest – Carte approx. £ 24
◆ Spacious, open-plan pub named after a former landlord's favourite attire. Menu has strong Lancastrian slant, with sourcing a top priority. Generous portions, friendly service and realistic prices.

at Langho North : 4.5 mi. on A 666 – ✉ Whalley

Northcote (Nigel Haworth) with rm

Northcote Rd, North : 0.5 mi. on A 59 at junction with A 666 ✉ BB6 8BE – ✆ (01254) 240 555 – www.northcote.com – Fax (01254) 246 568 – Closed 25 December
14 rm – 👤£ 195/210 👥£ 225/250
Rest – Menu £ 25 (lunch) – Carte £ 38/62
Spec. Langoustines with leeks and pea ice cream. Lamb with potato mille-feuille, samphire and basil salsa. 'Blackberry textures' with spearmint ice cream.
◆ Traceability and food miles are all-important to this team, with regional ingredients and local suppliers the stars of the show; some produce travelling only the few metres from Northcote's own organic gardens. Traditional dining room in red-brick Victorian house. Elegant, contemporary bedrooms boast designer touches.

at Mellor Northwest : 3.25 mi. by A 677 – ✉ Blackburn

Stanley House

Southwest : 0.75 mi. by A 677 and Further Lane ✉ BB2 7NP – ✆ (01254) 769 200 – www.stanleyhouse.co.uk – Fax (01254) 769 206 – Closed 1 week January
12 rm – 👤£ 178 👥£ 235/285
Rest *Cassis* – see restaurant listing
◆ 17C manor with superb rural views houses elegantly proportioned rooms defined by wonderfully rich colours. Bar and conference facilities in converted farmhouse.

Millstone

Church Lane ✉ BB2 7JR – ✆ (01254) 813 333 – www.shirehotels.com – Fax (01254) 812 628
22 rm – 👤£ 85/125 👥£ 99/125 – 1 suite **Rest** – *(bar lunch)* Menu £ 32
◆ Attractive little sandstone former coaching inn in quiet village. Lounge bar with log fire and comfy sofas. Cosy bedrooms: matching floral patterns, botanical prints. Elegant wood panelled dining room warmed by fire.

Cassis – at Stanley House Hotel

Southwest : 0.75 mi. by A 677 and Further Lane ✉ BB2 7NP – ✆ (01254) 769 200 – www.stanleyhouse.co.uk – Fax (01254) 769 206 – Closed 2 weeks January, 2 weeks August, Saturday lunch, Sunday dinner, Monday and Tuesday
Rest – Menu £ 30 – Carte dinner £ 34/46
◆ Independent from main hotel. Name derives from rich blackcurrant theme throughout! Vast raised mezzanine for apéritifs. Weekly evolving menus with vibrant Lancashire accent.

BLACKPOOL – Blackpool – 502 K22 – pop. 142 283 Great Britain **20** A2

London 246 mi. – Leeds 88 mi. – Liverpool 56 mi. – Manchester 51 mi.

Blackpool Airport : ✆ (0844) 4827171, S : 3 mi. by A 584

1 Clifton St ✆ (01253) 478222, tic@blackpool.gov.uk

Blackpool Park North Park Drive, ✆ (01253) 397 916

Poulton-le-Fylde Breck Rd, Myrtle Farm, ✆ (01253) 892 444

Tower★ **AC** AY **A**

Imperial

North Promenade ✉ FY1 2HB – ✆ (01253) 623 971 – www.barcelo-hotels.co.uk – Fax (01253) 751 784 AY**c**

173 rm – †£ 65/140 ††£ 75/150, ☕ £ 10 – 7 suites

Rest *Palm Court* – *(dinner only and Sunday lunch)* Menu £ 23 **s**

◆ Imposing, classic 19C promenade hotel. Grand columned lobby, well-appointed rooms, many with views. Photos in the convivial No.10 bar recall PMs and past party conferences. Elegant restaurant with smartly liveried staff.

Hilton Blackpool

rm, rest,

North Promenade ✉ FY1 2JQ – ✆ (01253) 623 434 – www.hilton.co.uk/blackpool – Fax (01253) 294 371 AY**x**

268 rm ☕ – †£ 245 ††£ 255 – 6 suites

Rest *The Promenade* – *(bar lunch Monday-Saturday)* Menu £ 22 – Carte £ 22/30

◆ Open-plan, marble-floored lobby and smartly equipped rooms in contemporary style, almost all with views over the sea-front. Informal dining after cocktail lounge aperitifs.

ENGLAND

Number One South Beach

rm,

4 Harrowside West ✉ FY4 1NW – ✆ (01253) 343 900 – www.numberonehotels.com – Fax (01253) 343 906 BZ**v**

13 rm ☕ – †£ 75/125 ††£ 135/160 – 1 suite

Rest – *(dinner only and Sunday lunch)* Carte £ 22/30

◆ Modernised hotel on promenade. Contemporary interior with stylish, individually themed bedrooms; two with 4 posters. Superb bathrooms with whirlpool baths, luxury tiling and TVs. Restaurant with black runners on wood tables and vivid colour schemes; monthly menus provide interest.

Number One St Lukes without rest

1 St Lukes Rd ✉ FY4 2EL – ✆ (01253) 343 901 – www.numberoneblackpool.com – Fax (01253) 343 901 AZ**a**

3 rm ☕ – †£ 70/100 ††£ 100/125

◆ Engagingly run, enticingly stylish guesthouse. The good value nature of the establishment is further enhanced by an elegant breakfast room and luxuriously appointed bedrooms.

at Thornton Northeast : 5.5 mi. by A 584 - BY - on B 5412 – ✉ Blackpool

Twelve

Marsh Mill, Fleetwood Rd North, North : 0.5 mi. on A 585 ✉ FY5 4JZ – ✆ (01253) 821 212 – www.twelve-restaurant.co.uk – Fax (01253) 821 212 – Closed first 2 weeks January and Monday

Rest – *(dinner only and lunch Sunday and December)* Menu £ 19 (weekdays)/26 (Saturday) – Carte £ 31/45

◆ Spacious, high-ceilinged restaurant, passionately run by dynamic owner and friendly team. Good value menus offer interesting, well-executed modern dishes with the odd innovative touch.

Each starred restaurant lists three specialities that are typical of its style of cuisine. These may not always be on the menu but in their place expect delicious seasonal dishes. Be sure to try them.

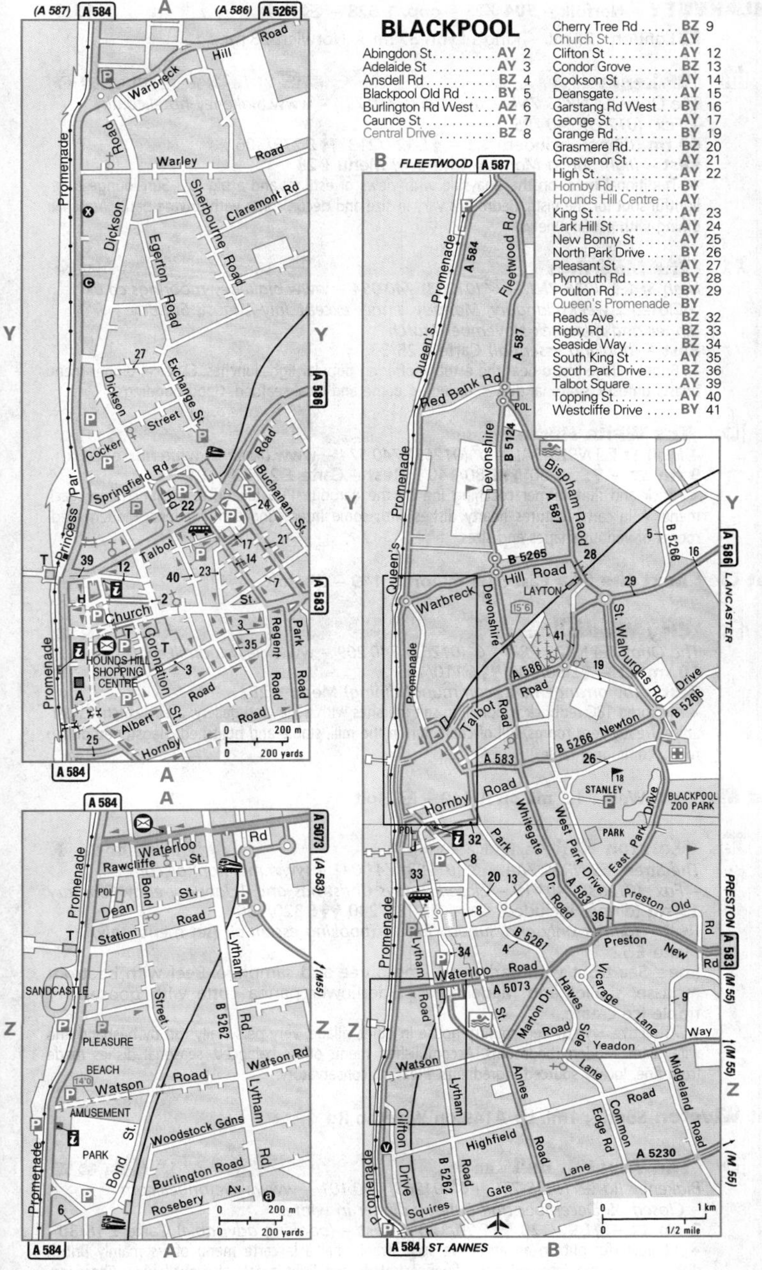
BLACKPOOL
Abingdon St. . . . . AY 2
Adelaide St . . . . AY 3
Ansdell Rd . . . . BZ 4
Blackpool Old Rd . . . . . BY 5
Burlington Rd West . . . AZ 6
Caunce St . . . . AY 7
Central Drive . . . . BZ 8
Cherry Tree Rd . . . . . . BZ 9
Church St. . . . . AY
Clifton St . . . . AY 12
Condor Grove . . . . BZ 13
Cookson St . . . . AY 14
Deansgate . . . . AY 15
Garstang Rd West . . . . BY 16
George St . . . . AY 17
Grange Rd . . . . BY 19
Grasmere Rd . . . . BZ 20
Grosvenor St . . . . AY 21
High St . . . . AY 22
Hornby Rd . . . . BY
Hounds Hill Centre . . . . AY
King St . . . . AY 23
Lark Hill St . . . . AY 24
New Bonny St . . . . AY 25
North Park Drive . . . . . BY 26
Pleasant St . . . . AY 27
Plymouth Rd . . . . BY 28
Poulton Rd . . . . BY 29
Queen's Promenade . . . BY
Reads Ave . . . . BZ 32
Rigby Rd . . . . BZ 33
Seaside Way . . . . BZ 34
South King St . . . . AY 35
South Park Drive . . . . . BZ 36
Talbot Square . . . . AY 39
Topping St . . . . AY 40
Westcliffe Drive . . . . . BY 41
FLEETWOOD
A 587
LANCASTER
A 586
PRESTON
A 583
(M 55)
ST. ANNES
A 584
HOUNDS HILL SHOPPING CENTRE
SANDCASTLE
PLEASURE BEACH
AMUSEMENT PARK
BLACKPOOL ZOO PARK
STANLEY PARK
LAYTON
ENGLAND

BLAKENEY – Norfolk – 504 X25 – pop. 1 628 – ✉ Holt 15 C1

London 127 mi. – King's Lynn 37 mi. – Norwich 28 mi.

Blakeney

The Quay ✉ NR25 7NE – ✆ (01263) 740 797 – www.blakeney-hotel.co.uk – Fax (01263) 740 795

64 rm (dinner included) – †£ 127/213 ††£ 278/306

Rest – *(light lunch Monday-Saturday)* Menu £ 28

◆ Traditional hotel on the quayside with views of estuary and a big sky! Sun lounge a delightful spot for the vista. Bedrooms vary in size and décor, some with private patio. Armchair dining with estuary views.

The Moorings

High St ✉ NR25 7NA – ✆ (01263) 740 054 – www.blakeney-moorings.co.uk – Closed 2 weeks January, Monday dinner except July-August, Sunday dinner and midweek November-March

Rest – *(booking essential)* Carte £ 25/33

◆ Bright village bistro near the estuary, offering popular light lunches. Classical dinner menu boasts unfussy, seasonal dishes, including game and local seafood. Good puddings.

The White Horse with rm

4 High St ✉ NR25 7AL – ✆ (01263) 740 574 – www.blakeneywhitehorse.co.uk

9 rm – †£ 50/80 ††£ 80/140 **Rest** – Carte £ 21/33

◆ Brick and flint former coaching inn by the harbour. Pub favourites on lunchtime snack menu. À la carte features hearty dishes with some interesting combinations. Modern bedrooms of various shapes and sizes.

ENGLAND

at Cley next the Sea East : 1.5 mi. on A 149 – ✉ Holt

Cley Windmill

The Quay ✉ NR25 7RP – ✆ (01263) 740 209 – www.cleywindmill.co.uk

10 rm – †£ 90/100 ††£ 110/155

Rest – *(by arrangement, communal dining)* Menu £ 28

◆ Restored 18C redbrick windmill in salt marshes with a viewing gallery: a birdwatcher's paradise. Neatly kept rooms, full of character, in the mill, stable and boatshed. Flagstoned dining room; communal table.

at Morston West : 1.5 mi. on A 149 – ✉ Holt

Morston Hall (Galton Blackiston)

The Street ✉ NR25 7AA – ✆ (01263) 741 041 – www.morstonhall.com – Fax (01263) 740 419 – Closed 2 days Christmas and 1 January-early February

13 rm (dinner included) – †£ 180/240 ††£ 320/360

Rest – *(dinner only and Sunday lunch) (booking essential) (set menu only)* Menu £ 52

Spec. Sea trout with garlic and lime purée and samphire. Beef with beetroot mousse, shallot and Madeira jus. Elderflower panna cotta with gooseberry ripple ice cream.

◆ Attractive, ivy covered country house in quiet village, very personally run by husband and wife team. Modern bedrooms. Accomplished menu offers balanced, seasonal dishes made from fine, locally sourced ingredients. Pleasant conservatory.

at Wiveton South : 1mi. by A149 on Wiveton Rd

The Wiveton Bell with rm

Blakeney Rd ✉ NR25 7TL – ✆ (01263) 740 101 – www.wivetonbell.com – Closed 25 December and Sunday dinner in winter

2 rm – †£ 90/120 ††£ 90/120 **Rest** – *(booking advisable)* Carte £ 18/30

◆ Characterful pub in an attractive spot. Traditional à la carte menu offers mainly British dishes with some international influence; salads and light meals also available. Charming, comfortable bedrooms.

BLANDFORD FORUM – Dorset – 503 N31 – pop. 9 854 4 C3

London 124 mi. – Bournemouth 17 mi. – Dorchester 17 mi. – Salisbury 24 mi.

1 Greyhound Yard ✆ (01258) 454770, blandfordtic@north-dorset.gov.uk

Ashley Wood Wimbourne Rd, ✆ (01258) 452 253

Town★

Kingston Lacy★★ AC, SE : 5.5 mi. by B 3082 – Royal Signals Museum★, NE : 2 mi. by B 3082. Milton Abbas★, SW : 8 mi. by A 354 – Sturminster Newton★, NW : 8 mi. by A 357

Portman Lodge without rest

Whitecliff Mill St ✉ DT11 7BP – ✆ (01258) 453 727 – www.portmanlodge.co.uk – Closed 24 December-3 January

3 rm – ♦£ 50 ♦♦£ 70

◆ Red brick Victorian house close to Georgian town centre; many original features. All rooms crammed with artefacts; individually decorated bedrooms with unique identities and styles.

at Iwerne Minster North : 6 mi. on A 350

The Talbot with rm

✉ DT11 8QN – ✆ (01747) 811 269 – www.the-talbot.com

5 rm – ♦£ 65/75 ♦♦£ 75/95 **Rest** – Carte £ 20/30

◆ Pleasant and unfussy mock-Elizabethan inn. Hearty and generous cooking features British classics at lunch and substantial, regularly-changing dishes in the evening. Rooms are comfortable, well-appointed and up-to-date.

at Farnham Northeast : 7.5 mi. by A 354 – ✉ Blandford Forum

Farnham Farm House without rest

North : 1m. by Shaftesbury rd ✉ DT11 8DG – ✆ (01725) 516 254 – www.farnhamfarmhouse.co.uk – Fax (01725) 516 306 – Closed 25-26 December

3 rm – ♦£ 60 ♦♦£ 80

◆ Attractive farmhouse in peaceful location. Simple, individually furnished bedrooms with country views. Swimming pool and therapy centre on site. Breakfast features local produce; picnics available.

The Museum Inn with rm

✉ DT11 8DE – ✆ (01725) 516 261 – www.museuminn.co.uk – Fax (01725) 516 988

8 rm – ♦£ 110 ♦♦£ 165 **Rest** – *(bookings not accepted)* Carte £ 27/36

◆ Part-thatched 17C country pub, in a picture postcard village. Menu offers British classics with a Mediterranean edge; cooking is seasonal, unfussy and local. Bedrooms range from small and cottagey, to spacious with four-posters.

at Chettle Northeast : 7.25 mi. by A 354 – ✉ Blandford Forum

Castleman with rm

✉ DT11 8DB – ✆ (01258) 830 096 – www.castlemanhotel.co.uk – Fax (01258) 830 051 – Closed February, 25-26 and 31 December

8 rm – ♦£ 60 ♦♦£ 95

Rest – *(dinner only and Sunday lunch)* Menu £ 21 – Carte £ 22/32

◆ Bland exterior hides impressive tiled hallway and elegant drawing rooms boasting superb Elizabethan wood carvings and vast oil paintings. Spacious bedrooms display traditional comforts. Dining room offers daily changing classics and garden views.

Shapwick Southeast : 7.5 mi. by B 3082

The Anchor

West St ✉ DT11 9LB – ✆ (01258) 857 269 – www.anchorshapwick.co.uk – Fax (01258) 858 840 – Closed 25 December

Rest – *(closed Sunday dinner)* Carte £ 19/28

◆ Traditionally furnished village pub, with flag floors, open fires, friendly staff and a cosy feel. Unfussy, modern cooking; daily changing menus feature game from local estates.

BLEDINGTON – Oxon. – 503 P28 – see Stow-on-the-Wold

BLOCKLEY – Gloucestershire – 503 O27 – pop. 1 668 – ✉ Moreton-In-Marsh
4 D1

London 91 mi. – Birmingham 39 mi. – Oxford 34 mi.

Lower Brook House

Lower St ✉ GL56 9DS – ✆ (01386) 700 286 – www.lowerbrookhouse.com – Fax (01386) 701 400 – Closed Christmas

6 rm – †£ 80/185 ††£ 80/185

Rest – *(closed Sunday) (dinner only) (booking essential for non-residents)* Carte £ 25/32

◆ Personally run, adjoining 17C Cotswold stone cottages with huge inglenooks, beams and flagged floors. Characterful and stylish from every aspect. Individually appointed rooms. Imaginative evening menus of local Cotswold produce.

BLUNDELLSANDS – Mersey. – 502 L23 – see Liverpool

BLUNSDON – Wilts. – 503 O29 – see Swindon

BLYTH – Nottinghamshire – 502 Q23 – pop. 1 867 – ✉ Worksop
16 B1

London 166 mi. – Doncaster 13 mi. – Lincoln 30 mi. – Nottingham 32 mi.

The Charnwood

rest,

Sheffield Rd, West : 0.75 mi. on A 634 ✉ S81 8HF – ✆ (01909) 591 610 – www.thecharnwood.com – Fax (01909) 591 427

45 rm – †£ 67/97 ††£ 84/153 **Rest** – Carte £ 27/45 **s**

◆ Well suited to the business traveller, this hotel offers consistently well-kept bedrooms. Its most recent additions are spacious, stylish, well-equipped and overlook the garden. A lounge bar offers informal dining; the large restaurant is smart with up-to-date décor.

BODIAM – East Sussex – 504 V30 Great Britain
8 B2

London 58 mi. – Cranbrook 7 mi. – Hastings 13 mi.

Castle★★

Battle Abbey★, S : 10 mi. by B 2244, B 2089, A 21 and minor rd – Rye★★, SW : 13 mi. by A 268

The Curlew

Junction Rd, Northwest : 1.5 mi. at junction with B 2244 ✉ TN32 5UY – ✆ (01580) 861 394 – www.thecurlewrestaurant.co.uk – Closed 2 weeks spring, 2 weeks autumn, 25-26 December, Monday and Tuesday

Rest – Carte £ 22/29

◆ This 17C inn has been transformed by the new owners; the interior has been given a striking, contemporary makeover. The concise but cleverly balanced menu follows the seasons and dishes are executed with aplomb.

BODMIN – Cornwall – 503 F32 – pop. 12 778
1 B2

London 270 mi. – Newquay 18 mi. – Plymouth 32 mi. – Truro 23 mi.

Shire Hall, Mount Folly ✆ (01208) 76616, bodmintic@visit.org.uk

St Petroc Church★

Bodmin Moor★★ - Lanhydrock★★, S : 3 mi. by B 3269 – Blisland★ (Church★), N : 5.5 mi. by A 30 and minor roads – Pencarrow★, NW : 4 mi. by A 389 and minor roads – Cardinham (Church★), NE : 4 mi. by A 30 and minor rd – St Mabyn (Church★), N : 5.5 mi. by A 389, B 3266 and minor rd. St Tudy★, N : 7 mi. by A 389, B 3266 and minor rd

Trehellas House

Washaway, Northwest: 3 mi. on A 389 ✉ PL30 3AD – ✆ (01208) 72 700 – www.trehellashouse.co.uk – Fax (01208) 73 336

12 rm – †£ 50/65 ††£ 65/160 **Rest** – Menu £ 10 (lunch) – Carte £ 25/37

◆ Relaxed, personally run country house with keen owners. Bedrooms divided between main house and converted stable. Cosy and cottagey feel without being chintzy. Traditional cooking; venison a speciality.

ENGLAND

Bokiddick Farm without rest

Lanivet, South : 5 mi. by A 30 following signs for Lanhydrock and Bokiddick ✉ PL30 5HP – ☎ (01208) 831 481 – www.bokiddickfarm.co.uk – Fax (01208) 831 481 – Closed Christmas and New Year

5 rm – †£ 45/50 ††£ 64/76

◆ Sizeable house on dairy farm: do take a quick tour. Warm welcome assured. Neat, well priced rooms with added amenities in old house; smart stable conversion for more rooms.

BODSHAM – Kent 9 C2

London 65 mi. – Ashford 10 mi. – Canterbury 10 mi.

Froggies at the Timber Batts

School Lane ✉ TN25 5JQ – ☎ (01233) 750 237 – www.thetimberbatts.co.uk – Fax (01233) 750 176 – Closed 24 December-3 January

Rest – French – Menu £ 20 (lunch) – Carte £ 27/40

◆ All things ranine are celebrated at this 15C pub, thanks to the jolly French owner with a sense of irony. Traditional beamed bar. Authentic French dishes and classic desserts.

BOLNHURST – Bedfordshire 12 A1

London 64 mi. – Bedford 8 mi. – St Neots 7 mi.

The Plough at Bolnhurst

Kimbolton Rd, South : 0.5 mi. on B 660 ✉ MK44 2EX – ☎ (01234) 376 274 – www.bolnhurst.com – Closed 2 weeks January, 31 December, Sunday dinner and Monday

Rest – Menu £ 17 (lunch) – Carte £ 28/42

◆ Restored, whitewashed pub with spacious, rustic interior, smart terrace and pleasant gardens. Assured service from smartly dressed staff. Wide-ranging, seasonal menu.

BOLTON ABBEY – North Yorkshire – 502 O22 – pop. 117 22 B2

– ✉ **Skipton** Great Britain

London 216 mi. – Harrogate 18 mi. – Leeds 23 mi. – Skipton 6 mi.

Bolton Priory★ **AC**

The Devonshire Arms Country House

✉ BD23 6AJ – ☎ (01756) 710 441 – www.devonshirehotels.co.uk – Fax (01756) 710 564

38 rm – †£ 190/335 ††£ 230/410 – 2 suites

Rest The Burlington and **The Brasserie** – *see restaurant listing*

◆ Fine period coaching inn, with antique-furnished guest areas and vast art collection. Compact bedrooms in extension, recently refurbished in bright, contemporary country house style. Refurbishment to continue in main house. Good spa and leisure. Smooth service.

The Burlington – at The Devonshire Arms Country House Hotel

✉ BD23 6AJ – ☎ (01756) 710 441 – www.devonshirehotels.co.uk – Fax (01756) 710 564

Rest – *(dinner only and Sunday lunch) (booking essential)* Menu £ 58

Spec. Foie gras terrine with fig purée and red wine jelly. Halibut with clams, cep gnocchi and tonka bean foam. 'Chocolate mayhem' with passion fruit and peanut ice cream.

◆ Elegant, antique-filled dining room with polished tables and oil paintings. Structured, formal service. Ambitious, creative cooking captures modern trends; elaborate dishes are artistically presented, displaying the chef's obvious passion.

The Brasserie – at The Devonshire Arms Country House Hotel

✉ BD23 6AJ – ☎ (01756) 710 710 – www.devonshirehotels.co.uk – Fax (01756) 710 564

Rest – Carte £ 20/50

◆ A contrast to the restaurant in atmosphere and design. This is a modern, vividly decorated brasserie; the kitchen produces carefully prepared, satisfying brasserie favourites.

BOLTON-BY-BOWLAND – Lancashire – 502 M/N22 Great Britain 20 B2

London 246 mi. – Blackburn 17 mi. – Skipton 15 mi.

Skipton - Castle★, E : 12 mi. by A 59 – Bolton Priory★, E : 17 mi. by A 59

Middle Flass Lodge
Settle Rd, North : 2.5 mi. by Clitheroe rd on Settle rd ✉ *BB7 4NY – ✆ (01200) 447 259 – www.middleflasslodge.co.uk – Fax (01200) 447 300*
7 rm – †£ 42/50 ††£ 62/75 **Rest** – *(by arrangement)* Menu £ 29
◆ Friendly, welcoming owners in a delightfully located barn conversion. Plenty of beams add to rustic effect. Pleasantly decorated, comfy rooms with countryside outlook. Blackboard's eclectic menu boasts local, seasonal backbone.

BONCHURCH – **Isle of Wight** – **504** P32 – **see Wight (Isle of)**

BOREHAM – **Essex** – **504** V27 – **see Chelmsford**

BOROUGHBRIDGE – **North Yorkshire** – **502** P21 – **pop. 3 311** **22** B2
London 215 mi. – Leeds 19 mi. – Middlesbrough 36 mi. – York 16 mi.
2 Fishergate ✆ (01423) 323 373

thediningroom
20 St James's Sq ✉ *YO51 9AR – ✆ (01423) 326 426 – www.thediningroomonline.co.uk – Fax (01423) 326 426 – Closed Sunday dinner and Monday*
Rest – *(dinner only and Sunday lunch) (booking essential)* Menu £ 28 – Carte £ 28/34
◆ Characterful cottage with beamed dining room. Vivid fireside sofas and Impressionist oils, as modern as the well-prepared dishes: duck on rocket and pesto features.

at Roecliffe **West : 1 mi.**

The Crown Inn
✉ *YO51 9LY – ✆ (01423) 322 300 – www.crowninnroecliffe.com – Fax (01423) 322 033 – Closed Sunday dinner*
Rest – Menu £ 19/22 – Carte £ 25/45
◆ 16C coaching inn with flagstones, beams and open fires. Locally sourced produce used in classical, carefully-crafted cooking, served in the bar and elegant restaurant.

ENGLAND

BORROWDALE – **Cumbria** – **502** K20 – **see Keswick**

BOSCASTLE – **Cornwall** – **503** F31 **1** B2
London 260 mi. – Bude 14 mi. – Exeter 59 mi. – Plymouth 43 mi.
Village★
Poundstock Church★ – Tintagel Old Post Office★

Boscastle House without rest
Tintagel Rd, South : 0.75 mi. on B 3263 ✉ *PL35 OAS – ✆ (01840) 250 654 – www.boscastlehouse.com – restricted opening in Winter*
6 rm – †£ 80 ††£ 120
◆ Modern styling in a detached Victorian house. Bedrooms are light and spacious, with roll-top baths and walk-in showers. Hearty breakfasts, cream teas and a calm, relaxing air.

Trerosewill Farm without rest
Paradise, South : 1 mi. off B 3263 ✉ *PL35 0BL – ✆ (01840) 250 545 – www.trerosewill.co.uk – Fax (01840) 250 727 – Closed November-mid February*
9 rm – †£ 40/60 ††£ 85/99
◆ Modern house on 50-acre working farm: fine views of the coast and good clifftop walks. Lovely conservatory breakfast room. Bedrooms in matching patterns, some with Jacuzzis.

Old Rectory without rest
St Juliot, Northeast : 2.5 mi. by B 3263 ✉ *PL35 0BT – ✆ (01840) 250 225 – www.stjuliot.com – Fax (01840) 250 225 – March-November*
4 rm – †£ 38/56 ††£ 82/90
◆ Communal breakfast room, with views of Victorian walled garden, from whence much of the produce comes. Characterful bedrooms; one in converted stables. Thomas Hardy stayed here.

BOSHAM – **W. Sussex** – **504** R31 – **see Chichester**

BOSTON SPA – West Yorkshire – 502 P22 – pop. 5 952 — 22 B2

London 127 mi. – Harrogate 12 mi. – Leeds 12 mi. – York 16 mi.

Four Gables without rest

Oaks Lane, West : 0.25 mi. by A 659 ✉ LS23 6DS – ✆ (01937) 845 592 – www.fourgables.co.uk – Closed Christmas and January

4 rm – †£ 50/60 ††£ 83/93

◆ Down a quiet private road, a 1900 house, after Lutyens: period fireplaces, stripped oak and terracotta tile floors. Traditional, individually decorated rooms. Mature garden.

BOUGHTON MONCHELSEA – Kent – pop. 2 863 — 8 B2

London 46 mi. – Southend-on-Sea 60 mi. – Basildon 48 mi. – Maidstone 4 mi.

The Mulberry Tree

Hermitage Lane, South : 1.5 mi. by Park Lane and East Hall Hill ✉ ME17 4DA – ✆ (01622) 749 082 – www.themulberrytreekent.co.uk – Closed 26 December, 1 January, Sunday dinner and Monday

Rest – Menu £ 16 (except Saturday dinner) – Carte £ 26/34

◆ Remotely situated, stylishly decorated, family-owned restaurant with enclosed garden. Daily-changing menus offer modern, tasty dishes, homemade using the best local produce.

BOURNE END – Hertfordshire – See Bedford

BOURNEMOUTH – Bournemouth – 503 O31 – pop. 167 527 — 4 D3

London 114 mi. – Bristol 76 mi. – Southampton 34 mi.

Bournemouth (Hurn) Airport : ✆ (01202) 364000, N : 5 mi. by Hurn - DV

Westover Rd ✆ (0845) 0511700, info@bournemouth.gov.uk

Queens Park Queens Park West Drive, ✆ (01202) 302 611

Meyrick Park Central Drive, ✆ (01202) 786 000

Compton Acres★★ (English Garden ≤★★★) **AC** AX – Russell-Cotes Art Gallery and Museum★★ **AC** DZ **M1** - Shelley Rooms **AC** EX **M2**

Poole★, W : 4 mi. by A 338 – Brownsea Island★ (Baden-Powell Stone ≤★★) **AC**, by boat from Sandbanks BX or Poole Quay – Christchurch★ (Priory Church★) E : 4.5 mi. on A 35. Corfe Castle★, SW : 18 mi. by A 35 and A 351 – Lulworth Cove★ (Blue Pool★) W : 8 mi. of Corfe Castle by B 3070 – Swanage★, E : 5 mi. of Corfe Castle by A 351

Plans pages 114, 115

Bournemouth Highcliff Marriott

St Michael's Rd, West Cliff — rm,

✉ BH2 5DU – ✆ (01202) 557 702 – www.bournenmouthhighcliffmarriott.co.uk – Fax (01202) 293 155 — CZ**z**

157 rm – †£ 155 ††£ 155/170 – 3 suites

Rest – *(dinner only and Sunday lunch)* Carte £ 25/29

◆ Imposing white clifftop landmark, linked by funicular to the beach. Elegant drawing rooms; bedrooms, in the grand tradition, and leisure centre are comprehensively equipped. Secure a bay view table in elegant formal restaurant.

Miramar

rm,

19 Grove Rd, East Overcliff ✉ BH1 3AL – ✆ (01202) 556 581 – www.miramar-bournemouth.com – Fax (01202) 291 242 — DZ**u**

43 rm – †£ 40/90 ††£ 80/130

Rest – *(closed Saturday lunch)* Menu £ 16/28

◆ Along the handsome lines of a grand Edwardian villa. Large, well cared for rooms, a few with curved balconies, in floral patterns. Library and a sun terrace facing the sea. Traditional menu.

ENGLAND

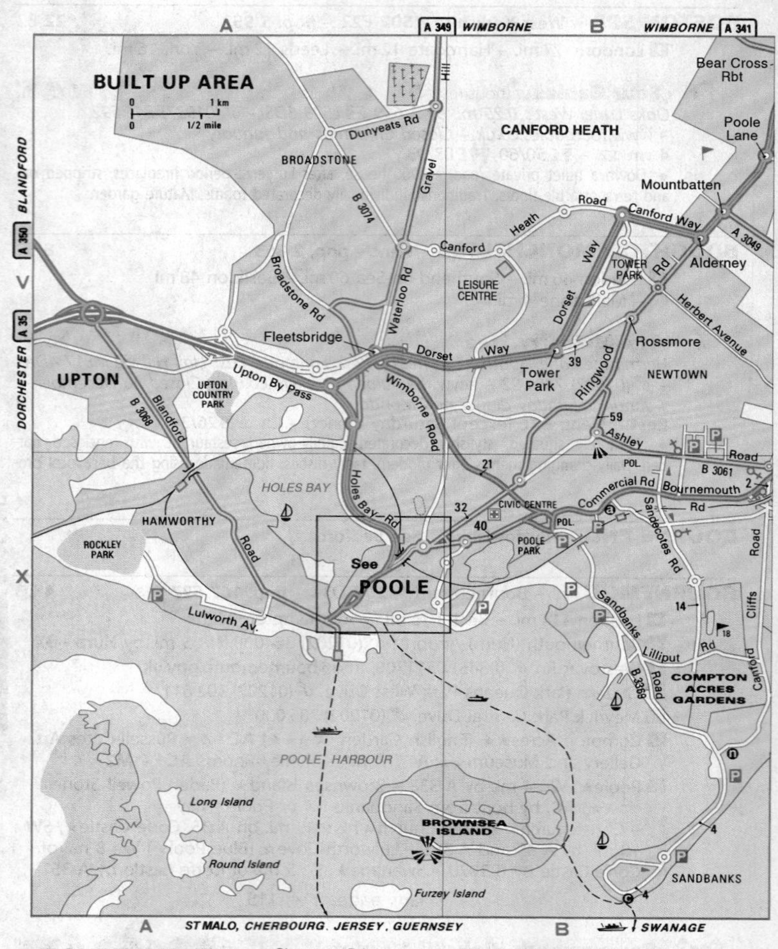

BOURNEMOUTH AND POOLE

Archway Rd . . . . . BX 2
Banks Rd . . . . . BX 4
Boscombe Overcliff Rd . . . . EX 6
Boscombe Spa Rd . . . . DX 7
Branksome Wood Rd . . . . CY 9
Chessel Ave . . . . . EX 10
Clarendon Rd . . . . . CX 12
Commercial Rd . . . . . CY 13
Compton Ave . . . . . BX 14
Cranleigh Rd . . . . . EV 16
Durley Rd . . . . . CZ 17
Ensbury Park Rd . . . . . CV 19
Exeter Rd . . . . . CDZ 20
Fernside Rd . . . . . ABX 21
Fir Vale Rd . . . . . DY 23
Gervis Pl . . . . . DY 24
Gloucester Rd . . . . . EV 26
Hampshire Centre . . . . . DV
Hinton Rd . . . . . DZ 27
Lansdowne Rd . . . . . DY 30
Lansdowne (The) . . . . . DY 28
Leven Ave . . . . . CX 31
Longfleet Rd . . . . . BX 32
Madeira Rd . . . . . DY 34
Manor Rd . . . . . EY 35
Meyrick Rd . . . . . EYZ 36
Old Christchurch Rd . . . . . DY
Old Wareham Rd . . . . . BV 39
Parkstone Rd . . . . . BX 40
Pinecliff Rd . . . . . CX 42
Post Office Rd . . . . . CY 43
Priory Rd . . . . . CZ 45
Queen's Rd . . . . . CX 46
Richmond Hill . . . . . CY 47
Richmond Park Rd . . . . . DV 48
Russell Cotes Rd . . . . . DZ 49
St Michael's Rd . . . . . CZ 51
St Paul's Rd . . . . . EY 52
St Peter's Rd . . . . . DY 53
St Stephen's Rd . . . . . CY 55
St Swithuns Rd South . . . . . EY 56
Seabourne Rd . . . . . EV 57
Seamoor Rd . . . . . CX 58
Sea View Rd . . . . . BV 59
Southbourne Grove . . . . . EX 61
Southbourne Overcliff Drive . . . . . EX 62
Sovereign Shopping Centre . EX
Square (The) . . . . . CY 63
Suffolk Rd . . . . . CY 64
Surrey Rd . . . . . CX 66
Triangle (The) . . . . . CY 67
Upper Hinton Rd . . . . . DZ 68
Wessex Way . . . . . CX 70
Western Rd . . . . . CX 73
Westover Rd . . . . . DZ 75
West Cliff Promenade . . . . . CZ 71

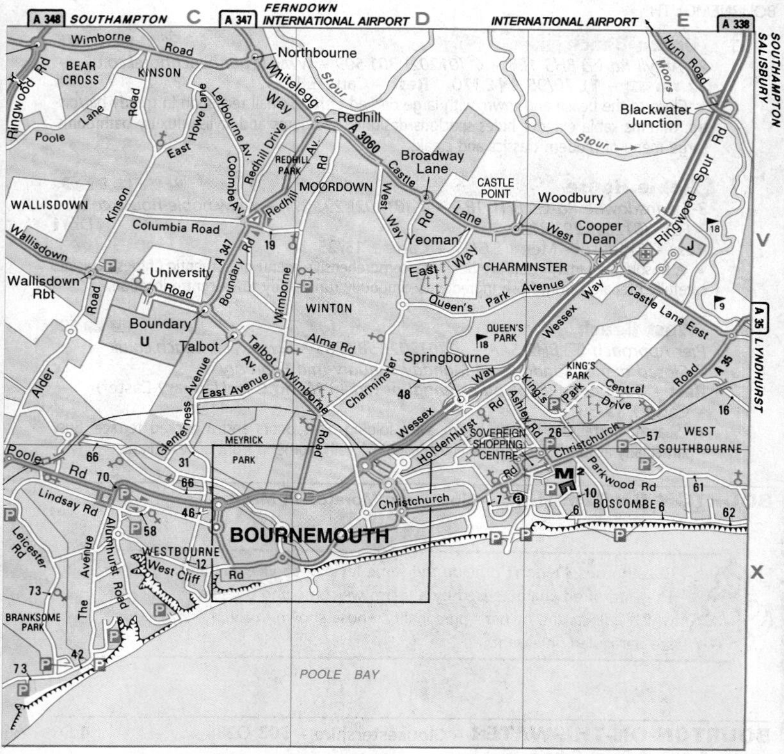

A 348 SOUTHAMPTON
C
A 347 FERNDOWN INTERNATIONAL AIRPORT
D
INTERNATIONAL AIRPORT
E
A 338 SOUTHAMPTON SALISBURY
Wimborne Road
BEAR CROSS
KINSON
Northbourne
Whitelegg Way
Stour
Ringwood Rd
Poole Lane
Road
Leybourne Av.
East Howe Lane
Redhill
A 3060
Hurn Road
Moors
Blackwater Junction
Stour
Spur Rd
REDHILL PARK
Redhill Drive
Av.
Rd
Broadway Lane
Castle
Coombe Av.
MOORDOWN
West Way
CASTLE POINT
Woodbury
WALLISDOWN
Kinson
Redhill
Rd
Lane
Columbia Road
A 347
Boundary Rd
19
Yeoman
West
Cooper Dean
Ringwood
J
18
V
Wallisdown
Wallisdown Rbt
Road
University
Road
Wimborne
East Way
CHARMINSTER
Wessex Way
Castle Lane East
9
WINTON
Queen's Park Avenue
Boundary
U
Talbot
Talbot Av.
Alma Rd
QUEEN'S PARK
18
A 35 LYNDHURST
Alder
Glenferness Avenue
East Avenue
Wimborne
Charminster
Springbourne
48
Wessex
Way
KING'S PARK
King's Park
Ashley Rd
Central Drive
Road
A 35
16
Rd
Holdenhurst
SOVEREIGN SHOPPING CENTRE
26
Christchurch
57
WEST SOUTHBOURNE
MEYRICK PARK
Poole
Rd
66
70
31
66
Road
Rd
M2
Parkwood Rd
61
Lindsay Rd
Christchurch
7
10
BOSCOMBE
6
6
62
46
58
Leicester Rd
Alumhurst Road
BOURNEMOUTH
The Avenue
WESTBOURNE
12
West Cliff
Rd
X
73
BRANKSOME PARK
42
73
POOLE BAY

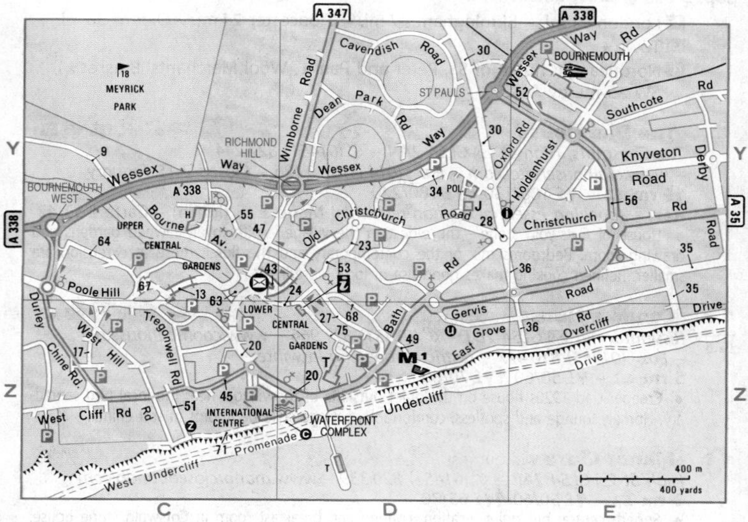

A 347
A 338
Cavendish Road
30
Wessex Way
Rd
BOURNEMOUTH
18
MEYRICK PARK
Wimborne Road
Dean Park Rd
ST PAULS
52
Rd
Southcote
Y
9
RICHMOND HILL
Way
30
Oxford Rd
Holdenhurst
Knyveton Road
Derby Road
Y
BOURNEMOUTH WEST
Wessex
Wessex
Way
A 338
34
POL
Rd
A 338
Bourne Av.
H
55
UPPER CENTRAL GARDENS
Old Christchurch
Road
J
28
Christchurch
56
A 35
47
23
64
43
53
Rd
36
35
Poole Hill
67
13
63
24
LOWER CENTRAL GARDENS
27
68
Bath Rd
Gervis Road
35
Drive
Durley Chine Rd.
West Hill
Tregonwell Rd
17
20
75
49
T
M1
East
Grove
36
Rd
Overcliff
Drive
Z
20
45
Z
West Cliff Rd
Rd
51
INTERNATIONAL CENTRE
Undercliff
WATERFRONT COMPLEX
71
Promenade
West Undercliff
T
0 400 m
0 400 yards
C
D
E

Urban Beach

23 Argyll Rd ✉ BH5 1EB – ✆ (01202) 301 509 – www.urbanbeachhotel.co.uk
12 rm – †£ 70/95 ††£ 170 **Rest** – Carte £ 17/32 DX**a**
◆ Close to the beach and town, with large decked terrace; small reception in trendy bar/bistro. Unremarkable exterior hides spacious designer bedrooms and stylish, luxury bathrooms. Large menu of modern classics and steaks.

Noble House

3-5 Lansdowne Rd ✉ BH1 1RZ – ✆ (01202) 291 277 – www.noble-house.co.uk – Fax (01202) 291 312 DEY**i**
Rest – Chinese – Menu £ 6/17 – Carte £ 13/25
◆ A hospitable family team are behind a comprehensive menu of authentic Chinese cuisine, carefully prepared from fresh ingredients. Smoothly run; handy town centre location.

West Beach

Pier Approach ✉ BH2 5AA – ✆ (01202) 587 785 – www.west-beach.co.uk – Closed dinner Sunday and Monday January-mid February DZ**c**
Rest – Seafood – *(booking essential at lunch)* Menu £ 16 (January-Easter) – Carte £ 19/39
◆ Seafood restaurant on the beach, with folding glass doors and a decked terrace. Busy - particularly at lunch. Fish and shellfish caught locally; some in front of restaurant.

BOURTON-ON-THE-HILL – Glos. – see Moreton-in-Marsh

Guesthouses don't provide the same level of service as hotels. They are often characterised by a warm welcome and a décor which reflects the owner's personality. Those shown in red are particularly pleasant.

BOURTON-ON-THE-WATER – Gloucestershire – 503 O28 **4** D1 – pop. 3 093 Great Britain

London 91 mi. – Birmingham 47 mi. – Gloucester 24 mi. – Oxford 36 mi.
Town★
Northleach (Church of SS. Peter and Paul★, Wool Merchants' Brasses★), SW : 5 mi. by A 429

The Dial House

The Chestnuts, High St ✉ GL54 2AN – ✆ (01451) 822 244 – www.dialhousehotel.com – Fax (01451) 810 126 – Closed 2-15 January
15 rm – †£ 100/130 ††£ 180/220
Rest – *(booking essential for non-residents)* Menu £ 15 (lunch) – Carte £ 33/42
◆ House of Cotswold stone - the oldest in the village - with lovely lawned gardens and drawing room. Bedrooms mix of the contemporary and the floral; those in extension are smaller. Refined cooking makes good use of local ingredients.

Coombe House without rest

Rissington Rd ✉ GL54 2DT – ✆ (01451) 821 966 – www.coombehouse.net – Fax (01451) 810 477 – restricted opening in winter
5 rm – †£ 50/60 ††£ 70/80
◆ Creeper-clad 1920s house on the quiet outskirts of the village, near the local bird sanctuary. Homely lounge and spotless, comfortable, cottage style bedrooms in soft chintz.

Manor Close without rest

High St ✉ GL54 2AP – ✆ (01451) 820 339 – www.manorclosedbandb.com
3 rm – †£ 50/60 ††£ 65/70
◆ Superb central but quiet location. Lounge and breakfast room in Cotswold stone house; comfortable floral rooms in purpose-built garden annexe, one on ground floor.

at Upper Slaughter **Northwest : 2.5 mi. by A 429 – ✉ Bourton-On-The-Water**

Lords of the Manor

✉ *GL54 2JD – ☎ (01451) 820 243 – www.lordsofthemanor.com – Fax (01451) 820 696*

24 rm – †£ 191 ††£ 220/303 – 2 suites

Rest – *(dinner only and Sunday lunch)* Menu £ 55

Spec. Lasagne of crab with fennel and white truffle. Loin and boulangère of lamb with morels and peas. Praline mousse with chocolate sorbet and sherry jelly.

◆ Charming and attractive 17C former rectory set in pretty Cotswold village, with neat and mature gardens. Comfortable sitting rooms and subtly contemporary bedrooms. Formal dining room where the classically based cooking is given a modern twist.

at Lower Slaughter **Northwest : 1.75 mi. by A 429 – ✉ Cheltenham**

Lower Slaughter Manor

✉ *GL54 2HP – ☎ (01451) 820 456 – www.lowerslaughter.co.uk – Fax (01451) 822 150*

19 rm – †£ 230/450 ††£ 330/850

Rest – Menu £ 22 (lunch) – Carte dinner £ 42/58

◆ Beautiful listed part 17C manor in warm Cotswold stone with lovely garden. Open fires and period detail throughout; furnishings and fabrics rich yet contemporary. Smart, boldly coloured bedrooms. Elegant dining room with French-influenced menu.

Washbourne Court

✉ *GL54 2HS – ☎ (01451) 822 143 – www.washbournecourt.co.uk – Fax (01451) 821 045*

26 rm – †£ 135/235 ††£ 135/250 – 4 suites

Rest – *(bar lunch Monday-Saturday)* Menu £ 45 – Carte £ 20/29

◆ Stone-built former manor house with pleasant cottage annexes. Stylish interior boasts marble floored reception, contemporary bedrooms, comfy lounges and low-beamed bar with terrace. Local produce a feature in the dark wood-furnished dining room.

BOVEY TRACEY – Devon – 503 I32 – pop. 4 514 – ✉ Newton Abbot 2 C2

London 214 mi. – Exeter 14 mi. – Plymouth 32 mi.

Stover Bovey Rd, Newton Abbot, ☎ (01626) 352 460

St Peter, St Paul and St Thomas of Canterbury Church★

Dartmoor National Park★★

Edgemoor

Haytor Rd, West : 1 mi. on B 3387 ✉ TQ13 9LE – ☎ (01626) 832 466 – www.edgemoor.co.uk – Fax (01626) 834 760

16 rm – †£ 95 ††£ 160 **Rest** – *(bar lunch)* Menu £ 35 **s** – Carte £ 25/36 **s**

◆ Country style, creeper-clad former school house. Lofty beamed, firelit lounge has deep chintz armchairs. Smart rooms - in main house or ex-schoolrooms - in floral prints. Elegantly proportioned dining room.

Brookfield House without rest

Challabrook Lane, Southwest : 0.75 mi. by Brimley rd ✉ TQ13 9DF – ☎ (01626) 836 181 – www.brookfield-house.com – Closed December and January

3 rm – †£ 50/54 ††£ 70/78

◆ Well-kept early Edwardian house in two acres of attractive gardens surrounded by Dartmoor. The three large bedrooms have expansive windows and are immaculately appointed.

at Haytor Vale **West : 3.5 mi. by B 3387 – ✉ Newton Abbot**

The Rock Inn with rm

✉ *TQ13 9XP – ☎ (01364) 661 305 – www.rock-inn.co.uk – Fax (01364) 661 242 – Closed 25-26 December*

9 rm – †£ 70 ††£ 117 **Rest** – Menu £ 15 (weekdays)/18 – Carte £ 20/23

◆ Attractive 18C former coaching inn. Rustic charm aplenty with log fires, beams and sloping floors. Simple bar menu; more elaborate restaurant menu. Bedrooms named after Grand National winners.

BOWNESS-ON-WINDERMERE – Cumbria – **502** L20 – see Windermere

BOX – Bath & North East Somerset – **503** N29 – see Bath

BRADFIELD – Essex – see Mistley

BRADFORD – West Yorkshire – **502** O22 – **pop. 293 717** Great Britain **22** B2

London 212 mi. – Leeds 9 mi. – Manchester 39 mi. – Middlesbrough 75 mi.
Leeds and Bradford Airport : (0113) 250 9696, NE : 6 mi. by A 658 BX
City Hall (01274) 433678, tourist.information@bradford.gov.uk
West Bowling Newall Hall, Rooley Lane, (01274) 393 207
Woodhall Hills Pudsley Woodhall Rd, Calverley, (0113) 256 4771
Bradford Moor Pollard Lane Scarr Hall, (01274) 640 202
East Brierley South View Rd, (01274) 681 023
Queensbury Brighouse Rd, (01274) 882 155
City★ – National Media Museum★ AZ **M**

Plan of Enlarged Area : see Leeds

Hilton Bradford
rm, rest, VISA AE

Hall Ings BD1 5SH – (01274) 734 734 – www.hilton.co.uk – Fax (01274) 306 146 BZ**e**
117 rm – £ 65/105 £ 75/115 – 4 suites
Rest *City 3* – Menu £ 15/19 – Carte £ 26/32
◆ City centre hotel, convenient for rail travellers. Don't be put off by dated 60s exterior. Well-equipped rooms; some look over City Hall. Comfortable cocktail lounge. Easy informality is the by-word in restaurant.

BRADFORD-ON-AVON – Wiltshire – **503** N29 – **pop. 9 072** **4** C2

London 118 mi. – Bristol 24 mi. – Salisbury 35 mi. – Swindon 33 mi.
50 St Margarets St (01225) 865797, tic@bradfordonavon.co.uk
Town★★ - Saxon Church of St Lawrence★★ - Tithe Barn★ – Bridge★
Great Chalfield Manor★ (All Saints★) **AC**, NE : 3 mi. by B 3109 – Westwood Manor★ **AC**, S : 1.5 mi. by B 3109 – Top Rank Tory (★). Bath★★★, NW : 7.5 mi. by A 363 and A 4 – Corsham Court★★ **AC**, NE : 6.5 mi. by B 3109 and A 4

Woolley Grange
P VISA AE

Woolley Green, Northeast : 0.75 mi. by B 3107 on Woolley St BA15 1TX – (01225) 864 705 – www.woolleygrangehotel.co.uk – Fax (01225) 864 059
19 rm (dinner included) – £ 145/220 £ 350/430 – 7 suites
Rest – Menu £ 38 (dinner) – Carte lunch £ 25/32
◆ Modern art, period furniture: innumerable charming details spread through the rooms of a beautiful Jacobean manor. This is a hotel very much geared to families. Classic British cooking in restaurant, conservatory or terrace.

The Swan
P VISA AE

1 Church St BA15 1LN – (01225) 868 686 – www.theswanbradford.co.uk – Fax (01225) 868 681
12 rm – £ 85/110 £ 90/140 **Rest** – Carte £ 19/30
◆ Smart former 16C coaching inn refurbished in modern browns and creams, with rear dining terrace. Stylish bedrooms have contemporary touches and up-to-date facilities. Large, wood furnished dining room.

Bradford Old Windmill
P VISA

4 Masons Lane, on A 363 BA15 1QN – (01225) 866 842 – www.bradfordoldwindmill.co.uk – Fax (01225) 866 648 – Closed December and January
3 rm – £ 79/99 £ 89/109
Rest – *(by arrangement, communal dining)* Menu £ 25
◆ 1807 windmill in redressed local stone; Gothic windows and restored bridge. Rooms and circular lounge, stacked with books and curios, share a homely, unaffected quirkiness. Flavourful vegetarian menus.

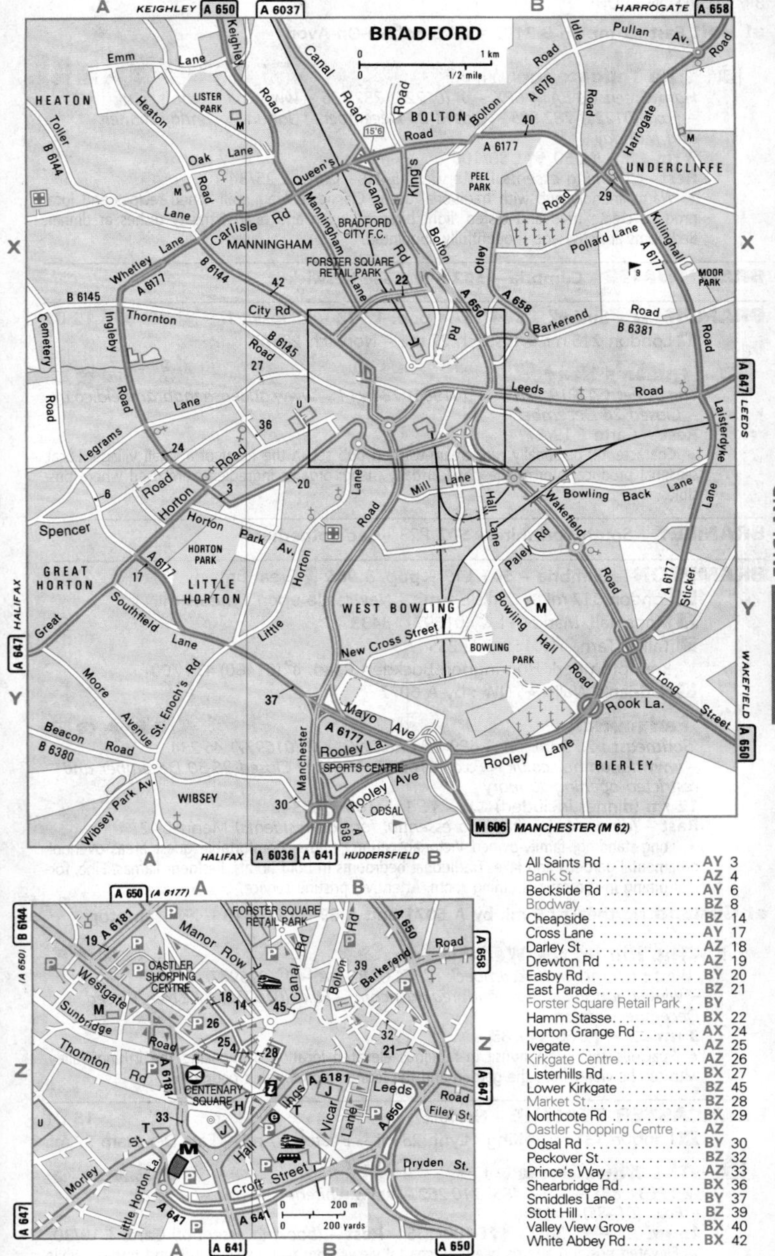

All Saints Rd	AY	3
Bank St	AZ	4
Beckside Rd	AY	6
Brodway	BZ	8
Cheapside	BZ	14
Cross Lane	AY	17
Darley St	AZ	18
Drewton Rd	AZ	19
Easby Rd	BY	20
East Parade	BZ	21
Forster Square Retail Park	BY	
Hamm Stasse	BX	22
Horton Grange Rd	AX	24
Ivegate	AZ	25
Kirkgate Centre	AZ	26
Listerhills Rd	BX	27
Lower Kirkgate	BZ	45
Market St	BZ	28
Northcote Rd	BX	29
Oastler Shopping Centre	AZ	
Odsal Rd	BY	30
Peckover St	BZ	32
Prince's Way	AZ	33
Shearbridge Rd	BX	36
Smiddles Lane	BY	37
Stott Hill	BZ	39
Valley View Grove	BX	40
White Abbey Rd	BX	42

at Holt East : 2 mi. on B 3107 – ✉ Bradford-On-Avon

The Tollgate Inn with rm
Ham Green ✉ BA14 6PX – ✆ (01225) 782 326 – www.tollgateholt.co.uk – Fax (01225) 782 805 – Closed 25 December, 1 January, Sunday dinner and Monday
4 rm – †£ 50 ††£ 80/100
Rest – *(booking essential)* Menu £ 15/19 – Carte £ 25/34
◆ Warm, friendly pub with traditional décor. Classic cooking, well-honed recipes and local produce create tried and tested 'light bites' at lunch and hearty, meaty dishes at dinner. Bedrooms are cosy and thoughtfully appointed.

BRAITHWAITE – Cumbria – **502** K20 – see Keswick

BRAMFIELD – Suffolk – **504** Y27 – pop. 1 778 – ✉ Ipswich **15** D2
London 215 mi. – Ipswich 27 mi. – Norwich 28 mi.

Queen's Head
The Street ✉ IP19 9HT – ✆ (01986) 784 214 – www.queensheadbramfield.co.uk – Closed 26 December
Rest – Carte £ 19/27
◆ Characterful, personally run, cream-washed pub set in the heart of a small village. Local, seasonal produce informs the classical daily menu; organic ingredients are used where possible.

BRAMLEY – South Yorkshire – **502** P23 – see Rotherham

BRAMPTON – Cumbria – **501** L19 – pop. 3 965 Great Britain **21** B1
London 317 mi. – Carlisle 9 mi. – Newcastle upon Tyne 49 mi.
Moot Hall, Market Pl ✆ (016977) 3433
Talkin Tarn, ✆ (0169) 772 255
Brampton Park Huntingdon Buckden Road, ✆ (01480) 434 700
Hadrian's Wall★★, NW : by A 6077

Farlam Hall
Southeast : 2.75 mi. on A 689 ✉ CA8 2NG – ✆ (016977) 46 234 – www.farlamhall.co.uk – Fax (016977) 46 683 – Closed 25-30 December and restricted opening January
12 rm (dinner included) – †£ 155/180 ††£ 340
Rest – *(dinner only) (booking essential for non-residents)* Menu £ 42
◆ Long-standing, family-owned Victorian country house. Comfortable guest areas overlook ornamental gardens and lake. Traditional bedrooms in bold florals. Resident llamas. Fine, formal dining in sumptuous dining room. Attentive, pristine service.

at Gilsland Northeast : 9 mi. by A 6071 and A 69 on B 6318 – ✉ Brampton

The Hill on the Wall without rest
West : 0.5 mi. on Kirkcambeck rd ✉ CA8 7DA – ✆ (016977) 47 214 – www.hadrians-wallbedandbreakfast.com – Fax (016977) 47 214 – Closed December-January
3 rm – †£ 60 ††£ 85
◆ Spacious 16C guest house in fabulous elevated location overlooking the Irthing Valley, with terrific views from the garden and the lounge. Comfortable bedrooms.

BRANCASTER STAITHE – Norfolk **15** C1
London 131 mi. – King's Lynn 25 mi. – Boston 57 mi. – East Dereham 27 mi.

The White Horse with rm
✉ PE31 8BY – ✆ (01485) 210 262 – www.whitehorsebrancaster.co.uk – Fax (01485) 210 930
15 rm – †£ 50/78 ††£ 100/156 **Rest** – *(booking essential)* Carte £ 19/30
◆ Elevated position affords beautiful coastal views from rear conservatory and terrace, while landscaped front terrace boasts parasols, heaters and lights. Varied menu with local seafood. Up-to-date, comfortable bedrooms.

ENGLAND

The Jolly Sailors
✉ PE31 8BJ Brancaster Staithe – ✆ (01485) 210 314 – www.jollysailorbrancaster.co.uk
Rest – Carte £ 14/25
◆ Characterful, rustic pub arranged around a courtyard. Simple menu ranges from baguettes and light bites to freshly made pizzas and pub classics; followed by tasty nursery puddings.

BRANDESBURTON – East Riding of Yorkshire

London 227 mi. – Leeds 73 mi. – Kingston upon Hull 15 mi. – Bradford 82 mi.

Burton Lodge
Southwest : 0.5 mi. on Leven rd ✉ YO25 8RU – ✆ (01964) 542 847 – www.burton-lodge.co.uk – Fax (01964) 544 771 – Closed 25-26 December
9 rm – †£ 40/50 ††£ 60/65
Rest – *(dinner only) (residents only)* Menu £ 17
◆ Personally run, extended 1930s house. Neat, modern bedrooms in soft pastels, some overlooking the golf course - perfect for an early round. A short drive to Beverley Minster. Neat dining room overlooks grounds.

BRANDS HATCH – Kent – 504 U29 – ✉ Dartford 8 B1

London 22 mi. – Maidstone 18 mi.
Fawkham Valley Dartford Fawkham, Gay Dawn Farm, ✆ (01474) 707 144

at Fawkham Green East : 1.5 mi. by A 20 – ✉ Ash Green

Brands Hatch Place
Brands Hatch Rd ✉ DA3 8NQ – ✆ (01474) 875 000 – www.handpicked.co.uk/brandshatchplace – Fax (01474) 879 652
38 rm – †£ 85/150 ††£ 95/260 **Rest** – Menu £ 32
◆ Sensitively extended Georgian house in 12 acres offering smart bedrooms, some in the annexe, with hi-tech facilities. Also, a range of conference and entertainment packages. Smart, contemporary restaurant.

BRANSCOMBE – Devon – 503 K31 – pop. 501 – ✉ Seaton 2 D2

London 167 mi. – Exeter 20 mi. – Lyme Regis 11 mi.
Village★
Seaton (<★★), NW : 3 m – Colyton★

Masons Arms with rm
✉ EX12 3DJ – ✆ (01297) 680 300 – www.masonsarms.co.uk – Fax (01297) 680 500
21 rm – †£ 56/80 ††£ 119/170
Rest – Menu £ 30 (dinner) – Carte £ 20/29
◆ Immensely charming 14C inn set in a picturesque village. Much of the produce is locally sourced, with crab landed on the nearby beach and local meats roasted on the spit over the fire. Individually styled bedrooms boast beams and antiques.

BRANSFORD – Worcs. – see Worcester

BRANSTON – Lincs. – 502 S24 – see Lincoln

BRAYE – C.I. – 503 Q33 – see Channel Islands (Alderney)

BRAY MARINA – Windsor & Maidenhead – see Bray-on-Thames

BRAY-ON-THAMES – Windsor and Maidenhead – 504 R29 – pop. 8 121 – ✉ Maidenhead 11 C3

London 34 mi. – Reading 13 mi.

Plan : see Maidenhead

XXXX **The Waterside Inn** (Alain Roux) with rm

✿✿✿ ✉ *SL6 2AT – ✆ (01628) 620 691 – www.waterside-inn.co.uk – Fax (01628) 784 710 – Closed 26 December-4 January* Xs

8 rm – †£ 190/290 ††£ 190/290 – 3 suites

Rest – French – *(closed Tuesday except dinner June-August and Monday) (booking essential)* Menu £ 54 (lunch)/109 – Carte £ 103/162

Spec. Tronçonnettes de homard poêlées minute au Porto blanc. Filets de lapereau grillés, sauce à l' armagnac et aux marrons glacés. Péché Gourmand selon "Alain" et "Michel".

◆ Few restaurants can match this glorious setting on the Thames, with the terrace an enchanting spot for an aperitif. Enjoy classic French cuisine, prepared with great care, in elegant surroundings. Service is charming and expertly organised. Luxurious bedrooms are spacious and chic.

XXX **Fat Duck** (Heston Blumenthal)

✿✿✿ *High St ✉ SL6 2AQ – ✆ (01628) 580 333 – www.fatduck.co.uk – Fax (01628) 776 188 – Closed dinner 18 December-11 January, Sunday dinner and Monday*

Rest – *(booking essential 2 months in advance) (set menu only)* Xe

Menu £ 130

Spec. Mock Turtle soup with 'Mad Hatter tea'. Powdered Anjou pigeon with blood pudding and confit of umbles. Flaming sorbet.

◆ Low-beamed, converted pub where history and science combine in an exciting, innovative alchemy of contrasting flavours and textures. It's very theatrical and involving; the attentive team are on hand to guide you through the experience.

XX **Caldesi in Campagna**

Old Mill Lane ✉ SL6 2BG – ✆ (01628) 788 500 – www.caldesi.com – Closed Sunday dinner and Monday Xx

Rest – Italian – Menu £ 16 (lunch) – Carte £ 24/45

◆ Welcoming former pub with smart interior, conservatory and decked garden with wood fired oven. Flavoursome Italian cooking displays Ligurian, Tuscan and Sicilian influences.

The Royal Oak

✿ *Paley Street, Southwest : 3.5 mi. by A 308, A 330 on B 3024 ✉ SL6 3JN – ✆ (01628) 620 541 – www.theroyaloakpaleystreet.com – Closed 25 December, 1 January and Sunday dinner*

Rest – Menu £ 20/25 – Carte £ 25/35

Spec. Fried Cornish sprats with mayonnaise. Rabbit and bacon pie. Rhubarb trifle.

◆ A warm and welcoming beamed dining pub, with service that gets the tone just right. The menu champions British produce and is very appealing. This is skilled, confident cooking which sensibly avoids over-elaboration; game is handled deftly.

The Hinds Head

High St ✉ SL6 2AB – ✆ (01628) 626 151 – www.hindsheadhotel.co.uk – Fax (01628) 623 394 – Closed 25-26 December Xe

Rest – *(booking essential)* Carte £ 28/46

◆ Charming pub in the heart of the village, with dark wood panelling, log fires and flag floors. Heart-warming traditional British dishes; some dating back to Tudor times.

at Bray Marina Southeast : 2 mi. by B 3208, A 308 - X - on Monkey Island Lane – ✉ Bray-On-Thames

X **Riverside Brasserie**

(follow road through the marina) ✉ SL6 2EB – ✆ (01628) 780 553 – www.riversidebrasserie.co.uk – Closed Monday-Thursday October-April

Rest – *(booking essential)* Carte £ 36/47

◆ Marina boathouse, idyllically set on the banks of the Thames. Very simply appointed interior and decked terrace. Inventive cooking in informal, busy and buzzy surroundings.

BREEDON ON THE HILL – Leics. – **see Castle Donington**

ENGLAND

BRENTWOOD – Essex – 504 V29 – pop. 47 593 — 13 C2

London 22 mi. – Chelmsford 11 mi. – Southend-on-Sea 21 mi.

44 High St ✆ (01277) 200300, enquiries@brentwood.gov.uk

Bentley G. & C.C. Ongar Rd, ✆ (01277) 373 179

Warley Park Little Warley Magpie Lane, ✆ (01277) 224 891

Marygreen Manor

London Rd, Southwest : 1.25 mi. on A 1023 ✉ CM14 4NR – ✆ (01277) 225 252 – www.marygreenmanor.co.uk – Fax (01277) 262 809

55 rm – †£ 135 ††£ 150, ☕ £ 14.50

Rest *Tudors* – see restaurant listing

◆ Charming Tudor building with wood panelled rooms and open fires. Bedrooms split between main house and courtyard - some named after Henry VIII's wives. Professionally run.

Tudors – at Marygreen Manor Hotel

London Rd, Southwest : 1.25 mi. on A 1023 ✉ CM14 4NR – ✆ (01277) 225 252 – Fax (01277) 262 809

Rest – *(closed Sunday dinner)* Menu £ 30/40 – Carte £ 14/40

◆ Spacious Tudor-style dining room with stained glass, wood beams and tapestries. Well-spaced, dressed tables and formal service. Appealing, modern food with a seasonal base.

at Great Warley Southwest : 2 mi. on B 186 – ✉ Brentwood

The Headley

The Common, Northeast : 0.5 mi. off B 186 ✉ CM13 3HS – ✆ (01277) 216 104 – www.theheadley.co.uk – Fax (01277) 224 063 – Closed Sunday dinner, Monday and Tuesday

Rest – Carte £ 17/25

◆ Large pub set over two floors. Well executed and tasty traditional pub dishes; simply cooked using good quality produce. Hearty, old-fashioned puddings and popular Sunday lunches.

BRIDGNORTH – Shropshire – 502 M26 – pop. 11 891 Great Britain — 18 B2

London 146 mi. – Birmingham 26 mi. – Shrewsbury 20 mi. – Worcester 29 mi.

The Library, Listley St ✆ (01746) 763257, bridgnorth.tourism@shropshire.gov.uk

Stanley Lane, ✆ (01746) 763 315

Ironbridge Gorge Museum★★ **AC** (The Iron Bridge★★ - Coalport China Museum★★ - Blists Hill Open Air Museum★★ - Museum of the Gorge and Visitor Centre★) NW : 8 mi. by B 4373

at Worfield Northeast : 4 mi. by A 454 – ✉ Bridgnorth

The Old Vicarage

✉ WV15 5JZ – ✆ (01746) 716 497 – www.theoldvicarageworfield.com – Fax (01746) 716 552

14 rm ☕ – †£ 85/115 ††£ 85/115

Rest – *(closed Monday and Tuesday lunch) (booking essential)* Menu £ 20/38

◆ Antiques, rare prints and rustic pottery: a personally run Edwardian parsonage in a rural setting with thoughtfully appointed bedrooms, some in the coach house. Delightful orangery dining room overlooking garden; modern British cooking.

BRIDGWATER – Somerset – 503 L30 – pop. 36 563 — 3 B2

London 160 mi. – Bristol 39 mi. – Taunton 11 mi.

King Sq ✆ (01278) 436438, bridgwater.tic@sedgemoor.gov.uk

Enmore Park Enmore, ✆ (01278) 672 100

Town★ - Castle Street★ – St Mary's★ – Admiral Blake Museum★ **AC**

Westonzoyland (St Mary's Church★★) SE : 4 mi. by A 372 – North Petherton (Church Tower★★) S : 3.5 mi. by A 38. Stogursey Priory Church★★, NW : 14 mi. by A 39

at Woolavington **Northeast : 5 mi. by A 39 on B 3141 – ✉ Bridgwater**

Chestnut House without rest
Hectors Stones Lower Road ✉ TA7 8EF – ✆ (01278) 683 658 – www.chestnuthousehotel.com – Fax (01278) 684 333 – Closed Christmas-New Year
7 rm – £ 70/72 £ 93/94
◆ Converted farmhouse, personally run; the exposed stone and beams in the homely lounge testify to its 16C origins. Rooms are neat, comfortable. Informal suppers on request.

at Cannington **Northwest : 3.5 mi. by A 39 – ✉ Bridgwater**

Blackmore Farm without rest
Southwest : 1.5 mi. by A 39 on Bradley Green rd ✉ TA5 2NE – ✆ (01278) 653 442 – www.dyerfarm.co.uk – Fax (01278) 653 427
6 rm – £ 45/50 £ 85/90
◆ Part 15C manor, now a working dairy farm, with great hall and chapel, set against a backdrop of the Quantocks. Bedrooms in the main house have the greater character.

BRIDPORT – Dorset – 503 L31 – pop. 12 977 — 3 B3

London 150 mi. – Exeter 38 mi. – Taunton 33 mi. – Weymouth 19 mi.
47 South St ✆ (01308) 424901, bridport.tic@westdorset-dc.gov.uk
Bridport and West Dorset West Bay East Cliff, ✆ (01308) 422 597
Mapperton Gardens★, N : 4 mi. by A 3066 and minor rd. Lyme Regis★ - The Cobb★, W : 11 mi. by A 35 and A 3052

ENGLAND

Roundham House without rest
Roundham Gdns, West Bay Rd, South : 1 mi. by B 3157 ✉ DT6 4BD – ✆ (01308) 422 753 – www.roundhamhouse.co.uk – Fax (01308) 421 500 – April-November
8 rm – £ 49/85 £ 85/118
◆ Sizeable Edwardian house displaying rich colours, period furnishings, comfy lounge and traditionally styled bedrooms with good comforts. Elevated position offers pleasant country views.

Britmead House without rest
West Bay Rd, South : 1 mi. on B 3157 ✉ DT6 4EG – ✆ (01308) 422 941 – www.britmeadhouse.co.uk – Fax (01308) 422 516 – Closed 24 -26 December and 31 December
8 rm – £ 40/52 £ 64/76
◆ On the road to West Bay and the Dorset Coast Path, a neat, redbrick Edwardian house with well-proportioned rooms and a comfortable lounge leading out to the garden.

Riverside
West Bay, South : 1.75 mi. by B 3157 ✉ DT6 4EZ – ✆ (01308) 422 011 – www.thefishrestaurant-westbay.co.uk – Fax (01308) 458 808 – 12 February-mid November and closed Monday except Bank Holidays
Rest – Seafood – *(lunch only and dinner Friday-Saturday) (booking essential)*
Menu £ 20 (weekday lunch) – Carte £ 23/37
◆ Long-standing seafood café with harbour views; accessed via a bridge. Good value daily menu offers extremely fresh, straightforward dishes crafted from local produce. Plenty of choice.

The Bull with rm
34 East St ✉ DT6 3LF – ✆ (01308) 422 878 – www.thebullhotel.co.uk – Fax (01308) 426 872
14 rm – £ 60/100 £ 95/180 **Rest** – Carte £ 28/45
◆ Boutique inn displaying a mix of period features and contemporary chic. Local fish and meat make up a mix of classic English and Mediterranean brasserie dishes. Uniquely styled, modern bedrooms boast feature walls and stylish bathrooms.

at Shipton Gorge **Southeast : 3 mi. by A 35 – ✉ Bridport**

Innsacre Farmhouse without rest
Shipton Lane, North : 1 mi. ✉ DT6 4LJ – ✆ (07534) 506 160 – www.innsacre.com – Closed 2 weeks Christmas
4 rm ☕ – **†**£ 60/95 **††**£ 95
◆ 17C farmhouse in acres of lawns and orchards. Simple comfortable lounge centred on old fireplace. Sizeable rooms in bold colours.

at Burton Bradstock **Southeast : 2 mi. by B 3157**

Norburton Hall without rest
Shipton Lane ✉ DT6 4NQ – ✆ (01308) 897 007 – www.norburtonhall.com – Closed 24-26 December
3 rm ☕ – **†**£ 90/100 **††**£ 115/200
◆ Spacious Edwardian Arts and Crafts house with coastal views and 6 acres of mature grounds. Woodwork, ornate carvings and period furniture abound; classical bedrooms, modern shower rooms.

BRIGGSWATH – **N. Yorks.** – **502** S20 – **see Whitby**

BRIGHOUSE – **West Yorkshire** – **502** O22 – **pop. 32 360** **22** B2

London 213 mi. – Bradford 12 mi. – Burnley 28 mi. – Leeds 15 mi.
9 Crow Nest Park Hove Edge Coach Rd, ✆ (01484) 401 121

XX **Brook's**
6 Bradford Rd ✉ HD6 1RW – ✆ (01484) 715 284 – www.brooks-restaurant.co.uk – Fax (01484) 712 641 – Closed 2 weeks summer, 10 days January, and Sunday
Rest – *(dinner only)* Menu £ 16 (early dinner Monday-Friday) – Carte £ 17/30
◆ Eclectic art collection fills the walls of this informal restaurant and wine bar with its vaguely Edwardian upstairs lounge. Robust, tasty cooking with 'Spam' on the menu!

ENGLAND

BRIGHSTONE – **Isle of Wight** – **504** P32 – **see Wight (Isle of)**

BRIGHTON AND HOVE – **Brighton and Hove** – **504** T31 **8** A3 – **pop. 134 293** Great Britain

London 53 mi. – Portsmouth 48 mi. – Southampton 61 mi.
Shoreham Airport : ✆ (01273) 467373, W : 8 mi. by A 27 AV
Royal Pavilion Shops ✆ (01273) 292595, brighton-tourism@brighton-hove.gov.uk
18 East Brighton Roedean Rd, ✆ (01273) 604 838
18 The Dyke Devil's Dyke Rd, Devil's Dyke, ✆ (01273) 857 296
18 Hollingbury Park Ditchling Rd, ✆ (01273) 552 010
18 Waterhall Waterhall Rd, ✆ (01273) 508 658
Town★★ - Royal Pavilion★★★ **AC** CZ – Seafront★★ – The Lanes★ BCZ – St Bartholomew's★ **AC** CX **B**
Devil's Dyke (←★) NW : 5 mi. by Dyke Rd (B 2121) BY

Plans on following pages

Grand
97-99 Kings Rd ✉ BN1 2FW – ✆ (01273) 224 300 – www.devere-hotels.com – Fax (01273) 720 613 BZ**v**
197 rm ☕ – **†**£ 90/260 **††**£ 120/270 – 4 suites
Rest ***Kings*** – *(closed Saturday lunch)* Menu £ 25 – Carte £ 25/45
◆ Imposing, white Victorian edifice with a prime place in the sun. Ornate marble, striking staircase, elegant rooms, indulgent cream teas in a quintessentially English lounge. Discreet, traditional grandeur distinguishes restaurant.

BRIGHTON AND HOVE

Adelaide Crescent . . . . AY 2
Brunswick Pl. . . . . AY 3
Brunswick Square . . . AYZ 4
Carlton Terrace. . . . . . . AV 5
Chatham Pl. . . . . BX 6
Churchill Square Shopping Centre . . . . BYZ
Denmark Rd . . . . BY 7
Eastern Rd . . . . CV 9
East St. . . . . CZ 8
George St . . . . AV 10
Gladstone Terrace . . . . CX 12
Gloucester Pl. . . . . CY 13
Gloucester Rd . . . . CY 14
Goldsmid Rd . . . . BX 15
Grand Junction Rd . . . . CZ 16
Hollingbury Park Ave . . BV 17
Hollingdean Rd. . . . . . . CV 18
Hove St. . . . . AV 19
London Rd CX
Marlborough Pl. . . . . . . CY 21
Montpelier Pl. . . . . BY 22
North St. . . . . CZ
Old Steine . . . . CZ 23
Pavillon Parade . . . . . . CZ 26
Richmond Pl. . . . . CY 27
Richmond Terrace . . . . CX 28
St George's Pl. . . . . CY 30
St Peter's Pl. . . . . CX 31
Terminus Rd . . . . BCX 32
Upper Lewes Rd . . . . . CX 33
Warren Rd . . . . CV 37
Waterloo Pl. . . . . CX 39
Wellington Rd. . . . . AV 40
Western Rd . . . . ABY
York Pl. . . . . CY 42

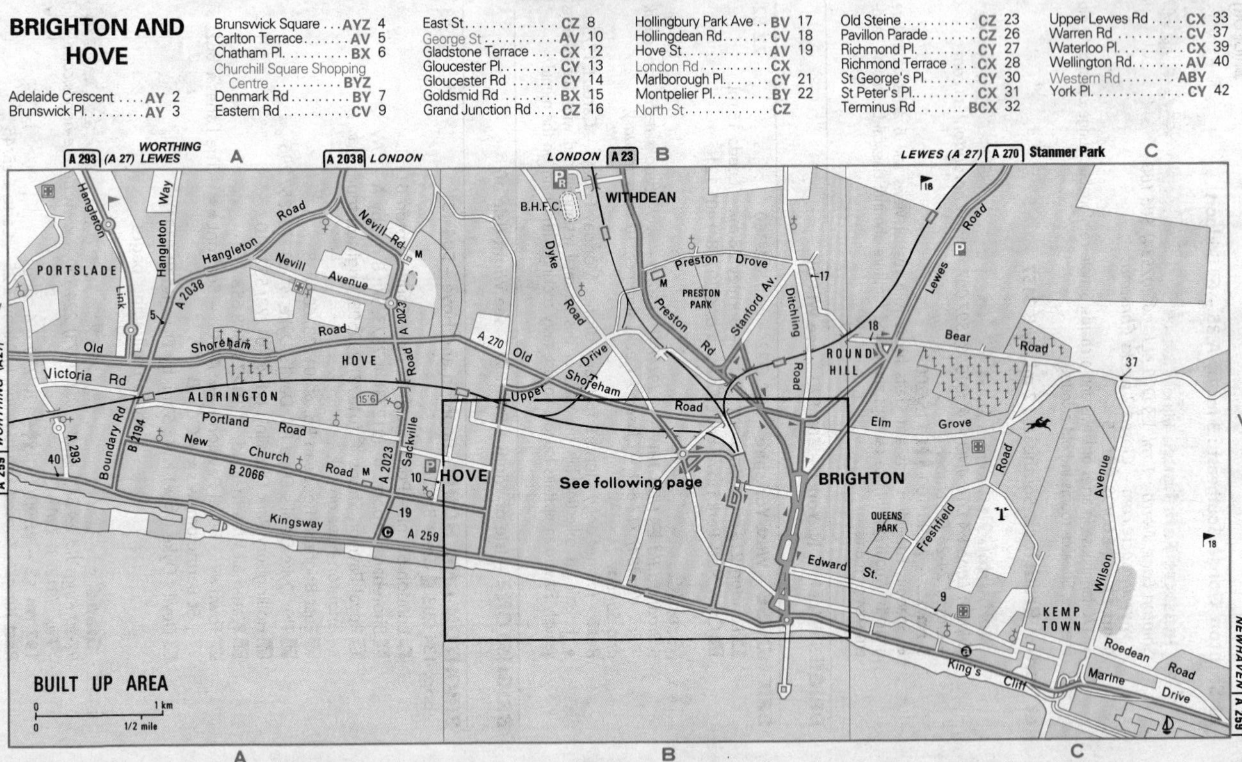

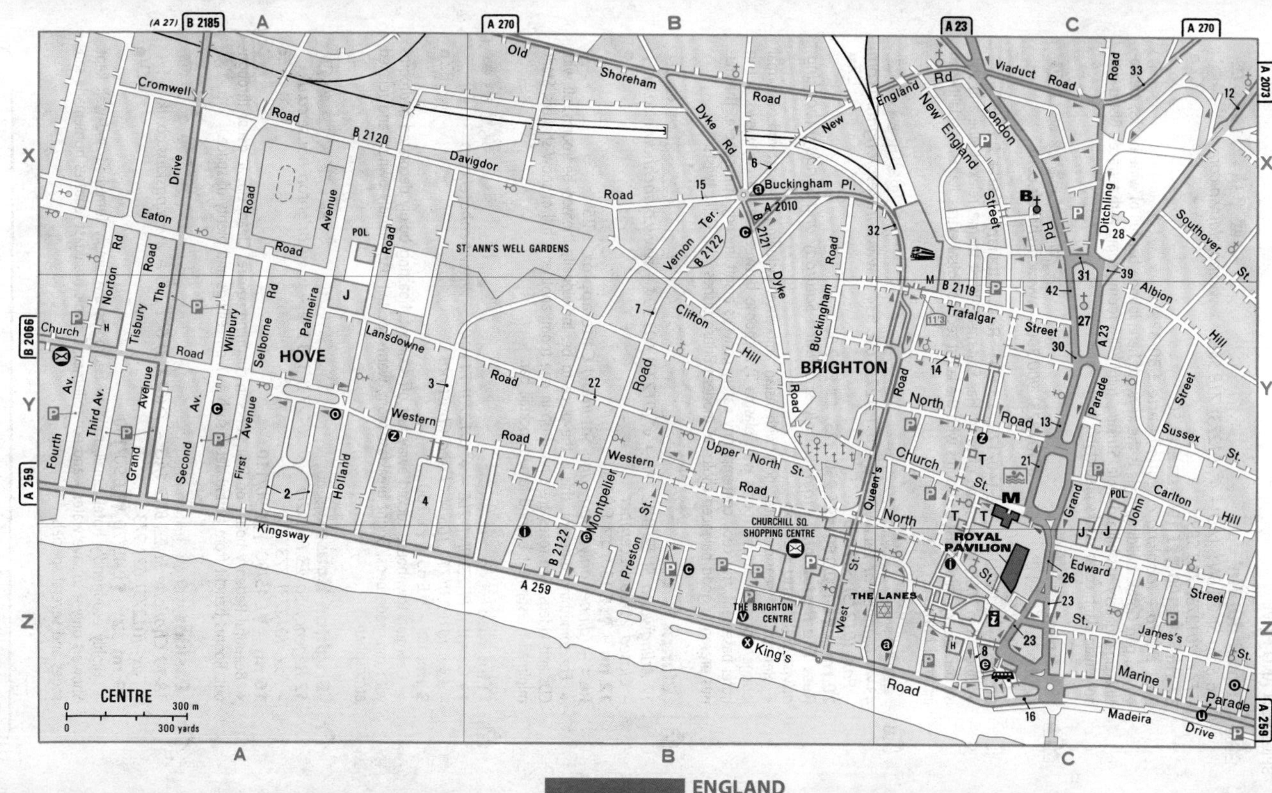
BRIGHTON
HOVE
ROYAL PAVILION
THE LANES
CHURCHILL SQ. SHOPPING CENTRE
THE BRIGHTON CENTRE
ST. ANN'S WELL GARDENS
CENTRE
0
300 m
0
300 yards
(A 27) B 2185
A 270
A 23
A 2073
A 259
B 2066
B 2120
B 2119
A 2010
B 2121
B 2122
A 23
A 259
London Rd
Ditchling Rd
Viaduct Road
New England Street
New England Rd
Dyke Rd
Dyke Road
Queen's Road
North Road
Church St.
North St.
Western Road
King's Road
Marine Parade
Madeira Drive
Kingsway
Old Shoreham Road
New Road
Cromwell Road
Eaton Road
Davigdor Road
Holland Road
Palmeira Avenue
First Avenue
Second Av.
Third Av.
Fourth Av.
Grand Avenue
The Drive
Church Road
Montpellier Road
Preston St.
Upper North St.
Clifton Hill
Vernon Ter.
Buckingham Pl.
Buckingham Road
Trafalgar Street
Sussex St.
Edward Street
Grand Parade
Carlton Hill
John St.
Albion Hill
Southover St.
St. James's St.
West St.
Lansdowne Road
Selborne Rd
Wilbury Road
Tisbury Road
Norton Rd
POL.
A
B
C
X
Y
Z

Hotel du Vin

2-6 Ship St ✉ *BN1 1AD – ✆ (01273) 718 588 – www.hotelduvin.com – Fax (01273) 718 599* CZ**a**

37 rm – †£ 190 ††£ 190, ☕ £ 13.50

Rest *Bistro* – *(booking essential)* Carte £ 30/37

◆ 19C part Gothic building. Style is the keyword here: lounge bar full of wine books; mezzanine cigar gallery has billiard table. Striking, minimalist rooms, some with terraces. Bistro with bohemian slant: cellar stocks predictably huge wine selection.

Myhotel Brighton

17 Jubilee St ✉ *BN1 1GE – ✆ (01273) 900 300 – www.myhotels.com – Fax (01273) 900 301* CY**z**

80 rm – †£ 140/175 ††£ 140/175, ☕ £ 4 **Rest** – Italian – Carte £ 21/30

◆ Opened in 2008, in the heart of town. Has East-meets-West theme; relaxed vibe and stylish bar. Quirky, minimalist bedrooms with the latest technological extras. Italian specialities in informal brasserie.

drakes

43-44 Marine Par ✉ *BN2 1PE – ✆ (01273) 696 934 – www.drakesofbrighton.com – Fax (01273) 684 805* CZ**u**

20 rm – †£ 100/150 ††£ 250/325, ☕ £ 12.50

Rest *The Restaurant* – *(dinner only and lunch Saturday and Sunday) (booking advisable)* Menu £ 20/36

◆ Refurbished seaside hotel, now with Asian ambience, including Thai artwork. Informal lounge/reception. Stylish rooms with plasma TVs: choose between sea or city views. Set in hotel basement, this cool, contemporary eatery conveys a soft, moody atmosphere. The menus present a good balanced choice of modern British dishes with Gallic twists.

ENGLAND

Blanch House

17 Atlingworth St ✉ *BN2 1PL – ✆ (01273) 603 504 – www.blanchhouse.co.uk – Closed 25-26 December* CZ**o**

12 rm – ††£ 130, ☕ £ 6.50

Rest – *(dinner only Friday and Saturday)* Carte approx. £ 25

◆ For something different, this is the place to be. Individually themed bedrooms, all with CDs and videos. Red roses are pinned up in one room; another is full of snow shakers. Stark, minimalist restaurant beyond famed cocktail bar.

The Neo without rest

19 Oriental Pl ✉ *BN1 2LL – ✆ (01273) 711 104 – www.neohotel.com – Fax (01273) 711 105 – Closed Christmas* BZ**e**

9 rm ☕ – †£ 65 ††£ 160

◆ Georgian townhouse tucked away just off seafront, boasting boldly decorated bedrooms with top-grade beds. Bright breakfast room, warm cocktail bar, friendly owners and relaxed atmosphere.

Brighton House without rest

52 Regency Sq ✉ *BN1 2FF – ✆ (01273) 323 282 – www.brighton-house.co.uk – Fax (01273) 773 307* BZ**c**

16 rm – †£ 45/90 ††£ 90/110

◆ Beautiful Regency house on four floors in charming square. Clean, classic décor throughout. Rooms benefit from period detail such as high ceilings and plenty of space.

Paskins without rest

18-19 Charlotte St ✉ *BN2 1AG – ✆ (01273) 601 203 – www.paskins.co.uk – Fax (01273) 621 973* CV**e**

19 rm ☕ – †£ 45/70 ††£ 90/130

◆ Highly eco-friendly hotel. Small, modern bedrooms are simply furnished and well kept. Showers only – to save water – and eco-toiletries. Organic breakfast features homemade sausages and several specials.

Good food at moderate prices? Look for the Bib Gourmand.

The Gingerman
21A Norfolk Sq ✉ BN1 2PD – ✆ (01273) 326 688 – www.gingermanrestaurants.com – Fax (01273) 326 688 – Closed 1 week Christmas-New Year and Monday BZ**i**

Rest – *(booking essential)* Menu £ 18/30

◆ Tucked away off the promenade; French and Mediterranean flavours to the fore in a confident, affordable, modern repertoire: genuine neighbourhood feel.

Terre à Terre
71 East St ✉ BN1 1HQ – ✆ (01273) 729 051 – www.terreaterre.co.uk – Fax (01273) 327 561 – Closed 25-26 December and Monday except Bank Holidays CZ**e**

Rest – Vegetarian – Menu £ 15 – Carte £ 26/30

◆ Hearty helpings of bold, original vegetarian cuisine lyrically evoked on an eclectic menu. Despite its popularity, still friendly, hip and suitably down-to-earth.

Sevendials
1 Buckingham Pl ✉ BN1 3TD – ✆ (01273) 885 555 – www.sevendialsrestaurant.co.uk – Closed 25-26 December and Sunday dinner

Rest – Menu £ 14 (lunch) – Carte £ 22/30 BX**a**

◆ Former bank on street corner: the vault now acts as function room. Light, airy feel with high ceiling. Modern menus with local ingredients admirably to fore. Good value lunch.

Due South
139 King's Rd Arches ✉ BN1 2FN – ✆ (01273) 821 218 – www.duesouth.co.uk – Closed 25-26 December BZ**x**

Rest – Carte £ 23/36

◆ Beside the beach, with lovely arch interior: best tables upstairs facing half-moon window overlooking sea. Organic prominence in modern menus using distinctly local produce.

Sam's of Brighton
1 Paston Place ✉ BN2 1HA – ✆ (01273) 676 222 – www.samsofbrighton.co.uk – Closed 25-26 December, 1 January and Monday CV**a**

Rest – Menu £ 15 (lunch) – Carte £ 21/28

◆ Simple neighbourhood eatery boasting large bar and 3 enormous candelabras. Simple menu of classical, seasonal dishes. Early brunch on offer at weekends and concise à la carte at noon.

Riddle and Finns
12b Meeting House Lane ✉ BN1 1HB – ✆ (01273) 323 008 – www.riddleandfinns.co.uk – Closed 25 December CZ**i**

Rest – Seafood – Menu £ 10 (2 course lunch) – Carte £ 24/45

◆ Informal and simply decorated, with white tiles, bar stools and high, marble-topped tables for communal dining. Well-executed, classical seafood dishes; polite, attentive service.

Blenio Bistro
87-93 Dyke Road ✉ BN1 3JE – ✆ (01273) 220 220 – www.bleniobistro.com – Closed Monday and Tuesday BX**c**

Rest – Carte £ 20/34

◆ Quirky bistro serving breakfast through to dinner, with inspired summer salads and hearty winter stews. Informally run with a smile, it features deli displays and a secluded terrace.

at Hove

The Claremont without rest
13 Second Ave ✉ BN3 2LL – ✆ (01273) 735 161 – www.theclaremont.eu – Fax (01273) 736 836 AY**c**

11 rm ☕ – †£ 80/120 ††£ 185

◆ Personally run Victorian town house with a neat garden; its tall windows and high ceilings lend a sense of space to the spotlessly kept, traditionally decorated bedrooms.

ENGLAND

The Meadow

64 Western Rd ✉ BN3 2JQ – ✆ (01273) 721 182 – www.themeadowrestaurant.co.uk – Fax (01273) 326 871 – Closed 25-26 December, Sunday dinner and Monday AY**o**

Rest – Menu £ 15 (lunch except Sunday and early dinner) – Carte £ 20/31

◆ Airy split-level dining room with shop. Name symbolises chef's vision to support local producers – the 'grass roots' of the restaurant. Beasts bought whole; some items from parents' garden or foraged for. Unfussy, classical cooking has French/Italian influences.

Graze

42 Western Road ✉ BN3 1JD – ✆ (01273) 823 707 – www.graze-restaurant.co.uk – Closed 25-26 December, 1 January and Monday AY**z**

Rest – Carte £ 24/31

◆ Modern restaurant with fresh, funky feel and clever details. Simply prepared, flavoursome 'English Tapas' dishes; create your own or choose a set menu. Some larger dishes available.

The Ginger Pig

3 Hove Street ✉ BN3 2TR – ✆ (01273) 736 123 – www.gingermanrestaurants.com – Closed 25 December AV**c**

Rest – *(bookings not accepted)* Carte £ 20/35

◆ Striking pub just off seafront. Contemporary interior with sofas and bold artwork. Spacious dining area and terrace. Keen service. Appealing menu; flavourful, filling food.

BRIGSTEER – Cumbria – see Kendal

BRIMFIELD – Herefordshire – **503** L27 – see Ludlow

BRIMSCOMBE – Glos. – **503** N28 – see Stroud

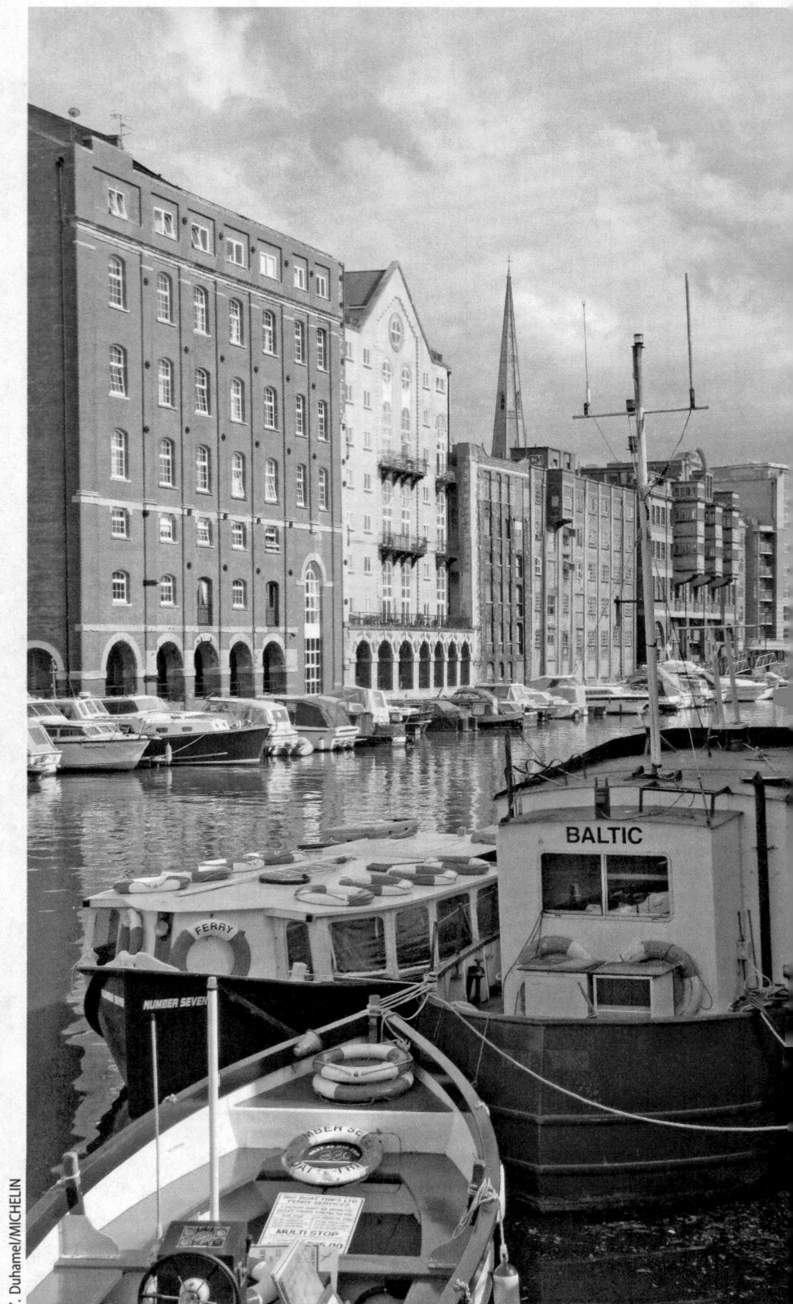

Y. Duhamel/MICHELIN

BRISTOL

County: City of Bristol
Michelin regional map: **503** M29
London 121 mi.
– Birmingham 91 mi.

Population: 420 556
Great Britain
Map reference: **4** C2

PRACTICAL INFORMATION

Tourist Information

Explore-at-Bristol, Harbourside (0333) 321 0101, ticharbourside@destinationbristol.co.uk

Airport

Bristol Airport : (0871) 334 4444, SW : 7 mi. by A 38 AX

Bridge

Severn Bridge (toll)

Golf Courses

Short Lodge GC Carsons Rd, (0117) 956 5501

Clifton Beggar Clifton Bush Lane, Failand, (01275) 393 474

Knowle, Fairway Brislington West Town Lane, (0117) 977 0660

Long Ashton Clarken Coombe, (01275) 392 229

Stockwood Vale Keynsham Stockwood Lane, (0117) 986 6505

SIGHTS

In town

City★★ – St Mary Redcliffe★★ DZ - At-Bristol★★ CZ - Brandon Hill★★ AX - Georgian House★★ AX **K** – Bristol Museum★★ CZ **M3** - Brunel's ss Great Britain and Maritime Heritage Centre★ **AC** AX **S2** – The Old City★ CYZ : Theatre Royal★★ CZ **T** - Merchant Seamen's Almshouses★ CZ **Q** – St Stephen's City★ CY **S1** - St John the Baptist★ CY – College Green★ CYZ (Bristol Cathedral★, Lord Mayor's Chapel★) – City Museum and Art Gallery★ AX **M1**

On the outskirts

Clifton★★ AX (Clifton Suspension Bridge★★ (toll), RC Cathedral of St Peter and St Paul★★ **F1**, Bristol Zoological Gardens★★ **AC**, Village★) – Blaise Hamlet★★ - Blaise Castle House Museum★, NW : 5 mi. by A 4018 and B 4057 AV

In the surrounding area

Bath★★★, SE : 13 mi. by A 4 BX – Chew Magna★ (Stanton Drew Stone Circles★ **AC**) S : 8 mi. by A 37 - BX - and B 3130 – Clevedon★ (Clevedon Court★ **AC**, ≤★) W : 11.5 mi. by A 370, B 3128 - AX - and B 3130

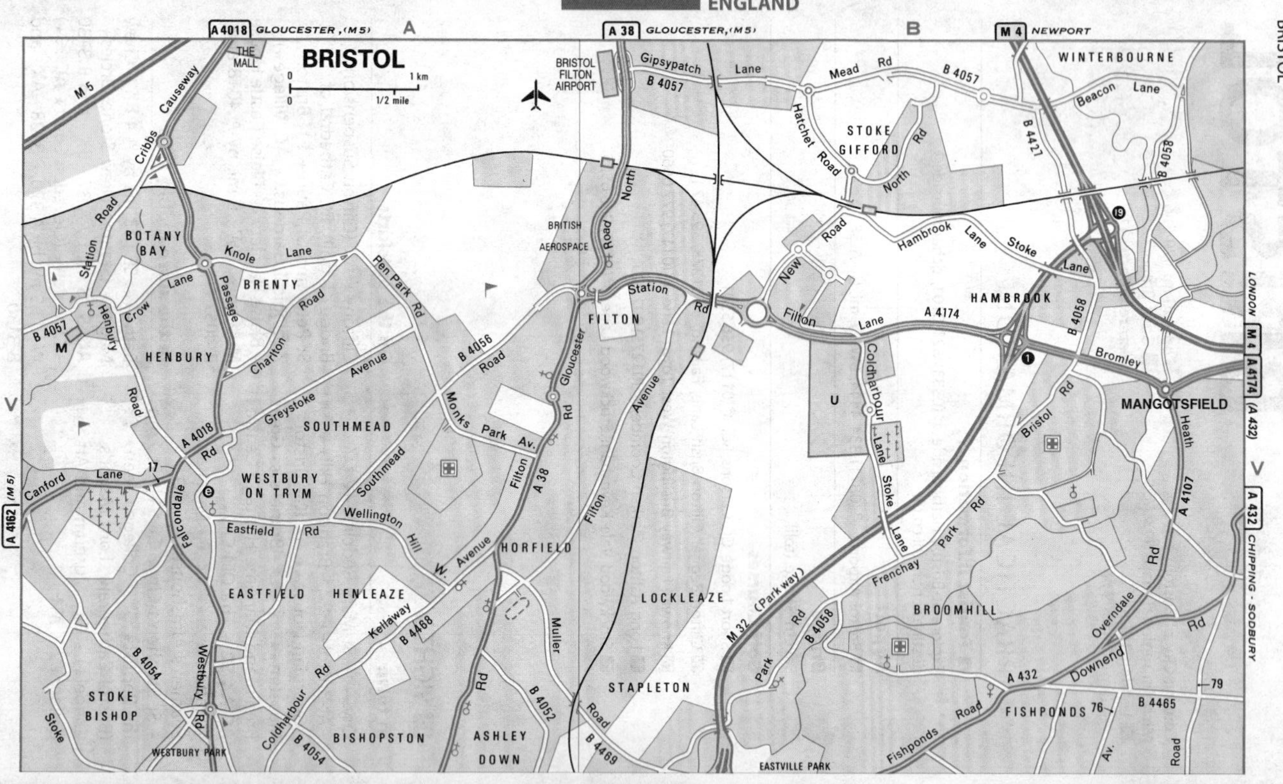
ENGLAND
BRISTOL
0 1 km
0 1/2 mile
A
B
A 4018 GLOUCESTER ,(M 5)
A 38 GLOUCESTER ,(M 5)
M 4 NEWPORT
LONDON M 4 A 4174 (A 432)
A 432 CHIPPING - SODBURY
A 4162 (M 5)
THE MALL
BRISTOL FILTON AIRPORT
BRITISH AEROSPACE
WINTERBOURNE
STOKE GIFFORD
HAMBROOK
MANGOTSFIELD
BOTANY BAY
BRENTY
HENBURY
FILTON
SOUTHMEAD
WESTBURY ON TRYM
HORFIELD
EASTFIELD
HENLEAZE
LOCKLEAZE
BROOMHILL
STOKE BISHOP
STAPLETON
FISHPONDS
BISHOPSTON
ASHLEY DOWN
WESTBURY PARK
EASTVILLE PARK
M 5
Cribbs Causeway
Station Road
Knole Lane
Passage
Crow Lane
Henbury Road
B 4057
M
Charlton Road
Pen Park Rd
B 4056 Road
Greystoke Avenue
Gipsypatch Lane
B 4057
Mead Rd
B 4057
Beacon Lane
B 4427
B 4058
Hatchet Road
North Rd
North Road
New Road
Hambrook Lane
Stoke Lane
Station Rd
Gloucester Rd
Filton Lane
A 4174
B 4058
Bromley Heath
A 4107
Coldharbour Lane
Stoke Lane
U
Bristol Rd
A 4018 Rd
Monks Park Av.
Southmead
Filton Avenue
A 38
Filton Avenue
Canford Lane
17
Falcondale
Eastfield Rd
Wellington Hill W.
Kellaway Avenue
B 4468
Muller Road
M 32 (Park way)
Frenchay Park Rd
Park Rd
B 4058
Overndale Rd
Downend Rd
A 432
79
76
B 4465
Av.
Road
Fishponds Road
B 4054
Westbury Rd
Coldharbour Rd
B 4054
B 4052
B 4469
Stoke
1
19

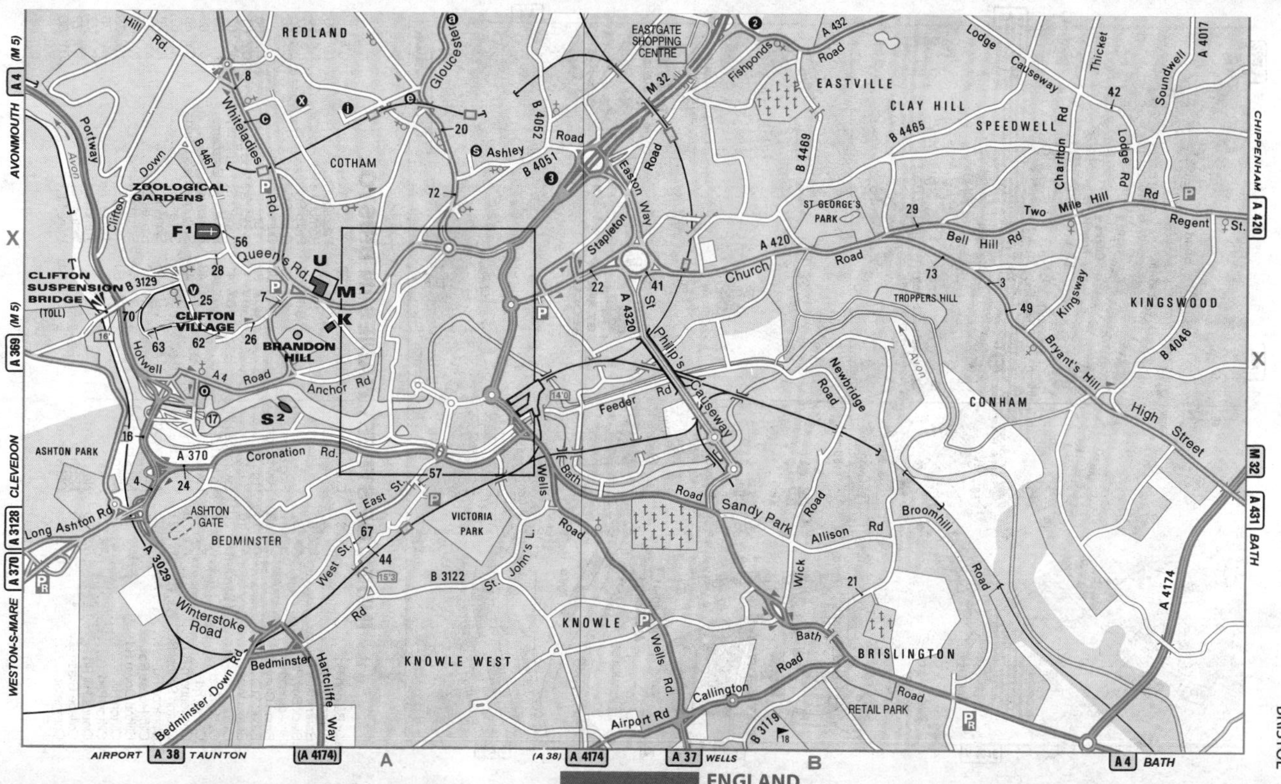
REDLAND
COTHAM
EASTGATE SHOPPING CENTRE
EASTVILLE
CLAY HILL
SPEEDWELL
KINGSWOOD
ST GEORGE'S PARK
TROPPERS HILL
CONHAM
ZOOLOGICAL GARDENS
CLIFTON SUSPENSION BRIDGE (TOLL)
CLIFTON VILLAGE
BRANDON HILL
ASHTON PARK
ASHTON GATE
BEDMINSTER
VICTORIA PARK
KNOWLE
KNOWLE WEST
BRISLINGTON
RETAIL PARK
Hill Rd.
Portway
Avon
Clifton Down
B 4467
Whiteladies Rd.
Gloucester
Ashley
B 4052
B 4051
Road
M 32
Fishponds
A 432
Road
Lodge Causeway
Thicket
Soundwell
A 4017
B 4465
B 4469
Charlton Rd
Lodge Rd
Two Mile Hill
Rd
Regent St.
A 420
Bell Hill Rd
Church Road
Easton Way
Stapleton
A 4320
St Philip's Causeway
Kingsway
Bryant's Hill
B 4046
High Street
Queen's Rd.
B 3129
Hotwell Road
A 4
Anchor Rd
Feeder Rd
Newbridge Road
Coronation Rd.
A 370
Wells Road
Bath Road
Sandy Park Road
Allison Rd
Broomhill Road
East St.
West St.
St. John's L.
B 3122
Rd
Long Ashton Rd
A 3029
Winterstoke Road
Bedminster Down Rd
Bedminster
Hartcliffe Way
Wick Road
Wells Rd.
Callington Road
Airport Rd
B 3119
A 4174
U
M1
K
F1
S2
AVONMOUTH A 4 (M 5)
A 369 (M 5)
CLEVEDON A 3128
WESTON-S-MARE A 370
AIRPORT A 38 TAUNTON
(A 4174)
(A 38) A 4174
A 37 WELLS
A 4 BATH
A 431 BATH
M 32
CHIPPENHAM A 420
A
B
ENGLAND

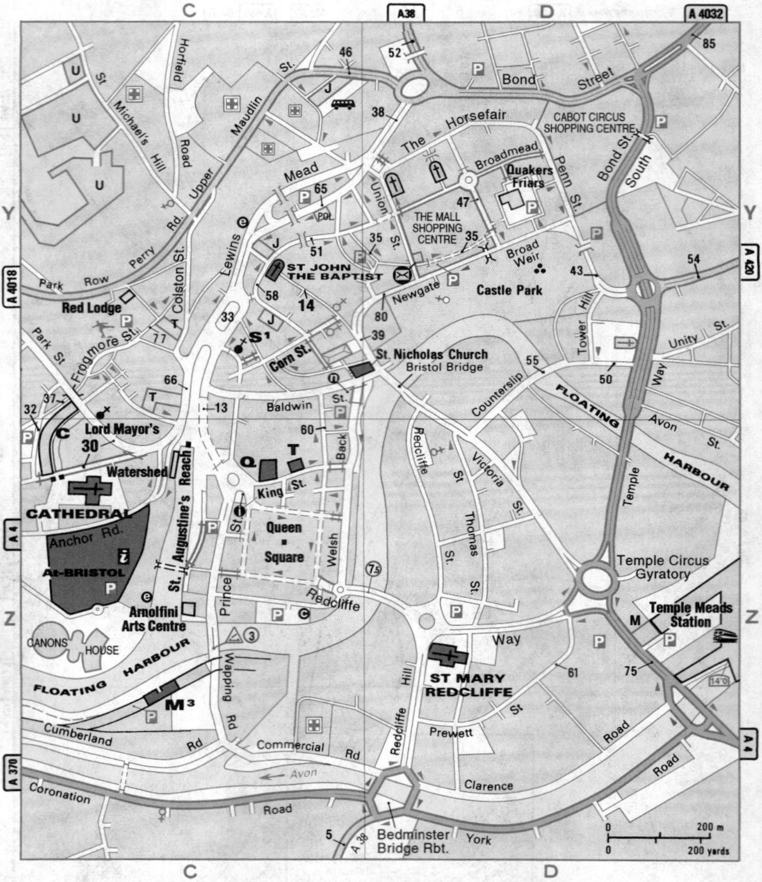

ENGLAND

INDEX OF STREET NAMES IN BRISTOL

Hotel du Vin

The Sugar House ✉ *BS1 2NU – ✆ (0117) 925 5577 – www.hotelduvin.com – Fax (0117) 925 1199* CY**e**

40 rm – 🚹£ 89/185 🚹🚹£ 89/200, ☕ £ 13.95

Rest ***Bistro*** – *(booking essential)* Menu £ 29 – Carte £ 21/38

◆ A massive chimney towers over the 18C sugar refinery; stylish loft rooms in minimalist tones: dark leather and wood, low-slung beds, Egyptian linen and subtle wine curios. Noisy, bustling bar and bistro; plenty of classics. Good wine list.

Mercure Brigstow Bristol

5-7 Welsh Back ✉ *BS1 4SP – ✆ (0117) 929 1030 – www.mercure.com – Fax (0117) 929 2030* CY**n**

115 rm – 🚹£ 159 🚹🚹£ 159, ☕ £ 13.95 – 1 suite

Rest ***Ellipse*** – Carte £ 17/26 **s**

◆ Smart city centre hotel with charming riverside position. Stylish public areas typified by lounges and mezzanine. 21C rooms, full of curves, bright colours and plasma TVs. Modern brasserie and bar overlooking river.

Casamia (Jonray and Peter Sanchez-Iglesias)

38 High St, Westbury-on-Trym, Northwest : 2 mi. by A 4018 ✉ *BS9 3DZ – ✆ (0117) 959 2884 – www.casamiarestaurant.co.uk – Fax (0117) 959 3658 – Closed 2 weeks August, 1 week January, Sunday, Monday and lunch Tuesday*

Rest – Italian – Menu £ 25/55 AV**e**

Spec. Pigeon with coffee and almonds. Roast quail with salsify, blueberries and tarragon. White peach with orange.

◆ Proudly and professionally run former trattoria; simply decorated, with linen-covered tables and leather-furnished bar for aperitifs. Skilful, innovative, flavourful cooking from ambitious brothers; Italian dishes with a twist. Well-paced, formal service.

ENGLAND

Bordeaux Quay (The Restaurant)

First Floor, V-Shed, Canons Way ✉ *BS1 5UH – ✆ (0117) 943 1200 – www.bordeaux-quay.co.uk – Fax (0117) 906 5567 – Closed 25-26 December, Monday and Sunday in August* CZ**e**

Rest – Menu £ 28 – Carte £ 25/42

◆ Harbourside three-in-one, consisting of deli, brasserie and restaurant. Owner is passionate about locally sourced organic and ethical produce. Cooking is fresh, honest and well-judged.

Bell's Diner

1 York Rd, Montpelier ✉ *BS6 5QB – ✆ (0117) 924 0357 – www.bellsdiner.co.uk – Fax (0117) 924 4280 – Closed 24-30 December, 1 January, lunch Saturday and Monday, Sunday and Bank Holidays* AX**s**

Rest – *(booking essential at dinner)* Menu £ 45 – Carte £ 27/37

◆ Shabby-chic neighbourhood restaurant, characterfully decorated with old bottles and flour sacks. Modern, French-inspired menus include a serious tasting selection – accompanied by wine flights.

Riverstation

The Grove, Harbourside ✉ *BS1 4RB – ✆ (0117) 914 4434 – www.riverstation.co.uk – Fax (0117) 934 9990 – Closed 24-26 December, 1 January and Sunday dinner* CZ**c**

Rest – Menu £ 15 *(lunch)* – Carte £ 24/37

◆ Great riverside location: watch canal boats pass by from the terrace. Bar offers all day dining with breakfast, brunch and meze plates. Upstairs café offers more substantial modern European fare.

Rockfish Grill

128 Whiteladies Rd ✉ *BS8 2RS – ✆ (0117) 973 73 84 – www.rockfishgrill.co.uk – Closed Sunday and Monday* AX**c**

Rest – Seafood – *(booking essential)* Menu £ 15/20 – Carte £ 23/56

◆ Well-run and busy, with polite, friendly service. Daily changing menus focus on fresh fish and seafood, with simple chargrilled fish the speciality. Owners' fishmongers is adjacent.

Culinaria
VISA MC

1 Chandos Rd, Redland ✉ BS6 6PG – ✆ (0117) 973 7999 – www.culinariabristol.co.uk – Closed 2 weeks summer, 1 week Easter, 1 week Christmas-New Year and Sunday-Wednesday AX**x**

Rest – Menu £ 20 (lunch) – Carte £ 27/33

◆ Combined deli and eatery; the personally run diner is informal with lots of light and space. Sound cooking behind a collection of Mediterranean, English and French dishes.

Greens' Dining Room
VISA MC

25 Zetland Rd ✉ BS6 7AH – ✆ (0117) 924 64 37 – www.greensdiningroom.com – Closed 1 week August,1 week Christmas, Sunday and Monday AX**e**

Rest – *(booking essential)* Menu £ 10 (2 course lunch)/28 – Carte £ 21/25

◆ Family run neighbourhood eatery, with intimate retro interior and convivial atmosphere. Unfussy British/Med dishes rely on natural flavours and carefully sourced produce.

The Albion Public House and Dining Rooms
VISA MC AE

Boyces Avenue, Clifton Village ✉ BS8 4AA – ✆ (0117) 973 3522 – www.thealbionclifton.co.uk – Fax (0117) 973 9768 – Closed 25-26 December, 1 January, Sunday dinner and Monday AX**v**

Rest – *(booking essential)* Menu £ 30 (dinner) – Carte £ 21/39

◆ Trendy Grade II listed pub at the heart of the village. Proudly British menu is seasonally influenced and offers appealing, mouthwatering dishes. Regular BBQs held on the pleasant terrace.

The Kensington Arms
VISA MC AE

35-37 Stanley Rd ✉ B56 6NP – ✆ (0117) 944 6444 – www.thekensingtonarms.co.uk – Fax (0117) 924 8095 – Closed 25 December and 1 January AX**i**

Rest – Carte £ 22/38

◆ Neglected boozer turned gastropub, with high ceilings and quirky décor. Modern, no-nonsense approach to food means that recreated pub classics come exactly as described.

The Pump House
P VISA MC AE

Merchants Rd ✉ BS8 4PZ – ✆ (0117) 927 2229 – www.the-pumphouse.com – Fax (0117) 927 9557 – Closed 25 December AX**o**

Rest – Menu £ 18 (lunch) – Carte £ 20/28

◆ Converted Victorian pumping station; stylish and modern after extensive refurbishment, with mezzanine restaurant and outside terrace. Menus offer an imaginative twist on classic dishes.

Robin Hood's Retreat
VISA MC AE

197 Gloucester Rd ✉ BS7 8BG – ✆ (0117) 924 8639 – www.robinhoodsretreat.co.uk AX**a**

Rest – *(booking advisable at dinner)* Menu £ 19 (lunch) – Carte £ 27/33

◆ Red-brick Victorian pub offering a good value daily-changing menu of original and interesting British classics, created using French techniques. Eight real ales available on tap.

BRITWELL SALOME – Oxfordshire – pop. 187 11 C2

▶ London 75 mi. – Oxford 21 mi. – Reading 19 mi.

The Goose
P VISA MC

✉ OX49 5LG – ✆ (01491) 612 304 – www.gooserestaurant.co.uk – Fax (01491) 613 945 – Closed 1-20 January, 16 August-1 September, 26-30 December and Monday-Tuesday

Rest – Menu £ 20 (lunch) – Carte £ 31/55

Spec. Pig's trotter with smoked ham hock and tomato salad. Roast lamb rump with seared liver and minted spring vegetables. Savarin of strawberries with yoghurt and mint syrup.

◆ Smart restaurant with charming service, comfy lounge and intimate dining room. Experienced chef leads a talented kitchen. Well-crafted dishes showcase local/foraged produce, mixing classical influences with an imaginative approach.

BROAD CAMPDEN – Glos. – see Chipping Campden

ENGLAND

BROADHEMBURY – Devon – 503 K31 – pop. 617 – ✉ Honiton 2 D2

London 191 mi. – Exeter 17 mi. – Honiton 5 mi. – Taunton 23 mi.

The Drewe Arms

✉ EX14 3NF – ✆ (01404) 841 267 – www.thedrewe.arms.com – Closed Monday
Rest – *(booking essential)* Carte £ 22/35

◆ Quintessential English pub in a beautiful cob and thatch village. Bar menu offers light bites and pub classics; restaurant features more modern, international dishes. Quality local produce.

BROAD OAK – Kent 9 D1

London 62 mi. – Hastings 8 mi. – Rye 7 mi.

Fairacres without rest

Udimore Rd, on B 2089 ✉ TN31 6DG – ✆ (01424) 883 236
– www.smoothhound.co.uk – Fax (01424) 883 236
– Closed Christmas - New Year
3 rm – †£ 60 ††£ 100

◆ Listed 17C cottage in picture-postcard pink. Big breakfasts under low beams. Individual rooms: one overlooks superb magnolia tree in garden. All have many thoughtful extras.

BROADWAY – Worcestershire – 503 O27 – pop. 2 496 Great Britain 19 C3

London 93 mi. – Birmingham 36 mi. – Cheltenham 15 mi. – Oxford 38 mi.
1 Cotswold Court ✆ (01386) 852937
Town★
Country Park (Broadway Tower ✳★★★), SE : 2 mi. by A 44 – Snowshill Manor★ (Terrace Garden★) **AC**, S : 2.5 m

The Lygon Arms

High St ✉ WR12 7DU – ✆ (01386) 852 255
– www.barcelo-hotels.co.uk/lygonarms – Fax (01386) 854 470
77 rm – †£ 124/174 ††£ 225/289 – 6 suites
Rest *Goblets* – see restaurant listing
Rest *The Great Hall* – *(dinner only and Sunday lunch)* Menu £ 25/43
– Carte approx. £ 63 **s**

◆ Superbly enticing, quintessentially English coaching inn with many 16C architectural details in its panelled, beamed interiors and rooms Charles I and Cromwell once stayed in. Refined dining and baronial splendours: heraldic friezes and minstrels' gallery.

The Broadway

The Green ✉ WR12 7AA – ✆ (01386) 852 401 – www.cotswold-inns-hotels.co.uk
– Fax (01386) 853 879
19 rm – †£ 108/147 ††£ 147/186
Rest *The Courtyard* – Menu £ 10/26 – Carte £ 22/30

◆ A 16C inn on the green, built as an abbot's retreat; sympathetically updated rooms in a pretty mix of rural patterns with an atmospheric, horse racing themed, timbered bar. Half-timbered restaurant with leaded windows.

The Olive Branch without rest

78 High St ✉ WR12 7AJ – ✆ (01386) 853 440
– www.theolivebranch-broadway.com
8 rm – †£ 58/72 ††£ 88/92

◆ A 1590s former staging post on the high street run by a friendly husband and wife team. Flagged floors, sandstone walls and compact bedrooms with a few charming touches.

Windrush House without rest

Station Rd ✉ WR12 7DE – ✆ (01386) 853 577 – www.broadway-windrush.co.uk
– Fax (01386) 852 850
5 rm – †£ 80/85 ††£ 90/95

◆ Personally run guesthouse and landscaped garden with an updated Edwardian elegance and subtle period style. Tastefully individual rooms; pleasant views to front and rear.

ENGLAND

Whiteacres without rest
Station Rd ✉ *WR12 7DE – ✆ (01386) 852 320 – www.broadwaybandb.com – Closed 1 week Christmas*
5 rm ☕ – 🚹£ 55/60 🚹🚹£ 70/75
◆ Spacious accommodation - homely, pleasantly updated and modestly priced - in a personally owned Victorian house, a short walk from the village centre.

Russell's with rm
20 High St ✉ *WR12 7DT – ✆ (01386) 853 555 – www.russellsofbroadway.co.uk – Fax (01386) 853 964*
7 rm ☕ – 🚹£ 85/155 🚹🚹£ 195/225
Rest – *(closed Sunday dinner and Bank Holiday Monday dinner)* Menu £ 15/18 – Carte £ 25/38
◆ Behind the splendid Cotswold stone façade lies a stylish modern restaurant with terrace front and rear. Seasonally influenced, regularly changing menus. Smart, comfy bedrooms.

Goblets – at The Lygon Arms
High St ✉ *WR12 7DU – ✆ (01386) 854 418 – www.barcleo-hotels.co.uk/lygonarms.co.uk – Fax (01386) 858 611*
Rest – *(booking essential)* Menu £ 25/38 – Carte approx. £ 63
◆ Characterfully firelit in rustic dark oak. Modern dining room at front more atmospheric than one to rear. Menus of light, tasty, seasonal dishes offered.

ENGLAND

at Buckland Southwest : 2.25 mi. by B 4632 – ✉ Broadway

Buckland Manor
✉ *WR12 7LY – ✆ (01386) 852 626 – www.bucklandmanor.com – Fax (01386) 853 557*
14 rm ☕ – 🚹£ 275 🚹🚹£ 285
Rest – *(booking essential for non-residents)* Menu £ 20 (lunch) – Carte £ 43/52
◆ Secluded part 13C country house with beautiful gardens. Individually furnished bedrooms boast high degree of luxury. Fine service throughout as old-world serenity prevails. Restaurant boasts elegant crystal, fine china and smooth service.

BROCKENHURST – Hampshire – 503 P31 – pop. 2 865 Great Britain 6 A2

London 99 mi. – Bournemouth 17 mi. – Southampton 14 mi. – Winchester 27 mi.

Brockenhurst Manor Sway Rd, ✆ (01590) 623 332

New Forest★★ (Rhinefield Ornamental Drive★★, Bolderwood Ornamental Drive★★)

Rhinefield House
Rhinefield Rd, Northwest : 3 mi. ✉ *SO42 7QB – ✆ (01590) 622 922 – www.rhinefieldhousehotel.co.uk – Fax (01590) 622 800*
50 rm ☕ – 🚹£ 125/250 🚹🚹£ 125/250 – 1 suite
Rest *Armada* – *(dinner only and Sunday lunch)* Menu £ 45
Rest *The Brasserie* – Menu £ 30 (dinner) – Carte £ 24/34
◆ Impressive country house with ornamental pond, parterres and yew maze, in 40 acres of tranquil forest parkland. Period features and furnishings abound, from ornate wood carvings to sleigh beds and roll-top baths. Individually-styled bedrooms have latest mod cons. Fine dining in Armada. Relaxed Brasserie with terrace.

New Park Manor
Lyndhurst Rd, North : 1.5 mi. on A 337 ✉ *SO42 7QH – ✆ (01590) 623 467 – www.newparkmanorhotel.co.uk – Fax (01590) 622 268*
24 rm ☕ – 🚹£ 99/230 🚹🚹£ 99/359
Rest *The Stag* – Menu £ 19/42 – Carte £ 35/42 **s**
◆ Extended, elegantly proportioned hunting lodge with equestrian centre for guided forest treks. Rooms, some in former servants' quarters, have four posters and parkland views. Candlelit fine dining.

The Cloud
Meerut Rd ✉ SO42 7TD – ✆ (01590) 622 165 – www.cloudhotel.co.uk – Fax (01590) 622 818 – Closed 27 December-15 January
18 rm (dinner included) – †£ 99/112 ††£ 212/224
Rest – Menu £ 16/30 **s**
◆ Well-kept, comfortable and personally owned, with something of a country cottage character. Simple, pine furnished accommodation; views over the wooded countryside. Intimate little restaurant with pleasant covered terrace.

Cottage Lodge without rest
Sway Rd ✉ SO42 7SH – ✆ (01590) 622 296 – www.cottagelodge.co.uk – Fax (01590) 623 014 – Closed 20 December-14 January
12 rm – †£ 50/100 ††£ 70/135
◆ 300-year old former forester's cottage in the heart of the village: family run and faultlessly kept. Low oak beamed ceiling, cosy snug bar and large, neatly appointed rooms.

Le Poussin at Whitley Ridge with rm
Beaulieu Rd, East : 1 mi. on B 3055 ✉ SO42 7QL – ✆ (01590) 622 354 – www.whitleyridge.co.uk – Fax (01590) 622 856
18 rm – †£ 95/150 ††£ 125/175
Rest – Menu £ 20 (lunch) – Carte £ 29/42
◆ Georgian house in 14 acres of mature gardens in a charming setting in the New Forest. Bedrooms are spacious and individually decorated. With the opening of Lime Wood, the menu here will become simpler and more in a brasserie style, with service also less formal.

Thatched Cottage with rm
16 Brookley Rd ✉ SO42 7RR – ✆ (01590) 623 090 – www.thatchedcottage.co.uk – Fax (01590) 623 479
5 rm – †£ 60/70 ††£ 60/150, £ 10
Rest – *(booking essential)* Carte £ 18/51
◆ 17C farmhouse and one-off rooms with a touch of eccentricity to their blend of curios, pictures and bright flowers. Open kitchen; elaborate, locally sourced menu.

at Sway Southwest : 3 mi. by B 3055 – ✉ Lymington

The Nurse's Cottage with rm
Station Rd ✉ SO41 6BA – ✆ (01590) 683 402 – www.nursescottage.co.uk – Closed 3 weeks February-March and 3 weeks November
5 rm (dinner included) – †£ 90/95 ††£ 200/210
Rest – *(dinner only) (booking essential)* Menu £ 29
◆ Personally run, welcoming conservatory restaurant with an intimate charm. Traditional menus make good use of Hampshire's larder. Pristine, comfy rooms with pretty details.

BROCKTON – **Shrops.** – **see Much Wenlock**

BROMFIELD – **Shrops.** – **503** L26 – **see Ludlow**

BROOK – **Hampshire** – **503** P31 – ✉ **Lyndhurst** **6** A2
London 92 mi. – Bournemouth 24 mi. – Southampton 14 mi.

Bell Inn
✉ SO43 7HE – ✆ (023) 8081 2214 – www.bellinnbramshaw.co.uk – Fax (023) 8081 3958
27 rm – †£ 70/120 ††£ 90/140 **Rest** – *(bar lunch)* Menu £ 35
◆ 18C former coaching inn located in the heart of the forest – with three golf courses close by. Bedrooms are in the process of being updated; Premium rooms are to be richly decorated. Pub classics on offer in rustic bar. More sophisticated fare in restaurant.

BROUGHTON – **Cambridgeshire** – **see Huntingdon**

BROXTON – Cheshire – 502 L24 – pop. 417 — 20 A3

London 197 mi. – Birmingham 68 mi. – Chester 12 mi. – Manchester 44 mi.

Cock O Barton

Barton Rd, Barton, West : 2 mi. on A 534 ✉ SY14 7HU – ✆ (01829) 782 277 – www.thecockobarton.co.uk – Fax (01829) 707 891 – Closed Monday except Bank Holidays and Christmas

Rest – Menu £ 20 (lunch) – Carte £ 25/35

◆ Part-15C pub exterior hides stylish restaurant with impressive terrace. Rich colours, stunning furnishings and luxurious fabrics abound. Appealing, generous dishes showcase local produce.

BRUNDALL – Norfolk – 504 Y26 – pop. 5 832 — 15 D2

London 118 mi. – Great Yarmouth 15 mi. – Norwich 8 mi.

The Lavender House

39 The Street ✉ NR13 5AA – ✆ (01603) 712 215 – www.thelavenderhouse.co.uk – Closed Sunday and Monday

Rest – *(dinner only) (booking essential)* Menu £ 40

◆ Characterful low-ceilinged thatched cottage with comfy lounge and bar, cosy dining rooms and impressive 8-seater table in kitchen. Original monthly menus display interesting modern twists.

BRUNTINGTHORPE – Leicestershire Great Britain — 16 B3

London 96 mi. – Leicester 10 mi. – Market Harborough 15 mi.

Leicester - Museum and Art Gallery★, Guildhall★ and St Mary de Castro Church★, N : 11 mi. by minor rd and A 5199

The Joiners

Church Walk ✉ LE17 5QH – ✆ (0116) 247 8258 – www.thejoinersarms.co.uk – Closed 25-26 December, 1 January, Sunday dinner, Monday and Bank Holidays

Rest – *(booking essential)* Menu £ 14 (weekdays) – Carte £ 21/28

◆ Neat and tidy whitewashed pub with characterful interior. Good value menus offer a mix of refined pub classics and brasserie-style dishes, cooked and presented in a straightforward manner.

BRUSHFORD – Somerset – 503 J30 – see Dulverton

BRUTON – Somerset – 503 M30 – pop. 2 982 — 4 C2

London 118 mi. – Bristol 27 mi. – Bournemouth 44 mi. – Salisbury 35 mi.

Stourhead★★★ **AC**, W : 8 mi. by B 3081

At The Chapel

High St ✉ BA10 0AE – ✆ (01749) 814 070 – www.atthechapel.co.uk – Fax (01749) 814 864 – Closed 25 December and Sunday dinner

Rest – Carte £ 19/33

◆ Informal, wood-floored restaurant in former chapel, with bakery to one side and wine shop to the other. Well-priced, daily changing menus offer rustic, Mediterranean-influenced dishes, with wood-fired pizzas a speciality in the evenings. Friendly service.

BRYHER – Cornwall – 503 A/B34 – see Scilly (Isles of)

BUCKDEN – Cambridgeshire – 504 T27 – pop. 2 385 – ✉ Huntingdon — 14 A2

London 65 mi. – Bedford 15 mi. – Cambridge 20 mi. – Northampton 31 mi.

The George

High St ✉ PE19 5XA – ✆ (01480) 812 300 – www.thegeorgebuckden.com – Fax (01480) 813 920

12 rm – †£ 90/100 ††£ 170

Rest ***Brasserie*** – see restaurant listing

◆ Delightfully restored former 19C coaching inn with stylish, contemporary look, typified by leather tub chairs and sofas. Smart bedrooms are all named after famous Georges.

Brasserie – at The George Hotel

High St ✉ PE19 5XA – ✆ (01480) 812 300 – www.thegeorgebuckden.com – Fax (01480) 813 920

Rest – Carte £ 28/39 **s**

◆ Spacious, modern brasserie serving a range from traditional English game to Mediterranean and Moroccan influenced dishes. French windows lead to courtyard, creating airy feel.

BUCKHORN WESTON – Dorset

4 C3

London 117 mi. – Poole 36 mi. – Bath 33 mi. – Weymouth 37 mi.

The Stapleton Arms with rm

Church Hill ✉ SP8 5HS – ✆ (01963) 370 396 – www.thestapletonarms.com – Fax (01963) 370 396

4 rm – †£ 72/96 ††£ 100/120

Rest – Carte £ 15/25

◆ Smart, stylish pub with elegant dining room; muddy boots, dogs and children all welcome. Wide-ranging menu offers traditional choices with some Mediterranean touches. Spacious, contemporary bedrooms, some with underfloor heating.

BUCKINGHAM – Buckinghamshire – 503 Q27 – pop. 12 512

11 C1

Great Britain

London 64 mi. – Birmingham 61 mi. – Northampton 20 mi. – Oxford 25 mi.

Silverstone Stowe Silverstone Rd, ✆ (01280) 850 005

Tingewick Rd, ✆ (01280) 815 566

Stowe Gardens★★, NW : 3 mi. by minor rd. Claydon House★ **AC**, S : 8 mi. by A 413

Villiers

3 Castle St ✉ MK18 1BS – ✆ (01280) 822 444 – www.oxfordshire-hotels.co.uk – Fax (01280) 822 113

43 rm – †£ 70/135 ††£ 105/160 – 3 suites

Rest *Villiers* – Menu £ 15/19 – Carte £ 28/37

◆ Professionally run hotel on central street. Spacious, bedrooms vary in style: some boasting original beams and eaves; all equally comfy with large, well-kept bathrooms. Modern restaurant offers appealing British menu. Locals often pop in to the lounges for coffee.

BUCKLAND – Glos. – 503 O27 – see Broadway (Worcs.)

BUCKLAND – Oxfordshire – 503 P28 – ✉ Faringdon

10 A2

London 78 mi. – Oxford 16 mi. – Swindon 15 mi.

The Lamb at Buckland

Lamb Lane ✉ SN7 8QN – ✆ (01367) 870 484 – www.thelambatbuckland.co.uk – Closed Sunday dinner and Monday

Rest – Carte £ 10/35

◆ Family-owned 17C pub decorated with ovine-inspired curios. Rear garden and sunken terrace. Heavily beamed restaurant; tasty traditional British cooking on blackboard menu.

BUCKLAND MARSH – Oxfordshire – pop. 2 243

10 A2

London 76 mi. – Faringdon 4 mi. – Oxford 15 mi.

The Trout at Tadpole Bridge with rm

✉ SN7 8RF – ✆ (01367) 870 382 – www.troutinn.co.uk – Fax (01367) 870 912 – Closed 25-26 December and Sunday dinner (November-April)

6 rm – †£ 75 ††£ 110

Rest – Carte £ 21/35

◆ Smart pub with attractive garden leading down to the Thames. Concise menu consists of classic Gallic dishes with contemporary touches; seafood and game often feature as specials. Comfy bedrooms exceed expectations. Private moorings available.

ENGLAND

BUDE – Cornwall – 503 G31 – pop. 3 681 1 B2

London 252 mi. – Exeter 51 mi. – Plymouth 50 mi. – Truro 53 mi.

Visitor Centre, The Crescent ✆ (01288) 354240, budetic@visitbude.info

Burn View, ✆ (01288) 352 006

The Breakwater ★★ – Compass Point (≤ ★)

Poughill ★ (church ★★), N : 2.5 mi. - E : Tamar River ★★ – Kilkhampton (Church ★), NE : 5.5 mi. by A 39 – Stratton (Church ★), E : 1.5 mi. – Launcells (Church ★), E : 3 mi. by A 3072 – Marhamchurch (St Morwenne's Church ★), SE : 2.5 mi. by A 39 – Poundstock ★ (≤ ★★, church ★, guildhouse ★), S : 4.5 mi. by A 39. Morwenstow (cliffs ★★, church ★), N : 8.5 mi. by A 39 and minor roads - Jacobstow (Church ★), S : 7 mi. by A 39

Falcon

Breakwater Rd ✉ EX23 8SD – ✆ (01288) 352 005 – www.falconhotel.com – Fax (01288) 356 359 – Closed 25 December

29 rm – †£ 60/75 ††£ 118/128 – 1 suite

Rest – Carte £ 20/28 **s**

◆ An imposing, personally run hotel with the proudly traditional character of a bygone age. Contemporary and classic blend in bedrooms. Separate private garden. Formal dining.

BUDLEIGH SALTERTON – Devon – 503 K32 – pop. 4 801 2 D2

London 182 mi. – Exeter 16 mi. – Plymouth 55 mi.

Fore St ✆ (01395) 445275, budleigh.tic@btconnect.com

East Devon Links Rd, Budleigh Salterton, ✆ (01395) 443 370

East Budleigh (Church ★), N : 2.5 mi. by A 376 – Bicton ★ (Gardens ★) **AC**, N : 3 mi. by A 376

The Long Range

5 Vales Rd, by Raleigh Rd ✉ EX9 6HS – ✆ (01395) 443 321 – www.thelongrangehotel.co.uk – Fax (01395) 442 132 – Closed New Year

7 rm – †£ 47/78 ††£ 100/116

Rest – *(by arrangement)* Menu £ 25

◆ Homely and unassuming guesthouse, personally run in quiet residential street. Sun lounge with bright aspect, overlooking broad lawn and neat borders. Simple, unfussy rooms. Tasty, locally sourced dishes in a comfy dining room.

BUNBURY – Ches. – 502 M24 – see Tarporley

BUNGAY – Suffolk – 504 Y26 – pop. 4 895 Great Britain 15 D2

London 108 mi. – Beccles 6 mi. – Ipswich 38 mi.

Norwich ★★ - Cathedral ★★, Castle Museum ★, Market Place ★, NW : 15 mi. by B 1332 and A 146

The Castle Inn with rm

35 Earsham Street – ✆ (01986) 892 283 – www.thecastleinn.net – Closed Sunday dinner

4 rm – †£ 50/55 ††£ 70/90 **Rest** – Carte £ 20/30

◆ Sky-blue pub with dining rooms and intimate rear bar. Fresh, simple and seasonal country based cooking; the Innkeeper's platter of local produce a perennial favourite. Homely, comfortable bedrooms.

at Earsham Southwest : 3 mi. by A 144 and A 143 – ✉ Bungay

Earsham Park Farm without rest

Old Railway Rd, on A 143 ✉ NR35 2AQ – ✆ (01986) 892 180 – www.earsham-parkfarm.co.uk – Fax (01986) 894 796

3 rm – †£ 46/68 ††£ 75/96

◆ Isolated red-brick Victorian farmhouse, surrounded by working farm which supplies the produce for breakfast. Well appointed rooms with rural names.

BURCOMBE – Wilts. – see Salisbury

ENGLAND

BURFORD – Oxfordshire – 503 P28 – pop. 1 171 — 10 A2

London 76 mi. – Birmingham 55 mi. – Gloucester 32 mi. – Oxford 20 mi.
The Brewery, Sheep St (01993) 823558, burford.vic@westoxon.gov.uk
, (01993) 822 583

Bay Tree

Sheep St OX18 4LW – (01993) 822 791 – www.cotswold-inns-hotels.co.uk/bay-tree – Fax (01993) 823 008
21 rm – £ 118/128 £ 163/222 **Rest** – Menu £ 16/28
◆ Characterful, creeper-clad 16C house with coaching inn style, antique furnishings and original features. Two front lounges with vast stone fireplaces. Comfortable bedrooms. Light, airy restaurant overlooking beautiful landscaped garden.

Burford House

99 High St OX18 4QA – (01993) 823 151 – www.burfordhouse.co.uk – Fax (01993) 823 240
8 rm – £ 115/165 £ 185
Rest – *(closed Sunday) (lunch only and dinner Thursday-Saturday)* Menu £ 16 (lunch) – Carte dinner £ 27/36
◆ Characterful 17C B&W timbered townhouse. Lounge and garden room have a subtle, contemporary edge, while comfy, individually decorated bedrooms are more traditional in style. Good breakfasts, homely lunches and gourmet dinners in informal restaurant.

Cotland House without rest

Fulbrook Hill, Fulbrook, Northeast : 0.5 mi. on A 361 OX18 4BH – (01993) 822 382 – www.cotlandhouse.com
4 rm – £ 40/70 £ 85/95
◆ Bright, modern house in Cotswold stone; its cool, light décor tinged with Gallic style. Neatly kept by friendly owner, with candles, magazines, fresh flowers and top-name toiletries.

ENGLAND

The Lamb Inn with rm

OX18 4LR – (01993) 823 155 – www.cotswold-inns-hotel.co.uk – Fax (01993) 822 228 – Closed 25 December
17 rm – £ 112/161 £ 191/250 **Rest** – Carte £ 33/45
◆ 15C weavers' cottage set in a charming town. Bar offers light bites and afternoon tea; the restaurant, a daily market and set menu. Ambitious cooking is robust and classically based. Bedrooms are cosy; Rosie has its own garden.

The Highway Inn with rm

117 High St OX18 4RG – (01993) 823 661 – www.thehighwayinn.co.uk – Closed first 2 weeks January
9 rm – £ 65/95 £ 85/140 **Rest** – Carte £ 25/32
◆ Characterful beamed inn dating from 1480. Simple, honest cooking of pub classics and delicious desserts, with an emphasis on local produce. Classic, cosy bedrooms.

at Swinbrook East : 2.75 mi. by A 40 – Burford

The Swan Inn with rm

OX18 4DY – (01993) 823 339 – www.theswannswinbrook.co.uk – Closed 25 December
6 rm – £ 70/100 £ 110/180 **Rest** – Carte £ 20/30
◆ English country pub on a lane next to the river. Menus balance traditional and modern British dishes, using local, seasonal produce as their base; game is from the nearby Estate. Beautifully luxurious new bedrooms.

BURGHCLERE – Hampshire – 503 Q29 — 6 B1

London 67 mi. – Newbury 4 mi. – Reading 30 mi.

Carnarvon Arms with rm

rm,

Winchester Rd, Whitway, South : 1.5 mi. by Highclere rd on Whitway rd RG20 9LE – (01635) 278 222 – www.carnarvonarms.com – Fax (01635) 278 444
23 rm – £ 89/95 £ 89/95 **Rest** – Menu £ 15 (lunch) – Carte £ 24/35
◆ Spacious modern dining pub serving up-to-date British cooking. Comfy sofas in bar; more formal dining area in converted barn with hieroglyphics on the walls. Compact, modern bedrooms.

BURLEYDAM – Ches. – see Whitchurch (Shrops.)

BURLTON – Shropshire – ✉ Shrewsbury 18 B1

London 235 mi. – Shrewsbury 10 mi. – Wrexham 20 mi.

The Burlton Inn with rm

✉ *SY4 5TB – ✆ (01939) 270 284 – www.burltoninn.com – Fax (01939) 270 928 – Closed 25 December*

6 rm – †£ 65 ††£ 85

Rest – *(light lunch Monday)* Menu £ 16 (dinner) – Carte £ 17/28

◆ Characterful 18C whitewashed inn that's personally run. Concise menu features unfussy classical cooking with a refined, contemporary touch; produce is local, seasonal and good quality. Neat, wood-furnished bedrooms boast large bathrooms.

BURNHAM MARKET – Norfolk – 504 W25 – pop. 898 Great Britain 15 C1

London 128 mi. – Cambridge 71 mi. – Norwich 36 mi.

Lambourne Dropmore Rd, ✆ (01628) 666 755

Holkham Hall★★ **AC**, E : 3 mi. by B 1155

The Hoste Arms

The Green ✉ PE31 8HD – ✆ (01328) 738 777 – www.hostearms.co.uk – Fax (01328) 730 103

33 rm – †£ 104/190 ††£ 128/286 – 1 suite

Rest *The Hoste Arms* – see restaurant listing

◆ Extended 17C inn in heart of pretty village. Stylish, comfortable bedrooms boast a high level of facilities and include the eye-catching Zulu wing with its South African themed décor.

Vine House without rest

The Green ✉ PE31 8HD – ✆ (01328) 738 777 – www.vinehouseboutiquehotel.co.uk

7 rm – †£ 128/241 ††£ 170/286

◆ Stylish, comfortable and elegant rooms with great bathrooms at this extended Georgian house. Evening butler service for drinks. Reception and meals at Hoste Arms opposite.

Railway Inn without rest

Creake Rd ✉ PE31 8HD – ✆ (01328) 738 777 – www.hostearms.co.uk

8 rm – †£ 69/133 ††£ 83/149

◆ Former station house with derelict platform and carriage to rear. Stylish, contemporary bedrooms boast bold feature walls, modern furniture, retro fittings and good facilities.

The Hoste Arms – at the Hoste Arms Hotel

The Green ✉ PE31 8HD – ✆ (01328) 738 777 – www.hostearms.co.uk – Fax (01328) 730 103

Rest – *(booking essential)* Carte £ 25/35 **s**

◆ Spacious dining areas include rustic bar and informal conservatory. Classically based menus feature global influences, with emphasis on local produce. Friendly, polite service.

at Burnham Thorpe Southeast : 1.25 mi. by B 1355 – ✉ Burnham Market

The Lord Nelson

Walsingham Rd ✉ PE31 8HL – ✆ (01328) 738 241 – www.nelsonslocal.co.uk – Fax (01328) 738 241 – Closed dinner 25-26 December and 1 January and dinner Monday except Bank Holidays

Rest – Carte £ 18/29

◆ Traditional whitewashed pub with low beams, flagged floors and an abundance of character, named after its most famous customer, who was born in the village. Hearty rustic cooking.

BURNHAM THORPE – Norfolk – 504 W25 – see Burnham Market

BURNSALL – North Yorkshire – 502 O21 – pop. 108 – ✉ Skipton 22 A2

London 223 mi. – Bradford 26 mi. – Leeds 29 mi.

The Red Lion

✉ *BD23 6BU – ☎ (01756) 720 204 – www.redlion.co.uk – Fax (01756) 720 292*

14 rm – †£ 65/100 ††£ 80/153 – 3 suites

Rest *The Restaurant* – see restaurant listing

◆ Part 16C inn on the River Wharfe, ideal for walks, fishing and shooting. Cosy bedrooms, some in adjacent cottage: all have 19C brass beds or overlook the village green.

Devonshire Fell

✉ *BD23 6BT – ☎ (01756) 729 000 – www.devonshirefell.co.uk – Fax (01756) 729 009*

10 rm – †£ 85/145 ††£ 90/210 – 2 suites **Rest** – Menu £ 16/29

◆ Once a club for 19C mill owners; strikingly updated by Lady Hartington with vivid colours and Hockney prints. Wide-ranging modern menu. Stylish rooms with Dales views.

The Restaurant – at The Red Lion Hotel

✉ *BD23 6BU – ☎ (01756) 720 204 – www.redlion.co.uk – Fax (01756) 720 292*

Rest – Menu £ 31 (dinner) – Carte £ 23/34

◆ Dales meat, game and local cheeses in robust, seasonal menu. Eat in the firelit, oak-panelled bar or the dining room with mullioned windows facing the green. Keen staff.

BURPHAM – W. Sussex – 504 S30 – see Arundel

BURRINGTON – Devon – 503 I31 – pop. 533 2 C1

London 260 mi. – Barnstaple 14 mi. – Exeter 28 mi. – Taunton 50 mi.

Northcote Manor

Northwest : 2 mi. on A 377 ✉ EX37 9LZ – ☎ (01769) 560 501 – www.northcotemanor.co.uk – Fax (01769) 560 770

10 rm – †£ 100/170 ††£ 155/255 – 1 suite

Rest – *(booking essential)* Menu £ 38 (dinner) **s** – Carte lunch approx. £ 19 **s**

◆ Creeper-clad hall above River Tew dating from 1716. Fine fabrics and antiques in elegant, individually styled rooms; attention to well-judged detail lends air of idyllic calm. Country house restaurant features eye-catching murals.

BURTON BRADSTOCK – Dorset – 503 L31 – See Bridport

BURTON-UPON-TRENT – Staffordshire – 502 O25 – pop. 43 784 19 C1

London 128 mi. – Birmingham 29 mi. – Leicester 27 mi. – Nottingham 27 mi.

Customer Service Centre, Market Place ☎ (01283) 508000, reception@eaststaffsbc.gov.uk

Branston G. & C.C. Burton Rd, ☎ (01283) 528 320

Craythorne Stretton Craythorne Rd, ☎ (01283) 564 329

at Stretton North : 3.25 mi. by A 5121 (A 38 Derby) – ✉ Burton-Upon-Trent

Dovecliff Hall

Dovecliff Rd ✉ DE13 0DJ – ☎ (01283) 531 818 – www.dovecliffhallhotel.co.uk – Fax (01283) 516 546

15 rm – †£ 95 ††£ 135/225

Rest – *(closed Sunday dinner)* Menu £ 19 (lunch) – Carte £ 25/44

◆ Imposing, listed 1790s house with lovely gardens and spacious rooms, nestling in an elevated position above the Trent. Airy bedrooms, most boasting garden vistas. Formal dining rooms in restaurant and delightful orangery.

BURY – Greater Manchester – 502 N23 – pop. 60 718 20 B2

London 211 mi. – Leeds 45 mi. – Liverpool 35 mi. – Manchester 9 mi.

The Met Art Centre, Market St ☎ (0161) 253 5111, touristinformation@bury.gov.uk

Greenmount, ☎ (01204) 883 712

ENGLAND

The Waggon

131 Bury and Rochdale Old Rd, Birtle, East : 2 mi. on B 6222 ✉ BL9 6UE – ✆ (01706) 622 955 – www.thewaggonatbirtle.co.uk – Closed 26 December-8 January, 1-15 August, Sunday dinner, Monday and Tuesday

Rest – *(dinner only and Sunday lunch)* Menu £ 17 (Wednesday-Friday) – Carte £ 22/31

◆ Unprepossessing façade hides a pleasantly decorated eatery with good value, no-nonsense cooking featuring a decidedly strong Lancashire base and the famous Bury Black Pudding.

BURY ST EDMUNDS – Suffolk – 504 W27 – pop. 36 218 15 C2

Great Britain

London 79 mi. – Cambridge 27 mi. – Ipswich 26 mi. – Norwich 41 mi.

6 Angel Hill ✆ (01284) 764667, tic@stedsbc.gov.uk

The Suffolk Golf and Spa Hotel Fornham St Genevieve, ✆ (01284) 706 777

Town★ - Abbey and Cathedral★

Ickworth House★ **AC**, SW : 3 mi. by A 143

Angel

rm, rm,

3 Angel Hill ✉ IP33 1LT – ✆ (01284) 714 000 – www.theangel.co.uk – Fax (01284) 714 001

73 rm – £ 90/150 £ 100/160 – 2 suites

Rest *The Eaterie* – Menu £ 16 (lunch) **s** – Carte £ 21/39 **s**

◆ 15C inn near the Abbey Gardens with a fine Georgian façade. Rooms offer a bright, modern take on classic style: a few, named after famous visitors, have four poster beds. The Eatery is in atmospheric 12C cellars.

Ravenwood Hall

East : 4 mi. by A 14 ✉ IP30 9JA – ✆ (01359) 270 345 – www.ravenwoodhall.co.uk – Fax (01359) 270 788

14 rm – £ 100 £ 100 **Rest** – Menu £ 37 – Carte £ 25/34

◆ Tudor dower house set in seven acres of calm lawns and woods. Welcoming lounge and individually designed bedrooms, more compact in the mews, are furnished with antiques. Restaurant with old wooden beams and inglenook fireplace.

Ounce House without rest

Northgate St ✉ IP33 1HP – ✆ (01284) 761 779 – www.ouncehouse.co.uk – Fax (01284) 768 315

5 rm – £ 80/95 £ 125/135

◆ Two 1870s houses knocked together; well furnished with Victorian elegance. Spacious, individually styled bedrooms; well-chosen antiques contribute to a characterful interior.

Maison Bleue

30-31 Churchgate St ✉ IP33 1RG – ✆ (01284) 760 623 – www.maisonbleue.co.uk – Fax (01284) 761 611 – Closed January, 2 weeks summer, Sunday and Monday

Rest – Seafood – Menu £ 17/26 – Carte £ 28/39

◆ 17C glass-fronted house with blue canopies and deceptively large, modern interior. Constantly evolving seafood-orientated menus display tasty, unfussy dishes. Service is formal and efficient.

at Ixworth Northeast : 7 mi. by A 143 – ✉ Bury St Edmunds

Theobalds

68 High St ✉ IP31 2HJ – ✆ (01359) 231 707 – www.theobaldsrestaurant.co.uk – Fax (01359) 231 707 – Closed 10 days late spring and Sunday dinner

Rest – *(dinner only and lunch Sunday, Wednesday and Friday)* Menu £ 27 (lunch) – Carte £ 31/35

◆ Beamed part 16C cottage with a cosy firelit lounge. Friendly service and well-judged seasonal menus combine heartwarming favourites and contemporary dishes.

ENGLAND

at Beyton East : 6 mi. by A 14 – ✉ Bury St Edmunds

Manorhouse without rest
The Green ✉ IP30 9AF – ✆ (01359) 270 960 – www.beyton.com
4 rm – †£ 50/55 ††£ 68/75
◆ Part 15C Suffolk longhouse with mature garden in idyllic spot overlooking village green. Two rooms are in converted barn; all have a rustic feel to them. Personally run.

at Horringer Southwest : 3 mi. on A 143 – ✉ Bury St Edmunds

The Ickworth
✉ IP29 5QE – ✆ (01284) 735 350 – www.lckworthhotel.co.uk – Fax (01284) 736 300
38 rm (dinner included) – †£ 180/328 ††£ 240/365 – 1 suite
Rest *Fredericks* – *(dinner only and lunch Sunday)* Menu £ 27/40
Rest *Conservatory* – Menu £ 20 (lunch) – Carte £ 23/33
◆ Ickworth House's east wing mixes modern and country house styles. Three airy drawing rooms; conservatory breakfasts. Comfy rooms with views. A favourite with young families. Smart Fredericks overlooks gardens. Informal family dining in Conservatory.

The Beehive
The Street ✉ IP29 5SN – ✆ (01284) 735 260 – www.beehivehorringer.co.uk – Fax (01284) 735 532 – Closed 25-26 December and Sunday dinner
Rest – Carte £ 18/25
◆ Pretty flintstone pub with cosy rooms and alcoves, keenly run by long-standing owners. Traditional pub dishes with the odd Euro-influence; local produce and seasonality to the fore.

ENGLAND

BUSHEY – Hertfordshire – 504 S29 – pop. 17 001 — 12 A2

London 18 mi. – Luton 21 mi. – Watford 3 mi.
Bushey Hall Bushey Hall Drive, ✆ (01923) 222 253
Bushey G. & C.C. High St, ✆ (020) 8950 2283

Plan : see Greater London (North-West) 1

st James
30 High St ✉ WD23 3HL – ✆ (020) 8950 2480 – www.stjamesrestaurant.co.uk – Fax (020) 8950 4107 – Closed 25 December, Sunday and Bank Holidays
Rest – Carte £ 27/32 BT**c**
◆ Long-standing, likeable restaurant with wood floored front room and bar, plus rear room for large parties. Appealing British menu shows real understanding of what guests want.

BUTTERMERE – Cumbria – 502 K20 – pop. 139 – ✉ Cockermouth — 21 A2

London 306 mi. – Carlisle 35 mi. – Kendal 43 mi.

Wood House
Northwest : 0.5 mi. on B 5289 ✉ CA13 9XA – ✆ (017687) 70 208 – www.wdhse.co.uk – Fax (017687) 70 241 – late March-November
3 rm – †£ 65 ††£ 100
Rest – *(by arrangement, communal dining)* Menu £ 29
◆ 16C house in a wonderfully serene lakeside setting with stunning views. Well-appointed lounge; antique furnished bedrooms. Meals cooked on the Aga using fresh seasonal, local ingredients and served family-style around an antique table.

BUXHALL – Suffolk – see Stowmarket

BUXTON – Derbyshire – 502 O24 – pop. 20 836 — 16 A1

London 172 mi. – Derby 38 mi. – Manchester 25 mi. – Stoke-on-Trent 24 mi.
The Crescent ✆ (01298) 25106, tourism@highpeak.gov.uk
Buxton and High Peak Townend, ✆ (01298) 26 263

Buxton's Victorian without rest
3A Broad Walk ✉ SK17 6JE – ✆ (01298) 78 759 – www.buxtonvictorian.co.uk – Fax (01298) 74 732 – Closed Christmas
7 rm – †£ 62/82 ††£ 84/88
◆ Charming Victorian house built in 1860 for the Duke of Devonshire. Cosy lounge and breakfast room with views over boating lake and bandstand. Bedrooms boast period furniture.

Grendon without rest
Bishops Lane ✉ SK17 6UN – ✆ (01298) 78 831 – www.grendonguesthouse.co.uk – Closed 3 January-1 February and 1 week May
5 rm – †£ 40/75 ††£ 85/90
◆ Cosy Edwardian house on edge of town, built for a wealthy mill owner in the 1900s, with period features and pleasant gardens. Comfortable, traditionally furnished bedrooms.

BYFORD – Herefordshire – 503 L27 – see Hereford

BYLAND ABBEY – N. Yorks. – 502 Q21 – see Helmsley

Prices quoted after the symbol † refer to the lowest rate in low season followed by the highest rate in high season, for a single room. The same principle applies to the symbol †† for a double room.

ENGLAND

CALLINGTON – Cornwall – 503 H32 – pop. 4 048 — 2 C2

London 237 mi. – Exeter 53 mi. – Plymouth 15 mi. – Truro 46 mi.

Langmans
3 Church St ✉ PL17 7RE – ✆ (01579) 384 933 – www.langmansrestaurant.co.uk – closed Sunday-Wednesday
Rest – *(dinner only) (booking essential) (set tasting menu only)* Menu £ 38
◆ Truly individual establishment: seven course tasting menus change monthly, employing skilful cooking with finesse; ingredients from small local suppliers. Booking essential.

CALLOW HILL – Worcestershire — 19 C3

London 120 mi. – Birmingham 26 mi. – Coventry 35 mi. – Wolverhampton 27 mi.

The Royal Forester
✉ DY14 9XW – ✆ (01299) 266 286 – www.royalforesterinn.co.uk
Rest – Menu £ 13 – Carte £ 18/35
◆ Traditional 15C pub that's undergone a sympathetic refurbishment. Appealing, down-to-earth menus feature a good value set meal or more wide-ranging à la carte. Modern, comfortable bedrooms, designed after foodstuffs.

CALNE – Wiltshire – 503 O29 – pop. 13 789 — 4 C2

London 91 mi. – Bristol 33 mi. – Southampton 63 mi. – Swindon 17 mi.
Bowood House★ **AC**, (Library ≤★) SW : 2 mi. by A 4 – Avebury★★ (The Stones★, Church★) E : 6 mi. by A 4

Bowood
Derry Hill, West : 3 mi. by A4 on Derry Hill rd . ✉ SN11 9PQ – ✆ (01249) 822 228 – www.bowood.org – Closed 25 December
43 rm – †£ 150/170 ††£ 170/240
Rest *Shelburne* – *(dinner only)* Carte £ 26/37 **s**
Rest *Clubhouse Brasserie* – Carte £ 19/30 **s**
◆ Smart, professionally run, purpose-built hotel in grounds of Lord and Lady Lansdowne's Estate. Contemporary country house styling. Spacious bedrooms; some with balconies. Modern British cooking in formal Shelburne, with attractive terrace. Brasserie menu in golf clubhouse.

Great Britain

London 55 mi. - Coventry 88 mi. - Ipswich 54 mi. - Kingston-upon-Hull 137 mi.

Cambridge City Airport : (01223) 373765, E : 2 mi. on A 1303 X

The Guildhall, Paes Hill (0871) 2268006, info@cambridge.org

Cambridge Menzies Hotel Bar Hill, (01954) 780 098

Town★★★ - St John's College★★★ **AC** Y - King's College★★ (King's College Chapel★★★) Z The Backs★★ YZ - Fitzwilliam Museum★★ Z **M1** - Trinity College★★ Y - Clare College★ Z **B** - Kettle's Yard★ Y **M2** - Queen's College★ **AC** Z

Audley End★★, S : 13 mi. on Trumpington Rd, A 1309, A 1301 and B 1383 - Imperial War Museum★, Duxford, S : 9 mi. on M 11

Plan on next page

Hotel du Vin

VISA AE

15-19 Trumpington St CB2 1QA - (01223) 227 330 - www.hotelduvin.com - Fax (01223) 227 331 Zu

41 rm - £ 155 £ 220/380, £ 13.50

Rest Bistro - *see restaurant listing*

◆ Row of ex-university owned 18C houses; now a smart, stylish hotel. Contemporary bedrooms feature wine theme; 'Brown Brothers' comes with its own cinema. Relaxing, clubby bar.

Hotel Felix

rm, P VISA AE

Whitehouse Lane, Huntingdon Rd, Northwest : 1.5 mi. by A 1307 CB3 0LX - (01223) 277 977 - www.hotelfelix.co.uk - Fax (01223) 277 973

52 rm - £ 190 £ 235/305, £ 7.50

Rest *Graffiti* - Menu £ 17 (lunch) - Carte dinner £ 27/38

◆ Privately owned Victorian mansion set in 3 acres of gardens with contemporary interior. Majority of bedrooms in extension; spacious and luxurious. Modern artwork decorates. Graffiti restaurant overlooks terrace and gardens.

Midsummer House (Daniel Clifford)

VISA AE

Midsummer Common CB4 1HA - (01223) 369 299 - www.midsummerhouse.co.uk - Fax (01223) 302 672 - Closed 1 week Easter, 2 weeks August, 2 weeks December, Tuesday lunch, Sunday and Monday Ya

Rest - Menu £ 30/65 - Carte £ 65/85

Spec. Caramelised sweetbreads with ox tongue and maple jelly. Braised turbot with scallops and asparagus. Roasted pineapple and coconut gateau with pineapple sorbet.

◆ Charming and idyllic location beside the River Cam; conservatory dining with fresh, bright feel. Visually impressive dishes reveal cooking that is confidently crafted; flavours are clear and pronounced. Service is formal and well-timed.

Alimentum

A/C VISA AE

152-154 Hills Rd CB2 8PB - (01223) 413 000 - www.restaurantalimentum.co.uk - Closed Christmas, Sunday dinner and Bank Holidays Xa

Rest - Menu £ 19 (until 7pm) - Carte £ 33/44

◆ Sleek, stylish restaurant with striking red and black décor and spacious cocktail bar. Modern menu has French base; dishes are clean and unfussy with some innovative touches.

22 Chesterton Road

A/C VISA AE

22 Chesterton Rd CB4 3AX - (01223) 351 880 - www.restaurant22.co.uk - Fax (01223) 323 814 - Closed 1 week Christmas-New Year, Sunday and Monday Yc

Rest - *(booking essential) (lunch by arrangement)* Menu £ 20/28

◆ Converted Victorian house with distinctive dining room decorated in rich colours. Monthly-changing classical menu; tasty, good value French-influenced dishes. Formal service.

CAMBRIDGE

Street	Square	No.
Bridge St	Y	2
Coldham's Lane	X	5
Corn Exchange St	Z	6
Downing St	Z	7
Free School Lane	Z	12
Grafton Centre	Y	
Hobson St	Y	14
King's Parade	Z	15
Lion Yard Centre	Z	
Madingley Rd	X	16
Magdalene St	Y	17
Market Hill	YZ	18
Market St	Y	19
Milton Rd	Y	20
Newmarket Rd	Y	21
Northampton St	Y	22
Parker St	Z	23
Peas Hill	Z	25
Pembroke St	Z	26
Petty Cury	Z	27
Rose Crescent	Y	28
St Andrew's St	Z	30
St John's St	Y	31
Short St	Y	32
Sidney St	Y	34
Trinity St	Y	36
Trumpington Rd	Z	37
Wheeler St	Z	39

COLLEGES

College	Square	Letter
Christ's	Y	A
Churchill	X	B
Clare	Z	B
Clare Hall	X	N
Corpus Christi	Z	G[1]
Darwin	Z	D
Downing	Z	E[1]
Emmanuel	Z	F
Fitzwilliam	X	G
Gonville and Caius	Y	G[2]
Hugues Hall	Z	K
Jesus	Y	K
King's	Z	
Lucy Cavendish	Y	O[1]
Magdalene	Y	N
Newnham	X	E[2]
New Hall	X	D
Pembroke	Z	N
Peterhouse	Z	O[2]
Queen's	Z	
Robinson	X	K
St Catharine's	Z	R
St Edmund's House	Y	U
St John's	Y	
Selwyn	X	F
Sidney Sussex	Y	P
Trinity	Y	
Trinity Hall	Y	V
Wolfson	X	U

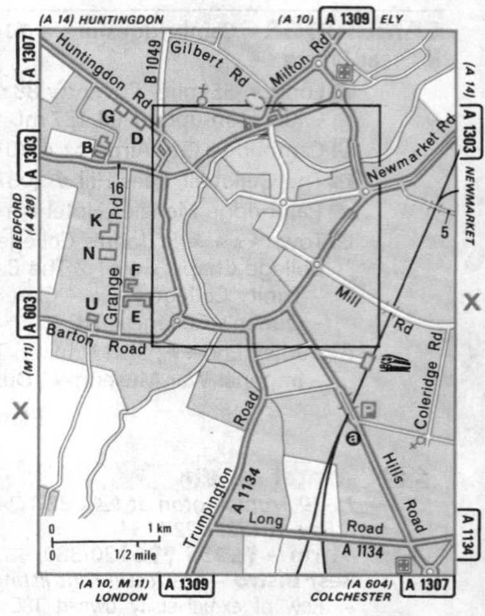

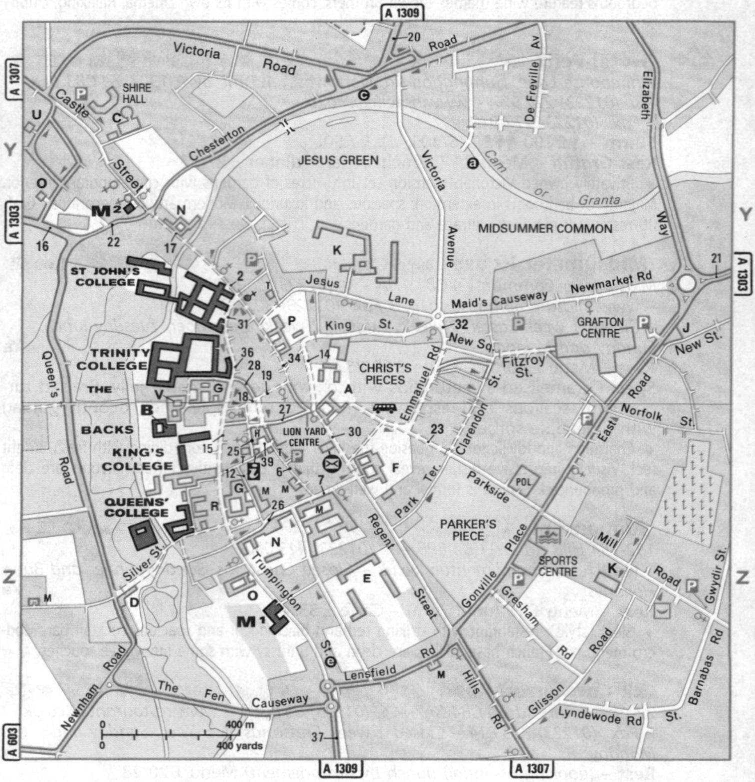

XX **Bistro** – at Hotel du Vin

15-19 Trumpington St ✉ *CB2 1QA* – ✆ *(01223) 227 330* – *www.hotelduvin.com* – *Fax (01223) 227 331* Z**u**

Rest – Menu £ 18 (lunch) – Carte £ 29/41

◆ Spacious brasserie with black banquettes and walls filled with wine memorabilia. Classic dishes presented in a modern style, with French undertones. Relaxed, buzzy ambience.

at Histon North : 3 mi. on B 1049 - X – ✉ Cambridge

XX **Phoenix**

20 The Green ✉ *CB4 9JA* – ✆ *(01223) 233 766* – *Closed 24-27 December*

Rest – Chinese – Menu £ 19/22 – Carte £ 39/84

◆ Popular Chinese restaurant in former pub on village green. Comfortable, homely inner. Polite, smartly attired staff. Vast menu with plenty of Peking and Sichuan favourites.

at Horningsea Northeast : 4 mi. by A 1303 - X - and B 1047 on Horningsea rd – ✉ Cambridge

Crown and Punchbowl with rm

High St ✉ *CB25 9JG* – ✆ *(01223) 860 643* – *www.thecrownandpunchbowl.co.uk* – *Fax (01223) 441 814* – *Closed 26-30 December, Sunday dinner and Bank Holiday Monday dinner*

5 rm – †£ 75 ††£ 95 **Rest** – Menu £ 15 (lunch) – Carte £ 24/33

◆ Homely dining pub with formal service. Dishes display European influences and arrive in a mix of classic and more ambitious styles. Daily fish specials and a mix and match sausage board. Simple, tidy bedrooms are handy for the airport.

at Little Wilbraham East : 7.25 mi. by A 1303 - X – ✉ Cambridge

The Hole in the Wall

2 High St ✉ *CB21 5JY* – ✆ *(01223) 812 282* – *www.the-holeinthewall.com* – *Closed 2 weeks in January, 2 weeks in October, 25 December, 26 December dinner, 1 January dinner, Sunday dinner and Monday*

Rest – Carte £ 23/33

◆ Remotely set 15C pub with plenty of charm. The confident kitchen produces good value, flavoursome British dishes and tasty puddings, using seasonal ingredients in classical ways.

at Little Shelford South : 5.5 mi. by A 1309 - X - off A 10 – ✉ Cambridge

XX **Sycamore House**

1 Church St ✉ *CB22 5HG* – ✆ *(01223) 843 396* – *Closed Christmas-New Year and Sunday-Tuesday*

Rest – *(dinner only) (booking essential)* Menu £ 26

◆ Converted 16C cottage in a sleepy hamlet. Long narrow dining room with thick walls, low ceiling and open fire. Frequently-changing, seasonal menu with hearty base.

at Madingley West : 4.5 mi. by A 1303 - X – ✉ Cambridge

The Three Horseshoes

High St ✉ *CB23 8AB* – ✆ *(01954) 210 221* – *www.threehorseshoesmadingley.co.uk* – *Fax (01954) 212 043*

Rest – *(booking advisable)* Carte £ 20/40

◆ Attractive thatched pub with bustling trattoria atmosphere. Concise bar menu and daily changing Italian à la carte, featuring straightforward combinations and fresh, tasty dishes.

at Hardwick West : 5 mi. by A 1303 - X – ✉ Cambridge

Wallis Farmhouse without rest

98 Main St ✉ *CB23 7QU* – ✆ *(01954) 210 347* – *www.wallisfarmhouse.co.uk* – *Fax (01954) 210 988*

4 rm – †£ 52/60 ††£ 72/80

◆ Remotely set Georgian house in picturesque village. Immaculately kept bedrooms in a converted barn across courtyard. Breakfast served in main house. Spacious rear garden.

CANNINGTON – **Somerset** – **503** K30 – **see Bridgwater**

CANTERBURY – Kent – **504** X30 – **pop. 43 552** Great Britain **9** D2

London 59 mi. – Brighton 76 mi. – Dover 15 mi. – Maidstone 28 mi.

12-13 Sun St, Buttermarket ✆ (01227) 378100, canterburyinformation@canterbury.gov.uk

City★★★ - Cathedral★★★ Y - St Augustine's Abbey★★ **AC** YZ **K** – King's School★ Y – Mercery Lane★ Y **12** - Christ Church Gate★ Y **D** – Museum of Canterbury★ **AC** Y **M1** – St Martin's Church★ Y **N** – West Gate Towers★ **AC** Y **R**

Abode Canterbury

High St ✉ CT1 2RX – ✆ (01227) 766 266 – www.abodehotels.co.uk – Fax (01227) 784 874 Y**a**

72 rm – †£ 99/150 ††£ 149/425, ☕ £ 13.50

Rest Michael Caines – see restaurant listing

◆ Centrally located, this smart hotel has undergone a vast top-to-toe transformation. A distinctive modern feel pertains, typified by sleek, airy bedrooms.

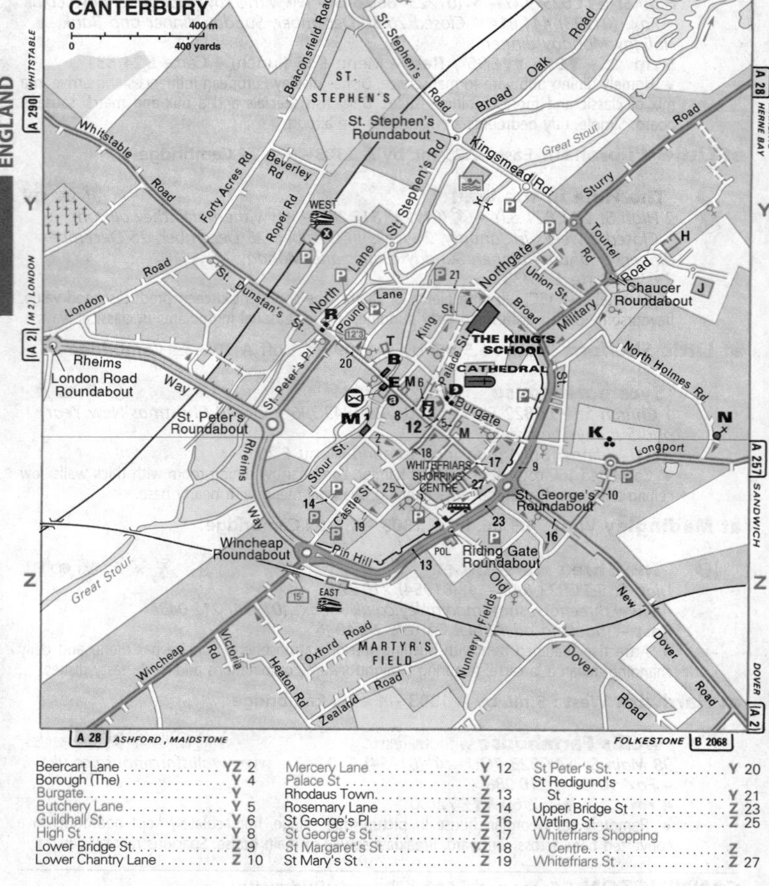

Beercart Lane	YZ 2	Mercery Lane	Y 12	St Peter's St.	Y 20
Borough (The)	Y 4	Palace St	Y	St Redigund's St	Y 21
Burgate	Y	Rhodaus Town	Z 13	Upper Bridge St	Z 23
Butchery Lane	Y 5	Rosemary Lane	Z 14	Watling St.	Z 25
Guildhall St.	Y 6	St George's Pl.	Z 16	Whitefriars Shopping Centre	Z
High St	Y 8	St George's St	Z 17	Whitefriars St.	Z 27
Lower Bridge St.	Z 9	St Margaret's St	YZ 18		
Lower Chantry Lane	Z 10	St Mary's St	Z 19		

ENGLAND

XX **Michael Caines** – at Abode Canterbury Hotel AC VISA MC AE ①

High St ✉ CT1 2RX – ☎ (01227) 826 684 – www.michaelcaines.com – Fax (01227) 784 874 Ya

Rest – *(Closed Sunday dinner)* Menu £ 12/25 – Carte £ 40/60

◆ Enjoy a glass of Champagne in smart bar before repairing to the upmarket restaurant to enjoy modern British cooking utilising a variety of styles and classical techniques.

X **The Goods Shed** P VISA MC AE

Station Rd West, St Dunstans ✉ CT2 8AN – ☎ (01227) 459 153 – www.thegoodsshed.net – Closed Sunday dinner and Monday Yx

Rest – Carte £ 29/34

◆ Once derelict railway shed, now a farmers' market that's open all day. Its eating area offers superbly fresh produce with no frills and real flavours very much to the fore.

at Tyler Hill North West : 4.5 mi. by A 28 and A 290 turning right into Tyler Hill rd in Blean.

The Ivy House P VISA MC

27 Hackington Rd ✉ CT2 9NE – ☎ (01227) 472 200 – Closed Sunday dinner and Monday

Rest – Carte £ 18/27

◆ Traditional pub close to the university. Dinner offers confident seasonal cooking, in substantial portions. Simpler lunch menu. Live music once a month on Sunday afternoons.

at Lower Hardres South : 3 mi. on B 2068 - Z – ✉ Canterbury

The Granville AC P VISA MC AE

Street End ✉ CT4 7AL – ☎ (01227) 700 402 – Fax (01227) 700 925 – Closed 25-26 December, Sunday dinner and Monday

Rest – Carte £ 21/35

◆ Open plan Scandinavian-style rooms, with exposed beams, leather sofas and a central fire. A concise menu keeps things commendably simple, with the focus on local produce.

CARBIS BAY – Cornwall – 503 D33 – see St Ives

CARLISLE – Cumbria – 501 L19 – pop. 71 773 Great Britain 21 B1

London 317 mi. – Blackpool 95 mi. – Edinburgh 101 mi. – Glasgow 100 mi.

Carlisle Airport ☎ (01228) 573641, NW : 5.5 mi. by A 7 - BY - and B 6264

Old Town Hall, Green Market ☎ (01228) 625600, tourism@carlisle-city.gov.uk

18 Aglionby, ☎ (01228) 513 029

18 Stony Holme St Aidan's Rd, ☎ (01228) 625 511

9 Dalston Hall Dalston, ☎ (01228) 710 165

Town★ - Cathedral★ (Painted Ceiling★) AY **E** – Tithe Barn★ BY **A**

Hadrian's Wall★★, N : by A 7 AY

Plan on next page

Cumbria Park AC rest, P VISA MC AE ①

32 Scotland Rd, North : 1 mi. on A 7 ✉ CA3 9DG – ☎ (01228) 522 887 – www.cumbriaparkhotel.co.uk – Fax (01228) 514 796 – Closed 25-26 December

47 rm – †£ 79 ††£ 100/150 **Rest** – *(bar lunch)* Carte £ 16/26 **s**

◆ Traditional hotel with well kept bedrooms; some with jacuzzi baths. Corridor walls filled with postcards and posters from owner's travels. Bottle green restaurant with Roman theme serves classic menu. Bar meals among the fishtanks in lounge/bar.

Number Thirty One VISA MC AE ①

31 Howard Place ✉ CA1 1HR – ☎ (01228) 597 080 – www.number31.co.uk – Fax (01228) 597 080 BYa

4 rm – †£ 65 ††£ 90

Rest – *(dinner only) (residents only by arrangement)* Menu £ 20 **s**

◆ Well-appointed Victorian townhouse with sumptuous lounge and immaculately-kept bedrooms. Richly decorated dining room with window onto plant-filled terrace.

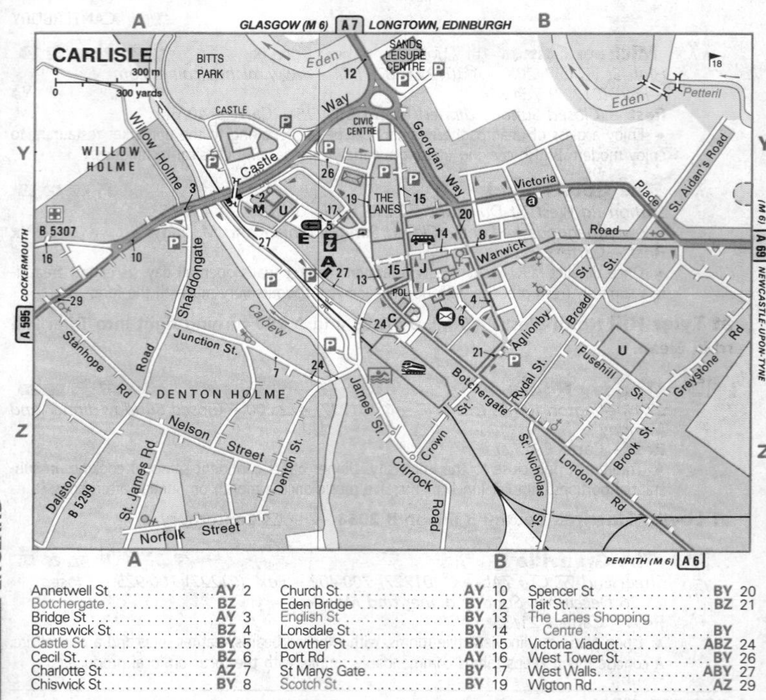

Annetwell St	AY	2	Church St	AY	10	Spencer St	BY	20
Botchergate	BZ		Eden Bridge	BY	12	Tait St	BZ	21
Bridge St	AY	3	English St	BY	13	The Lanes Shopping Centre	BY	
Brunswick St	BZ	4	Lonsdale St	BY	14	Victoria Viaduct	ABZ	24
Castle St	BY	5	Lowther St	BY	15	West Tower St	BY	26
Cecil St	BZ	6	Port Rd	AY	16	West Walls	ABY	27
Charlotte St	AZ	7	St Marys Gate	BY	17	Wigton Rd	AZ	29
Chiswick St	BY	8	Scotch St	BY	19			

ENGLAND

XX Gallo Rosso

Parkhouse Rd, Kingstown, Northwest : 2.75 mi. by A 7 ✉ CA6 4BY – ✆ (01228) 526 037 – www.gallorosso.co.uk – Fax (01228) 550 074 – Closed January and Tuesday

Rest – Italian – Menu £ 18 (Sunday lunch) – Carte £ 17/31

◆ Busy Italian restaurant with cosy lounge, linen-laid tables and a large open kitchen so you can watch chef at work. Good value cooking including freshly baked bread.

at High Crosby **Northeast : 5 mi. by A 7 - BY - and B 6264 off A 689 – ✉ Carlisle**

Crosby Lodge Country House

Crosby-on-Eden ✉ CA6 4QZ – ✆ (01228) 573 618 – www.crosbylodge.co.uk – Fax (01228) 573 428 – Closed Christmas-mid January

11 rm – †£ 90/95 ††£ 190

Rest – *(Sunday dinner residents only)* Menu £ 40 (dinner) – Carte £ 38/53

◆ Grade II listed, castellated house built in 1802. Warm ambience and welcoming hostess. Traditionally furnished lounge. Comfortable bedrooms with pleasant countryside outlook. Richly coloured dining room with polished brass around fireplace. Classic, homecooked food includes renowned sweet trolley.

CARLTON HUSTHWAITE – North Yorkshire – 502 Q21 — 22 B2

London 230 mi. – Leeds 51 mi. – Middlesbrough 32 mi. – York 20 mi.

Carlton Bore

✉ YO7 2BW – ✆ (01845) 501 265 – www.carltonbore.co.uk – Closed first 2 weeks January, Monday and Tuesday

Rest – Menu £ 15 (lunch) – Carte £ 22/30

◆ 17C inn set in a delightful village with rural views. Diverse, appealing menu of Yorkshire based produce; worthy of note are the Deli Platters and Yorkshire cheese selection.

CARLTON-IN-COVERDALE – N. Yorks. – 502 O21 – see Middleham

CARLYON BAY – Cornwall – 503 F33 – see St Austell

CARTERWAY HEADS – Northumberland – 501 O19 – ✉ Shotley Bridge

24 A2

London 272 mi. – Carlisle 59 mi. – Newcastle upon Tyne 21 mi.

Manor House Inn with rm

on A 68 ✉ DH8 9LX – ✆ (01207) 255 268 – www.themanorhouseinn.com

4 rm – ♦£ 43 ♦♦£ 65/75 **Rest** – Carte £ 17/31

◆ Stone-built pub, high up on the hills, with views down to the Derwent Reservoir. Menu of classic pub dishes; more variety on oft-changing specials boards. Local preserves and meats in shop. Comfortable bedrooms with peace-inducing views.

CARTHORPE – North Yorkshire

22 B1

London 228 mi. – Leeds 49 mi. – Middlesbrough 40 mi. – York 34 mi.

Fox and Hounds

✉ DL8 2LG – ✆ (01845) 567 433 – www.foxandhoundscarthorpe.co.uk – Fax (01845) 567 155 – Closed first week January and Monday

Rest – Menu £ 16 (lunch Tuesday-Thursday & dinner daily) – Carte £ 19/30

◆ Family run, ivy-clad stone pub with a real sense of history. Menus offer a huge array of choice, with meats from the local butcher, flour milled nearby and produce from the village dairy.

CARTMEL – Cumbria – 502 L21 – see Grange-over-Sands

CASTERTON – Cumbria – 502 M21 – see Kirkby Lonsdale

CASTLE CARY – Somerset – 503 M30 – pop. 3 056

4 C2

London 127 mi. – Bristol 28 mi. – Wells 13 mi.

Clanville Manor without rest

West : 2 mi. by B 3152 and A 371 on B 3153 ✉ BA7 7PJ – ✆ (01963) 350 124 – www.clanvillemanor.co.uk – Fax (01963) 350 719 – Closed Christmas and New Year

4 rm – ♦£ 45/90 ♦♦£ 90

◆ 18C house, charmingly cluttered. Heirlooms and antiques abound. Breakfasts served from the Aga. Walled garden boasts heated pool. Individual bedrooms, including four-poster.

at Lovington West : 4 mi. by B 3152 and A 371 on B 3153 – ✉ Castle Cary

The Pilgrims at Lovington with rm

rm,

✉ BA7 7PT – ✆ (01963) 240 597 – www.thepilgrimsatlovington.co.uk – Closed Sunday dinner, Monday and Tuesday lunch

5 rm – ♦£ 80 ♦♦£ 110 **Rest** – Carte £ 20/37

◆ Unremarkable appearance masks charming interior. British/Mediterranean menu uses local and homemade produce. Comfortable, contemporary bedrooms, luxurious bathrooms and substantial breakfasts.

CASTLE COMBE – Wiltshire – 503 N29 – pop. 347 – ✉ Chippenham

4 C2

London 110 mi. – Bristol 23 mi. – Chippenham 6 mi.

Village★★

Manor House H. and Golf Club

✉ SN14 7HR – ✆ (01249) 782 206 – www.exclusivehotels.co.uk – Fax (01249) 783 100

44 rm – ♦£ 180/230 ♦♦£ 180/230 – 4 suites

Rest ***The Bybrook*** – *(Closed Saturday lunch)* Menu £ 25 (lunch) – Carte £ 52/65

Spec. Scallops with sautéed potatoes and truffle. Slow cooked fillet of beef with cauliflower and mushroom ravioli. Roasted pineapple financier.

◆ Particularly peaceful manor in a sweeping green with trout in the river. Fine fabrics and oak panelling exude history. Luxurious bedrooms in mews cottages or main house. Smart restaurant; cooking is exact and confident.

Castle Inn

✉ SN14 7HN – ✆ (01249) 783 030 – www.castle-inn.info – Fax (01249) 782 315 – Closed 24-25 December

11 rm – †£ 70/150 ††£ 110/175 **Rest** – *(Bar menu)* Carte £ 19/31

◆ A hostelry dating back to the 12C in the middle of a delightful and historic village. Wooden beams and much character throughout. Breakfast in conservatory. Large and varied menu served in rustic bar.

CASTLE DONINGTON – Leicestershire – 502 P25 – pop. 5 977 — 16 B2

– ✉ Derby

London 123 mi. – Birmingham 38 mi. – Leicester 23 mi. – Nottingham 13 mi.

Nottingham East Midlands Airport : ✆ (0871) 919 9000, S : by B 6540 and A 453

Priest House on the River

Kings Mills ✉ *DE74 2RR* – ✆ *(01332) 810 649 – www.handpicked.co.uk/thepriesthouse – Fax (01332) 815 334*

39 rm – †£ 80/140 ††£ 100/165 – 3 suites

Rest *Brasserie* – Carte £ 25/40

◆ Stylish, contemporary hotel in tranquil riverside setting. Comfortable bedrooms - some with views of the river - decorated in neutral shades, with giant plasma screen TVs. Formally laid out restaurant with classical menu.

at Breedon on the Hill Southwest : 4 mi. by Breedon rd off A 453
– ✉ Castle Donington

The Three Horseshoes Inn

Main St ✉ *DE73 8AN* – ✆ *(01332) 695 129 – www.thehorseshoes.com – Closed 25-26 December, 1 January and Sunday dinner*

Rest – Carte £ 18/33

◆ Welcoming pub with open fire and interesting artefacts. Menu features local, seasonal produce and simple, honest dishes with an international edge; homemade classical puddings.

CATEL – C.I. – 503 P33 – see Channel Islands (Guernsey)

CAUNTON – Notts. – 502 R24 – see Newark-on-Trent

CERNE ABBAS – Dorset — 4 C3

London 132 mi. – Bristol - 60 mi. – Cardiff 115 mi. – Southampton 58 mi.

The New Inn

14 Long Street ✉ *DT2 7JF* – ✆ *(01300) 341 274 – www.newinncerneabbas.com – Fax (01300) 341 457 – Closed 1 week January*

Rest – Carte £ 18/30

◆ Sizeable pub set in picture postcard village, with exposed beams, decked terrace and vast garden. Freshly prepared, traditional dishes make good use of locally sourced produce.

CHADDESLEY CORBETT – Worcs. – 503 N26 – see Kidderminster

CHADWICK END – West Midlands – 503 O26 — 19 C2

London 106 mi. – Birmingham 13 mi. – Leicester 40 mi. – Stratford-upon-Avon 16 mi.

The Orange Tree

Warwick Road, on A 4141 ✉ *B93 0BN* – ✆ *(01564) 785 364 – www.lovelypubs.co.uk – Fax (01564) 782 988 – Closed Sunday dinner*

Rest – *(booking essential)* Carte £ 18/24

◆ Large, contemporary pub with neat gardens, spacious terrace and buzzing atmosphere. Wide-ranging menu offers several dishes in two sizes, with tasty spit roast chicken a speciality.

ENGLAND

CHAGFORD – Devon – 503 I31 – pop. 1 417 2 C2

London 218 mi. – Exeter 17 mi. – Plymouth 27 mi.

Dartmoor National Park★★

Gidleigh Park (Michael Caines)

Northwest : 2 mi. by Gidleigh Rd ✉ TQ13 8HH – ✆ (01647) 432 367 – www.gidleigh.com – Fax (01647) 432 574

23 rm – £ 295/435 £ 310/450 – 1 suite

Rest – *(booking essential)* Menu £ 36/95

Spec. Wild salmon with Oscietra caviar and salmon jelly. Rosé veal with button onions, broad beans and morels. Rhubarb mousse, crumble and sorbet.

◆ Lovingly restored and extremely comfortable Arts and Crafts house set in 100 acres. Luxurious bedrooms boast impressive bathrooms; some have a balcony. Formal restaurant, where classical French menus showcase skillfully prepared, quality local produce. Tasting menu for Michael Caines' signature dishes.

22 Mill Street with rm

22 Mill Street ✉ TQ13 8AW – ✆ (01647) 432 244 – www.22millst.com

2 rm – £ 79/99 £ 99/129, £ 12.50

Rest – *(booking essential)* Menu £ 20/40 s

◆ Smart, intimate restaurant on high street of scenic village; immaculately laid tables. Modern menu displays a strong French base and relies on locally sourced ingredients. Pleasant, contemporary bedrooms.

at Sandypark Northeast : 2.25 mi. on A 382 – ✉ Chagford

Mill End

on A 382 ✉ TQ13 8JN – ✆ (01647) 432 282 – www.millendhotel.com – Fax (01647) 433 106 – Closed 1-14 January

14 rm – £ 90/120 £ 90/160 – 2 suites

Rest – *(light lunch Monday-Saturday)* Menu £ 42 (dinner)

◆ Country house with mill wheel; river Teign runs through garden. Framed pictures, curios grace interiors. Upstairs bedrooms have views; those downstairs have private patios. Pretty restaurant, bright and comfortable.

Parford Well without rest

on Drewsteignton rd ✉ TQ13 8JW – ✆ (01647) 433 353 – www.parfordwell.co.uk – Closed Christmas and New Year

3 rm – £ 50/70 £ 90

◆ Tastefully maintained with superbly tended gardens. Elegant sitting room has plenty of books and French windows to garden. Two breakfast rooms. Homely, immaculate rooms.

at Easton Northeast : 1.5 mi. on A 382 – ✉ Chagford

Easton Court without rest

Easton Cross ✉ TQ13 8JL – ✆ (01647) 433 469 – www.easton.co.uk

5 rm – £ 53/58 £ 78/83

◆ Well appointed accommodation and a high ceilinged lounge overlooking the immaculate gardens. Home made marmalade a speciality. Friendly atmosphere.

Undecided between two equivalent establishments in the same town? Within each category, establishments are classified in our order of preference: the best first.

ENGLAND

CHANNEL ISLANDS – 503 L/M33

ALDERNEY – Alderney – 503 M32 — 5 B1

Aurigny Air Services ✆ (01481) 822886

States Office, Island Hall, Connaught Sq ✆ (01481) 823737, marketing@visitalderney.com

Braye Bay★ – Mannez Garenne (≤★ from Quesnard Lighthouse) – Telegraph Bay★ – Vallee des Trois Vaux★ – Clonque Bay★

BRAYE – Alderney — 5 B1

Braye Beach — rest, VISA AE

✉ *GY9 3XT – ✆ (01481) 824 300 – www.brayebeach.com – Fax (01481) 824 301*

27 rm – 🚹£ 80/120 🚹🚹£ 100/180

Rest – Carte £ 27/32 **s**

◆ Smart, contemporary hotel set on edge of beach. Vaulted basement houses a series of lounges, dining room and a 19-seat cinema. Modern European cooking with a subtle seafood slant.

First and Last — VISA AE

✉ *GY9 3TH – ✆ (01481) 823 162 – Closed October-Easter and Monday*

Rest – Seafood – *(dinner only)* Carte £ 25/34

◆ Positioned by the harbour with scenic views. Simple pine furniture, blue gingham tablecloths. Nautical theme prevails. Keen use of island produce with seafood base.

ST ANNE – Alderney — 5 B1

Farm Court without rest — VISA

Le Petit Val ✉ GY9 3UX – ✆ (01481) 822 075 – www.farmcourt-alderney.co.uk – Fax (01481) 822 075 – Closed Christmas and New Year

11 rm – 🚹£ 39/60 🚹🚹£ 78/98

◆ Converted stone farm buildings around cobbled courtyard and garden. Sitting room and breakfast room. Spacious well-appointed bedrooms with contemporary and antique furniture.

GUERNSEY – Guernsey – 503 L32 – pop. 58 867 — 5 A2

Guernsey Airport ✆ (01481) 237766, Aurigny Air ✆ (01481) 822 886

from St Peter Port to France (St Malo) and Jersey (St Helier) (Condor Ferries Ltd) 2 weekly – from St Peter Port to France (Dielette) (Manche Iles Express) (summer only) (60 mn) – from St Peter Port to Herm (Herm Seaway) (25 mn) – from St Peter Port to Sark (Isle of Sark Shipping Co. Ltd) (45 mn) – from St Peter Port to Jersey (St Helier) (HD Ferries) (1hr) – from St Peter Port to Jersey (St Helier) (Condor Ferries Ltd) daily

from St Peter Port to France (St Malo) and Jersey (St Helier) (Condor Ferries Ltd) – from St Peter Port to Jersey (St Helier) and Weymouth (Condor Ferries Ltd)

P.O. Box 23, North Esplanade ✆ (01481) 723552, enquiries@visitguernsey.com

Island★ - Pezeries Point★★ – Icart Point★★ – Côbo Bay★★ - St Martin's Point★★ – St Apolline's Chapel★ – Vale Castle★ – Fort Doyle★ – La Gran'mere du Chimquiere★ – Rocquaine Bay★ – Jerbourg Point★

CATEL/CASTEL – Guernsey — 5 A2

Cobo Bay — rest, VISA AE

Cobo Coast Rd ✉ GY5 7HB – ✆ (01481) 257 102 – www.cobobayhotel.com – Fax (01481) 254 542 – Closed January-February

36 rm – 🚹£ 49/95 🚹🚹£ 79/160

Rest – Menu £ 25 (dinner) **s** – Carte £ 25/34 **s**

◆ Modern hotel on peaceful, sandy Cobo Bay; an ideal location for families. The rooms are pleasant with bright décor and some have the delightful addition of seaview balconies. Romantic dining with views of sunsets.

FERMAIN BAY – Guernsey 5 A2

Fermain Valley

Fermain Lane ✉ *GY1 1ZZ – ☎ (01481) 235 666 – www.fermainvalley.com – Fax (01481) 235 413*

45 rm – †£ 110/140 ††£ 180/220

Rest *Valley Restaurant* – *(dinner only and lunch Saturday-Sunday)* Menu £ 35 **s**

Rest *Valley Brasserie* – Carte £ 26/34 **s**

◆ Fine sea views through the trees. Smart contemporary country house theme prevails: sleek lounges, decked terrace, library, and fresh, carefully appointed rooms with balconies. Fine dining in comfortable restaurant. Fresh fish and simple grills at the Brasserie.

FOREST – Guernsey – pop. 1 549 5 A2

Cafe d'Escalier

Le Gouffre, Southwest : 2 mi. ✉ *GY8 0BN – ☎ (01481) 264 121 – Fax (01481) 263 319*

Rest – Carte £ 20/32 **s**

◆ Lively eatery with easy going style. Wide menu offers homemade produce with Mediterranean influences; from breakfast and snacks through to afternoon tea and dinner. Buzzy, alert service.

VAZON BAY – Guernsey – ✉ Catel 5 A2

La Grande Mare

Vazon Coast Rd ✉ *GY5 7LL – ☎ (01481) 256 576 – www.lagrandemare.com – Fax (01481) 256 532*

12 rm – †£ 85/95 ††£ 170/190 – 13 suites – ††£ 218/290

Rest – Menu £ 18/23 – Carte dinner £ 21/34

◆ Resort complex, constantly evolving. Bedrooms are a good size, are well kept and boast every mod con; some have balconies. Family friendly, with indoor/outdoor activities. Formal dining room overlooks golf course.

ENGLAND

KINGS MILLS – Guernsey 5 A2

Fleur du Jardin

Castel ✉ *GY5 7JT – ☎ (01481) 257 996 – www.fleurdujardin.com – Fax (01481) 256 834*

15 rm – †£ 50 ††£ 128 **Rest** – Menu £ 13 (lunch) – Carte £ 15/25

◆ Characterful 15C inn. Majority of the bedrooms are fresh and modern, displaying neutral colours and a New England style. Traditional bar with more modern dining room uses local produce and good fish.

ST MARTIN – Guernsey – pop. 6 267 5 A2

St Peter Port 2 mi.

Bon Port

Moulin Huet Bay ✉ *GY4 6EW – ☎ (01481) 239 249 – www.bonport.com – Fax (01481) 239 596 – Closed 1 January-1 March*

23 rm – †£ 104/159 ††£ 115/199 – 1 suite

Rest *Bon Port* – *(bar lunch Monday-Saturday)* Menu £ 17/25 – Carte £ 20/37

◆ Perched on the top of the cliff, with a commanding view of the bay, this hotel is very keenly and personally run. Improving rooms vary in size and style and some have balconies. Relaxed dining in large, redecorated bistro.

Jerbourg

Jerbourg Point ✉ *GY4 6BJ – ☎ (01481) 238 826 – www.hoteljerboug.com – Fax (01481) 238 238 – Closed 5 January-28 February*

31 rm – †£ 44/109 ††£ 104/159 – 1 suite

Rest – Menu £ 18/22 – Carte £ 16/37 **s**

◆ In a prime position for walks to sandy bays. Popular terrace for afternoon teas. F with solar heated outdoor pool and garden patio. Most rooms have pleasant Finely presented, fish based cuisine.

La Barbarie
Saints Bay ✉ GY4 6ES – ✆ (01481) 235 217 – www.labarbariehotel.com – Fax (01481) 235 208 – Closed 1 November -12 March
21 rm – †£ 57/75 ††£ 75/126 – 1 suite
Rest – *(dinner only) (residents only bar lunch)* Menu £ 22 – Carte £ 21/32
◆ Stone-built former farmhouse with a welcoming, cottagey style. Characterful bar; well-kept pool and terrace. Bedrooms are traditional and comfortable. Seafood a speciality.

Saints Bay
Icart ✉ GY4 6JG – ✆ (01481) 238 888 – www.saintsbayhotel.com – Fax (01481) 235 558
35 rm – †£ 39/72 ††£ 58/124 **Rest** – Menu £ 20 – Carte £ 12/20
◆ Located on Icart Point, close to Fisherman's Harbour, the southern tip of the island and perfect for cliff top walks. Multilingual staff; neat bedrooms with all amenities. Broad choice of menus.

La Michele
Les Hubits ✉ GY4 6NB – ✆ (01481) 238 065 – www.lamichelehotel.com – Fax (01481) 239 492 – Easter-October
16 rm (dinner included) – †£ 44/65 ††£ 88/130
Rest – *(dinner only) (residents only)*
◆ Painted and canopied façade with conservatory lounge and secluded garden. Lovely seating area around the pool. Fermain bay is nearby; pleasant, unfussy bedrooms.

ENGLAND

Sunnydene Country
Rue des Marettes ✉ GY4 6JH – ✆ (01481) 236 870 – www.sunnydenecountryhotel.com – Fax (01481) 237 468 – April-October
20 rm – †£ 38/68 ††£ 66/86
Rest – *(dinner only)* Menu £ 18 – Carte approx. £ 18
◆ Neat and tidy hotel with pitch and putt to rear of garden! Comfortable, homely lounge; linen-laid dining room. Pretty pool and terrace area. Rooms in house or garden.

XX **The Auberge**
Jerbourg Rd ✉ GY4 6BH – ✆ (01481) 238 485 – www.theauberge.gg – Fax (01481) 230 967 – Closed 25-26 and 31 December, 1 January and Sunday dinner
Rest – *(booking essential)* Menu £ 15/19 – Carte £ 26/36
◆ Superbly located informal modern restaurant, with attractive terrace boasting tranquil sea and island views. Artistic dishes display bold flavours. Quality island-caught fish is a favourite.

ST PETER PORT – Guernsey 5 A2

18 Rohais St Pierre Park, ✆ (01481) 727 039
Town★★ - St Peter's Church★ Z – Hauteville House★ **AC** Z – Castle Cornet★ (<★) **AC** Z
Saumarez Park★ (Guernsey Folk Museum★), W : 2 mi. by road to Catel Z – Little Chapel★, SW : 2.25 mi. by Mount Durand road Z

Old Government House H. & Spa
St Ann's Pl ✉ GY1 2NU – ✆ (01481) 724 921 – www.theoghhotel.com – Fax (01481) 724 429 Y**a**
60 rm – †£ 190 ††£ 255
Rest *Governors* – *(booking essential)* Carte £ 35/45
Rest *The Brasserie* – ✆ (01481) 738 604 – Carte £ 30/40
◆ Now owned by Red Carnation Hotels with plans to improve this 18C house, first built for island governors. Already sitting room and leisure have been upgraded. Bedrooms planned next. Fine-dining in Governors. Informal Brasserie with local produce.

Duke of Richmond
Cambridge Park ✉ GY1 1UY – ✆ (01481) 726 221 – www.dukeofrichmond.com – Fax (01481) 728 945 Y**c**
73 rm – †£ 67/90 ††£ 98/118 – 1 suite
Rest – *(dinner only and lunch Saturday-Sunday)* Menu £ 14/22 **s** – Carte £ 31/41 **s**
◆ Boasts views over Candie Gardens. Refurbished bedrooms are nicely coordinated and have good amenities; those at the rear overlook the terrace. Large dining room; local seafood the speciality.

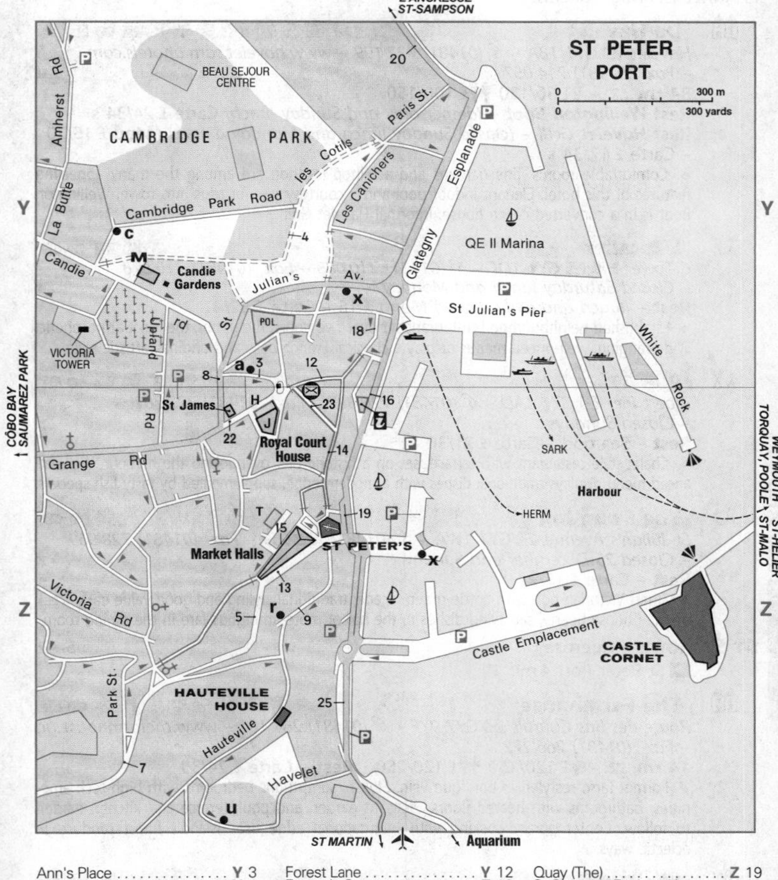

Les Rocquettes

Les Gravees, West : 1 mi. by St Julian's Ave and Grange Rd ✉ *GY1 1RN – ☎ (01481) 722 146 – www.rocquettes.sarniahotels.com – Fax (01481) 714 543*

51 rm – †£ 50/95 ††£ 100/140

Rest – *(bar lunch Monday-Saturday)* Menu £ 17 (dinner) – Carte £ 19/31

◆ Stately mansion with impressive health suite. Well-equipped bedrooms of various shapes and sizes. Superior rooms have balconies; others overlook the rear garden. Early suppers for children in dining room.

De Havelet

Havelet ✉ *GY1 1BA – ☎ (01481) 722 199 – www.havelet.sarniahotels.com – Fax (01481) 714 057* Z**u**

34 rm – ♦£ 50/120 ♦♦£ 100/150

Rest *Wellington Boot* – *(dinner only and Sunday lunch)* Carte £ 24/34 **s**

Rest *Havelet Grill* – *(closed Sunday lunch and Monday dinner)* Menu £ 15/20 – Carte £ 17/34 **s**

◆ Comfortable rooms, fine gardens and a hilltop location are among the many appealing features of this hotel. Elegant indoor pool and a courtesy bus for trips into town. Wellington Boot is in a converted coach house. Informal Havelet Grill.

L'Escalier

6 Tower Hill ✉ *GY1 1DF – ☎ (01481) 710 088 – Fax (01481) 710 878 – Closed Saturday lunch and Monday* Z**r**

Rest – *(lunch and early dinner)* Menu £ 16 – Carte £ 32/41

◆ Established neighbourhood restaurant set over two floors; the upper, the most atmospheric. Wide-ranging, well-priced menus display a classical French base and original, artistic style.

Pier 17

Albert Pier ✉ *GY1 1AD – ☎ (01481) 720 823 – Fax (01481) 722 702 – Closed Sundays* Z**x**

Rest – Seafood – Carte £ 21/30

◆ Chalet-style restaurant with terrace, set on a historic pier overlooking the harbour. Well-balanced menu displays traditional dishes with a modern edge, supplemented by tasty fish specials.

The Swan Inn

St Julian's Avenue ✉ *GY1 1WA – ☎ (01481) 728 969 – Fax (01481) 728 969 – Closed 25 December and Sunday* Y**x**

Rest – Carte £ 15/22

◆ Smart Victorian pub with bottle-green façade, traditional styling and good value early week menu. Choose hearty, satisfying dishes in the bar or more ambitious fare in the dining room.

ST SAVIOUR – Guernsey **5** A2

St Peter Port 4 mi.

The Farmhouse

Route des Bas Courtils ✉ *GY7 9YF – ☎ (01481) 264 181 – www.thefarmhouse.gg – Fax (01481) 266 272*

14 rm – ♦£ 120/150 ♦♦£ 120/250 **Rest** – Carte £ 24/35

◆ Former farm restyled in boutique vein. Stylish, sumptuous bedrooms with high-tech amenities; bathrooms with heated floors. Pleasant garden and pool; terrace and kitchen garden to follow. Contemporary cooking with international edge uses Island's finest produce in eclectic ways.

The Pavilion

Le Gron ✉ *GY7 9RN – ☎ (01481) 264 165 – Closed Christmas-mid January and Mondays in winter*

Rest – *(lunch only and dinner Saturday in summer)* Menu £ 15 **s** – Carte £ 22/29 **s**

◆ Farmhouse-style restaurant displaying exposed stone and beams. Menus offer something for everyone, from tea and cakes to full 3 courses. Fresh, simple, intelligent cooking. Desserts a must.

HERM – Herm – **503** M33

to Guernsey (St Peter Port) (Herm Seaway) (20 mn)

Le Grand Monceau★

White House

✉ *GY1 3HR – ☎ (01481) 722 159 – www.herm-island.com – Fax (01481) 710 066 – 26 March-November*

40 rm (dinner included) – ♦£ 88/154 ♦♦£ 176/272

Rest *Conservatory* – *(booking essential)* Menu £ 24/25

Rest *Ship Inn* – *(lunch only) (booking advisable)* Carte £ 18/26

◆ Hotel with real country house feel: offset by verdant hills, the beach extends to the door. Guernsey and Jethou can be viewed from the hushed lounge. Attractive rooms. Formal Conservatory with seafood emphasis. Relaxed Ship Inn.

JERSEY – **C.I.** – **503** L33 – **pop. 85 150** **5** B2

States of Jersey Airport : ✆ (01534) 446 000

from St Helier to France (St Malo) (Condor Ferries Ltd) (summer only) – from St Helier to France (St Malo) (Condor Ferries Ltd) 3 weekly - from Gorey to France (Carteret) (Manche Iles Express) (summer only) (60mn) – from St Helier to Guernsey (St Peter Port) (Condor Ferries Ltd) (50 mn) – from St Helier to Guernsey (St Peter Port) (Condor Ferries Ltd) daily

from St Helier to France (St Malo) and Guernsey (St Peter Port) (Condor Ferries Ltd) – from St Helier to Sark (Condor Ferries Ltd) (50 mn) – from St Helier to Guernsey (St Peter Port) and Weymouth (Condor Ferries Ltd)

Liberation Place, St Helier ✆ (01534) 448877, info@jersey.com

Island★★ - Jersey Zoo★★ **AC** – Jersey Museum★ - Eric Young Orchid Foundation★ – St Catherine's Bay★ (≤★★) – Grosnez Point★ - Devil's Hole★ – St Matthews Church, Millbrook (glasswork★) – La Hougue Bie★ (Neolithic tomb★ **AC**) - Waterworks Valley - Hamptonne Country Life Museum★ – St Catherine's Bay★ (≤★★) – Noirmont Point★

BEAUMONT – **St Peter** **5** B2

Bistro Soleil

La Route de la Haule ✉ JE3 7BA – ✆ (01534) 720 249 – Fax (01534) 625 621 – Closed 25-26 December, 1 January, Sunday dinner, Monday September-May and Bank Holidays

Rest – Menu £ 15/24 – Carte dinner £ 22/31

◆ Series of connected rooms with superb views over St Aubins Bay. Minimalist style: just a couple of modern pictures. Freshly prepared, bold menus with Mediterranean accent.

GOREY – **St Martin** – ✉ **St Martin** **5** B2

St Helier 4 mi.

Mont Orgueil Castle★ (≤★★) **AC** – Jersey Pottery★

Moorings

AC rest, VISA MC AE

Gorey Pier ✉ JE3 6EW – ✆ (01534) 853 633 – www.themooringshotel.com – Fax (01534) 857 618

15 rm – †£ 58/109 ††£ 115/147 **Rest** – Menu £ 18/23 – Carte £ 35/47

◆ Located at the base of Gorey Castle, overlooking the waterfront, once the heart of the oyster fishing industry. Well-priced; the first floor bedrooms have terraces. Pleasant decked area at front of restaurant.

Suma's

Gorey Hill ✉ JE3 6ET – ✆ (01534) 853 291 – www.sumasrestaurant.com – Fax (01534) 851 913 – Closed 22 December-20 January and Sunday dinner

Rest – *(booking essential) (lunch and early dinner)* Menu £ 19 **s** – Carte £ 30/50 **s**

◆ Modest façade conceals vibrant interior: head through to the terrace with its harbour/castle views. Modern European cooking uses island produce. Good value menus at lunch and in early evening.

Village Bistro

Gorey Village ✉ JE3 9EP – ✆ (01534) 853 429 – www.village-bistro.com – Closed Sunday dinner and Monday

Rest – Menu £ 16/19 – Carte £ 24/30

◆ Local produce sourced daily from small suppliers. Unpretentious feel; interesting choices to be made, particularly of seafood dishes.

The Bass and Lobster

Gorey Coast Road ✉ JE3 6EU – ✆ (01534) 859 590 – www.bassandlobster.com – Fax (01534) 858 719 – Closed 2 weeks early January, Monday lunch and Sunday

Rest – Menu £ 15 (lunch) – Carte £ 25/39

◆ Bright, modern pub close to beach. Seasonal island produce; fresh, tasty seafood and shellfish dominate the menu. Fantastic oysters; good value lunch menu. Smooth, effective service.

ENGLAND

GREEN ISLAND – St Clement 5 B2

Green Island

St Clement ✉ JE2 6LS – ✆ (01534) 857 787 – www.greenisland.je – Closed 20 December-1 week February, Sunday dinner and Monday

Rest – Seafood – *(booking essential)* Menu £ 18 (lunch) – Carte £ 30/42

◆ Charming, personally run restaurant with terrace and seaside kiosk. Internationally influenced dishes and seafood specials showcase island produce. Flavours are bold and perfectly judged.

GROUVILLE – Grouville 5 B2

St Helier 3 mi.

Cafe Poste

La Rue de la ville ES Renauds ✉ JE3 9FY – ✆ (01534) 859 696 – www.cafeposte.co.uk – Closed 2 weeks Spring/Summer, 2 weeks November, Monday and Tuesday

Rest – Menu £ 18 (lunch) – Carte (dinner and Sunday lunch) £ 27/39

◆ Popular neighbourhood restaurant – formerly a post office – with French country themed interior and cosy fire in winter. Eclectic menus include plenty of well-crafted seafood creations.

LA HAULE – St Peter – ✉ St Brelade 5 B2

La Haule Manor without rest

St Aubin's Bay ✉ JE3 8BS – ✆ (01534) 741 426 – www.lahaulemanor.com

10 rm – †£ 54/85 ††£ 90/122

◆ Attractive, extended Georgian house with fine coastal outlook. Period style sitting room; stylish breakfast room; large basement bar. Airy, well-kept bedrooms with good view.

Au Caprice

Route de la Haule, on A 1 ✉ JE3 8BA – ✆ (01534) 722 083 – www.aucapricejersey.com – Fax (01534) 280 058 – Mid-March to mid-November

12 rm – †£ 28/60 ††£ 54/74

Rest – *(by arrangement)* Menu £ 12 (dinner)

◆ Clean-lined white guesthouse with French windows; light and airy, providing homely good value rooms: two of them share large balcony at the front. Close to large sandy beach. Each morning, guests told dining room menu.

LA PULENTE – St Brelade – ✉ St Brelade 5 B2

St Helier 7 mi.

18 Les Mielles G. & C.C. St Ouens Bay, ✆ (01534) 482 787

Atlantic

Le Mont de la Pulente, on B 35 ✉ JE3 8HE – ✆ (01534) 744 101 – www.theatlantichotel.com – Fax (01534) 744 102 – Closed 3 January-5 February

49 rm – †£ 100/150 ††£ 200/300 – 1 suite

Rest *Ocean* – *(booking essential)* Menu £ 25/50 – Carte £ 50/60

Spec. Foie gras with mango, passion fruit and salted caramel. Brill with crab, asparagus and pea foam. Pear tarte Tatin with honey and lavender ice cream.

◆ Stylish hotel in stunning location with attentive team of personable staff. Public areas have relaxed, intimate feel and bedrooms are cool and fresh; some with patio, others a balcony. Elegant dining room serving delicious, well-crafted dishes, which display a real understanding of flavour. Smooth, professional service.

ROZEL BAY – St Martin – ✉ St Martin 5 B2

St Helier 6 mi.

Chateau La Chaire

Rozel Valley ✉ JE3 6AJ – ✆ (01534) 863 354 – www.chateau-la-chaire.co.uk – Fax (01534) 865 137

12 rm – ††£ 215/255 – 2 suites **Rest** – Menu £ 18/30 – Carte £ 35/45

◆ Imposing chateau dated 1843, rich in paintings and antiques: individually decorated bedrooms overlook the quiet wooded grounds. Ornate sitting room. Conservatory dining room; terrace popular in summer.

ENGLAND

ST AUBIN – St Brelade – ✉ St Brelade 5 B2

St Helier 4 mi.

Somerville rest,

Mont du Boulevard, South : 0.75 mi. via harbour ✉ JE3 8AD – ✆ (01534) 741 226 – www.dolanhotels.com – Fax (01534) 746 621

56 rm – £ 105/170 £ 149/189

Rest ***Tides*** – Menu £ 16/30 **s** – Carte approx. £ 38

◆ Delightful views of the harbour, bay and village. Evening entertainment laid on. Cheerful rooms, some in superior style. Cloth clad, classic dining room.

Cardington House without rest

Mont es Tours, South : 0.75 mi. via harbour (Just past the Somerville Hotel on the left-hand side) ✉ JE3 8AR – ✆ (01534) 748 000 – www.cardingtonhouse.com – Fax (01534) 748 007 – Closed January

5 rm – £ 150 £ 400

◆ Splendid Victorian house hidden away in delightful setting, with mature rear garden, great pool and steps down to a secluded beach. Chic, bold modern décor; comfy lounge with good view, airy breakfast room and stylish bedrooms.

Panorama without rest

La Rue du Crocquet ✉ JE3 8BZ – ✆ (01534) 742 429 – www.panoramajersey.com – Fax (01534) 745 940 – Closed 1 January-15 April and 15 October-31 December

14 rm – £ 61/105 £ 112/150

◆ Personally run hotel with conservatory, garden and bay views. Also boasts a teapot collection. The superior style bedrooms are very pleasant. All rooms boast good amenities.

Sabots d'or without rest

High St ✉ JE3 8BZ – ✆ (01534) 743 732 – www.sabotsdor.com – Fax (01534) 490 142 – Closed 22 December-5 January

12 rm – £ 25/68 £ 54/68

◆ Floral furnishings in homely and cosy bedrooms. Well located for shops, watersports; its cobbled high street position not far from picturesque harbour.

Salty Dog Bar and Bistro

Le Boulevard ✉ JE3 8AB – ✆ (01534) 742 760 – www.saltydogbistro.com – Fax (01534) 742 932 – Closed 24 December-08 January, lunch Monday-Thursday and lunch Monday in summer

Rest – Asian influences – Menu £ 22 – Carte £ 23/41

◆ Wood panelled walls and church pews create rustic feel in quirky, informal restaurant in St. Aubin's harbour. Menus blend local produce with New World and Asian influences.

ST BRELADE'S BAY – St Brelade – ✉ St Brelade 5 B2

St Helier 6 mi.

Fishermen's Chapel (frescoes★)

L'Horizon rm, rest,

✉ JE3 8EF – ✆ (01534) 743 101 – www.handpicked.co.uk/lhorizon – Fax (01534) 746 269

99 rm – £ 95/145 £ 190/230 – 7 suites

Rest ***The Grill*** – see restaurant listing

Rest ***Brasserie*** – *(closed Sunday)* Menu £ 34 (dinner) – Carte £ 28/41

◆ Period hotel right on the beach and consequently popular for its stunning views from the terrace and some of its tastefully decorated front bedrooms. Serene indoor pool. Informal brasserie adjacent to the sea.

St Brelade's Bay

La Route de la Baie ✉ JE3 8EF – ✆ (01534) 746 141 – www.stbreladesbayhotel.com – Fax (01534) 747 278 – Closed January-2 April and November-December

67 rm – £ 88/179 £ 206/304 – 3 suites

Rest – Menu £ 18/30 – Carte £ 28/37

◆ Traditional seafront hotel with mouth-watering views of bay and resplendent gardens with pool. Rattan furnished sitting room and spacious bedrooms. Friendly and family run. Front, sea-facing restaurant.

ENGLAND

Golden Sands

La Route de la Baie ✉ JE3 8EF – ✆ (01534) 741 241 – www.dolanhotels.com – Fax (01534) 499 366 – April-October

62 rm – †£ 46/123 ††£ 72/165

Rest – *(bar lunch)* Menu £ 24 (dinner) **s** – Carte £ 17/32 **s**

◆ With adjacent sweep of a sandy bay and many of the bedrooms south-facing with balconies, this hotel is a popular spot. Within easy reach of the airport and St Helier. Seasonal menus.

The Grill – at L'Horizon Hotel

✉ JE3 8EF – ✆ (01534) 743 101 – www.handpicked.co.uk/lhorizon – Fax (01534) 746 269 – Closed Tuesday and Wednesday

Rest – *(dinner only)* Menu £ 43 **s**

◆ Intimately styled grill room with tasteful cream and brown banquettes and framed photos of film stars. Seafood is the focus, but it faces competition from a strong suit of meat dishes.

Oyster Box

La Route de la Baie ✉ JE3 8EF – ✆ (01534) 743 311 – www.oysterbox.co.uk – Closed 25-26 December, Sunday dinner and Monday lunch

Rest – Carte £ 21/68

◆ Cool, modern restaurant on the beach with al fresco dining. Flexible menu ranges from sandwiches to 3 courses, featuring quality ingredients prepared in a fresh, simple manner.

ST HELIER – St Helier **5** B2

Jersey Museum★ **AC** Z - Elizabeth Castle (≤★) **AC** Z – Fort Regent (≤★ **AC**) Z

St Peter's Valley - German Underground Hospital★ **AC**, NW : 4 mi. by A 1, A 11 St Peter's Valley rd and C 112

Royal Yacht

Weighbridge ✉ JE2 3NF – ✆ (01534) 720 511 – www.theroyalyacht.com – Fax (01534) 767 729 Z**b**

108 rm – †£ 125 ††£ 205 – 2 suites

Rest *Sirocco* – *(dinner only and Sunday lunch)* Menu £ 25 – Carte £ 43/59

Rest *Cafe Zephyr* – Carte £ 24/46

Rest *The Grill* – Carte £ 16/32

◆ Striking hotel with contemporary interior and stunning spa. The most spacious bedrooms look towards harbour; the quietest over inner courtyard. Two stunning suites with hot tubs. Lively brasserie with pavement terrace. More formal dining in Sirocco restaurant. The Grill retains traditional feel.

Radisson Blu Waterfront

Rue de l'Etau ✉ JE2 3WF – ✆ (01534) 671 100 – www.radissonblu.com/hotel-jersey Z**c**

181 rm – †£ 95/135 ††£ 105/145 – 14 suites

Rest – Menu £ 25 (dinner) – Carte approx. £ 25 **s**

◆ Fantastic location overlooking the harbour. Very spacious bedrooms, light and contemporary in style; most of them with views. Vast fish tank in reception. Waterfront terrace. Contemporary brasserie style restaurant.

Grand

The Esplanade ✉ JE4 8WD – ✆ (01534) 722 301 – www.grandjersey.com – Fax (01534) 737 815 Y**u**

117 rm – †£ 125/150 ††£ 150/300 – 6 suites

Rest *Tassili* – *(closed Sunday-Wednesday) (dinner only)* Carte approx. £ 47 **s**

Rest *Victoria's* – *(dinner only and Sunday lunch)* Menu £ 20 – Carte approx. £ 25 **s**

◆ Impressive Victorian hotel with pitched white façade overlooking St Aubins Bay, given contemporary makeover. Strong leisure facilities and comfortable bedrooms. Tassili for formal dining. Brasserie style in Victoria's.

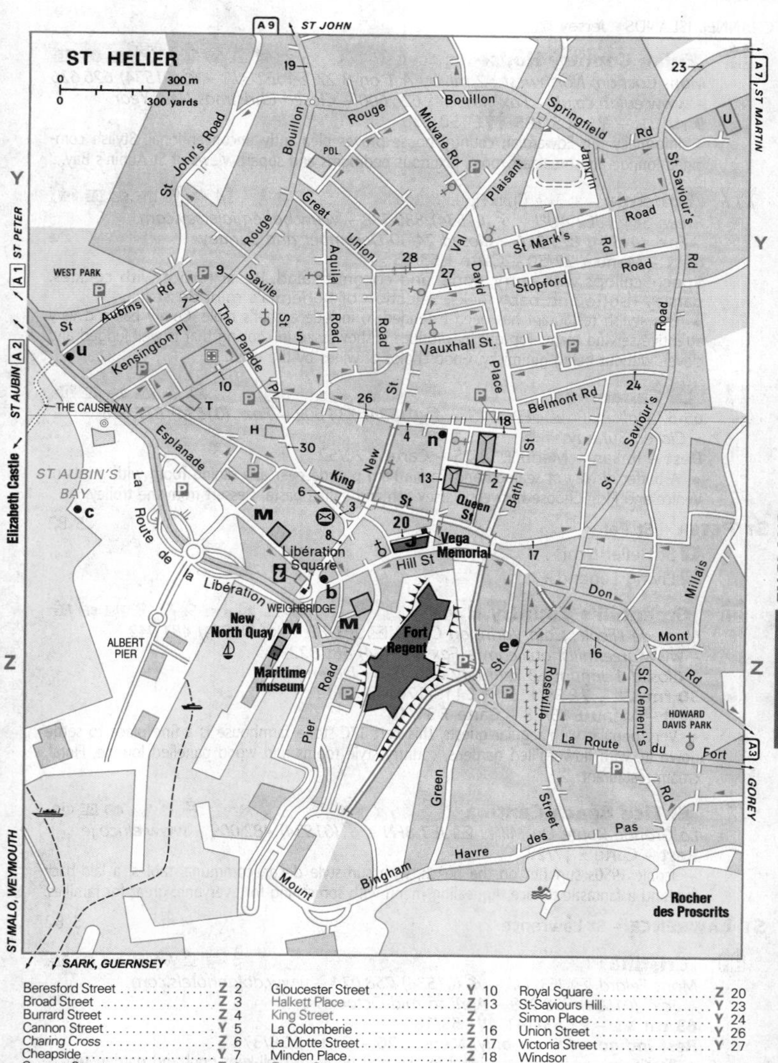

The Club Hotel & Spa

Green St ✉ JE2 4UH – ✆ (01534) 876 500 – www.theclubjersey.com
– Fax (01534) 720 371 – Closed 24-30 December **Ze**

42 rm – 🚹£ 99/215 🚹🚹£ 99/215 – 4 suites

Rest *Bohemia* – see restaurant listing

◆ Well-run, fresh, modern hotel boasting attractive outdoor bar and poolside terrace. Bedrooms differ considerably but all are sleek and contemporary with good amenities and luxurious bathrooms.

Eulah Country House without rest
Mont Cochon, Northwest : 2 mi. by A 1 on B 27 ✉ JE2 3JA – ✆ (01534) 626 626 – www.eulah.co.uk – Fax (01534) 626 600 – Closed Christmas-New Year
9 rm – †£ 105/185 ††£ 150/230
◆ Informally run Edwardian country house proves pleasantly unconventional. Stylish combined lounge and breakfast room, luxurious bedrooms and superb views of St Aubin's Bay.

Bohemia – at The Club Hotel & Spa
Green St ✉ JE2 4UH – ✆ (01534) 880 588 – www.bohemiajersey.com – Fax (01534) 875 054 – Closed 24-30 December and Sunday Z**e**
Rest – Menu £ 22/50 – Carte £ 53/63
Spec. Scallops with curry, apple and coconut salad. Roast turbot with cockles, parsley risotto and baby leeks. Selection of Bohemia's mini desserts.
◆ This stylish restaurant has been extended to include a chef's table. Comfy bar and very attentive serving team. Top quality produce is showcased in cooking that is well-judged and clever, without being gimmicky. Good choice of wines by the glass.

La Capannina
65-67 Halkett Pl ✉ JE2 4WG – ✆ (01534) 734 602 – Fax (01534) 877 628 – Closed Sunday Z**n**
Rest – Italian – Menu £ 18/25 – Carte £ 20/52
◆ A buffet display of seafood and Parma ham preside over airy dining room with prints of Venice and Pisa. Choose between Jersey fish and Italian pasta. Dessert from the trolley.

ST PETER – St Peter **5** B2

St Helier 5 mi.
Living Legend★

Greenhill's Country H.
Mont de l'Ecole, Coin Varin, on C 112 ✉ JE3 7EL – ✆ (01534) 481 042 – www.greenhillshotel.com – Fax (01534) 485 322 – Closed 1 January-2 February and 19-31 December
30 rm – †£ 58/115 ††£ 116/170 – 1 suite
Rest – Menu £ 15/28 – Carte £ 31/46
◆ Very popular with regular guests, this part 17C stone farmhouse is a fine place to settle down in, with flower-filled gardens, country style rooms and wood panelled lounge. Floral, cream restaurant.

El Tico Beach Cantina
La Grande Route Du Milles ✉ JE3 8FN – ✆ (01534) 482 009 – www.eltico.je
Rest – Carte £ 17/22
◆ Iconic 1950s surf hut on the beach, with surf-style décor, communal tables, a laid-back feel and a fantastic terrace. Appealing menu with something for everyone; great for families.

ST LAWRENCE – St Lawrence **5** B2

Cristina
Mont Felard ✉ JE3 1JA – ✆ (01534) 758 024 – www.dolanhotels.com – Fax (01534) 758 028 – April to mid-October
63 rm – †£ 53/141 ††£ 53/180
Rest *Indigo* – *(dinner only)* Menu £ 26 – Carte £ 28/37
◆ Traditional, white painted hotel in elevated position. Well-kept pool and garden terrace area. Spacious bar and wicker furnished lounge. Modern, pristine bedrooms. Tiled floors, suede fabrics add character to restaurant.

ST SAVIOUR – St Saviour **5** B2

St Helier 1 mi.

Longueville Manor
Longueville Rd, on A 3 ✉ JE2 7WF – ✆ (01534) 725 501 – www.longuevillemanor.com – Fax (01534) 731 613
28 rm – †£ 195/260 ††£ 330/460 – 2 suites **Rest** – Menu £ 21/55 **s**
◆ Exemplary part 14C manor for a special stay; every detail from furnishings to service is considered. Sumptuous rooms, delightful garden, poolside terrace. Panelled restaurant and terrace room overlooking garden; locally-inspired classics with modern twists.

ENGLAND

SARK – Sark – **503** L33

to Guernsey (St Peter Port) (Isle of Sark Shipping Co. Ltd) (summer only) (45 mn)

to Jersey (St Helier) (Condor Ferries Ltd) (50 mn)

Sark Tourism Visitor Centre ✆ (01481) 832345, office@sark.info

Island★★ - La Coupáe★★★ – Port du Moulin★★ – Creux Harbour★ – La Seigneurie★ **AC** – Pilcher Monument★ – Hog's Back★

Petit Champ

✉ GY9 0SF – ✆ (01481) 832 046 – www.hotelpetitchamp.co.uk – Fax (01481) 832 469 – April-September

10 rm (dinner included) – £ 71/143 £ 137/190

Rest – *(dinner only)* Carte £ 21/37

◆ Ideal for views of neighbouring islands, with three sun lounges to enjoy them from; neat, trim rooms. Quarry, from which hotel's stone comes, is site of solar heated pool. Dining room features Sark specialities.

La Sablonnerie with rm

Little Sark ✉ GY9 0SD – ✆ (01481) 832 061 – www.lasablonnerie.com – Fax (01481) 832 408 – Mid-April to mid-October

21 rm (dinner included) – £ 70/125 £ 135/250 – 1 suite

Rest – Menu £ 27/30 – Carte £ 25/37

◆ Immaculately whitewashed 16C former farmhouse: a long low building. Diners greeted from jetty by Victorian horse and carriage. Home-produced ingredients to fore. Smart rooms.

CHANNEL TUNNEL – **Kent** – **504** X30 – **see Folkestone**

CHAPEL-EN-LE-FRITH – **Derbyshire** – **504** O24 – **pop. 6 581** **16** A1

London 175 mi. – Sheffield 27 mi. – Manchester 21 mi. – Stoke-on-Trent 34 mi.

High Croft without rest

Manchester Rd, West : 0.75 mi. on B 5470 ✉ SK23 9UH – ✆ (01298) 814 843 – www.highcroft-guesthouse.co.uk

4 rm – £ 80 £ 100

◆ Edwardian house with period features and lovely mature garden. Comfortable bedrooms overlook surrounding hills and valleys; Atholl suite - a four poster with tub - is best.

CHAPELTOWN – **N. Yorks.** – **502** P23 – **see Sheffield**

CHARD – **Somerset** – **503** L31 – **pop. 12 008** **3** B3

London 157 mi. – Exeter 32 mi. – Lyme Regis 12 mi. – Taunton 18 mi.

The Guildhall, Fore St ✆ (01460) 65710, chardtic@chard.gov.uk

Bellplot House without rest

High St ✉ TA20 1QB – ✆ (01460) 62 600 – www.bellplothouse.co.uk – Fax (01460) 62 600

7 rm – £ 80 £ 90

◆ Impressive mid-Georgian house named after shape of original plot of land. Lounge with plush sofas and fitted bar. Bedrooms stylishly modern with bright yellow décor.

CHARLTON – **W. Sussex** – **504** R31 – **see Chichester**

CHARLTON – **Wiltshire** – **503** N29 – **see Malmesbury**

ENGLAND

CHARMOUTH – Dorset – 503 L31 – pop. 1 497 – ✉ Bridport 3 B3

London 157 mi. – Dorchester 22 mi. – Exeter 31 mi. – Taunton 27 mi.

White House

2 Hillside, The Street ✉ DT6 6PJ – ✆ (01297) 560 411 – www.whitehousehotel.com – restricted opening in winter

6 rm – †£ 60/90 ††£ 90/150

Rest – *(closed Sunday and Monday) (dinner only)* Menu £ 35

◆ Gleaming white Regency hotel a stone's throw from magnificent coastal scenery; popular with fossil hunters. Tasteful rooms, with pretty furnishings. Garden herbs and fruit used in home-cooked meals.

CHATHILL – Northumberland – see Alnwick

CHEDDAR – Somerset – 503 L30 – pop. 4 796 3 B2

London 157 mi. – Bristol 20 mi. – Caerdydd / Cardiff 70 mi. – Casnewydd / Newport 57 mi.

Batts Farm without rest

Latches Lane, South East : 2.5 m by A371 on Nyland Rd ✉ BS27 3UD – ✆ (01934) 741 469 – www.batts-farm.co.uk

4 rm – †£ 55 ††£ 65/90

◆ Friendly and welcoming – drinks on arrival and homemade biscuits in rooms. Pristine bedrooms offer thoughtful extras. Summer house looks onto peaceful garden. Excellent breakfast.

ENGLAND

CHEDDLETON – Staffordshire – 502 N24 – pop. 2 719 – ✉ Leek 19 C1

London 125 mi. – Birmingham 48 mi. – Derby 33 mi. – Manchester 42 mi.

Choir Cottage without rest

Ostlers Lane, via Hollow Lane (opposite Red Lion on A 520) ✉ ST13 7HS – ✆ (01538) 360 561 – www.choircottage.co.uk

3 rm – †£ 59/65 ††£ 70/75

◆ Personally run 17C stone cottage, formerly church owned, and let to the poor, rent used to buy choir gowns. Individually furnished bedrooms with four-posters.

CHELMSFORD – Essex – 504 V28 – pop. 99 962 13 C2

London 33 mi. – Cambridge 46 mi. – Ipswich 40 mi. – Southend-on-Sea 19 mi.

Unit 3, Dukes Walk, Duke St ✆ (01245) 283400, chelmsfordvisitor.information@firstgroup.com

Barda

30-32 Broomfield Rd ✉ CM1 1SW – ✆ (01245) 357 799 – www.barda-restaurant.com – Fax (01245) 350 333 – Closed 25, 26, 31 December and 1 January, Sunday dinner and Monday

Rest – Menu £ 17 – Carte £ 22/37

◆ Keenly run contemporary restaurant with large decked terrace. Simple, flavoursome dishes at lunch; more interesting, international cooking at dinner. Classical puddings display modern twists.

at Boreham Northeast : 3.5 mi. on B 1137 (Springfield Rd)

The Lion Inn

Main Rd ✉ CM3 3JA – ✆ (01245) 394 900 – www.lioninnhotel.co.uk – Fax (01245) 394 999 – Closed 25-27 December

15 rm – †£ 79 ††£ 140 **Rest** – Carte £ 20/32

◆ Keenly run, extended former pub with eco-friendly credentials and a French feel. Soundproofed bedrooms blend contemporary furnishings with antiques. Large open-plan lounge/brasserie with buzzy atmosphere; short menu of appealing, pub-style dishes.

CHELTENHAM – Gloucestershire – 503 N28 – pop. 98 875 4 C1

Great Britain

London 99 mi. – Birmingham 48 mi. – Bristol 40 mi. – Gloucester 9 mi.
77 Promenade (01242) 522878, tic@cheltenham.gov.uk
Cleeve Hill, (01242) 672 025
Cotswold Hills Ullenwood, (01242) 515 264
Town★
Sudeley Castle★ (Paintings★) **AC**, NE : 7 mi. by B 4632 A

Plan on next page

Hotel du Vin

Parabola Rd GL50 3AQ – (01242) 588 450 – www.hotelduvin.com – Fax (01242) 588 455 BY**c**

48 rm – £ 155/300 £ 155/300, £ 9.95 – 1 suite

Rest *Bistro* – Menu £ 16 (lunch) – Carte £ 24/35

◆ Stylish Regency house in smart area: lounge features chandelier made from wine glasses; bedrooms named after wines boast contemporary furnishings and wine-themed artwork. Bistro restaurant with paved terrace offers classic menus with French influences.

Hotel on the Park

38 Evesham Rd GL52 2AH – (01242) 518 898 – www.thehoteluk.co.uk – Fax (01242) 511 526 CY**r**

12 rm – £ 155 £ 295, £ 15

Rest *Parkers* – see restaurant listing

◆ Regency town house of distinction. Bedrooms are named after dukes and dignitaries; individually decorated with paintings, antiques, mirrors and lamps. Stately library.

Beaumont House without rest

56 Shurdington Rd GL53 0JE – (01242) 223 311 – www.bhhotel.co.uk – Fax (01242) 520 044 AX**u**

16 rm – £ 66/75 £ 174

◆ Keenly run Georgian house with comfy drawing room and bar; breakfast room overlooks lawned garden. Refurbished bedrooms are stylish and contemporary with excellent bathrooms.

Lypiatt House without rest

Lypiatt Rd GL50 2QW – (01242) 224 994 – www.staylypiatt.co.uk – Fax (01242) 224 996 BZ**c**

10 rm – £ 75 £ 110

◆ A privately owned, serene Victorian house with friendly service. Rooms on top floor with dormer roof tend to be smaller than those on the ground floor. Soft, pale colours.

Butlers without rest

Western Rd GL50 3RN – (01242) 570 771 – www.butlers-hotel.co.uk – Fax (01242) 528 724 BY**v**

9 rm – £ 60/65 £ 95

◆ Personally managed hotel where bedrooms constitute a peaceful haven with stylish drapes and canopies. Rooms named after famous butlers; some overlook wooded garden to rear.

Hilden Lodge without rest

271 London Rd, Charlton Kings GL52 6YG – (01242) 583 242 – www.hildenlodge.co.uk – Fax (01242) 263 511 – Closed Christmas- New Year AX**a**

9 rm – £ 49/59 £ 79

◆ Cream washed Regency house with small garden/terrace. Bedrooms are half light, half dark wood furnished, with smart, compact bathrooms and good facilities. Breakfast cooked to order.

Thirty Two without rest

32 Imperial Sq GL50 1QZ – (01242) 771 110 – www.thirtytwoltd.com – Fax (01242) 771 119 – closed 25-26 December BZ**e**

4 rm – £ 150 £ 165

◆ Immaculate Regency house overlooking grassy city square. Stylish, beautifully appointed bedrooms with furniture designed by owner; superb bathrooms. Excellent facilities and extra touches.

CHELTENHAM

Street	Grid	No.
Berkeley St	CYZ	4
Clarence St	CY	6
Crescent Terrace	BY	7
Deep St	AX	9
Dunalley St	CY	10
Henrietta St	CY	13
High St	BCY	
High St PRESTBURY	AX	14
Keynsham Rd	CZ	15
Knapp Rd	BY	16
Montpellier Ave	BZ	17
Montpellier Walk	BZ	18
North St	CY	20
Norwood Rd	BZ	21
Oriel Rd	CZ	22
Pittville St	CY	26
Portland St	CY	27
Promenade (The)	BZCY	28
Regent Arcade Shopping Centre	CY	
Regent St	CY	29
Rodney Rd	CY	30
Royal Well Rd	BCY	32
St James St	CY	33
St Johns Ave	CY	34
St Margaret's Rd	CY	35
Sandford Mill Rd	CZ	36
Sandford Terrace	CZ	37
Winchcombe St	CY	38

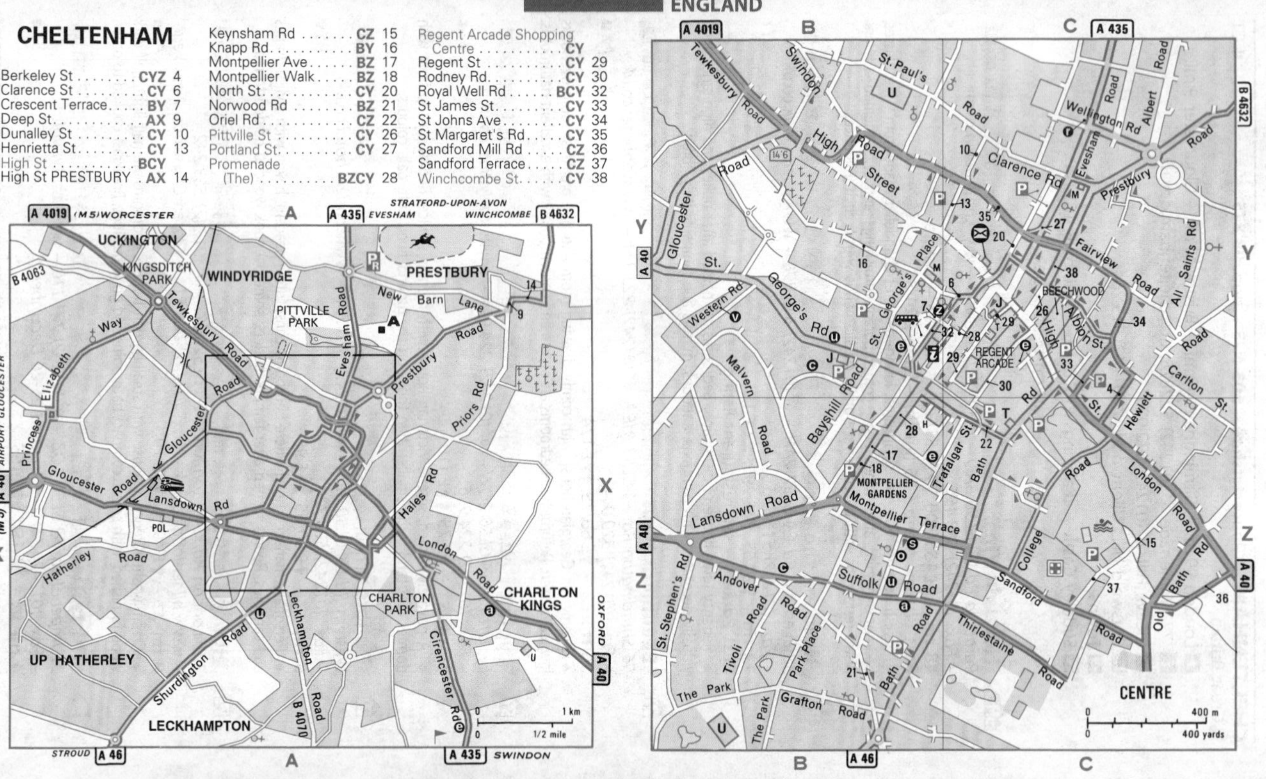

Hanover House without rest
65 St George's Rd ✉ GL50 3DU – ☎ (01242) 541 297 – www.hanoverhouse.org – Fax (01242) 541 297 BYu
3 rm – †£ 70 ††£ 90
◆ Early Victorian townhouse, perfectly located for seeing the city. Comfortable family lounge filled with books and portraits; spacious, tastefully furnished bedrooms. Organic breakfasts.

Georgian House without rest
77 Montpellier Terrace ✉ GL50 1XA – ☎ (01242) 515 577 – www.georgianhouse.net – Fax (01242) 545 929 – Closed Christmas and New Year BZs
3 rm – †£ 65/70 ††£ 85/105
◆ Smart, terraced Georgian house, hospitably run, in sought-after Montpelier area. Good-sized bedrooms decorated in authentic period style. Comfy, elegant communal rooms.

Le Champignon Sauvage (David Everitt-Matthias)
24-28 Suffolk Rd ✉ GL50 2AQ – ☎ (01242) 573 449 – www.lechampignonsauvage.com – Fax (01242) 254 365 – Closed 3 weeks June, 10 days Christmas, Sunday and Monday BZa
Rest – Menu £ 30/50
Spec. Seared scallops with pig's head carpaccio and pear. Lamb with roasted garlic purée and gnocchi. Bitter chocolate and olive tart with fennel ice cream.
◆ Firmly established restaurant with professional service from a well versed team. Confident, accomplished cooking is underscored by a classical base but dishes have personality and are visually impressive. Some ingredients foraged for by the chef.

Lumière
Clarence Parade ✉ GL50 3PA – ☎ (01242) 222 200 – www.lumiere.cc – Closed 2 weeks January, 2 weeks September, Tuesday lunch, Sunday and Monday BCYz
Rest – *(dinner only)* Menu £ 21/39
◆ Elegant, comfortable and personally run restaurant decorated in chic browns and leather. Cooking is a mix of the classical and the modern, making good use of local suppliers.

Parkers – at Hotel On the Park
38 Evesham Rd ✉ GL52 2AH – ☎ (01242) 518 898 – www.thehoteluk.co.uk – Fax (01242) 511 526 CYr
Rest – Carte £ 38/64 **s**
◆ A carefully decorated restaurant with mirrors, high ceilings, hand painted cornices and murals. Modern British cooking with classical undertones and a good range of wine.

The Daffodil
18-20 Suffolk Parade ✉ GL50 2AE – ☎ (01242) 700 055 – www.thedaffodil.com – Fax (01242) 700 088 – Closed first 2 weeks January, 25 December and Sunday BZu
Rest – Menu £ 16 (lunch) – Carte £ 25/34
◆ Originally a 1920s art deco cinema, now a restaurant with kitchen in former screen area and stylish lounge with intimate booths on balcony. Brasserie-style dishes display world-wide influences.

Royal Well Tavern
5 Royal Well Pl. Cheltenham – ☎ (01242) 221 212 – www.theroyalwelltavern.com – closed 25-26 December and Sunday BYe
Rest – Menu £ 13 (lunch) – Carte £ 29/49
◆ Tucked away in side street close to theatre. Bustling contemporary eatery; fusion of gentleman's club/brasserie. Rustic modern menu of carefully prepared dishes; many available in 2 sizes.

Brosh
8 Suffolk Parade, Montpellier ✉ GL50 2AB – ☎ (01242) 227 277 – www.broshrestaurant.co.uk – Closed 2 weeks January and Sunday-Tuesday
Rest – Mediterranean – *(dinner only)* Carte £ 23/37 BZo
◆ Cosy restaurant with atmospheric Moroccan-styled interior: evening candles and dimmed lights make for a great atmosphere. Specialist 'east' Mediterranean cooking with mezze.

Vanilla
9-10 Cambray Pl ✉ GL50 1JS – ☎ (01242) 228 228 – www.vanillainc.co.uk – Fax (01242) 228 228 – Closed 25-26 December, 1 January, and Sunday
Rest – Carte £ 18/33 CYe
◆ Centrally located, in Regency house basement; discreet, soft spot lighting, wooden floors, scoopback chairs. Staff serve light, modern dishes garnished with home-made sauces.

The Reservoir
London Road, Charlton Kings , Southeast : 3 mi. on A 40 ✉ GL54 4HG – ☎ (01242) 529 671 – www.thereservoirinn.co.uk – Closed Sunday dinner and Monday
Rest – Carte £ 18/29
◆ Large, open-plan pub on busy road opposite nature reserve. Good value pub classics made with locally sourced, seasonal produce. Efficient, friendly service. Flower-filled terrace.

at Cleeve Hill Northeast : 4 mi. on B 4632 - AX – ✉ Cheltenham

Cleeve Hill without rest
✉ GL52 3PR – ☎ (01242) 672 052 – www.cleevehill-hotel.co.uk – Fax (01242) 679 969
10 rm – †£ 45/65 ††£ 80/115
◆ Edwardian house in elevated spot; most bedrooms have views across Cleeve Common and the Malvern Hills. Breakfast room is in the conservatory; admire the landscape over coffee.

at Shurdington Southwest : 3.75 mi. on A 46 - AX – ✉ Cheltenham

ENGLAND

The Greenway
✉ GL51 4UG – ☎ (01242) 862 352 – www.thegreenway.co.uk – Fax (01242) 862 780
20 rm – †£ 245/335 ††£ 315/405 – 1 suite **Rest** – Menu £ 22/48
◆ Ivy-clad Elizabethan manor house set in large grounds and peaceful lawned gardens. Spacious, classically styled lounges and drawing rooms. Bedrooms have country house feel. Garden and lily pond on view from formal restaurant.

CHESTER – Cheshire – 502 L24 – pop. 80 121 Great Britain 20 A3

London 207 mi. – Birkenhead 7 mi. – Birmingham 91 mi. – Liverpool 21 mi.
Chester Visitor Centre, Vicars Lane ☎ (01244) 402111, tic@chester.gov.uk
Upton-by-Chester Upton Lane, ☎ (01244) 381 183
Curzon Park, ☎ (01244) 677 760
City★★ - The Rows★★ B – Cathedral★ B – City Walls★ B
Chester Zoo★ **AC**, N : 3 mi. by A 5116

Plans on following pages

The Chester Grosvenor and Spa
Eastgate ✉ CH1 1LT – ☎ (01244) 324 024 – www.chestergrosvenor.com – Fax (01244) 313 246 – Closed 25-26 December
76 rm – †£ 234 ††£ 234/374, £ 20 – 4 suites Ba
Rest *Simon Radley at The Chester Grosvenor* and ***La Brasserie*** – see restaurant listing
◆ 19C coaching inn with grand timbered façade; set close to cathedral in historic city centre. Lavish interior displays rich décor, impressive antiques and luxurious, individually styled bedrooms.

Green Bough
60 Hoole Rd, on A 56 ✉ CH2 3NL – ☎ (01244) 326 241 – www.greenbough.co.uk – Fax (01244) 326 265 – Closed 25 -26 December and 1 January At
13 rm – †£ 105 ††£ 195 – 2 suites
Rest *Olive Tree* – Menu £ 20 – Carte £ 38/47
◆ Personally run and very comfortable, boasting high quality decor; owner pays notable attention to detail. Individually styled, generously sized rooms with wrought iron beds. Dine formally in attractive surroundings.

New Blossoms

St John's St ✉ *CH1 1HL*
– ☏ (0870) 400 81 08
– www.macdonaldhotels.co.uk
– Fax (01244) 346 433

B**x**

66 rm – 🚹£ 69/180 🚹🚹£ 69/180, ☕ £ 8.75 – 1 suite **Rest** – Carte £ 20/34

◆ Centrally located 17C former coaching inn, with classical styling, high ceilings and a wrought iron staircase. Modern bedrooms have simple, clean designs and good facilities. Menu displays plenty of local, seasonal produce.

Oddfellows

20 Lower Bridge Street ✉ *CH1 1RS*
– ☏ (01244) 400 001
– www.oddfellows.biz

B**c**

4 rm ☕ – 🚹£ 125/175 🚹🚹£ 200
Rest *The Restaurant* – *(closed Sunday and Monday) (dinner only)* Carte £ 33/40
Rest *The Brasserie* – Menu £ 15 – Carte £ 25/36

◆ 17C Manor House with quirky mix off bizarre, whacky and fashionable furnishings. Stylish, well equipped bedrooms with great bathrooms. Sexy champagne bar. Restaurant with ceiling hung photo montages offers modern dinner menu, while relaxed brasserie boasts lovely terrace, pond and individual dining tents.

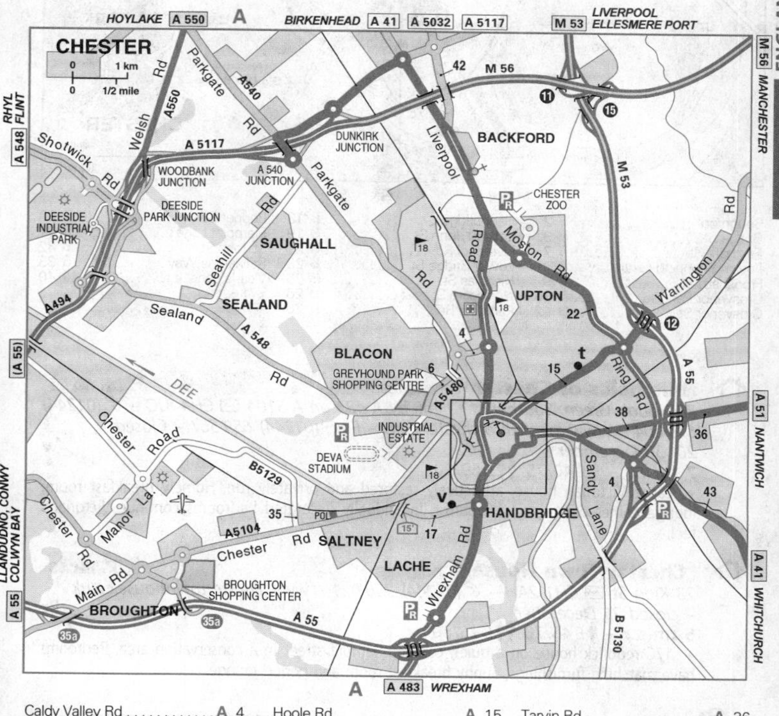

Caldy Valley Rd . . . . **A** 4
Countess Way . . . . **A** 5
Deva Link . . . . **A** 6
Greyhound Park Shopping Centre . . . . **A**
Hoole Rd . . . . **A** 15
Hough Green . . . . **A** 17
Long Lane . . . . **A** 22
Saltney Ferry Rd . . . . **A** 35
Tarvin Rd . . . . **A** 36
Vicar's Cross Rd . . . . **A** 38
Whitby Lane . . . . **A** 42
Whitchurch Rd . . . . **A** 43

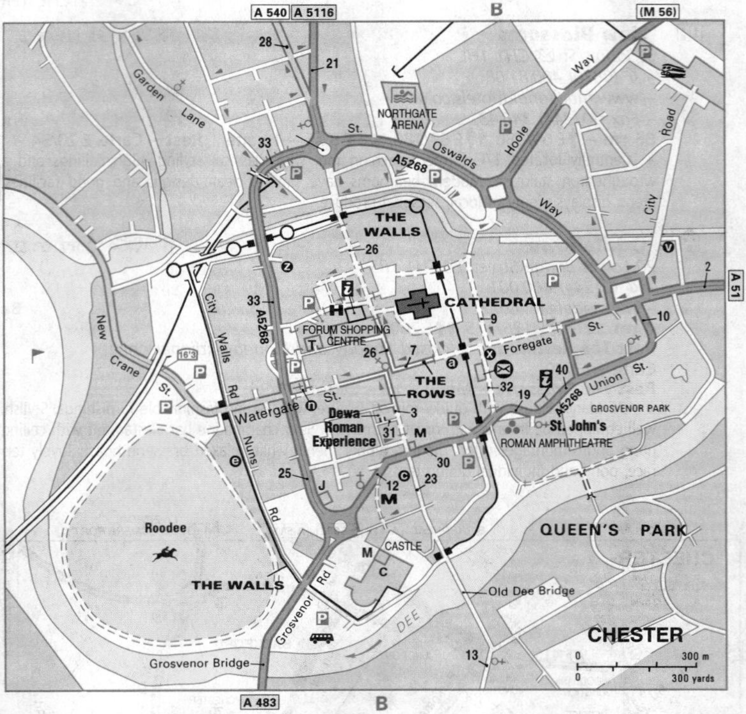

CHESTER

Street	Grid	No.
Boughton	B	2
Bridge St	B	3
Eastgate St	B	7
Forum Shopping centre	B	
Frodsham St	B	9
Grosvenor Park Rd	B	10
Grosvenor St	B	12
Handbridge	B	13
Little St John St	B	19
Liverpool Rd	B	21
Lower Bridge St	B	23
Nicholas St	B	25
Northgate St	B	26
Parkgate Rd	B	28
Pepper St	B	30
Pierpoint Lane	B	31
St John St	B	32
St Martins Way	B	33
Vicar's Lane	B	40
Watergate St	B	

Mitchell's of Chester without rest
28 Hough Green, Southwest : 1 mi. by A 483 on A 5104 ✉ CH4 8JQ – ✆ (01244) 679 004 – www.mitchellsofchester.com – Fax (01244) 659 567 – Closed 20- 30 December — A**v**
7 rm – 🛉£ 40/75 🛉🛉£ 69/90
◆ Large Victorian house, attractively restored and privately run. Homely breakfast room; lounge comes complete with parrot. Individually decorated bedrooms continue Victoriana feel.

Chester Town House without rest
23 King St ✉ CH1 2AH – ✆ (01244) 350 021 – www.chestertownhouse.co.uk – closed 25 December — B**z**
5 rm – 🛉£ 45/70 🛉🛉£ 75/80
◆ 17C redbrick house on a quiet, cobbled, lamplit street in a conservation area. Bedrooms have matching furnishings. Sunny breakfast room and period lounge.

Fancy a last minute break?
Check hotel websites to take advantage of price promotions.

Simon Radley at The Chester Grosvenor

Eastgate ✉ CH1 1LT – ☏ (01244) 324 024 – www.chestergrosvenor.com – Fax (01244) 313 246 – Closed 3-11 January, 25-26 December, Sunday and Monday **Ba**

Rest – *(dinner only)* Menu £ 69

Spec. Warm vichyssoise of squash with foie gras. Bellota reserva ham with 'all things pork'. Watermelon and cucumber freeze, iced yoghurt and mint.

◆ Smart restaurant with fabric-covered walls, plush furnishings, stylish cocktail lounge and formal but engaging service. Quality ingredients come together in classic combinations with innovative touches and attractive presentation.

Upstairs at the Grill

70 Watergate St ✉ CH1 2LA – ☏ (01244) 344 883 – www.upstairsatthegrill.co.uk – Fax (01244) 329 720 – Closed 25 December **Bn**

Rest – Beef specialities – *(dinner only and Sunday lunch)* Carte £ 21/39

◆ Buzzy, slightly wacky restaurant adorned with cow paraphernalia. Prime quality steaks – rib-eye, sirloin, chateaubriand, rare breeds – come with expert guidance. Sumptuous modern cocktail bar above.

La Brasserie – at The Chester Grosvenor and Spa Hotel

Eastgate ✉ CH1 1LT – ☏ (01244) 324 024 – www.chestergrosvenor.com – Fax (01244) 313 246 – Closed 25-26 December

Rest – Menu £ 20 (lunch Monday to Saturday) – Carte £ 32/49 **Ba**

◆ Attractive, classically styled Parisian brasserie with hand-painted glass skylight and pleasant buzzy ambience. Menus feature traditional British, French and Mediterranean dishes.

1539

The Racecourse ✉ CH1 2LY – ☏ (01244) 304 611 – www.restaurant1539.co.uk – closed 25-26 December **Be**

Rest – Carte £ 25/33

◆ Stylish and spacious modern brasserie set in a stand of the racecourse, with smartly furnished, decked terraces and panoramic views. Modern British cooking makes use of local produce.

The Old Harkers Arms

1 Russell St ✉ CH3 5AL – ☏ (01244) 344 525 – www.bandp.co.uk/harkers – Fax (01244) 344 812 **Bv**

Rest – Carte £ 20/29

◆ Characterful canalside pub in a Victorian warehouse. Cooking is rustic, unfussy and generous, and the daily-changing menu displays plenty of classics; over 100 whiskies are on offer.

CHESTER-LE-STREET – Durham – 502 P19 – pop. 36 049 — 24 B2

London 275 mi. – Durham 7 mi. – Newcastle upon Tyne 8 mi.

Lumley Park, ☏ (0191) 388 3218

Roseberry Grange Grange Villa, ☏ (0191) 370 0660

Lumley Castle

East : 1 mi. on B 1284 ✉ DH3 4NX – ☏ (0191) 389 1111 – www.lumleycastle.com – Fax (0191) 389 5871 – Closed 25-26 December and 2 January

73 rm – †£ 69/145 ††£ 105/250 – 1 suite

Rest *Black Knight* – *(closed Saturday lunch)* Menu £ 22/34 **s** – Carte dinner £ 27/46 **s**

◆ Norman castle, without additions, underscoring its uniqueness. Rich, gothic interiors of carved wood, chandeliers, statues, tapestries, rugs. Rooms imbued with atmosphere. Restaurant offers classical dishes with an original twist.

CHETNOLE – Dorset – see Sherborne

CHETTLE – Dorset – see Blandford Forum

CHEW MAGNA – Bath and North East Somerset – 503 M29 – pop. 1 187 — 4 C2

London 128 mi. – Bristol 9 mi. – Cardiff 52 mi. – Bournemouth 89 mi.

Pony & Trap

Knowle Hill, Newtown, South : 1.25 mi. on Bishop Stuttard rd ✉ BS40 8TQ – ✆ (01275) 332 627 – www.theponyandtrap.co.uk – Closed Sunday dinner in winter and Monday

Rest – *(booking essential)* Carte £ 16/28

◆ Cosy, friendly pub with fine views east. Well presented cooking shows a good understanding of ingredients and flavours. Menu has British bias, with plenty of pub classics.

Bear & Swan

13 South Parade ✉ BS40 8SL – ✆ (01275) 331 100 – www.bearandswan.co.uk – Closed 25 December dinner and Sunday dinner

Rest – Carte £ 25/32

◆ A combination of good food, real ales, friendly staff and a warm, genuine ambience attracts a loyal local following. Eat from the bar menu or in the candlelit restaurant.

A restaurant name printed in red denotes a Rising Star - an establishment showing great potential. It is in line for a higher award: a star or an additional star. They are included in the list of starred establishments at the beginning of the guide.

CHICHESTER – West Sussex – 504 R31 – pop. 27 477 Great Britain 7 C2

London 69 mi. – Brighton 31 mi. – Portsmouth 18 mi. – Southampton 30 mi.

29a South St ✆ (01243) 775888, chitic@chichester.gov.uk

Goodwood Kennel Hill, ✆ (01243) 755 133

Chichester Golf Centre Hunston Village, ✆ (01243) 533 833

City★★ – Cathedral★★ BZ **A** – St Mary's Hospital★ BY **D** – Pallant House★ **AC** BZ **M**

Fishbourne Roman Palace★★ (mosaics★) **AC** AZ **R**. Weald and Downland Open Air Museum★★ **AC**, N : 6 mi. by A 286 AY

CHICHESTER

Street	Grid	No.
Birdham Rd	AZ	2
Bognor Rd	AZ	3
Chapel St	BY	6
Chartres (Av. de)	BZ	7
Chichester Arundel Rd	AY	8
East Pallant	BZ	9
East St	BZ	
Florence Rd	AZ	10
Hornet (The)	BZ	12
Kingsham Rd	BZ	13
Lavant Rd	AY	14
Little London	BY	15
Market Rd	BZ	16
Northgate	BY	17
North Pallant	BZ	19
North St	BYZ	
Oaklands Way	BY	18
St Jame's	AZ	21
St John's St	BZ	23
St Martin's Square	BY	24
St Pancras	BY	25
St Paul's Rd	BY	27
Sherborne Rd	AZ	28
Southgate	BZ	29
South Pallant	BZ	31
South St	BZ	
Spitalfield Lane	BY	32
Stockbridge Rd	AZ	33
Tower St	BY	35
Via Ravenna	AZ	37
Westhampnett Rd	AYZ	38
West Pallant	BZ	39

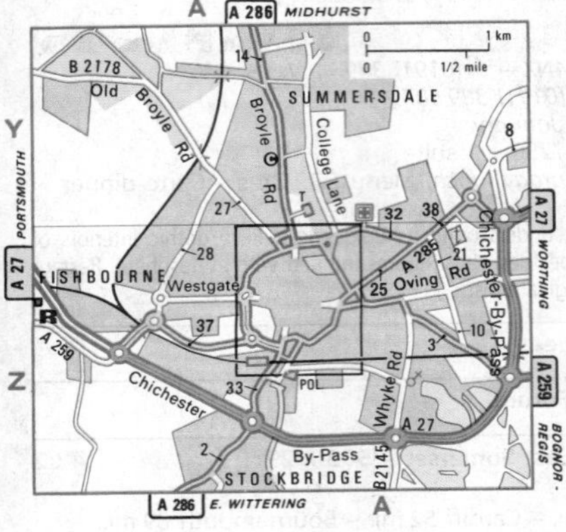

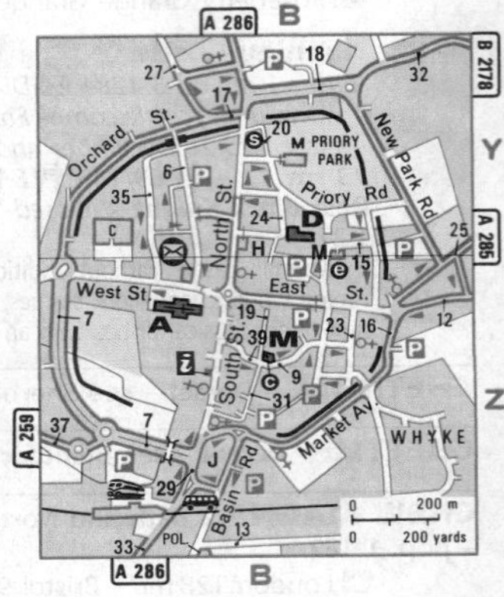

Crouchers Country H.

Birdham Rd, Apuldram, Southwest : 2.5 mi. on A 286 ✉ PO20 7EH – ✆ (01243) 784 995 – www.croucherscountryhotel.com – Fax (01243) 539 797

26 rm – †£ 75/95 ††£ 110/150

Rest – Menu £ 20/24 – Carte £ 26/38

◆ 1900s farmhouse surrounded by fields. Bedrooms are in a separate coach house, some on ground floor; furnished with matching floral fabrics. Admire waterfowl in nearby pond. Bright, modern dining room.

The Ship

North St ✉ PO19 1NH – ✆ (01243) 778 000 – www.theshiphotel.net – Fax (01243) 788 000 BY**s**

36 rm – †£ 75/150 ††£ 120/199 **Rest** – Carte £ 21/31

◆ Grade II listed building, formerly home to one of Nelson's men. Georgian and Regency features remain, including a cantilevered wrought iron staircase. Modern bedrooms display original cornices and fireplaces. Light, airy brasserie with modern menu; meat and game from nearby Goodwood Estate.

Comme ça

67 Broyle Rd, on A 286 ✉ PO19 6BD – ✆ (01243) 788 724 – www.commeca.co.uk – Fax (01243) 530 052 – Closed Christmas - New Year, Monday, Tuesday lunch and Sunday dinner AY**c**

Rest – French – Menu £ 24/35

◆ Stalwart of the local dining scene for many years. Classical French cooking ministered by Normand chef; family lunches on Sundays. Hops on exposed beams complete the décor.

Field and Fork at Pallant House Gallery

9 North Pallant ✉ PO19 1TJ – ✆ (01243) 770 827 – www.fieldandfork.co.uk – Closed 24-25 December, Sunday dinner, Monday and Tuesday BZ**c**

Rest – Modern – Menu £ 30 (dinner) – Carte lunch £ 22/40

◆ Bright, modern restaurant in striking Queen Anne building, with delightful courtyard. Light dishes at lunch; dinner a more formal affair. Fresh, seasonal produce used with care.

Cider House

Birdham Rd, Appledram, Southwest : 2.5 mi. on A 286 ✉ PO20 7EH – ✆ (01243) 779 345 – www.theciderhouse.biz – Closed 1-25 January

Rest – Carte £ 26/45

◆ Converted cow shed on cider farm; quirky exterior hides warm rustic inner with pine tables, sofas and log fire. Seasonal menus of earthy British dishes. Attentive, chatty service.

at Chilgrove North : 6.5 mi. by A 286 on B 2141

Fish House with rm

– ✆ (01243) 519 444 – www.thefishhouse.co.uk – Fax (01243) 519 499

15 rm – †£ 90/150 ††£ 130/160

Rest – Seafood – Menu £ 22/45 – Carte £ 28/44

Rest *Fish Bar* – Seafood – Menu £ 20 (Monday-Thursday) – Carte £ 24/34

◆ What was once The White Horse now has a stylish restaurant serving appealing seafood dishes beside a bustling, popular Fish bar. Its bedrooms are individually styled, boast every conceivable facility and are mostly located across a courtyard, beside the hot tubs under gazebos.

at Charlton North : 6.25 mi. by A 286 - AY – ✉ Chichester

The Fox Goes Free with rm

✉ PO18 0HU – ✆ (01243) 811 461 – www.thefoxgoesfree.com – Fax (01243) 811 712 – Closed 25 December

5 rm – †£ 60/100 ††£ 85/145 **Rest** – Carte £ 20/26

◆ Flint 17C inn retaining its character in the form of exposed stone walls, tile floors, beams and inglenook. Short, seasonal menus have a strong reliance on local produce. Comfortable, well-equipped bedrooms.

at East Lavant North : 2.5 mi. off A 286 - AY – ✉ Chichester

The Royal Oak Inn with rm
Pook Lane ✉ PO18 0AX – ☎ (01243) 527 434 – www.royaloakeastlavant.co.uk – Closed 25 December
10 rm – †£ 70/95 ††£ 150/300 **Rest** – Carte £ 25/45
◆ 18C inn with warm, rustic atmosphere combines the contemporary with the more traditional. Seasonal, modern cooking with game from the Goodwood Estate. Bedrooms – some above the bar, others in cottages and a barn – are furnished to a high standard.

at Mid Lavant North 2 mi. on A286

Rooks Hill without rest
Lavant Rd ✉ PO18 0BQ – ☎ (01243) 528 400 – www.rookshill.co.uk – Closed 27 December-10 January and 1 week Autumn
6 rm – †£ 75/110 ††£ 125/170
◆ Charming Grade II listed guesthouse with mix of contemporary styling and original features. Breakfast room opens into lovely terrace/garden. Well appointed bedrooms with attractive bathrooms. Large buffet breakfast.

The Earl of March
✉ PO18 0BQ – ☎ (01243) 533 993 – www.theearlofmarch.com – Fax (01243) 783 991 – Closed Sunday dinner October-April
Rest – Menu £ 25 (early dinner) – Carte £ 25/34
◆ Modern pub situated at the edge of the Goodwood Estate. Classic British à la carte menu, with daily-changing specials of game in winter and fish in summer; hearty, flavoursome cooking.

ENGLAND

at Tangmere East : 2 mi. by A 27 - AY – ✉ Chichester

Cassons
Arundel Rd, Northwest : 0.25 mi. off A 27 (westbound) ✉ PO18 0DU – ☎ (01243) 773 294 – www.cassonsrestaurant.co.uk – Fax (01243) 778 148 – Closed 2 weeks January, 25-26 December, 1 January, Tuesday lunch, Sunday dinner and Monday
Rest – Menu £ 21/27 (midweek) – Carte £ 35/50
◆ Eponymous owners run a homely and appealing neighbourhood restaurant where theme evenings (eg, India, New Zealand) gel with the locally renowned classical, seasonal cooking.

at Sidlesham South : 5 mi. on B 2145 - AZ

Landseer House without rest
Cow Lane, South: 1.5 mi. by B2145 and Keynor Lane. ✉ PO20 7LN – ☎ (01243) 641 525 – www.landseerhouse.co.uk
6 rm – †£ 95/110 ††£ 110/170
◆ Delightful, simply furnished family house with large conservatory and unusual furniture. Set in 4½ acres of gardens by a Nature Reserve and harbour; views to the Isle of Wight.

Crab & Lobster with rm
Mill Lane, South : 1 mi. by B 2145, then turn right onto Rookery Lane ✉ PO20 7NB – ☎ (01243) 641 233 – www.crab-lobster.co.uk
4 rm – †£ 75 ††£ 150 **Rest** – *(booking advisable)* Carte £ 24/41
◆ 18C pub situated on a nature reserve not far from the beach. British/Mediterranean menu features simply constructed, cleanly presented dishes and plenty of seafood. Spacious, contemporary rooms with sea or rural views.

at Bosham West : 4 mi. by A 259 - AZ – ✉ Chichester

Millstream rm, rest,
Bosham Lane ✉ PO18 8HL – ☎ (01243) 573 234 – www.millstream-hotel.co.uk – Fax (01243) 573 459
32 rm – †£ 79/123 ††£ 130/162 – 3 suites **Rest** – Menu £ 23/29
◆ Pretty hotel with garden that backs onto stream bobbing with ducks. Cosy bedrooms, individually co-ordinated fabric furnishings, sandwash fitted furniture and large windows. Seasonal, daily changing menus.

at West Stoke **Northwest : 2.75 mi. by B 2178 - AY - off B 2146 – ✉ Chichester**

XX ✿ **West Stoke House** with rm
Downs Rd ✉ PO18 9BN – ✆ (01243) 575 226 – www.weststokehouse.co.uk – Fax (01243) 574 655 – Closed 25-26 December
8 rm – †£ 125 ††£ 225
Rest – *(closed Monday and Tuesday) (booking essential)* Menu £ 25/45
Spec. Scallop with baby artichoke and Cumbrian ham salad. Slow cooked loin of veal with celeriac gratin. Tiramisu with cherry purée and ice cream.
◆ Part-17C manor furnished in a contemporary style, with elegant, art-filled lounge overlooking manicured gardens. Relaxed ambience for dining in the former ballroom; well-judged cooking uses modern techniques, with local produce and seasonality to the fore. Strikingly understated bedrooms boast all mod cons.

at Funtington **Northwest : 4.75 mi. by B 2178 - AY - on B 2146 – ✉ Chichester**

XX **Hallidays**
Watery Lane ✉ PO18 9LF – ✆ (01243) 575 331 – www.hallidays.info – Closed 1 week March, 2 weeks August, Monday, Tuesday, Saturday lunch and Sunday dinner
Rest – Menu £ 21/35 – Carte £ 25/35
◆ A row of part 13C thatched cottages; confident and keen chef delivers a lively medley of frequently changing set menus and à la carte. Modern meals sit alongside classics.

CHIDDINGFOLD – Surrey – 504 S30 – pop. 2 128 7 C2

London 47 mi. – Guildford 10 mi. – Haslemere 5 mi.

The Swan Inn with rm
Petworth Rd ✉ GU8 4TY – ✆ (01428) 682 073 – www.theswaninn.biz – Fax (01428) 683 259 – Closed Sunday dinner and Monday
11 rm – †£ 105 ††£ 105/150 **Rest** – Carte £ 23/30
◆ Majestic pub with a modern, stylish interior and popular terrace. Food is simple, unfussy and classical; specials change twice a day in line with the latest seasonal produce. Contemporary bedrooms with good bathrooms and mod cons.

CHIEVELEY – West Berkshire – 503 Q29 10 B3

London 60 mi. – Newbury 5 mi. – Swindon 25 mi.

XX **The Crab at Chieveley** with rm
Wantage Rd, West : 2.5 mi. by School Rd on B 4494 ✉ RG20 8UE – ✆ (01635) 247 550 – www.crabatchieveley.com – Fax (01635) 248 440
14 rm – †£ 120/160 ††£ 160/190
Rest – Menu £ 20 (lunch) – Carte £ 38/68
◆ Thatched former inn, a lively venue, on a country road with wheat fields. Choice of bistro or restaurant for seafood menu. Highly original bedrooms themed as famous hotels.

CHILGROVE – West Sussex – 504 R31 – see Chichester

CHILLATON – Devon – 503 H32 – see Tavistock

CHILLINGTON – Devon – 503 I33 2 C3

London 217 mi. – Plymouth 26 mi. – Torbay 20 mi. – Torquay 22 mi.

whitehouse
✉ TQ7 2JX – ✆ (01548) 580 505 – www.whitehousedevon.com
6 rm – †£ 180/200 ††£ 230/250 **Rest** – Carte £ 30/38
◆ Sizeable Georgian house with modern furnishings, relaxed atmosphere and beautiful gardens. Sumptuous, well appointed bedrooms, with large baths and handmade toiletries. Lovely dining room with casual, airy feel and appealing menu.

CHINNOR – Oxfordshire – 504 R28 – pop. 5 407 Great Britain 11 C2

London 45 mi. – Oxford 19 mi.

Ridgeway Path★★

ENGLAND

at Sprigg's Alley Southeast : 2.5 mi. by Bledlow Ridge rd – ✉ Chinnor

Sir Charles Napier
✉ OX39 4BX – ✆ (01494) 483 011 – www.sircharlesnapier.co.uk – Fax (01494) 485 311 – Closed 3 days Christmas, Sunday dinner and Monday
Rest – Carte £ 32/44
◆ Attractive flint pub in a small hillside hamlet, with pleasant outside terrace and delightful gardens. Refined, French based dishes are skilfully prepared and full of flavour.

at Kingston Blount Southwest : 1.75 mi. on B 4009 – ✉ Chinnor

Lakeside Town Farm without rest
Brook St, (off Sydenham rd) ✉ OX39 4RZ – ✆ (01844) 352 152 – www.townfarmcottage.co.uk – Fax (01844) 352 152
4 rm – †£ 60 ††£ 85/100
◆ Set in lovely gardens on a working farm: flora and fauna abound. Cosy bedrooms with well-coordinated décor and thoughtful touches. Family-style breakfasts include homemade bread and jam.

CHIPPENHAM – Wiltshire – 503 N29 – pop. 33 189 — 4 C2

London 106 mi. – Bristol 27 mi. – Southampton 64 mi. – Swindon 21 mi.
Yelde Hall, Market Place ✆ (01249) 665970, tourism@chippenham.gov.uk
Monkton Park (Par Three), ✆ (01249) 653 928
Yelde Hall★
Corsham Court★★ **AC**, SW : 4 mi. by A 4 – Sheldon Manor★ **AC**, W : 1.5 mi. by A 420 – Biddestone★, W : 3.5 mi. – Bowood House★ **AC** (Library ★) SE : 5 mi. by A 4 and A 342. Castle Combe★★, NW : 6 mi. by A 420 and B 4039

ENGLAND

at Stanton St Quintin North : 5 mi. by A 429 – ✉ Chippenham

Stanton Manor
✉ SN14 6DQ – ✆ (01666) 837 552 – www.stantonmanor.co.uk – Fax (01666) 837 022
22 rm – †£ 115 ††£ 215
Rest – Menu £ 15 (lunch) – Carte (dinner) £ 24/34
◆ Extended 19C manor in formal gardens; popular as a wedding venue. Appealing range of bedrooms, geared to corporate market; the deluxe rooms considerably better than the standards. Elegant restaurant uses produce from the garden.

CHIPPING CAMPDEN – Gloucestershire – 503 O27 – pop. 1 943 — 4 D1
Great Britain

London 93 mi. – Cheltenham 21 mi. – Oxford 37 mi. – Stratford-upon-Avon 12 mi.
Old Police Station ✆ (01386) 841206, visitchippingcampden@lineone.net
Town★
Hidcote Manor Garden★★ **AC**, NE : 2.5 m

Cotswold House rest,
The Square ✉ GL55 6AN – ✆ (01386) 840 330 – www.cotswoldhouse.com – Fax (01386) 840 310
25 rm – †£ 150 ††£ 500 – 3 suites
Rest Hicks' – *see restaurant listing*
Rest *Juliana's* – *(closed Sunday and Monday) (dinner only)* Menu £ 50
◆ Enviably stylish Regency town house with graceful spiral staircase winding upwards to luxurious rooms, some very modern, boasting every mod con imaginable. Impressive service. Formal though stylish Juliana's for accomplished cooking with an original style.

XX **The Kings** with rm

The Square ✉ GL55 6AW – ☎ (01386) 840 256 – www.kingscampden.co.uk – Fax (01386) 841 598

19 rm ☐ – †£ 165 ††£ 300 **Rest** – Carte £ 22/31

◆ Beautiful Cotswold stone house with champagne bar, beamed dining room and rear terrace. Large brasserie menu offers tasty, straightforward classics with modern Mediterranean influences. Stylish bedrooms display vivid colour schemes.

X **Hicks'** – at Cotswold House Hotel

The Square ✉ GL55 6AN – ☎ (01386) 840 330 – www.cotswoldhouse.com – Fax (01386) 840 310

Rest – *(booking essential)* Menu £ 20 (weekday lunch) – Carte £ 24/31

◆ Named after local benefactor. Booking advised; open all day serving locals and residents with modern varied menu. Morning coffees, afternoon teas, home-made cake available.

Eight Bells Inn with rm

Church St ✉ GL55 6JG – ☎ (01386) 840 371 – www.eightbellsinn.co.uk – Closed 25 December

7 rm ☐ – †£ 60/85 ††£ 85/125 **Rest** – Carte £ 22/32

◆ Atmospheric 14C pub with bustling bar and terraced garden. Menu offers an appealing blend of traditional and contemporary dishes, with specials chalked on the board. Bedrooms are warmly decorated and well looked after; room 7 has beams.

Undecided between two equivalent establishments in the same town? Within each category, establishments are classified in our order of preference: the best first.

at Mickleton North : 3.25 mi. by B 4035 and B 4081 on B 4632 – ✉ Chipping Campden

Three Ways House

✉ GL55 6SB – ☎ (01386) 438 429 – www.puddingclub.com – Fax (01386) 438 118

48 rm ☐ – †£ 80/115 ††£ 139/225

Rest – *(bar lunch Monday to Saturday)* Menu £ 35 (dinner)

◆ Built in 1870; renowned as home of the 'Pudding Club'. Two types of room, in original house or modern block, all very comfy and modern. Bar with antique tiled floor. Arcaded dining room; Pudding Club meets here to vote after tastings.

Nineveh Farm without rest

Southwest : 0.75 mi. by B4632 on B4081 ✉ GL55 6PS – ☎ (01386) 438 923 – www.stayinthecotswolds.co.uk

5 rm ☐ – †£ 65 ††£ 75

◆ Georgian farmhouse in pleasant garden. Warm welcome; local information in resident's lounge. Comfortable rooms with view in house or with French windows in garden house.

Myrtle House without rest

✉ GL55 6SA – ☎ (01386) 430 032 – www.myrtlehouse.co.uk

5 rm ☐ – †£ 45/55 ††£ 65/85

◆ Part Georgian house with large lawned garden. Bedrooms named and styled after flowers and plants, those on top floor most characterful.

at Paxford Southeast : 3 mi. by B 4035 – ✉ Chipping Campden

Churchill Arms with rm

✉ GL55 6XH – ☎ (01386) 594 000 – www.thechurchillarms.com – Fax (01386) 594 005

4 rm ☐ – †£ 55/75 ††£ 75/100

Rest – *(bookings not accepted)* Carte £ 22/35

◆ Popular Cotswold stone and brick pub; mellow interior. Good value menus chalked on blackboard. Organic local produce used. Comfortable bedrooms.

at Ebrington East : 2 mi. by B 4035

The Ebrington Arms with rm

✉ GL55 6NH – ✆ (01386) 593 223 – www.theebringtonarms.co.uk – Closed first week January, Sunday dinner and Monday except Bank Holidays

3 rm – †£ 85/90 ††£ 90/110 **Rest** – Carte £ 20/28

◆ Proper village local with beamed, flag-floored bar at its hub, set in charming chocolate box village. Robust, traditional dishes use local ingredients and up-to-date techniques. Bedrooms have countryside views; room three, with four-poster bed and luxury bathroom, is best.

at Broad Campden South : 1.25 mi. by B 4081 – ✉ **Chipping Campden**

Malt House without rest

✉ GL55 6UU – ✆ (01386) 840 295 – www.malt-house.co.uk – Fax (01386) 841 334 – Closed 1 week Christmas

7 rm – †£ 85 ††£ 140/160

◆ For a rare experience of the countryside idyll, this 16C malting house is a must. Cut flowers from the gardens on view in bedrooms decked out in fabrics to delight the eye.

CHIPPING NORTON – Oxfordshire – 503 P28 – pop. 5 688 — 10 A1

London 77 mi. – Oxford 22 mi. – Stow-on-the-Wold 9 mi.

The Masons Arms

Banbury Rd, Swerford, Northeast : 5 mi. on A 361 ✉ OX7 4AP – ✆ (01608) 683 212 – www.masons-arms.com – Fax (01608) 683 105 – Closed 25-26 December and Sunday dinner

Rest – Menu £ 17/25 – Carte £ 26/33

◆ Hugely popular, rurally-set modernised dining pub with countryside views. Well-presented, flavoursome dishes from wide-ranging menu, including British classics with a modern slant.

CHISELDON – Wilts. – 503 O29 – see Swindon

CHORLEY – Lancashire – 502 M23 – pop. 33 424 — 20 A2

London 222 – Blackpool 30 – Liverpool 33 – Manchester 26

Duxbury Park Duxbury Hall Rd, ✆ (01257) 265 380

Shaw Hill Hotel G. & C.C. Whittle-le-Woods Preston Rd, ✆ (01257) 269 221

XX **The Red Cat**

Blackburn Rd, Whittle-Le-Woods, Northeast : 2.5 m on A 674 – ✆ (01257) 263 966 – www.theredcat.co.uk – Closed Monday and Tuesday

Rest – Menu £ 18 (lunch) **s** – Carte dinner £ 26/42 **s**

◆ Restored pub with original beams, stone walls and brick fireplaces. Unfussy, modern dishes display good ingredients and sound cooking in well presented, classic combinations.

CHORLTON-CUM-HARDY – Gtr Manchester – 502 N23 – see Manchester

CHRISHALL – Essex

London 58 mi. – Barnet 44 mi. – Enfield 51 mi. – Luton 36 mi.

The Red Cow

11 High St ✉ SG8 8RN – ✆ (01763) 838 792 – www.theredcow.com – Closed Monday lunch

Rest – Carte £ 17/31

◆ Part 14C thatched inn; cosy and hugely characterful, with heavy beams and open fires. Mostly British dishes on simple seasonal menu. Bustling atmosphere and charming service.

CHRISTCHURCH – Dorset – 503 O31 – pop. 40 208 4 D3

London 111 mi. – Bournemouth 6 mi. – Salisbury 26 mi. – Southampton 24 mi.
49 High St ✆ (01202) 471780, enquiries@christchurchtourism.info
Highcliffe Castle Highcliffe-on-Sea 107 Lymington Rd, ✆ (01425) 272 953
Riverside Ave, ✆ (01202) 436 436
Town★ - Priory★
Hengistbury Head★ (≤★★) SW : 4.5 mi. by A 35 and B 3059

Captain's Club

Wick Ferry, Wick Lane ✉ BH23 1HU – ✆ (01202) 475 111 – www.captainsclubhotel.com – Fax (01202) 490 111
29 rm – †£ 149/189 ††£ 189/229
Rest Tides – *see restaurant listing*
◆ Trendy hotel displaying striking art deco and nautical influences. Floor to ceiling windows throughout; attractive river views. Smart, simply furnished bedrooms/suites. Stylish spa.

Christchurch Harbour

95 Mudeford, East : 2mi. ✉ BH23 3NT – ✆ (01202) 483 434 – www.christchurch-harbour-hotel.co.uk – Fax (01202) 479 004
64 rm – †£ 120/150 ††£ 145/245
Rest *Rhodes South* – see restaurant listing
Rest – Menu £ 16 (lunch) – Carte £ 29/33
◆ Busy hotel in a great spot, with pleasant drinks terrace and small spa. Contemporary styling and plush bedrooms; choose between Harbour or Inland, with a supplement for waterfront views. Restaurant offers classic cuisine.

The Kings

18 Castle St. ✉ BH23 1DT – ✆ (01202) 588 933 – www.thekings-christchurch.co.uk – Fax (01202) 588 930
20 rm – †£ 75/95 ††£ 95/150
Rest *Kings Rhodes* – Menu £ 14 (lunch) – Carte £ 24/31
◆ Lovingly restored late 17C former coaching inn, in the heart of the town, overlooking the priory, ruins and bowling green. Pretty, boutique style and well-appointed, contemporary bedrooms. Appealing ground floor bar and brasserie.

Druid House without rest

26 Sopers Lane ✉ BH23 1JE – ✆ (01202) 485 615 – www.druid-house.co.uk – Fax (01202) 473 484
10 rm – †£ 45/70 ††£ 60/90
◆ Bright, fresh interior in contrast to exterior. Cottagey breakfast room; light and airy conservatory sitting room, smart bar. Spacious bedrooms, two with balconies.

Rhodes South – at Christchurch Harbour Hotel

95 Mudeford, East : 2mi. ✉ BH23 3NT – ✆ (01202) 483 434 – www.rhodes-south.co.uk – Closed Sunday-Monday
Rest – Modern – Menu £ 25 (lunch) – Carte £ 28/37
◆ Contemporary, eco-friendly building with stylish interior, in fantastic waterside setting. Interesting seasonal menus have a slight seafood slant; refined, ambitious cooking.

Splinters

12 Church St ✉ BH23 1BW – ✆ (01202) 483 454 – www.splinters.uk.com – Closed 1-10 January, Sunday and Monday
Rest – Menu £ 15 (lunch)/26 (dinner Tuesday to Thursday) – Carte £ 26/39
◆ Well-run restaurant in cobbled street with bar, lounge and several cosy rooms; one with intimate booths. Classical cooking uses good ingredients and unfussy combinations. Interesting wine list.

Tides – at Captain's Club Hotel

rm,
Wick Ferry, Wick Lane ✉ BH23 1HU – ✆ (01202) 475 111 – www.captainsclubhotel.com – Fax (01202) 490 111
Rest – Menu £ 16/25 – Carte £ 26/36
◆ Stylish restaurant with water feature wall, oversized windows and river views. Modern, well judged cooking offers a wide choice, good combinations and some unusual formats.

ENGLAND

CHURCH ENSTONE – Oxfordshire – ✉ Chipping Norton 10 B1

London 72 mi. – Banbury 13 mi. – Oxford 38 mi.

The Crown Inn

Mill Lane ✉ OX7 4NN – ☎ (01608) 677 262 – www.crowninnenstone.co.uk – Closed 26 December, 1 January and Sunday dinner

Rest – Menu £ 18 (Sunday lunch) – Carte £ 19/30

◆ 17C inn set among pretty stone houses in a picturesque village. Meat, fruit and veg come from local farms and seafood is a speciality. Lunch offers pub favourites; puddings are homemade.

CHURCHILL – Oxfordshire – 503 P28 – pop. 502 – ✉ Chipping Norton 10 A1

London 79 mi. – Birmingham 46 mi. – Cheltenham 29 mi. – Oxford 23 mi.

The Chequers

Church Rd ✉ OX7 6NJ – ☎ (01608) 659 393

Rest – Menu £ 18 – Carte £ 20/30

◆ Traditional stone pub with unexpectedly stylish interior. Classical menus display the odd inventive touch but puddings are firmly rooted in the old school. Thursdays are roast duck nights.

The symbol guarantees a good night's sleep. In red ? The very essence of peace: only the sound of birdsong in the early morning...

ENGLAND

CHURCH STRETTON – Shropshire – 502 L26 – pop. 3 841 18 B2

Great Britain

London 166 mi. – Birmingham 46 mi. – Hereford 39 mi. – Shrewsbury 14 mi.

Trevor Hill, ☎ (01694) 722 281

Wenlock Edge★, E : by B 4371

Jinlye without rest

Castle Hill, All Stretton, North : 2.25 mi. by B 4370 turning left beside telephone box in All Stretton ✉ SY6 6JP – ☎ (01694) 723 243 – www.jinlye.co.uk – Fax (01694) 723 243

6 rm – †£ 65 ††£ 85/90

◆ Enjoy wonderful views of Long Mynd from this characterful crofter's cottage high in the hills, run by charming owner and daughter. Grandiose breakfast room. 19C conservatory.

The Studio

59 High St ✉ SY6 6BY – ☎ (01694) 722 672 – www.thestudiorestaurant.net – Closed 3 weeks January, 1 week spring, 1 week autumn, Christmas-New Year and Sunday-Tuesday

Rest – *(dinner only)* Menu £ 28

◆ Personally run former art studio; walls enhanced by local artwork. Pleasant rear terrace for sunny lunches. Tried-and-tested dishes: much care taken over local produce.

CIRENCESTER – Gloucestershire – 503 O28 – pop. 15 861 4 D1

Great Britain

London 97 mi. – Bristol 37 mi. – Gloucester 19 mi. – Oxford 37 mi.

Corinium Museum Park Street ☎ (01285) 654180, cirencestervic@cotswold.gov.uk

Bagendon Cheltenham Rd, ☎ (01285) 652 465

Town★ – Church of St John the Baptist★ – Corinium Museum★ (Mosaic pavements★) **AC**

Fairford : Church of St Mary★ (stained glass windows★★) E : 7 mi. by A 417

No 12 without rest
12 Park St ✉ GL7 2BW – ✆ (01285) 640 232 – www.no12cirencester.co.uk
4 rm – †£ 65 ††£ 90/95
◆ 16C property with Georgian façade, hidden away in the old alleyways. Delightful rear walled garden. Excellent organic breakfast. Stylish rooms charmingly blend old and new.

The Old Brewhouse without rest
7 London Rd ✉ GL7 2PU – ✆ (01285) 656 099 – www.theoldbrewhouse.com – Fax (01285) 656 099 – Closed 1 week Christmas
10 rm – †£ 50/65 ††£ 85
◆ Former 17C brewhouse with a cosy, cottagey ambience. Exposed stone in two breakfast rooms. Cast iron bedsteads adorn some of the rooms, all of which boast period character.

at Barnsley **Northeast : 4 mi. by A 429 on B 4425 – ✉ Cirencester**

Barnsley House
✉ GL7 5EE – ✆ (01285) 740 000 – www.barnsleyhouse.com – Fax (01285) 740 925
11 rm – †£ 295/570 ††£ 295/570 – 7 suites
Rest – *(booking essential for non-residents at dinner)* Menu £ 22 (lunch) – Carte dinner approx. £ 43
◆ Impressive 17C Cotswold manor house. Contemporary interior, with hi tech bedrooms; largest and most modern in annexed courtyard. Well kept gardens, hydrotherapy pool, cinema. Dining room has pleasant outlook. Modern, interesting menus.

Village Pub with rm
✉ GL7 5EF – ✆ (01285) 740 421 – www.thevillagepub.co.uk – Fax (01285) 740 925
7 rm – †£ 90 ††£ 90/160 **Rest** – Carte £ 22/31
◆ Characterful stone pub in a charming village. Dishes vary in style between pub and restaurant, rustic and refined; changing daily and even between services. Bedrooms feature beams, antique furniture and Victorian or four poster beds.

at Ewen **Southwest : 3.25 mi. by A 429 – ✉ Cirencester**

The Wild Duck Inn with rm
Drake's Island ✉ GL7 6BY – ✆ (01285) 770 310 – www.thewildduckinn.co.uk – Fax (01285) 770 924 – Closed 25 December dinner
12 rm – †£ 70 ††£ 135
Rest – Carte £ 20/30
◆ 16C stone pub with original features and plenty of character. Traditional menu features pub classics and old British favourites. Bedrooms in the original building are large and characterful, with high ceilings and a period feel.

at Sapperton **West : 5 mi. by A 419 – ✉ Cirencester**

The Bell
✉ GL7 6LE – ✆ (01285) 760 298 – www.foodatthebell.co.uk – Fax (01285) 760 761 – Closed 25 December
Rest – Carte £ 22/36
◆ Charming pub in a pretty village. Wide-ranging monthly menu and daily seafood specials take on a refined yet rustic style, relying on regional produce. Interesting wine list.

Prices quoted after the symbol † refer to the lowest rate in low season followed by the highest rate in high season, for a single room. The same principle applies to the symbol †† for a double room.

ENGLAND

CLACTON-ON-SEA – Essex – 504 X28 – pop. 51 284 13 D2

London 83 mi.

at St Osyth West : 4.5 mi. by A 133 and B 1027 – ✉

Park Hall without rest

Park Hall, East : 1.5 mi. on B 1027 ✉ CO16 8HG – ✆ (01255) 820 922 – www.parkhall.info

3 rm – £ 110 £ 150/190

◆ 14C antique-filled former monastery in 600 acres of arable farmland, with 5 acres of grounds, where peacocks roam free. Traditionally styled rooms come with many thoughtful extras.

CLANFIELD – Oxfordshire – 503 P28 – pop. 1 709 10 A2

London 75 mi. – Oxford 24 mi. – Swindon 16 mi.

Plough at Clanfield

Bourton Rd, on A 4095 ✉ OX18 2RB – ✆ (01367) 810 222 – www.theploughclanfield.co.uk – Closed 25-26 December

11 rm – £ 75/95 £ 95/195

Rest The Restaurant – *see restaurant listing*

◆ Charming hotel with delightful stone façade, located in the heart of a pretty village. Serene lounge with period fireplace. Comfortable, characterful bedrooms with a modern touch.

The Restaurant – at The Plough Hotel rm,

Bourton Rd, on A 4095 ✉ OX18 2RB – ✆ (01367) 810 222 – www.theploughclanfield.co.uk

Rest – Carte £ 21/34

◆ Accomplished modern cooking; strong on fish and game. Dining over several rooms at polished tables; pre and post-prandial drinks by the fire. Friendly, informal service.

CLAVERING – Essex – 504 U28 – pop. 1 663 – ✉ Saffron Walden 12 B2

London 44 mi. – Cambridge 25 mi. – Colchester 44 mi. – Luton 29 mi.

The Cricketers with rm rm,

✉ CB11 4QT – ✆ (01799) 550 442 – www.thecricketers.co.uk – Fax (01799) 550 882 – Closed 25-26 December

14 rm – £ 65 £ 110 **Rest** – Menu £ 30 (dinner) – Carte £ 23/30

◆ Attractive whitewashed pub exuding old-world charm. Straightforward cooking is precise and flavoursome. Local produce is key – all veg comes from their son Jamie Oliver's garden. Simple modern bedrooms in courtyard, more traditional rooms in the pavilion.

CLEEVE HILL – Glos. – 503 N28 – see Cheltenham

CLENT – Worcestershire – 504 N26 Great Britain 19 C2

London 127 mi. – Birmingham 12 mi. – Hagley 2 mi.

Black Country Museum★, N : 7 mi. by A 491 and A 4036 – Birmingham★ - Museum and Art Gallery★★, Aston Hall★★, NE : 10 mi. by A 491 and A 456

Bell & Cross

Holy Cross, West : 0.5 mi. off A 491 (northbound carriageway) (Bromsgrove rd) ✉ DY9 9QL – ✆ (01562) 730 319 – www.bellandcrossclent.co.uk – Fax (01562) 731 733 – Closed 25 December

Rest – Carte £ 18/25

◆ Early 19C village pub with gardens and dining terrace. Traditional public bar and five intimate dining rooms. Friendly service; blackboard specials and seasonal produce.

CLEY NEXT THE SEA – Norfolk – 504 X25 – see Blakeney

CLIFTON – Cumbria – 502 L20 – see Penrith

CLIPSHAM – Rutland – see Stamford

ENGLAND

CLITHEROE – Lancashire – 502 M22 – pop. 14 697 20 B2

London 64 mi. – Blackpool 35 mi. – Manchester 31 mi.

Council Offices, Church Walk ✆ (01200) 425566,tourism@ribblevalley.gov.uk

Whalley Rd, ✆ (01200) 422 618

Brooklyn without rest

32 Pimlico Rd ✉ BB7 2AH – ✆ (01200) 428 268 – www.brooklynguesthouse.co.uk – Fax (01200) 428 699

5 rm – †£ 35 ††£ 60

◆ Stone 19C house, two minutes' walk from town, with floral furnished rooms, quieter at the rear. Good base from which to explore the Trough of Bowland and Clitheroe Castle.

at Bashall Eaves Northwest : 3 mi. by B6243

The Red Pump Inn with rm

Clitheroe Road ✉ BB7 3DA – ✆ (01254) 826 227 – www.theredpumpinn.co.uk – Closed Monday except Bank Holidays

3 rm – †£ 55/75 ††£ 85/115

Rest – Menu £ 15 – Carte approx. £ 30

◆ One of the oldest inns in the Ribble Valley. The traditional menu is hearty and generous, featuring regional produce, including a variety of game dishes in season. Spacious, modern bedrooms with handmade furniture and oversized beds.

at Grindleton Northeast : 3 mi. by A 671

Duke of York Inn

Brow Top ✉ BB7 4QR – ✆ (01200) 441 266 – www.dukeofyorkgrindleton.com – Fax (01200) 441 250 – Closed 25 December and Monday except Bank Holidays when closed Tuesday

Rest – Menu £ 13 (before 7pm) – Carte £ 20/28

◆ Ivy-clad pub with large decked terrace, set in a pleasant hamlet. Great value lunch/early evening set menu and wide-ranging à la carte. Tasty, carefully prepared, seasonal cooking.

ENGLAND

CLOVELLY – Devon – 503 G31 – pop. 439 – ✉ Bideford 1 B1

London 241 mi. – Barnstaple 18 mi. – Exeter 52 mi. – Penzance 92 mi.

Village★★

SW : Tamar River★★. Hartland : Hartland Church★ - Hartland Quay★ (viewpoint★★) - Hartland Point ←★★★, W : 6.5 mi. by B 3237 and B 3248 – Morwenstow (Church★, cliffs★★), SW : 11.5 mi. by A 39

Red Lion

The Quay ✉ EX39 5TF – ✆ (01237) 431 237 – www.clovelly.co.uk – Fax (01237) 431 044

11 rm – †£ 62/83 ††£ 124/136

Rest – *(bar lunch)* Menu £ 30

◆ Cosy little hotel/inn on the quayside; a superb location. All rooms enjoy sea and harbour views and are dressed in soft, understated colours, providing a smart resting place. Simple dining room looks out to harbour.

CLOWS TOP – Worcestershire – pop. 1 164 18 B2

London 141 mi. – Bewdley 6 mi. – Stourport-on-Seven 10 mi.

The Colliers Arms

Tenbury Road, East : 0.5 mi. on A 456 ✉ DY14 9HA – ✆ (01299) 832 242 – www.colliersarms.com – Closed Sunday dinner

Rest – Menu £ 14 (dinner Monday-Thursday) – Carte £ 18/25

◆ Snug, traditional bar; open main bar with log fire and fishy wallpaper; airy rear dining room with views of garden. Hearty British classics - all fresh, seasonal and homemade.

CLUN – Shropshire – 503 K26 **18** A2

London 173 mi. – Church Stretton 16 mi. – Ludlow 16 mi.

Birches Mill without rest

Northwest : 3 mi. by A 488, Bicton rd, Mainstone rd and Burlow rd
SY7 8NL – (01588) 640 409 – www.birchesmill.co.uk
– April-October
3 rm – £ 70/75 £ 80/90

◆ High quality comforts in remote former corn mill: interior has characterful 17C/18C structures. Flagged lounge with lovely inglenook. Simple but tastefully decorated rooms.

COBHAM – Surrey – 504 S30 – pop. 1 586 **7** D1

London 24 mi. – Guildford 10 mi.

Plan : see Greater London (South-West) 5

at Stoke D'Abernon Southeast : 1.5 mi. on A 245 – Cobham

Woodlands Park

Woodlands Lane, on A 245 KT11 3QB – (01372) 843 933
– www.handpicked.co.uk/woodlandspark
– Fax (01372) 849 002
57 rm – £ 109/195 £ 119/205
Rest *Oak Room* – *(closed Sunday-Monday) (dinner only)* Carte £ 31/46 **s**
Rest *Bensons Brasserie* – Carte £ 18/23 **s**

◆ Designed in 1885 for son of founder of Bryant and May match company; one of first houses with electricity. Frequented by Prince of Wales and Lillie Langtry. Modish rooms. Appealingly welcoming Oak Room restaurant; also brasserie.

Guesthouses don't provide the same level of service as hotels. They are often characterised by a warm welcome and a décor which reflects the owner's personality. Those shown in red are particularly pleasant.

COCKERMOUTH – Cumbria – 501 J20 – pop. 7 446 **21** A2

London 306 mi. – Carlisle 25 mi. – Keswick 13 mi.
Town Hall, Market St (01900) 822634, cockermouthtic@co-net.com
Embleton, (017687) 76 223

Trout

Crown St CA13 0EJ – (01900) 823 591 – www.trouthotel.co.uk
– Fax (01900) 827 514
47 rm – £ 60 £ 124/185
Rest *The Restaurant* – *(dinner only and Sunday lunch)* Carte £ 29/41
Rest *The Terrace* – Carte £ 21/30

◆ Well run, extended hotel on banks of River Derwent. Refurbished, contemporary lounges and classically styled bedrooms; some in main house have original beams. The linen-laid Restaurant offers a daily set menu. The Terrace Bar and Bistro offers informal and al fresco dining, with a modern, international choice.

at Lorton Southeast : 4.25 mi. by B 5292 – Cockermouth

Winder Hall Country House

on B 5289 CA13 9UP – (01900) 85 107 – www.winderhall.co.uk
– Fax (01900) 85 479 – closed January
7 rm – £ 75/135 £ 145/185
Rest – *(dinner only) (booking essential for non-residents)* Menu £ 34 **s**

◆ Part-Jacobean manor house with mullioned windows and tranquil garden.Comfortable lounge and high quality bedrooms retain rich history of house and include two four posters. Oak panelled dining room overlooks garden. Local produce well-used in homemade dishes. Relaxed, friendly service.

New House Farm
South : 1.25 mi. on B 5289 ✉ CA13 9UU – ✆ (01900) 85 404 – www.newhouse-farm.com – Fax (01900) 85 478
5 rm – †£ 80/150 ††£ 140/170
Rest – *(by arrangement)* Menu £ 28
◆ Very well appointed, richly decorated guest house. Hot tub in garden, sumptuous bedrooms; one with double jacuzzi, two with four posters. Fine furnishings, roll top baths. Aga-cooked breakfasts and evenings meals.

The Old Vicarage
Church Lane, North : 0.25 mi. on Lorton Church rd ✉ CA13 9UN – ✆ (01900) 85 656 – www.oldvicarage.co.uk
8 rm – †£ 75/80 ††£ 120
Rest – *(by arrangement)* Menu £ 26
◆ Well kept Victorian house in beautiful countryside spot. Comfortable lounge. Hospitable owners. Sympathetically modernised bedrooms; four-postered Room 1 is the best. Cosy dining room; homecooked meals made with local produce.

COCKLEFORD – Gloucestershire – ✉ Cheltenham — 4 C1

London 95 mi. – Bristol 48 mi. – Cheltenham 7 mi.

The Green Dragon Inn with rm
✉ GL53 9NW – ✆ (01242) 870 271 – www.green-dragon-inn.co.uk – Fax (01242) 870 171 – Closed 25-26 December dinner and 1 January dinner
9 rm – †£ 70 ††£ 95
Rest – *(booking essential)* Carte £ 22/32
◆ 17C country inn of old Cotswold stone with beams, log fire and large outside terrace. Tasty meals employing good use of local ingredients. Smart rooms.

CODFORD ST MARY – Wiltshire – 504 N30 Great Britain — 4 C2

London 101 mi. – Bristol 38 mi. – Warminster 8 mi.
Stonehenge★★★ **AC**, E : 10.5 mi. by A 36 and A 303

The George
High St ✉ BA12 0NG – ✆ (01985) 850 270 – www.thegeorgecodford.co.uk – Closed Sunday dinner and Tuesday
Rest – Carte £ 21/35
◆ Unspectacular in outward appearance but spot-on with the cooking. The established chef has expertly mastered both British pub classics and more interesting, ambitious dishes.

COGGESHALL – Essex – 504 W28 – pop. 3 919 – ✉ Colchester — 13 C2

London 49 mi. – Braintree 6 mi. – Chelmsford 16 mi. – Colchester 9 mi.

XX **Baumanns Brasserie**
4-6 Stoneham St ✉ CO6 1TT – ✆ (01376) 561 453 – www.baumannsbrasserie.co.uk – Fax (01376) 563 762 – Closed first 2 weeks January, Monday and Tuesday
Rest – Menu £ 20/23 – Carte £ 31/35
◆ Characterful 16C building, its walls packed with pictures and prints. Tasty cooking, made using local produce, brings out classic flavour combinations. Speedy service.

at Pattiswick Northwest : 3 mi. by A 120 (Braintree Rd) – ✉ Coggeshall

The Compasses at Pattiswick
Compasses Rd ✉ CM77 8BG – ✆ (01376) 561 322 – www.thecompassesatpattiswick.co.uk – Fax (01376) 564 343 – Closed Sunday dinner October-Easter
Rest – Menu £ 13/18 – Carte £ 20/28
◆ Smart, rural pub with cheery service. Cooking is simple and honest, with plenty of effort put into sourcing local ingredients. Pheasant is from local shoots and venison from the woods behind.

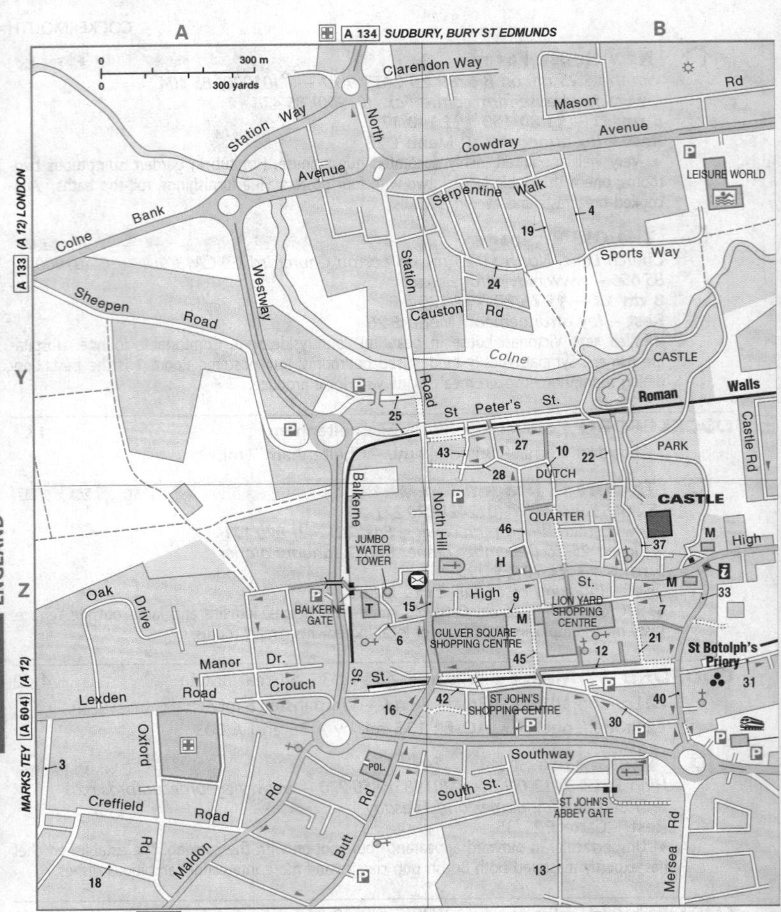

COLCHESTER – Essex – 504 W28 – pop. 104 390 Great Britain **13** D2

London 52 mi. – Cambridge 48 mi. – Ipswich 18 mi. – Luton 76 mi.

Visitor Information Centre, 1 Queens Street (01206) 282920, vic@colchester.gov.uk

Birch Grove Layer Rd, (01206) 734 276

Castle and Museum★ **AC** BZ

Rose and Crown

rm, VISA AE

East St CO1 2TZ – (01206) 866 677
– www.rose-and-crown.com
– Fax (01206) 866 616 CZ**d**

39 rm – †£ 99 ††£ 109/165, £ 10.95

Rest – Carte £ 17/28

◆ Part-15C coaching inn with period features and original stained glass. Bedrooms vary from family to business, to four-poster with a whirlpool bath. Characterful bar serves traditional pub fare. Contemporary restaurant offers classics with the odd Asian touch.

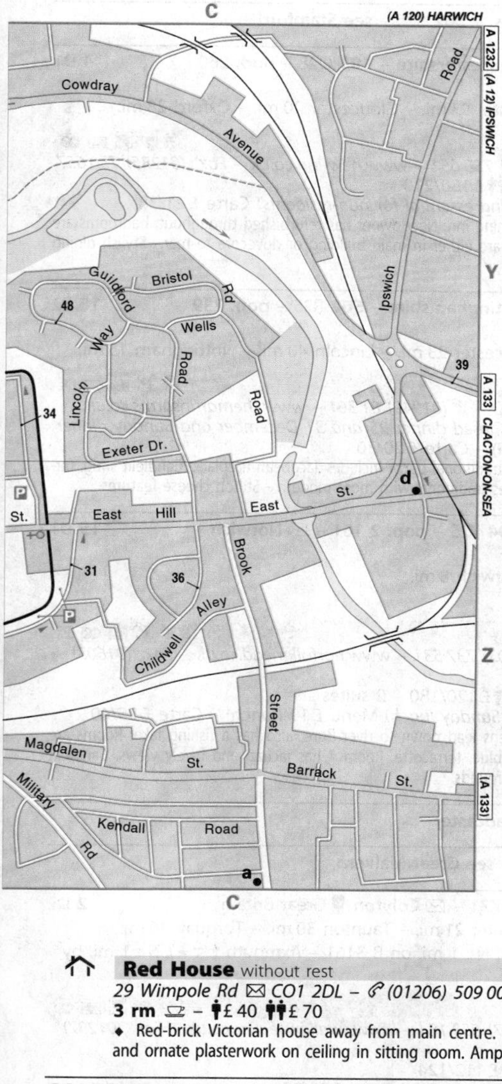

COLCHESTER

Street	Grid	No.
Beverley Rd	AZ	3
Catchpool Rd	BY	4
Church St	AZ	6
Culver Square Shopping Centre	BZ	
Culver St East	BZ	7
Culver St West	BZ	9
East Stockwell St	BYZ	10
Eld Lane	BZ	12
Flagstaff Rd	BZ	13
Headgate	ABZ	16
Head St	BZ	15
High St.	BZ	
Inglis Rd.	AZ	18
Kings Meadow Rd	BY	19
Lion Yard Shopping Centre	BZ	
Long Wyre St	BZ	21
Maidenburgh St	BYZ	22
Margaret Rd	BY	24
Middleborough	AY	25
Northgate St	BY	27
Nunn's Rd	BY	28
Osborne St	BZ	30
Priory St	BCZ	31
Queen St	BZ	33
Roman Rd	CY	34
Rosebery Ave	CY	36
Ryegate Rd	BYZ	37
St Andrews Ave	CY	39
St Botolph's St	BZ	40
St John's Shopping Centre	BZ	
St John's St.	BZ	42
Short Cut Rd	BY	43
Trinity St.	BZ	45
West Stockwell St	BYZ	46
Worcester Rd	CY	48

ENGLAND

Red House without rest

29 Wimpole Rd ✉ CO1 2DL – ✆ (01206) 509 005 CZ**a**

3 rm ☕ – 🚹£ 40 🚹🚹£ 70

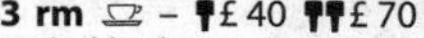

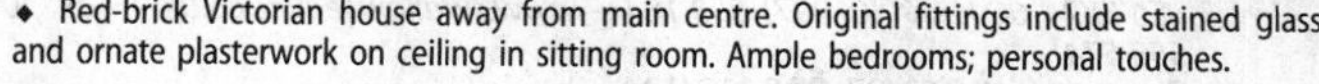

◆ Red-brick Victorian house away from main centre. Original fittings include stained glass and ornate plasterwork on ceiling in sitting room. Ample bedrooms; personal touches.

COLERNE – **Wilts.** – **503** M29 – **see Bath (Bath & North East Somerset)**

COLESBOURNE – **Gloucestershire** – **503** N28 **4** C-D1

London 104 mi. – Swindon 27 mi. – Gloucester 16 mi. – Cheltenham 7 mi.

The Colesbourne Inn with rm

✉ GL53 9NP – ✆ (01242) 870 376 – www.thecolesbourneinn.co.uk

9 rm ☕ – 🚹£ 55 🚹🚹£ 75 **Rest** – Carte £ 17/34

◆ Early 19C coaching inn, halfway between Cirencester and Cheltenham, featuring open fires, flagged floors and hanging hops and tankards. Unfussy bar menu; more elaborate à la carte. Antique-furnished bedrooms in former stables.

COLLYWESTON – Northants. – 502 S26 – see Stamford

COLN ST ALDWYNS – Gloucestershire – 503 O28 – pop. 260 4 D1
– ✉ Cirencester

London 101 mi. – Bristol 53 mi. – Gloucester 20 mi. – Oxford 28 mi.

New Inn At Coln

✉ GL7 5AN – ☎ (01285) 750 651 – www.new-inn.co.uk – Fax (01285) 750 657

13 rm – †£ 85/130 ††£ 150/210

Rest – *(bar lunch) (booking essential for non-residents)* Carte £ 21/38

◆ Pretty 16C Cotswold coaching inn. New owner has refurbished throughout; bedrooms are now bold and colourful and are either in main building or dovecote to rear. Stylish dining room with modern menu.

COLSTON BASSETT – Nottinghamshire – 502 R25 – pop. 239 16 B2
– ✉ Nottingham

London 129 mi. – Leicester 23 mi. – Lincoln 40 mi. – Nottingham 15 mi.

The Martins Arms

School Lane ✉ NG12 3FD – ☎ (01949) 81 361 – www.themartinsarms.co.uk – Fax (01949) 81 039 – Closed dinner 25 and 31 December and Sunday dinner

Rest – Menu £ 16 (lunch) – Carte £ 20/30

◆ Welcoming and well run; traditional décor includes Jacobean fireplace. Candlelit snug, formal dining room; menu mixes traditional with more modern - Stilton cheese features.

ENGLAND

COLTISHALL – Norfolk – 504 Y25 – pop. 2 161 – ✉ Norwich 15 D1
Great Britain

London 133 mi. – Norwich 8 mi.

Norfolk Broads★

Norfolk Mead

✉ NR12 7DN – ☎ (01603) 737 531 – www.norfolkmead.co.uk – Fax (01603) 737 521

11 rm – †£ 75/95 ††£ 120/180 – 2 suites

Rest – *(dinner only and Sunday lunch)* Menu £ 19 (lunch) – Carte £ 25/40

◆ Restful 18C manor; gardens lead down to river Bure; also has a fishing lake. Rooms are individually colour themed: blue, terracotta. Room 7 has jacuzzi and lovely views. Candlelit restaurant overlooking the grounds.

COLTON – N. Yorks. – see Tadcaster

COLWALL – Herefordshire – see Great Malvern

COLYFORD – Devon – 503 K31 – ✉ Colyton Great Britain 2 D2

London 168 mi. – Exeter 21 mi. – Taunton 30 mi. – Torquay 46 mi.

Colyton★ (Church★), N : 1 mi. on B 3161 – Axmouth (<★), S : 1 mi. by A 3052 and B 3172

Swallows Eaves

✉ EX24 6QJ – ☎ (01297) 553 184 – www.swallowseaves.co.uk – Fax (01297) 553 574

8 rm – †£ 63/87 ††£ 112/124

Rest – *(Closed Sunday) (dinner only)* Carte £ 20/30

◆ Unusual grey shale-coated 1920s house, with views from some rooms over the Axe Valley: listen out for birdsong on the marshes. Fully refurbished guest areas – bedrooms and bathrooms to follow. Menus feature locally sourced meats, fish and vegetables.

COMBE HAY – Bath & North East Somerset – see Bath

CONEYTHORPE – North Yorkshire – see Knaresborough

The sun's out? Then enjoy eating outside on the terrace:

CONGLETON – Cheshire – 502 N24 – pop. 25 400 Great Britain 20 B3

London 183 mi. – Liverpool 50 mi. – Manchester 25 mi. – Sheffield 46 mi.

Town Hall, High St ✆ (01260) 271095, congletontic@cheshireeast.gov.uk

Biddulph Rd, ✆ (01260) 273 540

Little Moreton Hall★★ **AC**, SW : 3 mi. by A 34

Sandhole Farm without rest

Hulme Walfield, North : 2.25 mi. on A 34 ✉ CW12 2JH – ✆ (01260) 224 419 – www.sandholefarm.co.uk – Fax (01260) 224 766

18 rm – £ 60 £ 80

◆ Former farm with its stable block converted into comfy, well-equipped bedrooms with a rustic feel. Breakfast taken in the farmhouse's conservatory overlooking the countryside.

Pecks

Newcastle Rd, Moreton, South : 2.75 mi. on A 34 ✉ CW12 4SB – ✆ (01260) 275 161 – www.pecksrest.co.uk – Fax (01260) 299 640 – Closed 25-30 December, Sunday dinner and Monday

Rest – Menu £ 18/29 (weekdays) – Carte Saturday dinner approx. £ 43

◆ Airy, modish restaurant with unique style. À la carte lunch; monthly changing 5/7 course set dinner at 8pm sharp. Traditional homemade dishes use good produce and arrive in generous portions.

L'Endroit

70-72 Lawton St ✉ CW12 1RS – ✆ (01260) 299 548 – www.lendroit.co.uk – Fax (01260) 299 548 – Closed 2 weeks February/March, 1 week June, 1 week September, Saturday lunch, Sunday and Monday

Rest – French – Carte £ 21/34

◆ Welcoming restaurant with warm décor, upmarket bistro-style and small patio. Seasonally changing à la carte displays tasty, well-done dishes with strong French undertones. Good value lunch.

Symbols shown in red indicate particularly charming establishments.

CONGRESBURY – North Somerset – 503 L29 3 B2

London 145 mi. – Bristol 13 mi. – Cardiff 56 mi. – Swansea 95 mi.

Cadbury House H. & Spa

Frost Hill, North : 1/2m. on B3133 ✉ BS49 5AD – ✆ (01934) 834 343 – www.cadbury.com – Fax (01934) 834 390

72 rm – £ 79/135 £ 79/145, £ 12.95

Rest *The Restaurant* – *(dinner only)* Menu £ 28 – Carte £ 30/41 **s**

Rest *The Lounge* – Carte £ 15/23 **s**

◆ 18C country house and 5 storey extension, plus impressive leisure club. Modern, stylish bedrooms with smart bathrooms; Executive rooms are larger with good northerly views. Large restaurant offers seasonal à la carte. The Lounge offers popular all day dining menu and has pleasant balcony terrace.

CONSTABLE BURTON – N. Yorks. – 502 O21 – see Leyburn

CONSTANTINE BAY – Cornwall – 503 E32 – see Padstow

COOKHAM – Windsor and Maidenhead – 504 R29 – pop. 5 304 – ✉ Maidenhead Great Britain 11 C3

London 32 mi. – High Wycombe 7 mi. – Oxford 31 mi. – Reading 16 mi.

to Marlow, Maidenhead and Windsor (Salter Bros. Ltd) (summer only)

Stanley Spencer Gallery★ **AC**

The White Oak

Pound Lane ✉ SL6 9QE – ✆ (01628) 423 043 – www.thewhiteoak.co.uk – Closed 26 December and Sunday dinner

Rest – Menu £ 15 (lunch) – Carte £ 23/35

◆ Red-brick pub close to common with bright, modern style and smart terrace. Professionally run by cheery team. Quality produce in unfussy pub dishes, with charcuterie/seafood to share.

COOKHAM DEAN – Windsor and Maidenhead Great Britain 11 C3

London 32 mi. – High Wycombe 7 mi. – Oxford 31 mi. – Reading 16 mi.

Windsor Castle★★★, Eton★★ and Windsor★, S : 5 mi. by B 4447, A 4 (westbound) and A 308

The Inn on the Green with rm

The Old Cricket Common ✉ SL6 9NZ – ✆ (01628) 482 638 – www.theinnonthegreen.com – Fax (01628) 487 474 – Closed Sunday dinner and Monday

9 rm – †£ 85/115 ††£ 85/150 **Rest** – *(booking essential)* Carte £ 20/40

◆ Part timbered inn with delightful patio terrace. Rustic bar; two dining rooms and conservatory: modern British cooking. Individually furnished rooms in the inn or annex.

CORBRIDGE – Northumberland – 501 N19 – pop. 2 800 Great Britain 24 A2

London 300 mi. – Hexham 3 mi. – Newcastle upon Tyne 18 mi.

Hill St ✆ (01434) 632815, corbridgetic@btconnect.com

Hadrian's Wall★★, N : 3 mi. by A 68 – Corstopitum★ **AC**, NW : 0.5 m

at Great Whittington North : 5.5 mi. by A 68 off B 6318 – ✉ Corbridge

Queens Head Inn

✉ NE19 2HP – ✆ (01434) 672 267 – www.the-queens-head-inn.co.uk – Closed Sunday dinner

Rest – Carte £ 17/28

◆ Dating from 1615, with cosy bar and bric à brac filled dining room. Menu offers everything from stotties to duck spring rolls, with lamb and beef from farm next door. Friendly service.

CORFE CASTLE – Dorset – 503 N32 – pop. 1 335 – ✉ Wareham 4 C3

London 129 mi. – Bournemouth 18 mi. – Weymouth 23 mi.

Castle★ (<★★) **AC**

Mortons House

45 East St ✉ BH20 5EE – ✆ (01929) 480 988 – www.mortonshouse.co.uk – Fax (01929) 480 820

18 rm – †£ 75/110 ††£ 140/150 – 2 suites

Rest – Menu £ 30 – Carte £ 30/43

◆ Elizabethan manor built in the shape of an "E" in Queen's honour. Wood panelled drawing room; range of bedrooms, some themed: the Victoria room has original Victorian bath. Colourful dining room with views over courtyard.

CORNHILL-ON-TWEED – Northumberland – 501 N17 – pop. 317 24 A1

Scotland

London 345 mi. – Edinburgh 49 mi. – Newcastle upon Tyne 59 mi.

Ladykirk (Kirk o'Steil★), NE : 6 mi. by A 698 and B 6470

Tillmouth Park

Northeast : 2.5 mi. on A 698 ✉ TD12 4UU – ✆ (01890) 882 255 – www.tillmouthpark.co.uk – Fax (01890) 882 540 – Closed 6 January-3 April

14 rm – †£ 75/100 ††£ 120/140

Rest *The Library* – Menu £ 20 (lunch) – Carte £ 37/60

Rest *Bistro* – Menu £ 14 – Carte £ 20/36

◆ In an area renowned for its fishing, a 19C country house in mature grounds and woodland. Inside one finds stained glass windows, grand staircases and antique furniture. Light meals in bistro. Large, panelled Library restaurant has good views of grounds.

Coach House rm, VISA

Crookham, East : 4 mi. on A 697 ✉ TD12 4TD – ✆ (01890) 820 293 – www.coachhousecrookham.com – Fax (01890) 820 284 – closed mid November-February

10 rm – †£ 45/85 ††£ 104

Rest – *(dinner only) (booking essential for non-residents)* Menu £ 23

◆ Converted from a collection of farm buildings, including a 1680s dower house, and set around a courtyard. Recently modernised, comfortable rooms with character.

CORSE LAWN – **Worcs.** – **see Tewkesbury (Glos.)**

CORSHAM – **Wiltshire** – **504** N29 – **pop. 11 318** **4** C2

London 107 mi. – Bristol 22 mi. – Chippenham 5 mi.

Heatherly Cottage without rest

Ladbrook Lane, Gastard, Southeast : 1.25 mi. by B 3353 ✉ SN13 9PE – ✆ (01249) 701 402 – www.heatherlycottage.co.uk – Closed December -March

3 rm – †£ 55/58 ††£ 72

◆ Part 17C stone cottage set down a quiet country road close to small village. Three very good value rooms: spacious, individually furnished and with good facilities.

CORTON DENHAM – **Somerset** – **see Sherborne**

COTTERED – **Hertfordshire** – **504** T28 – **pop. 1 788** **12** B2

London 46 mi. – Luton 24 mi. – Cambridge 29 mi. – Watford 43 mi.

The Bull of Cottered VISA

✉ SG9 9QP – ✆ (01763) 281 243

Rest – *(booking essential)* Carte £ 25/35

◆ Traditional, homely pub with flower baskets, polished horse brasses and log fires - a popular stop off point on way to Stansted Airport. Traditional menu offers eclectic mix.

COVENTRY – **West Midlands** – **503** P26 – **pop. 303 475** Great Britain **19** D2

London 100 mi. – Birmingham 18 mi. – Bristol 96 mi. – Leicester 24 mi.

St Michaels Tower, Priory Street ✆ (024) 7622 7264, tic@cvone.co.uk

Windmill Village Allesley Birmingham Rd, ✆ (024) 7640 4041

Sphinx Sphinx Drive, ✆ (024) 7645 1361

City★ - Cathedral★★★ **AC** AV – Old Cathedral★ AV **B** – Museum of British Road Transport★ **AC** AV **M2**

Plans on following pages

at Shilton **Northeast : 6.75 mi. by A 4600 - BX - on B 4065 – ✉ Coventry**

Barnacle Hall without rest

Shilton Lane, West : 1 mi. by B 4029 following signs for garden centre ✉ CV7 9LH – ✆ (024) 7661 2629 – www.barnaclehall.co.uk – Fax (024) 7661 2629 – closed 24 December-2 January

3 rm – †£ 45 ††£ 75

◆ Interesting part 16C farmhouse in rural location. Westerly facing 18C stone façade; remainder 16/17C. Beamed rooms have countryside outlook and farmhouse style furnishings.

at Balsall Common **West : 6.75 mi. by B 4101 - AY – ✉ Coventry**

The White Horse VISA AE

Kenilworth Road ✉ CV7 7DT – ✆ (01676) 533 207 – www.thewhitehorseatbc.co.uk – Fax (01676) 532 827

Rest – Carte £ 18/25

◆ Spacious, contemporary bar lounge with low backed leather chairs and art-adorned walls. Decked front terrace. Universal menu offers classics and rotisserie. Generous portions.

COVENTRY

Street	Grid	No.
Bayley Lane	AV	3
Bishop St.	AV	5
Broadgate	AV	6
Burges (The)	AV	7
Central Six Retail Park Shopping	AV	
Corporation St.	AV	
Earl St	AV	10
Fairfax St.	AV	12
Far Gosford St.	AV	13
Gallagher Retail Park	BX	
Gosford St.	AV	15
Greyfriars Lane	AV	16
Hales St.	AV	17
Hearsall Lane	AY	21
High St	AV	22
Ironmonger Rd	AV	23
Jordan Well	AV	26
Leicester Row	AV	29
Light Lane	AV	30
Little Park St	AV	31
Precincts Shopping	AV	
Primrose Hill St	AV	34
Queen Victoria Rd	AV	35
St Johns (Ringway)	AV	38
St Nicholas (Ringway)	AV	39
Swanswell (Ringway)	AV	40
Trinity St	AV	41
Upper Well St	AV	43
Vecqueray St	AV	45
Victoria St	AV	46
Warwick Rd	AV	49
White Friars (Ringway)	AV	54
White St	AV	51
Windsor St	AV	52

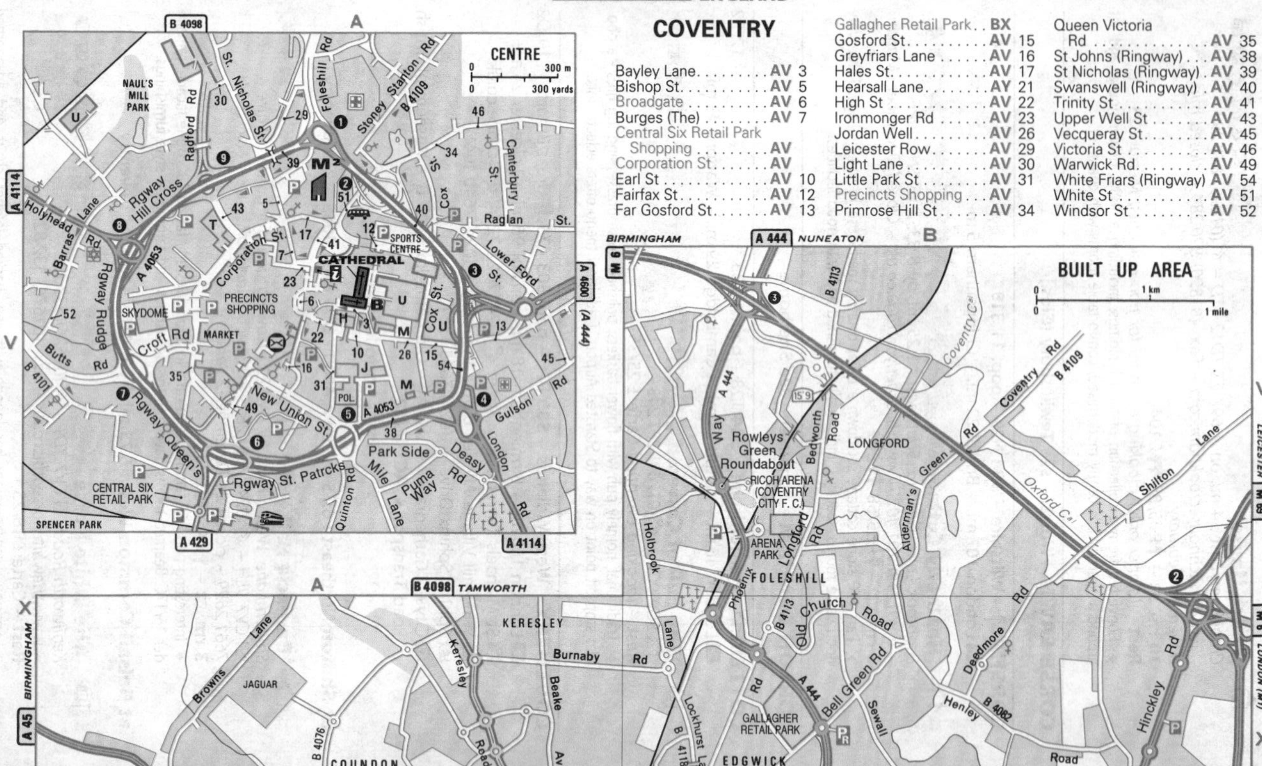

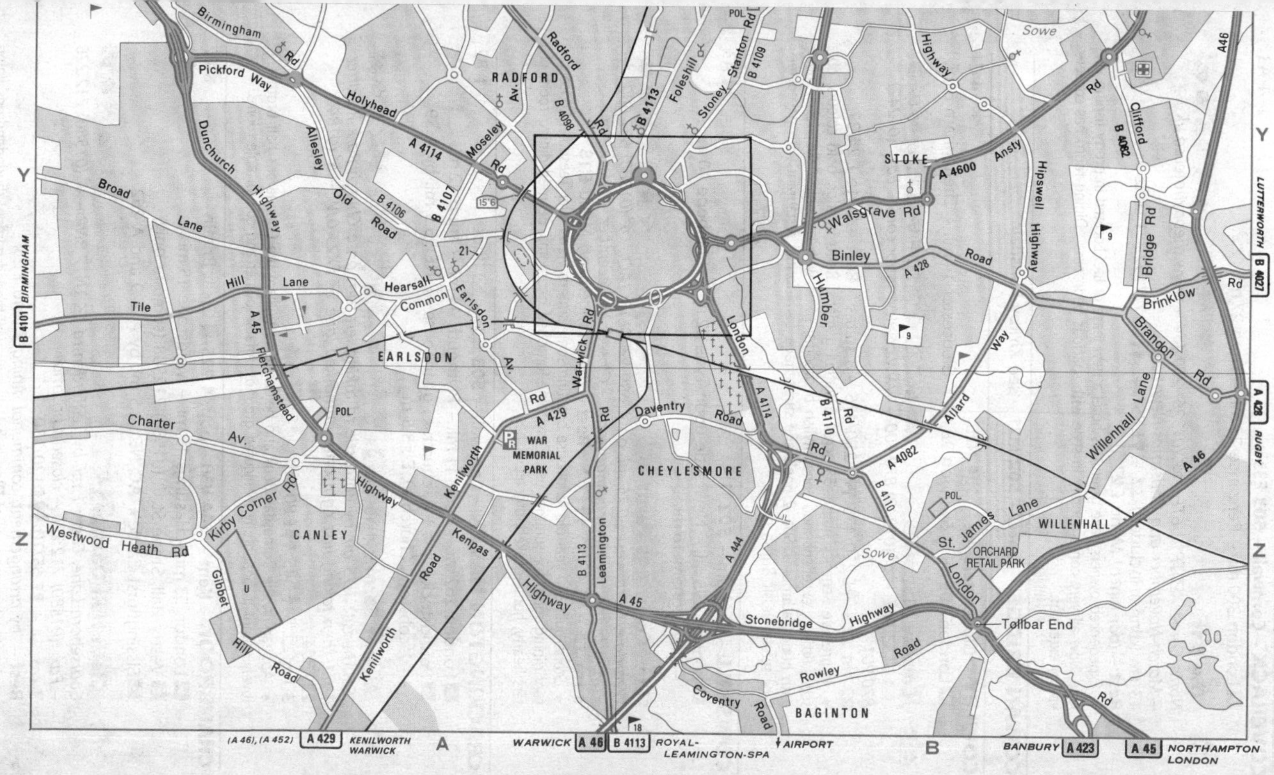
B 4101 BIRMINGHAM
LUTTERWORTH B 4027
A 428 RUGBY
(A 46), (A 452) A 429 KENILWORTH WARWICK
WARWICK A 46 B 4113 ROYAL-LEAMINGTON-SPA
AIRPORT
BANBURY A 423
A 45 NORTHAMPTON LONDON
RADFORD
STOKE
EARLSDON
CHEYLESMORE
CANLEY
WILLENHALL
BAGINTON
ORCHARD RETAIL PARK
WAR MEMORIAL PARK
Tollbar End
Birmingham Rd
Pickford Way
Holyhead Rd
A 4114
Moseley Av.
Radford Rd
B 4098
B 4113
Foleshill Rd
Stoney Stanton Rd
B 4109
Dunchurch Highway
Allesley Old Road
B 4106
B 4107
Broad Lane
Tile Hill Lane
Hearsall Common
Earlsdon Av.
A 45
Fletchamstead Highway
Charter Av.
Kirby Corner Rd
Westwood Heath Rd
Gibbet Hill Road
Kenilworth Rd
A 429
Kenilworth Road
Kenpas Highway
Warwick Rd
Leamington Rd
B 4113
Daventry Road
London Road
A 4114
A 444
Stonebridge Highway
Rowley Road
Coventry Road
Humber Rd
B 4110
Binley Road
A 428
Walsgrave Rd
A 4600
Ansty Rd
Hipswell Highway
Allard Way
A 4082
St. James Lane
London Rd
Willenhall Lane
Brandon Rd
Brinklow Rd
Bridge Rd
Clifford
B 4082
A 46
Sowe
POL.

ENGLAND

COVERACK – Cornwall – **503** E33 **1** A3

London 300 mi. – Penzance 25 mi. – Truro 27 mi.

The Bay

North Corner ✉ TR12 6TF – ✆ (01326) 280 464 – www.thebayhotel.co.uk – March-November and Christmas-New Year

13 rm (dinner included) – £ 85/142 £ 172/192 – 1 suite

Rest – *(bar lunch)* Menu £ 27

◆ Experienced owners have given this hotel a new lease of life. Located in pretty fishing village. Now all very contemporary in style with spacious bedrooms. Dining room has conservatory extension.

COWAN BRIDGE – Lancs. – **502** M21 – see Kirkby Lonsdale

COWLEY – Gloucestershire – **504** N28 **4** C1

London 105 mi. – Swindon 28 mi. – Gloucester 14 mi. – Cheltenham 6 mi.

Cowley Manor

✉ *GL53 9NL – ✆ (01242) 870 900 – www.cowleymanor.com – Fax (01242) 870 901*

22 rm – £ 250/475 £ 250/475 – 8 suites **Rest** – Carte £ 24/37

◆ Impressive Regency house. 55 acres; beautiful gardens. Retro interior, bold colours, obscure fittings, excellent mod cons. Stylish bedrooms, some with balconies/lake views, most with huge bathrooms. Spa, 2 pools and sun terrace. Semi-formal restaurant with paved terrace serves classic British dishes.

ENGLAND

COWSHILL – Durham – **502** N19 **24** A3

London 295 mi. – Newcastle upon Tyne 42 mi. – Stanhope 10 mi. – Wolsingham 16 mi.

Low Cornriggs Farm

Weardale, Northwest : 0.75 mi. on A 689 ✉ DL13 1AQ – ✆ (01388) 537 600 – www.britnett.net/lowcornriggsfarm – Closed 23 December - 3 January

3 rm – £ 42/45 £ 62 **Rest** – *(by arrangement)* Menu £ 18

◆ Stone-built 300 year-old farmhouse boasting some superb views over Teesdale. Conservatory dining room for summer use. Cosy, pine-furnished bedrooms. Beamed dining room offers hearty, home-cooked, organic dishes.

CRACKINGTON HAVEN – Cornwall – **503** G31 – ✉ **Bude** **1** B2

London 262 mi. – Bude 11 mi. – Plymouth 44 mi. – Truro 42 mi.

Poundstock★ (≤★★, church★, guildhouse★), NE : 5.5 mi. by A 39 – Jacobstow (Church★), E : 3.5 m

Manor Farm without rest

Southeast : 1.25 mi. by Boscastle rd taking left turn onto Church Park Rd after 1 mi. then taking first right onto unmarked lane ✉ EX23 0JW – ✆ (01840) 230 304

3 rm – £ 45 £ 80

◆ Appears in the Domesday Book and belonged to William the Conqueror's half brother. A lovely manor in beautifully manicured grounds. Affable owner and comfortable rooms.

CRANBROOK – Kent – **504** V30 – **pop. 4 225** Great Britain **8** B2

London 53 mi. – Hastings 19 mi. – Maidstone 15 mi.

Vestry Hall, Stone St ✆ (01580) 712538 (summer only)

Sissinghurst Castle★ **AC**, NE : 2.5 mi. by A 229 and A 262

Cloth Hall Oast

Coursehorn Lane, East : 1 mi. by Tenterden rd ✉ TN17 3NR – ✆ (01580) 712 220 – Fax (01580) 712 220 – closed Christmas

3 rm – £ 65/70 £ 120/130

Rest – *(by arrangement, communal dining)* Menu £ 25

◆ Run by former owner of Old Cloth Hall, with well-tended garden, rhododendrons lining the drive. Peaceful spot. Charming sitting room. Immaculate bedrooms exude personal style.

Apicius (Tim Johnson)
23 Stone St TN17 3HE – (01580) 714 666 – www.restaurant-apicius.co.uk – Closed 2 weeks summer, 2 weeks Christmas-New Year, Saturday lunch and Sunday dinner to Tuesday
Rest – Menu £ 27/30
Spec. Langoustine raviolo with vegetable and herb minestrone. Slow roast shoulder of pork with cabbage and apple. Poached pear with port sauce and Stilton ice cream.
◆ Named after Roman author of world's first cookbook. Cosy interior mixes original features with modern style. Passionate, well balanced, precise cooking uses local ingredients.

at Sissinghurst Northeast : 1.75 mi. by B 2189 on A 262 – Cranbrook

Rankins
The Street, on A 262 TN17 2JH – (01580) 713 964 – www.rankinsrestaurant.com – Closed Sunday dinner, Monday, Tuesday, and Wednesday-Saturday lunch
Rest – *(booking essential)* Menu £ 34
◆ Well-run village restaurant, immaculately kept by knowledgeable, personable owners. Concise set menus display hearty, traditional dishes with the odd Mediterranean touch. Desserts a speciality.

CRAYKE – N. Yorks. – see Easingwold

CREDITON – Devon – 503 J31 – pop. 7 092 2 C2

London 187 mi. – Torbay 32 mi. – Exeter 9 mi. – Torquay 30 mi.

Lamb Inn with rm
Northwest : 1.75 mi. EX17 4LW – (01363) 773 676 – www.lambinnsandford.co.uk
3 rm – £ 69/75 £ 89/95
Rest – Carte £ 16/23
◆ 16C period coaching inn; picturesque, pleasantly dated and full of charm. Classically based menu with strong French influences and dishes prepared in a simple, unassuming manner. Very spacious, recently converted bedrooms.

CREWE – Cheshire – 502 M24 – pop. 67 683 20 B3

London 174 mi. – Chester 24 mi. – Liverpool 49 mi. – Manchester 36 mi.
9 Queen's Park Queen's Park Drive, (01270) 662 378
18 Haslington Fields Rd, (01270) 584 227

Crewe Hall
Weston Road, Southeast : 1.75 mi. on A 5020 CW1 6UZ – (01270) 253 333 – www.qhotels.co.uk – Fax (01270) 253 322
113 rm – £ 77/122 £ 87/132 – 4 suites
Rest *Ilrá Brasserie* – (01270) 259 319 – Menu £ 18 (lunch) – Carte £ 25/42 **s**
◆ Impressive 17C mansion with formal gardens. Victorian décor featuring alabaster, marble and stained glass. Rooms offer luxurious comfort. Popular modern menu in the chic Brasserie.

CROCKERTON – Wiltshire – see Warminster

CROFT-ON-TEES – Durham – 502 P20 – see Darlington

CROMER – Norfolk – 504 X25 – pop. 8 836 15 D1

London 132 mi. – Norwich 23 mi.
Louden Rd (0871) 2003071, cromertic@north-norfolk.gov.uk
18 Royal Cromer Overstrand Rd, (01263) 512 884

Captains House without rest
5 The Crescent ✉ NR27 9EX – ✆ (01263) 515 434 – www.captains-house.co.uk
4 rm – 🛉£ 60 🛉🛉£ 140/200
◆ Immaculate Georgian house in seafront parade; tables outside for summer breakfast. Spacious, individually designed bedrooms with light seaside colours; excellent bathrooms.

at Overstrand Southeast : 2.5 mi. by B 1159 – ✉ Cromer

Sea Marge
16 High St ✉ NR27 0AB – ✆ (01263) 579 579 – www.mackenziehotels.com – Fax (01263) 579 524
25 rm – 🛉£ 91/156 🛉🛉£ 142/174 – 3 suites
Rest – *(bar lunch)* Carte £ 25/37
◆ Mock Elizabethan house built in 1908; gardens lead down to beach. Interior features panelled bar, minstrel gallery. Most bedrooms have sea views; newer ones with colonial feel. Restaurant offers views from a large leaded window.

at Northrepps Southeast : 3 mi. by A 149 and Northrepps rd – ✉ Cromer

Shrublands Farm without rest
✉ NR27 0AA – ✆ (01263) 579 297 – www.shrublandsfarm.com – Fax (01263) 579 297 – Closed 24-31 December
3 rm – 🛉£ 42/46 🛉🛉£ 64/72
◆ Part 18C arable farm in wooded gardens. Conservatory, lounge, neat rooms with cut flowers and garden views. Guests are encouraged to explore the farm.

ENGLAND

CROPSTON – Leicestershire – 502 Q25 — 16 B2

London 106 mi. – Birmingham 49 mi. – Sheffield 67 mi. – Leicester 6 mi.

Horseshoe Cottage Farm
Roecliffe Rd, Hallgates, Northwest : 1 mi. on Woodhouse Eaves rd ✉ LE7 7HQ – ✆ (0116) 235 00 38 – www.horseshoecottagefarm.com
3 rm – 🛉£ 63 🛉🛉£ 95 **Rest** – Menu £ 20
◆ Extended farmhouse in pleasant countryside location beside Bradgate Country Park. Comfortable lounge; homely touches in spacious, traditional bedrooms. Home-cooked food in communal dining room; local produce well used, including some from the vegetable garden.

CROSTHWAITE – Cumbria – 502 L21 – see Kendal

CROYDE – Devon – 503 H30 – ✉ Braunton — 2 C1

London 232 mi. – Barnstaple 10 mi. – Exeter 50 mi. – Taunton 61 mi.

Whiteleaf
Hobbs Hill ✉ EX33 1PN – ✆ (01271) 890 266 – www.thewhiteleaf.co.uk – Closed Christmas and January
5 rm – 🛉£ 58/62 🛉🛉£ 76/130 **Rest** – *(by arrangement)* Carte £ 26/34
◆ Homely guesthouse close to North Devon and Somerset coastal path; views of Baggy Point, Lundy Island. Co-ordinated accommodation with mini-bars: choose the four-poster room. Restaurant looks out onto garden.

CRUDWELL – Wilts. – 503 N29 – see Malmesbury

CUCKFIELD – West Sussex – 504 T30 – pop. 3 266 — 7 D2

London 40 mi. – Brighton 15 mi.

Ockenden Manor
Ockenden Lane ✉ RH17 5LD – ✆ (01444) 416 111 – www.ockenden-manor.co.uk – Fax (01444) 415 549
19 rm – 🛉£ 110/120 🛉🛉£ 332 – 3 suites
Rest – Modern – *(booking essential at lunch)* Menu £ 27 (lunch)/50
Spec. Scallops with gratin of razor clams and peas. Turbot with globe artichokes and langoustines. Cherry and almond clafoutis with crème fraîche ice cream.
◆ Secluded part 16C manor; heritage is on display in antique furnished bedrooms, many named after previous owners. Ideal for golfers, historians and the romantic. Appealing seasonal cooking, with a superb balance of flavours, served in formal yet relaxed surroundings. Impeccable service.

Cuckoo

1 Broad St ✉ RH17 5LJ – ✆ (01444) 414 184 – www.cuckoorestaurant.co.uk – Closed 25 December, Sunday dinner and Monday

Rest – Modern – Carte £ 21/32

◆ Charming 17C cottage in heart of pretty village, with log fire, fresh flowers, personable owner and informal ambience. Tasty, modern British cooking uses fresh, seasonal produce.

CUDDINGTON – **Buckinghamshire** – **503** M24 Great Britain **11** C2

London 48 mi. – Aylesbury 6 mi. – Oxford 17 mi.

Waddesdon Manor★★ **AC**, NE : 6 mi. via Cuddington Hill, Cannon's Hill, Waddesdon Hill and A 41

The Crown

Aylesbury Rd ✉ HP18 0BB – ✆ (01844) 292 222 – www.thecrowncuddington.co.uk – Closed Sunday dinner

Rest – Menu £ 17 – Carte £ 18/26

◆ Attractive thatched pub with traditional styling, welcoming atmosphere and friendly team. Seasonal menus display hearty comfort food in the winter and lighter dishes in the summer.

CULLINGWORTH – **W. Yorks.** – **502** O22 – **see Haworth**

CURY – **Cornwall** – **503** E33 – **see Helston**

CUTNALL GREEN – **Worcs.** – **503** N27 – **see Droitwich Spa**

CUXHAM – **Oxfordshire** – **504** Q29 **11** C2

London 49 mi. – Hillingdon 32 mi. – Reading 18 mi. – Milton Keynes 61 mi.

The Half Moon

✉ OX49 5NF – ✆ (01491) 614 151 – www.thehalf-moon.com – Closed Sunday dinner

Rest – Carte £ 21/28

◆ Sympathetically restored 17C whitewashed pub in a sleepy village. Twice-daily blackboard menu features local, ethical produce: veg from the kitchen garden and plenty of offal.

DALTON – **N. Yorks.** – **502** O20 – **see Richmond**

DANEHILL – **East Sussex** Great Britain **8** A2

London 53 mi. – Brighton 21 mi. – East Grinstead 7 mi.

Sheffield Park Garden★, S : 3 mi. on A 275

Coach & Horses

School Lane, Northeast : 0.75 mi. on Chelwood Common rd ✉ RH17 7JF – ✆ (01825) 740 369 – www.coachandhorses.danehill.biz – Fax (01825) 740 369 – Closed 25 December dinner, 26 December and Sunday dinner

Rest – Carte £ 20/30

◆ Charming firelit locals bar and more formal dining area in converted stables. Traditional menus utilise locally sourced ingredients and often include offal as well as more unusual cuts of meat.

DARGATE – **Kent** – **see Faversham**

DARLEY – **North Yorkshire** **22** B2

London 217 mi. – Harrogate 8 mi. – Ripon 16 mi.

Cold Cotes

Cold Cotes Rd, Felliscliffe, South : 2 mi. by Kettlesing rd, going straight over crossroads and on Harrogate rd ✉ HG3 2LW – ✆ (01423) 770 937 – www.coldcotes.com

6 rm – †£ 69 ††£ 79/93 **Rest** – *(by arrangement)* Menu £ 24

◆ Remotely set farmhouse in mature gardens; welcoming hosts and well-kept bedrooms, split between the house and the barn conversion. Dining room with pleasant country views; tasty home-cooking makes use of produce from the garden.

DARLEY ABBEY – Derbs. – 502 P25 – see Derby

DARLINGTON – Darlington – 502 P20 – pop. 86 082 — 22 B1

London 251 mi. – Leeds 61 mi. – Middlesbrough 14 mi. – Newcastle upon Tyne 35 mi.

Teesside Airport : ✆ (08712) 242426, E : 6 mi. by A 67

The Dolphin Centre, Horsemarket ✆ (01325) 388666, tic@darlington.gov.uk

Blackwell Grange Briar Close, ✆ (01325) 464 458

Stressholme Snipe Lane, ✆ (01325) 461 002

at Croft-on-Tees South : 4.25 mi. on A 167 – ✉ Darlington

Clow Beck House

Monk End Farm, West : 0.75 mi. by A 167 off Barton rd ✉ DL2 2SW – ✆ (01325) 721 075 – www.clowbeckhouse.co.uk – Fax (01325) 720 419 – closed 24 December-2 January

13 rm – †£ 85 ††£ 135

Rest – *(dinner only) (residents only)* Carte £ 28/41 **s**

◆ Collection of stone houses styled on an old farm building. The residence has a friendly, homely atmosphere. Spacious rooms with individual character. Tasty, home-cooked meals.

ENGLAND

at Hurworth-on-Tees South : 5.5 mi. by A 167

The Bay Horse

45 The Green ✉ DL2 2AA – ✆ (01325) 720 663 – www.thebayhorsehurworth.com – Fax (01325) 729 840 – Closed Sunday dinner

Rest – Menu £ 15 (lunch) – Carte £ 22/38

◆ Smart village pub with pleasant terrace and gardens. Wide-ranging menu offers largely hearty classics; presentation ranges from simple and rustic to more modern and intricate.

at Headlam Northwest : 8 mi. by A 67 – ✉ Gainford

Headlam Hall

✉ DL2 3HA – ✆ (01325) 730 238 – www.headlamhall.co.uk – Fax (01325) 730 790 – Closed 25 and 26 December

38 rm – †£ 90 ††£ 115 – 2 suites **Rest** – Carte £ 24/40

◆ Part Georgian, part Jacobean manor house in delightful, secluded countryside with charming walled gardens. Period interior furnishings and antiques. Good leisure facilities. Country house restaurant in four distinctively decorated rooms.

DARTMOUTH – Devon – 503 J32 – pop. 5 512 — 2 C3

London 236 mi. – Exeter 36 mi. – Plymouth 35 mi.

The Engine House, Mayor's Ave ✆ (01803) 834224, holidays@discoverdartmouth.com

Town★★ (<★) - Old Town - Butterwalk★ - Dartmouth Castle (<★★★) AC

Start Point (<★), S : 13 mi. (including 1 mi. on foot)

Dart Marina

rm, AC rest,

Sandquay ✉ TQ6 9PH – ✆ (01803) 832 580 – www.dartmarina.com – Fax (01803) 835 040

47 rm – †£ 95/185 ††£ 130/195 – 2 suites

Rest *River Restaurant* – *(dinner only and Sunday lunch)* Menu £ 33 (dinner)

Rest *Wildfire* – ✆ (01803) 837 180 – Carte £ 28/39

◆ Lovely location with excellent views over the Dart Marina. The hotel has smart, comfy bedrooms, many with balconies. Welcoming, bright, modern public areas. Stylish River Restaurant; terrace overlooks river. Modern, informal Wildfire offers eclectic menus.

Royal Castle

11 The Quay ✉ TQ6 9PS – ✆ (01803) 833 033 – www.royalcastle.co.uk – Fax (01803) 835 445

25 rm – †£ 95/105 ††£ 185/199

Rest – Menu £ 17/21 **s** – Carte £ 20/29 **s**

◆ Harbour views and 18C origins enhance this smart hotel with its cosy bar and open log fires. Each of the comfortable rooms is individually styled, some boast four-poster beds. Harbour-facing restaurant particularly proud of sourcing fresh fish.

The New Angel Rooms

51 Victoria Rd ✉ TQ6 9RT – ✆ (01803) 839 425 – www.thenewangel.co.uk – Fax (01803) 839 505 – Closed January

6 rm – †£ 85/115 ††£ 85/150

Rest ***The New Angel*** – see restaurant listing

◆ Characterful townhouse towards the edge of town with snug lounge and smart breakfast room. Immensely charming, individually designed bedrooms boast bold designs and a real sense of quality.

Broome Court without rest

Broomhill, West : 2 mi. by A 3122 and Venn Lane ✉ TQ6 0LD – ✆ (01803) 834 275 – Fax (01803) 833 260

3 rm – †£ 65/85 ††£ 120/150

◆ Pretty house in a stunning, secluded location. Two sitting rooms: one for winter, one for summer. Breakfast "en famille" in huge kitchen, complete with Aga. Cottagey bedrooms.

The New Angel (John Burton-Race)

2 South Embankment ✉ TQ6 9BH – ✆ (01803) 839 425 – www.thenewangel.co.uk – Fax (01803) 839 505 – Closed January, Sunday and Monday

Rest – *(booking essential)* Menu £ 25/30 – Carte £ 36/48

Spec. Dartmouth crab tortellini. Pan-fried wild sea bass with shrimp butter sauce. Chocolate fondant with vanilla ice cream.

◆ Split over two floors, with gold walls, chandeliers, pleasant estuary views and stylish cocktail bar above. Skilful, classical cooking has French undertones; well-sourced produce is local and seasonal. Bedrooms available a short walk away.

The Seahorse

5 South Embankment ✉ TQ6 9BH – ✆ (01803) 835 147 – www.seahorserestaurant.co.uk – Closed Tuesday lunch, Sunday and Monday

Rest – Seafood – *(booking essential)* Menu £ 20 (lunch) – Carte £ 27/39

◆ Picturesque location overlooking estuary/harbour; some al fresco tables. Classic bistro dishes with strong seafood slant; cooked in charcoal oven. Twice daily menu; simplicity is key.

Jan and Freddies Brasserie

10 Fairfax Place ✉ TQ6 9AD – ✆ (01803) 832 491 – www.janandfreddiesbrasserie.co.uk – Closed 1-21 January and Sunday

Rest – *(dinner only and lunch June to October) (booking advisable)* Carte £ 22/37

◆ Bright, stylish brasserie in the town centre, with welcoming service and a personal touch. Menus are classically based, with dishes crafted from local, seasonal produce.

The Floating Bridge

By Lower Ferry, Coombe Rd ✉ TQ6 9PQ – ✆ (01803) 832 354 – www.dartmarina.com – Closed 5-31 January, November to March Sunday dinner and Tuesday

Rest – Carte £ 15/25

◆ Unusually situated on a ferry slip road. Traditional, predominantly local menu features tasty, wholesome fare, with greater variety and fish specials available in the summer.

ENGLAND

at Kingswear East : via lower ferry – ✉ Dartmouth

Nonsuch House

Church Hill, from lower ferry take first right onto Church Hill before Steam Packet Inn ✉ TQ6 0BX – ✆ (01803) 752 829 – www.nonsuch-house.co.uk – Fax (01803) 752 357

4 rm – †£ 88/110 ††£ 113/145

Rest – *(closed Tuesday, Wednesday and Saturday) (dinner only) (residents only, set menu only, unlicensed)* Menu £ 35 **s**

◆ Charming, personably run Edwardian house stunningly sited above the river town. Smart conservatory terrace and large, well appointed bedrooms. Good, homely breakfasts. Fresh, local, seasonal cooking.

at Strete Southwest : 4 mi. on A 379 – ✉ Dartmouth

The Kings Arms

Dartmouth Rd ✉ TQ6 0RW – ✆ (01803) 770 377 – www.kingsarms-dartmouth.co.uk

Rest – Carte £ 22/35

◆ Dour exterior hides gem of a pub serving wide-ranging menu with focus on seafood; locally caught, simply cooked and very tasty. Delightful rear garden with fantastic coastal views.

at Blackawton West : 6 mi. by B 3122

The Normandy Arms

Chapel St ✉ TQ9 7BN – ✆ (01803) 712 884 – www.thenormandyarms.co.uk – Fax (01803) 712 734 – Closed 25 December, 1 January, 1 week in spring, Sunday dinner, Monday (except in August) and lunch Tuesday-Saturday

Rest – *(booking essential at dinner)* Carte £ 22/32

◆ Refurbished village pub, popular with locals and simple in style with comfy leather seats and two distinct dining areas. Straightforward cooking, homemade using local produce.

ENGLAND

DATCHWORTH – Hertfordshire – 504 T28 — 12 B2

London 31 mi. – Luton 15 mi. – Stevenage 6 mi.

Coltsfoot Country Retreat

Coltsfoot Lane, Bulls Green, South : 0.75 mi. by Bramfield Rd ✉ SG3 6SB – ✆ (01438) 212 800 – www.coltsfoot.com – Fax (01438) 212 840 – Closed 24 and 25 December

15 rm – †£ 135 ††£ 160

Rest – *(closed Sunday) (dinner only) (booking essential)* Carte £ 34/40

◆ Stylish hotel, once a working farm, in 40 rural acres. Lounge bar with log-burning stove. Highly individual rooms around courtyard have vaulted ceilings and rich furnishings. Main barn houses restaurant: concise modern menus employ good seasonal produce.

The Tilbury

Watton Rd ✉ SG3 6TB – ✆ (01438) 815 550 – www.thetilbury.co.uk – Fax (01438) 718 340 – Closed Sunday dinner

Rest – Menu £ 17/22 – Carte £ 25/35

◆ Red brick pub with flower baskets, terrace, garden and fresh, contemporary interior. Modern European menu offers honest, locally sourced food. Cookery school spans the globe.

DAVENTRY – Northamptonshire – 504 Q27 – pop. 21 731 — 16 B3

London 79 mi. – Coventry 23 mi. – Leicester 31 mi. – Northampton 13 mi.

9 Norton Rd, ✆ (01327) 702 829

27 Hellidon Lakes H. & C.C. Hellidon, ✆ (01327) 262 550

18 Staverton Park Staverton, ✆ (01327) 302 000

Fawsley Hall

Fawsley, South : 6.5 mi. by A 45 off A 361 ✉ NN11 3BA – ✆ (01327) 892 000 – www.fawsleyhall.com – Fax (01327) 892 001

53 rm – †£ 175 ††£ 325 – 5 suites – ††£ 350/475

Rest *Equilibrium* – *(Closed Sunday and Monday) (dinner only) (booking essential)* Menu £ 59

Rest *Bess's Brasserie* – Carte £ 20/32

◆ Set in 2,000 peaceful acres, a luxurious Tudor manor house boasting Georgian/Victorian wings, a grand hall and exclusive leisure club and spa. Well-appointed bedrooms: most characterful in main house; more contemporary in annexe. Ambitious, innovative menu in intimate Equilibrium. Brasserie classics in Bess's.

at Staverton Southwest : 2.75 mi. by A 45 off A 425 – ✉ Daventry

Colledges House
Oakham Lane, off Glebe Lane ✉ NN11 6JQ – ✆ (01327) 702 737 – www.colledgeshouse.co.uk – Closed 25 December
4 rm – ♦£ 68/70 ♦♦£ 102/106
Rest – *(by arrangement, communal dining)* Menu £ 32
◆ Part 17C house in a quiet village. Full of charm with antiques, curios, portraits and an inglenook fireplace. Homely rooms are in the main house and an adjacent cottage. Evening meals served at elegant oak table.

DAWLISH – Devon – 503 J32 – pop. 10 443 — 2 D2

London 184 mi. – Exeter 13 mi. – Teignmouth 3 mi.

Lammas Park House
3 Priory Rd, via High St and Strand Hill ✉ EX7 9JF – ✆ (01626) 888 064 – www.lammasparkhouse.co.uk – Fax (01626) 888 064
3 rm – ♦£ 70 ♦♦£ 90
Rest – *(by arrangement, communal dining)* Menu £ 19
◆ Lovely early 19C townhouse boasting a superb secluded rear terrace garden and handsome period details in situ. Clean, uncluttered rooms. Sit and admire views from observatory. Dinners served in communal style; owners are experienced restaurateurs.

DAYLESFORD Glos – Gloucestershire – 503 O28 – See Stow-on-the-Wold

DEAL – Kent – 504 Y30 – pop. 29 248 — 9 D2

London 78 mi. – Canterbury 19 mi. – Dover 8 mi. – Margate 16 mi.
The Landmark Centre, 129 High St ✆ (01304) 369576, info@deal.gov.uk
Walmer & Kingsdown Kingsdown The Leas, ✆ (01304) 373 256

Dunkerley's
19 Beach St ✉ CT14 7AH – ✆ (01304) 375 016 – www.dunkerleys.co.uk – Fax (01304) 380 187
16 rm – ♦£ 60/70 ♦♦£ 80/130
Rest *Restaurant* – see restaurant listing
◆ The hotel faces the beach and the Channel. Bedrooms are comfortably furnished and the principal rooms have jacuzzis. Comfortable bar offers a lighter menu than the restaurant.

Sutherland House
186 London Rd ✉ CT14 9PT – ✆ (01304) 362 853 – www.sutherlandhousehotel.co.uk – Fax (01304) 381 146
4 rm – ♦£ 55/57 ♦♦£ 75 **Rest** – *(by arrangement)* Menu £ 27
◆ An Edwardian house with garden in a quiet residential area. Stylish, welcoming bedrooms are individually decorated. Friendly, relaxed atmosphere. Refined dining room with homely ambience.

Restaurant – at Dunkerley's Hotel
19 Beach St ✉ CT14 7AH – ✆ (01304) 375 016 – www.dunkerleys.co.uk – Fax (01304) 380 187 – Closed dinner Sunday and Monday
Rest – Seafood – Menu £ 16/27
◆ With views of the Channel, the restaurant is best known for preparing locally caught seafood, although non-seafood options are also available. Wide ranging wine list.

at Worth Northwest : 5 mi. by A 258

Solley Farm House without rest
The Street ✉ CT14 0DG – ✆ (01304) 613 701 – www.solleyfarmhouse.co.uk – closed 25-26 December
3 rm – ♦£ 75 ♦♦£ 100
◆ 300 year old house, overlooking the village pond and church. Full of character and charm, with a very welcoming owner. Organic breakfasts served on the terrace in summer.

ENGLAND

DEDDINGTON – Oxfordshire – 503 Q28 – pop. 1 595 — 10 B1

London 72 mi. – Birmingham 46 mi. – Coventry 33 mi. – Oxford 18 mi.

Deddington Arms

Horsefair ✉ OX15 0SH – ☎ (01869) 338 364 – www.oxfordshire-hotels.co.uk – Fax (01869) 337 010

27 rm – †£ 55/90 ††£ 99/130 **Rest** – Menu £ 19 – Carte £ 24/30

◆ Traditional coaching inn with a smart, modish ambience, on the market place. Spacious modern bedrooms in rear extension. Stylish rooms, two four-postered, in the main house. The restaurant is decorated in a warm and contemporary style.

The Old Post House without rest

New St, on A4260 ✉ OX15 0SP – ☎ (01869) 338 978 – www.oldposthouse.co.uk

3 rm – †£ 55 ††£ 85

◆ Antiques abound in this beautifully kept guest house, with tea and cake on arrival and very comfortable bedrooms. Enjoy an Aga-cooked breakfast with homemade preserves in the delightful walled garden.

DEDHAM – Essex – 504 W28 – pop. 1 847 – ✉ Colchester — 13 D2

Great Britain

London 63 mi. – Chelmsford 30 mi. – Colchester 8 mi. – Ipswich 12 mi.

Stour Valley★ – Flatford Mill★, E : 6 mi. by B 1029, A 12 and B 1070

ENGLAND

Maison Talbooth

Stratford Rd, West : 0.5 mi. ✉ CO7 6HP – ☎ (01206) 322 150 – www.milsomhotels.com – Fax (01206) 322 309

12 rm – †£ 175 ††£ 350

Rest ***Le Talbooth*** – see restaurant listing

◆ Quiet, Victorian country house with intimate atmosphere, lawned gardens and views over river valley. Some rooms are smart and contemporary, others more traditional in style.

Milsoms

rm, rest,

Stratford Rd, West : 0.75 mi. ✉ CO7 6HW – ☎ (01206) 322 795 – www.milsomhotels.com – Fax (01206) 323 689

15 rm – †£ 85 ††£ 145, £ 15

Rest – *(bookings not accepted)* Carte £ 21/31

◆ Modern hotel overlooking Constable's Dedham Vale with attractive garden and stylish lounge. Bright, airy and welcoming rooms feature unfussy décor and modern colours. Likeably modish, wood-floored bistro.

Le Talbooth

Gun Hill, West : 1 mi. ✉ CO7 6HP – ☎ (01206) 323 150 – www.milsomhotels.com – Fax (01206) 322 309

Rest – *(closed Sunday dinner October-May)* Menu £ 28 (lunch) – Carte £ 37/52

◆ Part Tudor house in attractive riverside setting. Exposed beams and real fires contribute to the traditional atmosphere. Menus combine the classic and the more modern. Well chosen wine list.

Fountain House & Dedham Hall with rm

Brook St ✉ CO7 6AD – ☎ (01206) 323 027 – www.dedhamhall.co.uk – Fax (01206) 323 293 – Closed Christmas-New Year

5 rm – †£ 55 ††£ 95

Rest – *(Closed Sunday-Monday from November to January) (dinner only) (booking essential)* Menu £ 32

◆ In a quiet, country house dating back to 15C with traditional, uncluttered ambience. Weekly changing traditionally based set menu. Comfortable rooms also available.

The Sun Inn with rm

High St ✉ CO7 6DF – ☎ (01206) 323 351 – www.thesuninndedham.com – Closed 25-26 December

5 rm – †£ 68 ††£ 150 **Rest** – Menu £ 14 – Carte £ 18/28

◆ Sunny-coloured pub in idyllic village location. Italian-themed à la carte features simple, tasty dishes. Bar board menu offers sandwiches, terrines and tarts. Contemporary bedrooms.

DENHAM – Buckinghamshire – 504 S29 – pop. 2 269 Great Britain 11 D3

London 20 mi. – Buckingham 42 mi. – Oxford 41 mi.

Windsor Castle★★★, Eton★★ and Windsor★, S : 10 mi. by A 412

The Swan Inn

Village Rd ✉ UB9 5BH – ✆ (01895) 832 085 – www.swaninndenham.co.uk – Fax (01895) 835 516 – Closed 25-26 December

Rest – *(booking essential)* Carte £ 20/27

◆ Wisteria-clad, red-brick Georgian pub with pleasant terrace and gardens. Menus change with the seasons and offer plenty of interest; sides are appealing and pudding is a must.

DENMEAD – Hampshire – 503 Q31 – pop. 5 788 6 B2

London 70 mi. – Portsmouth 11 mi. – Southampton 27 mi.

Barnard's

Hambledon Rd ✉ PO7 6NU – ✆ (023) 9225 7788 – www.barnardsrestaurant.co.uk – Fax (023) 9225 7788 – Closed 1 week Christmas, Saturday lunch, Sunday and Monday

Rest – Menu £ 15 **s** – Carte £ 27/38 **s**

◆ Traditional neighbourhood restaurant with good local following. Husband and wife cook, supported by friendly team. Concise menus offer fresh, neatly presented, classically based dishes.

Good food at moderate prices? Look for the Bib Gourmand .

ENGLAND

DERBY – Derby – 502 P25 – pop. 229 407 Great Britain 16 B2

London 132 mi. – Birmingham 40 mi. – Coventry 49 mi. – Leicester 29 mi.

Nottingham East Midlands Airport, Castle Donington : ✆ (0871) 919 9000, SE : 12 mi. by A 6 X

Assembly Rooms, Market Pl ✆ (01332) 255802, tourism@derby.gov.uk

18 Sinfin Wilmore Rd, ✆ (01332) 766 323

18 Mickleover Uttoxeter Rd, ✆ (01332) 516 011

18 Kedleston Park Quardon Kedlston, ✆ (01332) 840 035

36 Breadsall Priory H. & C.C. Morley Moor Rd, ✆ (01332) 836 106

18 Allestree Park Allestree Allestree Hall, ✆ (01332) 550 616

City★ – Museum and Art Gallery★ (Collection of Derby Porcelain★) YZ **M1** – Royal Crown Derby Museum★ **AC** Z **M2**

Kedleston Hall★★ **AC**, NW : 4.5 mi. by Kedleston Rd X

Plan on next page

at Darley Abbey North : 2.5 mi. off A 6 - X – ✉ Derby

Darleys

Darley Abbey Mill ✉ DE22 1DZ – ✆ (01332) 364 987 – www.darleys.com – Fax (01332) 364 987 – closed 25 December-10 January and Sunday dinner

Rest – Menu £ 18 (lunch) – Carte (dinner) £ 33/38

◆ A converted cotton mill in an attractive riverside setting. The interior is modern, stylish and comfortable. High quality British cuisine of satisfying, classical character.

at Weston Underwood Northwest : 5.5 mi. by A 52 - X - and Kedleston Rd – ✉ Derby

Park View Farm without rest

✉ DE6 4PA – ✆ (01335) 360 352 – www.parkviewfarm.co.uk – Fax (01335) 360 352 – Closed Christmas

3 rm – †£ 50/60 ††£ 85/90

◆ Friendly couple run this elegant house on a working farm, in sight of Kedleston Hall. Antique-filled lounge with oils and a Victorian fireplace. Simple rooms in stripped pine.

DERBY

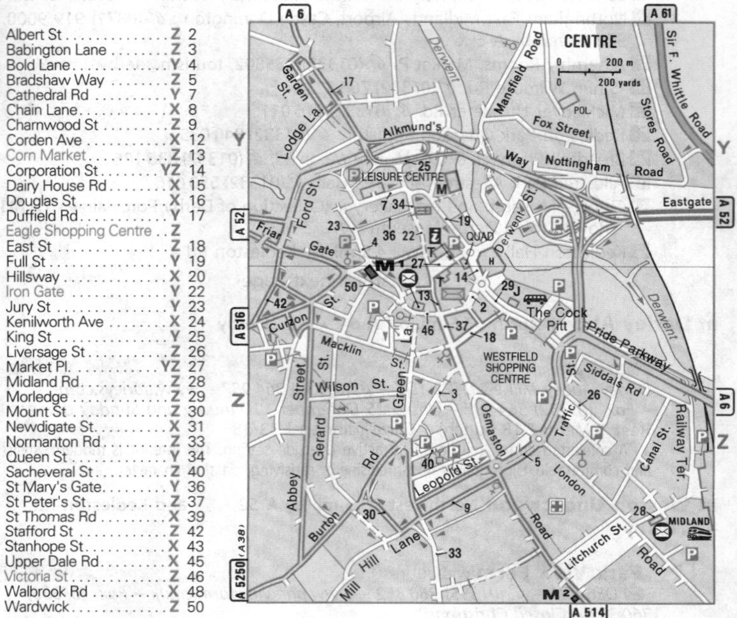

ENGLAND

DEVIZES – Wiltshire – 503 O29 – pop. 14 379 4 C2

London 98 mi. – Bristol 38 mi. – Salisbury 25 mi. – Southampton 50 mi.

Cromwell House, Market Pl ✆ (01380) 729408, all.tic's@wiltshire.gov.uk

Erlestoke, ✆ (01380) 831 069

St John's Church★★ – Market Place★ – Wiltshire Heritage Museum★ **AC**

Potterne (Porch House★★) S : 2.5 mi. by A 360 – E : Vale of Pewsey★. Stonehenge★★★ **AC**, SE : 16 mi. by A 360 and A 344 – Avebury★★ (The Stones★, Church★) NE : 7 mi. by A 361

at Marden Southeast : 6.5 mi. by A 342 – ✉ Devizes

The Millstream

✉ SN10 3RH – ✆ (01380) 848 308 – www.the-millstream.net – Fax (01380) 848 337 – Closed Monday (except bank holidays)

Rest – Carte £ 21/33

◆ Charming pub with chic country interior and delightfully eye-catching décor. Traditional pub dishes use local, seasonal ingredients, with contemporary influences and a French edge.

at Potterne South : 2.25 mi. on A 360 – ✉ Devizes

Blounts Court Farm without rest

Coxhill Lane ✉ SN10 5PH – ✆ (01380) 727 180 – www.blountscourtfarm.co.uk

3 rm – ♦£ 42/72 ♦♦£ 70/72

◆ Working farm personally run by charming owner: good value accommodation in blissful spot. Cosy rooms in converted barn are handsomely furnished with interesting artefacts.

at Rowde Northwest : 2 mi. by A 361 on A 342 – ✉ Devizes

The George & Dragon with rm

High Street ✉ SN10 2PN – ✆ (01380) 723 053 – www.thegeorgeanddragonrowde.co.uk – Closed Sunday dinner

3 rm – ♦£ 55/65 ♦♦£ 55/105

Rest – Seafood – *(booking essential)* Menu £ 18 (lunch) – Carte £ 25/40

◆ Unspectacular from the outside but warm and characterful inside. Excellent fish specials created from the daily catch accompany a menu of comforting British classics. Well-equipped, trendy-meets-old-world bedrooms.

DICKLEBURGH – Norfolk – 504 X26 – see Diss

DIDSBURY – Gtr Manchester – 502 N23 – see Manchester

DIPTFORD – Devon – 503 I32 – ✉ Totnes 2 C2

London 202 mi. – Plymouth 20 mi. – Torbay 16 mi. – Exeter 31 mi.

The Old Rectory

✉ TQ9 7NY – ✆ (01548) 821 575 – www.oldrectorydiptford.co.uk – Closed January, February and minimum 2 night stay

5 rm – ♦£ 65 ♦♦£ 110 **Rest** – *(by arrangement)* Menu £ 28

◆ Classic Georgian house of cavernous proportions with a three-acre garden. The lounge, though, is small and cosy. Airy rooms benefit from rural views; luxurious bathrooms. Food taken seriously: fine home-cooked meals served with pride.

DISS – Norfolk – 504 X26 – pop. 7 444 15 C2

London 98 mi. – Ipswich 25 mi. – Norwich 21 mi. – Thetford 17 mi.

Meres Mouth, Mere St ✆ (01379) 650523, dtic@s-norfolk.gov.uk

at Dickleburgh Northeast : 4.5 mi. by A 1066 off A 140 – ✉ Diss

Dickleburgh Hall Country House without rest

Semere Green Lane, North : 1 mi. ✉ IP21 4NT – ✆ (01379) 741 259 – www.dickhall.co.uk – March-October

3 rm – ♦£ 55 ♦♦£ 75/85

◆ 16C house still in private hands. Trim rooms in traditional patterns, beamed lounge with an inglenook fireplace; snooker room and golf course.

ENGLAND

DITCHEAT – Somerset

4 C2

London 124 mi. – Bath 29 mi.

The Manor House Inn with rm

BA4 6RB – (01749) 860 276 – www.manorhouseinn.co.uk – Closed 25 December

3 rm – †£ 50 ††£ 90 **Rest** – Menu £ 25 – Carte £ 18/28

◆ Welcoming, equestrian-themed pub set on the Somerset Levels. Traditional open fires and a restored skittle alley are coupled with honest classical cooking and locally sourced produce. Former stables house cosy bedrooms with good mod cons.

DOGMERSFIELD – Hampshire

7 C1

London 44 mi. – Farnham 6 mi. – Fleet 2 mi.

Four Seasons

Dogmersfield Park, Chalky Lane RG27 8TD – (01252) 853 000 – www.fourseasons.com/hampshire – Fax (01252) 853 010

111 rm – †£ 225/334 ††£ 225/334, £ 27 – 21 suites

Rest *Seasons* – *(closed Sunday dinner and Monday)* Menu £ 49 (weekday dinner) – Carte £ 42/63

◆ Part Georgian splendour in extensive woodlands; many original features in situ. Superb spa facilities: vast selection of leisure pursuits. Luxurious, highly equipped bedrooms. Restaurant has thoroughly modish, relaxing feel.

ENGLAND

The sun's out? Then enjoy eating outside on the terrace:

DONCASTER

Albion Pl.	C	3
Apley Rd	C	5
Balby Rd	C	8
Broxholme Lane	C	
Carr House Rd.	C	
Chequer Ave	C	12
Chequer Rd	C	
Christ Church Rd.	C	
Church Way	C	
Cleveland St	C	
Colonnades Shopping Centre	C	
Cunningham Rd	C	17
East Laith Gate	C	24
Frenchgate Shopping Centre	C	
Grey Friars Rd	C	
Hall Gate	C	
Highfield Rd.	C	
High St.	C	36
Milton Walk	C	40
Nether Hall Rd.	C	43
North Bridge Rd	C	44
Queen's Rd	C	46
St George's Bridge	C	
St Jame's Bridge	C	48
St Jame's St	C	
Silver St	C	
South Parade	C	
Thorne Rd	C	
Trafford Way	C	
Waterdale	C	
Waterdale Shopping Centre	C	
White Rose Way	C	70
Wood St.	C	

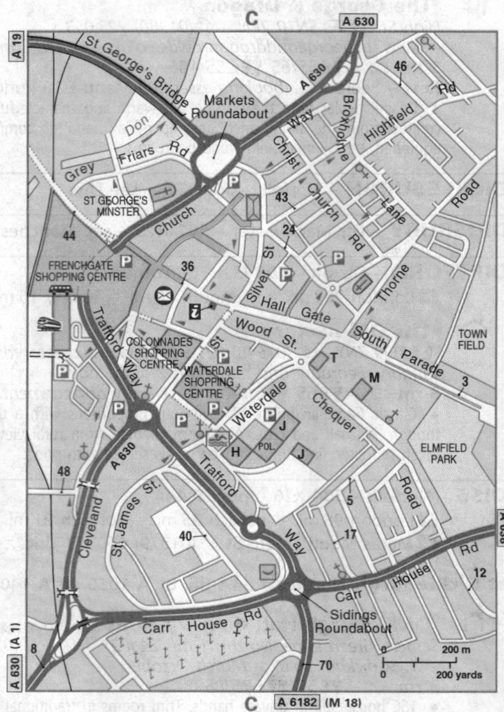

DONCASTER – South Yorkshire – 502 Q23 – pop. 67 977 23 C3

▶ London 173 mi. – Kingston-upon-Hull 46 mi. – Leeds 30 mi. – Nottingham 46 mi.
✈ Robin Hood Airport : ✆ (0871) 220 2210, SE : 7m off A638
ℹ 38-40 High St ✆ (01302) 734309, touristi.nformation@doncaster.gov.uk
18 Doncaster Town Moor Belle Vue Bawtry Rd, ✆ (01302) 533 778
18 Crookhill Park Conisborough, ✆ (01709) 862 979
18 Wheatley Amthorpe Rd, ✆ (01302) 831 655
9 Owston Park Owston Owston Lane, Carcroft, ✆ (01302) 330 821

Mount Pleasant

rm, AC rest, P VISA MC AE

Great North Rd, Southeast : 6 mi. on A 638 ✉ *DN11 0HW* – ✆ *(01302) 868 696* – *www.mountpleasant.co.uk* – *Fax (01302) 865 130*

54 rm – †£ 89/110 ††£ 160/175 – 2 suites **Rest *Garden*** – Carte £ 27/43

◆ Stone-built farmhouse with sympathetic extension. Traditionally styled throughout: wood panelled lounges and a small bar. Well-kept bedrooms, including one with a five-poster! Restaurant with garden views.

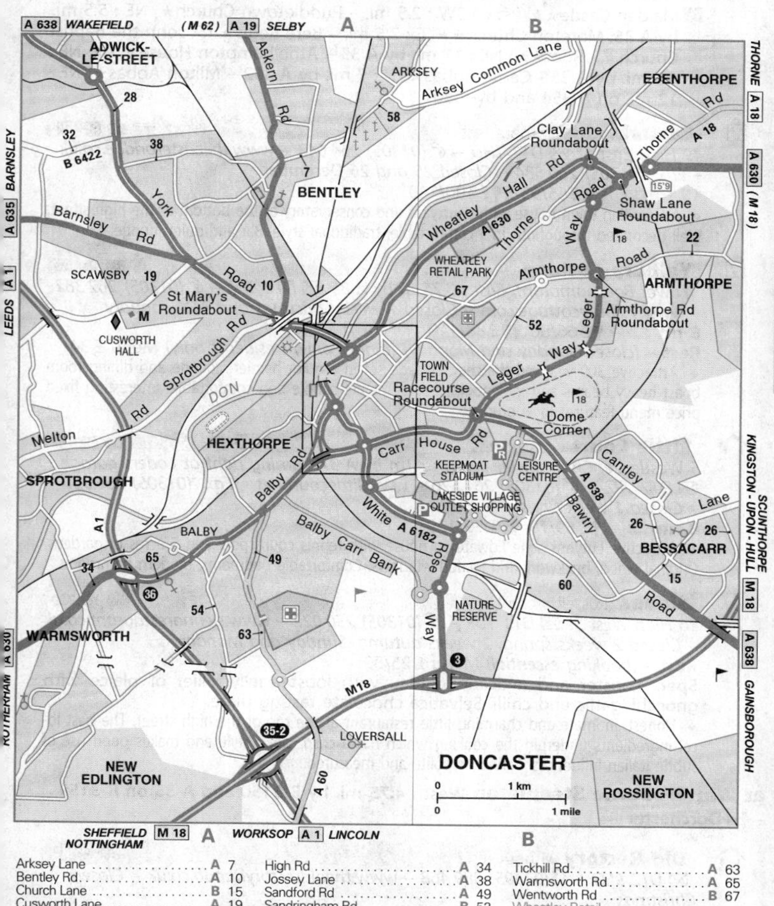

Arksey Lane	A	7
Bentley Rd	A	10
Church Lane	B	15
Cusworth Lane	A	19
Doncaster Rd	B	22
Goodison Boulevard	B	26
Great North Rd	A	28
Green Lane	A	32
High Rd	A	34
Jossey Lane	A	38
Sandford Rd	A	49
Sandringham Rd	B	52
Springwell Lane	A	54
Sprotbrough Rd	A	56
Station Rd	A	58
Stoops Lane	B	60
Tickhill Rd	A	63
Warmsworth Rd	A	65
Wentworth Rd	B	67
Wheatley Retail Park Shopping Centre	B	
Yorkshire Outlet Shopping Centre	B	

DONHEAD-ST-ANDREW – Wiltshire – 503 N30 4 C3

London 115 mi. – Bournemouth 34 mi. – Poole 32 mi. – Bath 37 mi.

Forester Inn

Lower Street ✉ SP7 9EE – ✆ (01747) 828 038 – Closed 25-26 December, Sunday dinner

Rest – Menu £ 16 (lunch) – Carte £ 20/32

◆ Thatched 13C stone pub with low beams and inglenooks. Modern British cooking, with Mediterranean/Asian influences: plenty of fish and seafood; locally sourced artisan cheeses.

DORCHESTER – Dorset – 503 M31 – pop. 16 171 4 C3

London 135 mi. – Bournemouth 27 mi. – Exeter 53 mi. – Southampton 53 mi.

11 Antelope Walk ✆ (01305) 267992, dorchester.tic@westdorset-dc.gov.uk

Came Down, ✆ (01305) 813 494

Town★ - Dorset County Museum★ **AC**

Maiden Castle★★ (<★) SW : 2.5 mi. – Puddletown Church★, NE : 5.5 mi. by A 35. Moreton Church★★, E : 7.5 mi. – Bere Regis★ (St John the Baptist Church★ - Roof★★) NE : 11 mi. by A 35 – Athelhampton House★ **AC**, NE : 6.5 mi. by A 35 - Cerne Abbas★, N : 7 mi. by A 352 – Milton Abbas★, NE : 12 mi. on A 354 and by-road

Casterbridge without rest

49 High East St ✉ DT1 1HU – ✆ (01305) 264 043 – www.thecasterbridge.co.uk – Fax (01305) 260 884 – Closed 25 and 26 December

15 rm – †£ 65/95 ††£ 100/140

◆ A Georgian town house with courtyard and conservatory at the bottom of the high street. Well decorated throughout in a comfortable, traditional style. Bar and quiet lounge.

Yalbury Cottage

(Lower Bockhampton), East : 3.75 m by A 35 ✉ DT2 8PZ – ✆ (01305) 262 382 – www.yalburycottage.com – Closed 1 week Christmas and 3-26 January

8 rm – †£ 66/80 ††£ 88/110

Rest – *(closed Sunday and Monday) (dinner only) (residents only)* Menu £ 34

◆ Attractive 300 year old thatched cottage set in a quiet hamlet. Lounge and dining room boast heavy beams and inglenooks. Bedrooms are simple and comfortable. Interesting fixed price menu features local produce.

Little Court without rest

5 Westleaze, Charminster , North : 1m by A 37, turning right at Loders garage ✉ DT2 9PZ – ✆ (01305) 261 576 – www.littlecourt.net – Fax (01305) 261 359 – Closed 1 week Christmas

8 rm – †£ 69/79 ††£ 79/129

◆ Attractive Lutyens style Edwardian house with tennis court, pool and 5 acres of gardens. Original wood, brickwork and leaded windows. Comfortable bedrooms; modern bathrooms.

Sienna (Russell Brown)

36 High West St ✉ DT1 1UP – ✆ (01305) 250 022 – www.siennarestaurant.co.uk – Closed 2 weeks spring, 2 weeks autumn, Sunday and Monday

Rest – *(booking essential)* Menu £ 25/39

Spec. Lobster and avocado gateau with lobster jelly. Fillet of plaice with gnocchi, garlic and chilli. Selvatica chocolate tasting plate.

◆ Honest, intimate and charming little restaurant at the top of the high street. The best local ingredients underpin the cooking which has a crisp, clean style and makes good use of subtle Italian influences. Service is polite and measured.

at Winterbourne Steepleton West : 4.75 mi. by B 3150 and A 35 on B 3159 – ✉ Dorchester

Old Rectory without rest

✉ DT2 9LG – ✆ (01305) 889 468 – www.theoldrectorybandb.co.uk – Closed Christmas

4 rm – †£ 60 ††£ 70/100

◆ Built in 1850 and having a characterful exterior. Situated in the middle of a charming village. Well kept, good sized rooms overlook the pleasant garden.

THE ARTISTRY OF CHAMPAGNE

MAISON FONDÉE EN 1776
BRUT PREMIER
LOUIS ROEDERER
CHAMPAGNE
BRUT
REIMS
12 % vol.
e 750 ml

DORRIDGE – West Midlands – 503 O26 – ✉ Birmingham **19 C2**

London 109 mi. – Birmingham 11 mi. – Warwick 11 mi.

XX **The Forest** with rm — AC rest, P VISA AE

25 Station Approach ✉ B93 8JA – ✆ (01564) 772 120 – www.forest-hotel.com – Fax (01564) 732 680 – Closed 25 December

12 rm – †£ 95/110 ††£ 120/140, ☕ £ 10

Rest – *(closed Sunday dinner)* Menu £ 16 (mid-week dinner) – Carte £ 21/29

◆ Attractive red-brick and timber former pub with a busy ambience. Food is its backbone: modern classics served in stylish bar and restaurant. Cool, modern bedrooms.

DOUGLAS – Isle of Man – 502 G21 – see Man (Isle of)

DOVER

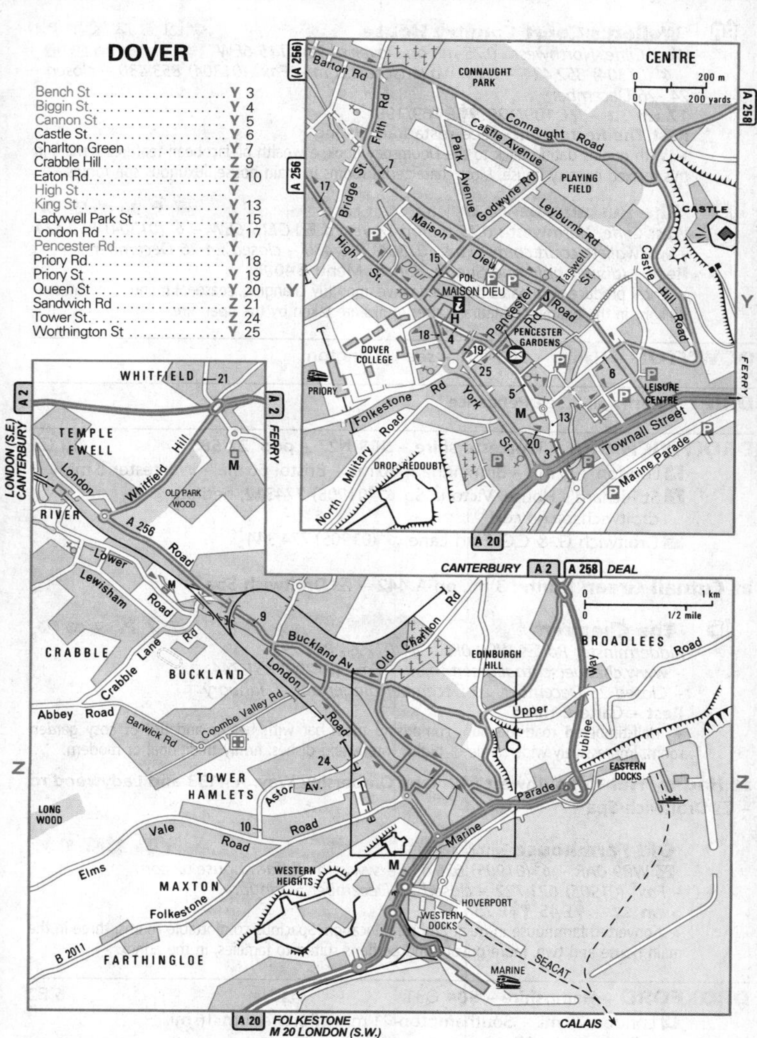

DOVER – Kent – 504 Y30 – pop. 34 087 Great Britain 9 D2

London 76 mi. – Brighton 84 mi.

to France (Calais) (P & O Stena Line) frequent services daily (1 h 15 mn) – to France (Calais) (SeaFrance S.A.) frequent services daily (1 h 30 mn) – to France (Boulogne) (SpeedFerries) 3-5 daily (50 mn)

The Old Town Gaol, Biggin ☎ (01304) 205108, tic@doveruk.com

Castle★★ **AC** Y

White Cliffs, Langdon Cliffs, NE : 1 mi. on A 2 Z and A 258

Plan on preceding page

at St Margaret's at Cliffe Northeast : 4 mi. by A 258 - Z – ✉ Dover

Wallett's Court Country House

West Cliffe, Northwest : 0.75 mi. on Dover rd ✉ CT15 6EW – ☎ (01304) 852 424 – www.wallettscourt.com – Fax (01304) 853 430 – closed 24 -26 December

17 rm – †£ 109/129 ††£ 169/199

Rest *The Restaurant* – see restaurant listing

◆ With origins dating back to the Doomsday Book, a wealth of Jacobean features remain in this relaxed country house. Most characterful rooms in main house; luxurious spa rooms.

The Restaurant – at Wallett's Court Hotel

West Cliffe, Northwest : 0.75 mi. on Dover rd ✉ CT15 6EW – ☎ (01304) 852 424 – ww.wallettscourt.com – Fax (01304) 853 430 – closed 24-26 December

Rest – *(dinner only and Sunday lunch)* Menu £ 40

◆ Local produce dominates the imaginative, monthly changing, seasonal menu. Dine by candlelight in the beamed restaurant after drinks are taken by the open fire.

ENGLAND

DOWNTON – Hants. – 503 P31 – see Lymington

DRIFT – Cornwall – see Penzance

DROITWICH SPA – Worcestershire – 503 N27 – pop. 22 585 19 C3

London 129 mi. – Birmingham 20 mi. – Bristol 66 mi. – Worcester 6 mi.

St Richard's House, Victoria Sq ☎ (01905) 774312, heritage@droitwichspa.gov.uk

18 Droitwich G. & C.C. Ford Lane, ☎ (01905) 774 344

at Cutnall Green North : 3 mi. on A 442 – ✉ Droitwich Spa

The Chequers

Kidderminster Rd ✉ WR9 0PJ – ☎ (01299) 851 292 – www.chequerscutnallgreen.co.uk – Fax (01299) 851 744 – Closed 25 December, 26 December dinner and 1 January

Rest – Carte £ 18/25

◆ Half-timbered roadside pub, comprising main bar with beams and fire or cosy garden room. Impressively wide range of highly interesting dishes, firmly traditional or modern.

at Hadley Heath Southwest : 4 mi. by Ombersley Way, A 4133 and Ladywood rd – ✉ Droitwich Spa

Old Farmhouse without rest

✉ WR9 0AR – ☎ (01905) 620 837 – www.theoldfarmhouse.uk.com – Fax (01905) 621 722 – closed 23 December-5 January

5 rm – †£ 45 ††£ 75

◆ Converted farmhouse in quiet and rural location. Spacious comfortable rooms, three in the main house and two, more private and perhaps suited to families, in the annex.

DROXFORD – Hampshire – 504 Q31 6 B2

London 79 mi. – Southampton 21 mi. – Portsmouth 16 mi. – Basingstoke 37 mi.

The Bakers Arms

High St ✉ SO32 3PA – ✆ (01489) 877 533 – www.thebakersarmsdroxford.com – Closed Sunday dinner and Monday

Rest – Carte £ 20/26

◆ Characterful pub with keen owners and a friendly team. Cooking is simple and unfussy, featuring British classics with a French/Mediterranean touch. Much of the produce is local.

DULVERTON – Somerset – 503 J30 – pop. 1 870 **3** A2

London 198 mi. – Barnstaple 27 mi. – Exeter 26 mi. – Minehead 18 mi.

Village★

Exmoor National Park★★ - Tarr Steps★★, NW : 6 mi. by B 3223

Ashwick House without rest

Northwest : 4.25 mi. by B 3223 turning left after second cattle grid ✉ TA22 9QD – ✆ (01398) 323 868 – www.ashwickhouse.com – Fax (01398) 323 868 – Closed Christmas

8 rm – †£ 75 ††£ 120

◆ Delightful, peaceful and secluded Edwardian country house in extensive gardens with pheasants and rabbits. Smartly appointed, airy rooms with thoughtful touches.

Woods

4 Banks Square ✉ TA22 9BU – ✆ (01398) 324 007 – Fax (01398) 323 366

Rest – Carte £ 15/30

◆ Delightful pub displaying charming décor and smart hand-made furniture. Classical cooking has a French slant and uses local, traceable produce; meat is from the owner's farm.

at Brushford South : 1.75 mi. on B 3222 – ✉ Dulverton

Three Acres Country House without rest

✉ TA22 9AR – ✆ (01398) 323 730 – www.threeacrescountryhouse.co.uk

6 rm – †£ 60 ††£ 120

◆ Keenly run and friendly 20C guesthouse. Super-comfy bedrooms are the strong point. There's an airy lounge, cosy bar and breakfasts are locally sourced.

DUNSLEY – N. Yorks. – see Whitby

DUNSTER – Somerset – 503 J30 – pop. 848 **3** A2

London 185 mi. – Minehead 3 mi. – Taunton 23 mi.

Town★★ - Castle★★ **AC** (upper rooms ≤★) - Water Mill★ **AC** - St George's Church★ - Dovecote★

Exmoor House without rest

12 West St ✉ TA24 6SN – ✆ (01643) 821 268 – www.exmoorhousedunster.co.uk – closed 25-26 December, January and February

6 rm – †£ 50 ††£ 65

◆ Georgian terraced house with cream exterior, enhanced by colourful window boxes. Spacious, comfy lounge and welcoming breakfast room. Chintz rooms with pleasing extra touches.

DURHAM – Durham – 501 P19 – pop. 42 939 Great Britain **24** B3

London 267 mi. – Leeds 77 mi. – Middlesbrough 23 mi. – Newcastle upon Tyne 20 mi.

2 Millennium Pl ✆ (0191) 384 3720, touristinfo@durhamcity.gov.uk

Mount Oswald South Rd, ✆ (0191) 386 7527

City★★★ - Cathedral★★★ (Nave★★★, Chapel of the Nine Altars★★★, Sanctuary Knocker★) B – Oriental Museum★★ **AC** (at Durham University by A 167) B – City and Riverside (Prebends' Bridge ≤★★★ A, Framwellgate Bridge ≤★★ B) – Monastic Buildings (Cathedral Treasury★, Central Tower ≤★) B – Castle★ (Norman chapel★) **AC** B

Hartlepool Historic Quay★, SE : 14 mi. by A 181, A 19 and A 179

Plan on next page

ENGLAND

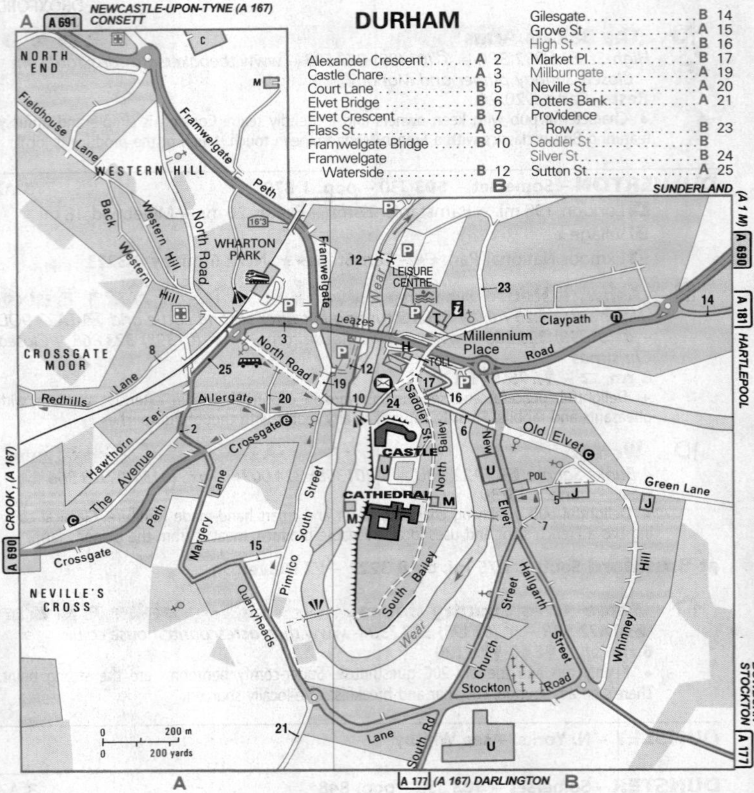

DURHAM

Fallen Angel

rm, AC, VISA, MC, AE

34 Old Elvet ✉ *DH1 3HN – ✆ (0191) 384 10 37 – www.fallenangelhotel.com – Fax (0191) 384 33 48* Bc

9 rm – †£ 80 ††£ 150/300 – 1 suite

Rest – *(closed dinner Sunday and Monday)* Carte £ 21/39

◆ A one-off: luxurious, individually themed bedrooms include 'Sci-Fi', which comes with Dalek and Tardis and the indulgent, red velvet 'Le Boudoir'. The garden rooms have terraces, hot tubs and a Rolls Royce. Accessible menu in informal conservatory restaurant.

Farnley Tower

P, VISA, MC, AE

The Avenue ✉ *DH1 4DX – ✆ (0191) 375 0011 – www.farnley-tower.co.uk – Fax (0191) 383 9694 – Closed 25-26 December,and 1 January* Ac

13 rm – †£ 60/75 ††£ 85/95

Rest *Gourmet Spot* – ✆ (0191) 384 6655 *(Closed Sunday and Monday)* Carte dinner only £ 32/44

◆ Spacious Victorian house in quiet residential area close to city centre. Modern, airy, well-equipped bedrooms with a good degree of comfort. Gourmet Spot, stylish and slick in black granite and leather, serves original, modern cuisine.

Cathedral View Town House without rest

VISA, MC

212 Lower Gilesgate ✉ *DH1 1QN – ✆ (0191) 386 9566 – www.cathedralview.com* Bn

6 rm – †£ 65/90 ††£ 80/100

◆ Alluring Georgian townhouse with terraced garden in older part of the city near the centre. Attractive breakfast room with good views. Spacious, individually named rooms.

Castle View without rest

4 Crossgate ✉ DH1 4PS – ✆ (0191) 386 8852 – www.castle-view.co.uk – Closed 3 weeks Christmas and New Year Ae

6 rm – £ 55/60 £ 80

◆ Attractive Georgian townhouse off steep cobbled hill, reputedly once the vicarage to adjacent church. Breakfast on terrace in summer. Individually furnished bedrooms.

Bistro 21

Aykley Heads House, Aykley Heads, Northwest : 1.5 mi. by A 691 and B 6532 ✉ DH1 5TS – ✆ (0191) 384 4354 – www.bistrotwentyone.co.uk – Fax (0191) 384 1149 – Closed 25-26 December, 1 January and Sunday dinner

Rest – *(booking essential)* Menu £ 18 (lunch and weekday dinner) – Carte £ 26/42

◆ Popular restaurant in former stables of 17C villa, with French farmhouse styling and enclosed courtyard. Fresh, uncomplicated cooking; neatly presented classics. Good value lunch/-midweek menu.

EARL STONHAM – Suffolk – 504 X27 15 C3

London 91 mi. – Ipswich 12 mi. – Colchester 33 mi. – Clacton-on-Sea 38 mi.

Bays Farm without rest

Forward Green, Northwest : 1 mi. by A1120 on Broad Green rd ✉ IP14 5HU – ✆ (01449) 711 286 – www.baysfarmsuffolk.co.uk

3 rm – £ 80 £ 90

◆ 17C former farmhouse in 4 acres of lawned gardens. Comfortable bedrooms with a country feel, 2 with garden views. Traditional, wood-filled guest areas. Breakfast outside in summer.

EARSHAM – Norfolk – 504 Y26 – see Bungay

EASINGWOLD – North Yorkshire – 502 Q21 – pop. 3 975 – ✉ York 23 C2

London 217 mi. – Leeds 38 mi. – Middlesbrough 37 mi. – York 14 mi.

Chapel Lane ✆ (01347) 821530, easingwold.touristinfo@virgin.net

Stillington Rd, ✆ (01347) 822 474

Old Vicarage without rest

Market Pl ✉ YO61 3AL – ✆ (01347) 821 015 – www.oldvicarage-easingwold.co.uk – Fax (01347) 821 015 – restricted opening in winter

4 rm – £ 60/75 £ 95/100

◆ Spacious, part Georgian country house with walled rose garden and adjacent croquet lawn. Immaculately kept throughout with fine period antiques in the elegant sitting room.

at Crayke East : 2 mi. on Helmsley Rd – ✉ York

The Durham Ox with rm

Westway ✉ YO61 4TE – ✆ (01347) 821 506 – www.thedurhamox.com – Fax (01347) 823 326 – Closed 25 December dinner

5 rm – £ 80 £ 150 **Rest** – *(booking essential)* Carte £ 15/35

◆ 300 year old, family run pub set in a sleepy hamlet. Regularly changing à la carte features hearty dishes of fresh seafood, local meats, Crayke game and tasty spit roast chicken. Bedrooms are set in old farm cottages; some are suites, some have jacuzzis.

EAST ALLINGTON – Devon 2 C3

London 210 mi. – Plymouth 24 mi. – Torbay 18 mi. – Exeter 38 mi.

Fortescue Arms with rm

✉ TQ9 7RA – ✆ (01548) 521 215 – www.fortescue-arms.co.uk – Closed Monday lunch

3 rm – £ 40 £ 60 **Rest** – Carte £ 25/30

◆ Ivy-clad pub with decked terrace, set in rural village. Beamed bar serves rustic pub dishes and warm organic bread, while focus is on more refined dishes in smart dining room. Simple bedrooms.

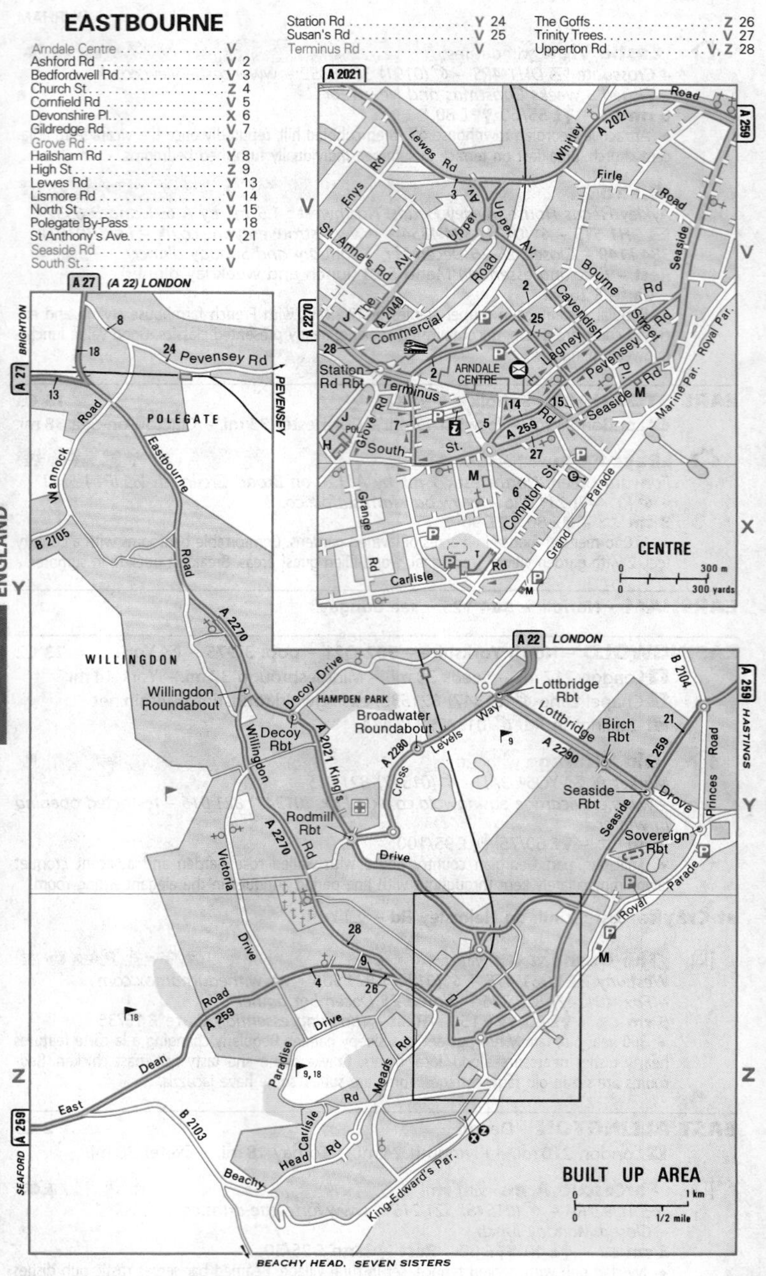
EASTBOURNE
Arndale Centre V
Ashford Rd V 2
Bedfordwell Rd V 3
Church St Z 4
Cornfield Rd V 5
Devonshire Pl. X 6
Gildredge Rd V 7
Grove Rd V
Hailsham Rd Y 8
High St Z 9
Lewes Rd Y 13
Lismore Rd V 14
North St V 15
Polegate By-Pass Y 18
St Anthony's Ave. Y 21
Seaside Rd V
South St. V
Station Rd Y 24
Susan's Rd V 25
Terminus Rd V
The Goffs Z 26
Trinity Trees V 27
Upperton Rd V, Z 28
CENTRE
ARNDALE CENTRE
Station Rd Rbt
BUILT UP AREA
POLEGATE
WILLINGDON
HAMPDEN PARK
Willingdon Roundabout
Decoy Rbt
Broadwater Roundabout
Lottbridge Rbt
Birch Rbt
Seaside Rbt
Rodmill Rbt
Sovereign Rbt
A 27 (A 22) LONDON
A 22 LONDON
BRIGHTON
PEVENSEY
HASTINGS
SEAFORD
BEACHY HEAD, SEVEN SISTERS
ENGLAND

EASTBOURNE – East Sussex – 504 U31 – pop. 106 562 Great Britain 8 B3

London 68 mi. – Brighton 25 mi. – Dover 61 mi. – Maidstone 49 mi.
Cornfield Rd ✆ (01323) 415450, tic@eastbourne.gov.uk
Royal Eastbourne Paradise Drive, ✆ (01323) 744 045
Eastbourne Downs East Dean Rd, ✆ (01323) 720 827
Eastbourne Golfing Park Lottbridge Drove, ✆ (01323) 520 400
Seafront★
Beachy Head★★★, SW : 3 mi. by B 2103 Z

Grand rm, rest, VISA AE
King Edward's Parade ✉ BN21 4EQ – ✆ (01323) 412 345 – www.grandeastbourne.com – Fax (01323) 412 233 Zx
131 rm – £ 160/505 £ 190/535 – 21 suites
Rest *Mirabelle* – see restaurant listing
Rest *Garden Restaurant* – Menu £ 20/36 – Carte £ 50/63
◆ Huge, pillared lobby with ornate plasterwork sets the tone of this opulently refurbished, Victorian hotel in prime seafront location. High levels of comfort throughout. Garden Restaurant exudes a light, comfy atmosphere.

Lansdowne rm, VISA AE
King Edward's Parade ✉ BN21 4EE – ✆ (01323) 725 174 – www.bw-lansdownehotel.co.uk – Fax (01323) 739 721 Zz
102 rm – £ 54/169 £ 141/179
Rest – *(bar lunch Monday-Saturday)* Carte dinner £ 14/26
◆ Traditional seaside hotel in the same family since 1912. Bedrooms are a mix of décor, either traditional or modern, some with sea views. Dining room has classic feel.

Brayscroft VISA AE
13 South Cliff Ave ✉ BN20 7AH – ✆ (01323) 647 005 – www.brayscrofthotel.co.uk Zn
6 rm – £ 36/50 £ 72/80
Rest – *(by arrangement)* Menu £ 18 – Carte £ 23/36
◆ Immaculately kept with individual style, antiques, original local art and comfy furnishings throughout. Well run by charming owners. Dining room overlooks a smart terrace.

XXXX **Mirabelle** – at Grand Hotel VISA AE
King Edward's Parade ✉ BN21 4EQ – ✆ (01323) 435 066 – Fax (01323) 412 233 – closed first 2 weeks January, Sunday and Monday Zx
Rest – *(booking essential)* Menu £ 22/37 – Carte £ 52/65
◆ Elegant, comfortable restaurant with a seasonally changing menu of original dishes. A bar lounge in the basement and wine list of impressive names.

at Jevington Northwest : 6 mi. by A 259 - Z - on Jevington Rd – ✉ Polegate

XX **Hungry Monk** VISA AE
The Street ✉ BN26 5QF – ✆ (01323) 482 178 – www.hungrymonk.co.uk – Fax (01323) 483 989 – Closed 24-26 December, Monday lunch and Bank Holidays
Rest – *(booking essential)* Menu £ 22/36
◆ Part 17C Elizabethan cottages with garden. Welcoming, relaxed atmosphere; antique chairs and log fires add to the charm. Menu offers good and hearty, traditional fare.

EAST CHILTINGTON – E. Sussex – see Lewes

EAST CHISENBURY – Wiltshire 4 D2

London 92 mi. – Bristol 51 mi. – Southampton 53 mi. – Reading 51 mi.

Red Lion Freehouse VISA
✉ SN9 6AQ – ✆ (01980) 671 124 – www.redlionfreehouse.com – Fax (01980) 671 136 – Closed 2 weeks January, 25 December, Tuesday lunch and Monday
Rest – *(booking advisable)* Carte £ 21/27
◆ Delightful thatched pub with pretty garden; run with honesty and passion. Daily changing, seasonal menu of well-priced, rustic, flavourful dishes. Cosy atmosphere; friendly service.

ENGLAND

EAST DEREHAM – Norfolk – 504 W25 – pop. 17 779 15 C1

London 109 mi. – Cambridge 57 mi. – King's Lynn 27 mi. – Norwich 16 mi.

at Wendling West : 5.5 mi. by A 47

Greenbanks Country H. with rm rm,

Swaffham Rd NR19 2AB – (01362) 687 742 – www.greenbankshotel.co.uk – Closed 1 week Christmas

9 rm – £ 75 £ 90/140

Rest – *(booking essential at lunch)* Carte £ 20/32 **s**

◆ Collection of yellow-washed buildings with red roofs, set in pleasant lawned grounds. Wood-furnished restaurant offers fresh, local produce and worldwide influences, especially Asian. Hotel boasts spacious, individually designed bedrooms, a pool and sauna.

EAST GARSTON – West Berkshire – see Lambourn

EASTGATE – Durham – 502 N19 24 A3

London 288 mi. – Bishop Auckland 20 mi. – Newcastle upon Tyne 35 mi. – Stanhope 3 mi.

Horsley Hall

Southeast : 1 mi. by A 689 DL13 2LJ – (01388) 517 239 – www.horsleyhall.co.uk – Fax (01388) 517 608 – Closed 23 December-2 January

7 rm – £ 65/75 £ 140

Rest – *(booking essential Sunday and for non residents)* Carte £ 16/29

◆ Attractive ivy-clad former hunting lodge with 14C origins, built for the Bishop of Durham. Impressive hall; superb stained glass; mix of simple, cosy bedrooms – two with Edwardian bathrooms. Baronial style dining room boasts impressive ornate ceiling.

EAST GRINSTEAD – West Sussex – 504 T30 – pop. 26 222 7 D2

London 48 mi. – Brighton 30 mi. – Eastbourne 32 mi. – Lewes 21 mi.

18 Copthorne Borers Arm Rd, (01342) 712 508

Gravetye Manor

Vowels Lane, Southwest : 4.5 mi. by B 2110 taking second turn left towards West Hoathly RH19 4LJ – (01342) 810 567 – www.gravetyemanor.co.uk – Fax (01342) 810 080

18 rm – £ 115/345 £ 175/345, £ 20

Rest – *(closed dinner 25 December to non-residents) (booking essential)* Menu £ 25 (lunch) – Carte £ 25/52

◆ Beautiful 16C manor house featuring polished oak, fine English fabrics, antiques and charming log fires. Beautiful grounds house gazebo for al fresco dining. Luxurious bedrooms, some with fine views. Classically based cooking; professional service.

EAST HOATHLY – East Sussex – 504 U31 – pop. 1 206 8 B3

London 60 mi. – Brighton 16 mi. – Eastbourne 13 mi. – Hastings 25 mi.

Old Whyly

London Rd, West : 0.5 mi., turning right after post box on right, taking centre gravel drive after approx. 400 metres BN8 6EL – (01825) 840 216 – www.oldwhyly.co.uk – Fax (01825) 840 738

3 rm – £ 65/85 £ 130

Rest – *(by arrangement, communal dining)* Menu £ 30

◆ Charming, secluded Georgian manor house decorated with antiques, oils and watercolours. Airy bedrooms individually styled. Delightful owner. Warm, informal dining room.

EAST KENNETT – Wiltshire – see Marlborough

EAST LAVANT – W. Sussex – see Chichester

EASTON – Devon – 503 I31 – see Chagford

EASTON – Hants. – see Winchester

ENGLAND

EASTON – Somerset – see Wells

EAST RUDHAM – Norfolk 15 C1

London 116 – Norwich 42 – Ipswich 72 – Peterborough 51

The Crown Inn with rm

The Green – (01485) 528 530 – www.thecrowneastrudham.co.uk – Closed 25 December

6 rm – £ 80 £ 80 **Rest** – Carte £ 23/30

◆ 15C pub with mix of period features and contemporary comforts, offering generous portions of tasty dishes on mainly British menu. Bright local and Antipodean service. Comfortable bedrooms boast modern bathrooms.

EAST WITTON – North Yorkshire – 502 O21 – Leyburn 22 B1

London 238 mi. – Leeds 45 mi. – Middlesbrough 30 mi. – York 39 mi.

The Blue Lion with rm

DL8 4SN – (01969) 624 273 – www.thebluelion.co.uk – Fax (01969) 624 189

15 rm – £ 68 £ 135 **Rest** – *(booking essential)* Carte £ 26/35

◆ Charming, characterful countryside pub. Daily-changing menu features a tasty mix of classic and modern dishes, all with seasonality and traceability at their core. Bedrooms – in the pub and outbuildings – are warm and cosy.

EBRINGTON – Gloucestershire – 504 O27 – see Chipping Campden

ECCLESTON – Lancashire – 502 L23 – pop. 4 708 20 A2

London 219 mi. – Birmingham 103 mi. – Liverpool 29 mi. – Preston 11 mi.

Parr Hall Farm without rest

Parr Lane PR7 5SL – (01257) 451 917 – www.parrhallfarm.com – Fax (01257) 453 749

10 rm – £ 40 £ 70

◆ Part 18C former farmhouse with neat lawned gardens in small, pleasant town. Bedrooms all in a converted barn; decorated with matching pine furniture and good bathrooms.

EGHAM – Surrey – 504 S29 – pop. 27 666 7 C1

London 29 mi. – Reading 21 mi.

Great Fosters

Stroude Rd, South : 1.25 mi. by B 388 TW20 9UR – (01784) 433 822 – www.greatfosters.co.uk – Fax (01784) 472 455

41 rm – £ 125/170 £ 170, £ 19.50 – 3 suites

Rest – *(closed Saturday lunch)* Menu £ 25/37 – Carte dinner approx. £ 49

◆ Elizabethan mansion with magnificent gardens. Delightfully original interior has tapestries, oak panelling and antiques. Bedooms in the main house especially notable. Two historic dining rooms: one an ancient tithe barn, the other in 16C French style.

Monsoon

20 High St TW20 9DT – (01784) 432 141 – www.monsoonrestaurant.co.uk – Fax (01784) 432 194

Rest – Indian – Menu £ 15 – Carte £ 16/25

◆ Smart, stylish restaurant that prides itself on immaculate upkeep and personable service. Contemporary artwork enlivens the walls. Freshly cooked, authentic Indian dishes.

ELDERSFIELD – Worcestershire – see Tewkesbury

ELLAND – West Yorkshire – 502 O22 – pop. 14 554 – Halifax 22 B3

London 204 mi. – Bradford 12 mi. – Burnley 29 mi. – Leeds 17 mi.

Hullen Edge Hammerstones Leach Lane, (01422) 372 505

La Cachette

31 Huddersfield Rd ✉ HX5 9AW – ✆ (01422) 378 833 – www.lacachette-elland.com – Fax (01422) 327 567 – Closed 2 weeks Summer, 1 week January, Sunday and most Bank Holidays

Rest – Menu £ 20 (dinner except Friday and Saturday after 7pm) – Carte £ 21/37

◆ A busy, bustling brasserie-style restaurant with sprinkling of French panache. Menu of eclectically blended interpretations served in the dining room or well-stocked wine bar.

ELSLACK – North Yorkshire – see Skipton

ELSTED – W. Sussex – 504 R31 – see Midhurst

ELSTOW – Beds. – 504 S27 – see Bedford

ELTISLEY – Cambridgeshire – 504 T27 14 A3

London 70 mi. – Leicester 62 mi.

The Eltisley

2 The Green ✉ PE19 6TG – ✆ (01480) 880 308 – www.theeltisley.co.uk – Closed Sunday dinner, Monday (except bank holidays)

Rest – Carte £ 23/33

◆ Chic and stylish gastropub beside a village green. Simple, unfussy cooking relies on quality, local produce to speak for itself; everything from starters to desserts is homemade.

ELTON – Cambridgeshire – 504 S26 14 A2

London 84 mi. – Peterborough 11 mi. – Bedford 40 mi. – Kettering 24 mi.

The Crown Inn with rm

8 Duck St ✉ PE8 6RQ – ✆ (01832) 280 232 – www.thecrowninn.org – Closed 25 December, 1-7 January, Sunday dinner, Monday (except bank holiday when open for lunch)

5 rm – †£ 60/90 ††£ 90/120

Rest – Menu £ 16 (weekday lunch) – Carte £ 25/34

◆ 17C thatched inn with a conservatory, terrace and plenty of character. Cooking is traditional and generous, with a touch of Italian influence; lunch sees lighter dishes. Smart, individually-styled bedrooms with spacious bathrooms.

ELY – Cambridgeshire – 504 U26 – pop. 13 954 Great Britain 14 B2

London 74 mi. – Cambridge 16 mi. – Norwich 60 mi.

Oliver Cromwell's House, 29 St Mary's St ✆ (01353) 662062, tic@eastcambs.gov.uk

18 107 Cambridge Rd, ✆ (01353) 662 751

Cathedral★★ **AC**

Wicken Fen★, SE : 9 mi. by A 10 and A 1123

The Boathouse

5-5A Annesdale ✉ CB7 4BN – ✆ (01353) 664 388 – www.cambscuisine.com – Fax (01353) 666 688

Rest – *(booking essential)* Menu £ 16 (lunch) – Carte £ 24/32

◆ A riverside setting makes for a charming ambience: bag a terrace table if you can. Airy, dark wood interior where worldwide menus benefit from numerous creative touches.

at Little Thetford South : 2.75 mi. off A 10 – ✉ Ely

Springfields without rest

Ely Road, North : 0.5 mi. on A 10 ✉ CB6 3HJ – ✆ (01353) 663 637 – Fax (01353) 663 130 – Closed 20 December-2 January

3 rm – †£ 55 ††£ 75

◆ Welcoming, bric-a-brac-filled bungalow in pleasant gardens: a perfect home from home. Comfy lounge with wood burning stove; immaculately kept bedrooms. Courtyard breakfast when weather allows.

at Sutton Gault West : 8 mi. by A 142 off B 1381 – ✉ Ely

The Anchor Inn with rm
✉ CB6 2BD – ✆ (01353) 778 537 – www.anchor-inn-restaurant.co.uk – Fax (01353) 776 180
4 rm – †£ 55 ††£ 155
Rest – Menu £ 16 (lunch) – Carte £ 20/30
◆ Riverside pub dating back to 1650 and the creation of the Hundred Foot Wash. Tempting main menu complemented by daily fish specials and occasionally oxen and zebra from the nearby estate. Neat, pine furnished bedrooms. Two suites; one with river views.

EMSWORTH – Hampshire – 504 R31 – pop. 18 310 — 6 B2

London 75 mi. – Brighton 37 mi. – Portsmouth 10 mi. – Southampton 22 mi.

36 on the Quay (Ramon Farthing) with rm
47 South St, The Quay ✉ PO10 7EG – ✆ (01243) 375 592 – www.36onthequay.co.uk – closed 3 weeks January,1 week May and 1 week October
4 rm – †£ 70/90 ††£ 95/110 – 2 suites
Rest – *(closed Sunday-Monday) (booking essential)* Menu £ 26/47
Spec. Red mullet with tomato caponata and anchovy beignet. Veal with dauphinoise potatoes and shallot cream. Iced peanut parfait with doughnuts and coffee cream.
◆ A former fisherman's house, situated on the quayside, with snug bar/lounge and attractive dining rooms in neutral hues. Well-executed, assured and tasty cooking with a traditional base. Smooth, professional service. Comfortable, contemporary bedrooms; Vanilla is the most luxurious, with the best view.

Fat Olives
30 South St ✉ PO10 7EH – ✆ (01243) 377 914 – www.fatolives.co.uk – closed 2 weeks June-July, 2 weeks Christmas, Sunday and Monday
Rest – *(booking essential)* Menu £ 19 (lunch) **s** – Carte £ 26/42 **s**
◆ Small terraced house with a welcoming ambience. Simply decorated with wood floor and rough plaster walls. Tasty modern British menu and, yes, fat olives are available!

Take note of the classification: you should not expect the same level of service in a X or 🏠 as in a XXXXX or 🏨.

EPSOM – Surrey – 504 T30 – pop. 64 493 — 7 D1

London 17 mi. – Guildford 16 mi.
Longdown Lane South Epsom Downs, ✆ (01372) 721 666
Horton Park G & C.C. Hook Rd, ✆ (020) 8393 8400

Chalk Lane
Chalk Lane, Southwest : 0.5 mi. by A 24 and Woodcote Rd ✉ KT18 7BB – ✆ (01372) 721 179 – www.chalklanehotel.com – Fax (01372) 727 878
22 rm – †£ 95/100 ††£ 185
Rest – Menu £ 18 (lunch) – Carte dinner £ 28/43
◆ At the foot of the Epsom Downs and near to the racecourse. Quality furnishings throughout; the neatly kept bedrooms are most comfortable. Smart, modern dining room.

Le Raj
211 Fir Tree Rd, Epsom Downs, Southeast : 2.25 mi. by B 289 and B 284 on B 291 ✉ KT17 3LB – ✆ (01737) 371 371 – www.lerajrestaurant.co.uk – Fax (01737) 211 903
Rest – Bangladeshi – Menu £ 20 (lunch) – Carte £ 30/48
◆ Original, interesting menu makes good use of fresh ingredients and brings a modern style to traditional Bangladeshi cuisine. Smart, vibrant, contemporary interior décor.

ENGLAND

ERMINGTON – Devon – 503 I32 2 C2

London 216 mi. – Plymouth 11 mi. – Salcombe 15 mi.

XX **Plantation House** with rm

Totnes Rd, Southwest : 0.5 mi. on A 3121 ✉ PL21 9NS – ✆ (01548) 831 100 – www.plantationhousehotel.co.uk

9 rm – 🛉£ 65/89 🛉🛉£ 150

Rest – *(closed Sunday and Monday to non-residents) (dinner only) (booking essential for non-residents)* Menu £ 38

◆ Appealing, converted Georgian rectory with smart gardens and terraced seating area. Personally run. Sound cooking of locally sourced ingredients. Individually styled bedrooms.

ERPINGHAM – Norfolk – 504 X25 – pop. 1 871 15 D1

London 123 mi. – Cromer 8 mi. – King's Lynn 46 mi. – Norwich 16 mi.

The Saracen's Head with rm

Wolterton, West : 1.5 mi. on Itteringham rd ✉ NR11 7LX – ✆ (01263) 768 909 – www.saracenshead-norfolk.co.uk – Fax (01263) 768 993 – Closed 25 December, 26 December dinner, Monday, Tuesday lunch (except after bank holidays)

6 rm – 🛉£ 50 🛉🛉£ 90 **Rest** – *(booking essential)* Carte £ 25/30

◆ Rurally set, idiosyncratic inn with long-standing owners; run with infectious enthusiasm. Daily changing blackboard menu features hearty, traditional dishes made using local produce. Spacious bedrooms.

ESCRICK – N. Yorks. – 502 Q22 – see York

ESHER – Surrey – 504 S29 – pop. 46 599 7 D1

London 20 mi. – Portsmouth 58 mi.

Thames Ditton & Esher Portsmouth Rd, ✆ (020) 8398 1551

Moore Place Portsmouth Rd, ✆ (01372) 463 533

Cranfield Golf at Sandown More Lane, ✆ (01372) 468 093

Plan : see Greater London (South-West) 5

XXX **George**

104 High St ✉ KT10 9QJ – ✆ (01372) 471 500 – www.george-esher.com – Fax (01372) 471 500 – Closed lunch Saturday and dinner Sunday-Monday

Rest – Carte £ 15/30

◆ Elegant and understated restaurant with added refinement of airy cocktail bar. Immaculately laid tables lend a formal air to modern dishes that change with the seasons.

XX **Good Earth**

14-18 High St ✉ KT10 9RT – ✆ (01372) 462 489 – Fax (01372) 460 668 – Closed 23-30 December BZ**e**

Rest – Chinese – Menu £ 30/36 – Carte £ 30/60

◆ A large Chinese restaurant with a smart, smooth style in décor and service. Well presented menu with much choice including vegetarian sections.

ETTINGTON – Warwickshire – 504 P27 – pop. 953 19 C3

London 95 mi. – Birmingham 41 mi. – Leicester 48 mi. – Coventry 23 mi.

The Chequers Inn

91 Banbury Rd ✉ CV37 7SR – ✆ (01789) 740 387 – www.the-chequers-ettington.co.uk – Closed Sunday dinner and Monday

Rest – Carte £ 18/27

◆ Chandeliers, brushed velvet furniture and Regency chairs set at chequered tables mean that this is not your typical pub. Cooking is classical in style, with well-matching flavours.

EVERSHOT – Dorset – 503 M31 – pop. 225 – ✉ Dorchester 4 C3

London 149 mi. – Bournemouth 39 mi. – Dorchester 12 mi. – Salisbury 53 mi.

Summer Lodge
9 Fore St ✉ DT2 0JR – ✆ (01935) 482 000
– www.summerlodgehotel.com – Fax (01935) 482 040
20 rm – †£ 225/455 ††£ 250/480 – 4 suites
Rest *The Restaurant* – *(booking essential to non residents)* Menu £ 27 (lunch) – Carte dinner £ 49/67
◆ Part Georgian dower house in quiet village, in the best tradition of stylish, English country hotels. Boasts a range of sleek, smart, up-to-date bedrooms. Elegant restaurant overlooking walled garden; excellent wine list.

Wooden Cabbage House
East Chelborough, West : 3.75 mi. by Beaminter rd. ✉ DT1 0QA – ✆ (01935) 83 362 – www.woodencabbage.co.uk
3 rm – †£ 65/75 ††£ 90 **Rest** – *(by arrangement)* Carte approx. £ 30
◆ This former shooting lodge offer peace and quiet, warm hospitality and views of the rolling hills. Spacious ground floor with breakfast by the Aga; cosy bedrooms. Dinner uses some home-grown produce.

The Acorn Inn with rm
28 Fore St ✉ DT2 0JW – ✆ (01935) 83 228 – www.acorn-inn.co.uk
– Fax (01935) 83 707
10 rm – †£ 60/100 ††£ 110/125 **Rest** – Carte £ 23/35
◆ Quintessentially English coaching inn referenced in 'Tess of the d'Urbervilles'. Menu displays traditional pub classics at lunch, with more interest and sophistication in the evening. Traditional English country bedrooms.

ENGLAND

EVESHAM – Worcestershire – 503 O27 – pop. 22 179 — 19 C3

London 99 mi. – Birmingham 30 mi. – Cheltenham 16 mi. – Coventry 32 mi.
The Almonry, Abbey Gate ✆ (01386) 446944, tic@almonry.ndo.co.uk

Evesham
Coopers Lane, off Waterside ✉ WR11 1DA – ✆ (01386) 765 566
– www.eveshamhotel.com – Fax (01386) 765 443 – Closed 25-26 December
40 rm – †£ 73/85 ††£ 120/142
Rest *Cedar* – Carte £ 17/29 **s**
◆ Idiosyncratic family run hotel in a quiet location. Guest families well catered for, with jolly japes at every turn. Individual rooms with cottage décor and eclectic themes. Unconventional menus in keeping with hotel style.

EWEN – Glos. – 503 O28 – see Cirencester

EXETER – Devon – 503 J31 – pop. 106 772 — 2 D2

London 201 mi. – Bournemouth 83 mi. – Bristol 83 mi. – Plymouth 46 mi.
Exeter Airport : ✆ (01392) 367433, E : 5 mi. by A 30 V
Dixs Field, Princesshay ✆ (01392) 665700, evit@exeter.gov.uk
Downes Crediton Hookway, ✆ (01363) 773 025
City★★ - Cathedral★★ Z – Royal Albert Memorial Museum★ Y
Killerton★★ **AC**, NE : 7 mi. by B 3181 V – Ottery St Mary★ (St Mary's★) E : 12 mi. by B 3183 - Y - A 30 and B 3174 – Crediton (Holy Cross Church★), NW : 9 mi. by A 377

Plans on next pages

Abode Exeter
The Royal Clarence, Cathedral Yard ✉ EX1 1HD – ✆ (01392) 319 955
– www.abodehotels.co.uk – Fax (01392) 439 423 Y**z**
52 rm – †£ 130/145 ††£ 270/330, £ 13.50 – 1 suite
Rest *Michael Caines* – see restaurant listing
◆ Georgian-style frontage; located on the doorstep of the cathedral. Boutique style hotel with a very modern, stylish interior. Understated bedrooms feature good mod cons.

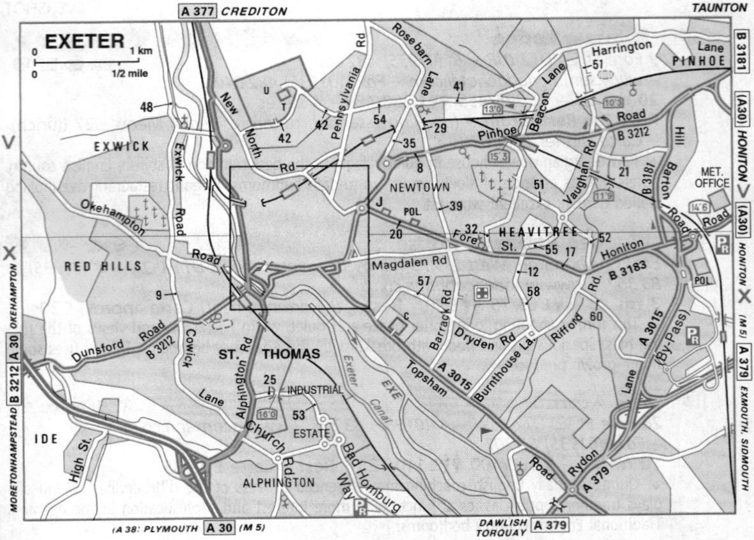

Street	Grid	No.
Blackboy Rd	V	8
Buddle Lane	X	9
Butts Rd	X	12
East Wonford Hill	X	17
Heavitree Rd	VX	20
Hill Lane	V	21
Marsh Barton Rd	X	25
Mount Pleasant Rd	V	29
North St HEAVITREE	X	32
Old Tiverton Rd	V	35
Polsloe Rd	V	39
Prince Charles Rd	V	41
Prince of Wales Rd	V	42
St Andrew's Rd	V	48
Summer Lane	V	51
Sweetbriar Lane	VX	52
Trusham Rd	X	53
Union Rd	V	54
Whipton Lane	X	55
Wonford Rd	X	57
Wonford St	X	58
Woodwater Lane	X	60

The Queens Court

VISA

Bystock Terrace ✉ *EX4 4HY – (01392) 272 709 – www.queenscourt-hotel.co.uk – Fax (01392) 491 390 – Closed 24 December-2 January* Y**n**

18 rm – £ 89 £ 109

Rest *Olive Tree* – *(closed Sunday lunch)* Carte £ 26/33

◆ A town house hotel located close to Central train station. Bright public areas decorated in a clean, modern style. Well-equipped, tidily furnished and co-ordinated bedrooms. Brightly painted, clean-lined restaurant.

Silversprings without rest

VISA

12 Richmond Rd ✉ *EX4 4JA – (01392) 494 040 – www.silversprings.co.uk – Fax (01392) 494 040 – Closed 20 December-4 January* Y**a**

10 rm – £ 60/85 £ 85/120

◆ Cream coloured Georgian terraced house in Roman part of town. Warm and friendly, with immaculately kept public areas. Varied palettes and cathedral views distinguish rooms.

Michael Caines – at Abode Exeter Hotel

VISA

The Royal Clarence, Cathedral Yard ✉ *EX1 1HD – (01392) 223 638 – www.michaelcaines.com – Fax (01392) 437 496* Y**z**

Rest – *(closed Sunday)* Menu £ 20 (lunch) – Carte £ 45/54

◆ Comfortable, contemporarily stylish restaurant overlooking Cathedral. Menu has good choice of well-balanced and confident modern British cooking. Pleasant, efficient service.

Angela's

VISA

38 New Bridge Street ✉ *EX4 3AH – (01392) 499 038 – www.angelasrestaurant.co.uk – Closed 1 week January,1 week spring, 1 week autumn, Tuesday lunch, Sunday and Monday* Z**a**

Rest – Menu £ 22 (lunch) – Carte £ 30/44

◆ Neighbourhood restaurant with welcoming feel. Plain décor with oils and prints; large well spaced tables. Extensive menu of local, seasonal fare; plenty of meat, fish and vegetarian choices.

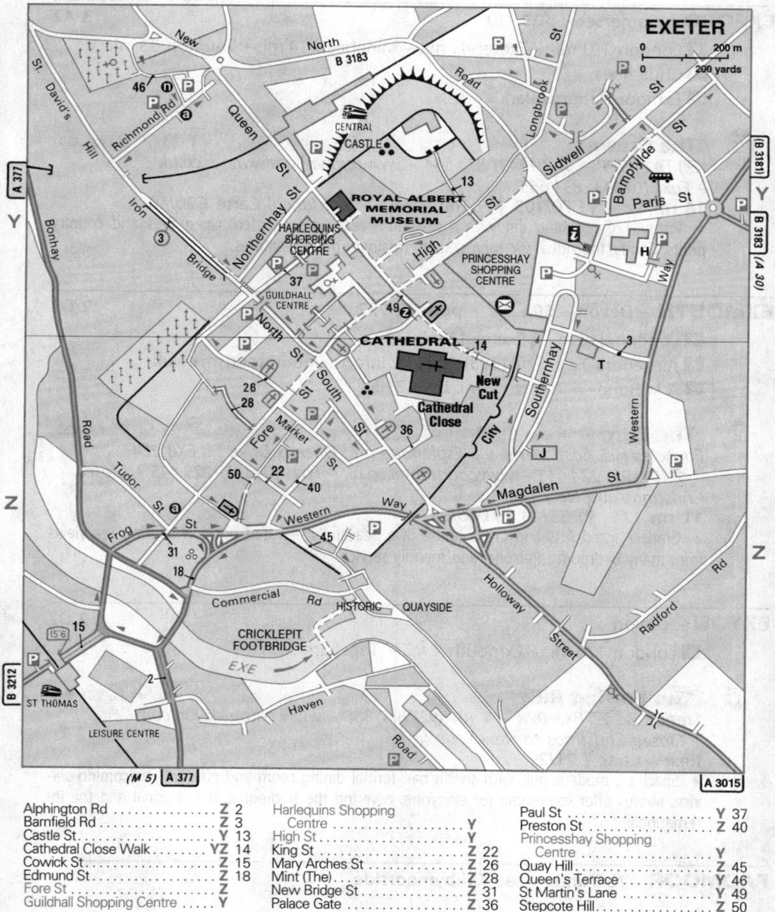

Alphington Rd .... Z 2
Barnfield Rd .... Z 3
Castle St .... Y 13
Cathedral Close Walk .... YZ 14
Cowick St .... Z 15
Edmund St .... Z 18
Fore St .... Z
Guildhall Shopping Centre .... Y
Harlequins Shopping Centre .... Y
High St .... Y
King St .... Z 22
Mary Arches St .... Z 26
Mint (The) .... Z 28
New Bridge St .... Z 31
Palace Gate .... Z 36
Paul St .... Y 37
Preston St .... Z 40
Princesshay Shopping Centre .... Y
Quay Hill .... Z 45
Queen's Terrace .... Y 46
St Martin's Lane .... Y 49
Stepcote Hill .... Z 50

at Rockbeare East : 7.5 mi. by A 30 - V – ✉ Exeter

Jack in the Green Inn

London Rd ✉ EX5 2EE – ✆ (01404) 822 240 – www.jackinthegreen.uk.com – Fax (01404) 823 445 – Closed 25 December to 5 January and Sunday

Rest – Menu £ 25 – Carte £ 25/35

◆ Characterful pub near Exeter airport, with leather-furnished lounge and beamed dining rooms. Unfussy, seasonal dishes, with good use of local ingredients. Friendly service.

at Kenton Southeast : 7 mi. by A 3015 - X - on A 379 – ✉ Exeter

XX Rodean

The Triangle ✉ EX6 8LS – ✆ (01626) 890 195 – www.rodeanrestaurant.co.uk – closed 2 weeks after Easter, Sunday dinner and Monday

Rest – *(dinner only and Sunday lunch)* Carte £ 28/39

◆ Family run early 20C butchers shop in pretty spot. Bar area for pre-prandials. Restaurant in two rooms with beams and local photos. Menus employ good use of local ingredients.

EXFORD – Somerset – 503 J30 — 3 A2

London 193 mi. – Exeter 41 mi. – Minehead 14 mi. – Taunton 33 mi.

Church★

Exmoor National Park★★

The Crown

TA24 7PP – (01643) 831 554 – www.crownhotelexmoor.co.uk – Fax (01643) 831 665

16 rm – †£ 70/105 ††£ 140 **Rest** – *(bar lunch)* Carte £ 20/40

◆ Pretty 17C coaching inn with a delightful rear water garden. Open fires and country prints. Comfy, individualistic rooms, some retaining period features.

EXMOUTH – Devon – 503 J32 – pop. 32 972 — 2 D2

London 210 mi. – Exeter 11 mi.

Alexandra Terr (01395) 222299, info@exmouthtourism.co.uk

A la Ronde★ **AC**, N : 2 mi. by B 3180

The Barn without rest

Foxholes Hill, East : 1 mi. via Esplanade and Queens Drive EX8 2DF – (01395) 224 411 – www.barnhotel.co.uk – Fax (01395) 225 445 – Closed Christmas and New Year

11 rm – †£ 35/48 ††£ 65/99

◆ Grade II listed Arts and Crafts house in a peacefully elevated position offering sea views from many bedrooms. Personal and friendly service.

EXTON – Devon — 2 D2

London 176 mi. – Exmouth 4 mi. – Topsham 3 mi.

The Puffing Billy

Station Rd EX3 0PR – (01392) 877 888 – www.eatoutdevon.com – Closed Christmas to New Year

Rest – Carte £ 21/29

◆ Spacious, modern pub with stylish bar, formal dining room and efficient, welcoming service. Menus offer something for everyone, covering the traditional, the regional and the international.

FADMOOR – N. Yorks. – see Kirkbymoorside

FAIRFORD – Gloucestershire – 503 O28 – pop. 2 960 Great Britain — 4 D1

London 88 mi. – Cirencester 9 mi. – Oxford 29 mi.

Church of St Mary★ (Stained glass windows★★)

Cirencester★ - Church of St John the Baptist★ - Corinium Museum★ (Mosaic Pavements★), W : 9 mi. on A 429, A 435, Spitalgate Lane and Dollar St – Swindon - Great Railway Museum★ **AC** - Railway Village Museum★ **AC**, S : 17 mi. on A 419, A 4312, A 4259 and B 4289

Allium

1 London St, Market Pl GL7 4AH – (01285) 712 200 – www.allium.uk.net – Closed 25-26 December, 2 weeks January, 2 weeks August, Tuesday lunch, Sunday dinner and Monday

Rest – Menu £ 23/39

◆ Keenly run neighbourhood restaurant with comfy lounge and small bar, colourful artwork and friendly, well-structured service. Set menus feature local produce; lunch provides good value.

FALMOUTH – Cornwall – 503 E33 – pop. 21 635 1 A3

London 308 mi. – Penzance 26 mi. – Plymouth 65 mi. – Truro 11 mi.

11 Market Strand, Prince of Wales Pier ✆ (01326) 312300, info@falmouthtic.co.uk

Swanpool Rd, ✆ (01326) 311 262

Budock Vean Hotel Mawnan Smith, ✆ (01326) 252 102

Town★ – Pendennis Castle★ (<★★) **AC** B

Glendurgan Garden★★ **AC** - Trebah Garden★, SW : 4.5 mi. by Swanpool Rd A – Mawnan Parish Church★ (<★★) S : 4 mi. by Swanpool Rd A – Cruise along Helford River★. Trelissick★★ (<★★) NW : 13 mi. by A 39 and B 3289 A – Carn Brea (<★★) NW : 10 mi. by A 393 A – Gweek (Setting★, Seal Sanctuary★) SW : 8 mi. by A 39 and Treverva rd – Wendron (Poldark Mine★) **AC**, SW : 12.5 mi. by A 39 - A - and A 394

Plan on next page

Greenbank

Harbourside ✉ TR11 2SR – ✆ (01326) 312 440 – www.greenbank-hotel.co.uk – Fax (01326) 211 362 Aa

59 rm – £ 85/105 £ 145/155 – 1 suite

Rest *Harbourside* – Carte £ 19/32

◆ Flagstones and sweeping staircase greet your arrival in this ex-17C coaching inn, just as they once did for Florence Nightingale and Kenneth Grahame. Rooms with harbour views. Fine vista of bay from modern restaurant.

St Michael's H & Spa

rm,

Gyllyngvase Beach ✉ TR11 4NB – ✆ (01326) 312 707 – www.stmichaelshotel.co.uk – Fax (01326) 211 772 Bc

61 rm – £ 57/159 £ 114/212

Rest – Menu £ 25 (dinner) – Carte £ 22/45

◆ Reinvestment and refurbishment ensure that the hotel remains fresh, bright and contemporary. Nautical theme throughout. Comfortable bedrooms, many with sea views. Restaurant looks down sloping gardens to bay beyond.

Dolvean House without rest

50 Melvill Rd ✉ TR11 4DQ – ✆ (01326) 313 658 – www.dolvean.co.uk – Fax (01326) 313 995 – Closed Christmas Bn

10 rm – £ 36/62 £ 72/94

◆ Smart cream property with local books and guides in parlour: exceptionally good detail wherever you look. Elegant, neatly laid breakfast room. Bright, well-kept bedrooms.

Chelsea House without rest

2 Emslie Rd ✉ TR11 4BG – ✆ (01326) 212 230 – www.chelseahousehotel.com Be

8 rm – £ 42/47 £ 78/90

◆ Large Victorian house in quiet residential area with partial sea-view at front. Neat breakfast room; well-appointed bedrooms, three with their own balconies.

Prospect House without rest

1 Church Rd, Penryn, Northwest : 2 mi. by A 39 on B 3292 ✉ TR10 8DA – ✆ (01326) 373 198 – www.prospecthouse.co.uk

3 rm – £ 40 £ 70/75

◆ Large Georgian guesthouse on Penryn river, set within walled garden, run by welcoming owner. Super breakfasts with local produce in abundance. Individually styled rooms.

The Three Mackerel

Swanpool Beach, South : 0.75 mi. off Pennance Rd ✉ TR11 5BG – ✆ (01326) 311 886 – www.thethreemackerel.com – Fax (01326) 316 014

Rest – Carte £ 22/49

◆ Casually informal beachside restaurant with white clapperboard façade. Super terrace or light interior. Seasonal, local ingredients provide the core of modern menus.

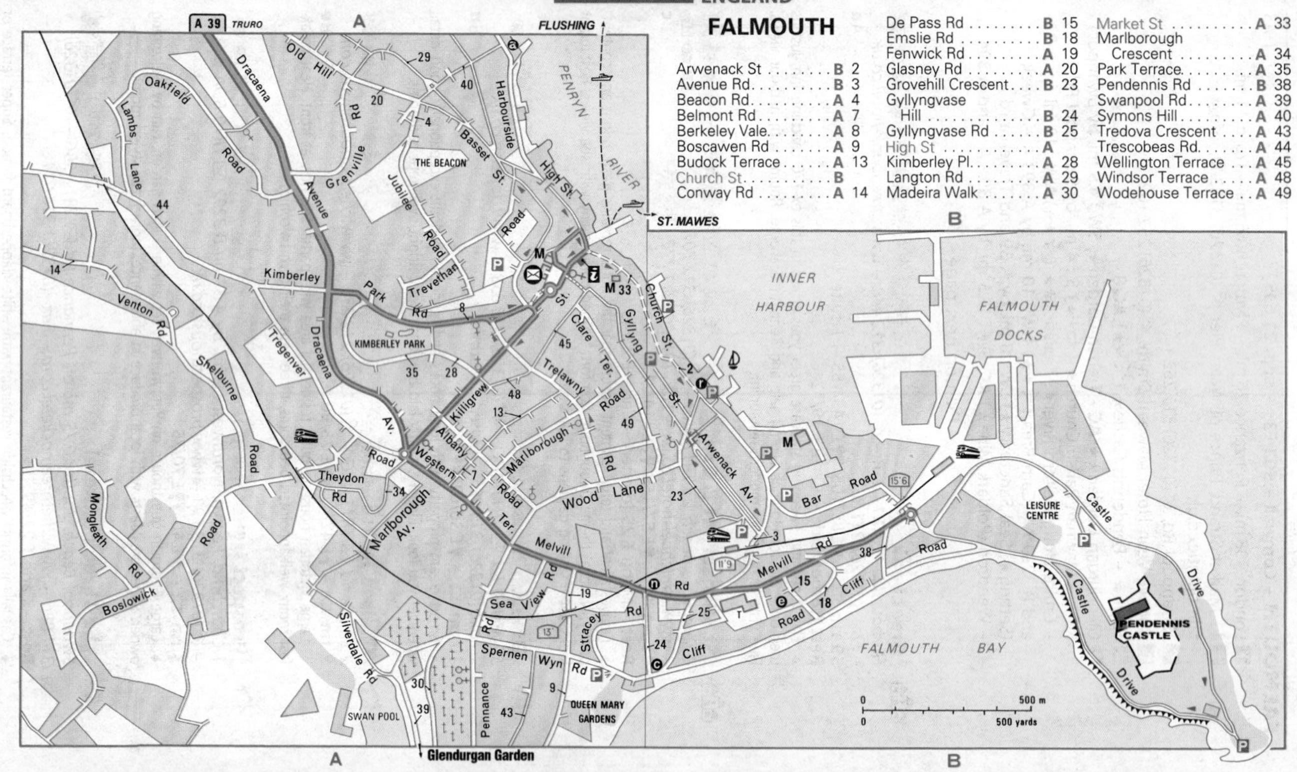
FALMOUTH
Arwenack St . . . . B 2
Avenue Rd. . . . . B 3
Beacon Rd. . . . . A 4
Belmont Rd . . . . A 7
Berkeley Vale. . . . . A 8
Boscawen Rd . . . . A 9
Budock Terrace . . . . . . A 13
Church St. . . . . B
Conway Rd . . . . A 14
De Pass Rd . . . . B 15
Emslie Rd . . . . B 18
Fenwick Rd . . . . A 19
Glasney Rd . . . . A 20
Grovehill Crescent . . . . B 23
Gyllyngvase Hill . . . . . . B 24
Gyllyngvase Rd . . . . . . B 25
High St . . . . A
Kimberley Pl. . . . . A 28
Langton Rd . . . . A 29
Madeira Walk . . . . A 30
Market St . . . . A 33
Marlborough Crescent . . . . A 34
Park Terrace. . . . . A 35
Pendennis Rd . . . . B 38
Swanpool Rd. . . . . A 39
Symons Hill . . . . A 40
Tredova Crescent . . . . A 43
Trescobeas Rd. . . . . . . A 44
Wellington Terrace . . . A 45
Windsor Terrace . . . . . A 48
Wodehouse Terrace . . A 49
A 39 TRURO
FLUSHING
ST. MAWES
PENRYN RIVER
INNER HARBOUR
FALMOUTH DOCKS
FALMOUTH BAY
THE BEACON
KIMBERLEY PARK
LEISURE CENTRE
PENDENNIS CASTLE
QUEEN MARY GARDENS
SWAN POOL
Glendurgan Garden
0 500 m
0 500 yards

Bistro de la Mer

28 Arwenack St – ☎ (01326) 316 509 – www.bistrodelamer.com – Closed Christmas, Sunday, lunch Monday and Sunday-Monday in October-April
Rest – Menu £ 17 (lunch) – Carte £ 25/38 **Br**
◆ Modest bistro with a subtle Mediterranean feel, set over two floors and decorated in sunny seaside colours of yellow and blue. Extensive seafood-oriented menu; honest cooking.

at Mylor Bridge North : 4.5 mi. by A 39 - A - and B 3292 on Mylor rd – ✉ Falmouth

Pandora Inn

Restronguet Creek, Northeast : 1 mi. by Passage Hill off Restronguet Hill ✉ TR11 5ST – ☎ (01326) 372 678 – www.pandorainn.com – Fax (01326) 378 958 – Closed 25 December
Rest – Carte £ 15/32
◆ Characterful 13C inn in scenic spot, with its own pontoon. Seasonally changing menus feature fish, seafood and salads in summer; with casseroles, stews and game in winter.

at Maenporth Beach South : 3.75 mi. by Pennance Rd

The Cove

Maenporth Beach ✉ TR11 5HN – ☎ (01326) 251 136 – www.thecovemaenporth.co.uk
Rest – Carte £ 22/31
◆ Within a modern building overlooking the beach and cove. Concise menu with daily specials; bright, unfussy cooking, with the occasional Asian note. Young, enthusiastic service.

FAREHAM – Hampshire – 503 Q31 – pop. 54 866 Great Britain 6 B2

London 77 mi. – Portsmouth 9 mi. – Southampton 13 mi. – Winchester 19 mi.
Westbury Manor, 84 West St ☎ (01329) 221342, farehamtic@tourismse.com
Portchester castle★ **AC**, SE : 2.5 mi. by A 27

Lauro's brasserie

8 High St ✉ PO16 7AN – ☎ (01329) 234 179 – www.laurosbrasserie.co.uk – Fax (01329) 822 776 – Closed 25 December, 1 January, Sunday dinner and Monday
Rest – Menu £ 13/26 (weekdays) – Carte £ 28/36
◆ Personally run 1820s townhouse. Cream and coral walls lead to a large open-plan kitchen. Daily set menu and weekly à la carte display flavoursome modern European dishes with an Asian edge.

FARNHAM – Dorset – 503 N31 – see Blandford Forum

FARNINGHAM – Kent – 504 U29 8 B1

London 22 mi. – Dartford 7 mi. – Maidstone 20 mi.

Beesfield Farm without rest

Beesfield Lane, off A 225 ✉ DA4 0LA – ☎ (01322) 863 900 – www.beesfieldfarm.co.uk – Fax (01322) 863 900 – Closed 12 December-12 January
3 rm – †£ 65/70 ††£ 80/90
◆ Peaceful valley setting, with attractive garden. Exudes character: oldest part is 400 year-old Kentish longhouse. Comfy sitting room; bedrooms boast beams and garden outlook.

FAR SAWREY – Cumbria – 502 L20 – see Hawkshead

FAVERSHAM – Kent – 504 W30 – pop. 18 222 9 C1

London 52 mi. – Dover 26 mi. – Maidstone 21 mi. – Margate 25 mi.
Fleur de Lis Heritage Centre, 13 Preston St ☎ (01795) 534542, ticfaversham@btconnect.com

ENGLAND

XXX ✿ **Read's** (David Pitchford) with rm

Macknade Manor, Canterbury Rd, East : 1 mi. on A 2 ✉ ME13 8XE – ☎ (01795) 535 344 – www.reads.com – Fax (01795) 591 200 – Closed 25-26 December, first week January, 2 weeks September, Sunday and Monday

6 rm ☕ – †£ 125/195 ††£ 165/195 **Rest** – Menu £ 24/52

Spec. Terrine of ham hock and confit chicken with piccalilli. Three styles of lamb with lentils, cabbage and celeriac. Plum soufflé with honeycomb ice cream and shortbread biscuits.

◆ Elegant red brick house with beautiful grounds. Confident, classically based dishes make the best of local produce, including fruit, vegetables and herbs from the walled garden. Comfortable bedrooms in country house style.

at Dargate **East : 6 mi. by A 2 off A 299 – ✉ Kent**

The Dove

Plum Pudding Lane ✉ ME13 9HB – ☎ (01227) 751 360 – Closed Sunday dinner and Monday

Rest – Carte £ 25/35

◆ Attractive Victorian red-brick pub boasting well-tended gardens complete with dovecotes. Menus offer heartwarming specials of the day, alongside appetising local and seasonal dishes.

at Oare **Northwest : 2.5 mi. by A2 off B2045**

Three Mariners

2 Church Road ✉ ME13 0QA – ☎ (01795) 533 633 – www.thethreemarinersoare.co.uk – Closed Monday (except Bank Holidays) and Tuesday dinner

Rest – Menu £ 15 (lunch) – Carte £ 21/28

◆ 500 year old pub by a small marina in a sleepy hamlet, with pleasant marsh views from the terrace. Constantly evolving menus offer an appealing mix of carefully prepared, flavoursome dishes.

FAWKHAM GREEN – **Kent** – **504** U29 – **see Brands Hatch**

FENCE – **Blackburn** – **502** N22 – **see Padiham**

FERMAIN BAY – **C.I.** – **503** L33 – **see Channel Islands (Guernsey)**

FERRENSBY – **N. Yorks.** – **see Knaresborough**

FLAUNDEN – **Hertfordshire** – **pop. 5 468** **12** A2

London 35 mi. – Reading 43 mi. – Luton 23 mi. – Milton Keynes 42 mi.

The Bricklayers Arms

Hogpits Bottom ✉ HP3 0PH – ☎ (01442) 833 322 – www.bricklayersarms.com – Fax (01442) 834 841 – Closed 25 December

Rest – Carte £ 26/33

◆ Smart pub tucked away in a small hamlet. There are no snacks on offer, just traditional, hearty, French-inspired dishes. Meat and fish are smoked in-house and old-school puddings follow.

FLETCHING – **East Sussex** – **504** U30/3 – **pop. 1 722** **8** A2

London 45 mi. – Brighton 20 mi. – Eastbourne 24 mi. – Maidstone 20 mi.

The Griffin Inn with rm

✉ TN22 3SS – ☎ (01825) 722 890 – www.thegriffininn.co.uk – Fax (01825) 722 810 – Closed 25 December

13 rm ☕ – †£ 70/80 ††£ 110/145

Rest – *(meals in bar Sunday dinner)* Menu £ 30 (Sunday lunch) – Carte £ 22/35

◆ 16C red and white brick pub with terrace and large garden. Daily-changing menu offers modern British dishes with some Italian influences; produce is locally sourced. Beamed bedrooms feature four-posters, rushmat flooring and hand-painted murals.

ENGLAND

FOLKESTONE – Kent – 504 X30 – pop. 45 273 Great Britain

London 76 mi. – Brighton 76 mi. – Dover 8 mi. – Maidstone 33 mi.

Access Channel Tunnel : Eurotunnel information and reservations ✆ (08705) 353535

Bouverie Place Shopping Centre ✆ (01303) 258594, cckirkham@gmail.com

The Leas★ (≤★) Z

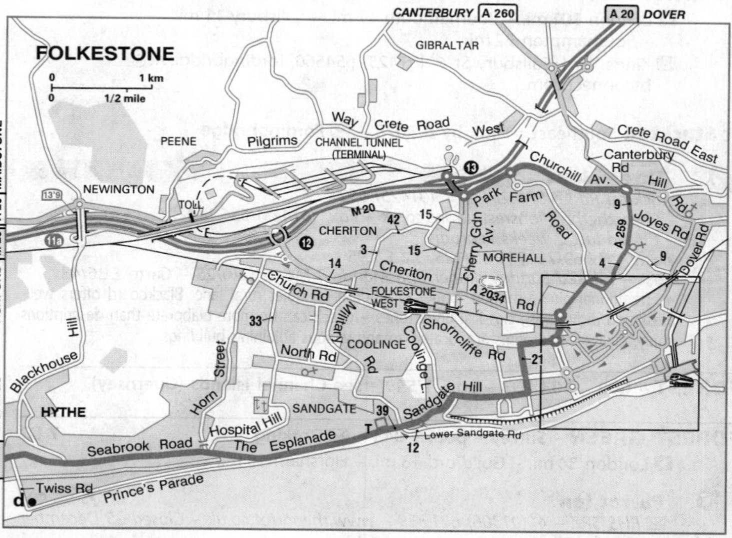

FOLKESTONE

FOLKESTONE

Street	Square	No.
Ashley Ave	X	3
Black Bull Rd	X, Y	4
Bouverie Pl.	Z	6
Bradstone Rd	Y	8
Canterbury Rd	X	9
Castle Rd	X	12
Cheriton High St	X	14
Cheriton Pl.	Z	13
Cherry Garden Lane	X	15
Clifton Crescent	Z	16
Clifton Rd	Z	17
Durlocks (The)	Y	20
Earl's Ave	X	21
Grace Hill	Y	22
Guildhall St	YZ	23
Harbour App. Rd	Z	25
Harbour St	Z	24
Langhorne Gardens	Z	27
Manor Rd	Z	28
Marine Terrace	Z	29
Middelburg Sq.	Z	30
North St	Y	32
Old High St	YZ	
Pond Hill Rd	X	33
Radnor Bridge Rd	Y	34
Remembrance (Rd of)	Z	35
Rendezvous St	Y	37
Ryland Pl.	Y	38
Sandgate High St	X	39
Sandgate Rd	Z	
Shorncliffe Rd	Y	41
Tilekiln Lane	X	42
Tontine St	Y	
Trinity Gardens	Z	43
Victoria Grove	Y	45
West Terrace	Z	47

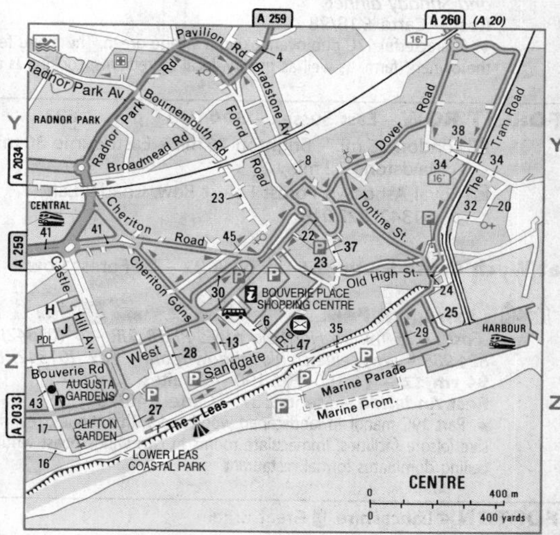

The Relish without rest

4 Augusta Gardens ✉ CT20 2RR – ✆ (01303) 850 952 – www.hotelrelish.co.uk – Fax (01303) 850 958 – Closed 22 December-2 January, minimum 2 night stay at weekends Zn

10 rm – †£ 65/90 ††£ 90/140

◆ Large Regency townhouse overlooking private parkland. Stylish black canopy to entrance; modish furnishings. Handy food and drink area at foot of stairs. Light, airy rooms.

FORDINGBRIDGE – Hampshire – 503 O31 – pop. 5 755 — 6 A2

London 101 mi. – Bournemouth 17 mi. – Salisbury 11 mi. – Southampton 22 mi.

Kings Yard, Salisbury St ✆ (01425) 654560, fordingbridgevic@btconnect.com

at Stuckton Southeast : 1 mi. by B 3078 – ✉ Fordingbridge

Three Lions with rm

Stuckton Rd ✉ SP6 2HF – ✆ (01425) 652 489 – www.thethreelionsrestaurant.co.uk – Fax (01425) 656 144 – Closed last 2 weeks February

7 rm – †£ 69/79 ††£ 85/125, £ 7.95

Rest – *(Closed Sunday dinner and Monday)* Menu £ 20/25 – Carte £ 36/43

◆ Traditional pine-furnished former farmhouse on quiet rural lane. Blackboard offers well-presented dishes with classical undertones – which can be more elaborate than descriptions imply. Pleasant bedrooms are located among various adjoining buildings.

FOREST – G02 – 503 P33 – pop. 1 549 – see Channel Islands (Guernsey)

FOREST GREEN – Surrey – pop. 1 843 – ✉ Dorking — 7 D2

London 34 mi. – Guildford 13 mi. – Horsham 10 mi.

Parrot Inn

✉ RH5 5RZ – ✆ (01306) 621 339 – www.theparrot.co.uk – Closed 25 December and Sunday dinner

Rest – Carte £ 18/28

◆ Characterful 17C pub overlooking a village green. The menu features plenty of meat from the owners' farm, as well as quality, local ingredients; cooking is unfussy and generous.

FOREST ROW – East Sussex – 504 U30 – pop. 3 623 — 8 A2

London 35 mi. – Brighton 26 mi. – Eastbourne 30 mi. – Maidstone 32 mi.

Royal Ashdown Forest Forest Row, Chapel Lane, ✆ (01342) 822 018

at Wych Cross South : 2.5 mi. on A 22 – ✉ Forest Row

Ashdown Park

East : 0.75 mi. on Hartfield rd ✉ RH18 5JR – ✆ (01342) 824 988 – www.elite.co.uk/ashdownpark – Fax (01342) 826 206

94 rm – †£ 160 ††£ 190 – 2 suites

Rest *Anderida* – Menu £ 37 – Carte £ 40/70

◆ Part 19C manor in landscaped woodland with antiques, real fires. Former convent. Extensive leisure facilities. Immaculate rooms in two wings boast writing desks, armchairs. Ornate ceiling dominates formal restaurant.

FORTON – Lancashire Great Britain — 20 A1

London 236 mi. – Blackpool 18 mi. – Manchester 45 mi.

Lancaster - Castle★, N : 5.5 mi. by A 6

The Bay Horse Inn with rm 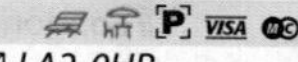

Bay Horse Lane, North : 1.25 mi. by A 6 on Quernmore rd ✉ LA2 0HR – ✆ (01524) 791 204 – www.bayhorseinn.com – Closed 25-26 December, 1 January, Sunday dinner and Monday

3 rm – 🚹£ 89 🚹🚹£ 89 **Rest** – Menu £ 21 (lunch) – Carte £ 18/28

◆ Cosy pub in a pleasant rural location, with characterful interior and attractive terrace. Seasonal, locally sourced produce is crafted into a mix of classic and modern dishes. Beautifully appointed bedrooms in the nearby corn store.

FOTHERINGHAY Northants – NTH – **504** S26 – see Oundle

see Oundle

FOWEY – Cornwall – **503** G32 – pop. 2 064 **1** B2

London 277 mi. – Newquay 24 mi. – Plymouth 34 mi. – Truro 22 mi.

5 South St ✆ (01726) 833616, info@fowey.co.uk

Town★★

Gribbin Head (<★★) 6 mi. rtn on foot – Bodinnick (<★★) - Lanteglos Church★, E : 5 mi. by ferry – Polruan (<★★) SE : 6 mi. by ferry – Polkerris★, W : 2 mi. by A 3082

Fowey Hall

Hanson Drive, West : 0.5 mi. off A 3082 ✉ PL23 1ET – ✆ (01726) 833 866 – www.foweyhallhotel.co.uk – Fax (01726) 834 100

25 rm – 🚹£ 135/235 🚹🚹£ 170/280 – 11 suites

Rest – *(light lunch Monday-Saturday)* Menu £ 40

◆ Imposing 19C country house within walled garden. Two spacious lounges with real fires, wicker furnished garden room. Smart, plush rooms. Special facilities for children. Impressive oak-panelled restaurant.

Old Quay House

28 Fore St ✉ PL23 1AQ – ✆ (01726) 833 302 – www.theoldquayhouse.com – Fax (01726) 833 668

11 rm – 🚹£ 100 🚹🚹£ 160/230

Rest – *(Closed lunch Tuesday)* Carte £ 24/34

◆ Former Victorian seamen's mission idyllically set on the waterfront. Stylish, contemporary lounge. Rear terrace overlooks the river. Smart, individually decorated bedrooms. Spacious restaurant with wicker and wood furniture, serving modern British dishes.

at Golant North : 3 mi. by B 3269 – ✉ Fowey

Cormorant

✉ PL23 1LL – ✆ (01726) 833 426 – www.cormoranthotel.co.uk – Fax (01726) 833 219 – Closed 3-31 January

14 rm – 🚹£ 45/65 🚹🚹£ 165/195

Rest – *(dinner only) (booking essential)* Menu £ 35 – Carte £ 29/41

◆ Stunningly located with wonderful views. All bedrooms have river vista, flatscreen TVs, fridges and large beds; several also have balconies. Comfortable lounge with fireplace. Pretty dining room with balcony terrace. Appealing menus.

FRAMLINGHAM – Suffolk – **504** Y27 – pop. 2 839 – ✉ Woodbridge **15** D3

London 92 mi. – Ipswich 19 mi. – Norwich 42 mi.

at Badingham Northeast : 3.25 mi. by B 1120 on A 1120 – ✉ Woodbridge

Colston Hall without rest

Badingham, North : 4.25 mi. by B 1120 off A 1120 ✉ IP13 8LB – ✆ (01728) 638 375 – www.colstonhall.com – Fax (01728) 638 084

6 rm – 🚹£ 50/110 🚹🚹£ 90/110

◆ Part Elizabethan farmhouse in rural location with lakes and garden. Comfy rooms - three of which are in stables - with character: plenty of timbers and small sitting areas.

FREATHY – Cornwall – see Millbrook

FRESSINGFIELD – Suffolk – 504 X26 — 15 D2

London 104 mi. – Ipswich 34 mi. – Lowestoft 27 mi.

XX **The Fox & Goose Inn**

Church Rd ✉ IP21 5PB – ✆ (01379) 586 247 – www.foxandgoose.net – Fax (01379) 586 106 – Closed 2 weeks early January, 27-31 December and Monday

Rest – *(booking essential)* Menu £ 16 (lunch) – Carte £ 24/34

◆ Spacious cream-washed former pub, run by ambitious young owners. Characterful dining rooms display exposed beams, stone floors and local artwork. Large menus offer traditional fare.

FRILSHAM – Newbury – see Yattendon

FRISTON – Suffolk – see Aldeburgh

FRITHSDEN – Herts. – see Hemel Hempstead

FRITTON – Norfolk — 15 D2

London 133 mi. – Great Yarmouth 8 mi. – Norwich 19 mi.

Fritton House

Church Lane ✉ NR31 9HA – ✆ (01493) 484 008 – www.adnams.co.uk

8 rm – †£ 120/160 ††£ 120/160 – 1 suite **Rest** – Carte £ 19/30

◆ Successful meeting point of 18C charm and contemporary boutique style. Elegant drawing room with sumptuous sofas and fresh flowers. Comfortable, sleek bedrooms. Dine on intriguing 21C dishes in relaxed, raftered surroundings.

FROGGATT EDGE – Derbyshire – 502 P24 — 16 A1

London 167 mi. – Bakewell 6 mi. – Sheffield 11 mi.

The Chequers Inn with rm

on A 625 ✉ S32 3ZJ – ✆ (01433) 630 231 – www.chequers-froggatt.com – Fax (01433) 631 072 – Closed 25 December

5 rm – †£ 75/95 ††£ 75/95 **Rest** – Carte £ 20/27

◆ Refurbished 16C Grade II listed building, retaining many period features. Wide-ranging, modern menus enhanced by accomplished cooking. Pleasant, cosy bedrooms.

FROME – Somerset – 503 M/N30 – pop. 24 171 — 4 C2

London 118 mi. – Bristol 24 mi. – Southampton 52 mi. – Swindon 44 mi.

Babington House

Babington, Northwest : 6.5 mi. by A 362 on Vobster rd ✉ BA11 3RW – ✆ (01373) 812 266 – www.babingtonhouse.co.uk – Fax (01373) 813 866

32 rm – †£ 195/700 ††£ 195/700, £ 14.50

Rest ***The Orangery*** – *(residents and members only)* Carte £ 25/45

◆ Country house with vivid difference: Georgian exterior; cool, trendy interior. Good health club, even a cinema. Modern, understated and recently refurbished bedrooms. Relaxed dining with modern menu.

XX **The Settle**

16 Cheap St, off Market Pl ✉ BA11 1BN – ✆ (01373) 465 975 – Fax (01373) 465 975 – Closed 1 week Christmas, 1 week August and Sunday-Wednesday

Rest – *(dinner only)* Menu £ 27

◆ Friendly first-floor restaurant with bar, set above tea shop in town centre. Concise, well-priced set menus offer succinct descriptions and feature local produce. Approachable chef often seen.

FUNTINGTON – W. Sussex – 504 R31 – see Chichester

FYFIELD – Oxfordshire – see Oxford

GATESHEAD – Tyne and Wear – 501 P19 – pop. 78 403 Great Britain **24** B2

London 282 mi. – Durham 16 mi. – Middlesbrough 38 mi. – Newcastle upon Tyne 1 mi.

Access Tyne Tunnel (toll)

Central Library, Prince Consort Rd ✆ (0191) 433 8420, l& ctouristinformationcentre@gateshead.gov.uk BX - The Sage, St Mary's Sq, Gateshead Quays ✆ (0191) 478 4222, tourism@gateshead.gov.uk AX

Ravensworth Wrekenton Angel View, Long Bank, ✆ (0191) 487 6014

Heworth Gingling Gate, ✆ (0191) 469 9832

Beamish : North of England Open Air Museum★★ **AC**, SW : 6 mi. by A 692 and A 6076 BX

Plan : see Newcastle upon Tyne

Stables Lodge without rest

South Farm, Lamesley, Southwest: 5 mi. by A 167 and Belle Vue Bank on A 692 ✉ NE11 0ET – ✆ (0191) 492 17 56 – www.thestableslodge.co.uk – Fax (0191) 410 61 92

3 rm – †£ 74 ††£ 138

◆ Rustic and cosy former farmhouse, just off the A1. Individually decorated, very comfortable bedrooms; the Red Room is the most luxurious; the Garden Room has its own hot tub.

Six

Baltic Centre for Contemporary Art, Gateshead Quays, South Shore Rd ✉ NE8 3BA – ✆ (0191) 440 49 48 – www.sixbaltic.com – Closed 25-26 Decmber, 1 January and Sunday dinner BX**x**

Rest – Menu £ 18 (lunch and early dinner) – Carte £ 24/34

◆ Fantastic location on top floor of Baltic Centre; floor to ceiling windows afford views of city's skyline, the Tyne and the Millennium bridge. Modern brasserie, with a menu to match.

at Low Fell South : 2 mi. on A 167 - BX – ✉ Gateshead

Eslington Villa

8 Station Rd, West : 0.75 mi. by Belle Vue Bank, turning left at T junction, right at roundabout then taking first turn right ✉ NE9 6DR – ✆ (0191) 487 6017 – www.eslingtonvilla.co.uk – Fax (0191) 420 0667 – Closed 25-28 December

18 rm – †£ 75 ††£ 95/100

Rest – *(closed Saturday lunch, Sunday dinner and Bank Holidays)* Menu £ 19/23

◆ Well-run, stylish, privately owned hotel 10 minutes' drive from city centre. Nicely furnished lounge bar leads from smart reception. Attractively styled, modern bedrooms. Two separate dining areas, one of which is a conservatory. Both are classically decorated and serve good range of traditionally based dishes with modern twists.

GEORGE GREEN – Buckinghamshire **11** D3

London 23

The Pinewood

Wexham Park Lane, Uxbridge Rd, on A412 – ✆ (01753) 896 400 – www.pinewoodhotel.co.uk – Fax (01753) 896 500 – Closed 24-27 December

49 rm – †£ 59/139 ††£ 69/149

Rest ***Eden*** – Carte £ 19/32 **s**

◆ Located on the A412 close to Slough; ideal for those on business or on a trip to Legoland. Functional, modern rooms with some flair. Modern dishes with a twist in Eden.

GILLINGHAM – Dorset – 503 N30 – pop. 8 630 **4** C3

London 116 mi. – Bournemouth 34 mi. – Bristol 46 mi. – Southampton 52 mi.

Stourhead★★★ **AC**, N : 9 mi. by B 3092, B 3095 and B 3092

Stock Hill Country House

Stock Hill, West : 1.5 mi. on B 3081 ✉ SP8 5NR – ☎ (01747) 823 626 – www.stockhillhouse.co.uk – Fax (01747) 825 628
9 rm (dinner included) – £ 145/185 £ 280/320
Rest – *(booking essential)* Menu £ 30/40
◆ Idyllically peaceful Victorian country house set in eleven acres of mature woodland. Classically furnished. Individually decorated bedrooms, including antique beds. Very comfortable restaurant with rich drapes, attentive service.

GILSLAND – **Cumbria** – **502** M19 – **see Brampton**

GISBURN – **Lancashire** – **502** N22 **20** B2

London 242 mi. – Bradford 28 mi. – Skipton 12 mi.

La Locanda

Main St ✉ BB7 4HH – ☎ (01200) 445 303 – www.lalocanda.co.uk – Closed 2 weeks autumn, 25 December and Monday except Bank Holidays
Rest – Italian – *(dinner only) (booking essential)* Menu £ 14 (weekdays) – Carte £ 18/29
◆ Charming flag-floored cottage in small hamlet. Authentic Italian cooking borrows influences from Lombardy/Piedmont, with produce largely imported. Tasty pasta and ice cream are homemade.

ENGLAND

GITTISHAM – **Devon** – **503** K31 – **see Honiton**

GLEWSTONE – **Herefordshire** – **see Ross-on-Wye**

GLOSSOP – **Derbyshire** – **502** O23 – **pop. 30 771** **16** A1

London 194 mi. – Manchester 18 mi. – Sheffield 25 mi.
Bank House, Henry St ☎ (01457) 855920, info@glossoptouristcentre.co.uk
Sheffield Rd, ☎ (01457) 865 247

The Wind in the Willows

Derbyshire Level, East : 1 mi. by A 57 ✉ SK13 7PT – ☎ (01457) 868 001 – www.windinthewillows.co.uk – Fax (01457) 853 354 – Closed 24-29 December
12 rm – £ 88/105 £ 130/155
Rest – *(dinner only) (residents only)* Menu £ 29 s
◆ Victorian country house in Peak District, named after trees in garden. Adjacent golf course. Snug, fully-panelled sitting room. Bedrooms individually styled with antiques. Eat on carved chairs at gleaming wooden tables.

GODSHILL – **Isle of Wight** – **504** Q32 – **see WIGHT (Isle of)**

GOLANT Cornwall – **Cornwall** – **503** G32 – **see Fowey**

GOLCAR – **W. Yorks.** – **see Huddersfield**

GOLDSBOROUGH – **North Yorkshire** – **see Whitby**

GOODNESTONE – **Kent** – **see Wingham**

GOREY – **C.I.** – **503** P33 – **see Channel Islands (Jersey)**

GORING – **Oxfordshire** – **503** Q29 – **pop. 4 193** Great Britain **10** B3

London 56 mi. – Oxford 16 mi. – Reading 12 mi.
Ridgeway Path★★

XX **Leatherne Bottel**

The Bridleway, North : 1.5 mi. by B 4009 ✉ RG8 0HS – ✆ (01491) 872 667 – www.leathernebottel.co.uk – Fax (01491) 875 308 – Closed Sunday dinner

Rest – *(booking essential)* Menu £ 19 (lunch)/30 (Sunday) – Carte £ 36/44

◆ Delightful Thameside restaurant with lovely summer terrace. Menus fuse traditional recipes with interesting, modern combinations. Tasting menu at dinner; leaves/herbs picked fresh from garden.

GOSFORTH – **Tyne and Wear** – **501** P18 – **see Newcastle upon Tyne**

GOUDHURST – **Kent** – **504** V30 – **pop. 2 498** **8** B2

London 50 mi. – Hastings 25 mi. – Maidstone 17 mi.

 **West Winchet** without rest

Winchet Hill, North : 2.5 mi. on B 2079 ✉ TN17 1JX – ✆ (01580) 212 024 – Fax (01580) 212 250 – Closed Christmas-New Year

3 rm – £ 55 £ 80

◆ Victorian house with large, attractive rear garden. Breakfast taken in vast and attractively decorated drawing room. Traditional bedrooms offer country style décor.

GOVETON – **Devon** – **503** I33 – **see Kingsbridge**

GRANGE-OVER-SANDS – **Cumbria** – **502** L21 – **pop. 4 835** **21** A3

Great Britain

London 268 mi. – Kendal 13 mi. – Lancaster 24 mi.

Victoria Hall, Main St ✆ (015395) 34026, grangetic@southlakeland.gov.uk

Meathop Rd, ✆ (015395) 33 180

Cartmel Priory★, NW : 3 m

Netherwood rm, rest,

Lindale Rd ✉ LA11 6ET – ✆ (015395) 32 552 – www.netherwood-hotel.co.uk – Fax (015395) 34 121

34 rm – £ 80/120 £ 120/200 **Rest** – Menu £ 18/32 **s**

◆ Unusual, castellated late 18C hotel offering fine view of Morecambe Bay. Atmospheric wood-panelled lounges, each boasting open log fire. Comfy rooms with good mod cons. Dine formally and enjoy superb bay vistas.

Clare House

Park Rd ✉ LA11 7HQ – ✆ (015395) 33 026 – www.clarehousehotel.co.uk – Fax (015395) 34 310 – March-November

18 rm (dinner included) – £ 84/147 £ 168

Rest – *(dinner only) (booking essential for non-residents)* Menu £ 32

◆ Longstanding family run hotel, its lovely lawned garden looking over Morecambe Bay. Two smartly furnished lounges. Traditionally styled rooms, most with bay views. Two pleasant dining rooms; daily changing five-course menus show care and interest.

at Cartmel **Northwest : 3 m – ✉ Grange-Over-Sands**

Aynsome Manor

North : 0.75 mi. by Cartmel Priory rd on Wood Broughton rd ✉ LA11 6HH – ✆ (015395) 36 653 – www.aynsomemanorhotel.co.uk – Fax (015395) 36 016 – Closed 25-26 December and 2-29 January

12 rm – £ 80/97 £ 90/126

Rest – *(Closed Sunday dinner to non-residents) (dinner only and Sunday lunch)* Menu £ 16/26

◆ Country house, personally run by two generations of the same family. Open fired snug bar and lounge with fine clocks. Sitting room has Priory view. Airy, traditional rooms. Dine on candle-lit, polished wood tables with silver.

Hill Farm without rest

Northwest : 1.5 mi. bearing to right of village shop in Market Square then left onto Cul-de-Sac rd after the racecourse ✉ LA11 7SS – ✆ (015395) 36 477 – *www.hillfarmbb.co.uk – February-October*

3 rm – †£ 40/45 ††£ 90/100

◆ Superb hospitality a feature of this 16C farmhouse with cottagey interior and lovely gardens: a peaceful setting. Individual colour schemes enhance the pretty bedrooms.

L'Enclume (Simon Rogan) with rm — rest, VISA AE

Cavendish St ✉ *LA11 6PZ* – ✆ *(015395) 36 362 – www.lenclume.co.uk*

12 rm – †£ 168 ††£ 198, £ 9.95

Rest – *(Closed lunch Monday-Wednesday) (booking essential)* Menu £ 25 (lunch) – Carte dinner £ 55/95

Spec. Razor clams with sea greens and asparagus. Squid ravioli with vodka and frogs legs. 'Expearamenthol frappé'.

◆ Converted smithy in sleepy village; stylish interior blends the rustic with the contemporary. 8/13/17 course set menus display creative, highly original dishes and inventive, contrasting combinations. Execution is very technical and presentation is impressive. Understated bedrooms offer good comforts.

Rogan and Company — VISA

The Square ✉ *LA11 6QD* – ✆ *(015395) 35 917 – www.roganandcompany.co.uk*

Rest – Carte £ 23/32

◆ Converted cottages in heart of rustic village. Modern interior with relaxed atmosphere, low level seating, raised stools and some antiques. Appealing menu offers real choice.

GRANTHAM – Lincolnshire – 502 S25 – pop. 34 592 Great Britain **17** C2

London 113 mi. – Leicester 31 mi. – Lincoln 29 mi. – Nottingham 24 mi.

The Guildhall Arts Centre, St Peter's Hill ✆ (01476) 406166, granthamtic@southkesteven.gov.uk

Belton Park Londonthorpe Rd, Belton Lane, ✆ (01476) 567 399

De Vere Belton Woods H., ✆ (01476) 593 200

St Wulfram's Church★

Belton House★ **AC**, N : 2.5 mi. by A 607. Belvoir Castle★★ **AC**, W : 6 mi. by A 607

at Hough-on-the-Hill North : 6.75 mi. by A 607 – ✉ Grantham

The Brownlow Arms with rm — rest, VISA

High Rd ✉ *NG32 2AZ* – ✆ *(01400) 250 234 – Closed 3 weeks January, 25-26 December, Sunday and Monday*

4 rm – †£ 65 ††£ 110

Rest – *(dinner only and Sunday lunch)* Carte £ 30/39

◆ Attractive part 17/19C inn in heart of rural Lincolnshire. Wood-panelled bar with deep armchairs. Formal dining: well executed modern British dishes. Very tasteful rooms.

at Woolsthorpe-by-Belvoir West : 7.5 mi. by A 607 – ✉ Grantham

The Chequers with rm — VISA AE

Main Street ✉ *NG32 1LU* – ✆ *(01476) 870 701 – www.chequersinn.net – Closed dinner 25-26 December and 1 January*

4 rm – †£ 49 ††£ 59 **Rest** – Menu £ 15/17 – Carte £ 21/33

◆ Attractive pub, orginally built as 17C farmhouse. Various nooks, crannies, exposed bricks and beams. Traditional English cuisine with emphasis on game. Simple, clean rooms.

at Harlaxton Southwest : 2.5 mi. on A 607 – ✉ Grantham

Gregory Arms — VISA

The Drift, Southwest : 2 m by A 607 ✉ *NG32 1AD* – ✆ *(01476) 577 076 – www.thegregory.co.uk – Closed dinner 25-26 December, 1 January and Sunday*

Rest – Carte £ 20/30 **s**

◆ Whitewashed, ivy-clad pub that's had an extensive refurbishment. Modern menu displays a selection of classic pub favourites, with the odd ambitious dish appearing at dinner.

at Great Gonerby Northwest : 2 mi. on B 1174 – ✉ Grantham

Harry's Place (Harry Hallam)

17 High St ✉ NG31 8JS – ✆ (01476) 561 780 – Closed 25 December-3 January, Sunday and Monday

Rest – *(booking essential)* Carte £ 52/62

Spec. Terrine of Filey crab. Lincolnshire salt marsh teal with blueberries. Wild blackberry soufflé.

◆ Long-standing, intimate restaurant consisting of just three tables; run by dedicated and delightful husband and wife team. Fresh flowers, candles and antiques abound. Classically based, hand-written menus offer well-judged, flavoursome dishes.

GRASMERE – Cumbria – 502 K20 – ✉ Ambleside ▮ Great Britain — 21 A2

London 282 mi. – Carlisle 43 mi. – Kendal 18 mi.

Dove Cottage★ **AC** AY **A**

Lake Windermere★★, SE : by A 591 AZ

Plans : see Ambleside

Rothay Garden

Broadgate ✉ LA22 9RJ – ✆ (01539) 435 334 – www.rothaygarden.com – Fax (01539) 435 723

30 rm (dinner included) – †£ 135/140 ††£ 230/240

Rest ***Rothay Garden*** – Menu £ 20/43

◆ A distinctive, modern hotel with delightful open bar and pleasant gardens. Stylish, contemporary bedrooms offer a host of extras. Formal, conservatory-style dining room offering complex cooking, which makes use of local, seasonal ingredients.

Dale Lodge

✉ LA22 9SW – ✆ (015394) 35 300 – www.dalelodgehotel.co.uk – Fax (015394) 35 570 – Closed 24-25 December

16 rm – †£ 80/100 ††£ 120/140

Rest ***The Lodge*** – *(booking essential at dinner)* Carte £ 24/33 **s**

◆ Family-owned hotel in delightful village, boasting spacious sitting rooms and contemporary bedrooms. The four newer duplex rooms have private courtyards and their own hot tub. Formal modern dining room, with seasonal, local food a speciality.

Moss Grove Organic without rest

✉ LA22 9SW – ✆ (015394) 35 251 – www.mossgrove.com – Fax (015394) 35 306 – Closed 24-25 December BZ**s**

11 rm – †£ 110/150 ††£ 155/195

◆ Uniquely organic hotel whose bedrooms offer top comforts; all have spa baths, some have four posters or balconies with rocking chairs. Mediterranean buffet in breakfast room.

Grasmere

Broadgate ✉ LA22 9TA – ✆ (015394) 35 277 – www.grasmerehotel.co.uk – Fax (015394) 35 277 – Closed 2 January-early February BZ**r**

13 rm – †£ 60/90 ††£ 130/150 – 1 suite

Rest – *(dinner only) (booking essential for non-residents)* Menu £ 30 **s**

◆ Small Victorian country house with pleasant acre of garden through which River Rothay flows. Snug, open-fired bar with good malt whisky selection. Individually styled rooms. Pleasant pine roofed rear dining room.

Lake View Country House without rest

Lake View Drive ✉ LA22 9TD – ✆ (015394) 35 384 – www.lakeview-grasmere.com BZ**c**

4 rm – ††£ 94/114

◆ Country house whose large garden boasts views of lake and a badger sett. Comfy bedrooms, two with spa baths. Breakfast includes homemade yoghurt, compotes and fruit platters.

Tweedies

Red Bank Rd ✉ LA22 9SW – ✆ (01539) 435 300 – www.dalelodgehotel.co.uk – Fax (01539) 435 570 – Closed 25 December dinner

Rest – Carte £ 23/34

◆ Charming, open-fired, flag-floored bar in heart of the Lakes. Substantial servings of pub favourites as well as more modern dishes, plus a vast array of regularly changing beers.

GRASSINGTON – North Yorkshire – 502 O21 – pop. 1 102 — 22 A2

– ✉ Skipton

London 240 mi. – Bradford 30 mi. – Burnley 28 mi. – Leeds 37 mi.

National Park Centre, Colvend, Hebden Rd ✆ (01756) 751690, grassington@yorkshiredales.org.uk

Ashfield House

Summers Fold, off Main St ✉ BD23 5AE – ✆ (01756) 752 584 – www.ashfieldhouse.co.uk – Fax (07092) 376 562 – Closed 9-31 January

8 rm – †£ 69/115 ††£ 97/123

Rest – *(closed dinner Wednesday and Sunday) (dinner only) (booking essential for non-residents)* Menu £ 34 **s**

◆ Sturdy 17C small stone hotel with beams and flagged floors: oozes period charm. Individually decorated, cottagey bedrooms with occasional exposed timber. Delightful garden. Tasty, locally-inspired dishes.

Grassington House

5 The Square ✉ BD23 5AQ – ✆ (01756) 752 406 – www.grassingtonhousehotel.co.uk – Closed 25 December

9 rm – †£ 65/75 ††£ 90/120

Rest *No 5 The Square* – Menu £ 16 (lunch) – Carte £ 26/35

◆ Refurbished Georgian house on cobbled street in busy village centre. Contemporary bar; terrace with smart cushioned furniture. Smart, modern bedrooms with good facilities. Restaurant offers large menu of classic British dishes with some worldwide influences.

Grassington Lodge without rest

8 Wood Lane ✉ BD23 5LU – ✆ (01756) 752 518 – www.grassingtonlodge.co.uk

11 rm – †£ 60 ††£ 110/150

◆ Modern guesthouse at gateway to Yorkshire Dales. Built over 100 years ago as home of village doctor. Gallery of local photos on display around the house. Stylish, smart rooms.

GREAT DUNMOW – Essex – 504 V28 – pop. 5 943 — 13 C2

London 42 mi. – Cambridge 27 mi. – Chelmsford 13 mi. – Colchester 24 mi.

The Starr with rm

Market Place ✉ CM6 1AX – ✆ (01371) 876 642 – www.the-starr.co.uk – Fax (01371) 876 337 – Closed 26 December-5 January and Monday

8 rm – †£ 90 ††£ 130 **Rest** – Menu £ 20 (lunch) – Carte £ 30/40

◆ Former 15C pub with rustic bar and fire. Characterful restaurant has exposed beams and conservatory. Strong, interesting cooking, traditionally inspired. Smart bedrooms.

Square 1

15 High St ✉ CM6 1AB – ✆ (01371) 859 922 – www.square1restaurant.co.uk – Closed 25 December, 1 January and Sunday dinner

Rest – Menu £ 15 (Monday dinner) – Carte £ 20/37

◆ Modern family-run restaurant in 14C monastic reading room. Stylish interior with vibrant artwork and open plan kitchen. Contemporary menu with subtle Mediterranean feel.

at Great Easton North : 2.75 mi. by B 184

The Green Man

Mile End Green, Northeast : 1 mi. by B 184 on Mile End Green rd ✉ CM6 2DN – ✆ (01371) 852 285 – www.thegreenmanrestaurant.com – Fax (01371) 852 216 – Closed Sunday dinner and Monday except Bank Holidays

Rest – Carte £ 28/44

◆ Contemporary, minimalist-style pub, 20 minutes from Stansted Airport. Ambitious cooking, classic desserts and attentive, assured service. Terrace and garden overlooking fields.

ENGLAND

at Aythorpe Roding Southwest : 5.5 mi. on B 184

Axe & Compasses

Dunmow Rd ✉ CM6 1PP – ✆ (01279) 876 648 – www.theaxeandcompasses.co.uk – Closed 25-26 December

Rest – Carte £ 20/25

◆ Characterful, cottage style pub complete with part-thatched roof and white picket fence. Tasty, attractively presented food; hearty pub favourites with their roots in the region.

GREAT EASTON – Essex – **504** U28 – see Great Dunmow

GREAT GONERBY – Lincs. – **502** S25 – see Grantham

GREAT HALLINGBURY – Essex – see Bishop's Stortford

GREAT MALVERN – Worcestershire – **503** N27 – pop. 35 588 **18** B3

London 127 mi. – Birmingham 34 mi. – Cardiff 66 mi. – Gloucester 24 mi.

21 Church St ✆ (01684) 892289, malvern.tic@malvernhills.gov.uk B

Plan on next page

Bredon House without rest

34 Worcester Rd ✉ WR14 4AA – ✆ (01684) 566 990 – www.bredonhouse.co.uk

10 rm – £ 55/65 £ 65/110 B**a**

◆ Elegant, Grade II listed Regency house with spectacular views. Personable owners make breakfast a special event. Most of the individually styled rooms enjoy the fine vista.

The Cotford

51 Graham Rd ✉ WR14 2HU – ✆ (01684) 572 427 – www.cotfordhotel.co.uk – Fax (01684) 572 952 B**s**

15 rm – £ 65/79 £ 115

Rest – *(dinner only and Sunday lunch)* Menu £ 28

◆ Recently refurbished Victorian gothic stone building in landscaped gardens; built in 1851 for the Bishop of Worcester. Modern but homely guest areas; cosy bedrooms. Modern dining room with garden views; seasonal menu of local, organic produce.

at Guarlford East : 2.5 mi. on B 4211

Plough and Harrow

Rhydd Rd, East : 0.5 mi. on B 4211 ✉ WR13 6NY – ✆ (01684) 310 453 – www.theploughandharrow.co.uk – Closed 25 December, Sunday dinner and Monday

Rest – Carte £ 20/35

◆ Modernised country pub with low-beamed bar and open fire; more formal dining room and large lawned garden. Unfussy cooking uses good quality produce, some from kitchen garden.

at Malvern Wells South : 2 mi. on A 449 – ✉ Malvern

Cottage in the Wood rest, rm,

Holywell Rd ✉ WR14 4LG – ✆ (01684) 588 860 – www.cottageinthewood.co.uk – Fax (01684) 560 662 A**z**

30 rm – £ 79/120 £ 99/190

Rest – Menu £ 14 (lunch) – Carte £ 30/40 **s**

◆ Early Victorian house, family owned and run, with superb view over surrounding vales. Very comfortable sitting room and bar. Individually furnished rooms in traditional style. Lovely restaurant with Oriental silk prints and Vale views.

at Colwall Southwest : 3 mi. on B 4218 – ✉ Great Malvern

Colwall Park

✉ WR13 6QG – ✆ (01684) 540 000 – www.colwall.co.uk – Fax (01684) 540 847

21 rm – £ 80/90 £ 120 – 1 suite A**v**

Rest ***Seasons*** – see restaurant listing

◆ Built in 1903, this personally run hotel has a distinct Edwardian feel. Play croquet in the garden or wander into the nearby Malvern Hills. Individually decorated bedrooms.

GREAT MALVERN

Street	Square	No.
Albert Rd South	B	3
Blackmore Park Rd	A	5
Church St.	B	
Clerkenwell Crescent	B	6
Cockshot Rd	B	8
Court Rd	B	12
Croft Bank	A	13
Happy Valley off St Ann's Rd	B	15
Imperial Rd	B	16
Jubilee Drive	A	17
Lygon Bank	B	18
Madresfield Rd	B	20
Moorlands Rd	B	22
North Malvern Rd	B	23
Orchard Rd	B	24
Richmond Rd	B	25
Townsend Way	A	26
Upper Welland Rd	A	27
Walwyn Rd	A	29
Wells Rd	A, B	30
Zetland Rd	B	31

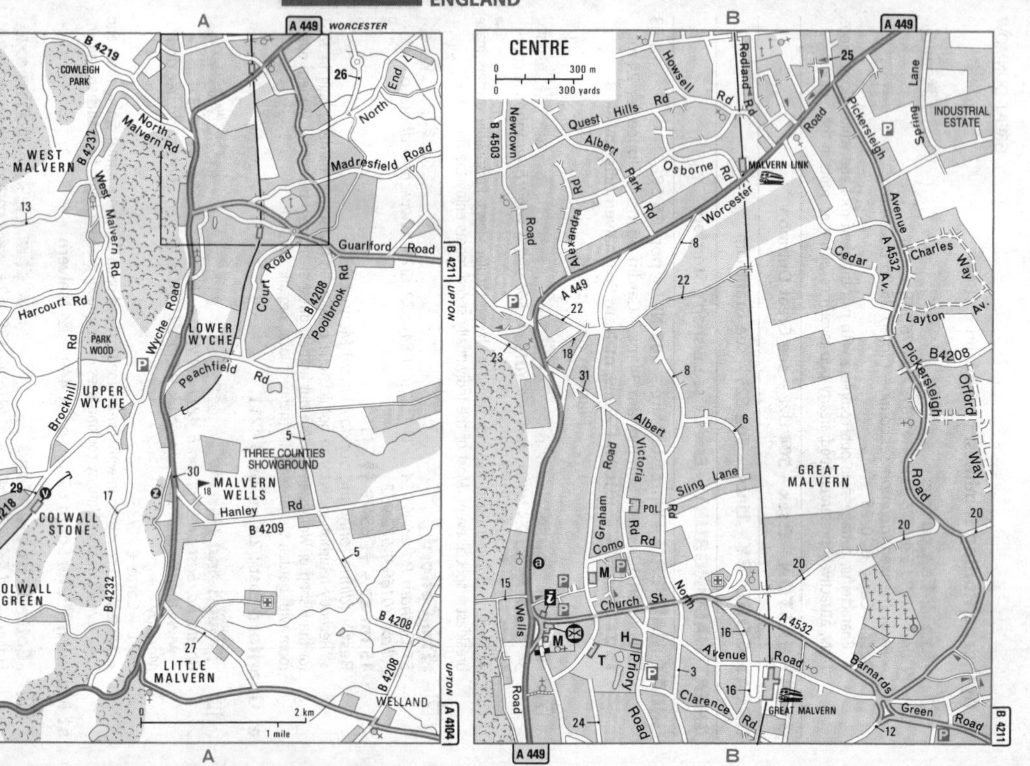

XX **Seasons** – at Colwall Park Hotel

✉ *WR13 6QG – ☎ (01684) 540 000 – www.colwall.co.uk – Fax (01684) 540 847* — A**v**

Rest – *(booking essential at lunch)* Menu £ 20 (lunch) **s** – Carte dinner £ 33/38 **s**

◆ Predominant oak panelling merges seamlessly with modern styling in a spacious location for formal dining. Accomplished and interesting modern British cooking.

at Acton Green Northwest : 7 mi. by A 449 - B -, B 4219, A 4103 on B 4220 – ✉ Bromyard

Hidelow House without rest

Acton Beauchamp, South : 0.75 mi. on B 4220 ✉ WR6 5AH – ☎ (01886) 884 547 – www.hidelow.co.uk – Fax (01886) 884 658

3 rm – †£ 45 ††£ 74/90

◆ Secluded, privately run guesthouse with pleasant views down the Leadon Valley. Sizeable bedrooms with a homely feel. Boudoir grand piano in the firelit lounge.

Fancy a last minute break?
Check hotel websites to take advantage of price promotions.

GREAT MILTON – Oxon. – 503 Q28 – see Oxford

GREAT MISSENDEN – Buckinghamshire – 504 R28 – pop. 7 980 — 11 C2

London 34 mi. – Aylesbury 10 mi. – Maidenhead 19 mi. – Oxford 35 mi.

XX **La Petite Auberge**

107 High St ✉ HP16 0BB – ☎ (01494) 865 370 – www.lapetiteauberge.co.uk – Closed 2 weeks Easter, 2 weeks Christmas and Sunday

Rest – French – *(dinner only)* Carte £ 29/38

◆ Neat, cottagey restaurant with painted wood chip paper and candles. Traditional chairs, crisp and tidy linen. Fresh and confident style of French cooking.

The Nags Head with rm

London Road, Southeast : 1m ✉ HP16 0DG – ☎ (01494) 862 200 – www.nagsheadbucks.com – Fax (01494) 862 945 – Closed 25 December

5 rm – †£ 90 ††£ 90/110

Rest – Carte £ 25/38

◆ Traditional 15C inn whose features include original oak beams and thick brick walls. Gallic charm mixes with British classics on interesting menus. Cheerful service. Stylish, modern bedrooms; number one is best. Tasty breakfast choice.

GREAT WARLEY – Essex – see Brentwood

GREAT WHITTINGTON – Northd. – 501 O18 – see Corbridge

GREAT WOLFORD – Warwickshire – 503 P27 — 19 C3

London 84 mi. – Birmingham 37 mi. – Cheltenham 26 mi.

The Fox & Hounds Inn with rm

✉ CV36 5NQ – ☎ (01608) 674 220 – www.thefoxandhoundsinn.com – Closed 6-20 January for meals, Sunday dinner and Monday

3 rm – †£ 50 ††£ 80 **Rest** – Carte £ 26/40

◆ Warm and welcoming, family-run pub with dried hops, log burner and cosy atmosphere. Concise blackboard menu; bold flavoursome cooking made from locally-sourced ingredients. Simple, neat, spacious bedrooms.

GREAT YARMOUTH – Norfolk – **504** Z26 – pop. 58 032 **15** D2

Great Britain

London 126 mi. – Cambridge 81 mi. – Ipswich 53 mi. – Norwich 20 mi.

25 Marine Parade ☎ (01493) 846345, tourism@great-yarmouth.gov.uk

Gorleston Warren Rd, ☎ (01493) 661 911

Beach House Caister-on-Sea, Great Yarmouth & Caister, ☎ (01493) 728 699

Norfolk Broads★

XX **Seafood**

85 North Quay ✉ NR30 1JF – ☎ (01493) 856 009 – www.theseafood.co.uk – Fax (01493) 332 256 – Closed 2 weeks Christmas, 2 weeks early June, Saturday lunch, Sunday and Bank Holidays

Rest – Seafood – Carte £ 26/45

◆ Long-standing restaurant on the edge of town, run by friendly owners. Traditional interior boasts intimate booths, a lobster tank and fresh fish display. Reliable, classical seafood dishes.

GREEN ISLAND – **503** P33 – see Channel Islands (Jersey)

GRETA BRIDGE – Durham – **502** O20 – see Barnard Castle

GRIMSTON – Norfolk – **504** V25 – see King's Lynn

GRINDLETON – Lancashire – **502** M22 – see Clitheroe

GRINSHILL – Shrops. – **503** L25 – see Shrewsbury

GROUVILLE – C.I. – **503** M33 – see Channel Islands (Jersey)

GUARLFORD – Worcestershire – see Great Malvern

GUERNSEY – C.I. – **503** O/P33 – see Channel Islands

GUILDFORD – Surrey – **504** S30 – pop. 69 400 Great Britain **7** C1

London 33 mi. – Brighton 43 mi. – Reading 27 mi. – Southampton 49 mi.

14 Tunsgate ☎ (01483) 444333, tic@guildford.gov.uk Y

Clandon Park★★, E : 3 mi. by A 246 Z – Hatchlands Park★, E : 6 mi. by A 246 Z. Painshill★★, Cobham, NE : 10 m – Polesden Lacey★, E : 13 mi. by A 246 Z and minor rd

X **Zinfandel**

4-5 Chapel St ✉ GU1 3UH – ☎ (01483) 455 155 – www.zinfandel.org.uk – Closed 25 December, 1 January and dinner Sunday and Monday Y**v**

Rest – Carte £ 19/30

◆ Modern laid-back restaurant set in characterful cobbled road between the castle and high street. Accessible menus offer something for everyone. Flickering candles set the mood in the evening.

at Shere East : 6.75 mi. by A 246 off A 25 - Z – ✉ Guildford

XX **Kinghams**

Gomshall Lane ✉ GU5 9HE – ☎ (01483) 202 168 – www.kinghams-restaurant.co.uk – Closed 25 December-4 January, Sunday dinner and Monday

Rest – *(booking essential)* Menu £ 23 (Tuesday-Thursday) – Carte £ 31/36

◆ Popular restaurant in 17C cottage in appealing village. Daily blackboard and fish specials are particularly good value. Adventurous modern menus with bold combinations.

ENGLAND

GUILDFORD

Bedford Rd . . . . Y 2
Bridge St . . . . Y 3
Castle St. . . . . Y 5
Chertsey St . . . . Y 6
Commercial Rd . . . . Y 8
Eastgate Gardens . . . . Y 9
Friary Bridge. . . . . Y 12
Friary Centre . . . . Y
High St. . . . . Y
Ladymead . . . . Z 13
Leapale Lane . . . . Y 15
Leapale Rd. . . . . Y 16
Leas Rd . . . . Y 17
Market St. . . . . Y 18
Mary Rd . . . . Y 19
Midleton Rd . . . . Z 20
Millbrook . . . . Y 21
New Inn Lane . . . . Z 22
North St . . . . Y
One Tree Hill Rd. . . . . Z 24
Onslow St . . . . Y 25
Park St . . . . Y 27
Quarry St . . . . Y 28
Stoughton Rd. . . . . Z 30
Trood's Lane. . . . . Z 31
Tunsgate . . . . Y 33
Tunsgate Shopping Centre . . . . Y
Warwick's Bench . . . . Y 34
Woodbridge Rd . . . . Z 37

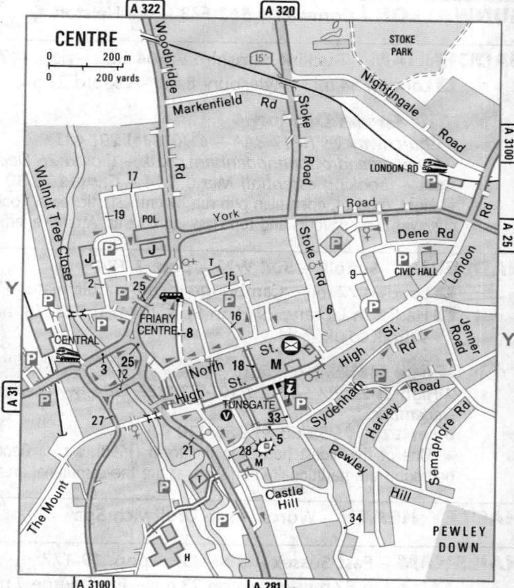

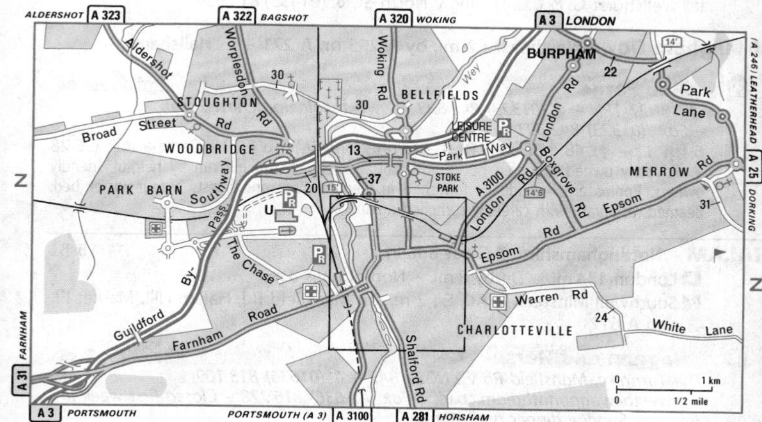

GULWORTHY – **Devon** – **503** H32 – **see Tavistock**

GUNNERSIDE – **North Yorkshire** – **502** N20 – ✉ **Darlington** **22** A1

London 268 mi. – Newcastle upon Tyne 60 mi. – Richmond 17 mi.

Oxnop Hall without rest

Low Oxnop, West : 1.5 mi. on B 6270 ✉ DL11 6JJ – ✆ (01748) 886 253 – www.oxnophall.com – Fax (01748) 886 253 – March-October

5 rm – †£ 40/55 ††£ 70/78

◆ Pleasant stone-built 17C farmhouse and working sheep farm in agreeable hillside position. Cosy little lounge. Bedrooms feature beams, mullion windows and rural views.

GUNWALLOE – Cornwall – 503 E33 – see Helston

HADDENHAM – Buckinghamshire – 504 R28 – pop. 4 720 11 C2

London 54 mi. – Aylesbury 8 mi. – Oxford 21 mi.

The Green Dragon

8 Churchway ✉ HP17 8AA – ✆ (01844) 291 403 – www.greendragonhaddenham.co.uk – Closed 26 December

Rest – *(booking essential)* Menu £ 14 – Carte £ 15/30

◆ Light, modern, open-plan pub run by enthusiastic team. Cooking is modern and adventurous, with bold flavours and top class ingredients. Attentive, efficient service.

HADLEIGH – Suffolk – 504 W27 – pop. 7 124 15 C3

London 72 mi. – Cambridge 49 mi. – Colchester 17 mi. – Ipswich 10 mi.

Hadleigh Library, 29 High St ✆ (01473) 823778, hadleigh.library@suffolk.co.uk

Edge Hall without rest

2 High St ✉ IP7 5AP – ✆ (01473) 822 458 – www.edgehall.co.uk – Closed 25-26 December

6 rm – †£ 55/68 ††£ 85/110

◆ One of the oldest houses in the town (1590), with a Georgian façade. Spacious, comfy bedrooms are traditionally furnished, as are the communal areas. Very well-kept gardens.

HADLEY HEATH – Worcs. – see Droitwich Spa

HAILSHAM – East Sussex – 504 U31 – pop. 19 177 8 B3

London 57 mi. – Brighton 23 mi. – Eastbourne 7 mi. – Hastings 20 mi.

Wellshurst G. & C.C. Hellingly North St, ✆ (01435) 813 636

at Magham Down Northeast : 2 mi. by A 295 on A 271 – ✉ Hailsham

Olde Forge

✉ BN27 1PN – ✆ (01323) 842 893 – www.theoldeforgehotel.co.uk – Fax (01323) 842 893

6 rm – †£ 48 ††£ 85 **Rest** – *(dinner only)* Menu £ 28 – Carte approx. £ 28

◆ Privately owned timbered house with cottage feel, charmingly run by helpful, friendly owners. Rooms are individually furnished in elegant pine; one boasts a four-poster bed. Beamed restaurant with carefully compiled menu.

HALAM – Nottinghamshire Great Britain 16 B1

London 134 mi. – Derby 8 mi. – Nottingham 8 mi.

Southwell Minster★★ **AC**, E : 2 mi. on Mansfield Rd, Halam Hill, Market Pl and A 612

Waggon and Horses

The Turnpike, Mansfield Rd ✉ NG22 8AE – ✆ (01636) 813 109 – www.thewaggonathalam.co.uk – Fax (01636) 816 228 – Closed first week in January, Sunday dinner and Monday

Rest – Menu £ 15 – Carte £ 20/40

◆ A bright and up-to-date pub. Daily blackboard menu features lots of fish and local meat dishes: sides of veg are free. Good value set menu at lunch, with OAP discount Tues-Sun.

HALFORD – Warwickshire – 503 P27 – pop. 301 19 C3

London 94 mi. – Oxford 43 mi. – Stratford-upon-Avon 8 mi.

Old Manor House without rest

Queens St ✉ CV36 5BT – ✆ (01789) 740 264 – www.oldmanor-halford.co.uk – Fax (01789) 740 609 – closed Christmas and New Year

3 rm – †£ 50/60 ††£ 90/100

◆ Characterful house in quiet residential area, well located for Stratford and the Cotswolds. Spacious garden next to River Stour. Well appointed drawing room and atmospheric bedrooms with rich fabrics.

The Halford Bridge with rm
Fosse Way ✉ CV36 5BN – ✆ (01789) 748 217 – www.thehalfordbridge.co.uk – Fax (01789) 748 159 – Closed Sunday dinner
10 rm ☕ – 🚹£ 75 🚹🚹£ 75
Rest – Menu £ 14 (Monday-Thursday) – Carte £ 16/25
◆ Imposing stone-built former coaching inn set on the Fosse Way. Classic combinations with a personal twist on seasonally changing menu. Atmospheric bar and enthusiastic service. Modern bedrooms with nutty names and original wood beams.

HALFWAY BRIDGE – W. Sussex – 504 R31 – see Petworth

HALIFAX – West Yorkshire – 502 O22 – pop. 83 570 22 B2

London 205 mi. – Bradford 8 mi. – Burnley 21 mi. – Leeds 15 mi.
Visitor Centre & Art Gallery, Piece Hall ✆ (01422) 368725, halifax@ytbtic.co.uk
18 Halifax Bradley Hall Holywell Green, ✆ (01422) 374 108
18 Halifax West End Highroad Well Paddock Lane, ✆ (01422) 341 878
9 Ryburn Sowerby Bridge Norland, ✆ (01422) 831 355
9 Lightcliffe Knowle Top Rd, ✆ (01422) 202 459
18 Ogden Union Lane, ✆ (01422) 244 171

Design House
Dean Clough (Gate 5) ✉ HX3 5AX – ✆ (01422) 383 242 – www.designhouserestaurant.co.uk – Fax (01422) 322 732 – Closed Saturday lunch and Sunday
Rest – Menu £ 21 (dinner) – Carte £ 28/44
◆ Located within converted mill on outskirts of town, an impressively stylish and modern restaurant with Philippe Starck furniture. Varied menu of contemporary British cooking.

Shibden Mill Inn with rm
Shibden Mill Fold, Northeast : 2.25mi. by A 58 and Kell Lane (turning left at Stump Cross public house) on Blake Hill Rd ✉ HX3 7UL – ✆ (01422) 365 840 – www.shibdenmillinn.com – Fax (01422) 362 971
11 rm ☕ – 🚹£ 79 🚹🚹£ 143 **Rest** – Carte £ 20/31
◆ Charming whitewashed country inn – formerly a corn mill – set in the valley. Extensive menu ranges from the traditional to the more modern. Events include fortnightly 'guinea pig' nights. Individually appointed bedrooms are comfy and cosy.

HALL GREEN – W. Mids. – 502 O26 – see Birmingham

HALNAKER – W. Sussex – see Chichester

HALTWHISTLE – Northumberland – 501 M19 – pop. 3 811 24 A2

Great Britain

London 335 mi. – Carlisle 22 mi. – Newcastle upon Tyne 37 mi.
Railway Station, Station Rd ✆ (01434) 322002, haltwhistletic@btconnect.com
18 Wallend Farm Greenhead, ✆ (01697) 747 367
Hadrian's Wall★★, N : 4.5 mi. by A 6079 – Housesteads★★ **AC**, NE : 6 mi. by B 6318 – Roman Army Museum★ **AC**, NW : 5 mi. by A 69 and B 6318 – Vindolanda (Museum★) **AC**, NE : 5 mi. by A 69 – Steel Rig (≤★) NE : 5.5 mi. by B 6318

Centre of Britain
Main St ✉ NE49 0BH – ✆ (01434) 322 422 – www.centre-of-britain.org.uk – Fax (01434) 322 655
12 rm ☕ – 🚹£ 69 🚹🚹£ 110 **Rest** – *(dinner only)* Menu £ 20
◆ Attractive hotel on busy main street. Oldest part, a pele tower, dates from 15C. Comfortable modern décor, including bedrooms, incorporates original architectural features. Glass-roofed restaurant with light, airy feel.

ENGLAND

Ashcroft without rest
Lantys Lonnen ✉ NE49 0DA – ☎ (01434) 320 213 – www.ashcroftguesthouse.co.uk – Fax (01434) 321 641 – Closed 25 December
8 rm ☕ – 🚹£ 38/60 🚹🚹£ 88
◆ Imposing Victorian house, formerly a vicarage, with beautifully kept gardens. Family run and attractively furnished throughout creating a welcoming atmosphere. Large bedrooms.

HAMBLE-LE-RICE – **Southampton** – **503** Q31 – **see Southampton**

HAMBLETON – **Rutland** – **see Oakham**

HANLEY SWAN – **Worcs.** – **503** N27 – **see Upton-upon-Severn**

HARDWICK – **Cambs.** – **see Cambridge**

HARLAXTON – **Lincs.** – **502** S25 – **see Grantham**

HAROME – **N. Yorks.** – **see Helmsley**

HARPENDEN – Hertfordshire – 504 S28 – pop. 28 452 — 12 A2

London 32 mi. – Luton 6 mi.
18 Harpenden Common East Common, ☎ (01582) 711 320
18 Hammonds End, ☎ (01582) 712 580

The Bean Tree
20A Leyton Rd ✉ AL5 2HU – ☎ (01582) 460 901 – www.thebeantree.com – Fax (01582) 460 826 – Closed 1 January, Saturday lunch, Sunday dinner and Monday
Rest – Menu £ 22 (mid-week dinner) – Carte £ 28/52
◆ Converted red-brick cottage with bean tree and smart terrace. Intimate, softly lit restaurant with sage green palette. Carefully sought ingredients; precise modern cooking.

The White Horse
Hatching Green, Southwest : 1 mi. by A 1081 on B 487 ✉ AL5 2JP – ☎ (01582) 469 290 – www.thewhitehorseharpenden.com – Closed 25 December
Rest – *(booking essential)* Menu £ 15 (lunch) – Carte £ 23
◆ Appealing 17C whitewashed pub with a cosy bar, formal restaurant and large terrace. Modern European dishes, with grazing boards and sharing plates. Polished, professional service.

The Fox
469 Luton Rd, Kingsbourne Green, Northwest : 2 mi. on A 1081 ✉ AL5 3QE – ☎ (01582) 713 817 – www.thefoxharpenden.co.uk
Rest – Carte £ 20/32
◆ Cosy country pub with a decked terrace and friendly atmosphere. With a wide ranging menu, popular rotisserie and list of daily specials, there's something for everyone.

HARROGATE – North Yorkshire – 502 P22 – pop. 66 178 — 22 B2

Great Britain

London 211 mi. – Bradford 18 mi. – Leeds 15 mi. – Newcastle upon Tyne 76 mi.
Royal Baths, Crescent Rd ☎ (01423) 537300, tic@harrogate.gov.uk
18 Forest Lane Head, ☎ (01423) 863 158
18 Pannal Follifoot Rd, ☎ (01423) 872 628
18 Oakdale, ☎ (01423) 567 162
9 Crimple Valley Hookstone Wood Rd, ☎ (01423) 883 485
Town★
Fountains Abbey★★★ **AC** :- Studley Royal **AC** (≤★ from Anne Boleyn's Seat) - Fountains Hall (Fa 0.5ade★), N : 13 mi. by A 61 and B 6265 AY – Harewood House★★ (The Gallery★) **AC**, S : 7.5 mi. by A 61 BZ

ENGLAND

HARROGATE

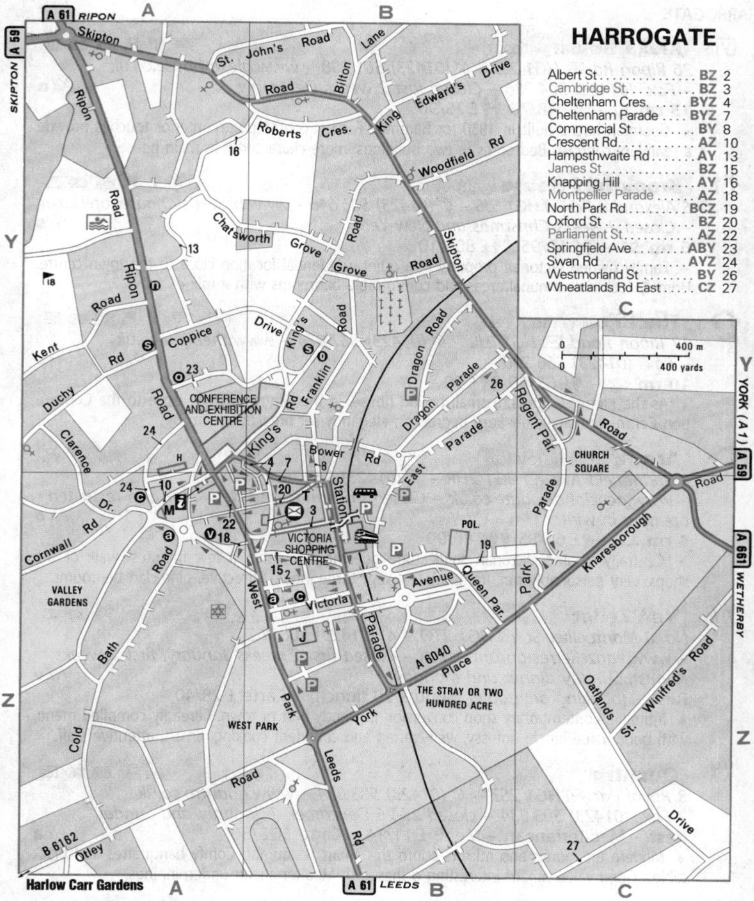

Hotel du Vin

Prospect Pl ✉ *HG1 1LB – ✆ (01423) 856 800 – www.hotelduvin.com – Fax (01423) 856 801*

BZ**a**

48 rm – 🚹£ 110/195 🚹🚹£ 110/195, ☕ £ 13.50

Rest *Bistro* – French – *(light lunch)* Carte £ 30/40

◆ Terrace of Georgian houses overlooking pleasant green. Individually appointed bedrooms with wine-theme decor and modern facilities. Buzzy, modern, stylish French bistro and private dining rooms. Good menu of Gallic influenced dishes.

Rudding Park

rm, rest,

Rudding Park, Follifoot, Southeast : 3.75 mi. by A 661 ✉ *HG3 1JH – ✆ (01423) 871 350 – www.ruddingpark.co.uk – Fax (01423) 872 286*

46 rm ☕ – 🚹£ 115/255 🚹🚹£ 136/285 – 3 suites

Rest *The Clocktower* – Menu £ 31 – Carte £ 36/46

◆ Grade I listed Georgian house in rural location with modern extension. Comfortable, elegant style throughout. Rooms are simple and classical with modern, colourful fabrics. Smart, contemporary brasserie with oak floors.

Alexa House without rest
26 Ripon Rd ✉ HG1 2JJ – ✆ (01423) 501 988 – www.alexa-house.co.uk – Fax (01423) 504 086 – Closed last 2 weeks December AY**n**
13 rm – †£ 48/75 ††£ 75/90
◆ Georgian house built in 1830 for Baron-de-Ferrier: contemporary interior touches provide a seamless contrast. Bedrooms in two buildings: more characterful in main house.

Brookfield House without rest
5 Alexandra Rd ✉ HG1 5JS – ✆ (01423) 506 646 – www.brookfieldhousehotel.co.uk – Closed 2 weeks Christmas and New Year BY**s**
6 rm – †£ 65/95 ††£ 80/110
◆ Family owned Victorian property in a quiet, residential location close to the town centre. Homely feel in communal areas and comfortable bedrooms with a mix of styles.

The Bijou without rest
17 Ripon Road ✉ HG1 2JL – ✆ (01423) 567 974 – www.thebijou.co.uk – Fax (01423) 566 200 AY**s**
10 rm – †£ 55/65 ††£ 90
◆ As the name suggests, a small period house, in the centre of town close to the Convention Centre. Immaculately kept bedrooms; elegantly set breakfast room.

Acacia without rest
3 Springfield Ave ✉ HG1 2HR – ✆ (01423) 560 752 – www.acaciaharrogate.co.uk – Closed Christmas and New Year and restricted opening in winter AY**o**
4 rm – †£ 60/85 ††£ 80/90
◆ Centrally located Victorian solid stone guesthouse, within a few minutes' walk of the shops; very personably run. Immaculately kept throughout. Attractive, pine-clad bedrooms.

Van Zeller
No. 8 Montpellier St ✉ HG1 2TQ – ✆ (01423) 508 762 – www.vanzellerrestaurants.co.uk – Closed first 2 weeks January, first 2 weeks August, Sunday dinner and Monday AZ**v**
Rest – *(booking advisable)* Menu £ 20 (lunch) – Carte £ 28/40
◆ Intimate, contemporary shop conversion in trendy part of town. Carefully compiled menu, with good value lunch; unfussy, well-crafted and confident cooking. Smart, attentive staff.

Quantro
3 Royal Par ✉ HG1 2SZ – ✆ (01423) 503 034 – www.quantro.co.uk – Fax (01423) 503 034 – closed 25-26 December, 1 January and Sunday
Rest – Mediterranean – Menu £ 11/14 – Carte £ 25/30 AZ**a**
◆ Modern art murals and mirrors adorn this smart restaurant. Comfy banquettes and black tables. Good value mix of interesting dishes with Mediterranean underpinnings.

Orchid
28 Swan Rd ✉ HG1 2SE – ✆ (01423) 560 425 – www.orchidrestaurant.co.uk – Fax (01423) 530 967 – Closed Saturday lunch AZ**c**
Rest – Menu £ 13/22 – Carte £ 22/38
◆ Unfussy, uncluttered restaurant with Asian styling. Polite, friendly service adds to the enjoyment of richly authentic dishes from a wide range of south-east Asian countries.

Sasso
8-10 Princes Sq ✉ HG1 1LX – ✆ (01423) 508 838 – Fax (01423) 508 838 – Closed 25-26 December, 1 January, Sunday and Bank Holidays BZ**c**
Rest – Italian – Carte £ 25/39
◆ In the basement of a 19C property. Antiques, ceramics and modern art embellish the interior. The menu offers a good choice of authentic Italian dishes with modern influences.

at Kettlesing West : 6.5 mi. by A 59 - AY – ✉ Harrogate

Knabbs Ash without rest
Skipton Rd, on A 59 ✉ HG3 2LT – ✆ (01423) 771 040 – www.knabbsash.co.uk
3 rm – †£ 50/55 ††£ 70/75
◆ Stone built cottage with spacious gardens and grounds. Cosy lounge; pine furnished breakfast room. Homely and simple, largely floral interior; rooms individually decorated.

ENGLAND

HARTINGTON – Derbyshire – 502 O24 – pop. 1 604 – ✉ Buxton 16 A1

London 168 mi. – Derby 36 mi. – Manchester 40 mi. – Sheffield 34 mi.

Biggin Hall

Biggin, Southeast : 2 mi. by B 5054 ✉ SK17 0DH – ☎ (01298) 84 451 – www.bigginhall.co.uk

20 rm – †£ 50/95 ††£ 126/136

Rest – *(booking essential)* Menu £ 10/20 **s** – Carte lunch approx. £ 16 **s**

◆ Charming house with much rustic personality and individuality. Stone floored lounges and open fires. Antique furnished bedrooms vary in size and shape. Elegant dining room with low beams.

HARTLAND – Devon – 503 G31 1 B1

London 221 mi. – Bude 15 mi. – Clovelly 4 mi.

Golden Park without rest

Southwest : 5 mi. following signs for Elmscott and Bude ✉ EX39 6EP – ☎ (01237) 441 254 – www.goldenpark.co.uk – Fax (01237) 441 254 – Closed 25 and 31 December and restricted opening in winter

3 rm – †£ 65 ††£ 65/90

◆ Walk to the North Devon coast from this delightfully set part 17C farmhouse. Style and character prevail, particularly in guests' lounge and beamed, smartly decorated rooms.

The Hart Inn

The Square ✉ EX39 6BL – ☎ (01237) 441 474 – www.thehartinn.com – Closed Sunday dinner and Monday

Rest – Carte £ 15/23

◆ Part 14 and 16C coaching inn with rustic, homely interior. Regularly changing menu features some Scandinavian influences but produce remains seasonal and local; generous portions.

ENGLAND

HARWELL – Oxfordshire – 503 Q29 – pop. 2 015 10 B3

London 64 mi. – Oxford 16 mi. – Reading 18 mi. – Swindon 22 mi.

Kingswell

Reading Rd, East : 0.75 mi. on A 417 ✉ OX11 0LZ – ☎ (01235) 833 043 – www.kingswell-hotel.com – Fax (01235) 833 193 – Closed 1 week Christmas

20 rm – †£ 99/105 ††£ 115/125 **Rest** – Menu £ 23/25 – Carte £ 21/45

◆ Large redbrick hotel located on the south Oxfordshire Downs. Convenient for Didcot rail and Oxford. Spacious, uniform, traditional bedrooms and pubby public areas. Classic menus served in traditional dining room.

HARWICH and DOVERCOURT – Essex – 504 X28 – pop. 20 130 13 D2

London 78 mi. – Chelmsford 41 mi. – Colchester 20 mi. – Ipswich 23 mi.

to Denmark (Esbjerg) (DFDS Seaways A/S) 3-4 weekly (20 h) – to The Netherlands (Hook of Holland) (Stena Line) 2 daily (3 h 30 mn)

Iconfield Park, Parkeston ☎ (01255) 506139, harwichtic@btconnect.com

Parkeston Station Rd, ☎ (01255) 503 616

Pier at Harwich

The Quay ✉ CO12 3HH – ☎ (01255) 241 212 – www.milsomhotels.com – Fax (01255) 551 922

14 rm – †£ 80 ††£ 185

Rest *Harbourside* – Seafood – Menu £ 25 (lunch) – Carte £ 25/45

Rest *Ha'Penny* – Carte £ 20/27

◆ Bright Victorian building located on the quayside giving many bedrooms views of the area's busy sea lanes. Décor is comfortably stylish and contemporary with a nautical theme. Seafood restaurant with North Sea outlook. Informal bistro.

A good night's sleep without spending a fortune? Look for Bib Hotel.

HASTINGS ST. LEONARDS

Albert Rd . . . . **BZ** 3
Bourne (The) . . . . **BY** 4
Cambridge Gardens . . . . . **BZ** 5
Castle Hill Rd . . . . **BZ** 8
Castle St . . . . **BZ** 7
Cornwallis Gardens . . . . . . **BZ** 9
Cornwallis Terrace . . . . . . **BZ** 10
Denmark Pl. . . . . **BZ** 13
Dorset Pl. . . . . **BZ** 15
Gensing Rd . . . . **AZ** 16
George St . . . . **BY** 18
Grosvenor Crescent . . . . . **AY** 19
Harold Pl. . . . . **BZ** 20
Havelock Rd . . . . **BZ** 21
King's Rd . . . . **AZ** 22
London Rd . . . . **AZ**
Marine Court . . . . **AZ** 23
Middle St . . . . **BZ** 24
Norman Rd . . . . **AZ**
Priory Meadow Shopping Centre . . . . **BZ**
Queen's Rd . . . . **BZ**
Robertson St . . . . **BZ** 27
Rock-a-Nore Rd . . . . **BY** 30
St Helen's Park Rd . . . . **BY** 31
Sedlescombe Rd South . . **AY** 32
Silchester Rd . . . . **AZ** 33
Warrior Square . . . . **AZ** 34
Wellington Pl. . . . . **BZ** 35
Wellington Square . . . . . . **BZ** 36
White Rock Road . . . . **BZ** 38

ENGLAND

HASTINGS and ST LEONARDS – East Sussex – 504 V31 – pop. 85 828 **8** B3

London 65 mi. – Brighton 37 mi. – Folkestone 37 mi. – Maidstone 34 mi.

Town Hall, Queen's Sq, Priory Meadow ✆ (0845) 2741001, hic@hastings.gov.uk

Beauport Park Golf Course St Leonards-on-Sea Battle Rd, ✆ (01424) 854 245

Tower House 1066 without rest

28 Tower Rd West ✉ TN38 ORG – ✆ (01424) 427 217 – www.towerhouse1066.co.uk – Fax (01424) 430 165 – Closed 3-15 January

10 rm – 🚹£ 45/70 🚹🚹£ 75/99 AY**c**

◆ Friendly and well run, a redbrick Victorian house in a residential area. Comfortably furnished with individually decorated bedrooms and a conservatory bar lounge area.

Zanzibar without rest

9 Eversfield Pl ✉ TN37 6BY – ✆ (01424) 460 109 – www.zanzibarhotel.co.uk

9 rm – 🚹£ 99/124 🚹🚹£ 215/240 AZ**c**

◆ Contemporary guest house with slightly unusual design. Bedrooms are named after countries and continents; South America is largest, with feature whirlpool bath and seaview.

St Clements

3 Mercatoria, St Leonards on Sea ✉ TN38 0EB – ✆ (01424) 200 355 – www.stclementsrestaurant.co.uk – Closed Sunday dinner and Monday

Rest – Menu £ 14/25 (Sunday lunch) – Carte £ 24/32 AZ**a**

◆ Charming, contemporary restaurant minutes from the sea. Classically based, seasonal menus showcase local produce, with seafood fresh off the boats. Relaxed, intimate mood.

Webbe's Rock-a-Nore

1 Rock-a-Nore ✉ TN34 3DW – ✆ (01424) 721 650 – www.webbesrestaurants.co.uk – Closed 25-26 December BY**x**

Rest – Seafood – Carte £ 20/37

◆ Bright, contemporary restaurant with horseshoe counter and open kitchen, in an enviable position across the beach from the fishing Stade. Unsurprisingly fresh fish and seafood.

HATCH BEAUCHAMP – Somerset – 503 K30 – see Taunton

HATFIELD HEATH – Essex – 504 U28 – see Bishop's Stortford (Herts.)

HATFIELD PEVEREL – Essex – 504 V28 – pop. 3 258 Great Britain **13** C2

London 39 mi. – Chelmsford 8 mi. – Maldon 12 mi.

Colchester - Castle and Museum★, E : 13 mi. by A 12

Blue Strawberry Bistrot

The Street ✉ CM3 2DW – ✆ (01245) 381 333 – www.bluestrawberrybistrot.co.uk – Fax (01245) 340 498 – Closed 26 December-1 January and Sunday dinner

Rest – Menu £ 17 (weekday lunch)/23 (Monday-Thursday dinner) – Carte £ 20/32

◆ Make your reservation by first name only in this characterful converted pub with inglenook and Victorian style. Rear dining terrace. Classic British cooking off large menus.

HATHERSAGE – Derbyshire – 502 P24 – pop. 1 582 – ✉ Sheffield (s. Yorks.) **16** A1

London 177 mi. – Derby 39 mi. – Manchester 34 mi. – Sheffield 11 mi.

Sickleholme Bamford, ✆ (01433) 651 306

The George

✉ S32 1BB – ✆ (01433) 650 436 – www.george-hotel.net – Fax (01433) 650 099

22 rm – 🚹£ 92/180 🚹🚹£ 126/153

Rest ***George's*** – Menu £ 35

◆ Built in 14C as an inn to serve the packhorse route. Sympathetically restored in rustic style, with oak beams and stone walls. Bedrooms have a bright, more modern feel. Rustically decorated, vibrant-hued dining room.

ENGLAND

The Walnut Club

Unit 6, The Square, Main Rd ✉ *S32 1BB* – ✆ *(01433) 651 155 – www.thewalnutclub.com – Closed Monday except Bank Holidays*

Rest – *(dinner only and lunch Friday-Sunday)* Carte £ 23/31

◆ Contemporary style restaurant found deep in Derbyshire walking country, serving generously portioned organic dishes. All day dining. Varied menus. Live jazz at weekends.

HAWES – North Yorkshire – 502 N21 – pop. 1 117 — 22 A1

London 253 mi. – Kendal 27 mi. – Leeds 72 mi. – Newcastle upon Tyne 76 mi.

Dales Countryside Museum, Station Yard ✆ (01969) 666210, hawes@yorkshiredales.org.uk

Stone House

Sedbusk, North : 1 mi. by Muker rd ✉ *DL8 3PT* – ✆ *(01969) 667 571 – www.stonehousehotel.com – Fax (01969) 667 720 – Closed January and mid-week in December*

23 rm – †£ 51/143 ††£ 143 **Rest** – *(dinner only)* Menu £ 33

◆ Built in 1908 as a family home. Interior decorated in traditional style; public areas include billiard room and oak panelled lounge. Some rooms with private conservatories. Dining room has exposed beams and wooden tables.

Cockett's

Market Pl ✉ *DL8 3RD* – ✆ *(01969) 667 312 – www.cocketts.co.uk – Fax (01969) 667 162 – Closed 25-26 December*

10 rm – †£ 45/50 ††£ 69/92

Rest – *(closed Tuesday) (dinner only)* Menu £ 20 – Carte £ 19/33

◆ Grade II listed building with a historic inscribed door lintel - reputedly the most photographed doorway in the country. Cosy, traditional atmosphere throughout. Dining room with enticing, age-old ambience.

HAWKSHEAD – Cumbria – 502 L20 – pop. 570 – ✉ Ambleside — 21 A2

Great Britain

London 283 mi. – Carlisle 52 mi. – Kendal 19 mi.

Main Street ✆ (015394) 36946 (summer only), enquiries@hawksheadtouristinfo.org.uk

Village★

Lake Windermere★★ – Coniston Water★ (Brantwood★, on east side), SW : by B 5285

at Near Sawrey Southeast : 2 mi. on B 5285 – ✉ Ambleside

Ees Wyke Country House

✉ *LA22 0JZ* – ✆ *(015394) 36 393 – www.eeswyke.co.uk – Restricted opening in winter*

8 rm – †£ 52/82 ††£ 104/132

Rest – *(dinner only) (booking essential)* Menu £ 33

◆ Panoramic views of Esthwaite Water and Grizedale Forest from this large, impressive Georgian house. Good sized bedrooms with distinctive, homely charm. Dining room's large windows afford lovely views.

at Far Sawrey Southeast : 2.5 mi. on B 5285 – ✉ Ambleside

West Vale without rest

✉ *LA22 0LQ* – ✆ *(015394) 42 817 – www.westvalecountryhouse.co.uk – Fax (015394) 45 302 – Closed 25 December and 10-28 January*

7 rm – †£ 70/90 ††£ 120/130

◆ Victorian house on edge of hamlet with attractive country views. A warm welcome to an interior with open-fired, stone-floored sitting room and snug bedrooms.

HAWNBY – North Yorkshire – 502 Q21 – ✉ Helmsley — 23 C1

London 245 mi. – Middlesbrough 27 mi. – Newcastle upon Tyne 69 mi. – York 30 mi.

ENGLAND

The Inn at Hawnby

YO62 5QS – (01439) 798 202 – *www.innathawnby.co.uk* – *Fax (01439) 798 344 – Closed 25 December*

9 rm – £ 69/79 £ 99 **Rest** – Carte £ 18/31

◆ Personally run small hotel in a very rural location with commanding views of nearby countryside - ideal for walking in the Dales. Snug bedrooms with a cottage feel. Tried-and-tested menus.

at Laskill Northeast : 2.25 mi. by Osmotherley rd – Hawnby

Laskill Grange without rest

Easterside YO62 5NB – (01439) 798 265 – www.laskillgrange.co.uk

7 rm – £ 45/75 £ 90/120

◆ A working farm with four cottagey bedrooms set in two converted Victorian stable blocks, surrounded by 1000 acres of rolling farmland. Breakfast served in sunny conservatory.

HAWORTH – West Yorkshire – 502 O22 – pop. 6 078 – Keighley 22 A2

Great Britain

London 213 mi. – Burnley 22 mi. – Leeds 22 mi. – Manchester 34 mi.

2-4 West Lane (01535) 642329, haworth@ytbtic.co.uk

Bront£ Parsonage MuseumAC

Ashmount Country House without rest

Mytholmes Lane BD22 8EZ – (01535) 645 726 – www.ashmounthaworth.co.uk – Fax (01535) 642 550

10 rm – £ 45/55 £ 175

◆ Built in 1870 by the physician to the Brontë sisters, this refurbished house has extremely comfortable bedrooms with period furniture and state-of-the-art bathrooms.

Old Registry without rest

4 Main St BD22 8DA – (01535) 646 503 – www.theoldregistryhaworth.co.uk – Closed 24-26 December

10 rm – £ 68 £ 100

◆ Stone house – a former registrar's office – on the cobbled main street. Bedrooms are individually themed, featuring rich fabrics and antique furniture. Breakfast of local produce.

Weaver's with rm rest,

15 West Lane BD22 8DU – (01535) 643 822 – www.weaversmallhotel.co.uk – Fax (01535) 644 832 – Closed 20 December - 10 January

3 rm – £ 65 £ 110

Rest – *(Closed Sunday, Monday and lunch Saturday and Tuesday)* Menu £ 18 (lunch) – Carte £ 23/31

◆ Former weavers cottages with an informal atmosphere and some charm. Characterful cluttered lounge with ornaments and artefacts. Homely cooking, surroundings and bedrooms.

HAYDON BRIDGE – Northd. – 501 N19 – see Hexham

HAYLING ISLAND – Hampshire – 504 R31 – pop. 14 842 6 B3

London 77 mi. – Brighton 45 mi. – Southampton 28 mi.

Beachlands, Seven Seafront (023) 9246 7111, tourism@havant.gov.uk

Links Lane, (023) 9246 4446

Cockle Warren Cottage without rest

36 Seafront PO11 9HL – (023) 9246 4961 – www.cocklewarren.co.uk

6 rm – £ 49/55 £ 70/89

◆ A pleasant cottage just across the road from the beach. Conservatory breakfast room overlooks pool. Comfortable, well-kept bedrooms. Families particularly welcome.

HAYTOR VALE – Devon – see Bovey Tracey

ENGLAND

HAYWARDS HEATH – West Sussex – 504 T31 – pop. 29 110 7 D2

Great Britain

London 41 mi. – Brighton 16 mi.

Lindfield East Mascalls Lane, ✆ (01444) 484 467

Sheffield Park Garden★, E : 5 mi. on A 272 and A 275

XX **Jeremy's at Borde Hill**

Borde Hill Gdns, North : 1.75 mi. by B 2028 on Balcombe Rd ✉ RH16 1XP – ✆ (01444) 441 102 – www.jeremysrestaurant.com – Fax (01494) 441 355 – closed 1-11 January, Sunday dinner and Monday except Bank Holidays

Rest – Carte £ 23/40

◆ Converted 19C stables with delightful views to Victorian walled garden. Contemporary interior with modern art. Confident, vibrant cooking in a light Mediterranean style.

HEACHAM – Norfolk – 504 V25 – pop. 4 611 14 B1

London 116 mi. – Hunstanton 2 mi. – King's Lynn 15 mi.

The Grove without rest

17 Collins Lane ✉ PE31 7DZ – ✆ (01485) 570 513 – www.thegroveandoldbarn.co.uk

3 rm – †£ 60 ††£ 75

◆ Victorian house set on high street continuation. Cosy, book-strewn guest lounge. Communal breakfasts. Two rooms homely and spotless; secluded stable room.

HEADLAM – Durham – 502 O20 – see Darlington

HEATHROW AIRPORT – Middx. – 504 S29 – see Hillingdon (Greater London)

HEBDEN BRIDGE – West Yorkshire – 502 N22 – pop. 4 086 22 A2

– ✉ West Yorkshire

London 223 mi. – Burnley 13 mi. – Leeds 24 mi. – Manchester 25 mi.

1 Bridge Gate ✆ (01422) 843831

Great Mount Wadsworth, ✆ (01422) 842 896

Holme House without rest

New Road ✉ HX7 8AD – ✆ (01422) 847 588

www.holmehousehebdenbridge.co.uk – Fax (01422) 847 354 – Closed 25 December

3 rm – †£ 55/60 ††£ 95

◆ Late Georgian house in town centre with gated parking and neat garden. Smart, comfortable, well furnished rooms. Bedrooms boast excellent facilities and spacious bathrooms.

HEDDON ON THE WALL – Northumberland 24 A2

London 288 mi. – Blaydon 7 mi. – Newcastle upon Tyne 8 mi.

Close House

Southwest : 2.25 mi. by B 6528 ✉ NE15 0HT – ✆ (01661) 852 255 – www.closehouse.co.uk – Fax (01661) 853 322 – Closed 2-15 January

19 rm (dinner included) – †£ 130 ††£ 200

Rest *Bewickes* – ✆ (01661) 835 099 – Menu £ 22 (lunch) **s** – Carte dinner £ 29/42 **s**

◆ Stunning Georgian mansion in 300 acres of mature grounds that stretch to the river. Original features blend with modern décor; front bedrooms have views, those to rear are more contemporary. Stylish restaurant offers interesting modern cooking and intimate air.

HEDLEY ON THE HILL – Northumberland 24 A2

London 293 mi. – Newcastle upon Tyne 16 mi. – Sunderland 26 mi. – South Shields 26 mi.

The Feathers Inn

✉ NE43 7SW – ✆ (01661) 843 607 – www.thefeathers.net – Closed first 2 weeks in January, Sunday dinner and Monday

Rest – Carte £ 15/28

◆ Attractive stone pub on a steep hill. Carefully sourced produce and straightforward British cooking produces tasty combinations of hearty, wholesome fare and good clear flavours.

ENGLAND

HELMSLEY – North Yorkshire – 502 Q21 – pop. 1 559 Great Britain 23 C1

London 239 mi. – Leeds 51 mi. – Middlesbrough 28 mi. – York 24 mi.

Helmsley Castle, Castlegate ✆ (01439) 770173, helmsley.tic@english-heritage.org.uk

Ampleforth College Castle Drive, Gilling East, ✆ (01439) 788 212

Rievaulx Abbey★★ **AC**, NW : 2.5 mi. by B 1257

The Black Swan

Market Pl ✉ YO62 5BJ – ✆ (01439) 770 466 – www.blackswan-helmsley.co.uk – Fax (01439) 770 174

45 rm – †£ 100/205 ††£ 140/240

Rest *The Rutland Room* – *(dinner only and Sunday lunch)* Menu £ 25 (Sunday lunch)/33 – Carte dinner £ 35/44

◆ Part 16C coaching inn in a historic market town; indeed it overlooks the market. Charming rustic interior with exposed beams. Many bedrooms with period fittings and features. Formal dining in classically furnished restaurant.

Feversham Arms

on B 1257 ✉ YO62 5AG – ✆ (01439) 770 766 – www.fevershamarmshotel.com – Fax (01439) 770 346

33 rm (dinner included) – †£ 160 ††£ 445

Rest *The Restaurant* – Menu £ 33 (dinner) – Carte £ 33/46

◆ A former coaching inn; its stone façade conceals surprisingly modern rooms of a quiet restful nature: walls, floors in muted colours, spot lighting, quality fabrics. Range of dining locations, including around the pool.

No.54 without rest

54 Bondgate ✉ YO62 5EZ – ✆ (01439) 771 533 – www.no54.co.uk – Closed Christmas and New Year

4 rm – †£ 40/65 ††£ 96/110

◆ Victorian terraced cottage, formerly the village vet's. Charming owner. Bedrooms are strong point: set around flagged courtyard, they're airy, bright and very well-equipped.

Carlton Lodge without rest

Bondgate ✉ YO62 5EY – ✆ (01439) 770 557 – www.carlton-lodge.com – Fax (01439) 772 378

8 rm – †£ 43/58 ††£ 80/90

◆ Late 19C house set just out of town. Homely and traditional air to the décor in the communal areas and the bedrooms, some of which have period features. Cosy breakfast room.

at Harome Southeast : 2.75 mi. by A 170 – ✉ York

The Pheasant

✉ YO62 5JG – ✆ (01439) 771 241 – www.thepheasanthotel.com – Fax (01439) 771 744 – Closed 24-25 December

12 rm – †£ 75/115 ††£ 150/170 – 2 suites

Rest – Menu £ 29 – Carte £ 30/41

◆ Ivy clad hotel in picturesque hamlet with a duck pond and mill stream close by. Now under the same ownership as The Star Inn. Charmingly decorated public areas; on-going upgrading of bedrooms. Conservatory dining room.

Cross House Lodge at The Star Inn

✉ YO62 5JE – ✆ (01439) 770 397 – www.thestaratharome.co.uk – Fax (01439) 771 833 – Closed 1 January

15 rm – †£ 100 ††£ 220

Rest *The Star Inn* – see restaurant listing

Rest *The Piggery* – *(booking essential) (residents only, set menu only)* Menu £ 45

◆ Converted farm building set opposite pub in pretty village. Open-plan, split-level lounge. Ultra-stylish, super-smart bedrooms in either main building, annex or local cottages. Communal dining and breakfast for residents in The Piggery.

ENGLAND

The Star Inn (Andrew Pern)
High St ✉ YO62 5JE – ✆ (01439) 770 397 – www.thestaratharome.co.uk – Fax (01439) 771 833 – Closed 1 January and Monday lunch
Rest – *(booking essential)* Carte £ 30/45 **s**
Spec. Foie gras 'toad in the hole'. Breaded lemon sole with kipper mayonnaise and tartare vinaigrette. Yorkshire curd tart.
◆ Recent extension to the dining room at this 700 year old inn, with a charming garden. Very satisfying cooking combines traditional Northern flavours with more up-to-date nuances, using local farm and estate produce.

at Ampleforth **Southwest : 4.5 mi. by A 170 off B 1257 – ✉ Helmsley**

Shallowdale House without rest
West : 0.5 mi. ✉ YO62 4DY – ✆ (01439) 788 325 – www.shallowdalehouse.co.uk – Fax (01439) 788 885 – Closed Christmas-New Year
3 rm – †£ 85 ††£ 115
◆ Modern guesthouse with spectacular views of the Howardian Hills; an area of outstanding beauty. Spacious rooms with large picture windows for the scenery. Warm and relaxed.

at Byland Abbey **Southwest : 6.5 mi. by A 170 – ✉ Helmsley**

The Abbey Inn with rm
✉ YO61 4BD – ✆ (01347) 868 204 – www.bylandabbeyinn.co.uk – Fax (01347) 868 678 – Closed 24 December dinner, 25 December, 31 December dinner, 1 January, Sunday dinner, Monday and Tuesday
3 rm – †£ 69 ††£ 99/149
Rest – *(booking essential)* Menu £ 16 (dinner) – Carte £ 19/26
◆ Delightful, sympathetically restored period pub, in a breathtaking location. Local, seasonal cooking uses simple techniques and relies on natural flavours to show through. Charming bedrooms, two with Abbey views; luxurious bathrooms.

at Oldstead **Southwest : 7.5 mi. by A 170**

Oldstead Grange without rest
✉ YO61 4BJ – ✆ (01347) 868 634 – www.oldsteadgrange.co.uk
3 rm – †£ 70/110 ††£ 80/120
◆ Comfort is paramount in this part 17C farmhouse on working farm. Cosy, warm lounge with real fire. Hand-made oak furniture adorns bedrooms which benefit from rural outlook.

The Black Swan with rm
✉ YO61 4BL – ✆ (01347) 868 387 – www.blackswanoldstead.co.uk – Closed 2 weeks in mid January and Monday lunch
4 rm – †£ 100 ††£ 140 **Rest** – Menu £ 16 – Carte £ 21/28
◆ Characterful stone-built pub with delightful ambience, set in remote location surrounded by farmland. Family-run, with smart, first floor dining room and rustic downstairs bar. Highly competent, modern cooking makes use of the finest local produce. Antique-furnished bedrooms boast modern fabrics and luxury bathrooms.

at Scawton **West 8.5 mi. by A 170 – ✉ Helmsley**

The Hare Inn
✉ YO7 2HG – ✆ (01845) 597 769 – www.thehareinn.co.uk – Closed Sunday dinner and Monday
Rest – Carte £ 20/30
◆ Warm, inviting and busy pub, parts of which date from 13C; in a remote setting, close to Rievaulx Abbey. Satisfying local food, with meat from Masham and poultry from Pateley Bridge.

HELSTON – Cornwall – 503 E33 – pop. 10 578 — 1 A3

London 306 mi. – Falmouth 13 mi. – Penzance 14 mi. – Truro 17 mi.
The Flora Day Furry Dance★★
Lizard Peninsula★ - Gunwalloe Fishing Cove★, S : 4 mi. by A 3083 and minor rd - Culdrose (Flambards Village Theme Park★), SE : 1 mi. - Wendron (Poldark Mine★), NE : 2.5 mi. by B 3297 - Gweek (Seal Sanctuary★), E : 4 mi. by A 394 and minor rd

Nansloe Manor

Meneage Rd, South : 1.5 mi. on A 3083 ✉ TR13 OSB – ☎ (01326) 558 400 – www.nansloe-manor.co.uk – Fax (01326) 558 401 – Closed 2 weeks January

15 rm – ♦£ 171/216 ♦♦£ 190/240

Rest – Menu £ 20 (weekday lunch)/25 (Sunday lunch) – Carte £ 29/37

◆ Modern country house set in 4 acres. Handmade French furniture, pastel décor and airy, continental feel. Subtly elegant bedrooms; some with balcony/terrace/views. Menus make use of produce from garden; classic combinations are presented in a contemporary style.

at Trelowarren Southeast : 4 mi. by A 394 and A 3083 on B 3293 – ✉ Helston

New Yard

Trelowarren Estate ✉ TR12 6AF – ☎ (01326) 221 595 – www.trelowarren.com – Fax (01326) 221 595 – Closed Monday October-May and Sunday dinner

Rest – *(booking advisable at dinner)* Menu £ 20/24 – Carte £ 26/32

◆ Converted country house stable yard adjoining craft gallery. Terrace view from modern tables and chairs. Dinner offers full menus of locally inspired dishes; lunch is simpler.

at Gunwalloe South : 5.5 mi. by A 394 off A 3083 – ✉ Helston

The Halzephron Inn with rm

✉ TR12 7QB – ☎ (01326) 240 406 – www.halzephron-inn.co.uk – Fax (01326) 241 442 – Closed 25 December

2 rm – ♦£ 40/50 ♦♦£ 60/90 **Rest** – Carte £ 20/30

◆ Traditional pub with coastal views and smuggling history serving good old-fashioned, no-nonsense home cooking. Low ceilings, old beams and cosy corners. Neat bedrooms.

at Cury South : 5 mi. by A394 and A3083

Colvennor Farmhouse without rest

West 1 mi. following sign for Poldu off A3083 and then sign for Nantithet ✉ TR12 7BJ – ☎ (01326) 241 208 – www.colvennorfarmhouse.com – March-October

3 rm – ♦£ 40/50 ♦♦£ 58/68

◆ The farmer has moved out into one of the barns and the farmhouse now provides spotless, simple accommodation. There's a pretty and colourful garden. Breakfast is a hearty affair.

HEMEL HEMPSTEAD – Hertfordshire – 504 S28 – pop. 83 118 — 12 A2

Great Britain

London 30 mi. – Aylesbury 16 mi. – Luton 10 mi. – Northampton 46 mi.

18 Little Hay Golf Complex Bovingdon Box Lane, ☎ (01442) 833 798

9 Boxmoor 18 Box Lane, ☎ (01442) 242 434

Whipsnade Wild Animal Park★

Restaurant 65

65 High St (Old Town) ✉ HP1 5AL – ☎ (01442) 239 010 – www.restaurant65.com – Closed first week January, 1 week July, Sunday dinner and Monday

Rest – *(booking advisable)* Menu £ 15/25

◆ Charming 17C building in old part of town; snug restaurant with white walls, black beams and homely, relaxed feel. Well executed modern British cooking with a classical base.

at Frithsden Northwest : 4.5 mi. by A 4146 – ✉ Hemel Hempstead

The Alford Arms

✉ HP1 3DD – ☎ (01442) 864 480 – www.alfordarmsfrithsden.co.uk – Fax (01442) 876 893 – Closed 25-26 December

Rest – Carte £ 20/27

◆ Attractive Victorian pub overlooking the village green. Traditional British menu follows the seasons: salads and fish in summer, game and comfort dishes in winter. Good classical desserts.

HEMINGFORD GREY – Cambs. – 504 T27 – see Huntingdon

ENGLAND

HENFIELD – West Sussex – 504 T31 – pop. 4 527 — 7 D2

London 47 mi. – Brighton 10 mi. – Worthing 11 mi.

The Ginger Fox

Albourne, Southwest 3 mi. on A281 ✉ BN6 9EA – ✆ (01273) 857 888 – www.gingermanrestaurants.com – Closed 25 December

Rest – Carte £ 20/35

◆ Whitewashed thatched pub. Daily changing à la carte and specials, with straightforward descriptions and rich, deep flavours; traditional and satisfying cooking with a twist.

at Wineham Northeast : 3.5 mi. by A 281, B 2116 and Wineham Lane – ✉ Henfield

Frylands without rest

West : 0.25 mi. taking left turn at telephone box ✉ BN5 9BP – ✆ (01403) 710 214 – www.frylands.co.uk – Closed 20 December - 1 January

3 rm – †£ 38 ††£ 60

◆ Part Elizabethan farmhouse in 250 acres with woodlands and fishing. Fresh homecooked breakfasts. Bedrooms exude charm and character with homely furnishings, original features.

HENLEY – West Sussex – see Midhurst

HENLEY-IN-ARDEN – Warwickshire – 503 O27 – pop. 2 797 — 19 C3

London 104 mi. – Birmingham 15 mi. – Stratford-upon-Avon 8 mi. – Warwick 8 mi.

Ardencote Manor H. & Country Club and Spa

Lye Green Rd, Claverdon, East : 3.75 mi. by A 4189 on Shrewley rd ✉ CV35 8LT – ✆ (01926) 843 111 – www.ardencote.com – Fax (01926) 842 646

76 rm – †£ 80/150 ††£ 120/195

Rest *The Lodge* – ✆ (01926) 843 939 – Menu £ 30 (dinner) – Carte £ 27/35

◆ Secluded manor house with modern extension and spacious leisure facilities, in formal gardens and grounds. Bedrooms are generally large and traditionally furnished. Informal dining room.

The Crabmill

Claverdon, East : 1 mi. on A 4189 ✉ B95 5EE – ✆ (01926) 843 342 – www.thecrabmill.co.uk – Closed 25 December, dinner 26 December, 1 January and Sunday

Rest – *(booking essential)* Menu £ 13 (dinner) – Carte £ 25/30

◆ Charming mix of the old and new; ancient beams blending with contemporary chocolate and pink décor. Relaxing summer room; summer terrace and garden. Modern Mediterranean menu.

at Tanworth-in-Arden Northwest : 4.5 mi. by A 3400 and Tanworth Rd – ✉ Henley-In-Arden

The Bell Inn with rm

The Green ✉ B94 5AL – ✆ (01564) 742 212 – www.thebellattanworthinarden.co.uk – Closed Sunday dinner

9 rm – †£ 50/60 ††£ 95/120 **Rest** – Menu £ 15 – Carte £ 18/27

◆ Modern, slightly kitsch dining pub with shop and post office in corner. Bold décor and feature walls contrast with traditional wood floors and old beams. Classical menus – seafood a speciality. Very contemporary bedrooms.

HENLEY-ON-THAMES – Oxfordshire – 504 R29 – pop. 10 513 — 11 C3

London 40 mi. – Oxford 23 mi. – Reading 9 mi.

to Reading (Salter Bros. Ltd) (summer only) daily (2 h 15 mn) – to Marlow (Salter Bros. Ltd) (summer only) daily (2 h 15 mn)

Town Hall, Market Place ✆ (01491) 578034, info@henleytowncouncil.gov.uk

Huntercombe Nuffield, ✆ (01491) 641 207

Hotel du Vin

New St ✉ RG9 2BP – ✆ (01491) 848 400 – www.hotelduvin.com – Fax (01491) 848 401

38 rm – †£ 145 ††£ 145/295, ☕ £ 13.50 – 2 suites

Rest ***Bistro*** – Menu £ 15 (lunch) – Carte £ 28/39

◆ Former brewery premises; now an easy-going, designer styled boutique hotel. Stunning rooms: studios with outdoor terrace and bath tub or airy doubles with great amenities. Bistro with resolutely Gallic style, French influenced menus and excellent wine list.

Falaise House without rest

37 Market Place ✉ RG9 2AA – ✆ (01491) 573 388 – www.falaisehouse.com – Fax (01491) 410 998

6 rm ☕ – †£ 85/95 ††£ 115

◆ Very well located 18C house boasting stylish, luxury bedrooms; some with chaises longues. Good breakfast choice includes homemade preserves and smoked salmon, cooked to order.

Luscombes at The Golden Ball

Lower Assendon, Northwest : 0.75 mi. by A 4130 on B 480 ✉ RG9 6AH – ✆ (01491) 574 157 – www.luscombes.co.uk – Closed 26 December

Rest – Carte £ 29/42

◆ Cosy restaurant, popular with locals, serving modern menu of tasty, simply cooked dishes. Smiley, attentive service. Lighter lunches, homemade preserves and afternoon cream teas.

at Lower Shiplake South : 2 mi. by A 4155 – ✉ Henley-On-Thames

Crowsley House

Crowsley Rd ✉ RG9 3JT – ✆ (01189) 406 708 – www.crowsleyhouse.co.uk – Fax (01189) 406 708

3 rm ☕ – †£ 75/95 ††£ 95/125

Rest – *(by arrangement, communal dining)* Menu £ 11/25

◆ Discreet guest house in secluded conservation area; two lively cats come as part of the family. Pristine, well-equipped bedrooms boast contemporary bathrooms. Breakfast is an extensive continental affair, with freshly baked pastries. Gourmet meals by arrangement.

ENGLAND

HEREFORD – **County of Herefordshire** – **503** L27 – **pop. 56 373** **18** B3

Great Britain

London 133 mi. – Birmingham 51 mi. – Cardiff 56 mi.

1 King St ✆ (01432) 268430, tic-hereford@herefordshire.gov.uk

Raven's Causeway Wormsley, ✆ (01432) 830 219

Belmont Lodge Belmont Ruckhall Lane, ✆ (01432) 352 666

Hereford Municipal Holmer Rd, ✆ (01432) 344 376

Burghill Valley Burghill Tillington Rd, ✆ (01432) 760 456

City★ - Cathedral★★ (Mappa Mundi★) A **A** – Old House★ A **B**

Kilpeck (Church of SS. Mary and David★★) SW : 8 mi. by A 465 B

Plan on next page

Brandon Lodge without rest

Ross Rd, South : 1.75 mi. on A 49 ✉ HR2 8BH – ✆ (01432) 355 621 – www.brandonlodge.co.uk – Fax (01432) 355 621

10 rm ☕ – †£ 45/60 ††£ 60/75

◆ A good value hotel with 18C origins, charmingly overseen by owner. Bedrooms in main building or adjacent annex: all are spacious, boasting a cheery warmth and good facilities.

The Stewing Pot

17 Church St ✉ HR1 2LR – ✆ (01432) 265 233 – www.stewingpot.co.uk – Closed Christmas-New Year, Sunday and Monday A**a**

Rest – Menu £ 16/20 – Carte £ 19/35

◆ Neighbourhood eatery tucked away down a narrow street, with plain décor and simple, homely furnishings. Taking on a bistro style, cooking is classical and reliably tasty.

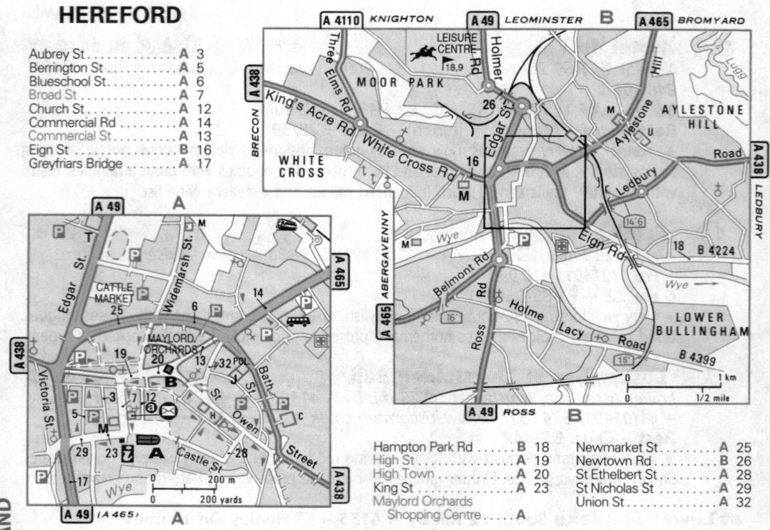

at Byford West : 7.5 mi. by A 438 - B – ✉ Hereford

🏠 **Old Rectory** without rest

✉ *HR4 7LD – ✆ (01981) 590 218 – www.theoldrectory.uk.com – March-November*

3 rm ☕ – 🚹£ 65 🚹🚹£ 79

◆ Rurally set Georgian-style 19C rectory with pleasant gardens. Spacious yet homely atmosphere and décor; the bedrooms are furnished in a simple, traditional style.

at Winforton Northwest : 15 mi. on A 438 – ✉ Hereford

🏠 **Winforton Court** without rest

✉ *HR3 6EA – ✆ (01544) 328 498 – www.winfortoncourt.co.uk – Fax (01544) 328 498 – Closed 20 December - 1 January*

3 rm ☕ – 🚹£ 70 🚹🚹£ 85/105

◆ Wonderfully characterful 16C house used as a circuit court by "Hanging" Judge Jeffries. Exudes personality with exposed beams, thick walls and uneven floors. Rustic rooms.

HERM – C.I. – 503 P33 – see Channel Islands

HERMITAGE – Dorset – see Sherborne

HERSTMONCEUX – East Sussex – 504 U31 – pop. 3 898 — 8 B3

London 63 mi. – Eastbourne 12 mi. – Hastings 14 mi. – Lewes 16 mi.

XXX **Sundial**

Gardner St ✉ BN27 4LA – ✆ (01323) 832 217 – www.sundialrestaurant.co.uk – Fax (01323) 832 909 – Closed Sunday dinner and Monday

Rest – French – Menu £ 23 – Carte £ 34/50

◆ Converted 16C cottage retaining leaded windows and a beamed ceiling. Comfortable chairs in a well spaced dining room. Menu is French with a classic, familiar style.

at Wartling Southeast : 3.75 mi. by A 271 and Wartling rd – ✉ Herstmonceux

Wartling Place without rest
✉ BN27 1RY – ✆ (01323) 832 590 – www.countryhouseaccommodation.co.uk
4 rm – †£ 75/85 ††£ 120/160
◆ Part Georgian house with three acres of gardens, sited in the village. Pleasantly furnished, with some antiques; two of the rooms have four-poster beds.

The Lamb Inn
Wartling Rd ✉ BN27 1RY – ✆ (01323) 832 116 – www.lambinnwartling.co.uk – Fax (01323) 832 637 – Closed Sunday dinner and Monday except Bank Holidays
Rest – Menu £ 15 – Carte £ 18/25
◆ Popular with locals, this early 16C pub offers a friendly welcome. Steeped in character with flag floors, fires and beams. Robust cooking uses quality, traceable ingredients.

HESSLE – **Kingston-upon-Hull** – **502** S22 – **see Kingston-upon-Hull**

HETTON – **North Yorkshire** – **502** N21 – **see Skipton**

HEXHAM – **Northumberland** – **501** N19 – **pop. 10 682** Great Britain **24** A2

London 304 mi. – Carlisle 37 mi. – Newcastle upon Tyne 21 mi.
Wentworth Car Park ✆ (01434) 652220
Spital Park, ✆ (01434) 603 072
De Vere Slaley Hall Slaley, ✆ (01434) 673 154
Tynedale Tyne Green, ✆ (01434) 608 154
Abbey★ (Saxon Crypt★★, Leschman chantry★)
Hadrian's Wall★★, N : 4.5 mi. by A 6079. Housesteads★★, NW : 12.5 mi. by A 6079 and B 6318

Beaumont
Beaumont St ✉ NE46 3LT – ✆ (01434) 602 331 – www.bw-beaumonthotel.co.uk – Fax (01434) 606 184
35 rm – †£ 70/90 ††£ 100/120
Rest *The Park* – Menu £ 13/20
◆ Victorian building of local stone overlooking park and the town's ancient abbey - which is visible from some of the comfortable rooms. Personally run with a warm atmosphere. Park restaurant on the first floor with views of the abbey.

Hallbank
Hallgate ✉ NE46 1XA – ✆ (01434) 606 656 – www.hallbankguesthouse.com – Fax (01434) 605 567
8 rm – †£ 50/80 ††£ 80/90 **Rest** – *(by arrangement)* Menu £ 18
◆ Red-brick Georgian house close to market square, set in the shadow of the old gaol. Fully refurbished rooms exhibit a warm, classic style with good modern facilities. Dine in adjacent, informal café/bistro.

West Close House without rest
Hextol Terrace, Southwest : 0.5 mi. off B 6305 ✉ NE46 2AD – ✆ (01434) 603 307 – Closed December-January
3 rm – †£ 30/45 ††£ 63
◆ Detached house in a residential area providing a high standard of simple, good value accommodation. Polished wood floors and immaculately kept.

Bouchon
4-6 Gilesgate ✉ NE46 3NJ – ✆ (01434) 609 943 – www.bouchonbistrot.co.uk – Closed Sunday, Monday and Bank Holidays
Rest – French – Menu £ 13 (lunch) – Carte £ 15/33
◆ In centre of town: simply styled ground floor with bar; plush intimate first floor dining room with opulent purple furnishings. Neatly presented and tasty authentic French cooking.

ENGLAND

The Rat Inn

Anick, Northeast : 1.75 mi. signposted off A 69 roundabout ✉ NE46 4LN – ✆ (01434) 602 814 – www.theratinn.com – Closed Sunday dinner and Monday

Rest – Carte £ 15/30

◆ Traditional pub with an open range and pleasant garden views. Daily-changing blackboard menu features wholesome cooking, with classic pub and more ambitious dishes – including some for two.

at Slaley Southeast : 5.5 mi. by B 6306 – ✉ Hexham

Slaley Hall

Southeast : 2.25 mi. ✉ NE47 0BY – ✆ (01434) 673 350 – www.devere.co.uk – Fax (01434) 673 962

132 rm – †£ 89/169 ††£ 89/169 – 7 suites

Rest ***Dukes Grill*** – *(Closed Sunday and Monday) (bar lunch Monday-Saturday)* Carte £ 38/72

Rest ***Hadrian's Brasserie*** – *(Closed Sunday dinner)* Menu £ 23/30 – Carte (dinner) £ 30/38

Rest ***The Claret Jug*** – Carte £ 22/33

◆ Spacious countryside leisure oasis boasting numerous recreational facilities, including a spa and two golf courses. Unwind in stylish guest areas and contemporary bedrooms; a few remain in classic style. Dishes from Josper Grill in opulent Dukes. Modern brasserie fare in Hadrian's. British classics in The Claret Jug.

at Haydon Bridge West : 7.5 mi. on A 69 – ✉ Hexham

Langley Castle

Langley-on-Tyne, South : 2 mi. by A 69 on A 686 ✉ NE47 5LU – ✆ (01434) 688 888 – www.langleycastle.com – Fax (01434) 684 019

27 rm – †£ 113/200 ††£ 113/200 **Rest** – Menu £ 20/39

◆ Stunning 14C castle in 12 acres. Stone walls, tapestries and heraldic shields give baronial feel. Luxurious bedrooms exhibit period features; some have window seats or four-posters. Stable rooms are simpler. Dining room offers adventurous, seasonally influenced menu.

ENGLAND

HEYTESBURY – Wilts. – 503 N30 – see Warminster

HIGH WYCOMBE – Buckinghamshire – 504 R29 – pop. 77 178 — 11 C2

Great Britain

London 34 mi. – Aylesbury 17 mi. – Oxford 26 mi. – Reading 18 mi.

The Library, 5 Eden Place ✆ (01494) 421892, tourism_enquiries@wycombe.gov.uk

Hazlemere G & C.C. Hazlemere Penn Rd, ✆ (01494) 719 300

Wycombe Heights Loudwater Rayners Ave, ✆ (01494) 816 686

Chiltern Hills★

Eat-Thai

14-15 Easton St ✉ HP11 1NT – ✆ (01494) 532 888 – www.eat-thai.co.uk – Fax (01494) 532 889 – Closed 25 December

Rest – Thai – Menu £ 15/26 – Carte £ 23/31

◆ Modern restaurant with wood floors and well-spaced tables. Three distinct areas serving fresh, tasty dishes with ingredients flown regularly from Thailand. Attentive service.

HIGHCLERE – Hampshire – 503 P29 – pop. 2 409 – ✉ Newbury — 6 B1

London 69 mi. – Newbury 5 mi. – Reading 25 mi.

The Yew Tree with rm

Hollington Cross, Andover Road, South : 1 mi. on A 343 ✉ RG20 9SE – ✆ (01635) 253 360 – www.theyewtree.net – Fax (01635) 255 035 – Closed 25-26 December dinner

6 rm – †£ 100 ††£ 100 **Rest** – Menu £ 19 (lunch) – Carte £ 27/50

◆ Smart 17C pub with a marble topped bar, owned by Marco Pierre White. Menu blends British frankness with French sophistication, ranging from pub classics to restaurant style dishes. Modern bedrooms with personality.

HIGHCLIFFE – Dorset – 503 O31 4 D3

London 112 mi. – Bournemouth 10 mi. – Salisbury 21 mi. – Southampton 26 mi.

Lord Bute

Lymington Rd ✉ *BH23 4JS* – ✆ *(01425) 278 884* – *www.lordbute.co.uk* – *Fax (01425) 279 258*
11 rm – †£ 98/108 ††£ 98/108 – 2 suites
Rest – *(Closed Sunday dinner and Monday)* Menu £ 17/32 – Carte approx. £ 31
◆ Modern property with a traditional style. Well designed, light, airy lounge. Bedrooms are well appointed and include safes and spa baths. Formal dining room adjacent to Orangery lounge.

HIGH CROSBY – Cumbria – see Carlisle

HIGHER BURWARDSLEY – Ches. – see Tattenhall

HIGH ONGAR – Essex 12 B2

London 30 mi.

The Wheatsheaf

King St, East : 2 mi. by A 414 on Blackmore rd ✉ *CM5 9NS* – ✆ *(01277) 822 220* – *www.thewheatsheafbrasserie.co.uk* – *Closed 26 December - 4 January, Sunday dinner and Monday*
Rest – *(booking essential)* Menu £ 15 (lunch) – Carte £ 23/34
◆ Former pub just outside village with fresh, light 'New England' style. Simple, flavoursome dishes use local produce; good value set price menu. Efficient, personable service.

HIGHWORTH – Swindon – 503 O29 – pop. 7 996 4 D1

London 85 mi. – Oxford 26 mi. – Swindon 6 mi.

Jesmonds of Highworth with rm

Jesmond House ✉ *SN6 7HJ* – ✆ *(01793) 762 364* – *www.jesmondsofhighworth.com* – *Fax (01793) 861 201*
10 rm – †£ 125 ††£ 125 **Rest** – *(dinner only)* Menu £ 33 – Carte £ 25/38
◆ Grade II listed building with contemporary interior and delightful rear terrace. Passionate, experienced kitchen team produce ambitious, artistic dishes with powerful flavours. Modern bedrooms are well-equipped and decorated in tasteful hues.

HINDON – Wiltshire – 503 N30 – pop. 493 4 C2

London 103 mi. – Shaftesbury 7 mi. – Warminster 10 mi.

The Lamb Inn with rm

High St ✉ *SP3 6DP* – ✆ *(01747) 820 573* – *www.lambathindon.co.uk*
17 rm – †£ 70/80 ††£ 90/110 **Rest** – Carte £ 18/33
◆ Scottish-themed bar with red décor and dark wood tables. Produce is predominantly local, with some Scottish contributions; dishes are a mix of British and Mediterranean. Traditional country bedrooms and furnishings.

HINDRINGHAM – Norfolk 15 C1

London 118 mi. – Fakenham 8 mi. – Holt 8 mi.

Field House without rest

Moorgate Rd ✉ *NR21 0PT* – ✆ *(01328) 878 726* – *www.fieldhousehindringham.co.uk*
3 rm – †£ 70/75 ††£ 80/100
◆ Well-kept flint stone house with pretty garden and summer house. Pristine lounge with books and magazines. Extensive breakfast menus. Carefully co-ordinated rooms with extras.

HINTLESHAM – Suffolk – 504 X27 – see Ipswich

HINTON ST GEORGE – Somerset **3** B3

London 138 mi. – Taunton 21 mi. – Weymouth 41 mi. – Yeovil 13 mi.

Lord Poulett Arms with rm

High St ✉ TA17 8SE – ☎ (01460) 73 149 – www.lordpoulettarms.com – Closed 26 December and 1 January

4 rm – †£ 59/88 ††£ 88 **Rest** – Carte £ 19/30

◆ Traditional pub with lavender framed terrace, boules pitch, secret garden and detailed country interior. Local, seasonal produce informs an interesting menu rooted in the Med. Smart, stylish bedrooms boast roll-top or slipper baths.

HISTON – Cambs. – **504** U27 – see Cambridge

HOCKLEY HEATH – West Midlands – **503** O26 – pop. 1 525 – ✉ Solihull **19** C2

London 117 mi. – Birmingham 11 mi. – Coventry 17 mi.

Nuthurst Grange Country House

Nuthurst Grange Lane, South : 0.75 mi. by A 3400 ✉ B94 5NL – ☎ (01564) 783 972 – www.nuthurst-grange.com – Fax (01564) 783 919

19 rm – †£ 139 ††£ 200

Rest ***The Restaurant*** – see restaurant listing

◆ Part Edwardian manor house, overlooking M40 and convenient for Birmingham airport. Classic English country décor throughout. Spacious rooms with high level of comfort.

The Restaurant – at Nuthurst Grange Country House Hotel

Nuthurst Grange Lane, South : 0.75 mi. by A 3400 ✉ B94 5NL – ☎ (01564) 783 972 – www.nuthurst-grange.co.uk – Fax (01564) 783 919

Rest – *(closed Sunday dinner)* Menu £ 19/45 – Carte £ 30/45

◆ Thoroughly traditional tone in the dining room's décor which contributes to a formal ambience. Seasonal menu draws on British and French traditions.

at Lapworth Southeast : 2 mi. on B 4439 – ✉ Warwick

The Boot Inn

Old Warwick Rd, on B 4439 ✉ B94 6JU – ☎ (01564) 782 464 – www.lovelypubs.co.uk

Rest – *(booking essential)* Carte £ 18/25

◆ Bustling modern dining pub, with traditional bucolic character at the front and spacious dining room to rear. Appealing rustic dishes supplemented by daily changing specials.

HOLBEACH – Lincolnshire – **502** U25 – pop. 7 247 **17** D2

London 117 mi. – Kingston-upon-Hull 81 mi. – Norwich 62 mi. – Nottingham 60 mi.

Pipwell Manor without rest

Washway Rd, Saracen's Head, Northwest : 1.5 mi. by A 17 ✉ PE12 8AY – ☎ (01406) 423 119 – Fax (01406) 423 119

4 rm – †£ 38 ††£ 56

◆ Georgian manor built on site of Cisterian Grange, close to solitude of the Wash. Garden railway for train spotters. Complimentary tea, cake on arrival. Country style rooms.

HOLFORD – Somerset – **503** K30 – pop. 307 – ✉ Bridgwater **3** B2

Great Britain

London 171 mi. – Bristol 48 mi. – Minehead 15 mi. – Taunton 22 mi.

Stogursey Priory Church★★, W : 4.5 m

Combe House

Southwest : 0.75 mi. by Youth Hostel rd ✉ TA5 1RZ – ☎ (01278) 741 382 – www.combehouse.co.uk – Fax (01278) 741 322

19 rm – †£ 75/109 ††£ 99/160 **Rest** – Menu £ 20 (lunch) – Carte £ 25/39

◆ Smart country house in secluded wooded valley, with lovely garden and waterwheel. Stylish, modern interior; bright bedrooms with contemporary Laura Ashley style fabrics and white furniture. Split-level restaurant offers classical cooking with a modern edge.

HOLKHAM – Norfolk – 504 W25 15 C1

London 124 mi. – King's Lynn 32 mi. – Norwich 39 mi.

The Victoria

Park Rd ✉ NR23 1RG – ☎ (01328) 711 008 – www.victoriaatholkham.co.uk – Fax (01328) 711 009

10 rm – †£ 100/140 ††£ 120/170

Rest *The Restaurant* – see restaurant listing

◆ Extended flint farmhouse boasting country outlook and large lawned gardens. Characterful, shabby-chic interior with individually styled bedrooms; some furniture from Indian subcontinent.

The Restaurant – at The Victoria Hotel

Park Rd ✉ NR23 1RG – ☎ (01328) 711 008 – www.victoriaatholkham.co.uk – Fax (01328) 711 009

Rest – Carte £ 30/35

◆ Choice of 2 Colonial-style dining rooms, conservatory or wood-furnished terrace. Seasonally evolving menus have unfussy, brasserie style: local produce to the fore. Friendly, attentive service.

HOLMFIRTH – West Yorkshire – 502 O23 – pop. 21 979 22 B3

London 187 mi. – Leeds 35 mi. – Sheffield 32 mi. – Manchester 25 mi.

Sunnybank without rest

78 Upperthong Lane, West : 0.5 mi. by A6024 ✉ HD9 3BQ – ☎ (01484) 684 065 – www.sunnybankguesthouse.co.uk – Closed 31 December

3 rm – †£ 60 ††£ 100

◆ Attractive Victorian house in mature gardens with smart bedrooms, good facilities and a modern edge; 2 rooms have great country views. Breakfast room boasts cushioned window seats.

HOLT – Norfolk – 504 X25 – pop. 3 550 15 C1

London 124 mi. – King's Lynn 34 mi. – Norwich 22 mi.

Byfords

Shirehall Plain ✉ NR25 6BG – ☎ (01263) 711 400 – www.byfords.org.uk – Fax (01263) 713 520

16 rm – †£ 95/105 ††£ 130/180

Rest – Menu £ 20 (dinner) – Carte £ 24/28

◆ Flint-fronted Grade II listed house that boasts something different: a well-stocked deli; rustic cellar café; and stunning rooms, with great bathrooms and under-floor heating.

Plantation House without rest

Old Cromer Rd, East 1.25 mi. by A148 on Kelling Hospital rd ✉ NR25 6AJ – ☎ (01263) 710 121 – www.plantation-house.net – Closed 22-28 December

4 rm – †£ 60/70 ††£ 90

◆ Red brick house just out of town, in exceptional mature gardens. Colonial style with heavy fabrics and objets d'art. Individually styled bedrooms with extra touches; most overlook garden.

Butlers

9 Appleyard ✉ NR25 6BN – ☎ (01263) 710 790 – www.butlersrestaurants.com – Closed 25-26 December and Sunday dinner

Rest – Carte £ 18/30

◆ Set in a pedestrianised area, with small terraces front and back. Classical menu displays a good mix of tasty, unfussy dishes, with regional produce and fresh local fish to the fore.

HOLT – Wilts. – 503 – see Bradford-on-Avon

HONITON – Devon – 503 K31 – pop. 11 213 2 D2

London 186 mi. – Exeter 17 mi. – Southampton 93 mi. – Taunton 18 mi.

Lace Walk Car Park ☎ (01404) 43716, honitontic@btconnect.com

All Hallows Museum★ **AC**

Ottery St Mary★ (St Mary's★) SW : 5 mi. by A 30 and B 3177. Faraway Countryside Park (≤★) **AC**, SE : 6.5 mi. by A 375 and B 3174

The Holt
178 High St ✉ EX14 1LA – ☎ (01404) 47 707 – www.theholt-honiton.com – Closed 25-26 December and 1 January
Rest – *(Closed Sunday-Monday)* Carte £ 20/26
◆ Rustic family-run pub providing a 'distinctive and sustainable taste of Devon'. Regularly changing menu of regional and homemade produce; local ales from the family brewery.

at Gittisham Southwest : 3 mi. by A 30 – ✉ Honiton

Combe House
✉ EX14 3AD – ☎ (01404) 540 400 – www.combehousedevon.com – Fax (01404) 46 004 – Closed last 2 weeks January
13 rm – †£ 155/175 ††£ 175/190 – 3 suites
Rest – *(booking essential for non-residents)* Menu £ 29/45
◆ Listed Elizabethan mansion set in glorious Devon countryside. Impressive Great Hall. Individually designed, stylish bedrooms with fine antiques and roaring fires. Unfussy cooking makes good use of local produce. Friendly service.

HOOK – Hampshire – 504 R30 – pop. 6 471 – ✉ Basingstoke 6 B1

London 47 mi. – Oxford 39 mi. – Reading 13 mi. – Southampton 31 mi.

Tylney Hall
Rotherwick , Northwest : 2.5 mi. by A30 and Newnham rd on Ridge Lane ✉ RG27 9AZ – ☎ (01256) 764 881 – www.tylneyhall.co.uk – Fax (01256) 768 141
103 rm – †£ 155/450 ††£ 205/500 – 14 suites
Rest ***Oak Room*** – Menu £ 25/37 – Carte approx. £ 47
◆ Grand and beautifully restored 19C mansion in delightful, extensive Gertrude Jekyll gardens. Country house rooms, some with private conservatories or suites over two floors. Classically English dining room with oak panelling and garden views.

The Hogget
London Road, at the junction of A 30 and A 287 ✉ RG27 9JJ – ☎ (01256) 763 009 – www.hogget.co.uk – Closed 25-26 December
Rest – Carte £ 21/28
◆ Located at junction of A30 and A287. Wholesome, honest cooking; sensibly priced and made using local produce: pie and mash or steak and chips through to crab cake or calves liver.

HOPE – Derbyshire – 502 O23 – ✉ Sheffield 16 A1

London 180 mi. – Derby 50 mi. – Manchester 31 mi. – Sheffield 15 mi.

Underleigh House without rest
Hope Valley, North : 1 mi. by Edale Rd ✉ S33 6RF – ☎ (01433) 621 372 – www.underleighhouse.co.uk – Fax (01433) 621 324 – Closed Christmas, New Year and January
5 rm – †£ 70 ††£ 90
◆ Converted Victorian property, rurally located and personally run, well located for the Peak District. Countryside views and a welcoming country ambience.

HOPE COVE – Devon – 503 I33 – see Salcombe

HORLEY – Surrey – 504 T30 – pop. 22 582 7 D2

London 27 mi. – Brighton 26 mi. – Royal Tunbridge Wells 22 mi.

Plan : see Gatwick

ENGLAND

Langshott Manor

Langshott, North : 0.5 mi. by A 23 turning right at Chequers H. onto Ladbroke Rd ✉ RH6 9LN – ✆ (01293) 786 680 – www.langshottmanor.com – Fax (01293) 825 872

21 rm – †£ 99/140 ††£ 109/190, ☕ £ 19.50 – 1 suite

Rest *Mulberry* – *(booking essential)* Menu £ 20/35 – Carte £ 30/40

◆ Part Elizabethan manor house set amidst gardens of roses, vines and ponds. For centuries the home of aristocrats, now a refined and harmonious country house hotel. Country house-style dining room with intimate ambience.

HORNCASTLE – Lincolnshire – 502 T24 – pop. 6 090 17 C1

London 143 mi. – Lincoln 22 mi. – Nottingham 62 mi.

The Library, Wharf Rd ✆ (01507) 601111, horncastleinfo@e-lindsey.gov.uk

Magpies

71-75 East St ✉ LN9 6AA – ✆ (01507) 527 004 – www.eatatthemagpies.co.uk – Fax (01507) 525 068 – Closed 28 December-13 January and Monday-Tuesday

Rest – Menu £ 25/38

◆ Renowned, family run restaurant in a converted 18C house. Snug, comfortable, beamed interior. Local ingredients used in accomplished, refined dishes in a modern style.

HORNDON-ON-THE-HILL – Thurrock – 504 V29 – pop. 1 612 13 C3

London 25 mi. – Chelmsford 22 mi. – Maidstone 34 mi. – Southend-on-Sea 16 mi.

The Bell with rm

High Rd ✉ SS17 8LD – ✆ (01375) 642 463 – www.bell-inn.co.uk – Fax (01375) 361 611 – Closed 25-26 December and Bank Holiday Mondays

15 rm – †£ 60 ††£ 60/85, ☕ £ 9.50 **Rest** – Carte £ 22/32

◆ 15C coaching inn, run by the same family for 50 years. Cooking is a step above your usual pub fare, displaying classically based dishes with some modern touches. Pub bedrooms styled after Victorian mistresses; those in Hill House display thoughtful extras.

HORNINGSEA – Cambs. – see Cambridge

HORNINGSHAM – Wiltshire – 504 N30 – see Warminster

HORN'S CROSS – Devon – 503 H31 – ✉ Bideford Great Britain 2 C1

London 222 mi. – Barnstaple 15 mi. – Exeter 46 mi.

Clovelly★★, W : 6.5 mi. on A 39 and B 3237 – Bideford : Bridge★★ - Burton Art Gallery★ **AC** - Lundy Island★★ (by ferry), NE : 7 mi. on a 39 and B 3235 – Hartland : Hartland Church★ - Hartland Quay★ (✻★★) - Hartland Point ←★★★, W : 9 mi. on A 39 and B 3248 – Great Torrington (Dartington Crystal★ **AC**), SE : 15 mi. on A 39 and A 386 – Rosemoor★, SE : 16 mi. on A 39, A 386 and B 3220

The Roundhouse without rest

West : 1 mi. on A 39 ✉ EX39 5DN – ✆ (01237) 451 687 – www.theroundhouse.co.uk – Fax (01237) 451 924

3 rm ☕ – †£ 40 ††£ 65

◆ Located on site of 13C corn mill, this friendly guesthouse offers cream teas on arrival! Spacious lounge and good quality breakfasts. Comfy, clean, well-kept bedrooms.

The Hoops Inn with rm

West : 0.5 mi. on A 39 ✉ EX39 5DL – ✆ (01237) 451 222 – www.hoopsinn.co.uk – Fax (01237) 451 247

13 rm ☕ – †£ 95/105 ††£ 95/105 **Rest** – Carte £ 15/30

◆ Quaint 13C inn with open fires, cosy snugs and a hidden well, plus restaurant for intimate candlelit dinners. Classic dishes such as cottage pie, beef Bourguignon and jam roly poly. Bedrooms in original inn boast four-posters and half-testers; those in coach house offer simpler comforts.

HORRINGER – Suffolk – 504 W27 – see Bury St Edmunds

HORSHAM – West Sussex – 504 T30 – pop. 47 804 — 7 D2

London 39 mi. – Brighton 23 mi. – Guildford 20 mi. – Lewes 25 mi.
9 Causeway ✆ (01403) 211661, tourist.information@horsham.gov.uk
Mannings Heath Fullers, Hammerpond Rd, Mannings Heath, ✆ (01403) 210 228

South Lodge

Brighton Rd, Lower Beeding, Southeast : 5 mi. on A 281 ✉ RH13 6PS – ✆ (01403) 891 711 – www.exclusivehotels.co.uk – Fax (01403) 891 766
86 rm – £ 230 £ 230, £ 16 – 3 suites
Rest *Camellia* – *(booking essential for non-residents)* Menu £ 20 *(lunch) (weekday)*/26 (Sunday) – Carte £ 37/55
Rest *The Pass* – Modern – *(lunch only , dinner Wednesday-Thursday and Sunday)* Menu £ 28/35

◆ Victorian mansion set in 93 acres, with period furnishings, heavy panelled walls and corporate feel. Traditional bedrooms in main house; more contemporary rooms in wing – some suites have jacuzzis/terraces. Fine dining with South Downs views in Camellia. Live kitchen action and elaborate, intricate cooking in The Pass.

Restaurant Tristan

Stans Way, off East St ✉ RH12 1HU – ✆ (01403) 255 688 – www.restauranttristan.co.uk – Closed 2 weeks summer, 2 weeks winter, 25 December, Sunday and Monday
Rest – Menu £ 15/36

◆ The dining happens in the beamed upstairs room of this period house. The cooking is seasonal but also elaborate in style; the kitchen is a fan of modern techniques. Service is quite formal.

at Rowhook Northwest : 4 mi. by A 264 and A 281 off A 29 – ✉ Horsham

The Chequers Inn

✉ RH12 3PY – ✆ (01403) 790 480 – www.nealsrestaurants.biz – Closed 25 December and Sunday dinner
Rest – Carte £ 25/32

◆ Delightful 18C inn with low beams, formal restaurant and relaxed atmosphere. Menus showcase local produce – including game from nearby estates – and fresh homemade puddings.

HOUGH-ON-THE-HILL – Lincs. – see Grantham

HOVE – Brighton and Hove – 504 T31 – see Brighton and Hove

HOVERINGHAM – Nottinghamshire – pop. 308 — 16 B2

London 135 mi. – Birmingham 77 mi. – Leeds 74 mi. – Sheffield 57 mi.

The Reindeer Inn

Main St ✉ NG14 7JR – ✆ (0115) 966 36 29 – www.thereindeerinn.com – Closed 2 weeks mid May, Sunday dinner, Monday and lunch Tuesday
Rest – Menu £ 7 (lunch) – Carte £ 19/29

◆ Modest looking pub with charming interior, set overlooking the cricket pitch in a pretty village. Classically based menus offer excellent value for money, particularly at lunchtime.

HUDDERSFIELD – West Yorkshire – 502 O23 – pop. 146 234 — 22 B3

London 191 mi. – Bradford 11 mi. – Leeds 15 mi. – Manchester 25 mi.
Huddersfield Library, Princes Alexandra Walk ✆ (01484) 223200, huddersfield.information@kirklees.gov.uk
Bradley Park Bradley Rd, ✆ (01484) 223 772
Woodsome Hall Fenay Bridge, ✆ (01484) 602 971
Outlane Slack Lane, Off New Hey Rd, ✆ (01422) 374 762
Meltham Thick Hollins Hall, ✆ (01484) 850 227
Fixby Hall Lightridge Rd, ✆ (01484) 426 203
Crosland Heath Felks Stile Rd, ✆ (01484) 653 216

Plans pages 277, 278

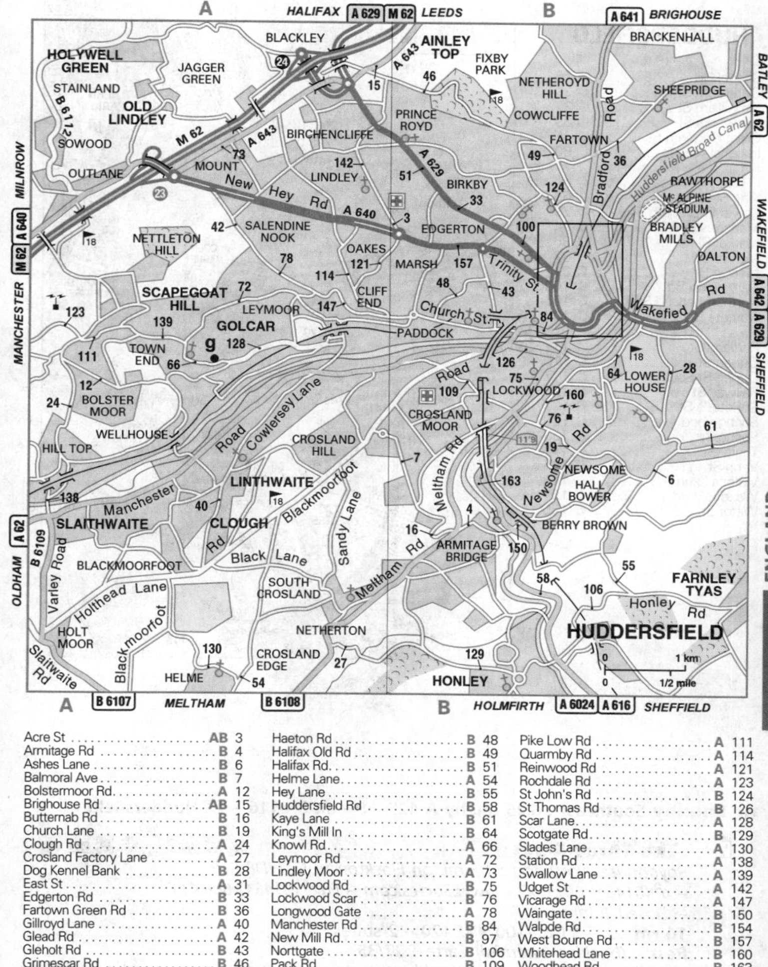

at Thunder Bridge Southeast : 5.75 mi. by A 629 - B – ✉ Huddersfield

Woodman Inn with rm

✉ *HD8 0PX* – ☎ *(01484) 605 778*
– *www.woodman-inn.co.uk*
– *Fax (01484) 604 110*
– *Closed 25 December dinner*

12 rm ☕ – 🚹£ 48 🚹🚹£ 74

Rest – Menu £ 16/19 – Carte approx. £ 29

◆ Traditional 19C pub set in a small hamlet in the valley. The classic British menus are extensive and change with the seasons. Lunch is simple and hearty, dinner more ambitious. Nearby cottage bedrooms are simple but well-kept.

HUDDERSFIELD

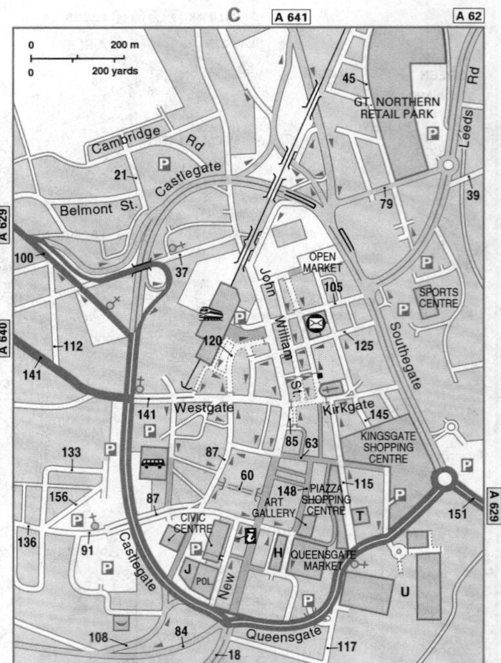

ENGLAND

at Shelley Southeast : 6.25 mi. by A 629 - B - on B 6116 – ✉ Huddersfield

The Three Acres rest, VISA

Roydhouse, Northeast : 1.5 mi. on Flockton rd ✉ HD8 8LR – ✆ (01484) 602 606 – www.3acres.com – Fax (01484) 608 411 – Closed 1 January

16 rm – †£ 80/100 ††£ 120 – 2 suites

Rest – *(booking essential)* Carte £ 27/35

◆ Well-established stone inn in rural location. Annex rooms more spacious and quiet; those in main house closer to the bar and dining room; all warm, modern and comfortable. Agreeably busy restaurant with open fires: fish dishes prepared at open seafood bar.

at Golcar West : 3.5 mi. by A 62 on B 6111 – ✉ Huddersfield

XXX **The Weavers Shed** with rm VISA

86-88 Knowl Road, Golcar ✉ HD7 4AN – ✆ (01484) 654 284 – www.weaversshed.co.uk – Fax (01484) 650 980 – Closed 2 weeks Christmas-New Year Ag

5 rm – †£ 90 ††£ 120

Rest – *(closed Saturday lunch, Sunday and Monday)* Menu £ 19 (lunch) – Carte £ 35/54

◆ Characterful 18C former cloth mill boasting exposed beams/stonework and Regency-style lounge. Concise, classical menus have a personal twist; quality produce is from allotment and nearby. Cottage bedrooms come with complimentary soft drinks and sherry.

HUNGERFORD – West Berkshire – 503 P29 – pop. 4 938 10 A3

London 74 mi. – Bristol 57 mi. – Oxford 28 mi. – Reading 26 mi.

Savernake Forest★★ (Grand Avenue★★★), W : 7 mi. by A 4 – Crofton Beam Engines★, SW : 8 mi. by A 338 and minor roads

Fishers Farm without rest

Shefford Woodlands, North : 4 mi. by A 4 and A 338 on B 4000 ✉ RG17 7AB – ☎ (01488) 648 466 – www.fishersfarm.co.uk – Fax (01488) 648 706

3 rm – †£ 50/60 ††£ 70/80

◆ Attractive redbrick farmhouse in a rural spot on a working farm. Well-appointed sitting room. Breakfast served family style. Individually styled rooms with country views.

at Kintbury Southeast : 3.75 mi. by A 4 – ✉ Hungerford

The Dundas Arms with rm

Station Rd ✉ RG17 9UT – ☎ (01488) 658 263 – www.dundasarms.co.uk – Fax (01488) 658 568 – Closed 25-26 December, 31 December dinner and Sunday dinner

5 rm – †£ 80 ††£ 90 **Rest** – Carte £ 19/30

◆ Traditional family-owned inn in splendid location between river and canal. Classic dishes on daily changing menu. Simply furnished bedrooms in former stables; all have French windows opening onto riverside terrace.

at Lambourn Woodlands North : 6 mi. by A 338 on B 4000

The Hare

✉ RG17 7SD – ☎ (01488) 71 386 – www.theharerestaurant.co.uk – Fax (01488) 71 186 – Closed 1 week spring, 2 weeks summer, 2 weeks winter, 25 December, Sunday dinner and Monday

Rest – *(booking essential)* Menu £ 20 (midweek)/26 – Carte (dinner) £ 20/40

◆ Attractive former pub with lawned garden, paved terrace, small lounge and three characterful dining rooms. Concise but interesting menus of flavoursome modern dishes crafted from local produce.

Is breakfast included? The cup symbol appears after the number of rooms.

HUNSDON – Hertfordshire 12 B2

London 26 mi. – Bishop's Stortford 8 mi. – Harlow 7 mi.

Fox and Hounds

2 High St ✉ SG12 8NH – ☎ (01279) 843 999 – www.foxandhounds-hunsdon.co.uk – Fax (01279) 841 092 – Closed Sunday dinner and Monday

Rest – Menu £ 14 (weekdays) – Carte £ 20/35

◆ Spacious pub featuring a rustic bar, smart dining room, large garden and terrace. Daily-changing menu displays a wide range of local seasonal produce, cooked simply and stylishly.

HUNSTANTON – Norfolk – 502 V25 – pop. 4 505 14 B1

London 120 mi. – Cambridge 60 mi. – Norwich 45 mi.

Town Hall, The Green ☎ (01485) 532610, hunstanton.tic@west-norfolk.gov.uk

Golf Course Rd, ☎ (01485) 532 811

Claremont without rest

35 Greevegate ✉ PE36 6AF – ☎ (01485) 533 171 – Mid-March to mid-November

7 rm – †£ 30/40 ††£ 60/70

◆ Classic seaside guesthouse in a Victorian building close to beach, shops and gardens. Well-kept, traditional interior and a toaster on each table at breakfast.

ENGLAND

XX **The Neptune** with rm

85 Old Hunstanton Rd, Old Hunstanton, Northeast : 1.5 mi. on A 149 – ✉ PE36 6HZ – ✆ (01485) 532 122 – www.theneptune.co.uk – Closed 26 December, 1-15 January, 1-15 November, Monday and Saturday lunch

7 rm (dinner included) – †£ 90/95 ††£ 160/180

Rest – *(dinner only and Sunday lunch) (lunch midweek by arrangement)*

Menu £ 24 – Carte £ 38/45

Spec. Mackerel, watermelon and crab salad. Beef with spinach purée, pickled onion and beef tea. Lemon custard with lemon grass ice cream and vanilla lemonade.

◆ Ivy-clad, red-brick 19C former coaching inn with flag-floored lounge, intimate dining room and New England styling. Concise, constantly evolving menu delivers refined, unfussy and flavoursome cooking, using high quality, local produce. Polite, efficient service led by ebullient owner. Bright and tidy bedrooms.

at Ringstead East : 3.75 mi. by A 149 – ✉ Hunstanton

The Gin Trap Inn with rm

6 High St ✉ PE36 5JU – ✆ (01485) 525 264 – www.gintrapinn.co.uk

3 rm – †£ 49/70 ††£ 78/140 **Rest** – Carte £ 20/28

◆ Attractive whitewashed inn with cosy front bar and spacious, wood-floored conservatory. Well-presented, value-for-money dishes mix the traditional and the more modern. Bedrooms boast wrought iron beds and roll top baths.

HUNTINGDON – **Cambridgeshire** – **504** T26 – **pop. 20 600** **14** A2

London 69 mi. – Bedford 21 mi. – Cambridge 16 mi.

Pathfinder HOuse, St. Mary's St ✆ (01480) 388588, hunts.tic@huntsdc.gov.uk

Hemingford Abbots Cambridge Rd, New Farm Lodge, ✆ (01480) 495 000

Old Bridge

1 High St ✉ PE29 3TQ – ✆ (01480) 424 300 – www.huntsbridge.com – Fax (01480) 411 017

24 rm – †£ 95/120 ††£ 120/190

Rest ***Terrace*** – see restaurant listing

◆ Long-standing, family-owned riverside hotel with small wine shop in reception: one owner is a Master of Wine. Contemporary bedrooms feature plenty of fabrics and spacious bathrooms.

XX **Terrace** – at Old Bridge Hotel

1 High St ✉ PE29 3TQ – ✆ (01480) 424 300 – www.huntsbridge.com – Fax (01480) 411 017

Rest – Menu £ 20 (lunch) – Carte £ 27/35

◆ Choose between formal wood-panelled dining room and more casual conservatory with terrace. Menus change every two days and feature traditional dishes with some Mediterranean influences.

at Broughton Northeast : 6 mi. by B 1514 off A 141 – ✉ Huntingdon

The Crown

Bridge Rd ✉ PE28 3AY – ✆ (01487) 824 428 – www.thecrowninnrestaurant.co.uk – Closed Monday and Tuesday

Rest – Menu £ 15 (lunch) – Carte £ 19/27

◆ Light and airy pub in pretty village offering good selection of real ales and some reasonably priced wines. Short and varied à la carte with Mediterranean leanings. Polite service.

at Hemingford Grey Southeast : 5 mi. by A 1198 off A 14 – ✉ Huntingdon

The Willow without rest

45 High St ✉ PE28 9BJ – ✆ (01480) 494 748 – www.thewillowguesthouse.co.uk – Fax (01480) 464 456 – Closed 25-26 December and 1 January

7 rm – †£ 49 ††£ 75

◆ Very personally run guesthouse in picturesque village location: its vivid yellow exterior makes it easy to spot. Good value, and close to The Cock. Immaculately kept bedrooms.

The Cock

47 High St ✉ PE28 9BJ – ☎ (01480) 463 609 – www.cambscuisine.com – Fax (01480) 461 747 – Closed 26 December
Rest – Menu £ 15 (weekday lunch) – Carte £ 20/31
◆ Homely 17C country pub with spacious dining room, run by an experienced team. Tried and tested pub cooking offers good value lunches, daily fish specials and a mix and match sausage board.

HUNWORTH – Norfolk — 15 C1

London 129 mi. – Norwich 25 mi. – East Dereham 17 mi. – Taverham 19 mi.

The Hunny Bell

The Green ✉ NR24 2AA Hunworth – ☎ (01263) 712 300 – www.thehunnybell.co.uk – Fax (01263) 710 161
Rest – Menu £ 20 (Sunday lunch) – Carte £ 25/35
◆ Renovated whitewashed pub with a smart country interior. Cooking is modern-European meets traditional pub and is local, seasonal and keenly priced. Much of the food is homemade.

HURLEY – Windsor and Maidenhead – pop. 1 712 — 11 C3

London 35 mi. – Maidenhead 5 mi. – Reading 18 mi.

Black Boys Inn with rm

Henley Rd, Southwest : 1.5 mi. on A 4130 ✉ SL6 5NQ – ☎ (01628) 824 212 – www.blackboysinn.co.uk – Closed 2 weeks Christmas, last 2 weeks August, Sunday dinner and Monday
8 rm – †£ 75/95 ††£ 95/110 **Rest** – Carte £ 25/38
◆ 16C pub with stylish modern interior, comfy lounge and wood burning stove. Cooking is well-crafted and flavoursome, with restaurant-style dishes. Friendly, knowledgeable service. Individually-styled bedrooms with excellent en suites.

HURST – Berks. – 503 Q29 – see Reading

HURSTBOURNE TARRANT – Hampshire – 503 P30 – pop. 700 – ✉ Andover — 6 B1

London 77 mi. – Bristol 77 mi. – Oxford 38 mi. – Southampton 33 mi.

Esseborne Manor

Northeast : 1.5 mi. on A 343 ✉ SP11 0ER – ☎ (01264) 736 444 – www.esseborne-manor.co.uk – Fax (01264) 736 725
19 rm – †£ 98/110 ††£ 150/180
Rest – Menu £ 15/18 **s** – Carte (dinner) £ 28/40 **s**
◆ 100 year old country house in attractive grounds with herb garden. Smart, well-appointed bedrooms, three in garden cottages. Ferndown room boasts a spa bath and private patio. Long, narrow dining room with large windows.

HURWORTH-ON-TEES – Darlington – 502 P20 – see Darlington

HUTTON-LE-HOLE – North Yorkshire – 502 R21 – pop. 162 — 23 C1

London 244 mi. – Scarborough 27 mi. – York 33 mi.

Burnley House without rest

✉ YO62 6UA – ☎ (01751) 417 548 – www.burnleyhouse.co.uk – March-October
7 rm – †£ 55/70 ††£ 85/95
◆ Attractive part 16C, part Georgian house, Grade II listed in a picturesque Moors village. Brown trout in beck winding through garden. Simple, individually styled bedrooms.

HYTHE – Kent – 504 X30 – pop. 14 766 — 9 D2

London 68 mi. – Folkestone 6 mi. – Hastings 33 mi. – Maidstone 31 mi.
Railway Station, Scanlons Bridge Rd ☎ (0871) 7162449
Sene Valley Folkestone Sene, ☎ (01303) 268 513

Plan : see Folkestone

ENGLAND

Hythe Imperial
Prince's Parade ✉ *CT21 6AE* – ✆ *(01303) 267 441*
– *www.mercure-uk.com* – *Fax (01303) 264 610*
100 rm – £ 70/135 £ 70/135, ☐ £ 13.95
Rest ***The Princes Room*** – *(dinner only and Sunday lunch) (bar lunch Monday -Saturday)* Menu £ 15/27 **s** – Carte £ 27/35 **s**

◆ Set in a 50 acre estate, this classic Victorian hotel retains the elegance of a former age. Wide range of bedrooms cater for everyone from families to business travellers. Spacious restaurant with classic style and menus to match.

Hythe Bay
Marine Parade ✉ *CT21 6AW* – ✆ *(01303) 233 844* – *www.thehythebay.co.uk*
– *Fax (01303) 233 845*
Rest – Seafood – Carte £ 21/45

◆ Originally built as tea rooms and in a great position just feet from the beach. Bright, airy room with views out to Channel. Seafood menus - ideal for lunch on a summer's day.

ICKLESHAM – East Sussex – 504 V/W31 — 9 C3

London 66 mi. – Brighton 42 mi. – Hastings 7 mi.

Manor Farm Oast
Windmill Lane, South : 0.5 mi. ✉ *TN36 4WL* – ✆ *(01424) 813 787*
– *www.manorfarmoast.co.uk* – *Closed 20 December-10 February*
3 rm ☐ – £ 89/99 £ 99
Rest – *(Friday and Saturday only)* Menu £ 30 (dinner)

◆ 19C former oast house retaining original features and surrounded by orchards. Welcoming beamed lounge with open fire. One of the comfy bedrooms is completely in the round! Home-cooked menus in circular dining room.

IGHTHAM COMMON – Kent – 504 U30 – see Sevenoaks

ILFRACOMBE – Devon – 503 H30 – pop. 10 508 Great Britain — 2 C1

London 218 mi. – Barnstaple 13 mi. – Exeter 53 mi.

Mortehoe★★ : St Mary's Church - Morte Point★, SW : 5.5 mi. on B 3343 – Lundy Island★★ (by ferry). Braunton : St Brannock's Church★, Braunton Burrows★, S : 8 mi. on A 361 – Barnstaple★ : Bridge★, S : 12 mi. on A 3123, B 3230, A 39, A 361 and B 3233

The Quay
11 The Quay ✉ *EX34 9EQ* – ✆ *(01271) 868 090* – *www.11thequay.co.uk*
– *Fax (01271) 865 599* – *Closed January, 25 December and Sunday dinner*
Rest – Carte £ 27/41

◆ Smart, three-floored restaurant packed with Damien Hirst artwork and surprisingly set in an old fishing port. Same menu served throughout, with seafood and local produce to the fore.

ILKLEY – West Yorkshire – 502 O22 – pop. 13 472 — 22 B2

London 210 mi. – Bradford 13 mi. – Harrogate 17 mi. – Leeds 16 mi.
Town Hall, Station Rd ✆ (01943) 602319, ilkleytic@bradford.gov.uk
Myddleton, ✆ (01943) 607 277

Rombalds
11 West View, Wells Rd ✉ *LS29 9JG* – ✆ *(01943) 603 201* – *www.rombalds.co.uk*
– *Fax (01943) 816 586* – *Closed 27 December - 4 January*
15 rm ☐ – £ 75/85 £ 110/128 – 4 suites
Rest – Menu £ 15/20 **s** – Carte £ 17/28 **s**

◆ Privately owned Georgian town house on edge of Moor. Elegant fixtures and fittings adorn its sitting room. Individually styled bedrooms have matching fabrics and drapes. Yorkshire produce to fore in cool blue restaurant.

ENGLAND

Box Tree (Simon Gueller)

37 Church St, on A 65 ✉ LS29 9DR – ✆ (01943) 608 484 – www.theboxtree.co.uk – Fax (01943) 607 186 – Closed 27-30 December, 1-7 January, Monday and Sunday dinner

Rest – *(dinner only and lunch Friday-Sunday)* Menu £ 28 (lunch) – Carte £ 49/59

Spec. Risotto of quail, peas and pancetta. Sea bass and clam chowder with Morteau sausage. Lemon tartlet with blood orange sorbet.

◆ Charming 18C sandstone cottage, adorned with antiques, paintings and ornaments. Classical menus with a French base, executed with confidence and a light touch when required; where flavour is never compromised by style.

ILMINGTON – Warwickshire – 504 O27 Great Britain — 19 C3

London 91 mi. – Birmingham 31 mi. – Oxford 34 mi. – Stratford-upon-Avon 9 mi.

Hidcote Manor Garden★★, SW : 2 mi. by minor rd – Chipping Campden★★, SW : 4 mi. by minor rd

Folly Farm Cottage

Back St ✉ CV36 4LJ – ✆ (01608) 682 425 – www.follyfarm.co.uk – Fax (01608) 682 425

3 rm – †£ 65 ††£ 84 **Rest** – *(by arrangement)* Carte £ 15/19 **s**

◆ Cosy, characterful cottage in small village, with friendly owners and lovely garden. Beams and heavy drapes abound. Some bedrooms have four-posters or whirlpool baths; two have small kitchens. Simple home-cooked dinners.

The Howard Arms with rm

Lower Green ✉ CV36 4LT – ✆ (01608) 682 226 – www.howardarms.com – Fax (01608) 682 874 – Closed 25 December dinner

8 rm – †£ 85 ††£ 140 **Rest** – Carte £ 20/31

◆ Gold stone English country inn, with a terrace, set on a peaceful village green. Wide-ranging, weekly changing menu is informed by seasonal produce from local farms and Estates. Cosy bedrooms with antique furniture.

INGLETON – North Yorkshire – 502 M21 – pop. 1 641 – ✉ Carnforth (Lancs.) — 22 A2

London 266 mi. – Kendal 21 mi. – Lancaster 18 mi. – Leeds 53 mi.

The Community Centre ✆ (015242) 41049, ingleton@ytbtic.co.uk

Riverside Lodge

24 Main St ✉ LA6 3HJ – ✆ (015242) 41 359 – www.riversideingleton.co.uk – Closed 24-25 December

7 rm – †£ 41 ††£ 62 **Rest** – *(by arrangement)* Menu £ 17

◆ Pleasant 19C house close to famous pot-holing caves. Conservatory dining room with great views across Yorkshire Dales. Informal gardens. Cosy sitting room and homely bedrooms.

INSTOW – Devon – 503 H30 – see Bideford

IPSWICH – Suffolk – 504 X27 – pop. 138 718 Great Britain — 15 C3

London 76 mi. – Norwich 43 mi.

St Stephens Church, St Stephens Lane ✆ (01473) 258070, tourist@ipswich.gov.uk

18 Rushmere Rushmere Heath, ✆ (01473) 725 648

27 Purdis Heath Bucklesham Rd, ✆ (01473) 728 941

27 Fynn Valley Witnesham, ✆ (01473) 785 267

Sutton Hoo★, NE : 12 mi. by A 12 Y and B 1083 from Woodbridge

Plan on next page

ENGLAND

IPSWICH

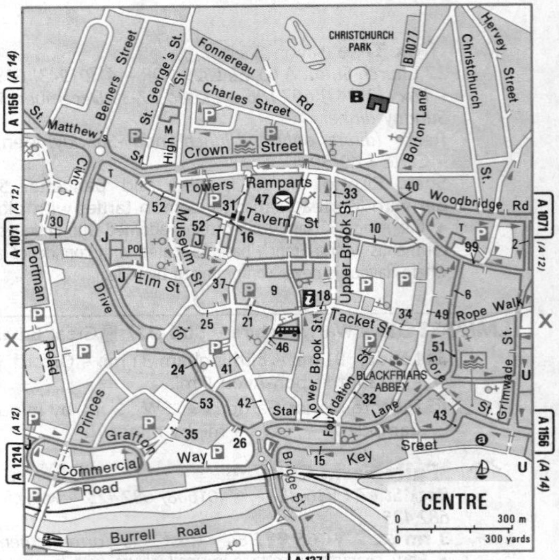

ENGLAND

A 14 (A 140) BURY
WHITTON
INDUSTRIAL ESTATE
Bury Rd
WHITE HOUSE
CASTLE HILL
BROOMHILL
ST. MARGARET'S
RUSHMERE
Lovetofts Dr.
B 1067
Bramford Rd
Norwich Rd A 1156
Dales Rd.
Henley Road
B 1077
Humber Doucy Lane
Valley Road
Park Rd
Westerfield Road
Tuddenham Road
Colchester Rd A 1214
Bramford Lane
Bramford Road
Sproughton Rd
CHRISTCHURCH PARK
Rushmere Road
Woodbridge Road A 1071
Spring Road
Cauldwell Hall Rd
ST. JOHN'S
Heath Road
CHANTRY
CHANTRY PARK
Hadleigh Road
Ranelagh Rd
ALEXANDRA PARK
ST. CLEMENT'S
Foxhall Road
Orwell
HOLYWELLS PARK
A 1156 Felixstowe Road
Bixley Road
London Road A 1214
Hawthorn Drive
SPRITES
STOKE PARK
Belstead Road
Stoke Park Drive
BRIDGE
Wherstead Road
Hawes St
Cliff Lane
Landseer Road
LANDSEER PARK
Clapgate Lane
Nacton Road
BOURNE PARK
GAINSBOROUGH
PRIORY HEATH
(A 12) (A 14) A 137 MANNINGTREE
(A 14)
A 1156 FELIXSTOWE
A 1214 (A 12) GREAT YARMOUTH
A 14 (A 12) HADLEIGH
A 1071 A 1214 (A 12) COLCHESTER
0 1 km
0 1/2 mile
Y
Z

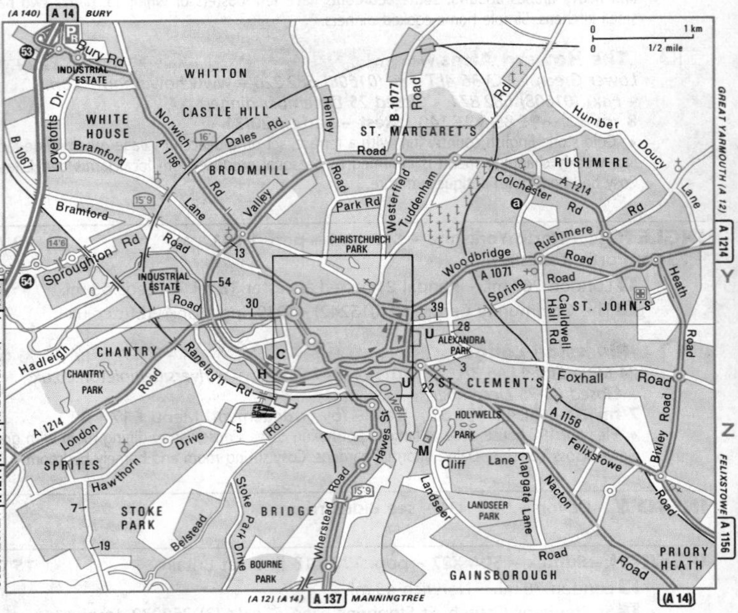

Salthouse Harbour

1 Neptune Quay ✉ *IP4 1AX – ✆ (01473) 226 789 – www.salthouseharbour.co.uk – Fax (01473) 226 927* Xa

68 rm – £ 100/160 £ 110/160 – 2 suites

Rest *The Eaterie* – Menu £ 16 (lunch) **s** – Carte £ 22/42 **s**

◆ Converted 6-storey former salt house overlooking the marina. Lounge with seagrass seats. Designer style bedrooms with modern facilities; some with good views; two penthouse suites. Modern brasserie with a Mediterranean touch.

Kesgrave Hall

Hall Rd, East : 4.75 mi. by A1214 on Bealings rd ✉ *IP5 2PU – ✆ (01473) 333 471 – www.kesgravehall.com – Fax (01473) 617 614*

15 rm – £ 161 £ 191, £ 15 **Rest** – Carte £ 20/36

◆ Characterful Georgian mansion with large terrace, set in mature grounds. Stylish bedrooms display bold décor and a mix of furniture; some even have baths in the room. Seasonally-changing modern European menus feature local, organic produce.

Sidegate Guest House without rest

121 Sidegate Lane ✉ *IP4 4JB – ✆ (01473) 728 714 – www.sidegateguesthouse.co.uk* Ya

6 rm – £ 55/60 £ 70

◆ Compact, friendly guesthouse in residential area. Comfy lounge with terraced doors onto garden. Neatly laid breakfast room. Bright, refurbished bedrooms.

at Hintlesham West : 5 mi. by A 1214 on A 1071 - Y – ✉ **Ipswich**

Hintlesham Hall

✉ *IP8 3NS – ✆ (01473) 652 334 – www.hintleshamhall.com – Fax (01473) 652 463*

33 rm – £ 120/199 £ 160/285

Rest – Menu £ 34 **s** – Carte approx. £ 45 **s**

◆ Grand and impressive Georgian manor house of 16C origins set in parkland with golf course. Stuart carved oak staircase. Ornate wedding room. Individually decorated rooms. Opulent room for fine dining.

IRBY – Merseyside – 502 K23 20 A3

London 212 mi. – Liverpool 12 mi. – Manchester 46 mi. – Stoke-on-Trent 56 mi.

XX Da Piero

5 Mill Hill Rd ✉ *CH61 4UB Merseyside – ✆ (0151) 648 7373 – www.dapiero.co.uk – Closed 2 weeks January, 2 weeks August, Sunday and Monday*

Rest – Italian – *(dinner only) (booking essential)* Carte £ 19/40

◆ Family-owned and run restaurant with homely, understated décor and intimate, pleasant feel. Carefully prepared, classical Italian cooking, with lots of rustic Sicilian dishes.

IRONBRIDGE – Telford and Wrekin – 503 M26 – pop. 1 560 18 B2

Great Britain

London 135 mi. – Birmingham 36 mi. – Shrewsbury 18 mi.

The Tollhouse ✆ (01952) 432166, tic@ironbridge.org.uk

Ironbridge Gorge Museum★★ **AC** (The Iron Bridge★★, Coalport China Museum★★, Blists Hill Open Air Museum★★, Museum of the Gorge and Visitor Centre★)

The Library House without rest

11 Severn Bank ✉ *TF8 7AN – ✆ (01952) 432 299 – www.libraryhouse.com*

4 rm – £ 65 £ 90

◆ Nicely hidden, albeit tricky to find, guesthouse with rear terrace. Homely sitting room. Cottage style breakfast room. Compact, comfy rooms, with a touch of style about them.

ENGLAND

XX **Restaurant Severn**

33 High Street ✉ TF8 7AG – ✆ (01952) 432 233 – www.restaurantseven.co.uk – Closed 2 weeks January, 1 week summer, Bank Holidays except Christmas, Sunday dinner, Monday and Tuesday
Rest – *(dinner only and Sunday lunch) (booking essential)* Carte £ 24/27
◆ Close to the Severn and world heritage site 'Ironbridge'. Pleasant, light and airy dining room with a real family feel. Experienced owners cook tasty, classically based dishes.

X **da Vinci**

26 High St ✉ TF8 7AD – ✆ (01952) 432 250 – www.davincisironbridge.co.uk – Closed 2 weeks Christmas and New Year, 1 week spring, Sunday and Monday
Rest – Italian – *(dinner only) (booking essential)* Carte £ 16/37
◆ Long-established, family-run osteria split over two floors, with deep red décor and tightly packed tables. Rustic, tasty, authentic Italian cooking with Tuscan specialities.

ISLE OF MAN – I.O.M. – 502 G21 – see Man (Isle of)

ITTERINGHAM – Norfolk – 504 X25 – ✉ Aylsham 15 C1

London 126 mi. – Cromer 11 mi. – Norwich 17 mi.

The Walpole Arms

The Common ✉ NR11 7AR – ✆ (01263) 587 258 – www.thewalpolearms.co.uk – Fax (01263) 587 074 – Closed 25 December and Sunday dinner
Rest – Carte £ 21/28
◆ 18C inn with characterful, beamed bar and more formal restaurant. Daily changing, Mediterranean-influenced menus of tasty, well-prepared dishes; snack menu offers pub classics.

ENGLAND

IVYCHURCH – Kent – 504 W30 Great Britain 9 C2

London 67 mi. – Ashford 11 mi. – Rye 10 mi.

Rye Old Town★★ : Mermaid St★ - St Mary's Church (≤★), SW : 9 mi. on A 2070 and A 259

Olde Moat House without rest

Northwest : 0.75 mi. on B 2070 ✉ TN29 0AZ – ✆ (01797) 344 700 – www.oldemoathouse.co.uk
3 rm – †£ 60 ††£ 60/80
◆ Blissfully characterful guesthouse with 15C origins, set in over three acres, encircled by small moat. Beamed sitting room with inglenook. Individual, homely styled rooms.

IWERNE MINSTER – Dorset – 504 N31 – see Blandford Forum

IXWORTH – Suffolk – 504 W27 – see Bury St Edmunds

JERSEY – C.I. – 503 O/P33 – see Channel Islands

JEVINGTON – E. Sussex – 504 U31 – see Eastbourne

KEGWORTH – Leicestershire – 502 Q25 – pop. 3 338 Great Britain 16 B2

London 123 mi. – Leicester 18 mi. – Loughborough 6 mi. – Nottingham 13 mi.

Calke Abbey★, SW : 7 mi. by A 6 (northbound) and A 453 (southbound) – Derby★ - Museum and Art Gallery★, Royal Crown Derby Museum★, NW : 9 mi. by A 50 – Nottingham Castle Museum★, N : 11 mi. by A 453 and A 52

Kegworth House

42 High St ✉ DE74 2DA – ✆ (01509) 672 575 – www.kegworthhouse.co.uk – Fax (01509) 670 645 – Closed Christmas
11 rm – †£ 50/150 ††£ 60/250
Rest – *(dinner only) (by arrangement, communal dining)* Menu £ 25
◆ Georgian manor house in village, secluded in walled garden. Fine interior with original decorative features. Individually-decorated bedrooms of charm and character. Home cooking by arrangement.

KELSALE – Suffolk – 504 Y27 – pop. 1 309 – ✉ Saxmundham 15 D3

London 103 mi. – Cambridge 68 mi. – Ipswich 23 mi. – Norwich 37 mi.

Mile Hill Barn without rest

North Green, North : 1.5 mi. on (main) A 12 ✉ IP17 2RG – ✆ (01728) 668 519 – www.mile-hill-barn.co.uk

3 rm – †£ 50 ††£ 80

◆ Converted 16C barn well placed for glorious Suffolk countryside. Timbered ceiling invokes rustic feel in pleasant lounge. Comfy bedrooms with pine and chintz furnishings.

KELVEDON – Essex – 504 W28 – pop. 4 593 13 C2

London 56 mi.

George & Dragon

Coggleshall Rd, Northwest : 2 mi. on B 1024 ✉ CO5 9PL – ✆ (01376) 561 797 – www.georgeanddragonkelvedon.co.uk – Closed 25 December, 1 January, Sunday and Monday

Rest – Carte £ 19/27

◆ Bright, welcoming restaurant with sleek, ultra-modern style, encompassing marble tiled floors, antique mirrors and art deco statuettes. Simple menu with locally caught fish specials.

KENDAL – Cumbria – 502 L21 – pop. 28 030 Great Britain 21 B2

London 270 mi. – Bradford 64 mi. – Burnley 63 mi. – Carlisle 49 mi.

Town Hall, Highgate ✆ (01539) 797516, kendaltic@southlakeland.gov.uk

18 The Heights, ✆ (01539) 723 499

Levens Hall and Garden★ AC, S : 4.5 mi. by A 591, A 590 and A 6. Lake Windermere★★, NW : 8 mi. by A 5284 and A 591

Beech House without rest

40 Greenside, by All Hallows Lane ✉ LA9 4LD – ✆ (01539) 720 385 – www.beechhouse-kendal.co.uk – Fax (01539) 724 082 – Closed Christmas

6 rm – †£ 60 ††£ 80/100

◆ Tasteful and stylish semi-detached Georgian villa. Open-plan lounge; communal breakfasts. Individually decorated rooms are particularly tasteful and comfortable.

Bridge Street Restaurant

1 Bridge St ✉ LA9 7DD – ✆ (01539) 738 855 – www.bridgestreetkendal.co.uk – Closed 25-26 December, Sunday dinner and Monday

Rest – Carte £ 22/33 s

◆ Sited within a Georgian building by the River Kent. Modern ground-floor lounge; dining upstairs in two rooms. Menus boast a distinct local accent.

at Sizergh Southwest : 3 mi. by A 591 – ✉ Kendal

The Strickland Arms

✉ LA8 8DZ – ✆ (01539) 561 010 – www.ainscoughs.co.uk – Fax (01539) 561 068

Rest – Carte £ 22/30

◆ Imposing grey pub with a large garden; neighbour to Sizergh Castle. Hearty homemade dishes arrive in huge portions and there's a good selection of real ales and wines by the glass.

at Brigsteer Southwest : 3.75 mi. by All Hallows Lane – ✉ Kendal

The Wheatsheaf with rm

✉ LA8 8AN – ✆ (015395) 68 254 – www.brigsteer.gb.com

3 rm – †£ 75 ††£ 85

Rest – *(booking essential)* Menu £ 15 (lunch) – Carte £ 20/24

◆ Refurbished 18C pub with a light, airy, contemporary feel. The seasonal menu is proudly Cumbrian with smoked salmon from Cartmel Valley and shrimps from Morecombe Bay. Classically-styled, pine-furnished bedrooms.

ENGLAND

at Crosthwaite West : 5.25 mi. by All Hallows Lane – ✉ Kendal

The Punch Bowl Inn with rm
✉ LA8 8HR Crosthwaite – ☎ (01539) 568 237 – www.the-punchbowl.co.uk – Fax (01539) 568 875
9 rm – £ 94/233 £ 125/310 **Rest** – Carte £ 20/35
◆ Laid back pub with glorious valley views and richly furnished, appealingly informal bar and restaurant. Tasty, classically created dishes make good use of local, seasonal ingredients. Luxurious bedrooms show great attention to detail.

KENILWORTH – Warwickshire – 503 P26 – pop. 22 218 Great Britain 19 C2

London 102 mi. – Birmingham 19 mi. – Coventry 5 mi. – Leicester 32 mi.

The Library, 11 Smalley Pl ☎ (01926) 748900, kenilworthlibrary@warwickshire.gov.uk

Castle★ **AC**

Loweridge House without rest
Hawkesworth Drive, Northeast : 1.25 mi. by Coventry rd (A429) off Tainters Hill Rd ✉ CV8 2GP – ☎ (01926) 859 522 – www.loweridgeguesthouse.co.uk – Fax (01926) 859 522
4 rm – £ 76 £ 91
◆ Spacious Victorian house, stylishly decorated in creams, golds and reds. Homely lounge and linen-laid breakfast room. Warmly furnished bedrooms boast a high level of facilities.

Victoria Lodge without rest
180 Warwick Rd ✉ CV8 1HU – ☎ (01926) 512 020 – www.victorialodgekenilworth.co.uk – Fax (01926) 858 703 – Closed 2 weeks Christmas and New Year
10 rm – £ 49/62 £ 80
◆ Keenly run, red-brick house with comfy lounge and linen-laid breakfast room. Immaculately kept, colourful bedrooms; some with balconies or patios. Complimentary bottled water; great breakfasts.

Petit Gourmand
101-103 Warwick Rd ✉ CV8 1HL – ☎ (01926) 864 567 – www.petit-gourmand.co.uk – Fax (01926) 864 510 – Closed Sunday dinner
Rest – Menu £ 16 – Carte £ 25/34
◆ Boasts contemporary feel, typified by striking mirrors and artwork. Good value, hearty, robust classically based dishes supplemented by tried-and-tested daily specials.

Bosquet
97a Warwick Rd ✉ CV8 1HP – ☎ (01926) 852 463 – www.restaurantbosquet.co.uk – Fax (01926) 852 463 – Closed 2 weeks August and 1 week Christmas
Rest – French – *(dinner only) (lunch by arrangement)* Menu £ 32 – Carte £ 35/41
◆ Contemporary feel to this established restaurant with wooden floors, well-spaced tables and stylish leather chairs. Confident, well-informed cooking displays a classical French base.

KENTON – Exeter – 503 J31 – see Exeter

KERNE BRIDGE – Herefordshire – 503 M28 – see Ross-on-Wye

KESWICK – Cumbria – 502 K20 – pop. 4 984 Great Britain 21 A2

London 294 mi. – Carlisle 31 mi. – Kendal 30 mi.

Moot Hall, Market Sq. ☎ (017687) 72645, keswicktic@lake-district.gov.uk

18 Threlkeld Hall, ☎ (017687) 79 324

Derwentwater★ X – Thirlmere (Castlerigg Stone Circle★), E : 1.5 mi. X **A**

KESWICK

Street	Grid	No.
Bank St	Z	2
Borrowdale Rd	Z	3
Brackenrigg Drive	Z	5
Brundholme Rd	X	6
Chestnut Hill	X	8
Church St	Z	10
Crosthwaite Rd	X	12
Derwent St	Z	13
High Hill	Z	14
Main St	Z	
Manor Brow	X	17
Market Square	Z	18
Museum Square	Z	19
Otley Rd	Z	20
Park Horse Yard	Z	21
Police Station Court	Z	22
Ratcliffe Pl.	Z	23
St Herbert St	Z	24
Standish St	Z	25
Station St	Z	26
The Crescent	Z	27
The Hawthorns	Y	29
The Headlands	Z	31
Tithebarn St	Z	32

A 66 WORKINGTON COCKERMOUTH — A 591 CARLISLE — PENRITH, M 6 — A 591 WINDERMERE — ROSTHWAITE B 5289 BUTTERMERE

PORTINSCALE, BRAITHWAITE, STAIR, DERWENTWATER, BRANDELHOW PARK, GREAT WOOD, HOGS EARTH, BORROWDALE, DERWENT FELLS, GRANGE

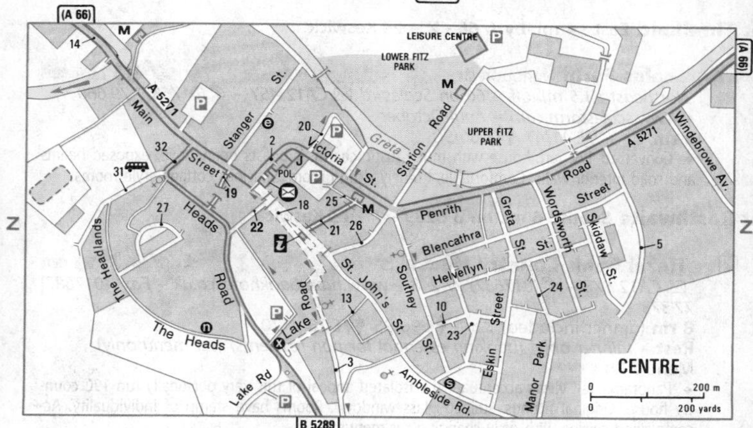

ENGLAND

Highfield ← A/C rest, P VISA MC AE

The Heads ✉ *CA12 5ER – ✆ (017687) 72 508 – www.highfieldkeswick.co.uk – Fax (017687) 80 837 – Closed January to mid-February* — Zn

18 rm (dinner included) – †£ 75 ††£ 150/190

Rest – *(dinner only)* Menu £ 45 **s**

◆ Substantial, keenly run 19C house with fine views across Derwent Water to Borrowdale Valley. Most bedrooms offer the vista; all are spacious and individually decorated. Traditional restaurant has big windows and imaginatively created dishes.

Lairbeck

Vicarage Hill ✉ CA12 5QB – ☎ (017687) 73 373 – www.lairbeckhotel-keswick.co.uk – Fax (0871) 661 25 52 – Restricted opening 9 November-10 March Xa

14 rm – £ 52/78 £ 121

Rest – *(dinner only) (residents only)* Menu £ 23 **s**

◆ Victorian house tucked away on north side of town, traditional in style, with immaculately-kept bedrooms. Room 4 is largest; four poster in room 7. Warm ambience in bar. Honest country cooking served in richly coloured dining room.

Abacourt House without rest

26 Stanger St ✉ CA12 5JU – ☎ (017687) 72 967 – www.abacourt.co.uk

5 rm – £ 64/65 Ze

◆ Converted Victorian town house close to town centre. Boasts original features such as pitch pine doors and staircase. Simple, cosy breakfast room. Immaculately kept bedrooms.

Acorn House without rest

Ambleside Rd ✉ CA12 4DL – ☎ (017687) 72 553 – www.acornhousehotel.co.uk – Closed 3 weeks December Zs

9 rm – £ 55 £ 70/84

◆ Characterful Georgian house in residential part of town. Well cared for gardens are a step away from elegant, comfortable lounge. Very bright, traditional, spacious bedrooms.

Morrel's

34 Lake Rd ✉ CA12 5DQ – ☎ (017687) 72 666 – www.morrels.co.uk – Closed 24-26 December, 1 week January and Monday Zx

Rest – *(dinner only)* Carte £ 20/35

◆ Pleasingly refurbished and personally run. Etched glass and vivid artwork dominate interior. Menus designed to appeal to all: an agreeable blend of traditional and modern.

ENGLAND

at Threlkeld East : 4 mi. by A 66 - X – ✉ Keswick

Scales Farm without rest

Northeast : 1.5 mi. off A 66 on Scales rd ✉ CA12 4SY – ☎ (017687) 79 660 – www.scalesfarm.com – April-October

6 rm – £ 41/47 £ 66/90

◆ Converted 17C farmhouse with much rustic charm. It boasts open stove, exposed beams and solid interior walls. Comfortable, homely sitting room. Spacious cottage style rooms.

at Rosthwaite South : 6 mi. on B 5289 - Y – ✉ Keswick

Hazel Bank Country House

✉ CA12 5XB – ☎ (017687) 77 248 – www.hazelbankhotel.co.uk – Fax (017687) 77 373

8 rm (dinner included) – £ 90/95 £ 160/170

Rest – *(dinner only) (booking essential for non-residents) (set menu only)* Menu £ 28 **s**

◆ Panoramic fell views accentuate the isolated appeal of this very personally run 19C country house. Original fittings; stained glass windows. Rooms have stamp of individuality. Accomplished cuisine with daily changing set menus.

at Portinscale West : 1.5 mi. by A 66 – ✉ Keswick

Swinside Lodge

Newlands, South : 1.5 mi. on Grange Rd ✉ CA12 5UE – ☎ (017687) 72 948 – www.swinsidelodge-hotel.co.uk – Fax (017687) 73 312 – closed Christmas

7 rm (dinner included) – £ 108 £ 250 Xc

Rest – *(dinner only) (booking essential for non-residents) (set menu only)* Menu £ 40 **s**

◆ Personally run 19C country house in beguilingly tranquil position close to extensive walks with mountain views. Two comfortable lounges; well furnished, traditional rooms. Intimate Victorian style dining room with large antique dresser.

at Braithwaite West : 2 mi. by A 66 - X - on B 5292 – ✉ Keswick

The Cottage in the Wood

Whinlatter Forest, Northwest : 1.75 mi. on B 5292 ✉ CA12 5TW – ✆ (017687) 78 409 – www.thecottageinthewood.co.uk – Closed January

9 rm – ♦£ 65/75 ♦♦£ 120/140

Rest – *(closed Monday) (light lunch Tuesday-Saturday)* Menu £ 28 (dinner) **s**

◆ Dramatically set 17C former coaching inn high up in large pine forest. Comfy, beamed lounge with fire. Smart, updated bedrooms look out over Skiddaw or the forest. Proudly local ingredients sourced for modern British cooking; mountain views.

KETTLESING – N. Yorks. – 502 P21 – see Harrogate

KETTLEWELL – North Yorkshire – 502 N21 – pop. 297 22 A2

London 246 mi. – Darlington 42 mi. – Harrogate 30 mi. – Lancaster 42 mi.

Littlebeck without rest

The Green, take turning at the Old Smithy shop by the bridge ✉ BD23 5RD – ✆ (01756) 760 378 – www.little-beck.co.uk – Restricted opening in winter

3 rm – ♦£ 45/50 ♦♦£ 68/75

◆ Characterful stone house from 13C with Georgian façade overlooking village maypole. Cosy lounge; extensive dales breakfast served. Attractively decorated bedrooms.

KEYSTON – Cambridgeshire – 504 S26 – pop. 257 – ✉ Huntingdon 14 A2

London 75 mi. – Cambridge 29 mi. – Northampton 24 mi.

The Pheasant

Village Loop Road ✉ PE17 0RE – ✆ (01832) 710 241 – www.thepheasant-keyston.co.uk – Closed Sunday dinner (September-April)

Rest – *(booking essential)* Menu £ 20 (lunch) – Carte £ 36/42

◆ Charming thatched 'destination dining' pub set in a sleepy hamlet. Seasonal daily menu features both classics and more international flavours, adopting a complete 'nose to tail' approach.

KIBWORTH BEAUCHAMP – Leicestershire – 504 Q/R26 – pop. 3 550 – ✉ Leicester 16 B2

London 85 mi. – Birmingham 49 mi. – Leicester 6 mi. – Northampton 17 mi.

Firenze

9 Station St ✉ LE8 0LN – ✆ (0116) 279 6260 – www.firenze.co.uk – Fax (0116) 279 3646 – closed Christmas, Sunday and Bank Holidays

Rest – Italian – *(booking essential)* Menu £ 23 (dinner) – Carte £ 29/41

◆ Smart neighbourhood restaurant displaying colourful modern fabrics and Mediterranean artwork. Extensive à la carte and tasting menus offer authentic Italian dishes; good value lunch.

KIBWORTH HARCOURT Leics. – Leicestershire – 504 R26 16 B2

London 101 mi. – Leicester 9 mi. – Coventry 36 mi. – Nottingham 41 mi.

Boboli

88 Main St ✉ LE8 0NQ – ✆ (0116) 279 3303 – www.bobolirestaurant.co.uk – Fax (0116) 279 3646 – closed Christmas, Monday and Sunday dinner

Rest – Italian – Menu £ 15 (lunch) – Carte £ 22/32

◆ Stylish Italian restaurant named after gardens in Florence. Fresh, simple and seasonally-changing cooking with bold flavours. Affordable wines and cheery, prompt service.

KIDDERMINSTER – Worcestershire – 503 N26 – pop. 55 348 18 B2

London 139 mi. – Birmingham 17 mi. – Shrewsbury 34 mi. – Worcester 15 mi.

at Chaddesley Corbett **Southeast : 4.5 mi. by A 448 – ✉ Kidderminster**

Brockencote Hall
on A 448 ✉ DY10 4PY – ✆ (01562) 777 876 – www.brockencotehall.com – Fax (01562) 777 872
17 rm – ♦£ 96/120 ♦♦£ 150/190
Rest ***The Restaurant*** – see restaurant listing
♦ 19C mansion, reminiscent of a French château, set in extensive grounds. Wide selection of comfy bedrooms with bold, modern décor and antiques. Spacious bathrooms; good facilities.

The Restaurant – at Brockencote Hall Hotel
on A 448 ✉ DY10 4PY – ✆ (01562) 777 876 – www.brockencotehall.com – Fax (01562) 777 872
Rest – French – Menu £ 22/40 **s** – Carte £ 35/49 **s**
♦ Choice of two rooms with classic French feel, rococo décor and formal service. Traditional French menus feature well-prepared Gallic ingredients. Vibrant, modern bar provides airy contrast.

KIDMORE END – **Oxon.** – **see Reading**

KINGHAM – Oxfordshire – **503** P28 – **pop. 1 434** **10** A1
London 81 mi. – Gloucester 32 mi. – Oxford 25 mi.

Mill House
✉ OX7 6UH – ✆ (01608) 658 188 – www.millhousehotel.co.uk – Fax (01608) 658 492
23 rm – ♦£ 95 ♦♦£ 140 **Rest** – Menu £ 13/28 – Carte £ 24/28
♦ Privately run house in 10 acres of lawned gardens with brook flowing through grounds. Spacious lounge with comfortable armchairs and books. Country house style bedrooms. Modern décor suffuses restaurant.

Moat End without rest
The Moat, by West St ✉ OX7 6XZ – ✆ (01608) 658 090 – www.moatend.co.uk – Closed Christmas and New Year
3 rm – ♦£ 50/65 ♦♦£ 70
♦ Cosy converted barn with garden, ponies and countryside views; luxury breakfasts include eggs from own hens. Neatly kept, compact rooms. Friendly owner has wealth of local knowledge.

The Kingham Plough with rm
The Green ✉ OX7 6YD – ✆ (01608) 658 327 – www.thekinghamplough.co.uk – Fax (01608) 658 327 – Closed 25 December
7 rm – ♦£ 70/80 ♦♦£ 85/110 **Rest** – Carte £ 30/45
♦ Quintessentially British pub overlooking the village green and serving carefully-prepared, gutsy pub food firmly rooted in the region. Stylish bedrooms boast pocket sprung beds and crisp Egyptian linen.

The Tollgate Inn with rm
Church St ✉ OX7 6YA – ✆ (01608) 658 389 – www.thetollgate.com – Closed Sunday dinner and Monday
9 rm – ♦£ 65 ♦♦£ 100 **Rest** – Carte £ 20/35
♦ Grade II listed inn in centre of unspoiled village. Easy-going lunch menu; more ambitious evening à la carte. Comfy seating and inglenooks, plus popular front terrace. Immaculately kept bedrooms have a warm, bright feel.

KINGSBRIDGE – **Devon** – **503** I33 – **pop. 5 521** **2** C3
London 236 mi. – Exeter 36 mi. – Plymouth 24 mi. – Torquay 21 mi.
The Quay ✆ (01548) 853195, advice@kingsbridgeinfo.co.uk
Thurlestone, ✆ (01548) 560 405
Town★ – Boat Trip to Salcombe★★ **AC**
Prawle Point (<★★★) SE : 10 mi. around coast by A 379

at Goveton Northeast : 2.5 mi. by A 381 – ✉ Kingsbridge

Buckland-Tout-Saints

Goveton, Northeast : 2.5 mi. by A 381 ✉ TQ7 2DS – ✆ (01548) 853 055 – www.tout-saints.co.uk – Fax (01548) 856 261 – closed 3-21 January

14 rm – †£ 90/105 ††£ 120/140 – 2 suites **Rest** – Menu £ 20/37

◆ Immaculate, impressive Queen Anne mansion with neat lawned gardens in rural location. Wood panelled lounge; all other areas full of antiques. Well-furnished bedrooms. Accomplished cooking in beautiful wood-panelled country house restaurant.

A restaurant name printed in red denotes a Rising Star - an establishment showing great potential. It is in line for a higher award: a star or an additional star. They are included in the list of starred establishments at the beginning of the guide.

KINGSKERSWELL – Devon – 503 J32 – pop. 4 624 – ✉ Torquay 2 C2

London 199 mi. – Exeter 18 mi. – Torquay 4 mi.

Bickley Mill with rm

Stoneycombe, West : 2 mi. ✉ TQ12 5LN – ✆ (01803) 873 201 – www.bickleymill.co.uk – Fax (01803) 875 129 – Closed 26-27 December and 1 January

9 rm – †£ 68 ††£ 80/90

Rest – Menu £ 15 (lunch Monday-Saturday) – Carte £ 19/30

◆ Converted flour mill dating back to 13C boasts pleasant garden and decked terrace. Modernised interior retains rustic stone walls and exposed beams. Modern British cooking. Contemporary bedrooms.

ENGLAND

KING'S LYNN – Norfolk – 502 V25 – pop. 40 921 Great Britain 14 B1

London 103 mi. – Cambridge 45 mi. – Leicester 75 mi. – Norwich 44 mi.

The Custom House, Purfleet Quay ✆ (01553) 763044, kings-lynn.tic@west-norfolk.gov.uk

Eagles Tilney All Saints School Rd, ✆ (01553) 827 147

Houghton Hall★★ AC, NE : 14.5 mi. by A 148 – Four Fenland Churches★ (Terrington St Clement, Walpole St Peter, West Walton, Walsoken) SW : by A 47

Bankhouse

King's Staithe Sq ✉ PE30 1RD – ✆ (01553) 660 492 – www.thebankhouse.co.uk

11 rm – †£ 80/90 ††£ 100/120 **Rest** – Carte £ 20/35

◆ Grade II listed Georgian house by River Ouse. Comfortable bedrooms in various shapes and sizes: all have good facilities and excellent bathrooms; some have a pleasant outlook. Stylish, contemporary bar and brasserie.

at Grimston East : 6.25 mi. by A 148 – ✉ King'S Lynn

Congham Hall

Lynn Rd ✉ PE32 1AH – ✆ (01485) 600 250 – www.conghamhallhotel.co.uk – Fax (01485) 601 191

12 rm – †£ 85/360 ††£ 165/255 – 2 suites

Rest ***Orangery*** – Menu £ 21/36 – Carte £ 44/52

◆ Immaculately peaceful cream-washed part Georgian house with formal flower garden. Classic country house style lounges with many antiques. Elegant bedrooms of varying sizes. Pleasant, classic restaurant using herb garden produce.

KINGS MILLS – C.I. – see Channel Islands (Guernsey)

KINGSTON BAGPUIZE – Oxon. – 503 P28 – see Oxford

KINGSTON BLOUNT – Oxon. – see Chinnor

KINGSTON-UPON-HULL – City of Kingston upon Hull – 502 S22 23 D2 – pop. 301 416 Great Britain

London 183 mi. – Leeds 61 mi. – Nottingham 94 mi. – Sheffield 68 mi.

Access Humber Bridge (toll)

Humberside Airport : ✆ (01652) 688456, S : 19 mi. by A 63

to The Netherlands (Rotterdam) (P & O North Sea Ferries) daily (11 h) – to Belgium (Zeebrugge) (P & O North Sea Ferries) 3-4 weekly (13 h 45 mn)

1 Paragon St ✆ (01482) 223559, hull.tic@vhey.co.uk

18 Springhead Park Willerby Rd, ✆ (01482) 656 309

18 Sutton Park Salthouse Rd, ✆ (01482) 374 242

Burton Constable★ **AC**, NE : 9 mi. by A 165 and B 1238 Z

X **Boars Nest** VISA MC AE

22-24 Princes Ave, Northwest : 1 mi. by Ferensway off West Spring Bank Rd ✉ HU5 3QA – ✆ (01482) 445 577 – www.theboarsnesthull.com – Closed 26 December and 1 January Zx

Rest – Menu £ 10/20 – Carte dinner £ 22/26

◆ Early 20C butchers, with original tiles and carcass rails in situ. Comfy, cluttered first-floor lounge. Eat hearty English dishes downstairs at mismatched tables and chairs.

at Hessle Southwest : 2 mi. by A 63 – ✉ Kingston-Upon-Hull

XXX **Artisan** VISA MC AE

22 The Weir ✉ HU13 0RU – ✆ (01482) 644 906 – www.artisanrestaurant.com – closed 1 week early January, 1 week summer, Sunday and Monday

Rest – *(dinner only) (booking essential) (lunch by arrangement)* Carte £ 39/45

◆ Personally and enthusiastically run neighbourhood restaurant with intimate atmosphere: husband cooks, wife serves. Twice-weekly Italian-based set and tasting menus utilise local ingredients.

KINGSWEAR – Devon – 503 J32 – see Dartmouth

KINGTON – County of Herefordshire – 503 K27 – pop. 2 597 18 A3

London 152 mi. – Birmingham 61 mi. – Hereford 19 mi. – Shrewsbury 54 mi.

at Titley Northeast : 3.5 mi. on B 4355 – ✉ Kington

The Stagg Inn (Steve Reynolds) with rm P VISA MC

✉ HR5 3RL – ✆ (01544) 230 221 – www.thestagg.co.uk – Fax (01544) 231 390 – Closed first 2 weeks in November, Sunday dinner and Monday

6 rm – †£ 70/100 ††£ 85/130 **Rest** – *(booking essential)* Carte £ 20/30

Spec. Pigeon breast with pistachio nut sauce. Fillet of beef with carrot, horseradish purée and Dauphinoise potatoes. Rhubarb jelly and compote.

◆ Rustic dining pub offers seasonally-changing menu featuring quality local produce, including the inn's own pigs and vegetables from the garden. Comfy rooms split between the pub and the old vicarage, two minutes walk down the road.

KINTBURY – Newbury – 503 P29 – see Hungerford

KIRKBY LONSDALE – Cumbria – 502 M21 – pop. 2 076 21 B3 – ✉ Carnforth (Lancs.)

London 259 mi. – Carlisle 62 mi. – Kendal 13 mi. – Lancaster 17 mi.

18 Scaleber Lane Barbon, ✆ (015242) 76 366

9 Casterton Sedbergh Rd, ✆ (015242) 71 592

Sun Inn with rm VISA MC

6 Market Street ✉ LA6 2AU – ✆ (015242) 71 965 – www.sun-inn.info – Fax (015242) 72 485 – Closed Monday lunch

11 rm – †£ 65/90 ††£ 120/160 **Rest** – Carte £ 22/27

◆ 17C inn in busy market town with lively locals bar and rustically refurbished restaurant. Tempting bar nibbles and tasty, seasonal dishes made with locally sourced produce. Good quality linen in modern, immaculately kept bedrooms.

ENGLAND

KINGSTON-UPON-HULL

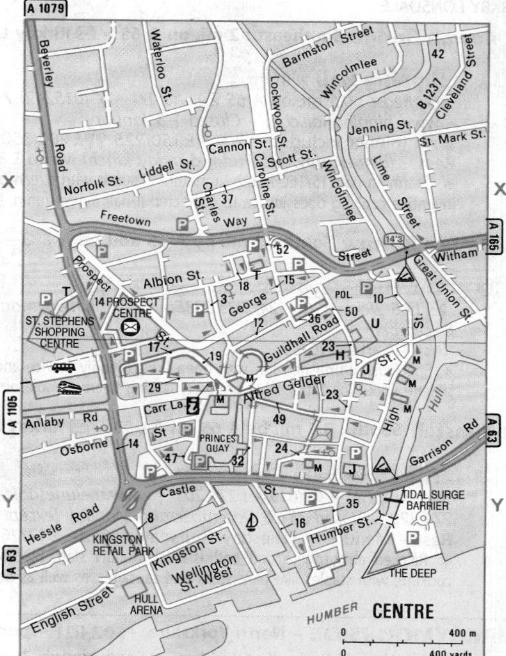

ENGLAND

BUILT UP AREA

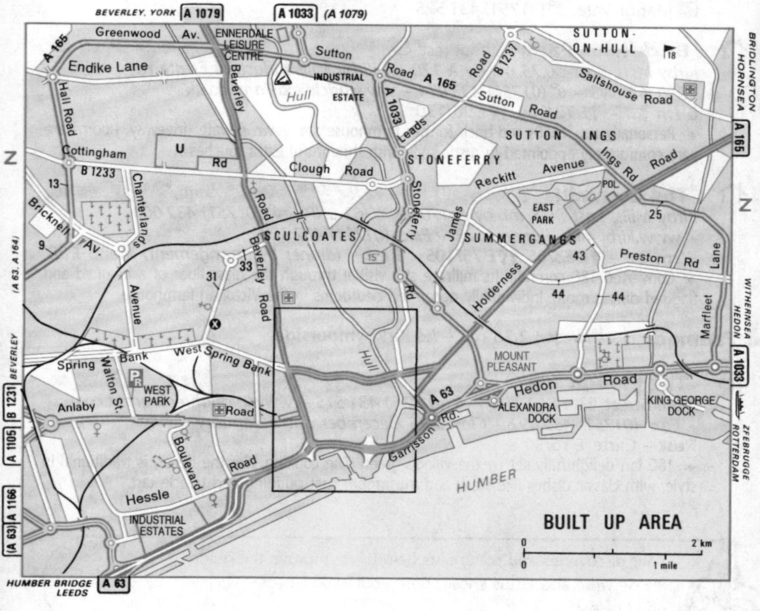

BEVERLEY, YORK A 1079 — A 1033 (A 1079)

Greenwood Av. · Endike Lane · Hall Road · Cottingham Rd · B 1233 · Chanterlands Avenue · Bricknell Av. · ENNERDALE LEISURE CENTRE · Beverley Road · Sutton Road A 165 · INDUSTRIAL ESTATE · Hull · A 1033 · Leads Rd · B 1237 · Sutton Road · Saltshouse Road · SUTTON-ON-HULL · SUTTON INGS · STONEFERRY · Stoneferry Rd · Clough Road · Reckitt Avenue · Ings Rd · EAST PARK · POL. · SCULCOATES · SUMMERGANGS · James · Holderness Road · Preston Rd · Marfleet Lane · Spring Bank · West Spring Bank · Walton St. · WEST PARK · Anlaby Road · Boulevard · Hessle Road · INDUSTRIAL ESTATES · MOUNT PLEASANT · Hedon Road · A 63 · ALEXANDRA DOCK · KING GEORGE DOCK · Garrison Rd. · HUMBER

BRIDLINGTON HORNSEA A 165 · WITHERNSEA HEDON A 1033 · ZEEBRUGGE ROTTERDAM · (A 63, A 164) BEVERLEY B 1231 · A 1105 · A 1166 · (A 63) · HUMBER BRIDGE LEEDS A 63

0 2 km
0 1 mile

at Cowan Bridge Southeast : 2 mi. on A 65 – ✉ Kirkby Lonsdale

XX **Hipping Hall** with rm — rm, P VISA

Southeast : 0.5 mi. on A 65 ✉ LA6 2JJ – ☎ (015242) 71 187 – www.hippinghall.com – Closed 1-8 January
9 rm (dinner included) – ♦£ 150/225 ♦♦£ 200/350
Rest – *(dinner only and Friday-Sunday lunch)* Menu £ 30/50
◆ Charming part 15/16C house in mature grounds with stream and flagged terrace. Modern, inventive cooking does justice to characterful hall dining room. Distinctly modish rooms.

at Nether Burrow South : 2 mi. by A 65 and on A 683 – ✉ Kirkby Lonsdale

The Highwayman — P VISA AE

✉ LA6 2RJ – ☎ (01524) 273 3338 – www.highwaymaninn.co.uk – Closed 25 December
Rest – Carte £ 16/33
◆ Spacious, refurbished inn with open fires, friendly service and stone terrace. Owners passionate about local, traceable produce, serving hearty, wholesome dishes.

at Tunstall South : 3.5 mi. by A 65 on A 683 – ✉ Kirkby Lonsdale

The Lunesdale Arms — P VISA

✉ LA6 2QN – ☎ (01524) 274 203 – www.thelunesdale.co.uk – Fax (01524) 274 229 – Closed 25-26 December and Monday (except bank holidays)
Rest – Menu £ 14 (Tuesday-Thursday) – Carte £ 17/26
◆ Relaxed atmosphere and enthusiastic, friendly staff. Blackboard menu of tasty, honest cooking, with staples like pies, steak and sausages, as well as delicious homemade puds

ENGLAND

KIRKBYMOORSIDE – North Yorkshire – 502 R21 – pop. 2 595 — 23 C1

London 244 mi. – Leeds 61 mi. – Scarborough 26 mi. – York 33 mi.
18 Manor Vale, ☎ (01751) 431 525

Brickfields Farm without rest — P VISA

Kirby Mills, East : 0.75 mi. by A 170 on Kirby Mills Industrial Estate rd
✉ YO62 6NS – ☎ (01751) 433 074 – www.brickfieldsfarm.co.uk
6 rm – ♦£ 72/104 ♦♦£ 90/130
◆ Personally run 1850s red-brick former farmhouse set down private driveway. Rooms are very comfortably appointed in rustic style with thoughtful extra touches.

The Cornmill — rm, P VISA

Kirby Mills, East : 0.5 mi. by A 170 ✉ YO62 6NP – ☎ (01751) 432 000 – www.kirbymills.demon.co.uk – Fax (01751) 432 300
5 rm – ♦£ 53/65 ♦♦£ 75/105 **Rest** – *(dinner by arrangement)* Menu £ 28
◆ Converted 18C cornmill, its millrace still visible through the glass floor of a beamed and flagged dining room. Individually decorated bedrooms in the Victorian farmhouse.

at Fadmoor Northwest : 2.25 mi. – ✉ Kirkbymoorside

The Plough Inn — P VISA

Main Street ✉ YO62 7HY – ☎ (01751) 431 515 – www.ploughrestaurant.co.uk – Fax (01751) 432 492 – Closed 25 December and 1 January
Rest – Carte £ 16/30
◆ 18C inn delightfully set by the village green. The cooking, like the décor, is traditional in style; with classic dishes like steak and mushroom suet pudding and treacle tart.

Your discoveries and comments help us to improve the guide.
Please write and let us know about your experiences - good or bad!

KIRKBY STEPHEN – Cumbria – **502** M20 – **pop. 1 832** **21** B2

London 296 mi. – Carlisle 46 mi. – Darlington 37 mi. – Kendal 28 mi.

Augill Castle

Northeast : 4.5 mi. by A 685 ✉ CA17 4DE – ☎ (01768) 341 937 – www.stayinacastle.com – Fax (01768) 342 287 – Closed Christmas

12 rm – **†**£ 80/115 **††**£ 160/230

Rest – *(Closed Sunday and Tuesday) (dinner only) (residents only, communal dining, set menu only)* Menu £ 35 **s**

◆ Carefully restored Victorian folly in neo-Gothic style with extensive gardens; fine antiques and curios abound. Comfy music room and library. Individually decorated rooms. Expansive dining room with ornate ceiling and Spode tableware.

The Black Swan with rm

Ravenstonedale, Southwest; 5m by A685. ✉ CA17 4NG – ☎ (01539) 623 204 – www.blackswanhotel.com – Fax (01539) 623 204

11 rm – **†**£ 47 **††**£ 75/110 **Rest** – Carte £ 15/25

◆ Family-owned Victorian inn with delightful garden by babbling Scandal Beck. Hearty, traditional cooking has comfort appeal; impressive selection of real ales. Cosy bedrooms with antique furnishings.

KIRKWHELPINGTON – Northumberland – **501** N/O18 – **pop. 353** **24** A2

– ✉ **Morpeth** Great Britain

London 305 mi. – Carlisle 46 mi. – Newcastle upon Tyne 20 mi.

Wallington House★ **AC**, E : 3.5 mi. by A 696 and B 6342

Shieldhall

Wallington, Southeast : 2.5 mi. by A 696 on B 6342 ✉ NE61 4AQ – ☎ (01830) 540 387 – www.shieldhallguesthouse.co.uk – Fax (01830) 540 490 – Closed January-March

4 rm – **†**£ 50/65 **††**£ 80 **Rest** – *(by arrangement)* Menu £ 25

◆ Converted farm buildings dating from 1695, with gardens. Well-furnished lounge/library. Spotless rooms in former stable block; furniture constructed by cabinet-making owner.

KIRTLINGTON – Oxfordshire – **503** Q28 **10** B2

London 70 mi. – Bicester 11 mi. – Oxford 16 mi.

The Dashwood

South Green, Heyford Rd ✉ OX5 3HJ – ☎ (01869) 352 707 – www.thedashwood.co.uk – Fax (01869) 351 432

12 rm – **†**£ 90/115 **††**£ 145

Rest – *(closed Sunday dinner)* Menu £ 13 (weekdays) – Carte dinner £ 26/35

◆ Grade II listed 16C building in local soft stone. Lounge with comfy leather armchairs. Bedrooms, boasting super contemporary décor, divided between main building and barn. Exposed stone dining room: impressive menus with modern European slant.

KNARESBOROUGH – North Yorkshire – **502** P21 – **pop. 13 380** **22** B2

London 217 – Bradford 21 – Harrogate 3 – Leeds 18

9 Castle Courtyard, Market Pl ☎ (01423) 866886 (limited winter opening, Nov- Mar), kntic@harrogate.gov.uk

Boroughbridge Rd, ☎ (01423) 862 690

Newton House without rest

5-7 York Place – ☎ (01423) 863 539 – www.newtonhouseyorkshire.com – Closed 1 week at Christmas

11 rm – **†**£ 50/85 **††**£ 100

◆ Extended mid-18C house boasts homely lounge with soft suites and smart, comfortable, individually decorated bedrooms; those on the first floor and in the annexe are larger.

ENGLAND

at Ferrensby **Northeast : 3 mi. on A 6055**

The General Tarleton Inn with rm

Boroughbridge Rd ✉ HG5 0PZ – ✆ (01423) 340 284 – www.generaltarleton.co.uk – Fax (01423) 340 288

13 rm – †£ 75/116 ††£ 95/150 **Rest** – Carte £ 25/32

◆ This 18C coaching inn has several dining areas inside and out. The menu has a strong seasonal Yorkshire base and features well-priced, tasty dishes and classics aplenty. Bedrooms are comfortable and well-kept.

at Coneythorpe **Northeast : 4.75 mi. by A 59**

The Tiger Inn

✉ HG5 0RY – ✆ (01423) 863 632 – www.tiger-inn.co.uk – Fax (01423) 330 439

Rest – Menu £ 17 – Carte

◆ Traditional red brick pub overlooking the green with formal rear dining room. Hearty, robust menu offers a modern take on classic British favourites; blackboard of mainly fish specials.

KNOWSTONE – **Devon** – **see South Molton**

KNUTSFORD – Cheshire – 502 M24 – pop. 12 656 — 20 B3

London 187 mi. – Chester 25 mi. – Liverpool 33 mi. – Manchester 18 mi.

Council Offices, Toft Rd ✆ (01565) 632611, ktic@cheshireeast.gov.uk

Longview

55 Manchester Rd, on A 50 ✉ WA16 0LX – ✆ (01565) 632 119 – www.longviewhotel.com – Fax (01565) 652 402 – Closed 23 November-4 January

29 rm – †£ 89/99 ††£ 132 – 3 suites

Rest – *(closed Sunday and Bank Holidays) (dinner only)* Carte £ 21/29

◆ Creeper-clad Victorian building close to town centre. Cosy bedrooms in main house ideal for corporate guests; quieter, more spacious rooms in annexe. Extra touches include hot water bottles. Snug cellar bar; comfy restaurant offering authentic Mediterranean cooking.

Belle Epoque Brasserie with rm

60 King St ✉ WA16 6DT – ✆ (01565) 633 060 – www.thebelleepoque.com – Fax (01565) 634 150 – Closed 25-26 December

6 rm – †£ 95 ††£ 115

Rest – *(closed Saturday lunch and Sunday dinner)* Menu £ 15/20 – Carte £ 25/34

◆ Bustling brasserie with Art Nouveau décor. Traditional and modern dishes with international touches using local produce. Contemporary style bedrooms with modern facilities.

at Mobberley **Northeast : 2.5 mi. by A 537 on B 5085 – ✉ Knutsford**

Hinton

Town Lane, on B 5085 ✉ WA16 7HH – ✆ (01565) 873 484 – www.thehinton.co.uk

6 rm – †£ 48 ††£ 62 **Rest** – *(by arrangement)* Menu £ 18

◆ Bay-windowed guesthouse with rear garden. Homely lounge; simple, uncluttered bedrooms with floral theme. Friendly owners. Local produce used in the kitchen.

The Frozen Mop

Faulkeners Lane ✉ WA16 7AL – ✆ (01565) 873 234 – www.thefrozenmop.co.uk

Rest – Menu £ 9 (lunch) – Carte £ 18/23

◆ Stylish, modern gastropub with an upmarket clientele. The modern menu features something for everyone, ranging from salads and sharing platters to pizzas, pastas and grills.

at Lach Dennis **Southwest : 7 mi. by A 50, B 5081 and B 5082 – ✉ Knutsford**

Duke of Portland

Penny's Lane ✉ CW9 8SY – ✆ (01606) 46 264 – www.dukeofportland.com

Rest – Menu £ 10 – Carte £ 22/35

◆ Spacious, airy, open-plan pub. Lengthy menus offer simply prepared dishes of carefully sourced local produce in tasty, satisfying portions; suppliers are credited in the dish descriptions.

KYNASTON – Herefordshire – see Ledbury

LACH DENNIS – Ches. – see Knutsford

LACOCK – Wiltshire – 503 N29 – pop. 1 068 – ✉ Chippenham 4 C2

London 109 mi. – Bath 16 mi. – Bristol 30 mi. – Chippenham 3 mi.

Village★★ - Lacock Abbey★ **AC** – High St★, St Cyriac★, Fox Talbot Museum of Photography★ **AC**

At The Sign of the Angel

6 Church St ✉ SN15 2LB – ✆ (01249) 730 230 – www.lacock.co.uk – Fax (01249) 730 527 – Closed Christmas

11 rm – †£ 82 ††£ 145 **Rest** – *(Closed Monday lunch)* Carte £ 28/42

◆ Part 14C and 15C former wool merchant's house in charming National Trust village. Relaxed and historic atmosphere. Antique furnished rooms, four in the garden cottage. Tremendously characterful dining room of hotel's vintage: traditional English dishes served.

LADOCK – Cornwall – 503 F33 1 B2

London 268 mi. – Exeter 84 mi. – Newquay 12 mi. – Penzance 37 mi.

Bissick Old Mill without rest

off B 3275 ✉ TR2 4PG – ✆ (01726) 882 557 – www.bissickoldmill.co.uk

4 rm – †£ 50/58 ††£ 85

◆ Charming stone-built 17C former mill. Much historic character with low beamed ceilings and stone fireplaces. Comfortable bedrooms. Breakfast room has much period charm.

LA HAULE – C.I. – 503 L33 – see Channel Islands (Jersey)

LAMBOURN – West Berkshire – pop. 2 955 10 A3

London 71 mi. – Bristol 60 mi. – Coventry 95 mi.

at East Garston Southeast : 3 mi. on Newbury Rd

Queen's Arms with rm

✉ RG17 7ET – ✆ (01488) 648 757 – wwwqueensarmshotel.co.uk – Fax (01488) 648 642

8 rm – †£ 95 ††£ 130 **Rest** – Carte £ 24/32

◆ Atmospheric, antique-furnished inn which celebrates country pursuits. Carefully prepared dishes include English classics such as fish pie, leg of lamb and Eton Mess. Superb bedrooms and a generous breakfast.

LAMBOURN WOODLANDS – Berks. – see Hungerford

LANCASTER – Lancashire – 502 L21 – pop. 45 952 Great Britain 20 A1

London 252 mi. – Blackpool 26 mi. – Bradford 62 mi. – Burnley 44 mi.

The Storey, Meeting House Lane ✆ (01524) 582394, lancastervic@lancaster.gov.uk

18 Ashton Hall Ashton-with-Stodday, ✆ (01524) 752 090

9 Lansil Caton Rd, ✆ (01524) 39 269

Castle★ **AC**

The Ashton

Wyresdale Rd, Southeast : 1.25 mi. by A 6 on Clitheroe rd ✉ LA1 3JJ – ✆ (01524) 68 460 – www.theashtonlancaster.com

5 rm – †£ 98/115 ††£ 125/165 **Rest** – *(by arrangement)* Menu £ 30

◆ Georgian house in lawned gardens; personally run by friendly owner. Good-sized bedrooms are decorated in bold colours and feature a blend of modern and antique furniture. Small, informal dining room; home-cooked comfort food makes good use of local produce.

ENGLAND

The Borough

3 Dalton Sq ✉ LA1 1PP – ✆ (01524) 64 170 – www.theboroughlancaster.co.uk – Closed 25 December and 1 January

Rest – Carte £ 17/29

◆ Victorian-fronted Georgian building with period flooring and leaded windows. Generous, regional dishes and 'create-your-own' Deli Boards use local, traceable produce.

LANGAR – **Nottinghamshire** – **502** R25 — **16** B2

London 132 mi. – Boston 45 mi. – Leicester 25 mi. – Lincoln 37 mi.

Langar Hall

✉ NG13 9HG – ✆ (01949) 860 559 – www.langarhall.co.uk – Fax (01949) 861 045

11 rm – £ 80/125 £ 125/185 – 1 suite

Rest – Menu £ 20 (lunch) – Carte dinner £ 25/45

◆ Georgian manor in pastoral setting, next to early English church; overlooks park, medieval fishponds. Antique filled rooms named after people featuring in house's history. Elegant, candle-lit, pillared dining room.

LANGHO – **Lancs.** – **502** M22 – **see Blackburn**

LANGPORT – **Somerset** – **503** L30 – **pop. 2 851** — **3** B3

London 134 mi. – Weston-super-Mare 31 mi. – Taunton 15 mi. – Yeovil 16 mi.

The Parsonage

Mulchelney, South : 2 mi. on Muchelney Pottery rd ✉ TA10 ODL – ✆ (01458) 259 058 – www.parsonagesomerset.co.uk – Closed Christmas and New Year

3 rm – £ 58 £ 95

Rest – *((communal dining) (by arrangement))* Menu £ 30

◆ Traditional Somerset longhouse in charming setting with airy, well-kept country bedrooms and lovely rear garden. Delightful hosts dine with their guests at family style meals crafted from fresh, local ingredients. Al fresco breakfast in summer.

LANGTHWAITE – **N. Yorks.** – **502** O20 – **see Reeth**

LA PULENTE – **C.I.** – **503** P33 – **see Channel Islands (Jersey)**

LAPWORTH – **Warks.** – **see Hockley Heath**

LASKILL **N. Yorks** – **North Yorkshire** – **502** Q21 – **see Hawnby**

LASTINGHAM – **North Yorkshire** – **502** R21 – **pop. 87** – ✉ **York** — **23** C1

London 244 mi. – Scarborough 26 mi. – York 32 mi.

Lastingham Grange

✉ YO62 6TH – ✆ (01751) 417 345 – www.lastinghamgrange.com – Fax (01751) 417 358 – mid March-mid November

11 rm – £ 100/160 £ 160/220

Rest – *(light lunch Monday-Saturday)* Carte £ 21/31

◆ A delightfully traditional country house atmosphere prevails throughout this extended, pleasantly old-fashioned, 17C farmhouse. Lovely gardens; well-appointed bedrooms. Dining room with rustic fare and rose garden view.

LAUNCESTON – **Cornwall** – **503** G32 – **pop. 7 135** — **1** B2

London 228 mi. – Bude 23 mi. – Exeter 47 mi. – Plymouth 27 mi.

18 Trethorne Kennards House, ✆ (01566) 86 903

Springer Spaniel

✉ PL15 9NS – ✆ (01579) 370 424 – www.thespringerspaniel.org.uk – Fax (01579) 370 424

Rest – Carte £ 19/27

◆ Sizeable 18C former coaching inn with a friendly, informal atmosphere. Wide-ranging classical menu uses local, traceable produce, including meat from the owners' nearby farm.

LAVENHAM – Suffolk – 504 W27 – pop. 1 231 – ✉ Sudbury 15 C3

Great Britain

London 66 mi. – Cambridge 39 mi. – Colchester 22 mi. – Ipswich 19 mi.

Lady St ✆ (01787) 248207, lavenhamtic@babergh.gov.uk

Town★★ – Church of St Peter and St Paul★

Swan

High St ✉ CO10 9QA – ✆ (01787) 247 477 – www.theswanatlavenham.co.uk – Fax (01787) 248 286

42 rm – †£ 75/135 ††£ 160/180 – 3 suites **Rest** – Menu £ 16/35

◆ Well-restored, part 14C, half timbered house with an engaging historical ambience. Each atmospheric bedroom is individually and stylishly decorated. Dining room has impressive timbered ceiling verging on the cavernous.

Lavenham Priory without rest

Water St ✉ CO10 9RW – ✆ (01787) 247 404 – www.lavenhampriory.co.uk – Fax (01787) 248 472 – Closed Christmas-New Year

6 rm – †£ 75 ††£ 155

◆ A Jacobean oak staircase and Elizabethan wall paintings are just two elements of this part 13C former priory, bursting with character. Bedrooms stylishly furnished with antiques.

The Great House with rm

Market Pl ✉ CO10 9QZ – ✆ (01787) 247 431 – www.greathouse.co.uk – Fax (01787) 248 007 – Closed 3 weeks January and 2 weeks Summer

3 rm – †£ 90/110 ††£ 160/195, £ 13 – 2 suites

Rest – French – *(Closed Sunday dinner, Monday and lunch Tuesday)* Menu £ 19/29 – Carte £ 25/45

◆ Impressive Georgian façade conceals 14C timbered house with eye-catching modern art and heated rear terrace. Classical French cooking displays modern twists. Service is well-paced and attentive. Contemporary, country house bedrooms boast old beams and modern hues.

The Angel with rm

Market Pl ✉ CO10 9QZ – ✆ (01787) 247 388 – www.maypolehotels.com – Fax (01787) 248 344

8 rm – †£ 85 ††£ 100, £ 6 **Rest** – Carte £ 20/29

◆ Popular 15C inn on market square, offering extensive range of seasonally changing, traditional dishes. Residents' lounge features impressive pargeted ceiling. Bedrooms have ancient timbers and modern facilities.

LEAMINGTON SPA – Warks. – 503 P27 – see Royal Leamington Spa

LECHLADE – Gloucestershire – 503 O28 – pop. 2 415 Great Britain 4 D1

London 84 mi. – Cirencester 13 mi. – Oxford 25 mi.

Fairford : Church of St Mary★ (stained glass windows★★), W : 4.5 mi. on A 417

at Southrop Northwest : 3 mi. on Eastleach rd – ✉ Lechlade

The Swan

✉ GL7 3NU – ✆ (01367) 850 205 – www.theswanatsouthrop.co.uk – Fax (01367) 850 517 – Closed 25-26 December and Sunday dinner

Rest – Menu £ 16 (Monday-Thursday) – Carte £ 23/34

◆ Ex-London restaurateur combines Italian-influenced cooking with pub classics at this delightful creeper-clad inn, set in a picture perfect Cotswold village. Charming service.

ENGLAND

LEDBURY – County of Herefordshire – 503 M27 – pop. 8 491 **18** B3

London 119 mi. – Hereford 14 mi. – Newport 46 mi. – Worcester 16 mi.

The Feathers

High St ✉ *HR8 1DS – ✆ (01531) 635 266 – www.feathers-ledbury.co.uk – Fax (01531) 638 955*

19 rm – 🛉£ 88/125 🛉🛉£ 130/150 – 3 suites

Rest *Quills* – *(Closed Monday-Thursday)* Carte £ 25/35

Rest *Fuggles* – Carte £ 25/35

◆ Impressive timbered 16C inn in centre of town. Much character with open fires and antique furnishings. Rooms vary in design, though they all lay claim to a stylish modernity. Intimate dining in Quills restaurant. Fuggles is decorated with hops.

The Malthouse

Church Lane ✉ *HR8 1DW – ✆ (01531) 634 443 – www.malthouse-ledbury.co.uk – Closed first week January, 1 week Autumn, 25 December, Sunday and Monday*

Rest – *(dinner only and Saturday lunch)* Carte £ 22/32

◆ Tucked away behind the butter market; rustic décor and attractive courtyard lend a classic country cottage aura. Monthly menu of carefully prepared dishes using local produce.

at Kynaston **West : 6.5 mi. by A 449, A 4172, Aylton Rd, on Fownhope Rd – ✉ Ledbury**

Hall End

✉ *HR8 2PD – ✆ (01531) 670 225 – www.hallendhouse.com – Fax (01531) 670 747 – Closed Christmas and New Year*

3 rm – 🛉🛉£ 95/120

Rest – *(booking essential) (communal dining, by arrangement)* Menu £ 25/35

◆ Lovingly restored, personally run, part Georgian home and livery stable in the countryside. Relax in the orangery and, suitably reposed, retire to lavishly furnished bedrooms.

at Trumpet **Northwest : 3.25 mi. on A 438 – ✉ Ledbury**

Verzon House

Hereford Rd ✉ *HR8 2PZ – ✆ (01531) 670 381 – www.verzonhouse.com – Fax (01531) 670 830 – Closed first 2 weeks January*

8 rm – 🛉£ 80/125 🛉🛉£ 125/135 **Rest** – Carte £ 23/40

◆ Extended Georgian redbrick house with stylish lounge bar, contemporary artwork and comfy seats. Modern bedrooms are named after cider apples; most have view over courtyard. Modern dishes served in restaurant, with decking for al fresco dining.

C. Labonne/MICHELIN

LEEDS

County: West Yorkshire
Michelin regional map: **502** P22
London 204 mi. – Liverpool 75 mi.
– Manchester 43 mi.
– Newcastle upon Tyne 95 mi.

Population: 443 247
Great Britain
Map reference: **22** B2

PRACTICAL INFORMATION

Tourist Information

The Arcade, City Station ✆ (0113) 242 5242, tourinfo@leeds.gov.uk

Airport

Leeds-Bradford Airport : ✆ (0113) 250 9696, NW : 8 mi. by A 65 and A 658 BT

Golf Courses

36 Temple Newsam Halton Temple Newsam Rd, ✆ (0113) 264 5624

18 Gotts Park Armley Armley Ridge Rd, ✆ (0113) 234 2019

18 Middleton Park Middleton Ring Rd, Beeston Park, ✆ (0113) 270 0449

27 Moor Allerton Wike Coal Rd, ✆ (0113) 266 1154

18 Howley Hall Morley Scotchman Lane, ✆ (01924) 350 100

9 Roundhay Park Lane, ✆ (0113) 266 2695

SIGHTS

In town

City★ - Royal Armouries Museum★★★ GZ - City Art Gallery★ **AC** GY **M**

On the outskirts

Kirkstall Abbey★ **AC**, NW : 3 mi. by A 65 GY – Temple Newsam★ (decorative arts★) **AC**, E : 5 mi. by A 64 and A 63 CU **D**

In the surrounding area

Harewood House★★ (The Gallery★) **AC**, N : 8 mi. by A 61 CT – Nostell Priory★, SE : 18 mi. by A 61 and A 638 – Yorkshire Sculpture Park★, S : 20 mi. by M 1 to junction 38 and 1 mi. north off A 637 – Brodsworth Hall★, SE : 25 mi. by M 1 to junction 40, A 638 and minor rd (right) in Upton

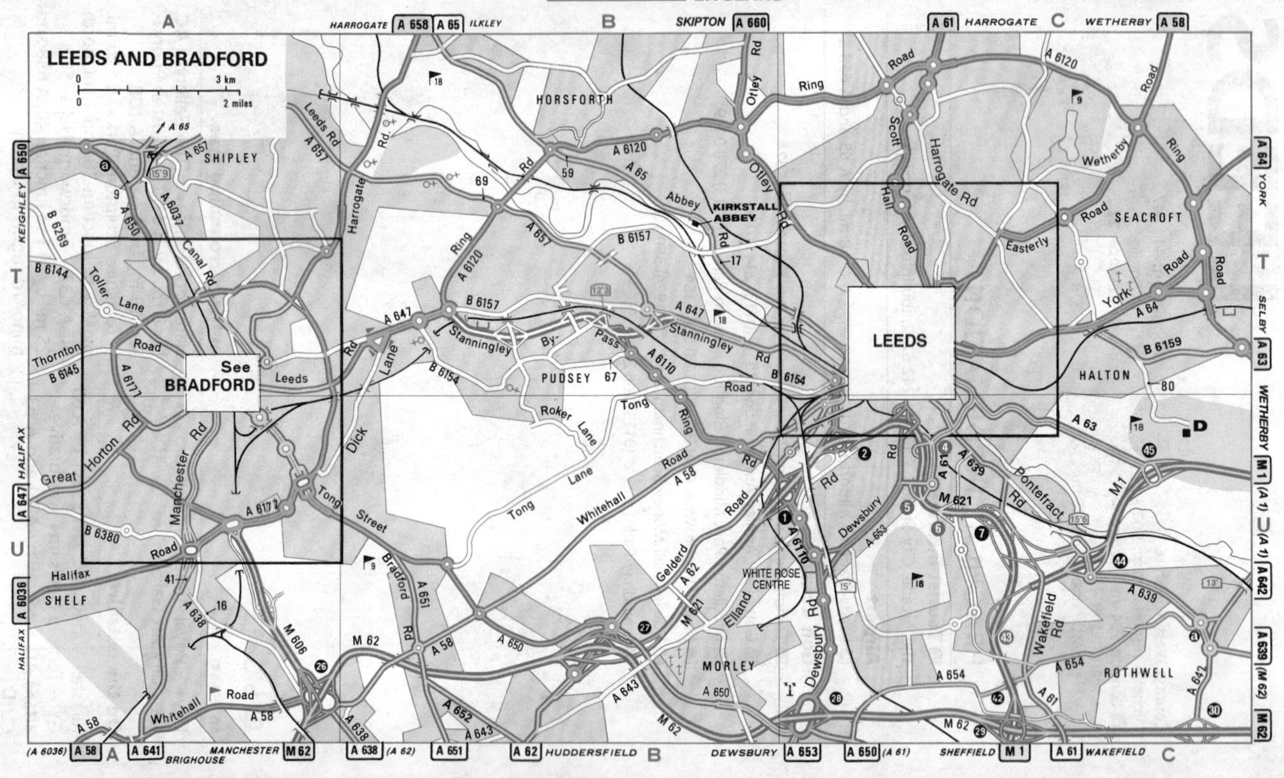
LEEDS AND BRADFORD
0 3 km
0 2 miles
HARROGATE A 658 A 65 ILKLEY
SKIPTON A 660
A 61 HARROGATE
WETHERBY A 58
A 64 YORK
SELBY A 63
WETHERBY M 1 (A 1) (A 1) A 642
A 639 (M 62) M 62
A 650 KEIGHLEY
A 647 HALIFAX
A 6036 HALIFAX
(A 6036) A 58
A 641 BRIGHOUSE
MANCHESTER M 62
A 638 (A 62)
A 651
A 62 HUDDERSFIELD
DEWSBURY A 653
A 650 (A 61)
SHEFFIELD M 1
A 61 WAKEFIELD
SHIPLEY
HORSFORTH
KIRKSTALL ABBEY
SEACROFT
HALTON
LEEDS
See BRADFORD
PUDSEY
WHITE ROSE CENTRE
MORLEY
ROTHWELL
SHELF

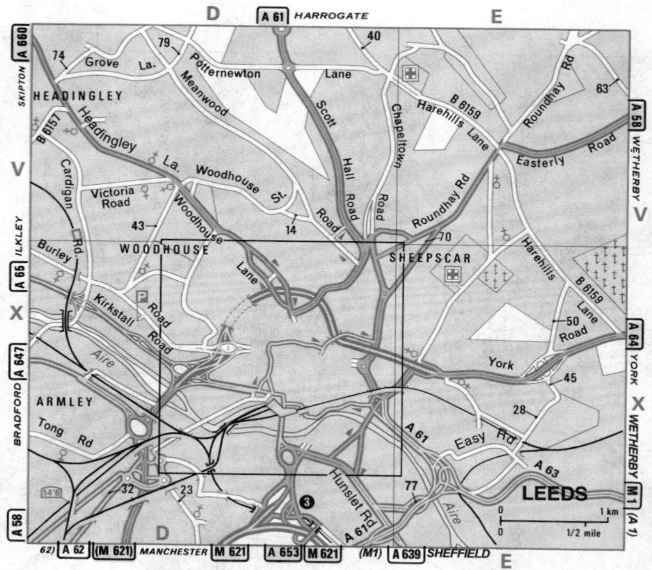

Bradford Rd . . . . AT 9
Cambridge Rd . . . . DV 14
Cleckheaton Rd . . . . AU 16
Commercial Rd . . . . BT 17
Domestic St . . . . DX 23
East Park Parade . . . . EX 28
Gelderd Rd . . . . DX 32
Harrogate Rd . . . . DV 40
Huddersfield Rd . . . . AU 41
Hyde Park Rd . . . . AV 43
Ivy St . . . . EX 45
Lupton Ave . . . . EX 51
New Rd Side . . . . BT 59
Oakwood Lane . . . . EV 63
Pudsey Rd . . . . BT 67
Rodley Lane . . . . BV 69
Roseville Rd . . . . EVX 70
Shaw Lane . . . . DV 74
South Accommodation Rd . . . . EX 77
Stainbeck Rd . . . . DV 79
Templenewsam Rd . . . . CT 80
White Rose Centre . . . . CU

Malmaison

rm, VISA AE

1 Swinegate ✉ LS1 4AG – ☎ (0113) 398 1000 – www.malmaison-leeds.com – Fax (0113) 398 1002 GZn

100 rm – †£ 140/170 ††£ 180, ☕ £ 13.95 – 1 suite

Rest – Menu £ 17 – Carte £ 30/44

♦ Relaxed, contemporary hotel hides behind imposing Victorian exterior. Vibrantly and individually decorated rooms are stylishly furnished, with modern facilities to the fore. Dine in modern interpretation of a French brasserie.

Quebecs without rest

VISA AE

9 Quebec St ✉ LS1 2HA – ☎ (0113) 244 8989 – www.theetoncollection.com – Fax (0113) 244 9090 – Closed 24-27 December FZa

43 rm – †£ 69/225 ††£ 69/225, ☕ £ 14.50 – 2 suites

♦ 19C former Liberal Club, now a modish, intimate boutique hotel. Original features include oak staircase and stained glass window depicting Yorkshire cities. Stylish rooms.

42 The Calls

VISA AE

42 The Calls ✉ LS2 7EW – ☎ (0113) 244 0099 – www.42thecalls.co.uk – Fax (0113) 234 4100 – Closed 3 days Christmas GZz

38 rm – †£ 89/190 ††£ 125/225, ☕ £ 14.50 – 3 suites

Rest *Brasserie Forty 4* – see restaurant listing

♦ Stylish, contemporary converted quayside grain mill retaining many of the original workings. Rooms facing river have best views; all well equipped with a host of extras.

Good food at moderate prices? Look for the Bib Gourmand.

ENGLAND

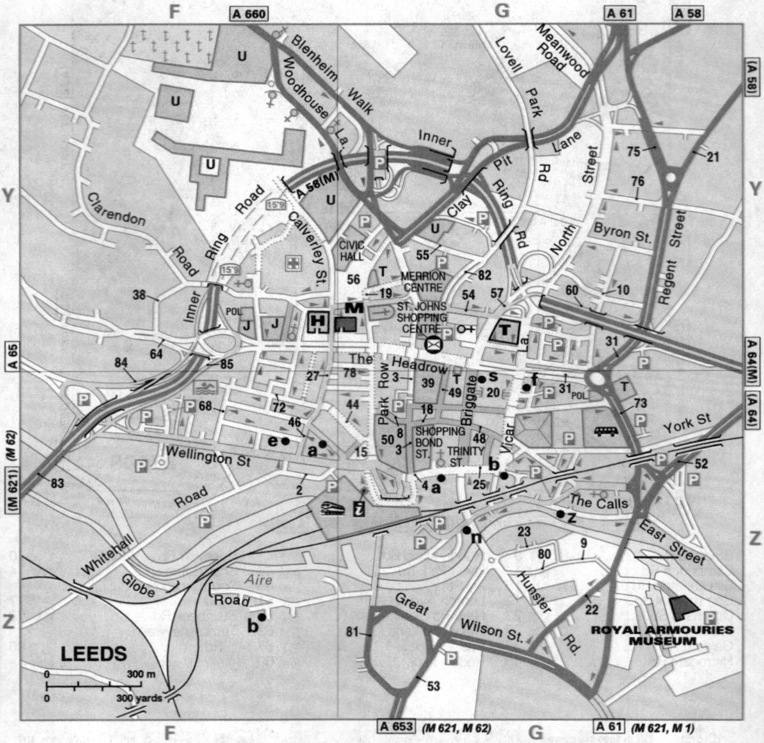

LEEDS

Street	Grid	No.	Street	Grid	No.	Street	Grid	No.
Aire St.	FZ	2	East Parade	FGZ	27	New York Rd	GY	60
Albion St	GZ	3	Hanover Way	FY	38	Park Lane	FY	64
Boar Lane	GZ	4	Headrow Centre	GZ	39	Queen St	FZ	68
Bond St	GZ	8	Headrow (The)	GY		St John's Centre	GY	
Bowman Lane	GZ	9	Infirmary St	GZ	44	St Paul's St	FZ	72
Bridge St	GY	10	King St	FZ	46	St Peter's St	GZ	73
Briggate	GZ		Kirkgate	GZ	48	Sheepscar St South	GY	75
City Square	GZ	15	Lands Lane	GZ	49	Skinner Lane	GY	76
Commercial St	GZ	18	Leeds Shopping Plaza	GZ	50	South Parade	FGZ	78
Cookridge St	GY	19	Marsh Lane	GZ	52	Trinity St Shopping Centre	GZ	
County Arcade	GZ	20	Meadow Lane	GZ	53	Victoria Rd	GZ	81
Cross Stamford St	GY	21	Merrion Centre	GY		Wade Lane	GY	82
Crown Point Rd	GZ	22	Merrion St	GY	54	Waterloo St	GZ	80
Dock St	GZ	23	Merrion Way	GY	55	Wellington Rd	FZ	83
Duncan St	GZ	25	Millennium Square	GY	56	Westgate	FZ	85
Eastgate	GZ	31	New Briggate	GY	57	West St	FZ	84

XXX **Anthony's** AC VISA MC

19 Boar Lane ✉ LS1 6EA – ✆ (0113) 245 5922 – www.anthonysrestaurant.co.uk – closed Christmas-New Year, Sunday and Monday GZ**a**

Rest – *(booking essential)* Menu £ 24/42

◆ Converted 19C property; ground floor lounge with Chesterfield sofas; minimalist basement dining room offers innovative menus with some intriguing combinations.

XX **No.3 York Place** AC VISA MC AE

3 York Pl ✉ LS1 2DR – ✆ (0113) 245 9922 – www.no3yorkplace.co.uk – Fax (0113) 245 9965 – Closed 25 December-6 January, Saturday lunch, Sunday and Bank Holidays FZ**e**

Rest – Menu £ 18 (lunch) – Carte £ 23/38

◆ A minimalist and discreet environment keeps the spotlight on the appealing cuisine. Classic flavours reinterpreted in a tasty range of brasserie style dishes.

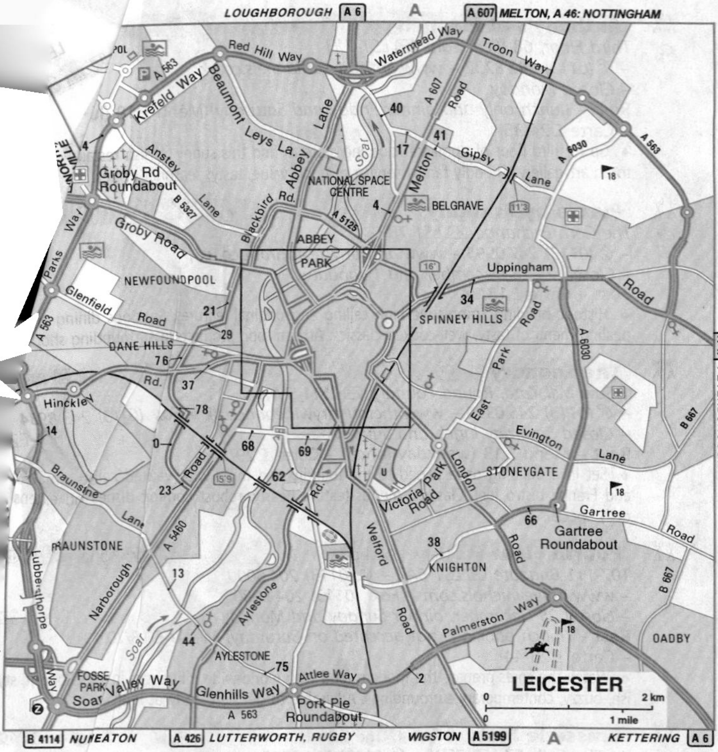

Asquith Way AY 2
Belgrave Rd AX 4
Braunstone Ave AY 10
Braunstone Lane East AY 13
Braunstone Way AY 14
Checketts Rd AX 17
Fosse Rd North AX 21
Fullhurst Ave AY 23
Glenfrith Way AX 24
Henley Rd AX 29
Humberstone Rd AX 34
King Richards Rd AY 37
Knighton Rd AY 38
Loughborough Rd AX 40
Marfitt St AX 41
Middleton St AY 44
Raw Dykes Rd AY 62
Stoughton Rd AY 66
Upperton Rd AY 68
Walnut St AY 69
Wigston Lane AY 75
Woodville Rd AY 76
Wyngate Drive AY 78

Leicester Marriott

Smith Way, Grove Park, Enderby, Southwest : 4 mi. by A 5460 off A 563 at junction 21 of M 1 ✉ LE19 1SW
– ✆ (0116) 282 0100 – www.leicestermarriott.co.uk
– Fax (0116) 282 0101 AYz

226 rm – †£ 129 ††£ 129 – 1 suite
Rest – Menu £ 22 (dinner)
– Carte £ 24/34

◆ Sleekly designed, comfortable hotel in useful location by junction 21 of M1. Coffee shop and bar. State-of-the-art gym. Standard and executive bedrooms. East meets west in contemporary restaurant; choice of buffet and eclectic à la carte.

The symbol guarantees a good night's sleep. In red ? The very essence of peace: only the sound of birdsong in the early morning…

XX **Anthony's at Flannels**
Third Floor, 68 Vicar Lane ✉ LS1 7JH – ✆ (0113) 242 8732 – www.anthonysatflannels.co.uk – Closed Monday GZ**f**
Rest – *(lunch only and dinner Friday and Saturday)* Menu £ 18 (lunch) – Carte £ 24/35
◆ Go to third floor of upmarket clothing store to find this sunny, stylish restaurant, adjacent to an art gallery. Friendly family service of good value, tasty, seasonal dishes.

XX **Piazza by Anthony**
The Corn Exchange ✉ LS1 7BR – ✆ (0113) 247 0995 – www.anthonysrestaurant.co.uk – Closed 25-26 December and 1 January GZ**b**
Rest – Carte £ 18/34
◆ Historic building; impressive high ceiling and original features. Spacious dining area; appealing menu of tasty, well-cooked classics. Artisan food products in surrounding shops.

XX **The Foundry**
1 Saw Mill Yard, Round Foundry ✉ LS11 5WH – ✆ (0113) 245 0390 – www.thefoundrywinebar.co.uk – Fax (0113) 243 8934 – Closed Saturday lunch and Sunday FZ**b**
Rest – Menu £ 13 (weekday lunch) – Carte £ 29/34
◆ Set in a building once joined to the foundry and mills, with vaulted ceiling, ornate bar and French bistro feel. Classical menus feature hearty, robust comfort dishes and extensive daily specials.

XX **Fourth Floor** – at Harvey Nichols
107-111 Briggate ✉ LS1 6AZ – ✆ (0113) 204 8000 – www.harveynichols.com – Fax (0113) 204 8080 – closed 25 December, dinner Sunday and Monday GZ**s**
Rest – *(lunch bookings not accepted on Saturday)* Menu £ 18/20 – Carte £ 25/44
◆ Watch the chefs prepare the modern food with world-wide influences in these bright, stylish, buzzy, contemporary surroundings. Advisable to get here early at lunch.

XX **Brasserie Forty 4** – at 42 The Calls Hotel
44 The Calls ✉ LS2 7EW – ✆ (0113) 234 3232 – www.brasserie44.com – Fax (0113) 234 3332 – Closed Sunday and Bank Holidays except Good Friday GZ**z**
Rest – Carte £ 26/29
◆ Former riverside warehouse with stylish bar; exudes atmosphere of buzzy informality. Smokehouse and char-grilled options in an eclectic range of dishes.

LEICESTER – Leicester – 502 Q26 – pop. 330 574 Great Britain **16** B2

London 107 mi. – Birmingham 43 mi. – Coventry 24 mi. – Nottingham 26 mi.

East Midlands Airport, Castle Donington : ✆ (0871) 9199000 NW : 22 mi. by A 50 - AX - and M 1

7-9 Every St, Town Hall Sq ✆ (0844) 888 5181(calls charged), info@goleicestershire.com

18 Leicestershire Evington Lane, ✆ (0116) 273 8825

18 Western Park Scudamore Rd, ✆ (0116) 287 5211

18 Humberstone Heights Gipsy Lane, ✆ (0116) 299 5570

18 Oadby Leicester Road Racecourse, ✆ (0116) 270 0215

9 Blaby Lutterworth Rd, ✆ (0116) 278 4804

Guildhall★ BY **B** – Museum and Art Gallery★ CY **M3** – St Mary de Castro Church★ BY **D**

National Space Centre★ N : 2 mi. by A 6 - AX - turning east into Corporation Rd and right into Exploration Drive

Plans pages 310, 311

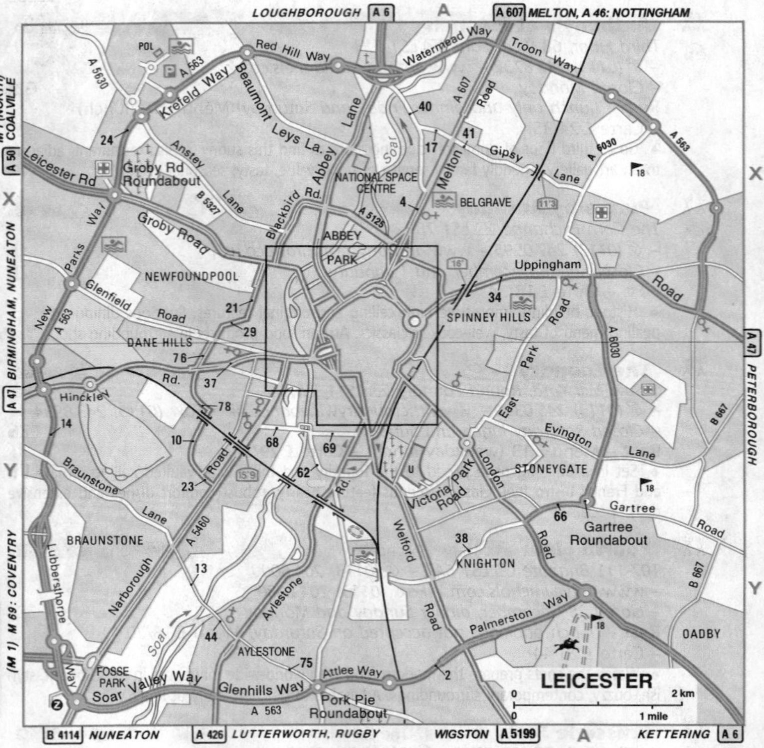

LEICESTER

Leicester Marriott

Smith Way, Grove Park, Enderby, Southwest : 4 mi. by A 5460 off A 563 at junction 21 of M 1 ✉ *LE19 1SW*
– ℰ (0116) 282 0100 – www.leicestermarriott.co.uk
– Fax (0116) 282 0101 AY**z**

226 rm – †£ 129 ††£ 129 – 1 suite
Rest – Menu £ 22 (dinner)
– Carte £ 24/34

◆ Sleekly designed, comfortable hotel in useful location by junction 21 of M1. Coffee shop and bar. State-of-the-art gym. Standard and executive bedrooms. East meets west in contemporary restaurant; choice of buffet and eclectic à la carte.

The symbol guarantees a good night's sleep. In red ? The very essence of peace: only the sound of birdsong in the early morning…

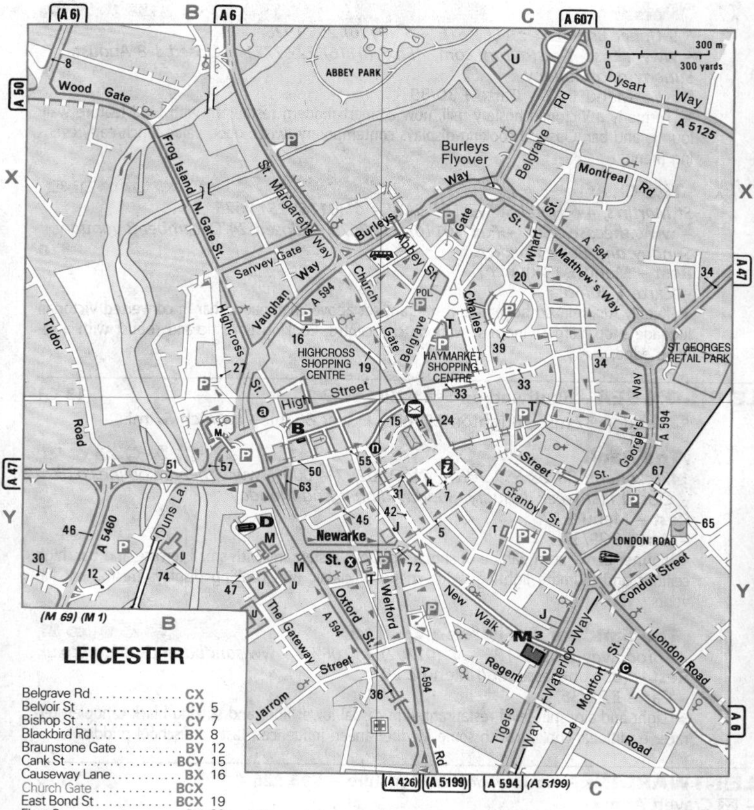

LEICESTER

The Belmont

De Montfort St ✉ *LE1 7GR – ☎ (0116) 254 4773 – www.belmonthotel.co.uk – Fax (0116) 247 0804* CY**c**

74 rm – 👤£ 60/130 👥£ 80/135, ☕ £ 12.95 – 1 suite

Rest *Cherry's* – *(Closed Saturday lunch and Sunday dinner)* Menu £ 16/25

◆ Friendly, family run hotel in city suburb, made up of a collection of houses – each with its own classical style. Bedrooms vary in shape and size: all have modern touches and good facilities. Contemporary bar with snack menu; formal restaurant offering traditional fare.

Hotel Maiyango

13-21 St. Nicholas Pl ✉ *LE1 4LD – ☎ (0116) 251 88 98 – www.maiyango.com – Fax (0116) 242 13 39* BY**a**

13 rm – 👤£ 160 👥£ 160, ☕ £ 8 – 1 suite

Rest – *(Closed Sunday lunch)* Menu £ 18/35 – Carte £ 30/40

◆ Stylish city centre hotel in converted shoe factory. Spacious rooms feature heavy wood furniture and modern facilities; 3rd floor bar overlooks rooftops. Ground floor restaurant with colonial feel serves well presented Mediterranean/Asian influenced cooking.

XX **Watsons**

5-9 Upper Brown St ✉ LE1 5TE – ✆ (0116) 255 1928 – www.watsons-restaurant.com – Fax (0116) 222 7771 – Closed 1-8 August, Sunday and Monday BY**x**

Rest – Menu £ 17 – Carte £ 30/39

◆ Formerly a Victorian hosiery mill, now a smart modern restaurant with bold feature wall, lounge and bar. Classical cooking displays contemporary twists; good value lunch/early evening menus.

XX **The Case**

St Martin's, 4-6 Hotel St ✉ LE1 5AW – ✆ (0116) 251 7675 – www.thecase.co.uk – Fax (0116) 251 7675 – Closed 24 December-3 January, Sunday and Bank Holidays BY**n**

Rest – Menu £ 13 (lunch) – Carte £ 20/40

◆ Keenly run, relaxed bohemian restaurant set above champagne bar in converted Victorian luggage shop. Large windows overlook city centre. Cooking is rustic and robust with a refined edge.

LEIGH-ON-SEA – Southend-on-Sea – 504 W29 — 13 C3

London 37 mi. – Brighton 85 mi. – Dover 86 mi. – Ipswich 57 mi.

XX **The Bank**

1470 London Rd ✉ SS9 2UR – ✆ (01702) 719 000 – www.thebankonline.co.uk – Closed first week January, Sunday dinner and Monday

Rest – Menu £ 17 – Carte £ 29/37

◆ Former bank set in parade of shops. Spacious restaurant with small terrace and bar, high ceilings and intimate lighting. Wide menu of classic 80's cooking displays fresh, neat flavours.

X **The Sandbar & Seafood Co. Ltd**

71 Broadway ✉ SS9 1PE – ✆ (01702) 480 067 – www.sandbarandseafood.co.uk

Rest – *(booking essential)* Menu £ 20 – Carte £ 21/36

◆ Light and airy split-level restaurant with casual lower floor and striking black canopied terrace. Traditional cooking with some Mediterranean influences; tasty old-school puddings.

LEINTWARDINE – County of Herefordshire – 503 L26 — 18 A2
– ✉ Craven Arms

London 156 mi. – Birmingham 55 mi. – Hereford 24 mi. – Worcester 40 mi.

Upper Buckton Farm

Buckton, West : 2 mi. by A 4113 and Buckton rd ✉ SY7 0JU – ✆ (01547) 540 634 – Fax (01547) 540 634 – Closed 25 December

3 rm – †£ 65 ††£ 90/100

Rest – *(by arrangement, communal dining)* Menu £ 28

◆ Fine Georgian farmhouse, part of a working farm, surrounded by countryside. Comfortable, simple, country feel with open fires in the lounge and characterful bedrooms. Traditional dining; local produce.

LENHAM – Kent – 504 W30 – pop. 2 191 – ✉ Maidstone — 9 C2

London 45 mi. – Folkestone 28 mi. – Maidstone 9 mi.

Chilston Park rm,

Sandway, South : 1.75 mi. off Broughton Malherbe rd ✉ ME17 2BE – ✆ (01622) 859 803 – www.handpicked.co.uk/chilstonpark – Fax (01622) 858 588

53 rm – †£ 85/125 ††£ 95/155 – 4 suites

Rest – *(Closed Saturday lunch)* Menu £ 18/28 – Carte dinner £ 37/41

◆ Part 17C mansion, set in parkland and furnished with antiques. Bedrooms are very individual and comfortable. Old stable conference facilities retain original stalls! Smart dining room and well-appointed sitting room.

ENGLAND

LEOMINSTER – County of Herefordshire – 503 L27 – pop. 10 440 18 B3

Great Britain

London 141 mi. – Birmingham 47 mi. – Hereford 13 mi. – Worcester 26 mi.

1 Corn Sq ✆ (01568) 616460, tic-leominster@herefordshire.gov.uk

Ford Bridge, ✆ (01568) 612 863

Berrington Hall★ **AC**, N : 3 mi. by A 49

at Leysters Northeast : 5 mi. by A 49 on A 4112 – ✉ Leominster

The Hills Farm without rest

✉ HR6 0HP – ✆ (01568) 750 205 – www.thehillsfarm.co.uk – March-October

3 rm – ♦£ 39/45 ♦♦£ 78/90

◆ An attractive ivy-clad farmhouse on a working farm. The interior is delightfully comfortable, from the cosy lounge to the country-cottage rooms, three in the converted barns.

LETCHWORTH – Hertfordshire – 504 T28 – pop. 32 932 12 B2

London 39 mi. – Luton 18 mi. – Stevenage 7 mi.

at Willian South : 1.75 mi. by A 6141 – ✉ Letchworth

The Fox

✉ SG6 2AE – ✆ (01462) 480 233 – www.foxatwillian.co.uk
– Fax (01462) 676 966 – Closed Sunday dinner

Rest – Carte £ 22/33

◆ Bright, airy pub that's always bustling. Lunch served throughout; dinner in the dining room only. Menu offers modern dishes with game in season and plenty of seafood; some Asian influences.

LEVINGTON – Suffolk 15 D3

London 75 mi. – Ipswich 5 mi. – Woodbridge 8 mi.

The Ship Inn

Church Lane ✉ IP10 0LQ – ✆ (01473) 659 573 – Fax (01473) 659 151
– Closed 25-26 December

Rest – *(bookings not accepted)* Carte £ 13/25

◆ Characterful thatched pub crammed with maritime curios. Seafood-orientated blackboard menus offer rustic, unfussy cooking. Lively atmosphere – arrive early; no bookings taken.

LEVISHAM – N. Yorks. – 502 R21 – see Pickering

LEWDOWN – Devon – 503 H32 2 C2

London 238 mi. – Exeter 37 mi. – Plymouth 29 mi.

Lydford★★, E : 4 m. Launceston★ - Castle★ (≤★) St Mary Magdalene★, W : 8 mi. by A 30 and A 388

Lewtrenchard Manor

South : 0.75 mi. by Lewtrenchard rd ✉ EX20 4PN – ✆ (01566) 783 222
– www.lewtrenchard.co.uk – Fax (01566) 783 332

13 rm – ♦£ 120/190 ♦♦£ 150/220 – 1 suite

Rest – *(booking essential for non-residents)* Menu £ 19/51

◆ A grand historical atmosphere pervades this delightfully secluded 17C manor house. Plenty of personality with antiques, artworks, ornate ceilings and panelling throughout. Two elegant dining rooms with stained glass windows.

LEWES – East Sussex – 504 U31 – pop. 15 988 Great Britain 8 A3

London 53 mi. – Brighton 8 mi. – Hastings 29 mi. – Maidstone 43 mi.

187 High St ✆ (01273) 483448, lewes.tic@lewes.gov.uk

Chapel Hill, ✆ (01273) 473 245

Town★ (High St★, Keere St★) – Castle (≤★) **AC**

Sheffield Park Garden★ **AC**, N : 9.5 mi. by A 275

Shelleys

High St ✉ BN7 1XS – ✆ (01273) 472 361 – www.the-shelleys.co.uk – Fax (01273) 483 152
18 rm – †£ 105/180 ††£ 200/300 – 1 suite
Rest – Menu £ 25 – Carte (dinner) £ 27/39
◆ Formerly an inn, and before that, a private house dating back to 1577 – owned by the great poet's family. Spacious, classically styled bedrooms include a four-poster and suite with garden views. Smart restaurant overlooks the lawns.

Millers without rest

134 High St ✉ BN7 1XS – ✆ (01273) 475 631 – www.millersbedandbreakfast.com – Closed 20 December-5 January, 4 and 5 November
3 rm – †£ 80 ††£ 90
◆ Characterful, small family home in a row of 16C houses that lead to the high street. Appealing personal feel in the individual bedrooms with books, trinkets and knick-knacks.

The Real Eating Company

18 Cliffe High St ✉ BN7 2AJ – ✆ (01273) 402 650 – www.real-eating.co.uk – closed Sunday and Monday dinner
Rest – Carte £ 24/29
◆ Friendly, informal deli-cum-bar in pretty, pedestrianised street. Fresh seasonal, local produce cooked in unfussy style to create tasty dishes, including plenty of British favourites.

at East Chiltington Northwest : 5.5 mi. by A 275 and B 2116 off Novington Lane – ✉ Lewes

The Jolly Sportsman

Chapel Lane ✉ BN7 3BA – ✆ (01273) 890 400 – www.thejollysportsman.com – Fax (01273) 890 400 – Closed 25-26 December
Rest – Carte £ 22/32
◆ Creeper-clad pub with raised rear garden and paved terrace. Menu displays simple dishes made from quality ingredients, with a subtle Mediterranean influence; fish is a strength.

ENGLAND

LEYBURN – North Yorkshire – 502 O21 – pop. 1 844 — 22 B1

London 251 mi. – Darlington 25 mi. – Kendal 43 mi. – Leeds 53 mi.
4 Central Chambers, Railway St ✆ (01748) 828747, tic.leyburn@richmondshire.gov.uk

Clyde House without rest

5 Railway St ✉ DL8 5AY – ✆ (01969) 623 941 – www.clydehouseleyburn.co.uk
6 rm – †£ 40/50 ††£ 75
◆ Recently refurbished to a high standard, this former coaching inn dates from mid-18C and is one of the oldest buildings in town. Hearty Yorkshire breakfasts to start the day.

The Dales Haven without rest

Market Pl ✉ DL8 5BJ – ✆ (01969) 623 814 – www.daleshaven.co.uk – Closed 2 weeks January
6 rm – †£ 45/49 ††£ 65/69
◆ Neat and tidy house in village centre. Pleasant rural views from breakfast room, which also displays artwork from local gallery. Colourful rooms include DVD and CD players.

The Sandpiper Inn with rm

Market Pl ✉ DL8 5AT – ✆ (01969) 622 206 – www.sandpiperinn.co.uk – Fax (01969) 625 367 – Closed 25-26 December, 1 January, Monday, and Tuesday in winter
2 rm – †£ 65 ††£ 80 **Rest** – Carte £ 21/33
◆ Charming 16C inn just off the square in busy market town. Frequently changing blackboard menus feature fine local produce; simpler dishes and sandwiches at lunchtime. Pleasant bedrooms have a homely feel.

at Constable Burton **East : 3.5 mi. on A 684 – ✉ Leyburn**

Wyvill Arms with rm
✉ *DL8 5LH* – ✆ *(01677) 450 581*
3 rm ☕ – 🚹£ 55 🚹🚹£ 75 **Rest** – Carte £ 24/36
◆ Intimate, ivy-clad stone pub with pleasant gardens, formerly an 18C farmhouse. Menus offer plenty of choice and feature local, traceable produce in carefully prepared, classical dishes. Simple, well-kept bedrooms.

LEYSTERS – **Herefordshire** – **503** M27 – **see Leominster**

LICHFIELD – **Staffordshire** – **502** O25 – **pop. 28 435** Great Britain **19** C2

London 128 mi. – Birmingham 16 mi. – Derby 23 mi. – Stoke-on-Trent 30 mi.
Lichfield Garrick, Castle Dyke ✆ (01543) 412112, info@visitlichfield.com
Lichfield Golf and Country Club Elmhurst, ✆ (01543) 417 333
City★ - Cathedral★★ **AC**

Swinfen Hall
Southeast : 2.25 mi. by A 5206 on A 38 ✉ *WS14 9RE* – ✆ *(01543) 481 494 – www.swinfenhallhotel.co.uk – Fax (01543) 480 341 – restricted opening between Christmas and New Year*
17 rm ☕ – 🚹£ 95/265 🚹🚹£ 295 – 1 suite
Rest *Four Seasons* – *(closed Saturday lunch)* Menu £ 43 (dinner) – Carte £ 25/29
◆ Very fine 18C house in 100 acres with beautiful façade, impressive stucco ceilings and elegant lounges furnished with taste and style. Bedrooms offer high levels of comfort. Modern menus served in superb oak-panelled restaurant with Grinling Gibbons carvings.

Chandlers Grande Brasserie
Corn Exchange, Conduit St ✉ *WS13 6JU* – ✆ *(01543) 416 688 – www.chandlersrestaurant.co.uk – Fax (01543) 417 887 – Closed Sunday dinner and Bank Holidays except 25 December*
Rest – Menu £ 14/18 – Carte £ 18/30
◆ On two floors in old cornmarket building. Tiled floors, prints and pin lights; a pleasant, relaxed atmosphere in which to enjoy a brasserie menu with good value lunch options.

LICKFOLD – **W. Sussex** – **see Petworth**

LIDGATE – **Suffolk** – **504** V27 – **see Newmarket**

LIFTON – **Devon** – **503** H32 – **pop. 964** **2** C2

London 238 mi. – Bude 24 mi. – Exeter 37 mi. – Launceston 4 mi.
Launceston★ - Castle★ (<★) St Mary Magdalene★, W : 4.5 mi. by A 30 and A 388

Arundell Arms
Fore St ✉ *PL16 0AA* – ✆ *(01566) 784 666 – www.arundellarms.com – Fax (01566) 784 494 – Closed 24-26 December*
21 rm ☕ – 🚹£ 105/125 🚹🚹£ 180 **Rest** – Menu £ 29/50
◆ Coaching inn, in a valley of five rivers, dating back to Saxon times. True English sporting hotel - popular with shooting parties and fishermen. Good country lodge style. English and French cuisine in opulently grand dining room.

Tinhay Mill with rm
Tinhay ✉ *PL16 0AJ* – ✆ *(01566) 784 201 – www.tinhaymillrestaurant.co.uk – Fax (01566) 784 201 – closed Sunday and Monday*
5 rm ☕ – 🚹£ 55/63 🚹🚹£ 85/95 **Rest** – *(dinner only)* Carte approx. £ 35
◆ Small converted mill: furnishings a mix of rustic and traditional, creating a cosy feel. Locally based, tasty cuisine from renowned Devonian owner/cook. Cottagey bedrooms.

LINCOLN – Lincolnshire – **502** S24 – **pop. 85 963** Great Britain **17** C1

London 140 mi. – Bradford 81 mi. – Cambridge 94 mi. – Kingston-upon-Hull 44 mi.

Humberside Airport : ✆ (01652) 688456, N : 32 mi. by A 15 - Y - M 180 and A 18

9 Castle Hill ✆ (01522) 873213, tourism@lincoln.gov.uk

Carholme Carholme Rd, ✆ (01522) 523 725

City★★ - Cathedral and Precincts★★★ **AC** Y – High Bridge★★ Z **9** – Usher Gallery★ **AC** YZ **M1** – Jew's House★ Y – Castle★ **AC** Y

Doddington Hall★ **AC**, W : 6 mi. by B 1003 - Z - and B 1190. Gainsborough Old Hall★ **AC**, NW : 19 mi. by A 57 - Z - and A 156

Bentley
rm, rest, VISA AE

Newark Rd, South Hykeham, Southwest : 5.75 mi. by A 15 on B 1434 at junction with A 46 ✉ LN6 9NH – ✆ (01522) 878 000 – www.thebentleyhotel.uk.com – Fax (01522) 878 001

80 rm – †£ 90 ††£ 105

Rest – Menu £ 13/22 **s** – Carte (dinner) £ 28/33 **s**

◆ Purpose-built hotel. Smart, modern feel with traditional touches throughout. Well kept bedrooms including Executive and more traditional styles. Well-run leisure club. Formal or relaxed dining alternatives.

Charlotte House without rest
rest, VISA AE

The Lawns, Union Rd ✉ LN1 3BJ – ✆ (01522) 541 000 – www.charlottehouselincoln.com – Fax (0871) 872 43 96 Y**v**

14 rm – †£ 145 ††£ 145, £ 9.50 – 6 suites

◆ Set next to a castle, a stylish and contemporary converted Georgian building with 8 acres of grounds; free town transfers. Super-cool, comfy rooms and luxurious bathrooms.

Bailhouse without rest
VISA AE

34 Bailgate ✉ LN1 3AP – ✆ (01522) 541 000 – www.bailhouse.co.uk – Fax (01522) 521 829 Y**c**

10 rm – ††£ 119, £ 9.50

◆ Beautiful 14C building with 19C additions. Intimate, relaxing feel enhanced by unobtrusive service, enclosed garden, and rooms oozing charm, some with 14C exposed beams.

Minster Lodge without rest
VISA AE

3 Church Lane ✉ LN2 1QJ – ✆ (01522) 513 220 – www.minsterlodge.co.uk – Closed 1 week Christmas Y**a**

6 rm – †£ 65 ††£ 75/85

◆ Converted house, close to the cathedral and castle, just by 3C Newport Arch with good access to the ring road. Immaculately kept throughout and run with a professional touch.

St Clements Lodge without rest

21 Langworthgate ✉ LN2 4AD – ✆ (01522) 521 532 – www.stclementslodge.co.uk – Fax (01522) 521 532 Y**u**

3 rm – †£ 48 ††£ 65

◆ A good value house in a convenient location, a short walk from the sights. Run by hospitable owners who keep three large, pleasantly decorated bedrooms.

Wig & Mitre
VISA AE

30-32 Steep Hill ✉ LN2 1LU – ✆ (01522) 535 190 – www.wigandmitre.com – Fax (01522) 532 402 Y**r**

Rest – Menu £ 15/20 – Carte £ 21/46

◆ First floor dining area, with characterful almost medieval decor, in a building which dates back to 14C. Skilfully prepared, confident, classic cooking.

ENGLAND

Good food at moderate prices? Look for the Bib Gourmand.

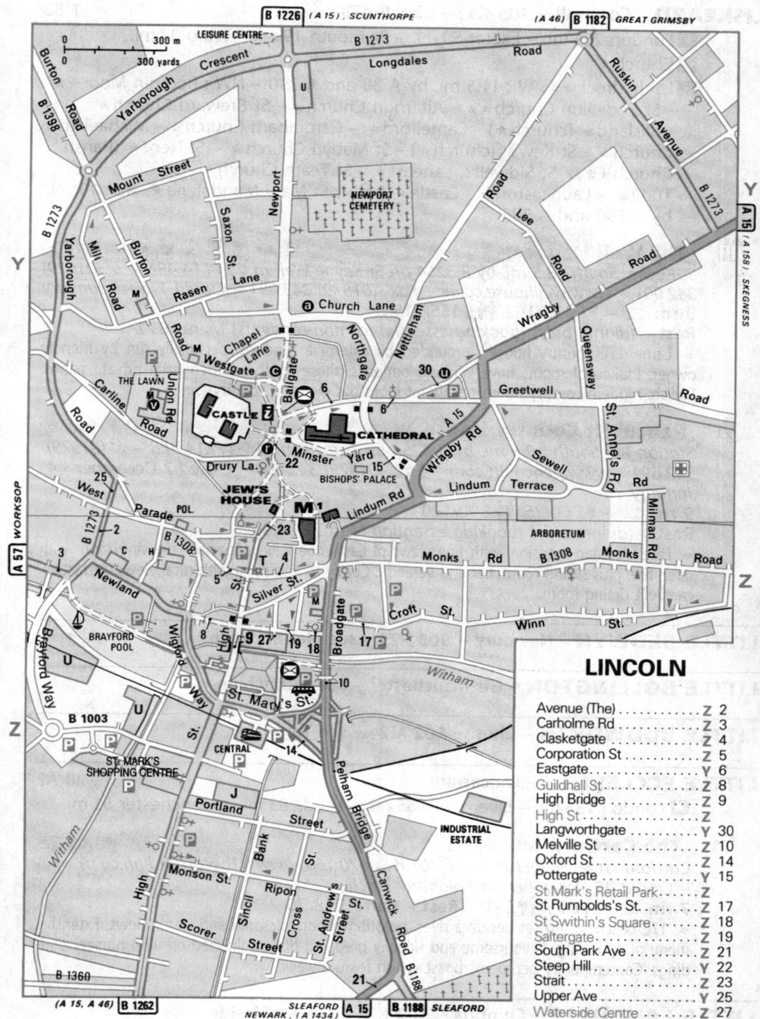

at Branston Southeast : 3.5 mi. by A 15 - Z - on B 1188 – ✉ Lincoln

Branston Hall

Lincoln Road ✉ LN4 1PD – ✆ (01522) 793 305 – www.branstonhall.com – Fax (01522) 790 734

50 rm – †£ 80 ††£ 110 – 1 suite

Rest – Menu £ 19/30 – Carte dinner £ 30/43

◆ Privately owned hall built in 1736, with additions. Stands in impressive grounds with lake. Bags of period charm, such as original wood panelling. Homely, comfortable rooms. Huge dining room has a formal feel and classical menus.

LISKEARD – Cornwall – 503 G32 – pop. 8 478 1 B2

London 261 mi. – Exeter 59 mi. – Plymouth 19 mi. – Truro 37 mi.

Church★

Lanhydrock★★, W : 11.5 mi. by A 38 and A 390 – NW : Bodmin Moor★★ - St Endellion Church★★ - Altarnun Church★ - St Breward Church★ - Blisland★ (church★) - Camelford★ – Cardinham Church★ - Michaelstow Church★ - St Kew★ (church★) - St Mabyn Church★ – St Neot★ (Parish Church★★) - St Sidwell's, Laneast★ - St Teath Church★ - St Tudy★ – Launceston★ - Castle★ (★) St Mary Magdalene★, NE : 19 mi. by A 390 and A 388

The Well House

St Keyne, South : 3.5 mi. by B 3254 on St Keyne Well rd ✉ PL14 4RN – ☎ (01579) 342 001 – www.wellhouse.co.uk – Fax (01579) 343 891 – Closed 1 week January

9 rm – †£ 139/162 ††£ 155/215

Rest – *(dinner only) (booking essential for non-residents)* Menu £ 27

◆ Large 19C country house surrounded by extensive grounds; personally run by friendly owner. Individual rooms have winning outlooks; those by the garden have private patios. Stylish, modern country house restaurant looks out over the countryside.

Pencubitt Country House

Station Rd, South : 0.5 mi. by B 3254 on Lamellion rd ✉ PL14 4EB – ☎ (01579) 342 694 – www.pencubitt.com – Fax (01579) 342 694 – Closed 7 December - 4 January

9 rm – †£ 60/75 ††£ 90/120

Rest – *(dinner only) (booking essential)* Menu £ 30 **s**

◆ Late Victorian mansion, with fine views of East Looe Valley. Spacious drawing room with open fire, plus sitting room, bar and veranda. Comfy rooms, most with rural views. Attractive, candlelit dining room.

LITTLE BEDWYN – Newbury – 503 P29 – see Marlborough

LITTLE BOLLINGTON – Gtr Manchester – see Altrincham

LITTLE BUDWORTH – Ches. – 502 M24 – see Tarporley

LITTLE ECCLESTON – Lancashire 20 A2

London 238 mi. – Liverpool - 55 mi. – Leeds 83 mi. – Manchester 51 mi.

The Cartford Inn with rm

Cartford Lane ✉ PR3 0YP – ☎ (01995) 670 166 – www.thecartfordinn.co.uk – Closed 25 December and Monday lunch

7 rm – †£ 65 ††£ 90 **Rest** – Carte £ 18/30

◆ 17C coaching inn set beside a river, boasting panoramic rural and water views. Extensive menu of appealing, flavoursome and skilfully prepared dishes, finished off with nursery puddings. Contemporary bedrooms boast stylish feature walls.

LITTLE LANGDALE – Cumbria – 502 K20 – see Ambleside

LITTLE LANGFORD – Wilts. – see Salisbury

LITTLE MARLOW – Buckinghamshire – see Marlow

LITTLE PETHERICK – Cornwall – 503 F32 – see Padstow

LITTLE SHELFORD – Cambs. – 504 U27 – see Cambridge

LITTLE THETFORD – Cambs. – see Ely

LITTLE WILBRAHAM – Cambs. – see Cambridge

LITTLEHAMPTON – West Sussex – **504** S31 – pop. 55 716 **7** C3

London 64 mi. – Brighton 18 mi. – Portsmouth 31 mi.

The Look and Sea Centre, 63-65 Surrey St (01903) 721866, littlehampton.vic@arun.gov.uk

Bailiffscourt & Spa

Climping St, Climping, West : 2.75 mi. by A 259
BN17 5RW – (01903) 723 511 – www.hshotels.co.uk
– Fax (01903) 723 107

39 rm – £ 240/340 £ 320/635

Rest – Menu £ 19/46

◆ Alluring reconstructed medieval house basking in acres of utterly peaceful grounds. Rich antiques and fine period features in an enchanting medieval ambience. Superb spa. Split-room dining area nestling amidst warmly tapestried walls.

Amberley Court without rest

Crookthorn Lane, Climping, West : 1.75 mi. by B 2187 off A 259 BN17 5SN – (01903) 725 131 – Fax (01903) 725 131 – Closed January, February and Christmas,

6 rm – £ 50 £ 89/105

◆ Converted farm barn with a tidy, homely atmosphere. Exposed beams, flourishing plants and a warm welcome. Simply decorated rooms, some in grounds, with traditional chintz.

C. Labonne/MICHELIN

LIVERPOOL

County: Merseyside
Michelin regional map: 502 L23
London 219 mi.
– Birmingham 103 mi.
– Leeds 75 mi. – Manchester 35 mi.

Population: 469 017
Great Britain
Map reference: 20 A3

PRACTICAL INFORMATION

Tourist Information

08 Place, 36-38 Whitechapel, ✆ (0151) 233 2459, 08place@liverpool.gov.uk

Airport

Liverpool John Lennon Airport: ✆ (0871) 521 8484, SE: 6 mi. by A 561 BX

Ferries and Shipping Lines

Tunnel

Mersey Tunnels (toll) AX

Golf Courses

27 Allerton Municipal Allerton Rd, ✆ (0151) 428 1046

18 Liverpool Municipal Kirby Ingoe Lane, ✆ (0151) 546 5435

9 Bowring Roby Rd, Bowring Park, ✆ (0151) 489 1901

SIGHTS

In town

City★ – The Walker★★ DY **M3** – Liverpool Cathedral★★ (Lady Chapel★) EZ – Metropolitan Cathedral of Christ the King★★ EY – Albert Dock★ CZ (Merseyside Maritime Museum★ **AC M2** - Tate Liverpool★)

In the surrounding area

Speke Hall★ **AC**, SE : 8 mi. by A 561 BX

LIVERPOOL

Street	Grid	No.
Aintree Lane	BV	2
Aintree Rd	AV	3
Allerton Rd	BX	5
Bailey Drive	AV	7
Belmont Rd	BX	8
Borough Rd	AX	11
Bowring Park Rd	BX	12
Breck Rd	ABX	13
Brewster St	AV	14
Bridge Rd	AV	16
Broad Green Rd	BX	18
Calderstones Rd	BX	21
Chester St	AX	24
Church St	DY	
Commercial Rd	AV	29
Copple House Lane	BV	33
County Rd	AV	34
Croxteth Hall Lane	BV	39
Croxteth Rd	BX	37
Durning Rd	BX	42
Dwerry House Lane	BV	43
Elmswood Rd	BX	44
Gainsborough Rd	BX	50
Great Howard St	AX, CY	56
Holt Rd	BX	61
Hornby Rd	AV	64
Kirkdale Rd	AV	71
Linacre Rd	AV	74
Lodge Lane	BX	77
Low Hill	ABX	79
Melrose Rd	AV	82
Mill Bank	BV	84

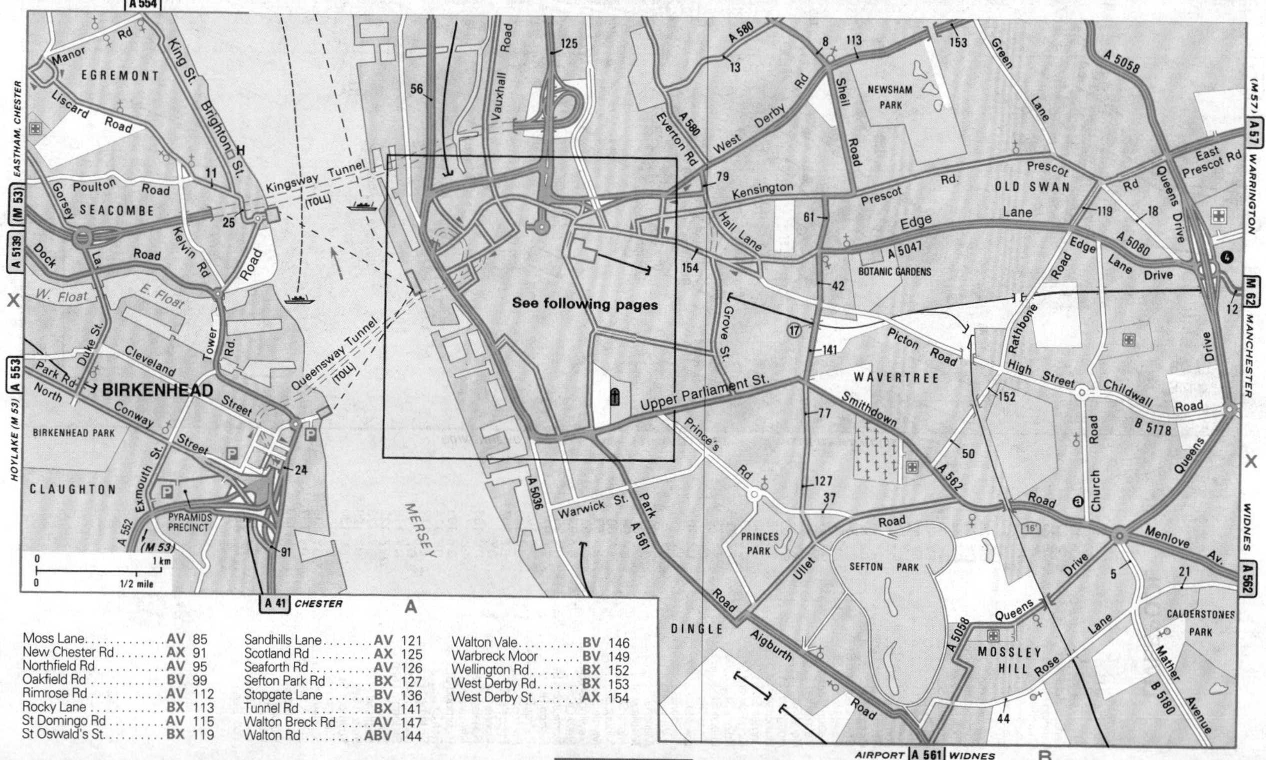

Street	Square	No.
Moss Lane	AV	85
New Chester Rd	AX	91
Northfield Rd	AV	95
Oakfield Rd	BV	99
Rimrose Rd	AV	112
Rocky Lane	BX	113
St Domingo Rd	AV	115
St Oswald's St	BX	119
Sandhills Lane	AV	121
Scotland Rd	AX	125
Seaforth Rd	AV	126
Sefton Park Rd	BX	127
Stopgate Lane	BV	136
Tunnel Rd	BX	141
Walton Breck Rd	AV	147
Walton Rd	ABV	144
Walton Vale	BV	146
Warbreck Moor	BV	149
Wellington Rd	BX	152
West Derby Rd	BX	153
West Derby St	AX	154

LIVERPOOL

Street	Grid	No.
Argyle St	DZ	6
Blackburne Pl.	EZ	10
Bold St.	DZ	
Brunswick Rd	EY	19
Canada Boulevard	CYZ	22
Canning Pl.	CZ	23
Churchill Way	DY	26
Church St	DY	
Clarence St	EYZ	27
Clayton Square Shopping Centre	DY	
College Lane	DZ	28
Commutation Row	DY	30
Cook St	CY	32
Crosshall St.	DY	36
Daulby St.	EY	40
Erskine St	EY	45
Fontenoy St	DY	48
Forrest St	DZ	49
George's Dock Lane	CY	51
Grafton St	DZ	53
Great Charlotte St	DY	54
Great Howard St	CY	56
Hatton Garden	DY	57
Haymarket	DY	58
Hood St.	DY	62
Houghton St	DY	65
Huskisson St	EZ	66
James St.	CY	68
King Edward St.	CY	69
Knight St	EZ	72
Leece St	EZ	73
Lime St	DY	
Liver St	CZ	76
London Rd	DEY	
Lord St	CDY	
Mansfield St.	DEY	80
Mathew St.	CDY	81
Moss St.	EY	86
Mount St	EZ	88
Myrtle St	EZ	89
Newington St	DZ	92
New Quay	CY	93
North John St	CY	96
Norton St.	EY	97
Parker St	DY	103
Prescot St	EY	105
Prince's Rd	EZ	107
Queen Square	DY	
Ranelagh St	DY	108
Renshaw St	DEZ	
Richmond St.	DY	109
Roe St	DY	114
St James Pl.	EZ	117
St John's Centre	DY	
St John's Lane	DY	118
School Lane	DYZ	122
Scotland Pl.	DY	123
Sefton St	DZ	129
Seymour St	EY	130
Skelhorne St	DY	133
Stanley St.	CDY	135
Suffolk St.	DZ	137
Tarleton St.	DY	139
Victoria St	DY	143
Water St	CY	150
William Brown St	DY	156
York St.	DZ	157

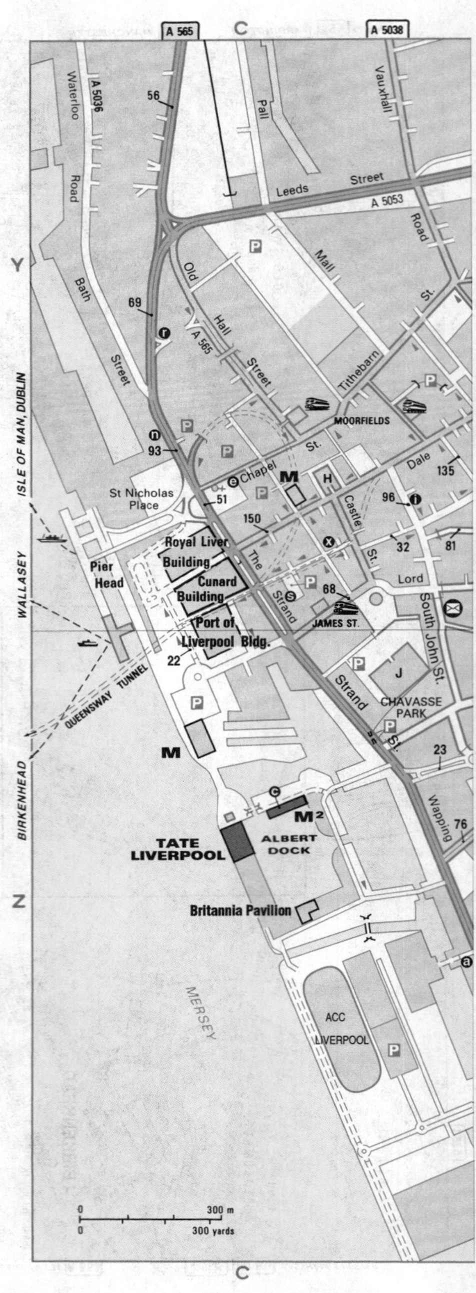

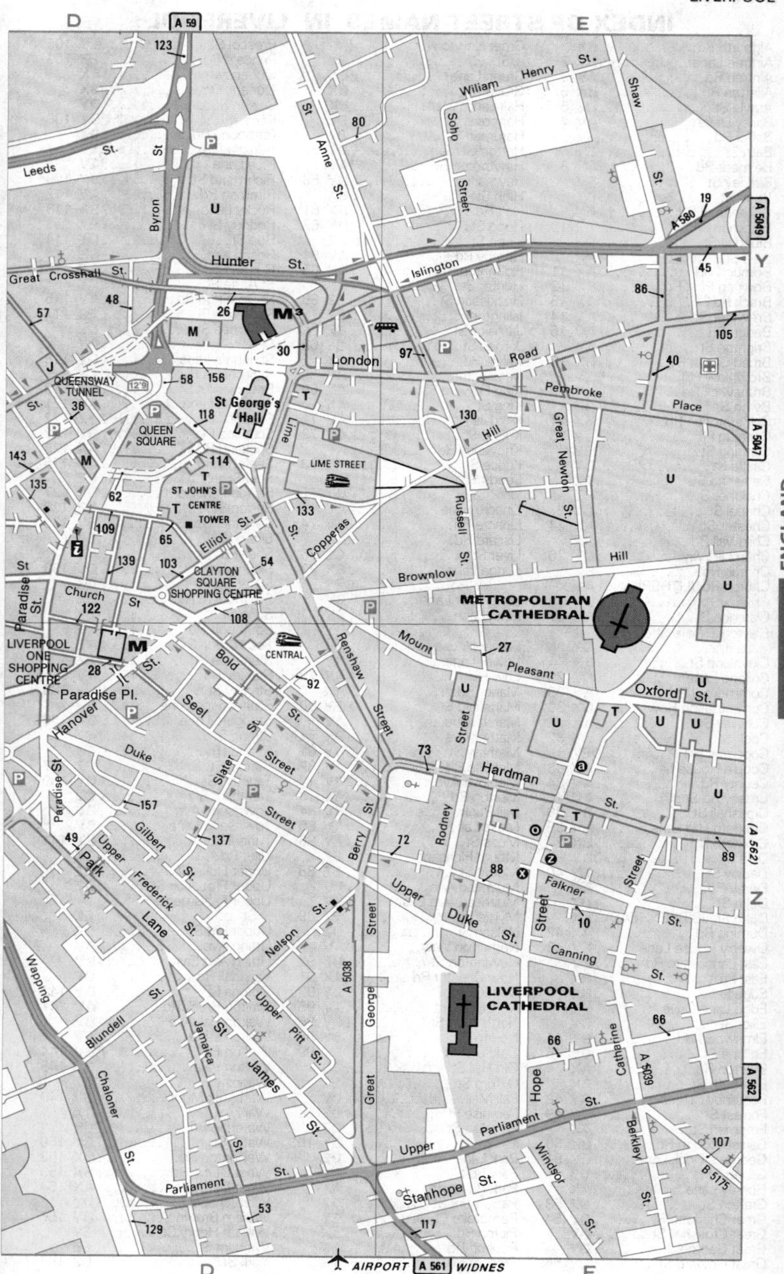
D
E
D
E
Y
Z
ENGLAND
METROPOLITAN CATHEDRAL
LIVERPOOL CATHEDRAL
St George's Hall
LIME STREET
CENTRAL
QUEEN SQUARE
QUEENSWAY TUNNEL
ST JOHN'S CENTRE TOWER
CLAYTON SQUARE SHOPPING CENTRE
LIVERPOOL ONE SHOPPING CENTRE
AIRPORT
A 561
WIDNES

INDEX OF STREET NAMES IN LIVERPOOL

ENGLAND

Malmaison

7 William Jessop Way, Princes Dock ✉ *L3 1QZ – ✆ (0151) 229 5000 – www.malmaison-liverpool.com – Fax (0151) 229 5002* CY**n**

130 rm – †£ 69/170 ††£ 69/170, ☕ £ 12.95 – 2 suites

Rest *Brasserie* – Menu £ 16 – Carte £ 19/33

◆ Eye-catching building in redeveloped area of city. Smart, up-to-date bedrooms; those on the waterside have best outlook. Plum evening lounge. Look out for Beatles memorabilia. Stylish brasserie with glass-fronted wine cellar serves extensive menu of classic French dishes.

Hope Street

40 Hope St ✉ *L1 9DA – ✆ (0151) 709 3000 – www.hopestreethotel.co.uk – Fax (0151) 709 2454* EZ**o**

89 rm – †£ 150 ††£ 150, ☕ £ 15.50 – 8 suites

Rest *The London Carriage Works* – see restaurant listing

◆ Boutique hotel in 'arty' location; formerly a carriage works. Stylish, understated bedrooms boast underfloor heating, quality furnishings and some rooftop/river views. Trendy bar open Thurs-Sat.

Hard Days Night

Central Buildings, North John St ✉ *L2 6RR – ✆ (0151) 236 19 64 – www.harddaysnighthotel.com – Fax (0151) 243 21 54* CY**i**

110 rm – †£ 105/280 ††£ 105/280, ☕ £ 12.50 – 2 suites

Rest *Blakes* – *(closed Sunday and Monday)* Menu £ 10 (lunch) – Carte £ 18/39

◆ Unique Beatles themed hotel; their story recounted in artwork from doorstep to rooftop, with every room featuring original works. Suites styled around Lennon and McCartney. Blakes restaurant features modern style brasserie menu.

Racquet Club

Hargreaves Buildings, 5 Chapel St ✉ *L3 9AG – ✆ (0151) 236 6676 – www.racquetclub.org – Fax (0151) 236 6870 – Closed Christmas and Bank Holidays* CY**e**

8 rm – †£ 110/150 ††£ 110/150, ☕ £ 12

Rest *Ziba* – see restaurant listing

◆ Ornate Victorian city centre building converted into club offering unusual accommodation. Leisure facilities are a particularly strong point. Simple, well-equipped rooms.

Panoramic

34th floor, West Tower, ✉ *L3 9PJ – ✆ (0151) 236 55 34 – www.panoramicliverpool.com – Fax (0151) 227 43 96 – Closed Saturday lunch, Sunday and Bank Holidays* CY**r**

Rest – Menu £ 20 (lunch) – Carte dinner £ 24/52

◆ Highest restaurant in the UK, with 360° views towards Wales, the coast, Liverpool and the Mersey below. Cooking is creative, ambitious and well executed; good value lunch.

60 Hope Street

60 Hope St ✉ *L1 9BZ – ✆ (0151) 707 6060 – www.60hopestreet.com – Fax (0151) 707 6016 – Closed Saturday lunch, Sunday and Bank Holidays* EZ**x**

Rest – Menu £ 20 (lunch) – Carte £ 33/50

◆ Attractive Grade II listed Georgian house concealing well-established modern brasserie with bold feature walls and informal basement wine bar. Interesting regional dishes provide good value.

The London Carriage Works – at Hope Street Hotel

40 Hope St ✉ *L1 9DA – ✆ (0151) 705 2222 – www.thelondoncarriageworks.co.uk – Fax (0151) 709 2454* EZ**o**

Rest – Menu £ 24 – Carte dinner Thursday-Sunday £ 46/54

◆ Spacious, open-plan brasserie dominated by impressive glass sculpture, with long bar, squashy sofas and relaxed ambience. Modern European brasserie dishes include some sharing plates.

ENGLAND

XX **Simply Heathcotes**

Beetham Plaza, 25 The Strand ✉ L2 0XL – ✆ (0151) 236 3536 – www.heathcotes.co.uk – Fax (0151) 236 3534 – Closed 25-26 December, 1 January and Bank Holidays CY**s**

Rest – Carte £ 20/35

◆ Modern brasserie hidden away in courtyard, behind striking sloped glass façade. Small bar overlooks The Strand and Liver building. Menus feature well-sourced, high quality local produce.

XX **The Restaurant bar and grill**

Halifax House, Brunswick St ✉ L2 0UU – ✆ (0151) 236 67 03 – www.therestaurantbarandgrill.co.uk – Fax (0151) 236 67 21 – Closed 25 December and 1 January CY**x**

Rest – Carte £ 23/42

◆ Spacious former banking hall, divided by huge glass wine racks. Large menu of homemade produce; mainly modern European fare, with some British classics and influences from Asia.

XX **Ziba** – at Racquet Club Hotel

Hargreaves Buildings, 5 Chapel St ✉ L3 9AG – ✆ (0151) 236 6676 – www.racquetclub.org – Fax (0151) 236 6870 – Closed Christmas, Saturday lunch, Sunday and Bank Holidays CY**e**

Rest – Menu £ 18 **s** – Carte £ 30/40 **s**

◆ Modern restaurant in old Victorian building with huge windows and artwork on walls. Small lunch menus, more extensive dinner menus, offering classic-based modern dishes.

ENGLAND

XX **Spire**

1 Church Rd ✉ L15 9EA – ✆ (0151) 734 5040 – www.spirerestaurant.co.uk – Fax (0151) 735 0058 – Closed 2 weeks January, Sunday, and lunch Monday and Saturday BX**a**

Rest – Menu £ 13/15 – Carte £ 22/31

◆ Named after its location in 'Church' Road: a simple neighbourhood eatery adorned with mirrors and abstract art. Homemade regional and modern European dishes. Good value set lunch/early dinner.

X **Host**

31 Hope St ✉ L1 9HX – ✆ (0151) 708 5831 – www.ho-st.co.uk – Fax (0151) 707 6016 – closed 25-26 December and 1 January EZ**z**

Rest – Asian – Carte £ 16/21

◆ Lively place with trendy bar and informal dining area of refectory-style tables. Wide range of Asian-inspired dishes, including Chinese, Japanese, Thai and Vietnamese. Good desserts.

X **Maritime Dining Room**

Merseyside Maritime Museum, 4th Floor ✉ L3 4AQ – ✆ (0151) 478 4056 – www.liverpoolmuseums.org.uk – Fax (0151) 478 4447 – Closed 25-26 December CZ**c**

Rest – *(lunch only) (booking advisable)* Carte £ 16/20

◆ Spacious brasserie located in superb museum, with great views of the Albert Dock/the Three Graces. Well-priced, appealing menu of tasty, modern brasserie dishes.

X **The Side Door**

29a Hope St ✉ L1 9BQ – ✆ (0151) 707 7888 – www.thesidedoor.co.uk – Fax (0151) 707 7888 – Closed 25-26 December, 1 January, Sunday and Bank Holidays EZ**a**

Rest – Menu £ 18 (dinner) – Carte £ 23/28

◆ Split-level bistro with attractive window boxes, warm décor and relaxed style: popular with locals and theatre-goers. Light lunch; modern European à la carte. Good value, fresh and simple.

at Blundellsands North : 7.5 mi. by A 565 - CY – ✉ **Liverpool**

The Blundellsands without rest

9 Elton Ave ✉ L23 8UN – ✆ (0151) 924 6947 – www.blundellsands.info – Fax (0151) 924 6947

4 rm – †£ 49/59 ††£ 79

◆ Large semi-detached guesthouse with residential setting. Comfortable guests' lounge; the bedrooms, chintz in style, are clean, well-kept and have lots of extra touches.

LIZARD – Cornwall – 503 E34 1 A3

London 326 mi. – Penzance 24 mi. – Truro 29 mi.

Lizard Peninsula★ - Mullion Cove★★ (Church★) - Kynance Cove★★ - Cadgwith★ - Coverack★ – Cury★ (Church★) - Gunwalloe Fishing Cove★ - St Keverne (Church★) - Landewednack★ (Church★) – Mawgan-in-Meneage (Church★) - Ruan Minor (Church★) - St Anthony-in-Meneage★

Housel Bay

Housel Bay ✉ *TR12 7PG – ✆ (01326) 290 417 – www.houselbay.com – Fax (01326) 290 359*

21 rm – £ 55/110 £ 79/140

Rest – *(bar lunch Monday-Saturday)* Carte £ 24/36

◆ Britain's most southerly mainland hotel, with spectacular views of Atlantic and Channel: the Cornish coastal path runs through its gardens. Comfortable bedrooms. Dining room affords dramatic sea and lighthouse views.

Landewednack House

Church Cove, East : 1 mi. by A 3083 ✉ *TR12 7PQ – ✆ (01326) 290 877 – www.landewednackhouse.com – Fax (01326) 290 192*

4 rm – £ 55/100 £ 110/190

Rest – *(communal dining)* Menu £ 33

◆ Part 17C former rectory and garden, overlooking Church Cove. Smart interiors stylishly furnished with antiques. Diners encouraged to discuss menus: best local produce to hand.

ENGLAND

C. Eymenier/MICHELIN

LONDON

Map reference: 12 B3

PRACTICAL INFORMATION

Tourist Information

Britain & London Visitor Centre, Thames Tower, Black Rd, W6 ✆ (020) 8846 9000, bvlcenquiry@visitlondon.com

Airports

Heathrow ✆ 0844 335 1801 **12** AX Terminal: Bus and Coach services run regularly, each day from Victoria. By Rail: Heathrow Express and Connect from Paddington Underground, daily every 20 minutes.

Gatwick ✆ 0844 335 1802 **13**: by A23 EZ and M23 - Terminal: Coach services from Victoria Coach Station run regularly each day. By Rail: Gatwick Express from Victoria Underground, daily every 15 minutes. Southern Trains every 15 minutes from Victoria, London Bridge and Clapham Junction

London City Airport ✆ (020) 7646 0088 **11** HV

Stansted, at Bishop's Stortford ✆ 0844 335 1803, NE: 34m **11** by M11 JT and A12O.

British Airways, Ticket sales and reservations, Paddington Station London, W2, ✆08700 8509 8500 **36** BX

Banks

Open, generally 9.30 am to 4.30 pm weekdays (except public holidays). You need ID (passport) for cashing cheques. Banks levy smaller commissions than hotels. Many 'Bureaux de Change' around Piccadilly open 7 days.

Medical Emergencies

To contact a doctor for first aid, emergency medical advice and chemists night service: ✆ 07000 372255.

Accident & Emergency: dial 999 for Ambulance, Police or Fire Services.

Post Offices

Open Monday to Friday 9am to 5.30 pm. Late collections made from Leicester Square.

Shopping

Most stores are found in Oxford Street (Selfridges, M & S), Regent Street (Hamleys, Libertys) and Knightsbridge (Harrods, Harvey Nichols). Open usually Monday to Saturday 9 am to 6 pm. Some open later (8 pm) once a week; Knightsbridge Wednesday, Oxford Street and Regent Street Thursday. Other areas worth visiting include Jermyn Street and Savile Row (mens outfitters), Bond Street (jewellers and haute couture).

Theatres

The "West End" has many major theatre performances and can generally be found around Shaftesbury Avenue. Most daily newspapers give details of performances. A half-price ticket booth is located in Leicester Square and is open Monday to Saturday 1 pm to 6.30 pm, Sunday and matinée days 12 noon to 6.30 pm. Restrictions apply.

Tipping

When a service charge is included in a bill it is not necessary to tip extra. If service is not included a discretionary 10% is normal.

Travel

As driving in London is difficult, it is advisable to take the Underground, a bus or taxi. Taxis can be hailed when the amber light is illuminated.

Congestion Charging

The congestion charge is £ 8 per day on all vehicles (except motor cycles and exempt vehicles) entering the central zone between 7.00 am and 6.00 pm - Monday to Friday except on Bank Holldays.

Payment can be made in advance, on the day, by post, on the Internet, by telephone (0845 900 1234) or at retail outlets.

A charge of up to £ 100 will be made for non-payment.

Further information is available on the Transport for London website - www.tfl.gov.uk

Localities outside the Greater London limits are listed alphabetically throughout the guide.

SIGHTS

Historical Buildings and Monuments

Palace of Westminster★★★: House of Lords★★, Westminster Hall★ (hammerbeam roof★★★), Robing Room★, Central Lobby★, House of Commons★, Big Ben★, Victoria Tower★ 39 ALX - Tower of London★★★ (Crown Jewels★★★, White Tower or Keep★★★, St John's Chapel★★) - British Airways London Eye (views★★★) 32 AMV.

Banqueting House★★ 31 ALV - Buckingham Palace★★ (Changing of the Guard, Royal Mews★★, Queen's Gallery★★) 38 AIX - Kensington Palace★★ 27 ABV - Lincoln's Inn★★ 32 AMT - Lloyds Building★★ 34 ARU - Royal Hospital Chelsea★★ 37 AGZ - St James's Palace★★ 30 AJV - Somerset House★★ 32 AMU - South Bank Arts Centre★★ (Royal Festival Hall★, National Theatre Royal★, County Hall★) 32 AMV - Spencer House★★ 30 AIV - The Temple★★ (Middle Temple Hall★★) 32 ANU - Tower Bridge★★ 34 ASV.

Albert Memorial★ 36 ADX - Apsley House★ 30 AHV - Burlington House★ 30 AIV - Charterhouse★ 19 UZD - George Inn★, Southwark 33 AQV - Gray's Inn★ 32 AMV - Guildhall★ (Lord Mayor's Show) 33 AQT - Shakespeare's Globe★ 33 APV - Dr Johnson's House★ 32 ANT - Leighton House★ 35 AAX - Linley Sambourne House★ 35 AAX - London Bridge★ 34 ARV - Mansion House★ (plate and insignia★★) 33 AQV - The Monument★ (⁂★) 34 ARU - Old Admiralty★ 31 AKV - Royal Albert Hall★ 36 ADX - Royal Exchange★ 34 ARU - Royal Opera House★ (Covent Garden) 31 ALU - Staple Inn★ 32 ANT - Theatre Royal★ (Haymarket) 31 AKV - Westminster Bridge★ 39 ALX.

Churches

The City Churches
St Paul's Cathedral★★★ (Dome ⋞★★★) 33 APU.

St Bartholomew the Great★★ (choir★) 33 APT - St Dunstan-in-the-East★ (Tower★) 34 ARU - St Mary-at-Hill★★ (plan★) 34 ARU - Temple Church★★ 32 ANU.

All Hallows-by-the-Tower (font cover★★, brasses★) 34 ARU - Christ Church★ 33 APT - Cole Abbey Presbyterian Church (spire★) 33 APU - St Andrew Undershaft (monuments★) 34 ARU - St Bride★ (steeple★★) 32 ANU - St Clement Eastcheap (pulpit★) 34 ARU - St Edmund the King and Martyr (spire★) 34 ARU - St Giles Cripplegate★ 33 AQT - St Helen

Bishopsgate★ (monuments★★) 34 ART - St James Garlickhythe (spire★, sword rests★) 33 AQU - St Magnus the Martyr (tower★, sword rest★) 34 ARU - St Margaret Lothbury★ (spire★, woodwork★, screen★, font★) 33 AQT - St Margaret Pattens (spire★, woodwork★) 34 ARU - St Martin-within-Ludgate (spire★, door cases★) 33 APU - St Mary Abchurch★ (reredos★★, spire★, dome★) 33 AQU - St Mary-le-Bow (steeple★★) 33 AQU - St Michael Paternoster Royal (spire★) 35 AQU - St Olave★ 34 ARU - St Peter upon Cornhill (screen★) 34 ARU - St Stephen Walbrook★ (steeple★, dome★) 33 AQU.

Other Churches

Westminster Abbey★★★ (Henry VII Chapel★★★, Chapel of Edward the Confessor★★, Chapter House★★, Poets' Corner★) 39 ALX.

Southwark Cathedral★★ 33 AQV.

Queen's Chapel★ 39 AJV - St Clement Danes★ 32 AMU - St James's★ 30 AJV - St Margaret's★ 39 ALX - St Martin-in-the-Fields★ 31 ALV - St Paul's★ (Covent Garden) 31 ALU - Westminster Roman Catholic Cathedral★ 39 ALX.

Parks

Regent's Park★★★ (terraces★★, Zoo★★) 11 QZC.

Hyde Park 29 AFV - Kensington Gardens★★ 28 ACV (Orangery★) 27 ABV - St James's Park★★31 AKV.

Streets and Squares

The City★★★ 33 AQT.

Bedford Square★★ 31 AKT - Belgrave Square★★ 37 AGX - Burlington Arcade★ 30 AIV - Covent Garden★★ (The Piazza★★) 31 ALU - The Mall★★ 31 AKV - Piccadilly★ 30 AIV - Trafalgar Square★★ 31 AKV - Whitehall★★ (Horse Guards★) 31 ALV.

Barbican★ 33 AQT - Bond Street★ 30 AIU - Canonbury Square★ 13 UZB - Carlton House Terrace★ 31 AKV - Cheyne Walk★ 23 PZG - Fitzroy Square★ 18 RZD - Jermyn Street★ 30 AJV - Leicester Square★ 31 AKU - Merrick Square★ 19 VZE - Montpelier Square★ 37 AFX - Neal's Yard★ 31 ALU - Piccadilly Arcade★ 30 AIV - Piccadilly Circus★ 31 AKU - Portman Square★ 29 AGT - Regent Street★ 30 AIU - Royal Opera Arcade★ 31 AKV - St James's Square★ 31 AJV - St James's Street★ 30 AIV - Shepherd Market★ 30 AHV - Trinity Church Square★ 19 VZE - Victoria Embankment Gardens★ 31 ALV - Waterloo Place★ 31 AKV.

Museums

British Museum★★★ 31 AKL - Imperial War Museum★★★ 40 ANY - National Gallery★★★ 31 AKV - Science Museum★★★ 36 ADX - Tate Britain★★★ 39 ALY - Victoria and Albert Museum★★★ 36 ADY - Wallace Collection★★★ 29 AGT.

Courtauld Institute Galleries★★ (Somerset House) 32 AMU - Gilbert Collection★★ (Somerset House) 32 AMU - Museum of London★★ 33 APT - National Portrait Gallery★★ 31 AKU - Natural History Museum★★ 36 ADY - Sir John Soane's Museum★★ 32 AMT - Tate Modern★★ (views★★★ from top floors) 33 APV.

Clock Museum★ (Guildhall) 33 AQT - London's Transport Museum★ 31 ALU - Madame Tussaud's Waxworks★ 17 QZD - National Army Museum★ 37 AGZ - Percival David Foundation of Chinese Art★ 18 SZD - Wellington Museum★ (Apsley House) 30 AHV.

Outer London

Blackheath 8 HX terraces and houses★, Eltham Palace★ **A**

Brentford 5 BX Syon Park★★, gardens★

Bromley 7 GXY The Crystal Palace Park★

Chiswick 6 CV Chiswick Mall★★, Chiswick House★ **D**, Hogarth's House★ **E**

Dulwich 11 Picture Gallery★ FX **X**

Greenwich 7 and 8 GHV Cutty Sark★★ GV **F**, Footway Tunnel (⋞ ★★), Fan Museum★ 10 GV **A**, National Maritime

Museum★★ (Queen's House★★) GV **M²**
Royal Naval College★★ (Painted Hall★, the Chapel★) GV **G**, The Park and Old Royal Observatory★ (Meridian Building: collection★★) HV **K**, Ranger's House★ (Wernher Collection) GX **N**
Hampstead Kenwood House★★ (Adam Library★★, paintings★★) 2 EU **P**, Fenton House★★ 11 PZA
Hampton Court 5 BY (The Palace★★★, gardens★★★, Fountain Court★, The Great Vine★)
Kew 6 CX Royal Botanic Gardens★★★: Palm House★★, Temperate House★, Kew Palace or Dutch House★★, Orangery★, Pagoda★, Japanese Gateway★
Hendon★ 2 Royal Air Force Museum★★ CT **M³**
Hounslow 5 BV Osterley Park★★
Lewisham 7 GX Horniman Museum★ **M⁴**
Richmond 5 and 6 CX Richmond Park★★, ❋★★★ CX, Richmond Hill❋★★ CX, Richmond Bridge★★ BX **R**, Richmond Green★★ BX **S**, (Maids of Honour Row★★, Trumpeter's House★), Asgill House★ BX **B**, Ham House★★ BX **V**
Shoreditch 14 XZ Beffrye Museum★ **M**
Tower Hamlets 7 GV Canary Wharf★★ B, Isle of Dogs★ St Katharine Dock★ 34 ASV
Twickenham 5 BX Marble Hill House★ **Z**, Strawberry Hill★ **A**

The maps in this section of the Guide are based upon the Ordnance Survey of Great Britain with the permission of the Controller of Her Majesty's Stationery Office.

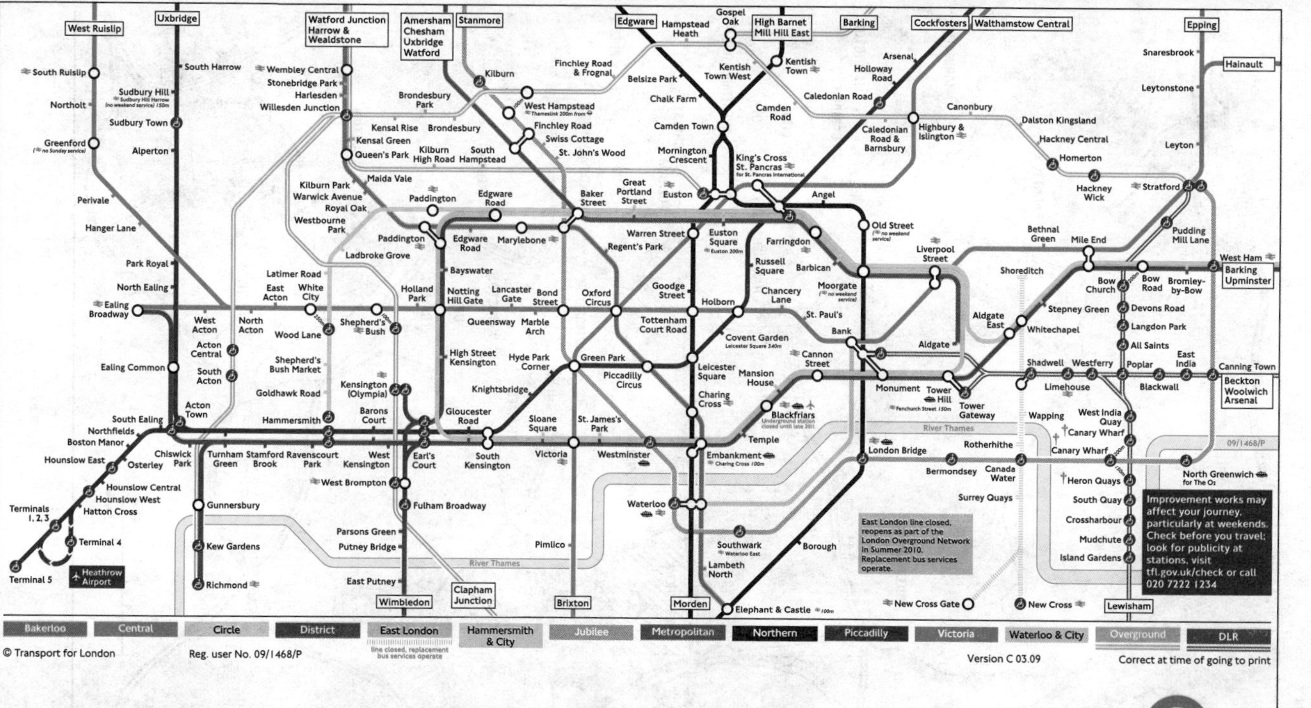
West Ruislip
Uxbridge
Watford Junction
Harrow & Wealdstone
Amersham
Chesham
Uxbridge
Watford
Stanmore
Edgware
Hampstead Heath
Gospel Oak
High Barnet
Mill Hill East
Barking
Cockfosters
Walthamstow Central
Epping
Hainault
Snaresbrook
Leytonstone
Leyton
South Ruislip
South Harrow
Sudbury Hill
Northolt
Sudbury Town
Greenford
Alperton
Perivale
Hanger Lane
Park Royal
North Ealing
Ealing Broadway
Wembley Central
Stonebridge Park
Harlesden
Willesden Junction
Kensal Rise
Brondesbury
Brondesbury Park
Kensal Green
Queen's Park
Kilburn High Road
South Hampstead
Kilburn
West Hampstead
Finchley Road & Frognal
Finchley Road
Swiss Cottage
St. John's Wood
Belsize Park
Chalk Farm
Kentish Town West
Kentish Town
Camden Town
Camden Road
Caledonian Road
Holloway Road
Arsenal
Caledonian Road & Barnsbury
Highbury & Islington
Canonbury
Dalston Kingsland
Hackney Central
Homerton
Hackney Wick
Stratford
Pudding Mill Lane
West Ham
Barking
Upminster
Mornington Crescent
King's Cross St. Pancras
Euston
Great Portland Street
Baker Street
Maida Vale
Kilburn Park
Warwick Avenue
Royal Oak
Westbourne Park
Paddington
Edgware Road
Marylebone
Ladbroke Grove
Latimer Road
Bayswater
Angel
Old Street
Warren Street
Euston Square
Regent's Park
Farringdon
Barbican
Russell Square
Liverpool Street
Bethnal Green
Mile End
Shoreditch
Bow Church
Bow Road
Bromley-by-Bow
Devons Road
Langdon Park
All Saints
East Acton
White City
Holland Park
Notting Hill Gate
Lancaster Gate
Bond Street
Oxford Circus
Goodge Street
Holborn
Chancery Lane
Moorgate
St. Paul's
Stepney Green
Whitechapel
Aldgate East
West Acton
North Acton
Wood Lane
Shepherd's Bush
Queensway
Marble Arch
Tottenham Court Road
Covent Garden
Bank
Aldgate
Acton Central
Ealing Common
South Acton
Shepherd's Bush Market
High Street Kensington
Hyde Park Corner
Green Park
Piccadilly Circus
Leicester Square
Mansion House
Cannon Street
Monument
Tower Hill
Tower Gateway
Shadwell
Westferry
Poplar
East India
Canning Town
Beckton
Woolwich Arsenal
Limehouse
Blackwall
Kensington (Olympia)
Goldhawk Road
Knightsbridge
Charing Cross
Blackfriars
Wapping
West India Quay
Canary Wharf
Acton Town
South Ealing
Northfields
Boston Manor
Hounslow East
Osterley
Chiswick Park
Hammersmith
Barons Court
Gloucester Road
Sloane Square
St. James's Park
Temple
River Thames
London Bridge
Rotherhithe
09/1468/P
Turnham Green
Stamford Brook
Ravenscourt Park
West Kensington
Earl's Court
South Kensington
Victoria
Westminster
Embankment
Bermondsey
Canada Water
Heron Quays
North Greenwich for The O2
Hounslow Central
Hounslow West
Hatton Cross
Terminals 1, 2, 3
Terminal 4
Terminal 5
Heathrow Airport
Gunnersbury
West Brompton
Fulham Broadway
Parsons Green
Putney Bridge
East Putney
Kew Gardens
Richmond
Pimlico
Waterloo
Southwark
Lambeth North
Borough
Surrey Quays
South Quay
Crossharbour
Mudchute
Island Gardens
Elephant & Castle
New Cross Gate
New Cross
Wimbledon
Clapham Junction
Brixton
Morden
Lewisham
East London line closed, reopens as part of the London Overground Network in Summer 2010. Replacement bus services operate.
Improvement works may affect your journey, particularly at weekends. Check before you travel; look for publicity at stations, visit tfl.gov.uk/check or call 020 7222 1234
Bakerloo
Central
Circle
District
East London
line closed, replacement bus services operate
Hammersmith & City
Jubilee
Metropolitan
Northern
Piccadilly
Victoria
Waterloo & City
Overground
DLR
© Transport for London
Reg. user No. 09/1468/P
Version C 03.09
Correct at time of going to print
MAYOR OF LONDON
Website
tfl.gov.uk
24 hour travel information
020 7222 1234
Transport for London
UNDERGROUND

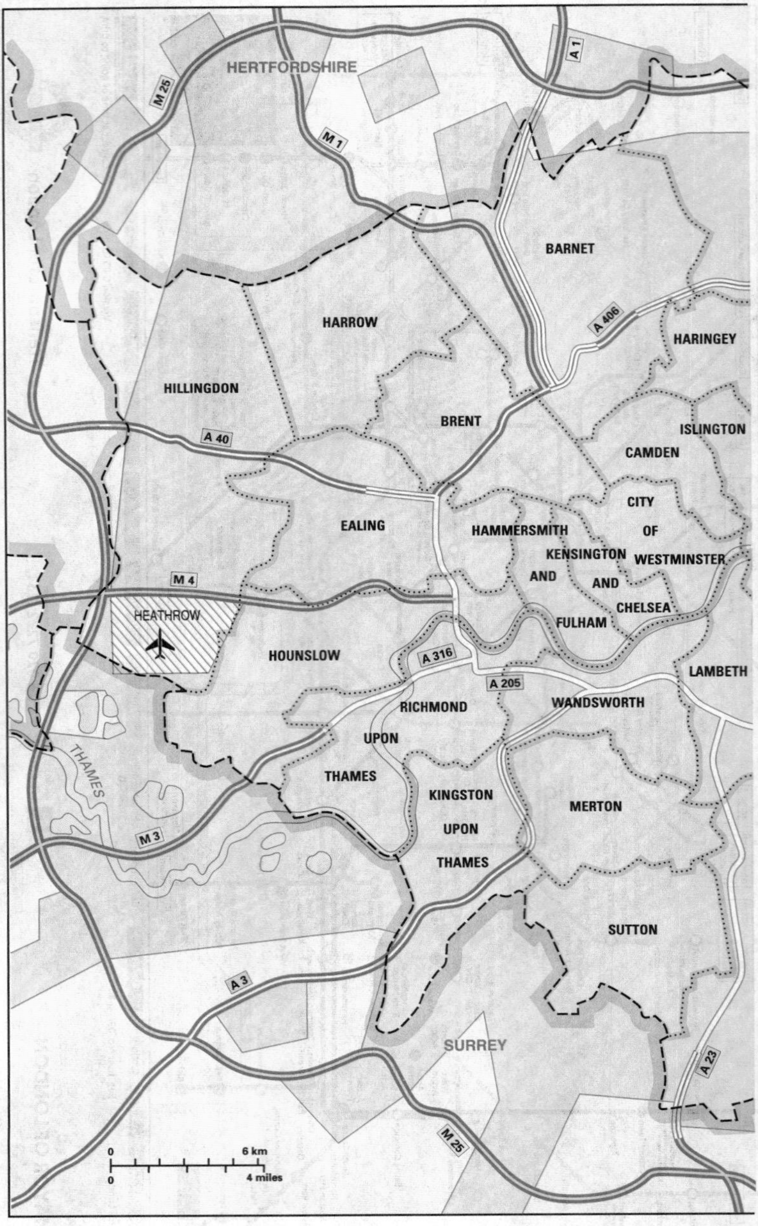

HERTFORDSHIRE

M 25

M 1

A 1

BARNET

A 406

HARROW

HARINGEY

HILLINGDON

BRENT

ISLINGTON

A 40

CAMDEN

CITY

EALING

HAMMERSMITH

OF

KENSINGTON

WESTMINSTER

AND

AND

M 4

CHELSEA

HEATHROW

FULHAM

HOUNSLOW

A 316

LAMBETH

A 205

RICHMOND

WANDSWORTH

UPON

THAMES

THAMES

KINGSTON

MERTON

UPON

M 3

THAMES

SUTTON

A 3

SURREY

A 23

M 25

0 6 km

0 4 miles

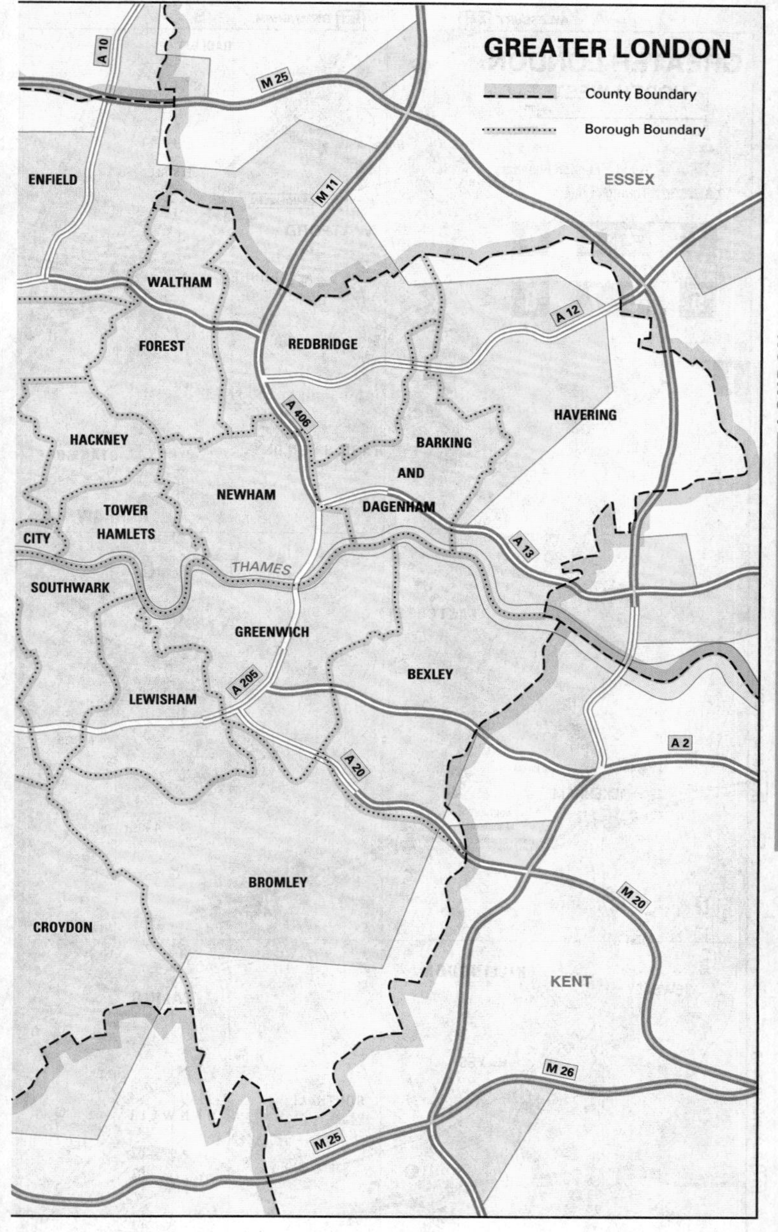
GREATER LONDON
County Boundary
Borough Boundary
ESSEX
ENFIELD
WALTHAM
FOREST
REDBRIDGE
HAVERING
HACKNEY
BARKING
AND
DAGENHAM
NEWHAM
TOWER
HAMLETS
CITY
THAMES
SOUTHWARK
GREENWICH
BEXLEY
LEWISHAM
BROMLEY
CROYDON
KENT
A 10
M 25
M 11
A 12
A 406
A 13
A 205
A 20
A 2
M 20
M 26

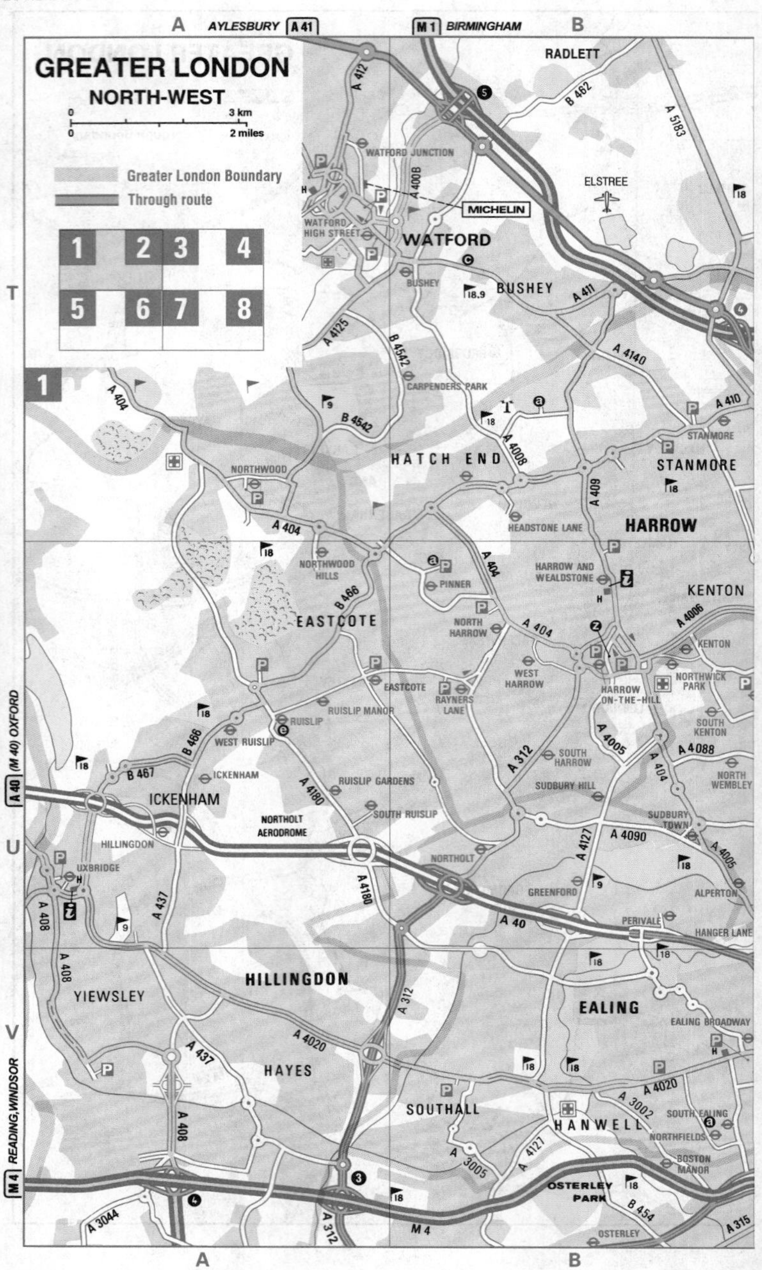
GREATER LONDON
NORTH-WEST
0 3 km
0 2 miles
Greater London Boundary
Through route
1 2 3 4
5 6 7 8
AYLESBURY A 41
M 1 BIRMINGHAM
A
B
T
U
V
LONDON
A 40 (M 40) OXFORD
M 4 READING, WINDSOR
RADLETT
WATFORD JUNCTION
MICHELIN
ELSTREE
WATFORD HIGH STREET
WATFORD
BUSHEY
CARPENDERS PARK
HATCH END
STANMORE
NORTHWOOD
HEADSTONE LANE
HARROW
NORTHWOOD HILLS
PINNER
HARROW AND WEALDSTONE
KENTON
EASTCOTE
NORTH HARROW
WEST HARROW
NORTHWICK PARK
RAYNERS LANE
HARROW ON-THE-HILL
RUISLIP MANOR
RUISLIP
WEST RUISLIP
SOUTH KENTON
SOUTH HARROW
ICKENHAM
RUISLIP GARDENS
SUDBURY HILL
NORTH WEMBLEY
NORTHOLT AERODROME
SOUTH RUISLIP
SUDBURY TOWN
HILLINGDON
NORTHOLT
UXBRIDGE
GREENFORD
ALPERTON
PERIVALE
HANGER LANE
YIEWSLEY
EALING
EALING BROADWAY
HAYES
SOUTHALL
HANWELL
SOUTH EALING
NORTHFIELDS
BOSTON MANOR
OSTERLEY PARK
OSTERLEY
M 4
A 412
A 400B
B 462
A 5183
A 411
A 4125
B 4542
A 4140
A 404
A 4008
A 410
A 409
B 466
A 4006
A 312
A 4005
A 4088
B 467
A 4180
A 4127
A 4090
A 437
A 408
A 40
A 4020
A 3002
A 3005
B 454
A 3044
A 315

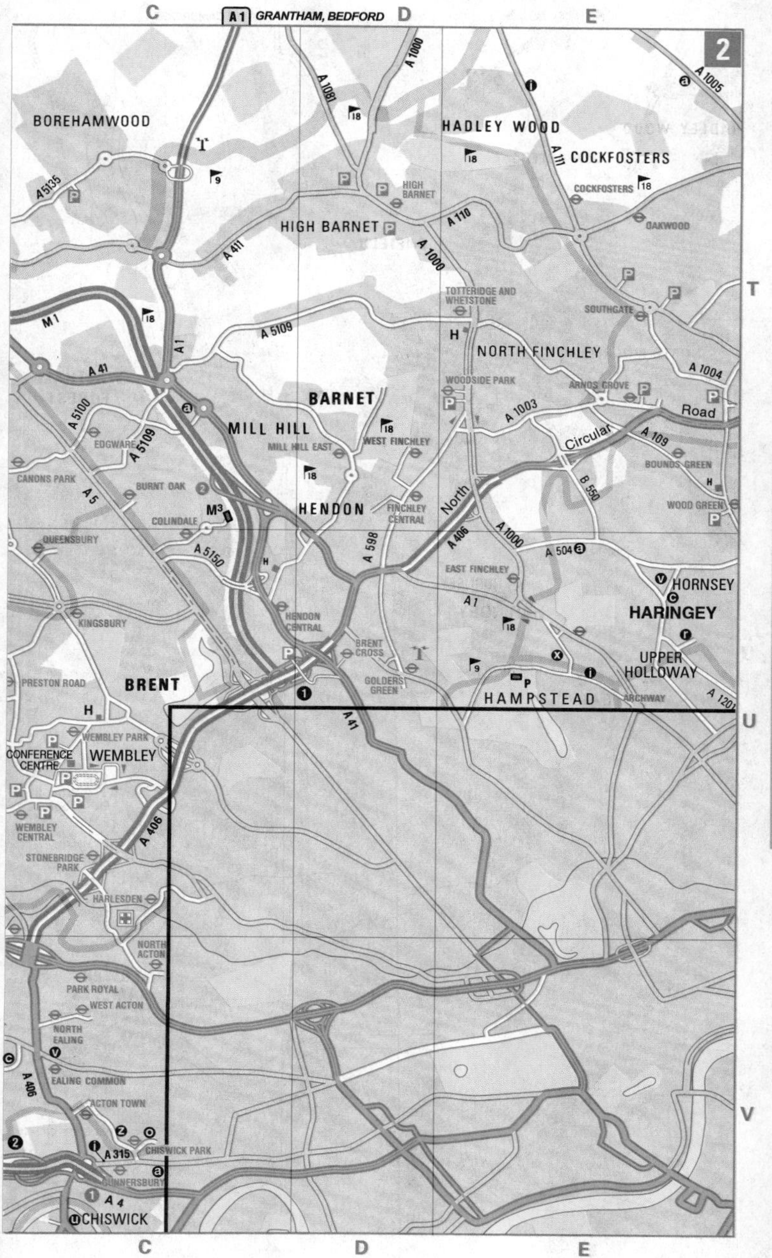
A1 GRANTHAM, BEDFORD
BOREHAMWOOD
HADLEY WOOD
COCKFOSTERS
HIGH BARNET
TOTTERIDGE AND WHETSTONE
SOUTHGATE
NORTH FINCHLEY
BARNET
MILL HILL
EDGWARE
HENDON
HORNSEY
HARINGEY
UPPER HOLLOWAY
BRENT
HAMPSTEAD
WEMBLEY
HARLESDEN
PARK ROYAL
WEST ACTON
NORTH EALING
EALING COMMON
ACTON TOWN
CHISWICK PARK
GUNNERSBURY
CHISWICK
LONDON

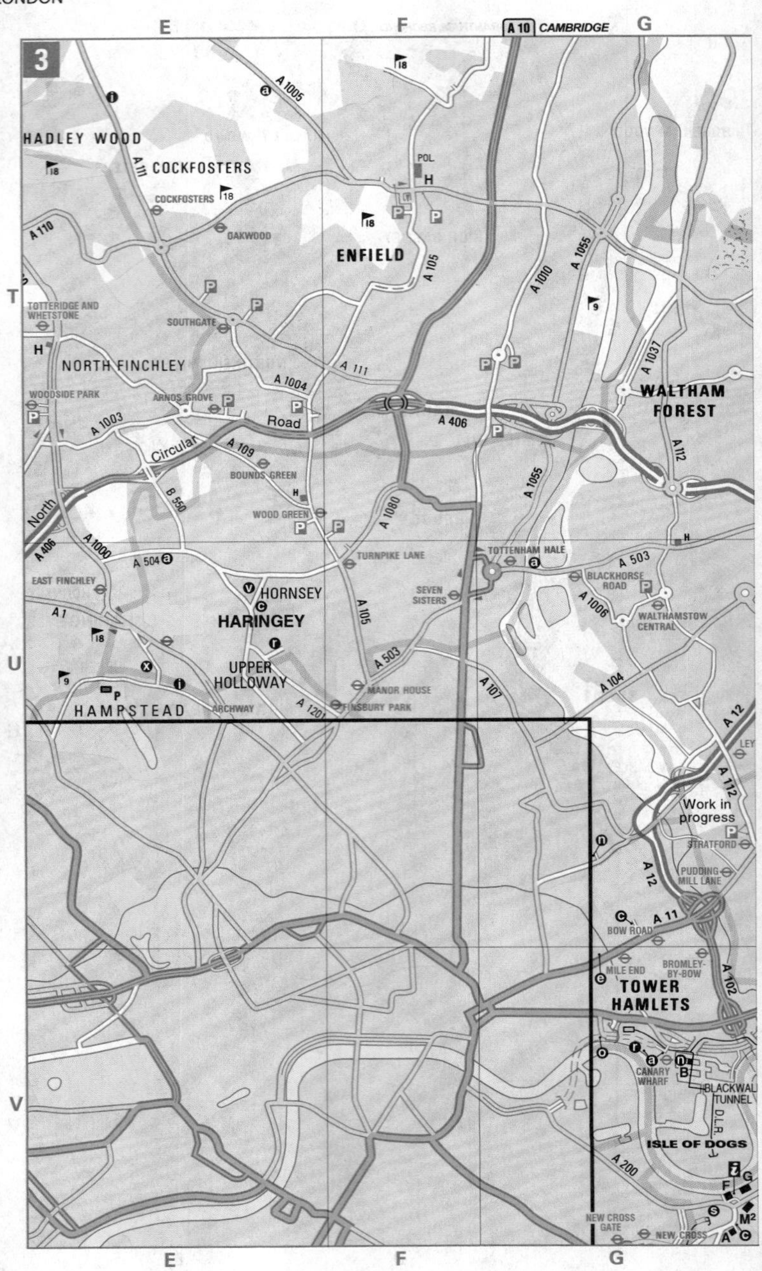
3
A 10 CAMBRIDGE
HADLEY WOOD
COCKFOSTERS
OAKWOOD
ENFIELD
TOTTERIDGE AND WHETSTONE
SOUTHGATE
NORTH FINCHLEY
WOODSIDE PARK
ARNOS GROVE
North Circular Road
BOUNDS GREEN
WOOD GREEN
TURNPIKE LANE
TOTTENHAM HALE
BLACKHORSE ROAD
WALTHAM FOREST
WALTHAMSTOW CENTRAL
SEVEN SISTERS
EAST FINCHLEY
HORNSEY
HARINGEY
UPPER HOLLOWAY
MANOR HOUSE
FINSBURY PARK
ARCHWAY
HAMPSTEAD
Work in progress
STRATFORD
PUDDING MILL LANE
BOW ROAD
MILE END
BROMLEY-BY-BOW
TOWER HAMLETS
CANARY WHARF
BLACKWALL TUNNEL
D.L.R.
ISLE OF DOGS
NEW CROSS GATE
NEW CROSS
LEY

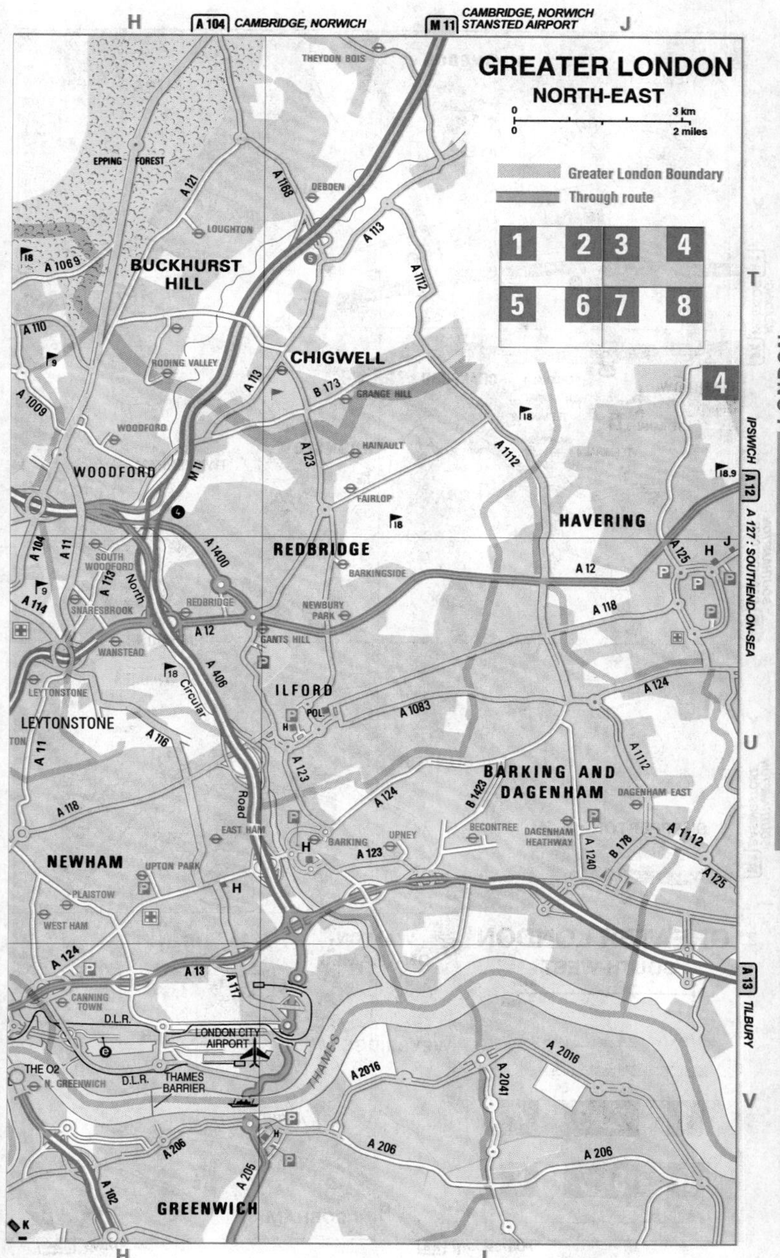
GREATER LONDON
NORTH-EAST
0 3 km
0 2 miles
Greater London Boundary
Through route
1 2 3 4
5 6 7 8
A 104 CAMBRIDGE, NORWICH
M 11 CAMBRIDGE, NORWICH STANSTED AIRPORT
IPSWICH A 12
A 127 : SOUTHEND-ON-SEA
A 13 TILBURY
THEYDON BOIS
EPPING FOREST
DEBDEN
LOUGHTON
BUCKHURST HILL
CHIGWELL
RODING VALLEY
GRANGE HILL
WOODFORD
HAINAULT
FAIRLOP
HAVERING
REDBRIDGE
SOUTH WOODFORD
BARKINGSIDE
SNARESBROOK
NEWBURY PARK
GANTS HILL
WANSTEAD
LEYTONSTONE
ILFORD
North Circular Road
BARKING AND DAGENHAM
DAGENHAM EAST
BECONTREE
DAGENHAM HEATHWAY
EAST HAM
BARKING
UPNEY
NEWHAM
UPTON PARK
PLAISTOW
WEST HAM
CANNING TOWN
D.L.R.
LONDON CITY AIRPORT
THE O2
N. GREENWICH
THAMES BARRIER
THAMES
GREENWICH
LONDON
H
J
T
U
V

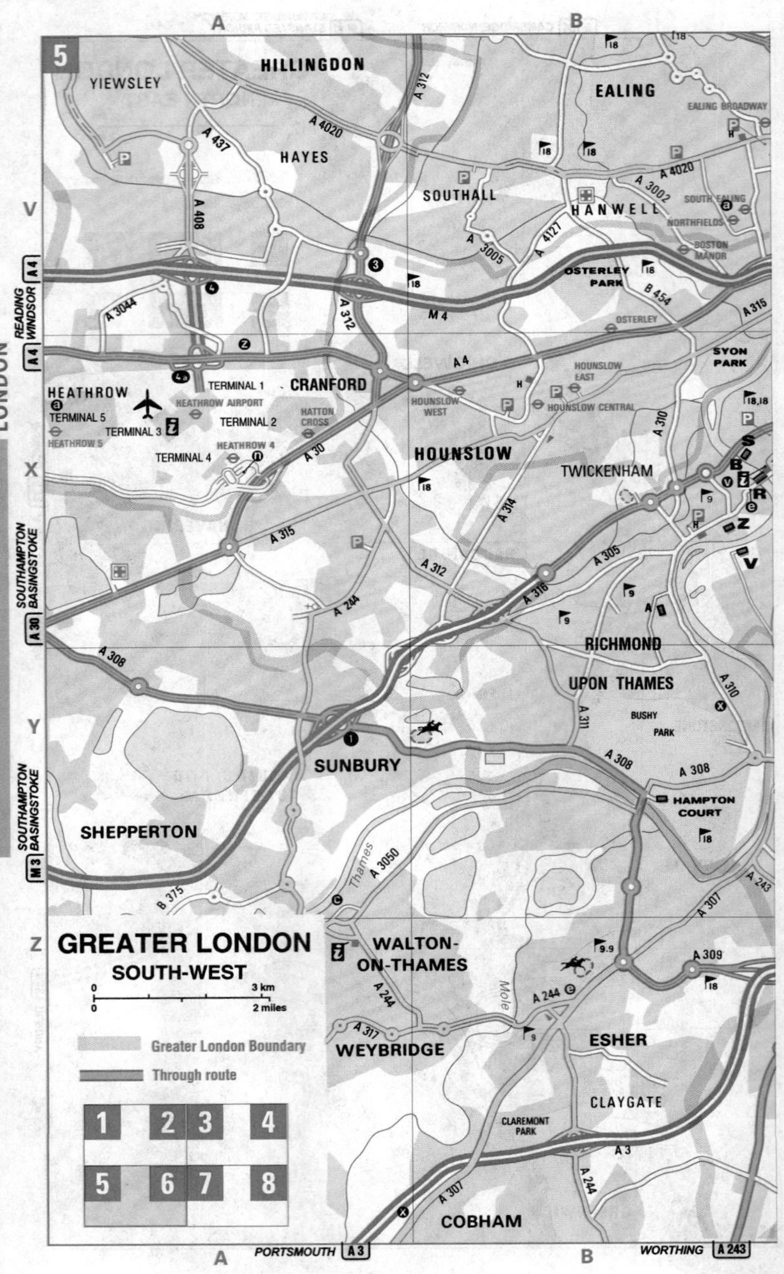
5
HILLINGDON
YIEWSLEY
EALING
EALING BROADWAY
HAYES
SOUTHALL
HANWELL
SOUTH EALING
NORTHFIELDS
BOSTON MANOR
OSTERLEY PARK
OSTERLEY
SYON PARK
HEATHROW
TERMINAL 1
CRANFORD
HEATHROW AIRPORT
TERMINAL 5
HEATHROW 5
TERMINAL 3
TERMINAL 2
HATTON CROSS
HEATHROW 4
TERMINAL 4
HOUNSLOW WEST
HOUNSLOW EAST
HOUNSLOW CENTRAL
HOUNSLOW
TWICKENHAM
RICHMOND
UPON THAMES
BUSHY PARK
SUNBURY
HAMPTON COURT
SHEPPERTON
Thames
WALTON-ON-THAMES
Mole
WEYBRIDGE
ESHER
CLAYGATE
CLAREMONT PARK
COBHAM
READING WINDSOR
SOUTHAMPTON BASINGSTOKE
SOUTHAMPTON BASINGSTOKE
PORTSMOUTH A 3
WORTHING A 243
GREATER LONDON
SOUTH-WEST
0 3 km
0 2 miles
Greater London Boundary
Through route
1 2 3 4
5 6 7 8
LONDON

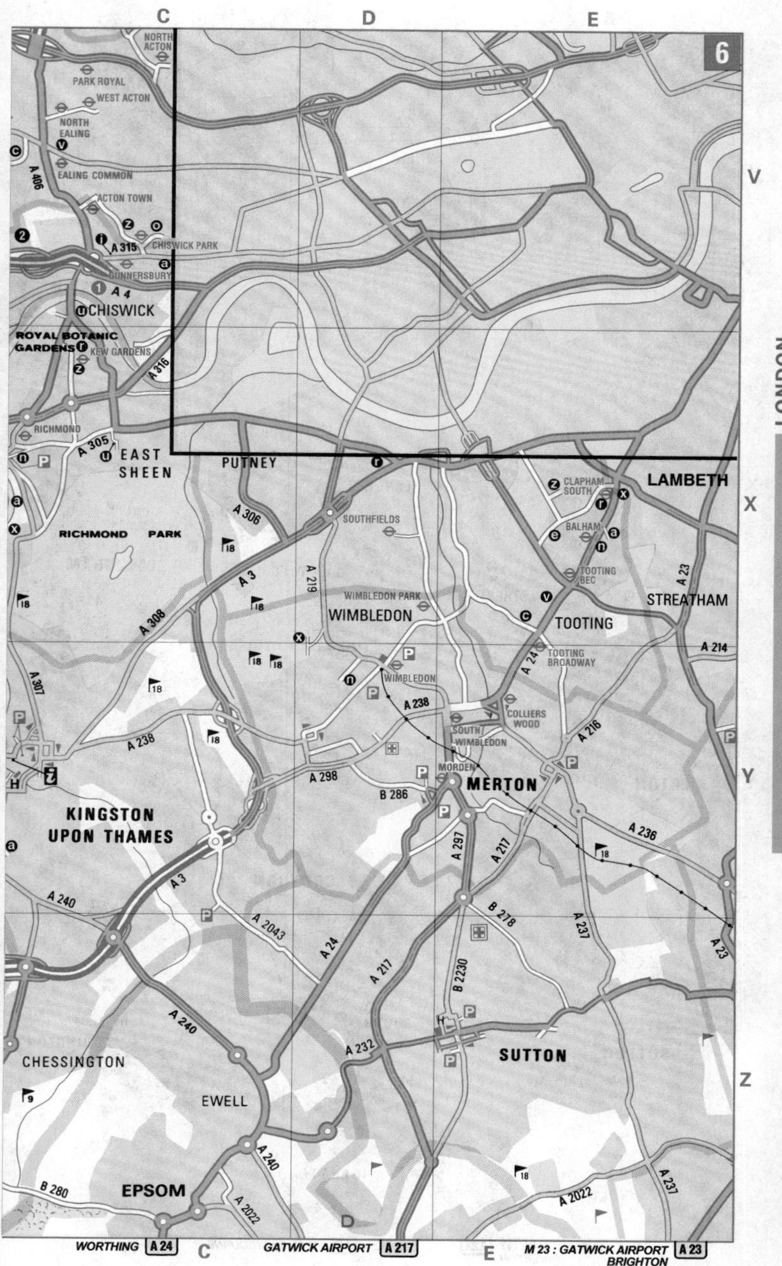

C
D
E
6
NORTH ACTON
PARK ROYAL
WEST ACTON
NORTH EALING
A 406
EALING COMMON
ACTON TOWN
A 315
CHISWICK PARK
GUNNERSBURY
A 4
CHISWICK
ROYAL BOTANIC GARDENS
KEW GARDENS
A 316
RICHMOND
A 305
EAST SHEEN
PUTNEY
LAMBETH
CLAPHAM SOUTH
BALHAM
A 306
SOUTHFIELDS
RICHMOND PARK
A 219
A 3
TOOTING BEC
A 23
STREATHAM
WIMBLEDON PARK
WIMBLEDON
A 308
TOOTING
A 214
A 24
TOOTING BROADWAY
A 307
WIMBLEDON
A 238
COLLIERS WOOD
A 238
SOUTH WIMBLEDON
A 216
A 298
MORDEN
MERTON
B 286
KINGSTON UPON THAMES
A 236
A 297
A 217
A 3
A 240
B 278
A 237
A 2043
A 23
A 24
A 217
B 2230
A 240
A 232
SUTTON
CHESSINGTON
EWELL
A 240
B 280
EPSOM
A 2022
A 2022
A 237
WORTHING A 24
C
GATWICK AIRPORT A 217
E
M 23 : GATWICK AIRPORT BRIGHTON A 23
V
X
Y
Z
LONDON

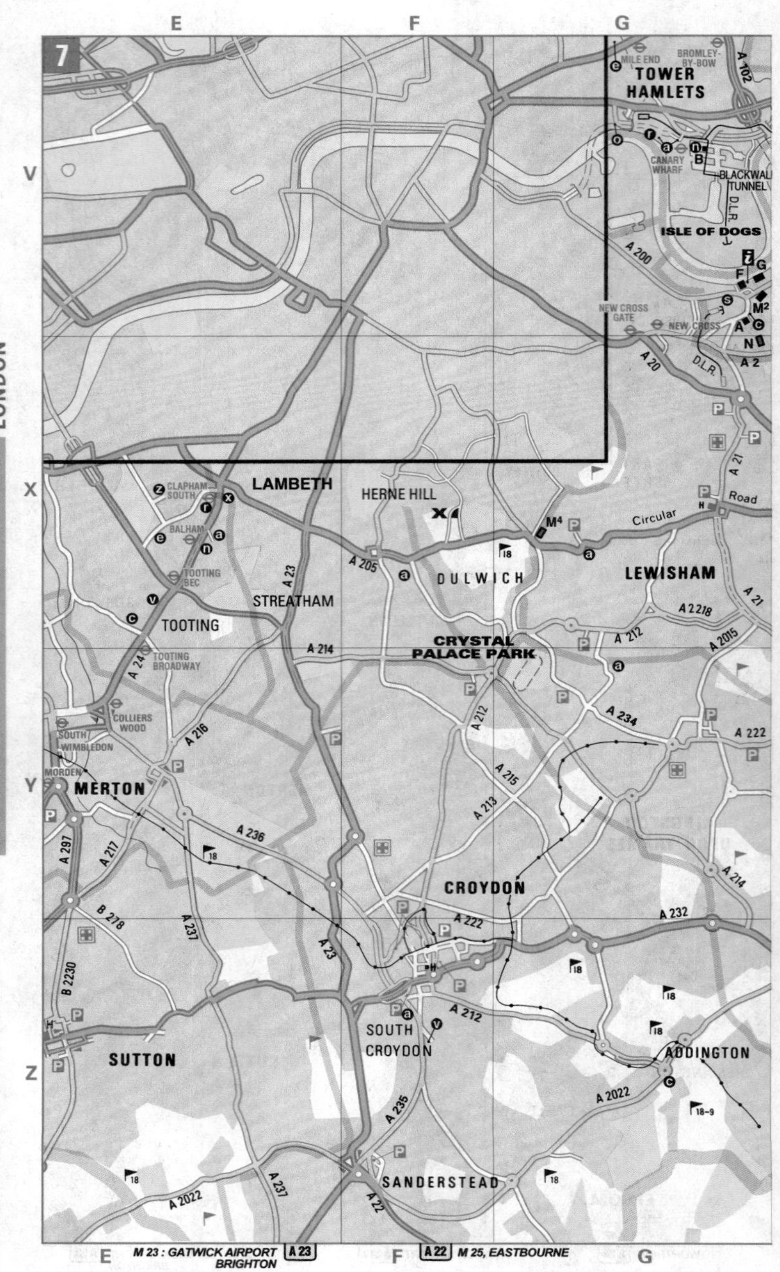

E
F
G
7
V
X
Y
Z
MILE END
BROMLEY-BY-BOW
TOWER HAMLETS
A 102
CANARY WHARF
BLACKWALL TUNNEL
D.L.R.
ISLE OF DOGS
A 200
NEW CROSS GATE
NEW CROSS
A 20
A 2
LAMBETH
CLAPHAM SOUTH
BALHAM
HERNE HILL
Circular
Road
A 21
TOOTING BEC
A 205
A 23
DULWICH
LEWISHAM
STREATHAM
TOOTING
A 2218
A 212
CRYSTAL PALACE PARK
A 2015
A 214
TOOTING BROADWAY
A 24
A 234
A 222
COLLIERS WOOD
SOUTH WIMBLEDON
A 216
A 215
MORDEN
MERTON
A 213
A 297
A 217
A 236
CROYDON
A 214
B 278
A 237
A 232
A 23
B 2230
A 212
SOUTH CROYDON
SUTTON
ADDINGTON
A 2022
A 235
SANDERSTEAD
A 2022
A 237
A 22
M 23 : GATWICK AIRPORT BRIGHTON
A 23
A 22
M 25, EASTBOURNE
LONDON

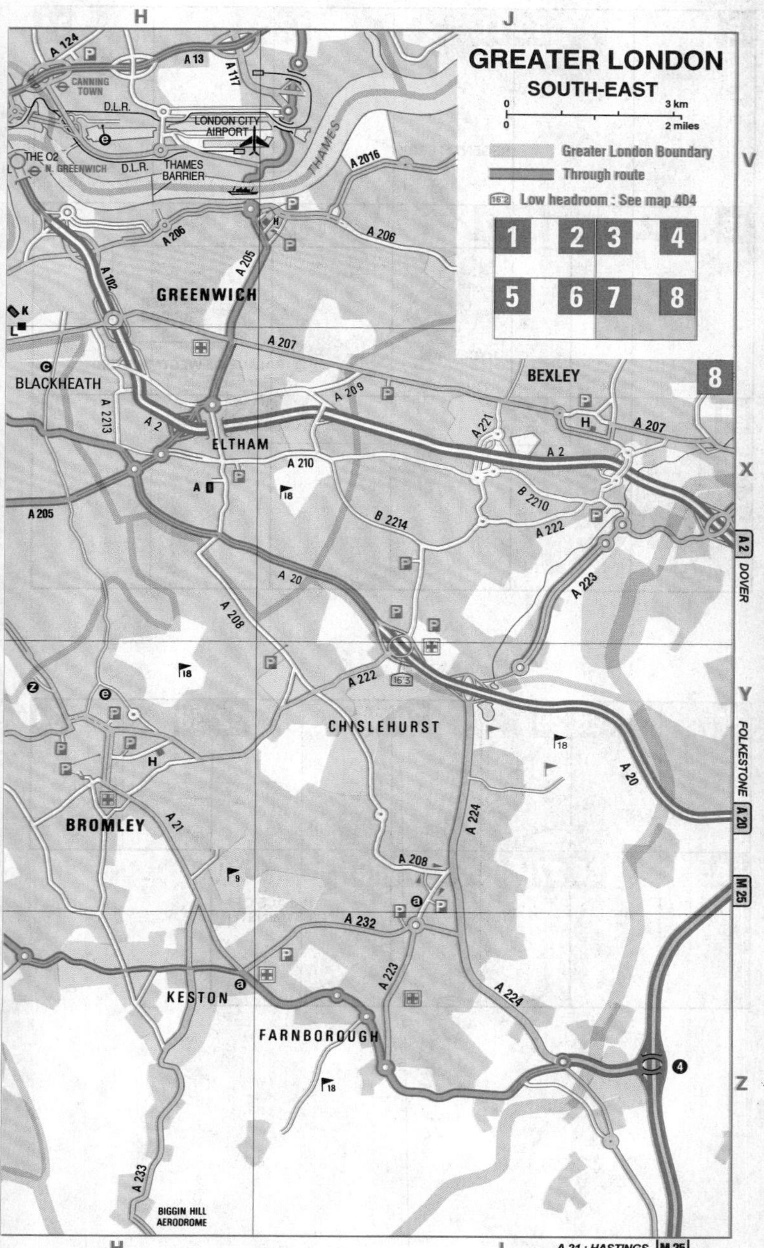
GREATER LONDON
SOUTH-EAST
0 3 km
0 2 miles
Greater London Boundary
Through route
Low headroom : See map 404
1 2 3 4
5 6 7 8
H
J
V
X
Y
Z
CANNING TOWN
D.L.R.
LONDON CITY AIRPORT
THE O2
N. GREENWICH
THAMES BARRIER
THAMES
GREENWICH
BLACKHEATH
ELTHAM
BEXLEY
CHISLEHURST
BROMLEY
KESTON
FARNBOROUGH
BIGGIN HILL AERODROME
A 124
A 13
A 117
A 2016
A 206
A 205
A 102
A 207
A 209
A 2213
A 2
A 210
A 221
B 2210
A 222
B 2214
A 20
A 208
A 223
A 224
A 21
A 232
A 233
A 2 DOVER
FOLKESTONE A 20
M 25
A 21 : HASTINGS M 25
8
LONDON

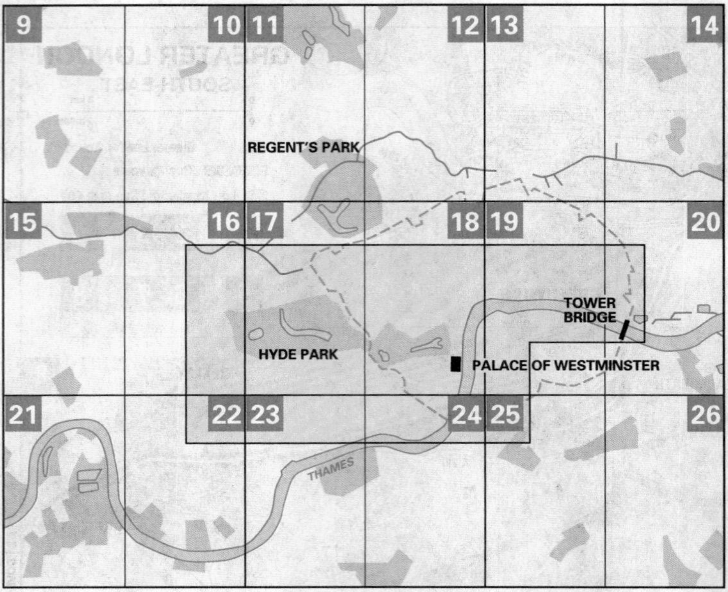
9
10
11
12
13
14
REGENT'S PARK
15
16
17
18
19
20
TOWER BRIDGE
HYDE PARK
PALACE OF WESTMINSTER
21
22
23
24
25
26
THAMES

27
28
29
30
31
32
33
34
THAMES
TOWER BRIDGE
HYDE PARK
35
36
37
38
39
40
PALACE OF WESTMINSTER

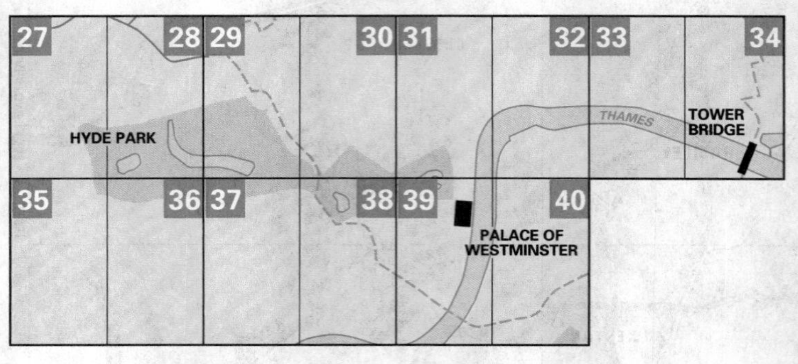

INDEX OF STREET NAMES IN LONDON CENTRE

PLAN 09

Street	Plan	Grid	No.
Acton Lane	9	KZB	
All Souls Ave	9	LZB	
Anson Rd	9	LZA	
Bathurst Gardens	9	LZB	
Brondesbury Park	9	LZB	
Brook Rd	9	KZA	
Burnley Rd	9	KZA	
Chamberlayne Rd	9	LZB	
Chapter Rd BRENT	9	LZA	
Church Rd BRENT	9	KZB	
Clifford Gardens	9	LZB	
Coles Green Rd	9	LZA	
College Rd	9	LZB	
Craven Park	9	KZB	351
Craven Park Rd	9	KZB	352
Crest Rd	9	KZA	
Cricklewood Broadway	9	LZA	
Denzil Rd	9	KZA	
Dollis Hill Lane	9	KZA	
Donnington Rd	9	LZB	
Doyle Gardens	9	LZB	
Dudden Hill Lane	9	KZA	
Edgware Rd BRENT	9	LZA	
Furness Rd	9	KZB	
Hardinge Rd	9	LZB	
Harlesden Rd	9	KZB	
Harley Rd	9	KZB	
Hawthorn Rd	9	LZB	357
Heber Rd	9	LZA	
High Rd BRENT	9	KZB	
High St	9	KZB	
Kendal Rd	9	LZA	
Longstone Ave	9	KZB	196
Manor Park Rd	9	KZB	
Mora Rd	9	LZA	
Mortimer Rd	9	LZC	
Mount Pleasant Rd	9	LZB	
Neasden Lane	9	KZA	
North Circular Rd	9	KZA	
North Park Ave	9	LZA	
Peter Ave	9	LZB	
Pound Lane	9	KZB	
Roundwood Rd	9	KZB	
Sherrick Green Rd	9	LZA	
Sidmouth Rd	9	LZB	
Sneyd Rd	9	LZA	
Tanfield Ave	9	KZA	
Walm Lane	9	LZB	
Wrottesley Rd	9	KZB	

PLAN 10

Street	Plan	Grid	No.
Asford Rd	10	MZA	425
Avenue (The) BRENT	10	MZB	
Aylestone Rd	10	MZB	
Belsize Rd	10	NZB	
Broadhurst Gardens	10	OZB	
Brondesbury Rd	10	NZB	
Brondesbury Villas	10	NZB	
Cambridge Rd	10	NZB	335
Carlton Vale	10	NZB	
Cavendish Ave	10	MZB	
Chatsworth Rd BRENT	10	MZB	
Chevening Rd	10	MZB	
Chichele Rd	10	MZA	
Christchurch Ave	10	MZB	
Claremont Rd	10	MZA	
Crediton Hill	10	NZA	
Cricklewood Lane	10	MZA	
Dyne Rd	10	MZB	
Frognal Lane	10	NZA	
Gascony Ave	10	NZB	
Greville Pl.	10	OZB	
Harvist Rd	10	MZB	
Heath Drive	10	NZA	
Hendon Way	10	MZA	
Hermitage Lane	10	NZA	
Iverson Rd	10	NZB	
Kilburn High Rd	10	NZB	
Kilburn Lane	10	MZB	
Kilburn Park Rd	10	NZC	
Kingswood Ave	10	MZB	
Lichfield Rd	10	MZA	
Lyndale Ave	10	NZA	
Mapesbury Rd	10	MZB	
Mill Lane	10	MZA	
Milman Rd	10	MZB	
Oxford Rd	10	NZB	336
Platt's Lane	10	NZA	
Priory Rd	10	NZB	
Quex Rd	10	NZB	
Randolph Ave	10	OZC	
Redington Rd	10	NZA	
Salusbury Rd	10	MZB	
Shoot Up Hill	10	MZA	
Teignmouth Rd	10	MZA	
Tiverton Rd	10	MZB	
Vale (The BARNET)	10	MZA	
Westbere Rd	10	MZA	
West End Lane	10	NZA	
West Heath Rd	10	NZA	
Willesden Lane	10	MZB	

PLAN 11

Street	Plan	Grid	No.
Abbey Rd	11	PZB	
Abercorn Pl.	11	PZB	277
Acacia Rd	11	PZB	
Adelaide Rd	11	QZB	
Agincourt Rd	11	QZA	362
Akenside Rd	11	PZA	22
Allitsen Rd	11	PZB	
Arkwright Rd	11	OZA	
Avenue Rd	11	PZB	
Belsize Ave	11	PZA	
Belsize Lane	11	PZB	
Belsize Park	11	PZB	19
Belsize Park Gardens	11	PZB	
Boundary Rd	11	OZB	
Canfield Gardens	11	OZB	
Carlton Hill	11	OZB	
Chalk Farm Rd	11	QZB	
Charlbert St	11	PZB	79
Circus Rd	11	PZB	
Constantine Rd	11	QZA	106
Downshire Hill	11	PZA	139
East Heath Rd	11	PZA	
Elsworthy Rd	11	PZB	
England's Lane	11	QZB	323
Eton Ave	11	PZB	
Fairfax Rd	11	PZB	
Fairhazel Gardens	11	OZB	
Finchley Rd	11	PZB	
Fitzjohn's Ave	11	PZA	
Fleet Rd	11	QZA	
Frognal	11	OZA	
Frognal Rise	11	PZA	171
Gayton Rd	11	PZA	324
Gloucester Ave	11	QZB	
Greencroft Gardens	11	OZB	
Grove End Rd	11	PZC	
Hamilton Terrace	11	OZB	
Hampstead Grove	11	PZA	208
Hampstead High St	11	PZA	209
Haverstock Hill	11	QZB	
Heath St	11	PZA	
Hollybush Hill	11	PZA	227
Keat's Grove	11	PZA	236
King Henry's Rd	11	PZB	297
Lancaster Grove	11	PZB	
Lawn Rd	11	QZA	
Loudoun Rd	11	PZB	
Lower Terrace	11	OZA	
Lyndhurst Rd	11	PZA	
Maida Vale	11	OZB	
Malden Rd	11	QZA	
Mansfield Rd	11	QZA	
Marlborough Pl.	11	PZB	
Nassington Rd	11	QZA	
Netherhall Gardens	11	PZA	
New End Square	11	PZA	305
North End Way	11	OZA	
Nutley Terrace	11	PZB	
Ordnance Hill	11	PZB	
Ornan Rd	11	PZA	
Outer Circle	11	QZB	
Parkhill Rd	11	QZA	
Parliament Hill	11	QZA	
Pond St	11	PZA	
Primrose Hill Rd	11	QZB	
Prince Albert Rd	11	QZB	
Prince of Wales Rd	11	QZB	
Queen's Grove	11	PZB	
Regent's Park Rd	11	QZB	
Rosslyn Hill	11	PZA	
St John's Wood Park	11	PZB	379
St. John's Wood High St.	11	PZB	29
Savernake Rd	11	QZA	
Southampton Rd	11	QZA	
South End Rd	11	PZA	
South Hill	11	PZA	390
Spaniards Rd	11	PZA	
Wellington Rd	11	PZB	
Well Walk	11	PZA	
Willoughby Rd	11	PZA	479
Willow Rd	11	PZA	

PLAN 12

Street	Plan	Grid	No.
Agar Grove	12	SZB	
Albany St	12	RZB	
Bartholomew Rd	12	RZB	16
Brewery Rd	12	SZB	
Busby Pl.	12	SZA	
Camden High St	12	RZB	
Camden Rd	12	RZB	
Camden St	12	RZB	
Carleton Rd	12	SZA	
Chetwynd Rd	12	RZA	
Copenhagen St	12	SZB	
Crowndale Rd	12	RZB	
Dalmeny Ave	12	SZA	
Dalmeny Rd	12	SZA	
Dartmouth Park Hill	12	RZA	
Delancey St	12	RZB	
Eversholt St	12	SZC	
Fortess Rd	12	RZA	
Gaisford St	12	RZB	
Hampstead Rd	12	RZB	
Highgate Rd	12	RZA	
Hillmarton Rd	12	SZA	
Holloway Rd	12	SZA	
Hornssey Rd	12	SZA	
Hungerford Rd	12	SZA	
Islip St	12	RZA	
Junction Rd	12	RZA	
Kentish Town Rd	12	RZB	
Lady Margaret Rd	12	RZA	
Leighton Rd	12	RZA	
Market Rd	12	SZB	
Midland Rd	12	SZB	
North Rd	12	SZB	
Ossulton St	12	SZC	
Pancras Rd	12	SZB	
Parkhurst Rd	12	SZA	
Parkway	12	RZB	
Park Village East	12	RZB	
Patshull Rd	12	RZB	
Pratt St	12	RZB	
Randolph St	12	RZB	366
Royal College St	12	RZB	
St Pancras Way	12	RZB	
Spring Pl.	12	RZA	
Swains Lane	12	RZA	

LONDON

Swinton St 12 TZC 417
Tollington Park 12 TZA
Tollington Way 12 SZA
Torriano Ave 12 SZA
Tufnell Park Rd 12 SZA
Wharfdale Rd 12 SZB 455
Willes Rd 12 RZB
York Way 12 SZB

PLAN 13

Albion Rd 13 VZA
Amwell St 13 UZC
Ardilaun Rd 13 VZA 333
Balls Pond Rd 13 VZB
Barnsbury Rd 13 UZB
Barnsbury St 13 UZB
Benwell Rd 13 UZA
Blackstock Rd 13 UZA
Bride St 13 UZB
Brownswood Rd 13 UZA
Caledonian Rd 13 TZA
Calshot St 13 TZB
Camden Passage 13 UZB 70
Canonbury Rd 13 UZB
Canonbury Square 13 UZB
Chapel Market 13 UZB 78
Clissold Crescent 13 VZA
Clissold Rd 13 VZA
Downham Rd 13 VZB
Drayton Park 13 UZA
Eagle Wharf Rd 13 VZB
East Rd 13 VZC
Englefield Rd 13 VZB
Essex Rd 13 VZB
Fonthill Rd 13 UZA
Gillespie Rd 13 UZA
Green Lanes 13 VZA
Grosvenor Ave 13 VZA
Halliford St 13 VZB
Hemingford Rd 13 UZB
Highbury Grove 13 UZA
Highbury Hill 13 UZA
Highbury New Park 13 VZA
Highbury Park 13 UZA
Highbury Pl 13 UZA
Hyde Rd 13 VZB 235
Isledon Rd 13 UZA
Liverpool Rd 13 UZB
Lordship Park 13 VZA
Lordship Rd 13 VZA
Mackenzie Rd 13 TZB
Matthias Rd 13 VZA
Mildmay Park 13 VZA
Mildmay Rd 13 VZA
Mountgrove Rd 13 UZA
New North Rd 13 VZB
Offord Rd 13 TZB
Penn St 13 VZB 343
Pentonville Rd 13 TZB
Penton Rise 13 TZB 344
Penton St 13 UZB 345
Petherton Rd 13 VZA
Pitfield St 13 VZC
Poole St 13 VZB 350
Prebend St 13 VZB
Queen's Drive 13 UZA
Richmond Ave 13 TZB
Riversdale Rd 13 VZA
Roman Way 13 TZB
St Paul's Rd 13 VZB
St Peter's St 13 UZB
St Thomas's Rd 13 UZA
Seven Sisters Rd 13 TZA
Shepherdess Walk 13 VZB
Southgate Rd 13 VZB
Spencer St 13 UZC 398
Stoke Newington Church St 13 VZA
Thornhill Rd 13 UZB
Upper St 13 UZB
Westbourne Rd 13 UZB 56
Westland Pl 13 VZC 478
Wharf Rd 13 VZB

PLAN 14

Albion Drive 14 XZB
Amhurst Rd 14 XZA
Barbauld Rd 14 XZA
Barretts Grove 14 XZA
Bishop's Way 14 YZB
Boleyn Rd 14 XZA
Bonner Rd 14 YZB
Bouverie Rd 14 XZA
Brooke Rd 14 XZA
Canrobert St 14 YZC
Cassland Rd 14 YZB
Cecilia Rd 14 XZA
Chatsworth Rd HACKNEY 14 YZA
Clapton Way 14 XZA
Cleveleys Rd 14 YZA
Clifden Rd 14 YZA
Columbia Rd 14 XZC
Cricketfield Rd 14 YZA 378
Dalston Lane 14 YZA
De Beauvoir Rd 14 XZB
Downs Park Rd 14 YZA
Downs Rd 14 YZA
Evering Rd 14 XZA
Forest Rd 14 XZB
Frampton Park Rd 14 YZB
Graham Rd 14 XZB
Hackney Rd 14 XZC
Homerton High St 14 YZA
Hoxton St 14 XZC
Kenninghall Rd 14 YZA
Kingsland Rd 14 XZB
King Henry's Walk 14 XZA 337
Kyverdale Rd 14 XZA
Lansdowne Drive 14 YZB
Lea Bridge Rd 14 YZA
Lower Clapton Rd 14 YZA
Mare St 14 YZB
Maury Rd 14 XZA
Median Rd 14 YZA
Middleton Rd 14 XZB
Millfields Rd 14 YZA
Morning Lane 14 YZB
Mount Pleasant Hill 14 YZA
Nevill Rd 14 XZA
Northwold Rd 14 XZA
Nuttall St 14 XZB
Old Bethnal Green Rd 14 XZC
Old Ford Rd 14 YZB
Pembury Rd 14 YZA
Powerscroft Rd 14 YZA
Pownall Drive 14 XZB
Prince George Rd 14 XZA
Pritchard's Rd 14 YZB
Queensbridge Rd 14 XZB
Rectory Rd 14 XZA
Richmond Rd 14 XZB
Ridley Rd 14 XZA
Sandringham Rd 14 XZA
Sewardstone Rd 14 YZB
Shacklewell Lane 14 XZA
Sheep Lane 14 YZB
Stoke Newington High St 14 XZA
Upper Clapton Rd 14 YZA
Victoria Park Rd 14 YZB
Walford Rd 14 XZA
Warner Pl 14 XZB
Well St 14 YZB
Whiston Rd 14 XZB
Whitmore Rd 14 XZB 464

PLAN 15

Abinger Rd 15 KZE
Ashfield Rd 15 KZE
Askew Rd 15 KZE
Avenue (The EALING) 15 KZE
Barlby Rd 15 LZD
Bienheim Rd 15 KZE
Bloemfontein Rd 15 LZE
Brackenbury Rd 15 LZE
Brassie Ave 15 KZD
Bromyard Ave 15 KZE
Bryony Rd 15 KZE
Cobbold Rd 15 KZE
Coningham Rd 15 LZE
Davisville Rd 15 KZE 462
Du Cane Rd 15 KZD
East Acton Lane 15 KZE
Emlyn Rd 15 KZE
Fairway (The) 15 KZD
Goldhawk Rd 15 LZE
Hammersmith Grove 15 LZE
Highlever Rd 15 LZD
Larden Rd 15 KZE
Lime Grove 15 LZE
Old Oak Common Lane 15 KZD
Old Oak Lane 15 KZC
Old Oak Rd 15 KZE
Paddenswick Rd 15 LZE
Percy Rd 15 LZE
St Quintin Ave 15 LZD
Sawley Rd 15 KZE
Serubs Lane 15 LZD
Sheperd's Bush Green 15 LZE 454
Shepherd's Bush Rd 15 LZF
South Africa Rd 15 LZE
Stamford Brook Rd 15 KZE 387
Steventon Rd 15 KZE
Uxbridge Rd 15 LZE
Vale (The EALING) 15 KZE
Victoria Rd 15 KZD
Western Ave 15 KZD
Westway 15 LZD
Wingate Rd 15 LZE 463
Wood Lane 15 LZD
Wormholt Rd 15 KZE
Wulfstan St 15 KZD
Yew Tree Rd 15 KZE

PLAN 16

Abbotsbury Rd 16 MZE
Addison Ave 16 MZE
Addison Crescent 16 MZE 3
Addison Rd 16 MZE
Blythe Rd 16 MZE
Bravington Rd 16 MZC
Chesterton Rd 16 MZD
Chippenham Rd 16 NZD 340
Clarendon Rd 16 MZE
Cornwall Crescent 16 MZD 107
Delaware Rd 16 NZD
Elgin Ave 16 NZD
Fernhead Rd 16 NZC
Fifth Ave 16 MZC
Golborne Rd 16 MZD
Holland Park 16 MZE
Holland Park Gardens 16 MZE 224
Holland Rd 16 MZE
Holland Villas Rd 16 MZE
Kensal Rd 16 MZD
Ladbroke Grove 16 MZD
Lancaster Rd 16 MZD
Lansdowne Walk 16 MZE 331
Lauderdale Rd 16 OZD
Masbro Rd 16 MZE
Olympia Way 16 MZE 326

Oxford Gardens 16 MZD
Royal Crescent 16 MZE 371
St Ann's Rd 16 MZE
St Mark's Rd 16 MZD
Shirland Rd 16 NZD
Sinclair Rd 16 MZE
Sixth Ave 16 MZC
Sutherland Ave 16 NZD
Walterton Rd 16 NZD 347
Warwick Ave 16 OZD
West Cross Route 16 MZE

PLAN 17

Allsop Pl. 17 QZD 4
Blomfield Rd 17 OZD
Broadley St 17 PZD
Clifton Gardens 17 PZD
Frampton St 17 PZD
Hall Rd 17 PZC
Lisson Grove 17 PZD
Maida Ave 17 PZD
North Carriage Drive 17 PZE
Park Rd 17 QZD
Rossmore Rd 17 QZD
St John's Wood Rd 17 PZD
Warrington Crescent 17 OZD 348

PLAN 18

Bernard St 18 SZD 25
Chester Rd 18 RZC
Euston Rd 18 RZD
Fitzroy Square 18 RZD
Great Ormond St 18 SZD
Guilford St 18 SZD
Herbrand St 18 SZD 218
Hunter St 18 SZD 233
Judd St 18 SZC
Park Crescent 18 RZD 28
Robert St 18 RZC
Russell Square 18 SZD
Sidmouth St 18 SZD 385
Tavistock Pl. 18 SZD
Tavistock Square 18 SZD 409
Upper Woburn Pl. 18 SZD 432
Woburn Pl. 18 SZD

PLAN 19

Bath St 19 VZC
Beech St 19 VZD
Borough Rd 19 UZE
Bowling Green Lane 19 UZD 43
Bunhill Row 19 VZD
Calthorpe St 19 TZD 65
Central St 19 VZC
Chiswell St 19 VZD
City Rd 19 VZC
Clerkenwell Rd 19 UZD 474
Corporation Row 19 UZD 110
Dufferin St 19 VZD 141
Elephant and Castle Shopping Centre 19 UZF
Falmouth Rd 19 VZE
Fann St 19 VZD 166
Goswell Rd 19 UZC
Great Dover St 19 VZE
Harper Rd 19 VZE
King's Cross Rd 19 TZC
Lever St 19 VZC
Lloyd Baker St 19 UZC 265
Long Lane SOUTHWARK 19 VZE
Merrick Square 19 VZE
Moreland St 19 VZC 293
Myddelton St 19 UZC 296
Newington Causeway 19 VZE 307
New Kent Rd 19 VZF
Old St 19 VZD
Paul St 19 VZD
Percival St 19 UZD
Pilgrimage St. 19 VZE 349
Rosebery Ave 19 UZD
St John St 19 UZC
Suffolk St. 19 VZE
Tabard St 19 VZE 408
Trinity Church Square 19 VZE
Trinity St 19 VZE
Whitecross St 19 VZD
Worship St 19 VZD

PLAN 20

Abbey St 20 XZE
Appold St 20 XZD 5
Back Church Rd 20 XZD
Bermondsey St. 20 XZE
Bethnal Green Rd 20 XZD
Bigland St 20 YZD
Brady St 20 YZD
Brick Lane 20 XZD
Brunel Rd 20 YZE
Cable St 20 YZD
Cambridge Heath Rd 20 YZD
Cannon Street Rd 20 YZD
Cavell St 20 YZD
Cephas St 20 YZD
Cheshire St 20 XZD
Christian St 20 YZD
Clements Rd 20 YZE
Club Row 20 XZD
Commercial Rd 20 YZD
Curtain Rd 20 XZD 126
Dock St 20 XZD
Drummond Rd 20 YZE
Fielgate St 20 XZD
Globe Rd 20 YZC
Grange Rd 20 XZE
Great Eastern St 20 XZD 192
Highway (The) 20 YZE
Jamaica Rd 20 XZE
Jublilee St 20 YZD
Lower Rd 20 YZE
Luke St 20 XZD
Mile End Rd 20 YZD
New Rd 20 YZD
Old Montague St 20 XZD
Pages Walk 20 XZF
Redman's Rd 20 YZD
Roman Rd 20 YZC
Rovel Rd 20 XZE 75
Salter Rd 20 YZE
Sclater St 20 XZD 470
Shoreditch High St 20 XZD 384
Sidney St 20 YZD
Spa Rd 20 XZE
Stepney Way 20 YZD
Surrey Quay's Rd 20 YZE 377
Tarling St 20 YZD
Thomas Moore St 20 XZE 365
Turin St 20 XZC
Vallance Rd 20 YZD
Vaughan Way 20 XZE
Wapping High St 20 YZE
Wapping Lane 20 YZE
Wapping Wall 20 YZE
Whitechapel Rd 20 XZD

PLAN 21

Banin St 21 LZF
Barnes High St 21 KZH 404
Bath Rd 21 KZF
Brook Green 21 LZF
Burlington Lane 21 KZG
Castelnau 21 LZG
Chancellor's Rd 21 LZG 21
Chiswick High Rd 21 KZG
Chiswick Lane 21 KZG
Chiswick Mall 21 KZG
Church Rd RICHMOND UPON THAMES 21 KZH
Dailing Rd 21 LZF 13
Devonshire Rd 21 KZG
Dorchester Grove 21 KZG 402
Dover House Rd 21 LZH
Erpingham Rd 21 LZH
Ferry Rd 21 KZG
Glenthorne Rd 21 LZF
Great West Rd 21 KZG
Gwendolen Ave 21 LZH
Hammersmith Bridge 21 LZG
Hammersmith Bridge Rd 21 LZG 431
Hertford Ave 21 KZH
Hotham Rd 21 LZH
Howards Lane 21 LZH
King St HAMMERSMITH 21 KZG
Lonsdale Rd 21 KZG
Lower Richmond Rd 21 LZH
Mill Hill Rd 21 KZH
Prebend Gardens 21 KZF
Priory Lane 21 KZH
Queen's Ride Lower 21 LZH
Rainville Rd 21 LZG
Rannoch Rd 21 LZG
Rocks Lane 21 LZH
Roehampton Lane 21 KZH
Station Rd 21 KZH
Stevenage Rd 21 LZG
Suffolk Rd 21 KZG
Talgarth Rd 21 LZG
Terrace (The) 21 KZH
Turnham Green Terrace 21 KZG 389
Upper Richmond Rd 21 LZH
Upper Richmond Rd West 21 KZH
Verdun Rd 21 KZG
Vine Rd 21 KZH
White Hart Lane 21 KZH

PLAN 22

Armoury Way 22 NZH 7
Bagley's Lane 22 OZH
Baron's Court Rd 22 MZG
Bishops Rd 22 NZG
Bishop's Park Rd 22 MZH
Broomhouse Lane 22 NZH
Carnwath Rd 22 NZH
Charlwood Rd 22 MZH
Clancarty Rd 22 NZH
Crabtree Lane 22 MZG 164
Dawes Rd 22 MZG
Disraeli Rd 22 MZH
Edith Rd 22 MZG
Estcourt Rd 22 MZG 203
Fairfield St 22 OZH 165
Fawe Park Rd 22 MZH
Filmer Rd 22 MZG
Finlay St 22 MZH
Fulham High St 22 MZH 172
Fulham Palace Rd 22 MZG
Gliddon Rd 22 MZG 182
Greyhound Rd 22 MZG
Gunterstone Rd 22 MZG
Halford Rd 22 NZG
Hammersmith Rd 22 MZG
Harwood Rd 22 NZG
Hugon Rd 22 NZH
Hurlingham Rd 22 NZH
Munster Rd 22 MZG
Musard Rd 22 MZG
New King's Rd 22 NZH
Oakhill Rd 22 NZH

Street	Plan	Grid	No.
Oxford Rd WANDSWORTH	22	MZH	
Parsons Green Lane	22	NZG	
Peterborough Rd	22	NZH	
Putney Bridge	22	MZH	
Putney Bridge Rd	22	MZH	
Putney High St	22	MZH	
Putney Hill	22	MZH	358
Queensmill Rd	22	MZG	450
Rylston Rd	22	MZG	
St Dunstan's Rd	22	MZG	
Star Rd	22	MZG	
Stephendale Rd	22	OZH	
Studdridge St	22	NZH	
Swandon Way	22	OZH	
Vanston Pl.	22	NZG	207
Wandsworth Bridge	22	OZH	437
Wandsworth Bridge Rd	22	NZH	
West Cromwell Rd.	22	NZG	
Woodlaw Rd	22	MZG	

PLAN 23

Street	Plan	Grid	No.
Albert Bridge	23	QZB	
Albert Bridge Rd	23	QZG	
Avenue (The)	23	QZH	
Battersea Bridge	23	PZG	
Battersea Bridge Rd	23	PZG	
Battersea Church Rd	23	PZG	
Battersea Park Rd	23	QZH	
Battersea Rise	23	PZH	
Cambridge Rd BATTERSEA	23	QZH	449
Carriage Drive East	23	QZG	
Carriage Drive North	23	QZG	
Carriage Drive South	23	QZG	
Cheyne Walk	23	PZG	
Clapham Common West Side	23	QZH	92
East Hill	23	PZH	155
Edith Grove	23	PZG	
Elspeth Rd	23	QZH	
Falcon Rd	23	PZH	
Gowrie Rd	23	QZH	
Gunter Grove	23	OZG	202
Imperial Rd	23	OZG	
Latchmere Rd	23	QZH	
Lavender Hill	23	QZH	
Lombard Rd	23	PZH	266
Lots Rd	23	OZG	
Marney Rd	23	QZH	
Northcote Rd	23	QZH	
North Side	23	PZH	316
Parade (The)	23	QZG	
Parkgate Rd	23	QZG	
Plough Rd	23	PZH	
Prince of Wales Drive	23	QZH	
St John's Hill	23	PZH	
St John's Rd	23	QZH	
Surrey Lane	23	PZH	
Townmead Rd	23	OZH	
Trinity Rd	23	PZH	441
Vicarage Crescent	23	PZH	433
Westbridge Rd	23	PZG	
York Rd WANDSWORTH	23	PZH	

PLAN 24

Street	Plan	Grid	No.
Acre Lane	24	SZH	
Bedford Rd	24	SZH	
Binfield Rd	24	SZH	
Bridgefoot	24	SZG	49
Cedars Rd	24	RZH	
Clapham Common North Side	24	RZH	428
Clapham High St.	24	SZH	
Clapham Manor St	24	SZH	
Clapham Park Hill	24	SZH	
Crescent Lane	24	SZH	
Fentiman Rd	24	TZG	
Jeffrey's Rd	24	SZH	
King's Ave	24	SZH	
Landor Rd	24	SZH	
Landsdowne Way	24	SZG	
Larkhall Lane	24	SZH	
Lingham St	24	SZH	
Long Rd	24	RZH	
Miles St	24	SZG	290
North St	24	RZH	
Old Town	24	RZH	426
Park Rd LAMBETH	24	SZH	
Queenstown Rd	24	RZH	
Queen's Circus	24	RZG	361
Rectory Grove	24	RZH	
Silverthorne Rd	24	RZH	
Triangle Place	24	SZH	
Union Rd	24	SZH	
Voltaire Rd	24	SZH	436
Wandsworth Rd	24	SZG	
Wilkinson St	24	TZG	420

PLAN 25

Street	Plan	Grid	No.
Akerman Rd	25	UZH	
Albany Rd	25	VZG	
Angell Drive	25	UZH	
Atlantic Rd	25	UZH	
Barrington Rd	25	UZH	
Benhill Rd	25	VZG	
Brixton Hill	25	UZH	
Brixton Rd	25	UZH	
Calais St	25	UZG	
Caldwell St	25	UZG	
Camberwell Grove	25	VZH	
Camberwell New Rd	25	UZG	
Camberwell Rd	25	VZG	
Carew St	25	VZH	
Champion Park	25	VZH	
Chapter Rd	25	UZG	
Church St Camberwell	25	VZG	
Clapham Rd	25	TZH	
Coldharbour Lane	25	UZH	
Comber Grove	25	VZG	
Denmark Hill	25	VZH	
Denmark Rd	25	VZH	
Dorset Rd	25	TZG	
East St	25	VZG	
Edmund St	25	VZG	
Effra Rd	25	UZH	
Elephant Rd	25	VZF	163
Elmington Rd	25	VZG	
Fawnbrake Ave	25	VZH	
Ferndene Rd	25	VZH	
Flint St	25	VZG	
Flodden Rd	25	VZG	
Foxley Rd	25	UZG	
Groveway	25	UZH	
Grove Lane	25	VZH	
Harleyford St	25	UZG	211
Herne Hill	25	VZH	
Herne Hill Rd	25	VZH	
Heygate St	25	VZF	
John Ruskin St	25	VZG	
Kellett Rd	25	UZH	
Knatchbull Rd	25	UZH	
Lilford Rd	25	UZH	
Lomond Grove	25	VZG	
Lothian Rd	25	UZG	
Loughborough Rd	25	UZH	
Manor Pl.	25	VZG	
Milkwood Rd	25	VZH	
Minet Rd	25	UZH	
Mostyn Rd	25	UZH	
Newington Butts	25	UZF	306
New Church Rd	25	VZG	
Penton Pl.	25	UZG	
Portland St	25	VZG	
Railton Rd	25	UZH	
Red Post Hill	25	VZH	
Rodney Rd	25	VZF	
Shakespeare Rd	25	UZH	
Sidney Rd	25	TZH	
Southampton Way	25	VZG	
Stocwell Park Rd	25	TZH	
Stocwell Rd	25	TZH	
Sunray Ave	25	VZH	
Thurlow St	25	VZG	
Vassall Rd	25	UZG	
Walworth Rd	25	VZG	
Warner Rd	25	VZH	
Wells Way	25	VZG	
Wiltshire Rd	25	UZH	
Wyndham Rd	25	VZG	

PLAN 26

Street	Plan	Grid
Ady's Rd	26	XZH
Asylum Rd	26	YZG
Avondale Rise	26	XZH
Avonley Rd	26	YZG
Barry Rd	26	YZH
Bellenden Rd	26	XZH
Bird In Bush Rd	26	YZG
Carlton Grove	26	YZG
Catlin St	26	YZG
Cheltenham Rd	26	YZH
Clayton Rd	26	YZH
Clifton Way	26	YZG
Cobourg Rd	26	XZG
Commercial Way	26	XZG
Consort Rd	26	YZH
Coopers Rd	26	XZG
Copeland Rd	26	YZH
Crystal Palace Rd	26	XZH
Dalwood St	26	XZG
Dog Kennel Hill	26	XZH
Dunton Rd	26	XZG
East Dulwich Grove	26	XZH
East Dulwich Rd	26	XZH
Evelina Rd	26	YZH
Galleywall Rd	26	YZG
Glengall Rd	26	XZG
Grove Hill Rd	26	XZH
Grove Vale	26	XZH
Hanover Park	26	XZH
Havil St	26	XZG
Heaton Rd	26	YZH
Hollydale Rd	26	YZH
Ilderton Rd	26	YZG
Kender St	26	YZG
Lausanne Rd	26	YZH
Linden Grove	26	YZH
Lordship Lane	26	XZH
Lyndhurst Grove	26	XZH
Lyndhurst Way	26	XZH
Lynton Rd	26	YZG
Mandela Way	26	XZF
Marlborough Grove	26	XZG
Mc Neil Rd	26	XZH
Meeting House Lane	26	YZG
Melbourne Grove	26	XZH
Naylord Rd	26	YZG
Neate St	26	XZG
Nunhead Grove	26	YZH
Nunhead Lane	26	YZH
Oglander Rd	26	XZH
Old Kent Rd	26	XZG
Peckham Hill St	26	XZH
Peckham Park Rd	26	XZG
Peckham Rd	26	XZH
Peckham Rye	26	YZH
Pomeroy St	26	YZG
Pytchley Rd	26	XZH
Queens Rd	26	YZH
Raymouth Rd	26	YZF
Reverdy Rd	26	XZG
Rolls Rd	26	XZG

Rotherhithe New Rd 26 YZG
Rye Lane 26 XZH
St George's Way 26 XZG
St James Rd 26 YZG
Shenley Rd 26 XZH
Southwark Park Rd 26 XZF
Stuart Rd 26 YZH
Summer Rd 26 XZG
Surrey Canal Rd 26 YZG
Trafalgar Ave 26 XZG
Verney Rd 26 YZG
Willowbrook Rd 26 XZG
Willow Walk 26 XZF
Yaldind Rd 26 XZF 369

PLAN 27

Artesian Rd 27 AAU
Aubrey Walk 27 AAV
Bark Pl. 27 ABU
Bayswater Rd 27 ABV
Bedford Gardens 27 AAV
Bishop's Bridge Rd 27 ABT
Bourne Terrace 27 ABT
Broad Walk (The) 27 ABV
Campden Grove 27 AAV
Campden Hill Rd 27 AAV
Campden Hill Square 27 AAV
Chepstow Crescent 27 AAU 84
Chepstow Pl. 27 AAU
Chepstow Rd 27 AAT
Chepstow Villas 27 AAU
Colville Rd 27 AAU
Colville Terrace 27 AAU
Dawson Pl. 27 AAU
Garway Rd 27 ABU
Gloucester Terrace 27 ABT
Great Western Rd 27 AAT
Harrow Rd 27 ABT
Hereford Rd 27 ABU
Holland Park Ave 27 AAV
Inverness Terrace 27 ABU
Kensington Church St 27 AAV
Kensington Gardens Square 27 ABU
Kensington Palace Gardens 27 ABV
Kensington Park Rd 27 AAU
Kensington Pl. 27 AAV
Ladbroke Rd 27 AAV
Ladbroke Square 27 AAV
Ledbury Rd 27 AAT
Leinster Square 27 ABU
Linden Gardens 27 AAU
Moscow Rd 27 ABU
Newton Rd 27 ABT
Notting Hill Gate 27 AAV
Orme Court 27 ABU 328
Ossington St 27 ABU
Palace Court 27 ABU
Palace Gardens Terrace 27 ABV
Palace Green 27 ABV
Pembridge Crescent 27 AAU
Pembridge Gardens 27 AAU
Pembridge Rd 27 AAU
Pembridge Square 27 AAU
Pembridge Villas 27 AAU
Porchester Gardens 27 ABU
Porchester Rd 27 ABT
Porchester Square 27 ABT 197
Portobello Rd 27 AAU
Queensborough Terrace 27 ABU
Queensway 27 ABU
St Luke's Rd 27 AAT
St Petersburgh Pl. 27 ABU
Sheffield Terrace 27 AAV
Talbot Rd 27 AAT
Tavistock Rd 27 AAT
Uxbridge St 27 AAV
Westbourne Gardens 27 ABT
Westbourne Grove 27 AAU
Westbourne Park Rd 27 AAT
Westbourne Park Villas 27 ABT

PLAN 28

Chilworth St 28 ACU
Church St 28 ADT
Cleveland Square 28 ACU
Cleveland Terrace 28 ACT
Craven Hill 28 ACU
Craven Rd 28 ACU
Craven Terrace 28 ACU
Devonshire Terrace 28 ACU 136
Eastbourne Terrace 28 ACT
Edgware Rd 28 ADT
Gloucester Square 28 ADU
Hyde Park Gardens 28 ADU
Lancaster Gate 28 ACU
Lancaster Terrace 28 ADU 257
Leinster Gardens 28 ACU
Leinster Terrace 28 ACU
London St 28 ADT
Norfolk Pl. 28 ADT
North Wharf Rd 28 ADT
Orsett Terrace 28 ACT
Porchester Terrace 28 ACU
Praed St 28 ADU
Queen Anne's Gate 28 ACU 94
Queen's Gardens 28 ACU
Radnor Pl. 28 ADT
Ring (The) 28 ADV
Sale Place 28 AET
South Wharf Rd 28 ADT
Spring St 28 ADU
Stanhope Terrace 28 ADU 158
Sussex Gardens 28 ADU
Sussex Pl. 28 ADU
Sussex Square 28 ADU
Westbourne Crescent 28 ADU 448
Westbourne St 28 ADU
Westbourne Terrace 28 ACT
Westbourne Terrace Rd 28 ACT 452

PLAN 29

Albion St 29 AFU
Aybrook St 29 AGT
Baker St 29 AGT
Bell St 29 AET
Blandford St 29 AGT
Bryanston Pl. 29 AFT
Bryanston Square 29 AFT 14
Bryanston St 29 AFU
Cambridge Square 29 AET 67
Chapel St 29 AET
Chiltern St 29 AGT
Clarendon Pl. 29 AEU 93
Connaught Square 29 AFU
Connaught St 29 AFU
Crawford Pl. 29 AFT
Crawford St 29 AFT
Culross St 29 AGU
Dorset St 29 AGT
Dunraven St 29 AGU 149
Enford St 29 AFT
George St 29 AFT
Gloucester Pl. 29 AGT
Granville Pl. 29 AGU 476
Great Cumberland Pl. 29 AFT
Green St 29 AGU
Harcourt St 29 AFT
Harrowby St 29 AFT
Hyde Park Square 29 AEU
Hyde Park St 29 AEU
Kendal St 29 AFU
Lees Pl. 29 AGU
Manchester Square 29 AGT 281
Manchester St 29 AGT
Marble Arch 29 AGU
Marylebone Rd 29 AFT
Montagu Pl. 29 AFT
Montagu Square 29 AGT 90
Mount St 29 AGV
Norfolk Crescent 29 AFT
North Audley St 29 AGU 314
North Row 29 AGU
Old Marylebone Rd 29 AFT
Orchard St 29 AGU
Oxford Square 29 AFU 332
Oxford St 29 AGU
Paddington St 29 AGT
Park Lane 29 AGU
Park St MAYFAIR 29 AGU
Portman Square 29 AGT
Portman St 29 AGU
Reeves Mews 29 AGV 103
Rotten Row 29 AEV
Serpentine Rd 29 AFV
Seymour St 29 AFU
Shouldham St 29 AFT
Southwick St 29 AET 156
Stanhope Pl. 29 AFU 400
Upper Berkeley St 29 AFU
Upper Brook St 29 AGU
Upper Grosvenor St 29 AGU
Upper Montagu St 29 AFT
Wigmore St 29 AGU
Woods Mews 29 AGU
York St 29 AFT

PLAN 30

Adam's Row 30 AHU
Albemarle St 30 AIU 225
Aldford St 30 AHV 2
Argyll St 30 AIU
Arlington St 30 AIV 6
Avery Row 30 AHU 12
Beak St 30 AIU
Berkeley Square 30 AHU
Berkeley St 30 AIV
Binney St 30 AHU
Bolton St 30 AIV
Brick St 30 AHV
Brook St 30 AHU
Brook's Mews 30 AHU
Bruton St 30 AIU
Burlington Arcade 30 AIV
Bury St 30 AIV
Carlos Pl. 30 AHU 35
Carnaby St 30 AIU
Cavendish Square 30 AHT
Chandos St 30 AIT 36
Charles St 30 AHV
Cleveland St 30 AIT
Clifford St 30 AIU 38
Conduit St 30 AIU
Cork St 30 AIU
Curzon St 30 AHV
Davies St 30 AHU
Deanery St 30 AHV 132
Devonshire St 30 AHT 48
Dover St 30 AIV
Duke St 30 AHU
Duke St ST. JAMES 30 AIV
Eastcastle St 30 AIT
Farm St MAYFAIR 30 AHV
Foley St 30 AIT
Gilbert St 30 AHU
Grafton St 30 AIU 62
Great Castle St 30 AIT 189
Great Marlborough St 30 AIU

Street	Plan	Grid	No.
Great Portland St	30	AIT	
Great Titchfield St	30	AIT	
Grosvenor Square	30	AHU	
Grosvenor St	30	AHU	
Half Moon St	30	AHV	81
Hamilton Pl.	30	AHV	205
Hanover Square	30	AIU	
Hanover St	30	AIU	
Harley St WESTMINSTER	30	AHT	
Hay's Mews	30	AHV	
Henrietta Pl.	30	AHT	
Hertford St	30	AHV	
Hill St	30	AHV	
Holles St	30	AIT	
Howland St	30	AIT	232
James St	30	AHT	
Kingly St	30	AIU	
King St ST. JAMES'S	30	AIV	
Langham St	30	AIT	
Little Portland St	30	AIT	228
Maddox St	30	AIU	
Margaret St	30	AIT	
Market Pl.	30	AIT	286
Marshall St	30	AIU	
Marylebone High St	30	AHT	
Marylebone Lane	30	AHT	287
Mortimer St	30	AIT	
Mount Row	30	AHU	
New Bond St	30	AHU	
New Cavendish St	30	AHT	
Old Bond St	30	AIV	
Old Burlington St	30	AIU	322
Old Park Lane	30	AHV	
Oxford Circus	30	AIT	
Piccadilly	30	AHV	
Piccadilly Arcade	30	AIV	
Poland St	30	AIT	
Portland Pl.	30	AIT	
Princes St	30	AQU	
Queen Anne St	30	AHT	
Queen's Walk	30	AIV	
Regent St	30	AIT	
Sackville St	30	AIU	
St George St	30	AIU	
St James's Pl.	30	AIV	116
St James's St	30	AIV	
Savile Row	30	AIU	
Shepherd Market	30	AHV	
Shepherd St	30	AHV	153
South Audley St	30	AHU	
South Molton St	30	AHU	
South St	30	AHV	
Stratton St	30	AIV	168
Thayer St	30	AHT	413
Tilney St	30	AHV	421
Vere St	30	AHU	
Vigo St	30	AIU	
Waverton St	30	AHV	178
Weighouse St	30	AHU	184
Welbeck St	30	AHT	
Wells St	30	AIT	
Weymouth St	30	AHT	
Wimpole St	30	AHT	

PLAN 31

Street	Plan	Grid	No.
Adam St	31	ALU	
Bateman St	31	AKU	18
Bayley St	31	AKT	260
Bedfordbury	31	ALU	243
Bedford Square	31	AKT	
Bedford St	31	ALU	
Berner's St	31	AJT	
Berwick St	31	AJT	26
Bloomsbury Square	31	ALT	
Bloomsbury St	31	AKT	
Bloomsbury Way	31	ALT	9
Boswell St	31	ALT	
Bow St	31	ALU	
Brewer St	31	AJU	
Broadwick St	31	AJU	
Bury Pl.	31	ALT	
Cambridge Circus	31	AKU	
Carlton Gardens	31	AKV	74
Carlton House Terrace	31	AKV	
Carting Lane	31	ALU	245
Chandos Pl.	31	ALU	
Charing Cross	31	ALV	
Charing Cross Rd	31	AKT	
Charles II St	31	AKV	
Charlotte St	31	AJT	
Cherries St	31	AKT	256
Cockspur St	31	AKV	39
Coventry St	31	AKU	
Cranbourn St	31	AKU	115
Craven St	31	ALV	
Dean St	31	AKT	
Denman St	31	AKU	133
Denmark St	31	AKT	134
Drury Lane	31	ALT	
Duke of York St	31	AJV	143
Duncannon St	31	ALV	147
D'Arblay St	31	AJU	
Earlham St	31	AKU	
Endell St	31	ALT	
Exeter St	31	ALU	
Floral St	31	ALU	
Frith St	31	AKU	
Garrick St	31	ALU	
Gerrard St	31	AKU	174
Glasshouse St SOHO	31	AJU	179
Golden Jubilee Bridge	31	ALV	
Golden Square	31	AJU	
Goodge St	31	AJT	
Gower St	31	AKT	
Great Queen St	31	ALT	
Great Russell St	31	AKT	
Great Windmill St	31	AKU	261
Greek St	31	AKU	
Hanway St	31	AKT	210
Haymarket	31	AKU	
Henrietta St	31	ALU	217
Horse Guards Ave	31	ALV	
Horse Guards Rd	31	AKV	
James St SOHO	31	AJU	
Jermyn St	31	AJV	
John Adam St	31	ALV	238
Kingsway	31	ALT	
King St STRAND	31	ALU	
Leicester Square	31	AKU	
Lexington St	31	AJU	
Lisle St	31	AKU	
Long Acre	31	ALU	
Macklin St	31	ALT	
Maiden Lane	31	ALU	83
Mall (The)	31	AKV	
Monmouth St	31	ALU	88
Museum St	31	ALT	
Neal St	31	ALU	
Newman St	31	AJT	
Newton St	31	ALT	
New Oxford St	31	AKT	
New Row	31	ALU	
Noel St	31	AJU	
Northumberland Ave	31	ALV	
Old Compton St	31	AKU	
Old Gloucester St	31	ALT	
Orange St	31	AKV	
Pall Mall	31	AJV	
Panton St	31	AKU	
Parker St	31	ALT	
Percy St	31	AKT	
Piccadilly Circus	31	AKU	
Richmond Terrace	31	ALV	234
Romilly St	31	AKU	368
Royal Opera Arcade	31	AKV	
Rupert St	31	AKU	
Russell St	31	ALU	
St Giles Circus	31	AKT	
St Giles High St	31	AKT	
St James's Square	31	AJV	
St Martins Lane	31	ALU	
Savoy Pl.	31	ALU	
Shaftesbury Ave	31	AKU	
Shelton St	31	ALU	
Shorts Gardens	31	ALU	
Soho Square	31	AKT	
Southampton Row	31	ALT	473
Southampton St	31	ALU	388
Store St	31	AKT	
Strand	31	ALV	
Tavistock St	31	ALU	
Tottenham Court Rd	31	AKT	
Trafalgar Square	31	AKV	
Upper St Martin's Lane	31	ALU	430
Villiers St	31	ALV	
Wardour St	31	AJU	
Warwick St	31	AJU	444
Waterloo Pl.	31	AKV	
Wellington St	31	ALU	187
Whitcomb St	31	AKU	191
Whitehall	31	ALV	
Whitehall Court	31	ALV	460
Whitehall Pl.	31	ALV	
Wild St	31	ALU	
William IV St	31	ALV	467

PLAN 32

Street	Plan	Grid	No.
Aldwych	32	AMU	
Arundel St	32	AMU	
Bedford Row	32	AMT	
Belvedere Rd	32	AMV	
Bouverie St	32	AMU	
Bream's Buildings	32	ANT	47
Carey St	32	AMU	
Chancery Lane	32	AMT	
Charterhouse St	32	ANT	
Cornwall Rd	32	ANV	
Cut (The)	32	ANV	
Essex St	32	AMU	
Farringdon Rd	32	ANT	
Fetter Lane	32	ANT	
Fleet St	32	ANU	
Furnival St	32	ANT	278
Gray's Inn Rd	32	ANT	
Greville St	32	ANT	
Halton Garden	32	ANT	
Hatfields	32	ANV	
High Holborn	32	AMT	
Holborn	32	ANT	
Holborn Viaduct	32	ANT	
John Carpenter St	32	ANU	17
Kemble St	32	AMU	
Lancaster Pl.	32	AMU	
Leather Lane	32	ANT	
Lincoln's Inn Fields	32	AMT	
New Fetter Lane	32	ANT	
New Square	32	AMT	
New St Square	32	ANT	282
Portugal St	32	AMU	
Procter St	32	AMT	273
Red Lion Square	32	AMT	
Red Lion St	32	AMT	
Roupel St	32	ANV	
St Andrews St	32	ANT	372
St Bride St	32	ANT	376
Sardinia St	32	AMT	381
Savoy St	32	AMU	270
Serle St	32	AMT	
Shoe Lane	32	ANT	
Stamford St	32	ANV	
Surrey St	32	AMU	175
Temple Ave	32	ANU	
Temple Pl.	32	AMU	

LONDON

Gloucester Rd 36 ACX
Grenville Pl. 36 ACY
Harcourt Terrace 36 ACZ 477
Harrington Gardens 36 ACY
Harrington Rd 36 ADY
Hollywood Rd 36 ACZ
Hyde Park Gate 36 ACX
Kensington Gore 36 ACX
King's Rd 36 ADZ
Launceston Pl. 36 ACX 259
Little Boltons (The) 36 ACZ
Manresa Rd 36 ADZ
Neville Terrace 36 ADZ 300
Old Church St 36 ADZ
Onslow Gardens 36 ADZ
Onslow Square 36 ADY
Palace Gate 36 ACX
Park Walk 36 ACZ
Pelham St 36 ADY
Prince Consort Rd 36 ADX
Prince's Gardens 36 ADX 356
Queensberry Pl. 36 ADY 360
Queen's Gate 36 ACX
Queen's Gate Gardens 36 ACY 198
Queen's Gate Pl. 36 ACY 363
Queen's Gate Terrace 36 ACX
Redcliffe Rd 36 ACZ
Roland Gardens 36 ACZ
South Parade 36 ADZ
Stanhope Gardens 36 ACY
Sumner Pl. 36 ADY
Sydney Pl. 36 ADY 405
Thurloe Pl. 36 ADY
Thurloe Square 36 ADY
Tregunter Rd 36 ACZ
Vale (The) 36 ADZ
Victoria Grove 36 ACX
Victoria Rd KENSINGTON 36 ACX
Wetherby Gardens 36 ACY

PLAN 37

Basil St 37 AFX
Beauchamp Pl. 37 AFX
Belgrave Square 37 AGX
Bourne St 37 AGY
Bray Pl. 37 AFY 45
Britten St 37 AEZ
Brompton Rd 37 AFX
Cadogan Gardens 37 AGY 23
Cadogan Gate 37 AGY 220
Cadogan Pl. 37 AGY
Cadogan Square 37 AGY
Cadogan St 37 AFY
Carriage Rd (The) 37 AFX
Chelsea Bridge Rd 37 AGZ
Chelsea Embankment 37 AGZ
Chelsea Manor St 37 AFZ
Cheltenham Terrace 37 AGZ
Chesham Pl. 37 AGX
Chesham St 37 AGY
Chester Row 37 AGY
Cheval Pl. 37 AFX
Christchurch St 37 AFZ
Draycott Ave 37 AFY
Draycott Pl. 37 AFY
Eaton Pl. 37 AGY
Egerton Gardens 37 AFY 160
Egerton Gardens Mews 37 AFY 162
Egerton Terrace 37 AFY 161
Elystan Pl. 37 AFZ
Elystan St 37 AEY
Ennismore Gardens 37 AEX
Flood St 37 AFZ
Franklin's Row 37 AGZ
Glebe Pl. 37 AEZ
Grosvenor Crescent 37 AGX
Hans Crescent 37 AFX
Hans Pl. 37 AFX
Hans Rd 37 AFX
Harriet St 37 AGX 214
Hasker St 37 AFY
Holbein Mews 37 AGZ 223
Holbein Pl. 37 AGY
Ixworth Pl. 37 AEY
Jubilee Pl. 37 AFZ
Knightsbridge 37 AFX
Lennox Gardens 37 AFY
Lennox Gardens Mews 37 AFY 263
Lower Sloane St 37 AGY
Lowndes Square 37 AGX
Lowndes St 37 AGX
Lyall St 37 AGY
Markham St 37 AFZ
Milner St 37 AFY
Montpelier Square 37 AFX
Montpelier St 37 AFX
Moore St 37 AFY
Mossop St 37 AFY
Oakley St 37 AEZ
Ormonde Gate 37 AGZ 329
Pimlico Rd 37 AGZ
Pont St 37 AFY
Radnor Walk 37 AFZ
Rawlings St 37 AFY
Redesdale St 37 AFZ 367
Royal Hospital Rd 37 AFZ
Rutland Gate 37 AEX
St Leonard's Terrace 37 AGZ
Shawfield St 37 AFZ
Sloane Ave 37 AFY
Sloane Square 37 AGY
Sloane St 37 AGX
Smith St 37 AFZ
South Terrace 37 AEY
Sydney St 37 AEZ
Symons St 37 AGY 407
Tedworth Square 37 AFZ
Tite St 37 AFZ
Trevor Pl. 37 AFX
Trevor Square 37 AFX
Walton St 37 AFY
West Halkin St 37 AGX
Whiteheads 37 AFY
William St 37 AGX 468
Wilton Pl. 37 AGX

PLAN 38

Alderney St 38 AIY
Belgrave Pl. 38 AHX
Belgrave Rd 38 AIY
Birdcage Walk 38 AIX
Bressenden Pl. 38 AIX
Buckingham Gate 38 AIX
Buckingham Palace Rd 38 AHY
Carlisle Pl. 38 AIY
Castle Lane 38 AIX
Chapel St BELGRAVIA 38 AHX
Charlwood St 38 AIZ
Chelsea Bridge 38 AHZ
Chester Square 38 AHY
Chester St 38 AHX
Churchill Gardens Rd 38 AIZ
Clarendon St 38 AIZ
Constitution Hill 38 AHX
Cumberland St 38 AIZ
Denbigh St 38 AIZ
Duke of Wellington Pl. 38 AHX 142
Eaton Square 38 AHY
Ebury Bridge 38 AHZ
Ebury Bridge Rd 38 AHZ
Ebury St 38 AHY
Eccleston Bridge 38 AHY 157
Eccleston Square 38 AIY
Eccleston St 38 AHY
Elizabeth St 38 AHY
Francis St 38 AIY
Gillingham St 38 AIY
Gloucester St 38 AIZ
Grosvenor Gardens 38 AHX
Grosvenor Pl. 38 AHX
Grosvenor Rd 38 AHZ
Guildhouse St 38 AIY 201
Halkin St 38 AHX
Hobart Pl. 38 AHX
Hudson's Pl. 38 AIY
Hugh St 38 AIY
Lower Belgrave St 38 AHY
Lower Grosvenor Pl. 38 AIX 274
Lupus St 38 AIZ
Palace St 38 AIX
St George's Drive 38 AIY
South Eaton Pl. 38 AHY
Sutherland St 38 AHZ
Terminus Pl. 38 AIY 412
Upper Belgrave St 38 AHX
Vauxhall Bridge Rd 38 AIY
Victoria St 38 AIX
Warwick Square 38 AIY
Warwick Way 38 AHZ
Wilton Rd 38 AIY
Wilton St 38 AHX

PLAN 39

Abingdon St 39 AKY
Albert Embankment 39 ALY
Artillery Row 39 AKX 8
Atterbury St 39 ALZ
Aylesford St 39 AKZ
Bessborough Gardens 39 AKZ
Bessborough St 39 AKZ 30
Bridge St 39 ALX
Broad Sanctuary 39 ALX 52
Caxton St 39 AKX
Chichester St 39 AJZ
Claverton St 39 AJZ
Dolphin Square 39 AJZ
Douglas St 39 AKY
Erasmus St 39 AKY
Glasshouse St LAMBETH 39 ALZ 108
Great College St 39 ALX
Great George St 39 AKX 193
Great Peter St 39 AKY
Great Smith St 39 AKX
Greencoat Pl. 39 AJY
Greycoat Pl. 39 AKY 200
Greycoat St 39 AKY
Horseferry Rd 39 AKY
Howick Pl. 39 AJY
John Islip St 39 AKZ
King Charles St 39 AKX
Lambeth Bridge 39 ALY
Marsham St 39 AKY
Millbank 39 ALZ
Monck St 39 AKY
Montpelier Walk 37 AFX
Moreton St 39 AJZ
Nine Elms Lane 39 AKZ
Old Pye St 39 AKX
Page St 39 AKY
Palmer St 39 AKX
Parlament Square 39 ALX
Parliament St 39 ALX
Parry St 39 ALZ 341
Petty France 39 AJX
Ponsonby Pl. 39 AKZ
Rampayne St 39 AKZ

Regency St . . . . 39 AKY
Rochester Row. . . . . 39 AJY
St Anne's St . . . . 39 AKX
St George's Square . 39 AKZ
South Lambeth Rd . . 39 ALZ 154
Storeys Gate . . . . 39 AKX
Tachbrook St. . . . . . . 39 AJY
Thirleby Rd . . . . 39 AJY 416
Thorney St. . . . . 39 ALY
Tinworth St . . . . 39 ALZ 129
Tothill St. . . . . 39 AKX
Tufton St . . . . 39 AKX
Vauxhall Bridge . . . . . 39 ALZ
Vincent Square . . . . . 39 AKY
Vincent St . . . . 39 AKY
Westminster Bridge. 39 ALX

PLAN 40

Baylis Rd . . . . 40 ANX
Black Prince Rd. . . . . 40 AMY
Braganza St. . . . . 40 AOZ
Brook Drive . . . . 40 ANY
Chester Way. . . . . . . 40 ANY
Clayton St . . . . 40 ANZ
Cleaver St . . . . 40 ANZ
Cooks St . . . . 40 AOZ
Courtenay St . . . . 40 AMZ
Dante Rd. . . . . 40 AOY
De Laune St . . . . 40 ANZ
Durham St. . . . . 40 AMZ 150
Fitzalan St . . . . 40 AMY
Garden Row . . . . 40 AOX 173
Harleyford Rd . . . . . . 40 AMZ
Hayles St. . . . . 40 AOY
Hercules Rd . . . . 40 AMX
Johnathan St. . . . . . . 40 AMZ
Juxon St . . . . 40 AMY
Kennington Lane . . . 40 AMZ
Kennington Oval. . . . 40 AMZ
Kennington Rd . . . . . 40 ANX
Kennington Park Rd 40 ANZ
Lambeth High St . . . 40 AMY
Lambeth Palace Rd . 40 AMX
Lambeth Rd . . . . 40 AMY
Lambeth Walk . . . . . 40 AMY
London Rd . . . . 40 AOX
Lower Marsh . . . . . . 40 AMX
Newburn St . . . . 40 AMZ
Pearman St. . . . . 40 ANX
Ravensdon St . . . . . . 40 ANZ 219
Renfrew Rd . . . . 40 ANY
St George's Rd . . . . . 40 ANX
Sancroft St . . . . 40 AMZ
Stannary St . . . . 40 ANZ
Tyers St . . . . 40 AMZ
Vauxhall St. . . . . 40 AMZ
Vauxhall Walk . . . . . . 40 AMZ
Walcot Square . . . . . 40 ANY
Walnut Tree Walk. . . 40 AMY
Webber St. . . . . 40 ANX
Westminster Bridge
Rd . . . . 40 AMX
West Square. . . . . . . 40 AOY
Wincoot St . . . . 40 ANY
York Rd . . . . 40 AMX

LONDON

K
L
9
Brent Reservoir
North Circular Road
A 406
NEASDEN JUNCTION
Crest Road
Avenue
Tanfield
Brook Rd
Coles Green Rd
Edgware Rd
A 5
Cricklewood
Dollis Hill Lane
GLADSTONE PARK
BRENT
Mora Rd
Sneyd Rd
Heber Rd
A 4088
Dudden Hill
Neasden Lane
Neasden
Kendal Rd
Anson Road
Park Ave North
Burnley Road
Sherrick Green Rd
Dollis Hill
Denzil Road
Chapter Road
Willesden Green
Walm Lane
WILLESDEN GREEN
High Road
Lane
A 407
357
Brondesbury Rd
Roundwood Road
Pound Lane
WILLESDEN CEMETERY
Peter Ave
KILBURN
Sidmouth
Mount Pleasant Rd
482
Church Road
ROUNDWOOD PARK
196
351
Donnington Road
Harlesden Road
Chamberlayne Road
A 404
352
Manor Park Rd
Doyle Road
Avenue
Hardinge Rd
480
Acton Lane
High Street
Wrottesley Road
Gdns
All Souls
College Rd
Clifford Gdns
Harley Road
Furness Road
Bathurst Gdns
KENSAL RISE
Harrow Road
Mortimer
Kensal Green
A 404
Harrow
Oak Lane
Willesden Junction
15
ZA
ZB
ZC
LONDON

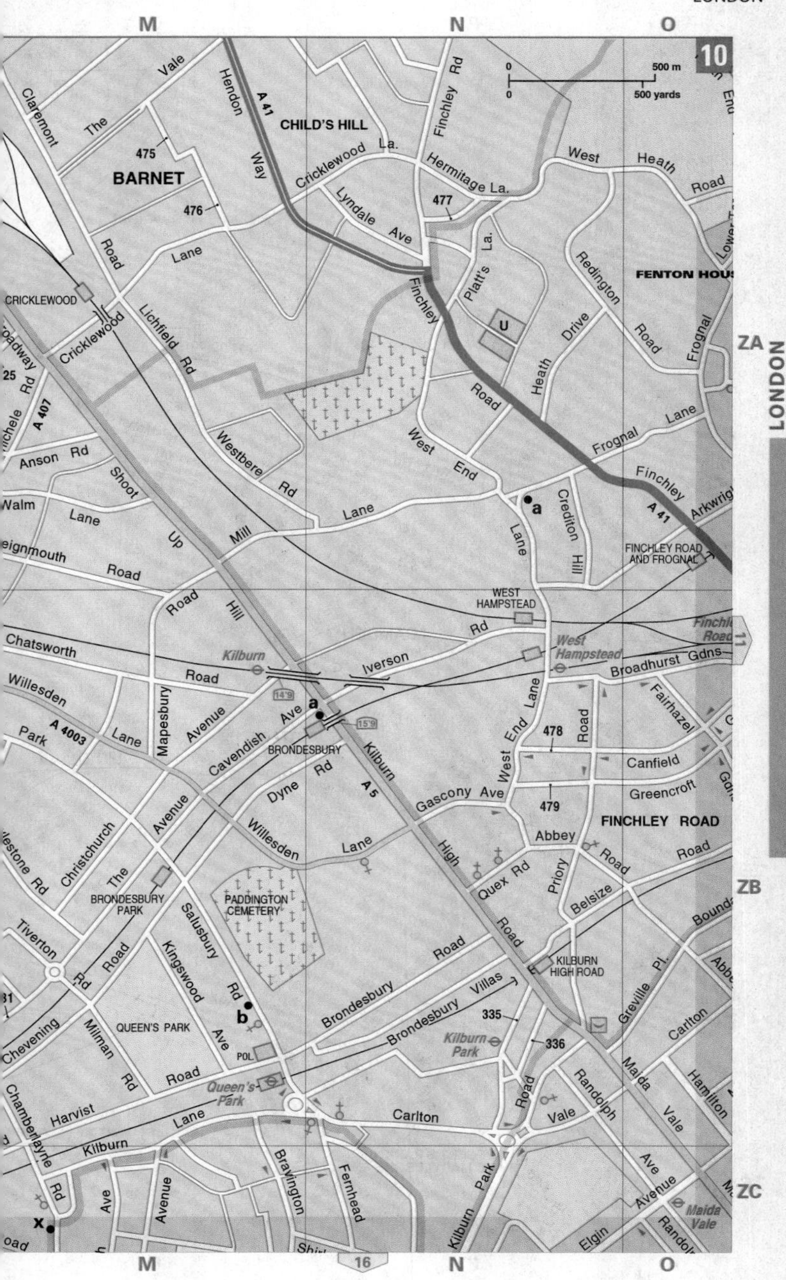
M
N
O
10
CHILD'S HILL
BARNET
CRICKLEWOOD
FENTON HOUSE
FINCHLEY ROAD AND FROGNAL
WEST HAMPSTEAD
Kilburn
West Hampstead
BRONDESBURY
FINCHLEY ROAD
BRONDESBURY PARK
PADDINGTON CEMETERY
KILBURN HIGH ROAD
QUEEN'S PARK
Kilburn Park
Queen's Park
Maida Vale
ZA
ZB
ZC
LONDON
16
11

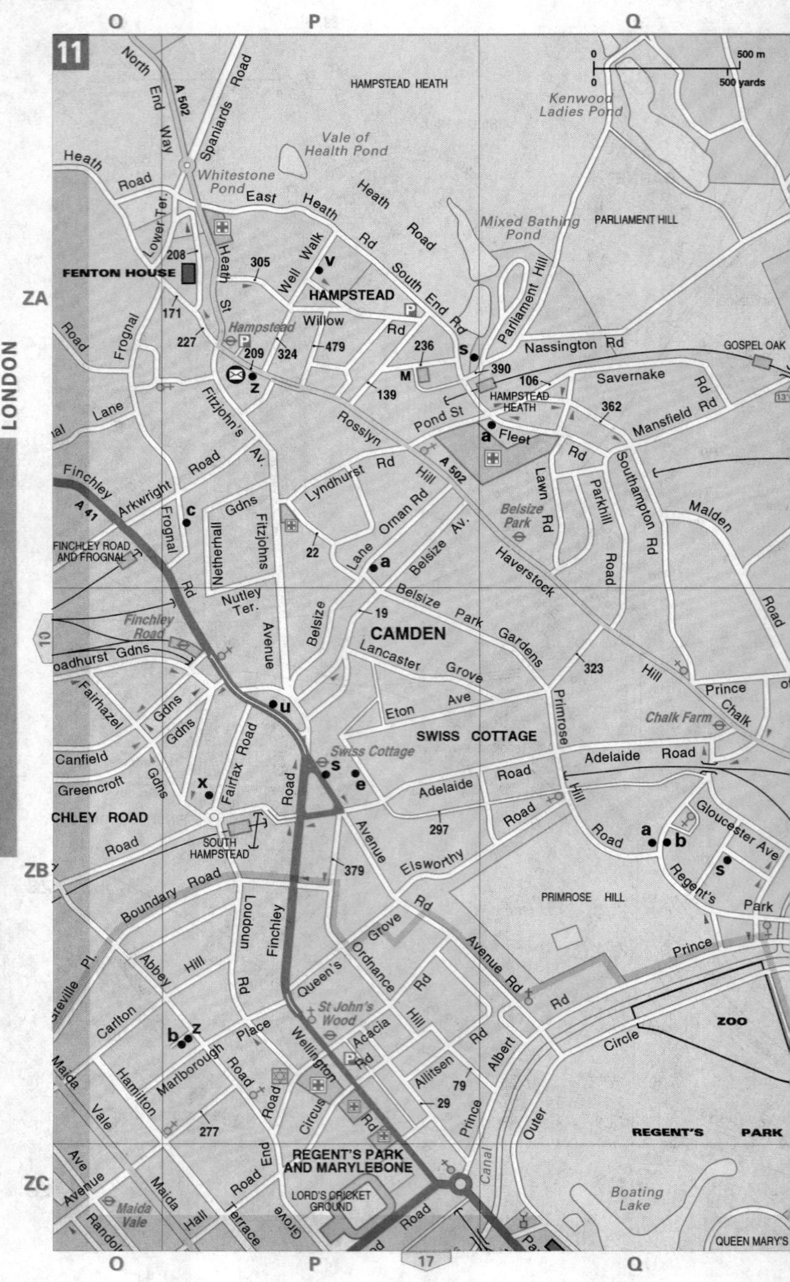
11
HAMPSTEAD HEATH
Kenwood Ladies Pond
Vale of Health Pond
Whitestone Pond
Mixed Bathing Pond
PARLIAMENT HILL
FENTON HOUSE
HAMPSTEAD
GOSPEL OAK
HAMPSTEAD HEATH
FINCHLEY ROAD AND FROGNAL
CAMDEN
SWISS COTTAGE
Swiss Cottage
Chalk Farm
Belsize Park
Finchley Road
SOUTH HAMPSTEAD
PRIMROSE HILL
ZOO
St John's Wood
REGENT'S PARK AND MARYLEBONE
LORD'S CRICKET GROUND
REGENT'S PARK
Boating Lake
QUEEN MARY'S
Maida Vale
Hampstead

R
S
T
12
DARTMOUTH PARK
Archway
Holloway Road
UPPER HOLLOWAY
A 1
Tollington Way
Tollington Park
Hornsey Road
Dartmouth Park Hill
Junction Road
Swains Lane
Chetwynd Road
Highgate Rd
Tufnell Park
Tufnell Park Road
Holloway Road
Seven Sisters Road
Hornsey Road
A 503
ZA
LONDON
Dalmeny Rd
Dalmeny Ave
Carleton Rd
Parkhurst Road
Caledonian Road
Fortess Road
Lady Margaret Rd
Leighton Rd
Kentish Town
Islip Street
Busby Place
Gaisford Street
Patshull Road
Torriano Ave
Camden Road
Hillmarton Road
Hungerford Road
ISLING
Caledonian Road
North Road
Market Road
Mackenzie Road
Brewery Road
York Way
A 5200
A 5203
CALEDONIAN AND BARNSBURY
Spring Place
Willes Road
KENTISH TOWN
Wales Road
A 400
Kentish Town Road
16
A 503
St Pancras Way
Agar Grove
Farm
CAMDEN ROAD
366
Offord
Royal College St
Camden Town
Parkway
Camden High St
Camden Rd
Pratt St
Richmond
ZB
Copenhagen St
Delancey St
Outer Circle
Park Village East
Albany Street
Mornington Crescent
Crowndale Rd
Eversholt Street
Pancras Rd
Hampstead Road
Midland Rd
KING'S CROSS
ST PANCRAS
455
Calshot St
Pentonville
King's
417
BRITISH LIBRARY
Ossulston St
TERRACES
REGENT'S PARK
Robert Street
Chester Rd
EUSTON
Euston Road
Judd
Cross
ZC
18

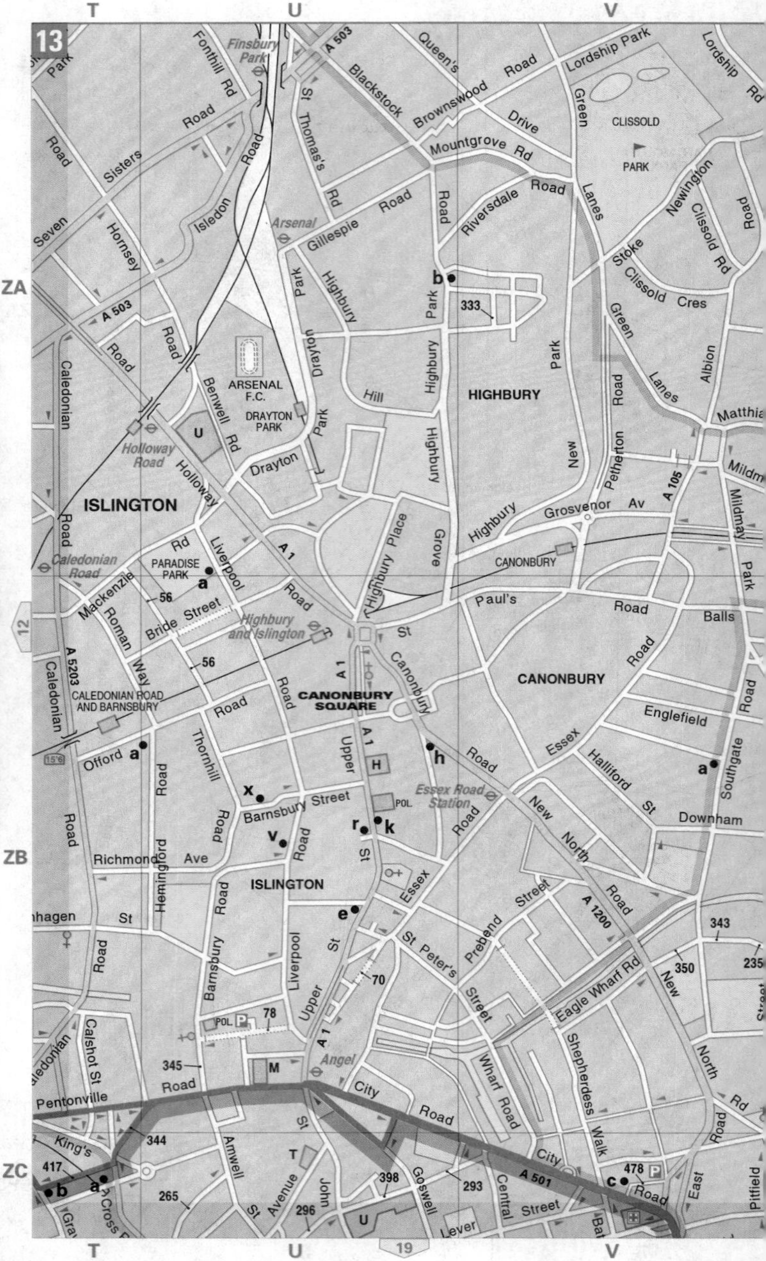
T
U
V
13
ZA
ZB
ZC
Finsbury Park
A 503
Queen's
Road
Lordship Park
Lordship Rd
Blackstock
Brownswood
Drive
Green
Lanes
CLISSOLD
PARK
Mountgrove Rd
Fonthill Rd
St Thomas's Rd
Road
Sisters
Seven
Road
Isledon
Arsenal
Gillespie
Road
Riversdale
Road
Stoke Newington
Clissold Rd
Road
Clissold Cres
Green Lanes
Hornsey
Road
A 503
Road
Road
Caledonian
Highbury
Park
Drayton
Park
Highbury
Park
b
333
ARSENAL F.C.
DRAYTON PARK
Benwell Rd
Hill
Highbury
HIGHBURY
New Park
Petherton Road
Albion
Matthias
Mildmay
U
Holloway Road
Holloway
Drayton
Highbury
A 105
ISLINGTON
Road
Highbury
Grosvenor Av
Mildmay Park
Caledonian Road
Rd
PARADISE PARK
Liverpool
Mackenzie
a
56
Highbury Place
Grove
CANONBURY
A 1
Road
Paul's
Road
Balls
12
Roman Way
Bride Street
Highbury and Islington
St
Canonbury
Road
A 5203
Caledonian
56
A 1
Road
CANONBURY SQUARE
CANONBURY
CALEDONIAN ROAD AND BARNSBURY
Road
Englefield
Road
15'6
Offord a
Thornhill
Upper
A 1
H
Road
h
Essex
Halliford
Southgate
a
Road
x
Essex Road Station
St
Barnsbury Street
POL.
Road
New
Downham
v
r k
Road
North
Road
Richmond Ave
St
ZB
Hemingford
Barnsbury
ISLINGTON
Essex
Street
A 1200
Road
Road
Prebend
343
hagen
St
e
St Peter's
350
235
Road
Liverpool
St
Eagle Wharf Rd
New
Barnsbury
Upper
70
Street
Street
POL. P
78
A 1
Shepherdess
Caledonian
Calshot St
Wharf Road
North
345
Road
M
Angel
Walk
Rd
Pentonville
City
Road
Road
St
King's
344
Amwell
T
City
417
A 501
478 P
b
a
265
Avenue
John
398
Goswell
293
Central
c
Road
East
Pitfield
Cross
St
296
U
Lever
Street
19

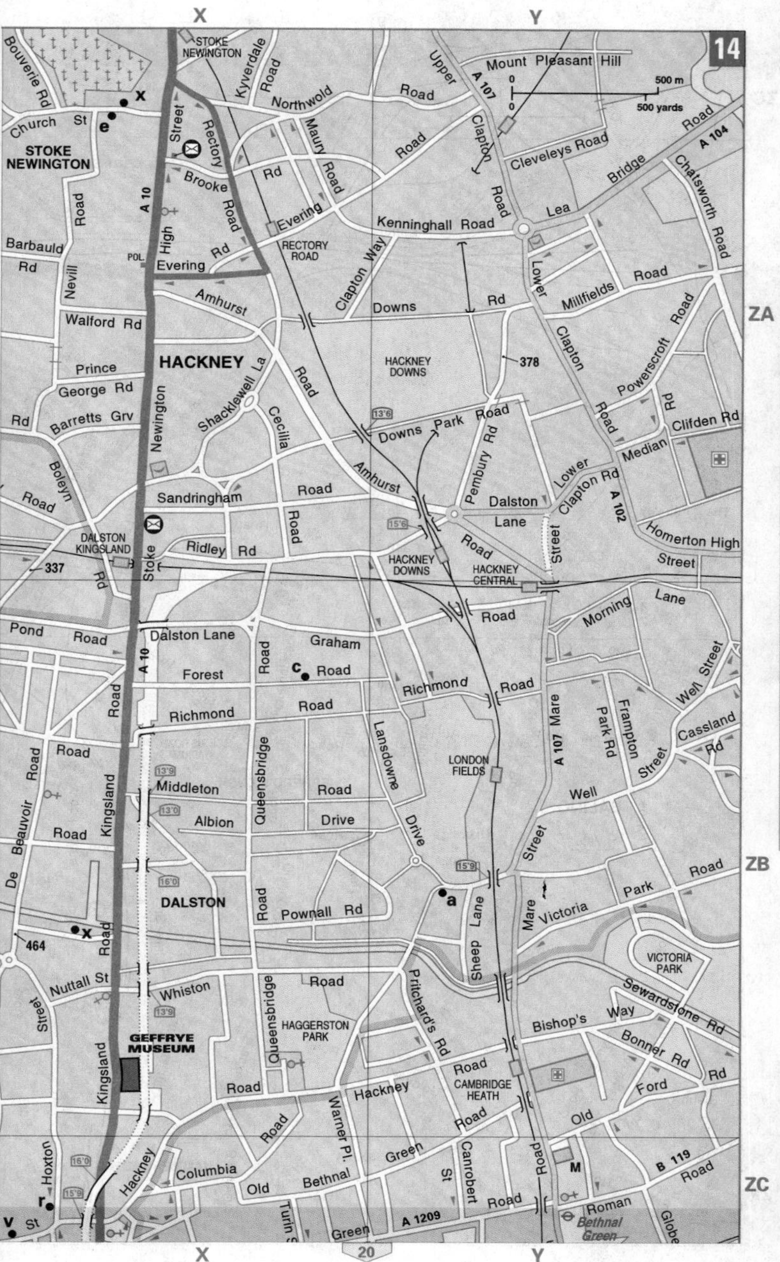
14
X
Y
ZA
ZB
ZC
20
STOKE NEWINGTON
HACKNEY
DALSTON
HACKNEY DOWNS
LONDON FIELDS
VICTORIA PARK
HAGGERSTON PARK
GEFFRYE MUSEUM
CAMBRIDGE HEATH
HACKNEY CENTRAL
DALSTON KINGSLAND
RECTORY ROAD
Bethnal Green
Mount Pleasant Hill
Upper Clapton Road
Cleveleys Road
Lea Bridge Road
Kenninghall Road
Chatsworth Road
Millfields Road
Lower Clapton Road
Clapton Road
Powerscroft Road
Clifden Rd
Median Rd
Homerton High Street
Morning Lane
Well Street
Cassland Rd
Frampton Park Rd
Mare Street
Victoria Park Road
Sewardstone Rd
Bishop's Way
Bonner Rd
Old Ford Rd
Roman Road
Globe Road
Cambridge Heath Road
Hackney Road
Bethnal Green Road
Old Bethnal Green Road
Columbia Road
Hackney Road
Hoxton St
Kingsland Road
Pritchard's Rd
Warner Pl.
Canrobert St
Whiston Road
Queensbridge Road
Nuttall St
Pownall Rd
Sheep Lane
Lansdowne Drive
Albion Drive
Middleton Road
Richmond Road
Forest Road
Graham Road
Dalston Lane
Pond Road
De Beauvoir Road
Ridley Rd
Sandringham Road
Amhurst Road
Downs Park Road
Pembury Rd
Downs Rd
Clapton Way
Cecilia Road
Shacklewell La
Stoke Newington High Street
Evering Rd
Rectory Road
Brooke Road
Northwold Road
Kyverdale Road
Maury Road
Church St
Bouverie Rd
Barbauld Rd
Nevill Road
Walford Rd
Prince George Rd
Barretts Grv
Boleyn Road
A 10
A 107
A 104
A 102
A 1209
B 119
378
337
464
500 m
500 yards
POL.
13'6
15'6
13'9
13'0
16'0
15'9

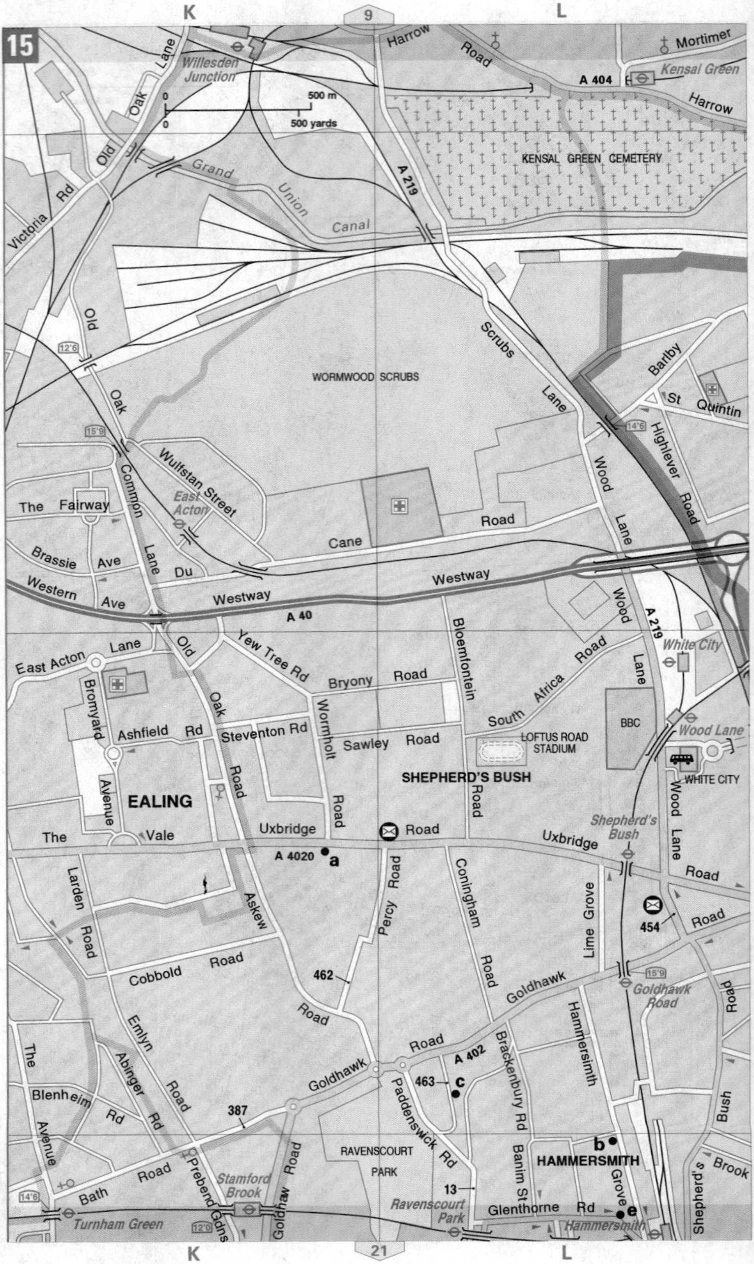

K 9 L

15

ZC

Willesden Junction

Old Oak Lane

0 500 m

0 500 yards

Harrow Road

Mortimer

A 404 Kensal Green

Harrow

KENSAL GREEN CEMETERY

Grand Union Canal

A 219

Victoria Rd

ZD

Old Oak

WORMWOOD SCRUBS

Scrubs Lane

Barlby

St Quintin

Highlever Road

Wood Lane

Wulfstan Street

East Acton

Common Lane

The Fairway

Brassie Ave

Du Cane Road

Western Ave

Westway

A 40

Bloemfontein Road

South Africa Road

White City

East Acton Lane

Old Oak Road

Yew Tree Rd

Bryony Road

Bromyard Avenue

Ashfield Rd

Steventon Rd

Wormholt Road

Sawley Road

LOFTUS ROAD STADIUM

BBC

Wood Lane

WHITE CITY

SHEPHERD'S BUSH

EALING

The Vale

Uxbridge Road

A 4020 a

Shepherd's Bush

Wood Lane

ZE

Larden Road

Askew Road

Percy Road

Coningham Road

Lime Grove

454

Cobbold Road

462

Goldhawk Road

Goldhawk Road

The Avenue

Emlyn Road

Abinger Rd

Blenheim Rd

387

A 402

463 c

Brackenbury Rd

Hammersmith Grove

Paddenswick Rd

RAVENSCOURT PARK

Banim St

b

HAMMERSMITH

Bush Road

Brook

Shepherd's

ZF

Bath Road

Prebend Gdns

Stamford Brook

Goldhawk Road

13

Ravenscourt Park

Glenthorne Rd

e

Turnham Green

Hammersmith

K 21 L

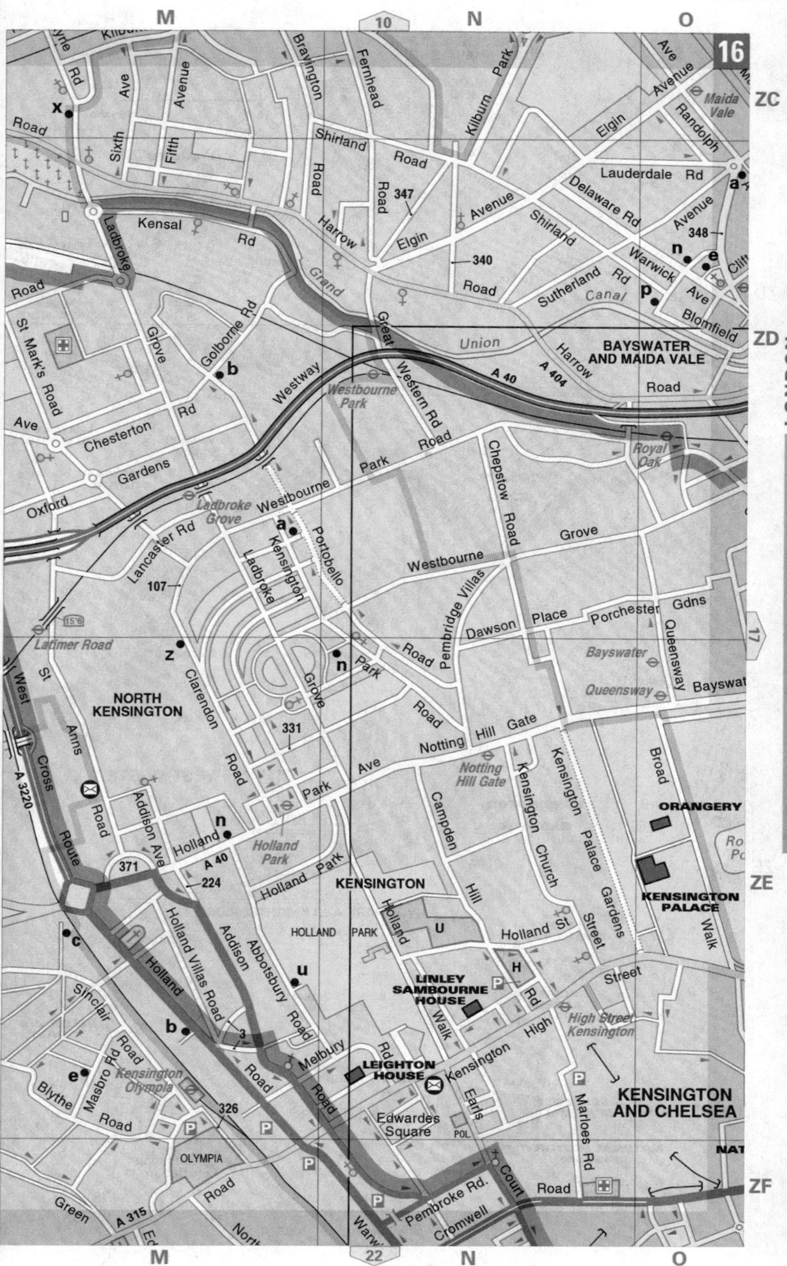

M
N
O
10
16
22
17
ZC
ZD
ZE
ZF
BAYSWATER AND MAIDA VALE
NORTH KENSINGTON
KENSINGTON
KENSINGTON AND CHELSEA
HOLLAND PARK
KENSINGTON PALACE
ORANGERY
LINLEY SAMBOURNE HOUSE
LEIGHTON HOUSE
OLYMPIA
Maida Vale
Westbourne Park
Royal Oak
Ladbroke Grove
Latimer Road
Bayswater
Queensway
Notting Hill Gate
Holland Park
High Street Kensington
Kensington Olympia
Grand Union Canal
Westway
A 40
A 404
A 3220
A 315
Shirland Road
Harrow Road
Elgin Avenue
Kensal Rd
Ladbroke Grove
Golborne Rd
Westbourne Park Road
Chepstow Road
Westbourne Grove
Portobello Road
Kensington Park Road
Pembridge Villas
Dawson Place
Porchester Gdns
Queensway
Notting Hill Gate
Holland Park Ave
Clarendon Road
Lancaster Rd
Chesterton Rd
Oxford Gardens
St Mark's Road
Kensington Church Street
Kensington Palace Gardens
Campden Hill
Holland St
Broad Walk
Kensington High Street
Holland Villas Road
Addison Road
Abbotsbury Road
Melbury Road
Edwardes Square
Earls Court Road
Marloes Rd
Pembroke Rd.
Cromwell Road
Blythe Road
Sinclair Road
Masbro Rd
West Cross Route
St Anns Road
Addison Ave
Lauderdale Rd
Delaware Rd
Sutherland Ave
Warwick Ave
Blomfield Rd
Randolph Avenue
Elgin Avenue
Kilburn Park
Fernhead Road
Bravington Road
Sixth Ave
Fifth Avenue
347
340
348
107
331
371
224
326
3

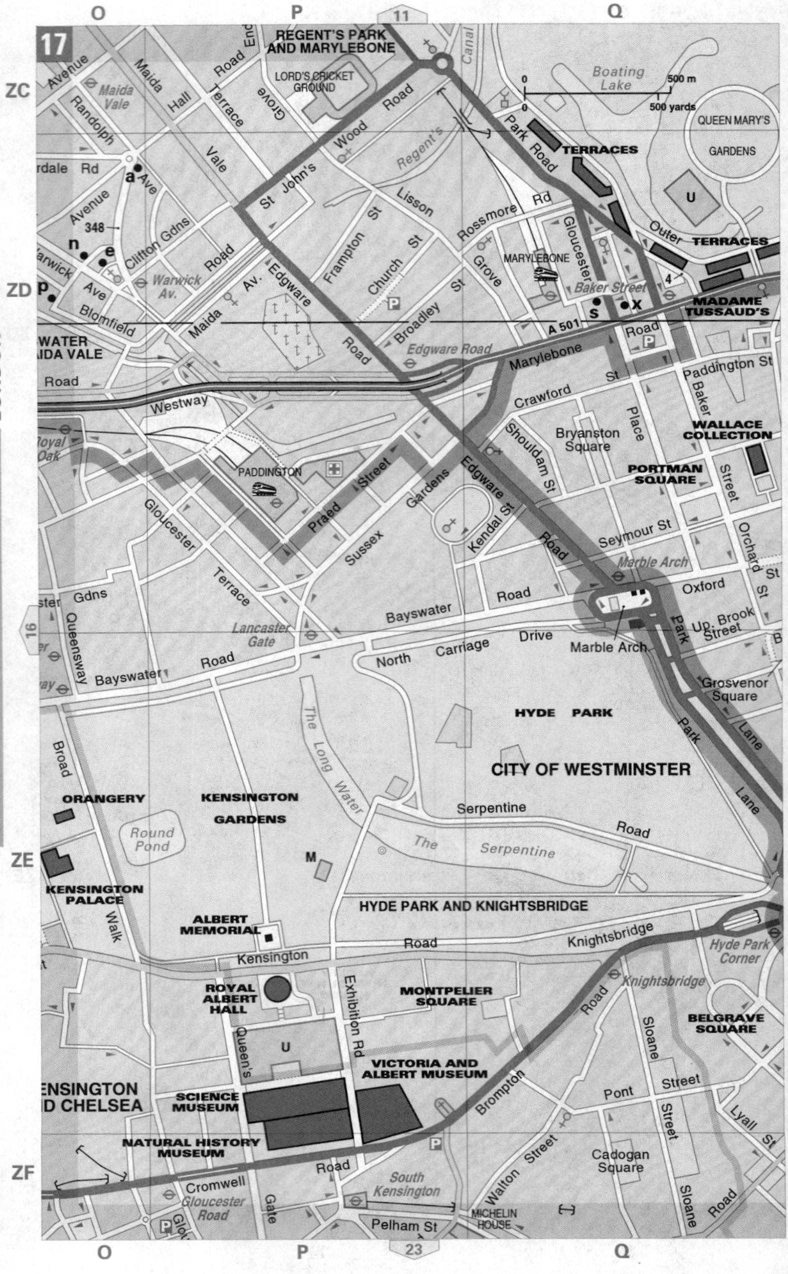

O P 11 Q

17

REGENT'S PARK AND MARYLEBONE

LORD'S CRICKET GROUND

Boating Lake

0 500 m

0 500 yards

QUEEN MARY'S GARDENS

TERRACES

Outer

TERRACES

U

Avenue

Maida Vale

Randolph

Maida

Hall

Road

Terrace

Grove

End

Vale

Wood

Road

St John's

Regent's

Canal

Park Road

rdale Rd

a

Ave

Avenue

348

n

e

Clifton Gdns

Warwick

Ave

Road

Warwick Av.

Lisson

Frampton St

Church St

Rossmore Rd

Grove

Gloucester

MARYLEBONE

Baker Street

4

s

x

MADAME TUSSAUD'S

p

Blomfield

Maida

Av.

Edgware

Road

Broadley St

P

A 501

Road

P

WATER

AIDA VALE

Road

Edgware Road

Marylebone

Road

St

Paddington St

Westway

Crawford

Baker

Royal Oak

Bryanston Square

Place

WALLACE COLLECTION

Shouldam St

PORTMAN SQUARE

Street

PADDINGTON

Praed

Street

Gardens

Edgware

Gloucester

Sussex

Kendal St

Road

Seymour St

Orchard St

Marble Arch

Terrace

Oxford St

Road

ster Gdns

Bayswater

Up. Brook Street

Queensway

Lancaster Gate

Drive

Park

Marble Arch

16

North

Carriage

Bayswater

Road

Grosvenor Square

HYDE PARK

The Long Water

Park

Lane

Broad

CITY OF WESTMINSTER

ORANGERY

KENSINGTON GARDENS

Serpentine

Road

Lane

Round Pond

The Serpentine

M

KENSINGTON PALACE

HYDE PARK AND KNIGHTSBRIDGE

Walk

ALBERT MEMORIAL

Road

Knightsbridge

Hyde Park Corner

Kensington

ROYAL ALBERT HALL

Exhibition Rd

MONTPELIER SQUARE

Road

Knightsbridge

BELGRAVE SQUARE

Sloane

U

Queen's

VICTORIA AND ALBERT MUSEUM

Brompton

ENSINGTON

D CHELSEA

SCIENCE MUSEUM

Pont

Street

Street

Lyall St

NATURAL HISTORY MUSEUM

P

Street

Cadogan Square

Road

Walton

Cromwell

South Kensington

Gloucester Road

Gate

Sloane

Road

MICHELIN HOUSE

Pelham St

Glo

P

O P 23 Q

ZC ZD ZE ZF

LONDON

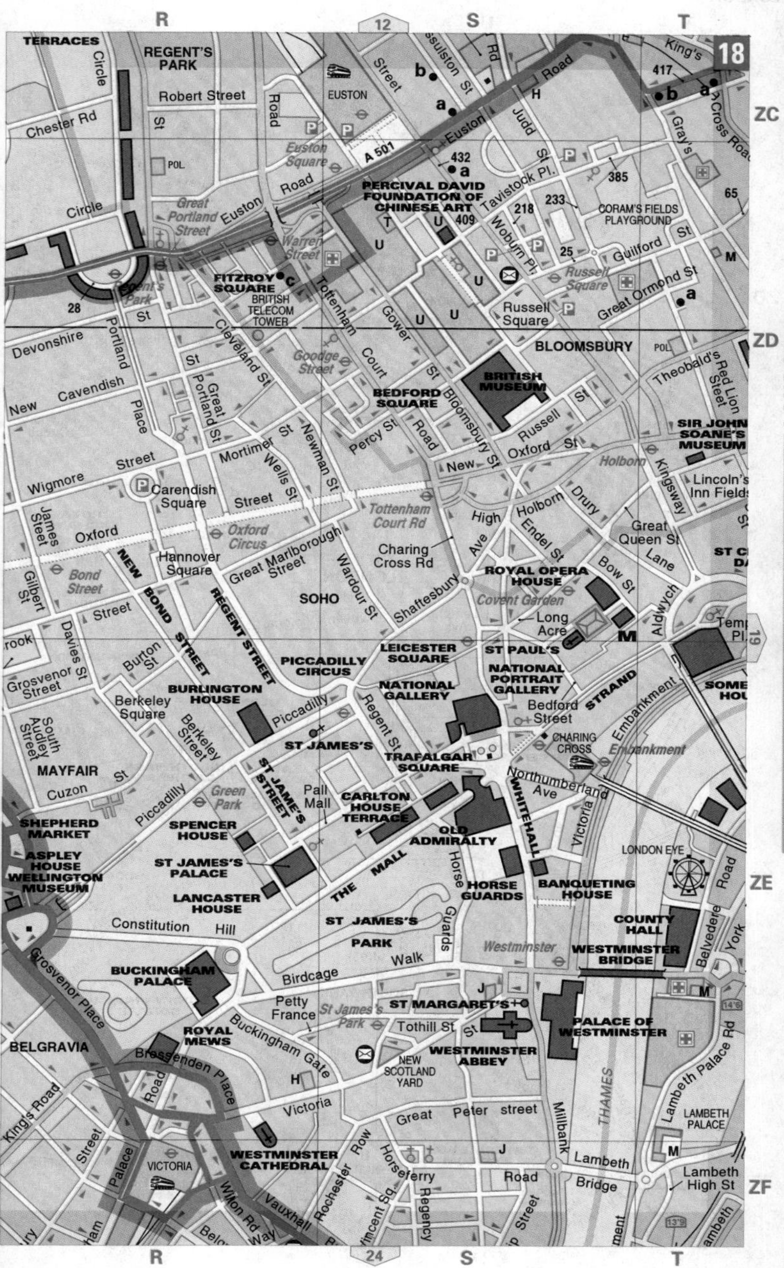

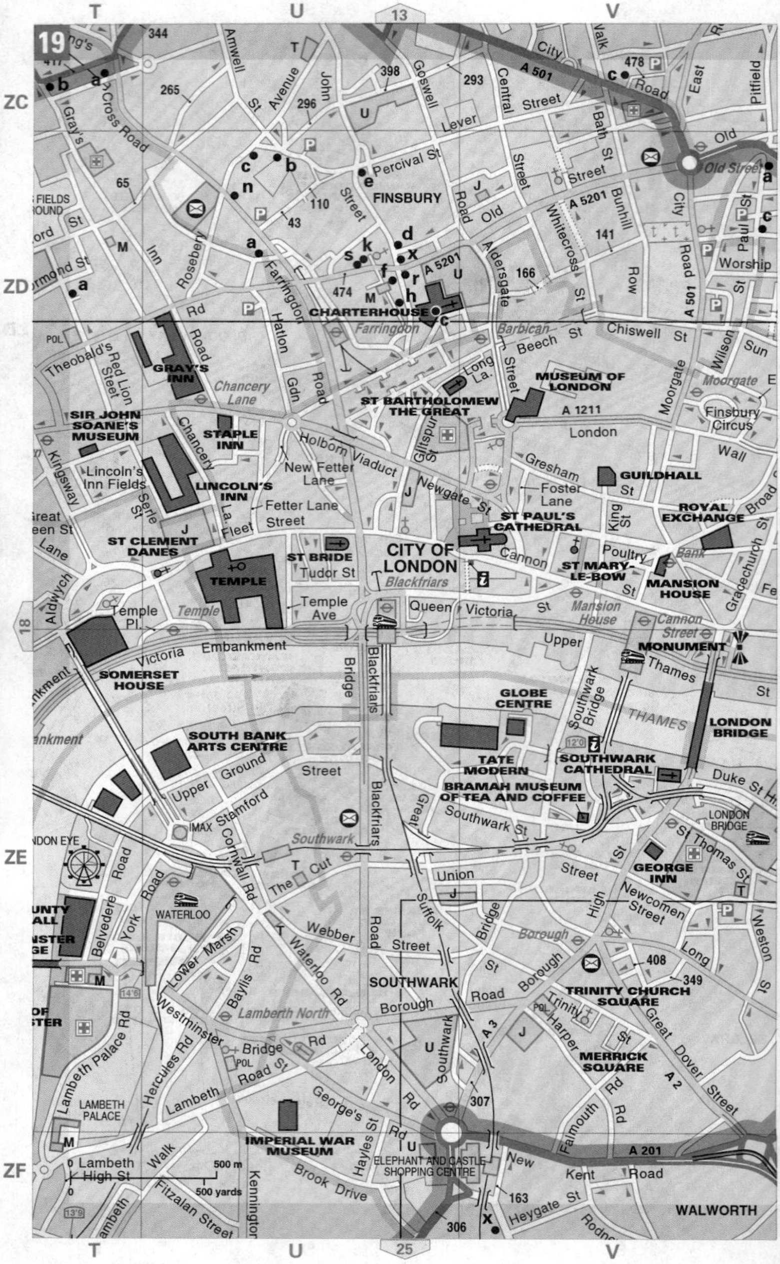
T
U
V
13
19
ZC
ZD
ZE
ZF
18
25
FINSBURY
CHARTERHOUSE
Farringdon
Barbican
MUSEUM OF LONDON
Chancery Lane
ST BARTHOLOMEW THE GREAT
Moorgate
Finsbury Circus
GRAY'S INN
SIR JOHN SOANE'S MUSEUM
STAPLE INN
LINCOLN'S INN
Lincoln's Inn Fields
GUILDHALL
ROYAL EXCHANGE
Bank
ST PAUL'S CATHEDRAL
ST CLEMENT DANES
TEMPLE
ST BRIDE
CITY OF LONDON
Blackfriars
ST MARY-LE-BOW
MANSION HOUSE
Mansion House
Cannon Street
Temple
MONUMENT
SOMERSET HOUSE
GLOBE CENTRE
THAMES
LONDON BRIDGE
SOUTH BANK ARTS CENTRE
TATE MODERN
SOUTHWARK CATHEDRAL
BRAMAH MUSEUM OF TEA AND COFFEE
IMAX
LONDON EYE
Southwark
GEORGE INN
WATERLOO
Borough
SOUTHWARK
TRINITY CHURCH SQUARE
Lambeth North
MERRICK SQUARE
LAMBETH PALACE
IMPERIAL WAR MUSEUM
ELEPHANT AND CASTLE SHOPPING CENTRE
WALWORTH
500 m
500 yards
A 501
A 5201
A 1211
A 3
A 2
A 201

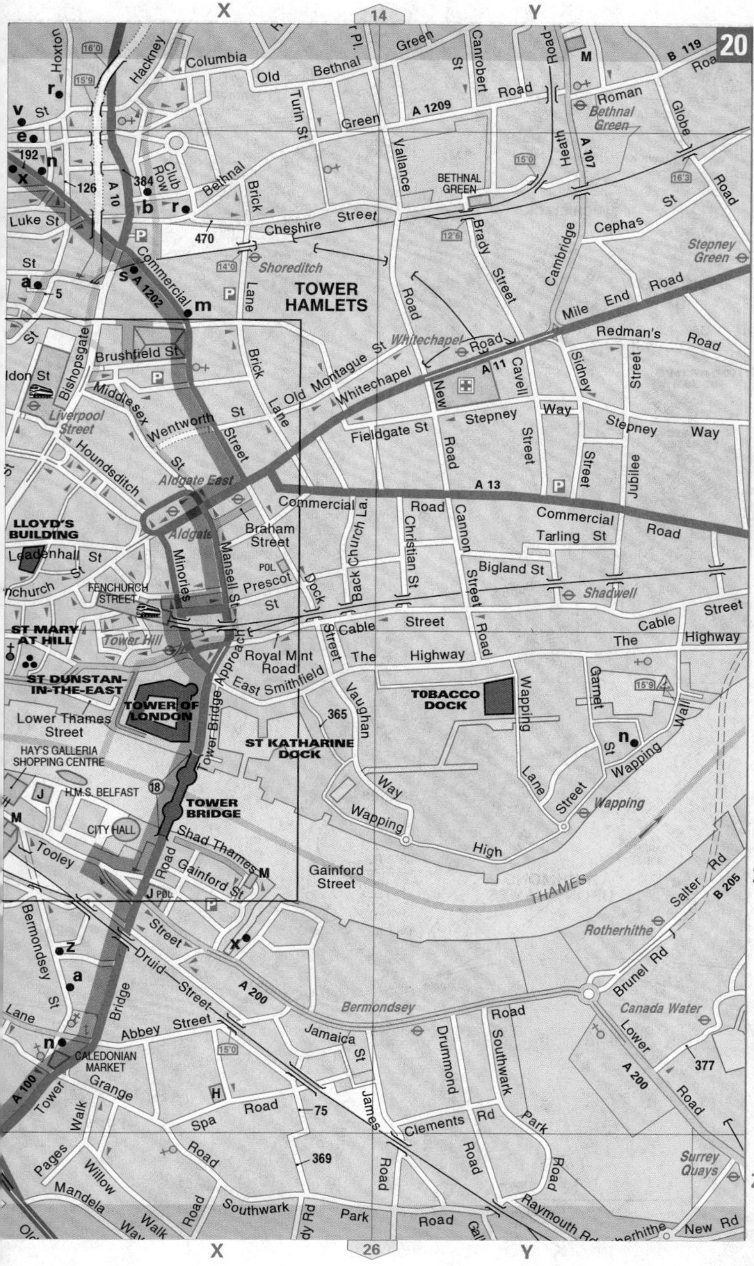

X Y 14 20

ZC ZD ZE ZF

LONDON

Hoxton
Hackney
Columbia
Old Bethnal Green
Green St
Canrobert
Road
B 119
Roman
Bethnal Green
Globe
Road
A 1209
Turin St
Green
Vallance
Club Row
Bethnal
Brick
A 10
384
126
192
Luke St
St
Cheshire Street
470
BETHNAL GREEN
Brady Street
Heath
A 107
Cambridge
Cephas St
Road
Stepney Green
Shoreditch
TOWER HAMLETS
Road
Lane
Commercial
A 1202
5
Mile End Road
Redman's Road
Sidney
Street
Brushfield St
Bishopsgate
ldon St
Middlesex
Liverpool Street
Wentworth St
Brick Lane
Old Montague St
Whitechapel
Whitechapel Road
A 11
New Road
Cavell
Stepney Way
Stepney Way
Fieldgate St
Street
Street
Jubilee
Road
Houndsditch
St
Aldgate East
Street
A 13
Commercial Road
Road
Cannon
Commercial
Tarling St
Road
Christian St
Back Church La.
Braham Street
LLOYD'S BUILDING
Leadenhall St
St
Aldgate
Minories
Mansell St
POL.
Prescot
St
Dock
Bigland St
Street
Shadwell
nchurch
FENCHURCH STREET
Street
Cable
Street
Cable
Street
ST MARY AT HILL
Tower Hill
Royal Mint Road
The Highway
The Highway
Road
East Smithfield
Approach
Tower Bridge
Vaughan
ST DUNSTAN-IN-THE-EAST
TOWER OF LONDON
Lower Thames Street
365
TOBACCO DOCK
Wapping
Garnet
Wall
HAY'S GALLERIA SHOPPING CENTRE
ST KATHARINE DOCK
St
n
Wapping
H.M.S. BELFAST
18
TOWER BRIDGE
Way
Lane
Street
Wapping
Wapping
High
CITY HALL
Tooley
Shad Thames
Road
Gainford St
Gainford Street
THAMES
Salter Rd
B 205
POL.
Street
Bermondsey
Rotherhithe
Druid
Street
A 200
Brunel Rd
St
Bridge
Lane
Bermondsey
Canada Water
Abbey Street
Jamaica St
Road
Drummond
Southwark
Lower
A 200
377
Road
CALEDONIAN MARKET
Grange
A 100
Tower
Walk
Road
Spa
75
James
Clements Rd
Park
Road
Surrey Quays
Pages
Road
369
Road
Road
Willow
Mandela Way
Walk
Road
Southwark Park Road
Raymouth Rd
New Rd
X 26 Y

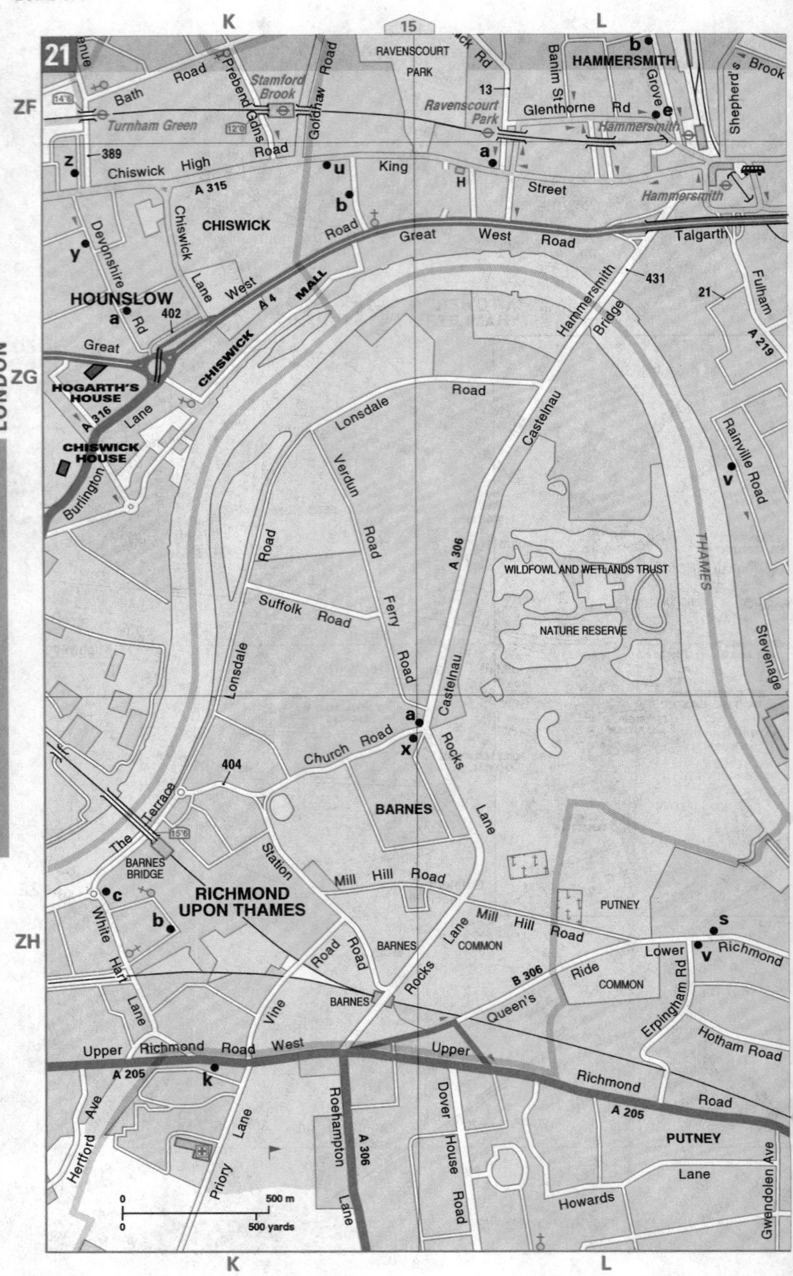

K
L
15
21
ZF
ZG
ZH
RAVENSCOURT PARK
HAMMERSMITH
Bath Road
Prebend Gdns
Stamford Brook
Goldhawk Road
Banim St
Grove
Shepherd's Brook
Turnham Green
Ravenscourt Park
Glenthorne Rd
Hammersmith
Chiswick High Road
King Street
A 315
CHISWICK
Chiswick Lane
Devonshire Rd
Great West Road
Talgarth
Hammersmith Bridge
Fulham
A 219
HOUNSLOW
A 4
MALL
West
CHISWICK
Great
HOGARTH'S HOUSE
A 316
Lane
CHISWICK HOUSE
Burlington
Lonsdale Road
Verdun Road
Castelnau
Rainville Road
A 306
WILDFOWL AND WETLANDS TRUST
NATURE RESERVE
THAMES
Suffolk Road
Ferry Road
Lonsdale
Stevenage
Church Road
Rocks Lane
BARNES
The Terrace
BARNES BRIDGE
Station Road
Mill Hill Road
RICHMOND UPON THAMES
PUTNEY
White Hart Lane
BARNES COMMON
Lower Richmond
Erpingham Rd
B 306
Queen's Ride
COMMON
Hotham Road
BARNES
Vine Road
Upper Richmond Road West
Upper Richmond Road
A 205
Roehampton Lane
A 306
Dover House Road
PUTNEY
Hertford Ave
Priory Lane
Howards Lane
Gwendolen Ave
0 500 m
0 500 yards
LONDON

M
N
O
16
22
ZF
ZG
ZH
LONDON
23
OLYMPIA
HAMMERSMITH AND FULHAM
EARL'S COURT
SOUTH KENSINGTON
FULHAM
EARL'S COURT EXHIBITION BLDG
BROMPTON
CEMETERY
CHELSEA F.C.
EEL BROOK COMMON
FULHAM PALACE GARDENS
SOUTH PARK
HURLINGHAM PARK
WANDSWORTH PARK
THAMES
PUTNEY
WANDSWORTH TOWN
West Kensington
Barons Court
Earl's Court
West Brompton
Fulham Broadway
Parsons Green
Putney Bridge
East Putney
Hammersmith Road
Talgarth Road
Cromwell Road
Pembroke Rd.
Warwick Road
North End Road
West Cromwell Road
Gunterstone Rd
Baron's Court Rd
St. Dunstan's Rd
Star Road
Greyhound Road
Lillie Road
Musard Road
Rylston Road
Halford Rd
Seagrave Rd
Old Brompton Road
Redcliffe Gardens
Finborough Road
Dawes Road
Munster Road
Filmer Road
Bishops Road
Parsons Green La.
Harwood Road
Fulham Road
King's Road
Lots Road
Imperial Road
Bagley's Lane
New King's Road
Wandsworth Bridge Road
Studdridge Street
Clancarty Road
Peterborough Road
Broomhouse Lane
Hurlingham Road
Hugon Rd
Stephendale Road
Townmead Road
Carnwath Road
Fulham Palace Road
Finlay Street
Bishop's Park Rd
Woodlawn Road
Putney Bridge
Putney High St
Putney Bridge Road
Charlwood Rd
Disraeli Rd
Oxford Road
Upper Richmond Rd
Fawe Park Road
Oakhill Road
Swandon Way
POL.
A 315
A 304
A 308
A 217
A 219
A 3209
182
164
450
203
207
202
172
437
358
7
165
14'6
15'0
15'
a
x
c
e
z
v
r
n

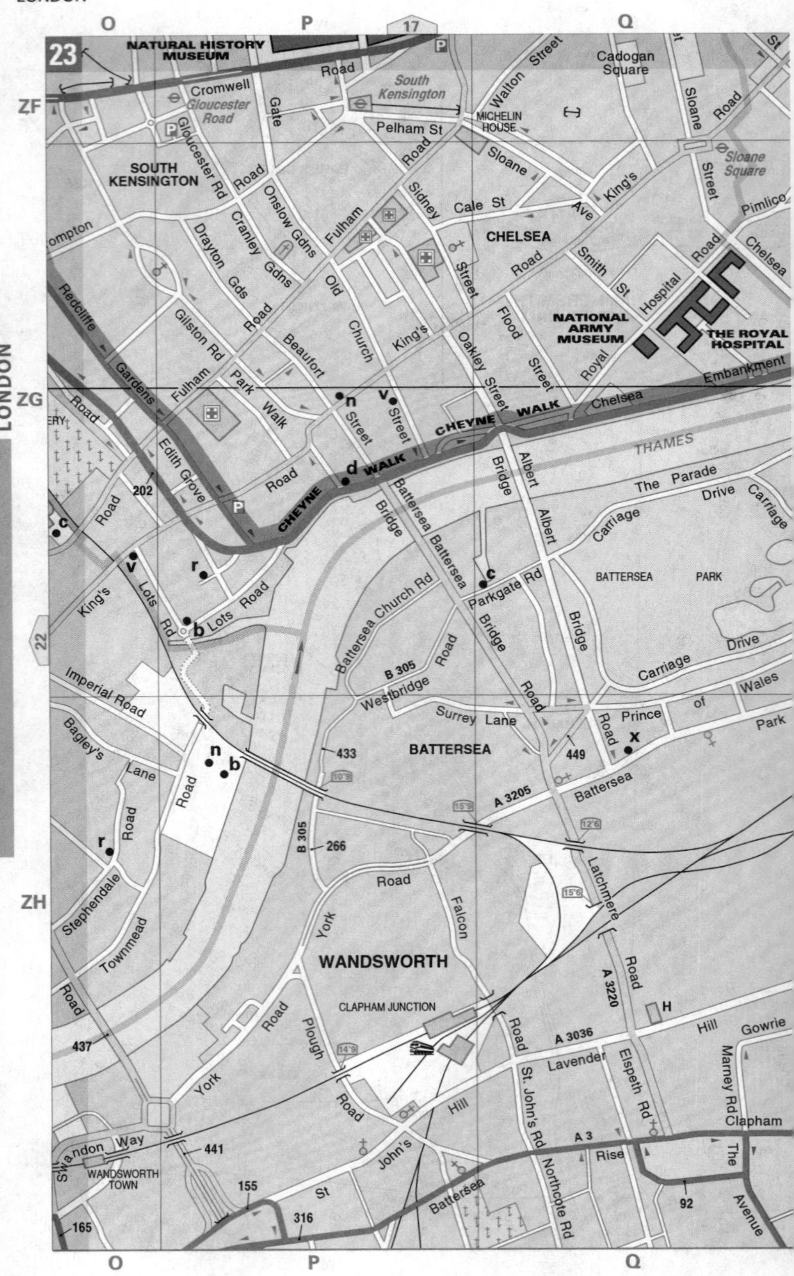
O
P
Q
17
23
NATURAL HISTORY MUSEUM
Cromwell
Gloucester Road
Road
Gate
South Kensington
Walton Street
Cadogan Square
Sloane Road
Pelham St
MICHELIN HOUSE
SOUTH KENSINGTON
Gloucester Rd
Onslow Gdns
Road
Sloane
King's
Sloane Square
Street
Sidney
Cale St
Ave
Pimlico
Fulham
CHELSEA
Smith
Chelsea
Drayton Gds
Cranley Gdns
Old Church
Street
Road
St
Hospital
Road
Redcliffe Gardens
Gilston Rd
Road
Beaufort
King's
Oakley
Flood Street
NATIONAL ARMY MUSEUM
THE ROYAL HOSPITAL
Royal
Embankment
Fulham
Park Walk
Street
Chelsea
CHEYNE WALK
ZF
ZG
ZH
Road
Edith Grove
THAMES
202
Road
CHEYNE WALK
Road
Bridge
Albert
Bridge
Battersea
The Parade
Drive
Carriage
Albert
Carriage
Battersea
BATTERSEA PARK
King's
Lots Rd
Lots Road
Battersea Church Rd
Parkgate Rd
Bridge
Bridge
22
Imperial Road
B 305
Road
Westbridge
Carriage
Drive
Road
Wales
of
Prince
Park
Surrey Lane
Road
Bagley's
Lane
BATTERSEA
433
449
Road
10'9
A 3205
Battersea
15'9
12'6
Road
B 305
266
Latchmere
15'6
Stephendale
Road
Townmead
York
Falcon
WANDSWORTH
Road
A 3220
Road
CLAPHAM JUNCTION
Road
Plough
Road
437
14'9
A 3036
Hill
Gowrie
Lavender
York
Road
Hill
St. John's Rd
Elspeth Rd
Marney Rd
Clapham
Swandon Way
441
John's
A 3
Rise
The
WANDSWORTH TOWN
155
St
Battersea
Northcote Rd
92
Avenue
165
316
LONDON

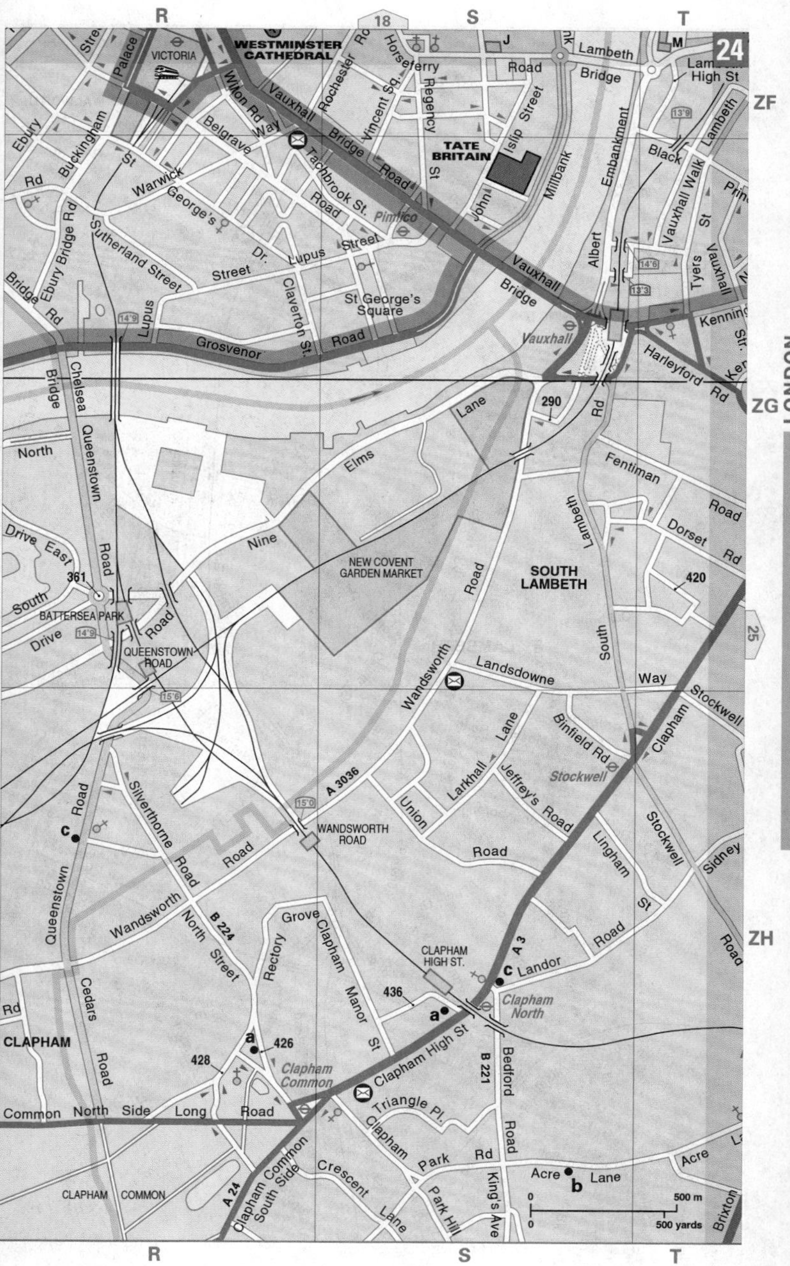

WESTMINSTER CATHEDRAL
VICTORIA
TATE BRITAIN
Pimlico
Vauxhall
St George's Square
NEW COVENT GARDEN MARKET
SOUTH LAMBETH
BATTERSEA PARK
QUEENSTOWN ROAD
WANDSWORTH ROAD
Stockwell
CLAPHAM HIGH ST.
Clapham North
Clapham Common
CLAPHAM
CLAPHAM COMMON
Vauxhall Bridge Road
Grosvenor Road
Nine Elms Lane
Wandsworth Road
Clapham High St
Clapham Road
Queenstown Road
Chelsea Bridge
Lambeth Bridge
Albert Embankment
Millbank
South Lambeth Road
Landsdowne Way
Stockwell Road
Bedford Road
Acre Lane
Common North Side
Long Road
Clapham Common South Side
Cedars Road
Harleyford Rd
Fentiman Road
Dorset Rd
Larkhall Lane
Binfield Rd
Jeffrey's Road
Union Road
Lingham St
Landor Road
Clapham Manor St
Rectory Grove
North Street
Silverthorne Road
Triangle Pl.
Clapham Park Rd
Crescent Lane
Park Hill
King's Ave
A 3036
A 3
A 24
B 224
B 221
500 m
500 yards

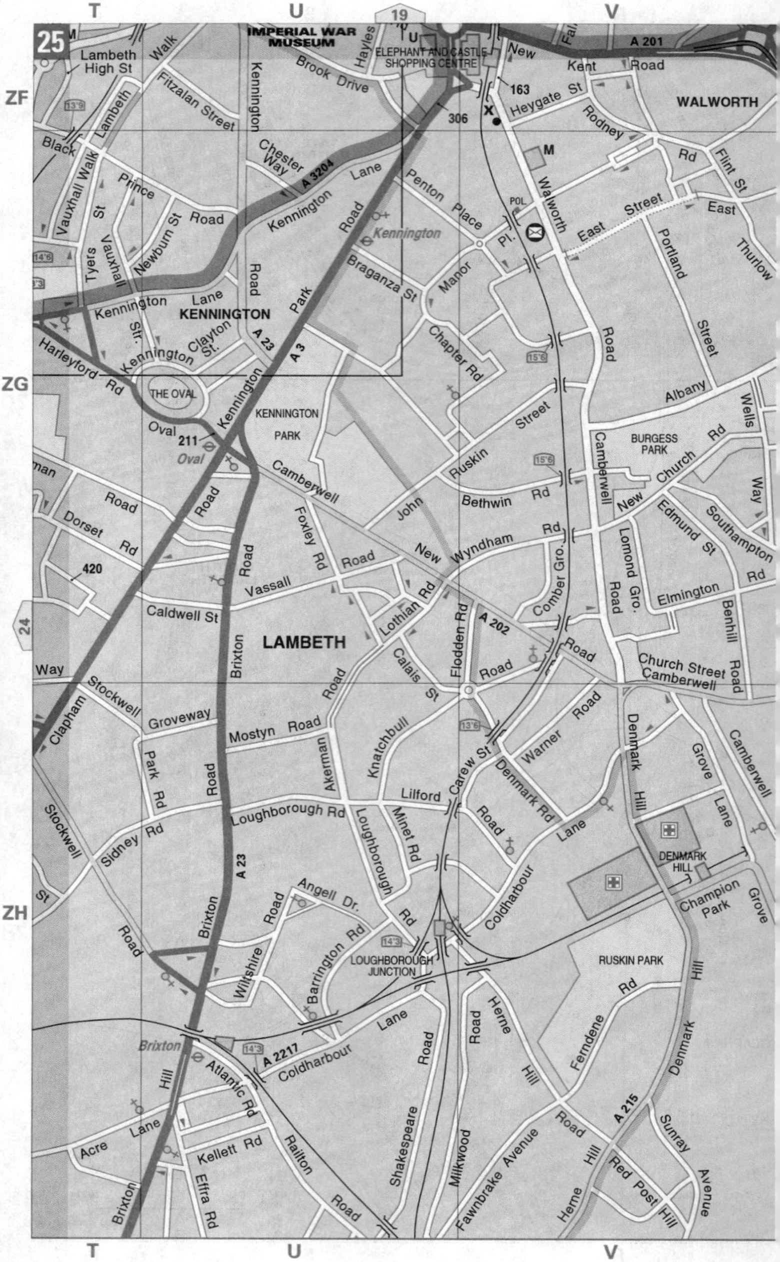

T U V

19 25

IMPERIAL WAR MUSEUM
ELEPHANT AND CASTLE SHOPPING CENTRE
WALWORTH
KENNINGTON
THE OVAL
KENNINGTON PARK
BURGESS PARK
LAMBETH
DENMARK HILL
RUSKIN PARK
LOUGHBOROUGH JUNCTION
Kennington
Oval
Brixton

Lambeth High St, Lambeth Walk, Fitzalan Street, Kennington Road, Brook Drive, Hayles, New Kent Road, A 201, Heygate St, Rodney Rd, Flint St, Black Prince Road, Vauxhall Walk, Tyers St, Vauxhall St, Newburn St, Chester Way, A 3204, Kennington Lane, Penton Place, Walworth Road, East Street, Portland Street, Thurlow, Braganza St, Manor Pl., Chapter Rd, Harleyford Rd, Kennington Oval, Clayton St., Kennington Park Road, A 23, A 3, Albany Road, Wells Way, Ruskin Street, Camberwell Road, New Church Rd, Bethwin Rd, John Ruskin Street, Edmund St, Southampton Rd, Camberwell New Road, Foxley Rd, New Wyndham Rd, Comber Gro., Lomond Gro., Elmington Rd, Benhill Road, Dorset Rd, Vassall Road, Lothian Rd, Flodden Rd, A 202, Caldwell St, Brixton Road, Calais St, Church Street Camberwell, Clapham Way, Stockwell Park Road, Groveway, Mostyn Road, Akerman Road, Knatchbull, Carew St, Warner Road, Denmark Rd, Denmark Hill, Grove Lane, Camberwell Grove, Park Rd, Lilford Road, Loughborough Rd, Minet Rd, Coldharbour Lane, Stockwell St, Sidney Rd, Angell Dr., Champion Park, Wiltshire Road, Barrington Rd, Herne Hill, Ferndene Rd, A 2217, Atlantic Rd, Shakespeare Road, Milkwood Road, Fawnbrake Avenue, A 215, Sunray Avenue, Red Post Hill, Brixton Hill, Acre Lane, Kellett Rd, Effra Rd, Railton Road

ZF ZG ZH

163 306 211 420 24

M POL.

T U V

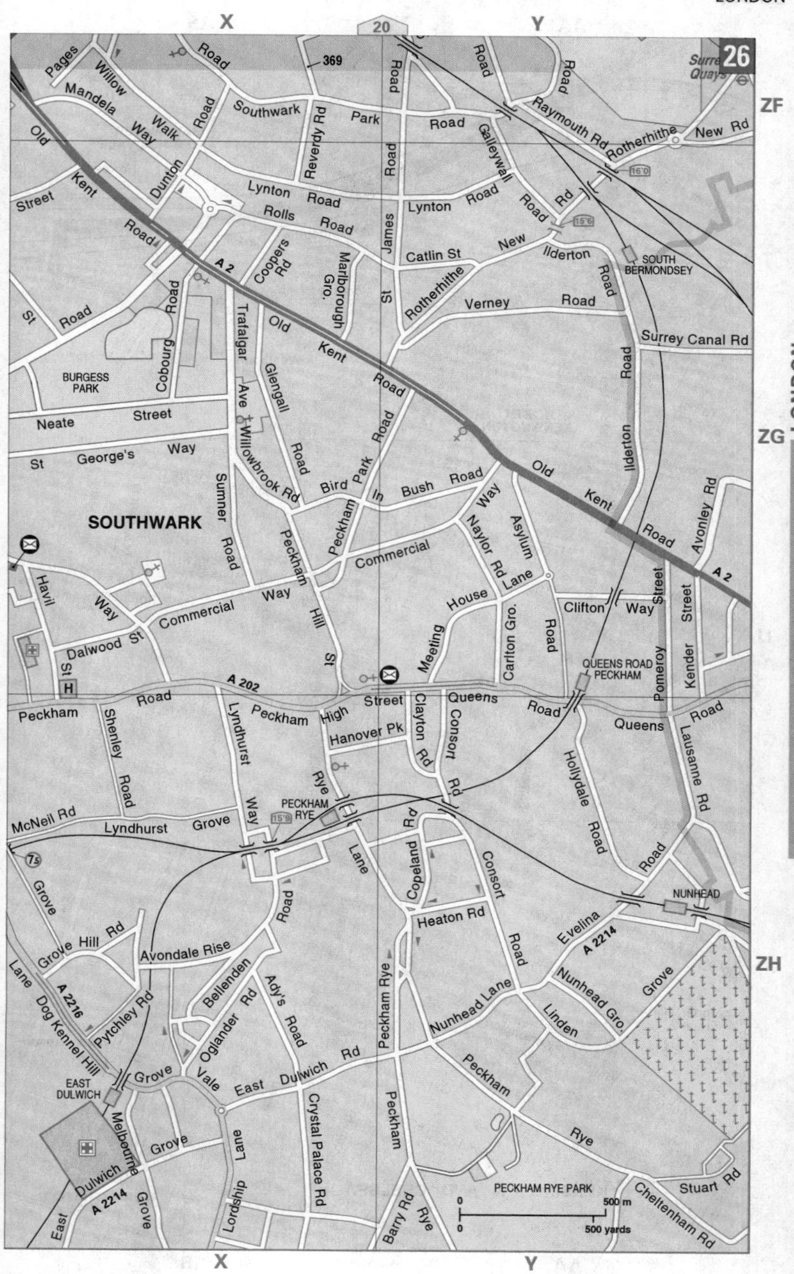
X
Y
20
26
ZF
ZG
ZH
SOUTHWARK
BURGESS PARK
SOUTH BERMONDSEY
QUEENS ROAD PECKHAM
PECKHAM RYE
NUNHEAD
EAST DULWICH
PECKHAM RYE PARK
Old Kent Road
A 2
A 202
A 2214
A 2216
Peckham Road
Peckham High Street
Queens Road
Commercial Way
Southwark Park Road
Lynton Road
Rolls Road
Ilderton Road
Rotherhithe New Road
Verney Road
Surrey Canal Rd
Rye Lane
East Dulwich Rd
Peckham Rye
Nunhead Lane
Lordship Lane
Crystal Palace Rd
Dog Kennel Hill
Grove Vale
Avondale Rise
Lyndhurst Grove
McNeil Rd
500 m
500 yards

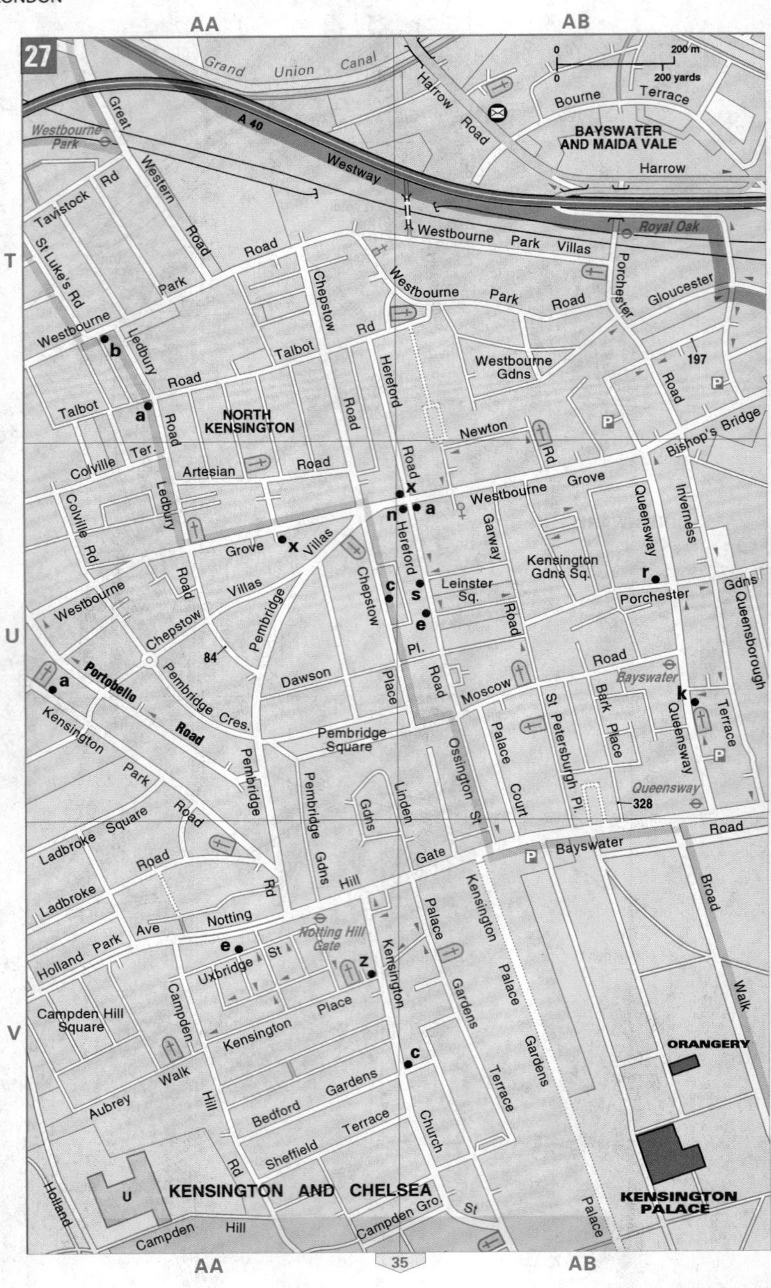

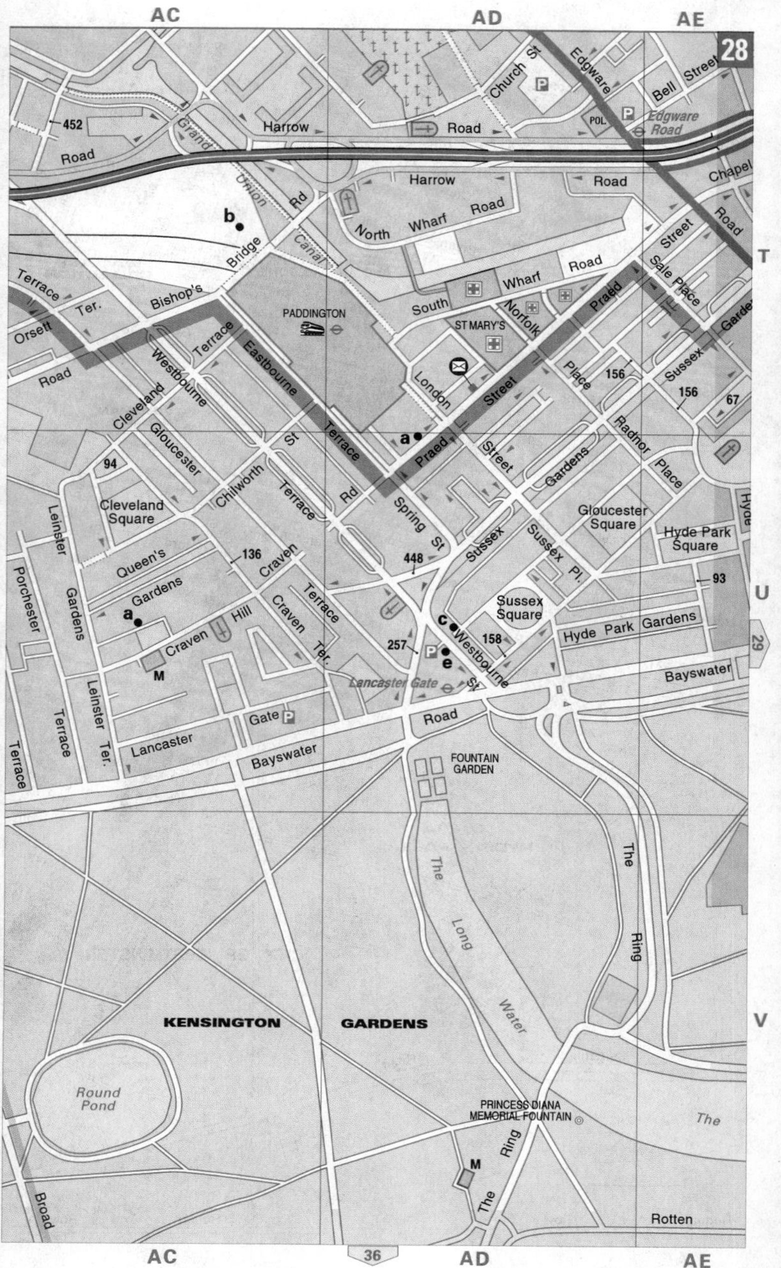
AC
AD
AE
28
T
U
V
29
36
Harrow Road
Church St
Edgware Road
Bell Street
POL.
Edgware Road
Chapel
Grand Union Canal
Harrow Road
North Wharf Road
Bishop's Bridge Rd
Terrace
Orsett Ter.
Road
Bishop's Terrace
Westbourne Terrace
Eastbourne Terrace
PADDINGTON
South Wharf Road
Norfolk
ST MARY'S
London
Praed Street
Sale Place
Sussex Gardens
Place
Cleveland
Gloucester
Chilworth St
Terrace Rd
Spring St
Radnor Place
Gloucester Square
Hyde Park Square
Hyde
Cleveland Square
Leinster Gardens
Porchester Terrace
Queen's Gardens
Craven Hill
Craven Terrace
Craven Ter.
Sussex
Sussex Pl.
Sussex Square
Hyde Park Gardens
Westbourne St
Bayswater Road
Lancaster Gate
Leinster Terrace
Leinster Ter.
Lancaster Gate
Bayswater Road
Terrace
FOUNTAIN GARDEN
The Long Water
The Ring
KENSINGTON GARDENS
Round Pond
PRINCESS DIANA MEMORIAL FOUNTAIN
The Ring
The
Rotten
Broad
M
a
b
c
e
452
94
136
448
257
158
156
67
93

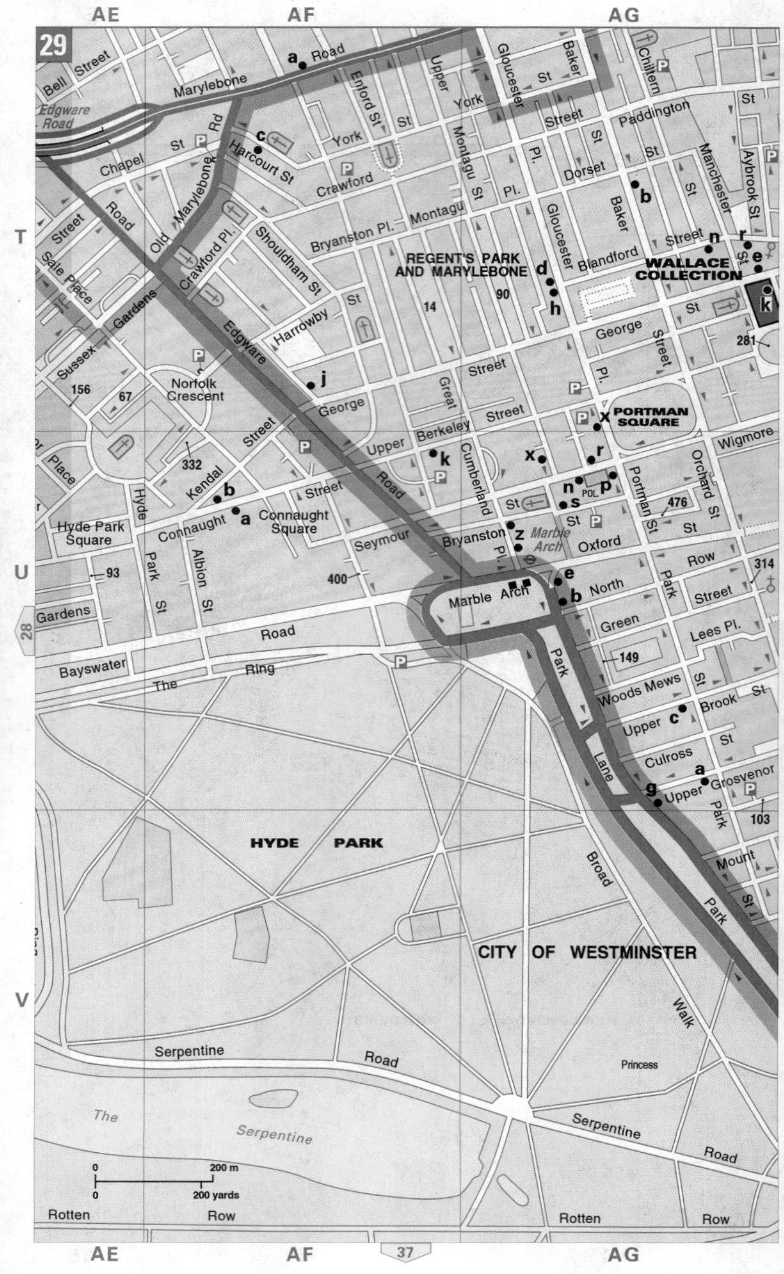
AE
AF
AG
29
T
U
V
28
37
Bell Street
Edgware Road
Marylebone Road
Chapel St
Old Marylebone Rd
Harcourt St
York St
Enford St
Upper York St
Gloucester Pl.
Baker St
Chiltern St
Paddington St
Manchester St
Aybrook St
Crawford St
Montagu St
Montagu Pl.
Dorset St
Bryanston Pl.
Shouldham St
Crawford Pl.
Sale Place
Sussex Gardens
Harrowby St
REGENT'S PARK AND MARYLEBONE
Blandford Street
WALLACE COLLECTION
George St
Norfolk Crescent
Kendal St
George Street
Great Cumberland Pl.
Upper Berkeley Street
Portman St
Orchard St
Wigmore St
PORTMAN SQUARE
Hyde Park Square
Hyde Park St
Albion St
Connaught Street
Connaught Square
Seymour St
Bryanston St
Marble Arch
Oxford St
North Row
Green Street
Lees Pl.
Gardens
Bayswater Road
The Ring
Park Lane
Woods Mews
Upper Brook St
Culross St
Upper Grosvenor St
Mount St
Park St
HYDE PARK
CITY OF WESTMINSTER
Broad Walk
Serpentine Road
The Serpentine
Princess
Rotten Row
POL
156
67
332
93
400
14
90
281
476
314
149
103
0
200 m
200 yards
LONDON

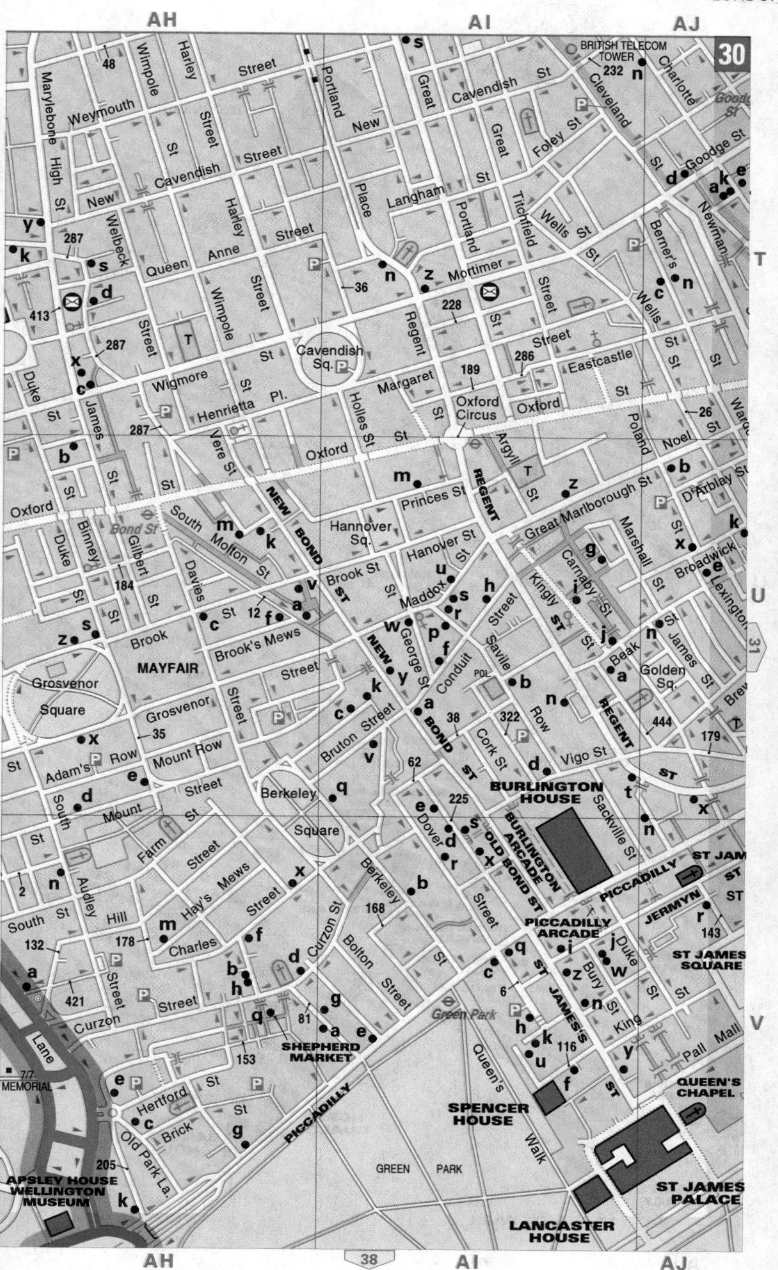
AH
AI
AJ
30
T
U
V
31
38
MAYFAIR
Grosvenor Square
Berkeley Square
Cavendish Sq.
Hannover Sq.
Golden Sq.
Oxford Circus
BURLINGTON HOUSE
BURLINGTON ARCADE
PICCADILLY ARCADE
SHEPHERD MARKET
SPENCER HOUSE
ST JAMES SQUARE
QUEEN'S CHAPEL
ST JAMES PALACE
LANCASTER HOUSE
APSLEY HOUSE WELLINGTON MUSEUM
GREEN PARK
BRITISH TELECOM TOWER
PICCADILLY
Oxford St
REGENT ST
NEW BOND ST
OLD BOND ST
JERMYN ST

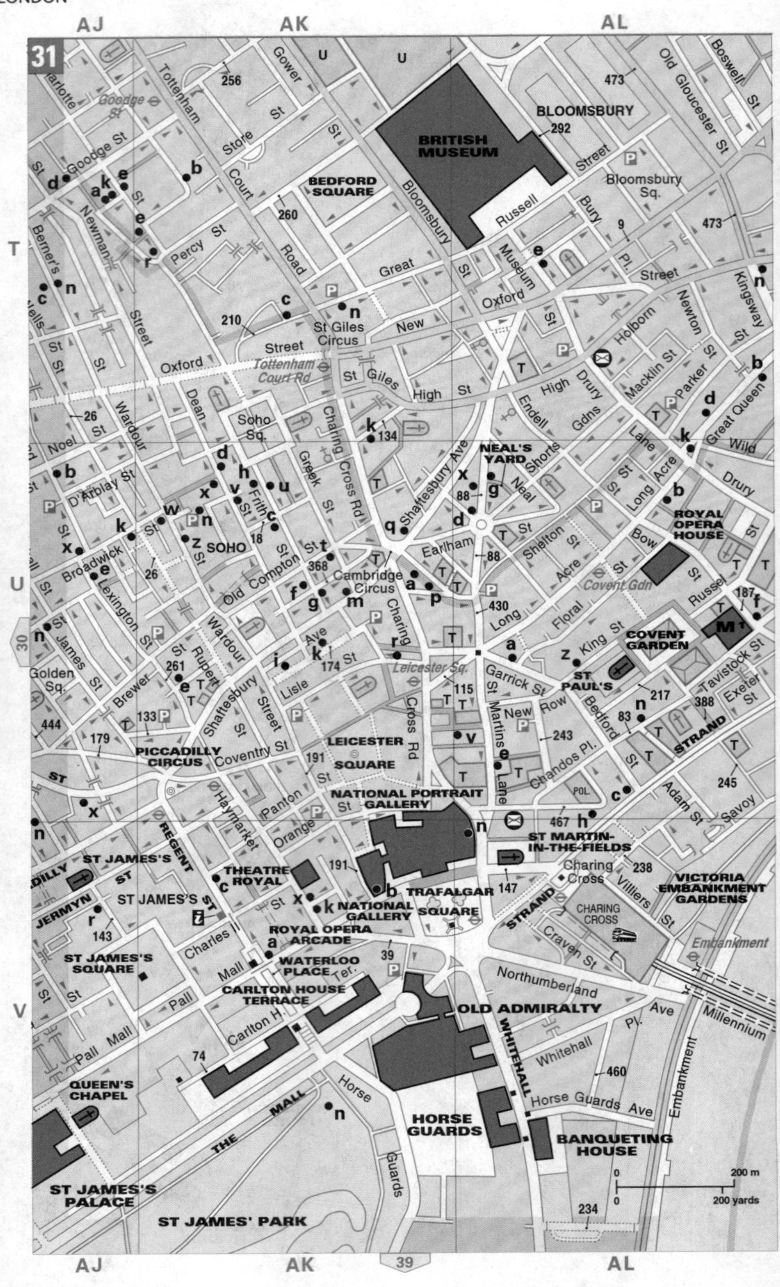

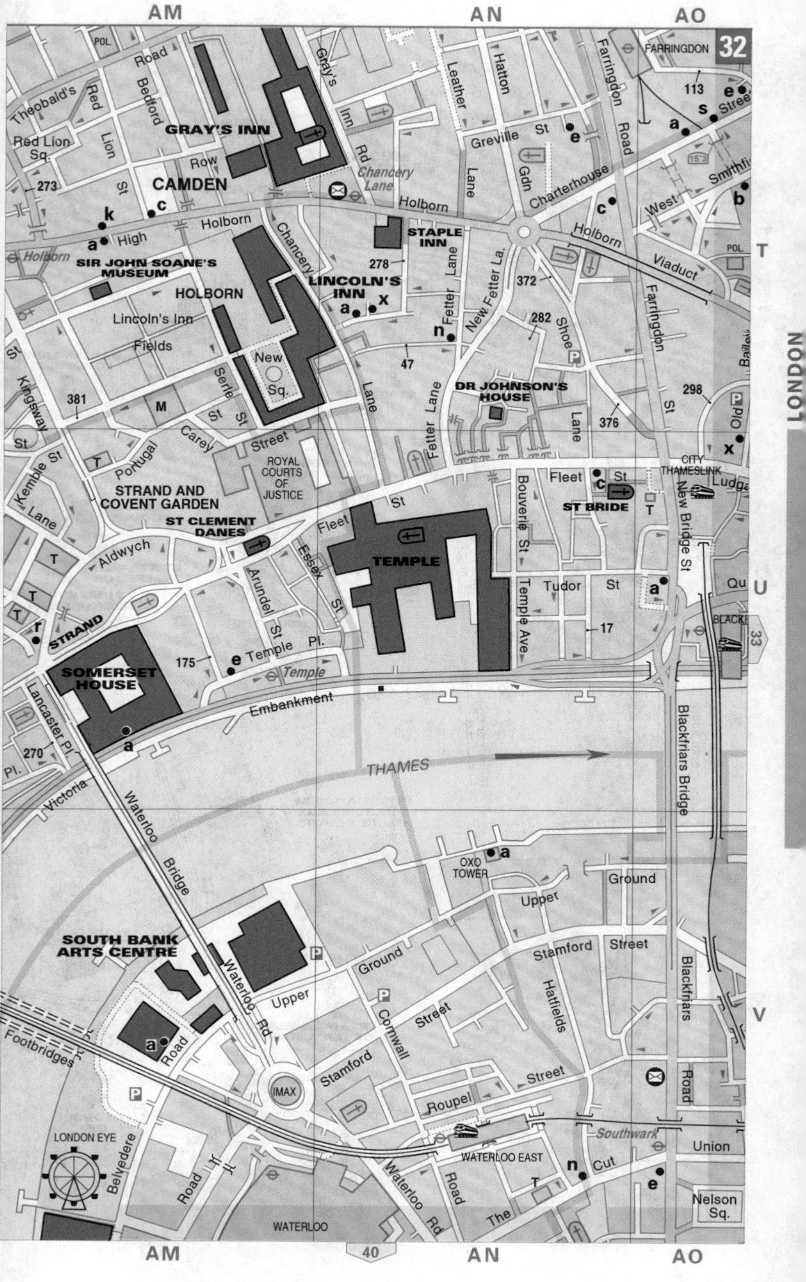

AM
AN
AO
32
FARRINGDON
GRAY'S INN
CAMDEN
SIR JOHN SOANE'S MUSEUM
HOLBORN
Lincoln's Inn Fields
STAPLE INN
LINCOLN'S INN
DR JOHNSON'S HOUSE
ROYAL COURTS OF JUSTICE
STRAND AND COVENT GARDEN
ST CLEMENT DANES
ST BRIDE
CITY THAMESLINK
TEMPLE
STRAND
SOMERSET HOUSE
THAMES
OXO TOWER
SOUTH BANK ARTS CENTRE
IMAX
LONDON EYE
WATERLOO EAST
WATERLOO
Theobald's Road
Red Lion Sq.
Red Lion St
Bedford Row
Gray's Inn Rd
Chancery Lane
Holborn
High Holborn
Leather Lane
Hatton Gdn
Greville St
Charterhouse St
Farringdon Road
Farringdon St
Holborn Viaduct
West Smithfield
Fetter Lane
New Fetter La.
Shoe Lane
Old Bailey
Kingsway
Serle St
Carey St
New Sq.
Portugal Street
Kemble St
Aldwych
Fleet St
Essex St
Arundel St
Temple Pl.
Bouverie St
Temple Ave.
Tudor St
New Bridge St
Ludgate
Lancaster Pl.
Victoria Embankment
Waterloo Bridge
Blackfriars Bridge
Upper Ground
Stamford Street
Hatfields
Cornwall Road
Waterloo Rd
Roupel Street
Belvedere Road
Southwark
The Cut
Union
Blackfriars Road
Nelson Sq.
Footbridges
T
U
V
33
40

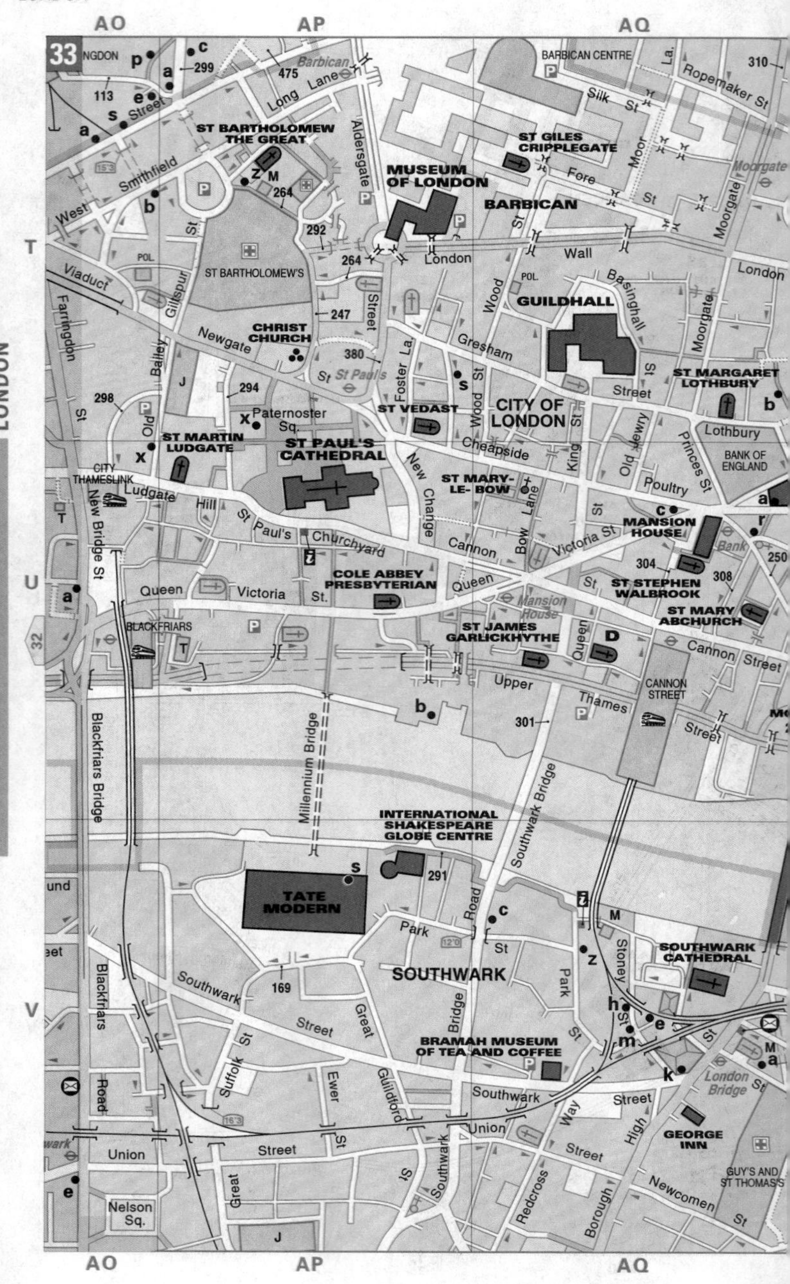
33
BARBICAN CENTRE
MUSEUM OF LONDON
BARBICAN
ST GILES CRIPPLEGATE
ST BARTHOLOMEW THE GREAT
ST BARTHOLOMEW'S
GUILDHALL
CHRIST CHURCH
ST PAUL'S CATHEDRAL
ST MARTIN LUDGATE
ST VEDAST
CITY OF LONDON
ST MARGARET LOTHBURY
BANK OF ENGLAND
ST MARY-LE-BOW
MANSION HOUSE
ST STEPHEN WALBROOK
ST MARY ABCHURCH
COLE ABBEY PRESBYTERIAN
ST JAMES GARLICKHYTHE
CANNON STREET
CITY THAMESLINK
BLACKFRIARS
INTERNATIONAL SHAKESPEARE GLOBE CENTRE
TATE MODERN
SOUTHWARK
SOUTHWARK CATHEDRAL
BRAMAH MUSEUM OF TEA AND COFFEE
GEORGE INN
GUY'S AND ST THOMAS'S
Millennium Bridge
Blackfriars Bridge
Southwark Bridge
Newgate
Cheapside
Poultry
Cannon Street
Upper Thames Street
Queen Victoria St.
Ludgate Hill
Southwark Street
Union Street
London Wall

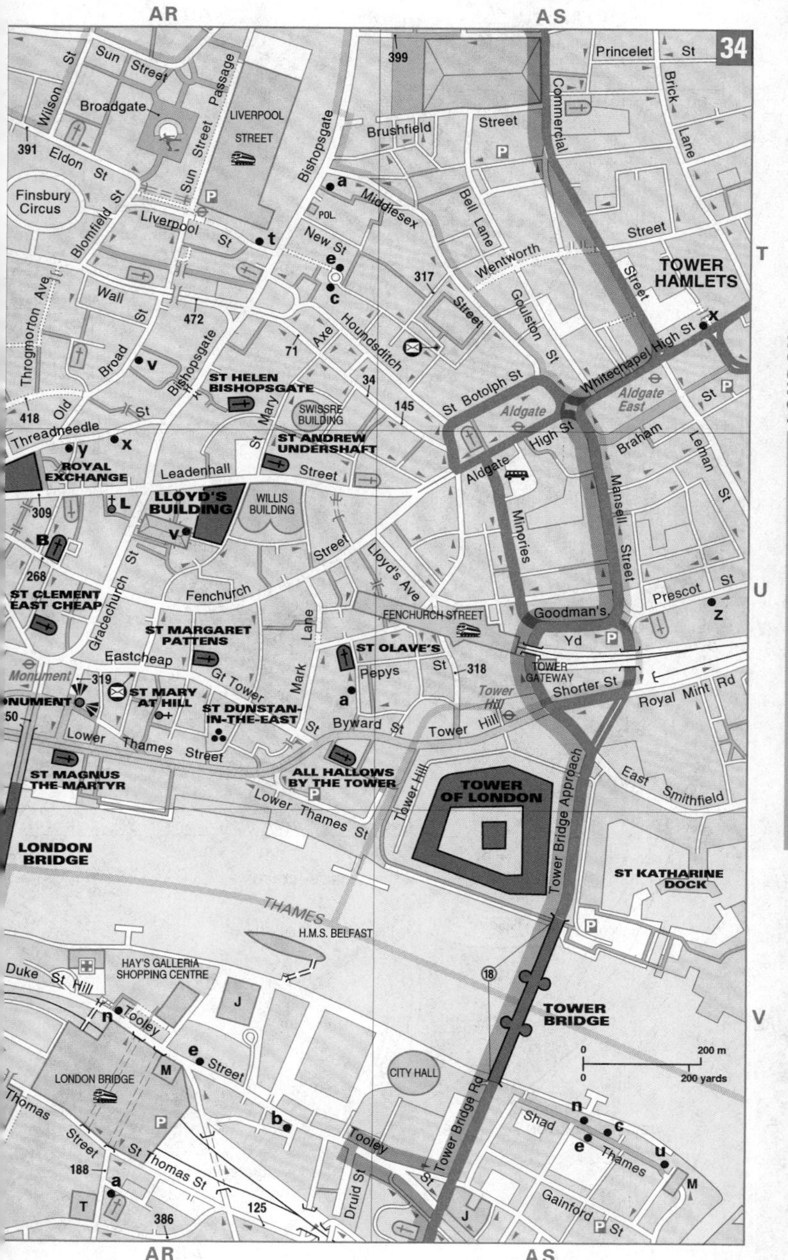
AR
AS
34
LIVERPOOL STREET
Bishopsgate
Broadgate
Finsbury Circus
Middlesex
Brushfield
Commercial
Princelet St
TOWER HAMLETS
Whitechapel High St
Aldgate
Aldgate East
ST HELEN BISHOPSGATE
ST ANDREW UNDERSHAFT
SWISSRE BUILDING
ROYAL EXCHANGE
LLOYD'S BUILDING
WILLIS BUILDING
Leadenhall Street
Fenchurch Street
Houndsditch
Minories
Mansell Street
Goodman's Yd
FENCHURCH STREET
ST CLEMENT EAST CHEAP
ST MARGARET PATTENS
ST OLAVE'S
TOWER GATEWAY
Tower Hill
Royal Mint Rd
ST MARY AT HILL
ST DUNSTAN-IN-THE-EAST
MONUMENT
ST MAGNUS THE MARTYR
ALL HALLOWS BY THE TOWER
TOWER OF LONDON
Tower Bridge Approach
East Smithfield
LONDON BRIDGE
THAMES
H.M.S. BELFAST
ST KATHARINE DOCK
HAY'S GALLERIA SHOPPING CENTRE
TOWER BRIDGE
CITY HALL
Tooley Street
Tower Bridge Rd
Shad Thames
Gainford St
St Thomas St
T
U
V
LONDON
0 200 m
0 200 yards

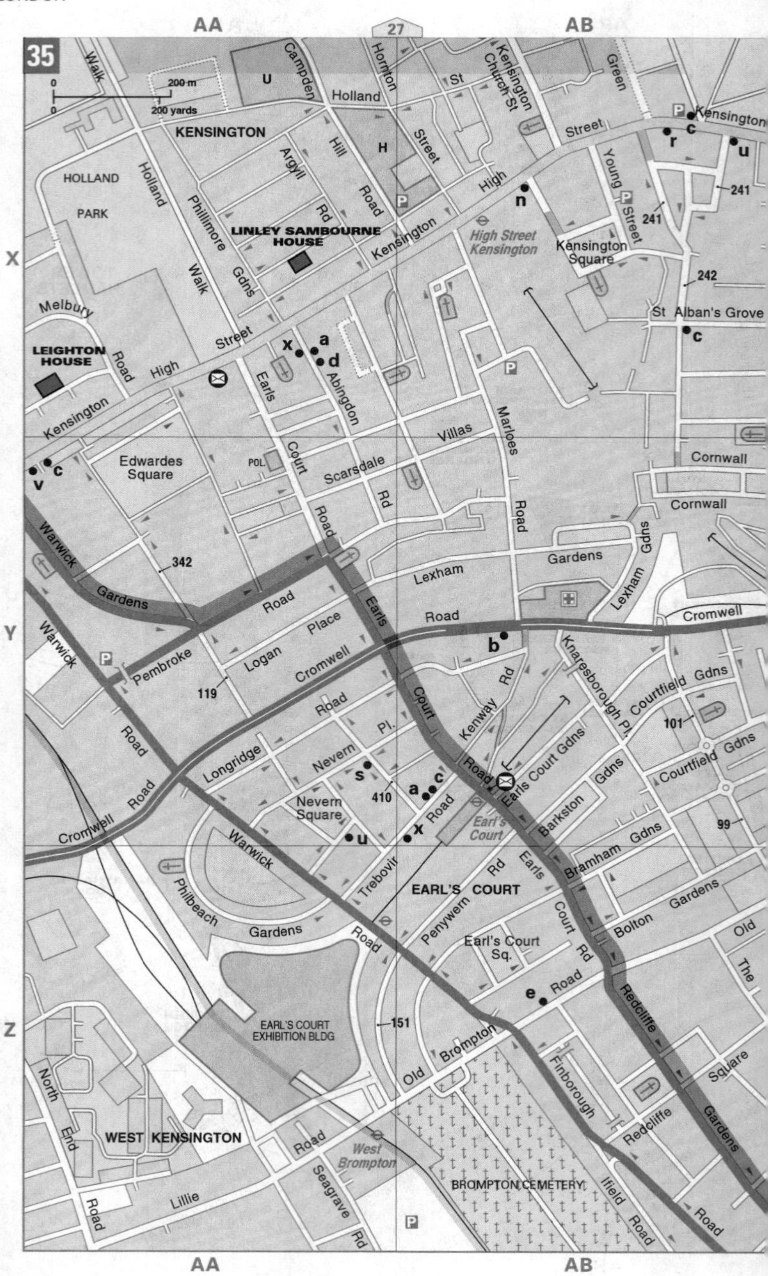
AA
27
AB
35
KENSINGTON
HOLLAND PARK
LINLEY SAMBOURNE HOUSE
LEIGHTON HOUSE
High Street Kensington
Kensington Square
Edwardes Square
EARL'S COURT
Earl's Court
Nevern Square
Earl's Court Sq.
EARL'S COURT EXHIBITION BLDG
WEST KENSINGTON
West Brompton
BROMPTON CEMETERY
X
Y
Z
LONDON

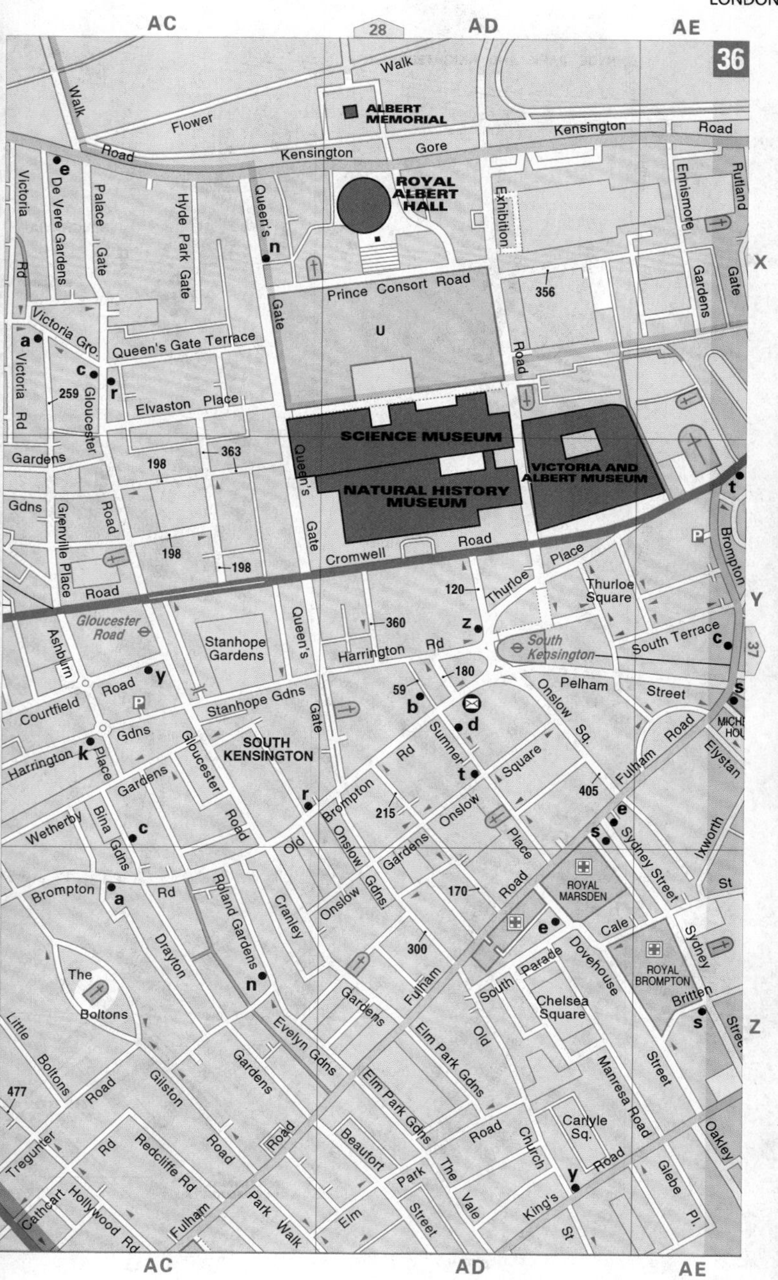
AC
AD
AE
28
36
ALBERT MEMORIAL
ROYAL ALBERT HALL
SCIENCE MUSEUM
NATURAL HISTORY MUSEUM
VICTORIA AND ALBERT MUSEUM
SOUTH KENSINGTON
ROYAL MARSDEN
ROYAL BROMPTON
Gloucester Road
South Kensington
Kensington Road
Kensington Gore
Flower Walk
Queen's Gate
Prince Consort Road
Exhibition Road
Cromwell Road
Thurloe Place
Thurloe Square
Harrington Rd
Pelham Street
Onslow Sq.
Fulham Road
Old Brompton Rd
Brompton Road
Sydney Street
The Boltons
Chelsea Square
Carlyle Sq.
King's Road
Manresa Road
Elm Park Gdns
X
Y
Z
37

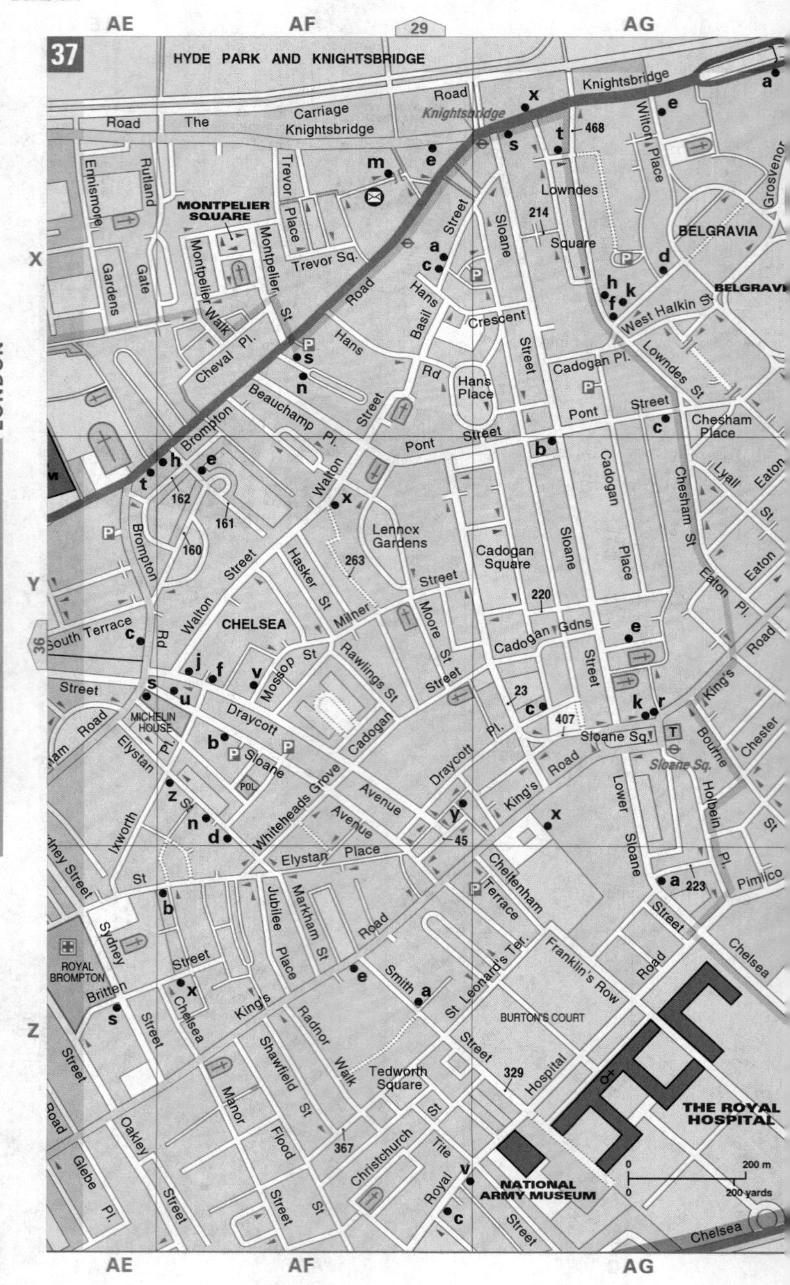
37
HYDE PARK AND KNIGHTSBRIDGE
AE
AF
AG
29
36
X
Y
Z
Knightsbridge
Road
The
Carriage
Knightsbridge
Road
Knightsbridge
468
Wilton Place
Grosvenor
Lowndes
214
Square
BELGRAVIA
BELGRAVI
West Halkin St
Ennismore
Gardens
Rutland
Gate
MONTPELIER
SQUARE
Montpelier Walk
Montpelier
St
Trevor
Place
Trevor Sq.
Road
Hans
Sloane
Street
Basil
Hans
Crescent
Street
Cheval Pl.
Brompton
Hans
Rd
Hans
Place
Cadogan Pl.
Lowndes St
Beauchamp
Pl.
Street
Pont
Street
Pont
Street
Chesham
Place
Cadogan
Chesham St
Lyall
Eaton
St
Walton
Lennox
Gardens
Cadogan
Square
Sloane
Place
Eaton
Eaton
Pl.
162
161
160
Brompton
Rd
263
Walton
Street
Hasker
St
Milner
Street
Moore
St
220
Cadogan Gdns
Street
Road
King's
Chester
South Terrace
CHELSEA
Mossop
St
Rawlings St
Street
Street
23
407
Sloane Sq.
Sloane Sq.
Bourne
Street
MICHELIN
HOUSE
Pl.
Draycott
Road
Elystan
Sloane
POL
Cadogan
Draycott
Pl.
Road
King's
Lower
Sloane
Holbein
Pl.
St
Avenue
Avenue
Whiteheads Grove
Ixworth
St
Pl.
45
Elystan
Place
Sydney Street
St
Cheltenham
Terrace
223
Pimlico
Street
Jubilee
Place
Markham
St
Road
Franklin's Row
Road
Chelsea
ROYAL
BROMPTON
Sydney
Street
Britten
Chelsea
King's
Smith
St Leonard's Ter.
BURTON'S COURT
Street
Street
Radnor
Walk
Shawfield
St
Tedworth
Square
329
Hospital
THE ROYAL
HOSPITAL
Road
Oakley
Manor
Flood
367
St
Christchurch
Tite
Royal
0
200 m
0
200 yards
NATIONAL
ARMY MUSEUM
Glebe
Pl.
Street
Street
St
Street
Chelsea
LONDON

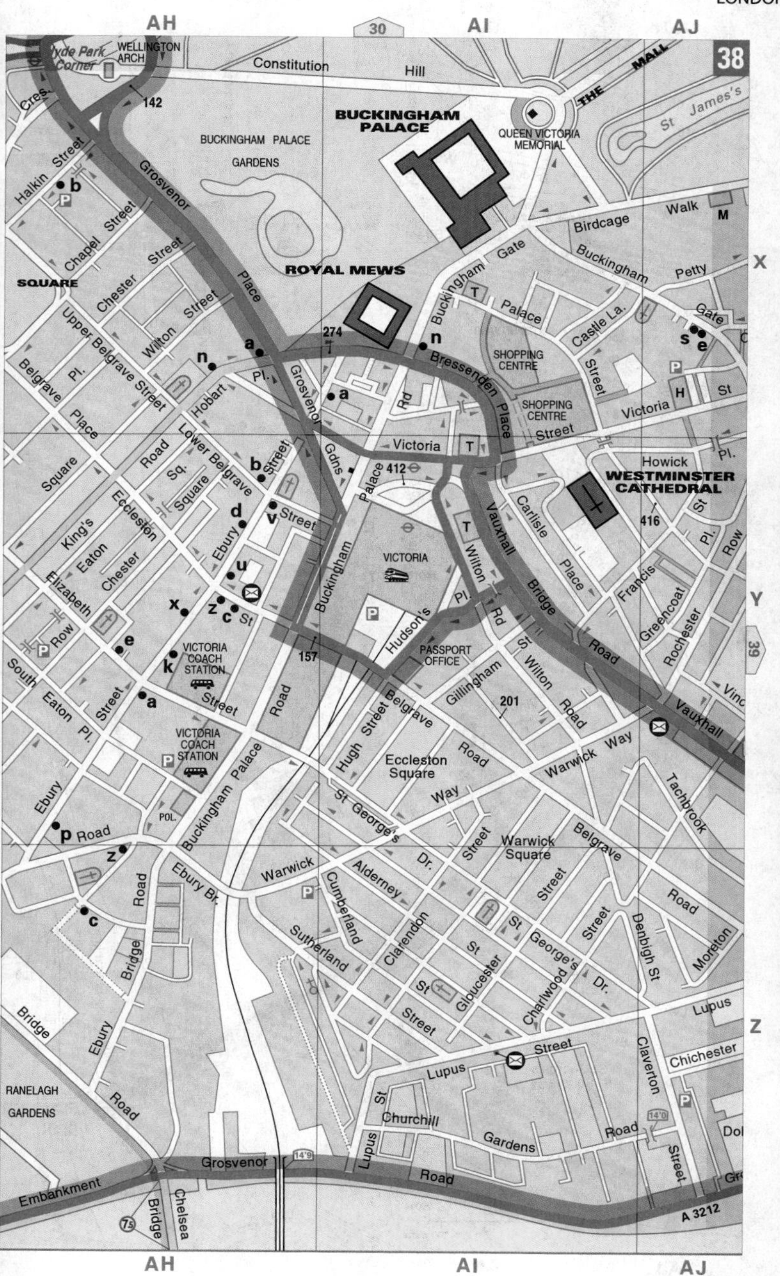

AH
AI
AJ
30
38
X
Y
Z
39
Hyde Park Corner
WELLINGTON ARCH
Constitution Hill
THE MALL
St James's
BUCKINGHAM PALACE
BUCKINGHAM PALACE GARDENS
QUEEN VICTORIA MEMORIAL
ROYAL MEWS
SHOPPING CENTRE
SHOPPING CENTRE
WESTMINSTER CATHEDRAL
VICTORIA
PASSPORT OFFICE
VICTORIA COACH STATION
VICTORIA COACH STATION
POL.
RANELAGH GARDENS
SQUARE
Eccleston Square
Warwick Square
Grosvenor Place
Grosvenor Gdns
Buckingham Palace Rd
Buckingham Gate
Birdcage Walk
Petty France
Victoria Street
Vauxhall Bridge Road
Belgrave Road
Warwick Way
Grosvenor Road
Chelsea Bridge
Embankment
A 3212
142
274
412
416
157
201

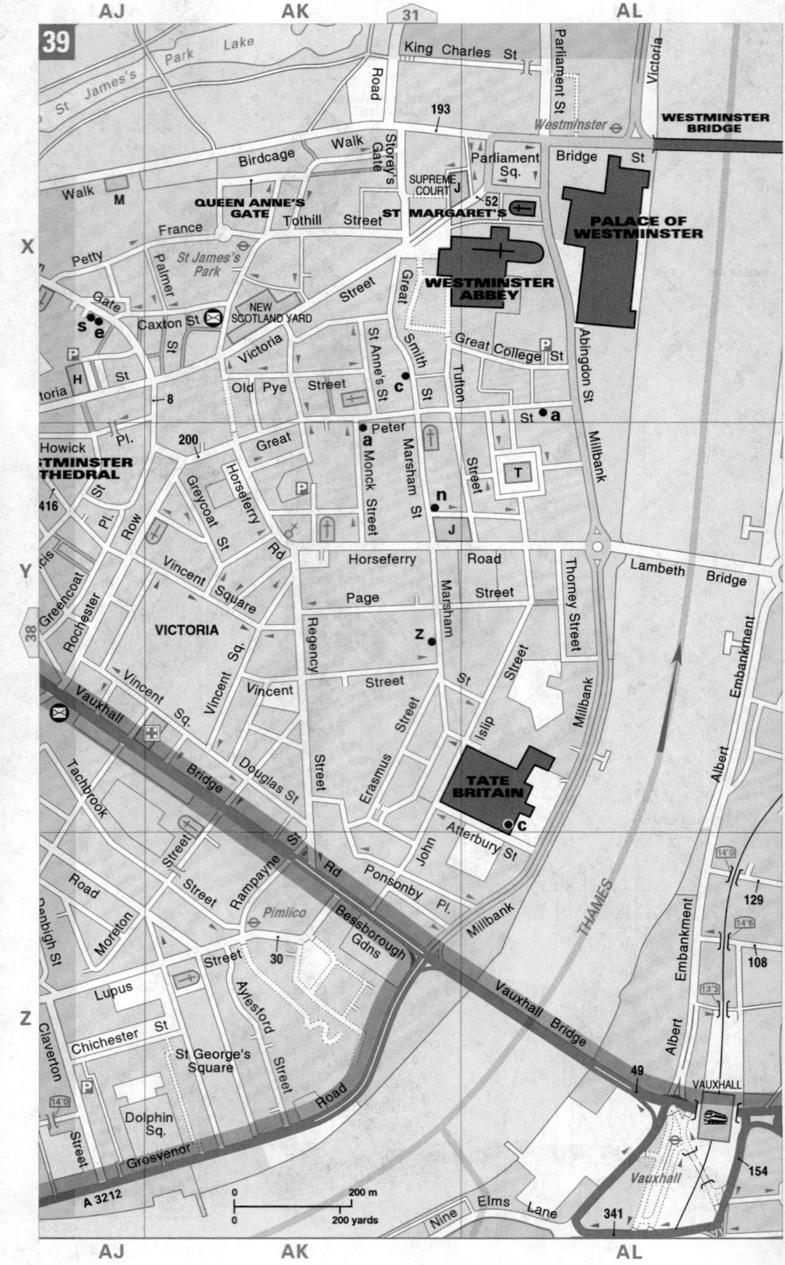

AJ
AK
AL
31
39
X
Y
Z
38
St James's Park Lake
King Charles St
Parliament St
Victoria
Road
193
Westminster
WESTMINSTER BRIDGE
Birdcage Walk
Storey's Gate
Parliament Sq.
Bridge St
SUPREME COURT
J
M
QUEEN ANNE'S GATE
Tothill Street
ST MARGARET'S
52
PALACE OF WESTMINSTER
France
Petty France
St James's Park
Palmer
Gate
WESTMINSTER ABBEY
Great Smith St
NEW SCOTLAND YARD
Caxton St
Victoria Street
Great College St
P
H
St
8
Old Pye Street
St Anne's St
Tufton
Abingdon St
Peter St
200
Great Peter
Howick Pl.
WESTMINSTER CATHEDRAL
416
Greycoat St
Horseferry Rd
Monck Street
Marsham St
Millbank
T
Row
Greycoat Pl.
Rochester
Vincent Square
Horseferry Road
Thorney Street
Lambeth Bridge
Page Street
Regency
VICTORIA
Vincent Sq.
Vincent Street
Marsham St
Erasmus Street
Islip Street
Embankment
Vauxhall Bridge Rd
Douglas St
Tachbrook Street
TATE BRITAIN
Atterbury St
John Islip
Albert Embankment
THAMES
Ponsonby Pl.
Millbank
Rampayne St
Moreton Street
Denbigh St
Pimlico
Bessborough Gdns
30
Lupus Street
Aylesford Street
Chichester St
Claverton Street
St George's Square
Dolphin Sq.
Grosvenor Road
A 3212
49
VAUXHALL
Vauxhall
Nine Elms Lane
341
154
129
108
14'0
14'6
13'3
0
200 m
200 yards

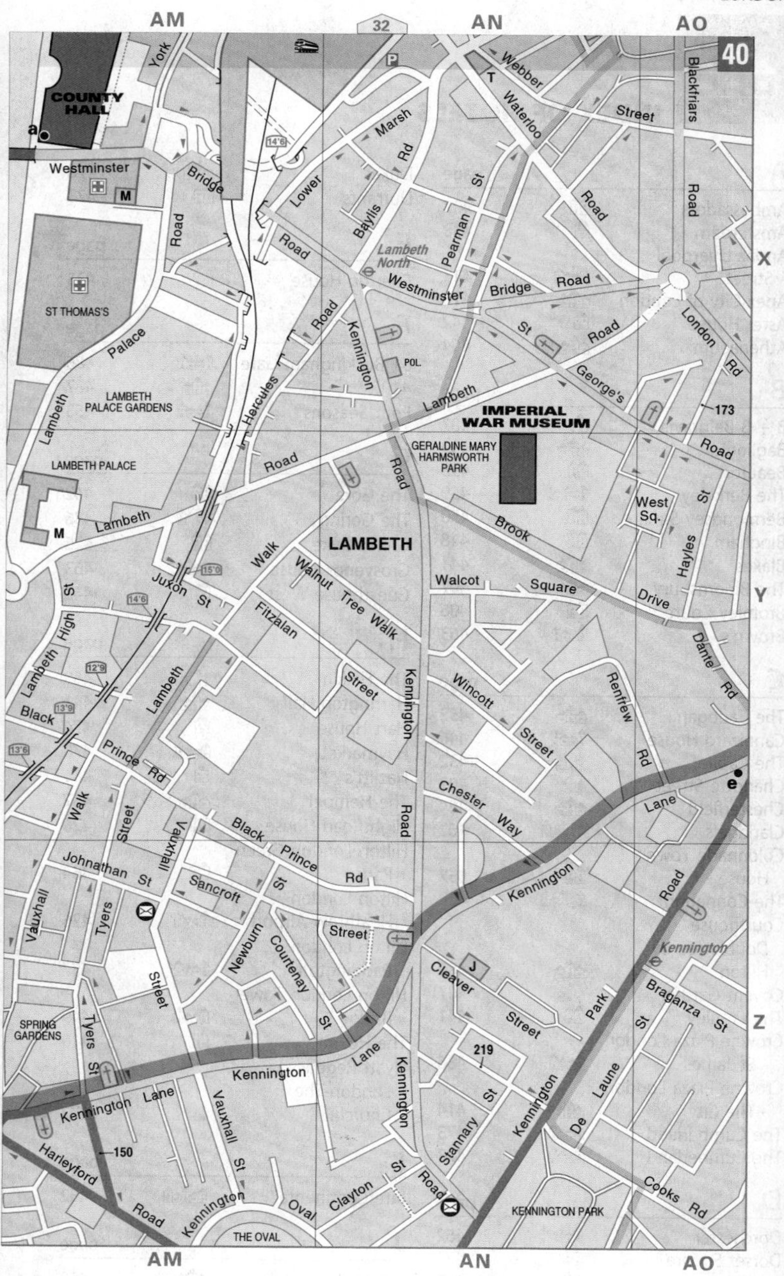
AM
32
AN
AO
40
COUNTY HALL
Westminster
M
ST THOMAS'S
LAMBETH PALACE GARDENS
LAMBETH PALACE
M
IMPERIAL WAR MUSEUM
GERALDINE MARY HARMSWORTH PARK
LAMBETH
Lambeth North
POL.
West Sq.
173
X
Y
Z
e
Kennington
J
219
150
SPRING GARDENS
KENNINGTON PARK
THE OVAL
a

INDEX OF HOTELS

K

L

M

N

O

P

R

S

T

W

Z

INDEX OF RESTAURANTS

A

B

C

D

E

F

LONDON

STARRED RESTAURANTS

✿✿✿		page
Alain Ducasse at The Dorchester N	XXXXX	464
Gordon Ramsay	XXXX	433

✿✿		page
L'Atelier de Joël Robuchon	X	485
Le Gavroche	XXXX	465
Hibiscus	XXX	466
The Ledbury N	XXX	443
Marcus Wareing at The Berkeley	XXXX	460
Pied à Terre	XXX	407
The Square	XXXX	465

✿		page
Amaya	XXX	460
Apsleys (at The Lanesborough) N	XXXX	460
Arbutus	X	483
L'Autre Pied	XX	475
Benares	XXX	467
Bingham Restaurant N	XX	448
Chapter One	XXX	406
Chez Bruce	XX	457
Club Gascon	XX	415
Galvin at Windows N	XXXX	465
The Glasshouse	XX	447
The Greenhouse	XXX	466
Hakkasan	XX	408
The Harwood Arms N	[pub]	422
Hélène Darroze at The Connaught	XXXX	465
Kai	XXX	466
Locanda Locatelli	XXX	474
Maze	XXX	466
Murano	XXX	466
Nahm	XX	461
Nobu (at The Metropolitan)	XX	470
Nobu Berkeley St	XX	468
Quilon	XXX	487
Rasoi	XX	435
Rhodes Twenty Four	XXX	414
Rhodes W1 (Restaurant)	XXXX	474
River Café	XX	422
Roussillon	XXX	487
St John	X	429
Semplice	XX	468
Sketch (The Lecture Room and Library)	XXXX	465
Tamarind N	XXX	467
Texture N	XX	475
Tom Aikens	XXX	434
La Trompette	XXX	426
Umu	XXX	467
Wild Honey	XX	468
Yauatcha	XX	481
Zafferano	XXX	461

BIB GOURMAND

Good food at moderate prices

PARTICULARLY PLEASANT HOTELS

(5 houses)	page
The Berkeley	459
Claridge's	462
The Connaught	462
Dorchester	462
Mandarin Oriental Hyde Park	461
The Ritz	477

(4 houses)	page
The Goring	486
One Aldwych	484
The Soho	480

(3 houses)	page
Blakes	441
The Capital	432
Charlotte Street	407
Covent Garden	407
Draycott	432
Dukes	478
The Halkin	460
The Milestone	439
The Pelham	441
Stafford	478

(2 houses)	page
Dorset Square	473
Egerton House	433
Knightsbridge	432
The Levin	433
Number Sixteen	441

PARTICULARLY PLEASANT RESTAURANTS

XXXXX	page
The Ritz Restaurant	478

XXXX	page
Hélène Darroze at The Connaught	465
Marcus Wareing at The Berkeley	460

XXX	page
Bibendum	434
Boundary	420
Cecconi's	467
Coq d'Argent	414
Quo Vadis	481
Scott's	467
The Wolseley	478

XX	page
Le Café Anglais	458
Le Caprice	479
J. Sheekey	485
Mon Plaisir	408
River Café	422
Rules	485
Wild Honey	468

X	page
L'Atelier de Joël Robuchon	485
Bibendum Oyster Bar	437
Bocca di Lupo	483
Dehesa	483
J. Sheekey Oyster Bar	486
Oxo Tower Brasserie	452
Petersham Nurseries Café	448

RESTAURANTS BY CUISINE TYPE

Innovative

International

Italian

Italian influences

LONDON
Boroughs and areas

Greater London is divided, for administrative purposes, into 32 boroughs plus **the City**: these sub-divide naturally into minor areas, usually grouped around former villages or quarters, which often maintain a distinctive character.

BRENT – Greater London – pop. 263 464 — 12 A3

Kensal Green

Paradise by way of Kensal Green

19 Kilburn Lane ✉ W10 4AE ⊖ Kensal Green. – ✆ (020) 8969 0098 – www.theparadise.co.uk – Closed August bank holiday — **10**MZC**x**

Rest – Menu £ 15/30 – Carte £ 24/31

◆ Decorated in a bohemian style with mismatched furniture, portraits and Murano chandeliers. Lighter lunch in bar, generously-sized portions of seasonal British fare in the rear restaurant.

Kilburn

North London Tavern

375 Kilburn High Rd ✉ NW6 7QB ⊖ Kilburn. – ✆ (020) 7625 6634 – www.realpubs.co.uk – Closed 25 December, lunch 26 December and 1 January and Monday — **10**NZB**a**

Rest – Carte £ 19/29

◆ Black exterior, popular bar for locals and a separate rear dining room with slight gothic feel. Appetising and gutsy gastropub staples with a wine list offering most bottles under £ 20.

Queen's Park

The Salusbury

50-52 Salusbury Road ✉ NW6 6NN ⊖ Queens Park. – ✆ (020) 7328 3286 – Closed 25-26 December, 1 January and Monday lunch — **10**MZB**b**

Rest – Menu £ 22/25

◆ Pleasingly down-to-earth pub, more shabby than chic. Italian influenced menu is a model of understatement; skilled kitchen produces generously sized dishes with plenty of flavour.

Willesden Green

Sushi-Say

33B Walm Lane ✉ NW2 5SH ⊖ Willesden Green – ✆ (020) 8459 2971 – Fax (020) 8907 3229 – Closed 25-26 December, 1 January, 2 weeks March-April, 1 week August, Monday and Tuesday following Bank Holiday

Rest – Japanese – *(dinner only and lunch Saturday-Sunday)* — **9**LZB**a**

Menu £ 17/37 – Carte £ 16/40

◆ Very popular with the locals, attracted by sweet service and an extensive selection of Japanese food. Sit at the counter to watch the skill of the owner as he prepares the sushi.

The Queensbury

110 Walm Lane Willesden Green ⊖ Willesden Green. – ✆ (020) 8452 0171 – www.thequeensbury.net — **9**LZA**a**

Rest – Carte £ 19/25

◆ Formerly called The Green, this reinvigorated pub has a brightly styled dining room beyond the bar and offers an appealing menu covering all bases. Weekend brunch and occasional live music.

BROMLEY – Greater London – pop. 280 305 — 12 B3

27 Orpington Golf Centre Sandy Lane, St Paul's Cray, ✆ (01689) 839 677

9 Magpie Hall lane Magpie Hall lane

BROMLEY

Bromley Court

Bromley Hill ✉ BR1 4JD – ✆ (020) 8461 8600 – www.bw-bromleycourthotel.co.uk – Fax (020) 8460 0899 **8**HY**z**

114 rm ☕ – 🛉£ 89/109 🛉🛉£ 105/120

Rest – *(closed Saturday lunch)* Menu £ 19/24

◆ A grand neo-Gothic mansion in three acres of well-tended garden. Popular with corporate guests for the large conference space. Constant redecoration ensures bedrooms remain bright. Conservatory or terrace dining available.

FARNBOROUGH

Chapter One

Farnborough Common, Locksbottom ✉ BR6 8NF – ✆ (01689) 854 848 – www.chaptersrestaurants.com – Fax (01689) 858 439 – Closed first week January **8**HZ**a**

Rest – Modern European – Menu £ 19 (lunch) – Carte £ 23/30

Spec. Salad of pigeon and pata negra with walnut dressing. Poached and roasted quail with foie gras and braised red cabbage. Lemon tart with crème fraîche sorbet.

◆ The skilled kitchen produces assured and precisely executed, modern European cooking at a fair price. The mock Tudor exterior belies the contemporary styling of the restaurant and bar within.

ORPINGTON

Xian

324 High St ✉ BR6 0NG – ✆ (01689) 871 881 – Fax (01689) 829 437 – Closed 2 weeks Spring, 25-26 December and Sunday lunch **8**JY**a**

Rest – Chinese – Menu £ 10/16 – Carte £ 17/25

◆ Modern, marbled interior with oriental artefacts make this personally run Chinese restaurant a firm favourite with locals. Look out for the Peking specialities.

SUNDRIDGE PARK

Crown

46 Plaistow Lane ✉ BR1 3PA Sundridge Park ⊖ Sundridge Park (rail). – ✆ (020) 8466 1313 – www.thecrownsundridgepark.co.uk – Closed Sunday dinner and Monday except Bank Holidays HY**e**

Rest – Menu £ 19 (Sunday lunch) – Carte £ 23/33

◆ This handsome, sizeable Victorian pub was gutted and transformed into a contemporary dining pub. Pub classics during the week; more adventurous cooking at weekends. Over 300 bottles on wine list.

CAMDEN – Greater London – pop. 198 020 **12** B3

BELSIZE PARK

XO

29 Belsize Lane ✉ NW3 5AS ⊖ Belsize Park – ✆ (020) 7433 0888 – www.rickerrestaurants.com/xo – Fax (020) 7794 3474 – Closed 25-26 December and 1 January **11**PZA**a**

Rest – Asian – Carte £ 19/36

◆ Stylish dining room with banquettes, revolving lights and mirrors. Vibrant atmosphere; popular with locals. Japanese, Korean, Thai and Chinese cooking; dishes are best shared.

Osteria Emilia

85b Fleet Road ✉ NW3 2QY ⊖ Belsize Park – ✆ (020) 7433 3317 – Closed 2 weeks summer, Christmas to New Year, Sunday and Monday **11**QZA**a**

Rest – Italian – Carte £ 26/35

◆ The name refers to Emilia-Romagna whose influences inform the cooking at this neighbourhood Italian. Spread over 2 floors, with bright, pared-down décor. The family also own the deli opposite.

Bloomsbury

Covent Garden

10 Monmouth St ✉ WC2H 9HB ⊖ Covent Garden – ✆ (020) 7806 1000 – www.coventgardenhotel.co.uk – Fax (020) 7806 1100 **31**ALU**x**

56 rm – †£ 264/323 ††£ 376, ☕ £ 19.50 – 2 suites

Rest *Brasserie Max* – *(booking essential)* Menu £ 25 – Carte £ 36/58

◆ Individually designed and stylish bedrooms, with CDs and VCRs discreetly concealed. Boasts a very comfortable first floor oak-panelled drawing room with its own honesty bar. Busy, warm and relaxed restaurant also offers afternoon tea.

Charlotte Street

15 Charlotte St ✉ W1T 1RJ ⊖ Goodge Street – ✆ (020) 7806 2000 – www.charlottestreethotel.co.uk – Fax (020) 7806 2002 **31**AKT**e**

48 rm – †£ 259/294 ††£ 364, ☕ £ 19 – 4 suites

Rest *Oscar* – Modern European – ✆ (020) 7907 4005 – Menu £ 22 – Carte £ 30/52

◆ Interior designed with a charming and understated English feel. Impeccably kept and individually decorated bedrooms. In-house screening room. Bright restaurant with large bar and European menu.

Montague on the Gardens

15 Montague St ✉ WC1B 5BJ ⊖ Holborn – ✆ (020) 7637 1001 – www.montaguehotel.com – Fax (020) 7637 2516 **31**ALT**a**

94 rm – †£ 144/265 ††£ 156/265, ☕ £ 17 – 6 suites

Rest *The Blue Door Bistro* – Menu £ 20/25 – Carte £ 29/47

◆ Cosy British feel to this period townhouse. Clubby bar and conservatory overlooking a secluded garden. Individually decorated bedrooms. Bistro divided into two small, pretty rooms.

The Bloomsbury

16-22 Gt Russell St ✉ WC1B 3NN ⊖ Tottenham Court Road – ✆ (020) 7347 1000 – www.doylecollection.com/bloomsbury – Fax (020) 7347 1001 **31**AKT**n**

153 rm – †£ 138/334 ††£ 138/334, ☕ £ 21

Rest *Landseer* – *(bar lunch)* Carte £ 30/42 **s**

◆ Refurbished in 2009. Neo-Georgian building by Edward Lutyens, built for YMCA in 1929. Smart comfortable interior, from the lobby to the bedrooms. Restaurant with mostly British menu.

Ambassadors

12 Upper Woburn Place ✉ WC1H 0HX ⊖ Euston – ✆ (020) 7693 5400 – www.ambassadors.co.uk – Fax (020) 7388 9930 **18**SZD**a**

100 rm – †£ 235 ††£ 235, ☕ £ 16

Rest *Number Twelve* – ✆ (020) 7693 5425 *(Closed Saturday lunch, Sunday, Monday and Bank Holidays)* Menu £ 18 – Carte £ 26/39

◆ Contemporary hotel near to Euston Station. Six floors of cleverly designed bedrooms with all mod cons; Premier rooms the most spacious. Several well-equipped meeting rooms. Ground floor restaurant has relaxed style and offers Italian menu.

Pied à Terre (Shane Osborn)

34 Charlotte St ✉ W1T 2NH ⊖ Goodge Street – ✆ (020) 7636 1178 – www.pied-a-terre.co.uk – Fax (020) 7916 1171 – Closed 24 December-5 January, Saturday lunch and Sunday **31**AJT**e**

Rest – Innovative – Menu £ 33 (lunch)/69 – Carte approx. £ 70

Spec. Crayfish and garlic gnocchi with Lardo di Colonnata. Suckling pig with beetroot, girolles and cider sauce. Bitter sweet chocolate tart, stout ice cream and macadamia nut cream.

◆ David Moore made the best of limited space to create a stylish and intimate restaurant that is very well established and professionally run. Shane Osborn's cooking is expertly rendered and elaborate in style but with clear flavours.

LONDON

XX **Mon Plaisir**

19-21 Monmouth St ✉ WC2H 9DD ⊖ Covent Garden – ✆ (020) 7836 7243 – www.monplaisir.co.uk – Fax (020) 7240 4774 – Closed 25 December-1 January, Saturday lunch, Sunday and Bank Holidays **31**ALU**g**

Rest – French – Menu £ 17 (lunch) – Carte £ 29/47

◆ London's oldest French restaurant and family-run for over fifty years. Divided into four rooms, all with a different feel but all proudly Gallic in their decoration.

XX **Incognico**

117 Shaftesbury Ave ✉ WC2H 8AD ⊖ Tottenham Court Road – ✆ (020) 7836 8866 – www.incognico.com – Fax (020) 7240 9525 – Closed Sunday and Bank Holidays **31**AKU**q**

Rest – French – Menu £ 20 – Carte £ 28/39

◆ Firmly established with clubby décor of wood panelling and brown leather chairs. Downstairs bar has a window into the kitchen, from where French and English classics are produced.

XX **Hakkasan**

8 Hanway Place ✉ W1T 1HD ⊖ Tottenham Court Road – ✆ (020) 7927 7000 – www.hakkasan.com – Fax (020) 7907 1889 – Closed 24-25 December

Rest – Chinese – Carte £ 32/109 **31**AKT**c**

Spec. Grilled quail with green mango and papaya salad. Stir-fried Mongolian style venison. Chocolate ganache.

◆ Cool and seductive subterranean restaurant, with an air of exclusivity. Innovation and originality have been added to the Cantonese base to create dishes with zip and depth. Lunchtime dim sum is a highlight.

XX **Roka**

37 Charlotte St ✉ W1T 1RR ⊖ Tottenham Court Road – ✆ (020) 7580 6464 – www.rokarestaurant.com – Fax (020) 7580 0220 – Closed 24-27 December and 1 January **31**AJT**k**

Rest – Japanese – Carte approx. £ 32

◆ Bright, atmospheric interior of teak and oak; bustling and trendy feel. Contemporary touches added to Japanese dishes; try specialities from the on-view Robata grill. Capable and chatty service.

XX **Sardo**

45 Grafton Way ✉ W1T 5DQ ⊖ Warren Street – ✆ (020) 7387 2521 – www.sardo-restaurant.com – Fax (020) 7387 2559 – Closed Christmas, Saturday lunch and Sunday **18**RZD**c**

Rest – Italian – Carte £ 26/34

◆ Simple, stylish interior run in a very warm and welcoming manner with very efficient service. Rustic Italian cooking with a Sardinian character and a modern tone.

XX **Fino**

33 Charlotte St (entrance on Rathbone St) ✉ W1T 1RR ⊖ Goodge Street – ✆ (020) 7813 8010 – www.finorestaurant.com – Fax (020) 7813 8011 – Closed 24-25 December, Saturday lunch, Sunday and Bank Holidays

Rest – Spanish – Carte £ 22/34 **31**AJT**a**

◆ Well-kept Spanish basement restaurant with stylish surroundings and plenty of atmosphere. Wide-ranging menu of authentic and carefully prepared dishes, best enjoyed when shared.

XX **Crazy Bear**

26-28 Whitfield St ✉ W1T 2RG ⊖ Goodge Street – ✆ (020) 7631 0088 – www.crazybeargroup.co.uk – Fax (020) 7631 1188 **31**AKT**b**

Rest – Asian – Menu £ 15 – Carte £ 24/50

◆ Exotic destination: downstairs bar geared to fashionable set; ground floor dining room is art deco inspired. Asian flavoured menus, with predominance towards Thai dishes.

XX **Archipelago**

110 Whitfield St ✉ W1T 5ED ⊖ Goodge Street – ✆ (020) 7383 3346 – www.archipelago-restaurant.co.uk – Fax (020) 7383 7181 – Closed 24-26 December, 1 January, Saturday lunch, Sunday and Bank Holiday Mondays

Rest – Innovative – Carte £ 30/40 **18**RZD**c**

◆ Exotic in menu and décor: crammed with knick-knacks from cages to Buddhas. Menu an eclectic mix of influences from around the world; unusual ingredients not for the faint-hearted.

Rasa Samudra

5 Charlotte St ✉ W1T 1RE ⊖ Goodge Street – ✆ (020) 7637 0222 – www.rasarestaurants.com – Fax (020) 7637 0224 – Closed 24 December-1 January, Sunday lunch and Bank Holidays **31AKTr**

Rest – Indian – Menu £ 23/30 – Carte £ 13/24

◆ Comfortably appointed with a collection of Indian silks and ornaments and perennially busy. The room at the back is more inviting. Authentic Keralan seafood and vegetarian specialities.

Cigala

54 Lamb's Conduit St ✉ WC1N 3LW ⊖ Russell Square – ✆ (020) 7405 1717 – www.cigala.co.uk – Fax (020) 7242 9949 – Closed 24-26 December, 1 January and Easter **19TZDa**

Rest – Spanish – *(booking essential)* Menu £ 18 (lunch) – Carte £ 24/35

◆ Spanish restaurant on corner of attractive street. Simply furnished; open-plan kitchen. Robust Iberian cooking, with some dishes designed for sharing; interesting drinks list.

Giaconda Dining Room

9 Denmark Street ✉ WC2H 8LS London ⊖ Tottenham Court Road – ✆ (020) 7240 3334 – www.giacondadining.com – Closed 1 week Christmas, 3 weeks August, Saturday, Sunday and Bank Holidays **31AKTk**

Rest – Modern European – *(booking essential)* Carte £ 24/28

◆ Aussie owners run a small, fun and very busy place in an unpromising location. The very well priced menu offers an appealing mix of gutsy, confident, no-nonsense food, with French and Italian influences.

Salt Yard

54 Goodge St ✉ W1T 4NA ⊖ Goodge Street – ✆ (020) 7637 0657 – www.saltyard.co.uk – Fax (020) 7580 7435 – Closed 10 days Christmas, Saturday lunch, Sunday and Bank Holidays **31AJTd**

Rest – Mediterranean – Carte £ 20/36

◆ Ground floor bar and buzzy basement restaurant specialising in good value plates of tasty Italian and Spanish dishes, ideal for sharing; charcuterie a speciality. Super wine list.

Tsunami

93 Charlotte St. ✉ W1T 4PY ⊖ Goodge Street – ✆ (020) 7637 0050 – www.tsunamirestaurant.co.uk – Fax (020) 7637 4411 – Closed 25 December, Saturday lunch and Sunday **30AITn**

Rest – Japanese – Menu £ 13 (lunch) – Carte £ 19/35

◆ Sister to the original in Clapham. Sweet, pretty place, with lacquered walls, floral motif and moody lighting. Contemporary Japanese cuisine is carefully prepared and sensibly priced.

Acorn House

69 Swinton St ✉ WC1X 9NT ⊖ King's Cross – ✆ (020) 7812 1842 – www.acornhouserestaurant.com – Closed 25 December, Sunday and Bank Holidays **18TZCb**

Rest – Modern European – Carte £ 25/36

◆ Eco-friendly training restaurant with a bright and appealing café-style feel and helpful service. Dishes are healthy, seasonal and generously proportioned, using organic ingredients.

Abeno

47 Museum St ✉ WC1A 1LY ⊖ Tottenham Court Road – ✆ (020) 7405 3211 – www.abeno.co.uk – Fax (020) 7405 3212 – Closed 1 January, 23-27 and 31 December **31ALTe**

Rest – Japanese – Menu £ 13 (lunch) – Carte £ 15/43

◆ Simple little place near British Museum. Specialises in okonomi-yaki: Japanese 'pancakes' cooked on a hotplate on each table. Choose your own filling and size of your pancake.

Prices quoted after the symbol 🚹 refer to the lowest rate in low season followed by the highest rate in high season, for a single room. The same principle applies to the symbol 🚹🚹 for a double room.

Camden Town

XX **York & Albany** with rm
127-129 Parkway ✉ NW1 7PS ⊖ Camden Town – ✆ (020) 7388 3344 – www.gordonramsay.com/yorkandalbany – Fax (020) 7592 1603 **12**RZB**s**
10 rm – †£ 175 ††£ 225, ☕ £ 12
Rest – Modern European – *(booking essential)* Menu £ 18 (lunch) – Carte £ 28/41
◆ 1820s John Nash former coaching inn, now part of Gordon Ramsay's empire. Smart bar and informal dining; lower level offers kitchen views. Cooking is refined without being fussy, and influences are European. Comfortable, individually decorated bedrooms.

X **Market**
43 Parkway ✉ NW1 7PN ⊖ Camden Town – ✆ (020) 7267 9700 – www.marketrestaurant.co.uk – Closed 25 December-2 January, Sunday dinner and Bank Holidays **12**RZB**x**
Rest – British – *(booking essential)* Menu £ 10 (2 course lunch weekdays) – Carte £ 25/29
◆ The highlights of the well-priced, daily menu are the classic British dishes, using market fresh ingredients. Simple comforts of exposed brick walls, zinc-topped tables and school chairs work well.

Prince Albert
163 Royal College St ✉ NW1 0SG ⊖ Camden Town. – ✆ (020) 7485 0270 – www.princealbertcamden.com – Fax (020) 7713 5994 **12**RZB**c**
Rest – *(booking essential)* Menu £ 11/12 – Carte £ 19/32
◆ Light, airy pub with welcoming neighbourhood feel. Simply prepared, satisfying dishes, with emphasis on freshness and traceability. Upstairs restaurant has own menu in evening.

Dartmouth Park

Bull and Last
168 Highgate Road ⊖ Tufnell Park. – ✆ (020) 7267 3641 – Closed 25 December
Rest – *(booking essential)* Carte £ 26/32 **12**RZA**a**
◆ Bright, breezy and enthusiastically run pub opposite Parliament Hill. Cooking is robust, generous and satisfying, with sourcing taken seriously; game and charcuterie the specialities.

Euston

Novotel London St. Pancras rm
100-110 Euston Rd ✉ NW1 2AJ ⊖ Euston – ✆ (020) 7666 9000 – www.novotel.com – Fax (020) 7666 9025 **18**SZC**a**
309 rm – †£ 260 ††£ 260, ☕ £ 14.95 – 3 suites
Rest – *(bar lunch Saturday and Sunday)* Menu £ 16/19 – Carte £ 27/36
◆ Halfway between Euston and Kings Cross, this hotel has good-sized bedrooms for a London hotel and those on the higher floors enjoy views over the city. Good business amenities. International menu and buffet breakfast.

XX **Snazz Sichuan**
37 Chalton St ✉ NW1 1JD ⊖ Euston – ✆ (020) 7388 0808 – www.newchinaclub.co.uk **12**SZC**b**
Rest – Chinese – Carte £ 10/40
◆ Authentic Sichuan atmosphere and cooking, with gallery and traditional tea room. Menu split into hot and cold dishes; the fiery Sichuan pepper helps heat you from inside out.

Hampstead

Langorf without rest
20 Frognal ✉ NW3 6AG ⊖ Finchley Road – ✆ (020) 7794 4483 – www.langorfhotel.com – Fax (020) 7435 9055 **11**PZA**c**
41 rm – †£ 82/98 ††£ 95/98, ☕ £ 6 – 5 suites
◆ Converted Edwardian house in a quiet residential area. Bright breakfast room overlooks secluded walled garden. Fresh bedrooms, many of which have high ceilings.

Goldfish

82 Hampstead High St. ✉ NW3 1RE ⊖ Hampstead – ☎ (020) 7794 6666 – www.goldfish-restaurant.co.uk – Closed 24-25 December **11**PZA**z**

Rest – Asian – Menu £ 16 (lunch) – Carte £ 15/30

◆ Sweet little place, divided into three differently decorated rooms. Mix of Chinese and other Asian countries; chef also adds own creations. Well-priced lunch menu, including popular weekend dim sum.

The Wells

30 Well Walk ✉ NW3 1BX ⊖ Hampstead. – ☎ (020) 7794 3785 – www.thewellshampstead.co.uk – Fax (020) 7794 6817 **11**PZA**v**

Rest – *(Closed Sunday lunch)* Carte £ 20/33

◆ Part country pub, part city sophisticate; busy ground floor, with more sedate upstairs restaurant. Cooking is hearty in flavour and sophisticated in look, with a pleasing British edge.

The Magdala

2A South Hill Park ✉ NW3 2SB ⊖ Belsize Park. – ☎ (020) 7435 2503 – www.the-magdala.com – Fax (020) 7435 6167 **11**PZA**s**

Rest – Carte £ 19/28

◆ Friendly pub on edge of Heath; turn right for drinking, left for eating. Concise but balanced menu with interesting snacks and sharing plates. Upstairs room used at weekends.

Hatton Garden

Bleeding Heart

Bleeding Heart Yard, off Greville St ✉ EC1N 8SJ ⊖ Farringdon – ☎ (020) 7242 8238 – www.bleedingheart.co.uk – Fax (020) 7831 1402 – Closed 23 December-4 January, Saturday, Sunday and Bank Holidays **32**ANT**e**

Rest – French – *(booking essential)* Carte £ 29/37

◆ Busy downstairs restaurant, popular with City suits. Fast-paced service, terrific wine list and well-practised cooking. Seasonally-changing French menu with traditional core.

Holborn

Renaissance Chancery Court

252 High Holborn ✉ WC1V 7EN ⊖ Holborn – ☎ (020) 7829 9888 – www.renaissancechancerycourt.co.uk. – Fax (020) 7829 9889 **32**AMT**a**

356 rm – †£ 276/357 ††£ 276/357, ☕ £ 24.50 – 2 suites

Rest ***Pearl*** – see restaurant listing

◆ Striking building built in 1914, now an imposing place to stay. Impressive marbled lobby and grand central courtyard. Very large bedrooms with comprehensive modern facilities.

Kingsway Hall

rm,

Great Queen St ✉ WC2B 5BX ⊖ Holborn – ☎ (020) 7309 0909 – www.kingswayhall.co.uk – Fax (020) 7309 9129 **31**ALT**b**

168 rm – †£ 119/299 ††£ 119/299, ☕ £ 15.95 – 2 suites

Rest – Menu £ 20 – Carte £ 20/25

◆ Large, corporate-minded hotel. Striking glass-framed and marbled lobby. Stylish ground floor bar. Well-appointed bedrooms with an extensive array of mod cons. European menus in smart, minimalist restaurant.

Pearl – at Renaissance Chancery Court Hotel

252 High Holborn ✉ WC1V 7EN ⊖ Holborn – ☎ (020) 7829 7000 – www.pearl-restaurant.com – Fax (020) 7829 9889 – Closed last 2 weeks August, Saturday lunch, Sunday and Bank Holidays **32**AMT**a**

Rest – French – Menu £ 29/55

◆ Impressive former banking hall, with walls clad in Italian marble and Corinthian columns. Waiters provide efficient service at well-spaced tables; cooking shows originality.

Matsuri - High Holborn

Mid City Pl, 71 High Holborn ✉ WC1V 6EA ⊖ Holborn – ☎ (020) 7430 1970 – www.matsuri-restaurant.com – Fax (020) 7430 1971 – Closed 25 December, 1 January, Sunday and Bank Holidays **32**AMT**c**

Rest – Japanese – Menu £ 29/35 – Carte £ 19/75

◆ Spacious, airy Japanese restaurant. Authentic menu served in main dining room, in basement teppan-yaki bar and at large sushi counter, where chefs demonstrate their skills.

XX **Asadal** AC VISA MC AE

227 High Holborn ✉ WC1V 7DA ⊖ Holborn – ✆ (020) 7430 9006 – www.asadal.co.uk – Closed 25-26 December, 1 January and Sunday lunch

Rest – Korean – Menu £ 12 (lunch) – Carte £ 13/20 **31**ALT**n**

◆ A hectic, unprepossessing location, but delivers the authenticity of a modest Korean café with the comfort and service of a proper restaurant. Good quality Korean cooking.

XX **Moti Mahal** AC VISA MC AE

45 Great Queen St ✉ WC2B 5AA ⊖ Holborn – ✆ (020) 7240 9329 – www.motimahal-uk.com – Fax (020) 7836 0790 – Closed 25-28 December, New Year, Saturday lunch and Sunday **31**ALU**k**

Rest – Indian – Menu £ 15/20 – Carte £ 31/42

◆ Bright and contemporary Indian restaurant spread over two floors. Chefs on view behind glass, with the tandoor oven the star of the show. Innovative and ambitious specialities. Keen service.

X **Great Queen Street** VISA MC

32 Great Queen St ✉ WC2B 5AA ⊖ Holborn – ✆ (020) 7242 0622 – Fax (020) 7404 9582 – Closed Christmas-New Year, Sunday dinner and Bank Holidays **31**ALT**d**

Rest – British – *(booking essential)* Menu £ 25 (Sunday lunch) – Carte £ 23/36

◆ The menu is a model of British understatement; the cooking, confident and satisfying with laudable prices and generous portions. Lively atmosphere and enthusiastic service.

X **Villandry Kitchen** AC MC AE

95-97 High Holborn ✉ WC1V 6LF ⊖ Holborn – ✆ (020) 7242 4580 – www.villandry.com – Closed 25 December **32**AMT**k**

Rest – French – Carte £ 18/30

◆ Open all day and offering everything from breakfast and afternoon tea to pizza, charcuterie and comforting French classics. Large, animated room with rustic feel and friendly service.

Primrose Hill

XX **Odette's** AC VISA MC AE

130 Regent's Park Rd ✉ NW1 8XL ⊖ Chalk Farm – ✆ (020) 7586 8569 – www.odettesprimrosehill.com – Fax (020) 7586 8362 – Closed Christmas and Monday **11**QZB**b**

Rest – Modern European – Menu £ 18 (lunch) – Carte £ 31/41

◆ Warm and inviting local institution, with enclosed rear terrace. Elaborate and sophisticated cooking which brings a little bit of the Welsh owner-chef's homeland to NW London.

XX **Sardo Canale** AC VISA MC AE

42 Gloucester Ave ✉ NW1 8JD ⊖ Chalk Farm – ✆ (020) 7722 2800 – www.sardocanale.com – Fax (020) 7722 0802 – Closed Christmas and Monday

Rest – Italian – Menu £ 13 (lunch) – Carte £ 25/33 **12**RZB**a**

◆ A series of five snug but individual dining rooms in conservatory style; delightful terrace with 200 year old olive tree. Appealing Italian menus with strong Sardinian accent.

X **L'Absinthe** AC VISA MC AE

40 Chalcot Road ✉ NW18LS ⊖ Chalk Farm – ✆ (020) 7483 4848 – Closed 2 weeks Christmas, August and Monday **11**QZB**s**

Rest – French – Menu £ 13 (weekday lunch) – Carte £ 19/28

◆ Lively and enthusiastically run French bistro, with tightly packed tables, spread over two floors. All the favourites, from Lyonnais salad to duck confit. Commendably priced French wine list.

The Engineer P VISA MC

65 Gloucester Ave ✉ NW1 8JH ⊖ Chalk Farm. – ✆ (020) 7722 0950 – www.the-engineer.com – Fax (020) 7483 0592 **11**QZB**z**

Rest – Carte £ 20/35

◆ Was at the vanguard of the gastropub movement and remains a classic. Kitchen shows a healthy respect for the provenance of its meats and balances modern influences with pub classics.

LONDON

Swiss Cottage

XX **Bradley's**

25 Winchester Rd ✉ NW3 3NR ⊖ Swiss Cottage – ✆ (020) 7722 3457 – www.bradleysnw3.co.uk – Fax (020) 7435 1392 – Closed 25 December, Easter, Saturday lunch and Sunday dinner **11**PZB**e**

Rest – Modern European – Menu £ 17/23 – Carte £ 27/36

◆ Warm pastel colours and modern artwork add a Mediterranean touch to this neighbourhood restaurant. Good value set menu; ingredients from across the British Isles.

XX **Eriki**

4-6 Northways Parade, Finchley Rd ✉ NW3 5EN ⊖ Swiss Cottage – ✆ (020) 7722 0606 – www.eriki.co.uk – Fax (020) 7722 8866 – Closed 25-26 December, 1 January, Saturday lunch and Bank Holidays

Rest – Indian – Carte £ 20/30 **11**PZB**u**

◆ The menu offers an invigorating gastronomic tour of all parts of India; vegetarians will be in clover. Vividly coloured, comfortable room with well-meaning service and lots of regulars.

XX **Singapore Garden**

83 Fairfax Road ✉ NW6 4DY ⊖ Swiss Cottage – ✆ (020) 7328 5314 – www.singaporegarden.co.uk – Fax (020) 7624 0656 – Closed Christmas

Rest – Asian – Menu £ 20/28 – Carte £ 27/46 **11**PZB**x**

◆ A smart, bright and comfortable room, with endearingly enthusiastic service. Your best bet is to pick vibrant and zesty dishes from the list of Singaporean and Malaysian specialities.

Tufnell Park

Junction Tavern

101 Fortess Rd ✉ NW5 1AG ⊖ Tufnell Park. – ✆ (020) 7485 9400 – www.junctiontavern.co.uk – Fax (020) 7485 9401 – Closed 24-26 December and 1 January **12**RZA**x**

Rest – Carte £ 21/27

◆ Sizeable pub with striking matt black façade. Dining room on one side, along with conservatory and busy bar. Well-balanced menu; flavoursome cooking. Interesting and regularly changing guest beers.

West Hampstead

X **Walnut**

280 West End Lane, Fortune Green ✉ NW6 1LJ ⊖ West Hampstead – ✆ (020) 7794 7772 – www.walnutwalnut.com – Closed Monday **10**NZA**a**

Rest – Traditional – *(dinner only)* Carte £ 25/34

◆ Eco-aware chef-owner in his raised, open kitchen offers classical cooking, where game and fish are the specialities. Relaxed and informal corner restaurant, with plenty of local regulars.

CITY OF LONDON – Greater London – pop. 7 172 091 **12** B3

Andaz Liverpool Street

Liverpool St ✉ EC2M 7QN ⊖ Liverpool Street – ✆ (020) 7961 1234 – www.andaz.com – Fax (020) 7961 1235 **34**ART**t**

264 rm – †£ 259/403 ††£ 259/403, ☐ £ 20 – 3 suites

Rest 1901 – *see restaurant listing*

Rest *Catch* – Seafood – ✆ (020) 7618 7200 *(closed Saturday and Sunday)* Menu £ 18 – Carte £ 34/45

Rest *Miyako* – Japanese – ✆ (020) 7618 7100 *(closed Saturday and Sunday) (booking essential)* Carte £ 20/39

◆ A contemporary and stylish interior hides behind the classic Victorian façade. Part of Hyatt group. Bright and spacious bedrooms with state-of-the-art facilities. Seafood at Catch, based within original hotel lobby. Miyako is a compact Japanese restaurant.

LONDON

Crowne Plaza London - The City

19 New Bridge St ✉ EC4V 6DB ⊖ St Paul's – ✆ (0871) 942 9190 – www.crowneplaza.com/londonthecity – Fax (020) 7438 8080
200 rm – ♦£ 180/256 ♦♦£ 180/256, ☕ £ 22.50 – 3 suites **32**AOU**a**
Rest *Refettorio* – ✆ (020) 7438 8052 *(Closed Saturday lunch, Sunday and Bank Holidays)* Menu £ 25 (dinner) – Carte £ 32/40

◆ Art deco façade by the river; interior enhanced by funky chocolate, cream and brown palette. Compact meeting room; well equipped fitness centre. Sizable, stylish rooms. Modish Refettorio for Italian cuisine.

Threadneedles

5 Threadneedle St ✉ EC2R 8AY ⊖ Bank – ✆ (020) 7657 8080 – www.theetoncollection.com – Fax (020) 7657 8100 **34**ARU**y**
68 rm – ♦£ 282/397 ♦♦£ 282/397, ☕ £ 19.50 – 1 suite
Rest *Bonds* – see restaurant listing

◆ A converted bank, dating from 1856, with a stunning stained-glass cupola in the lounge. Rooms are very stylish and individual featuring CD players and Egyptian cotton sheets.

Apex City of London

No 1, Seething Lane ✉ EC3N 4AX ⊖ Tower Hill – ✆ (020) 7702 2020 – www.apexhotels.co.uk – Fax (020) 7702 2217 **34**ARU**a**
179 rm – ♦£ 305 ♦♦£ 305, ☕ £ 17.95
Rest *Addendum* – ✆ (020) 7977 9500 – Carte £ 21/40

◆ Tucked away behind Tower of London, overlooking leafy square. Smart meeting facilities and well-equipped gym. Comfortable bedrooms and sleek bathrooms. Easy-going style in Addendum.

Rhodes Twenty Four

24th floor, Tower 42, 25 Old Broad St ✉ EC2N 1HQ ⊖ Liverpool Street – ✆ (020) 7877 7703 – www.rhodes24.co.uk – Fax (020) 7877 7788 – Closed Christmas-New Year, Saturday, Sunday and Bank Holidays
Rest – British – Carte £ 38/60 **34**ART**v**
Spec. Seared scallops with mashed potato and shallots. Saddle of venison with globe artichokes and truffle. Apricot tart with mint syrup and apricot sorbet.

◆ Panoramic views from this contemporary restaurant and bar, set on the 24th floor of Tower 42, the former Natwest building. Well balanced British dishes are appetisingly presented and display a healthy respect for the ingredients.

Coq d'Argent

✉ EC2R 8EJ ⊖ Bank – ✆ (020) 7395 5000 – www.coqdargent.co.uk – Fax (020) 7395 5050 – Closed Christmas, Easter and Bank Holidays
Rest – French – *(booking essential)* Menu £ 29 – Carte £ 31/46 **33**AQU**c**

◆ Take the dedicated lift to the top of this modern office block. Tables on the rooftop terrace have city views; busy bar. Gallic menus highlighted by popular shellfish dishes.

1901 – at Andaz Liverpool Street Hotel

Liverpool St ✉ EC2M 7QN ⊖ Liverpool Street – ✆ (020) 7618 7000 – www.andaz.com – Fax (020) 7618 5035 **34**ART**t**
Rest – French – *(closed Saturday lunch and Sunday)* Menu £ 22 (lunch) – Carte £ 32/41

◆ An impressive and imposing room, with an eye-catching cupola, cocktail bar and cheese and wine room. Kitchen makes proud use of British ingredients in refined and skilled cooking.

1 Lombard Street

1 Lombard St ✉ EC3V 9AA ⊖ Bank – ✆ (020) 7929 6611 – www.1lombardstreet.com – Fax (020) 7929 6622 – Closed Saturday, Sunday and Bank Holidays **33**AQU**r**
Rest – International – *(booking essential at lunch)* Carte £ 49/62

◆ Grade II listed banking hall; more formal rear room for elaborately presented, classical cooking using luxury ingredients. Busy, bustling and more casual front brasserie and bar.

XXX **Bonds** – at Threadneedles Hotel

5 Threadneedle St ✉ EC2R 8AY ⊖ Bank – ✆ (020) 7657 8088 – www.theetoncollection.com – Fax (020) 7657 8089 – Closed Saturday, Sunday and Bank Holidays **34**ARU**y**

Rest – Modern European – Menu £ 16 (lunch) – Carte £ 33/42

◆ Former banking hall from the 1850s, with pillars, marble and panelling. Experienced kitchen produced dishes with bold flavours; fish from Newhaven and slow-cooked meats the specialities.

XXX **Lutyens**

85 Fleet St ✉ EC4 1AE ⊖ St Paul's – ✆ (020) 7583 8385 – www.lutyens-restaurant.com – Fax (020) 7583 8386 – Closed lunch Saturday and Sunday **32**ANU**c**

Rest – Modern European – Carte £ 29/43

◆ The unmistakable hand of Sir Terence Conran: timeless and understated good looks mixed with functionality and an appealing Anglo-French menu with plenty of classics that include fruits de mer.

XX **Club Gascon** (Pascal Aussignac)

57 West Smithfield ✉ EC1A 9DS ⊖ Barbican – ✆ (020) 7796 0600 – www.clubgascon.com – Fax (020) 7796 0601 – Closed Christmas-New Year, Saturday lunch, Sunday and Bank Holidays **33**APT**z**

Rest – French – *(booking essential)* Menu £ 28/42 – Carte £ 43/68

Spec. Abalone and razor clams à la plancha with parsnip and seaweed tartare. Cappuccino of black pudding and lobster. Rhubarb and champagne sorbet, rose Chantilly.

◆ The gastronomy of Gascony and France's southwest are the starting points but the assured and intensely flavoured cooking also pushes at the boundaries. Marble and huge floral displays create suitably atmospheric surroundings.

XX **The Chancery**

9 Cursitor St ✉ EC4A 1LL ⊖ Chancery Lane – ✆ (020) 7831 4000 – www.thechancery.co.uk – Fax (020) 7831 4002 – Closed 25 December, Saturday and Sunday **32**ANT**a**

Rest – Modern European – Menu £ 34

◆ Near Law Courts, a small restaurant with basement bar. Contemporary interior with intimate style. Quality ingredients put to good use in accomplished, modern dishes.

XX **Mint Leaf Lounge**

12 Angel Court, Lothbury ✉ EC2R 7HB ⊖ Bank – ✆ (020) 7600 0992 – www.mintleaflounge.com – Fax (020) 7600 6628 – Closed 25-26 December, 1 January, Easter, Saturday and Sunday **33**AQT**b**

Rest – Indian – Menu £ 16 (lunch) – Carte £ 27/41

◆ Sister branch to the original in St James's. Slick and stylish, with busy bar. Well paced service of carefully prepared contemporary Indian food, with many of the influences from the south.

XX **Vivat Bacchus**

(basement) 47 Farringdon St ✉ EC4A 4LL ⊖ Farringdon – ✆ (020) 7353 2648 – www.vivatbacchus.co.uk – Fax (020) 7353 3025 – Closed 24 December-5 January, Saturday and Sunday **32**ANT**c**

Rest – Traditional – Menu £ 14/20 – Carte £ 19/35

◆ Platters and tapas served in the large bar; more intimate basement restaurant for meat dishes and South African specialities. Hugely impressive wine list with five cellars of wine.

XX **Vanilla Black**

17-18 Tooks Court ✉ EC4A 1LB ⊖ Chancery Lane – ✆ (020) 7242 2622 – www.vanillablack.co.uk – Closed 2 weeks Christmas, Saturday, Sunday and Bank Holiday Mondays **32**ANT**x**

Rest – Vegetarian – Menu £ 23/30 – Carte £ 23/30

◆ Proving that vegetarian food can be flavoursome and satisfying, with a menu that is varied and imaginative. This is a well run, friendly restaurant with understated décor, run by a husband and wife team.

LONDON

LONDON

XX **Cinnamon Kitchen**

9 Devonshire Square ✉ EC2M 4YL ⊖ Liverpool St – ✆ (020) 7626 5000 – www.cinnamon-kitchen.com – Fax (020) 7397 9611 – Closed 25-26 December, 1 January, Saturday lunch, Sunday and Bank Holidays **34**ART**e**

Rest – Indian – Menu £ 18 **s** – Carte £ 31/50 **s**

◆ Sister to The Cinnamon Club. Contemporary Indian cooking, with punchy flavours and arresting presentation. Sprightly service in large, modern surroundings. Watch the action from the Tandoor Bar.

XX **Kenza**

10 Devonshire Square ✉ EC2M 4YP ⊖ Liverpool Street – ✆ (020) 7929 5533 – www.kenza-restaurant.com – Fax (020) 7929 0303 – Closed 25 December-4 January, Saturday lunch, Sunday and Bank Holidays **34**ART**c**

Rest – Lebanese – Menu £ 28 – Carte £ 26/37

◆ Exotic basement restaurant, with lamps, carvings, pumping music and nightly belly dancing. Lebanese and Moroccan cooking are the menu influences and the cooking is authentic and accurate.

XX **Devonshire Terrace**

Devonshire Sq ✉ EC2M 4WY ⊖ Liverpool Street – ✆ (020) 7256 3233 – www.devonshireterrace.co.uk – Fax (020) 7256 3244 – Closed Saturday, Sunday and Bank Holidays **34**ART**c**

Rest – Modern European – Carte £ 18/39

◆ Brasserie-style cooking, where you choose the sauce and side dish to accompany your main course. Bright and busy restaurant with open kitchen and choice of two terraces, one within large atrium.

XX **Sauterelle**

The Royal Exchange ✉ EC3V 3LR ⊖ Bank – ✆ (020) 7618 2483 – www.restaurantsauterelle.com – Closed Saturday and Sunday **33**AQU**a**

Rest – French – Menu £ 21 – Carte £ 33/43

◆ Located on mezzanine level of Royal Exchange, a stunning 16C property with ornate columns and pillars. Appealing and rustic French menus attract plenty of lunchtime diners.

XX **The Mercer**

34 Threadneedle St ✉ EC2R 8AY ⊖ Bank – ✆ (020) 7628 0001 – www.themercer.co.uk – Fax (020) 7588 2822 – Closed 25 December-2 January, Saturday, Sunday and Bank Holidays **34**ARU**x**

Rest – Modern European – Carte £ 27/38

◆ Converted bank, with airy feel thanks to high ceilings and large windows. Brasserie style menu with appealing mix of classics and comfort food. Huge choice of wines available by glass or carafe.

XX **Boisdale of Bishopsgate**

Swedeland Court, 202 Bishopsgate ✉ EC2M 4NR ⊖ Liverpool Street – ✆ (020) 7283 1763 – www.boisdale.co.uk – Fax (020) 7283 1664 – Closed 25 December-4 January, Saturday, Sunday and Bank Holidays **34**ART**a**

Rest – Scottish – Menu £ 29/37 – Carte £ 26/43

◆ Through ground floor bar, serving oysters and champagne, to brick vaulted basement with red and tartan décor. Menu featuring Scottish produce. Live jazz most evenings.

XX **The White Swan**

108 Fetter Lane ✉ EC4A 1ES ⊖ Temple – ✆ (020) 7242 9696 – www.thewhiteswanlondon.com – Fax (020) 7404 2250 – Closed 25-26 December, Saturday and Sunday **32**ANT**n**

Rest – Modern European – Menu £ 29 (lunch) – Carte £ 30/36

◆ Smart dining room above pub just off Fleet Street: mirrored ceilings, colourful paintings on wall. Modern, daily changing menus, are good value for the heart of London.

A red **Rest** mention denotes an establishment with an award for culinary excellence, ✿ (star) or ☺ (Bib Gourmand).

XX **Manicomio**

6 Gutter Lane ✉ EC2V 8AS ⊖ St Paul's – ✆ (020) 7726 5010 – www.manicomio.co.uk – Fax (020) 7726 5011 – Closed Christmas-New Year, Saturday, Sunday and Bank Holidays **33**APT**s**

Rest – Italian – Carte £ 29/47

◆ Second branch to follow the first in Chelsea. Regional Italian fare, with top-notch ingredients. Bright and fresh first floor restaurant, with deli-café on the ground floor and bar on top floor.

XX **Luc's Brasserie**

17-22 Leadenhall Market ⊖ Bank – ✆ (020) 7621 0666 – www.lucsbrasserie.com – Fax (020) 7623 8516 – Closed 25 December-04 January, Friday-Monday dinner, Saturday-Sunday and Bank Holidays **34**ARU**v**

Rest – French – *(booking essential at lunch)* Menu £ 19 – Carte £ 29/41

◆ Looks down on the Victorian splendour of Leadenhall Market. First appeared in 1890 but re-invigorated in 2006. The menu is a paean to all things French and every classic dish is there.

XX **High Timber**

8 High Timber St ✉ EC4V 3PA ⊖ Mansion House – ✆ (020) 7248 1777 – www.hightimber.com – Closed 25 December-3 January, Saturday lunch and Sunday **33**APU**b**

Rest – Modern European – Menu £ 18 (lunch) – Carte £ 24/44

◆ Rustic look to the room, despite being in a modern block, with river views. Great wine cellar, with large choice from South Africa, owners' homeland. Cumbrian steaks the speciality.

X **Terranostra**

27 Old Bailey ✉ EC4M 7HS ⊖ St Paul's – ✆ (020) 3201 0077 – www.terranostrafood.co.uk – Closed Christmas, Easter, Saturday lunch, Sunday and Bank Holidays **33**AOU**x**

Rest – Italian – *(booking advisable at lunch)* Menu £ 18 – Carte £ 23/32

◆ Its informal, relaxed feel and sweet-natured service provides the ideal respite from bustle of The City and the trauma of the Old Bailey. Light, fresh food, with Sardinian leanings.

X **Paternoster Chop House**

Warwick Court, Paternoster Square ✉ EC4M 7DX ⊖ St Paul's – ✆ (020) 7029 9400 – www.paternosterchophouse.com – Fax (020) 7029 9409 – Closed 2 weeks Christmas, Saturday, Sunday dinner and Bank Holidays **33**APT**x**

Rest – British – Menu £ 25 – Carte £ 31/43

◆ On ground floor of office block, with large terrace. Classic and robust British cooking; menu a mix of traditional favourites, shellfish and comfort food. Busy and noisy.

CROYDON – Greater London – pop. 316 283 **12** B3

ADDINGTON

XX **Planet Spice**

88 Selsdon Park Rd ✉ CR2 8JT – ✆ (020) 8651 3300 – www.planet-spice.com – Closed 25 and 26 December **7**GZ**c**

Rest – Indian – Menu £ 20 – Carte £ 17/28

◆ Brasserie style Indian restaurant with fresh, vibrant décor and a modern feel. Attentive and helpful service. Traditional cooking with some innovative touches.

SOUTH CROYDON

XX **Le Cassoulet**

18 Selsdon Rd ✉ CR2 6PA – ✆ (020) 8633 1818 – www.lecassoulet.com – Fax (020) 8633 1815 – Closed 25-26 Dcember and 1-2 January **7**FZ**v**

Rest – French – Menu £ 17/20 – Carte £ 27/42

◆ Traditional French fare that represents decent value for money, with a more elaborate menu offered at dinner. Chic and elegant interior; carefully run, with attentive service.

Fish and Grill
48-50 South End ✉ CR0 1DP – ✆ (020) 8774 4060 – www.fishandgrill.co.uk – Fax (020) 8686 8002 – Closed 25 December **7**FZ**a**

Rest – Seafood – Menu £ 15 (lunch) – Carte £ 28/35

◆ Stylish and vibrant brasserie, with well-organised service and a bustling atmosphere. Appealing menu, with assorted seafood and grilled meats the specialities; good homemade desserts.

EALING – Greater London – pop. 300 948 **12** A3

West Middlesex Southall Greenford Rd, ✆ (020) 8574 3450

Horsenden Hill Woodland Rise

Acton Green

The Bollo
13-15 Bollo Lane ✉ W4 5LR ⊖ Chiswick Park. – ✆ (020) 8994 6037 – www.thebollohouse.co.uk **6**CV**z**

Rest – Carte £ 22/27

◆ Large Victorian pub with original glass cupola and oak panelling. Menu is a mix of generous pub classics and dishes with a southern Mediterranean influence. Look out for quiz nights and promotions.

Duke of Sussex
75 South Parade ✉ W4 5LF ⊖ Chiswick Park. – ✆ (020) 8742 8801 – Closed Monday lunch **6**CV**o**

Rest – Carte £ 20/27

◆ A grand Victorian pub with ornate décor. Appealingly rustic Spanish influences in the daily changing menu, with stews and cured meats a speciality; some dishes designed for sharing.

Ealing

Maxim
153-155 Northfield Ave ✉ W13 9QT ⊖ Northfields – ✆ (020) 8567 1719 – Fax (020) 8932 0717 – Closed 25-28 December and Sunday lunch

Rest – Chinese – Menu £ 16/23 – Carte £ 18/31 **s** **1**BV**a**

◆ Decorated with assorted oriental ornaments and pictures. Well-organised service from smartly attired staff. Authentic Chinese cooking from the extensive menu.

Charlotte's Place
16 St Matthew's Rd ✉ W5 3JT ⊖ Ealing Common – ✆ (020) 8567 7541 – www.charlottes.co.uk **2**CV**c**

Rest – Modern European – Menu £ 15 (lunch Monday-Saturday)/20 (Sunday) – Carte Monday to Saturday £ 24/31

◆ Friendly neighbourhood restaurant whose large windows and mirror ensure plenty of light. Modern European dishes and some brasserie classics come in decently-sized portions.

Sushi-Hiro
1 Station Par, Uxbridge Rd ✉ W5 3LD ⊖ Ealing Common – ✆ (020) 8896 3175 – Fax (020) 8896 3209 – Closed Monday **2**CV**v**

Rest – Japanese – *(booking advisable)* Carte approx. £ 26

◆ Don't let the unremarkable façade and modest interior put you off. Chef-owner works with quiet efficiency to offer first rate sushi at affordable prices, using excellent ingredients.

Kiraku
8 Station Par, Uxbridge Rd ✉ W5 3LD ⊖ Ealing Common – ✆ (020) 8992 2848 – www.kiraku.co.uk – Closed 1 week December, 1 week August, Monday and Tuesday following Bank Holidays **2**CV**v**

Rest – Japanese – Menu £ 13 (lunch) – Carte dinner £ 15/27

◆ The name of this cute little Japanese restaurant means 'relax and enjoy'; easy with such charming service. Extensive menu includes zensai, skewers, noodles, rice dishes and assorted sushi.

ENFIELD – Greater London – pop. 273 203 **12** B2

Leaside GC Edmonton Picketts Lock Lane, Lee Valley Leisure, ✆ (020) 8803 3611

LONDON

HADLEY WOOD

West Lodge Park
off Cockfosters Rd ✉ EN4 0PY – ✆ (020) 8216 3900 – www.bealeshotels.co.uk – Fax (020) 8216 3937 **3ETi**
59 rm – †£ 90/140 ††£ 140, ☕ £ 15
Rest *The Mary Beale* – ✆ (020) 8216 3906 – Menu £ 20/25 – Carte £ 29/41
◆ Family owned for over half a century, a country house in sweeping grounds with arboretum. Comfortable sitting rooms; neat, spacious bedrooms. Use of nearby leisure centre. Smart and comfortable, refurbished restaurant.

GREENWICH – Greater London – pop. 219 263 12 B3

GREENWICH

Spread Eagle
1-2 Stockwell St ✉ SE10 9FN ⊖ Greenwich (DLR) – ✆ (020) 8853 2333 – www.spreadeaglerestaurant.co.uk – Fax (020) 8293 1024 **7GVc**
Rest – French – Menu £ 30 (lunch) – Carte £ 29/49
◆ This converted pub is something of an institution. Cosy booth seating, wood panelling and a further upstairs room. Traditional French-influenced menu with attentive service.

Rivington Grill
178 Greenwich High Rd ✉ SE10 8NN ⊖ Greenwich (DLR) – ✆ (020) 8293 9270 – www.rivingtongrill.co.uk – Closed 25-26 December, 1 January, Monday, dinner 24 December,and lunch Tuesday and Wednesday **7GVs**
Rest – British – Menu £ 19/22 (lunch) – Carte £ 30/47
◆ Part of the Picturehouse complex; 21C rustic interior with closely set tables. Firmly English menus in bar and galleried restaurant. Banquets and market breakfasts on offer.

HACKNEY – Greater London – pop. 202 824 12 B3

HACKNEY

The Empress of India
130 Lauriston Rd, Victoria Park ✉ E9 7LH ⊖ Mile End. – ✆ (020) 8533 5123 – www.theempressofindia.com – Fax (020) 7404 2250 – Closed 25 December
Rest – Carte £ 19/29 **3GUn**
◆ Smart open-plan pub boasting mosaic floors and Indian murals. Classically based, seasonally-evolving menu blends the robust with the refined, using only the best rare breeds.

Cat & Mutton
76 Broadway Market ✉ E8 4QJ ⊖ Bethnal Green. – ✆ (020) 7254 5599 – www.catandmutton.co.uk – Fax (020) 7986 1444 – Closed 25-26 December, 1 January and Monday lunch **14YZBa**
Rest – British – Carte £ 22/60
◆ Early Victorian drinking pub that serves decent food; upstairs room used at weekends. Blackboard menu offers full-bodied, satisfying dishes; many ingredients from the local market.

Prince Arthur
95 Forest Rd ✉ E8 3BH ⊖ Bethnal Green. – ✆ (020) 7249 9996 – www.theprincearthurlondonfields.com – Fax (020) 7249 7074 – Closed 25-26 December, Monday-Tuesday lunch **14XZBc**
Rest – Carte £ 20/27
◆ An intimate local pub for local people, with plenty of character. Unpretentious and heartwarming menu, with classics like a pint of prawns and cottage pie; filling puddings.

HOXTON

The Hoxton
81 Great Eastern St ✉ EC2A 3HU ⊖ Old Street – ✆ (020) 7550 1000 – www.hoxtonhotels.com – Fax (020) 7550 1090 **20XZDx**
205 rm – †£ 57/199 ††£ 57/199, ☕ £ 10
Rest *Hoxton Grille* – Carte £ 22/35
◆ Urban lodge: industrial styled, clean lined modernism. "No ripoffs" mantra: cheap phone rate, free internet, complimentary 'lite pret' breakfast. Carefully considered rooms. Cooking style: New York deli meets French brasserie.

XX **Great Eastern Dining Room**

54 Great Eastern St ✉ EC2A 3QR ⊖ Old Street – ✆ (020) 7613 4545 – www.rickerrestaurants.com – Fax (020) 7613 4137 – Closed Sunday and Bank Holidays **20**XZD**n**

Rest – Asian – Menu £ 15/19 – Carte £ 15/45

◆ Half the place is a bar that's heaving in the evening. Dining area has candle-lit tables, contemporary chandeliers, and carefully prepared, seriously tasty pan-Asian cooking.

XX **Water House**

10 Orsman Rd ✉ N1 5QJ ⊖ Essex Road Station – ✆ (020) 7033 0123 – www.waterhouserestaurant – Closed 25 December-8 January, Sunday dinner and Monday **14**XZB**x**

Rest – Italian influences – Carte £ 15/22

◆ Sister to Acorn House, it shares its eco-friendly credentials and commitment to training local people. The menu is concise and seasonal; cooking has an Italian accent and flavours are natural.

X **Fifteen London**

13 Westland Pl ✉ N1 7LP ⊖ Old Street – ✆ (0871) 330 15 15 – www.fifteen.net – Fax (020) 7251 2749 – Closed dinner 24 and 25 December **13**VZC**c**

Rest – Italian – Menu £ 25 (weekday lunch)/60 – Carte £ 33/42

◆ Original branch of Jamie Oliver's charitable restaurants; run by trainees alongside full-time staff. Buzzy ground floor trattoria; more formal basement restaurant. Tasty, seasonal Italian food.

X **Hoxton Apprentice**

16 Hoxton Sq ✉ N1 6NT ⊖ Old Street – ✆ (020) 7749 2828 – www.hoxtonapprentice.com – Closed 23 December-3 January, Sunday dinner and Monday **20**XZC**r**

Rest – Modern European – Carte £ 20/27

◆ Set up as charitable enterprise in 19C former primary school; now stands on its own as accomplished restaurant where apprentices and pros cook interesting, seasonal dishes.

X **Real Greek Mezedopolio**

14-15 Hoxton Market ✉ N1 6HG ⊖ Old Street – ✆ (020) 7739 8212 – www.therealgreek.co.uk – Fax (020) 7739 4910 – Closed 25-26 December and 1 January **20**XZC**v**

Rest – Greek – Carte £ 15/20

◆ Very relaxed restaurant with emphasis on unstructured, shared eating experience. Fresh, healthy menu divided into cold and hot meze, souvlaki and large plates for 'sharers'.

SHOREDITCH

XXX **Boundary** with rm

2-4 Boundary St ✉ E2 7JE ⊖ Old St – ✆ (020) 7729 1051 – www.theboundary.co.uk – Fax (020) 7729 3061 – Closed Monday and Saturday lunch and Sunday dinner **20**XZD**b**

12 rm – †£ 184/230 ††£ 230/264, ☕ £ 12 – 5 suites

Rest – French – Menu £ 24 (lunch) – Carte £ 35/55

◆ Sir Terence Conran has taken a warehouse and created a 'caff' with a bakery and shop, a rooftop terrace and a stylish, good-looking French restaurant serving plenty of cross-Channel classics. Comfy and individual bedrooms.

XXX **L'Anima**

1 Snowden St ✉ EC2 2DA ⊖ Liverpool St – ✆ (0207) 422 7000 – www.lanima.co.uk – Fax (0207) 422 7077 – Closed 24 December dinner-4 January, Saturday lunch and Sunday **20**XZD**a**

Rest – Italian – *(booking essential)* Menu £ 37 (lunch) – Carte £ 26/58

◆ Very handsome room, with limestone and leather creating a sophisticated, glamorous environment. Precisely executed dishes with the emphasis on flavour; smooth but personable service.

LONDON

Rivington Grill

AK VISA MC AE D

28-30 Rivington St ✉ EC2A 3DZ ⊖ Old Street – ✆ (020) 7729 7053 – www.rivingtongrill.co.uk – Closed dinner 24 December, 25-26 December and 1 January **20**XZD**e**

Rest – British – Menu £ 19 (weekend lunch) – Carte £ 21/47

◆ Very appealing 'back to basics' British menu, with plenty of comforting classics including a section 'on toast'. This converted warehouse is popular with the local community of artists.

The Princess of Shoreditch

VISA MC AE

76-78 Paul St ✉ EC2A 4NE ⊖ Old Street. – ✆ (020) 7729 9270 – www.theprincessofshoreditch.com – Closed 24-26 December, Saturday lunch and Sunday dinner **19**VZD**a**

Rest – Carte £ 24/35

◆ Pies and platters in the busy ground floor bar; more ambitious but still flavoursome European-influenced cooking in the calmer upstairs room. Friendly service a feature.

The Fox

VISA MC AE

28 Paul St ✉ EC2A 4LB ⊖ Old Street. – ✆ (020) 7729 5708 – www.thefoxpublichouse.co.uk – Closed Christmas-New Year, Saturday lunch, Sunday dinner and Bank Holidays **19**VZD**c**

Rest – *(booking essential)* Carte £ 24/34

◆ Rough and ready pub with a great menu: this is found upstairs in the rather serene, but Gothic, restaurant. No nonsense dishes with bold, seasonal, unfussy, fresh flavours.

LONDON

Stoke Newington

Rasa

AK VISA MC AE

55 Stoke Newington Church St ✉ N16 0AR – ✆ (020) 7249 0344 – www.rasarestaurants.com – Closed 24-26 December and 1 January

Rest – Indian – *(dinner only and lunch Saturday and Sunday)* **14**XZA**e**
(booking essential) Menu £ 16 – Carte £ 9/13

◆ Busy Indian restaurant, an unpretentious environment in which to sample authentic vegetarian dishes from the south west of India. The "Feast" menu offers the best introduction.

Rasa Travancore

AK VISA MC AE

56 Stoke Newington Church St ✉ N16 0NB – ✆ (020) 7249 1340 – www.rasarestaurants.com – Closed 23-30 December **14**XZA**x**

Rest – Indian – *(dinner only)* Carte approx. £ 12

◆ Friendly, knowledgeable service a distinct bonus to diners getting to know the richness and variety of Keralan cooking. This branch celebrates the cooking of the region's Christian community.

HAMMERSMITH and FULHAM – Greater London – pop. 165 242 **12** B3

Fulham

Saran Rom

AK VISA MC AE D

The Boulevard, Imperial Wharf, Townmead Rd ✉ SW6 2UB ⊖ Fulham Broadway – ✆ (020) 7751 3111 – www.blueelephant.com/river – Closed 25-26 December **23**PZH**b**

Rest – Thai – *(dinner only and lunch July-August)* Menu £ 22/35 – Carte £ 26/48

◆ Owned by Blue Elephant group. Terrific riverside terrace and elegantly decorated interior, based on Thai Royal summer palace. Slight seafood bias to the appealing and balanced menu.

Memories of India on the River

AK VISA MC AE

7 The Boulevard, Imperial Wharf ✉ SW6 2UB ⊖ Fulham Broadway – ✆ (020) 7736 0077 – www.memoriesofindiaontheriver.co.uk – Fax (020) 7731 5222 – Closed 25 December **23**PZH**n**

Rest – Indian – Carte £ 22/36

◆ Indian fabrics adorn this sparkly restaurant, part of the wharf development. Vast palm useful for getting your bearings: interesting, original, well-presented Indian dishes.

XX **Blue Elephant**

4-6 Fulham Broadway ✉ SW6 1AA ⊖ Fulham Broadway – ✆ (020) 7385 6595 – www.blueelephant.com – Fax (020) 7386 7665 – Closed 25-26 December

Rest – Thai – *(dinner only and lunch July-August) (booking essential)* Menu £ 15/35 – Carte £ 26/48 **22**NZG**z**

◆ A London institution, with a gloriously unrestrained décor of plants, streams and bridges. Carefully prepared dishes from across Thailand. Curries are a strength and service is well-meaning.

XX **Mao Tai**

58 New Kings Rd, Parsons Green ✉ SW6 4LS ⊖ Parsons Green – ✆ (020) 7731 2520 – www.maotai.co.uk – Closed 25-26 December

Rest – Chinese – *(dinner only and Sunday lunch)* Carte £ 30/56 **22**NZH**e**

◆ A light and modern interior with wood flooring and framed artwork with an eastern theme. Well organised service. Chinese cuisine with Szechuan specialities.

The Farm

18 Farm Lane ✉ SW6 1PP ⊖ Fulham Broadway. – ✆ (020) 7381 3331 – www.thefarmfulham.co.uk – Closed 25 December **22**NZG**x**

Rest – Menu £ 25 – Carte £ 25/40

◆ Somewhat austere looking façade but welcoming fireplaces within. Ambitious menu displays international influences alongside more traditionally British dishes; beef is especially tender.

LONDON

The Harwood Arms

Walham Grove ⊖ Fulham Broadway. – ✆ (020) 7386 1847 – www.harwoodarms.com **22**NZG**a**

Rest – British – Carte £ 25/35

Spec. Potted rabbit with devils on horseback, celeriac and dandelion. Pigeon with air-dried ham, chicory and onions. Rhubarb doughnuts with orange curd and cream.

◆ This is a proper 'local' but one with really good food; you sit where you want. A seasonal British menu to please Mrs Beeton, with added inventiveness and verve from a skilled kitchen; even the bar snacks are good. Youthful, unflappable service.

Salisbury

21 Sherbrooke Rd ✉ SW6 2TZ ⊖ Fulham Broadway. – ✆ (020) 7381 4005 – www.thesalisbury.co.uk – Closed 25-26 December and 1 January **22**MZG**e**

Rest – Carte £ 16/25

◆ Relaunched in 2009 as a bright and colourful pub, with sliding glass dome over the dining room. Menu is a mix of small tasting plates, pasta, pies, pub favourites and imaginative puds.

Sands End

135-137 Stephendale Rd ✉ SW6 2PR ⊖ Fulham Broadway. – ✆ (020) 7731 7823 – www.thesandsend.co.uk – Closed 25 December

Rest – *(booking advisable)* Carte £ 23/31 **22**OZH**r**

◆ Busy and warmly run pub with junkshop-chic, country-comes-to-the-city feel. Appealing bar snacks; a concise, balanced menu produces carefully prepared and attractively presented dishes.

HAMMERSMITH

XX **River Café** (Ruth Rogers & Rose Gray)

Thames Wharf, Rainville Rd ✉ W6 9HA ⊖ Barons Court – ✆ (020) 7386 4200 – www.rivercafe.co.uk – Fax (020) 7386 4201 – Closed 25 December-1 January, Sunday dinner and Bank Holidays **21**LZG**r**

Rest – Italian – *(booking essential)* Carte £ 45/63

Spec. Char-grilled squid with red chilli and rocket. Wood-roasted turbot with capers, oregano and braised swiss chard. Panna cotta with grappa and raspberries

◆ The open kitchen let the superlative ingredients shine on the twice-daily changing menu; pasta a real highlight. Wood-fired oven dominates the stylish riverside room, with its contagiously effervescent atmosphere, helped along by charming, friendly service.

XX **Chez Kristof**

111 Hammersmith Grove, Brook Green ✉ W6 0NQ ⊖ Hammersmith – ✆ (020) 8741 1177 – www.chezkristof.co.uk – Closed Christmas **21**LZF**b**

Rest – French – Menu £ 18 – Carte £ 23/28

◆ Well worth seeking out in Brook Green: there's a deli, delightful terrace, and a menu of satisfying classics. Influences are mostly from within Europe, particularly France.

XX **Indian Zing**

236 King St ✉ W6 0RF ⊖ Ravenscourt Park – ✆ (020) 8748 5959 – www.indianzing.co.uk – Fax (020) 8748 2332 **21**LZG**a**

Rest – Indian – Menu £ 15 (lunch)/22 – Carte £ 23/42

◆ Proud and enthusiastic chef-owner is keen to satisfy his diners. Flavoursome and quite refined Indian cooking from across the continent. Colourful surroundings, with closely set tables.

X **Azou**

375 King St ✉ W6 9NJ ⊖ Stamford Brook – ✆ (020) 8563 7266 – www.azou.co.uk – Closed 25 December **21**KZG**u**

Rest – North African – Carte £ 19/29

◆ Silks, lanterns and rugs add to the atmosphere of this personally run, North African restaurant. Most come for the excellent tajines, with triple steamed couscous. Much is designed for sharing.

Anglesea Arms

35 Wingate Rd ✉ W6 0UR ⊖ Ravenscourt Park. – ✆ (020) 8749 1291 – www.anglesea-arms.com – Closed 25-27 December **15**LZE**c**

Rest – *(bookings not accepted)* Carte £ 17/46

◆ The twice daily changing menu of gutsy, wholesome food is served in both the glass-roofed restaurant with the open kitchen and the dark panelled bar. Good selection of wines by the glass

The Havelock Tavern

57 Masbro Rd, Brook Green ✉ W14 0LS ⊖ Kensington Olympia. – ✆ (020) 7603 5374 – www.thehavelocktavern.com – Closed 25-26 December

Rest – *(bookings not accepted)* Carte £ 21/26 **16**MZE**e**

◆ True and honest community pub that isn't afraid to hold onto its roots. Great value blackboard menu features modern, seasonal, gutsy dishes and proper heart-warming puddings.

Carpenter's Arms

91 Black Lion Lane ✉ W6 9BG ⊖ Stamford Brook. – ✆ (020) 8741 8386 – www.carpentersarmsw6.co.uk – Fax (020) 8741 6437 – Closed 1 week at Christmas **21**KZG**b**

Rest – *(booking essential)* Menu £ 16 (lunch) – Carte £ 27/33

◆ May not look like a pub but is a busy place with smart service. Good British ingredients to the fore, particularly the seasonal vegetables, in rustic and satisfying dishes.

The Dartmouth Castle

26 Glenthorne Road ✉ W6 0LS ⊖ Hammersmith. – ✆ (020) 8748 3614 – www.thedartmouthcastle.co.uk – Fax (020) 8748 3619 – Closed 25 December to 1 January, Holy Saturday and Easter Sunday **21**LZF**e**

Rest – Carte £ 20/28

◆ Busy, hospitable pub serving monthly-changing, Mediterranean-influenced menu. Cheery staff, regularly-changing cask ales and board games encourage the locals to linger.

Shepherd's Bush

K West

rm,

Richmond Way ✉ W14 0AX ⊖ Kensington Olympia – ✆ (020) 8008 6600 – www.k-west.co.uk – Fax (020) 8008 6650 **16**MZE**c**

214 rm – †£ 252 ††£ 367, ☐ £ 17.50 – 6 suites

Rest ***Kanteen*** – ✆ (020) 8008 6631 – Carte £ 21/25

◆ Former BBC offices, the interior is decorated in a smart, contemporary fashion. Bedrooms in understated modern style, deluxe rooms with work desks and DVD and CD facilities. Modish menus in trendy dining room.

LONDON

Princess Victoria

217 Uxbridge Rd ✉ W12 9DH ⊖ Shepherd's Bush. – ✆ (020) 8749 5886 – www.princessvictoria.co.uk – Fax (020) 8749 4886 – Closed 25-26 December

Rest – Menu £ 15 (lunch) – Carte £ 23/33 **15**KZE**a**

◆ Magnificent Victorian gin palace, with original plasterwork. The kitchen knows its butchery; pork board, homemade sausages and terrines all feature. Excellent wine list, with over 350 bottles.

HARINGEY – Greater London – pop. 216 507 **12** B3

Crouch End

Mountview without rest

31 Mount View Rd ✉ N4 4SS – ✆ (020) 8340 9222 – www.mountviewguesthouse.com **3**EU**r**

3 rm – £ 55 £ 70/90

◆ Redbrick Victorian house with a warm and stylish ambience engendered by the homely décor. One bedroom features an original fireplace and two overlook the quiet rear garden.

Bistro Aix

54 Topsfield Par, Tottenham Lane ✉ N8 8PT – ✆ (020) 8340 6346 – www.bistroaix.co.uk – Closed Monday **3**EU**v**

Rest – French – *(dinner only and lunch Saturday-Sunday)*

Menu £ 15 (lunch and weekday dinner) – Carte £ 19/33

◆ The simple wood furniture is complemented by plants and pictures. The owner chef's experience in France is reflected in the menu and the robust and hearty cooking.

The Queens Pub and Dining Room

26 Broadway Par ✉ N8 9DE – ✆ (020) 8340 2031 – www.thequeenscrouchend.co.uk **3**EU**c**

Rest – Carte approx. £ 25

◆ Striking example of a classic Victorian pub, from the original mahogany panelling to the stained glass windows and ornate ceiling. The menu is a mix of pub classics and Mediterranean influences.

Fortis Green

Clissold Arms

Fortis Green Rd ✉ N2 9HR ⊖ East Finchley. – ✆ (020) 8444 4224 – www.jobo-developments.com – Closed 1 January **3**EU**a**

Rest – Carte £ 21/34

◆ Reputedly the venue for The Kinks' first gig. Now modernised throughout, with a large rear terrace. Interesting menus, with terrines, whole sea bass and 32-day aged steaks the specialities.

Highgate

Rose and Crown

86 Highgate St ✉ N6 5HX ⊖ Archway – ✆ (020) 8340 0770 – www.roseandcrownhighgate.co.uk – Closed Sunday dinner and Monday lunch

Rest – Menu £ 20 (dinner) – Carte £ 21/30 **2**EU**i**

◆ Converted pub, smartly kitted out but not overly formal thanks to genial staff. Seasonally changing, European-influenced cooking, with competitively priced weekly-changing set menu.

The Bull

13 North Hill ✉ N6 4AB ⊖ Highgate. – ✆ (0845) 456 5033 – www.themeredithgroup.co.uk – Closed Monday in winter **2**EU**x**

Rest – Menu £ 15 – Carte £ 21/30

◆ Not your typical pub, The Bull offers seasonal and carefully prepared European food with a dominant French gene. Good breads. A bright room, clued-up service; more family-orientated at weekends.

TOTTENHAM

The Lock

Heron House, Hale Wharf, Ferry Lane ✉ N17 9NF ⊖ Tottenham Hale – ✆ (020) 8885 2829 – www.thelockrestaurant.com – Fax (020) 8885 1618 – Closed 31 December, Saturday lunch, Sunday dinner and Monday

Rest – Modern European – Menu £ 15 – Carte £ 22/33 **3**GU**a**

◆ Unpromising location for this starkly decorated restaurant. But the service is affable and the Mediterranean-influenced food is prepared with care and flair and represents value for money.

HARROW – Greater London – pop. 206 643 **12** A3

HARROW ON THE HILL

Incanto

41 High St ✉ HA1 3HT ⊖ Harrow on the Hill – ✆ (020) 8426 6767 – www.incanto.co.uk – Fax (020) 8423 5087 – Closed Easter, 25-26 December, Sunday dinner and Monday **1**BU**z**

Rest – Italian – Menu £ 19/23 – Carte £ 25/35

◆ Within Grade II former post office; split-level restaurant to rear of well stocked deli. Well paced service; Southern Italian bias to the rustic cooking, with quality produce to the fore.

HARROW WEALD

Grim's Dyke

Old Redding ✉ HA3 6SH – ✆ (020) 8385 3100 – www.grimsdyke.com – Fax (020) 8954 4560 **1**BT**a**

46 rm – †£ 60/95 ††£ 95/105

Rest *Gilberts* – *(Closed Saturday lunch)* Menu £ 14/27 – Carte £ 26/41

◆ Victorian mansion, former country residence of W.S.Gilbert. Rooms divided between main house and lodge, the former more characterful. Over 40 acres of garden and woodland. Restaurant with ornately carved fireplace.

PINNER

Friends

11 High St ✉ HA5 5PJ ⊖ Pinner – ✆ (020) 8866 0286 – www.friendsrestaurant.co.uk – Fax (020) 8866 0286 – Closed 25-26 December, Sunday dinner and Bank Holidays **1**BU**a**

Rest – Modern European – Menu £ 23/32

◆ Pretty beamed cottage, with some parts dating back 400 years. Inside, a welcoming glow from the log fire; personal service from owners and a fresh, regularly-changing menu.

HILLINGDON – Greater London – pop. 242 755 **12** A3

Haste Hill Northwood The Drive, ✆ (01923) 825 224

HEATHROW AIRPORT

Sofitel

Terminal 5, Heathrow Airport ✉ TW6 2GD – ✆ (020) 8757 7777 – www.sofitel.com – Fax (020) 8757 7788 **5**AX**a**

578 rm – †£ 114/396 ††£ 114/396, £ 21.50 – 27 suites

Rest *Brasserie Roux* – French – Menu £ 20 – Carte £ 27/39

Rest *Vivre* – Menu £ 25 (dinner) – Carte £ 25/38

◆ Smart and well run contemporary hotel, opened in 2008. Designed around a series of atriums, with direct access to T5. Crisply decorated, comfortable bedrooms with luxurious bathrooms. French brasserie classics. International menu in large Vivre.

London Heathrow Marriott

Bath Rd, Hayes ✉ UB3 5AN – ✆ (020) 8990 1100 – www.londonheathrowmarriott.co.uk – Fax (020) 8990 1110 **5**AX**z**

391 rm – †£ 183 ††£ 183, £ 16.95 – 2 suites

Rest *Tuscany* – Italian – *(Closed Sunday) (dinner only)* Menu £ 39 – Carte £ 29/43

Rest *Allie's grille* – Carte £ 25/37

◆ Built at the end of 20C, this modern, comfortable hotel is centred around a large atrium, with comprehensive business facilities: there is an exclusive Executive floor. Italian cuisine at bright and convivial Tuscany. Grill favourites at Allie's.

Hilton London Heathrow Airport
Terminal 4 ✉ *TW6 3AF* – ✆ *(020) 8759 7755*
– *www.hilton.co.uk/heathrow* – *Fax (020) 8759 7579* **5**AX**n**
355 rm – †£ 114/288 ††£ 114/288, ☐ £ 21 – 4 suites
Rest ***Brasserie*** – Modern – *(Closed lunch Saturday and Sunday) (buffet lunch)*
Menu £ 28/35 – Carte £ 41/52
Rest ***Zen Oriental*** – Chinese – ✆ (020) 8564 9609 – Menu £ 30
– Carte £ 31/42
◆ Group hotel with a striking modern exterior and linked to Terminal 4 by a covered walkway. Good sized bedrooms, with contemporary styled suites. Spacious Brasserie in vast atrium. Zen Oriental offers formal Chinese experience.

RUISLIP

Hawtrey's – at The Barn Hotel
West End Rd ✉ *HA4 6JB* ⊖ *Ruislip* – ✆ *(01895) 679 999*
– *www.thebarnhotel.co.uk* – *Fax (01895) 638 379* – *Closed Saturday lunch and Sunday dinner* **1**AU**e**
Rest – Modern European – Menu £ 16/29 – Carte £ 43/49
◆ Jacobean styled baronial hall: an extension to 16C Barn Hotel. Cloth clad tables, bright chandeliers. Fine dining - modern cooking that's confident and assured.

LONDON

HOUNSLOW – Greater London – pop. 212 341 **12** A3

The Treaty Centre, High St ✆ (0845) 456 2929, leisureshop-hct@lang.com
Wyke Green Isleworth Syon Lane, ✆ (020) 8560 8777
Airlinks Southall Lane, ✆ (020) 8561 1418
Hounslow Heath, Staines Rd, ✆ (020) 8570 5271

CHISWICK

Moran
626 Chiswick High Rd ✉ *W4 5RY* ⊖ *Gunnersbury* – ✆ *(020) 8996 5200*
– *www.moranhotels.com* – *Fax (020) 8996 5201* **6**CV**i**
118 rm ☐ – †£ 240 ††£ 250/350
Rest ***Napa*** – Menu £ 15/23 – Carte £ 23/43
◆ Converted office block with all-glass exterior, midway between Heathrow and West End. Decorated in a restrained contemporary style with bright and airy bedrooms. Two-tiered restaurant with terrace and modern menu.

High Road House
162 Chiswick High Rd ✉ *W4 1PR* ⊖ *Turnham Green* – ✆ *(020) 8742 1717*
– *www.highroadhouse.co.uk* – *Fax (020) 8987 8762* **21**KZG**e**
14 rm – †£ 145 ††£ 145, ☐ £ 15
Rest High Road Brasserie – *see restaurant listing*
◆ Cool, sleek hotel and club, the latter a slick place to lounge around or play games. Light, bright bedrooms with crisp linen. A carefully appointed, fairly-priced destination.

La Trompette
5-7 Devonshire Rd ✉ *W4 2EU* ⊖ *Turnham Green* – ✆ *(020) 8747 1836*
– *www.latrompette.co.uk* – *Fax (020) 8995 8097* – *Closed 25-26 December*
Rest – Modern European – *(booking essential)* Menu £ 24 **21**KZG**y**
(weekday lunch 25/30 weekends)/38 (dinner)
Spec. Foie gras and chicken liver parfait with toasted brioche. Herb crusted saddle of lamb with shallot purée and baby artichokes. Lemon tart with Italian meringue and blackcurrant sorbet.
◆ Enthusiastically run and smart neighbourhood restaurant, sister to Chez Bruce. Small front terrace and light, comfortable interior. Balanced menu and confident kitchen produce robust, spirited dishes. Good value early evening menus.

High Road Brasserie – at High Road House
162 Chiswick High Rd ✉ *W4 1PR* ⊖ *Turnham Green* – ✆ *(020) 8742 1717*
– *www.highroadhouse.co.uk* – *Fax (020) 8987 8762* **21**KZG**e**
Rest – Traditional – Carte £ 21/42
◆ Confidently run and stylish. Marble-topped bar and Belgian tiled dining area provide sleek backdrop to well-priced, satisfying menus full of interesting brasserie dishes.

XX **Le Vacherin** A/C VISA AE

76-77 South Par. ✉ W4 5LF ⊖ Chiswick Park – ✆ (020) 8742 2121 – www.levacherin.com – Fax (020) 8742 0799 – Closed Monday lunch except December and Bank Holidays **6**CV**o**

Rest – French – Menu £ 17 (lunch) – Carte dinner £ 34/46

♦ Smart and authentic French brasserie, complete with belle époque prints. Satisfying menu of carefully prepared classics, from snails to cassoulet, including baked Vacherin. All French wine list.

X **Fish Hook** A/C VISA AE

6-8 Elliott Rd ✉ W4 1PE ⊖ Turnham Green – ✆ (020) 8742 0766 – www.fishhook.co.uk – Fax (020) 8742 3374 – closed 25-26 December

Rest – Seafood – Menu £ 15 (lunch) – Carte £ 31/43 **21**KZG**z**

♦ Warm, intimate and local feel to this seafood restaurant. Owner-chef adds the occasional Asian note to the crisp, clean and classical cooking. Good value lunch and early evening menu.

X **Sam's Brasserie** A/C VISA AE

11 Barley Mow Passage ✉ W4 4PH ⊖ Turnham Green – ✆ (020) 8987 0555 – www.samsbrasserie.co.uk – Fax (020) 8987 7389 – Closed 24-28 December

Rest – Mediterranean – Menu £ 15 (weekday lunch)/18 (Sunday-Thursday dinner) – Carte £ 25/37 **2**CV**a**

♦ Bustling and fun brasserie with large bar, in former Sanderson wallpaper mill. Appealing menu leans towards the Med; cooking is flavoursome. Service is young and keen and the wine affordable.

The Devonshire VISA AE

126 Devonshire Rd ✉ W4 2JJ ⊖ Turnham Green. – ✆ (020) 7592 7962 – www.gordonramsay.com – Fax (020) 7592 1603 – Closed Monday-Tuesday and lunch Wednesday-Thursday **21**KZG**a**

Rest – Menu £ 19 (dinner) – Carte £ 23/30

♦ Was the second member of Gordon Ramsay's burgeoning pub group. Appealing snacks like cockles and scotch eggs in the bar; pub classics, pies, soups and more elaborate dishes in the neat restaurant.

ISLINGTON – Greater London – pop. 175 797 **12** B3

ARCHWAY

X **500** VISA AE

782 Holloway Rd ✉ N19 3JH ⊖ Archway – ✆ (020) 7272 3406 – www.500restaurant.co.uk – Closed 2 weeks summer, 10 days Christmas, Sunday lunch and Monday **12**SZA**y**

Rest – Italian – *(booking essential)* Carte £ 20/24

♦ Small, fun and well-priced Italian that's always busy. Good pastas and bread; the veal chop and rabbit are specialities. The passion of the ebullient owner and keen chef are evident.

St John's Tavern VISA AE

91 Junction Rd ✉ N19 5QU ⊖ Archway – ✆ (020) 7272 1587 – Fax (020) 7272 1587 – Closed 25-26 December and lunch Monday-Thursday **12**RZA**s**

Rest – Carte £ 18/29

♦ Daily changing menu in the dining room at the back of the pub. Cosy atmosphere, with dark colours and fireplace. Rustic cooking from open kitchen and blackboard menu.

BARNSBURY

XX **Morgan M** A/C VISA

489 Liverpool Rd ✉ N7 8NS ⊖ Highbury and Islington – ✆ (020) 7609 3560 – www.morganm.com – Fax (020) 8292 5699 – Closed 24-30 December, Sunday dinner, Monday and lunch Tuesday and Saturday **13**UZA**a**

Rest – French – Menu £ 27/39 – Carte £ 39/45

♦ Simple restaurant in a converted pub. Smartly laid tables complemented by formal service. Modern dishes based on classical French combinations.

LONDON

Fig
169 Hemingford Rd ✉ N1 1DA ⊖ Caledonian Road – ☎ (020) 7609 3009 – www.fig-restaurant.co.uk – Closed Sunday **13**UZB**a**

Rest – Modern European – *(dinner only and lunch Friday-Saturday)* Menu £ 19 (lunch) – Carte £ 28/38

◆ Well-travelled Danish chef-owner uses Scandinavian influences and other world cuisines to create light, fresh and flavoursome dishes. Warm, cosy and inviting neighbourhood feel.

Canonbury

The House
63-69 Canonbury Rd ✉ N1 2DG ⊖ Highbury and Islington. – ☎ (020) 7704 7410 – www.themeredithgroup.co.uk – Fax (020) 7704 9388 – Closed Monday lunch **13**UZB**h**

Rest – Menu £ 15 (lunch) – Carte £ 26/35

◆ A smart looking pub with an attractive terrace; but one that still feels like a genuine local. The cooking is crisp and confident and there's an emphasis on good quality, organic ingredients.

Clerkenwell

Malmaison
18-21 Charterhouse Sq ✉ EC1M 6AH ⊖ Barbican – ☎ (020) 7012 3700 – www.malmaison.com – Fax (020) 7012 3702 – Closed 23-28 December

97 rm – †£ 215 ††£ 215/495, ☕ £ 17.95 **19**UZD**o**

Rest *Brasserie* – *(closed Saturday lunch)* Menu £ 18 – Carte £ 25/44

◆ Striking early 20C red-brick building overlooking pleasant square. Stylish, comfy public areas. Bedrooms in vivid, bold colours, with plenty of extra touches. Modern brasserie employing meats from Smithfield.

The Rookery without rest
12 Peters Lane, Cowcross St ✉ EC1M 6DS ⊖ Barbican – ☎ (020) 7336 0931 – www.rookeryhotel.com – Fax (020) 7336 0931 – Closed 24-26 December

32 rm – †£ 137/253 ††£ 206/253 – 1 suite **33**AOT**p**

◆ A row of charmingly restored 18C houses. Wood panelling, stone-flagged flooring, open fires and antique furniture. Highly individual bedrooms, with Victorian bathrooms.

Eastside Inn
40 St John St ✉ EC1M 4AY ⊖ Barbican – ☎ (020) 7490 9230 – www.esilondon.com – Fax (020) 7490 9234 – Closed 9-18 April, 23 August-5 September, 24 December-9 January, Saturday, Sunday and Bank Holidays

Rest – Innovative – Menu £ 35/70 **33**APT**c**

Rest *Bistro* – Modern European – ☎ (020) 7490 9240 – Carte £ 24/38

◆ Impressive open kitchen with formal 'fine dining' restaurant on one side and a more relaxed 'bistro moderne' on the other. Expect technically skilled, original and elaborate constructions.

The Clerkenwell Dining Room
69-73 St John St ✉ EC1M 4AN ⊖ Farringdon – ☎ (020) 7253 9000 – www.theclerkenwell.com – Fax (020) 7253 3322 – Closed 25 December, Saturday lunch, Sunday and Bank Holidays **19**UZD**h**

Rest – French – Carte £ 25/35

◆ Former pub, now a stylish modern restaurant with etched glass façade. Three adjoining dining areas with bar provide setting for contemporary cooking with its roots in France.

Smiths of Smithfield
Top Floor, 67-77 Charterhouse St ✉ EC1M 6HJ ⊖ Barbican – ☎ (020) 7251 7950 – www.smithsofsmithfield.co.uk – Fax (020) 7236 5666 – Closed 24 December-2 January and Saturday lunch **33**AOT**s**

Rest – Modern European – Carte £ 35/47

Rest *The Dining Room* – *(closed Saturday lunch, Sunday and Bank Holidays)* Carte £ 22/28

◆ On three floors where the higher you go the more formal it becomes. Busy, bustling atmosphere and modern menu. Good views of the market from the top floor terrace. The Dining Room with mirrors and dark blue walls.

XX **Portal**

88 St John St ✉ EC1M 4EH ⊖ Farringdon – ✆ (020) 7253 6950 – www.portalrestaurant.com – Fax (020) 7490 5836 – Closed 1-6 January, Saturday lunch, Sunday and Bank Holidays **19**UZD**r**

Rest – Mediterranean – Menu £ 26 (lunch) – Carte £ 27/47

◆ Portugal and southern Europe are the main influences, with fish and pork dishes the house specialities. Busy front bar and a chic, semi-industrial feel to the rear restaurant. Helpful service.

XX **The Larder**

91-93 St John St ✉ EC1M 4NU ⊖ Farringdon – ✆ (020) 7608 1558 – www.thelarderrestaurant.com – Closed 24 December-2 January, Easter, Sunday, Monday lunch and Bank Holidays **19**UZD**f**

Rest – Modern European – Menu £ 17 (lunch) – Carte £ 23/34

◆ Large, glass-fronted restaurant with stark, noisy, industrial feel and own bakery selling breads and pastries. Unfussy food has an English accent with some European influences.

X **St John**

26 St John St ✉ EC1M 4AY ⊖ Barbican – ✆ (020) 7251 0848 – www.stjohnrestaurant.com – Fax (020) 7251 4090 – Closed Christmas- New Year, Easter, Saturday lunch, Sunday dinner and Bank Holidays **33**APT**c**

Rest – British – *(booking essential)* Carte £ 22/39

Spec. Roast bone marrow and parsley salad. Middle white pork, swede and pickled walnut. Eccles cake and Lancashire cheese.

◆ 'Nose to tail eating' is how they describe their cooking at this busy, bright, converted 19C smokehouse. Strong on offal, game and unusual cuts; gloriously British, highly seasonal, appealingly simple and very satisfying.

LONDON

X **Hix Oyster and Chop House**

36-37 Greenhill Rents ✉ EC1M 6BN ⊖ Farringdon – ✆ (0207) 017 1930 – www.hixoysterandchophouse.co.uk – Fax (0207) 549 3584 – Closed 25-26 December, 1 January, Saturday lunch and Bank Holidays **33**AOT**e**

Rest – British – Menu £ 35 (Sunday lunch) – Carte £ 28/58

◆ Appropriately utilitarian surroundings put the focus on seasonal and often underused British ingredients. Cooking is satisfying and unfussy, with plenty of oysters and aged beef served on the bone.

X **Vinoteca**

7 St John St ✉ EC1M 4AA ⊖ Farringdon – ✆ (020) 7253 8786 – www.vinoteca.co.uk – Closed 23 December - 3 January and Sunday dinner

Rest – Modern European – Carte £ 20/30 **33**APT**a**

◆ This cosy and passionately run 'bar and wine shop' is always busy and full of life. Thrilling wine list is constantly evolving; the classic and vibrant dishes are the ideal accompaniment.

X **Comptoir Gascon**

61-63 Charterhouse St ✉ EC1M 6HJ ⊖ Farringdon – ✆ (020) 7608 0851 – www.comptoirgascon.com – Fax (020) 7608 0871 – Closed Christmas-New Year, Sunday and Monday **33**AOT**a**

Rest – French – *(booking essential)* Carte £ 16/26

◆ Buzzy restaurant; sister to Club Gascon. Rustic and satisfying specialities from the SW of France include wine, cheese, bread and especially duck. Further produce on display to take home.

The Coach & Horses

26-28 Ray St ✉ EC1R 3DJ ⊖ Farringdon. – ✆ (020) 7837 1336 – www.thecoachandhorses.com – Fax (020) 7278 1478 – Closed Christmas to New Year, Easter, Saturday lunch, Sunday dinner and Bank Holidays

Rest – Italian influences – Carte £ 22/28 **19**UZD**a**

◆ Characterful Victorian pub, recently refurbished and moving with the times. Pleasant and well-run dining room with strong Mediterranean influence on the menu. Appealing snack menu in the bar.

Finsbury

The Zetter

St John's Square, 86-88 Clerkenwell Rd ✉ EC1M 5RJ ⊖ Farringdon – ✆ (020) 7324 4444 – www.thezetter.com – Fax (020) 7324 4445 **19**UZD**s**

59 rm – †£ 170/270 ††£ 170/270, ☕ £ 9.50

Rest – *(closed 24-28 December)* Menu £ 16 (lunch) – Carte £ 21/37

◆ Discreetly trendy modern design in the well-equipped bedrooms and rooftop studios of a converted 19C warehouse:pleasant extras from old paperbacks to flat screen TV/DVDs. Light, informal restaurant serves modern Mediterranean dishes and weekend brunches.

Quality Chop House

92- 94 Farringdon Rd ✉ EC1R 3EA ⊖ Farringdon – ✆ (020) 7837 5093 – www.qualitychophouse.co.uk – Fax (020) 7833 8748 – Closed 25 December

Rest – British – Carte £ 23/39 **19**UZD**n**

◆ On the window is etched 'Progressive working class caterers'. This is borne out with the individual café-style booths and a menu ranging from jellied eels to caviar.

Moro

34-36 Exmouth Market ✉ EC1R 4QE ⊖ Farringdon – ✆ (020) 7833 8336 – www.moro.co.uk – Fax (020) 7833 9338 – Closed Easter, 1 week Christmas-New Year and Bank Holidays **19**UZD**b**

Rest – Mediterranean – *(booking essential)* Carte £ 28/36

◆ Daily changing menu an eclectic mix of Mediterranean, Moroccan and Spanish. Friendly T-shirted staff. Informal surroundings with bare tables and a large zinc bar.

The Ambassador

55 Exmouth Market ✉ EC1R 4QL ⊖ Farringdon – ✆ (020) 7837 0009 – www.theambassadorcafe.co.uk – Closed Bank Holidays **19**UZD**c**

Rest – Modern European – Menu £ 16 – Carte £ 19/33

◆ Lino and melamine give a refreshing retro appeal to this cool, buzzy diner. Seasonally pertinent ingredients inform all day Eurocentric menus offering range of honest, earthy dishes.

Medcalf

40 Exmouth Market ✉ EC1R 4QE ⊖ Farringdon – ✆ (020) 7833 3533 – www.medcalfbar.co.uk – Closed 23 December-5 January, Sunday dinner and Bank Holidays **19**UZD**b**

Rest – British – *(booking essential)* Carte £ 22/34

◆ Bustling, no-frills former butcher's shop with lively atmosphere. Satisfying robust cooking, with the emphasis on seasonal, British ingredients. Good range of beer and wine by the glass.

Cicada

132-134 St John St ✉ EC1V 4JT ⊖ Farringdon – ✆ (020) 7608 1550 – www.rickerrestaurants.com – Fax (020) 8608 1551 – Closed Sunday and Bank Holidays **19**UZD**d**

Rest – Asian – Menu £ 11/15 – Carte approx. £ 23

◆ Set in a culinary hotbed, this buzzy restaurant and vibrant bar is spacious, lively and popular for its south east Asian dishes. You can even just pop in for one course and a beer.

The Modern Pantry

47-48 St John's Sq ✉ EC1V 4JJ ⊖ Farringdon – ✆ (020) 7553 9210 – www.themodernpantry.co.uk – Closed 24-28 December and 1 January

Rest – International – *(booking advisable)* Menu £ 23 (lunch) – Carte £ 22/37 **19**UZD**k**

◆ Zesty, vivacious cooking stars at Anna Hansen's restaurant, housed within a Georgian building. Café-style ground floor more fun than upstairs. Good value menu; fusion without being convoluted.

The Peasant

240 St John St ✉ EC1V 4PH ⊖ Farringdon. – ✆ (020) 7336 7726 – www.thepeasant.co.uk – Fax (020) 7490 1089 – Closed 25 December to 1 January and Bank Holidays except Good Friday **19**UZD**e**

Rest – *(booking essential)* Menu £ 35 (dinner) – Carte £ 23/30

◆ Classic Victorian pub involved in the vanguard of the original gastropub movement. Robust, hearty fare downstairs and more original dishes in the formal upstairs restaurant.

The Well

180 St John St ✉ EC1V 4JY ⊖ Farringdon. – ✆ (020) 7251 9363 – www.downthewell.com – Fax (020) 7253 9683 – Closed 25 December

Rest – Carte £ 20/40 **19**UZD**x**

◆ Compact pub with sliding glass doors and popular pavement benches. Modern dishes range from potted shrimps to foie gras and chicken liver parfait. Classic puddings; splendid cheeses.

Highbury

Au Lac

82 Highbury Park ✉ N5 2XE ⊖ Arsenal – ✆ (020) 7704 9187 – Fax (020) 7704 9187 **13**UZA**b**

Rest – Vietnamese – *(dinner only and lunch Thursday and Friday)* Carte £ 8/21

◆ Cosy Vietnamese restaurant, with brightly coloured walls and painted fans. Large menus with authentic dishes usefully highlighted. Fresh flavours; good value.

Islington

Almeida

30 Almeida St ✉ N1 1AD ⊖ Angel – ✆ (020) 7354 4777 – www.almeida-restaurant.co.uk – Fax (020) 7354 2777 – Closed 1 January, Monday lunch and Sunday dinner **13**UZB**r**

Rest – French – Menu £ 32 (dinner) – Carte lunch £ 18/28

◆ Crisply decorated restaurant dating from 1891. Classically inspired menus with plenty of choice; good value lunch. Interesting French regional wines. Overwhelmingly busy pre/post theatre.

Metrogusto

13 Theberton St ✉ N1 0QY ⊖ Angel – ✆ (020) 7226 9400 – www.metrogusto.co.uk – Fax (020) 7226 9400 – Closed 25-26 December and 1 January **13**UZB**e**

Rest – Italian – *(dinner only and lunch Friday-Sunday)* Menu £ 19 (dinner) – Carte £ 24/36

◆ A gem amongst all the chain restaurants in Islington. Warm hospitality and competitively priced, seasonal and contemporary Italian cooking with daily specials. Lively, eye-catching artwork.

Ottolenghi

287 Upper St ✉ N1 2TZ ⊖ Highbury and Islington – ✆ (020) 7288 1454 – www.ottolenghi.co.uk – Fax (020) 7704 1456 – Closed 25-26 December, 1 January and Sunday dinner **13**UZB**k**

Rest – Mediterranean – *(booking essential)* Carte £ 29/34

◆ This attractive deli morphs into a little restaurant at night, with communal tables and chatty service. Fresh, flavoursome dishes with influences from across all parts of the Med.

The Drapers Arms

44 Barnsbury St ✉ N1 1ER ⊖ Highbury and Islington. – ✆ (020) 7619 0348 – www.thedrapersarms.com **13**UZB**x**

Rest – British – Carte £ 18/30

◆ Handsome Georgian pub, revived and re-opened in 2009. The food is all about seasonality and flavour; 'proper' British dishes and less familiar cuts. Same menu in the bar and upstairs dining room.

The Northgate

113 Southgate Rd ✉ N1 3JS ⊖ Dalston Kingsland (rail). – ✆ (020) 7359 7392 – Fax (020) 7359 7393 **13**VZB**a**

Rest – *(dinner only and lunch Saturday and Sunday)* Carte £ 20/27

◆ Cavernous corner pub; busy front bar with tables laid for dining at the back. Large blackboard menu lists mostly Mediterranean-influenced dishes with the emphasis on flavour. Relaxed service.

The Barnsbury
209-211 Liverpool Rd ✉ N1 1LX ⊖ Highbury and Islington. – ✆ (020) 7607 5519 – www.thebarnsbury.co.uk – Fax (020) 7607 3256 – Closed 24-26 December and 1 January **13**UZB**v**
Rest – Carte £ 26/29
◆ Looks more like a pub from the inside, with locals, a large central bar, soundtrack and small rear garden. Satisfying European-based cooking, with classic combinations of flavours.

King's Cross

Konstam at the Prince Albert
2 Acton St ✉ WC1X 9NA ⊖ King's Cross St Pancras – ✆ (020) 7833 5040 – www.konstam.co.uk – Closed 24 December-2 January, Saturday lunch and Bank Holidays **18**TZC**a**
Rest – Traditional – Carte £ 26/35
◆ Avert your gaze from the hugely wondrous light display to enjoy interesting dishes sourced totally from within boundaries of London Transport network! Chef has own allotment.

LONDON

KENSINGTON and CHELSEA (Royal Borough of) **12** B3
– Greater London – pop. 158 439

Chelsea

Sheraton Park Tower
101 Knightsbridge ✉ SW1X 7RN ⊖ Knightsbridge – ✆ (020) 7235 8050 – www.luxurycollection.com/parktowerlondon – Fax (020) 7235 8231 – Closed 25-26 December and 1 January **37**AGX**t**
275 rm – †£ 430 ††£ 600, ☐ £ 25 – 5 suites
Rest *One-O-One* – see restaurant listing
◆ Built in the 1970s in a unique cylindrical shape. Well-equipped bedrooms are all identical in size. Top floor executive rooms have commanding views of Hyde Park and City.

The Capital
22-24 Basil St ✉ SW3 1AT ⊖ Knightsbridge – ✆ (020) 7589 5171 – www.capitalhotel.co.uk – Fax (020) 7225 0011 **37**AFX**a**
49 rm – †£ 265 ††£ 420, ☐ £ 20 – 8 suites
Rest – *(booking essential)* Menu £ 33/63
◆ A thoroughly British hotel, privately owned and in a great location. Experienced staff provide conscientious service and the atmosphere is discreet and elegant. Individually styled bedrooms use a number of different designers. There were plans for a new dining concept as we went to print.

Draycott without rest
26 Cadogan Gdns ✉ SW3 2RP ⊖ Sloane Square – ✆ (020) 7730 6466 – www.draycotthotel.com – Fax (020) 7730 0236 **37**AGY**c**
35 rm – †£ 179/219 ††£ 363, ☐ £ 19.95 – 11 suites
◆ Charming, discreet 19C house with elegant sitting room overlooking tranquil garden for afternoon tea. Bedrooms are individually decorated in a country house style and are named after writers or actors.

The Cadogan
75 Sloane St ✉ SW1X 9SG ⊖ Knightsbridge – ✆ (020) 7235 7141 – www.cadogan.com – Fax (020) 7245 0994 **37**AGY**b**
63 rm – †£ 294/340 ††£ 409, ☐ £ 24.50
Rest *Langtry's* – *(closed Sunday dinner)* Menu £ 35 – Carte £ 30/42
◆ An Edwardian townhouse, made famous by two former residents – Oscar Wilde and Lillie Langtry. Quiet drawing room for afternoon tea; bedrooms are varied and comfortable. Discreet restaurant; traditional menu.

Knightsbridge
10 Beaufort Gdns ✉ SW3 1PT ⊖ Knightsbridge – ✆ (020) 7584 6300 – www.knightsbridgehotel.com – Fax (020) 7584 6355 **37**AFX**s**
44 rm – †£ 196/242 ††£ 340, ☐ £ 17.50 **Rest** – *(room service only)*
◆ Attractively furnished townhouse with a very stylish, discreet feel. Every bedroom is immaculately appointed and has an individuality of its own; fine detailing throughout.

Egerton House

17-19 Egerton Terrace ✉ SW3 2BX ⊖ South Kensington – ✆ (020) 7589 2412 – www.egertonhousehotel.com – Fax (020) 7584 6540 **37**AFY**e**

27 rm – †£ 294/363 ††£ 294/363, ☕ £ 24.50 – 1 suite

Rest – *(room service only)* Carte £ 25/34

◆ Discreet, compact but comfortable townhouse in a good location, recently refurbished throughout and owned by Red Carnation group. High levels of personal service make the hotel stand out.

The Levin

28 Basil St ✉ SW3 1AS ⊖ Knightsbridge – ✆ (020) 7589 6286 – www.thelevinhotel.co.uk – Fax (020) 7823 7826 **37**AFX**c**

12 rm – †£ 305 ††£ 305, ☕ £ 16.50

Rest *Le Metro* – *(Closed Sunday in summer)* Carte £ 26/31

◆ Impressive façade, contemporary interior and comfortable bedrooms in subtle art deco style, boasting marvellous champagne mini bars. Sister to The Capital hotel. Informal brasserie includes blackboard menu and pies of the week.

Beaufort without rest

33 Beaufort Gdns ✉ SW3 1PP ⊖ Knightsbridge – ✆ (020) 7584 5252 – www.thebeaufort.co.uk – Fax (020) 7589 2834 **37**AFX**n**

29 rm – †£ 173/253 ††£ 322/334, ☕ £ 19.50

◆ A vast collection of English floral watercolours adorn this 19C townhouse in a useful location. Modern and co-ordinated rooms. Tariff includes all drinks and afternoon tea.

Myhotel Chelsea

35 Ixworth Pl ✉ SW3 3QX ⊖ South Kensington – ✆ (020) 7225 7500 – www.myhotels.com – Fax (020) 7225 7555 **37**AFY**z**

44 rm – †£ 205/235 ††£ 235, ☕ £ 18 – 1 suite

Rest – Carte £ 17/26

◆ Restored Victorian property in a fairly quiet and smart side street. Modern and well-equipped rooms are ideal for the corporate traveller. Smart dining room for modern menus.

Sydney House without rest

9-11 Sydney St ✉ SW3 6PU ⊖ South Kensington – ✆ (020) 7376 7711 – www.sydneyhousechelsea.com – Fax (020) 7376 4233 – Closed 24-29 December **36**ADY**s**

21 rm – †£ 125/195 ††£ 155/275, ☕ £ 9.95

◆ Stylish, discreet and compact Georgian townhouse made brighter through mirrors and light wood. Thoughtfully designed bedrooms; Room 43 has its own terrace. Part of Abode group.

The Sloane Square

7-12 Sloane Sq ✉ SW1W 8EG ⊖ Sloane Square – ✆ (020) 7896 9988 – www.sloanesquarehotel.co.uk – Fax (020) 7751 4211 **37**AGY**k**

102 rm – †£ 194/228 ††£ 282, ☕ £ 12.50

Rest Chelsea Brasserie – see restaurant listing

◆ Red-brick hotel opened in 2007, boasts bright, contemporary décor. Stylish, co-ordinated bedrooms, with laptops; library of DVDs and games available. Rooms at back slightly quieter.

Gordon Ramsay

✿✿✿ *68-69 Royal Hospital Rd ✉ SW3 4HP ⊖ Sloane Square – ✆ (020) 7352 4441 – www.gordonramsay.com – Fax (020) 7352 3334 – Closed 25-26 December, 1 January, Saturday and Sunday* **37**AFZ**c**

Rest – French – *(booking essential)* Menu £ 45/90

Spec. Pressed foie gras with Madeira jelly, smoked duck, peach and almond crumble. Roasted fillet of turbot with langoustines, linguine and wild mushrooms. Cherry soufflé with chocolate sorbet and crystallised pistachios.

◆ Clare Smyth is at the helm of Gordon Ramsay's flagship; her cooking has added a subtle sense of rural sincerity to the sophisticated dishes. The elegant simplicity of the room works well and the service is smooth, organised and unobtrusive.

XXX **Bibendum**

Michelin House, 81 Fulham Rd ✉ SW3 6RD ⊖ South Kensington – ☎ (020) 7581 5817 – www.bibendum.co.uk – Fax (020) 7823 7925 – Closed 24-26 December and 1 January **37**AEY**s**

Rest – French – Menu £ 30 (lunch and Sunday dinner) – Carte £ 40/60

◆ Has maintained a loyal following for over 20 years, with its French food that comes with a British accent. Located on the 1st floor of a London landmark – Michelin's former HQ, dating from 1911.

XXX ✿ **Tom Aikens**

43 Elystan St ✉ SW3 3NT ⊖ South Kensington – ☎ (020) 7584 2003 – www.tomaikens.co.uk – Fax (020) 7589 2107 – Closed 25-26 December, New Year, Easter Monday, Saturday lunch, Sunday, Monday and Bank Holidays

Rest – Innovative – Menu £ 29 (lunch) – Carte £ 29/65 **37**AFY**n**

Spec. Tartare of scallops with almond gazpacho. Fillet of beef, summer truffle and red wine sauce. Pistachio meringue, parfait and cassonade.

◆ Neat and elegant dining room, with well co-ordinated service. Seasonal ingredients, largely from the British Isles, are used in dishes that show plenty of originality and skill, with fish the kitchen's strength.

XXX **Fifth Floor** – at Harvey Nichols

109-125 Knightsbridge ✉ SW1X 7RJ ⊖ Knightsbridge – ☎ (020) 7235 5250 – www.harveynichols.com – Fax (020) 7823 2207 – Closed Christmas, Easter and Sunday dinner **37**AGX**s**

Rest – Modern European – Menu £ 20 (lunch) – Carte £ 29/58

◆ Stylish, colour-changing surroundings on Harvey Nichols' fifth floor, reached via its own lift. Modern cooking with some originality and the emphasis on France. Good wine list.

XXX **Toto's**

Walton House, Walton St ✉ SW3 2JH ⊖ Knightsbridge – ☎ (020) 7589 0075 – Fax (020) 7581 9668 – Closed 25-27 December **37**AFY**x**

Rest – Italian – *(booking essential at dinner)* Menu £ 24 (lunch) – Carte £ 34/45

◆ Old-fashioned in the best sense, with caring service. Ground floor has the better atmosphere. Earthy and rustic Italian cooking, with handmade pasta a speciality.

XXX **Awana**

85 Sloane Ave ✉ SW3 3DX ⊖ South Kensington – ☎ (020) 7584 8880 – www.awana.co.uk – Fax (020) 7584 6188 – Closed 25-26 December and 1 January **37**AFY**b**

Rest – Malaysian – *(booking essential)* Menu £ 15 (lunch) – Carte £ 21/44

◆ Traditional Malay elements adorn this restaurant, which has its own stylish cocktail bar. Invigorating Malaysian specialities are smartly presented; satay chef has separate counter.

XXX **Chutney Mary**

535 King's Rd ✉ SW10 0SZ ⊖ Fulham Broadway – ☎ (020) 7351 3113 – www.realindianfood.com – Fax (020) 7351 7694 – Closed dinner 25 December

Rest – Indian – *(dinner only and lunch Saturday-Sunday)* **22**OZG**v**

Menu £ 22 (lunch) – Carte £ 29/39

◆ Soft lighting and sepia etchings hold sway at this forever popular restaurant. Extensive menu of specialities from all corners of India. Complementary wine list.

XXX **One-O-One** – at Sheraton Park Tower Hotel

101 Knightsbridge ✉ SW1X 7RN ⊖ Knightsbridge – ☎ (020) 7290 7101 – www.oneoonerestaurant.com – Fax (020) 7235 6196 – Closed 25-26 December and 1 January **37**AGX**t**

Rest – Seafood – Menu £ 19/38 – Carte £ 49/62

◆ Smart ground floor restaurant; lacking a little in atmosphere but the seafood is good. Much of the produce from Brittany and Norway; don't miss the King crab legs. Small tasting plates also offered.

Good food at moderate prices? Look for the Bib Gourmand.

XX **Chelsea Brasserie** – at The Sloane Square Hotel

7-12 Sloane Sq. ✉ SW1W 8EG ⊖ Sloane Square – ✆ (020) 7896 9988 – www.sloanesquarehotel.co.uk – Fax (020) 7751 4211 **37**AGY**k**

Rest – French – *(closed Sunday dinner)* Menu £ 25 – Carte £ 32/40

◆ You pass through the busy bar to get to the smartly lit brasserie, with exposed brick, mirrors and tiles. Cooking has a strong French base. Good value theatre menu and brisk service.

XX **Daphne's**

112 Draycott Ave ✉ SW3 3AE ⊖ South Kensington – ✆ (020) 7589 4257 – www.daphnes-restaurant.co.uk – Fax (020) 7225 2766 – Closed 25-26 December and 1 January **37**AFY**j**

Rest – Italian – *(booking essential)* Menu £ 19 (lunch) – Carte £ 31/50

◆ Established over 40 years ago and a Chelsea institution with 'celebrity' following. Reliable formula of tired and tested Italian classics in a room with a warm, Tuscan feel.

XX ✿ **Rasoi** (Vineet Bhatia)

10 Lincoln St ✉ SW3 2TS ⊖ Sloane Square – ✆ (020) 7225 1881 – www.rasoirestaurant.co.uk – Fax (020) 7581 0220 – Closed 25 -26 December, 1 January, Saturday lunch and Sunday **37**AFY**y**

Rest – Indian – Menu £ 26/55

Spec. Grilled prawn, coconut and chilli panna cotta with brown shrimp chutney. Baked sea bass, tandoori crushed potatoes and crispy okra. Blueberry and black cardamom kulfi.

◆ Innovative and creative Indian cuisine in the incongruous setting of a typical Chelsea townhouse. Ring the doorbell and you'll be greeted by an exotic aroma that hints of what's to follow.

XX **Racine**

239 Brompton Rd ✉ SW3 2EP ⊖ South Kensington – ✆ (020) 7584 4477 – www.racine-restaurant.com – Fax (020) 7584 4900 – Closed 25 December

Rest – French – Menu £ 18/20 (lunch and early dinner) – Carte £ 28/44 **37**AEY**t**

◆ Dark leather banquettes, large mirrors and wood floors create the atmosphere of a genuine Parisienne brasserie. Tasty, well-crafted, regional French fare.

XX **Papillon**

96 Draycott Ave ✉ SW3 3AD ⊖ South Kensington – ✆ (020) 7225 2555 – www.papillonchelsea.co.uk – Fax (020) 7225 2554 – Closed Sunday dinner

Rest – French – Menu £ 20 (lunch) – Carte £ 35/47 **37**AFY**f**

◆ Classic French regional fare, from fish soup to Chateaubriand, all feature at this well-run brasserie. French windows, lamps and a fleur-de-lys motif add to the authenticity.

XX **Bluebird**

350 King's Rd ✉ SW3 5UU ⊖ Sloane Square – ✆ (020) 7559 1000 – www.bluebird-restaurant.com – Fax (020) 7559 1115 **23**PZG**n**

Rest – British – Menu £ 21 – Carte £ 32/52

◆ Former industrial space incorporates everything from a wine store to a private members club. Large, buzzy restaurant champions British produce in an appealing menu that has something for everyone.

XX **Poissonnerie de l'Avenue**

82 Sloane Ave ✉ SW3 3DZ ⊖ South Kensington – ✆ (020) 7589 2457 /5774 – www.poissonneriedelavenue.co.uk – Fax (020) 7581 3360 – Closed 25 December and 1 January **37**AFY**u**

Rest – French – Menu £ 26 (lunch) – Carte £ 28/43

◆ A Chelsea institution with a loyal following. Classically decorated and comfortable. Emphasis on well-sourced and very fresh seafood, in dishes with a Mediterranean accent.

XX **Le Cercle**

1 Wilbraham Pl ✉ SW1X 9AE ⊖ Sloane Square – ✆ (020) 7901 9999 – www.lecercle.co.uk – Fax (020) 7901 9111 – Closed Christmas - New Year, Sunday and Monday **37**AGY**e**

Rest – French – Menu £ 15/18 – Carte £ 20/35

◆ Discreetly signed basement restaurant down residential side street. High, spacious room with chocolate banquettes. Tapas style French menus; accomplished cooking.

XX **Le Colombier**

145 Dovehouse St ✉ SW3 6LB ⊖ South Kensington – ✆ (020) 7351 1155 – www.le-colombier-restaurant.co.uk – Fax (020) 7351 5124 **36**ADZ**e**

Rest – French – Menu £ 25 (lunch) – Carte £ 29/43

◆ Proudly Gallic corner restaurant in an affluent residential area. Attractive enclosed terrace. Bright and cheerful surroundings and service of traditional French cooking.

XX **Painted Heron**

112 Cheyne Walk ✉ SW10 0DJ ⊖ Gloucester Road – ✆ (020) 7351 5232 – www.thepaintedheron.com – closed 25 December, 1 January and Saturday lunch **23**PZG**d**

Rest – Indian – Menu £ 32 – Carte £ 33/40

◆ Well-supported locally and quite formally run Indian restaurant. Nooks and crannies create an intimate atmosphere. Fish and game dishes are the highlight of the contemporary cooking.

XX **Caraffini**

61-63 Lower Sloane St ✉ SW1W 8DH ⊖ Sloane Square – ✆ (020) 7259 0235 – www.caraffini.co.uk – Fax (020) 7259 0236 – Closed 25 December, Easter, Sunday and Bank Holidays **37**AGZ**a**

Rest – Italian – *(booking essential)* Carte £ 23/39

◆ The omnipresent and ebullient owner oversees the friendly service in this attractive neighbourhood restaurant. Authentic and robust Italian cooking; informal atmosphere.

XX **Marco**

Stamford Bridge, Fulham Rd ✉ SW6 1HS ⊖ Fulham Broadway – ✆ (020) 7915 2929 – www.marcorestaurant.co.uk – Fax (020) 7915 2931 – Closed 25 December, Sunday and Monday except match days **22**OZG**c**

Rest – Traditional – *(dinner only)* Carte £ 34/59

◆ Marco Pierre White's restaurant at Chelsea Football Club offers an appealing range of classics, from British favourites to satisfying French and Italian fare. Comfortable and well-run room.

XX **Carpaccio**

4 Sydney St ✉ SW3 6PP ⊖ South Kensington – ✆ (020) 7352 3435 – www.carpacciorestaurant.co.uk – Fax (020) 7622 8304 – Closed Bank Holidays

Rest – Italian – Carte £ 24/35 **36**ADY**e**

◆ Lively local Italian with an animated service crew; blokey decoration courtesy of stills from Bond movies and Ayrton Senna's cockpit. All-encompassing menu ranges from pizza to carpaccio.

XX **Eight over Eight**

392 King's Rd ✉ SW3 5UZ ⊖ Gloucester Road – ✆ (020) 7349 9934 – www.rickerrestaurants.com – Fax (020) 7351 5157 – Closed 25-26 December, 1 January and Sunday lunch **23**PZG**n**

Rest – Asian – Menu £ 15 (lunch) – Carte £ 27/39

◆ Lively modern restaurant in converted pub; bar in front and dining room at rear. Eclectic Asian menu; strong flavours and unusual combinations. (Major fire here as we went to print.)

XX **Good Earth**

233 Brompton Rd ✉ SW3 2EP ⊖ Knightsbridge – ✆ (020) 7584 3658 – www.goodearthgroup.co.uk – Fax (020) 7823 8769 – Closed 23-31 December

Rest – Chinese – Menu £ 12/36 – Carte £ 26/37 **37**AFY**h**

◆ The basement is busier and more popular than the ground floor. Extensive menu makes good use of quality ingredients and offers appealing choice between classic and more unusual dishes.

XX **The Botanist**

7 Sloane Square ✉ SW1W 8EE ⊖ Sloane Square – ✆ (020) 7730 0077 – www.thebotanistonsloanesquare.com – Fax (020) 7730 7177 – Closed 25 December **37**AGY**r**

Rest – Modern European – Carte £ 28/41

◆ Busy bar, popular with after-work crowd; the swish and stylish restaurant occupies the other half of this corner site. Crisp and clean cooking, with influences kept within Europe.

LONDON

Bibendum Oyster Bar

Michelin House, 81 Fulham Rd ✉ SW3 6RD ⊖ South Kensington – ✆ (020) 7589 1480 – www.bibendum.co.uk – Fax (020) 7823 7925 – Closed 24-26 December and 1 January **37**AEY**s**

Rest – Seafood – *(bookings not accepted)* Carte £ 20/33

◆ Oysters, potted shrimps and a shared plateau de fruits de mer are the highlights at this continental-style café, with its mosaic floor and colourful ceramic tiles. Wine list includes 460ml pots.

Foxtrot Oscar

79 Royal Hospital Rd ✉ SW3 4HN ⊖ Sloane Square – ✆ (020) 7352 4448 – www.gordonramsay.com – Fax (020) 7592 1603 – Closed 10 days Christmas , Monday-Tuesday and lunch Wednesday-Thursday **37**AFZ**v**

Rest – Traditional – *(booking essential)* Carte £ 26/34

◆ A real Chelsea institution, now under the ownership of the Gordon Ramsay group. Expect authentic comfort food from cassoulet and coq au vin to burgers and eggs Benedict and all at sensible prices.

Manicomio

85 Duke of York Sq, King's Rd ✉ SW3 4LY ⊖ Sloane Square – ✆ (020) 7730 3366 – www.manicomio.co.uk – Fax (020) 7730 3377 – closed 25-26 December and 1 January **37**AGY**x**

Rest – Italian – Carte £ 28/41

◆ Outside, a delightful terrace overlooks the trendy square. Inside, a clean, modern, informal style prevails. Rustic Italian menus. Next door, a café and superbly stocked deli.

Aubaine

260-262 Brompton Rd ✉ SW3 2AS ⊖ South Kensington – ✆ (020) 7052 0100 – www.aubaine.co.uk – Fax (020) 7052 0622 **37**AEY**c**

Rest – French – Carte £ 22/44

◆ 'Boulangerie, patisserie, restaurant'. Pass the bakery aromas to an all-day eatery with 'distressed' country feel. Well-judged menus range from croque monsieur to coq au vin.

Tom's Kitchen

27 Cale St ✉ SW3 3QP ⊖ South Kensington – ✆ (020) 7349 0202 – www.tomskitchen.co.uk – Fax (020) 7823 3652 – Closed 25 December and 1 January **37**AFZ**b**

Rest – French – Carte £ 27/52

◆ A converted pub, whose white tiles and mirrors help to give it an industrial feel. Appealing and wholesome dishes come in man-sized portions. The eponymous Tom is Tom Aikens.

The Admiral Codrington

17 Mossop St ✉ SW3 2LY ⊖ South Kensington. – ✆ (020) 7581 0005 – www.theadmiralcodrington.com – Fax (020) 7589 2452 – Closed 25-26 December **37**AFY**v**

Rest – Carte £ 24/34

◆ Local landmark pub, with separate dining room complete with retractable roof. Menu is an appealing mix of satisfying British and European classics. The bar gets busy in the evenings.

Chelsea Ram

32 Burnaby St ✉ SW10 0PL ⊖ Fulham Broadway. – ✆ (020) 7351 4008

Rest – Menu £ 18 (dinner) – Carte £ 19/24 **23**PZG**r**

◆ A stalwart of the London pub scene. Full table service of honest home cooking and comforting classics, from lamb chops to cottage pies and heartwarming puddings. Over 20 wines by the glass.

The Cadogan Arms

298 King's Rd ✉ SW3 5UG ⊖ South Kensington – ✆ (020) 7352 6500 – www.thecadoganarmschelsea.com **36**ADZ**y**

Rest – *(booking advisable at dinner)* Carte £ 24/37

◆ Part of the Martin Brothers bourgeoning pub group. This is a proper pub, with billiard tables upstairs and a gusty, full-on menu. Stuffed and mounted animals stare down as you eat.

LONDON

Builders Arms

13 Britten St ✉ SW3 3TY ⊖ South Kensington. – ✆ (020) 7349 9040 – www.geronimo-inns.co.uk **37**AFZ**x**

Rest – *(bookings not accepted)* Carte £ 25/30

◆ Lively and busy pub, popular with the locals. Rustic and satisfying cooking, with blackboard daily specials; the popular peri-peri chicken dish is for sharing. Regular wine promotions.

The Pig's Ear

35 Old Church St ✉ SW3 5BS ⊖ Sloane Square. – ✆ (020) 7352 2908 – www.thepigsear.com – Fax (020) 7352 9321 – Closed Sunday dinner **23**PZG**v**

Rest – Carte £ 25/40

◆ Busy bar, romantic panelled dining room and cosy, curtained-off Blue Room with fire. Modern British meets Mediterranean menu; dishes like beef marrow or lamb stew and dumplings.

The Phoenix

23 Smith St ✉ SW3 4EE ⊖ Sloane Square. – ✆ (020) 7730 9182 – www.geronimo-inns.co.uk – Closed 25-26 December **37**AFZ**a**

Rest – Carte £ 23/30

◆ The main bar is popular with locals but go through to the dining room at the back which was redecorated in 2008. Expect proper pub food with interesting and seasonal daily specials.

Lots Road Pub & Dining Room

114 Lots Rd ✉ SW10 0RJ ⊖ Fulham Broadway. – ✆ (020) 7352 6645 – www.lotsroadpub.com **23**PZG**b**

Rest – Carte £ 20/31

◆ Lively semicircular shaped pub, close to Chelsea Harbour. Hearty and satisfying classics, from mussels to Perthshire côte de boeuf and a tart of the day. Service keeps it bright and cheery.

Earl's Court

K + K George

1-15 Templeton Pl ✉ SW5 9NB ⊖ Earl's Court – ✆ (020) 7598 8700 – www.kkhotels.com – Fax (020) 7370 2285 **35**AAY**s**

154 rm ☕ – 🚹£ 230 🚹🚹£ 300 **Rest** – Carte £ 20/34

◆ Five converted 19C houses overlooking large rear garden. Scandinavian-style rooms with low beds, white walls and light wood furniture. Breakfast room has the garden view. Informal dining in the bar.

Twenty Nevern Square without rest

20 Nevern Sq ✉ SW5 9PD ⊖ Earl's Court – ✆ (020) 7565 9555 – www.twentyneversquare.co.uk – Fax (020) 7565 9444 **35**AAY**u**

20 rm – 🚹£ 100/160 🚹🚹£ 160/190, ☕ £ 9

◆ In an attractive Victorian garden square, an individually designed, privately owned townhouse. Original pieces of furniture and some rooms with their own terrace.

Mayflower without rest

26-28 Trebovir Rd ✉ SW5 9NJ ⊖ Earl's Court – ✆ (020) 7370 0991 – www.mayflowerhotel.co.uk – Fax (020) 7370 0994 **35**ABY**x**

46 rm – 🚹£ 79/109 🚹🚹£ 105/115, ☕ £ 9 – 4 suites

◆ Conveniently placed, friendly establishment with a secluded rear breakfast terrace and basement breakfast room. Individually styled rooms with Asian influence.

Amsterdam without rest

7 and 9 Trebovir Rd ✉ SW5 9LS ⊖ Earl's Court – ✆ (020) 7370 2814 – www.amsterdam-hotel.com – Fax (020) 7244 7608 **35**ABY**c**

19 rm – 🚹£ 75/94 🚹🚹£ 96/99, ☕ £ 2 – 8 suites

◆ Basement breakfast room and a small secluded garden. The brightly decorated bedrooms are light and airy. Some have smart wood floors; some boast their own balcony.

Rushmore without rest

11 Trebovir Rd ✉ SW5 9LS ⊖ Earl's Court – ✆ (020) 7370 3839 – www.rushmore-hotel.co.uk – Fax (020) 7370 0274 **35**ABY**a**

22 rm ☕ – 🚹£ 69/89 🚹🚹£ 89/129

◆ Behind its Victorian façade lies an hotel popular with tourists. Individually decorated bedrooms in a variety of shapes and sizes. Piazza-style conservatory breakfast room.

XX **Langan's Coq d'Or**

254-260 Old Brompton Rd ✉ SW5 9HR ⊖ Earl's Court – ✆ (020) 7259 2599 – www.langansrestaurants.co.uk – Fax (020) 7370 7735 – Closed 25-26 December and 1 January **35**ABZ**e**

Rest – Traditional – Menu £ 26 – Carte approx. £ 29

◆ Classic, buzzy brasserie and excellent value menu to match. Walls adorned with pictures of celebrities: look out for more from the enclosed pavement terrace. Smooth service.

KENSINGTON

Royal Garden

2-24 Kensington High St ✉ W8 4PT ⊖ High Street Kensington – ✆ (020) 7937 8000 – www.royalgardenhotel.co.uk – Fax (020) 7361 1991

376 rm – †£ 241 ††£ 275, ☕ £ 19.50 – 20 suites **35**ABX**c**

Rest *Min Jiang* – see restaurant listing

Rest *Park Terrace* – ✆ (020) 7361 0602 – Menu £ 20/31 **s**

◆ A tall, modern hotel with many of its rooms enjoying enviable views over the adjacent Kensington Gardens. All the modern amenities and services, with well-drilled staff. Bright, spacious Park Terrace offers British, Asian and modern European cuisine.

The Milestone

1-2 Kensington Court ✉ W8 5DL ⊖ High Street Kensington – ✆ (020) 7917 1000 – www.milestonehotel.com – Fax (020) 7917 1010

63 rm – †£ 271/322 ††£ 305/357, ☕ £ 25 – 6 suites **35**ABX**u**

Rest – *(booking essential for non-residents)* Menu £ 27 – Carte £ 39/62

◆ Elegant hotel with decorative Victorian façade and English feel. Charming oak-panelled lounge and snug bar. Meticulously decorated bedrooms with period detail. Panelled dining room with charming little oratory for privacy seekers.

Baglioni

60 Hyde Park Gate ✉ SW7 5BB ⊖ High Street Kensington – ✆ (020) 7368 5700 – www.baglionihotels.com – Fax (020) 7368 5701 **36**ACX**e**

52 rm – †£ 455/593 ††£ 593, ☕ £ 25 – 15 suites

Rest *Brunello* – ✆ (020) 7368 5900 – Menu £ 24 (lunch) – Carte £ 46/68

◆ Opposite Kensington Palace, this hotel boasts an ornate interior and a trendy basement bar. Small gym/sauna. Stylish bedrooms come in cool shades and boast impressive facilities. Restaurant specialises in rustic Italian cooking.

XXX **Launceston Place**

1a Launceston Pl ✉ W8 5RL ⊖ Gloucester Road – ✆ (020) 7937 6912 – www.launcestonplace-restaurant.co.uk – Fax (020) 7938 2412 – Closed 24-30 December, 1 January, 4 January, Monday lunch and Bank Holidays

Rest – Modern European – Menu £ 18/42 **36**ACX**a**

◆ Relaunched and reinvigorated, with dark walls and moody lighting, but still with that local feel. Cooking is original and deftly executed and uses ingredients largely from the British Isles.

XXX **Belvedere**

Holland House, off Abbotsbury Rd ✉ W8 6LU ⊖ Holland Park – ✆ (020) 7602 1238 – www.belvedererestaurant.co.uk – Fax (020) 7610 4382 – Closed 26 December, 1 January and Sunday dinner **16**MZE**u**

Rest – French – Menu £ 20 (lunch) – Carte £ 26/49

◆ Former 19C orangery in a delightful position in the middle of the park. On two floors with a bar and balcony terrace. Huge vases of flowers. Modern take on classic dishes.

XXX **Min Jiang** – at Royal Garden Hotel

10th Floor, 2-24 Kensington High St ✉ W8 4PT ⊖ High Street Kensington – ✆ (020) 7361 1988 – www.minjiang.co.uk – Fax (020) 7361 1991

Rest – Chinese – Menu £ 20/48 – Carte £ 40/61 **35**ABX**c**

◆ Stylish and comfortable Chinese restaurant on the 10th floor of the hotel, with terrific views. Lunchtime dim sum a strength; the Beijing duck is a speciality and comes roasted in a wood-fired oven.

XX **Babylon** – at The Roof Gardens

99 Kensington High St (entrance on Derry St) ✉ W8 5SA ⊖ High Street Kensington – ✆ (020) 7368 3993 – www.roofgardens.virgin.com – Fax (020) 7368 3995 – Closed 24 December - 2 January and Sunday dinner

Rest – Modern European – Menu £ 20 (lunch) – Carte £ 46/57 **35**ABX**n**

◆ Situated on the roof of this pleasant London building affording attractive views of the London skyline. Stylish modern décor in keeping with the contemporary, British cooking.

XX **Clarke's**

124 Kensington Church St ✉ W8 4BH ⊖ Notting Hill Gate – ✆ (020) 7221 9225 – www.sallyclarke.com – Fax (020) 7229 4564 – Closed 2 weeks Christmas-New Year and Bank Holidays **27**ABV**c**

Rest – Modern European – Menu £ 40 (dinner) – Carte lunch £ 29/35

◆ Forever popular restaurant, now serving a choice of dishes boasting trademark fresh, seasonal ingredients and famed lightness of touch. Loyal following for over 20 years.

XX **Zaika**

1 Kensington High St ✉ W8 5NP ⊖ High Street Kensington – ✆ (020) 7795 6533 – www.zaika-restaurant.co.uk – Fax (020) 7937 8854 – Closed 25-26 December, 1-2 January and Monday lunch **35**ABX**r**

Rest – Indian – Menu £ 25 (lunch) – Carte £ 30/40

◆ A converted bank, sympathetically restored, with original features and Indian artefacts adding plenty of colour. Well-organised service of modern and quite innovative Indian dishes.

XX **Whits**

21 Abingdon Rd ✉ W8 6AH ⊖ High Street Kensington – ✆ (020) 7938 1122 – www.whits.co.uk – Fax (020) 7938 1122 – Closed 23 December-6 January, Sunday and Monday **35**AAX**d**

Rest – Modern European – Menu £ 19/24 – Carte dinner £ 29/38

◆ Run by friendly owner. Bar runs length of lower level. Most diners migrate upstairs with its modish artwork and intimate tables. Modern cooking with generous portions.

XX **Memories of China**

353 Kensington High St ⊖ High Street Kensington – ✆ (020) 7603 6951 – www.memories-of-china.co.uk – Fax (020) 7603 0848 – Closed Christmas-New Year and Sunday lunch **35**AAY**v**

Rest – Chinese – *(booking essential)* Carte £ 26/48

◆ Subtle lighting and brightly coloured high-back chairs add to the modern feel of this Chinese restaurant. Screens separate the tables. Plenty of choice from extensive menu.

XX **Timo**

343 Kensington High St ✉ W8 6NW ⊖ High Street Kensington – ✆ (020) 7603 3888 – www.timorestaurant.net – Fax (020) 7603 8111 – Closed 25 December, Sunday and Bank Holidays **35**AAY**c**

Rest – Italian – Menu £ 18 (lunch) – Carte dinner £ 29/44

◆ Modern, personally run restaurant with unadorned walls and comfortable seating in brown suede banquettes. Italian menus of contemporary dishes and daily changing specials.

XX **L Restaurant & Bar**

2 Abingdon Rd ✉ W8 6AF ⊖ High Street Kensington – ✆ (020) 7795 6969 – www.l-restaurant.co.uk – Fax (020) 7795 6699 – Closed Monday lunch and Bank Holidays **35**AAX**x**

Rest – Spanish – Carte £ 26/34

◆ Wonderfully airy glass-roofed dining room with tastefully designed woodwork and mirrors. Authentic Iberian menus with an emphasis on tapas matched by good value wine list.

X **Kensington Place**

201-209 Kensington Church St ✉ W8 7LX ⊖ Notting Hill Gate – ✆ (020) 7727 3184 – www.kensingtonplace-restaurant.co.uk – Fax (020) 7792 8388 – Restricted opening Christmas-New Year **27**AAV**z**

Rest – Modern European – *(booking essential)* Menu £ 17/23 – Carte £ 31/42

◆ A cosmopolitan crowd still head for this establishment that set the trend for large, bustling and informal restaurants. Professionally run with skilled modern cooking.

Cibo

3 Russell Gdns ✉ W14 8EZ ⊖ Kensington Olympia – ✆ (020) 7371 6271 – www.ciborestaurant.net – Fax (020) 7602 1371 – Closed Christmas-New Year, Saturday lunch and Sunday dinner **16**MZE**b**

Rest – Italian – Carte £ 25/39

◆ Long-standing neighbourhood Italian with local following. More space at the back of the room. Robust, satisfying cooking; the huge grilled shellfish and seafood platter a speciality.

Malabar

27 Uxbridge St ✉ W8 7TQ ⊖ Notting Hill Gate – ✆ (020) 7727 8800 – www.malabar-restaurant.co.uk – Closed 1 week Christmas and August Bank Holiday **27**AAV**e**

Rest – Indian – *(buffet lunch Sunday)* Menu £ 24 **s** – Carte £ 23/44 **s**

◆ Indian restaurant in a residential location. Three rooms with individual personalities and informal service. Extensive range of good value dishes; particularly appealing vegetarian choice.

Wódka

12 St Albans Grove ✉ W8 5PN ⊖ High Street Kensington – ✆ (020) 7937 6513 – www.wodka.co.uk – Fax (020) 7937 8621 – Closed 25-26 December

Rest – Polish – *(dinner only and lunch October-December)* **35**ABX**c**

Menu £ 19 – Carte £ 23/30

◆ Warmly run, long-standing neighbourhood Polish restaurant. Robust and satisfying dishes, with plenty of game, alongside heartening soups; but desserts also reveal a lightness of touch.

South Kensington

The Pelham

15 Cromwell Pl ✉ SW7 2LA ⊖ South Kensington – ✆ (020) 7589 8288 – www.pelhamhotel.co.uk – Fax (020) 7584 8444 **36**ADY**z**

51 rm – †£ 182 ††£ 299/322, ☕ £ 17.50 – 1 suite

Rest *Bistro Fifteen* – *(Closed 25 December)* Menu £ 19/23 – Carte £ 35/46

◆ Immaculately kept, with willing staff and a discreet atmosphere. A mix of English country house and city town house; with panelled sitting room and library. Colourful all day bistro; candlelit at dinner, with European menu.

Blakes

rest,

33 Roland Gdns ✉ SW7 3PF ⊖ Gloucester Road – ✆ (020) 7370 6701 – www.blakeshotels.com – Fax (020) 7373 0442 **36**ACZ**n**

40 rm – †£ 173/225 ††£ 253/524, ☕ £ 25 – 8 suites **Rest** – Carte £ 60/69

◆ Behind the Victorian façade lies one of London's first 'boutique' hotels. Dramatic, bold and eclectic décor, with oriental influences and antiques from around the globe. Fashionable restaurant with bamboo and black walls.

NH Harrington Hall

5-25 Harrington Gdns ✉ SW7 4JB ⊖ Gloucester Road – ✆ (020) 7396 9696 – www.nh-hotels.com – Fax (020) 7396 1719 **36**ACY**n**

200 rm – †£ 115 ††£ 115/185, ☕ £ 18

Rest *Five 25* – Menu £ 16 – Carte £ 21/37

◆ Occupying 10 adjoining Victorian terraced houses and set over six floors. Contemporary guest areas; classically styled bedrooms with floral prints, plasma TVs and modern amenities. Smart restaurant offers wide-ranging menu.

Number Sixteen without rest

16 Sumner Pl ✉ SW7 3EG ⊖ South Kensington – ✆ (020) 7589 5232 – www.numbersixteenhotel.co.uk – Fax (020) 7584 8615 **36**ADY**d**

42 rm – †£ 141/235 ††£ 317, ☕ £ 17.50

◆ Enticingly refurbished 19C town houses in smart area. Discreet entrance, comfy sitting room and charming breakfast terrace. Bedrooms in English country house style.

The Cranley without rest

10 Bina Gardens ✉ SW5 0LA ⊖ Gloucester Road – ✆ (020) 7373 0123 – www.cranley.franklynhotels.com – Fax (020) 7373 9497 **36**ACY**c**

38 rm – †£ 138/276 ††£ 161/305, ☕ £ 25 – 1 suite

◆ Delightful Regency townhouse combines charm and period details with modern comforts and technology. Individually styled bedrooms; some with four-posters. Room service available.

LONDON

The Rockwell

181-183 Cromwell Rd ✉ SW5 0SF ⊖ Earl's Court – ✆ (020) 7244 2000 – www.therockwell.com – Fax (020) 7244 2001 **35**ABY**b**

40 rm – †£ 120 ††£ 176, ☕ £ 12.50 **Rest** – Carte £ 23/37

◆ Two Victorian houses with open, modern lobby and secluded, south-facing garden terrace. Bedrooms come in bold warm colours; 'Garden rooms' come with their own patios. Small dining room offers easy menu of modern European staples.

The Gore

190 Queen's Gate ✉ SW7 5EX ⊖ Gloucester Road – ✆ (020) 7584 6601 – www.gorehotel.com – Fax (020) 7589 8127 **36**ACX**n**

50 rm – †£ 207 ††£ 242, ☕ £ 16.95

Rest *190 Queensgate* – *(booking essential)* Menu £ 20/24 – Carte £ 26/42

◆ Idiosyncratic Victorian house, with lobby covered with pictures and prints. Individually styled bedrooms have discreet mod cons and charming bathrooms. Informal bistro with European menu.

Aster House without rest

3 Sumner Pl ✉ SW7 3EE ⊖ South Kensington – ✆ (020) 7581 5888 – www.asterhouse.com – Fax (020) 7584 4925 **36**ADY**t**

13 rm ☕ – †£ 92/156 ††£ 138/173

◆ End of terrace Victorian house with a pretty little rear garden and first floor conservatory. Ground floor rooms available. Useful location for visiting many tourist attractions.

Bombay Brasserie

Courtfield Rd ✉ SW7 4QH ⊖ Gloucester Road – ✆ (020) 7370 4040 – www.bombaybrasserielondon.com – Fax (020) 7835 1669 – Closed 25-26 December **36**ACY**y**

Rest – Indian – *(booking advisable at dinner)* Menu £ 22 (weekday lunch buffet) – Carte £ 34/47

◆ Plush new look for this well-run, well-known and comfortable Indian restaurant; very smart bar and conservatory with a show kitchen. More creative dishes now sit alongside the more traditional.

L'Etranger

36 Gloucester Rd ✉ SW7 4QT ⊖ Gloucester Road – ✆ (020) 7584 1118 – www.circagroupltd.co.uk – Fax (020) 7584 8886 – Closed 25 December and Saturday lunch **36**ACX**c**

Rest – Innovative – *(booking essential)* Menu £ 20 (lunch) – Carte £ 33/89

◆ Silks and lilacs create a stylish, atmospheric feel; ask for a corner table. Interesting menus incorporate techniques and flavours from Japanese cooking. Impressive wine and sake lists.

Pasha

1 Gloucester Rd ✉ SW7 4PP ⊖ Gloucester Road – ✆ (020) 7589 7969 – www.pasha-restaurant.co.uk – Fax (020) 7581 9996 – Closed 24-25 December and 1 January **36**ACX**r**

Rest – Moroccan – Menu £ 28 – Carte £ 24/42

◆ Relax over ground floor cocktails, then descend to mosaic floored restaurant where the rose-petal strewn tables are the ideal accompaniment to tasty Moroccan home cooking.

Cambio de Tercio

163 Old Brompton Rd ✉ SW5 0LJ ⊖ Gloucester Road – ✆ (020) 7244 8970 – www.cambiodetercio.co.uk – Fax (020) 7373 2359 – closed 2 weeks Christmas

Rest – Spanish – Carte £ 27/39 **36**ACZ**a**

◆ Good ingredients and authentic Spanish flavours; desserts are more contemporary. Choose tapas or regular menu. Service improves the more you visit. Owner also has tapas bar across the road.

Bangkok

9 Bute St ✉ SW7 3EY ⊖ South Kensington – ✆ (020) 7584 8529 – www.bankokrestaurant.co.uk – Closed Christmas-New Year, Sunday and Bank Holidays **36**ADY**b**

Rest – Thai – Carte £ 20/32

◆ This simple Thai bistro has been a popular local haunt for nearly 40 years. Guests can watch the chefs at work, preparing inexpensive and authentic dishes from the succinct menu.

Bumpkin

102 Old Brompton Road ✉ SW7 3RD ⊖ Gloucester Road – ☎ (020) 7341 0802 – www.bumpkinuk.com – Fax (020) 7835 0714 **36**ACY**r**

Rest – British – Carte £ 26/38

◆ Sister to the Notting Hill original with the same pub-like informality and friendly service. The kitchen champions British seasonal produce; the simpler dishes are the best ones.

NORTH KENSINGTON

The Portobello without rest

22 Stanley Gdns ✉ W11 2NG ⊖ Notting Hill Gate – ☎ (020) 7727 2777 – www.portobellohotel.co.uk – Fax (020) 7792 9641 – Closed 24-29 December

21 rm – †£ 150/200 ††£ 200/355, ☕ £ 17.50 **16**NZE**n**

◆ An attractive Victorian townhouse in an elegant terrace. Original and theatrical décor. Circular beds, half-testers, Victorian baths: no two bedrooms are the same.

Guesthouse West

163-165 Westbourne Grove ✉ W11 2RS ⊖ Notting Hill Gate – ☎ (020) 7792 9800 – www.guesthousewest.com – Fax (020) 7792 9797

20 rm – †£ 190/196 ††£ 190/196 **Rest** – Carte £ 22/32 **27**AAU**x**

◆ Attractive Edwardian house in the heart of Notting Hill, close to its shops and restaurants. Contemporary bedrooms boast the latest in audio visual gadgetry. Chic Parlour Bar for all day light dishes in a tapas style.

The Ledbury

127 Ledbury Rd ✉ W11 2AQ ⊖ Notting Hill Gate – ☎ (020) 7792 9090 – www.theledbury.com – Fax (020) 7792 9191 – Closed lunch over Christmas and 28-31 August **27**AAT**a**

Rest – French – Menu £ 25 (lunch £ 40 Sunday)/60 (dinner) – Carte lunch £ 38/47

Spec. Pheasant and herb tea with pheasant canapés. Skate wing in brown butter with asparagus and langoustines. Passion fruit soufflé with Sauternes ice cream.

◆ Elegant, understated surroundings with professional, well-organised service but it still has a neighbourhood feel. Highly skilled kitchen with an inherent understanding of flavour; great ingredients, especially game in season.

Notting Hill Brasserie

92 Kensington Park Rd ✉ W11 2PN ⊖ Notting Hill Gate – ☎ (020) 7229 4481 – www.nottinghillbrasserie.com – Fax (020) 7221 1246 – Closed 27-29 December

Rest – French – Menu £ 23/30 (lunch) – Carte £ 40/53 **27**AAU**a**

◆ Modern, comfortable restaurant with quiet, formal atmosphere, set over four small rooms. Authentic African artwork on walls. Contemporary dishes with European influence.

Edera

148 Holland Park Ave ✉ W11 4UE ⊖ Holland Park – ☎ (020) 7221 6090 – Fax (020) 7313 9700 **16**MZE**n**

Rest – Italian – Carte £ 31/44

◆ Split-level restaurant with outdoor tables. Modern Italian cooking uses some unusual ingredients and combinations. Sardinian specialities include Bottarga and homemade pastas.

E&O

14 Blenheim Crescent ✉ W11 1NN ⊖ Ladbroke Grove – ☎ (020) 7229 5454 – www.rickerrestaurants.com – Fax (020) 7229 5522 – Closed 25-26 December and August Bank Holiday **16**MZD**a**

Rest – Asian – Carte £ 22/44

◆ Mean, moody and cool: does that describe the surroundings or the A-list diners? Minimalist chic meets high sound levels. Menus scour Far East, with dishes meant for sharing.

Take note of the classification: you should not expect the same level of service in a X or 🏠 as in a XXXXX or 🏨.

LONDON

Bumpkin

209 Westbourne Park Rd ✉ W11 1EA ⊖ Westbourne Park – ✆ (020) 7243 9818 – www.bumpkinuk.com – Fax (020) 7229 1826 – Closed 25-26 December, 1 January and August Bank Holiday **27**AAT**b**

Rest – British – Menu £ 12 (2 course lunch) – Carte £ 24/39

Rest *Brasserie* – Menu £ 12 (2 course lunch) – Carte £ 29/40

◆ Converted pea-green pub with casual, clubby feel and wholesome philosophy of cooking seasonal, carefully sourced and organic food. Whisky tasting and private dining on top floors. First floor restaurant offers modern Mediterranean menu.

The Fat Badger

310 Portobello Road ✉ W10 5TA ⊖ Ladbroke Grove. – ✆ (020) 8969 4500 – www.thefatbadger.com **16**MZD**b**

Rest – British – Carte £ 20/29

◆ Large rustic pub with old sofas, chandeliers, upstairs dining room and some intriguing wallpaper. Seasonal and earthy British food, with whole beasts delivered to the kitchen.

LONDON

KINGSTON UPON THAMES – Greater London – pop. 146 873 12 A3

18 Hampton Court Palace Hampton Wick, ✆ (020) 8977 2423

Surbiton

The French Table

85 Maple Rd ✉ KT6 4AW – ✆ (020) 8399 2365 – www.thefrenchtable.co.uk – Fax (020) 8390 5353 – Closed 25-27 December, 1-11 January, Monday except in December and Sunday dinner **6**CY**a**

Rest – Mediterranean – Menu £ 23 (lunch) – Carte dinner £ 32/38

◆ Run by a husband and wife team; a narrow room with a lively, local atmosphere. Gutsy and satisfying French-Mediterranean cooking. Saturday morning cookery lessons.

LAMBETH – Greater London – pop. 267 785 12 B3

Brixton

Upstairs

89b Acre Lane ✉ SW2 5TN ⊖ Clapham North – ✆ (020) 7733 8855 – www.upstairslondon.com – Closed Easter 04-12 April, 15-31 August, 20 December-4 January, Sunday and Monday **24**SZH**b**

Rest – Modern European – *(dinner only)* Menu £ 26

◆ Entrance buzzer, then narrow stairs to first floor bar and second floor restaurant. Cosy, with simple, stylish décor. A mix of French and English cooking; neat and accurate.

Clapham Common

Trinity

4 The Polygon ✉ SW4 0JG ⊖ Clapham Common – ✆ (020) 7622 1199 – www.trinityrestaurant.co.uk – Fax (020) 7622 1166 – Closed 24-30 December, 1-3 January, Monday lunch and Sunday dinner **24**RZH**a**

Rest – Innovative – Menu £ 20 (Monday-Thursday) – Carte dinner £ 30/48

◆ Contemporary, stylish and bright restaurant with abstract art, crisp linen tablecloths and relaxed atmosphere. Original menu offers precise, artfully presented modern cooking.

Four O Nine

409 Clapham Rd, entrance on Landor Rd ✉ SW9 9BT ⊖ Clapham North – ✆ (020) 7737 0722 – www.fouronine.co.uk – Closed 24-26 December

Rest – Modern European – *(dinner only and Sunday lunch)* **24**SZH**c**

Carte £ 28/35

◆ Intimate, stylish first floor restaurant with secretive entrance. Crisp, unfussy, appetisingly presented food, with natural flavours to the fore. French/Italian influences.

Tsunami
Unit 3, 5-7 Voltaire Rd ✉ SW4 6DQ ⊖ Clapham North – ✆ (020) 7978 1610 – www.tsunamirestaurant.co.uk – Fax (020) 7978 1591 – Closed 24-26 December and 1 January **24**SZH**a**
Rest – Japanese – *(dinner only and lunch Saturday-Sunday)* Carte £ 22/31
◆ Stylish and lively surroundings in which to enjoy innovative and original modern Japanese cooking, with large, local following. A second branch now in Charlotte Street.

KENNINGTON

Lobster Pot
3 Kennington Lane ✉ SE11 4RG ⊖ Kennington – ✆ (020) 7582 5556 – www.lobsterpotrestaurant.co.uk – Closed Sunday and Monday **40**AOY**e**
Rest – French – Carte £ 34/54
◆ Family-run, with exuberant décor of fish tanks, portholes and even the sound of seagulls. Classic seafood menu with fruits de mer, plenty of oysters and daily specials. Good crêpes too.

SOUTHBANK

London Marriott H. County Hall 
Westminster Bridge Rd ✉ SE1 7PB ⊖ Westminster – ✆ (020) 7928 5200 – www.marriottcountyhall.com – Fax (020) 7928 5300
195 rm – †£ 448 ††£ 448, ☐ £ 20.95 – 5 suites **40**AMX**a**
Rest *County Hall* – ✆ (020) 7902 8000 *(closed 26 December)* Menu £ 28 – Carte £ 32/43
◆ Occupying the historic County Hall building. Many of the spacious and comfortable bedrooms enjoy river and Parliament outlook. Impressive leisure facilities. World famous views from restaurant.

Skylon
1 Southbank Centre, Belvedere Rd ✉ SE1 8XX ⊖ Waterloo – ✆ (020) 7654 7800 – www.skylonrestaurant.co.uk – Fax (020) 7654 7801 – Closed 25 December **32**AMV**a**
Rest – Modern European – Menu £ 18/43 – Carte £ 25/35
◆ 1950s style dining flagship in Royal Festival Hall. Grill with bar, river views and easy-to-eat menu. Restaurant offers more ambitious dishes, which means higher prices.

WEST DULWICH

The Rosendale
65 Rosendale Rd ⊖ West Dulwich (rail). – ✆ (020) 8670 0812 – www.therosendale.co.uk – Closed 1 January **7**FX**a**
Rest – Menu £ 24 (Thursday-Sunday) – Carte £ 14/29
◆ Huge, high-ceilinged former coaching inn with buzzy atmosphere and smart rear terrace. Local produce well-used; even the bread and butter are homemade. Outstanding wine list.

LEWISHAM – Greater London – pop. 248 922 **12** B3

BLACKHEATH

Chapters
43-45 Montpelier Vale ✉ SE3 0TJ – ✆ (020) 8333 2666 – www.chaptersrestaurants.com – Fax (020) 8355 8399 – Closed early January **8**HX**c**
Rest – Modern European – Carte £ 18/43
◆ A contemporary and bustling all day brasserie and bar at the top of town. Large, appealingly priced menu with British and Mediterranean influences, with meats cooked over charcoal a speciality.

FOREST HILL

The Dartmouth Arms
7 Dartmouth Road ✉ SE23 3HN ⊖ Forest Hill (rail). – ✆ (020) 8488 3117 – www.thedartmoutharms.com – Fax (020) 8699 9946 – Closed 25-26 December and 1 January **7**GX**a**
Rest – British – Menu £ 17 (dinner Monday-Thursday) – Carte £ 19/29
◆ Across the road from the train station, offering an appealing mix of dishes, commendable in their Britishness and inventiveness, and with a healthy regard for seasonality.

LONDON HEATHROW AIRPORT – see Hillingdon, London p. 87

MERTON – Greater London – pop. 187 908 12 B3

WIMBLEDON

Cannizaro House
West Side, Wimbledon Common ✉ SW19 4UE ⊖ Wimbledon – ✆ (020) 8879 1464 – www.cannizarohouse.com – Fax (020) 8879 7338 **6**DXY**x**
44 rm – †£ 395 ††£ 485 – 2 suites
Rest – Menu £ 26/29 – Carte except Sunday £ 30/40
◆ Part-Georgian mansion in a charming spot on the common. Appealing drawing room popular for afternoon tea. Rooms in original house are antique-furnished, some with balconies. Refined restaurant overlooks splendid formal garden.

Light House
75-77 Ridgway ✉ SW19 4ST ⊖ Wimbledon – ✆ (020) 8944 6338 – www.lighthousewimbledon.com – Fax (020) 8946 4440 – Closed 24-28 December and Sunday dinner **6**DY**n**
Rest – International – Menu £ 18 (lunch)/19 (midweek dinner before 7.30pm) – Carte £ 27/39
◆ Bright and modern neighbourhood restaurant with open-plan kitchen. Informal service of a weekly changing and diverse menu of progressive Italian/fusion dishes.

RICHMOND-UPON-THAMES – Greater London – pop. 172 335 12 B3

Old Town Hall, Whittaker Ave 020 8940 9125, info@visitrichmond.co.uk
Richmond Park Roehampton Gate, ✆ (020) 8876 3205
Sudbrook Park

BARNES

Sonny's
94 Church Rd ✉ SW13 0DQ – ✆ (020) 8748 0393 – www.sonnys.co.uk – Fax (020) 8748 2698 – Closed Sunday dinner and Bank Holidays
Rest – Modern European – Menu £ 19 – Carte £ 26/32 **21**KZH**x**
◆ Bright, modern and informal neighbourhood restaurant. Balanced set menu, with good choice of easy-to-eat dishes with European influences. Plenty of wines by the glass.

Riva
169 Church Rd ✉ SW13 9HR – ✆ (020) 8748 0434 – Fax (020) 8748 0434 – Closed last 2 weeks August, Christmas - New Year, Saturday lunch and Bank Holidays **21**LZH**a**
Rest – Italian – Carte £ 29/46
◆ A restaurant built on customer loyalty; the regulars are showered with attention from the eponymous owner. Gutsy, no-nonsense dishes, full of flavour. Interesting all-Italian wine list.

Le Provence
7 White Hart Lane ✉ SW13 0PX – ✆ (020) 8878 4092 – www.leprovence.co.uk – Closed Monday **21**KZH**c**
Rest – Mediterranean – Menu £ 15 (lunch) – Carte £ 21/31
◆ Sensibly priced menu mixes satisfying French classics with others of more Mediterranean provenance; set menu changes daily. Busy local atmosphere; ask for one of the cosy booths.

The Brown Dog
28 Cross Street ✉ SW13 0AP ⊖ Barnes Bridge (Rail). – ✆ (020) 8392 2200 – www.thebrowndog.co.uk – Closed 25-26 December **21**KZH**b**
Rest – Carte £ 22/29
◆ Horseshoe bar, snug lounge and separate dining room; charming décor includes cast iron fireplaces, antique furniture and space age lamps. Seasonal menu; tasty, moreish food.

East Sheen

Mango & Silk

199 Upper Richmond Rd West ✉ SW14 8 QT – ✆ (020) 8876 6220 – www.mangoandsilk.co.uk – Fax (020) 8878 2056 – Closed Monday

Rest – Indian – *(dinner only and Sunday lunch)* Carte approx. £ 21 **21**KZH**k**

◆ An air of calm pervades the restaurant, thanks to the charming owner. Udit Sarkhel is the chef and his cooking is as expertly crafted as ever. The generous prices make over-ordering the easy option.

The Victoria with rm

✉ SW14 7RT ⊖ Mortlake (rail). – ✆ (020) 8876 4238 – www.thevictoria.net – Fax (020) 8878 3464 – Closed 2 days between Christmas and New Year

7 rm – £ 105 ££ 115 **Rest** – Carte £ 23/38 **6**CX**u**

◆ The same menu is served in the relaxed bar and the conservatory restaurant with its wood-burning stove. Earthy, flavoursome cooking; rotisserie on the large terrace in summer. Brightly decorated bedrooms.

Kew

The Glasshouse

14 Station Parade ✉ TW9 3PZ ⊖ Kew Gardens – ✆ (020) 8940 6777 – www.glasshouserestaurant.co.uk – Fax (020) 8940 3833 – Closed 24-26 December and 1 January **6**CX**z**

Rest – Modern European – Menu £ 24/38

Spec. Confit salmon with onion seed wafers. Rump of lamb with spiced cous cous, falafels and coriander. Apple financier with butterscotch sauce and crème fraîche.

◆ Celebrated 10 years in 2009. Bright and relaxed interior, with palpable sense of neighbourhood and affable service. Balanced dishes are full of flavour, from a varied and appealing menu influenced by France and other southern European countries.

Kew Grill

10b Kew Green ✉ TW9 3BH ⊖ Kew Gardens – ✆ (020) 8948 4433 – www.awtrestaurants.com – Fax (020) 8605 3532 – Closed Monday lunch

Rest – Beef specialities – *(booking essential)* Menu £ 15 (lunch) – Carte £ 22/51 **6**CV**u**

◆ Just off Kew Green, this long, narrow restaurant has a Mediterranean style and feel. Grilled specialities employ top-rate ingredients: the beef is hung for 35 days.

A Taste of McClements

8 Station Approach ✉ TQ9 3QB ⊖ Kew Gardens – ✆ (020) 8940 6617 – www.tasteofmclements.com **6**CX**r**

Rest – Traditional – Menu £ 18/45

◆ 'Fine dining' courtesy of local restaurateur John McClements, in what was once his fish shop. Classically based cooking, with set menu of many courses. Thoughtfully compiled wine list.

Ma Cuisine

The Old Post Office, 9 Station Approach ✉ TW9 3QB ⊖ Kew Gardens – ✆ (020) 8332 1923 – www.macuisinekew.co.uk **6**CX**r**

Rest – French – Menu £ 15/18 – Carte lunch £ 20/30

◆ Formerly Kew's post office building; it now features tables on the pavement, an arched roof and red gingham tablecloths. Good value, classic French dishes are sure to satisfy.

Richmond

Petersham

Nightingale Lane ✉ TW10 6UZ – ✆ (020) 8939 1084 – www.petershamhotel.co.uk – Fax (020) 8939 1002 – Closed 24-26 December

60 rm – £ 135/160 ££ 170 – 1 suite **6**CX**c**

Rest ***The Restaurant at The Petersham*** – see restaurant listing

◆ Extended over the years, a fine example of Victorian Gothic architecture. Impressive Portland stone, self-supporting staircase. Most comfortable rooms overlook the Thames.

LONDON

Bingham

61-63 Petersham Rd – (020) 8940 0902 – www.thebingham.co.uk – Fax (020) 8948 8737 **6**CX**c**

15 rm – £ 219/328 £ 219/328, £ 15

Rest Bingham Restaurant – *see restaurant listing*

◆ A pair of conjoined and restored Georgian townhouses; a short walk from Richmond centre. Ask for a room overlooking the river and garden. Contemporary styled bedrooms; some with four-posters.

The Restaurant at The Petersham – at Petersham Hotel

Nightingale Lane ✉ TW10 6UZ – (020) 8939 1084/8940 7471 – www.petershamhotel.co.uk – Fax (020) 8939 1002 – Closed 24-26 December and Sunday **6**CX**c**

Rest – French – Menu £ 26 (lunch) – Carte £ 31/47

◆ Tables by the window have spectacular views across royal parkland and the winding Thames. Formal surroundings in which to enjoy classic and modern cooking. See the cellars.

Bingham Restaurant – at Bingham Hotel

61-63 Petersham Road ✉ TW1O 6UT – (020) 8940 0902 – www.thebingham.co.uk – Fax (020) 8948 8737 **6**CX**c**

Rest – Modern European – *(Closed Sunday dinner)* Menu £ 23/39

Spec. Brill fillet with scallop, ricotta gnocchi and poached grapes. Sea trout with broad beans, foie gras and pickled mushrooms. Chocolate tart with orange chantilly and sorbet.

◆ On a summer's day, sit on the balcony terrace overlooking the garden and the Thames. Well-meaning and courteous service; comfortable room, slightly frayed. Cooking that is accomplished and precise; delicate in presentation but assured in flavour.

Petersham Nurseries Café

Church Lane (off Petersham Rd) ✉ TW10 7AG – (020) 8605 3627 – www.petershamnurseries.com – Closed Easter and 25 December **6**CX**x**

Rest – Italian influences – *(lunch only)* Carte £ 33/50

◆ Uniquely set in glasshouse (or outside, if sunny), with earthy implements and charming Indian artefacts. Flavourful cooking with Italian influences; friendly service from welly-shod staff.

Swagat

86 Hill Rise ✉ TW10 6UB ⊖ Richmond – (0208) 940 7557 – swagatindiancuisine.co.uk – Closed Sunday **6**CX**i**

Rest – Indian – *(dinner only)* Menu £ 25 – Carte £ 28/31

◆ Well-meaning service and an appealing menu have made this Indian restaurant popular with locals so it's worth booking. Plenty of classics and vegetarian choices; try the less familiar.

Matsuba

10 Red Lion St ✉ TW9 1RW – (020) 8605 3513 – www.matsuba.co.uk – Closed 25-26 December, 1 January and Sunday **6**CX**n**

Rest – Japanese – Menu £ 35/45 – Carte £ 15/24

◆ Family-run Japanese restaurant with just 11 tables; understated but well-kept appearance. Extensive menu offers wide range of Japanese dishes, along with bulgogi, a Korean barbecue dish.

TEDDINGTON

Simply Thai

196 Kingston Rd ✉ TW11 9JD – (020) 8943 9747 – www.simplythai-restaurant.co.uk – Closed Easter, 25 December and Sunday lunch **5**BY**x**

Rest – Thai – *(booking essential at lunch)* Menu £ 18 – Carte £ 24/28

◆ Owner does the cooking and her passion is palpable. Modern twists are added to traditional dishes; seafood is the highlight and there's an emphasis on healthy eating. Charming service.

Fancy a last minute break?
Check hotel websites to take advantage of price promotions.

TWICKENHAM

A Cena

418 Richmond Rd ✉ TW1 2EB ⊖ Richmond – ✆ (020) 8288 0108 – www.acena.co.uk – Fax (020) 8940 5346 – Closed 24-26 December, Sunday dinner and Monday lunch **5**BX**e**

Rest – Italian – Carte £ 25/34

◆ Rustic and quite intimate feel to this well-run neighbourhood Italian restaurant. Appealing, seasonal menu covers most of Italy and the generously sized dishes are full of flavour.

The Grill Room

2 Whitton Rd – ✆ (020) 8891 0803 – www.thegrillroomtw1.co.uk **5**BX**a**

Rest – Beef specialities – Carte £ 22/33

◆ Classic steakhouse menu, with cuts sourced from across the UK and all hung on the premises for between 32 and 42 days. Other favourite British dishes available. Try reserving one of the booths.

Tangawizi

406 Richmond Rd, Richmond Bridge ✉ TW1 2EB ⊖ Richmond – ✆ (020) 8891 3737 – www.tangawizi.co.uk – Fax (020) 8891 3737 – Closed 25 December

Rest – Indian – *(dinner only)* Carte £ 14/28 **5**BX**e**

◆ Name means Ginger in Swahili. Sleek décor in warm purple with subtle Indian touches. Well-priced, nicely balanced, slowly evolving menus take their influence from north India.

Brula

43 Crown Rd, St Margarets ✉ TW1 3EJ – ✆ (020) 8892 0602 – www.brula.co.uk – Fax (020) 8892 7727 – Closed 25-30 December, Mondays in August and Sunday dinner **5**BX**v**

Rest – French – *(booking essential)* Menu £ 15 (lunch) – Carte £ 20/29

◆ French brasserie in look, with mirrors and chandeliers. Good value, well-crafted cooking is largely French but now comes with other European influences. Friendly service and popular with locals.

Ma Cuisine

6 Whitton Rd ✉ TW1 1BJ – ✆ (020) 8607 9849 – www.macuisinetw1.co.uk

Rest – French – Menu £ 15 (lunch) – Carte £ 20/30 **5**BX**a**

◆ Small neighbourhood bistro-style restaurant offering particularly good value and classic French country cooking. Check out the blackboard specials. Part of a small group.

SOUTHWARK – Greater London – pop. 243 749 **12** B3

ℹ Level 2, Tate Modern, Bankside ✆ (020) 7401 5266, tourisminfo@southwark.gov.uk

BERMONDSEY

Hilton London Tower Bridge

5 More London Place, Tooley St ✉ SE1 2BY ⊖ London Bridge – ✆ (020) 3002 4300 – www.hilton.co.uk/towerbridge – Fax (020) 3002 4350 **34**ARV**e**

245 rm – †£ 240/355 ††£ 240/355, ☕ £ 19.50 **Rest** – Carte £ 30/45

◆ Usefully located new-style Hilton hotel with boldly decorated open-plan lobby. Contemporary bedrooms boast well-designed features; 4 floors of executive rooms. Dine on classics and comfort food in restaurant with outdoor seating.

London Bridge

8-18 London Bridge St ✉ SE1 9SG ⊖ London Bridge – ✆ (020) 7855 2200 – www.londonbridgehotel.com – Fax (020) 7855 2233 **33**AQV**a**

138 rm – †£ 232 ††£ 232, ☕ £ 15 – 3 suites

Rest *Georgetown* – Malaysian – Menu £ 17 (lunch) – Carte £ 21/44

Rest *Londinium* – *(dinner only)* Carte £ 25/35

◆ In one of the oldest parts of London, independently owned with an ornate façade dating from 1915. Modern interior with classically decorated bedrooms and an impressive gym. Georgetown for appealing Malaysian cuisine. Londinium for brasserie dining.

Bermondsey Square

Bermondsey Sq, Tower Bridge Rd ✉ SE1 3UN ⊖ London Bridge – ✆ (0870) 111 2525 – www.bermondseysquarehotel.co.uk – Fax (0870) 111 2526 **20**XZE**n**

79 rm – †£ 119/169 ††£ 119/169, ☕ £ 10

Rest ***Alfie's*** – English – Menu £ 10/15 – Carte £ 24/29

◆ Opened in 2009 in hip, regenerated square. Cleverly designed hotel, with subtle '60s influence and fun feel. Well-equipped rooms, including four loft suites. English menu in Alfie's makes good use of local food markets.

Le Pont de la Tour

36d Shad Thames, Butlers Wharf ✉ SE1 2YE ⊖ London Bridge – ✆ (020) 7403 8403 – www.lepontdelatour.co.uk – Fax (020) 7940 1835

Rest – French – Menu £ 32/43 **34**ASV**c**

◆ Elegant and stylish room commanding spectacular views of the Thames and Tower Bridge. Formal and detailed service. Modern menu with an informal bar attached.

Bengal Clipper

Cardamom Building, Shad Thames, Butlers Wharf ✉ SE1 2YR ⊖ London Bridge – ✆ (020) 7357 9001 – www.bengalclipper.co.uk – Fax (020) 7357 9002

Rest – Indian – Menu £ 15 – Carte £ 23/29 **34**ASV**e**

◆ Housed in a Thameside converted warehouse, a smart Indian restaurant with original brickwork and steel supports. Menu features Bengali and Goan dishes. Evening pianist.

Vivat Bacchus London Bridge

4 Hays Lane (basement) ✉ SE1 2HB ⊖ London Bridge – ✆ (0207) 234 0891 – www.vivatbacchus.co.uk – Fax (0207) 357 7021 – Closed Christmas-New Year, Sunday and Bank Holidays **34**ARV**n**

Rest – Traditional – Menu £ 12 (lunch) – Carte £ 21/34

◆ South African element to both the menu and the very impressive wine list. International platters in ground floor wine bar; robust cooking in the basement restaurant, with its great cheese room.

Blueprint Café

Design Museum, Shad Thames, Butlers Wharf ✉ SE1 2YD ⊖ London Bridge – ✆ (020) 7378 7031 – www.danddlondon.com – Closed 25 December and Sunday dinner **34**ASV**u**

Rest – Modern European – Menu £ 23/28 **s** – Carte £ 26/40 **s**

◆ Above the Design Museum, with impressive views of the river and bridge: handy binoculars on tables. Eager and energetic service, modern British menus: robust and rustic.

Magdalen

152 Tooley St ✉ SE1 2TU ⊖ London Bridge – ✆ (020) 7403 1342 – www.magdalenrestaurant.co.uk – Fax (020) 7403 9950 – Closed last 2 weeks August, 24 December - 4 January, Saturday lunch and Sunday **34**ARV**b**

Rest – British – Menu £ 19 (lunch) – Carte £ 27/45

◆ Appealing bistro-style restaurant set over two floors, with aubergine-coloured walls and chandeliers. Seasonal menus offer precise, well-executed and simply presented cooking.

Village East

171-173 Bermondsey St ✉ SE1 3UW ⊖ London Bridge – ✆ (020) 7357 6082 – www.villageeast.co.uk – Fax (020) 7403 3360 – Closed 24-27 December

Rest – Modern European – Menu £ 13 (2 course lunch)/30 – Carte £ 26/37 **20**XZE**a**

◆ In a glass-fronted block sandwiched by Georgian townhouses, this trendy restaurant has two loud, buzzy bars and dining areas serving ample portions of modern British fare.

Cantina Del Ponte

36c Shad Thames, Butlers Wharf ✉ SE1 2YE ⊖ London Bridge – ✆ (020) 7403 5403 – www.cantina.co.uk **34**ASV**c**

Rest – Italian – Menu £ 14/19 – Carte £ 25/37

◆ An Italian stalwart, refurbished late in 2007. Simple menu offers an appealing mix of classic dishes, with a good value set menu until 7pm. Riverside setting with pleasant terrace.

Butlers Wharf Chop House

36e Shad Thames, Butlers Wharf ✉ SE1 2YE ⊖ London Bridge – ✆ (020) 7403 3403 – www.chophouse.co.uk – Fax (020) 7940 1855 – Closed 1-3 January and Sunday dinner in winter **34**ASV**n**

Rest – British – Menu £ 26 – Carte £ 28/47

◆ Grab a table on the terrace in summer and dine in the shadow of Tower Bridge. Rustic feel to the interior; noisy and fun. The menu focuses on traditional English ingredients and dishes.

Champor-Champor

62-64 Weston St ✉ SE1 3QJ ⊖ London Bridge – ✆ (020) 7403 4600 – www.champor-champor.com – Closed 1 week Easter, 1 week Christmas, Sunday and Bank Holidays **34**ARV**a**

Rest – Asian – *(dinner only) (booking essential)* Menu £ 32

◆ Brims over with colourful Asian décor and artefacts including serene Buddha and sacred cow. Two intimate dining rooms: tasty, appealing mix of Malay, Chinese and Thai cuisine.

The Garrison

99-101 Bermondsey St ✉ SE1 3XB ⊖ London Bridge. – ✆ (020) 7089 9355 – www.thegarrison.co.uk – Closed 25-26 December and 1 January **20**XZE**z**

Rest – *(booking essential at dinner)* Menu £ 14 – Carte £ 28/45

◆ Part shabby-chic gastropub, part boho brasserie, with booths, bustling vibe and mini cinema for private dining. Wholesome, homemade, no-nonsense cooking and organic ales.

Elephant and Castle

Dragon Castle

114 Walworth Rd ✉ SE17 1JL ⊖ Elephant and Castle – ✆ (020) 7277 3388 – www.dragoncastle.eu – Closed 24-25 December **25**VZF**x**

Rest – Chinese – Menu £ 23 – Carte £ 20/44

◆ Large blue building with red studded door and decoratively understated interior. Generous plates of authentic Cantonese food plus popular dim sum menu. Attentive service.

Southwark

Southwark Rose

43-47 Southwark Bridge Rd ✉ SE1 9HH ⊖ London Bridge – ✆ (020) 7015 1480 – www.southwarkrosehotel.co.uk – Fax (020) 7015 1481 **33**AQV**c**

78 rm – †£ 95/190 ††£ 95/190, ☕ £ 12.95 – 6 suites

Rest – *(dinner only)* Carte £ 10/21 **s**

◆ Purpose-built budget hotel south of the City, near the Globe Theatre. Top floor dining room with bar. Uniform style, reasonably spacious bedrooms with writing desks.

Oxo Tower

Oxo Tower Wharf, (8th floor), Barge House St ✉ SE1 9PH ⊖ Southwark – ✆ (020) 7803 3888 – www.harveynichols.com – Fax (020) 7803 3838 – Closed 25-26 and dinner 24 December **32**ANV**a**

Rest – Carte £ 34/53

Rest ***Oxo Tower Brasserie*** – see restaurant listing

◆ Top of a converted factory, providing stunning views of the Thames and beyond. Stylish, minimalist interior with huge windows. Modern, mostly European, cuisine.

Roast

The Floral Hall, Borough Market ✉ SE1 1TL ⊖ London Bridge – ✆ (0845) 034 7300 – www.roast-restaurant.com – Fax (0845) 034 7301 – Closed 25-26 December, 1-2 January and Sunday dinner **33**AQV**e**

Rest – British – *(booking essential)* Carte £ 32/63

◆ Set into the roof of Borough Market's Floral Hall. Extensive cocktail list in bar; split-level restaurant has views to St Paul's. Robust English cooking uses market produce.

Baltic

74 Blackfriars Rd ✉ SE1 8HA ⊖ Southwark – ✆ (020) 7928 1111 – www.balticrestaurant.co.uk – Fax (020) 7928 8487 – Closed 25-26 December

Rest – Eastern European – Menu £ 18 – Carte £ 20/30 **33**AOV**e**

◆ Set in a Grade II listed 18C former coach house. Enjoy authentic and hearty east European and Baltic influenced food. Interesting vodka selection and live jazz on Sundays.

Oxo Tower Brasserie

(8th floor), Oxo Tower Wharf, Barge House St ✉ SE1 9PH ⊖ Southwark – ✆ (020) 7803 3888 – www.harveynichols.com – Fax (020) 7803 3838 – Closed 25 -26 and dinner 24 December **32**ANV**a**

Rest – Menu £ 25 (lunch) – Carte £ 26/45

◆ Same views but less formal and more fun than the restaurant. Open-plan kitchen produces a modern, easy to eat and quite light menu. In summer, try to secure a table on the terrace.

Cantina Vinopolis

No.1 Bank End ✉ SE1 9BU ⊖ London Bridge – ✆ (020) 7940 8333 – www.cantinavinopolis.com – Fax (020) 7089 9339 – closed Sunday dinner and Bank Holidays **33**AQV**z**

Rest – International – Menu £ 30 – Carte £ 23/34

◆ Large, solid brick vaulted room under Victorian railway arches, with an adjacent wine museum. Modern menu with a huge selection of wines by the glass.

Tate Modern (Restaurant)

Tate Modern, 7th Floor, Bankside ✉ SE1 9TG ⊖ Southwark – ✆ (020) 7887 8888 – www.tate.org.uk/modern/eatanddrink – Fax (020) 7401 5171 – Closed 24-26 December **33**APV**s**

Rest – British – *(lunch only and dinner Friday-Saturday)* Menu £ 20 (lunch) – Carte dinner £ 23/33

◆ 7th floor restaurant with floor to ceilings windows on two sides and large mural. Appealing mix of light and zesty dishes, with seasonal produce. Good choice of wines and non-alcoholic drinks.

Tapas Brindisa

18-20 Southwark St, Borough Market ✉ SE1 1TJ ⊖ London Bridge – ✆ (020) 7357 8880 – www.brindisatapaskitchens.com **33**AQV**k**

Rest – Spanish – *(bookings not accepted)* Carte £ 21/35

◆ Prime quality Spanish produce sold in owner's shops and this bustling eatery on edge of Borough Market. Freshly prepared, tasty tapas: waiters will assist with your choice.

Wright Brothers

11 Stoney St, Borough Market ✉ SE1 9AD ⊖ London Bridge – ✆ (020) 7403 9554 – www.wrightbros.eu.com – Fax (020) 7403 9558 – Closed Christmas - New Year, Sunday and Bank Holidays **33**AQV**m**

Rest – Seafood – Carte £ 20/33

◆ Classic style oyster and porter house – a large number of porter ales on offer. Simple settings afford a welcoming ambience to enjoy huge range of oysters and prime shellfish.

Brew Wharf

Brew Wharf Yard, Stoney St ✉ SE1 9AD ⊖ London Bridge – ✆ (020) 7378 6601 – www.brewwharf.com – Fax (020) 7940 5997 – Closed Christmas-New Year and Sunday **33**AQV**h**

Rest – Traditional – Carte £ 19/29

◆ Bustling market eatery and micro-brewery housed in three huge railway arches. The beers and concise wine list are the reasons most people come here; menus are quite simple.

The Anchor & Hope

36 The Cut ✉ SE1 8LP ⊖ Southwark. – ✆ (020) 7928 9898 – Fax (020) 7928 4595 – Closed Sunday dinner and Monday lunch

Rest – British – *(bookings not accepted)* Carte £ 20/35 **32**ANV**n**

◆ Close to Waterloo and both Vic theatres; no reservations so get here early to avoid waiting. Rustic feel of bare floorboards and simple furniture is matched perfectly by the bold and earthy cooking.

Each starred restaurant lists three specialities that are typical of its style of cuisine. These may not always be on the menu but in their place expect delicious seasonal dishes. Be sure to try them.

Bow

The Morgan Arms

43 Morgan St ✉ E3 5AA ⊖ Bow Road. – ✆ (020) 8980 6389 – www.geronimo-inns.co.uk – Closed 25-26 December **3GUc**

Rest – *(bookings not accepted)* Carte £ 20/31

◆ Characterful pub with mismatch of furniture and shabby-chic appeal. Constantly evolving menu offers robust cooking, using some unusual and sometimes unfamiliar ingredients.

Canary Wharf

Four Seasons

Westferry Circus ✉ E14 8RS ⊖ Canary Wharf – ✆ (020) 7510 1999 – www.fourseasons.com/canarywharf – Fax (020) 7510 1998 **3GVa**

128 rm – 🚹£ 259/288 🚹🚹£ 259/288, ☕ £ 25 – 14 suites

Rest *Quadrato* – see restaurant listing

◆ Sleek and stylish international hotel with striking river and city views. Atrium lobby leading to modern bedrooms boasting every conceivable extra. Detailed and professional service.

Quadrato – at Four Seasons Hotel

Westferry Circus ✉ E14 8RS ⊖ Canary Wharf – ✆ (020) 7510 1999 – Fax (020) 7510 1998 **3GVa**

Rest – Italian – Menu £ 25 – Carte £ 27/44

◆ Striking, modern restaurant with terrace overlooking river. Sleek, stylish dining room with glass-fronted open-plan kitchen. Menu of northern Italian dishes; swift service.

Dockmaster's House

1 Hertsmere Road – ✆ (020) 7345 0345 – www.dockmastershouse.com – Closed Saturday lunch and Sunday **3GVr**

Rest – Indian – *(booking advisable)* Menu £ 21 (lunch and early dinner 6pm-7.15pm) – Carte £ 29/39

◆ A contemporary overhaul of a three storey Georgian house in the shadow of Canary Wharf's skyscrapers has created this slick operation. Elaborate Indian cooking, although sometimes a little pretentious.

Plateau

Canada Place, (4th floor) Canada Square ✉ E14 5ER ⊖ Canary Wharf – ✆ (020) 7715 7100 – www.plateaurestaurant.co.uk – Fax (020) 7715 7110 – Closed 25-26 December, 1 January, Sunday and Bank Holidays **3GVn**

Rest – Modern European – Menu £ 35 – Carte £ 29/40

◆ Impressive open-plan space with dramatic glass walls and ceilings and striking 1970s design. Rotisserie meats in the Grill; globally-influenced dishes in formal restaurant.

The Gun

27 Coldharbour ✉ E14 9NS ⊖ Blackwall (DLR). – ✆ (020) 7515 5222 – www.thegundocklands.com – Fax (020) 7515 4407 – Closed 25 December **7GVx**

Rest – Carte £ 21/30

◆ A restored 18C pub in cobbled street with proud history and views of the O2 Arena. European influences to dishes and daily fish from Billingsgate the best choice. Professional service.

Limehouse

The Narrow

44 Narrow Street ✉ E14 8DP ⊖ Limehouse (DLR). – ✆ (020) 7592 7950 – www.gordonramsay.com – Fax (020) 7592 1603 **3GVo**

Rest – *(booking essential)* Carte £ 21/27

◆ Grade II listed former dockmaster's house on the river; part of Gordon Ramsay's group. Menu specialises in British favourites, from shrimps to sardines, braised beef to trifle.

MILE END

L'Oasis

237 Mile End Rd ✉ E1 4AA ⊖ Stepney Green. – ✆ (020) 7702 7051 – www.loasisstepney.co.uk **3**GVU**e**

Rest – Carte £ 20/30

◆ Affable owner keeps this narrow, neighbourhood Victorian pub warm and welcoming. Cooking combines satisfyingly stout dishes like sausages and pies with more European influences like meze.

SPITALFIELDS

Les Trois Garcons

1 Club Row ✉ E1 6JX ⊖ Shoreditch – ✆ (020) 7613 1924 – www.lestroisgarcons.com – Fax (020) 7012 1236 – Closed 16-31 August, 23 December-10 January, Sunday and most Bank Holidays **20**XZD**r**

Rest – French – *(dinner only and lunch in December)* Menu £ 31 – Carte £ 50/68

◆ Extraordinarily eccentric, with stuffed animals, twinkling beads, assorted chandeliers and ceiling handbags. The French food is more traditional and governed by the seasons.

Hawksmoor

157 Commercial Rd ✉ E1 6BJ ⊖ Shoreditch – ✆ (020) 7247 7392 – www.thehawksmoor.com – Closed 25 December, Saturday lunch, Sunday and Bank Holidays **20**XZD**s**

Rest – Beef specialities – *(booking advisable)* Carte £ 27/70

◆ Unremarkable surroundings and ordinary starters and puds but no matter: this is all about great British beef, hung for 35 days, from Longhorn cattle in the heart of the Yorkshire Moors.

St John Bread and Wine

94-96 Commercial St ✉ E1 6LZ ⊖ Shoreditch – ✆ (020) 7251 0848 – www.stjohnbreadandwine.com – Fax (020) 7247 8924 – Closed Christmas-New Year and Bank Holidays **20**XZD**m**

Rest – British – Carte £ 23/27

◆ Part-wine shop/bakery and local restaurant. Highly seasonal and appealing menu changes twice a day; cooking is British, uncomplicated and very satisfying. Try the less familiar dishes.

WAPPING

Wapping Food

Wapping Wall ✉ E1W 3SG ⊖ Wapping – ✆ (020) 7680 2080 – www.thewappingproject.com – Closed 23 December-3 January, Sunday dinner and Bank Holidays **20**YZE**n**

Rest – Modern European – Carte £ 25/39

◆ Something a little unusual; a combination of restaurant and gallery in a converted hydraulic power station. Enjoy the unfussy, modern menu surrounded by turbines and art.

WHITECHAPEL

Cafe Spice Namaste

16 Prescot St ✉ E1 8AZ ⊖ Tower Hill – ✆ (020) 7488 9242 – www.cafespice.co.uk – Fax (020) 7481 0508 – Closed Christmas-New Year, Saturday lunch, Sunday and Bank Holidays **34**ASU**z**

Rest – Indian – Menu £ 30 – Carte £ 25/37

◆ A riot of colour from the brightly painted walls to the flowing drapes. Sweet natured service adds to the engaging feel. Fragrant and competitively priced Indian cooking.

Whitechapel Gallery Dining Room

77-82 Whitechapel High St ✉ E1 7QX Whitechapel ⊖ Aldgate East – ✆ (020) 7522 7896 – www.whitechapelgallery.com – Fax (020) 7522 7896 – Closed 24 December-2 January, Sunday dinner and Monday **34**AST**x**

Rest – Mediterranean – *(booking advisable)* Menu £ 20 (lunch) – Carte £ 26/31

◆ The Gallery was founded in 1901 and expanded in 2009 with the creation of this sweet, tightly packed restaurant. Concise seasonal menu; British produce with Mediterranean flavours.

BALHAM

Brasserie James

47 Balham Hill ✉ SW12 9DR ⊖ Clapham South – ✆ (020) 8772 0057 – www.brasseriejames.com – Closed one week Christmas and Sunday dinner

Rest – Modern European – Menu £ 14/16 – Carte £ 26/32 **6**EX**x**

◆ Crisp and neat brasserie owned and run by former Conran/D&D chef. Something for everyone on the seasonal menu, from moules to pasta. Weekend brunches; good value set menus; wines by carafe.

Lamberts

2 Station Parade ✉ SW12 9AZ ⊖ Balham – ✆ (020) 8675 2233 – www.lambertsrestaurant.com – Closed 25-26 December, 1-2 January, Sunday dinner and Monday **6**EX**n**

Rest – Traditional – *(dinner only and lunch Saturday-Sunday)* Carte £ 26/36

◆ Simple restaurant offering unfussy, generous dishes of quality produce in a casual environment. Sensibly priced, seasonal à la carte menu; classical cooking, modern presentation.

Harrison's

15-19 Bedford Hill ✉ SW12 9EX ⊖ Balham – ✆ (020) 8675 6900 – www.harrisonsbalham.co.uk – Fax (020) 8673 3965 – Closed 24-27 December

Rest – Mediterranean – Menu £ 17 – Carte £ 21/33 **6**EX**a**

◆ Sister to Sam's Brasserie in Chiswick. Open all day, with an appealing list of favourites, from fishcakes to Cumberland sausages. Weekend brunches; kids' menu; good value weekday set menus.

The Avalon

16 Balham Hill ✉ SW12 9EB ⊖ Clapham South. – ✆ (020) 8675 8613 – www.theavalonlondon.com – Closed 25-26 December **6**EX**r**

Rest – *(booking advisable)* Carte £ 21/32

◆ Fully renovated pub that has a suitably mythical edge to its aesthetic. Tiled rear dining room with plenty of bustle. Menu combines British and Mediterranean influences in no-nonsense cooking.

BATTERSEA

Chada

208-210 Battersea Park Rd ✉ SW11 4ND – ✆ (020) 7622 2209 – www.chadathai.com – Fax (020) 7924 2791 – Closed Sunday and Bank Holidays **23**QZH**x**

Rest – Thai – *(dinner only)* Carte £ 23/32

◆ Weather notwithstanding, the Thai ornaments and charming staff in traditional silk costumes transport you to Bangkok. Carefully prepared and authentic dishes.

Ransome's Dock

35-37 Parkgate Rd ✉ SW11 4NP – ✆ (020) 7223 1611 – www.ransomesdock.co.uk – Fax (020) 7924 2614 – Closed Christmas, August Bank Holiday and Sunday dinner **23**QZG**c**

Rest – Modern European – Carte £ 22/41

◆ Secreted in a warehouse development, with a dockside terrace in summer. Vivid blue interior, crowded with pictures. Chef patron produces reliable brasserie-style cuisine.

Tom Ilić

123 Queenstown Rd ✉ SW8 3RH – ✆ (020) 7622 0555 – www.tomilic.com – Closed dinner 25-31 December, Sunday dinner, Monday and Tuesday lunch

Rest – Traditional – *(booking essential)* Menu £ 17/22 – Carte £ 22/30 **24**RZH**c**

◆ Bold flavours, plenty of offal and quite a lot of pork are features of this popular, neighbourhood restaurant. Simply decorated with closely set tables and a semi-open kitchen.

The Butcher & Grill

39-41 Parkgate Rd ✉ SW11 4NP – ✆ (020) 7924 3999 – www.thebutcherandgrill.com – Fax (020) 7223 7977 – Closed 25-26 December and dinner Sunday and Bank Holidays **23**QZG**c**

Rest – Traditional – Menu £ 15 (weekdays) – Carte £ 12/49

◆ Former warehouse converted into butcher's-cum-deli-cum-steakhouse. Tables on two levels; comes alive in the evenings. Quality raw ingredients, from lamb burgers and cutlets to rib-eyes and T-bones.

The Bolingbroke

174 Northcote Rd ✉ SW11 6RE ⊖ Clapham Junction (rail). – ✆ (020) 7228 4040 – www.thebolingbroke.com – Fax (020) 7228 2285 – Closed 25-26 December

Rest – Carte £ 21/29 **6**EX**z**

◆ Smart, locally popular pub whose more diminutive size adds extra charm. Glass-roofed dining room sees flavoursome dishes with a mostly British accent; more choice at dinner. Child friendly.

Putney

Enoteca Turi

28 Putney High St ✉ SW15 1SQ ⊖ Putney Bridge – ✆ (020) 8785 4449 – www.enotecaturi.com – Fax (020) 8780 5409 – Closed 25-26 December, 1 January, Sunday and lunch Bank Holidays **22**MZH**n**

Rest – Italian – *(lunch)* Menu £ 18/27 (Monday-Thursday) – Carte £ 31/39

◆ A long-standing owner-run Italian restaurant. Earthy cooking focuses on the northerly regions of Italy. Interesting wine list, with plenty by the glass and carafe.

L'Auberge

22 Upper Richmond Rd ✉ SW15 2RX – ✆ (020) 8874 3593 – www.ardillys.com – Closed Christmas, Sunday and Monday **6**DX**r**

Rest – French – *(dinner only)* Menu £ 17 – Carte £ 25/32

◆ Locally renowned neighbourhood restaurant. Art nouveau prints of famous champagne houses set tone for frequently changing, authentic French dishes; personable service.

The Phoenix

Pentlow St ✉ SW15 1LY – ✆ (020) 8780 3131 – www.sonnys.co.uk – Closed dinner Sunday and Bank Holidays **21**LZH**s**

Rest – Italian influences – Menu £ 18 – Carte £ 25/33

◆ Light and bright interior with French windows leading out onto a spacious terrace. Unfussy and considerate service. An eclectic element to the modern Mediterranean menu.

The Spencer Arms

237 Lower Richmond Road ✉ SW15 1HJ ⊖ East Putney. – ✆ (020) 8788 0640 – www.thespencerarms.co.uk – Fax (020) 8788 2216 – Closed 25 December and 1 January **21**LZH**V**

Rest – Menu £ 13/20 – Carte £ 18/25

◆ Classic Victorian pub with appealingly unassuming manner. Cooking is gutsy and satisfying with Mediterranean influences. Small plates of 'English Tapas' act as nibbles or sharing plates.

Prince of Wales

138 Upper Richmond Rd ✉ SW15 2SP ⊖ East Putney. – ✆ (020) 8788 1552 – www.princeofwalesputney.co.uk – Closed 25 December and 1 January

Rest – Carte £ 25/40 **22**MZH**z**

◆ Scottish owner aims to make it a 'country pub in the city'. Robust and largely British cooking, with plenty of game in season, usual cuts, stews and terrines. Sunday night is quiz night.

Tooting

Kastoori

188 Upper Tooting Rd ✉ SW17 7EJ ⊖ Tooting Bec – ✆ (020) 8767 7027 – www.kastoorirestaurant.com – Closed 25-26 December and lunch Monday and Tuesday **6**EX**v**

Rest – Indian – Carte £ 14/19

◆ The family proudly celebrate their Gujarati heritage by offering a wide selection of vegetarian dishes. Enthusiastic service makes up for the modest look of this long-standing restaurant.

Wandsworth

Chez Bruce (Bruce Poole)

2 Bellevue Rd ✉ SW17 7EG ⊖ Tooting Bec – ✆ (020) 8672 0114 – www.chezbruce.co.uk – Fax (020) 8767 6648 – Closed 24-26 December and 1 January **6EXe**

Rest – French – *(booking essential)* Menu £ 26/40

Spec. Hake with courgette flower, escabèche of mackerel and coriander. Pork with choucroute, crispy belly and boudin blanc. Apricot and almond tart with amaretto ice cream.

◆ Simply decorated neighbourhood restaurant serving confident classical French cooking with a touch of the Mediterranean. Animated, informal atmosphere; well-organised service.

WESTMINSTER (City of) – Greater London – pop. 181 766 **12 B3**

Bayswater and Maida Vale

Hilton London Paddington

rm, VISA AE

146 Praed St ✉ W2 1EE ⊖ Paddington – ✆ (020) 7850 0500 – www.hilton.co.uk/paddington – Fax (020) 7850 0600 **28ADUa**

344 rm – †£ 321 ††£ 321, ☕ £ 19.95 – 20 suites

Rest ***The Brasserie*** – *(closed Saturday lunch)* Menu £ 20 – Carte £ 26/35

◆ Early Victorian railway hotel, sympathetically restored in contemporary style with art deco details. Co-ordinated bedrooms with hi-tech facilities continue the modern style. Contemporary brasserie offers modern menu.

Lancaster London

P VISA AE

Lancaster Ter ✉ W2 2TY ⊖ Lancaster Gate – ✆ (020) 7262 6737 – www.lancasterlondon.com – Fax (020) 7724 3191 **28ADUe**

394 rm – †£ 357 ††£ 357, ☕ £ 23 – 22 suites

Rest Island and **Nipa** – see restaurant listing

◆ Formerly called the Royal Lancaster. Imposing 1960s purpose-built hotel overlooking Hyde Park. Extensive conference facilities. Well-equipped bedrooms are decorated in traditional style.

The Hempel

rm, VISA AE

31-35 Craven Hill Gdns ✉ W2 3EA ⊖ Queensway – ✆ (020) 7298 9000 – www.the-hempel.co.uk – Fax (020) 7402 4666 – Closed 25-28 December

44 rm – †£ 183/298 ††£ 183/298, ☕ £ 21.50 – 6 suites **28ACUa**

Rest – *(Closed Sunday) (dinner only)* Carte £ 34/44

◆ A striking example of minimalist design. Individually appointed bedrooms are understated yet very comfortable. Relaxed ambience. Trendy restaurant with European menu.

Colonnade Town House without rest

VISA AE

2 Warrington Cres ✉ W9 1ER ⊖ Warwick Avenue – ✆ (020) 7286 1052 – www.theetoncollection.com – Fax (020) 7286 1057 **17OZDe**

43 rm – †£ 127/196 ††£ 150/196, ☕ £ 12.50

◆ Former hospital in quiet yet central location. Bedrooms range in size according to grade; all are comfy and classically furnished with good amenities. Tapas served in bar/on pleasant terrace.

New Linden without rest

VISA AE

58-60 Leinster Sq ✉ W2 4PS ⊖ Bayswater – ✆ (020) 7221 4321 – www.themayflowercollection.com – Fax (020) 7727 3156 **27ABUe**

50 rm – †£ 79/109 ††£ 105/115

◆ Smart four storey white stucco façade. Basement breakfast room with sunny aspect. Bedrooms are its strength: flat screen TVs and wooden floors; two split-level family rooms.

Miller's without rest

VISA AE

111A Westbourne Grove (entrance on Hereford Rd) ✉ W2 4UW ⊖ Bayswater – ✆ (020) 7243 1024 – www.millershotel.com – Fax (020) 7243 1064

8 rm – †£ 173/202 ††£ 265 **27ABUa**

◆ Victorian house brimming with antiques and knick-knacks. Charming sitting room provides the setting for a relaxed breakfast. Individual, theatrical rooms named after poets.

XX **Le Café Anglais**

8 Porchester Gdns ✉ W2 4BD ⊖ Bayswater – ✆ (020) 7221 1415 – www.lecafeanglais.co.uk – Closed 25-26 December and 1 January

Rest – Modern European – Menu £ 20/25 – Carte £ 28/45 **27**ABU**r**

◆ Big, bustling and contemporary brasserie with art deco styling, within Whiteley's shopping centre. Large and very appealing selection of classic brasserie food; the rotisserie is the centrepiece.

XX **Angelus**

4 Bathurst St ✉ W2 2SD ⊖ Lancaster Gate – ✆ (020) 7402 0083 – www.angelusrestaurant.co.uk – Fax (020) 7402 5383 – Closed Christmas-New Year **28**ADU**c**

Rest – French – Menu £ 36/38 – Carte £ 36/52

◆ In the style of a French brasserie, with studded leather banquettes, huge art nouveau mirror, Murano chandeliers and lounge bar. Unfussy, French dishes; clean, precise cooking.

XX **Island** – at Lancaster London Hotel

Lancaster Ter ✉ W2 2TY ⊖ Lancaster Gate – ✆ (020) 7551 6070 – www.islandrestaurant.co.uk – Fax (020) 7551 6071 **28**ADU**e**

Rest – Modern European – Carte £ 27/46

◆ Modern, stylish restaurant with buzzy open kitchen. Full length windows allow good views of adjacent Hyde Park. Seasonally based, modern menus with wide range of dishes.

XX **Nipa** – at Lancaster London Hotel

Lancaster Ter ✉ W2 2TY ⊖ Lancaster Gate – ✆ (020) 7551 6039 – www.niparestaurant.co.uk – Fax (020) 7724 3191 – Closed Christmas-New Year, Saturday lunch, Sunday and Bank Holidays **28**ADU**e**

Rest – Thai – Menu £ 15/27 – Carte £ 26/37

◆ On the 1st floor and overlooking Hyde Park. Authentic and ornately decorated restaurant offers subtly spiced Thai cuisine. Keen to please staff in traditional silk costumes.

XX **Trenta**

30 Connaught St ✉ W2 2AF ⊖ Marble Arch – ✆ (020) 7262 9623 – Fax (020) 7262 9636 – Closed Christmas-New Year, Sunday and Bank Holidays

Rest – Italian – *(dinner only and lunch Thursday and Friday)* **29**AFU**b**

Carte £ 23/31

◆ Only 7 tables on ground floor and 5 more downstairs; red and cream with comfy leather seats. Uncomplicated Italian cooking on constantly changing menu.

XX **Pearl Liang**

8 Sheldon Sq., Paddington Central ✉ W2 6EZ ⊖ Paddington – ✆ (020) 7289 7000 – www.pearlliang.co.uk – Closed 24-25 December

Rest – Chinese – Menu £ 23 – Carte £ 25/53 **28**ACT**b**

◆ Spacious, business-orientated Chinese restaurant within a corporate development. Extensive choice from a variety of set menus; try the more unusual dishes like jellyfish or pig's trotter.

X **Assaggi**

39 Chepstow Pl, (above Chepstow pub) ✉ W2 4TS ⊖ Bayswater – ✆ (020) 7792 5501 – www.assaggi.com – Closed 2 weeks Christmas, Sunday and Bank Holidays **27**AAU**c**

Rest – Italian – *(booking essential)* Carte approx. £ 44

◆ Pared-down simplicity to this room above a pub, where regulars are given fulsome welcomes. Cooking relies on the quality of the ingredients and the wine list is exclusively Italian.

X **Hereford Road**

3 Hereford Road ✉ W2 4AB ⊖ Bayswater – ✆ (020) 7727 1144 – www.herefordroad.org – Closed 24, 26, 31 December and 1 January

Rest – British – *(booking essential)* Menu £ 16 (lunch) **27**ABU**s**

– Carte £ 27/30

◆ Converted butcher's shop that specialises in classic British dishes and recipes, with first rate, seasonal ingredients. Booths for six people are the prize seats. Friendly and relaxed feel.

Arturo

23 Connaught St ✉ W2 2AY ⊖ Marble Arch – ✆ (020) 7706 3388 – www.arturorestaurant.co.uk – Fax (020) 7402 9195 – Closed 25-26 December, 1 January, Easter, Saturday and Sunday lunch **29**AFU**a**

Rest – Italian – Menu £ 17 – Carte £ 20/33

◆ On a smart street near Hyde Park: sleek, modish feel imbues interior with intimate, elegant informality. Tuscan and Sicilian dishes cooked with confidence and originality.

Kiasu

48 Queensway ✉ W2 3RY ⊖ Bayswater – ✆ (020) 7727 8810 – www.kiasu.co.uk – Fax (020) 7727 7220 **27**ABU**k**

Rest – Asian – Menu £ 6 (weekday lunch) – Carte £ 15/33

◆ Its name means 'afraid to be second best'. Malaysian owner; some dishes are hot and spicy, others light and fragrant; all designed for sharing. Brightly decorated; good fun.

Urban Turban

98 Westbourne Grove ✉ W2 5RU ⊖ Bayswater – ✆ (020) 7243 4200 – www.urbanturban.uk.com – Fax (020) 7243 4080 **27**ABU**x**

Rest – Indian – Menu £ 10 (lunch) – Carte £ 22/27

◆ Mumbai street food is the inspiration behind this venture from Vineet Bhatia. Order a number of dishes to share. Ground floor for the bustle and bar; the downstairs area is calmer.

El Pirata De Tapas

115 Westbourne Grove ✉ W2 4UP ⊖ Bayswater – ✆ (020) 7727 5000 – www.elpiratadetapas.co.uk – Closed early January and Bank Holidays

Rest – Spanish – Carte £ 14/23 **27**ABU**n**

◆ Contemporary yet warm Spanish restaurant with a genuine neighbourhood feel. Authentic flavours from a well-priced and appealing selection of tapas, ideal for sharing with friends.

Prince Alfred & Formosa Dining Room

5A Formosa St ✉ W9 1EE ⊖ Warwick Avenue. – ✆ (020) 7286 3287 – www.theprincealfred.com **17**OZD**n**

Rest – Carte £ 21/35

◆ Characterful and classic Victorian pub, with a large, more modern dining room in side extension. Open kitchen and a mix of British specialities and European classics. Friendly service.

The Warrington

93 Warrington Cres ✉ W9 1EH ⊖ Maida Vale. – ✆ (020) 7592 7960 – www.gordonramsay.com – Fax (020) 7592 1603 **17**OZD**a**

Rest – Carte £ 20/27 *(dinner only and lunch Friday-Sunday)*

◆ Imposing, classic Victorian pub, owned by Gordon Ramsay, with traditional feel to the ground floor bar. Upstairs is the smarter dining room with appealing menu of French and British classics.

The Waterway

54 Formosa St ✉ W9 2JU ⊖ Warwick Avenue. – ✆ (020) 7266 3557 – www.thewaterway.co.uk – Fax (020) 7266 3547 **17**OZD**p**

Rest – Carte £ 30/40

◆ Terrific decked terrace by the canal its most appealing feature. Contemporary interior with busy cocktail bar; menu in separate dining room mixes the classics with more ambitious dishes.

BELGRAVIA

The Berkeley

Wilton Pl ✉ SW1X 7RL ⊖ Knightsbridge – ✆ (020) 7235 6000 – www.the-berkeley.co.uk – Fax (020) 7235 4330 **37**AGX**e**

189 rm – 🛉£ 552/658 🛉🛉£ 658, ☕ £ 26 – 25 suites

Rest *Marcus Wareing at The Berkeley* – see restaurant listing

Rest *Boxwood café* – ✆ (020) 7592 1226 – Menu £ 21 (lunch) – Carte £ 31/56

◆ Discreet and rejuvenated hotel with rooftop pool and opulently decorated bedrooms. Relax in the gilded and panelled Caramel Room or have a drink in the cool Blue Bar. Modern cooking in glitzy Boxwood Café.

The Lanesborough

Hyde Park Corner ✉ SW1X 7TA ⊖ Hyde Park Corner – ✆ (020) 7259 5599 – www.lanesborough.com – Fax (020) 7259 5606 **37**AGX**a**

86 rm – †£ 409/547 ††£ 547, ☕ £ 30 – 9 suites

Rest Aspleys – *see restaurant listing*

◆ Converted in the 1990s from 18C St George's Hospital. Butler service offered. Regency-era inspired decoration; lavishly appointed rooms with impressive technological extras.

The Halkin

5 Halkin St ✉ SW1X 7DJ ⊖ Hyde Park Corner – ✆ (020) 7333 1000 – www.halkin.como.bz – Fax (020) 7333 1100 **38**AHX**b**

35 rm – †£ 259/449 ††£ 374/564, ☕ £ 25 – 6 suites

Rest *Nahm* – see restaurant listing

◆ Opened in 1991 as London's first boutique hotel and still looking sharp today. Thoughtfully conceived bedrooms with silk walls and marbled bathrooms; everything at the touch of a button. Abundant Armani-clad staff. Small, discreet bar.

Jumeirah Lowndes

21 Lowndes St ✉ SW1X 9ES ⊖ Knightsbridge – ✆ (020) 7823 1234 – www.jumeirahlowndeshotel.com – Fax (020) 7235 1154 **37**AGX**h**

87 rm – ††£ 598, ☕ £ 27 – 14 suites

Rest *Mimosa* – Menu £ 18 (lunch) – Carte approx. £ 33

◆ Compact yet friendly modern corporate hotel within this exclusive residential area. Good levels of personal service offered. Close to the famous shops of Knightsbridge. Modern restaurant opens onto street terrace.

Marcus Wareing at The Berkeley

Wilton Pl ✉ SW1X 7RL ⊖ Knightsbridge – ✆ (020) 7235 1200 – www.marcus-wareing.com – Fax (020) 7235 1266 – Closed Saturday lunch and Sunday **37**AGX**e**

Rest – French – Menu £ 35/75

Spec. Foie gras with apricot compote and amaretti crumble. Sea bass with langoustines, smoked eel and asparagus. Iced lime mousse with pineapple carpaccio.

◆ Marcus Wareing's cooking is creative, sophisticated and backed by sound classical techniques. The restaurant is sumptuously appointed, and service is smooth and well-organised. The chef's table is one of the best in town.

Apsleys – at The Lanesborough Hotel

Hyde Park Corner ✉ SW1X 7TA ⊖ Hyde Park Corner – ✆ (020) 7259 5599 – www.apsleys.co.uk – Fax (020) 7333 7255 **37**AGX**a**

Rest – Italian – Menu £ 26 (lunch) – Carte £ 47/74

Spec. Sea bass with cannolo, celery and melon. Roast pigeon with pearl onions and a mustard seed sauce. Crunchy chocolate dome with salted pine nut ice cream.

◆ Under the guidance of celebrated chef Heinz Beck from Rome's La Pergola. Exquisite and precise Italian cooking, in a grand and eye-catching room designed by Adam Tihany. The serving team are polished but the atmosphere animated.

Amaya

Halkin Arcade, 19 Motcomb St ✉ SW1X 8JT ⊖ Knightsbridge – ✆ (020) 7823 1166 – www.realindianfood.com – Fax (020) 7259 6464 – Closed 25 December **37**AGX**k**

Rest – Indian – Menu £ 25/39 – Carte £ 32/65

Spec. Oysters with coconut and ginger. Tandoori duck with tamarind glaze. Pineapple tarte tatin.

◆ Light, piquant and aromatic Indian cooking specialising in kebabs from a tawa skillet, sigri grill or tandoor oven. Chic comfortable surroundings, modern and subtly exotic.

Good food and accommodation at moderate prices? Look for the Bib symbols: red Bib Gourmand for food, blue Bib Hotel for accommodation.

Zafferano

15 Lowndes St SW1X 9EY Knightsbridge – (020) 7235 5800
– www.zafferanorestaurant.com – Fax (020) 7235 1971
– Closed Christmas-New Year **37**AGX**f**

Rest – Italian – *(booking essential)* Menu £ 45 (dinner)
– Carte lunch £ 45/60

Spec. Roasted onion with cheese fondue and white truffle. Flat spaghetti with tomato and lobster. Chocolate fondant with gianduia chocolate ice cream.

◆ Pasta is the star of the show at this perennially busy Italian restaurant. The cooking is reliable and assured and the menus balanced. The stylish surroundings are comfortable but also full of bustle; the bar is an appealing adjunct.

Nahm – at The Halkin Hotel

5 Halkin St SW1X 7DJ Hyde Park Corner – (020) 7333 1234
– www.halkin.como.bz – Fax (020) 7333 1100 **38**AHX**b**

Rest – Thai – *(Closed lunch Saturday and Sunday) (booking advisable)*
Menu £ 30 (lunch)/55 – Carte £ 39/46

Spec. Salted chicken wafers, longans and Thai basil. Pork belly braised with peanuts. Coconut cake with rambutans and perfumed syrup.

◆ Discreet, comfortable dining room; sleek understated décor. Sophisticated cooking showcases the harmony of Thai cooking achieved through careful combinations of textures and flavours.

Mango Tree

46 Grosvenor Pl SW1X 7EQ Victoria – (020) 7823 1888
– www.mangotree.org.uk – Fax (020) 7838 9275
– Closed 25 December and 1 January **38**AHX**a**

Rest – Thai – Menu £ 20 (lunch)
– Carte £ 30/36

◆ Expect clued-up and efficient service in this large, contemporarily styled and ever popular Thai restaurant. The kitchen presents the authentic dishes in a modern style.

Noura Brasserie

16 Hobart Pl SW1W 0HH Victoria – (020) 7235 9444 – www.noura.co.uk
– Fax (020) 7235 9244 **38**AHX**n**

Rest – Lebanese – Menu £ 20/30
– Carte £ 24/39

◆ Dine in either the bright bar or the comfortable, contemporary restaurant. Authentic, modern Lebanese cooking specialises in chargrilled meats and meze.

The Pantechnicon Rooms

10 Motcomb St SW1X 8LA Knightsbridge. – (020) 7730 6074
– www.thepantechnicon.com – Fax (020) 7730 6055
– Closed 25 December to 1 January **37**AGX**d**

Rest – Carte £ 28/40

◆ Same owners as the nearby Thomas Cubitt; a smart pub with more formal dining room upstairs. Shellfish and seafood a speciality. Bright, comfortable surroundings with enthusiastic service.

HYDE PARK AND KNIGHTSBRIDGE

Mandarin Oriental Hyde Park

rm,

66 Knightsbridge SW1X 7LA Knightsbridge
– (020) 7235 2000 – www.mandarinoriental.com/london – Fax (020) 7235 2001 **37**AGX**x**

173 rm – £ 435 £ 555, £ 29 – 25 suites

Rest – *(Change of concept during 2010)*

◆ Built in 1889 this classic hotel, with striking façade, remains one of London's grandest. Many of the luxurious and impeccably kept bedrooms enjoy views of Hyde Park. Plans for two new restaurants from internationally acclaimed chefs in 2010.

Knightsbridge Green without rest
159 Knightsbridge ✉ SW1X 7PD ⊖ Knightsbridge – ✆ (020) 7584 6274 – www.thekghotel.com – Fax (020) 7225 1635 – Closed 25-26 December **37**AFX**z**
16 rm – †£ 150/180 ††£ 200/250 – 12 suites
◆ Just yards from Hyde Park and all the smartest shops. Small lounge; breakfast served in the well-proportioned bedrooms spread over six floors. Privately owned.

Zuma
5 Raphael St ✉ SW7 1DL ⊖ Knightsbridge – ✆ (020) 7584 1010 – www.zumarestaurant.com – Fax (020) 7584 5005 – Closed 25-26 December and 1 January **37**AFX**m**
Rest – Japanese – Carte approx. £ 26
◆ Eye-catching design that blends East with West. Bustling atmosphere; fashionable clientele; popular sushi bar. Varied and interesting contemporary Japanese food.

Mr Chow
151 Knightsbridge ✉ SW1X 7PA ⊖ Knightsbridge – ✆ (020) 7589 7347 – www.mrchow.com – Fax (020) 7584 5780 – Closed 24 to 26 December, 1 January, Easter Monday and Monday lunch **37**AFX**e**
Rest – Chinese – Menu £ 23/38 – Carte £ 42/63
◆ Long-standing Chinese restaurant, opened in 1968. Smart clientele, stylish and comfortable surroundings and prompt service from Italian waiters. Carefully prepared and satisfying food.

MAYFAIR

Dorchester
Park Lane ✉ W1K 1QA ⊖ Hyde Park Corner – ✆ (020) 7629 8888 – www.thedorchester.com – Fax (020) 7629 8080 **30**AHV**a**
200 rm – †£ 340/570 ††£ 524/857, ☕ £ 29.50 – 49 suites
Rest Alain Ducasse at The Dorchester and **China Tang** – *see restaurant listing*
Rest *The Grill* – Menu £ 25/29 – Carte £ 48/69
◆ A sumptuously decorated, luxury hotel offering every possible facility. Impressive marbled and pillared promenade. Rooms quintessentially English in style. Exemplary levels of service. Exuberant tartan décor in The Grill.

Claridge's
Brook St ✉ W1K 4HR ⊖ Bond Street – ✆ (020) 7629 8860 – www.claridges.co.uk – Fax (020) 7499 2210 **30**AHU**c**
143 rm – †£ 564/736 ††£ 736, ☕ £ 31 – 60 suites
Rest *Gordon Ramsay at Claridge's* – see restaurant listing
◆ Rightly celebrated for its Art Deco and one of London's finest hotels. Exceptionally well-appointed and sumptuous bedrooms, all with butler service. Magnificent Foyer for afternoon tea.

The Connaught
Carlos Place ✉ W1K 2AL ⊖ Bond St – ✆ (020) 3147 7200 – www.the-connaught.co.uk – Fax (020) 7314 3537 – Closed 1 week January and 1 week August **30**AHU**e**
95 rm – †£ 480/610 ††£ 610, ☕ £ 28 – 27 suites
Rest *Hélène Darroze at The Connaught* – see restaurant listing
Rest *Espelette* – Carte £ 44/63
◆ This famous hotel reopened in 2008 after a major renovation. Luxury bedrooms updated in style and mod cons while retaining that elegant British feel. Choice of two stylish bars. Espelette for all day, informal dining.

InterContinental
1 Hamilton Place, Park Lane ✉ W1J 7QY ⊖ Hyde Park Corner – ✆ (020) 7409 3131 – www.london.intercontinental.com – Fax (020) 7493 3476
399 rm – †£ 229/390 ††£ 229/390, ☕ £ 27 – 48 suites **30**AHV**k**
Rest *Theo Randall* – see restaurant listing
Rest *Cookbook Café* – Menu £ 25 (lunch) – Carte £ 28/44
◆ International hotel relaunched in 2007 after major refit. English-style bedrooms with hi-tech equipment and large, open-plan lobby. Cookbook Café invites visiting chefs to showcase their talents.

London Hilton

22 Park Lane ✉ *W1K 1BE* ⊖ *Hyde Park Corner*
– ✆ (020) 7493 8000 – www.hilton.co.uk/londonparklane
– Fax (020) 7208 4061 **30**AHV**e**

397 rm – †£ 241/482 ††£ 241/482, ☕ £ 24.50 – 56 suites
Rest *Galvin at Windows* – see restaurant listing
Rest *Trader Vics* – *(closed lunch Saturday and Sunday)* Menu £ 24 (lunch) – Carte £ 33/53
Rest *Podium* – Menu £ 22/29 – Carte £ 26/54

◆ This 28 storey tower is one of the city's tallest hotels, providing impressive views from the upper floors. Club floor bedrooms are particularly comfortable. Exotic Trader Vics with bamboo and plants. Modern European food in Podium.

Grosvenor House

Park Lane ✉ *W1K 7TN* ⊖ *Marble Arch – ✆ (020) 7499 6363*
– www.londongrosvenorhouse.co.uk – Fax (020) 7493 3341 **29**AGU**g**

378 rm – †£ 344 ††£ 344, ☕ £ 27.50 – 55 suites
Rest *Bord'eaux* – French – Menu £ 25 – Carte £ 28/46

◆ Refurbished hotel in commanding position by Hyde Park. Uniform, comfortable bedrooms in classic Marriott styling. Boasts the largest ballroom in Europe. Brasserie specialises in dishes from SW France.

Westbury

Bond St ✉ *W1S 2YF* ⊖ *Bond Street – ✆ (020) 7629 7755*
– www.westburymayfair.com – Fax (020) 7495 1163 **30**AIU**a**

232 rm – †£ 149/494 ††£ 149/494, ☕ £ 23.50 – 13 suites
Rest – *(closed Saturday lunch and Sunday dinner)* Menu £ 30 – Carte £ 45/65

◆ Caused a commotion with its New York styling when it opened in the 1950s; now fully refurbished. Smart, comfortable bedrooms; art deco suites. Elegant, well-known Polo bar. Bright, fresh restaurant; extensive private dining facilities.

Brown's

Albemarle St ✉ *W1S 4BP* ⊖ *Green Park – ✆ (020) 7493 6020*
– www.roccofortecollection.com – Fax (020) 7493 9381 **30**AIV**d**

105 rm – †£ 229/547 ††£ 322/604, ☕ £ 27 – 12 suites
Rest *The Albemarle* – British – ✆ (020) 7518 4004 – Menu £ 30 – Carte £ 28/56

◆ This urbane hotel with an illustrious past offers a swish bar featuring Terence Donovan prints, up-to-the minute bedrooms and a quintessentially English sitting room for tea. Wood panelled dining room with traditional British cooking.

London Marriott H. Park Lane

140 Park Lane ✉ *W1K 7AA* ⊖ *Marble Arch*
– ✆ (020) 7493 7000 – www.marriott.com/lonpl
– Fax (020) 7493 8333 **29**AGU**b**

148 rm – †£ 282/363 ††£ 282/363, ☕ £ 22.95 – 9 suites
Rest *140 Park Lane* – Menu £ 15/25 – Carte £ 32/52

◆ This international hotel is usefully located close to the shops of Oxford Street and Hyde Park. Well-kept basement health club. Smart, generously sized bedrooms are well-equipped. Attractive restaurant overlooks Marble Arch.

The Metropolitan

Old Park Lane ✉ *W1K 1LB* ⊖ *Hyde Park Corner – ✆ (020) 7447 1000*
– www.metropolitan.como.bz – Fax (020) 7447 1100 **30**AHV**c**

147 rm – †£ 432 ††£ 432, ☕ £ 30 – 3 suites
Rest *Nobu* – see restaurant listing

◆ Minimalist interior and a voguish reputation has made this hotel and its Met Bar the favoured choice of pop stars and celebrities. Sleek design and fashionably attired staff set it apart.

Athenaeum

116 Piccadilly ✉ W1J 7BJ ⊖ Hyde Park Corner – ☎ (020) 7499 3464 – www.athenaeumhotel.com – Fax (020) 7493 1860 **30**AHV**g**
145 rm – ††£ 340/403, ☕ £ 27 – 12 suites
Rest *Damask* – Menu £ 19/27 – Carte £ 42/58
◆ Built in 1925 as a luxury apartment block and currently undergoing an extensive renovation. Individually designed suites are in an adjacent Edwardian townhouse. Conservatory roofed, contemporary dining room.

Chesterfield

35 Charles St ✉ W1J 5EB ⊖ Green Park – ☎ (020) 7491 2622 – www.chesterfieldmayfair.com – Fax (020) 7491 4793 **30**AHV**f**
103 rm – †£ 340/374 ††£ 374, ☕ £ 22 – 4 suites
Rest – Menu £ 20/26 – Carte £ 33/67
◆ An assuredly English feel to this Georgian house. Discreet lobby leads to a clubby bar and wood panelled library. Individually decorated bedrooms, with some antique pieces. Intimate and pretty restaurant.

London Marriott H. Grosvenor Square

Grosvenor Sq ✉ W1K 6JP ⊖ Bond Street – ☎ (020) 7493 1232 – www.marriottgrosvenorsquare.com – Fax (020) 7514 1528
224 rm – †£ 275/333 ††£ 275/333, ☕ £ 22 – 12 suites **30**AHU**s**
Rest *Maze Grill* – see restaurant listing
◆ A well-appointed international group hotel that benefits from an excellent location in the heart of Mayfair. Many of the bedrooms specifically equipped for the business traveller.

Washington Mayfair

5-7 Curzon St ✉ W1J 5HE ⊖ Green Park – ☎ (020) 7499 7000 – www.washington-mayfair.co.uk – Fax (020) 7495 6172 **30**AHV**d**
166 rm – †£ 173/374 ††£ 173/374, ☕ £ 19.50 – 5 suites
Rest – Menu £ 23 – Carte £ 29/49
◆ Location is hard to beat. Hotel blends a classical style with modern amenities. Large lounge and contemporary bedrooms. Piano bar annexe to formal dining room.

Hilton London Green Park

Half Moon St ✉ W1J 7BN ⊖ Green Park – ☎ (020) 7629 7522 – www.hilton.co.uk/greenpark – Fax (020) 7491 8971 **30**AIV**a**
162 rm – †£ 114/305 ††£ 137/317, ☕ £ 19.95
Rest – *(bar lunch weekends)* Menu £ 20 **s** – Carte £ 31/36 **s**
◆ A row of sympathetically adjoined townhouses, dating from the 1730s. Well-maintained bedrooms share the same décor but vary in size and shape. Monet prints decorate light, airy dining room.

Alain Ducasse at The Dorchester

Park Lane ✉ W1K 1QA ⊖ Hyde Park Corner – ☎ (020) 7629 8866 – www.alainducasse-dorchester.com – Fax (020) 7629 8686 – Closed 1-23 August, dinner 25 December, 26-30 and lunch 31 December, 1-4 January, Saturday lunch, Sunday and Monday **30**AHV**a**
Rest – French – Menu £ 45 (lunch) – Carte £ 45/75
Spec. Roasted chicken and lobster with sweetbreads. Fillet of beef and foie gras Rossini with'sacristain' potatoes. 'Baba like in Monte-Carlo'.
◆ Luxury and extravagance are the hallmarks of this Alain Ducasse outpost. Dining room is elegant without being staid; food is modern and refined yet satisfying and balanced. Service is formal and well-organised.

Guesthouses don't provide the same level of service as hotels. They are often characterised by a warm welcome and a décor which reflects the owner's personality. Those shown in red are particularly pleasant.

XXXX ✿✿ Le Gavroche (Michel Roux Jnr)

A/C VISA MC AE D

43 Upper Brook St ✉ W1K 7QR ⊖ Marble Arch – ✆ (020) 7408 0881 – www.le-gavroche.co.uk – Fax (020) 7491 4387 – Closed Christmas and New Year, Saturday lunch, Sunday and Bank Holidays **29AGUc**

Rest – French – *(booking essential)* Menu £ 48 (lunch) – Carte £ 59/137

Spec. Hot duck foie gras and crispy duck pancake flavoured with cinnamon. Roast saddle of rabbit with crispy potatoes and Parmesan. Bitter chocolate and praline 'indulgence'.

◆ Classic and indulgent French cuisine is the draw at Michel Roux Jnr's renowned London institution. The large, smart basement room has a clubby, masculine feel; service is formal and structured.

XXXX ✿✿ The Square (Philip Howard)

A/C VISA MC AE D

6-10 Bruton St ✉ W1J 6PU ⊖ Green Park – ✆ (020) 7495 7100 – www.squarerestaurant.com – Fax (020) 7495 7150 – Closed 25 December, 1 January and lunch Saturday, Sunday and Bank Holidays **30AIUv**

Rest – French – Menu £ 35/75

Spec. Langoustine with Parmesan gnocchi and truffle. Beef with red wine ravioli and smoked black pepper. Brillat-Savarin cheesecake with passion fruit and mango.

◆ Smart, busy restaurant; comfortable and never overformal. Cooking is thoughtful and honest, with a dextrous balance of flavours and textures. Prompt, efficient service.

XXXX ✿ Hélène Darroze at The Connaught

VISA MC AE

Carlos Place ✉ W1K 2AL ⊖ Bond St – ✆ (020) 3147 7200 – www.the-connaught.co.uk – Fax (020) 7314 3537 – Closed 1 week January, 1 week August, Sunday dinner and Monday **30AHUe**

Rest – French – *(booking essential)* Menu £ 35/75

Spec. Gillardeau oyster tartare with Aquitaine caviar jelly. Pigeon 'flambé au capucin' with green pea mousseline. Carupano chocolate cream with lavender praline.

◆ The influences are from Landes and SW of France; the accomplished cooking is creative and flavours are bold and confident. Formal and elegant room; original mahogany panelling.

XXXX ✿ Sketch (The Lecture Room & Library)

A/C VISA MC AE D

First Floor, 9 Conduit St ✉ W1S 2XG ⊖ Oxford Street – ✆ (020) 7659 4500 – www.sketch.uk.com – Fax (020) 7629 1683 – Closed 25-30 December, 17-30 August, Saturday lunch, Sunday, Monday and Bank Holidays

Rest – French – *(booking essential)* Menu £ 35/95 – Carte £ 64/100 **30AIUh**

Spec. Langoustines 'addressed in five ways'. Fillet of Bavarian Simmental beef. Pierre Gagnaire's 'grand dessert'.

◆ A work of animated art, full of energy, vitality and colour; an experience of true sensory stimulation. Ambitious, highly elaborate and skilled cooking; try the tasting menu.

XXXX ✿ Galvin at Windows – at London Hilton Hotel

A/C VISA MC AE D

22 Park Lane ✉ W1K 1BE ⊖ Hyde Park Corner – ✆ (020) 7208 4021 – www.galvinatwindows.com – Fax (020) 7208 4144 – Closed Saturday lunch and Sunday dinner **30AHVe**

Rest – French – Menu £ 25/58

Spec. Foie gras with pain d'épice and hazelnuts. Fillet and peppered short rib of beef with Swiss chard and shallots. Strawberry vacherin with basil and champagne.

◆ Spectacular views from the 28th floor of the Hilton are not the only draw: the room is contemporary and cleverly laid out, service is attentive and efficient and the cooking is confident, detailed, balanced and satisfying.

XXXX Gordon Ramsay at Claridge's

A/C VISA MC AE D

Brook St ✉ W1K 4HR ⊖ Bond St – ✆ (020) 7499 0099 – www.gordonramsay.com – Fax (020) 7499 3099 **30AHUc**

Rest – Modern European – *(booking essential)* Menu £ 30/70

◆ Grand and impressive room within the elegant surroundings of Claridge's hotel. Service is ceremonial and structured and the cooking is classically based. Popular Chef's Table in the kitchen.

XXXX **China Tang** – at Dorchester Hotel

Park Lane ✉ *W1A 2HJ* ⊖ *Hyde Park Corner* – ✆ *(020) 7629 9988 – www.thedorchester.com – Fax (020) 7629 9595 – Closed 25 December*

Rest – Chinese – Menu £ 15 (lunch) – Carte £ 40/70 **30**AHV**a**

◆ A striking mix of art deco, Oriental motifs, hand-painted fabrics, mirrors and marbled table tops. Carefully prepared, traditional Cantonese dishes using quality ingredients.

XXX ✿✿ **Hibiscus** (Claude Bosi)

29 Maddox St ✉ *W1S 2PA* ⊖ *Oxford Circus* – ✆ *(020) 7629 2999 – www.hibiscusrestaurant.co.uk – Fax (020) 7514 9552 – Closed 10 days Christmas-New Year, Sunday, Monday and Saturday lunch except 15 November-23 December* **30**AIU**s**

Rest – Innovative – Menu £ 25/85

Spec. Sweetbreads with oak smoked goat's cheese and onion fondue. Chicken stuffed with crayfish, girolles and green mango. Tart of sweet peas, mint and sheep's whey with coconut ice cream.

◆ Claude Bosi's cooking is creative and bold, but with a sound, classical base; desserts are a real highlight. Attractive room combines French oak with Welsh slate as a reminder of his previous restaurant in Ludlow. Formal and conscientious service.

XXX ✿ **The Greenhouse**

27a Hay's Mews ✉ *W1J 5NY* ⊖ *Hyde Park Corner* – ✆ *(020) 7499 3331 – www.greenhouserestaurant.co.uk – Fax (020) 7499 5368 – Closed 24 December -5 January, Saturday lunch, Sunday and Bank Holidays* **30**AHV**m**

Rest – Innovative – Menu £ 29/65

Spec. Foie gras with cherries, tonka bean cream and kirsch jelly. Pigeon with sesame seeds, baby spinach and pommes soufflé. 'Snix' - chocolate, salted caramel and peanuts.

◆ Smart, elegant restaurant broken up into sections by glass screens. Innovative selection of elaborately presented dishes, underpinned with sound French culinary techniques.

XXX ✿ **Murano**

20 Queen St ✉ *W1J 5PR* ⊖ *Green Park* – ✆ *(020) 7592 1222 – www.angelahartnett.com – Fax (020) 7592 1213 – Closed Sunday*

Rest – Italian influences – Menu £ 25/55 **30**AHV**b**

Spec. Scallops with gnocchi, apple and cucumber chutney. Côte de veau with asparagus and mushrooms, hazelnut velouté. Caramelia chocolate mousse, Sacher sponge and chocolate ice cream.

◆ Angela Hartnett's bright and stylish restaurant, in collaboration with Gordon Ramsay, provides a luminous setting for her refined and balanced cooking, with its strong Italian influences.

XXX ✿ **Maze**

10-13 Grosvenor Sq ✉ *W1K 6JP* ⊖ *Bond Street* – ✆ *(020) 7107 0000 – www.gordonramsay.com – Fax (020) 7592 1603* **30**AHU**z**

Rest – Innovative – Menu £ 23 (lunch) – Carte £ 49/69

Spec. Crab salad with pickled mooli, apple jelly and bloody mary sorbet. Pigeon with ganache, blueberries and red wine. Chocolate delice with honey, Banyuls and olive oil ice cream.

◆ Choose a variety of small but expertly formed dishes at this sleek and stylish contemporary restaurant. The cooking is innovative, balanced and precise; service is well-organised.

XXX ✿ **Kai**

65 South Audley St ✉ *W1K 2QU* ⊖ *Hyde Park Corner* – ✆ *(020) 7493 8988 – www.kaimayfair.co.uk – Fax (020) 7493 1456 – Closed 25-26 December and 1 January* **30**AHV**n**

Rest – Chinese – *(booking essential)* Menu £ 22 (lunch) – Carte £ 38/91

Spec. Wasabi prawns with mango and basil seeds. Lamb with Sichuan peppercorns, mushroom and bamboo shoot. Peranakan mango cake with coconut sugar milkshake.

◆ Carefully prepared Chinese food, from a menu that mixes the classics with more innovative dishes; flavours are clean and assured. Spread over two floors, with sweet natured service and smart surroundings.

XXX **Benares** (Atul Kochhar)

12a Berkeley Square House ✉ W1J 6BS ⊖ Green Park – ✆ (020) 7629 8886 – www.benaresrestaurant.com – Fax (020) 7499 2430 **30**AIU**q**

Rest – Indian – Menu £ 25 (lunch) – Carte £ 45/122

Spec. Soft shell crab with squid salad. Grilled roe deer fillet with yellow pumpkin risotto. Rose panna cotta with raspberry mousse.

◆ A smart and stylish, first floor Indian restaurant. Many of the regional dishes are given innovative twists but flavours remain authentic. Convivial atmosphere and pleasant service.

XXX **Tamarind**

20 Queen St ✉ W1J 5PR ⊖ Green Park – ✆ (020) 7629 3561 – www.tamarindrestaurant.com – Fax (020) 7499 5034 – Closed 25 December, 1 January and Saturday lunch **30**AHV**h**

Rest – Indian – Menu £ 19/52 – Carte £ 38/63

Spec. Scallops with star anise and smoked peppers. Lamb shank with spices, yoghurt and chillies. Grilled pineapple with rose petal ice cream.

◆ Makes the best use of its basement location, with smoked mirrors, gilded columns and a somewhat exclusive feel. Appealing and balanced Indian cooking; kebabs and curries are the specialities, complemented by carefully prepared vegetable dishes.

XXX **Umu**

14-16 Bruton Pl ✉ W1J 6LX ⊖ Bond Street – ✆ (020) 7499 8881 – www.umurestaurant.com – Fax (020) 7016 5120 – Closed 24 December-7 January, Saturday lunch, Sunday and Bank Holidays **30**AIU**k**

Rest – Japanese – Menu £ 21 (lunch) – Carte £ 33/76

Spec. Sweet shrimp with sake jelly and caviar. Grilled skill fish teriyaki, citrus flavoured radish and wasabi. Chocolate fondant with white miso ice cream.

◆ Stylish, discreet interior using natural materials, with central sushi bar. Extensive choice of Japanese dishes; choose one of the seasonal kaiseki menus for the full experience. Over 160 different labels of sake.

XXX **Scott's**

20 Mount St ✉ W1K 2HE ⊖ Bond St – ✆ (020) 7495 7309 – www.scotts-restaurant.com – Fax (020) 7647 6326 – Closed 25-26 December and 1 January **30**AHU**d**

Rest – Seafood – Carte £ 41/69

◆ A landmark London institution reborn. Stylish yet traditional; oak panelling juxtaposed with vibrant artwork from young British artists. Top quality seafood, kept simple.

XXX **Cecconi's**

5a Burlington Gdns ✉ W1S 3EP ⊖ Green Park – ✆ (020) 7434 1500 – www.cecconis.com – Fax (020) 7434 2020 – Closed 25 December **30**AIU**d**

Rest – Italian – *(booking essential)* Carte £ 22/45

◆ A chic bar and a stylish, modern dining venue, invariably busy throughout the day. Famed for its Bellinis.The menus call on the Italian classics, with a page of Super Tuscans to choose from. Popular weekend brunches.

XXX **Corrigan's Mayfair**

28 Upper Grosvenor Street ✉ W1K 7EH London ⊖ Marble Arch – ✆ (020) 7499 9943 – www.corrigansmayfair.com – Fax (020) 7499 9321 – Closed 24 to 27 December, 1 January and Saturday lunch **29**AGU**a**

Rest – British – Menu £ 27 (lunch) – Carte £ 30/48

◆ Richard Corrigan's flagship celebrates British and Irish cooking, with game a speciality. The room is comfortable, clubby and quite glamorous and feels as though it has been around for years.

XXX **Bentley's (Grill)**

11-15 Swallow St ✉ W1B 4DG ⊖ Piccadilly Circus – ✆ (020) 7734 4756 – www.bentleys.org – Fax (020) 7758 4140 – Closed 25 December and 1 January **30**AJU**n**

Rest – British – Menu £ 20 (lunch) – Carte £ 33/45

◆ Entrance into striking bar; panelled staircase to richly decorated restaurant. Carefully sourced seafood or meat dishes enhanced by clean, crisp cooking. Unruffled service.

XXX **Theo Randall** – at InterContinental Hotel

1 Hamilton Place, Park Lane ✉ W1J 7QY ⊖ Hyde Park Corner – ✆ (020) 7409 3131 – www.london.intercontinental.com – Fax (020) 7493 3476 – Closed Saturday lunch, Sunday and Bank Holidays **30**AHV**k**

Rest – Italian – Menu £ 27 (lunch and early/late dinner) – Carte £ 45/55

◆ Stylish and spacious ground floor restaurant; helpful and chatty service. Rustic, seasonal Italian dishes focus on the best ingredients; wood oven the speciality.

XXX **Sartoria**

20 Savile Row ✉ W1S 3PR ⊖ Green Park – ✆ (020) 7534 7000 – www.danddlondon.com – Fax (020) 7534 7070 – Closed 25 December, Sunday, Saturday lunch and Bank Holidays **30**AIU**b**

Rest – Italian – Menu £ 24 – Carte £ 29/39

◆ In the street renowned for English tailoring, a coolly sophisticated restaurant to suit those looking for classic Italian cooking with modern touches.

XXX **Avista**

Millennium Mayfair H, 39 Grosvenor Sq ✉ W1K 2HP ⊖ Bond Street – ✆ (020) 7596 3399 – www.avistarestaurant.com – Fax (020) 7596 3443 – Closed 25 December, Saturday lunch, Sunday and Bank Holidays **30**AHU**x**

Rest – Italian – Menu £ 20 (lunch) – Carte £ 30/49

◆ A large room, softened by neutral shades, within the Millennium Hotel. The menu traverses Italy and the cooking marries the rustic with the more refined. Pasta dishes are a highlight.

XX ✿ **Wild Honey**

12 St George St ✉ W1S 2FB ⊖ Oxford Circus – ✆ (020) 7758 9160 – www.wildhoneyrestaurant.co.uk – Fax (020) 7493 4549 – Closed 25-26 December and 1 January **30**AIU**w**

Rest – Modern European – Menu £ 19 (lunch) – Carte £ 29/39 **s**

Spec. Rabbit and foie gras boudin blanc with peas. Cod with potato gnocchi and sea purslane. Cherry clafoutis with almond sorbet.

◆ Skilled kitchen uses seasonal ingredients at their peak to create dishes full of flavour and free from ostentation. Attractive oak-panelled room, with booth seating for larger groups. Personable and unobtrusive service.

XX ✿ **Semplice** (Marco Torri)

9-10 Blenheim St ✉ W1S 1LJ ⊖ Bond Street – ✆ (020) 7495 1509 – www.ristorantesemplice.com – Fax (020) 7493 7074 – Closed 2 weeks Christmas, 4 days Easter, Saturday lunch and Sunday **30**AHU**k**

Rest – Italian – *(booking essential at dinner)* Menu £ 19 (lunch) – Carte £ 33/38

Spec. Fassone beef carpaccio. Milk-fed veal wrapped in Parma ham with mushrooms, courgettes and tomato. Domori chocolate fondant.

◆ Plenty of regulars are always in evidence in this comfortable and stylish restaurant, decorated with ebony, leather and gold. The enthusiasm of the young owners is palpable; the kitchen uses small, specialist suppliers in unfussy, flavoursome dishes.

XX ✿ **Nobu Berkeley St**

15 Berkeley St ✉ W1J 8DY ⊖ Green Park – ✆ (020) 7290 9222 – www.noburestaurants.com/berkeley – Fax (020) 7290 9223 – Closed 25 December, and lunch Saturday and Sunday **30**AIV**b**

Rest – Japanese – Carte £ 44/65

Spec. Yellowtail sashimi with jalapeno. Black cod with miso. Chocolate bento box with green tea ice cream.

◆ In a prime position off Berkeley Square: downstairs 'destination' bar and above, a top quality, soft-hued restaurant. Innovative Japanese dishes with original combinations.

XX **Maze Grill** – at London Marriott H. Grosvenor Square rm, A/C

10-13 Grosvenor Sq ✉ W1K 6JP ⊖ Bond Street VISA MC AE
– ✆ (020) 7495 2211 – www.gordonramsay.com – Fax (020) 7592 1603
Rest – Beef specialities – Menu £ 18 (lunch) – Carte £ 34/61 **30**AHU**s**
◆ Opened in 2008 as an addendum to Maze. Menu specialises in steaks, from Hereford grass-fed to Wagyu 9th grade, with a variety of sauces and side dishes available as accompaniments.

XX **Bellamy's** A/C VISA MC AE

18 Bruton Pl ✉ W1J 6LY ⊖ Bond Street – ✆ (020) 7491 2727
– www.bellamysrestaurant.co.uk – Fax (020) 7491 9990 – Closed Saturday lunch, Sunday and Bank Holidays **30**AIU**c**
Rest – French – Menu £ 29 – Carte £ 35/58
◆ French deli/brasserie tucked down a smart mews. Go past the caviar and cheeses into the restaurant proper for a very traditional, but well-executed, range of Gallic classics.

XX **Patterson's** A/C VISA MC AE

4 Mill St ✉ W1S 2AX ⊖ Oxford Street – ✆ (020) 7499 1308
– www.pattersonsrestaurant.com – Fax (020) 7491 2122
– Closed 25-26 December **30**AIU**p**
Rest – Modern European – Menu £ 23 (lunch) – Carte £ 23/45
◆ Stylish modern interior in black and white. Elegant tables and attentive service. Modern British cooking with concise wine list and sensible prices.

LONDON

XX **Alloro** A/C VISA MC AE

19-20 Dover St ✉ W1S 4LU ⊖ Green Park – ✆ (020) 7495 4768
– www.alloro-restaurant.co.uk – Fax (020) 7629 5348 – Closed 25 December, Saturday lunch and Sunday **30**AIV**r**
Rest – Italian – Menu £ 32/35
◆ Confidently run and smartly dressed Italian with an appealing and sensibly priced menu of easy-to-eat dishes. All breads and pasta made in-house. Boisterous and busy adjacent baretto.

XX **Goodman** A/C VISA MC AE

26 Maddox Street ✉ W1S 1QH ⊖ Oxford Circus – ✆ (020) 7499 3776
– www.goodmanrestaurants.com – Closed Easter, 25 December, 1 January and Sunday **30**AIU**u**
Rest – Beef specialities – *(booking essential)* Menu £ 15 (lunch) – Carte £ 28/47
◆ A worthy attempt at recreating a New York steakhouse; all leather and wood and macho swagger. Beef is dry or wet aged in house and comes with a choice of four sauces; rib-eye the speciality.

XX **Dolada** A/C VISA MC AE

13 Albemarle St ✉ W1S 4HJ Mayfair ⊖ Green Park – ✆ (020) 7409 1011
– www.dolada.co.uk – Fax (020) 7493 0081 – Closed Christmas and New Year, Saturday lunch and Sunday **30**AIV**x**
Rest – Italian – Menu £ 21/26 – Carte £ 30/42
◆ Smart basement restaurant lightened by confident and thoughtful service. Dishes from across Italy; the deconstructed spaghetti carbonara a speciality. Even more originality in the tasting menu.

XX **Hush** A/C VISA MC AE

8 Lancashire Court, Brook St ✉ W1S 1EY ⊖ Bond Street – ✆ (020) 7659 1500
– www.hush.co.uk – Fax (020) 7659 1501 – Closed 25-27 December, 1 January and Sunday **30**AHU**v**
Rest – Modern European – *(booking essential)* Carte £ 28/41
◆ Accessible brasserie-style menu served in a large, busy room; smart destination bar upstairs and plenty of private dining. Tucked away in a charming courtyard, with a summer terrace.

XX **Fakhreldine** A/C VISA MC AE

85 Piccadilly ✉ W1J 7NB ⊖ Green Park – ✆ (020) 7493 3424
– www.fakhreldine.co.uk – Fax (020) 7495 1977 **30**AIV**e**
Rest – Lebanese – Menu £ 14/25 – Carte £ 25/40
◆ Long-standing restaurant with great view of Green Park. Large selection of classic meze dishes and more modern European-style menu of original Lebanese dishes.

XX **Nobu** – at The Metropolitan Hotel

19 Old Park Lane ✉ W1Y 1LB ⊖ Hyde Park Corner – ✆ (020) 7447 4747 – www.noburestaurants.com – Fax (020) 7447 4749 – Closed 25 December and 1 January **30**AHV**c**

Rest – Japanese – *(booking essential)* Menu £ 50/90 – Carte £ 70/90

Spec. Yellowtail sashimi with jalapeno and yuzu soy dressing. Black cod with miso. Chocolate bento box with green tea ice cream.

◆ Its celebrity clientele ensure this remains one of the more glamorous spots. Staff are fully conversant in the innovative menu that adds South American influences to Japanese cooking. Has spawned many imitators.

XX **Via Condotti**

23 Conduit St ✉ W1S 2XS ⊖ Oxford Circus – ✆ (020) 7493 7050 – www.viacondotti.co.uk – Fax (020) 7409 7985 – Closed Christmas, New Year, Sunday and Bank Holidays **30**AIU**f**

Rest – Italian – Menu £ 28 – Carte £ 25/39

◆ Reliable and keenly run Italian, as warm and welcoming as the pretty façade suggests. Balanced and appetising cooking, using influences from the north of Italy, and all fairly priced.

XX **Taman Gang**

141 Park Lane ✉ W1K 7AA ⊖ Marble Arch – ✆ (020) 7518 3160 – www.tamangang.com – Fax (020) 7518 3161 – Closed Sunday, Monday and Bank Holidays **29**AGU**e**

Rest – Asian – *(dinner only)* Carte £ 25/73

◆ Basement restaurant with largish bar and lounge area. Stylish but intimate décor. Informal and intelligent service. Pan-Asian dishes presented in exciting modern manner.

XX **Sumosan**

26 Albemarle St ✉ W1S 4HY ⊖ Green Park – ✆ (020) 7495 5999 – www.sumosan.com – Fax (020) 7355 1247 – Closed 25-26 and 31 December, lunch Saturday, Sunday and Bank Holidays **30**AIU**e**

Rest – Japanese – Menu £ 23 (lunch) – Carte £ 32/59

◆ Aims to attract the smart set, with its cocktail list, modern interpretations of Japanese flavours and too-cool-to-smile service. Skilled kitchen deftly executes a wide-ranging menu.

XX **Mews of Mayfair**

10-11 Lancashire Court, Brook St (first floor) ✉ W1S 1EY ⊖ Bond Street – ✆ (020) 7518 9388 – www.mewsofmayfair.com – Fax (020) 7518 9389 – Closed 25-26 December and Sunday **30**AHU**a**

Rest – Modern European – Menu £ 19 (lunch) – Carte £ 29/36

◆ This pretty restaurant, bright in summer and warm in winter, is on the first floor of a mews house, once used as storage rooms for Savile Row. Seasonal menus offer something for everyone.

XX **Chor Bizarre**

16 Albemarle St ✉ W1S 4HW ⊖ Green Park – ✆ (020) 7629 9802 – www.chorbizarre.com – Fax (020) 7493 7756 – Closed Sunday lunch

Rest – Indian – Menu £ 18 (lunch) – Carte £ 30/45 **30**AIV**s**

◆ Eccentric and colourful décor of trinkets, curios and antiques; the name translates as 'thieves' market'. The menu is long and chatty; dishes from more northerly parts of India are the highlight.

XX **Sketch (The Gallery)**

9 Conduit St ✉ W1S 2XG ⊖ Oxford Street – ✆ (020) 7659 4500 – www.sketch.uk.com – Fax (020) 7629 1683 – Closed 25-26 December, Sunday, Monday lunch and Bank Holidays **30**AIU**h**

Rest – International – *(dinner only) (booking essential)* Carte £ 32/52

◆ On the ground floor of the Sketch building: daytime video art gallery metamorphoses into evening brasserie with ambient wall projections and light menus with eclectic range.

Cocoon

65 Regent St ✉ W1B 4EA ⊖ Piccadilly Circus – ✆ (020) 7494 7600 – www.cocoon-restaurants.com – Fax (020) 7494 7607 – Closed Saturday lunch and Sunday **30**AJU**x**

Rest – Asian – Menu £ 25/50 – Carte £ 28/45

◆ Trendy restaurant, based on a prime Regent Street site. Silk nets cleverly divide long, winding room. Bold, eclectic menus cover a wide spectrum of Asian dishes.

Momo

25 Heddon St ✉ W1B 4BH ⊖ Oxford Circus – ✆ (020) 7434 4040 – www.momoresto.com – Fax (020) 7287 0404 – Closed 25 December, 1 January and Sunday lunch **30**AIU**n**

Rest – Moroccan – Menu £ 19/45 – Carte £ 20/43

◆ Lanterns, rugs, trinkets and music contribute to the authentic Moroccan atmosphere; come in a group to better appreciate it. The more traditional dishes are the kitchen's strength.

Veeraswamy

Victory House, 99 Regent St, entrance on Swallow St ✉ W1B 4RS ⊖ Piccadilly Circus – ✆ (020) 7734 1401 – www.realindianfood.com – Fax (020) 7439 8434 – Closed dinner 25 December **30**AIU**t**

Rest – Indian – Menu £ 21 (lunch) – Carte £ 32/44

◆ May have opened back in 1926 but feels fresh and is awash with vibrant colours and always full of bustle. Skilled kitchen cleverly mixes the traditional with more contemporary creations.

La Petite Maison

54 Brooks Mews ✉ W1K 4EG ⊖ Bond Street – ✆ (020) 7495 4774 – www.lpmlondon.co.uk – Closed 25-26 December **30**AHU**f**

Rest – French – Carte £ 32/98 **s**

◆ Open-plan restaurant; sister to the eponymous Nice original. Healthy French Mediterranean cooking with a seafood slant. 20 starters to choose from; sharing is encouraged.

Kiku

17 Half Moon St ✉ W1J 7BE ⊖ Green Park – ✆ (020) 7499 4208 – www.kikurestaurant.co.uk – Fax (020) 7409 3259 – Closed 25 December, 1 January, lunch Sunday and Bank Holidays **30**AIV**g**

Rest – Japanese – Menu £ 18/46 – Carte £ 33/55

◆ Bright and fresh feel thanks to minimalistic décor of stone and natural wood. A plethora of menus, a fierce adherence to seasonality and an authentic emphasis on presentation.

Bar Trattoria Semplice

22 Woodstock St ✉ W1C 2AR ⊖ Bond Street – ✆ (020) 7491 8638 – www.bartrattoriasemplice.com **30**AHU**m**

Rest – Italian – Menu £ 16 (lunch) – Carte £ 24/29

◆ Baby sister to Semplice a few yards away, offering simpler, well-priced cooking in a relaxed and fun room. Specialities from a different region of Italy are featured each month. All-day menu in bar.

Chisou

4 Princes St ✉ W1B 2LE ⊖ Oxford Circus – ✆ (020) 7629 3931 – www.chisou.co.uk – Fax (020) 7629 5255 – Closed 24-31 December, Sunday and Bank Holidays except Easter **30**AIU**m**

Rest – Japanese – Menu £ 17 (lunch) – Carte £ 28/46

◆ In Mayfair's Japanese quarter; simple slate flooring and polished wood tables. Cosy sushi bar to rear. Elaborate menus of modern/classic Japanese dishes. Gets very busy.

Bentley's (Oyster Bar)

11-15 Swallow St ✉ W1B 4DG ⊖ Piccadilly Circus – ✆ (020) 7734 4756 – www.bentleys.org – Fax (020) 7758 4140 **30**AJU**n**

Rest – Seafood – Menu £ 20 (lunch) – Carte £ 33/45

◆ Sit at the counter to watch white-jacketed staff open oysters by the bucket load. Interesting seafood menus feature tasty fish pies; lots of daily specials on blackboard.

Automat
33 Dover St ✉ W1S 4NF ⊖ Green Park – ✆ (020) 7499 3033 – www.automat-london.com – Fax (020) 7499 2682 – Closed 25-26 December and 1 January **30**AIV**r**

Rest – American – Carte £ 39/52

◆ Buzzing New York style brasserie in three areas: a café, a 'dining car' with deep leather banquettes, and actual brasserie itself. Classic dishes from burgers to cheesecake.

The Cafe at Sotheby's
34-35 New Bond St ✉ W1A 2AA ⊖ Bond Street – ✆ (020) 7293 5077 – www.sothebys.com – Fax (020) 7293 6993 – Closed 24 December-4 January, Saturday and Sunday **30**AIU**y**

Rest – Modern European – *(lunch only) (booking essential)* Carte £ 25/33 **s**

◆ A velvet rope separates this simple room from the main lobby of this famous auction house. Pleasant service from staff in aprons. Menu is short but well-chosen and light.

Le Boudin Blanc
5 Trebeck St ⊖ Green Park – ✆ (020) 7499 3292 – www.boudinblanc.co.uk – Fax (020) 7495 6973 – Closed 24-26 December **30**AHV**q**

Rest – French – Menu £ 15 (lunch) – Carte £ 27/47

◆ Very busy restaurant with a simple bistro style; the first floor is marginally less frantic than the ground floor. Robust and satisfying French classics have authentic flavour.

The Only Running Footman
5 Charles St ✉ W1J 5DF ⊖ Green Park. – ✆ (020) 7499 2988 – www.therunningfootman.biz – Fax (020) 7629 8061 **30**AHV**x**

Rest – Menu £ 15 – Carte £ 26/35

◆ Charming, historic pub whose small, atmospheric ground floor is always busy, with a first-come-first-served rule. Upstairs you can book, it's plusher and the menu more ambitious.

Regent's Park and Marylebone

Landmark London
222 Marylebone Rd ✉ NW1 6JQ ⊖ Edgware Rd – ✆ (020) 7631 8000 – www.landmarklondon.co.uk – Fax (020) 7631 8080 **29**AFT**a**

290 rm – †£ 195/633 ††£ 195/633, ☐ £ 28 – 9 suites

Rest *Winter Garden* – Menu £ 35 (lunch) **s** – Carte £ 36/67 **s**

◆ Imposing Victorian Gothic building with a vast glass-enclosed atrium, overlooked by many of the modern, well-equipped bedrooms. Winter Garden popular for afternoon tea.

Hyatt Regency London-The Churchill
30 Portman Sq ✉ W1H 7BH ⊖ Marble Arch – ✆ (020) 7486 5800 – www.london.churchill.hyatt.com – Fax (020) 7486 1255 **29**AGT**x**

404 rm – †£ 213/460 ††£ 213/460, ☐ £ 25 – 40 suites

Rest *The Montagu* – ✆ (020) 7299 2037 – Menu £ 22/25 – Carte £ 35/47

◆ Smart property overlooking attractive square. Elegant marbled lobby. Well-appointed and recently refurbished rooms have the international traveller in mind. Restaurant provides popular Sunday brunch entertainment.

Langham
1c Portland Pl, Regent St ✉ W1B 1JA ⊖ Oxford Circus – ✆ (020) 7636 1000 – www.langhamhotels.com – Fax (020) 7323 2340 **29**AGT**n**

359 rm – †£ 218/466 ††£ 218/466, ☐ £ 30 – 21 suites

Rest *The Landau* – ✆ (020) 7965 0165 *(Closed Saturday lunch and Sunday)* Menu £ 34 – Carte £ 40/61

◆ Opened in 1865 and relaunched in 2009 following a major refurbishment. Impressive art deco Palm Court; comfortable bedrooms and notable leisure facilities. The Landau is an eye-catching and ornate room, with a wide-ranging menu.

The Cumberland

Great Cumberland Place ✉ *W1H 4DL* ⊖ *Marble Arch – ✆ (0870) 333 92 80 – www.guoman.com – Fax (0870) 333 92 81* **29**AGU**z**

1010 rm – **†**£ 138/299 **††**£ 138/334

Rest Rhodes W1 Restaurant and **Rhodes W1 Brasserie** – *see restaurant listing*

◆ Huge, well-located, conference and group oriented hotel whose lobby boasts modern art, sculpture and running water panels. Distinctive bedrooms with a host of impressive extras.

Sanderson

50 Berners St ✉ *W1T 3NG* ⊖ *Oxford Circus – ✆ (020) 7300 1400 – www.morganshotelgroup.com – Fax (020) 7300 1401* **31**AJT**c**

150 rm – **†**£ 414/627 **††**£ 414/627, £ 25

Rest *Suka* – Carte £ 35/45

◆ Designed by Philipe Starck and still attracting a suitably fashionable crowd. Purple Bar dark and moody; Long Bar bright and stylish. Pure white bedrooms with idiosyncratic design touches. Malaysian dishes designed for sharing in Suka.

The Leonard

15 Seymour St ✉ *W1H 7JW* ⊖ *Marble Arch – ✆ (020) 7935 2010 – www.theleonard.com – Fax (020) 7935 6700* **29**AGU**n**

32 rm – **†**£ 115/190 **††**£ 167/190, £ 15 – 16 suites

Rest – Menu £ 16 (dinner) – Carte £ 23/30

◆ Around the corner from Selfridges, an attractive Georgian townhouse: antiques and oil paintings abound. Well-appointed rooms in classic country house style. Small dining room adjoins bar.

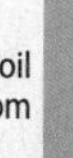

London Marriott H. Marble Arch

rm,

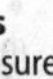

134 George St ✉ *W1H 5DN* ⊖ *Marble Arch – ✆ (020) 7725 5923 – www.londonmarriottmarblearch.co.uk – Fax (020) 7725 5924* **29**AFT**j**

240 rm – **†**£ 304/351 **††**£ 304/351, £ 18.95

Rest *Mediterrano* – ✆ *(020) 7723 1277 (dinner only)* Carte £ 24/39 **s**

◆ Centrally located and modern. Offers comprehensive conference facilities. Leisure centre underground. An ideal base for both corporate and leisure guests. Mediterranean-influenced cooking.

Dorset Square

39 Dorset Sq ✉ *NW1 6QN* ⊖ *Marylebone – ✆ (020) 7723 7874 – www.dorsetsquare.co.uk – Fax (020) 7724 3328* **17**QZD**s**

37 rm – **†**£ 173/322 **††**£ 322, £ 15.50

Rest *Osteria Dell' Orologio* – *(closed Saturday lunch and Sunday) (booking essential)* Menu £ 22

◆ Converted Regency townhouses in a charming square which was the site of the original Lord's cricket ground. A warm and welcoming country house in the city with individually decorated rooms. Pretty basement Italian restaurant.

Durrants

rest,

26-32 George St ✉ *W1H 5BJ* ⊖ *Bond Street – ✆ (020) 7935 8131 – www.durrantshotel.co.uk – Fax (020) 7487 3510* **29**AGT**e**

92 rm – **†**£ 125 **††**£ 175, £ 17 – 4 suites

Rest – *(Closed dinner 25 December)* Menu £ 20 – Carte £ 31/41

◆ Traditional, privately owned hotel with friendly, long-standing staff. Newly refurbished bedrooms are brighter in style but still English in character. Clubby dining room for mix of British classics and lighter, European dishes.

The Mandeville

rm,

Mandeville Pl ✉ *W1U 2BE* ⊖ *Bond Street – ✆ (020) 7935 5599 – www.mandeville.co.uk – Fax (020) 7935 9588* **30**AHT**x**

142 rm – **†**£ 340/363 **††**£ 363, £ 21.50 – 7 suites

Rest *de Ville* – *(Closed Sunday dinner)* Menu £ 16 (lunch) – Carte £ 26/37

◆ Usefully located hotel with marbled reception leading into a very colourful and comfortable bar. Stylish rooms have flatscreen TVs and make good use of the space available. Modern British cuisine served in bright de Ville restaurant.

The Sumner without rest
54 Upper Berkeley St ✉ W1H 7QR ⊖ Marble Arch – ✆ (020) 7723 2244 – www.thesumner.com – Fax (0870) 705 8767 **29**AFU**k**
20 rm ☕ – †£ 190 ††£ 190
◆ Two Georgian terrace houses in central location. Comfy, stylish sitting room; basement breakfast room. Largest bedrooms, 101 and 201, benefit from having full-length windows.

Hart House without rest
51 Gloucester Pl ✉ W1U 8JF ⊖ Marble Arch – ✆ (020) 7935 2288 – www.harthouse.co.uk – Fax (020) 7935 8516 **29**AGT**d**
15 rm ☕ – †£ 103/110 ††£ 127/173
◆ Within an attractive Georgian terrace and run by the same family for over 35 years. Warm and welcoming service; well-kept, competitively priced bedrooms over three floors.

St George without rest
49 Gloucester Pl ✉ W1U 8JE ⊖ Marble Arch – ✆ (020) 7486 8586 – www.stgeorge-hotel.net – Fax (020) 7486 6567 **29**AGT**h**
19 rm – †£ 85/95 ††£ 125/130, ☕ £ 5
◆ Terraced house on a busy street, usefully located within walking distance of many attractions. Offers a warm welcome and comfortable bedrooms which are spotlessly maintained.

LONDON

Rhodes W1 (Restaurant) – at The Cumberland Hotel
Great Cumberland Place ✉ W1H 7DL ⊖ Marble Arch – ✆ (020) 7616 5930 – www.rhodesw1.com – Fax (020) 7479 3888 – Closed Christmas, 1 week August, Sunday-Tuesday and Bank Holidays **29**AGU**z**
Rest – French – *(booking advisable)* Menu £ 24/50
Spec. Salad of artichokes with wild mushrooms, truffle and duck egg. Salmon with parsley gnocchi, snails and roast garlic. Apricot soufflé with white chocolate ice cream and apricot sauce.
◆ Just 12 tables in a warm and textured room designed by Kelly Hoppen. Influences are more European than usual for a Gary Rhodes restaurant but with the same emphasis on clear, uncluttered flavours.

Locanda Locatelli
8 Seymour St ✉ W1H 7JZ ⊖ Marble Arch – ✆ (020) 7935 9088 – www.locandalocatelli.com – Fax (020) 7935 1149 – Closed Bank Holidays **29**AGU**r**
Rest – Italian – Carte £ 39/57
Spec. Pheasant ravioli. Rabbit with Parma ham, radicchio and polenta. Tasting of Amedei chocolate.
◆ Slick and dapper-looking Italian with a celebrity following and a sophisticated atmosphere. Plenty of interest on the extensive menu, with cooking that is confident, balanced and expertly rendered; pastas and desserts are the stand-out courses.

Latium
21 Berners St, Fitzrovia ✉ W1T 3LP ⊖ Oxford Circus – ✆ (020) 7323 9123 – www.latiumrestaurant.com – Fax (020) 7323 3205 – Closed 25-26 December, 1 January, Saturday lunch and Sunday **31**AJT**n**
Rest – Italian – Menu £ 20/30
◆ Bright and contemporary surroundings but with warm and welcoming service. Owner-chef from Lazio but dishes come from across Italy, often using British produce. Ravioli is the house speciality.

Galvin Bistrot de Luxe
66 Baker St ✉ W1U 7DJ ⊖ Baker Street – ✆ (020) 7935 4007 – www.galvinrestaurants.com – Fax (020) 7486 1735 – Closed 25-26 December and 1 January **29**AGT**b**
Rest – French – Menu £ 16 – Carte £ 23/35
◆ Firmly established modern Gallic bistro with ceiling fans, globe lights and wood panelled walls. Satisfying and precisely cooked classic French dishes from the Galvin brothers.

XX ✿ **Texture** (Agnar Sverrisson) AC VISA MC AE

34 Portman Square ✉ W1H 7BY ⊖ Marble Arch – ☎ (020) 7224 0028 – www.texture-restaurant.co.uk – Closed 1 week Christmas, first 2 weeks August, Sunday and Monday **29**AGU**p**

Rest – Innovative – Menu £ 22 (lunch) – Carte £ 38/55

Spec. Pigeon with sweetcorn, bacon popcorn and red wine. Icelandic cod with chorizo, squid and artichokes. Strawberries with granola and milk ice cream.

◆ Technically skilled but light and invigorating cooking from Icelandic chef-owner, who uses ingredients from home. Bright restaurant with high ceiling and popular adjoining champagne bar. Pleasant service from keen staff, ready with a smile.

XX ✿ **L'Autre Pied** (Marcus Eaves) AC VISA MC AE

5-7 Blandford Street ✉ W1U 3DB ⊖ Bond Street – ☎ (020) 7486 9696 – www.lautrepied.co.uk – Fax (020) 7486 5067 – Closed 23-29 December

Rest – Modern European – Menu £ 21 (lunch) – Carte £ 37/55 **30**AHT**k**

Spec. Seared foie gras, artichokes and pineapple sorbet. Rabbit with confit tomato, Dauphine potatoes and smoked eel. Baked Alaska with basil ice cream and strawberries.

◆ A more informal sibling to Pied à Terre, with red leather seating, closely set tables and relaxed atmosphere. But cooking is just as ambitious: it is original, creative and technically adroit.

XX **Zayna** AC VISA MC AE

25 New Quebec Rd ✉ W1H 7SF ⊖ Marble Arch – ☎ (020) 7723 2229 – www.zaynarestaurant.co.uk – Fax (0870) 042 00 22 **29**AGU**x**

Rest – Indian – Carte £ 29/40

◆ Enthusiastically run, elegant restaurant spread over two floors, with keen owner. Interesting north Indian and Pakistani delicacies; kitchen only uses halal meat and free-range chicken.

XX **Ozer** AC VISA MC AE

5 Langham Pl, Regent St ✉ W1B 3DG ⊖ Oxford Circus – ☎ (020) 7323 0505 – www.ozer.co.uk – Fax (020) 7323 0111 **30**AIT**z**

Rest – Turkish – Menu £ 11/15 – Carte £ 26/41 **s**

◆ The large front bar is always busy but go through to the equally popular but comfortable restaurant to enjoy authentic Turkish food. Wide range of appealing hot and cold meze is the draw.

XX **Rhodes W1 Brasserie** – at The Cumberland Hotel AC VISA MC AE

Great Cumberland Pl ✉ W1H 7DL ⊖ Marble Arch – ☎ (020) 7616 5930 – www.rhodesw1.com – Fax (020) 7479 3888 **29**AGU**z**

Rest – Modern European – Menu £ 17 (lunch) – Carte £ 26/38

◆ Large brasserie on the ground floor of the Cumberland hotel, with keen, helpful service and equally big bar. Expect Gary Rhodes' signature dishes, alongside others of a more European persuasion.

XX **The Providores** AC VISA MC AE

109 Marylebone High St ✉ W1U 4RX ⊖ Bond Street – ☎ (020) 7935 6175 – www.theprovidores.co.uk – Fax (020) 7935 6877 – Closed 25 to 29 December and 1-2 January **30**AHT**y**

Rest – Innovative – Menu £ 42 (dinner) – Carte (lunch) £ 35/50

◆ Packed ground floor for tapas; upstairs for innovative fusion cooking, with spices and ingredients from around the world, including Australasia. Starter-sized dishes at dinner allow for greater choice.

XX **La Porte des Indes** AC VISA MC AE

32 Bryanston St ✉ W1H 7EG ⊖ Marble Arch – ☎ (020) 7224 0055 – www.laportedesindes.com – Fax (020) 7224 1144 – Closed 25-26 December and 1 January **29**AGU**s**

Rest – Indian – Menu £ 15/28 – Carte £ 22/42

◆ Don't be fooled by the discreet entrance: inside there is a spectacularly unrestrained display of palm trees, murals and waterfalls. French-influenced Indian cuisine.

LONDON

XX **Levant** A/C VISA MC AE D

Jason Court, 76 Wigmore St ✉ W1U 2SJ ⊖ Bond Street – ☎ (020) 7224 1111 – www.levant.co.uk – Fax (020) 7486 1216 **30**AHT**c**

Rest – Lebanese – Menu £ 28 (dinner) – Carte £ 30/40

◆ Belly dancing, lanterns and a low-slung bar all add up to an exotic dining experience. The Lebanese food is satisfying and authentic, carefully prepared and ideal for sharing in groups.

XX **Villandry** A/C VISA MC AE D

170 Great Portland St ✉ W1W 5QB ⊖ Regent's Park – ☎ (020) 7631 3131 – www.villandry.com – Fax (020) 7631 3030 – Closed 25-26 and 31 December, 1 January and Sunday dinner **30**AIT**s**

Rest – French – Carte £ 25/41

◆ The senses are heightened by passing through the well-stocked deli to the dining room behind. Bare walls, wooden tables and a menu offering simple, tasty dishes.

XX **L'Aventure** VISA MC AE

3 Blenheim Terrace ✉ NW8 0EH ⊖ St John's Wood – ☎ (020) 7624 6232 – Fax (020) 7625 5548 – Closed 15-31 August, first week January, Saturday lunch, Sunday and Bank Holidays **11**PZB**b**

Rest – French – Menu £ 20/38

◆ Behind the pretty tree-lined entrance you'll find a charming neighbourhood restaurant. Relaxed atmosphere and service by personable owner. Authentic French cuisine.

XX **Phoenix Palace** A/C VISA MC AE

5 Glentworth St ✉ NW1 5PG ⊖ Baker Street – ☎ (020) 7486 3515 – www.phoenixpalace.co.uk – Fax (020) 7486 3401 – Closed 25 December

Rest – Chinese – Carte £ 22/37 **17**QZD**x**

◆ Tucked away near Baker Street; lots of photos of celebrities who've eaten here. Huge room for 200 diners where authentic, fresh, well-prepared Chinese dishes are served.

XX **Vineria** A/C VISA MC AE

1 Blenheim Terrace ✉ NW8 0EH ⊖ St John's Wood – ☎ (020) 7328 5014 – www.vineria.it – Closed Monday **11**PZB**z**

Rest – Italian – Menu £ 20 (lunch) – Carte £ 28/39

◆ Pleasant enclosed front terrace; conservatory section and white walls ensure a bright interior. Undemanding menu covers all parts of Italy, with pasta dishes the kitchen's strength.

X **Trishna** A/C VISA MC AE

15-17 Blandford St ✉ W1U 3DG ⊖ Baker Street – ☎ (020) 7935 5624 – www.trishnalondon.com – Fax (020) 7935 9259 **29**AGT**r**

Rest – Indian – Menu £ 17 (lunch) – Carte £ 27/43

◆ A franchise of the celebrated Mumbai restaurant. Specialises in fish and seafood dishes, with brown crab with butter garlic being a highlight. Bright surroundings allow the focus to be the food.

X **Michael Moore** VISA MC AE D

19 Blandford St ✉ W1U 3DH ⊖ Baker Street – ☎ (020) 7224 1898 – www.michaelmoorerestaurant.com – Fax (020) 7224 0970 – Closed Christmas-New Year, Saturday lunch, Sunday and Bank Holidays

Rest – International – Menu £ 18 (lunch) – Carte £ 33/49 **29**AGT**r**

◆ Warm glow emanates not just from mustard façade but also effusive welcome within. Cosy, locally renowned favourite, with global cuisine served by friendly, efficient staff.

X **The Wallace** VISA MC AE

Hertford House, Manchester Sq ✉ W1U 3BN ⊖ Bond St – ☎ (020) 7563 9505 – www.thewallacerestaurant.com – Closed 25 December **29**AGT**k**

Rest – French – *(lunch only and dinner Friday-Saturday)* Carte £ 26/32

◆ Large glass-roofed courtyard on the ground floor of Hertford House and the splendid Wallace Collection. French-influenced menu, with fruits de mer section; terrines are the house speciality.

Union Café

96 Marylebone Lane ✉ W1U 2QA ⊖ Bond Street – ✆ (020) 7486 4860 – www.brinkleys.com – Fax (020) 7935 1537 – Closed Sunday dinner and Bank Holidays **30**AHT**d**

Rest – International – Carte £ 31/38

◆ A quasi-industrial feel, with exposed ducts, open kitchen and bustling atmosphere. Menu full of global influences, so expect anything from dim sum to risotto, burgers to pork belly.

Caffé Caldesi

1st Floor, 118 Marylebone Lane ✉ W1U 2QF ⊖ Bond Street – ✆ (020) 7487 0754 – www.caldesi.com – Fax (020) 7935 8832 – Closed 25-26 December, 1 January and Sunday lunch **30**AHT**s**

Rest – Italian – Carte £ 24/41

◆ Converted pub with a simple modern interior in which to enjoy tasty, uncomplicated Italian dishes. Downstairs is a lively bar with a deli counter serving pizzas and pastas.

Dinings

22 Harcourt St. ✉ W1H 4HH ⊖ Marylebone – ✆ (020) 7723 0666 – www.dinings.co.uk – Fax (020) 7723 3222 – Closed lunch Saturday, Sunday and Bank Holidays **29**AFT**c**

Rest – Japanese – *(booking essential)* Carte £ 29/40

◆ Resembles an after-work Japanese izakaya, or pub, with chummy atmosphere and loud music. Food is a mix of small plates of delicate dishes, a blend of modern and the more traditional.

Il Baretto

43 Blandford St ✉ W1U 7HF ⊖ Baker Street – ✆ (020) 7486 7340 – www.ilbaretto.co.uk – Closed 25 December-1 January and Sunday

Rest – Italian – Carte £ 20/45 **29**AGT**n**

◆ The wood-fired oven is the star of the show at this neighbourhood Italian. The extensive menu has something for everyone, although prices vary a lot. The basement room has a lively atmosphere.

Chada Chada

16-17 Picton Pl ✉ W1U 1BP ⊖ Bond Street – ✆ (020) 7935 8212 – www.chadathai.com – Fax (020) 7924 2791 – Closed Sunday and Bank Holidays **30**AHU**b**

Rest – Thai – Menu £ 14/21 – Carte £ 23/32

◆ Authentic and fragrant Thai cooking; the good value menu offers some interesting departures from the norm. Service is eager to please in the compact and cosy rooms.

St James's

The Ritz

150 Piccadilly ✉ W1J 9BR ⊖ Green Park – ✆ (020) 7493 8181 – www.theritzlondon.com – Fax (020) 7493 2687 **30**AIV**c**

116 rm – †£ 288/714 ††£ 311/714, ☕ £ 32 – 17 suites

Rest *The Ritz Restaurant* – see restaurant listing

◆ World famous hotel, opened 1906 as a fine example of Louis XVI architecture and decoration. Elegant Palm Court famed for its afternoon tea. Many of the lavishly appointed and luxurious rooms and suites overlook the park.

Sofitel St James London

6 Waterloo Pl ✉ SW1Y 4AN ⊖ Piccadilly Circus – ✆ (020) 7747 2200 – www.sofitel.com – Fax (020) 7747 2210 **31**AKV**a**

179 rm – †£ 230/397 ††£ 253/397, ☕ £ 23.50 – 6 suites

Rest *Brasserie Roux* – see restaurant listing

◆ Grade II listed building in smart Pall Mall location. Classically English interiors include floral Rose Lounge and club-style St James bar. Comfortable, well-fitted bedrooms.

LONDON

Haymarket
1 Suffolk Place ✉ SW1Y 4BP ⊖ Piccadilly Circus – ✆ (020) 7470 4000 – www.haymarkethotel.com – Fax (020) 7470 4001 **31**AKV**d**
47 rm – †£ 294 ††£ 382, ☕ £ 18.50 – 3 suites
Rest *Brumus* – ✆ (020) 7451 1012 – Menu £ 20 – Carte £ 24/49
◆ Smart, spacious hotel in John Nash Regency building, with stylish blend of modern and antique furnishings. Large, comfortable bedrooms in soothing colours. Impressive pool. Brumus bar and restaurant puts focus on Italian cooking.

Dukes
35 St James's Pl ✉ SW1A 1NY ⊖ Green Park – ✆ (020) 7491 4840 – www.dukeshotel.com – Fax (020) 7493 1264 **30**AIV**f**
84 rm – †£ 190/368 ††£ 190/512, ☕ £ 24.50 – 6 suites
Rest – Menu £ 18/20 – Carte £ 29/37
◆ The most recent redecoration retained the discreet, traditionally British feel of this hotel in a central but quiet location. Dukes bar famous for its martinis. Elegant bedrooms with country house feel. Discreet dining room.

Stafford
16-18 St James's Pl ✉ SW1A 1NJ ⊖ Green Park – ✆ (020) 7493 0111 – www.thestaffordhotel.co.uk – Fax (020) 7493 7121 **30**AIV**u**
73 rm – †£ 363/391 ††£ 506/552, ☕ £ 25 – 15 suites
Rest – *(closed Saturday lunch)* Menu £ 30 (lunch) – Carte dinner £ 55/74
◆ A genteel atmosphere prevails in this discreet 'country house in the city'. Bedrooms divided between main house, converted 18C stables and newer Mews. Traditional and intimate dining room.

St James's Hotel and Club
7-8 Park Place ✉ SW1A 1LS ⊖ Green Park – ✆ (020) 7316 1600 – www.stjameshotelandclub.com – Fax (020) 7316 1603 **30**AIV**k**
50 rm – †£ 248/386 ††£ 282/478, ☕ £ 22 – 10 suites
Rest *Seven Park Place* – *(closed Sunday and Monday) (booking essential)* Menu £ 30/45
◆ 1890s house in cul-de-sac, formerly a private club, reopened as a hotel in 2008. Modern, boutique–style interior with over 400 paintings. Fine finish to compact, but well-equipped bedrooms. Refined cooking by chef William Drabble in restaurant with limited space.

The Ritz Restaurant – at The Ritz Hotel
150 Piccadilly ✉ W1J 9BR ⊖ Green Park – ✆ (020) 7493 8181 – www.theritzlondon.com – Fax (020) 7493 2687 **30**AIV**c**
Rest – Traditional – Menu £ 37/46 – Carte £ 48/98 **s**
◆ Grand and lavish restaurant, with Louis XVI decoration, trompe l'oeil and ornate gilding. Delightful terrace over Green Park. Structured, formal service. Classic, traditional dishes are the highlight of the menu. Jacket and tie required.

The Wolseley
160 Piccadilly ✉ W1J 9EB ⊖ Green Park – ✆ (020) 7499 6996 – www.thewolseley.com – Fax (020) 7499 6888 – Closed 25 December, 1 January, August Bank Holiday and dinner 24 and 31 December **30**AIV**q**
Rest – Modern European – *(booking essential)* Carte £ 21/47
◆ Feels like a grand European coffee house, with pillars and high vaulted ceiling. Appealing menus range from caviar to a hot dog. Open from breakfast and boasts a celebrity following.

St Alban
4-12 Regent St ✉ SW1Y 4PE ⊖ Piccadilly Circus – ✆ (020) 7499 8558 – www.stalban.net – Fax (020) 7499 6888 – Closed 25-26 December, 1 January, Sunday dinner and August Bank Holiday **31**AKV**c**
Rest – Mediterranean – Carte £ 25/57
◆ Light, airy restaurant with colourful booth seating and feeling of space. Weekly changing southern European menu; specialities from the wood-fired oven and charcoal grill.

XXX **Sake No Hana**

23 St James's St ✉ SW1A 1HA ⊖ Green Park – ✆ (020) 7925 8988 – www.sakenohana.com – Fax (020) 7925 8999 – Closed 24-25 December and Sunday lunch **30**AIV**n**

Rest – Japanese – Carte £ 20/60

◆ Stylish first floor restaurant reached by elevator, where cedar wood décor goes some way to disguising an ugly '60s building. Mix of traditional and modern Japanese food; ground floor sushi bar.

XX **Le Caprice**

Arlington House, Arlington St ✉ SW1A 1RJ ⊖ Green Park – ✆ (020) 7629 2239 – www.le-caprice.co.uk – Fax (020) 7493 9040 – Closed 24-26 December and 1 January **30**AIV**h**

Rest – Modern European – Menu £ 20 – Carte £ 33/53

◆ Still attracting a fashionable clientele and as busy as ever. Dine at the bar or in the smoothly run restaurant. Food combines timeless classics with modern dishes.

XX **Quaglino's**

16 Bury St ✉ SW1Y 6AL ⊖ Green Park – ✆ (020) 7930 6767 – www.quaglinos.co.uk – Fax (020) 7930 2732 – Closed 25 December, Sunday and Bank Holidays **30**AIV**j**

Rest – Modern European – *(booking essential)* Menu £ 20 – Carte £ 33/46

◆ Descend the sweeping staircase from the stylish bar into the capacious dining room where a busy and buzzy atmosphere prevails. Accessible menu, with something for everyone.

XX **Mint Leaf**

Suffolk Pl ✉ SW1Y 4HX ⊖ Piccadilly Circus – ✆ (020) 7930 9020 – www.mintleafrestaurant.com – Fax (020) 7930 6205 – Closed 25-26 December, 1 January, lunch Saturday and Sunday **31**AKV**k**

Rest – Indian – Menu £ 17 (lunch) – Carte £ 31/55

◆ Cavernous and moodily lit basement restaurant incorporating trendy bar with lounge music and extensive cocktail list. Contemporary Indian cooking with curries the highlight.

XX **Brasserie St Jacques**

33 St James's Street ✉ SW1A 1HD ⊖ Green Park – ✆ (020) 7839 1007 – www.brasseriestjacques.co.uk – Fax (020) 7839 3204 – Closed Christmas, New Year and Saturday lunch **30**AIV**z**

Rest – French – Carte £ 30/50

◆ With its high ceiling and narrow layout, it may lack the buzz one finds in a typical French brasserie, but is nearer the mark with a menu that features all the classic brasserie favourites.

XX **Franco's**

61 Jermyn St ✉ SW1Y 6LX ⊖ Green Park – ✆ (020) 7499 2211 – www.francoslondon.com – Fax (020) 7495 1375 – Closed Sunday and Bank Holidays **30**AIV**i**

Rest – Italian – *(booking essential)* Menu £ 25 (lunch) – Carte £ 35/51

◆ Great all day menu at 'the café'. Further in, regulars have taken to the last refurbishment. Classic Italian cooking allows bold but refined flavours to shine through.

XX **Avenue**

7-9 St James's St ✉ SW1A 1EE ⊖ Green Park – ✆ (020) 7321 2111 – www.theavenue-restaurant.co.uk – Fax (020) 7321 2500 – Closed Sunday

Rest – Modern European – Menu £ 23 – Carte dinner £ 24/36 **30**AIV**y**

◆ Large, brash restaurant, with sheer white décor and a very popular bar. All-encompassing menu, with everything from caviar to burgers. Service comes with an urgency not always required.

XX **Matsuri - St James's**

15 Bury St ✉ SW1Y 6AL ⊖ Green Park – ✆ (020) 7839 1101 – www.matsuri-restaurant.com – Fax (020) 7930 7010 – Closed 25 December

Rest – Japanese – Carte £ 29/69 **30**AIV**w**

◆ Sweet natured service at this traditional Japanese stalwart. Teppan-yaki is their speciality, with Scottish beef the highlight; sushi counter also available. Good value lunch menus.

LONDON

XX **Brasserie Roux** – at Sofitel St James London
8 Pall Mall ✉ SW1Y 5NG ⊖ Piccadilly Circus – ✆ (020) 7968 2900 – www.brasserieroux.com – Fax (020) 7747 2251 **31**AKV**a**
Rest – French – Menu £ 20/21 – Carte £ 32/49
◆ Informal, smart, classic brasserie style with large windows making the most of the location. Large menu of French classics with many daily specials; comprehensive wine list.

X **Al Duca**
4-5 Duke of York St ✉ SW1Y 6LA ⊖ Piccadilly Circus – ✆ (020) 7839 3090 – www.alduca_restaurant.co.uk – Fax (020) 7839 4050 – Closed one week Christmas, Sunday and Bank Holidays **31**AJV**r**
Rest – Italian – Menu £ 28
◆ Bright, busy restaurant that's always full of life. Friendly and approachable service of robust and rustic Italian dishes; the set priced menu is good value, especially in this neighbourhood.

X **Inn the Park**
St James's Park ✉ SW1A 2BJ ⊖ Charing Cross – ✆ (020) 7451 9999 – www.innthepark.com – Fax (020) 7451 9998 – Closed 25 December
Rest – British – Menu £ 15 (dinner) – Carte £ 30/36 **31**AKV**n**
◆ Oliver Peyton's eco-friendly restaurant in the middle of the park, with a terrific terrace. British menu uses many small suppliers. Cooking is straightforward and wholesome.

X **Portrait**
3rd Floor, National Portrait Gallery, St Martin's Pl ✉ WC2H 0HE ⊖ Charing Cross – ✆ (020) 7312 2490 – www.searcys.co.uk – Closed 24-26 December **31**ALV**n**
Rest – Modern European – *(lunch only and dinner Saturday-Sunday) (booking essential)* Menu £ 23 – Carte £ 31/40
◆ On the top floor of National Portrait Gallery with rooftop local landmark views: a charming spot for lunch. Modern British/European dishes; weekend brunch.

X **The National Dining Rooms**
Sainsbury Wing, The National Gallery, Trafalgar Sq ✉ WC2N 5DN ⊖ Charing Cross – ✆ (020) 7747 2525 – www.thenationaldiningrooms.co.uk – Closed 25-26 December and 1 January **31**AKV**b**
Rest – British – *(lunch only and dinner Friday)* Menu £ 24 – Carte approx. £ 32
◆ Set on the East Wing's first floor, you can tuck into cakes in the bakery or grab a prime corner table in the restaurant for great views and proudly seasonal British menus.

Soho

The Soho rm,
4 Richmond Mews ✉ W1D 3DH ⊖ Tottenham Court Road – ✆ (020) 7559 3000 – www.sohohotel.com – Fax (020) 7559 3003 **31**AKU**n**
89 rm – †£ 322 ††£ 403, ☕ £ 18.50 – 2 suites
Rest *Refuel* – ✆ (020) 7559 3007 – Menu £ 20 – Carte £ 34/52
◆ Stylish and very fashionable hotel boasts two screening rooms, comfy drawing room and up-to-the-minute bedrooms, some vivid, others more muted, all boasting hi-tech extras. Contemporary bar and restaurant.

Courthouse Doubletree by Hilton rm,
19-21 Great Marlborough St ✉ W1F 7HL ⊖ Oxford Circus – ✆ (020) 7297 5555 – www.courthouse-hotel.com – Fax (020) 7297 5566 **30**AIU**z**
108 rm – †£ 196/403 ††£ 253/518, ☕ £ 22.50 – 1 suite
Rest *Silk* – Indian – *(Closed 10 days Christmas, Sunday and Monday) (dinner only)* Menu £ 25 – Carte £ 26/43
Rest *The Carnaby* – Menu £ 15/20 – Carte £ 22/30
◆ Striking Grade II listed ex magistrates' court: interior fused imaginatively with original features; for example, the bar incorporates three former cells. Stylish rooms. Silk's fusion cuisine influenced by the Silk Route. Informal Carnaby offers extensive choice.

Sanctum Soho

20 Warwick St ✉ W1B 5NF ⊖ Piccadilly Circus – ☎ (020) 7292 6100 – www.sanctumsoho.com – Fax (020) 7434 3074 **30**AIU**a**

30 rm – †£ 202 ††£ 202/403, ☕ £ 11.50

Rest *No. 20* – *(Closed Sunday dinner)* Menu £ 20 – Carte £ 24/45

◆ Plenty of glitz and bling at this funky, self-styled rock 'n' roll hotel, with some innovative touches such as TVs behind mirrors. Rooftop lounge and hot tub. Relaxed and comfortable dining with plenty of classic dishes.

Hazlitt's without rest

6 Frith St ✉ W1D 3JA ⊖ Tottenham Court Road – ☎ (020) 7434 1771 – www.hazlittshotel.com – Fax (020) 7439 1524 **31**AKU**u**

29 rm – †£ 183/253 ††£ 195/253 – 3 suites

◆ Three adjoining early 18C townhouses and former home of the eponymous essayist. Idiosyncratic bedrooms, many with antique furniture and Victorian baths; ask for one of the newer ones.

Quo Vadis

26-29 Dean St ✉ W1D 3LL ⊖ Tottenham Court Road – ☎ (020) 7437 9585 – www.quovadis.co.uk – Fax (020) 7734 7593 – Closed 24-25 December and Bank Holidays **31**AKU**v**

Rest – British – Menu £ 20 (lunch) – Carte £ 33/47

◆ Dating from the 1920s and renewed in 2008; a veritable Soho institution with an art deco feel. Instantly appealing menu of carefully prepared classics, from grilled Hereford beef to assorted seafood.

Red Fort

77 Dean St ✉ W1D 3SH ⊖ Tottenham Court Road – ☎ (020) 7437 2525 – www.redfort.co.uk – Fax (020) 7434 0721 – Closed 25 December and lunch Saturday, Sunday and Bank Holidays **31**AKU**x**

Rest – Indian – *(booking advisable at dinner)* Menu £ 20/35 – Carte £ 35/42

◆ Smart, stylish restaurant with modern water feature and glass ceiling to rear. Seasonally changing menus of authentic dishes handed down over generations.

Yauatcha

15 Broadwick St ✉ W1F 0DL ⊖ Tottenham Court Road – ☎ (020) 7494 8888 – www.yauatcha.com – Fax (020) 7287 6959 – Closed 24-25 December **31**AJU**k**

Rest – Chinese – Carte £ 21/67

Spec. King crab dumpling. Crispy duck with Thai spring onion and cucumber. Roasted pineapple with praline parfait and ice cream.

◆ Refined, delicate and delicious dim sum; ideal for sharing in a group. Stylish surroundings spread over two floors: the lighter, brighter ground floor or the darker, more atmospheric basement. Afternoon teas also a speciality.

Bob Bob Ricard

1 Upper James St ✉ W1F 9DF ⊖ Oxford Circus – ☎ (020) 3145 1000 – www.bobbobricard.com – Fax (020) 7851 9308 **31**AJU**n**

Rest – Modern European – Carte £ 26/49

◆ Enigmatically decorated and flamboyant grand café, with a menu that offers everything from caviar and jelly, to beef Wellington or a bowl of cornflakes. Open from early to very late.

Floridita

100 Wardour St ✉ W1F 0TN ⊖ Tottenham Court Road – ☎ (020) 7314 4000 – www.floriditalondon.com – Fax (020) 7314 4040 – Closed 25-26 December, 1 January, Sunday, Monday and Bank Holidays **31**AKU**z**

Rest – Latin American – *(dinner only and lunch in December)* Menu £ 39 – Carte £ 27/63

◆ Mediterranean tapas on the ground floor; the huge downstairs for live music, dancing and Latin American specialities, from Cuban spice to Argentinean beef. Great cocktails and a party atmosphere.

XX **Haozhan**

8 Gerrard St ✉ W1D 5PJ ⊖ Leicester Square – ✆ (0207) 434 38 38 – www.haozhan.co.uk – Fax (0207) 434 99 91 – Closed 24-25 December

Rest – Chinese – Menu £ 10 (lunch) – Carte £ 21/41 **31**AKU**k**

◆ It bucks the trend of Chinatown mediocrity by offering well-judged, original and balanced Cantonese dishes, with Taiwanese and Malaysian specialities. Contemporary, stylish décor and helpful service.

XX **Café Lazeez**

21 Dean St ✉ W1D 3TN ⊖ Tottenham Court Road – ✆ (020) 7434 9393 – www.lazeez.sohocom – Fax (020) 7434 0022 – Closed 25 December, 1 January and Sunday **31**AKU**d**

Rest – Indian – Carte £ 27/35

◆ Adjoining the Soho Theatre; the bar hums before shows. Downstairs restaurant is popular for pre and post-theatre meals of modern Indian fare. Ask for one of the booths.

XX **Benja**

17 Beak St ✉ W1F 9RW ⊖ Oxford Circus – ✆ (020) 7287 0555 – www.benjarestaurant.com – Fax (020) 7287 0056 – Closed 25 December, 1 January, lunch Sunday and Bank Holidays **30**AIU**j**

Rest – Thai – *(booking essential at dinner)* Menu £ 30 (dinner) – Carte £ 25/39

◆ Soho townhouse divided into three sleek and colourful floors including an intimate basement bar. Thai food is carefully prepared and full of punchy flavours. Service is very charming.

LONDON

XX **Vasco and Piero's Pavilion**

15 Poland St ✉ W1F 8QE ⊖ Tottenham Court Road – ✆ (020) 7437 8774 – www.vascosfood.com – Fax (020) 7437 0467 – Closed Saturday lunch, Sunday and Bank Holidays **31**AJU**b**

Rest – Italian – *(booking essential at lunch)* Menu £ 32 (dinner) – Carte lunch £ 27/38

◆ A long-standing, family-run Italian restaurant with a loyal local following. Pleasant service under the owners' guidance. Warm décor and traditional cooking.

XX **La Trouvaille**

12A Newburgh St ✉ W1F 7RR ⊖ Oxford Circus – ✆ (020) 7287 8488 – www.latrouvaille.co.uk – Fax (020) 7434 4170 – Closed 25 December, Saturday lunch, Sunday, Monday dinner and Bank Holidays **30**AIU**g**

Rest – French – Menu £ 20/35

◆ Atmospheric restaurant located just off Carnaby Street. Hearty, robust French cooking with a rustic character. French wine list with the emphasis on southern regions.

XX **Stanza**

97-107 Shaftesbury Ave ✉ W1D 5DY ⊖ Leicester Square – ✆ (020) 7494 3020 – www.stanzalondon.com – Fax (020) 7494 3050 – Closed Sundays and Bank Holidays **31**AKU**m**

Rest – Modern European – Carte £ 21/38

◆ This first floor restaurant is very popular for pre/post theatre dining; the à la carte can get a little pricey. Gutsy, modern cooking with bold flavours; friendly and efficient service.

XX **Plum Valley**

20 Gerrard St ✉ W1D 6JQ ⊖ Leicester Square – ✆ (020) 7494 4366 – Fax (020) 7494 4367 – Closed 25 December **31**AKU**i**

Rest – Chinese – Carte £ 21/44

◆ Its striking black façade make this modern Chinese restaurant easy to spot in Chinatown. Mostly Cantonese cooking, with occasional forays into Vietnam and Thailand; dim sum is the strength.

Each starred restaurant lists three specialities that are typical of its style of cuisine. These may not always be on the menu but in their place expect delicious seasonal dishes. Be sure to try them.

Arbutus (Anthony Demetre)

63-64 Frith St ✉ W1D 3JW ⊖ Tottenham Court Road – ✆ (020) 7734 4545 – www.arbutusrestaurant.co.uk – Fax (020) 7287 8624 – Closed 25-26 December and 1 January **31**AKU**h**

Rest – Modern European – Menu £ 16 (lunch) – Carte £ 28/38

Spec. Squid and mackerel burger with parsley and razor clams. Saddle of rabbit, cottage pie and broad beans. White peach with thyme and strawberry sorbet.

◆ A clever kitchen that really understands flavour creates uncomplicated bistro-style dishes which really satisfy; offal is often the highlight. Always bustling but the service copes and is evenly paced.

Bocca di Lupo

12 Archer St ✉ WID 7BB ⊖ Piccadilly Circus – ✆ (020) 7734 2223 – www.boccadilupo.com – Closed Sunday **31**AKU**e**

Rest – Italian – *(booking essential)* Carte £ 23/31

◆ Deservedly busy and great fun; but atmosphere, food and service are all best when sitting at the marble counter, watching the chefs. Specialities from across Italy are available in large or small sizes; they're full of flavour and vitality.

Dehesa

25 Ganton St ✉ W1F 9BP ⊖ Oxford Circus – ✆ (020) 7494 4170 – www.dehesa.co.uk – Fax (020) 7494 4175 – Closed 1 week Christmas and Sunday dinner **30**AIU**i**

Rest – Mediterranean – Carte £ 20/30

◆ Repeats the success of its sister restaurant, Salt Yard, by offering tasty, good value Spanish and Italian tapas. Unhurried atmosphere in appealing corner location. Terrific drinks list too.

Cafe Boheme

13 Old Compton St ✉ W1D 5JQ ⊖ Leicester Square – ✆ (020) 7734 0623 – www.cafeboheme.co.uk – Fax (020) 7434 3775 – Closed 25 December

Rest – French – Carte £ 24/36 **31**AKU**t**

◆ Expect classic Gallic comfort food and a zinc-topped bar surrounded by wine drinkers. Remade as a Parisian brasserie in 2008, ideal for pre/post theatre meals. Open from dawn to the wee small hours.

Tierra Brindisa

46 Broadwick St ✉ W1F 7AF ⊖ Tottenham Court Rd – ✆ (020) 7534 1690 – www.brindisatapaskitchens.com – Fax (020) 7534 1699 – Closed Sunday

Rest – Spanish – *(booking essential at dinner)* Menu £ 30 – Carte £ 21/28 **31**AJU**x**

◆ Sister to Tapas Brindisa in Borough Market; this is a slightly more structured affair but still as busy and enjoyable. Focus is on natural flavours, uncluttered plates and quality Spanish produce.

Aurora

49 Lexington St ✉ W1F 9AP ⊖ Piccadilly Circus – ✆ (020) 7494 0514 – www.aurorasoho.co.uk – Closed 25-26 December and Bank Holidays

Rest – Modern European – *(booking essential)* Carte approx. £ 26 **31**AJU**e**

◆ An informal, no-nonsense, bohemian-style bistro with a small but pretty walled garden terrace. Short but balanced menu; simple fresh food. Pleasant, languid atmosphere.

Barrafina

54 Frith St ✉ W1D 3SL ⊖ Tottenham Court Rd – ✆ (020) 7813 8016 – www.barrafina.co.uk – Fax (020) 7734 7593 **31**AKU**c**

Rest – Spanish – *(bookings not accepted)* Carte £ 22/35 **s**

◆ Centred around a counter with seating for 20, come here if you want authentic Spanish tapas served in a buzzy atmosphere. Seafood is a speciality and the Jabugo ham a must.

Bar Shu

28 Frith St ✉ W1D 5LF ⊖ Leicester Square – ✆ (020) 7287 8822 – Fax (020) 7287 8858 – Closed 25 December **31**AKU**g**

Rest – Chinese – *(booking advisable)* Carte £ 28/38

◆ The fiery flavours of authentic Sichuan cooking are the draw here; dishes have some unusual names but help is at hand as menu has pictures. Best atmosphere is on the ground floor.

LONDON

Imli

167-169 Wardour St ✉ W1F 8WR ⊖ Tottenham Court Road – ✆ (020) 7287 4243 – www.imli.co.uk – Fax (020) 7287 4245 **31**AKU**w**

Rest – Indian – Menu £ 10/12 – Carte £ 18/24

◆ Long, spacious interior is a busy, buzzy place. Good value, fresh and tasty Indian tapas-style dishes prove a popular currency. Same owners as Tamarind.

Ba Shan

24 Romilly St ✉ W1D 5AH ⊖ Leicester Square – ✆ (020) 7287 3266 – Fax (020) 7494 4228 – Closed Christmas **31**AKU**f**

Rest – Chinese – *(booking advisable)* Carte £ 18/28 **s**

◆ 3-4 tables in each of the five rooms. Open all day, serving a mix of 'snack' and 'home-style' dishes, some with Sichuan leanings, others from northern areas and Henan province.

Baozi Inn

25 Newport Court ✉ WC2H 7JS ⊖ Leicester Square – ✆ (020) 7287 6877 – Closed 24-25 December **31**AKU**r**

Rest – Chinese – Carte £ 19/25

◆ Baozi, or steamed filled buns, are a good way to start, followed by some fiery Sichuan specialities. Simple, honest and friendly restaurant, just off the main strip of Chinatown.

LONDON

Strand and Covent Garden

One Aldwych

1 Aldwych ✉ WC2B 4RH ⊖ Temple – ✆ (020) 7300 1000 – www.onealdwych.com – Fax (020) 7300 1001 **32**AMU**r**

93 rm – †£ 242/449 ††£ 242/541, ☕ £ 24.75 – 12 suites

Rest *Axis* – see restaurant listing

Rest *Indigo* – Carte £ 28/43

◆ Former 19C bank, now a stylish hotel with lots of artwork; the lobby changes its look seasonally and doubles as a bar. Stylish, contemporary bedrooms with the latest mod cons; the deluxe rooms and suites are particularly desirable. Impressive leisure facilities. Light, accessible menu at Indigo.

Swissôtel The Howard

Temple Pl ✉ WC2R 2PR ⊖ Temple – ✆ (020) 7836 3555 – www.swissotel.com/london – Fax (020) 7379 4547 **32**AMU**e**

187 rm – †£ 409 ††£ 432, ☕ £ 23.50 – 2 suites

Rest *12 Temple Place* – ✆ (020) 7300 1700 – Menu £ 25 (lunch) – Carte £ 34/48

◆ Discreet elegance is the order of the day at this handsomely appointed hotel. Many of the comfortable rooms enjoy balcony views of the Thames. Attentive service. Large terrace to restaurant serving modern European dishes.

St Martins Lane

45 St Martin's Lane ✉ WC2N 3HX ⊖ Charing Cross – ✆ (020) 7300 5500 – www.morganshotelgroup.com – Fax (020) 7300 5501 **31**ALU**e**

202 rm – †£ 363/685 ††£ 363/685, ☕ £ 25 – 2 suites

Rest *Asia de Cuba* – *(Closed Sunday dinner)* Carte £ 38/55

◆ The unmistakable hand of Philippe Starck evident at this most contemporary of hotels. Unique and stylish, from the starkly modern lobby to the state-of-the-art rooms. 350 varieties of rum and tasty Asian dishes at fashionable Asia de Cuba.

The Ivy

1-5 West St ✉ WC2H 9NQ ⊖ Leicester Square – ✆ (020) 7836 4751 – www.the-ivy.co.uk – Closed 24-26 December and 1 January **31**AKU**p**

Rest – International – Carte £ 32/51

◆ One of the original celebrity hang-out restaurants; still pulling them in. Appealing menu, from shepherd's pie to fishcakes and nursery puddings. Staff go about their business with alacrity.

XXX **Axis** – at One Aldwych Hotel

1 Aldwych ✉ WC2B 4RH ⊖ Temple – ☎ (020) 7300 0300 – www.onealdwych.com – Fax (020) 7300 0301 – Closed Easter weekend, Christmas, Saturday lunch, Sunday and Bank Holidays **31**AMU**r**

Rest – British – Menu £ 20 (lunch) – Carte £ 30/39

◆ Spiral staircase down to this modern restaurant with very high ceiling; new fabrics and bamboo-effect façade in front of futuristic mural. British ingredients to the fore in carefully crafted dishes.

XX **J. Sheekey**

28-32 St Martin's Court ✉ WC2 4AL ⊖ Leicester Square – ☎ (020) 7240 2565 – www.j-sheekey.co.uk – Fax (020) 7497 0891 – Closed 25-26 December and 1 January **31**ALU**v**

Rest – Seafood – *(booking essential)* Menu £ 26 (weekend lunch) – Carte £ 30/55

◆ Festooned with photographs of actors and linked to the theatrical world since opening in 1890. Wood panels and alcove tables add famed intimacy. Accomplished seafood cooking.

XX **Rules**

35 Maiden Lane ✉ WC2E 7LB ⊖ Leicester Square – ☎ (020) 7836 5314 – www.rules.co.uk – Fax (020) 7497 1081 – Closed 4 days Christmas

Rest – British – *(booking essential)* Carte £ 30/47 **31**ALU**n**

◆ London's oldest restaurant boasts a fine collection of antique cartoons, drawings and paintings. Tradition continues in the menu, specialising in game from its own estate.

XX **Clos Maggiore**

33 King St ✉ WC2E 8JD ⊖ Leicester Square – ☎ (020) 7379 9696 – www.closmaggiore.com – Fax (020) 7379 6767 **31**ALU**z**

Rest – French – Menu £ 20 (lunch) – Carte £ 30/43

◆ Walls covered with flowering branches create delightful woodland feel to rear dining area with retractable glass roof. French cooking shows flair, creativity and ambition.

XX **Admiralty**

Somerset House, The Strand ✉ WC2R 1LA ⊖ Temple – ☎ (020) 7845 4646 – www.theadmiraltyrestaurant.com – Fax (020) 7845 4658 – Closed Sunday

Rest – French – *(booking essential)* Carte £ 23/33 **32**AMU**a**

◆ Wonderful setting - in the south building of the magnificent 18C Somerset House. Divided into two bright rooms. French cooking with a contemporary edge and nods towards the Med.

XX **The Forge**

14 Garrick Street ✉ WC2E 9BJ ⊖ Leicester Square – ☎ (020) 7379 1432 – www.theforgerestaurant.co.uk – Fax (020) 7379 1530 – Closed 24 to 26 December **31**ALU**a**

Rest – Modern European – Menu £ 17 (lunch) – Carte £ 29/38

◆ Long and appealing menu, from eggs Benedict to Dover sole; good value theatre menus and last orders at midnight. Most influences from within Europe. Large room with downstairs bar.

XX **Le Deuxième**

65a Long Acre ✉ WC2E 9JH ⊖ Covent Garden – ☎ (020) 7379 0033 – www.ledeuxieme.com – Fax (020) 7379 0066 – Closed 25-26 December

Rest – Modern European – Menu £ 17 (lunch) – Carte £ 30/32 **31**ALU**b**

◆ Caters well for theatregoers: opens early, closes late. Buzzy eatery, simply decorated in white with subtle lighting. International menu but emphasis within Europe.

X **L'Atelier de Joël Robuchon**

✿✿ *13-15 West St ✉ WC2H 9NE ⊖ Leicester Square – ☎ (020) 7010 8600 – www.joel-robuchon.com – Fax (020) 7010 8601* **31**AKU**a**

Rest – French – Menu £ 25 *(lunch and early dinner)* – Carte £ 34/81

Rest *La Cuisine* – French – *(Closed Sunday) (dinner only)* Carte £ 38/85

Spec. Langoustine fritters with basil sauce. Quail stuffed with foie gras, truffle mash. Araguani chocolate with white chocolate ice cream.

◆ Ground floor Atelier with counter seating and chefs on view; upstairs the more structured La Cuisine. Wonderfully precise, creative and occasionally playful cooking; dishes may look delicate but pack a punch. Cool top floor lounge bar.

J. Sheekey Oyster Bar

28-32 St Martin's Court ✉ WC2 4AL ⊖ Leicester Square – ✆ (020) 7240 2565 – www.j-sheeky.co.uk – Fax (020) 7497 0891 – Closed 25-26 December and 1 January **31**ALU**v**

Rest – Seafood – Carte £ 26/32

◆ An addendum to J. Sheekey, created by knocking through into next door. Open all day and so easier to get a seat, with the same quality seafood but with slightly smaller portions and cheaper prices.

Terroirs

5 William IV St ✉ WC2N 4DW ⊖ Charing Cross – ✆ (020) 7036 0660 – www.terroirswinebar.com **31**ALU**h**

Rest – French – *(Closed Sunday and Bank Holidays)* Carte £ 22/28

◆ Informal bistro/wine bar with a fun atmosphere and exhilarating menu of mostly French fare, with additional Spanish and Italian flavours. Equally thoughtful and well-priced wine list.

Le Café du Jardin

28 Wellington St ✉ WC2E 7BD ⊖ Covent Garden – ✆ (020) 7836 8769 – www.lecafedujardin.com – Fax (020) 7836 4123 – Closed 25-26 December

Rest – Mediterranean – Menu £ 17 (lunch) – Carte £ 27/33 **31**ALU**f**

◆ Spread over two floors, with the bustle on the ground floor. Sunny, mostly Mediterranean cooking. Very busy early and late evening thanks to the good value theatre menus which change weekly.

Bedford & Strand

1a Bedford St ✉ WC2E 9HH ⊖ Charing Cross – ✆ (020) 7836 3033 – www.bedford-strand.com – Closed 25 December-1 January, Saturday lunch, Sunday and Bank Holidays **31**ALU**c**

Rest – British – *(booking essential)* Carte £ 22/32

◆ Basement bistro/wine bar with simple décor and easy-going atmosphere; kitchen sources well and has a light touch with Italian, French and British dishes.

Victoria

The Goring

15 Beeston Pl, Grosvenor Gdns ✉ SW1W 0JW ⊖ Victoria – ✆ (020) 7396 9000 – www.thegoring.com – Fax (020) 7834 4393 **38**AIX**a**

65 rm – †£ 229/426 ††£ 275/472, ☕ £ 23 – 6 suites

Rest – British – *(Closed Saturday lunch)* Menu £ 35/48

◆ Opened in 1910 as a quintessentially English hotel. The fourth generation of Goring is now at the helm. Many of the attractive rooms overlook a peaceful garden. Elegantly appointed restaurant with an appropriately British menu.

Crowne Plaza London - St James

45 Buckingham Gate ✉ SW1E 6AF ⊖ St James's Park – ✆ (020) 7834 6655 – www.london.crowneplaza.com – Fax (020) 7630 7587

321 rm – †£ 409 ††£ 409, ☕ £ 14.25 – 19 suites **39**AJX**e**

Rest Quilon and **Bank** – see restaurant listing

Rest *Bistro 51* – Menu £ 18/22 – Carte £ 33/47

◆ Built in 1897 as serviced accommodation for visiting aristocrats. Behind the impressive Edwardian façade lies an equally elegant interior. Quietest rooms overlook courtyard. Bright and informal café-style restaurant.

51 Buckingham Gate

51 Buckingham Gate ✉ SW1E 6AF ⊖ St James's Park – ✆ (020) 7769 7766 – www.51-buckinghamgate.com – Fax (020) 7233 5014 **39**AJX**s**

89 suites – ††£ 475, ☕ £ 22

Rest Quilon and **Bank** – see restaurant listing

◆ In the courtyard of the Crowne Plaza hotel but offering greater levels of comfort and service. Contemporary in style, suites range from one to seven bedrooms. Butler service available.

LONDON

41 without rest

41 Buckingham Palace Rd ✉ SW1W 0PS ⊖ Victoria – ✆ (020) 7300 0041 – www.41hotel.com – Fax (020) 7300 0141 **38**AIX**n**

29 rm – †£ 240/379 ††£ 264/402, ☕ £ 25 – 1 suite

◆ Smart and discreet addendum to The Rubens hotel next door. Attractively decorated and quiet lounge where breakfast is served; comfortable bedrooms boast fireplaces and plenty of extras.

The Rubens at The Palace

39 Buckingham Palace Rd ✉ SW1W 0PS ⊖ Victoria – ✆ (020) 7834 6600 – www.rubenshotel.com – Fax (020) 7828 5401 **38**AIX**n**

160 rm – †£ 126/298 ††£ 149/298, ☕ £ 18.50 – 1 suite

Rest *Old Masters* – *(Closed lunch Saturday and Sunday)* Menu £ 28

Rest *Library* – *(dinner only)* Menu £ 35 – Carte £ 34/59

Rest *bbar* – ✆ (020) 7958 7000 *(Closed Saturday, Sunday and Bank Holidays)* Menu £ 21 – Carte £ 25/35

◆ Discreet, comfortable hotel in great location for visitors to London. Constant reinvestment ensures bright and contemporary bedrooms. Old Masters for grills. Fine dining in cosy Library. Casual dining in bbar.

LONDON

Tophams without rest

24-32 Ebury Street ✉ SW1W 0LU ⊖ Victoria – ✆ (020) 7730 3313 – www.tophamshotel.com – Fax (020) 7730 0008 **38**AHY**d**

48 rm – †£ 180/275 ††£ 195/275, ☕ £ 14.95

◆ A row of five pretty terraced houses, in a good spot for tourists and recently refurbished. Neat bedrooms with large bathrooms and good mod cons. Comfortable breakfast room.

B + B Belgravia without rest

64-66 Ebury St ✉ SW1W 9QD ⊖ Victoria – ✆ (020) 7259 8570 – www.bb-belgravia.com – Fax (020) 7259 8591 **38**AHY**x**

17 rm ☕ – †£ 99 ††£ 135

◆ Two houses, three floors, and, considering the location, representing good value accommodation. Sleek, clean-lined bedrooms. Breakfast overlooking little garden terrace.

Lord Milner without rest

111 Ebury Street ✉ SW1W 9QU ⊖ Victoria – ✆ (020) 7881 9880 – www.lordmilner.com – Fax (020) 7730 8027 **38**AHY**k**

10 rm – †£ 90/145 ††£ 135/165, ☕ £ 14 – 1 suite

◆ A four storey terraced house, with individually decorated bedrooms, three with four-poster beds and all with marble bathrooms. Garden Suite the best room, with its own patio. No public areas.

Roussillon (Alex Gauthier)

16 St Barnabas St ✉ SW1W 8PE ⊖ Sloane Square – ✆ (020) 7730 5550 – www.roussillon.co.uk – Fax (020) 7824 8617 – Closed Christmas to New Year, Saturday lunch and Sunday **38**AHZ**c**

Rest – French – Menu £ 35/55

Spec. Black truffle risotto with Parmesan tuiles. Sea bass with artichokes and confit tomatoes. Louis XV crunchy praline and chocolate.

◆ A true neighbourhood restaurant with loyal regulars. Chef searches for the best ingredients and such is the emphasis on seasonality that we are reminded of what things really taste of; vegetables are excellent. Wine list has gems from France's SW.

Quilon – at Crowne Plaza London - St James Hotel

41 Buckingham Gate ✉ SW1 6AF ⊖ St James's Park – ✆ (020) 7821 1899 – www.quilon.co.uk – Fax (020) 7233 9597 – Closed Saturday lunch

Rest – Indian – Menu £ 22/37 – Carte dinner £ 37/47 **39**AJX**e**

Spec. Spiced oysters and lentils with onion relish. Koondapur halibut curry and tamarind gravy. Spiced dark chocolate and hazelnut mousse.

◆ Vibrant and well-balanced Indian dishes, many of which originate from the south west coast of India but are given a 'Western' twist . Skilled use of spices, appealing seafood specialities and well-organised service.

XXX **The Cinnamon Club**

30-32 Great Smith St ✉ SW1P 3BU ⊖ St James's Park – ✆ (020) 7222 2555 – www.cinnamonclub.com – Fax (020) 7222 1333 – Closed 26 December, Sunday and Bank Holidays **39**AKX**c**

Rest – Indian – Menu £ 19 – Carte £ 30/53

◆ Housed in former Westminster Library: exterior has ornate detail, interior is stylish and modern. Walls are lined with books. New Wave Indian cooking with plenty of choice.

XXX **Santini**

29 Ebury St ✉ SW1W 0NZ ⊖ Victoria – ✆ (020) 7730 4094 – www.santini-restaurant.com – Fax (020) 7730 0544 – Closed 23-27 December, 1 January , Easter, lunch Saturday and Sunday **38**AHY**v**

Rest – Italian – Menu £ 25 (dinner) – Carte £ 29/54

◆ Smart, crisp and cool Italian restaurant, with a large, impressive terrace and old-school service. Menu has subtle Venetian accent but is not inexpensive; pastas and desserts are good.

XXX **Shepherd's**

Marsham Court, Marsham St ✉ SW1P 4LA ⊖ Pimlico – ✆ (020) 7834 9552 – www.langansrestaurants.co.uk – Fax (020) 7233 6047 – Closed 25 December, Saturday, Sunday and Bank Holidays **39**AKY**z**

Rest – British – *(booking essential)* Menu £ 35

◆ A truly English restaurant where game and traditional puddings are a highlight. Popular with those from Westminster – the booths offer a degree of privacy.

XX **Atami**

37 Monck St (entrance on Great Peter St) ✉ SW1P 2BL ⊖ Pimlico – ✆ (020) 7222 2218 – www.atami-restaurant.com – Fax (020) 7222 2788 – Closed Saturday lunch and Sunday **39**AKY**a**

Rest – Japanese – Menu £ 23/45 – Carte approx. £ 22

◆ Clean, modern lines illuminated by vast ceiling orbs induce a sense of calm. Menus true to Japanese roots feature sushi and sashimi but also turn down interesting modern highways.

XX **Il Convivio**

143 Ebury St ✉ SW1W 9QN ⊖ Sloane Square – ✆ (020) 7730 4099 – www.etruscarestaurants.com – Fax (020) 7730 4103 – Closed 26 December-4 January, Sunday and Bank Holidays **38**AHY**a**

Rest – Italian – Carte £ 33/47

◆ A retractable roof provides alfresco dining to part of this comfortable and modern restaurant. Contemporary and traditional Italian menu with homemade pasta specialities.

XX **Boisdale**

15 Eccleston St ✉ SW1W 9LX ⊖ Victoria – ✆ (020) 7730 6922 – www.boisdale.co.uk – Fax (020) 7730 0548 – Closed 1 week Christmas, Saturday lunch and Sunday **38**AHY**c**

Rest – Scottish – Carte £ 26/89

◆ A proudly Scottish restaurant with acres of tartan and a charmingly higgledy-piggledy layout. Stand-outs are the smoked salmon and the 28-day aged Aberdeenshire cuts of beef. Live nightly jazz.

XX **Rex Whistler**

Tate Britain, Millbank ✉ SW1P 4RG ⊖ Pimlico – ✆ (020) 7887 8825 – www.tate.org.uk/britain/eatanddrink – Fax (020) 7887 8892 – Closed 24-26 December **39**ALY**c**

Rest – British – *(lunch only) (booking essential)* Menu £ 20 – Carte £ 31/38

◆ As with upstairs, it celebrates Britain, with a daily catch from Newlyn and fruity desserts the specialities. Comfortable room, with striking Rex Whistler mural. Terrific wine list.

XX **Ken Lo's Memories of China**

65-69 Ebury St ✉ SW1W 0NZ ⊖ Victoria – ✆ (020) 7730 7734 – www.londonfinedininggroup.com – Fax (020) 7730 2992 – Closed Christmas-New Year, Sunday lunch and Bank Holidays **38**AHY**u**

Rest – Chinese – Menu £ 20/32 **s** – Carte £ 24/60 **s**

◆ An air of tranquillity pervades this traditionally furnished room. Lattice screens add extra privacy. Extensive Chinese menu: bold flavours with a clean, fresh style.

XX **Quirinale**

North Court, 1 Great Peter St ⊖ Westminster – ✆ (020) 7222 7080 – www.quirinale.co.uk – Closed August, 1 week Christmas - New Year, Saturday lunch and Sunday **39**ALX**a**

Rest – Italian – Menu £ 23 (lunch) – Carte £ 32/45

◆ Light and bright Italian restaurant with contemporary, minimalist feel typified by cream leather banquettes. Seasonally changing menu encompasses all things Italian.

XX **Bank** – at Crown Plaza London-St James Hotel

45 Buckingham Gate ✉ SW1E 6BS ⊖ St James's Park – ✆ (020) 7630 6644 – www.bankrestaurants.com – Fax (020) 7630 5663 – Closed Saturday lunch, Sunday and Bank Holidays **39**AJX**e**

Rest – Modern European – *(booking essential at lunch)* Carte £ 34/49

◆ Behind the understated entrance lies a vibrant and busy interior. Pass through one of Europe's longest bars to reach the conservatory restaurant, where you'll find a varied, accessible menu.

XX **Osteria Dell' Angolo**

47 Marsham St. ✉ SW1P 3DR ⊖ St. James's Park – ✆ (020) 3268 1077 – www.osteriadellangolo.co.uk – Fax (020) 3268 1073 – Closed 25 December, Saturday lunch, Sunday and Bank Holidays **39**AKY**n**

Rest – Italian – Menu £ 20 (lunch) – Carte £ 29/49

◆ Expert restaurateur Claudio Pulze opened this sunny Italian restaurant opposite the Home Office in 2009. Tuscan element to the cooking, along with some creativity; service is keen and friendly.

X **Olivo**

21 Eccleston St ✉ SW1W 9LX ⊖ Victoria – ✆ (020) 7730 2505 – www.olivorestaurant.com – Fax (020) 7823 5377 – Closed Bank Holidays and lunch Saturday and Sunday **38**AHY**z**

Rest – Italian – Menu £ 23 (lunch) – Carte dinner £ 32/36

◆ Carefully prepared, authentic Sardinian specialities are the highlight at this popular Italian restaurant. Simply decorated in blues and yellows, with an atmosphere of bonhomie.

X **La Poule au Pot**

231 Ebury St ✉ SW1W 8UT ⊖ Sloane Square – ✆ (020) 7730 7763 – Fax (020) 7259 9651 – Closed 25-26 December and 1 January **38**AHY**p**

Rest – French – Menu £ 23 (lunch) – Carte £ 32/45

◆ An old favourite of many. The subdued lighting and friendly informality make this one of London's more romantic restaurants. Classic French menu with extensive plats du jour.

X **Olivomare**

10 Lower Belgrave St ✉ SW1W 0LJ ⊖ Victoria – ✆ (020) 7730 9022 – www.olivorestaurants.com – Fax (020) 7823 5377 – Closed Bank Holidays

Rest – Seafood – Carte £ 34/42 **38**AHY**b**

◆ Understated and stylish piscatorial decoration and seafood with a Sardinian base. Fortnightly changing menu, with high quality produce, much of which is available in shop next door.

The Ebury

11 Pimlico Rd ✉ SW1W 8NA ⊖ Sloane Square. – ✆ (020) 7730 6784 – www.theebury.co.uk – Fax (020) 7730 6149 – Closed 25-26 December

Rest – Menu £ 17 (lunch) – Carte £ 30/45 **38**AHZ**z**

◆ Smart and stylish room, with an appealing menu ranging from burgers to black bream. Low-slung tables around popular central bar; efficient service. Upstairs is used for private parties.

The Thomas Cubitt

44 Elizabeth Street ✉ SW1W 9PA ⊖ Sloane Square. – ✆ (020) 7730 6060 – www.thethomascubitt.co.uk – Fax (020) 7730 6055 – Closed 24 December to 1 January **38**AHY**e**

Rest – *(booking essential)* Menu £ 25 (lunch) – Carte £ 28/40

◆ A pub of two halves: choose the busy ground floor bar with its accessible menu or upstairs for more ambitious, quite elaborate cooking with courteous service and a less frenetic environment.

LONG COMPTON – Warks. – see Shipston-on-Stour

LONG CRENDON – Buckinghamshire – 504 Q/R28 – pop. 2 383 – ✉ Aylesbury 11 C2

London 50 mi. – Aylesbury 11 mi. – Oxford 15 mi.

XX **Angel** with rm

47 Bicester Rd ✉ HP18 9EE – ✆ (01844) 208 268 – Fax (01844) 202 497 – Closed Sunday dinner

4 rm – †£ 70 ††£ 95 **Rest** – Menu £ 20 (lunch) – Carte £ 28/43

◆ Characterful former pub with low ceilings, leather furnished lounge bar and airy conservatory. Oft-changing menus offer tasty modern British cooking, with well-chosen wine list. Stylish bedrooms, all individually decorated. 3 is the cosiest, 4 the biggest.

LONG MELFORD – Suffolk – 504 W27 – pop. 2 734 Great Britain 15 C3

London 62 mi. – Cambridge 34 mi. – Colchester 18 mi. – Ipswich 24 mi.

Melford Hall★ **AC**

Black Lion

Church Walk, The Green ✉ CO10 9DN – ✆ (01787) 312 356 – www.blacklionhotel.net – Fax (01787) 374 557

9 rm – †£ 100 ††£ 169 – 1 suite **Rest** – Carte £ 25/34

◆ 17C Georgian inn overlooking village green. Named after wines, bedrooms are smart, stylish and individually designed; good facilities and traditional bathrooms. Formal restaurant with enclosed rear terrace features extensive, popular menu.

X **Scutchers**

Westgate St, on A 1092 ✉ CO10 9DP – ✆ (01787) 310 200 – www.scutchers.com – Fax (01787) 375 700 – Closed Christmas, Sunday, Monday and Bank Holidays

Rest – Menu £ 24 – Carte £ 38/45

◆ Former medieval Hall House now contains an informal and unpretentious restaurant serving a range of creative modern dishes using good quality ingredients.

LONG SUTTON – Somerset – 503 L30 – ✉ Langport 3 B3

London 132 mi. – Bridgwater 16 mi. – Yeovil 10 mi.

The Devonshire Arms with rm

✉ TA10 9LP – ✆ (01458) 241 271 – www.thedevonshirearms.com – Fax (01458) 241 037 – Closed 25-26 December

9 rm – †£ 70 ††£ 80/120 **Rest** – Carte £ 23/30

◆ Spacious hunting lodge with modern décor, front terrace and garden. Mix of French and English dishes with a good value menu at lunch and a concise à la carte for dinner. Modern bedrooms with neutral shades and rattan furniture.

LONGHORSLEY – Northd. – 501 – see Morpeth

LONGRIDGE – Lancashire – 502 M22 – pop. 7 491 20 A2

London 241 mi. – Blackburn 12 mi. – Burnley 18 mi.

XX **The Longridge Restaurant**

104-106 Higher Rd, Northeast : 0.5 mi. by B 5269 following signs for Jeffrey Hill ✉ PR3 3SY – ✆ (01772) 784 969 – www.heathcotes.co.uk – Fax (01772) 785 713 – Closed 1 January, 4-6 January and Monday

Rest – Menu £ 19 (lunch) – Carte £ 31/48

◆ Stylish, subtly hued restaurant with changing character: bright by day and intimate at night. Highly seasonal, regional cooking uses quality ingredients to create neat, flavoursome dishes.

X **Thyme**

1-3 Inglewhite Rd ✉ PR3 3JR – ✆ (01772) 786 888 – Fax (01772) 784 138 – Closed 1-8 January and Monday

Rest – Menu £ 11/14 (lunch and early dinner) – Carte £ 22/28

◆ Simple high street eatery adorned with pretty hanging baskets outside and modern artwork inside. Local produce a feature: interesting Lancastrian cheese menu. Good value lunch/early dinner.

LONGSTOCK – Hampshire – 503 P30 – see Stockbridge

LONGTOWN – Cumbria – 502 L18 **21** A1

London 326 mi. – Carlisle 9 mi. – Newcastle upon Tyne 61 mi.

Bessiestown Farm

Catlowdy, Northeast : 8 mi. by Netherby St on B 6318 ✉ CA6 5QP – ✆ (01228) 577 219 – www.bessiestown.co.uk – Fax (01228) 577 019 – Closed 25 December
5 rm – †£ 49/57 ††£ 80 **Rest** – *(by arrangement)* Menu £ 18

◆ Comfortable, warm accommodation in homely, modern farmhouse conversion in a rural location on a working farm. Décor has a traditional British tone, well-kept throughout. Home-cooked food served in airy dining room.

LOOE – Cornwall – 503 G32 – pop. 5 280 **1** B2

London 264 mi. – Plymouth 23 mi. – Truro 39 mi.
The Guildhall, Fore St ✆ (01503) 262072, looetic@btconnect.com
Bin Down, ✆ (01503) 240 239
Whitsand Bay Hotel Torpoint Portwrinkle, ✆ (01503) 230 276
Town★ – Monkey Sanctuary★ **AC**

Barclay House

St Martins Rd, East Looe, East : 0.5 mi. by A 387 on B 3253 ✉ PL13 1LP – ✆ (01503) 262 929 – www.barclayhouse.co.uk – Fax (01503) 262 632
10 rm – †£ 75/105 ††£ 150/170 – 1 suite
Rest *The Restaurant* – see restaurant listing

◆ Smart but relaxed and welcoming hotel near harbour. Gardens overlooking estuary. Snug sitting room and bar. Individually decorated bedrooms.

Beach House without rest

Marine Dr, Hannafore, Southwest : 0.75 mi. by Quay Rd ✉ PL13 2DH – ✆ (01503) 262 598 – www.thebeachhouselooe.co.uk – Fax (01503) 262 298 – Closed Christmas
5 rm – †£ 75/120 ††£ 100/130

◆ Large detached house with front garden. Immaculate bedrooms: three have sea vistas; 'Fistral' with balcony is best. Breakfast room upstairs; arched window with views over bay.

Bucklawren Farm without rest

St Martin-by-Looe, Northeast : 3.5 mi. by A 387 and B 3253 turning right onto single track road signposted to Monkey Sanctuary ✉ PL13 1NZ – ✆ (01503) 240 738 – www.bucklawren.co.uk – Fax (01503) 240 481 – March-October
7 rm – †£ 35/50 ††£ 60/75

◆ Characterful farmhouse within 500 acre working farm. Large conservatory overlooks pleasant garden. Spotlessly kept interior with simple, country house-style bedrooms.

The Restaurant – at Barclay House Hotel

St Martins Rd, East Looe, East : 0.5 mi. by A 387 on B 3253 ✉ PL13 1LP – ✆ (01503) 262 929 – www.barclayhouse.co.uk – Fax (01503) 262 632
Rest – *(Closed Sunday dinner) (dinner only and Sunday lunch June-October)* Menu £ 35

◆ Extensive views of estuary. Matching mustard coloured walls and table cloths. Attentive well-informed service. Eclectic menu using fresh local produce, particularly seafood.

Trawlers on the Quay

The Quay, East Looe ✉ PL13 1AH – ✆ (01503) 263 593 – www.trawlersrestaurant.co.uk – Closed Sunday and Monday
Rest – Seafood – *(dinner only)* Carte £ 28/33

◆ Personally run restaurant in a pretty setting on the quay. Faux marble table tops; clean, neutral décor. Balanced menu of local seafood and meat dishes. Home-made bread, too.

LORTON – Cumbria – 502 K20 – see Cockermouth

LOUGHBOROUGH – Leicestershire – 502 – pop. 55 258 — 16 B2

London 117 mi. – Birmingham 41 mi. – Leicester 11 mi. – Nottingham 15 mi.

Town Hall, Market Pl ☎ (01509) 231914, tic@charnwoodbc.gov.uk

Lingdale Woodhouse Eaves Joe Moore's Lane, ☎ (01509) 890 703

at Belton West : 6 mi. by A 6 on B 5324 – ✉ Loughborough

The Queen's Head with rm

2 Long St ✉ LE12 9TP – ☎ (01530) 222 359 – www.thequeenshead.org – Closed 25 December and Sunday dinner

6 rm – †£ 65 ††£ 100 **Rest** – Menu £ 16/23 – Carte £ 23/35

◆ Stylish two-roomed restaurant and cool lounge and bar in calming cream tones, with chocolate leather furniture. Seasonally-evolving menus make proud use of local produce. Bright, contemporary bedrooms of varying sizes.

at Woodhouse Eaves South : 4.5 mi. by A 6 via Woodhouse – ✉ Loughborough

The Woodhouse

43 Maplewell Rd ✉ LE12 8RG – ☎ (01509) 890 318 – www.thewoodhouse.co.uk – Fax (01509) 890 718 – Closed Sunday dinner and Monday

Rest – Menu £ 15/18 – Carte £ 34/42

◆ Smart village restaurant with comfy lounge, bold modern colours and eye-catching art. Concise, understated menu relies on quality local produce: classical combinations have a personal twist.

ENGLAND

LOUTH – Lincolnshire – 502 T/U23 – pop. 15 930 — 17 D1

London 156 mi. – Boston 34 mi. – Great Grimsby 17 mi. – Lincoln 26 mi.

Town Hall, Cannon St. ☎ (01507) 601111, louthinfo@e-lindsey.gov.uk

Brackenborough

Cordeaux Corner, Brackenborough, North : 2 mi. by A 16 ✉ LN11 0SZ – ☎ (01507) 609 169 – www.oakridgehotels.co.uk – Fax (01507) 609 413

24 rm – †£ 82/97 ††£ 97

Rest – Menu £ 25 (dinner) – Carte £ 20/39

◆ Family owned hotel run with a warm and personal style. Public areas have a relaxed feel and bedrooms are spacious, individually designed and boast a host of extras. Homely dining.

LOVINGTON – Somerset – 503 M30 – see Castle Cary

LOW FELL – Tyne and Wear – see Gateshead

LOW ROW – North Yorkshire – 502 N20 – see Reeth

LOWER FROYLE – Hampshire – see Alton

LOWER HARDRES – Kent – 504 X30 – see Canterbury

LOWER ODDINGTON – Glos. – see Stow-on-the-Wold

LOWER SHIPLAKE – Oxfordshire – 504 R29 – see Henley-on-Thames

LOWER SLAUGHTER – Glos. – 503 – see Bourton-on-the-Water

LOWER SWELL – Glos. – see Stow-on-the-Wold

LOWER VOBSTER – Somerset – pop. 2 222 – ✉ Radstock 4 C2

London 119 mi. – Bath 16 mi. – Frome 5 mi.

The Vobster Inn with rm

✉ BA3 5RJ – ✆ (01373) 812 920 – www.vobsterinn.co.uk – Fax (01373) 812 247 – Closed Sunday dinner and Monday lunch

3 rm – †£ 55/65 ††£ 85/95 **Rest** – Carte £ 22/28

◆ Hands-on Spanish owners combine Mediterranean ingredients and local produce. Cooking has an honest, rustic edge, with fish specials from St Mawes. Modern, well-equipped bedrooms; the family room overlooks the garden.

LOWER WHITLEY – Cheshire – 502 M24 20 A3

London 199 mi. – Liverpool 25 mi. – Manchester 24 mi. – Warrington 7 mi.

Chetwode Arms

Street Lane ✉ WA4 4EN – ✆ (01925) 730 203 – www.chetwodearms.com – Fax (01925) 730 203 – Closed 26 December

Rest – Menu £ 12 (Sunday lunch) – Carte £ 25/65

◆ Cosy inn with a terrace and bowling green. Wide-ranging à la carte features British and Austrian cooking, as well as dishes cooked on hot rocks; including kudu, crocodile and zebra.

LOWESTOFT – Suffolk – 504 Z26 – pop. 68 340 Great Britain 15 D2

London 116 mi. – Ipswich 43 mi. – Norwich 30 mi.

East Point Pavillion, Royal Plain ✆ (01502) 533600, touristinfo@waveny.gov.uk

Rookery Park Carlton Colville, ✆ (01502) 509 190

Norfolk Broads★

at Oulton Broad West : 2 mi. by A 146 – ✉ Lowestoft

Ivy House Country

Ivy Lane, Southwest : 1.5 mi. by A 146 ✉ NR33 8HY – ✆ (01502) 501 353 – www.ivyhousecountryhotel.co.uk – Fax (01502) 501 539 – Closed 20 December to 3 January

19 rm – †£ 99/115 ††£ 170 – 1 suite

Rest ***The Crooked Barn*** – see restaurant listing

◆ Converted farm in rural seclusion down an unmade lane. Well kept gardens and grounds. Spacious bedrooms, in converted barns, have bright, fresh décor.

The Crooked Barn – at Ivy House Country Hotel

Ivy Lane, Southwest : 1.5 mi. by A 146 ✉ NR33 8HY – ✆ (01502) 501 353 – www.ivyhousecountryhotel.co.uk – Fax (01502) 501 539 – Closed 20 December to 3 January

Rest – Menu £ 28 – Carte £ 29/45 **s**

◆ Thatched part 18C former hay loft, the focus of Ivy House Farm's characterful setting. Delightful crooked beamed interior. Modern British fare using fresh, local produce.

LUDFORD – Lincolnshire 17 C1

London 174 mi. – Sheffield 74 mi. – Kingston upon Hull 43 mi. – Nottingham 59 mi.

The Black Horse Inn

Magna Mile ✉ LN8 6AJ – ✆ (01507) 313 645 – Fax (01507) 313 645 – Closed 2 weeks January, Sunday dinner and Monday

Rest – Carte £ 16/27

◆ 18C pub with open fires, simple wooden tables and understated, homely décor. Tasty, honest food freshly made from seasonal, local produce. Comforting nursery puddings.

LUDLOW – Shropshire – 503 L26 – pop. 9 548 Great Britain 18 B2

London 162 mi. – Birmingham 39 mi. – Hereford 24 mi. – Shrewsbury 29 mi.

Castle St ✆ (01584) 875053, ludlow.tourism@shropshire.gov.uk

Town★ Z – Castle★ **AC** – Feathers Hotel★ – St Laurence's Parish Church★ (Misericords★) **S**

Stokesay Castle★ **AC**, NW : 6.5 mi. by A 49

Plan on next page

ENGLAND

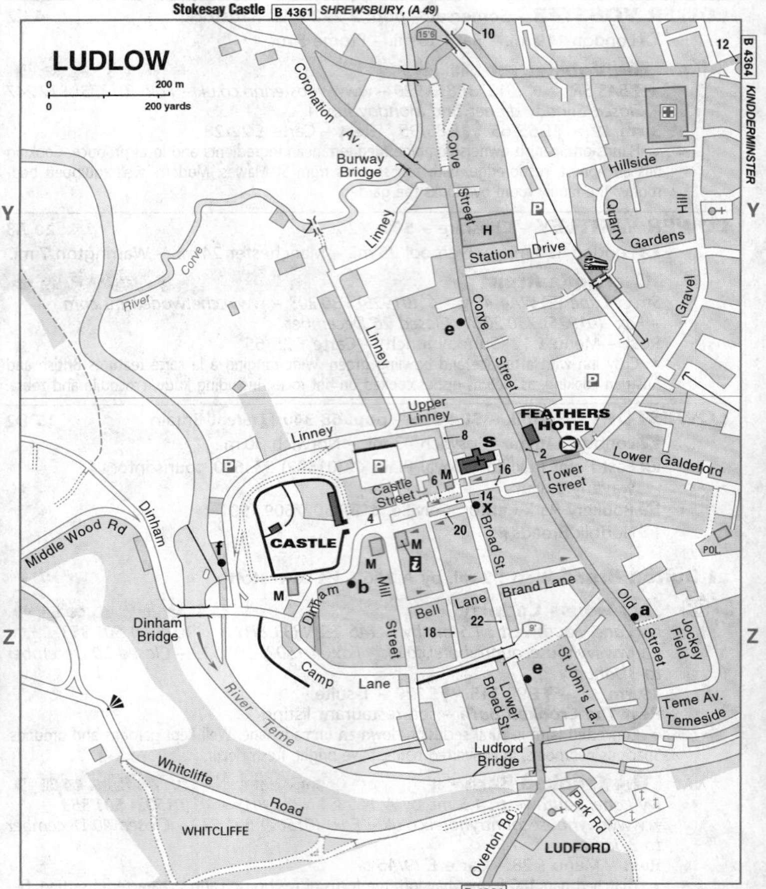

Stokesay Castle B 4361 *SHREWSBURY, (A 49)*

LUDLOW

0 200 m
0 200 yards

B 4364 KIDDERMINSTER

HEREFORD B 4361 (A 49)

Bull Ring	**Z** 2	Fishmore Rd	**Y** 10	Lower Raven Lane	**Z** 18
Castle Square	**Z** 4	Henley Rd	**Y** 12	Market St	**Z** 20
Church St	**Z** 6	High St	**Z** 14	Silk Mill	**Z** 22
College St	**Z** 8	King St	**Z** 16		

Overton Grange

Old Hereford Rd, South : 1.75 mi. by B 4361 ✉ *SY8 4AD* – ✆ *(01584) 873 500* – *www.overtongrangehotel.com* – *Fax (01584) 873 524*
14 rm – †£ 95/140 ††£ 140/240
Rest – *(booking essential for non-residents) (lunch by arrangement)* Menu £ 33/43
◆ Edwardian country house with good views of the surrounding countryside. Comfortable lounges. Attentive service and well-kept, individual rooms. Accomplished, inventive modern cuisine with a French base.

When you make a booking, check the price and category of the room.

Dinham Hall

Dinham ✉ SY8 1EJ – ✆ (01584) 876 464 – www.dinhamhall.co.uk – Fax (01584) 876 019 Zb

13 rm – £ 95/160 £ 140

Rest – Menu £ 13 (lunch) – Carte £ 29/37

◆ 18C manor house, with pretty walled garden, situated by Ludlow Castle in the heart of charming medieval town. Period furnishings and individual rooms. Informal dining with crisp, bright décor.

Fishmore Hall

FIshmore Rd, North : 1.5 mi. via Corve St ✉ SY8 3DP – ✆ (01584) 875 148 – www.fishmorehall.co.uk

15 rm – £ 100/210 £ 100/250

Rest – Menu £ 25/47 – Carte dinner £ 32/44

◆ Elegantly restored Georgian house – former girls' school – set out of town in half an acre of land. Very modern designer feel, boasting bold wallpaper and flat screen plasma TVs. Two smart dining rooms serve French based menu.

De Grey's Town House without rest

Broad St ✉ SY8 1NG – ✆ (01584) 872 764 – www.degreys.co.uk – Closed 25 December-3 January Zx

9 rm – £ 90 £ 120

◆ Dating back to 1570 this building retains all its good old English style and charm. Bedrooms are spacious, very individual and feature quality hand made oak furniture.

The Bringewood

Burrington, Southwest : 7.5 mi. by B4361 on Burrington Rd – ✆ (01568) 770 033 – www.thebringewood.co.uk

11 rm – £ 85 £ 95/125

Rest – *(Closed Monday and Tuesday)* Menu £ 30

◆ Converted cow sheds/stables on remotely situated 250 acre working farm. Delightful rear terrace with countryside views and modern feel throughout; very comfy bedrooms. Open, airy dining room with weekly seasonal menus and home grown veg.

ENGLAND

Bromley Court without rest

18-20 Lower Broad St ✉ SY8 1PQ – ✆ (01584) 876 996 – www.ludlowhotels.com – Closed last 2 weeks January Ze

3 rm – £ 75/90 £ 100/110

◆ Delightful Tudor cottage converted to provide three well-furnished suites of bed and living room: high quality comfort. Breakfast and check-in opposite at 73 Lower Broad St.

La Bécasse

17 Corve St ✉ SY8 1DA – ✆ (01584) 872 325 – www.labecasse.co.uk – Closed 24 December-6 January, Sunday dinner, Monday and Tuesday lunch Ye

Rest – Menu £ 26/55

Spec. Crab with celeriac and coconut royale. Roast loin and confit fillet of lamb with liquorice. Caramel soufflé with white chocolate ice cream and raspberry jelly.

◆ 17C former coaching inn; its characterful dining room split into three intimate areas, with linen-laid tables and attractive listed wood panelling. Intricate, elaborate, classically based cooking uses luxury ingredients. Attentive, formal service.

Mr Underhill's at Dinham Weir (Chris Bradley) with rm

Dinham Bridge ✉ SY8 1EH – ✆ (01584) 874 431 – www.mr-underhills.co.uk – Closed 1 week summer, 1 week winter, 25 and 26 December, Monday and Tuesday Zf

4 rm – £ 110/170 £ 135/170 – 2 suites

Rest – *(dinner only) (booking essential) (set menu only)* Menu £ 50/58

Spec. Smoked haddock and scallops with tomato pasta. Venison and capers with raisin and herb gnocchi. Hot apricot fondant tart with apricot ice cream.

◆ Yellow painted riverside house, away from town centre. Daily set menu with classical base makes particularly good use of local meats and cheeses. Comfortable and stylishly decorated bedrooms.

Koo
127 Old St ✉ SY8 1NU – ✆ (01584) 878 462 – www.koo-ook.co.uk – Fax (01584) 878 462 – Closed 25-26 December, 1 January, Sunday, Monday and Tuesday in winter Za
Rest – Japanese – *(dinner only)* Menu £ 26 – Carte £ 20/24
◆ Friendly atmosphere in a simply styled interior decorated with banners and artefacts. Good value meals from a regularly changing menu of authentic and tasty Japanese dishes.

at Woofferton South : 4 mi. by B 4361 - Z - on A 49 – ✉ Ludlow

Ravenscourt Manor without rest
on A 49 ✉ SY8 4AL – ✆ (01584) 711 905 – Closed January-March
3 rm – †£ 50 ††£ 70/75
◆ Characterful black and white timbered 16C manor house in two and a half acres of lawned gardens. Friendly welcome; comfy lounge. Individually decorated, period style rooms.

at Brimfield South : 4.5 mi. by B 4361 - Z - off A 49 – ✉ Ludlow

The Roebuck Inn with rm
✉ SY8 4NE – ✆ (01584) 711 230 – www.theroebuckinnludlow.co.uk – Closed Sunday dinner
3 rm – †£ 65 ††£ 85 **Rest** – *(booking essential)* Carte £ 17/36
◆ 15C country pub with homely appeal, serving well prepared, locally sourced food in bar and formal dining room; flavourful French classics the highlights. Friendly service. Warm, comfortable bedrooms.

at Bromfield Northwest : 2.5 mi. on A 49 - Y – ✉ Ludlow

The Clive with rm
✉ SY8 2JR – ✆ (01584) 856 565 – www.theclive.co.uk – Fax (01584) 856 661 – Closed 25 and 26 December
15 rm – †£ 60/85 ††£ 85/110 **Rest** – Carte £ 21/31
◆ Large converted pub with modern décor in vivid colours. Restaurant, bar, café and bistro areas. Menu of internationally inspired traditional dishes. Very good modern bedrooms.

ENGLAND

LUTON – Luton – 504 S28 – pop. 185 543 Great Britain 12 A2

London 35 mi. – Cambridge 36 mi. – Ipswich 93 mi. – Oxford 45 mi.
Luton International Airport : ✆ (01582) 405100, E : 1.5 mi. X
Central Library, St George's Sq ✆ (01582) 401579, tourist.information@luton.gov.uk
Stockwood Park London Rd, ✆ (01582) 413 704
Whipsnade Wild Animal Park★, West : 8 mi. by B 489, signed from M 1 (junction 9) and M 25 (junction 21) X

Luton Hoo
The Mansion House, Southeast : 2.5 mi. by A505 on A1081 ✉ LU1 3TQ – ✆ (01582) 734 437 – www.lutonhoo.com – Fax (01582) 485 438
207 rm – †£ 220 ††£ 220 – 21 suites
Rest *Wernher* – *(closed Saturday lunch)* Menu £ 30/42 – Carte £ 37/52
Rest *Adam's Brasserie* – *(Closed Sunday dinner, Monday and Tuesday)* Menu £ 25/30 – Carte £ 27/41
◆ Stunning 18C house set in over 1,000 acres of gardens, some designed by Capability Brown. Main mansion boasts numerous comfortable sitting rooms and characterful bedrooms. Formal, marble-filled Wernher restaurant offers traditional menu. Geared towards families, Adam's brasserie is simpler.

LUXBOROUGH – Somerset – 503 J30 – ✉ Watchet 3 A2

London 205 mi. – Exeter 42 mi. – Minehead 9 mi. – Taunton 25 mi.

The Royal Oak Inn of Luxborough with rm
Exmoor National Park ✉ TA23 0SH – ✆ (01984) 640 319 – www.theroyaloakinnluxborough.co.uk – Fax (01984) 641 561 – Closed 25 December
11 rm – †£ 55/80 ††£ 90/100 **Rest** – Carte £ 13/27
◆ Red sandstone pub in an extremely beautiful location. Seasonal menu offers substantial dishes of classically prepared, boldly flavoured foods, with an international edge. Bedrooms are compact but charming.

LYDDINGTON – Rutland – see Uppingham

LYDFORD – Devon – 503 H32 – pop. 1 734 – ✉ Okehampton 2 C2

London 234 mi. – Exeter 33 mi. – Plymouth 25 mi.

Village★★

Dartmoor National Park★★

Moor View House

Vale Down, Northeast : 1.5 mi. on A 386 ✉ EX20 4BB – ✆ (01822) 820 220 – Fax (01822) 820 220 – Closed Christmas-New Year

4 rm – †£ 45/50 ††£ 70/85

Rest – *(by arrangement, communal dining)* Menu £ 25

◆ Victorian country house with attractive garden. Relaxed and friendly atmosphere with real fires; traditionally furnished with antique pieces. Thoughtful, personal touches. Dine with fellow guests at antique table.

The Dartmoor Inn with rm

Moorside, East : 1 mi. on A 386 ✉ EX20 4AY – ✆ (01822) 820 221 – www.dartmoorinn.com – Fax (01822) 820 494 – Closed Sunday dinner and Monday lunch

3 rm – †£ 85/95 ††£ 110/125

Rest – Menu £ 20 (Tuesday-Thursday) – Carte £ 25/40

◆ Pleasant service and a relaxed ambience amidst gently rustic surroundings. Modern menu using local ingredients influenced by Mediterranean and local styles. Smart rooms.

LYME REGIS – Dorset – 503 L31 – pop. 4 406 3 B3

London 160 mi. – Dorchester 25 mi. – Exeter 31 mi. – Taunton 27 mi.

Guildhall Cottage, Church St ✆ (01297) 442138, lymeregis.tic@westdorset-dc.gov.uk

Timber Hill, ✆ (01297) 442 963

Town★ – The Cobb★

Alexandra

Pound St ✉ DT7 3HZ – ✆ (01297) 442 010 – www.hotelalexandra.co.uk – Fax (01297) 443 229 – Closed late December-late January

25 rm – †£ 90/205 ††£ 225/235

Rest – Menu £ 38 (dinner) – Carte lunch £ 20/31

◆ A busy, family run hotel with traditional style at the top of the town. Set in manicured gardens with views of the sea. Comfortable lounge and south facing conservatory. Tasty, home-cooked menus.

Hix Oyster and Fish House

Lister Gardens ✉ DT7 3JP – ✆ (01297) 446 910 – www.restaurantsetcltd.co.uk – Closed 25-26 December, January, Tuesday in winter and Monday

Rest – Seafood – Menu £ 21 (weekday lunch) **s** – Carte £ 28/50 **s**

◆ Small eatery in a terrace by the new gardens; superb views over the bay and cob. Rustic, simple and understated. Daily seafood menu with real understanding of less is more.

LYMINGTON – Hampshire – 504 P31 – pop. 14 227 6 A3

London 103 mi. – Bournemouth 18 mi. – Southampton 19 mi. – Winchester 32 mi.

to the Isle of Wight (Yarmouth) (Wightlink Ltd) frequent services daily (30 mn)

St Barb Museum and Visitor Centre, New St (01590) 689000, information@nfdc.gov.uk

Stanwell House

14-15 High St ✉ SO41 9AA – ✆ (01590) 677 123 – www.stanwellhouse.com – Fax (01590) 677 756

23 rm – †£ 89 ††£ 138 – 4 suites

Rest *Bistro* – Menu £ 13/27 **s** – Carte £ 27/44 **s**

Rest *Seafood at Stanwells* – Carte £ 27/42 **s**

◆ Well-run, centrally located Georgian house. Comfortable, individually decorated bedrooms include some four-posters; those in the original house are more characterful. Informal bistro overlooks terrace. Fresh seafood and attentive service in Stanwells.

The Mill at Gordleton rest,

Silver St, Hordle, Northwest : 3.5 mi. by A 337 off Sway Rd ✉ SO41 6DJ – ✆ (01590) 682 219 – www.themillatgordleton.co.uk – Fax (01590) 683 073 – Closed 25 December

6 rm – †£ 95/115 ††£ 130 – 1 suite

Rest – Menu £ 16/25 – Carte £ 19/41

◆ Delightfully located part 17C water mill on edge of New Forest, in well-kept gardens. Comfortable, traditionally styled interior with a pubby bar and clean-lined rooms. Terrace available for alfresco dining.

Egan's

24 Gosport St ✉ SO41 9BG – ✆ (01590) 676 165 – Closed 25 December-12 January, Sunday and Monday

Rest – *(booking essential)* Menu £ 16 (lunch) – Carte dinner £ 27/34

◆ Bustling whitewashed bistro-style restaurant set near the High Street. Fresh, simple cooking with modern elements; plenty of seafood and game in season. Pleasant, efficient service.

at Downton West : 3 mi. on A 337 – ✉ Lymington

The Olde Barn without rest

Christchurch Rd, East : 0.5 mi. on A 337 ✉ SO41 0LA – ✆ (01590) 644 939 – www.theoldebarn.co.uk – Fax (01590) 644 939

3 rm – †£ 50/60 ††£ 70/75

◆ Unsurprisingly, a converted 17C barn with large, chintzy lounge and wood burner. Some bedrooms in barn annex: a mix of modern style and exposed brick, all spotlessly clean.

ENGLAND

LYMM – Warrington – 502 M23 – pop. 9 554 — 20 B3

London 190 mi. – Liverpool 26 mi. – Leeds 62 mi. – Sheffield 68 mi.

The Church Green

Higher Lane, on A 56 ✉ WA13 0AP – ✆ (01925) 752 068 – www.thechurchgreen.co.uk – Closed 25 December and Sunday dinner

Rest – *(booking essential)* Carte £ 25/39

◆ Keenly run Victorian pub with smart, open-plan bar and restaurant. Well-crafted, flavourful dishes more akin to restaurant dining on à la carte; some pubby dishes at lunch.

LYNDHURST – Hampshire – 503 – pop. 2 281 Great Britain — 6 A2

London 95 mi. – Bournemouth 20 mi. – Southampton 10 mi. – Winchester 23 mi.

New Forest Museum and Visitor Centre, Main Car Park (023) 8028 2269

Dibden Golf Centre Main Rd, ✆ (023) 8020 7508

New Forest Southampton Rd, ✆ (023) 8028 2752

New Forest★★ (Bolderwood Ornamental Drive★★, Rhinefield Ornamental Drive★★)

Lime Wood

Beaulieu Rd, Southeast : 1 mi. by A 35 on B 3056 ✉ SO43 7FZ – ✆ (023) 8028 7177 – www.limewood.co.uk – Fax (023) 8028 7199

15 rm – †£ 125/225 ††£ 225/300, £ 15 – 14 suites – ††£ 350/750

Rest *The Dining Room by Alex Aitken* – Menu £ 25 (lunch) – Carte £ 48/58

Rest *The Scullery* – Carte £ 26/35

◆ Luxurious extended Regency country house in the New Forest. Stylish, contemporary bedrooms; many with forest views. Spa and leisure facilities due to open Spring 2010. Fine dining by Alex Aitken in The Dining Room. Relaxed, all day dining in The Scullery.

Fra Noi

74 High St ✉ SO43 7BJ – ✆ (023) 8028 3745 – www.franoi.co.uk – Closed 1 week January, 25 December, Sunday dinner and Monday

Rest – Italian – *(booking essential)* Menu £ 13 (lunch) – Carte £ 20/31

◆ Delightful modern trattoria on the High St, with floor to ceiling windows and funky décor. Menu showcases cooking from the Emilia-Romagna region. Relaxed, friendly atmosphere.

LYNMOUTH – Devon – 503 I30 – see Lynton

LYNTON – Devon – 503 I30 – pop. 1 870 2 C1

London 206 mi. – Exeter 59 mi. – Taunton 44 mi.

Town Hall, Lee Rd ✆ (01598) 752225, info@lyntourism.co.uk

Town★ (<★)

Valley of the Rocks★, W : 1 mi. – Watersmeet★, E : 1.5 mi. by A 39. Exmoor National Park★★ – Doone Valley★, SE : 7.5 mi. by A 39 (access from Oare on foot)

Lynton Cottage

North Walk Hill ✉ EX35 6ED – ✆ (01598) 752 342 – www.lyntoncottage.com – Fax (01598) 754 016 – Closed 1 December-15 January and restricted opening in winter

16 rm – †£ 62 ††£ 136 **Rest** – *(bar lunch)* Menu £ 32

◆ Stunning vistas of the bay and Countisbury Hill from this personally run, cliff top hotel. All bedrooms to a good standard - superior rooms command the best views. Outside the restaurant, stunning sea views. Inside, local art on the walls.

Hewitt's - Villa Spaldi

North Walk ✉ EX35 6HJ – ✆ (01598) 752 293 – www.hewittshotel.com – Fax (01598) 752 489 – 15 March-15 October

7 rm – †£ 85/120 ††£ 130/180 – 1 suite

Rest – Menu £ 25/35 **s** – Carte £ 35/45 **s**

◆ Splendid 19C Arts & Crafts house in tranquil wooded cliffside setting. Stained glass window by Burne Jones and library filled with antiques. Stylish rooms with sea views. Oak panelled dining room; charming service.

Victoria Lodge without rest

30-31 Lee Rd ✉ EX35 6BS – ✆ (01598) 753 203 – www.victorialodge.co.uk – Fax (01598) 753 203 – 19 March-October

8 rm – †£ 119 ††£ 140

◆ Large 19C house decorated with period photographs, prints and Victoriana. Traditional décor in communal areas and bedrooms which are comfortable and inviting.

St Vincent

Market St, Castle Hill ✉ EX35 6JA – ✆ (01598) 752 244 – www.st-vincent-hotel.co.uk – Easter-October

5 rm – †£ 75/80 ††£ 75/80 **Rest** – *(by arrangement)* Menu £ 28

◆ Grade II listed building with charming Belgian owners 200 metres from Coastal Path. Lovely Edwardian lounge with crackling fire. Neat, simple, clean bedrooms. Cloth-clad dining room: owners proud of French/Mediterranean menus.

at Lynmouth

Shelley's without rest

8 Watersmeet Rd ✉ EX35 6EP – ✆ (01598) 753 219 – www.shelleyshotel.co.uk – Fax (01598) 753 219 – March-October

11 rm – †£ 70 ††£ 100

◆ Centrally located hotel named after eponymous poet who honeymooned here in 1812. Stylish public areas. Very comfortable bedrooms with good views of picturesque locale.

The Heatherville

Tors Park, by Tors Rd ✉ EX35 6NB – ✆ (01598) 752 327 – www.heatherville.co.uk – Fax (01598) 752 634 – March-October

6 rm – †£ 30 ††£ 94 **Rest** – *(by arrangement)* Menu £ 25

◆ Victorian house perched above the town. Well kept throughout with bright, warm décor. Rooms with bold fabrics and woodland views: room 6 has the best outlook. Home-cooked meals employ fresh, local produce.

at Martinhoe West : 4.25 mi. via Coast rd (toll) – ✉ Barnstaple

Old Rectory

✉ EX31 4QT – ✆ (01598) 763 368 – www.oldrectoryhotel.co.uk – 20 March-end of October

8 rm – †£ 120 ††£ 140 **Rest** – *(dinner only) (residents only)* Menu £ 33

◆ Built in 19C for rector of Martinhoe's 11C church. Quiet country retreat in charming three acre garden with cascading brook. Bright and co-ordinated bedrooms. Classic country house dining room.

ENGLAND

LYTHAM – Lancashire – 502 L22 – see Lytham St Annes

LYTHAM ST ANNE'S – Lancashire – 502 L22 – pop. 41 327 20 A2

London 237 mi. – Blackpool 7 mi. – Liverpool 44 mi. – Preston 13 mi.

Town Hall, St Annes Rd West (01253) 725610, touristinfo@flyde.gov.uk

Fairhaven Ansdell, Oakwood Avenue, (01253) 736 741

St Annes Old Links Highbury Rd, (01253) 723 597

at Lytham

Clifton Arms

West Beach FY8 5QJ – (01253) 739 898 – www.cliftonarms-lytham.com – Fax (01253) 730 657

45 rm – †£ 63/100 ††£ 125/185

Rest – *(bar lunch Monday-Saturday)* Menu £ 30 – Carte £ 20/36

◆ Former inn with strong associations with local championship golf course. Traditional country house public areas. Cottage-style rooms, front ones with great views. Restaurant's popular window tables overlook Lytham Green.

The Hastings

26 Hastings Pl. FY8 5LZ – (01253) 732 400 – www.hastingslytham.co.uk – Closed Monday

Rest – Carte £ 20/31

◆ Red-brick restaurant with modern bar, intimate ground floor dining room and brighter first floor, featuring exposed rafters and glass skylight. Wide-ranging menu with a regional slant.

ENGLAND

at St Anne's

The Grand

South Promenade FY8 1NB – (01253) 721 288 – www.the-grand.co.uk – Fax (01253) 714 459 – Closed 23-26 December

53 rm – †£ 145 ††£ 160, £ 6.50

Rest *Café Grand* – (01253) 643 413 – Carte £ 23/34

◆ Impressive, turreted Victorian hotel on promenade. Warm, much improved interior. Spacious rooms, most with good views, turret rooms have particularly good aspect. Rich crimson restaurant overlooks the sea.

Greens Bistro

3-9 St Andrews Road South - Lower Ground Floor FY8 1SX – (01253) 789 990 – www.greensbistro.co.uk – Closed 1 week Spring, 1 week Autumn, 25-26 December, Sunday and Monday

Rest – *(dinner only)* Menu £ 16 (Tuesday-Friday) – Carte £ 23/27

◆ Worth the effort to find, this simple, pleasant bistro, hidden beneath some shops, has linen clad tables, friendly service, and good value, well executed modern British menus.

MACCLESFIELD – Cheshire – 502 N24 – pop. 50 688 20 B3

London 186 mi. – Chester 38 mi. – Manchester 18 mi. – Stoke-on-Trent 21 mi.

Town Hall (0871) 7162640

The Tytherington Club, (01625) 506 000

Shrigley Hall Pott Shrigley Shrigley Park, (01625) 575 757

Sutton Hall

Bullocks Lane, Southeast : 2 mi. by A 523 off Sutton rd SK11 0HE - (01260) 253 211 – www.suttonhall.co.uk – Fax (01260) 252 538 – Closed 25 December

Rest – Carte £ 17/28

◆ A huge out-of-town pub whose previous incarnations include hotel and nunnery. Daily changing menus offer plenty of interest, with traditional, unfussy cooking. Pleasant grounds surround.

MADINGLEY – Cambs. – 504 U27 – see Cambridge

MAENPORTH BEACH – Cornwall – see Falmouth

MAGHAM DOWN – E. Sussex – see Hailsham

MAIDEN BRADLEY – Wiltshire – 503 N30 – pop. 335 — 4 C2

London 114 mi. – Bristol 36 mi. – Cardiff 77 mi. – Southampton 75 mi.

The Somerset Arms with rm

Church St ✉ BA12 7HW – ☎ (01985) 844 207
– www.thesomersetarms.co.uk
5 rm – £ 76/95 £ 84/105
Rest – *(closed Sunday dinner, Monday and restricted opening in January)*
Carte £ 21/32

◆ Proudly run pub, popular with locals. Oft-changing menu uses local produce, including eggs from own hens and herbs and veg from garden. Rustic, flavourful cooking, with steaks a speciality. Polite, well-paced service. Excellent bedrooms boast modern facilities.

MAIDENCOMBE – Devon – 503 J32 – see Torquay

Fancy a last minute break?
Check hotel websites to take advantage of price promotions.

MAIDENHEAD – Windsor and Maidenhead – 504 R29 – pop. 58 848 — 11 C3

London 33 mi. – Oxford 32 mi. – Reading 13 mi.
to Marlow, Cookham and Windsor (Salter Bros. Ltd) (summer only) (3 h 45 mn)
The Library, St Ives Rd ☎ (01628) 796502, maidenhead.tic@rbwm.gov.uk
Bird Hills Hawthorn Hill Drift Rd, ☎ (01628) 771 030
Shoppenhangers Rd, ☎ (01628) 624 693

Plan on next page

Fredrick's

Shoppenhangers Rd ✉ SL6 2PZ – ☎ (01628) 581 000
– www.fredricks-hotel.co.uk – Fax (01628) 771 054
– Closed 23-30 December — X**c**
33 rm – £ 109/295 £ 129/295 – 1 suite
Rest *Fredrick's* – see restaurant listing

◆ Redbrick former inn with well-equipped spa facilities. Ornate, marble reception with smoked mirrors. Conservatory with wicker chairs. Very comfy, individually styled rooms.

Walton Cottage

Marlow Rd ✉ SL6 7LT – ☎ (01628) 624 394
– www.waltoncottagehotel.co.uk – Fax (01628) 773 851
– Closed 24 December-2 January — Y**e**
69 rm – £ 99/130 £ 130/160 – 3 suites
Rest – *(dinner only)* Menu £ 20 – Carte £ 10/20 **s**

◆ A collection of brick built, bay-windowed houses and annexed blocks near town centre. Poet's Parlour lounge is cosy with beams and brick. Aimed at the business traveller. Restaurant prides itself in traditional home cooking.

Fredrick's – at Fredrick's Hotel

Shoppenhangers Rd ✉ SL6 2PZ – ☎ (01628) 581 000
– www.fredricks-hotel.co.uk – Fax (01628) 771 054
– Closed 23-30 December and Saturday lunch — X**c**
Rest – Menu £ 25/39 – Carte £ 31/48 **s**

◆ Ornate paintings, smoked mirrors and distressed pine greet diners in this large restaurant. Chandeliers, full-length windows add to classic feel. Elaborate British menus.

MAIDENHEAD

Bad Godesberg Way . . . . . Y 2
Belmont Park Ave . . . . V 3
Blackamoor Lane . . . . V 5
Boyn Hill Ave . . . . Z 6
Braywick Rd . . . . Z 7
Bridge St . . . . Y 9
College Rd . . . . V 13
Cookham Rd . . . . Y 14
Crescent (The) . . . . Y 15
Ferry Rd . . . . X 17
Frascati Way . . . . YZ 18
Furze Platt Rd . . . . V 20
Grenfell Pl. . . . . Z 21
Gringer Hill . . . . V 22
Harrow Lane . . . . V 24
High St . . . . Y
High St BRAY-ON-THAMES . . . . X 25
King's Grove . . . . Z 27
Linden Ave . . . . V 28
Lower Cookham Rd . . . . . . V 29
Manor Lane . . . . X 31
Market St . . . . Y 32
Nicholson's Walk Shopping Centre . . . . . . YZ
Norreys Drive . . . . X 35
Oldfield Rd . . . . V 36
Ray Mill Rd West . . . . V 39
Ray St . . . . V 38
St Ives Rd . . . . Y 41
St Mark Rd . . . . V 42
Stafferton Way . . . . Z 43
Upper Bray Rd . . . . X 45

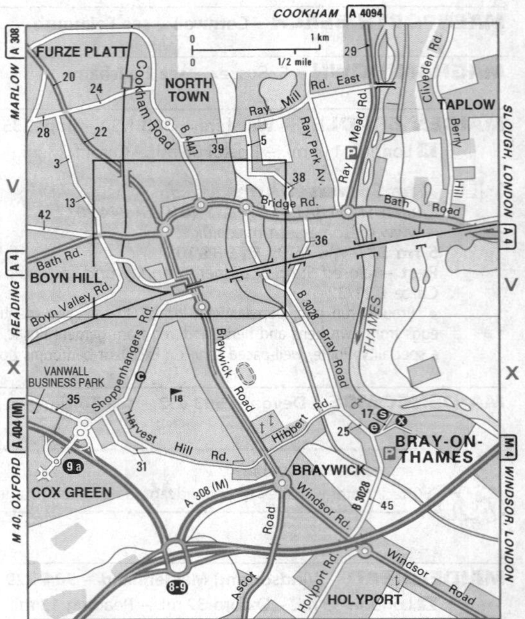

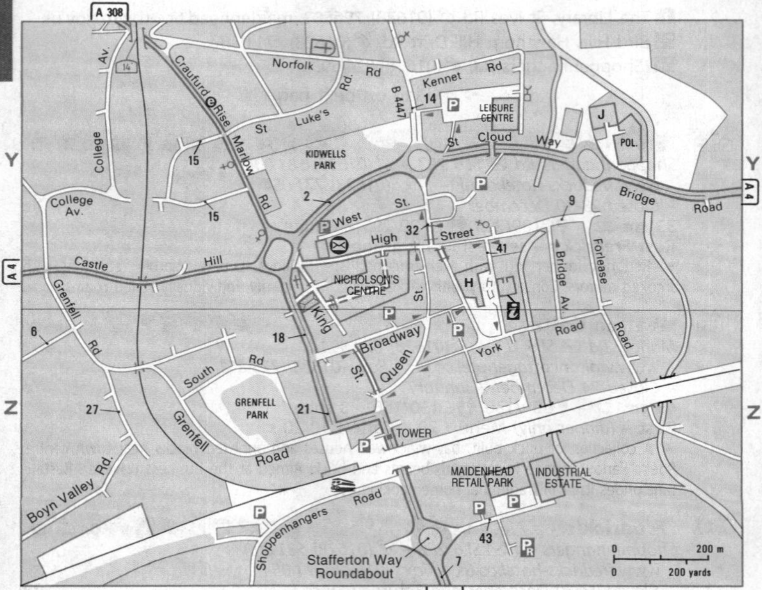

A 308
Craufurd Rise
College Av.
Norfolk Rd
B 4447
Kennet Rd
LEISURE CENTRE
St Luke's
Marlow Rd
KIDWELLS PARK
St Cloud Way
POL.
Bridge Road
A 4
West St.
High Street
Castle Hill
NICHOLSON'S CENTRE
King St.
Grenfell Rd
Bridge Av.
Forlease Road
York Road
Broadway
Queen St.
South Rd
GRENFELL PARK
Grenfell Road
TOWER
Boyn Valley Rd.
Shoppenhangers Road
MAIDENHEAD RETAIL PARK
INDUSTRIAL ESTATE
Stafferton Way Roundabout
200 m
200 yards

ENGLAND

MAIDEN NEWTON – Dorset – 503 M31 4 C3

London 144 mi. – Exeter 55 mi. – Taunton 37 mi. – Weymouth 16 mi.

XX **Le Petit Canard** VISA AE

Dorchester Rd ✉ DT2 0BE – ☎ (01300) 320 536 – www.le-petit-canard.co.uk – Fax (01300) 321 286 – Closed dinner Sunday and Monday

Rest – *(dinner only and Sunday lunch by arrangement)* Menu £ 31/36

◆ Pleasant stone-built cottage in middle of charming village. Plenty of candles, well-spaced tables and soft music. English dishes with French and Oriental touches.

MAIDENSGROVE – Oxfordshire – pop. 1 572 – ✉ Henley-On-Thames 11 C3

London 43 mi. – Oxford 23 mi. – Reading 15 mi.

The Five Horseshoes P VISA

✉ RG9 6EX – ☎ (01491) 641 282 – www.thefivehorseshoes.co.uk – Fax (01491) 641 086 – Closed Sunday dinner

Rest – Carte £ 20/30

◆ Walkers' paradise serving doorstop sandwiches and comforting classics, with regular hog roasts and popular summer barbecues. Beamed bar and suntrap restaurant with countryside views.

MAIDSTONE – Kent – 504 V30 – pop. 89 684 Great Britain 8 B2

London 36 mi. – Brighton 64 mi. – Cambridge 84 mi. – Colchester 72 mi.

Town Hall, High St ☎ (01622) 602169, tourism@maidstone.gov.uk

Tudor Park Hotel Bearsted Ashford Rd, ☎ (01622) 734 334

Cobtree Manor Park Boxley Chatham Rd, ☎ (01622) 753 276

Leeds Castle★ **AC**, SE : 4.5 mi. by A 20 and B 2163

at Bearsted East : 3 mi. by A 249 off A 20 – ✉ Maidstone

XX **Soufflé** P VISA AE

The Green ✉ ME14 4DN – ☎ (01622) 737 065 – www.soufflerestaurant.net – Fax (01622) 737 065 – Closed Saturday lunch, Sunday dinner and Monday

Rest – Menu £ 15/25 – Carte £ 31/40

◆ Converted 16C house on village green with terrace. Timbered interior. Period features include old bread oven in one wall. Modern dishes with interesting mix of ingredients.

X **Fish On The Green** P VISA

Church Lane ✉ ME14 4EJ – ☎ (01622) 738 300 – www.fishonthegreen.com – Fax (01233) 820 074 – Closed 25 December-25 January, Sunday dinner and Monday

Rest – Seafood – Menu £ 16 (lunch) – Carte £ 28/41

◆ Well-run, contemporary restaurant with pleasant terrace, tucked away in corner of the green. Focus on fresh fish, with a few local meat dishes. Good value lunch menu; friendly service.

at West Peckham Southwest : 7.75 mi. by A 26 off B 2016 – ✉ Maidstone

The Swan on the Green P VISA AE

✉ ME18 5JW – ☎ (01622) 812 271 – www.swan-on-the-green.co.uk – Fax (0870) 056 0556 – Closed 25 December and dinner Sunday and Monday

Rest – Carte £ 21/26

◆ With attached micro-brewery, this is a pub for serious ale-lovers. Simply furnished, it overlooks the village green and church. No-nonsense, hearty dishes use local produce.

MALMESBURY – Wiltshire – 503 N29 – pop. 5 094 4 C2

London 108 mi. – Bristol 28 mi. – Gloucester 24 mi. – Swindon 19 mi.

Town Hall, Cross Hayes ☎ (01666) 823748, tic@malmesbury.gov.uk

Town★ – Market Cross★★ – Abbey★

Whatley Manor

Easton Grey, West : 2.25 mi. on B 4040 ✉ SN12 0RB – ✆ (01666) 822 888 – www.whatleymanor.com – Fax (01666) 826 120

15 rm – ††£ 295/495 – 8 suites

Rest Le Mazot – *see restaurant listing*

Rest *The Dining Room* – *(Closed Monday and Tuesday) (dinner only) (booking essential for non-residents)* Menu £ 69/85 **s**

Spec. Langoustines with caramelised bacon and soy. Lamb roasted with spices, coconut and pea purée. Mango cannelloni with mint ice cream and pink grapefruit.

◆ Cotswold stone buildings set in beautiful gardens. Chic, contemporary, luxurious bedrooms; sumptuous bathrooms. Stunning spa, top class business centre and cinema. The Dining Room offers comfortable surroundings in which to enjoy technically-skilled and innovative cooking, with charming service.

The Old Bell

Abbey Row ✉ SN16 0BW – ✆ (01666) 822 344 – www.oldbellhotel.com – Fax (01666) 825 145

34 rm – †£ 90/99 ††£ 220/235

Rest *The Restaurant* – see restaurant listing

◆ Hugely characterful part-13C former abbots' hostel in pleasant gardens, set next to the abbey. Intimate bar. Mix of bedroom styles: bold and fashionable in main house, more classical in annexe.

ENGLAND

Le Mazot – at Whatley Manor Hotel

Easton Grey, West : 2.25 mi. on B 4040 ✉ SN12 0RB – ✆ (01666) 822 888 – www.whatleymanor.com – Fax (01666) 826 120

Rest – Menu £ 22 (lunch) **s** – Carte £ 33/40 **s**

◆ Gold wood Swiss chalet restaurant, offering casual dining on comfy banquettes. Including some Swiss specialities, cooking is refined, light and skilled. Polite, careful service.

The Restaurant – at The Old Bell Hotel

Abbey Row ✉ SN16 0BW – ✆ (01666) 822 344 – www.oldbellhotel.com – Fax (01666) 825 145 – Closed Sunday and Monday dinner

Rest – *(light lunch) (booking essential at dinner)* Menu £ 35 (dinner)

◆ Imposing, richly coloured dining room displaying old portraits and fine china. Skilled kitchen offers brasserie-style lunch and fine dining in evening. Refined, artful dishes; attentive service.

at Crudwell North : 4 mi. on A 429 – ✉ Malmesbury

The Rectory

✉ SN16 9EP – ✆ (01666) 577 194 – www.therectoryhotel.com – Fax (01666) 577 853

12 rm – †£ 95/105 ††£ 165/175 **Rest** – *(dinner only)* Carte £ 27/34

◆ 17C stone-built former Rectory with formal garden. A little quirky but personally run. Comfortable, individually-styled bedrooms with many modern extras, some with spa baths. Airy oak-panelled dining room; modern seasonal cooking.

The Potting Shed

The Street ✉ SN16 9EW – ✆ (01666) 577 833 – www.thepottingshedpub.com – Closed Sunday dinner

Rest – Carte £ 17/27

◆ Relaxed country dining pub with gardening theme and organic herb and vegetable beds at rear. Seasonal produce and rustic, wholesome dishes served in generous portions.

at Charlton Northeast : 2.5 mi. on B 4040 – ✉ Chichester

The Horse and Groom with rm

The Street, on B 4040 ✉ SN16 9DL – ✆ (01666) 823 904 – www.horseandgroominn.com

5 rm – †£ 90/100 ††£ 90/100 **Rest** – Menu £ 17 (lunch) – Carte £ 20/30

◆ 16C Cotswold stone pub with outside bar. Local, seasonal ingredients inform the wide-ranging menu of sandwiches, platters, British classics and more contemporary dishes. Beautifully appointed, stylish bedrooms with sumptuous bathrooms.

MALPAS – Cheshire – **502** L24 – **pop. 3 684** **20** A3

London 177 mi. – Birmingham 60 mi. – Chester 15 mi. – Shrewsbury 26 mi.

at Tilston Northwest : 3 mi. on Tilston Rd – ✉ Malpas

Tilston Lodge without rest

✉ SY14 7DR – ✆ (01829) 250 223 – Fax (01829) 250 223

3 rm – ♦£ 48/52 ♦♦£ 76/88

◆ A former Victorian hunting lodge with delightful gardens and grounds, personally run in a very pleasant style by the charming owner. Cosy, individually appointed bedrooms.

MALVERN WELLS – Worcs. – **503** N27 – see Great Malvern

MAN (Isle of) – I.O.M. – **502** G21 – **pop. 80 058** Great Britain

from Douglas to Belfast (Isle of Man Steam Packet Co. Ltd) (summer only) (2 h 45 mn) – from Douglas to Republic of Ireland (Dublin) (Isle of Man Steam Packet Co. Ltd) (2 h 45 mn/4 h) – from Douglas to Heysham (Isle of Man Steam Packet Co.) (2 h/3 h 30 mn) – from Douglas to Liverpool (Isle of Man Steam Packet Co. Ltd) (2 h 30 mn/4 h)

Laxey Wheel★★ - Snaefell★ (✻★★★) - Cregneash Folk Museum★

DOUGLAS – Douglas – **pop. 26 218** **20** B1

Ronaldsway Airport : ✆ (01624) 821600, SW : 7 mi.

Sea Terminal Buildings ✆ (01624) 686766, tourism@gov.im

Douglas Pulrose Park, ✆ (01624) 675 952

King Edward Bay Onchan Groudle Rd, ✆ (01624) 620 430

Sefton rm,

Harris Promenade ✉ IM1 2RW – ✆ (01624) 645 500 – www.seftonhotel.co.im – Fax (01624) 676 004

89 rm – ♦£ 85/105 ♦♦£ 135 – 3 suites

Rest *The Gallery* – *(lunch residents only)* Carte dinner £ 35/65 **s**

◆ Victorian fronted promenade hotel, built around unique atrium water garden. Comfy, airy bedrooms may have balconies, look out to sea or have internal water garden views. Gallery restaurant with its boldly coloured Manx art, offers flambé dishes as its speciality.

The Regency

Queens Promenade ✉ IM2 4NN – ✆ (01624) 680 680 – www.regency.im – Fax (01624) 680 690

34 rm – ♦£ 75/99 ♦♦£ 119 – 4 suites

Rest *Five Continents* – *(dinner only)* Menu £ 26 – Carte £ 26/44

◆ Perfect for business travellers: mobile phone loan, PCs with free internet in every bedroom and special office suites, combined with traditional seaside styling and Douglas Bay views. Oak panelled restaurant boasts original collection of Island pictures.

Admiral House without rest

12 Loch Promenade ✉ IM1 2LX – ✆ (01624) 629 551 – www.admiralhouse.com – Fax (01624) 675 021

23 rm – ♦£ 115 ♦♦£ 125

◆ Set on the promenade, an impressive Victorian building with turret and views over Douglas Bay. Spacious, modern bedrooms; breakfast served in stylish coffee shop. Close to ferry terminal.

Penta without rest

Queens Promenade ✉ IM9 4NE – ✆ (01624) 680 680 – www.regency.im – Fax (01624) 680 690

22 rm – ♦£ 49 ♦♦£ 59

◆ Set on the promenade, with views over Douglas Bay. Large, well equipped bedrooms each have a computer with free internet access. Wine themed, Mediterranean style breakfast room.

XXX **Ciappelli's**

Admirals House, 12-13 Loch Promenade ✉ IM1 2LX – ☎ (01624) 677 442 – www.ciappellis.com – Fax (01624) 671 305 – Closed Saturday lunch and Sunday

Rest – Menu £ 25 (lunch) – Carte £ 37/55

◆ Stylish, sophisticated restaurant; unique on the Island. Modern, well judged cooking uses local ingredients in good combinations. Dishes arrive well presented with clear flavours.

XX **Macfarlane's**

24 Duke Street ✉ IM1 2AY – ☎ (01624) 624 777 – www.macfarlanes.im – Closed 2 weeks August, 1 week Christmas, Saturday lunch, Sunday and Monday

Rest – Carte £ 27/46

◆ Simple, honest restaurant in heart of town, with leather topped tables and high-sided booths. Unfussy, regularly changing menu relies on fresh local produce, with shellfish to the fore.

PORT ERIN – **Port Erin – pop. 3 575** **20** B1

Rowany Cottier without rest

Spaldrick ✉ IM9 6PE – ☎ (01624) 832 287 – www.rowanycottier.com

5 rm ☕ – 🚹£ 45/75 🚹🚹£ 75/90

◆ Beautifully sited by peaceful Bradda Glen. Pleasant guest areas with views over Port Erin and Calf of Man. Spacious, well kept bedrooms. Locally sourced breakfast; homemade bread.

PORT ST MARY – **Port St Mary – pop. 1 913** **20** B1

Aaron House without rest

The Promenade ✉ IM9 5DE – ☎ (01624) 835 702 – www.aaronhouse.co.uk – Fax (01624) 837 731 – Closed 20 December-7 January

6 rm ☕ – 🚹£ 49/98 🚹🚹£ 98/118

◆ Charming guesthouse with bay/harbour views. Strong Victorian feel, with period furniture and owner in replica housemaid's dress. Comfy, immaculate bedrooms. Afternoon tea on arrival. Interesting breakfast choices.

Ballahane House without rest

Truggan Rd, West : 0.75 mi by Cregneish rd ✉ IM9 5LD – ☎ (01624) 834 238 – www.ballahane.co.uk

3 rm ☕ – 🚹£ 58/75 🚹🚹£ 90/110

◆ Hidden behind farm buildings on country lane, with distant views of Bradda Head. Individually themed bedrooms, quality furnishings, stylish bathrooms. Organic Island breakfast produce.

RAMSEY – **Ramsey – pop. 7 309** **20** B1

The River House without rest

North : 0.25 mi. turning left immediately after bridge ✉ IM8 3DA – ☎ (01624) 816 412

3 rm ☕ – 🚹£ 60/69 🚹🚹£ 85/95

◆ Attractive country house with pleasant gardens. Tastefully furnished throughout, with comfy drawing room, antiques and objets d'art. Three stylishly furnished bedrooms with matching bathrooms.

C. Labonne/MICHELIN

MANCHESTER

County: Greater Manchester
Michelin regional map: **502** N23
London 202 mi.
– Birmingham 86 mi.
– Glasgow 221 mi. – Leeds 43 mi.

Population: 394 269
Great Britain
Map reference: **20** B2

PRACTICAL INFORMATION

Tourist Information

Manchester Visitor Centre, Town Hall Extension, Lloyd St ✆ (0871) 222 8223, touristinformation@visitmanchester.co.uk

Salford T.I.C., Pier 8, Salford Quays ✆ (0161) 848 8601, tic@salford.gov.uk

Airport

Manchester International Airport : ✆ (08712) 710 711, S : 10 mi. by A 5103 - AX - and M 56

Golf Courses

Heaton Park Prestwich, ✆ (0161) 654 9899

Houldsworth Park Stockport Houldsworth St, Reddish, ✆ (0161) 442 1712

Chorlton-cum-Hardy Barlow Hall Rd, Barlow Hall, ✆ (0161) 881 3139

William Wroe Flixton Pennybridge Lane, ✆ (0161) 748 8680

SIGHTS

See

City★ - Castlefield Heritage Park★ CZ – Town Hall★ CZ – Manchester Art Gallery★ CZ **M2** – Cathedral★ (stalls and canopies★) CY – Museum of Science and Industry★ CZ **M** – Urbis★ CY – Imperial War Museum North★, Trafford Park AX **M**

Env.

Whitworth Art Gallery★, S : 1.5 m

Exc.

Quarry Bank Mill★, S : 10 mi. off B 5166, exit 5 from M 56

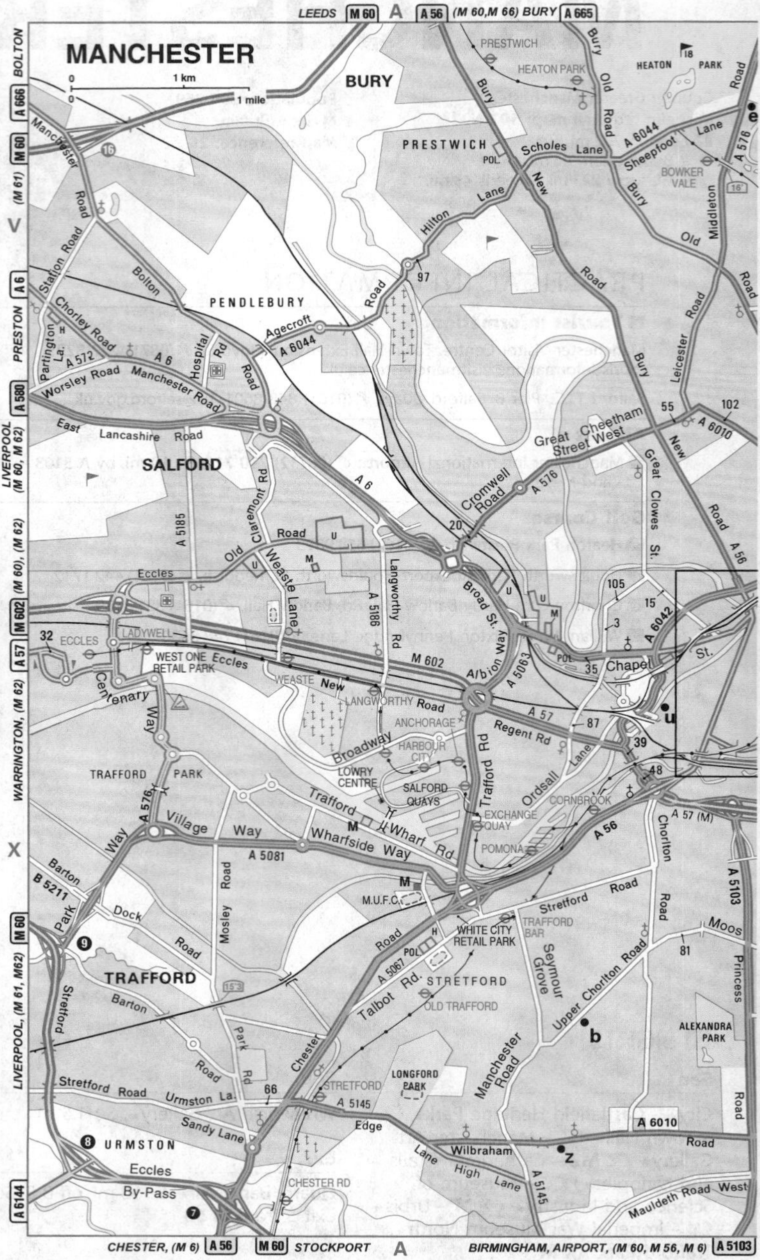

MANCHESTER

0 1 km
0 1 mile

LEEDS M 60 A A 56 (M 60, M 66) BURY A 665

BOLTON A 666 M 60 (M 61) V A 6 PRESTON A 580 LIVERPOOL (M 60, M 62) (M 60), (M 62) M 602 A 57 WARRINGTON, (M 62) X M 60 LIVERPOOL, (M 61, M62) A 6144

CHESTER, (M 6) A 56 M 60 STOCKPORT A BIRMINGHAM, AIRPORT, (M 60, M 56, M 6) A 5103

ENGLAND

BURY
PRESTWICH
HEATON PARK
HEATON PARK
PRESTWICH
POL
Scholes Lane
A 6044
Sheepfoot Lane
BOWKER VALE
Bury Old Road
Bury New Road
Middleton Old Road
A 576
Hilton Lane
Agecroft Road
A 6044
PENDLEBURY
Manchester Road
Station Road
Bolton Road
Chorley Road
Partington La.
A 572
A 6
Worsley Road
Manchester Road
Hospital Rd
East Lancashire Road
SALFORD
Claremont Rd
Old Road
Weaste Lane
A 5185
A 5186
Langworthy Rd
Cromwell Road
A 576
Great Cheetham Street West
A 6010
Leicester Road
Great Clowes St.
New Road
A 56
Broad St.
Albion Way
A 5063
A 6042
Chapel St.
Eccles
ECCLES
LADYWELL
WEST ONE RETAIL PARK
Eccles New Road
WEASTE
LANGWORTHY
M 602
A 57
Regent Rd
Ordsall Lane
Centenary Way
ANCHORAGE
HARBOUR CITY
Broadway
LOWRY CENTRE
SALFORD QUAYS
TRAFFORD PARK
A 576
Village Way
Trafford Wharf Rd
Trafford Rd
EXCHANGE QUAY
POMONA
CORNBROOK
A 56
A 57 (M)
Wharfside Way
A 5081
Mosley Road
M.U.F.C.
Barton Park
B 5211
Dock Road
Stretford Road
TRAFFORD BAR
WHITE CITY RETAIL PARK
Chorlton Road
A 5103
Moss
Princess Road
Seymour Grove
Upper Chorlton Road
TRAFFORD
Stretford
Barton Road
Park Rd
Chester Road
A 5067
Talbot Rd.
STRETFORD
OLD TRAFFORD
ALEXANDRA PARK
Manchester Road
LONGFORD PARK
STRETFORD
Stretford Road
Urmston La.
Sandy Lane
A 5145
Edge Lane
A 6010
Wilbraham Road
URMSTON
Eccles By-Pass
High Lane
A 5145
CHESTER RD
Mauldeth Road West

16 18 16' 97 55 102 20 105 15 3 35 32 87 39 48 81 66 15'3

b e u z

9 8 7

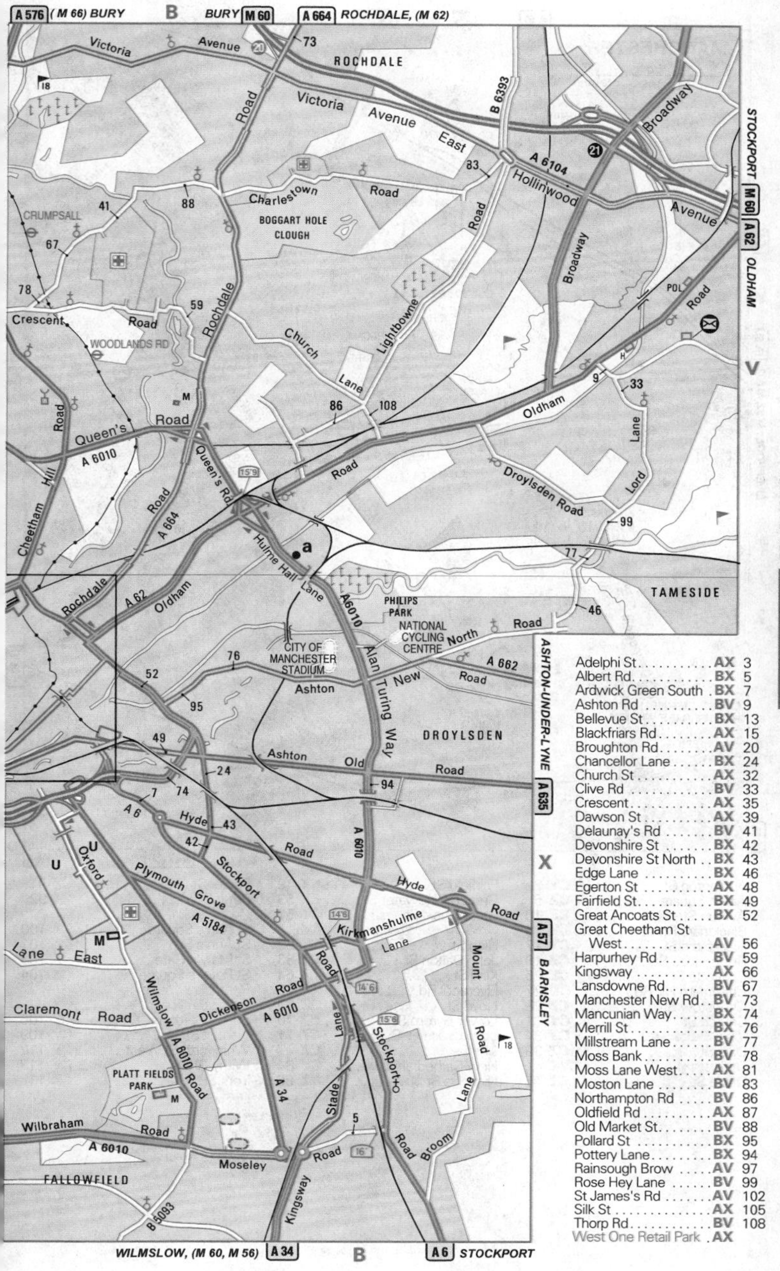
A 576 (M 66) BURY
B
BURY M 60
A 664 ROCHDALE, (M 62)
73
ROCHDALE
Victoria Avenue
Victoria Avenue East
B 6393
Broadway
21
STOCKPORT M 60 A 62 OLDHAM
A 6104
Hollinwood Avenue
83
Charlestown Road
88
41
CRUMPSALL
67
BOGGART HOLE CLOUGH
Rochdale Road
Broadway
POL
Road
78
Crescent
Road
59
WOODLANDS RD
Church Lane
Lightbowne Road
V
9
33
Oldham Road
Lane
M
86
108
Queen's Road
A 6010
Cheetham Hill Road
Queen's Rd
A 664
Road
Droylsden Road
Lord
99
ENGLAND
a
Hulme Hall Lane
77
TAMESIDE
Rochdale
A 62
Oldham
A6010
PHILIPS PARK
NATIONAL CYCLING CENTRE
Road
46
CITY OF MANCHESTER STADIUM
North
76
Alan Turing Way
A 662
52
Ashton New Road
95
ASHTON-UNDER-LYNE
49
DROYLSDEN
Ashton Old Road
24
74
94
7
A 635
A 6
Hyde
43
42
Road
X
A 6010
U
U
Oxford
Stockport
Hyde Road
Plymouth Grove
A 5184
Kirkmanshulme Lane
A 57 BARNSLEY
M
Lane East
Mount Road
Wilmslow
Road
Dickenson Road
A 6010
Claremont Road
Lane
Stockport
18
A 6010
PLATT FIELDS PARK
Road
A 34
Stade
Lane
M
5
Wilbraham Road
Road
A 6010
Moseley Road
Road
Broom
FALLOWFIELD
Kingsway
B 5093
WILMSLOW, (M 60, M 56) A 34
B
A 6 STOCKPORT

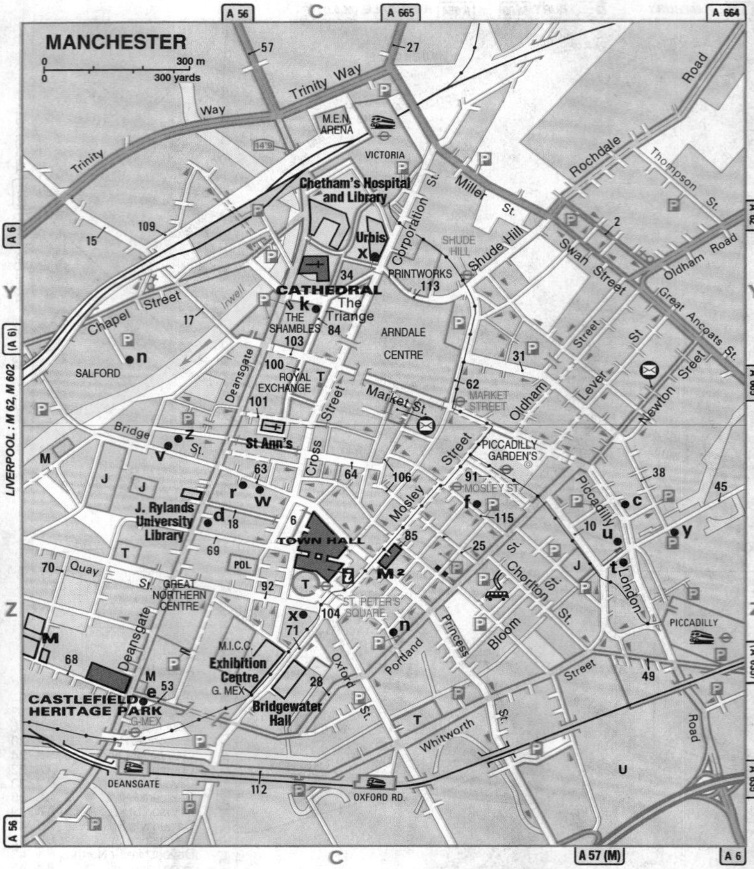

Addington St. . . . . CY 2
Albert Square . . . . CZ 6
Aytoun St. . . . . CZ 10
Blackfriars Rd . . . . CY 15
Blackfriars St. . . . . CY 17
Brazennoze St. . . . . CZ 18
Charlotte St . . . . CZ 25
Cheetham Hill Rd . . . . CY 27
Chepstow St. . . . . CZ 28
Church St . . . . CY 31
Corn Exchange . . . . CY 34
Dale St. . . . . CZ 38
Deansgate . . . . CYZ
Ducie St. . . . . CZ 45
Fairfield St . . . . CZ 49
Great Bridgewater St . . . . . CZ 53
Great Ducie St . . . . CY 57
Great Northern centre . . . . CZ
High St . . . . CY 62
John Dalton St . . . . CZ 63
King St. . . . . CZ 64
Liverpool Rd . . . . CZ 68-
Lloyd St . . . . CZ 69
Lower Byrom St . . . . CZ 70
Lower Mosley St . . . . CZ 71
Mosley St . . . . CZ
New Cathedral St . . . . CY 84
Nicholas St . . . . CZ 85
Parker St . . . . CZ 91
Peter St . . . . CZ 92
Princess St . . . . CZ
St Ann's Square . . . . CY 100
St Ann's St . . . . CY 101
St Mary's Gate . . . . CY 103
St Peter's Square . . . . CZ 104
Shambles Shopping Centre (The) . . . . CY
Spring Gardens . . . . CZ 106
Viaduct St . . . . CY 109
Whitworth St West . . . . . . CZ 112
Withy Grove . . . . CY 113
York St. . . . . CZ 115

The Lowry

50 Dearmans Pl, Chapel Wharf, Salford ✉ M3 5LH – ✆ (0161) 827 4000 – www.roccofortecollection.com – Fax (0161) 827 4001 CY**n**

158 rm – **🚹£ 350 🚻£ 350**, ☕ £ 18.50 – 7 suites

Rest ***The River*** – see restaurant listing

◆ Stylish and hugely spacious, with excellent facilities, impressive spa and minimalist feel: art displays and exhibitions feature throughout. Smart bedrooms with oversized widows; some river views.

The Midland

16 Peter St ✉ M60 2DS – ✆ (0161) 236 3333 – www.qhotels.co.uk – Fax (0161) 932 4100 CZ**x**

298 rm – **🚹£ 250 🚻£ 250**, ☕ £ 15 – 15 suites

Rest ***The French*** – see restaurant listing

◆ Grand Edwardian hotel in city centre, boasting comfy guest areas and great leisure facilities. Take afternoon tea in lounge or sup cocktails in bar. Spacious bedrooms; suites with city views.

Hilton

303 Deansgate ✉ M3 4LQ – ✆ (0161) 870 16 00 – www.hilton.co.uk/manchesterdeansgate – Fax (0161) 870 16 50 CZ**e**

275 rm – **🚹£ 349 🚻£ 349**, ☕ £ 10 – 4 suites

Rest – Menu £ 17/25 – Carte £ 28/76

◆ 23 floors of a striking glass skyscraper. Smart atrium lobby with elevated walkways; glass bottomed pool above. Comfortable, contemporary bedrooms with views. Superb 360° outlook from Cloud bar. Stylish Podium restaurant offers modern brasserie menu of European dishes.

Malmaison

Piccadilly ✉ M1 3AQ – ✆ (0161) 278 1000 – www.malmaison.com – Fax (0161) 278 1002 CZ**u**

160 rm – **🚹£ 170 🚻£ 170**, ☕ £ 13.95 – 7 suites

Rest ***Brasserie*** – Menu £ 17 – Carte £ 24/42

◆ Former cotton warehouse and dolls' hospital boasting seductive red and black Moulin Rouge style décor and sensuous spa. Comfy bedrooms. Uniquely designed suites include Man Utd theme and mini cinema dark room. Cocktails in bar; tasty classics in brasserie.

Abode

107 Piccadilly ✉ M1 2DB – ✆ (0161) 247 77 44 – www.abodehotels.co.uk – Fax (0161) 247 77 47 – Closed 25 December and 1 January CZ**c**

61 rm – **🚹£ 79/135 🚻£ 79/145**, ☕ £ 13.50 – 1 suite

Rest ***Michael Caines*** – see restaurant listing

◆ Classic Victorian cotton merchant's warehouse with iron columns and girders still in situ. Relaxed boutique ambience with modern, trendy open plan rooms and stylish bathrooms.

Marriott Manchester Victoria and Albert

Water St ✉ M3 4JB – ✆ (0161) 838 1188 – www.manchestermarriottva.co.uk – Fax (0161) 834 2484 AX**u**

144 rm – **🚹£ 99/139 🚻£ 99/139**, ☕ £ 16.95 – 1 suite

Rest – *(bar lunch)* Menu £ 21 **s** – Carte £ 19/35 **s**

◆ Restored 19C warehouses on the banks of the River Irwell, with exposed brick and original beams and columns. Large and well-equipped bedrooms. Restaurant proud of its timbered warehouse origins.

City Inn

One Piccadilly Place, 1 Auburn Street ✉ M1 3DG – ✆ (0161) 242 10 00 – www.cityinn.com – Fax (0161) 242 10 01 CZ**t**

284 rm – **🚹£ 225 🚻£ 225**, ☕ £ 13.95 – 1 suite

Rest ***Elements*** – ✆ (0161) 242 10 20 – Menu £ 15/17 – Carte £ 24/40

◆ Contemporary glass building with spacious, airy interior and local art on display. Modern bedrooms boast pale hues, iMac computers and excellent entertainment facilities. Showers only. Smart, stylish restaurant with appealing, wide ranging menu.

Novotel Manchester Centre rm, AC VISA AE
21 Dickinson St ✉ M1 4LX – ☎ (0161) 235 2200 – www.novotel.com – Fax (0161) 235 2210 CZ**n**
164 rm – †£ 65/125 ††£ 65/125, ☕ £ 13 **Rest** – Carte £ 24/37
◆ The open-plan lobby boasts a spacious, stylish bar and residents can take advantage of an exclusive exercise area. Decently equipped, tidily appointed bedrooms. Compact dining room with grill-style menus.

XXXX **The French** – at The Midland Hotel AC P VISA AE
Peter St ✉ M60 2DS – ☎ (0161) 236 3333 – www.qhotels.co.uk – Fax (0161) 932 4100 – Closed Sunday and Monday CZ**x**
Rest – *(dinner only)* Carte £ 32/56 **s**
◆ Elegant, high-ceilinged room dating from 1903, displaying opulent Louis XV styling, ornate carvings, gilded paintings and rich fabrics. Well-judged, classical French dishes; quality ingredients.

XXX **The River** – at The Lowry Hotel AC P VISA AE
50 Dearmans Pl, Chapel Wharf, Salford ✉ M3 5LH – ☎ (0161) 827 4000 – www.roccofortecollection.com – Fax (0161) 827 4001 CY**n**
Rest – Menu £ 23 – Carte £ 36/54
◆ Airy first-floor restaurant with full length windows and river views. Vast mirrors, modern artwork and decorative plates fill the walls. Seasonal British menus feature proudly local produce.

XXX **Wings** AC VISA AE
1 Lincoln Sq ✉ M2 5LN – ☎ (0161) 834 9000 – www.wingsrestaurant.co.uk – Closed 25 December CZ**d**
Rest – Chinese – Menu £ 30 – Carte £ 23/54
◆ Well-run restaurant off busy square. Narrow room with linen-clad tables, comfy booths, terracotta army replicas and Hong Kong skyline murals. Extensive menu of authentic Cantonese dim sum.

XXX **Vermilion** AC P VISA AE
Hulme Hall Lane/Lord North Street ✉ M40 8AD – ☎ (0161) 202 00 55 – www.vermilioncinnabar.com – Fax (0161) 205 82 22 – Closed 1 January and Saturday lunch BV**a**
Rest – Asian – Menu £ 10/25 **s** – Carte £ 30/52 **s**
◆ Destination restaurant on city fringes; rich colours and impressive furnishings. Original, interesting, and sophisticated menu features Thai, Japanese, Malaysian and Chinese influences.

XX **Michael Caines** – at Abode Hotel AC VISA AE
107 Piccadilly ✉ M1 2DB – ☎ (0161) 247 77 44 – www.abodehotels.co.uk – Fax (0161) 247 77 47 – Closed Sunday CZ**c**
Rest – Menu £ 12/25 – Carte £ 23/34
◆ Stylish restaurant in hotel basement. Modern, sophisticated cooking with a well-judged French base and quality ingredients; good value 'grazing' menu of interesting tapas dishes.

XX **Ithaca** AC VISA AE
36 John Dalton Street ✉ M2 6LE – ☎ (0161) 833 49 70 – www.ithacamanchester.com – Closed 25 December, 1 January and Sunday lunch CY**w**
Rest – Japanese – Menu £ 13 – Carte £ 19/88
◆ Traditional Victorian façade masks fashionable 4 floor bar/restaurant with silver walls, black sparkly tiles and mirrored lights. Modern Japanese menu displays good use of ingredients.

XX **Second Floor - Restaurant** – at Harvey Nichols AC VISA AE
21 New Cathedral St ✉ M1 1AD – ☎ (0161) 828 8898 – www.harveynichols.com – Fax (0161) 828 8815 – Closed 25 December, Easter, dinner Sunday and Monday CY**k**
Rest – Menu £ 25 (lunch) – Carte £ 33/36
◆ Smart restaurant with glossy black panelling, stylish colour-changing lighting and oversized windows; city views. Elaborate modern European menu with interesting twists; good presentation.

ENGLAND

XX **Grado**

New York St ✉ M1 4BD – ☎ (0161) 238 97 90 – www.heathcotes.co.uk – Fax (0161) 228 65 35 – Closed 25-26 December, 4-5 January, Sunday and Bank Holidays CZ**f**

Rest – Spanish – Menu £ 16 (lunch) **s** – Carte £ 22/27 **s**

◆ Set in an office block in heart of the city, with long bar for tapas dining or tables for à la carte. Menus offer classic Spanish dishes and a daily-changing charcoal oven special.

XX **The Modern**

URBIS, 6th Floor, Cathedral Gardens ✉ M4 3BG – ☎ (0161) 605 82 82 – www.themodernmcr.co.uk – Closed 25-26 December, 1 January and Sunday dinner CY**x**

Rest – Menu £ 15 (lunch) – Carte £ 23/40

◆ Set on the 5th floor of an impressive glass building, with beautiful views. Seasonally-changing modern British menu is local and regional where possible; good value set lunch.

XX **Koreana**

Kings House, 40a King St West ✉ M3 2WY – ☎ (0161) 832 4330 – www.koreana.co.uk – Fax (0161) 832 2293 – Closed 1 week August, 25-26 December, 1 January, Saturday lunch, Sunday and Bank Holidays CZ**z**

Rest – Korean – Carte £ 12/30

◆ Authentic, family-run restaurant; Korean girls serve in traditional dresses. À la carte and set menus can be confusing; ask owners for help. Cooking is fresh, light and largely homemade.

XX **The Restaurant Bar and Grill**

14 John Dalton St ✉ M2 6JR – ☎ (0161) 839 1999 – www.individualrestaurants.co.uk – Fax (0161) 835 1886 – Closed 25 December CZ**r**

Rest – Carte £ 26/35

◆ Striking building boasting stylish suspended staircase leading to spacious restaurant with oversized windows. Extensive menu offers modern brasserie dishes; influences from Asia/the Med.

X **Luso**

63 Bridge St ✉ M3 3BQ – ☎ (0161) 839 55 50 – www.lusorestaurant.co.uk – Closed 24-31 December and Sunday CZ**v**

Rest – Portuguese – Menu £ 12 (lunch)/20 (early dinner) – Carte £ 26/40

◆ Inspired by the Roman name for Portugal – Lusitania – the owner's homeland. Large à la carte reflects this heritage and adds some international influences; tapas style 'Pesticos' at lunch.

X **Palmiro**

197 Upper Chorlton Rd, South : 2 mi. by A 56 off Chorlton Rd ✉ M16 0BH – ☎ (0161) 860 7330 – www.palmiro.net – Fax (0161) 861 7464 – Closed 25-26 December and 1 January AX**b**

Rest – Italian – *(dinner only and Saturday lunch)* Carte £ 21/27 **s**

◆ Spartan interior with grey mottled walls and halogen lighting: a highly regarded neighbourhood Italian eatery boasting good value rustic dishes cooked with maximum simplicity.

X **Second Floor - Brasserie** – at Harvey Nichols

21 New Cathedral St ✉ M1 1AD – ☎ (0161) 828 8898 – www.harveynichols.com – Fax (0161) 828 8815 – Closed 25 December, Easter, dinner Sunday and Monday CY**k**

Rest – Carte £ 21/28

◆ Relaxed brasserie and bar. Black and stainless steel furniture sits under colour-changing strip lighting. Informal menu of coffees, snacks and light meals. Popular with shoppers.

ENGLAND

Hotels, guesthouses and restaurants change every year, so change your Michelin guide every year!

at Didsbury South : 5.5 mi. by 5103 - AX - on A 5145 – ✉ Manchester

Didsbury House

Didsbury Park, South : 1.5 mi. on A 5145 ✉ M20 5LJ – ✆ (0161) 448 2200 – www.didsburyhouse.com – Fax (0161) 448 2525

23 rm – †£ 95/140 ††£ 95/140, ☕ £ 14.50 – 4 suites

Rest – *(room service only)* Carte £ 24/30

◆ Grade II listed 19C house: grand wooden staircase, superb stained glass window. Otherwise, stylish and modern with roof-top hot tubs. Spacious, individually designed rooms.

Eleven Didsbury Park

11 Didsbury Park, South : 0.5 mi. by A 5145 ✉ M20 5LH – ✆ (0161) 448 7711 – www.elevendidsburypark.com – Fax (0161) 448 8282

20 rm – †£ 95/140 ††£ 95/140, ☕ £ 14.50 – 1 suite

Rest – *(room service only)* Carte £ 24/34

◆ The cool contemporary design in this Victorian town house creates a serene and relaxing atmosphere. Good-sized bedrooms decorated with flair and style. Personally run.

Café Jem&I

1c School Lane ✉ M20 6SA – ✆ (0161) 445 3996 – jemandirestaurant.co.uk – Fax (0161) 448 8661 – Closed 25 December and Bank Holidays

Rest – Carte £ 23/37

◆ Simple, unpretentious cream coloured building tucked away off the high street. Open-plan kitchen; homely, bistro feel. Good value, tasty modern classics.

ENGLAND

at West Didsbury South : 5.5 mi. by A 5103 - AX - on A 5145 – ✉ Manchester

Rhubarb

167 Burton Rd ✉ M20 2LN – ✆ (0161) 448 8887 – www.rhubarbrestaurant.co.uk – Closed 25-26 December

Rest – *(dinner only and Sunday lunch)* Carte £ 22/28

◆ Suburban eatery with small pavement terrace, where neutral hues are offset by large canvasses and a colourful feature wall. Large, seasonally changing menus display an eclectic mix of dishes.

at Manchester International Airport South : 9 mi. by A 5103 - AX - off M 56 – ✉ Manchester

Moss Nook

Ringway Rd, Moss Nook, East : 1.25 mi. on Cheadle rd ✉ M22 5NA – ✆ (0161) 437 4778 – www.manchesterairportrestaurant.co.uk – Fax (0161) 498 8089 – Closed 25-26 December, 2-10 January, Saturday lunch, Sunday and Monday

Rest – Menu £ 21/39 – Carte £ 38/46

◆ Established restaurant in red-brick house: entrance to rear, past garden and pergola-covered terrace. Traditional décor, rich fabrics, wood panelling and stained glass. Classical French cooking.

at Chorlton-Cum-Hardy Southwest : 5 mi. by A 5103 - AX - on A 6010 – ✉ Manchester

Abbey Lodge without rest

501 Wilbraham Rd ✉ M21 0UJ – ✆ (0161) 862 9266 – www.abbey-lodge.co.uk AX**z**

4 rm – †£ 45/65 ††£ 65/70, ☕ £ 7.50

◆ Attractive Edwardian house boasting many original features including stained glass windows. Owner provides charming hospitality and pine fitted rooms are immaculately kept.

MANCHESTER INTERNATIONAL AIRPORT Gtr Manchester – Greater Manchester – 503 N23 – see Manchester

MANSFIELD – Nottinghamshire – 502 Q24 – pop. 69 987 16 B1

London 143 mi. – Chesterfield 12 mi. – Worksop 14 mi.

No.4 Wood Street

4 Wood St ✉ NG18 1QA – ✆ (01623) 424 824 – www.4woodstreet.co.uk – Closed 26 December, 1 January, Saturday lunch, Sunday dinner and Monday

Rest – Menu £ 16 – Carte £ 23/38

◆ Solid brick restaurant hidden away in town centre. Relax in lounge bar with comfy armchairs before enjoying well-executed, modern, seasonal dishes in rustic dining room.

MARAZION – Cornwall – 503 D33 – pop. 1 381 – ✉ Penzance 1 A3

London 318 mi. – Penzance 3 mi. – Truro 26 mi.

Praa Sands Penzance, ✆ (01736) 763 445

St Michael's Mount★★ (<★★) – Ludgvan★ (Church★) N : 2 mi. by A 30 – Chysauster Village★, N : 2 mi. by A 30 – Gulval★ (Church★) W : 2.5 m – Prussia Cove★, SE : 5.5 mi. by A 30 and minor rd

Mount Haven

Turnpike Rd, East : 0.25 mi. ✉ TR17 0DQ – ✆ (01736) 710 249 – www.mounthaven.co.uk – Fax (01736) 711 658 – Closed mid-December to 12 February

18 rm – †£ 70/160 ††£ 170/200

Rest – *(bar lunch)* Carte £ 28/35

◆ Small hotel overlooking St Michael's Bay. Spacious bar and lounge featuring Indian crafts and fabrics. Contemporary rooms with modern amenities, some with balcony and view. Bright attractive dining room; menu mixes modern and traditional.

at Perranuthnoe Southeast : 1.75 mi. by A 394 – ✉ Penzance

Ednovean Farm without rest

✉ TR20 9LZ – ✆ (01736) 711 883 – www.ednoveanfarm.co.uk – Closed Christmas-New Year

3 rm – †£ 85/115 ††£ 90/115

◆ Very spacious, characterful converted 17C granite barn offering peace, tranquillity and Mounts Bay views. Fine choice at breakfast on oak table. Charming, individual rooms.

Victoria Inn with rm

✉ TR20 9NP – ✆ (01736) 710 309 – www.victoriainn-penzance.co.uk – Closed 25-26 December, 1 week January, Sunday dinner and Monday in winter

2 rm – †£ 45 ††£ 70

Rest – Carte £ 22/33

◆ Rustic, country pub serving a classical menu of local, seasonal produce and very fresh fish. Allegedly the oldest inn in Cornwall, it has simple rooms with a nautical theme.

at St Hilary East : 2.5 mi. by Turnpike Rd on B 3280 – ✉ Penzance

Ennys without rest

Trewhella Lane ✉ TR20 9BZ – ✆ (01736) 740 262 – www.ennys.co.uk – Fax (01736) 740 055 – April-October

5 rm – †£ 75/125 ††£ 95/135

◆ Blissful 17C manor house on working farm. Spacious breakfast room and large farmhouse kitchen for afternoon tea. Redecoration has made the bedrooms brighter. Good size sitting room.

ENGLAND

MARCHAM – Oxfordshire – 503 P29 – see Abingdon

MARDEN – Wilts. – see Devizes

MARGATE – Kent – 504 Y29 – pop. 58 465 9 D1

London 74 mi. – Canterbury 17 mi. – Dover 21 mi. – Maidstone 43 mi.
12-13 The Parade (0872) 646111

Indian Princess

44 King St ✉ CT9 1QE – (01843) 231 504 – www.theindianprincess.co.uk – Closed Monday lunch
Rest – Indian – Menu £ 20 (lunch) – Carte £ 25/41
◆ Former pub in the Old Town; now a quirky Indian restaurant. Concise seasonal menu showcases Kentish produce in an original style, with well-balanced flavours and subtle spicing.

MARKET DRAYTON – Shropshire – 502 M25 – pop. 10 407 18 B1

London 159 mi. – Nantwich 13 mi. – Shrewsbury 21 mi.

Goldstone Hall

South : 4.5 mi. on A 529 ✉ TF9 2NA – (01630) 661 202 – www.goldstonehall.com – Fax (01630) 661 585
12 rm – £ 80/88 £ 130/162
Rest – Carte £ 25/37 **s**
◆ 16C red-brick country house that's been extensively added to over the ages. Five acres of formal garden: PG Wodehouse enjoyed its shade! Modern rooms with huge beds. Contemporary twists on daily changing menus.

MARKET HARBOROUGH – Leicestershire – 504 R26 – pop. 20 127 16 B3

London 88 mi. – Birmingham 47 mi. – Leicester 15 mi. – Northampton 17 mi.
Council Offices, Adam and Eve St (01858) 828282
Great Oxendon Rd, (01858) 463 684

at Thorpe Langton North : 3.75 mi. by A 4304 and Great Bowden rd – ✉ Market Harborough

The Bakers Arms

Main St ✉ LE16 7TS – (01858) 545 201 – www.thebakersarms.co.uk – Fax (01858) 545 924 – Closed first week in January, Tuesday-Friday lunch, Sunday dinner and Monday
Rest – *(booking essential)* Carte £ 20/35
◆ Thatched, yellow-washed pub with characterful interior. Blackboard menu evolves constantly throughout the day, displaying pub classics, reliable combinations and comforting desserts.

MARLBOROUGH – Wiltshire – 503 O29 – pop. 7 713 4 D2

London 84 mi. – Bristol 47 mi. – Southampton 40 mi. – Swindon 12 mi.
The Library, High St (01225) 774 222, all.tic's@kennet.gov.uk
The Common, (01672) 512 147
Town★
Savernake Forest★★ (Grand Avenue★★★), SE : 2 mi. by A 4 – Whitehorse (<★), NW : 5 m – West Kennett Long Barrow★, Silbury Hill★, W : 6 mi. by A 4. Ridgeway Path★★ – Avebury★★ (The Stones★, Church★), W : 7 mi. by A 4 – Crofton Beam Engines★ **AC**, SE : 9 mi. by A 346 – Wilton Windmill★ **AC**, SE : 9 mi. by A 346, A 338 and minor rd

X **Coles**

27 Kingsbury Hill ✉ SN8 1JA – ✆ (01672) 515 004
– www.colesrestaurant.co.uk – Fax (01672) 512 069
– Closed 25-28 December and Bank Holidays
Rest – Carte £ 27/37

◆ Shots of 70s film stars adorn a busy, bay-windowed former pub which retains its firelit bar. Friendly staff and elaborate but robust cuisine with an array of daily specials.

at Ramsbury **Northeast : 7.25 mi. by A 346 – ✉ Marlborough**

The Bell

The Square ✉ SN8 2PE – ✆ (01672) 520 230
– www.thebellramsbury.com – Fax (01672) 520 832
– Closed 25 December and Monday dinner
Rest – Menu £ 15/20 – Carte £ 22/32

◆ Whitewashed Victorian pub with atmospheric bar and pleasant dining room. Constantly evolving menus are divided into easy-to-read sections, with tempting local steaks the newest feature.

at Little Bedwyn **East : 9.5 mi. by A 4 – ✉ Marlborough**

The Harrow at Little Bedwyn (Roger Jones)

✉ SN8 3JP – ✆ (01672) 870 871 – www.harrowatlittlebedwyn.co.uk
– Closed 2 weeks August, 2 weeks Christmas, Sunday dinner, Monday and Tuesday
Rest – Menu £ 30/40 – Carte £ 44/46
Spec. Cured wild salmon with smoked sea salt. Roast grey leg partridge with cabbage, apple and Sauternes. Chocolate and Madeira tiramisu.

◆ A contemporary makeover means understated elegance, with neutral hues and smartly laid tables. The flavourful seasonal cooking is presented in a modern style, whilst retaining its classical base. Comprehensive wine list; regular wine evenings.

at East Kennett **West : 5.25 mi. by A4**

The Old Forge without rest

✉ SN8 4EY – ✆ (01672) 861 686
– www.theoldforge-avebury.co.uk
4 rm – †£ 50/60 ††£ 60/70

◆ Converted former smithy with a relaxing, homely feel. Comfortable bedrooms have classic country house style; the family room has pleasant countryside views. Communal breakfast.

MARLDON – Devon – **503** J32 – **pop. 1 798** **2** C2

London 193 mi. – Newton Abbott 7 mi. – Paignton 3 mi.

Church House Inn

Village Rd ✉ TQ3 1SL – ✆ (01803) 558 279
– www.churchhousemarldon.com
Rest – Carte £ 22/33

◆ Charming 18C pub displaying original Georgian windows and plenty of nooks and crannies. Cooking is traditional and tasty, featuring quality regional produce in generous helpings.

Don't confuse the couvert rating X with the stars ✿!
Couverts defines comfort and service, while stars are awarded for the best cuisine across all categories of comfort.

MARLOW – Buckinghamshire – 504 R29 – pop. 17 522 11 C3

London 35 mi. – Aylesbury 22 mi. – Oxford 29 mi. – Reading 14 mi.

to Henley-on-Thames (Salter Bros. Ltd) (summer only) (2 h 15 mn) – to Maidenhead, Cookham and Windsor (Salter Bros. Ltd) (summer only)

31 High St ☎ (01628) 483597, tourism_enquiries@wycombe.gov.uk

Danesfield House

rest,

Henley Rd, Southwest : 2.5 mi. on A 4155
✉ SL7 2EY – ☎ (01628) 891 010 – www.danesfieldhouse.co.uk – Fax (01628) 890 408

83 rm – †£ 150/220 ††£ 150/245, £ 11.50 – 1 suite

Rest *Oak Room* – *(Closed 2 weeks Christmas, 2 weeks August and Sunday - Tuesday lunch)* Menu £ 29 (lunch Wednesday-Friday)/55

Rest *Orangery* – Carte £ 29/37

♦ Stunning house and gardens in Italian Renaissance style with breathtaking views of Thames. Grand lounge with country house feel. Comfy rooms; state-of-art health spa. Intimate Oak Room restaurant. Orangery is a charming terrace brasserie.

Compleat Angler

Marlow Bridge, Bisham Rd ✉ SL7 1RG – ☎ (0844) 879 9128 – www.macdonaldhotels.co.uk/compleatangler – Fax (01628) 486 388

61 rm – †£ 100/255 ††£ 100/255 – 3 suites

Rest *Aubergine at the Compleat Angler* – ☎ (01628) 405 405 *(closed Sunday dinner and Monday)* Menu £ 29/55

Rest *Bowaters* – Menu £ 23 – Carte £ 33/41

♦ Smart riverside hotel boasting superb views, set in enviable location between bridge and weir. Bedrooms mix classical furnishings with contemporary fabrics: some have waterfront balconies; feature rooms are best. Ambitious French menu in Aubergine. More traditional British fare in contemporary Bowaters.

ENGLAND

XX The Vanilla Pod

31 West St ✉ SL7 2LS – ☎ (01628) 898 101 – www.thevanillapod.co.uk – Fax (01628) 898 108 – Closed Easter, 24 December-8 January, Sunday, Monday and Bank Holidays

Rest – *(booking essential)* Menu £ 20/40 **s**

♦ Discreet, well-established address with plush furnishings and just a few tables; formerly home to T. S. Eliot. Ambitious cooking boasts French foundations, original touches and artistic flair.

The Hand and Flowers (Tom Kerridge) with rm

126 West St ✉ SL7 2BP – ☎ (01628) 482 277 – www.thehandandflowers.co.uk – Fax (01628) 401 913 – Closed 24-26 December, 31 December lunch, 31 January dinner and Sunday dinner

4 rm – †£ 140 ††£ 190

Rest – *(booking essential)* Carte £ 30/37

Spec. Moules marinière with stout and brown bread. Honey roast duck tart with cabbage and chanterelles. Pistachio sponge with melon sorbet and marzipan.

♦ Chef-owner produces highly skilled cooking and pushes at the boundaries without forgetting this is a pub; technique is key. Staff keep their composure under pressure and enthusiastic amateurs can even spend a day shadowing in the kitchen. Neighbouring cottages house pretty bedrooms, one with a Jacuzzi.

The Royal Oak

Frieth Rd, Bovingdon Green, West : 1.25 mi. by A 4155 ✉ SL7 2JF – ☎ (01628) 488 611 – www.royaloakmarlow.co.uk – Fax (01628) 478 680 – Closed 25-26 December

Rest – Carte £ 20/27

♦ Part-17C, country-chic pub with herb garden, petanque pitch and pleasant terrace. Set close to the M40 and M4: an ideal London getaway. Largely British menu with the odd Asian influence.

The Cheerful Soul

Henley Rd, Southwest : 1 mi. on A 4155 ✉ SL7 2DF – ✆ (01628) 483 343 – Fax (01628) 478 990 – Closed Sunday dinner and Monday

Rest – *(booking advisable)* Menu £ 16 (lunch) – Carte £ 20/28

◆ Characterful 17C pub run by winners of TV programme 'The Restaurant'. Fresh, bright interior and smiley staff. Well-executed, simply presented dishes; good value lunch menu.

at Little Marlow East : 3 mi. on A 4155

The Queens Head

Pound Lane ✉ SL7 3SR – ✆ (01628) 482 927 – www.marlowslittlesecret.co.uk

Rest – Carte £ 23/35

◆ 16C pub popular with walkers. Lunch menu offers ploughman's and fish and chips; dinner menu raises bar with duck liver parfait and pan-fried sea bass. Poised, friendly service.

MARPLE – Greater Manchester – 502 N23 – pop. 18 475 — 20 B3

London 190 mi. – Chesterfield 35 mi. – Manchester 11 mi.

Springfield without rest

99 Station Rd ✉ SK6 6PA – ✆ (0161) 449 0721 – www.springfieldhotelmarple.co.uk

7 rm – †£ 57 ††£ 77

◆ Part Victorian house with sympathetic extensions and pleasant rural views. Conservatory breakfast room; individually styled bedrooms. Useful for visits to Peak District.

MARSDEN – West Yorkshire – 502 O23 – pop. 3 499 – ✉ Huddersfield — 22 A3

London 195 mi. – Leeds 22 mi. – Manchester 18 mi. – Sheffield 30 mi.

Olive Branch with rm

Manchester Rd, Northeast : 1 mi. on A 62 ✉ HD7 6LU – ✆ (01484) 844 487 – www.olivebranch.uk.com – Closed first 2 weeks January and 26 December

3 rm – †£ 55 ††£ 70, £ 12.50

Rest – *(dinner only and Sunday lunch)* Menu £ 19 (weekday dinner) – Carte £ 26/40

◆ Characterful drovers inn, with terrace and secluded garden. Large classical menu is split between meat and seafood, with hearty specials displayed on large post-it notes. Bedrooms are modern, comfortable and individually themed.

MARSTON MEYSEY – Wiltshire — 4 D1

London 91 mi. – Birmingham 82 mi. – Bristol 56 mi. – Coventry 85 mi.

The Old Spotted Cow with rm

The Street ✉ SN6 6LQ – ✆ (01285) 810 264 – www.theoldspottedcow.co.uk – Closed Monday except Bank Holidays

1 rm – †£ 50 ††£ 75 **Rest** – Carte £ 18/28

◆ Enthusiastically run country pub serving seasonal, rustic cooking, which combines hearty British classics with worldly spices. Sunday roasts, summer barbecues and monthly spice nights. One comfortable, contemporary bedroom.

MARTINHOE – Devon – see Lynton

MARTOCK – Somerset – 503 L31 – pop. 4 309 — 3 B3

London 148 mi. – Taunton 19 mi. – Yeovil 6 mi.

Village★ - All Saints★★

Montacute House★★ **AC**, SE : 4 mi. – Muchelney★★ (Parish Church★★), NW : 4.5 mi. by B 3165 – Ham Hill (≤★★), S : 2 mi. by minor roads. Barrington Court★ **AC**, SW : 7.5 mi. by B 3165 and A 303

The Hollies

Bower Hinton, South : 1 mi. on B 3165 ✉ TA12 6LG – ☏ (01935) 822 232 – www.thehollieshotel.co.uk – Fax (01935) 822 249
48 rm – †£ 90 ††£ 108/140 – 3 suites
Rest – *(dinner only)* Carte £ 21/33 **s**
◆ Impressive former 17C farmhouse in small village near grand Montacute House. Separate annex has large, well-equipped, up-to-date bedrooms with good comforts and facilities. Characterful oak beamed, boothed restaurant and lounge in the farmhouse.

MARTON – Shropshire Great Britain 18 A1

London 174 mi. – Birmingham 57 mi. – Shrewsbury 16 mi.
Powis Castle★★★, NW : 7 mi. by B 4386 and A 490

The Sun Inn

✉ SY21 8JP – ☏ (01938) 561 211 – www.suninn.org.uk – Closed Sunday dinner (except last Sunday in the month), Monday and lunch Tuesday
Rest – Carte £ 15/33
◆ Welcoming country pub on the English-Welsh border. A regularly changing British/ Mediterranean menu and a fresh fish board feature in the restaurant, with specials in the bar.

MASHAM – North Yorkshire – 502 P21 – pop. 1 171 – ✉ Ripon 22 B1

London 231 mi. – Leeds 38 mi. – Middlesbrough 37 mi. – York 32 mi.

Swinton Park

Swinton, Southwest : 1 mi. ✉ HG4 4JH – ☏ (01765) 680 900 – www.swintonpark.com – Fax (01765) 680 901
26 rm (dinner included) – ††£ 340 – 4 suites
Rest *Samuels* – *(Closed Monday and Tuesday lunch)* Menu £ 24/42
◆ 17C castle with Georgian and Victorian additions, on a 20,000 acre estate and deer park. Luxurious, antique filled lounges. Very comfortable, individually styled bedrooms. Grand dining room with ornate gold leaf ceiling and garden views.

Bank Villa

on A 6108 ✉ HG4 4DB – ☏ (01765) 689 605 – www.bankvilla.com
6 rm – †£ 50/55 ††£ 85/95
Rest – *(by arrangement)* Carte £ 21/24
◆ Stone-built Georgian villa with Victorian additions. Two lounges and conservatory; delightful, 'sun-trap' stepped garden. Cosy, cottagey rooms: some are in the eaves! Home-cooked menus in pastel dining room/tea room.

Vennell's

7 Silver St ✉ HG4 4DX – ☏ (01765) 689 000 – www.vennellsrestaurant.co.uk – Closed 26 December-8 January, Sunday dinner and Monday
Rest – *(dinner only and Sunday lunch) (booking essential)* Menu £ 25 **s**
◆ Local art for sale at this personally run local eaterie with comfy basement bar. Bold, confident cooking executed with care and precision. Popular annual 'lobster week'.

MATFEN – Northumberland – 501 O18 – pop. 500 24 A2

London 309 mi. – Carlisle 42 mi. – Newcastle upon Tyne 24 mi.

Matfen Hall

✉ NE20 0RH – ☏ (01661) 886 500 – www.matfenhall.com – Fax (01661) 886 055
53 rm – †£ 125/150 ††£ 185
Rest *Library and Print Room* – *(dinner only and Sunday lunch)* Menu £ 30 – Carte £ 33/44
◆ 19C country mansion built by Thomas Ruckman, master of Gothic design. Set in 500 acres with superb Grand Hall, fine paintings, plush drawing room and mix of bedroom styles. Characterful Library dining room has display of original books.

ENGLAND

MATLOCK – Derbyshire – 502 P24 – pop. 11 265 Great Britain 16 B1

London 153 mi. – Derby 17 mi. – Manchester 46 mi. – Nottingham 24 mi.

Crown Sq ✆ (01629) 583388, matlockinfo@derbyshiredales.gov.uk

Hardwick Hall★★ **AC**, E : 12.5 mi. by A 615 and B 6014 – Crich Tramway Village★ **AC**, S : 12 mi. by A 6 and B 5036

at Birchover Northwest : 7.5 mi. by A 6 – ✉ Matlock

The Druid Inn

Main St ✉ DE4 2BL – ✆ (01629) 650 302 – www.thedruidinn.co.uk – Closed 25 December and Sunday dinner

Rest – Menu £ 14 (weekdays) – Carte £ 25/38

◆ A rustic bar and modern, airy dining room are echoed by classic British favourites and more ambitious restaurant style dishes, including some for two; food is wholesome and tasty.

MAWGAN PORTH – Cornwall – 503 E32 – see Newquay

MAWNAN SMITH – Cornwall – 503 E33 – see Falmouth

MEDBOURNE – Leicestershire – 504 R26 16 B2

London 93 mi. – Corby 9 mi. – Leicester 16 mi.

Homestead House without rest

Ashley Rd ✉ LE16 8DL – ✆ (01858) 565 724 – www.homesteadhouse.co.uk

3 rm – †£ 35 ††£ 55

◆ Personally run, spotlessly kept guest house with comfortable, leather-furnished lounge and traditionally styled, homely bedrooms; two with a pleasant countryside outlook.

Horse & Trumpet with rm

Old Green ✉ LE16 8DX – ✆ (01858) 565 000 – www.horseandtrumpet.com – Fax (01858) 565 551 – Closed 26 December, 1-8 January, Sunday dinner and Monday

4 rm – †£ 75 ††£ 75

Rest – Menu £ 20 (lunch) – Carte £ 35/42

◆ Attractive 18C thatched building set by village bowling green, with courtyard, characterful beamed lounges and intimate dining rooms. Refined, flavoursome modern cooking; two tasting menus available. Cottage-style bedrooms in former stables.

MELLOR – Lancs. – see Blackburn

MELLS – Somerset – 503 M30 – pop. 2 222 4 C2

London 117 mi. – Bath 16 mi. – Frome 3 mi.

The Talbot Inn with rm

Selwood St ✉ BA11 3PN – ✆ (01373) 812 254 – www.talbotinn.com – Fax (01373) 813 599

8 rm – †£ 95 ††£ 95/145

Rest – Menu £ 13/16 – Carte £ 23/33

◆ Traditional coaching inn with a courtyard, secluded terrace and pergola. Country style cooking is hearty, robust and uses homemade produce; wide-ranging menu. Bedrooms are classical, some modest.

MELTON MOWBRAY – Leicestershire – 502 R25 – pop. 25 554 16 B2

London 113 mi. – Leicester 15 mi. – Northampton 45 mi. – Nottingham 18 mi.

Council Offices, Nottingham Rd ✆ (01664) 480992, customerservices@melton.gov.uk

18 Thorpe Arnold Waltham Rd, ✆ (01664) 562 118

Stapleford Park

East : 5 mi. by B 676 on Stapleford rd ✉ LE14 2EF – ✆ (01572) 787 000 – www.staplefordpark.com – Fax (01572) 787 001

55 rm – †£ 220 ††£ 240/288

Rest *Grinling Gibbons Dining Room* – *(dinner only and Sunday lunch) (booking essential)* Menu £ 24/47 – Carte £ 47/62

Rest *Pavilion Brasserie* – *(April-end October)* Carte £ 23/29

◆ Astoundingly beautiful stately home in 500 glorious acres, exuding a grandeur rarely surpassed. Extensive leisure facilities; uniquely designed rooms of sumptuous elegance. Ornate rococo dining room a superb example of master craftsman's work. Smart brasserie.

at Stathern North : 8 mi. by A 607 – ✉ Melton Mowbray

Red Lion Inn

2 Red Lion St ✉ LE14 4HS – ✆ (01949) 860 868 – www.theredlioninn.co.uk – Fax (01949) 861 579 – Closed Sunday dinner

Rest – *(booking essential)* Menu £ 16/18 – Carte £ 19/32

◆ Large, whitewashed village pub. Menus offer straightforward cooking and refined pub classics with the odd international twist. Produce is sourced from their allotment and local suppliers.

MERIDEN – W. Mids. – **503** P26 – see Coventry

MEVAGISSEY – Cornwall – **503** F33 – pop. 2 221 — 1 B3

London 287 mi. – Newquay 21 mi. – Plymouth 44 mi. – Truro 20 mi.

Town★★

NW : Lost Gardens of Heligan★

Trevalsa Court

School Hill, East : 0.5 mi. on B 3273 (St Austell rd) ✉ PL26 6TH – ✆ (01726) 842 468 – www.trevalsa-hotel.co.uk – Fax (01726) 844 482 – February-November

13 rm – †£ 70/176 ††£ 200/220

Rest – *(dinner only)* Menu £ 30

◆ Charming 1930s building with lovely garden which has access to Polstreath Beach. Homely morning room. Owners have brightened up the bedrooms and added contemporary furnishings. Oak-panelled dining room with daily menu, devised using best available produce.

Kerryanna without rest

Treleaven Farm ✉ PL26 6SA – ✆ (01726) 843 558 – www.kerryanna.co.uk – Fax (01726) 843 558 – Easter-September

3 rm – ††£ 74

◆ Purpose-built bungalow within farm providing pleasant ambience. Useful for Lost Gardens of Heligan. Spacious front sitting room. Immaculately kept, sizeable, chintz bedrooms.

MICKLEHAM – Surrey – **504** T30 – pop. 484 — 7 D1

London 21 mi. – Brighton 32 mi. – Guildford 14 mi. – Worthing 34 mi.

The King William IV

Byttom Hill, North : 0.5 mi. by A 24 ✉ RH5 6EL – ✆ (01372) 372 590 – www.king-williamiv.com – Closed Sunday dinner

Rest – Carte £ 19/29

◆ Traditional homemade pies and simply-cooked, fresh vegetables: robust, hearty cooking perfect for refuelling after a walk in the Surrey countryside. Lovely terraced garden.

MICKLETON – Glos. – **503** O27 – see Chipping Campden

MIDDLE WINTERSLOW – Wilts. – **503** O30 – see Salisbury

MIDDLEHAM – North Yorkshire – 502 O21 – pop. 754 22 B1

London 233 mi. – Kendal 45 mi. – Leeds 47 mi. – Newcastle upon Tyne 63 mi.

at Carlton-in-Coverdale Southwest : 4.5 mi. by Coverham rd – ✉ Leyburn

Abbots Thorn

✉ DL8 4AY – ✆ (01969) 640 620 – www.abbotsthorn.co.uk – Closed December-January

3 rm – †£ 40/74 ††£ 60/74

Rest – *(by arrangement, communal dining)* Menu £ 23

◆ Well priced, comfortable, quiet guesthouse in attractive rural village. Handy for visits to Moors. Cosy sitting room. Sizeable bedrooms which are homely and well-kept. Fresh, local produce to fore at dinner.

Foresters Arms with rm

✉ DL8 4BB – ✆ (01969) 640 272 – www.forestersarms-carlton.co.uk – Fax (01969) 640 272 – restricted opening in winter

3 rm – †£ 65 ††£ 79

Rest – Carte £ 15/20

◆ Compact 17C stone-built inn. Flagged floor bar with beams and open fire. Timbered restaurant where modern dishes utilise fresh, local produce. Pleasant, cottagey rooms.

MIDDLETON-IN-TEESDALE – Durham – 502 N20 – pop. 1 143 24 A3

London 447 mi. – Carlisle 91 mi. – Leeds 124 mi. – Middlesbrough 70 mi.

10 Market Pl ✆ (01833) 641001, tic@middletonplus.myzen.co.uk

Grove Lodge

Hude, Northwest : 0.5 mi. on B 6277 ✉ DL12 0QW – ✆ (01833) 640 798 – www.grovelodgeteesdale.co.uk

3 rm – †£ 48/52 ††£ 79/82

Rest – Menu £ 22 – Carte £ 18/29

◆ Victorian former shooting lodge perched on a hill where the two front facing rooms have the best views. Neat and friendly house, traditionally decorated. Home-cooked dinners are proudly served.

MIDHURST – West Sussex – 504 R31 – pop. 6 120 7 C2

London 57 mi. – Brighton 38 mi. – Chichester 12 mi. – Southampton 41 mi.

North St ✆ (01730) 817322, midtic@chichester.gov.uk

Spread Eagle

South St ✉ GU29 9NH – ✆ (01730) 816 911 – www.hshotels.co.uk – Fax (01730) 815 668

37 rm – †£ 135/212 ††£ 180/221 – 2 suites

Rest – Menu £ 20/39 **s**

◆ 15C hostelry boasting lovely characterful bar with uneven oak flooring and roaring fire. Many antiques. Good leisure facilities. Rooms have country house décor and style. A very traditional ambience pervades restaurant.

at Henley North : 4.5 mi. by A286

Duke of Cumberland

✉ GU27 3HQ – ✆ (01428) 652 280 – Closed 25-26 December and 1 January

Rest – Carte approx. £ 30

◆ Hidden gem of a pub with delightful, low-beamed interior, huge fireplace and tiered gardens with babbling brooks. Appealing menu of carefully prepared, seasonal dishes. Charming service.

ENGLAND

at Bepton Southwest : 2.5 mi. by A 286 on Bepton rd – ✉ Midhurst

Park House

✉ GU29 0JB – ☎ (01730) 819 000 – www.parkhousehotel.com – Fax (01730) 819 099 – Closed 25-26 December

14 rm – †£ 145/225 ††£ 145/285 – 1 suite

Rest – *(booking essential at lunch)* Menu £ 25/35

◆ Comfortable, privately owned country house. Charming lounge with chintz armchairs, antique paintings, heavy drapes. Bar with honesty policy. Rooms are bright and colourful. Classical dining room with antique tables and chairs.

at Elsted Southwest : 5 mi. by A 272 on Elsted rd – ✉ Midhurst

Three Horseshoes

✉ GU29 0JY – ☎ (01730) 825 746

Rest – Carte £ 22/31

◆ Simply furnished, cosy beamed pub with large south-facing garden. Enormous portions of wholesome, hearty cooking in the form of casseroles and pies; chatty, informal service.

at Redford West : 3 mi. by A272 then following signs for Redford

Redford Cottage without rest

✉ GU29 OQF – ☎ (01428) 741 242 – Fax (01428) 741 242 – Closed 24-26 and 31 December and 1 January

5 rm – †£ 65 ††£ 95

◆ Charming 15C cottage in delightful gardens. Uniquely styled, attractively furnished bedrooms; china, books and pictures abound. Hearty breakfast from the Aga can be taken on the terrace.

ENGLAND

at Stedham West : 2 mi. by A 272 – ✉ Midhurst

Nava Thai at The Hamilton Arms

School Lane ✉ GU29 0NZ – ☎ (01730) 812 555 – www.thehamiltonarms.co.uk – Fax (01730) 817 459 – Closed Monday except Bank Holidays

Rest – Thai – Menu £ 25 – Carte £ 20/30

◆ Extensive menu of tasty Thai dishes served among authentic oriental artefacts and incense in this traditional village inn. Fragrant, flavoursome cooking and polite service.

at Trotton West : 3.25 mi. on A 272 – ✉ West Sussex

The Keepers Arms

✉ GU31 5ER – ☎ (01730) 813 724 – www.keepersarms.co.uk – Closed 25-26 December

Rest – Carte £ 22/28

◆ Refurbished hillside pub set back from the main road, with cosy bar and sofas and two feature tables. Good value, flavoursome modern British dishes on concise à la carte menu.

MID LAVANT – West Sussex – see Chichester

MIDSOMER NORTON – Bath and North East Somerset – 503 M30 4 C2

London 125 mi. – Bath 11 mi. – Wells 12 mi.

XX The Moody Goose at the Old Priory with rm

Church Sq ✉ BA3 2HX – ☎ (01761) 416 784 – www.theoldpriory.co.uk – Fax (01761) 417 851 – Closed 24-27 and 31 December and Sunday

6 rm – †£ 85/95 ††£ 120/145

Rest – Menu £ 29/33 – Carte dinner £ 37/43

◆ 12C former priory, by a church, with enviable walled garden. Flagged floors, beams and vast fireplaces create impressive interior. Interesting modern cooking. Comfy rooms.

MILFORD-ON-SEA – Hampshire – 503 P31 – pop. 4 229 – ✉ Lymington 6 A3

London 109 mi. – Bournemouth 15 mi. – Southampton 24 mi. – Winchester 37 mi.

Westover Hall
Park Lane ✉ SO41 0PT – ✆ (01590) 643 044 – www.westoverhallhotel.com – Fax (01590) 644 490
11 rm (dinner included) – £ 168/220 £ 200/290 – 3 suites
Rest – Menu £ 20/42 **s**
◆ Characterful 19C mansion in delightful spot overlooking Christchurch Bay. Comfortable sitting room and impressive hall and minstrels gallery. Bedrooms have personality. Ornate dining room: decorative ceiling, stained glass, panelling.

MILLBROOK – Cornwall – 503 H32 — 2 C2

London 235 mi. – Liskeard 16 mi. – Plymouth 23 mi.

at Freathy West : 3 mi. by B 3247, Whitsand Bay Rd on Treninnow Cliff Rd – ✉ Millbrook

The View
East : 1 mi. ✉ PL10 1JY – ✆ (01752) 822 345 – www.theview-restaurant.co.uk – Closed 2 weeks February, Monday except Bank Holidays and Tuesday
Rest – Seafood – Carte £ 22/32 **s**
◆ Converted café: best views are from front terrace. Basic interior smartened up in evenings. Interesting, understated, seafood oriented menus: cooking is clean and delicious.

MILTON – Oxon. – see Banbury

MILTON ABBOT – Devon – 503 H32 – see Tavistock

MILTON BRYAN – Beds. – 504 S28 – see Woburn

MILTON KEYNES – Milton Keynes – 504 R27 – pop. 156 148 — 11 C1

London 56 mi. – Bedford 16 mi. – Birmingham 72 mi. – Northampton 18 mi.
The Chapel, The Knoll, Newport Pagnell (01908) 614 638, info@destinationmiltonkeynes.co.uk
18 Abbey Hill Two Mile Ash Monks Way, ✆ (01908) 563 845
18 Tattenhoe Bletchley Tattenhoe Lane, ✆ (01908) 631 113
27 Wavendon Golf Centre Wavendon Lower End Rd, ✆ (01908) 281 811

Plans pages 528, 529, 530, 531

Brasserie Blanc
Chelsea House, 301 Avebury Blvd ✉ MK9 2GA – ✆ (01908) 546 590 – www.brasserieblanc.com – Fax (01908) 546 591 – Closed 25 December EZ**c**
Rest – French – *(booking essential)* Menu £ 15 – Carte £ 22/43
◆ Striking modern building with a bustling trade – part of the Raymond Blanc chain. Menu features refined French brasserie dishes, mainly classics, with some house specialities.

at Newton Longville Southwest : 6 mi. by A 421 - AX – ✉ Milton Keynes

The Crooked Billet
2 Westbrook End ✉ MK17 0DF – ✆ (01908) 373 936 – www.thebillet.co.uk – Closed Sunday dinner and Monday lunch
Rest – *(booking advisable)* Menu £ 19/23 – Carte £ 25/50
◆ Charming 17C thatched pub with smart yet informal interior. Modern, seasonal dishes are crafted from local produce and a seven course tasting menu is available at dinner. Excellent wine list.

HORIZONTAL ROADS

Bletcham Way (H10) CX
Chaffron Way (H7) . . . . BX, CV
Childs Way (H6) . . . . BX, CV
Dansteed Way (H4) . . . . ABV
Groveway (H9) CVX
Millers Way (H2) . . . . AV
Monks Way (H3) . . . . ABV
Portway (H5) . . . . BCV
Ridgeway (H1) . . . . AV
Standing Way (H8) . . . . BX, CV

MILTON KEYNES

Buckingham Rd . . . . BX
London Rd . . . . CUV
Manor Rd CX
Marsh End Rd . . . . CU
Newport Rd . . . . BV
Northampton Rd . . . . AU
Stoke Rd CX
Stratford Rd . . . . AV
Whaddon Way . . . . BX
Wolverton Rd . . . . BU

VERTICAL ROADS

Brickhill St (V10) . . . . BU, CX
Fulmer St (V3) . . . . ABX
Grafton St (V6) . . . . BVX
Great Monks St (V5) . . . . AV
Marlborough St (V8) . . . . . . BV, CX
Overstreet (V9) . . . . BV
Saxon St (V7) . . . . BVX
Snelshall St (V1) . . . . BX
Tattenhoe St (V2) . . . . ABX
Tongwell St (V11) CVX
Watling St (V4) . . . . AV, BX

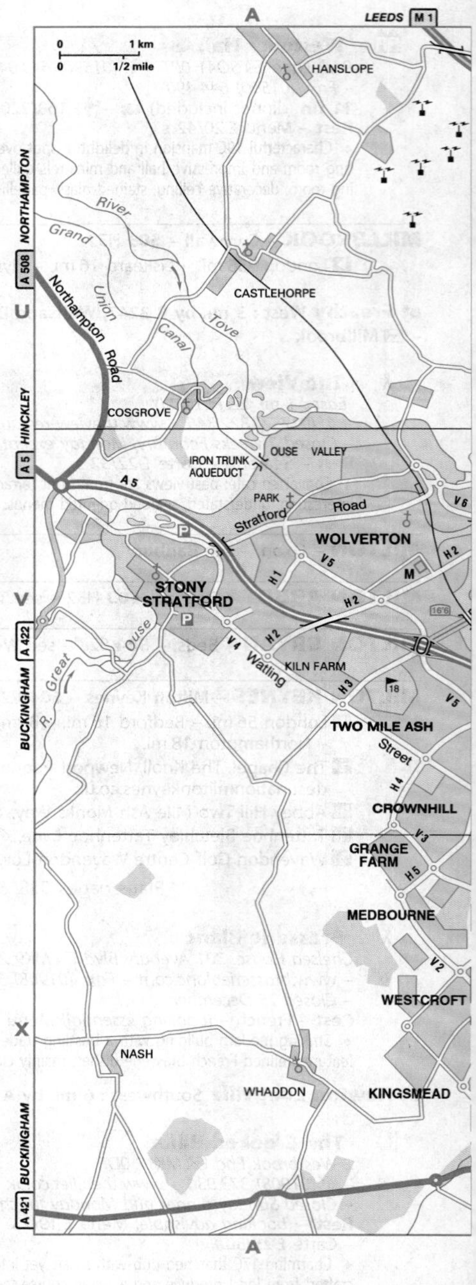

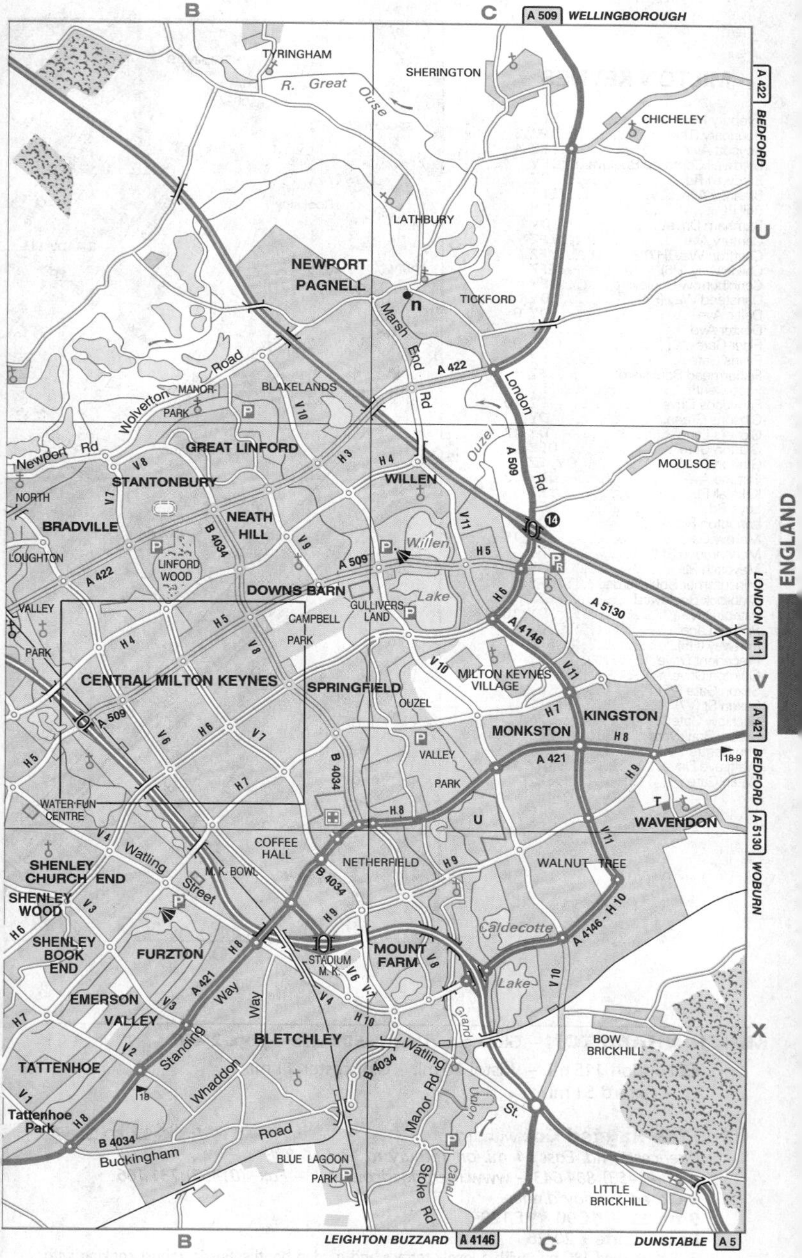

B C A 509 WELLINGBOROUGH

TYRINGHAM

SHERINGTON

R. Great Ouse

CHICHELEY

A 422 BEDFORD

LATHBURY

U

NEWPORT PAGNELL

TICKFORD

Marsh End Rd

A 422

London Rd

A 509

Wolverton Road

MANOR PARK

BLAKELANDS

V 10

Ouzel

Newport Rd

GREAT LINFORD

H 3

H 4

WILLEN

MOULSOE

V 8

STANTONBURY

NORTH

V 7

NEATH HILL

B 4034

V 11

14

BRADVILLE

LOUGHTON

V 9

Willen Lake

H 5

A 422

LINFORD WOOD

A 509

DOWNS BARN

H 6

A 5130

GULLIVERS LAND

VALLEY PARK

H 5

CAMPBELL PARK

A 4146

LONDON M 1

ENGLAND

H 4

V 8

V 10

MILTON KEYNES VILLAGE

V 11

CENTRAL MILTON KEYNES

SPRINGFIELD

V

OUZEL

H 7

KINGSTON

A 509

MONKSTON

A 421 BEDFORD

H 5

V 6

H 6

V 7

VALLEY PARK

A 421

H 8

18-9

B 4034

H 9

H 7

WATER FUN CENTRE

H 8

U

WAVENDON

V 11

A 5130 WOBURN

V 4

COFFEE HALL

Watling Street

NETHERFIELD

H 9

WALNUT TREE

SHENLEY CHURCH END

M. K. BOWL

B 4034

SHENLEY WOOD

V 3

H 9

A 4146 - H 10

H 6

SHENLEY BOOK END

FURZTON

H 8

STADIUM M. K.

MOUNT FARM

V 8

Caldecotte Lake

V 6

V 1

A 421

Way

Way

V 4

V 10

EMERSON VALLEY

V 3

Standing

H 10

Grand

H 7

BLETCHLEY

Watling

BOW BRICKHILL

X

V 2

B 4034

TATTENHOE

Whaddon

Manor Rd

Union Canal

18

St.

V 1

Tattenhoe Park

H 8

Road

B 4034

Buckingham

BLUE LAGOON PARK

Stoke Rd

LITTLE BRICKHILL

B LEIGHTON BUZZARD A 4146 C DUNSTABLE A 5

ENGLAND

MILTON KEYNES

- Avebury Boulevard . . . . EFY
- Boundary (The) . . . . FZ 3
- Boycott Ave . . . . EZ 4
- Bradwell Common Boulevard . DEY
- Bradwell Rd . . . . DZ
- Brearley Ave . . . . EFZ
- Brill Pl. DY
- Burnham Drive . . . . DY
- Century Ave . . . . EFZ
- Chaffron Way (H7) . . . . FZ
- Childs Way (H6) . . . . EFZ
- Conniburrow Boulevard . . . . EY
- Dansteed Way (H4) . . . . DY
- Deltic Ave . . . . DY 6
- Dexter Ave . . . . FZ 7
- Elder Gate . . . . DZ 9
- Evans Gate . . . . EZ
- Fishermead Boulevard . . . . FZ
- Food Centre . . . . FY
- Fulwoods Drive . . . . FZ 10
- Gibsons Green . . . . DY
- Glovers Lane . . . . DY 12
- Grafton Gate . . . . DEZ
- Grafton St (V6) . . . . DY, EZ
- Ibstone Ave . . . . DEY 13
- Kirkstall Pl. . . . . EZ
- Leys Rd . . . . DZ
- Loughton Rd . . . . DY
- Mallow Gate . . . . EY 15
- Marlborough St (V8) . . . . FY
- Mayditch Pl. . . . . DY
- Midsummer Boulevard . . . . EFY
- Oldbrook Boulevard . . . . EFZ
- Patriot Drive . . . . DY 16
- Pitcher Lane . . . . DZ
- Portway (H5) . . . . EFY
- Precedent Drive . . . . DY 18
- Quinton Drive . . . . DY
- Saxon Gate (V7) . . . . EY
- Saxon St (V7) . . . . EY, FZ
- Secklow Gate . . . . FY
- Silbury Boulevard . . . . EFY
- The Centre : MK . . . . EFY
- Walgrave Drive . . . . DY 19
- Witan Gate . . . . EZ

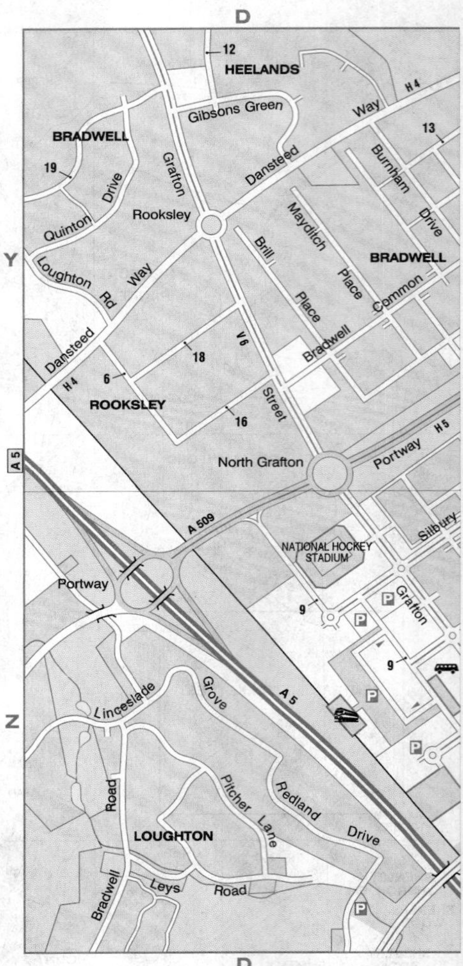

MINCHINHAMPTON – Gloucestershire – 503 N28 – pop. 2 446 4 C1

London 115 mi. – Bristol 26 mi. – Gloucester 11 mi. – Oxford 51 mi.

The Ragged Cot with rm

Cirencester Rd, East : 1 mi. on Tetbury rd GL6 8PE – (01453) 884 643 – www.theraggedcot.co.uk – Fax (01453) 731 166 – Closed Sunday dinner

9 rm – †£ 90 ††£ 120

Rest – Carte £ 20/26

◆ Refurbished 18C pub with a lovely terrace and garden booths. Rustic, robust cooking with local produce sees lighter dishes at lunch and a more structured à la carte at dinner. Pleasant bedrooms with neutral colours and modern facilities.

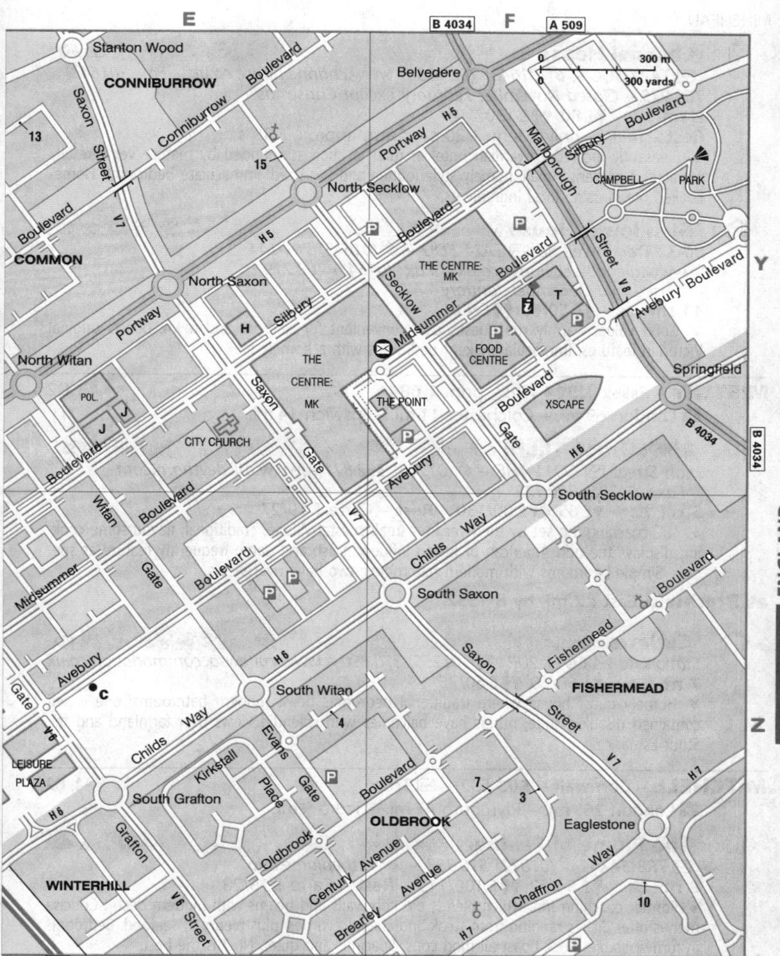

MINEHEAD – Somerset – 503 J30 – pop. 11 699 **3** A2

▶ London 187 mi. – Bristol 64 mi. – Exeter 43 mi. – Taunton 25 mi.

ℹ Visitor Information Centre, Warren Rd ✆ (01643) 702624, visitor@westsomerset.gov.uk

⛳18 The Warren Warren Rd, ✆ (01643) 702 057

👁 Town★ - Higher Town (Church Steps★, St Michael's★)

Dunster★★ - Castle★★ **AC** (upper rooms ≤★) Water Mill★ **AC**, St George's Church★, Dovecote★, SE : 2.5 mi. by A 39 – Selworthy★ (Church★, ≤★★) W : 4.5 mi. by A 39. Exmoor National Park★★ – Cleeve Abbey★★ **AC**, SE : 6.5 mi. by A 39

Channel House

✉ TA24 5QG – ☎ (01643) 703 229 – www.channelhouse.co.uk – Fax (01643) 708 925 – Closed November-February except Christmas

8 rm – £ 80 £ 130

Rest – *(dinner only)* Menu £ 20 **s** – Carte approx. £ 35 **s**

◆ Pleasantly located Edwardian hotel in rural location surrounded by mature yet carefully manicured gardens. Small, homely style lounge and fair sized, immaculate bedrooms. Home-cooked meals using local ingredients.

Glendower House without rest

30-32 Tregonwell Rd ✉ TA24 5DU – ☎ (01643) 707 144 – www.glendower-house.co.uk – Fax (01643) 708 719 – Closed mid-December-January

11 rm – £ 50/60 £ 90

◆ Good value, warmly run guesthouse, convenient for seafront and town; boasts original Victorian features. Immaculately kept bedrooms with a homely feel.

MISTLEY – Essex – 504 X28 – pop. 1 684 — 13 D2

London 69 mi. – Colchester 11 mi. – Ipswich 14 mi.

The Mistley Thorn with rm

High Street ✉ CO11 1HE – ☎ (01206) 392 821 – www.mistleythorn.com – Fax (01206) 390 122

5 rm – £ 65 £ 80/130 **Rest** – Carte £ 19/27

◆ 18C coaching inn set by the river in a small coastal village. Traditional, flavoursome cooking displays the odd American or Italian influence; fish and game frequently feature as specials. Simple bedrooms with modern bathrooms; two have river views.

at Bradfield East : 2 mi. by B 1352

Curlews without rest

Station Rd ✉ CO11 2UP – ☎ (01255) 870 890 – www.curlewsaccommodation.co.uk

7 rm – £ 50/60 £ 60/75

◆ Homely guest house where traditional bedrooms boast modern bathrooms; one is self contained disabled suite; others have balconies with splendid views over farmland and the Stour Estuary.

MITCHELL – Cornwall – 503 E32 – ✉ Truro — 1 B2

London 265 mi. – Plymouth 47 mi. – Truro 9 mi.

The Plume of Feathers with rm

✉ TR8 5AX – ☎ (01872) 510 387 – www.theplume.info

8 rm – £ 54/62 £ 100/115 **Rest** – Carte £ 15/28

◆ Former coaching inn, which blends old cob walls and beams with modern décor. Concise menus offer dishes ranging from steak and chips to curries, plus plenty of seafood. Bedrooms in former stable block boast all mod cons. Spacious and quiet, No.7 is the best.

MITTON – Lancs. – 502 M22 – see Whalley

MOBBERLEY – Ches. – 502 N24 – see Knutsford

MOCCAS – County of Herefordshire – 503 L27 — 18 A3

London 171 mi. – Hereford 13 mi. – Cwmbrân 45 mi. – Great Malvern 36 mi.

Moccas Court

✉ HR2 9LH – ☎ (01981) 500 019 – www.moccas-court.co.uk – Fax (01981) 500 095 – Closed 25-26 December and restricted opening January-March

5 rm – £ 137/219

Rest – *(Closed Sunday-Monday) (dinner only) (by arrangement, communal dining, set menu only)* Menu £ 45

◆ Breathtakingly beautiful Grade I listed Georgian house in 100 acres of grounds on terraced banks over the Wye. Antique filled interior; bedrooms furnished to high standard. Estate sourced produce served in ornate Round Room.

ENGLAND

MONK FRYSTON – North Yorkshire – 502 Q22 – pop. 1 548 – ✉ Lumby 22 B2

London 190 mi. – Kingston-upon-Hull 42 mi. – Leeds 13 mi. – York 20 mi.

Monk Fryston Hall

Main St ✉ LS25 5DU – ✆ (01977) 682 369 – www.monkfrystonhotel.co.uk – Fax (01977) 683 544

29 rm – †£ 79/89 ††£ 135

Rest – Menu £ 29 (dinner) – Carte lunch £ 18/29

◆ Very characterful, possibly haunted, manor house dating from the 1300s with many later additions. Spacious grounds. Baronial style hall with antiques. Imposing rooms. Comfortable dining room with baronial touches.

MONKS ELEIGH – Suffolk – 504 W27 15 C3

London 72 mi. – Cambridge 47 mi. – Colchester 17 mi. – Ipswich 16 mi.

The Swan

The Street ✉ IP7 7AU – ✆ (01449) 741 391 – www.monkseleigh.com – Closed 25-26 December, Sunday dinner and Monday

Rest – Menu £ 18 – Carte £ 19/29

◆ Attractive honey yellow pub with a thatched roof. Relying on local produce, menus change daily, comprising of classic and refined pub dishes with some Italian influences.

MONKTON COMBE – Bath and North East Somerset – see Bath

MORECAMBE – Lancashire – 502 L21 – pop. 49 569 20 A1

London 247 mi. – Preston 27 mi. – Blackpool 39 mi. – Blackburn 34 mi.

Midland

Marine Road West ✉ LA4 4BU – ✆ (01524) 424 000 – www.elh.co.uk

43 rm – †£ 87/99 ††£ 159/219 – 1 suite

Rest – Menu £ 25 (lunch) – Carte dinner £ 32/38

◆ Great location gives the hotel fantastic views of the bay and mountains. Fully restored with superb art deco style enhanced by modern design. Bold colours in the bedrooms. Terrific bay views from the restaurant.

MORETONHAMPSTEAD – Devon – 503 I32 – pop. 1 380 – ✉ Newton Abbot 2 C2

London 213 mi. – Exeter 13 mi. – Plymouth 30 mi.

18 Bovey Castle North Bovey, ✆ (01647) 445 009

Dartmoor National Park★★

The White Hart

Station Rd ✉ TQ13 8NF – ✆ (01647) 441 340 – www.whitehartdartmoor.co.uk – Fax (01647) 441 341

28 rm – †£ 85 ††£ 140 **Rest** – *(bar lunch)* Menu £ 23 – Carte £ 25/34

◆ 17C Grade II listed former coaching inn in the town. Charming country furnished residents lounge. Pleasant 'locals' bar. Attractively refurbished rooms are strong point. Clothed dining room with Glorious Devon posters on the wall.

Moorcote without rest

Northwest : 0.25 mi. on A 382 ✉ TQ13 8LS – ✆ (01647) 440 966 – www.moorcotehouse.co.uk – Closed November-February

4 rm – †£ 48 ††£ 62

◆ Perched on hill above Moretonhampstead, this Victorian guesthouse has mature gardens and well-kept bedrooms with stunning views of Dartmoor. Cosy breakfast room and lounge.

The White Horse Inn

7 George St ✉ TQ13 8PG – ✆ (01647) 440 267 – www.whitehorsedevon.co.uk – Closed Monday

Rest – Carte £ 18/30

◆ 17C stone pub set in a busy market village. Well-balanced menu features tasty, unfussy dishes made from local produce, ranging from British classics to more Mediterranean fare.

MORETON-IN-MARSH – Gloucestershire – 503 O28 – pop. 3 198 4 D1

Great Britain

London 86 mi. – Birmingham 40 mi. – Gloucester 31 mi. – Oxford 29 mi.

Chastleton House★★, SE : 5 mi. by A 44

Manor House rest,
High St ✉ GL56 0LJ – ✆ (01608) 650 501 – www.cotswold-inns-hotels.co.uk/manor – Fax (01608) 651 481
34 rm – †£ 115/155 ††£ 142/181
Rest *Mulberry* – *(dinner only and Sunday lunch)* Menu £ 20/38 **s**
◆ Part-16C Cotswold stone house hides chic, stylish interior with vibrant furnishings. Numerous comfy guest areas; beautiful grounds. Quirky, individually decorated bedrooms ooze style. Relaxed brasserie and bar for afternoon tea and cocktails; sophisticated Mulberry for dinner.

The Old School without rest
Little Compton, East : 4 mi. on A 44 ✉ GL56 0SL – ✆ (01608) 674 588 – www.theoldschoolbedandbreakfast.com
4 rm – †£ 60/80 ††£ 90/110
◆ Attractive, well kept Victorian building with large, neat garden. Period features such as A-frame ceilings and stained glass windows are complemented by modern furnishings.

at Bourton-on-the-Hill West : 2 mi. on A 44 – ✉ Moreton-In-Marsh

Horse & Groom with rm
✉ GL56 9AQ – ✆ (01386) 700 413 – www.horseandgroom.info – Fax (01386) 700 413 – Closed 25 December and Sunday dinner
5 rm – †£ 75 ††£ 160 **Rest** – *(booking essential)* Carte £ 19/32
◆ Grade II listed yellow-stone building with a friendly atmosphere. Menu features hearty, unfussy cooking and ranges from classic pub dishes to more restaurant style offerings. Modern bedrooms, each individually styled.

ENGLAND

MORPETH – Northumberland – 501 O18 – pop. 13 555 — 24 B2

London 301 mi. – Edinburgh 93 mi. – Newcastle upon Tyne 15 mi.
The Chantry, Bridge St ✆ (01670) 500700, morpeth.tic@northumberland.gov.uk
The Clubhouse, ✆ (01670) 504 942

Black Door Bar & Dining Rooms
59 Bridge St ✉ NE61 1PQ – ✆ (01670) 516 200 – www.blackdoorgroup.co.uk – Closed Sunday dinner
Rest – Menu £ 13 (lunch) – Carte £ 22/33
◆ Informal dining and bar on rustic ground floor; fashionable first floor room with feature walls in chocolate flock. Smart private room above. Appealing menu of classic dishes.

at Longhorsley Northwest : 6.5 mi. by A 192 on A 697 – ✉ Morpeth

Thistleyhaugh Farm
Northwest : 3.75 mi. by A 697 and Todburn rd taking first right turn ✉ NE65 8RG – ✆ (01665) 570 629 – www.thistleyhaugh.co.uk – Fax (01665) 570 629 – Closed 25 December and January
5 rm – †£ 53/75 ††£ 80
Rest – *(by arrangement, communal dining)* Menu £ 20
◆ Attractive Georgian farmhouse on working farm in a pleasant rural area. The River Coquet flows through the grounds. Comfortable, cosy bedrooms in traditional style. Dine overlooking garden.

MORSTON – Norfolk – see Blakeney

MORTEHOE – Devon – 503 H30 – see Woolacombe

MOULSFORD – Oxfordshire – pop. 491 — 10 B3

London 53 mi. – Newbury 16 mi. – Reading 13 mi.

The Beetle & Wedge Boathouse with rm
Ferry Lane ✉ OX10 9JF – ✆ (01491) 651 381 – www.beetleandwedge.co.uk – Fax (01491) 651 376 – Closed 1 week January
3 rm – †£ 75 ††£ 90 **Rest** – *(booking essential)* Carte £ 26/34
◆ Busy Thameside restaurant with charming terrace; dine in light conservatory or more rustic char grill. Classic menu with plenty of choice, including dishes from the grill. Comfortable bedrooms in Ferryman's Cottage; one has his-and-hers roll-top baths.

MOULTON – North Yorkshire – 502 P20 – pop. 197 – ✉ Richmond 22 B1

London 243 mi. – Leeds 53 mi. – Middlesbrough 25 mi. – Newcastle upon Tyne 43 mi.

Black Bull Inn

✉ DL10 6QJ – *(01325) 377 289 – www.blackbullmoulton.com – Fax (01325) 377 422 – Closed Sunday dinner*

Rest – Seafood – Menu £ 20 (Monday-Thursday) – Carte £ 29/49

◆ Old country pub with variety of dining areas, including an original Brighton Belle Pullman carriage from 1932 and conservatory with huge grapevine. Seafood a speciality.

MOUSEHOLE – Cornwall – 503 D33 – ✉ Penzance 1 A3

London 321 mi. – Penzance 3 mi. – Truro 29 mi.

Village★

Penwith★★ – Lamorna (The Merry Maidens and The Pipers Standing Stone★) SW : 3 mi. by B 3315. Land's End★ (cliff scenery★★★) W : 9 mi. by B 3315

The Old Coastguard without rest

The Parade ✉ TR19 6PR – (01736) 731 222 – www.oldcoastguardhotel.co.uk – Fax (01736) 731 720 – Closed 10 January-4 March

14 rm – †£ 143/158 ††£ 190/210

◆ Creamwash hotel in unspoilt village with good views of Mounts Bay. Spacious lounge has sun terrace overlooking water. Modern rooms: Premier variety are best for the vista.

Cornish Range with rm

6 Chapel St ✉ TR19 6SB – (01736) 731 488 – www.cornishrange.co.uk – Closed 2 weeks January-February

3 rm – ††£ 80/110

Rest – Seafood – *(booking essential)* Carte £ 24/36

◆ Converted 18C pilchard processing cottage hidden away in narrow street. Cottagey inner filled with Cornish artwork. Excellent local seafood dishes. Very comfortable rooms.

2 Fore Street

2 Fore St ✉ TR19 6PF – (01736) 731 164 – www.2forestreet.co.uk – Closed 4 January-10 February and Monday in winter

Rest – Seafood – *(booking essential at dinner)* Carte £ 21/32

◆ Cosy, bright bistro in pretty harbourside setting; popular with locals and tourists. Menu based on the best of the day's catch; simple, unfussy preparation. Casual, friendly service.

MUCH WENLOCK – Shropshire – 502 M26 – pop. 1 959 18 B2

Great Britain

London 154 mi. – Birmingham 34 mi. – Shrewsbury 12 mi. – Worcester 37 mi.

The Museum, High St (01952) 727679, muchwenlock.tourism@shropshire.gov.uk

Priory★ **AC**

Ironbridge Gorge Museum★★ **AC** (The Iron Bridge★★ - Coalport China Museum★★ - Blists Hill Open Air Museum★★ - Museum of the Gorge and Visitor Centre★) NE : 4.5 mi. by A 4169 and B 4380

at Brockton Southwest : 5 mi. on B 4378 – ✉ Much Wenlock

The Feathers at Brockton with rm

✉ TF13 6JR – (01746) 785 202 – www.feathersatbrockton.co.uk – Closed 25 December, 1 January, Monday and lunch Tuesday

4 rm – †£ 50 ††£ 75

Rest – Menu £ 10 (Tuesday-Sunday dinner) – Carte £ 15/25

◆ Rustic 16C pub in prime walking country, with snug, characterful inner and relaxing atmosphere. Traditional British dishes use local produce. Comfortable, country style bedrooms.

MUNSLOW – Shropshire – 503 L26 — 18 B2

London 166 mi. – Ludlow 10 mi. – Shrewsbury 21 mi.

The Crown Country Inn with rm

SY7 9ET – (01584) 841 205 – www.crowncountryinn.co.uk – Closed 25 December, Sunday dinner and Monday

3 rm – £ 55 £ 90 **Rest** – Carte £ 23/30

◆ Exposed beams, flagstone floors and inglenook fireplaces bear witness to this rustic pub's longevity. Wide-ranging menu of flavoursome dishes made with locally sourced produce. Comfortable, individually styled bedrooms.

MURCOTT – Oxfordshire – pop. 1 293 – Kidlington — 10 B2

London 70 mi. – Oxford 14 mi. – Witney 20 mi.

The Nut Tree (Mike North)

Main St OX5 2RE – (01865) 331 253 – www.nuttreeinn.co.uk – Closed Sunday dinner

Rest – Menu £ 18 (Monday-Thursday) – Carte £ 31/43

Spec. Home smoked salmon with horseradish and salmon skin biscuit. Confit of Nut Tree raised pork with celeriac purée apple. Passion fruit soufflé and sorbet with glazed cream.

◆ Traditional thatched village pub with loyal local following and a busy bar. Pigs and cows are raised at the back and used in many of the fresh, satisfying, flavoursome dishes; fantastic homemade bread. Service is well-organised and efficient.

MYLOR BRIDGE – Cornwall – 503 E33 – see Falmouth

NANTWICH – Cheshire – 502 M24 – pop. 13 447 — 20 A3

London 176 mi. – Chester 20 mi. – Liverpool 45 mi. – Manchester 40 mi.

Nantwich Civic Hall, Market St (01270) 610983, Nantwich.tic@cheshireeast.gov.uk

Alvaston Hall Middlewich Rd, (01270) 628 473

Rookery Hall

rm

Worleston, North : 2.5 mi. by A 51 on B 5074 CW5 6DQ – (0845) 0727 533 – www.handpickedhotels.co.uk/rookeryhall – Fax (0845) 0727 534

68 rm – £ 95/155 £ 120/190 – 2 suites

Rest – *(dinner only and lunch Sunday in December) (booking essential)* Menu £ 34 **s** – Carte £ 37/51 **s**

◆ Main house dates from 19C, with pleasant grounds, but with recent additions and extensions. Geared more towards corporate market. Impressive spa. Comfortable and modern bedrooms. Wood panelled restaurant.

NATIONAL EXHIBITION CENTRE – W. Mids. – 503 O26 – see Birmingham

NEAR SAWREY – Cumbria – 502 L20 – see Hawkshead

NETHER BURROW – Cumbria – see Kirkby Lonsdale

NETLEY MARSH – Hampshire – 503 P31 – see Southampton

NETTLEBED – Oxfordshire – 504 R29 — 11 C3

London 44 mi. – Oxford 20 mi. – Reading 10 mi.

White Hart

28 High St RG9 5DD – (01491) 641 245 – www.whitehartnettlebed.com – Fax (01491) 649 018

12 rm – £ 125 £ 145

Rest – *(Closed Sunday dinner)* Menu £ 18 – Carte £ 20/31

◆ Recently refurbished part 17C inn boasts spacious, modern bedrooms, all uniquely styled with a certain 'designer' appeal, some in original hotel, others in adjacent new block. Minimalist Bistro.

NETTLETON SHRUB – Wilts. – 503 N29 – see Castle Combe

NEWARK-ON-TRENT – Nottinghamshire – 502 R24 – pop. 35 454 17 C1

Great Britain

London 127 mi. – Lincoln 16 mi. – Nottingham 20 mi. – Sheffield 42 mi.
Coddington, Newark, (01636) 626 282
St Mary Magdalene★

Grange

73 London Rd, South : 0.5 mi. on Grantham rd (B 6326) ✉ NG24 1RZ – (01636) 703 399 – www.grangenewark.co.uk – Fax (01636) 702 328 – Closed 24 December-2 January
19 rm – £ 79/110 £ 110/155
Rest *Cutlers* – *(closed Sunday dinner) (dinner only and Sunday lunch)*
Carte £ 23/29

◆ Small, personally run hotel with tranquil landscaped garden, set in residential area not far from the town. Traditional bedrooms vary in size but all are cosy and comfy; some have four-posters. Classical menu served in restaurant, amongst antique china and cutlery.

at Caunton Northwest : 7 mi. by A 616 – ✉ Newark-On-Trent

Caunton Beck

Main St ✉ NG23 6AB – (01636) 636 793 – www.wigandmitre.com – Fax (01636) 636 828
Rest – Menu £ 15 – Carte £ 24/38

◆ Welcoming modern pub, with stone-floored bar, beamed ceilings, flower-filled front terrace and restaurant serving classic pub dishes. Popular weekend breakfast destination.

NEWBIGGIN – Cumbria – 502 L19 – see Penrith

NEWBURY – West Berkshire – 503 Q29 – pop. 32 675 10 B3

London 67 mi. – Bristol 66 mi. – Oxford 28 mi. – Reading 17 mi.
The Wharf (01635) 30267, tourism@westberks.gov.uk
Newbury and Crookham Greenham Common Bury's Bank Rd, (01635) 40 035
Donnington Valley Donnington Snelsmore House, Snelsmore Common, (01635) 568 140

Plans pages 538, 539

The Vineyard at Stockcross

Stockcross, Northwest : 2 mi. by A 4 on B 4000 ✉ RG20 8JU – (01635) 528 770 – www.the-vineyard.co.uk – Fax (01635) 528 398
34 rm – £ 299, £ 18.50 – 15 suites – £ 349 AV**b**
Rest – Menu £ 68 **s**

◆ Outside, a pool bearing bowls of fire encapsulates bright art-filled interiors. Luxurious suites with woven fabrics. Very good service. Super spa. Modern or country house style rooms. A change of chef as we went to print.

Donnington Valley H. & Spa

Old Oxford Rd, Donnington, North : 1.75 mi. by A 4 off B 4494 ✉ RG14 3AG – (01635) 551 199 – www.donningtonvalley.co.uk – Fax (01635) 551 123 AV**a**
111 rm – £ 119/200 £ 139/230, £ 14.50
Rest *Winepress* – Menu £ 23/27 **s** – Carte £ 32/50 **s**

◆ Smart bedrooms in purpose-built country hotel with 18-hole golf course. Newer Executive rooms are the smartest. Excellent spa and leisure facilities. Large bar. Wine-themed restaurant.

The Square

5-6 Weavers Walk, Northbrook St ✉ RG14 1AL – (01635) 44 805 – www.thesquarenewbury.co.uk – Fax (01635) 523 114 – Closed Sunday
Rest – Menu £ 15 (early evening) – Carte £ 20/39 BZ**a**

◆ Keenly run restaurant in pleasant mews, with warm décor, colourful artwork and pleasant front terrace. Good-sized menu offers classically based dishes; lunchtime snacks prove popular.

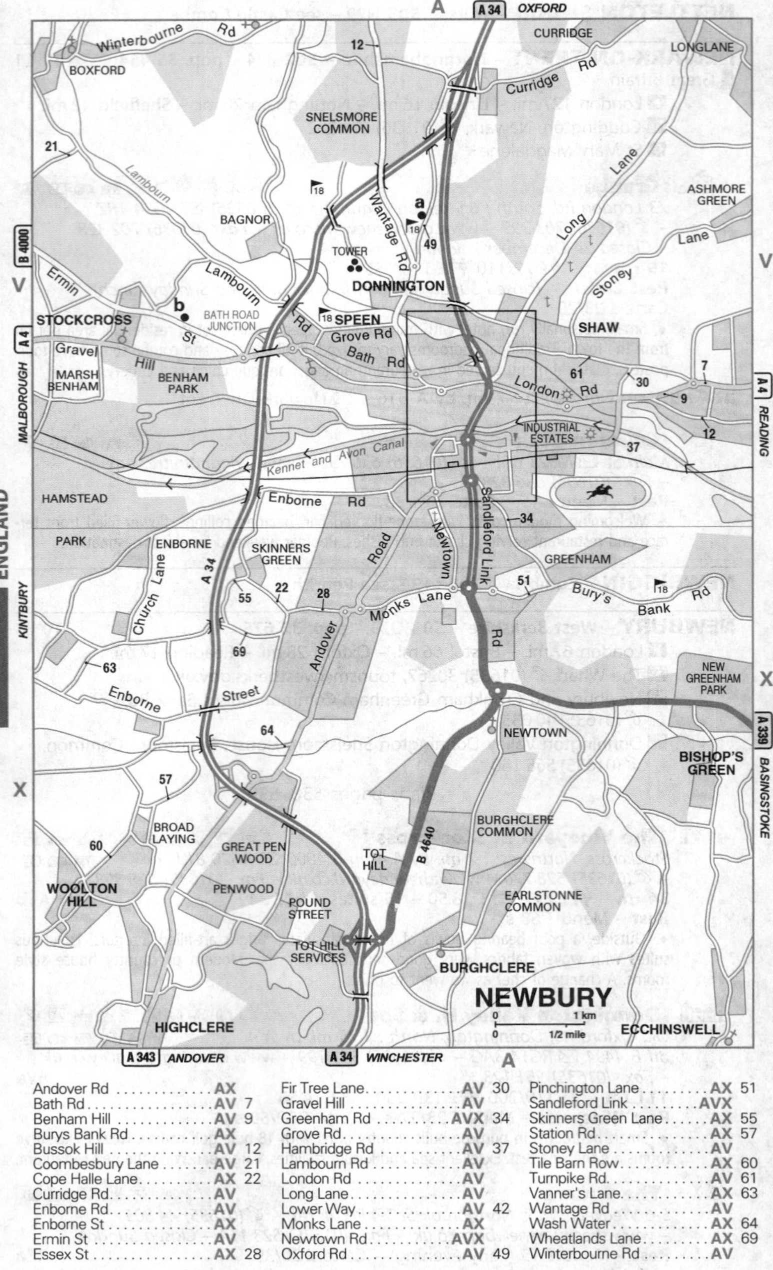

Andover Rd **AX**	Fir Tree Lane **AV** 30	Pinchington Lane **AX** 51
Bath Rd **AV** 7	Gravel Hill **AV**	Sandleford Link **AVX**
Benham Hill **AV** 9	Greenham Rd **AVX** 34	Skinners Green Lane **AX** 55
Burys Bank Rd **AX**	Grove Rd **AV**	Station Rd **AX** 57
Bussok Hill **AV** 12	Hambridge Rd **AV** 37	Stoney Lane **AV**
Coombesbury Lane **AV** 21	Lambourn Rd **AV**	Tile Barn Row **AX** 60
Cope Halle Lane **AX** 22	London Rd **AV**	Turnpike Rd **AV** 61
Curridge Rd **AV**	Long Lane **AV**	Vanner's Lane **AX** 63
Enborne Rd **AV**	Lower Way **AV** 42	Wantage Rd **AV**
Enborne St **AX**	Monks Lane **AX**	Wash Water **AX** 64
Ermin St **AV**	Newtown Rd **AVX**	Wheatlands Lane **AX** 69
Essex St **AX** 28	Oxford Rd **AV** 49	Winterbourne Rd **AV**

NEWBURY

Street	Grid	No.
Almond Ave	BY	3
Andover Rd	BZ	4
Bartholomew St	BZ	6
Bone Lane	BZ	10
Carnegie Rd	BZ	13
Castle Grove	BY	15
Cheap St	BZ	16
Chesterfield Rd	BZ	18
Craven Rd	BZ	24
Dolman Rd	BY	25
Donnington Link	BY	27
Greenham Hill	BZ	31
Greenham Rd	BZ	33
Hambridge Rd	BZ	36
Kennett Shopping Centre	BZ	
Kiln Rd	BY	40
Kings Rd	BZ	
London Rd	BY	
Love Lane	BY	
Maple Crescent	BY	43
Market St	BZ	45
Mill Lane	BZ	
Newtown Rd	BZ	48
New Rd	BZ	46
Northbrook St	BYZ	
Northcroft Lane	BZ	
Old Bath Rd	BY	
Oxford Rd	BY	
Park Way	BYZ	50
Pound St	BZ	
Queens Rd	BZ	
Racecourse Rd	BZ	
Rockingham Rd	BZ	52
St Johns Rd	BZ	
Sandleford Link	BZ	54
Shaw Hill	BY	
Shaw Rd	BY	
Station Rd	BZ	
Strawberry Hill	BY	58
Western Ave	BY	
West St	BZ	66
Wharf St	BZ	67

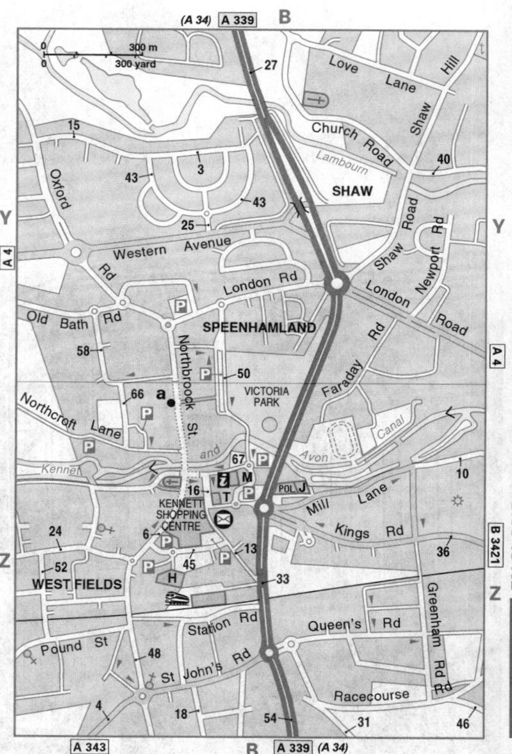

NEWBY BRIDGE – **Cumbria** – **502** L21 – ✉ **Ulverston** Great Britain **21** A3

London 270 mi. – Kendal 16 mi. – Lancaster 27 mi.

Lake Windermere★★

Lakeside

rm, VISA AE

Lakeside, Northeast : 1 mi. on Hawkshead rd ✉ LA12 8AT – ☎ (015395) 30 001 www.Lakesidehotel.co.uk – Fax (015395) 31 699 – Closed 22 December-10 January

74 rm – †£ 140/290 ††£ 320/410 – 3 suites

Rest *Lakeview* – *(dinner only)* Menu £ 45 **s**

Rest *John Ruskins Brasserie* – *(dinner only)* Menu £ 38 **s**

◆ Delightfully situated on the shores of Lake Windermere. Plenty of charm and character. Work out at the state-of-the-art leisure centre then sleep in fitted, modern bedrooms. Lakeview offers smart ambience. Bright, informal John Ruskins Brasserie.

The Knoll

VISA

Lakeside, Northeast : 1.25 mi. on Hawkshead rd ✉ LA12 8AU – ☎ (015395) 31 347 – www.theknoll-lakeside.co.uk – Fax (015395) 30 850 – Closed 23 December-2 January

8 rm – †£ 85/98 ††£ 125/138

Rest – *(dinner only) (booking essential for non-residents)* Menu £ 25

◆ Late Victorian country house close to popular lakeside, with welcoming owners, comfortable lounge and contemporary bedrooms; room 4 is the best. Extensive breakfast menu. Linen clad dining room; local produce proudly used.

NEWBY WISKE – **N. Yorks.** – **502** P21 – see Northallerton

Steve Wright/Fotolia.com

NEWCASTLE UPON TYNE

County: Tyne and Wear
Michelin regional map: 501
London 276 mi.
– Edinburgh 105 mi. – Leeds 95 mi.

Population: 189 863
Great Britain
Map reference: 24 B2

PRACTICAL INFORMATION

Tourist Information

8-9 Central Arcade ✆ (0191) 277 8000, tourist.info@newcastle.gov.uk

Guild Hall Visitors Centre, Quayside (0191) 277 2444

Airport

Newcastle Airport : ✆ (0871) 882 1121, NW : 5 mi. by A 696 AV

Ferries and Shipping Lines

to Norway (Bergen, Haugesund and Stavanger) (Fjord Line) (approx 26 h) – to The Netherlands (Amsterdam) (DFDS Seaways A/S) daily (15 h)

Tunnel

Tyne Tunnel (toll)

Golf Courses

Broadway East Gosforth, ✆(0191) 285 0553

City of Newcatle Gosforth Three Mill Bridge, ✆(0191) 285 1775

Wallsend Bigges Main Rheydt Ave,, NE : by A1058, ✆(0191) 262 1973

Whickham Fellside Rd, Hollinside Park, ✆(0191) 488 1576

SIGHTS

In town

City★ – Grey Street★ CZ – Quayside★ CZ : Composition★, All Saints Church★ (interior★) – Castle Keep★ **AC** CZ – Laing Art Gallery and Museum★ **AC** CY **M1** – Museum of Antiquities★ CY **M2** – LIFE Interactive World★ CZ – Gateshead Millennium Bridge★ CZ

On the outskirts

Hadrian's Wall★★, W : by A 69 AV

In the surrounding area

Beamish : North of England Open-Air Museum★★ **AC**, SW : 7 mi. by A 692 and A 6076 AX – Seaton Delaval Hall★ **AC**, NE : 11 mi. by A 189 - BV - and A 190

NEWCASTLE-UPON-TYNE

Street	Grid	No.
Adelaide Terrace	AX	2
Atkinson Rd	AX	3
Bath St	BX	4
Bensham Rd	AX	6
Benton Bank	BV	8
Buddle St	BV	13
Byker Bridge	BV	15
Church Ave	AV	16
Church Rd	AV	18
Clayton Rd	BV	21
Coldwell Lane	BX	22
Coldwell St	BX	24
Condercum Rd	AX	26
Fossway	BV	31
Haddrick's Mill Rd	BV	36
High St West	BV	37
Jesmond Dene Rd	BV	39
Killingworth Rd	BV	42
Lobley Hill Rd	AX	45
Matthew Bank	BV	49
Neptune Rd	BV	51
Redheugh Bridge	AX	62
Red Hall Drive	BV	61
Saltwell Rd	BX	69
Shipdon Rd	AX	71
Springfield Rd	AV	72
Station Rd	BX	73
Stephenson Rd	BV	74
Sunderland Rd	BX	76
Sutton St	BV	77
Swalwell Bank	ABX	79
Waverdale Ave	BV	83
West Farm Ave	BV	87
Whickham Bank	AX	89
Windy Nook Rd	BX	91

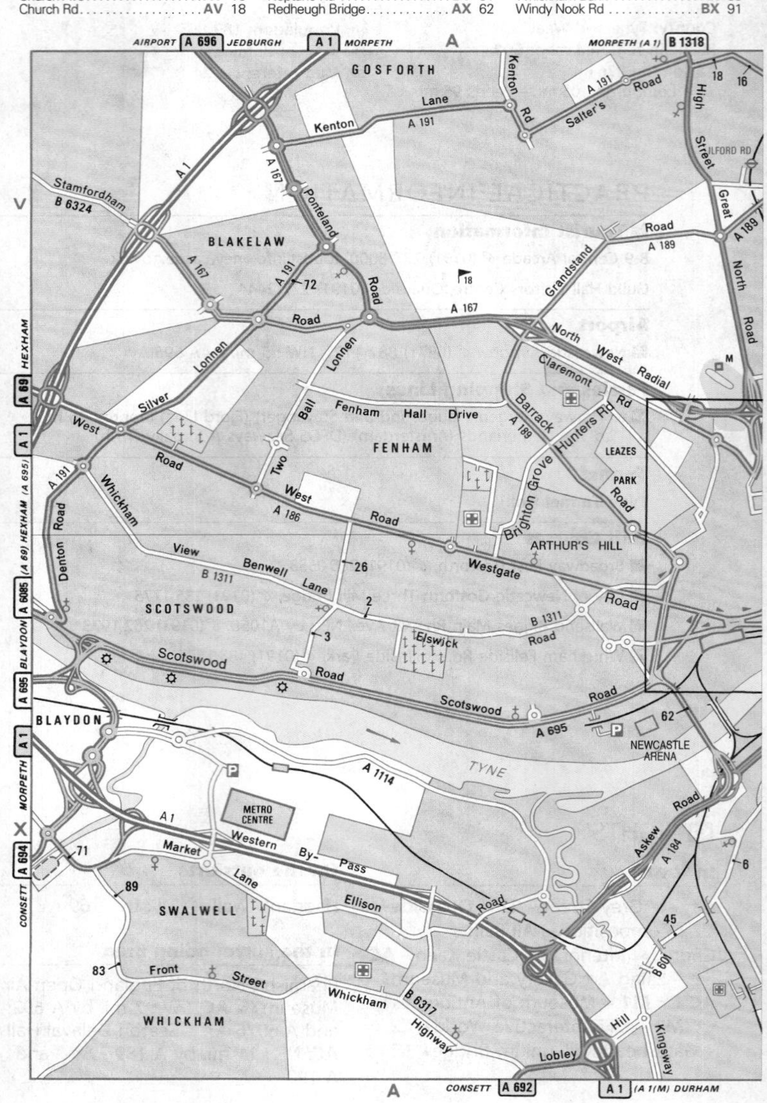

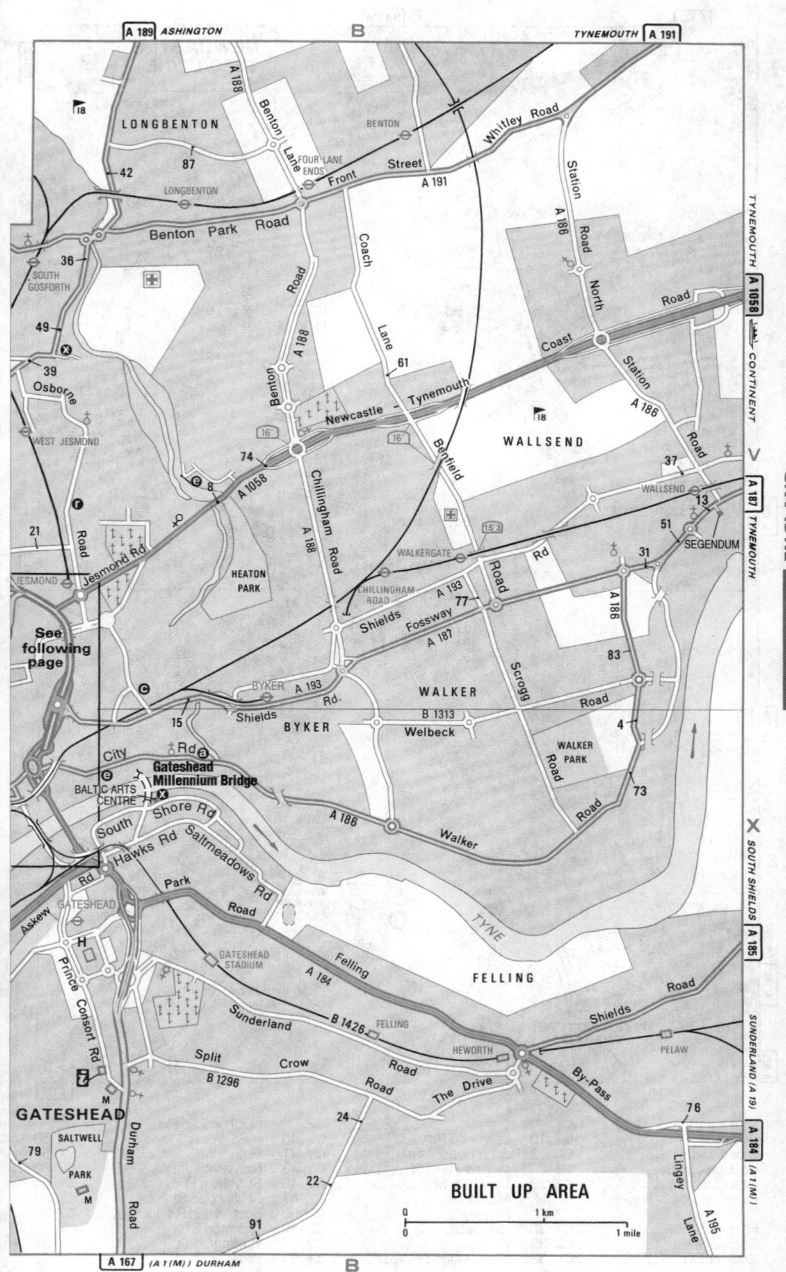
A 189 ASHINGTON
B
TYNEMOUTH A 191
LONGBENTON
BENTON
Benton Lane
A 188
FOUR LANE ENDS
Front Street
A 191
Whitley Road
87
42
LONGBENTON
Benton Park Road
36
SOUTH GOSFORTH
Station Road
A 186
North Road
Coach Lane
Benton Road
A 188
49
39
Osborne
WEST JESMOND
61
Coast Road
Station Road
A 186
Newcastle - Tynemouth
WALLSEND
Benfield Road
74
8
A 1058
Chillingham Road
A 188
21
Road
Jesmond Rd
JESMOND
HEATON PARK
37
WALLSEND
13
51
SEGENDUM
31
WALKERGATE
CHILLINGHAM ROAD
A 193
Shields
Fossway
A 187
77
Rd
A 186
83
See following page
BYKER
A 193
Rd.
Shields
15
WALKER
Scrogg Road
BYKER
B 1313
Welbeck
Road
4
City Rd
Gateshead Millennium Bridge
BALTIC ARTS CENTRE
WALKER PARK
Road
73
South Shore Rd
Hawks Rd
Saltmeadows Rd
A 186
Walker Road
Rd
Askew
GATESHEAD
Park Road
TYNE
H
Prince Consort Rd
GATESHEAD STADIUM
A 184
Felling
FELLING
Sunderland
B 1426
FELLING
Road
Shields Road
HEWORTH
PELAW
Split Crow Road
B 1296
The Drive
By-Pass
M
GATESHEAD
24
76
SALTWELL PARK
M
79
Durham Road
22
BUILT UP AREA
0 1 km
0 1 mile
91
Lingey Lane
A 195
A 167 (A 1(M)) DURHAM
B
TYNEMOUTH A 1058
CONTINENT
V
A 187 TYNEMOUTH
X
SOUTH SHIELDS A 185
SUNDERLAND (A 19)
A 184 (A 1(M))

ENGLAND

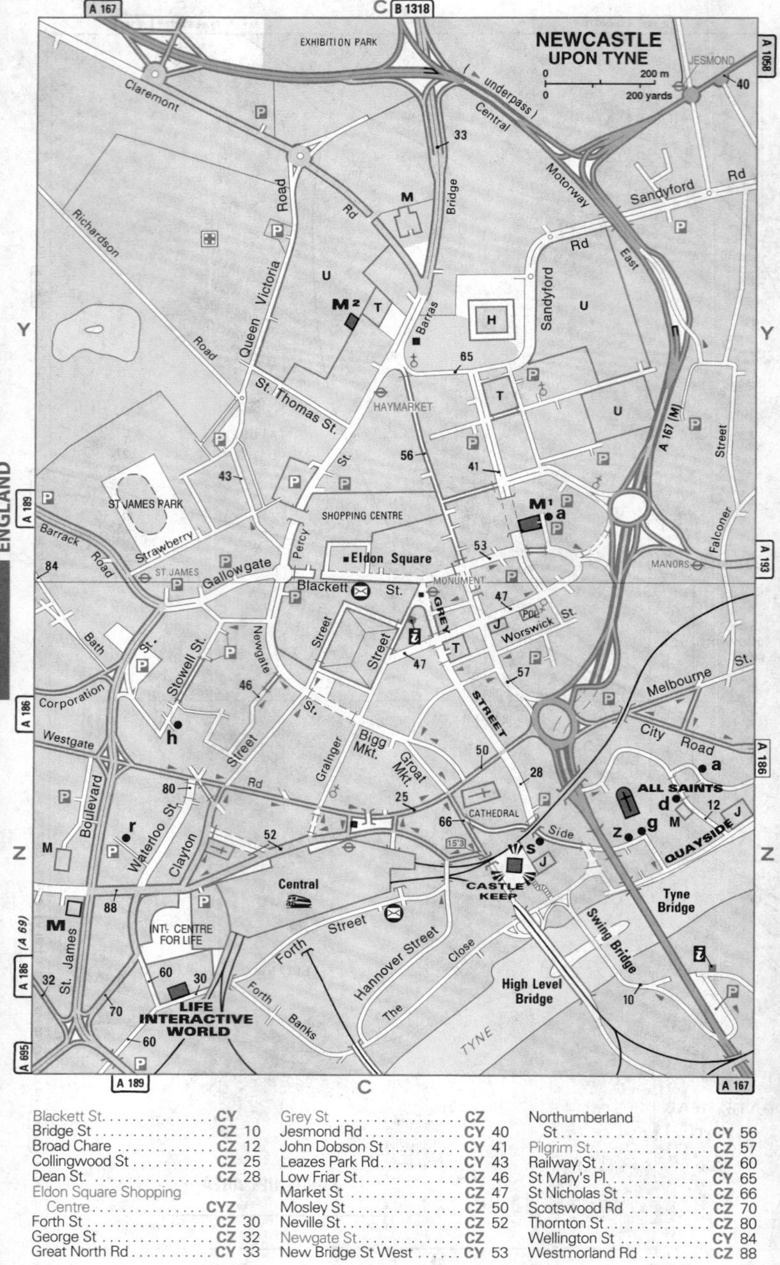

Blackett St. . . . . CY
Bridge St . . . . CZ 10
Broad Chare . . . . CZ 12
Collingwood St . . . . CZ 25
Dean St. . . . . CZ 28
Eldon Square Shopping Centre . . . . CYZ
Forth St . . . . CZ 30
George St . . . . CZ 32
Great North Rd . . . . CY 33
Grey St . . . . CZ
Jesmond Rd . . . . CY 40
John Dobson St . . . . . . CY 41
Leazes Park Rd . . . . . . CY 43
Low Friar St . . . . CZ 46
Market St . . . . CZ 47
Mosley St . . . . CZ 50
Neville St . . . . CZ 52
Newgate St . . . . CZ
New Bridge St West . . . . CY 53
Northumberland St . . . . CY 56
Pilgrim St . . . . CZ 57
Railway St . . . . CZ 60
St Mary's Pl. . . . . CY 65
St Nicholas St . . . . CZ 66
Scotswood Rd . . . . CZ 70
Thornton St . . . . CZ 80
Wellington St . . . . CY 84
Westmorland Rd . . . . . . CZ 88

Jesmond Dene House
Jesmond Dene Rd, Northeast: 1.5 mi. by B 1318 off A 189 ✉ NE2 2EY – ✆ (0191) 212 3000 – www.jesmonddenehouse.co.uk – Fax (0191) 212 3001
40 rm – £ 165/175 £ 250, £ 16 BV**x**
Rest – Menu £ 24 (lunch Monday-Saturday)/25 (Sunday) – Carte £ 39/67
◆ 19C house attractively located in a tranquil dene. Subtle modern touches blend with period features to create a cosy atmosphere. Well-appointed bedrooms differ in décor and outlook. Carefully judged modern cooking is crafted from regional ingredients.

Hotel du Vin
Allan House, City Rd ✉ NE1 2BE – ✆ (0191) 229 22 00 – www.hotelduvin.com – Fax (0191) 229 22 01 BX**a**
42 rm – £ 160 £ 160, £ 13.50
Rest *Bistro* – Carte £ 30/43
◆ Former home of the Tyne Tees Steam Shipping Co., overlooking the river and decorated with photos of ship building scenes. Stylish, chic bedrooms have wine themes; some have feature baths, others boast terraces. Classic brasserie dishes and impressive wine list in Bistro.

Malmaison
Quayside ✉ NE1 3DX – ✆ (0191) 245 5000 – www.malmaison.com – Fax (0191) 245 4545 BX**e**
120 rm – £ 170 £ 170, £ 13.50 – 2 suites
Rest *Brasserie* – *(bar lunch)* Menu £ 16 – Carte approx. £ 28
◆ Unstuffy and contemporary hotel hides within this quayside former Co-operative building. Vibrantly and individually decorated rooms; some overlook Millennium Bridge. Brasserie has modern interpretation of French style.

Fisherman's Lodge
Jesmond Dene, Jesmond ✉ NE7 7BQ – ✆ (0191) 281 3281 – www.fishermanslodge.co.uk – Fax (0191) 281 6410 – Closed 25 December
Rest – Menu £ 19 (lunch and early dinner) – Carte £ 31/43 BV**e**
◆ Attractive Victorian house secreted in a narrow wooded valley yet close to city centre. Series of well-appointed, stylish rooms. Modern British cooking with seafood bias.

Café 21
Trinity Gardens ✉ NE1 2HH – ✆ (0191) 222 0755 – www.cafetwentyone.co.uk – Fax (0191) 221 0761 – Closed 25-26 December and 1 January CZ**a**
Rest – Menu £ 18 (lunch) – Carte £ 30/47
◆ Stylish, open-plan brasserie where subtle greys contrast with bold floral fabrics. Appealing classics display French undertones; best value menus at lunch/early dinner. Efficient service.

Amer's
34 Osborne Rd, Jesmond ✉ NE2 2AJ – ✆ (0191) 281 5377 – www.jesmondhotel.co.uk – Fax (0191) 212 0783 – Closed Monday lunch, Sunday and Bank Holidays BV**r**
Rest – *(booking essential)* Menu £ 12 (lunch) – Carte £ 22/32
◆ Popular ground floor restaurant in smart location. Cosy, stylish lounge/bar sets you up for good value dishes that are modern in style and prepared with skill and flair.

Grainger Rooms
7 Higham Pl ✉ NE1 8AF – ✆ (0191) 232 4949 – www.graingerrooms.co.uk – Closed 1 week Christmas CY**a**
Rest – Menu £ 15/28
◆ Red brick Georgian townhouse with first floor dining, eye-catching chandeliers and rustic photos. Hearty, flavoursome British cooking uses excellent produce. Polite service.

Brasserie Black Door
The Biscuit Factory, 16 Stoddart St ✉ NE2 1AN – ✆ (0191) 260 5411 – www.blackdoorgroup.co.uk – Fax (0191) 260 5422 – Closed 25 December, 1 January and Sunday dinner BV**c**
Rest – Menu £ 13/25 – Carte £ 22/28
◆ Art gallery restaurant set in a 1930s former biscuit factory. Through modish lounge to airy dining space with industrial ambience, wall art and recognisable brasserie dishes.

ENGLAND

XX **Rasa**
27 Queen St. ✉ NE1 3UG – ✆ (0191) 232 77 99 – www.rasarestaurants.com – Closed 25 December, Sunday and Bank Holidays CZ**g**
Rest – Indian – Menu £ 22 – Carte £ 16/23
◆ Extensive menu of authentic Keralan cooking; friendly, knowledgable staff are happy to explain dishes. Vegetarians particularly well catered for. Very good value lunch menus.

X **Pan Haggerty**
21 Queen St – ✆ (0191) 221 09 04 – www.panhaggerty.com – Closed 25-26 December, 1 January and Sunday dinner CZ**z**
Rest – Menu £ 15 (lunch) – Carte dinner £ 23/31
◆ Situated on the quayside; modern and stylish, with a rustic edge. Mix of regional and British dishes made with locally sourced ingredients; well presented, with precise flavours.

X **Caffé Vivo**
29 Broad Chare ✉ NE1 3DQ – ✆ (0191) 232 13 31 – www.caffevivo.co.uk – Closed Sunday, Monday and Bank Holidays CZ**d**
Rest – Italian – Menu £ 17 (lunch and early dinner) – Carte £ 19/28
◆ Housed within a quayside warehouse, along with a theatre. Simpler café during the day gives way to a bustling dinner. Much of the produce imported from Italy; the cooking is simple and satisfying.

X **Barn Asia**
Waterloo Square, St James's Boulevard ✉ NE1 4DN – ✆ (0191) 221 10 00 – www.barnasia.com – Fax (0191) 221 10 12 – Closed 24-26 December, 1 January, Sunday and Monday CZ**r**
Rest – South-East Asian – *(dinner only and Friday lunch)* Carte £ 20/31
◆ Stark furnishings vibrantly decorated with interesting artwork and bright lanterns. Wide-ranging SE Asian menu offers dishes from Vietnamese classics to some Thai and Japanese.

X **Blackfriars**
Friars St ✉ NE1 4XN – ✆ (0191) 261 5945 – www.blackfriarsrestaurant.co.uk – Closed Sunday dinner and Bank Holidays CZ**h**
Rest – Menu £ 15 (lunch) – Carte £ 26/28
◆ Late 13C stone built monks' refectory still serving food in a split level beamed restaurant. Relaxed atmosphere with friendly informal service. Interesting and original menu.

ENGLAND

at Gosforth North : 2.5 mi. by B 1318 - AV – ✉ Newcastle Upon Tyne

Newcastle Marriott H. Gosforth Park
High Gosforth Park, North : 2 mi. on B 1318 at junction with A 1056 ✉ NE3 5HN – ✆ (0191) 236 4111 – www.marriott.co.uk/nclgf – Fax (0870) 400 73 88
173 rm – †£ 115 ††£ 115, ☕ £ 14.95 – 5 suites
Rest *Plate* – *(closed Sunday dinner) (bar lunch Monday-Saturday)* Menu £ 25/33
◆ Set next to the renowned racecourse; the most famous hotel in the city. Large, angular building with traditional styling, extensive conference/leisure facilities and bedrooms boasting good mod cons. Equestrian-themed restaurant offers classical à la carte.

at Ponteland Northwest : 8.25 mi. by A 167 on A 696 - AV – ✉ Newcastle Upon Tyne

X **Cafe Lowrey**
33-35 Broadway, Darras Hall Estate, Southwest : 1.5 mi. by B 6323 off Darras Hall Estate rd ✉ NE20 9PW – ✆ (01661) 820 357 – www.cafelowrey.co.uk – Fax (01661) 820 357 – Closed Monday and Bank Holidays
Rest – *(dinner only and lunch Saturday and Sunday) (booking essential)* Carte £ 22/35
◆ Small restaurant in shopping parade with wooden chairs and cloth-laid tables. Blackboard menus offering modern British cooking using local produce.

NEWICK – East Sussex – **504** U31 – **pop. 2 129** — **8** A2

London 57 mi. – Brighton 14 mi. – Eastbourne 20 mi. – Hastings 34 mi.

Newick Park

Southeast : 1.5 mi. following signs for Newick Park ✉ BN8 4SB – ☎ (01825) 723 633 – www.newickpark.co.uk – Fax (01825) 723 969 – Closed 31 December-4 January

15 rm – £ 125 ££ 165 – 1 suite

Rest – *(booking essential for non-residents)* Menu £ 22/43

◆ Georgian manor in 200 acres; views of Longford river and South Downs. Stately hallway and lounge. Unique rooms, some with original fireplaces, all with Egyptian cotton sheets. Dine in relaxed formality on high-back crimson chairs.

272

20-22 High St ✉ BN8 4LQ – ☎ (01825) 721 272 – www.272restaurant.co.uk – Closed 25-26 December, Monday, Sunday dinner and Tuesday lunch

Rest – Carte £ 22/38

◆ Well-run restaurant with an easy-going, relaxed feel. Chairs from Italy, modern art on walls. Frequently changing menus offer a winning blend of British and European flavours.

NEWMARKET – Suffolk – **504** V27 – **pop. 16 947** — **14** B2

London 64 mi. – Cambridge 13 mi. – Ipswich 40 mi. – Norwich 48 mi.

Palace House, Palace St ☎ (01638) 667200, tic.newmarket@forest-heath.gov.uk

Links Cambridge Rd, ☎ (01638) 663 000

at Lidgate Southeast : 7 mi. on B 1063 – ✉ Newmarket

The Star Inn

The Street ✉ CB8 9PP – ☎ (01638) 500 275 – Closed 25-26 December, 1 January and Monday lunch

Rest – Menu £ 14/18 – Carte £ 25/30

◆ Quintessentially English inn, with ancient beams and inglenooks. Mainly Spanish menu offers rustic cooking including local game and plenty of fish dishes. Well-paced service.

NEW MILTON – Hampshire – **503** P31 – **pop. 24 324** — **6** A3

London 106 mi. – Bournemouth 12 mi. – Southampton 21 mi. – Winchester 34 mi.

Barton-on-Sea Milford Rd, ☎ (01425) 615 308

Chewton Glen

Christchurch Rd, West : 2 mi. by A 337 and Ringwood Rd on Chewton Farm Rd ✉ BH25 6QS – ☎ (01425) 275 341 – www.chewtonglen.com – Fax (01425) 272 310

48 rm – £ 313/341 ££ 313/567, £ 25 – 10 suites

Rest ***Marryat Room and Conservatory*** – Menu £ 25/65 **s** – Carte £ 45/57 **s**

◆ 19C country house in 130 acres of New Forest parkland. Luxurious bedrooms and grand suites blend the classic with the contemporary; most have terraces/balconies. Impressive leisure facilities include croquet, archery and clay pigeon shooting. Conservatory dining room offers accomplished cooking.

NEWPORT PAGNELL – Milton Keynes – **504** R27 – **pop. 14 739** — **11** C1

London 57 mi. – Bedford 13 mi. – Luton 21 mi. – Northampton 15 mi.

Plan : see Milton Keynes

Robinsons

18-20 St John St ✉ MK16 8HJ – ☎ (01908) 611 400 – www.robinsonsrestaurant.co.uk – Fax (01908) 216 900 – Closed 26 December, 1 January, Saturday lunch, Sunday and Bank Holidays CU**n**

Rest – Menu £ 14/20 – Carte £ 31/37

◆ Smart restaurant combining exposed brick and wood floors with neutral hues and contemporary furnishings. Great value, seasonal menus display an interesting mix of British/European dishes.

ENGLAND

NEWPORT – Telford and Wrekin – 502 M25 – pop. 12 137 18 B1

London 148 mi. – Stafford 12 mi. – Telford 9 mi.

The Fox

Pave Lane, Chetwynd Aston, South : 1.5 mi. by Wolverhampton rd (A 41)
✉ TF10 9LQ – ✆ (01952) 815 940 – www.fox-newport.co.uk – Fax (01952) 815 941
Rest – Carte £ 18/30

◆ Characterful whitewashed pub boasting a large patio and pleasant gardens. Extensive daily changing menu offers a choice of light bites and pub classics; cooking is reliable and robust.

NEWQUAY – Cornwall – 503 E32 – pop. 19 562 1 A2

London 291 mi. – Exeter 83 mi. – Penzance 34 mi. – Plymouth 48 mi.
Newquay Airport : ✆ (01637) 860600 Y
Municipal Offices, Marcus Hill ✆ (01637) 854020, newquay.tic@cornwall.gov.uk
Tower Rd, ✆ (01637) 872 091
Treloy, ✆ (01637) 878 554
Merlin Mawgan Porth, ✆ (01841) 540 222
Penhale Point and Kelsey Head★ (←★★), SW : by A 3075 Y – Trerice★ **AC**, SE : 3.5 mi. by A 392 - Y - and A 3058. St Agnes - St Agnes Beacon★★ (✳★★), SW : 12.5 mi. by A 3075 - Y - and B 3285

The Bristol

Narrowcliff ✉ TR7 2PQ – ✆ (01637) 870 275 – www.hotelbristol.co.uk – Fax (01637) 879 347 – Closed 2 weeks January and Christmas Zr
73 rm – †£ 85/120 ††£ 135/165 – 1 suite
Rest – *(closed Sunday) (bar lunch Monday-Saturday)* Menu £ 18/26 – Carte £ 26/35

◆ Classic seaside hotel built in 1933, well established and family run. Wide range of bedrooms from singles to family suites. Elements of art deco. Large conference facilities. The dining room overlooks Atlantic.

Trebarwith

Trebarwith Crescent ✉ TR7 1BZ – ✆ (01637) 872 288 – www.trebarwith-hotel.co.uk – Fax (01637) 875 431 – 11 April - October
41 rm – †£ 39/69 ††£ 78/139 Za
Rest – *(bar lunch)* Menu £ 18 **s** – Carte £ 18/28 **s**

◆ Superb bay and coastline views from this renowned seaside hotel. Has its own cinema, plus evening discos and dances. You'll get the stunning vistas from traditional bedrooms. Dine by the sea beneath Wedgwood-style ceiling.

at Watergate Bay Northeast : 3 mi. by A 3059 on B 3276 – ✉ Newquay

Fifteen Cornwall

On The Beach ✉ TR8 4AA – ✆ (01637) 861 000 – www.fifteencornwall.co.uk
Rest – Italian – *(booking essential)* Menu £ 26/55 – Carte lunch £ 27/45

◆ Phenomenally successful converted café in a golden idyll. Jamie Oliver's academy youngsters offer Cornwall-meets-Italy menus in a cavernous room bathed in West Coast hues. Dinner is 5 course tasting menu.

at Mawgan Porth Northeast : 6 mi. by A 3059 on B 3276

The Scarlet

Tredragon Rd ✉ TR8 4DQ – ✆ (01637) 861 800 – www.scarlethotel.co.uk – Fax (01637) 861 801 – Closed 4 January-12 February
37 rm – †£ 160/250 ††£ 180/270
Rest *The Restaurant* – Menu £ 20 (lunch) – Carte £ 30/39

◆ Stunning location to this eco-friendly and decidedly cool hotel: there's a path to the beach and every room has a terrace and sea views. Bedrooms in natural tones with organic bedding. Great spa. Kitchen makes intelligent use of local produce.

NEWQUAY

0 — 1 km
0 — 1/2 mile

TOWAN HEAD
NEWQUAY BAY
FISTRAL BAY
FISTRAL BEACH
Pentire Av.
The Gannel
CRANTOCK
Mellanvrane Roundabout
ST-COLUMB MINOR
Henver Road
Trevenson Road
TRENCREEK
B 3276
A 3059
A 3058
WADEBRIDGE
BODMIN
A 392
REDRUTH
Y
2
14
15

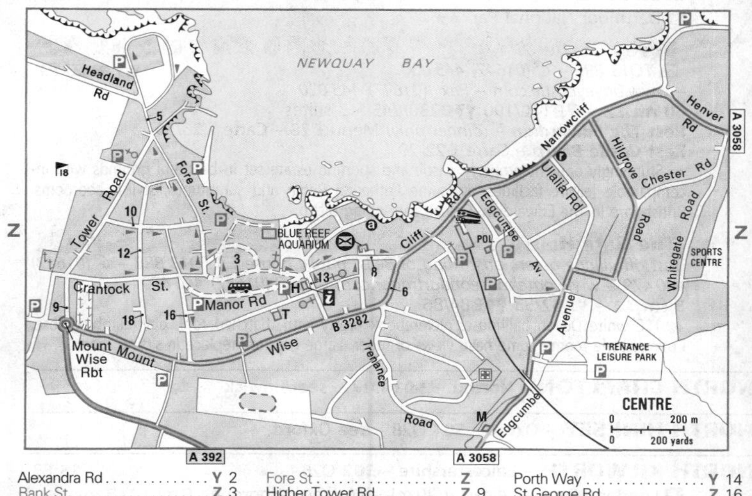

Alexandra Rd . . . . Y 2
Bank St. . . . . Z 3
Beacon Rd . . . . Z 5
Berry Rd . . . . Z 6
East St . . . . Z 8
Fore St . . . . Z
Higher Tower Rd . . . . Z 9
Hope Terrace . . . . Z 10
Jubilee St . . . . Z 12
Marcus Hill . . . . Z 13
Porth Way . . . . Y 14
St George Rd . . . . Z 16
St John's Rd. . . . . Z 18
Trevemper Rd . . . . Y 15

NEW ROMNEY – **Kent** – **504** W31 **9** C2

London 71 mi. – Brighton 60 mi. – Folkestone 17 mi. – Maidstone 36 mi.

Romney Bay House

Coast Rd, Littlestone, East : 2.25 mi. by B 2071 ✉ TN28 8QY – ✆ (01797) 364 747 – Fax (01797) 367 156 – Closed 1 week Christmas and 3-10 January

10 rm – †£ 69 ††£ 164

Rest – *(Closed Sunday, Monday and Thursday) (dinner only) (booking essential for non-residents) (set menu only)* Menu £ 43

◆ Beach panorama for late actress Hedda Hopper's house, built by Portmeirion architect Clough Williams-Ellis. Individual rooms; sitting room with telescope and bookcases. Enjoy drinks on terrace before conservatory dining.

NEWTON LONGVILLE – **Bucks.** – **504** R28 – **see Milton Keynes**

NEWTON-ON-OUSE – **North Yorkshire** – **502** Q22 – **see York**

NEWTON POPPLEFORD – **Devon** – **503** K31 – **see Sidmouth**

NITON – Isle of Wight – 504 Q32 – see Wight (Isle of)

NOMANSLAND – Hampshire – 503 P31 4 D3

London 96 mi. – Bournemouth 26 mi. – Salisbury 13 mi. – Southampton 14 mi.

XX **Les Mirabelles**

Forest Edge Rd ✉ SP5 2BN – ✆ (01794) 390 205 – www.lesmirabelles.com – Fax (01794) 390 106 – Closed 25 December-mid January, Sunday and Monday

Rest – French – Menu £ 20 (dinner and Tuesday-Thursday lunch) – Carte £ 27/40

◆ Unpretentious little French restaurant overlooking the village common. Superb wine list. Extensive menu of good value, classic Gallic cuisine.

NORTH BOVEY – Devon – 503 I32 – pop. 254 – ✉ Newton Abbot 2 C2

London 214 mi. – Exeter 13 mi. – Plymouth 34 mi. – Torquay 21 mi.

Dartmoor National Park★★

Bovey Castle

✉ TQ13 8RE – ✆ (01647) 445 000 – www.boveycastle.com – Fax (01647) 445 020

60 rm – †£ 140/190 ††£ 230/245 – 3 suites

Rest *The Edwardian* – *(dinner only)* Menu £ 28 – Carte £ 26/50

Rest *Castle Bistro* – Carte £ 22/29

◆ Stunningly opulent property: castle and sporting estate set in beautiful grounds with incomparable leisure facilities, awesome Cathedral Room and sumptuous, stylish bedrooms. British fare in The Edwardian. Casual, easy-going bistro.

The Gate House without rest

just off village green, past "Ring of Bells" public house ✉ TQ13 8RB – ✆ (01647) 440 479 – www.gatehouseondartmoor.com – Fax (01647) 440 479

3 rm – †£ 52/53 ††£ 84/86

◆ 15C white Devon hallhouse; picturebook pretty with thatched roof, pink climbing rose. Country style rooms; some have views of moor. Large granite fireplace in sitting room.

NORTH CHARLTON – Northd. – 501 O17 – see Alnwick

NORTH HINKSEY – Oxon. – 504 Q28 – see Oxford

NORTH KILWORTH – Leicestershire – 502 Q26 16 B3

London 95 mi. – Leicester 20 mi. – Market Harborough 9 mi.

Kilworth House

Lutterworth Rd, West : 0.5 mi. on A 4304 ✉ LE17 6JE – ✆ (01858) 880 058 – www.kilworthhouse.co.uk – Fax (01858) 880 349

41 rm – †£ 150 ††£ 165 – 3 suites

Rest *The Wordsworth* – Menu £ 40 (dinner) – Carte £ 26/45

Rest *The Orangery* – Carte £ 23/35

◆ 19C extended house set in 38 acres of parkland, with original staircase, stained glass windows and open air theatre. Individually appointed rooms, some with commanding views. Ornate Wordsworth with courtyard vista. Light meals in beautiful Orangery.

NORTH LEIGH – Oxfordshire – 504 P28 – see Witney

NORTH LOPHAM – Norfolk – 504 W26 15 C2

London 98 mi. – Norwich 34 mi. – Ipswich 31 mi. – Bury Saint Edmunds 20 mi.

Church Farm House

Church Rd ✉ IP22 2LP – ✆ (01379) 687 270 – www.churchfarmhouse.org – Fax (01379) 687 270 – Closed January

3 rm – †£ 48/58 ††£ 96 **Rest** – Menu £ 27

◆ Characterful thatched farmhouse with lovely garden, simple facilities, homely feel and personal touches. Individually styled bedrooms look to the church. Home cooked meals use local produce, with breakfast served outside in summer.

NORTH SHIELDS – Tyne and Wear – 502 P18 – pop. 39 042 — 24 B2

London 288 mi. – Newcastle upon Tyne 9 mi. – Sunderland 14 mi. – Middlesbrough 39 mi.

Magnesia Bank

Camden St ✉ NE30 1NH – ✆ (0191) 257 48 31 – www.magnesiabank.com – Fax (0191) 260 54 22 – Closed Sunday dinner

Rest – Carte £ 18/30

◆ Spacious Georgian building set above the Tyne. Good quality classics served in the bar, more substantial dishes in the dining room; fish is from the quay 100m away. Regular live music.

NORTH WALSHAM – Norfolk – 503 Y25 – pop. 11 845 — 15 D1

Great Britain

London 125 mi. – Norwich 16 mi.

Blicking Hall★★ **AC**, W : 8.5 mi. by B 1145, A 140 and B 1354

Beechwood

20 Cromer Rd ✉ NR28 0HD – ✆ (01692) 403 231 – www.beechwood-hotel.co.uk – Fax (01692) 407 284

17 rm – £ 76 £ 90/160

Rest – *(dinner only and Sunday lunch)* Menu £ 21/35 **s**

◆ Privately owned, peacefully set, part 19C hotel where Agatha Christie once stayed. Thoughtfully appointed bedrooms; newer ones are larger. Attentive service. Handsome dining room with flowers.

NORTHALLERTON – North Yorkshire – 502 P20 – pop. 15 517 — 22 B1

London 238 mi. – Leeds 48 mi. – Middlesbrough 24 mi. – Newcastle upon Tyne 56 mi.

Applegarth ✆ (01609) 776864

at Staddlebridge Northeast : 7.5 mi. by A 684 on A 19 at junction with A 172 – ✉ Northallerton

McCoys Bistro at The Tontine with rm

on southbound carriageway (A 19) ✉ DL6 3JB – ✆ (01609) 882 671 – www.mccoystontine.co.uk – Fax (01609) 882 660 – Closed 25-26 December and 1-2 January

6 rm – £ 95 £ 120

Rest – *(booking essential)* Menu £ 17 (lunch)/19 (early dinner) – Carte £ 28/46

◆ Yorkshire meets France in long-standing restaurant with mirrors, wood panelling, framed memorabilia. Snug bar to plot coups in. Large bedrooms, unique in decorative style.

at Newby Wiske South : 2.5 mi. by A 167 – ✉ Northallerton

Solberge Hall

Northwest : 1.25 mi. on Warlaby rd ✉ DL7 9ER – ✆ (01609) 779 191 – www.solbergehall.co.uk – Fax (01609) 780 472

23 rm – £ 65/95 £ 95/130 – 1 suite

Rest – Menu £ 12 (lunch) – Carte £ 26/40

Rest *Silks* – *(Closed 25 December)* Carte £ 21/35

◆ Tranquil grounds surround this graceful Georgian house, situated in the heart of the countryside. Popular for weddings; bedrooms in main house or stable block. Local ingredients well employed in flavoursome menus.

NORTHAMPTON – Northamptonshire – 504 R27 – pop. 189 474 — 16 B3

Great Britain

London 69 mi. – Cambridge 53 mi. – Coventry 34 mi. – Leicester 42 mi.

The Royal and Derngate Theatre Foyer, Guildhall Rd ✆ (01604) 622677, northampton.tic@northamptonshireenterprise.ltd.uk

Delapre Nene Valley Way, Eagle Drive, ✆ (01604) 764 036

Collingtree Park Windingbrook Lane, ✆ (01604) 700 000

All Saints, Brixworth★, N : 7 mi. on A 508 Y

Plan on next page

ENGLAND

NORTHAMPTON

Street	Grid	No.
Abington Square	X	2
Abington St	X	
Bewick Rd	Y	4
Billing Rd	X	5
Bridge St	X	6
Campbell St	X	7
Castillian St	X	8
Charnwood Ave	Y	10
Church Lane	X	12
Cliftonville Rd	Z	13
College St	X	14
Derngate	X	15
Drapery	X	18
Gold St	X	
Greyfriars	X	23
Grosvenor Centre	X	
Guildhall Rd	X	24
Hazelwood Rd	X	25
Horse Shoe St	X	28
Kettering Rd	X	30
Kingsthorpe Grove	Y	34
Lower Mounts	X	35
Oaklands Drive	Y	38
Overstone Rd	X	39
Park Ave North	Y	40
Park Ave South	Z	43
Rushmere Rd	Z	44
St James Retail Park	X	
St Andrew's Rd	Y	45
St Edmund's Rd	X	48
St Edmund's St	Z	49
St James's Rd	Z	50
St John's St	X	51
St Leonard's Rd	Z	52
St Michael's Rd	X	53
St Peters Way Centre	X	
Sheep St	X	54
Silver St	X	55
Spencer Bridge Rd	X, Z	57
Towcester Rd	Z	58
Upper Mounts	X	59
Waveney Way	Y	60
Weston Favell Centre	Y	
West Bridge	X	62
Windrush Way	Y	63

ENGLAND

Dang's

205 Wellingborough Rd ✉ NN1 4ED – ✆ (01604) 607 060 – www.dangs.co.uk – Closed 25-26 December and Monday Z**n**

Rest – Vietnamese – *(dinner only)* Menu £ 12 (Sunday-Thursday) – Carte £ 17/22 **s**

◆ Immaculately furnished, contemporary Vietnamese restaurant. Passionately run, food is fresh, tasty, good value and mostly homemade. Noodle bowls are a speciality.

NORTHAW – Hertfordshire – 504 T28 **12** B2

London 22 mi.

The Sun at Northaw

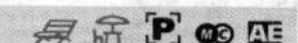

1 Judges Hill ✉ EN6 4NL – ✆ (01707) 655 507 – www.thesunatnorthaw.co.uk – Fax (01707) 665 379 – Closed Sunday dinner and Monday except Bank Holidays

Rest – Carte £ 24/36

◆ Whitewashed 17C inn by village green; dine in bar or either dining room. Hearty, traditional, flavoursome cooking: dishes use East of England produce, and a map points out suppliers.

NORTHLEACH – Gloucestershire – 503 O28 – pop. 1 923 **4** D1

London 87 mi. – Birmingham 73 mi. – Bristol 54 mi. – Coventry 47 mi.

The Wheatsheaf Inn

West End ✉ GL50 3EZ – ✆ (01451) 860 244 – www.cotswoldswheatsheaf.com

Rest – Menu £ 13 (lunch) – Carte £ 19/30

◆ Characterful 17C former coaching inn set in historic village, with stone-floored bar and open fires. Daily changing menus offer mostly pub classics; refined, flavoursome cooking.

NORTHREPPS – Norfolk – 504 Y25 – see Cromer

NORTON – Shrops. – see Telford

NORTON ST PHILIP – Somerset – 503 N30 – pop. 820 – ✉ Bath **4** C2

London 113 mi. – Bristol 22 mi. – Southampton 55 mi. – Swindon 40 mi.

The Plaine without rest

✉ *BA2 7LT – ✆ (01373) 834 723 – www.theplaine.co.uk – Fax (01373) 834 723*

3 rm – †£ 75/110 ††£ 95/115

◆ 16C stone cottages opposite George Inn on site of original market place. Beams, stone walls denote historic origins. Fresh, bright interior. Welcoming owners.

NORWICH – Norfolk – 504 Y26 – pop. 174 047 Great Britain **15** D2

London 109 mi. – Kingston-upon-Hull 148 mi. – Leicester 117 mi. – Nottingham 120 mi.

Norwich Airport : ✆ (0844) 748 0112, N : 3.5 mi. by A 140 V

The Forum, Millennium Plain ✆ (01603) 213999, tourism@norwich.gov.uk

Royal Norwich Hellesdon Drayton High Rd, ✆ (01603) 425 712

Marriott Sprowston Manor Hotel Wroxham Rd, ✆ (0870) 400 72 29

Costessy Park Costessey, ✆ (01603) 746 333

Bawburgh Marlingford Rd, Glen Lodge, ✆ (01603) 740 404

City★★ - Cathedral★★ Y – Castle (Museum and Art Gallery★ **AC**) Z – Market Place★ Z

Sainsbury Centre for Visual Arts★ **AC**, W : 3 mi. by B 1108 X. Blicking Hall★★ **AC**, N : 11 mi. by A 140 - V - and B 1354 – NE : Norfolk Broads★

Plans on following pages

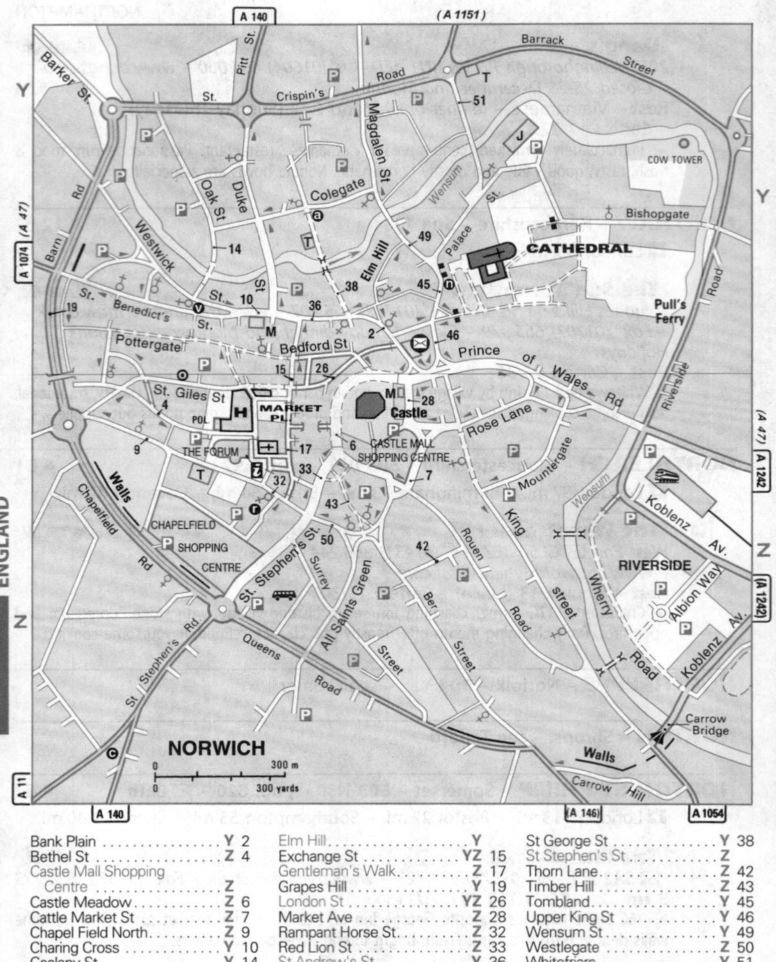

Bank Plain . . . . Y 2
Bethel St . . . . Z 4
Castle Mall Shopping Centre . . . . Z
Castle Meadow . . . . Z 6
Cattle Market St . . . . Z 7
Chapel Field North . . . . Z 9
Charing Cross . . . . Y 10
Coslany St . . . . Y 14
Elm Hill . . . . Y
Exchange St . . . . YZ 15
Gentleman's Walk . . . . Z 17
Grapes Hill . . . . Y 19
London St . . . . YZ 26
Market Ave . . . . Z 28
Rampant Horse St . . . . Z 32
Red Lion St . . . . Z 33
St Andrew's St . . . . Y 36
St George St . . . . Y 38
St Stephen's St . . . . Z
Thorn Lane . . . . Z 42
Timber Hill . . . . Z 43
Tombland . . . . Y 45
Upper King St . . . . Y 46
Wensum St . . . . Y 49
Westlegate . . . . Z 50
Whitefriars . . . . Y 51

Marriott Sprowston Manor H. & Country Club

Wroxham Rd, rest,
Northeast : 3.25 mi. on A 1151 ✉ NR7 8RP
– ✆ (01603) 410 871 – www.marriottsprowstonmanor.co.uk
– Fax (01603) 423 911
93 rm – †£ 120/130 ††£ 140 – 1 suite
Rest *1559* – *(Closed Sunday dinner) (dinner only and Sunday lunch)*
Menu £ 15/25 – Carte £ 28/43
Rest *Zest* – Carte £ 21/34 **s**

◆ Red-brick Elizabethan manor house in rural location, with championship golf course. Smart, contemporary bedrooms boast high level of facilities; most have countryside outlook. Formal restaurant 1559 named after year manor house built. All day menus in Zest.

Barrack St	V 3	Heigham St	V 22	Mile End Rd	X 29
Bowthorpe Rd	V 5	Ketts Hill	V 23	Riverside Rd	V 34
Farrow Rd	V 16	Lakenham Rd	X 24	St Augustine's St	V 37
Guardian Rd	V 21	Long John Hill	X 27	Waterloo Rd	V 48

St Giles House

rm, rest,

41-45 St Giles St ✉ NR2 1JR – ✆ (01603) 275 180 – www.stgileshousehotel.com – Fax (0845) 299 1905 YZo

23 rm – £ 120 £ 130 – 1 suite

Rest – Menu £ 19 – Carte dinner £ 23/37

◆ Boutique hotel with impressive façade in heart of old town. Superb art deco interior with open plan bar/lounge. Individually decorated bedrooms boast modern facilities. Brasserie style menu.

Annesley House

6 Newmarket Rd ✉ NR2 2LA – ✆ (01603) 624 553 – www.bw-annesleyhouse.co.uk – Fax (01603) 621 577 – Closed 25-26 December and 1 January Zc

26 rm – £ 48/85 £ 70/95, £ 9.50 **Rest** – *(light lunch)* Menu £ 32

◆ A relaxed atmosphere prevails at this established hotel set within three Georgian houses. Some of the generously proportioned bedrooms overlook the feature water garden. Conservatory restaurant.

Arbor Linden Lodge without rest

557 Earlham Rd ✉ NR4 7HW – ✆ (01603) 462 308 – www.guesthousenorwich.com Xr

6 rm – £ 38/45 £ 58

◆ Close to both university and hospitals. Friendly and family run guesthouse. Enjoy a relaxed breakfast in the conservatory. Clean, comfortable bedrooms.

ENGLAND

XX **By Appointment** with rm

25-29 St Georges St ✉ NR3 1AB – ✆ (01603) 630 730 – www.byappointmentnorwich.co.uk – Fax (01603) 630 730 – Closed 25-26 December Y**a**

5 rm – †£ 80/95 ††£ 140

Rest – *(Closed Sunday-Monday) (dinner only)* Carte £ 35/37

◆ Pretty, antique furnished restaurant. Interesting, traditional dishes off blackboard with theatrical service. Characterful bedrooms include a host of thoughtful extras.

X **1 Up at the Mad Moose Arms**

2 Warwick St, off Dover St ✉ NR2 3LD – ✆ (01603) 627 687 – www.themadmoose.co.uk – Fax (01603) 633 945 – Closed 25 December

Rest – *(dinner only and Sunday lunch)* Menu £ 16 – Carte £ 22/28 **s** X**n**

◆ Housed in a Victorian pub, with bar downstairs and friendly, informal dining room above. Appealing menus feature tasty British and southern European dishes; good use of local ingredients.

X **Tatler's**

21 Tombland ✉ NR3 1RF – ✆ (01603) 766 670 – www.tatlers.com – Fax (01603) 764 296 – Closed 25 December, Sunday and Monday Y**n**

Rest – Menu £ 16 – Carte £ 22/34

◆ Characterful shabby-chic restaurant set by the cathedral in the historic city centre; formerly a Georgian merchant's house. Rustic cooking has a refined edge, with good value menus early week.

X **St Benedicts**

9 St Benedicts St ✉ NR2 4PE – ✆ (01603) 765 377 – www.rafflesrestaurants.co.uk – Fax (01603) 666 919 – Closed 25-31 December, Sunday and Monday

Rest – Menu £ 12/24 – Carte £ 22/27 Y**v**

◆ Attractive high street eatery in fashionable area. Simple bistro-style interior with green panelled walls and friendly service. Neatly presented, tasty cooking; good value midweek menus.

X **Mackintosh's Canteen**

Unit 410, Chaplefield Plain, (First Floor) ✉ NR2 1SZ – ✆ (01603) 305 280 – www.mackintoshscanteen.co.uk – Fax (01603) 305 281 Z**r**

Rest – Carte £ 22/31

◆ Smart modern brasserie boasting full length windows, combined with an all day terraced café: a shoppers' haven. Friendly, efficient team serve tasty, freshly prepared modern dishes.

at Stoke Holy Cross South : 5.75 mi. by A 140 - X – ✉ Norwich

Wildebeest Arms

82-86 Norwich Rd ✉ NR14 8QJ – ✆ (01508) 492 497 – www.thewildebeest.co.uk – Fax (01508) 494 946 – Closed 25-26 December

Rest – *(booking essential)* Menu £ 17/20 – Carte £ 25/37

◆ Rustic pub with tree trunk tables and wild animal artefacts. Good value set menus and ambitious à la carte offering seasonal European dishes. Well organised, friendly service.

NOSS MAYO – Devon – 503 H33 2 C3

London 242 mi. – Plymouth 12 mi. – Yealmpton 3 mi.

Saltram House★★, NW : 7 mi. by B 3186 and A 379 – Plymouth★, NW : 9 mi. by B 3186 and A 379

The Ship Inn

✉ PL8 1EW – ✆ (01752) 872 387 – www.nossmayo.com – Fax (01752) 873 294

Rest – Carte £ 21/33

◆ Very large and busy pub with waterside views and maritime memorabilia. Classic dishes mix with international flavours on the à la carte. Bar menu features pub favourites.

ENGLAND

NOTTINGHAM – City of Nottingham – **502** Q25 – pop. 249 584 **16** B2

Great Britain

London 135 mi. – Birmingham 50 mi. – Leeds 74 mi. – Leicester 27 mi.

Nottingham East Midlands Airport, Castle Donington : (0871) 9199000 SW : 15 mi. by A 453 AZ

1-4 Smithy Row (08444) 775678, touristinfo@nottinghamcity.gov.uk

Bulwell Forest Hucknall Rd, (0115) 977 0576

Wollaton Park, (0115) 978 7574

Mapperley Central Ave, Plains Rd, (0115) 955 6672

Nottingham City Bulwell Norwich Gardens, (0115) 927 2767

Beeston Fields Beeston, (0115) 925 7062

Ruddington Grange Ruddington Wilford Rd, (0115) 984 6141

Edwalton Wellin Lane, (0115) 923 4775

Cotgrave Place G. & C.C. Stragglethorpe Cotgrave, Nr Cotgrave Village, (0115) 933 3344

Castle Museum★ (alabasters★) **AC**, CZ **M**

Wollaton Hall★ **AC**, W : 2.5 mi. by Ilkeston Rd, A 609 AZ **M.** Southwell Minster★★, NE : 14 mi. by A 612 BZ - Newstead Abbey★ **AC**, N : 11 mi. by A 60, A 611 - AY - and B 683 – Mr Straw's House★, Worksop, N : 20 mi. signed from B 6045 (past Bassetlaw Hospital) – St Mary Magdalene★, Newark-on-Trent, NE : 20 mi. by A 612 BZ

Plans pages 558, 559

Park Plaza

rm, VISA AE

41 Maid Marian Way ✉ NG1 6GD – (0115) 947 7200 – www.parkplazanottingham.com – Fax (0115) 947 7300 CY**v**

177 rm – †£ 62/149 ††£ 72/159, £ 12 – 1 suite

Rest *Chino Latino* – *(closed 24-27 December, Sunday and Bank Holidays)* Carte £ 27/52 **s**

◆ Converted city centre office block with stylish and contemporary decor. Choice of meeting rooms. Spacious stylish bedrooms with many extras. Formal Chino Latino Japanese restaurant.

Welbeck

rm, VISA AE

Talbot St ✉ NG1 5GS – (0115) 841 1000 – www.welbeck-hotel.co.uk – Fax (0115) 841 1001 – Closed 23 December-2 January CY**s**

96 rm – †£ 115 ††£ 115, £ 10.75

Rest – *(closed Sunday dinner) (dinner only and Sunday lunch)* Menu £ 19 – Carte £ 18/28

◆ Bright modern hotel in city centre close to theatre. Colourful cushions and pared-down style in bedrooms. Three conference rooms for hire. Fifth floor dining room gives fine views of city.

Hart's

VISA AE

Standard Hill, Park Row ✉ NG1 6FN – (0115) 988 1900 – www.hartsnottingham.co.uk – Fax (0115) 947 7600 CZ**e**

30 rm – †£ 120 ††£ 120, £ 13.50 – 2 suites

Rest *Hart's* – see restaurant listing

◆ Modern boutique hotel built on the ramparts of a medieval castle. Comfy bedrooms have courtyard or skyline views; some have French doors and a private garden. Breakfast in contemporary bar.

Lace Market

VISA AE

29-31 High Pavement ✉ NG1 1HE – (0115) 852 3232 – www.lacemarkethotel.co.uk – Fax (0115) 852 3223 DZ**a**

42 rm – †£ 79/149 ††£ 109/159

Rest *Merchants* – see restaurant listing

◆ Located in old lacemaking quarter, but nothing lacy about interiors; crisp rooms with minimalist designs, unpatterned fabrics. A stylish place to rest one's head.

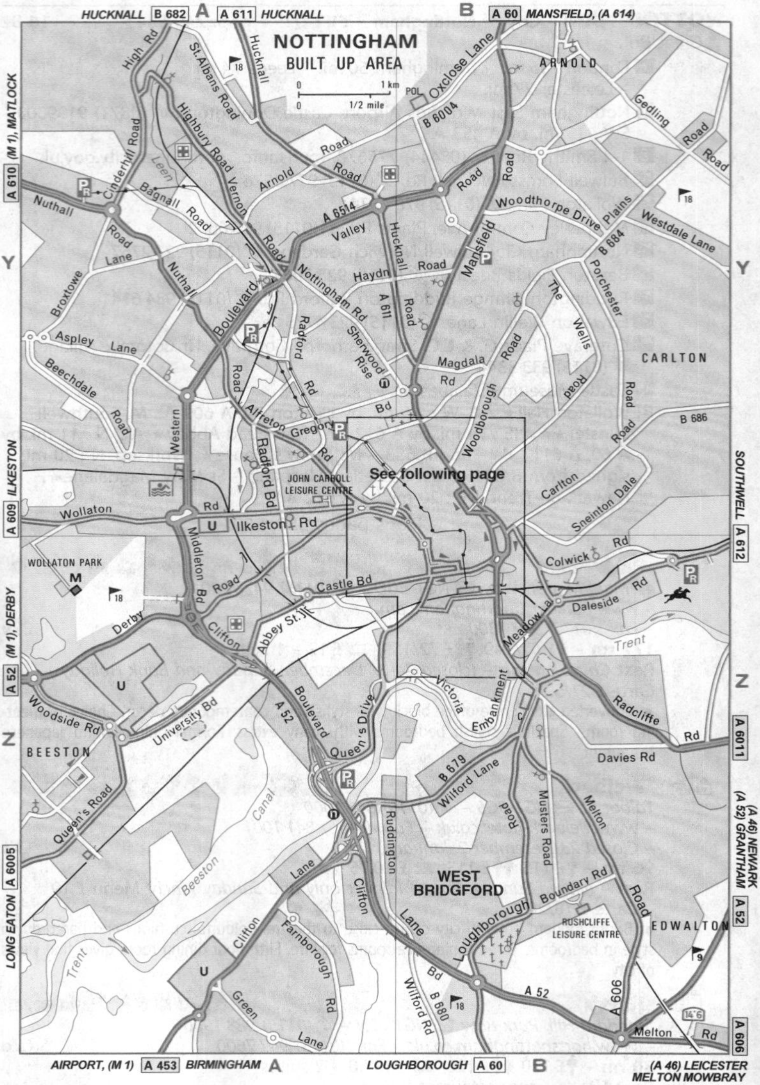

Greenwood Lodge City without rest

5 Third Ave, Sherwood Rise ✉ *NG7 6JH* – ✆ *(0115) 962 1206*
– www.greenwoodlodgecityguesthouse.co.uk – Fax (0115) 962 1206
– Closed 24-28 December AY**n**

6 rm – £ 48/63 £ 80/95

◆ Regency house with elegant reception offset by paintings, antiques. Conservatory breakfast room from which to view birdlife. Period beds, lovely fabrics in pretty rooms.

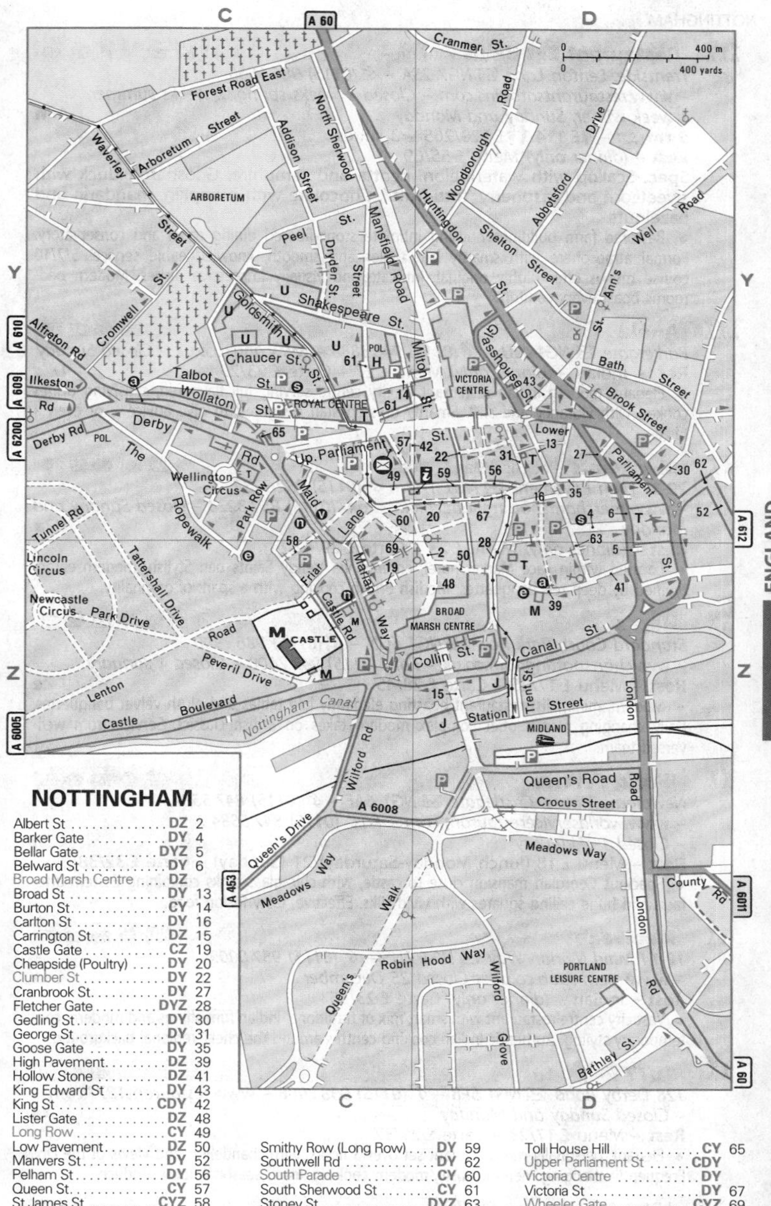

NOTTINGHAM

Albert St . . . . DZ 2
Barker Gate . . . . DY 4
Bellar Gate . . . . DYZ 5
Belward St . . . . DY 6
Broad Marsh Centre . . . . . . DZ
Broad St . . . . DY 13
Burton St. . . . . CY 14
Carlton St . . . . DY 16
Carrington St. . . . . DZ 15
Castle Gate . . . . CZ 19
Cheapside (Poultry) . . . . . DY 20
Clumber St . . . . DY 22
Cranbrook St. . . . . DY 27
Fletcher Gate . . . . DYZ 28
Gedling St. . . . . DY 30
George St . . . . DY 31
Goose Gate . . . . DY 35
High Pavement . . . . DZ 39
Hollow Stone . . . . DZ 41
King Edward St . . . . DY 43
King St . . . . CDY 42
Lister Gate . . . . DZ 48
Long Row . . . . CY 49
Low Pavement . . . . DZ 50
Manvers St . . . . DY 52
Pelham St . . . . DY 56
Queen St. . . . . CY 57
St James St . . . . CYZ 58
Smithy Row (Long Row) . . . . DY 59
Southwell Rd . . . . DY 62
South Parade . . . . CY 60
South Sherwood St . . . . CY 61
Stoney St . . . . DYZ 63
Toll House Hill . . . . CY 65
Upper Parliament St . . . . . . CDY
Victoria Centre . . . . DY
Victoria St . . . . DY 67
Wheeler Gate . . . . CYZ 69

ENGLAND

XXX ✿ **Restaurant Sat Bains** with rm — rest, P, VISA

Trentside, Lenton Lane ✉ NG7 2SA – ✆ (0115) 986 6566 – www.restaurantsatbains.com – Closed 2 weeks spring, 2 weeks summer, 1 week winter, Sunday and Monday AZ**n**

5 rm – †£ 114 ††£ 129/265 – 3 suites

Rest – *(dinner only)* Menu £ 55/69

Spec. Scallop with watermelon, ricotta and samphire. Goosnargh duck with sweetcorn and raspberry 'tutti-frutti'. Chocolate with pumpkin, mandarin and hazelnuts.

◆ Restored farm buildings housing intimate stone-floored dining room and conservatory. Formal atmosphere with smartly laid tables and smooth, knowledgeable service. 5/7/10 course menus offer highly original, intricate and visually impressive dishes. Modern bedrooms boast every comfort.

XXX **Anoki** — VISA AE

Barkergate ✉ NG1 1JU – ✆ (0115) 948 3888 – www.anoki.co.uk – Closed Sunday

Rest – Indian – *(dinner only)* Menu £ 27 – Carte £ 23/29 DY**s**

◆ Elegant, modern Indian restaurant in city centre serving full flavoured, satisfying dishes cooked with vibrancy and skill. Smartly dressed staff delighted to give advice – or even a taster.

XX **Merchants** – at Lace Market Hotel — AC VISA AE

29-31 High Pavement ✉ NG1 1HE – ✆ (0115) 852 3232 – www.merchantsnottingham.co.uk – Fax (0115) 852 3223 – closed Sunday and Monday DZ**a**

Rest – *(dinner only)* Menu £ 23 – Carte £ 29/42

◆ Located within Lace Market hotel, entered via trendy Saints bar. Stylish, modern eatery typified by deep red banquettes. Modish British cooking with a spark of originality.

XX **Hart's** — AC VISA AE

Standard Court, Park Row ✉ NG1 6GN – ✆ (0115) 988 1900 – www.hartsnottingham.co.uk – Fax (0115) 947 7600 – Closed 1 January

Rest – Menu £ 17/25 – Carte £ 28/45 CZ**e**

◆ Modern, minimalist restaurant boasting elegantly laid tables and plush velvet banquettes. Daily changing menus offer complex modern takes on British classics. Service from well-versed team.

XX **World Service** — VISA AE

Newdigate House, Castlegate ✉ NG1 6AF – ✆ (0115) 847 5587 – www.worldservicerestaurant.com – Fax (0115) 847 5584 – Closed 1-7 January CZ**n**

Rest – Menu £ 18 (lunch Monday-Saturday)/21 (Sunday) – Carte £ 32/38

◆ Spacious Georgian mansion close to castle, with chic glass tanks containing Eastern artefacts and huge ceiling squares with vivid silks. Effective, tasty fusion food.

XX **MemSaab** — AC VISA AE

12-14 Maid Marian Way ✉ NG1 6HS – ✆ (0115) 957 0009 – www.mem-saab.co.uk – Closed 25 December CY**n**

Rest – Indian – *(dinner only)* Carte £ 23/35

◆ Vast city centre restaurant with smart mix of traditional Indian furnishings and modern, contemporary styling. Authentic Indian cooking centres around the chefs' regional backgrounds.

XX **1877** — VISA AE

128 Derby Road ✉ NG1 5FB – ✆ (0115) 958 8008 – www.restaurant1877.com – Closed Sunday and Monday CY**a**

Rest – Menu £ 17/23 – Carte £ 29/37

◆ Elegant, personally run restaurant set over 3 floors, with chandeliers and views of the city. Frequently changing menu of tasty, modern cooking, using seasonal, local produce.

X **4550 Miles from Delhi** — AC VISA AE

41 Mount St ✉ NG1 6HE – ✆ (0115) 947 5111 – www.milesfromdelhi.com – Fax (0115) 947 4555 – Closed lunch Saturday and Sunday CY**n**

Rest – Indian – Menu £ 20 (lunch) – Carte £ 16/35

◆ Stylish, up-to-date and very spacious restaurant incorporating a three storey glazed atrium and modish bar. Freshly prepared, skilfully cooked, authentic Indian cuisine.

ENGLAND

Iberico World Tapas

High Pavement ✉ NG1 1HN – ✆ (0115) 941 0410 – www.ibericotapas.com – Closed 25 December, 1 January, Sunday and Monday DZ**e**

Rest – Menu £ 10 (lunch) – Carte £ 17/21

◆ Moorish tiles and fretwork in vaults of Grade II listed building in heart of Lace Market. Tasty tapas with a twist: half the menu is Spanish, half is Asian. Relaxed, buzzy ambience.

Cock and Hoop

29-31 High Pavement ✉ NG1 1HE – ✆ (0115) 852 3231 – www.cockandhoop.co.uk DZ**a**

Rest – Carte £ 17/22

◆ Characterful 18C pub run by the next door Lace Market Hotel. Printed and blackboard menus offer sandwiches and all the traditional pub favourites, in satisfying portions.

at Plumtree Southeast : 5.75 mi. by A 60 - BZ - off A 606 – ✉ Nottingham

Perkins

Old Railway Station, Station Rd ✉ NG12 5NA – ✆ (0115) 937 3695 – www.perkinsrestaurant.co.uk – Fax (0115) 937 6405 – Closed 2-17 January and Sunday dinner

Rest – Menu £ 16 (Monday-Saturday lunch)/20 (Monday-Thursday dinner) – Carte £ 27/35

◆ Longstanding restaurant named after owners; once a railway station. Dine in conservatory or relax in bar, a former waiting room. Classical cooking makes use of local ingredients.

at Sherwood Business Park Northwest : 10 mi. by A 611 - AY - off A 608 – ✉ Nottingham

Dakota

rm,

Lakeview Drive ✉ NG15 0DA – ✆ (01623) 727 670 – www.dakotanottingham.co.uk – Fax (01623) 727 677

92 rm – †£ 69/150 ††£ 69/150, ☕ £ 11

Rest ***Grill*** – Carte £ 23/37

◆ Hard-to-miss hotel just off the M1 - it's a big black cube! Lobby with plush sofas, bookshelves and Dakota aircraft montage. Spacious rooms with kingsize beds and plasma TVs. Modern British grill style menus.

at Stapleford Southwest : 5.5 mi. by A 52 - AZ - ✉ Nottingham

Crème

12 Toton Lane ✉ NG9 7HA – ✆ (0115) 939 7422 – www.cremerestaurant.co.uk – Fax (0115) 939 7453 – Closed 26 December-7 January, Monday, Saturday lunch and Sunday dinner

Rest – Menu £ 15 – Carte Saturday dinner £ 15/29

◆ Smart, well run restaurant offering well-presented, modern British cooking served by friendly staff. Long lounge area with comfy sofas; airy, formally-laid dining room.

NUNEATON – Warwickshire – 503 P26 – pop. 70 721 **19** D2

London 102 mi. – Birmingham 25 mi. – Coventry 17 mi.

Leathermill Grange

Leathermill Lane, Caldecote, Northwest : 3.5 mi. by B 4114 on B 4111 ✉ CV10 0RX – ✆ (01827) 714 637 – www.leathermillgrange.co.uk – Fax (01827) 716 422 – Closed Christmas-New Year

3 rm ☕ – †£ 60 ††£ 90

Rest – *(by arrangement, communal dining)* Menu £ 25

◆ Imposing Victorian farmhouse in peaceful rural spot. Spacious, spotless bedrooms - one four poster. Homebaking and tea on arrival. Guest lounge and conservatory with garden view. Meals homecooked on Aga use fruit and vegetables grown in garden. Fine tableware.

ENGLAND

OAKHAM – Rutland – 502 R25 – pop. 9 620 Great Britain 17 C2

London 103 mi. – Leicester 26 mi. – Northampton 35 mi. – Nottingham 28 mi.

Rutland County Museum, Catmose St (01572) 758441, museum@rutland.gov.uk

Oakham Castle★

Rutland Water★, E : by A 606 – Normanton Church★ **AC**, SE : 5 mi. by A 603 and minor road East

Barnsdale Lodge

The Avenue, Rutland Water, East : 2.5 mi. on A 606 ✉ LE15 8AH – (01572) 724 678 – www.barnsdalelodge.co.uk – Fax (01572) 724 961

44 rm – £ 85/100 £ 125/145

Rest *Restaurant* – Menu £ 15 (lunch) – Carte £ 23/38

◆ Privately owned, converted farmhouse with mature gardens. Ample, modern rooms, a large bar flagged in York stone and extensive meeting facilities in renovated stables. Flavours of the season to fore in the Restaurant.

Lord Nelson's House H. and Nicks Restaurant with rm

Market Pl ✉ LE15 6DT – (01572) 723 199 – www.nicksrestaurant.co.uk – Fax (01572) 723 199 – Closed 25 December-5 January, Sunday-Tuesday and Wednesday dinner

4 rm – £ 65/89 £ 75/115 **Rest** – Menu £ 20 – Carte £ 22/42

◆ 17C townhouse in corner of busy market square. Two wood-furnished dining rooms: one with inglenook; one overlooking the marketplace. Choose from informal brasserie or fine dining menus. Characterful, individually styled first-floor bedrooms. Traditional guest areas.

ENGLAND

at Hambleton East : 3 mi. by A 606 – ✉ Oakham

Hambleton Hall

✉ LE15 8TH – (01572) 756 991 – www.hambletonhall.com – Fax (01572) 724 721

16 rm – £ 175/205 £ 310/375, £ 16.50 – 1 suite

Rest – Menu £ 26/39 – Carte £ 58/76

Spec. Guinea fowl, foie gras and ham hock terrine with piccalilli. Assiette of rabbit with barley risotto and liquorice. Chocolate and olive oil truffle with salted caramel, pistachios and baked banana.

◆ Looking over Rutland Water, a beautiful Victorian manor house with gardens, still run by its founding family. Charming period interiors and immaculate, antique filled bedrooms. Cooking is confident and continues to evolve; it is based on classic techniques but with modern touches.

Finch's Arms with rm

Ketton Rd ✉ LE15 8TL – (01572) 756 575 – www.finchsarms.co.uk – Fax (01572) 771 142

6 rm – £ 95 £ 150 **Rest** – Menu £ 15/19 – Carte £ 20/30

◆ Attractive 17C sandstone inn boasting contemporary Mediterranean-style rooms and a large terrace with beautiful Rutland Water views. Menus feature both classic and modern British dishes. Bedrooms are exceedingly stylish.

OAKSEY – Wiltshire – 503 N29 4 C1

London 98 mi. – Cirencester 8 mi. – Stroud 20 mi.

The Wheatsheaf at Oaksey

Wheatsheaf Lane ✉ SN16 9TB – (01666) 577 348 – www.thecompletechef.co.uk – Closed Sunday dinner and Monday

Rest – Carte £ 19/27

◆ Popular with the locals, this traditional Cotswold-stone pub displays a constantly evolving blackboard menu of classic, flavourful and wholesome dishes, with proper puddings to follow.

OARE – Kent – 504 W30 – see Faversham

OBORNE – Dorset – 503 M31 – see Sherborne

OCKLEY – Surrey – 504 S30 — 7 D2

London 31 mi. – Brighton 32 mi. – Guildford 23 mi. – Lewes 36 mi.

Gatton Manor Hotel G. & C.C. Standon Lane, (01306) 627 555

Bryce's

Old School House, Stane St, on A 29 ✉ RH5 5TH – (01306) 627 430 – www.bryces.co.uk – Fax (01306) 628 274 – Closed 25-26 December, 1 January, and Sunday dinner in winter

Rest – Seafood – Menu £ 15 – Carte £ 31/36

◆ Contemporary bar and restaurant with copper-topped bar and high-backed leather chairs. Market-fresh seafood, simply cooked and full of flavour. Friendly team provide attentive service.

ODIHAM – Hampshire – 504 R30 – pop. 2 908 – ✉ Hook — 7 C1

London 51 mi. – Reading 16 mi. – Southampton 37 mi. – Winchester 25 mi.

St John

83 High St ✉ RG29 1LB – (01256) 702 697 – www.stjohn-restaurant.co.uk – Fax (01256) 702 697 – Closed 25 December and Sunday

Rest – Menu £ 22 (lunch) – Carte £ 26/43

◆ Refurbished and stylish restaurant boasts vivid artwork, suspended arcs of wood from the ceiling and comfy leather banquettes. Eclectic menus with classical base.

OLD BURGHCLERE – Hampshire – 504 Q29 – ✉ Newbury — 6 B1

London 77 mi. – Bristol 76 mi. – Newbury 10 mi. – Reading 27 mi.

Dew Pond

✉ RG20 9LH – (01635) 278 408 – www.dewpond.co.uk – Fax (01635) 278 580 – Closed 2 weeks Christmas-New Year, Sunday and Monday

Rest – *(dinner only)* Menu £ 32

◆ This traditionally decorated cottage, set in fields and parkland, overlooks Watership Down and houses a collection of local art. Tasty Anglo-gallic menu.

OLDHAM – Greater Manchester – 502 N23 – pop. 103 544 — 20 B2

London 212 mi. – Leeds 36 mi. – Manchester 7 mi. – Sheffield 38 mi.

v (0161) 777 3064, tourist@oldham.gov.uk

Crompton and Royton Royton High Barn, (0161) 624 2154

Werneth Garden Suburb Green Lane, (0161) 624 1190

Lees New Rd, (0161) 624 4986

Plan : see Manchester

The White Hart Inn with rm

51 Stockport Rd, Lydgate, East : 3 mi. by A 669 on A 6050 ✉ OL4 4JJ – (01457) 872 566 – www.thewhitehart.co.uk – Fax (01457) 875 190 – Closed 26 December, 1 January and Tuesday

12 rm – †£ 95 ††£ 128

Rest ***The White Hart Inn*** – see restaurant listing

Rest – *(dinner only and Sunday lunch)* Carte £ 22/35

◆ Smart, contemporary restaurant set in a pleasant pub overlooking the moors. A good value fixed price menu features carefully prepared modern British cooking. Bedrooms, named after local dignitaries, are cosy and comfortable.

Dinnerstone

99-101 High St, Uppermill, Saddleworth, East : 4 mi. on A 669 ✉ OL3 6BD – (01457) 875 544 – www.dinnerstone.co.uk – Fax (01457) 875 190 – Closed 26 December, 1 January and Monday

Rest – Carte £ 14/33

◆ Airy modern restaurant in centre of busy village with semi-open kitchen, vibrant art and relaxed feel. Large menu has Mediterranean base yet retains its Northern accent.

ENGLAND

The White Hart Inn

51 Stockport Rd, Lydgate, East : 3 mi. by A 669 on A 6050 ✉ OL4 4JJ – ✆ (01457) 872 566 – www.thewhitehart.co.uk – Fax (01457) 875 190 – Closed 26 December, 1 January, Sunday and Tuesday dinner

Rest – Menu £ 20 (Wednesday-Saturday) – Carte £ 21/35

◆ Popular pub set on the moors, with old timber, open fires, exposed brickwork and framed photos of the owner's travels. Satisfying brasserie-style classics feature local produce.

OLDSTEAD – **North Yorkshire** – **502** Q21 – **see Helmsley**

OLD WARDEN – **Beds.** – **504** S27 – **see Biggleswade**

OLTON – **W. Mids.** – **502** O26 – **see Solihull**

OMBERSLEY – **Worcestershire** – **503** N27 – **pop. 2 089** **18** B3

London 148 mi. – Birmingham 42 mi. – Leominster 33 mi.

Bishopswood Rd, ✆ (01905) 620 747

The Venture In

Main St ✉ WR9 0EW – ✆ (01905) 620 552 – Fax (01905) 620 552 – Closed 1 week Christmas, 2 weeks February, 2 weeks August, Sunday dinner and Monday

Rest – Menu £ 26/36

◆ Charming, restored Tudor inn, traditional from its broad inglenook to its fringed Victorian lights. Modern, flavourful menu, well judged and locally sourced. Friendly staff.

ORFORD – **Suffolk** – **504** Y27 – **pop. 1 153** – ✉ **Woodbridge** **15** D3

London 103 mi. – Ipswich 22 mi. – Norwich 52 mi.

The Crown and Castle

✉ IP12 2LJ – ✆ (01394) 450 205 – www.crownandcastle.co.uk – Closed 3-6 January

19 rm – †£ 99 ††£ 155/205 – 1 suite

Rest The Trinity – see restaurant listing

◆ 19C redbrick hotel standing proudly next to 12C Orford Castle. Retro-styled bar. Stylish modern rooms, some facing the Ness; best rooms are in the garden wing.

The Trinity – at The Crown and Castle Hotel

✉ IP12 2LJ – ✆ (01394) 450 205 – www.crownandcastle.co.uk – Closed 3-6 January

Rest – *(booking essential)* Carte £ 28/33

◆ Relaxed, stylish restaurant featuring brick fireplaces, abstract artwork and red banquettes. Classic combinations make vibrant use of local produce. Friendly service.

OSMOTHERLEY – **North Yorkshire** – **502** Q20 – **pop. 1 217** – ✉ **Northallerton** **22** B1

London 245 mi. – Darlington 25 mi. – Leeds 49 mi. – Middlesbrough 20 mi.

The Golden Lion with rm

6 West End ✉ DL6 3AA – ✆ (01609) 883 526 – www.goldenlionosmotherley.co.uk – Closed 25 December, lunch Monday and Tuesday

3 rm – †£ 60 ††£ 90 **Rest** – Carte £ 20/24

◆ Set in a delightful village, with a warm, rustic, fire-lit interior. Staff make you feel instantly at ease; unpretentious, classic cooking leaves you relaxed, sated and satisfied. Modern bedrooms have good showers.

OSWESTRY – **Shropshire** – **502** K25 – **pop. 16 660** **18** A1

London 182 mi. – Chester 28 mi. – Shrewsbury 18 mi.

Mile End Services ✆ (01691) 662488, oswestrytourism@shropshire.gov.uk

Aston Park, ✆ (01691) 610 535

Llanymynech Pant, ✆ (01691) 830 983

The Walls

Welsh Walls ✉ SY11 1AW – ✆ (01691) 670 970 – www.the-walls.co.uk – Fax (01691) 653 820 – Closed 1 January

Rest – Carte £ 23/33

◆ Built in 1841 as a school; now a buzzy restaurant. High ceiling with wooden rafters; original wood flooring. Friendly atmosphere. Varied menu offers some adventurous options.

at Trefonen Southwest : 2.5 mi. on Trefonen rd – ✉ Oswestry

The Pentre

Southwest : 1.75 mi. by Treflach rd off New Well Lane ✉ SY10 9EE – ✆ (01691) 653 952 – www.thepentre.com – Closed 1 week Christmas

3 rm – †£ 40/50 ††£ 66/72

Rest – *(by arrangement, communal dining)* Menu £ 23

◆ Restored 16C farmhouse with superb views over Tanat Valley. Heavily timbered inglenook and wood-burning stove in lounge. Sloping floors enhance rooms of tremendous character. Home-cooked dinners served with fellow guests.

at Rhydycroesau West : 3.25 mi. on B 4580 – ✉ Oswestry

Pen-Y-Dyffryn Country H.

✉ SY10 7JD – ✆ (01691) 653 700 – www.peny.co.uk – Closed 2-15 January

12 rm – †£ 85 ††£ 114/164

Rest – *(dinner only) (booking essential for non-residents)* Menu £ 35

◆ Peaceful 19C listed rectory in five-acre informal gardens near Offa's Dyke. Cosy lounge, friendly ambience; good-sized, individually styled rooms, four in the coach house. Home-cooked dishes utilising organic ingredients.

OULTON BROAD – Suffolk – 504 Z26 – see Lowestoft

OUNDLE – Northamptonshire – 504 S26 – pop. 5 219 17 C3
– ✉ Peterborough

London 89 mi. – Leicester 37 mi. – Northampton 30 mi.

14 West St ✆ (01832) 274333, oundletic@east-northamptonshire.gov.uk

Benefield Rd, ✆ (01832) 273 267

at Fotheringhay North : 3.75 mi. by A 427 off A 605 – ✉ Peterborough (cambs.)

Castle Farm without rest

✉ PE8 5HZ – ✆ (01832) 226 200 – www.castlefarm-guesthouse.co.uk

5 rm – †£ 40/43 ††£ 70/75

◆ Large 19C wisteria-clad former farmhouse, with lawned gardens leading down to the river. Comfy open-fired lounge with country views and traditionally styled bedrooms; two are in the wing.

The Falcon Inn

✉ PE8 5HZ – ✆ (01832) 226 254 – www.thefalcon-inn.co.uk – Fax (01832) 226 046

Rest – Carte £ 25/40

◆ Attractive ivy-clad inn with neat garden and terrace, set in a pretty village. Good-sized menus include unusual combinations and some interesting modern takes on traditional dishes.

OVERSTRAND – Norfolk – 504 Y25 – see Cromer

OVINGTON – Hants. – see Winchester

ENGLAND

OXFORD – Oxfordshire – **503** Q28 – **pop. 143 016** Great Britain **10** B2

London 59 mi. – Birmingham 63 mi. – Brighton 105 mi. – Bristol 73 mi.

Access Swinford Bridge (toll)

to Abingdon Bridge (Salter Bros. Ltd) (summer only) daily (2 h)

15-16 Broad St ✆ (01865) 252200, tic@oxford.gov.uk

City★★★ - Christ Church★★ (Hall★★ **AC**, Tom Quad★, Tom Tower★, Cathedral★ **AC** - Choir Roof★) BZ – Merton College★★ **AC** BZ - Magdalen College★★ BZ – Ashmolean Museum★★ BY **M1** – Bodleian Library★★ (Ceiling★★, Lierne Vaulting★) **AC** BZ **A1** – St John's College★ BY - The Queen's College★ BZ – Lincoln College★ BZ - Trinity College (Chapel★) BY – New College (Chapel★) **AC**, BZ – Radcliffe Camera★ BZ **P1** – Sheldonian Theatre★ **AC**, BZ **T** – University Museum of National History★ BY **M4** – Pitt Rivers Museum★ BY **M3**

Iffley Church★ AZ **A**. Woodstock : Blenheim Palace★★★ (Park★★★) **AC**, NW : 8 mi. by A 4144 and A 34 AY

Plans pages 567, 568

Randolph

Beaumont St ✉ OX1 2LN – ✆ (0844) 879 91 32 – www.macdonaldhotels.co.uk – Fax (01865) 791 678 BY**n**

142 rm – £ 119/275 £ 129/275, £ 13.50 – 9 suites

Rest *The Restaurant at the Randolph* – ✆ (0870) 400 82 00 *(dinner only and lunch Saturday and Sunday)* Menu £ 30 – Carte £ 33/44

◆ Grand Victorian edifice. Lounge bar: deep burgundy, polished wood and chandeliers. Handsome rooms in a blend of rich fabrics; some, more spacious, have half-tester beds. Spacious, linen-clad Restaurant.

Malmaison

3 Oxford Castle ✉ OX1 1AY – ✆ (01865) 268 400 – www.malmaison.com – Fax (01865) 268 402 BZ**a**

91 rm – £ 170/240 £ 170/240, £ 13.95 – 3 suites

Rest *Brasserie* – Menu £ 14/16 – Carte £ 27/38

◆ Unique accommodation by castle: this was a prison from 13C to 1996! Former visitors' room now moody lounge. Stunning rooms in converted cells or former house of correction! Brasserie in old admin area: modern British menu with fine French edge.

Old Bank

92-94 High St ✉ OX1 4BN – ✆ (01865) 799 599 – www.oldbank-hotel.co.uk – Fax (01865) 799 598 BZ**s**

41 rm – £ 170/210 £ 185/350, £ 12.95 – 1 suite

Rest *Quod* – ✆ (01865) 202 505 – Menu £ 13 (weekday lunch)/25 – Carte £ 23/37

◆ Elegantly understated, clean-lined interiors and the neo-Classical façade of the city's first bank - an astute combination. Rooms in modern wood and leather. Lively Italian-influenced brasserie.

Old Parsonage

1 Banbury Rd ✉ OX2 6NN – ✆ (01865) 310 210 – www.oldparsonage-hotel.co.uk – Fax (01865) 311 262 BY**e**

30 rm – £ 125/210 £ 125/210, £ 14

Rest – Menu £ 17 (weekday lunch) – Carte (Saturday-Sunday lunch and dinner) £ 30/38

◆ Discreet address with airy, minimalist feel. Characterful guest areas include a library, richly coloured bar-lounge and terrace. Some of the stylish bedrooms boast balconies/gardens. Afternoon tea is followed by contemporary Mediterranean dinner: jazz on Fridays.

Remont without rest

367 Banbury Rd ✉ OX2 7PL – ✆ (01865) 311 020 – www.remont-oxford.co.uk – Fax (01865) 552 080 – Closed 16 December-10 January AY**c**

25 rm – £ 84/119 £ 138

◆ Stylish hotel on outskirts of city. Crisp, contemporary bedrooms; superior rooms have sofas; rear room quietest. Light, airy breakfast room with buffet counter overlooks garden.

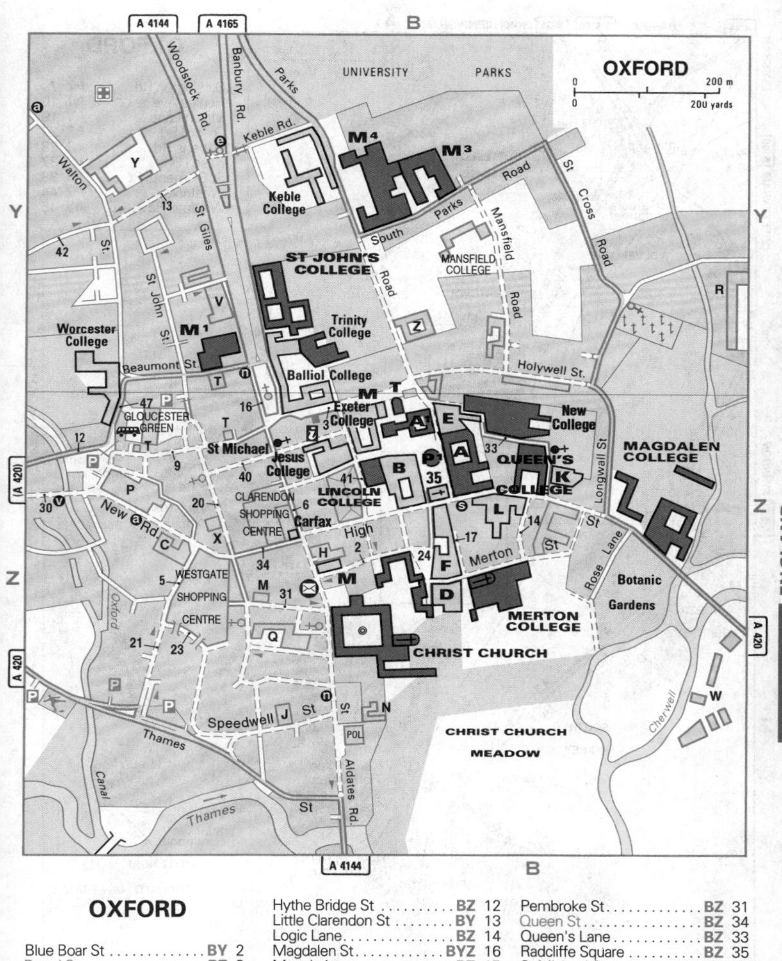

OXFORD

Blue Boar St	BY	2
Broad St	BZ	3
Castle St	BZ	5
Clarendon Shopping Centre	BZ	
Cornmarket St	BZ	6
George St	BZ	9
High St	BZ	
Hythe Bridge St	BZ	12
Little Clarendon St	BY	13
Logic Lane	BZ	14
Magdalen St	BYZ	16
Magpie Lane	BZ	17
New Inn Hall St	BZ	20
Norfolk St	BZ	21
Old Greyfriars St	BZ	23
Oriel Square	BZ	24
Park End St	BZ	30
Pembroke St	BZ	31
Queen St	BZ	34
Queen's Lane	BZ	33
Radcliffe Square	BZ	35
St Michael St	BZ	40
Turl St	BZ	41
Walton Crescent	BY	42
Westgate Shopping Centre	BZ	
Worcester St	BZ	47

COLLEGES

All Souls	BZ	A
Balliol	BY	
Brasenose	BZ	B
Christ Church	BZ	
Corpus Christi	BZ	D
Exeter	BZ	
Hertford	BZ	E
Jesus	BZ	
Keble	BY	
Lady Margaret Hall	AY	Z
Linacre	BZ	N
Lincoln	BZ	
Magdalen	BZ	
Mansfield	BY	
Merton	BZ	
New	BZ	
Nuffield	BZ	P
Oriel	BZ	F
Pembroke	BZ	Q
Queen's	BZ	
St Anne's	AY	K
St Anthony's	AY	L
St Catherine's	BY	R
St Cross	BY	V
St Edmund Hall	BZ	K
St Hilda's	BZ	W
St Hugh's	AY	P
St John's	BY	
St Peter's	BZ	X
Sommerville	BY	Y
Trinity	BY	
University	BZ	L
Wadham	BY	Z
Wolfson	AY	X
Worcester	BY	

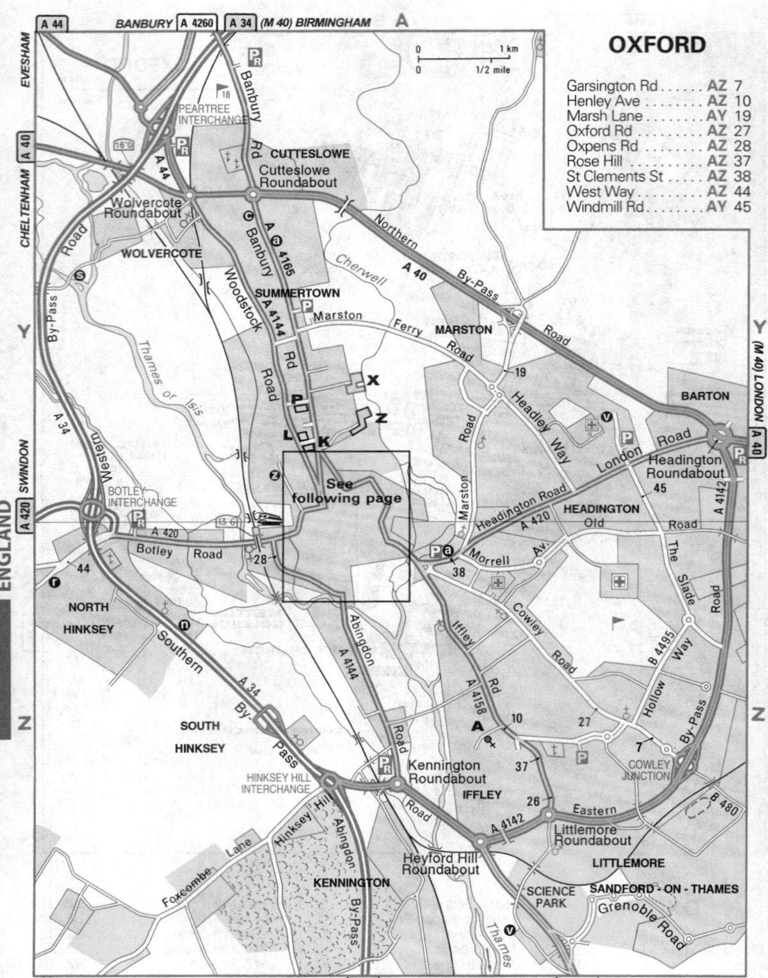

Burlington House without rest

374 Banbury Rd ✉ OX2 7PP – ☎ (01865) 513 513 – www.burlington-house.co.uk – Fax (01865) 311 785 – Closed 20 December-2 January AY**a**

12 rm – †£ 65/87 ††£ 85/110

◆ Handsome former merchant's house dating from 1889, with smart lounge, Japanese courtyard and modern bedrooms (compact singles). Breakfast includes homemade bread and granola, served on blue china.

Cotswold House without rest

363 Banbury Rd ✉ OX2 7PL – ☎ (01865) 310 558 – www.cotswoldhouse.co.uk – Fax (01865) 310 558 AY**c**

8 rm – †£ 62/72 ††£ 90/120

◆ Modern, Cotswold stone house, hung with baskets of flowers in summer. Affordable, spotless en suite rooms in pretty, traditional style; friendly ambience. Non smoking.

XX **4550 Miles from Delhi** VISA MC AE

40-41 Park End St ✉ – ✆ (01865) 244 922 – www.milesfromdelhi.com/oxford – Closed lunch Saturday and Sunday BZ**v**

Rest – Indian – Menu £ 20 (lunch) – Carte £ 16/35

◆ Capacious restaurant with open kitchen and friendly staff. Fantastic choice includes sizzling Tandoori specialities, Tawa dishes from the Punjab and good vegetarian selection.

XX **Shanghai 30's** VISA MC AE

82 St Aldates ✉ OX1 1RA – ✆ (01865) 242 230 – www.shanghai30s.com – Fax (01865) 790 219 – Closed Monday lunch BZ**n**

Rest – Chinese – Carte £ 11/23

◆ Colonial-style restaurant in characterful 15C building; sit in more intimate wood panelled room. Menu focuses on fiery Sichuan and Shanghainese cooking. Friendly, eager staff.

X **Brasserie Blanc** A/C VISA MC AE

71-72 Walton St ✉ OX2 6AG – ✆ (01865) 510 999 – www.brasserieblanc.com – Fax (01865) 510 700 – Closed 25 December AY**z**

Rest – French – Menu £ 14/18 – Carte £ 19/41

◆ Busy, informal brasserie; striking interior and sharp service. Good value menus focus on French country cooking; with dishes like Toulouse sausage and mash or beef Bourguignon.

X **Branca** A/C VISA MC AE

111 Walton St ✉ OX2 6AJ – ✆ (01865) 556 111 – www.branca-restaurants.com – Fax (01865) 556 501 BY**a**

Rest – Italian – Carte £ 22/28

◆ Modern restaurant with casual, friendly feel and minimalist décor. Vibrant, simple, fresh Italian influenced dishes: antipasti taster plates, pasta and pizza are specialities.

ENGLAND

X **Fishers** A/C VISA MC AE

36-37 St Clements ✉ OX4 1AB – ✆ (01865) 243 003 – www.fishers-restaurant.com – Closed 25-26 December and 1 January

Rest – Seafood – Menu £ 20 – Carte £ 24/33 AZ**a**

◆ Well-established seafood restaurant on eastern side of city, with paper-topped tables, rustic décor and lively, informal atmosphere. Daily changing menus; friendly service.

The Black Boy P VISA MC AE

91 Old High St, Headington ✉ OX3 9HT – ✆ (01865) 741 137 – www.theblackboy.uk.com – Closed 24 December to 31 December, Sunday dinner and Monday AY**v**

Rest – Carte £ 18/23

◆ Sizeable pub just off Headington village serving sensibly priced pub classics with a French edge. Homemade breads and pizzas; popular Sunday roasts. Thursday jazz night.

at Stanton St John Northeast : 5.5 mi. by A 420 and Barton crematorium rd on B 4027 – ✉ Oxford

The Talkhouse with rm P VISA MC AE

Wheatley Rd ✉ OX33 1EX – ✆ (01865) 351 648 – www.talkhouse.co.uk

4 rm – †£ 65 ††£ 75

Rest – Menu £ 12 – Carte £ 22/35

◆ Characterful, part-thatched Cotswold stone pub with spacious patio. Sizeable menu ranges from pub classics to more elaborate offerings; excellent desserts and homemade ice cream. Comfy, cottage-style bedrooms are set across the courtyard.

Good food and accommodation at moderate prices? Look for the Bib symbols: red Bib Gourmand for food, blue Bib Hotel for accommodation.

at Sandford-on-Thames Southeast : 5 mi. by A 4158 – ✉ Oxford

Oxford Thames Four Pillars
rm, rest,

Henley Rd ✉ OX4 4GX – ✆ (01865) 334 444 – www.four-pillars.co.uk – Fax (01865) 777 372 AZ**v**

62 rm – 🛉£ 110/160 🛉🛉£ 140/190

Rest ***The River Room*** – *(Closed Saturday lunch)* Carte £ 27/33 **s**

◆ Modern sandstone hotel set in 30 acres of peaceful parkland leading to the Thames. Bright Connoisseur rooms are the best; some have garden views and balconies. Lovely pool. Great outlook from The River Room, which serves both light and elaborate dishes.

at Toot Baldon Southeast : 5.5 mi. by B 480 - AZ – ✉ Oxford

The Mole Inn

✉ OX44 9NG – ✆ (01865) 340 001 – www.themoleinn.com – Fax (01865) 343 011 – Closed 25 December and 1 January

Rest – Carte £ 23/30

◆ Popular pub with pleasant terrace and beautiful landscaped gardens. Appealing menu suits all tastes and appetites. Sourcing is taken seriously, so when ingredients are gone, they're gone.

at North Hinksey Southwest : 3.5 mi. by A 420 – ✉ Oxford

Gables without rest

6 Cumnor Hill ✉ OX2 9HA – ✆ (01865) 862 153 – www.gables-guesthouse.co.uk – Fax (01865) 864 054 – Closed 22-31 December AZ**r**

5 rm – 🛉£ 55/65 🛉🛉£ 75/90

◆ Proudly run guest house with welcoming owner and thoughtful touches in its immaculately kept rooms. Relaxing conservatory looks out onto pretty garden. Flexible arrival times.

The Fishes

✉ OX2 0NA – ✆ (01865) 249 796 – www.fishesoxford.co.uk – Closed 25 December AZ**n**

Rest – Carte £ 19/40

◆ Lively, family-friendly pub with pretty riverside garden, perfect for picnics. Food is fresh, free range and available all day. Wednesday is steak night; Sunday means a roast.

at Fyfield Southwest : 6.5 mi. by A 420 AZ – ✉ Abingdon

The White Hart

Main Road ✉ OX13 5LW – ✆ (01865) 390 585 – www.whitehart-fyfield.com – Closed Sunday dinner and Monday

Rest – Menu £ 18 (lunch) – Carte £ 25/32

◆ 15C former chantry house with impressive flag-floored, vaulted dining room. Menus display honest British cooking, internationally influenced sharing boards and excellent desserts.

at Kingston Bagpuize Southwest : 7 mi. by A 420 AZ – ✉ Oxford

Fallowfields Country House

Faringdon Rd ✉ OX13 5BH – ✆ (01865) 820 416 – www.fallowfields.com – Fax (01865) 821 275

10 rm – 🛉£ 100/140 🛉🛉£ 155/170

Rest – Menu £ 15 (lunch) – Carte £ 20/51

◆ 19C manor house with lawned garden and fire-lit lounge. Spacious, individually styled bedrooms boast lovely views; most have spa baths. The elephant emblem appears throughout. Modern menus list the miles or yards the produce has travelled; much is home-grown.

at Wolvercote Northwest : 2.5 mi. by A 4144 (Woodstock Rd) on Godstow Rd

Trout Inn

195 Godstow Rd ✉ OX2 8PN – ✆ (01865) 510 930 – www.thetroutoxford.co.uk

Rest – *(booking advisable)* Carte £ 18/29 AY**s**

◆ Modernised inn of Cotswold stone made famous by Inspector Morse, with idyllic riverside location and splendid terrace. Menu offers pastas, salads, steaks, pizzas and the like.

at Great Milton Southeast : 12 mi. by A 40 off A 329 - AY – ✉ Oxford

Le Manoir aux Quat' Saisons (Raymond Blanc)

Church Rd ✉ OX44 7PD – ✆ (01844) 278 881 – www.manoir.com – Fax (01844) 278 847

25 rm – †£ 410/460 ††£ 580/640, ☕ £ 16 – 7 suites

Rest – French – Menu £ 49 (weekday lunch) **s** – Carte £ 103/115 **s**

Spec. Plancha seared lobster with red pepper and cardamom jus. Duck breast with lavender honey, pickled radish and fresh blackcurrants. Croustade pastry with caramelised apples, honey and ginger ice cream.

◆ Comfort and luxury are the cornerstones of Raymond Blanc's country house hotel which continues to evolve thanks to constant reinvestment. Sumptuous lounges and bedrooms, both classic and modern, are surrounded by delightful gardens. Unerringly precise preparation of French-inspired cuisine, using exemplary ingredients.

OXHILL – Warwickshire – **503** P27 – **pop. 303** — **19** C3

London 90 mi. – Banbury 11 mi. – Birmingham 37 mi.

Oxbourne House

✉ CV35 0RA – ✆ (01295) 688 202 – www.oxbournehouse.com

3 rm ☕ – †£ 45/60 ††£ 65/85

Rest – *(by arrangement, communal dining)* Menu £ 25

◆ Late 20C house oozing charm, individuality and fine rural views; splendid gardens. Antiques abound, complemented by the finest soft furnishings. Stylishly appointed bedrooms. Spacious dining room: plenty of ingredients grown in house grounds.

ENGLAND

PADIHAM – Lancashire – **502** N22 – **pop. 11 091** — **20** B2

London 230 mi. – Burnley 6 mi. – Clitheroe 8 mi.

at Fence Northeast : 3 mi. by A 6068 – ✉ Burnley

Fence Gate Inn

Wheatley Lane Rd ✉ BB12 9EE – ✆ (01282) 618 101 – www.fencegate.co.uk – Fax (01282) 615 432

Rest – Carte £ 21/35

Rest *The Topiary* – Carte £ 25/33

◆ Spacious 17C inn divided into two areas. Pleasant oak panelled bar offers sandwiches, gourmet pies and tasty varieties of homemade sausage; stylish brasserie boasts more ambitious fare.

PADSTOW – Cornwall – **503** F32 – **pop. 2 449** — **1** B2

London 288 mi. – Exeter 78 mi. – Plymouth 45 mi. – Truro 23 mi.

Red Brick Building, North Quay ✆ (01841) 533449, padstowtic@btconnect.com

Trevose Constantine Bay, ✆ (01841) 520 208

Town★ - Prideaux Place★

Trevone (Cornwall Coast Path★★) W : 3 mi. by B 3276 – Trevose Head★ (≤★★) W : 6 mi. by B 3276. Bedruthan Steps★, SW : 7 mi. by B 3276 – Pencarrow★, SE : 11 mi. by A 389

Plan on next page

The Metropole

Station Rd ✉ PL28 8DB – ✆ (01841) 532 486 – www.the-metropole.co.uk – Fax (01841) 532 867 BY**a**

58 rm ☕ – †£ 82/147 ††£ 184/216

Rest – *(bar lunch Monday-Saturday)* Menu £ 30 (dinner) **s**

◆ Grand 19C hotel perched above this quaint fishing town. Exceptional views of Camel Estuary. Well-furnished sitting room. Comfortable bedrooms in smart, co-ordinated style. Traditional dining; local produce.

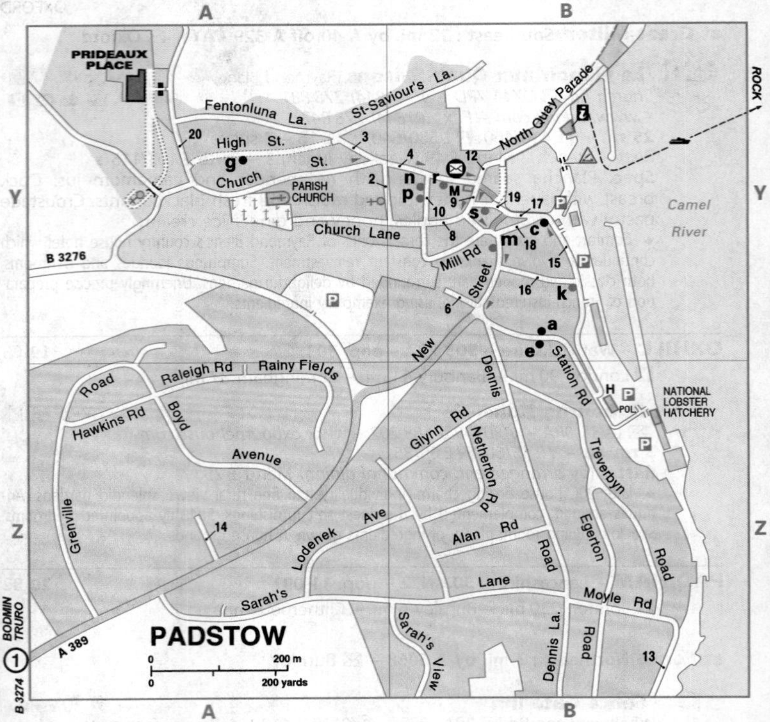

PADSTOW

Street	Grid	No.
Barry's Lane	ABY	2
Cross St	AY	3
Duke St	BY	4
Hill St	BY	6
Lanadwell St.	BY	8
Market Pl	BY	9
Middle St	BY	10
Mill Square	BY	12
Porthilly View	BZ	13
Raleigh Close	AZ	14
Riverside	BY	15
St Edmund's Lane	BY	16
South Quay	BY	17
Strand St	BY	18
The Strand	BY	19
Tregirls Lane	AY	20

Old Custom House Inn rest, VISA

South Quay ✉ PL28 8BL – ✆ (01841) 532 359 – oldcustomhousepadstow.co.uk – Fax (01841) 533 372 BY**c**

23 rm – †£ 80/115 ††£ 115/175

Rest *Pescadou* – Seafood – *(booking essential)* Carte £ 30/33

◆ Listed, slate-built former grain store and exciseman's house: spacious and comfortable throughout. Front and side rooms have views of the quayside and Camel Estuary. Seafood emphasis in bustling, glass-fronted restaurant.

Woodlands Country House without rest VISA

Treator, West : 1.25 mi. on B 3276 ✉ PL28 8RU – ✆ (01841) 532 426 – www.woodlands-padstow.co.uk – Fax (01841) 533 353 – Closed Christmas-1 February

8 rm – †£ 71/79 ††£ 122/136

◆ Personally run Victorian country house with well-kept garden. Large lounge in classic traditional style; views sweeping down to Trevone Bay. Co-ordinated bedrooms.

Treverbyn House without rest

Station Rd ✉ PL28 8DA – ✆ (01841) 532 855 – www.treverbynhouse.com – Fax (01841) 532 855 – Closed December and January BY**e**

5 rm – †£ 99 ††£ 110

◆ Something of a grand style with views of the Camel Estuary. Large rooms retain open fireplaces and have comfortable, uncluttered décor: The Turret room is the one to ask for.

ENGLAND

Althea Library without rest
27 High St ✉ PL28 8BB – ✆ (01841) 532 717 – www.althealibrary.co.uk – Fax (01841) 532 717 – Closed 22-26 December, 1-21 January and 21 August-5 September AY**g**
3 rm – ££ 92
◆ Grade II listed former school library with very friendly feel. Neat terrace; homely breakfast room/lounge with food cooked on the Aga. Cosy, individually styled beamed rooms.

The Seafood with rm
Riverside ✉ PL28 8BY – ✆ (01841) 532 700 – www.rickstein.com – Fax (01841) 532 942 – Closed dinner 24 December-lunch 27 December and 1 May
20 rm – £ 135/270 £ 135/270 BY**k**
Rest – Seafood – *(booking essential)* Menu £ 29 (lunch in winter) – Carte £ 40/52
◆ Converted granary owned by Rick Stein, with large stainless steel sushi bar, fibre optic lighting and modern artwork. Daily selection of tasty fish/seafood, from the simple to more exotic. New England style bedrooms, some with terraces, balconies and bay views.

St Petroc's with rm
4 New St ✉ PL28 8EA – ✆ (01841) 532 700 – www.rickstein.com – Fax (01841) 532 942 – Closed dinner 24 December-lunch 27 December and 1 May
10 rm – £ 135/270 £ 135/270 – 2 suites BY**m**
Rest – Seafood – *(booking essential)* Menu £ 18 (lunch in winter) – Carte £ 29/33
◆ Handsome white-fronted house on a steep hill, where confidently prepared modern dishes with local, seasonal produce take centre stage. Stylish, individual bedrooms.

ENGLAND

Paul Ainsworth at No.6
6 Middle St ✉ PL28 8AP – ✆ (01841) 532 093 – www.number6inpadstow.co.uk – Fax (01841) 532 093 – Closed 4-26 January, Sunday and Monday October-May except Bank Holidays BY**n**
Rest – Menu £ 14 (lunch) **s** – Carte £ 28/34 **s**
◆ Targeting the top end of the market, this converted cottage has striking black and white floors, early evening as well as ambitious menus featuring elaborate, complex dishes.

Custard
1A The Strand ✉ PL28 8AJ – ✆ (01841) 532 565 – www.custarddiner.com – Closed 11 January-9 February, 25-26 December, Sunday dinner and Monday October-March BY**s**
Rest – Carte £ 22/30
◆ Comfortable, homely eatery. Good value menu ranges from breakfast and afternoon tea to full 3 courses; simple, flavoursome cooking features British classics with some modern twists.

Rick Stein's Café with rm
10 Middle St ✉ PL28 8AP – ✆ (01841) 532 700 – www.rickstein.com – Fax (01841) 532 942 – Closed dinner 24 December-lunch 27 December and 1 May BY**p**
3 rm – £ 90/135 £ 90/135
Rest – *(booking essential at dinner)* Menu £ 22 (dinner) – Carte approx. £ 24
◆ Contemporary, unfussy bistro with modern, well-priced Mediterranean influenced cuisine employing the best local and seasonal ingredients. Well-appointed bedrooms.

Margot's
11 Duke St ✉ PL28 8AB – ✆ (01841) 533 441 – www.margots.co.uk – Closed January, Sunday-Monday and restricted opening Christmas-New Year
Rest – *(booking essential at dinner)* Menu £ 22/29 BY**r**
◆ Informal bistro-style restaurant with a friendly welcoming atmosphere. Varied menu capitalises on finest, fresh, local ingredients and bold, characterful flavours.

A good night's sleep without spending a fortune? Look for Bib Hotel.

at Little Petherick South : 3 mi. on A 389 – ✉ Wadebridge

Molesworth Manor without rest

✉ *PL27 7QT – ☎ (01841) 540 292 – www.molesworth.co.uk*
– Closed November-January
9 rm – †£ 65/70 ††£ 80/110
◆ Part 17C and 19C former rectory. Charming individual establishment with inviting country house atmosphere amid antique furniture and curios. Rooms furnished in period style.

Old Mill House without rest

✉ *PL27 7QT – ☎ (01841) 540 388*
– www.theoldmillhouse.com – Fax (01841) 540 406
– March-October
7 rm – †£ 80/85 ††£ 115/120
◆ Rural curios on display in a listed, family owned 16C cornmill with working water wheel. Homely, individually decorated rooms, some overlooking the millrace and neat garden.

at St Merryn West : 2.5 mi. by A 389 on B 3276 – 503 F32

Rosel & Co.

The Dog House ✉ PL28 8NF – ☎ (01841) 521 289 – www.roselandco.co.uk
– Closed January-February, Sunday and Monday
Rest – *(dinner only)* Menu £ 30
◆ Simply styled, brightly lit restaurant with chunky wooden tables, open kitchen and warm, relaxed ambience. Concise menu of precise, flavourful cooking: well-sourced ingredients used to create classic combinations with interesting modern twists.

The Cornish Arms

Churchtown ✉ PL28 8ND – ☎ (01841) 520 288
– www.rickstein.com
Rest – Carte £ 16/30
◆ A real locals pub, surprisingly leased by Rick Stein. Sound, sensibly priced cooking offer typical pub dishes and a few fish specials; and doesn't exclude the regulars. Smart terrace.

at Constantine Bay West : 4 mi. by B 3276 – ✉ Padstow

Treglos

rm, rest,

✉ *PL28 8JH – ☎ (01841) 520 727*
– www.tregloshotel.com – Fax (01841) 521 163
– Closed December-March
39 rm (dinner included) – †£ 95/170 ††£ 190/226 – 5 suites
Rest – *(bar lunch Monday-Saturday)* Menu £ 30 (dinner)
◆ An extensive, family run building surrounded by garden. Facilities include games rooms, children's play area and a lounge bar. Consistently decorated, bright, neat bedrooms. Smart attire the code in very comfortable dining room.

PAIGNTON – Torbay – 503 J32 – pop. 47 398 — 2 C2

London 226 mi. – Exeter 26 mi. – Plymouth 29 mi.
Cinema House,The Esplanade (01803) 558 383, paignton.tic@torbay.gov.uk
Torbay★ - Kirkham House★ **AC** Y **B**
Paignton Zoo★★ **AC**, SW : 0.5 mi. by A 3022 AY (see Plan of Torbay) – Cockington★, N : 3 mi. by A 3022 and minor roads

Plan of Built up Area : see Torbay

Redcliffe

rest,

4 Marine Drive ✉ TQ3 2NL – ☎ (01803) 526 397 – www.redcliffehotel.co.uk
– Fax (01803) 528 030 Y**n**
68 rm – †£ 58/120 ††£ 116/130
Rest – *(bar lunch Monday-Saturday)* Menu £ 20 – Carte £ 24/30
◆ Smoothly run family owned hotel, handily set on the seafront, a favourite of author Dick Francis. Children's play area and putting green options. Airy, pine furnished rooms. Admire the sea views from spacious, neat restaurant.

ENGLAND

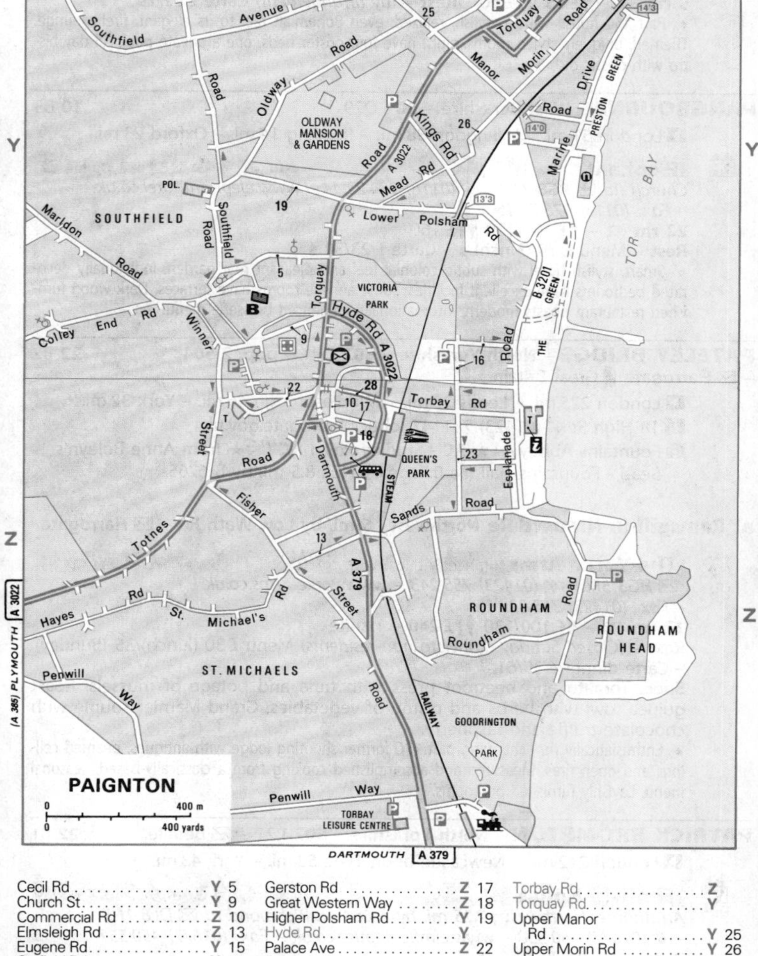

Cecil Rd	Y	5	
Church St	Y	9	
Commercial Rd	Z	10	
Elmsleigh Rd	Z	13	
Eugene Rd	Y	15	
Garfield Rd	Y	16	
Gerston Rd	Z	17	
Great Western Way	Z	18	
Higher Polsham Rd	Y	19	
Hyde Rd	Y		
Palace Ave	Z	22	
Queen's Rd	Z	23	
Torbay Rd	Z		
Torquay Rd	Y		
Upper Manor Rd	Y	25	
Upper Morin Rd	Y	26	
Victoria Rd	Z	28	

PAINSWICK – Gloucestershire – 503 N28 – pop. 1 666 Great Britain 4 C1

London 107 mi. – Bristol 35 mi. – Cheltenham 10 mi. – Gloucester 7 mi.

Town★

Cotswolds 88

Kemps Lane ✉ GL6 6YB – ☎ (01452) 813 688 – www.cotswolds88hotel.com – Fax (01452) 814 059 – Closed 4-14 January

18 rm – †£ 165/185 ††£ 295/395 **Rest** – Carte £ 24/41

◆ Stone Regency style house with neat garden and terrace. Bold stylish colours, quirky furnishings and striking fixtures abound. Eclectic bedrooms; modern bathrooms. Restaurant offers modern menu of organic produce.

Cardynham House

The Cross, by Bisley St and St Marys St ✉ *GL6 6XX – ✆ (01452) 814 006 – www.cardynham.co.uk – Fax (01452) 812 321*

9 rm – £ 65 £ 90 **Rest** – *(by arrangement)* Carte £ 22/29

◆ Part 15C house with a stylish, relaxed, even Bohemian feel to its elegant, firelit lounge. Themed, uniquely styled rooms: eight have four-poster beds, one a private pool. All day bistro with classic dishes.

PANGBOURNE – **West Berkshire** – **504** Q29 **10** B3

London 51 mi. – Hillingdon 38 mi. – Reading 14 mi. – Oxford 23 mi.

Elephant

Church Rd ✉ *RG8 7AR – ✆ (0118) 984 22 44 – www.elephanthotel.co.uk – Fax (0118) 976 73 46*

22 rm – £ 100/120 £ 160

Rest – Menu £ 10 (lunch) **s** – Carte £ 23/30 **s**

◆ Smart, stylish hotel with subtle colonial feel and pleasant rear garden. Individually decorated bedrooms have excellent facilities; some annexe rooms have terraces. Dark wood furnished restaurant boasts modern, internationally influenced brasserie menu.

PATELEY BRIDGE – **North Yorkshire** – **502** O21 – **pop. 2 504** **22** B2
– ✉ **Harrogate** Great Britain

London 225 mi. – Leeds 28 mi. – Middlesbrough 46 mi. – York 32 mi.

18 High St ✆ (01423) 711147, pbtic@harrogate.gov.uk

Fountains Abbey★★★ **AC** - Studley Royal **AC** (<★ from Anne Boleyn's Seat) - Fountains Hall (Fa 0.5ade★), NE : 8.5 mi. by B 6265

at Ramsgill-in-Nidderdale **Northwest : 5 mi. by Low Wath Rd** – ✉ **Harrogate**

The Yorke Arms (Frances Atkins) with rm

✉ *HG3 5RL – ✆ (01423) 755 243 – www.yorke-arms.co.uk – Fax (01423) 755 330*

12 rm – £ 100/130 £ 240 – 1 suite

Rest – *(Closed Sunday dinner to non-residents)* Menu £ 30 (lunch)/35 (Sunday) – Carte dinner £ 35/61

Spec. Tomato and beetroot press with tuna and potage of mussels. Roast guinea fowl with herbs and pistou of vegetables. Grand Marnier soufflé with chocolate truffle and raspberry.

◆ Enthusiatically run, charming part 17C former shooting lodge with antiques, beamed ceilings and open fires. Measured and accomplished cooking from a classically-based, seasonal menu. Lavishly furnished bedrooms.

PATRICK BROMPTON – **North Yorkshire** – **502** P21 – ✉ **Bedale** **22** B1

London 242 mi. – Newcastle upon Tyne 58 mi. – York 43 mi.

Elmfield House

Arrathorne, Northwest : 2.25 mi. by A 684 on Richmond rd ✉ *DL8 1NE – ✆ (01677) 450 558 – www.elmfieldhouse.co.uk – Fax (01677) 450 557*

7 rm – £ 70 £ 85

Rest – *(Closed Sunday) (dinner only) (booking essential) (residents only)* Menu £ 21 **s**

◆ Spacious, neatly fitted accommodation in a peaceful, personally run hotel, set in acres of gardens and open countryside. Try your luck at the adjacent fishing lake. Tasty, home-cooked meals.

PATTISWICK – **Essex** – **see Coggeshall**

PAULERSPURY – **Northants.** – **503** R27 – **see Towcester**

PAXFORD – **Gloucestershire** – **504** O27 – **see Chipping Camden**

PEMBRIDGE – County of Herefordshire – 503 L27 18 A3

London 162 mi. – Hereford 15 mi. – Leominster 7 mi.

Lowe Farm

West : 3.25 mi. by A 44 following signs through Marston village ✉ HR6 9JD – ✆ (01544) 388 395 – www.lowe-farm.co.uk – Fax (01544) 388 395 – Closed 21-27 December

5 rm – †£ 40 ††£ 80/110 **Rest** – *(by arrangement)* Menu £ 23

◆ Working farm: farmhouse dates from 13C; renovated barn from 14C with pleasant lounge and countryside views. Rooms in house and barn are cosy, comfortable and of a good size. Dining room boasts chunky pine tables, exposed brick and beams.

PENN – Buckinghamshire – 504 R/S29 – pop. 3 779 11 D2

London 31 mi. – High Wycombe 4 mi. – Oxford 36 mi.

The Old Queens Head

Hammersley Lane ✉ HP10 8EY – ✆ (01494) 813 371 – www.oldqueensheadpenn.co.uk – Fax (01494) 816 145 – Closed 25-26 December

Rest – Carte £ 20/27

◆ Lively pub with characterful rustic feel, part-dating back to 1666; head for the old barn. Menus offer generous, hearty dishes and some appealing sides. Homemade puddings are a must.

PENRITH – Cumbria – 501 L19 – pop. 14 471 21 B2

London 290 mi. – Carlisle 24 mi. – Kendal 31 mi. – Lancaster 48 mi.

Robinsons School, Middlegate ✆ (01768) 867466, pen.tic@eden.gov.uk - Rheged, Redhills, Penrith ✆ (01768) 860034, tic@rheged.com

Salkeld Rd, ✆ (01768) 891 919

Brooklands without rest

2 Portland Place ✉ CA11 7QN – ✆ (01768) 863 395 – www.brooklandsguesthouse.com – Fax (01768) 863 395 – Closed 2 weeks December-January

7 rm – †£ 35/60 ††£ 80

◆ Traditonal Victorian terraced house a minute's walk from the shops: many original features restored. Pleasantly furnished breakfast room. Locally made pine enhances bedrooms.

at Yanwath Southwest : 2.5 mi. by A 6 on B 5320 – ✉ Penrith

The Yanwath Gate Inn

✉ CA10 2LF – ✆ (01768) 862 386 – www.yanwathgate.com – Closed 25 December

Rest – Menu £ 14 (weekday lunch) – Carte £ 20/40

◆ Originally a toll gate, this is now a cosy pub. Cooking is carefully balanced and displays finesse, without being showy; everything is homemade and local produce is paramount.

at Newbiggin West : 3.5 mi. by A 66 – ✉ Penrith

The Old School

✉ CA11 0HT – ✆ (01768) 483 709 – www.theold-school.com – Fax (01768) 483 709 – Closed 1 week Christmas and 2 weeks spring

3 rm – †£ 35/55 ††£ 70/75

Rest – *(by arrangement, communal dining)* Menu £ 20

◆ Well sited off two major roads, this 19C former school house has been tastefully converted with an open-fired lounge and rooms individually decorated to a high standard.

at Temple Sowerby East : 6.75 mi. by A 66 – ✉ Penrith

Temple Sowerby House

✉ CA10 1RZ – ✆ (01768) 361 578 – www.templesowerby.com – Fax (01768) 361 958 – Closed 21-29 December

12 rm – †£ 90/120 ††£ 140/170 **Rest** – *(dinner only)* Menu £ 40

◆ Listed building with Georgian frontage, run with enthusiasm and charm. Refurbished bedrooms are stylishly decorated and include spa baths and body jet showers. Dining room overlooks walled garden. Menu offers concise, modern selection, cooked using fine seasonal produce.

ENGLAND

at Clifton Southeast : 3 mi on A6

George and Dragon with rm
✉ CA10 2ER – ✆ (01768) 865 381
– www.georgeanddragonclifton.co.uk
10 rm – ♦£ 64 ♦♦£ 125 **Rest** – Carte £ 21/35
◆ 18C coaching inn belonging to local landowners, the Lowther family. Simple, effective cooking; organic meats, seasonal game and vegetables come fresh from the surrounding Estate. Comfortable, modern bedrooms are decorated in bold colours.

PENZANCE – Cornwall – 503 D33 – pop. 20 255 1 A3

London 319 mi. – Exeter 113 mi. – Plymouth 77 mi. – Taunton 155 mi.

Access Access to the Isles of Scilly by helicopter, British International Heliport (01736) 364296, Fax (01736) 363871

to the Isles of Scilly (Hugh Town) (Isles of Scilly Steamship Co. Ltd) (summer only) (approx. 2 h 40 mn)

Station Rd ✆ (01736) 362 207, penzancetic@cornwall.gov.uk

Town★ - Outlook★★★ – Western Promenade (≤★★★) YZ – National Lighthouse Centre★ **AC** Y – Chapel St★ Y – Maritime Museum★ **AC** Y **M1** – Penlee House Gallery and Museum★, **AC**

St Buryan★★ (church tower★★), SW : 5 mi. by A 30 and B 3283 - Penwith★★ – Trengwainton Garden★★, NW : 2 mi. – Sancreed - Church★★ (Celtic Crosses★★) - Carn Euny★, W : 3.5 mi. by A 30 Z – St Michael's Mount★★ (≤★★), E : 4 mi. by B 3311 - Y - and A 30 – Gulval★ (Church★), NE : 1 mi. - Ludgvan★ (Church★), NE : 3.5 mi. by A 30 - Chysauster Village★, N : 3.5 mi. by A 30, B 3311 and minor rd – Newlyn★ - Pilchard Works★, SW : 1.5 mi. by B 3315 Z - Lanyon Quoit★, NW : 3.5 mi. by St Clare Street – Men-an-Tol★, NW : 5 mi. by B 3312 - Madron Church★, NW : 1.5 mi. by St Clare Street Y. Morvah (≤★★), NW : 6.5 mi. by St Clare Street Y – Zennor (Church★), NW : 6 mi. by B 3311 Y – Prussia Cove★, E : 8 mi. by B 3311 - Y - and A 394 – Land's End★ (cliff scenery★★★), SW : 10 mi. by A 30 Z – Porthcurno★, SW : 8.5 mi. by A 30, B 3283 and minor rd

Hotel Penzance ≤ AC rest, P VISA MC AE
Britons Hill ✉ *TR18 3AE – ✆ (01736) 363 117*
– www.hotelpenzance.com – Fax (01736) 350 970
– Closed 2-15 January Yc
25 rm – ♦£ 80/140 ♦♦£ 175/180
Rest ***Bay*** – ✆ (01736) 366 890 *(Closed Saturday lunch) (booking essential for non-residents)* Menu £ 16/29 – Carte £ 33/47
◆ Adjoining Edwardian merchants' houses, overlooking the bay and St Michael's Mount. Several lounges, pleasant garden terrace and outdoor pool. Mix of classic and contemporary bedrooms. Menus highlight local produce – every third Sunday, lunch comes from within 25 miles.

The Abbey without rest P VISA MC AE
Abbey St ✉ *TR18 4AR – ✆ (01736) 366 906 – www.theabbeyonline.co.uk*
– Closed January Yu
6 rm – ♦£ 75/120 ♦♦£ 150/210 – 2 suites
◆ Powder blue painted 17C house with lovely Victorian gardens. Attractive antique furnishings include historical pictures. Country house atmosphere and characterful bedrooms.

Beachfield ≤ VISA MC AE
The Promenade ✉ *TR18 4NW – ✆ (01736) 362 067*
– www.beachfield.co.uk – Fax (01736) 331 100
– Closed Christmas-New Year Za
18 rm – ♦£ 55/85 ♦♦£ 119/139
Rest – *(dinner only)* Menu £ 23 – Carte £ 21/31
◆ Classic seaside hotel with good views. Well-kept public areas include traditional lounge. Comfy bedrooms are well maintained and have a neat, bright feel. Traditional, varied menus, featuring fish specials.

ENGLAND

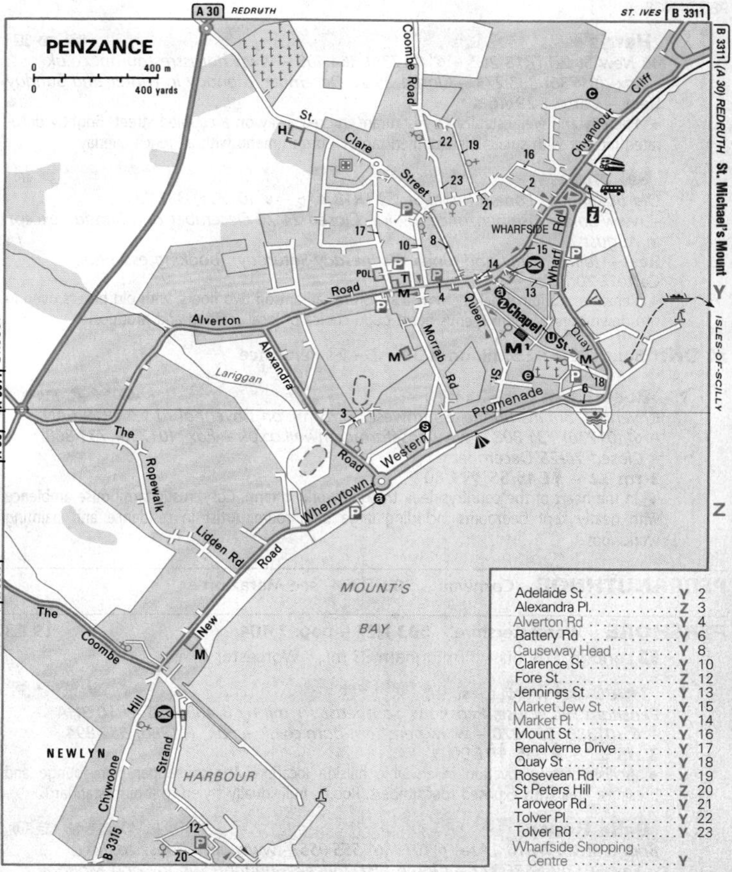

PENZANCE

Street	Grid	No.
Adelaide St	Y	2
Alexandra Pl.	Z	3
Alverton Rd	Y	4
Battery Rd	Y	6
Causeway Head	Y	8
Clarence St	Y	10
Fore St	Z	12
Jennings St	Y	13
Market Jew St	Y	15
Market Pl.	Y	14
Mount St	Y	16
Penalverne Drive	Y	17
Quay St	Y	18
Rosevean Rd	Y	19
St Peters Hill	Z	20
Taroveor Rd	Y	21
Tolver Pl.	Y	22
Tolver Rd	Y	23
Wharfside Shopping Centre	Y	

Chy-An-Mor without rest
15 Regent Terrace ✉ TR18 4DW – ✆ (01736) 363 441 – www.chyanmor.co.uk – Closed December-February Ye
9 rm – £ 38/42 £ 78/90
◆ Located on a terrace of houses overlooking the promenade. Thoroughly well kept throughout. Comfy, well-furnished bedrooms. Wake up to a good choice at breakfast.

The Summer House
Cornwall Terrace ✉ TR18 4HL – ✆ (01736) 363 744 – www.summerhouse-cornwall.com – Fax (01736) 360 959 – April-October Zs
5 rm – £ 110/150 £ 120/150
Rest – *(by arrangement)* Menu £ 35
◆ There's a friendly atmosphere to this listed Regency House in bright blues and yellows. Pleasant patio garden. Residents can enjoy Mediterranean influenced cooking.

The sun's out? Then enjoy eating outside on the terrace:

XX **Harris's**

46 New St ✉ TR18 2LZ – ☎ (01736) 364 408 – www.harrissrestaurant.co.uk – Fax (01736) 333 273 – Closed 25-26 December, Monday in winter and Sunday

Rest – Carte £ 29/46 **s** Y**a**

◆ Friendly and well-established restaurant, tucked away on a cobbled street. Brightly decorated interior with smart linen clothed tables. Cornish menu with a French overlay.

X **Bakehouse**

Old Bakehouse Lane, Chapel St ✉ TR18 4AE – ☎ (01736) 331 331 – www.bakehouse-penzance.co.uk – Closed 24-26 December and Sunday except in August Y**z**

Rest – *(dinner only and lunch Wednesday-Saturday) (booking essential)* Carte £ 20/38

◆ Penzance's original bakery, now a stylish restaurant on two floors, with old bakers oven in situ downstairs. Modern menus boast good choice of local seafood and produce.

at Drift Southwest : 2.5 mi. on A 30 - Z – ✉ Penzance

Rose Farm without rest

Chyenhal, Buryas Bridge, Southwest : 0.75 mi. on Chyenhal rd ✉ TR19 6AN – ☎ (01736) 731 808 – www.rosefarmcornwall.co.uk – Fax (01736) 731 808 – Closed 24-25 December

3 rm – †£ 45/55 ††£ 80

◆ In the heart of the countryside, a tranquil working farm. Cosy, rustic farmhouse ambience with neatly kept bedrooms including large barn room. Artist in residence and painting workshops.

PERRANUTHNOE – Cornwall – 503 D33 – see Marazion

PERSHORE – Worcestershire – 503 N27 – pop. 7 104 19 C3

London 106 mi. – Birmingham 33 mi. – Worcester 8 mi.

The Barn without rest

Pensham Hill House, Pensham, Southeast : 1 mi. by B 4084 ✉ WR10 3HA – ☎ (01386) 555 270 – www.pensham-barn.co.uk – Fax (01386) 552 894

3 rm – †£ 55 ††£ 90

◆ Stylish barn renovation in enviable hillside location. Attractive open-plan lounge and breakfast area with exposed roof timbers. Rooms individually styled to a high standard.

XX **Belle House**

Bridge St ✉ WR10 1AJ – ☎ (01386) 555 055 – www.belle-house.co.uk – Fax (01386) 555 377 – Closed first 2 weeks January, Sunday and Monday

Rest – Menu £ 21/29 **s**

◆ 16C and 18C high street building with some very characterful parts, including heavily beamed bar. Accomplished cooking on modern menus using carefully sourced ingredients.

PETERBOROUGH – Peterborough – 502 T26 – pop. 136 292 14 A2

Great Britain

London 85 mi. – Cambridge 35 mi. – Leicester 41 mi. – Lincoln 51 mi.

Bridge St ☎ (01733) 452336, tic@peterborough.gov.uk

Thorpe Wood Nene Parkway, ☎ (01733) 267 701

Peterborough Milton Milton Ferry, ☎ (01733) 380 489

Orton Meadows Ham Lane, ☎ (01733) 237 478

Cathedral★★ **AC** Y

X **Jim's Bistro**

52 Broadway ✉ PE1 1SB – ☎ (01733) 341 122 – www.jimsyard.biz – Closed first week January, last week July, first week August, last week December, Sunday and Monday Y**a**

Rest – *(booking essential)* Carte £ 19/27 **s**

◆ Bright room with quirky mural, bar and open-plan kitchen; choose banquette seating under the mirror. Daily changing menu of tasty, wholesome, seasonal dishes. Friendly service.

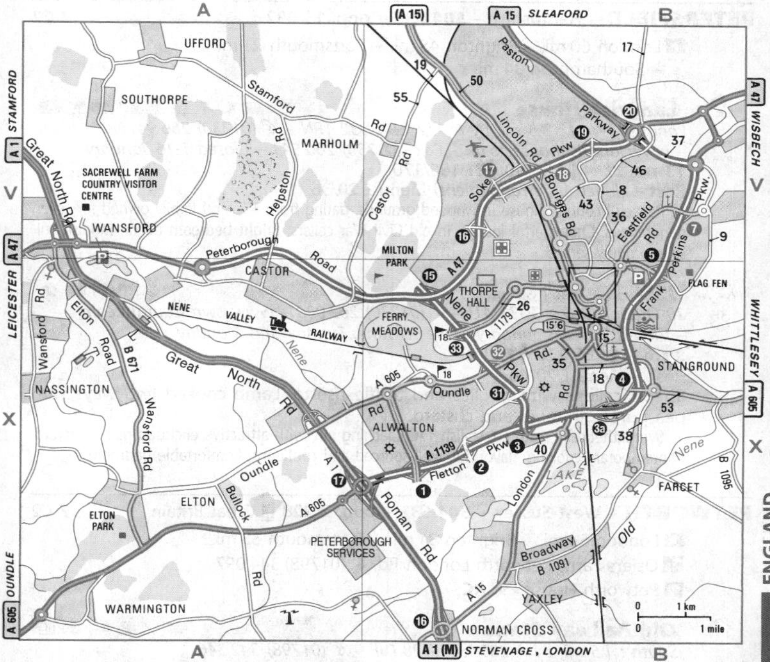

A (A 15) A 15 SLEAFORD B
UFFORD
SOUTHORPE
Stamford Rd
MARHOLM
Helpston Rd
Castor Rd
Paston Parkway
Lincoln Rd
Soke Pkw
Bourges Bd
Eastfield Rd
Frank Perkins Pkw.
A 1 STAMFORD
Great North Rd
SACREWELL FARM COUNTRY VISITOR CENTRE
WANSFORD
A 47 LEICESTER
Peterborough Road
CASTOR
MILTON PARK
A 47
THORPE HALL
Nene Pkw
A 1179
FLAG FEN
A 47 WISBECH
NENE VALLEY RAILWAY
FERRY MEADOWS
Wansford Rd
Elton Road
B 671
Great North Rd
NASSINGTON
A 605 Oundle Rd
New Rd.
London Rd
STANGROUND
WHITTLESEY A 605
ALWALTON
A 1139 Fletton Pkw
Oundle Rd
A 1
Roman Rd
ELTON
Bullock Rd
A 605
LAKE
Nene
FARCET
B 1095
ELTON PARK
PETERBOROUGH SERVICES
Broadway B 1091
Old
A 605 OUNDLE
A 15
WARMINGTON
YAXLEY
NORMAN CROSS
A 1 (M) STEVENAGE, LONDON
0 1 km
0 1 mile
V X

ENGLAND

PETERBOROUGH

Bridge St . . . . Z
Cattle Market Rd . . . . Y 2
Church St . . . . YZ
City Rd . . . . Y 3
Cowgate . . . . Y 5
Cross St. . . . . Z 6
Dogsthorpe Rd . . . . BV 8
Edgerley Drain Rd . . . . BV 9
Embankment Rd . . . . Z 12
Exchange St . . . . Y 13
Fletton Ave . . . . BX 15
Geneva St . . . . Y 16
Guntons Rd . . . . BV 17
High St . . . . BX 18
Hurn Rd . . . . BV 19
Longthorpe Parkway . . . . . . BX 26
Long Causeway . . . . Y 25
Market Way . . . . Y 28
Midgate . . . . Y 29
New Rd . . . . BX 35
Park Rd. . . . . BV 36
Paston Parkway . . . . BV 37
Peterborough Rd . . . . BX 38
Phorpres Way . . . . BX 40
Queensgate Shopping Centre . . . . Y
Rivergate . . . . Z 42
Rivergate Shopping Centre . . . . Z
St Paul's Rd . . . . BV 43
Thorpe Rd . . . . Y 45
Welland Rd . . . . BV 46
Wentworth St. . . . . Z 48
Werrington Parkway . . . . . . BV 50
Wheelyard . . . . Y 52
Whittlesey Rd . . . . BX 53
Woodcroft Rd . . . . BV 55

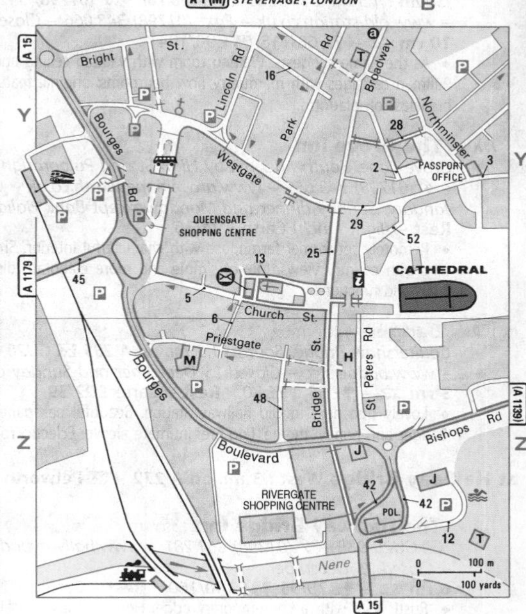

PETERSFIELD – Hampshire – 504 R30 – pop. 13 092 7 C2

London 60 mi. – Brighton 45 mi. – Portsmouth 21 mi. – Southampton 34 mi.

Langrish House

Langrish, West : 3.5 mi. by A 272 ✉ GU32 1RN – ✆ (01730) 266 941 – www.langrishhouse.co.uk – Fax (01730) 260 543 – Closed 1-16 January

13 rm – †£ 80/90 ††£ 155/170

Rest – *(lunch by arrangement)* Menu £ 20/36

◆ Peaceful country house in wooded grounds, dating from 17C and family owned for seven generations. Characterful lounge in old Civil War cellars. Bright bedroom décor. Modish cuisine, proudly served.

JSW (Jake Watkins) with rm

20 Dragon St ✉ GU31 4JJ – ✆ (01730) 262 030 – www.jswrestaurant.com – Closed 2 weeks January, 2 weeks June, Sunday and Monday

3 rm – †£ 65/110 ††£ 110

Rest – Menu £ 20/48

Spec. Scallops with girolles and truffle risotto. Lamb cooked two ways with pea purée. Rhubarb and custard.

◆ Sympathetically restored, stylish 17C coaching inn, with attractive enclosed rear courtyard. Contemporary cooking: flavourful, well-sourced and confident. Comfortable bedrooms.

ENGLAND

PETWORTH – West Sussex – 504 S31 – pop. 2 298 Great Britain 7 C2

London 54 mi. – Brighton 31 mi. – Portsmouth 33 mi.

Osiers Farm Petworth London Rd, ✆ (01798) 344 097

Petworth House★★ **AC**

Old Railway Station without rest

South : 1.5 mi. by A 285 ✉ GU28 0JF – ✆ (01798) 342 346 – www.old-station.co.uk – Fax (01798) 343 066 – Closed 24-26 December

10 rm – †£ 68/118 ††£ 90/194

◆ As the name suggests. Waiting room with vaulted ceiling and ticket office now a lounge, Pullman carriages with marquetry now bedrooms; original features abound. Cake on arrival; breakfast on platform.

The Grove Inn

Grove Lane, South : 0.5 mi. by High St and Pulborough rd ✉ GU28 0HY – ✆ (01798) 343 659 – www.groveinnpetworth.co.uk – Closed 1 week January, Sunday dinner and Monday except Bank Holiday lunch

Rest – *(light lunch)* Carte £ 24/36

◆ Remotely set former farmhouse with characterful interior. Small open-fired bar; conservatory with country views. Mix of simple and more elaborate dishes. Outside kitchen/bar for BBQs and functions.

Badgers with rm

Coultershaw Bridge, South : 1.5 mi. on A 285 ✉ GU28 0JF – ✆ (01798) 342 651 – www.badgers.cc – Closed 25 December and Sunday dinner (October to April)

3 rm – †£ 55 ††£ 80 **Rest** – Carte £ 22/39

◆ Lovely pub next to Old Railway Station. Beautiful oak panelled bar has old photos and 'badger and honey' theme. Log fire; intimate alcove. Eclectic, robust menus. Comfy rooms.

at Halfway Bridge West : 3 mi. on A 272 – ✉ Petworth

The Halfway Bridge Inn with rm

✉ GU28 9BP – ✆ (01798) 861 281 – www.halfwaybridge.co.uk – Closed 25 December

6 rm – †£ 75/95 ††£ 140/160 **Rest** – Carte £ 22/30

◆ Rustic pub with a contemporary edge. Honest, British cooking arrives in hearty, flavoursome portions; daily specials list pub classics and proper puddings. Comfortable, modern bedrooms with good bathrooms.

at Lickfold Northwest : 6 mi. by A 272 – ✉ Petworth

The Lickfold Inn
✉ GU28 9EY – ☎ (01798) 861 285 – www.evanspubs.co.uk
– Closed 25 December and Sunday dinner
Rest – Carte £ 23/42
◆ Characterful 15C red-brick pub owned by Chris Evans. Fairly ambitious restaurant style dishes and a good cheese selection. Dinner menu slightly more extensive than lunch.

PICKERING – North Yorkshire – 502 R21 – pop. 6 616 23 C1

London 237 mi. – Middlesbrough 43 mi. – Scarborough 19 mi. – York 25 mi.
The Ropery ☎ (01751) 473791, pickeringtic@btconnect.com

White Swan Inn
Market Pl ✉ YO18 7AA – ☎ (01751) 472 288 – www.white-swan.co.uk – Fax (01751) 475 554
20 rm – †£ 110/130 ††£ 145/175 – 1 suite **Rest** – Carte £ 21/38
◆ Long-standing former coaching halt in a popular market town. Lovely lounge and comfortable bedrooms - the new ones in the courtyard are very stylish with contemporary touches. Traditional dining room offers lengthy menu.

17 Burgate without rest
17 Burgate ✉ YO18 7AU – ☎ (01751) 473 463 – www.17burgate.co.uk – Fax (01751) 473 463 – Closed 19-27 December
5 rm – †£ 90 ††£ 105
◆ Painstakingly restored 17C town house, the décor smoothly spanning 400 years. Sitting room bar; sizzling breakfasts; superbly appointed rooms, two with larger seating areas.

Bramwood
19 Hall Garth ✉ YO18 7AW – ☎ (01751) 474 066 – www.bramwoodguesthouse.co.uk
8 rm – †£ 48/65 ††£ 80 **Rest** – *(by arrangement)* Menu £ 25
◆ Georgian town house with sheltered garden. Personally run with curios of rural life dotted around a firelit lounge. Cosy bedrooms in homely, cottagey style.

Old Manse
Middleton Rd ✉ YO18 8AL – ☎ (01751) 476 484 – www.oldmansepickering.co.uk – Fax (01751) 477 124 – Closed 24-30 December
10 rm – †£ 49/59 ††£ 85 **Rest** – *(by arrangement)* Menu £ 20
◆ A welcoming ambience and modestly priced rooms, spacious and spotless, make this personally run house an ideal base for touring the moors. Secluded rear garden and orchard. Informal conservatory dining room.

at Levisham Northeast : 6.5 mi. by A 169 – ✉ Pickering

The Moorlands Country House
✉ YO18 7NL – ☎ (01751) 460 229 – www.moorlandslevisham.co.uk – Fax (01751) 460 470 – March-October, minimum 2 night stay
4 rm – †£ 90/100 ††£ 130/150 **Rest** – *(by arrangement)* Menu £ 27
◆ Restored 19C house with attractive gardens in the heart of the North York Moors National Park. There are fine views to be enjoyed here. Rooms furnished to high standard. Traditional, home-cooked meals in pretty dining room.

at Sinnington Northwest : 4 mi. by A 170 – ✉ York

Fox and Hounds with rm
Main St ✉ YO62 6SQ – ☎ (01751) 431 577 – www.thefoxandhoundsinn.co.uk – Fax (01751) 432 791 – Closed 25-26 December
10 rm – †£ 49/69 ††£ 70/120 **Rest** – Carte £ 20/30
◆ Handsome and sturdy 18C coaching inn in pretty village; substantial interior has plenty of charm. Flexible menus, with local specialities the popular choice. Comfortable, cottagey bedrooms are popular at weekends.

ENGLAND

PICKHILL – North Yorkshire – 502 P21 – pop. 412 – ✉ Thirsk 22 B1

London 229 mi. – Leeds 41 mi. – Middlesbrough 30 mi. – York 34 mi.

Nags Head Country Inn

✉ YO7 4JG – ☎ (01845) 567 391 – www.nagsheadpickhill.co.uk – Fax (01845) 567 212 – Closed 25 December

14 rm – †£ 65/70 ††£ 85/95 – 1 suite **Rest** – Carte £ 18/34

◆ Atmospheric 300 year old inn in an ancient hamlet, an easy drive to Thirsk and Ripon races. Neat rooms in soft floral fabrics. Over 800 ties on display in the rustic bar. Rural restaurant adorned with bookshelves and patterned rugs.

PIDDLETRENTHIDE – Dorset – pop. 691 – ✉ DT2 4 C3

London 129 mi. – Bristol 54 mi. – Cardiff 120 mi. – Southampton 55 mi.

The European Inn with rm

South 0.5 mi. on B3143 ✉ DT2 7QT – ☎ (01300) 348 308 – www.european-inn.co.uk – Closed 1 week January-February, Sunday dinner and Monday

2 rm – †£ 55 ††£ 80 **Rest** – *(booking advisable at dinner)* Carte £ 20/29

◆ Relaxing inn loved by the locals. Concise menu features fresh, seasonal and sustainable local produce, some from the owners' nearby farm. Tasty, traditional puddings. Stylish bedrooms and a hearty breakfast.

PILLERTON PRIORS – Warks. – 503 P27 – see Stratford-upon-Avon

PILTDOWN – East Sussex – pop. 1 517 8 A2

London 41 mi. – Brighton 21 mi. – Uckfield 3 mi.

The Peacock Inn

Shortbridge ✉ TN22 3XA – ☎ (01825) 762 463 – www.peacock-inn.co.uk – Fax (01825) 762 463 – Closed 25-26 and 31 December

Rest – Carte £ 20/34

◆ 18C former alehouse, adorned with photos of celebrity visitors. Menu features straightforward pub food, including steaks and grills and often fresh fish specials.

PLUMTREE – Notts. – see Nottingham

PLYMOUTH – Plymouth – 503 H32 – pop. 243 795 2 C2

London 242 mi. – Bristol 124 mi. – Southampton 161 mi.

Access Tamar Bridge (toll) AY

Plymouth City (Roborough) Airport : ☎ (01752) 204090, N : 3.5 mi. by A 386 ABY

to France (Roscoff) (Brittany Ferries) 1-3 daily (6 h) – to Spain (Santander) (Brittany Ferries) 2 weekly (approx 24 h)

Plymouth Mayflower, 3-5 The Barbican ☎ (01752) 306330, barbicantic@plymouth.gov.uk

18 Staddon Heights Plymstock, ☎ (01752) 402 475

9 Elfordleigh Hotel G. & C.C. Plympton Colebrook, ☎ (01752) 348 425

Town★ - Smeaton's Tower (≤★★) **AC** BZ **T1** – Plymouth Dome★ **AC** BZ – Royal Citadel (ramparts ≤★★) **AC** BZ – City Museum and Art Gallery★ BZ **M1**

Saltram House★★ **AC**, E : 3.5 mi. BY **A** - Tamar River★★ – Anthony House★ **AC**, W : 5 mi. by A 374 – Mount Edgcumbe (≤★) **AC**, SW : 2 mi. by passenger ferry from Stonehouse AZ. NE : Dartmoor National Park★★ – Buckland Abbey★★ **AC**, N : 7.5 mi. by A 386 ABY

Plans pages 586, 587

Holiday Inn
Armada Way ✉ PL1 2HJ – ✆ (01752) 639 988 – www.holidayinn.co.uk – Fax (01752) 673 816 BZ**s**
211 rm – £ 69/89 £ 69/89
Rest – *(dinner only and Sunday lunch)* Menu £ 20 **s** – Carte £ 24/37 **s**
◆ Substantial purpose-built hotel enjoys a panorama of the city skyline and the Plymouth Sound. Neatly laid-out, well-equipped bedrooms; extensive leisure club. Modern restaurant on top floor to make most of view.

Bowling Green without rest
9-10 Osborne Pl, Lockyer St, The Hoe ✉ PL1 2PU – ✆ (01752) 209 090 – www.thebowlingreenplymouth.com – Fax (01752) 209 092 BZ**r**
12 rm – £ 47/58 £ 68
◆ Georgian house, half overlooking Hoe, near site of Drake's legendary game. High-ceilinged rooms in pine and modern fabrics; some have power showers. Stroll to promenade.

Tanners
Prysten House, Finewell St ✉ PL1 2AE – ✆ (01752) 252 001 – www.tannersrestaurant.com – Fax (01752) 252 105 – Closed 25-26 December, 31 December-8 January, Sunday and Monday BZ**n**
Rest – *(booking essential)* Menu £ 23/39
◆ Characterful 15C house, reputedly Plymouth's oldest building: mullioned windows, tapestries, exposed stone and an illuminated water well. Modern, interesting cooking.

Artillery Tower
Firestone Bay ✉ PL1 3QR – ✆ (01752) 257 610 – www.artillerytower.co.uk – Closed 10 days in August, 10 days at Christmas, Sunday and Monday AZ**a**
Rest – *(lunch only) (booking essential at lunch)* Menu £ 25/35
◆ Uniquely located in 500 year-old circular tower, built to defend the city. Courteous service of mostly well executed local dishes: blackboard fish specialities.

Chloe's
Gill Akaster House Princess St – ✆ (01752) 201 523 – www.chloesrestaurant.co.uk – Fax (01752) 843 913 – Closed 24 December-3 January, Sunday and Monday BZ**a**
Rest – Menu £ 17/35
◆ Airy, open plan restaurant with simple neighbourhood feel, neutral décor and hanging Hessian lights. Tasty dishes display a classical French base. Live pianist every night.

Barbican Kitchen
Black Friars Distillery, 60 Southside St ✉ PL1 2LQ – ✆ (01752) 604 448 – www.barbicankitchen.com – Fax (01752) 604 445 – Closed 25-26 and dinner 31 December BZ**u**
Rest – Carte £ 18/31
◆ Established eatery in famous Gin Distillery, with funky inner in vibrant lime, pink and lilac, rough stone walls and modern art. Well-versed team in bright T-shirts serve brasserie-style dishes.

at Plympton St Maurice East : 6 mi. by A 374 on B 3416 - BY – ✉ Plymouth

St Elizabeth's House
Longbrook St – ✆ (01752) 344 840 – www.stelizabeths.co.uk – Fax (01752) 331 426
13 rm – £ 159 £ 159 – 2 suites
Rest – Menu £ 15 **s** (lunch) – Carte dinner £ 17/35 **s**
◆ Immaculate cream-washed former convent, now a stylish boutique hotel; lounge is dressed in period décor while light bedrooms are contemporary, with up-to-date facilities. Formal dining room offers classically based cooking with a modern twist.

Don't confuse the couvert rating with the stars!
Couverts defines comfort and service, while stars are awarded for the best cuisine across all categories of comfort.

ENGLAND

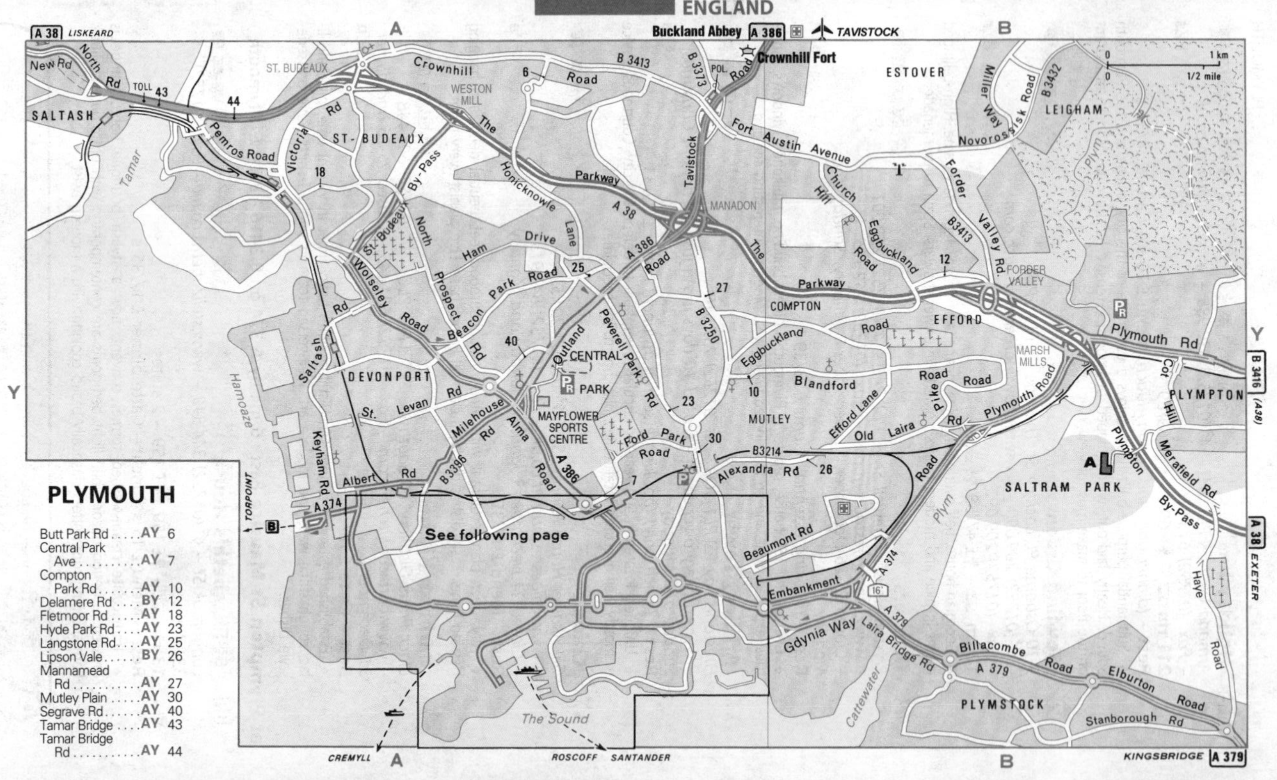

PLYMOUTH

Butt Park Rd	AY	6
Central Park Ave	AY	7
Compton Park Rd	AY	10
Delamere Rd	BY	12
Fletmoor Rd	AY	18
Hyde Park Rd	AY	23
Langstone Rd	AY	25
Lipson Vale	BY	26
Mannamead Rd	AY	27
Mutley Plain	AY	30
Segrave Rd	AY	40
Tamar Bridge	AY	43
Tamar Bridge Rd	AY	44

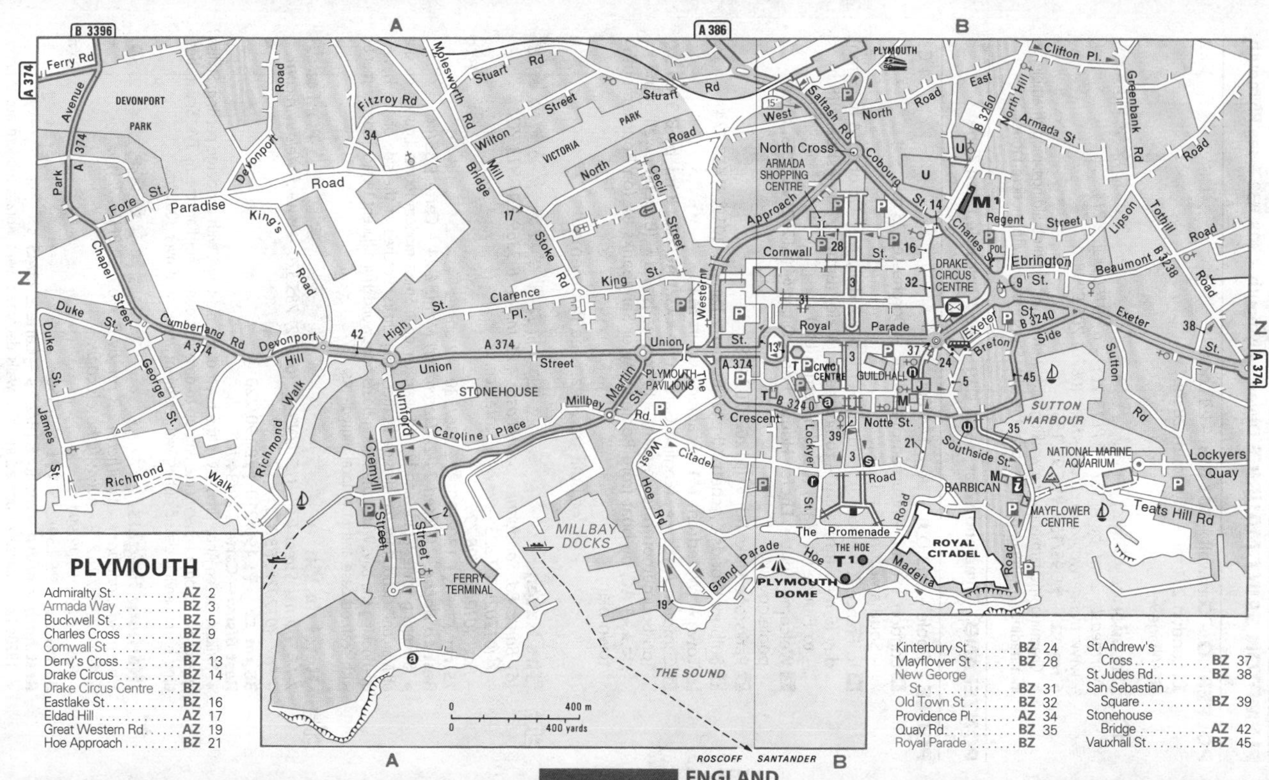
PLYMOUTH
Admiralty St . . . . AZ 2
Armada Way . . . . BZ 3
Buckwell St . . . . BZ 5
Charles Cross . . . . BZ 9
Cornwall St . . . . BZ
Derry's Cross . . . . BZ 13
Drake Circus . . . . BZ 14
Drake Circus Centre . . . BZ
Eastlake St . . . . BZ 16
Eldad Hill . . . . AZ 17
Great Western Rd . . . . . AZ 19
Hoe Approach . . . . BZ 21
Kinterbury St . . . . BZ 24
Mayflower St . . . . BZ 28
New George St . . . . BZ 31
Old Town St . . . . BZ 32
Providence Pl . . . . AZ 34
Quay Rd . . . . BZ 35
Royal Parade . . . . BZ
St Andrew's Cross . . . . . BZ 37
St Judes Rd . . . . BZ 38
San Sebastian Square . . . BZ 39
Stonehouse Bridge . . . . . AZ 42
Vauxhall St . . . . BZ 45
A
B
Z
B 3396
A 386
A 374
Ferry Rd
DEVONPORT PARK
VICTORIA PARK
North Cross
ARMADA SHOPPING CENTRE
DRAKE CIRCUS CENTRE
CIVIC CENTRE
GUILDHALL
PLYMOUTH PAVILIONS
STONEHOUSE
SUTTON HARBOUR
NATIONAL MARINE AQUARIUM
BARBICAN
MAYFLOWER CENTRE
ROYAL CITADEL
THE HOE
PLYMOUTH DOME
MILLBAY DOCKS
FERRY TERMINAL
THE SOUND
ROSCOFF
SANTANDER
400 m
400 yards
ENGLAND

PLYMPTON SAINT MAURICE Devon – Plymouth – 503 H32 – see Plymouth

POLPERRO – Cornwall – 503 G33 – ✉ Looe 1 B2

London 271 mi. – Plymouth 28 mi.

Village★

Trenderway Farm without rest

Northeast : 2 mi. by A 387 ✉ PL13 2LY – ✆ (01503) 272 214
– www.trenderwayfarm.co.uk – Fax (0870) 705 9998

6 rm – £ 95/155 £ 95/155

◆ Charming 16C farmhouse on working farm with converted outbuildings: modish ambience in a traditional setting. Breakfast over the lake. Stylish rooms with modern fabrics.

PONTELAND – Tyne and Wear – 501 O19 – see Newcastle upon Tyne

POOLE – Poole – 503 O31 – pop. 144 800 4 C3

London 116 mi. – Bournemouth 4 mi. – Dorchester 23 mi. – Southampton 36 mi.

to France (Cherbourg) (Brittany Ferries) 1-2 daily May-October (4 h 15 mn) day (5 h 45 mn) night – to France (St Malo) (Brittany Ferries) daily (8 h) – to France (St Malo) (Condor Ferries Ltd)

Welcome Centre, Enefco House, Poole Quay ✆ (01202) 253253, info@poole.gov.uk

Parkstone Links Rd, ✆ (01202) 707 138

Bulbury Woods Lytchett Minster Bulberry Lane, ✆ (01929) 459 574

Town★ (Waterfront **M1** , Scaplen's Court **M2**)

Compton Acres★★, (English Garden ★★★) **AC**, SE : 3 mi. by B 3369 BX (on Bournemouth town plan) – Brownsea Island★ (Baden-Powell Stone ★★) **AC**, by boat from Poole Quay or Sandbanks BX (on Bournemouth town plan)

Plan of Built up Area : see Bournemouth BX

The Haven

rest, VISA AE

161 Banks Rd, Sandbanks, Southeast : 4.25 mi. on B 3369 ✉ BH13 7QL
– ✆ (01202) 707 333 – www.fjbhotels.co.uk
– Fax (01202) 708 796 BX**c**

75 rm – £ 130/290 £ 236/530 – 2 suites

Rest *La Roche* – *(Closed 24-27 December)* Menu £ 24 – Carte £ 35/46

◆ Sweeping white façade and heated seawater pool. Smart modern rooms. Lounge on site of Marconi's laboratory has fireside leather wing chairs. Perched at the side of the Haven, overlooking the bay. Watch the fishing boats from wonderful adjacent terrace. Eclectic menus with seafood base and tasty local ingredients.

Hotel du Vin

VISA AE

7-11 Thames Street ✉ BH15 1JN – ✆ (01202) 785 570 – www.hotelduvin.com
– Fax (01202) 785 571 **a**

38 rm – £ 190/210 £ 190/220

Rest *Bistro* – Carte £ 29/34

◆ Striking Queen Anne property in the heart of the old town, with concierge parking. Stylish interior based on a wine theme and up-to-date bedrooms with flat screens TVs. Smart, bustling bistro serving classic dishes, with excellent wine list of over 300 bins.

Harbour Heights

VISA AE

Haven Rd, Sandbanks, Southeast : 3 mi. by B 3369 ✉ BH13 7LW
– ✆ (01202) 707 272 – www.fjbhotels.co.uk
– Fax (01202) 708 594 BX**n**

38 rm – £ 130/215 £ 260/360

Rest *harbar bistro* – Menu £ 18/27 **s** – Carte £ 23/45 **s**

◆ 1920s hotel stylishly updated in 2003; walls decorated with vibrant modern art. Swanky, smart bedrooms boast modern interiors and all mod cons: request room with a sea view. Bistro-styled restaurant with very popular terrace.

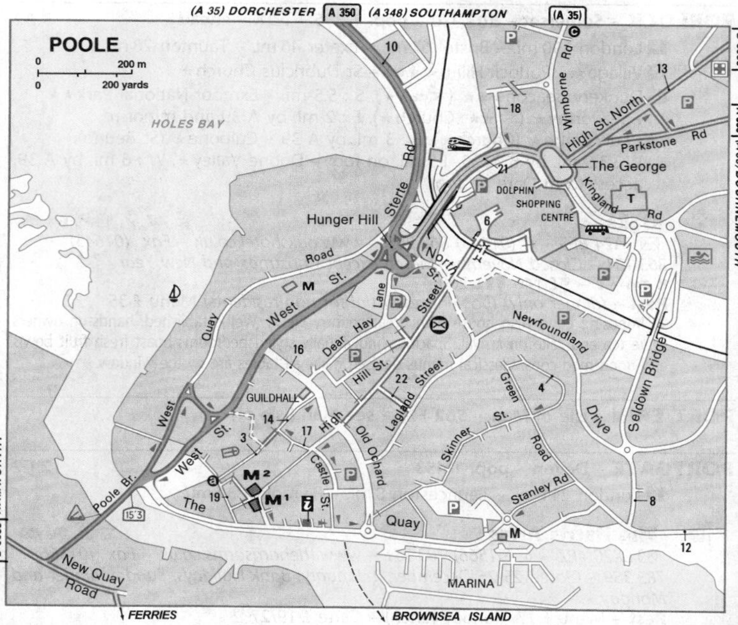

Church St	3	Furnell Rd	8	New Orchard	16
Dolphin Quay Shopping Centre		High St		New St	17
Emerson Rd	4	Holes Bay Rd	10	Serpentine Rd	18
Falkland Square	6	Labrador Drive	12	Thames St	19
Fishermans Rd	7	Longfleet Rd	13	Towngate Bridge	21
		Market St	14	Westons Lane	22

Cranborne House without rest

45 Shaftesbury Rd ✉ BH15 2LU – ✆ (01202) 685 200 – www.cranborne-house.co.uk c

5 rm – 🛉£ 49/69 🛉🛉£ 69/89

◆ Victorian house with original features and pleasant, modern style. Bedrooms – in quiet rear wing of house – boast handmade pine furniture and modern bathrooms. Separate guest entrance.

XX **Isabel's** VISA AE

32 Station Rd, Lower Parkstone ✉ BH14 8UD – ✆ (01202) 747 885 – www.isabelsrestaurant.co.uk – Fax (01202) 747 885 – Closed dinner 25-28 December, 1 January, Sunday and Monday BX**a**

Rest – *(dinner only) (booking essential)* Menu £ 22 (weekdays)/30 (Saturday) – Carte £ 26/35

◆ Long-established neighbourhood restaurant; old shelves recall its origins as a Victorian pharmacy. Intimate wooden booths. Classically inspired menu with a rich Gallic tone.

The Cow A/C VISA

58 Station Road, Ashley Cross ✉ BH14 8UD – ✆ (01202) 749 569 – www.thecowpub.co.uk – Fax (01202) 307 493 – Closed Sunday dinner

Rest – Carte £ 23/30 BX**a**

◆ Vibrant suburban pub with bar and bistro areas. Dishes are lighter at lunch and more ambitious in the evening: ingredients are good quality, expertly prepared and well-presented.

POOLEY BRIDGE – Cumbria – **501** L20 – see Ullswater

PORLOCK – Somerset – 503 J30 – pop. 1 395 – ✉ Minehead 3 A2

London 190 mi. – Bristol 67 mi. – Exeter 46 mi. – Taunton 28 mi.

Village★ - Porlock Hill (≤★★) – St Dubricius Church★

Dunkery Beacon★★★ (≤★★★), S : 5.5 mi. – Exmoor National Park★★ - Selworthy★ (≤★★, Church★), E : 2 mi. by A 39 and minor rd - Luccombe★ (Church★), E : 3 mi. by A 39 – Culbone★ (St Beuno), W : 3.5 mi. by B 3225, 1.5 mi. on foot – Doone Valley★, W : 6 mi. by A 39, access from Oare on foot

Oaks

✉ TA24 8ES – (01643) 862 265 – www.oakshotel.co.uk – Fax (01643) 863 131 – Closed November-March except Christmas and New Year

8 rm – £ 140 £ 200

Rest – *(dinner only) (booking essential for non-residents)* Menu £ 35

◆ Imposing Edwardian house with great country views. Well-established, hands-on owners serve tea and cake on arrival. Spacious, individually styled bedrooms boast fresh fruit bowls and good mod cons. Classical menus devised daily; all tables are by the window.

PORT ERIN – Isle of Man – 502 F21 – see Man (Isle of)

PORTGATE – Devon – pop. 1 453 2 C2

London 211 mi. – Launceston 8 mi. – Plymouth 34 mi.

The Harris Arms

✉ EX20 4PZ – (01566) 783 331 – www.theharrisarms.co.uk – Fax (01566) 783 359 – Closed 25-26 December, 1 January, Bank Holidays, Sunday dinner and Monday

Rest – Menu £ 17 (Sunday lunch) – Carte £ 19/27

◆ Traditional 16C pub offers friendly welcome, relaxed ambience, decked terrace and excellent wine list. Robust, confident cooking uses local, seasonal ingredients.

PORTHLEVEN – Cornwall – pop. 3 190 1 A3

London 284 mi. – Helston 3 mi. – Penzance 12 mi.

Kota with rm

Harbour Head ✉ TR13 9JA – (01326) 562 407 – www.kotarestaurant.co.uk – Fax (01326) 562 407 – Closed 25 December and 1 January-12 February

2 rm – £ 50/70 £ 65/90

Rest – *(Closed Sunday except Bank Holidays) (dinner only and lunch Friday-Saturday)* Carte £ 22/33

◆ Cottagey converted 18C harbourside granary. Characterful restaurant - thick walls, tiled floors - serves modern Asian inspired dishes with local fish specials. Simple rooms.

PORTINSCALE – Cumbria – see Keswick

PORTSCATHO – Cornwall – 503 F33 – ✉ Truro 1 B3

London 298 mi. – Plymouth 55 mi. – Truro 16 mi.

St Just-in-Roseland Church★★, W : 4 mi. by A 3078 – St Anthony-in-Roseland (≤★★) S : 3.5 m

Rosevine

Rosevine, North : 2 mi. by A 3078 ✉ TR2 5EW – (01872) 580 206 – www.rosevine.co.uk – Fax (01872) 580 230 – Closed 7 January-7 February and 2 weeks in November

12 suites – £ 145/350, £ 10

Rest – *(Closed Sunday dinner) (bar lunch)* Carte £ 27/37

◆ Surrounded by attractive gardens, this family owned hotel offers traditional, homely comforts. Rooms are well looked after and a friendly air prevails. Pretty restaurant makes use of local ingredients.

Driftwood
Rosevine, North : 2 mi. by A 3078 ✉ TR2 5EW – ✆ (01872) 580 644
www.driftwoodhotel.co.uk – Fax (01872) 580 801 – Closed 11 January-4 February
15 rm – †£ 212/221 ††£ 250/260
Rest – *(dinner only) (booking essential)* Menu £ 42
◆ Stylish décor and a neutral, contemporary feel make this an enviable spot to lay one's head. Attractive decking affords fine sea views. Smart bedrooms with pristine style. Distinctive modern dining room with fine vistas.

PORTSMOUTH and SOUTHSEA – Portsmouth – 503 Q31 – pop. 187 056 Great Britain

6 B3

London 78 mi. – Brighton 48 mi. – Salisbury 44 mi. – Southampton 21 mi.

to the Isle of Wight (Ryde) (Wightlink Ltd) frequent services daily (15 mn) – from Southsea to the Isle of Wight (Ryde) (Hovertravel Ltd) frequent services daily (10 mn)

to France (St Malo) (Brittany Ferries) daily (8 h 45 mn) day (10 h 45 mn) night
– to France (Caen) (Brittany Ferries) 2-4 daily (6 h) day (6 h 45 mn) night
– to France (Cherbourg) (Brittany Ferries) 2 daily (5 h) day, (7 h) night
– to France (Le Havre) (LD Lines) daily (5 h 30 mn/7 h 30 mn)
– to France (Cherbourg) (Brittany Ferries) 1-2 daily (2 h 45 mn)
– to France (Caen) (Brittany Ferries) 2-4 daily (3 h 45 mn)
– to Spain (Bilbao) (P & O European Ferries Ltd) 1-2 weekly (35 h)
– to Guernsey (St Peter Port) and Jersey (St Helier) (Condor Ferries Ltd) daily except Sunday (10 hrs)
– to the Isle of Wight (Fishbourne) (Wightlink Ltd) frequent services daily (35 mn)

Clarence Esplanade, Southsea ✆ (023) 9282 6722, vis@portsmouthcc.gov.uk.

Southsea Burrfields Rd, ✆ (023) 9266 8667

Crookhorn Lane Waterlooville Widley, ✆ (023) 9237 2210

Southwick Park Southwick Pinsley Drive, ✆ (023) 9238 0131

City★ – Naval Portsmouth BY : H.M.S. Victory★★★ **AC**, The Mary Rose★★, Royal Naval Museum★★ **AC** – Old Portsmouth★ BYZ : The Point (≤★★) - St Thomas Cathedral★ – Southsea (Castle★ **AC**) AZ – Royal Marines Museum, Eastney★ **AC**, AZ **M1**

Portchester Castle★ **AC**, NW : 5.5 mi. by A 3 and A 27 AY

Plans pages 592, 593

The Retreat without rest
35 Grove Road South, Southsea ✉ PO5 3QS – ✆ (023) 9235 3701 – www.theretreatguesthouse.co.uk
CZ **e**
4 rm – †£ 105 ††£ 105
◆ Grade II listed Victorian corner house in residential area. Original features include terrazzo flooring and stained glass windows. Simple, spacious bedrooms; modern bathrooms.

Fortitude Cottage without rest
51 Broad St, Old Portsmouth ✉ PO1 2JD – ✆ (023) 9282 3748 – www.fortitudecottage.co.uk – Fax (023) 9282 3748 – Closed December
6 rm – †£ 50/115 ††£ 85/115
BY **c**
◆ Pretty little quayside townhouse named after an 18C battleship. First floor breakfast room with views of ferry terminal. Room 4 has great roof terrace. Charming owners.

Bistro Montparnasse
103 Palmerston Rd, Southsea ✉ PO5 3PS – ✆ (023) 9281 6754 – www.bistromontparnasse.co.uk – Closed 25-26 December, 1 week February, 1 week September, Sunday and Monday
CZ **a**
Rest – Menu £ 34
◆ Passionately run suburban restaurant. Simple, understated style with neutral hues and nature photographs. Menus provide interest, featuring original combinations and clean, precise cooking.

ENGLAND

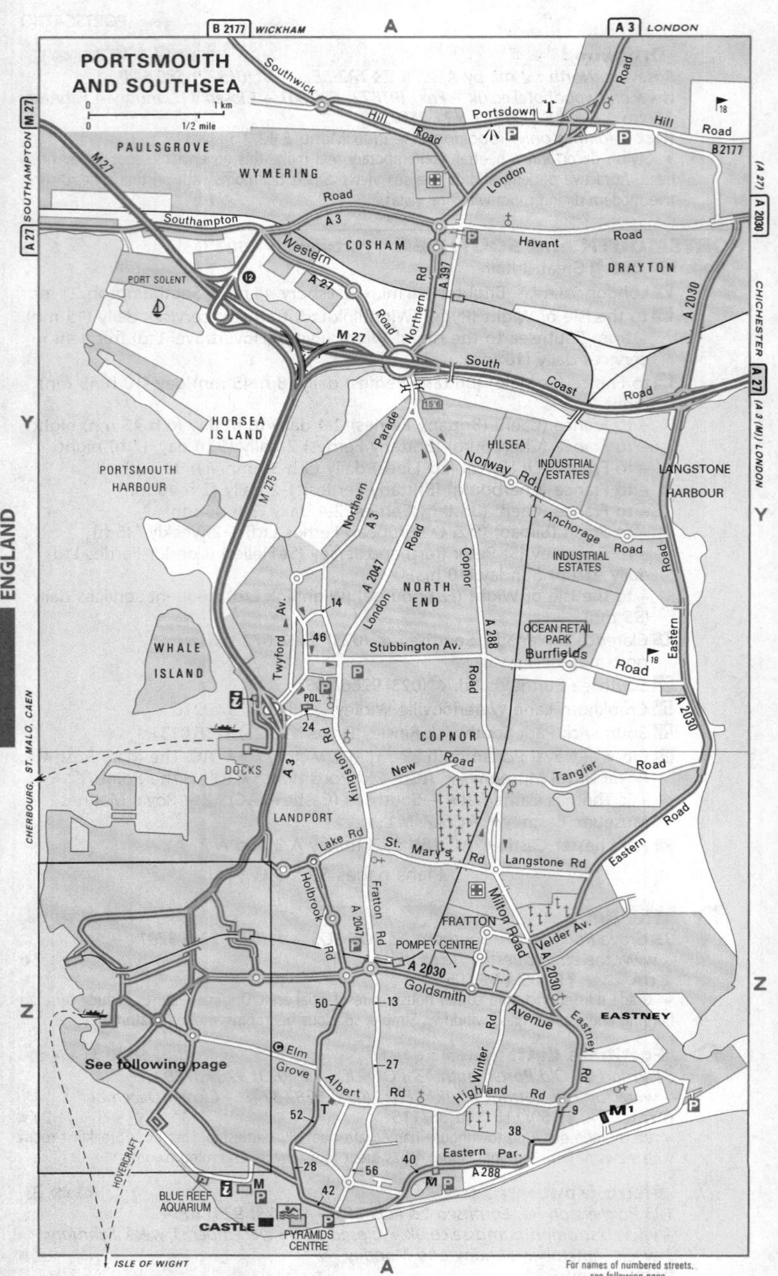
PORTSMOUTH AND SOUTHSEA
0 1 km
0 1/2 mile
B 2177 WICKHAM
A
A 3 LONDON
M 27 SOUTHAMPTON
A 27
(A 27) A 2030
CHICHESTER
A 27 (A 3 (M)) LONDON
CHERBOURG, ST. MALO, CAEN
ISLE OF WIGHT
HOVERCRAFT
Y
Z
PAULSGROVE
WYMERING
COSHAM
DRAYTON
PORT SOLENT
HORSEA ISLAND
PORTSMOUTH HARBOUR
HILSEA
INDUSTRIAL ESTATES
LANGSTONE HARBOUR
NORTH END
OCEAN RETAIL PARK
WHALE ISLAND
COPNOR
DOCKS
LANDPORT
FRATTON
POMPEY CENTRE
EASTNEY
BLUE REEF AQUARIUM
CASTLE
PYRAMIDS CENTRE
Southwick Hill Road
Portsdown Hill Road
B2177
London Road
Southampton Road
A 3
Havant Road
Western Road
A 27
Northern Rd
A 397
A 2030
M 27
South Coast Road
Northern Parade
Norway Rd.
Anchorage Road
Eastern Road
M 275
A 3
London Road
A 2047
Copnor Road
A 288
Twyford Av.
Stubbington Av.
Burrfields Road
POL.
Kingston Rd
New Road
Tangier Road
Lake Rd
St. Mary's Rd
Langstone Rd
Holbrook Rd
Fratton Rd
Milton Road
Velder Av.
A 2030
Goldsmith Avenue
Winter Rd
Eastney Rd
Elm Grove
Albert Rd
Highland Rd
Eastern Par.
A 288
See following page
M
M1
T
14
46
24
50
13
27
52
28
56
42
40
38
9
12
15'6
18
For names of numbered streets, see following page.

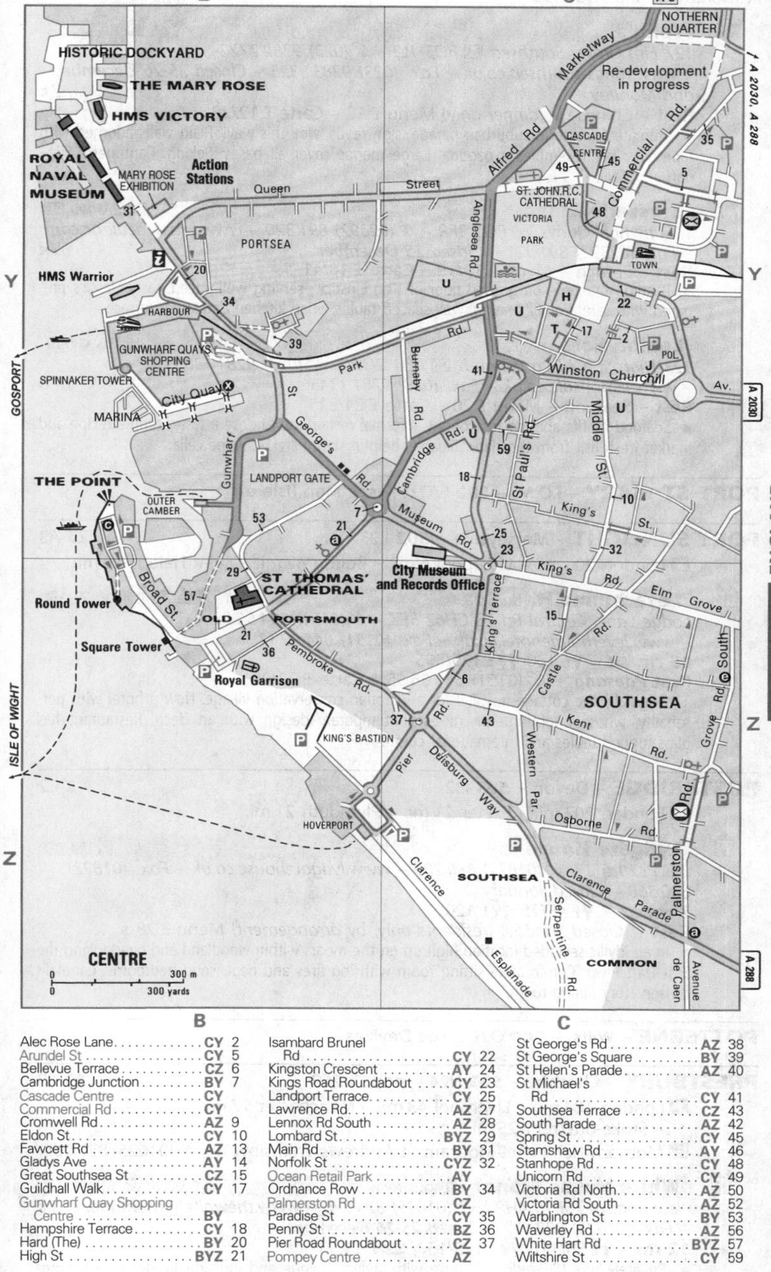

Alec Rose Lane	CY	2
Arundel St	CY	5
Bellevue Terrace	CZ	6
Cambridge Junction	BY	7
Cascade Centre	CY	
Commercial Rd	CY	
Cromwell Rd	AZ	9
Eldon St	CY	10
Fawcett Rd	AZ	13
Gladys Ave	AY	14
Great Southsea St	CZ	15
Guildhall Walk	CY	17
Gunwharf Quay Shopping Centre	BY	
Hampshire Terrace	CY	18
Hard (The)	BY	20
High St	BYZ	21
Isambard Brunel Rd	CY	22
Kingston Crescent	AY	24
Kings Road Roundabout	CY	23
Landport Terrace	CY	25
Lawrence Rd	AZ	27
Lennox Rd South	AZ	28
Lombard St	BYZ	29
Main Rd	BY	31
Norfolk St	CYZ	32
Ocean Retail Park	AY	
Ordnance Row	BY	34
Palmerston Rd	CZ	
Paradise St	CY	35
Penny St	BZ	36
Pier Road Roundabout	CZ	37
Pompey Centre	AZ	
St George's Rd	AZ	38
St George's Square	BY	39
St Helen's Parade	AZ	40
St Michael's Rd	CY	41
Southsea Terrace	CZ	43
South Parade	AZ	42
Spring St	CY	45
Stamshaw Rd	AY	46
Stanhope Rd	CY	48
Unicorn Rd	CY	49
Victoria Rd North	AZ	50
Victoria Rd South	AZ	52
Warblington St	BY	53
Waverley Rd	AZ	56
White Hart Rd	BYZ	57
Wiltshire St	CY	59

XX **Tang's**

127 Elm Grove, Southsea ✉ PO5 1LJ – ✆ (023) 9282 2722 – www.tangs-southsea.co.uk – Fax (023) 9283 8323 – Closed 25-26 December and Monday AZ**c**

Rest – Chinese – *(dinner only)* Menu £ 17 – Carte £ 12/28

◆ Intimate Chinese in suburban parade: sign reads 'wok this way!' Plain walls adorned with tapestries; bar resembles a pagoda. Large menus cover all bases: Peking, Cantonese, Sichuan and Thai.

XX **Brasserie Blanc**

1 Gunwharf Quays ✉ PO1 3FR – ✆ (02392) 891 320 – www.brasserieblanc.com – Fax (02392) 891 321 – Closed 25 December BY**x**

Rest – French – Menu £ 15/18 – Carte £ 18/41

◆ Bustling brasserie on ground floor of 'The Lipstick', serving well-priced, tasty classics prepared with care. Comfy seating, well-spaced tables, open kitchen and super terrace.

X **Lemon Sole**

123 High St, Old Portsmouth ✉ PO1 2HW – ✆ (023) 9281 1303 – www.lemonsole.co.uk – Fax (023) 9281 1345 BY**a**

Rest – Seafood – Menu £ 20 – Carte £ 24/31

◆ Seafood motifs abound in a bright, informal restaurant. Choose a tasty, simple recipe and market-fresh fish from the slab. Likeable, helpful staff. Part 14C wine cellar.

PORT ST MARY – I.O.M. – 502 F/G21 – see Man (Isle of)

PORT SUNLIGHT – Merseyside – 502 L23 — 20 A3

London 206 mi. – Liverpool 6 mi. – Bolton 42 mi. – Saint Helens 20 mi.

Leverhulme H. & Spa

Lodge Lane, Central Rd ✉ CH62 5EZ – ✆ (0151) 644 55 55 – www.leverhulmehotel.co.uk – Fax (0151) 644 99 11

15 rm ☕ – †£ 160 ††£ 175/395

Rest ***Paesano*** – ✆ (0151) 644 66 55 – Carte £ 22/29

◆ Originally the cottage hospital for a Victorian conservation village. Now a hotel with personality, whose bright interior mixes contemporary design with art deco. Restaurant has glass-topped tables and international cuisine.

POSTBRIDGE – Devon – 503 I32 — 2 C2

London 207 mi. – Exeter 21 mi. – Plymouth 21 mi.

Lydgate House

✉ PL20 6TJ – ✆ (01822) 880 209 – www.lydgatehouse.co.uk – Fax (01822) 880 360 – Closed January

7 rm ☕ – †£ 45/75 ††£ 120

Rest – *(Closed Sunday) (residents only, by arrangement)* Menu £ 28 **s**

◆ In an idyllic secluded location high up on the moors within woodland and overlooking the East Dart River. Comfortable sitting room with log fires and neat, snug bedrooms. Candlelit conservatory dining room.

POTTERNE – Wilts. – 503 O29 – see Devizes

PRESTBURY – Cheshire – 502 N24 – pop. 3 269 — 20 B3

London 184 mi. – Liverpool 43 mi. – Manchester 17 mi. – Stoke-on-Trent 25 mi.

Mottram Hall Hotel Mottram St Andrews Wilmslow Rd, ✆ (01625) 820 064

White House Manor without rest

New Road ✉ SK10 4HP – ✆ (01625) 829 376 – www.thewhitehousemanor.co.uk – Fax (01625) 828 627 – Closed 25-26 December

12 rm – †£ 50/110 ††£ 125/150, ☕ £ 11.50

◆ Privately run 18C redbrick house with stylish, unique and individually decorated rooms which provide every luxury. Breakfast in your room or in the conservatory.

The Bridge
The Village ✉ SK10 4DQ – ✆ (01625) 829 326 – www.bridge-hotel.co.uk – Fax (01625) 827 557
23 rm – †£ 50/90 ††£ 90, ☕ £ 9.75 – 1 suite
Rest – *(Closed Sunday dinner)* Menu £ 14 – Carte £ 22/32
◆ Dating back to the 1600s, a sympathetically extended hotel on the river Bollin. Classic, subtly co-ordinated décor in rooms, more characterful in the old timbered house. Live music at weekends in the beamed, galleried hall of the restaurant.

PRESTON – **Lancashire** – **502** L22 **20** A2

London 226 mi. – Blackpool 18 mi. – Burnley 22 mi. – Liverpool 30 mi.
The Guildhall, Lancaster Rd ✆ (01772) 253731, tourism@preston.gov.uk
Fulwood Fulwood Hall Lane, ✆ (01772) 700 011
Ingol Tanterton Hall Rd, ✆ (01772) 734 556
Ashton & Lea Lea Tudor Ave, Blackpool Rd, ✆ (01772) 735 282
Penwortham Blundell Lane, ✆ (01772) 744 630

Inside Out
100 Higher Walton Rd, Walton-le-Dale, Southeast : 1.75 mi. by A 6 on A 675 ✉ PR5 4HR – ✆ (01772) 251 366 – www.insideoutrestaurant.co.uk – Fax (01772) 258 918 – Closed first 2 weeks January, 1 week in autumn and Monday
Rest – Menu £ 16 – Carte £ 22/29
◆ Inside - a chic and stylish restaurant; 'out' - a lovely decked terrace with heaters overlooking a garden. Well sourced, quality ingredients assembled with love and flair.

PULFORD – **Ches.** – **502** L24 – **see Chester**

PULHAM MARKET – **Norfolk** – **504** X26 – **pop. 919** – ✉ **Diss** **15** C2

London 106 mi. – Cambridge 58 mi. – Ipswich 29 mi. – Norwich 16 mi.

Old Bakery without rest
Church Walk ✉ IP21 4SL – ✆ (01379) 676 492 – www.theoldbakery.net – Fax (01379) 676 492
3 rm ☕ – †£ 45/65 ††£ 65/80
◆ Characterful pink-hued Elizabethan house on village green. Spacious timbered rooms hold antiques and have plenty of personality. Pretty garden with summer house.

PURTON – **Wiltshire** – **503** O29 – **pop. 3 328** – ✉ **Swindon** **4** D2

London 94 mi. – Bristol 41 mi. – Gloucester 31 mi. – Oxford 38 mi.

Pear Tree at Purton
Church End, South : 0.5 mi. by Church St on Lydiard Millicent rd ✉ SN5 4ED – ✆ (01793) 772 100 – www.peartreepurton.co.uk – Fax (01793) 772 369 – Closed 26-30 December
15 rm ☕ – †£ 115/145 ††£ 115/145 – 2 suites **Rest** – Menu £ 20/35 **s**
◆ Personally run, extended 16C sandstone vicarage in mature seven-acre garden. Spacious flower-filled lounge. Rooms with traditional comforts and thoughtful extras. Conservatory restaurant overlooks wild flower borders.

RADNAGE – **Bucks.** – **see Stokenchurch**

RAINHAM – **Medway** – **504** U29 **9** C1

London 14 mi. – Basildon 16 mi. – Dartford 9 mi.

The Barn
507 Lower Rainham Rd, North : 1.75 mi. by Station Rd ✉ ME8 7TN – ✆ (01634) 361 363 – www.thebarnrestaurant.co.uk – Closed 25-26 December, Saturday lunch, Sunday dinner and Bank Holidays
Rest – Menu £ 15/22 – Carte £ 15/41
◆ Rurally set, heavily beamed 17C barn with beamed dining room and cosy upstairs lounge. Elaborate cooking uses locally sourced, seasonal produce. Ideal for special occasions.

ENGLAND

RAMSBOTTOM – Greater Manchester – 502 N23 – pop. 17 352 — 20 B2

London 223 mi. – Blackpool 39 mi. – Burnley 12 mi. – Leeds 46 mi.

ramsons

18 Market Pl ✉ BL0 9HT – ☎ (01706) 825 070 – www.ramsons-restaurant.com – Closed Monday, Sunday dinner and Tuesday lunch

Rest – Italian influences – Menu £ 30 (lunch)/40 (Tuesday-Thursday dinner) – Carte £ 30/44

◆ Passionately run and slightly quirky, this well-regarded eatery offers mostly Italian influenced cooking utilising refined ingredients. Accompanying fine wine list.

RAMSBURY – Wilts. – 503 P29 – see Marlborough

RAMSEY – Isle of Man – 502 G21 – see Man (Isle of)

RAMSGATE – Kent – pop. 37 967 – ✉ CT11 Kent — 9 D1

London 77 mi. – Southend-on-Sea 89 mi. – Ipswich 128 mi.

Age & Sons

Charlotte Court ✉ CT118HE – ☎ (01843) 851 515 – www.ageandsons.co.uk – Closed 25-26 December, Monday-Tuesday and Sunday dinner

Rest – Carte £ 20/31

◆ Attractive converted wine warehouse in centre of town. Sexy basement bar; rustic ground floor café; more formal 1st floor restaurant and lovely terrace. Interesting modern menu of gutsy, flavourful cooking. Charming service.

RAMSGILL-IN-NIDDERDALE – N. Yorks. – 502 021 – see Pateley Bridge

RANTON GREEN – Staffordshire – 502 N25 — 19 C1

London 150 mi. – Birmingham 36 mi. – Stoke-on-Trent 19 mi. – Wolverhampton 32 mi.

Hand and Cleaver

Butt Lane ✉ ST18 9JZ – ☎ (01785) 822 367 – www.handandcleaver.co.uk – Closed Sunday dinner in winter and Monday except Bank Holidays

Rest – Menu £ 15 (lunch) – Carte £ 20/28

◆ Popular, very spacious 17C pub with snug bar, open fires, embossed plaster walls and a 1970s feel. Regularly changing menu offers traditional pub dishes, made using local produce.

RAWTENSTALL – Lancashire – 502 N22 – pop. 21 797 — 20 B2

London 232 mi. – Accrington 9 mi. – Burnley 12 mi.

The Dining Room

8-12 Burnley Rd ✉ BB4 8EW – ☎ (01706) 210 567 – www.thediningroomrestaurant.co.uk – Closed 1 week January, Tuesday and lunch Wednesday-Thursday

Rest – *(booking essential)* Menu £ 17 (lunch)/20 (Sunday lunch) – Carte approx. £ 39

◆ Stylish restaurant with comfy lounge and bar. Fixed price menu demonstrates owners' passion and skill. Neat, modern dishes use classic combinations yet introduce creative, inventive touches.

RAYLEIGH – Essex – 504 V29 – pop. 30 629 — 13 C3

London 35 mi. – Chelmsford 13 mi. – Southend-on-Sea 6 mi.

at Thundersley South : 1.25 mi. on A 129 – ✉ Rayleigh

The Woodmans Arms

Rayleigh Rd ✉ SS7 3TA – ☎ (01268) 775 799 – www.thewoodmansarms.co.uk – Fax (01268) 590 689

Rest – Carte £ 18/28

◆ Comfy sofas for drinkers; smart restaurant for diners. Seasonal cooking is hearty and flavourful; traditional in the main with lighter choices at lunch. A cheerful young team.

READING – Reading – 503 Q29 – pop. 232 662

London 43 mi. – Brighton 79 mi. – Bristol 78 mi. – Croydon 47 mi.
Access Whitchurch Bridge (toll)
to Henley-on-Thames (Salter Bros. Ltd) (summer only)
Calcot Park Calcot Bath Rd, (0118) 942 7124

Plan on next page

Millennium Madejski
rm,
Madejski Stadium, South : 1.5 mi. by A 33 RG2 0FL – (0118) 925 3500 – www.millenniumhotels.co.uk – Fax (0118) 925 3501 Xv
201 rm – £ 69/200 £ 69/200, £ 15.75 – 10 suites
Rest *Cilantro* – *(closed Sunday and Monday) (dinner only)* Menu £ 50
Rest *Le Café* – *(closed Saturday lunch - except match days)* Menu £ 15 (lunch) – Carte £ 24/35
◆ Purpose-built hotel, in modern retail park; part of the Madejski sports stadium. Imposing atrium lounge-bar and marble floored lobby. Stylish, inviting rooms. Impressively smart Cilantro. Informal Le Café is open plan to atrium lounge.

The Forbury
rm, rest,
26 The Forbury RG1 3EJ – (0800) 078 97 89 – www.theforburyhotel.co.uk – Fax (0118) 959 0806 Yc
23 rm – £ 230 £ 230, £ 10
Rest *Cerise* – Carte £ 33/46
◆ Former civic hall overlooking Forbury Square Gardens; now a very stylish town house hotel. Eye-catching artwork features in all the stunningly individualistic bedrooms. Stylish basement cocktail bar/restaurant where clean, crisp, modern cooking holds sway.

Malmaison
rm,
Great Western Hse, 18-20 Station Rd RG1 1JX – (0118) 956 2300 – www.malmaison.com – Fax (0118) 956 2301 – Closed 1 week Christmas
75 rm – £ 175 £ 175, £ 14.95 Ye
Rest *Brasserie* – *(Closed Saturday lunch)* Menu £ 17 – Carte £ 29/41
◆ Modernised Victorian railway hotel with contemporary furnishings, busy cafe and smart bar. Spacious, stylish bedrooms boast high level of facilities. Railway theme throughout. Industrial feel Brasserie serves contemporary, French influenced cooking.

Beech House without rest
60 Bath Rd RG30 2AY – (0118) 959 1901 – www.beechhousehotel.com – Fax (0118) 958 3200 Xa
15 rm – £ 59/85 £ 85/95
◆ Red brick Victorian house with neat garden, terrace and summer house. Traditionally furnished with antiques and period ornaments. Pleasant, well equipped bedrooms with showers.

Forbury's
1 Forbury Sq, The Forbury RG1 3BB – (0118) 957 4044 – www.forburys.com – Fax (0118) 956 9191 – Closed 26-27 December, 1-2 January and Sunday
Rest – Menu £ 16/21 – Carte £ 32/40 Ya
◆ Modern eatery near law courts. Relaxing area of comfy leather seats. Spacious dining room enhanced by bold prints of wine labels. Eclectic menus with Gallic starting point.

LSQ2
Lime Sq., 220 South Oak Way, Green Park, South : 2 mi. by A 33 RG2 6UP – (0118) 987 3702 – www.lsq2.co.uk – Closed Sunday Xc
Rest – Carte £ 25/39
◆ Bright, airy restaurant with full length windows and terrace, set in suburban business park. Flavoursome cooking mixes British classics with modern Asian and international brasserie dishes.

London Street Brasserie
2-4 London St RG1 4PN – (0118) 950 5036 – www.londonstbrasserie.co.uk – Closed 25-26 December Zc
Rest – *(booking essential)* Menu £ 18 (lunch) – Carte £ 28/38
◆ Lively and modern: a polite, friendly team serve appetising British classics and international dishes. Deck terrace and first-floor window tables overlook the river Kennett.

ENGLAND

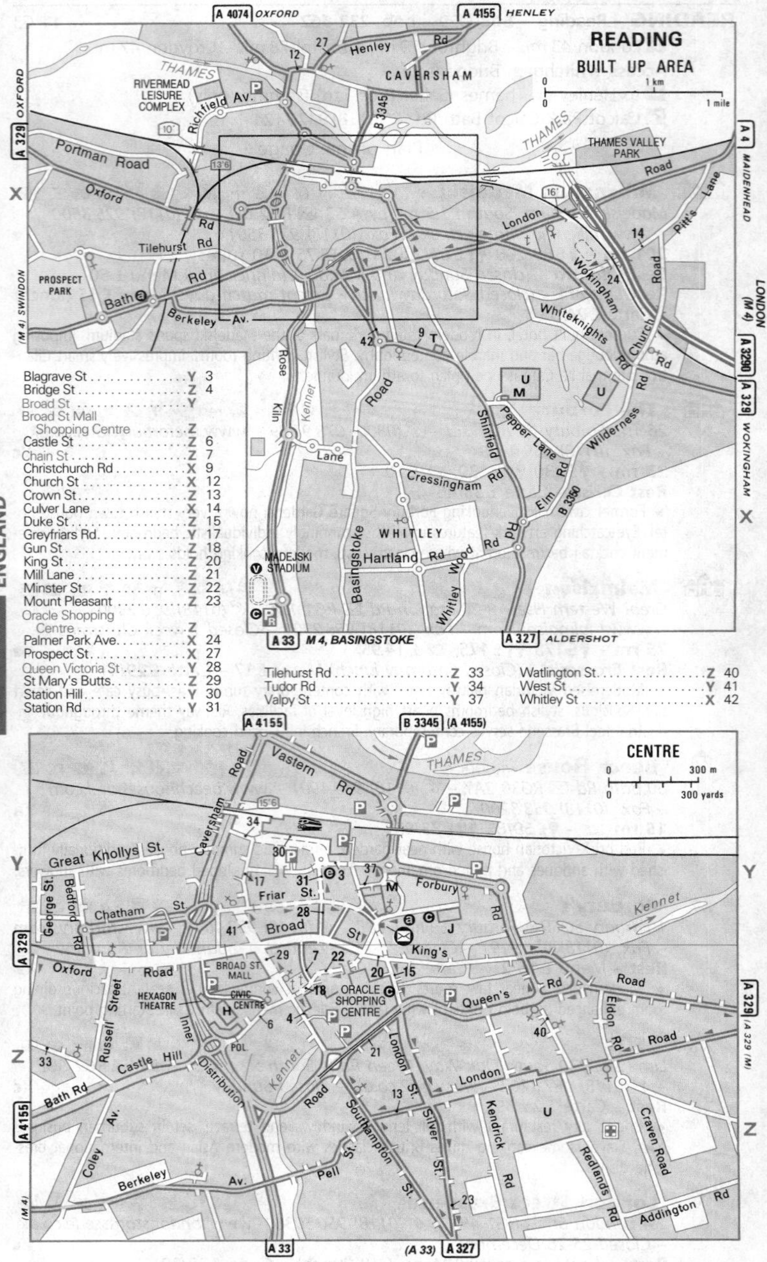
READING
BUILT UP AREA
0 1 km
0 1 mile
A 4074 OXFORD
A 4155 HENLEY
A 329 OXFORD
(M 4) SWINDON
A 4 MAIDENHEAD
LONDON (M 4)
A 3290
A 329 WOKINGHAM
A 33 M 4, BASINGSTOKE
A 327 ALDERSHOT
THAMES
CAVERSHAM
RIVERMEAD LEISURE COMPLEX
Richfield Av.
B 3345
Henley Rd
THAMES VALLEY PARK
Portman Road
Oxford Rd
Tilehurst Rd
Bath Rd
PROSPECT PARK
Berkeley Av.
London Road
Wokingham Road
Whiteknights Rd
Church Rd
Pitt's Lane
Rose Kiln Lane
Kennet
Shinfield Rd
Pepper Lane
Wilderness Rd
Cressingham Rd
Elm Rd
B 3350
WHITLEY
Hartland Rd
Whitley Wood Rd
Basingstoke Road
MADEJSKI STADIUM
Blagrave St Y 3
Bridge St Z 4
Broad St Y
Broad St Mall Shopping Centre Z
Castle St Z 6
Chain St Z 7
Christchurch Rd X 9
Church St X 12
Crown St Z 13
Culver Lane X 14
Duke St Z 15
Greyfriars Rd Y 17
Gun St Z 18
King St Z 20
Mill Lane Z 21
Minster St Z 22
Mount Pleasant Z 23
Oracle Shopping Centre Z
Palmer Park Ave. X 24
Prospect St X 27
Queen Victoria St Y 28
St Mary's Butts Z 29
Station Hill Y 30
Station Rd Y 31
Tilehurst Rd Z 33
Tudor Rd Y 34
Valpy St Y 37
Watlington St Z 40
West St Y 41
Whitley St X 42
CENTRE
0 300 m
0 300 yards
A 4155
B 3345 (A 4155)
A 329
A 329 (A 329 (M))
A 4155
(M 4)
A 33
(A 33) A 327
Vastern Rd
Caversham Road
Great Knollys St.
George St.
Bedford Rd
Chatham St.
Friar St.
Broad St.
Forbury Rd
King's Rd
Queen's Rd
Kennet
Oxford Road
BROAD ST. MALL
HEXAGON THEATRE
CIVIC CENTRE
ORACLE SHOPPING CENTRE
Russell Street
Inner Distribution Road
Castle Hill
Bath Rd
Coley Av.
Berkeley Av.
Pell St.
Southampton St.
London St.
Silver St.
London Road
Kendrick Rd
Redlands Rd
Craven Road
Eldon Rd
Addington Rd
Road

at Kidmore End North : 5 mi. by A 4155 - X - off B 481 – ✉ Reading

The New Inn with rm
Chalkhouse Green Rd ✉ RG4 9AU – ☎ (0118) 972 3115 – www.thenewinn.co.uk – Closed Sunday dinner
6 rm – †£ 65 ††£ 85 **Rest** – Menu £ 12 – Carte £ 20/30
◆ 16C inn with rough floorboards, beams and open fires and delightful canopied terrace. Smart, updated restaurant serves adventurous fare. Stylish, comfy, well-equipped rooms.

at Hurst East : 5 mi. by A 329 - X - on B 3030 – ✉ Reading

The Castle at Hurst
Church Hill ✉ RG10 0SJ – ☎ (0118) 934 0034 – www.castlerestaurant.co.uk – Fax (0118) 934 0334
Rest – Menu £ 18 (lunch) – Carte £ 22/36
◆ Charming 16C monk's wash-house. Part panelled dining room with wattle and daub on display and a cosy snug. Classical French menu enhanced by modern interpretations.

at Shinfield South : 4.25 mi. on A 327 - X – ✉ Reading

L'Ortolan (Alan Murchison)
Church Lane ✉ RG2 9BY – ☎ (0118) 988 8500 – www.lortolan.com – Fax (0118) 988 9338 – Closed 24 December-7 January, Sunday and Monday
Rest – Menu £ 26 (lunch)/38 (dinner midweek) – Carte £ 27/57
Spec. Foie gras and pain d'épices sandwich with quince chutney. Saddle of venison with spiced red cabbage and blackberries. Tiramisu.
◆ Red brick former vicarage with lawned gardens and stylish lounge and conservatory. Bright, comfortable dining room; classically based cooking with some original touches and pretty presentation. Smart, busy private dining rooms.

at Sonning-on-Thames Northeast : 4.25 by A 4 on B 4446

French Horn with rm
rm, rest,
✉ RG4 6TN – ☎ (0118) 969 22 04 – www.thefrenchhorn.co.uk – Fax (0118) 944 22 10 – Closed 25-31 December
16 rm – †£ 125 ††£ 170 **Rest** – *(booking essential)* Carte £ 34/61 s
◆ Long-standing family owned restaurant in pretty riverside setting. Bay windowed dining room overlooks lovely garden and offers classical French menus crafted from seasonal ingredients. Comfy, traditional bedrooms; some in an annexe, some with views.

ENGLAND

REDDITCH – Worcestershire – 503 O27 – pop. 74 803 — 19 C2

London 111 mi. – Birmingham 15 mi. – Cheltenham 33 mi. – Stratford-upon-Avon 15 mi.
Palace Theatre, Alcester St ☎ (01527) 60806, info.centre@redditchbc.gov.uk
18 Abbey Hotel G. & C.C. Dagnell End Rd, ☎ (01527) 406 600
18 Lower Grinsty Callow Hill Green Lane, ☎ (01527) 543 079
9 Pitcheroak Plymouth Rd, ☎ (01527) 541 054

Old Rectory
Ipsley Lane, Ipsley ✉ B98 0AP – ☎ (01527) 523 000 – www.theoldrectory-hotel.co.uk – Fax (01527) 517 003
10 rm – †£ 109 ††£ 139
Rest – *(booking essential for non-residents)* Menu £ 15/25
◆ Converted early Georgian rectory surrounded by pleasant mature gardens creating a quiet and secluded haven. Smart, traditional interior décor and individually styled rooms. Charming Georgian style conservatory restaurant.

REDFORD – West Sussex – see Midhurst

REETH – North Yorkshire – 502 O20 – pop. 939 – ✉ Richmond — 22 B1

London 253 mi. – Leeds 53 mi. – Middlesbrough 36 mi. – Newcastle upon Tyne 61 mi.
Hudson House, The Green ☎ (01748) 884059,reeth@yorkshiredales.org.uk

The Burgoyne

On The Green ✉ DL11 6SN – ✆ (01748) 884 292 – www.theburgoyne.co.uk – Fax (01748) 884 292 – Closed 2 January-12 February
8 rm – †£ 105/137 ††£ 145/185 – 1 suite
Rest – *(dinner only) (booking essential for non-residents)* Menu £ 33
◆ Late Georgian hotel overlooking the green with views of the Dales. A charming, personally run, traditionally furnished house with well-appointed, individually styled rooms. Deep green dining room complements surrounding fells.

at Langthwaite Northwest : 3.25 mi. on Langthwaite rd – ✉ Reeth

The Charles Bathurst Inn with rm

✉ DL11 6EN – ✆ (01748) 884 567 – www.cbinn.co.uk – Fax (01748) 884 599 – Closed 25 December
19 rm – †£ 98/123 ††£ 98/123 **Rest** – Carte £ 18/30
◆ Characterful 18C hostelry set in a peaceful hillside village, boasting commanding rural views. The daily menu, inscribed on a mirror, offers refined yet hearty classical British dishes. Bedrooms are spacious and extremely comfy.

at Low Row West : 4 mi. on B 6270

The Punch Bowl Inn with rm

✉ DL11 6PF – ✆ (01748) 886 233 – www.pbinn.co.uk – Fax (01748) 886 945 – Closed 25 December
11 rm – †£ 98/120 ††£ 98/120 **Rest** – Carte £ 18/25
◆ Modernised, but retaining a wealth of rustic charm, this 17C stone inn in the heart of Swaledale is a popular stop off point for walkers. Menus have a strong sense of the seasons. Bedrooms are stylish, spacious and supremely comfortable.

ENGLAND

REIGATE – Surrey – 504 T30 – pop. 47 602 7 D2

London 26 mi. – Brighton 33 mi. – Guildford 20 mi. – Maidstone 38 mi.

Tony Tobin @ The Dining Room

59a High St ✉ RH2 9AE – ✆ (01737) 226 650 – www.tonytobinrestaurants.co.uk – Fax (01737) 226 650 – Closed 23 December-3 January, Saturday lunch, Sunday dinner and Bank Holidays
Rest – Menu £ 19 (except Saturday) – Carte £ 37/46
◆ Contemporary first floor restaurant with pale hues and comfy lounge/bar above. Classical set lunch, more modern à la carte and 5 course tasting menu; the latter with wine recommendations.

The Westerly

2-4 London Rd ✉ RH2 9AN – ✆ (01737) 222 733 – www.thewesterly.co.uk – Closed 1-8 January, Sunday, Monday and lunch Saturday and Tuesday
Rest – *(booking essential at dinner)* Menu £ 20 (lunch) – Carte £ 28/34
◆ Modern, simply decorated restaurant. Skilful kitchen, passionate about the seasons; intelligent menu and understated, wholesome cooking at honest prices. Welcoming service.

La Barbe

71 Bell St ✉ RH2 7AN – ✆ (01737) 241 966 – www.labarbe.co.uk – Fax (01737) 226 387 – Closed Saturday lunch, Sunday dinner and Bank Holidays
Rest – French – Menu £ 24/34
◆ Friendly bistro with Gallic atmosphere and welcoming ambience. Regularly changing menus offer good choice of traditional French cuisine - classical and provincial in style.

RETFORD – Nottinghamshire – 502 R24 – pop. 20 679 16 B1

London 148 mi. – Lincoln 23 mi. – Nottingham 31 mi. – Sheffield 27 mi.
40 Grove St (01777) 860780, retford.tourist@bassetlaw.gov.uk

The Barns without rest

Morton Farm, Babworth, Southwest : 2.25 mi. by A 6420 ✉ DN22 8HA – ✆ (01777) 706 336 – www.thebarns.co.uk – Closed Christmas and New Year
6 rm – †£ 39 ††£ 64/82
◆ Privately owned and run converted part 18C farmhouse on a quiet country road. Informal, old-fashioned, cottage décor throughout. Beams within and lawned gardens without.

RHYDYCROESAU – Shrops. – 502 K25 – see Oswestry

RICHMOND – North Yorkshire – 502 O20 – pop. 8 178 Great Britain 22 B1

London 243 mi. – Leeds 53 mi. – Middlesbrough 26 mi. – Newcastle upon Tyne 44 mi.

Friary Gardens, Victoria Rd ✆ (01748) 828 742, richmond@ytbtic.co.uk

Bend Hagg, ✆ (01748) 825 319

Catterick Leyburn Rd, ✆ (01748) 833 268

Town★ - Castle★ **AC** – Georgian Theatre Royal and Museum★

The Bowes Museum★, Barnard Castle, NW : 15 mi. by B 6274, A 66 and minor rd (right) – Raby Castle★, NE : 6 mi. of Barnard Castle by A 688

Millgate House without rest

3 Millgate ✉ DL10 4JN – ✆ (01748) 823 571 – www.millgatehouse.com – Fax (01748) 850 701

3 rm – †£ 95 ††£ 125

◆ Georgian townhouse with fine elevated views of River Swale and Richmond Castle. Award winning terraced garden. Antique furnished interior. Bedrooms are tastefully restrained.

West End without rest

45 Reeth Rd, West : 0.5 mi. on A 6108 ✉ DL10 4EX – ✆ (01748) 824 783 – www.stayatwestend.co.uk

5 rm – †£ 30/50 ††£ 60/70

◆ Pleasantly located mid 19C house with well kept gardens, close to the River Swale. Small sitting room; spacious, immaculately kept rear breakfast room. Comfortable, homely bedrooms.

at Dalton Northwest : 6.75 mi. by Ravensworth rd and Gayles rd – ✉ Richmond

The Travellers Rest

✉ DL11 7HU – ✆ (01833) 621 225 – Closed 25-26 December, 1 January, 1 week in November, Sunday dinner and Monday

Rest – *(dinner only and Sunday lunch)* Carte £ 17/31

◆ Community pub serving remote village. Blackboard menus offer fresh, homemade dishes, including tasty terrines, fishcakes and the popular duck with orange sauce. Friendly service.

RINGSTEAD – Norfolk – 504 V25 – see Hunstanton

RINGWOOD – Hampshire – 503 O31 – pop. 13 387 6 A2

London 102 mi. – Bournemouth 11 mi. – Salisbury 17 mi. – Southampton 20 mi.

The Furlong ✆ (01425) 470896, information@nfdc.gov.uk

Moortown Lodge without rest

244 Christchurch Rd, South : 1 mi. on B 3347 ✉ BH24 3AS – ✆ (01425) 471 404 – www.moortownlodge.co.uk – Fax (01425) 476 527

7 rm – †£ 76/84 ††£ 84/94

◆ House dating from the 1760s, located on the edge of the New Forest. Family run, traditional atmosphere with a cosy lounge and chintz-furnished rooms of varying sizes.

RIPLEY – North Yorkshire – 502 P21 – pop. 193 – ✉ Harrogate 22 B2

London 213 mi. – Bradford 21 mi. – Leeds 18 mi. – Newcastle upon Tyne 79 mi.

The Boar's Head

✉ HG3 3AY – ✆ (01423) 771 888 – www.boarsheadripley.co.uk – Fax (01423) 771 509

25 rm – †£ 105 ††£ 150

Rest *The Restaurant* – Menu £ 18/30 – Carte £ 22/34

Rest *The Bistro* – Carte £ 18/27

◆ 18C coaching inn within estate village of Ripley Castle, reputedly furnished from castle's attics. Comfy, stylish, unique rooms are individually furnished; some in courtyard or adjacent house. Classically based, seasonal dishes in The Restaurant. More informal dining in The Bistro.

RIPLEY – Surrey – **504** S30 – **pop. 2 041** **7** C1

London 28 mi. – Guildford 6 mi.

Talbot Inn

High St. ✉ GU23 6BB – ✆ (01483) 225 188 – www.thetalbotinn.com

39 rm – £ 99/129 £ 159, £ 5.95

Rest The Restaurant – *see restaurant listing*

◆ Lovingly restored 15C coaching inn, where Nelson would meet his mistress. Characterful beamed rooms in main house; more contemporary in new wing. All have flat screens and good facilities.

Drake's (Steve Drake)

The Clock House, High St ✉ GU23 6AQ – ✆ (01483) 224 777 – www.drakesrestaurant.co.uk – Fax (01483) 222 940 – Closed Christmas, 2 weeks August, 10 days January, Saturday lunch, Sunday and Monday

Rest – Menu £ 26/46

Spec. Quail with liver parfait and pickled radish. John Dory with pea, ham and liquorice sauce. Salted peanut caramel, biscotti and malt barley ice cream.

◆ Georgian restaurant's red brick façade dominated by large clock. Intimate lounges and relaxing, open plan dining room with local gallery art on walls. Simple, seasonal menu; kitchen makes use of modern techniques and interesting combinations. Well-established team provide formal service.

The Restaurant – at Talbot Inn

High St. ✉ GU23 6BB – ✆ (01483) 225 188 – www.thetalbotinn.com – Fax (01483) 221 332

Rest – Menu £ 15/35 – Carte £ 25/55

◆ Contemporary, brasserie-style restaurant with copper ceiling and glass doors onto secluded terrace/garden. Menu showcases local, seasonal produce in modern British dishes.

ENGLAND

RIPON – North Yorkshire – **502** P21 – **pop. 16 468** Great Britain **22** B2

London 222 mi. – Leeds 26 mi. – Middlesbrough 35 mi. – York 23 mi.

Minster Rd ✆ (01765) 604625, ripontic@harrogate.gov.uk

Ripon City Palace Rd, ✆ (01765) 603 640

Town★ - Cathedral★ (Saxon Crypt) **AC**

Fountains Abbey★★★ **AC** :- Studley Royal **AC** (<★ from Anne Boleyn's Seat) - Fountains Hall (Fa 0.5ade★), SW : 2.5 mi. by B 6265 – Newby Hall (Tapestries★) **AC**, SE : 3.5 mi. by B 6265

The Old Deanery

Minster Rd ✉ HG4 1QS – ✆ (01765) 600 003 – www.theolddeanery.co.uk – Fax (01765) 600 027 – Closed 25 December-1 January

11 rm – £ 95/130 £ 100/160

Rest – *(Closed Sunday dinner)* Menu £ 16/33 – Carte approx. £ 20

◆ Eponymously named hotel opposite cathedral. Stylish interior blends seamlessly with older charms. Afternoon tea in secluded garden. 18C oak staircase leads to modern rooms. Appealing seasonal cooking in spacious dining room.

Sharow Cross House

Dishforth Rd, Sharow, Northeast : 1.75 mi. by A 61 on Sharow rd ✉ HG4 5BQ – ✆ (01765) 609 866 – www.sharowcrosshouse.com – Closed 2 weeks Christmas and New Year

3 rm – £ 55/65 £ 75/85 **Rest** – *(by arrangement)* Menu £ 22

◆ Idyllically set 19C house, built for mill owner. Capacious hall with welcoming fire. Spacious bedrooms: the master room is huge and offers Cathedral views on clear days.

at Aldfield **Southwest : 3.75 mi. by B 6265 – ✉ Ripon**

Bay Tree Farm

✉ HG4 3BE – ✆ (01765) 620 394 – www.baytreefarm.co.uk – Fax (01765) 620 394

6 rm – £ 45/60 £ 76/90 **Rest** – *(by arrangement)* Menu £ 16

◆ 18C sandstone barn with rural views, set on a working farm. Lounge with wood burning stove and French windows opening into garden; bright, spacious bedrooms with modern bathrooms. Homely food could include beef from the farm.

RISHWORTH – W. Yorks. – see Sowerby Bridge

ROADE – Northamptonshire – 504 R27 – pop. 2 254 **16** B3

London 66 mi. – Coventry 36 mi. – Leicester 42 mi. – Northampton 5 mi.

XX **Roade House** with rm — AC rest, P VISA AE

16 High St ✉ NN7 2NW – ☎ (01604) 863 372 – www.roadehousehotel.co.uk – Fax (01604) 862 421 – Closed 26 December-3 January

10 rm – £ 65/79 ££ 86/100

Rest – *(Closed Sunday dinner)* Menu £ 23/31

◆ Personally run, former village pub and schoolhouse, with two lounges and a simple linen-laid dining room. Crafted from local produce, monthly set menus offer classical cooking with modern touches. Pleasant bedrooms are furnished in pine.

ROCHDALE – Greater Manchester – 502 N23 – pop. 95 796 **20** B2

London 224 mi. – Blackpool 40 mi. – Burnley 11 mi. – Leeds 45 mi.

Touchstones, The Esplanade ☎ (01706) 924928, tic@link4life.org

18 Bagslate Edenfield Rd, ☎ (01706) 643 818

18 Marland Bolton Rd, Springfield Park, ☎ (01706) 649 801

27 Castle Hawk Castleton Chadwick Lane, ☎ (01706) 640 841

XX **Nutters** — P VISA AE

Edenfield Rd, Norden, West : 3.5 mi. on A 680 ✉ OL12 7TT – ☎ (01706) 650 167 – www.nuttersrestaurant.com – Fax (01706) 650 167 – Closed 27-30 December, 2-3 January and Monday

Rest – Menu £ 17/22 (lunch) – Carte £ 24/38

◆ Views of the lyrical gardens contrast with a menu of often complex modern British dishes with international twists and influences. Best views at either end of the room.

ROCK – Cornwall – 503 F32 – pop. 4 593 – ✉ Wadebridge **1** B2

London 266 mi. – Newquay 24 mi. – Tintagel 14 mi. – Truro 32 mi.

Pencarrow★, SE : 8.5 mi. by B 3314 and A 389

St Enodoc — P VISA AE

✉ PL27 6LA – ☎ (01208) 863 394 – www.enodoc-hotel.co.uk – Fax (01208) 863 970 – Closed 8 December-2nd February

16 rm – £ 95/185 ££ 130/235 – 4 suites

Rest – *(Nathan Outlaw due to open in spring 2010)*

◆ Tasteful and very comfortable New England style hotel, popular with families and golfers, with stunning views over the bay to Padstow. As we went to press: Michelin starred chef Nathan Outlaw plans to relocate his restaurant here from Fowey.

XX **L'Estuaire** — VISA

Rock Rd ✉ PL27 6JS – ☎ (01208) 862 622 – www.lestuairerestaurant.com – Fax (01208) 862 622 – Closed 1 week Christmas, 2 weeks January, 2 weeks November and Monday-Tuesday except Bank Holidays

Rest – *(booking advisable)* Menu £ 23 (lunch) – Carte £ 29/51

◆ Pleasant restaurant with small terrace, in popular seaside town. Concise à la carte features modern, seasonal flavours, including tasty cured meats and delicious homemade bread and ice cream.

at Trebetherick North : 1 mi. by Trewint Lane – 503 F32

St Moritz — P VISA AE

Trebetherick ✉ PL27 6SD – ☎ (01208) 862 242 – www.stmoritzhotel.co.uk – Fax (01208) 862 262

30 rm – £ 72/135 ££ 120/210 – 15 suites

Rest – Menu £ 22 (lunch) – Carte dinner £ 26/36

◆ Art deco style hotel with leisure club, swimming pool and 6 room spa. Smartly furnished bedrooms; spacious bathrooms. Suites have a lounge, kitchen and estuary views. Restaurant displays a simple, flavoursome menu of unfussy dishes.

ROCKBEARE – Devon – see Exeter

ROECLIFFE – North Yorkshire – see Boroughbridge

ROGATE – West Sussex – 504 R30 – pop. 1 785 – ✉ Petersfield (hants.) 7 C2

London 63 mi. – Brighton 42 mi. – Guildford 29 mi. – Portsmouth 23 mi.

Mizzards Farm without rest

Southwest : 1 mi. by Harting rd ✉ GU31 5HS – ☎ (01730) 821 656 – Fax (01730) 821 655 – Minimum 2 night stay, closed Christmas and New Year

3 rm – †£ 65 ††£ 88/90

◆ 17C farmhouse with delightful landscaped gardens, which include a lake, bordered by River Rother. Views of woods and farmland. Fine fabrics and antiques in appealing rooms.

ROMALDKIRK – Durham – 502 N20 – see Barnard Castle

ROMSEY – Hampshire – 503 P31 – pop. 17 386 Great Britain 6 A2

London 82 mi. – Bournemouth 28 mi. – Salisbury 16 mi. – Southampton 8 mi.

13 Church St ☎ (01794) 512987, romseytic@testvalley.gov.uk

18 Dunwood Manor Awbridge Danes Rd, ☎ (01794) 340 549

18 Nursling, ☎ (023) 8073 4637

27 Wellow East Wellow Ryedown Lane, ☎ (01794) 322 872

Abbey★ (interior★★)

Broadlands★ AC, S : 1 m

Ranvilles Farm House without rest

Ower, Southwest : 2 mi. on A 3090 (southbound carriageway) ✉ SO51 6AA – ☎ (023) 8081 4481 – www.ranvilles.com – Fax (023) 8081 4481

5 rm – †£ 30/45 ††£ 55/70

◆ Attractive part 16C farmhouse set within five acres of garden and fields. Welcoming country style décor and furniture throughout, including the well-kept bedrooms.

Highfield House

Newtown Rd, Awbridge, Northwest : 3.5 mi. by A 3090 (old A 31) off A 27 ✉ SO51 0GG – ☎ (01794) 340 727 – www.highfieldhampshire.co.uk

3 rm – †£ 50/65 ††£ 80

Rest – *(by arrangement, communal dining)* Menu £ 18

◆ Modern house with gardens, in a tranquil location just out of Awbridge village. Accommodation is comfortable with good facilities. Real fires in the guest lounge. Communal dining with garden views.

The Three Tuns VISA AE

58 Middlebridge St ✉ SO51 8HL – ☎ (01794) 512 639 – www.thethreetunsromsey.co.uk – Closed 26 December and Monday lunch

Rest – Menu £ 8 (lunch) – Carte £ 15/25

◆ Cosy period feel in thickly beamed, 300-year-old pub. Lunch menus offer pub favourites, while the evening à la carte moves things up a notch. Friendly service and real ales.

ROSS-ON-WYE – County of Herefordshire – 503 M28 – pop. 10 085 18 B3

Great Britain

London 118 mi. – Gloucester 15 mi. – Hereford 15 mi. – Newport 35 mi.

Swan House, Edde Cross St ☎ (01989) 562768, tic-ross@herefordshire.gov.uk

Market House★ – Yat Rock (≤★)

SW : Wye Valley★ – Goodrich Castle★ AC, SW : 3.5 mi. by A 40

The Chase VISA AE

Gloucester Rd ✉ HR9 5LH – ☎ (01989) 763 161 – www.chasehotel.co.uk – Fax (01989) 768 330 – Closed 25-27 December

36 rm – †£ 65/175 ††£ 135/195 **Rest** – Menu £ 14/19 – Carte £ 26/37

◆ Elegant Georgian country house, close to town centre. Ground floor areas have been given a contemporary makeover. Range of bedroom styles with traditional décor. Restaurant exudes airy, period feel.

ENGLAND

Wilton Court

Wilton Lane, West : 0.75 mi. by B 4260 (A 49 Hereford) ✉ HR9 6AQ – ✆ (01989) 562 569 – www.wiltoncourthotel.com – Fax (01989) 768 460 – Closed 3-20 January

10 rm – £ 80/125 £ 115/155

Rest *Mulberry* – Menu £ 18 (lunch) – Carte £ 30/40

◆ Attractive, part-Elizabethan house on the banks of the River Wye. 16C wood panelling in situ in bar and two of the bedrooms: others have a distinctly William Morris influence. Light, airy conservatory restaurant boasts Lloyd Loom furniture and garden views.

The Bridge at Wilton with rm

Wilton ✉ HR9 6AA – ✆ (01989) 562 655 – www.bridge-house-hotel.com – Fax (01989) 567 652

9 rm – £ 80 £ 120 **Rest** – Menu £ 16 **s** (lunch) – Carte £ 31/45 **s**

◆ On the banks of the Wye, boasting a kitchen garden supplying ingredients for the owners' passionate belief in home cooking. Also, a homely bar and well-maintained bedrooms.

The Lough Pool at Sellack

Sellack, Northwest : 3.25 mi. by B 4260 and A 49 on Hoarwithy rd ✉ HR9 6LX – ✆ (01989) 730 236 – www.loughpool.co.uk – Fax (01981) 570 322 – Closed 25 December, Sunday dinner and Monday except Bank Holidays

Rest – Carte £ 21/28

◆ Characterful 16C black and white timbered inn, set in a beautiful, rural spot. Great value traditional menu changes daily, featuring fresh, local produce from just down the road.

Mill Race

Walford ✉ HR9 5QS – ✆ (01989) 562 891 – www.millrace.info

Rest – Carte £ 12/27

◆ Spacious, modern pub with large terrace and regular events. Seasonal British menu focuses on simplicity, with the sourcing of humanely reared, sustainable produce being paramount.

at Glewstone Southwest : 3.25 mi. by A 40 – ✉ Ross-On-Wye

Glewstone Court

✉ HR9 6AW – ✆ (01989) 770 367 – www.glewstonecourt.com – Fax (01989) 770 282 – Closed 25-26 December

8 rm – £ 60/80 £ 120 **Rest** – Menu £ 14 **s** (lunch) – Carte £ 24/35 **s**

◆ Part Georgian and Victorian country house with impressive cedar of Lebanon in grounds. Sweeping staircase leads to uncluttered rooms. Family run with charming eccentricity. Antique-strewn dining room.

at Kerne Bridge South : 3.75 mi. on B 4234 – ✉ Ross-On-Wye

Lumleys without rest

✉ HR9 5QT – ✆ (01600) 890 040 – www.thelumleys.co.uk

3 rm – £ 50 £ 75

◆ Welcoming and personally run guesthouse in sympathetically converted Victorian house. Ideally located for Wye Valley and Forest of Dean. Pine decorated cottage style rooms.

ROSTHWAITE – Cumbria – **502** K20 – see Keswick

ROTHBURY – Northumberland – **501** O18 – pop. 1 963 – ✉ Morpeth **24** A2

Great Britain

London 311 mi. – Edinburgh 84 mi. – Newcastle upon Tyne 29 mi.

Coquetdale Centre, Church St ✆ (01669) 620887, tic.rothbury@nnpa.org.uk

Cragside House★ (interior★) AC

Farm Cottage without rest

Thropton, West : 2.25 mi. on B 6341 ✉ NE65 7NA – ✆ (01669) 620 831 – www.farmcottageguesthouse.co.uk – Fax (01669) 620 831 – Closed 23 December-2 January

5 rm – £ 50/65 £ 80/84

◆ 18C stone cottage and gardens; owner was actually born here. Two comfy lounges filled with family prints and curios. Individually styled rooms with plenty of extra touches.

ENGLAND

Thropton Demesne Farmhouse without rest

Thropton, West : 2.25 mi. on B 6341 ✉ NE65 7LT – ☎ (01669) 620 196 – www.throptondemesne.co.uk – Easter-October

4 rm – £ 60 £ 70

◆ Early 19C stone-built former farmhouse; unbroken Coquet Valley views. Lounge defined by quality décor. Artwork on walls by owner. Individually styled rooms with lovely vistas.

ROTHERHAM – South Yorkshire – 502 P23 – pop. 117 262 — 22 B3

London 166 mi. – Kingston-upon-Hull 61 mi. – Leeds 36 mi. – Sheffield 6 mi.

40 Bridgegate ☎ (01709) 835904, tic@rotherham.gov.uk

Thrybergh Park, ☎ (01709) 850 466

Grange Park Kimberworth Upper Wortley Rd, ☎ (01709) 558 884

Phoenix Brinsworth Pavilion Lane, ☎ (01709) 363 788

at Bramley East : 4.5 mi. by A 6021 off A 631 – ✉ Rotherham

Elton rm, rest,

Main St, Bramley ✉ S66 2SF – ☎ (01709) 545 681 – www.bw-eltonhotel.co.uk – Fax (01709) 549 100

29 rm – £ 52/82 £ 72/96

Rest – Menu £ 14/23 **s** – Carte £ 25/29 **s**

◆ Solid stone house with extensions, in the centre of village. Traditionally styled public areas include conservatory lounge. Extension rooms have a more modern style. Richly styled dining room with warm burgundy walls.

ENGLAND

ROWDE – Wilts. – 503 N29 – see Devizes

ROWHOOK – W. Sussex – see Horsham

ROWSLEY – Derbyshire – 502 P24 – pop. 451 – ✉ Matlock — 16 A1

Great Britain

London 157 mi. – Derby 23 mi. – Manchester 40 mi. – Nottingham 30 mi.

Chatsworth★★★ (Park and Garden★★★) **AC**, N : by B 6012

East Lodge rm, rest,

✉ DE4 2EF – ☎ (01629) 734 474 – www.eastlodge.com – Fax (01629) 733 949

12 rm – £ 80/160 £ 80/160

Rest – Carte £ 22/36

◆ Elegant 17C country house set in ten acres of well kept grounds, once the lodge to Haddon Hall. Rooms are each individually decorated and superior rooms have garden views. Simple dining room with terrace.

The Peacock

Bakewell Rd ✉ DE4 2EB – ☎ (01629) 733 518 – www.thepeacockatrowsley.com – Fax (01629) 732 671 – Closed 24-26 December

16 rm – £ 75/125 £ 195/230, £ 7

Rest – Carte £ 39/54

◆ Characterful, antique furnished, 17C house with gardens leading down to the River Derwent. Rooms, a variety of shapes and sizes, are antique or reproduction furnished. Restaurant divided between three smart rooms.

ROWTON – Ches. – see Chester

London 99 mi. - Birmingham 23 mi. - Coventry 9 mi. - Leicester 33 mi.

The Royal Pump Rooms, The Parade ✆ (01926) 742762, leamingtontic@shakespeare-country.co.uk

Leamington and County Whitnash Golf Lane, ✆ (01926) 425 961

Mallory Court

Harbury Lane, Bishop's Tachbrook, South : 2.25 mi. by B 4087 (Tachbrook Rd)
✉ CV33 9QB - ✆ (01926) 330 214 - www.mallory.co.uk - Fax (01926) 451 714
30 rm ☕ - **†**£ 95/325 **††**£ 149/395
Rest *The Brasserie at Mallory* - see restaurant listing
Rest *The Dining Room* - *(Closed Saturday lunch) (booking essential)*
Menu £ 28 (weekday lunch)/35 (Sunday lunch) - Carte dinner £ 40/55
Spec. Foie gras 'bon bon' with smoked duck and sherry jelly. Loin and bolognaise of venison. Crème brûlée with strawberries and mascarpone ice cream.

◆ Part Edwardian country house in Lutyens style; extensive landscaped gardens. Finest quality antiques and furnishings throughout public areas and individually styled bedrooms. Refined, classically-based cooking in elegant, panelled restaurant; formal and well-organised service.

Adams without rest

22 Avenue Rd ✉ CV31 3PQ - ✆ (01926) 450 742 - www.adams-hotel.co.uk
- Fax (01926) 313 110 - Closed 24 December-3 January V**n**
14 rm ☕ - **†**£ 60/90 **††**£ 85/90

◆ Delightful house of the Regency period with plenty of charm and character: original features include ceiling mouldings. Immaculate and similarly attractive bedrooms.

York House without rest

9 York Rd ✉ CV31 3PR - ✆ (01926) 424 671 - www.yorkhousehotel.biz
- Fax (01926) 832 272 - Closed 23 December-1 January V**u**
8 rm ☕ - **†**£ 36/55 **††**£ 65/70

◆ Victorian house on a pleasant parade, retains characterful fittings such as stained glass windows. Views of River Leam. Simply furnished rooms in period style.

ROYAL LEAMINGTON SPA

Adelaide Rd V
Avenue Rd . . . . V 2
Bath St . . . . V 3
Beauchamp Ave . . . . U
Beauchamp Hill . . . . U 4
Binswood St . . . . U 6
Brandon Parade . . . . U 10
Church Hill . . . . UV 16
Clarendon Ave. . . . . U
Clarendon Pl. . . . . U 18
Dale St . . . . UV
Hamilton Terrace . . . . V 21
High St . . . . V 22
Holly Walk . . . . U
Kenilworth Rd . . . . U
Leam Terrace V
Leicester St . . . . U
Lillington Ave . . . . U
Lillington Rd . . . . U
Lower Ave . . . . V 28
Newbold Terrace . . . . V 30
Northumberland Rd . . . . U 33
Old Warwick Rd V
Parade . . . . UV
Priory Terrace . . . . V 37
Radford Rd V
Regent Grove . . . . UV 40
Regent St . . . . UV
Royal Priors Shopping Centre . . . . U
Rugby Rd . . . . U
Russell Terrace V
Spencer St . . . . V 44
Tachbrook Rd . . . . V 47
Victoria Terrace . . . . V 49
Warwick St . . . . U
Willes Rd . . . . UV

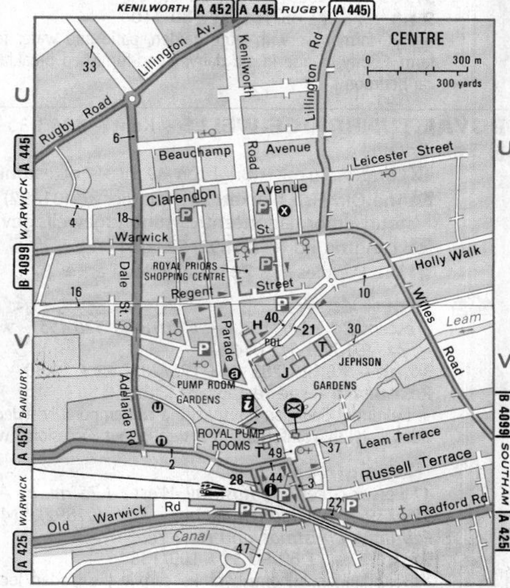

XX **Restaurant 23**

23 Dormer Place ✉ CV32 5AA – ✆ (01926) 422 422 – www.restaurant23.co.uk – Fax (01926) 422 246 – Closed 25-26 December, 2 weeks January, last 2 weeks August, Sunday and Monday Va

Rest – Menu £ 19 (lunch)/23 (dinner weekdays) – Carte £ 37/44

◆ Ever spoken to a working chef in a restaurant? You can here, in elegantly appointed surroundings, where classically based, seasonal, modern dishes are concocted by the owner.

XX **Oscar's**

39 Chandos St ✉ CV32 4RL – ✆ (01926) 452 807 – www.oscarsfrenchbistro.co.uk – Closed 25-26 December, Sunday and Monday Ux

Rest – French – *(booking essential)* Menu £ 16/26

◆ Friendly, informal and unpretentious, divided between three cosy rooms on two floors; best atmosphere on ground floor. Expect good value and authentic French bistro cooking.

XX **The Emperors**

Bath Place ✉ CV31 3BP – ✆ (01926) 313 030 – Fax (01926) 435 966 – Closed 25-26 December, 1 January and Sunday Vi

Rest – Chinese – Carte £ 19/27 **s**

◆ Former warehouse, now a spacious Chinese restaurant with smart red, gold and black décor. Emperors' jackets hang on the walls. Large menus mix popular and authentic dishes with seasonal specials.

XX **The Brasserie at Mallory** at Mallory Court Hotel

Harbury Lane, Bishop's Tachbrook, South : 2.25 mi. by B 4087 (Tachbrook Rd) ✉ CV33 9QB – ✆ (01926) 453 939 – www.mallory.co.uk – Fax (01926) 451 714 – closed Monday-Tuesday and Sunday dinner

Rest – *(booking essential)* Menu £ 20/25 – Carte £ 27/36

◆ In hotel annex; step into bar with eye-catching Art Deco style. Conservatory dining room overlooks pretty walled garden and terrace. Modern British cooking in a buzzy setting.

at Weston under Wetherley Northeast : 4.5 mi. by A 445 on B 4453 – ✉ Royal Leamington Spa

Wethele Manor Farm without rest

✉ CV33 9BZ – ✆ (01926) 831 772 – www.wethelemanor.com – Fax (01926) 315 359 – Closed 1 week Christmas

9 rm – †£ 65/105 ††£ 80/110

◆ 16C farmhouse with large garden, patio and water feature, set in 250 acres of working farm. Comfy lounge in old dairy; wood-furnished breakfast room complete with well. Classical bedrooms.

ENGLAND

ROYAL TUNBRIDGE WELLS – Kent – 504 U30 – pop. 60 095 — 8 B2

Great Britain

London 36 mi. – Brighton 33 mi. – Folkestone 46 mi. – Hastings 27 mi.

The Old Fish Market, The Pantiles ✆ (01892) 515675, touristinformationcentre@tunbridgewells.gov.uk

Langton Rd, ✆ (01892) 523 034

The Pantiles★ B **26** – Calverley Park★ B

Hotel du Vin

Crescent Rd ✉ TN1 2LY – ✆ (01892) 526 455 – www.hotelduvin.com – Fax (01892) 512 044 Bc

34 rm – †£ 125/285 ††£ 125/285, £ 14.50

Rest *Bistro* – see restaurant listing

◆ Delightful Georgian house with a contemporarily styled interior themed around wine; provides a stylish, comfortable feel throughout. Occasional wine-based events.

Danehurst without rest

41 Lower Green Rd, Rusthall, West : 1.75 mi. by A 264 ✉ TN4 8TW – ✆ (01892) 527 739 – www.danehurst.net – Fax (01892) 514 804 – Closed first 2 weeks February, Christmas and New Year Ae

5 rm – †£ 60/90 ††£ 109/135

◆ Victorian family home, with koi carp in the garden, located in residential area of town. Mix of homely furniture and furnishings and a conservatory breakfast room.

ROYAL TUNBRIDGE WELLS

Street	Ref	Street	Ref	Street	Ref
Benhall Mill Rd	**A** 3	Hall's Hole Rd	**A** 13	Pantiles (The)	**B** 26
Bishop's Down	**A** 4	High Rocks Lane	**A** 16	Prospect Rd	**A** 27
Calverley Rd	**B**	High St	**B** 14	Royal Victoria Pl. Shopping Centre	**B**
Crescent Rd	**B** 9	Hungershall Park Rd	**A** 17	Rusthall Rd	**A** 28
Fir Tree Rd	**A** 10	Lansdowne Rd	**B** 18	St John's Rd	**B** 29
Grosvenor Rd	**B** 12	Lower Green Rd	**A** 20	Tea Garden Lane	**A** 30
		Major York's Rd	**A** 21	Vale Rd	**B** 33
		Monson Rd	**B** 22	Victoria Rd	**B** 34
		Mount Ephraim	**A, B** 23	Warwick Park	**B** 35
		Mount Ephraim Rd	**B** 24		
		Mount Pleasant Rd	**B** 25		

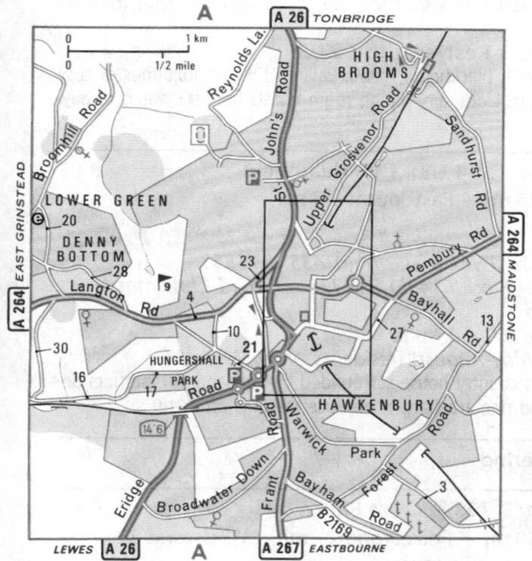

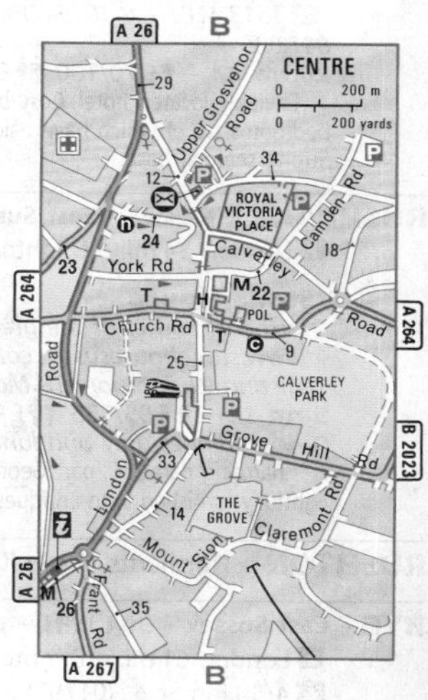

ENGLAND

Thackeray's

85 London Rd ✉ TN1 1EA – ☎ (01892) 511 921 – www.thackerays-restaurant.co.uk – Fax (01892) 527 561 – Closed Sunday dinner and Monday Bn

Rest – Menu £ 18/27 – Carte £ 38/49

◆ Grade II listed 17C house with handsome Oriental terrace. Modern interior contrasts pleasingly with façade. The classically based cooking employs first rate ingredients.

Bistro – at Hotel du Vin

✉ TN1 2LY – ☎ (01892) 526 455 – www.hotelduvin.com – Fax (01892) 512 044

Rest – *(booking essential)* Carte £ 23/39 Bc

◆ Classically styled with dark wood floors and furniture and wine memorabilia. Terrace for lunch. Interesting modern menu. Informal and efficient service.

at Speldhurst North : 3.5 mi. by A 26 - A – ✉ Royal Tunbridge Wells

George & Dragon

Speldhurst Hill ✉ TN3 0NN – ☎ (01892) 863 125 – www.speldhurst.com – Fax (01892) 863 216 – Closed Sunday dinner

Rest – Carte £ 20/28

◆ Warm and welcoming 13C pub with lovely terrace. Cooking is rustic and forthright, and they're proud of the range and quality of their local ingredients; heart-warming puddings.

ROYSTON – Hertfordshire – 504 T27 – pop. 14 570 — 12 B1

London 48 mi.

The Cabinet at Reed

High St, South : 3 mi. by A 10 ✉ SG8 8AH – ☎ (01763) 848 366 – www.thecabinetatreed.co.uk – Closed 26 December, 1 January and Monday

Rest – Menu £ 15/25 – Carte £ 25/45

◆ White clapperboard pub with pleasant restaurant and delightful snug. Cooking is flavoursome but not always what it seems, as traditional dishes are given a more modern twist.

ROZEL BAY – C.I. – **503** P33 – **see Channel Islands (Jersey)**

RUAN-HIGH-LANES – Cornwall – **503** F33 – **see Veryan**

RUNSWICK BAY – North Yorkshire – ✉ Whitby **23** C1

London 285 mi. – Middlesbrough 24 mi. – Whitby 9 mi.

Cliffemount

✉ TS13 5HU – ☎ (01947) 840 103 – www.cliffemounthotel.co.uk – Fax (01947) 841 025

20 rm – ♦£ 70/100 ♦♦£ 135 **Rest** – Carte £ 23/39

◆ Enviably located hotel. Cosy bar with blackboard menu. Balanced mix of luxurious or cosy bedrooms, 10 of which have balconies. Light, airy dining room boasts fantastic views of bay. Strong seafood base.

RUSHLAKE GREEN – East Sussex – **504** U31 – ✉ Heathfield **8** B2

London 54 mi. – Brighton 26 mi. – Eastbourne 13 mi.

Stone House

Northeast corner of the green ✉ TN21 9QJ – ☎ (01435) 830 553 – www.stonehousesussex.co.uk – Fax (01435) 830 726 – Closed Christmas-New Year and 21 February-18 March

5 rm – ♦£ 95/135 ♦♦£ 195/260 – 1 suite

Rest – *(dinner only and lunch May-August) (residents only)* Menu £ 28

◆ Charming part 15C, part Georgian country house surrounded by parkland. All interiors delightfully furnished with antiques and fine art. Garden produce features on menu.

RUSHTON – Northants. – **see Kettering**

RYE – East Sussex – **504** W31 – **pop. 3 708** Great Britain **9** C2

London 61 mi. – Brighton 49 mi. – Folkestone 27 mi. – Maidstone 33 mi.

4/5 Lion St ☎ (01797) 229049, ryetic@tourismse.com

Old Town★★ : Mermaid Street★, St Mary's Church (★)

The George in Rye

98 High St ✉ TN31 7JT – ☎ (01797) 222 114 – www.thegeorgeinrye.com – Fax (01797) 224 065

24 rm – ♦£ 95/125 ♦♦£ 175/275

Rest – Menu £ 17 (lunch) – Carte dinner £ 25/46

◆ Part 16C coaching inn; appealing mix of contemporary design and original features. Variously-sized bedrooms have state-of-the-art TVs and quality linen. Pleasant courtyard. Trendy restaurant offers Mediterranean dishes made with locally sourced produce and good choice of wines by glass.

Mermaid Inn

Mermaid St ✉ TN31 7EY – ☎ (01797) 223 065 – www.mermaidinn.com – Fax (01797) 225 069

31 rm – ♦£ 80/150 ♦♦£ 200/240 **Rest** – Menu £ 25/34 – Carte £ 46/54

◆ Historic inn dating from 15C. Immense character, from the timbered exterior on a cobbled street to the heavily beamed, antique furnished interior warmed by roaring log fires. Two dining options: both exude age and character.

Jeake's House without rest

Mermaid St ✉ TN31 7ET – ☎ (01797) 222 828 – www.jeakeshouse.com – Fax (01797) 222 623

11 rm – ♦£ 64/80 ♦♦£ 102/128

◆ Down a cobbled lane, a part 17C house, once a wool store and a Quaker meeting place. Welcoming atmosphere amid antiques, sloping floors and beams. Pretty, traditional rooms.

Oaklands without rest

Udimore Rd, Southwest : 1.25 mi. on B 2089 ✉ TN31 6AB – ☎ (01797) 229 734 – www.oaklands-rye.co.uk – Fax (01797) 229 734

3 rm – ♦£ 60/70 ♦♦£ 84/100

◆ Restored Edwardian guest house with countryside views run by welcoming hosts. Stylish breakfast room with old Arabic door as table. Spotless bedrooms include two four posters.

Durrant House without rest

2 Market St ✉ TN31 7LA – ✆ (01797) 223 182 – www.durranthouse.com

5 rm ☕ – 🚹£ 78 🚹🚹£ 120

◆ Grade I listed house of unknown age. Neat breakfast room with daily breakfast specials. Bright lounge looks down East Street. Carefully appointed, immaculate modern rooms.

Willow Tree House without rest

113 Winchelsea Rd, South : 0.5 mi. on A 259 ✉ TN31 7EL – ✆ (01797) 227 820 – www.willow-tree-house.com

6 rm ☕ – 🚹£ 70 🚹🚹£ 120

◆ Lovingly restored 18C house close to harbour. Light colours and modern fabrics sit beside exposed brickwork and original fireplaces. Bedrooms boast excellent bathrooms with power showers. Good breakfasts.

Flushing Inn

4 Market St ✉ TN31 7LA – ✆ (01797) 223 292 – www.theflushinginn.com – Closed first two weeks January, first two weeks June, 26 December, Monday and Tuesday

Rest – Seafood – Menu £ 19 (lunch) – Carte £ 15/37

◆ A neighbourhood institution, this 15C inn with heavily timbered and panelled dining area features a superb 16C fresco. The seafood oriented menu has a local, traditional tone.

Webbe's at The Fish Café

17 Tower St ✉ TN31 7AT – ✆ (01797) 222 226 – www.webbesrestaurants.co.uk – Fax (01797) 229 260 – Closed 25-26 December and Mondays in winter

Rest – Seafood – *(booking essential at dinner)* Carte £ 22/32 **s**

◆ Large converted warehouse: terracotta painted ground floor for seafood lunches and eclectic options. Dinner upstairs features more serious piscine menus. Tangible buzziness.

Globe Inn

10 Military Rd, North : off A 268 ✉ TN31 7NX – ✆ (01797) 227 918 – Closed Monday

Rest – *(booking essential)* Carte £ 20/30

◆ Traditional weatherboard inn with contemporary interior. Deli boards, tapas style dishes and pub classics available at lunch; more formally laid out menu of substantial dishes at dinner.

ENGLAND

SAFFRON WALDEN – Essex – 504 U27 – pop. 14 313 — 12 B1

London 43 mi. – Bishop's Stortford 12 mi. – Cambridge 18 mi.

the restaurant

Victoria House, 2 Church St ✉ CB10 1JW – ✆ (01799) 526 444 – www.trocs.co.uk – Closed 2 weeks Easter, 1 week summer, Sunday and Monday

Rest – *(dinner only)* Menu £ 17 (weekdays) **s** – Carte £ 22/33 **s**

◆ Cosy basement restaurant in town centre, displaying stone floors, exposed brick and modern art. Stylishly presented dishes boast well-defined flavours and some interesting Mediterranean touches.

Dish

13a King St ✉ CB10 1HE – ✆ (01799) 513 300 – www.dishrestaurant.co.uk – Fax (01799) 531 699 – Closed Sunday dinner

Rest – Menu £ 18/20 (except dinner Friday-Saturday) – Carte dinner Friday-Saturday £ 26/35

◆ First floor restaurant within characterful beamed house in town centre. Modern oil paintings exude jazzy theme. Classically based dishes take on adventurous note at dinner.

Guesthouses don't provide the same level of service as hotels. They are often characterised by a warm welcome and a décor which reflects the owner's personality. Those shown in red are particularly pleasant.

ST ALBANS – Hertfordshire – 504 T28 – pop. 82 429 Great Britain 12 A2

London 27 mi. – Cambridge 41 mi. – Luton 10 mi.

Town Hall, Market Pl ✆ (01727) 864511, tic@stalbans.gov.uk

18 Batchwood Hall Batchwood Drive, ✆ (01727) 833 349

27 Redbourn Kinsbourne Green Lane, ✆ (01582) 793 493

City★ - Cathedral★ BZ – Verulamium★ (Museum★ **AC** AY)

Hatfield House★★ **AC**, E : 6 mi. by A 1057

St Michael's Manor

rm, VISA AE

St Michael's Village, Fishpool St ✉ *AL3 4RY* – ✆ *(01727) 864 444*
– www.stmichaelsmanor.com – Fax (01727) 848 909 AY**d**
29 rm – ♦£ 125/180 ♦♦£ 250 – 1 suite
Rest *The Lake* – *(closed 25 December)* Menu £ 25 (lunch) – Carte £ 25/36

◆ This part 16C, part William and Mary manor house overlooks a lake. Elegant bedrooms are named after trees; some are suites with sitting rooms, all are luxurious and stylish. Conservatory dining room with splendid vistas.

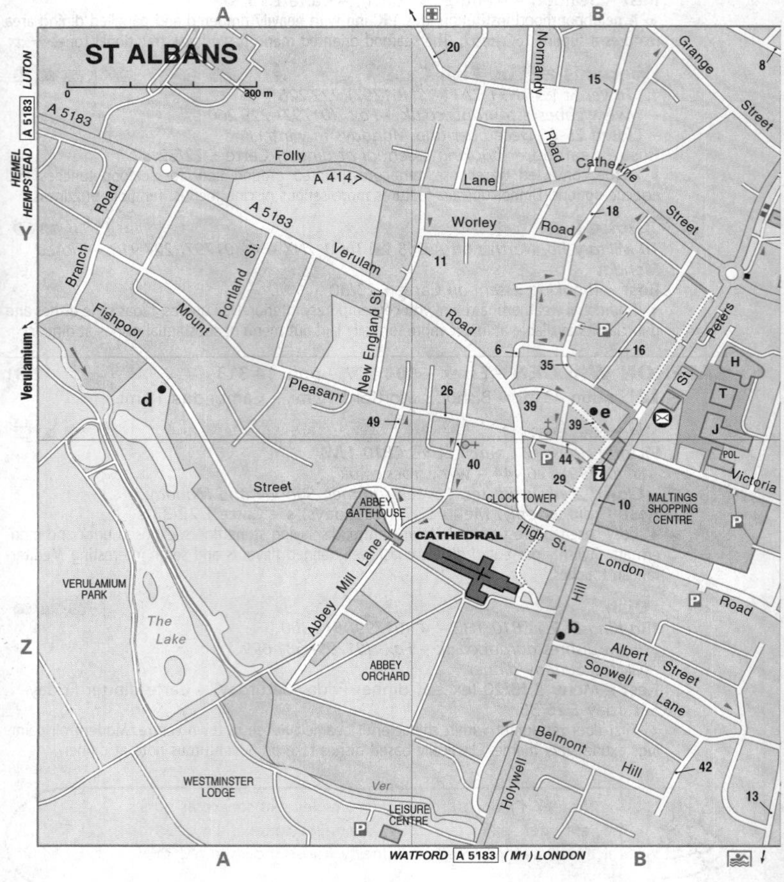

Ardmore House

54 Lemsford Rd ✉ *AL1 3PR – ✆ (01727) 859 313*
– www.ardmorehousehotel.co.uk – Fax (01727) 859 313 CY**a**
40 rm ☕ – 🧍£ 63/75 🧍🧍£ 75/95
Rest *Belvedere* – Italian – ✆ (01727) 841 444 *(Closed Sunday dinner, Monday lunch and Bank Holidays)* Menu £ 15 (weekday lunch)/20 (dinner) – Carte £ 23/39
◆ Two part-Edwardian, part-Victorian properties in quiet residential road. Traditional guest areas and terrace overlook gardens. Simple, well-kept bedrooms have bright, airy feel and good desk space. Spacious Italian-themed conservatory restaurant.

Sukiyaki

6 Spencer St ✉ *AL3 5EG – ✆ (01727) 865 009 – Closed 2 weeks in summer, 1 week Christmas, Sunday, Monday and Tuesday lunch* BY**e**
Rest – Japanese – Menu £ 8/22 – Carte £ 16/21
◆ A pared-down style, minimally decorated restaurant with simple, precise helpings of Japanese food. No noodles or sushi, expect instead sukiyaki (a beef dish), and tempura.

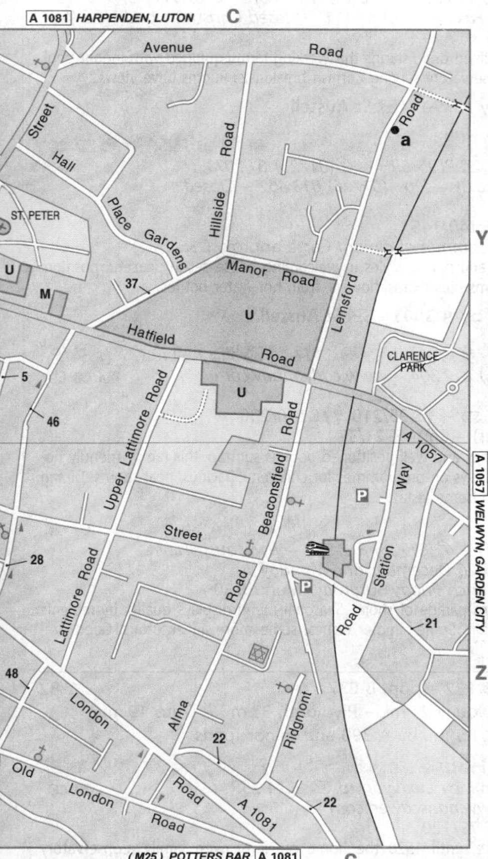

Abbey Mill Lane . . . AZ
Albert St. . . . BZ
Alma Rd. . . . CZ
Avenue Rd . . . CY
Beaconsfield Rd. . . . CYZ
Belmont Hill. . . . BZ
Branch Rd . . . AY
Bricket Rd . . . BCYZ 5
Britton Ave . . . BY 6
Carlisle Ave. . . . BCY 8
Catherine St . . . BY
Chequer St . . . BZ 10
Church Crescent . . . ABY 11
Cottonmill Lane . . . BCZ 13
Dalton St . . . BY 15
Drovers Way. . . . BY 16
Etna Rd. . . . BY 18
Fishpool St . . . AYZ
Folly Ave . . . BY 20
Folly Lane. . . . ABY
Grange St . . . BY
Grimston Rd . . . CZ 21
Grosvenor Rd . . . CZ 22
Hall Pl. Gardens . . . CY
Hatfield Rd . . . CY
High St. . . . BZ
Hillside Rd. . . . CY
Holywell Hill. . . . BZ
Lattimore Rd. . . . CZ
Lemsford Rd. . . . CY
London Rd . . . BCZ
Lower Dagnall St . . . BYZ 26
Maltings Shopping Centre . . . BZ
Manor Rd . . . CY
Market Pl. . . . BZ 29
Marlborough Rd . . . CZ 28
Mount Pleasant. . . . AY
New England St . . . AY
Normandy Rd . . . BY
Old London Rd . . . CZ
Portland St. . . . AY
Ridgemont Rd. . . . CZ
Russell Ave . . . BY 35
St Peter's Rd. . . . CY 37
St Peter's St. . . . BCY
Sopwell Lane . . . BZ
Spencer St . . . BY 39
Spicer St College . . . BYZ 40
Station Way. . . . CZ
Thorpe Rd . . . BZ 42
Upper Dagnall St . . . BYZ 44
Upper Lattimore Rd. . . . CYZ
Upper Marlborough Rd . . . CYZ 46
Verulam Rd . . . ABY
Victoria St . . . BCZ
Watson's Walk . . . CZ 48
Welclose St . . . AYZ 49
Worley Rd. . . . BY

ENGLAND

ST ANNE – 503 Q33 – see Channel Islands (Alderney)

ST ANNE'S – Lancs. – 502 K22 – see Lytham St Anne's

ST AUBIN – C.I. – 503 P33 – see Channel Islands (Jersey)

ST AUSTELL – Cornwall – 503 F32 – pop. 22 658 **1** B2

London 281 mi. – Newquay 16 mi. – Plymouth 38 mi. – Truro 14 mi.

Carlyon Bay, ☎ (01726) 814 250

Holy Trinity Church★

St Austell Bay★★ (Gribbin Head★★) E : by A 390 and A 3082 – Carthew : Wheal Martyn China Clay Heritage Centre★★ **AC**, N : 2 mi. by A 391 – Mevagissey★★ - Lost Gardens of Heligan★, S : 5 mi. by B 3273 – Charlestown★, SE : 2 mi. by A 390 - Eden Project★★, NE : 3 mi. by A 390 at St Blazey Gate. Trewithen★★★ **AC**, NE : 7 mi. by A 390 – Lanhydrock★★, NE : 11 mi. by A 390 and B 3269 – Polkerris★, E : 7 mi. by A 390 and A 3082

Poltarrow Farm without rest

St Mewan, Southwest : 1.75 mi. by A 390 ✉ PL26 7DR – ☎ (01726) 67 111 – www.poltarrow.co.uk – Fax (01726) 67 111 – Closed Christmas and New Year

5 rm – †£ 50 ††£ 75

◆ Tucked away down a tree-lined drive stands this working farm equipped with indoor pool, elegant sitting room and conservatory serving Cornish breakfasts. Rooms have views.

ENGLAND

at Tregrehan East : 2.5 mi. by A 390 – ✉ St Austell

Anchorage House

Nettles Corner, Boscundle ✉ PL25 3RH – ☎ (01726) 814 071 – www.anchoragehouse.co.uk – Fax (01726) 813 462 – Closed December-February

5 rm – †£ 85/90 ††£ 140/145

Rest – *(by arrangement, communal dining)* Carte approx. £ 35

◆ Intriguing mix of modern and period styles in welcoming house set in peaceful position. Antique beds in spacious rooms plus extras: flowers, fruit, hot water bottles.

at Carlyon Bay East : 2.5 mi. by A 3601 – ✉ St Austell

Carlyon Bay

rest,

✉ PL25 3RD – ☎ (01726) 812 304 – www.carlyonbay.com – Fax (01726) 814 938

86 rm (dinner included) – †£ 95/210 ††£ 170/280

Rest – Menu £ 37 (dinner) – Carte £ 21/37

◆ With superb views across bay and well-positioned pool as suntrap, this family friendly hotel has golf course access and lays on programmes for children. Spacious, neat rooms. Dining room with live music and handsome vistas.

Austell's

10 Beach Rd. ✉ PL25 3PH – ☎ (01726) 813 888 – www.austells.net – Closed 1-14 January, 25-26 December and Monday

Rest – *(dinner only and lunch Friday-Saturday)* Menu £ 30

◆ Light, airy eatery in modern parade of shops. Seasonal menu displays quality ingredients used with flair and imagination. Some simpler dishes, some more adventurous. Good presentation.

ST BLAZEY – Cornwall – 503 F32 – pop. 8 837 **1** B2

London 276 mi. – Newquay 21 mi. – Plymouth 33 mi. – Truro 19 mi.

Eden Project★★, NW; 1.5 mi. by A 390 and minor roads

Nanscawen Manor House without rest

Prideaux Rd, West : 0.75 mi. by Luxulyan rd ✉ PL24 2SR – ☎ (01726) 814 488 – www.nanscawen.com

3 rm – †£ 50/88 ††£ 79/120

◆ Sumptuous country house, until 1520 the home of Nanscawen family. Conservatory breakfast room set in fragrant gardens. Welcoming bedrooms; outdoor spa bath. Non smoking.

ST BRELADE'S BAY – C.I. – 503 P33 – see Channel Islands (Jersey)

ST HELIER – C.I. – 503 P33 – see Channel Islands (Jersey)

ST HILARY – Cornwall – see Marazion

ST IVES – Cornwall – 503 D33 – pop. 9 866 **1** A3

▶ London 319 mi. – Penzance 10 mi. – Truro 25 mi.

i The Guildhall, Street-an-Pol ✆ (01736) 796297, stivestic@cornwall.gov.uk

Golf 18 Tregenna Castle H., ✆ (01736) 795 254

Golf 18 West Cornwall Lelant, ✆ (01736) 753 401

Sights: Town★★ - Barbara Hepworth Museum★★ **AC** Y **M1** – Tate St Ives★★ (View ★★) - St Nicholas Chapel (View ★★) Y – Parish Church★ Y **A**

Excursions: S : Penwith★★ Y. St Michael's Mount★★ (View ★★) S : 10 mi. by B 3306 - Y - B 3311, B 3309 and A 30

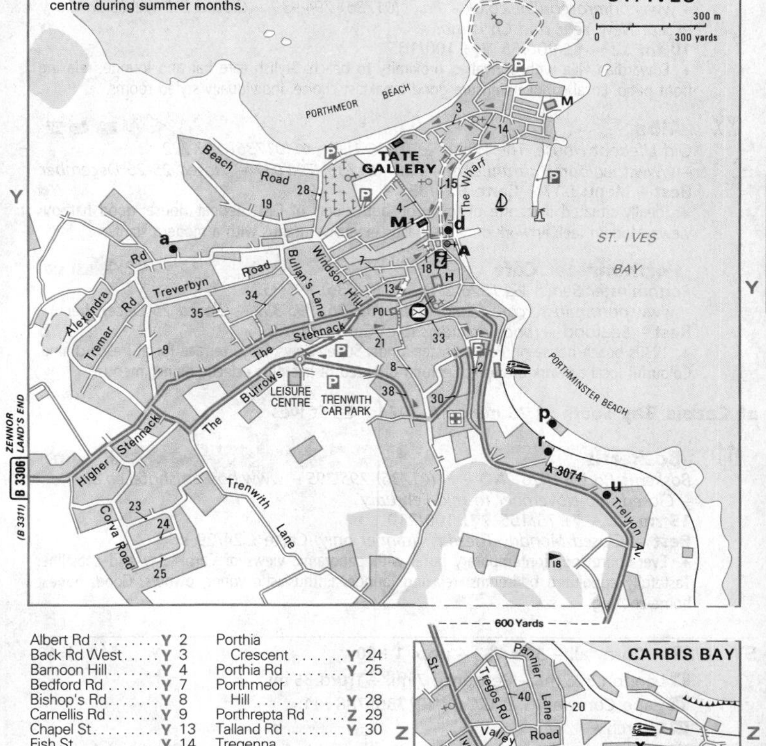

ENGLAND

The Garrack
Burthallan Lane ✉ TR26 3AA – ✆ (01736) 796 199 – www.garrack.com – Fax (01736) 798 955 – Closed 1 week Christmas Y**a**
18 rm (dinner included) – †£ 78/170 ††£ 190/210
Rest *The Restaurant* – *(dinner only and Sunday lunch)* Menu £ 27 – Carte £ 25/35
◆ Well-established hotel with pleasant gardens close to Tate. Plenty of homely touches. Spacious pool and sauna. Individually designed bedrooms, many with feature beds. Very popular dining room serves Cornish specialities.

Blue Hayes without rest
Trelyon Ave ✉ TR26 2AD – ✆ (01736) 797 129 – www.bluehayes.co.uk – Fax (01736) 799 098 – March-October Y**u**
6 rm – †£ 100/140 ††£ 190/210
◆ 19C house with super view from terrace over the harbour; access to coast path from garden. Hi-tech interior. Single course supper available. Well-appointed bedrooms.

Primrose Valley without rest
Porthminster Beach ✉ TR26 2ED – ✆ (01736) 794 939 – www.primroseonline.co.uk – Fax (01736) 794 939 – Closed 2-3 weeks January except New Year and Christmas Y**r**
10 rm – †£ 90/155 ††£ 100/165
◆ Edwardian villa with unrivalled proximity to beach. Stylish café bar and lounge; relaxing front patio. Local suppliers ensure good breakfast choice. Individually styled rooms.

ENGLAND

Alba
Old Lifeboat House, The Wharf ✉ TR26 1LF – ✆ (01736) 797 222 – www.thealbarestaurant.com – Fax (01736) 798 937 – Closed 25-26 December
Rest – Menu £ 17 – Carte £ 24/33 Y**d**
◆ Ideally situated in centre of town, on both floors of Old Lifeboat House; good harbour views. Modern feel; artwork on walls. Tasty, extensive menus with a modern slant.

Porthminster Cafe
Porthminster Beach ✉ TR26 2EB – ✆ (01736) 795 352 – www.porthminstercafe.co.uk – Fax (01736) 795 352 – Closed 25 December
Rest – Seafood – *(booking advisable)* Carte £ 25/36 Y**p**
◆ 1930s beach house on Porthminster sands. Super views: large terrace for al fresco dining. Colourful local artwork on walls. Seafood oriented dishes plus eclectic dinner menus.

at Carbis Bay South : 1.75 mi. on A 3074 – ✉ St Ives

Boskerris
Boskerris Rd ✉ TR26 2NQ – ✆ (01736) 795 295 – www.boskerrishotel.co.uk – Closed mid-November to mid-February Z**x**
15 rm – †£ 75/155 ††£ 100/210
Rest – *(Closed Monday-Tuesday) (dinner only)* Carte £ 24/29 **s**
◆ Ever-improving, contemporary hotel with panoramic views of Carbis Bay and coastline. Tastefully appointed bedrooms; relaxing lounge. Enthusiastic young owners. Good, honest home-cooking.

ST JUST – Cornwall – 503 C33 – pop. 1 890 **1** A3

London 325 mi. – Penzance 7 mi. – Truro 35 mi.

Cape Cornwall G. & C.C., ✆ (01736) 788 611

Church★

Penwith★★ – Sancreed - Church★★ (Celtic Crosses★★), SE : 3 mi. by A 3071 – St Buryan★★ (Church Tower★★), SE : 5.5 mi. by B 3306 and A 30 – Land's End★ (cliff scenery★★★), S : 5.5 mi. by B 3306 and A 30 – Cape Cornwall★ (<★★), W : 1.5 mi. - Morvah (<★★), NE : 4.5 mi. by B 3306 – Geevor Tin Mine★ **AC**, N : 3 mi. by B 3306 – Carn Euny★, SE : 3 mi. by A 3071 - Wayside Cross★ - Sennen Cove★ (<★), S : 5.5 mi. by B 3306 and A 30. Porthcurno★, S : 9.5 mi. by B 3306, A 30 and B 3315

Boscean Country House without rest

Northwest : 0.5 mi. by Boswedden Rd ✉ TR19 7QP – ✆ (01736) 788 748 – www.bosceancountryhouse.co.uk – April-October

12 rm – †£ 110 ††£ 110, ☕ £ 6.50

◆ Originally a doctor's residence; this Edwardian house is surrounded by 3 acres of walled gardens, a haven for wildlife. Wealth of oak panelling indoors; most rooms have views.

ST KEVERNE – Cornwall – 503 E33 – pop. 1 843 1 A3

London 302 mi. – Penzance 26 mi. – Truro 28 mi.

Old Temperance House without rest

The Square ✉ TR12 6NA – ✆ (01326) 280 986 – www.oldtemperancehouse.co.uk – Closed January and 24-26 December

4 rm ☕ – †£ 55 ††£ 80

◆ 'Roses round the door' charm, in idyllic spot on pretty square. Spotlessly neat lounge. Excellent, out-of-the-ordinary breakfasts. Fresh, bright, carefully co-ordinated rooms.

The Greenhouse

6 High Street ✉ TR12 6NN – ✆ (01326) 280 800 – www.tgor.co.uk – Closed 3 weeks January, Monday and Tuesday in winter

Rest – *(dinner only and Sunday lunch)* Carte £ 18/28

◆ Simple, sweet restaurant run by husband and wife, who use as much local produce as possible, from beer to salt. The cooking is tasty, wholesome and heart-warming.

ST KEW – Cornwall – See Wadebridge

ST LAWRENCE – C.I. – 503 P33 – see Channel Islands (Jersey)

ST MARGARET'S AT CLIFFE – Kent – 504 Y30 – see Dover

ST MARTIN – C.I. – 503 P33 – see Channel Islands (Guernsey)

ST MARTIN'S – Cornwall – 503 B34 – see Scilly (Isles of)

ST MARY'S – Cornwall – 503 B34 – see Scilly (Isles of)

ST MAWES – Cornwall – 503 E33 – ✉ Truro 1 B3

London 299 mi. – Plymouth 56 mi. – Truro 18 mi.

Town★ - Castle★ **AC** (<★)

St Just-in-Roseland Church★★, N : 2.5 mi. by A 3078

Tresanton

27 Lower Castle Rd ✉ TR2 5DR – ✆ (01326) 270 055 – www.tresanton.com – Fax (01326) 270 053 – Closed 2 weeks January

27 rm ☕ – †£ 225/355 ††£ 225/355 – 2 suites

Rest – *(booking essential for non-residents)* Menu £ 35/42

◆ Enduringly trendy former 1940s yachtsman's club with cinema. Watercolours on pale walls; gleaming crisp rooms with views; contemporary lounge and attentive service. Dining room boasts open terrace with harbour views and modern seafood dishes.

Idle Rocks

Harbourside, 1 Tredenham Rd ✉ TR2 5AN – ✆ (01326) 270 771 – www.idlerocks.co.uk – Fax (01326) 270 062

27 rm ☕ – ††£ 226/295

Rest *The Water's Edge* – *(closed Christmas-New Year) (light lunch)* Menu £ 30 – Carte £ 23/32

◆ Fine waterfront hotel with splendid views of the harbour and fishermen's cottages. Deep comfortable chairs in lounge and bright bedrooms, many with sea views. Restaurant with terrace overlooks the sea.

ST MERRYN – Cornwall – 503 F32 – see Padstow

ST OSYTH – Essex – 504 X28 – see Clacton-on-Sea

ST PETER – C.I. – 503 P33 – see Channel Islands (Jersey)

ST PETER PORT – C.I. – **503** P33 – see Channel Islands (Guernsey)

ST SAVIOUR – Guernsey – **503** P33 – see Channel Islands (Guernsey)

ST SAVIOUR – Saint Saviour – **503** P33 – see Channel Islands (Jersey)

SALCOMBE – Devon – 503 I33 – pop. 1 893 — 2 C3

London 243 mi. – Exeter 43 mi. – Plymouth 27 mi. – Torquay 28 mi.

Council Hall, Market St (01548) 843927, info@salcombeinformation.co.uk

Sharpitor (Overbecks Museum and Garden★) (★★) **AC**, S : 2 mi. by South Sands Z. Prawle Point (★★★) E : 16 mi. around coast by A 381 - Y - and A 379

Marine

Cliff Rd TQ8 8JH – (01548) 844 444 – www.marinehotelsalcombe.com – Fax (01548) 843 109 — Ye

52 rm – £ 75/145 £ 150/217 – 1 suite

Rest – *(dinner only and Sunday lunch)* Menu £ 17/35

◆ Spectacular position on water's edge overlooking the estuary. Hotel makes the most of this; many bedrooms have balconies whilst centrally located rooms share the best views. Bright, roomy restaurant looks onto the water.

Tides Reach

South Sands TQ8 8LJ – (01548) 843 466 – www.tidesreach.com – Fax (01548) 843 954 – February-November — Zx

32 rm (dinner included) – £ 77/230 £ 160/320

Rest – *(bar lunch)* Menu £ 34 **s**

◆ Traditional, personally run hotel set in pleasant sandy cove on Salcombe Estuary. Lilac and green rooms boast floral fabrics and flowers; many have balconies and a fine view. Restaurant overlooks attractive gardens and pond.

SALCOMBE

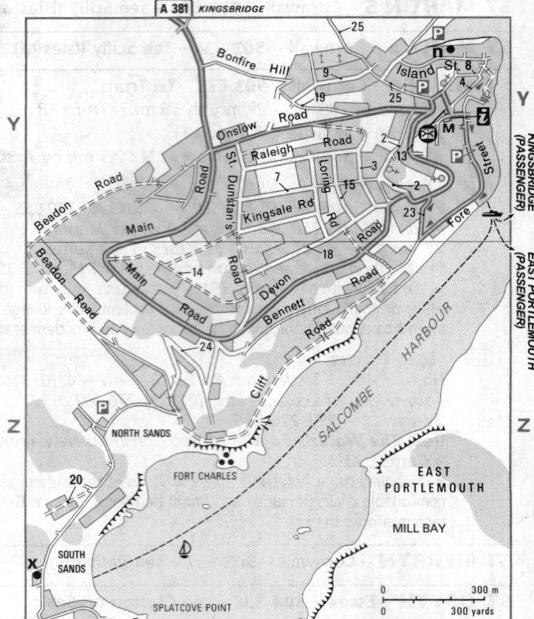

X **The Oyster Shack** VISA MC

Hannaford's Landing, Island St – ✆ (01548) 843 596
– www.oystershack.co.uk Yn

Rest – Carte £ 24/36

◆ Set in modern arcade amongst chandleries and sail makers. Central bar with stools, open dining room and terrace with harbour/estuary views. Seafood menu centred around oyster dishes.

at Soar Mill Cove Southwest : 4.25 mi. by A 381 - Y - via Malborough village – ✉ Salcombe

Soar Mill Cove VISA MC

✉ TQ7 3DS – ✆ (01548) 561 566 – www.soarmillcove.co.uk – Fax (01548) 561 223 – February-October

22 rm – †£ 105/195 ††£ 130/220

Rest – *(booking essential for non-residents)* Menu £ 29 (dinner) **s** – Carte lunch £ 22/27 **s**

◆ Family run local stone and slate hotel on one level in delightful and secluded coastal setting; rooms have terraces and chintz furnishings. Geared for families. Classically styled dining room.

at Hope Cove West : 4 mi. by A 381 - Y - via Malborough village – ✉ Kingsbridge

Lantern Lodge P VISA MC

by Grand View Rd ✉ TQ7 3HE – ✆ (01548) 561 280
– www.lantern-lodge.co.uk – Fax (01548) 561 736
– March to mid-November

14 rm (dinner included) – †£ 90/143 ††£ 120/190

Rest – *(dinner only) (booking essential for non-residents)* Menu £ 25

◆ Named after its lantern window, reputedly designed to guide sailors home, this welcoming, traditional clifftop hotel overlooks Hope Cove. Front bedrooms have views. Pretty dining room with small, adjacent bar.

ENGLAND

SALE – Greater Manchester – **502** N23 – pop. 55 234 – ✉ Manchester **20** B3

London 212 mi. – Liverpool 36 mi. – Manchester 6 mi. – Sheffield 43 mi.

18 Sale Lodge Golf Rd, ✆ (0161) 973 1638

Cornerstones without rest P VISA MC

230 Washway Rd, (on A 56) ✉ M33 4RA – ✆ (0161) 283 6909
– www.cornerstonesguesthouse.com
– Closed 25 December-1 January

9 rm – †£ 42 ††£ 60, £ 6.50

◆ Built in 1871 for the Lord Mayor, this restored Victorian house is personally run. A medley of rooms: spacious with varied décor and fabrics. Homely breakfast room.

X **The Fat Loaf** VISA MC AE

62 Green Lane, Ashton on Mersey, West : 0.5 mi by B 5166
– ✆ (0161) 972 03 97 – www.thefatloaf.co.uk
– Closed 1 January and Sunday

Rest – Menu £ 18 (weekdays) – Carte £ 22/32

◆ Keenly run neighbourhood eatery, hidden away on a small residential parade. Cooking is clean, fresh and flavoursome, with emphasis on locally sourced, seasonal produce.

Guesthouses don't provide the same level of service as hotels. They are often characterised by a warm welcome and a décor which reflects the owner's personality. Those shown in red are particularly pleasant.

SALISBURY – **Wiltshire** – **503** O30 – **pop. 43 355** **4** D3

London 91 mi. – Bournemouth 28 mi. – Bristol 53 mi. – Southampton 23 mi.

Fish Row ✆ (01722) 334956, visitorinfo@wiltshire.gov.uk

Salisbury & South Wilts. Netherhampton, ✆ (01722) 742 645

High Post Great Durnford, ✆ (01722) 782 356

City★★ - Cathedral★★★ **AC** Z – Salisbury and South Wiltshire Museum★ **AC** Z **M2** – Close★ Z : Mompesson House★ **AC** Z **A** – Sarum St Thomas Church★ Y **B** – Redcoats in the Wardrobe★ Z **M1**

Wilton Village★ (Wilton House★★ **AC**, Wilton Carpet Factory★ **AC**), W : 3 mi. by A 30 Y – Old Sarum★ **AC**, N : 2 mi. by A 345 Y – Woodford (Heale House Garden★) **AC**, NW : 4.5 mi. by Stratford Rd Y. Stonehenge★★★ **AC**, NW : 10 mi. by A 345 - Y - and A 303 – Wardour Castle★ **AC**, W : 15 mi. by A 30 Y

Cricket Field House without rest

Wilton Rd, West : 1.25 mi. on A 36 ✉ SP2 9NS – ✆ (01722) 322 595 – www.cricketfieldhouse.co.uk – Fax (01722) 322 595

14 rm – ♦£ 50/75 ♦♦£ 65/95

◆ Personally run extended house overlooking the County Cricket Ground. Bedrooms are prettily decorated with pictures and floral touches; majority of rooms are in the annex.

2 Park Lane without rest

2 Park Lane, North : 1.25 mi. by A 345 ✉ SP1 3NP – ✆ (01722) 321 001 – www.2parklane.co.uk – Fax (01722) 321 001 – Closed 25-26 and 31 December

6 rm – ♦£ 60/70 ♦♦£ 70/80

◆ Refurbished Victorian house, whose original features include eye-catching parquet floor in entrance. Spacious bedrooms offer a good level of facilities including flat screen TVs.

St Anns House without rest

32-34 St Ann St ✉ SP1 2DP – ✆ (01722) 335 657 – www.stannshouse.co.uk – Closed 20 December-8 January Ze

8 rm – ♦£ 55/75 ♦♦£ 75/120

◆ Traditional Georgian townhouse with immaculate bedrooms, sash windows and original fireplaces. Large breakfast menu offers well sourced options. Honesty bar and private dining available.

Anokaa

60 Fisherton St ✉ SP2 7RB – ✆ (01772) 414 142 – www.anokaa.com – Fax (01772) 414 142 Ye

Rest – Indian – *(buffet lunch)* Carte £ 17/49

◆ Lives up to being "something out of the ordinary", with eye-catching interior and staff in silky full-length gowns. Indian dishes mix modern and classical styles with aplomb.

The Gastrobistro at the Pheasant Inn

19 Salt Lane ✉ SP1 1DT – ✆ (01722) 414 926 – www.gastrobistro.co.uk – Closed 25 December dinner, 1 January, dinner Sunday and Monday Y**o**

Rest – Menu £ 14 – Carte £ 20/35

◆ Ivy-clad, red-brick pub with a decked terrace and neat garden. Flavoursome cooking displays honest country foundations and good combinations; excellent homemade puddings.

at Middle Winterslow Northeast : 6.5 mi. by A 30 - Y – ✉ Salisbury

The Beadles without rest

Middleton ✉ SP5 1QS – ✆ (01980) 862 922 – www.guestaccom.co.uk/754.htm – Fax (01980) 863 565 – Easter-November

3 rm – ♦£ 45/50 ♦♦£ 75/80

◆ Recently built from 100-year old bricks and Georgian in style; geese clack in garden. Flower-filled rooms with extra touches: pictures, reading lamps, comfortable chairs.

Enjoy good food without spending a fortune! Look out for the Bib Gourmand symbol to find restaurants offering fine cuisine at special prices !

SALISBURY

- Bedwin St . . . . Y 3
- Blue Boar Row . . . . Y 5
- Bourne Hill . . . . Y 6
- Bridge St . . . . YZ 7
- Brown St . . . . Z 8
- Butcher Row . . . . Y 9
- Catherine St . . . . Z 12
- Crane Bridge Rd . . . . Z 14
- Crane St . . . . Z 13
- Endless St . . . . Y 16
- Estcourt Rd . . . . Y 17
- Greencroft St . . . . Y 18
- High St . . . . Z 19
- Maltings Shopping Centre (The) . . . . Y
- Milford Hill . . . . Z 20
- Milford St . . . . Y 22
- Minster St . . . . Y 23
- New Canal . . . . Z 25
- Old George Mall Shopping Centre . . . . Z
- Queen St . . . . Y 29
- St Ann St . . . . Z 30
- St John St . . . . Z 32
- St Mark's Rd . . . . Y 33
- St Nicholas Rd . . . . Z 36
- Scots Lane . . . . Y 37
- Silver St . . . . YZ 38
- West Walk . . . . Z 39
- Winchester St . . . . Y 40

at Whiteparish Southeast : 7.5 mi. by A 36 - Z - on A 27 – ✉ Salisbury

Newton Farmhouse without rest

Southampton Rd, Southwest : 1.5 mi. on A 36 ✉ SP5 2QL
– ✆ (01794) 884 416 – www.newtonfarmhouse.com
– Fax (01794) 884 105

9 rm – †£ 70 ††£ 110

◆ Step back in time in this 16C farmhouse, gifted to Nelson's family after Battle of Trafalgar. Original bread oven in inglenook fireplace, oak beams and well. Garden rooms the nicest.

at Burcombe West : 5.25 mi. by A 36 - Y - off A 30 – ✉ Salisbury

The Ship Inn
Burcombe Lane ✉ SP2 0EJ – ✆ (01722) 743 182 – www.theshipburcombe.co.uk
Rest – Carte £ 23/32
◆ Old and new blend seamlessly, while large windows overlook a superb riverside garden. Cooking is generous and flavoursome – British and Mediterranean – with twice-daily specials.

at Teffont West : 10.25 mi. by A 36 - Y - and A 30 on B 3089 – ✉ Salisbury

Howard's House
Teffont Evias ✉ SP3 5RJ – ✆ (01722) 716 392 – www.howardshousehotel.co.uk – Fax (01722) 716 820 – Closed Christmas
9 rm – †£ 110 ††£ 185
Rest – *(booking essential for non-residents)* Menu £ 27/28 – Carte (dinner) £ 30/46
◆ Personally run, part 17C dower house boasting fine gardens in a quaint, quiet village. Comfortable lounge and pleasant bedrooms with village or garden vistas. Garden herbs and vegetables grace accomplished cooking.

at Little Langford Northwest : 8 mi. by A 36 - Y - and Great Wishford rd – ✉ Salisbury

Little Langford Farmhouse without rest
✉ SP3 4NP – ✆ (01722) 790 205 – www.littlelangford.co.uk – Fax (01722) 790 086 – Restricted opening in winter
3 rm – †£ 60/80 ††£ 75/80
◆ An unusual Victorian Gothic farmhouse with turret, crenellations and lancet windows. Period style interiors throughout. Spacious, well-furnished bedrooms with rural views.

ENGLAND

at Upper Woodford North : 6.75 mi. by A 360

The Bridge Inn
✉ SP4 6NU – ✆ (01722) 782 323 – www.thebridgewoodford.co.uk
Rest – Carte £ 23/33
◆ Light, airy pub on banks of the River Avon, its garden an al fresco delight. Light bites lunch menu and classic à la carte; fresh, tasty dishes neatly presented on wood or slate.

SANDFORD-ON-THAMES – Oxon. – see Oxford

SANDFORD ORCAS – Dorset – **503** M31 – see Sherborne

SANDIWAY – Cheshire – **502** M24 – pop. 4 299 – ✉ Northwich **20** A3

London 191 mi. – Liverpool 34 mi. – Manchester 22 mi. – Stoke-on-Trent 26 mi.

Nunsmere Hall
Tarporley Rd, Southwest : 1.5 mi. by A 556 on A 49 ✉ CW8 2ES – ✆ (01606) 889 100 – www.nunsmere.co.uk – Fax (01606) 889 055
36 rm – †£ 135 ††£ 135
Rest *The Crystal* – Menu £ 22/30 – Carte dinner £ 41/51
◆ Secluded, on a wooded peninsular, originally built in 1900. Deep-seated sofas and sumptuous drawing rooms. Tasteful, individually furnished bedrooms exude quality and comfort. Dine in the classical style on imaginative and accomplished cuisine.

SANDSEND – N. Yorks. – **502** R/S20 – see Whitby

SANDWICH – Kent – **504** Y30 – pop. 4 398 Great Britain **9** D2

London 72 mi. – Canterbury 13 mi. – Dover 12 mi.
Guildhall ✆ (01304) 613565, info@ticsandwich.wanadoo.co.uk
Town★

The Bell at Sandwich
The Quay ✉ *CT13 9EF* – ✆ *(01304) 613 388* – *www.bellhotelsandwich.co.uk* – *Fax (01304) 615 308*
34 rm – †£ 90/109 ††£ 130
Rest *The Old Dining Room* – Menu £ 15 (lunch) – Carte £ 25/32
◆ Situated by River Stour with original Victorian fittings in situ. Refurbishment has resulted in stunning transformation of bedrooms: now cool, elegant, stylish and welcoming. Pleasant brasserie with strong seafood base.

SANDYPARK – **Devon** – **503** I31 – **see Chagford**

SAPPERTON – **Glos.** – **503** N28 – **see Cirencester**

SARK – C.I. – **503** P33 – **see Channel Islands**

SAWDON – **N. Yorks.** – **see Scarborough**

SCARBOROUGH – **North Yorkshire** – **502** S21 – **pop. 38 364** **23** D1
Great Britain

London 253 mi. – Kingston-upon-Hull 47 mi. – Leeds 67 mi. – Middlesbrough 52 mi.

Brunswick, Westborough - Harbourside, Sandside ✆ (01723) 383636, tourismbureau@scarborough.gov.uk

Scarborough North Cliff North Cliff Ave, Burniston Rd, NW : 2 mi. by A 165, ✆ (01723) 355 397

Scarborough South Cliff Deepdale Ave, S : 1 mi. by A 165, off Filey Rd, ✆ (01723) 374 737

Robin Hood's Bay★, N : 16 mi. on A 171 and minor rd to the right (signposted) – Whitby Abbey★, N : 21 mi. on A 171 – Sledmere House★, S : 21 mi. on A 645, B 1249 and B 1253 (right)

Plan on next page

Beiderbecke's
1-3 The Crescent ✉ *YO11 2PW* – ✆ *(01723) 365 766* – *www.beiderbeckes.com* – *Fax (01723) 367 433* Z**s**
26 rm – †£ 85/120 ††£ 115/160 – 1 suite **Rest** – Carte £ 22/32
◆ Named after the jazz musician. Although housed in a restored Georgian building, the rooms' décor is balanced between period style and contemporary feel with bright colours. Colourful, contemporary brasserie.

The Royal
St Nicholas St ✉ *YO11 2HE* – ✆ *(01723) 364 333* – *www.englishrosehotels.co.uk* – *Fax (01723) 500 618* Z**a**
118 rm – †£ 65/119 ††£ 120/200 **Rest** – Menu £ 15/30
◆ One of the town's grand old ladies; 1830s elegance exemplified by unforgettable main staircase. Mix of original or contemporary bedroom styles. Formal ambience in grand dining room.

The Crown Spa H.
8-10 Esplanade ✉ *YO11 2AG* – ✆ *(01723) 357 400* – *www.crownspahotel.com* – *Fax (01723) 357 404* Z**i**
114 rm (dinner included) – †£ 72/248 ††£ 136/296 – 1 suite
Rest *Taste* – ✆ (01723) 357 439 – Menu £ 30 **s** – Carte £ 29/37 **s**
◆ 19C landmark - the town's first resort hotel, on the esplanade overlooking the bay. Spacious lounges in the classic style. Large bedrooms, many with fine sea views. Popular Taste serves family favourites.

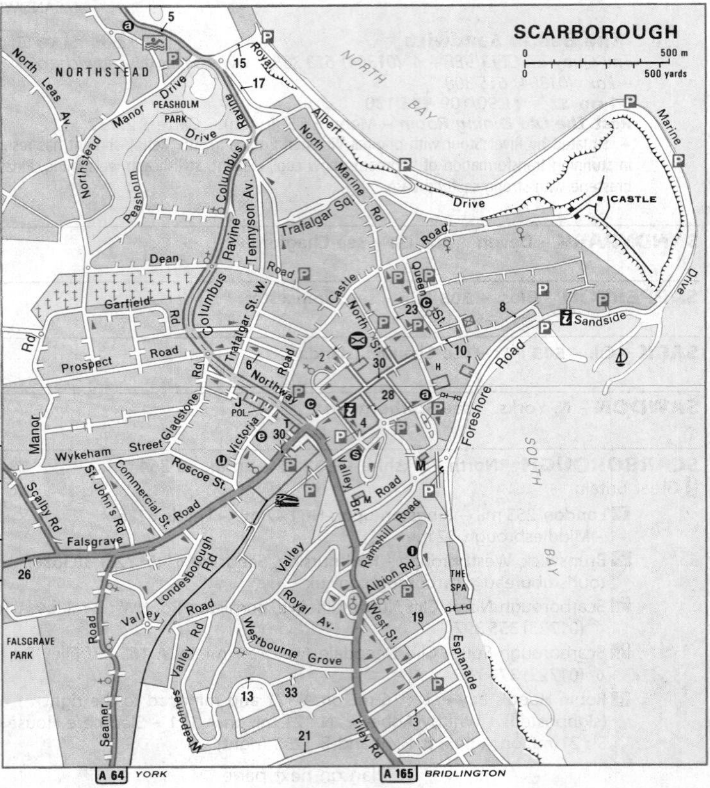

SCARBOROUGH

Ox Pasture Hall

Lady Edith's Drive, Raincliffe Woods, West : 3.25 mi. by A 171 following signs for Raincliffe Woods ✉ *YO12 5TD – ☎ (01723) 365 295 – www.oxpasturehall.com – Fax (01723) 355 156*

21 rm – †£ 89/140 ††£ 119/195

Rest – *(Bar meals Sunday-Monday)* Carte approx. £ 39 **s**

◆ Deep in the countryside, yet close to the sea. A charming part-17C farmhouse: most bedrooms offer pleasant views, some around an attractive wisteria-clad courtyard. Dining room has uniform feel.

Alexander

33 Burniston Rd ✉ *YO12 6PG – ☎ (01723) 363 178 – www.alexanderhotelscarborough.co.uk – March-October* Y**a**

8 rm – †£ 40/52 ††£ 70/82

Rest – *(Closed Sunday) (dinner only) (residents only)* Menu £ 18 **s**

◆ Red-brick 1930s house situated close to North Bay attractions. Smartly furnished lounge. Bedrooms vary in size and are all pleasantly decorated and comfortable.

Windmill without rest
Mill St, by Victoria Rd ✉ YO11 1SZ – ☎ (01723) 372 735 – www.windmill-hotel.co.uk – Fax (01723) 377 190 – Closed 25 December Zu
11 rm – ♦£ 60/76 ♦♦£ 100
◆ For a unique place to stay, look no further than this restored 18C windmill with fascinating 3000 piece toy museum. All rooms built round courtyard; some with direct access.

Lanterna
33 Queen St ✉ YO11 1HQ – ☎ (01723) 363 616 – www.lanterna-ristorante.co.uk – Fax (01723) 363 616 – Closed 2 weeks February, 2 weeks October-November, 25-26 December, 1 January and Sunday Yc
Rest – Italian – *(dinner only)* Carte £ 34/106
◆ Scarborough's best known restaurant: a landmark for decades. Endearing trattoria style "clutter". Classic Italian menu, plus a renowned selection of truffle dishes.

Pepper's
Stephen Joseph Theatre, (1st Floor) Westborough ✉ YO11 1OW – ☎ (01723) 500 642 – www.peppersrestaurant.co.uk – Closed 2 weeks January and 25-26 December Zc
Rest – *(dinner only and lunch when a matinée)* Menu £ 17 (early dinner) – Carte £ 32/41
◆ Smart, personally run restaurant. Good cooking and extremely passionate sourcing – owner visits farms to assess animal's welfare, as well as butchering techniques.

The Green Room
138 Victoria Rd ✉ YO11 1SL – ☎ (01723) 501 801 – www.thegreenroomrestaurant.com – Closed 26 December, Sunday and Monday Ze
Rest – *(dinner only)* Menu £ 17 (weekdays) – Carte £ 27/37
◆ Pleasant family run bistro; son cooks and mum is out front serving. Great care is taken to use only locally sourced produce and ingredients. Cooking is modern and imaginative.

at Sawdon **Southwest : 9.75 mi. by A 170 - Z – ✉ Scarborough**

The Anvil Inn with rm
Main St ✉ YO13 9DY – ☎ (01723) 859 896 – www.theanvilinnsawdon.co.uk – Closed 25-26 December, 1 January, Sunday dinner and Monday
1 rm **Rest** – Carte £ 19/28
◆ Formerly a smithy, with bellows, tools, forge and anvil still in bar. Classical cooking features locally sourced produce and the odd international influence. Intimate restaurant. Smart bedroom in converted next door barn.

When you make a booking, check the price and category of the room.

SCAWTON – **N. Yorks.** – **502** Q21 – **see Helmsley**

SCILLY (Isles of) – **Cornwall** – **503** A/B34 **1** A3

London 295 mi. – Camborne 23 mi. – Saint Austell 52 mi. – Falmouth 36 mi.

Access Helicopter service from St Mary's and Tresco to Penzance : ☎ (01736) 363871

St Mary's Airport : ☎ (01720) 422677, E : 1.5 mi. from Hugh Town

from Hugh Town to Penzance (Isles of Scilly Steamship Co. Ltd) (summer only) (2 h 40 mn)

Hugh Street, St Mary's ☎ (01720) 424031, tic@scilly.gov.uk

Islands★ - The Archipelago (≤★★★)

St Agnes : Horsepoint★

BRYHER – Cornwall – pop. 78 – ✉ 1 A3

Watch Hill (← ★) – Hell Bay★

Hell Bay

✉ *TR23 0PR – ☎ (01720) 422 947 – www.hellbay.co.uk – Fax (01720) 423 004 – March-October*

11 rm (dinner included) – £ 155/600 £ 310/600 – 14 suites – £ 310/600

Rest – *(booking essential for non-residents)* Menu £ 35 (dinner) **s** – Carte lunch approx. £ 29 **s**

◆ Totally renovated, with a charming style that's relaxed, modern, comfy and colourful. Courtyard terraces, a vast lounge/bar and clean-lined rooms add to an idyllic appeal. Dining room with garden views and daily changing menu.

Bank Cottage without rest

✉ *TR23 0PR – ☎ (01720) 422 612 – www.bank-cottage.com – Fax (01720) 422 612 – April-October*

4 rm – £ 45/52 £ 90/104

◆ A modern guesthouse in lush sub-tropical gardens, complete with koi fish pond. A peaceful haven with floral bedrooms and a cosy little boxroom where you can buy seafood.

TRESCO – Cornwall – pop. 167 – ✉ 1 A3

Island★ - Abbey Gardens★★ **AC** (Lighthouse Way ← ★★)

ENGLAND

The Island

Old Grimsby ✉ TR24 0PU – ☎ (01720) 422 883 – www.tresco.co.uk – Fax (01720) 423 008 – March-October

45 rm (dinner included) – £ 210/338 £ 280/450 – 2 suites

Rest – *(bar lunch)* Menu £ 39 (dinner) – Carte £ 19/32

◆ A heated pool, sub-tropical gardens, panoramic views to be had at this luxurious hotel. Enthusiastic owners collect art for interiors. Well appointed garden rooms. Light, welcoming dining room boasts sea vistas and friendly staff.

New Inn

New Grimsby ✉ TR24 0QQ – ☎ (01720) 423 006 – www.tresco.co.uk – Fax (01720) 423 200

16 rm – £ 70/150 £ 140/230

Rest – *(booking essential for non-residents)* Carte £ 20/35

◆ This stone built former inn makes a hospitable stopping off point. Friendly, bustling ambience in lounges and bars; very pleasant garden terrace. Comfortable bedrooms. Same menu can be taken in the restaurant or the bar.

ST MARTIN'S – Cornwall – pop. 113 1 A3

St Martin's Head (← ★★)

St Martin's on the Isle

✉ *TR25 0QW – ☎ (01720) 422 092 – www.stmartinshotel.co.uk – Fax (01720) 422 298 – late March-September*

27 rm – £ 125/195 £ 250/390 – 3 suites

Rest Teän – see restaurant listing

Rest *Bistro* – *(closed Monday dinner)* Carte £ 25/32

◆ Set on the quayside with unrivalled views of white beaches and blue sea; a truly idyllic island setting. Snooze peacefully in snug bedrooms. Bistro, with terrace and eclectic menu, is perfect for lunch.

XXX Teän – at St Martin's on the Isle Hotel

✉ *TR25 0QW – ☎ (01720) 422 092 – www.stmartinshotel.co.uk – Fax (01720) 422 298 – late March-September*

Rest – *(dinner only) (booking essential)* Menu £ 45 **s**

◆ The restaurant offers fantastic views. The kitchen focuses on carefully-prepared, seasonal dishes which make the best of local produce, including home grown vegetables and herbs.

ST MARY'S – Cornwall – pop. 1 607 1 A3

Carn Morval, ✆ (01720) 422 692

Gig racing★★ - Garrison Walk★ (≤★★) – Peninnis Head★ – Hugh Town - Museum★

Star Castle

The Garrison ✉ TR21 0JA – ✆ (01720) 422 317 – www.star-castle.co.uk – Fax (01720) 422 343 – Closed 2 January-14 February and 1-22 December

34 rm (dinner included) – †£ 88/170 ††£ 238/352 – 4 suites

Rest *Castle Dining Room* – *(dinner only)* Menu £ 29/35

Rest *Conservatory* – Seafood – *(dinner only)* Menu £ 29/35

◆ Elizabethan castle built in 1593 in the shape of an eight pointed star, surrounded by dry moat. There are harbour views; palms, echiums in garden. Airy rooms; subtle colours. Medieval wall tapestry highlight of Castle Dining Room. Seafood menus in Conservatory.

Atlantic

rm, VISA

Hugh St, Hugh Town ✉ TR21 0PL – ✆ (01720) 422 417 – www.atlantichotelscilly.co.uk – Fax (01720) 423 009 – 12 February-13 November

25 rm – †£ 95/140 ††£ 240/270

Rest – *(bar lunch)* Menu £ 20 – Carte £ 21/26

◆ A traditional white, comfortable hotel with views of St Mary's harbour and bobbing boats. Some bedrooms in extension but all rooms now have a more contemporary feel. Traditional dinner menu.

Evergreen Cottage without rest

Parade, Hugh Town ✉ TR21 0LP – ✆ (01720) 422 711 – www.evergreencottageguesthouse.co.uk – Closed 2 weeks Christmas-New Year

5 rm – †£ 38/60 ††£ 75/78

◆ A 300-year old captain's cottage; very pleasant, with window boxes, a few minutes walk from the quay. Plenty of local literature in low beamed lounge. Compact, tidy rooms.

SEAHAM – Durham – 501 P/Q19 – pop. 21 153 24 B2

London 284 mi. – Carlisle 77 mi. – Leeds 84 mi. – Middlesbrough 24 mi.

Seaham Hall

rm, AC, P, VISA, AE

Lord Byron's Walk, North : 1.25 mi. by B 1287 ✉ SR7 7AG – ✆ (0191) 516 1400 – www.seaham-hall.co.uk – Fax (0191) 516 1410

16 rm – †£ 195/300 ††£ 195/300 – 2 suites

Rest The White Room – *(dinner only and Sunday lunch) (booking essential for non-residents)* Menu £ 40/60

Rest *Ozone* – *(Closed Sunday and Monday dinner)* Menu £ 17 (lunch) – Carte £ 22/24

◆ Impressive extended coastal mansion with portico entrance, modern styling, spacious sitting room and superb oriental spa. Bedrooms are large, boasting luxury bathrooms and impressive technology. Fine dining in The White Room. Stylish, tranquil Ozone – located in the Spa – serves a blend of Asian and European food.

SEAHOUSES – Northumberland – 501 P17 Great Britain 24 B1

London 328 mi. – Edinburgh 80 mi. – Newcastle upon Tyne 46 mi.

Car Park, Seafield Rd ✆ (01665) 720884,(April- Oct) seahouses.tic@northumberland.gov.uk

Beadnell Rd, ✆ (01665) 720 794

Farne Islands★ (by boat from harbour)

Olde Ship

9 Main St ✉ NE68 7RD – ☎ (01665) 720 200 – www.seahouses.co.uk – Fax (01665) 721 383 – Closed first 3 weeks January, last week November and December

13 rm – †£ 50/116 ††£ 100/116 – 5 suites

Rest – *(bar lunch Monday-Saturday)* Carte £ 16/29

◆ Cosy, part-18C family-run inn, close to thriving harbour – with old ships' decking floors, nautical bric-a-brac and great harbour views from wardroom. Comfy, individually designed bedrooms. Characterful bar and classical dining room.

SEASALTER – **Kent** – **504** X29 – **see Whitstable**

SEAVIEW – **I.O.W.** – **503** Q31 – **see Wight (Isle of)**

SEDLESCOMBE – **East Sussex** – **504** V31 – **pop. 1 631** – ✉ **Battle** **8** B3

London 56 mi. – Hastings 7 mi. – Lewes 26 mi. – Maidstone 27 mi.

Brickwall

The Green ✉ TN33 0QA – ☎ (01424) 870 253 – www.brickwallhotel.com – Fax (01424) 870 785

25 rm – †£ 50/115 ††£ 85/135

Rest – Menu £ 25 (Sunday-Thursday)/28 (Friday-Saturday) – Carte lunch £ 17/26

◆ Part Tudor mansion at top of village green, built for local ironmaster in 1597. Well placed for beauty spots. Range of rooms include family, four-poster and ground floor. Dining room boasts characterful low beamed ceiling.

SETTLE – **North Yorkshire** – **502** N21 – **pop. 3 621** **22** A2

London 238 mi. – Bradford 34 mi. – Kendal 30 mi. – Leeds 41 mi.

Town Hall, Cheapside ☎ (01729) 825192, settle@ytbtic.co.uk

Giggleswick, ☎ (01729) 825 288

Little House

17 Duke St ✉ BD24 9DJ – ☎ (01729) 823 963 – www.littlehouserestaurant.co.uk – Closed 2 weeks January, 1 week September, Sunday except mid-summer, Monday and Tuesday

Rest – *(dinner only) (booking essential)* Carte £ 22/29

◆ Former 19C gate house, a 'little house' of stone that was once a cobblers. Well-kept, rustic style within a compact space. Traditional and classic styles of cooking prevail.

SEVENOAKS – **Kent** – **504** U30 – **pop. 26 699** Great Britain **8** B1

London 26 mi. – Guildford 40 mi. – Maidstone 17 mi.

Buckhurst Lane ☎ (01732) 450305, tic@sevenoakstown.gov.uk

Woodlands Manor Tinkerpot Lane, ☎ (01959) 523 806

Darenth Valley Shoreham Station Rd, ☎ (01959) 522 944

Knole★★ **AC**, SE : 0.5 mi. – Ightham Mote★★ **AC**, E : 5 mi. by A 25

Sun Do

61 High St ✉ TN13 1JF – ☎ (01732) 453 299 – Fax (01732) 454 860 – Closed 25-26 December

Rest – Chinese – Menu £ 10/29 – Carte £ 18/29

◆ Meaning "Happiness", with attentive staff and oriental setting, you can expect authentic Chinese food here. Extensive choice, including various set menus.

at Ightham Common Southeast : 5 mi. by A 25 on Common Rd – ✉ Sevenoaks

Harrow Inn

Common Rd ✉ TN15 9EB – ☎ (01732) 885 912 – Fax (01732) 885 912 – Closed 26-30 December, Sunday dinner and Monday

Rest – Carte £ 20/32

◆ 17C stone and brick pub with welcoming fire and candles on every table. Hearty, rustic dishes served in traditional bar and more formal restaurant. Small back terrace.

ENGLAND

SHAFTESBURY – Dorset – 503 N30 – pop. 6 665 4 C3

London 115 mi. – Bournemouth 31 mi. – Bristol 47 mi. – Dorchester 29 mi.
8 Bell St ✆ (01747) 853514, tourism@shaftesburydorset.com
Gold Hill★ (≤★) – Local History Museum★ **AC**
Wardour Castle★ **AC**, NE : 5 m

The Retreat without rest

47 Bell St ✉ SP7 8AE – ✆ (01747) 850 372 – www.the-retreat.co.uk – Closed January
10 rm – †£ 52/70 ††£ 90
◆ Georgian townhouse in good location - central but not noisy. Spotlessly clean throughout. Individually decorated bedrooms; several overlook the rear, so particularly quiet.

XX La Fleur de Lys with rm

Bleke St ✉ SP7 8AW – ✆ (01747) 853 717 – www.lafleurdelys.co.uk – Fax (01747) 853 130 – Closed lunch Monday-Tuesday and dinner Sunday
7 rm – †£ 75/100 ††£ 100/175
Rest – Menu £ 30 (dinner) – Carte £ 30/43
◆ Smart, personally run restaurant in 1870s ivy-covered house close to centre of town. Comfortable bar with plenty of sofas. Flavourful home cooking and friendly, attentive service. Well-kept bedrooms, named after grape varieties.

XX Le Chanterelle

Sherborne Causeway, West : 3 mi. on A 30 ✉ SP7 9PX – ✆ (01747) 852 821 – Fax (01747) 852 821 – Closed Monday
Rest – Menu £ 18 (lunch) – Carte £ 20/30
◆ Whitewashed wisteria clad building just off the A30, with the occasional beam and large inglenook. French based menu boasts good ingredients and some unusual combinations; good value lunch.

SHALDON – Devon – 503 J32 – pop. 1 628 2 D2

London 188 mi. – Exeter 16 mi. – Torquay 7 mi. – Paignton 13 mi.

X ODE

21 Fore St ✉ TQ14 0DE – ✆ (01626) 873 977 – www.odetruefood.co.uk – Closed October, 25 December, Sunday-Tuesday, lunch Wednesday and Saturday and Bank Holidays
Rest – Organic – *(booking essential)* Menu £ 22 (lunch) – Carte dinner £ 35/45
◆ Intimate neighbourhood restaurant in glass-fronted Georgian house – leave time to park. Cooking has a strong seafaring base and often involves water baths. Produce is local and 100% organic.

SHANKLIN – I.O.W. – 503 Q32 – see Wight (Isle of)

SHAPWICK – Dorset – see Blandford Forum

SHEDFIELD – Hampshire – 503 Q31 – pop. 3 558 – ✉ Southampton 6 B2

London 75 mi. – Portsmouth 13 mi. – Southampton 10 mi.
Meon Valley Shedfield Sandy Lane, off A 334, ✆ (01329) 833 455

XX Vatika

Botley Rd, Wickham Vineyard, on A334 ✉ SO32 2HL – ✆ (01329) 830 405 – www.vatikarestaurant.co.uk – Closed dinner 25-26 and 27 December, 1 January, Monday and Tuesday
Rest – *(booking advisable at dinner)* Menu £ 25/40
◆ Sleek, contemporary restaurant overlooking delightful vineyard. Refined fusion cooking uses modern techniques to create unusual, highly artistic British and Indian combinations.

ENGLAND

SHEFFIELD – South Yorkshire – 502 P23 – pop. 439 866 Great Britain 22 B3

London 174 mi. – Leeds 36 mi. – Liverpool 80 mi. – Manchester 41 mi.
14 Norfolk Row ☎ (0114) 221 1900, visitor@yorkshiresouth.com
Tinsley Park Darnall High Hazel Park, ☎ (0114) 203 7435
Beauchief Abbey Lane, ☎ (0114) 236 7274
Birley Wood Birley Lane, ☎ (0114) 264 7262
Concord Park Shiregreen Lane, ☎ (0114) 257 7378
Abbeydale Dore Twentywell Lane, ☎ (0114) 236 0763
Lees Hall Norton Hemsworth Rd, ☎ (0114) 255 4402
Cutlers' Hall★ CZ **A** – Cathedral Church of SS. Peter and Paul CZ **B** : Shrewsbury Chapel (Tomb★)
Magna★ **AC**, NE : 3 mi. by A 6178 - BY - and Bessemer Way

Plans pages 631, 632

Leopold

Leopold Sq ✉ S1 1GZ – ☎ (0114) 252 40 00 – www.leopoldhotels.com – Fax (0114) 252 40 01 – Closed 24 December-3 January CZ**a**
76 rm – †£ 90/169 ††£ 90/169, ☕ £ 10.50 – 14 suites
Rest ***1880*** – *(meals in bar)* Carte £ 28/45 **s**
◆ Former Boys Grammar School, now an elegant boutique townhouse with stylish, contemporary bedrooms, state-of-the-art facilities and old school photos on the walls. Light meals served in the bar.

The Westbourne without rest

25 Westbourne Rd ✉ S10 2QQ – ☎ (0114) 266 0109 – www.westbournehousehotel.com – Fax (0114) 266 7778 – Closed Christmas AZ**c**
8 rm ☕ – †£ 50/75 ††£ 79/95
◆ Red brick Victorian house in residential area; lovely breakfast room and rear bedrooms overlook mature gardens. Individually styled bedrooms boast original features and good facilities.

Quarry House without rest

Rivelin Glen Quarry, Rivelin Valley Rd, Northwest : 4.5 mi. by A 61 on A 6101 ✉ S6 5SE – ☎ (0114) 234 0382 – www.quarryhouse.org.uk
3 rm ☕ – †£ 50 ††£ 90
◆ Stone built, former Quarry Master's house in a pretty wooded valley close to town. Bright, contemporary bedrooms with quality furnishings, good facilities and extra touches. Homely lounge.

Old Vicarage (Tessa Bramley)

Marsh Lane, Ridgeway Moor, Southeast : 6.75 mi. by A 6135 (signed Hyde Park) and B 6054 turning right at Ridgeway Arms ✉ S12 3XW – ☎ (0114) 247 5814 – www.theoldvicarage.co.uk – Closed first two weeks August, 26 December-6 January, Saturday lunch, Sunday, Monday and Bank Holidays
Rest – *(lunch by arrangement)* Menu £ 40/60 – Carte approx. £ 60
Spec. Turbot with bubble and squeak and cob nuts. Roast partridge stuffed with black pudding, dried grapes and pine nuts. Blackberry and crème de mure sorbet with honey parfait.
◆ Victorian vicarage in mature gardens. Traditional, homely lounge; abstract art in more modern dining room. Innovative cooking makes vibrant use of local/home grown ingredients.

Rafters

220 Oakbrook Rd, Nether Green, Southwest : 2.5 mi. by A 625 and Fulwood rd, turning left at mini roundabout, on right at traffic lights ✉ S11 7ED – ☎ (0114) 230 4819 – www.raftersrestaurant.co.uk – Fax (0114) 230 4819 – Closed 1 week January, 1 week August, 25-26 December, Sunday and Tuesday
Rest – *(dinner only)* Menu £ 36
◆ Small first floor restaurant above residential shops, displaying exposed brickwork and vibrant decor. Classical menu with some Asian influences; produce sourced from within 100 miles.

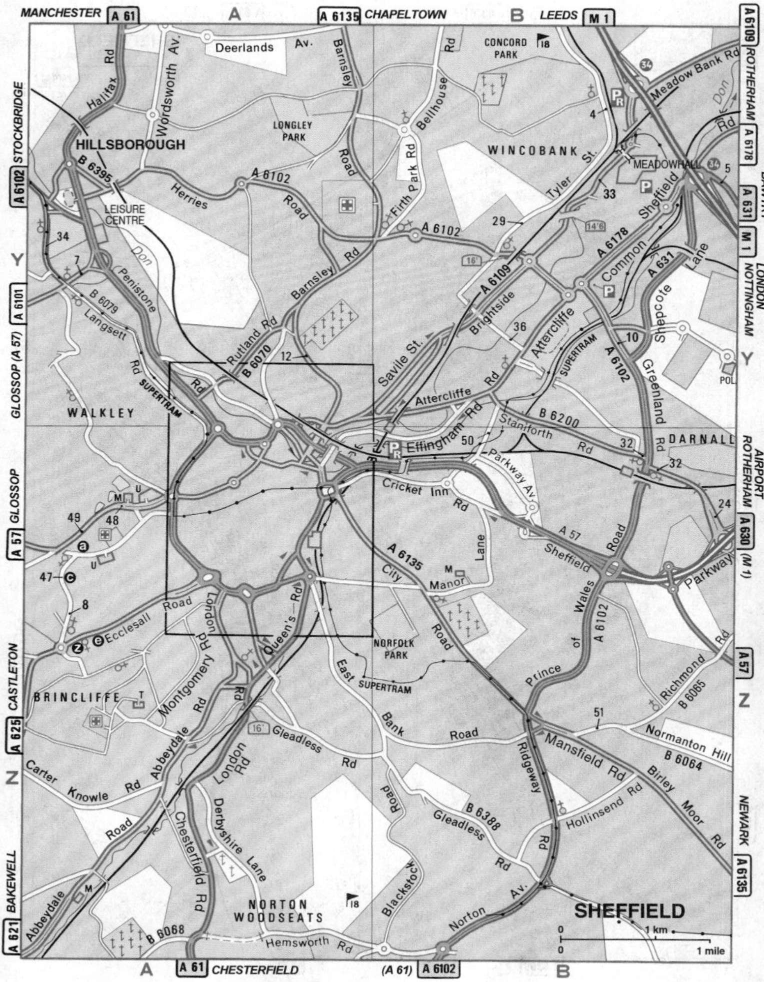

SHEFFIELD

Barrow Rd . . . . **BY** 4
Bawtry Rd . . . . **BY** 5
Bradfield Rd . . . . **AY** 7
Brocco Bank . . . . **AZ** 8
Broughton Lane . . . . **BY** 10
Burngreave Rd . . . . **AY** 12
Handsworth Rd . . . . **BZ** 24
Holywell Rd. . . . . **BY** 29
Main Rd. . . . . **BZ** 32
Meadowhall Shopping Centre . . . . **BY**
Meadow Hall Rd . . . . **BY** 33
Middlewood Rd . . . . **AY** 34
Newhall Rd . . . . **BY** 36
Westbourne Rd . . . . **AZ** 47
Western Bank. . . . . **AZ** 48
Whitham Rd . . . . **AZ** 49
Woodbourn Rd. . . . . **BYZ** 50
Woodhouse Rd. . . . . **BZ** 51

XX Artisan

VISA MO AE D

32-34 Sandygate Rd, West : 2.25 mi. by A 57, turning left at Crosspool Tavern ✉ S10 5RY – ✆ (0114) 266 6096 – www.artisanofsheffield.co.uk – Fax (0114) 266 0279

Rest – Menu £ 16/26 **s** – Carte £ 22/37 **s**

◆ Refined yet rustic restaurant with terrace, red leather banquettes and walls crammed with mirrors, wine racks and menus. Classic British brasserie cooking displays a personal touch.

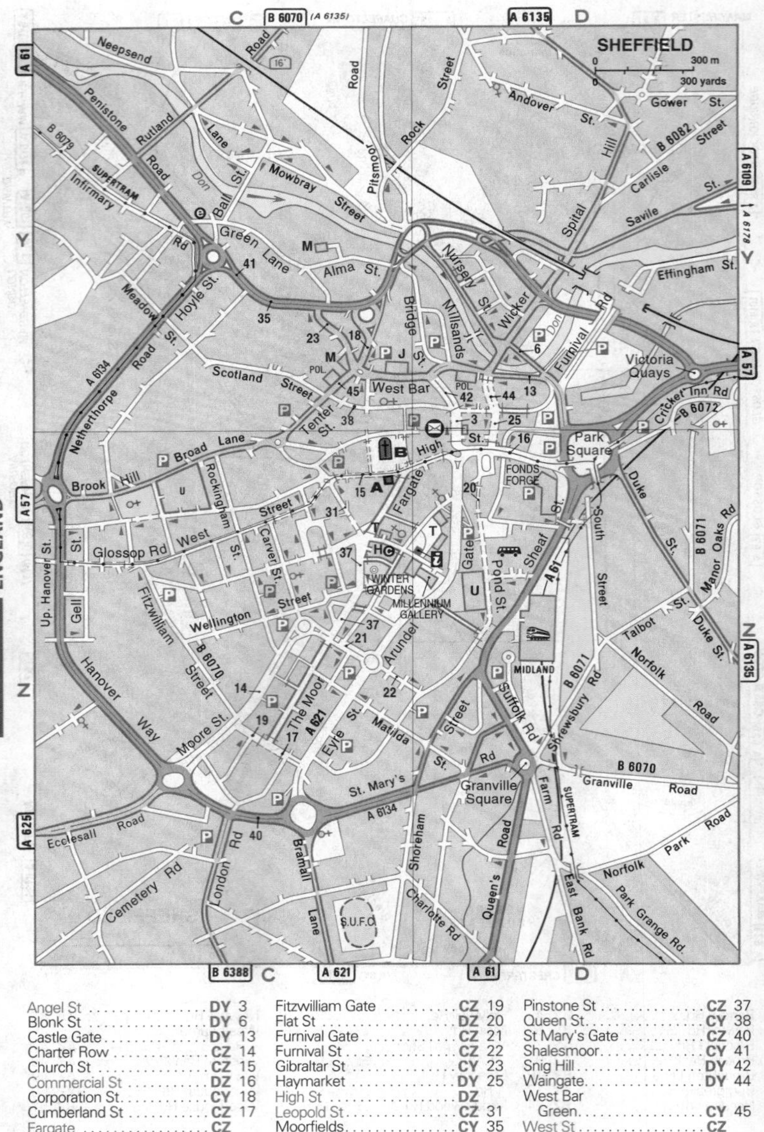

Angel St .... DY 3	Fitzwilliam Gate .... CZ 19	Pinstone St .... CZ 37
Blonk St .... DY 6	Flat St .... DZ 20	Queen St. .... CY 38
Castle Gate .... DY 13	Furnival Gate .... CZ 21	St Mary's Gate .... CZ 40
Charter Row .... CZ 14	Furnival St .... CZ 22	Shalesmoor .... CY 41
Church St .... CZ 15	Gibraltar St .... CY 23	Snig Hill .... DY 42
Commercial St .... DZ 16	Haymarket .... DY 25	Waingate .... DY 44
Corporation St. .... CY 18	High St .... DZ	West Bar Green .... CY 45
Cumberland St .... CZ 17	Leopold St .... CZ 31	West St .... CZ
Fargate .... CZ	Moorfields .... CY 35	

XX **The Walnut Club** VISA MC

557 Ecclesall Rd ✉ S11 8PR – ✆ (0114) 267 65 66 – www.thewalnutclub.com – Closed Monday AZz

Rest – Menu £ 20 – Carte £ 20/33

◆ Large open plan room with central island bar, vibrant atmosphere and regular live music. Good value menu displays international flavours, grills and platters. Fri and Sat, over 25s only in bar area.

X **Canteen** AC VISA MC AE

(first floor) 32-34 Sandygate Rd, West : 2.75 mi. by A 57 turning left at Crosspool Tavern ✉ S10 5RY – ✆ (0114) 266 6096 – www.catchofsheffield.co.uk – Closed 25 December

Rest – *(booking essential)* Menu £ 12

◆ Simply decorated canteen-style restaurant, where an all-purpose, daily changing blackboard menu offers something for everyone. Hearty dishes use good produce and are well-priced.

X **Thyme Cafe** VISA MC

490-492 Glossop Rd ✉ S10 2QA – ✆ (0114) 266 74 34 – www.thymecafe.co.uk – Fax (0114) 266 74 34 – Closed 25-26 December and 1 January AZa

Rest – *(bookings not accepted)* Carte £ 19/27 **s**

◆ Busy café in city suburbs with simple, rustic style. Large menus display classic British dishes in generous portions, with influences from Asia/the Med. Coffee and cakes 3-5pm.

X **Nonna's** VISA MC AE

535-541 Ecclesall Rd ✉ S11 8PR – ✆ (0114) 268 6166 – www.nonnas.co.uk – Closed 25 December and 1 January AZe

Rest – Italian – Menu £ 15/25 **s** – Carte £ 18/32 **s**

◆ Popular eatery with bar, deli and wine shop. Food ranges from pastries to the full 3 courses. Extensive Italian menus offer classic, homemade, flavoursome dishes; themed monthly specials.

The Milestone VISA MC AE

84 Green Lane ✉ S3 8SE – ✆ (0114) 272 8327 – www.the-milestone.co.uk – Closed 25-26 December CYe

Rest – Menu £ 17/20 – Carte £ 17/24

◆ Spacious 18C pub in industrial area of the city. Emphasis firmly on seasonal, organic, locally sourced produce. Hearty gastro menu downstairs; more formal first floor dining.

at Chapeltown North : 6 mi. on A 6135 - AY – ✉ Sheffield

XX **Greenhead House** P VISA MC

84 Burncross Rd ✉ S35 1SF – ✆ (0114) 246 9004 – www.greenheadhouse.com – Fax (0114) 246 9004 – Closed 2 weeks Easter, 2 weeks August, 1 week Christmas and Sunday-Tuesday

Rest – *(dinner only and Friday lunch) (booking essential)* Menu £ 44 (dinner) – Carte lunch approx. £ 20

◆ Traditional suburban house with homely, velvet furnished lounge displaying ornaments/antiques. Simple dining room; friendly service. Concise menu of home-cooked, largely classical dishes.

at Totley Southwest : 5.5 mi. on A 621 - AZ – ✉ Sheffield

The Cricket Inn P VISA MC

Penny Lane ✉ S17 3AZ – ✆ (0114) 236 5256 – www.cricketinn.co.uk – Closed 25 December

Rest – Menu £ 12 – Carte £ 18/26

◆ Popular village pub with extensive Yorkshire-based menu covering bar snacks through to grills and roasts. Hearty, robust cooking with local beers recommended for each dish.

ENGLAND

SHEFFORD – Bedfordshire – **504** S27 – pop. 3 319 **12** A1

London 48 mi. – Bedford 10 mi. – Luton 16 mi. – Northampton 37 mi.

The Black Horse with rm

Ireland, Northwest : 1.75 mi. by Northbridge St and B 658 on Ireland rd ✉ SG17 5QL – ✆ (01462) 811 398 – www.blackhorseireland.com – Fax (01462) 817 238 – Closed 25-26 December, 1 January and Sunday dinner

2 rm – †£ 55 ††£ 55 **Rest** – Carte £ 25/30

◆ Traditional façade masks an ultra-modern interior with marble floors, granite bar and hi-tech fittings. Eclectic menu ranges from pizza and pies to confit of duck and sea bass. Delightfully cosy bedrooms.

SHELLEY – W. Yorks. – **502** O23 – see Huddersfield

SHEPTON MALLET – Somerset – **503** M30 – pop. 8 830 **4** C2

London 127 mi. – Bristol 20 mi. – Southampton 63 mi. – Taunton 31 mi.

The Mendip Gurney Slade, ✆ (01749) 840 570

Town★ - SS. Peter and Paul's Church★

Downside Abbey★ (Abbey Church★) N : 5.5 mi. by A 37 and A 367. Longleat House★★★ **AC**, E : 15 mi. by A 361 and B 3092 – Wells★★ - Cathedral★★★, Vicars' Close★, Bishop's Palace★ **AC** (<★★) W : 6 mi. by A 371 – Wookey Hole★ (Caves★ **AC**, Papermill★) W : 6.5 mi. by B 371 – Glastonbury★★ - Abbey★★ (Abbot's Kitchen★) **AC**, St John the Baptist★★, Somerset Rural Life Museum★ **AC** – Glastonbury Tor★ (<★★★) SW : 9 mi. by B 3136 and A 361 - Nunney★, E : 8.5 mi. by A 361

Charlton House

rm, rest,

East : 1 mi. on A 361 (Frome rd) ✉ BA4 4PR – ✆ (01749) 342 008 – www.charltonhouse.com – Fax (01749) 346 362

26 rm – †£ 120/185 ††£ 200/420 **Rest** – Menu £ 21 – Carte £ 29/44

◆ Grand 17C house owned by founders of Mulberry Company; a smart, boutique style prevails touched by informality. Antiques in luxury bedrooms: Adam and Eve carved four-poster. Well used local produce to the fore in conservatory dining room.

SHERBORNE – Dorset – **503** M31 – pop. 9 350 **4** C3

London 128 mi. – Bournemouth 39 mi. – Dorchester 19 mi. – Salisbury 36 mi.

3 Tilton Court, Digby Rd ✆ (01935) 815341, sherborne.tic@westdorset-dc.gov.uk

Higher Clatcombe, ✆ (01935) 812 274

Town★ - Abbey★★ - Castle★ **AC**

Sandford Orcas Manor House★ **AC**, NW : 4 mi. by B 3148 – Purse Caundle Manor★ **AC**, NE : 5 mi. by A 30. Cadbury Castle (<★★) N : 8 mi. by A 30 – Parish Church★, Crewkerne, W : 14 mi. on A 30

The Eastbury

Long St ✉ DT9 3BY – ✆ (01935) 813 131 – www.theeastburyhotel.co.uk – Fax (01935) 817 296

23 rm – †£ 69/89 ††£ 170 **Rest** – Menu £ 22/33 – Carte £ 19/29

◆ Traditional town house, a former gentleman's residence, built in 1740 with peaceful walled garden. Well-kept rooms named after country flowers. 15C abbey is nearby. Bright restaurant looking onto garden.

The Green

On The Green ✉ DT9 3HY – ✆ (01935) 813 821 – www.thegreensherborne.co.uk – Closed Sunday and Monday

Rest – Menu £ 20/33

◆ Pretty Grade II listing at the top of the hill in town centre with stone floor and inglenook. A bistro feel predominates; dishes are traditional with a strong seasonal base.

ENGLAND

at Corton Denham North : 3.75 mi. by B 3145 – ✉ Sherborne

The Queen's Arms with rm
✉ *DT9 4LR – ☎ (01963) 220 317 – www.thequeensarms.com*
5 rm – †£ 85 ††£ 85/130 **Rest** – Carte £ 20/25
◆ A comfy, firelit bar is at the hub of this 18C inn, which serves hearty, flavoursome cooking in big bowls. They keep their own pigs and chickens, with the focus on local, seasonal produce. Modern, stylish bedrooms with flat screen TVs and smart bathrooms.

at Oborne Northeast : 2 mi. by A 30 – ✉ Sherborne

The Grange rm,
✉ *DT9 4LA – ☎ (01935) 813 463 – www.thegrangeatoborne.co.uk – Fax (01935) 817 464*
18 rm – †£ 90 ††£ 150
Rest – *(Closed Sunday dinner) (light lunch)* Menu £ 31 (dinner)
◆ A 200-year old country house with floodlit gardens. Rooms are a treat: some modern, some traditional, all large; some have patio access; others have balconies. Friendly owner. Dorset and Somerset ingredients zealously used in dining room.

at Hermitage South : 7.5 mi. by A 352 – ✉ Sherborne

Almshouse Farm without rest
✉ *DT9 6HA – ☎ (01963) 210 296 – Fax (01963) 210 296 – March-October*
3 rm – †£ 35 ††£ 60
◆ Part 16C former monastery, now a working farm, surrounded by rural landscape. Original features include inglenook fireplace in cosy breakfast room. Pretty, neat bedrooms.

at Sandford Orcas North : 4.25 mi. by B3148

The Alders without rest
✉ *DT9 4SB – ☎ (01963) 220 666 – www.thealdersbb.com*
3 rm – †£ 45/58 ††£ 55/68
◆ Characterful stone house in attractive walled garden, near to 13C church. Pleasant, traditionally furnished bedrooms. Torches for evening pub visits and aromatherapy treatments available.

at Chetnole Southeast : 7 mi. by A 352

The Chetnole Inn with rm
Chetnole ✉ DT9 6NU – ☎ (01935) 872 337 – www.thechetnoleinn.co.uk
3 rm – †£ 60 ††£ 85 **Rest** – Carte £ 20/25
◆ Sofa-furnished locals' bar with dartboard and skittle alley; cosy beamed dining room with wood-burner and understated style. Simple, tasty, value-for-money cooking. Pleasant, pine-furnished bedrooms.

SHERE – Surrey – **504** S30 – see Guildford

SHERINGHAM – Norfolk – **504** X25 – pop. 7 143 **15** C1
London 136 mi. – Cromer 5 mi. – Norwich 27 mi.

The Dales Country House
Lodge Hill, Upper Sheringham, Southwest : 1.25 mi. by A 149 on B 1157
✉ *NR26 8TJ – ☎ (01263) 824 555 – www.mackenziehotels.com – Fax (01263) 822 647*
20 rm – †£ 95/150 ††£ 150/172
Rest *Upchers* – Menu £ 18/24 – Carte £ 25/37
◆ Substantial 19C country house whose rich décor affords much comfort. Famous gardens conveniently adjacent. Original oak staircase in situ. Traditional bedrooms overlook the grounds. Wood-panelled restaurant with superb oak-carved inglenook.

Fairlawns without rest
26 Hooks Hill Rd ✉ NR26 8NL – ☎ (01263) 824 717 – www.fairlawns-sheringham.co.uk – Closed mid-December and January
5 rm – †£ 60 ††£ 90
◆ Attractive late Victorian house in peaceful area with large, well kept garden, comfy lounge and honesty bar. Spacious, modem bedrooms, some with sea/garden views; excellent bathrooms.

ENGLAND

SHERWOOD BUSINESS PARK – Nottingham – see Nottingham

SHILTON – W. Mids. – 503 P26 – see Coventry

SHINFIELD – Reading – 504 R29 – see Reading

SHIPLEY – West Yorkshire – 502 O22 – pop. 28 162 22 B2

London 216 mi. – Bradford 4 mi. – Leeds 12 mi.

Northcliffe High Bank Lane, (01274) 584 085

Bingley Beckfoot Lane, Cottingley Bridge, (01274) 568 652

Zaara's

34-38 Bradford Road BD18 3NT – (01274) 588 114 – www.zaaras.com

Rest – *(dinner only)* Carte £ 16/20 AT**a**

◆ Funky, modern restaurant with bright décor and lots of neon. Tasty, authentic Indian cooking, with an emphasis on Punjabi dishes. Efficient service from smartly dressed team.

SHIPSTON-ON-STOUR – Warwickshire – 503 P27 – pop. 4 456 19 C3

London 85 mi. – Oxford 30 mi. – Stratford-upon-Avon 12 mi.

at Long Compton South : 5 mi. on A 3400 – pop. 1 994 – Shipston-On-Stour

The Red Lion with rm

on A 3400 CV36 5JS – (01608) 684 221 – www.redlion-longcompton.co.uk – Fax (01608) 684 968

5 rm – †£ 55 ††£ 80/90 **Rest** – Menu £ 15 (dinner) – Carte £ 25/32

◆ 18C former coaching inn with flag floors, log fires and a warm, modern feel. Seasonal menu of tasty, home-cooked pub classics, with more adventurous daily specials. Stylish, contemporary bedrooms.

SHIPTON GORGE – Dorset – see Bridport

SHOCKLACH – Cheshire 20 A3

London 193 mi. – Liverpool 42 mi. – Stoke-on-Trent 37 mi. – Saint Helens 45 mi.

The Bull

Worthenbury Road SY14 7BL – (01829) 250 239 – www.thebullshocklach.com – Closed 25 December

Rest – Menu £ 13 – Carte £ 23/34

◆ Smart village restaurant with large terrace and modern, stylish feel. Gorgeous tiled floor; plenty of antiques and curios. Menu of tasty dishes with a seasonal, traceable base.

SHOTTLE – Derbs. – see Belper

SHREWSBURY – Shropshire – 502 L25 – pop. 67 126 Great Britain 18 B2

London 164 mi. – Birmingham 48 mi. – Chester 43 mi. – Derby 67 mi.

Rowley's House, Barker St (01743) 281200, visitorinfo@shropshire.gov.uk

Condover, (01743) 872 977

Meole Brace, (01743) 364 050

Abbey★ **D**

Ironbridge Gorge Museum★★ **AC** (The Iron Bridge★★ - Coalport China Museum★★ - Blists Hill Open Air Museum★★ – Museum of the Gorge and Visitor Centre★) SE : 12 mi. by A 5 and B 4380

Prince Rupert

rm, rest,

Butcher Row SY1 1UQ – (01743) 499 955 – www.prince-rupert-hotel.co.uk – Fax (01743) 357 306 **n**

68 rm – †£ 69/85 ††£ 99, £ 12.50 – 2 suites

Rest *Royalist* – *(Closed Sunday dinner and Monday)* Carte £ 24/35 **s**

Rest *Chambers* – (01743) 233 818 – Carte £ 21/25 **s**

◆ 12C home of Prince Rupert, in the shadow of the cathedral. A collection of old buildings, some 15C, affords tremendous character. Rooms vary in age: the oldest are the best. Baronial style Royalist. Olde Worlde atmosphere of Chambers.

ENGLAND

SHREWSBURY

Barker St.	2	Coleham Head	13	Pride Hill	26
Beeches Lane	3	Darwin Centre	15	Princess St	27
Belmont	4	Dogpole	16	St Chad's Terrace	29
Bridge St.	6	High St	18	St John's Hill	30
Castle Foregate	7	Kingsland Bridge	19	St Mary's St	31
Castle Gates	8	Mardol	20	Shoplatch	33
Castle St	9	Mardol Quay	22	Smithfield Rd	34
Chester St	10	Moreton Crescent	23	Wyle Cop	38
Claremont Bank	12	Murivance	24		

ENGLAND

Pinewood House without rest

Shelton Park, The Mount, Northwest : 1.5 mi. on A 458 ✉ SY3 8BL – ☎ (01743) 364 200 – Closed 23-28 December

3 rm ☕ – †£ 48 ††£ 60/66

◆ A Regency house surrounded by wooded gardens. A homely, intimate atmosphere pervades the drawing room with its sofas and fresh flowers, whilst bedrooms are charmingly decorated.

Tudor House without rest

2 Fish St ✉ SY1 1UR – ☎ (01743) 351 735 – www.tudorhouseshrewsbury.co.uk – Fax (01743) 351 735 **e**

4 rm ☕ – †£ 69/95 ††£ 89/120

◆ On a picturesque medieval street in a historic part of Shrewsbury, this compact 15C house retains its antiquated charm in its cosy sitting room and simple bedrooms.

Good food at moderate prices? Look for the Bib Gourmand ☺.

X **Mad Jack's** with rm

15 St.Mary's St ✉ SY1 1EQ – ✆ (01743) 358 870 – www.madjacks.uk.com – Fax (01743) 344 422 – Closed 25 December **a**

4 rm – †£ 70/100 ††£ 80/145

Rest – *(Closed Sunday dinner)* Menu £ 17/22 – Carte £ 23/37

◆ Centrally located in the heart of a busy market town. Spacious main dining area, snug and hidden courtyard, with plain décor and marble tables. Good service, slightly eclectic menu. Modern, comfy bedrooms.

The Armoury

Victoria Quay, Welsh Bridge ✉ SY1 1HH – ✆ (01743) 340 525 – www.armoury-shrewsbury.co.uk – Fax (01743) 340 526 **c**

Rest – Carte £ 19/32

◆ Former 18C riverside warehouse with huge open-plan interior; sturdy brick walls full of old pictures and bookshelves. Daily changing menus offer a wide range of dishes.

at Albrighton North : 3 mi. on A 528 – ✉ Shrewsbury

Albright Hussey Manor

Ellesmere Rd ✉ SY4 3AF – ✆ (01939) 290 571 – www.albrighthussey.co.uk – Fax (01939) 291 143

25 rm – †£ 70/85 ††£ 99/120 – 1 suite

Rest – Menu £ 25 (dinner) **s** – Carte £ 29/36 **s**

◆ Most impressive part 16C moated manor house. Fountains, stone walls and bridge in lawned gardens. The five rooms in the original house have oak panelling and huge fireplaces. Hugely characterful, heavily beamed 16C dining room.

ENGLAND

at Grinshill North : 7.75 mi. by A 49 – ✉ Shrewsbury

XX **The Inn at Grinshill** with rm

The High St ✉ SY4 3BL – ✆ (01939) 220 410 – www.theinnatgrinshill.co.uk – Fax (01939) 220 327 – Closed Sunday dinner, Monday and dinner Bank Holidays

6 rm – †£ 60/90 ††£ 120 **Rest** – Carte £ 20/43

◆ 18C stable block in small village: a cosy bar with sofas awaits, while beyond a light and airy, modern restaurant serves a wide range of menus. Spacious, stylish bedrooms.

at Atcham Southeast : 3 mi. by A 5064 on B 4380 – ✉ Shropshire

The Mytton and Mermaid

✉ SY5 6QG – ✆ (01743) 761 220 – www.myttonandmermaid.co.uk – Fax (01743) 761 297 – Closed 25 December

16 rm – †£ 85 ††£ 90/175

Rest The Restaurant – *see restaurant listing*

◆ Impressive Georgian riverside house with neat lawned gardens. Characterful, traditionally styled bedrooms in main house, some with views; smaller, more contemporary rooms in old stables.

X **The Restaurant** – at The Mytton and Mermaid Hotel

✉ SY5 6QG – ✆ (01743) 761 220 – www.myttonandmermaid.co.uk – Fax (01743) 761 292 – Closed 25 December

Rest – Carte £ 26/32

◆ Choice of three dining areas: casual bar, more formal dining room or pleasant outside terraces. Same menu served throughout, offering tasty classically based dishes and daily specials.

at Acton Burnell Southeast : 7.5 mi. by A 458 – ✉ Shrewsbury

Acton Pigot without rest

Acton Pigot, Northeast : 1.75 mi. by Kenley rd ✉ SY5 7PH – ✆ (01694) 731 209 – www.actonpigot.co.uk – Fax (01694) 731 399 – Closed 25 December

3 rm – †£ 50 ††£ 75

◆ 17C farmhouse on working farm. Wealth of pursuits includes heated pool, fishing lake and tennis court. Age of house handsomely apparent in guest areas. Pleasant, cosy rooms.

SHREWTON – Wiltshire – 503 O30 – pop. 1 648 — 4 D2

London 91 mi. – Bristol 53 mi. – Southampton 52 mi. – Reading 69 mi.

The Manor

Southeast : 0.5 mi. on A 360 ✉ SP3 4HF – ✆ (01980) 620 216 – www.rollestonemanor.com

7 rm – †£ 60/115 ††£ 80/130

Rest – *(booking essential at lunch)* Menu £ 25

◆ Grade II listed former farmhouse set on main road, just out of the village. Good-sized, antique-furnished bedrooms offer modern facilities. Traditional lounge. Two-roomed restaurant for classic dishes at linen-laid tables.

SHURDINGTON – Glos. – 503 N28 – see Cheltenham

SIBFORD GOWER – Oxon. – see Banbury

SIDFORD – Devon – 503 K31 – see Sidmouth

SIDLESHAM – West Sussex – see Chicester

SIDMOUTH – Devon – 503 K31 – pop. 12 066 — 2 D2

London 176 mi. – Exeter 14 mi. – Taunton 27 mi. – Weymouth 45 mi.

Ham Lane ✆ (01395) 516441, sidmouthtic@eclipse.co.uk

18 Cotmaton Rd, ✆ (01395) 513 451

Bicton★ (Gardens★) **AC**, SW : 5 m

Riviera

rest,

The Esplanade ✉ EX10 8AY – ✆ (01395) 515 201 – www.hotelriviera.co.uk – Fax (01395) 577 775 – Closed 2 January-February

26 rm – †£ 120/177 ††£ 240/332 **Rest** – Menu £ 27/39 – Carte £ 42/50

◆ An established seafront hotel with fine Regency façade and bow fronted windows. Peach and pink bedrooms with floral touches and friendly staff make for a comfortable stay. Formal dining salon affords views across Lyme Bay.

Old Farmhouse

Hillside Rd, off Salcombe Rd ✉ EX10 8JG – ✆ (01395) 512 284 – March-October

6 rm – †£ 30/66 ††£ 60/72 **Rest** – *(by arrangement)* Menu £ 14

◆ Utterly charming 16C ex-cider mill and farmhouse with low ceilings, heavy beams, numerous inglenooks, cosy lounge and pleasant rooms that boast rafters and sloping roofs. Dinner served in rustic dining room.

at Sidford North : 2 mi. – ✉ Sidmouth

Salty Monk with rm

Church St, on A 3052 ✉ EX10 9QP – ✆ (01395) 513 174 – www.saltymonk.co.uk – Closed 2 weeks November and January

5 rm – †£ 70 ††£ 180/200

Rest – *(dinner only and lunch Thursday-Sunday) (booking essential)* Menu £ 30 (dinner) – Carte lunch £ 27/36

◆ Former 16C salt house where monks stayed en route to Exeter Cathedral. Fine lounge with deep leather armchairs. Modern cooking in conservatory restaurant. Pleasant bedrooms.

at Newton Poppleford Northwest : 4 mi. by B 3176 on A 3052 – ✉ Sidmouth

Moores'

6 Greenbank, High St ✉ EX10 0EB – ✆ (01395) 568 100 – www.mooresrestaurant.co.uk – Closed first 2 weeks January, Sunday dinner, Monday and Bank Holidays

Rest – Menu £ 15/28 **s**

◆ Two pretty 18C cottages set back from the main road are the setting for this busy, personally run restaurant with conservatory extension. Modern, locally sourced dishes.

SINNINGTON – N. Yorks. – 502 R21 – see Pickering

SISSINGHURST – Kent – 504 V30 – see Cranbrook

SITTINGBOURNE – Kent – 504 W29 – pop. 39 974 9 C1

London 44 mi. – Canterbury 18 mi. – Maidstone 15 mi. – Sheerness 9 mi.

Hempstead House

London Rd, Bapchild, East : 2 mi. on A 2 ✉ ME9 9PP – ✆ (01795) 428 020 – www.hempsteadhouse.co.uk – Fax (01795) 436 362

27 rm – £ 80/110 £ 100/150

Rest *Lakes* – *(residents only Sunday dinner)* Menu £ 18 (lunch) – Carte £ 25/37

◆ Part-Victorian former estate house in four acres of landscaped gardens, surrounded by open countryside. Classical interior boasts antiques, open fires and warm bedrooms in floral designs. Eat on terrace or in elegant dining room with crystal chandeliers.

SIZERGH – Cumbria – see Kendal

SKELWITH BRIDGE – Cumbria – 502 K20 – see Ambleside

SKIPTON – North Yorkshire – 502 N22 – pop. 14 313 Great Britain 22 A2

London 217 mi. – Kendal 45 mi. – Leeds 26 mi. – Preston 36 mi.

35 Coach St ✆ (01756) 792809, skipton@ytbtic.co.uk

Short Lee Lane, off NW Bypass, ✆ (01756) 793 922

Castle★ AC

Carlton House without rest

46 Keighley Rd ✉ BD23 2NB – ✆ (01756) 700 921 – www.carltonhouse.rapidal.co.uk

5 rm – £ 30/40 £ 60

◆ Victorian terraced house near centre of town. Pleasantly furnished in sympathetic style. Attractive dining room serves full English breakfast. Individually decorated bedrooms.

The Bull

Broughton, West : 3 mi. on A 59 ✉ BD23 3AE – ✆ (01756) 792 065 – www.thebullatbroughton.co.uk – Fax (01756) 792 065

Rest – Carte £ 20/30

◆ Part of Ribble Valley Inns, a burgeoning pub company which proudly promotes local and very British ingredients and dishes. This solid, sizeable pub boasts log fires, beams and stone floors.

at Hetton North : 5.75 mi. by B 6265 – ✉ Skipton

Angel Inn and Barn Lodgings with rm

✉ BD23 6LT – ✆ (01756) 730 263 – www.angelhetton.co.uk – Fax (01756) 730 363 – Closed 1 week January and 25 December

5 rm – £ 115/165 £ 130/180

Rest – *(Closed Sunday dinner) (dinner only and Sunday lunch) (booking essential)* Carte £ 25/35

◆ Well regarded restaurant with stone walls, beams and roaring log fire. Fine quality, locally sourced produce. Bedrooms with antique furniture and modern appointments.

Angel Inn

✉ BD23 6LT – ✆ (01756) 730 263 – www.angelhetton.co.uk – Fax (01756) 730 363 – Closed 1 week January and 25 December

Rest – *(booking essential)* Carte £ 28/34

◆ Remotely set 18C stone inn that's become a Yorkshire institution: the wine cave is worth a visit. Menus offer something for everyone, featuring local produce in tasty, satisfying dishes.

at Elslack West : 5 mi. by A 59 and A 56 – ✉ Skipton

The Tempest Arms

✉ BD23 3AY – ✆ (01282) 842 450 – www.tempestarms.co.uk – Fax (01282) 843 331

21 rm – £ 63 £ 85/140 **Rest** – Carte £ 19/36

◆ Extended 18C stone inn with characterful beams and traditional feel. Smart bedrooms; those in annexed block are best - spacious, most with balconies, two with outdoor hot tubs. Open plan bar and dining room. Huge choice on menus.

SLALEY – Northd. – 501 N19 – see Hexham

SLAPTON - Devon - 503 J33 — 2 C3

London 223 mi. - Dartmouth 7 mi. - Plymouth 29 mi.

Dartmouth★★, N : 7 mi. by A 379 - Kingsbridge★, W : 7 mi. by A 379

The Tower Inn with rm

Church Rd ✉ TQ7 2PN - ✆ (01548) 580 216 - www.thetowerinn.com - Closed Sunday dinner and Monday, November to April

3 rm - †£ 50/55 ††£ 70/75 **Rest** - Carte £ 17/30

◆ Built in 1347 as cottages for men working on local chantry. Beams, flag floors, stone walls: all very characterful. Surprisingly modern menus. Simple annex bedrooms.

SNAINTON - North Yorkshire - 502 S21 — 23 C2

London 241 mi. - Pickering 8 mi. - Scarborough 10 mi.

Coachman Inn with rm

Pickering Road West, West : 0.5 mi. by A 170 on B 1258 ✉ YO13 9PL - ✆ (01723) 859 231 - www.coachmaninn.co.uk - Fax (01723) 850 008 - Closed 25 December, 1 January, Monday and lunch Tuesday

3 rm - †£ 50 ††£ 75 **Rest** - Carte £ 22/35

◆ Family-run Grade II listed former Georgian coaching inn. Warm, traditional bar and elegant dining room make good use of local ingredients in classic dishes. Individually styled bedrooms.

SNAPE - Suffolk - 504 Y27 - pop. 1 509 — 15 D3

London 113 mi. - Ipswich 19 mi. - Norwich 50 mi.

The Crown Inn

Bridge Rd ✉ IP17 1SL - ✆ (01728) 688 324 - Closed Monday in winter

Rest - Carte £ 15/25

◆ Characterful 400 year old pub on the village outskirts. Produce is local, home-grown, or home-reared. Lunch offers sandwiches and snacks while dinner is more substantial; proper puddings.

SNETTISHAM - Norfolk - 504 V25 - pop. 2 145 — 14 B1

London 113 mi. - King's Lynn 13 mi. - Norwich 44 mi.

The Rose and Crown with rm

Old Church Rd ✉ PE31 7LX - ✆ (01485) 541 382 - www.roseandcrownsnettisham.co.uk - Fax (01485) 543 172

16 rm - †£ 70/100 ††£ 80/110 **Rest** - Carte £ 18/28

◆ A warren of rooms with uneven floors and low beamed ceilings. Gutsy cooking uses locally sourced produce, with globally influenced dishes alongside trusty pub classics. Modern bedrooms are decorated in sunny colours, with a good level of facilities.

SOAR MILL COVE - Devon - see Salcombe

SOLIHULL - West Midlands - 503 O26 - pop. 94 753 — 19 C2

London 109 mi. - Birmingham 7 mi. - Coventry 13 mi. - Warwick 13 mi.

Central Library, Homer Rd ✆ (0121) 704 6130, artsbook@solihull.gov.uk

The Town House

727 Warwick Rd ✉ B91 3DA - ✆ (0121) 704 1567 - www.thetown-house.com - Fax (0121) 713 2189 - Closed 1 January

Rest - Menu £ 13/16 (weekdays) - Carte £ 28/37

◆ Once a salubrious nightclub with town centre location. Stylish open-plan interior boasts large dining area with leather banquettes. Soundly prepared modern dishes.

Metro Bar and Grill

680-684 Warwick Rd ✉ B91 3DX - ✆ (0121) 705 9495 - www.metrobarandgrill.co.uk - Fax (0121) 705 4754 - Closed 25-26 December and Sunday

Rest - Menu £ 18 - Carte £ 24/35

◆ Locally renowned town centre bar/restaurant that combines buzzy informality with appealing range of brasserie dishes. Dine alongside busy bar: don't expect a quiet night out!

ENGLAND

at Olton Northwest : 2.5 mi. on A 41 – ✉ Solihull

XX **Rajnagar** A/C VISA MC AE

256 Lyndon Rd ✉ B92 7QW – ☎ (0121) 742 8140 – www.rajnagar.com – Fax (0121) 743 3147

Rest – Indian – *(dinner only)* Menu £ 15 – Carte £ 20/30

◆ A busy, modern neighbourhood favourite, privately owned, offering authentic, regional specialities of Indian cuisine. Service is flexible and friendly.

SOMERTON – Somerset – 503 L30 – pop. 4 133 — 3 B2

London 138 mi. – Bristol 32 mi. – Taunton 17 mi.

Town★ - Market Place★ (cross★) – St Michael's Church★

Long Sutton★ (Church★★) SW : 2.5 mi. by B 3165 – Huish Episcopi (St Mary's Church Tower★★) SW : 4.5 mi. by B 3153 – Lytes Cary★, SE : 3.5 mi. by B 3151 – Street - The Shoe Museum★, N : 5 mi. by B 3151. Muchelney★★ (Parish Church★★) SW : 6.5 mi. by B 3153 and A 372 – High Ham (<★★, St Andrew's Church★), NW : 9 mi. by B 3153, A 372 and minor rd – Midelney Manor★ **AC**, SW : 9 mi. by B 3153 and A 378

Lynch Country House without rest < P VISA MC AE

4 Behind Berry ✉ TA11 7PD – ☎ (01458) 272 316 – www.thelynchcountryhouse.co.uk – Fax (01458) 272 590

9 rm – †£ 70 ††£ 100

◆ Stands on a crest overlooking the Cary Valley. The grounds of this Regency house are equally rich with unusual shrubs, trees and lake. Coach house rooms more modern.

SONNING-ON-THAMES – Wokingham – 504 R29 – see Reading

SOUTH DALTON – East Riding – see Beverley

SOUTH LEIGH – Oxon. – 503 P28 – see Witney

SOUTH MOLTON – Devon – 503 I30 – pop. 4 093 — 2 C1

London 197 mi. – Barnstaple 11 mi. – Bristol 81 mi.

Kerscott Farm < P

Ash Mill, Southeast : 5 mi. by A 361 on B 3227 ✉ EX36 4QG – ☎ (01769) 550 262 – www.devon-bandb.co.uk – Fax (01769) 550 910 – Closed Christmas and New Year

3 rm – †£ 45/55 ††£ 70

Rest – *(communal dining, by arrangement)* Menu £ 17

◆ Beautiful, personally run 14C/17C farmhouse with fine views to Exmoor. Watch out for lambs and geese. Bags of internal character: beams and vast inglenooks. Charming rooms. Communal farmhouse dinners using farm's own produce.

at Knowstone Southeast : 9.5 mi. by A 361 – ✉ South Molton

The Masons Arms (Mark Dodson) P VISA MC AE

✉ EX36 4RY – ☎ (01398) 341 231 – www.masonsarmsdevon.co.uk – Closed first week in January, Sunday dinner and Monday

Rest – *(booking essential)* Menu £ 34 (Sunday lunch) – Carte £ 26/42

Spec. Seared scallops with Thai salad. Roulade of pork belly with red cabbage and apple compote. Trio of rhubarb.

◆ Our Pub of the Year 2010 is a pretty 13C thatched inn with cosy bar and bright dining room featuring celestial ceiling mural. Sophisticated cooking of French and British classics using local produce. Pronounced, assured flavours.

ENGLAND

SOUTH RAUCEBY – Lincolnshire – **502** S24/2 – **pop. 335** **17** C2

London 131 – Sheffield 68 – Leicester 54 – Kingston upon Hull 69

The Bustard Inn

44 Main St – ✆ (01529) 488 250 – www.thebustardinn.co.uk – Closed 1 January, Sunday dinner and Monday

Rest – Menu £ 15 (lunch) – Carte £ 20/40

◆ Sympathetically restored stone pub in a peaceful hamlet. Appealing blackboard of seasonal, homemade dishes in characterful bar; more substantial, structured menu in beamed restaurant.

SOUTHAMPTON – Southampton – **503** P31 – **pop. 234 224** **6** B2

Great Britain

London 87 mi. – Bristol 79 mi. – Plymouth 161 mi.

Access Itchen Bridge (toll) AZ

Southampton/Eastleigh Airport : ✆ (0844) 481 7777, N : 4 mi. BY

to Hythe (White Horse Ferries Ltd) frequent services daily (12 mn) – to the Isle of Wight (Cowes) (Red Funnel Ferries) frequent services daily (approx. 22 mn)

to the Isle of Wight (East Cowes) (Red Funnel Ferries) frequent services daily (55 mn)

9 Civic Centre Rd ✆ (023) 8083 3333, tourist.information@southampton.gov.uk

27 Southampton Municipal Bassett Golf Course Rd, ✆ (023) 8076 0546

18 Stoneham Bassett Monks Wood Close, ✆ (023) 8076 9272

18 Chilworth Main Rd, ✆ (023) 8074 0544

Old Southampton AZ : Bargate★ **B** - Tudor House Museum★ **M1**

ENGLAND

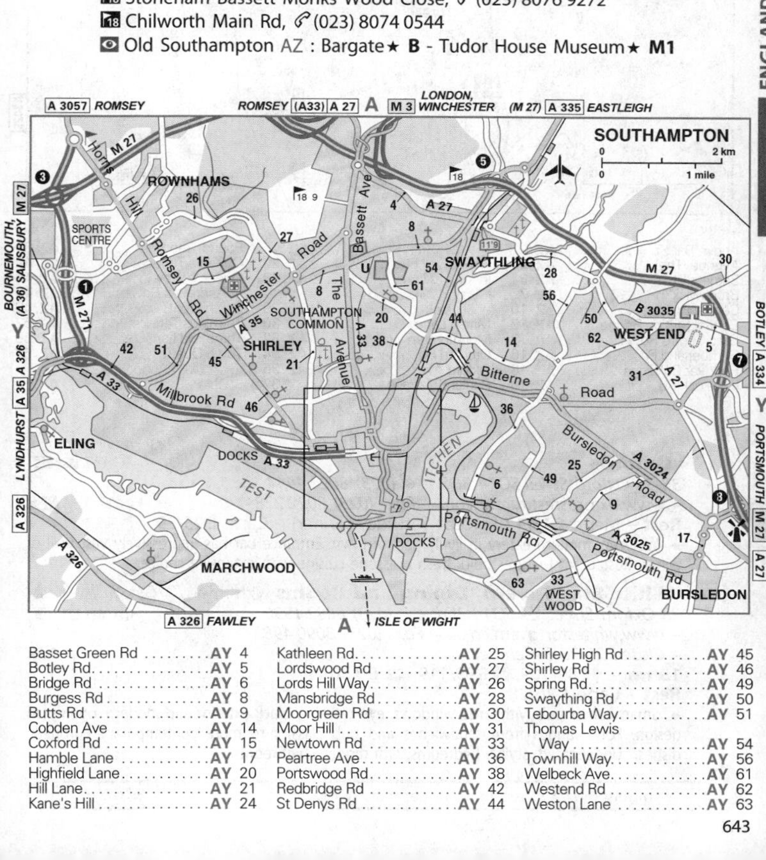

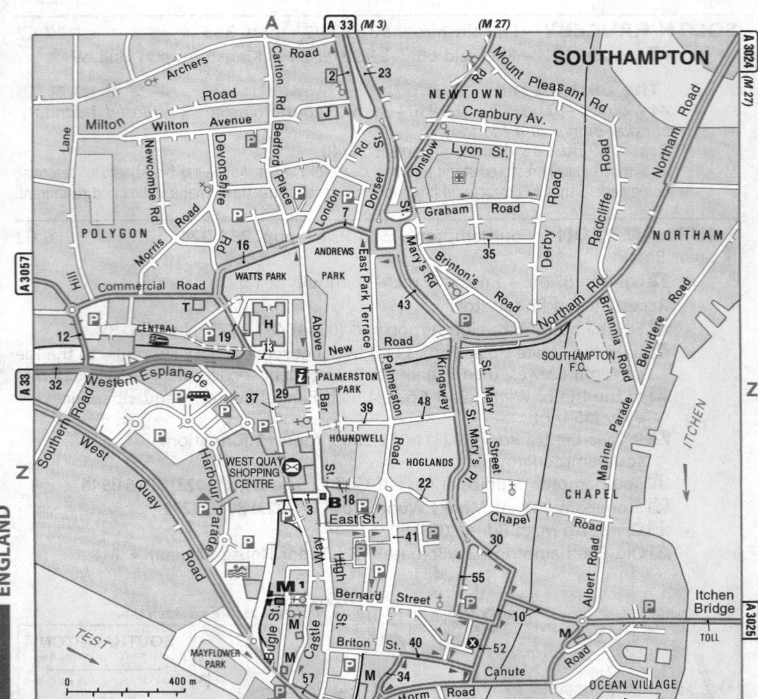

Oxfords

35-36 Oxford St ✉ SO14 3DS – ✆ (023) 8022 4444 – www.oxfordsrestaurant.com – Fax (023) 8022 2284 AZx

Rest – Menu £ 15/17 (except Saturday dinner) – Carte £ 25/29

◆ Well-run, modern eatery in lively part of town. Entrance bar has impressively vast wall of wines. Restaurant features bold, fresh brasserie cuisine with extensive choice.

White Star Tavern, Dining and Rooms with rm

28 Oxford Street ✉ SO14 3DJ – ✆ (023) 8082 1990 – www.whitestartavern.co.uk – Fax (023) 8090 4982 – Closed 25-26 December AZx

13 rm – †£ 89/109 ††£ 99/119, ☕ £ 3.50

Rest – Carte £ 20/28

◆ Smart corner pub with large windows, eye-catching black exterior and modern, open plan design. Food ranges from sandwiches and pub classics to more contemporary European dishes. Understated, stylish bedrooms with modern bathrooms.

Symbols shown in red indicate particularly charming establishments.

at Hamble-le-Rice **Southeast : 5 mi. by A 3025 - A - on B 3397 – ✉ Southampton**

The Bugle
High St ✉ SO31 4HA – ✆ (023) 8045 3000 – www.buglehamble.co.uk – Fax (023) 8045 3051
Rest – *(booking essential)* Carte £ 22 **s**
◆ Part 12C inn on Southampton Water, with exposed beams and brickwork, stone and oak floors and a wood burning stove. Serves a traditional menu and appealing bar bites.

at Netley Marsh **West : 6.5 mi. by A 33 off A 336**

Hotel TerraVina
174 Woodlands Rd ✉ SO40 7GL – ✆ (023) 8029 3784 – www.hotelterravina.co.uk – Fax (023) 8029 3627 – Closed 29-30 December
11 rm – †£ 140/250 ††£ 140/250, ☕ £ 12.50
Rest – Menu £ 28 (lunch) – Carte dinner £ 30/41
◆ Attractive Victorian house with extensions beautifully clad in cedar, and friendly, hands-on Anglo-French owners. Comfy, boutique-style bedrooms; some with terraces. Classic British and French dishes; precise, well judged cooking. Superb wine list and cellars. Wonderful colonial style roofed terrace.

Is breakfast included? The cup symbol ☕ appears after the number of rooms.

SOUTHEND-ON-SEA – Southend-on-Sea – 504 W29 – pop. 160 257 — 13 C3

London 39 mi. – Cambridge 69 mi. – Croydon 46 mi. – Dover 85 mi.
Southend-on-Sea Airport : ✆ (01702) 608100, N : 2 m
Western Esplanade ✆ (01702) 215120, vic@southend.gov.uk
Belfairs Leigh-on-Sea Eastwood Road North, ✆ (01702) 525 345
Ballards Gore G. & C.C. Gore Rd, Canewdon, ✆ (01702) 258 917
Garon Park Golf Complex Garon Park, Eastern Ave, ✆ (01702) 601 701

Beaches without rest
192 Eastern Esplanade, Thorpe Bay ✉ SS1 3AA – ✆ (01702) 586 124 – www.beachesguesthouse.co.uk
7 rm – †£ 40/70 ††£ 80/90
◆ A sunny guesthouse on Thorpe Bay with panorama of Thames Estuary. Continental buffet breakfast. Individually styled rooms: four have sea views; two have balconies.

Pebbles without rest
190 Eastern Esplanade, Thorpe Bay ✉ SS1 3AA – ✆ (01702) 582 329 – Fax (01702) 582 329
7 rm ☕ – †£ 45/50 ††£ 65/75
◆ Friendly guesthouse on the Esplanade overlooking estuary; away from bustle of town but within easy walking distance. Rooftop garden and sea views from most bedrooms.

Pier View without rest
5 Royal Terrace ✉ SS1 1DY – ✆ (01702) 437 900 – www.pierviewguesthouse.co.uk – Fax (01702) 437 901 – Closed 1 week Christmas
9 rm – †£ 58/80 ††£ 95
◆ Set in Georgian terrace close to centre of town, with superb views of cliffs, pier and estuary. Bedrooms decorated in pastel shades, with flat screen TVs and Egyptian bedding.

SOUTHPORT – Merseyside – 502 K23 – pop. 91 404 — 20 A2

London 221 mi. – Liverpool 25 mi. – Manchester 38 mi. – Preston 19 mi.
112 Lord St ✆ (01704) 533333, info@visitsouthport.com
Southport Golf Links Park Road West, ✆ (01704) 535 286

ENGLAND

The Vincent

98 Lord Street ✉ *PR8 1JR – ☎ (01704) 883 800 – www.thevincenthotel.com – Fax (01704) 883 830*

59 rm – 🛉 £ 85/195 🛉🛉 £ 85/195 – 1 suite

Rest *V-Deli/Cafe* – Menu £ 18 (Sunday lunch) – Carte £ 19/44

◆ Striking modern glass, steel and stone boutique hotel, unique to the area. Compact but very stylish with chic lobby and bar. Contemporary bedrooms in dark colours. Informal dining; menu with global influences.

Cambridge House

4 Cambridge Rd, Northeast : 1.5 mi. on A 565 ✉ *PR9 9NG – ☎ (01704) 538 372 – www.cambridgehousehotel.co.uk – Fax (01704) 547 183*

16 rm – 🛉 £ 49/60 🛉🛉 £ 75/110

Rest – *(dinner only and Sunday lunch) (booking essential for non residents)* Menu £ 25 **s** – Carte £ 25/30 **s**

◆ Personally run and sizeable Victorian town house; lavishly furnished lounge and cosy bar. Very comfortably appointed period rooms in main house. Comfortable, Regency-style dining room.

Lynwood House without rest

11A Leicester St ✉ *PR9 0ER – ☎ (01704) 540 794 – www.lynwoodhotel.com – Fax (01704) 500 724*

10 rm – 🛉 £ 35/50 🛉🛉 £ 70/85

◆ Only a couple of minutes' walk from busy Lord Street, this 19C terraced house retains period style in its lounge and neat breakfast room. Pleasantly individual bedrooms.

Warehouse Brasserie

30 West St ✉ *PR8 1QN – ☎ (01704) 544 662 – www.warehouse-brasserie.co.uk – Fax (01704) 500 074 – Closed 25-26 December and 1 January*

Rest – Menu £ 16 (lunch)/18 (weekday dinner) – Carte £ 21/31

◆ Former warehouse, now a sleek modern restaurant with Salvador Dali prints and buzzy atmosphere. The open-plan kitchen offers modern cooking with interesting daily specials.

ENGLAND

SOUTHROP – Glos. – 503 O28 – see Lechlade

SOUTHWOLD – Suffolk – 504 Z27 – pop. 3 858 15 D2

London 108 mi. – Great Yarmouth 24 mi. – Ipswich 35 mi. – Norwich 34 mi.

69 High St ☎ (01502) 724729, southwold.tic@waveney.gov.uk

The Common, ☎ (01502) 723 234

Swan

Market Pl ✉ *IP18 6EG – ☎ (01502) 722 186 – www.adnams.co.uk – Fax (01502) 724 800*

40 rm – 🛉 £ 103/110 🛉🛉 £ 135/180 – 2 suites

Rest – Menu £ 21/30 – Carte £ 27/36

◆ Restored coaching inn by Adnams Brewery. Antique filled interiors: 17C portrait of local heiress in hallway. Vintage rooms in main house; garden rooms built round the green. Tall windows define elegant restaurant.

The Crown with rm

90 High St ✉ *IP18 6DP – ☎ (01502) 722 275 – www.adnams.co.uk – Fax (01502) 727 263*

14 rm – 🛉 £ 138 🛉🛉 £ 138/218 – 1 suite **Rest** – Carte £ 26/34

◆ Smart, Georgian-fronted inn with buzzing atmosphere and nautically themed locals bar. Modern, seasonal menu served in all areas. Contemporary, individually styled bedrooms; those at the rear are the quietest.

The Randolph with rm

41 Wangford Rd, Reydon, Northwest : 1 mi. by A 1095 on B 1126 ✉ *IP18 6PZ – ☎ (01502) 723 603 – www.therandolph.co.uk – Fax (01502) 722 194*

10 rm – 🛉 £ 65 🛉🛉 £ 85/105

Rest – Menu £ 19 (Sunday lunch) – Carte £ 19/27

◆ Sizeable red-brick and part-timbered pub with grand Victorian façade and pleasant terrace. Good-sized menus feature local, seasonal produce in classic pub dishes with a refined edge. Bedrooms are spacious and well-kept.

SOWERBY BRIDGE – West Yorkshire – 502 O22 – pop. 9 901 — 22 A2
– ✉ Halifax

London 211 mi. – Bradford 10 mi. – Burnley 35 mi. – Manchester 32 mi.

The Millbank

Mill Bank, Southwest : 2.25 mi. by A 58 ✉ HX6 3DY – ✆ (01422) 825 588 – www.themillbank.com – Closed first week in January and Monday

Rest – *(booking essential)* Carte £ 20/32

◆ Contemporary pub, boasting a conservatory with views over the Ryburn Valley. The extensive menu offers sophisticated pub grub and features knowledgeably prepared, quality produce.

at Rishworth Southwest : 4 mi. by A 58 on A 672 – ✉ Sowerby Bridge

The Old Bore

Oldham Rd, South : 0.5 mi. on A 672 ✉ HX6 4QU – ✆ (01422) 822 291 – www.oldbore.co.uk – Closed first 2 weeks in January, Monday and Tuesday

Rest – Menu £ 15 – Carte £ 25/35

◆ Inviting pub with busy walls, smart dining rooms and delightful terrace. Monthly-changing menus offer classical and more ambitious British dishes, made from quality ingredients.

SPALDING – Lincolnshire – 502 T25 – pop. 22 081 — 17 C2

London 108 mi. – Peterborough 23 mi. – Stamford 19 mi.

at Surfleet Seas End North : 5.75 mi. by A 16 – ✉ Spalding

The Ship Inn with rm

154 Reservoir Rd ✉ PE11 4DH – ✆ (01775) 680 547 – Fax (01775) 680 541

4 rm – †£ 45 ††£ 55/65 **Rest** – Carte £ 15/30

◆ Spacious pub with upstairs terrace and excellent jetty views. Menu features timeless British classics and homemade old-school puddings, crafted from quality, local ingredients. Bedrooms are large and simply furnished.

SPARSHOLT – Hants. – 503 P30 – see Winchester

SPEEN – Buckinghamshire – 504 R28 – ✉ Princes Risborough — 11 C2

London 41 mi. – Aylesbury 15 mi. – Oxford 33 mi. – Reading 25 mi.

Old Plow (Restaurant)

Flowers Bottom, West : 0.5 mi. by Chapel Hill and Highwood Bottom ✉ HP27 0PZ – ✆ (01494) 488 300 – www.yeoldplough.co.uk – Fax (01494) 488 702 – Closed August, 1 week late May, Christmas-New Year, Sunday and Monday

Rest – Menu £ 30/34

◆ Characterful 17C building with oak beams and log fires, set in peaceful Chiltern Hills hamlet. Extensive 2/3 course set menus feature traditional French dishes, classical sauces and fish specials.

Bistro – at Old Plow

Flowers Bottom, West : 0.5 mi. by Chapel Hill and Highwood Bottom ✉ HP27 0PZ – ✆ (01494) 488 300 – www.yeoldplough.co.uk – Fax (01494) 488 702 – Closed August, 1 week late May, Christmas-New Year, Sunday and Monday

Rest – *(booking essential)* Menu £ 15 (lunch and weekday dinner) – Carte £ 24/36

◆ Cosy low-ceilinged bistro with lovely views from garden. Flexible blackboard menu features quality meats and fresh Brixham fish. Choice of à la carte or set menu; and tapas Saturday lunchtime.

SPELDHURST – Kent – 504 U30 – see Royal Tunbridge Wells

SPRIGG'S ALLEY – Oxon. – see Chinnor

STADDLEBRIDGE – N. Yorks. – see Northallerton

STADHAMPTON – Oxfordshire – 503 Q28 – pop. 718 10 B2

London 53 mi. – Aylesbury 18 mi. – Oxford 10 mi.

Crazy Bear with rm

Bear Lane, off Wallingford rd ✉ OX44 7UR – ✆ (01865) 890 714 – www.crazybeargroup.co.uk – Fax (01865) 400 481

17 rm – †£ 185 ††£ 345

Rest – Menu £ 19 **s** (lunch) – Carte £ 28/45 **s**

Rest *Thai Thai* – Thai – *(closed Sunday lunch) (booking essential)* Carte £ 25/45

◆ Wacky eatery with red London bus reception, smart glasshouse and huge toy bear in trendy bar. Flamboyant English restaurant serves British and French brasserie dishes. More intimate room offers authentic Thai cuisine. Glamorous, individually styled bedrooms boast chic designer furnishings; some have infinity baths.

STAFFORD – Staffordshire – 502 N25 – pop. 63 681 19 C1

London 142 mi. – Birmingham 26 mi. – Derby 32 mi. – Shrewsbury 31 mi.

Eastgate St ✆ (0871) 7161932, tic@staffordbc.gov.uk

Stafford Castle Newport Rd, ✆ (01785) 223 821

Moat House

rm, rest,

Lower Penkridge Rd, Acton Trussell, South: 3.75 mi. by A 449 ✉ ST17 0RJ – ✆ (01785) 712 217 – www.moathouse.co.uk – Fax (01785) 715 344 – Closed 25 December and 1 January

40 rm – †£ 130 ††£ 150 – 1 suite

Rest *The Conservatory* – Menu £ 20 (lunch) – Carte £ 33/42

◆ Timbered 15C moated manor house with modern extensions and lawned gardens, within sight of the M6. Characterful rustic bar. Colourful rooms with individual style. Bright, airy conservatory restaurant overlooks canal.

STAITHES – North Yorkshire – 502 R20 – ✉ Saltburn (Cleveland) 23 C1

London 269 mi. – Middlesbrough 22 mi. – Scarborough 31 mi.

Endeavour with rm

1 High St ✉ TS13 5BH – ✆ (01947) 840 825 – www.endeavour-restaurant.co.uk – Closed end November-March, Sunday and Monday

4 rm – †£ 85/95 ††£ 85/95

Rest – Seafood – *(dinner only and lunch Friday-Saturday) (booking essential)* Menu £ 25/33

◆ Named after Captain Cook's sailing ship: a compact former fisherman's cottage serving tasty menus, with emphasis on locally caught fish. Neat, well-appointed bedrooms.

STAMFORD – Lincolnshire – 502 S26 – pop. 19 525 Great Britain 17 C2

London 92 mi. – Leicester 31 mi. – Lincoln 50 mi. – Nottingham 45 mi.

The Arts Centre, 27 St Mary's St ✆ (01780) 755611, stamfordtic@southkesteven.gov.uk

Town★★ - St Martin's Church★ – Lord Burghley's Hospital★ – Browne's Hospital★ **AC**

Burghley House★★ **AC**, SE : 1.5 mi. by B 1443

The George of Stamford

71 St Martin's ✉ PE9 2LB – ✆ (01780) 750 750 – www.georgehotelofstamford.com – Fax (01780) 750 701

46 rm – †£ 98/115 ††£ 133/191 – 1 suite

Rest – Carte £ 39/58

Rest *Garden Room* – Carte £ 29/59 **s**

◆ Historic inn, over 900 years old. Crusading knights stayed here en route to Jerusalem. Walled garden and courtyard with 17C mulberry tree. Original bedrooms; designer décor. Oak panelled dining room exudes elegance. Garden Room boasts leafy courtyard.

Jim's Yard

3 Ironmonger St, off Broad St ✉ PE9 1PL – ✆ (01780) 756 080 – www.jimsyard.biz – Closed 20 July-7 August, 21 December-8 January, Sunday and Monday

Rest – Menu £ 17 (lunch) – Carte £ 21/31

◆ Two 18C houses in a courtyard: conservatory or first-floor dining options. Smart tableware enhances enjoyment of great value menus employing well-executed, classic cooking.

IN HOC SIGNO VINCES
RAMOS PINTO
Est. 1880

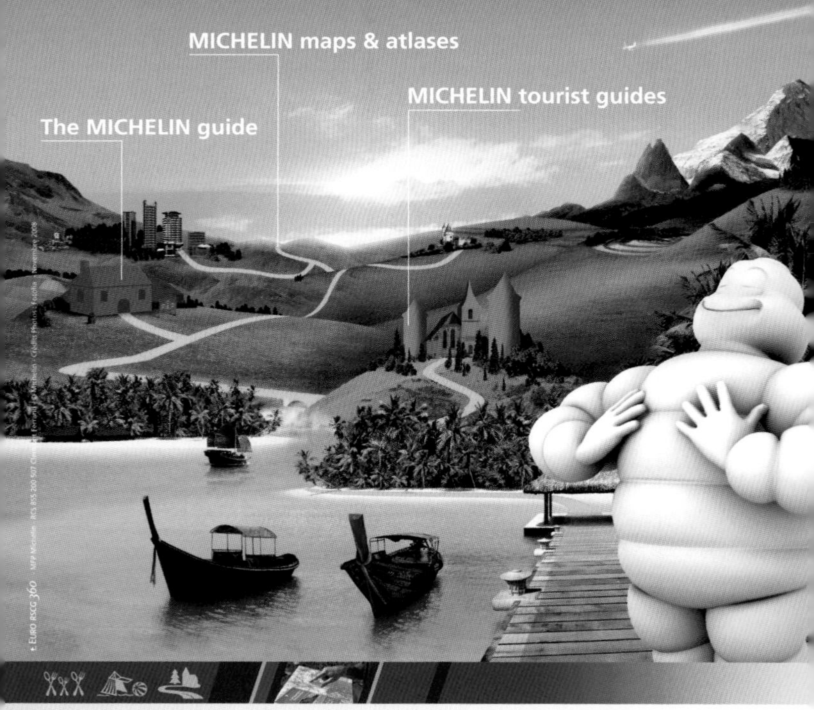

at Collyweston **Southwest : 3.5 mi. on A 43 – ✉ Stamford**

The Collyweston Slater with rm

87-89 Main Road ✉ PE9 3PQ – ✆ (01780) 444 288
– www.collywestonslater.co.uk
5 rm – £ 60/75 £ 85/120 **Rest** – Carte £ 15/25
◆ Charming stone pub with a modern interior. Cooking is European and displays local produce, careful preparation and bold flavours: concise main menu is supported heavily by specials. Bedrooms are comfortable and stylish.

at Clipsham **Northwest : 9.5 mi. by B 1081 off A 1 – ✉ Stamford**

The Olive Branch & Beech House (Sean Hope) with rm

Main St ✉ LE15 7SH – ✆ (01780) 410 355 rm,
– www.theolivebranchpub.com – Fax (01780) 410 000 – Closed lunch 25 December, lunch 31 December and 1 January
6 rm – £ 85/95 £ 150/170
Rest – *(booking essential)* Menu £ 20/25 – Carte £ 26/38
Spec. Potted shrimp and prawn terrine. Honey roast duck breast with beetroot and spiced black cherries. Carrot cake with pistachio ice cream.
◆ Soundly judged, flavoursome cooking, varied and modern, in cosy firelit pub with simple pews and sepia prints. Rooms, over the road in Georgian house, are sassy and stylish.

STANDISH – **Greater Manchester** – **502** M23 – **pop. 14 350** **20** A2
– ✉ **Wigan**

London 210 mi. – Liverpool 25 mi. – Manchester 21 mi. – Preston 15 mi.

at Wrightington Bar **Northwest : 3.5 mi. by A 5209 on B 5250 – ✉ Wigan**

The Mulberry Tree

9 Wood Lane ✉ WN6 9SE – ✆ (01257) 451 400 – www.themulberrytree.info – Fax (01257) 451 400
Rest – Carte £ 16/45
◆ Spacious 19C pub with popular bar and smart linen-laid dining room. Two different menus display generous portions of highly regional produce and some good value mid-week deals.

STANSTED MOUNTFITCHET – **Essex** – **504** U28 – **see Bishop's Stortford (Herts.)**

STANTON – **Suffolk** – **504** W27 – **pop. 2 073** **15** C2

London 88 mi. – Cambridge 38 mi. – Ipswich 40 mi. – King's Lynn 38 mi.

The Leaping Hare

Wyken Vineyards, South : 1.25 mi. by Wyken Rd ✉ IP31 2DW – ✆ (01359) 250 287 – www.wykenvineyards.co.uk – Fax (01359) 253 022 – Closed 25 December-5 January
Rest – *(lunch only and dinner Friday-Saturday) (booking essential)* Menu £ 17 (lunch) – Carte £ 25/40
◆ 17C long barn in working farm and vineyard. Hare-themed pictures and tapestries decorate a beamed restaurant and café. Tasty dishes underpinned by local, organic produce.

STANTON ST QUINTIN – **Wilts.** – **503** N29 – **see Chippenham**

STANTON ST JOHN – **Oxon.** – **503** Q28 – **see Oxford**

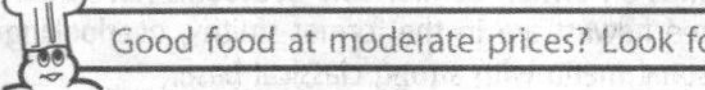

STANWICK – Northamptonshire – pop. 1 924 17 C3

London 83 mi. – Northampton 18 mi. – Milton Keynes 36 mi. – Peterborough 27 mi.

Luxury Lodge

West St ✉ NN9 6QY – ✆ (01933) 622 233 – www.thecourtyard.me.uk – Fax (01933) 622 276

12 rm – †£ 65 ††£ 79

Rest – *(by arrangement)* Menu £ 18 (lunch) – Carte £ 18/30

◆ Cosy, traditional bedrooms in main house; bright, contemporary bedrooms in converted stable block. Lounge opens into pleasant courtyard and neat gardens. Light, airy conservatory restaurant offers dishes with a Mediterranean slant.

STAPLEFORD – Nottinghamshire – 504 Q25 – see Nottingham

STATHERN – Leics. – see Melton Mowbray

STAVERTON – Devon – 503 I32 – pop. 682 – ✉ Totnes 2 C2

London 220 mi. – Exeter 20 mi. – Torquay 33 mi.

Kingston House

Northwest : 1 mi. on Kingston rd ✉ TQ9 6AR – ✆ (01803) 762 235 – www.kingston-estate.com – Fax (01803) 762 444 – Closed Christmas and New Year

3 rm – †£ 110/190 ††£ 180/200

Rest – *(dinner only) (residents only, set menu only)* Menu £ 38 **s**

◆ A spectacular Georgian mansion in sweeping moorland. Unique period details include painted china closet, marquetry staircase, authentic wallpapers. Variety of antique beds.

STAVERTON – Northants. – 504 Q27 – see Daventry

STEDHAM – W. Sussex – 504 R31 – see Midhurst

STEYNING – West Sussex – 504 T31 – pop. 8 692 7 D2

London 52 mi. – Brighton 12 mi. – Worthing 10 mi.

at Ashurst North : 3.5 mi. on B 2135 – ✉ Steyning

The Fountain Inn

✉ BN44 3AP – ✆ (01403) 710 219

Rest – Carte £ 20/25

◆ 16C inn overflowing with character in form of beamed ceilings, flagstone floors, open fires, garden pond and skittle alley. Down-to-earth cooking is fresh and full of flavour.

STILTON – Cambridgeshire – 504 T26 – pop. 2 500 – ✉ Peterborough 14 A2

London 76 mi. – Cambridge 30 mi. – Northampton 43 mi. – Peterborough 6 mi.

Bell Inn

Great North Rd ✉ PE7 3RA – ✆ (01733) 241 066 – www.thebellstilton.co.uk – Fax (01733) 245 173 – Closed 25 December

22 rm – †£ 74 ††£ 131

Rest *Village Bar* – see restaurant listing

Rest *Galleried Restaurant* – *(closed Saturday lunch and Sunday dinner)* Menu £ 28

◆ Historic coaching inn with hospitable, hands-on owner. Comfortable bedrooms have traditional feel: some have four-posters; the three newest are in the former smithy, overlooking the garden. First floor restaurant offers seasonal menu with strong classical base.

ENGLAND

Village Bar (at Bell Inn)
Great North Rd ✉ PE7 3RA – ✆ (01733) 241 066 – www.thebellstilton.co.uk – Fax (01733) 245 173 – Closed 25 December
Rest – Carte £ 20/29
◆ 17C coaching inn where Stilton cheese was born. Choose from a characterful bar or more modern bistro area. Served throughout, the classical menu is a step above your usual pub fare.

STOCKBRIDGE – Hampshire – 503 P30 – pop. 570 — 6 B2

London 75 mi. – Salisbury 14 mi. – Southampton 19 mi. – Winchester 9 mi.

The Greyhound with rm
31 High St ✉ SO20 6EY – ✆ (01264) 810 833 – www.thegreyhound.info – Closed 24-26 and 31 December, 1 January and Sunday dinner
8 rm – †£ 70 ††£ 90/120 **Rest** – Carte £ 25/40
◆ Pretty pub with relaxing open-fired bar and sophisticated dining area. Classical menu displays satisfying combinations with a modern edge, which arrive appetisingly presented. Bedrooms are modern and stylish, with huge showers.

at Longstock North : 1.5 mi. on A 3057 – ✉ Stockbridge

The Peat Spade Inn with rm
Village Street ✉ SO20 6DR – ✆ (01264) 810 612 – www.peatspadeinn.co.uk – Fax (01264) 811 078 – Closed 25 December for food
6 rm – †£ 130 ††£ 130 **Rest** – *(booking essential)* Carte £ 24/34
◆ The ultimate shooting and fishing pub, with country pursuit décor and furnishings. Cooking is proper, proud and local, featuring flavoursome, well-presented British pub classics. Bedrooms are modern and stylish.

ENGLAND

STOKE BY NAYLAND – Suffolk – 504 W28 — 15 C3

London 70 mi. – Bury St Edmunds 24 mi. – Cambridge 54 mi. – Colchester 11 mi.

The Crown with rm
✉ CO6 4SE – ✆ (01206) 262 001 – www.crowninn.net – Fax (01206) 264 026 – Closed 25-26 December
11 rm – †£ 80 ††£ 200 **Rest** – Carte £ 20/33
◆ Spacious 16C pub with smart wood-furnished patio; set in a hillside village overlooking the valley. Menus feature locally sourced, seasonal produce, a daily catch and seafood specials. Spacious bedrooms boast country views; some have French windows and a terrace.

STOKE D'ABERNON – Surrey – 504 S30 – see Cobham

STOKE GABRIEL – Devon – 503 J32 – see Totnes

STOKE HOLY CROSS – Norfolk – 504 X26 – see Norwich

STOKE-ON-TRENT – Stoke-on-Trent – 502 N24 – pop. 259 252 — 19 C1

Great Britain

London 162 mi. – Birmingham 46 mi. – Leicester 59 mi. – Liverpool 58 mi.

Victoria Hall, The Cultural Quarter, City Centre ✆ (01782) 236000, stoke.tic@stoke.gov.uk

Greenway Hall Stockton Brook, ✆ (01782) 503 158

Parkhall Weston Coyney Hulme Rd, ✆ (01782) 599 584

The Potteries Museum and Art Gallery★ Y **M** – Gladstone Pottery Museum★ **AC** V

The Wedgwood Story★ **AC**, S : 7 mi. on A 500, A 34 and minor rd V. Little Moreton Hall★★ **AC**, N : 10 mi. by A 500 on A 34 U – Biddulph Grange Garden★, N : 7 mi. by A 52, A 50 and A 527 U

Plans on following pages

STOKE-ON-TRENT NEWCASTLE-UNDER-LYME

Alexandra Rd . . . . **U** 3
Bedford Rd . . . . **U** 4
Brownhills Rd . . . . **U** 12
Church Lane . . . . **U** 19
Cobridge Rd . . . . **U** 21
Davenport St. . . . . **U** 23
Elder Rd . . . . **U** 24
Etruria Vale Rd . . . . **U** 27
Grove Rd. . . . . **V** 30
Hanley Rd . . . . **U** 31
Heron St . . . . **V** 34
Higherland. . . . . **V** 37
High St . . . . **U** 35
Manor St. . . . . **V** 44
Mayne St . . . . **V** 45
Moorland Rd. . . . . **U** 48
Porthill Rd . . . . **U** 59
Snow Hill . . . . **U** 63
Stoke Rd. . . . . **U** 68
Strand (The) . . . . **V** 69
Victoria Park Rd . . . . **U** 75
Victoria Pl. Link . . . . **V** 76
Watlands View . . . . **U** 77
Williamson St . . . . **U** 78
Wolstanton Link Rd . . . . **U** 80

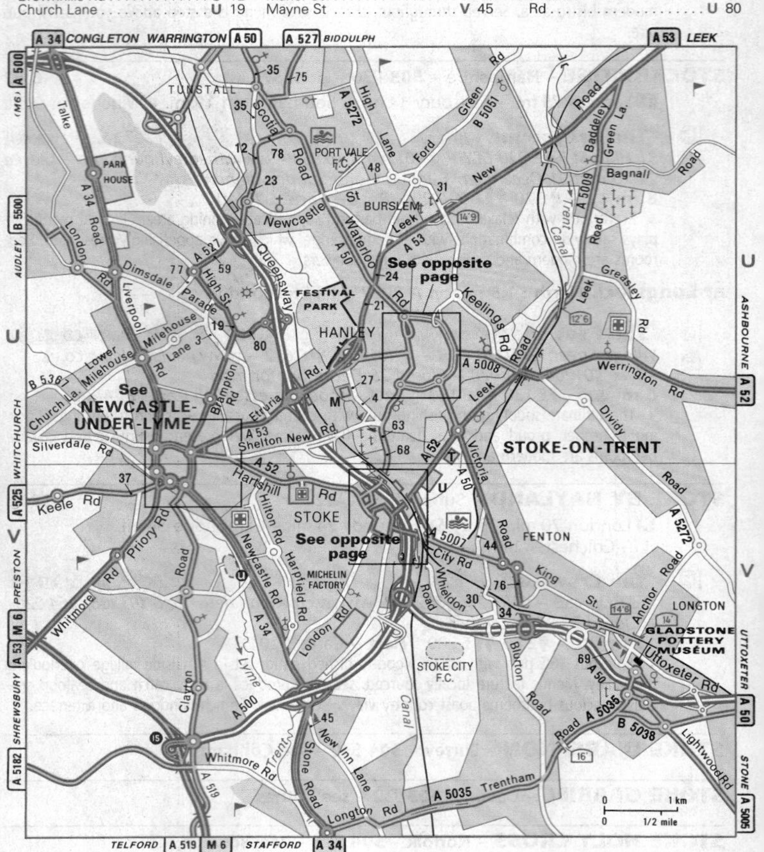

The Manor at Hanchurch

Newcastle Road ✉ *ST4 8SD*
– ✆ *(01782) 643 030*
– *www.hanchurchmanor.co.uk*
– *Fax (01782) 643 714* Vx
6 rm – 🛉£ 100/150 🛉🛉£ 100/150
Rest *Maldini's* – Italian – *(closed Sunday dinner)* Menu £ 16 (lunch) – Carte £ 28/30

◆ A fine period house whose stylish bedrooms boast thick carpets, quality furnishings and smart modern bathrooms, some with spa baths. Spacious bar displays plush fabrics. Classic Italian cooking in Maldini's.

ENGLAND

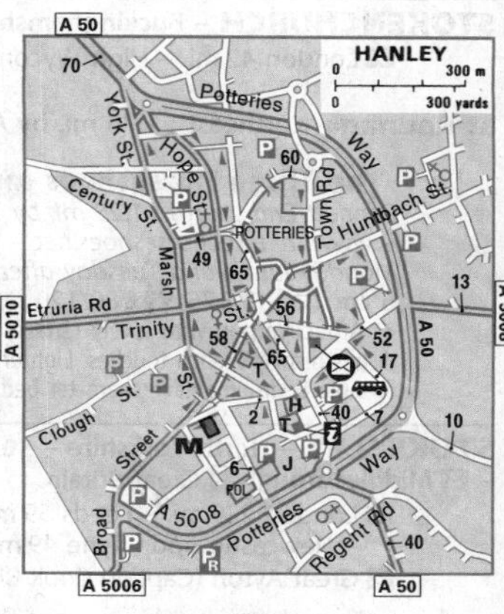

HANLEY		
Albion St	Y	2
Bethesda St	Y	6
Birch Terrace	Y	7
Botteslow St	Y	10
Bucknall New Rd	Y	13
Charles St	Y	17
Lichfield St	Y	40
New Hall St	Y	49
Old Hall St	Y	52
Parliament Row	Y	55
Percy St	Y	56
Piccadilly	Y	58
Potteries Shopping Centre	Y	
Quadrant Rd	Y	60
Stafford St	Y	65
Vale Pl.	Y	70

STOKE-ON-TRENT		
Campbell Pl.	X	14
Church St	X	
Elenora St	X	26
Fleming Rd	X	28
Hartshill Rd	X	33
London Rd	X	42
Shelton Old Rd	X	62
Station Rd	X	66
Vale St	X	72

ENGLAND

STOKE POGES – Buckinghamshire – 504 S29 – pop. 4 112 — 11 D3

London 30 mi. – Aylesbury 28 mi. – Oxford 44 mi.

Stoke Park Park Rd, ✆ (01753) 717 171

Stoke Park

Park Rd ✉ SL2 4PG – ✆ (01753) 717 171 – www.stokepark.com – Fax (01753) 717 181 – Closed first week January

49 rm – †£ 325 ††£ 325, ☐ £ 18.50

Rest *The Dining Room* – Menu £ 25/40

◆ Grand, palatial hotel in huge grounds, with golf course, extensive sporting activities and impressive spa. Choice of smart classical or stunning contemporary bedrooms. Lounge offers all day brasserie menu. Stylish restaurant displays classical à la carte.

Stoke Place

rm,

Stoke Green, South : 0.5 mi. by B 416 ✉ SL2 4HT – ✆ (01753) 534 790 – www.stokeplace.co.uk – Fax (01753) 512 743

29 rm ☐ – †£ 225 ††£ 300/350

Rest *The Garden Room* – Carte £ 23/39

◆ 17C Queen Anne mansion, by a lake, in 22 acres of grounds. Chic, quirky guest areas display bold print wallpapers and original furnishings; sleek, modern bedrooms boast clean lines and stylish beds. Contemporary menu served in both the Garden and Vyse Rooms.

STOKE ROW – Oxfordshire — 11 C3

London 45 mi. – Henley-on-Thames 6 mi. – Reading 10 mi.

The Cherry Tree Inn with rm

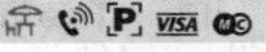

✉ RG9 5QA – ✆ (01491) 680 430 – www.thecherrytreeinn.com – Closed 25 December and Sunday dinner

4 rm ☐ – †£ 95 ††£ 95 **Rest** – Carte £ 25/40

◆ 400 year old Grade II listed pub with slightly funky feel. Fresh, zesty menu displays worldwide flavours: dishes range from traditional to adventurous, with mussels a permanent fixture. Bedrooms are modern, bright and spacious.

STOKENCHURCH – Buckinghamshire – 504 R29 – pop. 3 949 11 C2

London 42 mi. – High Wycombe 10 mi. – Oxford 18 mi.

at Radnage Northeast : 1.75 mi. by A 40 – ✉ Stokenchurch

The Three Horseshoes Inn with rm

Bennett End, North : 1.25 mi. by Town End rd ✉ HP14 4EB – ✆ (01494) 483 273 – www.thethreehorseshoes.net – Fax (01494) 485 464 – Closed Sunday dinner, Monday lunch and Tuesday after Bank Holiday Monday

6 rm – †£ 75 ††£ 80/120 **Rest** – Menu £ 17 (lunch) – Carte £ 24/35

◆ Attractive pub with lovely terrace, set in a fantastic hillside location. Classically prepared dishes display French touches. Lighter offerings at lunch; à la carte or tapas at dinner. Comfortable bedrooms have character beds and modern bathrooms. Molières is best.

STOKESLEY – North Yorkshire – 502 Q20 – pop. 4 725 23 C1
– ✉ Middlesbrough Great Britain

London 239 mi. – Leeds 59 mi. – Middlesbrough 8 mi.
– Newcastle upon Tyne 49 mi.

Great Ayton (Captain Cook Birthplace Museum★ AC), NE : 2.5 mi. on A 173

Chapter's with rm

rest,

27 High St ✉ TS9 5AD – ✆ (01642) 711 888 – www.chaptershotel.co.uk – Fax (01642) 713 387 – Closed 14-19 September, 25-26 December and 1 January

13 rm – †£ 66/85 ††£ 89/99

Rest – *(Closed Sunday dinner)* Carte £ 25/40 **s**

◆ Solid, mellow brick Victorian house with colour washed rooms. Bistro style dining with strong Mediterranean colour scheme. Eclectic menu: classics and more modern dishes.

STON EASTON – Somerset – 503 M30 – pop. 579 4 C2
– ✉ Bath (Bath & North East Somerset)

London 131 mi. – Bath 12 mi. – Bristol 11 mi. – Wells 7 mi.

Ston Easton Park

✉ BA3 4DF – ✆ (01761) 241 631 – www.stoneaston.co.uk – Fax (01761) 241 377

20 rm – †£ 145/190 ††£ 225/475 – 2 suites

Rest *The Sorrel* – *(booking essential for non-residents)* Menu £ 23 (lunch) – Carte £ 42/57

◆ Aristocratic Palladian mansion; grounds designed by Humphrey Repton, given subtle contemporary styling. Lavish rooms: Grand Saloon with Kentian plasterwork. Formal restaurant served by a Victorian kitchen garden.

STORRINGTON – West Sussex – 504 S31 – pop. 7 727 7 C2

London 54 mi. – Brighton 20 mi. – Portsmouth 36 mi.

Old Forge

6 Church St ✉ RH20 4LA – ✆ (01903) 743 402 – www.fine-dining.co.uk – Fax (01903) 742 540 – Closed 2 weeks spring, 1 week autumn, Christmas, Saturday lunch, Sunday dinner and Monday-Wednesday

Rest – Menu £ 19/34

◆ Appealing whitewashed and brick cottages with three dining rooms bearing all hallmarks of flavoursome traditional cuisine. Array of cheeses; fine wine from small producers.

STOWMARKET – Suffolk – 504 W27 – pop. 15 059 15 C3

London 95 mi. – Ipswich 14 mi. – Colchester 35 mi. – Clacton-on-Sea 40 mi.

at Buxhall West : 3.75 mi. by B 115 – ✉ Stowmarket

The Buxhall Crown

Mill Road ✉ IP14 3DW – ✆ (01449) 736 521 – Closed 25-26 December and Sunday dinner

Rest – *(booking advisable)* Menu £ 19 (lunch) – Carte £ 18/30

◆ Part 16C pub with characterful bar, contemporary dining room and charming terrace. Appealing, constantly evolving menu reflects the owners' passion for simplicity, freshness and seasonality.

STOW-ON-THE-WOLD – Gloucestershire – 503 O28 – pop. 2 074 4 D1

Great Britain

London 86 mi. – Birmingham 44 mi. – Gloucester 27 mi. – Oxford 30 mi.

Chastleton House★★, NE : 6.5 mi. by A 436 and A 44

Grapevine

Sheep St ✉ GL54 1AU – ✆ (01451) 830 344 – www.vines.co.uk – Fax (01451) 832 278

22 rm – †£ 70/85 ††£ 110/160

Rest *The Conservatory* – Menu £ 19/33

Rest *Lavigna* – Carte £ 18/22

◆ Among the antique shops, two extended 17C houses. Rooms in bright, modern décor with a nod to tradition, half with beams and bare stone. Timbered bar; sepia photos of Stow. In Conservatory black grapes hang from spreading vine. Easy-going, informal Lavigna.

The Royalist

Digbeth St ✉ GL56 1BN – ✆ (01451) 830 670 – www.theroyalisthotel.com – Fax (01451) 870 048

14 rm – †£ 65/120 ††£ 100/180

Rest *Eagle & Child* – Carte £ 18/25

Rest *947 AD* – Menu £ 35 (dinner) – Carte lunch £ 23/29

◆ Historic high street inn - reputedly England's oldest. Comfortable, stylish rooms, individual in shape and décor and quieter at the rear. Two-room bar in exposed stone. Robust cooking in the attached stone pub. Fine dining in the intimate, beamed restaurant with ingelnook fireplace.

Fosse Manor

Fosse Way, South : 1.25 mi. on A 429 ✉ GL54 1JX – ✆ (01451) 830 354 – www.fossemanor.co.uk – Fax (01451) 832 486

19 rm – †£ 95 ††£ 194/230 **Rest** – Carte £ 28/35

◆ Former coaching inn on the main road. Contemporary public areas with informal feel. Up-to-date bedrooms, some of which are set in the coach house. Lunch available in bar. Classically proportioned dining room with menu of Mediterranean favourites.

Number Nine without rest

9 Park St ✉ GL54 1AQ – ✆ (01451) 870 333 – www.number-nine.info

3 rm – †£ 45/55 ††£ 65/75

◆ Ivy-clad 18C Cotswold stone house run by friendly owners on the high street. Winding staircase leads to the large bedrooms which occupy each floor.

The Old Butchers

Park St ✉ GL54 1AQ – ✆ (01451) 831 700 – www.theoldbutchers.com – Fax (01451) 831 388

Rest – Menu £ 14 (lunch) – Carte £ 24/31

◆ Former butcher's shop of Cotswold stone: closely set tables in a very busy, modern restaurant. Daily changing, affordable, modish menus feature prominent use of local produce.

The White Hart Inn with rm

The Square ✉ GL54 1AF – ✆ (01451) 830 674 – www.whitehartstow.com – Fax (01451) 870 525 – Closed 4 days in May and 4 days in October

5 rm – †£ 100 ††£ 120 **Rest** – Menu £ 15 – Carte £ 22/25

◆ 13C property on town square with stylish, contemporary interior. Cooking is classic, understated and very tasty, with seafood to the fore. Good value set menu. Cosy, modern bedrooms; 'Stag' is the best.

at Upper Oddington East : 2 mi. by A 436 – ✉ Stow-on-the-Wold

Horse & Groom Village Inn with rm

✉ GL56 0XH – ✆ (01451) 830 584 – www.horseandgroom.uk.com

7 rm – †£ 69/89 ††£ 89/109 **Rest** – Carte £ 20/30

◆ Popular, welcoming pub, with open fire and characterful beams. Substantial menu displays carefully sourced produce, including venison from nearby estates and veg from the village. Bedrooms have a pleasant, cottagey feel.

at Daylesford East : 3.5 mi. by A 436 – ✉ Stow-on-the-Wold

The Cafe at Daylesford Organic

✉ *GL56 0YG – ☎ (01608) 731 700 – www.daylesfordorganic.com – Fax (01608) 731 701 – Closed 25-26 December and 1 January*

Rest – Organic – *(lunch only) (bookings not accepted)* Carte £ 24/29

◆ Beautifully designed farm shop, spa, yoga centre and two-floor café, which becomes very busy as customers tuck into tasty dishes whose ingredients are all organically sourced.

at Bledington Southeast : 4 mi. by A 436 on B 4450 – ✉ Kingham

The Kings Head Inn with rm

The Green ✉ OX7 6XQ – ☎ (01608) 658 365 – www.kingsheadinn.net – Fax (01608) 658 902 – Closed 25-26 December

12 rm – †£ 60 ††£ 125 **Rest** – Carte £ 20/28

◆ 15C stone inn with low-ceilinged, beamed bar and comfortable dining room. Traditional dishes with odd international influence; robust, rustic cooking. Smart bedrooms; those in pub more characterful; those in annex more stylish.

at Lower Oddington East : 3 mi. by A 436 – ✉ Stow-on-the-Wold

The Fox Inn with rm

✉ *GL56 0UR – ☎ (01451) 870 555 – www.foxinn.net – Fax (01451) 870 666 – Closed 25 December*

3 rm – †£ 95 ††£ 95 **Rest** – *(booking essential)* Carte £ 20/32

◆ 16C ivy dressed pub in a charming village. Flag floors, beams, fireplaces, nooks, crannies, books and candlelight. Hearty English fare. Sumptuously decorated rooms.

ENGLAND

at Lower Swell West : 1.25 mi. on B 4068 – ✉ Stow-on-the-Wold

Rectory Farmhouse without rest

by Rectory Barns Rd ✉ GL54 1LH – ☎ (01451) 832 351 – Closed Christmas and New Year

3 rm – †£ 65 ††£ 98

◆ 17C former farmhouse of Cotswold stone. Bedrooms are very comfortable and decorated in distinctive cottage style. Breakfast in kitchen, conservatory or, in summer, on the terrace.

STRATFORD-UPON-AVON – Warwickshire – 503 P27 — 19 C3

– **pop. 22 187** Great Britain

London 96 mi. – Birmingham 23 mi. – Coventry 18 mi. – Leicester 44 mi.

Bridgefoot ☎ (0870) 160 7930, info@shakespeare-country.co.uk

Tiddington Rd, ☎ (01789) 205 749

Menzies Welcombe Hotel & GC Warwick Rd, ☎ (01789) 413 800

Stratford Oaks Snitterfield Bearley Rd, ☎ (01789) 731 980

Town★★ - Shakespeare's Birthplace★ **AC**, AB

Mary Arden's House★ **AC**, NW : 4 mi. by A 3400 A. Ragley Hall★ **AC**, W : 9 mi. by A 422 A

Ettington Park

Alderminster, Southeast : 6.25 mi. on A 3400 ✉ CV37 8BU – ☎ (0845) 072 7454 – www.handpicked.co.uk – Fax (0845) 072 7455

43 rm – †£ 105/205 ††£ 145/225 – 5 suites

Rest – Menu £ 35 **s** – Carte £ 33/39 **s**

◆ Impressive Gothic mansion surrounded by lovely gardens and wooded grounds. Large, characterful guest areas boast impressive ornate ceilings. Smart, stylish bedrooms have modern facilities. Formal restaurant offers classical British menus.

Welcombe H. Spa and Golf Club

Warwick Rd, Northeast : 1.5 mi. on A 439 ✉ CV37 0NR – ☎ (01789) 295 252 – www.menzieshotels.co.uk – Fax (01789) 414 666

73 rm – †£ 85/110 ††£ 110/185 – 5 suites

Rest *Trevelyan* – *(Closed Saturday lunch)* Menu £ 21/30 **s** – Carte £ 31/46 **s**

◆ Imposing Jacobean-style house built in 1866, with attractive grounds, superb spa/leisure club and classical guest areas. Choose from corporate, or traditional, antique-filled bedrooms. Formal dining room overlooks the gardens and water features.

STRATFORD-UPON-AVON

Banbury Rd	B	2
Bell Court Shopping Centre	A	39
Benson Rd	B	3
Bridge Foot	B	6
Bridge St	B	8
Chapel Lane	A	13
Chapel St	A	14
Church St	A	16
Clopton Bridge	B	18
College Lane	A	19
Ely St	A	22
Evesham Pl.	A	24
Great William St	A	25
Greenhill St	A	27
Guild St	A	28
Henley St	A	29
High St	A	31
Rother St	A	32
Scholars Lane	A	33
Sheep St	AB	35
Tiddington Rd	B	38
Trinity St	A	40
Warwick Rd	B	42
Waterside	B	43
Windsor St	A	45
Wood St	A	47

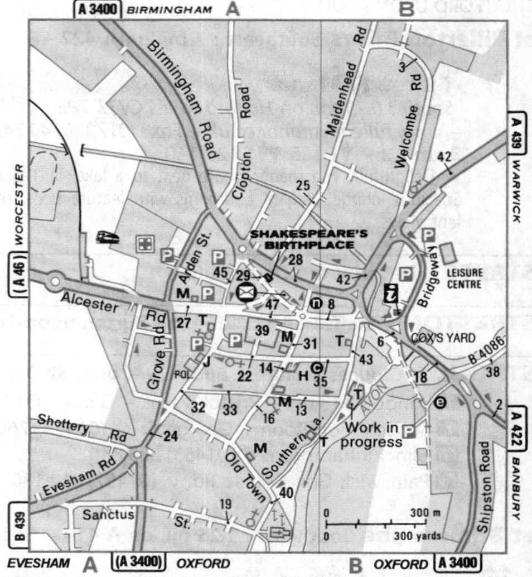

Cherry Trees without rest

Swan's Nest Lane ✉ CV37 7LS – ✆ (01789) 292 989
– www.cherrytrees-stratford.co.uk – Fax (01789) 292 989 Be
3 rm – ♦£ 55/65 ♦♦£ 115

◆ Smart, proudly run guest house in peaceful location. Spacious bedrooms boast quality furnishings, state-of-the-art showers, conservatory seating areas and thoughtful extras. Cake served on arrival.

White Sails without rest

85 Evesham Rd, Southwest : 1 mi. on B 439 ✉ CV37 9BE – ✆ (01789) 264 326
– www.white-sails.co.uk – Closed January-February
4 rm – ♦♦£ 95/115

◆ Friendly guest house boasting excellent bedrooms; all individually furnished and with a high level of facilities, including superb bathrooms. Leather furnished lounge with local info.

Malbec Petit Bistro

6 Union St ✉ CV37 6QT – ✆ (01789) 269 106 – www.malbecrestaurant.co.uk
Fax (01789) 269 106 – Closed 1 week October, 1 week Christmas, Sunday and Monday
Rest – Menu £ 15 (lunch) – Carte £ 22/30 An

◆ Smart restaurant with intimate, barrel-ceilinged, basement bistro and excellent service. Concise, constantly evolving menus offer rustic, flavoursome dishes with a refined edge; set lunch option provides the best value.

Lambs

12 Sheep St ✉ CV37 6EF – ✆ (01789) 292 554 – www.lambsrestaurant.co.uk
Fax (01789) 297 212 – Closed 25-26 December, Sunday dinner and Monday lunch
Rest – Menu £ 15/20 – Carte £ 22/34 Bc

◆ Attractive 16C timbered house, with characterful beams and original features on first floor. Concise menu offers refined modern dishes and fish specials, with good value pre-theatre options.

at Alveston East : 2 mi. by B 4086 - B – ✉ Stratford-upon-Avon

The Baraset Barn

1 Pimlico Lane, on B 4086 ✉ CV37 7RJ – ✆ (01789) 295 510
– www.lovelypubs.co.uk – Closed Sunday dinner
Rest – Menu £ 15 – Carte £ 20/30

◆ Modern, stylish pub with glass-fronted kitchen, hidden inside a traditional exterior. Cooking is assured and flavoursome and the modern menu offers something for everyone.

at Pillerton Priors Southeast : 7 mi. on A 422 - B – ✉ Stratford-upon-Avon

Fulready Manor without rest
South : 0.75 mi. on Halford rd ✉ CV37 7PE – ✆ (01789) 740 152 – www.fulreadymanor.co.uk – Fax (01789) 740 247
3 rm – †£ 125 ††£ 125/140
◆ Delightfully run manor house next to a lake, in 125 acres of peaceful arable farmland. Spacious lounge. Elegant bedrooms with feature beds, smart bathrooms and extras. Excellent views.

STRETE – Devon – see Dartmouth

STRETTON – Staffs. – **502** P25 – see Burton-upon-Trent

STROUD – Gloucestershire – **503** N28 – **pop. 32 052** 4 C1

London 113 mi. – Bristol 30 mi. – Gloucester 9 mi.
Subscription Rooms, George St ✆ (01453) 760960, tic@stroud.gov.uk
Minchinhampton, ✆ (01453) 833 840
Painswick Golf Course Rd, ✆ (01452) 812 180

at Brimscombe Southeast : 2.25 mi. on A 419 – ✉ Stroud

Burleigh Court
Burleigh Lane, South : 0.5 mi. by Burleigh rd via The Roundabouts ✉ GL5 2PF – ✆ (01453) 883 804 – www.burleighcourthotel.co.uk – Fax (01453) 886 870 – Closed 25-26 December
18 rm – †£ 105 ††£ 190
Rest – Menu £ 25 (lunch) – Carte (dinner) £ 34/41
◆ Regency house with mature garden, on edge of a steep hill overlooking Golden Valley. Swimming pool and terrace at the rear a real suntrap. Smart bedrooms with views. Comfortable dining room overlooks the gardens.

STUCKTON – Hants. – see Fordingbridge

STUDLAND – Dorset – **503** O32 – **pop. 471** 4 C3

London 135 mi. – Bournemouth 25 mi. – Southampton 53 mi. – Weymouth 29 mi.

Shell Bay
Ferry Rd, North : 3 mi. or via car ferry from Sandbanks ✉ BH19 3BA – ✆ (01929) 450 363 – www.shellbay.net – Fax (01929) 450 570 – April-December
Rest – Seafood – *(booking essential at dinner)* Carte £ 18/32
◆ Popular restaurant superbly situated on Poole harbour beach, with vast windows and terrace providing stunning panoramic views. Light lunch; more adventurous dinner. Local seafood a speciality.

STURMINSTER NEWTON – Dorset – **503** N31 – **pop. 2 317** 4 C3

London 123 mi. – Bournemouth 30 mi. – Bristol 49 mi. – Salisbury 28 mi.
Mill★ AC

Plumber Manor
Southwest : 1.75 mi. by A 357 on Hazelbury Bryan rd ✉ DT10 2AF – ✆ (01258) 472 507 – www.plumbermanor.com – Fax (01258) 473 370 – Closed February
16 rm – †£ 100/115 ††£ 180
Rest – *(dinner only and Sunday lunch)* Menu £ 24/30
◆ Manor house in a peaceful, secluded spot, owned by the same family since it was built in the 17C. The bedrooms are well kept and some have antique furniture. Choice of three dining rooms; traditional cooking.

ENGLAND

SUMMERCOURT – Cornwall – **503** F32 – ✉ **Newquay** **1** B2

London 263 mi. – Newquay 9 mi. – Plymouth 45 mi.

Viners

Carvynick, 1.5 mi. northwest off the junction of A 30 and A 3058. ✉ TR8 5AF – ✆ (01872) 510 544 – www.vinersrestaurant.co.uk – Fax (01872) 510 468 – Closed Sunday dinner, Monday, and Tuesday-Saturday lunch in winter

Rest – Menu £ 19 – Carte £ 32/38

◆ Rustic, stone-built inn with informal atmosphere and enthusiastic staff. Old favourites and more ambitious offerings share the menu, and dishes make good use of local produce.

SUNBURY ON THAMES – Surrey – **504** S29 – **pop. 27 415** **7** C1

London 16 mi. – Croydon 38 mi. – Barnet 44 mi. – Ealing 10 mi.

Indian Zest

21 Thames St ✉ TW16 5QF – ✆ (01932) 765 000 – www.indianzest.co.uk – Fax (01932) 765 000

Rest – Indian – Menu £ 12/18 – Carte £ 21/26

◆ Original in its decoration and food. 450 year old building; a series of small rooms set around a bar; subtle colonial feel. Interesting mix of modern Indian and traditional regional cuisine.

SUNNINGDALE – Windsor and Maidenhead – **504** S29 **11** D3

London 33 mi. – Croydon 39 mi. – Barnet 46 mi. – Ealing 22 mi.

Bluebells

Shrubbs Hill, London Rd, Northeast : 0.75 mi. on A 30 ✉ SL5 0LE – ✆ (01344) 622 722 – www.bluebells-restaurant.com – Fax (01344) 620 990 – Closed 1-13 January, 25-26 December, Sunday dinner, Monday and Bank Holidays

Rest – Menu £ 16 (lunch) – Carte dinner £ 31/50

◆ Smart, well-manicured façade matched by sophisticated interior of deep green. Large rear terrace, deck and garden. Modern British cooking with original starting point.

SUNNINGHILL – Windsor & Maidenhead – **504** S29 – **see Ascot**

SUNNISIDE – Tyne and Wear – ✉ **NE16 5** **24** B2

London 283 mi. – Newcastle upon Tyne 6 mi. – Sunderland 16 mi. – Middlesbrough 41 mi.

Hedley Hall without rest

Hedley Lane, South : 2 m by A 6076 ✉ NE16 5EH – ✆ (01207) 231 835 – www.hedleyhall.com

4 rm – † £ 52/60 †† £ 80

◆ Pleasant former farmhouse in quiet rural location close to Beamish, with spacious conservatory and sitting room. Rooms are large, with good levels of comfort and country views.

SURFLEET SEAS END – Lincs. – **502** T25 – **see Spalding**

SUTTON COLDFIELD – West Midlands – **503** O26 – **pop. 105 452** **19** C2

London 124 mi. – Birmingham 8 mi. – Coventry 29 mi. – Nottingham 47 mi.

18 Pype Hayes Walmley Eachelhurst Rd, ✆ (0121) 351 1014

18 Boldmere Monmouth Dr., ✆ (0121) 354 3379

18 110 Thornhill Rd, ✆ (0121) 580 7878

36 The Belfry Wishaw Lichfield Rd, ✆ (01675) 470 301

Plan : see Birmingham pp. 2 and 3

The Belfry rm, rest,
Wishaw, East : 6.5 mi. by A 453 on A 446 ✉ B76 9PR
– ✆ (01675) 470 301 – www.thebelfry.com – Fax (01675) 470 256
– Closed 25-26 December
313 rm – †£ 129 ††£ 149 – 11 suites
Rest *French Restaurant* – *(closed Sunday and Monday) (dinner only)*
Carte £ 24/30
Rest *Atrium* – *(light lunch Monday-Saturday)* Menu £ 25
◆ Famed for championship golf course, this large hotel has an unashamedly leisure oriented slant, including a superb AquaSpa. Sizeable rooms; superior variety overlook courses. Formal French Restaurant has golfing vistas. Atrium dominated by glass dome ceiling.

SUTTON COURTENAY – Oxfordshire – pop. 2 413 — 10 B2

London 72 mi. – Bristol 77 mi. – Coventry 70 mi.

The Fish
4 Appleford Rd ✉ OX14 4NQ – ✆ (01235) 848 242
– www.thefishatsuttoncourtenay.co.uk – Fax (01235) 848 014 – Closed January, Sunday dinner and Monday
Rest – Menu £ 16 (Tuesday-Saturday lunch) – Carte £ 23/27
◆ Robust, seasonal country cooking: escargots and crème brûlée meet steak and kidney pie and profiteroles on Franco-Anglo menu. Neat garden and bright conservatory. Charming service.

SUTTON GAULT – Cambs. – 504 U26 – see Ely

SUTTON-ON-THE-FOREST – North Yorkshire – 502 P21 – pop. 281 — 23 C2

London 230 mi. – Kingston-upon-Hull 50 mi. – Leeds 52 mi.
– Scarborough 40 mi.

Rose & Crown
Main St ✉ YO61 1DP – ✆ (01347) 811 333 – www.rosecrown.co.uk
– Fax (01347) 811 333 – Closed first week in January, Sunday dinner and Monday
Rest – *(booking essential)* Menu £ 20 – Carte £ 25/35
◆ Always a welcoming atmosphere at this village pub, with its cosy bar and busy dining room. Variety of menus ensures something for everyone; good food and local specialities. Large terrace and gazebo.

The Blackwell Ox Inn with rm
Huby Rd ✉ YO61 1DT – ✆ (01347) 810 328 – www.blackwelloxinn.co.uk
– Fax (01347) 812 738 – Closed 1 January, 25 December and Sunday dinner
7 rm – †£ 65 ††£ 110 **Rest** – Menu £ 14 **s** – Carte £ 14/30 **s**
◆ 19C brick-built pub with welcoming atmosphere. Cooking is hearty, straightforward and satisfying; menus feature old favourites, some Gallic influences and the odd more ambitious dish. Bedrooms are finished to a high standard; some boast four-posters.

SWANAGE – Dorset – 503 O32 – pop. 11 097 — 4 C3

London 130 mi. – Bournemouth 22 mi. – Dorchester 26 mi.
– Southampton 52 mi.

The White House, Shore Rd ✆ (01929) 422885, mail@swanage.gov.uk

Isle of Purbeck Studland, ✆ (01929) 450 361

Town★

St Aldhelm's Head★★ (≤★★★), SW : 4 mi. by B 3069 – Durlston Country Park (≤★★), S : 1 mi. – Studland (Old Harry Rocks★★, Studland Beach (≤★), St Nicholas Church★), N : 3 mi. – Worth Matravers (Anvil Point Lighthouse ≤★★), S : 2 mi. – Great Globe★, S : 1.25 m. Corfe Castle★ (≤★★) **AC**, NW : 6 mi. by A 351 – Blue Pool★, NW : 9 mi. by A 351 and minor roads – Lulworth Cove★, W : 18 mi. by A 351 and B 3070

ENGLAND

Cauldron Bistro
VISA MC

5 High St ✉ *BH19 2LN* – ✆ *(01929) 422 671*
– Closed first 2 weeks January, first 2 weeks December and Monday-Wednesday
Rest – *(light lunch)* Carte £ 20/38

◆ Quaint and cosy; boothed tables, mix and match furniture. Quality ingredients, local fish, generous portions cooked with care. Unusual vegetarian dishes.

SWAY – **Hants.** – **503** P31 – **see Brockenhurst**

SWINBROOK – **Oxon.** – **503** P28 – **see Burford**

SWINDON – Swindon – 503 O29 – pop. 155 432 4 D2

London 83 mi. – Bournemouth 69 mi. – Bristol 40 mi. – Coventry 66 mi.
37 Regent St ✆ (01793) 530328, infocentre@swindon.gov.uk
27 Broome Manor Pipers Way, ✆ (01793) 532 403
18 Shrivenham Park Shrivenham Penny Hooks, ✆ (01793) 783 853
18 The Wiltshire G & CC Wootton Bassett Vastern, ✆ (01793) 849 999
18 Wrag Barn G & C.C. Highworth Shrivenham Rd, ✆ (01793) 861 327
Great Western Railway Museum★ **AC** – Railway Village Museum★ **AC** Y **M**
Lydiard Park (St Mary's★) W : 4 mi. U. Ridgeway Path★★, S : 8.5 mi. by A 4361 – Whitehorse (≤★)E : 7.5 mi. by A 4312, A 420 and B 400 off B 4057

SWINDON

Street	Grid	No.
Beckhampton St	Y	3
Bridge St	Y	7
Brunel Shopping Centre	YZ	
Canal Walk	Y	9
Cricklade St	Z	13
Cross St	Z	15
Deacon St	Z	16
Dryden St	Z	19
Edmund St	Z	21
Faringdon Rd	Y	22
Farnsby St	YZ	24
High St	Z	27
Islington St	Y	29
London St	Y	31
Milton Rd	YZ	33
North St	Z	39
North Star Ave	Y	37
Ocotal Way	Y	40
Prospect Hill	Z	45
Regent St	YZ	46
Sheppard St	Y	49
Southampton St	Y	54
South St	Z	52
Spring Gardens	Y	55
The Parade	Y	58
Upham Rd	Z	60
Warwick Rd	Z	63
Wood St	Z	67

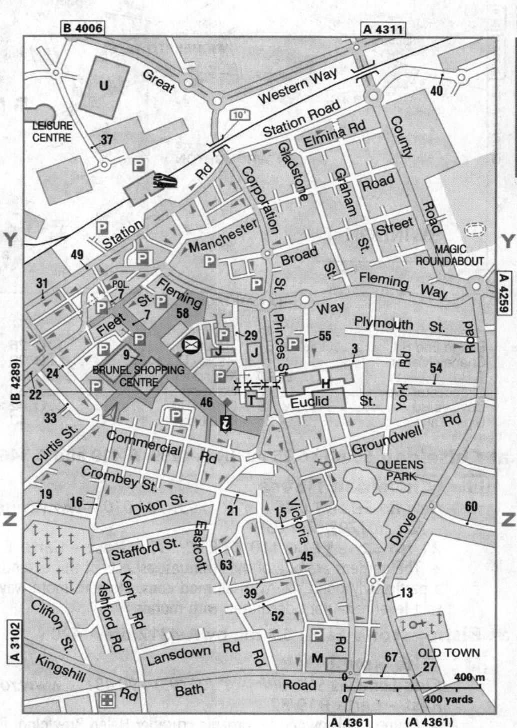

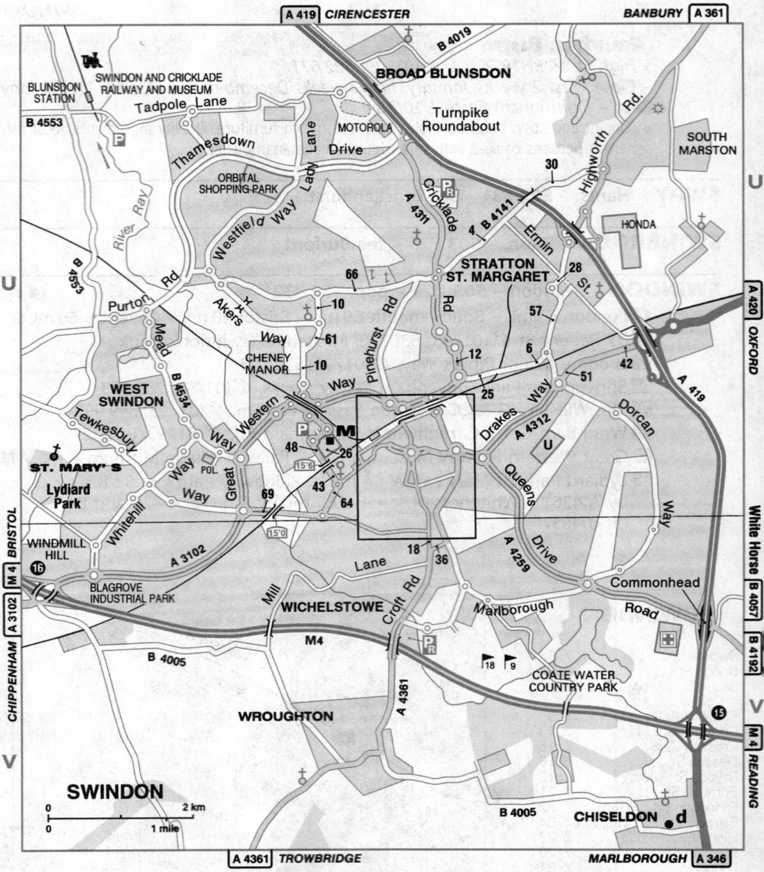

Street	Grid	No.
Beechcroft Rd	U	4
Bridge End Rd	U	6
Cheney Manor Rd	U	10
Cirencester Way	U	12
Devises Rd	V	18
Gipsy Lane	U	25
Great Western Retail Outlet	U	26
Hobley Drive	U	28
Kingsdown Rd	U	30
Newport St	V	36
Oxford Rd	U	42
Park Lane	U	43
Rodbourne Rd	U	48
Slade Drive	U	51
Swindon Rd	U	57
Vicarage Rd	U	61
Westcott Pl.	U	64
Whitworth Rd	U	66
Wootton Basset Rd	U	69

at Chiseldon South : 6.25 mi. by A 4259, A 419 and A 346 on B 4005 – ✉ Swindon

Chiseldon House

New Rd ✉ SN4 0NE – ✆ (01793) 741 010 – www.chiseldonhousehotel.co.uk – Fax (01793) 741 059 **Vd**

21 rm – £ 60/110 £ 90/130 **Rest** – Carte £ 20/32

◆ The gardens are one of the strongest aspects of this extended Georgian house. Rooms are a particularly good size with all mod cons. Close to motorway and easily accessible. Ornate, split-level restaurant decorated with murals.

at Bishopstone East : 5.5 mi. by A 4312 off A 420

The Royal Oak

Cues Lane ✉ SN6 8PP – ✆ (01793) 790 481 – www.royaloakbishopstone.co.uk

Rest – Carte £ 19/32

◆ Country pub owned by organic crusader Helen Browning. Produce is from her farm or local suppliers and is largely organic and fair-trade: cooking is hearty, seasonal and creative.

SYMONDS YAT WEST – County of Herefordshire – 503 M28 – ✉ Ross-On-Wye ▮ Great Britain 18 B3

London 126 mi. – Gloucester 23 mi. – Hereford 17 mi. – Newport 31 mi.

Town★ – Yat Rock (≤★)

S : Wye Valley★

Norton House without rest

Whitchurch ✉ HR9 6DJ – ✆ (01600) 890 046 – www.norton-house.com – Fax (01600) 890 045 – Closed 25-26 December

3 rm – †£ 50 ††£ 70/80

◆ Built of local stone, this 18C farmhouse of 15C origins boasts quaint interiors. Rooms with antique beds in patchwork quilts and flowers. Tea, cake on arrival.

Guesthouses don't provide the same level of service as hotels. They are often characterised by a warm welcome and a décor which reflects the owner's personality. Those shown in red are particularly pleasant.

TADCASTER – North Yorkshire – 502 Q22 – pop. 6 548 22 B2

London 206 mi. – Harrogate 16 mi. – Leeds 14 mi. – York 11 mi.

at Colton Northeast : 3 mi. by A 659 and A 64 – ✉ Tadcaster

Ye Old Sun Inn with rm

Main Street ✉ LS24 8EP – ✆ (01904) 744 261 – www.yeoldsuninn.co.uk – Closed 3 weeks in January, 26 December and Monday lunch

3 rm – †£ 75 ††£ 120

Rest – Menu £ 17 (lunch) – Carte £ 20/30

◆ Rustic, family-run pub with warming open fires and a small deli. Owners are great ambassadors of local suppliers and seasonal produce, and give regular cookery demonstrations. Smart bedrooms are located in the house next door.

TANGMERE – W. Sussex – 504 R31 – see Chichester

TANWORTH-IN-ARDEN – Warks. – 503 O26 – see Henley-in-Arden

TAPLOW – Buckinghamshire – 504 R29 11 C3

London 33 mi. – Maidenhead 2 mi. – Oxford 36 mi. – Reading 12 mi.

Cliveden

North : 2 mi. by Berry Hill ✉ SL6 0JF – ✆ (01628) 668 561 – www.clivedenhouse.co.uk – Fax (01628) 661 837

31 rm – †£ 242/472 ††£ 242/472 – 8 suites

Rest *Waldo's* – *(dinner only) (booking essential)* Menu £ 68

Rest *Terrace* – Menu £ 38/59

◆ Breathtakingly stunning 19C stately home in National Trust gardens. Ornate, sumptuous public areas, filled with antiques. Exquisitely appointed rooms the last word in luxury. Waldo's is discreet and formal; luxury ingredients are used in ambitious creations. View parterre and Thames in top class style from Terrace.

TARPORLEY – Cheshire – 502 L/M24 – pop. 2 634 20 A3

London 186 mi. – Chester 11 mi. – Liverpool 27 mi. – Shrewsbury 36 mi.

Portal G & C.C. Cobblers Cross Lane, ✆ (01829) 733 933

Portal Premier Forest Rd, ✆ (01829) 733 884

ENGLAND

at Little Budworth Northeast : 3.5 mi. on A 49 – ✉ Tarporley

Cabbage Hall

Forest Road ✉ CW6 9ES – ☎ (01829) 760 292 – www.cabbagehallrestaurant.com – Fax (01829) 760 292 – Closed 4-19 January

Rest – Menu £ 17 (weekday lunch) – Carte £ 31/40

◆ Smart former pub in 11 acres of land, serving flavourful, satisfying, modern dishes which make good use of regional ingredients. Effective service from a well-versed team.

at Bunbury South : 3.25 mi. by A 49 – ✉ Tarporley

Dysart Arms

Bowes Gate Rd, by Bunbury Mill rd ✉ CW6 9PH – ☎ (01829) 260 183 – www.dysartarms-bunbury.co.uk – Fax (01829) 261 050

Rest – Carte £ 15/25

◆ Traditional red brick pub with French windows, terrace and garden. Daily changing menu displays a mix of fresh, tasty British and Mediterranean dishes, and classical puddings.

at Willington Northwest : 3.5 mi. by A 51 – ✉ Tarporley

Willington Hall

✉ CW6 0NB – ☎ (01829) 752 321 – www.willingtonhall.co.uk – Fax (01829) 752 596 – Closed 25-26 December

10 rm – †£ 80 ††£ 130

Rest – *(Closed Sunday dinner and Bank Holiday Mondays)* Menu £ 18/25 – Carte (dinner) £ 24/30

◆ Imposing 19C country house with ornate façade in mature grounds; many original features remain, including vast hall and impressive staircase. Most rooms have rural outlook. Intimate dinners served in classically proportioned surroundings.

ENGLAND

TARR STEPS – Somerset – 503 J30 — 3 A2

London 191 mi. – Taunton 31 mi. – Tiverton 20 mi.

Tarr Steps ★★ (Clapper Bridge ★★)

Tarr Farm Inn with rm

✉ TA22 9PY – ☎ (01643) 851 507 – www.tarrfarm.co.uk – Fax (01643) 851 111

9 rm – †£ 75/90 ††£ 150 **Rest** – Carte £ 22/30

◆ Beside a river, in idyllic countryside, this is a true destination pub. Food ranges from cream teas and sandwiches to three courses at lunch, with more ambitious dishes at dinner. Bedrooms are elegant, luxurious and extremely well-equipped.

TATTENHALL – Cheshire – 502 L24 – pop. 1 860 — 20 A3

London 200 mi. – Birmingham 71 mi. – Chester 10 mi. – Liverpool 29 mi.

Higher Huxley Hall without rest

North : 2.25 mi. on Huxley rd ✉ CH3 9BZ – ☎ (01829) 781 484 – www.huxleyhall.co.uk – Closed Christmas

5 rm – †£ 50/75 ††£ 80/95

◆ This historic manor house, sited on a former farm, dates from 14C and is attractively furnished with antiques. Bedrooms are comfortable and well equipped.

at Higher Burwardsley Southeast : 1 mi. – ✉ Tattenhall

The Pheasant Inn with rm

✉ CH3 9PF – ☎ (01829) 770 434 – www.thepheasantinn.co.uk – Fax (01829) 771 097

12 rm – †£ 65/75 ††£ 85/140 **Rest** – Carte £ 22/35

◆ Sits on a hill in the flat Cheshire Plains; lovely garden and terrace. Daily changing menu features local produce, ranging from afternoon tea, to deli boards and pub classics. Bedrooms are compact, stylish and comfortable; most have views.

TAUNTON – Somerset – **503** K30 – **pop. 58 241** **3** B3

London 168 mi. – Bournemouth 69 mi. – Bristol 50 mi. – Exeter 37 mi.

The Library, Paul St ☎ (01823) 336344, tauntontic@tauntondeane.gov.uk

Taunton Vale Creech Heathfield, ☎ (01823) 412 220

Vivary Vivary Park, ☎ (01823) 289 274

Taunton and Pickeridge Corfe, ☎ (01823) 421 537

Town★ - St Mary Magdalene★ V – Somerset County Museum★ **AC** V **M** – St James'★ U – Hammett St★ V **25** – The Crescent★ V – Bath Place★ V **3**

Trull (Church★), S : 2.5 mi. by A 38 – Hestercombe Gardens★, N : 5 mi. by A 3259 BY and minor roads to Cheddon Fitzpaine. Bishops Lydeard★ (Church★), NW : 6 mi. – Wellington : Church★, Wellington Monument (≤★★), SW : 7.5 mi. by A 38 – Combe Florey★, NW : 8 mi. – Gaulden Manor★ **AC**, NW : 10 mi. by A 358 and B 3227

Plan on next page

The Castle

Castle Green ✉ TA1 1NF – ☎ (01823) 272 671 – www.the-castle-hotel.com – Fax (01823) 336 066 V**a**

44 rm – †£ 140/170 ††£ 230/335, ☕ £ 15.50

Rest – *(Closed Sunday and Monday)* Carte £ 28/50

◆ Traditionally renowned, family owned British hotel: afternoon tea a speciality. 12C origins with Norman garden. Wisteria-clad and castellated. Individually styled rooms. Classic British cooking uses top quality West Country produce.

Meryan House

Bishop's Hull Rd, West : 0.75 mi. by A 38 ✉ TA1 5EG – ☎ (01823) 337 445 – www.meryanhouse.co.uk – Fax (01823) 322 355 AZ**c**

12 rm ☕ – †£ 60/80 ††£ 80/85

Rest – *(dinner only) (booking essential for non-residents)* Menu £ 26

◆ Privately owned extended house on town outskirts. Comfortable sitting room has adjacent patio garden and small bar with jukebox. Well-kept, individually styled rooms. Intimate dining room with large inglenook.

The Willow Tree

3 Tower Lane ✉ TA1 4AR – ☎ (01823) 352 835 – www.willowtreerestaurant.co.uk – Closed January, August, Sunday and Monday V**c**

Rest – *(dinner only)* Menu £ 23 (Tuesday and Wednesday)/30 (Thursday to Saturday)

◆ Converted 17C town house in central location. Exposed beams and large inglenook fireplaces. Friendly service. Appealing menu of modern seasonal cooking with a classical base.

Brazz

Castle Bow ✉ TA1 1NF – ☎ (01823) 252 000 – www.brazz.co.uk – Fax (01823) 336 066 – closed dinner 25 December V**e**

Rest – Carte £ 20/33

◆ Bright and breezy bistro style eatery to rear of The Castle hotel. Large, bustling bar area. Main restaurant has large aquarium, concave ceiling and brasserie favourites.

at Hatch Beauchamp Southeast : 6 mi. by A 358 - BZ – ✉ Taunton

Farthings

Village Rd ✉ TA3 6SG – ☎ (01823) 480 664 – www.farthingshotel.co.uk – Fax (01823) 481 118

12 rm ☕ – †£ 75/130 ††£ 95/195 **Rest** – Menu £ 32/37 **s** – Carte £ 30/48 **s**

◆ Georgian country house with pleasant, spacious gardens in pretty village. Personally run, with small lounge and well-stocked bar. Sizeable, individually decorated rooms. Smart dining room; local produce to fore.

TAUNTON

Bath Pl. . . . . **V** 3
Billetfield . . . . **V** 6
Billet St. . . . . **V** 4
Birch Grove . . . . **U** 7
Bishop's Hull Rd . . . . **AZ** 9
Bridge St . . . . **U** 12
Bridge (The) . . . . **U** 10
Burton Pl. . . . . **V** 13
Cann St . . . . **V** 15
Chritchard Parkway . . . . . . **BYZ** 45
Cleveland St . . . . **U** 16
Comeytrowe Lane . . . . **AZ** 18
Corporation St . . . . **V** 19
County Walk Shopping Centre . . . . . . **V**
Duke St . . . . **V** 21
East St . . . . **V**
Fore St . . . . **V** 22
Hamilton Rd . . . . **BZ** 24
Hammet St . . . . **V** 25
High St . . . . **V**
Hurdle Way . . . . **V** 27
Ilminster Rd . . . . **BZ** 28
Magdalene St . . . . **V** 30
Middleway . . . . **AZ** 31
North St . . . . **V** 33
Obridge Viaduct . . . . **BY** 34
Old Market Shopping Centre . . . . . . **V**
Portland St. . . . . **U** 36
Priory Ave . . . . **U** 37
Shoreditch Rd . . . . **BZ** 39
Shuttern . . . . **V** 40
Silver St South . . . . **V, Z** 42
Upper High St . . . . **V** 43
Upper Wood St. . . . . **U** 44
Wellington New Rd . . . . **AZ** 46
Wilton St . . . . **V** 48
Winchester St . . . . **U** 49
Wood St . . . . **U** 51

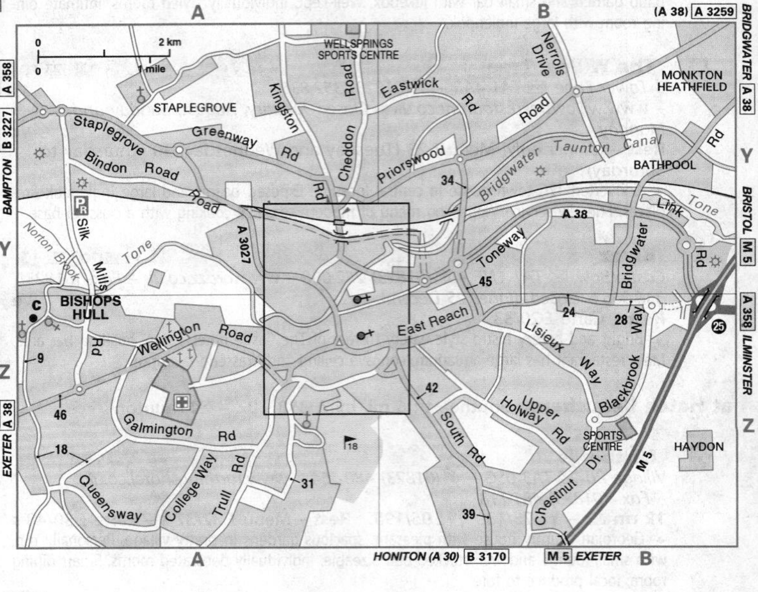

ENGLAND

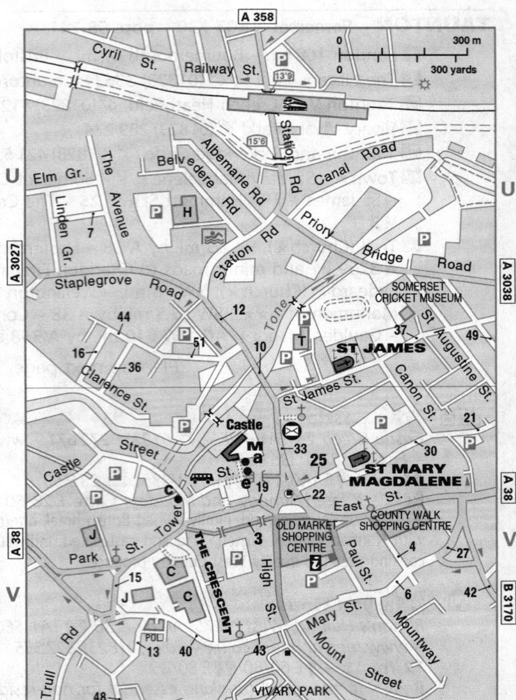

0
2 km
0
1 mile
MINEHEAD A 358
B 3227
BAMPTON
EXETER A 38
BRIDGWATER A 38
BRISTOL M 5
A 358 ILMINSTER
HONITON (A 30) B 3170
M 5 EXETER
WELLSPRINGS SPORTS CENTRE
STAPLEGROVE
MONKTON HEATHFIELD
BATHPOOL
BISHOPS HULL
HAYDON
SPORTS CENTRE
Staplegrove Road
Greenway Rd
Bindon Road
Kingston Road
Cheddon Rd
Eastwick Rd
Nerrols Drive
Priorswood Road
Taunton Canal
Bridgwater
Link Rd
Toneway
East Reach
Lisieux Way
Bridgwater Way
Blackbrook Way
Upper Holway Rd
Chestnut Dr.
South Rd
Wellington Road
Galmington Rd
College Way
Trull Rd
Queensway
Silk Mills Rd
Norton Brook
Tone
A 3027
A 38
M 5
Y
Z
A
B

at West Bagborough **Northwest : 10.5 mi. by A 358 - AY - ✉ Taunton**

Tilbury Farm without rest
East : 0.75 mi. ✉ TA4 3DY – ☎ (01823) 432 391
3 rm – †£ 40/45 ††£ 65
◆ Impressively characterful 18C house with terrific views of Vale of Taunton. Welcoming lounge boasts log fire. Well-kept, spacious bedrooms all with beams and good views.

The Rising Sun Inn with rm
✉ TA4 3EF – ☎ (01823) 432 575 – www.risingsun.info – Closed Sunday dinner in winter
2 rm – †£ 55 ††£ 85 **Rest** – Carte £ 14/25
◆ Warm, intimate inn with a 'village pub' atmosphere. Local ingredients contribute to a well-balanced mix of modern and traditional dishes, with plenty of care taken in the kitchen.

at West Hatch **Southeast : 5 mi. by A38**

The Farmers Inn with rm
Higher West Hatch ✉ TA3 5RS – ☎ (01823) 480 480 – www.farmersinnwesthatch.co.uk – Fax (01823) 481 177
5 rm – †£ 85 ††£ 130 **Rest** – Menu £ 15 (lunch) – Carte £ 25/30
◆ A soft-stone inn with welcoming owners serving local or home-brewed ales and ciders alongside an ambitious British/European menu. Luxurious bedrooms and bathrooms; most with sitting areas and views.

ENGLAND

TAVISTOCK – **Devon** – **503** H32 – **pop. 11 018** **2** C2

London 239 mi. – Exeter 38 mi. – Plymouth 16 mi.
Town Hall, Bedford Sq ☎ (01822) 612938, tavistocktic@westdevon.gov.uk
Down Rd, ☎ (01822) 612 344
Hurdwick Tavistock Hamlets, ☎ (01822) 612 746
Morwellham★ **AC**, SW : 4.5 m. E : Dartmoor National Park★★ – Buckland Abbey★★ **AC**, S : 7 mi. by A 386 – Lydford★★, N : 8.5 mi. by A 386

Browns
80 West St ✉ PL19 8AQ – ☎ (01822) 618 686 – www.brownsdevon.co.uk – Fax (01822) 618 646
20 rm – †£ 70/129 ††£ 109/149, £ 7.50
Rest – Menu £ 20/40 – Carte £ 26/39
◆ Former coaching inn and oldest licensed premises in town; now a stylish and contemporary hotel. The mews rooms have a particularly comfortable feel to them. Busy, friendly, informal brasserie.

April Cottage
12 Mount Tavy Rd ✉ PL19 9JB – ☎ (01822) 613 280 – www.aprilcottagetavistock.co.uk
3 rm – †£ 45/65 ††£ 60/70 **Rest** – Menu £ 18
◆ Compact but homely Victorian cottage. Meals taken in rear conservatory overlooking River Tavy. Curios adorn small lounge. Carefully furnished rooms with varnished pine.

at Gulworthy **West : 3 mi. on A 390 – ✉ Tavistock**

The Horn of Plenty with rm
Gulworthy, West : 4 mi. by A 390 off Chipshop rd ✉ PL19 8JD – ☎ (01822) 832 528 – www.thehornofplenty.co.uk – Fax (01822) 834 390 – Closed 24-26 December
10 rm – †£ 190 ††£ 200 **Rest** – French – Menu £ 27/47
◆ Stylish, contemporary restaurant featuring local artwork, in enchanting, creeper-clad country house. Classic cooking uses local ingredients. Polite service. Modern country house style bedrooms; those in annex have terrace.

at Milton Abbot Northwest : 6 mi. on B 3362 – ✉ Tavistock

Hotel Endsleigh
Southwest : 1 mi. ✉ PL19 0PQ – ✆ (01822) 870 000 – www.hotelendsleigh.com – Fax (01822) 870 578 – Closed 18-31 January
13 rm – †£ 180 ††£ 300 – 2 suites
Rest – Menu £ 30/40 **s** – Carte £ 21/40 **s**
◆ Painstakingly restored Regency lodge in magnificent Devonian gardens and grounds. Stylish lounge and refined bedrooms are imbued with an engaging, understated elegance. Interesting, classically based dishes served in two minimalist dining rooms.

at Chillaton Northwest : 6.25 mi. by Chillaton rd – ✉ Tavistock

Tor Cottage without rest
Southwest : 0.25 mi. by Tavistock rd, turning right at bridle path sign, down unmarked track for 0.5 mi. ✉ PL16 0JE – ✆ (01822) 860 248 – www.torcottage.co.uk – Fax (01822) 860 126 – Closed mid December to 1 February
5 rm – †£ 94 ††£ 140
◆ Lovely cottage and peaceful gardens in 28 hillside acres. Terrace or conservatory breakfast. Individual rooms, most spread around garden, with open fires or wood stoves.

TEFFONT – Wilts. – see Salisbury

TEIGNMOUTH – Devon – **503** J32 – **pop. 14 799** **2** D2

London 216 mi. – Exeter 16 mi. – Torquay 8 mi.
The Den, Sea Front ✆ (01626) 215666, teigntic@teignbridge.gov.uk

Thomas Luny House without rest
Teign St, follow signs for the Quays, off the A 381 ✉ TQ14 8EG – ✆ (01626) 772 976 – www.thomas-luny-house.co.uk
4 rm – †£ 68/70 ††£ 85/98
◆ Personally run Georgian house with sheltered walled garden. Smart breakfast room with antique pieces. Well furnished drawing room. Stylish, individually appointed bedrooms.

TELFORD – Telford and Wrekin – **502** M25 – **pop. 138 241** **18** B2
Great Britain

London 152 mi. – Birmingham 33 mi. – Shrewsbury 12 mi. – Stoke-on-Trent 29 mi.
Wrekin Square ✆ (01952) 238008, tourist-info@telfordshopping.co.uk
Telford Sutton Heights Great Hay, ✆ (01952) 429 977
Wrekin Wellington, ✆ (01952) 244 032
The Shropshire Muxton Muxton Grange, ✆ (01952) 677 800
Ironbridge Gorge Museum★★ **AC** (The Iron Bridge★★, Coalport China Museum★★, Blists Hill Open Air Museum★★, Museum of the River and Visitor Centre★) S : 5 mi. by B 4373. Weston Park★★ **AC**, E : 7 mi. by A 5

Dovecote Grange without rest
Bratton Rd, Northwest : 6.75 mi. by A 442 and B 5063 (following signs for Admaston) off B 4394 ✉ TF5 0BS – ✆ (01952) 243 739 – www.dovecotegrange.co.uk
5 rm – †£ 50 ††£ 70/80
◆ Attractive guesthouse, garden and terrace enjoying views over the local fields. Combined lounge and breakfast area with modern leather furniture. Large, comfy, modish rooms.

at Norton South : 7 mi. on A 442 – ✉ Shifnal

Hundred House with rm
Bridgnorth Rd ✉ TF11 9EE – ✆ (01952) 580 240 – www.hundredhouse.co.uk – Fax (01952) 580 260
10 rm – †£ 61/85 ††£ 90/133 **Rest** – Carte £ 25/40
◆ Characterful, family-run redbrick inn with exposed beams, stained glass and a huge herb garden. Carefully sourced dishes are robust and original. Sizeable rooms in 19C style, some with canopied beds and swings.

ENGLAND

TEMPLE SOWERBY – Cumbria – 502 M20 – see Penrith

TENTERDEN – Kent – 504 W30 – pop. 6 977 9 C2

London 57 mi. – Folkestone 26 mi. – Hastings 21 mi. – Maidstone 19 mi.

Town Hall, High St ✆ (01580) 763572, tentic@ashford.gov.uk

Richard Phillips at Chapel Down

Tenterden Vinyard, Small Hythe, South: 2.5 mi. on B 2082
✉ TN30 7NG Tenterden – ✆ (01580) 761 616
– www.richardphillipsatchapeldown.co.uk

Rest – Modern – *(lunch only and dinner Thursday-Saturday)* Menu £ 15 (lunch) – Carte £ 29/40

◆ Spacious modern restaurant and funky bar on 1st floor of a barn conversion; terrace has countryside views. Good value lunch menu and more elaborate à la carte showcase seasonal produce.

TETBURY – Gloucestershire – 503 N29 – pop. 5 250 Great Britain 4 C1

London 113 mi. – Bristol 27 mi. – Gloucester 19 mi. – Swindon 24 mi.

33 Church St ✆ (01666) 503552, tourism@tetbury.org

Westonbirt, ✆ (01666) 880 242

Westonbirt Arboretum★ **AC**, SW : 2.5 mi. by A 433

Calcot Manor

Calcot, West : 3.5 mi. on A 4135 ✉ GL8 8YJ – ✆ (01666) 890 391
– www.calcotmanor.co.uk – Fax (01666) 890 394

34 rm – †£ 207 ††£ 230 – 1 suite

Rest *The Gumstool Inn* – see restaurant listing

Rest *Conservatory* – *(booking essential) (lunch)* Menu £ 19/25 **s** – Carte £ 33/57 **s**

◆ Impressive Cotswold farmhouse, gardens and meadows with converted ancient barns and stables. Superb spa. Variety of luxuriously appointed rooms with contemporary flourishes. Stylish Conservatory serves interesting modern dishes.

The Chef's Table

49 Long St ✉ GL8 8AA – ✆ (01666) 504 466
– Closed 25-26 December, 1 January, Sunday and dinner Monday-Tuesday

Rest – Carte £ 31/40 **s**

◆ Glass-fronted deli shop with busy, informal restaurant to the rear; mix of tables and high stools. Daily blackboard menu displays rustic, generous dishes of local, organic produce.

The Gumstool Inn – at Calcot Manor Hotel

West : 3.5 mi. on A 4135 ✉ GL8 8YJ – ✆ (01666) 890 391
– www.calcotmanor.co.uk – Fax (01666) 890 394

Rest – *(booking essential)* Carte £ 25/35

◆ Converted farm out-building on the Calcot Estate, which dates back to the 14C. Cooking is seasonal, rustic and hearty, with a wide-ranging menu and extensive daily specials.

The Trouble House

Cirencester Rd, Northeast : 2 mi. on A 433 ✉ GL8 8SG – ✆ (01666) 502 206
– www.thetroublehouse.co.uk – Closed 1 week January, Sunday dinner and Monday

Rest – Carte £ 19/35

◆ Although unremarkable in appearance, this pub conceals a characterful, cosy inner. Cooking is unfussy, using the best ingredients and keeping flavours natural and complementary.

TEWKESBURY – Gloucestershire – 503 N28 – pop. 9 978 Great Britain 4 C1

London 108 mi. – Birmingham 39 mi. – Gloucester 11 mi.

100 Church St ✆ (01684) 855040, outofthehat@tewkesbury.gov.uk

Tewkesbury Park Hotel Lincoln Green Lane, ✆ (01684) 295 405

Town★ – Abbey★★ (Nave★★, vault★)

St Mary's, Deerhurst★, SW : 4 mi. by A 38 and B 4213

at Corse Lawn Southwest : 6 mi. by A 38 and A 438 on B 4211 – ✉ Gloucester

Corse Lawn House
✉ GL19 4LZ – ✆ (01452) 780 771 – www.corselawn.com – Fax (01452) 780 840 – Closed 25-26 December
15 rm ☕ – 🚹£ 100 🚹🚹£ 160 – 3 suites
Rest *The Restaurant* – Menu £ 26/33 – Carte £ 31/37
Rest *Bistro* – Menu £ 16/19 – Carte £ 31/37
◆ Elegant Queen Anne Grade II listed house, set back from village green and fronted by former 'coach wash'. Two comfortable lounges and classic country house style rooms. Formal restaurant with period décor and framed prints, nicely set overlooking rear garden. Classic style of dishes; quality wine list. Informal Bistro.

at Eldersfield Southwest : 8.5 mi. by A 38, A 438 and B 4211

The Butchers Arms
Lime St, Southeast : 1 mi. ✉ GL19 4NX – ✆ (01452) 840 381 – www.thebutchersarms.net – Closed first week January, 25-26 December, Sunday dinner, Monday, and Tuesday lunch
Rest – *(booking essential)* Carte £ 28/36
◆ Traditional pub run by a husband and wife team. Concise regularly-changing menu features local or homemade produce and refined cooking, but hurry, only 25 diners can be accommodated.

ENGLAND

Good food at moderate prices? Look for the Bib Gourmand.

THAXTED – Essex – **504** V28 – **pop. 2 066** **13** C2
London 44 mi. – Cambridge 24 mi. – Colchester 31 mi. – Chelmsford 20 mi.

Crossways without rest
32 Town St ✉ CM6 2LA – ✆ (01371) 830 348 – www.crosswaysthaxted.co.uk
3 rm ☕ – 🚹£ 40 🚹🚹£ 60
◆ Passionately run 16C house in picturesque market town, with pleasant breakfast room and small open-fired lounge. Spotless bedrooms furnished in period style. Good, old-fashioned hospitality.

THIRSK – North Yorkshire – **502** P21 – **pop. 9 099** **22** B1
London 227 mi. – Leeds 37 mi. – Middlesbrough 24 mi. – York 24 mi.
49 Market Pl ✆ (01845) 522755, thirsktic@hambleton.gov.uk
Thirsk & Northallerton Thornton-Le-Street, ✆ (01845) 525 115

Golden Fleece
42 Market Pl ✉ YO7 1LL – ✆ (01845) 523 108 – www.goldenfleecehotel.com – Fax (01845) 523 996
23 rm ☕ – 🚹£ 70/75 🚹🚹£ 100
Rest – *(bar lunch Monday-Saturday)* Carte £ 21/30
◆ Sizeable Grade II listed 16C coaching inn located in centre of market town. Dick Turpin was a regular visitor. Spacious, comfortable lounge. Well-kept, inviting rooms. Yorkshire flavours are a staple of restaurant.

Spital Hill
York Rd, Southeast : 1.75 mi. on A 19, entrance between 2 white posts ✉ YO7 3AE – ✆ (01845) 522 273 – www.spitalhill.co.uk – Fax (01845) 524 970 – Closed 24-26 and 31 December
3 rm ☕ – 🚹£ 58/69 🚹🚹£ 90/110
Rest – *(by arrangement, communal dining)* Menu £ 35
◆ Expansive early Victorian house surrounded by nearly two acres of secluded gardens. Fully tiled entrance hall and comfortable sitting room. Spacious rooms, warmly furnished. Communal dining at mealtimes.

at Topcliffe **Southwest : 4.5 mi. by A 168 – ✉ Thirsk**

Angel Inn

Long St ✉ YO7 3RW – ✆ (01845) 577 237 – www.topccliffeangelinn.co.uk – Fax (01845) 578 000

15 rm – †£ 55/65 ††£ 75 **Rest** – Carte £ 15/26 **s**

◆ Enlarged hostelry dating back to early 17C in tiny village. Spacious lounge and characterful bar. Popular with business travellers. Sizeable bedrooms have pine furniture. Bright décor enlivens dining room.

at Asenby **Southwest : 5.25 mi. by A 168 – ✉ Thirsk**

Crab Manor

Dishforth Rd ✉ YO7 3QL – ✆ (01845) 577 286 – www.crabandlobster.co.uk – Fax (01845) 577 109

14 rm – †£ 90 ††£ 230 – 2 suites

Rest ***Crab and Lobster*** – see restaurant listing

◆ Split between an 18C Georgian Manor and individual Scandinavian log cabins, the stylish bedrooms are themed around famous hotels of the world. All have sharing or private hot tubs.

Crab and Lobster – at Crab Manor Hotel

Dishforth Rd ✉ YO7 3QL – ✆ (01845) 577 286 – www.crabandlobster.com – Fax (01845) 577 109

Rest – Seafood – Menu £ 13/35 – Carte £ 25/52

◆ Charming thatched pub with characterful, quirky interior. Extensive menu features plenty of seafood – from fish soup to whole lobster – as well as traditional British dishes.

ENGLAND

THORNBURY – South Gloucestershire – 503 M29 – pop. 11 969 – ✉ Bristol

4 C1

London 128 mi. – Bristol 12 mi. – Gloucester 23 mi. – Swindon 43 mi.

Thornbury Castle

Castle St ✉ BS35 1HH – ✆ (01454) 281 182 – www.thornburycastle.co.uk – Fax (01454) 416 188

24 rm – †£ 100/400 ††£ 350/790 – 3 suites

Rest – Menu £ 25/48

◆ 16C castle built by Henry VIII with gardens and vineyard. Two lounges boast plenty of antiques. Rooms of stately comfort; several bathrooms resplendent in marble. Restaurant exudes formal aura.

THORNHAM MAGNA – Suffolk – 504 X27 – ✉ Eye

15 C2

London 96 mi. – Cambridge 47 mi. – Ipswich 20 mi. – Norwich 30 mi.

at Yaxley **Northeast : 2.25 mi. by Eye rd and A 140 – ✉ Eye**

The Bull Auberge

Ipswich Rd, on A140 ✉ IP23 8BZ – ✆ (01379) 783 604 – www.the-auberge.co.uk – Fax (01379) 788 486

11 rm – †£ 60/80 ††£ 100/120

Rest – *(closed Saturday lunch, Sunday and Monday)* Menu £ 25 (dinner) – Carte £ 19/33

◆ 15C inn by busy road; rustic origins enhanced by brick walls, beams and open fire. Original, well presented, modern menus prepared with care. Stylish, well appointed rooms.

THORNTON – Lancs. – 502 K22 – see Blackpool

THORPE LANGTON – Leics. – see Market Harborough

THRELKELD – Cumbria – 502 K20 – see Keswick

THRUSCROSS – North Yorkshire 22 B2

London 223 mi. – Leeds 22 mi. – Bradford 23 mi. – Huddersfield 37 mi.

The Stone House Inn

HG3 4AH – (01943) 880 325 – *www.stonehouseinn.co.uk*

Rest – Carte £ 12/27

◆ 300 year old coaching inn set high in the Yorkshire dales. A real family pub, with a kids menu designed by the owners' children and a wide-ranging main menu of local, seasonal fare.

THUNDER BRIDGE – W. Yorks. – see Huddersfield

THUNDERSLEY – Essex – 504 V29 – see Rayleigh

THURSFORD GREEN – Norfolk 15 C1

London 120 mi. – Fakenham 7 mi. – Norwich 29 mi.

Holly Lodge

The Street NR21 0AS – (01328) 878 465 – www.hollylodgeguesthouse.co.uk

3 rm – £ 90 ££ 120 **Rest** – Menu £ 19

◆ Stylishly furnished 18C house set in delightful garden. Welcome includes Pimms by the pond or afternoon tea. Excellent breakfast. Well-appointed bedrooms in converted stables. Home-cooked evening meals.

ENGLAND

THWING – East Riding of Yorkshire 23 D2

London 228 mi. – Bridlington 10 mi. – York 16 mi.

The Falling Stone

Main St YO25 3DS – (01262) 470 403 – Closed Sunday dinner and Tuesday

Rest – Carte £ 14/25

◆ Traditional firelit bar, comfy lounge and smart, linen-clad restaurant. Blackboard menu of classic pub dishes and fine selection of local ales from the Wold Brewery. Chatty service.

TICKTON – East Riding of Yorkshire – 502 S22 – see Beverley

TILSTON – Cheshire – 502 L24 – see Malpas

TITCHWELL – Norfolk – 504 V25 – pop. 99 15 C1

London 128 mi. – King's Lynn 25 mi. – Boston 56 mi. – Wisbech 36 mi.

Titchwell Manor

PE31 8BB – (01485) 210 221 – www.titchwellmanor.com – Fax (01485) 210 104

27 rm – £ 130/200 ££ 190/250

Rest – Menu £ 16 (lunch) – Carte £ 29/40

◆ Victorian, red bricked former farmhouse. Bedrooms in the main house more traditional; those in converted outbuildings more modern and the best look over the lavender garden. Traditional menus in conservatory restaurant.

TITLEY – Herefordshire – 503 L27 – see Kington

TIVERTON – Devon – 503 J31 – pop. 16 772 2 D2

London 191 mi. – Bristol 64 mi. – Exeter 15 mi. – Plymouth 63 mi.

Hornhill without rest

Exeter Hill, East : 0.5 mi. by A 396 and Butterleigh rd EX16 4PL – (01884) 253 352 – www.hornhill-farmhouse.co.uk

3 rm – £ 35/40 ££ 60/70

◆ Georgian house on hilltop boasting pleasant views of the Exe Valley. Well-furnished drawing room with real fire. Attractively styled bedrooms with antiques.

TOLLARD ROYAL - Wiltshire **4** C3

London 118 mi. – Bristol 63 mi. – Southampton 40 mi. – Portsmouth 59 mi.

King John Inn with rm

SP5 5PS – (01725) 516 207 – www.kingjohninn.co.uk

8 rm – £ 90/150 £ 90/150 **Rest** – Carte £ 20/31

◆ Red-brick Victorian pub in pretty village; smart, spacious and open-plan. Daily changing, classically based menus, with game a speciality in season. Comfortable, contemporary bedrooms mix modern facilities with antique furniture; some in coach house opposite.

TOOT BALDON - Oxon. - see Oxford

TOPCLIFFE - N. Yorks. - **502** P21 - see Thirsk

TOPSHAM - Devon - **503** J31 - pop. 3 545 - Exeter **2** D2

London 175 mi. – Torbay 26 mi. – Exeter 4 mi. – Torquay 24 mi.

The Galley

41 Fore St EX3 0HU – (01392) 876 078 – www.galleyrestaurant.co.uk – Fax (01392) 876 333 – Closed Sunday and Monday

Rest – Seafood – Carte £ 28/42

◆ Idiosyncratic and gloriously eccentric, every nook and cranny filled with bric-a-brac or foody paraphernalia. Original, tasty, locally sourced piscine dishes.

La Petite Maison

35 Fore St EX3 0HR – (01392) 873 660 – www.lapetitemaison.co.uk – Fax (01392) 873 660 – Closed 1 week spring, 2 weeks autumn, Sunday and Monday

Rest – *(booking essential at lunch)* Menu £ 36

◆ Cosy two-roomed restaurant in charming village by River Clyst. Flavourful, classic dishes are presented in a modern style and come in generous portions. Friendly, welcoming owners.

TORQUAY - Torbay - **503** J32 - pop. 62 968 **2** C-D2

London 223 mi. – Exeter 23 mi. – Plymouth 32 mi.

5 Vaughan Parade (01803) 211211, torquay.tic@torbay.gov.uk

St Marychurch Petitor Rd, (01803) 327 471

Torbay★ – Kent's Cavern★ **AC** CX **A**

Paignton Zoo★★ **AC**, SE : 3 mi. by A 3022 - Cockington★, W : 1 mi. AX

Plans pages 674, 675

The Imperial

rm, rest,

Park Hill Rd TQ1 2DG – (01803) 294 301 – www.paramount-hotels.co.uk – Fax (01803) 298 293 CZ**a**

139 rm – £ 81/182 £ 93/194 – 13 suites

Rest *Regatta* – *(dinner only)* Menu £ 29

◆ Landmark hotel's super clifftop position is part of Torquay skyline. Palm Court lounge has classic style. Excellent leisure facilities. Rooms provide stunning bay views. Regatta's style emulates cruise liner luxury.

The Palace

Babbacombe Rd TQ1 3TG – (01803) 200 200 – www.palacetorquay.co.uk – Fax (01803) 299 899 CX**u**

135 rm – £ 60/85 £ 150 – 6 suites

Rest – *(dinner only)* Menu £ 28 **s** – Carte £ 28/39 **s**

◆ Large, traditional hotel in 25 acres of gardens with sub-tropical woodland and charming terraces. Well-furnished lounge. Excellent leisure facilities. Comfortable rooms. Spacious restaurant exudes air of fine dining.

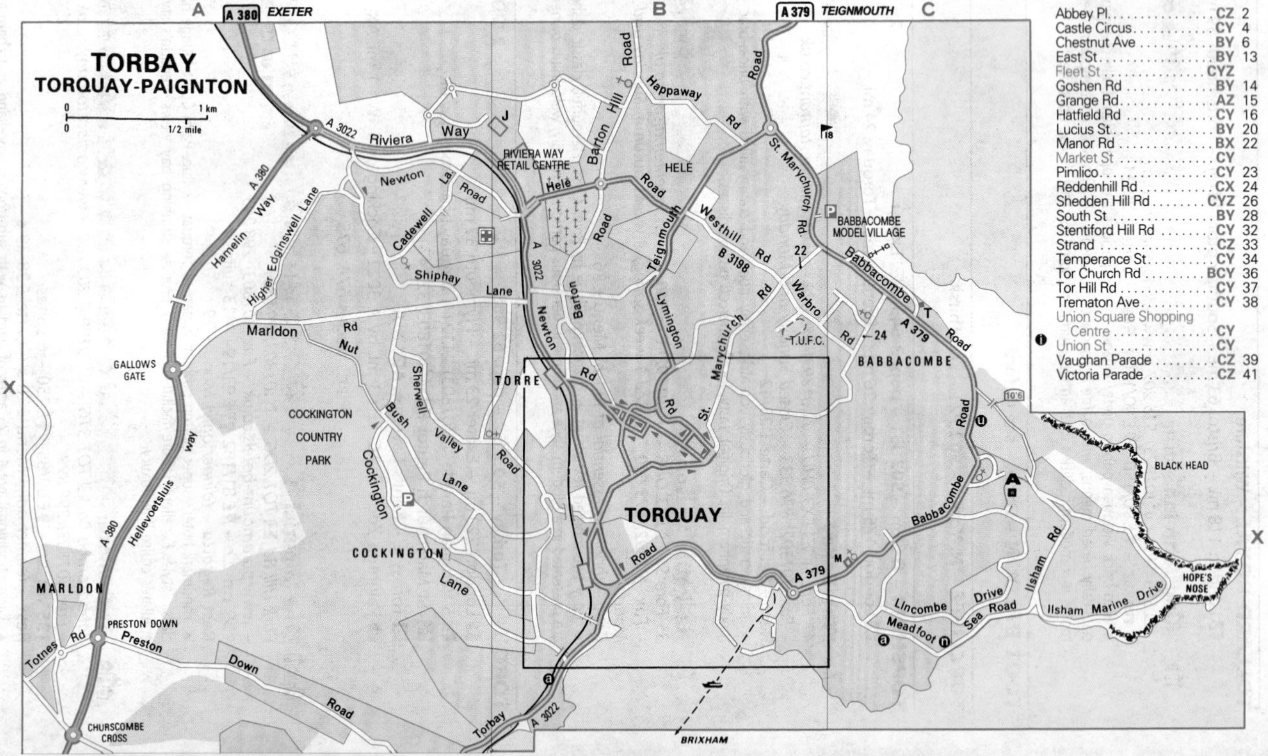

TORBAY
TORQUAY-PAIGNTON

0 — 1 km
0 — 1/2 mile

A 380 EXETER
A 379 TEIGNMOUTH

A B C

TORBAY, TORQUAY-PAIGNTON, Riviera Way, A 3022, A 380, Hamelin Way, Higher Edginswell Lane, Newton La., Road, Cadewell, Shiphay, Lane, Marldon Rd, Nut, GALLOWS GATE, COCKINGTON COUNTRY PARK, Bush, Sherwell, Valley, Road, Cockington, Lane, COCKINGTON, Lane, Hellevoetsluis, way, A 380, MARLDON, Totnes Rd, PRESTON DOWN, Preston, Down, Road, CHURSCOMBE CROSS, J, RIVIERA WAY RETAIL CENTRE, Hele, Barton Hill Road, Happaway Rd, Road, HELE, Road, Teignmouth, Barton, Newton, A 3022, TORRE, Rd, Lymington, Westhill, B 3198, Rd, Marychurch, St., Rd, St. Marychurch Rd., Road, 18, BABBACOMBE MODEL VILLAGE, 22, Warbro, Rd, T.U.F.C., 24, Babbacombe, T, A 379, Road, BABBACOMBE, 10'6, Road, Babbacombe, A, BLACK HEAD, Ilsham Rd, HOPE'S NOSE, Ilsham Marine Drive, Lincombe, Drive, Sea, Road, Meadfoot, TORQUAY, Road, A 379, M, BRIXHAM, A 3022, Torbay, X, X

Street	Grid	No.
Abbey Pl.	CZ	2
Castle Circus	CY	4
Chestnut Ave	BY	6
East St	BY	13
Fleet St	CYZ	
Goshen Rd	BY	14
Grange Rd	AZ	15
Hatfield Rd	CY	16
Lucius St	BY	20
Manor Rd	BX	22
Market St	CY	
Pimlico	CY	23
Reddenhill Rd	CX	24
Shedden Hill Rd	CYZ	26
South St	BY	28
Stentiford Hill Rd	CY	32
Strand	CZ	33
Temperance St	CY	34
Tor Church Rd	BCY	36
Tor Hill Rd	CY	37
Trematon Ave	CY	38
Union Square Shopping Centre	CY	
Union St	CY	
Vaughan Parade	CZ	39
Victoria Parade	CZ	41

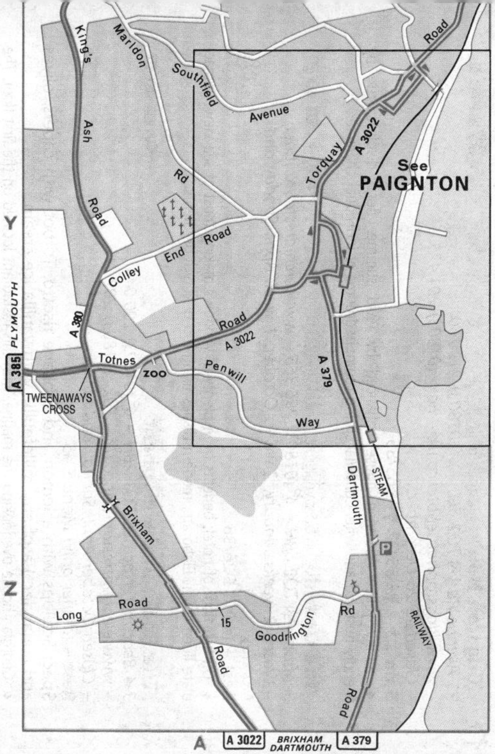

TORQUAY
CENTRE

0 400 m
0 400 yards

UPTON
TORRE
CHELSTON
UPTON PARK
UNION SQUARE
RIVIERA CENTRE
ABBEY GARDENS
PRINCESS GARDENS
LIVING COASTS
POL.
H
M
T
TORRE
TORQUAY
BRIXHAM

Newton Road
Avenue
Lymington Road
Union
St. Marychurch Rd
Windsor Road
Ellacombe Church Rd
Princes Rd
Hoxton Rd
Market St.
Union Street
Abbey Road
Belgrave Road
Mill Lane
Mill Rd
Old Mill Rd
Croft Road
Warren Rd
St.Luke's Rd North
Fleet
Falkland Road
The King's Drive
Rathmore Rd
Walnut Road
Seaway Lane
Torbay Road
A 379 Torbay Road
A 3022
A 379

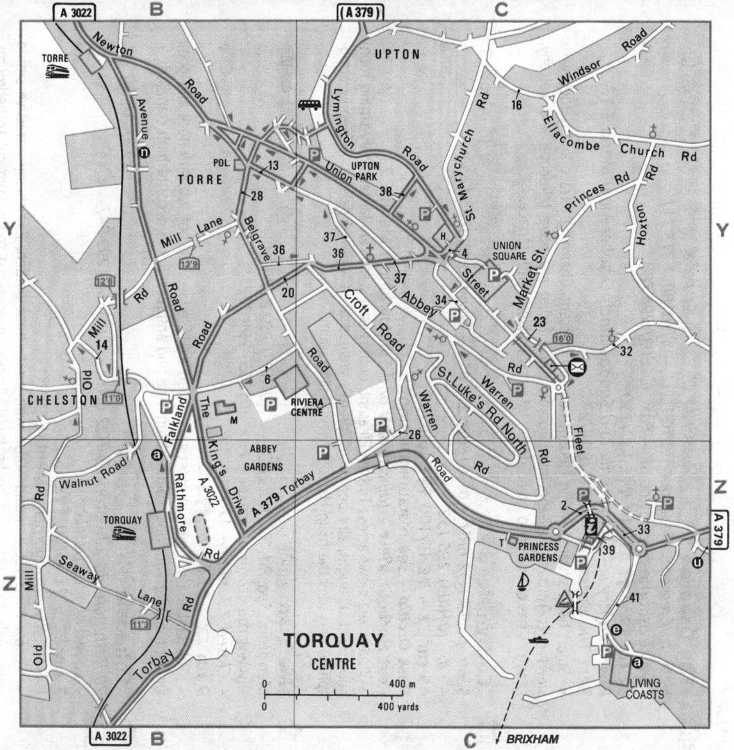

16 13 28 38 4 37 36 20 34 23 32 6 26 14 2 33 39 41
13'9 12'6 11'0 16'0 11'3

Y Z B C

See
PAIGNTON

King's Ash Road
Marldon
Southfield Avenue
Colley End Road
Totnes Road
A 3022
A 380
A 385
PLYMOUTH
TWEENAWAYS CROSS
ZOO
Penwill Way
Torquay Road
A 379
Dartmouth Road
STEAM RAILWAY
Brixham Road
Long Road
Goodrington Rd
15
A 3022 BRIXHAM DARTMOUTH A 379

A

The Osborne

Hesketh Crescent, Meadfoot ✉ TQ1 2LL – ✆ (01803) 213 311 – www.osborne-torquay.co.uk – Fax (01803) 296 788 CX**n**

32 rm – £ 65/110 £ 130/230

Rest *Langtry's* – *(dinner only and Sunday lunch October-May)* Menu £ 17/27

Rest *The Brasserie* – Carte £ 18/27

◆ Smart hotel situated within elegant Regency crescent. Charming terrace and garden with views over Torbay. Well-appointed rooms: those facing sea have telescope and balcony. Langtry's has classic deep green décor. Informal Brasserie with terrace.

Corbyn Head

Seafront ✉ TQ2 6RH – ✆ (01803) 213 611 – www.corbynhead.com – Fax (01803) 296 152 BX**a**

45 rm – £ 45/100 £ 160/250

Rest *Orchid* – see restaurant listing

Rest *Harbour View* – *(dinner only and Sunday lunch)* Menu £ 23

◆ Boasts sea views across Torbay. Pleasant, enthusiastic staff. Very large, comfy sitting room and cosy bar. Bright, airy bedrooms, prettily created from a pastel palette. A friendly atmosphere pervades the main Harbour View dining room.

Marstan without rest

Meadfoot Sea Rd ✉ TQ1 2LQ – ✆ (01803) 292 837 – www.marstanhotel.co.uk – Fax (01803) 299 202 – Closed 2 January- 12 February CX**a**

9 rm – £ 65/75 £ 120/142

◆ Substantial 19C house in quiet area; given a 21C edge with hot tub, sun deck and pool. Opulent interior with gold coloured furniture and antiques. Room décor of high standard.

ENGLAND

Colindale

20 Rathmore Rd, Chelston ✉ TQ2 6NY – ✆ (01803) 293 947 – www.colindalehotel.co.uk BZ**a**

7 rm – £ 45/50 £ 65/75

Rest – *(by arrangement)* Menu £ 18

◆ Yellow hued 19C terraced house with pretty front garden. Particularly attractive sitting room with deep sofas and books. Welsh dresser in breakfast room. Immaculate bedrooms. Homecooked dishes have a French accent.

Kingston House without rest

75 Avenue Rd ✉ TQ2 5LL – ✆ (01803) 212 760 – www.kingstonhousehotel.co.uk – Fax (01803) 201 425 – Closed 25-26 December BY**n**

5 rm – £ 55/72 £ 65/85

◆ Sunny yellow Victorian house enhanced by vivid summer floral displays; run by friendly husband and wife. Convivial sitting room; bedrooms of individual character.

The Orchid – at Corbyn Head Hotel

Seafront ✉ TQ2 6RH – ✆ (01803) 296 366 – www.orchidrestaurant.net – Closed 2 weeks January, 2 weeks October, 1 week April, Sunday and Monday BX**a**

Rest – Menu £ 26/38

◆ On first floor of hotel; benefits from plenty of windows making most of sea view. Immaculate linen cover. Elaborate, modern dishes using top quality ingredients.

The Room in the Elephant

3-4 Beacon Terrace ✉ TQ1 2BH – ✆ (01803) 200 044 – www.elephantrestaurant.co.uk – Fax (01803) 202 717 – Closed October-April, Sunday and Monday CZ**e**

Rest – *(dinner only)* Menu £ 45

Spec. Scallops with a lemon and cabbage risotto. Turbot with capers, olives and coriander. Raspberry millefeuille with vanilla ice cream.

◆ Georgian house overlooking the marina, with this restaurant located on the first floor. The confident cooking makes good use of quality local produce; dishes are never too complicated in their make-up.

The Brasserie

Ground Floor, 3-4 Beacon Terrace ✉ TQ1 2BH – ✆ (01803) 200 044 – www.elephantrestaurant.co.uk – Fax (01803) 202 717 – Closed 3 weeks January, Sunday and Monday CZ**e**

Rest – Menu £ 20/28

◆ Smart split level restaurant with slight colonial feel, on ground floor of Victorian property. Large choice of classic brasserie dishes made using local produce. Polite service.

Number 7

Beacon Terrace ✉ TQ1 2BH – ✆ (01803) 295 055 – www.no7-fish.com – Closed 2 weeks February, 1 week November, Christmas-New Year, Monday in winter and Sunday except dinner July-September CZ**e**

Rest – Seafood – *(dinner only and lunch Wednesday-Saturday) (booking advisable)* Carte £ 30/37

◆ On harbour front in centre of town: modest, friendly, family run restaurant specialising in simply prepared fresh fish, mostly from Brixham. Fishing themes enhance ambience.

The Orange Tree

14-16 Parkhill Rd – ✆ (01803) 213 936 – www.orangetreerestaurant.co.uk – Closed 1 week January, 2 weeks November, 26 December, 31 January, Sunday and Bank Holiday Mondays CZ**u**

Rest – *(dinner only) (booking essential)* Carte £ 26/39

◆ Intimate neighbourhood eatery hidden away from the town, with homely décor and a modern, comfortable feel. Classical cooking displays a French base and uses local, seasonal produce.

at Babbacombe Northeast : 2 mi. on A 379

The Cary Arms

Babbacombe Beach, East : 0.25 mi. by Beach rd. ✉ TQ1 3LX – ✆ (01803) 327 110 – www.caryarms.co.uk – Fax (01803) 323 221 CX**i**

Rest – Carte approx. £ 25 **s**

◆ Idyllic location built into rocks with terraces down to shore. Ultra-comfy, nautically styled residents lounge and modern, boutique-chic bedrooms in New England style, with roll-top baths looking out to sea. Stone/slate-floored bar serving traditional pub dishes.

at Maidencombe North : 3.5 mi. by A 379 - BX – ✉ Torquay

Orestone Manor

Rockhouse Lane ✉ TQ1 4SX – ✆ (01803) 328 098 – www.orestonemanor.com – Fax (01803) 328 336 – Closed 1-23 January

12 rm – †£ 99/149 ††£ 225/250

Rest – Menu £ 18 (lunch) – Carte £ 30/42

◆ Country house in the woods! Terrace overlooks mature gardens. Conservatory exudes exotic charm. Individual rooms; ask for one in the attic. Pleasant dining with interesting modern English cooking underpinned by tasty local seafood plus herbs, fruit and veg from the kitchen garden.

TOTLAND – I.O.W. – **503** P31 – **see Wight (Isle of)**

TOTLEY – S. Yorks. – **502** P24 – **see Sheffield**

TOTNES – Devon – **503** I32 – **pop. 7 929** **2** C2

London 224 mi. – Exeter 24 mi. – Plymouth 23 mi. – Torquay 9 mi.

The Town Mill, Coronation Rd ✆ (01803) 863168, enquire@totnesinformation.co.uk

Dartmouth G & C.C. Blackawton, ✆ (01803) 712 686

Town★ – Elizabethan Museum★ - St Mary's★ – Butterwalk★ – Castle (≤★★★) **AC**

Paignton Zoo★★ **AC**, E : 4.5 mi. by A 385 and A 3022 – British Photographic Museum, Bowden House★ **AC**, S : 1 mi. by A 381 – Dartington Hall (High Cross House★), NW : 2 mi. on A 385 and A 384. Dartmouth★★ (Castle ≤★★★), SE : 12 mi. by A 381 and A 3122

Royal Seven Stars

The Plains ✉ TQ9 5DD – ✆ (01803) 862 125 – www.royalsevenstars.co.uk – Fax (01803) 867 929
21 rm – †£ 50/79 ††£ 109
Rest – *(dinner only and Sunday lunch)* Carte £ 18/28
◆ 17C former coaching inn in centre of town. Lounge with smart colonial edge, contemporary, light and fresh bedrooms; some have jacuzzi baths, Agatha Christie has a four poster. TQ9 a dining room in converted stables.

at Stoke Gabriel Southeast : 4 mi. by A 385 – ✉ Totnes

The Steam Packet Inn with rm

St Peter's Quay ✉ TQ9 5EW – ✆ (01803) 863 880 – www.steampacketinn.co.uk
4 rm – †£ 60 ††£ 80 **Rest** – Carte £ 17/27
◆ Deservedly popular pub with vast terrace, set on the River Dart, close to the town centre. Eclectic, wide-ranging menu has something for everyone, with fresh fish a speciality. Bedrooms are elegant, cosy and snug, with a contemporary feel.

TOWCESTER – Northamptonshire – 503 R27 – pop. 8 073 — 16 B3

London 70 mi. – Birmingham 50 mi. – Northampton 9 mi. – Oxford 36 mi.
Whittelbury Park G. & C.C. Whittlebury, ✆ (01327) 850 000

Farthingstone Hotel Farthingstone, ✆ (01327) 361 291

at Paulerspury Southeast : 3.25 mi. by A 5 – ✉ Towcester

Vine House with rm

100 High St ✉ NN12 7NA – ✆ (01327) 811 267 – www.vinehousehotel.com – Fax (01327) 811 309 – Closed 1 week Christmas, Monday lunch and Sunday
6 rm – †£ 65/95 ††£ 95/105 **Rest** – Menu £ 30
◆ Keenly run 17C stone cottage with lovely garden, traditional lounges and split-level dining room. Concise set menus feature refined, flavoursome dishes with a classical base and modern edge. Individually styled, period bedrooms are named after grape vines.

TREBETHERICK – Cornwall – see Rock

TREFONEN – Shrops. – 502 K25 – see Oswestry

TREGREHAN – Cornwall – 503 F32 – see St Austell

TRELOWARREN – Cornwall – see Helston

TRESCO – Cornwall – 503 B34 – see Scilly (Isles of)

TROTTON – West Sussex – see Midhurst

TROUTBECK – Cumbria – 502 L20 – see Windermere

TROWBRIDGE – Wiltshire – 503 N30 – pop. 34 401 — 4 C2

London 115 mi. – Bristol 27 mi. – Southampton 55 mi. – Swindon 32 mi.
St Stephen's Pl ✆ (01225) 710535, tic@trowbridge.gov.uk
Westwood Manor★, NW : 3 mi. by A 363 – Farleigh Hungerford★ (St Leonard's Chapel★) **AC**, W : 4 m. Longleat House★★★ **AC**, SW : 12 mi. by A 363, A 350 and A 362 - Bratton Castle (≤★★) SE : 7.5 mi. by A 363 and B 3098 – Steeple Ashton★ (The Green★) E : 6 mi. – Edington (St Mary, St Katherine and All Saints★) SE : 7.5 m

Old Manor

Trowle Common, Northwest : 1 mi. on A 363 ✉ BA14 9BL – ✆ (01225) 777 393 – www.oldmanorhotel.com – Fax (01225) 765 443
19 rm (dinner included) – †£ 70/90 ††£ 190
Rest – *(dinner only)* Menu £ 29
◆ Attractive Grade II listed Queen Anne house with 15C origins. Lovely gardens and pleasant lounges: wealth of beams adds to charm. Most bedrooms - some four poster - in annex. Spacious restaurant with welcoming ambience.

ENGLAND

XX **Red or White**

Evolution House, 46 Castle St ✉ BA14 8AY – ✆ (01225) 781 666 – www.redorwhite.biz – Fax (01225) 776 505 – Closed last week August, Sunday and Bank Holidays

Rest – Italian – Menu £ 14/22 – Carte £ 22/35

◆ Bright, modern restaurant, personally run by two brothers, with small Italian deli at the front. Classic Italian cooking, with more ambitious dishes at dinner. Friendly service.

TRUMPET – **Herefordshire** – **see Ledbury**

TRURO – **Cornwall** – **503** E33 – **pop. 20 920** **1** B3

London 295 mi. – Exeter 87 mi. – Penzance 26 mi. – Plymouth 52 mi.

Municipal Buildings, Boscawen St ✆ (01872) 274555, tic@truro.gov.uk

Treliske, ✆ (01872) 272 640

Killiow Kea Killiow, ✆ (01872) 270 246

Royal Cornwall Museum★★ **AC**

Trelissick Garden★★ (≤★★) **AC**, S : 4 mi. by A 39 – Feock (Church★) S : 5 mi. by A 39 and B 3289. Trewithen★★★, NE : 7.5 mi. by A 39 and A 390 – Probus★ (tower★ - garden★) NE : 9 mi. by A 39 and A 390

Mannings rm,

Lemon St ✉ TR1 2QB – ✆ (01872) 270 345 – www.manningshotels.co.uk – Fax (01872) 242 453 – Closed 24-26 December

43 rm – †£ 79/95 ††£ 95

Rest ***Mannings*** – ✆ (01872) 247 900 *(Closed Sunday lunch)* Carte £ 23/41

◆ The name came after Prince Albert stayed in 1846: the Royal Arms stands proudly above the entrance. Comfortable, stylish lounges; modern bedrooms. Cuisine with global influences.

XX **Tabb's**

85 Kenwyn St ✉ TR1 3BZ – ✆ (01872) 262 110 – www.tabbs.co.uk – Closed Sunday and Monday

Rest – *(dinner only)* Carte £ 31/37

◆ Stylish restaurant with lilac walls, flint floors and well-spaced, cloth-covered tables. Hearty, well-constructed dishes show good understanding of flavours. Relaxed atmosphere.

X **Saffron**

5 Quay St ✉ TR1 2HB – ✆ (01872) 263 771 – www.saffronrestauranttruro.co.uk – Closed 25-26 December, Sunday, Monday dinner January-June and Bank Holiday Monday

Rest – Menu £ 20 (dinner) – Carte £ 26/34

◆ Bright exterior with colourful hanging baskets and attractive brightly coloured interior with a rustic tone. Varied Cornish menus to be enjoyed at any hour of the day.

TUNBRIDGE WELLS – **Kent** – **504** U30 – **see Royal Tunbridge Wells**

TUNSTALL – **Lancashire** – **see Kirkby Lonsdale**

TURNERS HILL – **West Sussex** – **504** T30 – **pop. 1 534** **7** D2

London 33 mi. – Brighton 24 mi. – Crawley 7 mi.

Alexander House

East St, East : 1 mi. on B 2110 ✉ RH10 4QD – ✆ (01342) 714 914 – www.alexanderhouse.co.uk – Fax (01342) 859 759

36 rm – †£ 165/200 ††£ 230 – 2 suites

Rest ***Reflections Brasserie*** – Carte £ 34/44

◆ Set in extensive gardens, a stunning, classically comfortable country house, once owned by the family of poet Percy Shelley. Luxuriously appointed, quite modern bedrooms. Informal air at Reflections.

ENGLAND

TURVILLE – Buckinghamshire – ✉ Henley-On-Thames 11 C2

London 45 mi. – Oxford 22 mi. – Reading 17 mi.

The Bull & Butcher

✉ RG9 6QU – ✆ (01491) 638 283 – www.thebullandbutcher.com – Fax (01491) 638 836

Rest – *(booking advisable)* Carte £ 21/28

◆ Characterful 16C pub boasting pleasant country views, located in a tranquil village that's been the setting for many TV shows. Cooking is generous and robust; regular theme nights feature.

TWO BRIDGES – Devon – 503 I32 – ✉ Yelverton 2 C2

London 226 mi. – Exeter 25 mi. – Plymouth 17 mi.

Dartmoor National Park★★

Prince Hall

East : 1 mi. on B 3357 ✉ PL20 6SA – ✆ (01822) 890 403 – www.princehall.co.uk – Fax (01822) 890 676

9 rm – †£ 80/150 ††£ 140/170

Rest – *(light lunch) (booking essential for non-residents)* Menu £ 37

◆ Unique 18C country house, traditional in style, set alone in heart of Dartmoor. Magnificent view over West Dart River to rolling hills. Individually styled rooms. Local dishes proudly served in rustic restaurant.

TYLER HILL – Kent – see Canterbury

TYNEMOUTH – Tyne and Wear – 501 P18 – pop. 17 056 24 B2

London 290 mi. – Newcastle upon Tyne 8 mi. – Sunderland 7 mi.

Grand

Grand Parade ✉ NE30 4ER – ✆ (0191) 293 6666 – www.grandhotel-uk.com – Fax (0191) 293 6665

45 rm – †£ 79/89 ††£ 89/175

Rest *Grand* – *(closed Sunday dinner)* Menu £ 13/25

◆ Impressive Victorian hotel built as home for Duchess of Northumberland. Commanding views over coastline. Atmospheric lounges and bars. Well-equipped rooms with fine views. Classical dining room with imposing drapes, floral displays and ceiling cornices.

Martineau Guest House without rest

57 Front St ✉ NE30 4BX – ✆ (0191) 296 0746 – www.martineau-house.co.uk

4 rm – †£ 55/70 ††£ 80

◆ 18C Georgian stone terraced house in main street, named after Harriet Martineau. Breakfast in open plan kitchen. Homely spacious individually styled rooms, two with view.

Brasserie 1883

3-5 Percy Park Rd ✉ NE30 4LZ – ✆ (0191) 257 8500 – www.brasserie1883.com – Closed 25 December and Sunday

Rest – *(booking essential)* Menu £ 14 (lunch and early dinner) – Carte £ 18/33

◆ Relaxed split-level brasserie: its traditional façade belying a warm, contemporary interior. Eclectic menus display a mix of influences, from classical north east British to modern international.

UCKFIELD – East Sussex – 504 U31 – pop. 15 374 8 A2

London 45 mi. – Brighton 17 mi. – Eastbourne 20 mi. – Maidstone 34 mi.

Horsted Place

Little Horsted, South : 2.5 mi. by B 2102 and A 22 on A 26 ✉ TN22 5TS – ✆ (01825) 750 581 – www.horstedplace.co.uk – Fax (01825) 750 459 – Closed first week January

15 rm – †£ 140/175 ††£ 140/175 – 5 suites

Rest – *(Closed Saturday lunch)* Menu £ 20 (lunch) – Carte approx. £ 40

◆ Imposing country house from the height of the Victorian Gothic revival; handsome Pugin-inspired drawing rooms and luxurious bedrooms overlook formal gardens and parkland. Pristine restaurant with tall 19C archways and windows.

Buxted Park
Buxted, Northeast : 2 mi. on A 272 ✉ TN22 4AY – ✆ (0845) 072 7412 – www.handpicked.co.uk/buxtedpark – Fax (0845) 072 7413
43 rm – £ 105/175 £ 115/185 – 1 suite
Rest *Dining Room* – Menu £ 20/32 – Carte approx. £ 44
◆ 18C Palladian mansion in 300 acres with ornate public areas exuding much charm: spacious, period lounges. Rooms, modern in style, in original house or garden wing. Modern British cooking in the Dining Room.

ULLINGSWICK – County of Herefordshire – 503 M27 – pop. 237 – ✉ Hereford

18 B3

London 134 mi. – Hereford 12 mi. – Shrewsbury 52 mi. – Worcester 19 mi.

Three Crowns Inn with rm
Bleak Acre, East : 1.25 mi. ✉ HR1 3JQ – ✆ (01432) 820 279 – www.threecrownsinn.com – Fax (08700) 515 338 – Closed 25-26 December and Monday
1 rm – £ 95 **Rest** – Menu £ 15 (lunch) – Carte approx. £ 26
◆ Pleasant part-timbered pub on a quiet country road: hops hang from the beams. Eclectic assortment of benches and pews. Rustic, robust dishes on daily changing menus. One smart, contemporary bedroom.

ULLSWATER – Cumbria – 502 L20 – pop. 1 199 – ✉ Penrith

21 B2

London 296 mi. – Carlisle 25 mi. – Kendal 31 mi. – Penrith 6 mi.

Beckside Car Park, Glenridding, Penrith ✆ (017684) 82414, ullswatertic@lake-district.gov.uk

at Pooley Bridge on B 5320 – ✉ Penrith

Sharrow Bay Country House
South : 2 mi. on Howtown rd ✉ CA10 2LZ – ✆ (017684) 86 301 – www.sharrowbay.co.uk – Fax (017684) 86 349
21 rm (dinner included) – £ 160/275 £ 400/520 – 3 suites
Rest – *(booking essential)* Menu £ 32/70 **s** – Carte approx. £ 32 **s**
Spec. Soufflé Suissesse of stilton with spinach. Tournedos of Aberdeen Angus beef with oxtail ravioli. Francis Coulson's sticky toffee sponge with ice cream.
◆ Victorian country house in idyllic spot on shores of Lake Ullswater. Richly appointed, antique-filled interior. Traditional bedrooms blend luxury and old-fashioned charm. Charming dining room where the classical cooking comes in generous portions.

at Watermillock on A 592 – ✉ Penrith

Rampsbeck Country House
✉ CA11 0LP – ✆ (017684) 86 442 – www.rampsbeck.co.uk – Fax (017684) 86 688 – Closed 4-8 January
18 rm – £ 95/155 £ 140/290 – 1 suite
Rest *The Restaurant* – see restaurant listing
◆ Personally run country house with peaceful gardens and homely guest areas. Very comfortable deluxe bedrooms, some with balconies; standard rooms more traditionally furnished.

The Restaurant – at Rampsbeck Country House Hotel
✉ CA11 0LP – ✆ (017684) 86 442 – www.rampsbeck.co.uk – Fax (017684) 86 688 – Closed 4-8 January
Rest – *(booking essential) (lunch by arrangement)* Menu £ 29/50 **s**
◆ Refurbished house retains traditional character, with polished silver, fresh flowers and lake views. Seasonal menu combines modern with more traditional. Unobtrusive service.

ULVERSTON – Cumbria – 502 K21 – pop. 11 210

21 A3

London 278 mi. – Kendal 25 mi. – Lancaster 36 mi.

Coronation Hall, County Sq ✆ (01229) 587140, ulverstontic@southlakeland.gov.uk

The Bay Horse with rm
Canal Foot, East : 2.25 mi. by A 5087, turning left at Morecambe Rd and beyond Industrial area, on the coast ✉ *LA12 9EL – ☏ (01229) 583 972 – www.thebayhorsehotel.co.uk – Fax (01229) 580 502 – Closed Monday lunch*
9 rm – †£ 80 ††£ 90/120 **Rest** – Menu £ 29 (dinner) – Carte £ 20/30
◆ Pleasant 18C former post house overlooking Morecambe Bay sands. A range of menus offer plenty of choice, featuring both classic pub and restaurant-style dishes. Traditional bedrooms with nice touches; those to the front have balcony views.

UPPER ODDINGTON – Glos. – see Stow-on-the-Wold

UPPER SLAUGHTER – Glos. – 503 O28 – see Bourton-on-the-Water

UPPER WOODFORD – Wiltshire – 503 O30 – see Salisbury

UPPINGHAM – Rutland – 504 R26 – pop. 3 947 17 C2

London 101 mi. – Leicester 19 mi. – Northampton 28 mi. – Nottingham 35 mi.

Lake Isle with rm — rest,
16 High St East ✉ *LE15 9PZ – ☏ (01572) 822 951 – www.lakeisle.co.uk – Fax (01572) 824 400 – Closed 27 December-4 January, Sunday dinner and Monday lunch*
12 rm – †£ 65 ††£ 100 **Rest** – *(light lunch)* Carte £ 25/38
◆ Pleasant town centre property, accessed via narrow passageway. Heavy wood-furnished dining room; concise, classically based menu of quality produce displaying unfussy modern touches. Bedrooms boast good facilities/extras: superior are largest, with whirlpool baths.

ENGLAND

at Lyddington South : 2 mi. by A 6003 – ✉ Uppingham

Old White Hart with rm
51 Main Street ✉ *LE15 9LR – ☏ (01572) 821 703 – www.oldwhitehart.co.uk – Fax (01572) 821 965 – Closed 25 December and Sunday dinner (September-April)*
10 rm – †£ 60/70 ††£ 80/95 **Rest** – Menu £ 14 – Carte £ 22/30
◆ Traditional coaching inn with neat garden and canopy covered terrace. Monthly changing menus display simple, unfussy pub classics. Regular petanque evenings offer game play and dinner. Stylish, modern bedrooms boast smart bathrooms.

UPTON SCUDAMORE – Wilts. – 503 N30 – see Warminster

UPTON-UPON-SEVERN – Worcestershire – 503 N27 – pop. 1 789 18 B3

London 116 mi. – Hereford 25 mi. – Stratford-upon-Avon 29 mi. – Worcester 11 mi.

4 High St ☏ (01684) 594200, upton.tic@malvernhills.gov.uk

at Hanley Swan Northwest : 3 mi. by B 4211 on B 4209 – ✉ Upton-Upon-Severn

Yew Tree House without rest
✉ *WR8 0DN – ☏ (01684) 310 736 – www.yewtreehouse.co.uk – Fax (01684) 311 709*
3 rm – †£ 45 ††£ 75
◆ Imposing cream coloured Georgian guesthouse, built in 1780, in centre of pleasant village. One mile from Three Counties Showground. Cosy lounge; individually styled rooms.

URMSTON – Greater Manchester – 502 M23 – pop. 40 964 20 B2

London 204 mi. – Manchester 9 mi. – Sale 4 mi.

Isinglass
46 Flixton Rd ✉ *M41 5AB – ☏ (0161) 749 8400 – www.isinglassrestaurant.com – Closed 26 December, 1 January and Monday*
Rest – *(dinner only and lunch Saturday-Sunday)* Menu £ 15 (weekday dinner) – Carte £ 18/42
◆ Hidden away in Manchester suburb, this is a neighbourhood favourite. Very personally run, with warm rustic interior. Unusual dishes underpinned by a strong Lancastrian base.

UTTOXETER – Staffordshire – 503 O25 – pop. 12 023 19 C1

London 150 mi. – Birmingham 41 mi. – Stafford 16 mi.

at Beamhurst Northwest : 3 mi. on A 522 – ✉ Uttoxeter

XX **Gilmore at Strine's Farm**

✉ ST14 5DZ – ✆ (01889) 507 100 – www.restaurantgilmore.com – Fax (01889) 507 238 – Closed 1 week January, 1 week Easter, 1 week August, 1 week October-November, Monday, Tuesday, Sunday dinner and lunch Saturday and Wednesday

Rest – *(booking essential)* Menu £ 28/40

◆ Personally run converted farmhouse in classic rural setting. Three separate, beamed, cottage style dining rooms. New approach to classic dishes: fine local ingredients used.

VAZON BAY – C.I. – 503 P33 – see Channel Islands (Guernsey)

VENTNOR – I.O.W. – 503 Q32 – see Wight (Isle of)

VERYAN – Cornwall – 503 F33 – pop. 877 – ✉ Truro 1 B3

London 291 mi. – St Austell 13 mi. – Truro 13 mi.

Village★

Nare rest,

Carne Beach, Southwest : 1.25 mi. ✉ TR2 5PF – ✆ (01872) 501 111 – www.narehotel.co.uk – Fax (01872) 501 856

33 rm – †£ 120/262 ††£ 350/430 – 4 suites

Rest *The Dining Room* – *(dinner only and Sunday lunch)* Menu £ 30/45

Rest *Quarterdeck* – Carte £ 19/39

◆ On the curve of Carne Bay, surrounded by National Trust land; superb beach. Inside, owner's Cornish art collection in evidence. Most rooms have patios and balconies. The Dining Room boasts high windows and sea views; dinner dress code. Informal Quarterdeck.

VIRGINSTOW – Devon – 503 H31 2 C2

London 227 mi. – Bideford 25 mi. – Exeter 41 mi. – Launceston 11 mi.

Percy's

Coombeshead Estate, Southwest : 1.25 mi. on Tower Hill rd ✉ EX21 5EA – ✆ (01409) 211 236 – www.percys.co.uk – Fax (01409) 211 460

7 rm – †£ 120/150 ††£ 170/210

Rest Percy's – see restaurant listing

◆ Rural location surrounded by 130 acres of land and forest which include woodland trails and animals. Airy, modern rooms in granary or bungalow boast range of charming extras.

XX **Percy's** – at Percy's Hotel

Coombeshead Estate, Southwest : 1.25 mi. on Tower Hill rd ✉ EX21 5EA – ✆ (01409) 211 236 – www.percys.co.uk – Fax (01409) 211 460

Rest – *(dinner only)* Menu £ 40

◆ Modern rear extension with deep sofas alongside chic ash and zinc bar. Restaurant has an understated style. Locally sourced, organic produce and homegrown vegetables.

WADDESDON – Buckinghamshire – 504 R28 – pop. 1 865 11 C2
– ✉ Aylesbury Great Britain

London 51 mi. – Aylesbury 5 mi. – Northampton 32 mi. – Oxford 31 mi.

Chiltern Hills★

Waddesdon Manor★★, S : 0.5 mi. by a 41 and minor rd – Claydon House★, N : by minor rd

XX **The Five Arrows** with rm

High St ✉ HP18 0JE – ✆ (01296) 651 727 – www.thefivearrows.com – Fax (01296) 655 716

10 rm – †£ 50/95 ††£ 80/125 – 1 suite

Rest – Menu £ 15 (weekday lunch) – Carte £ 25/36

◆ Beautiful 19C inn on Rothschild estate, an influence apparent in pub crest and wine cellar. Striking architecture, stylish dining, relaxed ambience, Anglo-Mediterranean menu. Individually decorated bedrooms - some four posters - divided between main house and courtyard, the latter being smaller but quieter.

ENGLAND

WADEBRIDGE – Cornwall – 503 F32 – pop. 6 222 1 B2

London 245 mi. – Plymouth 41 mi. – Torbay 68 mi. – Torquay 88 mi.

at St Kew Northeast : 4.5 mi. by A 39

St Kew Inn

✉ PL30 3HB – ✆ (01208) 841 259 – www.stkewinn.co.uk

Rest – Carte £ 18/32

◆ Characterful country pub in quintessentially English location. Wide-ranging menu of fresh, tasty dishes and St Austell beer in wooden casks. Attractive garden with picnic tables and heaters.

WALBERSWICK – Suffolk – 504 Y27 – pop. 1 648 15 D2

London 115 mi. – Norwich 31 mi. – Ipswich 31 mi. – Lowestoft 16 mi.

The Anchor

Main St ✉ IP18 6UA – ✆ (01502) 722 112 – www.anchoratwalberswick.com – Fax (01502) 724 464 – Closed 25 December

Rest – Carte £ 20/30

◆ Large pub with a sizeable garden and seaward views. Hearty, flavoursome cooking uses local or homemade produce where possible; seafood features highly. Excellent beer and wine.

ENGLAND

WALBERTON – W. Sussex – see Arundel

WALLINGFORD – Oxfordshire – 503 Q29 – pop. 8 019 Great Britain 10 B3

London 54 mi. – Oxford 12 mi. – Reading 16 mi.

Town Hall, Market Pl ✆ (01491) 826972, ticwallingford@freenet.co.uk

Ridgeway Path★★

North Moreton House without rest

North Moreton, West : 4 mi. by A 4130 ✉ OX11 9AT – ✆ (01235) 813 283 – www.northmoretonhouse.co.uk – Fax (01235) 511 305

3 rm – †£ 48/55 ††£ 75/85

◆ Grade II listed house in mature lawned gardens with fine 17C barn. Spacious, individually decorated bedrooms. Breakfast on local organic produce at vast antique table.

The Partridge

32 St Mary's St ✉ OX10 0ET – ✆ (01491) 825 005 – www.partridge-inn.com – Fax (01491) 837 153 – Closed Sunday dinner

Rest – Menu £ 15 **s** – Carte £ 17/38 **s**

◆ Former pub, now a stylish, contemporary restaurant, with separate lounge, garden and raised rear terrace. Well-priced market menu offered alongside interesting à la carte of European dishes: cooking is flavourful, confident and accomplished. Efficient service.

WALTON – W. Yorks. – 502 Q22 – see Wetherby

WANTAGE – Oxfordshire – 504 P29 – pop. 9 452 10 B3

London 71 mi. – Oxford 16 mi. – Reading 24 mi. – Swindon 21 mi.

Vale and Downland Museum, 19 Church St ✆ (01235) 760176, tourism@wantage.com

The Boar's Head with rm

Church St, Ardington, East : 2.5 mi. by A 417 ✉ OX12 8QA – ✆ (01235) 833 254 – www.boarsheadardington.co.uk – Closed 25-26 December and 1 January

3 rm – †£ 80 ††£ 140

Rest – Menu £ 18 (lunch) – Carte £ 25/38

◆ Attractive 18C part-timbered pub set in a picture perfect Victorian model village. Wide-ranging menus offer something for everyone, from a 'Rapide' lunch to a gourmet tasting menu. Bedrooms are modern, stylish and spacious.

WAREHAM – Dorset – 503 N31 – pop. 2 568 4 C3

London 123 mi. – Bournemouth 13 mi. – Weymouth 19 mi.

Holy Trinity Church, South St ☎ (01929) 552740, tic@purbeck-dc.gov.uk

Town★ – St Martin's★★

Blue Pool★ **AC**, S : 3.5 mi. by A 351 – Bovington Tank Museum★ **AC**, Woolbridge Manor★, W : 5 mi. by A 352. Moreton Church★★, W : 9.5 mi. by A 352 – Corfe Castle★ (≤★★) **AC**, SE : 6 mi. by A 351 – Lulworth Cove★, SW : 10 mi. by A 352 and B 3070 – Bere Regis★ (St John the Baptist Church★), NW : 6.5 mi. by minor rd

The Priory

Church Green ✉ BH20 4ND – ☎ (01929) 551 666 – www.theprioryhotel.co.uk – Fax (01929) 554 519

16 rm – †£ 180 ††£ 275 – 2 suites

Rest – Menu £ 28 (Sunday lunch)/40 (dinner) – Carte lunch £ 31/40

◆ Charming, privately run part 16C priory, friendly and discreetly cosy. Well-equipped rooms. Manicured four-acre gardens lead down to River Frome: luxury suites in boathouse. Charming restaurant beneath stone vaults of undercroft.

Gold Court House

St John's Hill ✉ BH20 4LZ – ☎ (01929) 553 320 – www.goldcourthouse.co.uk – Fax (01929) 553 320

3 rm – †£ 50 ††£ 75

Rest – *(by arrangement, communal dining)* Menu £ 20

◆ Affable hosts are justly proud of this pretty 1760s house on a quiet square. Classically charming sitting room and bedrooms; well-chosen books and antiques. Dine communally while viewing delightful courtyard garden.

WAREN MILL – Northd. – 501 O17 – see Bamburgh

WARKWORTH – Northumberland – 502 P17 24 B2

London 316 mi. – Alnwick 7 mi. – Morpeth 24 mi.

Roxbro House without rest

5 Castle Terrace ✉ NE65 0UP – ☎ (01665) 711 416 – www.roxbrohouse.co.uk – Closed 23 December-2 January

3 rm – †£ 50/90 ††£ 120

◆ A discreet style enhances this 19C stone house in the shadow of Warkworth castle. Stylish lounge in harmony with very smart boutique bedrooms, two of which face the castle.

WARMINSTER – Wiltshire – 503 N30 – pop. 17 486 4 C2

London 111 mi. – Bristol 29 mi. – Exeter 74 mi. – Southampton 47 mi.

Central Car Park ☎ (01985) 218548, visitwarminster@btconnect.com

Longleat House★★★ **AC**, SW : 3 m. Stonehenge★★★ **AC**, E : 18 mi. by A 36 and A 303 – Bratton Castle (≤★★) NE : 6 mi. by A 350 and B 3098

at Upton Scudamore North : 2.5 mi. by A 350 – ✉ Warminster

The Angel Inn with rm

✉ BA12 0AG – ☎ (01985) 213 225 – www.theangelinn.co.uk – Fax (01985) 218 182 – Closed 25-26 December and 1 January

10 rm – †£ 80 ††£ 88 **Rest** – Menu £ 15 (lunch) – Carte £ 20/30

◆ Village pub with a country-cottage interior and decked terrace. Hearty à la carte menu with blackboard specials, daily fresh fish dishes, homemade bread and ice creams. Comfortable, modern rooms with individually co-ordinated furnishings.

at Heytesbury Southeast : 3.75 mi. by B 3414 – ✉ Warminster

The Resting Post without rest

67 High St ✉ BA12 0ED – ☎ (01985) 840 204 – www.therestingpost.co.uk

3 rm – †£ 50/60 ††£ 70/75

◆ Immaculately kept Grade II listed building dating back to 17C – originally a post office and general store run by the same couple. Individually styled bedrooms, one with a 6ft bed.

ENGLAND

The Angel Inn

High St ✉ BA12 0ED – ✆ (01985) 840 330
– www.theangelatheytesbury.co.uk
Rest – Carte £ 18/26
◆ Exposed beams and brickwork combined with bold, modern styling. Concise menu features big dishes and local produce, including legendary well-hung steaks and generous sharing boards.

at Crockerton **South : 2 mi. by A 350**

Bath Arms with rm

Clay St, on Shear Water rd. ✉ BA12 8AJ – ✆ (01985) 212 262
– www.batharmscrockerton.co.uk
2 rm – †£ 80/95 ††£ 80/95 **Rest** – Carte £ 21/27
◆ Down-to-earth pub with big ambitions, situated on Longleat Estate. Daily changing menu features classic pub dishes, snacks and grills alongside more modern fare. Two ultra-spacious, contemporary bedrooms.

at Horningsham **Southwest : 5 mi. by A 362 – ✉ Wiltshire**

The Bath Arms with rm

Longleat ✉ BA12 7LY – ✆ (01985) 844 308 – www.batharms.co.uk
– Fax (01985) 845 187
15 rm – †£ 85/140 ††£ 95/150
Rest – Menu £ 14/30 – Carte approx. £ 30
◆ Stylish creeper-clad pub next to the Longleat Estate. Modern, honest British menu uses produce sourced from within 50 miles; dishes are presented in a straightforward manner. Unique bedrooms with eccentric design themes.

ENGLAND

WARTLING – **E. Sussex** – **504** V31 – **see Herstmonceux**

WARWICK – **Warwickshire** – **503** P27 – **pop. 23 350** Great Britain **19** C3

London 96 mi. – Birmingham 20 mi. – Coventry 11 mi.
– Leicester 34 mi.

The Court House, Jury St ✆ (01926) 492212, touristinfo@warwick-uk.co.uk

Warwick Racecourse, ✆ (01926) 494 316

Town★ - Castle★★ **AC** Y – Leycester Hospital★ **AC** Y **B** – Collegiate Church of St Mary★ (Tomb★) Y **A**

Charter House without rest

87 West St ✉ CV34 6AH – ✆ (01926) 496 965
– www.charterhouseguesthouse.com
– Closed 25 December Y**c**
3 rm – †£ 65 ††£ 85/95
◆ Timbered 15C house not far from the castle. Comfortable, delicately ordered rooms with a personal touch: pretty counterpanes and posies of dried flowers. Tasty breakfasts.

Park Cottage without rest

113 West St ✉ CV34 6AH – ✆ (01926) 410 319 – www.parkcottagewarwick.co.uk
– Fax (01926) 497 994 Y**e**
7 rm – †£ 52/62 ††£ 75/85
◆ Between the shops and restaurants of West Street and the River Avon, a listed part Tudor house offering a homely lounge and sizeable, traditionally appointed bedrooms.

Saffron Gold

Unit 1, Westgate House, Market St ✉ CV34 4DE
– ✆ (01926) 402 061 – www.saffronwarwick.co.uk
– Closed 25 December Y**n**
Rest – Indian – *(dinner only)* Menu £ 20 – Carte £ 16/30
◆ Split-level dining room hung with sitars and prints from the subcontinent. Piquant seafood and Goan dishes are the specialities of a freshly prepared Indian repertoire.

WARWICK-ROYAL LEAMINGTON SPA

Birmingham Rd	Z	7
Bowling Green St	Y	9
Brook St	Y	12
Butts (The)	Y	13
Castle Hill	Y	15
Church St	Y	17
High St	Y	23
Jury St	Y	
Lakin Rd	Y	25
Linen St	Y	26
Market Pl.	Y	29
Old Square	Y	35
Old Warwick Rd	Z	36
Radford Rd	Z	39
Rock (The)	Y	32
St John's Rd	Y	42
St Nicholas Church St	Y	43
Shires Retail Park	Z	
Smith St	Y	
Swan St	Y	46
Theatre St	Y	48
West St	Y	50

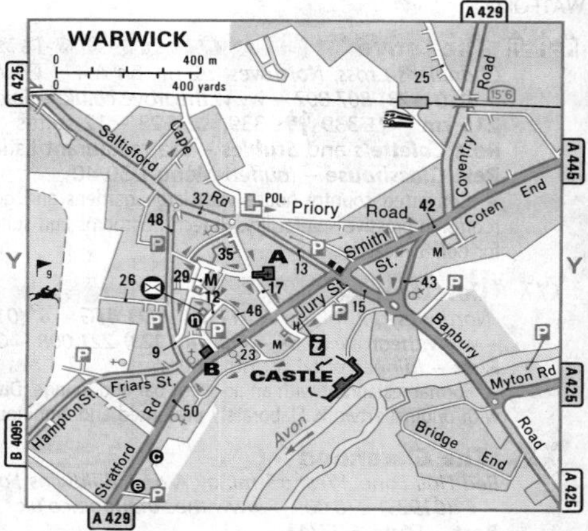

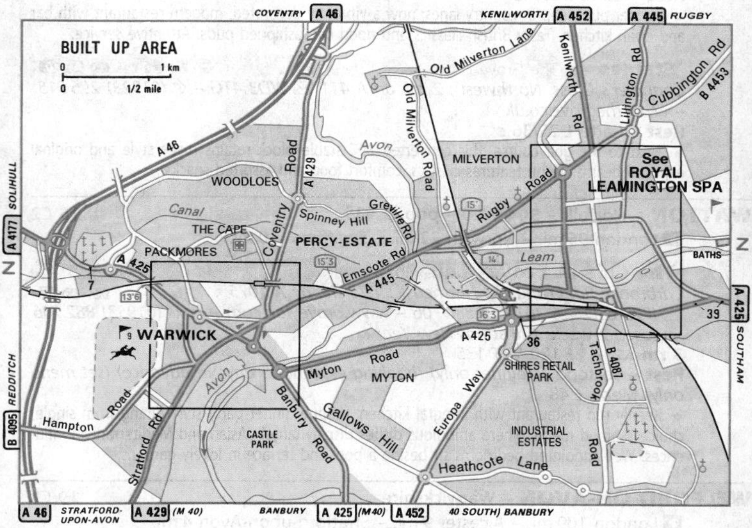

WATERGATE BAY – Cornwall – 503 E32 – see Newquay

WATERMILLOCK – Cumbria – 502 L20 – see Ullswater

WATFORD – Hertfordshire – 504 S29 – pop. 120 960 12 A2

London 21 mi. – Aylesbury 23 mi.

West Herts. Cassiobury Park, ✆ (01923) 236 484

Oxhey Park South Oxhey Prestwick Rd, ✆ (01923) 248 213

Plan : see Greater London (North-West) 2

The Grove

Chandler's Cross, Northwest : 2 mi. on A 411 ✉ WD3 4TG – ✆ (01923) 807 807 – www.thegrove.co.uk – Fax (01923) 221 008

215 rm – †£ 339 ††£ 339, ☕ £ 23 – 12 suites

Rest *Colette's* and ***Stables*** – see restaurant listing

Rest *Glasshouse* – *(buffet)* Menu £ 30/40

◆ Converted country house with large gardens and golf course. Modern décor in public rooms. Impressive spa facility. Hi-tech bedrooms and suites in modern extension. Glasshouse for buffet meals.

Colette's – at The Grove Hotel

Northwest : 2 mi. on A 411 ✉ WD3 4TG – ✆ (01923) 296 010 – www.thegrove.co.uk – Fax (01923) 221 008 – Closed Sunday and Monday

Rest – *(dinner only)* Menu £ 60 **s**

◆ Formal restaurant with an adjacent bar and lounge. Divided into two rooms and decorated with original artwork. Elaborately presented and ambitious cooking.

The Clarendon

Red Hall Lane, West : 5 mi. by A 412, Baldwins Lane and Sarratt rd ✉ WD3 4LU – ✆ (01923) 270 009 – www.theclarendon.co.uk

Rest – Carte £ 27/43

◆ Former pub deep in country lanes; now a vibrantly decorated, modern restaurant with bar and open kitchen. Tasty British classics and good old-fashioned puds. Attentive service.

Stables – at The Grove Hotel

Chandler's Cross, Northwest : 2 mi. on A 411 ✉ WD3 4TG – ✆ (01923) 296 015 – www.thegrove.co.uk

Rest – Carte £ 25/36 **s**

◆ Next to the golf course, this converted 19C stable block retains rustic style and original exposed beams. Menu features classics, comfort food and assorted snacks.

ENGLAND

WATTON – Norfolk – 504 W26 – pop. 7 435 — 15 C2

London 95 mi. – Norwich 22 mi. – Swaffham 10 mi.

The Café at Brovey Lair with rm

Carbrooke Rd, Ovington, Northeast : 1.75 mi. by A 1075 ✉ IP25 6SD – ✆ (01953) 882 706 – www.broveylair.com – Fax (01953) 882 706 – Closed 2 weeks Christmas-New Year

3 rm ☕ – †£ 120 ††£ 135

Rest – Seafood – *(dinner only) (booking essential 2 days in advance) (set menu only)* Menu £ 48

◆ Keenly run restaurant with integral kitchen. Unique dinner party style dining from single-choice seafood menu, where ambitious dishes display largely Asian and Mediterranean influences. Well-appointed bedrooms sit beside a pool and terrace in lovely gardens.

WELFORD-ON-AVON – Warwickshire — 19 C3

London 109 mi. – Alcester 9 mi. – Stratford-upon-Avon 4 mi.

The Bell Inn

Binton Rd ✉ CV37 8EB – ✆ (01789) 750 353 – www.thebellwelford.co.uk – Fax (01789) 750 893

Rest – Carte £ 21/30

◆ Part 17C inn in neat village near Stratford. Attractive dining terrace. Flagged and beamed bar with open fire. Eclectic mix of dishes: local suppliers printed on back of menu.

WELLINGHAM – Norfolk — 15 C1

London 120 mi. – King's Lynn 29 mi. – Norwich 28 mi.

Manor House Farm without rest

✉ PE32 2TH – ✆ (01328) 838 227 – www.manor-house-farm.co.uk – Fax (01328) 838 348

3 rm ☕ – †£ 65/70 ††£ 90/120

◆ Idyllic setting beside church, surrounded by gardens and working farm. Family style breakfast; home grown bacon and sausage. Charming rooms in the house or comfortable annexe.

WELLINGTON – County of Herefordshire – 503 L27 **18** B3

London 161 mi. – Gloucester 38 mi. – Worcester 31 mi. – Hereford 6 mi.

The Wellington

HR4 8AT – (01432) 830 367 – www.wellingtonpub.co.uk
– Closed 25 December, Sunday dinner and Monday lunch
Rest – Carte £ 24/32

♦ An extremely popular, much-loved neighbourhood pub. In line with their highly seasonal ethos, menus change daily and feature classic combinations of local, traceable produce.

WELLS – Somerset – 503 M30 – pop. 10 406 **4** C2

London 132 mi. – Bristol 20 mi. – Southampton 68 mi. – Taunton 28 mi.
Town Hall, Market Pl (01749) 672552, touristinfo@wells.gov.uk
East Horrington Rd, (01749) 675 005
City★★ – Cathedral★★★ – Bishop's Palace★ (★★) **AC** – St Cuthbert★
Glastonbury★★ - Abbey★★ (Abbot's Kitchen★) **AC**, St John the Baptist★★, Somerset Rural Life Museum★ **AC**, Glastonbury Tor★ (★★★), SW : 5.5 mi. by A 39 – Wookey Hole★ (Caves★ **AC**, Papermill★), NW : 2 m. Cheddar Gorge★★ (Gorge★★, Caves★, Jacob's Ladder ★) - St Andrew's Church★, NW : 7 mi. by A 371 – Axbridge★★ (King John's Hunting Lodge★, St John the Baptist Church★), NW : 8.5 mi. by A 371

The Swan

11 Sadler St BA5 2RX – (01749) 836 300 – www.swanhotelwells.co.uk
– Fax (01749) 836 301
50 rm – £ 90/102 £ 114/170 – 1 suite
Rest – Menu £ 15 (lunch) – Carte dinner £ 25/33

♦ Refurbished to a very good standard, this friendly former posting inn faces the Cathedral's west front. Two firelit lounges; stylish, individually decorated rooms. Stunning Cathedral suite. Restaurant boasts framed antique clothing and oak panelling.

Beryl without rest

East : 1.25 mi. by B 3139 off Hawkers Lane BA5 3JP – (01749) 678 738
– www.beryl-wells.co.uk – Fax (01749) 670 508 – Closed 24-25 December
10 rm – £ 65/85 £ 100/130

♦ Neo-gothic former hunting lodge in formal gardens run in idiosyncratic style. Impeccable antique-filled drawing room. Traditional rooms, larger on first floor. Charming hosts.

The Old Spot

12 Sadler St BA5 2SE – (01749) 689 099 – Closed 1 week Christmas,
Monday, Sunday dinner and Tuesday lunch
Rest – Menu £ 15/28 **s**

♦ Restaurant's rear leads straight onto stunning Cathedral grounds. Relaxing interior spot on for enjoying gloriously unfussy, mouth-wateringly tasty dishes. Good value, too.

at Wookey Hole Northwest : 1.75 mi. by A 371 – Wells

Miller's at Glencot House

Glencot Lane BA5 1BH – (01749) 677 160 – www.glencothouse.co.uk
– Fax (01749) 670 210
15 rm – £ 135/165 £ 165/295
Rest – *(booking essential for non-residents)* Menu £ 18/33

♦ 19C mansion in Jacobean style, bursting with personality and now owned by Martin Miller who has filled the house with antiques. Rooms all refurbished; relaxed atmosphere throughout. French inspired menu with good local produce.

at Easton Northwest : 3 mi. on A 371 – Wells

Beaconsfield Farm without rest

on A 371 BA5 1DU – (01749) 870 308 – www.beaconsfieldfarm.co.uk
– Closed 23 December-2 January
3 rm – £ 60/70 £ 70/85

♦ In the foothills of the Mendips, a renovated farmhouse offering well-fitted, cottage-style rooms. Generous breakfasts in the parlour overlooking the four-acre grounds.

ENGLAND

WELLS-NEXT-THE-SEA – Norfolk – 504 W25 – pop. 2 451 15 C1

London 122 mi. – Cromer 22 mi. – Norwich 38 mi.

The Crown

The Buttlands ✉ NR23 1EX – ✆ (01328) 710 209
– www.thecrownhotelwells.co.uk – Fax (01328) 711 432
12 rm – ♦£ 90/135 ♦♦£ 110/155
Rest *Restaurant* – *(dinner only and Sunday lunch)* Carte £ 30/35
Rest *Bar* – *(bookings not accepted)* Menu £ 13 (Sunday-Thursday)
– Carte £ 13/38

◆ 16C cream and blue painted former coaching inn overlooking village green. Spacious modern bedrooms boast good facilities; those at front boast pleasant green views. Small linen-laid dining room offers classical fare. Large leather-furnished bar and rustic brasserie serve weekly menus with more international influences.

Machrimore without rest

Burnt St, on A149 ✉ NR23 1HS – ✆ (01328) 711 653 – www.machrimore.co.uk
3 rm – ♦£ 50/60 ♦♦£ 78

◆ Converted farm buildings with delightful gardens and illuminated water features. Accessed via the garden, bedrooms have quality furniture, good facilities, their own patio and seating.

at Wighton Southeast : 2.5 mi. by A149

Meadowview without rest

53 High St ✉ NR23 1PF – ✆ (01328) 821 527 – www.meadow-view.net
5 rm – ♦£ 60 ♦♦£ 80/100

◆ Set in peaceful village, with neat garden, hot tub, comfy furniture and gazebo overlooking meadow. Smart, modern interior with comfy furnishings; good facilities. Breakfast cooked on Aga.

WELWYN – Hertfordshire – 504 T28 – pop. 10 512 12 B2

London 31 mi. – Bedford 31 mi. – Cambridge 31 mi.

Tewin Bury Farm rest,

Southeast : 3.5 mi. by A 1000 on B 1000 ✉ AL6 0JB – ✆ (01438) 717 793
– www.tewinbury.co.uk – Fax (01438) 840 440
39 rm – ♦£ 140 ♦♦£ 155
Rest – Menu £ 13 (Sunday-Thursday) – Carte £ 25/30

◆ Consisting of a range of converted farm buildings on 400-acre working farm. 17C tythe barn used as function room located next to river. Individual rooms have beamed ceilings. Restaurant located in timbered farm building.

WELWYN GARDEN CITY – Hertfordshire – 504 T28 – pop. 43 512 12 B2

London 22 mi. – Luton 21 mi.

Panshanger Golf Complex Old Herns Lane, ✆ (01707) 333 312

Auberge du Lac

Brocket Hall, West : 3 mi. by A 6129 on B 653 ✉ AL8 7XG – ✆ (01707) 368 888
– www.brocket-hall.co.uk – Fax (01707) 368 898
– Closed 27 December - 5 January, Sunday and Monday
Rest – Menu £ 30 (weekdays)/55
Spec. Caramelised scallops with pomegranate, orange and carrot. Roast lamb with artichoke and balsamic glazed sweetbreads. Millefeuille of caramel parfait with sautéed apples and cider dressing.

◆ You get buzzed in at the gates to reach this part 18C former hunting lodge in the grounds of Brocket Hall; a charming setting with its lakeside terrace. The cooking is technically adept and the focus is on flavours; excellent cheeseboard.

WENDLING – Norfolk – 504 W25 – see East Dereham

WENTBRIDGE – West Yorkshire – 502 Q23 – ✉ Pontefract — 22 B3

London 183 mi. – Leeds 19 mi. – Nottingham 55 mi. – Sheffield 28 mi.

Wentbridge House

Old Great North Rd ✉ WF8 3JJ – ✆ (01977) 620 444 – www.wentbridgehouse.co.uk – Fax (01977) 620 148

41 rm – £ 100 £ 170/210

Rest *Fleur de Lys* – *(dinner only and Sunday lunch)* Carte £ 34/51

Rest *Wentbridge Brasserie* – Carte £ 25/43

◆ Once owned by the late Queen Mother's family, a part 18C bay-windowed house decorated in traditional colours. Sizeable rooms, some overlooking the lawned grounds. Fleur de Lys adjacent to smart firelit bar. Informal Wentbridge Brasserie.

WEST BAGBOROUGH – Somerset – 503 K30 – see Taunton

WEST DIDSBURY – Gtr Manchester – see Manchester

WEST END – Surrey – 504 S29 – pop. 4 135 – ✉ Guildford — 7 C1

London 37 mi. – Bracknell 7 mi. – Camberley 5 mi. – Guildford 8 mi.

The Inn @ West End

42 Guildford Road, on A 322 ✉ GU24 9PW – ✆ (01276) 858 652 – www.the-inn.co.uk

Rest – Menu £ 25 (Sunday lunch)/33 (Friday-Saturday dinner) – Carte £ 28/33

◆ Pretty pub with a 'tea shop' atmosphere, lovely garden and terrace. Really fresh local produce and simple techniques create a wholesome, traditional menu. Good range of wines.

WEST HATCH – Somerset – see Taunton

WEST KIRBY – Merseyside – 502 K23 Great Britain — 20 A3

London 219 mi. – Chester 19 mi. – Liverpool 12 mi.

Liverpool★ - Cathedrals★★, The Walker★★, Merseyside Maritime Museum★ and Albert Dock★, E : 13.5 mi. by A 553

Peel Hey without rest

Frankby Rd, Frankby, East : 2.25 mi. by A 540 on B 5139 ✉ CH48 1PP – ✆ (0151) 677 9077 – www.peelhey.com – Fax (0151) 604 1999

9 rm – £ 65/75 £ 85/95

◆ Personally run, 19C house with attractive bedrooms; those to the rear are quieter, with countryside views. Comfortable conservatory and pleasant lawned garden. Pubs for dinner close by.

42 Caldy Road without rest

42 Caldy Road, Southeast : 1.25 mi. on B 5141 ✉ CH48 2HQ – ✆ (0151) 625 87 40 – www.warrencott.demon.co.uk – Fax (0151) 625 41 15 – Closed Christmas and New Year

4 rm – £ 65/75 £ 85/95

◆ Creeper-clad guesthouse with attractive garden and estuary views, set on smart residential road. Crisp, white, up to date bedrooms, two with sea views; modern bathrooms.

WEST MALLING – Kent – 504 V30 – pop. 2 144 — 8 B1

London 35 mi. – Maidstone 7 mi. – Royal Tunbridge Wells 14 mi.

Addington Maidstone, ✆ (01732) 844 785

Scott House without rest

37 High St ✉ ME19 6QH – ✆ (01732) 841 380 – www.scott-house.co.uk – Fax (01732) 522 367 – Closed Christmas-New Year

4 rm – £ 79 £ 89

◆ Comfy rooms in period style and a relaxing first-floor lounge share this part Georgian town house with a fine interior décor shop, run by the same warm husband and wife team.

The Swan

35 Swan St ✉ ME19 6JU – ✆ (01732) 521 910 – www.theswanwestmalling.co.uk – Fax (01732) 522 898 – Closed 26 December and 1 January

Rest – Carte £ 28/37

◆ Radically renovated 16C pub in modern pine. Stylish lounge: leopard-print carpet, purple cushions. Modish menu at sensible prices; informal, very efficient service.

ENGLAND

WEST MEON – Hampshire – 504 Q30 6 B2

London 74 mi. – Southampton 27 mi. – Portsmouth 21 mi. – Basingstoke 32 mi.

The Thomas Lord

High Street ✉ GU32 1LN – ✆ (01730) 829 244 – www.thethomaslord.co.uk
Rest – Carte £ 22/28

◆ Named after the founder of Lord's, with a cricketing theme. Constantly evolving menus and a passion for local produce; cooking is generous and robust, British with a hint of Mediterranean.

WEST PECKHAM – Kent – see Maidstone

WEST STOKE – W. Sussex – see Chichester

WEST TANFIELD – North Yorkshire – 502 P21 – pop. 551 – ✉ Ripon 22 B2

London 237 mi. – Darlington 29 mi. – Leeds 32 mi. – Middlesbrough 39 mi.

The Old Coach House without rest

2 Stable Cottage, Southeast : 1 mi. on A 6108 ✉ HG4 3HT – ✆ (01765) 634 900 – www.oldcoachhouse.info – Closed 2 January- 10 February
8 rm – †£ 45/79 ††£ 89

◆ Nestled between the Dales and the Moors, a smart 18C house with 'country living' feel. Spacious, modern bedrooms furnished by local, independent suppliers; some boast beams/-wetrooms.

WESTBURY – Wiltshire – 503 N30 – pop. 11 135 4 C2

London 111 mi. – Trowbridge 5 mi. – Warminster 4 mi.

Garden House

rest,

26 Edward St ✉ BA13 3BD – ✆ (01373) 859 995 – www.thegardenhotel.co.uk – Closed 25-26 December and 1 January
8 rm – †£ 80/110 ††£ 120
Rest – *(dinner only and Sunday lunch)* Carte £ 18/31 **s**

◆ Welcoming former town post office with comfy lounge and friendly bar. Spacious bedrooms blend the classic and the contemporary; 3 annexe rooms nearby. All boast spa baths. Restaurant uses local produce to create traditional dishes.

WESTFIELD – East Sussex – 504 V31 – pop. 1 509 8 B3

London 66 mi. – Brighton 38 mi. – Folkestone 45 mi. – Maidstone 30 mi.

The Wild Mushroom

Woodgate House, Westfield Lane, Southwest : 0.5 mi. on A 28 ✉ TN35 4SB – ✆ (01424) 751 137 – www.webbesrestaurants.co.uk – Fax (01424) 753 405 – Closed 1 week August, 1 week October, 25-26 December, Sunday dinner and Monday
Rest – *(booking essential)* Menu £ 19 (lunch) – Carte dinner £ 24/34

◆ Bustling and hospitable with modern interior and conservatory lounge. Flavourful, well-priced dishes from a varied, interesting menu. Loyal local following: be sure to book.

WESTON-SUPER-MARE – North Somerset – 503 K29 – pop. 78 044 3 B2

London 147 mi. – Bristol 24 mi. – Taunton 32 mi.

Beach Lawns ✆ (01934) 888800, westontouristinfo@n-somerset.gov.uk

Worlebury Monks Hill, ✆ (01934) 625 789

Seafront (≤★★) BZ

Axbridge★★ (King John's Hunting Lodge★, St John the Baptist Church★) SE : 9 mi. by A 371 - BY - and A 38 – Cheddar Gorge★★ (Gorge★★, Caves★, Jacob's Ladder ✻★) – Clevedon★ (≤★★, Clevedon Court★), NE : 10 mi. by A 370 and M 5 – St Andrew's Church★, SE : 10.5 mi. by A 371

Albert Quadrant	BZ 2	Royal Parade	BZ 11
Flowerdown Bridge	BY 4	Sovereign Centre	BZ
High St.	BZ 7	Upper Bristol Rd	BY 12
Meadow St.	BZ 8	Upper Church Rd	AY 13
Oxford St.	BZ 9	Walliscote Rd	BZ 14
Regent St.	BZ 10	Waterloo St.	BZ 15
		Windwhistle Rd	AZ 16

The Beachlands

17 Uphill Road North ✉ *BS23 4NG – ✆ (01934) 621 401 – www.beachlandshotel.com – Fax (01934) 621 966 – Closed 24-29 December*

23 rm – £ 65/100 £ 134/140 AZ**c**

Rest – *(dinner only and Sunday lunch)* Menu £ 22

◆ Well-established and family run, convenient for beach and golf course. Rooms in traditional prints; some, south-facing, have veranda doors giving on to a secluded garden. Formal dining room overlooks pleasant gardens.

The symbol 🍇 denotes a particularly interesting wine list.

ENGLAND

Queenswood without rest
Victoria Park, off Upper Church Rd ✉ BS23 2HZ – ✆ (01934) 416 141 – www.queenswoodhotel.com – Fax (01934) 621 759 – Closed Christmas
18 rm – †£ 55/80 ††£ 75/100 BZ**s**
◆ Sizeable, 19C-style house, well kept by friendly, long-standing owners. Red velour lounge sofas and neat rooms in the time-honoured tradition of the British seaside holiday.

Duets
103 Upper Bristol Road ✉ BS22 8ND – ✆ (01934) 413 428 – www.duets.co.uk – Closed 1 week February, 2 weeks August, Sunday dinner, Saturday lunch, Monday and Tuesday BY**a**
Rest – Menu £ 19/28 – Carte £ 31/34
◆ Diligent and unfussy service sets the tone in this traditionally styled restaurant, deservedly a neighbourhood favourite. Ably judged cooking on a tasty classical base.

The Cove
Birnbeck Rd ✉ BS23 2BX – ✆ (01934) 418 217 – www.the-cove.co.uk – Closed 25 December, Sunday dinner and Monday except Bank Holidays AY**e**
Rest – Menu £ 13 (lunch) – Carte £ 22/31
◆ Seafront eatery with striking lines, contemporary styling and bay views. Modern, seasonal menu displays European flair and seafood slant; most produce from within 20 miles. Tapas 3-9pm.

WESTON UNDER WETHERLEY – **Warks.** – **see Royal Leamington Spa**

WESTON UNDERWOOD – **Derbs.** – **see Derby**

WETHERBY – **West Yorkshire** – **502** P22 – **pop. 10 562** Great Britain **22** B2

London 208 mi. – Harrogate 8 mi. – Leeds 13 mi. – York 14 mi.
The Library, 17 Westgate ✆ (01937) 582151, wetherbytic@leedslearning.net
Linton Linton Lane, ✆ (01937) 580 089
Harewood House★★ (The Gallery★) **AC**, SW : 5.5 mi. by A 58 and A 659

Wood Hall
Trip Lane, Linton, Southwest : 3 mi. by A 661 and Linton Rd ✉ LS22 4JA – ✆ (01937) 587 271 – www.handpicked.co.uk – Fax (01937) 584 353
44 rm – †£ 115/185 ††£ 185/255
Rest – *(dinner only and Sunday lunch)* Menu £ 35 **s** – Carte £ 48/61 **s**
◆ Peacefully set part Jacobean and Georgian manor in 100 acres of woods and gardens. Refurbished contemporary public areas; well-appointed bedrooms. Popular wedding venue. Elegant dining room with candelabras and tall sash windows.

at Walton East : 4 mi. by B 1224 – ✉ **Wetherby**

The Fox and Hounds
Hall Park Road ✉ LS23 7DQ – ✆ (01937) 842 192 – www.thefoxandhoundswalton.com
Rest – *(booking essential)* Menu £ 18 (lunch) – Carte £ 17/30
◆ Characterful, low-beamed stone pub with a cosy snug, home to stuffed fox, Basil. Hearty, robust cooking; classic British dishes. Friendly atmosphere and polite, chatty service.

WEYMOUTH – **Dorset** – **503** M32 – **pop. 48 279** **4** C3

London 142 mi. – Bournemouth 35 mi. – Bristol 68 mi. – Exeter 59 mi.
to Guernsey (St Peter Port) and Jersey (St Helier) (Condor Ferries Ltd)
The King's Statue, The Esplanade ✆ (01305) 785747, tic@weymouth.gov.uk
Links Rd, ✆ (0844) 980 9909
Town★ – Timewalk★ **AC** – Nothe Fort (≤★) **AC** – Boat Trip★ (Weymouth Bay and Portland Harbour) **AC**
Chesil Beach★★ – Portland★ - Portland Bill (✻★★) S : 2.5 mi. by A 354. Maiden Castle★★ (≤★) N : 6.5 mi. by A 354 – Sub-Tropical Gardens★ **AC**, St Catherine's Chapel★) NW : 9 mi. by B 3157

ENGLAND

Chandlers without rest
4 Westerhall Rd ✉ DT4 7SZ – ✆ (01305) 771 341 – www.chandlershotel.com – Fax (01305) 830 122 – Closed mid December to mid January
10 rm – †£ 60/110 ††£ 155
◆ Substantial Victorian house with comfy, stylish interior. Every bedroom has a unique focus point – maybe a spa bath or striking colour scheme.

Bay View without rest
35 The Esplanade ✉ DT4 8DH – ✆ (01305) 782 083 – www.bayview-weymouth.co.uk – Fax (01305) 782 083 – Closed December
8 rm – †£ 40/50 ††£ 50/60
◆ Generously sized en suite rooms, many with four-poster beds or broad bay windows, in a sizeable townhouse with views over the bay. Neatly kept basement lounge.

Perry's
4 Trinity Rd, The Old Harbour ✉ DT4 8TJ – ✆ (01305) 785 799 – www.perrysrestaurant.co.uk – Fax (01305) 787 002 – Closed 25-26 December, Saturday lunch and Monday
Rest – Seafood – Menu £ 16 (lunch) – Carte £ 25/35
◆ Townhouse on the quay houses keenly run restaurant serving tasty modern dishes, including the freshest local seafood. Thoughtfully complied wine list, with some unusual choices.

WHALLEY – Lancashire – 502 M22 – pop. 3 230 – ✉ Blackburn 20 B2

London 233 mi. – Blackpool 32 mi. – Burnley 12 mi. – Manchester 28 mi.
Long Leese Barn Clerkhill, ✆ (01254) 822 236

at Mitton Northwest : 2.5 mi. on B 6246 – ✉ Whalley

The Three Fishes
Mitton Road ✉ BB7 9PQ – ✆ (01254) 826 888 – www.thethreefishes.com – Fax (01254) 826 026 – Closed 25 December
Rest – *(bookings not accepted)* Carte £ 18/31
◆ Spacious 17C pub with modern styling set in a small hamlet by the River Ribble. Featuring local and handmade produce, the wide-ranging, regional menu lists the provenance of every dish.

WHITBY – North Yorkshire – 502 S20 – pop. 13 594 Great Britain 23 C1

London 257 mi. – Middlesbrough 31 mi. – Scarborough 21 mi. – York 45 mi.
Langborne Rd ✆ (01723) 383637, tourismbureau@scarborough.gov.uk
Low Straggleton Sandsend Rd, ✆ (01947) 600 660
Abbey★

Bagdale Hall
1 Bagdale ✉ YO21 1QL – ✆ (01947) 602 958 – www.bagdale.co.uk – Fax (01947) 820 714
14 rm (dinner included) – †£ 60/70 ††£ 100/150
Rest – *(dinner only and Sunday lunch)* Carte approx. £ 28
◆ Tudor manor with fine fireplaces in carved wood and 19C Delft tiles; panelled rooms with mullioned windows; four-posters in period style bedrooms. Annexe for more modern rooms. Dining room boasts timbered ceiling and massive wooden fireplace.

Cross Butts Stable
Guisborough Rd, West : 1.75 mi. on A 171 (Teeside rd) ✉ YO21 1TL – ✆ (01947) 820 986 – www.cross-butts.co.uk
9 rm – †£ 60 ††£ 130 **Rest** – Carte £ 15/25 **s**
◆ Extended farmhouse on working farm personally run by a welcoming family. Superb bedrooms, set round courtyard with water feature, have flag floors and warm, sumptuous aura. Smart, informal restaurant areas over two floors: a mix of suites, sofas and tables.

Green's

13 Bridge St ✉ YO22 4BG – ✆ (01947) 600 284 – www.greensofwhitby.com – Closed 25-26 December and 1 January

Rest – Seafood – *(dinner only and lunch Friday-Sunday) (booking essential)* Menu £ 41 – Carte £ 21/39

◆ Set in town centre, close to quayside, with a rustic, informal ambience. Constantly changing seafood menus are simply cooked and employ much produce freshly landed at Whitby.

Red Chard Lounge and Grill

22-23 Flowergate ✉ YO21 3BA – ✆ (01947) 606 660 – www.redchard.com – Closed first week and midweek January, 1 week March, Monday and lunch Saturday-Tuesday

Rest – Beef specialities – Carte £ 25/38

◆ Modern town centre bar/lounge/dining room in one; funky and relaxing, with art-covered walls. Wide ranging menu with local produce to the fore; quality 21 day hung beef.

at Briggswath Southwest : 3.5 mi. by A 171 (Teesdie rd), A 169 on B 1410 – ✉ Whitby

The Lawns without rest

73 Carr Hill Lane ✉ YO21 1RS – ✆ (01947) 810 310 – www.thelawnsbedandbreakfastwhitby.co.uk – Fax (01947) 810 310 – Closed Christmas and New Year

3 rm – †£ 70 ††£ 70

◆ Sizeable, converted house above a south-facing garden and verge of evergreens. Stripped wooden floors, understated décor. Spotless rooms. Fine views of moors and Esk valley.

ENGLAND

at Sandsend Northwest : 3 mi. on A 174 – ✉ Whitby

Estbek House with rm

East Row ✉ YO21 3SY – ✆ (01947) 893 424 – www.estbekhouse.co.uk – Fax (01947) 893 623 – Closed 3 January-7 February

4 rm – †£ 65/100 ††£ 140/180

Rest – Seafood – *(dinner only)* Carte £ 33/47

◆ This personally run Regency house, adjacent to beach, boasts delightful terrace, basement bar, smart restaurant serving local, wild seafood, and utterly charming rooms.

at Goldsborough Northwest : 6 mi. by A 174

Fox & Hounds

– ✆ (01947) 893 372 – www.foxandhoundsgoldsborough.co.uk – Closed 2 weeks January, Christmas, Sunday dinner, Monday, Tuesday and Bank Holidays

Rest – *(booking essential)* Carte £ 26/38

◆ Cosy pubby restaurant in a coastal hamlet, run by a team of two. Constantly evolving blackboard menu features local produce and unfussy cooking. Seasonality is paramount and fresh fish a speciality.

WHITCHURCH – Shropshire – 502 L25 – pop. 8 673 18 B1

London 168 mi. – Nantwich 11 mi. – Wrexham 15 mi.

at Burleydam East : 4.25 mi. on A 525 – ✉ Whitchurch

The Combermere Arms

✉ SY13 4AT – ✆ (01948) 871 223 – www.combermerearms-burleydam.co.uk – Fax (01948) 661 371

Rest – Carte £ 20/28

◆ 16C country inn with flagged floors, snug corners and old beams. Informal menu with plenty of choice, including sandwiches at lunch. Interesting wine list and cheese selection.

WHITEHAVEN – Cumbria – 502 J20 – pop. 24 978 21 A2

London 332 mi. – Carlisle 39 mi. – Keswick 28 mi. – Penrith 47 mi.

Zest

Low Rd, South : 0.5 mi. on B 5345 (St Bees) ✉ CA28 9HS – ✆ (01946) 692 848 – www.zestwhitehaven.com – Closed 25 December-6 January and Sunday-Tuesday

Rest – *(dinner only)* Carte £ 25/30

◆ Don't be put off by the unprepossessing exterior: inside is a smart, stylish eatery and bar with brown leather sofas. Eclectic range of modern menus with numerous influences.

WHITEPARISH – Wilts. – 503 P30 – see Salisbury

WHITEWELL – Lancashire – 502 M22 – pop. 5 617 – ✉ Clitheroe 20 B2

London 281 mi. – Lancaster 31 mi. – Leeds 55 mi. – Manchester 41 mi.

The Inn at Whitewell with rm

Forest of Bowland ✉ BB7 3AT – ✆ (01200) 448 222 – www.innatwhitewell.com – Fax (01200) 448 298

23 rm – †£ 77 ††£ 203 – 1 suite **Rest** – Carte £ 15/32

◆ Attractive 14C inn boasting panoramic valley views, set above the river in the heart of the Trough of Bowland. Menus are largely classical with the odd international touch. Spacious bedrooms; some with four-posters and antique baths; some more contemporary.

WHITSTABLE – Kent – 504 X29 – pop. 30 195 9 C1

London 68 mi. – Dover 24 mi. – Maidstone 37 mi. – Margate 12 mi.

7 Oxford St ✆ (0871) 7162449, whitstableinformation@canterbury.gov.uk

Continental

29 Beach Walk, East : 0.5 mi. by Sea St and Harbour St ✉ CT5 2BP – ✆ (01227) 280 280 – www.hotelcontinental.co.uk – Fax (01227) 284 114

30 rm – †£ 63/83 ††£ 85/145 **Rest** – *(bar lunch)* Carte £ 24/39 **s**

◆ Laid-back, privately owned hotel with an unadorned 30s-style façade overlooking the sea; simply furnished, plain-walled rooms - picture windows and warm colours. Split-level bistro with "no frills" approach.

Whitstable Oyster Fishery Co.

Royal Native Oyster Stores, The Horsebridge ✉ CT5 1BU – ✆ (01227) 276 856 – www.oysterfishery.co.uk – Fax (01227) 770 829 – Closed 25-26 December and 31 December and Monday dinner

Rest – Seafood – *(booking essential)* Carte £ 30/40

◆ Relaxed and unfussy converted beach warehouse; seafood on display in open kitchen; oysters and moules-frites draw a trendy young set at weekends. Arthouse cinema upstairs.

Jo Jo's

209 Tankerton Rd, East : 1.5 mi. by Sea St and Harbour St ✉ CT5 2AT – ✆ (01227) 274 591 – www.jojosrestaurant.co.uk – Closed mid December-late January and Sunday-Tuesday

Rest – *(dinner only and Saturday lunch) (booking essential)* Carte approx. £ 18

◆ Neighbourhood eatery in residential parade. Concise Mediterranean menu of meze/tapas with daily specials; lots of fish and meat. Veg and herbs from kitchen garden. Closed 1 week in 6.

Pearson's Arms

The Horsebridge, Sea Wall ✉ CT5 1BT – ✆ (01227) 272 005 – www.pearsonsarms.com

Rest – Carte £ 23/33

◆ Spacious 18C seaside pub with rustic feel; watch sunset from first floor dining room. Appealing blackboard menu offers predominantly seafood, with local game in winter, bread baked in-house and homely puds. Tasty food; engaging service.

at Seasalter Southwest : 2 mi. by B 2205 – ✉ Whitstable

The Sportsman (Steve Harris)

Faversham Rd, Southwest : 2 mi. following coast rd ✉ CT5 4BP – ✆ (01227) 273 370 – www.thesportsmanseasalter.co.uk – Closed 25-26 December, Sunday dinner and Monday

Rest – Carte £ 23/34

Spec. 'Salmagundi'- seasonal English salad. Farm pork belly and apple sauce. Jasmine tea junket with rosehip syrup and breakfast crunch.

◆ Passionate, self-taught chef uses freshest food from local landscape to create simple, yet meticulously executed, dishes full of flavour. Emphasis on seafood; homemade elements include salt, butter and bread.

WHITTLESFORD – **Cambridgeshire** – **504** U27 **14** B3

London 50 mi. – Cambridge 11 mi. – Peterborough 46 mi.

The Tickell

1 North Rd ✉ CB2 4NZ – ✆ (01223) 833 128 – www.thetickell.co.uk – Fax (01223) 835 907 – Closed Sunday dinner and Monday

Rest – Menu £ 37 – Carte (lunch) £ 20/39

◆ Richly ornate 300 year-old exterior with conservatory and terrace. Quirky feel pervades: emerald green walls, yellow ceiling. Rich, classic meals from the Gallic repertoire.

WHITWELL-ON-THE-HILL – **North Yorkshire** – **502** R21 – **pop. 136** **23** C2 – ✉ **York**

London 240 mi. – Kingston-upon-Hull 47 mi. – Scarborough 29 mi. – York 13 mi.

The Stone Trough Inn

Kirkham Abbey, East : 1.75 mi. by A 64 on Kirkham Priory rd ✉ YO60 7JS – ✆ (01653) 618 713 – www.stonetroughinn.co.uk – Fax (01653) 618 819

Rest – Carte approx £ 20

◆ Attractive stone pub overlooking the river and the ruins of Kirkham Abbey. Cooking is straightforward and hearty, with a strong classical base and a mix of local and cosmopolitan influences.

WHORLTON – **Durham** – **see Barnard Castle**

WICKFORD – **Essex** – **504** V29 – **see Basildon**

WIGHT (Isle of) – **Isle of Wight** – **503** P/Q31 – **pop. 138 500** Great Britain

from Ryde to Portsmouth (Hovertravel Ltd) frequent services daily (10 mn) – from Ryde to Portsmouth (Wightlink Ltd) frequent services daily (15 mn) – from East Cowes to Southampton (Red Funnel Ferries) frequent services daily (22 mn)

from East Cowes to Southampton (Red Funnel Ferries) frequent services daily (1 h) – from Yarmouth to Lymington (Wightlink Ltd) frequent services daily (30 mn) – from Fishbourne to Portsmouth (Wightlink Ltd) frequent services daily (35 mn)

Island★★

Osborne House, East Cowes★★ **AC** – Carisbrooke Castle, Newport★★ **AC** (Keep ≤★) – Brading★ (Roman Villa★ **AC**, St Mary's Church★, Nunwell House★ **AC**) – Shorwell : St Peter's Church★ (wall paintings★)

BONCHURCH – **Isle of Wight** – ✉ **Isle Of Wight** **6** B3

The Pond Café

Bonchurch ✉ PO38 1RG – ✆ (01983) 855 666 – www.pondcafe.com – Closed 2 weeks January, Tuesday and Wednesday

Rest – Carte £ 27/35

◆ Intimate restaurant, with duck pond, in sleepy hamlet. Cosy sunlit terrace. Island's larder utilised to the full for seasonal dishes in unfussy, halogen lit surroundings.

BRIGHSTONE – Isle of Wight 6 B3

The Lodge without rest

Main Rd ✉ PO30 4DJ – ☎ (01983) 741 272 – www.thelodgebrighstone.com – Fax (01983) 741 272 – Closed Christmas and New Year

7 rm – 🛉£ 50/60 🛉🛉£ 70/75

◆ Victorian country house set in two and a half acres: quiet location. Real fire centrepiece of large sitting room. Completely co-ordinated rooms of varnished pine.

GODSHILL – Isle of Wight

The Taverners

High Street ✉ PO38 3HZ – ☎ (01983) 840 707 – www.thetavernersgodshill.co.uk – Fax (01983) 840 517 – Closed 2 weeks early January, Sunday dinner except Bank Holiday weekends and school summer holidays

Rest – Carte £ 16/25

◆ Fresh, flavoursome food and friendly service at popular pub in pretty village. Classic dishes on menu, plus seasonal blackboard specials. Spacious interior; sprawling gardens.

NITON – Isle of Wight 6 B3

The Hermitage

North : 3 m by Newport rd (A3020) – ☎ (01983) 730 010 – www.hermitage-iow.co.uk

10 rm – 🛉£ 45/90 🛉🛉£ 45/95 **Rest** – *(dinner only)* Menu £ 18

◆ 19C country house in 12 acres of gardens; flora and fauna abound. Traditional bedrooms, named after their antique furniture. The best boast impressive period beds and luxury bathrooms. Dishes home-cooked using local produce; attentive staff.

SEAVIEW – Isle of Wight – pop. 2 286 – ✉ Isle Of Wight 6 B3

Priory Bay

Priory Drive, Southeast : 1.5 mi. by B 3330 ✉ PO34 5BU – ☎ (01983) 613 146 – www.priorybay.co.uk – Fax (01983) 616 539

18 rm – 🛉£ 115/225 🛉🛉£ 200/270 – 2 suites

Rest *The Restaurant* – Menu £ 35 (dinner) – Carte £ 27/40

◆ Medieval priory with Georgian additions, surrounded by woodland. High ceilinged drawing room and bar area with leaded windows. Characterful rooms. Main Restaurant has views of the garden.

Seaview

High St ✉ PO34 5EX – ☎ (01983) 612 711 – www.seaviewhotel.co.uk – Fax (01983) 613 721 – Closed 21-26 December

25 rm – 🛉£ 75/120 🛉🛉£ 145/199 – 3 suites

Rest *The Restaurant and Sunshine Room* – see restaurant listing

◆ Victorian hotel with smart genuine style. Integral part of the community, on street leading to seafront. Bold modern bedrooms and nautically styled, welcoming public areas.

The Restaurant and Sunshine Room – at The Seaview Hotel

High St ✉ PO34 5EX – ☎ (01983) 612 711 – www.seaviewhotel.co.uk – Fax (01983) 613 721 – Closed 21-26 December

Rest – *(dinner only and lunch Saturday and Sunday) (meals in bar Sunday dinner except Bank Holidays) (booking essential)* Carte £ 29/38

◆ Traditional dining room with contemporary conservatory. Boasts rare model ship collection. Very visual, modern, elaborate dishes make the best of seasonal island produce.

SHANKLIN – Isle of Wight – pop. 8 055 – ✉ Isle Of Wight 6 B3

Newport 9 mi.

67 High St ☎ (01983) 813813, info@islandbreaks.co.uk

The Fairway Lake Sandown, ☎ (01983) 403 217

Rylstone Manor

Rylstone Gdns ✉ PO37 6RG – ☎ (01983) 862 806 – www.rylstone-manor.co.uk – Fax (01983) 862 806 – Closed January

9 rm – 🛉£ 70/110 🛉🛉£ 145/175 **Rest** – *(dinner only)* Menu £ 28 **s**

◆ Part 19C former gentleman's residence set in the town's cliff-top gardens. Interior has a comfortable period feel. Well furnished, individually styled bedrooms. Characterful Victorian hued dining room.

ENGLAND

Grange Bank House without rest
Grange Rd ✉ PO37 6NN – ☎ (01983) 862 337 – www.grangebank.co.uk – Closed December and January
9 rm – †£ 29/45 ††£ 58/70
◆ Extended Victorian house near high street. Comfortable, simple and immaculately kept with friendly, domestic ambience. Good value accommodation.

Foxhills without rest
30 Victoria Ave ✉ PO37 6LS – ☎ (01983) 862 329 – www.foxhillsofshanklin.co.uk – Fax (01983) 866 666 – March-October
8 rm – †£ 65/75 ††£ 88/118
◆ Attractive house in leafy avenue with woodland to the rear. Bright lounge with fireplace. Bedrooms in pastel shades. Unusual jacuzzi, spa and beauty treatments.

TOTLAND – Isle of Wight – pop. 7 317 – ✉ Isle Of Wight 6 A3

Newport 13 mi.

Sentry Mead
Madeira Rd ✉ PO39 0BJ – ☎ (01983) 753 212 – www.sentrymead.co.uk – Fax (01983) 754 710 – Closed 24-27 December
12 rm – †£ 45/55 ††£ 90/110
Rest – *(Closed Monday-Tuesday) (dinner only and Sunday lunch)* Carte £ 23/29
◆ Detached Victorian house with quiet garden 100 yards from beach. Traditional interiors include bar area and conservatory lounge. Comfortable rooms furnished with light wood. Popular menus in dining room.

ENGLAND

VENTNOR – Isle of Wight – pop. 6 257 – ✉ Isle Of Wight 6 B3

Newport 10 mi.
Steephill Down Rd, ☎ (01983) 853 326

Royal
Belgrave Rd ✉ PO38 1JJ – ☎ (01983) 852 186 – www.royalhoteliow.co.uk – Fax (01983) 855 395
54 rm – †£ 128/193 ††£ 240/260
Rest – *(dinner only and Sunday lunch October-June)* Menu £ 38
◆ Largest hotel on the island, a Victorian property, in the classic style of English seaside hotels. Traditional décor throughout the public areas and comfortable bedrooms. Light lunches in conservatory; classic meals in capacious dining room.

The Hambrough with rm — rest,
Hambrough Rd ✉ PO38 1SQ – ☎ (01983) 856 333 – www.thehambrough.com – Fax (01983) 857 260 – Closed 2 weeks early January, 1 week end April and 1 week early November
7 rm – †£ 182/196 ††£ 280/300
Rest – *(closed Sunday and Monday)* Menu £ 24/45
Spec. Ravioli of lobster and braised veal with pickled vegetables and lobster bisque. Rabbit with button mushrooms and fondant potato. Cylinder of white chocolate and passion fruit with tropical fruits.
◆ Striking Victorian cliff top villa with contemporary interior and fantastic sea views. Confident chef uses classical techniques and top quality ingredients in interesting and appealing combinations to create refined and precise dishes. Immaculate bedrooms boast quality linen and come in understated neutral hues.

YARMOUTH – Isle of Wight – ✉ Isle Of Wight 6 A3

Newport 10 mi.
The Quay, PO41 0PQ (01983) 813 813

The George
Quay St ✉ PO41 0PE – ☎ (01983) 760 331 – www.thegeorge.co.uk – Fax (01983) 760 425
18 rm – †£ 138 ††£ 229/287
Rest *The Brasserie* – see restaurant listing
◆ 17C quayside hotel in shadow of Yarmouth Castle. Flagged central hall and extensive wood panelling. Traditionally decorated bedrooms; best are 'balcony suites' with views of Solent.

The Brasserie – at The George Hotel
Quay St ✉ PO41 0PE – ✆ (01983) 760 331 – www.thegeorge.co.uk – Fax (01983) 760 425
Rest – Menu £ 27 (lunch) **s** – Carte £ 24/36 **s**
◆ Stylish, informal brasserie restaurant overlooking terrace and garden, with views out to sea. Mediterranean-influenced menu makes good use of seasonal, local produce.

WIGHTON – Norfolk – 504 W25 – see Wells-Next-The-Sea

WILLESLEY – Wiltshire – 503 N29 4 C2

London 115 mi. – Bristol 23 mi. – Swindon 37 mi. – Gloucester 38 mi.

Beaufort House without rest
✉ GL8 8QU – ✆ (01666) 880 444
4 rm – †£ 75 ††£ 89
◆ Part 17C former inn and staging post with an attractive garden. Much improved and modernised by current owner. Smart bedrooms; those at the rear look over garden and are quieter.

WILLIAN – Herts. – see Letchworth

WILLINGTON – Ches. – see Tarporley

WILMINGTON – Kent – 504 V29 – see Dartford

WILMSLOW – Cheshire – 502 N24 – pop. 28 604 20 B3

London 189 mi. – Liverpool 38 mi. – Manchester 12 mi. – Stoke-on-Trent 27 mi.
Great Warford Mobberley, ✆ (01565) 872 148

Stanneylands
Stanneylands Rd, North : 1 mi. by A 34 ✉ SK9 4EY – ✆ (01625) 525 225 – www.primahotels.co.uk – Fax (01625) 537 282
54 rm – †£ 150 ††£ 150, £ 14.50 – 1 suite
Rest ***The Restaurant*** – *(residents only Sunday dinner)* Menu £ 18/30 – Carte £ 35/50
◆ Attractive 19C redbrick hotel standing in mature grounds; exudes pleasant, country house style. Two characterful lounges and comfortable, traditional bedrooms. Comfy oak-panelled surroundings for diners.

WIMBORNE MINSTER – Dorset – 503 O31 – pop. 14 844 4 C3

London 112 mi. – Bournemouth 10 mi. – Dorchester 23 mi. – Salisbury 27 mi.
29 High St ✆ (01202) 886116, wimbornetic@eastdorset.gov.uk
Town★ - Minster★ – Priest's House Museum★ **AC**
Kingston Lacy★★ **AC**, NW : 3 mi. by B 3082

Les Bouviers with rm
Arrowsmith Rd, Canford Magna, Southeast : 2.25 mi. by A 349 on A 341 ✉ BH21 3BD – ✆ (01202) 889 555 – www.lesbouviers.co.uk – Fax (01202) 639 428
6 rm – †£ 183 ††£ 215 **Rest** – *(Closed Sunday dinner)* Menu £ 20/44
◆ Plush yet homely restaurant affording views to acres of mature grounds. Formal feel lightened by personable service. Complex dishes with modern twists. Stylish bedrooms.

WINCHCOMBE – Gloucestershire – 503 O28 – pop. 3 682 4 D1

London 100 mi. – Birmingham 43 mi. – Gloucester 26 mi. – Oxford 43 mi.
Town Hall, High St ✆ (01242) 602925, winchcombetic@tewkesbury.gov.uk

Isbourne Manor House without rest
Castle St ✉ GL54 5JA – ✆ (01242) 602 281 – www.isbourne-manor.co.uk – Fax (01242) 602 281 – Closed 3 days Christmas
3 rm – †£ 80/90 ††£ 100
◆ Wisteria-clad Georgian and Elizabethan manor. Cosy drawing room: antique furniture and open fire. One room has a four-poster bed, one a roof top terrace. Riverside garden.

ENGLAND

Westward without rest

Sudeley Lodge, East : 1.5 mi. by Castle St on Sudeley Lodge/Parks/Farm rd
GL54 5JB – (01242) 604 372 – www.westward-sudeley.co.uk – Fax (01242) 604 640 – Closed Christmas and New Year
3 rm – £ 65 £ 100
◆ Secluded, personally run 18C farmhouse: elegant, wood-floored drawing room and charming sitting room, bedrooms share fine views of 550-acre estate and mature gardens.

5 North St (Marcus Ashenford)

5 North St GL54 5LH – (01242) 604 566 – Fax (01242) 603 788 – Closed 2 weeks January, 1 week end of August, Tuesday lunch, Sunday dinner and Monday
Rest – Menu £ 25/45 – Carte (dinner) £ 35/45
Spec. Scallop,ham hock and leek terrine with celeriac and parsley purée. Best end and slow cooked breast of lamb with rosemary carrots. Chocolate and passion fruit.
◆ Husband and wife team run this cosy 17C timbered restaurant and its low-beamed ceiling adds to the warm and traditional feel. The seasons inform the cooking; dishes using classic combinations are the highlight.

Wesley House with rm

High St GL54 5LJ – (01242) 602 366 – www.wesleyhouse.co.uk – Fax (01242) 609 046
5 rm – £ 65 £ 80/95
Rest – *(Closed Sunday dinner)* Menu £ 16/38 – Carte £ 26/42
◆ Hugely characterful part 15C house: dine amongst the beams or in the stylish glass-roofed extension. Tasty modern British cooking with original twists. Smilingly quaint rooms.

ENGLAND

Wesley House Bar & Grill

20 High St GL54 5LJ – (01242) 602 366 – www.wesleyhouse.co.uk – Fax (01242) 609 046 – Closed Sunday and Monday
Rest – Carte £ 15/30
◆ Located on busy high street, this is a buzzy place to be, with trendy bar, comfy lounge, and wood-floored dining area serving authentic Spanish tapas beneath the big mirrors.

The White Hart Inn with rm

High St GL54 5LJ – (01242) 602 359 – www.wineandsausage.com – Fax (01242) 602 703
11 rm – £ 60/75 £ 85/115 **Rest** – Menu £ 15 (lunch) – Carte £ 20/30
◆ Whitewashed former coaching inn with rustic feel. Hearty homemade dishes; sausages have their own menu. Friendly, chatty atmosphere and service. Well-stocked wine shop. Comfortable bedrooms have a traditional feel; the rear rooms are quieter.

WINCHELSEA – East Sussex – 504 W31 Great Britain 9 C3

London 64 mi. – Brighton 46 mi. – Folkestone 30 mi.
Town★ – St Thomas Church (effigies★)

Strand House

Tanyard's Lane, East : 0.25 mi. on A 259 TN36 4JT – (01797) 226 276 – www.thestrandhouse.co.uk – Fax (01797) 224 806
10 rm – £ 55/65 £ 90/150 **Rest** – *(by arrangement)* Menu £ 30
◆ 14C and 15C half-timbered house of low beams and inglenook fireplaces: carefully tended rear garden shaded by tall trees, snug lounge; well-kept rooms in traditional style. Simple homecooking.

WINCHESTER – Hampshire – 503 P30 – pop. 41 420 Great Britain 6 B2

London 72 mi. – Bristol 76 mi. – Oxford 52 mi. – Southampton 12 mi.
Guildhall, High Street (01962) 840500, tourism@winchester.gov.uk
City★★ - Cathedral★★★ **AC** B – Winchester College★ **AC** B **B** – Castle Great Hall★ B **D** – God Begot House★ B **A**
St Cross Hospital★★ **AC** A

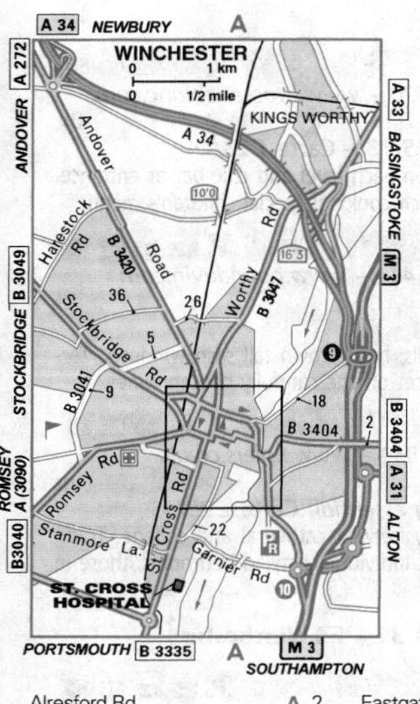

Hotel du Vin

14 Southgate St ✉ SO23 9EF – ✆ (01962) 841 414 – www.hotelduvin.com
– Fax (01962) 842 458 **Bi**

24 rm – †£ 140/225 ††£ 140/225, ☕ £ 13.50

Rest *Bistro* – see restaurant listing

♦ Elegant bedrooms, each with CD player, mini bar and distinct décor reflecting its wine house sponsors, in a 1715 redbrick house. Smart Champagne bar with inviting sofas.

Giffard House without rest

50 Christchurch Rd ✉ SO23 9SU – ✆ (01962) 852 628 – www.giffardhotel.co.uk
– Fax (01962) 856 722 – Closed 24 December-1 January **Bs**

13 rm ☕ – †£ 69/83 ††£ 99/125

♦ Imposing part Victorian, part Edwardian house. Well-furnished throughout; comfortable sitting room with large fireplace. Immaculate rooms with good facilities.

29 Christchurch Road without rest

29 Christchurch Road – ✆ (01962) 868 661 – www.fetherstondilke.com
– Fax (01962) 868 661 **Bv**

3 rm ☕ – †£ 50/60 ††£ 75/85

♦ 21C Regency style guesthouse in attractive residential area. Tastefully furnished guest areas display classical artwork. 3 comfy bedrooms; 2 with shower, 1 with private bathroom.

The Black Rat

88 Chesil Street ✉ SO23 0HX – ✆ (01962) 844 465 – www.theblackrat.co.uk
– Closed 2 weeks Easter, 1 week October-November and 2 weeks December

Rest – British – *(dinner only and lunch Saturday-Sunday)* **Ba**

Carte £ 28/36 **s**

♦ Hugely atmospheric, rustic restaurant with busy walls and unique garden huts. Nightly changing modern British menu boasts produce from within 50 miles and veg/herbs from allotment. Generous, flavoursome cooking.

Brasserie Blanc
19-20 Jewry St ✉ SO23 8RZ – ✆ (01962) 810 870 – www.brasserieblanc.com – Closed 25 December Bx
Rest – French – *(booking advisable)* Menu £ 15/18 – Carte £ 23/44
◆ Bustling restaurant set over 2 floors, with terrace on each level and chic bar at entrance. Seasonal menu displays simply prepared classical French cooking; special children's menu.

Bistro – at Hotel du Vin
14 Southgate St ✉ SO23 9EF – ✆ (01962) 841 414 – www.hotelduvin.com – Fax (01962) 842 458 Bi
Rest – *(booking essential)* Carte £ 35/46
◆ Oenophile memorabilia covers panelled cream walls; hops crown tall sash windows. Terrace under broad sunshades. Classic modern flavours set off the carefully chosen wines.

The Wykeham Arms with rm
75 Kingsgate St ✉ SO23 9PE – ✆ (01962) 853 834 – www.fullers.co.uk – Closed 25 December Bu
14 rm ☕ – †£ 65 ††£ 115 **Rest** – *(booking essential)* Carte £ 25/35
◆ Characterful, curio-crammed 18C inn, hidden away betwixt cathedral and college. Traditional lunch menu; more elaborate evening à la carte. Individually-styled bedrooms, those in annex are quieter, with their own terrace garden.

at Ovington East : 5.75 mi. by B 3404 - A - and A 31 – ✉ Winchester

The Bush Inn
✉ *SO24 0RE – ✆ (01962) 732 764 – www.wadworth.co.uk – Fax (01962) 735 130*
Rest – Carte £ 17/34
◆ Friendly, family-run 18C inn hidden away in idyllic spot on banks of River Itchen, its walls cluttered with curios and taxidermy. Wholesome, unfussy dishes on blackboard menus.

at Sparsholt Northwest : 3.5 mi. by B 3049 - A – ✉ Winchester

Lainston House
✉ *SO21 2LT – ✆ (01962) 776 088 – www.exclusivehotels.co.uk – Fax (01962) 776 672*
48 rm – †£ 135/230 ††£ 265, ☕ £ 20 – 2 suites
Rest *Avenue* – Carte £ 48/59
◆ Charming 17C manor with pretty grounds, parks and old herb garden. Traditionally styled lounge, cedar-panelled bar and up-to-date gym. Rooms, some more modern, vary in size. Dark wood dining room overlooks lawn.

Plough Inn
Main Road ✉ SO21 2NW – ✆ (01962) 776 353 – Fax (01962) 776 400 – Closed 25 December
Rest – *(booking essential)* Carte £ 22/27
◆ Traditionally styled, open plan inn serving good old pub favourites as well as more elaborate dishes. Delightful lawned garden with countryside views and children's play area.

at Easton Northeast : 4 mi. by A 3090 - A - off B 3047 – ✉ Winchester

The Chestnut Horse
✉ *SO21 1EG – ✆ (01962) 779 257 – www.thechestnuthorse.com – Closed 25 December, 26 December dinner, 1 January dinner and Sunday dinner in winter*
Rest – Carte £ 26/33
◆ 16C pub with colourful décor; choose from the red room, green room or pretty terrace. Extensive menu displays pub classics alongside more modern dishes and interesting specials.

WINDERMERE – Cumbria – 502 L20 – pop. 7 941 ▮ Great Britain 21 A2

▶ London 274 mi. – Blackpool 55 mi. – Carlisle 46 mi. – Kendal 10 mi.
ℹ Victoria St ✆ (015394) 46499, windermeretic@southlakeland.gov.uk
Lake Windermere★★ – Brockhole National Park Centre★ **AC**, NW : 2 mi. by A 591

ENGLAND

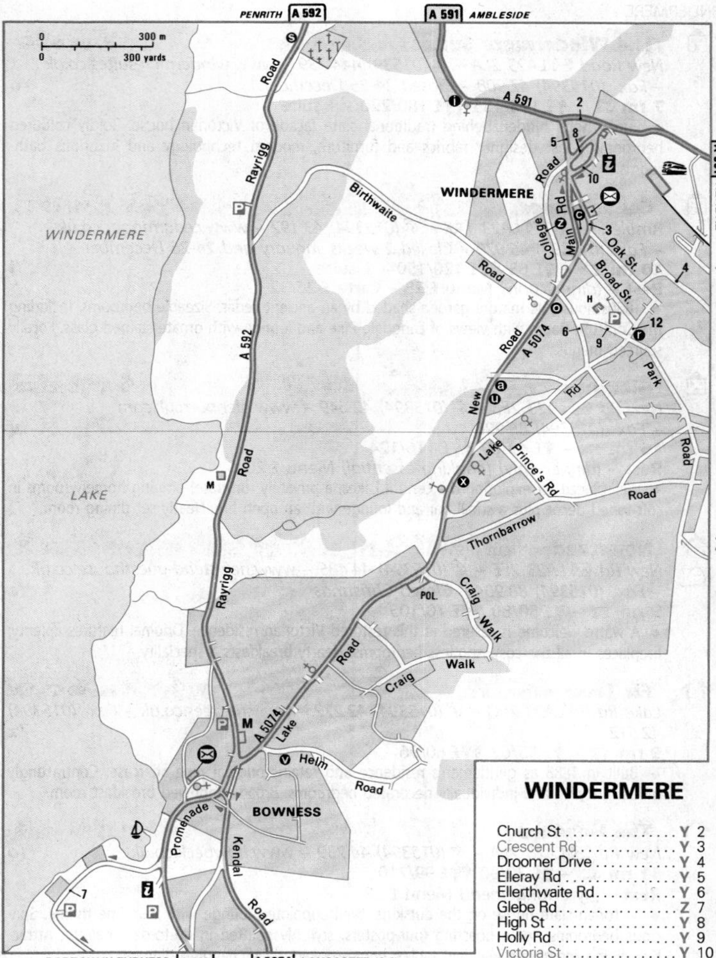

WINDERMERE

Church St . . . . Y 2
Crescent Rd . . . . Y 3
Droomer Drive . . . . Y 4
Elleray Rd . . . . Y 5
Ellerthwaite Rd . . . . Y 6
Glebe Rd . . . . Z 7
High St . . . . Y 8
Holly Rd . . . . Y 9
Victoria St . . . . Y 10
Woodland Rd . . . . Y 12

Holbeck Ghyll

Holbeck Lane, Northwest : 3.25 mi. by A 591 ✉ *LA23 1LU – ☎ (015394) 32 375 – www.holbeckghyll.com – Fax (015394) 34 743 – Closed 2 weeks early January*

27 rm (dinner included) – **†**£ 175/295 **††**£ 310/450 – 5 suites

Rest – *(booking essential at lunch)* Menu £ 30/53

Spec. Terrine of guinea fowl, leek and prune. Best end of lamb with olive gnocchi, confit peppers and aubergine. Spiced strawberry yoghurt cannelloni with vanilla cheesecake.

◆ Charming Victorian hunting lodge with pleasant gardens and stunning views. Individually decorated bedrooms combine country house style with a contemporary edge. Cooking is confident and precise; appealing menus are complemented by an exceptional wine list.

The Windermere Suites without rest

New Road ✉ LA23 2LA – ☎ (01539) 444 739 – www.windermeresuites.co.uk – Fax (015394) 47 908 – Closed 24-25 December Yo

7 rm – †£ 125/155 ††£ 180/220 – 1 suite

◆ Funky hotel hidden behind traditional slate façade of Victorian house. Boldly coloured bedrooms boast designer fabrics and furniture, modern technology and luxurious bathrooms.

Cedar Manor

Ambleside Rd ✉ LA23 1AX – ☎ (015394) 43 192 – www.cedarmanor.co.uk – Fax (015394) 45 970 – Closed 2 weeks January and 24-26 December

10 rm – †£ 63 ††£ 120/150 – 1 suite Yi

Rest – *(dinner only)* Menu £ 28 – Carte £ 26/32

◆ 1860s house, its mature garden shaded by an ancient cedar. Sizeable bedrooms, including the Coniston Room with views of Langdale Pike and lounge with ornate stained glass. Locally sourced menus.

Glenburn

New Rd ✉ LA23 2EE – ☎ (015394) 42 649 – www.glenburn.uk.com – Fax (015394) 88 998 Yu

16 rm – †£ 49/69 ††£ 116/124

Rest – *(dinner only) (booking essential)* Menu £ 20 **s**

◆ Well-placed for exploring the central Lakes, a privately run hotel offering homely rooms in soft-toned décor plus a small bar and lounge with an open fire. Neatly set dining room.

ENGLAND

Newstead without rest

New Rd ✉ LA23 2EE – ☎ (015394) 44 485 – www.newstead-guesthouse.co.uk – Fax (015394) 88 904 – Closed Christmas Ya

9 rm – †£ 50/80 ††£ 70/105

◆ A warm welcome is assured at this restored Victorian residence. Original features aplenty; fireplaces in all the cosy, spotless bedrooms. Hearty breakfasts a speciality.

Fir Trees without rest

Lake Rd ✉ LA23 2EQ – ☎ (015394) 42 272 – www.fir-trees.co.uk – Fax (015394) 42 512 Zx

9 rm – †£ 55/62 ††£ 80/96

◆ Built in 1888 as gentleman's residence and retains original pine staircase. Contrastingly modern, stylish and individually decorated bedrooms. Broad-windowed breakfast room.

The Howbeck

New Rd ✉ LA23 2LA – ☎ (015394) 44 739 – www.howbeck.co.uk Yo

11 rm – †£ 70/90 ††£ 99/210

Rest – *(by arrangement)* Menu £ 28

◆ Victorian slate house on the outskirts. Well appointed lounge with maritime theme. Spacious bedrooms, some boasting four-posters, stylishly painted in up-to-date palette. Attractive dining room with well-laid tables: home-cooked, daily changing dinners.

1 Park Rd

1 Park Rd ✉ LA23 2AN – ☎ (015394) 42 107 – www.1parkroad.com – Fax (015394) 48 997 – Closed Christmas Yr

6 rm – †£ 80/100 ††£ 100/120

Rest – *(by arrangement)* Menu £ 25

◆ Large lakeland property built in 1883, with relaxing guest lounge and piano; resident dog, Maggie, and well-equipped bedrooms (those on the top floor are the best). Fresh cooking served in modern dining room.

Miller Howe with rm

rest,

Rayrigg Rd ✉ LA23 1EY – ☎ (015394) 42 536 – www.millerhowe.com – Fax (015394) 45 664 – Closed 2 weeks January Ys

13 rm (dinner included) – †£ 80/150 ††£ 270/290 – 2 suites

Rest – *(booking essential)* Menu £ 24/40 – Carte £ 24/42

◆ Renowned, elegantly furnished lakeside villa with handsomely fitted rooms. Modern Italianate restaurant; distinct Northern character to classic, seasonal dishes. Smart bedrooms.

XX **Jerichos at the Waverley** with rm

College Rd ✉ LA23 1BX – ✆ (015394) 42 522 – www.jerichos.co.uk – Fax (015394) 88 899 – Closed 3 weeks mid-January, 1-15 November, 24-26 December, 1 January and Thursday Yz

10 rm – £ 40/65 £ 75/120 **Rest** – *(dinner only)* Carte £ 27/42

◆ Spacious dining room with eclectic, modern décor located in Victorian house full of period features, with cosy lounge. Seasonal menu makes good use of local produce. Comfortable, modern bedrooms; some with great views of the Lakes.

X **Francine's**

27 Main Rd ✉ LA23 1DX – ✆ (015394) 44 088 – www.francinesrestaurantwindermere.co.uk – Fax (015394) 44 088 – Closed 2 weeks end January, 2 weeks end November, 25-26 December, 1 January, dinner Sunday-Tuesday and Monday Yc

Rest – *(booking essential at dinner)* Menu £ 18 (dinner) – Carte approx. £ 48

◆ Unpretentious bistro/coffee house with light décor, well-spaced tables and an informal feel, offers traditional French-influenced cooking. Eponymous owner bakes the cakes.

If you are looking for particularly pleasant accommodation, book a hotel shown in red : ...

at Bowness-on-Windermere South : 1 mi. - Z - ✉ Windermere

Gilpin Lodge

Crook Rd, Southeast : 2.5 mi. by A 5074 on B 5284 ✉ LA23 3NE – ✆ (015394) 88 818 – www.gilpinlodge.co.uk – Fax (015394) 88 058

20 rm (dinner included) – £ 185/220 £ 440

Rest – *(booking essential for non-residents)* Menu £ 28/53 – Carte lunch £ 25/39

◆ Extended country house with comfortable, very English sitting room and delightful Oriental bar and terrace. Most bedrooms have contemporary décor; private hot tubs in Garden suites. Four individually styled dining rooms. Cooking combines classic technique and modern influences.

Linthwaite House

Crook Rd, South : 0.75 mi. by A 5074 on B 5284 ✉ LA23 3JA – ✆ (015394) 88 600 – www.linthwaite.com – Fax (015394) 88 601

31 rm (dinner included) – £ 184/260 £ 204/370

Rest – *(closed Monday lunch)* Menu £ 22/50 **s**

◆ Set in superb elevated position with stunning views of Lake Windermere. Chic, modern rooms. Cane chairs and louvred blinds give conservatory teas an almost colonial feel. Refined modern cooking in restaurant boasting vast mirror collection!

Lindeth Howe

Lindeth Drive, Longtail Hill, South : 1.25 mi. by A 592 off B 5284 ✉ LA23 3JF – ✆ (015394) 45 759 – www.lindeth-howe.co.uk – Fax (015394) 46 368 – Closed 3-14 January

34 rm – £ 75/128 £ 250 – 1 suite

Rest ***The Dining Room*** – *(light lunch Monday-Saturday)* Menu £ 40 – Carte £ 30/46

◆ Once owned by Beatrix Potter, this extended and updated house surveys a broad sweep of Lakeland scenery from its upper floors. Mix of bedroom styles; modernisation under way. Large, formal dining room with garden views.

Storrs Hall

South : 2 mi. on A 592 ✉ LA23 3LG – ✆ (015394) 47 111 – www.elh.co.uk – Fax (015394) 47 555

29 rm – £ 122 £ 328 – 1 suite

Rest ***The Terrace*** – Menu £ 20/43 **s** – Carte £ 44/51 **s**

◆ Oils, antiques and fine fabrics fill an elegant Georgian mansion. Traditional orangery, 19C bar in dark wood and stained glass and comfortable, individually decorated rooms. Ornate dining room overlooks lawns and lake.

ENGLAND

Fayrer Garden House rest,
Lyth Valley Rd, South : 1 mi. on A 5074 ✉ LA23 3JP – ☎ (015394) 88 195 – www.fayrergarden.com – Fax (015394) 45 986 – Closed first 2 weeks January
28 rm (dinner included) – ♦£ 75/148 ♦♦£ 280/300
Rest *The Terrace* – *(dinner only) (booking essential for non-residents)* Menu £ 40
◆ Extensive house with five acres of grounds and beautiful gardens. Clubby bar and pleasantly homely lounge. Cosy rooms show the owners' feel for thoughtful detail. Wonderful views to be gained from The Terrace.

Angel Inn rest,
Helm Rd ✉ LA23 3BU – ☎ (015394) 44 080 – www.the-angelinn.com – Fax (015394) 46 003 – Closed 25 December Z**v**
14 rm – ♦£ 65/110 ♦♦£ 90/180 **Rest** – Carte £ 20/33
◆ Homely, good-sized rooms in an enlarged early 18C cottage, set in a secluded spot yet close to town. Cosy, unpretentious bar, its armchairs centred on an open fire. Dining room has columned archway and landscape murals.

Low House
South : 1 mi. by A 5074 and B 5284 on Heathwaite rd ✉ LA23 3NA – ☎ (015394) 43 156 – www.lowhouse.co.uk – Closed Christmas
3 rm – ♦£ 40/60 ♦♦£ 100/120 **Rest** – *(by arrangement)* Menu £ 30
◆ Charming 17C country house with fine furnishings, log burner, organic breakfasts and welcoming feel. Bedrooms boast top comforts and one can borrow the boat or the Bentley.

Fair Rigg without rest
Ferry View, South : 0.5 mi. on A 5074 ✉ LA23 3JB – ☎ (015394) 43 941 – www.fairrigg.co.uk – Closed 2 January-11 February
6 rm – ♦£ 45/55 ♦♦£ 60/90
◆ 19C property with pleasing views over the lake to the hills. Hearty Cumbrian breakfasts guaranteed, accompanied by the fine vista. Original fireplaces enhance comfy rooms.

ENGLAND

at Troutbeck North : 4 mi. by A 592 - Y – ✉ Windermere

The Queen's Head with rm
North : 0.75 mi. on A 592 ✉ LA23 1PW – ☎ (01539) 432 174 – www.queensheadhotel.com – Fax (01539) 431 938
15 rm – ♦£ 110/140 ♦♦£ 110/140 **Rest** – Menu £ 20 – Carte £ 25/38
◆ Atmospheric pub with Elizabethan details, set amongst Lakeland scenery. Wide ranging menu features traditional, wholesome cooking and a delicious assortment of homemade bread. Two bedrooms have great fell views.

at Winster South : 4 mi. on A 5074 – ✉ Windermere

Brown Horse Inn with rm
on A 5074 ✉ LA23 3NR – ☎ (01539) 443 443 – www.thebrownhorseinn.co.uk
9 rm – ♦£ 35/45 ♦♦£ 80/90 **Rest** – Carte £ 20/30
◆ Traditional 1850s coaching inn with real fires and candlelit tables. Robust, flavourful dishes classically prepared with prime local produce. Wine tastings and race nights. Light modern bedrooms are simply decorated yet comfortable.

WINDLESHAM – Surrey – 504 S29 – pop. 4 103 **7** C1

London 40 mi. – Reading 18 mi. – Southampton 53 mi.

The Bee
School Rd ✉ GU20 6PD – ☎ (01276) 479 244 – www.thebeepub.co.uk – Closed Sunday dinner
Rest – Menu £ 16 (weekday lunch) – Carte £ 20/35
◆ Stylish, modern pub with buzzing atmosphere. Daily changing menus showcase seasonal, local produce in precisely cooked dishes. Good value two course lunch. Summer barbecues.

The Brickmakers

Chertsey Rd, East : 1 mi. on B 386 ✉ GU20 6HT
– ☎ (01276) 472 267 – www.thebrickmakerswindlesham.co.uk
– Fax (01276) 451 014
Rest – Carte £ 20/30
◆ Red-brick pub with restaurant, conservatory and sizeable garden. Straightforward bar dishes or more substantial à la carte; all well-cooked and full of flavour.

WINDSOR – Windsor and Maidenhead – 504 S29 – pop. 30 568 — 11 D3

Great Britain

London 28 mi. – Reading 19 mi. – Southampton 59 mi.
to Marlow, Maidenhead and Cookham (Salter Bros. Ltd) (summer only)
The Old Booking Hall, Central Station, Thames St ☎ (01753) 743900, windsor.tic@rbwm.gov.uk
Town★ – Castle★★★ : St George's Chapel★★★ **AC** (stalls★★★), State Apartments★★ **AC**, North Terrace (≤★★) Z – Eton College★★ **AC** (College Chapel★★, Wall paintings★) Z
Windsor Park★ **AC** Y

Plan on next page

The Mercure Castle

18 High St ✉ SL4 1LJ – ☎ (01753) 851 577
– www.mercure.com – Fax (01753) 856 930
– Closed 25 December Z**c**
106 rm – †£ 310 ††£ 310 – 2 suites
Rest *18* – Carte £ 19/33
◆ Former inn built by monks, now a terraced property with Georgian façade. Décor in traditional style. Modern rooms in converted stables, more characterful ones in old building. Very comfortable 18 with modern menus.

Sir Christopher Wren's House

rest,
Thames St ✉ SL4 1PX – ☎ (01753) 861 354
– www.sirchristopherwren.co.uk – Fax (01753) 442 490 Z**e**
93 rm – †£ 80/230 ††£ 85/230, £ 11.50 – 2 suites
Rest *Strok's* – Menu £ 29 (lunch) **s** – Carte £ 36/55 **s**
◆ Built by Wren as his family home in 1676, he supposedly haunts his old rooms. On banks of Thames close to station and Windsor Castle. Antique furnished in original building. Restaurant has views of Thames and elegant dining terrace.

Royal Adelaide

46 Kings Rd ✉ SL4 2AG – ☎ (01753) 863 916 – www.theroyaladelaide.com
– Fax (01753) 830 682 Z**v**
42 rm – †£ 69/145 ††£ 89/199
Rest – Carte £ 16/28
◆ Three adjoining Georgian houses with light blue painted façade. Just outside town centre. Rooms vary in shapes and sizes, all in individual traditional style. Dining room offers daily changing, international menus.

The Christopher

110 High St, Eton ✉ SL4 6AN – ☎ (01753) 852 359 – www.thechristopher.co.uk
– Fax (01753) 830 914 Z**a**
33 rm – †£ 113/174 ††£ 149/174, £ 12
Rest – Carte £ 20/26
◆ Refurbished 17C former coaching inn close to Eton College and perfect for walking to the castle. Contemporary bedrooms split between main building and mews annex. Simple homecooking.

Windsor Grill

65 St Leonards Rd ✉ SL4 3BX – ☎ (01753) 859 658
– www.awtrestaurants.com Z**x**
Rest – Beef specialities – Carte £ 21/46
◆ Rustic Victorian property owned by Antony Worrall Thompson. Wide menu displays classic comfort dishes, including well flavoured hung beef and pork/chicken from his farm.

ENGLAND

WINDSOR

Bexley St	Z	2
Bolton Rd	Y	3
Castle Hill	Z	4
Charles St.	Z	5
Claremont Rd.	Z	6
Clarence Crescent	Z	7
Clewer Crescent Rd	Z	8
Datchet Rd	Z	9
Goswell Rd	Z	10
Grove Rd	Z	12
High St	Z	13
High St DATCHET	Y	14
Horton Rd	Y	16
Keats Lane	Z	17
King Edward Court Centre	Z	
Peascod St	Z	19
Ragstone Rd	Y	20
River St.	Z	21
Sheet St Rd	Y	22
Stovell Rd.	Z	23
Thames Ave	Z	24
Thames St	Z	25
Trinity Pl.	Z	27
Windsor Bridge	Z	28
Windsor Rd	Y	29

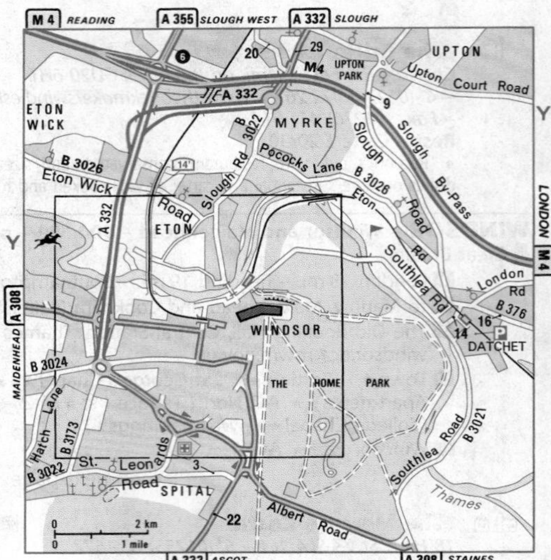

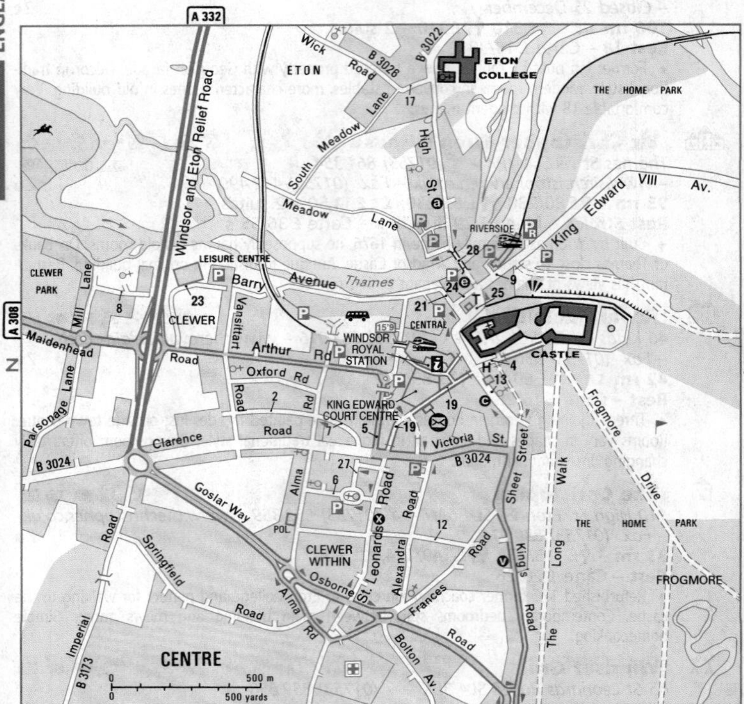

CENTRE

ENGLAND

WINEHAM – W. Sussex – **504** T31 – **see Henfield**

WINFORTON – County of Herefordshire – **503** L27 – **see Hereford**

WINGHAM – Kent – **504** X30 – **pop. 1 618** **9** D2

London 67 mi. – Canterbury 7 mi. – Dover 16 mi.

at Goodnestone South : 2 mi. by B 2046 – ✉ Wingham

The Fitzwalter Arms

The Street ✉ CT3 1PJ – ℘ (01304) 840 303 – www.thefitzwalterarms.co.uk – Closed 25 December, 1 January, Sunday dinner and Tuesday

Rest – Carte £ 16/28

◆ Striking brick pub with castellated exterior and mullioned windows. Darts, billiards and open fire in characterful beamed bar create feel of village local. Large beer garden.

WINSFORD – Somerset – **503** J30 – **pop. 270** – ✉ Minehead **3** A2

London 194 mi. – Exeter 31 mi. – Minehead 10 mi. – Taunton 32 mi.

Village★

Exmoor National Park★★

Karslake House

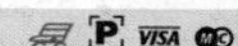

Halse Lane ✉ TA24 7JE – ℘ (01643) 851 242 – www.karslakehouse.co.uk – Fax (01643) 851 242 – Closed February to Easter and 1 week Christmas

6 rm – †£ 90 ††£ 130

Rest – *(Closed Sunday-Monday) (dinner only)* Menu £ 33

◆ Personally run 15C malthouse with lovely gardens and immaculate, thoughtfully styled bedrooms. Good home-cooked fare on daily changing menu, with fine use of local produce.

The Royal Oak Inn with rm

Exmoor National Park ✉ TA24 7JE – ℘ (01643) 851 455 – www.royaloakexmoor.co.uk

8 rm – †£ 70 ††£ 150 **Rest** – Menu £ 25 (dinner) – Carte £ 18/28

◆ Delightful 12C thatched pub set by a ford in a picturesque Exmoor village. Arriving exactly as described, British dishes use homemade, local and seasonal produce. Smart, individually styled bedrooms; private in-room therapy treatments available.

WINSTER – Cumbria – **502** L20 – **see Windermere**

WINSTER – Derbyshire – **502** P24 – **pop. 1 787** **16** A1

London 153 mi. – Derby 25 mi. – Matlock 4 mi.

The Dower House without rest

Main St ✉ DE4 2DH – ℘ (01629) 650 931 – www.thedowerhousewinster.com – Fax (01629) 650 391 – Closed Christmas and New Year

3 rm – †£ 70/75 ††£ 95/100

◆ Attractive stone house dating from 16C, with lovely walled garden, cosy lounge and spacious, well-kept bedrooms; choose the four poster for its view of the historic village.

WINTERBOURNE STEEPLETON – Dorset – **503** M31 – **see Dorchester**

WINTERINGHAM – North Lincolnshire – **502** S22 – **pop. 4 714** **23** C3 – ✉ Scunthorpe

London 176 mi. – Kingston-upon-Hull 16 mi. – Sheffield 67 mi.

Winteringham Fields with rm

1 Silver St ✉ DN15 9ND – ℘ (01724) 733 096 – www.winteringhamfields.com – Fax (01724) 733 898 – Closed 3 weeks August and Christmas

8 rm – †£ 115/160 ††£ 155/220, £ 20 – 2 suites

Rest – *(closed Sunday-Monday) (booking essential for non-residents)* Menu £ 40 – Carte approx. £ 75

◆ 16C house with beamed ceilings, and original range with fire. Cosy, cottagey atmosphere. Carefully executed menu, served in choice of dining rooms. Characterful bedrooms.

ENGLAND

WITNEY – Oxfordshire – 503 P28 – pop. 22 765 10 B2

London 69 mi. – Gloucester 39 mi. – Oxford 13 mi.

Town Centre Shop, 3 Welch Way ✆ (01993) 775802, witney.vic@westoxon.gov.uk

The Fleece with rm

11 Church Green ✉ OX28 4AZ – ✆ (01993) 892 270 – www.fleecewitney.co.uk – Closed 25 December

10 rm – †£ 80 ††£ 90

Rest – Menu £ 16 (lunch) – Carte £ 18/30

◆ Smart Georgian pub with worthy values, set overlooking the green. Using local, seasonal, free range produce, menus offer a choice of dish size and appealing 'create your own' deli boards. Bedrooms are bright, modern and spacious.

at North Leigh Northeast : 3 mi. by A 4095 – ✉ Oxfordshire

Gorselands Hall without rest

Boddington Lane, North : 0.75 mi. by A 4095 on East End rd ✉ OX29 6PU – ✆ (01993) 882 292 – www.gorselandshall.com – Fax (01993) 881 895 – Closed 25-26 December and New Year

6 rm – †£ 42/50 ††£ 68

◆ Spacious house in countryside setting, halfway between Woodstock and Witney. Sitting room with French windows, snooker table, books and games. Neat bedrooms in uniform style.

ENGLAND

at South Leigh Southeast : 3 mi. by A 40 – ✉ Witney

Mason Arms

✉ OX29 6XN – ✆ (01993) 702 485 – Closed August, 4 days Christmas, Sunday dinner and Monday

Rest – Carte £ 29/65

◆ Privately owned 15C thatched inn with unique style and much individuality. Dimly lit, with intimate atmosphere. French influenced traditional cooking and extensive wine list.

The sun's out? Then enjoy eating outside on the terrace:

WIVETON – Norfolk – see Blakeney

WOBURN – Bedfordshire – 504 S28 – pop. 1 534 – ✉ Milton Keynes 12 A2

Great Britain

London 49 mi. – Bedford 13 mi. – Luton 13 mi. – Northampton 24 mi.

Woburn Abbey★★

Inn at Woburn rm, rest,

George St ✉ MK17 9PX – ✆ (01525) 290 441 – www.theinnatwoburn.com – Fax (01525) 290 432

52 rm – †£ 115/165 ††£ 135/165 – 5 suites

Rest *Olivier's* – *(closed Sunday lunch)* Menu £ 15 (lunch) – Carte dinner £ 21/35

◆ 18C coaching inn, part of Woburn Estate with its abbey and 3000 acre park. Pleasant modern furnishings and interior décor. Tastefully decorated rooms: book a Cottage suite. Classic dishes in contemporary Olivier's.

The Birch

20 Newport Rd, North : 0.5 mi. on A 5130 ✉ MK17 9HX – ✆ (01525) 290 295 – www.birchwoburn.com – Fax (01525) 290 899 – Closed 25-26 December, 1 January and Sunday dinner

Rest – *(booking essential)* Carte £ 28/37

◆ Smart, well run pub whose traditional façade masks a bright, modern interior with contemporary furnishings. Menu offers old favourites, daily specials and grills by the ounce.

at Milton Bryan Southeast : 2.5 mi. by A 4012 – ✉ Woburn

The Red Lion

Toddington Rd ✉ MK17 9HS – ✆ (01525) 210 044 – www.redlion-miltonbryan.co.uk – Closed 25-26 December, 1 January and Monday in winter

Rest – Carte £ 22/29

◆ Smart red-brick country pub with pleasant terrace and beautiful hanging baskets. Traditional menus feature quality produce from local artisan suppliers and fish from the Brixham day boats.

Don't confuse the couvert rating with the stars!
Couverts defines comfort and service, while stars are awarded for the best cuisine across all categories of comfort.

WOLD NEWTON – East Riding of Yorkshire

23 D2

London 229 mi. – Bridlington 25 mi. – Scarborough 13 mi.

Wold Cottage without rest

South : 0.5 mi. on Thwing rd ✉ YO25 3HL – ✆ (01262) 470 696 – www.woldcottage.com – Fax (01262) 470 696 – Closed Christmas

5 rm – £ 60 £ 120

◆ Georgian former farmhouse set in many rural acres; a country house style prevails with antique furniture in all areas. Spacious, individually named rooms: two in barn annex.

WOLSINGHAM – Durham – 502 O19 – pop. 2 020

24 A3

London 269 mi. – Newcastle upon Tyne 38 mi. – Sunderland 30 mi. – Middlesbrough 34 mi.

The Mill Race

✉ DL13 3AP – ✆ (01388) 526 551 – www.themillracehotel.co.uk – Closed 26 December, 1 January, Monday and Sunday dinner

Rest – *(dinner only and lunch Friday and Sunday)* Menu £ 16 (dinner) – Carte £ 20/35

◆ Situated in centre of picturesque town; the gateway to Weardale. Well-presented, flavourful restaurant-style dishes. Good value fixed price menu midweek and early Saturday evenings.

WOLVERCOTE – Oxfordshire – 504 Q28 – see Oxford

WOLVERHAMPTON – West Midlands – 502 N26 – pop. 251 462

19 C2

London 132 mi. – Birmingham 15 mi. – Liverpool 89 mi. – Shrewsbury 30 mi.

18 Queen Sq ✆ (01902) 312051, visitorinfo@wolverhampton.gov.uk

Plan of Enlarged Area : see Birmingham pp. 4 and 5

Plans on following pages

Novotel rm,

Union St ✉ WV1 3JN – ✆ (01902) 871 100 – www.novotel.com – Fax (01902) 870 054

Ba

132 rm – £ 49/125 £ 49/125, £ 13

Rest *Elements* – Carte £ 24/38 **s**

◆ Conveniently located in the centre of town near to train station. Purpose-built lodge hotel with well fitted modern furnishings. Suitable for business and leisure stopovers. Large windows give bright feel to restaurant.

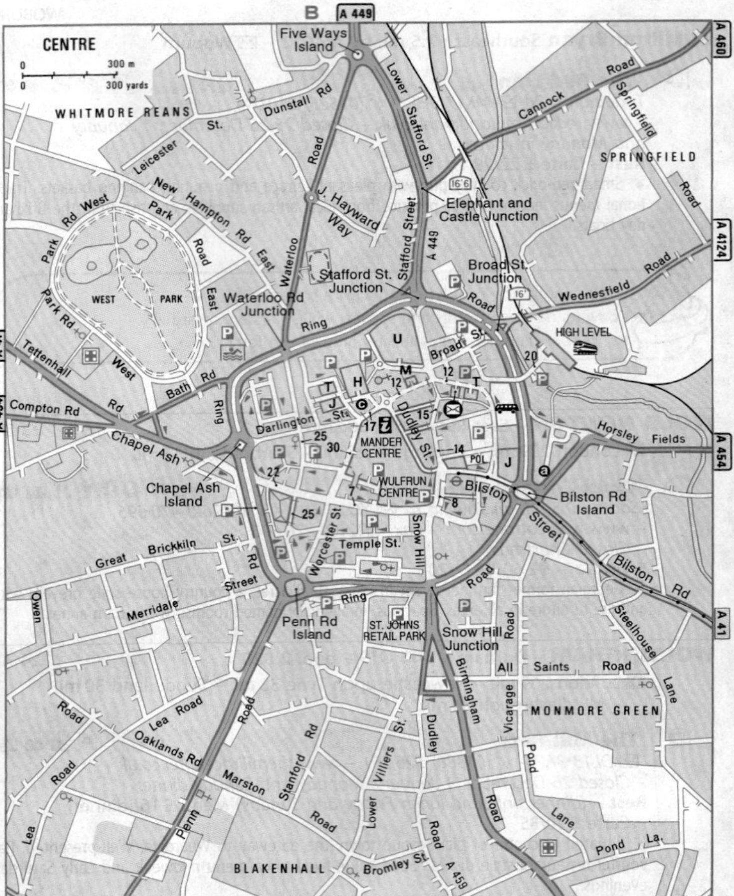

ENGLAND

CENTRE

0 300 m
0 300 yards

B A 449 A 460 A 4124 A 41 A 454 A 4123 B A 449

Five Ways Island
WHITMORE REANS
Dunstall Rd
Lower Stafford St.
Cannock Road
Springfield Road
SPRINGFIELD
Leicester St.
New Hampton Rd East
Park Rd West
J. Hayward Way
Elephant and Castle Junction
Stafford Street
WEST PARK
Waterloo Road
Stafford St. Junction
Broad St. Junction
Wednesfield Road
Waterloo Rd Junction
Ring
Broad St.
HIGH LEVEL
Park Rd West
Tettenhall Rd
Bath Rd
Ring
U H M T T
Darlington St.
Dudley St.
MANDER CENTRE
WULFRUN CENTRE
Compton Rd
Chapel Ash
Chapel Ash Island
Horsley Fields
POL
Bilston Street
Bilston Rd Island
Bilston Rd
Great Brickkiln St.
Worcester St.
Temple St.
Snow Hill
Ring Rd
Ring
Merridale Street
Penn Rd Island
ST. JOHNS RETAIL PARK
Snow Hill Junction
Road
Steelhouse Lane
Owen Road
All Saints Road
Birmingham Road
Vicarage Road
MONMORE GREEN
Lea Road
Oaklands Rd
Penn Road
Stanford Rd
Villiers St.
Dudley Road
Pond Lane
Marston Road
Lower Road
Lea Road
BLAKENHALL
Bromley St.
A 459
Pond La.

Bilash

No 2 Cheapside ✉ WV1 1TU
– ✆ (01902) 427 762
– www.thebilash@co.uk
– Fax (01902) 311 991
– Closed 25-26 December and Sunday Bc

Rest – Indian – Menu £ 12 (lunch) – Carte £ 28/41

◆ In a pleasant square, and easily identified by its bright yellow façade and modish interior. Family owned; well established, locally renowned Indian/Bangladeshi cooking.

Fancy a last minute break?
Check hotel websites to take advantage of price promotions.

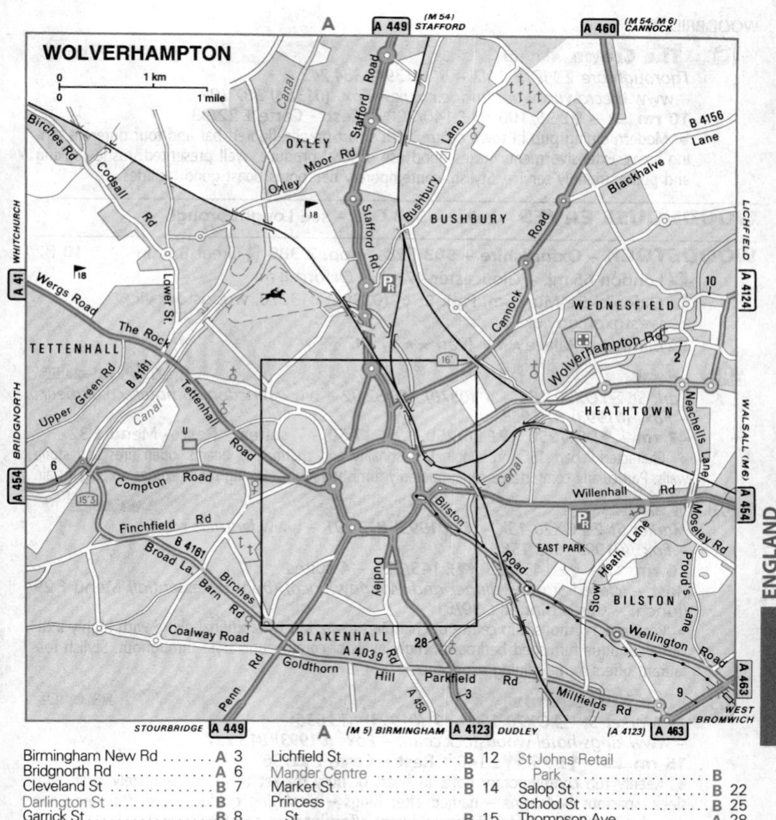

Birmingham New Rd	A 3	Lichfield St	B 12	St Johns Retail Park	B
Bridgnorth Rd	A 6	Mander Centre	B	Salop St	B 22
Cleveland St	B 7	Market St	B 14	School St	B 25
Darlington St	B	Princess St	B 15	Thompson Ave	A 28
Garrick St	B 8	Queen Square	B 17	Victoria St	B 30
High St	A 9	Railway Drive	B 20	Wulfrun Centre	B
Lichfield Rd	A 10				

WOOBURN COMMON – Bucks. – see Beaconsfield

WOODBRIDGE – Suffolk – 504 X27 – pop. 10 956 15 D3

London 81 mi. – Great Yarmouth 45 mi. – Ipswich 8 mi. – Norwich 47 mi.

Cretingham Grove Farm, ✆ (01728) 685 275

Seckford Great Bealings Seckford Hall Rd, ✆ (01394) 388 000

Seckford Hall

rm, rest, VISA AE

Southwest : 1.25 mi. by A 12 ✉ IP13 6NU – ✆ (01394) 385 678 – www.seckford.co.uk – Fax (01394) 380 610 – Closed 25 December

25 rm – †£ 80/90 ††£ 120/190, ☕ £ 13.95 – 7 suites

Rest – *(Closed Monday lunch)* Menu £ 17/33 **s**

◆ Reputedly once visited by Elizabeth I, a part Tudor country house set in attractive gardens. Charming traditionally panelled public areas. Comfortable bedrooms. Local lobster proudly served in smart dining room.

The Riverside

VISA AE

Quayside ✉ IP12 1BH – ✆ (01394) 382 587 – www.theriverside.co.uk – Fax (01394) 382 656 – Closed 25-26 December, 1 January and Sunday dinner

Rest – *(booking essential)* Menu £ 30 (dinner) – Carte £ 26/41

◆ Not just a restaurant, but a cinema too! Floor to ceiling windows and busy terrace. Appealing menus offer modern, well-presented cooking. Set menu includes ticket for film.

The Crown with rm

Thoroughfare ✉ IP12 1AD – ✆ (01394) 384 242 – www.thecrownatwoodbridge.co.uk – Fax (01384) 387 192

10 rm ☕ – 🚹£ 95/100 🚹🚹£ 140/200 **Rest** – Carte £ 22/38

◆ Modern dining pub in town centre, with smart granite-floored bar and four different dining areas. Extensive menu makes good use of local produce. Well presented, rustic cooking and polite, friendly service. Stylish, contemporary bedrooms boast good facilities.

WOODHOUSE EAVES – Leics. – 503 Q25 – see Loughborough

WOODSTOCK – Oxfordshire – 503 P28 – pop. 2 389 Great Britain 10 B2

London 65 mi. – Gloucester 47 mi. – Oxford 8 mi.

Oxfordshire Museum, Park St ✆ (01993) 813276, woodstock.vic@westoxon.gov.uk

Blenheim Palace★★★ (Park★★★) **AC**

Bear

rm, VISA AE

Park St ✉ OX20 1SZ – ✆ (0870) 400 82 02 – www.macdonald-hotels.co.uk/bear – Fax (01993) 810 968

47 rm – 🚹£ 86/250 🚹🚹£ 86/250, ☕ £ 17.50 – 7 suites **Rest** – Menu £ 32

◆ Characterful part 16C inn. Original personality and charm; oak beams, open fires and stone walls. Particularly comfortable contemporarily furnished rooms. Dining room exudes an elegant air.

Feathers

VISA AE

Market St ✉ OX20 1SX – ✆ (01993) 812 291 – www.feathers.co.uk – Fax (01993) 813 158

16 rm ☕ – 🚹£ 145/225 🚹🚹£ 145/225 – 4 suites

Rest – *(closed Sunday dinner and Monday lunch) (booking essential)* Menu £ 29 (lunch) – Carte dinner £ 39/51

◆ Restored 17C houses in centre of charming town. Much traditional allure with highly individual, antique furnished bedrooms. High levels of comfort and style throughout. Stylish restaurant offers formal dining experience.

The Kings Arms

VISA AE

19 Market St ✉ OX20 1SU – ✆ (01993) 813 636 – www.kings-hotel-woodstock.co.uk – Fax (01993) 813 737

15 rm ☕ – 🚹£ 75 🚹🚹£ 140 **Rest** – Carte £ 22/36

◆ Keenly run contemporary hotel in heart of busy market town. Immaculately kept, with sleek, spacious bedrooms – named after Kings – displaying golden wood, starched linen and plump cushions. Informal bar-restaurant offers local, seasonal British dishes.

WOOFFERTON – Shrops. – see Ludlow

WOOKEY HOLE – Somerset – 503 L30 – see Wells

WOOLACOMBE – Devon – 503 H30 2 C1

London 237 mi. – Barnstaple 15 mi. – Exeter 55 mi.

The Esplanade ✆ (01271) 870553, info@woolacombetourism.co.uk

Exmoor National Park★★ - Mortehoe★★ (St Mary's Church★, Morte Point - vantage point★) N : 0.5 mi. – Ilfracombe : Hillsborough (≤★★) **AC**, Capstone Hill★ (≤★), St Nicholas' Chapel (≤★) **AC**, NE : 5.5 mi. by B 3343 and A 361. Braunton★ (St Brannock's Church★, Braunton Burrows★), S : 8 mi. by B 3343 and A 361

at Mortehoe North : 0.5 mi. – ✉ Woolacombe

Cleeve House

rm, VISA

✉ EX34 7ED – ✆ (01271) 870 719 – www.cleevehouse.co.uk – Fax (01271) 870 719 – April-October

6 rm ☕ – 🚹£ 58/60 🚹🚹£ 86/90

Rest – *(by arrangement)* Menu £ 22 – Carte £ 25/33

◆ Bright and welcoming feel in décor and atmosphere. Very comfortable lounge and individually styled bedrooms with co-ordinated fabrics. Rear rooms with great country views. Neat dining room; walls hung with local artwork.

ENGLAND

WOOLAVINGTON – Somerset – 503 L30 – see Bridgwater

WOOLER – Northumberland – 502 N17 – pop. 1 857 — 24 A1

London 330 mi. – Alnwick 17 mi. – Berwick-on-Tweed 17 mi.

Firwood without rest

Middleton Hall, South : 1.75 mi. by Earle rd on Middleton Hall rd ✉ NE71 6RD – ✆ (01668) 283 699 – www.firwoodhouse.co.uk – Closed December-January

3 rm – †£ 60/70 ††£ 85

◆ 19C former hunting lodge with beautiful tiled hall, set in tranquil spot overlooking the Cheviots. Comfy bay-windowed guest areas great for sighting red squirrels/wild birds. Spacious bedrooms.

WOOLHAMPTON – West Berkshire – 503 Q29 Great Britain — 10 B3

London 56 mi. – Newbury 8 mi. – Thatcham 4 mi.

Basildon Park★, NE : 10 mi. by A 4, A 340 and A 417

The Angel

Bath Rd ✉ RG7 5RT – ✆ (0118) 971 3307 – www.thea4angel.com – Closed 25-26 December and Sunday dinner

Rest – Carte £ 21/26

◆ Ivy-covered pub with distinctive interior of hanging hops, rows of jars and a ceiling lined with wine bottles. Hearty cooking; lunchtime sandwiches; more varied à la carte.

WOOLHOPE – County of Herefordshire — 18 B3

London 138 mi. – Birmingham 70 mi. – Bristol 66 mi. – Coventry 81 mi.

The Butchers Arms

✉ HR1 4RF – ✆ (01432) 860 281 – www.butchersarmswoolhope.co.uk – Closed 2 weeks January, Sunday dinner and Monday except Bank Holidays

Rest – English – Carte £ 21/25

◆ Stephen Bull's third pub in the area is an attractive 16C inn by a brook with a pretty garden. Charming bars with beams and open fires and a more formal dining room. Honest, well-priced, regional cooking; local lamb and cheese the highlights.

WOOLSTHORPE-BY-BELVOIR – Lincs. – 502 R25 – see Grantham

WORCESTER – Worcestershire – 503 N27 – pop. 94 029 Great Britain — 18 B3

London 124 mi. – Birmingham 26 mi. – Bristol 61 mi. – Cardiff 74 mi.

The Guildhall, High St ✆ (01905) 726311, touristinfo@cityofworcester.gov.uk

Perdiswell Park Bilford Rd, ✆ (01905) 754 668

City★ – Cathedral★★ – Royal Worcester Porcelain Works★ (Museum of Worcester Porcelain★) M

The Elgar Trail★

Plan on next page

Glasshouse

Sidbury ✉ WR1 2HU – ✆ (01905) 611 120 – www.theglasshouse.co.uk – Closed Sunday dinner — a

Rest – Menu £ 15 (lunch) – Carte £ 30/43

◆ Leather furnished lounge. Stylish chocolate and blue hued dining areas; the first floor has glass wall and views of city. Brasserie style menu offers modern British dishes.

Brown's

24 Quay St ✉ WR1 2JJ – ✆ (01905) 26 263 – www.brownsrestaurant.co.uk – Fax (01905) 25 768 – Closed 26 December, 1 January and Sunday dinner

Rest – Menu £ 15 (lunch) – Carte £ 36/49 — x

◆ Converted riverside corn mill. Spacious, open interior as befits the building's origins. Impressive collection of modern artwork. Mainly British dishes are renowned locally.

ENGLAND

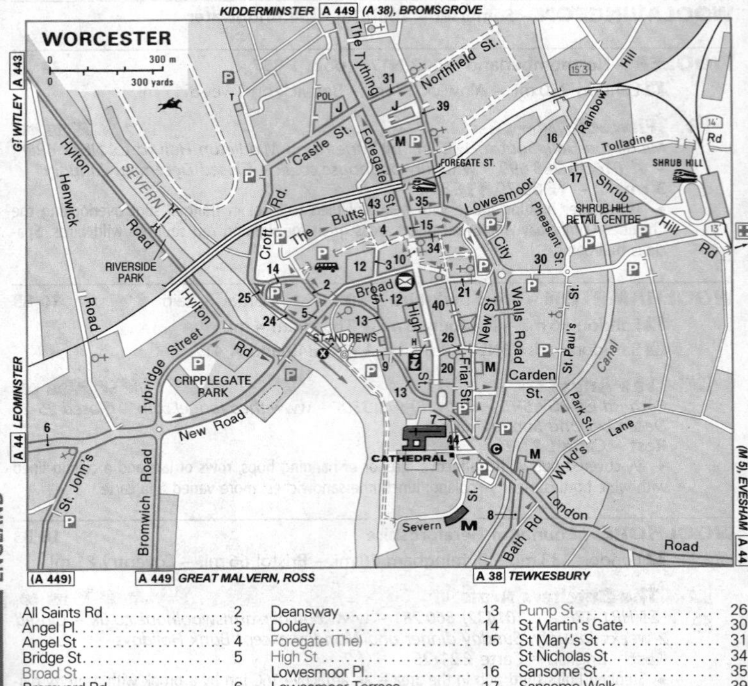

at Bransford West : 4 mi. by A 44 on A 4103 – ✉ Worcester

Bear and Ragged Staff
Station Rd, Southeast : 0.5 mi. on Powick rd ✉ WR6 5JH – ☎ (01886) 833 399 – www.bear.uk.com – Fax (01886) 833 106 – Closed dinner 25 December and 1 January, Monday in winter and dinner Sunday
Rest – Menu £ 15 (Tuesday-Saturday lunch) – Carte £ 20/30
◆ Traditional inn on quiet country lane; its front dominated by two oak trees. Bar menu of pub classics; more substantial dishes in linen-clad dining room. Vegetables from kitchen garden.

WORFIELD – **Shrops.** – **see Bridgnorth**

WORKSOP – **Nottinghamshire** – **502** Q24 – **pop. 39 072** **16** B1

London 160 mi. – Sheffield 20 mi. – Nottingham 37 mi. – Rotherham 17 mi.

Browns without rest
The Old Orchard Cottage, Holbeck Lane, Southwest : 4.5 mi. by A 60 ✉ S80 3NF – ☎ (01909) 720 659 – www.brownsholbeck.co.uk – Fax (01909) 720 659 – Closed Christmas
3 rm – †£ 57/65 ††£ 84
◆ Cosy, comfortable, individually-decorated bedrooms in cottage dating from 1730 and named after the owners. Mature orchard and tranquil garden. Comprehensive breakfast.

WORTH – **Kent** – **504** Y30 – **see Deal**

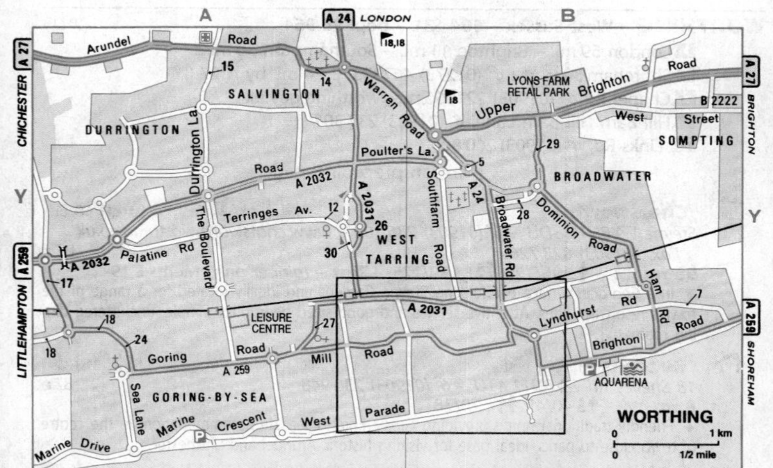

A
B
Y
A 24 LONDON
A 27 CHICHESTER
A 27 BRIGHTON
A 259 LITTLEHAMPTON
A 259 SHOREHAM
Arundel Road
SALVINGTON
DURRINGTON
Durrington La.
Warren Road
LYONS FARM RETAIL PARK
Upper Brighton Road
B 2222
West Street
SOMPTING
Poulter's La.
BROADWATER
Road
A 2032
A 2031
Southfarm Road
A 24
Broadwater Rd
Dominion Road
Terringes Av.
WEST TARRING
Palatine Rd
The Boulevard
A 2032
Ham Rd
Lyndhurst Rd
A 2031
LEISURE CENTRE
Goring Road
A 259
Mill Road
Brighton Road
AQUARENA
GORING-BY-SEA
Sea Lane
Marine Crescent
West Parade
Marine Drive
WORTHING
0 1 km
0 1/2 mile

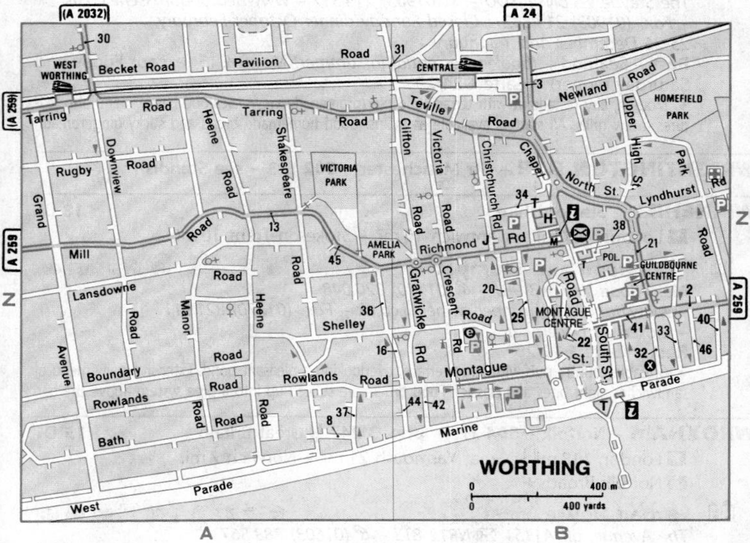
(A 2032)
A 24
A 259
A 259
A 259
N
WEST WORTHING
Becket Road
Pavilion Road
CENTRAL
Newland Road
HOMEFIELD PARK
Tarring Road
Tarring Road
Teville Road
Heene Road
Downview Road
Rugby
Shakespeare
VICTORIA PARK
Clifton Road
Victoria Road
Christchurch Rd
Chapel Road
North St.
Upper High St.
Park Rd
Lyndhurst Rd
Grand Avenue
Mill Road
AMELIA PARK
Richmond Rd
Road
Lansdowne Road
Manor Road
Heene Road
Road
Gratwicke Rd
Crescent Road
Shelley Road
MONTAGUE CENTRE
South St.
GUILDBOURNE CENTRE
POL
Boundary Road
Rowlands Road
Rowlands Road
Montague St.
Bath Road
Marine Parade
Parade
West Parade
WORTHING
0 400 m
0 400 yards
A
B

- Brighton Rd . . . . BZ 2
- Broadwater Rd . . . . BZ 3
- Broadwater St West . . . . BY 5
- Brougham Rd . . . . BY 7
- Brunswick Rd . . . . AZ 8
- Chapel Rd . . . . BZ
- Church Rd . . . . AY 12
- Cowper Rd . . . . AZ 13
- Crockhurst Hill . . . . AY 14
- Durrington Hill . . . . AY 15
- Eriswell Rd . . . . ABZ 16
- Goring St . . . . AY 17
- Goring Way . . . . AY 18
- Grafton Rd . . . . BZ 20
- Guildbourne Centre . . . . BZ
- High St . . . . BZ 21
- Liverpool Rd . . . . BZ 22
- Lyons Farm Retail Park . . . . BY
- Montague Centre Shopping Centre . . . . BZ
- Montague St . . . . BZ
- Mulberry Lane . . . . AY 24
- Portland Rd . . . . BZ 25
- Rectory Rd . . . . AY 26
- Reigate Rd . . . . AY 27
- Sompting Ave . . . . BY 28
- Sompting Rd . . . . BY 29
- South Farm Rd . . . . ABZ 31
- South St WEST TARRING . . . . AY, AZ 30
- South St WORTHING . . . . BZ
- Steyne Garden . . . . BZ 33
- Steyne (The) . . . . BZ 32
- Stoke Abbott Rd . . . . BZ 34
- Tennyson Rd . . . . AZ 36
- Thorn Rd . . . . AZ 37
- Union Pl . . . . BZ 38
- Warwick Rd . . . . BZ 40
- Warwick St . . . . BZ 41
- Western Pl . . . . BZ 44
- West St . . . . BZ 42
- Wykeham Rd . . . . AZ 45
- York Rd . . . . BZ 46

WORTHING – West Sussex – 504 S31 – pop. 96 964 — 7 D3

London 59 mi. – Brighton 11 mi. – Southampton 50 mi.
Shoreham Airport : (01273) 467373, E : 4 mi. by A 27 BY
Chapel Rd (01903) 221066, tic@worthing.gov.uk
Hill Barn Hill Barn Lane, (01903) 237 301
Links Rd, (01903) 260 801

Plan on preceding page

Chatsworth
rm, rest, VISA AE

Steyne BN11 3DU – (01903) 236 103 – www.chatsworthworthing.co.uk – Fax (01903) 823 726 BZ**x**

98 rm – £ 95/125 £ 130/175 **Rest** – *(dinner only)* Menu £ 19

◆ In a Georgian terrace overlooking Steyne Gardens and ideally located for a range of the town's resort activities. Attentive service and good sized bedrooms. Simple, uncluttered dining room.

Beacons without rest
VISA

18 Shelley Rd BN11 1TU – (01903) 230 948 BZ**e**

8 rm – £ 40/45 £ 70/78

◆ Friendly traditional home providing classic English seaside accommodation. In the centre of town close to parks. Ideal base for visiting historic Arundel and Chichester.

Bryce's
VISA

The Steyne BN11 3DU – (01903) 214 317 – www.seafoodbrasserie.co.uk – Fax (01903) 213 842 – Closed Sunday dinner October-February, 25-26 December and 1 January

Rest – Seafood – *(booking essential in summer)* Menu £ 15 (except Friday and Saturday dinner) – Carte £ 24/29

◆ Modern, airy restaurant with terrace and pier/promenade views. Seafood based menu also features a few grills. All starters available as mains. Good homemade bread and sticky gingerbread.

WRIGHTINGTON BAR – Gtr Manchester – 502 L23 – see Standish

WRINEHILL – Staffordshire — 18 B1

London 167 mi. – Nantwich 10 mi. – Stoke-on-Trent 10 mi.

The Hand and Trumpet
VISA

Main Road CW3 9BJ – (01270) 820 048 – www.hand-and-trumpet-wrinehill.co.uk – Fax (01270) 821 911 – Closed 25 December

Rest – Carte £ 19/28

◆ Sizeable country pub with large terrace, overlooking a pleasant pond. Extensive daily menu of sandwiches, light bites and classics. Food orders are sucked up into a pipe system above the bar.

WROXHAM – Norfolk – 504 Y25 – pop. 3 247 Great Britain — 15 D1

London 118 mi. – Great Yarmouth 21 mi. – Norwich 7 mi.
Norfolk Broads★

Broad House
VISA AE

The Avenue, off A1151 NR12 8TS – (01603) 783 567 – www.broadhousehotel.co.uk

9 rm – £ 300 £ 450 – 1 suite

Rest *Trafford's* – Menu £ 21/45 – Carte £ 30/45

◆ Elegant Queen Anne house with extensive gardens and private jetty on Wroxham Broad. Bedrooms boast excellent comforts, good views and superb bathrooms; attic rooms most characterful. Dining room features traditional, daily changing menus with a personal twist, using local or garden produce.

WYCH CROSS – E. Sussex – 504 U30 – see Forest Row

WYE – Kent – 504 W30 – pop. 2 066 – Ashford — 9 C2

London 60 mi. – Canterbury 10 mi. – Dover 28 mi. – Hastings 34 mi.

XX **Wife of Bath** with rm

4 Upper Bridge St ✉ TN25 5AF – ✆ (01233) 812 232 – www.thewifeofbath.com – Closed 25 December

5 rm ☕ – †£ 65 ††£ 95

Rest – *(Closed Tuesday lunch, Sunday dinner and Monday)* Menu £ 19 (weekday lunch) – Carte £ 25/32

◆ A lovely timber-framed house built in 1760. Fine cloth tables. Well chosen menu of satisfying dishes. Full or Continental breakfast after staying in comfy, soft-toned rooms.

YANWATH – Cumbria – see Penrith

YARM – Stockton-on-Tees – 502 P20 – pop. 8 929 — 24 B3

London 242 mi. – Middlesbrough 8 mi. – Newcastle upon Tyne 47 mi.

Judges Country House

Kirklevington Hall, Kirklevington, South : 1.5 mi. on A 67 ✉ TS15 9LW – ✆ (01642) 789 000 – www.judgeshotel.co.uk – Fax (01642) 787 692

21 rm ☕ – †£ 95/183 ††£ 120/214 **Rest** – Menu £ 18/28 – Carte £ 44/60

◆ Former Victorian judge's residence surrounded by gardens. Welcoming panelled bar and spacious lounge filled with antiques and curios. Attractive rooms with a host of extras. Conservatory dining room overlooks the gardens.

YARMOUTH – I.O.W. – 503 P31 – see Wight (Isle of)

YARPOLE – County of Herefordshire — 18 B2

London 166 mi. – Worcester 31 mi. – Shrewsbury 38 mi. – Hereford 18 mi.

The Bell Inn

Green Lane ✉ HR6 0BD – ✆ (01568) 780 359 – www.thebellinnyarpole.co.uk – Closed Sunday dinner October-June and Monday

Rest – Carte £ 19/24

◆ Characterful black and white timbered inn with a real sense of identity. Cooking mixes French and British, featuring classic bar dishes alongside those of a more ambitious nature.

YATTENDON – West Berkshire – 503 Q29 – pop. 288 – ✉ Newbury — 10 B3

London 61 mi. – Oxford 23 mi. – Reading 12 mi.

The Royal Oak with rm

The Square ✉ RG18 0UG – ✆ (01635) 201 325 – www.royaloakyattendon.com

5 rm ☕ – †£ 110 ††£ 130

Rest – *(booking advisable)* Menu £ 19 (lunch) – Carte £ 30/39

◆ Beautiful former coaching inn in picture postcard village just off the M4, with beamed bar at its hub. Flavoursome cooking displays fine French technique. Classically-styled bedrooms.

at Frilsham South : 1 mi. by Frilsham rd on Bucklebury rd – ✉ Yattendon

The Pot Kiln

✉ RG18 0XX – ✆ (01635) 201 366 – www.potkiln.org – Fax (01635) 201 366 – Closed 25 December and Tuesday

Rest – Menu £ 20 (weekday lunch) – Carte £ 25/30

◆ 17C red brick pub country pub. Food is fresh, local and homemade; 90% of game and all river fish are caught by the owner. Dishes range from pub favourites with a modern/local twist to more restaurant style.

YAXLEY – Suffolk – see Thornham Magna

YEALMPTON – Devon – 503 H/I32 — 2 C2

London 211 mi. – Ivybridge 7 mi. – Plymouth 8 mi.

XX **The Seafood**

Market St ✉ PL8 2EB – ✆ (01752) 880 502 – www.theroseandcrown.co.uk – Fax (01752) 881 058 – Closed 25 December, Sunday and Monday

Rest – Seafood – Menu £ 15 (lunch and Tuesday-Friday dinner 6pm-7pm) – Carte £ 25/36

◆ Former cowshed, now a fashionable 'New England' style restaurant, featuring stylish black and white fishing photos. Simple selection of seafood at lunch; more depth at dinner.

Rose & Crown

Market St ✉ PL8 2EB – ✆ (01752) 880 223 – www.theroseandcrown.co.uk
Rest – Menu £ 13 (lunch) – Carte £ 20/33
◆ Vast, pink pub displaying a pleasant mix of old and new. Daily changing menu ranges from light bites to full 3 courses; flavoursome dishes boast ambitious presentation. Efficient service.

YEOVIL – Somerset – 503 M31 – pop. 41 871 3 B3

London 136 mi. – Exeter 48 mi. – Southampton 72 mi. – Taunton 26 mi.

Hendford ✆ (01935) 845946, yeoviltic@southsomerset.gov.uk Cart Gate Picnic Site, stoke sub-hamdon ✆ (01935) 829333 (seasonal opening), cartgate.tic@southsomerset.gov.uk

Sherborne Rd, ✆ (01935) 422 965

St John the Baptist★

Monacute House★★ **AC**, W : 4 mi. on A 3088 – Fleet Air Arm Museum, Yeovilton★★ **AC**, NW : 5 mi. by A 37 – Tintinhull House Garden★ **AC**, NW: 5.5 mi. – Ham Hill (≤★★) W : 5.5 mi. by A 3088 – Stoke sub Hamdon (parish church★) W : 5.25 mi. by A 3088. Muchelney★★ (parish church★★) NW : 14 mi. by A 3088, A 303 and B 3165 – Lytes Cary★, N : 7.5 mi. by A 37, B 3151 and A 372 – Sandford Orcas Manor House★, NW : 8 mi. by A 359 – Cadbury Castle (≤★★) NE : 10.5 mi. by A 359 – East Lambrook Manor★ **AC**, W : 12 mi. by A 3088 and A 303

Lanes

rm, VISA AE

West Coker, Southwest : 3 mi. on A 30 ✉ BA22 9AJ – ✆ (01935) 862 555 – www.laneshotel.net – Fax (01935) 864 260
29 rm – †£ 90 ††£ 120 **Rest** – *(closed Saturday lunch)* Carte £ 18/27
◆ 18C stone former rectory in walled grounds. Stylish modern interior with chocolate and red leather predominant. Stretch out in relaxed lounge. Airy, modish bedrooms. Modern classics served in restaurant.

at Barwick South : 2 mi. by A 30 off A 37 – ✉ Yeovil

Little Barwick House with rm

rest, AE

✉ BA22 9TD – ✆ (01935) 423 902 – www.littlebarwickhouse.co.uk – Fax (01935) 420 908 – Closed 26 December-9 January
6 rm – †£ 100 ††£ 230 **Rest** – *(closed Monday, Tuesday lunch and Sunday dinner) (booking essential)* Menu £ 25/38
◆ Charming Georgian dower house in a secluded spot, run by a delightful and hospitable couple. The cooking is robust, gutsy and visually bold but without gimmicks. Comfortable, stylish and immaculately kept bedrooms.

YORK – York – 502 Q22 – pop. 137 505 Great Britain 23 C2

London 203 mi. – Kingston-upon-Hull 38 mi. – Leeds 26 mi. – Middlesbrough 51 mi.

Museum St ✆ (01904) 550099, info@visityork.org.

Strensall Lords Moor Lane, ✆ (01904) 491 840

Heworth Muncastergate Muncaster House, ✆ (01904) 424 618

City★★★ – Minster★★★ (Stained Glass★★★, Chapter House★★, Choir Screen★★) CDY – National Railway Museum★★★ CY – The Walls★★ CDXYZ – Castle Museum★ **AC** DZ **M2** – Jorvik Viking Centre★ **AC** DY **M1** – Fairfax House★ **AC** DY **A** – The Shambles★ DY **54**

Middlethorpe Hall

rm, VISA AE

Bishopthorpe Rd, South : 1.75 mi. ✉ YO23 2GB – ✆ (01904) 641 241 – www.middlethorpe.com – Fax (01904) 620 176
21 rm – †£ 130/175 ††£ 190/260, £ 6.95 – 8 suites
Rest – *(booking essential for non-residents)* Menu £ 23 (lunch) **s** – Carte dinner £ 36/55 **s**
◆ Impressive William and Mary country house dating from 1699. Elegantly and carefully restored; abundantly furnished with antiques. Most characterful rooms in main house. Wood-panelled, three-roomed restaurant with period feel.

ENGLAND

YORK

ENGLAND

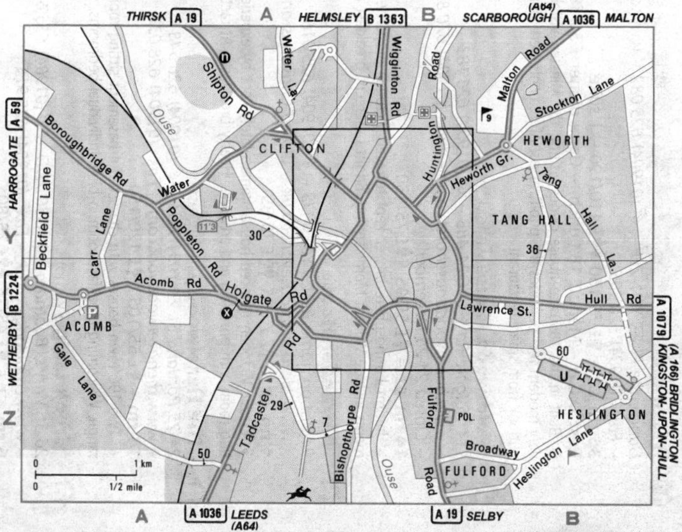

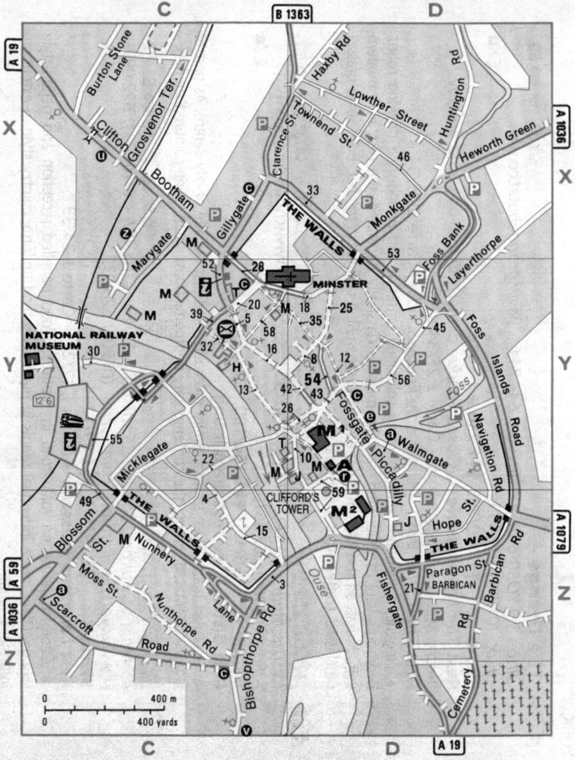

The Grange

Clifton ✉ YO30 6AA – ✆ (01904) 644 744 – www.grangehotel.co.uk – Fax (01904) 612 453 CX**u**

35 rm – ♦£ 120/195 ♦♦£ 230 – 1 suite

Rest *The Ivy Brasserie* – *(Closed Sunday dinner) (dinner only and Sunday lunch)* Menu £ 16 (lunch) **s** – Carte £ 25/34 **s**

Rest *The Cellar Bar* – *(dinner only Friday-Sunday)* Carte £ 25/34 **s**

◆ Regency townhouse with imposing columned entrance and period-style drawing room. Bedrooms vary in shape and size, the majority classically decorated, the rest, in a modern vein. Murals on the walls in the brasserie; low barrelled ceilings in the bar. Both serve brasserie classics crafted from fresh, local produce.

Hotel du Vin

89 The Mount ✉ YO24 1AX – ✆ (01904) 557 350 – www.hotelduvin.com – Fax (01904) 567 361 CZ**a**

44 rm – ♦£ 150/190 ♦♦£ 150/190, £ 13.50

Rest Bistro – see restaurant listing

◆ Georgian house close to Knavesmire racecourse and just outside of city centre. As part of a 'wine-orientated' group, the contemporary bedrooms boast smart, wine-coloured themes.

York Pavilion

45 Main St, Fulford, South : 1.5 mi. on A 19 ✉ YO10 4PJ – ✆ (01904) 622 099 – www.yorkpavilionhotel.com – Fax (01904) 626 939

57 rm – ♦£ 79/115 ♦♦£ 89/125

Rest *Langtons Brasserie* – Menu £ 17/27 – Carte £ 24/33

◆ Georgian house on main road in suburbs. Wood panelled reception and period-style lounge. Older, more individual rooms in main house and uniform, chintzy style in extension. Informal dining.

Dean Court

rest,

Duncombe Pl ✉ YO1 7EF – ✆ (01904) 625 082 – www.deancourt-york.co.uk – Fax (01904) 620 305 CY**c**

36 rm – ♦£ 75/160 ♦♦£ 110/190 – 1 suite

Rest *D.C.H* – Menu £ 18 (lunch) – Carte dinner £ 30/38

◆ Built in the 1850s to house clerics visiting the Minster, visible from most rooms. Now a very modern feel pervades the public areas. Aforementioned rooms more traditional. Minster outlook from smart restaurant.

Holmwood House without rest

114 Holgate Rd ✉ YO24 4BB – ✆ (01904) 626 183 – www.holmwoodhousehotel.co.uk – Fax (01904) 670 899 – Closed 24-26 December AZ**x**

14 rm – ♦£ 55/95 ♦♦£ 75/130

◆ Informal atmosphere in well-kept terraced Victorian property. Individually decorated bedrooms include William Morris styling. Bright basement breakfast room.

Alexander House without rest

94 Bishopthorpe Rd ✉ Y023 1JS – ✆ (01904) 625 016 – www.alexanderhouseyork.co.uk – Closed Christmas and New Year

4 rm – ♦£ 75/85 ♦♦£ 75/85 CZ**v**

◆ Classic Victorian terraced house, immaculately kept by experienced owners. Delightful sitting room with porcelain and artworks. Hearty breakfasts. Attractive bedrooms.

The Hazelwood without rest

24-25 Portland St ✉ Y031 7EH – ✆ (01904) 626 548 – www.thehazelwoodyork.com – Fax (01904) 628 032 CX**c**

14 rm – ♦£ 55/105 ♦♦£ 120/150

◆ Two 19C town houses with characterful basement sitting room featuring original cooking range. Welcoming breakfast room in blue. Individual bedrooms, some with four posters.

Crook Lodge without rest

26 St Mary's, Bootham ✉ YO30 7DD – ✆ (01904) 655 614 – www.crooklodge.co.uk – Fax (01904) 625 915 CX**z**

6 rm – ♦£ 45/75 ♦♦£ 75/80

◆ Privately owned, attractive Victorian redbrick house in quiet location. Basement breakfast room with original cooking range. Some rooms compact, all pleasantly decorated.

ENGLAND

Bronte without rest
22 Grosvenor Terrace ✉ YO30 7AG – ✆ (01904) 621 066 – www.bronte-guesthouse.com – Fax (01904) 653 434 – Closed 20-27 December
6 rm – †£ 40/60 ††£ 60/80 CX**n**
◆ Cosy little Victorian terraced house with pretty exterior, decorated in keeping with period nature of property. Charming breakfast room has antique furnishings. Comfy rooms.

Melton's
7 Scarcroft Rd ✉ YO23 1ND – ✆ (01904) 634 341 – www.meltonrestaurant.co.uk – Fax (01904) 635 115 – Closed 2 weeks Christmas, Sunday and Monday CZ**c**
Rest – *(booking essential)* Menu £ 23 (lunch and early dinner) – Carte £ 26/34
◆ Glass fronted restaurant with mural decorated walls and neighbourhood feel. Smart, crisp tone in both service and table cover. Good modern British food with some originality.

J. Baker's
7 Fossgate ✉ YO1 9TA – ✆ (01904) 622 688 – www.jbakers.co.uk – Fax (01904) 671 931 – Closed Sunday and Monday DY**c**
Rest – Menu £ 12/29 – Carte lunch approx. £ 21
◆ Contemporary restaurant in city centre. Spacious first floor 'chocolate' lounge for coffee and truffles. Informal dining room; good value, modern dishes use regional produce.

Bistro – at Hotel du Vin
89 The Mount ✉ YO24 1AX – ✆ (01904) 567 350 – www.hotelduvin.com – Fax (01904) 567 361 CZ**a**
Rest – French – Carte £ 29/39
◆ Typical bustling Bistro offering modern French dishes as well as all the old favourites. Set in Hotel du Vin, it offers a good selection of wines by the glass.

Blue Bicycle with rm
34 Fossgate ✉ YO1 9TA – ✆ (01904) 673 990 – www.thebluebicycle.com – Fax (01904) 677 688 – Closed 1-10 January and 24-26 December
5 rm – †£ 165 ††£ 165 **Rest** – *(dinner only and lunch Thursday-Sunday and December) (booking essential)* Carte £ 22/47 DY**e**
◆ Delightfully cluttered, atmospheric restaurant full of objets d'art, ornaments and pictures. Wood floors and heavy, old, pine tables. Bustling and busy; British cuisine. Spacious modern bedrooms, luxuriously appointed.

31 Castlegate
31 Castlegate ✉ YO1 9RN – ✆ (01904) 621 404 – www.31castlegate.co.uk – Closed 25-26 December, 1 January and Monday DY**r**
Rest – Menu £ 14 (except Saturday after 7pm) – Carte dinner £ 22/32
◆ Superbly located former home of Georgian architect. Impressive period décor in situ. First floor, high ceilinged dining room for well-priced, tasty dishes on eclectic menus.

Melton's Too
25 Walmgate ✉ YO1 9TX – ✆ (01904) 629 222 – www.meltonstoo.co.uk – Fax (01904) 636 677 – Closed dinner 24 and 31 December, 25-26 December and 1 January
Rest – Menu £ 13 (2 courses until 7pm) – Carte £ 20/25 DY**a**
◆ Café-bistro 'descendant' of Melton's restaurant. Located in former saddlers shop with oak beams and exposed brick walls. Good value eclectic dishes, with tapas a speciality.

at Newton-on-Ouse Northwest : 8 mi. by A 19

The Dawnay Arms
✉ YO30 2BR – ✆ (01347) 848 345 – www.thedawnayatnewton.co.uk – Closed 1 January, Sunday dinner and Monday except Bank Holidays
Rest – Menu £ 15/16 – Carte £ 20/35
◆ Spacious 18C inn boasting handsome rustic style, with beamed ceilings and roaring fires. Tasty, good value dishes on seasonal menus. Dining room looks out over River Ouse.

ZENNOR – Cornwall – 503 D33 1 A3

London 305 mi. – Penzance 11 mi. – St Ives 5 mi.

The Gurnard's Head with rm
Treen, West : 1.5 mi. on B 3306 ✉ TR26 3DE – ✆ (01736) 796 928 – www.gurnardshead.co.uk – Closed 4 days January
7 rm – †£ 75/85 ††£ 100/140 **Rest** – *(restricted lunch Monday)* Carte £ 20/24
◆ Welcoming, shabby-chic pub in a charming area. Modern cooking uses local produce and displays the odd Mediterranean touch. Interesting wines by the glass. Comfy bedrooms come with a good breakfast but no TVs, internet or mobile phone signal.

ENGLAND

O. Forir/MICHELIN

Scotland

ABERDEEN – Aberdeen City – 501 N12 – pop. 184 788 Scotland 28 D1

Edinburgh 130 mi. – Dundee 67 mi.

Aberdeen Airport, Dyce : (0844) 481 6666, NW : 7 mi. by A 96 X

to Shetland Islands (Lerwick) and via Orkney Islands (Stromness) (P and O Scottish Ferries) 1-2 daily

23 Union St (01224) 288828, aberdeen@visitscotland.com

Hazelhead Hazelhead Park, (01224) 321 830

Royal Aberdeen Bridge of Don Links Rd, (01224) 702 571

Balnagask St Fitticks Rd, (01224) 871 286

King's Links Golf Rd, (01224) 632 269

Portlethen Badentoy Rd, (01224) 781 090

Murcar Links Bridge of Don, (01224) 704 354

Auchmill West Heatheryfold Bonnyview Rd, (01224) 715 214

City★★ - Old Aberdeen★★ X – St Machar's Cathedral★★ (West Front★★★, Heraldic Ceiling★★★) X **A** – Art Gallery★★ (Macdonald Collection★★) Y **M** – Mercat Cross★★ Y **B** – King's College Chapel★ (Crown Spire★★★, medieval fittings★★★) X **D** – Provost Skene's House★ (painted ceilings★★) Y **E** – Maritime Museum★ Z **M1** – Marischal College★ Y **U**

Brig o' Balgownie★, by Don St X. SW : Deeside★★ - Crathes Castle★★ (Gardens★★★) **AC**, SW : 16 mi. by A 93 X – Dunnottar Castle★★ **AC** (site★★★), S : 18 mi. by A 90 X – Pitmedden Garden★★, N : 14 mi. by A 90 on B 999 X – Castle Fraser★ (exterior★★) **AC**, W : 16 mi. by A 944 X - Fyvie Castle★, NW : 26.5 mi. on A 947

Plans pages 729, 730

SCOTLAND

The Marcliffe H. and Spa

rest, VISA AE

North Deeside Rd AB15 9YA – (01224) 861 000 – www.marcliffe.com – Fax (01224) 868 860 X**r**

40 rm – £ 225 £ 245 – 2 suites

Rest The Conservatory – see restaurant listing

◆ Spacious, professionally run modern country house, popular with business travellers. Eight acres of pleasant grounds. Individually decorated rooms with antique furniture. Large spa.

Mercure Ardoe House H. and Spa

VISA AE

South Deeside Rd, Blairs, Southwest : 5 mi. on B 9077 AB12 5YP – (01224) 860 600 – www.mercure-uk.com – Fax (01224) 860 644

107 rm – £ 180 £ 180, £ 15.95 – 2 suites

Rest *Blairs* – *(bar lunch Monday-Friday)* Menu £ 34

◆ Imposing 18C Scottish baronial style mansion with annexes. Country house character aligned to excellent leisure facilities. Modern bedrooms, many overlooking the grounds. Formal, wood-panelled Blairs.

Malmaison

VISA AE

49-53 Queens Rd AB15 4YP Aberdeen – (01224) 327 370 – www.malmasion.com – Fax (01224) 327 371 X**v**

80 rm – £ 160 £ 160/375, £ 14

Rest *The Brasserie* – Menu £ 18 – Carte £ 26/36

◆ Period building with modern facilities, out of city centre. Cosy, very comfortable, well-furnished bedrooms; the sexy suites have their own balconies. A huge inner and two private dining rooms in the superb Brasserie, where cooking has fiercely Scottish base.

Atholl

rm, VISA AE

54 King's Gate AB15 4YN – (01224) 323 505 – www.atholl-aberdeen.com – Fax (01224) 321 555 – closed 1 January X**s**

34 rm – £ 60/120 £ 90/140 **Rest** – Carte £ 16/36

◆ Baronial style hotel set in leafy suburbs; well run by friendly staff. Traditional lounge bar; well-priced, up-to-date rooms. A useful address for visitors to the city. Dining room specialises in tried-and-tested Scottish cooking.

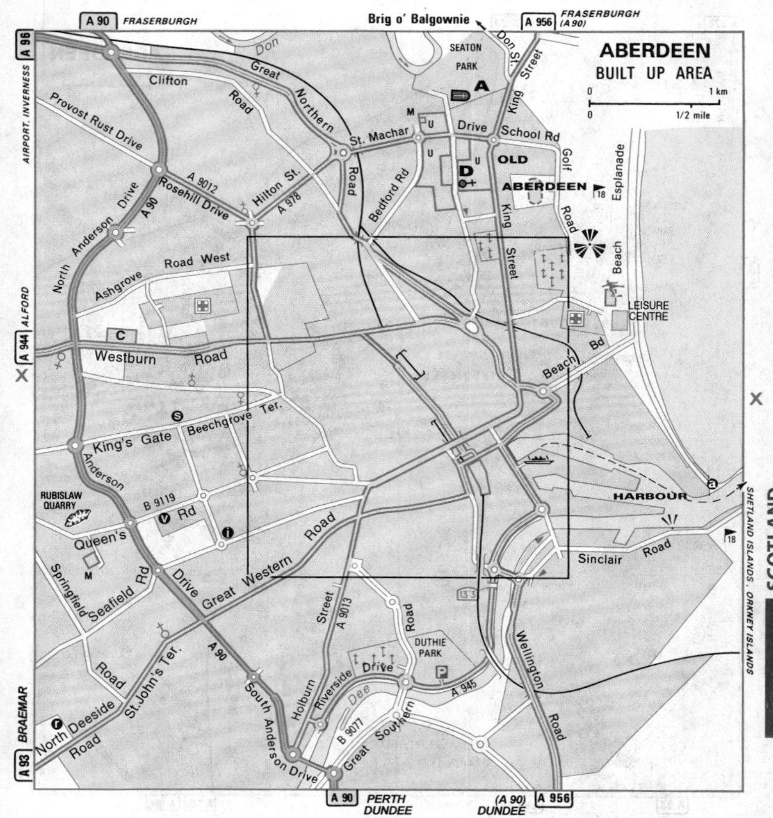

Conservatory – at The Marcliffe Hotel and Spa

North Deeside Rd ✉ AB15 9YA – ☎ (01224) 861 000 – www.marcliffe.com – Fax (01224) 868 860 Xr

Rest – Menu £ 29 (Sunday lunch) **s** – Carte £ 30/67 **s**

◆ Spacious conservatory dining room with large open kitchen. Fiercely Scottish menu; hearty tasty dishes, including superbly flavourful steaks. Warm service and a relaxing atmosphere.

Silver Darling

Pocra Quay, North Pier ✉ AB11 5DQ – ☎ (01224) 576 229 – www.thesilverdarling.co.uk – Fax (01224) 588 119 – Closed 2 weeks Christmas-New Year, Saturday lunch and Sunday Xa

Rest – Seafood – Menu £ 20 (lunch) – Carte dinner £ 36/44

◆ Former customs house attractively set at port entrance; panoramic views across harbour and coastline. Attentive service of superb quality seafood prepared in imaginative ways.

Nargile

77-79 Skene St ✉ AB10 1QD – ☎ (01224) 636 093 – www.rendezvousatnargile.co.uk – Fax (01224) 636 202 – closed 25 December, 1 January and lunch Monday-Thursday and Sunday Ya

Rest – Turkish – Menu £ 24 (dinner) – Carte £ 22/29

◆ Traditionally decorated Turkish restaurant with subdued lighting from Turkish lamps. Open-plan kitchen allows the diner to watch the chefs prepare the authentic dishes.

ABERDEEN

Street	Grid	No.
Bon Accord Centre	Y	
Broad St	Y	6
Castle St	Y	7
College St.	Z	9
Craigie Loanings	Y	12
Denburn Rd.	YZ	14
East North St	Y	16
George St	Y	
Great Southern Rd	Z	18
Guild St.	Z	19
Justice St	Y	21
Millburn St	Z	23
Rosemount Terrace	Y	25
Rosemount Viaduct	Y	26
St Andrew St	Y	28
St Nicholas Centre	Y	29
St Nicholas St	YZ	30
School Hill	YZ	32
South Esplanade West	Z	33
South Mount St.	Y	34
Springbank Terrace	Z	35
Spring Garden	Y	36
Trinity Centre	Z	
Trinity Quay	Z	37
Union St	Z	
Union Terrace.	Z	39
Upperkirkgate	Y	40
Victoria St.	Z	42
Waverley Pl.	Z	43
Wellington Pl.	Z	45
Woolmanhill	Y	48

X **Rendezvous at Nargile** AC VISA MC AE

106-108 Forest Ave ✉ AB15 4UP
– ✆ (01224) 323 700
– www.rendezvousatnargile.co.uk
– Fax (01224) 312 202
– Closed 1, 4-7 January and 25 December
Rest – Turkish – Menu £ 22/28 – Carte £ 21/34

Xi

◆ Bright, refreshing neighbourhood restaurant set opposite the Rendezvous Gallery. All day menus offer plenty of choice, with cooking influenced by the Mediterranean, and in particular, Turkey.

ABERFELDY – Perth and Kinross – 501 I14 – pop. 1 895 28 C2

Edinburgh 75 mi. – Dunkeld 17 mi. – Pitlochry 14 mi.

at Fortingall West : 8 mi. by B 846 and Fortingall rd

Fortingall

PH15 2NQ – (01887) 830 367 – www.fortingallhotel.com

10 rm – £ 99 £ 198

Rest – Menu £ 35 (dinner) – Carte lunch approx. £ 18 **s**

◆ Refurbished arts and crafts style house on private estate. Bedrooms, named after local estates, have a contemporary style with a touch of tweed; those at front boasting views. Daily-changing menu served in antique-furnished restaurant.

Fancy a last minute break?
Check hotel websites to take advantage of price promotions.

ABERLOUR – Moray – 501 K11 – pop. 785 Scotland 28 C1

Edinburgh 192 mi. – Aberdeen 60 mi. – Elgin 15 mi. – Inverness 55 mi.

Rothes Blackhall, (01340) 831 443

Dufftown (Glenfiddich Distillery★), SE : 6 mi. by A 95 and A 941

Dowans

Southwest : 0.75 mi. by A 95 AB38 9LS – (01340) 871 488 – www.dowanshotel.com – Fax (01340) 871 038

19 rm – £ 65/90 £ 100/140

Rest – Carte £ 21/38

◆ Welcoming, informal establishment with classic Scottish country house style. Inviting public areas. Comfortably smart rooms; those at the front have the best views. Two roomed restaurant.

SCOTLAND

ABOYNE – Aberdeenshire – 501 L12 – pop. 2 202 Scotland 28 D1

Edinburgh 131 mi. – Aberdeen 30 mi. – Dundee 68 mi.

Formanston Park, (013398) 86 328

Craigievar Castle★ **AC**, NE : 12 mi. by B 9094, B 9119 and A 980

Struan Hall without rest

Ballater Rd AB34 5HY – (013398) 87 241 – www.struanhall.co.uk – Fax (013398) 87 241 – Closed January and December

3 rm – £ 42/50 £ 84

◆ An agreeable and welcoming guesthouse with attractive garden. Well kept throughout. Large sitting room and antique breakfast table. Simple, comfy bedrooms.

ABRIACHAN – Highland – 501 G11 – pop. 120 30 C2

London 573 mi. – Edinburgh 168 mi. – Inverness 11 mi. – Elgin 50 mi.

Loch Ness Lodge

Brachla, on A 82 IV3 8LA – (01456) 459 469 – www.loch-ness-lodge.com – Fax (01456) 459 439 – Closed January, 25 and 26 December

7 rm – £ 120/140 £ 190/240

Rest – *(booking essential to non residents dinner only)* Menu £ 45

◆ Comfortable, modern country house overlooking Loch Ness; warmly decorated, spacious bedrooms boast a high level of facilities. Sauna and hot tub for guests. Daily changing 5 course menu uses Scottish produce; cooking is flavourful and classically based. Linen laid dining room with excellent views; attentive service.

ACHILTIBUIE – Highland – 501 D9 **30** C1

Edinburgh 243 mi. – Inverness 84 mi. – Ullapool 25 mi.

Summer Isles

IV26 2YG – (01854) 622 282 – www.summerisleshotel.com – Fax (01854) 622 251 – 26 March-31 October

10 rm – £ 110 £ 140/260 – 3 suites

Rest ***Summer Isles Bar*** – see restaurant listing

Rest – *(booking essential) (set menu only at dinner, light seafood lunch)* Menu £ 54

Spec. Scallops with leeks and white wine. Venison with butternut squash and vegetables. Apricot and amaretto pudding.

◆ Remotely located hotel, with magnificent views over the eponymous islands. Individually styled, comfortable bedrooms split between main house and various converted outbuildings. Efficient service in pleasant restaurant. Local produce well used in menu of traditional dishes, with emphasis firmly on seafood.

Summer Isles (Bar) – at Summer Isles Hotel

IV26 2YG – (01854) 622 282 – www.summerisleshotel.com – Fax (01854) 622 251 – 26 March-31 October

Rest – Seafood – *(bookings not accepted)* Carte £ 20/30 **s**

◆ Simple two-roomed set up, with locals bar and lawn for al fresco dining. Menus are seafood orientated, with some snacks and traditional pub dishes. Daily changing specials add interest.

SCOTLAND

ALYTH – Perth and Kinross – 501 J14 – pop. 2 301 **28** C2

Edinburgh 63 mi. – Aberdeen 69 mi. – Dundee 16 mi. – Perth 21 mi.

Pitcrocknie, (01828) 632 268

Tigh Na Leigh

22-24 Airlie St PH11 8AJ – (01828) 632 372 – www.tighnaleigh.co.uk – Fax (01828) 632 279 – 12 February-19 December

5 rm – £ 47/71 £ 100/120

Rest – *(dinner only) (residents only booking essential)* Menu £ 25

◆ Extremely spacious, modern bedrooms in this comfortable and contemporary conversion, which retains many original features. Look out for Tom and Eddie, the cats. Dining room overlooks kitchen garden, church and carp pond. Daily-changing dinner menu and small wine list.

ANNBANK – South Ayrshire – 501 G17 – pop. 854 **25** B2

Edinburgh 84 mi. – Ayr 6 mi. – Dumfries 54 mi. – Dumfries 38 mi.

Enterkine

Southeast : 0.5 mi. on B 742 (Coylton rd) KA6 5AL – (01292) 520 580 – www.enterkine.com – Fax (01292) 521 582

13 rm (dinner included) – £ 125 £ 250 – 1 suite

Rest – *(booking essential)* Menu £ 19/45

◆ 1930s country house surrounded by extensive gardens and woodlands. Spacious, comfortable lounges. Luxurious bedrooms; one with large roof terrace. Charming library. Formal restaurant with views over River Ayr serves modern cooking; popular with non-residents.

ANSTRUTHER – Fife – 501 L15 – pop. 3 442 Scotland **28** D2

Edinburgh 46 mi. – Dundee 23 mi. – Dunfermline 34 mi.

Scottish Fisheries Museum, Harbourhead (01333) 311073 (April-October), anstruther@visitscotland.com

Marsfield Shore Rd, (01333) 310 956

Scottish Fisheries Museum★★ **AC**

The East Neuk★★ – Crail★★ (Old Centre★★, Upper Crail★) NE : 4 mi. by A 917. Kellie Castle★ **AC**, NW : 7 mi. by B 9171, B 942 and A 917

The Spindrift

Pittenweem Rd ✉ *KY10 3DT – ✆ (01333) 310 573 – www.thespindrift.co.uk – Fax (01333) 310 573 – Closed January and Christmas*
8 rm – 🚹£ 45/55 🚹🚹£ 64/80 **Rest** – *(by arrangement)* Menu £ 22
◆ Victorian house originally owned by tea clipper captain whose bedroom replicates a master's cabin. Comfortable period style throughout and local kippers for breakfast. 19C style dining room reflects house's age.

Cellar

24 East Green ✉ *KY10 3AA – ✆ (01333) 310 378 – www.cellaranstruther.co.uk – Fax (01333) 312 544 – Closed Monday in winter and Sunday*
Rest – Seafood – *(booking essential)* Menu £ 24/38
◆ Long-standing restaurant hidden behind the Fisheries Museum, with atmospheric beamed interior, candlelit tables and open fire. Fine seafood from the local coast is served simply and precisely.

APPLECROSS – Highland – 501 C11 — 29 B2

London 639 mi. – Edinburgh 234 mi. – Gairloch 56 mi. – Portree 76 mi.

The Potting Shed

Applecross Walled Garden, Northeast : 0.5 mi. ✉ *IV54 8ND – ✆ (01520) 744 440 – www.applecrossgarden.co.uk – Restricted opening in winter*
Rest – Carte £ 14/29
◆ Lovely 17C walled kitchen garden whose restaurant has grown from a tearoom. Its simple structure belies its tasty dishes, fresh from owner's fishing boat or the garden itself.

Applecross Inn with rm

Shore St ✉ *IV54 8LR – ✆ (01520) 744 262 – www.applecrossinn.uk.com – closed 1 January and 25 December*
7 rm – 🚹£ 100 🚹🚹£ 110 **Rest** – *(booking essential)* Carte £ 15/30
◆ Charming Highland inn set in an extremely remote location, boasting stunning water and hill views. Menus feature local, seasonal produce from the nearby estate and bay; seafood a speciality. Set in old fishermen's cottages, smart, comfy bedrooms boast sea views.

SCOTLAND

ARBROATH – Angus – 501 M14 – pop. 22 785 — 28 D2

Edinburgh 72 mi. – Dundee 17 mi. – Montrose 12 mi.

The Old Vicarage without rest

2 Seaton Rd, Northeast : 0.75 mi. by A 92 and Hayshead Rd ✉ *DD11 5DX – ✆ (01241) 430 475 – www.theoldvicaragebandb.co.uk*
3 rm – 🚹£ 55/60 🚹🚹£ 80/85
◆ Detached 19C house, of large proportions, clothed in Victorian style throughout. Antique furnished bedrooms: ask for view of Arbroath Abbey.

ARCHIESTOWN – Moray – 501 K11 – ✉ Aberlour (Aberdeenshire) — 28 C1

Edinburgh 194 mi. – Aberdeen 62 mi. – Inverness 49 mi.

Archiestown

The Square ✉ *AB38 7QL – ✆ (01340) 810 218 – www.archiestownhotel.co.uk – Fax (01340) 810 239 – Closed 3 January-10 February and 23-29 December*
11 rm – 🚹£ 60/85 🚹🚹£ 120/140
Rest ***Bistro*** – Carte £ 27/37
◆ Welcoming hotel hidden away in a small hamlet; ideally located for shooters/fishermen. Spacious, comfy sitting rooms with warming open fires. Cosy bedrooms, many boasting country views. Daily changing dishes in laid-back bistro.

ARDEONAIG – Perth and Kinross – 501 H14 – see Killin (Stirling)

ARDHASAIG – Western Isles Outer Hebrides – 501 Z10 – see Lewis and Harris (Isle of)

ARDRISHAIG – Argyll and Bute – 501 D15 – pop. 1 283 – ✉ Lochgilphead — 27 B2

Edinburgh 132 mi. – Glasgow 86 mi. – Oban 40 mi.

Allt-na-Craig

Tarbert Rd, on A 83 ✉ PA30 8EP – ✆ (01546) 603 245 – www.allt-na-craig.co.uk – Closed Christmas and New Year

5 rm – £ 45/75 £ 90/120 **Rest** – *(by arrangement)* Menu £ 25

◆ Spacious, modernised Victorian house with lovely gardens, once the childhood home of author Kenneth Grahame. Front bedrooms have good views over loch. Simple, traditional dining room where breakfasts and evening meals are served.

ARDUAINE – **Argyll and Bute** – **501** D15 – ✉ **Oban** Scotland **27** B2

Edinburgh 142 mi. – Oban 20 mi.

Loch Awe★★, E : 12 mi. by A 816 and B 840

Loch Melfort

✉ *PA34 4XG – ✆ (01852) 200 233 – www.lochmelfort.co.uk – Fax (01852) 200 214 – Closed 4-19 January*

25 rm (dinner included) – £ 89/115 £ 138/258

Rest ***Arduaine*** – Seafood – *(dinner only)* Menu £ 35 **s** – Carte £ 22/31 **s**

Rest ***Chartroom*** – Carte £ 16/36

◆ Comfortable hotel next to famed Arduaine gardens with stunning southerly views of Sound of Jura. Largest rooms in original house. Daily changing menu and tables with views in formal Arduaine. Light, airy Chartroom has terrace and contemporary style.

ARRAN (Isle of) – **North Ayrshire** – **501** E17 – **pop. 5 058** Scotland **25** A2

London 449 mi. – Edinburgh 95 mi. – Glasgow 45 mi. – Paisley 31 mi.

from Brodick to Ardrossan (Caledonian MacBrayne Ltd) 4-6 daily (55 mn) – from Lochranza to Kintyre Peninsula (Claonaig) (Caledonian MacBrayne Ltd) frequent services daily (30 mn) – from Brodick to Isle of Bute (Rothesay) (Caledonian MacBrayne Ltd) 3 weekly (2 h 5 mn)

Island★★ - Brodick Castle★★ **AC**

BRODICK – **North Ayrshire** – **pop. 621** **25** A2

The Pier ✆ (01770) 303776, brodick@visitscotland.com

Brodick, ✆ (01770) 302 349

Machrie Bay, ✆ (01770) 850 232

Kilmichael Country House

Glen Cloy, West : 1 mi. by Shore Rd, taking left turn opposite Golf Club ✉ KA27 8BY – ✆ (01770) 302 219 – www.kilmichael.com – Fax (01770) 302 068 – Easter-October

5 rm – £ 76/95 £ 144/180 – 3 suites

Rest – *(Closed Tuesday) (dinner only) (booking essential)* Menu £ 42

◆ Reputedly the oldest house on the Isle of Arran, in peaceful location with immaculate lawned grounds. Comfortable country house style and individually decorated bedrooms. Welcoming owners. Restaurant housed in extension. Daily-changing menus.

Alltan without rest

Knowe Rd, West : 0.5 mi. by Shore Rd taking left at Golf Club ✉ KA27 8BY – ✆ (01770) 302 937 – www.alltanarran.co.uk – March-October

3 rm – £ 80 £ 80

◆ Friendly, modern guest house outside village. Comfortable rear lounge with woodburning stove overlooks garden and river. Raised decked balcony with wrought iron furniture.

LOCHRANZA

Apple Lodge

✉ *KA27 8HJ – ✆ (01770) 830 229 – Fax (01770) 830 229 – Closed Christmas and New Year, minimum 3 night stay in high season*

4 rm – £ 55 £ 82/90 **Rest** – *(by arrangement)* Menu £ 26

◆ Extended period house with small garden and pleasing views, in centre of quiet village. Homely cottage-style décor with antique furniture and a welcoming atmosphere. Food is home-cooked and uses island and home produce in good, hearty, varied dishes.

ASCOG – **Argyll and Bute** – **501** E16 – **see Bute (Isle of)**

AUCHENCAIRN – Dumfries and Galloway – 501 I19 — 25 B3
– ✉ Castle Douglas

Edinburgh 94 mi. – Dumfries 21 mi. – Stranraer 60 mi.

Balcary Bay
Southeast : 2 mi. on Balcary rd ✉ DG7 1QZ – ✆ (01556) 640 217 – www.balcary-bay-hotel.co.uk – Fax (01556) 640 272 – closed 1 December-30 January

20 rm – £ 70/100 £ 138/160

Rest – *(lunch by arrangement)* Menu £ 20 (Sunday lunch)/37 (dinner) **s** – Carte approx. £ 35 **s**

◆ Perched on the eponymous bay with magnificent views of Auchencairn Bay and Solway Firth. Comfortable, family run hotel. Bedrooms have bay or garden views. Restaurant decorated in keeping with the hotel's traditional style; window tables much in request.

Balcary Mews without rest
Balcary Bay, Southeast : 2 mi. on Balcary rd ✉ DG7 1QZ – ✆ (01556) 640 276 – www.balcarymews.co.uk – Fax (01556) 640 276 – Closed Christmas-New Year

3 rm – £ 55 £ 80

◆ Well-priced, smuggler-built 18C property with lovely views. Warm welcome enhances overall homely feel, typified by comfy lounge overlooking pretty garden. Quality rooms.

AUCHTERARDER – Perth and Kinross – 501 I15 – pop. 3 945 — 28 C2
Scotland

Edinburgh 55 mi. – Glasgow 45 mi. – Perth 14 mi.

18 Ochil Rd, ✆ (01764) 662 804

9 Dunning Rollo Park, ✆ (01764) 684 747

Tullibardine Chapel★, NW : 2 m

Gleneagles
Southwest : 2 mi. by A 824 on A 823 ✉ PH3 1NF – ✆ (01764) 662 231 – www.gleneagles.com – Fax (01764) 662 134

216 rm – £ 310/410 £ 430/570 – 16 suites

Rest *Andrew Fairlie at Gleneagles* – see restaurant listing

Rest *Strathearn* – *(dinner only and Sunday lunch)* Menu £ 40/56

Rest *Deseo* – Carte £ 36/48

◆ World famous for its championship golf courses and extensive leisure facilities. Graceful art deco and constant reinvestment ensure the impressive grandeur of this early 20C mansion remains. Strathearn is elegant art deco dining room. Deseo offers Mediterranean dishes in informal atmosphere.

Andrew Fairlie at Gleneagles
Southwest : 2 mi. by A 824 on A 823 ✉ PH3 1NF – ✆ (01764) 694 267 – www.andrew.fairlie.com – Fax (01764) 694 163 – Closed 3 weeks January, 24-25 December and Sunday

Rest – *(dinner only)* Menu £ 75

Spec. Home smoked lobster, lime and herb butter. Peelham Farm veal breast, loin and sweetbreads. Raspberries with Banyuls, brownie and hot chocolate.

◆ Discreet, minimalist restaurant, decorated with still life, food themed oil paintings. Precise, well-presented cooking utilises prime Scottish ingredients. Welcoming staff.

AULTBEA – Highland – 501 D10 — 29 B2

London 636 mi. – Edinburgh 231 mi. – Gairloch 13 mi. – Ullapool 45 mi.

Mellondale without rest
47 Mellon Charles, Northwest : 3 mi. on Mellon Charles rd ✉ IV22 2JL – ✆ (01445) 731 326 – www.mellondale.co.uk – Fax (01445) 731 326 – March-October

4 rm – £ 40/45 £ 60/70

◆ Remotely located whitewashed house with neat garden. Immaculately kept dining room and homely lounge look to Loch Ewe. Smart, modern bedrooms with bright décor, two with views.

AVIEMORE – Highland – 501 I12 – pop. 2 397 Scotland 30 D3

Edinburgh 129 mi. – Inverness 29 mi. – Perth 85 mi.

Unit 7, Grampian Rd ✆ (08452) 255121, aviemore@visitscotland.com

Town★

The Cairngorms★★ (★★★) - ★★★ from Cairn Gorm, SE : 11 mi. by B 970 – Landmark Visitor Centre (The Highlander★) **AC**, N : 7 mi. by A 9 – Highland Wildlife Park★ **AC**, SW : 7 mi. by A 9

Corrour House without rest

Rothiemurchus, Southeast : 1 mi. on B 970 ✉ PH22 1QH – ✆ (01479) 810 220 – www.corrourhouse.co.uk – Fax (01479) 811 500 – Restricted opening in winter

8 rm – †£ 55/65 ††£ 84/96

◆ Victorian dower house in charming setting surrounded by neat lawned garden. Rooms are comfortably furnished with reproduction furniture - those on top floor have best views.

The Old Minister's Guest House without rest

Rothiemurchus, Southeast : 1 mi. on B 970 ✉ PH22 1QH – ✆ (01479) 812 181 – www.theoldministershouse.co.uk – Fax (01479) 811 925

4 rm – †£ 45/65 ††£ 96

◆ Early 20C house on outskirts of town, with a river at the bottom of its pretty garden. Nicely-laid breakfast room. Spacious bedrooms, finished to high standard.

AYR – South Ayrshire – 501 G17 – pop. 46 431 Scotland 25 A2

Edinburgh 81 mi. – Glasgow 35 mi.

22 Sandgate ✆ (01292) 290300, ayr@visitscotland.com

18 Seafield Doonfoot Rd, Belleisle Park, ✆ (01292) 441 258

18 Dalmilling Westwood Ave, ✆ (01292) 263 893

9 Doon Valley Patna Hillside, ✆ (01292) 531 607

Alloway★ (Burns Cottage and Museum★ **AC**) S : 3 mi. by B 7024 BZ. Culzean Castle★ **AC** (setting★★★, Oval Staircase★★) SW : 13 mi. by A 719 BZ

Fairfield House rest,

12 Fairfield Rd ✉ KA7 2AS – ✆ (01292) 267 461 – www.fairfieldhotel.co.uk – Fax (01292) 261 456 AY**a**

44 rm – †£ 89/119 ††£ 109/189

Rest *Martins Bar & Grill* – Menu £ 16 (lunch) – Carte £ 26/38

◆ Former holiday retreat for Glasgow tea merchant, refurbished in contemporary browns and beiges. Bedrooms in main house have sea view. Those in extension well-equipped but smaller. Restaurant offers traditional cooking, popular with locals.

No.26 The Crescent without rest

26 Bellevue Crescent ✉ KA7 2DR – ✆ (01292) 287 329 – www.26crescent.co.uk

5 rm – †£ 50/70 ††£ 70/80 BZ**c**

◆ Superior, well-priced guest house with mix of traditional and modern décor. Comfortable and well-run, with individually-furnished bedrooms – best one at front has four poster.

Coila without rest

10 Holmston Rd ✉ KA7 3BB – ✆ (01292) 262 642 – www.coila.co.uk – Closed Christmas and New Year AY**u**

4 rm – †£ 40/50 ††£ 55/75

◆ Spotlessly-kept house proudly decorated with owners' personal ornaments and family photos. Warm, homely lounge. Good-sized bedrooms with king-size beds and modern facilities.

Fouters

2a Academy St ✉ KA7 1HS – ✆ (01292) 261 391 – www.fouters.co.uk – Fax (01292) 619 323 – Closed 25 December, 1 January, Sunday and Monday

Rest – Carte £ 16/37 AY**e**

◆ Vaulted basement restaurant with low ceilings and flagged floors. Menu has something for everyone; classic, unfussy cooking using quality local produce. Effective service.

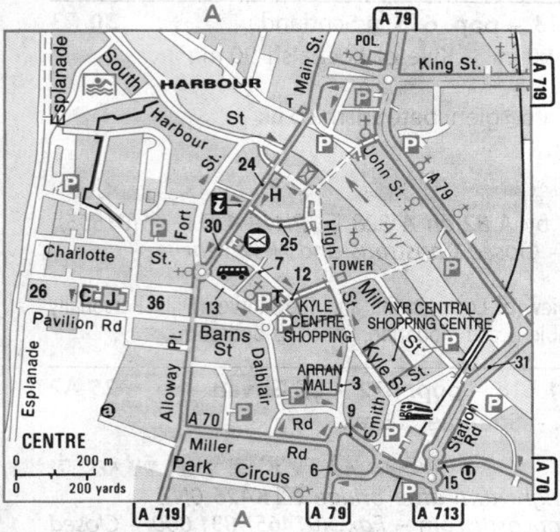

AYR AND PRESTWICK

Street	Grid	No.
Allison St	BZ	2
Alloway St	AY	3
Arran Mall	AY	
Beresford Terrace	AY	6
Boswell Park	AY	7
Burns' Statue Square	AY	9
Carrick Rd	BZ	10
Carrick St	AY	12
Fullarton St	AY	13
Heathfield Retail Park	BY	
High Rd	BYZ	14
High St	AY	
Holmston Rd	AY	15
Mac Call's Ave	BZ	20
Newmarket St	AY	25
New Bridge St	AY	24
St Germain-en-Laye (Pl. de)	AY	26
St Leonard's Rd	BZ	27
St Quivox Rd	BY	28
Sandgate	AY	30
Victoria Bridge	AY	31
Waggon Rd	BZ	33
Walker Rd	BZ	34
Wellington Square	AY	36

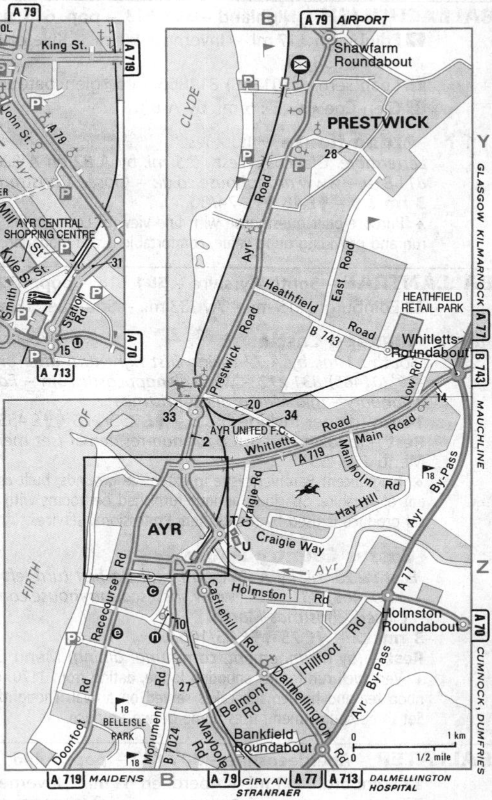

SCOTLAND

at Dunfoot/Doonfoot Southwest : 2.5 mi. on A 719 - BZ – ✉ Ayr

Greenan Lodge without rest

39 Dunure Rd, on A 719 ✉ KA7 4HR – ✆ (01292) 443 939 – www.greenanlodge.com

3 rm – †£ 45 ††£ 70

◆ Modern and Mediterranean in style with friendly owner. Roomy lounge; guests welcome to have a tinkle on the ivories. Light bedrooms with flat screen TVs. Good base for golf.

BADACHRO – Highland – 501 C10 – pop. 58 – ✉ Gairloch 29 B2

Edinburgh 224 mi. – Inverness 71 mi. – Ullapool 61 mi.

Badachro Inn

✉ IV21 2AA – ✆ (01445) 741 255 – www.badachroinn.com – Fax (01445) 741 319 – Closed 25-26 December

Rest – Carte £ 20 approx

◆ Rustic lochside pub boasting a decked terrace and great views. Menus feature local produce – in particular fresh seafood – with dishes ranging from pub snacks to more substantial fare.

Good food at moderate prices? Look for the Bib Gourmand.

BALLACHULISH – Highland – 501 E13 – pop. 615 Scotland 30 C3

Edinburgh 117 mi. – Inverness 80 mi. – Kyle of Lochalsh 90 mi. – Oban 38 mi.

Loan sern ☎ (01855) 811866, info@glencoetourism.co.uk

Glen Coe★★, E : 6 mi. by A 82

Ardno House without rest

Lettermore, Glencoe, West : 3.5 mi. by A 82 on A 828 ✉ PH49 4JD – ☎ (01855) 811 830 – www.ardnohouse.co.uk – Closed Christmas and New Year

3 rm – †£ 48 ††£ 74/80

◆ Purpose-built guesthouse with fine view of Loch Linnhe and the Morven Hills. Personally run and providing good value, comfortable accommodation. Spacious bedrooms.

BALLANTRAE – South Ayrshire – 501 E18 – pop. 672 – ✉ Girvan 25 A2

Edinburgh 115 mi. – Ayr 33 mi. – Stranraer 18 mi.

Glenapp Castle

South : 1 mi. by A 77 taking first right turn after bridge ✉ KA26 0NZ – ☎ (01465) 831 212 – www.glenappcastle.com – Fax (01465) 831 000 – Closed 2 January - mid March and Christmas

14 rm (dinner included) – †£ 255/275 ††£ 455/595 – 3 suites

Rest – *(booking essential for non-residents) (set menu only at dinner)* Menu £ 35/55

◆ Magnificent Baronial castle in extensive grounds; built as home for Deputy Lord Lieutenant of Ayrshire. Spacious, antique-furnished bedrooms with tall Victorian windows. Much local produce is used by the kitchen. Professional service.

Cosses Country House

East : 2.25 mi. by A 77 (South) taking first turn left after bridge ✉ KA26 0LR – ☎ (01465) 831 363 – www.cossescountryhouse.com – Fax (01465) 831 598 – Closed Christmas-March

3 rm – †£ 75 ††£ 85/100

Rest – *(by arrangement, communal dining)* Menu £ 30

◆ Very well run former shooting lodge, dating from 1670. Warm lounge with log fire; afternoon tea and homemade cakes served on arrival. Thoughtful extras provided in bedrooms. Set three course menu uses home grown produce.

BALLATER – Aberdeenshire – 501 K12 – pop. 1 446 28 C1

Edinburgh 111 mi. – Aberdeen 41 mi. – Inverness 70 mi. – Perth 67 mi.

Old Royal Station, Station Square ☎ (013397) 55306, ballater@visitscotland.com

Victoria Rd, ☎ (013397) 55 567

Darroch Learg

Braemar Rd ✉ AB35 5UX – ☎ (013397) 55 443 – www.darrochlearg.co.uk – Fax (013397) 55 252 – Closed last 3 weeks January and Christmas

12 rm (dinner included) – †£ 135/185 ††£ 210/310

Rest *The Conservatory* – see restaurant listing

◆ Country house hotel: enjoy superb views from its elevated position. Plush lounges with soft suites, open fires and antiques. Enticing bedrooms: upper floors have best outlook.

The Auld Kirk

Braemar Rd ✉ AB35 5RQ – ☎ (01339) 755 762 – www.theauldkirk.com – Closed 25-26 December

6 rm – †£ 70 ††£ 140 **Rest** – *(Closed Sunday) (dinner only)* Menu £ 35

◆ Hotel in former church with contemporary style bar, lounge and breakfast room. Well equipped bedrooms, with superb bathrooms. Restaurant in former side chapel has vaulted ceiling and chandeliers and serves traditional menu.

Moorside House without rest

26 Braemar Rd ✉ AB35 5RL – ☎ (013397) 55 492 – www.moorsidehouse.co.uk – Fax (013397) 55 492 – Easter-mid October

9 rm – †£ 45 ††£ 60

◆ Detached Victorian pink stone guesthouse on main road just outside town centre. Neat garden. Vividly coloured breakfast room. Sizeable, well-furnished rooms.

The Conservatory – at Darroch Learg Hotel
Braemar Rd ✉ AB35 5UX – ✆ (013397) 55 443 – www.darrochlearg.co.uk – Fax (013397) 55 252 – Closed Christmas and last 3 weeks January
Rest – *(dinner only and Sunday lunch)* Menu £ 45
◆ Attractive conservatory restaurant with a fine view from its garden location: comfortable dining enhanced by attentive service. Notably impressive wine list.

The Green Inn with rm
9 Victoria Rd ✉ AB35 5QQ – ✆ (013397) 55 701 – www.green-inn.com – Closed 2 weeks January and 2 weeks November
3 rm – †£ 50 ††£ 70/90, ☕ £ 10
Rest – *(Closed Sunday-Monday) (dinner only)* Menu £ 40
◆ Former temperance hall, opposite the green, boasting comfy lounges and pleasant conservatory. Interesting, well sourced and accomplished modern British cooking. Cosy rooms.

BALLOCH – West Dunbartonshire – 501 G15 – ✉ Alexandria — 25 B1

Scotland

Edinburgh 72 mi. – Glasgow 20 mi. – Stirling 30 mi.
The Old Station Building, Balloch Rd ✆ (08707) 200607, info@balloch.visitscotland.com
N : Loch Lomond★★

Cameron House
Loch Lomond, Northwest : 1.5 mi. by A 811 on A 82 ✉ G83 8QZ – ✆ (01389) 755 565 – www.devere.co.uk – Fax (01389) 759 522
128 rm ☕ – †£ 280 ††£ 280 – 12 suites
Rest *Martin Wishart at Loch Lomond* – see restaurant listing
Rest *Camerons Grill* – *(dinner only)* Carte £ 29/50
◆ Extensive Victorian house superbly situated on shores of Loch Lomond. Impressive leisure facilities. Luxurious rooms with four posters and panoramic views. Camerons Grill has a contemporary feel.

Martin Wishart at Loch Lomond – at Cameron House Hotel
Loch Lomond, Northwest : 1.5 mi. by A 811 on A 82 ✉ G83 8QZ – ✆ (01389) 722 504 – www.martinwishartlochlomond.co.uk – Fax (01389) 759 522 – Closed 1 January, 18 January-9 February, 10-18 May, Monday and Tuesday
Rest – *(dinner only and Sunday lunch)* Menu £ 25/50
◆ Intimate restaurant with views of the mountains and loch; plush, contemporary styling, comfy central banquettes, formal service and well-presented, modern cooking.

BALLYGRANT – Argyll and Bute – 501 B16 – see Islay (Isle of)

BALMACARA – Highland — 29 B2

London 582 mi. – Edinburgh 198 mi. – Inverness 75 mi.

Balmacara Mains without rest
Glaick , West : 0.75 mi. by A 87 ✉ IV40 8DN – ✆ (01599) 566 240 – www.ontheloch.com
8 rm ☕ – †£ 65/88 ††£ 95/120
◆ Superb lochside location, between Eilean Donan Castle and Skye Bridge. Stylish bedrooms vary in size, some cosy, some huge; most have loch views. Large lounge with open fire.

BALMEDIE – Aberdeenshire – 501 N12 – pop. 1 653 — 28 D1

Edinburgh 137 mi. – Aberdeen 7 mi. – Peterhead 24 mi.

Cock and Bull
Ellon Rd, Blairton, North : 1 mi. on A 90 ✉ AB23 8XY – ✆ (01358) 743 249 – www.thecockandbull.co.uk – Fax (01358) 742 466
Rest – Carte £ 20/35
◆ Quirky pub with a profusion of knick-knacks; dine in cosy lounge, formal dining room or airy conservatory. Big, hearty portions of honest, manly food, with nothing too fancy or fiddly.

BALTASOUND – Shetland Islands – **501** R1 – see Shetland Islands (Island of Unst)

BANAVIE – Highland – **501** E13 – see Fort William

BANCHORY – Aberdeenshire – **501** M12 – **pop. 6 034** Scotland **28** D2

Edinburgh 118 mi. – Aberdeen 17 mi. – Dundee 55 mi. – Inverness 94 mi.

Bridge St (01330) 822000 (Easter-October), banchory@visitscotland.com

Kinneskie Kinneskie Rd, (01330) 822 365

Torphins Bog Rd, (013398) 82 115

Crathes Castle★★ (Gardens★★★) **AC**, E : 3 mi. by A 93 – Cairn o'Mount Road★ (≤★★), S : by B 974. Dunnottar Castle★★ (site★★★) **AC**, SW : 15.5 mi. by A 93 and A 957 – Aberdeen★★, NE : 17 mi. by A 93

Raemoir House

North : 2.5 mi. on A 980 ✉ AB31 4ED – (01330) 824 884 – www.raemoir.com – Fax (01330) 822 171

20 rm (dinner included) – †£ 120/150 ††£ 190

Rest – Menu £ 35 (dinner) – Carte lunch £ 20/35

◆ Enviably located 18C Highland mansion with 17C "ha-hoose" (hall house) as popular alternative to main house. Country house ambience: antiques abound. Very comfortable rooms. The "Oval" dining room luxuriates with Victorian tapestry walls.

Banchory Lodge

Dee St ✉ AB31 5HS – (01330) 822 625 – www.banchorylodge.co.uk – Fax (01330) 825 019

22 rm – †£ 95/125 ††£ 170 **Rest** – Menu £ 36 (dinner) – Carte £ 21/40

◆ Part 16C former coaching inn delightfully situated on River Dee. Country house style accentuated by antiques and china. Individually decorated bedrooms. Dee views and floral displays enhance the attraction of the dining room.

BARRA (Isle of) – Western Isles – **501** X12/13 – ✉ Castlebay **29** A3

CASTLEBAY – Western Isles **29** A3

Castlebay

✉ HS9 5XD – (01871) 810 223 – www.castlebayhotel.com – Fax (01871) 810 455 – Closed 22 December-10 January

15 rm – †£ 48/77 ††£ 120/142 **Rest** – *(bar lunch)* Carte £ 16/32

◆ Personally run, early 20C hotel situated in prominent position overlooking Kisimul Castle and Isle of Vatersay. Cosy sitting room and spacious bar. Homely, well-kept rooms. Linen-clad dining room with excellent bay view and traditional fare.

Grianamul without rest

✉ HS9 5XD – (01871) 810 416 – www.members.aol.com/macneilronnie – April-October

3 rm – †£ 40 ††£ 60

◆ Purpose-built guesthouse, convenient for local amenities; adjacent to heritage centre. Comfortable, homely lounge. Very sunny breakfast room. Sizeable, well-kept rooms.

NORTH BAY – Western Isles **29** A3

Heathbank

✉ HS9 5YQ – (01871) 890 266 – www.barrahotel.co.uk – Fax (01871) 890 266 – Closed 3 weeks January

5 rm – †£ 57/90 ††£ 84/90

Rest – *(bar lunch) (booking essential in winter)* Carte £ 15/29

◆ Former 19C schoolhouse on a quiet road. Relax in ample space, including a terrace to admire the landscape. Airy bedrooms, in light lemon hues with DVDs, are the strong point. Home-cooked menus in bar and intimate dining room.

BENDERLOCH – Argyll and Bute – **501** D14 – see Connel

BERNISDALE – Highland – **501** A/B11 – see Skye (Isle of)

BISHOPTON – Renfrewshire – 501 G16 25 B1

Edinburgh 59 mi. – Dumbarton 9 mi. – Glasgow 13 mi.

Mar Hall

rm,

Earl of Mar Estate, Northeast : 1 mi. on B 815 ✉ PA7 5NW – (0141) 812 9999 – www.marhall.com – Fax (0141) 812 9997

50 rm – £ 120/205 £ 140/205 – 3 suites

Rest *Cristal* – Menu £ 40 – Carte £ 29/44

♦ Stunning Gothic mansion with period charm, boasting well-equipped gym, impressive spa, and championship golf course. Stylish interior; chic, superior bedrooms. 250 acres of parkland stretch to the Clyde. High-ceilinged Cristal offers classical fine dining and unusual combinations.

BLAIRGOWRIE – Perth and Kinross – 501 J14 – pop. 7 965 Scotland 28 C2

Edinburgh 60 mi. – Dundee 19 mi. – Perth 16 mi.

26 Wellmeadow (01250) 872960, blairgowrie@visitscotland.com

Scone Palace★★ AC, S : 12 mi. by A 93

Kinloch House

West : 3 mi. on A 923 ✉ PH10 6SG – (01250) 884 237 – www.kinlochhouse.com – Fax (01250) 884 333 – Closed 14-29 December

17 rm – £ 100/225 £ 210/310 – 1 suite **Rest** – Menu £ 25/50

♦ Wonderfully tranquil, ivy-clad 19C country house set in its own grounds. Appealingly traditional lounges. Conservatory and leisure centre. Large, smart, well-furnished rooms. Restaurant with bright yellow décor and Scottish influenced cooking.

Heathpark House without rest

Coupar Angus Rd, Rosemount, Southeast : 0.75 mi. on A 923 ✉ PH10 6JT – (01250) 870 700 – www.heathparkhouse.com – Fax (01250) 870 700 – Closed 1 January, 1 week in autumn and 25 December

3 rm – £ 43/45 £ 75

♦ Substantial Victorian guesthouse in a quiet residential spot with mature gardens. Spacious lounge; breakfasts taken in welcoming dining room. Large, individually styled rooms.

Gilmore House without rest

Perth Rd, Southwest : 0.5 mi. on A 93 ✉ PH10 6EJ – (01250) 872 791 – www.gilmorehouse.co.uk – Closed Christmas

3 rm – £ 60/70

♦ Traditional stone-built guesthouse only a few minutes' walk from town, well run by owners. Comfortable front lounge and breakfast room. Cosy and keenly priced accommodation.

BONNYRIGG – Midlothian – 501 K16 – pop. 14 457 26 C1

Edinburgh 8 mi. – Galashiels 27 mi. – Glasgow 50 mi.

Dalhousie Castle

Southeast : 1.25 mi. on B 704 ✉ EH19 3JB – (01875) 820 153 – www.dalhousiecastle.co.uk – Fax (01875) 823 365

36 rm – £ 85/185 £ 125/295 – 2 suites

Rest *Dungeon* – *(dinner only) (booking essential for non-residents)* Menu £ 47 **s**

Rest *The Orangery* – Carte £ 31/32 **s**

♦ 13C castle on the banks of the South Esk with spacious, medieval style rooms and historically-themed bedrooms. Popular venue for weddings, with falconry centre in grounds. Hugely impressive barrel-vaulted Dungeon features suits of armour. The Orangery overlooks river and parkland, and offers a less formal menu.

BOWMORE – Argyll and Bute – 501 B16 – see Islay (Isle of)

BRAEMAR – Aberdeenshire – 501 J12 – pop. 500 Scotland 28 C2

Edinburgh 85 mi. – Aberdeen 58 mi. – Dundee 51 mi. – Perth 51 mi.

The Mews, Mar Rd (013397) 41600, braemar@visitscotland.com

Cluniebank Rd, (013397) 41 618

Lin O'Dee★, W : 5 m

SCOTLAND

Callater Lodge without rest
9 Glenshee Rd ✉ AB35 5YQ – ✆ (013397) 41 275 – www.hotel-braemar.co.uk – closed 21-28 December
6 rm – †£ 40/55 ††£ 75
◆ Stone house in large garden on the road to Glenshee. Lounge with leather chairs and library with inglenook. Pleasant spacious bedrooms, some with view across the valley.

BREASCLETE – **Western Isles Outer Hebrides** – **501** Z9 – **see Lewis and Harris (Isle of)**

BRIDGEND OF LINTRATHEN – **Angus** – **501** K13 – ✉ **Kirriemuir** **28** C2

Edinburgh 70 – Dundee 20 – Pitlochry 37

Lochside Lodge with rm
– ✆ (01575) 560 340 – www.lochsidelodge.com – Fax (01575) 560 251 – Closed 1-31 January , 2 weeks October, 25-26 December, Sunday and Monday
6 rm – †£ 75 ††£ 100/120 **Rest** – *(dinner only)* Menu £ 35
◆ Spacious stone building set beside a picturesque loch and glen. Formal restaurant offers ambitious, imaginative menu served at smart linen-clad tables. Well-kept bedrooms are split between the courtyard and hayloft.

The Steading
✉ DD8 5JJ – ✆ (01575) 560 340 – www.lochsidelodge.com – Fax (01575) 560 251 – Closed first 3 weeks in January, 2 weeks in early October, 25-27 December, Sunday and Monday
Rest – Menu £ 13/25
◆ Informal counterpart to Lochside Lodge. Sharing the same kitchen, dishes range from steady classics to more imaginative offerings. Tasty homemade bread, ice cream and desserts.

SCOTLAND

BROADFORD – **Highland** – **501** C12 – **see Skye (Isle of)**

BRODICK – **North Ayrshire** – **501** E17 – **see Arran (Isle of)**

BRORA – **Highland** – **501** I9 – **pop. 1 140** **30** D2

Edinburgh 234 mi. – Inverness 78 mi. – Wick 49 mi.
Golf Rd, ✆ (01408) 621 417

Royal Marine
Golf Rd ✉ KW9 6QS – ✆ (01408) 621 252 – www.royalmarinebrora.com – Fax (01408) 621 181
22 rm – †£ 89/135 ††£ 194 **Rest** – Carte £ 21/33
◆ Originally a laird's home. Traditional lounge with log fire. Good leisure facilities plus snooker room and unlimited golf. Refurbished, modern bedrooms. Cuisine reflects Highland location.

BROUGHTY FERRY – **Dundee** – **501** L14 – **see Dundee**

BUNCHREW – **Highland** – **see Inverness**

BURRAY – **Orkney Islands** – **501** L7 – **see Orkney Islands**

BUTE (Isle of) – **Argyll and Bute** – **501** E16 – **pop. 7 354** **27** B3

from Rothesay to Wemyss Bay (Mainland) (Caledonian MacBrayne Ltd) frequent services daily (35 mn)
– from Rhubodach to Colintraive (Mainland) (Caledonian MacBrayne Ltd) frequent services daily (5 mn)

ASCOG – **Argyll and Bute** **27** B3

Balmory Hall without rest
Balmory Rd ✉ PA20 9LL – ✆ (01700) 500 669 – www.balmoryhall.com – February-October
4 rm – †£ 100 ††£ 170
◆ Impressive, carefully restored mid 19C Italianate mansion. Columned hall and well-furnished lounge. Tastefully furnished bedrooms. Breakfast at an antique table.

CADBOLL – Highland – see Tain

CAIRNBAAN – Argyll and Bute – **501** D15 – see Lochgilphead

CALLANDER – Stirling – **501** H15 – **pop. 2 754** Scotland **28** C2

Edinburgh 52 mi. – Glasgow 43 mi. – Oban 71 mi. – Perth 41 mi.

Rob Roy and Trossachs Visitor Centre, Ancaster Sq (08707) 200628, callander@visitscotland.com

Aveland Rd, (01877) 330 090

Town★

The Trossachs★★★ (Loch Katrine★★) – Hilltop Viewpoint★★★ (★★★) W : 10 mi. by A 821

Roman Camp

Main St FK17 8BG – (01877) 330 003 – www.romancamphotel.co.uk – Fax (01877) 331 533

11 rm – £ 85/125 £ 185/195 – 3 suites

Rest *The Restaurant* – see restaurant listing

◆ Attractive 17C former hunting lodge by Roman settlement. Characterful interior with beautiful drawing room, antique-filled library and chapel. Classical bedrooms boast bold floral designs.

Brook Linn without rest

Leny Feus FK17 8AU – (01877) 330 103 – www.brooklinn-scotland.co.uk – Fax (01877) 330 103 – Easter-October

4 rm – £ 70/80

◆ Victorian house in a fairly secluded rural location. Homely style lounge and wood furnished dining room for breakfast. Traditional, well-kept bedrooms.

Lubnaig without rest

Leny Feus FK17 8AS – (01877) 330 376 – www.lubnaighouse.co.uk – Fax (01877) 330 376 – May-mid October

8 rm – £ 50/57 £ 70/84

◆ Built in 1864, a characterful Victorian house on the outskirts of town. Well-kept mature gardens visible from communal rooms. Homely bedrooms, two in converted stables.

The Restaurant – at Roman Camp Hotel

Main St FK17 8BG – (01877) 330 003 – www.romancamphotel.co.uk – Fax (01877) 331 533

Rest – Menu £ 29/49 – Carte dinner £ 44/64

◆ Spacious country house restaurant with unique ceiling and impressive flower displays. Daily changing set menu and concise à la carte offer ambitious modern dishes of local, seasonal produce.

Mhor Fish

75-77 Main Street FK17 8DX – (01877) 330 213 – www.mhor.net – Fax (01877) 330 282 – Closed Monday

Rest – Seafood – Menu £ 12/25 **s** – Carte £ 11/26 **s**

◆ Simple, busy, well-run eatery on main street; popular with locals. Great variety of fish, homemade pies and chips cooked in beef dripping. A touch more serious in the evening.

CARDROSS – Argyll and Bute – **501** G16 – **pop. 1 925** Scotland **25** A-B1

Edinburgh 63 mi. – Glasgow 17 mi. – Helensburgh 5 mi.

The Clyde Estuary★

Kirkton House without rest

Darleith Rd G82 5EZ – (01389) 841 951 – www.kirktonhouse.co.uk – Fax (01389) 841 868 – Closed January and December

6 rm – £ 45 £ 70

◆ Former farmhouse with origins in 18C; quiet, elevated spot overlooking North Clyde. Ideal stop-off between Glasgow airport and Highlands. Bedrooms all have country views.

CARINISH – Western Isles – **501** Y11 – see Uist (Isles of)

CARNOUSTIE – Angus – 501 L14 – pop. 10 561 — 28 D2

Edinburgh 68 mi. – Aberdeen 59 mi. – Dundee 12 mi.

Carnoustie Library, 21 High St ✆ (01241) 859620, carnoustie.library@angus.gov.uk

Monifieth Golf Links Princes St, Medal Starter's Box, ✆ (01382) 532 767

Burnside Links Par, ✆ (01241) 802 290

Panmure Barry, ✆ (01241) 855 120

Buddon Links Links Par, ✆ (01241) 802 280

The Old Manor without rest

Panbride, Northeast : 1.25 mi. by A 930 on Panbride Rd ✉ DD7 6JP – ✆ (01241) 854 804 – www.oldmanorcarnoustie.com – Fax (01241) 855 327 – Closed Christmas and New Year

5 rm – †£ 60/70 ††£ 75/80

◆ Substantial 18C house five minutes' drive from championship golf course. Good views of Tay Estuary. Hearty Scottish breakfast guaranteed. Smart rooms, some with brass beds.

CARRADALE – Argyll and Bute – 501 D17 – see Kintyre (Peninsula)

CASTLEBAY – Western Isles – 501 X12/1 – see Barra (Isle of)

CASTLE DOUGLAS – Dumfries and Galloway – 501 I19 – pop. 3 671 — 25 B3

Scotland

Edinburgh 98 mi. – Ayr 49 mi. – Dumfries 18 mi. – Stranraer 57 mi.

Market Hill ✆ (01556) 502611 (Easter-October), castledouglastic@visitscotland.com

Abercromby Rd, ✆ (01556) 502 801

Threave Garden★★ **AC**, SW : 2.5 mi. by A 75 – Threave Castle★ **AC**, W : 1 m

Douglas House without rest

63 Queen St ✉ DG7 1HS – ✆ (01556) 503 262 – www.douglas-house.com

4 rm – †£ 35/65 ††£ 75/90

◆ Attractive stone built house dating from 1880, with some original features. Extensive choice at breakfast. Uncluttered, individually decorated bedrooms. Very personable owners.

Smithy House without rest

The Buchan, Southwest : 0.75 m on A 75 (Stranraer rd) ✉ DG7 1TH – ✆ (01556) 503 841 – www.smithyhouse.co.uk – Closed Christmas and New Year

3 rm – †£ 60/70 ††£ 75

◆ Converted 14C smithy in large garden 10 minutes walk from town. Communal breakfast table. Guests' lounge featuring original forge. Pleasant bedrooms facing garden or loch.

CAWDOR – Highland – 501 I11 – pop. 812 – ✉ Inverness — 30 D2

Edinburgh 170 mi. – Aberdeen 100 mi. – Inverness 14 mi.

Cawdor Tavern

The Lane ✉ IV12 5XP – ✆ (01667) 404 777 – www.cawdortavern.info – Fax (01667) 454 584 – Closed 25 December and 1 January

Rest – *(booking essential)* Carte £ 17/25

◆ Charming, personally run whitewashed pub – formerly the joiners' workshop of Cawdor Castle. Wide-ranging menu offers a good selection of frequently changing, classically based dishes.

CHIRNSIDE – Scottish Borders – 501 N16 – pop. 1 204 – ✉ Duns — 26 D1

Edinburgh 52 mi. – Berwick-upon-Tweed 8 mi. – Glasgow 95 mi. – Newcastle upon Tyne 70 mi.

Chirnside Hall

East : 1.25 mi. on A 6105 ✉ TD11 3LD – ✆ (01890) 818 219 – www.chirnsidehallhotel.com – Fax (01890) 818 231 – Closed March

10 rm – 🚹£ 85 🚻£ 150

Rest – *(dinner only) (booking essential for non-residents)* Menu £ 30

◆ Large, imposing, Victorian country house in a rural location. Well appointed interiors with good quality period atmosphere. Individually decorated bedrooms. Smart place settings in a traditionally appointed dining room.

CLEAT – Orkney Islands – 501 K/L6 – see Orkney Islands (Island of Westray) – ✉ Orkney Islands

---

COLONSAY (Isle of) – Argyll and Bute – 501 B15 – pop. 106 — 27 A2

London 502 mi. – Edinburgh 129 mi. – Greenock 98 mi.

from Scalasaig to Oban (Caledonian MacBrayne Ltd) 3 weekly (2 h) – from Scalasaig to Kintyre Peninsula (Kennacraig) via Isle of Islay (Port Askaig) (Caledonian MacBrayne Ltd) weekly

18 Colonsay, ✆ (01951) 200 290

SCALASAIG – Argyll and Bute – ✉ Colonsay — 27 A2

The Colonsay

✉ PA61 7YP – ✆ (01951) 200 316 – www.colonsayestate.co.uk – Fax (01951) 200 353 – March-October, Christmas and New Year

9 rm – 🚹£ 65/110 🚻£ 90/110, £ 6.50 **Rest** – *(bar lunch)* Carte £ 21/29

◆ Listed building from mid-18C; a thoroughly rural, remote setting. Public areas include excellent photos of local scenes and the only bar on the island. Bright, modern rooms. Welcoming, informal dining room.

SCOTLAND

COMRIE – Perth and Kinross – 501 I14 – pop. 1 926 — 28 C2

Edinburgh 66 mi. – Glasgow 56 mi. – Oban 70 mi. – Perth 24 mi.

9 Comrie Laggan Braes, ✆ (01764) 670 055

The Royal

Melville Sq ✉ PH6 2DN – ✆ (01764) 679 200 – www.royalhotel.co.uk – Fax (01764) 679 219

11 rm – 🚹£ 80 🚻£ 130/170

Rest *Royal* – Menu £ 28 (dinner) – Carte £ 21/28

◆ 18C coaching inn in centre of town: Queen Victoria once stayed here. Stylish, contemporary feel, especially individually decorated bedrooms, with four posters and antiques. Restaurant with two rooms: conservatory brasserie or intimate dining room.

CONNEL – Argyll and Bute – 501 D14 – ✉ Oban — 27 B2

Edinburgh 118 mi. – Glasgow 88 mi. – Inverness 113 mi. – Oban 5 mi.

Ards House without rest

on A 85 ✉ PA37 1PT – ✆ (01631) 710 255 – www.ardshouse.com – Fax (01631) 710 857 – Closed Christmas and New Year

4 rm – 🚹£ 55/60 🚻£ 78/92

◆ Victorian house overlooking Loch Etive. Well run with a smart and elegant atmosphere. Traditional décor and appointments throughout communal areas and bedrooms.

The Oyster Inn with rm

✉ PA37 1PJ – ✆ (01631) 710 666 – www.oysterinn.co.uk – Fax (01631) 710 042

16 rm – 🚹£ 23 🚻£ 44/59 **Rest** – Seafood – Carte £ 20/40 **s**

◆ Cosy 18C pub with exposed stone walls, log fires and outside terrace. Good, honest cooking with the focus on seafood. Always popular with the locals. Mix of pine furnished bedrooms and bunk rooms.

at Benderloch North : 2.5 mi. by A 828 – ✉ Connel

Dun Na Mara without rest

✉ PA37 1RT – ✆ (01631) 720 233 – www.dunnamara.com – Closed December and January

7 rm – ♦£ 50/70 ♦♦£ 90/115

◆ Fully restored Edwardian home with fine views. Minimalistic, intimate interior. Pleasant gardens lead to idyllic private beach. Individual, modish rooms boast clean lines.

CRAIGNURE – **Argyll and Bute** – **501** C14 – **see Mull (Isle of)**

CRAILING – **Borders** – **501** M17 – **see Jedburgh**

CRIEFF – **Perth and Kinross** – **501** I14 – **pop. 6 579** Scotland **28** C2

Edinburgh 60 mi. – Glasgow 50 mi. – Oban 76 mi. – Perth 18 mi.

Town Hall, High St ✆ (01764) 652578, criefftic@visitscotland.com

Perth Rd, ✆ (01764) 652 909

Muthill Peat Rd, ✆ (01764) 681 523

Town★

Drummond Castle Gardens★ **AC**, S : 2 mi. by A 822. Scone Palace★★ **AC**, E : 16 mi. by A 85 and A 93

Merlindale

Perth Rd, on A 85 ✉ PH7 3EQ – ✆ (01764) 655 205 – www.merlindale.co.uk – Fax (01764) 655 205 – Closed mid December-mid January

3 rm – ♦£ 40/55 ♦♦£ 75/85

Rest – *(by arrangement, communal dining)* Menu £ 35

◆ Traditional, stone-built house close to the town. Well-equipped bedrooms are individually decorated and very comfortable. Accomplished evening meals at a communal table.

Yann's at Glenearn House with rm

Perth Rd, on A 85 ✉ PH7 3EQ – ✆ (01764) 650 111 – www.yannsatglenearnhouse.com – Closed 1 week Spring, 2 weeks Autumn, 25-26 December, Monday and Tuesday

5 rm – ♦£ 50/55 ♦♦£ 70/80 **Rest** – French – Carte £ 20/30

◆ Busy, keenly run, bistro-style restaurant with informal lounge. Well-priced, French cooking makes good use of Scottish produce; Savoyard sharing dishes a speciality. Polite, swift service. Comfortable bedrooms with good facilities and a relaxed, bohemian style.

CRINAN – **Argyll and Bute** – **501** D15 – ✉ **Lochgilphead** Scotland **27** B2

Edinburgh 137 mi. – Glasgow 91 mi. – Oban 36 mi.

Hamlet★

Kilmory Knap (Macmillan's Cross★) SW : 14 m

Crinan

✉ PA31 8SR – ✆ (01546) 830 261 – www.crinanhotel.com – Fax (01546) 830 292 – Closed 4-31 January and 23-28 December

20 rm (dinner included) – ♦£ 120/140 ♦♦£ 250/360

Rest *Westward* – *(dinner only)* Menu £ 45

Rest *The Mainbrace* – Carte £ 20/45

◆ Superbly located, well-run hotel with commanding views of Loch Crinan and Sound of Jura. Simply furnished bedrooms set over 3 floors; best on 3rd floor are spacious with large windows. Emphasis on fresh seafood in Westward Restaurant. Interesting bar menu in The Mainbrace.

CROSSFORD – **Fife** – **501** J15 – **see Dunfermline**

CULLODEN – **Highland** – **501** H11 – **see Inverness**

CUPAR – Fife – 501 K15 – pop. 8 506 28 C2

Edinburgh 45 mi. – Dundee 15 mi. – Perth 23 mi.

Ostler's Close

25 Bonnygate ✉ KY15 4BU – ✆ (01334) 655 574 – www.ostlerclose.co.uk – Fax (01334) 654 036 – Closed 1-2 January, 2 weeks Easter, 2 weeks mid October, 25-26 December, Sunday and Monday

Rest – *(dinner only and Saturday lunch)* Carte £ 25/41

◆ Personally run, welcoming restaurant with snug cottage feel and characterful low ceilings; hidden away down an alley. Particular attention given to prime Scottish meat and local fish.

CURRIE – City of Edinburgh – 501 K16 – See Edinburgh

DALRY – North Ayrshire – 501 F16 25 A1

Edinburgh 70 mi. – Ayr 21 mi. – Glasgow 25 mi.

Lochwood Farm Steading without rest

Southwest : 5 mi. by A 737 and the Saltcoats rd ✉ KA21 6NG – ✆ (01294) 552 529 – www.lochwoodfarm.co.uk

5 rm – £ 50 £ 80

◆ Excellent hospitality at a good value farmhouse on one hundred acres of dairy farm. Fine views of country and coast from outside hot tub. Pleasant, well-kept little bedrooms.

Braidwoods (Keith Braidwood)

Drumastle Mill Cottage, Southwest : 1.5 mi. by A 737 on Saltcoats rd ✉ KA24 4LN – ✆ (01294) 833 544 – www.braidwoods.co.uk – Fax (01294) 833 553 – Closed 1-19 January, first 2 weeks September, 25-31 December, Monday and Tuesday lunch, dinner Sunday and Sunday lunch from May-September

Rest – *(booking essential)* Menu £ 25/40

Spec. Scallops, crushed peas and Parma ham. Loin and shoulder of lamb with spinach and rosemary jus. Heather honey parfait with Tayberry coulis.

◆ Well-established crofter's cottage in remote location; very personally run by husband and wife team. Two-part dining room with homely feel. Seasonal, regional produce is the cornerstone of the flavoursome classical dishes. Smooth service.

SCOTLAND

DINGWALL – Highland – 501 G11 – pop. 5 026 30 C2

Edinburgh 172 mi. – Inverness 14 mi.

Cafe India Brasserie

Lockhart House, Tulloch St ✉ IV15 9JZ – ✆ (01349) 862 552 – closed 25 December

Rest – Indian – Menu £ 9 (lunch) – Carte £ 23/33

◆ Bustling, locally regarded Indian restaurant, handily located in town centre. Updated décor is fresh and modern. Authentically prepared, tasty regional Indian food.

DOONFOOT – South Ayrshire – 501 G17 – see Ayr

DORNOCH – Highland – 501 H10 – pop. 1 206 Scotland 30 D2

Edinburgh 219 mi. – Inverness 63 mi. – Wick 65 mi.

Sheriff Court House, Castle St ✆ (08452) 255121, dornoch@visitscotland.com

Royal Dornoch Golf Rd, ✆ (01862) 810 219

Town★

Highfield House without rest

Evelix Rd ✉ IV25 3HR – ✆ (01862) 810 909 – www.highfieldhouse.co.uk – February-October

3 rm – £ 55 £ 80

◆ Purpose-built guesthouse with garden and fine Highland views. Small, spruce lounge; neat and tidy breakfast room. Bedrooms offer ample comforts: one has whirlpool bath.

2 Quail without rest

Castle St ✉ IV25 3SN – ✆ (01862) 811 811 – www.2quail.com – Closed 2 weeks spring and 1 week Christmas

3 rm – £ 70/110 £ 80/110

◆ Terraced townhouse on main street of busy village; traditional in style, with an intimate feel. Antique-furnished bedrooms boast good facilities. Small library; comfortable lounge.

DOUNBY – Orkney Islands – 501 K6 – see Orkney Islands

DRUMBEG – Highland – 501 E9 – ✉ Highland 30 C1

Edinburgh 262 mi. – Inverness 105 mi. – Ullapool 48 mi.

Blar na Leisg at Drumbeg House

take first right on entering village from Kylesku direction ✉ IV27 4NW – ✆ (01571) 833 325 – www.blarnaleisg.com – Fax (01571) 833 325

4 rm (dinner included) – £ 100/140 £ 200/230

Rest – *(by arrangement)* Menu £ 40

◆ Edwardian house in tranquil spot, with neat lawned gardens and impressive view. Stylish and modern, it boasts a collection of Scottish art, a state-of-the-art kitchen and good-sized rooms with contemporary furniture and bold fabrics. Set menu of home-cooked local produce.

DRUMNADROCHIT – Highland – 501 G11 – pop. 813 – ✉ Milton 30 C2

Scotland

Edinburgh 172 mi. – Inverness 16 mi. – Kyle of Lochalsh 66 mi.

Loch Ness★★ – Loch Ness Monster Exhibition★ **AC** – The Great Glen★

Drumbuie Farm without rest

Drumbuie, East : 0.75 mi. by A 82 ✉ IV63 6XP – ✆ (01456) 450 634 – www.loch-ness-farm.co.uk – Fax (01456) 450 459 – Closed Christmas

3 rm – £ 42/45 £ 62/68

◆ Immaculate purpose-built guesthouse on working farm with Highland cattle. Pleasant breakfast room has Loch Ness views. Good collection of malt whiskies. Spacious bedrooms.

DUISDALEMORE – Highland – see Skye (Isle of)

DULNAIN BRIDGE – Highland – 501 J12 – see Grantown-on-Spey

DUMFRIES – Dumfries and Galloway – 501 J18 – pop. 31 146 26 C3

Scotland

Edinburgh 80 mi. – Ayr 59 mi. – Carlisle 34 mi. – Glasgow 79 mi.

64 Whitesands ✆ (01387) 253862, dumfriestic@visitscotland.com A

Dumfries & Galloway Maxwelltown 2 Laurieston Ave, ✆ (01387) 253 582

Dumfries & County Edinburgh Rd, Nunfield, ✆ (01387) 253 585

Crichton Bankend Rd, ✆ (01387) 247 894

Town★ – Midsteeple★ A **A**

Lincluden College (Tomb★) **AC**, N : 1.5 mi. by College St A. Drumlanrig Castle★★ (cabinets★) **AC**, NW : 16.5 mi. by A 76 A – Shambellie House Museum of Costume (Costume Collection★) S : 7.25 mi. by A 710 A - Sweetheart Abbey★ **AC**, S : 8 mi. by A 710 A – Caerlaverock Castle★ (Renaissance fa 0.5ade★★) **AC**, SE : 9 mi. by B 725 B – Glenkiln (Sculptures★) W : 9 mi. by A 780 - A - and A 75

Hazeldean House without rest

4 Moffat Rd ✉ DG1 1NJ – ✆ (01387) 266 178 – www.hazeldeanhouse.com – Fax (01387) 266 178 B**u**

7 rm – £ 35/45 £ 60

◆ Interestingly furnished 19C villa. Entrance door has original stained glass. Characterful antiques and Victoriana in lounge. Conservatory breakfast room. Spacious bedrooms.

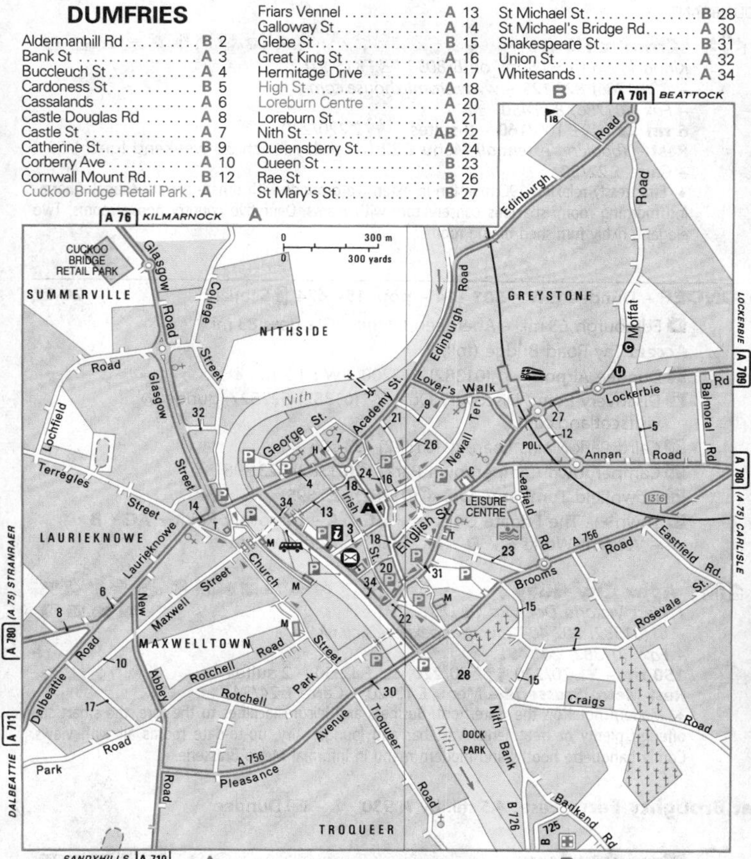

🏠 Hamilton House without rest

12 Moffat Rd ✉ DG1 1NJ – ✆ (01387) 266 606
– www.hamiltonhousedumfries.co.uk
– Fax (01387) 262 060
– Closed Christmas and New Year — **Bc**

7 rm ☕ – 🚹£ 35/45 🚹🚹£ 56/60

◆ Converted Victorian townhouse furnished in light colours, with uncluttered, modern feel. Bright breakfast room and small open-plan lounge with plenty of local info. Personable owners.

DUNAIN PARK – **Highland** – **see Inverness**

DUNBLANE – **Stirling** – **501** I15 – **pop. 7 911** 📗 Scotland — **28** C2

▶ Edinburgh 42 mi. – Glasgow 33 mi. – Perth 29 mi.

👁 Town★ – Cathedral★★ (west front★★)

⊙ Doune★ (castle★ **AC**) W : 4.5 mi. by A 820

Cromlix House

Kinbuck, North : 3.5 mi. on B 8033 ✉ FK15 9JT
– ✆ (01786) 822 125 – www.cromlixhouse.com
– Fax (01786) 825 450
6 rm – £ 100/160 – 8 suites – £ 220/240
Rest – *(booking essential)* Menu £ 22 (weekday lunch 30 weekend lunch)/50
– Carte £ 22/50

◆ Effortlessly relaxing 19C mansion in extensive grounds with ornate private chapel. Charming morning room; spacious conservatory with plants. Definitive country house rooms. Two elegant, richly furnished dining rooms.

DUNDEE – **Dundee City** – **501** L14 – **pop. 154 674** Scotland **28** C2

Edinburgh 63 mi. – Aberdeen 67 mi. – Glasgow 83 mi.

Access Tay Road Bridge (toll) Y

Dundee Airport : ✆ (01382) 662200, SW : 1.5 mi. Z

Discovery Point, Discovery Quay ✆ (01382) 527527, dundee@visitscotland.com

Caird Park Mains Loan, ✆ (01382) 453 606

Camperdown Camperdown Park, ✆ (01382) 623 398

Downfield Turnberry Ave, ✆ (01382) 825 595

Town★ - The Frigate Unicorn★ **AC** Y **A** – Discovery Point★ **AC** Y **B** – Verdant Works★ Z **D** – McManus Galleries★ Y **M**

Apex City Quay

1 West Victoria Dock Rd ✉ DD1 3JP
– ✆ (01382) 202 404 – www.apexhotels.co.uk
– Fax (01382) 201 401 Y**a**
150 rm – £ 70/220 £ 70/220, £ 12.50 – 2 suites
Rest ***Metro Brasserie*** – Menu £ 13/20 – Carte £ 24/34

◆ Modern hotel on the waterfront. Business and leisure facilities to the fore, the smart spa offering plenty of treatments. Vast bar and lounge. Airy, up-to-date rooms all with views. Comfy banquette booths and modern menu in informal Metro Brasserie.

at Broughty Ferry East : 4.5 mi. by A 930 - Z – ✉ Dundee

Broughty Ferry

16 West Queen St ✉ DD5 1AR – ✆ (01382) 480 027
– www.hotelbroughtyferry.co.uk – Fax (01382) 739 426
16 rm – £ 68/80 £ 88/112
Rest ***Bombay Brasserie*** – Indian – Carte £ 24/31 **s**

◆ Family owned and friendly modern hotel beside the main road. The spacious, individually decorated bedrooms are furnished to a high standard. Brasserie serves elaborate, authentic Indian and European-influenced menus.

DUNFERMLINE – **Fife** – **501** J15 – **pop. 39 229** Scotland **28** C3

Edinburgh 16 mi. – Dundee 48 mi. – Motherwell 39 mi.

1 High St ✆ (01383) 720999, dunfermline@visitscotland.com

Canmore Venturefair Ave, ✆ (01383) 724 969

Pitreavie Queensferry Rd, ✆ (01383) 722 591

Pitfirrane Crossford, ✆ (01383) 723 534

Saline Kinneddar Hill, ✆ (01383) 852 591

Town★ - Abbey★ (Abbey Church★★) **AC**

Forth Bridges★★, S : 5 mi. by A 823 and B 980. Culross★★ (Village★★★, Palace★★ **AC**, Study★ **AC**), W : 7 mi. by A 994 and B 9037

SCOTLAND

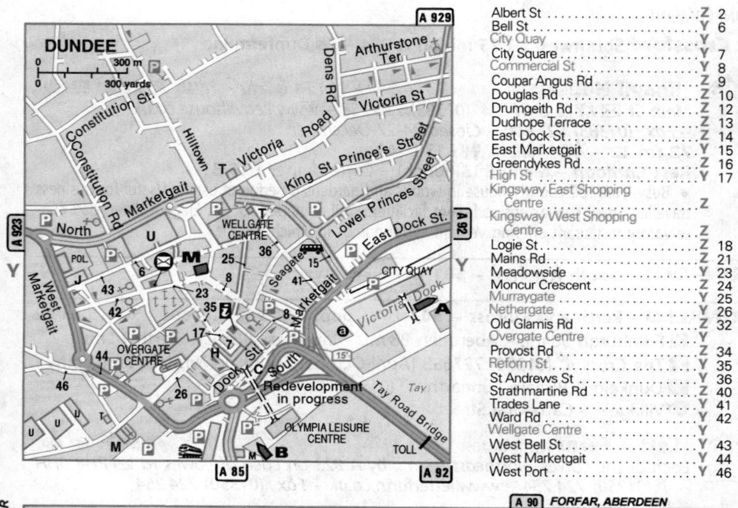

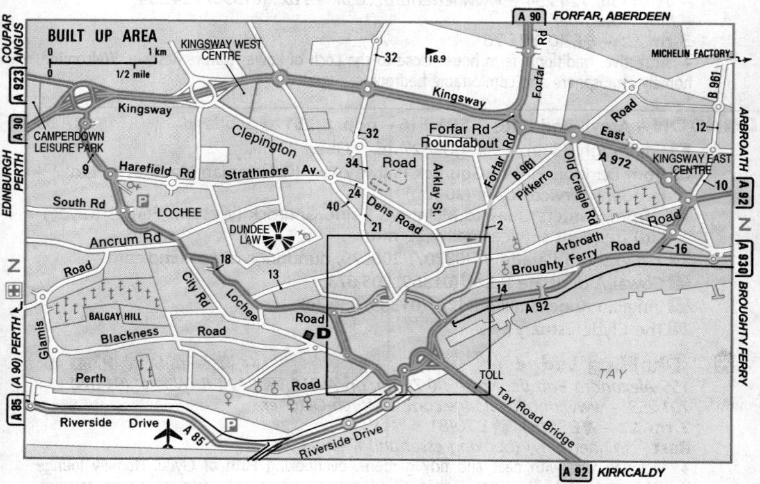

Garvock House

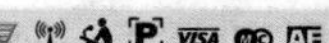

St John's Drive, Transy, East : 0.75 mi. by A 907 off Garvock Hill
✉ KY12 7TU – ✆ (01383) 621 067 – www.garvock.co.uk
– Fax (01383) 621 168
26 rm – 🛉£ 70/93 🛉🛉£ 90/148
Rest – Menu £ 21 (lunch) – Carte dinner £ 22/38
◆ Privately owned Victorian house in woodland setting with classically decorated public areas. Contrastingly, most of the attractive, modish rooms are in a modern extension. Comfortable, smartly decorated dining room.

Good food at moderate prices? Look for the Bib Gourmand ☺.

at Crossford Southwest : 1.75 mi. on A 994 – ✉ Dunfermline

Keavil House

Main St ✉ KY12 8NN – ✆ (01383) 736 258 – www.keavilhouse.co.uk – Fax (01383) 621 600 – Closed 24-27 December

72 rm – £ 110/115 £ 130/140

Rest *Cardoon* – Menu £ 13 (lunch) – Carte dinner £ 19/31 **s**

◆ Busy, part 16C country house in woods and gardens on edge of estate. Useful for business traveller. Small bar, extensive leisure facilities. Well-equipped rooms. Elegant, linen-clad conservatory restaurant offering verdant surroundings in which to dine.

DUNFOOT – **South Ayrshire** – **501** G17 – **see Ayr**

DUNKELD – **Perth and Kinross** – **501** J14 – **pop. 1 005** Scotland **28** C2

Edinburgh 58 mi. – Aberdeen 88 mi. – Inverness 98 mi. – Perth 14 mi.

The Cross ✆ (01350) 727688 (April-October), dunkeld@visitscotland.com

Dunkeld & Birnam Fungarth, ✆ (01350) 727 524

Village★ - Cathedral Street★

Letter Farm without rest

Loch of the Lowes, Northeast : 3 mi. by A 923 on Loch of Lowes rd ✉ PH8 0HH – ✆ (01350) 724 254 – www.letterfarm.co.uk – Fax (01350) 724 254 – May-November

3 rm – £ 40 £ 76

◆ Attractive, traditional farm house close to the Loch of Lowes Nature Reserve. Welcoming, homely atmosphere and comfortable bedrooms.

DUNOON – **Argyll and Bute** – **501** F16 – **pop. 8 251** Scotland **27** B3

Edinburgh 73 mi. – Glasgow 27 mi. – Oban 77 mi.

from Dunoon Pier to Gourock Railway Pier (Caledonian MacBrayne Ltd) frequent services daily (20 mn)
– from Hunters Quay to McInroy's Point, Gourock (Western Ferries (Clyde) Ltd) frequent services daily (20 mn)

7 Alexandra Parade ✆ (08707) 200629, dunoon@visitscotland.com

Cowal Ardenslate Rd, ✆ (01369) 705 673

Innellan Knockamillie Rd, ✆ (01369) 830 242

The Clyde Estuary★

Dhailling Lodge

155 Alexandra Parade, North : 0.75 mi. on A 815 ✉ PA23 8AW – ✆ (01369) 701 253 – www.dhaillinglodge.com – March-October

7 rm – £ 35/81 £ 70/81

Rest – *(dinner only) (booking essential)* Menu £ 20

◆ Victorian villa with neat and tidy gardens, overlooking Firth of Clyde. Homely lounge boasts books and local guides. Individually decorated rooms with welcoming extra touches. Smart dining room with good views from all tables.

DUNVEGAN – **Highland** – **501** A11 – **see Skye (Isle of)**

DURNESS – **Highland** – **501** F8 – ✉ **Highland** **30** C1

Edinburgh 266 mi. – Thurso 78 mi. – Ullapool 71 mi.

Durine ✆ (0845) 2255121 (April-October)

Durness Balnakeil, ✆ (01971) 511 364

Mackay's

✉ IV27 4PN – ✆ (01971) 511 202 – www.visitmackays.com – Fax (01971) 511 321 – Easter-October

7 rm – £ 118/130 £ 118/130 **Rest** – Carte £ 25/38

◆ Smart grey house in most North Westerly village of the British Isles. Modern, comfortable bedrooms, pleasant bathrooms and good facilities. Small, cosy guest lounge. Rustic dining room serves concise menu of traditionally based dishes with a Scottish base.

SCOTLAND

DUROR – Highland – 501 E14 29 B3

▶ Edinburgh 131 mi. – Ballachulish 7 mi. – Oban 26 mi.

Bealach House

Salachan Glen, Southeast : 4.5 mi. by A 828 ✉ PA38 4BW – ✆ (01631) 740 298 – www.bealach-house.co.uk – closed January and December

3 rm – †£ 65 ††£ 100

Rest – *(by arrangement, communal dining)* Menu £ 28

◆ Down a one-and-a-half mile rural track for total privacy. This former crofter's house, set in eight acres, is immaculate, with snug conservatory and smart, well-kept rooms. Communal dining: daily changing menus have strong local base.

DYKE – Moray – 501 J11 – see Forres

EDDLESTON – Scottish Borders – 501 K16 – see Peebles

▶ Edinburgh 20 – Galashiels 22 – Peebles 4

EDINBANE – Highland – 501 A11 – see Skye (Isle of)

M.-P. Renier/MICHELIN

EDINBURGH

County: City of Edinburgh
Michelin regional map: **501** K16
Glasgow 46 mi.
– Newcastle upon Tyne 105 mi.

Population: 430 082
Scotland
Map reference: **26** C1

PRACTICAL INFORMATION

Tourist Information

Edinburgh & Scotland Information Centre, 3 Princes St ✆ (08452) 255 121, info@visitscotland.com

Edinburgh International Airport, ✆ (0870) 040 0007, edinburgh.airport@visitscotland.com

Airport

Edinburgh Airport : ✆ (0844) 481 8989, W : 6 mi. by A 8 AV

Golf Courses

Braid Hills Braid Hills Rd, ✆(0131) 447 6666

Carrick Knowe Glendevon Park, ✆(0131) 337 10 96

Duddingston Duddingston Road West, ✆(0131) 661 7688

Silverknowes Parkway, ✆(0131) 336 3843

Liberton 297 Gilmerton Rd, Kingston Grange, ✆(0131) 664 3009

Marriott Dalmahoy Hotel & C.C. Kriknewton, ✆(0131) 335 80 10

Portobello Stanley St, ✆(0131) 669 4361

SIGHTS

In town

City★★★ - Edinburgh International Festival★★★ (August) - Royal Museum of Scotland★★★ EZ **M2** – National Gallery of Scotland★★ DY **M4** - Royal Botanic Garden★★★ AV – The Castle★★ **AC** DYZ : Site★★★ - Palace Block (Honours of Scotland★★★) - St Margaret's Chapel (※★★★) - Great Hall (Hammerbeam Roof★★) – ⩤★★ from Argyle and Mill's Mount DZ - Abbey and Palace of Holyroodhouse★★ **AC** (Plasterwork Ceilings★★★, ※★★ from Arthur's Seat) BV – Royal Mile★★ : St Giles' Cathedral★★ (Crown Spire★★★) EYZ - Gladstone's Land★ **AC** EYZ **A** - Canongate Talbooth★ EY **B** – New Town★★ (Charlotte Square★★★ CY **14** - The Georgian House★ **AC** CY **D** – Scottish National Portrait Gallery★ EY **M6** - Dundas House★ EY **E**) – Scottish National Gallery of Modern Art★ AV **M1** - Victoria Street★ EZ **84** – Scott Monument★ (⩤★) **AC** EY **F** - Craigmillar Castle★ **AC**, SE : 3 mi. by A 7 BX – - Calton Hill (※★★★ **AC** from Nelson's Monument) EY – Dean Gallery★ AV opposite **M1** - Royal Yacht Britannia★ BV

On the outskirts

Edinburgh Zoo★★ **AC** AV – Hill End Ski Centre (※★★) **AC**, S : 5.5 mi. by A 702 BX – The Royal Observatory (West Tower ⩤★) **AC** BX – Ingleston, Scottish Agricultural Museum★, W : 6.5 mi. by A 8 AV

In the surrounding area

Rosslyn Chapel★★ **AC** (Apprentice Pillar★★★) S : 7.5 mi. by A 701 - BX - and B 7006 – Forth Bridges★★, NW : 9.5 mi. by A 90 AV – Hopetoun House★★ **AC**, NW : 11.5 mi. by A 90 - AV - and A 904 – Dalmeny★ - Dalmeny House★ **AC**, St Cuthbert's Church★ (Norman South Doorway★★) NW : 7 mi. by A 90 AV – Crichton Castle (Italianate courtyard range★) **AC**, SE : 10 mi. by A 7 - X - and B 6372

EDINBURGH

Street	Grid	No.
Bernard Terrace	EZ	3
Bread St	DZ	6
Bristo Pl.	EZ	7
Candlemaker Row	EZ	9
Castlehill	DZ	10
Castle St	DY	
Chambers St	EZ	12
Chapel St	EZ	13
Charlotte Square	CY	14
Deanhaugh St	CY	23
Douglas Gardens	CY	25
Drummond St	EZ	27
Forrest Rd	EZ	31
Frederick St	DY	
Gardner's Crescent	CZ	32
George IV Bridge	EZ	33
George St	DY	
Grassmarket	DZ	35
Hanover St	DY	
High St	EYZ	37
Home St	DZ	38
Hope St	CY	39
Johnston Terrace	DZ	42
King's Bridge	DZ	44
King's Stables Rd	DZ	45
Lawnmarket	EYZ	46
Leith St	EY	47
Leven St	DZ	48
Lothian St	EZ	51
Mound (The)	DY	55
North Bridge	EY	61
North St Andrew St	EY	66
Princes St	DY	
Raeburn Pl.	CY	69
Randolph Crescent	CY	71
St Andrew Square	EY	73
St James Centre	EY	
St Mary's St	EY	75
Shandwick Pl.	CYZ	77
South Charlotte St	DY	78
South St David St	DEY	79
Spittal St	DZ	83
Victoria St	EZ	84
Waterloo Pl.	EY	87
Waverley Bridge	EY	89
Waverley Market	EY	
West Maitland St	CZ	92

Traffic subject to disruption due to tram construction

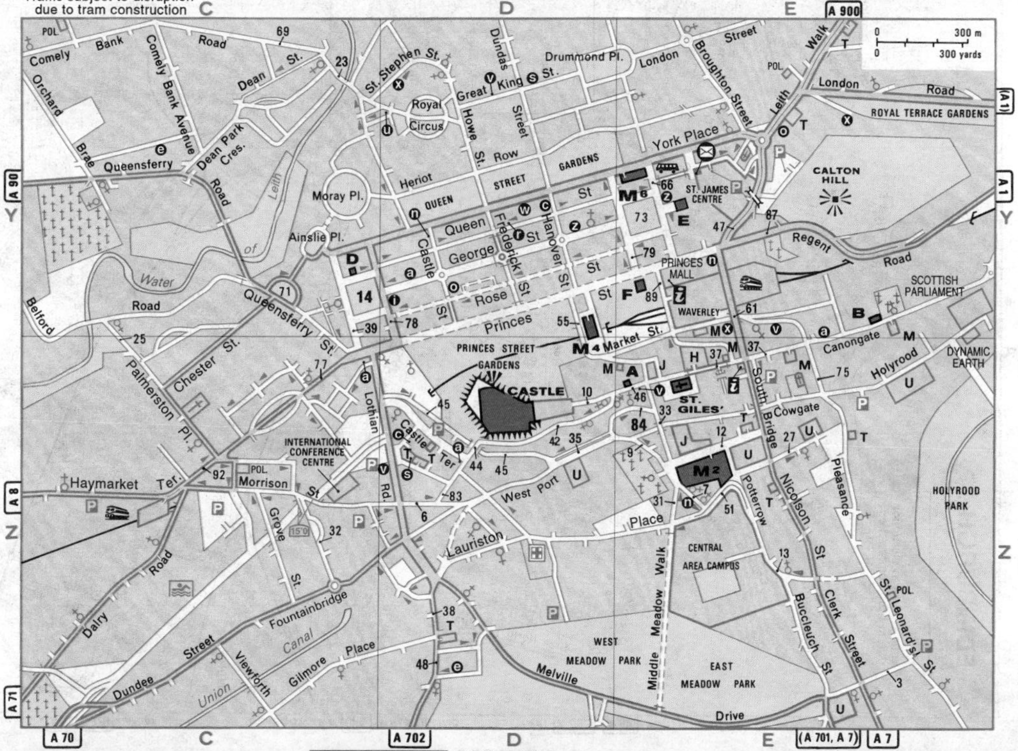

SCOTLAND

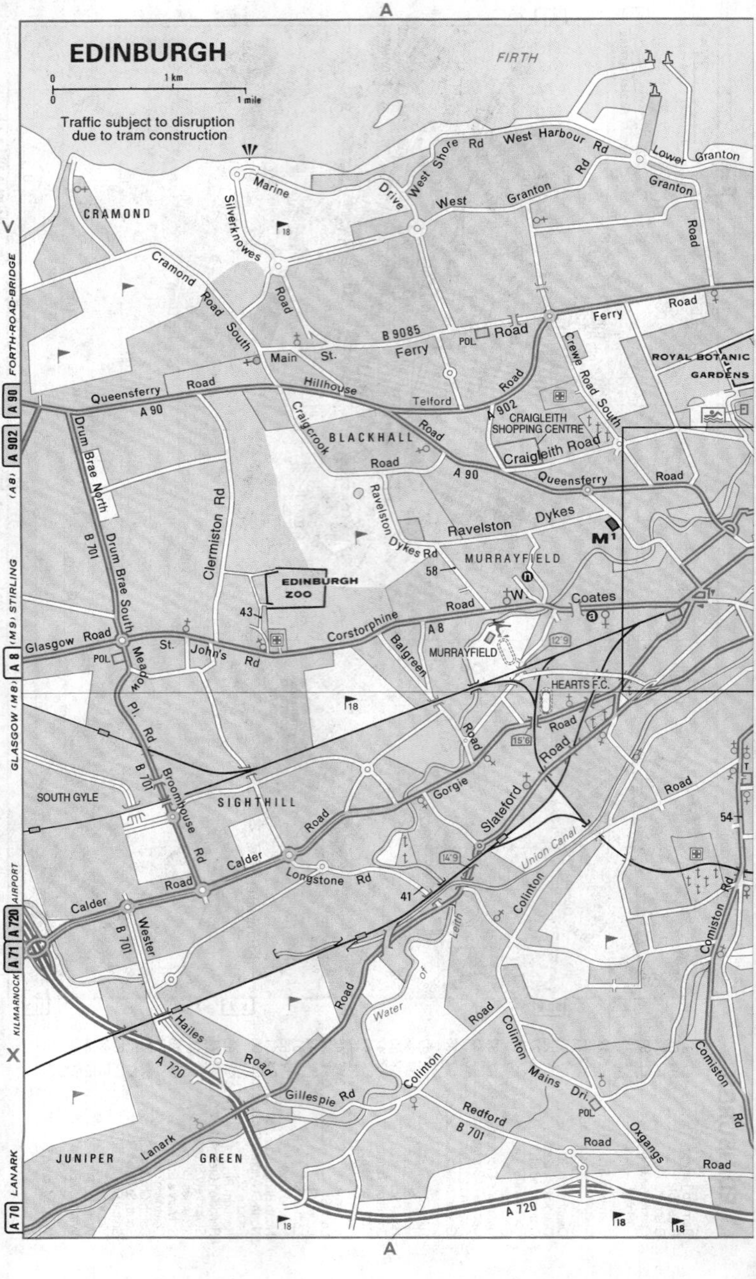

A

EDINBURGH

0 1 km
0 1 mile

Traffic subject to disruption due to tram construction

FIRTH

West Shore Rd, West Harbour Rd, Lower Granton, Granton Road, West Granton Rd, Marine Drive, Silverknowes Road, CRAMOND, Cramond Road South, Main St., B 9085 Ferry Road, POL., Hillhouse Road, Telford Road, A 902, Crewe Road South, ROYAL BOTANIC GARDENS, Queensferry Road, A 90, CRAIGLEITH SHOPPING CENTRE, Craigleith Road, Craigcrook Road, BLACKHALL, Drum Brae North, Drum Brae South, B 701, Clermiston Rd, Ravelston Dykes Rd, Ravelston Dykes, M1, MURRAYFIELD, 58, EDINBURGH ZOO, 43, Coates, W., a, n, Corstorphine Road, A 8, Glasgow Road, St. John's Rd, Meadow Pl. Rd, Balgreen Road, MURRAYFIELD, 12'9, HEARTS F.C., 15'6, Gorgie Road, Slateford Road, SOUTH GYLE, Broomhouse Rd, SIGHTHILL, Calder Road, Longstone Rd, 14'9, Union Canal, 41, Wester Hailes Road, Colinton Road, Water of Leith, Comiston Rd, 54, A 720, Colinton Mains Dri., Oxgangs Road, Redford Road, B 701, Gillespie Rd, Lanark Road, JUNIPER GREEN, 18

V

X

FORTH-ROAD-BRIDGE A 90

A 902 (A 8)

(M 9) STIRLING

GLASGOW (M 8) A 8

AIRPORT A 720

KILMARNOCK A 71

LANARK A 70

SCOTLAND

A

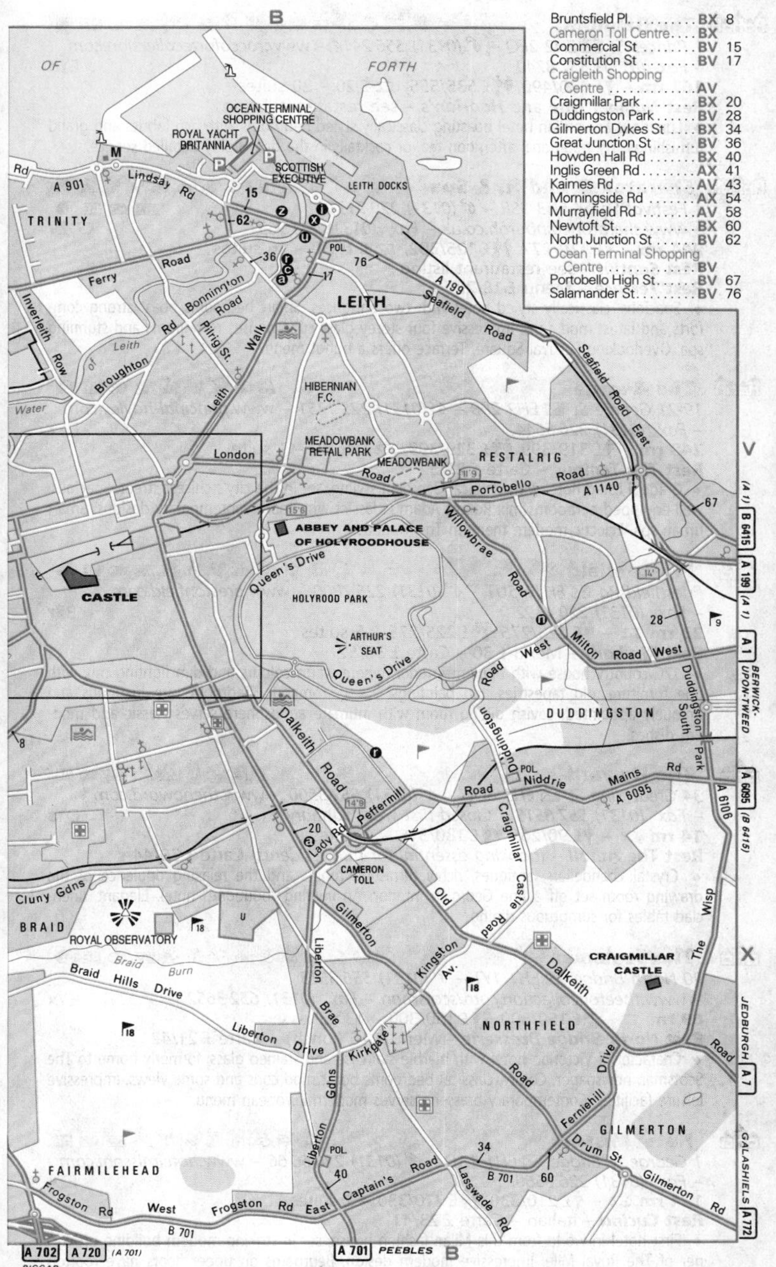

Bruntsfield Pl.	BX	8
Cameron Toll Centre	BX	
Commercial St	BV	15
Constitution St	BV	17
Craigleith Shopping Centre	AV	
Craigmillar Park	BX	20
Duddingston Park	BV	28
Gilmerton Dykes St	BX	34
Great Junction St	BV	36
Howden Hall Rd	BX	40
Inglis Green Rd	AX	41
Kaimes Rd	AV	43
Morningside Rd	AX	54
Murrayfield Rd	AV	58
Newtoft St	BX	60
North Junction St	BV	62
Ocean Terminal Shopping Centre	BV	
Portobello High St	BV	67
Salamander St	BV	76

SCOTLAND

The Balmoral

1 Princes St ✉ *EH2 2EQ – ✆ (0131) 556 2414 – www.roccofortecollection.com – Fax (0131) 557 8740* EY**n**

167 rm – †£ 470/490 ††£ 535/555, ☕ £ 20 – 20 suites

Rest *Number One* and *Hadrian's* – see restaurant listing

◆ Luxurious Edwardian hotel boasting classically styled bedrooms with rich fabrics and grand furnishings. Try traditional afternoon tea, or cocktails in the bar. Highly detailed service.

Sheraton Grand H. & Spa

1 Festival Sq ✉ *EH3 9SR – ✆ (0131) 229 9131 – www.sheratonedinburgh.co.uk – Fax (0131) 221 9631* CDZ**v**

244 rm – †£ 110/277 ††£ 125/302, ☕ £ 19.50 – 16 suites

Rest *Santini* – see restaurant listing

Rest *Terrace* – Menu £ 18/22

◆ Spacious, classically styled hotel with two entrances. Smart bedrooms boast strong comforts and latest mod cons. Impressive four storey glass cube houses restaurants and stunning spa. Overlooking Festival Square, Terrace offers a buffet menu.

The George

19-21 George St ✉ *EH2 2PB – ✆ (0131) 225 1251 – www.principal-hayley.com – Fax (0131) 226 5644* DY**z**

248 rm – †£ 319/399 ††£ 329/399, ☕ £ 16.50 – 1 suite

Rest *The Tempus* – Carte £ 22/32

◆ Grade II listed hotel with classical Georgian styling, set in the city's chicest street. Spacious, well-equipped bedrooms mix Robert Adam's classics with more contemporary designs. Smart urban spa. Eclectic modern menu in The Tempus.

SCOTLAND

Prestonfield

Priestfield Rd ✉ *EH16 5UT – ✆ (0131) 225 7800 – www.prestonfield.com – Fax (0131) 220 4392* BX**r**

23 rm ☕ – †£ 225/275 ††£ 225/275 – 5 suites

Rest *Rhubarb* – Menu £ 30 – Carte £ 38/52

◆ 17C country house with opulent interior, where warm colours and dim lighting mix with fine furniture, old tapestries and paintings – very romantic. Bedrooms are luxurious and uniquely appointed. Lavish dining room with intimate atmosphere serves classic and modern dishes.

The Howard

34 Great King St ✉ *EH3 6QH – ✆ (0131) 557 3500 – www.thehoward.com – Fax (0131) 557 6515 – Closed first week January* DY**s**

14 rm ☕ – †£ 90/265 ††£ 180/315 – 4 suites

Rest *The Atholl* – *(booking essential for non-residents)* Carte £ 30/44 **s**

◆ Crystal chandeliers, antiques, richly furnished rooms and the relaxing opulence of the drawing room set off a fine Georgian interior. An inviting "boutique" hotel. Elegant, linen-clad tables for sumptuous dining.

The Scotsman

20 North Bridge ✉ *EH1 1YT – ✆ (0131) 556 5565 – www.theetoncollection.com/scotsman – Fax (0131) 652 3652* EY**x**

69 rm ☕ – †£ 150/300 ††£ 150/300 – 13 suites

Rest *North Bridge Brasserie* – Menu £ 16 (lunch) – Carte £ 21/42

◆ Characterful Victorian hotel with marble staircase and stained glass; formerly home to The Scotsman newspaper. Comfy, classical bedrooms boast mod cons and some views. Impressive leisure facilities. Contemporary brasserie serves modern European menu.

Hotel Missoni

1 George IV Bridge ✉ *EH1 1AD – ✆ (0131) 220 66 66 – www.hotelmissoni.com – Fax (0131) 226 6660* EZ**v**

134 rm ☕ – †£ 210/330 ††£ 210/330 – 2 suites

Rest *Cucina* – Italian – Carte £ 23/41

◆ First hotel in world from this Milan fashion house; set in striking modern building on corner of The Royal Mile. Impressive modern design. Bedrooms on upper floors have rooftop views. Vibrant bar. Classic Italian cooking eaten at huge sharing tables in Cucina.

Channings

15 South Learmonth Gdns ✉ *EH4 1EZ – ✆ (0131) 274 7401 – www.channings.co.uk – Fax (0131) 274 7405* CY**e**

38 rm – **†**£ 125/220 **††**£ 180/250 – 3 suites

Rest – Carte £ 19/32

◆ Cosy Edwardian townhouse, tastefully furnished and run by friendly team. Individually appointed bedrooms: newer rooms are spacious, contemporary and themed after Shackleton, who lived nearby. Formal basement restaurant serves Gallic dishes.

Hotel du Vin

11 Bristo Pl ✉ *EH1 1EZ – ✆ (0131) 247 49 00 – www.hotelduvin.com – Fax (0131) 247 49 01* EZ**n**

47 rm – **†**£ 135 **††**£ 135/255, £ 13.50

Rest ***Bistro*** – Carte £ 20/38

◆ Boutique hotel located in city's former asylum, with contemporary, wine-themed bedrooms. Search out the murals featuring a caricature of Burke and Hare, and the whisky snug with its 300 spirits. Bistro offers superb wine list and a classic European menu.

Tigerlily

125 George St ✉ *EH2 4JN – ✆ (0131) 225 5005 – www.tigerlilyedinburgh.co.uk – Fax (0131) 225 7046 – Closed 25 December* DY**a**

33 rm – **†**£ 125/225 **††**£ 125/395 **Rest** – Carte £ 23/38

◆ Coverted Georgian townhouse boasting hip interior, including pink furnished bar, buzzy basement nightclub and glamourous, well-appointed bedrooms. Busy dining room offers wide choice of dishes, with Asian tendencies.

The Glasshouse without rest

2 Greenside Pl ✉ *EH1 3AA – ✆ (0131) 525 8200 – www.theetoncollection.com – Fax (0131) 525 8205 – Closed 23-26 December* EY**o**

65 rm – **†**£ 295 **††**£ 295/450, £ 16.50

◆ Contemporary glass hotel with 150 year old church façade. Stylish bedrooms have floor to ceiling windows and some balconies. Impressive two acre roof garden; honesty bar and 3 course room service.

The Roxburghe

38 Charlotte Sq ✉ *EH2 4HQ – ✆ (0844) 879 9063 – www.macdonaldhotels.co.uk/roxburghe – Fax (0131) 240 5555* DY**i**

197 rm – **†**£ 70/260 **††**£ 80/270, £ 13.50 – 1 suite

Rest – *(bar lunch)* Carte £ 21/31

◆ Characterful Georgian hotel overlooking Charlotte Square. Spacious, individually styled bedrooms in main house; quieter, more contemporary rooms in annexe – feature rooms offer heightened luxury. Airy restaurant boasts large windows and views of square.

Christopher North House

6-10 Gloucester Place ✉ *EH3 6EF – ✆ (0131) 225 2720 – www.christopher-north.co.uk – Fax (0131) 220 4706* CY**u**

28 rm – **†**£ 98/158 **††**£ 118/168

Rest – *(closed Sunday dinner) (dinner only)* Carte £ 16/29

◆ Luxurious adjoining townhouses with romantic interiors and stunning restored staircases. Decorated in gold, black and silver colour schemes, bedrooms boast top class furnishings and jacuzzis. Characterful dining room located in original house.

The Rutland

1-3 Rutland St ✉ *EH1 2AE – ✆ (0131) 229 34 02 – www.therutlandhotel.com – Fax (0131) 229 97 16* CZ**a**

12 rm – **†**£ 125/200 **††**£ 125/175, £ 10

Rest – Menu £ 13/16 (except weekends) – Carte £ 22/39

◆ Boutique hotel with commanding position at top of Princes Street. Stylish, modern bedrooms have bold décor, flat screen TVs and large, slate-floored shower rooms. Intimate basement lounge. Contemporary restaurant uses plenty of Scottish produce in its classic dishes.

Kildonan Lodge

27 Craigmillar Park ✉ *EH16 5PE* – ✆ *(0131) 667 2793*
– *www.kildonanlodgehotel.co.uk* – *Fax (0131) 667 9777* BX**a**
12 rm – £ 65/118 £ 98/159
Rest *Mathew's* – *(dinner only, booking essential)* Menu £ 19 – Carte £ 25/34
◆ Well-managed detached Victorian house on main road into city. Spacious and traditionally furnished, with cosy fire-lit drawing room and comfy bedrooms; some with four-posters and jacuzzis. Mathew's offers classical dining and plenty of Scottish produce.

Davenport House without rest

58 Great King St ✉ *EH3 6QY* – ✆ *(0131) 558 8495* – *www.davenport-house.com*
– *Fax (0131) 558 8496* – *Closed Christmas* DY**v**
6 rm – £ 65/75 £ 75/110
◆ Luxurious Georgian townhouse restored to its former glory. Cosy sitting room and spacious breakfast room. Bedrooms are at the top of the house and are decorated to a very high standard, with bathrooms to match.

Kew House without rest

1 Kew Terrace, Murrayfield ✉ *EH12 5JE* – ✆ *(0131) 313 0700*
– *www.kewhouse.com* – *Fax (0131) 313 0747* AV**a**
8 rm – £ 75/125 £ 90/180
◆ Personally run stone-built terraced house; larger than it looks from outside. Bedrooms are immaculately kept and up-to-date. Comfortable sitting room with free use of computer.

Elmview without rest

✉ *EH3 9LN* – ✆ *(0131) 228 1973* – *www.elmview.co.uk*
– *April-October* DZ**e**
5 rm – £ 60/100 £ 80/120
◆ Occupies the basement of a Victorian house in pretty terrace overlooking The Meadows. Bedrooms are spotlessly kept and are very large, with modern bathrooms. Owners are very welcoming.

The Beverley without rest

40 Murrayfield Ave ✉ *EH12 6AY* – ✆ *(0131) 337 1128* – *www.thebeverley.com*
– *Fax (0131) 313 3275* – *Closed 24-27 December* AV**n**
8 rm – £ 40/80 £ 70/100
◆ Elegant 19C bay windowed house in quiet, tree-lined avenue close to the rugby stadium. Good value, individually appointed rooms with modern facilties and thoughtful extras.

Number One – at The Balmoral Hotel

1 Princes St ✉ *EH2 2EQ* – ✆ *(0131) 557 6727*
– *www.restaurantnumberone.com* – *Fax (0131) 557 3747*
– *Closed 2-12 January and 26 December* EY**n**
Rest – Modern – *(dinner only)* Menu £ 58
Spec. Scallops with cabbage purée, pancetta and truffle. Fillet of beef with oxtail ravioli, squash purée and leeks. Passion fruit soufflé with coconut sorbet.
◆ Stylish restaurant in a grand hotel, displaying bold red walls hung with fine art, well-spaced tables and deep corner banquettes. Ambitious cooking uses quality Scottish produce to create elaborate, precisely executed dishes. Assured, attentive service.

21212 (Paul Kitching) with rm

rest,

3 Royal Terrace ✉ *EH7 5AB* – ✆ *(0845) 222 12 12* – *www.21212restaurant.co.uk*
– *Fax (0131) 523 10 38* EY**x**
4 rm – £ 250/325 £ 250/325
Rest – Inventive – *(closed Sunday and Monday)* Menu £ 30 (lunch)/60 (5 course dinner) **s**
Spec. Chicken, haggis and bacon, with blue cheese flapjack. Halibut and smoked salmon with cous cous and strawberries. Baked lemon curd, sticky rice.
◆ Smart Georgian townhouse with high-ceilinged dining room, contemporary décor and an open kitchen. The restaurant's name reflects the number of dishes per course; skilful and innovative cooking offers some quirky combinations. Opulent 1st floor sitting room and luxurious bedrooms.

SCOTLAND

XXX **Abstract**

33-35 Castle Terrace ✉ EH1 2EL – ✆ (0131) 229 1222 – www.abstractrestaurant.com – Fax (0131) 228 2398 – Closed Sunday and Monday DZ**a**

Rest – Modern European – Menu £ 25 (weekday dinner) – Carte £ 29/42

◆ Idiosyncratic decoration of faux-snakeskin covered tables, gold ceiling and flowery walls. France underpins the modern cooking which sometimes uses some unusual combinations.

XXX **Oloroso**

33 Castle St ✉ EH2 3DN – ✆ (0131) 226 7614 – www.oloroso.co.uk – Fax (0131) 226 7185 – Closed 25-26 December DY**o**

Rest – Innovative – Carte £ 33/52

◆ Contemporary rooftop restaurant with buzzy atmosphere and good service. Huge glass windows and superb terrace boast city, river and castle views. Bar and grill menus display modern cooking.

XXX **Hadrian's** – at The Balmoral Hotel

2 North Bridge ✉ EH1 1TR – ✆ (0131) 557 5000 – www.roccofortecollection.com – Fax (0131) 557 3747 EY**n**

Rest – Modern European – Menu £ 20 (lunch) – Carte £ 22/47

◆ Delightful restaurant where lime green colour scheme offsets dark floors and brown leather chairs. Brasserie classics display plenty of Scottish produce; excellent value 3 course set menu.

XX **Atrium**

10 Cambridge St ✉ EH1 2ED – ✆ (0131) 228 8882 – www.atriumrestaurant.co.uk – Fax (0131) 228 8808 – Closed 1-2 January, 24-26 December, Saturday lunch and Sunday except during Edinburgh festival DZ**c**

Rest – Modern European – Menu £ 18 (lunch) – Carte £ 31/43

◆ Located inside the Traverse Theatre, an adventurous repertoire enjoyed on tables made of wooden railway sleepers. Twisted copper lamps subtly light the ultra-modern interior.

XX **The Dining Room**

The Scotch Malt Whisky Society, 28 Queen St ✉ EH52 1JX – ✆ (0131) 220 20 44 – www.smws.co.uk – Fax (0131) 225 35 72 – Closed Sunday and dinner Monday and Tuesday DY**w**

Rest – Modern European – *(booking essential)* Carte £ 23/34

◆ Set in fine Georgian building. Informal bistro by day, offering classic menu; linen and lights by night, with accomplished, modern dishes. Unsurprisingly superb range of whiskies.

XX **Forth Floor - Restaurant (at Harvey Nichols)**

30-34 St Andrew Sq ✉ EH2 2AD – ✆ (0131) 524 8350 – www.harveynichols.com – Fax (0131) 524 8351 – Closed 1 January, 25 December, dinner Sunday and Monday EY**z**

Rest – Modern European – Menu £ 18/25 – Carte £ 23/39

◆ Wonderful skyline views from huge room-length window; great sunsets. Bar divides it into formal area with pricier modern European menu, and more causal brasserie; good Scottish ingredients.

XX **Santini** – at Sheraton Grand Hotel & Spa.

8 Conference Sq ✉ EH3 8AN – ✆ (0131) 221 7788 – www.santiniedinburgh.co.uk – Fax (0131) 221 9631 – Closed Saturday lunch and Sunday CDZ**v**

Rest – Italian – Menu £ 8/19 – Carte £ 23/46

◆ Smart restaurant in huge glass cube. Dining room split in two: the right side more relaxed with piazza views and pleasant terrace. Wide-ranging menu of Italian classics; good value set selection.

SCOTLAND

XX **The Stockbridge** VISA MC AE

54 St Stephens St ✉ EH3 5AL – ✆ (0131) 226 6766 – www.thestockbridgerestaurant.com – Closed 1-14 January, 24-26 December and Monday CY**x**

Rest – Classic – *(dinner only and lunch Saturday-Sunday)* Menu £ 16/22 – Carte £ 34/42

◆ Intimate neighbourhood restaurant, its dark green walls hung with colourful Scottish art. Friendly staff serve a mix of classical and more modern dishes, precisely prepared.

X **Wedgwood** VISA MC AE

267 Canongate ✉ EH8 8BQ – ✆ (0131) 558 87 37 – www.wedgwoodtherestaurant.co.uk – Fax (0560) 205 89 78 – Closed 3 weeks January and 25-26 December EY**a**

Rest – Modern European – Menu £ 14 (lunch) – Carte £ 28/41

◆ Neat restaurant with bold white and crimson décor, hidden away at bottom of Royal Mile. Personally run, with friendly staff. Well presented, seasonal dishes; generous portions.

X **The Dogs** VISA MC AE

110 Hanover St. ✉ EH2 1DR – ✆ (0131) 220 1208 – www.thedogsonline.co.uk – Closed 1 January and 25-26 December DY**c**

Rest – British – Carte £ 16/20

◆ Set on the first floor of a classic Georgian mid-terrace; impressive staircase, simple décor, high-ceilings. Robust, good value comfort food crafted from local, seasonal produce.

SCOTLAND

X **Tony's Table** VISA MC AE

58a North Castle St ✉ EH2 3LU – ✆ (0131) 226 67 43 – www.tonystable.com – Fax (0131) 226 76 14 – Closed 1-15 January, 25 December, Sunday and Monday DY**n**

Rest – Modern European – Menu £ 20 (lunch) – Carte dinner approx. £ 20

◆ Informal eatery, with deli shop and bakery; pigs quite a feature of its eclectic décor. Great value menu draws its influence from around Europe, with tasty terrines or tortellini alongside haggis, fish pie or curry. Friendly service.

X **Blue** AC VISA MC AE

10 Cambridge St ✉ EH1 2ED – ✆ (0131) 221 1222 – www.bluescotland.com – Fax (0131) 228 8808 – Closed 1 January, 24-26 and 31 December and Sunday except during Edinburgh festival DZ**c**

Rest – Modern European – Carte £ 22/32

◆ Strikes a modern note with bright, curving walls, glass and simple settings. A café-bar with a light, concise and affordable menu drawing a young clientele. Bustling feel.

X **Zucca** AC VISA MC AE

15-17 Grindlay St ✉ EH3 9AX – ✆ (0131) 221 93 23 – www.zuccarestaurant.co.uk – Closed 1 January, 25 December, Sunday and Monday DZ**s**

Rest – Italian – *(booking essential)* Menu £ 7/14 **s** – Carte £ 16/29 **s**

◆ Friendly, well-run restaurant adjacent to Lyceum Theatre. Head upstairs for classic Italian dishes and all-Italian wine list, with great value pre-theatre menus. Book or come after 8pm.

X **Amore Dogs** VISA MC AE

104 Hanover St ✉ EH2 1DR – ✆ (0131) 220 51 55 – www.amoredogs.co.uk DY**c**

Rest – Italian – Carte £ 12/20

◆ Sister to 'The Dogs' next door, with similar canine-themed décor. Simple, spacious and open-plan, with a buzzy atmosphere and friendly service. Good value, rustic Italian dishes.

X **La Garrigue** AC VISA MC AE

31 Jeffrey St ✉ EH1 1DH – ✆ (0131) 557 3032 – www.lagarrigue.co.uk – Fax (0131) 557 30 32 – Closed Sunday EY**v**

Rest – French – Menu £ 15/28

◆ Very pleasant restaurant near the Royal Mile: beautiful handmade wood tables add warmth to rustic décor. Authentic French regional cooking with classical touches.

X **Le Café Saint-Honoré** VISA MC AE

34 North West Thistle Street Lane ✉ EH2 1EA – ☎ (0131) 226 2211 – www.cafesthonore.com – Fax (0131) 477 2716 – Closed Christmas and New Year DY**r**

Rest – French – *(booking essential)* Menu £ 22 (except Friday and Saturday after 8pm) – Carte £ 23/37

◆ Longstanding city favourite tucked away off Frederick St; a bustling, bistro furnished in a classic French style. Good value, daily changing menu with a pronounced Gallic flavour.

at Leith

Malmaison rm, VISA MC AE

1 Tower Pl ✉ EH6 7DB – ☎ (0131) 468 5000 – www.malmaison.com – Fax (0131) 468 5002 BV**i**

100 rm – †£ 90/220 ††£ 90/310, ☕ £ 13.95

Rest *Brasserie* – Menu £ 16 **s** – Carte £ 25/41 **s**

◆ Imposing quayside sailors' mission converted in strikingly elegant style. Good-sized rooms, thoughtfully appointed, combine more traditional comfort with up-to-date overtones. Sophisticated brasserie with finely wrought iron.

XXX ✿ **Martin Wishart** VISA MC AE

54 The Shore ✉ EH6 6RA – ☎ (0131) 553 3557 – www.martin-wishart.co.uk – Fax (0131) 467 7091 – Closed 1-19 January, 25-26 and 31 December, Sunday and Monday

Rest – Innovative – *(booking essential)* Menu £ 25 (weekday lunch)/60 BV**u**

Spec. Tarte fine of sardines, shallots and lemon. Lobster with spinach, pepper and mustard. Valrhona Manjari chocolate and raspberries.

◆ Discrete façade leads to tastefully decorated room with bold, modern designs. Underpinned by a classical base, well presented dishes display carefully judged modern touches and excellent ingredients. Two tasting menus available.

XX ✿ **The Kitchin** (Tom Kitchin) AC VISA MC AE

78 Commercial Quay ✉ EH6 6LX – ☎ (0131) 555 1755 – www.thekitchin.com – Fax (0131) 553 0608 – Closed Christmas and New Year, Sunday and Monday BV**z**

Rest – French – Menu £ 25 (lunch) – Carte £ 50/62

Spec. Razorfish with chorizo and lemon confit. Pork belly with snails, garlic and parsley. Apple sorbet with salted toffee and champagne soup.

◆ Converted dockside warehouse overlooking the quay. Expect refreshingly honest, very flavoursome and unfussy cooking from menus offering considerable choice. Seasonality, freshness and provenance are at the heart of the chef's philosophy.

XX ✿ **Plumed Horse** (Tony Borthwick) VISA MC AE

50-54 Henderson St ✉ EH6 6DE – ☎ (0131) 554 5556 – www.plumedhorse.co.uk – Closed 1 week Easter, 2 weeks July, 1 week October, Sunday and Monday

Rest – Modern – Menu £ 23 (weekday lunch)/43 **s** BV**a**

Spec. Crab quiche with scallop and spiced crab sauce. Rosé veal with truffled mashed potato and girolles. Fudge and ginger parfait, vanilla, lime and 'Sailor Jerry' granita.

◆ Personally run restaurant with ornate ceiling, vivid paintings, an intimate feel and formal service. Well-crafted, classical cooking with strong, bold flavours and good use of Scottish ingredients.

XX **The Vintners Rooms** VISA MC AE

The Vaults, 87 Giles St ✉ EH6 6BZ – ☎ (0131) 554 6767 – www.thevintersrooms.com – Fax (0131) 555 5653 – Closed 23 December-6 January, Sunday and Monday BV**r**

Rest – Mediterranean – Menu £ 23 (lunch) – Carte £ 38/45

◆ Atmospheric 18C bonded spirits warehouse with high ceilings, stone floor, rug-covered walls and candlelit side-room with ornate plasterwork. French/Mediterranean cooking.

SCOTLAND

Cafe Fish

60 Henderson St ✉ EH6 6DE – ✆ (0131) 538 6131 – www.cafefish.net – Closed 1 January, Sunday dinner and Monday BV**c**

Rest – Seafood – Menu £ 23 (dinner) – Carte lunch £ 17/29

◆ Light, modern, quasi-industrial style, with brushed aluminium bar and open-plan kitchen. Short menus of simply cooked seafood; good value fresh fish from sustainable Scottish sources.

The Ship on the Shore

24-26 The Shore ✉ EH6 6QN – ✆ (0131) 555 0409 – www.theshipontheshore.co.uk – Closed 24-26 December BV**x**

Rest – Seafood – Carte £ 20/35

◆ Smart period building on the quayside, modelled on the Royal Yacht Britannia and filled with nautical memorabilia. Seafood menu offers fresh, simply prepared, classical dishes.

The Kings Wark

36 The Shore ✉ EH6 6QU – ✆ (0131) 554 9260 – www.kingswark.com BV**u**

Rest – Traditional – Carte £ 15/26

◆ Brightly coloured pub with old-fashioned interior, set on the quayside. Hand-written menus offer hearty, classical dishes; blackboard displays freshly prepared, locally sourced specials.

SCOTLAND

at Currie Southwest : 5 m on A 70

Violet Bank House without rest

167 Lanark Road West ✉ EH14 5NZ – ✆ (0131) 451 51 03 – www.violetbankhouse.co.uk

3 rm ☕ – 🧍£ 80/110 🧍🧍£ 110/130

◆ Comfortable, well-run cottage with charming, individually decorated bedrooms and attractive garden running down to river. Impressive Scottish breakfast features lots of choice.

at Kirknewton Southwest : 7 mi. on A 71 - AX – ✉ Edinburgh

Dalmahoy H. & Country Club

✉ EH27 8EB – ✆ (0131) 333 1845 – www.marriottdalmahoy.co.uk – Fax (0131) 333 1433 rm, rest,

212 rm ☕ – 🧍£ 120/180 🧍🧍£ 120/180 – 3 suites

Rest *Pentland* – *(dinner only)* Carte £28/42

Rest *The Long Weekend* – Carte £ 17/41

◆ Extended Georgian mansion in 1000 acres with 2 Championship golf courses. Comprehensive leisure club, smart rooms and a clubby cocktail lounge. Tranquil atmosphere with elegant comfort in Pentland restaurant. Informal modern dining at The Long Weekend.

at Ingliston West : 7 mi. on A 8 – ✉ EH28 8

Norton House

West : 6 mi. on A 89 ✉ EH28 8LX – ✆ (0131) 333 12 75 – www.handpicked.co.uk/nortonhouse – Fax (0131) 333 53 05 rm, rest,

79 rm ☕ – 🧍£ 90/150 🧍🧍£ 100/160 – 4 suites

Rest *Ushers* – *(Closed Sunday and Monday) (dinner only)* Carte £ 41/49

Rest *Brasserie* – Carte £ 25/30

◆ 19C country house in mature grounds, with impressive oak staircase and superb spa. Classic bedrooms in original house. Large, luxurious junior suites in extension; most have balconies. Classic cooking with seasonal Scottish produce in intimate Ushers. Stylish, modern Brasserie.

EDNAM – Borders – see Kelso

ELGIN – Moray – 501 K11 – pop. 20 829 Scotland — 28 C1

Edinburgh 198 mi. – Aberdeen 68 mi. – Fraserburgh 61 mi. – Inverness 39 mi.

Elgin Library, Cooper Park ☎ (01343) 562 608, elgin@visitscotland.com

Moray Lossiemouth Stotfield Rd, ☎ (01343) 812 018

Hardhillock Birnie Rd, ☎ (01343) 542 338

Hopeman Moray, ☎ (01343) 830 578

Town★ - Cathedral★ (Chapter house★★)**AC**

Glenfiddich Distillery★, SE : 10 mi. by A 941

Mansion House

The Haugh, via Haugh Rd ✉ IV30 1AW – ☎ (01343) 548 811 – www.mansionhousehotel.co.uk – Fax (01343) 547 916 – Closed 25 December

23 rm – 🚹£ 89/100 🚹🚹£ 149/192

Rest – Menu £ 23 (lunch) – Carte (dinner) £ 19/35

◆ 19C Baronial mansion surrounded by lawned gardens. Country house-style interior. Rooms in main house most characterful, those in purpose-built annexe more modern. The formal restaurant is decorated in warm yellows and blues.

The Pines without rest

East Rd, East : 0.5 mi. on A 96 ✉ IV30 1XG – ☎ (01343) 552 495 – www.thepinesguesthouse.com – Fax (01343) 552 495

5 rm – 🚹£ 55/75 🚹🚹£ 65/75

◆ Detached Victorian house with a friendly and warm ambience amidst comfy, homely décor. Bedrooms are of a good size and furnished with colourful, modern fabrics.

at Urquhart East : 5 mi. by A 96 – ✉ Elgin

Parrandier

The Old Church of Urquhart, Meft Rd, Northwest : 0.25 mi. by Main St and Meft Rd ✉ IV30 8NH – ☎ (01343) 843 063 – www.oldchurch.eu – Fax (01343) 843 063

4 rm – 🚹£ 41 🚹🚹£ 62/68

Rest – *(by arrangement, communal dining)* Menu £ 14

◆ Former 19C church in quiet rural location converted to provide open plan lounge and split level dining area. Comfortable bedrooms with original church features.

ELIE – Fife – 501 L15 – pop. 942 — 28 D2

Edinburgh 44 mi. – Dundee 24 mi. – St Andrews 13 mi.

Sangster's (Bruce Sangster)

51 High St ✉ KY9 1BZ – ☎ (01333) 331 001 – www.sangsters.co.uk – Fax (01333) 331 001 – Closed January, 1 week November, 25-26 December, Sunday, Monday and Tuesday lunch also Tuesday dinner and Wednesday lunch in winter.

Rest – *(booking essential)* Menu £ 21/36

Spec. Scallops with chilli, ginger and coriander. Pigeon and venison with red cabbage and wild mushrooms. Raspberry soufflé and yoghurt ice cream.

◆ This sweet little restaurant is run by a husband and wife team. The understated decoration includes a collection of local artwork on the walls. The cooking is detailed, finely tuned and informed by the seasons.

Don't confuse the couvert rating X with the stars ✿! Couverts defines comfort and service, while stars are awarded for the best cuisine across all categories of comfort.

SCOTLAND

ERISKA (Isle of) – **Argyll and Bute** – **501** D14 – ✉ **Oban** **27** B2

▶ Edinburgh 127 mi. – Glasgow 104 mi. – Oban 12 mi.

Isle of Eriska

rm, rest,

Benderloch ✉ PA37 1SD – ✆ (01631) 720 371 – www.eriska-hotel.co.uk – Fax (01631) 720 531 – Closed January

23 rm – †£ 160/240 ††£ 325/450 – 7 suites

Rest – *(light lunch residents only) (booking essential)* Menu £ 40 (dinner) **s** – Carte lunch £ 19/30 **s**

◆ On a private island, a wonderfully secluded 19C Scottish Baronial mansion with dramatic views of Lismore and mountains. Highest levels of country house comfort and style. Elegant dining.

EUROCENTRAL – **Glasgow** – **see Glasgow**

FAIRLIE – **North Ayrshire** – **501** F16 – **pop. 1 510** **25** A1

▶ Edinburgh 75 mi. – Ayr 50 mi. – Glasgow 36 mi.

Fins

Fencebay Fisheries, Fencefoot Farm, South : 1.5 mi. on A 78 ✉ KA29 0EG – ✆ (01475) 568 989 – www.fencebay.co.uk – Fax (01475) 568 921 – Closed 1 week January, 25-26 December, Monday and Sunday dinner

Rest – Seafood – *(booking essential)* Carte £ 19/31

◆ Converted farm buildings house a simple, flag-floored restaurant, craft shops and a traditional beech smokery. Friendly service and fresh seasonal seafood.

FLODIGARRY – **Highland** – **501** B11 – **see Skye (Isle of)**

FORGANDENNY – **Perth. and Kinross** – **501** J14 – **see Perth**

FORRES – **Moray** – **501** J11 – **pop. 8 967** Scotland **28** C1

▶ Edinburgh 165 mi. – Aberdeen 80 mi. – Inverness 27 mi.

116 High St ✆ (01309) 672938 (Easter-October), forres@visitscotland.com

Muiryshade, ✆ (01309) 672 949

Sueno's Stone★★, N : 0.5 mi. by A 940 on A 96 – Brodie Castle★ **AC**, W : 3 mi. by A 96. Elgin★ (Cathedral★, chapter house★★ **AC**), E : 10.25 mi. by A 96

Knockomie

rm,

Grantown Rd, South : 1.5 mi. on A 940 ✉ IV36 2SG – ✆ (01309) 673 146 – www.knockomie.co.uk – Fax (01309) 673 290

15 rm – †£ 115 ††£ 210

Rest ***The Grill Room*** – Menu £ 38 (dinner) – Carte £ 23/36

◆ Extended Arts and Crafts house in comfortable seclusion off a rural road. Country house atmosphere. Bedrooms in main house older and more characterful. Contemporary restaurant offers seasonally changing menu of local, seasonal produce.

Ramnee

Victoria Rd ✉ IV36 3BN – ✆ (01309) 672 410 – www.ramneehotel.com – Fax (01309) 673 392 – Closed 1-3 January and 25-26 December

19 rm – †£ 85/130 ††£ 100/160 – 1 suite

Rest ***Hamlyns*** – Carte £ 16/30 **s**

◆ Family owned Edwardian building in town centre with extensive lawned grounds. Welcoming public areas include panelled reception and pubby bar. Warmly traditional bedrooms. Formal dining room in traditional style.

at Dyke **West : 3.75 mi. by A 96** – ✉ **Forres**

The Old Kirk without rest

Northeast : 0.5 mi. ✉ IV36 2TL – ✆ (01309) 641 414 – www.oldkirk.co.uk

3 rm – †£ 47/55 ††£ 64/80

◆ Former 19C church in country location. Stained glass window in first floor lounge; wood furnished breakfast room. Pleasantly furnished bedrooms with original stonework.

FORT AUGUSTUS – Highland – ✉ PH32 30 C3

London 543 mi. – Edinburgh 159 mi. – Inverness 34 mi. – Fort William 32 mi.

Lovat Arms

✉ PH32 4DU – ☎ (01456) 459 250 – www.lovatarms-hotel.com – Fax (01320) 366 677

29 rm – £ 105/175 ££ 120/250

Rest – Menu £ 35 (dinner) – Carte £ 20/40

◆ Professionally run Victorian house with traditional lounge and lawned gardens, set in pleasant village at southern end of Loch Ness. Variously sized bedrooms have a contemporary feel and good facilities. Smart, modern brasserie offers classic cooking.

FORTINGALL – Perth and Kinross – 501 H14 – see Aberfeldy

FORTROSE – Highland – 501 H11 – pop. 1 174 30 C2

London 574 mi. – Edinburgh 168 mi. – Inverness 14 mi. – Nairn 27 mi.

Water's Edge without rest

Canonbury Terrace, on A 832 ✉ IV10 8TT – ☎ (01381) 621 202 – www.watersedge.uk.com – Fax (08704) 296 806 – restricted opening in winter

3 rm – £ 90/99 ££ 100/110

◆ Personally run guest house with attractive gardens and superb views over the Moray Firth. Immaculately kept guest areas. Three 1st floor rooms have French windows onto terrace.

FORT WILLIAM – Highland – 501 E13 – pop. 9 908 Scotland 30 C3

Edinburgh 133 mi. – Glasgow 104 mi. – Inverness 68 mi. – Oban 50 mi.

15 High St ☎ (0845) 2255121, info@visitscotland.com

18 North Rd, ☎ (01397) 704 464

Town★

The Road to the Isles★★ (Neptune's Staircase (≤★★), Glenfinnan★ ≤★, Arisaig★, Silver Sands of Morar★, Mallaig★), NW : 46 mi. by A 830 – Ardnamurchan Peninsula★★ - Ardnamurchan Point (≤★★), NW : 65 mi. by A 830, A 861 and B 8007 - SE : Ben Nevis★★ (≤★★) - Glen Nevis★

Inverlochy Castle

Torlundy, Northeast : 3 mi. on A 82 ✉ PH33 6SN – ☎ (01397) 702 177 – www.inverlochycastlehotel.com – Fax (01397) 702 953

17 rm – £ 295/380 ££ 380/540 – 1 suite

Rest – *(booking essential for non-residents)* Menu £ 35/64

Spec. Lobster with asparagus, fennel and orange dressing. Turbot with ox cheek tortellini and lime jus. Pear and pistachio torte with pistachio ice cream.

◆ World renowned, castellated house in beautiful grounds with superb views. Sumptuous sitting rooms; impressive Great Hall. Individually styled bedrooms, luxuriously furnished. Cooking has classical roots with touches of modernity and uses top quality, Scottish produce. Jacket and tie required at dinner.

Distillery House without rest

Nevis Bridge, North Rd ✉ PH33 6LR – ☎ (01397) 700 103 – www.stayinfortwilliam.co.uk – Closed 23-30 December

10 rm – £ 45/84 ££ 75/84

◆ Conveniently located a short walk from the centre of town, formerly part of Glenlochy distillery. Cosy guests' lounge and comfortable rooms, some with views of Ben Nevis.

The Grange without rest

Grange Rd, South : 0.75 mi. by A 82 and Ashburn Lane ✉ PH33 6JF – ☎ (01397) 705 516 – www.thegrange-scotland.co.uk – March-October

3 rm – £ 98 ££ 120

◆ Large Victorian house with attractive garden, in an elevated position in a quiet residential part of town. Very comfortable and tastefully furnished with many antiques.

SCOTLAND

Crolinnhe without rest
Grange Rd, South : 0.75 mi. by A 82 and Ashburn Lane ✉ PH33 6JF – ☎ (01397) 702 709 – www.crolinnhe.co.uk – Easter-October
3 rm – †£ 127 ††£ 127
◆ Very comfortably and attractively furnished Victorian house, run with a real personal touch. Relaxing guests' sitting room and well furnished bedrooms.

Lochan Cottage without rest
Lochyside, North : 2.5 mi. by A 82, A 830 on B 8006 ✉ PH33 7NX – ☎ (01397) 702 695 – www.fortwilliam-guesthouse.co.uk – February-October
6 rm – †£ 37/66 ††£ 54/66
◆ Spotlessly kept, whitewashed cottage with homely public areas. Breakfast taken in conservatory overlooking delightfully landscaped gardens. Neat, well-kept rooms.

Ashburn House without rest
18 Achintore Rd, South : 0.5 mi. on A 82 ✉ PH33 6RQ – ☎ (01397) 706 000 – www.highland5star.co.uk – Fax (01397) 702 024
7 rm – †£ 45/100 ††£ 90/110
◆ Attractive Victorian house overlooking Loch Linnhe, on the main road into town which is a short walk away. Well furnished bedrooms and a comfortable conservatory lounge.

SCOTLAND

Lawriestone without rest
Achintore Rd, South : 0.5 mi. on A 82 ✉ PH33 6RQ – ☎ (01397) 700 777 – www.lawriestone.co.uk – Fax (01397) 700 777 – closed 25-26 December and 1-2 January
5 rm – ††£ 70/80
◆ Victorian house overlooking Loch Linnhe; not far from town centre, ideal for touring Western Highlands. Especially proud of Scottish breakfasts. Airy rooms; some with views.

The Gantocks without rest
Achintore Rd, South 1 mi. on A 82 – ☎ (01397) 702 050 – www.fortwilliam5star.co.uk – Closed Christmas and New Year
3 rm – †£ 80/100 ††£ 90/110
◆ Spacious whitewashed bungalow with Loch views. Modern bedrooms have king size beds and large baths; 1 overlooks the Loch. Handmade shortbread on arrival. Unusual homemade breakfasts.

Lime Tree An Ealdhain with rm
Achintore Rd ✉ PH33 6RQ – ☎ (01397) 701 806 – www.limetreefortwilliam.co.uk – Closed November and 24-26 December
9 rm – †£ 60/100 ††£ 80/100
Rest – *(light lunch)* Menu £ 28 (dinner)
◆ Former manse, now a restaurant, art gallery and hotel. Traditional menu showcases local, seasonal produce in wholesome, hearty dishes. Comfortable, contemporary lounges. Stylish bedrooms; some with Loch views.

Crannog
Town Pier ✉ PH33 6DB – ☎ (01397) 705 589 – www.crannog.net – Fax (01397) 708 666 – Closed 1 January, dinner 24 and 31 December and 25 December
Rest – Seafood – *(booking essential)* Carte £ 29/39
◆ Lochside dining on Fort William town pier; choose a window table for the view. Interior of bright reds and yellows with some Celtic artwork. Locally sourced seafood dishes.

GALSON – **Western Isles Outer Hebrides** – **501** A8 – **see Lewis and Harris (Isle of)**

GATTONSIDE – **Borders** – **see Melrose**

GIGHA (Isle of) – Argyll and Bute – 501 C16 — 27 A3

Edinburgh 168 mi.

to Tayinloan (Caledonian MacBrayne Ltd) 8-10 daily (20 mn)

Gigha

PA41 7AA – (01583) 505 254 – www.gigha.org.uk – Fax (01583) 505 244 – Closed 25 December

13 rm – £ 43/65 £ 85/185

Rest – *(bar lunch) (booking essential for non-residents)* Carte £ 17/30

◆ 18C whitewashed house on island owned by residents; views over Ardminish Bay to Kintyre. Cosy pine-panelled bar. Elegant lounge. Simple, clean and tidy rooms. Inviting restaurant with exposed stone walls and pine tables.

GLAMIS – Angus – 501 K/L14 – pop. 648 – Forfar — 28 C2

Edinburgh 69 mi. – Dundee 13 mi. – Forfar 7 mi.

Town★ – Castle★★

Meigle Museum★ **AC** W : 7 mi. by A 94

Castleton House

West : 3.25 mi. on A 94 DD8 1SJ – (01307) 840 340 – www.castletonglamis.co.uk – Fax (01307) 840 506 – Closed Christmas and New Year

6 rm – £ 90/120 £ 140/190 **Rest** – Carte £ 20/31 **s**

◆ Moat still visible in gardens of this 20C country house built on site of medieval fortress. Appealing lounges, cosy bar. Individually designed, attractively appointed rooms. Stylish conservatory restaurant looks out to garden.

O. Forir/MICHELIN

GLASGOW

County: Glasgow City
Michelin regional map: **501** H16
Edinburgh 46 mi.
– Manchester 221 mi.

Population: 629 501
Scotland
Map reference: **25** B1

PRACTICAL INFORMATION

Tourist Information

11 George Sq (0141) 204 4400, glasgow@visitscotland.com

Glasgow Airport, Tourist Information Desk (0141) 848 4440, glasgowairport@visitscotland.com

Airports

Glasgow Airport : (0844) 481 5555, W : 8 mi. by M 8, AV

Access to Oban by helicopter

Golf courses

18 Littlehill Auchinairn Rd, (0141) 276 07 04

18 Rouken Glen Thornlibank Stewarton Rd, (0141) 638 7044

18 Linn Park Simshill Rd, (0141) 633 0377

Lethamhill Cumbernauld Rd, (0141) 770 6220

9 Alexandra Park Dennistoun, (0141) 276 0600

9 King's Park Croftfoot 150a Croftpark Ave, (0141) 630 1597

9 Knightswood Lincoln Ave, (0141) 959 6358

SIGHTS

In town

City★★★ – Cathedral★★★ (<★) DZ - The Burrell Collection★★★ AX **M1** – Hunterian Art Gallery★★ (Whistler Collection★★★ - Mackintosh Wing★★★) AC CY **M4** – Museum of Transport★★ (Scottish Built Cars★★★, The Clyde Room of Ship Models★★★) AV **M6** – Art Gallery and Museum Kelvingrove★★ CY – Pollok House★ (The Paintings★★) AX **D** – Tolbooth Steeple★ DZ - Hunterian Museum (Coin and Medal Collection★) CY **M5** – City Chambers★ DZ **C** – Glasgow School of Art★ AC CY **M3** – Necropolis (<★ of Cathedral) DYZ – Gallery of Modern Art★ – Glasgow (National) Science Centre★, Pacific Quay AV

On the outskirts

Paisley Museum and Art Gallery (Paisley Shawl Section★), W : 4 mi. by M 8 AV

In the surrounding area

The Trossachs★★★, N : 31 mi. by A 879 - BV -, A 81 and A 821 – Loch Lomond★★, NW : 19 mi. by A 82 AV – New Lanark★★, SE : 20 mi. by M 74 and A 72 BX

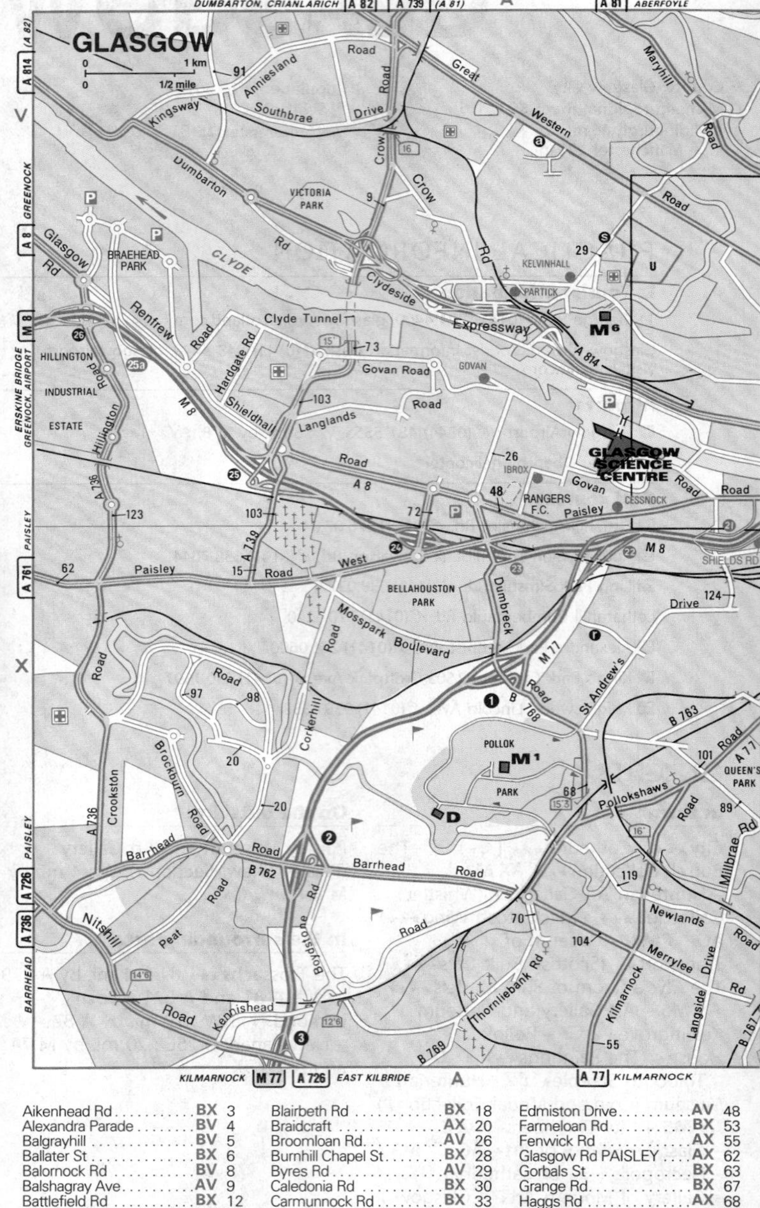

Aikenhead Rd . . . . BX 3
Alexandra Parade . . . . BV 4
Balgrayhill . . . . BV 5
Ballater St . . . . BX 6
Balornock Rd . . . . BV 8
Balshagray Ave. . . . . AV 9
Battlefield Rd . . . . BX 12
Berryknowes Rd . . . . AX 15
Bilsland Drive . . . . BV 16

Blairbeth Rd . . . . BX 18
Braidcraft . . . . AX 20
Broomloan Rd. . . . . AV 26
Burnhill Chapel St. . . . . BX 28
Byres Rd . . . . AV 29
Caledonia Rd . . . . BX 30
Carmunnock Rd . . . . BX 33
Cook St . . . . BV 38
Cumbernauld Rd . . . . BV 40

Edmiston Drive. . . . . AV 48
Farmeloan Rd . . . . BX 53
Fenwick Rd . . . . AX 55
Glasgow Rd PAISLEY . . . . . AX 62
Gorbals St . . . . BX 63
Grange Rd. . . . . BX 67
Haggs Rd . . . . AX 68
Harriet St. . . . . AX 70
Helen St . . . . AV 72

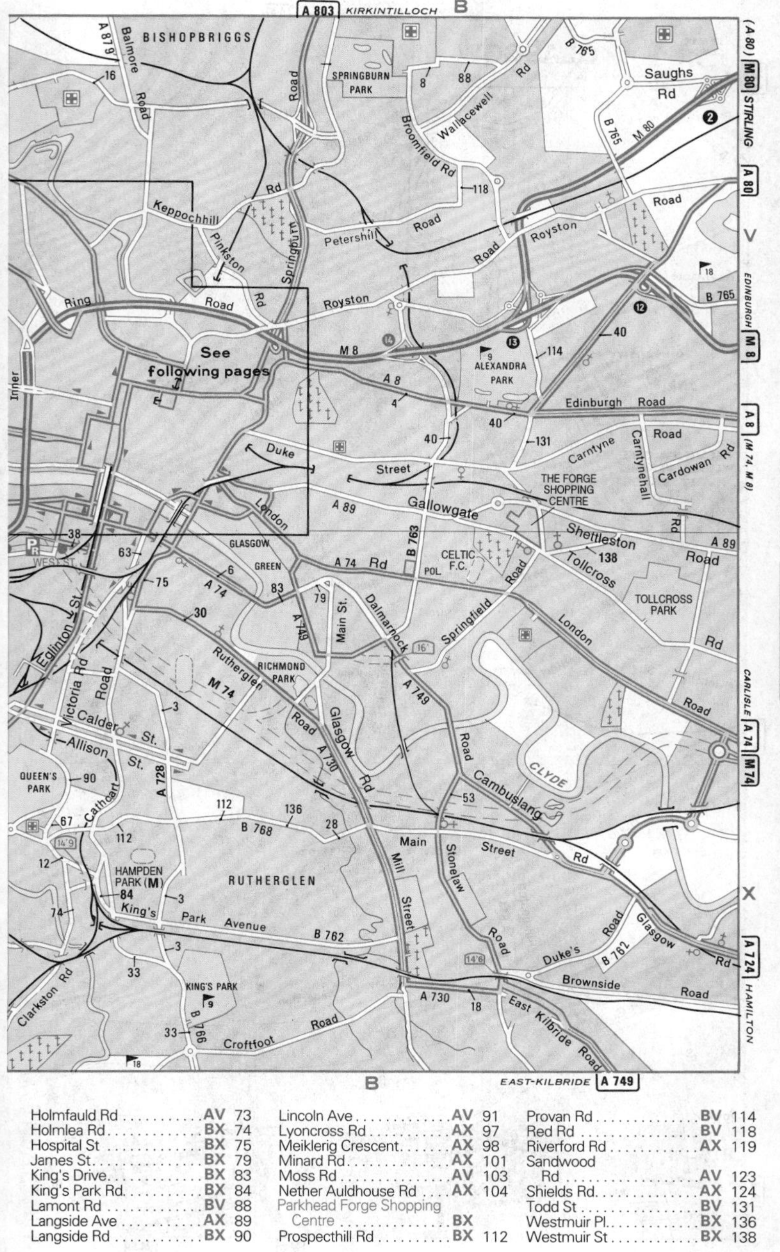

Holmfauld Rd . . . . AV 73
Holmlea Rd. . . . . BX 74
Hospital St . . . . BX 75
James St. . . . . BX 79
King's Drive. . . . . BX 83
King's Park Rd. . . . . BX 84
Lamont Rd . . . . BV 88
Langside Ave . . . . AX 89
Langside Rd . . . . BX 90
Lincoln Ave . . . . AV 91
Lyoncross Rd . . . . AX 97
Meiklerig Crescent. . . . . . AX 98
Minard Rd. . . . . AX 101
Moss Rd . . . . AV 103
Nether Auldhouse Rd . . . AX 104
Parkhead Forge Shopping Centre . . . . BX
Prospecthill Rd . . . . BX 112
Provan Rd . . . . BV 114
Red Rd . . . . BV 118
Riverford Rd . . . . AX 119
Sandwood Rd . . . . AV 123
Shields Rd. . . . . AX 124
Todd St . . . . BV 131
Westmuir Pl. . . . . BX 136
Westmuir St . . . . BX 138

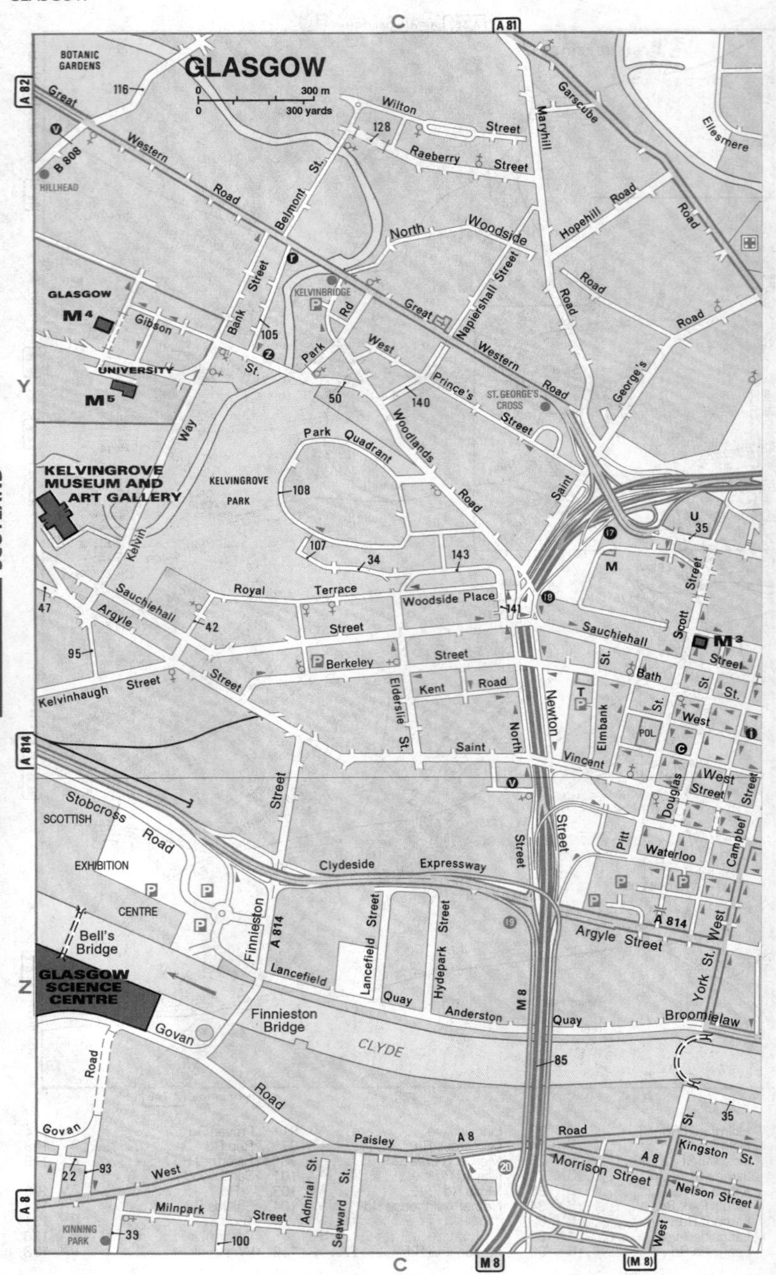
GLASGOW
0 300 m
0 300 yards
BOTANIC GARDENS
HILLHEAD
KELVINBRIDGE
GLASGOW UNIVERSITY
KELVINGROVE MUSEUM AND ART GALLERY
KELVINGROVE PARK
ST. GEORGE'S CROSS
SCOTTISH EXHIBITION CENTRE
Bell's Bridge
GLASGOW SCIENCE CENTRE
Finnieston Bridge
CLYDE
KINNING PARK
Great Western Road
Wilton Street
Raeberry Street
Maryhill Road
Garscube Road
Ellesmere
Hopehill Road
North Woodside Road
Napiershall Street
Belmont St.
Bank Street
Gibson St.
Park Rd
West Prince's Street
George's Road
Woodlands Road
Park Quadrant
Saint George's Road
Kelvin Way
Royal Terrace
Woodside Place
Sauchiehall Street
Argyle Street
Berkeley Street
Kelvinhaugh Street
Kent Road
Elderslie St.
Saint Vincent Street
North Street
Newton Street
Elmbank St.
Bath St.
Scott Street
West St.
Douglas St.
West Street
Campbell Street
Pitt St.
Waterloo
Stobcross Road
Finnieston Street
Clydeside Expressway
Lancefield Street
Lancefield Quay
Hydepark Street
Anderston Quay
Broomielaw
York St.
West St.
Govan Road
Paisley Road West
Morrison Street
Kingston St.
Nelson Street
Milnpark Street
Admiral St.
Seaward St.
A 81
A 82
B 808
A 814
A 8
M 8
(M 8)
C
Y
Z
M⁴
M⁵
M³
M
U
T
POL
116
128
105
50
140
108
107
34
143
141
35
47
42
95
85
93
22
39
100

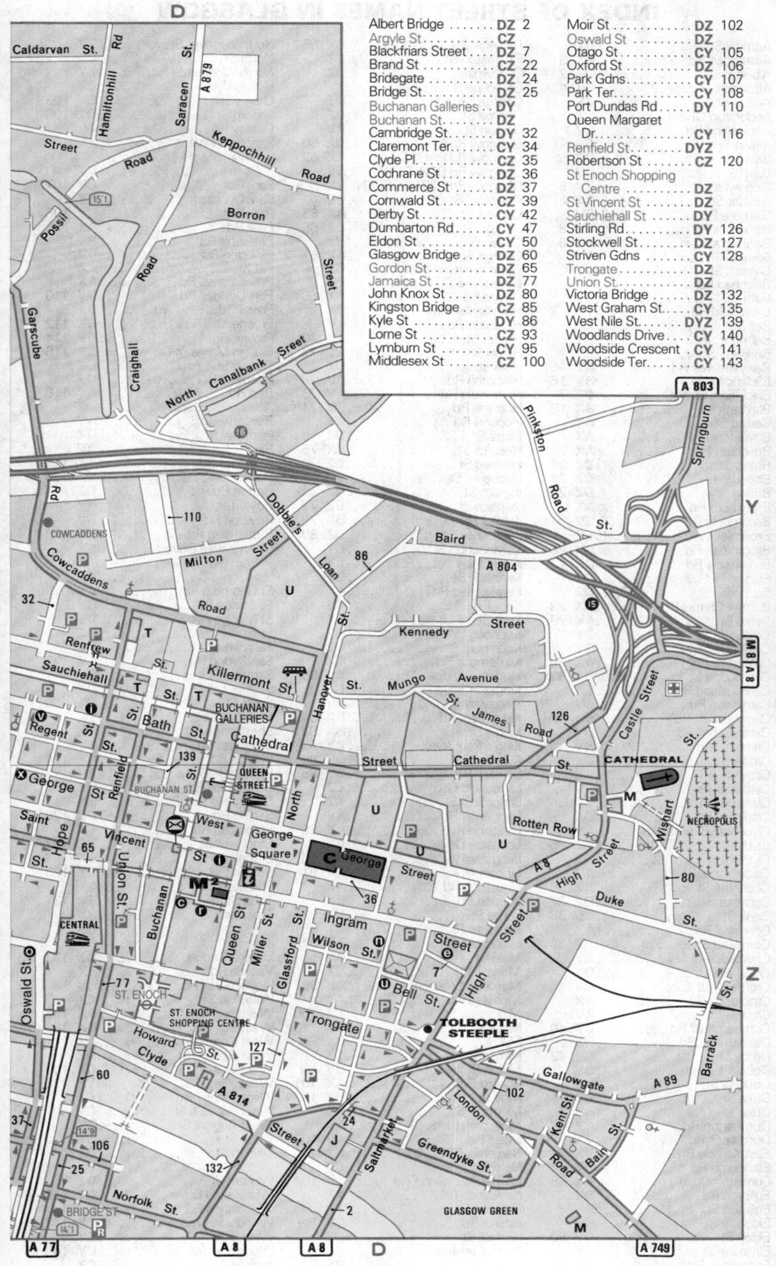
D
Albert Bridge . . . . DZ 2
Argyle St. . . . . CZ
Blackfriars Street . . . . DZ 7
Brand St . . . . CZ 22
Bridgegate . . . . DZ 24
Bridge St. . . . . DZ 25
Buchanan Galleries . . . DY
Buchanan St. . . . . DZ
Cambridge St. . . . . . . DY 32
Claremont Ter. . . . . . . CY 34
Clyde Pl. . . . . CZ 35
Cochrane St . . . . DZ 36
Commerce St . . . . DZ 37
Cornwald St . . . . CZ 39
Derby St . . . . CY 42
Dumbarton Rd . . . . . . CY 47
Eldon St . . . . CY 50
Glasgow Bridge . . . . . DZ 60
Gordon St. . . . . DZ 65
Jamaica St . . . . DZ 77
John Knox St . . . . DZ 80
Kingston Bridge . . . . . CZ 85
Kyle St . . . . DY 86
Lorne St . . . . CZ 93
Lymburn St . . . . CY 95
Middlesex St . . . . CZ 100
Moir St . . . . DZ 102
Oswald St . . . . DZ
Otago St . . . . CY 105
Oxford St . . . . DZ 106
Park Gdns . . . . CY 107
Park Ter. . . . . CY 108
Port Dundas Rd . . . . . DY 110
Queen Margaret Dr. . . . CY 116
Renfield St . . . . DYZ
Robertson St . . . . CZ 120
St Enoch Shopping Centre . . . . . . DZ
St Vincent St . . . . DZ
Sauchiehall St . . . . . . DY
Stirling Rd . . . . DY 126
Stockwell St . . . . DZ 127
Striven Gdns . . . . CY 128
Trongate . . . . DZ
Union St. . . . . DZ
Victoria Bridge . . . . . . DZ 132
West Graham St. . . . . . CY 135
West Nile St. . . . . DYZ 139
Woodlands Drive . . . . . CY 140
Woodside Crescent . . . CY 141
Woodside Ter. . . . . CY 143
Caldarvan St.
Hamiltonhill Rd
Saracen St.
A 879
Keppochhill Road
Possil Road
Borron Street
Garscube Rd
Craighall Road
North Canalbank Sreet
A 803
Pinkston Road
Springburn
Baird St.
A 804
Dobbie's Loan
Milton Street
COWCADDENS
Cowcaddens Road
Kennedy Street
Renfrew St.
Sauchiehall St.
Killermont St.
BUCHANAN GALLERIES
Hanover St.
St. Mungo Avenue
St. James Road
Castle Street
Bath St.
Regent St.
Cathedral Street
CATHEDRAL
NECROPOLIS
QUEEN STREET
BUCHANAN ST.
George St
Saint Vincent St.
Hope St.
Renfield St.
West George St
George Square
North St.
Rotten Row
Wishart St.
George Street
High Street
Duke St.
Union St.
Buchanan St.
Queen St.
Miller St.
Glassford St.
Ingram Street
Wilson St.
Bell St.
CENTRAL
Oswald St.
ST. ENOCH
ST. ENOCH SHOPPING CENTRE
Trongate
TOLBOOTH STEEPLE
Howard St.
Clyde St.
A 814
Gallowgate
A 89
Barrack St.
London Road
Kent St.
Bain St.
Saltmarket
Greendyke St.
Norfolk St.
BRIDGE ST
GLASGOW GREEN
A 77
A 8
A 749
M 8
Y
Z

INDEX OF STREET NAMES IN GLASGOW

SCOTLAND

Hotel du Vin at One Devonshire Gardens

rm, VISA AE

1 Devonshire Gardens ✉ G12 OUX – ☎ (0141) 339 2001 – www.hotelduvin.com – Fax (0141) 337 1663 AV**a**

45 rm – †£ 150/325 ††£ 150/325, ☕ £ 17 – 4 suites

Rest *Bistro* – *(Closed Saturday lunch)* Menu £ 18 (lunch) – Carte £ 30/53

◆ Collection of adjoining 19C houses in terrace, refurbished with attention to detail. Warm, intimate and comfortable bedrooms are named after wines. High levels of service. Smart Bistro offers classic grill menu as well as more innovative carte.

Radisson Blu Glasgow

rm, AC VISA AE

301 Argyle St ✉ G2 8DL – ☎ (0141) 204 3333 – Fax (0141) 204 3344 DZ**o**

246 rm – †£ 135 ††£ 145, ☕ £ 16 – 1 suite

Rest *Collage* – Mediterranean – Menu £ 20 – Carte £ 20/35

◆ Stylish modern commercial hotel with impressive open-plan interior; set in central location close to the station. Three styles of bedroom – all offering good levels of comfort. Spacious dining room with central buffet area and all-encompassing menu.

Malmaison

rm, VISA AE

278 West George St ✉ G2 4LL – ☎ (0141) 572 1000 – www.malmaison.com – Fax (0141) 572 1002 CY**c**

68 rm – †£ 150 ††£ 150, ☕ £ 13.95 – 4 suites

Rest *The Brasserie* – Menu £ 16 – Carte £ 29/41

◆ Visually arresting former Masonic chapel. Comfortable, well-proportioned rooms seem effortlessly stylish with bold patterns and colours and thoughtful extra attentions. Informal Brasserie with French themed menu and Champagne bar.

Abode Glasgow

rm, AC VISA AE

129 Bath St ✉ G2 2SZ – ☎ (0141) 221 6789 – www.abodehotels.co.uk – Fax (0141) 221 6777 DY**v**

60 rm – †£ 89/140 ††£ 89/195, ☕ £ 13.50

Rest *Michael Caines* – see restaurant listing

Rest *Bar MC & Grill* – Menu £ 11 (lunch) – Carte £ 25/41

◆ Near Mackintosh's School of Art, an early 20C building decorated with a daring modern palette: striking colour schemes and lighting in the spacious, elegantly fitted rooms. All-day dining in stylish bar and grill.

Sherbrooke Castle

rm, AC rest, P VISA AE

11 Sherbrooke Ave, Pollokshields ✉ G41 4PG – ☎ (0141) 427 4227 – www.sherbrooke.co.uk – Fax (0141) 427 5685 AX**r**

16 rm ☕ – †£ 95/105 ††£ 155/175 – 2 suites

Rest *Morrisons* – Menu £ 13 (lunch) – Carte £ 15/35

◆ Late 19C baronial Romanticism given free rein inside and out. The hall is richly furnished and imposing; rooms in the old castle have a comfortable country house refinement. Panelled Victorian dining room with open fire.

XXX Brian Maule at Chardon d'Or

VISA AE

176 West Regent St ✉ G2 4RL – ☎ (0141) 248 3801 – www.brianmaule.com – Fax (0141) 248 3901 – Closed 2 weeks January, 2 weeks end July, 25-26 December, Saturday lunch, Sunday and Bank Holidays CY**i**

Rest – Modern – Menu £ 20 (lunch) – Carte £ 38/51

◆ Sizeable Georgian house in suburbs, boasting original pillars, ornate carved ceiling and modern art. Well-spaced linen-clad tables; formal service from well-versed team. Classic Scottish cooking.

XXX Rogano

AC VISA AE

11 Exchange Place ✉ G1 3AN – ☎ (0141) 248 4055 – www.roganoglasgow.com – Closed 1 January DZ**c**

Rest – Seafood – Menu £ 20 (lunch) – Carte £ 30/48

◆ Long-standing Glasgow institution; art deco, with original panelling, stained glass windows and etched mirrors. Classic menus lean towards local seafood. The langoustines are a must.

XXX **Two Fat Ladies at The Buttery**

652 Argyle St ✉ G3 8UF – ✆ (0141) 221 8188 – www.twofatladiesrestaurant.com – Fax (0141) 221 0901 CZ**v**

Rest – Menu £ 16 (lunch) – Carte £ 29/41

◆ Wood-panelled restaurant with banquette seating and tartan furnishings; an old classic revived. Tasty, seasonal cooking; charming, attentive service and a great range of whiskies.

XX **Michael Caines** – at Abode Glasgow Hotel

129 Bath St ✉ G2 2SZ – ✆ (0141) 221 6789 – www.michaelcaines.co.uk – Fax (0141) 221 6789 – Closed 10-24 January, 2 weeks mid-July, Sunday and Monday DY**v**

Rest – Modern – Menu £ 13 (lunch) – Carte £ 39/46

◆ Smart, stylish restaurant in boutique hotel, a mirrored wall creating impression of size. Quality décor matched by clean, unfussy cooking prepared with finesse and skill.

XX **La Vallee Blanche**

360 Byres Road – ✆ (0141) 334 3333 – www.lavalleeblanche.com – Fax (0141) 334 3334 – Closed Monday CY**v**

Rest – French – Menu £ 13 (lunch) – Carte £ 24/33

◆ 1st floor restaurant-cum-ski-lodge, with wood-clad walls, stag antler lights and myriad candles. Classical cooking with a seasonal French base. Formal service from a jolly team.

XX **The Grill Room at The Square**

Second Floor, 29 Royal Exchange Sq ✉ G1 3AJ – ✆ (0141) 225 5615 – www.29glasgow.com – Fax (0141) 225 5611 DZ**r**

Rest – Steakhouse – *(booking advisable)* Menu £ 16 (lunch) – Carte £ 26/50

◆ 2nd floor of impressive Georgian building on Royal Exchange Square. Appealing menu focuses on seafood and 28-day hung Scottish steak, with choice of sauce and chunky chips.

XX **Urban**

23-25 St Vincent Place ✉ G1 2DT – ✆ (0141) 248 5636 – www.urbanbrasserie.co.uk – Fax (0141) 248 5720 – Closed 1-2 January and 25-26 December DZ**i**

Rest – Modern – Menu £ 20 – Carte £ 27/45

◆ Imposing 19C building in heart of city centre. Stylish, modern interior with individual booths and illuminated glass ceiling. Modern English cooking. Live piano at weekends.

XX **Manna**

104 Bath St ✉ G2 2EN – ✆ (0141) 332 6678 – www.mannarestaurant.co.uk – Fax (0141) 332 6549 – Closed 1-2 January, 25-26 December and Sunday lunch DY**i**

Rest – Mediterranean – Menu £ 16 – Carte £ 24/46

◆ Parrot motifs recur everywhere, even on the door handles! Well-spaced tables and mirrored walls add a sense of space to the basement. A free-ranging fusion style prevails.

XX **Gamba**

225a West George St ✉ G2 2ND – ✆ (0141) 572 0899 – www.gamba.co.uk – Fax (0141) 572 0896 – Closed 1-2 January, 25-26 December and Sunday lunch DZ**x**

Rest – Seafood – Menu £ 20 (lunch) – Carte £ 22/39

◆ Extensive and appealing seafood menu; simple and effective cooking from chef-owner, with lemon sole a speciality. Comfortable dining room with good service from well-versed team.

XX **La Parmigiana**

447 Great Western Rd, Kelvinbridge ✉ G12 8HH – ✆ (0141) 334 0686 – www.laparmigiana.co.uk – Fax (0141) 357 5595 – Closed 1 January, 25-26 December and Sunday CY**r**

Rest – Italian – *(booking essential)* Menu £ 15 (lunch) – Carte £ 31/42

◆ Compact, pleasantly decorated traditional eatery with a lively atmosphere and good local reputation. Obliging, professional service and a sound, authentic Italian repertoire.

SCOTLAND

The Dhabba

44 Candleriggs ✉ G1 1LE – ☎ (0141) 553 1249 – www.thedhabba.com – Fax (0141) 553 1730 – Closed 1 January and 25 December DZ**u**

Rest – Indian – Menu £ 10 (lunch) – Carte £ 17/29

◆ In the heart of the Merchant City, this large, modern restaurant boasts bold colours and huge wall photos. Concentrates on authentic, accomplished North Indian cooking.

Stravaigin

28 Gibson St, (basement) ✉ G12 8NX – ☎ (0141) 334 2665 – www.stravaigin.com – Fax (0141) 334 4099 – Closed 25 December and 1 January CY**z**

Rest – *(dinner only and lunch Friday-Sunday)* Carte £ 19/37

◆ Basement restaurant with bright murals. A refined instinct for genuinely global cuisine produces surprising but well-prepared combinations - ask about pre-theatre menus.

Stravaigin 2

8 Ruthven Lane, off Byres Rd ✉ G12 9BG – ☎ (0141) 334 7165 – www.stravaigin.com – Fax (0141) 357 4785 – Closed 1-2 January, 25 December and lunch 26 December AV**s**

Rest – Modern – Menu £ 13 (lunch Monday-Saturday) – Carte £ 24/33

◆ Lilac painted cottage tucked away in an alley off Byres Road. Simple, unfussy, modern bistro-style interior, spread over two floors. Eclectic menu offers something for everyone.

Dakhin

First Floor, 89 Candleriggs ✉ G1 1NP – ☎ (0141) 553 2585 – www.dakhin.com – Fax (0141) 553 2492 – Closed 1 January and 25 December DZ**n**

Rest – South Indian – Menu £ 10 (lunch) – Carte £ 16/30

◆ Large open plan first floor restaurant in redeveloped area of city serving authentic, flavoursome South Indian cooking. Friendly, informal atmosphere; knowledgable service.

The Shandon Belles

652 Argyle Street ✉ G3 8UF – ☎ (0141) 221 8188 – www.twofatladiesrestaurant.com – Fax (0141) 221 0901 CZ**v**

Rest – Scottish – *(booking advisable)* Carte £ 15/20

◆ Rustic restaurant in the basement of The Buttery, with exposed brick walls, church pews and simply laid tables. Tasty, unfussy dishes with a hearty base. Friendly service.

Babbity Bowster

16-18 Blackfriars St ✉ G1 1PE – ☎ (0141) 552 5055 – Fax (0141) 552 7774 – Closed 25 December and 1 January DZ**e**

Rest – Traditional – Carte £ 15/23

◆ Double-fronted Georgian pub with fiercely Scottish interior; close to the Merchant City. Honest, seasonal cooking features traditional Scottish favourites; restaurant menu is more elaborate.

at Eurocentral East : 12 mi. by M 8 off A 8 – ✉ Glasgow

Dakota

✉ ML1 4WJ – ☎ (0870) 220 82 81 – www.dakotaeurocentral.co.uk – Fax (01698) 835 445 – closed 25-26, 31 December and 1-2 January

90 rm – †£ 95 ††£ 95

Rest *Grill* – Carte £ 30/34

◆ Stylish, modern hotel with sleek, masculine feel. Well-thought out bedrooms have king-sized beds and plasma TVs. Comfortable lounge popular for afternoon tea. Open plan bar and grill offers good selection of modern cooking.

GLENDEVON – Perth and Kinross – 501 I/J15 **28** C2

Edinburgh 37 mi. – Perth 26 mi. – Stirling 19 mi.

An Lochan Country Inn with rm

✉ FK14 7JY – ☎ (01259) 781 252 – www.anlochan.co.uk

13 rm – †£ 85 ††£ 100 **Rest** – Menu £ 13/20 – Carte £ 20/30

◆ 18C drovers' inn in picturesque glen with cosy beamed bar and great choice of beer and whisky. Quality Perthshire produce includes Highland beef and locally stalked venison. Traditional bedrooms feature a flicker of tartan.

SCOTLAND

GLENROTHES – Fife – 501 K15 – pop. 38 679 Scotland 28 C2

Edinburgh 33 mi. – Dundee 25 mi. – Stirling 36 mi.

18 Thornton Station Rd, (01592) 771 173

18 Golf Course Rd, (01592) 758 686

18 Balbirnie Park Markinch, (01592) 612 095

9 Auchterderran Cardenden Woodend Rd, (01592) 721 579

9 Leslie Balsillie Laws, (01592) 620 040

Falkland★ (Palace of Falkland★ **AC**, Gardens★ **AC**) N : 5.5 mi. by A 92 and A 912

Balbirnie House

Balbirnie Park, Markinch, Northeast : 1.75 mi. by A 911 and A 92 on B 9130
KY7 6NE – (01592) 610 066 – www.balbirnie.co.uk – Fax (01592) 610 529
30 rm – £ 95/130 £ 210
Rest *Orangery* – *(closed Monday and Tuesday)* Menu £ 16/33 – Carte Lunch £ 19/26
Rest *Bistro* – Menu £ 13 – Carte £ 19/32

◆ Highly imposing part Georgian mansion in Capability Brown-styled grounds. Several lounges and library bar with period style and individually furnished country house rooms. Contemporary glass-roofed restaurant serves classics with a modern twist. Basement bistro offers French-influenced favourites.

GRANTOWN-ON-SPEY – Highland – 501 J12 – pop. 2 166 30 D2

Edinburgh 143 mi. – Inverness 34 mi. – Perth 99 mi.

54 High St (01479) 872773 (Seasonal), grantown@host.co.uk

18 Golf Course Rd, (01479) 872 079

9 Abernethy Nethy Bridge, (01479) 821 305

Culdearn House

Woodlands Terrace PH26 3JU – (01479) 872 106 – www.culdearn.com – Fax (01479) 873 641
6 rm (dinner included) – £ 90/100 £ 190/220
Rest – *(dinner only) (booking essential for non-residents)* Menu £ 34 **s**

◆ Personally run Victorian granite stone hotel offering a high degree of luxury, including beautifully furnished drawing room and very tastefully furnished bedrooms. Formally attired dining room; good Scottish home cooking.

The Pines

Woodside Ave PH26 3JR – (01479) 872 092 – www.thepinesgrantown.co.uk – April-October
5 rm – £ 65/75 £ 130
Rest – *(dinner only) (residents only, set menu only)* Menu £ 35

◆ Top level hospitality in an attractive 19C house with lovely rear garden leading onto woods and Spey. Elegant lounges display fine collection of artwork. Bedrooms are individually appointed. Candlelit dinners, full of Scottish flavours, are a special event.

The Glass House

Grant Rd PH26 3LD – (01479) 872 980 – www.theglasshouse.grantown.co.uk – Fax (01479) 872 980 – Closed 1-2 January, 2 weeks November, 25-26 December, Monday, Sunday dinner and Tuesday lunch
Rest – Menu £ 20 (lunch) – Carte dinner £ 28/39

◆ Conservatory style dining in a house extension near the high street. Light-filled interior overlooks the garden. Amiable owner serves tasty, seasonal modern British dishes.

GRULINE – Argyll and Bute – see Mull (Isle of)

GUILDTOWN – Perth and Kinross – 501 J14 – see Perth

GULLANE – East Lothian – 501 L15 – pop. 2 172 Scotland 26 C1

Edinburgh 19 mi. – North Berwick 5 mi.

Dirleton★ (Castle★) NE : 2 mi. by A 198

XX **La Potinière**

Main St ✉ EH31 2AA – ✆ (01620) 843 214 – www.la-potiniere.co.uk – Fax (01620) 843 214 – Closed 3 weeks January, 1 week October, 25-26 December, Sunday dinner October-April, Monday and Tuesday
Rest – *(booking essential)* Menu £ 23/40
◆ Sweet restaurant dressed in pink and white, serving fresh, seasonal cooking. Regularly changing menus of traditional dishes, with ingredients from local suppliers. Good value lunch.

HARRAY – **Orkney Islands** – **501** K6 – **see Orkney Islands (Mainland)**

HARRIS (Isle of) – **Western Isles Outer Hebrides** – **501** Z10 – **see Lewis and Harris (Isle of)**

INGLISTON – **City of Edinburgh** – **501** J16 – **see Edinburgh**

INVERGARRY – **Highland** – **501** F12 – ✉ **Inverness** Scotland **30** C3

Edinburgh 159 mi. – Fort William 25 mi. – Inverness 43 mi. – Kyle of Lochalsh 50 mi.
The Great Glen★

Glengarry Castle

on A 82 ✉ PH35 4HW – ✆ (01809) 501 254 – www.glengarry.net – Fax (01809) 501 207 – 19 March-8 November
26 rm – †£ 63/98 ††£ 150/170
Rest – *(light lunch Monday-Saturday)* Menu £ 29 **s** – Carte approx. £ 23 **s**
◆ On shores of Loch Oich, and named after eponymous Victorian castle whose ruin stands in grounds. Warm country house feel throughout; many bedrooms retain original fittings. Dining room shares the warm, country house style of the hotel.

SCOTLAND

INVERKEILOR – **Angus** – **501** M14 – **pop. 902** – ✉ **Arbroath** **28** D2

Edinburgh 85 mi. – Aberdeen 32 mi. – Dundee 22 mi.

XX **Gordon's** with rm

32 Main St ✉ DD11 5RN – ✆ (01241) 830 364 – www.gordonsrestaurant.co.uk – Closed 2 weeks January
4 rm – †£ 75 ††£ 120
Rest – *(Closed Monday, Tuesday and Saturday lunch to non residents) (booking essential)* Menu £ 27/44 **s**
◆ Family owned restaurant in small village. Welcoming atmosphere, beams, open fires and rugs on the wood floors. Good cooking with some innovative touches. Well-kept bedrooms.

INVERMORISTON – **Highland** – **501** G12 **30** C2

London 550 mi. – Edinburgh 166 mi. – Inverness 28 mi. – Dingwall 42 mi.

Tigh na Bruach without rest

Southwest : 0.5 mi. on A 82 ✉ IV63 7YE – ✆ (01320) 351 349 – www.tighnabruach.com – March-November
3 rm – †£ 75/85 ††£ 90/110
◆ Name means 'house on the bank'. Located by Loch Ness, it boasts splendid loch/mountain views and beautiful gardens. Very comfy bedrooms have pleasant terraces which overlook the lake.

INVERNESS – **Highland** – **501** H11 – **pop. 40 949** Scotland **30** C2

Edinburgh 156 mi. – Aberdeen 107 mi. – Dundee 134 mi.
Inverness Airport, Dalcross : ✆ (01667) 464000, NE : 8 mi. by A 96 Y
Castle Wynd ✆ (01463) 234353 Y, invernesstic@host.co.uk
18 Culcabock Rd, ✆ (01463) 239 882
18 Torvean Glenurquhart Rd, ✆ (01463) 225 651
Town★ – Museum and Art Gallery★ Y **M**
Loch Ness★★, SW : by A 82 Z – Clava Cairns★, E : 9 mi. by Culcabock Rd, B 9006 and B 851 Z – Cawdor Castle★ **AC**, NE : 14 mi. by A 96 and B 9090 Y

Plan on next page

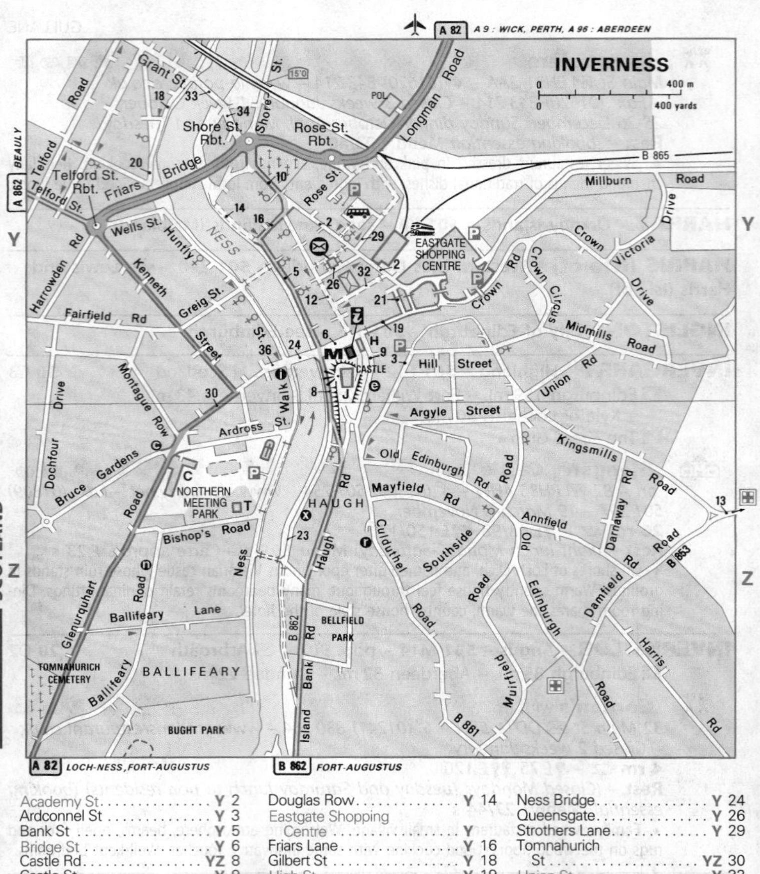

SCOTLAND

Academy St	Y 2	Douglas Row	Y 14	Ness Bridge	Y 24
Ardconnel St	Y 3	Eastgate Shopping Centre	Y	Queensgate	Y 26
Bank St	Y 5	Friars Lane	Y 16	Strothers Lane	Y 29
Bridge St	Y 6	Gilbert St	Y 18	Tomnahurich St	YZ 30
Castle Rd	YZ 8	High St	Y 19	Union St	Y 32
Castle St	Y 9	Huntly Pl.	Y 20	Waterloo Bridge	Y 33
Chapel St	Y 10	Inglis St	Y 21	Waterloo Pl.	Y 34
Church St	Y 12	Ness Bank	Z 23	Young St	Y 36
Culcabock Rd	Z 13				

Rocpool Reserve

Culduthel Rd ✉ IV2 4AG – ✆ (01463) 240 089 – www.rocpool.com – Fax (01463) 248 431 Zr

11 rm – **†£ 137/156 ††£ 288/356**

Rest Chez Roux – *see restaurant listing*

◆ Ultra-stylish boutique hotel with elegant, modern furnishings and sexy bar. Chic, comfortable bedrooms; some with their own terrace and hot tub. Attentive, professional service.

Glenmoriston Town House

20 Ness Bank ✉ IV2 4SF – ✆ (01463) 223 777 – www.glenmoristontownhouse.com – Fax (01463) 712 378 Zx

30 rm – **†£ 95/115 ††£ 170/210**

Rest *Abstract* – see restaurant listing

Rest *Contrast* – Carte £ 16/39 **s**

◆ Chic, stylish town house. Modern cocktail bar a trendy meeting point. Bedrooms are individualistic, those on the front enjoying river views; those at the rear are quieter. Locally sourced cooking at Contrast.

Ballifeary House without rest
10 Ballifeary Rd ✉ IV3 5PJ – ☎ (01463) 235 572 – www.ballifearyguesthouse.co.uk – Fax (01463) 717 583 – Closed 24-27 December **Zn**
7 rm – †£ 35/70 ††£ 70/80
◆ Pleasant house set away from town centre, with homely sitting room and comfortable, immaculately kept bedrooms. Smart breakfast room with crisp linen and polished glassware.

Moyness House without rest
6 Bruce Gdns ✉ IV3 5EN – ☎ (01463) 233 836 – www.moyness.co.uk – Fax (01463) 233 836 **Zc**
6 rm – †£ 65/95 ††£ 94/100
◆ Immaculately clipped hedges frame this attractive Victorian villa. Bedrooms vary in shape and size but all are comfortable, individually decorated and fully en suite.

Abstract – at Glenmoriston Town House Hotel
20 Ness Bank ✉ IV2 4SF – ☎ (01463) 223 777 – www.abstractrestaurant.com – Fax (01463) 712 378 – Closed Sunday and Monday **Zx**
Rest – *(dinner only)* Menu £ 27 (weekdays) **s** – Carte £ 40/50 **s**
◆ Restaurant, bar and conservatory with considerable style. Vast wall mirror offsets abstract ink pictures. Accomplished cooking with Gallic accent is impressively original.

Rocpool
1 Ness Walk ✉ IV3 5NE – ☎ (01463) 717 274 – www.rocpoolrestaurant.com – Closed 1-2 January, 25-26 December, Sunday lunch and Sunday dinner October-April **Yi**
Rest – Carte £ 22/33
◆ On the banks of the River Ness, this modern, cosmopolitan restaurant has a stylish ambience, popular with business diners. Modern cooking with a British/Mediterranean axis.

Chez Roux – at Rocpool Reserve Hotel
Culduthel Rd ✉ IV2 4AG – ☎ (01463) 240 089 – www.rocpool.com – Fax (01463) 248 431 **Zr**
Rest – Menu £ 13 (lunch) – Carte £ 25/33
◆ Smart, stylish restaurant; its walls filled with photos of the Roux brothers' early days. Classic flavourful French cooking; smooth, attentive service from a professional team.

Café 1
Castle St ✉ IV2 3EA – ☎ (01463) 226 200 – www.cafe1.net – Fax (01463) 716 363 – Closed 1 January, 25-26 December and Sunday **Ye**
Rest – Carte £ 23/34 **s**
◆ Personally run bistro opposite the castle with an informal touch, enhanced by tiled flooring and modish chairs. Local ingredients feature in regularly changing modern menus.

at Culloden East : 3 mi. by A 96 - Y – ✉ Inverness

Culloden House
✉ IV2 7BZ – ☎ (01463) 790 461 – www.cullodenhouse.co.uk – Fax (01463) 792 181 – Closed 24-26 December
25 rm – †£ 85/210 ††£ 125/250 – 3 suites
Rest *Adams Dining Room* – Menu £ 48 (dinner) – Carte £ 32/50
◆ Imposing Georgian country house in 40 acres, requisitioned by Bonnie Prince Charlie in 1746. Drawing rooms boast ornate wall-hung plaster friezes. Antique-furnished rooms. Adam's plaster reliefs adorn walls and ceiling of grand dining room; traditional menu.

at Bunchrew West : 3 mi. on A 862 - Y – ✉ Inverness

Bunchrew House
✉ IV3 8TA – ☎ (01463) 234 917 – www.bunchrewhousehotel.com – Fax (01463) 710 620 – Closed Christmas
16 rm – †£ 110/149 ††£ 160/270 **Rest** – Menu £ 25/40
◆ Unhurried relaxation is assured at this 17C Scottish mansion nestling in a tranquil spot on the shores of Bealy Firth. Drawing room is wood panelled; bedrooms restful. Gardens seen through the windows provide a pleasant backdrop to spacious dining room.

SCOTLAND

ISLAY (Isle of) – Argyll and Bute – 501 B16 — 27 A3

Port Ellen Airport : ✆ (01496) 302361

from Port Askaig to Isle of Jura (Feolin) (Caledonian MacBrayne Ltd) frequent services daily (approx. 4 mn)
– from Port Ellen or Port Askaig to Kintyre Peninsula (Kennacraig) (Caledonian MacBrayne Ltd) 1-2 daily
– from Port Askaig to Oban via Isle of Colonsay (Scalasaig) (Caledonian MacBrayne Ltd) weekly
– from Port Askaig to Isle of Colonsay (Scalasaig) and Kintyre Peninsula (Kennacraig) (Caledonian MacBrayne Ltd) weekly

The Square, Main St, Bowmore ✆ (01496) 810254, bowmore@visitscotland.com

Port Ellen 25 Charlotte St, ✆ (01496) 300 094

BALLYGRANT – Argyll and Bute — 27 A3

Kilmeny

Southwest : 0.5 mi. on A 846 ✉ PA45 7QW – ✆ (01496) 840 668 – www.kilmeny.co.uk – Fax (01496) 840 668 – Closed Christmas and New Year

5 rm – †£ 80/95 ††£ 120/142

Rest – *(by arrangement, communal dining)* Menu £ 35

◆ 19C converted farmhouse on a working farm. Its elevated position affords far reaching countryside views. Best of Scottish hospitality, home-cooking and comfort.

BOWMORE – Argyll and Bute — 27 A3

Harbour Inn with rm

The Square ✉ PA43 7JR – ✆ (01496) 810 330 – www.harbour-inn.com – Fax (01496) 810 990

7 rm – †£ 120/150 ††£ 150 **Rest** – Carte £ 30/50

◆ Attractive whitewashed inn in busy little town, short walk from distillery. Panelled bar and a dining room with bay views. Menus centre on Islay produce. Bright bedrooms.

PORT CHARLOTTE – Argyll and Bute — 27 A3

Port Charlotte

Main St ✉ PA48 7TU – ✆ (01496) 850 360 – www.portcharlotte.co.uk – Fax (01496) 850 361 – Closed 24-26 December

10 rm – †£ 95 ††£ 160/265 **Rest** – *(bar lunch)* Carte £ 18/33

◆ Simple, well-modernised, Victorian building in attractive conservation village. Pine panelled bar and relaxing lounge with open fires. Rooms furnished with fine old pieces. Attractive wood furnished restaurant with stone walls and views over the bay.

PORT ELLEN – Argyll and Bute — 27 A3

Glenegedale House

Northwest : 4.75 mi. on A 846 ✉ PA42 7AR – ✆ (01496) 300 400 – www.glenegedalehouse.co.uk

8 rm – †£ 90 ††£ 106 **Rest** – *(by arrangement)* Menu £ 35

◆ Refurbished in elegantly sympathetic style, this stalwart house proffers neutral tones with quality soft furnishings. Antiques abound. Well-equipped rooms. Handy for airport. Spacious dining room with homely cooked fare.

Glenmachrie Farmhouse without rest

Northwest : 4.5 mi. on A 846 ✉ PA42 7AQ – ✆ (01496) 302 560 – www.glenmachrie.com – Fax (01496) 302 560

5 rm – †£ 75 ††£ 90

◆ Modern farmhouse on a working farm a short drive from a number of Islay's distilleries and Duich Nature Reserve. Run on "green" low-impact policies. Warm welcoming rooms.

JEDBURGH – Scottish Borders – 501 M17 – pop. 4 090 Scotland — 26 D2

Edinburgh 48 mi. – Carlisle 54 mi. – Newcastle upon Tyne 57 mi.

Murray's Green ✆ (01835) 863170, jedburgh@visitscotland.com

Jedburgh Dunion Rd, ✆ (01835) 863 587

Town★ - Abbey★★ **AC** – Mary Queen of Scots House Visitor Centre★ **AC** – The Canongate Bridge★

Waterloo Monument (✳★★) N : 4 mi. by A 68 and B 6400

SCOTLAND

The Spinney without rest

Langlee, South : 2 mi. on A 68 ✉ TD8 6PB – ✆ (01835) 863 525 – www.thespinney-jedburgh.co.uk – March-October

3 rm – ££ 60/66

◆ Good value accommodation with homely atmosphere and ambience. Traditional feel from the gardens to the lounge. Bedrooms of a good size overlooking the attractive gardens.

Hundalee House without rest

South : 1.5 mi. by A 68 ✉ TD8 6PA – ✆ (01835) 863 011 – www.accommodation-scotland.org – Fax (01835) 863 011 – Closed February

5 rm – £ 30/45 £ 58/60

◆ 18C country lodge in a rural location, with good gardens featuring mature topiary. Country house feel and a warm welcome. Distinctive period décor and some antiques.

at Crailing **Northeast : 4 mi. by A 68 on A 698 – ✉ Jedburgh**

Crailing Old School

on B 6400 ✉ TD8 6TL – ✆ (01835) 850 382 – www.crailingoldschool.co.uk – Closed 1 week Spring, 2 weeks Autumn, Christmas and New Year

4 rm – £ 39/50 £ 65/80

Rest – *(by arrangement, communal dining)* Menu £ 25

◆ Former village school well sited for touring and golfing. Attractive guests' lounge also used for communal breakfast. Comfortable bedrooms in the house and the garden lodge. Home-cooked dinners.

KELSO – **Scottish Borders** – **501** M17 – **pop. 5 116** Scotland **26** D2

Edinburgh 44 mi. – Hawick 21 mi. – Newcastle upon Tyne 68 mi.

Town House, The Square ✆ (01835) 863170 (mornings only in winter), bordersinfo@visitscotland.com

Golf Course Rd, ✆ (01573) 223 009

Town★ - The Square★★ – ★ from Kelso Bridge

Tweed Valley★★ - Floors Castle★ **AC**, NW : 1.5 mi. by A 6089. Mellerstain★★ (Ceilings★★★, Library★★★) **AC**, NW : 6 mi. by A 6089 – Waterloo Monument (★★), SW : 7 mi. by A 698 and B 6400 – Jedburgh Abbey★★ **AC**, SW : 8.5 mi. by A 698 - Dryburgh Abbey★★ **AC** (setting★★★), SW : 10.5 mi. by A 6089, B 6397 and B 6404 – Scott's View★★, W : 11 mi. by A 6089, B 6397, B 6404 and B 6356 – Smailholm Tower★ (★★), NW : 6 mi. by A 6089 and B 6397 - Lady Kirk (Kirk o'Steil★), NE : 16 mi. by A 698, A 697, A 6112 and B 6437

The Roxburghe

Heiton, Southwest : 3.5 mi. by A 698 ✉ TD5 8JZ – ✆ (01573) 450 331 – www.roxburghe.net – Fax (01573) 450 611

20 rm – £ 130/145 £ 164/272 – 2 suites

Rest – Menu £ 40 (dinner) **s** – Carte lunch approx. £ 18 **s**

◆ Wonderfully characterful Jacobean style mansion built in 1853. Sitting rooms with log fires and fresh flowers. Lovely conservatory, attractive library bar. Luxurious rooms. Warmly hued, formal restaurant with collection of horse racing pictures.

Ednam House

Bridge St ✉ TD5 7HT – ✆ (01573) 224 168 – www.ednamhouse.com – Fax (01573) 226 319 – Closed 20 December-7 January

32 rm – £ 69/128 £ 87/155

Rest – *(bar lunch Monday-Saturday)* Carte £ 15/28 **s**

◆ Dominant Georgian mansion on Tweed. Distinctive décor exudes period appeal. Three impressively ornate lounges. Bar with fishing theme. Traditional rooms. Spacious dining room with relaxed atmosphere, overlooking gardens and river.

The Cobbles Inn

7 Bowmont St ✉ TD57JH – ✆ (01573) 223 548 – www.thecobblesinn.co.uk – Fax (01573) 223 548 – Closed Sunday dinner and Monday

Rest – Menu £ 17 (Sunday lunch) – Carte £ 19/30

◆ Characterful 19C coaching inn set off a quaint cobbled market square. Appealing daily dishes display a strong seasonal base and plenty of fresh local produce; good value early evening menu.

SCOTLAND

at Ednam North : 2.25 mi. on B 6461 – ✉ Kelso

Edenwater House
off Stichill rd ✉ TD5 7QL – ☎ (01573) 224 070
– www.edenwaterhouse.co.uk – Fax (01573) 226 615
– Closed January and December
4 rm – †£ 65/75 ††£ 100/110
Rest – *(Closed Sunday-Monday) (dinner only) (booking essential)* Menu £ 35
◆ Charming house in rural location next to 17C kirk. Beautiful gardens with stream and meadows beyond. Antique filled lounges. Rooms boast fine quality furnishings. Elegant dining room serving traditionally based meals using local produce.

KENMORE – **Perth and Kinross** – **501** I14 – **pop. 596** Scotland **28** C2

Edinburgh 82 mi. – Dundee 60 mi. – Oban 71 mi. – Perth 38 mi.
18 Taymouth Castle Aberfeldy, ☎ (01887) 830 228
27 Mains of Taymouth, ☎ (01887) 830 226
Village★
Loch Tay★★. Ben Lawers★★, SW : 8 mi. by A 827

Kenmore rest,
The Square ✉ PH15 2NU – ☎ (01887) 830 205 – www.kenmorehotel.com
– Fax (01887) 830 262
40 rm – †£ 95/109 ††£ 125/135
Rest *Taymouth* – Carte £ 21/36
◆ Scotland's oldest inn. Standing on the Tay, it is now a smart, white-fronted hotel with Poet's Parlour featuring original pencilled verse by Burns. Cosy, well-kept rooms. Restaurant with panoramic river views.

SCOTLAND

KILBERRY – **Argyll and Bute** – **501** D16 – **see Kintyre (Peninsula)**

KILCHRENAN – **Argyll and Bute** – **501** E14 – ✉ **Taynuilt** Scotland **27** B2

Edinburgh 117 mi. – Glasgow 87 mi. – Oban 18 mi.
Loch Awe★★, E : 1.25 m

Ardanaiseig
Northeast : 4 mi. ✉ PA35 1HE – ☎ (01866) 833 333 – www.ardanaiseig.com
– Fax (01866) 833 222 – Closed 2 January-1 March
17 rm – †£ 96/167 ††£ 220/360 – 1 suite
Rest – *(booking essential for non-residents)* Menu £ 25/50
◆ Substantial country house in extensive informal gardens beside Loch Awe. Undisturbed peace. Impressively elegant interior; antiques to the fore. Tasteful bedrooms. Dining room boasts views to loch; classic country house cooking.

Roineabhal rm,
✉ PA35 1HD – ☎ (01866) 833 207 – www.roineabhal.com – Fax (01866)
833 477 – Easter-November
3 rm – †£ 65 ††£ 100 **Rest** – *(by arrangement)* Menu £ 40
◆ Large stone house, built by the owners, enviably located by rushing stream and close to Loch Awe. Rusticity prevails in welcoming interior; spacious rooms with homely extras. By arrangement five-course communal dinner, home-cooked using local produce.

KILDRUMMY – **Aberdeenshire** – **501** L12 – ✉ **Alford** Scotland **28** D1

Edinburgh 137 mi. – Aberdeen 35 mi.
Castle★ **AC**
Huntly Castle (Heraldic carvings★★★) N : 15 mi. by A 97 – Craigievar Castle★, SE : 13 mi. by A 97, A 944 and A 980

Kildrummy Castle
South : 1.25 mi. on A 97 ✉ AB33 8RA – ✆ (019755) 71 288 – www.kildrummycastlehotel.co.uk – Fax (019755) 71 345 – Closed 3-21 January and 1 week November
16 rm – †£ 90/120 ††£ 213/223
Rest ***The Dining Room*** – *(Closed Monday lunch)* Menu £ 35 (dinner) – Carte lunch approx. £ 19
◆ Imposing, stone built 19C mansion in superb grounds with fine view of original 13C castle. Baronial, country house style abounds: lounges flaunt antiques. Variable rooms. Delightfully wood-panelled dining room; homely Scottish cooking.

KILLIECRANKIE – **Perth and Kinross** – **501** I13 – **see Pitlochry**

KILLIN – **Stirling** – **501** H14 – **pop. 666** Scotland **27** B2

Edinburgh 72 mi. – Dundee 65 mi. – Oban 54 mi. – Perth 43 mi.
The Old Mill, Falls of Dochart ✆ (08707) 200627, (April- Oct) killin.sdtourism@btconnect.com
Killin, ✆ (01567) 820 312
Loch Tay★★, Ben Lawers★★, NE : 8 mi. by A 827

at Ardeonaig **Northeast : 6.75 mi. – ✉ Killin (Stirling)**

Ardeonaig rm,
South Road Loch Tay ✉ FK21 8SU – ✆ (01567) 820 400 – www.ardeonaighotel.co.uk
26 rm (dinner included) – †£ 100/125 ††£ 180/350
Rest ***The Restaurant*** – Menu £ 35 (dinner) – Carte £ 26/42
◆ Wonderful setting beside Loch Tay. Enthusiastic owner has stamped his own style and service is professional yet unobtrusive. Cosy bar, chic sitting room and charming library. Deluxe rooms in extension. Kitchen merges South African influences with local ingredients.

KILMORY – **North Ayrshire** – **501** E17 – **see Arran (Isle of)**

KINCLAVEN – **Perth and Kinross** – **501** J14 – **pop. 394** – ✉ **Stanley** **28** C2

Edinburgh 56 mi. – Perth 12 mi.

Ballathie House rm,
Stanley ✉ PH1 4QN – ✆ (01250) 883 268 – www.ballathiehousehotel.com – Fax (01250) 883 396 – Closed 1-10 February
39 rm (dinner included) – †£ 130/165 ††£ 260/280 – 3 suites
Rest – Menu £ 22/45
◆ Imposing mid 19C former shooting lodge on banks of Tay, imbued with tranquil, charming atmosphere. Elegant, individually furnished bedrooms with a floral theme. Richly alluring restaurant overlooking river.

KINGUSSIE – **Highland** – **501** H12 – **pop. 1 410** Scotland **30** C3

Edinburgh 117 mi. – Inverness 41 mi. – Perth 73 mi.
Gynack Rd, ✆ (01540) 661 600
Highland Wildlife Park★ **AC**, NE : 4 mi. by A 9. Aviemore★, NE : 11 mi. by A 9 – The Cairngorms★★ (★★★) - ★★★ from Cairn Gorm, NE : 18 mi. by B 970

Hermitage

Spey St ✉ PH21 1HN – ✆ (01540) 662 137 – www.thehermitage-scotland.com – Fax (01540) 662 177
5 rm – †£ 40/55 ††£ 60/80 **Rest** – *(by arrangement)* Menu £ 20
◆ Pleasant Victorian detached house with views of Cairngorms. Attractive lawned garden. Homely, welcoming lounge with log fire. Colourful, floral rooms. Garden views from conservatory style dining room.

SCOTLAND

The Cross at Kingussie with rm

Tweed Mill Brae, Ardbroilach Rd ✉ PH21 1LB – ☎ (01540) 661 166 – www.thecross.co.uk – Fax (01540) 661 080 – Closed 3 weeks January, 1 week Autumn, Christmas, Sunday and Monday

8 rm (dinner included) – †£ 160/190 ††£ 220/280

Rest – *(dinner only) (booking essential)* Menu £ 50 **s**

◆ Personally run converted tweed mill restaurant in four acres of waterside grounds with beamed ceilings and modern artwork. Modish Scottish cuisine. Comfortable rooms.

KINROSS – Perth and Kinross – 501 J15 – pop. 4 681 — 28 C2

Edinburgh 28 mi. – Dunfermline 13 mi. – Perth 18 mi. – Stirling 25 mi.

Kinross Information Centre, Loch Leven Nature Reserve ☎ (01577) 863680 (closed weekends October-April), kinrosstic@perthshire.co.uk

Green Hotel 2 The Muirs, ☎ (01577) 863 407

Milnathort South St, ☎ (01577) 864 069

Bishopshire Kinnesswood Woodmarch

The Green

2 Muirs ✉ KY13 8AS – ☎ (01577) 863 467 – www.green-hotel.com – Fax (01577) 863 180 – Closed 24-28 December

46 rm – †£ 70/100 ††£ 95/155

Rest *Basil's* – *(dinner only)* Menu £ 30

◆ 18C former coaching inn in neat grounds off village high street. Spacious, welcoming lounge. Try your hand at curling. Comfortable, modern rooms. Bright, airy modern restaurant with modish menus to match.

SCOTLAND

KINTYRE (Peninsula) – Argyll and Bute – 501 D16 Scotland — 27 B3

Campbeltown Airport : ☎ (01586) 553797

from Claonaig to Isle of Arran (Lochranza) (Caledonian MacBrayne Ltd) frequent services daily (30 mn)
– from Kennacraig to Isle of Islay (Port Ellen or Port Askaig) (Caledonian MacBrayne Ltd) 1-3 daily
– from Kennacraig to Oban via Isle of Colonsay (Scalasaig) and Isle of Islay (Port Askaig) 3 weekly

Machrihanish Campbeltown, ☎ (01586) 810 213

Dunaverty Campbeltown Southend, ☎ (01586) 830 677

Gigha Isle of Gigha, ☎ (01583) 505 242

Carradale★ – Saddell (Collection of grave slabs★)

CARRADALE – Argyll and Bute — 27 B3

Dunvalanree

Port Righ Bay ✉ PA28 6SE – ☎ (01583) 431 226 – www.dunvalanree.com – Closed Christmas

5 rm (dinner included) – †£ 107 ††£ 172

Rest – *(dinner only)* Menu £ 28

◆ 1930s house on the bay facing Arran and Kilbrannan Sound. Comfortable firelit lounge, "Arts and Crafts" stained glass entrance and well-fitted rooms, one in Mackintosh style. Intimate dining room takes up the period style.

KILBERRY – Argyll and Bute — 27 A3

The Kilberry Inn with rm

✉ PA29 6YD – ☎ (01880) 770 223 – www.kilberryinn.com – Closed January-mid March and Monday

4 rm – ††£ 95 **Rest** – *(booking essential at dinner)* Carte £ 20/31

◆ Remotely set restaurant with open fires, wooden beams and local art displayed on its stone walls. Menus have a traditional base, with lots of locally sourced seafood in summer and game in winter. The comfortable bedrooms are named after nearby islands; simply yet elegantly furnished, with a welcoming feel.

KIRKBEAN – Dumfries and Galloway – 501 J19 Scotland — 26 C3

Edinburgh 92 mi. – Dumfries 13 mi. – Kirkcudbright 29 mi.

Sweetheart Abbey★, N : 5 mi. by A 710. Threave Garden★★ and Threave Castle★, W : 20 mi. by A 710 and A 745

Cavens

DG2 8AA – (01387) 880 234 – www.cavens.com – Fax (01387) 880 467 – Closed January and February

8 rm – £ 80/130 £ 80/190 **Rest** – *(dinner only)* Menu £ 35 **s**

◆ 18C house with extensions set in mature gardens. Very comfortable lounges opening onto terrace. Spacious well furnished bedrooms. Simple refreshing meals using local produce.

KIRKCOLM – Dumfries and Galloway – 501 E19 – see Stranraer

KIRKCUDBRIGHT – Dumfries and Galloway – 501 H19 – pop. 3 447 — 25 B3

Scotland

Edinburgh 108 mi. – Dumfries 28 mi. – Stranraer 50 mi.

Harbour Sq (01557) 330494 (Easter-October), kirkcudbright@visitscotland.com

Stirling Crescent, (01557) 330 314

Town★

Dundrennan Abbey★ **AC**, SE : 5 mi. by A 711

Selkirk Arms

High St DG6 4JG – (01557) 330 402 – www.selkirkarmshotel.co.uk – Fax (01557) 331 639

17 rm – £ 65/95 £ 90/110 **Rest** – Menu £ 26 (dinner) – Carte £ 23/33

◆ Traditional coaching inn in centre of quaint town; Burns reputedly wrote 'The Selkirk Grace' here. Rustic interior. Large bar serving simple food. Good sized rooms. Comfortable dining room with seasonal, classically based menu.

Gladstone House

48 High St DG6 4JX – (01557) 331 734 – www.kirkcudbrightgladstone.co.uk – Fax (01557) 331 734 – Closed Christmas

3 rm – £ 45/50 £ 70 **Rest** – *(by arrangement)* Menu £ 25

◆ Attractive Georgian style merchant's house with welcoming owners. Spacious, comfortably furnished sitting room. Traditional bedrooms in pastel shades; two are built into the eaves. Cosy ground floor dining room; set menu features local produce.

KIRKMICHAEL – Perth and Kinross – 501 J13 — 28 C2

Edinburgh 73 mi. – Aberdeen 85 mi. – Inverness 102 mi. – Perth 29 mi.

The Strathardle Inn with rm

on A 924 PH10 7NS – (01250) 881 224 – www.strathardleinn.co.uk – Fax (01250) 881 373 – Closed 2 weeks January

8 rm – £ 50 £ 70 **Rest** – Carte £ 19/22

◆ 18C drover's inn serving robust cooking with a Scottish twist. Concise lunch menu of pub favourites. Dinner menu might feature smoked salmon or local venison. Simple, modern bedrooms.

KIRKNEWTON – Edinburgh – 501 J16 – see Edinburgh

KIRKWALL – Orkney Islands – 501 L7 – see Orkney Islands

KIRK YETHOLM – Scottish Borders — 26 D2

London 346 mi. – Edinburgh 57 mi. – Hawick 26 mi. – Galashiels 27 mi.

Mill House without rest

Main St TD5 8PE – (01573) 420 604 – www.millhouseyetholm.co.uk – Fax (01573) 420 644

3 rm – £ 50 £ 90

◆ Converted grain mill with a spacious and immaculately presented interior, full of homely, warm touches. Well appointed bedrooms add the final touch to a most appealing house.

SCOTLAND

KIRRIEMUIR – Angus – 501 K13 – pop. 5 963 28 C2

Edinburgh 65 mi. – Aberdeen 50 mi. – Dundee 16 mi. – Perth 30 mi.

Purgavie Farm

Lintrathen, West : 5.5 mi. on B 951 ✉ DD8 5HZ – ✆ (01575) 560 213 – www.purgavie.co.uk – Fax (01575) 560 213

3 rm – †£ 35 ††£ 60

Rest – *(by arrangement, communal dining)* Menu £ 15

◆ Farmhouse on working farm at foot of Glen Isla, part of lovely Glens of Angus. Homely lounge with open fire. Large, comfortable rooms with panoramic views. Meals are taken communally in the comfortable dining room.

KYLESKU – Highland – 501 E9 Scotland 30 C1

Edinburgh 256 mi. – Inverness 100 mi. – Ullapool 34 mi.

Loch Assynt★★, S : 6 mi. by A 894

Kylesku

✉ IV27 4HW – ✆ (01971) 502 231 – www.kyleskuhotel.co.uk – Closed mid-October to 1 March

8 rm – †£ 60 ††£ 94

Rest Kylesku (Bar) – *see restaurant listing*

Rest – Menu £ 29 (dinner) – Carte £ 18/27

◆ Delightfully located 17C coaching inn, set beside 2 sea-lochs in a peaceful village. Spectacular panoramic views from cosy lounge, restaurant and most of the homely bedrooms. Cooking centres around fresh Highland game and locally landed seafood.

Kylesku (Bar) – at Kylesku Hotel

✉ IV27 4HW – ✆ (01971) 502 231 – www.kyleskuhotel.co.uk – Closed mid-October to 1 March

Rest – Menu £ 29 (dinner) – Carte £ 18/29

◆ Wonderfully located beside two-sea lochs, with outside seating and spectacular mountain views. Wide menu offers fresh Highland meats, and seafood landed daily on the neighbouring slipway.

LAIRG – Highland – 501 G9 – pop. 857 30 C2

Edinburgh 218 mi. – Inverness 61 mi. – Wick 72 mi.

Ferrycroft Countryside Centre, Sutherland ✆ (01549) 402160 (April-October), ferrycroft@croftersrestaurant.fsnet.co.uk

Park House

✉ IV27 4AU – ✆ (01549) 402 208 – www.parkhousesporting.com – Fax (01549) 402 693 – Closed 20 December-3 January

4 rm – †£ 35/55 ††£ 70/80 **Rest** – *(by arrangement)* Menu £ 22

◆ Victorian house, just set back from Loch Shin, comfortable and well furnished with high ceilings and views of the loch. Good spacious bedrooms. Country pursuits organised. Hunting and fishing activities of the establishment reflected in the home-cooked menus.

LANGASS – Western Isles – see Uist (Isles of)

LEITH – Edinburgh – 501 K16 – see Edinburgh

LERWICK – Shetland Islands – 501 Q3 – see Shetland Islands (Mainland)

LEVERBURGH – Western Isles Outer Hebrides – 501 Y10 – see Lewis and Harris (Isle of)

LEWIS and HARRIS (Isle of) – 501 A9 Scotland

from Stornoway to Ullapool (Mainland) (Caledonian MacBrayne Ltd) 2/3 daily (2 h 40 mn)
– from Kyles Scalpay to the Isle of Scalpay (Caledonian MacBrayne Ltd) (10 mn)
– from Tarbert to Isle of Skye (Uig) (Caledonian MacBrayne Ltd) 1-2 daily (1 h 45 mn)
– from Tarbert to Portavadie (Caledonian MacBrayne Ltd) (summer only) frequent services daily (25 mn)
– from Leverburgh to North Uist (Otternish) (Caledonian MacBrayne Ltd) (3-4 daily) (1 h 10 mn)

Callanish Standing Stones★★ – Carloway Broch★ – St Clement's Church, Rodel (tomb★)

LEWIS – Western Isles

BREASCLETE – Western Isles 29 B1

Eshcol

21 Breasclete HS2 9ED – (01851) 621 357 – www.eshcol.com – Fax (01851) 621 357 – March-October

3 rm – £ 50 £ 80 **Rest** – *(by arrangement)* Menu £ 22

◆ Friendly, family run house in rural location, set against a backdrop of delightful scenery. Immaculately kept throughout with a homely atmosphere and views from most rooms. Dinners served at Loch Roag next door.

Loch Roag

22A Breasclete HS2 9EF – (01851) 621 357 – www.lochroag.com – Fax (01851) 621 357

4 rm – £ 40/60 £ 70/100 **Rest** – *(by arrangement)* Menu £ 22

◆ Charming rural location with super views. Run by same family as Eshcol! Bedrooms are decorated in traditional style and the house as a whole has a snug welcoming atmosphere. Simple uncluttered dining room with lovely loch view.

GALSON – Western Isles 29 B1

Galson Farm

South Galson HS2 0SH – (01851) 850 492 – www.galsonfarm.co.uk – Fax (01851) 850 492

4 rm – £ 46 £ 100

Rest – *(by arrangement, communal dining)* Menu £ 26

◆ Characterful working farm in a very remote location. Close to the ocean and ideally placed for exploring the north of the island. Cosy, comfortable, well-kept bedrooms. Freshly prepared home cooking in traditionally styled dining room.

STORNOWAY – Western Isles 29 B1

26 Cromwell St (01851) 703088, stornaway@visitscotland.com

Lady Lever Park, (01851) 702 240

Cabarfeidh rest,

Manor Park, North : 0.5 mi. on A 859 HS1 2EU – (01851) 702 604 – www.cabarfeidh-hotels.co.uk – Fax (01851) 705 572 – Closed 1 January, 24-26, 30 and 31 December

46 rm – £ 120/140 £ 160

Rest – Menu £ 14 (lunch) – Carte dinner £ 28/42

◆ Modern purpose-built hotel surrounded by gardens and close to golf course. Up-to-date, well-equipped bedrooms. Range of banqueting and conference facilities. Restaurant is divided into four areas including conservatory, bistro and garden rooms.

Braighe House without rest

20 Braighe Rd, Southeast : 3 mi. on A 866 HS2 0BQ – (01851) 705 287 – www.braighehouse.co.uk

5 rm – £ 75/110 £ 110/130

◆ Spacious proportions allied to enviable coastal outlook. Style and taste predominate in the large, comfy lounge and airy bedrooms. Hearty breakfasts set you up for the day.

SCOTLAND

HARRIS – Western Isles

ARDHASAIG – Western Isles 29 A1

Ardhasaig House with rm

HS3 3AJ – (01859) 502 500 – www.ardhasaig.co.uk – Fax (01859) 502 077 – *Closed November*

6 rm – £ 40/120 £ 90/160

Rest – *(dinner only) (booking essential for non-residents) (set menu only)* Menu £ 48

◆ Purpose built house with wild, dramatic views. Smart dining room with daily changing menu; accomplished dishes feature seasonal island produce. Well-kept bedrooms.

LEVERBURGH – Western Isles 29 A2

Carminish

1a Strond, South : 1 mi. on Srandda rd HS5 3UD – (01859) 520 400 – www.carminish.com – *restricted opening in winter*

3 rm – £ 30/50 £ 60/68

Rest – *(by arrangement, communal dining)* Menu £ 21

◆ Idyllically located guesthouse with spectacular views of the Carminish Islands and Sound of Harris. Comfortable lounge. Well-kept rooms. Hearty cooking.

SCALPAY – Western Isles 29 B2

Hirta House without rest

HS4 3XZ – (01859) 540 394 – www.hirtahouse.co.uk – Fax (01859) 540 394

3 rm – £ 40/50 £ 70

◆ Enter Scalpay by impressive modern bridge and admire the hills of Harris from this stylish guesthouse with its bold wall colours, vivid artwork and nautically inspired rooms.

SCARISTA – Western Isles 29 A2

Scarista House

HS3 3HX – (01859) 550 238 – www.scaristahouse.com – Fax (01859) 550 277 – *March-late December*

5 rm – £ 140 £ 199

Rest – *(dinner only) (booking essential for non-residents) (set menu only)* Menu £ 40

◆ Sympathetically restored part 18C former manse, commanding position affords delightful views of Scarista Bay. Elegant library and inviting antique furnished bedrooms. Strong local flavour to the daily changing menu.

TARBERT – Western Isles – pop. 1 338 – Harris 29 A2

Ceol na Mara without rest

7 Direcleit HS3 3DP – (01859) 502 464 – www.ceolnamara.com

4 rm – £ 50/70 £ 80/90

◆ Wonderful views and a loch's edge setting enhance the allure of this idyllically set house with smart decking area, peaceful garden, lovely lounge and simple, spacious rooms.

LEWISTON – Highland – 501 G12 Scotland 30 C2

Edinburgh 173 mi. – Inverness 17 mi.

Loch Ness★★ – The Great Glen★

Woodlands without rest

East Lewiston IV63 6UJ – (01456) 450 356 – www.woodlands-lochness.co.uk – Fax (01456) 450 927 – *March-November*

4 rm – £ 40/60 £ 60/70

◆ Spacious, purpose-built guesthouse with large garden and decked terrace; situated just away from the village centre. Bedrooms are airy, comfortable and immaculately kept.

Loch Ness Inn with rm

IV63 6UW – (01456) 450 991 – www.staylochness.co.uk

12 rm – £ 57/89 £ 75/99 **Rest** – Carte £ 17/30

◆ Honest local pub with traditional bar, contemporary dining room and smart wood-furnished rear terrace. Pub classics on the blackboard at lunch, more restaurant-style dishes at dinner. Individually styled bedrooms have a country feel.

SCOTLAND

LINLITHGOW – West Lothian – **501** J16 – **pop. 13 370** Scotland **26** C1

Edinburgh 19 mi. – Falkirk 9 mi. – Glasgow 35 mi.

County Buildings, High St (01506) 775320 (April-October), linlithgow@visitscotland.com

Braehead, (01506) 842 585

West Lothian Airngath Hill, (01506) 826 030

Town★★ – Palace★★ **AC** : Courtyard (fountain★★), Great Hall (Hooded Fireplace★★), Gateway★ – Old Town★ – St Michaels★

Cairnpapple Hill★ **AC**, SW : 5 mi. by A 706 – House of the Binns (plasterwork ceilings★) **AC**, NE : 4.5 mi. by A 803 and A 904. Hopetoun House★★ **AC**, E : 7 mi. by A 706 and A 904 – Abercorn Parish Church (Hopetoun Loft★★) NE : 7 mi. by A 803 and A 904

Arden House without rest

Belsyde, Southwest : 2.25 mi. on A 706 ✉ EH49 6QE – (01506) 670 172 – www.ardencountryhouse.com – Fax (01506) 670 172 – Closed 25 December

3 rm – £ 58/110 £ 80/110

◆ Charmingly run guesthouse set in peaceful location with lovely rural views. Thoughtful extras include scones and shortbread on arrival. Rooms boast a luxurious style.

XXX Champany Inn with rm

Champany, Northeast : 2 mi. on A 803 at junction with A 904 ✉ EH49 7LU – (01506) 834 532 – www.champany.com – Fax (01506) 834 302 – Closed 1-2 January, 25-26 December, Saturday lunch and Sunday

16 rm – £ 120 £ 135

Rest – Beef specialities – Menu £ 40 (dinner) – Carte £ 50/67

Spec. Hot smoked salmon with sherry hollandaise. Rib eye of Aberdeen Angus beef. Cheesecake with seasonal berries.

◆ This personally run restaurant specialises in offering superb, succulently-flavoured and expertly cooked prime Scotch beef. The excellent South African wine list provides the perfect accompaniment. Handsomely equipped bedrooms are themed around tartan colour schemes.

XX Livingston's

52 High St ✉ EH49 7AE – (01506) 846 565 – www.livingstons-restaurant.co.uk – Closed first 2 weeks January, third week June, third week October, Sunday and Monday

Rest – Menu £ 20/37

◆ Friendly restaurant tucked away off high street. Menus offer good value meals using fresh regional produce; comfortable dining room, conservatory and summer terrace.

X The Chop and Ale House – at Champany Inn

Champany, Northeast : 2 mi. on A 803 at junction with A 904 ✉ EH49 7LU – (01506) 834 532 – www.champany.com – Fax (01506) 834 302 – Closed 25-26 December and 1 January

Rest – Carte £ 25/38

◆ Former bar of Champany Inn: a more relaxed alternative to its restaurant. Stone walls filled with shotguns and animal heads. Meat is all-important; try the homemade burgers.

LOANS – South Ayrshire – **501** G17 – see Troon

LOCHALINE – Highland – **501** C14 **29** B3

Edinburgh 162 mi. – Craignure 6 mi. – Oban 7 mi.

X Whitehouse

✉ PA34 5XT – (01967) 421 777 – www.thewhitehouserestaurant.co.uk – Fax (01967) 421 220 – Closed mid January-Easter, November-mid December, Monday and Sunday dinner

Rest – Carte £ 20/26

◆ Remote setting adds to welcoming feel endorsed by hands-on owners. Two lovely, cosy, wood-lined dining rooms where the ethos of seasonal and local cooking shines through.

SCOTLAND

LOCHEARNHEAD – Stirling – 501 H14 Scotland 28 C2

Edinburgh 65 mi. – Glasgow 56 mi. – Oban 57 mi. – Perth 36 mi.

at Balquhidder Southwest : 5 mi. by A84 – Stirling

Monachyle Mhor
West : 4 mi. FK19 8PQ – (01877) 384 622 – www.mhor.net – Fax (01877) 384 305 – Closed 7 January-5 February
14 rm – £ 275 £ 275
Rest – *(booking essential for non residents)* Menu £ 49 (dinner) – Carte lunch £ 28/45
◆ Passionately run, remote hotel with its own working farm. Bedrooms in direct contrast to the farmhouse feel as they are modern and stylish; bathrooms are particularly smart. Owner-chef uses much of the farm's produce in his modern dishes.

LOCHINVER – Highland – 501 E9 – pop. 470 – Lairg Scotland 30 C1

Edinburgh 251 mi. – Inverness 95 mi. – Wick 105 mi.
Assynt Visitor Centre, Kirk Lane (01506) 832 222 (April-October), lochinver@visitscotland.com
Village★
Loch Assynt★★, E : 6 mi. by A 837

Inver Lodge
Iolaire Rd IV27 4LU – (01571) 844 496 – www.inverlodge.com – Fax (01571) 844 395 – April-December
20 rm – £ 110/120 £ 200 **Rest** – *(bar lunch)* Menu £ 50
◆ Family owned hotel set in hillside above the village, surrounded by unspoilt wilderness. Choice of spacious lounges. All the bedrooms have good views. Restaurant boasts wonderful outlook.

Ruddyglow Park Country House
Assynt, Northeast : 6.75 mi. on A 837 IV27 4HB – (01571) 822 216 – www.ruddyglowpark.com – Fax (01571) 822 216
3 rm – £ 130/140 £ 200 **Rest** – *(by arrangement)* Menu £ 45
◆ Honey yellow house in superb location; excellent Loch and mountain views. Two traditional bedrooms and one – in a log cabin – more modern. Good facilities and extra touches. Communal dining; home cooked dishes with a Scottish base.

Davar without rest
Baddidarroch Rd, West : 0.5 mi. on Baddidarroch rd IV27 4LJ – (01571) 844 501
3 rm – £ 40 £ 60/64
◆ Purpose-built guesthouse in an excellent position which affords wonderful views of Loch Inver Bay and Suilven. Homely and simple with well-kept bedrooms and communal breakfast.

The Albannach (Colin Craig and Lesley Crosfield) with rm
Baddidarroch, West : 1 mi. by Baddidarroch rd IV27 4LP – (01571) 844 407 – Fax (01571) 844 285 – Closed 3 January-1 March
5 rm (dinner included) – £ 130/200 £ 250/360
Rest – *(Closed Monday dinner to non residents) (dinner only) (booking essential for non-residents) (set menu only)* Menu £ 55
Spec. Ragoût of langoustine with lobster and ginger. Salmon with samphire and caper sauce. Citrus soufflé with bitter chocolate ice cream.
◆ A substantial 19C house with exceptional mountain views. The owners cook together and offer a daily-changing traditional 5 course menu based around superb ingredients at a set time. Atmospheric, candlelit dining room. Stylish, contemporary bedrooms vary in size.

LOCHMADDY – Western Isles Outer Hebrides – 501 Y11 – see Uist (Isles of)

LOCHRANZA – North Ayrshire – 501 E16 – see Arran (Isle of)

LOCKERBIE – Dumfries and Galloway – 501 J18 – pop. 4 009 26 C3

Edinburgh 74 mi. – Carlisle 27 mi. – Dumfries 13 mi. – Glasgow 73 mi.
Corrie Rd, (01576) 203 363
Lochmaben Castlehill Gate, (01387) 810 552

Dryfesdale Country House
Northwest : 1 mi. by Glasgow rd off B 7076 ✉ DG11 2SF – ✆ (01576) 202 427 – www.dryfesdalehotel.co.uk – Fax (01576) 204 187 – Closed 21-28 December
28 rm – 🛉£ 65/89 🛉🛉£ 105/150 **Rest** – Carte £ 18/32
◆ Extended, commercially oriented 17C house in a rural setting with pleasant countryside views. Lounge bar with fine selection of malts. Rooms are modish and smart. Enjoy the vistas from dining room.

MELROSE – Scottish Borders – 501 L17 – pop. 1 656 Scotland 26 D2

Edinburgh 38 mi. – Hawick 19 mi. – Newcastle upon Tyne 70 mi.
Abbey House, Abbey St ✆ (01835) 863170, melrose@visitscotland.com
Melrose Dingleton Dingleton Rd, ✆ (01896) 822 855
Town★ - Abbey★★ (decorative sculpture★★★) **AC**
Eildon Hills (✳★★★) – Scott's View★★ – Abbotsford★★ **AC**, W : 4.5 mi. by A 6091 and B 6360 – Dryburgh Abbey★★ **AC** (setting★★★), SE : 4 mi. by A 6091 – Tweed Valley★★. Bowhill★★ **AC**, SW : 11.5 mi. by A 6091, A 7 and A 708 – Thirlestane Castle (plasterwork ceilings★★) **AC**, NE : 21 mi. by A 6091 and A 68

Burts
Market Sq ✉ TD6 9PL – ✆ (01896) 822 285 – www.burtshotel.co.uk – Fax (01896) 822 870 – Closed 2-6 January and 25-26 December
20 rm – 🛉£ 70/120 🛉🛉£ 130/140 **Rest** – Carte £ 27/35 s
◆ One-time coaching inn on main square - traditionally appointed and family run. Unpretentious rooms behind a neat black and white façade, brightened by pretty window boxes. Cosy, clubby restaurant.

The Townhouse
Market Sq ✉ TD6 9PQ – ✆ (01896) 822 645 – www.thetownhousemelrose.co.uk – Fax (01896) 823 474 – Closed first week January
11 rm – 🛉£ 90/128 🛉🛉£ 116/128
Rest – Menu £ 24/32 – Carte £ 19/33
Rest *Brasserie* – Menu £ 24/32 – Carte £ 19/34
◆ This 17C townhouse has a spruce, clean-lined appeal throughout. The bedrooms continue the theme of simple, well-kept attention to detail. Warm and intimate restaurant or informal brasserie options.

at Gattonside North : 2 mi. by B 6374 on B 6360 – ✉ Melrose

Fauhope House without rest
East : 0.25 mi. by B 6360 taking unmarked lane to the right of Monkswood Rd at edge of village ✉ TD6 9LU – ✆ (01896) 823 184 – www.fauhopehouse.com – Fax (01896) 823 184
3 rm – 🛉£ 75 🛉🛉£ 110
◆ Melrose Abbey just visible through the trees of this charming 19C country house with its antiques and fine furniture. Valley views at breakfast. Flower strewn, stylish rooms.

MEMUS – Angus 28 D2

London 497 mi. – Edinburgh 86 mi. – Aberdeen 52 mi. – Dundee 25 mi.

Drovers
✉ DD8 3TY – ✆ (01307) 860 322 – www.the-drovers.com
Rest – Menu £ 25/30 – Carte £ 20/30
◆ Remote Highland inn with cosy bar, set on the fringes of a peaceful hamlet. Cooking is hearty and warming, offering plenty of comfort food. Set restaurant menu is more elaborate.

MOFFAT – Dumfries and Galloway – 501 J17 – pop. 2 135 Scotland 26 C2

Edinburgh 61 mi. – Carlisle 43 mi. – Dumfries 22 mi. – Glasgow 60 mi.
Churchgate ✆ (01683) 220620 (Easter-October), moffat@visitscotland.com
Coatshill, ✆ (01683) 220 020
Grey Mare's Tail★★, NE : 9 mi. by A 708

SCOTLAND

Hartfell House

Hartfell Crescent ✉ *DG10 9AL – ✆ (01683) 220 153 – www.hartfellhouse.co.uk – Closed 2 weeks January, 1 week Autumn and 25 December*
7 rm ☕ – 🚹£ 40/50 🚹🚹£ 70
Rest *The Lime Tree* – *(Closed Sunday dinner and Monday) (dinner only and Sunday lunch)* Menu £ 27
◆ Welcoming house with immense charm. Plenty of original fittings on display, including ornate cornicing and marquettry on the doors. Good sized bedrooms have a homely feel. Large dining room with huge windows and wood panelling serves appealing, brasserie menu.

Bridge House

Well Rd, East : 0.75 mi. by Selkirk rd (A 708) taking left hand turn before bridge ✉ *DG10 9JT – ✆ (01683) 220 558 – www.bridgehousemoffat.co.uk – Closed 25 December-mid February*
7 rm ☕ – 🚹£ 55 🚹🚹£ 75 **Rest** – *(by arrangement)* Menu £ 28
◆ Personally run early Victorian guesthouse. Lots of room to stretch out in comfy, modish lounge overlooking garden. Front two bedrooms have best views, one boasts four poster. Local, seasonal menus in linen-laid dining room.

Well View

Ballplay Rd, East : 0.75 mi. by Selkirk rd (A 708) ✉ *DG10 9JU – ✆ (01683) 220 184 – www.wellview.co.uk – Fax (01683) 220 088*
3 rm ☕ – 🚹£ 80 🚹🚹£ 120
Rest – *(by arrangement, communal dining)* Menu £ 20/38
◆ Well established, family run 19C house. The bedrooms are the strong point: traditionally furnished, they're of a good size and most comfortable.

SCOTLAND

Fancy a last minute break?
Check hotel websites to take advantage of price promotions.

MONTROSE – Angus – 501 M13 – pop. 10 845 Scotland 28 D2

Edinburgh 92 mi. – Aberdeen 39 mi. – Dundee 29 mi.
Montrose Museum, Panmure Place ✆ (01674) 673232 (Seasonal), montrose.museum@angus.gov.uk
36 Traill Drive, ✆ (01674) 672 932
Edzell Castle★ (The Pleasance★★★) **AC**, NW : 17 mi. by A 935 and B 966 – Cairn O'Mount Road★ (≤★★) N : 17 mi. by B 966 and B 974 – Brechin (Round Tower★) W : 7 mi. by A 935 – Aberlemno (Aberlemno Stones★, Pictish sculptured stones★) W : 13 mi. by A 935 and B 9134

36 The Mall without rest

36 The Mall, North : 0.5 mi. by A 92 at junction with North Esk Road ✉ *DD10 8SS – ✆ (01674) 673 646 – www.36themall.co.uk – Fax (01674) 673 646*
3 rm ☕ – 🚹£ 45/60 🚹🚹£ 56/70
◆ Bay windowed 19C former manse with pleasant conservatory lounge. Impressive plate collection the talking point of communal breakfast room. Well-kept rooms with high ceilings.

MUIR OF ORD – Highland – 501 G11 – pop. 1 812 30 C2

Edinburgh 173 mi. – Inverness 10 mi. – Wick 121 mi.
18 Great North Rd, ✆ (01463) 870 825

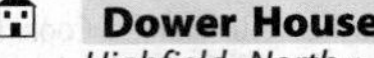

Dower House

Highfield, North : 1 mi. on A 862 ✉ *IV6 7XN – ✆ (01463) 870 090 – www.thedowerhouse.co.uk – Fax (01463) 870 090 – Closed 2 weeks November and 25 December*
3 rm ☕ – 🚹£ 65/85 🚹🚹£ 120/165 – 1 suite
Rest – *(set menu only, lunch by arrangement)* Menu 38 **s**
◆ Personally run, part 17C house in mature garden. Stacked bookshelves, soft fireside armchairs, cosy bedrooms and fresh flowers: a relaxed but well-ordered country home. Dining room offers careful cooking of fine fresh ingredients.

MULL (Isle of) – Argyll and Bute – 501 B/C14 – pop. 1 841 Scotland **27** A2

from Fionnphort to Isle of Iona (Caledonian MacBrayne Ltd) frequent services daily (10 mn) – from Pierowall to Papa Westray (Orkney Ferries Ltd) (summer only) (25 mn)

from Craignure to Oban (Caledonian MacBrayne Ltd) frequent services daily (45 mn) – from Fishnish to Lochaline (Mainland) (Caledonian MacBrayne Ltd) frequent services daily (15 mn) – from Tobermory to Isle of Tiree (Scarinish) via Isle of Coll (Arinagour) (Caledonian MacBrayne Ltd) 3 weekly (2 h 30 mn) – from Tobermory to Kilchoan (Caledonian MacBrayne Ltd) 4 daily (summer only) (35 mn)

The Pier, Craignure ✆ (08707) 200610, mull@visitscotland.com- Main Street, Tobermory ✆ (01688) 302182 (April-October), tobermory@visitscotland.com

Craignure Scallastle, ✆ (01688) 302 517

Island★ - Calgary Bay★★ – Torosay Castle **AC** (Gardens★ ★)

Isle of Iona★ (Maclean's Cross★, St Oran's Chapel★, St Martin's High Cross★, Infirmary Museum★ **AC** (Cross of St John★))

CRAIGNURE – Argyll and Bute **27** B2

Birchgrove without rest

Lochdon, Southeast : 3 mi. on A 849 ✉ PA64 6AP – ✆ (01680) 812 364 – www.birchgrovebandb.co.uk – 27 March-4 October

3 rm – £ 65 £ 75

◆ Modern guesthouse with landscaped gardens in peaceful setting with good views. Close to ferry pier. Clean, well-kept rooms, all boasting pleasant island outlook.

GRULINE – Argyll and Bute **27** A2

Gruline Home Farm

✉ PA71 6HR – ✆ (01680) 300 581 – www.gruline.com – Closed Christmas and New Year

3 rm (dinner included) – £ 160 £ 200

Rest – *(by arrangement, communal dining)* Menu £ 40

◆ Spot deer, eagles and buzzards in utter tranquillity at this delightful farm, located off the beaten track with fine views over nearby mountains. Beautifully appointed rooms. Creative cooking brings out true flavour of island produce.

TIRORAN – Argyll and Bute **27** A2

Tiroran House

✉ PA69 6ES – ✆ (01681) 705 232 – www.tiroran.com – Fax (01681) 705 240 – restricted opening in winter

7 rm – £ 152/162 £ 162

Rest – *(dinner only) (residents only)* Menu £ 42 **s**

◆ Tastefully furnished, very comfortable country house in remote location with superb views across Loch Scridain. Choice of two charming sitting rooms. Individually decorated bedrooms; some with garden and loch views. Home-cooked dinners in vine-covered conservatory-style dining room.

TOBERMORY – Argyll and Bute – pop. 980 **27** A2

Erray Rd, ✆ (01688) 302 387

Tobermory rm,

53 Main St ✉ PA75 6NT – ✆ (01688) 302 091 – www.thetobermoryhotel.com – Fax (01688) 302 254 – Closed 7 January-7 February and Christmas

16 rm – £ 38/98 £ 90/122

Rest *Waters Edge* – *(dinner only) (booking essential for non-residents)* Menu £ 32

◆ Pink-painted, converted fishing cottages - cosy, well-run and informal - on the pretty quayside. Soft toned bedrooms in cottage style, most overlooking the bay. Intimate setting: linen-clad tables and subtly nautical décor.

Sonas House without rest

The Fairways, North : 0.5 mi. by Black Brae and Erray Rd following signs for the golf club ✉ PA75 6PS – ☎ (01688) 302 304 – www.sonashouse.co.uk – Fax (01688) 302 103

3 rm – £ 70/100 £ 90/125

◆ In elevated position above Tobermory, with views over the Sound of Mull. Choose a room in the house or the annexe studio; all come with a host of extras and superb views. Luxury swimming pool.

Brockville without rest

Raeric Rd, by Back Brae ✉ PA75 6RS – ☎ (01688) 302 741 – www.brockville-tobermory.co.uk – Fax (01688) 302 741

3 rm – £ 40/70 £ 70/80

◆ Modern guesthouse in the residential part of town. The communal breakfast room has good views over the sea. Cottagey rooms have extra touches including local information and CDs.

Highland Cottage with rm

Breadalbane St, via B 8073 ✉ PA75 6PD – ☎ (01688) 302 030 – www.highlandcottage.co.uk – March-October

6 rm – £ 125 £ 185

Rest – *(dinner only) (booking essential for non-residents)* Menu £ 45

◆ Modern cottage near the harbour. Prettily set dining room shows the same care and attention as the locally sourced menu. Individually styled rooms with good views.

The sun's out? Then enjoy eating outside on the terrace:

SCOTLAND

NAIRN – Highland – 501 I11 – pop. 8 418 Scotland — 30 D2

Edinburgh 172 mi. – Aberdeen 91 mi. – Inverness 16 mi.

Seabank Rd, ☎ (01667) 453 208

Nairn Dunbar Lochloy Rd, ☎ (01667) 452 741

Forres (Sueno's Stone★★) E : 11 mi. by A 96 and B 9011 - Cawdor Castle★ **AC**, S : 5.5 mi. by B 9090 – Brodie Castle★ **AC**, E : 6 mi. by A 96. Fort George★, W : 8 mi. by A 96, B 9092 and B 9006

Golf View rest,

The Seafront ✉ IV12 4HD – ☎ (01667) 452 301 – www.golfviewhotel.com – Fax (01667) 455 267

41 rm – £ 85/170 £ 120/220 – 1 suite

Rest *Restaurant* – *(dinner only)* Menu £ 27

Rest *Conservatory* – Carte £ 19/34

◆ Non-golfers may prefer the vista of the Moray Firth from one of the sea-view rooms or a poolside lounger. Smart, traditional accommodation, up-to-date gym and beauty salon. Half-panelled dining room. Stylish, spacious conservatory restaurant.

Boath House rm,

Auldearn, East : 2 mi. on A 96 ✉ IV12 5TE – ☎ (01667) 454 896 – www.boath-house.com – Fax (01667) 455 469 – Closed 3-27 January

8 rm – £ 180/250 £ 280/320 **Rest** – *(booking essential)* Menu £ 29/65

Spec. Scallops with leek, truffle and egg cream. Lobster with peas and potato terrine. Angelica rice with redcurrant yoghurt and sorbet.

◆ 1820s neo-classical mansion, owned by a charming couple, hosts modern Highland art collections. Intimate, elegant bedrooms; some have half-tester beds/views of the trout lake. Smart, contemporary bathrooms. Formally laid dining room has garden views; accomplished cooking, with vivid presentation and subtle flavours.

Bracadale House without rest

Albert St ✉ IV12 4HF – ☎ (01667) 452 547 – www.bracadalehouse.com – mid March-mid October

3 rm – £ 40/60 £ 55/60

◆ This elegant Victorian house, near the beach, is enthusiastically run by a friendly owner. There's an attractive first floor lounge and rooms finished with a tasteful palette.

NEWTON STEWART – Dumfries and Galloway – 501 G19 – pop. 3 573 Scotland 25 B3

Edinburgh 131 mi. – Dumfries 51 mi. – Glasgow 87 mi. – Stranraer 24 mi.

Dashwood Sq ✆ (01671) 402431 (June- Sept), newtonstewarttic@visitscotland.com

Minnigaff Kirroughtree Ave, ✆ (01671) 402 172

Wigtownshire County Glenluce Mains of Park, ✆ (01581) 300 420

Galloway Forest Park★, Queen's Way★ (Newton Stewart to New Galloway) N : 19 mi. by A 712

Kirroughtree House

Northeast : 1.5 mi. by A 75 on A 712 ✉ *DG8 6AN – ✆ (01671) 402 141 – www.kirroughtreehouse.co.uk – Fax (01671) 402 425 – Closed 2 January-mid February*

15 rm – £ 95/145 £ 240/250 – 2 suites

Rest – *(booking essential for non-residents)* Menu £ 35 (dinner) **s** – Carte lunch £ 21/29 **s**

◆ Grand 1719 mansion dominates acres of sculpted garden. Well-proportioned bedrooms; firelit lounge with antiques, period oils and French windows leading to the croquet lawn. Elegant fine dining, in keeping with formal grandeur of the house.

Rowallan

Corsbie Rd, via Jubilee Rd off Dashwood Sq ✉ *DG8 6JB – ✆ (01671) 402 520 – www.rowallan.co.uk – Fax (01671) 402 520*

6 rm – £ 45/55 £ 70/78 **Rest** – *(by arrangement)* Menu £ 20

◆ Victorian house in attractive large garden not far from town centre. Large lounge with bar; meals served in conservatory. Brightly decorated bedrooms.

NORTH BAY – Western Isles – see Barra (Isle of)

NORTH BERWICK – East Lothian – 501 L15 – pop. 6 223 Scotland 26 D1

Edinburgh 24 mi. – Newcastle upon Tyne 102 mi.

1 Quality St ✆ (01620) 892197

North Berwick Beach Rd, West Links, ✆ (01620) 890 312

Glen East Links, Tantallon Terrace, ✆ (01620) 892 726

North Berwick Law (✲★★★) S : 1 mi. - Tantallon Castle★★ (clifftop site★★★) **AC**, E : 3.5 mi. by A 198 – Dirleton★ (Castle★ **AC**) SW : 2.5 mi. by A 198. Museum of Flight★, S : 6 mi. by B 1347 – Preston Mill★, S : 8.5 mi. by A 198 and B 1047 – Tyninghame★, S : 7 mi. by A 198 – Coastal road from North Berwick to Portseton★, SW : 13 mi. by A 198 and B 1348

Glebe House without rest

Law Rd ✉ *EH39 4PL – ✆ (01620) 892 608 – www.glebehouse-nb.co.uk – Closed Christmas*

3 rm – £ 70/75 £ 90/100

◆ Owned by a likeable couple, a classically charming 1780s manse in secluded gardens. En suite rooms are pleasantly unfussy and well-kept. Breakfasts at a long communal table.

NORTH QUEENSFERRY – Fife – 501 J15 – pop. 1 102 28 C3

Edinburgh 13 mi. – Dunfermline 6 mi. – Glasgow 45 mi.

The Wee Restaurant

17 Main St ✉ *KY11 1JT – ✆ (01383) 616 263 – www.theweerestaurant.co.uk – Closed Sunday dinner and Monday*

Rest – Menu £ 19 (lunch) **s** – Carte dinner £ 27/34 **s**

◆ Affable couple run this light and cosy little restaurant with just 7 tables, virtually under the Forth rail bridge. Good fresh Scottish ingredients uses in classic, neatly prepared dishes.

NORTH UIST – Western Isles Outer Hebrides – 501 X/Y10 – see Uist (Isles of)

SCOTLAND

OBAN – Argyll and Bute – 501 D14 – pop. 8 120 Scotland 27 B2

Edinburgh 123 mi. – Dundee 116 mi. – Glasgow 93 mi. – Inverness 118 mi.

Access Access to Glasgow by helicopter

to Isle of Mull (Craignure) (Caledonian MacBrayne Ltd) (45 mn) – to Isle of Tiree (Scarinish) via Isle of Mull (Tobermory) and Isle of Coll (Arinagour) (Caledonian MacBrayne Ltd) – to Isle of Islay (Port Askaig) and Kintyre Peninsula (Kennacraig) via Isle of Colonsay (Scalasaig) (Caledonian MacBrayne Ltd) (summer only) – to Isle of Lismore (Achnacroish) (Caledonian MacBrayne Ltd) 2-3 daily (except Sunday) (55 mn) – to Isle of Colonsay (Scalasaig) (Caledonian MacBrayne Ltd) 3 weekly (2 h)

Church Building, Argyll Sq (08707) 200630, oban@visitscotland.com

Glencruitten Glencruitten Rd, (01631) 562 868

Loch Awe★★, SE : 17 mi. by A 85 – Bonawe Furnace★, E : 12 mi. by A 85 – Cruachan Power Station★ **AC**, E : 16 mi. by A 85 – Seal and Marine Centre★ **AC**, N : 14 mi. by A 828

Manor House

Gallanach Rd ✉ PA34 4LS – (01631) 562 087 – www.manorhouseoban.com – Fax (01631) 563 053 – Closed 25-26 December

11 rm – £ 107/155 £ 140/195

Rest – *(lunch by arrangement)* Menu £ 23/36 – Carte £ 16/37

◆ Period furniture and colour schemes bring out the character of this 18C dower house, once part of the Argyll ducal estate. Individual rooms, most with fine views of the bay. Green and tartan restaurant warmed by an ancient range.

The Barriemore without rest

Corran Esplanade ✉ PA34 5AQ – (01631) 566 356 – www.barriemore-hotel.co.uk – Fax (01631) 571 084 – Closed 4 January-7 February and 20-29 December

11 rm – £ 47/79 £ 70/96

◆ Gabled 1890s house overlooking town and islands. A comfortable blend of modern and period styling - front bedrooms are larger and look towards Oban Bay, Kerrera and Mull.

Glenburnie House without rest

Corran Esplanade ✉ PA34 5AQ – (01631) 562 089 – www.glenburnie.co.uk – Fax (01631) 562 089 – March-November

12 rm – £ 45/85 £ 80/100

◆ Bay-windowed Victorian house has enviable views over the bay. Pleasant lounge with a hint of homely informality and usefully equipped rooms, one with a four-poster bed.

Alltavona without rest

Corran Esplanade ✉ PA34 5AQ – (01631) 565 067 – www.alltavona.co.uk – Fax (01631) 565 067 – Closed 14-26 December

10 rm – £ 35/80 £ 70/95

◆ 19C villa on smart esplanade with fine views of Oban Bay. Attractively furnished interiors in keeping with the house's age. Fine oak staircase and individually styled rooms.

Coast

104 George St ✉ PA34 5NT – (01631) 569 900 – www.coastoban.com – Closed January, 25 December, Sunday dinner October-March and Sunday lunch

Rest – Menu £ 15 (lunch) – Carte £ 23/38

◆ Former bank building in town centre. Contemporary interior of stripped wood floors and khaki coloured walls. Appealing modern menus including plenty of fish and shellfish.

The Waterfront

No 1, The Pier ✉ PA34 4LW – (01631) 563 110 – www.waterfrontoban.co.uk – Fax (01631) 562 853 – Closed 25 December

Rest – Seafood – Carte £ 23/37

◆ Converted quayside mission with fine views of harbour and bay; airy, open-plan interior. Flavourful but simple seafood: blackboard specials feature the day's fresh catch.

Ee-usk at The North Pier

The North Pier ✉ *PA34 5DQ – ✆ (01631) 565 666 – www.eeusk.com – Fax (01631) 570 282 – Closed 25-26 December and 1 January*

Rest – Seafood – Carte £ 23/33

◆ A smart addition to the pier with its harbour proximity; excellent views of the bay add a relaxing charm. Fresh seafood menus with daily specials.

OLDMELDRUM – **Aberdeenshire** – **501** N11 – **pop. 2 003** Scotland **28** D1

Edinburgh 140 mi. – Aberdeen 17 mi. – Inverness 87 mi.

Oldmeldrum Kirkbrae, ✆ (01651) 872 648

Haddo House★, NE : 9 mi. by B 9170 on B 9005

Cromlet Hill without rest

South Rd ✉ *AB51 0AB – ✆ (01651) 872 315 – www.cromlethill.co.uk – Fax (01651) 872 164*

3 rm – £ 50 £ 70/80

◆ Half Georgian, half Victorian house with attractive front garden. Characterful sitting room; smart, airy, well-equipped rooms. Communal breakfast at antique dining table.

ONICH – **Highland** – **501** E13 – ✉ **Fort William** **29** B3

Edinburgh 123 mi. – Glasgow 93 mi. – Inverness 79 mi. – Oban 39 mi.

Lochleven Seafood Café

Lockleven, Southeast 6.5 mi. by A82 on B863 ✉ *PH33 6SA – ✆ (01855) 821 048 – www.lochlevenseafoodcafe.co.uk – Restricted opening October-March*

Rest – Seafood – *(booking advisable at dinner)* Carte £ 28/35 **s**

◆ Stunning Lochside location looking toward Glencoe Mountains. Extremely fresh, simply prepared seafood; shellfish platter and razor clams a speciality. Themed evenings in winter.

SCOTLAND

Guesthouses don't provide the same level of service as hotels. They are often characterised by a warm welcome and a décor which reflects the owner's personality. Those shown in red are particularly pleasant.

ORKNEY ISLANDS – 501 K/L7 – pop. 19 800 Scotland

see Kirkwall

from Burwick (South Ronaldsay) to John O'Groats (John O'Groats Ferries) 2-4 daily (40 mn) (summer only)

service between Isle of Hoy (Longhope), Isle of Hoy (Lyness), Isle of Flotta and Houton (Orkney Ferries Ltd)

– from Stromness to Scrabster (P & O Scottish Ferries) (1-3 daily) (2 h)

– from Stromness to Shetland Islands (Lerwick) and Aberdeen (Northlink Ferries) 1-2 daily

– from Kirkwall to Westray, Stronsay via Eday and Sanday (Orkney Ferries Ltd)

– from Tingwall to Wyre via Egilsay and Rousay (Orkney Ferries Ltd)

– from Kirkwall to Shapinsay (Orkney Ferries Ltd) (25 mn)

– from Stromness to Isle of Hoy (Moness) and Graemsay (Orkney Ferries Ltd)

– from Kirkwall to North Ronaldsay (Orkney Ferries Ltd) weekly (2 h 40 mn)

– from Kirkwall to Invergordon (Orcargo Ltd) daily (8 h 30 mn)

– from Houton to Isle of Hoy (Lyness), Flotta and Longhope (Orkney Ferries Ltd)

Old Man of Hoy★★★ – Islands★★ – Maes Howe★★ **AC** – Skara Brae★★ **AC** – Kirkbuster Museum and Corrigal Farm Museum★ **AC** – Brough of Birsay★ **AC** – Birsay (≤★) – Ring of Brodgar★ – Unstan Cairn★

MAINLAND – Orkney Islands

London 683 mi. – Edinburgh 278 mi.

BURRAY – Orkney Islands 31 A3

Sands

KW17 2SS – (01856) 731 298 – www.thesandshotel.co.uk – Fax (01856) 731 303 – Closed 25-26 December and 1-3 January

8 rm – £ 70/80 £ 90/95 – 2 suites **Rest** – *(bar lunch)* Carte £ 13/26

◆ Harbourside hotel – previously a fish store – in small coastal hamlet overlooking the Scapa Flow. Modern in style, with pleasant bedrooms, smart bathrooms and harbour/bay views. Nautical themed restaurant features fresh Orkney produce; plenty of local fish.

DOUNBY – Orkney Islands 31 A3

Ashleigh without rest

Howaback Rd, South : 0.75 mi. by A986 KW17 2JA – (01856) 771 378 – www.ashleigh-orkney.com – Fax (01856) 771 378 – Closed 23 December-5 January

4 rm – £ 33/48 £ 66/72

◆ Purpose built guesthouse in rural central Island location. Smart bedrooms with warm fabrics, good facilities and modern bathrooms. Lounge has pleasant loch and mountain views; neat garden.

HARRAY – Orkney Islands 31 A3

SCOTLAND

Merkister

off A 986 KW17 2LF – (01856) 771 366 – www.merkister.com – Fax (01856) 771 515 – Closed 24 December-4 January

16 rm – £ 35/75 £ 70/110

Rest – *(bar lunch Monday-Saturday) (booking essential)* Menu £ 24 – Carte £ 18/40

◆ Cream washed hotel in rural location, overlooking Loch Harray. Comfy lounge with leather sofas, small library and honesty bar. Spacious bedrooms with good facilities and views. Lounge bar offers snacks, more formal restaurant offers traditional menu and plenty of seafood.

Holland House without rest

on St Michael's Church rd KW17 2LQ – (01856) 771 400 – www.hollandhouseorkney.co.uk – Closed 18 December-11 January

3 rm – £ 48/60 £ 96

◆ Smart, very comfy late Victorian guesthouse, formerly a manse. Modern bedrooms – named after local Lochs – display warm hues and good front views. Good facilities, quality extra touches.

KIRKWALL – Orkney Islands – pop. 6 206 Scotland 31 A3

Kirkwall Airport : (01856) 886210, S : 3.5 m

West Castle St (01856) 872856, info@visitorkney.com

Grainbank, (01856) 872 457

Kirkwall★★ - St Magnus Cathedral★★ – Western Mainland★★, Eastern Mainland (Italian Chapel★) - Earl's Palace★ **AC** – Tankerness House Museum★ **AC** – Orkney Farm and Folk Museum★

Ayre

Ayre Rd KW15 1QX – (01856) 873 001 – www.ayrehotel.co.uk – Fax (01856) 876 289

33 rm – £ 65/85 £ 90/120 **Rest** – Carte £ 19/32 **s**

◆ Originally 3 Victorian houses, now a traditionally styled town centre hotel. Individually designed bedrooms display co-ordinating décor and fabrics; front rooms have sea/harbour views. Traditional restaurant; menu split between steak, chicken and seafood.

Avalon House without rest

Carness Rd, Northeast : 1.5 mi. by Shore Street KW15 1UE – (01856) 876 665 – www.avalon-house.co.uk – Closed 2 weeks Christmas

5 rm – £ 43/50 £ 64/70

◆ Purpose built guesthouse in small residential area just out of town. Spacious bedrooms boast modern décor and quality furniture; showers only (bath in family room). Pleasant breakfast room.

XX **Foveran** with rm

St Ola, Southwest : 3 mi. on A 964 ✉ KW15 1SF – ☎ (01856) 872 389 – www.foveranhotel.co.uk – Fax (01856) 876 430 – restricted opening October-April

8 rm – †£ 73/90 ††£ 110 **Rest** – *(dinner only)* Carte £ 24/35

◆ Pleasant hotel overlooking the Scapa Flow, in quiet, out of town location. Smart, immaculately kept bedrooms boast homely décor, simple colour schemes and good bathrooms. Large restaurant boasts excellent views and traditional menu of local produce; daily seafood specials.

ST MARGARET'S HOPE – Orkney Islands — 31 A3

XX **Creel** with rm

Front Rd ✉ KW17 2SL – ☎ (01856) 831 311 – www.thecreel.co.uk – mid April-mid October

3 rm – †£ 70/80 ††£ 105/120

Rest – Seafood – *(Closed Monday and Tuesday) (dinner only)* Carte £ 36/43

◆ Neat yellow washed building in seafront village. Restaurant boasts colourful artwork, nautical ornaments and sea views. Daily changing, seafood based menus feature fresh, tasty produce and some unusual fish. Modern bedrooms with good bathrooms and views over St Margaret's Hope Bay.

STROMNESS – Orkney Islands Scotland — 31 A3

Town★ - Pier Gallery (collection of abstract art★)

X **Hamnavoe**

35 Graham Pl, off Victoria St ✉ KW16 3BY – ☎ (01856) 850 606 – restricted opening in winter

Rest – *(Closed Monday) (dinner only) (booking essential)* Carte £ 27/35

◆ Set on a narrow street in a small harbourside town, with welcoming coal fire and walls filled with oil paintings of local scenes. Local Orkadian produce informs the traditional menus.

ISLE OF WESTRAY – Orkney Islands — 31 A2

CLEAT – ✉ Orkney Islands — 31 A2

Cleaton House

✉ KW17 2DB – ☎ (01857) 677 508 – www.cleatonhouse.com

6 rm – †£ 55/68 ††£ 85/120

Rest – *(bar lunch) (booking essential for non-residents)* Menu £ 38 **s**

◆ Mid Victorian former Lairds mansion; set on a peninsula, with panoramic views. Comfy, classical guest areas boast heavy fabrics and antique furniture – a style echoed in the bedrooms. Rear lounge bar offers informal dining with a concise, seafood based menu.

PIEROWALL – Orkney Islands – 501 L6 — 31 A2

No 1 Broughton

✉ KW17 2DA – ☎ (01857) 677 726 – www.no1broughton.co.uk – Closed October, Christmas and New Year

3 rm – †£ 35/60 ††£ 60 **Rest** – *(by arrangement)* Menu £ 18

◆ Pleasant whitewashed house overlooking Pierowall Bay. Comfy lounge; dining room with views. Bedrooms boast good facilities and modern bathrooms. Home cooked breakfast of Island produce.

PEAT INN – Fife — 28 D2

London 462 mi. – Edinburgh 45 mi. – Dundee 17 mi. – Kirkcaldy 19 mi.

XXX ✿ **The Peat Inn** (Geoffrey Smeddle) with rm

✉ KY15 5LH – ☎ (01334) 840 206 – www.thepeatinn.co.uk – Fax (01334) 840 530 – Closed 2 weeks January, 25-26 December, Sunday and Monday

8 rm – †£ 115/145 ††£ 165/195

Rest – *(booking essential)* Menu £ 15/34 – Carte £ 28/45

Spec. Marinaded salmon with lobster, coriander and lime. Seared rib-eye and braised short rib of beef with girolles and Madeira jus. Pavé of chocolate with caramel ice cream.

◆ Passionately run, former inn found in the heart of the Fife countryside. Roaring fire in the lounge; three cosy dining rooms with beams. The accomplished, classically based cooking, with just a hint of the modern, uses fine Scottish produce. Comfortable annexed bedrooms overlook the lovely back garden.

SCOTLAND

PEEBLES – Scottish Borders – 501 K17 – pop. 8 065 Scotland 26 C2

Edinburgh 24 mi. – Glasgow 53 mi. – Hawick 31 mi.

High St ✆ (01835) 863170, bordersinfo@visitscotland.com

Kirkland St, ✆ (01721) 720 197

Tweed Valley★★. Traquair House★★ **AC**, SE : 7 mi. by B 7062 – Rosslyn Chapel★★ **AC**, N : 16.5 mi. by A 703, A 6094, B 7026 and B 7003

Cringletie House

Edinburgh Rd, North : 3 mi. on A 703 ✉ EH45 8PL – ✆ (01721) 725 750 – www.cringletie.com – Fax (01721) 725 751 – Closed 3-27 January

12 rm – †£ 160/180 ††£ 200/220 – 1 suite

Rest – *(dinner only and Sunday lunch)* Menu £ 43

◆ Smoothly run and handsomely furnished Victorian hotel in country house style with contemporary edge. Rooms are modern, well-equipped and peaceful. Spacious, formal restaurant with a trompe l'oeil ceiling.

Rowanbrae without rest

103 Northgate ✉ EH45 8BU – ✆ (01721) 721 630 – Fax (01721) 723 324 – Closed Christmas-7 January

3 rm – †£ 40 ††£ 60

◆ Built for the manager of a 19C woollen mill. Pleasant, affordable rooms, well kept by a cheerful couple. Fortifying breakfasts with posies of garden flowers on each table.

SCOTLAND

at Eddleston North : 4.5 mi. on A 703

The Horseshoe Inn with rm

Edinburgh Rd ✉ EH45 8QP – ✆ (01721) 730 225 – www.horseshoeinn.co.uk – Fax (01721) 730 268 – Closed Monday except Bank Holidays and Tuesday following Bank Holidays

8 rm – †£ 70 ††£ 100/140

Rest – Menu £ 20 (lunch) – Carte dinner £ 33/55

Rest *Bistro* – Carte £ 19/35

◆ It's easy to drive past this roadside former pub but stop off for serious cooking from experienced French chef or lighter dishes in adjacent bistro. Simple, comfy bedrooms.

PERTH – Perth and Kinross – 501 J14 – pop. 43 450 Scotland 28 C2

Edinburgh 44 mi. – Aberdeen 86 mi. – Dundee 22 mi. – Dunfermline 29 mi.

Lower City Mills, West Mill St ✆ (01738) 450600, perth@visitscotland.com

Craigie Hill Cherrybank, ✆ (01738) 620 829

King James VI Moncreiffe Island, ✆ (01738) 625 170

Murrayshall New Scone, ✆ (01738) 554 804

North Inch, c/o Perth & Kinross Council 35 Kinncoll St, ✆ (01738) 636 481

City★ – Black Watch Regimental Museum★ Y **M1** – Georgian Terraces★ Y – Museum and Art Gallery★ Y **M2**

Scone Palace★★ **AC**, N : 2 mi. by A 93 Y – Branklyn Garden★ **AC**, SE : 1 mi. by A 85 Z – Kinnoull Hill (≤★) SE : 1.25 mi. by A 85 Z – Huntingtower Castle★ **AC**, NW : 3 mi. by A 85 Y – Elcho Castle★ **AC**, SE : 4 mi. by A 912 - Z - and Rhynd rd. Abernethy (11C Round Tower★), SE : 8 mi. by A 912 - Z - and A 913

Huntingtower

rm,

Crieff Rd, West : 3.5 mi. by A 85 ✉ PH1 3JT – ✆ (01738) 583 771 – www.huntingtowerhotel.co.uk – Fax (01738) 583 777

34 rm – †£ 79/99 ††£ 139/159

Rest *Oak Room* – *(bar lunch)* Menu £ 15/20

◆ Late Victorian half-timbered country house named after nearby castle. Choose bedrooms in the more traditional old house or modern, executive rooms. Restaurant with views towards lawn and stream.

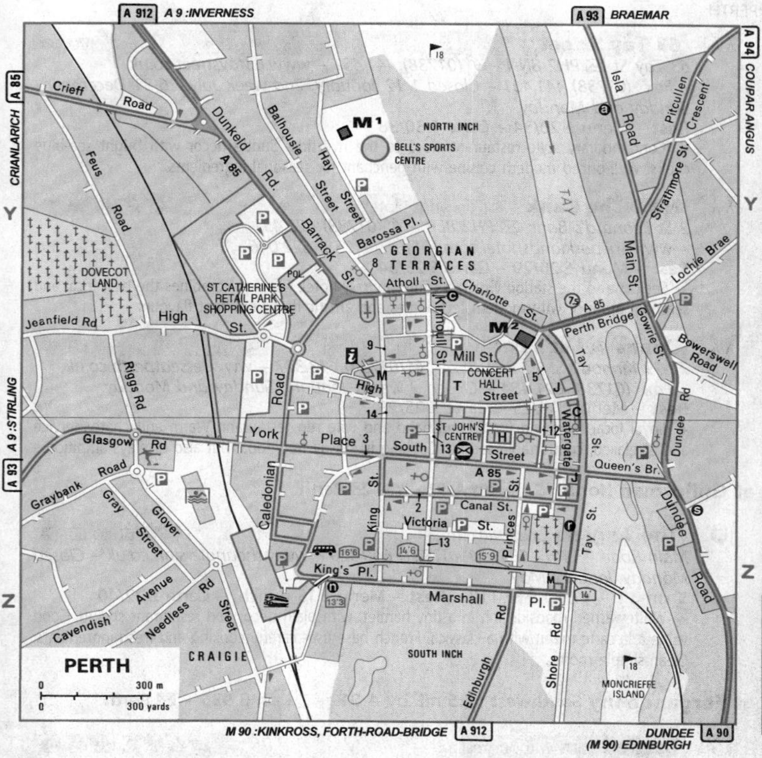

PERTH

Charterhouse Lane . . . . Z 2	Melville St . . . . Y 8	St John's Centre . . . . Z
County Pl. . . . . Z 3	North Methven St . . . . Y 9	Scott St . . . . Z 13
George St . . . . Y 5	St Catherine's Retail Park . . . . . Y	South Methven St . . . . Y 14
High St . . . . Y	St John St . . . . Z 12	South St . . . . Z

Parklands

2 St Leonard's Bank ✉ PH2 8EB – ✆ (01738) 622 451
– www.theparklandshotel.com – Fax (01738) 622 046 Z**n**
15 rm ☕ – 🚹£ 84/124 🚹🚹£ 109/199
Rest *No.1 The Bank* – see restaurant listing
◆ Modern hotel set opposite the railway station. Contemporary bedrooms – some overlooking the garden – boast spacious bathrooms and good facilities; great for business travellers.

Beechgrove without rest

Dundee Rd ✉ PH2 7AQ – ✆ (01738) 636 147 – Fax (01738) 636 147
7 rm ☕ – 🚹£ 50/80 🚹🚹£ 60/100 Z**s**
◆ Virginia creeper clad Georgian manse, immaculately kept. Bedrooms are spacious and boast mahogany furniture and added extras; comfy firelit lounge in traditional décor.

Taythorpe without rest

Isla Rd, North : 1 mi. on A 93 ✉ PH2 7HQ – ✆ (01738) 447 994
– www.taythorpe.co.uk – Fax (01738) 447 994 – Closed 25 December
3 rm ☕ – 🚹£ 42 🚹🚹£ 70 Y**a**
◆ Immaculately kept, modern guesthouse close to Scone Palace. Good value accommodation. Welcoming, homely lounge. Cosy, communal breakfasts. Warmly inviting, well-kept bedrooms.

XX **63 Tay Street** VISA MC

63 Tay St ✉ PH2 8NN – ☎ (01738) 441 451 – www.63taystreet.co.uk – Fax (01738) 441 461 – Closed 1-12 January, 2nd week July, 26-31 December, Sunday and Monday Z**r**

Rest – Menu £ 20/34 – Carte £ 30/38

◆ Contemporary style restaurant close to the riverside. Subtle décor with bright sea-blue chairs. Well-priced modern cuisine with penchant for seasonal ingredients.

XX **No.1 The Bank** – at Parklands Hotel P VISA MC

2 St Leonard's Bank ✉ PH2 8EB – ☎ (01738) 622 451 – www.theparklandshotel.com – Fax (01738) 622 046 Z**n**

Rest – Menu £ 20/29 – Carte £ 25/34

◆ Set close to the station within a contemporary hotel. Cooking combines the best local and seasonal produce with modern techniques and artistic flair. Confident flavours.

XX **Deans @ Let's Eat** VISA MC

77-79 Kinnoull St ✉ PH1 5EZ – ☎ (01738) 643 377 – www.letseatperth.co.uk – Fax (01738) 621 464 – Closed 2 weeks January, Sunday and Monday

Rest – Menu £ 14/25 – Carte £ 25/29 Y**c**

◆ Loyal local following for this husband and wife run restaurant. Warm and chatty service and a relaxed, comfortable setting. Cooking is mostly traditional but also displays ambition.

SCOTLAND

at Guildtown North : 5 mi. on A 93 - Y – ✉ Perth

The Anglers Inn with rm P VISA MC AE

Main Road ✉ PH2 6BS – ☎ (01821) 640 329 – www.theanglersinn.co.uk – Closed Monday January-May

5 rm – †£ 50 ††£ 110 **Rest** – Menu £ 15 (lunch) – Carte £ 22/40

◆ Whitewashed roadside inn in a tiny hamlet, with plain décor and restaurant styling. Good value à la carte menu with a classical French base uses careful cooking and fresh ingredients. Clean simple rooms.

at Forgandenny Southwest : 6.5 mi. by A 912 - Z - on B 935 – ✉ Perth

Battledown without rest P VISA MC

by Station Rd on Church and School rd ✉ PH2 9EL – ☎ (01738) 812 471 – www.accommodationperthshire.com – Fax (01738) 812 471

3 rm – †£ 35/40 ††£ 65/70

◆ Immaculately whitewashed, part 18C cottage in quiet village. Lovely garden; owner's paintings on show. Cosy, pine-furnished breakfast room. Neat, tidy rooms, all on ground level.

PIEROWALL – **Orkney Islands** – **501** K6 – **see Orkney Islands (Isle of Westray)**

PITLOCHRY – **Perth and Kinross** – **501** I13 – **pop. 2 564** Scotland **28** C2

Edinburgh 71 mi. – Inverness 85 mi. – Perth 27 mi.

22 Atholl Rd ☎ (01796) 472215, pitlochry@visitscotland.com

Pitlochry Estate Office, ☎ (01796) 472 792

Town★

Blair Castle★★ **AC**, NW : 7 mi. by A 9 A – Queen's View★★, W : 7 mi. by B 8019 A – Falls of Bruar★, NW : 11 mi. by A 9 A

Green Park rm, P VISA MC

Clunie Bridge Rd ✉ PH16 5JY – ☎ (01796) 473 248 – www.thegreenpark.co.uk – Fax (01796) 473 520 A**a**

51 rm (dinner included) – †£ 69/94 ††£ 138/194

Rest – *(light lunch residents only) (booking essential at dinner for non-residents)* Menu £ 25

◆ Family run 1860s summer retreat on Loch Faskally. Rooms in the old house are decorated in floral patterns; impressive up-to-date wing has good, contemporary facilities. Unhurried dinners at lochside setting.

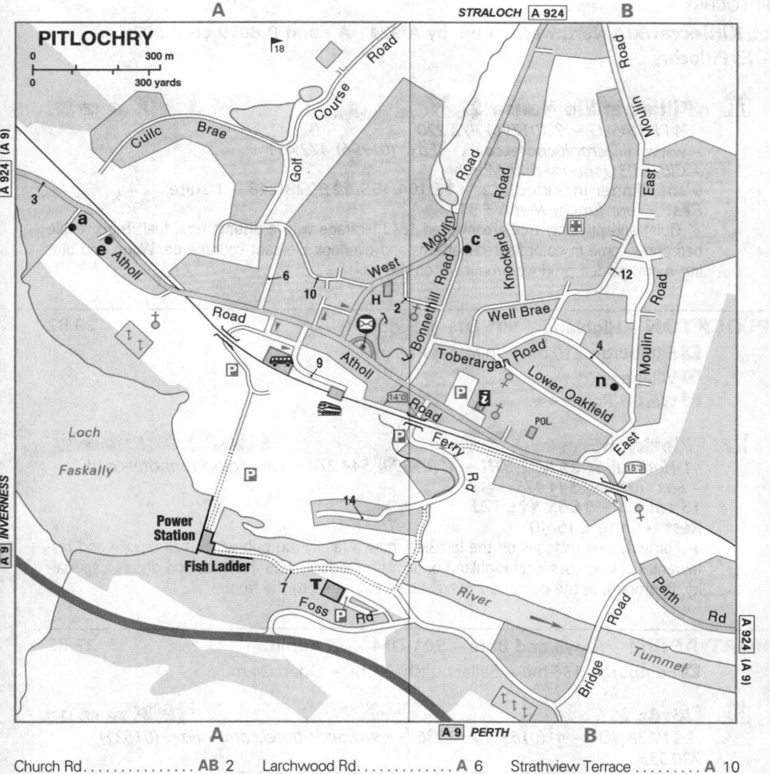

Church Rd . . . . AB 2
Clunie Bridge Rd . . . . A 3
Higher Oakfield . . . . B 4
Larchwood Rd . . . . A 6
Port Na Craig Rd . . . . A 7
Station Rd . . . . A 9
Strathview Terrace . . . . A 10
Tom Na Moan Rd . . . . B 12
Tummel Crescent . . . . A 14

Craigatin House and Courtyard without rest

165 Atholl Rd ✉ PH16 5QL – ☎ (01796) 472 478 – www.craigatinhouse.co.uk – Closed 1-27 December — A**e**

12 rm – 🕴£ 60/75 🕴🕴£ 75/85 – 1 suite

◆ 19C detached house with converted stables. Smart, stylish décor, including comfy conservatory lounge and breakfast room. Eye-catchingly inviting rooms, some in the annexe.

Beinn Bhracaigh without rest

Higher Oakfield ✉ PH16 5HT – ☎ (01796) 470 355 – www.beinnbhracaigh.com – Restricted opening mid November-mid February — B**n**

10 rm – 🕴£ 60/75 🕴🕴£ 75/90

◆ Affordable, spacious, refurbished bedrooms - with good town views from front - in a local stone house of late 19C origin. Impressive range of whiskies in residents' bar.

Dunmurray Lodge without rest

72 Bonnethill Rd ✉ PH16 5ED – ☎ (01796) 473 624 – www.dunmurray.co.uk – Fax (01796) 473 624 – Restricted opening in winter — B**c**

4 rm – 🕴£ 45/60 🕴🕴£ 60/70

◆ Pretty, immaculately kept 19C cottage, once a doctor's surgery. Relax in homely sitting room's squashy sofas. Bedrooms are small and cosy with soothing cream colour scheme.

at Killiecrankie Northwest : 4 mi. by A 924 - A - and B 8019 on B 8079 – ✉ Pitlochry

Killiecrankie House

✉ PH16 5LG – ✆ (01796) 473 220 – www.killiecrankiehotel.co.uk – Fax (01796) 472 451 – Closed 3 January-mid March

9 rm (dinner included) – †£ 104/155 ††£ 228/248 – 1 suite

Rest – *(bar lunch)* Menu £ 31

◆ Quiet and privately run, a converted 1840 vicarage with a distinct rural feel. The sizeable bedrooms come in co-ordinated patterns and overlook pleasant countryside. Warm, red dining room; garden produce prominent on menus.

PLOCKTON – **Highland** – **501** D11 Scotland **29** B2

Edinburgh 210 mi. – Inverness 88 mi.

Village★

Wester Ross★★★

Plockton with rm

41 Harbour St ✉ IV52 8TN – ✆ (01599) 544 274 – www.plocktonhotel.co.uk – Fax (01599) 544 475

15 rm – †£ 55 ††£ 120

Rest – Carte £ 15/40

◆ Formerly two cottages on the lochside, now a family-run pub with small terrace and restaurant. Cooking uses local Highland or Scottish produce, with fresh seafood dishes a speciality. Bedrooms, in the pub and annexe, boast bay views to the front.

PORT APPIN – **Argyll and Bute** – **501** D14 – ✉ **Appin** **27** B2

Edinburgh 136 mi. – Ballachulish 20 mi. – Oban 24 mi.

Airds

✉ PA38 4DF – ✆ (01631) 730 236 – www.airds-hotel.com – Fax (01631) 730 535

11 rm (dinner included) – †£ 190/305 ††£ 305/445

Rest – *(booking essential for non-residents)* Menu £ 53 – Carte lunch £ 27/33

◆ Former ferry inn with superb views of Loch Linnhe and mountains. Charming rooms - antiques and floral fabrics. Firelit, old-world sitting rooms hung with landscapes. Smartly set tables, picture windows looking across the water in the restaurant.

PORT CHARLOTTE – **Argyll and Bute** – **501** A16 – **see Islay (Isle of)**

PORT ELLEN – **Argyll and Bute** – **501** B17 – **see Islay (Isle of)**

PORTMAHOMACK – **Highland** – **501** I10 **30** D2

Edinburgh 194 mi. – Dornoch 21 mi. – Tain 12 mi.

The Oystercatcher with rm

Main St ✉ IV20 1YB – ✆ (01862) 871 560 – www.the-oystercatcher.co.uk – Fax (01862) 871 777 – restricted opening in winter

3 rm – †£ 43/70 ††£ 98

Rest – Seafood – *(Closed Monday and Tuesday) (booking essential)* Menu £ 28 – Carte £ 28/63

◆ Personally run bistro and piscatorially themed main dining room in a lovely setting. Numerous seafood menus, offering a vast choice and some unusual combinations. Simple bedrooms.

SCOTLAND

PORTPATRICK – Dumfries and Galloway – 501 E19 – pop. 585 – ✉ Stranraer **25** A3

Edinburgh 141 mi. – Ayr 60 mi. – Dumfries 80 mi. – Stranraer 9 mi.

Golf Course Rd, ✆ (01776) 810 273

Knockinaam Lodge

Southeast : 5 mi. by A 77 off B 7042 ✉ DG9 9AD – ✆ (01776) 810 471 – www.knockinaamlodge.com – Fax (01776) 810 435

10 rm (dinner included) – £ 305/345 ££ 380/420

Rest – *(booking essential for non-residents) (set menu only)* Menu £ 39/55

Spec. Steamed sea bass with gazpacho. Fillet of Angus beef with baby garden vegetables, garlic beignet and truffle. Summer pudding with clotted cream ice cream.

◆ Family-run Victorian house, with a warm, relaxing feel; idyllically situated in its own private cove. Country house style bedrooms, with two contemporary suites in the eaves. Well-executed, classic dishes are refreshingly simple in their construction, using superb local produce, including much from the garden.

Campbells

1 South Crescent ✉ DG9 8JR – ✆ (01776) 810 314 – www.campbellsrestaurant.co.uk – Fax (01776) 810 361 – Closed 2 weeks January-February, 1 week November, 25 December and Monday

Rest – Seafood – Menu £ 14 (Sunday) – Carte £ 19/32

◆ Personally run attractive harbourside restaurant with modern rustic feel throughout. Tasty, appealing menus, full of seafood specialities and Scottish ingredients.

PORTREE – Highland – 501 B11 – see Skye (Isle of)

QUOTHQUAN – South Lanarkshire – 501 J27 – ✉ Biggar Scotland **26** C2

Edinburgh 32 mi. – Dumfries 50 mi. – Glasgow 36 mi.

Biggar★ (Gladstone Court Museum★ **AC** – Greenhill Covenanting Museum★ **AC**) SE : 4.5 mi. by B 7016

Shieldhill Castle

Northeast : 0.75 mi. ✉ ML12 6NA – ✆ (01899) 220 035 – www.shieldhill.co.uk – Fax (01899) 221 092

26 rm – £ 75 ££ 103/268

Rest *Chancellors* – Menu £ 20 – Carte £ 26/55

◆ Part 12C fortified manor with 16C additions and invitingly comfortable panelled lounge. Large rooms, individually furnished, some with vast sunken baths; those in courtyard are most modern and best. Accomplished cooking in 16C dining room with high carved ceilings.

RANNOCH STATION – Perth and Kinross – 501 G13 **27** B2

Edinburgh 108 mi. – Kinloch Rannoch 17 mi. – Pitlochry 36 mi.

Moor of Rannoch

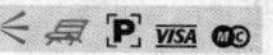

✉ PH17 2QA – ✆ (01882) 633 238 – www.moorofrannoch.co.uk – 14 February-October

5 rm – £ 57/96 ££ 96

Rest – *(dinner only) (booking essential for non-residents)* Carte £ 25/32 **s**

◆ Immaculately whitewashed 19C property "in the middle of nowhere", next to railway station with link to London! Comfy, sofa-strewn lounges. Rustic rooms with antiques. Home-cooked menus in characterful dining room with conservatory.

Each starred restaurant lists three specialities that are typical of its style of cuisine. These may not always be on the menu but in their place expect delicious seasonal dishes. Be sure to try them.

SCOTLAND

ST ANDREWS – Fife – 501 L14 – pop. 14 209 Scotland 28 D2

Edinburgh 51 mi. – Dundee 14 mi. – Stirling 51 mi.

70 Market St ✆ (01334) 472021, standrews@visitscotland.com

Duke's Craigtoun Park, ✆ (01334) 474 371

City★★ - Cathedral★ (✻★★) **AC** B – West Port★ A

Leuchars (parish church★), NW : 6 mi. by A 91 and A 919. The East Neuk★★, SE : 9 mi. by A 917 and B 9131 B – Crail★★ (Old Centre★★, Upper Crail★) SE : 9 mi. by A 917 B – Kellie Castle★ **AC**, S : 9 mi. by B 9131 and B 9171 B – Ceres★, SW : 9 mi. by B 939 - E : Inland Fife★ A

Old Course H. Golf Resort and Spa

rm, VISA AE Ab

Old Station Rd ✉ KY16 9SP – ✆ (01334) 474 371 – www.oldcoursehotel.co.uk – Fax (01334) 477 668

116 rm – †£ 205/360 ††£ 235/390 – 21 suites

Rest *Road Hole* – *(closed 3 January-20 February, Sunday and Monday) (dinner only)* Carte £ 40/57

Rest *Sands Grill* – Carte £ 26/71

◆ Famed for its golf course and its unrivalled views of the bay. Relax into richly furnished formal interiors and enjoy luxurious pampering in the impressive spa. Bedrooms are a mix of the modern and classic. Road Hole Grill has a fine view of the 17th hole. Sands Grill has a classic brasserie menu.

Fairmont St Andrews

rm, VISA AE

Southeast : 3 mi. on A 917 ✉ KY16 8PN – ✆ (01334) 837 000 – www.fairmont.com/standrews – Fax (01334) 471 115

192 rm – †£ 119/299 ††£ 119/299 – 6 suites

Rest *The Squire* – Menu £ 30

Rest *Esperante* – *(closed Monday-Tuesday) (dinner only)* Menu £ 43

◆ Considerable refurbishment at this large, golf oriented, purpose-built resort hotel. Wonderful Tayside views and pristine fairways. Impressive spa. Spacious, comfortable and well-equipped bedrooms. Informal Squire popular with golfers. Mediterranean influenced Esperante.

ST ANDREWS

Abbey St . . . . . B 2
Abbey Walk . . . . . B 3
Alexandra Pl. . . . . A 5
Alfred Pl. . . . . A 6
Bridge St. . . . . A 7
Butts Wynd . . . . . B 9
Castle St . . . . . B 10
Church St . . . . . AB 13
Ellice Pl. . . . . A 15
Gibson Pl. . . . . A 17
Gillespie Terrace . . . . . A 18
Greenside Pl. . . . . B 20
Gregory Lane . . . . . B 21
Gregory Pl. . . . . B 22
Greyfriars Garden . . . . . A 24
Hepburn Gardens . . . . . A 25
Link Crescent . . . . . A 27
Murray Park . . . . . A 28
Murray Pl. . . . . A 29
Pilmour Links . . . . . A 31
Pilmour Pl. . . . . A 32
Playfair Terrace . . . . . A 34
Queen's Gardens . . . . . A 35
Queen's Terrace . . . . . B 36
St Mary's Pl. . . . . A 37
Union St . . . . . B 38

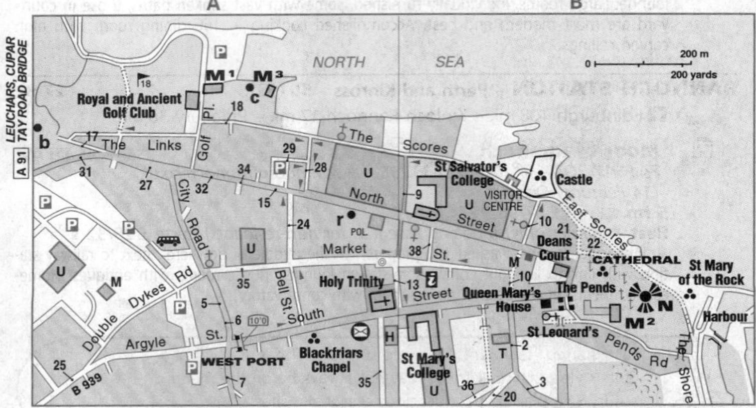

Rufflets Country House — Strathkinness Low Rd, West : 1.5 mi. on B 939 ✉ KY16 9TX – ✆ (01334) 472 594 – www.rufflets.co.uk – Fax (01334) 478 703

22 rm – †£ 100/210 ††£ 150/250 – 2 suites

Rest ***Terrace*** – *(dinner only and Sunday lunch)* Carte £ 24/43

Rest ***Music Room*** – *(Closed Sunday lunch and dinner Friday-Saturday)* Menu £ 16/18

◆ Handsome 1920s house set in ornamental gardens. Traditional drawing room with cosy fireside sofas. Thoughtfully appointed bedrooms that mix classic and contemporary styles. Terrace restaurant offers fine vantage point to view the lawns. Informal lunches in Music Room, with its mock bookshelf wallpaper.

18 Queens Terrace without rest — *18 Queens Terrace, by Queens Gardens ✉ KY16 9QF – ✆ (01334) 478 849 – www.18queensterrace.com – Fax (01334) 470 283 – Closed Christmas and New Year*

4 rm – †£ 70/75 ††£ 90/95

◆ Victorian townhouse, retaining much of its original character, with attractive drawing room and spacious, tastefully decorated bedrooms. Pleasantly located, with a secluded cottage garden.

Aslar House without rest — *120 North St ✉ KY16 9AF – ✆ (01334) 473 460 – www.aslar.com – Closed 4-18 January and 1 week Christmas* — A**r**

6 rm – †£ 45/85 ††£ 90/100

◆ Victorian house, privately run in a welcoming spirit. Homely, pine furnished rooms, all en suite, are larger on the top floor; most overlook a quiet rear garden. Good value.

The Seafood — *The Scores ✉ KY16 9AB – ✆ (01334) 479 475 – www.theseafoodrestaurant.com – Fax (01334) 479 476 – Closed 25-26 December and 1 January* — A**c**

Rest – Seafood – *(booking essential)* Menu £ 26/45

◆ Overhanging the town's beach, with super views, as all four sides are made of glass. A very pleasant attitude and attention to detail accompanies agreeable, top quality, regularly changing seafood menus.

Take note of the classification: you should not expect the same level of service in a X or 🏠 as in a XXXXX or 🏠🏠🏠.

SCOTLAND

ST BOSWELLS – Scottish Borders – 501 L17 – pop. 1 199 — 26 D2

– ✉ Melrose ▮ Scotland

▶ Edinburgh 39 mi. – Glasgow 79 mi. – Hawick 17 mi. – Newcastle upon Tyne 66 mi.

St Boswells, ✆ (01835) 823 527

Dryburgh Abbey★★ **AC** (setting★★★), NW : 4 mi. by B 6404 and B 6356 – Tweed Valley★★. Bowhill★★ **AC**, SW : 11.5 mi. by A 699 and A 708

Whitehouse — *Northeast : 3 mi. on B 6404 ✉ TD6 0ED – ✆ (01573) 460 343 – www.whitehousecountryhouse.com*

3 rm – †£ 65/75 ††£ 100/110 **Rest** – *(by arrangement)* Menu £ 29

◆ Appreciate the good rural views from enticingly comfortable country house style lounge in this 19C former dower house. Nourishing breakfast specials. Airy, welcoming rooms. Home-cooked meals in dining room overlooking the fields.

Clint Lodge — *North : 2.25 mi. by B 6404 on B 6356 ✉ TD6 0DZ – ✆ (01835) 822 027 – www.clintlodge.co.uk – Fax (01835) 822 656*

5 rm – †£ 50/70 ††£ 110 **Rest** – *(by arrangement)* Menu £ 33

◆ Personally run Victorian shooting lodge with sweeping prospects of the Tweed Valley and Cheviots. Antiques, open fires, fishing memorabilia and comfortable, classic rooms. A choice of tables allows for private or communal dining.

ST FILLANS – Perth and Kinross – 501 H14 — 28 C2

Edinburgh 65 mi. – Lochearnhead 8 mi. – Perth 29 mi.

Achray House

PH6 2NF – (01764) 685 231 – www.achray-house.co.uk – Fax (01764) 685 320 – Closed 3-24 January

8 rm (dinner included) – £ 90/105 £ 130/160 **Rest** – Carte £ 20/30

◆ Well run, former Edwardian villa with a stunning Loch Earn view. A homely warmth pervades all areas. Bedrooms are clean and simple; some are suitable for families. Freshly prepared seafood a feature of dining room menus.

The Four Seasons

Lochside PH6 2NF – (01764) 685 333 – www.thefourseasonshotel.co.uk – Fax (01764) 685 444 – Closed January, February and midweek March, November and early December

12 rm – £ 55/95 £ 110/130

Rest – Menu £ 35 (dinner) – Carte £ 20/30

◆ Small hotel in enviable location beside Loch Earn, with welcoming atmosphere, neat bedrooms and slightly retro edge; front facing rooms have Loch views. Cosy bar and lounge. Bistro open for lunch, restaurant for 4 course dinner.

ST MARGARET'S HOPE – Orkney Islands – 501 L7 – see Orkney Islands

ST MONANS – Fife – 501 L15 – pop. 3 965 — 28 D2

Edinburgh 47 mi. – Dundee 26 mi. – Perth 40 mi. – Stirling 56 mi.

The Seafood

16 West End KY10 2BX – (01333) 730 327 – www.theseafoodrestaurant.com – Fax (01333) 730 508 – Closed 1 week January, Monday and Tuesday

Rest – Seafood – *(booking essential)* Menu £ 26/38

◆ Former pub with nautical memorabilia in a delightful spot overlooking the harbour. Comfortable lounge leads into neatly set restaurant. Local fish prepared with care and precision.

SANQUHAR – Dumfries and Galloway – 501 I17 – pop. 2 028 — 25 B2

London 368 mi. – Edinburgh 58 mi. – East Kilbride 51 mi. – Hamilton 43 mi.

Blackaddie House with rm

Blackaddie Rd DG4 6JJ – (01659) 50 270 – www.blackaddiehotel.co.uk – Fax (01659) 50 900

9 rm – £ 55/70 £ 90/125 **Rest** – Carte £ 31/46

◆ Manor house, with homely feel, on banks of River Nith. Classical cooking with seasonal base, plenty of choice and strong seafood element. Bedrooms named after whisky distilleries.

SCALASAIG – Argyll and Bute – 501 B15 – see Colonsay (Isle of)

SCALPAY – Western Isles – 501 A10 – see Lewis and Harris (Isle of)

SCARISTA – Western Isles Outer Hebrides – 501 Y10 – see Lewis and Harris (Isle of)

SCOURIE – Highland – 501 E8 – Lairg Scotland — 30 C1

Edinburgh 263 mi. – Inverness 107 mi.

Cape Wrath★★★ (★★) AC, N : 31 mi. (including ferry crossing) by A 894 and A 838 – Loch Assynt★★, S : 17 mi. by A 894

Eddrachilles

Badcall Bay, South : 2.5 mi. on A 894 IV27 4TH – (01971) 502 080 – www.eddrachilles.com – Fax (01971) 502 477 – mid March-mid October

11 rm – £ 70/73 £ 94/100 **Rest** – *(bar lunch)* Menu £ 30 **s**

◆ Isolated hotel, converted from small part 18C former manse, magnificently set at the head of Badcall Bay and its islands. Conservatory lounge. Traditional, well-kept rooms. Dining room with stone walls and flagstone floors.

SCRABSTER – Highland – 501 J8 – see Thurso

SHETLAND ISLANDS – 501 P/Q3 – pop. 21 988 Scotland

Sumburgh Airport : ✆ (01950) 460905, S : 25 mi. of Lerwick by A 970 - Tingwall Airport: 01595) 840246, NW: 6m. of Lerwick by A971

from Foula to Walls (Shetland Islands Council) 1-2 weekly (2 h 30 mn) – from Fair Isle to Sumburgh (Shetland Islands Council) 1-2 weekly (2 h 40 mn)

from Lerwick (Mainland) to Aberdeen and via Orkney Islands (Stromness) (P and O Scottish Ferries)
– from Vidlin to Skerries (Shetland Islands Council) booking essential 3-4 weekly (1 h 30 mn)
– from Lerwick (Mainland) to Skerries (Shetland Islands Council) 2 weekly (booking essential) (2 h 30 mn)
– from Lerwick (Mainland) to Bressay (Shetland Islands Council) frequent services daily (7 mn)
– from Laxo (Mainland) to Isle of Whalsay (Symbister) (Shetland Islands Council) frequent services daily (30 mn)
– from Toft (Mainland) to Isle of Yell (Ulsta) (Shetland Islands Council) frequent services daily (20 mn)
– from Isle of Yell (Gutcher) to Isle of Fetlar (Oddsta) and via Isle of Unst (Belmont) (Shetland Islands Council)
– from Fair Isle to Sumburgh (Mainland) (Shetland Islands Council) 3 weekly (2 h 40 mn)

Islands★ - Up Helly Aa (last Tuesday in January) – Mousa Broch★★★ **AC** (Mousa Island) – Jarlshof★★ - Lerwick to Jarlshof★ (<★) – Shetland Croft House Museum★ **AC**

SCOTLAND

MAINLAND – Shetland Islands — 31 B2

London 559 mi. – Edinburgh 148 mi.

LERWICK – Shetland Islands – pop. 6 830 Scotland — 31 B2

The Market Cross, Lerwick ✆ (08452) 255 121, info@visitshetland.com
Shetland Gott Dale, ✆ (01595) 840 369
Clickhimin Broch★
Gulber Wick (<★), S : 2 mi. by A 970

Kveldsro House

Greenfield Pl ✉ ZE1 0AQ – ✆ (01595) 692 195 – www.shetlandhotels.com – Fax (01595) 696 595 – Closed 1-2 January and 25-26 December
17 rm – ♦£ 98 ♦♦£ 120
Rest – *(bar lunch Monday-Saturday, carvery lunch Sunday)* Carte £ 20/35 **s**
◆ Neat, modern style in evidence throughout this smoothly run hotel - its name comes from the Norse for "evening peace". Tidy rooms, well-equipped and furnished in pale wood. Classically smart and formally set restaurant.

Glen Orchy House

20 Knab Rd ✉ ZE1 0AX – ✆ (01595) 692 031 – www.guesthouselerwick.com – Fax (01595) 692 031
23 rm – ♦£ 55 ♦♦£ 80
Rest – Thai – *(dinner only) (booking essential) (residents only)* Carte £ 15/17 **s**
◆ Built as a convent in the 1900s and sympathetically extended. Colourful public areas. Bright honesty bar. Spotless bedrooms with neat modern fabrics and fittings. Restaurant offers authentic Thai menus.

VEENSGARTH – Shetland Islands — 31 B2

Herrislea House

✉ ZE2 9SB – ✆ (01595) 840 208 – www.herrisleahouse.co.uk – Fax (01595) 840 630 – Restricted opening in winter
9 rm – ♦£ 70/120 ♦♦£ 100/130
Rest – *(dinner only) (booking essential for non-residents)* Carte £ 20/31 **s**
◆ Purpose-built hotel run by native islanders; a homely hall, with mounted antlers, leads to tidy bedrooms, pleasantly furnished in solid pine, and an angling themed bar. Neatly laid out but fairly informal restaurant.

ISLAND OF UNST – Shetland Islands 31 B1

BALTASOUND – Shetland Islands

Buness House

East : 0.5 mi. by A 968 and Springpark Rd ✉ ZE2 9DS – ✆ (01957) 711 315 – www.users.zetnet.co.uk/buness-house – Fax (01957) 711 815 – Restricted opening December-March

3 rm – £ 75 £ 120/125

Rest – *(by arrangement, communal dining)* Menu £ 37

◆ Whitewashed house of 16C origin. Cosy, well-stocked library. Comfortable rooms facing Balta Sound, one decorated with Victorian prints and découpages. Nearby nature reserve. Willow-pattern china and sea views from the conservatory dining room.

Guesthouses don't provide the same level of service as hotels. They are often characterised by a warm welcome and a décor which reflects the owner's personality. Those shown in red are particularly pleasant.

SCOTLAND

SHIELDAIG – Highland – 501 D11 – ✉ Strathcarron Scotland 29 B2

Edinburgh 226 mi. – Inverness 70 mi. – Kyle of Lochalsh 36 mi.

Wester Ross★★★

Tigh An Eilean

✉ IV54 8XN – ✆ (01520) 755 251 – www.tighaneilean.co.uk – Fax (01520) 755 321 – Mid-March to November

11 rm – £ 75/100 £ 160

Rest – *(booking essential for non-residents) (bar lunch)* Menu £ 40/44

◆ In a sleepy lochside village, an attractive, personally run 19C inn with fine views of the Shieldaig Islands. Cosy, well-kept bedrooms and a comfy lounge with a homely feel. Linen-clad dining room showing eclectic variety of art; Scottish produce to the fore.

SKIRLING – Scottish Borders – 501 J17 – ✉ Biggar Scotland 26 C2

Edinburgh 29 mi. – Glasgow 45 mi. – Peebles 16 mi.

Biggar★ - Gladstone Court Museum★, Greenhill Covenanting Museum★, S : 3 mi. by A 72 and A 702. New Lanark★★, NW : 16 mi. by A 72 and A 73

Skirling House

✉ ML12 6HD – ✆ (01899) 860 274 – www.skirlinghouse.com – Fax (01899) 860 255 – Closed January, February and 1 week November

5 rm – £ 90 £ 130 **Rest** – *(by arrangement)* Menu £ 35

◆ Attractive Arts and Crafts house (1908). 16C Florentine carved ceiling in drawing room. Comfortable bedrooms with modern conveniences. Daily dinner menu using fresh produce.

SKYE (Isle of) – Highland – 501 B11 – pop. 9 232 Scotland 29 B2

from Mallaig to Isles of Eigg, Muck, Rhum and Canna (Caledonian MacBrayne Ltd) (summer only) – from Mallaig to Armadale (Caledonian MacBrayne Ltd) (summer only) 1-2 weekly (30 mn)

from Mallaig to Armadale (Caledonian MacBrayne Ltd) 1-5 daily (30 mn) – from Uig to North Uist (Lochmaddy) or Isle of Harris (Tarbert) (Caledonian MacBrayne Ltd) 1-3 daily (1 h 50 mn) – from Sconser to Isle of Raasay (Caledonian MacBrayne Ltd) 9-10 daily (except Sunday) (15 mn)

Island★★ - The Cuillins★★★ – Skye Museum of Island Life★ **AC**

N : Trotternish Peninsula★★ – W : Duirinish Peninsula★ – Portree★

BERNISDALE – Highland

The Spoons without rest

75 Aird Bernisdale ✉ *IV51 9NU* – ✆ *(01470) 532 217* – *www.thespoonsonskye.com* – *Closed 24-29 December*

3 rm – †£ 90/110 ††£ 120/140

◆ Luxurious, purpose-built guest house in unspoilt hamlet, with airy, wood-floored lounge and Scandinavian-style breakfast room. Bedrooms are individually decorated in a crisp, modern style. 3 course breakfasts, with eggs from the charming owners' chickens.

BROADFORD – Highland **29** B2

Tigh an Dochais

13 Harrapool, on A 87 ✉ *IV49 9AQ* – ✆ *(01471) 820 022* – *www.skyebedandbreakfast.co.uk* – *March-November*

3 rm – †£ 70 ††£ 80 **Rest** – *(by arrangement)* Menu £ 25

◆ Striking house with award-winning architecture, overlooking the bay and peninsula. Modern, minimalist-style bedrooms have superb views and good facilities, including underfloor heating. Relaxed, home-cooked meals by arrangement.

DUISDALEMORE – Highland **29** B2

Duisdale House

Sleat, on A 851. ✉ *IV43 8QW* – ✆ *(01471) 833 202* – *www.duisdale.com*

18 rm – †£ 60/150 ††£ 140/230 – 1 suite **Rest** – Carte £ 22/47 **s**

◆ Stylish, up-to-date hotel with lawned gardens, hot tub and coastal views. Comfortable bedrooms boast bold décor, excellent bathrooms and a pleasing blend of contemporary and antique furniture. Modern cooking makes good use of local produce. Smart uniformed staff.

DUNVEGAN – Highland **29** B2

Roskhill House without rest

Roskhill, Southeast : 2.5 mi. by A 863 ✉ *IV55 8ZD* – ✆ *(01470) 521 317* – *www.roskhillhouse.co.uk* – *Restricted opening November-February*

5 rm – †£ 45/55 ††£ 64/76

◆ Expect bright, contemporary bedrooms and smart bathrooms at this friendly, personally run 19C croft house, which has been extended. The peaceful location is another feature.

The Three Chimneys & The House Over-By with rm

✉ *IV55 8ZT* – ✆ *(01470) 511 258* – *www.threechimneys.co.uk* – *Fax (01470) 511 358* – *Closed 3 weeks January*

6 rm – †£ 275 ††£ 275

Rest – Seafood – *(booking essential)* Menu £ 35/60

◆ Internationally renowned crofter's cottage restaurant on Loch Dunvegan shores. Accomplished Skye seafood dishes, plus Highland lamb, beef and game. Sumptuous bedrooms.

EDINBANE – Highland **29** B2

Greshornish House

North : 3.75 mi. by A 850 in direction of Dunvegan ✉ *IV51 9PN* – ✆ *(01470) 582 266* – *www.greshornishhouse.com* – *Fax (01470) 582 345* – *Restricted opening in winter*

8 rm (dinner included) – †£ 135/165 ††£ 230/265

Rest – *(booking essential)* Menu £ 38 – Carte £ 22/34

◆ Utter tranquillity: a beautifully sited hotel in 10 acres of grounds, with cluttered sitting rooms, snooker room, smart bedrooms with a view - and Skye's only tennis court! Conservatory breakfasts; Western Isle ingredients to fore in the dining room.

FLODIGARRY – Highland – ✉ Staffin **29** B2

Flodigarry Country House

✉ *IV51 9HZ* – ✆ *(01470) 552 203* – *www.flodigarry.co.uk* – *Fax (01470) 552 301* – *Closed 8 November-21 December and January*

18 rm – †£ 110/130 ††£ 160/200

Rest – *(bar lunch Monday-Saturday)* Carte £ 31/56 **s**

◆ Extended and traditionally decorated Victorian house, with pretty cottage annexe which was once home to Flora Macdonald. Characterful bar and comfortable drawing room. Rooms divided between the two. Semi-panelled candlelit restaurant.

SCOTLAND

PORTREE – Highland – pop. 1 917 **29** B2

Bayfield House, Bayfield Rd ☎ (08452) 255121

Cuillin Hills

Northeast : 0.75 mi. by A 855 ✉ IV51 9QU – ☎ (01478) 612 003 – www.cuillinhills-hotel-skye.co.uk – Fax (01478) 613 092
26 rm – †£ 180 ††£ 200/300
Rest – *(bar lunch Monday-Saturday, buffet lunch Sunday)* Menu £ 35 **s** – Carte £ 18/28 **s**
◆ Enlarged 19C hunting lodge in 15-acre grounds above lochside with fine views. Drawing room and bar boast a contemporary style. In contrast, bedrooms are more traditional. Smart and spacious dining room with views of Portree Bay.

Bosville

Bosville Ter ✉ IV51 9DG – ☎ (01478) 612 846 – www.macleodhotels.co.uk/bosville – Fax (01478) 613 434
19 rm – †£ 69/120 ††£ 88/128
Rest *Chandlery* – see restaurant listing
Rest *Bistro* – Carte £ 17/31
◆ Well-established, busy hotel overlooking harbour and hills. First-floor sitting room and tidy, modern accommodation in co-ordinated décor. Buzzy ground floor bistro.

Almondbank without rest

Viewfield Rd, Southwest : 0.75 mi. on A 87 ✉ IV51 9EU – ☎ (01478) 612 696 – Fax (01478) 613 114
4 rm – †£ 55/65 ††£ 65/75
◆ Situated away from the town centre, this purpose built house has been well looked after by the friendly owner. Spotless bedrooms; superb views across Portree Bay.

The Chandlery – at Bosville Hotel

Bosville Ter ✉ IV51 9DG – ☎ (01478) 612 846 – www.macleodhotels.co.uk – Fax (01478) 613 434
Rest – Menu £ 40 – Carte approx. £ 22
◆ A purple colour scheme distinguishes this formal but relaxed restaurant from the adjacent bistro. Skilfully executed dishes display a proven touch of orginality and flair.

SLEAT – Highland **30** C1

Kinloch Lodge

✉ IV43 8QY – ☎ (01471) 833 214 – www.kinloch-lodge.co.uk – Fax (01471) 833 277
13 rm (dinner included) – †£ 150/190 ††£ 250/300 – 1 suite
Rest – *(booking essential for non-residents)* Menu £ 25/52 **s**
Spec. Roast monkfish with pork cheeks and caramelised passion fruit. Halibut with deep-fried red pepper gnocchi, mussels and saffron. Carrot and vanilla mousse with pistachio marshmallows.
◆ An historic 17C hunting lodge on Loch Na Dal. Antiques abound, with a very handsome and comfortable drawing room. The bedrooms are spacious and reflect the charm of the house. Expert use of top quality produce in accomplished dishes given a contemporary twist.

STRUAN – Highland **29** B2

Ullinish Country Lodge

West : 1.5 mi. by A 863 ✉ IV56 8FD – ☎ (01470) 572 214 – www.theisleofskye.co.uk – Fax (01470) 572 341 – Closed January and 1 week November
6 rm – †£ 120 ††£ 160
Rest – *(light lunch) (booking essential for non-residents)* Menu £ 50
◆ Country lodge comforts in superb windswept spot with fine views. Traditional sitting room; each bedroom has a distinct style with luxury fabrics and character beds built of wood. Skye ingredients put to compelling, highly original use in creative modern dishes.

TEANGUE – Highland 29 B3

Toravaig House

Knock Bay, on A 851 ✉ IV44 8RE – ✆ (01471) 820 200 – www.skyehotel.co.uk – Fax (01471) 833 231
9 rm – †£ 60/150 ††£ 100/290
Rest – *(booking essential for non-residents)* Menu £ 22/35 **s** – Carte £ 24/40 **s**
◆ Comfortable and stylish country house on the road to Mallaig ferry. Small but perfectly formed lounge. Bedrooms designed to a high standard and service is keen and willing. Skye produce to the fore in two restaurant rooms.

WATERNISH – Highland 29 A2

Loch Bay Seafood

1 MacLeod Terrace, Stein ✉ IV55 8GA – ✆ (01470) 592 235 – www.lochbay-seafood-restaurant.co.uk – Fax (01470) 592 235 – Closed 6 January-Easter and November-Christmas
Rest – Seafood – *(Closed Sunday and Monday) (booking essential)*
Carte £ 22/34
◆ Small and atmospheric cottage restaurant with simple wooden tables and benches. The freshest local seafood, including halibut, sole and turbot, is carefully prepared.

Stein Inn with rm

MacLeod Ter, Stein ✉ IV55 8GA – ✆ (01470) 592 362 – www.stein-inn.co.uk
5 rm – †£ 37 ††£ 75/100
Rest – Seafood – *(residents only Monday dinner except Bank Holidays)*
Carte £ 16/25
◆ Set in a tiny fishing village, this characterful inn is the oldest on Skye. Menus are formed around the latest local produce available, with lighter toasties and salads on offer at lunch. Bedrooms are simple and well-kept, with bay views.

SLEAT – Highland – see Skye (Isle of)

SORN – East Ayrshire – 501 H17 25 B2

Edinburgh 67 mi. – Ayr 15 mi. – Glasgow 35 mi.

The Sorn Inn with rm

35 Main St ✉ KA5 6HU – ✆ (01290) 551 305 – www.sorninn.com – Fax (01290) 553 470 – Closed Sunday dinner and Monday
4 rm – †£ 40/45 ††£ 90/95 **Rest** – Menu £ 19/24 – Carte £ 20/29
◆ Simple whitewashed inn; very much a family affair. Robust cooking offered in the snug bar and more refined, knowledgeably executed dishes with a Mediterranean edge in the dining room. Neat, simple bedrooms are good value.

SPEAN BRIDGE – Highland – 501 F13 30 C3

Edinburgh 143 mi. – Fort William 10 mi. – Glasgow 94 mi. – Inverness 58 mi.
The Kingdom of Scotland, by Fort William, Inverness-shire ✆ (0845) 2255121 (April-October), info@visitscotland.com
Spean Bridge GC Station Rd, ✆ 077 471 47 090

Corriegour Lodge

Loch Lochy, North : 8.75 mi. on A 82 ✉ PH34 4EA – ✆ (01397) 712 685 – www.corriegour.com – Fax (01397) 712 696 – March-October and New Year
11 rm – †£ 80/90 ††£ 159/179
Rest – *(dinner only) (booking essential for non-residents)* Menu £ 48
◆ Enthusiastically run 19C hunting lodge in woods and gardens above Loch Lochy. Bright, individually decorated rooms and a cosy bar and lounge share a warm, traditional feel. Formally set dining room with wide picture windows.

Distant Hills without rest

Roybridge Rd, East : 0.5 mi. on A86 ✉ PH34 4EU – ✆ (01397) 712 452 – www.distanthills.com
7 rm – †£ 47/75 ††£ 75/85
◆ Welcoming guesthouse with comfy, contemporary furnishings. Lounge boasts French windows onto terrace and colourful garden; small stream nearby. Tea on arrival. Wide ranging breakfast.

SCOTLAND

Corriechoille Lodge

East : 2.75 mi. on Corriechoille rd ✉ PH34 4EY – ✆ (01397) 712 002 – www.corriechoille.com – Closed November-March, Sunday and Monday

4 rm – £ 48 £ 76 **Rest** – *(by arrangement)* Menu £ 28

◆ Off the beaten track in quiet estate land, a part 18C lodge: stylishly modern lounge, spacious en suite rooms: those facing south have fine views of the Grey Corries.

Russell's at Smiddy House with rm

Roybridge Rd ✉ PH34 4EU – ✆ (01397) 712 335 – www.smiddyhouse.co.uk – Fax (01397) 712 043 – Closed 1 week Spring, 2 weeks November and Monday-Tuesday during winter

4 rm – £ 70/80 £ 70/85

Rest – *(dinner only) (booking essential)* Menu £ 33 **s**

◆ Spacious Victorian house in small Highland village with intimate, candlelit dining rooms and attentive service. Weekly-changing menu with strong, locally sourced seafood base. Immaculately-kept, individually decorated bedrooms.

Old Pines with rm

Northwest : 1.5 mi. by A 82 on B 8004 ✉ PH34 4EG – ✆ (01397) 712 324 – www.oldpines.co.uk – Closed Christmas and New Year

7 rm – £ 45/70 £ 90/110

Rest – *(booking essential for non-residents)* Carte £ 27/35

◆ There's almost a dinner party atmosphere at this warm, simple restaurant. The emphasis is firmly on the seasonal and the organic. The staff are very friendly. The bedrooms are well-kept.

SPITTAL OF GLENSHEE – Perth and Kinross – 501 J13 28 C2

– ✉ **Blairgowrie** Scotland

Edinburgh 69 mi. – Aberdeen 74 mi. – Dundee 35 mi.

Glenshee (✱★★) (chairlift **AC**)

Dalmunzie Castle

✉ PH10 7QG – ✆ (01250) 885 224 – www.dalmunzie.com – Fax (01250) 885 225 – Closed December

17 rm (dinner included) – £ 120/155 £ 210/270

Rest – *(bar lunch)* Menu £ 42

◆ Edwardian hunting lodge in a magnificent spot, encircled by mountains. Traditional rooms mix antique and pine furniture. Bar with cosy panelled alcove and leather chairs. Modern dining room with views down the valley.

STEVENSTON – North Ayrshire – 501 F17 – pop. 9 129 25 A2

Edinburgh 82 mi. – Ayr 19 mi. – Glasgow 36 mi.

Ardeer Farm Steading without rest

Ardeer Mains Farm, East : 0.75 mi. by A 738 and B 752, on no through rd ✉ KA20 3DD – ✆ (01294) 465 438 – www.ardeersteading.co.uk

6 rm – £ 32/35 £ 45/48

◆ Comfortable family-owned guest house has contemporary furnishings, with bright cushions and bed throws. Pleasant breakfast room and modern lounge with cream leather sofas.

STIRLING – Stirling – 501 I15 – pop. 32 673 Scotland 28 C2

Edinburgh 37 mi. – Dunfermline 23 mi. – Falkirk 14 mi. – Glasgow 28 mi.

41 Dumbarton Rd ✆ (08707) 200620, stirling@visitscotland.com- Pirnhall, Motorway Service Area, junction 9, M 9/ M80 ✆ (01786) 814111 (April-October), info@pirnhall.visitscotland.com

Town★★ – Castle★★ **AC** (Site★★★, external elevations★★★, Stirling Heads★★, Argyll and Sutherland Highlanders Regimental Museum★) B – Argyll's Lodging★ (Renaissance decoration★) B **A** – Church of the Holy Rude★ B **B**

Wallace Monument (✱★★) NE : 2.5 mi. by A 9 - A - and B 998. Dunblane★ (Cathedral★★, West Front★★), N : 6.5 mi. by A 9 A

STIRLING

Barnton St. . . . . **B** 2
Borestone Crescent . . . . . . **A** 3
Causewayhead Rd . . . . . **A, B** 4
Cornton Rd. . . . . **A** 7
Corn Exchange Rd . . . . **B** 5
Coxithill Rd . . . . **A** 8
Drummond Pl. . . . . **B** 9
Dumbarton Rd . . . . **B** 10
Goosecroft Rd . . . . **B** 12
King St . . . . **B** 13
Leisure Centre . . . . **B**
Murray Pl. . . . . **B** 15
Newhouse . . . . **A** 16
Park Pl. . . . . **A** 18
Port St. . . . . **B**
Queen St . . . . **B** 20
Randolph Terrace . . . . **A** 22
St John St. . . . . **B** 23
St Mary's Wynd . . . . **B** 24
Seaforth Pl. . . . . **B** 25
Shirra's Brae Rd . . . . **A** 26
Spittal St . . . . **B** 27
Thistle Centre . . . . **B**
Union St . . . . **B** 28
Upper Craigs. . . . . **B** 29
Weaver Row. . . . . **A** 31

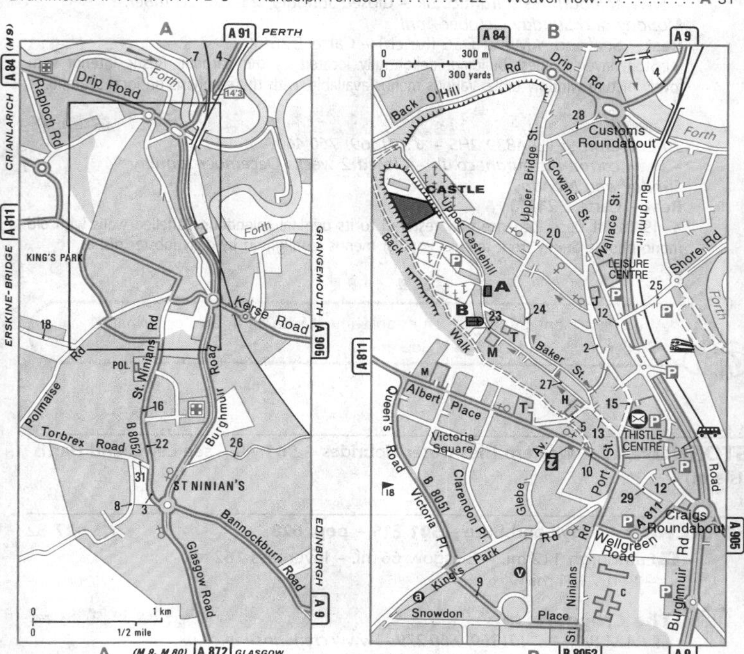

Park Lodge

32 Park Ter ✉ FK8 2JS – ✆ (01786) 474 862 – www.parklodge.net – Fax (01786) 449 748 – Closed 1-2 January and 25-26 December B**a**

9 rm ☕ – 👤£ 60/85 👥£ 80/95

Rest – *(Closed Sunday and Monday)* Menu £ 15/25 **s**

◆ Creeper-clad Georgian and Victorian house, still in private hands and furnished with an enviable collection of antiques. Compact but well-equipped rooms with a stylish feel. Intimate dining room overlooking a pretty garden.

Number 10 without rest

Gladstone Pl ✉ FK8 2NN – ✆ (01786) 472 681 – www.cameron-10.co.uk

3 rm ☕ – 👤£ 45/50 👥£ 60 B**v**

◆ Surprisingly spacious 19C terrace house in a pleasant suburb. Pine furnished en suite bedrooms are characteristically well kept and comfortable. Friendly owner.

West Plean House without rest

South : 3.5 mi. on A 872 (Denny rd) ✉ FK7 8HA – ✆ (01786) 812 208 – www.westpleanhouse.com – Fax (01786) 480 550 – Closed 18 December-18 January

3 rm ☕ – 👤£ 45/50 👥£ 70/75

◆ Attractive country house dating from 1801; the estate includes a working farm. Drawing rooms filled with antiques and family heirlooms. Individually decorated bedrooms are warm and traditional.

STONEHAVEN – Aberdeenshire – 501 N13 – pop. 9 577 Scotland 28 D2

Edinburgh 109 mi. – Aberdeen 16 mi. – Montrose 22 mi.

Dunnottar Castle★★, S : 1.5 mi. by A 92

XX **Tolbooth**

Old Pier, Harbour ✉ AB39 2JU – ✆ (01569) 762 287 – www.tolbooth-restaurant.co.uk – Closed January, 25-26 December, Monday and Sunday October-April

Rest – Seafood – Menu £ 16 (lunch) – Carte £ 26/39

◆ Stonehaven's oldest building, delightfully located by the harbour. Rustic interior with lovely picture window table. Various menus available, with the emphasis on local seafood.

XX **Carron**

20 Cameron St ✉ AB39 2HS – ✆ (01569) 760 460 – www.carron-restaurant.co.uk – Closed 2 weeks December-January, Sunday and Monday

Rest – Carte £ 21/30

◆ 1930s Art Deco elegance fully restored to its original splendour. Panelled walls with old mono photos. Sunny front terrace. Popular menus highlighted by daily lobster dishes.

A red **Rest** mention denotes an establishment with an award for culinary excellence, ✿ (star) or ☺ (Bib Gourmand).

SCOTLAND

STORNOWAY – Western Isles Outer Hebrides – 501 A9 – see Lewis and Harris (Isle of)

STRACHUR – Argyll and Bute – 501 E15 – pop. 628 27 B2

Edinburgh 112 mi. – Glasgow 66 mi. – Inverness 162 mi. – Perth 101 mi.

The Creggans Inn

✉ PA27 8BX – ✆ (01369) 860 279 – www.creggans-inn.co.uk

14 rm – †£ 75/95 ††£ 100/140 – 1 suite

Rest – Menu £ 37 (dinner) – Carte £ 20/30

◆ Locally renowned inn, with splendid views over Loch Fyne. Cosy bar with busy pub dining trade and two lounges, one with fine outlook. Individually styled, comfy rooms. Large dining room with wood floor and warm colour scheme.

X **Inver Cottage**

Strathlaclan, Southwest : 6.5 mi. by A 886 on B 8000 ✉ PA27 8BU – ✆ (01369) 860 537 – www.invercottage.co.uk – Closed January-March, Sunday dinner and Monday-Tuesday except Bank Holidays

Rest – Carte £ 21/30

◆ Wonderfully located former crofters' cottage with fine views over loch and mountains. The simple little restaurant, with its own craft shop, serves tasty Scottish based menus.

STRANRAER – Dumfries and Galloway – 501 E19 – pop. 10 851 25 A3

Scotland

Edinburgh 132 mi. – Ayr 51 mi. – Dumfries 75 mi.

to Northern Ireland (Belfast) (Stena Line) (1 h 45 mn) – to Northern Ireland (Belfast) (Stena Line) 4-5 daily (1 h 45 mn/3 h 15 mn)

28 Harbour St ✆ (01776) 702595, stranraertic@visitscotland.com

Creachmore Leswalt, ✆ (01776) 870 245

Logan Botanic Garden★ **AC**, S : 11 mi. by A 77, A 716 and B 7065

at Kirkcolm Northwest : 6 mi. by A 718 – ✉ Stranraer

Corsewall Lighthouse rm, VISA MC AE

Corsewall Point, Northwest : 4.25 mi. by B 738 ✉ DG9 0QG – ☎ (01776) 853 220 – www.lighthousehotel.co.uk – Fax (01776) 854 231

5 rm (dinner included) – †£ 130/150 ††£ 200/280 – 4 suites

Rest – Menu £ 33 (dinner) – Carte £ 20/34

◆ Sensitively converted and family run, a 19C working lighthouse at the mouth of Loch Ryan. Snug bedrooms in traditional fabrics - views of the sea or the windswept promontory. Simple, characterful restaurant with seascapes and old black beams.

STRATHPEFFER – **Highland** – **501** G11 – **pop. 918** **30** C2

Edinburgh 174 mi. – Inverness 18 mi.

Pump Room Museum ☎ (01997) 421415, (June- Sept), info@visitscotland.com

Strathpeffer Spa Golf Course Rd, ☎ (01997) 421 219

Craigvar without rest VISA MC

The Square ✉ IV14 9DL – ☎ (01997) 421 622 – www.craigvar.com – closed 2 weeks mid-November and 20 December-7 January

3 rm – †£ 40/55 ††£ 70/80

◆ Georgian house overlooking main square of pleasant former spa town. Charming owner guarantees an agreeable stay. Bedrooms are crammed with antiques and original fittings.

STRATHYRE – **Stirling** – **501** H15 – ✉ **Callander** Scotland **27** B2

Edinburgh 62 mi. – Glasgow 53 mi. – Perth 42 mi.

The Trossachs★★★ (Loch Katrine★★) SW : 14 mi. by A 84 and A 821 – Hilltop viewpoint★★★ (✻★★★) SW : 16.5 mi. by A 84 and A 821

XX **Creagan House** with rm VISA MC AE

on A 84 ✉ FK18 8ND – ☎ (01877) 384 638 – www.creaganhouse.co.uk – Fax (01877) 384 319 – Closed February, 10-25 November and 24-26 December

5 rm – †£ 70 ††£ 120

Rest – *(Closed Wednesday and Thursday) (dinner only) (booking essential)* Menu £ 30

◆ Personally run baronial dining room in 17C former farmhouse. Concise fixed price menu of fine seasonal Scottish produce; classical dishes prepared with care. 'Smokie and a Pokie,' a speciality. Watch red squirrels in the garden from the cosy bedrooms.

STROMNESS – **Orkney Islands** – **501** K7 – **see Orkney Islands**

STRONTIAN – **Highland** – **501** D13 **29** B3

Edinburgh 139 mi. – Fort William 23 mi. – Oban 66 mi.

Acharacle ☎ (08452) 255121 (April-October), strontian@visitscotland.com

Kilcamb Lodge VISA MC

✉ PH36 4HY – ☎ (01967) 402 257 – www.kilcamblodge.co.uk – Fax (01967) 402 041 – Closed January

10 rm (dinner included) – †£ 151/196 ††£ 248/349

Rest – *(booking essential for non-residents at dinner)* Menu £ 48 (dinner) – Carte lunch approx. £ 22

◆ A spectacular location in 19 acres of lawn and woodland, leading down to a private shore on Loch Sunart. The idyll continues indoors: immaculate bedrooms; thoughtful extras. Savour views from large windows and tuck into roast grouse.

STRUAN – **Highland** – **see Skye (Isle of)**

SWINTON – **Scottish Borders** – **501** N16 – **pop. 472** – ✉ **Duns** **26** D2

Edinburgh 49 mi. – Berwick-upon-Tweed 13 mi. – Glasgow 93 mi. – Newcastle upon Tyne 66 mi.

The Wheatsheaf with rm

Main Street ✉ TD11 3JJ – ☎ (01890) 860 257 – www.wheatsheaf-swinton.co.uk – Fax (01890) 860 688 – Closed 25-26 and 31 December and second week January

10 rm – †£ 65/75 ††£ 98/112 **Rest** – Carte £ 18/38

◆ Solid stone inn overlooking the village green. The bar menu offers light pub classics; the à la carte displays more adventure. Both feature local produce, including meat from nearby farms. Bedrooms are spacious, cosy and well-equipped.

TAIN – Highland – 501 H10 – pop. 4 540 — 30 D2

Edinburgh 191 mi. – Inverness 35 mi. – Wick 91 mi.

Tain Chapel Rd, ☎ (01862) 892 314

Tarbat Portmahomack, ☎ (01862) 871 278

Golf View House without rest

13 Knockbreck Rd ✉ IV19 1BN – ☎ (01862) 892 856 – www.golf-view.co.uk – Fax (01862) 892 856 – 15 march-30 November

5 rm – †£ 45/55 ††£ 65/75

◆ Built as a manse, a local sandstone house overlooking the Firth and the fairways. Bright rooms are well kept and tidy. Lawn and flowers shaded by beech trees.

at Cadboll Southeast : 8.5 mi. by A 9 and B 9165 (Portmahomack rd) off Hilton rd – ✉ Tain

Glenmorangie House

Fearn ✉ IV20 1XP – ☎ (01862) 871 671 – www.theglenmorangiehouse.com – Fax (01862) 871 625 – closed January

9 rm (dinner included) – †£ 195 ††£ 380 – 3 suites

Rest – *(dinner only) (booking essential for non-residents) (communal dining, set menu only)* Menu £ 50 **s**

◆ Restored 17C property owned by the famous distillery. Bedrooms in converted cottages have agreeable modern style. Those in main house, more traditional. Classically based cooking, with Scottish produce to the fore. Relaxed, attentive service from uniformed staff.

TALMINE – Highland – 501 G8 – ✉ Lairg — 30 C1

Edinburgh 245 mi. – Inverness 86 mi. – Thurso 48 mi.

Cloisters without rest

Church Holme ✉ IV27 4YP – ☎ (01847) 601 286 – www.cloistertal.demon.co.uk – Fax (01847) 601 286 – Closed 1 January and 25 December

3 rm – †£ 33 ††£ 55

◆ Pleasantly located guesthouse, with guest areas in converted church. Simple but trim and spotless rooms in annexe; superb views of Rabbit Islands and Tongue Bay.

TARBERT – Western Isles Outer Hebrides – 501 Z10 – see Lewis and Harris (Isle of)

TARBET – Argyll and Bute – 501 F15 – ✉ Arrochar — 27 B2

Edinburgh 88 mi. – Glasgow 42 mi. – Inverness 138 mi. – Perth 78 mi.

Lomond View Country House without rest

on A 82 ✉ G83 7DG – ☎ (01301) 702 477 – www.lomondview.co.uk – Fax (01301) 702 477

3 rm – †£ 50/75 ††£ 80/85

◆ Purpose-built guesthouse which lives up to its name: there are stunning loch views. Spacious sitting room. Light and airy breakfast room. Sizeable, modern bedrooms.

SCOTLAND

TAYVALLICH – Argyll and Bute – 501 D15 – ✉ Lochgilphead 27 B2

Edinburgh 148 mi. – Glasgow 103 mi. – Inverness 157 mi.

Tayvallich Inn

✉ *PA31 8PL – ✆ (01546) 870 282 – www.tayvallichinn.co.uk – Fax (01546) 830 116 – Closed mid-January to mid-February, Monday-Tuesday November to Easter and 25-26 December*

Rest – Carte £ 17/30

◆ Enthusiastically run inn set by a sheltered harbour in a secluded village. Menu offers plenty of seafood in summer and game in the winter, with a good choice of daily specials.

TEANGUE – Highland – see Skye (Isle of)

THORNHILL – Dumfries and Galloway – 501 I18 – pop. 1 633 25 B2

Scotland

Edinburgh 64 mi. – Ayr 44 mi. – Dumfries 15 mi. – Glasgow 63 mi.

Drumlanrig Castle★★ (cabinets★) **AC**, NW : 4 mi. by A 76

Gillbank House without rest

8 East Morton St ✉ DG3 5LZ – ✆ (01848) 330 597 – www.gillbank.co.uk – Fax (01848) 331 713

6 rm – £ 50 £ 70

◆ Victorian stone built personally run house just off town square. Guests' sitting room and airy breakfast room. Spacious, well-furnished bedrooms with bright décor.

THURSO – Highland – 501 J8 – pop. 7 737 Scotland 30 D1

Edinburgh 289 mi. – Inverness 133 mi. – Wick 21 mi.

from Scrabster to Stromness (Orkney Islands) (P and O Scottish Ferries) (2 h)

Riverside ✆ (0845) 2255121 (April-October), thurso@visitscotland.com

Newlands of Geise, ✆ (01847) 893 807

Strathy Point★ (★★★) W : 22 mi. by A 836

Forss House

Forss, West : 5.5 mi. on A 836 ✉ KW14 7XY – ✆ (01847) 861 201 – www.forsshousehotel.co.uk – Fax (01847) 861 301 – Closed 24 December-3 January

14 rm – £ 110 £ 160 **Rest** – *(dinner only)* Carte £ 29/39

◆ Traditional décor sets off the interior of this 19C house, smoothly run in a friendly style. Peaceful location. Annexed rooms are the more contemporary. Vast choice of malts in restaurant bar.

Murray House

1 Campbell St ✉ KW14 7HD – ✆ (01847) 895 759 – www.murrayhousebb.com – Closed 18 December-11 January

5 rm – £ 25/60 £ 60/70 **Rest** – *(by arrangement)* Menu £ 15

◆ A centrally located and family owned Victorian town house. Pine furnished bedrooms are colourfully decorated and carefully maintained. Modern dining room with home-cooked evening meals.

at Scrabster Northwest : 2.25 mi. on A 9

The Captain's Galley

The Harbour ✉ KW14 7UJ – ✆ (01847) 894 999 – www.captainsgalley.co.uk – Closed Sunday and Monday

Rest – Seafood – *(dinner only) (booking essential)* Menu £ 43

◆ Former ice house and salmon station, boasting a concise menu of unfussy, flavoursome, largely seafood dishes. Landed in the harbour, fish is strictly seasonal and sustainable.

TIGHNABRUAICH – Argyll and Bute – 501 E16 — 27 B3

Edinburgh 113 mi. – Glasgow 63 mi. – Oban 66 mi.

An Lochan

PA21 2BE – (01700) 811 239 – www.anlochan.co.uk – Fax (01700) 811 300 – Closed 2 weeks Christmas

11 rm – £ 110/190 £ 110/190 **Rest** – Carte £ 23/40 **s**

◆ Privately owned 19C hotel with firelit shinty bar, in an unspoilt village overlooking the Kyles of Bute. Deep burgundy walls, vivid landscapes and modernised bedrooms. Formal restaurant with fine loch views. Innovative cooking from a dynamic young team.

TIRORAN – Argyll and Bute – 501 B14 – see Mull (Isle of)

TOBERMORY – Argyll and Bute – 501 B14 – see Mull (Isle of)

TONGUE – Highland – 501 G8 – pop. 552 – Lairg Scotland — 30 C1

Edinburgh 257 mi. – Inverness 101 mi. – Thurso 43 mi.

Cape Wrath★★★ (★★) W : 44 mi. (including ferry crossing) by A 838 – Ben Loyal★★, S : 8 mi. by A 836 – Ben Hope★ (★★★) SW : 15 mi. by A 838 – Strathy Point★ (★★★) E : 22 mi. by A 836 – Torrisdale Bay★ (★★) NE : 8 mi. by A 836

Tongue

Main St IV27 4XD – (01847) 611 206 – www.tonguehotel.co.uk – Fax (01847) 611 345 – Closed 31 January-7 March

18 rm – £ 60/75 £ 100/120 **Rest** – *(bar lunch)* Carte £ 20/37

◆ Former hunting lodge of the Duke of Sutherland overlooking Kyle of Tongue. Smart interiors include intimate bar and beamed lounge. Bedrooms are more contemporary in style. Restaurant with fireplace and antique dressers.

TORRIDON – Highland – 501 D11 – Achnasheen Scotland — 29 B2

Edinburgh 234 mi. – Inverness 62 mi. – Kyle of Lochalsh 44 mi.

Wester Ross★★★

The Torridon

South : 1.5 mi. on A 896 IV22 2EY – (01445) 791 242 – www.thetorridon.com – Fax (01445) 712 253 – Closed 2 January-4 February, Monday and Tuesday November-March

18 rm (dinner included) – £ 153/295 £ 430/505 – 1 suite

Rest – *(bar lunch) (booking essential)* Menu £ 45

◆ Family-owned and run former hunting lodge; remotely set, with wonderful views of Loch Torridon and mountains. Ornate ceilings, peat fires and Highland curios. Some very contemporary bedrooms; others more classic in style. Traditional wood-panelled restaurant uses fine local produce, some from the grounds.

The Torridon Inn

South : 1.5 mi. on A 896 IV22 2EY – (01445) 791 242 – www.thetorridon.com – Fax (01445) 712 253 – April-November

12 rm – £ 87 £ 87 **Rest** – Carte £ 17/31

◆ Peaceful, rural location in grounds of Torridon House. Spacious, functional bedrooms in annexe; the larger ones ideal for families. Characterful, rustic restaurant serving classic pub dishes.

TROON – South Ayrshire – 501 G17 – pop. 14 766 — 25 A2

Edinburgh 77 mi. – Ayr 7 mi. – Glasgow 31 mi.

to Northern Ireland (Larne) (P and O Irish Sea) 2 daily

Troon Municipal Harling Drive, (01292) 312 464

Lochgreen House

Monktonhill Rd, Southwood, Southeast : 2 mi. on B 749 KA10 7EN – (01292) 313 343 – www.costley-hotels.co.uk – Fax (01292) 318 661

37 rm – £ 105/190 £ 175/215 – 1 suite

Rest ***Tapestry*** – see restaurant listing

◆ Attractive, coastal Edwardian house in mature grounds. Lounges exude luxurious country house feel. Large rooms, modern or traditional, have a good eye for welcoming detail.

XXX **Tapestry** – at Lochgreen House Hotel

Monktonhill Rd, Southwood, Southeast : 2 mi. on B 749 ✉ KA10 7EN – ✆ (01292) 313 343 – Fax (01292) 318 661

Rest – Carte £ 25/43

◆ Spacious dining room with baronial feel. Elegant chandeliers; large pottery cockerels. Classical, modern cooking, with a strong Scottish base.

at Loans East : 2 mi. on A 759 – ✉ Troon

Highgrove House

Old Loans Rd, East : 0.25 mi. on Dundonald rd ✉ KA10 7HL – ✆ (01292) 312 511 – www.costleyhotels.co.uk – Fax (01292) 318 228

9 rm (dinner included) – †£ 90 ††£ 120/145

Rest – Menu £ 20/25 – Carte £ 20/30

◆ Immaculate whitewashed hotel in elevated position, offering superb coastal panorama. Comfy floral bedrooms; 1 and 2 have the best views. Tartan carpets remind you where you are. Large restaurant with floor to ceiling windows and granite coloumns. Popular, long-established menus.

TURNBERRY – South Ayrshire – 501 F18 – ✉ Girvan Scotland 25 A2

Edinburgh 97 mi. – Ayr 15 mi. – Glasgow 51 mi. – Stranraer 36 mi.

Culzean Castle★ **AC** (setting★★★, Oval Staircase★★) NE : 5 mi. by A 719

Turnberry rm, rest

on A 719 ✉ KA26 9LT – ✆ (01655) 331 000 – www.luxurycollection.com/turnberry – Fax (01655) 331 706 – Closed 1-7 and 10-14 January

207 rm – †£ 260/374 ††£ 280/394 – 4 suites

Rest *1906* – *(dinner only)* Carte £ 50/55

Rest *Tappie Toorie* – *(lunch only)* Carte £ 16/28

Rest *Ailsa Bar and Lounge* – Carte £ 25/29

◆ This celebrated Edwardian hotel with panoramic views of the coast and world famous golf courses was fully refurbished in 2009. Extensive spa facilities; luxuriously appointed bedrooms. Classic brasserie in 1906. Informal Tappie Toorie Grill for golfers. All-day dining in Ailsa.

UDNY GREEN – Aberdeenshire 28 D1

London - 554 mi. – Edinburgh 143 mi. – Aberdeen 15 mi. – Arbroath 67 mi.

XX **Eat on the Green**

✉ AB41 7RS – ✆ (01651) 842 337 – www.eatonthegreen.co.uk – Fax (01651) 843 362 – Closed Monday, Tuesday and Saturday lunch

Rest – Menu £ 22 (lunch)/45 (Saturday dinner) – Carte dinner approx. £ 36

◆ Converted pub by the village green, with snug seating area and two smart dining rooms. Accomplished, flavourful dishes make good use of seasonal, local produce. Polished service.

UIST (Isles of) – 501 X/Y11 – pop. 3 510

from Lochmaddy to Isle of Skye (Uig) (Caledonian MacBrayne Ltd) 1-3 daily (1 h 50 mn)

– from Otternish to Isle of Harris (Leverburgh) (Caledonian MacBrayne Ltd) (1 h 10 mn)

NORTH UIST – Western Isles 29 A2

CARINISH – Western Isles 29 A2

Temple View

✉ HS6 5EJ – ✆ (01876) 580 676 – www.templeviewhotel.co.uk – Fax (01876) 580 682

10 rm – †£ 55/75 ††£ 95/105

Rest – *(bar lunch)* Menu £ 24 **s** – Carte £ 20/27 **s**

◆ Extended Victorian house on main route from north to south. Pleasantly refurbished, it offers a smart sitting room, cosy bar with conservatory, and up-to-date bedrooms. Extensive local specialities the highlight of small dining room.

LANGASS – Western Isles

Langass Lodge

✉ HS6 5HA – ✆ (01876) 580 285 – www.langasslodge.co.uk – Fax (01876) 580 385 – Closed February, 25 December and 1 January
11 rm – †£ 55/80 ††£ 110/130
Rest – *(dinner only and Sunday lunch)* Menu £ 34
◆ Former Victorian shooting lodge boasting superb views, classical comforts, a modish conservatory extension, and bedrooms styled from traditional to clean-lined modernity. Superior cooking of fine Hebridean produce from land and sea.

LOCHMADDY – Western Isles 29 A2

Tigh Dearg

✉ HS6 5AE – ✆ (01876) 500 700 – www.tighdearghotel.co.uk
8 rm – †£ 79/89 ††£ 80/160 **Rest** – Carte £ 17/32
◆ 'The Red House', visible from a long distance, is an outpost of utterly stylish chic. Modish bar matched by well-equipped gym, sauna and steam room, and sleek 21C bedrooms. Hebridean produce well sourced in designer-style restaurant.

ULLAPOOL – Highland – 501 E10 – pop. 1 308 Scotland 30 C2

Edinburgh 215 mi. – Inverness 59 mi.
to Isle of Lewis (Stornoway) (Caledonian MacBrayne Ltd) (2 h 40 mn)
20 Argyle St ✆ (0845) 2255121, ullapool@visitscotland.com
Town★
Wester Ross★★★ - Loch Broom★★. Falls of Measach★★, S : 11 mi. by A 835 and A 832 - Corrieshalloch Gorge★, SE : 10 mi. by A 835 – Northwards to Lochinver★★, Morefield (←★★ of Ullapool), ←★ Loch Broom

Point Cottage without rest

22 West Shore St ✉ IV26 2UR – ✆ (01854) 612 494 – www.pointcottage.co.uk – March-October
3 rm – †£ 30/60 ††£ 50/70
◆ Converted fisherman's cottage of 18C origin. Rooms in bright modern fabrics enjoy beautiful views across Loch Broom to the hills. Substantial breakfasts. Convenient for ferry.

Ardvreck without rest

Morefield Brae, Northwest : 2 mi. by A 835 ✉ IV26 2TH – ✆ (01854) 612 028 – www.smoothhound.co.uk/hotels – Fax (01854) 613 000 – March-October
10 rm – †£ 35/70 ††£ 70/80
◆ Peacefully located house boasting fine views of loch and mountains. Well appointed breakfast room with splendid vistas. Spacious rooms: some with particularly fine outlooks.

Tanglewood House

on A 835 ✉ IV26 2TB – ✆ (01854) 612 059 – www.tanglewoodhouse.co.uk – Closed Christmas, New Year and Easter
3 rm – †£ 80 ††£ 110
Rest – *(by arrangement, communal dining)* Menu £ 36
◆ Blissfully located guesthouse on heather covered headland. Drawing room has a 20 foot window overlooking loch. Homely, traditional rooms, all with vistas. Home cooked meals make use of local produce.

UNST (Isle of) – Shetland Islands – 501 R1 – see Shetland Islands

URQUHART – Moray – see Elgin

VEENSGARTH – Shetland Islands – see Shetland Islands (Mainland)

WALKERBURN – Scottish Borders – pop. 647 **26** C2

Edinburgh 30 mi. – Galashiels 23 mi. – Peebles 8 mi.

Windlestraw Lodge

Tweed Valley, on A 72 ✉ EH43 6AA – ✆ (01896) 870 636 – www.windlestraw.co.uk – Fax (01896) 870 639 – closed 2 weeks Spring, 1 week Autumn, Christmas and New Year

6 rm (dinner included) – £ 125 £ 230/270

Rest – *(dinner only) (booking essential for non-residents)* Menu £ 43

◆ Edwardian country house in picturesque Tweed Valley: lovely views guaranteed. Period style lounges serviced by well-stocked bar. Half the good-sized rooms enjoy the vista. Linen-clad dining room.

WATERNISH – Highland – 501 A11 – see Skye (Isle of)

WESTRAY (Isle of) – Orkney Islands – 501 K/L6 – see Orkney Islands

WHITING BAY – North Ayrshire – 501 E17 – see Arran (Isle of)

WICK – Highland – 501 K8 – pop. 9 713 Scotland **30** D1

Edinburgh 282 mi. – Inverness 126 mi.

Wick Airport : ✆ (01955) 602215, N : 1 m

Whitechapel Rd ✆ (0845) 2255121, info@visitscotland.com

Reiss, ✆ (01955) 602 726

Duncansby Head★ (Stacks of Duncansby★★) N : 14 mi. by A 9 – Grey Cairns of Camster★ (Long Cairn★★) S : 17 mi. by A 9 – The Hill O'Many Stanes★, S : 10 mi. by A 9

The Clachan without rest

13 Randolph Place, South Rd, South : 0.75 mi. on A 99 ✉ KW1 5NJ – ✆ (01955) 605 384 – www.theclachan.co.uk – Closed Christmas and New Year

3 rm – £ 50/55 £ 60/65

◆ This detached 1930s house on the town's southern outskirts provides homely en suite accommodation in pastels and floral patterns. Charming owner.

Bord De L'Eau

2 Market St (Riverside) ✉ KW1 4AR – ✆ (01955) 604 400 – Closed first 2 weeks January, 25-26 December, Sunday lunch and Monday

Rest – French – Carte £ 23/35

◆ Totally relaxed little riverside eatery with French owner. Friendly, attentive service of an often-changing, distinctly Gallic repertoire. Keenly priced dishes.

Y. Duhamel/MICHELIN

ABERAERON (Aber Aeron) – Ceredigion – 503 H27 – pop. 1 520 — 33 B3

Cardiff 90 mi. – Aberystwyth 16 mi. – Fishguard 41 mi.

Ty Mawr Mansion Country House

Cilcennin, East : 4.5 mi. by A 482 ✉ SA48 8DB – ✆ (01570) 470 033 – www.tymawrmansion.co.uk – Closed 1-17 January

8 rm – ♦£ 90/180 ♦♦£ 180/320 – 1 suite

Rest – *(Closed Sunday) (dinner only)* Menu £ 25 (Monday-Thursday) – Carte £ 25/45

◆ Grade II listed Georgian stone mansion in 12 acres of grounds. Three sumptuous reception rooms matched by luxurious bedrooms, which are oversized and full of top facilities. Chefs rear pigs for locally renowned restaurant boasting bold edge to cooking.

Llys Aeron without rest

Lampeter Rd, on A 482 ✉ SA46 0ED – ✆ (01545) 570 276 – www.llysaeron.co.uk

3 rm – ♦£ 45/60 ♦♦£ 75/105

◆ Imposing Georgian house on main road. Hearty Aga cooked breakfasts overlooking well established rear walled garden. Comfy lounge; light, airy rooms in clean pastel shades.

3 Pen Cei without rest

3 Quay Parade ✉ SA46 0BT – ✆ (01545) 571 147 – www.pencei.co.uk

5 rm – ♦£ 75/90 ♦♦£ 90/130

◆ Brightly painted, modern-style guest house on harbour front, featuring spacious bedrooms named after nearby rivers. Aeron has bathroom with free-standing bath and large walk-in shower.

Harbourmaster with rm

Quay Par ✉ SA46 0BA – ✆ (01545) 570 755 – www.harbour-master.com – Closed 25 December, Monday lunch (October-May)

13 rm – ♦£ 50/60 ♦♦£ 110/250 **Rest** – Menu £ 18 (lunch) – Carte £ 20/35

◆ Refurbished and enlarged through the acquisition of the adjacent aquarium. Restaurant with Welsh black beef and seafood a feature; more informal bar. Comfortable and brightly decorated bedrooms.

WALES

ABERDOVEY (Aberdyfi) – Gwynedd – 503 H26 – pop. 869 — 32 B2

London 230 mi. – Dolgellau 25 mi. – Shrewsbury 66 mi.

Snowdonia National Park★★★

Llety Bodfor without rest

Bodfor Terrace ✉ LL35 0EA – ✆ (01654) 767 475 – www.lletybodfor.co.uk – Fax (01654) 767 836 – Closed 5-29 December

8 rm – ♦£ 50/105 ♦♦£ 125/160

◆ Two 19C seafront houses, now a guest house with a difference: a relaxed atmosphere prevails but the design is stylish and contemporary. Spacious New England themed bedrooms boast bay views.

at Pennal Northeast : 6.5 mi. on A 493 – ✉ Aberdovey

Penmaendyfi without rest

Cwrt, Southwest : 1.25 mi. by A 493 ✉ SY20 9LD – ✆ (01654) 791 246 – www.penmaendyfi.co.uk – March-October

6 rm – ♦£ 60 ♦♦£ 80/100

◆ Attractive 18C country house in quiet rural location, with distant estuary views, beautiful wooden veranda and comfy lounge. Spacious bedrooms boast sleigh beds and smart modern bathrooms.

ABERGAVENNY (Y-Fenni) – Monmouthshire – 503 L28 – pop. 14 055 — 33 C4

London 163 mi. – Cardiff 31 mi. – Gloucester 43 mi. – Newport 19 mi.

Swan Meadow, Monmouth Rd ✆ (01873) 853254, abergavennyic@breconbeacons.org

Monmouthshire Llanfoist, ✆ (01873) 852 606

Town★ - St Mary's Church★ (Monuments★★)

Brecon Beacons National Park★★ – Blaenavon Ironworks★, SW : 5 mi. by A 465 and B 4246. Raglan Castle★ **AC**, SE : 9 mi. by A 40

Llansantffraed Court

Llanvihangel Gobion, Southeast : 6.5 mi. by A 40 and B 4598 off old Raglan rd ✉ NP7 9BA – ✆ (01873) 840 678 – www.llch.co.uk – Fax (01873) 840 674

21 rm – †£ 86/115 ††£ 115/175 **Rest** – Menu £ 20/30 – Carte £ 29/36

◆ Historic country house beside ornamental pond and fountain, in 19 acres of grounds. Large lounges and bar. Dark-hued bedrooms with smart bathrooms: room 19 has double aspect mountain/valley views. Classical menus showcase local ingredients.

The Angel

15 Cross St ✉ NP7 5EN – ✆ (01873) 857 121 – www.angelhotelabergavenny.com – Fax (01873) 858 059

32 rm – †£ 65/100 ††£ 130 **Rest** – Carte £ 22/38

◆ Georgian former coaching inn run by friendly, attentive team. Smart exterior and very modern guest areas: traditionally styled bedrooms undergoing refurbishment. Contemporary bar and restaurant with courtyard offer extensive bistro menu and popular afternoon teas.

The Hardwick

Old Raglan Rd, Southeast : 2 mi. by A 40 on B 4598 ✉ NP7 9AA – ✆ (01873) 854 220 – www.thehardwick.co.uk – Closed 25-26 December, Sunday dinner and Monday (except bank holidays)

Rest – *(booking essential)* Menu £ 21 (lunch) – Carte £ 29/40

◆ Simple, unassuming, whitewashed pub with mountain views. Simplicity and the use of local produce are paramount here and lengthy menus feature influences from Britain and the Med.

at Llanddewi Skirrid Northeast : 3.25 mi. on B 4521

The Walnut Tree (Shaun Hill)

✉ NP7 8AW – ✆ (01873) 852 797 – www.thewalnuttreeinn.co.uk – Closed 1 week Christmas, Sunday and Monday

Rest – *(booking essential)* Menu £ 27 (lunch) – Carte £ 35/38

Spec. Tête de veau boudin with sweetbreads. Turbot with clams and chive beurre blanc. Orange and almond cake.

◆ A reinvigorated, long-standing Welsh institution set in a valley. Welcoming staff and always bustling with regulars. It takes skill to make cooking look this simple; it's seasonal and each dish bursts with flavour.

at Cross Ash Northeast : 8.25 mi. on B 4521

1861

✉ NP7 8PB – ✆ (0845) 388 1861 – www.18-61.co.uk – Closed first week January, Sunday dinner and Monday

Rest – Menu £ 22/30 – Carte £ 30/38

◆ Former pub; now a cosy restaurant, with contemporary furnishings and exposed brick fireplace. Classically based menus make use of good quality local produce. Personable service.

at Nant-Y-Derry Southeast : 6.5 mi. by A 40 off A 4042 – ✉ Abergavenny

The Foxhunter

✉ NP7 9DD – ✆ (01873) 881 101 – www.thefoxhunter.com – Closed 25-26 December, 1 January, Sunday dinner, Monday

Rest – Menu £ 25 (lunch) – Carte £ 29/36

◆ Former station master's house with fresh, bright feel, flagstone floors and wood burning stoves. Dishes range in style from classic British to fusion and come in large, hearty portions.

at Llanover South : 5.5 mi. by A 40 off A 4042

Llansabbath Country House without rest

✉ NP7 9BY – ✆ (01873) 840 068 – www.llansabbathcountryhouse.co.uk – Closed 25 December

5 rm – †£ 50 ††£ 80

◆ Former farmhouse renovated in a modern style. Large lounge with wood burning stove; conservatory breakfast with eggs from hens who roam the garden. Comfortable bedrooms have all mod cons.

WALES

ABERGELE – Conwy – 503 J24 – pop. 17 574 32 C1

London 229 mi. – Cardiff 182 mi. – Liverpool 51 mi. – Manchester 75 mi.

at Betws-yn-Rhos Southwest : 4.25 mi. by A 548 on B 5381

Ffarm Country House
LL22 8AR – (01492) 680 448 – www.ffarmcountryhouse.co.uk – Closed Christmas
8 rm – £ 85/95 £ 135
Rest – *(dinner only Thursday-Saturday)* Menu £ 30
◆ Gothic-style country house; stylish, comfortable and personally run. Beautiful tiled hall with vaulted wood ceiling. Tastefully furnished bedrooms named after wine regions. Seasonal menus make the most of local produce; open to non-residents as well as guests.

ABERSOCH – Gwynedd – 502 G25 – pop. 805 – Pwllheli 32 B2

London 265 mi. – Caernarfon 28 mi. – Shrewsbury 101 mi.

Golf Rd, (01758) 712 636

Lleyn Peninsula★★ – Plas-yn-Rhiw★ **AC**, W : 6 mi. by minor roads. Bardsey Island★, SW : 15 mi. by A 499 and B 4413 – Mynydd Mawr★, SW : 17 mi. by A 499, B 4413 and minor roads

XX **Venetia** with rm
Lon Sarn Bach LL53 7EB – (01758) 713 354 – www.venetiawales.com – Closed 25-26 December and 1 January-14 February
5 rm – £ 103/133 £ 118/148
Rest – Italian – *(dinner only)* Carte £ 25/35
◆ Smart, modernised detached house boasts minimalist bar/lounge and stark white dining room. Classic Italian dishes, well presented in a distinctly modern style, with fish a speciality. Friendly, efficient service. Comfortable, well-equipped bedrooms.

WALES

at Bwlchtocyn South : 2 mi. – Pwllheli

Porth Tocyn
LL53 7BU – (01758) 713 303 – www.porth-tocyn-hotel.co.uk – Fax (01758) 713 538 – Easter-October
17 rm – £ 68/80 £ 130/170, £ 6
Rest – *(bar lunch Monday-Saturday, buffet lunch Sunday)* Menu £ 40
◆ Set high on the headland overlooking Cardigan Bay, a traditional hotel in the family for 3 generations. Comfy lounges. Mix of classic and more modern bedrooms; some with balconies/sea views. Modern menus display interesting, soundly executed dishes.

ABERYSTWYTH (Aberestuuth) – Ceredigion – 503 H26 – pop. 15 935 32 B2

London 238 mi. – Chester 98 mi. – Fishguard 58 mi. – Shrewsbury 74 mi.

Terrace Rd (01970) 612125, aberystwythtic@ceredigion.gov.uk

Bryn-y-Mor, (01970) 615 104

Town★★ - The Seafront★ – National Library of Wales (Permanent Exhibition★)

Vale of Rheidol★★ (Railway★★ **AC**) - St Padarn's Church★, SE : 1 mi. by A 44. Devil's Bridge (Pontarfynach)★, E : 12 mi. by A 4120 – Strata Florida Abbey★ **AC** (West Door★), SE : 15 mi. by B 4340 and minor rd

Gwesty Cymru
19 Marine Ter SY23 2AZ – (01970) 612 252 – www.gwestycymru.com – Closed 1 week at Christmas
8 rm – £ 65/100 £ 115/135 **Rest** – *(by arrangement)* Carte £ 29/35
◆ Georgian Grade II listed building on promenade, with front terrace and sea views. Thoughtfully designed bedrooms are colour themed in décor and furnishings; impressive bathrooms. Small dining room serves traditional dishes made from local produce.

ANGLESEY (Isle of) (Sir Ynys Môn) – Isle of Anglesey – 503 G/H24 – pop. 68 900

London 253 mi. – Birkenhead 74 mi. – Holyhead 25 mi.
Baron Hill, ☎ (01248) 810 231
Town★★ - Castle★ AC
Anglesey★★ – Penmon Priory★, NE : 4 mi. by B 5109 and minor roads. Plas Newydd★ AC, SW : 7 mi. by A 545 and A 4080

BEAUMARIS – Isle of Anglesey – ✉ Isle Of Anglesey 32 B1

Ye Olde Bull's Head Inn

Castle St ✉ LL58 8AP – ☎ (01248) 810 329 – www.bullsheadinn.co.uk – Fax (01248) 811 294 – Closed 25-26 December and 1 January
13 rm – 🚹£ 80/90 🚹🚹£ 110/160
Rest *The Loft* – see restaurant listing
Rest *Brasserie* – *(bookings not accepted)* Carte £ 15/28
◆ Welcoming 17C coaching inn; its characterful, beamed bar a marked contrast to the chic, stylish lounge. Bedrooms, named after Dickens' characters, also mix the traditional with the contemporary. The Brasserie offers a wide-ranging menu with a Mediterranean slant.

The Townhouse without rest

10 Castle St ✉ LL58 8AP – ☎ (01248) 810 329 – www.townhousewales.co.uk – Fax (01248) 811 294 – Closed 25-26 December and 1 January
13 rm – 🚹£ 80/90 🚹🚹£ 100/160
◆ Stylish 16C townhouse, with striking bedrooms boasting an extensive range of modern facilities, including media hubs. Comprehensive continental breakfast served in your room.

Cleifiog without rest

Townsend ✉ LL58 8BH – ☎ (01248) 811 507 – www.cleifiogbandb.co.uk – Closed Christmas-New Year
3 rm – 🚹£ 65 🚹🚹£ 95
◆ Attractively furnished 16C seafront townhouse, with neat garden and lovely outlook. Owner's art and needlework feature throughout, along with antique tapestries. Great levels of comfort.

The Loft – at Ye Olde Bull's Head Inn

Castle St ✉ LL58 8AP – ☎ (01248) 810 329 – www.bullsheadinn.co.uk – Fax (01248) 811 294 – Closed 25-26 December, 1 January and Sunday dinner
Rest – *(dinner only and Sunday lunch)* Menu £ 40
◆ Stylish, contemporary restaurant with exposed beams, bold crimson end walls and linen-clad tables. Well-presented, ambitious cooking uses many local ingredients. Efficient service.

BENLLECH – Isle of Anglesey – pop. 2 306 – ✉ Isle Of Anglesey 32 B1

Hafod without rest

Amlwch Rd ✉ LL74 8SR – ☎ (01248) 853 092 – Closed 25 December
3 rm – 🚹£ 45/50 🚹🚹£ 65
◆ Sensitively renovated 19C house with lawned garden and views of sea and bays. Comfortably finished bedrooms, well maintained by the charming owner.

CEMAES (Cemais) – Isle of Anglesey – ✉ Isle Of Anglesey 32 B1

Hafod Country House without rest

South : 0.5 mi. on Llanfechell rd ✉ LL67 ODS – ☎ (01407) 711 645 – April-October
3 rm – 🚹£ 40 🚹🚹£ 65
◆ Pleasant Edwardian guesthouse with very welcoming owner on outskirts of picturesque fishing village. Comfortable sitting room. The bedrooms are in immaculately kept order.

LLANERCHYMEDD – Isle of Anglesey – ✉ Isle Of Anglesey — 32 B1

Llwydiarth Fawr without rest

North : 1 mi. on B 5111 ✉ LL71 8DF – ✆ (01248) 470 321 – www.llwydiarthfawr.com – Closed Christmas

4 rm – †£ 40/65 ††£ 85/100

◆ Sizeable Georgian house in 1,000 acres of farmland. Country house feel with impressive hallway/landing, plush drawing room and fine views. Individually decorated bedrooms boast extras.

MENAI BRIDGE (Porthaethwy) – Isle of Anglesey – ✉ Isle Of Anglesey — 32 B1

Neuadd Lwyd

Penmynydd, Northwest : 4.75 mi. by B 5420 on Eglwys St Gredifael Church rd ✉ LL61 5BX – ✆ (01248) 715 005 – www.neuaddlwyd.co.uk – Closed 22 November-21 January

4 rm (dinner included) – †£ 135/195 ††£ 185/245

Rest – *(by arrangement)* Menu £ 39

◆ This fine 19C rectory, set in a beautiful rural location, has had a sleek and stylish refit, lending it a luxurious air. Elegant interiors are matched by stunning bedrooms. Freshest Welsh ingredients incorporated into tasty evening meals.

RHOSCOLYN – Isle of Anglesey – ✉ Isle Of Anglesey

The White Eagle

✉ LL65 2NJ – ✆ (01407) 860 267 – www.white-eagle.co.uk – Fax (01407) 861 623 – Closed 25 December

Rest – Carte £ 20/27

◆ Spacious pub with cosy bar, modern dining room, decked terrace and sea views. Monthly menu offers everything from sandwiches and salads, to pub classics and more sophisticated fare.

VALLEY – Isle of Anglesey – ✉ Isle Of Anglesey

Cleifiog Uchaf

off Spencer Rd ✉ LL65 3AB – ✆ (01407) 741 888 – www.cleifioguchaf.co.uk

6 rm – †£ 64/74 ††£ 105/145 – 2 suites

Rest – *(closed Sunday and Monday) (dinner only)* Carte £ 19/51

◆ Restored 16C longhouse, simply and stylishly furnished. Bedrooms boast character beds and every mod con including flat screens, DVDs and Roberts radios. Slate-floored, bistro-style dining room for classical combinations of locally sourced, seasonal ingredients.

WALES

BALA – Gwynedd – pop. 1 980 – ✉ Gwynedd — 32 B2

London - 213 mi. – Cardiff 160 mi. – Liverpool 75 mi. – Stoke-on-Trent 84 mi.

Abercelyn Country House without rest

Llanycil, Southwest : 1 mi. on A 494 ✉ LL23 7YF – ✆ (01678) 521 109 – www.abercelyn.co.uk – Closed January and December

3 rm – †£ 55/60 ††£ 80/90

◆ Attractive former rectory, with pleasant garden and brook. Warmly decorated bedrooms, named after surrounding mountains. Eggs from owners' hens, plus homemade jams and breads.

BARMOUTH (Abermaw) – Gwynedd – 502 H25 – pop. 2 306 — 32 B2

London 231 mi. – Chester 74 mi. – Dolgellau 10 mi. – Shrewsbury 67 mi.

The Station, Station Rd ✆ (01341) 280787, (summer only) barmouth.tic@gwynedd.gov.uk

Town★ - Bridge★ **AC**

Snowdonia National Park★★★

Llwyndu Farmhouse

Northwest : 2.25 mi. on A 496 ✉ *LL42 1RR – ✆ (01341) 280 144 – www.llwyndu-farmhouse.co.uk*

7 rm – **†**£ 50/110 **††**£ 100/110 **Rest** – *(by arrangement)* Menu £ 29

◆ Grade II listed 16C farmhouse below the Rhinog Mountains, overlooking Cardigan Bay. Traditional beams, inglenooks and quirky, characterful features abound. Using quality Welsh produce, candlelit dinners combine the traditional with the modern.

BARRY (Barri) – The Vale of Glamorgan – 503 K29 – pop. 50 661 — 33 C4

London 167 mi. – Cardiff 10 mi. – Swansea 39 mi.

The Promenade, The Triangle, Barry Island ✆ (01446) 747171, barrytic@valeofglamorgan.gov.uk

RAF St Athan St Athan Clive Rd, ✆ (01446) 751 043

Egerton Grey Country House

Southwest : 4.5 mi. by B 4226 and A 4226 and Porthkerry rd via Cardiff Airport ✉ *CF62 3BZ – ✆ (01446) 711 666 – www.egertongrey.co.uk – Fax (01446) 711 690*

10 rm – **†**£ 90/150 **††**£ 140/180 **Rest** – Menu £ 17/32 **s**

◆ A secluded country house with a restful library and drawing room. Part Victorian rectory. Bedrooms overlook gardens with views down to Porthkerry Park and the sea. Intimate dining room with paintings and antiques.

BEAUMARIS – Isle of Anglesey – 504 H24 – see Anglesey (Isle of)

BEDDGELERT (Bedkelerd) – Gwynedd – 502 H24 – pop. 535 — 32 B1

London 249 mi. – Caernarfon 13 mi. – Chester 73 mi.

Snowdonia National Park★★★ - Aberglaslyn Pass★, S : 1.5 mi. on A 498

Sygun Fawr Country House

Northeast : 0.75 mi. by A 498 ✉ *LL55 4NE – ✆ (01766) 890 258 – www.sygunfawr.co.uk – Closed January*

11 rm – **†**£ 40/60 **††**£ 105

Rest – *(Closed Sunday-Monday to non-residents) (dinner only) (booking essential)* Menu £ 26

◆ Part 16C stone built house in Gwynant Valley. Superbly located, an elevated spot which affords exceptional views of Snowdon, particularly from double deluxe rooms. Dine in conservatory extension or traditional room in house.

BENLLECH – Isle of Anglesey – 502 H24 – see Anglesey (Isle of)

BETWS GARMON – Gwynedd — 32 B1

Cardiff 194 mi. – Betws-y-Coed 25 mi. – Caernarfon 5 mi.

Betws Inn

Northwest : 1 mi. on A 4085 ✉ *LL54 7YY – ✆ (01286) 650 324 – www.betws-inn.co.uk*

3 rm – **†**£ 50/70 **††**£ 70/90 **Rest** – *(by arrangement)* Carte £ 20/25

◆ Former village coaching inn with characterful beamed lounge. After a day's trekking, sleep in well-priced, good sized rooms with quality wood furniture and smart fabrics. Home-cooked local produce proudly served in rustic dining room.

BETWS-Y-COED – Conwy – 502 I24 – pop. 848 — 32 B1

London 226 mi. – Holyhead 44 mi. – Shrewsbury 62 mi.

Royal Oak Stables ✆ (01690) 710426, tic.byc@eryri-npa.gov.uk

Clubhouse, ✆ (01690) 710 556

Town★

Snowdonia National Park★★★. Blaenau Ffestiniog★ (Llechwedd Slate Caverns★ **AC**), SW : 10.5 mi. by A 470 – The Glyders and Nant Ffrancon (Cwm Idwal★), W : 14 mi. by A 5

WALES

Tan-y-Foel Country House

East : 2.5 mi. by A 5, A 470 and Capel Garmon rd on Llanwrst rd ✉ LL26 ORE – ✆ (01690) 710 507 – www.tyfhotel.co.uk – Fax (01690) 710 681 – Closed December and restricted opening in January

6 rm – †£ 110/155 ††£ 145/240

Rest – *(dinner only) (booking essential)* Menu £ 45

◆ Personally run, part 16C country house, stylishly decorated in modern vein. Stunning views of Vale of Conwy and Snowdonia. Lovely rooms revel in the quality and elegance of the establishment. Contemporary rear room makes up the restaurant.

Bryn Bella without rest

Lôn Muriau, Llanrwst Rd, Northeast : 1 mi. by A 5 on A 470 ✉ LL24 0HD – ✆ (01690) 710 627 – www.bryn-bella.co.uk

5 rm – †£ 65/75 ††£ 65/75

◆ Comfy, well-kept guest house with pleasant garden, valley views and every conceivable extra in the bedrooms. Keen owners provide reliable local info. Fresh, tasty eggs from their rescued hens.

Pengwern without rest

Allt Dinas, Southeast : 1.5 mi. on A 5 ✉ LL24 0HF – ✆ (01690) 710 480 – www.snowdoniaaccommodation.com – Closed Christmas

3 rm – †£ 60 ††£ 72/82

◆ Former Victorian artist 'colony' with a comfy, homely and stylish lounge, warmly decorated breakfast room and individually appointed bedrooms, two with superb valley vistas.

Llannerch Goch without rest

Capel Garmon, East : 2 mi. by A 5 and A 470 on Capel Gorman rd ✉ LL26 0RL – ✆ (01690) 710 261 – www.betwsycoed.co.uk – Easter-September

3 rm – †£ 45/48 ††£ 68/72

◆ Remotely located 17C vicarage boasting pleasant mountain views. Rustic wood-furnished interior; pleasant sun lounge overlooking garden and stream. Brightly coloured country-style bedrooms.

WALES

at Penmachno **Southwest : 4.75 mi. by A 5 on B 4406 – ✉ Betws-Y-Coed**

Penmachno Hall

on Ty Mawr rd ✉ LL24 0PU – ✆ (01690) 760 410 – www.penmachnohall.co.uk – Fax (01690) 760 410 – Closed Christmas-New Year

3 rm – †£ 90 ††£ 90

Rest – *(by arrangement, communal dining)* Menu £ 35

◆ Former rectory built in 1862 with neat garden; super country setting. Sunny morning room where breakfast is served. Modern, bright bedrooms personally styled by the owners. Tasty home-cooking in deep burgundy communal dining room.

BETWS-YN-RHOS – Conwy – 502 J24 – see Abergele

BODUAN – Gwynedd – see Pwllheli

BONVILSTON (Tresimwn) – The Vale of Glamorgan – 503 J29 — 33 C4

London 164 mi. – Cardiff 9 mi. – Swansea 25 mi.

The Great Barn without rest

Lillypot, Northwest : 1 mi. by A 48 off Tre-Dodridge rd ✉ CF5 6TR – ✆ (01446) 781 010 – www.greatbarn.com – Fax (01446) 781 185

6 rm – †£ 45/50 ††£ 75/85

◆ Converted corn barn, personally run in simple country home style. Pleasant antiques, pine and white furniture in rooms. Great traditional breakfasts; relax in conservatory.

BRECON – Powys – 503 J28 – pop. 7 901 — 33 C3

London 171 mi. – Cardiff 40 mi. – Carmarthen 31 mi. – Gloucester 65 mi.

Cattle Market Car Park ✆ (01874) 622485, brectic@powys.gov.uk

Cradoc, Penoyre Park, ✆ (01874) 623 658

Newton Park Llanfaes, ✆ (01874) 622 004

Town★ - Cathedral★ **AC** – Penyclawdd Court★

Brecon Beacons National Park★★. Llanthony Priory★★, S : 8 mi. of Hay-on-Wye by B 4423 - Dan-yr-Ogof Showcaves★ **AC**, SW : 20 mi. by A 40 and A 4067 – Pen-y-Fan★★, SW : by A 470

Canal Bank without rest

Southeast : 0.5 mi. by B 4601 turning right over bridge onto unmarked road after petrol station ✉ LD3 7HG – ✆ (01874) 623 464 – www.accommodation-breconbeacons.co.uk – Closed 24-25 December

3 rm – †£ 85 ††£ 90

◆ Delightfully stylish and peaceful 18C canalside cottage. Charming garden with pergola and access to Usk. Organic breakfasts. Immaculate rooms with extra attention to detail.

Cantre Selyf without rest

5 Lion St ✉ LD3 7AU – ✆ (01874) 622 904 – www.cantreselyf.co.uk – Fax (01874) 625 951 – Closed Christmas and New Year

3 rm – †£ 60 ††£ 82

◆ Charming, centrally located 17C townhouse with peaceful garden, period bedrooms and modern shower rooms. Contemporary colours blend with original Georgian features and antiques throughout.

Felin Glais

Aberyscir, West : 4 mi. by Upper Chapel rd off Cradoc Golf Course rd turning right immediately after bridge ✉ LD3 9NP – ✆ (01874) 623 107 – www.felinglais.co.uk – Fax (01874) 623 107

4 rm – †£ 75 ††£ 85

Rest – *(by arrangement, communal dining)* Menu £ 35

◆ 17C house and barn in tranquil hamlet. Spacious interior with pleasant 'lived in' feel; rooms filled with books and knick-knacks. Homely bedrooms; good toiletries; towels/bedding from Harrods. Lengthy menu of modern classics: order dinner two days ahead.

The Felin Fach Griffin with rm

Felin Fach, Northeast : 4.75 mi. by B 4602 off A 470 ✉ LD3 0UB – ✆ (01874) 620 111 – www.felinfachgriffin.co.uk – Closed 1 week January and 25 December

7 rm – †£ 70/85 ††£ 115/150

Rest – Menu £ 19/28 – Carte £ 30/38

◆ Rather unique pub with extremely laid back atmosphere. Following the motto "simple things, done well", dishes are straightforward, tasty and arrive in refined, well presented portions. Bedrooms boast super-comfy beds and excellent bedding.

BRIDGEND (Pen-y-Bont) – Bridgend – 503 J29 – pop. 39 429 — 33 B4

London 177 mi. – Cardiff 20 mi. – Swansea 23 mi.

Bridgend Designer Outlet Village, The Derwen, junction 36, M 4 ✆ (01656) 654906, bridgendtic@bridgend.gov.uk

at Southerndown Southwest : 5.5 mi. by A 4265 on B 4524 – ✉ Vale Of Glamorgan

La Plie

Beach Rd ✉ CF32 0RP – ✆ (01656) 880 127 – www.laplierestaurant.co.uk – Fax (01656) 724 282 – Closed 2 weeks October, 1 week January, 26-27 December, Sunday dinner, Monday and lunch Tuesday

Rest – *(booking advisable) (restricted opening in winter)* Menu £ 22/42 **s**

◆ Meaning 'The Plaice'; simple restaurant perched above the cliffs in tiny hamlet. Set course menus display modern, well presented dishes. Seafood, game and offal feature highly.

WALES

at Laleston West : 2 mi. on A 473 – ✉ Bridgend

Great House

High St, on A 473 ✉ CF32 0HP – ✆ (01656) 657 644 – www.great-house-laleston.co.uk – Fax (01656) 668 892 – Closed Christmas and New Year

12 rm – †£ 100 ††£ 145

Rest *Leicester's* – *(Closed Sunday dinner and Bank Holidays)* Menu £ 13 (lunch) **s** – Carte £ 20/34 **s**

◆ 15C Grade II listed building, believed to have been a gift from Elizabeth I to the Earl of Leicester. Personally run - attention to detail particularly evident in the rooms. Comfortable dining courtesy of exposed beams, original windows and owner's personal touches and nuances. Imaginative, seasonal menus using finest local and Welsh produce.

BWLCHTOCYN – Gwynedd – 502 G25 – see Abersoch

CAERNARFON – Gwynedd – 502 H24 – pop. 9 726 32 B1

London 249 mi. – Birkenhead 76 mi. – Chester 68 mi. – Holyhead 30 mi.

Oriel Pendeitsh, Castle St. ✆ (01286) 672232, caernarfon.tic@gwynedd.gov.uk

Aberforeshore Llanfaglan, ✆ (01286) 673 783

Town★★ - Castle★★★ AC

Snowdonia National Park★★★

WALES

Plas Dinas

South : 2 mi. on A 487 ✉ LL54 7YF – ✆ (01286) 830 214 – www.plasdinas.co.uk – Closed Christmas and New Year

10 rm – †£ 89/109 ††£ 99/119

Rest – *(Closed Sunday and Monday) (dinner only) (residents only)* Menu £ 30

◆ Personally run country house: the family home of Lord Snowdon; antiques and portraits abound. Bedrooms range from the simply furnished to a four-poster suite; some are more contemporary, with striking feature walls. Small, regularly changing menu of home-cooked dishes.

at Seion Northeast : 5.5 mi. by A 4086 and B 4366 on Seion rd – ✉ Gwynedd

Ty'n Rhos Country House with rm

Southwest : 0.25 mi. ✉ LL55 3AE – ✆ (01248) 670 489 – www.tynrhos.co.uk – Fax (01248) 671 772

14 rm – †£ 65/110 ††£ 100/180

Rest – *(booking essential at lunch)* Menu £ 23/38

◆ Formal restaurant with contemporary furnishings, French windows and views over Anglesey. Classic country house cooking uses local, seasonal produce to create hearty old favourites. Modern bedrooms, some with views/terraces.

at Groeslon South : 3 mi. by A 487

Y Goeden Eirin

Dolydd, North : 0.5 mi. ✉ LL54 7EF – ✆ (01286) 830 942 – www.ygoedeneirin.co.uk – Closed 20 December-6 January

3 rm – †£ 65/75 ††£ 90/100 **Rest** – *(by arrangement)* Menu £ 28

◆ Attractive stone house between mountains and sea. Picture windows in lounge; interesting artwork and furniture. Charming bedrooms – those in annexe have stable doors and slate-floored bathrooms. Dining room boasts original oils, grand piano and fresh, seasonal dishes.

at Llandwrog South : 4.25 mi. by A 487 on A 499

Rhiwafallen with rm

rest,

North : 1 mi. on A 499 ✉ LL54 5SW – ✆ (01286) 830 172 – www.rhiwafallen.co.uk – Closed 1 week September, 25-26 December, Sunday dinner and Monday

5 rm – †£ 80/120 ††£ 100/150

Rest – *(dinner only and Sunday lunch)* Menu £ 20 (lunch)/35

◆ 19C farmhouse run by enthusiastic young couple; dine in slate-floored conservatory with pleasant view. Seasonal, monthly changing menu; well presented, modern-style dishes based on classic combinations. Stylish, contemporary bedrooms, with bathrooms to match.

CAERSWS – Powys – **502** J26 **32** C2

London 194 mi. – Aberystwyth 39 mi. – Chester 63 mi. – Shrewsbury 42 mi.

at Pontdolgoch Northwest : 1.5 mi. on A 470 – ✉ Newtown

The Talkhouse with rm

✉ *SY17 5JE – ☎ (01686) 688 919 – www.talkhouse.co.uk – Closed first 2 weeks November and 24-26 December*

3 rm – †£ 70 ††£ 125

Rest – *(Closed Monday-Tuesday except for residents and lunch Wednesday and Thursday) (booking essential)* Carte £ 22/30

◆ 17C coaching inn with comfy lounge and cosy bar; dining room overlooks garden. Daily changing menu offers hearty portions and bold flavours. Cottage-style bedrooms with antique furniture; Myfanwy is the best.

Y. Duhamel/MICHELIN

CARDIFF

County: Cardiff
Michelin regional map: **503** K29
London 155 mi.
– Birmingham 110 mi.
– Bristol 46 mi. – Coventry 124 mi.

Population: 292 150
Wales
Map reference: **33** C4

PRACTICAL INFORMATION

Tourist Information

The Old Library, The Hayes, Working St ✆(0870) 1211258, visitor@cardiff.gov.uk

Airport

Cardiff (Wales) Airport : ✆ (01446) 711111, SW : 8 mi. by A 48 AX

Golf Courses

Dinas Powis Old Highwalls, ✆(029) 2051 2727

SIGHTS

In town

City★★★ - National Museum and Gallery★★★ **AC** (Evolution of Wales★★, Picture galleries★★) BY – Castle★ **AC** BZ – Llandaff Cathedral★ AV **B** – Cardiff Bay★ (Techniquest★ **AC**) AX

On the outskirts

Museum of Welsh Life★★ **AC**, St Fagan's, W : 5 mi. by A 4161 AV – Castell Coch★★ **AC**, NW : 5 mi. by A 470 AV

In the surrounding area

Caerphilly Castle★★ **AC**, N : 7 mi. by A 469 AV – Dyffryn Gardens★ **AC**, W : 8 mi. by A 48 AX

CARDIFF BAY

Britannia Quay . . . . **CU** 2
Bute Crescent . . . . **CT** 4
Clarence Embankment . . . **CT** 8
Dudley St . . . . **CU** 9
Hemingway Rd. . . . . **CT** 12
Lloyd George Ave . . . . **CT** 14
Mermaid Quay Shopping Centre. . . . . **CU**
Mount Stuart Square . . . . **CT** 15
Pomeroy St. . . . . **CT** 17
Windsor Esplanade . . . . . **CU** 19

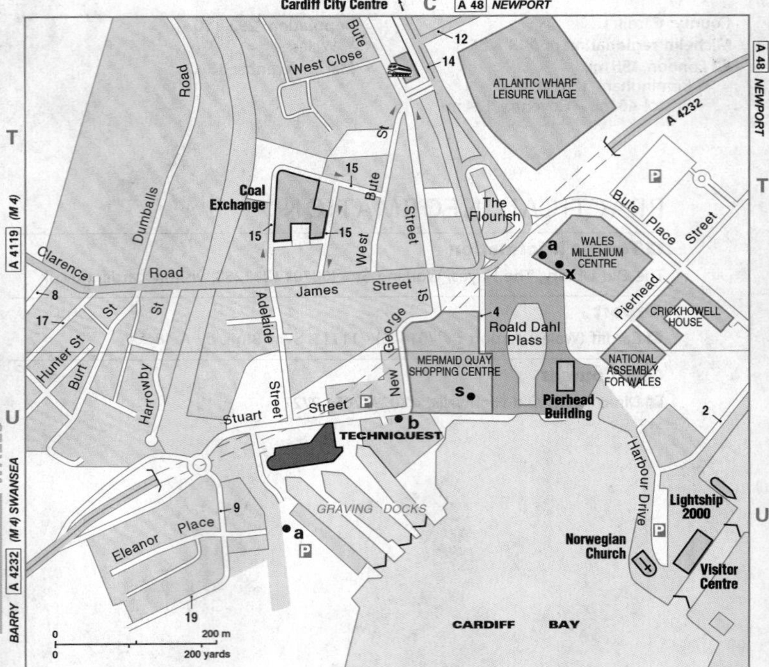

The St David's H. & Spa

Havannah St, Cardiff Bay, South : 1.75 mi. by Bute St
✉ CF10 5SD – ✆ (029) 2045 4045
– www.principal-hayley.com/thestdavids
– Fax (029) 2031 3051 CU**a**

120 rm – ♀£ 290 ♀♀£ 320, ☕ £ 18.50 – 12 suites
Rest *Tides Grill* – Carte £ 25/33

◆ Striking modern hotel with panoramic views across waterfront. High-tech meeting rooms and fitness club. Well-proportioned rooms, all with balconies, in minimalist style. Informal Tides Grill.

Hilton Cardiff

Kingsway ✉ CF10 3HH – ✆ (029) 2064 6300
– www.hilton.co.uk/cardiff
– Fax (029) 2064 6333 BZ**x**

193 rm ☕ – ♀£ 90/360 ♀♀£ 100/370 – 4 suites
Rest *Razzi* – Menu £ 19/27 **s**

◆ State-of-the-art meeting rooms and leisure facilities feature in this imposingly modern corporate hotel. Spacious, comfy bedrooms boast fine views of castle or City Hall. Popular menu in conservatory-style restaurant.

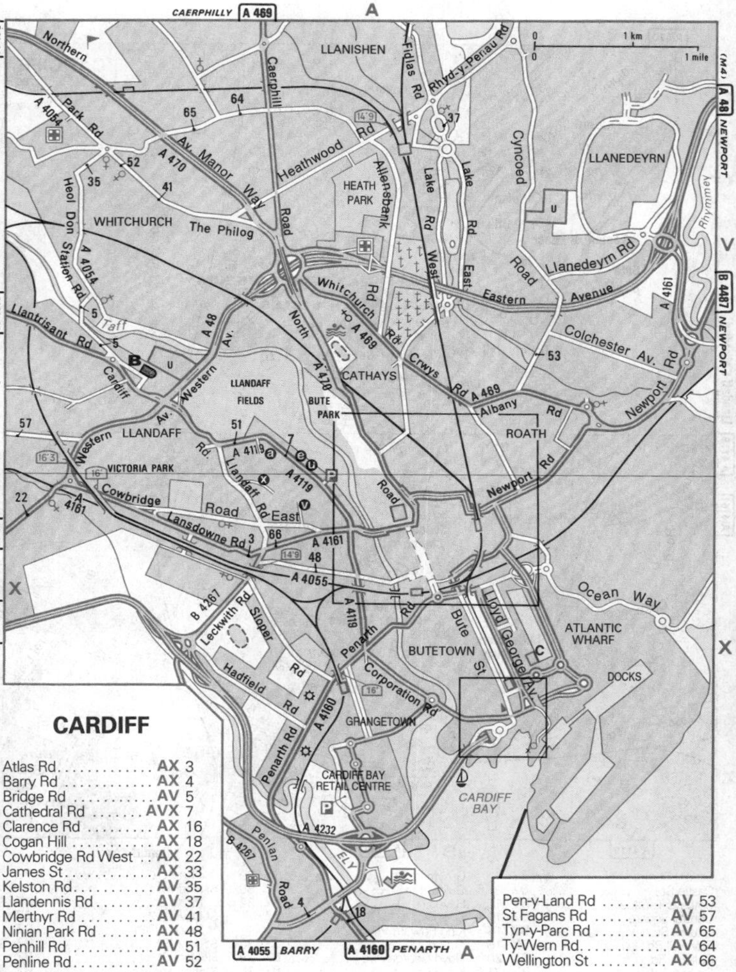

CARDIFF

Street	Grid	No.
Atlas Rd	AX	3
Barry Rd	AX	4
Bridge Rd	AV	5
Cathedral Rd	AVX	7
Clarence Rd	AX	16
Cogan Hill	AX	18
Cowbridge Rd West	AX	22
James St	AX	33
Kelston Rd	AV	35
Llandennis Rd	AV	37
Merthyr Rd	AV	41
Ninian Park Rd	AX	48
Penhill Rd	AV	51
Penline Rd	AV	52
Pen-y-Land Rd	AV	53
St Fagans Rd	AV	57
Tyn-y-Parc Rd	AV	65
Ty-Wern Rd	AV	64
Wellington St	AX	66

Park Plaza

Greyfriars Rd ✉ *CF10 3AL* – ✆ *(029) 2011 1111*
– www.parkplazacardiff.com
– Fax (029) 2011 1112 BY**s**

129 rm – †£ 80/180 ††£ 90/270, ☕ £ 13

Rest ***Laguna Kitchen and Bar*** – see restaurant listing

◆ Fresh, modern hotel: spacious throughout with large lounge and good conference facilities. Vast leisure centre boasts 8 treatment rooms. Contemporary bedrooms range from standard to open-plan suites.

Good food at moderate prices? Look for the Bib Gourmand ☺.

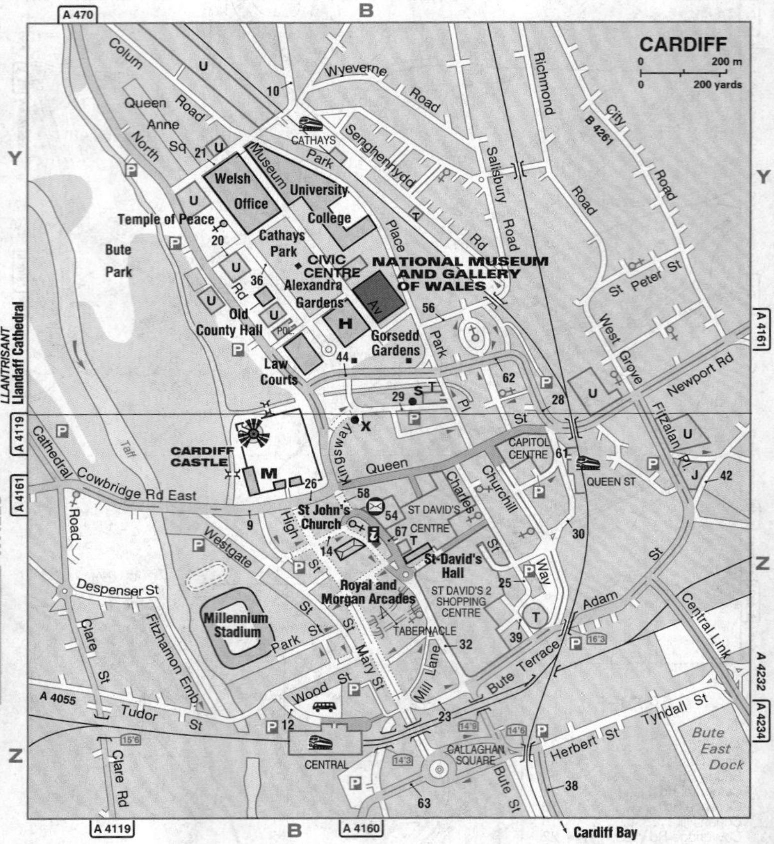

CARDIFF

Capitol Centre . . . . BZ
Castle St . . . . BZ 9
Cathays Terrace . . . . BY 10
Central Square . . . . BZ 12
Church St . . . . BZ 14
City Hall Rd . . . . BY 15
College Rd . . . . BY 20
Corbett Rd . . . . BY 21
Customhouse St . . . . BZ 23
David St . . . . BZ 25
Duke St . . . . BZ 26
Dumfries Pl. . . . . BY 28
Greyfriars Rd . . . . BY 29
Guilford St . . . . BZ 30
Hayes (The) . . . . BZ 32
High St . . . . BZ
King Edward VII Ave . . . . BY 36
Lloyd George Ave . . . . BZ 38
Mary Ann St . . . . BZ 39
Moira Terrace . . . . BZ 42
Nantes (Boulevard de) . . . . BY 44
Queens Arcade Shopping Centre . . . . BZ 54
Queen St . . . . BZ
St Andrews Pl. . . . . BY 56
St-David's 2 . . . . BZ
St David's Centre . . . . BZ
St John St . . . . BZ 58
St Mary St . . . . BZ
Station Terrace . . . . BZ 61
Stuttgarter Strasse . . . . BY 62
Tresillian Way . . . . BZ 63
Working St . . . . BZ 67

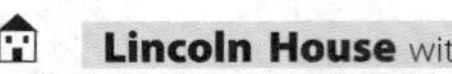

Lincoln House without rest

118-120 Cathedral Rd ✉ CF11 9LQ
– ✆ (029) 2039 5558
– www.lincolnhotel.co.uk
– Fax (029) 2023 0537 AV**e**

23 rm – 🚹£ 65/85 🚹🚹£ 120/150

◆ Two lovingly restored houses with original features still in situ. Comfy bedrooms boast contemporary fabrics and wallpapers; some have period furniture/four-posters. Ultra-modern attic penthouse.

The Town House without rest
70 Cathedral Rd ✉ CF11 9LL – ☎ (029) 2023 9399 – www.thetownhousecardiff.co.uk – Fax (029) 2022 3214 AV**u**
8 rm ☕ – 👤£ 50/70 👥£ 73/83
◆ Carefully restored Victorian house, hospitably run by owners. Light and airy bedrooms have some thoughtful touches and are well appointed: ones at front are the most spacious.

Le Gallois
✉ CF11 9NR – ☎ (029) 2034 1264 – www.legallois.co.uk – Fax (029) 2023 7911 – Closed Christmas-New Year, Sunday dinner and Monday AX**x**
Rest – Menu £ 25/35
◆ Bright and relaxed restaurant where keen owners provide both the friendly service and the assured modern European cooking. Gallic and Welsh combinations with inventive edge.

Laguna Kitchen and Bar – at Park Plaza Hotel
Greyfriars Rd ✉ CF10 3AL – ☎ (029) 2011 1103 – www.lagunakitchenandbar.com BY**s**
Rest – Menu £ 15 (lunch) – Carte £ 17/38
◆ On ground floor of hotel, this smart, modern restaurant serves an intriguing mix of local or international dishes.There's a bar, too, with an area of booths for casual dining.

Woods Brasserie
The Pilotage Building, Stuart St, Cardiff Bay, South : 1.5 mi. by Bute St ✉ CF10 5BW – ☎ (029) 2049 2400 – www.woods-brasserie.com – Fax (029) 2048 1998 – Closed 25 December and Sunday dinner from October-June
Rest – *(booking essential at dinner)* Menu £ 17 (lunch) – Carte £ 25/38 CU**b**
◆ Modern brasserie dishes and European influences from an open kitchen. Bay view from the first-floor terrace. Popular for business lunches and bay visitors in the evening.

Garçon
9 Upper Mermaid Quay, South : 1.5 mi. by Bute St ✉ CF10 5BZ – ☎ (029) 2049 0990 – www.garcon-resto.co.uk – Fax (029) 2048 8516 – Closed 1 January, 24-26 December and Sunday dinner November-March CU**s**
Rest – Menu £ 16 (lunch) – Carte £ 25/42
◆ Classic brasserie style, with leather banquettes, mirrors and a large bar counter. Extensive menus offer filling and flavourful French classics. Friendly, efficient service.

Patagonia
11 Kings Rd ✉ CF11 9BZ – ☎ (029) 2019 0265 – www.patagonia-restaurant.co.uk – Closed 2 weeks Christmas, Sunday and Monday AX**v**
Rest – *(dinner only)* Menu £ 29
◆ Friendly neighbourhood restaurant set over two floors, with brightly coloured walls and eclectic artwork. Short menu offers wholesome and tasty modern European cooking.

The New Conway
53 Conway Rd ✉ CF11 9NW – ☎ (029) 2022 4373 – www.theconway.co.uk
Rest – Carte £ 15/30 AV**a**
◆ Neighbourhood pub with pleasingly simple approach to food which sees fresh, seasonal, local produce used to create tasty pub classics like toad in the hole or apple and raisin crumble.

at Penarth **South : 3 mi. by A 4160 - AX – ✉ Cardiff**

Holm House
Marine Parade Penarth – ☎ (029) 2070 1572 – www.holmhouse.com – Fax (029) 2070 9875
12 rm (dinner included) ☕ – 👤£ 165/185 👥£ 255/415
Rest ***Neale's*** – *(Closed lunch Monday and Tuesday)* Menu £ 19/40
◆ Built in 1920s for son of local shipbuilder. Part Art Deco, part modern styling, displaying flock wallpapers and bold colours; some bedrooms boast feature baths and oversized windows. Restaurant with views to distant Holm Islands; weekly menus of simple, wholesome combinations.

XX **The Olive Tree**

21 Glebe St ✉ CF64 1EE – ✆ (029) 2070 7077 – www.the-olive-tree.net – Closed Sunday dinner and Monday

Rest – *(dinner only and Sunday lunch)* Menu £ 17 – Carte £ 25/37

◆ Rewarding discovery tucked away in the centre of town. Relaxing feel augmented by vivid artwork. Warm, friendly service of good value, seasonal, frequently changing dishes.

CARMARTHEN – Carmarthenshire – **503** H28 – **pop. 14 648** **33** B3

London 219 mi. – Fishguard 47 mi. – Haverfordwest 32 mi. – Swansea 27 mi.

113 Lammas St ✆ (01267) 231557, carmarthentic@carmarthenshire.gov.uk

Kidwelly Castle★ – National Botanic Garden★

at Felingwm Uchaf Northeast : 8 mi. by A 40 on B 4310 – ✉ Carmarthen

Allt y Golau Uchaf without rest

North : 0.5 mi. on B 4310 ✉ SA32 7BB – ✆ (01267) 290 455 – www.alltygolau.com – Fax (01267) 290 743 – Closed 23 December - 2 January

3 rm – †£ 45 ††£ 65

◆ Georgian farmhouse in uplifting elevated position, perfect for walkers. Tranquil garden bursts to life in spring. Home-baked breakfasts of repute. Neat, pretty, compact rooms.

at Nantgaredig East : 5 mi. on A 40 – ✉ Carmarthen

Y Polyn

South : 1 mi. by B4310 on B4300 ✉ SA32 7LH – ✆ (01267) 290 000 – www.ypolyn.co.uk – Closed 25-26 December, 1 January, Sunday dinner, and Monday

Rest – Menu £ 13/29 – Carte £ 20/32

◆ Welcoming dining pub in a great rural location by a stream. Cooking is classically based but with modern touches. Hearty and wholesome dishes, with a greater choice at dinner.

CEMAES – Isle of Anglesey – **502** G23 – see Anglesey (Isle of)

COLWYN BAY (Bae Colwyn) – Conwy – **502** I24 – **pop. 30 269** **32** B1

London 237 mi. – Birkenhead 50 mi. – Chester 42 mi. – Holyhead 41 mi.

Information Point, Cayley Promenade, Rhos-on-Sea ✆ (01492) 548778

18 Abergele Tan-y-Goppa Rd, ✆ (01745) 824 034

9 Old Colwyn Woodland Ave, ✆ (01492) 515 581

Welsh Mountain Zoo★ **AC** (<★)

Bodnant Garden★★ **AC**, SW : 6 mi. by A 55 and A 470

Rathlin Country House without rest

48 Kings Rd, Southwest : 0.25 mi. on B 5113 ✉ LL29 7YH – ✆ (01492) 532 173 – www.rathlincountryhouse.co.uk – Fax (0871) 661 9887 – Closed 24-25 December

3 rm – †£ 65/85 ††£ 85

◆ Large Arts and Crafts house in mature gardens, boasting ornate ceilings, leaded windows and parquet floors. Individually furnished bedrooms; one with steam shower. Good breakfasts.

Pen-y-Bryn

Pen-y-Bryn Rd, Upper Colwyn Bay, Southwest : 1 mi. by B 5113 ✉ LL29 6DD – ✆ (01492) 533 360 – www.penybryn-colwynbay.co.uk

Rest – Carte £ 19/26

◆ Modern, laid back pub set on a residential street; its unassuming façade concealing impressive bay views. Extensive daily menu ranges from pub classics to more adventurous fare.

WALES

at Rhos-on-Sea Northwest : 1 mi. – ✉ Colwyn Bay

Plas Rhos without rest
Cayley Promenade ✉ LL28 4EP – ☎ (01492) 543 698 – www.plasrhos.co.uk – Fax (01492) 540 088 – Closed January and December
7 rm – †£ 48/75 ††£ 70/98
◆ 19C house on first promenade from Colwyn Bay. Homely front lounge with bay view. Breakfasts feature local butcher's produce. Immaculately kept rooms: superior ones to front.

CONWY – Conwy – 502 I24 – pop. 3 847 — 32 B1

London 241 mi. – Caernarfon 22 mi. – Chester 46 mi. – Holyhead 37 mi.
Conwy Castle Visitor Centre ☎ (01492) 592248, conwytic@conwy.gov.uk
Penmaenmawr Conway Old Rd, ☎ (01492) 623 330
Town★★ - Castle★★ **AC** – Town Walls★★ - Plas Mawr★★
Snowdonia National Park★★★ – Bodnant Garden★★ **AC**, S : 8 mi. by A 55 and A 470 – Conwy Crossing (suspension bridge★)

Castle
High St ✉ LL32 8DB – ☎ (01492) 582 800 – www.castlewales.co.uk – Fax (01492) 582 300
27 rm – †£ 92/118 ††£ 180/195 – 1 suite
Rest ***Dawson's*** – Menu £ 24 – Carte £ 21/26
◆ Adjoining brick and flint coaching inns within walled town, on site of former Cistercian abbey. Comfy fire-lit country house sitting room; mix of classic/modern bedrooms. Some castle views. Contemporary dining room offers extensive menu of brasserie classics.

The Groes Inn with rm
South : 3 mi. on B 5106 ✉ LL32 8TN – ☎ (01492) 650 545 – www.groesinn.com – Fax (01492) 650 855
14 rm – †£ 85 ††£ 157 **Rest** – Carte £ 25/35
◆ Characterful inn, beautifully set overlooking the estuary, in the foothills of Snowdonia. Local Welsh and British dishes arrive in neat, generous portions; more adventurous restaurant menu. Tastefully-styled bedrooms boasts views; some have terraces and balconies.

at Llansanffraid Glan Conwy Southeast : 2.5 mi. by A 547 on A 470 – ✉ Conwy

Old Rectory Country House without rest
Llanrwst Rd, on A 470 ✉ LL28 5LF – ☎ (01492) 580 611 – www.oldrectorycountryhouse.co.uk – Restricted opening in winter
6 rm – †£ 79/99 ††£ 139/159 – 1 suite
◆ Personally run country house with attractive gardens and estuary views. Beautifully furnished Georgian-style sitting room displays china and antiques. Bedrooms, split between the house and annexe, boast comfy feature beds and luxury bathrooms. Good breakfasts.

at Rowen South : 3.5 mi. by B 5106

Tir Y Coed
✉ LL32 8TP – ☎ (01492) 650 219 – www.tirycoed.com – restricted opening in winter
7 rm – †£ 91 ††£ 150 **Rest** – *(dinner only)* Menu £ 29
◆ In secluded valley at foothills of Snowdonia, with balcony terrace overlooking mature garden. Tastefully furnished bedrooms. Intimate, candlelit dining room features fine collection of Victorian lithographs. Daily changing menu reflects the best of local produce.

COWBRIDGE (Y Bont Faen) – The Vale of Glamorgan – 503 J29 – pop. 3 616 — 33 B4

London 170 mi. – Cardiff 15 mi. – Swansea 30 mi.

WALES

Huddarts

69 High St ✉ CF71 7AF – ✆ (01446) 774 645 – www.huddartsrestaurant.co.uk – Fax (01446) 772 215 – closed 1 week spring, 1 week autumn, 26 December-5 January, Sunday dinner and Monday

Rest – Menu £ 20 (Sunday lunch)/25 (dinner weekdays) **s** – Carte £ 28/32 **s**

◆ Intimate, family run restaurant located on high street of this ancient market town. Welsh tapestries on wall. Skilfully executed traditional dishes with modern influences.

CRICCIETH – Gwynedd – 502 H25 – pop. 1 826 — 32 B2

London 249 mi. – Caernarfon 17 mi. – Shrewsbury 85 mi.

Ednyfed Hill, ✆ (01766) 522 154

Lleyn Peninsula★★ – Ffestiniog Railway★★

Mynydd Ednyfed Country House

Caernarfon Rd, Northwest : 0.75 mi. on B 4411 ✉ LL52 0PH – ✆ (01766) 523 269 – www.criccieth.net – Fax (01766) 522 929 – Closed 23 December-4 January

8 rm – †£ 78 ††£ 120 **Rest** – *(dinner only)* Carte £ 20/27 **s**

◆ Cosy, personally run 17C country house in eight acres of gardens and woodland. Traditional bedrooms – some with four-posters and fine bay views; all with stylish modern bathrooms. Dinner served in conservatory, which also boasts great outlook.

CRICKHOWELL (Crucywel) – Powys – 503 K28 – pop. 2 166 — 33 C4

London 169 mi. – Abergavenny 6 mi. – Brecon 14 mi. – Cardiff 40 mi.

Resource and Information Centre, Beaufort St ✆ (01873) 811970, tic@crickhowellinfo.org.uk

Brecon Beacons National Park★★. Llanthony Priory★★, NE : 10 mi. by minor roads

Gliffaes Country House

West : 3.75 mi. by A 40 ✉ NP8 1RH – ✆ (01874) 730 371 – www.gliffaeshotel.com – Fax (01874) 730 463 – closed 2-31 January

23 rm – †£ 85/96 ††£ 230

Rest – *(light lunch Monday-Saturday)* Menu £ 35 **s**

◆ 19C country house and gardens on banks of Usk, offering great tranquillity. Welcoming bar, lounge and conservatory. Popular for outdoor pursuits. Luxuriously individual rooms. Bold, country house dining room has pleasant garden views.

The Bear

High St ✉ NP8 1BW – ✆ (01873) 810 408 – www.bearhotel.co.uk – Fax (01873) 811 696 – Closed 25 December

34 rm – †£ 70 ††£ 153 – 1 suite

Rest *The Bear* – see restaurant listing

◆ Well-maintained 15C coaching inn full of nooks and crannies. Stylish bedrooms, some with jacuzzis; most characterful are in main house and feature beams, four-posters and fireplaces.

Glangrwyney Court

South : 2 mi. on A 40 ✉ NP8 1ES – ✆ (01873) 811 288 – www.glancourt.co.uk – Fax (01873) 810 317

8 rm – †£ 65/95 ††£ 85/125 **Rest** – *(by arrangement)* Menu £ 32

◆ Spacious Georgian house with sizeable garden and warm welcome. Large front lounge in chintz with antiques and trinkets. Pleasantly cluttered, well-kept rooms.

Ty Gwyn without rest

Brecon Rd ✉ NP8 1DG – ✆ (01873) 811 625 – www.tygwyn.com

3 rm – †£ 40/45 ††£ 68/70

◆ A homely place boasting spotlessly kept, simply furnished bedrooms, with comfort and character. Well-tended garden with stream. Enthusiastic owner has vast local knowledge.

Nantyffin Cider Mill Inn

Brecon Rd, West : 1 mi. on A 40 ✉ NP8 1SG – ✆ (01873) 810 775 – www.cidermill.co.uk – Fax (01873) 810 986 – Closed Monday except Bank Holidays and Sunday dinner (October to Easter)
Rest – Menu £ 17 (lunch) – Carte £ 22/30
◆ Converted 16C cider mill featuring original cider press. Predominantly Mediterranean dishes; blackboard of fish specials and set menu of old favourites. Cider and real ales on tap.

The Bear

High St ✉ NP8 1BW – ✆ (01873) 810 408 – www.bearhotel.co.uk – Fax (01873) 811 696 – Closed 25 December
Rest – Carte £ 17/25
◆ Keenly run coaching inn serving classical, tried-and-tested menu available both in characterful bar and more formal restaurant. Swift, assured service from young, cheery team.

CROSS ASH – Monmouthshire – see Abergavenny

CROSSGATES – Powys – 503 J27 – see Llandrindod Wells

DEGANWY – Conwy – 502 I24 – see Llandudno

DOLFOR – Powys – 503 K26 — 32 C2

London 199 – Cardiff 93 – Oswestry 34 – Ludlow 39

Old Vicarage

North : 1.5 mi. off A 483 – ✆ (01686) 629 051 – www.theoldvicaragedolfor.co.uk
3 rm – †£ 65 ††£ 95 **Rest** – *(by arrangement)* Menu £ 28
◆ Characterful 19C detached house with large gardens; formerly a vicarage. Cosy bedrooms, named after nearby rivers, mix period furniture with modern colours. Concise menu of home-cooked dishes features local produce and veg from garden. Preserves/chutneys for sale.

DOLGELLAU – Gwynedd – 502 I25 – pop. 2 407 — 32 B2

London 221 mi. – Birkenhead 72 mi. – Chester 64 mi. – Shrewsbury 57 mi.
Ty Meirion, Eldon Sq ✆ (01341) 422888, tic.dolgellau@eryri-npa.gov.uk
Hengwrt Estate Pencefn Rd, ✆ (01341) 422 603
Town★
Snowdonia National Park★★★ - Cadair Idris★★★ - Precipice Walk★, NE : 3 mi. on minor roads

Penmaenuchaf Hall

Penmaenpool, West : 1.75 mi. on A 493 (Tywyn Rd) ✉ LL40 1YB – ✆ (01341) 422 129 – www.penhall.co.uk – Fax (01341) 422 787
14 rm – †£ 95/145 ††£ 150/230
Rest – Menu £ 18/40 – Carte dinner £ 40/45
◆ From a handsome drawing room, enjoy the enviable position of this Victorian mansion with its Rhinog Mountain and Mawddach Estuary vistas. Bedrooms are tastefully furnished. Dine in smart garden room with outside terrace.

Ffynnon without rest

Love Lane, (off Cader Rd) ✉ LL40 1RR – ✆ (01341) 421 774 – www.ffynnontownhouse.com – Fax (01341) 421 779 – Closed Christmas
5 rm – †£ 120 ††£ 190
◆ A haven of luxury; lovingly restored and modernised, yet retaining many original features. Stylish sitting room and spacious, tastefully decorated suites, boasting every mod con.

Tyddyn Mawr without rest

Islawdref, Cader Rd, Southwest : 2.5 mi. by Tywyn rd on Cader Idris rd ✉ LL40 1TL – ✆ (01341) 422 331 – www.wales-guesthouse.co.uk – February - November
3 rm – †£ 55 ††£ 68
◆ Set on secluded working sheep farm, stunningly situated beneath Cader Idris mountain. Immaculate bedrooms boast superb views and plenty of extras; one has a balcony, another, a terrace. 5 course breakfast taken beside impressive inglenook. Great hospitality.

WALES

at Llanelltyd **Northwest : 2.25 mi. by A 470 on A 496**

Mawddach

LL40 2TA – (01341) 424 020 – www.mawddach.com – closed 1 week January, 1 week Spring, 1 week Autumn, Monday, Tuesday and Sunday dinner

Rest – Menu £ 17 (Sunday lunch) – Carte £ 24/30

◆ Stylish modern barn conversion on family farm; 1st floor dining room dominated by glass wall with superb view. Well-priced, straightforward cooking; more adventurous dinner menu.

EAST ABERTHAW (Aberddawan) – The Vale of Glamorgan 33 B-C4

– **503** J29 – **Barry**

London 180 mi. – Cardiff 20 mi. – Swansea 33 mi.

The Blue Anchor Inn

CF62 3DD – (01446) 750 329 – www.blueanchoraberthaw.com – Closed Sunday dinner

Rest – Carte £ 16/28

◆ Thatched stone-built pub dating back to 1380, with characterful bar and vast upstairs restaurant. Traditional, wholesome dishes boast straightforward presentation and plenty of flavour.

FELINGWM UCHAF – Carmarthenshire – see Carmarthen

FISHGUARD – Pembrokeshire – 503 F28 – pop. 3 193 33 A3

London 265 mi. – Cardiff 114 mi. – Gloucester 176 mi. – Holyhead 169 mi.

to Republic of Ireland (Rosslare) (Stena Line) 2-4 daily (1 h 50 mn/ 3 h 30 mn)

Town Hall, The Square (01437) 776636, fishguard.tic@pembrokeshire.gov.uk - Ocean Lab, The Parrog, Goodwick (01348) 872037, fishguardharbour.tic@pembrokshire.gov.uk

Pembrokeshire Coast National Park★★

Manor Town House without rest

11 Main St SA65 9HG – (01348) 873 260 – www.manortownhouse.com – Fax (01348) 873 260 – Closed January and Christmas

6 rm – †£ 55/75 ††£ 95

◆ Georgian Grade II listed house. Bedrooms are individually styled and furnished with antiques, choose from Victorian and Art Deco; some with harbour and sea views.

at Welsh Hook **Southwest : 7.5 mi. by A 40 – Haverfordwest**

Stone Hall with rm

SA62 5NS – (01348) 840 212 – www.stonehall-mansion.co.uk – Fax (01348) 840 815 – Closed 1 week Spring, 1 week Winter, 25-26 December, Sunday and Monday

5 rm – †£ 85 ††£ 105

Rest – *(dinner only) (booking essential)* Menu £ 31 – Carte approx. £ 37

◆ Charming part-14C manor house with 17C additions. Tranquil setting and personal hospitality. Home-cooked, French-style dishes using prime seasonal produce. Comfy rooms.

GRESFORD (Groes-ffordd) – Wrexham – 502 L24 – see Wrexham

GROESLON – Gwynedd – see Caernarfon

HARLECH – Gwynedd – 502 H25 – pop. 1 233 32 B2

London 241 mi. – Chester 72 mi. – Dolgellau 21 mi.

High St (01766) 780658, tic.harlech@aryri-npa.gov.uk

Royal St David's, (01766) 780 203

Castle★★ **AC**

Snowdonia National Park★★★

WALES

XX **Castle Cottage** with rm

Pen Llech, off B 4573 ✉ LL46 2YL – ✆ (01766) 780 479 – www.castlecottageharlech.co.uk – Closed 3 weeks November

7 rm – †£ 75/115 ††£ 150

Rest – *(dinner only) (booking essential)* Menu £ 36

◆ Attractive cottage behind Harlech Castle, with cosy yet surprisingly contemporary interior. Classical, daily changing menus display passionately sourced local produce and modern touches. Bedrooms are spacious and comfy; some have stunning castle/mountain views.

HAVERFORDWEST (Hwlffordd) – Pembrokeshire – 503 F28 – pop. 13 367 — 33 A3

London 250 mi. – Fishguard 15 mi. – Swansea 57 mi.

Old Bridge ✆ (01437) 763110, haverfordwest.tic@pembrokeshire.gov.uk

Arnolds Down, ✆ (01437) 763 565

Scolton Museum and Country Park★

Pembrokeshire Coast National Park★★. Skomer Island and Skokholm Island★, SW : 14 mi. by B 4327 and minor roads

Lower Haythog Farm

Spittal, Northeast : 5 mi. on B 4329 ✉ SA62 5QL – ✆ (01437) 731 279 – www.lowerhaythogfarm.co.uk – Fax (01437) 731 279

5 rm – †£ 35/55 ††£ 75/85 **Rest** – *(by arrangement)* Menu £ 23

◆ Friendly atmosphere, traditional comforts and a warm welcome at this 250 acre working dairy farm with accessible woodland walks. Well kept and comfortable throughout. Dining room in homely, country style reflected in hearty, home-cooked food.

The Paddock

✉ SA62 5QL – ✆ (01437) 731 531 – www.thepaddockwales.co.uk

3 rm – †£ 65/75 ††£ 80/90 **Rest** – *(by arrangement)* Menu £ 28

◆ Very modern new build guest house set on working farm; minimalist ground floor bedrooms feature chunky furniture and Egyptian cotton bedding. Comfy lounge with books, magazines and board games. Set 2 or 3 course dinner makes good use of local produce.

HAWARDEN (Penarlâg) – Flintshire – 502 K24 – pop. 1 858 — 32 C1

London 205 mi. – Chester 9 mi. – Liverpool 17 mi. – Shrewsbury 45 mi.

X **The Hawarden Brasserie**

68 The Highway ✉ CH5 3DH – ✆ (01244) 536 353 – www.thehawardenbrasserie.com – Fax (01244) 520 888 – Closed 1 January and Saturday lunch

Rest – *(booking advisable)* Carte £ 19/31

◆ Long-standing neighbourhood restaurant run by experienced owners and popular with the locals. Light lunch; bistro classics at dinner. Dishes are good value, tasty and neatly presented.

HAY-ON-WYE (Y Gelli) – Powys – 503 K27 – pop. 1 846 — 33 C3

London 154 mi. – Brecon 16 mi. – Cardiff 59 mi. – Hereford 21 mi.

Craft Centre, Oxford Rd ✆ (01497) 820144, post@hay-on-wye.co.uk

Rhosgoch Builth Wells, ✆ (01497) 851 251

Town★

Brecon Beacons National Park★★. Llanthony Priory★★, SE : 12 mi. by minor roads

Old Black Lion with rm

26 Lion St ✉ HR3 5AD – ✆ (01497) 820 841 – www.oldblacklion.co.uk – Fax (01497) 822 960

10 rm – †£ 48 ††£ 95 **Rest** – Carte £ 21/31

◆ Characterful part-13C inn with lots of old world charm. Traditional menu offers tasty, honest dishes, hearty portions and plenty of choice, with more favourites on the board. Bedrooms boast either antiques furnishings or rich colours and modern bathrooms.

WALES

Three Tuns
4 Broad St ✉ HR3 5DB – ✆ (01497) 821 855 – www.three-tuns.com – Fax (01497) 821 955 – Closed 25-26 December, Monday, Tuesday and Sunday dinner
Rest – Carte £ 20/28
◆ Grade II listed 16C pub, reputedly the oldest building in the town. Bar and terrace offer blackboard classics; formal upstairs dining room displays more Italian influences.

at Llanigon Southwest : 2.5 mi. by B 4350 – ✉ Hay-on-Wye

Old Post Office without rest
✉ HR3 5QA – ✆ (01497) 820 008 – www.oldpost-office.co.uk – Closed December and January
3 rm – †£ 55/70 ††£ 70/75
◆ Dating from 17C, a converted inn. Near the "book town" of Hay-on-Wye. Smart modern ambience blends with characterful charm. Pine furnished rooms with polished floors.

HOWEY – Powys – see Llandrindod Wells

KNIGHTON (Trefyclawdd) – Powys – 503 K26 – pop. 2 851 — 33 C3

London 162 mi. – Birmingham 59 mi. – Hereford 31 mi. – Shrewsbury 35 mi.
Offa's Dyke Centre, West St ✆ (01547) 528753, oda@offasdyke.demon.co.uk
Ffrydd Wood, ✆ (01547) 528 646
Town★
Offa's Dyke★, NW : 9.5 m

Milebrook House
Ludlow Rd, Milebrook, East : 2 mi. on A 4113 ✉ LD7 1LT – ✆ (01547) 528 632 – www.milebrookhouse.co.uk – Fax (01547) 520 509
10 rm – †£ 77 ††£ 122
Rest – *(closed Monday lunch)* Menu £ 16/34 **s** – Carte £ 23/32 **s**
◆ Located in the Teme Valley; good for exploring the Welsh Marches. Possesses a fine, formal garden well stocked with exotic plants. Rooms are large and pleasingly decorated. The kitchen garden provides most of the vegetables which appear in the restaurant.

LAKE VYRNWY – Powys – 502 J25 – ✉ Llanwddyn — 32 C2

London 204 mi. – Chester 52 mi. – Llanfyllin 10 mi. – Shrewsbury 40 mi.
The Shop in the Corner, Vyrnwy Craft Workshops ✆ (01691) 870346
Lake★

Lake Vyrnwy rm,
✉ SY10 0LY – ✆ (01691) 870 692 – www.lakevyrnwyhotel.co.uk – Fax (01691) 870 259
51 rm – †£ 120/125 ††£ 200/210 – 1 suite
Rest – Menu £ 18/40 – Carte £ 20/38
◆ Victorian country house built from locally quarried stone overlooking the lake; an RSPB sanctuary and sporting estate, ideal for game enthusiasts. Rooms have timeless chic. Spectacular lakeside views from the restaurant are matched by accomplished cooking.

LALESTON – Bridgend – 503 J29 – see Bridgend

LAMPHEY (Llandyfai) – Pembrokeshire – 503 F28 – see Pembroke

LAUGHARNE – Carmarthenshire – 503 G28 **33** B4

London 230 mi. – Cardiff 80 mi. – Carmarthen 13 mi.

Hurst House rest, VISA AE

East Marsh, South : 3 mi. by A 4066 taking left turn on unmarked road opposite Hill Crest house ✉ SA33 4RS – ℰ (01994) 427 417 – www.hurst-house.co.uk – Fax (01994) 427 840 – Closed 1 week January

18 rm – £ 265 £ 265

Rest – *(booking advisable for non-residents)* Menu £ 20 – Carte dinner £ 25/31

◆ Former farmhouse set by the marshes in Dylan Thomas country; a restful hotel to suit the modern young traveller. State-of-the-art rooms boast natural materials and thoughtful extras. Small spa. Keenly priced, traditional menus in restaurant overlooking terrace and gardens.

LLANARMON DYFFRYN CEIRIOG – Wrexham – 502 K25 **32** C2

– ✉ Llangollen (Denbighshire)

London 196 mi. – Chester 33 mi. – Shrewsbury 32 mi.

The Hand at Llanarmon with rm rm, VISA

✉ *LL20 7LD – ℰ (01691) 600 666 – www.thehandhotel.co.uk – Fax (01691) 600 262*

13 rm – £ 44/70 £ 85/120

Rest – Menu £ 18 (Sunday lunch) – Carte £ 20/32

◆ Rustic, personally run inn providing a warm welcome and wholesome meals to travellers through the lush Ceiriog Valley. Generous portions of fresh, flavoursome cooking. Cosy bedrooms with hill views and recently modernised bathrooms.

LLANDDEWI SKIRRID – Monmouthshire – see Abergavenny

LLANDEILO – Carmarthenshire – 503 I28 – pop. 1 731 **33** B3

London 218 mi. – Brecon 34 mi. – Carmarthen 15 mi. – Swansea 25 mi.

Town★ - Dinefwr Park★ **AC**

Brecon Beacons National Park★★ - Black Mountain★, SE : by minor roads – Carreg Cennen Castle★ **AC**, SE : 4 mi. by A 483 and minor roads

Plough Inn rm, VISA AE

Rhosmaen, North : 1 mi. on A 40 ✉ SA19 6NP – ℰ (01558) 823 431 – www.ploughrhosmaen.com – Fax (01558) 823 969 – Closed 26 December

14 rm – £ 60/80 £ 80/120 **Rest** – Menu £ 13/15 – Carte £ 19/28

◆ Powder blue building boasting contemporary interior and pleasant country views to the rear. Modern bedrooms are spacious, comfy and well-equipped: 305 has a whirlpool bath. Snacks, light lunches and more substantial dinners served in large vaulted restaurant.

at Salem North : 3 mi. by A 40 off Pen y banc rd – ✉ Llandeilo

The Angel VISA

✉ *SA197LY – ℰ (01558) 823 394 – www.angelsalem.co.uk – Closed 1 week spring, Sunday dinner, Monday and Tuesday lunch*

Rest – Carte £ 20/35

◆ Village pub with inviting bar lounge and formal, Edwardian style dining room. Traditional cooking, enlivened by Asian and Italian influences and some interesting combinations.

LLANDENNY – Monmouthshire – 503 L28 – see Usk

LLANDOVERY – Carmarthenshire – 503 I28 – pop. 2 235 **33** B3

London 207 mi. – Cardiff 61 mi. – Swansea 37 mi. – Merthyr Tydfil 34 mi.

New White Lion rm, VISA

43 Stone St ✉ SA20 0BZ – ℰ (01550) 720 685 – www.newwhitelion.co.uk

6 rm – £ 80 £ 110

Rest – *(dinner only) (booking essential residents only)* Menu £ 25 **s**

◆ Stylish grade II listed hotel with individually designed bedrooms named after characters from local folklore, and cool sitting room with honesty bar. Cosy dining room; homemade dishes make good use made of local, seasonal produce.

LLANDRILLO – Denbighshire – 502 J25 – pop. 1 048 – ✉ Corwen 32 C2

London 210 mi. – Chester 40 mi. – Dolgellau 26 mi. – Shrewsbury 46 mi.

XXX **Tyddyn Llan** (Bryan Webb) with rm rm, P VISA

✉ *LL21 OST – ☎ (01490) 440 264 – www.tyddynllan.co.uk – Fax (01490) 440 414 – Closed last 2 weeks January*

13 rm (dinner included) – †£ 130 ††£ 200/300

Rest – *(dinner only and lunch Friday-Sunday) (booking essential)*

Menu £ 28/45

Spec. Scallops with vegetable relish and beurre blanc. Rack of lamb with spiced aubergine. Prune and almond tart with mascarpone ice cream.

◆ Personally run country house with pretty gardens. Dine in one of two spacious rooms. Menu offers considerable choice; cooking is classical in style and dishes are expertly balanced, using sensible combinations. Tidy, well-equipped bedrooms.

LLANDRINDOD WELLS – Powys – 503 J27 – pop. 5 024 33 C3

London 204 mi. – Brecon 29 mi. – Carmarthen 60 mi. – Shrewsbury 58 mi.

Old Town Hall, Memorial Gardens ☎ (01597) 822600, llandrindodtic@btconnect.com

Llandrindod Wells The Clubhouse, ☎ (01597) 823 873

Elan Valley★★ (Dol-y-Mynach and Claerwen Dam and Reservoir★★, Caban Coch Dam and Reservoir★, Garreg-ddu Viaduct★, Pen-y-Garreg Reservoir and Dam★, Craig Goch Dam and Reservoir★), NW : 12 mi. by A 4081, A 470 and B 4518

Metropole rm, AC rest, P VISA AE

Temple St ✉ LD1 5DY – ☎ (01597) 823 700 – www.metropole.co.uk – Fax (01597) 824 828

118 rm – †£ 110/130 ††£ 120/140 – 2 suites

Rest *Radnor* – *(dinner only)* Carte £ 26/32

Rest *Spencer's* – Carte £ 22/30 **s**

◆ Brightly painted hotel run for many years by Baird-Murray family. Some modern bedrooms; others more traditional. Pool in Victorian-style conservatory. Menu in formal Radnor showcases local produce. All day menu in Spencer's; a contemporary bar and brasserie.

at Crossgates Northeast : 3.5 mi. on A 483 – ✉ Llandrindod Wells

Guidfa House P VISA

✉ *LD1 6RF – ☎ (01597) 851 241 – www.guidfahouse.co.uk – Fax (01597) 851 875*

6 rm – †£ 65/75 ††£ 90/105 **Rest** – *(by arrangement)* Menu £ 30

◆ Georgian house with white painted façade and pleasant garden to relax in. Indoors, find spacious, bright bedrooms. A friendly welcome is given with tips on local activities. Seasonally changing menu of zesty home cooking in traditionally decorated dining room.

at Howey South : 1.5 mi. by A 483 – ✉ Llandrindod Wells

Acorn Court Country House without rest P

Chapel Rd, Northeast : 0.5 mi. ✉ LD1 5PB – ☎ (01597) 823 543 – www.acorncourt.co.uk – Fax (01597) 823 543 – Closed 25 December

4 rm – †£ 36/50 ††£ 70/78

◆ Chalet-style house in lovely countryside; guests can fish in the lake. Bedrooms are large with many extra touches: hairdryers, stationery, soft toys - homely and welcoming.

LLANDUDNO – Conwy – 502 I24 – pop. 14 872 32 B1

London 243 mi. – Birkenhead 55 mi. – Chester 47 mi. – Holyhead 43 mi.

Library Building, Mostyn St ☎ (01492) 577577, llandudnotic@conwy.gov.uk

Rhos-on-Sea Penrhyn Bay, ☎ (01492) 549 641

72 Bryniau Rd West Shore, ☎ (01492) 875 325

Hospital Rd, ☎ (01492) 876 450

Town★ - Pier★ B – The Great Orme★ (panorama★★, Tramway★, Ancient Copper Mines★ **AC**) AB

Bodnant Garden★★ **AC**, S : 7 mi. by A 470 B

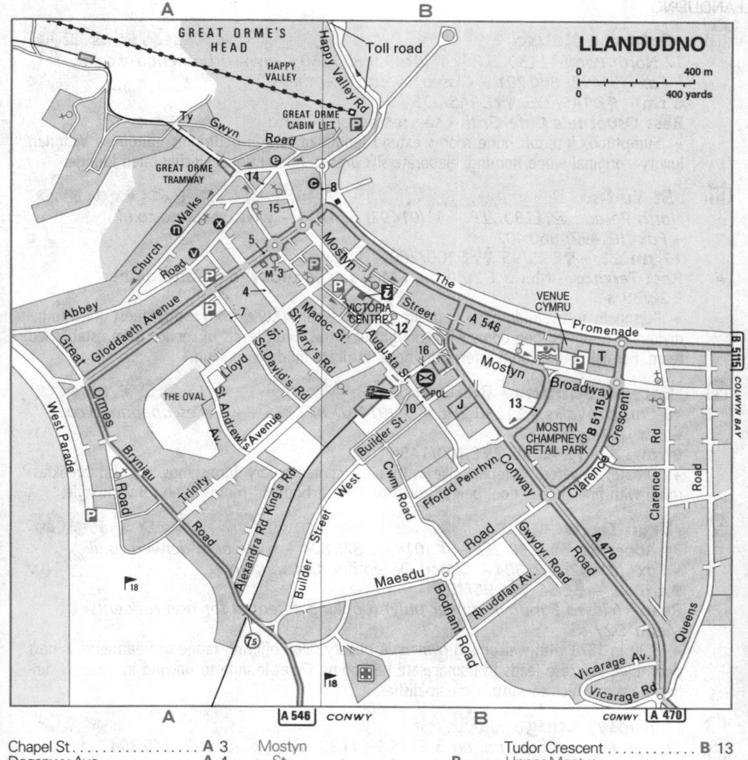

Chapel St	A 3	Mostyn St	B	Tudor Crescent	B 13
Deganwy Ave	A 4	North Parade	AB 8	Upper Mostyn St	A 15
Gloddaeth St	A 5	Oxford Rd	B 10	Vaughan St	B 16
Maelgwyn Rd	A 7	Trinity Square	B 12	Victoria Centre	B
Mostyn Champneys Retail Park	B	Tudno St	A 14		

Bodysgallen Hall

Southeast : 2 mi. on A 470 ✉ *LL30 1RS – ✆ (01492) 584 466 – www.bodysgallen.com – Fax (01492) 582 519*

rm, VISA MC AE

18 rm – 🚹£ 140 🚹🚹£ 175/405, ☕ £ 7 – 18 suites

Rest *The Dining Room* – *(Closed Sunday dinner and Monday October-May) (booking essential)* Menu £ 22/39

Rest *1620* – *(Closed Sunday from June-October)* Carte £ 26/30 **s**

◆ Beautiful country house with 13C tower, stunning gardens and tasteful spa. Characterful wood panelled main lounge with inglenook. Antique-furnished bedrooms, some with splendid views towards Snowdon. Formal Dining Room overlooks gardens. 1620 serves brasserie classics.

The Empire

rm, VISA MC AE

73 Church Walks ✉ *LL30 2HE – ✆ (01492) 860 555 – www.empirehotel.co.uk – Fax (01492) 860 791 – Closed 19-30 December* A**e**

46 rm ☕ – 🚹£ 65/90 🚹🚹£ 95/130 – 1 suite

Rest *Watkins and Co.* – *(dinner only and Sunday lunch)* Menu £ 15/21

◆ Grand columned façade leads to Victorian interior hung with chandeliers and Russell Flint prints. Bedrooms feature brass/cast iron beds, antiques and contrasting hi-tech mod cons. Set on site of former wine merchants, Watkins and Co. offers fine dining.

Osborne House

17 North Par ✉ LL30 2LP – ✆ (01492) 860 330 – www.osbornehouse.co.uk – Fax (01492) 860 791 – Closed 19-30 December A**c**

6 rm – †£ 145/225 ††£ 145/225

Rest *Osborne's Cafe Grill* – see restaurant listing

◆ Sumptuous interior: huge rooms extend length of house; bedrooms epitomise Victorian luxury - original wood flooring, elaborate silk drapes, fine antiques. Richly hued lounge.

St Tudno

North Parade ✉ LL30 2LP – ✆ (01492) 874 411 – www.st-tudno.co.uk – Fax (01492) 860 407 A**c**

17 rm – †£ 75/95 ††£ 100/260 – 1 suite

Rest *Terrace* – Menu £ 20 (lunch Monday-Saturday) **s** – Carte dinner £ 28/38 **s**

◆ Personally run seaside hotel opposite pier. Classical in style, from comfy guest areas to individually designed bedrooms with thoughtful extras. High levels of service from established team. Formal dining room offers ambitious, intricate modern cooking.

Escape Boutique B&B without rest

48 Church Walks ✉ LL30 2HL – ✆ (01492) 877 776 – www.escapebandb.co.uk – Fax (01492) 878 777 A**n**

9 rm – †£ 70/95 ††£ 100/145

◆ Ornate, elevated Victorian villa with ultra contemporary furnishings. Modish breakfast room with fine choice. Cool beige/brown or 'French boudoir' rooms. B and B with style.

WALES

Bryn Derwen

34 Abbey Rd ✉ LL30 2EE – ✆ (01492) 876 804 – www.bryn-derwen.co.uk – Fax (01492) 876 804 – Closed December and January A**v**

9 rm – †£ 54 ††£ 96/104

Rest – *(closed Sunday) (dinner only) (booking essential for non-residents)* Menu £ 27 **s**

◆ Built in 1878 with welcoming owners. A beauty salon offering range of treatments is next door. Pine staircase leads to immaculate bedrooms. Quiet lounge to unwind in. Homely dining room in which to sample classic dishes.

Lympley Lodge without rest

Colwyn Rd, East : 2.5 mi. on B 5115 ✉ LL30 3AL – ✆ (01492) 549 304 – www.lympleylodge.co.uk – Closed mid December-February

3 rm – †£ 50/55 ††£ 80/90

◆ Charming Victorian house built in 1870. Traditional, homely feel, with antique furniture, wrought iron beds and thoughtful extras – including every toiletry imaginable. Hearty breakfast.

Abbey Lodge without rest

14 Abbey Rd ✉ LL30 2EA – ✆ (01492) 878 042 – www.abbeylodgeuk.com – Closed January and February A**x**

4 rm – †£ 38 ††£ 70/75

◆ Built as a gentlemen's residence in early 1850s; a pretty, gabled house with terraced garden where you're made to feel at home. Smart drawing room and cosy, comfy bedrooms.

Sefton Court without rest

49 Church Walks ✉ LL30 2HL – ✆ (01492) 875 235 – www.seftoncourt-hotel.co.uk – Fax (01492) 879 560 – Easter-October

10 rm – †£ 45 ††£ 70 A**n**

◆ Substantial Victorian house in elevated position, affording good town views. Original features include pretty stained glass and interesting friezes. Contemporary bedrooms provide a pleasant contrast.

Osborne's Cafe Grill – at Osborne House Hotel

17 North Par ✉ LL30 2LP – ✆ (01492) 860 330 – www.osbornehouse.co.uk – Fax (01492) 860 791 – Closed 19-30 December A**c**

Rest – Menu £ 18 – Carte £ 18/31

◆ Impressive, ornate main dining room with velvet drapes and ornate gold lighting. Eclectic, modern menus, and the bustling informal style of a bistro; enthusiastic service.

at Deganwy South : 2.75 mi. on A 546 - A - ✉ Llandudno

Quay H. & Spa
Deganwy Quay ✉ LL31 9DJ – ✆ (01492) 564 100 – www.quayhotel.com – Fax (01492) 564 115
55 rm – 🛉£ 125 🛉🛉£ 180/230, ☕ £ 13 – 19 suites
Rest *Vue* – Carte £ 35/61
◆ Stylish hotel on Conwy estuary, boasting superb harbour/castle views, large guest areas, extensive facilities and excellent spa. Spacious, contemporary bedrooms include 3 private towers. Nautically-themed first floor restaurant offers modern cuisine and stunning outlook.

Nikki Ip's
57 Station Rd ✉ LL31 9DF – ✆ (01492) 596 611 – Closed 1 January and 25 December
Rest – Chinese – *(booking essential)* Menu £ 12/28 – Carte £ 20/26
◆ Choice of casual eatery/bar or friendly restaurant with estuary views. Dim sum and concise set menu at lunch; extensive à la carte and specials at dinner. Fresh, tasty ingredients; good flavours.

LLANDWROG – **Gwynedd** – **503** H24 – **see Caernarfon**

LLANDYRNOG – **Denbighshire** – **503** J/K24 — **32** C1
▶ Cardiff 158 mi. – Denbigh 7 mi. – Ruthin 6 mi.

Pentre Mawr
North : 1.25 mi. by B 5429 taking left hand fork after 0.75 mi. ✉ LL16 4LA – ✆ (01824) 790 732 – www.pentremawrcountryhouse.co.uk – Closed 25 December
7 rm ☕ – 🛉£ 100/120 🛉🛉£ 150/160 **Rest** – *(by arrangement)* Menu £ 30
◆ Set in 200 acres. Choice of 17C farmhouse with cosy open-fired lounges, country house atmosphere and antique-furnished bedrooms, or luxury African-themed canvas lodges with private terraces and hot tubs. Dinner served in wood-floored conservatory; local ingredients a feature.

LLANELLTYD – **Gwynedd** – **503** I25 – **see Dolgellau**

LLANERCHYMEDD – **Isle of Anglesey** – **502** G24 – **see Anglesey (Isle of)**

LLAN FFESTINIOG – **Gwynedd** — **32** B2
▶ London 234 mi. – Bangor 35 mi. – Wrexham 52 mi.
◙ Llechwedd Slate Caverns★ **AC** N : 4 mi. by A 470

Cae'r Blaidd Country House
North : 0.75 mi. by A 470 on Blaenau Rd ✉ LL41 4PH – ✆ (01766) 762 765 – www.caerblaidd.fsnet.co.uk – Fax (01766) 762 765 – Closed January
3 rm ☕ – 🛉£ 49 🛉🛉£ 75 **Rest** – *(communal dining)* Menu £ 20
◆ Sizeable Victorian house in remote setting, boasting panoramic mountain views. Spacious guest areas; light, airy bedrooms – two with superb outlooks. Welcoming owners are mountain guides. Daily changing dishes of local produce served at large communal table.

LLANFIHANGEL – **Powys** – **502** J25 – **see Llanfyllin**

LLANFYLLIN – **Powys** – **502** K25 – **pop. 1 267** — **32** C2
▶ London 188 mi. – Chester 42 mi. – Shrewsbury 24 mi. – Welshpool 11 mi.
◙ Pistyll Rhaeadr★, NW : 8 mi. by A 490, B 4391, B 4580 and minor roads

Seeds
5 Penybryn Cottages, High St ✉ SY22 5AP – ✆ (01691) 648 604 – closed Christmas, Sunday-Tuesday and lunch Wednesday
Rest – *(restricted opening in winter)* Menu £ 26 (Saturday dinner) – Carte £ 18/30
◆ Converted 16C red-brick cottages in sleepy town, run by hands-on husband and wife team. Simple, rustic interior featuring old kitchen range; matched by unfussy, flavoursome, classical dishes.

at Llanfihangel Southwest : 5 mi. by A 490 and B 4393 on B 4382 – ✉ Llanfyllin

Cyfie Farm
South : 1.5 mi. by B 4382 ✉ SY22 5JE – ✆ (01691) 648 451
– www.cyfiefarm.co.uk – Fax (01691) 648 363
– mid February-mid November
4 rm – ♦£ 85/90 ♦♦£ 100/120
Rest – *(by arrangement, communal dining)* Menu £ 25
◆ 17C longhouse, now a sheep farm, with super views of Meifod Valley. One room has distinctly quaint feel. Luxurious new cottages: outdoor hot tub affords great vistas. Cordon Bleu trained owners serve at communal table.

LLANGAMMARCH WELLS – Powys – 503 J27 — 33 B3

London 200 mi. – Brecon 17 mi. – Builth Wells 8 mi. – Cardiff 58 mi.

Lake Country House and Spa
East : 0.75 mi. ✉ LD4 4BS – ✆ (01591) 620 202 – www.lakecountryhouse.co.uk – Fax (01591) 620 457
22 rm – ♦£ 125/195 ♦♦£ 225/245 – 8 suites
Rest – *(booking essential)* Menu £ 19/40 s
◆ 19C country house in mature grounds. Welsh teas a speciality. Rooms in house or lodge full of antiques, flowers and extravagant fabrics. Tranquil spa adds to the experience. Candlelit dining; super wine list.

LLANGOLLEN – Denbighshire – 502 K25 – pop. 2 930 — 32 C2

London 194 mi. – Chester 23 mi. – Holyhead 76 mi. – Shrewsbury 30 mi.
Y Chapel, Castle St ✆ (01978) 860828, llangollen@nwtic.com
Vale of Llangollen Holyhead Rd, ✆ (01978) 860 906
Town★ - Railway★ **AC** - Plas Newydd★ **AC**
Pontcysyllte Aqueduct★★, E : 4 mi. by A 539 - Castell Dinas Bran★, N : by footpath – Valle Crucis Abbey★ **AC**, N : 2 mi. by A 542. Chirk Castle★★ **AC** (wrought iron gates★), SE : 7.5 mi. by A 5 – Rug Chapel★ **AC**, W : 11 mi. by A 5 and A 494

Gales
18 Bridge St ✉ LL20 8PF – ✆ (01978) 860 089 – www.galesofllangollen.co.uk – Fax (01978) 861 313 – Closed 24 December-2 January
13 rm – ♦£ 60 ♦♦£ 80, £ 5 – 2 suites
Rest – *(Closed Sunday)* Carte £ 20/26
◆ Pair of family-run, brick-built townhouses with characterful wine theme throughout. Spacious beamed bedrooms boast modern bathrooms and complimentary port. Below are a wine/kitchenware shop and atmospheric wood-panelled wine bar with wide-ranging blackboard menu.

Oakmere without rest
Regent St, on A 5 ✉ LL20 8HS – ✆ (01978) 861 126
– www.oakmere.llangollen.co.uk
6 rm – ♦£ 60 ♦♦£ 75
◆ A restored Victorian house with an immaculate garden. Indoors are polished pitch pine furnishings, a breakfast room with conservatory area and tidy bedrooms.

LLANGRANNOG – Ceredigion – 503 G27 — 33 B3

London 241 mi. – Caerdydd / Cardiff 96 mi.
– Aberystwyth / Aberyswyth 30 mi. – Caerfyrddin / Carmarthen 28 mi.

The Grange
Pentregat, Southeast : 3 mi. by B 4321 on A 487 ✉ SA44 6HW – ✆ (01239) 654 121 – www.grangecountryhouse.co.uk – Fax (01239) 654 121
4 rm – ♦£ 55/65 ♦♦£ 85 **Rest** – *(by arrangement)* Menu £ 20
◆ Originally the manor house of the adjacent estate. Traditionally furnished guest areas; afternoon tea from real silver teapot on arrival. Well-maintained bedrooms boast roll-top baths. Dinner features locally sourced meat/fish and home-grown veg.

LLANIGON – Powys – 503 K27 – see Hay-on-Wye

LLANOVER – Monmouthshire – see Abergavenny

LLANRHIDIAN – Swansea – 503 H29 – see Swansea

LLANSANFFRAID GLAN CONWY – Conwy – 502 I24 – see Conwy

LLANTWIT MAJOR (Llanilltud Fawr) – The Vale of Glamorgan – 503 J29 – pop. 13 366 33 B4

London 175 mi. – Cardiff 18 mi. – Swansea 33 mi.

West House

West St ✉ CF61 1SP – ☎ (01446) 792 406 – www.westhouse-hotel.co.uk – Fax (01446) 796 147

21 rm – †£ 63/70 ††£ 85/120

Rest – *(dinner only and lunch Friday-Sunday)* Carte £ 21/33 **s**

◆ 16C building with pleasant walled garden, set in old part of town. Cosy lounge with wood burning stove. Bedrooms currently being refurbished in contemporary style: period furniture will remain. Dining room showcases local, seasonal produce.

LLANUWCHLLYN – Gwynedd – 503 I/J25 32 B2

Cardiff 147 mi. – Dolgellau 13 mi. – Llangollen 27 mi.

Eifionydd without rest

✉ LL23 7UB – ☎ (01678) 540 622 – www.visitbala.com – March-October

3 rm – †£ 40/60 ††£ 76/84

◆ Comfy guest house in small hamlet, boasting beautiful rear views across a stream to the mountains beyond. Pleasant sun lounge, conservatory and breakfast room. Immaculately kept, individually decorated bedrooms with compact modern bathrooms.

LLANWENARTH – Monmouthshire – see Abergavenny

LLANWRTYD WELLS – Powys – 503 J27 – pop. 649 33 B3

London 214 mi. – Brecon 32 mi. – Cardiff 68 mi. – Carmarthen 39 mi.

Ty Barcud, The Square ☎ (01591) 610666, enquiries@llanwrtyd.com

Abergwesyn-Tregaron Mountain Road★, NW : 19 mi. on minor roads

Lasswade Country House

Station Rd ✉ LD5 4RW – ☎ (01591) 610 515 – www.lasswadehotel.co.uk – Fax (01591) 610 611 – Closed 25 December

8 rm – †£ 55/75 ††£ 95/110 **Rest** – *(dinner only)* Menu £ 32

◆ Keenly run detached house close to town, with book-filled lounge and conservatory breakfast room. Traditional décor gradually being replaced by more modern styles; light hues in bedrooms. Concise menu features their own hot-smoked salmon and other local produce.

Carlton Riverside with rm

Irfon Cres ✉ LD5 4ST – ☎ (01591) 610 248 – www.carltonriverside.co.uk – Closed 22-30 December

4 rm – †£ 40/60 ††£ 75/100

Rest – *(Closed Sunday dinner) (dinner only and Sunday lunch) (booking essential)* Menu £ 25 (dinner) – Carte £ 30/48

◆ 400 yards from the old premises, overlooking the River Irfon. Skilled cooking based on traditional combinations uses quality ingredients. Two comfy lounges and courteous host. Simple, well-priced bedrooms.

LLYSWEN – Powys – 503 K27 – ✉ Brecon 33 C3

London 188 mi. – Brecon 8 mi. – Cardiff 48 mi. – Worcester 53 mi.

Brecon Beacons National Park★★

Llangoed Hall
Northwest : 1.25 mi. on A 470 ✉ LD3 0YP – ✆ (01874) 754 525 – www.llangoedhall.com – Fax (01874) 754 545
23 rm – £ 175/190 £ 210/400
Rest – *(booking essential for non-residents)* Menu £ 25/45 **s**
◆ Homely country house by river, built by Williams-Ellis and owned by family of late Bernard and Laura Ashley. Spacious rooms mix period and modern furnishings. Impressive art collection includes Whistler. Restaurant serves classical dishes with a modern edge.

MACHYNLLETH – Powys – 503 I26 – pop. 2 147 32 B2

London 220 mi. – Shrewsbury 56 mi. – Welshpool 37 mi.
Royal House, Penrallt St ✆ (01654) 702401, mactic@powys.gov.uk
Felingerrig, ✆ (01654) 702 000
Town★ - Celtica★ **AC**
Snowdonia National Park★★★ - Centre for Alternative Technology★★ **AC**, N : 3 mi. by A 487

Ynyshir Hall
Eglwysfach, Southwest : 6 mi. on A 487 ✉ SY20 8TA – ✆ (01654) 781 209 – www.ynyshir-hall.co.uk – Fax (01654) 781 366
6 rm – £ 180/220 £ 285/375 – 3 suites
Rest – *(booking essential) (light lunch Monday and Tuesday)* Menu £ 65 (dinner) – Carte lunch £ 31/44
Spec. Scallop and langoustine carpaccio, tomato jelly and caviar. Assiette of lamb with broad beans and onion cream. Pumpkin seed soufflé with chocolate sauce.
◆ Part Georgian house set within 1000 acre RSPB reserve. Bright, individually appointed bedrooms, cosy drawing room with art, antiques and Welsh pottery. Charming and very attentive service. Adroit cooking skilfully blends the classic with the modern.

MENAI BRIDGE – Isle of Anglesey – 502 H24 – see Anglesey (Isle of)

Guesthouses don't provide the same level of service as hotels. They are often characterised by a warm welcome and a décor which reflects the owner's personality. Those shown in red are particularly pleasant.

MOLD (Yr Wyddgrug) – Flintshire – 502 K24 – pop. 9 568 32 C1

London 211 mi. – Chester 12 mi. – Liverpool 22 mi. – Shrewsbury 45 mi.
Library and Museum , Earl Rd ✆ (01352) 759331, mold@nwtic.com
18 Pantmywyn Clicain Rd, ✆ (01352) 740 318
27 Old Padeswood Station Rd, Old Padeswood, ✆ (01244) 547 701
18 Padeswood & Buckley Station Lane, The Caia, ✆ (01244) 550 537
9 Caerwys, ✆ (01352) 721 222
St Mary's Church★

Tower without rest
Nercwys, South : 1 mi. by B 5444, Nercwys rd on Treuddyn rd ✉ CH7 4EW – ✆ (01352) 700 220 – www.towerwales.co.uk – Closed 20 December-31 January
3 rm – £ 55 £ 105
◆ Impressive fortified house with pond and extensive grounds, dating from 1465 and in family almost as long. Huge high-ceilinged bedrooms boast character beds, antiques and vast modern showers.

Glasfryn
Raikes Lane, Sychdyn, North : 1 mi. by A 5119 on Civic Centre rd (Theatr Clwyd) ✉ CH7 6LR – ✆ (01352) 750 500 – www.glasfryn-mold.co.uk – Fax (01352) 751 923 – Closed 25 December
Rest – Carte £ 18/31
◆ Sizeable red-brick pub with Arts and Crafts styling and pleasant town outlook. Menu offers plenty of choice from pub to culinary classics. Portions are generous and service is swift.

WALES

MONMOUTH (Trefynwy) – Monmouthshire – 503 L28 – pop. 8 547 33 C4

London 135 mi. – Abergavenny 19 mi. – Cardiff 40 mi.

Town★

at Whitebrook South : 8.25 mi. by A 466 – ✉ Monmouth

XXX **The Crown at Whitebrook** with rm

✉ *NP25 4TX – ☎ (01600) 860 254 – www.crownatwhitebrook.co.uk – Fax (01600) 860 607 – Closed 2 weeks Christmas*

8 rm – ♦£ 80/100 ♦♦£ 115/140

Rest – *(Closed Sunday dinner) (booking essential)* Menu £ 28/45

Spec. Langoustine with leek, fennel and white chocolate. Quail with beetroot, watercress and celeriac. Spiced pineapple with tonka bean, coconut and sherry.

◆ Attentively run by smart, personable staff. Lounge bar with deep leather sofas and immaculately laid dining room. The kitchen effectively employs modern techniques to produce original, flavoursome dishes. Smart bedrooms in contemporary colours.

at Rockfield Northwest : 2.5 mi. on B 4233 – ✉ Monmouth

X **Stonemill**

West : 1 mi. on B 4233 ✉ NP25 5SW – ☎ (01600) 716 273 – www.thestonemill.co.uk – Closed 1-14 January, Sunday dinner and Monday

Rest – Menu £ 15/19 – Carte £ 26/39

◆ Converted 16C stone cider mill with exposed timbers; leather sofa in sitting area/bar. Attentive service. Well sourced modern seasonal dishes using small local suppliers.

MONTGOMERY (Trefaldwyn) – Powys – 503 K26 – pop. 1 059 32 C2

London 194 mi. – Birmingham 71 mi. – Chester 53 mi. – Shrewsbury 30 mi.

Town★

Little Brompton Farm without rest

Southeast : 2 mi. on B 4385 ✉ SY15 6HY – ☎ (01686) 668 371 – www.littlebromptonfarm.co.uk

3 rm – ♦£ 35 ♦♦£ 70

◆ Part 17C cottage on working farm, run by friendly couple: husband's lived here all his life! Cosy beamed lounge and inglenook. Hearty breakfast. Traditionally appointed rooms.

MUMBLES (The) – Swansea – 503 I29 – see Swansea

NANTGAREDIG – Carmarthenshire – 503 H28 – see Carmarthen

NANT-Y-DERRY – Monmouthshire – see Abergavenny

NARBERTH – Pembrokeshire – 503 F28 – pop. 1 869 33 A4

London 234 mi. – Caerdydd / Cardiff 88 mi. – Abertawe / Swansea 51 mi. – Rhondda 79 mi.

 **The Grove**

Molleston, South : 2 mi. by A 478 on Herons Brook rd ✉ SA67 8BX – ☎ (01834) 860 915 – www.thegrove-narberth.co.uk

12 rm – ♦£ 130 ♦♦£ 150/260

Rest – *(booking essential at lunch)* Carte £ 24/35 **s**

◆ Part-Georgian, part-Victorian house in charming rural location. Bedrooms blend bold walls and fabrics with traditional furnishings; spacious bathrooms boast every modern amenity. Monthly changing menus offer traditional dishes with a few Italian influences.

WALES

NEWPORT – Newport – 503 L29 – pop. 116 143 — 33 C4

London 145 mi. – Bristol 31 mi. – Cardiff 12 mi. – Gloucester 48 mi.

Museum and Art Gallery, John Frost Sq ✆ (01633) 842962, newport.tic@newport.gov.uk

Caerleon Broadway, ✆ (01633) 420 342

Parc Coedkernew Church Lane, ✆ (01633) 680 933

Museum and Art Gallery★ AX **M** - Transporter Bridge★ **AC** AY - Civic Centre (murals★) AX

Caerleon Roman Fortress★★ **AC** (Fortress Baths★ - Legionary Museum★ - Amphitheatre★), NE : 2.5 mi. by B 4596 AX – Tredegar House★★ (Grounds★ - Stables★), SW : 2.5 mi. by A 48 AY. Penhow Castle★, E : 8 mi. by A 48 AX

Celtic Manor Resort

Coldra Woods, East : 3 mi. on A 48 ✉ NP18 1HQ
– ✆ (01633) 413 000 – www.celtic-manor.com – Fax (01633) 412 910
298 rm – †£ 280 ††£ 280, ☕ £ 18 – 32 suites
Rest *The Crown at Celtic Manor* – *(closed Sunday and Monday)* Menu £ 38/48
Rest *Rafters* – Menu £ 17 (lunch) – Carte £ 22/44
Rest *The Olive Tree* – *(dinner only and Sunday lunch)* Menu £ 30

◆ Modern resort-style hotel in 1,400 acres. Large conference rooms, 3 golf courses, extensive leisure facilities and small shopping mall. Classical bedrooms; impressive presidential suites. Modern fine dining in The Crown. Favourites and grills in informal Rafters. Buffet and carvery in Olive Tree.

WALES

NEWPORT (Trefdraeth) – Pembrokeshire – 503 F27 – pop. 1 162 — 33 A3

London 258 mi. – Fishguard 7 mi.

Bank Cottages, Long St ✆ (01239) 820912 (summer only), newporttic@pembrokeshirecoast.org.uk

Newport Links, ✆ (01239) 820 244

Pembrokeshire Coast National Park★★

Cnapan

East St, on A 487 ✉ SA42 0SY – ✆ (01239) 820 575 – www.cnapan.co.uk
– Fax (01239) 820 878 – April-mid-December
5 rm ☕ – †£ 88 ††£ 98
Rest – *(closed Tuesday) (dinner only) (booking essential)* Menu £ 32

◆ Keenly run, well-maintained house with traditionally furnished lounge and bar. Fresh, compact bedrooms with white walls, coloured throws and slightly old-fashioned feel. Candle-lit restaurant opens onto spacious garden and offers extensive home-cooked menu.

Llysmeddyg with rm

East St ✉ SA42 0SY – ✆ (01239) 820 008 – www.llysmeddyg.com
8 rm ☕ – †£ 85/135 ††£ 150
Rest – *(Closed Monday lunch) (booking essential at lunch)* Menu £ 19 (lunch) – Carte £ 31/42

◆ Earnestly laid-back style; lunch offered in the cellar bar. Dinner, with fine art surroundings, has more of a modern edge. Bright bedrooms with good bathrooms.

NEWTOWN – Powys – pop. 10 358 – ✉ Blaenau Gwent — 32 C2

London 194 mi. – Cardiff 98 mi. – Birmingham 81 mi. – Wolverhampton 69 mi.

Highgate without rest

Bettws Cedewain, Northeast : 2.5 mi. by B 4568 on Llanfair Rd. ✉ SY16 3LF
– ✆ (01686) 623 763 – www.highgate-accommodation.co.uk – Fax (01686) 629 194
5 rm ☕ – †£ 35/50 ††£ 70/85

◆ Built in 1631, with colourful gardens, stables for your horse and superb views across rolling fields. Tastefully furnished, it boasts good-sized bedrooms and a warm, welcoming feel.

PEMBROKE (Penfro) – **Pembrokeshire** – **503** F28 – **pop. 7 214** **33** A4

London 252 mi. – Carmarthen 32 mi. – Fishguard 26 mi.

Access Cleddau Bridge (toll)

to Republic of Ireland (Rosslare) (Irish Ferries) 2 daily (4 h) – to Republic of Ireland (Cork) (Swansea Cork Ferries) daily (8 h 30 mn)

Pembroke Visitor Centre, Commons Rd ☎ (01646) 622388 (summer only), pembroke.tic@pembrokeshire.gov.uk

Pembroke Dock Military Rd, ☎ (01646) 621 453

Town★★ - Castle★★ **AC**

Pembrokeshire Coast National Park★★ - Carew Castle★ **AC**, NE : 4 mi. by A 4075. Bosherston (St Govan's Chapel★), S : 7 mi. by B 4319 and minor roads – Stack Rocks★, SW : 9 mi. by B 4319 and minor roads

at Lamphey East : 1.75 mi. on A 4139 – ✉ Pembroke

Lamphey Court

✉ *SA71 5NT – ☎ (01646) 672 273 – www.lampheycourt.co.uk – Fax (01646) 672 480*

39 rm – †£ 92/99 ††£ 105/150 **Rest** – Carte £ 17/37 **s**

◆ Large Georgian mansion surrounded by parkland, built by Charles Mathias in an idyllic location. Well furnished throughout with fine mahogany in the co-ordinated bedrooms. Formal restaurant with a good country house-style menu.

PENARTH – **Cardiff** – **503** K29 – **see Cardiff**

PENMACHNO – **Conwy** – **502** I24 – **see Betws-y-Coed**

PENNAL – **Gwynedd** – **503** I26 – **see Aberdovey**

PENTYRCH – **Cardiff** – **503** K29 – **see Cardiff**

PONTDOLGOCH – **Powys** – **see Caersws**

PORTHCAWL – **Bridgend** – **503** I29 – **pop. 15 640** **33** B4

London 183 mi. – Cardiff 28 mi. – Swansea 18 mi.

The Old Police Station, John St ☎ (01656) 786639, porthcawltic@bridgend.gov.uk

Glamorgan Heritage Coast★

Foam Edge without rest

9 West Dr ✉ CF36 3LS – ☎ (01656) 782 866 – www.foam-edge.co.uk

3 rm – †£ 40/50 ††£ 70/85

◆ Unassuming house by the promenade masks stylish, modern interior with superb Bristol Channel views. A family home in essence, with comfy lounge and communal breakfast. Bedrooms in pastel hues.

PORTHGAIN – **Pembrokeshire** – **see St Davids**

PORTHMADOG – **Gwynedd** – **503** H25 – **pop. 3 008** **32** B2

Cardiff 162 mi. – Blanau Ffestiniog 12 mi. – Caernarfon 19 mi.

Plas Tan-yr-Allt

Tremadog, North : 1.5 mi. by A 487 on A 498 ✉ LL49 9RG – ☎ (01766) 514 545 – www.tanyrallt.co.uk – Closed February and Monday-Wednesday October to March

6 rm – †£ 120 ††£ 175

Rest – *(closed Monday-Tuesday) (dinner only) (booking essential) (communal dining)* Menu £ 39 **s**

◆ Personally run country house in 50 acres: superb bay views from terrace. Beautiful drawing room, stylish library, relaxed, idiosyncratic feel. Chic bedrooms; heated slate floors in bathrooms. Communal dining at vast table, from classical, daily changing menus.

PORTMEIRION – **Gwynedd** – **502** H25 **32** B2

London 245 mi. – Caernarfon 23 mi. – Colwyn Bay 40 mi. – Dolgellau 24 mi.

Village★★★ **AC**

Snowdonia National Park★★★ - Lleyn Peninsula★★ – Ffestiniog Railway★★ **AC**

Portmeirion

LL48 6ET – (01766) 770 000 – www.portmerion-village.com – Fax (01766) 771 331

28 rm – £ 135/265 £ 170/300 – 14 suites

Rest – *(booking essential for non-residents)* Menu £ 25/40

◆ Set in private Italianate village in extensive gardens and woodland designed by Sir Clough Williams-Ellis. Delightful views of village and estuary. Antique furnished rooms. Restaurant offers lovely views of the estuary and an open and light style of décor.

Castell Deudraeth rest,

LL48 6EN – (01766) 772 400 – www.portmerion-village.com – Fax (01766) 771 771

9 rm – £ 265 £ 190/300 – 2 suites

Rest ***Grill*** – Carte £ 17/29

◆ Impressive crenellated manor house displaying original stone fireplace. Relaxed, informal atmosphere; fine Snowdonia views. Huge bedrooms boast chic, contemporary décor and kitchen areas. Choose from brasserie classics in conservatory/pleasant walled garden.

PWLLHELI – **Gwynedd** – **502** G25 – **pop. 3 861** **32** B2

London 261 mi. – Aberystwyth 73 mi. – Caernarfon 21 mi.

Min Y Don, Station Sq (01758) 613000, pwllheli.tic@gwynedd.gov.uk

Golf Rd, (01758) 701 644

Lleyn Peninsula★★

Plas Bodegroes with rm

Northwest : 1.75 mi. on A 497 LL53 5TH – (01758) 612 363 – www.bodegroes.co.uk – Fax (01758) 701 247 – 11 March-29 November

11 rm – £ 50/150 £ 170

Rest – *(closed Sunday dinner and Monday except Bank Holidays) (dinner only and Sunday lunch) (booking essential)* Menu £ 43

◆ Delightful Grade II listed Georgian house in secluded gardens. Local art decorates the pale green dining room. Classically based cooking, using good quality local ingredients. Contemporary, Scandinavian style bedrooms.

at Boduan **Northwest : 3.75 mi. on A 497 – Pwllheli**

The Old Rectory without rest

LL53 6DT – (01758) 721 519 – www.theoldrectory.net – Fax (01758) 721 519 – Closed 1 week Christmas

3 rm – £ 65/90 £ 90/100

◆ Lovely part-Georgian family home with paddock, run by charming owner. Comfy lounge with carved wooden fireplace; cakes on arrival. Tasteful bedrooms boast period furnishings and garden views.

RHOSCOLYN – **Isle of Anglesey** – **503** G24 – **see Anglesey (Isle of)**

RHOS-ON-SEA (Llandrillo-yn-Rhos) – **Conwy** – **502** I24 – **see Colwyn Bay**

RHYL – **Denbighshire** – **502** J24 – **pop. 24 889** **32** C1

Cardiff 182 mi. – Chester 34 mi. – Llandudno 18 mi.

Rhuddlan Castle★★, S : 3 mi. by A 525 – Bodelwyddan★★, S : 5 mi. by A 525 and minor rd – St Asaph Cathedral★, S : 5 mi. by A 525. Llandudno★, W : 16 mi. by A 548, A 55 and B 5115

XX **Barratt's at Ty'n Rhyl** with rm

167 Vale Rd, South : 0.5 mi. on A 525 ✉ LL18 2PH – ✆ (01745) 344 138 – www.barrattsoftynrhyl.co.uk – Fax (01745) 344 138

3 rm ☕ – 🚹£ 67 🚹🚹£ 90

Rest – *(dinner only and Sunday lunch) (booking essential)* Menu £ 15/25 **s** – Carte approx. £ 36 **s**

◆ Rhyl's oldest house boasts comfortable lounges with rich oak panelling. Dine in either the conservatory or original house. Ambitious cooking on classic base. Individual rooms.

ROCKFIELD – Monmouthshire – 503 L28 – see Monmouth

ROWEN – Conwy – see Conwy

RUTHIN (Rhuthun) – Denbighshire – 502 K24 – pop. 5 218 — 32 C1

London 210 mi. – Birkenhead 31 mi. – Chester 23 mi. – Liverpool 34 mi.

Ruthin-Pwllglas, ✆ (01824) 702 296

Llandyrnog (St Dyfnog's Church★), Llanrhaeder-yng-Nghinmeirch (Jesse Window★★), N : 5.5 mi. by A 494 and B 5429. Denbigh★, NW : 7 mi. on A 525

Firgrove

Llanfwrog, West : 1.25 mi. by A 494 on B 5105 ✉ LL15 2LL – ✆ (01824) 702 677 – www.firgrovecountryhouse.co.uk – Fax (01824) 702 677 – March-15 November

3 rm ☕ – 🚹£ 55 🚹🚹£ 80

Rest – *(by arrangement, communal dining)* Menu £ 30

◆ Attractive stone-built house in pleasant gardens. Sit by cosy inglenook in winter or in delightful glasshouse in summer. Comfy four-poster bedrooms and self-contained cottage offer valley views. Communal dinners feature locally sourced farm produce.

Eyarth Station without rest

Llanfair Dyffryn Clwyd, South : 1.75 mi. by A 525 ✉ LL15 2EE – ✆ (01824) 703 643 – www.eyarthstation.co.uk – Fax (0871) 714 67 43

6 rm ☕ – 🚹£ 50 🚹🚹£ 72

◆ Former railway station: platform at heart of house, tracks under conservatory. Simple pine-furnished bedrooms feature railway memorabilia. Panoramic windows in lounge afford great rural views.

XX **Manorhaus** with rm

Well St ✉ LL15 1AH – ✆ (01824) 704 830 – www.manorhaus.com – Fax (01824) 707 333 – Closed 1 week Christmas

8 rm ☕ – 🚹£ 110 🚹🚹£ 150 **Rest** – *(dinner only)* Menu £ 30

◆ Classical Georgian property with conservatory extension; weekly changing menu features locally sourced ingredients. Each bedroom individually styled to correspond to the work of one of the contemporary Welsh artists exhibited here. Small gym and mini-cinema.

ST ASAPH – Denbighshire – 503 J24 – pop. 3 491 — 32 C1

London 223 mi. – Cardiff 176 mi. – Liverpool 46 mi. – Manchester 69 mi.

Tan-yr-Onnen without rest

Waen, East : 1.5 mi. by A 55 and B 5429 on Tremeirchion rd ✉ LL17 0DU – ✆ (01745) 583 821 – www.northwalesbreaks.co.uk – Closed Christmas and New Year

6 rm ☕ – 🚹£ 65 🚹🚹£ 85/120

◆ Just off the A55, this spacious house offers stylish, up-to-date bedrooms, well-equipped with silent fridges, DVD players and digital TVs. Large conservatory and lounge; full Welsh breakfast.

ST CLEARS – Carmarthenshire – 503 G28 – pop. 1 587 — 33 B3

London 221 mi. – Caerdydd / Cardiff 76 mi. – Abertawe / Swansea 37 mi. – Llanelli 33 mi.

Coedllys Country House without rest

Llangynin, Northwest : 3.5 mi. by A 40 turning first left after 30 mph sign on entering village. ✉ *SA33 4JY – ✆ (01994) 231 455 – www.coedllyscountryhouse.co.uk – Fax (01944) 231 441 – Closed 23-27 December*

3 rm – £ 58/68 £ 90/100

◆ Idyllic country house and animal sanctuary with picture-perfect façade. Delightful owner keeps everything immaculate. Superb breakfasts. Rooms with unerring eye for detail.

ST DAVIDS (Tyddewi) – Pembrokeshire – 503 E28 – pop. 1 959 — 33 A3

– ✉ Haverfordwest

London 266 mi. – Carmarthen 46 mi. – Fishguard 16 mi.

Oriel Y Parc ✆ (01437) 720392, orielyparc@pembrokeshirecoast.org.uk

St Davids City Whitesands Bay, ✆ (01437) 721 751

Town★ – Cathedral★★ - Bishop's Palace★ **AC**

Pembrokeshire Coast National Park★★

Warpool Court

Southwest : 0.5 mi. by Porth Clais rd ✉ *SA62 6BN – ✆ (01437) 720 300 – www.warpoolcourthotel.com – Fax (01437) 720 676 – closed January and last 2 weeks November*

21 rm – £ 105/140 £ 340/360

Rest – Menu £ 40 (dinner) **s** – Carte (lunch) £ 26/38 **s**

◆ Over 3000 hand-painted tiles of Celtic or heraldic design decorate the interior of this 19C house. Modern bedrooms, some with views over neat lawned gardens to the sea. Daily changing classic menus accompanied by fine views.

Ramsey House

Lower Moor, Southwest : 0.5 mi. on Porth Clais rd ✉ *SA62 6RP – ✆ (01437) 720 321 – www.ramseyhouse.co.uk – closed 24-26 December and restricted opening November-January*

6 rm – £ 70/120 £ 100/120 **Rest** – *(by arrangement)* Menu £ 35

◆ Unassuming bungalow hiding stylish, contemporary interior with superb comforts, small lounge and bar. Bedrooms display modern colour schemes and state-of-the-art shower rooms. Traditional menus offer tasty three course dinners.

The Waterings without rest

Anchor Drive, High St, East : 0.25 mi. on A 487 ✉ *SA62 6QH – ✆ (01437) 720 876 – www.waterings.co.uk – Fax (01437) 720 876*

5 rm – £ 50/80 £ 75/80

◆ Set in peaceful landscaped gardens and named after a sheltered cove on Ramsey Island. Spacious rooms, furnished in solid pine, around a central courtyard. Likeable hosts.

Cwtch

22 High St ✉ *SA62 6SD – ✆ (01437) 720 491 – www.cwtchrestaurant.co.uk – Closed Monday October-June*

Rest – *(dinner only) (booking advisable)* Menu £ 28

◆ Simple, friendly restaurant. Daily menu features hearty portions of honest British classics, crafted from local produce and arriving with large side of veg; old school desserts.

at Porthgain Northeast : 7.75 mi. by A 487 – ✉ St Davids

The Shed

The Quay ✉ *SA62 5BN – ✆ (01348) 831 518 – www.theshedporthgain.co.uk – Closed Tuesday and restricted opening in winter*

Rest – Seafood – *(booking essential)* Carte £ 30/36

◆ At the tip of the harbour in a charming spot, this locally renowned rustic eatery started life as a lobster pot store and now serves simply prepared, tasty seafood dishes.

SALEM – Carmarthenshire – see Llandeilo

SAUNDERSFOOT – Pembrokeshire – 503 F28 – pop. 2 946 — 33 A4

London 241 mi. – Cardiff 90 mi. – Pembroke 12 mi.

St Brides Spa

St Brides Hill ✉ SA69 9NH – ☎ (01834) 812 304 – www.stbridesspahotel.com – Fax (01834) 811 766

40 rm – †£ 190 ††£ 250/280

Rest *Cliff* – Carte £ 29/52 **s**

◆ Occupying a great position over Carmarthen Bay, with breathtaking spa equipped to the highest spec. Fabulous terraces and outdoor infinity pool. Superbly designed bedrooms. Modern European cooking in fine dining restaurant with informal style.

SEION – Gwynedd – see Caernarfon

SHIRENEWTON – Monmouthshire – 503 L29 – see Chepstow

SKENFRITH – Monmouthshire — 33 C4

London 135 mi. – Hereford 16 mi. – Ross-on-Wye 11 mi.

The Bell at Skenfrith with rm

✉ NP7 8UH – ☎ (01600) 750 235 – www.skenfrith.co.uk – Fax (01600) 750 525 – Closed last week January, first week February and Tuesday November-Easter

11 rm – †£ 75/120 ††£ 220

Rest – *(booking essential)* Menu £ 23 (Sunday lunch) £ 29 (dinner) – Carte £ 20/29

◆ Well-run pub in verdant valley offering clean, fresh cooking of classic dishes with an innovative twist. Excellent choice of champagnes; warm and unobtrusive service. Understated elegance in super-comfy bedrooms.

SOUTHERNDOWN – Bridgend – 503 J29 – see Bridgend

SWANSEA – Swansea – 503 I29 – pop. 169 880 — 33 B4

London 191 mi. – Birmingham 136 mi. – Bristol 82 mi. – Cardiff 40 mi.

Plymouth St ☎ (01792) 468321, tourism@swansea.gov.uk

18 Morriston 160 Clasemont Rd, ☎ (01792) 796 528

18 Clyne Mayals 120 Owls Lodge Lane, ☎ (01792) 401 989

18 Langland Bay, ☎ (01792) 361 721

18 Fairwood Park Fairwood Blackhills Lane, ☎ (01792) 297 849

9 Inco Clydach, ☎ (01792) 841 257

9 Allt-y-Graban Pontllin Allt-y-Graban Rd, ☎ (01792) 885 757

9 Palleg Swansea Valley Lower Cwmtwrch, ☎ (01639) 842 193

Town★ - Maritime Quarter★ B – Maritime and Industrial Museum★ B – Glynn Vivian Art Gallery★ B – Guildhall (British Empire Panels★ A **H**)

Gower Peninsula★★ (Rhossili★★), W : by A 4067 A. The Wildfowl and Wetlands Trust★, Llanelli, NW : 6.5 mi. by A 483 and A 484 A

Plans pages 870, 871

Morgans

Somerset Place ✉ SA1 1RR – ☎ (01792) 484 848 – www.morganshotel.co.uk – Fax (01792) 484 849 — B**b**

41 rm – †£ 90/250 ††£ 90/250 **Rest** – Menu £ 17/25

◆ Converted hotel near docks. Contemporary feel: neutral colours, leather sofas. Splendid original features include soaring cupola. Very stylish rooms. Modish cooking in sleek surroundings.

Didier & Stephanie's

56 St Helens Rd ✉ SA1 4BE – ☎ (01792) 655 603 – Fax (01792) 470 563 – closed Christmas and New Year, Sunday and Monday — A**a**

Rest – French – *(booking essential)* Menu £ 17 (lunch) – Carte (dinner) £ 28/30

◆ Cosy, neighbourhood-styled restaurant with a strong Gallic influence. Welcoming owners provide tasty, good value, seasonally changing menus with lots of French ingredients.

SWANSEA

Clase Rd.	A	12
Martin St	A	24
Pen-y-Graig Rd.	A	30
Plasmarl By-Pass	A	32
Ravenhill Rd.	A	35
St Helen's Rd.	A	40
Station Rd	A	37
Terrace Rd	A	45
Uplands Crescent	A	49
Walter Rd.	A	52
Woodfield St	A	60

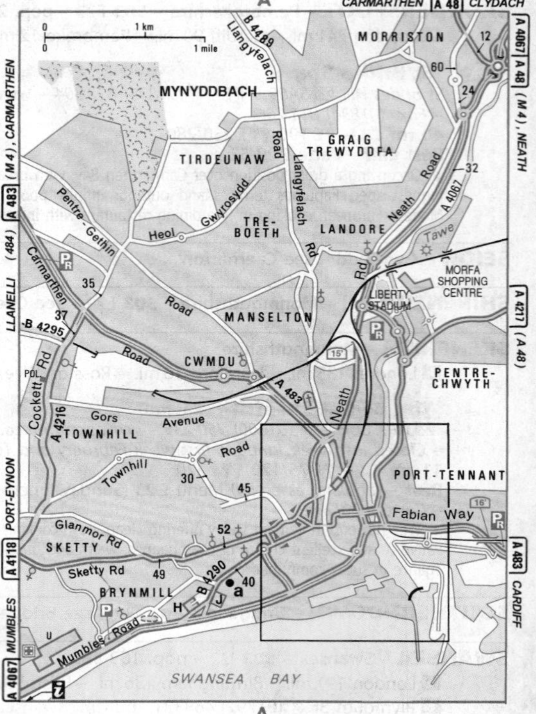

at The Mumbles Southwest : 7.75 mi. by A 4067 - A – ✉ Swansea

Darcy's

698 Mumbles Rd ✉ SA3 4EH
– ✆ (01792) 361 616 – www.darcysrestaurant.com
– Closed 1-16 January, 25-26 December, Monday and lunch Tuesday and Sunday

Rest – Menu £ 17 (lunch) – Carte £ 21/39

◆ Simple, friendly restaurant serving tasty dishes in a mix of styles; some are quite classic, others more modern. Slate and exposed brick give a rustic feel. Good value lunch menu.

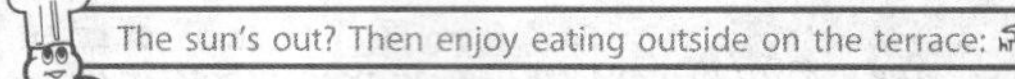

at Llanrhidian West : 10.5 mi. by A 4118 - A - B 4271 – ✉ Reynoldston

Fairyhill

Reynoldston, West : 2.5 mi. by Llangennith Rd ✉ SA3 1BS
– ✆ (01792) 390 139 – www.fairyhill.net – Fax (01792) 391 358
– Closed 1-27 January and 26 December

8 rm – †£ 155 ††£ 275

Rest – Menu £ 20/45 **s** – Carte (lunch) £ 26/38 **s**

◆ Georgian country house in extensive parkland and gardens. Mix includes sleek lounge, eclectic bedrooms, treatment and meeting rooms, all set within general modish ambience. Gower produce dominates seasonal menus.

WALES

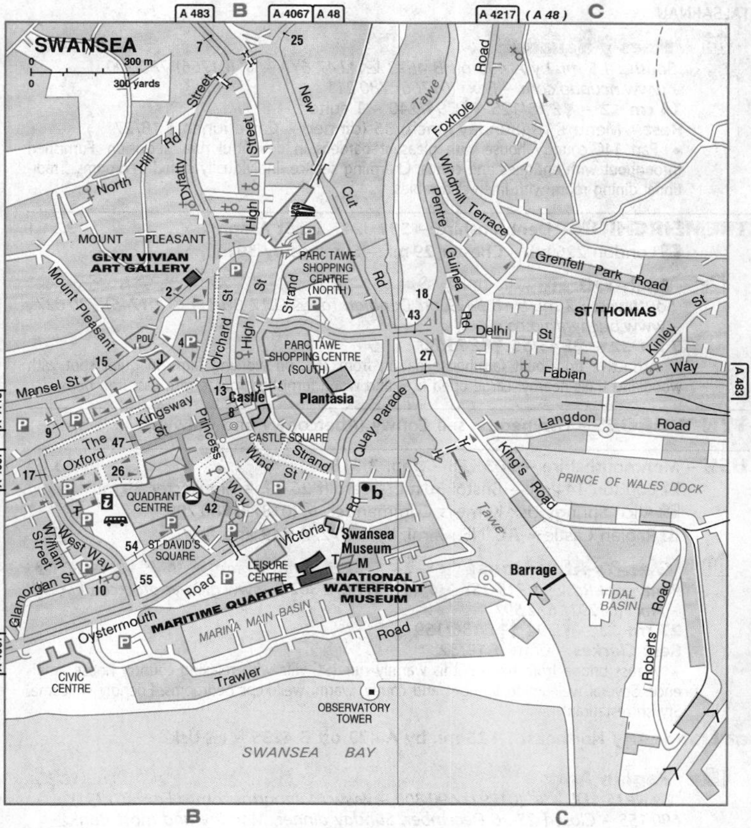

SWANSEA

Street	Grid	No.
Alexandra Rd	B	2
Belle Vue Way	B	4
Carmarthen Rd	B	7
Castle St	B	8
Christina St	B	9
Clarence Terrace	B	10
College St	B	13
De la Beche St	B	15
Dillwyn St	B	17
East Bank Way	C	18
Grove Pl.	B	22
Kingsway (The)	B	
Nearth Rd	B	25
Nelson St	B	26
New Cut Bridge	C	27
Oxford St	B	
Parc Tawe Shopping Centre	B	
Princess Way	B	
Quadrant Centre	B	
St David's Square	B	
St Mary's Square	B	42
Tawe Bridge	C	43
Union St	B	47
Wellington St	B	54
West Way	B	55

XX The Welcome To Town

P VISA

✉ SA3 1EH – ✆ (01792) 390 015
– *www.thewelcometotown.co.uk*
– *Fax (01792) 390 015*
– *Closed 1 week October, 25-26 December, 1 January, Sunday and Monday*

Rest – *(booking essential)* Menu £ 20/30

◆ Converted pub set on picturesque peninsula. Cosy, traditional interior with good service of seasonal dishes cooked with real quality from wide choice menu.

TALSARNAU – Gwynedd – 502 H25 – pop. 647 – ✉ Harlech — 32 B2

London 236 mi. – Caernafon 33 mi. – Chester 67 mi. – Dolgellau 25 mi.

Snowdonia National Park★★★

Maes-y-Neuadd

South : 1.5 mi. by A 496 off B 4573 ✉ LL47 6YA – ✆ (01766) 780 200 – www.neuadd.com – Fax (01766) 780 211
14 rm – †£ 75/125 ††£ 94/240 – 1 suite
Rest – Menu £ 18 (Sunday lunch)/35 (dinner) – Carte lunch £ 18/27
◆ Part 14C country house with pleasant gardens in delightful rural seclusion. Furnished throughout with antiques and curios. Charming service. Individually styled bedrooms. Traditional dining room with linen-clad tables.

TREMEIRCHION – **Denbighshire** – **502** J24 – ✉ **St Asaph** **32** C1

London 225 mi. – Chester 29 mi. – Shrewsbury 59 mi.

Bach-Y-Graig without rest

Southwest : 2 mi. by B 5429 off Denbigh rd ✉ LL17 0UH – ✆ (01745) 730 627 – www.bachygraig.co.uk
3 rm – †£ 45/55 ††£ 75/80
◆ Attractive brick-built farmhouse dating from 16C, on working farm. In quiet spot with woodland trails nearby. Large open fires and wood furnished rooms with cast iron beds.

TYN-Y-GROES – **Gwynedd** – **see Conwy (Aberconwy and Colwyn)**

USK – **Monmouthshire** – **503** L28 – **pop. 2 318** **33** C4

London 144 mi. – Bristol 30 mi. – Cardiff 26 mi. – Gloucester 39 mi.

Alice Springs Usk Kemeys Commander, ✆ (01873) 880 708

Raglan Castle★ **AC**, NE : 7 mi. by A 472, A 449 and A 40

Glen-Yr-Afon House rm, rest,

Pontypool Rd ✉ NP15 1SY – ✆ (01291) 672 302 – www.glen-yr-afon.co.uk – Fax (01291) 672 597
27 rm – †£ 94 ††£ 136/159
Rest *Clarkes* – Carte £ 19/32
◆ Across bridge from town is this warmly run 19C villa with relaxing country house ambience. Several welcoming lounges and comfy, warm, well-kept bedrooms. Friendly welcome. Stylish restaurant.

at Llandenny **Northeast : 4.25 mi. by A 472 off B 4235 – ✉ Usk**

Raglan Arms

✉ NP15 1DL – ✆ (01291) 690 800 – www.raglanarms.com – Fax (01291) 690 155 – Closed 25-26 December, Sunday dinner, Monday and most Bank Holidays
Rest – Carte £ 22/31
◆ Cosy village pub with fireside sofas and simply laid tables. Local produce employed in a range of cooking styles; lunchtime main courses offer particularly good value.

VALLEY – **Isle of Anglesey** – **503** G24 – **see Anglesey (Isle of)**

WELSH HOOK – **Pembrokeshire** – **503** F28 – **see Fishguard**

WHITEBROOK – **Monmouthshire** – **see Monmouth**

WOLF'S CASTLE (Cas-Blaidd) – **Pembrokeshire** – **503** F28 – **pop. 616** **33** A3
– ✉ **Haverfordwest**

London 258 mi. – Fishguard 7 mi. – Haverfordwest 8 mi.

Pembrokeshire Coast National Park★★

Wolfscastle Country H. rest,

✉ SA62 5LZ – ✆ (01437) 741 225 – www.wolfscastle.com – Fax (01437) 741 383 – Closed 24-26 December
20 rm – †£ 75/105 ††£ 95/135
Rest – *(lunch by arrangement Monday-Saturday)* Menu £ 14 – Carte £ 21/32
◆ Spacious, family run country house; tidy rooms in traditional soft chintz, modern conference room and simply styled bar with a mix of cushioned settles and old wooden chairs. Dining room with neatly laid tables in pink linens.

WALES

WREXHAM (Wrecsam) – Wrexham – 502 L24 – pop. 42 576 32 C1

London 192 mi. – Chester 12 mi. – Liverpool 35 mi. – Shrewsbury 28 mi.

Lambpit St ✆ (01978) 292015, tic@wrexham.gov.uk

Chirk, ✆ (01691) 774 407

Clays Golf Centre Bryn Estyn Rd, ✆ (01978) 661 406

Moss Valley Moss Rd, ✆ (01978) 720 518

Pen-y-Cae Ruabon Rd, ✆ (01978) 810 108

Plassey Oaks Golf Complex Eyton, ✆ (01978) 780 020

St Giles Church★

Erddig★★ **AC** (Gardens★★), SW : 2 m – Gresford (All Saints Church★), N : 4 mi. by A 5152 and B 5445

at Gresford Northeast : 3 mi. by A 483 on B 5445

Pant-yr-Ochain

Old Wrexham Rd, South : 1 mi. ✉ LL12 8TY – ✆ (01978) 853 525 – www.brunningandprice.co.uk – Fax (01978) 853 505 – Closed 25 December

Rest – Carte £ 19/28

◆ Classic country manor house with mature, manicured gardens and a lake. Daily changing menu offers hearty, wholesome dishes ranging from pub classics to more modern fare. Over 12s only.

WALES

Ireland

O. Forir/MICHELIN

Northern Ireland

ANNAHILT (Eanach Eilte) – Down – 712 N/O4 – see Hillsborough

BALLINTOY – Moyle – 712 M2 35 C1

Belfast - 59 mi. – Ballycastle 8 mi. – Londonderry 48 mi.

Whitepark House without rest

150 Whitepark Rd, West : 1.5 mi. on A2 ✉ BT54 6NH – ✆ (028) 2073 1482 – www.whiteparkhouse.com

3 rm – £ 75 £ 100

◆ Charming 18C house with personable owner. Comfy, open-fired lounge and individually decorated bedrooms filled with antiques, plants, books and art. Breakfast around communal table.

BALLYCLARE (Bealach Cláir) – Newtownabbey – 712 N/O3 35 D2 – pop. 8 770

Belfast 14 mi. – Newtownabbey 6 mi. – Lisburn 23 mi.

Oregano

29 Ballyrobert Rd, South : 3.25 mi. by A 57 on B 56 ✉ BT39 9RY – ✆ (028) 9084 0099 – www.oreganorestaurant.co.uk – Fax (028) 9084 0033 – Closed 25 December, 1 January, 12-20 July, Saturday lunch, Sunday dinner and Monday

Rest – Menu £ 15 (lunch) – Carte £ 23/34

◆ Whitewashed Victorian house hides stylish restaurant with leather-furnished bar/lounge. Good value modern British cooking uses local produce. European influences; clean, unfussy flavours.

BALLYMENA (An Baile Meánach) – Ballymena – 712 N3 35 C2 – pop. 28 717 Ireland

Belfast 27 mi. – Dundalk 78 mi. – Larne 21 mi. – Londonderry 51 mi.

1-29 Bridge St ✆ (028) 2563 5900, tourist.information@ballymena.gov.uk

128 Raceview Rd, ✆ (028) 2586 1207

Antrim Glens★★★ - Murlough Bay★★★ (Fair Head ≤★★★), NE : 32 mi. by A 26, A 44, A 2 and minor road - Glengariff Forest Park★★ **AC** (Waterfall★★), NW : 13 mi. by A 43 – Glengariff★, NE : 18 mi. by A 43 - Glendun★, NE : 19 mi. by A 43, B 14 and A2 – Antrim (Round Tower★) S : 9.5 mi. by A 26

at Galgorm West : 3 mi. on A 42 – ✉

Galgorm Resort and Spa rest,

136 Fenaghy Rd, West : 1.5 mi. on Cullybacky rd ✉ BT42 1EA – ✆ (028) 2588 1001 – www.galgorm.com – Fax (028) 2588 0080

75 rm – £ 145 £ 145/295

Rest *River Room* – *(closed Sunday-Wednesday) (dinner only and Sunday lunch)* Carte £ 32/45

Rest *Gillies* – Carte £ 20/46

◆ Victorian manor house in smart grounds. Stylish lounges, huge function rooms, superb spa/leisure club. Modern bedrooms with excellent facilities in annexes; more traditional rooms in main house. Classical fine dining in River Room. Informal and al fresco dining in Gillies steak house.

BANGOR (Beannchar) – North Down – 712 O/P4 – pop. 58 388 35 D2 Ireland

Belfast 15 mi. – Newtownards 5 mi.

34 Quay St ✆ (028) 9127 0069, tic@northdown.gov.uk

North Down Heritage Centre★

Ulster Folk and Transport Museum★★ **AC**, W : 8 mi. by A 2. Newtownards : Movilla Priory (Cross Slabs★) S : 4 mi. by A 21 - Mount Stewart★★★ **AC**, SE : 90 mi. by A 21 and A 20 – Scrabo Tower (≤★★) S : 6.5 mi. by A 21 – Ballycopeland Windmill★, SE : 10 mi. by B 21 and A 2, turning right at Millisle – Strangford Lough★ (Castle Espie Centre★ **AC** - Nendrum Monastery★) - Grey Abbey★ **AC**, SE : 20 mi. by A 2, A 21 and A 20

Clandeboye Lodge

10 Estate Rd, Clandeboye, Southwest : 3 mi. by A 2 and Dundonald rd following signs for Blackwood Golf Centre ✉ BT19 1UR – ✆ (028) 9185 2500 – www.clandeboyelodge.com – Fax (028) 9185 2772 – Closed 24-26 December

43 rm – †£ 75/105 ††£ 85/175

Rest *Clanbrasserie* – *(bar lunch Monday-Saturday)* Carte £ 19/31 **s**

◆ On site of former estate school house, surrounded by 4 acres of woodland. Well placed for country and coast. Meetings and weddings in separate extension. Contemporary rooms. Restaurant boasts minimal, stylish décor. Modish menus.

Cairn Bay Lodge without rest

278 Seacliffe Rd, East : 1.25 mi. by Quay St ✉ BT20 5HS – ✆ (028) 9146 7636 – www.cairnbaylodge.com – Fax (028) 9145 7728 – closed 3 weeks January

3 rm – †£ 60/70 ††£ 70/80

◆ Large Edwardian house overlooking the bay. Neat garden, comfy guest areas, unusual objets d'art and small beauty/therapy facility. Spacious, individually styled bedrooms boast plenty of extras.

Shelleven House without rest

59-61 Princetown Rd ✉ BT20 3TA – ✆ (028) 9127 1777 – www.shellevenhouse.com – Fax (028) 9127 1777

11 rm – †£ 36/50 ††£ 75/80

◆ Personally run, end of terrace, double front Victorian house; short stroll to marina. Large, uniformly appointed rooms: ask for a large one at the front. Homely, good value.

The Boat House

Seacliff Rd ✉ BT20 5HA – ✆ (028) 9146 9253 – www.theboathouseni.co.uk – Closed 2 weeks spring, 2 weeks autumn, Monday except Bank Holidays and Tuesday

Rest – Menu £ 22/25 – Carte £ 26/35

◆ Harbour front former lifeboat station housing intimate, linen-laid restaurant run by two brothers. Classically based cooking with some French/Italian influences. Good use of local produce.

Jeffers by the Marina

7 Grays Hill ✉ BT20 3BB – ✆ (028) 9185 9555 – www.jeffersbythemarina.com – Closed 25-26 December and Monday except Bank Holidays

Rest – Carte £ 24/30

◆ Narrow, glass-fronted restaurant opposite marina, with mirrored wall and black, granite-topped tables. Modern cooking makes good use of indigenous produce. Polite, friendly service.

Coyle's

44 High St ✉ BT20 5AZ – ✆ (028) 9127 0362 – www.coylesbistro.co.uk – Fax (028) 9127 0362 – Closed 25 December

Rest – Carte £ 23/32

◆ Friendly, laid-back, typically Irish pub; a great place for a quiet drink and a good meal. Bar menu offers classics and some international influences; bistro menu steps things up a gear.

O. Forir/MICHELIN

BELFAST (Béal Feirste)

County: Belfast
Michelin regional map: **712** O4
Dublin 103 mi.
– Londonderry 70 mi.

Population: 276 459
Ireland
Map reference: **35** D2

PRACTICAL INFORMATION

Tourist Information

47 Donegal Pl (028) 9024 6609, info@belfastvisitor.com

Belfast International Airport, Information desk (028) 9448 4677

George Best Belfast City Airport, Sydenham Bypass (028) 9093 5372

Airports

Belfast International Airport, Aldergrove : (028) 9448 4848, W : 15.5 mi. by A 52 AY

George Best Belfast City Airport : (028) 9093 9093

Ferries and Shipping Lines

to Isle of Man (Douglas) (Isle of Man Steam Packet Co. Ltd) (summer only) (2 h 45 mn)
– to Stranraer (Stena Line) 4-5 daily (1 h 30 mn/3 h 15 mn), (Seacat Scotland) March-January (90 mn)
– to Liverpool (Norfolkline Irish Sea) daily (8 h 30 mn)

Golf Courses

18 Balmoral 518 Lisburn Rd, (028) 9038 1514

18 Belvoir Park Newtonbreda 73 Church Rd, (028) 9049 1693

18 Fortwilliam Downview Ave, (028) 9037 0770

18 The Nock Club Dundonald Summerfield, (028) 9048 2249

18 Shandon Park 73 Shandon Park, (028) 9080 5030

9 Cliftonville Westland Rd, (028) 9022 8585

9 Ormeau 50 Park Road, (028) 9064 1069

SIGHTS

In town

City★ - Ulster Museum★★ (Spanish Armada Treasure★★, Shrine of St Patrick's Hand★) AZ **M1** – City Hall★ BY – Donegall Square★ BY **20** – Botanic Gardens (Palm House★) AZ – St Anne's Cathedral★ BX – Crown Liquor Saloon★ BY – Sinclair Seamen's Church★ BX – St Malachy's Church★ BY

On the outskirts

Belfast Zoological Gardens★★ **AC**, N : 5 mi. by A 6 AY

In the surounding area

Carrickfergus (Castle★★ **AC**, St Nicholas' Church★) NE : 9.5 mi. by A 2 – Talnotry Cottage Bird Garden, Crumlin★ **AC**, W : 13.5 mi. by A 52

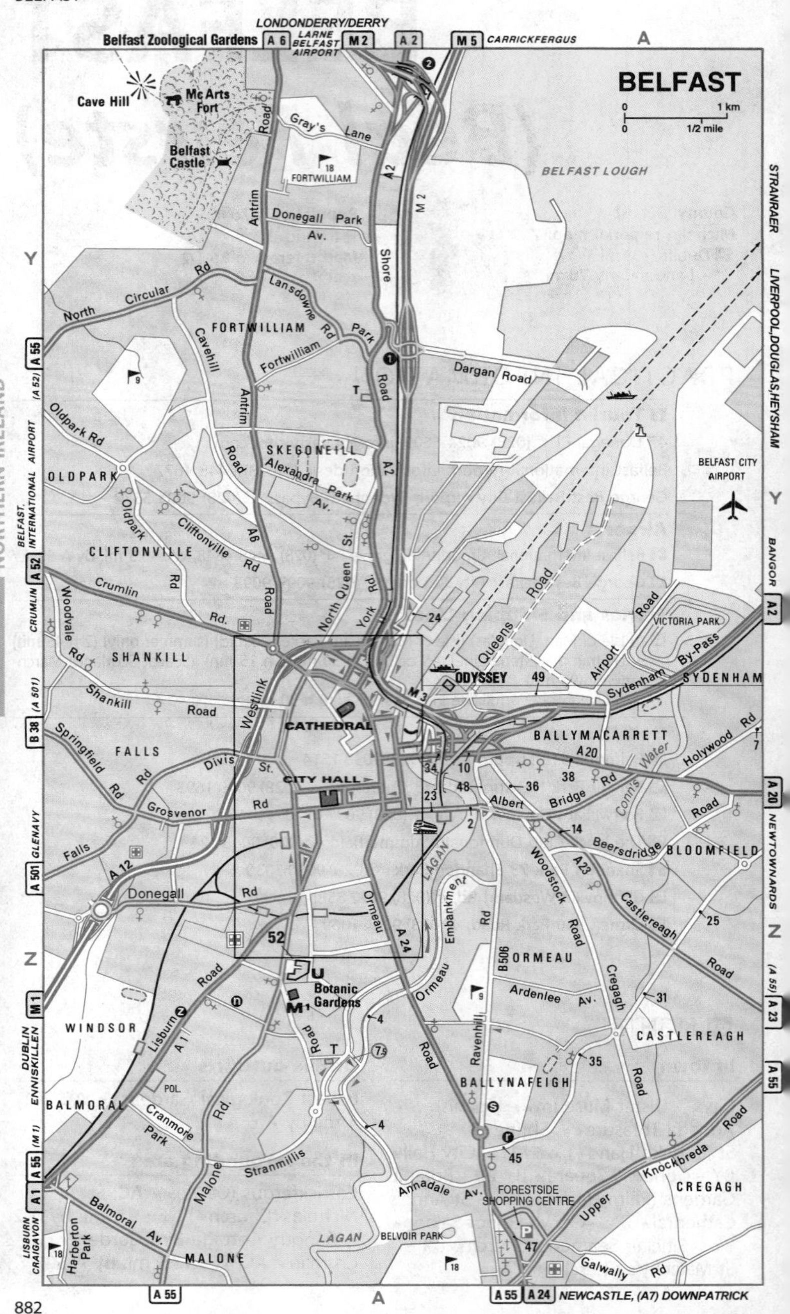
BELFAST
LONDONDERRY/DERRY
Belfast Zoological Gardens
LARNE BELFAST AIRPORT
CARRICKFERGUS
Cave Hill
McArts Fort
Belfast Castle
FORTWILLIAM
BELFAST LOUGH
STRANRAER
LIVERPOOL,DOUGLAS,HEYSHAM
BELFAST CITY AIRPORT
NORTHERN IRELAND
BELFAST, INTERNATIONAL AIRPORT
CRUMLIN
GLENAVY
DUBLIN ENNISKILLEN
LISBURN CRAIGAVON
BANGOR
NEWTOWNARDS
NEWCASTLE, (A7) DOWNPATRICK
OLDPARK
CLIFTONVILLE
SKEGONEILL
SHANKILL
FALLS
CATHEDRAL
CITY HALL
ODYSSEY
BALLYMACARRETT
SYDENHAM
VICTORIA PARK
BLOOMFIELD
ORMEAU
WINDSOR
BALMORAL
Botanic Gardens
CASTLEREAGH
BALLYNAFEIGH
MALONE
CREGAGH
FORESTSIDE SHOPPING CENTRE
BELVOIR PARK
LAGAN
Conn's Water
North Circular Rd
Antrim Road
Gray's Lane
Donegall Park Av.
Shore Road
Lansdowne Rd
Fortwilliam Park
Cavehill Road
Dargan Road
Oldpark Rd
Alexandra Park Av.
North Queen St.
York Rd.
Cliftonville Rd
Crumlin Rd.
Woodvale Rd
Shankill Road
Springfield Rd
Westlink
Divis St.
Grosvenor Rd
Falls
Donegall Rd
Queens Road
Airport Road
Sydenham By-Pass
Holywood Rd
Albert Bridge Rd
Beersbridge Road
Woodstock Road
Castlereagh Road
Ormeau Road
Embankment
Ravenhill Rd
Ardenlee Av.
Cregagh Road
Lisburn Road
Malone Rd.
Cranmore Park
Stranmillis Road
Annadale Av.
Balmoral Av.
Harberton Park
Upper Knockbreda Road
Galwally Rd
POL.
A 6
M 2
A 2
M 5
A 55
(A 52)
A 52
(A 501)
B 38
A 501
A 12
M 1
(M 1)
A 1
A 24
A 20
A 23
(A 55)
B506
M 3
M1
U
T
P
A
Y
Z
0
1 km
1/2 mile
18
9
24
49
34
10
48
36
38
23
2
14
25
7
52
31
35
4
45
47

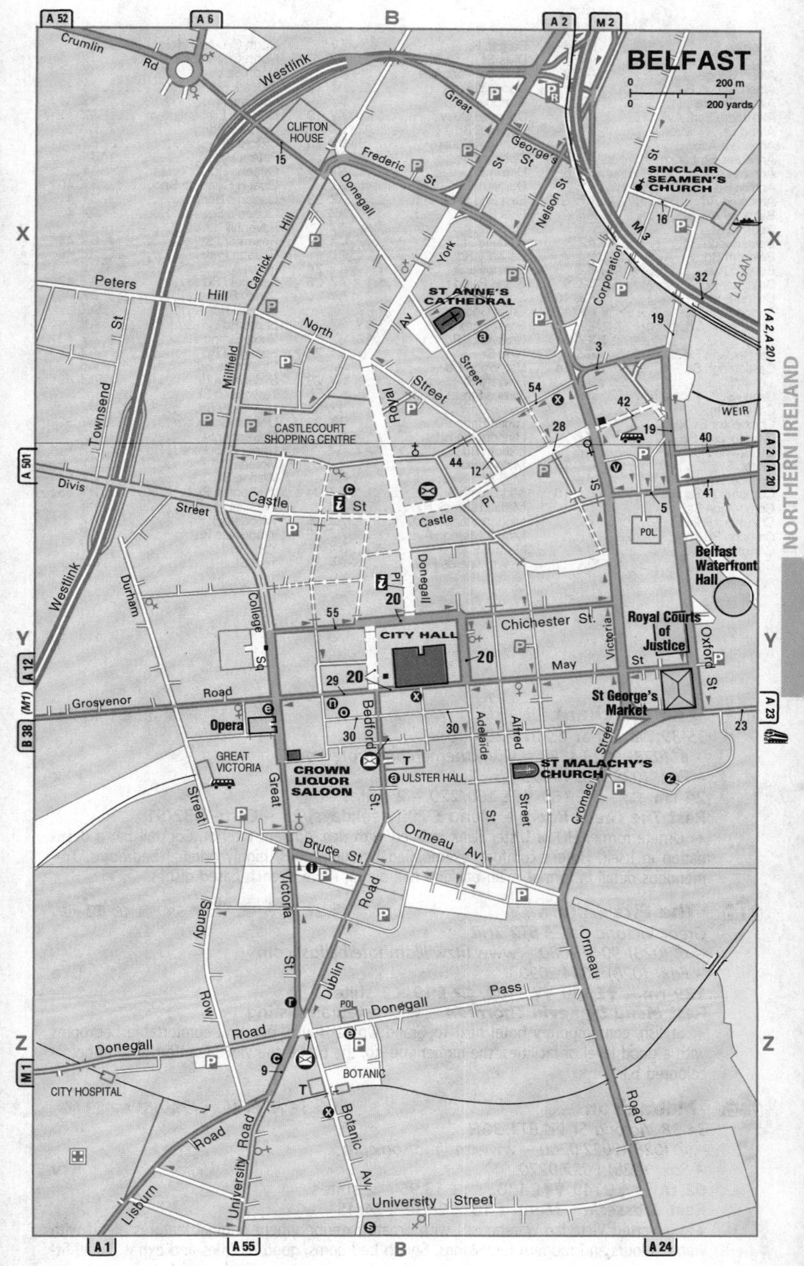
BELFAST
0 200 m
0 200 yards
A 52
A 6
A 2
M 2
B
X
Y
Z
Crumlin Rd
Westlink
CLIFTON HOUSE
Great George's St
Frederic St
Donegall
York St
Nelson St
SINCLAIR SEAMEN'S CHURCH
M 3
LAGAN
Corporation St
Carrick Hill
Peters Hill
North Street
Royal Av
ST ANNE'S CATHEDRAL
Millfield
Townsend St
CASTLECOURT SHOPPING CENTRE
WEIR
A 501
Divis Street
Castle St
Castle Pl
Donegall Pl
Victoria St
Belfast Waterfront Hall
POL.
Durham
College Sq
CITY HALL
Chichester St.
Royal Courts of Justice
Oxford St
May St
Grosvenor Road
St George's Market
Opera
Bedford St.
Adelaide St
Alfred Street
Cromac Street
GREAT VICTORIA
CROWN LIQUOR SALOON
ULSTER HALL
ST MALACHY'S CHURCH
Great Victoria St.
Bruce St.
Ormeau Av.
Sandy Row
Dublin Road
Ormeau Road
Donegall Pass
Donegall Road
CITY HOSPITAL
BOTANIC
Botanic Av.
University Road
Lisburn Road
University Street
A 12
(M1)
B 38
A 23
(A 2, A 20)
A 2
A 20
M 1
A 1
A 55
A 24
NORTHERN IRELAND

INDEX OF STREET NAMES IN BELFAST

Adelaïde St . . . BY
Airport Rd . . . AY
Albert Bridge . . . AZ 2
Albert Bridge Rd . . . AZ
Albert Square . . . BX 3
Alexandre Park Ave . . . AY
Alfred St . . . BY
Annadale Ave . . . AZ
Annadale Embankment . . . AZ 4
Ann St . . . BY 5
Antrim Rd . . . AY
Ardenlee Rd . . . AZ
Balmoral Ave . . . AZ
Bedford St . . . BY
Beersdridge Rd . . . AZ
Belmont Rd . . . BZ 7
Botanic Ave . . . BZ
Bradbury Pl . . . BZ 9
Bridge End . . . AZ 10
Bridge St . . . BY 12
Castlecourt Shopping Centre . . . BXY
Castlereagh Rd . . . AZ
Castlereagh St . . . AZ 14
Castle Pl . . . BY
Castle St . . . BY
Cavehill Rd . . . AY
Chichester St . . . BX
City Hospital St . . . BZ
Cliftonville Rd . . . AY
Clifton St . . . BX 15
College Square . . . BY
Corporation Square . . . BX 16
Corporation St . . . BX
Cranmore Park . . . AZ
Cregagh Rd . . . AZ
Cromac St . . . BY
Crumlin Rd . . . AY, BX
Dargan Rd . . . AY
Divis St . . . BY
Donegall Park Ave . . . AY
Donegall Pass . . . BZ
Donegall Pl . . . BY
Donegall Quay . . . BXY 19
Donegall Rd . . . AZ, BZ
Donegall Square . . . BY 20
Donegall St . . . BX
Dublin Rd . . . BZ
Durham St . . . BY
East Bridge St . . . AZ 23
Falls Rd . . . AZ
Forestside Shopping Centre . . . AZ
Frederic St . . . BX
Galwally Rd . . . AZ
Garmoyle St . . . AY 24
Grand Parade . . . AZ 25
Gray's Lane . . . AY
Great George's St . . . BX
Great Victoria St . . . BY, BZ
Grosvenor Rd . . . AZ, BY
High St . . . BXY 28
Holywood Rd . . . AZ
Howard St . . . BY 29
James Street South . . . BY 30
Ladas Drive . . . BY 31
Lagan Bridge . . . BX 32
Lansdowne Rd . . . AY
Lisburn Rd . . . AZ, BZ
Malone Rd . . . AZ
May St . . . BX
Middlepath St . . . AZ 34
Millfield Carrick Hill . . . BXY
Mountpottinger Rd . . . AZ 36
Mount Merrion Ave . . . AZ 35
Nelson St . . . BX
Newtownards Rd . . . AZ 38
North Circular Rd . . . AY
North Queen St . . . AY
North St . . . BX
Oldpark Rd . . . AY
Ormeau Ave . . . BZ
Ormeau Embankment . . . AZ
Ormeau Rd . . . AZ, BZ
Oxford St . . . BY
Peters Hill . . . BX
Queens Rd . . . AY
Queen Elizabeth Bridge . . . BY 40
Queen's Bridge . . . BY 41
Queen's Square . . . BX 42
Ravenhill . . . AZ
Rosemary St . . . BY 44
Rosetta Park . . . AZ 45
Royal Ave . . . BXY
Saintfield Rd . . . AZ 47
Sandy Row . . . BZ
Shankill Rd . . . AZ
Shore Rd . . . AY
Short Strand . . . AZ 48
Springfiel Rd . . . AZ
Stranmillis Rd . . . AZ
Sydenham Rd . . . AZ 49
Townsend St . . . BX
University Rd . . . BZ
University Square . . . AZ 52
University St . . . BZ
Upper Knockbreda Rd . . . AZ
Victoria St . . . BY
Waring St . . . BX 54
Wellington Pl . . . BY 55
Westlink . . . BY
Woodstock Rd . . . AZ
Woodvalle Rd . . . AY
York Rd . . . AY
York St . . . BX

The Merchant

35-39 Waring St ✉ *BT1 2DY*
– ✆ (028) 9023 4888 – www.themerchanthotel.com
– Fax (028) 9024 7775 BX**x**

24 rm ☕ – 👤£ 160 👥£ 160/220 – 2 suites
Rest *The Great Room* – Menu £ 20 (weekdays)/25 – Carte £ 32/51

◆ Ornate former HQ of Ulster Bank imbued with rich, opulent interior. Cocktail bar a destination in itself. Hotel's comforts exemplified by sumptuous, highly original bedrooms. Tremendous detail in former main banking hall dining room. French based dishes.

The Fitzwilliam

Great Victoria St ✉ *BT2 7HR*
– ✆ (028) 9044 2080 – www.fitzwilliamhotelbelfast.com
– Fax (028) 9044 2090 BY**e**

129 rm – 👤£ 180 👥£ 180, ☕ £ 19 – 1 suite
Rest *Menu by Kevin Thornton* – see restaurant listing

◆ Stylish, contemporary hotel next to Grand Opera House, boasting comfortable bedrooms with a good level of facilities; the higher you go, the better the view. Comfort food in boldly coloured bar.

Malmaison

rest,

34-38 Victoria St ✉ *BT1 3GH*
– ✆ (028) 9022 0200 – www.malmaison.com
– Fax (028) 9022 0220 BY**v**

62 rm – 👤£ 140 👥£ 170, ☕ £ 13.95 – 2 suites
Rest *Brasserie* – Menu £ 16 – Carte £ 24/45

◆ Converted Victorian warehouses with ornate exterior, where original features blend with warm colours and modern furnishings. Stylish bedrooms, good facilities and extras. Small fitness/meeting rooms; stylish bar. Pleasant French brasserie serving classical fare.

Radisson Blu

3 Cromac Pl, Cromac Wood ✉ BT7 2JB – ✆ (028) 9043 4065 – www.radissonblu.co.uk/belfast – Fax (028) 9043 4066 BY**z**

119 rm – 🚹£ 89/160 🚹🚹£ 89/160, ☕ £ 14.95 – 1 suite

Rest *Filini* – Italian influences – *(closed Sunday)* Menu £ 15/20 – Carte £ 22/36

◆ Stylish, modern hotel on the site of former gasworks. Smart, up-to-date facilities. Two room styles - Urban or Nordic; both boast fine views over city and waterfront. Restaurant/bar with floor-to-ceiling windows and part-open kitchen.

Ten Square

10 Donegall Sq South ✉ BT1 5JD – ✆ (028) 9024 1001 – www.tensquare.co.uk – Fax (028) 9024 3210 – Closed 25 December BY**x**

23 rm ☕ – 🚹£ 170 🚹🚹£ 170/265

Rest *Grill Room* – Carte £ 23/41

◆ Large Victorian building in central location behind city hall, with busy conference facility. Stylish bedrooms display contemporary feature walls, good facilities and smart bathrooms. Spacious informal bar/restaurant offers accessible menu.

Malone Lodge rest,

60 Eglantine Ave ✉ BT9 6DY – ✆ (028) 9038 8000 – www.malonelodgehotelbelfast.com – Fax (028) 9038 8088 AZ**n**

58 rm ☕ – 🚹£ 160 🚹🚹£ 160 – 35 suites – 🚹🚹£ 99/200

Rest *The Green Door* – *(closed Sunday dinner)* Carte £ 18/22

◆ Well-run, privately owned hotel in peaceful 19C terrace. Bedrooms display good facilities, with smart corporate bedrooms in main house and executive rooms/apartments in various annexes. Wood-furnished bar; simple restaurant offering classical menus.

The Crescent Townhouse rest,

13 Lower Crescent ✉ BT7 1NR – ✆ (028) 9032 3349 – www.crescenttownhouse.com – Fax (028) 9032 0646 – Closed 25-26 December, 1 January and 12-13 July BZ**x**

17 rm ☕ – 🚹£ 75 🚹🚹£ 100

Rest *Metro Brasserie* – 13 Lower Cres *(bar lunch)* Carte £ 23/33

◆ Centrally located Regency style townhouse on corner site, where original features blend well with modern facilities. Spacious bedrooms boast quality décor/furnishings and smart bathrooms. Dark wood bar; informal brasserie offering popular menus.

Benedicts rest,

7-21 Bradbury Pl, Shaftesbury Sq ✉ BT7 1RQ – ✆ (028) 9059 1999 – www.benedictshotel.co.uk – Fax (028) 9059 1990 – Closed 24-25 December and 11-12 July BZ**c**

32 rm ☕ – 🚹£ 70 🚹🚹£ 80/90 **Rest** – Menu £ 20 (dinner) **s** – Carte £ 20/25 **s**

◆ A lively, strikingly designed bar with nightly entertainment can be found at the heart of this busy commercial hotel. Well-appointed bedrooms above offer modern facilities. Relaxed, popular restaurant.

Ravenhill House without rest

690 Ravenhill Rd ✉ BT6 0BZ – ✆ (028) 9020 7444 – www.ravenhillhouse.com – Fax (028) 9028 2590 – Closed 2 weeks Christmas-New Year and 2 weeks early July AZ**s**

5 rm ☕ – 🚹£ 50/55 🚹🚹£ 75

◆ Personally run detached 19C house, attractively furnished in keeping with its age. The largely organic breakfast is a highlight. Good sized rooms with bold shades predominant.

Roseleigh House without rest

19 Rosetta Park, South : 1.5 mi. by A 24 (Ormeau Rd) ✉ BT6 0DL – ✆ (028) 9064 4414 – www.roseleighhouse.co.uk – Closed Christmas-New Year and Easter AZ**r**

9 rm ☕ – 🚹£ 45/50 🚹🚹£ 65

◆ Imposing Victorian house close to the Belvoir Park golf course and in a fairly quiet residential suburb. Brightly decorated and well-kept bedrooms with modern amenities.

XXX **Deanes** [AC] [VISA] [MC] [AE]

34-40 Howard St ✉ BT1 6PF – ✆ (028) 9033 1134 – www.michaeldeane.co.uk – Fax (028) 9056 0001 – Closed 25-26 December, 1 January, 12 July, Sunday and Monday

Rest – Menu £ 22 (lunch) – Carte £ 34/44 BY**n**

Spec. Pigeon breast and confit leg pastilla, orange and cocoa. Lamb with pissaladière and artichoke barigoule. Strawberry soup and parfait with watermelon sorbet.

◆ Smart grey building with bright modern interior, full length windows and stylish leather-furnished lounge. Good sized à la carte and understated tasting menu feature top quality produce in precise, flavoursome, classically based dishes. Attentive service.

XX **James Street South** [AC] [VISA] [MC] [AE]

21 James St South ✉ BT2 7GA – ✆ (028) 9043 4310 – www.jamesstreetsouth.co.uk – Fax (028) 9043 4310 – Closed 25-26 December, 1 January, Easter, 12 July and Sunday lunch BY**o**

Rest – Menu £ 17/19 – Carte £ 27/38

◆ Smart backstreet restaurant with Victorian façade, slate-floored bar and bright, modern dining room. Good-sized menus offer tasty dishes of simply cooked local produce. Efficient service.

XX **Menu by Kevin Thornton** – at The Fitzwilliam Hotel [VISA] [MC] [AE] [DC]

Great Victoria St ✉ BT27HR – ✆ (028) 9044 2080 – www.fitzwilliamhotelbelfast.com – Fax (028) 9044 2090 BY**r**

Rest – Carte £ 12/34

◆ Three-roomed restaurant on 1st floor of stylish hotel; large centre table seats one large party or several smaller; if you're a couple, choose a booth. Classic dishes cooked in modern Irish style.

XX **Cayenne** [AC] [VISA] [MC] [AE] [DC]

7 Ascot House, Shaftesbury Sq ✉ BT2 7DB – ✆ (028) 9033 1532 – www.cayenne-restaurant.co.uk – Fax (028) 9026 1575 – Closed 25-26 December, 1 January, 12-13 July and Monday-Wednesday lunch

Rest – Asian influences – *(booking essential)* Menu £ 16/20 – Carte £ 25/36 BZ**r**

◆ Striking modern artwork and a lively atmosphere feature in this busy, relaxed and stylish restaurant. Carefully prepared selection of creative Asian influenced dishes.

XX **Shu** [AC] [VISA] [MC] [AE]

253 Lisburn Rd ✉ BT9 7EN – ✆ (028) 9038 1655 – www.shu-restaurant.com – Fax (028) 9068 1632 – Closed 1 January, 12-13 July, 24-26 December and Sunday AZ**z**

Rest – Menu £ 15/27 – Carte £ 22/35

◆ Modern L-shaped restaurant in affluent residential district, with cream/dark wood décor and lively atmosphere. Modern British cooking is guided by seasonality and availability of local produce.

X **No 27** [AC] [VISA] [MC] [AE]

27 Talbot St ✉ BT1 2LD – ✆ (028) 9031 2884 – www.no27.co.uk – Fax (028) 9031 2979 – Closed 25-26 December, 1 January, May Day, 12-13 July and dinner Sunday-Monday BX**a**

Rest – Carte £ 17/42

◆ Bustling restaurant opposite cathedral; sleekly styled with wooden floor, modern lighting and open kitchen. Simple lunch choices; daily changing dinner menu of modern British cooking.

X **Deanes Deli** [AC] [VISA] [MC] [AE]

42-44 Bedford St ✉ BT2 7FF – ✆ (028) 9024 8800 – www.michaeldeane.co.uk – Closed 25-26 December, 1 January, Monday and Tuesday at Easter, May Day, 12-13 July and Sunday BY**a**

Rest – Carte £ 23/32

◆ Spacious, glass-fronted city centre restaurant serving a mix of comfort food and globally influenced dishes, with a good choice of daily specials. Bustling, chatty atmosphere.

Ginger Bistro

7-8 Hope St ✉ *BT12 5EE* – ✆ *(028) 9024 4421* – *www.gingerbistro.com* – *Closed 25-26 December, 12-13 July, Bank Holidays. Sunday and lunch Monday*

Rest – Carte approx. £ 33 BYZ**i**

◆ Keenly run neighbourhood eatery with modern artwork for sale and bespoke fish-themed paintings. Eclectic menus display Irish produce and worldwide influences; good value lunch/pre-theatre.

The Ginger Tree

23 Donegall Pass ✉ *BT7 1DQ* – ✆ *(028) 9032 7151* – *www.ni.gingertree.co.uk* – *Closed 24-26 December, 12-13 July and Sunday lunch* BZ**e**

Rest – Japanese – Menu £ 10/28 – Carte £ 16/29

◆ Simple glass fronted restaurant with black-clothed tables, framed Japanese clothing on walls and Asian-themed fittings. Extensive menus include various set options and à la carte; authentic cooking.

Molly's Yard

1 College Green Mews, Botanic Ave ✉ *BT7 1LW* – ✆ *(028) 9032 2600* – *www.mollysyard.com* – *Closed 24-27 December, 1 January and Sunday*

Rest – *(booking essential)* Carte £ 17/24 BZ**s**

◆ Friendly split-level bistro in former coach house/stables. Cosier downstairs, with exposed brickwork and courtyard. Menus display fresh, unfussy, modern bistro fare; simpler dishes at lunch.

Mourne Seafood Bar

34 Bank St ✉ *BT1 1HJ* – ✆ *(028) 9024 8544* – *www.mourneseafood.com* – *Closed 24-26 December, 1 January, 17 March and dinner Sunday-Monday* BY**c**

Rest – Seafood – *(booking essential at dinner lunch bookings not accepted)* Carte £ 15/25

◆ Classic seafood menu supplemented by daily specials; mussels are a speciality, served in black enamel pots. Gets very busy, so arrive early, or be prepared to wait.

Prices quoted after the symbol 🚹 refer to the lowest rate in low season followed by the highest rate in high season, for a single room. The same principle applies to the symbol 🚹🚹 for a double room.

BUSHMILLS (Muileann na Buaise) – Moyle – 712 M2 – pop. 1 319 35 C1

– ✉ **Bushmills** Ireland

▶ Belfast 57 mi. – Ballycastle 12 mi. – Coleraine 10 mi.

Bushfoot Portballintrae 50 Bushfoot Rd, ✆ (028) 2073 1317

Giant's Causeway★★★ (Hamilton's Seat ≤★★) N : 2 mi. by A 2 and minor road - Dunluce Castle★★ **AC** W : 3 mi. by A 2 – Carrick-a-rede Rope Bridge★★★ **AC**, E : 8 mi. by A 2 – Magilligan Strand★★, W : 18 mi. by A 2, A 29 and A 2 - Gortmore Viewpoint★★, SW : 23 mi. by A 2, A 29, A 23 and minor road from Downhill – Downhill★ (Mussenden Temple★), W : 15 mi. by A 2, A 29 and A 2

Bushmills Inn

9 Dunluce Rd ✉ *BT57 8QG* – ✆ *(028) 2073 3000* – *www.bushmillsinn.com* – *Fax (028) 2073 2048*

32 rm – 🚹£ 118/168 🚹🚹£ 218/268

Rest ***The Restaurant*** – *(carvery lunch Sunday)* Carte £ 20/34

◆ Part-17C whitewashed inn. Original building features traditionally styled bedrooms, a circular library, turf fires and oil lamps. Extensions play host to more modern bedrooms and seating areas. Extensive classical menu served in cosy restaurant and on terrace.

NORTHERN IRELAND

COLERAINE (Cúil Raithin) – Coleraine – 712 L2 – pop. 24 089 35 C1

Ireland

Belfast 53 mi. – Ballymena 25 mi. – Londonderry 31 mi. – Omagh 65 mi.

Railway Rd ✆ (028) 7034 4723, info@northcoastni.com

Castlerock 65 Circular Rd, ✆ (028) 7084 8314

Brown Trout 209 Agivey Rd, Aghadowey, ✆ (028) 7086 8209

Giant's Causeway★★★ (Hamilton's Seat ≤★★), NE : 14 mi. by A 29 and A2 - Dunluce Castle★★ **AC**, NE : 8 mi. by A 29 and A 2 – Carrick-a-rede-Rope Bridge★★★ **AC**, NE : 18 mi. by A 29 and A2 – Benvarden★ **AC** E : 5 mi. by B 67 – Magilligan Strand★★, NW : 8 mi. by A 2 - Gortmore Viewpoint★★, NW : 12 mi. by A 2 and minor road from Downhill - Downhill★**AC** (Mussenden Temple★), NE : 7 mi. by A 2

Greenhill House without rest

24 Greenhill Rd, Aghadowey, South : 9 mi. by A 29 on B 66 ✉ BT51 4EU – ✆ (028) 7086 8241 – www.greenhill-house.co.uk – Fax (028) 7086 8365 – March-October

6 rm – †£ 40 ††£ 60

◆ An agreeably clean-lined Georgian house with large windows overlooking fields. Game and course fishing available locally. Neat bedrooms replete with extra touches.

COMBER (An Comar) – Ards – 712 O4 – pop. 8 933 35 D2

Belfast 10 mi. – Newtownards 5 mi. – Lisburn 17 mi.

Anna's House without rest

Tullynagee, 35 Lisbarnett Rd, Southeast : 3.5 mi. by A 22 ✉ BT23 6AW – ✆ (028) 9754 1566 – www.annashouse.com – closed Christmas-New Year

4 rm – †£ 65 ††£ 90

◆ Farmhouse with cosy lounge and comfy bedrooms with lovely vistas. Glass-walled extension has geo-thermal heating and lake views. Organic breakfasts utilise produce from garden.

CRUMLIN (Cromghlinn) – Antrim – 712 N4 – pop. 4 259 35 C2

Belfast 14 mi. – Ballymena 20 mi.

Caldhame Lodge without rest

102 Moira Rd, Nutts Corner, Southeast : 1.25 mi. on A 26 ✉ BT29 4HG – ✆ (028) 9442 3099 – www.caldhamelodge.co.uk – Fax (028) 9442 3313

8 rm – †£ 45/48 ††£ 65/70

◆ Spic and span, with thoroughly polished, wood furnished hall, complete with grandfather clock. Immaculate, co-ordinated, individualistic rooms; bridal suite with whirlpool.

DERRY/LONDONDERRY (Doire) – Londonderry – 712 K2/3 – see Londonderry

DONAGHADEE (Domhnach Daoi) – Ards – 712 P4 – pop. 6 470 35 D2

Ireland

Belfast 18 mi. – Ballymena 44 mi.

Warren Rd, ✆ (028) 9188 3624

Ballycopeland Windmill★ **AC** S : 4 mi. by A 2 and B 172. Mount Stewart★★★ **AC**, SW : 10 mi. by A 2 and minor road SW – Movilla (cross slabs★), Newtownards, SW : 7 mi. by B 172

Grace Neill's

33 High St ✉ BT21 0AH – ✆ (028) 9188 4595 – www.graceneills.com – Fax (028) 9188 9631 – Closed 25 December

Rest – Carte £ 23/35

◆ Characterful beamed pub – the oldest in Ireland – decorated with antiques and old pictures. Extensive, largely classical menu, with express lunches and daily fish and seafood specials.

Pier 36 with rm

36 The Parade ✉ BT21 0HE – ☎ (028) 9188 4466 – www.pier36.co.uk – Fax (028) 9188 4636 – Closed 25 December

7 rm – †£ 50 ††£ 90 **Rest** – Menu £ 13 – Carte £ 20/35

◆ Spacious harbourside pub, set opposite a lighthouse. Extensive menus feature a mix of classic, modern and international influences, and plenty of fresh, local seafood. Good weekday deals. Simple, comfy bedrooms boast sea views.

DOWNPATRICK (Dún Pádraig) – Down – 712 O4/5 – pop. 10 316 35 D3

Ireland

Belfast 23 mi. – Newry 31 mi. – Newtownards 22 mi.

Cathedral★ **AC** - Down County Museum★ **AC**

Struell Wells★ **AC**, SE : 2 mi. by B 1 - Ardglass★ (Jordan's Castle**AC**), SE : 7 mi. by B 1 – Inch Abbey★ **AC**, NW : 2 mi. by A 7 – Quoile Countryside Centre★ **AC**, E : 2 mi. by A 25 – Castle Ward★★ **AC** (Audley's Castle★), E : 8 mi. by A 25

Pheasants' Hill Farm without rest

37 Killyleagh Rd, North : 3 mi. on A 22 ✉ BT30 9BL – ☎ (028) 4461 7246 – www.pheasantshill.com – closed 8 December - 4 January

3 rm – †£ 55 ††£ 90

◆ Purpose-built house surrounded by an organic smallholding with livestock which provides many ingredients for hearty breakfasts. Homely, pine furnished bedrooms.

DUNDRUM (Dún Droma) – Down – 712 O5 – pop. 1 065 Ireland 35 D3

Belfast 29 mi. – Downpatrick 9 mi. – Newcastle 4 mi.

Castle★ **AC**

Castlewellan Forest Park★★ **AC**, W : 4 mi. by B 180 and A 50 - Tollymore Forest Park★ **AC**, W : 3 mi. by B 180 - Drumena Cashel and Souterrain★, W : 4 mi. by B 180

The Carriage House without rest

71 Main St ✉ BT33 0LU – ☎ (028) 4375 1635 – www.carriagehousedundrum.com

3 rm – †£ 40/50 ††£ 70/80

◆ Welcoming, lilac-washed terraced house with colourful window boxes and attractive rear garden. Comfy, traditionally styled guest areas. Simple bedrooms with plain décor and antique furniture.

Buck's Head Inn

77-79 Main St ✉ BT33 0LU – ☎ (028) 4375 1868 – www.bucksheadrestaurant.com – Closed 24-25 December and Monday (October-April)

Rest – Seafood – Menu £ 29 (dinner) – Carte £ 16/28

◆ Informal restaurant with attractive terrace and garden. Lounge for pre-meal drinks; choice of dining rooms. Good-sized menus of unfussy, traditional cooking with a local seafood base.

Mourne Seafood Bar

10 Main St ✉ BT33 0LU – ☎ (028) 4375 1377 – www.mourneseafood.com – Closed Monday-Wednesday (October to April)

Rest – Seafood – *(booking essential in summer)* Menu £ 25 (Saturday dinner) – Carte £ 17/27

◆ Informal, rustic restaurant, set on main street; wood-furnished interior with coastal oil paintings. Classical seafood cooking, with oysters/mussels from owners' beds a speciality.

Each starred restaurant lists three specialities that are typical of its style of cuisine. These may not always be on the menu but in their place expect delicious seasonal dishes. Be sure to try them.

NORTHERN IRELAND

DUNGANNON (Dún Geanainn) – Dungannon – 712 L4 35 C2
– pop. 11 139 Ireland

Belfast 42 mi. – Ballymena 37 mi. – Dundalk 47 mi. – Londonderry 60 mi.

The Argory★, S : 5 mi. by A 29 and east by minor rd. Ardboe Cross★, NW : 17 mi. by A 45, B 161 and B 73 – Springhill★ **AC**, NE : 24 mi. by A 29 – Sperrin Mountains★ : Wellbrook Beetling Mill★ **AC**, NW : 22 mi. by A 29 and A 505 - Beaghmore Stone Circles★, NW : 24 mi. by A 29 and A 505

Grange Lodge

7 Grange Rd, Moy, Southeast : 3.5 mi. by A 29 ✉ BT71 7EJ – ✆ (028) 8778 4212 – www.grangelodgecountryhouse.com – Fax (028) 8778 4313 – Closed 20 December - 1 February

5 rm – †£ 60/69 ††£ 85/89

Rest – *(by arrangement)* Menu £ 35

◆ Attractive Georgian country house surrounded by well-kept mature gardens with a peaceful ambience. Fine hospitality and period furnishings. Tastefully decorated bedrooms. Large dining room furnished with elegant antiques and fine tableware.

ENNISKILLEN (Inis Ceithleann) – Fermanagh – 712 J4 – pop. 13 599 34 A2
Ireland

Belfast 87 mi. – Londonderry 59 mi.

Wellington Rd ✆ (028) 6632 3110, tic@fermanagh.gov.uk

Castlecoole, ✆ (028) 6632 5250

Castle Coole★★★ **AC**, SE : 1 m – Florence Court★★ **AC**, SW : 8 mi. by A 4 and A 32 – Marble Arch Caves and Forest Nature Reserve★ **AC**, SW : 10 mi. by A 4 and A 32. NW by A 26 : Lough Erne★★ : Cliffs of Magho Viewpoint★★★ **AC**- Tully Castle★ **AC** – N by A 32, B 72, A 35 and A 47 : Devenish Island★ **AC** - Castle Archdale Forest Park★ **AC** - White Island★ - Janus Figure★

Lough Erne Golf Resort

Belleek Rd, Northwest : 4 mi. on A 46 ✉ BT93 7ED – ✆ (028) 6632 3230 – www.locherne golfresort.com – Fax (028) 6634 5721

89 rm – †£ 95/230 ††£ 115/250 – 31 suites – ††£ 215/420

Rest *Catalina* – *(dinner only and Sunday lunch)* Menu £ 40

Rest *Lochside Clubhouse Bar* – Carte £ 20/37

◆ Busy hotel in golf resort on peninsula between Castle Hume Lough and Lough Erne: a spacious, modern building boasting heritage style, with features such as wood panelling and antique furniture. Fine dining with lough views in Catalina. Informal brasserie in the Clubhouse.

Manor House

Killadeas, North : 7.5 mi. by A 32 on B 82 ✉ BT94 1NY – ✆ (028) 6862 2200 – www.manorhouseresorthotel.com – Fax (028) 6862 1545

81 rm – †£ 67/130 ††£ 75/130 – 2 suites

Rest – Menu £ 18/28

◆ Impressive manor house overlooking Lough Erne. Characterful guest areas; well-equipped leisure and meeting facilities. Traditional bedrooms in main house, more modern rooms in extensions. Formal dining room boasts ornate plasterwork and offers classical menus.

Cedars

301 Killadeas Rd, Irvingstown, North : 10 mi. by A 32 on B 82 ✉ BT94 1PG – ✆ (028) 6862 1493 – www.cedarsguesthouse.com – Fax (028) 6862 8335 – closed 1 week Christmas

10 rm – †£ 40/55 ††£ 60/100

Rest *Rectory Bistro* – *(closed Monday-Tuesday) (dinner only and Sunday lunch)* Menu £ 15 – Carte £ 22/29

◆ Good value, converted 19C former rectory with pleasant gardens. Exudes impression of spaciousness; country style décor. Individually styled bedrooms: ask for numbers 2 or 5. Country style bistro serves hearty cuisine.

GALGORM Antrim – Ballymena – 712 N3 – see Ballymena

HILLSBOROUGH (Cromghlinn) – Lisburn – 712 N4 – pop. 3 400 — 35 C2

Ireland

Belfast 12 mi.

The Courthouse, The Square ✆ (028) 9268 9717, tic.hillsborough@lisburn.gov.uk

Town★ – Fort★

Rowallane Gardens★ **AC**, Saintfield, E : 10 mi. by B 178 and B 6. The Argory★, W : 25 mi. by A 1 and M 1

The Plough Inn

3 The Square ✉ BT26 6AG – ✆ (028) 9268 2985 – Fax (028) 9268 2472 – Closed 25-26 December

Rest – Menu £ 15/25 – Carte £ 15/28

◆ Family run 18C coaching inn that's three establishments in one: a café, bar with adjoining dining room, and bistro. Dishes range from light snacks and pub classics to modern international fare.

at Annahilt Southeast : 4 mi. on B 177 – ✉ Hillsborough

Fortwilliam without rest

210 Ballynahinch Rd, Northwest : 0.25 mi. on B 177 ✉ BT26 6BH – ✆ (028) 9268 2255 – www.fortwilliamcountryhouse.com – Fax (028) 9268 9608

4 rm – †£ 50 ††£ 70

◆ Attractive bay-windowed farmhouse with neat gardens – keenly run and comfortable throughout. Individually designed bedrooms boast pleasant outlooks and extras; two have private bathrooms.

The Pheasant

410 Upper Ballynahinch Rd, North : 1 mi. on Lisburn rd ✉ BT26 6NR – ✆ (028) 9263 8056 – www.thepheasantrestaurant.co.uk – Fax (028) 9263 8026 – Closed 25-26 December, 12-13 July

Rest – Menu £ 13 (lunch) £ 20 (dinner) – Carte £ 20/28

◆ Sizeable yellow-washed pub with gothic styling and typical Irish feel. Menus offer local, seasonal produce, with seafood a speciality in summer and game featuring highly in the winter.

HOLYWOOD (Ard Mhic Nasca) – North Down – 712 O4 — 35 D2

– pop. 12 037 Ireland

Belfast 7 mi. – Bangor 6 mi.

Holywood Demesne Rd, Nuns Walk, ✆ (028) 9042 2138

Cultra : Ulster Folk and Transport Museum★★ **AC**, NE : 1 mi. by A 2

Culloden

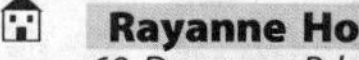

rest,

142 Bangor Rd, East : 1.5 mi. on A 2 ✉ BT18 0EX – ✆ (028) 9042 1066 – www.hastingshotels.com – Fax (028) 9042 6777

102 rm – †£ 185/210 ††£ 230/250, £ 20 – 3 suites

Rest *Mitre* – *(dinner only and Sunday lunch)* Menu £ 40

Rest *Cultra Inn* – ✆ (028) 9042 5840 – Carte £ 24/28

◆ Gothic mansion overlooking Belfast Lough. Spacious guest areas boast open fires and antiques. Bedrooms range from characterful to stylish and contemporary. Smart spa/leisure facilities. Mitre offers classical menus and good views. Informal Cultra Inn offers simpler fare.

Rayanne House

60 Demesne Rd, by My Lady's Mile Rd ✉ BT18 9EX – ✆ (028) 9042 5859 – www.rayannehouse.com – Fax (028) 9042 5859 – closed 24-25 December

11 rm – †£ 70/95 ††£ 110/130

Rest – *(dinner only) (residents only)* Menu £ 45

◆ Victorian red-brick house in peaceful residential area. Homely, antique-filled guest areas. Stylish contemporary bedrooms with country house feel, good facilities, smart bathrooms and extras. Formal dining room with seasonal menu; interesting breakfasts.

Beech Hill without rest

23 Ballymoney Rd, Craigantlet, Southeast : 4.5 mi. by A 2 on Craigantlet rd ✉ BT23 4TG – ✆ (028) 9042 5892 – www.beech-hill.net

3 rm – †£ 55 ††£ 90

◆ Country house in rural location. Pleasant clutter of trinkets and antiques in guest areas which include a conservatory. Neat, traditionally styled bedrooms: a very fine home.

Fontana

61A High St ✉ BT18 9AE – ✆ (028) 9080 9908 – Closed 25 December, 1 January, Saturday lunch, Sunday dinner and Monday

Rest – *(Sunday brunch)* Menu £ 15/18 – Carte £ 16/37

◆ Smart first floor restaurant in town centre, accessed via narrow passageway. Modern British cooking displays some Mediterranean influences. Good value set lunch and midweek dinner.

KILLINCHY – Ards 35 D2

– Belfast 16 mi. – Newtownards 11 mi. – Lisburn 17 mi.

Balloo House - Restaurant

1 Comber Rd, West : 0.75 mi. on A 22 ✉ BT23 6PA – ✆ (028) 9754 1210 – www.balloohouse.com – Fax (028) 9754 1683 – Closed 25 December, 1 January, Sunday and Monday

Rest – *(dinner only) (booking essential)* Carte £ 30/42

◆ Intimate first floor restaurant with high beamed ceilings and linen-laid tables. Flavourful classic cooking has modern touches; hearty yet refined dishes feature local produce.

LARNE (Latharna) – Larne – 712 O3 – pop. 18 228 Ireland 35 D2

Belfast 23 mi. – Ballymena 20 mi.

to Fleetwood (Stena Line) daily (8 h) – to Cairnryan (P & O Irish Sea) 3-5 daily (1 h/2 h 15 mn)

Narrow Gauge Rd ✆ (028) 2826 0088, larnetourism@btconnect.com

Cairndhu Ballygally 192 Coast Rd, ✆ (028) 2858 3954

SE : Island Magee (Ballylumford Dolmen★), by ferry and 2 mi. by B 90 or 18 mi. by A 2 and B 90. NW : Antrim Glens★★★ - Murlough Bay★★★ (Fair Head ★★★), N : 46 m by A 2 and minor road – Glenariff Forest Park★★ **AC** (Waterfall★★), N : 30 mi. by A 2 and A 43 - Glenariff★, N : 25 mi. by A 2 - Glendun★, N : 30 mi. by A 2 – Carrickfergus (Castle★★ - St Nicholas' Church★), SW : 15 mi. by A 2

Manor House without rest

23 Olderfleet Rd, Harbour Highway ✉ BT40 1AS – ✆ (028) 2827 3305 – www.themanorguesthouse.com – Fax (028) 2826 0505 – Closed 25-26 December

8 rm – †£ 30/35 ††£ 55/60

◆ Spacious Victorian terraced house two minutes from ferry terminal. Well-furnished lounge with beautifully varnished wood floors. Small breakfast room. Cosy, homely bedrooms.

LIMAVADY (Léim an Mhadaidh) – Limavady – 712 L2 – pop. 12 135 Ireland 34 B1

Belfast 62 mi. – Ballymena 39 mi. – Coleraine 13 mi. – Londonderry 17 mi.

Council Offices, 7 Connell St ✆ (028) 7776 0307, tourism@limavady.gov.uk

Benone Par Three Benone 53 Benone Ave, ✆ (028) 7775 0555

Sperrin Mountains★ : Roe Valley Country Park★ **AC**, S : 2 mi. by B 68 - Glenshane Pass★, S : 15 mi. by B 68 and A 6

Lime Tree

60 Catherine St ✉ BT49 9DB – ✆ (028) 7776 4300 – www.limetreerest.com – Closed 1 week Spring, 1 week July, 25-26 December, Sunday and Monday

Rest – *(dinner only)* Menu £ 18 (early dinner mid week) – Carte £ 26/38

◆ Keenly run neighbourhood restaurant, where a traditional exterior hides smart modern hues. Good-sized menus of unfussy classical dishes, with seafood a speciality. Friendly, detailed service.

LONDONDERRY/DERRY (Doire) – Derry – 712 K2/3 – pop. 83 699 34 B1

Ireland

Belfast 70 mi. – Dublin 146 mi.

City of Derry Airport : ✆ (028) 7181 0784, E : 6 mi. by A 2

44 Foyle St ✆ (028) 7126 7284, info@derryvisitor.com

City of Derry 49 Victoria Rd, ✆ (028) 7134 6369

Town★ - City Walls and Gates★★ – Guildhall★ **AC** – Long Tower Church★ – St Columb's Cathedral★ **AC** – Tower Museum★ **AC**

Grianan of Aileach★★ (≤★★) (Republic of Ireland) NW : 5 mi. by A 2 and N 13. Ulster-American Folk Park★★, S : 33 mi. by A 5 - Ulster History Park★ **AC**, S : 32 mi. by A 5 and minor road – Sperrin Mountains★ : Glenshane Pass★ (≤★★), SE : 24 mi. by A 6 - Sawel Mountain Drive★ (≤★★), S : 22 mi. by A 5 and minor roads via Park – Roe Valley Country Park★ **AC**, E : 15 mi. by A 2 and B 68 – Beaghmore Stone Circles★, S : 52 mi. by A 5, A 505 and minor road

City

rest, VISA AE

Queens Quay ✉ BT48 7AS – ✆ (028) 7136 5800 – www.cityhotelderry.com – Fax (028) 7136 5801 – Closed 24 - 26 December

144 rm – **†£ 79/149 ††£ 86/156** – 1 suite

Rest *Thompson's on the River* – *(bar lunch Monday-Saturday)* Menu £ 22 **s** – Carte £ 25/33 **s**

◆ Hotel in purpose-built modern style. Well located, close to the city centre and the quay. Smart rooms ordered for the business traveller. Useful conference facilities. Modern restaurant overlooks water.

Beech Hill Country House

VISA AE

32 Ardmore Rd, Southeast : 3.5 mi. by A 6 ✉ BT47 3QP – ✆ (028) 7134 9279 – www.beech-hill.com – Fax (028) 7134 5366 – closed 24 - 25 December

25 rm – **†£ 95/105 ††£ 115/135** – 2 suites

Rest *The Ardmore* – Menu £ 20/30 **s** – Carte dinner £ 32/42 **s**

◆ 18C country house, now personally run but once a US marine camp; one lounge is filled with memorabilia. Accommodation varies from vast rooms to more traditional, rural ones. Restaurant housed within conservatory and old billiard room. Fine garden.

Ramada H. Da Vinci's

rest, VISA AE

15 Culmore Rd, North : 1 mi. following signs for Foyle Bridge ✉ BT48 8JB – ✆ (028) 7127 9111 – www.davincishotel.com – Fax (028) 7127 9222 – closed 24 - 25 December

70 rm – **†£ 100/120 ††£ 100/120,** £ 8.95

Rest *The Grill Room* – *(dinner only and Sunday lunch)* Menu £ 22 – Carte £ 19/33

◆ Set beside a characterful Irish pub – now the trendy hotel bar – at the northern edge of the city. Photos of stars who've stayed here fill one wall. Well-equipped, uniform bedrooms improve with grade. Charming brasserie displays rustic beams and exposed brickwork.

MAGHERA (Machaire Rátha) – Magherafelt – 712 L3 – pop. 3 711 35 C2

Belfast 40 mi. – Ballymena 19 mi. – Coleraine 21 mi. – Londonderry 32 mi.

Ardtara Country House

VISA AE

8 Gorteade Rd, Upperlands, North : 3.25 mi. by A 29 off B 75 ✉ BT46 5SA – ✆ (028) 7964 4490 – www.ardtara.com – Fax (028) 7964 5080

9 rm – **†£ 75/85 ††£ 140/160**

Rest – *(booking essential for non-residents) (lunch by arrangement)* Menu £ 20/32 – Carte £ 20/32

◆ 19C house with a charming atmosphere. The interior features "objets trouvés" collected from owner's travels; original fireplaces set off the individually styled bedrooms. Restaurant set in former billiard room with hunting mural and panelled walls.

A red **Rest** mention denotes an establishment with an award for culinary excellence, ✿ (star) or ☺ (Bib Gourmand).

NORTHERN IRELAND

NEWCASTLE (An Caisleán Nua) – Down – 712 O5 – pop. 7 444 35 D3

Ireland

Belfast 32 mi. – Londonderry 101 mi.

10-14 Central Promenade ✆ (028) 4372 2222, newcastle.tic@downdc.gov.uk

Castlewellan Forest Park★★ **AC**, NW : 4 mi. by A 50 – Tolymore Forest Park★ **AC**, W : 3 mi. by B 180 – Dundrum Castle★ **AC**, NE : 4 mi. by A 2. Silent Valley Reservoir★ (≤★) - Spelga Pass and Dam★ - Kilbroney ForestPark (viewpoint★) – Annalong Marine Park and Cornmill★ **AC**, S : 8 mi. by A 2 – Downpatrick : Cathedral★ **AC**, Down Country Museum★ **AC**, NE : 20 mi. by A 2 and A 25

Slieve Donard

Downs Rd ✉ *BT33 0AH* – ✆ *(028) 4372 1066* – *www.hastingshotels.com* – *Fax (028) 4372 1166*

176 rm – †£ 140/185 ††£ 200/260

Rest *Oak* – Menu £ 30/38

Rest *Percy French* – Carte £ 12/22

◆ Grand railway hotel boasting marble-floored lobby, interesting museum, superb leisure facilities and excellent sea/mountain views. Spacious bedrooms in classic or contemporary styles; good mod cons. Formal Oak offers classical menu. More accessible fare in casual bar-restaurant Percy French.

Burrendale H. & Country Club

rest,

51 Castlewellan Rd, North : 1 mi. on A 50 ✉ *BT33 0JY* – ✆ *(028) 4372 2599* – *www.burrendale.com* – *Fax (028) 4372 2328*

67 rm – †£ 80 ††£ 120 – 1 suite

Rest *Vine* – *(dinner only and Sunday lunch)* Carte £ 24/27 **s**

Rest *Cottage Kitchen* – Menu £ 15/20 **s** – Carte £ 18/26 **s**

◆ Set between the Mourne Mountains and Irish Sea, with the Royal County Down Golf Course nearby. Leisure oriented. Range of rooms from small to very spacious. Linen-clad Vine for traditional dining. Homely cooking to the fore at Cottage Kitchen.

NEWTOWNARDS (Baile Nua na hArda) – Ards – 712 O4 – pop. 27 821 35 D2

Belfast 10 mi. – Bangor 144 mi. – Downpatrick 22 mi.

Edenvale House without rest

130 Portaferry Rd, Southeast : 2.75 mi. on A 20 ✉ *BT22 2AH* – ✆ *(028) 9181 4881* – *www.edenvalehouse.com*

3 rm – †£ 50 ††£ 90

◆ Attractive Georgian farmhouse with pleasant mountain views. Traditionally decorated, with comfy drawing room and wicker-furnished sun room. Spacious, homely bedrooms boast good facilities.

PORTRUSH (Port Rois) – Coleraine – 712 L2 – pop. 6 372 Ireland 35 C1

Belfast 58 mi. – Coleraine 4 mi. – Londonderry 35 mi.

Sandhill Drive ✆ (028) 7082 3333 (March-October), portrushtic@btconnect.com

Royal Portrush Dunluce Rd, ✆ (028) 7082 2311

Giant's Causeway★★★ (Hamilton's Seat ≤★★, E: 9 m by A 2) - Carrick-a-rede Rope Bridge★★★, E: 14 mi. by A 2 and B 15 - Dunluce Castle★★ **AC**, E: 3 mi. by A 2 – Gortmore Viewpoint★★, E: 14 mi. by A 29, A 2 and minor road - Magilligan Strand★★, E: 13 mi. by A 29 and A 2 – Downhill★ (Mussenden Temple★), E: 12 mi. by A 29 and A 2

Beulah without rest

16 Causeway St ✉ *BT56 8AB* – ✆ *(028) 7082 2413* – *www.beulahguesthouse.com* – *closed 1 week Christmas*

10 rm – †£ 33/60 ††£ 65

◆ Terraced Victorian house in perfect central location. Sound Irish breakfasts. Homely guest lounge. Colourful, co-ordinated and immaculately kept modern bedrooms.

PORTSTEWART (Port Stióbhaird) – **Coleraine** – **712** L2 **35** C1

Belfast 60 mi. – Ballymena 32 mi. – Coleraine 6 mi.

The York

2 Station Rd, on A2 ✉ BT55 7DA – ✆ (028) 7083 3594 – www.theyorkportstewart.co.uk – Fax (028) 7083 2223

8 rm – †£ 110 ††£ 140 **Rest** – Carte £ 14/26

◆ Smart, contemporary hotel overlooking the North Coast. Stylish bedrooms offer all mod cons; the two front rooms are the largest, with terraces and excellent views. Trendy, marble-floored bar. Ground floor restaurant with extensive menus and a large terrace.

WARRENPOINT (An Pointe) – **Newry and Mourne** – **712** N5 – **pop. 7 000** **35** C3

Belfast 44 mi. – Newry 7 mi. – Lisburn 37 mi.

Restaurant 23

23 Church St ✉ BT34 3HN – ✆ (028) 4175 3222 – www.restaurant23.com – Fax (028) 4177 4323 – Closed 24-26 December, Tuesday and Monday except Bank Holidays

Rest – Menu £ 18 (dinner) **s** – Carte £ 24/32 **s**

◆ A very stylish interior makes most of intimate space. Easy-going, good value brasserie style lunches; evening dishes - adopting a more original slant - are more serious.

O. Forir/MICHELIN

Republic of Ireland

ACHILL ISLAND (Acaill) – Mayo – **712** B5/6 Ireland **36** A2

Dublin 288 km – Castlebar 54 km – Galway 144 km

Achill Sound ☎ (098) 45384, (July- Sept) achill.touristoffice@failteireland.ie

Achill Island Keel, ☎ (098) 43 456

Island★

DOOGORT (Dumha Goirt) – Mayo – ✉ Achill Island

Gray's

– ☎ (098) 43 244 – Easter-September

14 rm – € 50/61 € 100/110 **Rest** – *(by arrangement)* Menu € 32

◆ A row of tranquil whitewashed cottages with a homely atmosphere; popular with artists. Cosy sitting rooms with fireplaces and simple but spotless bedrooms. Local scene paintings adorn dining room walls.

KEEL – Mayo – ✉ Achill Island

Achill Cliff House

– ☎ (098) 43 400 – www.achillcliff.com – Fax (098) 43 007

10 rm – € 120/150 € 120/160

Rest – *(dinner only and Sunday lunch)* Menu € 28 – Carte € 31/38

◆ Whitewashed modern building against a backdrop of countryside and ocean. Within walking distance of Keel beach. Well-kept, spacious bedrooms with modern furnishings. Spacious restaurant with sea views.

ADARE (Áth Dara) – Limerick – **712** F10 – **pop. 982** Ireland **38** B2

Dublin 210 km – Killarney 95 km – Limerick 16 km

Heritage Centre, Mains St ☎ (061) 396255, touristofficeadare@shannondevelopment.ie

Town★ – Adare Friary★ - Adare Parish Church★

Rathkeale (Castle Matrix★ **AC** - Irish Palatine Heritage Centre★) W : 12 km by N 21 – Newcastle West★, W : 26 km by N 21 – Glin Castle★ **AC**, W : 46.5 km by N 21, R 518 and N 69

Adare Manor H. and Golf Resort

– ☎ (061) 396 566 – www.adaremanor.com
– Fax (061) 396 124 – closed 24-26 December

62 rm – € 290/493 € 290/493

Rest *The Oakroom* – *(dinner only)* Carte € 42/69 **s**

Rest *The Carraigehouse* – Carte € 32/51 **s**

◆ Part 19C Gothic mansion on banks of River Maigue in extensive parkland. Impressively elaborate interiors and capacious lounges. Most distinctive rooms in the oldest parts. Oak-panelled dining room overlooks river. Informal Carraigehouse.

Dunraven Arms

Main St – ☎ (061) 605 900 – www.dunravenhotel.com – Fax (061) 396 541

86 rm – € 135/200, €25

Rest *Maigue Restaurant* – ☎ (061) 396 633 *(dinner only and Sunday lunch)* Carte € 33/41

◆ Considerably extended 18C building opposite town's charming thatched cottages. Understated country house style. Comfortable bedrooms in bright magnolia. Well-equipped gym. Burgundy décor, antique chairs and historical paintings create a classic traditional air. Menus offer some eclectic choice on an Irish backbone. Formal yet friendly service.

XX The Wild Geese

Rose Cottage – ☎ (061) 396 451 – www.thewild-geese.com
– closed 24-26 December, 3-20 January, Sunday in winter and Monday

Rest – *(dinner only) (booking essential)* Menu € 35 – Carte € 35/47

◆ Traditional 18C cottage on main street. Friendly service and cosy welcoming atmosphere. Varied menu with classic and international influences uses much fresh local produce.

White Sage

Main Street – ✆ (061) 396 004 – www.thewhitesagerestaurant.com – closed 10 January-10 February, 24-26 December and Monday

Rest – *(dinner only) (booking advisable)* Menu € 30 – Carte € 34/45

◆ Set in a row of thatched cottages, with a spacious, candlelit inner and small rear terrace. Experienced chef creates tasty European dishes using regional produce. Charming service.

ARAN ISLANDS (Oileáin Árann) – Galway – 712 C/D8 – pop. 1 280 — 38 B1

Ireland

Dublin 260 km – Galway 43 km – Limerick 145 km – Ennis 111 km

Access Access by boat or aeroplane from Galway city or by boat from Kilkieran, Rossaveel or Fisherstreet (Clare) and by aeroplane from Inverin

Cill Ronain, Inis Mor ✆ (099) 61263, aran@failteireland.ie

Islands★ – Inishmore (Dún Aonghasa★★★)

INISHMORE – Galway – ✉ Aran Islands

Óstán Árann

Kilronan – ✆ (099) 61 104 – www.aranislandshotel.com – Fax (099) 61 225

22 rm – € 59/99 € 98/158 **Rest** – Menu € 20/25 – Carte € 22/31

◆ Comfortable, family-owned hotel with great view of harbour. Bustling bar with live music most nights in the season. Spacious, up-to-date bedrooms decorated in bright colours. Traditional dishes served in wood-floored restaurant.

Pier House

Kilronan – ✆ (099) 61 417 – www.pierhousearan.com – Fax (099) 61 122 – 17 March - October

10 rm – € 55/75 € 90/120

Rest *The Restaurant* – see restaurant listing

◆ Purpose-built hotel, perfectly located at the end of the pier with an attractive outlook from residents lounge. Cosy bedrooms furnished in a comfortable, modern style. Some family rooms.

Ard Einne Guesthouse

Killeany – ✆ (099) 61 126 – www.ardeinne.com – Fax (099) 61 388 – February-November

8 rm – € 90 € 120 **Rest** – *(by arrangement)* Menu € 27

◆ Purpose-built chalet-style establishment in isolated spot with superb views of Killeany Bay. Homely atmosphere amidst traditional appointments. Simple, comfortable bedrooms. Spacious dining room provides home-cooked meals.

The Restaurant – at Pier House Hotel

Kilronan – ✆ (099) 61 417 – www.pierhouserestaurant.com – Fax (099) 61 811 – 17 March - October

Rest – *(light lunch)* Menu € 29 – Carte € 30/47

◆ Well-regarded restaurant with cosy ambience. Light lunches replaced by more serious dinner menus, with a strong selection of local seafood. Tasty, homely cooking with the odd Asian influence.

INISHMAAN – Galway – ✉ Aran Islands

Inis Meáin Restaurant & Suites with rm

– ✆ (086) 826 60 26 – www.inismeain.com – early April-mid September, 2 night minimum stay

3 rm – € 185 € 250

Rest – *(closed Sunday and Monday) (dinner only) (booking essential)* Carte € 30/61

◆ Striking stone building in futuristic design owned and run by charming native of this unspoilt island. Unpretentious modern cooking exploits finest local ingredients, including seafood caught in currachs and delicious home-grown potatoes. Minimalist bedrooms feature natural furnishings. Breakfast delivered to room.

ARDMORE (Aird Mhór) – Waterford – 712 I12 – pop. 412 39 C3

Dublin 240 km – Waterford 71 km – Cork 60 km – Kilkenny 123 km

Cliff House

– *(024) 87 800 – www.thecliffhousehotel.com – Fax (024) 87 820 – restricted opening January and December*

36 rm – € 150/225 € 170/200 – 3 suites

Rest The House – *see restaurant listing*

Rest *Bar* – Carte € 32/43

◆ No expense was spared with this ground-breaking hotel built into the cliffs; contemporary in style but using local materials. Bedrooms come with all mod cons and state-of-the-art bathrooms; all have views and some have balconies. All day menu served in Bar.

The House – at Cliff House Hotel

– *(024) 87 800 – www.thecliffhousehotel.com – Fax (024) 87 820 – Closed Monday and restricted opening January and December*

Rest – *(dinner only)* Menu € 63

Spec. Smoked salmon lolly, 'mi-cuit' and herb cream. Duck breast with sweet potato tart and beetroot. Dark chocolate mousse with sea salt, pistachio and white coffee ice cream

◆ Innovative, imaginative dishes cooked with style and skill using local ingredients; some from chef's own vegetable garden. Full length windows give diners stunning views of the bay. Linen-laid tables, gleaming glassware and professional service.

ARTHURSTOWN (Colmán) – Wexford – 712 L11 – pop. 159 39 D2

Dublin 166 km – Cork 159 km – Limerick 162 km – Waterford 42 km

Dunbrody Country House

rm,

– *(051) 389 600 – www.dunbrodyhouse.com*

– Fax (051) 389 601 – closed 19-27 December

16 rm – € 110/360 € 325/360 – 6 suites

Rest – *(bar lunch Monday-Saturday) (booking essential for non-residents) (residents only Sunday dinner)* Menu € 55/65

◆ Fine country house hotel with a pristine, elegant style, set within a part-Georgian former hunting lodge affording much peace. Smart, comfortable bedrooms. Elegant dining room serving modern-style menu, with Mediterranean and Asian influences. Bar lunch starts at 2pm.

ASHBOURNE (Cill Dhéagláin) – Meath – 712 M7 – pop. 8 528 37 D3

Dublin 21 km – Drogheda 26 km – Navan 27 km

Broadmeadow Country House without rest

Bullstown, Southeast : 4 km by R 135 on R 125 (Swords rd)

– (01) 835 2823 – www.irishcountryhouse.com – Fax (01) 835 2819 – closed 23 December-4 January

8 rm – € 50/60 € 100/150

◆ Substantial creeper-clad guesthouse and equestrian centre in rural area yet close to airport. Light and airy breakfast room overlooks garden. Spacious rooms have country views.

ASHFORD (Áth na Fuinseog) – Wicklow – 712 N8 – pop. 1 349 39 D2

Dublin 43 km – Rathdrum 17 km – Wicklow 6 km

Ballyknocken House

Glenealy, South : 4.75 km on L 1096 – (0404) 44 627 – www.ballyknocken.com – Fax (0404) 44 696 – closed Christmas and New Year

7 rm – € 59/75 € 110/118 **Rest** – *(by arrangement)* Menu € 45

◆ Part-Victorian guesthouse on a working farm, with adjoining cookery school. Comfy bedrooms are furnished with antiques, and some have claw-foot baths. Light, airy dining room. Set daily changing menu of traditional Irish cooking.

ATHLONE (Baile Átha Luain) – Westmeath – 712 I7 – pop. 17 544 37 C3

Ireland

Dublin 120 km – Galway 92 km – Limerick 120 km – Roscommon 32 km

Athlone Castle, St Peter's Sq ☎ (090) 647 2107 (April-October), athlone@failteireland.ie

Hodson Bay, ☎ (090) 649 20 73

Clonmacnois★★★ (Grave Slabs★, Cross of the Scriptures★) S : 21 km by N 6 and N 62 – N : Lough Ree (Ballykeeran Viewpoint★)

Sheraton Athlone

Gleeson St – ☎ (090) 645 1000 – www.sheraton.com/athlone – Fax (090) 645 1001

164 rm – € 69/159 € 138/318 – 1 suite

Rest – *(dinner only and Sunday lunch)* Menu € 35 – Carte € 29/46

◆ Contemporary international hotel masked by unspectacular exterior. Impressive leisure and spa facilities. Good-sized bedrooms: the higher the floor, the bigger the room. Traditional menu of classics.

Shelmalier House without rest

Retreat Rd, Cartrontroy, East : 2.5 km by Dublin rd (N 6) – ☎ (090) 647 22 45 – www.shelmalierhouse.com – Fax (090) 647 31 90 – March-October

7 rm – € 50 € 72

◆ Modern house with large garden in a quiet residential area of town. Homely décor throughout, including comfortable bedrooms which are well kept.

Left Bank Bistro

Fry Pl – ☎ (090) 649 44 46 – www.leftbankbistro.com – Fax (090) 649 45 09 – closed 25 December-2 January, Sunday and Monday

Rest – Menu € 28 (dinner) – Carte € 24/43

◆ Glass-fronted with open-plan wine store and bright, modern bistro buzzing with regulars. Salads and foccacias, plus modern Irish dishes and fish specials in the evening.

Kin Khao

Abbey Lane – ☎ (090) 649 88 05 – www.kinkhaothai.ie – Fax (090) 648 98 35 – closed 24-26 December

Rest – Thai – Carte € 29/32 **s**

◆ Friendly Thai restaurant set over two floors, with vivid yellow exterior and simply furnished dining area. Wide-ranging à la carte menu; be adventurous and opt for 'Janya's favourites'.

at Glassan Northeast : 8 km on N 55 – ✉ Athlone

Wineport Lodge

rm,

Southwest : 1.5 km – ☎ (090) 643 90 10 – www.wineport.ie – closed 24-26 December

28 rm – € 125/155 € 170/210 – 1 suite

Rest – *(dinner only and Sunday lunch)* Menu € 44 **s** – Carte € 47/59 **s**

◆ Beautifully located by Lough Ree. Come in from the delightful terrace and sip champagne in stylish bar. Superb rooms of limed oak and ash boast balconies and lough views. Smart restaurant with separate galleried area for private parties.

Glasson Golf H. & Country Club

West : 2.75 km – ☎ (090) 648 51 20 – www.glassongolfhotel.ie – Fax (090) 648 54 44

rm,

65 rm – € 60/150 € 80/300

Rest – *(bar lunch)* Menu € 35 **s** – Carte € 24/38 **s**

◆ Family owned hotel commands fine views of Lough Ree and its attractive golf course. Modern bedrooms are spacious with superior rooms making most of view. Original Georgian house restaurant with wonderful outlook.

Glasson Stone Lodge without rest

– ☎ (090) 648 50 04 – www.glassonstonelodge.com – May-October

6 rm – € 50 € 80

◆ A warm welcome and notable breakfasts with home-baked breads and locally sourced organic bacon. Bedrooms and communal areas are airy and tastefully furnished.

Harbour House without rest

Southwest : 2 km – ☎ (090) 648 50 63 – www.harbourhouse.ie – April-October

6 rm – 🚹 € 50 🚹🚹 € 76

◆ Sited in quiet rural spot a stone's throw from Lough Ree. Traditionally styled lounge with stone chimney breast; adjoining breakfast room. Comfy bedrooms overlook garden.

AUGHRIM (Eachroim) – Wicklow – 712 N9 – pop. 1 145 — 39 D2

Dublin 74 km – Waterford 124 km – Wexford 96 km

The Battle of Aughrim Visitors Centre, Ballinasloe ☎ (090) 9763939 (summer only)

Brooklodge H & Wells Spa

Macreddin Village, North : 3.25 km – ☎ (0402) 36 444 – www.brooklodge.com – Fax (0402) 36 580

89 rm – 🚹 € 135/160 🚹🚹 € 80/240 – 1 suite

Rest *Strawberry Tree* – *(dinner only)* Menu € 65

Rest *Armento* – *(closed Sunday and Monday) (dinner only)* Menu € 30

Rest *Orchard Cafe* – Carte € 18/20

◆ 180 acre estate in secluded Wicklow valley featuring well-appointed, contemporary bedrooms with spacious bathrooms, a state-of-the-art spa and restaurants serving solely organic food. Ornate, linen-clad Strawberry Tree offers a traditional menu. Italian dishes in Armento. Orchard Café for a light lunch.

AVOCA (Abhóca) – Wicklow – 712 N9 – pop. 734 Ireland — 39 D2

Dublin 75 km – Waterford 116 km – Wexford 88 km

Avondale★, N : by R 752 – Meeting of the Waters★, N : by R 752

Keppel's Farmhouse without rest

Ballanagh, South : 3.25 km by unmarked rd – ☎ (0402) 35 168 – www.keppelsfarmhouse.com – Fax (0402) 35 168 – mid May-October

5 rm – 🚹 € 50/55 🚹🚹 € 80/85

◆ Farmhouse set in seclusion at end of long drive on working dairy farm. Attractively simple modern and traditional bedrooms; those in front have far-reaching rural views.

BAGENALSTOWN (Muine Bheag) – Carlow – 712 L9 – pop. 2 532 — 39 D2

Dublin 101 km – Carlow 16 km – Kilkenny 21 km – Wexford 59 km

Kilgraney Country House

South : 6.5 km by R 705 (Borris Rd) – ☎ (059) 977 52 83 – www.kilgraneyhouse.com – Fax (059) 977 55 95 – closed January, February, December and Monday-Wednesday March-November

8 rm – 🚹 € 120 🚹🚹 € 280 – 2 suites

Rest – *(dinner only) (booking essential)* Menu € 52 **s**

◆ 18C house with individual interiors featuring Far Eastern artefacts from owners' travels. Sitting room in dramatic colours, paintings resting against wall. Stylish rooms. Communal dining in smart surroundings.

BALLINA (Béal an Átha) – Mayo – 712 E5 – pop. 10 490 Ireland — 36 B2

Dublin 241 km – Galway 117 km – Roscommon 103 km – Sligo 59 km

Cathedral Rd ☎ (096) 70848 (April-October), ballina.touristoffice@failteireland.ie

Mossgrove Shanaghy, ☎ (096) 21 050

Rosserk Abbey★, N : 6.5 km by R 314. Moyne Abbey★, N : 11.25 km by R 314 - Pontoon Bridge View (≤★), S : 19.25 km by N 26 and R 310 – Downpatrick Head★, N : 32 km by R 314

REPUBLIC OF IRELAND

The Ice House

The Quay Village, Northeast : 2.5 km by N 59 – ✆ (096) 23 500 – www.theicehouse.ie – Fax (096) 23 598 – closed 25-26 December
32 rm ☕ – † € 95/125 †† € 150/195 – 6 suites
Rest – *(dinner only and Sunday lunch)* Menu € 39 – Carte € 39/58
♦ A former ice vault for local fishermen with two modern extensions. Terrific river views. The bedrooms a quirky mix of the old and the new; some with full-length windows. Modern menus in restaurant.

Crockets on the Quay with rm

The Quay, Northeast : 2.5 km by N 59 – ✆ (096) 75 930 – www.crocketsonthequay.ie – Fax (096) 70 069 – Closed 25 December and Good Friday
8 rm ☕ – † € 45 †† € 80
Rest – *(dinner only and Sunday lunch)* Carte € 23/39
♦ Friendly, atmospheric Irish pub on the river, with plasma screens, terrace and dining area in beamed former boat house. Hearty, fresh cooking uses quality ingredients. Modest bedrooms; 6, 7 and 8 are the quietest.

BALLINADEE (Baile na Daidhche) – Cork – 712 G12 – see Kinsale

BALLINASLOE (Béal Átha na Sluaighe) – Galway – 712 H8 **36 B3**
– **pop. 6 303** Ireland

Dublin 146 km – Galway 66 km – Limerick 106 km – Roscommon 58 km
Bridge St, (0909) 642604 (July-Oct), ballinasloe@failteireland.ie
Rossgloss, ✆ (0905) 42 126
Mountbellew, ✆ (090) 967 92 59
Clonfert Cathedral★ (west doorway★★), SW : by R 355 and minor roads. Turoe Stone, Bullaun★, SW : 29 km by R 348 and R 350 – Loughrea (St Brendan's Cathedral★), SW : 29 km by N 6 – Clonmacnoise★★★ (grave slabs★, Cross of the Scriptures★) E : 21 km by R 357 and R 444

Moycarn Lodge

Shannonbridge Rd, Southeast : 2.5 km by N 6 off R 357 – ✆ (090) 964 5050 – www.moycarnlodge.ie – Fax (090) 964 4760 – Closed 25-26 December
15 rm ☕ – † € 39/99 †† € 78/99 **Rest** – Menu € 15/25 – Carte € 19/33
♦ Pleasant rural spot next to River Suck, with berthing available for boats and family cruisers for hire. Light, simply furnished bedrooms; some with river view. Hospitable owners. Rustically-styled restaurant.

BALLINCOLLIG (Baile an Chollaigh) Cork – Cork – 712 D12 **38 B3**
– **pop. 16 339**

Dublin 168 km – Cork 6 km – Carrigaline 17 km – Cobh 20 km

Oriel House

West : 1 km on A 608 – ✆ (021) 420 84 00 – www.corkluxuryhotels.com – Fax (021) 487 58 80 – closed 25-26 December
76 rm ☕ – † € 110 †† € 140 – 2 suites
Rest – *(bar lunch Monday-Saturday)* Menu € 25 **s** – Carte € 36/46 **s**
♦ Former manor house with modern extensions boasts smart spa, conference suite and contemporary bar. Most bedrooms are in the new wings; those at the rear are quieter. Simple menu served in smart, airy restaurant.

BALLINGARRY (Baile an Gharraí) – Limerick – 712 F10 – pop. 441 **38 B2**
Ireland

Dublin 227 km – Killarney 90 km – Limerick 29 km
Kilmallock★ (Kilmallock Abbey★, Collegiate Church★), SE : 24 km by R 518 – Lough Gur Interpretive Centre★ **AC**, NE : 29 km by R 519, minor road to Croom, R 516 and R 512 – Monasteranenagh Abbey★, NE : 24 km by R 519 and minor road to Croom

Mustard Seed at Echo Lodge
– *(069) 68 508 – www.mustardseed.ie – Fax (069) 68 511*
– closed first 2 weeks February and 24-26 December
14 rm – € 120 € 180 – 2 suites
Rest – *(dinner only) (booking essential for non-residents)* Menu € 63
◆ Converted convent with very neat gardens and peaceful appeal. Cosy lounge with fireplace and beautiful fresh flowers. Individually furnished rooms with mix of antiques. Meals enlivened by home-grown herbs and organic farm produce.

BALLINROBE (Baile an Róba) – Mayo – 712 E7 – pop. 2 098 36 B3

Dublin 163 km – Castlebar 18 km – Galway 31 km – Westport 20 km

JJ Gannons with rm
Main St – (094) 954 1008 – www.jjgannons.com – Fax (094) 952 0018
– Closed 25 December and Good Friday
10 rm – € 69 € 120/200 **Rest** – Menu € 12/45 – Carte € 12/45
◆ Run by third generation of the eponymous family, with atmospheric front bar and smart, spacious restaurant. Satisfyingly traditional dishes, fish specials and eager service. Spacious, comfortable bedrooms have a bright, minimalist style.

BALLSBRIDGE (Droichead na Dothra) – Dublin – 712 N8 – see Dublin

BALLYBOFEY (Bealach Féich) – Donegal – 712 I3 – pop. 4 176 37 C1

Dublin 238 km – Londonderry 48 km – Sligo 93 km
Ballybofey & Stranorlar The Glebe, (074) 31 093

Kee's
Main St, Stranorlar, Northeast : 0.75 km on N 15 – (074) 913 10 18
– www.keeshotel.ie – Fax (074) 913 19 17
53 rm – € 96/106 € 158/178 **Rest** – Carte € 25/50 **s**
◆ Long-standing, family-run hotel in town centre. Bedrooms in newer building are more spacious and modern. Atmospheric bar and raised lounge area. Popular favourites served in informal, wood-furnished restaurant.

BALLYBUNION (Baile an Bhuinneánaigh) – Kerry – 712 D10 – pop. 1 365 Ireland

Dublin 283 km – Limerick 90 km – Tralee 42 km
Ballybunnion Sandhill Rd, (068) 27 146
Rattoo Round Tower★, S : 10 km by R 551. Ardfert★, S : 29 km by R 551, R 556 and minor road W – Banna Strand★, S : 28 km by R 551 – Carrigafoyle Castle★, NE : 21 km by R 551 – Glin Castle★ **AC**, E : 30.5 km by R 551 and N 69

Teach de Broc Country House
Link Rd, South : 2.5 km on Golf Club rd – (068) 27 581
– www.ballybuniongolf.com – Fax (068) 27 919 – March-October
14 rm – € 80/100 € 130/160
Rest – *(closed Monday) (light lunch)* Carte € 27/46
◆ Clean, tidy guesthouse with coastal proximity and great appeal to golfers as it's adjacent to the famous Ballybunion golf course. Home cooked meals. Neat, spacious rooms.

The 19th Lodge without rest
Golf Links Rd, South : 2.75 km by Golf Club rd – (068) 27 592
– www.ballybuniongolflodge.com – Fax (068) 27 830 – February-November
14 rm – € 70/130 € 100/170
◆ Orange washed house aimed at golfers playing at adjacent course. First floor lounge with honesty bar and comfy sofas. Linen-clad breakfast room. Luxurious rooms.

BALLYCASTLE (Baile an Chaisil) – Mayo – 712 D5 – pop. 215 36 B2

Ireland
Dublin 267 km – Galway 140 km – Sligo 88 km
Cáide Fields★, **AC**, NE : 8 km by R 314

Stella Maris

Northwest : 3 km by R 314 – (096) 43 322 – www.stellamarisireland.com – Fax (096) 43 965 – May-September

12 rm – € 165 € 250

Rest – *(dinner only) (booking essential)* Carte € 35/53

◆ Former coastguard station and fort in a great spot overlooking the bay. Public areas include a long conservatory. Attractive rooms with antique and contemporary furnishings. Modern menus in stylish dining room.

BALLYCONNELL (Báal Atha Conaill) – Cavan – 712 J5 – pop. 747 37 C2

Dublin 143 km – Drogheda 122 km – Enniskillen 37 km

Slieve Russell, (049) 952 6458

Slieve Russell

Southeast : 2.75 km on N 87 – (049) 952 6444 – www.quinnhotels.com – Fax (049) 952 6474

220 rm – € 90/109 € 130/158 – 2 suites

Rest *Conall Cearnach* – (049) 952 5016 *(dinner only and Sunday lunch)* Carte € 35/48

Rest *Setanta* – (049) 952 5014 *(closed Sunday lunch)* Menu € 19 (lunch) – Carte € 29/45

◆ Impressive façade in mock-Georgian style, with neo-classical lobby. Bedrooms overlooking grounds are large and luxurious with every modern convenience. Restaurants named after Irish folk heroes. Classical dishes in formal Conall Cearnach. Relaxed, stylish Setanta offers eclectic Mediterranean menu.

BALLYCOTTON (Baile Choitín) – Cork – 712 H12 – pop. 412 39 C3

Ireland

Dublin 265 km – Cork 43 km – Waterford 106 km

Cloyne Cathedral★, NW : by R 629

Bayview

– (021) 464 67 46 – www.thebayviewhotel.com – Fax (021) 464 60 75 – April-October

33 rm – € 85/120 € 170/190 – 2 suites

Rest – *(bar lunch Monday-Saturday)* Menu € 47 – Carte € 44/50

◆ A series of cottages in an elevated position with fine views of bay, harbour and island. Bar and lounge in library style with sofas. Spacious, comfy rooms with ocean views. Warm, inviting dining room.

BALLYDAVID (Baile na nGall) – Kerry – 712 A11 – ✉ Dingle 38 A2

Dublin 362 km – Dingle 11 km – Tralee 58 km

Old Pier

An Fheothanach, North : 3 km on Feomanagh rd – (066) 915 52 42 – www.oldpier.com – closed 25 December

6 rm – € 40/50 € 70/85 **Rest** – *(by arrangement)* Carte € 26/45

◆ Run by the charming owner, a pretty clifftop house surveying the harbour and the Three Sisters. Immaculate rooms with bright bedspreads and cherrywood floors.

BALLYFARNAN (Béal Átha Fearnáin) – Roscommon – 712 H5 – pop. 182 37 C2

Dublin 111 km – Roscommon 42 km – Sligo 21 km – Longford 38 km

Kilronan Castle

South East : 3.5 km on Keadew rd – (071) 961 80 00 – www.kilronancastle.ie – Fax (071) 961 80 01

84 rm – € 79/209 € 89/219

Rest *Douglas Hyde* – *(dinner only and Sunday lunch)* Menu € 50

◆ Imposing restored castle, with wood panelling, antiques, portraits and a suit of armour. Opulent red and gold bedrooms offer a high level of comfort. Impressive hydrotherapy centre. Grand dining room; traditional menu uses local produce.

REPUBLIC OF IRELAND

BALLYLICKEY (Béal Átha Leice) – Cork – 712 D12 – ✉ Bantry 38 A3

Ireland

Dublin 347 km – Cork 88 km – Killarney 72 km

Bantry Bay Donemark, ✆ (027) 50 579

Bantry Bay★ - Bantry House★ **AC**, S : 5 km by R 584. Glengarriff★ (Ilnacullin★★, access by boat) NW : 13 km by N 71 - Healy Pass★★ (≤★★) W : 37 km by N 71, R 572 and R 574 – Slieve Miskish Mountains (≤★★) W : 46.75 km by N 71 and R 572 – Lauragh (Derreen Gardens★ **AC**) NW : 44 km by N 71, R 572 and R 574 – Allihies (copper mines★) W : 66.75 km by N 71, R 572 and R 575 – Garnish Island (≤★) W : 70.75 km by N 71 and R 572

Seaview House

– ✆ (027) 50 462 – www.seaviewhousehotel.com – Fax (027) 51 555 – mid March-mid November

25 rm – € 65/95 € 140/190

Rest – *(dinner only and Sunday lunch)* Menu € 45

♦ Tall, well-run, whitewashed Victorian house set amidst lush gardens which tumble down to Bantry Bay. Traditional lounges with bar and spacious, individually designed rooms. Warmly decorated dining room.

Ballylickey House without rest

– ✆ (027) 50 071 – www.ballylickeymanorhouse.com – May-August

6 rm – € 65/75 € 80/110

♦ Impressive hotel with attractive gardens set amongst Bantry Bay's ragged inlets. Spacious, cosy bedrooms, named after flowers and birds. Breakfast room with fireside armchairs.

BALLYLIFFIN (Baile Lifín) – Donegal – 712 J2 – pop. 357 37 C1

Dublin 174 km – Lifford 46 km – Letterkenny 39 km

Ballyliffin Lodge

Shore Rd – ✆ (074) 937 82 00 – www.ballyliffinlodge.com – Fax (074) 937 89 85 – closed 25 December

40 rm – € 110 € 200/230

Rest – *(bar lunch Monday-Saturday)* Carte € 33/47 **s**

♦ Modern, purpose-built hotel with rural/beach views. Comfortable lounges and good quality spa. Well-appointed bedrooms; the front-facing ones are larger and look towards Malin Head. Small, formal restaurant offers traditional menus.

BALLYMACARBRY (Baile Mhac Cairbre) – Waterford – 712 I11 39 C2

– pop. 436 – ✉ Clonmel Ireland

Dublin 190 km – Cork 79 km – Waterford 63 km

Clonmel★ (St Mary's Church★, County Museum★ **AC**), N : 16 km by R 671 – Lismore★ (Castle Gardens★ **AC**, St Carthage's Cathedral★), SW : 26 km by R 671and N 72 – W : Nier Valley Scenic Route★★

Hanora's Cottage

Nire Valley, East : 6.5 km by Nire Drive rd and Nire Valley Lakes rd – ✆ (052) 613 61 34 – www.hanorascottage.com – Fax (052) 613 65 40 – closed 1 week Christmas

10 rm – € 75 € 150

Rest – *(closed Sunday dinner) (dinner only and Sunday lunch) (booking essential for non-residents)* Menu € 50

♦ Pleasant 19C farmhouse with purpose-built extensions in quiet location at foot of mountains. Very extensive and impressive breakfast buffet. Stylish rooms, all with jacuzzis. Locally renowned menus, brimming with fresh produce.

Glasha Farmhouse

Northwest : 4 km by R 671 – ✆ (052) 636 108 – www.glashafarmhouse.com – Fax (052) 636 108

6 rm – € 50 € 80/90

Rest – *(closed Sunday) (by arrangement)* Menu € 26 – Carte € 25/45

♦ Immaculate farmhouse rurally set on working farm. Garden water feature is focal point. Spacious conservatory. Wonderful breakfasts with huge choice. Neat, tidy rooms.

Cnoc-na-Ri without rest

Nire Valley, East : 6 km on Nire Drive rd – (052) 36 239 – February-October
4 rm – € 45 € 70

◆ Purpose-built guesthouse situated in the heart of the unspoilt Nire Valley, a perfect location for walking holidays. Immaculately kept, clean and spacious bedrooms.

BALLYMORE EUSTACE (An Baile Mór) – Kildare – pop. 725 39 D1

Dublin 48 km – Naas 12 km – Drogheda 99 km

Ballymore Inn

– (045) 864 585 – www.ballymoreinn.com – Fax (045) 864 747
– Closed 25 December and Good Friday
Rest – Menu € 22/30 – Carte € 34/58

◆ Remote village pub with spacious bar and Parisian brasserie-style dining area. Generous portions include tasty homemade bread, pizzas, tarts and pastries. Small artisan producers favoured.

BALLYMOTE (Baile an Mhóta) – Sligo – 712 G5 – pop. 1 229 – ✉ Sligo 36 B2

Dublin 199 km – Longford 77 km – Sligo 24 km

Ballymote Ballinascarrow, (071) 83 504

Mill House without rest

Keenaghan – (071) 918 34 49 – April-September
6 rm – € 35/45 € 70

◆ Simple guesthouse situated on edge of busy market town. Very friendly welcome. Small, comfortable sitting room. Light, airy breakfast room. Spacious, immaculate bedrooms.

BALLYNAHINCH (Baile na hInse) – Galway – 712 C7 – ✉ Recess 36 A3

Ireland

Dublin 225 km – Galway 66 km – Westport 79 km

Connemara★★★ – Roundstone★, S : by R 341 – Cashel★, SE : by R 341 and R 340

Ballynahinch Castle

– (095) 31 006 – www.ballynahinch-castle.com – Fax (095) 31 085
– Closed 31 January-25 February and 17-27 December
37 rm – € 145/190 € 205/210 – 3 suites
Rest – *(dinner only) (booking essential for non-residents)* Menu € 60 **s**

◆ Grey stone, part 17C castle in magnificent grounds with fine river views. Two large sitting rooms, characterful bar frequented by fishermen. Spacious rooms with antiques. Inviting dining room with stunning river views.

BALLYNAMULT (Béal na Molt) – Waterford – pop. 179 39 C2

Dublin 194 km – Clonmel 21 km – Waterford 63 km

Sliabh gCua Farmhouse without rest

Tooraneena, Southeast : 2 km – (058) 47 120 – www.sliabhgcua.com
– May-October
3 rm – € 50 € 90

◆ Creeper clad early 19C house in quiet hamlet with rural views. Tea and scones on arrival. Comfy lounge with real fire. Individually decorated rooms boast period furniture.

BALLYVAUGHAN (Baile Uí Bheacháin) – Clare – 712 E8 – pop. 224 38 B1

Ireland

Dublin 240 km – Ennis 55 km – Galway 46 km

The Burren★★ (Scenic Route★★, Aillwee Cave★ **AC** (Waterfall★★), Corcomroe Abbey★, Poulnabrone Portal Tomb★) – Kilfenora (Crosses★, Burren Centre★ **AC**), S : 25 km N 67 and R 476. Cliffs of Moher★★★, S : 32 km by N 67 and R 478

Gregans Castle

Southwest : 6 km on N 67 – ✆ (065) 707 7005 – www.gregans.ie – Fax (065) 707 7111 – 12 February-28 November

16 rm – € 152/192 € 195/235 – 4 suites

Rest – *(bar lunch)* Carte € 38/65 **s**

◆ Idyllically positioned, family owned hotel with fine views to The Burren and Galway Bay. Relaxing sitting room, cosy bar lounge, country house-style bedrooms. Sizeable conservatory dining room specialising in seasonal, regional dishes.

Drumcreehy House without rest

Northeast : 2 km on N 67 – ✆ (065) 707 73 77 – www.drumcreehyhouse.com – Fax (065) 707 73 79 – closed 22-26 December

12 rm – € 60/100 € 84/100

◆ Efficiently run, pristine house overlooking Galway Bay. Stylish lounge with honesty bar. Bedrooms, named after flowers, are excellent value: spacious, comfortable and furnished in German stripped oak. Great choice at breakfast.

Ballyvaughan Lodge without rest

– ✆ (065) 707 72 92 – www.ballyvaughanlodge.com – Fax (065) 707 72 87 – Closed 24-26 December

11 rm – € 40/50 € 70/90

◆ Red hued guesthouse, attractively furnished throughout. Light and airy sitting room with large windows. Home-made bread and jams for breakfast. Clean, tidy bedrooms.

Cappabhaile House without rest

Southwest : 1.5 km on N 67 – ✆ (065) 707 72 60 – www.cappabhaile.com – March-October

10 rm – € 70/90 € 80/105

◆ Stone clad bungalow with pleasant gardens and good views across the Burren. Spacious open-plan lounge-cum-breakfast room with central fireplace. Very large, spotless rooms.

Take note of the classification: you should not expect the same level of service in a X or 🏠 as in a XXXXX or 🏰.

REPUBLIC OF IRELAND

BALTIMORE (Dún na Séad) – **Cork** – **712** D13 – **pop. 377** Ireland **38** A3

Dublin 344 km – Cork 95 km – Killarney 124 km

Sherkin Island★ (by ferry) – Castletownshend★, E : 20 km by R 595 and R 596 – Glandore★, E : 26 km by R 595, N 71 and R 597

Casey's of Baltimore rest,

East : 0.75 km on R 595 – ✆ (028) 20 197 – www.caseysofbaltimore.com – Fax (028) 20 509 – closed 20-27 December

14 rm – € 103/115 € 158/182 **Rest** – Carte € 33/49 **s**

◆ Popular hotel near sea-shore. Cosy bar with open fires and traditional music at weekends, with beer garden overlooking bay. Large, well-decorated rooms with pine furniture. Great sea views from dining room.

Baltimore Townhouse without rest

– ✆ (028) 20 197 – www.baltimoretownhouse.com – Fax (028) 20 509 – closed 20-27 December

6 rm – € 120/160 € 120/160

◆ Six open plan suites comprising bedroom, living area, small kitchen and bathroom. Check in at Casey's on your way into the village; breakfast is also served there.

Slipway without rest

The Cove, East : 0.75 km – ✆ (028) 20 134 – www.theslipway.com – Fax (028) 20 134 – April-October

4 rm – € 60/70 € 75/80

◆ Relaxed, informal guesthouse with yellow façade and lovely views of local harbour, particularly from veranda outside breakfast room. Simple, individualistic, well-kept rooms.

BANDON (Droichead na Bandan) – Cork – 712 F12 – pop. 5 822 38 B3

Dublin 181 km – Cork 20 km – Carrigaline 28 km – Cobh 33 km

Poacher's Inn

Clonakilty Rd, Southwest : 1.5 km on N 71 – (023) 884 1159 – Closed 25 December and Good Friday

Rest – Carte € 22/36

◆ Busy refurbished pub with downstairs bar, sofas and wood burning stove; simple menu served all day. Small restaurant upstairs offers larger selection, including lots of fish.

BANTRY (Beanntraí) Cork – Cork – 712 D12 38 A3

Dublin 215 km – Cork 53 km – Killarney 49 km – Macroom 34 km

O'Connor's

The Square – (035327) 50 221 – www.oconnorseafood.com – Closed Easter, 24-26 December, lunch Saturday in summer and Sundays

Rest – Menu € 30 (early evening) – Carte dinner € 34/48

◆ Popular seafood restaurant on edge of the harbour, with rustic stone floor, granite-topped tables and maritime décor. Tasty, classically cooked local seafood. Pleasant service.

BARNA (Bearna) – Galway – 712 E8 – pop. 12 795 36 B3

Dublin 227 km – Galway 9 km

The Twelve

Barna Crossroads – (091) 597 000 – www.thetwelvehotel.ie – Fax (091) 597 003

38 rm – € 90/130 € 99/149 – 10 suites

Rest *West* – *(closed Monday) (dinner only)* Menu € 25 **s** – Carte € 35/39 **s**

Rest *The Pins* – Menu € 20 **s** – Carte € 26/28 **s**

◆ Boutique hotel whose bedrooms are stylish and modern with quality furniture, up-to-date technology and designer toiletries. Original menu offered in elegant West restaurant. The Pins offers an interesting menu of European dishes in an informal atmosphere.

O'Grady's on the Pier

– (091) 592 223 – www.ogradysonthepier.com – Fax (091) 590 677 – closed 24-26 December

Rest – Seafood – *(booking essential)* Carte € 34/50

◆ Converted quayside pub on two floors with great views of Galway Bay. Cheerful, attentive staff and daily menus of simple, flavourful seafood have earned good local reputation.

BARRELLS CROSS – Cork – 712 G12 – see Kinsale

BEAUFORT (Lios an Phúca) – Kerry – 712 D11 – see Killarney

BIRR (Biorra) – Offaly – 712 I8 – pop. 5 081 Ireland 39 C1

Dublin 140 km – Athlone 45 km – Kilkenny 79 km – Limerick 79 km

The Civic Office, Wilmer Rd (057) 912 0923

The Glenns, (057) 912 00 82

Town★ – Birr Castle Demesne★★ **AC** (Telescope★★)

Clonfert Cathedral★ (West doorway★★), NW : 24 km by R 439, R 356 and minor roads – Portumna★ (Castle★ **AC**), W : 24 km by R 489 – Roscrea★ (Damer House★ **AC**) S : 19.25 km by N 62 – Slieve Bloom Mountinas★, E : 21 km by R 440

The Maltings without rest

Castle St – (057) 91 21 345 – Fax (057) 91 22 073

10 rm – € 50/55 € 80

◆ Characterful 19C hotel on riverside near Birr Castle, originally built to store malt for Guinness. Cosy bar and lounge. Bedrooms enriched by flowery fabrics and drapes.

BLACKLION (An Blaic) – Cavan – 712 I5 – pop. 174 34 A3

Dublin 194 km – Drogheda 170 km – Enniskillen 19 km

Blacklion Toam, (071) 985 30 24

XXX **MacNean House** with rm — AC rest, VISA MC

Main St – ☎ (071) 985 30 22 – www.macneanrestaurant.com – Fax (071) 985 34 04 – closed January and 22-28 December

10 rm ☕ – 👤 € 95 👥 € 140

Rest – *(closed Wednesday except June-September, Monday and Tuesday) (dinner only and Sunday lunch) (booking essential)* Menu € 70

◆ Stylish, modern restaurant in smart townhouse, with plush seating, linen-clad tables and subtle cream décor. Refined, complex dishes use good quality seasonal and local ingredients. Keenly run, with friendly local staff. Comfortable, contemporary bedrooms.

BLARNEY (An Bhlarna) – Cork – 712 G12 – pop. 2 400 – ✉ Cork — 38 B3

Ireland

Dublin 268 km – Cork 9 km

Town Centre (021) 4381624, (May- Sept) blarneytio@failteireland.ie

Blarney Castle★★ **AC** – Blarney Castle House★ **AC**

🏠 **Killarney House** without rest — P

Station Rd, Northeast : 1.5 km – ☎ (021) 438 18 41 – www.killarneyhouseblarney.com – Fax (021) 438 18 41

6 rm ☕ – 👤 € 45/50 👥 € 66/74

◆ Spacious, modern guesthouse set above attractive village. Very comfortable lounge. Breakfast room equipped to high standard. Sizeable, immaculately kept rooms.

at Tower West : 3.25 km on R 617 – ✉ Cork

🏠 **Ashlee Lodge** — AC P VISA MC AE

– ☎ (021) 438 53 46 – www.ashleelodge.com – Fax (021) 438 57 26 – closed 20 December-20 January

10 rm ☕ – 👤 € 65/95 👥 € 75/140 **Rest** – *(dinner only)* Carte approx. € 34 **s**

◆ Relaxing modern house, ideally located for Blarney Castle. Breakfast room with extensive menu. Outdoor Canadian hot tub. Very well-equipped rooms, some with whirlpool baths.

BORRIS – Carlow – 712 L10 – pop. 582 — 39 D2

Dublin 121 km – Carlow 36 km – Waterford 66 km

🏠 **Step House** — P VISA MC

– ☎ (059) 977 3209 – www.stephousehotel.ie – Fax (059) 977 3395

19 rm – 👤 € 65/85 👥 € 110/160 – 1 suite

Rest *Cellar* – Menu € 28 (early dinner) **s** – Carte € 22/51 **s**

◆ Extended Georgian townhouse offers spacious, modern bedrooms decorated in cool pastel shades. All have freestanding roll-top baths; the penthouse has floor to ceiling windows and a terrace overlooking the mountains. Traditional cooking served in Cellar.

BOYLE (Mainistir na Búille) – Roscommon – 712 H6 – pop. 2 522 — 36 B2

Ireland

Dublin 175 km – Longford 53 km – Sligo 45 km

King House (071) 966 2145, (May- Sept) boyle.touristoffice@failteireland.ie

King House★ **AC**

Boyle Abbey★ **AC**, E : 2 km by N 4 – Lough Key Forest Park★ **AC**, E : 3.25 km by N 4. Arigna Scenic Drive★ (≤★), NE : 20 km by N 4, R 280 and R 207 – Curlew Mountains (≤★), NW : 3.5 km by N 4

🏠 **Rosdarrig House** without rest — P VISA MC

Carrick Rd – ☎ (071) 966 20 40 – www.rosdarrig.com – April-October

5 rm ☕ – 👤 € 45/50 👥 € 70/75

◆ Comfortable, well-kept guesthouse with friendly owners. Attractive lounge and appealing wood-floored breakfast room. Good sized, smartly decorated rooms overlooking garden.

BUNDORAN (Bun Dobhráin) – Donegal – 712 H4 – pop. 1 964 37 C2
Ireland

Dublin 259 km – Donegal 27 km – Sligo 37 km

The Bridge, Main St ✆ (071) 9842539 (April-October)

Creevykeel Court Cairn★, S : 5 km by N 15 – Rossnowlagh Strand★★, N : 8.5 km by N 15 and R 231

Fitzgerald's

– ✆ (071) 984 13 36 – www.fitzgeraldshotel.com – Fax (071) 984 21 21 – restricted opening in winter

16 rm – € 65/85 € 100/150

Rest ***The Bistro*** – *(closed Monday-Tuesday to non-residents July-August) (dinner only)* Carte € 27/38 **s**

◆ Family owned hotel in centre of popular seaside town overlooking Donegal Bay. Reception rooms warmed by wood-burning stove. Sumptuous sofas abound. Sea-facing front bedrooms. Linen-clad, informal Bistro with carefully compiled menu.

BUNRATTY (Bun Raite) – Clare – 712 F9 Ireland 38 B2

Dublin 207 km – Ennis 24 km – Limerick 13 km

Town★★ – Bunratty Castle★★

Bunratty Manor

rm,

– ✆ (061) 707 984 – www.bunrattymanor.net – Fax (061) 360 588 – Closed 1 week Christmas

22 rm – € 79/99 € 99/120

Rest – *(dinner only and Sunday lunch)* Carte € 30/45

◆ Purpose-built, tourist-oriented hotel in village centre. Comfy lounge with chintz suites; Neat, modern rooms in colourful fabrics and drapes. Smart terrace fringed by pleasant garden. Traditional menus.

Bunratty Grove without rest

Castle Rd, North : 2.5 km – ✆ (061) 369 579 – www.bunrattygrove.com – Fax (061) 369 561 – Closed 15 December-1 February

6 rm – € 40/60 € 50/60

◆ Pink painted guesthouse on country road with peaceful ambience. Large lounge-cum-library and pleasant, cottagey breakfast room. Immaculate rooms with polished wood floors.

Guesthouses don't provide the same level of service as hotels. They are often characterised by a warm welcome and a décor which reflects the owner's personality. Those shown in red are particularly pleasant.

BUTLERSTOWN (Baile an Bhuitléaraigh) – Waterford – see Waterford

CAHERDANIEL (Cathair Dónall) – Kerry – 712 B12 – pop. 352 38 A3
– ✉ Killarney Ireland

Dublin 383 km – Killarney 77 km

Ring of Kerry★★ – Derrynane National Historic Park★★ – Skellig Islands★★ **AC**, by boat – Sneem★, E : 19 km by N 70 – Staigue Fort★, E : 8 km by N 70 and minor road

Iskeroon without rest

West : 8 mi. by N 70 and Bunavalla Pier rd taking left turn at junction then turning left onto track immediately before pier – ✆ (066) 947 51 19 – www.iskeroon.com – Fax (066) 947 54 88 – April-September, minimum stay 2 nights

3 rm – € 160 € 160

◆ A "design icon", this low-lying house looking out to Derrynane Harbour was built in 1930s by the Earl of Dunraven. Lush gardens; boldly designed, vividly coloured bedrooms.

CAHERLISTRANE (Cathair Loistreáin) – Galway – 712 E7 36 B3

Dublin 256 km – Ballina 74 km – Galway 42 km

Lisdonagh House

Northwest : 2.5 km by Shrule rd – (093) 31 163 – www.lisdonagh.com – Fax (093) 31 528 – May-November

8 rm – € 120/150 € 140/280 – 2 suites **Rest** – Carte € 39/49

◆ Georgian house overlooking Lough Hacket; row across to island in the middle. A grand entrance hall with fine murals leads to antique filled rooms named after Irish artists. Locally caught fish predominant in dining room.

CAHERSIVEEN (Cathair Saidhbhín) – Kerry – 712 B12 – pop. 1 294 38 A2

Ireland

Dublin 355 km – Killarney 64 km

Ring of Kerry★★

O'Neill's (The Point) Seafood Bar

Renard Point, Southwest : 2.75 km by N 70 – (066) 947 2165 – Fax (066) 947 2165 – March-October

Rest – *(bookings not accepted)* Carte € 28/38

◆ A warm welcome and freshly prepared seafood await at this simply furnished pub, situated on the western edge of the Iveragh Peninsula. Concise menu. Maritime décor.

CAMPILE (Ceann Poill) – Wexford – 712 L11 – pop. 347 Ireland 39 D2

Dublin 154 km – Waterford 35 km – Wexford 37 km

Dunbrody Abbey★, S : 3.25 km by R 733 – J F Kennedy Arboretum★, N : 3.25 km by R 733. Tintern Abbey★, SE : 12.75 km by R 733 – Duncannon Fort★, S : 12.75 km by R 733

Kilmokea Country Manor rm,

West : 8 km by R 733 and Great Island rd – (051) 388 109 – www.kilmokea.com – Fax (051) 388 776 – February-October

6 rm – € 75/180 € 150/300

Rest – *(booking essential for non-residents)* Menu € 54 (dinner) **s** – Carte lunch € 20/32 **s**

◆ Former Georgian rectory in large public gardens. Elegantly furnished. Games room, tennis and fishing. Comfortable bedrooms in house and converted stable block. Formal dining room with polished tables and period style; breakfast in conservatory.

CAPPOQUIN (Ceapach Choinn) – Waterford – 712 I11 – pop. 740 39 C2

Ireland

Dublin 219 km – Cork 56 km – Waterford 64 km

Lismore★ (Lismore Castle Gardens★ **AC**, St Carthage's Cathedral★), W : 6.5 km by N 72. The Gap★ (★) NW : 14.5 km by R 669

Richmond House with rm

Southeast : 0.75 km on N 72 – (058) 54 278 – www.richmondhouse.net – Fax (058) 54 988 – Closed 20 December-20 January, Sunday and Monday

9 rm – € 160/220 **Rest** – *(dinner only)* Menu € 58

◆ Built for Earl of Cork and Burlington in 1704; retains Georgian style with stately, cove-ceilinged dining room: local produce to the fore. Individually decorated period rooms.

at Millstreet East : 11.25 km by N 72 on R 671 – ✉ Cappoquin

Castle Country House without rest

– (058) 68 049 – www.castlecountryhouse.com – April-October

5 rm – € 50/70 € 100

◆ Extended farmhouse on working dairy and beef farm with 15C origins. Rural location and lovely gardens. Individual bedrooms with cottage style decor.

CARAGH LAKE (Loch Cárthaí) – Kerry – 712 C11 Ireland **38** A2

Dublin 341 km – Killarney 35 km – Tralee 40 km
Dooks Glenbeigh, ✆ (066) 976 82 05
Lough Caragh★
Iveragh Peninsula★★ (Ring of Kerry★★)

Ard-Na-Sidhe

– ✆ (066) 976 91 05 – www.ardnasidhe.com – Fax (066) 976 92 82 – May-mid October
18 rm – € 150/270 € 170/300
Rest – *(dinner only) (booking essential for non-residents)* Carte € 35/56 **s**
◆ Built 1880 by an English Lady who called it "House of Fairies". Elizabethan in style; gardens lead down to lake. Possesses atmosphere of private home. Antique filled rooms. Tasteful dining room with intimate feel.

Carrig Country House

– ✆ (066) 976 91 00 – www.carrighouse.com – March-November
17 rm – € 125/140 € 150/250
Rest – *(dinner only) (booking essential for non-residents)* Menu € 38 – Carte € 30/47
◆ Down a wooded drive, the yellow ochre façade of the house immediately strikes you. Its loughside setting assures good views. Ground floor rooms have their own private patio. Caragh Lough outlook from dining room windows.

CARLINGFORD (Cairlinn) – Louth – 712 N5 – pop. 623 Ireland **37** D2

Dublin 106 km – Dundalk 21 km
Town★
Windy Gap★, NW : 12.75 km by R 173 – Proleek Dolmen★, SW : 14.5 km by R 173

Four Seasons

rest,

– ✆ (042) 937 35 30 – www.4seasonshotelcarlingford.ie – Fax (042) 937 35 31 – closed 23-26 December
59 rm – € 95/129 € 99/150
Rest – *(bar lunch Monday-Saturday)* Menu € 35 – Carte € 28/41
◆ Purpose-built hotel on outskirts of scenic market town. Extensive conference facilities; smart leisure centre. Spacious and well-equipped bedrooms. Popular bar leading to intimate dining room with Irish menus.

Beaufort House without rest

– ✆ (042) 937 38 79 – www.beauforthouse.net – Fax (042) 937 38 78
6 rm – € 65/120 € 120
◆ Modern house attractively sited on shores of Carlingford Lough. Very comfortable, spacious rooms with sea or mountain views. Substantial breakfasts served overlooking lough.

CARLOW (Ceatharlach) – Carlow – 712 L9 – pop. 20 724 **39** D2

Dublin 80 km – Kilkenny 37 km – Wexford 75 km
College St ✆ (059) 9131554, carlowtouristoffice@failteireland.ie
Carlow Dublin Rd, Deer Park, ✆ (059) 913 16 95

Seven Oaks

Athy Rd – ✆ (059) 913 13 08 – www.sevenoakshotel.com – Fax (059) 913 21 55 – closed 25-26 December
89 rm – € 80/90 € 120/160
Rest – *(closed Saturday lunch)* Menu € 25/38 **s** – Carte dinner € 24/37 **s**
◆ Close to the sights of the River Barrow walk, this neat hotel in a residential area makes a good resting place. Well-kept rooms: ask for those in the new wing. Intimate booths in tranquil dining room.

REPUBLIC OF IRELAND

Barrowville Town House without rest

Kilkenny Rd, South : 0.75 km on N 9 – (059) 914 33 24 – www.barrowville.com – Fax (059) 914 19 53 – closed 24-25 December

7 rm – € 39/55 € 100/140

◆ Delightful Georgian property filled with beautiful furniture, including a grand piano in the drawing room. Conservatory breakfast room looks out over the garden. Spacious, homely bedrooms.

CARNAROSS (Carn na Ros) – **Meath** – **712** L6 – **Kells** **37** D3

Dublin 69 km – Cavan 43 km – Drogheda 48 km

The Forge

Pottlereagh, Northwest : 5.5 km by N 3 on Oldcastle rd – (046) 924 50 03 – www.theforgerestaurant.ie – Fax (046) 924 59 17 – closed 2 weeks August, 24-26 and 31 December, 1 January, Sunday dinner, Monday and Tuesday

Rest – *(dinner only and Sunday lunch)* Menu € 45 (mid week)/50 (weekends) – Carte € 45/56

◆ Former forge tucked away in rural isolation. Family run, traditionally styled restaurant serving tried-and-tested dishes with modern twist: ample, good value choice.

CARNE – **Wexford** – **712** M11 **39** D3

Dublin 169 km – Waterford 82 km – Wexford 21 km

The Lobster Pot

– (053) 913 1110 – Fax (053) 913 1401 – Closed 17 January-10 February, 25-26 December, Good Friday and Monday except Bank Holidays

Rest – Seafood – Carte € 35/50

◆ Long-standing, popular pub quirkily cluttered with nautical knick-knacks. Wide-ranging seafood menu offers the freshest fish available; precisely cooked and simply served.

CARRICKMACROSS (Carraig Mhachaire Rois) – **Monaghan** – **712** L6 – **pop. 4 387** Ireland **37** D2

Dublin 92 km – Dundalk 22 km

Nuremore Hotel & CC, (042) 966 14 38

Dún a' Rí Forest Park★, SW : 8 km by R 179 – St Mochta's House★, E : 7 km by R 178 and minor road S

Nuremore

South : 1.5 km on N 2 – (042) 966 14 38 – www.nuremore.com – Fax (042) 966 18 53

72 rm – € 135/160 € 195/230

Rest *The Restaurant* – see restaurant listing

◆ Much extended Victorian house in attractive grounds; a rural retreat in which to swim, ride or practice golf. Comfortable rooms, most with views over countryside.

The Restaurant – at Nuremore Hotel

South : 1.5 km on N 2 – (042) 966 14 38 – www.nuremore.com – Fax (042) 966 18 53 – closed Saturday lunch

Rest – Menu € 31/52 **s**

◆ Split-level dining room; tables laid with white linen, bone china and stylish glassware. Menu of seasonal dishes influenced by French fine dining. Attentive service.

CARRICK-ON-SHANNON (Cora Droma Rúisc) – **Leitrim** – **712** H6 – **pop. 3 163** Ireland **37** C2

Dublin 156 km – Ballina 80 km – Galway 119 km – Roscommon 42 km

Old Barrel Store, The Marina (0719) 620170 (April-October), leitrim@failteireland.ie

Carrick-on-Shannon Woodbrook, (071) 966 7015

Town★

Lough Rynn Demesne★

REPUBLIC OF IRELAND

The Landmark rm, rest,

on N 4 – (071) 962 22 22 – www.thelandmarkhotel.com – Fax (071) 962 22 33 – Closed 25 December

60 rm – € 90/125 € 130/198

Rest *Boardwalk* – Carte € 23/37 **s**

◆ Next to the Shannon, with a water feature in reception and water-themed pictures throughout. Traditional style bedrooms; some overlooking the river. Stylish cocktail lounges with stunning modern design. Boardwalk boasts pleasant river views.

Ciúin House rm,

Hartley, North : 1 km. by R 280 on L 3400 – (071) 967 14 88 – www.ciuinhouse.com – Fax (071) 967 14 87 – Closed 24-27 December

15 rm – € 50/70 € 95/130

Rest – *(dinner only) (booking essential) (residents only)* Carte € 23/45 **s**

◆ Purpose-built house suitable for both tourists and business travellers; 10min walk from centre of town. Stylish, comfortable lounge with bar. Modern bedrooms; two with Jacuzzi baths. Small, contemporary-style restaurant serving unfussy dishes.

Hollywell without rest

Liberty Hill, off N 4, taking first left over bridge – (071) 962 11 24 – Fax (071) 962 11 24 – closed Christmas and midweek in winter

4 rm – € 65/75 € 125/140

◆ A charming part 18C house in a peaceful spot by the river. Read up on area in a well-appointed lounge, take breakfast in dining room run by hospitable owner. Neat rooms.

The Oarsman

Bridge St – (071) 962 1733 – www.theoarsman.com – Fax (071) 962 1734 – Closed 25 December, Good Friday, Sunday and Monday except Bank Holidays

Rest – Menu € 20/35 – Carte € 18/22

◆ Friendly, family-run pub with lively, local feel, set on busy, town centre street. Eclectic menus offer wide range; from snacks and salads through to restaurant-style dishes.

CARRIGALINE (Carraig Uí Leighin) – Cork – 712 G12 – pop. 12 835 — 38 B3

Dublin 262 km – Cork 14 km

Fernhill, (021) 437 2226

Carrigaline Court rm, rest,

Cork Rd – (021) 485 21 00 – www.carrigcourt.com – Fax (021) 437 11 03 – closed 25 December

89 rm – € 95/140 € 140/220 – 2 suites

Rest – *(dinner only) (meals served in bar Sunday-Thursday)* Carte approx. € 45 **s**

◆ Modern hotel with airy interiors; rooms are spacious, with all mod cons, whilst leisure centre boasts a 20m pool, steam room, sauna. Corporate friendly with large ballroom. Local products to the fore in stylish restaurant.

Raffeen Lodge without rest

Ringaskiddy Rd, Monkstown, Northeast : 4 km by R 611 and N 28 off R 610 – (021) 437 16 32 – www.raffeenlodge.com – Fax (021) 437 16 32 – closed 20 December-4 January

6 rm – € 40/45 € 60/70

◆ A short drive from the fishing village of Ringaskiddy and Cork airport. A neat and tidy, good value house; rooms are uniformly decorated in pastel shades, simple in style.

CARRIGANS (An Carraigain) – Donegal – 712 J3 – pop. 191 — 37 C1

Dublin 225 km – Donegal 66 km – Letterkenny 230 km – Sligo 124 km

Mount Royd without rest

– (074) 914 01 63 – www.mountroyd.com – Fax (074) 914 04 00 – March-October

4 rm – € 40 € 60

◆ Genuinely hospitable owners keep this creeper-clad period house in excellent order. En suite rooms are cosy and individually styled. Traditional, pleasantly cluttered lounge.

REPUBLIC OF IRELAND

CASHEL (An Caiseal) – Galway – 712 C7 Ireland 36 A3

Dublin 278 km – Galway 66 km

Town★

Connemara★★★

Cashel House

– ✆ (095) 31 001 – www.cashel-house-hotel.com – Fax (095) 31 077
– Closed mid January-mid February

29 rm – 🚹 € 95/240 🚹🚹 € 230/310

Rest – *(bar lunch Monday-Saturday) (booking essential for non-residents)*
Menu € 65 **s**

◆ Built 1840; a very comfortable and restful country house, warmly decorated with delightful gardens. General de Gaulle stayed in one of the luxurious country house rooms. Dining room, with Queen Anne style chairs, opens into elegant conservatory.

CASHEL (Caiseal) – Tipperary – 712 I10 – pop. 2 936 Ireland 39 C2

Dublin 162 km – Cork 96 km – Kilkenny 55 km – Limerick 58 km

Heritage Centre, Town Hall, Main St ✆ (062) 62511, cashelhc@iol.ie

Town★★★ – Rock of Cashel★★★ **AC** – Cormac's Chapel★★ – Round Tower★ – Museum★ – Cashel Palace Gardens★ – GPA Bolton Library★ **AC**

Holy Cross Abbey★★, N : 14.5 km by R 660 – Athassel Priory★, W : 8 km by N 74. Caher (Castle★★, Swiss Cottage★), S : 18 km by N 8 – Glen of Aherlow★, W : 21 km by N 74 and R 664

Cashel Palace

Main St – ✆ (062) 62 707 – www.cashel-palace.ie – Fax (062) 61 521 – Closed 24-27 December

19 rm – 🚹 € 95/130 🚹🚹 € 130/238

Rest – *(carvery lunch Monday-Saturday)* Menu € 49 – Carte € 25/45

◆ A stately Queen Anne house, once home to an Archbishop, in walled gardens with path leading up to Cashel Rock. Inside, an extensive, pillared lounge and capacious rooms. Harmonious dining room: vaulted ceilings, open fire and light, bright colours.

Baileys of Cashel

rm,

Main St – ✆ (062) 61 937 – www.baileys-ireland.com – Fax (062) 63 957 – Closed 25-26 December and 1 January

20 rm – 🚹 € 80 🚹🚹 € 140 **Rest** – Carte € 22/43

◆ Extended Georgian townhouse, used as grain store during Irish famine. Contemporary bedrooms are furnished to a high standard. Small lounge with library; bar area in basement. Restaurant with open plan kitchen serves modern European cooking.

Aulber House without rest

Deerpark, Golden Rd, West : 0.75 km on N 74 – ✆ (062) 63 713 – www.aulberhouse.com – Fax (062) 63 715 – Closed 3 December-3 January

12 rm – 🚹 € 50/60 🚹🚹 € 80/100

◆ Modern house in Georgian style with lawned gardens; five minutes from town centre. Comfy, leather furnished lounge. Smart, individually styled rooms.

Chez Hans

Rockside, Moor Lane St – ✆ (062) 61 177 – www.chezhans.net – Fax (062) 61 177 – Closed 2 weeks January, 2 weeks September, Sunday and Monday

Rest – *(dinner only) (booking essential)* Carte € 35/65

◆ A converted synod hall with stained glass windows, near Cashel Rock: an unusual setting for a restaurant. Carefully prepared and cooked meals, using local ingredients.

Cafe Hans

Rockside, Moore Lane St – ✆ (062) 63 660 – closed 2 weeks January, 1 week September, Sunday and Monday

Rest – *(lunch only) (bookings not accepted)* Carte € 27/31

◆ Next door to Chez Hans; white emulsioned walls, open kitchen and glass roof. Simple, tasty dishes are prepared with good, local ingredients. Come early as you can't book.

CASTLEBALDWIN (Béal Átha na gCarraigíní) – Sligo – 712 G5 36 B2
– ✉ Boyle (roscommon) Ireland

Dublin 190 km – Longford 67 km – Sligo 24 km

Carrowkeel Megalithic Cemetery (≤★★), S : 4.75 km. Arigna Scenic Drive★, N : 3.25 km by N 4 - Lough Key Forest Park★ AC, SE : 16 km by N 4 – View of Lough Allen★, N : 14.5 km by N 4 on R 280 – Mountain Drive★, N : 9.5 km on N 4 – Boyle Abbey★ AC, SE : 12.75 km by N 4 - King House★, SE : 12.75 km by N 4

Cromleach Lodge

Ballindoon, Southeast : 5.5 km – ☎ (071) 916 51 55 – www.cromleach.com – Fax (071) 916 54 55 – Closed 20-27 December

57 rm – € 150/180 € 240/300

Rest *Moira's* – see restaurant listing

◆ Remotely located hotel in fine position overlooking Lough Arrow. Large, luxurious bedrooms; some modern, some classic; deluxe rooms with views and either balcony or terrace are well worth the extra.

Moira's – at Cromleach Lodge Hotel

Ballindoon, Southeast : 5.5 km – ☎ (071) 916 51 55 – www.cromleach.com – Fax (071) 916 54 55 – Closed 20-27 December

Rest – Menu € 55 (dinner) – Carte approx. € 55

◆ Spacious, contemporary restaurant with views to Lough Arrow. Rear booths ideal for large groups. Fixed price menu of modern Irish cooking, with local produce to the fore.

CASTLEGREGORY (Caisleán Ghriaire) – Kerry – 712 B11 – pop. 205 38 A2

Dublin 330 km – Dingle 24 km – Killarney 54 km

The Shores Country House without rest

Conor Pass Rd, Kilcummin, Southwest : 6 km on Brandon rd – ☎ (066) 713 91 95 – www.shorescountryhouse.com – Fax (066) 713 91 96

6 rm – € 55/90 € 70/90

◆ Between Stradbally Mountain and a long sandy beach, a modern guest house run by the friendly longstanding owner. Immaculate, comfortable rooms, some with antique beds.

CASTLELYONS (Caisleán Ó Liatháin) – Cork – 712 H11 – pop. 203 38 B2

Dublin 219 km – Cork 30 km – Killarney 104 km – Limerick 64 km

Ballyvolane House

Southeast : 5.5 km by Midleton rd on Britway rd – ☎ (025) 36 349 – www.ballyvolanehouse.ie – Fax (025) 36 781 – closed 24 December-4 January

6 rm – € 135 € 210/220

Rest – *(by arrangement, communal dining)* Menu € 35/55

◆ Stately 18C Italianate mansion mentioned in local legend, with lakes in parkland. Name means "place of springing heifers". Antique-filled rooms, some with Victorian baths. Dining room with silver candlesticks and balanced dishes.

CASTLEMARTYR (Baile na Martra) Cork – Cork – 712 H12 39 C3
– pop. 978

Dublin 174 km – Cork 20 km – Ballincollig 25 km – Carrigaline 24 km

Castlemartyr

– ☎ (021) 464 4050 – www.castlemartyrresort.com – Fax (021) 464 4051

83 rm – € 195/290 € 195/459, € 25 – 26 suites

Rest *Bell Tower* – Menu € 45 (dinner) **s** – Carte € 31/54 **s**

Rest *Garden Room* – Menu € 65 (dinner) **s** – Carte € 53/70 **s**

◆ Grand 17C manor house in 220 acres, with river, castle ruins, golf course and spa. Maximum luxury; from the meeting room and lounge to the contemporary bedrooms and suites. Traditional fine dining in the Bell Tower. Breakfast or lunch in the Garden Room, overlooking the formal gardens and fountain.

CASTLEPOLLARD (Baile na gCros) – Westmeath – 712 K6 37 C3
– pop. 1 004

Dublin 63 km – Mullingar 13 km – Tullamore 37 km – Édenderry 36 km

Lough Bishop House

Derrynagarra, Collinstown, Southeast : 6 km by R 394 taking left turn on unmarked rd opposite church and school after 4 km – ☎ (044) 966 13 13 – www.loughbishophouse.com – Fax (044) 966 13 13 – Closed Christmas-New Year

3 rm – € 60/70 € 110

Rest – *(by arrangement, communal dining)* Menu € 30

◆ Renovated 19C farmhouse on south-facing hillside. Well-kept, with homely lounge and simple, antique-furnished bedrooms; the two larger with countryside views. Home cooked dishes made with local produce, including meat and eggs from the farm and fruit from the orchard.

CASTLETOWNBERE (Baile Chaisleáin Bhéarra) – Cork – 712 C13 – pop. 868 Ireland — 38 A3

Dublin 360 km – Cork 130 km – Killarney 93 km

Berehaven Millcove, ☎ (027) 70 700

Ring of Beara★, W : by R 572 (Allihies, mines★ - Garnish Bay ≤★) – Slieve Miskish Mountains (≤★)

Rodeen without rest

East : 3.25 km by R 572 – ☎ (027) 70 158 – www.rodeencountryhouse.com – March-October

6 rm – € 40/50 € 70/80

◆ Owner used to run a horticulture business and this is evident in the variety of shrubs in the garden. Rooms are compact but nicely decorated; some look out to Bantry Bay.

CASTLETOWNSHEND (Baile an Chaisleáin) – Cork – 712 E13 – pop. 188 Ireland — 38 B3

Dublin 346 km – Cork 95 km – Killarney 116 km

Glandore★, NE : 10 km R 596 – Sherkin Island★ **AC**, W : 15 km by R 596 and R 595 and ferry

Mary Ann's

Main St – ☎ (028) 36 146 – www.westcorkweek.com/maryanns/ – Closed 25-27 December and Monday in winter

Rest – *(bookings not accepted)* Carte € 25/45

◆ A pleasant 19C pub in pretty village. Tempting dishes are distinguished by the fact that almost everything is homemade. Sunny terrace is popular for lunch.

CAVAN (An Cabhán) – Cavan – 712 J6 – pop. 7 883 Ireland — 37 C2

Dublin 114 km – Drogheda 93 km – Enniskillen 64 km

Central Library, 1st Floor, Farnham St ☎ (049) 4331942 (April-September), cavan@failteireland.ie

Killykeen Forest Park★, W : 9.5 km by R 198

Radisson Blu Farnham Estate

Farnham Estate, Northwest : 3.75 km on R 198 – ☎ (049) 437 77 00 – www.farnhamestatecom – Fax (049) 437 77 01

154 rm – € 105/195 € 130/220 – 4 suites

Rest *Botanica* – *(dinner only and Sunday lunch)* Menu € 40 **s** – Carte € 34/47 **s**

◆ Period charm and acres of mature parkland in this renovated 400-year old mansion, offset by 21C hotel with meeting facilities, wellness centre and snazzy, well-equipped rooms. Local, seasonal produce in light, airy Botanica.

Cavan Crystal

Dublin Rd, East : 1.5 km on N 3 – ☎ (049) 436 0600 – www.cavancrystalhotel.com – Fax (049) 436 0699 – Closed 24-25 December

85 rm – € 100/130 € 170/190

Rest *Opus One* – see restaurant listing

◆ Modern hotel next to Cavan Crystal factory. Vast atrium is distinctive and stylish. Extensive meeting and leisure facilities. Comfy, well-equipped, modish bedrooms.

REPUBLIC OF IRELAND

XX **Opus One** – at Cavan Crystal Hotel
Dublin Rd, East : 1.5 km on N 3 – ✆ (049) 436 0600 – www.cavancrystalhotel.com – Fax (049) 436 0699 – Closed 24-25 December
Rest – *(light lunch)* Carte € 33/46 **s**
◆ Contemporary restaurant on first floor of hotel. Simple lunch menu; more elaborate dinner menu offers well-crafted, modern dishes, with some unusual combinations of flavour and texture.

XX **The Oak Room**
62 Main Street – ✆ (049) 437 14 14 – www.theoakroom.ie – Closed 24-27 December, Sunday except Bank Holidays and Monday
Rest – *(dinner only)* Menu € 25 **s** – Carte € 35/45 **s**
◆ Two-roomed restaurant above 'Smith and Wilson' bar on high street. Experienced chef uses local ingredients to produce an eclectic array of dishes, including some with Asian influences.

at Cloverhill North : 12 km by N 3 on N 54 – ✉ Belturbet

XX **The Olde Post Inn** with rm rest,
– ✆ (047) 55 555 – www.theoldepostinn.com – Fax (047) 55 111 – Closed 24-27 December and Monday
6 rm – € 55/65 € 100/130
Rest – *(dinner only and Sunday lunch)* Menu € 35 **s** – Carte € 40/55 **s**
◆ Keenly run former village post office; now a characterful restaurant with large rafters and exposed stone and brick. Attractive wooden conservatory. Seasonally changing menu of well presented, modern Irish cooking. Stylish, modern bedrooms.

CELBRIDGE – Kildare – 712 M7 – pop. 17 262 — 39 D1

Dublin 21 km – Naas 26 km – Drogheda 71 km

XX **La Serre**
The Village at Lyons, South : 4.5 km. by Ardclough rd. – ✆ (01) 630 3500 – www.villageatlyons.com – Fax (01) 630 35 05 – Closed 25 December, Monday and Tuesday
Rest – Menu € 30/45 – Carte approx. € 45
◆ Delightful restaurant in 17C Turner designed conservatory, with rustic courtyard for outdoor dining. Emphasis is on simplicity, with fish pies, steak and chips or oysters.

CLAREMORRIS (Clár Chlainne Mhuiris) – Mayo – 712 E/F6 – pop. 2 595 — 36 B2

Dublin 149 km – Castlebar 18 km – Galway 39 km – Newbridge 41 km

McWilliam Park rm, rest,
Knock Rd, East : 2 km on N 60 – ✆ (094) 937 8000 – www.mcwilliampark.ie – Fax (094) 937 8001
101 rm – € 95/130 € 170/210 – 2 suites
Rest – *(carvery lunch Monday-Saturday)* Menu € 38 **s** – Carte € 30/45 **s**
◆ Named after a local 18C landowner, this busy, purpose built hotel is located on the outskirts of town, convenient for the N17, Knock and the airport. Modern bedrooms. Stylish restaurant offers dishes made using local produce.

CLIFDEN (An Clochán) – Galway – 712 B7 – pop. 1 497 Ireland — 36 A3

Dublin 291 km – Ballina 124 km – Galway 79 km

Galway Rd ✆ (095) 21163 (March-October), clifdentouristoffice@failteireland.ie

Connemara★★★, NE : by N 59 – Sky Road★★ (≤ ★★), NE : by N 59 – Connemara National Park★, NE : 1.5 km by N 59 – Killary Harbour★, NE : 35 km by N 59 – Kylemore Abbey★ **AC**, N : 18 km by N 59

Clifden Station House
– ✆ (095) 21 699 – www.clifdenstationhouse.com
– Fax (095) 21 667
78 rm – € 88/140 € 100/240
Rest – *(closed weekdays November-February) (bar lunch)* Menu € 30
– Carte € 30/45
◆ A modern hotel on site of the Galway-Clifden railway line closed in 1935. Now forms part of a complex which includes a museum. Good sized rooms in cheerful colours. Traditional fare offered in restaurant.

Ardagh
Ballyconneely Rd, South : 2.75 km on R 341 – ✆ (095) 21 384
– www.ardaghhotel.com – Fax (095) 21 314 – 2 April-26 October
14 rm – € 55/125 € 120/200 – 3 suites
Rest – *(dinner only)* Carte € 41/62
◆ Family run hotel on edge of Ardbear Bay. A welcoming, domestically furnished interior with turf fires, piano, pictures and plants. Bedrooms are large, especially superiors. Fresh, pine dining room with views.

REPUBLIC OF IRELAND

Dolphin Beach Country House
Lower Sky Rd, West : 5.5 km by Sky Rd – ✆ (095) 21 204
– www.dolphinbeachhouse.com – Fax (095) 22 935 – 13 February-5 November
9 rm – € 80/105 € 150/180 **Rest** – *(residents only)* Menu € 40 **s**
◆ Terracotta coloured former farmhouse, perched on side of hill with stunning views of bay. Delightful sitting room with huge windows to accommodate vista. Attractive rooms. Tasty, home-cooked meals.

The Quay House without rest
Beach Rd – ✆ (095) 21 369 – www.thequayhouse.com – Fax (095) 21 608
– Mid-March-November
14 rm – € 100/120 € 130/150
◆ Once a harbour master's residence, then a Franciscan monastery. Rooms are divided between the main house: bohemian in style, and new annex: spacious with kitchenettes.

Sea Mist House without rest
– ✆ (095) 21 441 – www.seamisthouse.com – Closed Christmas and restricted opening in winter
6 rm – € 55/65 € 90/100
◆ 20C terraced stone house with sloping garden in town centre. Good choice at breakfast in cheerful room. Lounge at front and in conservatory. Spacious, modern bedrooms.

Buttermilk Lodge without rest
Westport Rd – ✆ (095) 21 951 – www.buttermilklodge.com – Fax (095) 21 953
11 rm – € 50/75 € 80/100
◆ Yellow painted, name refers to nearby lough, a theme which is continued inside as each room bears the name of a lough. Daily breakfast specials; maps provided for exploring.

CLOGHEEN (An Chloichín) – Tipperary – 712 I11 – pop. 509 — 39 C2

Dublin 122 km – Tipperary 23 km – Clonmel 21 km – Dungarvan 28 km

XX **Old Convent** with rm
Mount Anglesby, Southeast : 0.5 km on R 668 (Lismore rd) – ✆ (052) 746 55 65
– www.theoldconvent.ie – Closed 23 December-February and Sunday-Wednesday
6 rm – € 120/140 € 170/180
Rest – *(dinner only) (booking essential) (set menu only)* Menu € 65
◆ Home to the Sisters of Mercy for over 100 years, this converted convent retains a serene feel. Dine in the candlelit former chapel on seasonal 8 course tasting menu. Comfortable bedrooms, decorated in calming colours.

CLONAKILTY (Cloich na Coillte) – Cork – 712 F13 – pop. 4 154 38 B3
Ireland

Dublin 310 km – Cork 51 km

25 Ashe St ✆ (023) 8833226, clonakiltytio@failteireland.ie

Dunmore Muckross, ✆ (023) 34 644

West Cork Regional Museum★ AC

Courtmacsherry★, E : 12 km by R 600 and R 601 – Timoleague Friary★, E : 8 km by R 600. Carbery Coast★ (Drombeg Stone Circle★, Glandore★, Castletownshend★) by N 71 and R 597

Inchydoney Island Lodge & Spa

South : 5.25 km by N 71 following signs for Inchydoney Beach – ✆ *(023) 883 31 43* – *www.inchydoneyisland.com* – *Fax (023) 883 52 29* – *Closed 24-26 December*

AC rest, VISA

63 rm – € 150/200 € 200/220 – 4 suites

Rest *The Gulfstream* – ✆ (023) 882 11 19 *(dinner only and Sunday lunch)* Menu €65 **s**

Rest *Dunes Bistro* – ✆ (023) 882 11 16 – Carte € 23/45 **s**

◆ Set on a headland looking out to sea. Range of leisure facilities; treatments - aquamarine spa, underwater massages - are especially good. Big, bright bedrooms with extras. The Gulfstream has fine sea views. The Dunes Bistro has a hearty, nautical theme.

An Súgan

VISA

41 Wolfe Tone St – ✆ *(023) 883 3719* – *www.ansugan.com* – *Fax (023) 883 3825* – *Closed 25-26 December and Good Friday*

Rest – Carte € 25/45

◆ Personally run, salmon-pink pub with characterful dining rooms and charm aplenty. Menus are based around daily arrivals of fresh local fish and seafood but some meat dishes also feature.

Each starred restaurant lists three specialities that are typical of its style of cuisine. These may not always be on the menu but in their place expect delicious seasonal dishes. Be sure to try them.

CLONDALKIN (Cluain Dolcáin) – Dublin – 712 M8 – see Dublin

CLONEGALL (Cluain na nGall) Carlow – Carlow – 712 M9 – pop. 231 39 D2

Dublin 73 km – Carlow 20 km – Kilkenny 39 km – Wexford 30 km

Sha Roe Bistro

VISA

Main St – ✆ *(053) 937 56 36* – *Closed January, 1 week April, 1 week October, Sunday dinner, Monday and Tuesday*

Rest – *(dinner only and Sunday lunch) (booking essential)* Carte € 32/44

◆ Spacious sitting room, comfy sofas, rustic artwork and candles help create relaxing feel. Simple dining room with inglenook fireplace; seasonal cooking uses local ingredients.

CLONTARF (Cluain Tarbh) – Dublin – 712 N7 – see Dublin

CLOVERHILL (Droim Caiside) – Cavan – 712 J5 – see Cavan

CONG (Conga) – Mayo – 712 E7 – pop. 150 Ireland 36 A3

Dublin 257 km – Ballina 79 km – Galway 45 km

Old Courthouse (094) 9546542 (March-October), congtouristoffice@failteireland.ie

Town★

Lough Corrib★★. Ross Errilly Abbey★ (Tower ★) – Joyce Country★★ (Lough Nafooey★) W : by R 345

REPUBLIC OF IRELAND

Ashford Castle

– ☎ (094) 954 60 03 – www.ashford.ie – Fax (094) 954 62 60

78 rm – 🛉 € 165/375 🛉🛉 € 175/395 – 5 suites

Rest *George V Room* – *(dinner only and Sunday lunch) (residents only)*
Menu € 68 – Carte € 56/98

Rest *Cullens* – *(closed October-Easter and Wednesday-Thursday)*
Carte € 23/55 **s**

◆ Hugely imposing restored castle in formal grounds on Lough Corrib. Suits of armour and period antiques in a clubby lounge. Handsomely furnished country house rooms. George V imbued with air of genteel formality. Cullens serves bistro-style menu in informal atmosphere.

Lisloughrey Lodge

The Quay, Southeast : 2 km by R 346 – ☎ (094) 954 54 00 – www.lisloughrey.ie – Fax (094) 954 54 24 – Closed 24-26 December

41 rm – 🛉 € 200/250 🛉🛉 € 200/250 – 9 suites

Rest *Salt* – *(closed Monday and Tuesday)* Menu € 65

◆ Traditional exterior belies modernity of this stylish boutique hotel, with its sexy black and red lounge. Bedrooms set around courtyard; 'Duplex', the most comfortable. First floor restaurant boasts Lough view; modern menus use local produce and offer some unusual combinations.

Michaeleen's Manor without rest

Quay Rd, Southeast : 1.5 km by R 346 – ☎ (094) 954 60 89 – www.quietman-cong.com – Fax (094) 954 64 48

11 rm – 🛉 € 55 🛉🛉 € 85

◆ Named after the lead character in the film 'The Quiet Man,' filmed in the village; comfortable, brightly decorated bedrooms follow suit. Homely lounges; airy breakfast room.

Ballywarren House

East : 3.5 km on R 346 – ☎ (094) 954 69 89 – www.ballywarrenhouse.com – Fax (094) 954 69 89 – Closed 1 week Spring and 1 week Autumn

3 rm – 🛉 € 98/136 🛉🛉 € 148 **Rest** – *(by arrangement)* Menu € 46

◆ Passionately run by a charming couple who ensure each guest's stay is special. Open fires, galleried landing and oak staircase. Bedrooms boast luxurious linen and lovely views. Aga-cooked breakfast and tasty homemade dinners.

Good food and accommodation at moderate prices? Look for the Bib symbols: red Bib Gourmand for food, blue Bib Hotel for accommodation.

CORK (Corcaigh) – Cork – 712 G12 – pop. 119 418 Ireland 38 B3

Dublin 248 km

Cork Airport : ☎ (021) 4313131, S : 6.5 km by L 42 X

to France (Roscoff) (Brittany Ferries) weekly (14 h/16 h) – to Pembroke (Swansea Cork Ferries) 2-6 weekly (8 h 30 mn)

Cork City, Grand Parade ☎ (021) 4255100, corktio@failteireland.ie

Douglas, ☎ (021) 489 10 86

Mahon Blackrock Cloverhill, ☎ (021) 429 25 43

Monkstown Parkgarriffe, ☎ (021) 484 13 76

Little Island, ☎ (021) 435 34 51

City★★ – Shandon Bells★★ Y, St Fin Barre's Cathedral★★ **AC** Z, Cork Public Museum★ X **M** – Grand Parade★ Z, South Mall★ Z, St Patrick Street★ Z, Crawford Art Gallery★ Y – Elizabethan Fort★ Z

Dunkathel House★ **AC**, E : 9.25 km by N 8 and N 25 X. Fota Island★ (Fota House★★ **AC**, Fota Wildlife Park★ **AC**), E : 13 km by N 8 and N 25 X – Cobh★ (St Colman's Cathedral★, Lusitania Memorial★) SE : 24 km by N 8, N 25 and R 624 X

Plans pages 923, 924

REPUBLIC OF IRELAND

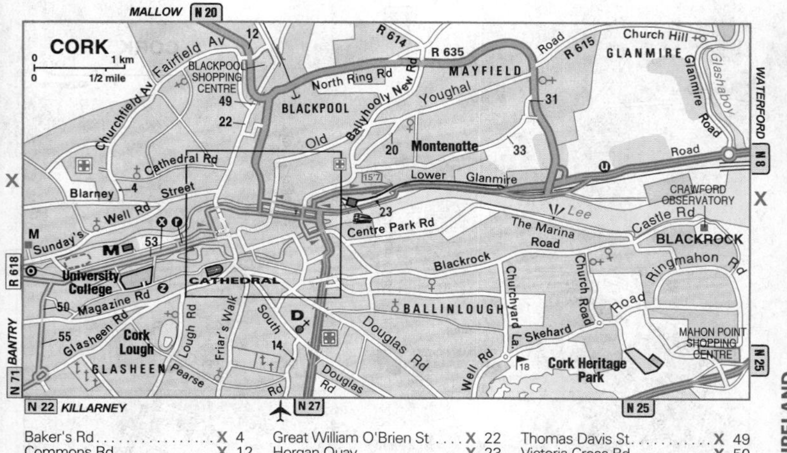

Baker's Rd . . . X 4	Great William O'Brien St . . . X 22	Thomas Davis St. . . . X 49
Commons Rd . . . X 12	Horgan Quay . . . X 23	Victoria Cross Rd. . . . X 50
Curragh Rd . . . X 14	Lower Mayfield Rd . . . X 31	Western Rd . . . X 53
Gardiner's Hill . . . X 20	Middle Glanmire Rd . . . X 33	Wilton Rd. . . . X 55

Hayfield Manor

Perrott Ave, College Rd – ☎ (021) 484 59 00 – www.hayfieldmanor.ie – Fax (021) 431 68 39 Xz

84 rm – € 380 € 380 – 4 suites

Rest *Orchids* – *(closed Sunday and Monday) (dinner only) (booking essential)* Menu € 65 **s** – Carte € 59/69 **s**

Rest *Perrotts* – Menu € 32 (lunch) **s** – Carte € 34/60 **s**

◆ Purpose-built yet Georgian in character. Stately interiors and harmoniously styled bedrooms with marble bathrooms and quality furniture - armchairs, coffee tables and desks. Twin dining options to suit all tastes.

The Kingsley

Victoria Cross – ☎ (021) 480 05 55 – www.kingsleyhotel.com – Fax (021) 480 05 26 Xo

129 rm – € 139/200 € 175/280 – 2 suites

Rest *Otters* – Menu € 30/50 – Carte € 45/78

◆ An inviting spot by river Lee, once site of Lee baths: outdoor hot tub and indoor pool takes their place. Relax in smart rooms or take tea in the lounge overlooking the weir. Airy restaurant has private booths and banquettes.

Lancaster Lodge without rest

Lancaster Quay, Western Rd – ☎ (021) 425 11 25 – www.lancasterlodge.com – Fax (021) 425 11 26 – Closed 24-28 December Zi

48 rm – € 89/129 € 99/149

◆ Purpose-built hotel with crisp, modern interior. Bedrooms are chintz-free, pleasingly and sparingly decorated. Largest rooms on the fourth floor; rear rooms are quieter.

Crawford House without rest

Western Rd – ☎ (021) 427 90 00 – www.crawfordguesthouse.com – Fax (021) 427 99 27 – Closed mid-December to mid-January Xx

12 rm – € 55/70 € 80/110

◆ Victorian-style building offering bright, airy and comfortable guesthouse accommodation. Modern interiors with a choice of wood floors or carpeting in guest rooms.

Garnish House without rest

Western Rd – ☎ (021) 427 51 11 – www.garnish.ie – Fax (021) 427 38 72

26 rm – € 80/95 € 100/140 Xr

◆ Justifiably proud of gourmet breakfast: 30 options include pancakes and porridge. Guests are welcomed with home-made scones in cosy rooms; those at the rear have quiet aspect.

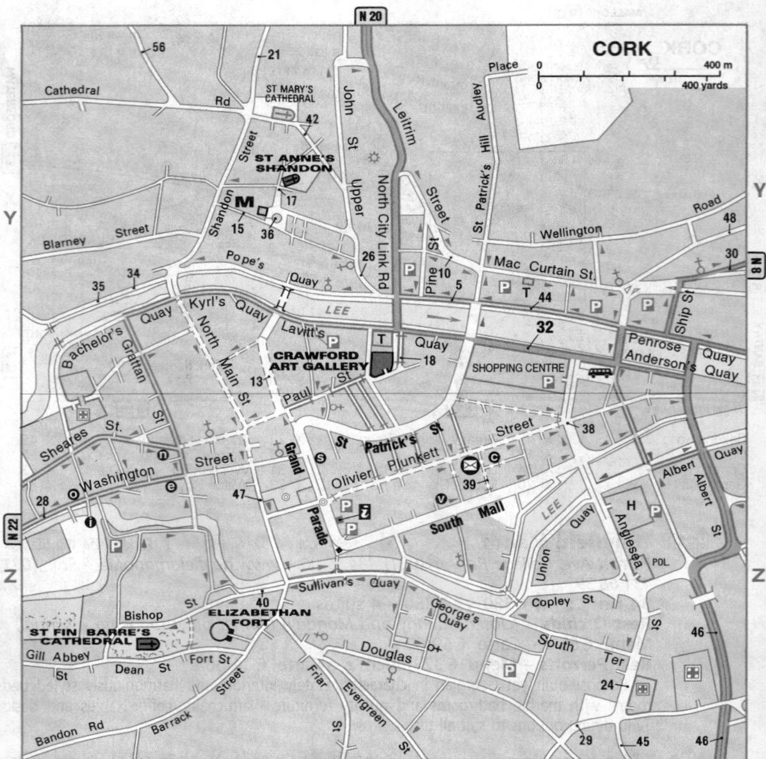

Buttermarket . . . . Y 36	Langford Row . . . . Z 29	Pembroke St . . . . Z 39
Camden Pl. . . . . Y 5	Lower Glanmire Rd. . . . . Y 30	Proby's Quay . . . . Z 40
Coburg St. . . . . Y 10	Merchant Quay Shopping Centre . . . . . . Y	Roman St. . . . . Y 42
Corn Market St . . . . Y 13	Merchant's Quay. . . . . Y 32	St Patrick's Quay. . . . . Y 44
Dominic St. . . . . Y 15	Newsom's Quay . . . . Y 34	St Patrick's St. . . . . Z
Eason Hill . . . . Y 17	North Main Street . . . . YZ	Southern Rd. . . . . Z 45
Emmet Pl. . . . . Y 18	North Mall . . . . Y 35	South City Link Rd . . . . Z 46
Gerald Griffin St . . . . Y 21	Olivier Plunkett St . . . . Z	South Main St . . . . Z 47
Infirmary Rd . . . . Z 24	Parnell Pl. . . . . Z 38	Summer Hill. . . . . Y 48
John Redmond St . . . . Y 26		Wolfe Tone St . . . . Y 56
Lancaster Quay . . . . Z 28		

XXX **Flemings** with rm

Silver Grange House, Tivoli, East : 4.5 km on N 8 – ✆ (021) 482 16 21 – www.flemingsrestaurant.ie – Fax (021) 482 18 00 – Closed 24-27 December Xu

3 rm – 🛉 € 80/90 🛉🛉 € 110

Rest – *(closed Sunday dinner and Monday lunch in summer)* Menu € 35 (dinner) – Carte € 47/61

◆ Classical cuisine, French bias; uses local produce, organically home-grown vegetables, herbs. Two dining rooms in keeping with Georgian character of house. Period furnished bedrooms.

XX **Jacques**

Phoenix St – ✆ (021) 427 73 87 – www.jacquesrestaurant.ie – Closed 25 December, Sunday and Bank Holidays Zc

Rest – *(dinner only)* Menu € 25 (Monday-Wednesday)/35 (Thursday-Saturday) – Carte € 36/50

◆ A long, warmly decorated room with modern tables on which old Irish classics are delivered. Farm ducks, wild game, fresh fish and organic vegetables are used in the cooking.

XX **Les Gourmandises** VISA MC AE D

17 Cook St – ✆ (021) 425 19 59 – www.lesgourmandises.ie – Fax (021) 489 90 05 – Closed 2 weeks March, 2 weeks August, Sunday and Monday Zv

Rest – French – *(dinner only) (booking essential)* Menu € 29/40 **s**

◆ Relaxed city centre restaurant boasting stained glass door, skylight and comfy lounge bar with red banquettes and modern art. Irish produce employed on classic French menus.

X **Isaacs Restaurant** VISA MC AE D

48 MacCurtain St – ✆ (021) 450 38 05 – Fax (021) 455 13 48 – Closed Sunday and lunch Bank Holidays Yu

Rest – *(booking essential)* Menu € 17 (lunch) – Carte € 27/42 **s**

◆ Tall brick arches and modern art in converted warehouse: buzzy, friendly and informal. Modern and traditional brasserie dishes plus home-made desserts and blackboard specials.

X **Cafe Paradiso** with rm VISA MC

16 Lancaster Quay, Western Rd – ✆ (021) 427 79 39 – www.cafeparadiso.ie – Closed 1 week Christmas Zo

3 rm – † € 160 †† € 160

Rest – Vegetarian – *(closed Sunday and Monday) (dinner only and lunch Friday and Saturday) (booking essential)* Carte € 30/47

◆ A growing following means booking is essential at this relaxed vegetarian restaurant. Colourful and inventive international combinations; blackboard list of organic wines. Spacious bedrooms in bright colours; the back one is the quiestest.

X **Fenn's Quay** A/C VISA MC AE

5 Sheares St – ✆ (021) 427 95 27 – www.fennsquay.ie – Fax (021) 427 95 26 – Closed Sunday and Bank Holidays Zn

Rest – Carte € 30/47

◆ In a renovated 18C terrace in historic part of the city, this informal café-restaurant boasts modern art on display. Popular for mid-morning coffees and, light lunches.

X **Farmgate Cafe** VISA MC D

English Market, First Floor, Princes St – ✆ (021) 427 81 34 – Fax (021) 427 81 34 – Closed 24 December-3 January, Sunday and Bank Holidays Zs

Rest – *(lunch only)* Carte € 18/30

◆ Long-standing café on 1st floor of the English Market. Small daily changing menu of food from the stalls below or from the counties of Munster; all simple, homemade and fresh.

at Cork Airport South : 6.5 km by N 27 - X – ✉ Cork

International Airport rm, A/C P VISA MC AE

(Gate 2) – ✆ (021) 454 9800 – www.corkinternationalairporthotel.com – Fax (021) 454 9999 – Closed 24-26 December

146 rm – † € 200 †† € 200, ☕ €15

Rest – *(closed dinner Sunday and Monday) (carvery lunch)* Menu € 35 – Carte € 35/48

◆ Quirky hotel with aviation theme and various eateries. Decent-sized bedrooms come in Deluxe and Executive versions. The superb Pullman lounge resembles the cabin of a plane. Modern restaurant has interesting smoking terrace.

CORK AIRPORT (Aerfort Chorcai) **Cork** – **Cork** – **712** G12 – **see Cork**

The symbol guarantees a good night's sleep. In red ? The very essence of peace: only the sound of birdsong in the early morning...

CORROFIN (Cora Finne) – Clare – 712 E9 – pop. 485 38 B1

Dublin 228 km – Gort 24 km – Limerick 51 km

Fergus View without rest

Kilnaboy, North : 3.25 km on R 476 – ☎ (065) 683 76 06 – www.fergusview.com – Fax (065) 683 76 06 – March-20 November

6 rm – € 53 € 78

◆ Originally built for the hospitable owner's grandfather as a schoolhouse, with good countryside views. Conservatory entrance into cosy lounge. Pristine bedrooms with compact bathrooms.

CROOKHAVEN (An Cruachán) – Cork – 712 C13 – pop. 1 669 38 A3

Dublin 373 km – Bantry 40 km – Cork 120 km

Galley Cove House without rest

West : 0.75 km on R 591 – ☎ (028) 35 137 – www.galleycovehouse.com – Fax (028) 35 137 – March-October

4 rm – € 45/60 € 75/90

◆ Perched overlooking eponymous bay and its pleasant harbour. Conservatory breakfast room has bamboo seating. Rooms are neat and tidy, and enhanced by colourful fabrics.

CROSSMOLINA (Crois Mhaoilíona) – Mayo – 712 E5 – pop. 930 36 B2

Ireland

Dublin 252 km – Ballina 10 km

Errew Abbey★, SE : 9.5 km by R 315. Cáide Fields★ **AC**, N : 24 km by R 315 and R 314 W – Killala★, NE : 16 km by R 315 and minor road – Moyne Abbey★, NE : 18 km by R 115, minor road to Killala, R 314 and minor road – Rosserk Abbey★, NE : 18 km by R 115, minor road to Killala, R 314 and minor road

Enniscoe House

Castlehill, South : 3.25 km on R 315 – ☎ (096) 31 112 – www.enniscoe.com – Fax (096) 31 773 – Closed 7 January-31 March

6 rm – € 130/150 € 220/260

Rest – *(dinner only) (booking essential for non-residents)* Menu € 44/50 **s**

◆ Georgian manor, overlooking Lough Conn, on Enniscoe estate with walled garden and heritage centre. Hallway boasts original family tree; antique beds in flower-filled rooms. Home cooked country dishes served in the dining room.

DALKEY (Deilginis) – Dún Laoghaire-Rathdown – 712 N8 – pop. 8 076 39 D1

Ireland

Dublin 13 km – Bray 9 km

Killiney Bay (★★), S : by coast road

Jaipur

21 Castle St – ☎ (01) 285 0552 – www.jaipur.ie – Fax (01) 284 0900 – closed 25 December

Rest – Indian – *(dinner only)* Carte € 34/47

◆ Central location and smart, lively, brightly coloured, modern décor. Well-spaced, linen-clad tables. Warm, friendly ambience. Contemporary Indian dishes.

DINGLE (An Daingean) – Kerry – 712 B11 – pop. 1 772 Ireland 38 A2

Dublin 347 km – Killarney 82 km – Limerick 153 km

The Quay ☎ (066) 9151188, dingletio@failteireland.ie

Town★ – St Mary's Church★ – Diseart (stained glass★ **AC**)

Gallarus Oratory★★, NW : 8 km by R 559 – NE : Connor Pass★★ – Kilmalkedar★, NW : 9 km by R 559. Dingle Peninsula★★ – Connor Pass★★, NE : 8 km by minor road – Stradbally Strand★★, NE : 17 km via Connor Pass – Corca Dhuibhne Regional Museum★ **AC**, NW : 13 km by R 559 – Blasket Islands★, W : 21 km by R 559 and ferry from Dunquin

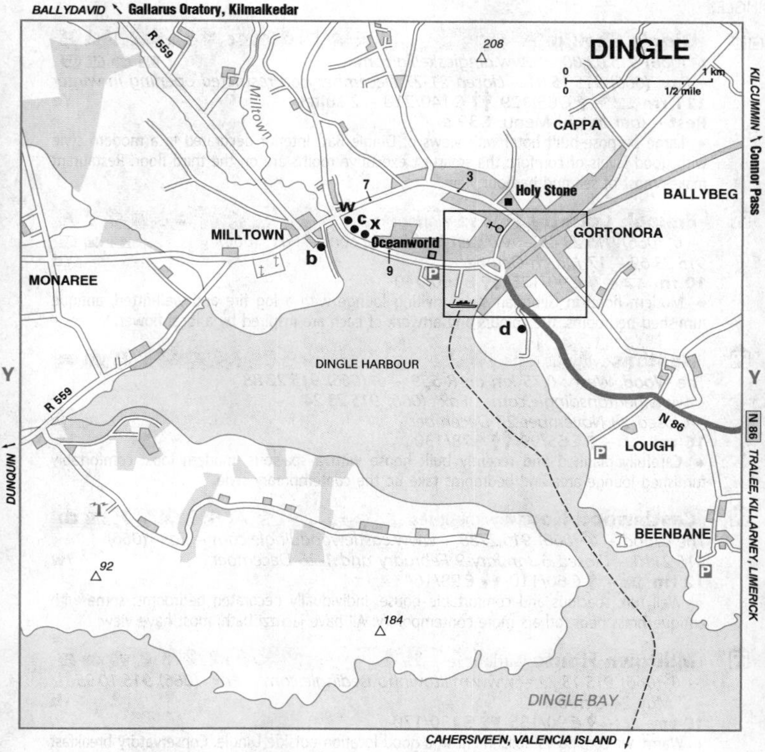

BALLYDAVID ↖ Gallarus Oratory, Kilmalkedar

DINGLE

0 1 km
0 1/2 mile

R 559
208
Milltown
CAPPA
KILCUMMIN ↖ Connor Pass
BALLYBEG
3
7
Holy Stone
W
c
x
MILLTOWN
GORTONORA
b
Oceanworld
9
MONAREE
d
DINGLE HARBOUR
Y
Y
R 559
N 86
N 86 TRALEE, KILLARNEY, LIMERICK
LOUGH
DUNQUIN ↖
BEENBANE
92
184
DINGLE BAY
CAHERSIVEEN, VALENCIA ISLAND ↙

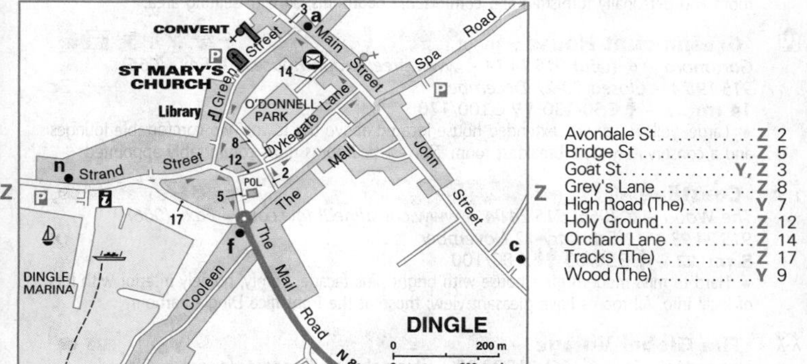

Avondale St . . . . Z 2
Bridge St . . . . Z 5
Goat St. . . . . Y, Z 3
Grey's Lane . . . . Z 8
High Road (The) . . . . Y 7
Holy Ground. . . . . Z 12
Orchard Lane . . . . Z 14
Tracks (The) . . . . Z 17
Wood (The). . . . . Y 9

Dingle Skellig

(066) 915 02 00 – www.dingleskellig.com
– Fax (066) 915 15 01 – closed 21-27 December and restricted opening in winter
111 rm – € 85/129 € 140/210 – 2 suites Y**e**
Rest – *(bar lunch)* Menu € 39 **s**
◆ Large purpose-built hotel with views of Dingle Bay. Interior decorated in a modern style with good levels of comfort: the smartest executive rooms are on the third floor. Restaurant makes most of sea and harbour view.

Emlagh Country House without rest

– (066) 915 23 45 – www.emlaghhouse.com – Fax (066) 915 23 69 – 17 March-October Y**d**
10 rm – € 90/125 € 160/240
◆ Modern hotel in Georgian style. Inviting lounge with a log fire and well-fitted, antique furnished bedrooms: the colours and artwork of each are inspired by a local flower.

Heatons without rest

The Wood, West : 0.75 km on R 559 – (066) 915 22 88 – www.heatonsdingle.com – Fax (066) 915 23 24 – Closed 28 November-27 December Y**c**
16 rm – € 65/99 € 78/130
◆ Carefully planned and recently built house with a spacious, modern look: comfortably furnished lounge area and bedrooms take up the contemporary style.

Castlewood House without rest

The Wood – (066) 915 2788 – www.castlewooddingle.com – Fax (066) 915 2110 – Closed 6 January-9 February and 1-26 December Y**w**
12 rm – € 60/110 € 98/164
◆ Well run, spacious and comfortable house. Individually decorated bedrooms; some with antique brass beds, others more contemporary. All have jacuzzi bath; most have view.

Milltown House without rest

– (066) 915 13 72 – www.milltownhousedingle.com – Fax (066) 915 10 95 – 7 May-24 October Y**b**
10 rm – € 90/135 € 130/170
◆ Warm, welcoming establishment in a good location outside Dingle. Conservatory breakfast room and personally furnished and comfortable bedrooms, all with seating area.

Greenmount House without rest

Gortonora – (066) 915 14 14 – www.greenmounthouse.ie – Fax (066) 915 19 74 – Closed 20-27 December Z**c**
14 rm – € 50/130 € 100/170
◆ Large, yellow painted, extended house located above the town. Two comfortable lounges and a conservatory-style breakfast room. Newest bedrooms most comfortably appointed.

Coastline without rest

The Wood – (066) 915 24 94 – www.coastlinedingle.com – Fax (066) 915 24 93 – 12 February-12 November Y**x**
8 rm – € 50/60 € 80/100
◆ Hard to miss modern guesthouse with bright pink façade. Comfy, homely interior with lots of local info. All rooms have pleasant view; those at the front face Dingle harbour.

The Global Village

Upper Main St – (66) 915 23 25 – www.globalvillagedingle.com – Closed mid-November to mid-March and Tuesday Z**a**
Rest – *(booking essential)* Menu € 28 (early dinner) **s** – Carte € 42/53 **s**
◆ Homely restaurant, where owner brings global influences from his travels to the wide-ranging menu, with its emphasis on seafood. Good use of local produce; fantastic fresh fish dishes.

A red **Rest** mention denotes an establishment with an award for culinary excellence, ✿ (star) or ☺ (Bib Gourmand).

REPUBLIC OF IRELAND

The Chart House

The Mall – ✆ (066) 915 22 55 – www.thecharthousedingle.com – Fax (066) 915 22 55 – Closed Christmas, 6 January-6 February and restricted opening in winter Zf

Rest – *(dinner only) (booking essential)* Menu € 35 – Carte € 39/46

◆ Attractive cottage close to a main route into town. Snug interior with exposed flint walls and wooden ceiling. Modern flourish applied to local ingredients.

Out of the Blue

Waterside – ✆ (066) 915 08 11 – www.outoftheblue.ie – Closed November-15 March and Wednesday Zn

Rest – Seafood – *(dinner only) (booking essential)* Carte € 38/49 **s**

◆ Simple, brightly painted building, with a relaxing, rustic charm, located 50yds from harbour. Daily changing menu of classic fish dishes. Jolly service from a well-versed local team.

DONEGAL (Dún na nGall) – Donegal – 712 H4 – pop. 2 339 Ireland 37 C1

Dublin 264 km – Londonderry 77 km – Sligo 64 km

Donegal Airport ✆ (074) 9548284

Quay St ✆ (074) 9721148, claire.harkin@failteireland.ie

Donegal Castle★ **AC**

Donegal Coast★★ - Cliffs of Bunglass★★, W : 48.25 km by N 56 and R 263 – Glencolmcille Folk Village★★ **AC**, W : 53 km by N 56 and R 263 – Rossnowlagh Strand★★, S : 35.5 km by N 15 and R 231 – Trabane Strand★, W : 58 km by N 56 and R 263

Solis Lough Eske Castle rest,

Northeast : 6.5 km by N15 (Killybegs rd) – ✆ (074) 9725 100 – www.solisloughheskecastle.com – Fax (074) 9723 762 – Closed Monday-Thursday November-March

94 rm – € 175/425 € 275/425 – 1 suite

Rest *Cedars* – *(dinner only)* Menu € 55 – Carte € 34/54

◆ Rebuilt 17C castle with a driveway that skirts the lough. The many extensions detract somewhat from the character but the bedrooms are comfortable and contemporary in style. Superb wellness centre. Bright, modern and stylish restaurant; traditional menu.

Harvey's Point rest,

Lough Eske, Northeast : 7.25 km by T 27 (Killybegs rd) – ✆ (074) 972 22 08 – www.harveyspoint.com – Fax (074) 972 23 52 – Closed Sunday-Wednesday November-Easter except Christmas

66 rm – € 95/195 € 178/320 – 4 suites

Rest *The Restaurant* – see restaurant listing

Rest *The Steakhouse* – *(Friday-Sunday) (dinner only)* Carte € 30/55 **s**

◆ Sprawling, classically styled hotel in restful loughside setting, with wood-panelled rooms and leather-furnished lounge. Bedrooms in new wing have high level of facilities; those in courtyard more traditional in style. Classic dishes and pleasant views in The Steakhouse.

Ardeevin without rest

Lough Eske, Barnesmore, Northeast : 9 km by N 15 following signs for Lough Eske Drive – ✆ (074) 972 17 90 – www.members.tripod.com/ardeevin – Fax (074) 972 17 90 – 17 March-November

6 rm – € 45/50 € 70/80

◆ Inviting, individual rooms, almost all with superb views of Lough Eske and the quiet countryside. Hearty Irish breakfasts with fresh bread baked by the long-standing owners.

The Restaurant – at Harvey's Point Hotel

Lough Eske, Northeast : 7.25 km by T 27 (Killybegs rd) – ✆ (074) 972 22 08 – www.harveyspoint.com – Fax (074) 972 23 52 – Closed Sunday-Wednesday November-Easter except Christmas

Rest – Menu € 35/59 **s** – Carte € 28/43 **s**

◆ Large restaurant with semicircular glass side providing lovely lough views. Traditional cooking, local ingredients and a few international touches. Attentive, formal service.

REPUBLIC OF IRELAND

at Laghy South : 5.5 km on N 15 – ✉ Donegal

Coxtown Manor without rest

South : 3 km. on Ballintra rd – ✆ (074) 973 4575 – www.coxtownmanor.com – Fax (074) 973 4576 – Mid-February to end-October

9 rm – ♀ € 70 ♀♀ € 70/140

◆ Attractive, ivy-clad Georgian house boasting comfy lounge and high-ceilinged breakfast room. Classic bedrooms in main house; those in converted stables have a more modern feel.

DONNYBROOK (Domhnach Broc) – Dublin – 712 N8 – see Dublin

DOOGORT (Dumha Goirt) – Mayo – 712 B5/6 – see Achill Island

DOOLIN (Dúlainm) – Clare – 712 D8 Ireland 38 B1

Dublin 275 km – Galway 69 km – Limerick 80 km

The Burren★★ (Cliffs of Moher★★★, Scenic Route★★, Aillwee Cave★ **AC** (Waterfall★★), Poulnabrone Portal Tomb★, Corcomroe Abbey★, Kilfenora Crosses★, Burren Centre★ **AC**)

Tír Gan Éan

– ✆ (065) 707 57 26 – www.tirganean.ie – Fax (065) 707 57 34 – Closed January,1 week Christmas and mid week November-February

12 rm – ♀ € 80/150 ♀♀ € 130/180

Rest – *(bar lunch Monday-Saturday)* Carte € 39/47

◆ Stylish boutique hotel on main through road, with contemporary open plan bar. Bedrooms come in creams and browns, with flat screens, fridges and modern art. Accessible menu; local produce.

Ballyvara House without rest

Southeast : 1 km – ✆ (065) 707 44 67 – www.ballyvarahouse.ie – Fax (065) 707 48 68 – May-September

9 rm – ♀ € 60/100 ♀♀ € 100/150 – 2 suites

◆ Pleasant rural views from this 19C former farm cottage, close to tourist village. Comfy lounge with squashy sofas; outside a smart decked courtyard. Bright, impressive rooms.

XX **Cullinan's** with rm

– ✆ (065) 707 41 83 – www.cullinansdoolin.com – Fax (065) 707 42 39 – Accommodation closed 13 December-26 February,

8 rm – ♀ € 40/80 ♀♀ € 80/100

Rest – *(Closed 26 October-April, Sunday and Wednesday) (dinner only) (booking essential)* Carte € 35/47

◆ Simple wood-floored restaurant serving contemporary dishes which make good use of local produce. Friendly service and charming setting with garden views and fresh flowers. Immaculate, pine-furnished bedrooms; some overlooking a little river.

DROGHEDA (Droichead Átha) – Louth – 712 M6 – pop. 35 090 37 D3

Ireland

Dublin 46 km – Dundalk 35 km

Mayoralty St ✆ (041) 9837070, tourism@drogheda.ie

Seapoint Termonfeckin, ✆ (041) 982 23 33

Towneley Hall Tullyallen, ✆ (041) 984 2229

Town★ – Drogheda Museum★ – St Laurence Gate★

Monasterboice★★, N : 10.5 km by N 1 – Boyne Valley★★, on N 51 – Termonfeckin★, NE : 8 km by R 166. Newgrange★★★, W : 5 km by N 51 on N 2 – Mellifont Old Abbey★ **AC** - Knowth★

The D

rest,

Scotch Hall, Marsh Rd – ✆ (041) 987 77 00 – www.thed.com – Fax (041) 987 77 02 – Closed 23-30 December

104 rm – ♀ € 99/169 ♀♀ € 99/169 **Rest** – Menu € 25 **s** – Carte € 20/35 **s**

◆ Stylish hotel adjacent to shopping centre on banks of the Boyne. Modish, minimalistic interiors include two comfy bars and spacious bedrooms with a cool, clinical appeal. Popular menus in the airy dining room.

Scholars Townhouse

King St, by West St and Lawrence St turning left at Lawrence's Gate – ☎ (041) 983 54 10 – www.scholarshotel.com – Fax (041) 987 77 52 – Closed 25-26 December

19 rm – € 65/90 € 130/150 **Rest** – Menu € 25 – Carte € 27/53

◆ Wood panelling and ornate coving reflect Victorian style of this tastefully refurbished 19C townhouse. Some bedrooms have original stained glass windows; good level of facilities. Formal restaurant serves classically-based menus. Dine under ceiling murals commemorating the Battle of the Boyne.

DRUMSHANBO (Droim Seanbhó) – Leitrim – 712 H5 – pop. 665 — 37 C2

Ireland

Dublin 166 km – Carrick-on-Shannon 14 km – Sligo 48 km

Arigna Scenic Drive★ (≤★), N : 8 km by R 280

Ramada H. and Suites at Lough Allen

Carrig Na Brac, on Keadew rd rest,
– ☎ (071) 964 01 00 – www.ramadahotelleitrim.com – Fax (071) 964 01 01 – Closed 25-27 December

74 rm – € 79/105 € 140/175

Rest *Rushes* – *(bar lunch Monday-Saturday)* Menu € 33 **s** – Carte € 32/44 **s**

◆ Purpose-built hotel, beside Lough Allen, with part-stone exterior. Airy, up-to-the-minute bar. Pleasant terrace includes hot tub. Well-equipped spa. Minimalist, modern rooms. Dining room boasts stylish blond wood and seasonal menus.

O. Forir/MICHELIN

DUBLIN
(Baile Átha Cliath)

County: Dublin
Michelin regional map: **712** N7
▶ Belfast 166 km – Cork 248 km
– Londonderry 235 km

Population: 1 045 769
Ireland
Map reference: **39** D1

PRACTICAL INFORMATION

Tourist Information

Suffolk St, (01) 605 7700, information@dublintourism.ie

Airport

Dublin Airport : ☎ (01) 814 1111, N : 9 km by N 1 BS

Ferries

to Holyhead (Irish Ferries) 4 daily (3 h 15 mn)
– to Holyhead (Stena Line) 1-2 daily (3 h 45 mn)
– to the Isle of Man (Douglas) (Isle of Man Steam Packet Co. Ltd) (2 h 45 mn/4 h 45 mn)
– to Liverpool (P & O Irish Sea) (8 h)

Golf Courses

- Elm Park Donnybrook, Nutley House, ☎ (01) 269 3438
- Milltown Lower Churchtown Rd, ☎ (01) 497 6090
- Royal Dublin Dollymount North Bull Island, ☎ (01) 833 6346
- Forrest Little Cloghran, ☎ (01) 840 17 63
- Lucan Celbridge Rd, ☎ (01) 628 2106
- Edmondstown, ☎ (01) 493 24 61
- Coldwinters St Margaret's, Newtown house, ☎ (01) 864 0324

SIGHTS

In town

Suffolk St - Arrivals Hall, Dublin Airport - The Square Shopping Centre, TallaghtCity★★★ - Trinity College★★ JY - Old Library★★★ (Treasury★★★, Long Room★★) – Dublin Castle★★ (Chester Beatty Library★★★) HY - Christ Church Cathedral★★ HY - St Patrick's Cathedral★★ HZ - Marsh's Library★★ HZ – National Museum★★ (The Treasury★★) KZ - National Gallery★★ KZ - Newman House★★ JZ - Bank of Ireland★★ JY – Custom House★★ KX - Kilmainham Gaol Museum★★ AT **M6** - Kilmainham Hospital★★ AT – Phoenix Park★★ AS - National Botanic Gardens★★ BS - Marino Casino★★ CS – Tailors' Hall★ HY - City Hall★ HY - Temple Bar★ HJY - Liffey Bridge★ JY – Merrion Square★ KZ - Number Twenty-Nine★ KZ **D** - Grafton Street★ JYZ - Powerscourt Centre★ JY – Rotunda Hospital Chapel★ JX - O'Connell Street★ (GPO Building★) JX - Hugh Lane Municipal Gallery of Modern Art★ JX **M4** – Pro-Cathedral★ JX - Bluecoat School★ BS **F** - Guinness Museum★ BT **M7** - Rathfarnham Castle★ AT – Zoological Gardens★ AS – Ceol★ BS **n**

On the outskirts

The Ben of Howth★ (≤★), NE : 9.5 km by R 105 CS

In the surrounding area

Powerscourt★★ (Waterfall★★ **AC**), S : 22.5 km by N 11 and R 117 EV – Russborough House★★★, SW : 35.5 km by N 81 BT

DUBLIN

Street	Grid	No.
Adelaïde Rd	BT	3
Alfie Byrne Rd	CS	5
Bath Ave	CT	9
Benburb St	BS	15
Berkeley Rd	BS	16
Botanic Rd	BS	19
Canal Rd	BT	30
Clanbrassil St	BT	40
Conyngham Rd	AS	48
Denmark St	BS	52
Donnybrook Rd	CT	54
Dorset St	BS	55
Drimnagh Rd	AT	57
Eglinton Rd	CT	63
Grand Parade	BT	72
Inchicore Rd	AT	79
Infirmary Rd	AS	81
James St	BT	84
Leeson St Upper	BT	94
Macken St	BST	99
Morehampton Rd	BT	108
Mount St Upper	BT	112
Palmerston Park	BT	123
Phibsborough Rd	BS	132
Rathmines Rd Upper	BT	135
Ringsend Rd	CT	139
St Agnes Rd	AT	141
St Alphonsus Rd	BS	144
St John's Rd West	AS	147
Sandford Rd	BT	151
Shelbourne Rd	CT	157
Shrewsbury Rd	CT	159
South Circular Rd	AS	162
Suir Rd	AT	168
Terenure Rd East	BT	172
Thomas St West	BT	174
Victoria Quay	BS	178
Western Way	BS	184
Wolfe Tone Quay	BS	195

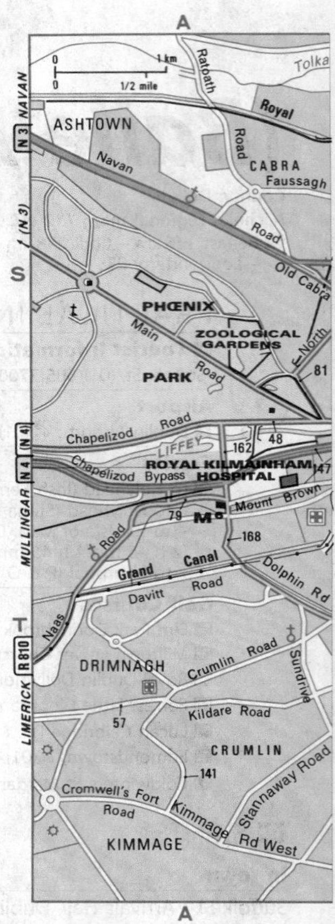

The Shelbourne

27 St Stephen's Green
– ✆ (01) 663 4500 – www.theshelbourne.ie
– Fax (01) 661 6006 JZ**c**
243 rm – € 189/279 € 199/289, € 29 – 19 suites
Rest *The Saddle Room* – see restaurant listing

◆ A delightful refit of a grand old hotel, with elegant meeting rooms and sumptuous bedrooms offering a host of extras. The historic Horseshoe Bar and Lord Mayor's Room remain.

The Merrion

Upper Merrion St
– ✆ (01) 603 0600 – www.merrionhotel.com
– Fax (01) 603 0700 KZ**e**
133 rm – € 460 € 480, € 29 – 10 suites
Rest *The Cellar* – see restaurant listing
Rest *The Cellar Bar* – *(closed Sunday)* Carte € 26/34

◆ Elegant hotel boasting opulent lounges and stylish cocktail bar. Spacious bedrooms – some with original features, some more corporate in style – boast smart marble bathrooms and good facilities. Characterful barrel-ceilinged bar offers concise carvery menu.

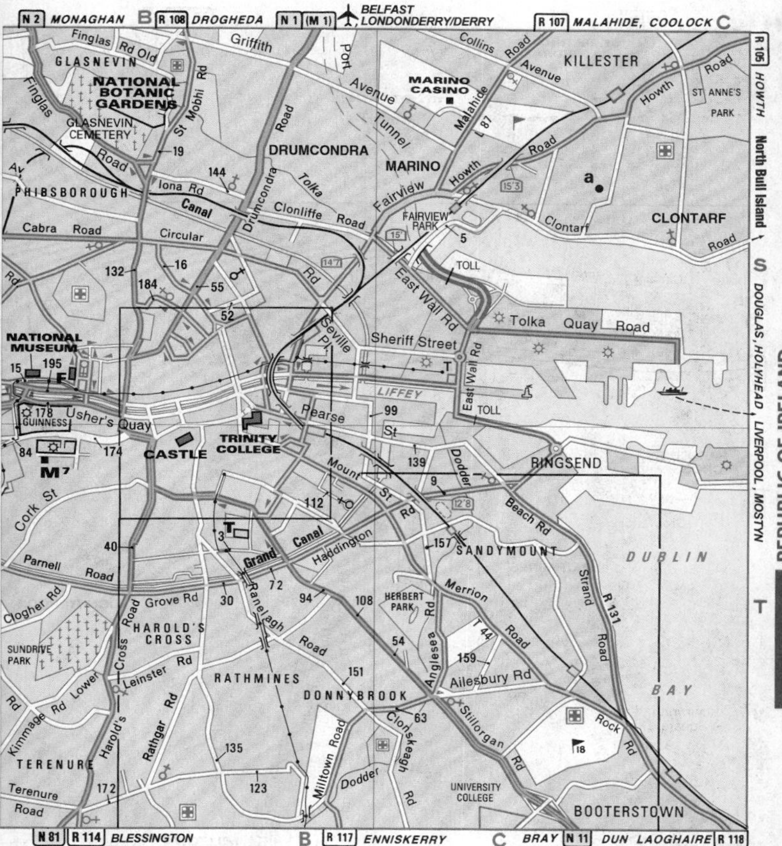

The Westin

Westmoreland St
– (01) 645 1000 – www.thewestindublin.com
– Fax (01) 645 1234 JY**n**

153 rm – € 179/489 € 179/489, €27 – 10 suites

Rest *The Exchange* – *(closed Sunday and Monday) (dinner only and Sunday lunch)* Carte € 33/59

Rest *The Mint* – Carte € 25/38

◆ Once a bank; now a smart hotel set over 6 period buildings, with comfy lounges, impressive conference rooms and good facilities. Georgian-style bedrooms boast heavy fabrics and marble bathrooms. Modern European cooking in semi-formal Exchange. Classic pub dishes in The Mint (formerly the bank's vaults).

Dylan

Eastmoreland Pl – (01) 660 3000 – www.dylan.ie – Fax (01) 660 3005 – Closed 25-26 December EU**a**

44 rm – € 199/395 € 199/395, €27 **Rest** – Carte € 36/62

◆ Modern boutique hotel with vibrant use of colour. Supremely comfortable, individually decorated bedrooms boast an opulent feel and a host of unexpected extras. French-influenced menus served in warm, stylish dining room.

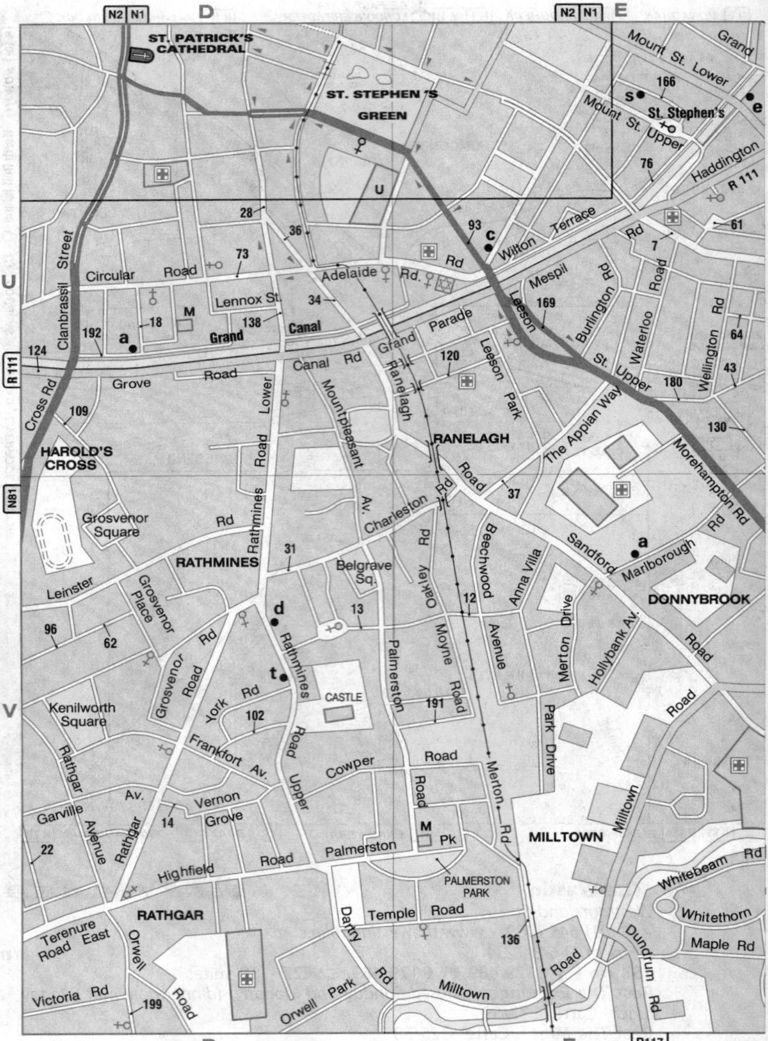

Street	Grid	No.
Ailesbury Drive	FV	4
Baggot St Upper	EU	7
Beechwood Rd	EV	12
Beech Hill Ave	FV	10
Belgrave Rd	DV	13
Belleville Ave	DV	14
Bloomfield Ave	DU	18
Brighton Rd	DV	22
Camden St	DU	28
Castlewood Ave	DV	31
Charlemont St	DU	34
Charlotte St	DU	36
Chelmsford Rd	EV	37
Church Ave	FU	39
Clyde Rd	EFU	43
Eastmoreland Pl	EU	61
Effra Rd	DU	62
Elgin Rd	EFU	64
Harrington St	DU	73
Herbert Pl	EU	76
Irishtown Rd	FU	82
Lansdowne Rd	FU	90
Lea Rd	GU	91
Leeson St Lower	EU	93
Leinster Rd West	DV	96
Londonbridge Rd	FU	97
Maxwell Rd	DV	102

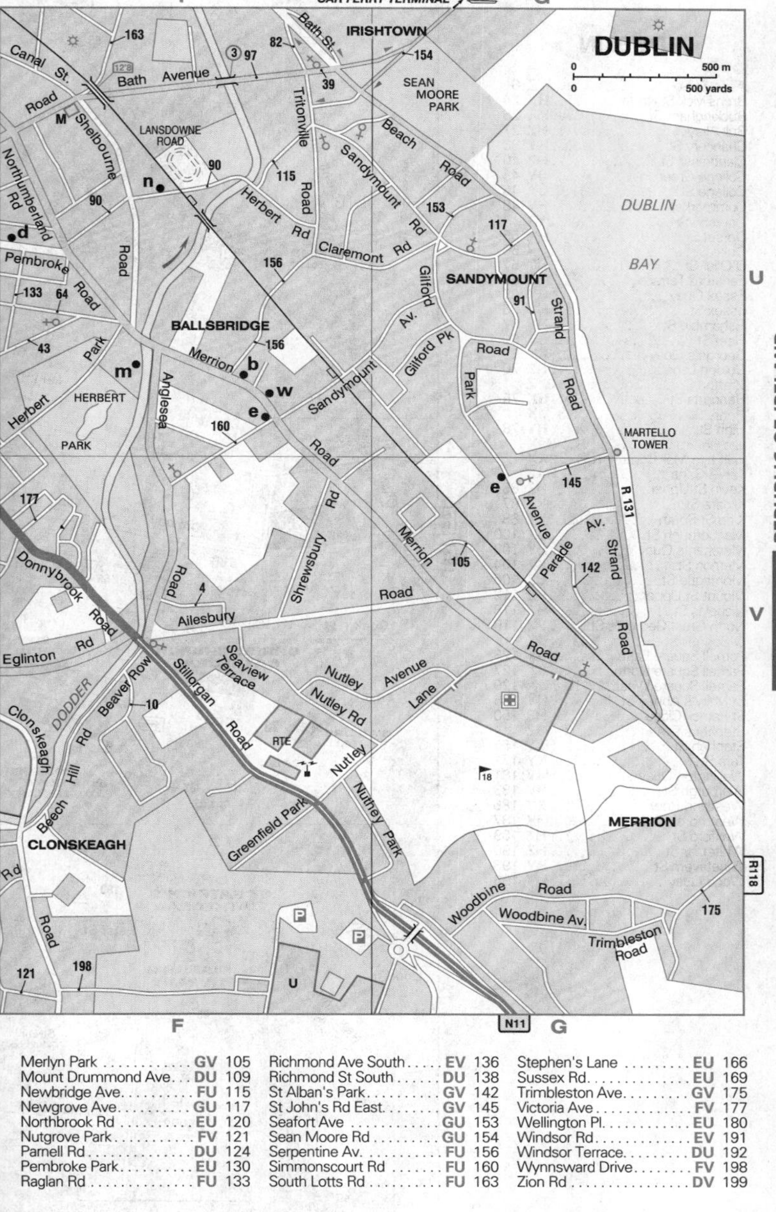

Merlyn Park . . . . **GV** 105	Richmond Ave South . . . . . **EV** 136	Stephen's Lane . . . . **EU** 166
Mount Drummond Ave. . . **DU** 109	Richmond St South . . . . . . **DU** 138	Sussex Rd. . . . . **EU** 169
Newbridge Ave. . . . . **FU** 115	St Alban's Park. . . . . **GV** 142	Trimbleston Ave. . . . . **GV** 175
Newgrove Ave. . . . . **GU** 117	St John's Rd East. . . . . **GV** 145	Victoria Ave . . . . **FV** 177
Northbrook Rd . . . . **EU** 120	Seafort Ave . . . . **GU** 153	Wellington Pl. . . . . **EU** 180
Nutgrove Park . . . . **FV** 121	Sean Moore Rd . . . . **GU** 154	Windsor Rd. . . . . **EV** 191
Parnell Rd. . . . . **DU** 124	Serpentine Av. . . . . **FU** 156	Windsor Terrace. . . . . **DU** 192
Pembroke Park. . . . . **EU** 130	Simmonscourt Rd . . . . **FU** 160	Wynnsward Drive. . . . . **FV** 198
Raglan Rd . . . . **FU** 133	South Lotts Rd . . . . **FU** 163	Zion Rd . . . . **DV** 199

DUBLIN

Street	Grid	No.
Anne St South	JYZ	6
Brunswick St North	HX	24
Buckingham St	KX	25
Bull Alley	HZ	27
Chancery St	HY	33
Clanbrassil St	HZ	40
College Green	JY	45
College St	JY	46
Cornmarket	HY	49
Dawson St	JYZ	
Dorset St	HX	55
Duke St	JY	58
D'Olier St	JY	51
Earlsford Terrace	JZ	60
Essex Quay	HY	65
Essex St	HY	66
Fishamble St	HY	67
Fleet St	JY	68
George's Quay	KY	69
Golden Lane	HZ	70
Grafton St	JYZ	
Henrietta St	HX	75
Henry St	JX	
High St	HY	78
Ilac Centre	HJX	
Irish Life Mall Centre	JKX	
Jervis Centre	HJX	
Kevin St Upper	HZ	85
Kildare St	JKZ	87
King St South	JZ	88
Marlborough St	JX	100
Merchants Quay	HY	103
Merrion St	KZ	104
Montague St	JZ	106
Mount St Upper	KZ	112
Nicholas St	HY	118
North Great George's St	JX	119
O'Connell St	JX	
Parnell Square East	JX	126
Parnell Square North	JX	127
Parnell Square West	HJX	129
St Mary's Abbey St	HY	148
St Patrick Close	HZ	150
Stephens Green	JZ	
Stephen St	HJY	165
Tara St	KY	171
Wellington Quay	HJY	181
Werburgh St	HY	183
Westland Row	KY	186
Westmoreland St	JY	187
Wexford St	HZ	189
Whitefriar St	HZ	190
Winetavern St	HY	193
Wood Quay	HY	196

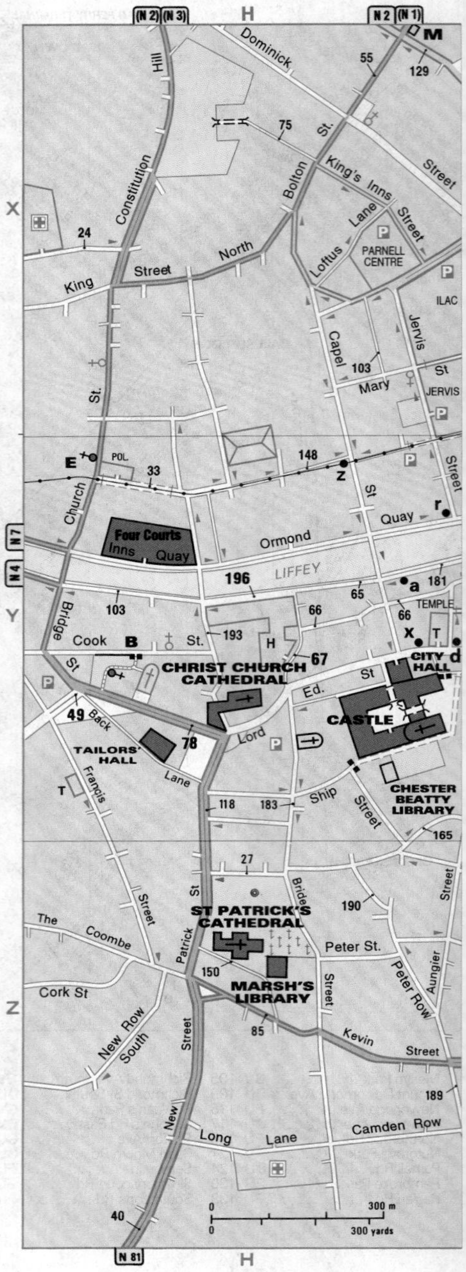

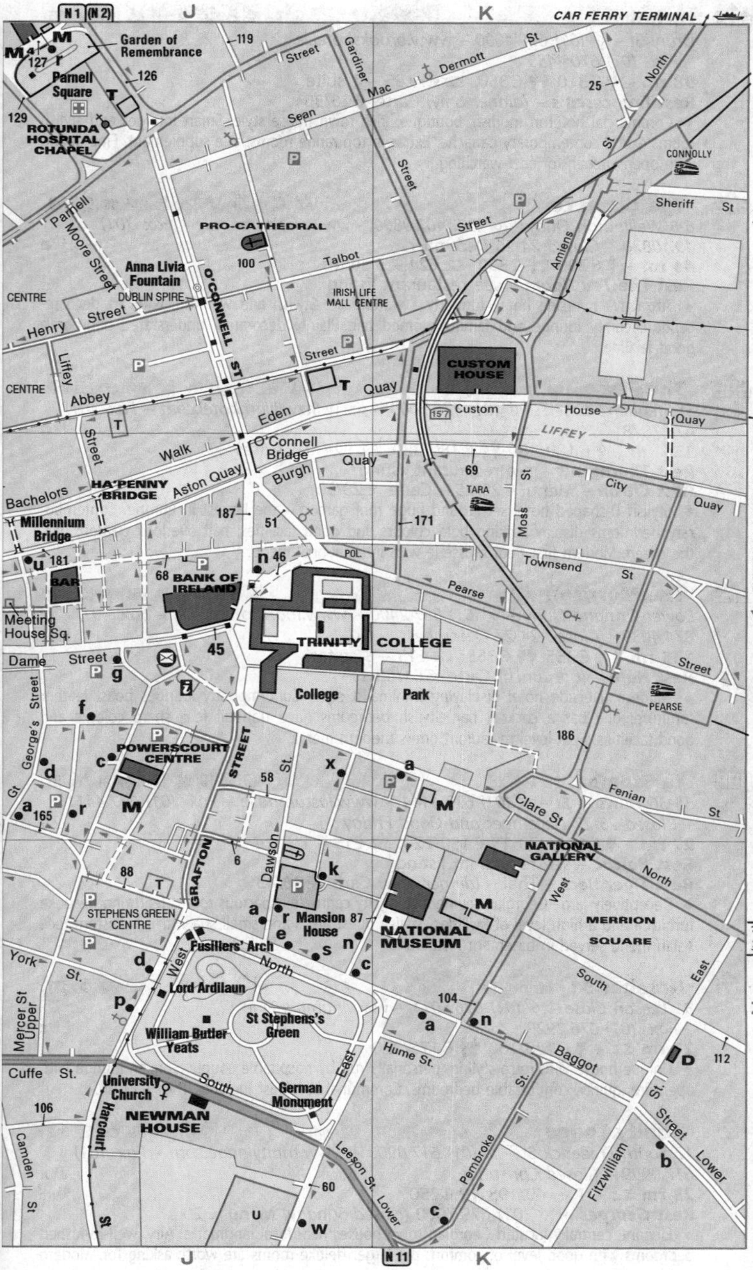

N 1 (N 2)
J
K
CAR FERRY TERMINAL
Garden of Remembrance
Parnell Square
ROTUNDA HOSPITAL CHAPEL
Sean Mac Dermott Street
Gardiner Street
North St
Sheriff St
CONNOLLY
PRO-CATHEDRAL
Talbot Street
Anna Livia Fountain
DUBLIN SPIRE
O'CONNELL ST
IRISH LIFE MALL CENTRE
Amiens St
Moore Street
Parnell St
Henry Street
CENTRE
Liffey Street
Abbey Street
Eden Quay
CUSTOM HOUSE
Custom House Quay
LIFFEY
O'Connell Bridge
Burgh Quay
Aston Quay
Bachelors Walk
HA'PENNY BRIDGE
Millennium Bridge
TARA
Moss St
City Quay
Townsend St
Pearse Street
POL.
BANK OF IRELAND
BAR
Meeting House Sq.
TRINITY COLLEGE
College Park
Dame Street
PEARSE
George's Street
POWERSCOURT CENTRE
GRAFTON STREET
Dawson St.
Clare St
Fenian St
NATIONAL GALLERY
Mansion House
NATIONAL MUSEUM
MERRION SQUARE
West
North
South
East
STEPHENS GREEN CENTRE
York St.
Fusiliers' Arch
Lord Ardilaun
St Stephens's Green
William Butler Yeats
Mercer St Upper
Cuffe St.
University Church
NEWMAN HOUSE
German Monument
Hume St.
Baggot Street Lower
Pembroke St.
Fitzwilliam St.
Leeson St. Lower
Harcourt St
Camden St
N 11
T 44
X
Y
Z
REPUBLIC OF IRELAND

Brooks

Drury St – ✆ (01) 670 4000 – www.brookshotel.ie – Fax (01) 670 4455 JY**r**

98 rm – † € 310 †† € 350, ☕ €19.95 – 1 suite

Rest *Francesca's* – *(dinner only)* Carte € 26/36

◆ Commercial hotel in modish, boutique, Irish town house style. Smart lounges and stylish rooms exude contemporary panache. Extras in top range rooms, at a supplement. Fine dining with open kitchen for chef-watching.

The Clarence

6-8 Wellington Quay – ✆ (01) 407 0800 – www.theclarence.ie – Fax (01) 407 0820 – Closed 24-26 December HY**a**

44 rm – † € 390 †† € 390, ☕ €24 – 5 suites

Rest *The Tea Room* – see restaurant listing

◆ Attractive riverside hotel, formerly a warehouse. Stylish and well-run, with art deco reception, comfy lounge and famous domed bar. Plainly decorated, understated bedrooms; good facilities.

The Fitzwilliam

St Stephen's Green – ✆ (01) 478 7000 – www.fitzwilliamhotel.com – Fax (01) 478 7878 JZ**d**

136 rm – † € 180/380 †† € 180/380, ☕ €24 – 3 suites

Rest *Thornton's* – see restaurant listing

Rest *Citron* – Menu € 20/25 – Carte € 28/50

◆ Stylish U-shaped hotel set around huge roof garden – the largest in Europe. Contemporary bedrooms display striking bold colours and good facilities; half overlook garden; half, the green. Modern first floor brasserie with international menu.

The Morrison

Lower Ormond Quay – ✆ (01) 887 2400 – www.morrisonhotel.ie – Fax (01) 874 4039 – Closed 24-27 December HY**r**

135 rm – † € 355 †† € 355, ☕ €15 – 3 suites

Rest *Halo* – *(bar lunch)* Carte € 51/65 **s**

◆ Modern riverside hotel displaying minimalist style. Contemporary lounges boast leather furniture: one has a cocktail bar. Stylish bedrooms have tranquil feel, sharp colours and good facilities. Split-level restaurant offers modern menu.

La Stampa

35-36 Dawson St – ✆ (01) 677 4444 – www.lastampa.ie – Fax (01) 677 4411 – Closed 25-27 December and Good Friday JZ**a**

27 rm – † € 120/220 †† € 150/220, ☕ €15 – 1 suite

Rest *Balzac* – see restaurant listing

Rest *Tiger Becs* – Thai – *(dinner only)* Carte € 36/43

◆ Deceptively large Georgian townhouse in city centre, its spacious rooms featuring bespoke furniture and a high level of facilities. Stylish guest areas and small spa with Far Eastern feel. Asian menu served in basement restaurant.

Number 31 without rest

31 Leeson Close – ✆ (01) 676 5011 – www.number31.ie – Fax (01) 676 2929 EU**c**

21 rm ☕ – † € 120/160 †† € 175/220

◆ Unique house with retro styling, personally run by hospitable couple. Sunken lounge with open fire; quirky, comfortable bedrooms. Communal breakfast includes The Full Irish.

Trinity Lodge

12 South Frederick St – ✆ (01) 617 0900 – www.trinitylodge.com – Fax (01) 617 0999 – Closed Christmas JY**x**

23 rm ☕ – † € 140/195 †† € 250

Rest *Georges* – ✆ (01) 679 7000 *(closed Sunday)* Menu € 20 **s**

◆ Elegant, centrally located Georgian town houses near local landmarks. Airy, well-furnished bedrooms with good level of comfort: the larger deluxe rooms are worth asking for. Modern restaurant and popular wine bar.

Eliza Lodge

23-24 Wellington Quay – ☎ (01) 671 8044 – www.elizalodge.com – Fax (01) 671 8362 – Closed 20-29 December JY**u**

18 rm – 🛉 € 76/160 🛉🛉 € 80/160

Rest *Italian Corner* – Italian – ☎ (01) 671 9114 – Carte € 23/38

◆ Friendly, family-owned hotel ideally situated for lively Temple Bar area. Uniform bedrooms; those at the top have the best outlook over the city and river; two have balconies. Bright restaurant serves popular Italian menus overlooking the Liffey.

Patrick Guilbaud (Guillaume Lebrun)

21 Upper Merrion St – ☎ (01) 676 4192 – www.restaurantpatrickguilbaud.ie – Fax (01) 661 0052 – Closed 25-26 December, 17 March, Good Friday, Sunday and Monday

Rest – French – Menu € 50 (lunch) **s** – Carte € 96/149 **s** KZ**e**

Spec. Crab cannelloni with pineapple and pickled ginger. Duck 'Peppered Bigarade' with caramelised legs, orange and almond crumble. Yuzu soufflé.

◆ Smart, stylish and personally run restaurant within a restored and sympathetically extended Georgian house; decorated with contemporary Irish art. Accomplished and harmonious cooking, with cleverly complementing flavours and textures.

Shanahan's on the Green

119 St Stephen's Green – ☎ (01) 407 0939 – www.shanahans.ie – Fax (01) 407 0940 – Closed Christmas, Sunday and Good Friday

Rest – Beef specialities – *(dinner only and lunch Friday) (booking essential)* Menu € 45/55 – Carte approx. € 100 JZ**p**

◆ Sumptuous Georgian town house; upper floor window tables survey the Green. Supreme comfort enhances your enjoyment of strong seafood dishes and choice cuts of Irish beef.

Thornton's – at The Fitzwilliam Hotel

128 St Stephen's Green – ☎ (01) 478 7008 – www.thorntonsrestaurant.com – Fax (01) 478 7009 – Closed 1 week Christmas, Sunday, Monday, lunch Tuesday, Wednesday and Bank Holidays JZ**d**

Rest – Modern – Menu € 45/49 **s** – Carte € 101/120 **s**

Spec. Foie gras terrine with hazelnut sauce. Duck with pommes Maxim and girolle sauce. Chocolate fondant with bergamot marshmallow and balsamic.

◆ Elegant hotel restaurant where smart glass panels divide the room; eye-catching food photos adorn the walls. Choice of classical à la carte, or modern tasting menu displaying innovative texture and flavour combinations. Knowledgeable service.

L'Ecrivain (Derry Clarke)

109A Lower Baggot St – ☎ (01) 661 1919 – www.lecrivain.com – Fax (01) 661 0617 – Closed Christmas-New Year, Saturday lunch, Sunday and Bank Holidays KZ**b**

Rest – Contemporary – *(booking essential)* Menu € 25/85 – Carte dinner € 65/79

Spec. Scallops with frog's leg beignet, morels and garlic foam. Suckling pig with tortellini and baby vegetable salad. Lemon tart with raspberry granité and mascarpone.

◆ Three-floored, former warehouse with piano bar, whiskey-themed private dining room, mezzanine and attractive terrace. Refined cooking arrives with modern touches and contemporary presentation. Service is formal but comes with personality.

Chapter One (Ross Lewis)

The Dublin Writers Museum, 18-19 Parnell Sq – ☎ (01) 873 2266 – www.chapteronerestaurant.com – Fax (01) 873 2330 – Closed first 2 weeks August, 2 weeks Christmas, Sunday and Monday JX**r**

Rest – Modern – *(booking essential)* Menu € 38 (lunch) **s** – Carte dinner € 60/68 **s**

Spec. Langoustine and smoked bacon spring roll with red pepper purée. Chicken with sweetcorn, chanterelles and ricotta gnocchi. Warm chocolate mousse with orange and Campari jelly.

◆ Long-established, popular restaurant in basement of historic building; contemporary lounge/bar and two smart dining rooms. Seasonal, classically-based cooking demonstrates skill and understanding. Attentive, formal service.

XXX **Bentley's Oyster Bar & Grill** with rm — AC rest, VISA MC AE

22 St. Stephen's Green – ✆ (01) 638 39 39 – www.bentleysdublin.com – Fax (01) 638 39 00 – Closed 25-27 December — JZs

9 rm – † € 99/160 †† € 99/200, ☕ €10

Rest – Seafood – *(booking advisable)* Menu € 25 (lunch) **s** – Carte € 37/79 **s**

◆ Imposing Georgian house in main city square. Large formally laid dining room and marble topped oyster bar with stools. Menus display tasty dishes crafted from quality produce. Stylish, traditional bedrooms; the best overlook the green.

XXX **The Saddle Room** – at The Shelbourne Hotel — AC VISA MC AE

27 St Stephen's Green – ✆ (01) 663 4500 – www.theshelbourne.ie – Fax (01) 651 6066 — JZc

Rest – Grills – Menu € 19/40 **s** – Carte dinner € 44/66 **s**

◆ Smart restaurant in heart of hotel with delightful seafood bar. Grill/seafood menu offers quality Irish produce including superior 21 day hung steaks. Two private dining rooms.

XX **Pichet** — AC VISA MC

14-15 Trinity St – ✆ (01) 677 10 60 – www.pichetrestaurant.com – Closed 1-11 January, 25-27 December and Bank Holidays — JYg

Rest – Modern European – *(booking advisable)* Menu € 25 (lunch and early dinner) – Carte € 29/47

◆ Popular brasserie with buzzy atmosphere; its long narrow room dominated by an open-plan kitchen counter. Front bar/café and heated terrace. Neat, flavoursome modern European cooking, with good value, daily changing menus.

XX **Pearl Brasserie** — AC VISA MC AE

20 Merrion St Upper – ✆ (01) 661 3572 – www.pearl-brasserie.com – Fax (01) 661 3629 – Closed 25 December and Sunday — KZn

Rest – French – Menu € 22 (2 course lunch) – Carte € 28/50

◆ A metal staircase leads down to this intimate, newly refurbished, vaulted brasserie where Franco-Irish dishes are served at smart, linen-laid tables. Amiable, helpful service.

XX **Dax** — VISA MC AE

23 Pembroke Street Upper – ✆ (01) 676 1494 – www.dax.ie – Closed 2 weeks August, 1 week Easter, Saturday lunch, Sunday and Monday — KZc

Rest – French – *(booking essential)* Menu € 29 (lunch)/39 (dinner Tuesday-Thursday) – Carte € 48/98

◆ Hidden away in basement of Georgian terrace, with rustic inner, immaculately laid tables, wine cellar and bar serving tapas. Knowledgable staff serve French influenced menus.

XX **One Pico** — AC VISA MC AE

5-6 Molesworth Pl – ✆ (01) 676 0300 – www.onepico.com – Fax (01) 676 0411 – Closed 25 December, Sunday and Bank Holidays — JZk

Rest – Modern – Menu € 20/39

◆ Wide-ranging cuisine, classic and traditional by turns, always with an original, eclectic edge. Décor and service share a pleasant formality, crisp, modern and stylish.

XX **Dobbin's** — AC VISA MC AE

15 Stephen's Lane, (off Stephen's Place) off Lower Mount St – ✆ (01) 661 9536 – www.dobbins.ie – Fax (01) 661 3331 – Closed 25 December-2 January, Saturday lunch, dinner Sunday and Monday and Bank Holidays — EUs

Rest – Traditional – *(booking essential)* Menu € 25 (lunch) – Carte € 44/56

◆ Smart, well-established restaurant in residential area. Small bar with booths leads to spacious, neatly laid dining room with warm, modern décor. Large menu displays international influences.

XX Locks

Number 1, Windsor Terrace – ✆ (01) 454 3391 – www.locksrestaurant.ie – Fax (01) 453 8352 – Closed Sunday dinner DU **a**

Rest – French – *(dinner only and lunch Saturday and Sunday)* Menu € 35 – Carte € 39/59

◆ Quirky modern restaurant by the canal boasting stylish inner with wooden floor, comfy leather seating and dining split over 2 floors. French menu includes some regional dishes.

XX The Cellar – at The Merrion Hotel

Upper Merrion St – ✆ (01) 603 0630 – www.merrionhotel.com – Fax (01) 603 0700 – Closed Saturday lunch KZ **e**

Rest – Menu € 20/30 – Carte € 36/67 **s**

◆ Set in hotel cellars, a formal restaurant with linen-laid tables, high-backed chairs and characterful curved ceiling. Good-sized menus of modern Irish cooking feature local, regional produce.

XX The Tea Room – at The Clarence Hotel

6-8 Wellington Quay – ✆ (01) 407 0813 – Fax (01) 407 0826 – Closed 24-26 December, Sunday and Monday HY **a**

Rest – Modern – *(dinner only) (booking essential)* Menu € 26 – Carte € 30/46

◆ Spacious hotel restaurant, where small mezzanine level overlooks larger main room with central banquette island. Ambitious cooking displays Gallic influences. Polite, formal service.

XX Les Frères Jacques

74 Dame St – ✆ (01) 679 4555 – www.lesfreresjacques.com – Fax (01) 679 4725 – Closed 24 December-2 January, Saturday lunch, Sunday and Bank Holidays

Rest – French – Menu € 23/38 – Carte € 58/70 HY **x**

◆ Long-standing restaurant on narrow cobbled alley, with typical French styling and team. Classical Gallic cooking with seafood a speciality: daily fresh fish and lobster tank on display.

XX Peploe's

16 St Stephen's Green – ✆ (01) 676 3144 – www.peploes.com – Fax (01) 676 3154 – Closed 25-29 December, Monday lunch and Bank Holidays JZ **e**

Rest – Mediterranean – *(booking essential)* Menu € 25 (lunch and early dinner) – Carte € 29/50

◆ Well-run, atmospheric brasserie named after Scottish artist and set in former bank vault. Small bar; main room with smart mural and linen-laid tables. Extensive menu with influences from the Med.

XX Bleu Bistro

Joshua House, Dawson St – ✆ (01) 676 7015 – www.bleu.ie – Fax (01) 676 7027 – Closed 25-26 December, Sunday and Bank Holidays JZ **r**

Rest – Modern European – Menu € 20 (lunch)/25 – Carte € 31/46

◆ Stylish, modern eatery on a bustling street. Smart and contemporary interior, with framed mirrors a feature. The appealing, varied menu keeps its influences within Europe.

XX Town Bar and Grill

21 Kildare St – ✆ (01) 662 4800 – www.townbarandgrill.com – Fax (01) 662 3857 – Closed 25-26 December and Good Friday JZ **n**

Rest – Italian influences – *(booking essential)* Menu € 25 (lunch) – Carte dinner € 46/58

◆ Located in wine merchant's old cellars: brick pillars divide a large space; fresh flowers and candles add a personal touch. Italian flair in bold cooking with innovative edge.

XX Fallon & Byrne

First Floor, 11-17 Exchequer St – ✆ (01) 472 1000 – www.fallonandbyrne.com – Fax (01) 472 1016 – Closed 25 December, Good Friday and Sunday dinner

Rest – Bistro – Menu € 30 (dinner) – Carte € 24/56 JY **f**

◆ Food emporium boasting vast basement wine cellar, ground floor full of fresh quality produce, and first floor French style bistro with banquettes, mirrors and tasty bistro food.

XX **Balzac** – at La Stampa Hotel VISA AE

35-36 Dawson St – (01) 677 8611 – www.lastampa.ie – Fax (01) 677 4411 – closed Sunday JZ**a**

Rest – French – *(dinner only)* Menu €25 – Carte €32/50

◆ Spacious restaurant in former dance hall, with high glass ceiling, linen-laid tables and banquette seating. Comfy lounge bar and appealing French themed menus.

XX **Bang Café** A/C VISA AE

11 Merrion Row – (01) 676 0898 – www.bangrestaurant.com – Fax (01) 676 0899 – Closed 25 December-2 January and Sunday KZ**a**

Rest – Modern – *(booking essential)* Menu €29 (lunch and early dinner) – Carte dinner €38/51

◆ Stylish three-floor restaurant with bar, open kitchen and enclosed rear terrace. Closely set linen-laid tables and mix of low-backed chairs/banquettes. Modern Irish cooking to the fore.

XX **Jaipur** VISA AE

41 South Great George's St – (01) 677 0999 – www.jaipur.ie – Fax (01) 677 0979 – Closed 25-26 December JY**a**

Rest – Indian – *(dinner only)* Menu €35 – Carte €34/47

◆ Long-standing restaurant set over two floors, with orange and red hues, stainless steel staircase and full length windows. Extensive menu displays interesting flavours from all over India.

X **The Pig's Ear** VISA AE

4 Nassau St – (01) 670 38 65 – www.thepigsear.ie – Fax (01) 670 38 68 – Closed first week January, 25 December, Sunday and Bank Holidays

Rest – Modern European – Menu €20 (lunch) – Carte €32/46 KY**a**

◆ Bistro-style restaurant set in Georgian city centre house with striking pink door. Well-priced, refined bistro cooking with French influences and Irish produce. Service with personality.

X **La Maison** A/C VISA

15 Castlemarket – (01) 672 7258 – www.lamaisonrestaurant.ie – Fax (01) 672 7238 – Closed 2 weeks Christmas-New Year and Sunday JY**c**

Rest – French – *(bookings not accepted)* Carte €27/41

◆ A simple and appealing French bistro, decorated with original posters. Personable service and a menu of carefully prepared and seasonal Gallic classics at a good price.

X **Mermaid Café** A/C VISA AE

69-70 Dame St – (01) 670 8236 – www.mermaid.ie – Fax (01) 607 4426 – Closed 24-26 December, 1 January and Good Friday HY**d**

Rest – Modern – *(Sunday brunch) (booking essential)* Carte €29/45

◆ This informal restaurant with unfussy décor and bustling atmosphere offers an interesting and well cooked selection of robust modern dishes. Efficient service.

X **L'Gueuleton** VISA

1 Fade St – (01) 675 3708 – Closed 25-26 and 31 December, 1 January

Rest – French – *(bookings not accepted)* Carte €30/42 JY**d**

◆ Busy, highly renowned recent arrival. Rustic style: mish-mash of roughed-up chairs and tables with candles or Parisian lamps. Authentic French country dishes full of flavour.

at Ballsbridge

Four Seasons A/C P VISA AE

Simmonscourt Rd – (01) 665 4000 – www.fourseasons.com/dublin – Fax (01) 665 4099 FU**e**

157 rm – †€195/270 ††€225/325, □ €29 – 40 suites – ††€530/655

Rest *Seasons* – Menu €32/69 – Carte €40/60

Rest *The Cafe* – *(dinner only)* Carte €38/75

◆ Set in grounds of the RDS arena. Elegant guest areas, state-of-the-art meeting rooms and impressive ballrooms boast ornate décor, antiques and Irish art. Spacious bedrooms; plenty of extras. Fine dining with fountain/garden views in Seasons. All day family focus in The Café.

REPUBLIC OF IRELAND

Herbert Park
– ✆ (01) 667 2200 – *www.herbertparkhotel.ie* – Fax (01) 667 2595
151 rm – 🛉 € 250/360 🛉🛉 € 385, ☕ €19.50 – 2 suites FU**m**
Rest *The Pavilion* – Carte € 30/45
◆ Contemporary hotel overlooking suburban park, with smart marble-floored reception, stylish seating areas and chic bar. Modern bedrooms display quality furnishings and marble bathrooms. Sizeable, formal restaurant offers interesting menu.

Merrion Hall without rest
54-56 Merrion Rd – ✆ *(01) 668 1426* – *www.halpinsprivatehotels.com* – *Fax (01) 668 4280* FU**b**
34 rm ☕ – 🛉 € 169/189 🛉🛉 € 199/219
◆ Red-brick Victorian house boasts spacious, antique-furnished guest areas with a Georgian feel. Comfortable, stylish bedrooms have a traditional edge; those to rear are quieter.

Ariel House without rest
50-54 Lansdowne Rd – ✆ *(01) 668 5512* – *www.ariel-house.net* – *Fax (01) 668 5845* – *Closed 22-27 December* FU**n**
37 rm ☕ – 🛉 € 150 🛉🛉 € 250
◆ Personally run Victorian townhouse with comfy, traditionally styled guest areas and antique furnishings. Warmly decorated bedrooms have modern facilities and smart bathrooms; some four-posters.

Aberdeen Lodge without rest
53-55 Park Ave – ✆ *(01) 283 8155* – *www.halpinsprivatehotels.com* – *Fax (01) 283 7877* GV**e**
17 rm ☕ – 🛉 € 169/189 🛉🛉 € 199/219
◆ Two Victorian townhouses in smart suburban setting, knocked through into one impressive hotel. Comfy lounge, warm homely atmosphere and well-equipped bedrooms – some with garden views.

Pembroke Townhouse without rest
90 Pembroke Rd – ✆ *(01) 660 0277* – *www.pembroketownhouse.ie* – *Fax (01) 660 0291* – *Closed 22 December- 3 January* FU**d**
48 rm – 🛉 € 199 🛉🛉 € 310, ☕ €15
◆ Formerly three Georgian houses, now a friendly hotel with traditional styling, comfy lounge and sunny breakfast room. Bedrooms vary in shape and size: duplex rooms are the cosiest.

Glenogra House without rest
64 Merrion Rd – ✆ *(01) 668 3661* – *www.glenogra.com* – *Fax (01) 668 3698* – *Closed 24-27 December* FU**w**
12 rm ☕ – 🛉 € 99/139 🛉🛉 € 99/199
◆ Personally run red-brick Victorian house with informal reception, comfy lounge and homely furnishings. Simply decorated bedrooms vary in shape and size; all boast modern facilities.

at Donnybrook

Marble Hall without rest
81 Marlborough Rd – ✆ *(01) 497 7350* – *www.marblehall.net* – *February-November* EV**a**
3 rm ☕ – 🛉 € 55 🛉🛉 € 80/90
◆ Georgian townhouse with effusive welcome guaranteed. Individually styled throughout, with plenty of antiques and quality soft furnishings. Stylish, warmly decorated bedrooms.

at Rathmines

Zen
89 Upper Rathmines Rd – ✆ *(01) 497 94 28* – *Fax (01) 491 17 28* – *Closed 25-27 December* DV**t**
Rest – Chinese – *(dinner only and Friday lunch)* Menu € 20 – Carte € 18/34
◆ Renowned family run Chinese restaurant in the unusual setting of an old church hall. Imaginative, authentic oriental cuisine with particular emphasis on spicy Szechuan dishes.

REPUBLIC OF IRELAND

at Dublin Airport North : 10.5 km by N 1 - BS - and M 1 – ✉ Dublin

Carlton H. Dublin Airport

Old Airport Rd, Cloughran, on R 132 Santry rd – ✆ (01) 866 7500 – www.carlton.ie/dublinairport – Fax (01) 862 3114
117 rm – † € 89/259 †† € 89/259, ☕ €16.50 – 1 suite
Rest *Kittyhawks* – Carte € 23/48 **s**
◆ Modern commercial hotel with spacious marbled reception and comfy guest areas. Uniform bedrooms display good facilities and smart bathrooms. Some rooms overlook airfield; some have balconies. Informal all-day brasserie offers popular menu.

Bewleys

Baskin Lane, East : 1.5 km on A 32 – ✆ (01) 871 1000 – www.bewleyshotels.com – Fax (01) 871 1299 – Closed 25 December
466 rm – † € 59/79 †† € 59/79, ☕ €9.50
Rest *The Brasserie* – Menu € 19 (lunch) **s** – Carte dinner € 27/36 **s**
◆ Immense eight floor hotel, ten minutes from the airport, with selection of small meeting rooms. Immaculately kept bedrooms; good value for money. Wide-ranging menu served in The Brasserie.

at Clontarf Northeast : 5.5 km by R 105 – ✉ Dublin

Clontarf Castle

Castle Ave – ✆ (01) 833 2321 – www.clontarfcastle.ie – Fax (01) 833 0418
108 rm ☕ – † € 360 †† € 370 – 3 suites CS**a**
Rest *Fahrenheit Grill* – *(bar lunch)* Carte € 28/46 **s**
◆ Set in an historic castle, partly dating back to 1172. Striking medieval style entrance lobby. Modern rooms and characterful luxury suites, all with cutting edge facilities. Restaurant boasts grand medieval style décor reminiscent of a knights' banqueting hall; fresh local meats and seafood feature.

at Sandyford Southeast : 12 km by N 11 and R 112 off R 133 - CT – ✉ Dublin

The Beacon

Beacon Court, Sandyford Business Region – ✆ (01) 291 5000 – www.thebeacon.com – Fax (01) 291 5005 – Closed 24-25 December
87 rm ☕ – † € 110/150 †† € 120/160 – 1 suite
Rest *My Thai* – Thai – Menu € 25/45 **s** – Carte € 29/40 **s**
◆ Ultra-stylish hotel with uniquely quirky entrance lobby featuring a chandelier on the floor and bed with central seating! Modish bar, low-key meeting rooms, sleek bedrooms. Funky, relaxed restaurant serving authentic Asian dishes.

at Foxrock Southeast : 13 km by N 11 - CT – ✉ Dublin

Bistro One

3 Brighton Rd – ✆ (01) 289 7711 – www.bistro-one.ie – Fax (01) 207 0742 – Closed 25 December-2 January, Sunday and Monday
Rest – *(booking essential)* Menu € 24 (lunch) – Carte € 28/47
◆ Long-standing neighbourhood restaurant; popular with the locals. Daily lunch and monthly dinner menus display a mix of Irish and Mediterranean influences. Good use of local produce.

at Dundrum Southeast : 8 km by N 11 - CT – ✉ Dublin

Harvey Nichols First Floor Restaurant

Harvey Nichols, Town Square, Sandyford Rd – ✆ (01) 291 0488 – www.harveynichols.com – Fax (01) 291 0489 – Closed 25-26 December, Sunday and Monday
Rest – Menu € 25/30
◆ Up the lift to ultra-stylish bar and plush, designer-led restaurant. Attentive, professional service. Dishes are modern, seasonal and confident with a fine dining feel.

Ananda

Town Square – ✆ (01) 296 00 99 – www.anandarestarant.ie – Fax (01) 296 00 33 – Closed 25 December
Rest – Indian – Menu € 25/38 **s** – Carte € 28/46 **s**
◆ Meaning 'bliss' in ancient Sanskrit. Stylish restaurant located in city centre arcade. Beautiful décor, attractive fretwork and gorgeous lighting. Flavourful modern Indian cuisine.

DUBLIN AIRPORT (Aerfort Bhaile Átha Cliath) – Dublin – 712 N7 – see Dublin

DUNBOYNE (Dún Búinne) – Meath – 712 M7 – pop. 5 713 37 D3

Dublin 17 km – Drogheda 45 km – Newbridge 54 km

Dunboyne Castle

– (01) 801 35 00 – *www.dunboynecastlehotel.com* – Fax (01) 436 68 01

141 rm – € 140/155 € 165/180 – 4 suites

Rest – *(bar lunch Monday-Saturday)* Carte € 33/54

◆ Georgian house with vast, modern extensions, set in 26 acres. Ornate ceilings typify style in original house; now used for conferences. Some bedrooms have balconies; most overlook grounds. Discreet, stylish spa. Large, formal restaurant serves classic Irish dishes.

DUNCANNON (Dún Canann) – Wexford – 712 L11 – pop. 291 39 D2

Ireland

Dublin 167 km – New Ross 26 km – Waterford 48 km

Fort★ AC

Dunbrody Abbey★ AC, N : 9 km by R 733 – Kilmokea Gardens★ AC, N : 11 km by R 733 – Tintern Abbey★ AC, E : 8 km by R 737 and R 733. Kennedy Arboretum★ AC, N : 21 km by R 733

Aldridge Lodge with rm

South : 1 km by Hook Head Rd – (051) 389 116 – www.aldridgelodge.com – Fax (051) 389 116 – Closed 2 weeks January, 3 days Christmas and Monday-Tuesday

3 rm – € 55 € 100

Rest – *(dinner only) (booking essential)* Menu € 39 **s**

◆ Close to the beach, a smart, cheery restaurant with gardens serving good value, quality local menus: lobster a speciality as owner's dad's a lobster fisherman! Cosy rooms.

Sqigl

Quay Rd – (051) 389 700 – www.sqiglrestaurant.com – Closed January

Rest – *(dinner only) (booking essential)* Menu € 25 – Carte € 31/48

◆ Stone-built restaurant; a converted barn standing adjacent to a popular bar in this coastal village. Faux leopard skin banquettes. Modern European cuisine with amiable service.

DUNDALK (Dún Dealgan) – Louth – 712 M5/6 – pop. 35 085 37 D2

Ireland

Dublin 82 km – Drogheda 35 km

Killinbeg Killin Park, (042) 933 93 03

Dún a' Rí Forest Park★, W : 34 km by R 178 and R 179 – Proleek Dolmen★, N : 8 km by N 1 R 173

Crowne Plaza

Green Park, South : 2.5 km. on N 52 – (042) 939 49 00 – www.cpdundalk.ie – Fax (042) 939 49 55 – Closed 25 December

128 rm – € 84/104 € 99/119, € 15 – 1 suite

Rest – *(bar lunch Monday-Saturday)* Menu € 35 – Carte € 28/40

◆ Modern 14 storey hotel tower block with stylish ground floor bar/lounge and good conference facilities. Uniform bedrooms boast views of surrounding countryside. Top floor restaurant offers seasonally changing menu of classic dishes and has superb 360° vista.

Rosemount without rest

Dublin Rd, South : 2.5 km on R 132 – (042) 933 58 78 – www.rosemountireland.com – Fax (042) 933 58 78 – Closed 3 days Christmas

9 rm – € 45/50 € 65

◆ A modern house a short drive from the town with good access to the M1. Well-appointed guests' lounge and attractive breakfast room. Comfortably furnished bedrooms.

REPUBLIC OF IRELAND

XX **Rosso**

5 Roden Pl – ✆ (042) 935 6502 – www.rossorestaurant.com – Fax (042) 935 6503 – Closed 25-26 December, 1 January, Saturday lunch, Sunday dinner and Monday

Rest – Menu € 26 (dinner) – Carte € 31/47

◆ Traditional on the outside, contemporary on the inside, with stylish furnishings and banquette seating. Front windows overlook cathedral. Classic cooking with a modern twist.

at Jenkinstown Northeast : 9 km by N 52 on R 173

Fitzpatricks

Rockmarshall, Southeast : 1 km – ✆ (042) 937 61 93 – www.fitzpatricks-restaurant.com – Fax (042) 937 62 74 – Closed Monday in winter except Bank Holidays

Rest – Menu € 25 (dinner) – Carte € 30/43

◆ Hugely characterful pub with beautiful flower displays and intriguing memorabilia. Extensive menu of hearty, flavoursome dishes and plenty of classics; local seafood and steaks a speciality.

DUNDRUM (Dún Droma) – Dublin – 712 N8 – see Dublin

DUNFANAGHY (Dún Fionnachaidh) – Donegal – 712 I2 – pop. 316 — 37 C1

– ✉ Letterkenny Ireland

Dublin 277 km – Donegal 87 km – Londonderry 69 km

Dunfanaghy Letterkenny, ✆ (074) 913 6335

Horn Head Scenic Route★, N : 4 km. Doe Castle★, SE : 11.25 km by N 56 – The Rosses★, SW : 40.25 km by N 56 and R 259

Arnolds — rest,

Main St – ✆ (074) 913 62 08 – www.arnoldshotel.com – Fax (074) 913 63 52 – 26 March-October

30 rm – € 55/100 € 110/150

Rest *Sea Scapes* – *(bar lunch)* Menu € 35 – Carte € 24/39

◆ Pleasant traditional coaching inn with a variety of extensions. Spacious lounge area and a charming bar with open fires. Family run with traditional bedrooms. Informal Sea Scapes serves wide-ranging menus.

XX **The Mill** with rm — rest,

Southwest : 0.75 km on N 56 – ✆ (074) 913 69 85 – www.themillrestaurant.com – Fax (074) 913 69 85 – Closed January, February and midweek March, November and December

6 rm – € 70 € 100 **Rest** – *(closed Monday) (dinner only)* Menu € 45

◆ Former Flax mill on New Lake with Mount Muckish view. Locally renowned and warmly run; enhanced by personally decorated ambience. Traditional cooking served in split-level, linen-laid dining room. Unfussy bedrooms with simple facilities.

DUNGARVAN (Dún Garbhán) – Waterford – 712 J11 – pop. 8 362 — 39 C3

Ireland

Dublin 190 km – Cork 71 km – Waterford 48 km

The Courthouse ✆ (058) 41741, info@dungarvantourism.com

Knocknagrannagh, ✆ (058) 41 605

Gold Coast Ballinacourty, ✆ (058) 42 249

East Bank (Augustinian priory, ★)

Ringville (★), S : 13 km by N 25 and R 674 – Helvick Head★ (★), SE : 13 km by N 25 and R 674

Gortnadiha Lodge without rest

South : 6.5 km by N 25 off R 674 – ✆ (058) 46 142 – www.gortnadihalodge.com – Closed 10 December-10 January

3 rm – € 50 € 90

◆ Friendly guesthouse set in its own glen with fine bay views, a first floor terrace for afternoon tea, homemade jams and breads for breakfast, and antique furnished bedrooms.

XX **Tannery** with rm — AC rest, VISA MC AE DC

10 Quay St, via Parnell St – ✆ (058) 45 420 – www.tannery.ie – Fax (058) 45 814 – Closed 2 weeks January, 25 December and Sunday except July and August

14 rm – † € 60/70 †† € 100/120

Rest – *(dinner only and lunch Friday and Sunday)* Menu € 29 (early weekday dinner) – Carte approx. € 53

◆ Characterful 19C former tannery; high-ceilinged dining room with informal ambience. Imaginative modern menus centre round produce from kitchen garden. Super cooking school. Stylish, comfortable bedrooms in adjacent townhouse.

DUNKINEELY (Dún Cionnaola) – Donegal – 712 G4 – pop. 363 — 37 C1

Dublin 156 km – Lifford 42 km – Sligo 53 km – Ballybofey 28 km

XX **Castle Murray House** with rm — P VISA MC

St John's Point, Southwest : 1.5 km by N 56 on St John's Point rd – ✆ (074) 973 70 22 – www.castlemurray.com – Fax (074) 973 73 30 – Closed early January-mid February

10 rm – † € 80/90 †† € 130/150

Rest – *(dinner only and Sunday lunch, light lunch in Summer)* Menu € 32/53

◆ In delightful, picturesque position with view of sea and sunsets from the lounges and the pleasant dining room. Good local seafood. Comfortable and contemporary styled bedrooms.

Good food at moderate prices? Look for the Bib Gourmand.

DUN LAOGHAIRE (Dún Laoghaire) – Dún Laoghaire-Rathdown – 712 N8 – pop. 23 857 Ireland — 39 D1

Dublin 14 km

to Holyhead (Stena Line) 4-5 daily (1 h 40 mn)

v (01) 6057 700, info@dlrtourism.com

Dun Laoghaire Eglinton Park, ✆ (01) 280 3916

★★ of Killiney Bay from coast road south of Sorrento Point

Plan on next page

XX **Rasam** — VISA MC

1st Floor (above Eagle House pub), 18-19 Glasthule Rd – ✆ (01) 230 0600 – www.rasam.ie – Fax (01) 230 1000 – Closed 25-26 December — **e**

Rest – Indian – *(dinner only)* Carte € 40/55

◆ Located above Eagle House pub, this airy, modern, stylish restaurant shimmers with silky green wallpaper. Interesting, authentic dishes covering all regions of India.

X **Cavistons** — AC VISA MC AE DC

58-59 Glasthule Rd – ✆ (01) 280 9245 – www.cavistons.com – Fax (01) 284 4054 – Closed 23-29 December, Sunday and Monday — **a**

Rest – Seafood – *(lunch only and dinner Friday and Saturday) (booking essential)* Carte € 34/48

◆ Simple, informal restaurant attached to the well-established seafood shop which specialises in finest piscine produce. Mermaid friezes and quality crustacean cuisine.

X **Tribes** — AC VISA MC AE

57a Glasthule Rd – ✆ (01) 236 5971 – www.tribes.ie – Fax (01) 236 5971 – Closed 25-26 December and 1 January — **x**

Rest – *(dinner only and Sunday lunch)* Menu € 24 – Carte € 30/37

◆ Personally run neighbourhood restaurant next to Cavistons. Smart, original interior harmonises seamlessly with creative modern European menus that evolve slowly over time.

REPUBLIC OF IRELAND

DUNLAVIN (Dún Luáin) – Wicklow – 712 L8 – pop. 849 — 39 D2

Dublin 50 km – Kilkenny 71 km – Wexford 98 km

18 Rathsallagh, ✆ (045) 403 316

Rathsallagh House

Southwest : 3.25 km on Grangecon Rd – ✆ (045) 403 112
– www.rathsallagh.com – Fax (045) 403 343

28 rm – 🚹 € 175 🚹🚹 € 190/290 – 1 suite

Rest – *(bar lunch Monday-Saturday)* Menu € 65

◆ 18C converted stables set in extensive grounds and golf course. Picturesque walled garden. Characterful, country house-style public areas and cosy, individual bedrooms. Kitchen garden provides ingredients for welcoming dining room.

DUNMORE EAST (Dún Mór) – Waterford – 712 L11 – pop. 1 547 — 39 C2

– ✉ Waterford Ireland

Dublin 174 km – Waterford 19 km

18 Dunmore East, ✆ (051) 383 151

Village★

The Beach without rest

1 Lower Village – ✆ (051) 383 316 – www.dunmorebeachguesthouse.com
– Fax (051) 383 319 – March-October

7 rm – 🚹 € 50/70 🚹🚹 € 80/90

◆ Modern house close to the beach. Wonderful views from conservatory breakfast/lounge area. Very spacious bedrooms with pine furniture and modern facilities; some with balcony.

DURRUS (Dúras) – **Cork** – **712** D13 – **pop. 313** **38** A3

Dublin 338 km – Cork 90 km – Killarney 85 km

XX **Blairs Cove** with rm

Southwest : 1.5 km on R 591 – (027) 62 913 – www.blairscove.ie – Fax (027) 61 487 – restricted opening in winter

4 rm – €105/160 €190/260

Rest – *(closed Sunday dinner and Monday) (dinner only and Sunday lunch) (booking essential)* Menu €58 – Carte €33/46

◆ Cosy bar with roaring fire leads to converted 17C barn. Imposing chandelier and candelabras; grand piano doubles as sweet trolley. Meats are a speciality, cooked in open grill. Fine Georgian house with outbuildings and sea views, set around a courtyard. Spacious, modern suites come with own kitchens and dining areas.

X **Good Things Cafe**

Ahakista Rd, West : 0.75 km on Ahakista rd – (027) 61 426 – www.thegoodthingscafe.com – Fax (027) 61 426 – late June-September and Easter

Rest – *(closed Tuesday and Wednesday)* Carte €28/49 **s**

◆ Simple and unpretentious. Walls filled with shelves full of books and foods of all kinds for sale. Open-plan kitchen serves accomplished dishes full of quality local produce.

ENNIS (Inis) – **Clare** – **712** F9 – **pop. 24 253** Ireland **38** B2

Dublin 228 km – Galway 67 km – Limerick 35 km – Roscommon 148 km

Arthurs Row (065) 6828366, touristofficeennis@shannondevelopment.ie

Drumbiggle Rd, (065) 682 40 74

Ennis Friary★ **AC**

Dysert O'Dea★, N : 9.75 km by N 85 and R 476, turning left after 6.5 km and right after 1.5 km - Quin Franciscan Friary★, SE : 10.5 km by R 469 – Knappogue Castle★ **AC**, SE : 12.75 km by R 469 – Corrofin (Clare Heritage Centre★ **AC**), N : 13.75 km by N 85 and R 476 – Craggaunowen Centre★ **AC**, SE : 17.75 km by R 469 - Kilmacduagh Churches and Round Tower★, NE : 17.75 km by N 18 – Kilrush★ (Scattery Island★ by boat) SW : 43.5 km by N 68 - Bridge of Ross, Kilkee★, SW : 57 km by N 68 and N 67

Temple Gate

The Square – (065) 682 33 00 – www.templegatehotel.com – Fax (065) 682 33 22 – Closed 24-26 December

68 rm – €69/129 €89/149 – 2 suites

Rest *Legends* – *(carvery lunch Monday-Saturday)* Carte €26/43

◆ A professional yet friendly mood prevails at this privately run hotel in modern, subtly neo-Gothic style. Panelled library and well-fitted rooms in traditional patterns. Legends serves carefully presented modern dishes in informal surroundings.

ENNISCORTHY (Inis Córthaidh) – **Wexford** – **712** M10 – **pop. 9 538** **39** D2

Ireland

Dublin 122 km – Kilkenny 74 km – Waterford 54 km – Wexford 24 km

1798 Rebellion Centre, Millpark Rd (0539) 234699, info@1798centre.ie

Knockmarshal, (053) 923 31 91

Enniscorthy Castle★ (County Museum★)

Ferns★, NE : 13 km by N 11 – Mount Leinster★, N : 27.25 km by N 11

Monart rest,

The Still, Northwest : 3 km by N 11 (Dublin rd) – (053) 923 8999 – www.monart.ie – Closed 19-27 December

68 rm – €215/295 €350/490 – 2 suites

Rest *The Restaurant* – *(dinner only and Sunday lunch)* Menu €35 (except Saturday) – Carte €38/69

Rest *Garden Lounge* – Carte €27/42 **s**

◆ Spa resort in 100 acres; enter via the elegant Georgian house and experience various therapies in state-of-the-art treatment rooms. Bedrooms all have views; many have balconies. Formal dining in The Restaurant. Enjoy lighter dishes in the Garden Lounge or out on the terrace.

Ballinkeele House

Ballymurn, Southeast : 10.5 km by unmarked road on Curracloe rd – (053) 91 38 105 – www.ballinkeele.com – Fax (053) 91 38 468 – February-November

5 rm – € 100/110 € 170/180

Rest – *(by arrangement, communal dining)* Menu € 48

◆ High ceilinged, firelit lounge plus sizeable rooms with period-style furniture and countryside views add to the charm of a quiet 1840 manor, well run by experienced owners. Dining room enriched by candlelight and period oils.

ENNISKERRY (Áth an Sceire) – Wicklow – 712 N8 – pop. 1 881 — 39 D1

Ireland

Dublin 25 km – Wicklow 32 km

Powerscourt Powerscourt Estate, (01) 204 6033

Powerscourt★★ **AC** (Waterfall★★, **AC**)

Ritz Carlton

West : 2 km. by Powerscourt rd – (01) 274 8888 – www.ritzcarlton.com – Fax (01) 274 9999

76 rm – € 250 € 390, €29 – 124 suites – € 350/5000

Rest ***Gordon Ramsay at Powerscourt*** – *(01) 274 9377 (dinner only and lunch Saturday and Sunday)* Menu € 40 – Carte € 40/95

Rest ***The Sugar Loaf*** – Carte € 33/52

◆ Opened in 2008 within the Powerscourt House Estate, a vast and impressive structure with lots of leisure activities. Many rooms are suites; bathrooms are luxurious. Formal restaurant with mountain views and mix of Gordon Ramsay dishes and reinterpreted Irish classics. Relaxed Sugar Loaf.

REPUBLIC OF IRELAND

Take note of the classification: you should not expect the same level of service in a ✗ or 🏠 as in a ✗✗✗✗✗ or 🏨.

ENNISTIMON (Inis Díomáin) – Clare – 712 E9 – pop. 813 Ireland — 38 B1

Dublin 254 km – Galway 83 km – Limerick 63 km

The Burren★★ : Cliffs of Moher★★★, Scenic Route★★, Aillwee Cave★ **AC** (waterfall★★), Corcomroe Abbey★, Kilfenora High Crosses★, Burren Centre★ **AC**

Grovemount House without rest

Lahinch Rd, West : 0.75 km on N 67 – (065) 707 14 31 – www.grovemount-ennistymon.com – Fax (065) 707 18 23 – May-October

6 rm – € 45/55 € 70/80

◆ Spotless bedrooms in warm oak and a homely lounge in this modern guesthouse, run by the friendly owner. A short drive to the sandy beach at Lahinch and the Cliffs of Moher.

FETHARD (Fiodh Ard) – Tipperary – 712 I10 – pop. 1 374 Ireland — 39 C2

Dublin 161 km – Cashel 16 km – Clonmel 13 km

Cashel★★★ : Rock of Cashel★★★ **AC** (Cormac's Chapel★★, Round Tower★), Museum★ **AC**, Cashel Palace Gardens★, GPA Bolton Library★ **AC**, NW : 15 km by R 692 – Clonmel★ : County Museum★ **AC**, St Mary's Church★, S : 13 km by R 689

Mobarnane House

North : 8 km by Cashel rd on Ballinure rd – (052) 613 19 62 – www.mobarnanehouse.com – Fax (052) 613 19 62 – March-October

4 rm – € 100 € 150

Rest – *(by arrangement, communal dining)* Menu € 45

◆ Very personally run classic Georgian house with mature gardens in quiet rural setting, tastefully restored to reflect its age. Ask for a bedroom with its own sitting room. Beautiful dining room for menus agreed in advance.

FOTA ISLAND (Oileán Fhóta) – Cork – 712 H12 — 38 B3

Dublin 263 km – Cork 17 km – Limerick 118 km – Waterford 110 km

Fota Island

– (021) 467 3000 – www.fotaisland.ie – Fax (021) 467 3456 – closed 24-28 December

123 rm – € 330, €16.50 – 8 suites

Rest *The Cove* – *(dinner only Friday and Saturday)* Carte € 48/71

Rest *Fota* – *(bar lunch)* Carte € 28/43

◆ All-encompassing resort location within Ireland's only wildlife park boasting Wellness Centre with 'walking river' and 18 hole golf course. Stylish rooms from the top drawer. The Cove is a very formal place to dine. Fota's appealing menus suit all tastes.

Undecided between two equivalent establishments in the same town? Within each category, establishments are classified in our order of preference: the best first.

FOXROCK (Carraig an tSionnaigh) – Dublin – 712 N7 – see Dublin

FURBOGH/FURBO (Na Forbacha) – Galway – 712 E8 – pop. 1 236 — 36 A3

Dublin 228 km – Galway 11 km

Connemara Coast

– (091) 592 108 – www.sinnotthotels.com – Fax (091) 592 065

141 rm – € 130/200 € 178/350 – 1 suite

Rest *The Gallery* – *(bar lunch)* Menu € 40 **s** – Carte € 40/50 **s**

◆ Sprawling hotel geared to families, with super views of Galway Bay, The Burren and Aran from the spacious bedrooms. Comprehensive leisure facilities. Club for kids. Two dining options; The Gallery for adults only.

GALWAY (Gaillimh) – Galway – 712 E8 – pop. 72 414 Ireland — 36 B3

Dublin 217 km – Limerick 103 km – Sligo 145 km

Carnmore Airport : (091) 755569, NE : 6.5 km

Discover Ireland Centre, Aras Failte, Forster St (091) 537700, irelandwestinfo@failteireland.ie Salthill Promenade (091) 520500 (May-August)

Galway Salthill Blackrock, (091) 522 033

City★★ – St Nicholas' Church★ BY - Roman Catholic Cathedral★ AY – Eyre Square : Bank of Ireland Building (sword and mace★) BY

NW : Lough Corrib★★. W : by boat, Aran Islands (Inishmore - Dun Aenghus★★★) BZ - Thoor Ballylee★, SE : 33.75 km by N 6 and N 18 D – Dunguaire Castle, Kinvarra★ **AC**, S : 25.75 km by N 6, N 18 and N 67 D – Aughnanure Castle★, NW : 25.75 km by N 59 - Oughterard★ (★★), NW : 29 km by N 59 - Knockmoy Abbey★, NE : 30.5 km by N 17 and N 63 D – Coole Park (Autograph Tree★), SE : 33.75 km by N 6 and N 18 D - St Mary's Cathedral, Tuam★, NE : 33.75 km by N 17 D – Loughrea (St Brendan's Cathedral★), SE : 35.5 km by N 6 D - Turoe Stone★, SE : 35.5 km by N 6 and north by R 350

Plans pages 954, 955

Glenlo Abbey

Bushypark, Northwest : 5.25 km on N 59 – (091) 526 666 – www.glenlo.com – Fax (091) 527 800 – *Closed 23-27 December*

42 rm – € 189/315 € 250/400, €22 – 4 suites

Rest *River Room* – *(dinner only Thursday-Sunday)* Menu € 35 – Carte € 36/54

Rest *Pullman* – *(dinner only Monday-Saturday)* Carte € 37/52

◆ Imposing 18C grey stone country house with impressive grounds and church/bay views. Very comfortable lounge, leading into chapel. Spacious, traditional rooms. Formal River Room boasts golf course views. Pullman, a converted railway carriage, offers modern dishes with an Asian base.

REPUBLIC OF IRELAND

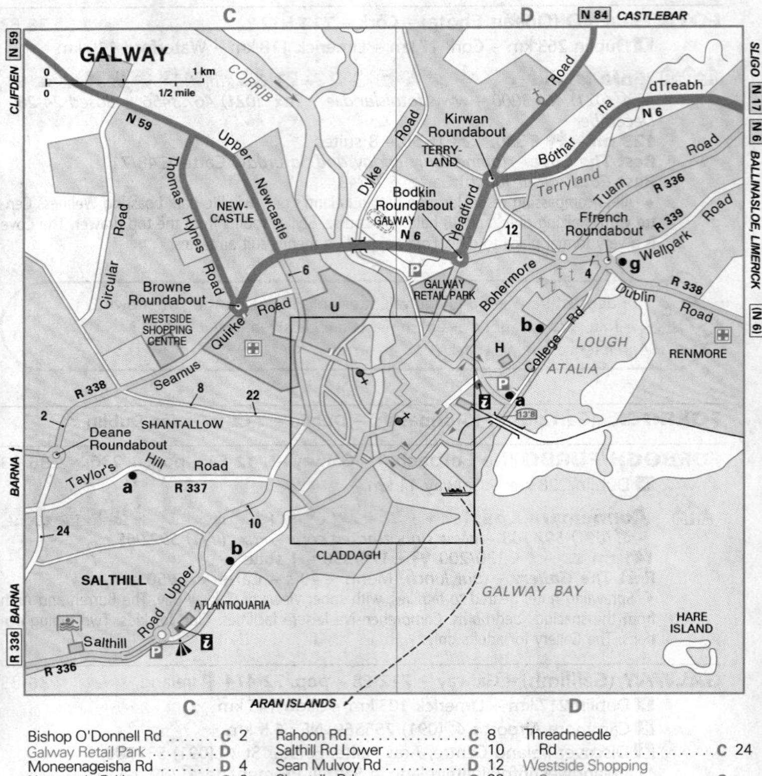

Bishop O'Donnell Rd . . . . C 2
Galway Retail Park . . . . D
Moneenageisha Rd . . . . D 4
Newcastle Rd Lower . . . . C 6
Rahoon Rd. . . . . C 8
Salthill Rd Lower . . . . C 10
Sean Mulvoy Rd . . . . D 12
Shantalla Rd. . . . . C 22
Threadneedle Rd . . . . C 24
Westside Shopping Centre C

Radisson Blu

Lough Atalia Rd
– ✆ (091) 538 300
– www.radissonhotelgalway.com
– Fax (091) 538 380 **Da**

259 rm – € 110/350 € 130/350 – 2 suites
Rest *Marinas* – Carte € 25/54

◆ Striking atrium leads to ultra-modern meeting facilities and very comfortable and refurbished accommodation. Higher spec rooms on the 5th floor have glass balconies. International dining; accessible, rapid lunch menu.

The G

rm,

Wellpark, Dublin Rd
– ✆ (091) 865 200
– www.theghotel.ie
– Fax (091) 865 203
– Closed 23-25 December **Dg**

100 rm – € 130/370 € 150/410 – 1 suite
Rest *Matz at the G* – *(dinner only)* Menu € 55 – Carte € 37/56 **s**

◆ Uber-hip boutique hotel with cutting edge design from renowned milliner Philip Treacy. Vividly assured sitting room styles; décor imbued with fashion shoot portraits. Cool, slinky bedrooms. Stunning spa. Modern Irish cooking in colourful restaurant.

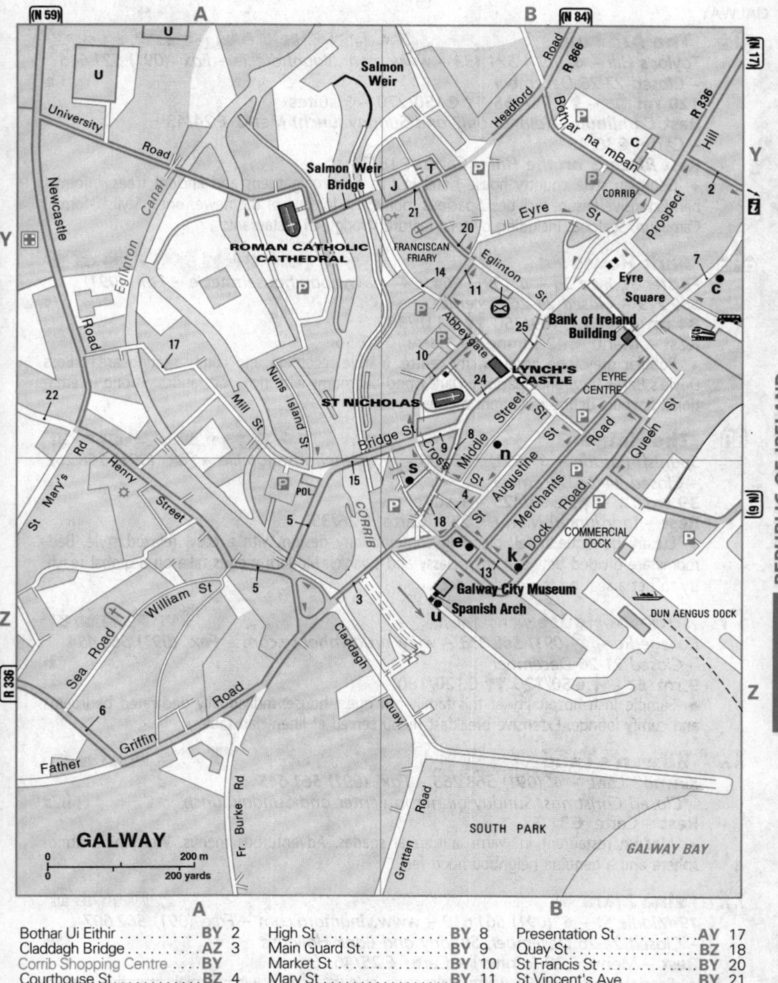

Bothar Ui Eithir	BY	2	High St	BY	8	Presentation St	AY	17
Claddagh Bridge	AZ	3	Main Guard St.	BY	9	Quay St	BZ	18
Corrib Shopping Centre	BY		Market St	BY	10	St Francis St	BY	20
Courthouse St.	BZ	4	Mary St	BY	11	St Vincent's Ave	BY	21
Dominick St	AZ	5	Newton Smith	BY	14	Shantalla Rd	AY	22
Father Griffin Ave	AZ	6	New Dock St.	BZ	13	Shop St	BY	24
Forster St	BY	7	O'Brien Bridge	AY	15	William St	BY	25

Clayton

Ballybrit, East : 4 km on N 6
– (091) 721 900
– www.clayton.ie
– Fax (091) 721 901
– Closed 23-27 December

196 rm – € 150/350 € 250/350

Rest – *(bar lunch)* Menu € 45 – Carte € 35/43

◆ Striking angular building on edge of city, with stylish, modern interior and bar with buffet carvery. Smart white bedrooms have a minimalistic feel, with dark wood furniture. Large first floor restaurant offers traditional menu.

The Ardilaun
rest,

Taylor's Hill – (091) 521 433 – www.theardilaunhotel.ie – Fax (091) 521 546 – Closed 22-26 December C**a**

120 rm – € 75/155 € 150/270 – 5 suites

Rest *Camilaun* – *(dinner only and Sunday lunch)* Menu € 24/43 – Carte € 36/45

Rest *Blazer's on the Hill* – Carte € 18/34

◆ Georgian style country house hotel in five acres of gardens and ancient trees. Informal bar. Extensive leisure facilities. Spacious rooms; ask for one of the newer ones. Stylish, formal Camilaun. Seafood, including oysters, feature strongly in restaurant.

Park House

Forster St, Eyre Sq – (091) 564 924 – www.parkhousehotel.ie – Fax (091) 569 219 – Closed 24-26 December BY**c**

84 rm – € 109/250 € 118/380

Rest – Menu € 42 (dinner) – Carte € 30/56

◆ Popular greystone hotel in city centre. Marble reception and comfy seating areas. Boss Doyle's Bar is busy and spacious. Dark wood bedrooms with rich, soft fabrics. Strong international flavours define restaurant menus.

The House
rm,

Spanish Parade – (091) 538 900 – www.thehousehotel.ie – Fax (091) 568 262 – Closed 24-27 December BZ**e**

39 rm – € 99/425 – 1 suite

Rest – *(bar lunch)* Menu € 25 – Carte € 26/35

◆ Luxury boutique hotel, blending contemporary design with a cosy, relaxed style. Bedrooms are divided between cosy, classy and swanky. Modern menus take on a global reach; try to get a seat on the outdoor deck.

Ardawn House without rest

College Rd – (091) 568 833 – www.ardawnhouse.com – Fax (091) 563 454 – Closed 21-26 December D**b**

9 rm – € 50/120 € 120/180

◆ Sample Irish hospitality at this family-run guest house. Individually decorated bedrooms and comfy lounge. Extensive breakfast menu served at linen-clad tables.

Kirwan's Lane

Kirwan's Lane – (091) 568 266 – Fax (091) 561 645 – Closed Christmas, Sunday dinner in winter and Sunday lunch BZ**s**

Rest – Carte € 31/53

◆ Modern restaurant in warm, autumnal shades. Adventurous menus. Welcoming atmosphere and a genuine neighbourhood feel.

Vina Mara

19 Middle St – (091) 561 610 – www.vinamara.com – Fax (091) 562 607 – Closed 24-26 December, Sunday and Bank Holidays BY**n**

Rest – Menu € 28 (dinner) – Carte € 25/46

◆ Spacious restaurant in warm welcoming colours - smart yet informal; attentive service. Mediterranean style dishes with Irish and other touches. Affordable but limited lunch choice.

Ard Bia at Nimmos

Spanish Arch – (091) 561 114 – www.ardbia.com – Closed Monday

Rest – *(light lunch) (booking essential at dinner)* Carte € 24/36 BZ**u**

◆ Simple restaurant in two-storey building with buzzy, bohemain feel. Generous, full-flavoured dishes have Mediterranean and Irish influences. Lighter lunches; upstairs used at weekends.

Sheridan's on the Docks

Dock St (first floor) – (091) 564 905 – www.sheridansonthedocks.com – Fax (091) 564 095 – Closed Christmas - New Year, Sunday and Monday

Rest – *(booking advisable dinner only)* Carte € 40/48 BZ**k**

◆ Head for candlelit upstairs dining room for flavourful, seasonal food; passionately and respectfully prepared, with some ingredients foraged for by chef. Atmospheric ground floor pub.

GARRYKENNEDY – Tipperary – 712 G9 — 39 C2

Dublin 176 km – Killaloe 14 km – Youghal 2 km

Larkins

– (067) 23 232 – www.larkinspub.com – Fax (067) 23 933
– Closed 25 December, Good Friday, and Monday-Friday lunch (November-April)
Rest – Carte € 32/38

♦ Thatched whitewashed inn - bigger inside than it looks from the outside - sparks nostalgia with classic adverts and tins of food. Honest hearty cooking comes in generous portions.

GARRYVOE (Garraí Uí Bhuaigh) – Cork – 712 H12 – pop. 560 — 39 C3
– ✉ Castlemartyr

Dublin 259 km – Cork 37 km – Waterford 100 km

Garryvoe

– (021) 464 67 18 – www.garryvoehotel.com – Fax (021) 464 68 24 – Closed 24-25 December
65 rm – € 85/120 € 170/190 – 1 suite
Rest – *(closed Monday and Tuesday in winter) (bar lunch Monday-Saturday)* Menu € 44 – Carte € 45/56

♦ Traditionally styled hotel adjacent to the beach with good sea views, to be enjoyed in characterful locals bar. A purpose-built, up-to-date wing features smart, modern rooms. Bright, colourful, contemporary restaurant.

GLASLOUGH (Glasloch) – Monaghan – 712 L5 – see Monaghan

GLASSAN (Glasán) – Westmeath – 712 I7 – see Athlone

GOLEEN – Cork – pop. 238 — 38 A3

Dublin 381 km – Cork 124 km – Tralee 143 km

The Heron's Cove

The Harbour – (028) 35 225 – www.heronscove.com – Fax (028) 35 422
– Closed Christmas-New Year
5 rm – € 70 € 90
Rest – *(by arrangement)* Menu € 30 – Carte € 32/47

♦ Hidden away in pretty location on the waterfront, with simple, comfortable bedrooms and harbour views. Open dining room has pleasant vista. Local seafood menu of flavourful, seasonal dishes.

GOREY (Guaire) – Wexford – 712 N9 – pop. 7 193 Ireland — 39 D2

Dublin 93 km – Waterford 88 km – Wexford 61 km
Main St (055) 942 1248, info@northwexford.com
Courtown Kiltennel, (055) 25 166
Ferns★, SW : 17.75 km by N 11

Marlfield House

Courtown Rd, Southeast : 1.5 km on R 742 – (053) 942 11 24
– www.marlfieldhouse.com – Fax (053) 942 15 72 – Closed January - February and restricted opening October-December
19 rm – € 120/145 € 255/275
Rest – *(dinner only and Sunday lunch) (booking essential for non-residents)* Menu € 67

♦ Luxuriously comfortable Regency mansion, with extensive gardens and woods. Utterly charming public areas with fine antiques and splendid fabrics. Thoughtfully furnished rooms. Very comfortable conservatory restaurant utilising produce from the garden.

Kin Khao

3 Main St – (053) 943 0677 – www.kinkhaothai.ie – Fax (053) 943 0676
– Closed 24-26 December and Monday
Rest – Thai – *(dinner only)* Menu € 26 – Carte € 29/32

♦ No-frills restaurant above shops serving elaborate, well presented cooking. Extensive menu, with some daily specials; cheery service and a good wine list. Choose a table at the front.

GRAIGUENAMANAGH (Gráig na Manach) – Kilkenny – 712 L10 39 D2 – pop. 1 376 Ireland

Dublin 125 km – Kilkenny 34 km – Waterford 42 km – Wexford 26 km

Duiske Abbey★★ **AC**

Jerpoint Abbey★★ **AC**, W : 15 km by R 703 and N 9 – Inistioge★, SW : 8 km by minor road – Kilfane Glen and Waterfall★ **AC**, SW : 17 km by R 703 and N 9

Waterside with rm

The Quay – (059) 972 42 46 – www.watersideguesthouse.com – Fax (059) 972 47 33 – Closed January, 24-26 December and Sunday-Thursday in winter

10 rm – € 65/69 € 98/110

Rest – *(dinner only and Sunday lunch)* Carte € 29/43 **s**

◆ Converted 19C cornstore on banks of river Barrow, at foot of Brandon Hill. Base for hill-walkers. Modern cooking with Mediterranean flourishes. Beamed rooms with river views.

GREYSTONES (Na Clocha Liatha) – Wicklow – 712 N8 – pop. 14 569 39 D1 Ireland

Dublin 35 km

Greystones, (01) 287 4136

Killruddery House and Gardens★ **AC**, N : 5 km by R 761 – Powerscourt★★ (Waterfall★★) **AC**, NW : 10 km by R 761, minor road, M 11 and minor road via Enniskerry. Wicklow Mountains★★

Chakra by Jaipur

Meridan Point Centre, First Floor, Church Rd – (01) 201 7222 – Fax (01) 201 7220 – Closed 25 December

Rest – Indian – *(dinner only and Sunday lunch)* Menu € 30 – Carte € 33/47

◆ Red and ochre restaurant overlooked by elephant god, Ganesh, on 1st floor of modern shopping centre. Vibrant Indian cooking represents all regions; a blend of old and new.

GWEEDORE (Gaoth Dobhair) – Donegal – 712 H2 37 C1

Dublin 278 km – Donegal 72 km – Letterkenny 43 km – Sligo 135 km

Gweedore Court

on N 56 – (074) 953 2900 – www.anchuirt-hotel.ie – Fax (074) 953 2929 – Closed 1 week Christmas

66 rm – € 79/200 € 170/220

Rest – *(bar lunch Monday-Saturday)* Menu € 25/35 – Carte € 28/38

◆ Rebuilt 19C house sharing grounds with a Gaelic craft centre. Spacious accommodation in classic patterns; east-facing rooms enjoy superb views of Glenreagh National Park. Classic menu matched by traditional surroundings and period-inspired décor.

HORSE AND JOCKEY (An Marcach) – Tipperary – 712 I10 39 C2

Dublin 146 km – Cashel 14 km – Thurles 9 km

Horse and Jockey rm,

– (0504) 44 192 – www.horseandjockeyhotel.com – Fax (0504) 44 747 – Closed 25 December

65 rm – € 95 € 180 – 1 suite **Rest** – Carte € 28/43 **s**

◆ Much extended hotel with stylish, state-of-the-art meeting rooms, superb spa and great gift shop. Bar full of horse racing pictures on walls. Spacious, contemporary bedrooms. Easy going dining room with traditional menus.

HOWTH (Binn Éadair) – Fingal – 712 N7 – pop. 8 186 – ✉ Dublin 39 D1 Ireland

Dublin 16 km

Deer Park Hotel Howth Castle, (01) 832 6039

The Cliffs★ (≤★)

Inisradharc without rest

Balkill Rd, North : 0.75 km – (01) 832 23 06 – closed 12 December-6 January

3 rm – € 70/80 € 80/90

◆ High above the pretty fishing village with views of the harbour and Eye Island. Conservatory breakfast room and spacious en suite bedrooms share a homely style.

XX **Aqua**

1 West Pier – ☎ (01) 832 0690 – www.aqua.ie – Fax (01) 832 0687 – Closed 25-26 December and Monday except Bank Holidays

Rest – Seafood – Menu €30 (lunch and early dinner) – Carte €44/75

◆ Glass sided, first floor restaurant in former yacht club, with super bay views. Intimate bar filled with local photos, whetting the appetite for accomplished dishes of fresh seafood.

XX **King Sitric** with rm

East Pier – ☎ (01) 832 5235 – www.kingsitric.ie – Fax (01) 839 2442 – Closed Christmas

8 rm – †€145 ††€205

Rest – Seafood – *(closed Tuesday, Monday in winter and Bank Holidays) (dinner only and Sunday lunch)* Menu €35 – Carte €35/61

◆ Established in 1971 and one of Ireland's original seafood restaurants. Enjoy locally caught produce in first floor dining room with bay views. Modern, comfy bedrooms.

INISHCRONE (Inis Crabhann) – Sligo – 712 E5 – pop. 829 Ireland 36 B2

Dublin 257 km – Ballina 13 km – Galway 127 km – Sligo 55 km

Rosserk Abbey★, W : 16 km by R 297, N 59 and R 314 – Moyne Abbey★, W : 19 km by R 297, N 59 and R 314. Killala★, W : 21 km by R 297, N 59 and R 314

Ceol na Mara without rest

Main St – ☎ (096) 36 351 – www.ceol-na-mara.com – Closed 20-27 December and restricted opening in winter

9 rm – †€50 ††€80

◆ At the centre of town, a sizeable guest house kept spotless by the friendly longstanding owners. Simply appointed bedrooms are all en suite, with sea views to the rear.

INISHMAAN (Inis Meáin) – Galway – 712 D8 – see Aran Islands

INISHMORE (Árainn) – Galway – 712 C/D8 – see Aran Islands

INISTIOGE (Inis Tíog) – Kilkenny – 712 K10 – pop. 263 39 C2

Dublin 82 km – Kilkenny 16 km – Waterford 19 km – Wexford 33 km

X **Bassetts at Woodstock**

Woodstock Gardens, Northwest : 3 km – ☎ (056) 775 8820 – www.bassetts.ie – Closed 3 weeks January, Monday, Tuesday and Sunday dinner

Rest – Menu €29 (dinner) – Carte €24/45

◆ Personally run restaurant at entrance to Woodstock gardens. Homely inner with delightful terrace. Food is ethical, seasonal and traceable, and the owner rears his own pigs.

JENKINSTOWN (Baile Sheinicín) – Louth – see Dundalk

KANTURK (Ceann Toirc) – Cork – 712 F11 – pop. 1 915 Ireland 38 B2

Dublin 259 km – Cork 53 km – Killarney 50 km – Limerick 71 km

Fairy Hill, ☎ (029) 50 534

Town★ - Castle★

Glenlohane without rest

East : 4 km by R 576 and Charlville rd on Cecilstown rd – ☎ (029) 50 014 – www.glenlohane.com

3 rm – †€75 ††€150

◆ In the family for over 250 years, a Georgian country house at the centre of wooded parkland and a working farm. Library and cosy, en suite rooms overlooking the fields.

KEEL = An Caol – Mayo – 712 B5/6 – see Achill Island

REPUBLIC OF IRELAND

KENMARE (Neidín) – **Kerry** – **712** D12 – **pop. 1 701** Ireland **38** A3

Dublin 338 km – Cork 93 km – Killarney 32 km

Heritage Centre ✆ (064) 664 1233 (April-October), kenmaretio@failteireland.ie AY

Kenmare, ✆ (064) 41 291

Town★

Ring of Kerry★★ - Healy Pass★★ (≤★★), SW : 30.5 km by R 571 and R 574 AY – Mountain Road to Glengarriff (≤★★) S : by N 71 AY - Slieve Miskish Mountains (≤★★), SW : 48.25 km by R 571 AY – Gougane Barra Forest Park★★, SE : 16 km AY - Lauragh (Derreen Gardens★ **AC**), SW : 23.5 km by R 571 AY – Allihies (Copper Mines★), SW : 57 km by R 571 and R 575 AY – Garnish Island (≤★), SW : 68.5 km by R 571, R 575 and R 572 AY

Park

– ✆ *(064) 664 12 00 – www.parkkenmare.com – Fax (064) 664 14 02*

– May-26 October, Christmas and New Year BY**k**

46 rm – € 220/364 € 290/364 **Rest** – *(dinner only)* Menu € 68

◆ Privately run country house boasts many paintings and antiques. Superb spa facilities. Inviting, classically tasteful rooms; many offer superb views of Kenmare Bay and hills. Grand, bay-windowed dining room; local produce to fore.

Sheen Falls Lodge

Southeast : 2 km by N 71 – ✆ (064) 664 16 00

– www.sheenfallslodge.ie – Fax (064) 664 13 86

– Closed 2 January-5 February

57 rm – € 310/455 € 310/455, € 24 – 9 suites – € 465/1870

Rest *La Cascade* – *(dinner only)* Carte € 61/86

◆ Modern, purpose-built hotel in idyllic location, with superb views of the famous falls. Spacious bedrooms have everything you could want. Extensive spa, gym and stables. Floodlit river views at La Cascade. Attentive, formal service.

KENMARE

Back Lane . . . . BY 2
Cromwell's Bridge . . . . . . AY
Davitt's Place. . . . . AY
Downing's Row . . . . BY 5
East Park St. . . . . AY 7
Finnihy Bridge . . . . AY
Henry St . . . . AY
Henry's Lane . . . . ABY 8
Killarney Rd . . . . AY
Main St . . . . BY
Market St . . . . AY
New St . . . . AY
Old Bridge St. . . . . AY 12
Railway Rd . . . . BY
Rock St . . . . BY 14
Shelborne St. . . . . BY
The Square . . . . AY

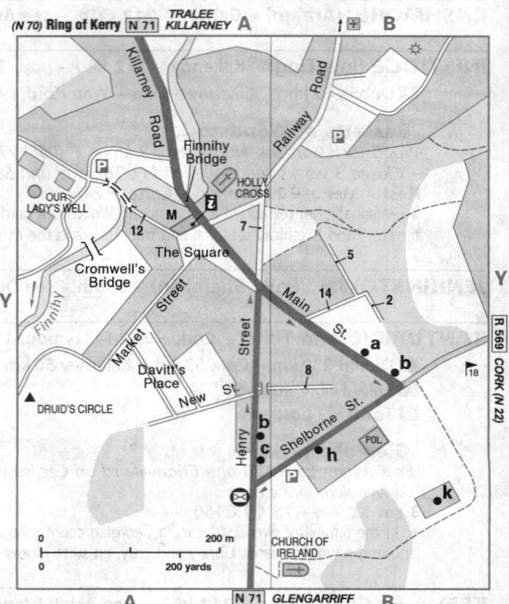

REPUBLIC OF IRELAND

Brook Lane

Gortamullen, North : 1 km by N 71 on N 70 – ☎ (064) 664 2077 – www.brooklanehotel.com – Fax (064) 664 0869 – Closed 24-26 December
20 rm – € 75/110 € 120/190
Rest ***Casey's Bistro*** – Carte € 20/33
◆ Homely charms with a contemporary, designer edge, within easy walking distance of the town centre. The main strength here are the airy bedrooms, which are delightfully comfy with a host of extras. Spacious, formal dining room; menu offers something for everyone.

Shelburne Lodge without rest

East : 0.75 km on R 569 (Cork Rd) – ☎ (064) 664 10 13 – www.shelburnelodge.com – Fax (064) 664 21 35 – mid-March - mid-November
9 rm – € 75/120 € 100/170
◆ Georgian farmhouse with pleasant lawns and herb garden. Antiques stylishly combined with contemporary colours and modern art. Firelit lounge and cosy rooms. Affable hosts.

Sallyport House without rest

South : 0.5 km on N 71 – ☎ (064) 664 20 66 – www.sallyporthouse.com – Fax (064) 664 20 67 – April-October
5 rm – € 80/100 € 100/150
◆ 1930s house in garden and orchard. Wood floored hall, full of books and local information, leads to pristine, antique furnished bedrooms and a pretty front sitting room.

The Lime Tree

Shelbourne St – ☎ (064) 664 12 25 – www.limetreerestaurant.com – Fax (064) 664 18 39 – weekends only in winter BY**h**
Rest – *(dinner only)* Carte € 32/45
◆ Tasty, unelaborate modern Irish cooking in a 19C former schoolhouse: stone walls, modern art on walls and in first-floor gallery. Busy, affordable and unfailingly friendly.

Mulcahys

36 Henry St – ☎ (064) 42 383 – Fax (064) 42 383 – Closed 24-26 December
Rest – *(dinner only)* Carte € 34/49 AY**c**
◆ Stylish wine racks, high-backed chairs, polished tables and friendly, attentive service set the tone here. Modern dishes appeal to the eye and palate alike.

D'Arcy's

Main St – ☎ (064) 664 15 89 – weekends only in winter BY**b**
Rest – *(dinner only) (booking essential)* Menu € 29 **s** – Carte € 32/42 **s**
◆ Restaurant set in striking, green-painted former bank. Pop in for oysters or fresh Kerry seafood at oyster bar or modern Irish menu in restaurant, with open fire and candles.

Leath Phingin Eile

35 Main St – ☎ (064) 664 15 59 – www.leathphingineile.com – Fax (064) 664 08 69 – Closed 24-26 December and Tuesday in winter BY**a**
Rest – *(dinner only and lunch in summer) (booking essential)* Menu € 25 – Carte € 25/43
◆ Simply styled restaurant set over two floors serving classical dishes which follow the seasons. Excellent breads and tapenade. Popular with locals, its name means 'halfpenny'.

Packies

Henry St – ☎ (064) 664 15 08 – www.kenmarerestaurants.com – Closed February and Monday AY**b**
Rest – *(dinner only) (booking essential)* Carte € 25/49
◆ Locally popular, personally run little place with understated rustic feel. Handwritten menu of fresh, modern Irish dishes prepared with care and super local seafood. Friendly staff.

KILBRITTAIN (Cill Briotáin) – Cork – 712 F12 – pop. 185 — 38 B3

Dublin 289 km – Cork 38 km – Killarney 96 km

The Glen without rest

Southwest : 6.5 km by un-marked rd off R 600 – ☎ (023) 884 98 62 – www.glencountryhouse.com – Fax (023) 884 98 62 – Easter-October
5 rm – € 65/75 € 120/130
◆ 130 year-old family house, part of working farm close to beach. Delicious organic farmhouse breakfasts. Lovingly restored bedrooms elegantly furnished to a high standard.

REPUBLIC OF IRELAND

XX **Casino House**

Coolmain Bay, Southeast : 3.5 km by unmarked rd on R 600 – (023) 88 49 944 – www.casinohouse.ie – Fax (023) 88 49 945 – Closed January-17 March, Wednesday and mid-week November and December

Rest – *(dinner only and Sunday lunch)* Carte € 34/52 **s**

◆ A stylish and contemporary makeover has given this spacious former farmhouse a bright new look and a cool extension. The cooking has an Italian base, using local produce and the restaurant has a relaxing feel.

KILCOLGAN (Cill Cholgáin) – **Galway** – **712** F8 – ✉ **Oranmore** **36** B3

Dublin 220 km – Galway 17 km

Moran's Oyster Cottage

The Weir, Northwest : 2 km by N 18 – (091) 796 113 – www.moransoystercottage.com – Fax (091) 796 150 – Closed 24-26 December and Good Friday

Rest – Seafood – Carte € 25/40

◆ Likeable thatched pub in sleepy village. Settle down in one of the beamed snugs and parlours to enjoy prime local seafood - simple and fresh - or soups, salads and sandwiches.

Good food at moderate prices? Look for the Bib Gourmand.

KILKEE (Cill Chaoi) – **Clare** – **712** D9 – **pop. 1 325** Ireland **38** A-B2

Dublin 285 km – Galway 124 km – Limerick 93 km

The Square (065) 9056112 (June-early September), tourisminfo@shannondevelopments.ie

Kilkee East End, (065) 905 60 48

Kilrush★ (Scattery Island★ by boat), SE : 16 mi. by N 67 – SW : Loop Head Peninsula (Bridge of Ross★)

Stella Maris

– (065) 905 64 55 – www.stellamarishotel.com – Fax (065) 906 00 06 – Closed 25 December

20 rm – † € 65/120 †† € 100/140

Rest – Carte € 20/45

◆ Family-run hotel in centre of bustling seaside town, whose refurbished bedrooms offer a surprising amount of space. Terrace, with view of bay, is popular spot from which to people-watch. Enjoy traditional fare in the atmospheric bar or on the veranda.

Halpin's Townhouse

Erin St – (065) 905 60 32 – www.halpinsprivatehotels.com – Fax (065) 905 63 17 – March-October

12 rm – † € 129/139 †† € 169/179

Rest – *(bar lunch Monday-Saturday)* Menu € 26 – Carte € 22/37

◆ Attractive terraced house offering good value accommodation and a warm welcome. Pub-style bar in the basement and uniform bedrooms with fitted furniture. Traditionally appointed ground floor restaurant.

KILKENNY (Cill Chainnigh) – **Kilkenny** – **712** K10 – **pop. 22 179** **39** C2
Ireland

Dublin 114 km – Cork 138 km – Killarney 185 km – Limerick 111 km

Shee Alms House (056) 7751500, kevin.dowling@failteireland.ie

Glendine, (056) 776 5400

Callan Geraldine, (056) 772 5136

Castlecomer Drumgoole, (056) 444 1139

Town★★ – St Canice's Cathedral★★ – Kilkenny Castle and Park★★ **AC** – Black Abbey★ – Rothe House★

Jerpoint Abbey★★ **AC**, S : 19.25 km by R 700 and N 9 – Kilfane Glen and Waterfall★ **AC**, S : 21 km by R 700 and N 9 – Kells Priory★, S : 12.5 km by R 697 – Dunmore Cave★ **AC**, N: 11.25 km by N 77 and N 78

Kilkenny rm, rest,

College Rd, Southwest : 1.25 km at junction with N 76 – ✆ (056) 776 20 00 – www.hotelkilkenny.ie – Fax (056) 776 59 84

138 rm – € 110/190 € 175/270

Rest *Taste* – *(closed Monday-Thursday lunch)* Menu € 38 (dinner) – Carte € 25/49

◆ Unremarkable exterior contrasts with the thoughtfully designed and contemporary interior. Bedrooms are brightly decorated. Well-equipped leisure centre and large meeting rooms available. Italian menu served in split level dining room.

Butler House without rest

15-16 Patrick St – ✆ (056) 776 57 07 – www.butler.ie – Fax (056) 776 56 26 – Closed 23-30 December

12 rm – € 80/155 € 120/200 – 1 suite

◆ Substantial part Georgian house. Spacious accommodation with 1970s-style furnishings - superior bow-fronted bedrooms to the rear overlook neat, geometric lawned gardens.

Blanchville House

Dunbell, Maddoxtown, Southeast : 10.5 km by N 10 turning right 0.75 km after the Pike Inn – ✆ (056) 772 71 97 – www.blanchville.ie – Fax (056) 772 76 36 – March-October

6 rm – € 70 € 130 **Rest** – *(by arrangement)* Menu € 50

◆ Antique-furnished former manor house with Peel Tower in garden and large, firelit drawing room. Spacious bedrooms, with homemade tea and cakes on arrival. Dinner available on request, or transport offered to restaurants in Kilkenny.

Fanad House without rest

Castle Rd, South : 0.75 km on R 700 – ✆ (056) 776 41 26 – www.fanadhouse.com – Fax (056) 775 60 01

8 rm – € 50/70 € 80/120

◆ Modern, purpose-built, green painted house looking out towards the castle. A warm welcome and bright, well-appointed bedrooms await the visitor.

Campagne

5 The Arches – ✆ (056) 777 2858 – www.campagne.ie – Fax (056) 777 2875 – Closed 1 week Christmas, 10 days January, 10 days October, Monday and Tuesday

Rest – *(dinner only and lunch Friday and Sunday) (booking advisable)* Menu € 28 **s** – Carte € 35/48 **s**

◆ Hidden close to the railway arches, away from the city centre. Crescent shaped dining room with bright contemporary art. Modern French and Irish cooking; tasty, unfussy dishes.

Zuni with rm

26 Patrick St – ✆ (056) 772 39 99 – www.zuni.ie – Fax (056) 775 64 00 – Closed 23-27 December

13 rm – € 65/75 € 100/130 **Rest** – Carte € 33/40

◆ Chic modern design in leather and dark wood draws the smart set to this former theatre. Friendly service; bold, generous and eclectic cooking. Stylish, good-value rooms.

Ristorante Rinuccini

1 The Parade – ✆ (056) 776 15 75 – www.rinuccini.com – Fax (056) 775 12 88 – Closed 25-26 December

Rest – Italian – Menu € 28 (early dinner) – Carte € 32/51

◆ This family owned restaurant is bigger than it looks and has long been a local favourite. They come for the classic Italian cooking and thoughtful service. It's named after the 17C papal nuncio.

KILLALOE (Cill Dalua) – **Clare** – **712** G9 – **pop. 1 035** Ireland **38** B2

Dublin 175 km – Ennis 51 km – Limerick 21 km – Tullamore 93 km

The Bridge ✆ (061) 376866, (May- Sept) tourisminfo@shannon-dev.ie

Town★ – St Flannan's Cathedral★

Graves of the Leinstermen (★), N : 7.25 km by R 494 – Castleconnell★, S : 16 km by R 494 and R 466 – Clare Glens★, S : 24 km by R 494, R 504 and R 503. Nenagh (Castle★), NE : 19.25 km by R 496 and N 7 – Holy Island★ **AC**, N : 25.75 km by R 463 and boat from Tuamgraney

XX **Cherry Tree**

Lakeside, Ballina, following signs for Lakeside H. – ✆ (061) 375 688 – www.cherrytreerestaurant.ie – Fax (061) 375 689 – Closed last week January, first week February, 25-26 December, Tuesday in winter, Sunday and Monday

Rest – *(dinner only and Sunday lunch)* Menu € 39 – Carte € 34/49

◆ Contemporary, relaxing interior, polite staff and a wide range of original, well-sourced modern Irish dishes on offer from an open kitchen. Seasonal produce of the essence.

Enjoy good food without spending a fortune! Look out for the Bib Gourmand symbol to find restaurants offering fine cuisine at special prices !

KILLARNEY (Cill Airne) – **Kerry** – **712** D11 – **pop. 14 603** Ireland **38** A2

- Dublin 304 km – Cork 87 km – Limerick 111 km – Waterford 180 km
- Kerry (Farranfore) Airport : ✆ (066) 976 4644, N : 15.25 km by N 22
- Beech Rd ✆ (064) 663 1633, killarneytio@failteireland.ie
- Mahoney's Point, ✆ (064) 31 034
- Town★★ – St Mary's Cathedral★ CX
- Killarney National Park★★★ (Muckross Friary★, Muckross House and Farms★) AZ - Gap of Dunloe★★, SW : 9.5 km by R 562 AZ – Ross Castle★ **AC**, S : 1.5 km by N 71 and minor rd – Torc Waterfall★, S : 8 km by N 71 BZ. Ring of Kerry★★ – Ladies View★★, SW : 19.25 km by N 71 BZ – Moll's Gap★, SW : 25 km by N 71 BZ

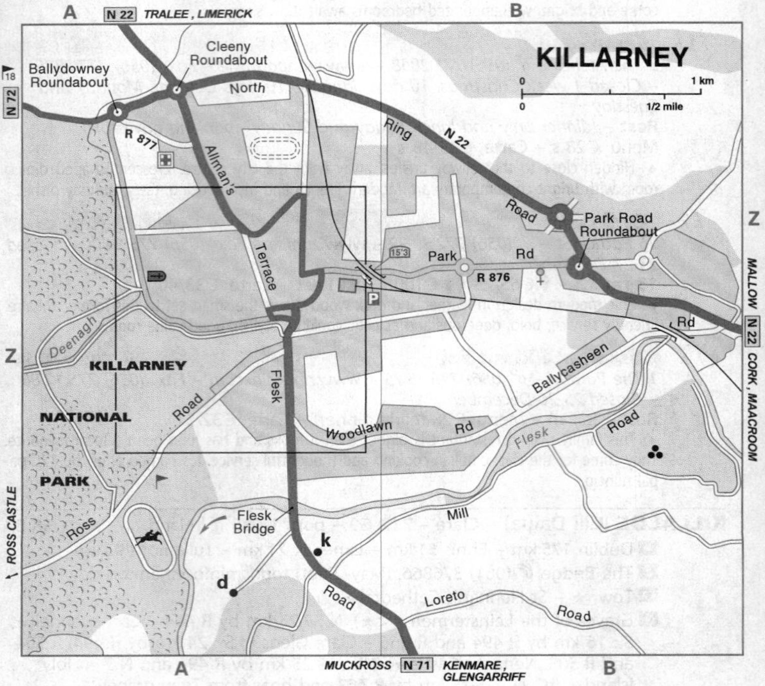

A
N 22 TRALEE , LIMERICK
B
KILLARNEY
0
1 km
0
1/2 mile
Cleeny Roundabout
Ballydowney Roundabout
North
Ring
N 22
Road
R 877
Allman's
Terrace
Park Road Roundabout
Park
Rd
R 876
P
Z
MALLOW
N 22
CORK, MAACROOM
Rd
Deenagh
KILLARNEY
NATIONAL
PARK
Road
Flesk
Ballycasheen
Woodlawn
Rd
Flesk
Road
Ross
Flesk Bridge
Mill
k
d
Road
Loreto
Road
ROSS CASTLE
N 72
A
MUCKROSS N 71 KENMARE , GLENGARRIFF
B

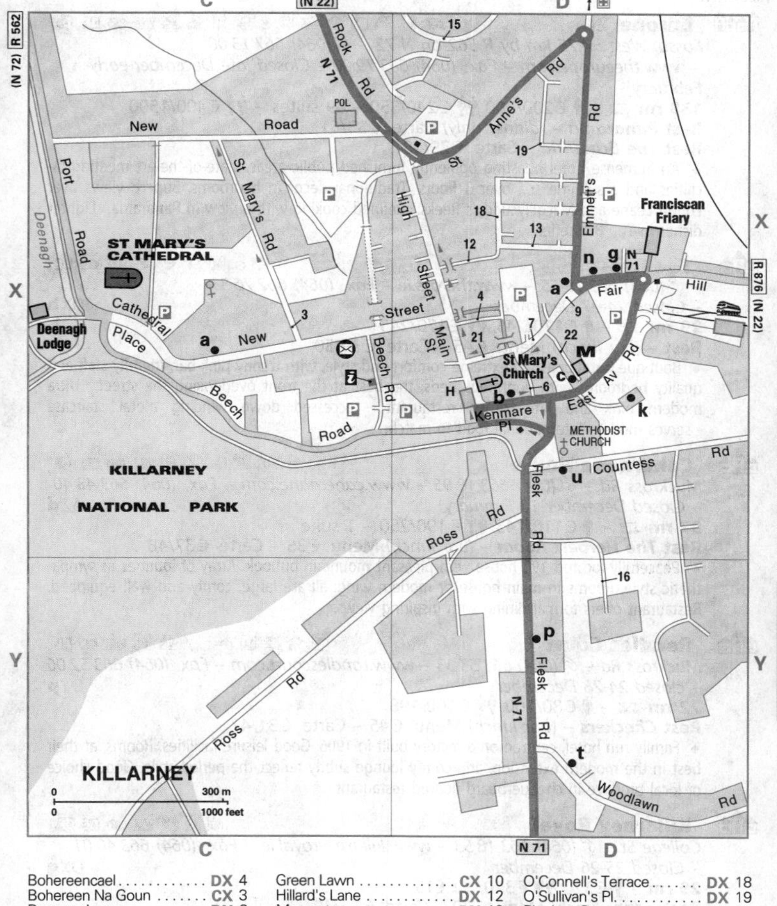

Bohereencael . . . . **DX** 4	Green Lawn . . . . **CX** 10	O'Connell's Terrace . . . . . . **DX** 18
Bohereen Na Goun . . . . . . **CX** 3	Hillard's Lane . . . . **DX** 12	O'Sullivan's Pl. . . . . **DX** 19
Brewery Lane. . . . . **DX** 6	Mangerton . . . . **DX** 13	Plunkett St . . . . **DX** 21
College Square . . . . **DX** 7	Marian Terrace . . . . **DX** 15	St Anthony's Pl. . . . . **DX** 22
College St. . . . . **DX** 9	Muckross Drive . . . . **DXY** 16	

Killarney Park

– ✆ (064) 663 55 55 – www.killarneyparkhotel.ie – Fax (064) 663 52 66 – Closed 24-26 December DX**k**

65 rm – 🛉 € 275/400 🛉🛉 € 275/400 – 3 suites

Rest *Park* – *(bar lunch)* Menu € 55 – Carte € 43/56

◆ Smart modern hotel. Firelit library, panelled billiard room and the bedrooms' décor and fine details balance old-world styling and contemporary convenience. Armchair dining beneath sparkling chandeliers and Corinthian capitals.

Aghadoe Heights H. and Spa

Northwest : 4.5 km by N 22 – ✆ (064) 663 17 66 – www.aghadoeheights.com – Fax (064) 663 13 45 – restricted opening in winter

72 rm – 🛉 € 160/250 🛉🛉 € 250/350 – 2 suites

Rest *Lake Room* – see restaurant listing

◆ Striking glass-fronted hotel: stylish bar, modern health and fitness centre and contemporary rooms, many with sumptuous sofas. Balconied front rooms offer views of the lough.

Europe

Fossa, West : 4.75 km by R 562 on N 72 – (064) 667 13 00 – www.theeurope.com – Fax (064) 663 79 00 – Closed late December-early February

138 rm – € 200/300 € 240/350 – 49 suites – € 400/1500

Rest *Panorama* – *(dinner only)* Carte € 33/61

Rest *The Brasserie* – Carte € 29/48

◆ An immense hotel boasting opulently furnished public areas, state-of-the-art meeting facilities and a sublime spa over 3 floors. Traditional décor in bedrooms. Superb views over Lough Leane and Macgillycuddy's Reeks. Refined cooking with a view in Panorama. Lighter dishes in The Brasserie.

The Ross

– (064) 663 18 55 – www.theross.ie – Fax (064) 662 76 33 – Closed 24-27 December DX**b**

29 rm – € 170/245 € 170/245

Rest – *(bar lunch)* Menu € 45 – Carte € 39/50

◆ Boutique hotel boasting extreme comfort and style, with trendy pink bar, friendly staff and quality bedrooms with enormous beds; the best at the front overlooking the street. Ultra modern pink and lime green restaurant - accessed down winding metal staircase - serves modern international food to match.

Cahernane House

Muckross Rd – (064) 663 18 95 – www.cahernane.com – Fax (064) 663 43 40 – Closed December-13 February AZ**d**

37 rm – € 110/145 € 190/250 – 1 suite

Rest *The Herbert Room* – *(bar lunch)* Menu € 35 – Carte € 37/48

◆ Peacefully located 19C house with pleasant mountain outlook. Array of lounges in sympathetic style. Rooms in main house or modern wing: all are large, comfy and well equipped. Restaurant offers formal dining with inspiring views.

Randles Court

rest,

Muckross Rd – (064) 663 53 33 – www.randlescourt.com – Fax (064) 663 52 06 – closed 24-28 December DY**p**

72 rm – € 80/160 € 100/198

Rest *Checkers* – *(bar lunch)* Menu € 45 – Carte € 31/47

◆ Family run hotel, centred on a rectory built in 1906. Good leisure facilities. Rooms, at their best in the modern extension, and comfy lounge subtly reflect the period style. Good choice of local produce in chequerboard floored restaurant.

Killarney Royal

College St – (064) 663 18 53 – www.killarneyroyal.ie – Fax (064) 663 40 01 – Closed 25-26 December DX**g**

29 rm – € 320 € 320, €15

Rest – *(bar lunch)* Menu € 30 – Carte € 25/40

◆ Smart yet cosy lounge with an open fire, spacious, individually decorated rooms and a traditional bar in a town house hotel, built at the turn of the 20th century. Classic, candlelit dining room with flowing white linen.

Fairview

rest,

College St – (064) 663 41 64 – www.fairviewkillarney.com – Fax (064) 667 17 77 – Closed 24-25 December DX**a**

29 rm – € 49/110 € 70/170

Rest – *(closed Monday and Tuesday) (dinner only)* Carte € 25/35 **s**

◆ Stylish townhouse with smart, leather furnished lounge. Bright, up-to-date bedrooms exude distinctively individualistic flourishes; penthouse has whirlpool bath and roof terrace. Modern restaurant serves traditional menu of local meat and fish.

Killarney Lodge without rest

Countess Rd – (064) 663 64 99 – www.killarneylodge.net – Fax (064) 663 10 70 – March-October DX**u**

16 rm – € 70/100 € 100/140

◆ Run by a likeable couple, a purpose-built hotel offering comfortable, thoughtfully furnished rooms. Within easy walking distance of the town centre.

Earls Court House without rest
Woodlawn Junction, Muckross Rd – ✆ (064) 66 34 009 – www.killarney-earlscourt.ie – Fax (064) 66 34 366 – March-14 November
30 rm – € 100/120 € 120/140 DY**t**
◆ Behind an unassuming façade, reproduction furniture combines well with modern facilities in spotlessly kept rooms. Tasty breakfasts served at antique dining tables.

Kathleens Country House without rest
Madams Height, Tralee Rd, North : 3.25 km on N 22 – ✆ (064) 663 28 10 – www.kathleens.net – Fax (064) 663 23 40 – May-September
17 rm – € 50/90 € 75/140
◆ Cosy lounge with broad, pine-backed armchairs facing an open fire and neat bedrooms in traditional patterns - an extended house run by the eponymous owner for over 20 years.

Lake Room – Aghadoe Heights H. and Spa
Northwest : 4.5 km by N 22 – ✆ (064) 663 17 66 – www.aghadoeheights.com – Fax (064) 663 13 45 – restricted opening in winter
Rest – *(bar lunch Monday-Saturday)* Menu € 46 – Carte € 34/58
◆ Luxurious dining room with commanding countryside views. Classic, technically skilled cooking make good use of seasonal, regional ingredients. Effective, professional service.

Chapter Forty
40 New St – ✆ (064) 66 71 833 – www.chapter40.ie CX**a**
Rest – *(dinner only)* Menu € 35 – Carte € 35/49
◆ Refurbished restaurant in contemporary browns and creams with small bar area and window looking into kitchen. Large menu includes some eclectic combinations. Great soda bread.

Cucina Italiana
17 St Anthonys Place – ✆ (064) 662 65 75 – Fax (064) 662 65 76 DX**c**
Rest – Italian – *(dinner only)* Carte € 34/55
◆ Stylish, modern restaurant set over three floors, in centre of town. Fresh, authentic Italian cooking; hearty, with a strong Neapolitan feel. Effective service from smart Italian staff.

Don't confuse the couvert rating with the stars! Couverts defines comfort and service, while stars are awarded for the best cuisine across all categories of comfort.

at Beaufort **West : 9.75 km by R 562 - AZ - off N 72 – ✉ Killarney**

Dunloe Castle
Southeast : 1.5 km on Dunloe Golf Course rd – ✆ (064) 664 41 11 – www.thedunloe.com – Fax (064) 664 45 83 – April-October
100 rm – € 170/250 € 210/290 – 2 suites
Rest – *(light lunch)* Carte € 26/61 **s**
◆ Creeper-clad modern hotel offers sizeable, well-equipped rooms and smart conference suites, not forgetting an impressive view of the Gap of Dunloe and Macgilllicuddy's Reeks. Restaurant serves Irish classic dishes.

KILLENARD – Laois 39 C-D1

Dublin 48 km – Portlaoise 19 km – Naas 25 km – Carlow 36 km

The Heritage
– ✆ (057) 864 55 00 – www.theheritage.com – Fax (057) 864 23 50 – Closed 21-27 December
94 rm – € 120/230 € 200/245 – 25 suites
Rest *The Arlington* – *(closed Wednesday and Sunday) (dinner only)* Menu € 40 – Carte € 45/58
Rest *Greens* – Carte € 46/53
Rest *Sol Oriens* – *(dinner only)* Carte € 27/37 **s**
◆ Stunning hotel surrounded by extensive gardens and golf course. State-of-the-art meeting facilities and superb spa. Capacious, elegant bedrooms offer supreme comforts. Formal dining in The Arlington. More of a brasserie feel to Greens, in the leisure centre. Pizza, pasta, salad and steaks in informal Sol Oriens.

REPUBLIC OF IRELAND

KILLORGLIN (Cill Orglan) – Kerry – 712 C11 – pop. 1 627 Ireland 38 A2

Dublin 333 km – Killarney 19 km – Tralee 26 km

Killorglin Stealroe, ✆ (669) 761 979

Lough Caragh★, SW : 9 km by N 70 and minor road S. Ring of Kerry★★

Grove Lodge without rest

Killarney Rd, East : 0.75 km on N 72 – ✆ (066) 976 11 57 – www.grovelodge.com – Fax (066) 976 27 26 – Closed 23-30 December

10 rm – € 45/60 € 75/90

◆ Comfortable, well-fitted rooms - one with four-poster bed and private patio - in a smoothly run riverside house. Try smoked salmon and eggs or a full Irish breakfast.

KILMALLOCK (Cill Mocheallóg) – Limerick – 712 G10 – pop. 1 443 38 B2

Ireland

Dublin 212 km – Limerick 34 km – Tipperary 32 km

Abbey★ - Collegiate Church★

Lough Gur Interpretive Centre★ AC, N : 16 km by R 512 and minor road – Monasteranenagh Abbey★, N : 24 km by R 512 to Holycross and minor road W

Flemingstown House

Southeast : 4 km on R 512 – ✆ (063) 98 093 – www.flemingstown.com – Fax (063) 98 546 – March-October

5 rm – € 70 € 120 **Rest** – *(by arrangement)* Menu € 45

◆ Creeper clad, extended 19C house in centre of 200 acre working farm. The attractively decorated bedrooms boast countryside vistas and pieces of antique furniture. Satisfying homemade fare served in comfy dining room.

KILMESSAN (Cill Mheasáin) – Meath – 712 L/M7 – pop. 341 37 D3

Dublin 38 km – Navan 16 km – Trim 11 km

The Station House

– ✆ (046) 902 52 39 – www.thestationhousehotel.com – Fax (046) 902 55 88

20 rm – € 59/99 € 69/190 **Rest** – Menu € 20/25 – Carte € 22/50

◆ Former 19C railway station. Bedrooms spread around between station house and converted engine shed! The Signal Suite, the original signal box, now offers four poster comforts. Appealing restaurant using local ingredients.

KINLOUGH (Cionn Locha) – Leitrim – 712 H4 – pop. 690 37 C2

Dublin 220 km – Ballyshannon 11 km – Sligo 34 km

Courthouse with rm

Main St – ✆ (071) 984 23 91 – www.thecourthouserest.com – Fax (071) 984 28 24 – Closed Christmas and Monday-Wednesday in winter

4 rm – € 37/45 € 74/80

Rest – Italian influences – *(dinner only and Sunday lunch)* Menu € 28 (early dinner) **s** – Carte € 35/45 **s**

◆ Simple, unassuming, pink-painted former courthouse has terracotta palette and wall-mounted gargoyles. Prominent Italian menus include home-made breads, pasta, desserts.

KINNEGAD (Cionn Átha Gad) – Westmeath – 712 K7 – pop. 2 245 37 C3

Dublin 61 km – Mullingar 20 km – Tullamore 41 km

Hilamar rm, rest,

Main St – ✆ (044) 939 17 19 – www.hilamarhotel.com – Fax (044) 939 17 18 – Closed 25 December

45 rm – € 65/99 € 99/160

Rest – *(carvery lunch Sunday)* Carte € 28/46

◆ Trendy hotel with relaxed feel. Stylish bedrooms decorated in bright, modern colours, with quality furniture and up-to-date facilities. Flat screens in bar. Pavement terrace. Modern restaurant.

KINSALE (Cionne tSáile) – Cork – 712 G12 – pop. 4 099 Ireland

Dublin 286 km – Cork 27 km

Pier Rd ✆ (021) 4772234, kinsaletio@eircom.net

Town★★ – St Multose Church★ Y – Kinsale Regional Museum★ AC Y M1

Kinsale Harbour★ (≤★ from St Catherine's Anglican Church, Charles Fort★). Carbery Coast★, W : 61 km by R 600

Perryville House without rest

Long Quay – ✆ (021) 477 27 31
– www.perryvillehouse.com
– Fax (021) 477 22 98
– April-October

18 rm – † € 120 †† € 250

◆ Delightful Georgian house on the shores of the bay. Antiques, open fires and period charm throughout; lovely sitting room. Bedrooms are spacious and stylish. Service is keen and friendly.

Yf

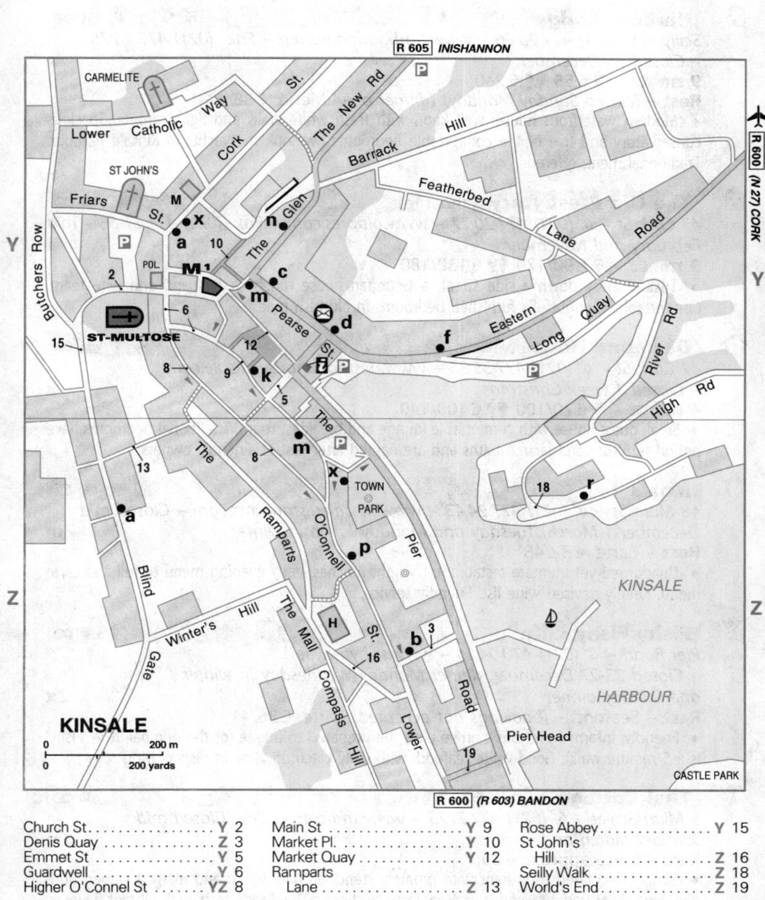

Church St	Y 2	Main St	Y 9	Rose Abbey	Y 15
Denis Quay	Z 3	Market Pl.	Y 10	St John's Hill	Z 16
Emmet St	Y 5	Market Quay	Y 12	Seilly Walk	Z 18
Guardwell	Y 6	Ramparts Lane	Z 13	World's End	Z 19
Higher O'Connel St	YZ 8				

Blue Haven
rest,

3 Pearse St – ✆ (021) 477 22 09 – www.bluehavencollection.com – Fax (021) 477 42 68 – Closed 24-25 December Y**c**

17 rm – € 65/100 € 80/195

Rest *Blu* – *(dinner only)* Menu € 25 – Carte € 28/48

Rest *Blue Haven* – Carte € 19/33

◆ Well established hotel in centre of town boasts refurbished public areas and floral bedrooms of varying size, named after wine estates; the largest at the front. Blu serves a traditional British menu. Wood panelled Blue Haven looks like the interior of a yacht, and has small terrace.

Old Bank House without rest

11 Pearse St – ✆ (021) 477 40 75 – www.oldbankhousekinsale.com – Fax (021) 477 42 96 – Closed 25 December Y**d**

18 rm – € 110/160 € 200/230

◆ Personally and enthusiastically run town house: cosy lounge and comfortable, neatly kept accommodation - bedrooms above the post office are slightly larger.

Harbour Lodge

Scilly – ✆ (021) 477 23 76 – www.harbourlodge.com – Fax (021) 477 26 75 – Closed 25 December Z**r**

9 rm – € 55 € 240

Rest – *(closed Sunday-Monday) (dinner only)* Menu € 38

◆ Modern waterfront house; well kept, with fresh white walls and light carpets. Spacious conservatory and five of the comfortable bedrooms overlook the yachts in Kinsale harbour. Traditional menu offered.

The Old Presbytery without rest

43 Cork St – ✆ (021) 477 20 27 – www.oldpres.com – Fax (021) 477 21 66 – mid February-mid November Y**a**

9 rm – € 90/170 € 130/180

◆ Tucked away down a side street, a Georgian house run by a husband and wife team. Comfortable, thoughtfully furnished bedrooms in old Irish pine.

Desmond House without rest

42 Cork St – ✆ (021) 477 35 35 – www.desmondhousekinsale.com – Closed 1 week Christmas Y**x**

4 rm – € 70/100 € 100/140

◆ Small guest house with comfortable lounge and breakfast room. Traditional bedrooms have period furniture and jacuzzi baths and are named after castles. Friendly owners.

Max's

48 Main St – ✆ (021) 477 24 43 – www.kinsalerestaurants.com – Closed mid December-1 March, Tuesday and Monday lunch in winter Z**m**

Rest – Carte € 32/48

◆ Unadorned yet intimate restaurant: try light lunches, early evening menu or full à la carte menu. Keenly devised wine list. Friendly service.

Fishy Fishy Cafe

Pier Road – ✆ (021) 470 04 15 – www.fishyfishy.ie – Closed 23-27 December, dinner Monday-Wednesday in winter and Sunday dinner Z**x**

Rest – Seafood – *(bookings not accepted)* Carte € 36/41

◆ Friendly, informal and busy: arrive early, be prepared to queue (or the original little 'Fishy' is a 5 minute walk). Good-value seafood, with daily catch on view in display fridges.

Thai Cottage

6 Mian Street – ✆ (021) 477 7775 – www.thaicottage.ie – Closed mid January-March and Tuesday Y**m**

Rest – Carte approx. € 30

◆ Simply decorated restaurant with ornately stencilled dark wood and many a carved Buddha. Smartly attired, graceful staff. Very tasty, authentic Thai food; fresh, with vibrant flavours.

Bulman

East : 2 km by R 600 – ✆ (021) 477 21 31 – www.toddies.com – closed Sunday dinner and Monday

Rest – Carte € 19/29 **s**

◆ Rustic pub with open fire, nautical theme and view of Kinsale and bay. Daily changing menu focuses on local seafood; lunch in bar, dinner in more formal first floor restaurant.

at Barrells Cross **Southwest : 5.75 km on R 600 - Z – ✉ Kinsale**

Rivermount House without rest

Northeast : 0.75 km – ✆ (021) 477 80 33 – www.rivermount.com – Fax (021) 477 82 25 – March-November

6 rm – € 50/90 € 70/90

◆ This purpose-built guesthouse has been given a head-to-toe refurbishment and is now slick and understated, with lots of designery touches. Run by a friendly and conscientious couple.

at Ballinadee **West : 12 km by R 600 - Z – ✉ Kinsale**

Glebe Country House without rest

– ✆ (021) 477 82 94 – www.glebecountryhouse.com – Fax (021) 477 84 56 – Closed Christmas

4 rm – € 60/70 € 90/110

◆ Creeper-clad Georgian rectory. Handsomely furnished drawing room; well-chosen fabrics and fine wooden beds in pretty rooms, one with french windows on to the garden.

KNIGHTS TOWN (An Chois) – Kerry – 712 B12 – see Valencia Island

KNOCK (An Cnoc) – Mayo – 712 F6 – pop. 745 Ireland 36 B2

Dublin 212 – Galway 74 – Westport 51

Ireland West Airport, Knock : ✆ (094) 9368100, NE : 14.5 km by N 17

Town Centre ✆ (094) 9388193 (May-September), knock.touristoffice@failteireland.ie

Basilica of our Lady, Queen of Ireland★

Museum of Country Life★★ **AC**, NW : 26 km by R 323, R 321 and N 5

Hotels see : ***Cong*** *SW : 58 km by N 17, R 331 R 334 and R 345*

LAGHY (An Lathaigh) – Donegal – 712 H4 – see Donegal

LAHINCH (An Leacht) – Clare – 712 D9 – pop. 607 Ireland 38 B1

Dublin 260 km – Galway 79 km – Limerick 66 km

Lahinch, ✆ (065) 708 10 03

Spanish Point Miltown Malbay, ✆ (065) 708 42 19

Cliffs of Moher★★★ – Kilfenora (Burren Centre★ **AC**, High Crosses★), NE : 11 km by N 85 and R 481

Vaughan Lodge

Ennistymon Rd – ✆ (065) 708 11 11 – www.vaughanlodge.ie – Fax (065) 708 10 11 – April-October

20 rm – € 120/160 € 140/300

Rest – *(closed Monday) (dinner only)* Menu € 47 – Carte € 36/72

◆ Stylish reception area and comfortable lounge and bar offering large array of malts and satellite TV to keep abreast of the golf. Modern bedrooms of a good size; one balcony. Contemporary restaurant decorated with photos of local coastline.

Moy House

Southwest : 4 km on N 67 (Milltown Malbay rd) – ✆ (065) 708 28 00 – www.moyhouse.com – Fax (065) 708 25 00 – Closed 3 January-12 February

8 rm – € 145/255 € 240/280 – 1 suite

Rest – *(closed Sunday and Monday in winter) (dinner only) (residents only)* Menu € 55

◆ Early 19C country house in lovely spot away from town and with delightful views of Lahinch Bay. Genuine country house atmosphere with antiques and curios; charming bedrooms. Stylishly understated dining room.

REPUBLIC OF IRELAND

Dough Mor Lodge without rest
Station Rd – ☎ (065) 708 20 63 – www.doughmorlodge.com – Fax (065) 707 13 84 – March-October
6 rm ☕ – 🚹 € 55/70 👫 € 90/110
◆ Attractive, well-kept guesthouse with large front garden, a minute's walk from the town centre. Cosy lounge; Gingham-clad breakfast room. Spacious bedrooms in white or cream.

LEENANE (An Líonán) – Galway – 712 C7 – ✉ Clifden 📗 Ireland 36 A3

▶ Dublin 278 km – Ballina 90 km – Galway 66 km
◉ Killary Harbour★
Ⓖ Joyce Country★★ – Lough Nafooey★, SE : 10.5 km by R 336 – Aasleagh Falls★, NE : 4 km. Connemara★★★ – Lough Corrib★★, SE : 16 km by R 336 and R 345 – Doo Lough Pass★, NW : 14.5 km by N 59 and R 335

Delphi Lodge
Northwest : 13.25 km by N 59 on Louisburgh rd – ☎ (095) 42 222 – www.delphilodge.ie – Fax (095) 42 296 – Closed Christmas and New Year
12 rm ☕ – 🚹 € 165 👫 € 264
Rest – *(dinner only) (residents only, communal dining, set menu only)* Menu € 49
◆ Georgian sporting lodge in a stunning loughside setting with extensive gardens and grounds. Haven for fishermen. Country house feel and simple bedrooms. Communal dining table: fisherman with the day's best catch sits at its head.

LEIGHLINBRIDGE (Leithghlinn an Droichid) Carlow – Carlow – 712 L9 – pop. 674 39 D2

▶ Dublin 63 km – Carlow 8 km – Kilkenny 16 km – Athy 22 km

Lord Bagenal
Main St – ☎ (059) 977 40 00 – www.lordbagenal.com – Fax (059) 972 26 29 – Closed 24-26 December
39 rm ☕ – 🚹 € 65/85 👫 € 130/190
Rest – *(carving lunch)* Menu € 35 – Carte € 26/36
◆ Impressive hotel on banks of River Barrow; originally a coaching inn, now with vast new extension. Characterful bar with excellent collection of Irish art. Spacious bedrooms. Traditional menus in Lord Bagenal bar and restaurant.

LETTERFRACK (Leitir Fraic) – Galway – 712 C7 📗 Ireland 36 A3

▶ Dublin 304 km – Ballina 111 km – Galway 91 km
Ⓖ Connemara★★★ - Sky Road★★ (≤★★) – Connemara National Park★ – Kylemore Abbey★, E : 4.75 km by N 59

Rosleague Manor
West : 2.5 km on N 59 – ☎ (095) 41 101 – www.rosleague.com – Fax (095) 41 168 – 15 March-15 November
20 rm ☕ – 🚹 € 95/145 👫 € 85/110 **Rest** – *(dinner only)* Carte € 32/48
◆ Imposing, part 19C manor in a secluded, elevated position affording delightful views of Ballynakill harbour and mountains. Antique furnished, old fashioned comfort. Country house-style dining room: distinctive artwork on walls.

LETTERKENNY (Leitir Ceanainn) – Donegal – 712 I3 – pop. 17 586 37 C1
📗 Ireland

▶ Dublin 241 km – Londonderry 34 km – Sligo 116 km
ℹ Neil T Blaney Rd ☎ (074) 9121160, letterkenny@failteireland.ie
⛳18 Dunfanaghy, ☎ (074) 913 6335
Ⓖ Glenveagh National Park★★ (Gardens★★), NW : 19.25 km by R 250, R 251 and R 254 – Grianan of Aileach★★ (≤★★) NE : 28 km by N 13 – Church Hill (Glebe House and Gallery★ **AC**) NW : 16 km by R 250

Radisson Blu rest,

Paddy Harte Rd – (074) 919 44 44 – www.radissonblu.ie/letterkenny – Fax (074) 919 44 55

114 rm – € 125/169 € 159/200

Rest – *(bar lunch)* Menu € 20 – Carte € 34/47

◆ Corporate accommodation in edge of town. Bar serves a daily changing menu; rooms are identically appointed: all are clean, modern and spacious. Business class has extras. Dinner in restaurant offers modern international choice.

An important business lunch or dinner with friends?
The symbol indicates restaurants with private rooms.

LIMERICK (Luimneach) – **Limerick** – **712** G9 – **pop. 90 757** Ireland **38** B2

Dublin 193 km – Cork 93 km

Shannon Airport : (061) 712000, W : 25.75 km by N 18 Z

Arthur's Quay (061) 317522 Y, limericktouristoffice@shannondev.ie

City★★ - St Mary's Cathedral★ Y – Hunt Museum★★ **AC** Y - Georgian House★ **AC** Z – King John's Castle★ **AC** Y - Limerick Museum★ Z **M2** – John Square★ Z **20** – St John's Cathedral★ Z

Bunratty Castle★★ **AC**, W : 12 km by N 18 – Cratloe Wood (<★) NW : 8 km by N 18 Z. Castleconnell★, E : 11.25 km by N 7 - Lough Gur Interpretive Centre★ **AC**, S : 17.75 km by R 512 and R 514 Z – Clare Glens★, E : 21 km by N 7 and R 503 Y – Monasteranenagh Abbey★, S : 21 km by N 20 Z

Plan on next page

Limerick Strand

Ennis Rd – (061) 421 800 – www.strandlimerick.ie – Fax (061) 421 866 – Closed 25-26 December Y**z**

184 rm – € 89/149 € 159/250

Rest ***River Restaurant*** – Menu € 25/30 **s** – Carte € 28/46 **s**

◆ Extensive function and leisure facilities. Modern bedrooms come in dark wood and autumnal browns and oranges; Junior suites have balconies. Terrace bar overlooks River Shannon. River restaurant serves mix of traditional and more modern dishes.

Absolute H. & Spa

Sir Harry's Mall – (061) 463 600 – www.absolutehotel.com – Fax (061) 463 601 Y**a**

99 rm – € 99/139 € 139/169

Rest – Menu € 25 (dinner) – Carte € 22/45

◆ Stylish, modern hotel and spa on outskirts of city centre; designed like an old mill to reflect the area's industrial heritage. Clever use of space in light-coloured bedrooms. Restaurant serves traditional menu and overlooks river.

Radisson Blu H. & Spa rest,

Ennis Rd, Northwest : 6.5 km on N 18 – (061) 456 200 – www.radissonblu.ie/hotel-limerick – Fax (061) 327 418

152 rm – € 89/149 € 89/149, €15 – 2 suites

Rest ***Porters*** – *(buffet lunch)* Menu € 30 **s** – Carte € 38/49 **s**

◆ Modern hotel with tastefully used chrome and wood interiors. Well-equipped conference rooms and a leisure centre which includes tennis court. Smart, state-of-the-art bedrooms. Informal Porters restaurant with traditional menus.

No 1 Pery Square

Pery Square – (061) 402 402 – www.oneperysquare.com – Fax (061) 313 060 – Closed 24-26 December Z**a**

19 rm – € 155 € 165 – 1 suite

Rest ***Brasserie No1*** – see restaurant listing

◆ Charming, personally run house in the historic Georgian quarter of the city. Beautiful spa facility and wine shop in cellar. Well-proportioned, luxuriously appointed bedrooms.

REPUBLIC OF IRELAND

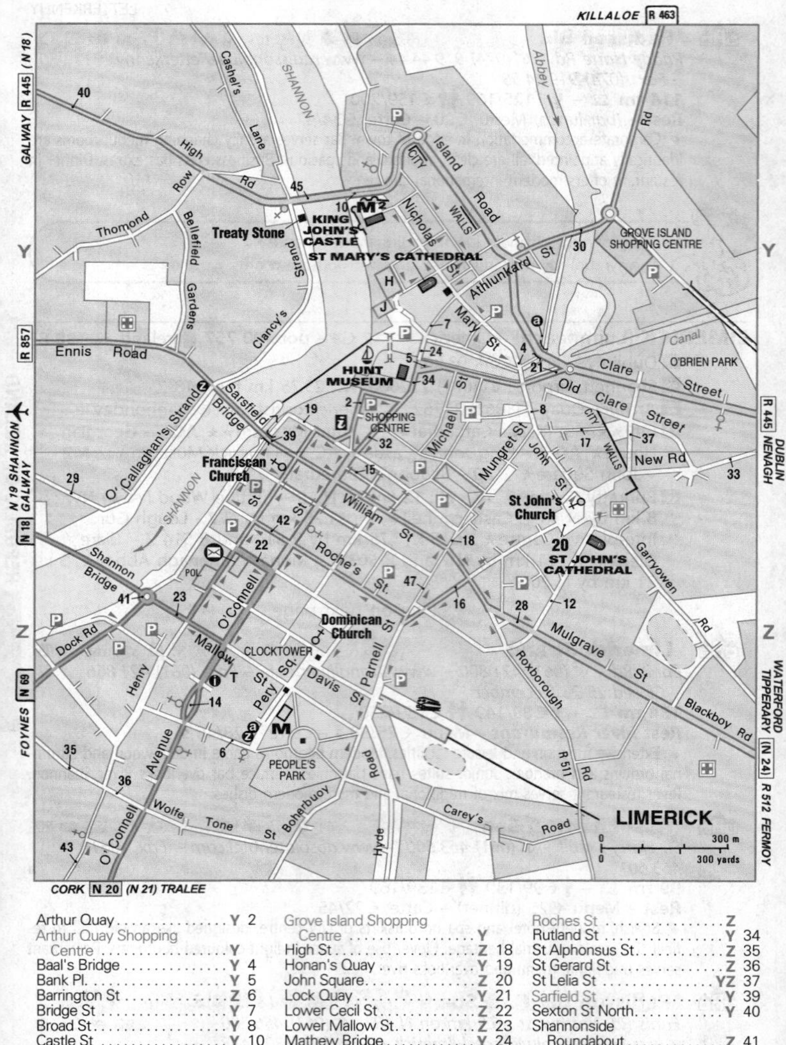

Arthur Quay . . . . Y 2
Arthur Quay Shopping Centre . . . . Y
Baal's Bridge . . . . Y 4
Bank Pl. . . . . Y 5
Barrington St . . . . Z 6
Bridge St . . . . Y 7
Broad St . . . . Y 8
Castle St . . . . Y 10
Cathedral Pl. . . . . Z 12
Charlotte's Quay . . . . Y 13
Cruises St. . . . . Z 15
Gerald Griffen St . . . . Z 16
Grattan St. . . . . Y 17
Grove Island Shopping Centre . . . . Y
High St . . . . Z 18
Honan's Quay . . . . Y 19
John Square . . . . Z 20
Lock Quay . . . . Y 21
Lower Cecil St . . . . Z 22
Lower Mallow St . . . . Z 23
Mathew Bridge . . . . Y 24
Newtown Mahon . . . . Z 28
North Circular Rd . . . . Z 29
O'Connell St . . . . Z
O'Dwyer Bridge . . . . Y 30
Patrick St . . . . YZ 32
Penniwell Rd . . . . Z 33
Roches St . . . . Z
Rutland St . . . . Y 34
St Alphonsus St . . . . Z 35
St Gerard St . . . . Z 36
St Lelia St . . . . YZ 37
Sarfield St . . . . Y 39
Sexton St North . . . . Y 40
Shannonside Roundabout . . . . Z 41
Shannon St . . . . Z 42
South Circular Rd. . . . . Z 43
The Crescent . . . . Z 14
Thomond Bridge . . . . Y 45
Wickham St . . . . Z 47
William St . . . . Z

XX **Market Square Brasserie** VISA MC AE

74 O'Connel St – (061) 316 311 – Closed 24 December-3 January, Sunday and Monday Zi

Rest – *(dinner only) (booking essential)* Menu €50 – Carte €35/50

◆ Atmospheric restaurant with cosy, clothed tables, candles and flowers. Extensive, seasonally-changing menu; beef is popular and desserts particularly good. Hearty portions.

Brasserie No1 at No 1 Pery Square Hotel
Pery Square – ☎ (061) 402 402 – www.oneperysquare.com – Fax (061) 313 060 – Closed 24-26 December Za
Rest – *(closed Sunday dinner)* Menu € 25 – Carte € 25/58
◆ Set on first floor of hotel, with well-spaced tables, Georgian-style furniture and semi-open kitchen. Tasty bistro dishes with a modern slant. Good service from a well-versed team.

LISCANNOR (Lios Ceannúir) – **Clare** – **712** D9 – **pop. 71** Ireland **38** B1

Dublin 272 km – Ennistimmon 9 km – Limerick 72 km

Cliffs of Moher★★★, NW : 8 km by R 478 – Kilfenora (Burren Centre★ **AC**, High Crosses★), NE : 18 km by R 478, N 67 and R 481

Vaughan's Anchor Inn
Main Street – ☎ (065) 708 1548 – www.vaughans.ie – Fax (065) 708 1548 – Closed 25 December
Rest – Seafood – Carte € 22/35
◆ Lively, characterful family-run pub in picturesque fishing village near Cliffs of Moher. Emphasis on seafood, with pub favourites at lunch; more elaborate meals in the evenings.

LISDOONVARNA (Lios Dúin Bhearna) – **Clare** – **712** E8 – **pop. 767** **38** B1
Ireland

Dublin 268 km – Galway 63 km – Limerick 75 km

The Burren★★ (Cliffs of Moher★★★, Scenic Route★★, Aillwee Cave★ **AC** (Waterfall★★), Corcomroe Abbey★, Kilfenora Crosses★)

Sheedy's Country House
Sulphir Hill – ☎ (065) 707 40 26 – www.sheedys.com – Fax (065) 707 45 55 – Easter-October
11 rm – † € 105/160 †† € 140/160
Rest ***The Restaurant*** – see restaurant listing
◆ Classic late 19C mustard painted property in an elevated position. Public areas centre around the bright, wicker furnished sun lounge. Neat, well-equipped bedrooms.

The Restaurant – at Sheedy's Country House House
Sulphir Hill – ☎ (065) 707 40 26 – www.sheedys.com – Fax (065) 707 45 55 – Easter-October
Rest – *(dinner only) (booking essential for non-residents)* Carte € 40/50 **s**
◆ Attractive, comfortable restaurant at the front of the building. Linen covered tables and smart place settings. Interesting menus using freshest, local produce.

Wild Honey Inn with rm
South : 0.5 km on Ennistimon rd – ☎ (065) 707 43 00 – www.wildhoneyinn.com – Fax (065) 707 44 90 – Closed 25 December, Good Friday and restricted opening in Winter
14 rm – † € 50/65 †† € 70/100 **Rest** – Carte € 23/38
◆ Atmospheric, family-run inn with characterful, fire-lit bar. Light lunches and more interesting dinner menu, with some particularly tasty specials: traditional, satisfying dishes, neatly presented. Simply furnished bedrooms boast up-to-date facilities.

LISMORE (Lios Mór) – **Waterford** – **712** I11 – **pop. 1 240** **39** C2

Dublin 227 km – Cork 56 km – Fermoy 26 km

Lismore House rm,
Main St – ☎ (058) 72 966 – www.lismorehousehotel.com – Fax (058) 53 068 – Closed 25-26 December and January
29 rm – † € 60/90 †† € 80/140, € 12.50 **Rest** – *(bar lunch)* Carte € 28/47 **s**
◆ Georgian house with purpose built rear. Bedrooms are all brand new with up-to-date facilities including plasmas and playstations; several overlook the Millennium Gardens. Intimate dining room.

O'Brien Chop House

Main St – ✆ (058) 53 810 – www.obrienchophouse.ie – Fax (058) 53 812 – Closed Monday, Tuesday and Sunday dinner

Rest – Menu € 19 (lunch) – Carte € 26/39

◆ Timeless Victorian bar leads through to rustic restaurant, with bare wooden floorboards and whitewashed walls. Very appealing, value-for-money menu of wholesome Irish dishes which make excellent use of locally sourced produce. Polite, friendly service.

LISTOWEL (Lios Tuathail) – Kerry – 712 D10 – pop. 4 338 Ireland 38 B2

Dublin 270 km – Killarney 54 km – Limerick 75 km – Tralee 27 km

St John's Church ✆ (068) 22590 (June-September), listoweltio@failteireland.ie

Ardfert★ **AC**, SW : 32 km by N 69 and minor roads via Abbeydorney – Banna Strand★, SW : 35 km by N 69 and minor roads via Abbeydorney – Carrigafoyle Castle★, N : 17 km by R 552 and minor road – Glin Castle★ **AC**, N : 24 km by N 69 – Rattoo Round Tower★, W : 19 km by R 553, R 554 and R 551

Allo's Bar with rm

41 Church St – ✆ (068) 22 880 – Fax (068) 22 803 – Closed 25 December, Sunday, Monday and Bank Holidays

3 rm – † € 60/80 †† € 80/100 **Rest** – *(booking essential)* Carte € 20/45

◆ Brightly-painted pub with covered terrace and cosy, citrus snug; once a handy hidey-hole for the local priest to sup a swift drink. Plenty of old favourites on the menu. Comfortable, antique-furnished bedrooms - but no breakfast served.

LITTLE ISLAND (An tOileán Beag) – Cork – 712 G/H12 – see Cork

---

LONGFORD (An Longfort) – Longford – 712 I6 – pop. 8 836 37 C3

Dublin 124 km – Drogheda 120 km – Galway 112 km – Limerick 175 km

Market Square ✆ (043) 42577, info@longfordtourism.com

Viewmount House

Dublin Rd, Southeast : 1.5 km by R 393 – ✆ (043) 334 19 19 – www.viewmounthouse.com – Fax (043) 334 29 06

15 rm – † € 50/70 †† € 100/140 – 5 suites

Rest *VM* – *(closed 25 December, Good Friday, Monday, Tuesday and Sunday dinner) (dinner only and Sunday lunch)* Menu € 53

◆ Impressive Georgian house in four acres; breakfast room has ornate vaulted ceiling, lounge is reached by fine staircase. Rooms boast antique beds and period furniture. Formal VM restaurant in converted stable block offers à la carte menu of modern dishes.

MALAHIDE (Mullach Íde) – Fingal – 712 N7 – pop. 14 937 Ireland 39 D1

Dublin 14 km – Drogheda 38 km

Beechwood The Grange, ✆ (01) 846 1611

Castle★★

Newbridge House★ **AC**, N : 8 km by R 106, M1 and minor road

Bon Appétit (Oliver Dunne)

(First Floor) No.9 St James Terrace – ✆ (01) 845 0314 – www.bonappetit.ie – Fax (01) 845 5365 – Closed 3-18 January, 1-16 August, Sunday and Monday

Rest – French – *(dinner only and Friday lunch) (booking essential)* Menu € 50

Spec. Citrus cured salmon with beetroot bavarois and summer truffle. Lamb cutlet with confit belly, aubergine and white onion purée. Chocolate & orange cannelloni with white chocolate mousse, orange and olive oil sorbet

◆ Set in delightful converted Georgian terrace. Sumptuous, subtly lit bar; elegant, formally set dining room with fine china and linen. Cooking uses classic combinations and has a French accent. Formal service, with good attention to detail.

REPUBLIC OF IRELAND

Jaipur

5 St James Terrace – ✆ (01) 845 5455 – www.jaipur.ie – Fax (01) 845 5456 – Closed 25 December

Rest – Indian – *(dinner only)* Carte € 30/49

◆ Friendly basement restaurant in Georgian terraced parade. Well-run by efficient, welcoming staff. Simple but lively and modern décor. Contemporary Indian cooking.

The Brasserie at Bon Appétit

(basement) No.9 St James Terrace – ✆ (01) 845 0314 – www.bonappetit.ie – Fax (01) 835 5365 – Closed 25-26 December, Good Friday and Monday

Rest – *(dinner only and Sunday lunch) (booking essential)* Carte € 33/41

◆ In basement of Georgian terraced house – a popular alternative to the more formal 'Bon Appétit' upstairs – serving classical brasserie dishes such as moules or steak frites.

MALLOW (Mala) – Cork – 712 F11 – pop. 10 241 Ireland 38 B2

Dublin 240 km – Cork 34 km – Killarney 64 km – Limerick 66 km

Ballyellis, ✆ (022) 21 145

Town★ – St James' Church★

Annes Grove Gardens★, E : 17.75 km by N 72 and minor rd – Buttevant Friary★, N : 11.25 km by N 20 – Doneraile Wildlife Park★ **AC**, NE : 9.5 km by N 20 and R 581 – Kanturk★ (Castle★), W : 16 km by N 72 and R 576

Longueville House

West : 5.5 km by N 72 – ✆ (022) 47 156 – www.longuevillehouse.ie – Fax (022) 47 459 – Closed January and February

20 rm – † € 75/140 †† € 160/260

Rest *Presidents* – *(closed Monday and Tuesday) (dinner only and Sunday lunch) (booking essential)* Menu € 40/65

◆ Part Georgian manor; exudes history from oak trees planted in formation of battle lines at Waterloo and views of Dromineen Castle to richly ornate, antique-filled bedrooms. Restaurant offers gourmet cuisine.

MIDLETON (Mainistir na Corann) – Cork – 712 H12 – pop. 10 048 39 C3

Dublin 268 km – Cork 22 km – Limerick 123 km – Waterford 102 km

Farmgate Restaurant and Country Store

Midleton – ✆ (021) 463 2771 – www.farmgate.ie – Closed 24 December-3 January, Sunday and Bank Holidays

Rest – *(closed Monday-Wednesday dinner)* Carte € 21/50

◆ Busy and appealingly rustic, with entrance through shop and local art on display. Market-bought produce, simply cooked; perhaps an Irish stew, some tasty squid or a freshly baked tart.

MILLSTREET (Sráid an Mhuilinn) – Waterford – 712 I11 – see Cappoquin

---

MOHILL (Maothail) – Leitrim – 712 I6 – pop. 931

Dublin 98 km – Carrick-on-Shannon 11 km – Cavan 41 km – Castlerea 44 km

Lough Rynn Castle

rm,

East : 4 km by R 201 and Drumlish rd – ✆ (071) 963 27 00 – www.loughrynn.ie – Fax (071) 963 27 10

40 rm – † € 89/135 †† € 155/215 – 2 suites

Rest *The Sandstone* – Menu € 32/42 **s** – Carte € 43/72 **s**

◆ Extended 18C house on large estate. Bedrooms in main house and converted stables have warm décor and a high level of facilities. Baronial Hall features huge original fireplace. French influenced menus served in formal, intimate dining room.

MONAGHAN (Muineachán) – Monaghan – 712 L5 – pop. 6 710 37 D2

Dublin 133 km – Belfast 69 km – Drogheda 87 km – Dundalk 35 km

Clones Rd ✆ (047) 81122 (June-September), northwestinfo@failteireland.ie

REPUBLIC OF IRELAND

at Glaslough Northeast : 9.5 km by N 12 on R 185 – ✉ Monaghan

Castle Leslie
Castle Leslie Estate – ✆ (047) 88 100 – www.castleleslie.com – Fax (047) 88 256 – Closed 24-27 December
20 rm – € 120/180 € 160/320
Rest – *(dinner only)* Menu € 55 – Carte € 45/75
◆ Impressive castle set in large grounds: home to 4th generation of the Leslie family. Ornate, comfortable, antique-furnished guest areas and individually styled bedrooms. Intimate, linen-laid dining room overlooking the lough; classically based menus.

The Lodge at Castle Leslie Estate
– ✆ (047) 88 100 – www.castleleslie.com – Fax (047) 88 256 – Closed 24-27 December
29 rm – € 90/140 € 120/220 – 1 suite
Rest *Snaffles* – *(dinner only)* Menu € 48 – Carte € 31/55
◆ Victorian former hunting lodge in 1000 acres with equestrian centre. Plenty of antiques and equine-themed pictures; relaxed and informal atmosphere. Stylish and contemporary bedrooms, some with balconies. Snaffles mezzanine brasserie has open kitchen and serves Mediterranean meets Irish cooking.

REPUBLIC OF IRELAND

MULLINGAR (An Muileann gCearr) – Westmeath – 712 J/K7 37 C3

– pop. 18 416 Ireland

Dublin 79 km – Drogheda 58 km

Market Sq. ✆ (0449) 348650, eastandmidlandsinfo@failteireland.ie

Belvedere House and Gardens★ **AC**, S : 5.5 km by N 52. Fore Abbey★, NE : 27.25 km by R 394 – Multyfarnhan Franciscan Friary★, N : 12.75 km by N 4 – Tullynally★ **AC**, N : 21 km by N 4 and R 394

Mullingar Park rm, rest,
Dublin Rd, East : 2.5 km on Dublin Rd (N 4) – ✆ (044) 933 7500 – www.mullingarparkhotel.com – Fax (044) 933 5937 – Closed 25-26 December
94 rm – € 100/160 € 150/250 – 1 suite
Rest – *(buffet lunch)* Menu € 24/30 – Carte (dinner) € 33/47 **s**
◆ Spacious modern hotel with a strong appeal to business and leisure travellers: there's a hydrotherapy pool and host of treatment rooms. Airy, light bedrooms with mod cons. Smart, airy restaurant with international menus.

Marlinstown Court without rest
Dublin Rd, East : 2.5 km on Dublin Rd (N 4) – ✆ (044) 934 00 53 – www.marlinstowncourt.com – Fax (044) 934 00 57 – Closed 23-27 December
5 rm – € 45/50 € 75/80
◆ Clean, tidy guesthouse close to junction with N4. Modern rear extension. Light and airy pine-floored lounge and breakfast room overlooking garden. Brightly furnished bedrooms.

MULRANNY (An Mhala Raithní) – Mayo – 712 C6 36 A2

Dublin 270 km – Castlebar 35 km – Westport 29 km

Mulranny Park rm, rest,
on N 59 – ✆ (098) 36 000 – www.mulrannyparkhotel.ie – Fax (098) 36 899 – Closed 25 December and 3-28 January
39 rm – € 75/130 € 150/210 – 21 suites
Rest *Nephin* – see restaurant listing
Rest *Waterfront Bistro* – *(bar lunch Monday-Saturday)* Carte € 25/36
◆ Purpose-built business oriented hotel behind 19C façade: lovely Clew Bay views. Impressive leisure and conference facilities. Airy rooms with slightly minimalist interiors. Waterfront Bistro has informal, relaxing ambience.

Nephin – at Mulranny Park Hotel
on N 59 – ✆ (098) 36 000 – www.mulrannyparkhotel.ie – Fax (098) 36 899 – Closed 25 December and 3-28 January
Rest – *(dinner only)* Menu € 49 – Carte € 40/49
◆ Large, lively restaurant with fine southerly views. Modern, intricately presented cooking offers interesting combinations based around well sourced, quality ingredients.

NAAS (An Nás) – Kildare – 712 L/M8 – pop. 20 044 Ireland 39 D1

Dublin 30 km – Kilkenny 83 km – Tullamore 85 km

Kerdiffstown Naas, (045) 874 644

Russborough★★★ **AC**, S : 16 km by R 410 and minor road – Castletown House★★ **AC**, NE : 24 km by R 407 and R 403

Killashee House H. & Villa Spa rm, rest,

South : 1.5 km on R 448 (Kilcullen Rd) – (045) 879 277 – www.killasheehouse.com – Fax (045) 879 266 – Closed 24-26 December

129 rm – € 140 € 275 – 12 suites

Rest *Turners* – *(dinner only Friday-Saturday)* Menu € 35/45

Rest *Jack's* – Carte € 22/32

◆ Imposing part 1860s hunting lodge in acres of parkland. Rooms in the original house are most characterful: French antique furniture, original panelling and fireplaces. Elegant Turners overlooking garden. Informal Jack's.

Vie de Châteaux

The Harbour – (045) 888 478 – www.viedechateaux.ie – Fax (045) 888 478 – Closed 25 December-10 January, lunch Saturday and Sunday and Bank Holidays

Rest – *(booking essential)* Menu € 25/29 – Carte € 32/49

◆ Stylish, popular restaurant with open-plan kitchen and a brasserie feel. Concise, keenly priced menu moves with the seasons; mainly French dishes but with some Mediterranean influences.

NAVAN (An Uaimh) – Meath – 712 L7 – pop. 24 851 Ireland 37 D3

Dublin 48 km – Drogheda 26 km – Dundalk 51 km

Moor Park Mooretown, (046) 27 661

Royal Tara Bellinter, (046) 902 5244

Brú na Bóinne : Newgrange★★★ **AC**, Knowth★, E : 16 km by minor road to Donore – Bective Abbey★, S : 6.5 km by R 161 – Tara★ **AC**, S : 8 km by N 3. Kells★ (Round Tower and High Crosses★★, St Columba's House★), NW : by N 3 – Trim★ (castle★★), SW : 12.75 km by R 161

Ma Dwyers without rest

Dublin Rd, South : 1.25 km on N 3 – (046) 907 79 92 – Fax (046) 907 79 95

28 rm – € 40/50 € 100

◆ Yellow-painted, mock-Georgian house; comfortable guest lounge, modern breakfast room. Hospitality trays in equally bright, simple bedrooms.

NEWMARKET-ON-FERGUS (Cora Chaitlín) – Clare – 712 F7 38 B2 – pop. 1 542 Ireland

Dublin 219 km – Ennis 13 km – Limerick 24 km

Dromoland Castle, (061) 368 444

Bunratty Castle★★ **AC**, S : 10 km by N 18 – Craggaunowen Centre★ **AC**, NE : 15 km by minor road towards Moymore – Knappogue Castle★ **AC**, NE : 12 km N 18 and minor roads via Quin – Quin Friary★ **AC**, N : 10 km by N 18 and minor road to Quin

Dromoland Castle

Northwest : 2.5 km – (061) 368 144 – www.dromoland.ie – Fax (061) 363 355 – Closed 25-26 December

93 rm – € 195/350 € 195/518, €25 – 5 suites

Rest *Earl of Thomond* – *(bar lunch)* Carte € 26/53

Rest *Fig Tree* – *(bar lunch)* Carte € 26/53

◆ Restored 16C castle with 375 acres of woodland and golf course. Sumptuous rooms with plenty of thoughtful extras. Waterford crystal chandeliers and gilded mirrors in the Earl of Thomond restaurant. More informal style in the Fig Tree, popular with golfers.

NEWPORT (Baile Uí Fhiacháin) – **Mayo** – **712** D6 – **pop. 590** **36** A2

Ireland

Dublin 264 km – Ballina 59 km – Galway 96 km

James St, Westport (098) 25711, westport@failteireland.ie

Burrishoole Abbey★, NW : 3.25 km by N 59 – Furnace Lough★, NW : 4.75 km by N 59. Achill Island★, W : 35 km by N 59 and R 319

Newport House

– *(098) 41 222 – www.newporthouse.ie – Fax (098) 41 613 – 18 March-October*

16 rm – € 100/125 € 200/250

Rest – *(dinner only)* Menu € 68 **s** – Carte € 40/50 **s**

◆ Mellow ivy-clad Georgian mansion; grand staircase up to gallery and drawing room. Bedrooms in main house or courtyard; some in self-contained units ideal for families and those with dogs. Enjoy the fresh Newport estate produce used in the dishes served in the elegant dining room.

OUGHTERARD (Uachtar Ard) – **Galway** – **712** E7 – **pop. 1 305** **36** A3

Ireland

Dublin 240 km – Galway 27 km

Main Street (091) 552808, oughterardoffice@eircom.net

Gortreevagh, (091) 552 131

Town★

Lough Corrib★★ (Shore road - NW - ★★) – Aughnanure Castle★ **AC**, SE : 3.25 km by N 59

Currarevagh House

Northwest : 6.5 km on Glann rd – (091) 552 312 – www.currarevagh.com – Fax (091) 552 731 – March-October

12 rm – € 95/110 € 190/220

Rest – *(dinner only) (set menu only)* Menu € 50

◆ Victorian manor on Lough Corrib, set in 180 acres. Period décor throughout plus much fishing memorabilia. Two lovely sitting rooms. Comfortable, well-kept rooms. Four course dinner menu makes good use of garden produce.

Railway Lodge without rest

West : 0.75 km by Costello rd taking first right onto unmarked road – (091) 552 945 – www.railwaylodge.net

4 rm – € 70 € 100/110

◆ Elegantly furnished modern guest house in remote farm location. Plenty of choice at breakfast. Open fires, books and magazines; TV only in lounge. Beautifully kept bedrooms.

Waterfall Lodge without rest

West : 0.75 km on N 59 – (091) 552 168 – www.waterfalllodge.net

6 rm – € 50 € 80

◆ Two minutes from the centre, a well-priced guesthouse rebuilt with gleaming wood and original Victorian fittings. A good fishing river flows through the charming gardens.

PARKNASILLA (Páirc na Saileach) – **Kerry** – **712** C12 Ireland **38** A3

Dublin 360 km – Cork 116 km – Killarney 55 km

Sneem★, NW : 4 km by N 70. Ring of Kerry★★ : Derrynane National Historic Park★★, W : 25.75 km by N 70 – Staigue Fort★, W : 21 km by N 70

Parknasilla

rest,

– *(064) 45 122 – www.parknasillahotel.ie – Fax (064) 45 323 – Closed 2 January-2 April*

69 rm – € 110/199 € 149/199 – 9 suites

Rest *Pigmaylion* – *(dinner only) (booking essential for non residents)* Carte € 35/54 **s**

◆ Set in 500 acres and built by the railway. Huge sums have been spent, with state-of-the-art spa and leisure facilities. Bedrooms kept fairly light; bigger ones in main house. Traditionally formal restaurant; lighter lunches in bar.

PASSAGE EAST (An Pasáiste) – WD Waterford – pop. 644

Dublin 181 km – Waterford 14 km – Kilkenny 64 km – Carlow 96 km

Parkswood

on R 683 – (051) 380 863 – www.parkswood.com

4 rm – € 80 € 90 **Rest** – *(by arrangement)* Menu € 30/35

◆ Delightful hosts give a friendly welcome, with tea and scones, to their 17C house, with super views and charming garden. Immaculate bedrooms are colour themed, with balconies. Tasty homecooking; the choice depends on the latest catch and what's available locally.

PORTLAOISE (Port Laoise) – Laois – 712 K8 – pop. 14 613 — 39 C2

Dublin 88 km – Carlow 40 km – Waterford 101 km

Ivyleigh House without rest

Bank Pl, Church St – (057) 862 20 81 – www.ivyleigh.com – Fax (057) 866 33 43 – Closed 1 week Christmas

6 rm – € 60/90 € 110/160

◆ Attractive Georgian listed house with gardens. Breakfast a feature: owner makes it all herself from fresh produce. Charming period drawing room. Airy bedrooms with antiques.

PORTMAGEE (An Caladh) – Kerry – 712 A12 – pop. 375 Ireland — 38 A2

Dublin 365 km – Killarney 72 km – Tralee 82 km

Ring of Kerry★★

Moorings

rest,

– (066) 947 71 08 – www.moorings.ie – Fax (066) 947 72 20 – Closed 2 weeks at Christmas

16 rm – € 60/70 € 90/140

Rest – *(closed November-mid March and Monday except Bank Holidays) (bar lunch)* Carte € 31/60

◆ Pub-style hotel in the high street of this attractive village. Spacious, nautical themed bar and trim upstairs lounge. Bedrooms with views over harbour and its fishing boats. Stone-walled, candlelit dining room with seafaring curios.

PORTMARNOCK (Port Mearnóg) – Fingal – 712 N7 – pop. 8 979 — 39 D1

Ireland

Dublin 8 km – Drogheda 45 km

Malahide Castle★★ **AC**, N : 4 km by R 124 – Ben of Howth★, S : 8 km by R 124 – Newbridge House★ **AC**, N : 16 km by R 124, M 1 and minor road east

Portmarnock H. and Golf Links

rest,

Strand Rd – (01) 846 0611 – www.portmarnock.com – Fax (01) 846 2442 – Closed 24-26 December

138 rm – € 79/169 € 89/179 – 3 suites

Rest *The Osborne* – *(closed Sunday and Monday) (dinner only)*

Menu € 25/38 **s** – Carte dinner € 38/43 **s**

◆ Large golf-oriented hotel with challenging 18-hole course. Original fittings embellish characterful, semi-panelled Jamesons Bar. Very comfortable, individually styled rooms. Smart brasserie with traditional menus.

RATHDRUM – Wicklow – 712 N9 – pop. 2 235 — 39 D2

Dublin 60 km – Wicklow 17 km – Drogheda 127 km

Bates

3 Market St – (0404) 29 988 – www.batesrestaurant.ie – Closed Monday and Bank Holidays

Rest – Menu € 20/25 – Carte dinner € 26/45

◆ Champions local produce, with counter selling local cheese, home-cured meats and Italian staples. Various menus offer mostly Italian dishes, with bold flavours and hearty portions.

RATHMELTON (Ráth Mealtain) – Donegal – 712 J2 – pop. 2 119 — 37 C1

Ireland

Dublin 248 km – Donegal 59 km – Londonderry 43 km – Sligo 122 km

Town★

Ardeen without rest

turning by the Town Hall – (074) 915 12 43 – www.ardeenhouse.com – Fax (074) 915 12 43 – Easter-October

5 rm – € 45/55 € 90

◆ Simple Victorian house, with very welcoming owner, on edge of village. Homely ambience in lounge and breakfast room. Immaculately kept bedrooms.

RATHMINES (Ráth Maonais) – Dublin – 712 N8 – see Dublin

RATHMULLAN (Ráth Maoláin) – Donegal – 712 J2 – pop. 469 37 C1

– ✉ Letterkenny Ireland

Dublin 265 km – Londonderry 58 km – Sligo 140 km

Otway Saltpans, (074) 915 1665

Knockalla Viewpoint★, N : 12.75 km by R 247 – Rathmelton★, SW : 11.25 km by R 247

Rathmullan House

North : 0.5 mi. on R 247 – (074) 915 81 88 – www.rathmullanhouse.com – Fax (074) 915 82 00 – Closed 10 January-5 February, midweek November-December and 23-27 December

34 rm – € 75/150 € 160/240

Rest *Rathmullan House* – *(bar lunch)* Menu € 55 – Carte € 45/55

◆ Part 19C country house with fine gardens in secluded site on Lough Swilly. Choose a lounge as pleasant spot for lunch. Stylish, individualistic rooms: newer ones very comfy. Restaurant boasts serious dinner menus at linen-clad tables.

RATHNEW (Ráth Naoi) – Wicklow – 712 N8 – see Wicklow

RIVERSTOWN (Baile idir Dhá Abhainn) – Sligo – 712 G5 – pop. 310 36 B2

Dublin 198 km – Sligo 21 km

Coopershill

– (071) 916 51 08 – www.coopershill.com – April-October

8 rm – € 144/171 € 236/272

Rest – *(dinner only) (booking essential for non-residents)* Menu € 59

◆ Magnificent Georgian country house set within 500 acre estate. Home to six generations of one family. Antique furnished communal areas and rooms exude charm and character. Family portraits, antique silver adorn dining room.

ROSCOMMON (Ros Comáin) – Roscommon – 712 H7 – pop. 5 017 36 B3

Ireland

Dublin 151 km – Galway 92 km – Limerick 151 km

Harrison Hall (090) 6626342 (June-August), roscommon.touristoffice@failteireland.ie

Moate Park, (09066) 26 382

Castle★

Castlestrange Stone★, SW : 11.25 km by N 63 and R 362 – Strokestown★ (Famine Museum★ **AC**, Strokestown Park House★ **AC**), N : 19.25 km by N 61 and R 368 – Castlerea : Clonalis House★ **AC**, NW : 30.5 km by N 60

Abbey

on N 63 (Galway rd) – (090) 662 62 40 – www.abbeyhotel.ie – Fax (090) 662 60 21 – Closed 24-26 December

50 rm – € 160/180 € 280/300

Rest – Menu € 50 (dinner) – Carte € 29/41 **s**

◆ Part 19C house with modern extensions, convenient central location and surrounded by attractive gardens. Excellent leisure facilities. Comfortable bedrooms. Spacious restaurant overlooks ruins of Abbey.

Westway without rest
Galway Rd, Southwest : 1.25 km on N 63
– ✆ (090) 662 69 27 – www.westwayguests.com
– March - October
5 rm – €40 €60
◆ Modern guesthouse with friendly welcome near town centre. Comfy, traditional residents' lounge. Breakfast room with conservatory extension. Brightly decorated rooms.

Undecided between two equivalent establishments in the same town? Within each category, establishments are classified in our order of preference: the best first.

ROSSLARE (Ros Láir) – **Wexford** – **712** M11 – **pop. 1 359** Ireland **39** D2

Dublin 167 km – Waterford 80 km – Wexford 19 km

Kilrane ✆ (053) 33232 (April-September)

Rosslare Strand, ✆ (053) 913 2203

Irish Agricultural Museum, Johnstowon Castle★★ **AC**, NW : 12 km by R 740, N 25 and minor road. Kilmore Quay★, SW : 24 km by R 736 and R 739 – Saltee Islands★, SW : 24 km by R 736, R 739 and ferry

Kelly's Resort rest,
– ✆ (053) 91 32 114 – www.kellys.ie – Fax (053) 91 32 222 VISA AE
– Closed 5 December - mid February
121 rm – €88/138 €176/208
Rest *Beaches* – Menu €28/48
Rest *La Marine* – Carte €34/40 **s**
◆ Large, purpose-built hotel on the beachfront of this popular holiday town. Good range of leisure facilities; well-appointed rooms. Kelly's dining room offers a classic popular menu. La Marine is a French inspired, bistro-style restaurant.

ROSSLARE HARBOUR (Calafort Ros Láir) – **Wexford** – **712** N11 – **pop. 1 041** **39** D2

Dublin 169 km – Waterford 82 km – Wexford 21 km

to France (Cherbourg and Roscoff) (Irish Ferries) (17 h/15 h) – to Fishguard (Stena Line) 1-4 daily (1 h 40 mn/3 h 30 mn) – to Pembroke (Irish Ferries) 2 daily (3 h 45 mn)

Kilrane ✆ (053) 33232 (April-October)

at Tagoat West : 4 km on N 25 – ✉ Rosslare

Churchtown House P VISA
North : 0.75 km on Rosslare rd – ✆ (053) 913 2555
– www.churchtownhouse.com – Fax (053) 913 2577
– May-October
12 rm – €75/120 €130/160
Rest – *(closed Sunday and Monday) (dinner only) (booking essential) (residents only)* Menu €39
◆ Part 18C house with extension, set in spacious, well-kept garden. Traditional country house-style lounge and wood furnished dining room. Individually decorated rooms. Fresh country cooking in the Irish tradition.

ROUNDSTONE (Cloch na Rón) – **Galway** – **712** C7 – **pop. 207** **36** A3 Ireland

Dublin 293 km – Galway 76 km – Ennis 144 km

Town★

Connemara★★★: Sky Road, Clifden★★, W : 24 km by R 341 and minor road – Cashel★, E : 15 km by R 341 – Connemara National Park★ **AC**, N : 40 km by R 341 and N 59 – Kylemore Abbey★ **AC**, N : 44 km by R 341 and N 59

REPUBLIC OF IRELAND

O'Dowds

– *(095) 35 809 – www.odowdsbar.com – Closed 25 December*
Rest – Seafood – *(booking advisable)* Carte € 27/41
◆ Busy pub in pretty harbourside town; popular with tourists and locals alike. Owned by the O'Dowd family for over 100 years, it specialises in fresh, simply cooked seafood.

SANDYFORD (Áth an Ghainimh) – Dublin – 712 N8 – see Dublin

SHANAGARRY (An Seangharraí) – Cork – 712 H12 – pop. 297 39 C3

– Midleton Ireland

Dublin 262 km – Cork 40 km – Waterford 103 km

Cloyne Cathedral★, NW : 6.5 km by R 629

Ballymaloe House

Northwest : 2.75 km on L 35 – (021) 465 25 31 – www.ballymaloe.ie – Fax (021) 465 20 21 – Closed 24-26 December and 2 weeks January
30 rm – € 160/175 € 280/295
Rest – *(buffet Sunday dinner) (booking essential)* Menu € 40/75
◆ Hugely welcoming part 16C, part Georgian country house surrounded by 400 acres of farmland. Characterful sitting room with cavernous ceiling. Warm, comfortable bedrooms. Characterful dining room divided into assorted areas.

SKERRIES (Na Sceirí) – Fingal – 712 N7 – pop. 9 535 Ireland 39 D1

Dublin 30 km – Drogheda 24 km

Skerries Mills (01) 849 5208, skerriesmills@indigo.ie

Skerries Hacketstown, (01) 849 1567

Malahide Castle★★ **AC**, S : 23 km by R 127, M 1 and R 106 – Ben of Howth (★), S : 23 km by R 127, M 1 and R 106 – Newbridge House★ **AC**, S : 16 km by R 217 and minor road

Redbank House with rm

5-7 Church St – (01) 849 1005 – www.redbank.ie – Fax (01) 849 1598
18 rm – € 50/75 € 90/120
Rest – Seafood – *(Closed Sunday dinner) (dinner only and Sunday lunch)* Menu € 25 – Carte € 46/60
◆ One of Ireland's most well-renowned and long-standing restaurants. Fresh seafood from Skerries harbour is served simply or in more elaborate fashion. Smart, comfy bedrooms.

SLIGO (Sligeach) – Sligo – 712 G5 – pop. 19 402 Ireland 36 B2

Dublin 214 km – Belfast 203 km – Dundalk 170 km – Londonderry 138 km

Sligo Airport, Strandhill : (071) 9168280

Aras Reddan, Temple St (071) 9161201, northwestinfo@failteireland.ie

Rosses Point, (071) 917 7134

Town★★ – Abbey★ **AC** – Model Arts and the Niland Gallery★ **AC**

SE : Lough Gill★★ – Carrowmore Megalithic Cemetery★ **AC**, SW : 4.75 km – Knocknarea★ (★★) SW : 9.5 km by R 292. Drumcliff★, N : by N 15 - Parke's Castle★ **AC**, E : 14.5 km by R 286 – Glencar Waterfall★, NE : 14.5 km by N 16 – Creevykeel Court Cairn★, N : 25.75 km by N 15

Clarion rm, rest,

Clarion Rd, Northeast : 3 km by N 16 – (071) 911 90 00 – www.clarionhotelsligo.com – Fax (071) 911 90 01 – Closed 20-27 December
163 rm – € 250 € 250, €16 – 149 suites
Rest *Kudos* – Carte € 28/48
Rest *Sinergie* – *(dinner only)* Carte € 28/48 **s**
◆ Extensive Victorian building with granite façade: now the height of modernity with excellent leisure club and impressive, spacious bedrooms; large choice of smart suites. Informal Asian inspired Kudos. Modern European menus at Sinergie.

Tree Tops without rest
Cleveragh Rd, South : 1.25 km by Dublin rd – ☎ (071) 916 01 60 – www.sligobandb.com – Fax (071) 916 23 01 – Closed Christmas and New Year
5 rm – € 48/50 € 74/76
◆ Pleasant guesthouse in residential area. Stunning collection of Irish art. Cosy public areas include small lounge and simple breakfast room. Neat, comfortable rooms.

Montmartre
Market Yard – ☎ (071) 916 99 01 – www.montmartrerestaurant.ie – Fax (071) 914 00 65 – Closed 24-26 December, 11 January-1 February and Monday
Rest – *(dinner only)* Menu € 30 (Tuesday-Thursday)/37 – Carte € 30/44 **s**
◆ Smart, modern restaurant near cathedral with small bar at entrance and plenty of light from windows. Efficient, formal staff serve broadly influenced classic French food.

STRAFFAN (Teach Srafáin) – **Kildare** – **712** M8 – **pop. 439** Ireland **39** D1

Dublin 24 km – Mullingar 75 km
Naas Kerdiffstown, ☎ (045) 874 644
Castletown House, Celbridge★ **AC**, NW : 7 km by R 406 and R 403

The K Club
– ☎ (01) 601 7200 – www.kclub.ie – Fax (01) 601 7297 – Closed January
60 rm – € 395/595 € 395/595 – 9 suites
Rest *Byerley Turk* – *(closed Sunday-Monday, weekends only in winter) (dinner only) (booking essential for non-residents)* Menu € 75/95
Rest *Legends* – *(dinner only and Sunday lunch)* Carte € 50/80
Rest *River Room* – *(closed lunch Monday-Tuesday)* Menu € 35/49 – Carte € 50/82
◆ Part early 19C country house overlooking River Liffey, with gardens, arboretum and championship golf course. Huge leisure centre. Exquisitely sumptuous rooms. Opulent food in the formal Byerley Turk. Informal Legends has views of the golf course. Accessible menu offered in The River Room.

Barberstown Castle
North : 0.75 km – ☎ (01) 628 8157 – www.barberstowncastle.ie – Fax (01) 627 7027 – Closed 3 days at Christmas and January
59 rm – € 150 € 280
Rest – *(dinner only) (booking essential)* Menu € 35/45 – Carte € 45/55
◆ Whitewashed Elizabethan and Victorian house with 13C castle keep and gardens. Country house style lounges exude style. Individually decorated, very comfortable bedrooms. Dine in characterful, stone-clad keep.

TAGOAT (Teach Gót) – **Wexford** – **712** M11 – **see Rosslare Harbour**

TAHILLA (Tathuile) – **Kerry** – **712** C12 – **pop. 193** Ireland **38** A3

Dublin 357 km – Cork 112 km – Killarney 51 km
Ring of Kerry★★ – Sneem★, NW : 6.5 km by N 70

Tahilla Cove without rest
– ☎ (064) 66 45 204 – www.tahillacove.com – Fax (064) 66 45 104 – May-19 October
9 rm – € 85/95 € 120/150
◆ Two houses surrounded by oak forest, with Caha Mountains as a backdrop and garden sweeping down to Coongar harbour. Some bedrooms have balconies from which to savour views.

TERMONBARRY – **Roscommon** – **712** I6 – **pop. 518** Ireland **37** C3

Dublin 130 km – Galway 137 km – Roscommon 35 km – Sligo 100 km
Strokestown★ (Famine Museum★ **AC**, Strokestown Park House★ **AC**), NW : by N 5

Keenan's
– ✆ (043) 332 6098 – *www.keenans.ie* – Fax (043) 332 6180
– *Closed 25-26 December*
12 rm – € 65/75 € 99/110
Rest – Menu € 25/35 – Carte lunch € 27/45
◆ Modern hotel on the banks of the Shannon, with cosy residents lounge. Stylish bedrooms have flat screens and showers; some have river views; some also have balconies. Large contemporary restaurant offers à la carte menu; characterful bar serves pub classics.

THOMASTOWN (Baile Mhic Andáin) – Kilkenny – 712 K10 — 39 C2

– **pop. 1 837** – ✉ **Kilkenny** Ireland

Dublin 124 km – Kilkenny 17 km – Waterford 48 km – Wexford 61 km

Jerpoint Abbey★★, SW : 3 km by N9 – Graiguenamanagh★ (Duiske Abbey★★ **AC**), E : 16 km by R 703 – Inistioge★, SE : 8 km by R 700 – Kilfane Glen and Waterfall★ **AC**, SE : 5 km by N 9

Abbey House without rest
Jerpoint Abbey, Southwest : 2 km on N 9 – ✆ (056) 772 41 66
– *www.abbeyhousejerpoint.com* – Fax (056) 772 41 92
– *Closed 20-30 December*
7 rm – € 50/70 € 85
◆ Neat inside and out, this whitewashed house in well-kept gardens offers simple but spacious rooms and pretty wood furnished breakfast room. Read up on area in lounge.

THURLES (Durlas) – Tipperary – 712 I9 – pop. 7 682 Ireland — 39 C2

Dublin 148 km – Cork 114 km – Kilkenny 48 km – Limerick 75 km

Turtulla, ✆ (0504) 21 983

Holy Cross Abbey★★ **AC**, SW : 8 km by R 660

Inch House
– ✆ (0504) 51 348 – *www.inchhouse.ie* – Fax (0504) 51 754 – *Closed 2 weeks Christmas and 2 weeks Easter*
5 rm – € 70/80 € 120/130
Rest – *(closed Sunday-Monday) (dinner only) (booking essential for non-residents)* Menu € 60 – Carte dinner € 50/60
◆ 1720s country house on a working farm; lovely rural views. Handsomely restored with a fine eye for decorative period detail. Individually styled en suite bedrooms. Classically proportioned yet intimate dining room.

TOORMORE (An Tuar Mór) – Cork – 712 D13 – pop. 207 – ✉ Goleen — 38 A3

Dublin 355 km – Cork 109 km – Killarney 104 km

Fortview House without rest
Gurtyowen, Northeast : 2.5 km on Durrus rd (R 591) – ✆ (028) 35 324
– *www.fortviewhousegoleen.com* – *April-September*
5 rm – € 50 € 100
◆ Stone built farmhouse; antique country pine furniture in coir carpeted rooms and brass, iron bedsteads. Fresh vegetable juice, home-made museli, potato cake for breakfast.

Rock Cottage
Barnatonicane, Northeast : 3.25 km on Durrus rd (R 591) – ✆ (028) 35 538
– *www.rockcottage.ie* – Fax (028) 35 538
3 rm – € 100 € 140 **Rest** – *(by arrangement)* Menu € 50
◆ Georgian former hunting lodge idyllically set in 17 acres of parkland. Very well appointed lounge: modern art on walls. Immaculate, light and airy bedrooms.

TOWER – Cork – 712 G12 – see Blarney

TRALEE (Trá Lí) – Kerry – 712 C11 – pop. 22 744 Ireland — 38 A2

Dublin 297 km – Killarney 32 km – Limerick 103 km

Ashe Memorial Hall, Denny St (066) 7121288, traleetouristoffice@failteireland.ie

Kerry - The Kingdom★ **AC**

Blennerville Windmill★ **AC**, SW : 3.25 km by N 86 – Ardfert★, NW : 8 km by R 551. Banna Strand★, NW : 12.75 km by R 551 - Crag Cave★ **AC**, W : 21 km by N 21 – Rattoo Round Tower★, N : 19.25 km by R 556

Fels Point

Fels Point, East : 2 km on N 70 – (066) 719 9100 – www.felspointhotel.ie – Fax (066) 711 9987 – Closed 23-26 December

166 rm – € 75/130 € 85/190, €15.95

Rest *Morels* – (066) 711 9986 – Menu € 30 (dinner) – Carte € 23/42

◆ Corporate hotel on outskirts of city centre with contemporary style throughout. Bedrooms come in three grades; all are a good size, Executive come with a balcony and view. Traditional dishes served in Morels restaurant.

The Meadowlands

Oakpark, Northeast : 1.25 km on N 69 – (066) 718 04 44 – www.meadowlandshotel.com – Fax (066) 718 09 64 – Closed 24-26 December

56 rm – € 100/130 € 200/210 – 2 suites

Rest – *(closed Sunday dinner) (bar lunch)* Menu € 30 (dinner) – Carte € 32/47

◆ Smart, terracotta hotel, a good base for exploring area. Inside are warmly decorated, air conditioned rooms and mellow library lounge with open fire and grandfather clock. Proprietor owns fishing boats, so seafood takes centre stage in dining room.

The Grand

rest,

Denny St – (066) 712 14 99 – www.grandhoteltralee.com – Fax (066) 712 28 77 – Closed 25 December

44 rm – € 60/90 € 120/180 **Rest** – Menu € 25 **s** – Carte € 25/40 **s**

◆ Established 1928; enjoys a central position in town. Rooms are decorated with mahogany furniture whilst the popular bar, once a post office, bears hallmarks of bygone era. Appetising dinners in restaurant with historic ambience.

Brook Manor Lodge without rest

Fenit Rd, Spa, Northwest : 3.5 km by R 551 on R 558 – (066) 712 04 06 – www.brookmanorlodge.com – Fax (066) 712 75 52

8 rm – € 65/95 € 100/140

◆ Modern purpose-built manor in meadowland looking across to the Slieve Mish mountains: good for walks and angling. Breakfast in conservatory. Immaculate bedrooms.

TRAMORE (Trá Mhór) – Waterford – 712 K11 – pop. 9 634 Ireland — 39 C2

Dublin 170 km – Waterford 9 km

(051) 381572 (June-August)

Dunmore East★, E : 18 km by R 675, R 685 and R 684

Glenorney without rest

Newtown, Southwest : 1.5 km by R 675 – (051) 381 056 – www.glenorney.com – Fax (051) 381 103 – March-November

6 rm – € 50/90 € 80/90

◆ On a hill overlooking Tramore Bay. Inside are personally decorated rooms: family photographs and curios; sun lounge with plenty of books. Rear rooms have lovely bay views.

TRIM (Baile Átha Troim) – Meath – 712 L7 – pop. 6 870 Ireland — 37 D3

Dublin 43 km – Drogheda 42 km – Tullamore 69 km

Old Town Hall, Castle St (046) 9437227, trimvisitorcentre@eircom.net

County Meath Newtownmoynagh, (046) 943 1463

Trim Castle★★ – Town★

Bective Abbey★, NE : 6.5 km by R 161

REPUBLIC OF IRELAND

Trim Castle

Castle St – ✆ (046) 948 3000 – www.trimcastlehotel.com – Fax (046) 948 3077 – closed 25 December
68 rm – € 135/165 € 150/180
Rest *Jules* – Menu € 20/35 – Carte € 31/47
◆ Newly-built hotel. Decently-sized, contemporary bedrooms; those at the front overlook Trim Castle, as does the third floor roof terrace. Ideal venue for wedding receptions. All-day café serves light dishes. More formal dining in first floor restaurant.

Highfield House without rest

Maudlins Rd – ✆ (046) 943 63 86 – www.highfieldguesthouse.com – Fax (046) 943 81 82 – closed 23 December-4 January
8 rm – € 55 € 80/88
◆ 19C former maternity home in lawned gardens overlooking Trim Castle and River Boyne. Sizeable bedrooms in cheerful colours offer a welcome respite after sightseeing.

The symbol guarantees a good night's sleep. In red ? The very essence of peace: only the sound of birdsong in the early morning...

REPUBLIC OF IRELAND

TULLY CROSS – Galway – 712 C7 — 36 A3

Dublin 301 km – Galway 85 km – Letterfrack 3 km

Maol Reidh

– ✆ (095) 43 844 – www.maolreidhhotel.com – Fax (095) 43 784 – November-January weekends only
12 rm – € 65/75 € 90/130
Rest – *(bar lunch)* Menu € 30 (dinner) – Carte € 30/35 **s**
◆ This good value, personally run hotel was built with local stone and a noteworthy attention to detail. Cosy rear bar and sitting room. Good sized bedrooms. Stylish restaurant with modern menus.

TWOMILEBORRIS (Buiríos Léith) – Tipperary – 712 I9 – see Thurles

VALENCIA ISLAND (Dairbhre) – Kerry – 712 A/B12 – pop. 650 — 38 A2

Dublin 381 km – Killarney 88 km – Tralee 92 km

KNIGHTS TOWN – Kerry — 38 A2

Glanleam House

Glanleam, West : 2 km taking right fork at top of Market St – ✆ (066) 947 61 76 – www.glanleam.com – Mid-March to October
5 rm – € 60/130 € 140/260 – 1 suite
Rest – *(dinner only) (booking essential for non-residents) (communal dining)* Menu € 50
◆ Part 17C and 18C country house in extensive sub-tropical gardens, superbly located off West Kerry coast. Art Deco interiors. Spacious drawing room. Individually styled rooms. Communal dining; produce grown in hotel's 19C walled gardens.

WATERFORD (Port Láirge) – Waterford – 712 K11 – pop. 49 213 — 39 C2

Ireland

Dublin 154 km – Cork 117 km – Limerick 124 km

Waterford Airport, Killowen : ✆ (051) 846600

The Granary, The Quay ✆ (051) 875823 Y, southeastinfo@failteireland.ie
Crystal Visitor Centre, Cork Rd ✆ (051) 358397 (seasonal), WaterfordCrystal@failteireland.ie

Newrath, ✆ (051) 876 748

Town★ - City Walls★ – Waterford Treasures★ **AC** Y

Waterford Crystal★, SW : 2.5 km by N 25 Y. Duncannon★, E : 19.25 km by R 683, ferry from Passage East and R 374 (south) Z – Dunmore East★, SE : 19.25 km by R 684 Z – Tintern Abbey★, E : 21 km by R 683, ferry from Passage East, R 733 and R 734 (south) Z

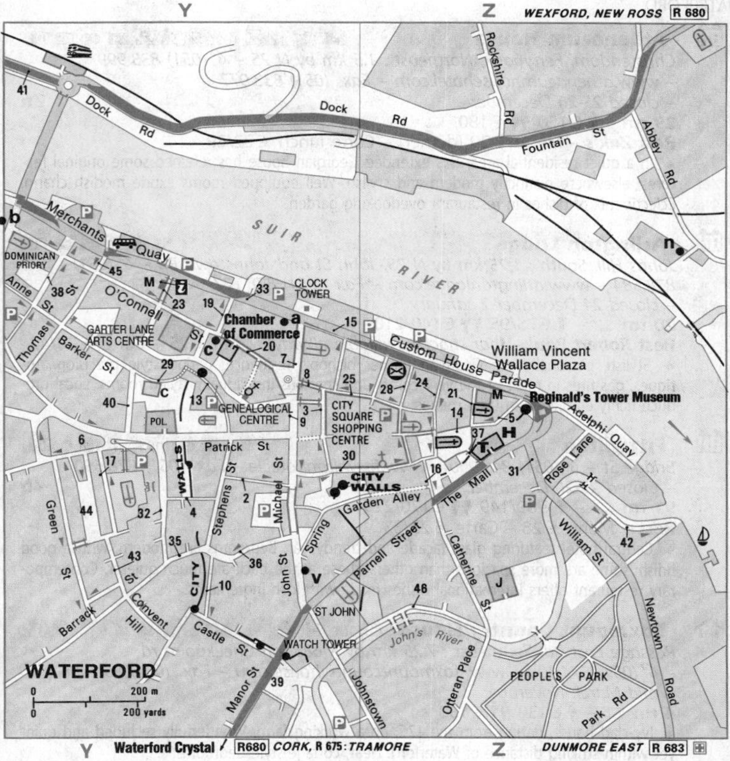

WATERFORD

Street	Grid	No.
Alexander St	Y	2
Arundel Square	Y	3
Bachelors Walk	Y	4
Bailey's New St	Z	5
Ballybricken Green	Y	6
Barronstrand St	Y	7
Blackfriars St	Y	8
Broad St	Y	9
Brown's Lane	Y	10
Carrigeen Park	Y	13
Cathedral Square	Z	14
City Square Shopping Centre	YZ	
Coal Quay	Y	15
Colbeck St	Z	16
Five Alley Lane	Y	17
George St	Y	20
Gladstone St	Y	19
Greyfriar's St	Z	21
Hanover St	Y	23
Henrietta St	Z	24
High St	YZ	25
Jenkin's Lane	Y	27
Keiser St	Z	28
King's Terrace	Y	29
Lady Lane	YZ	30
Lombard St	Z	31
Mayors Walk	Y	32
Meagher's Quay	Y	33
Newgate St	Y	35
New St	Y	36
Palace Lane	Z	37
Penrose Lane	Y	38
Railway Square	Y	39
St Patrick Terrace	Y	40
Sally Park	Y	41
Scotch Quay	Z	42
Shortcourse	Y	43
Trinity Square	Y	44
Vulcan St	Y	45
Water Side	Z	46

Waterford Castle H. and Golf Club

The Island, Ballinakill, East : 4 km by R 683, Ballinakill Rd and private ferry – ☎ *(051) 878 203* – *www.waterfordcastle.com* – *Fax (051) 879 316* – *closed 24-26 December*

14 rm – € 105/172 € 128/214 – 5 suites

Rest ***The Munster Dining Room*** – *(bar lunch Monday-Saturday)* Menu €65

◆ Part 15C and 19C castle in charmingly secluded, historic river island setting. Classic country house ambience amid antiques and period features. Comfortable, elegant rooms. Oak panelled dining room with ornate ceilings and evening pianist.

Athenaeum House

Christendom, Ferrybank, Northeast : 1.5 km by N 25 – (051) 833 999 – www.athenaeumhousehotel.com – Fax (051) 833 977 – closed 25-26 December Z**n**

29 rm – € 150 € 180, €15

Rest *Zak's* – Menu € 29 (dinner) – Carte lunch € 22/29

◆ In a quiet residential area, this extended Georgian house has retained some original features; elsewhere distinctly modern and stylish. Well equipped rooms exude modish charm. Eclectic mix of dishes in restaurant overlooking garden.

Arlington Lodge

Johns Hill, South : 1.25 km by N 25, John St and Johnstown Rd – (051) 878 584 – www.arlingtonlodge.com – Fax (051) 878 127 – closed 24 December-2 January

20 rm – € 75/95 € 140/210

Rest *Robert Paul* – *(bar snacks available all day)* Menu € 25 – Carte € 28/42

◆ Stylish, personally run Georgian former bishop's residence: period style precision. Antiques, gas fires in most of the very comfy and spacious individually styled rooms. Local produce richly employed in tasty menus.

Fitzwilton

Bridge St – (051) 846 900 – www.fitzwiltonhotel.ie – Fax (051) 878 650 – Closed 23-26 December Y**b**

91 rm – € 89/149 € 170/229

Rest – Menu € 28 – Carte € 23/33

◆ Central hotel featuring glass façade and trendy bar. Bedrooms are modern, with a good finish: some are more spacious than others; those at the back are much quieter. Contemporary restaurant offers international dishes made with Irish ingredients.

Foxmount Country House without rest

Passage East Rd, Southeast : 7.25 km by R 683, off Cheekpoint rd – (051) 874 308 – www.foxmountcountryhouse.com – Fax (051) 854 906 – mid March-November

4 rm – € 130 € 130

◆ Ivy-clad house, dating from the 17C, on a working farm. Wonderfully secluded and quiet yet within striking distance of Waterford. Neat, cottage-style bedrooms.

La Bohème

2 George's St – (051) 875 645 – www.labohemerestaurant.ie – Fax (051) 875 645 – closed Christmas, 10 days summer, end July-early August, Sunday, Monday and Bank Holidays Y**c**

Rest – French – *(dinner only) (booking essential)* Menu € 37 – Carte € 41/56

◆ Careful restoration of this historic building has created an atmospheric, candlelit dining room. Classic French cooking, traditionally prepared, includes daily market specials.

Bodéga

54 John St – (051) 844 177 – www.bodegawaterford.com – Fax (051) 844 177 – closed 25-26 December, 1 January, Good Friday, Sunday (except Bank holidays) and lunch Saturday Y**v**

Rest – Menu € 25/30 – Carte € 29/43

◆ Tucked away in the heart of the city. Purple exterior; orange interior, augmented by mosaics and wall murals. Classic rustic French menus or warming lunchtime dishes.

WATERVILLE (An Coireán) – Kerry – 712 B12 – pop. 546 Ireland 38 A3

Dublin 383 km – Killarney 77 km

Main St. (066) 9474646 (June-September)

Ring of Kerry Golf Links Rd, (066) 947 41 02

Ring of Kerry★★ – Skellig Islands★★, W: 12.75 km by N 70, R 567 and ferry from Ballinskelligs – Derrynane National Historic Park★★ **AC**, S: 14.5 km by N70 – Leacanabuaile Fort (<★★), N: 21 km by N 70

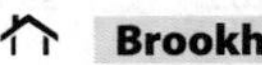

Brookhaven House without rest

New Line Rd, North : 1.25 km on N 70 – (066) 947 44 31 – www.brookhavenhouse.com – Fax (066) 947 47 24 – March-November

6 rm – € 65/100 € 120

◆ Spacious modern guesthouse overlooking Waterville golf course; large and neat, with restful lounge and cottage style bedrooms. Proud of its home-baked breakfasts.

WESTPORT (Cathair na Mart) – Mayo – 712 D6 – pop. 5 475 — 36 A2

 Ireland

Dublin 262 km – Galway 80 km – Sligo 104 km

James St (098) 25711, westport@failteireland.ie

Town★★ (Centre★) – Westport House★★ **AC**

Ballintubber Abbey★, SE : 21 km by R 330. SW : Murrisk Peninsula★★ – Croagh Patrick★, W : 9.5 km by R 335 – Bunlahinch Clapper Bridge★, W : 25.75 km by R 335 - Doo Lough Pass★, W : 38.5 km by R 335 – Aasleagh Falls★, S : 35.5 km by N 59

Carlton Atlantic Coast rm,

The Quay, West : 1.5 km by R 335 – (098) 29 000 – www.carltonatlanticcoasthotel.com – Fax (098) 29 111 – closed 22-29 December

84 rm – € 79/175 € 98/300 – 1 suite

Rest *Blue Wave* – *(dinner only)* Menu € 42

◆ Striking 18C mill conversion on shores of Clew Bay. Enjoy a seaweed treatment in the hydrotherapy jet bath or a drink in the lively Harbourmaster bar. Well-kept bedrooms. Top-floor restaurant with harbour and bay views.

Ardmore Country House

The Quay, West : 2.5 km on R 335 – (098) 25 994 – www.ardmorecountryhouse.com – Fax (098) 27 795 – March-October

13 rm – € 100/130 € 130/180

Rest – *(dinner only) (booking essential residents only on Sunday)* Menu € 40 – Carte € 35/55

◆ Attractive, personally run hotel in commanding setting with views across gardens and Clew Bay. Neat, comfortable bedrooms have a sumptuous yet homely feel. Passionate chef-owner produces traditional dishes using local ingredients.

Westport Country Lodge rm,

Aghagower, Southeast : 4 km by R 330 Cathair na Mart / Westport – (098) 56 030 – www.westportlodge.ie – Fax (098) 56 040

20 rm – € 40/75 € 90/140

Rest – Menu € 20 (dinner) – Carte € 20/28

◆ Hotel set in 36 acres, with 9 hole golf course. Rooms have big beds, flat screens and mod cons; many also have countryside views out towards Croagh Patrick. Contemporary bar and dining room. Unpretentious homemade food, with classics given a modern touch.

Augusta Lodge without rest

Golf Links Rd, North : 0.75 km off N 59 – (098) 28 900 – www.augustalodge.ie – Fax (098) 28 995 – closed 23-26 December

10 rm – € 45/70 € 70/100

◆ Family run, purpose-built guesthouse, convenient for Westport Golf Club; play the piano in the lounge while admiring the golfing memorabilia. Homely, simple bedrooms.

Quay West without rest

Quay Rd, West : 0.75 km – (098) 27 863 – www.quaywestport.com – Fax (098) 28 379

6 rm – € 40/50 € 70/80

◆ Purpose-built guesthouse located within walking distance of the town centre. Simply appointed throughout providing sensibly priced, well kept rooms.

Sheebeen

Rosbeg, West : 3 km on R 335 – (098) 26 528 – www.croninssheebeen.com – Fax (098) 24 396 – Closed lunch weekdays November-mid March

Rest – Carte € 22/40

◆ Thatched roadside pub to west of town. Cosy front bar has some tables but main dining is upstairs. Fresh, accurate cooking; go for the fresh local fish and seafood specials.

REPUBLIC OF IRELAND

WEXFORD (Loch Garman) – Wexford – 712 M10 – pop. 18 163 39 D2

Ireland

Dublin 141 km – Kilkenny 79 km – Waterford 61 km

Crescent Quay ✆ (053) 23111

Mulgannon, ✆ (053) 42 238

Town★ - Main Street★ YZ - Franciscan Friary★ Z – St Iberius' Church★ Y D - Twin Churches★ Z

Irish Agricultural Museum, Johnstown Castle★★ **AC**, SW : 7.25 km X – Irish National Heritage Park, Ferrycarrig★ **AC**, NW : 4 km by N 11 V – Curracloe★, NE : 8 km by R 741 and R 743 V. Kilmore Quay★, SW : 24 km by N 25 and R 739 (Saltee Islands★ - access by boat) X – Enniscorthy Castle★ (County Museum★ **AC**) N : 24 km by N 11 V

Whites

rm,

Abbey St – ✆ (053) 912 2311 – www.whitesofwexford.ie – Fax (053) 914 5000 – Closed 24-26 December Ya

152 rm – € 190 €330

Rest *Whites* – *(dinner only)* Menu €25 – Carte approx. €25

◆ Smart new hotel built around a paved central courtyard. Spacious and modern, with a busy bar, popular meeting rooms, superb leisure facilities and very comfortable bedrooms. Traditional menu served in contemporary dining room.

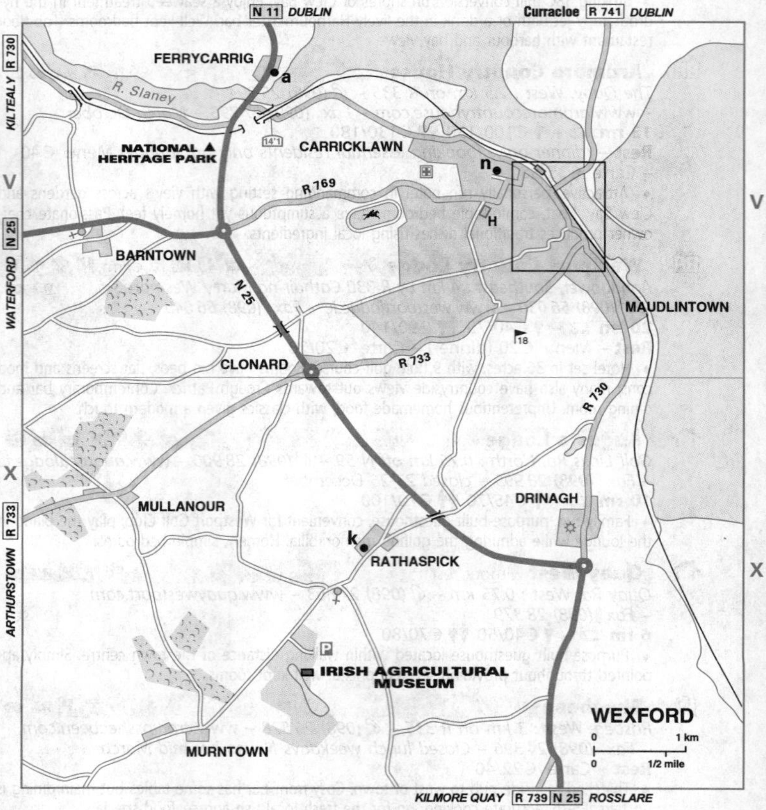

N 11 DUBLIN
Curracloe R 741 DUBLIN
KILTEALY R 730
FERRYCARRIG
a
R. Slaney
NATIONAL HERITAGE PARK
14'1
CARRICKLAWN
n
V
R 769
H
WATERFORD N 25
BARNTOWN
N 25
MAUDLINTOWN
CLONARD
R 733
X
ARTHURSTOWN R 733
MULLANOUR
R 730
DRINAGH
k
RATHASPICK
P
IRISH AGRICULTURAL MUSEUM
WEXFORD
0 1 km
0 1/2 mile
MURNTOWN
KILMORE QUAY R 739 N 25 ROSSLARE

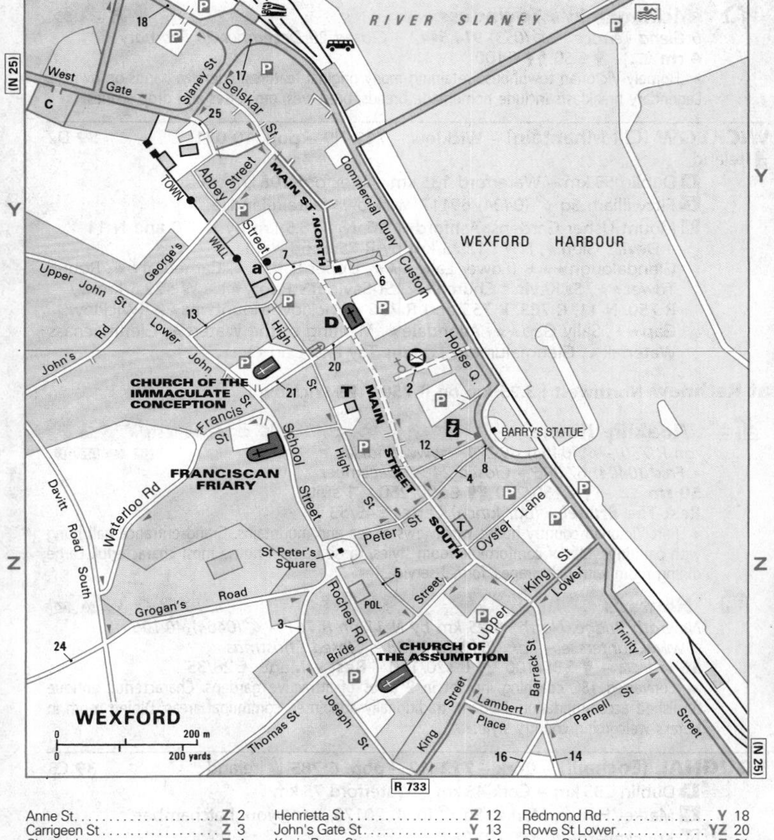

Anne St.	Z	2	Henrietta St	Z	12	Redmond Rd	Y	18
Carrigeen St	Z	3	John's Gate St	Y	13	Rowe St Lower	YZ	20
Cinema Lane	Z	4	Kevin Barry St	Z	14	Rowe St Upper	Z	21
Clifford St	Z	5	Main St North	Y		Selskar St	Y	
Common Quay St	Y	6	Main St South	Z		Summerhill Rd	Z	24
Cornmarket	Y	7	Michael St	Z	16	Temperance Row	Y	25
Crescent Quay	Z	8	Redmond Pl.	Y	17			

Ferrycarrig

rm, rest,

Ferrycarrig, Northwest : 4.5 km on N 11
– (053) 91 20 999 – www.ferrycarrighotel.com
– Fax (053) 91 20 982 Va

98 rm – € 90/135 € 170/250 – 4 suites

Rest ***Reeds*** – *(booking essential at lunch)* Menu € 30 – Carte € 30/43

◆ Imposing hotel idyllically set on River Slaney and estuary. Public areas on enchanting waterfront curve. Good leisure facilities. Modern rooms with super views and balconies. Lively, informal Reeds.

Rathaspeck Manor without rest

Rathaspeck, Southwest : 6.5 km by Rosslare Rd off Bridgetown rd
– (053) 914 16 72 – www.rathaspeckmanor.com
– March-November Xk

4 rm – € 45/60 € 90/120

◆ Georgian country house with 18-hole golf course half a mile from Johnstone Castle. Period furnishings adorn the public rooms. Comfortable, spacious bedrooms.

McMenamin's Townouse without rest

6 Glena Terrace – (053) 914 6442 – Closed 20 December-20 February

4 rm – € 60 € 100 Xn

◆ Homely Victorian townhouse retaining many original features. Friendly, hands-on owners. Legendary breakfasts include homemade breads, preserves, omelettes and drop scones.

WICKLOW (Cill Mhantáin) – Wicklow – 712 N9 – pop. 10 071 — 39 D2

Ireland

Dublin 53 km – Waterford 135 km – Wexford 108 km

Fitzwilliam Sq (0404) 69117, wicklow@failteireland.ie

Mount Usher Gardens, Ashford★ **AC**, NW : 6.5 km by R 750 and N 11 – Devil's Glen★, NW : 12.75 km by R 750 and N 11. Glendalough★★★ (Lower Lake★★★, Upper Lake★★, Cathedral★★, Round Tower★★, St Kevin's Church★★, St Saviour's Priory★) – W : 22.5 km by R 750, N 11, R 763, R 755 and R 756 – Wicklow Mountains★★ (Wicklow Gap★★, Sally Gap★★, Avondale★, Meeting of the Waters★, Glenmacnass Waterfall★, Glenmalur★, – Loughs Tay and Dan★)

at Rathnew Northwest : 3.25 km on R 750 – Wicklow

Tinakilly House — rm, rest

on R 750 – (0404) 69 274 – www.tinakilly.ie – Fax (0404) 67 806 – Closed 24-27 December

50 rm – € 150/200 € 200/250 – 1 suite

Rest *The Brunel* – *(bar lunch)* Carte € 45/53

◆ Part Victorian country house with views of sea and mountains. Grand entrance hall hung with paintings. Mix of comfortable room styles, those in main house most characterful. Large dining room with rich drapes, formal service.

Hunter's

Newrath Bridge, North : 1.25 km by N 11 on R 761 – (0404) 40 106 – www.hunters.ie – Fax (0404) 40 338 – Closed Christmas

16 rm – € 85/100 € 120/170 **Rest** – Menu € 28/35

◆ Converted 18C coaching inn set in 2 acres of attractive gardens. Characterful, antique furnished accommodation. Elegant, traditionally appointed communal areas. Dining room in hotel's welcoming country style.

YOUGHAL (Eochaill) – Cork – 712 I12 – pop. 6 785 Ireland — 39 C3

Dublin 235 km – Cork 48 km – Waterford 75 km

Market House, Market Sq (024) 20170, info@youghalchamber.ie

Knockaverry, (024) 92 787

Town★ – St Mary's Collegiate Church★★ – Town Walls★ - Clock Gate★

Helvick Head★ (★), NE : 35.5 km by N 25 and R 674 – Ringville (★), NE : 32.25 km by N 25 and R 674 – Ardmore★ - Round Tower★ - Cathedral★ (arcade★), N : 16 km by N 25 and R 674 – Whiting Bay★, SE : 19.25 km by N 25, R 673 and the coast road

Aherne's with rm — rm

163 North Main St – (024) 92 424 – www.ahernes.com – Fax (024) 93 633 – Closed 23-28 December

12 rm – € 125/130 € 170/210

Rest – Seafood – *(bar lunch)* Menu € 45 – Carte € 27/52

◆ A sitting room fireplace greets you at this family-run restaurant. Choose between a formal dining room or cosy bar. It's all about the seafood which is all the better for being simply prepared.

- → *Discover the best restaurant ?*
- → *Find the nearest hotel ?*
- → *Find your bearings using our maps and guides ?*
- → *Understand the symbols used in the guide...*

Follow the red Bibs !

Advice on restaurants from **Chef Bib**.

Tips and advice from **Clever Bib** on finding your way around the guide and on the road.

Advice on hotels from **Bellboy Bib**.

Major hotel groups

Central reservation telephone numbers

ACCOR HOTELS (MERCURE & NOVOTEL)	0208 2834500
CHOICE HOTELS	0800 444444 *(Freephone)*
DE VERE HOTELS PLC	0870 6063606
DOYLE COLLECTION	0870 9072222
HILTON HOTELS	08705 515151
HOLIDAY INN & CROWNE PLAZA WORLDWIDE	0800 897121 *(Freephone)*
HYATT HOTELS WORLDWIDE	0845 8881234
INTERCONTINENTAL HOTELS	0800 0289387 *(Freephone)*
MACDONALD HOTELS PLC	08457 585593
MARRIOTT HOTELS	0800 221222 *(Freephone)*
MILLENNIUM & COPTHORNE HOTELS PLC	0845 3020001
RADISSON HOTELS WORLDWIDE	0800 374411 *(Freephone)*
SHERATON HOTELS & RESORTS WORLDWIDE	0800 353535 *(Freephone)*

International Dialling Codes

Note: When making an international call, do not dial the first (0) of the city code (except for calls to Italy).

from \ to	A	B	CH	CZ	D	DK	E	FIN	F	GB	GR
A Austria		0032	0041	00420	0049	0045	0034	00358	0033	0044	0030
B Belgium	0043		0041	00420	0049	0045	0034	00358	0033	0044	0030
CH Switzerland	0043	0032		00420	0049	0045	0034	00358	0033	0044	0030
CZ Czech Republic	0043	0032	0041		0049	0045	0034	00358	0033	0044	0030
D Germany	0043	0032	0041	00420		0045	0034	00358	0033	0044	0030
DK Denmark	0043	0032	0041	00420	0049		0034	00358	0033	0044	0030
E Spain	0043	0032	0041	00420	0049	0045		00358	0033	0044	0030
FIN Finland	0043	0032	0041	00420	0049	0045	0034		0033	0044	0030
F France	0043	0032	0041	00420	0049	0045	0034	00358		0044	0030
GB United Kingdom	0043	0032	0041	00420	0049	0045	0034	00358	0033		0030
GR Greece	0043	0032	0041	00420	0049	0045	0034	00358	0033	0044	
H Hungary	0043	0032	0041	00420	0049	0045	0034	00358	0033	0044	0030
I Italy	0043	0032	0041	00420	0049	0045	0034	00358	0033	0044	0030
IRL Ireland	0043	0032	0041	00420	0049	0045	0034	00358	0033	0044	0030
J Japan	00143	00132	00141	001420	00149	00145	00134	001358	00133	00144	00130
L Luxembourg	0043	0032	0041	00420	0049	0045	0034	00358	0033	0044	0030
N Norway	0043	0032	0041	00420	0049	0045	0034	00358	0033	0044	0030
NL Netherlands	0043	0032	0041	00420	0049	0045	0034	00358	0033	0044	0030
PL Poland	0043	0032	0041	00420	0049	0045	0034	00358	0033	0044	0030
P Portugal	0043	0032	0041	00420	0049	0045	0034	00358	0033	0044	0030
RUS Russia	81043	81032	81041	6420	81049	81045	*	810358	81033	81044	*
S Sweden	0043	0032	0041	00420	0049	0045	0034	00358	0033	0044	0030
USA	01143	01132	01141	001420	01149	01145	01134	01358	01133	01144	01130

** Direct dialling not possible*

H	I	IRL	J	L	N	NL	PL	P	RUS	S	USA	
0036	0039	00353	0081	00352	0047	0031	0048	00351	007	0046	001	**A Austria**
0036	0039	00353	0081	00352	0047	0031	0048	00351	007	0046	001	**B Belgium**
0036	0039	00353	0081	00352	0047	0031	0048	00351	007	0046	001	**CH Switzerland**
0036	0039	00353	0081	00352	0047	0031	0048	00351	007	0046	001	**CZ Czech Republic**
0036	0039	00353	0081	00352	0047	0031	0048	00351	007	0046	001	**D Germany**
0036	0039	00353	0081	00352	0047	0031	0048	00351	007	0046	001	**DK Denmark**
0036	0039	00353	0081	00352	0047	0031	0048	00351	007	0046	001	**E Spain**
0036	0039	00353	0081	00352	0047	0031	0048	00351	007	0046	001	**FIN Finland**
0036	0039	00353	0081	00352	0047	0031	0048	00351	007	0046	001	**F France**
0036	0039	00353	0081	00352	0047	0031	0048	00351	007	0046	001	**GB United Kingdom**
0036	0039	00353	0081	00352	0047	0031	0048	00351	007	0046	001	**GR Greece**
	0039	00353	0081	00352	0047	0031	0048	00351	007	0046	001	**H Hungary**
0036		00353	0081	00352	0047	0031	0048	00351	*	0046	001	**I Italy**
0036	0039		0081	00352	0047	0031	0048	00351	007	0046	001	**IRL Ireland**
00136	00139	001353		001352	00147	00131	00148	001351	*	001146	0011	**J Japan**
0036	0039	00353	0081		0047	0031	0048	00351	007	0046	001	**L Luxembourg**
0036	0039	00353	0081	00352		0031	0048	00351	007	0046	001	**N Norway**
0036	0039	00353	0081	00352	0047		0048	00351	007	0046	001	**NL Netherlands**
0036	0039	00353	0081	00352	0047	0031		00351	007	0046	001	**PL Poland**
0036	0039	00353	0081	00352	0047	0031	048		007	0046	001	**P Portugal**
81036	*	*	*	*	*	81031	1048	*		*	*	**RUS Russia**
0036	0039	00353	0081	00352	0047	0031	0048	00351	007		001	**S Sweden**
01136	01139	011353	01181	011352	01147	01131	01148	011351	*	011146		**USA**

Index of towns

O. Forir/MICHELIN

C

D

H

M

Page

N Page

O Page

P Page

Q Page

R Page

S Page

T Page

U Page

V Page

W Page

Y — Page

Z — Page

Maps

Regional maps of listed towns

Places with at least one

- ● hotel or restaurant
- ✿ starred establishment
- « Bib Gourmand » restaurant
- « Bib Hotel »
- particularly pleasant restaurant
- traditional pub serving good food
- particularly pleasant hotel
- particularly pleasant guesthouse
- particularly quiet hotel

Distances in miles

(except for the Republic of Ireland: km). The distance is given from each town to other nearby towns and to the capital of each region as grouped in the guide. To avoid excessive repetition some distances have only been quoted once – you may therefore have to look under both town headings.
The distances quoted are not necessarily the shortest but have been based on the roads which afford the best driving conditions and are therefore the most practical.

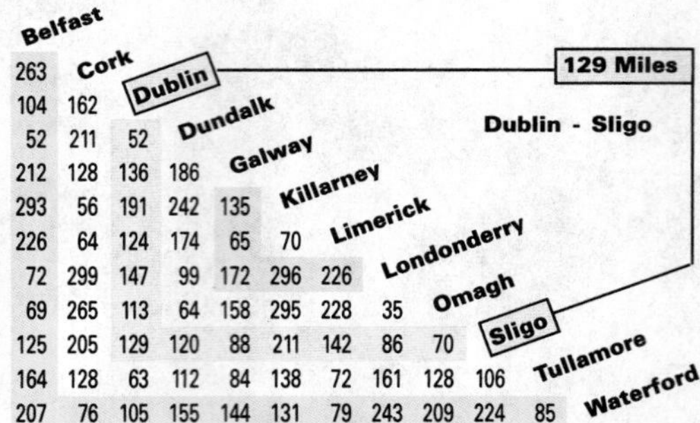

	Belfast	Cork	Dublin	Dundalk	Galway	Killarney	Limerick	Londonderry	Omagh	Sligo	Tullamore
Cork	263										
Dublin	104	162									
Dundalk	52	211	52								
Galway	212	128	136	186							
Killarney	293	56	191	242	135						
Limerick	226	64	124	174	65	70					
Londonderry	72	299	147	99	172	296	226				
Omagh	69	265	113	64	158	295	228	35			
Sligo	125	205	129	120	88	211	142	86	70		
Tullamore	164	128	63	112	84	138	72	161	128	106	
Waterford	207	76	105	155	144	131	79	243	209	224	85

Distances between major towns

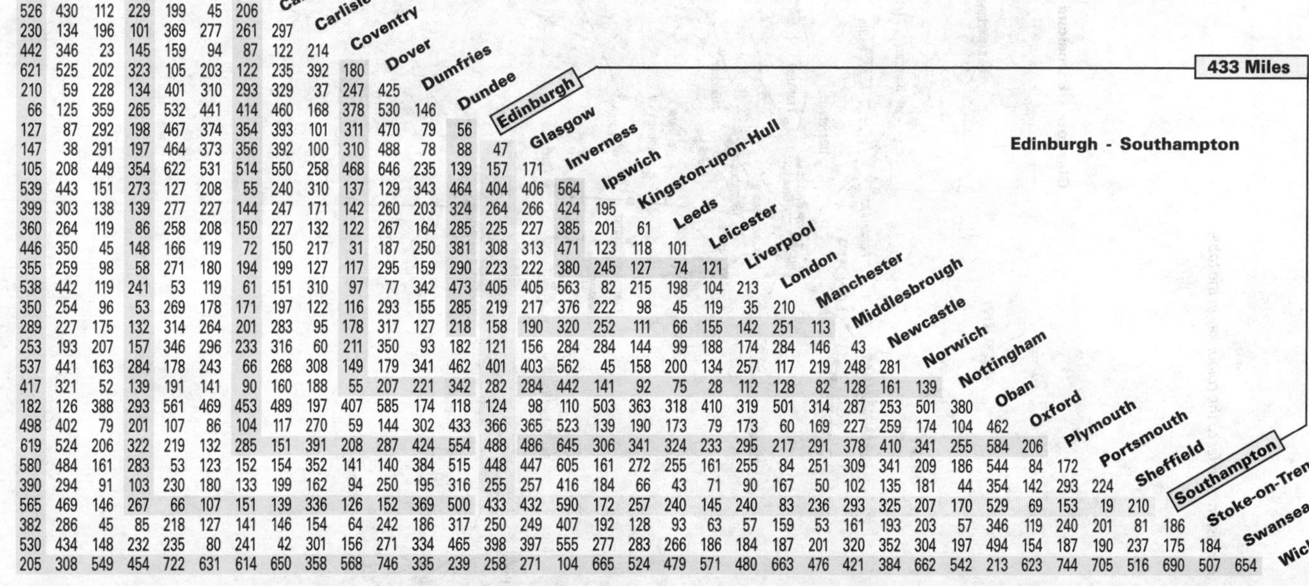

	Aberdeen	Ayr	Birmingham	Blackpool	Brighton	Bristol	Cambridge	Cardiff	Carlisle	Coventry	Dover	Dumfries	Dundee	Edinburgh	Glasgow	Inverness	Ipswich	Kingston-upon-Hull	Leeds	Leicester	Liverpool	London	Manchester	Middlesbrough	Newcastle	Norwich	Nottingham	Oban	Oxford	Plymouth	Portsmouth	Sheffield	Southampton	Stoke-on-Trent	Swansea
Ayr	182																																		
Birmingham	424	328																																	
Blackpool	329	233	127																																
Brighton	597	501	178	300																															
Bristol	505	410	92	208	166																														
Cambridge	488	392	100	222	122	187																													
Cardiff	526	430	112	229	199	45	206																												
Carlisle	230	134	196	101	369	277	261	297																											
Coventry	442	346	23	145	159	94	87	122	214																										
Dover	621	525	202	323	105	203	122	235	392	180																									
Dumfries	210	59	228	134	401	310	293	329	37	247	425																								
Dundee	66	125	359	265	532	441	414	460	168	378	530	146																							
Edinburgh	127	87	292	198	467	374	354	393	101	311	470	79	56																						
Glasgow	147	38	291	197	464	373	356	392	100	310	488	78	88	47																					
Inverness	105	208	449	354	622	531	514	550	258	468	646	235	139	157	171																				
Ipswich	539	443	151	273	127	208	55	240	310	137	129	343	464	404	406	564																			
Kingston-upon-Hull	399	303	138	139	277	227	144	247	171	142	260	203	324	264	266	424	195																		
Leeds	360	264	119	86	258	208	150	227	132	122	267	164	285	225	227	385	201	61																	
Leicester	446	350	45	148	166	119	72	150	217	31	187	250	381	308	313	471	123	118	101																
Liverpool	355	259	98	58	271	180	194	199	127	117	295	159	290	223	222	380	245	127	74	121															
London	538	442	119	241	53	119	61	151	310	97	77	342	473	405	405	563	82	215	198	104	213														
Manchester	350	254	96	53	269	178	171	197	122	116	293	155	285	219	217	376	222	98	45	119	35	210													
Middlesbrough	289	227	175	132	314	264	201	283	95	178	317	127	218	158	190	320	252	111	66	155	142	251	113												
Newcastle	253	193	207	157	346	296	233	316	60	211	350	93	182	121	156	284	284	144	99	188	174	284	146	43											
Norwich	537	441	163	284	178	243	66	268	308	149	179	341	462	401	403	562	45	158	200	134	257	117	219	248	281										
Nottingham	417	321	52	139	191	141	90	160	188	55	207	221	342	282	284	442	141	92	75	28	112	128	82	128	161	139									
Oban	182	126	388	293	561	469	453	489	197	407	585	174	118	124	98	110	503	363	318	410	319	501	314	287	253	501	380								
Oxford	498	402	79	201	107	86	104	117	270	59	144	302	433	366	365	523	139	190	173	79	173	60	169	227	259	174	104	462							
Plymouth	619	524	206	322	219	132	285	151	391	208	287	424	554	488	486	645	306	341	324	233	295	217	291	378	410	341	255	584	206						
Portsmouth	580	484	161	283	53	123	152	154	352	141	140	384	515	448	447	605	161	272	255	161	255	84	251	309	341	209	186	544	84	172					
Sheffield	390	294	91	103	230	180	133	199	162	94	250	195	316	255	257	416	184	66	43	71	90	167	50	102	135	181	44	354	142	293	224				
Southampton	565	469	146	267	66	107	151	139	336	126	152	369	500	433	432	590	172	257	240	145	240	83	236	293	325	207	170	529	69	153	19	210			
Stoke-on-Trent	382	286	45	85	218	127	141	146	154	64	242	186	317	250	249	407	192	128	93	63	57	159	53	161	193	203	57	346	119	240	201	81	186		
Swansea	530	434	148	232	235	80	241	42	301	156	271	334	465	398	397	555	277	283	266	186	184	187	201	320	352	304	197	494	154	187	190	237	175	184	
Wick	205	308	549	454	722	631	614	650	358	568	746	335	239	258	271	104	665	524	479	571	480	663	476	421	384	662	542	213	623	744	705	516	690	507	654

For distances refer to the colour key in the table

● FOLKESTONE (CHANNEL TUNNEL)
● SOUTHAMPTON
● TYNEMOUTH

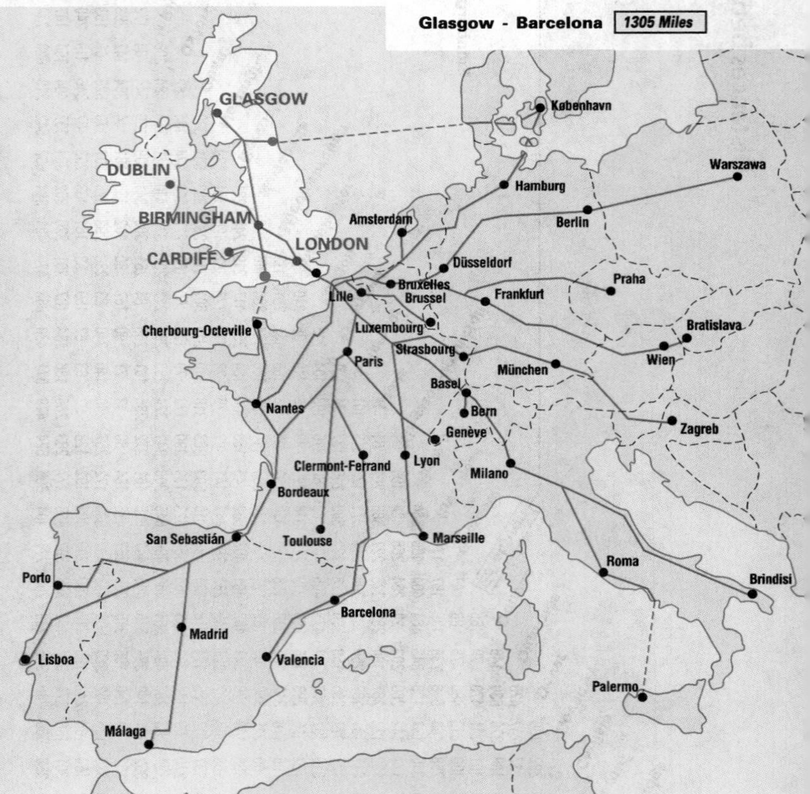

Birmingham	Cardiff	Dublin	Glasgow	London	
230	456	397	334	297	**Amsterdam**
1018	1051	1185	1305	892	**Barcelona**
647	680	816	934	522	**Basel**
774	807	941	724	648	**Berlin**
725	759	893	995	600	**Bern**
723	757	891	1010	598	**Bordeaux**
1060	1093	1227	1346	934	**Bratislava**
1493	1526	1660	1780	1367	**Brindisi**
320	353	487	606	194	**Bruxelles-Brussel**
161	148	329	448	86	**Cherbourg**
637	671	805	924	512	**Clermont-Ferrand**
445	479	613	732	320	**Düsseldorf**
566	600	734	853	441	**Frankfurt am Main**
665	737	832	951	539	**Genève**
509	699	677	605	540	**Hamburg**
701	891	868	796	732	**København**
265	298	432	551	139	**Lille**
1446	1479	1613	1732	1320	**Lisboa**
452	486	620	739	327	**Luxembourg**

Birmingham	Cardiff	Dublin	Glasgow	London	
667	701	835	954	542	**Lyon**
1153	1186	1320	1440	1027	**Madrid**
1488	1521	1655	1775	1362	**Málaga**
861	895	1029	1148	736	**Marseille**
875	908	1042	1161	749	**Milano**
800	833	967	1086	674	**München**
564	597	731	851	274	**Nantes**
1789	1822	1956	2076	1664	**Palermo**
370	403	537	656	244	**Paris**
1349	1382	1516	1635	1223	**Porto**
880	913	1047	1166	754	**Praha**
1240	1274	1408	1527	1115	**Roma**
867	900	1034	1154	741	**San Sebastián**
580	614	748	867	455	**Strasbourg**
795	828	962	1082	669	**Toulouse**
1230	1263	1397	1517	1104	**Valencia**
1118	1151	1286	1069	993	**Warszawa**
1007	1040	1174	1294	881	**Wien**
1118	1151	1285	1404	992	**Zagreb**

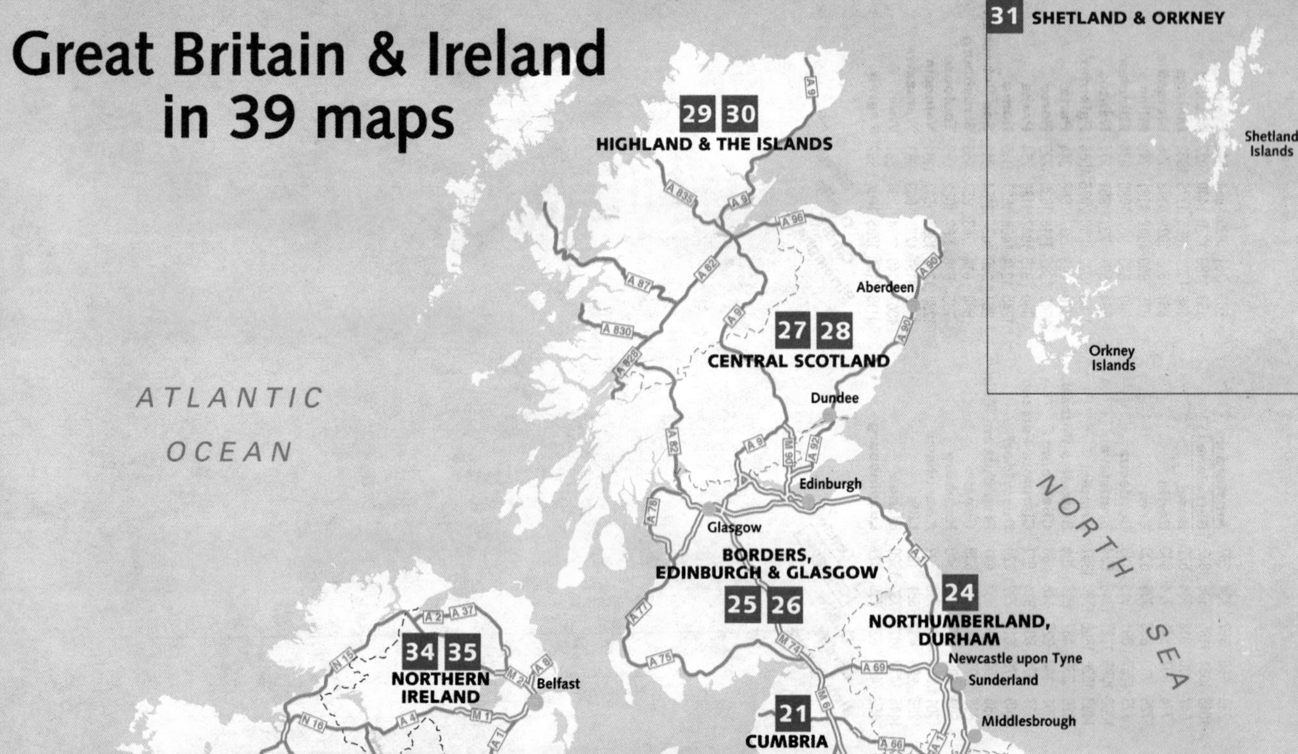
Great Britain & Ireland
in 39 maps
31 SHETLAND & ORKNEY
Shetland Islands
Orkney Islands
29 30
HIGHLAND & THE ISLANDS
27 28
CENTRAL SCOTLAND
Aberdeen
Dundee
Edinburgh
Glasgow
BORDERS,
EDINBURGH & GLASGOW
25 26
24
NORTHUMBERLAND,
DURHAM
Newcastle upon Tyne
Sunderland
Middlesbrough
21
CUMBRIA
34 35
NORTHERN
IRELAND
Belfast
ATLANTIC
OCEAN
NORTH SEA
A 9
A 835
A 96
A 82
A 87
A 830
A 828
A 90
A 92
M 90
A 78
A 77
A 75
M 74
M 6
A 69
A 1
A 66
A 2
A 37
N 15
N 16
A 4
M 1
M 2
A 8

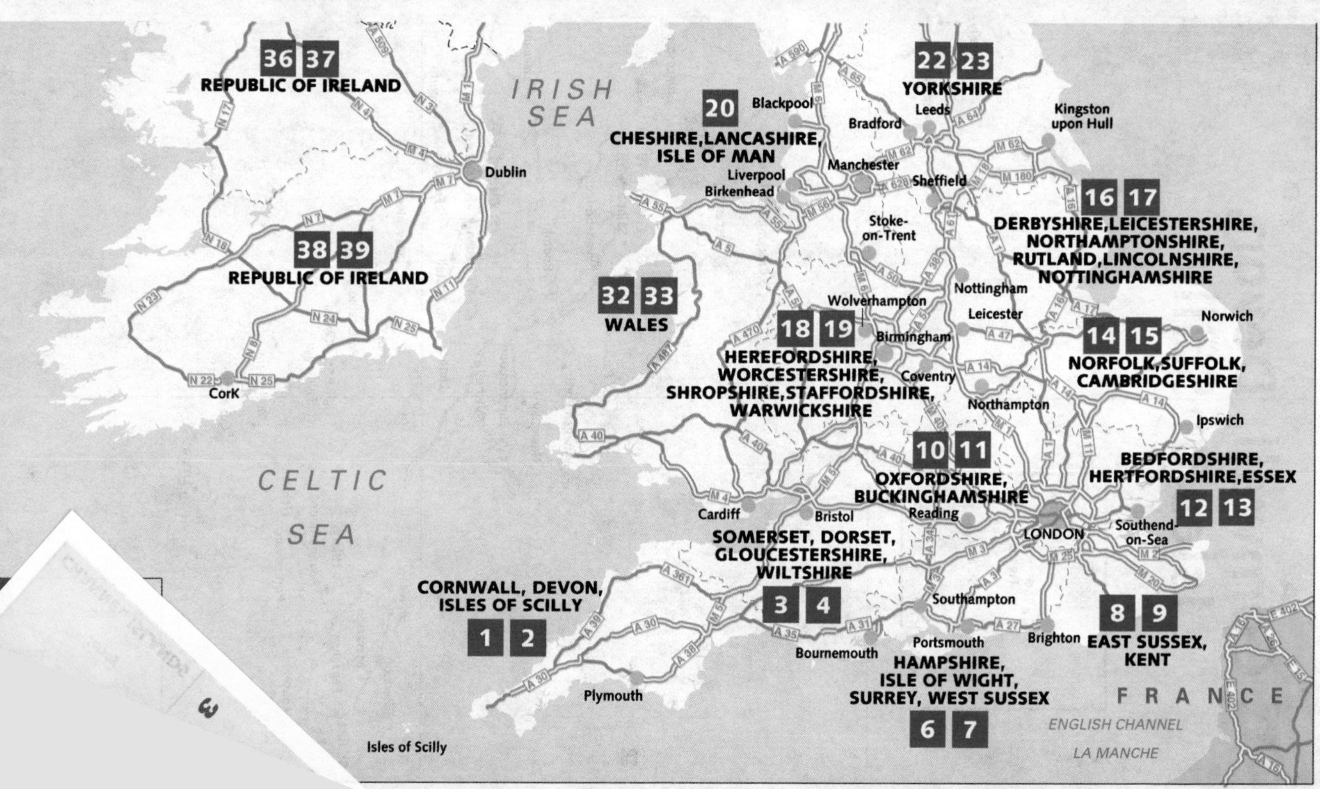

36 37
REPUBLIC OF IRELAND
38 39
REPUBLIC OF IRELAND
Dublin
Cork
IRISH SEA
CELTIC SEA
20
CHESHIRE, LANCASHIRE, ISLE OF MAN
22 23
YORKSHIRE
32 33
WALES
16 17
DERBYSHIRE, LEICESTERSHIRE, NORTHAMPTONSHIRE, RUTLAND, LINCOLNSHIRE, NOTTINGHAMSHIRE
18 19
HEREFORDSHIRE, WORCESTERSHIRE, SHROPSHIRE, STAFFORDSHIRE, WARWICKSHIRE
14 15
NORFOLK, SUFFOLK, CAMBRIDGESHIRE
10 11
OXFORDSHIRE, BUCKINGHAMSHIRE
BEDFORDSHIRE, HERTFORDSHIRE, ESSEX
12 13
SOMERSET, DORSET, GLOUCESTERSHIRE, WILTSHIRE
3 4
CORNWALL, DEVON, ISLES OF SCILLY
1 2
8 9
EAST SUSSEX, KENT
HAMPSHIRE, ISLE OF WIGHT, SURREY, WEST SUSSEX
6 7
Blackpool
Leeds
Bradford
Kingston upon Hull
Manchester
Liverpool
Birkenhead
Sheffield
Stoke-on-Trent
Nottingham
Wolverhampton
Leicester
Birmingham
Coventry
Northampton
Norwich
Ipswich
Cardiff
Bristol
Reading
LONDON
Southend-on-Sea
Southampton
Portsmouth
Brighton
Bournemouth
Plymouth
Isles of Scilly
FRANCE
ENGLISH CHANNEL
LA MANCHE

1 Cornwall, Devon, Isles of Scilly

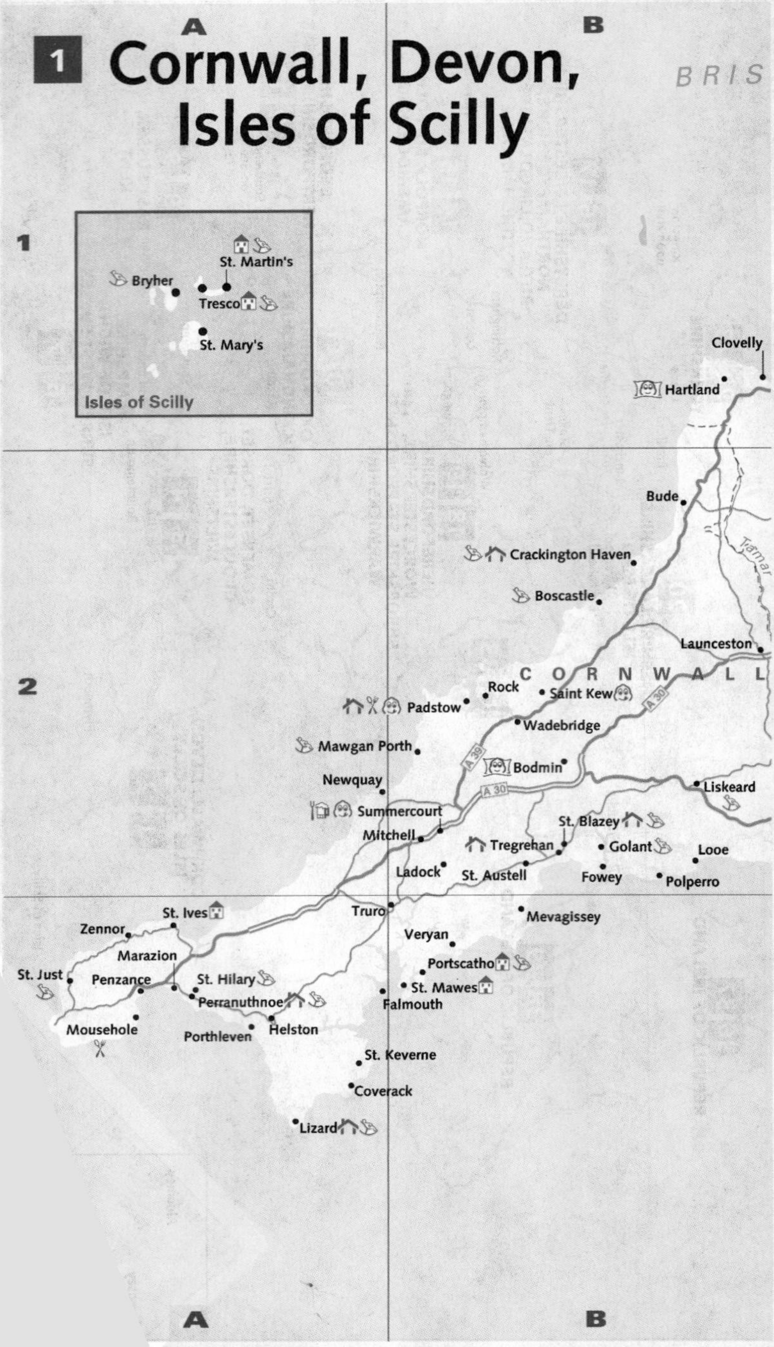

A B

1

Isles of Scilly

St. Martin's

Bryher

Tresco

St. Mary's

BRIS

Clovelly

Hartland

2

Bude

Crackington Haven

Tamar

Boscastle

Launceston

CORNWALL

Rock

Saint Kew

A 30

Padstow

Wadebridge

Mawgan Porth

A 39

Bodmin

Newquay

A 30

Liskeard

Summercourt

St. Blazey

Mitchell

Tregrehan

Golant

Looe

Ladock

St. Austell

Fowey

Polperro

St. Ives

Truro

Mevagissey

Zennor

Veryan

Marazion

Portscatho

St. Just

Penzance

St. Hilary

St. Mawes

Perranuthnoe

Falmouth

Mousehole

Porthleven

Helston

St. Keverne

Coverack

Lizard

A B

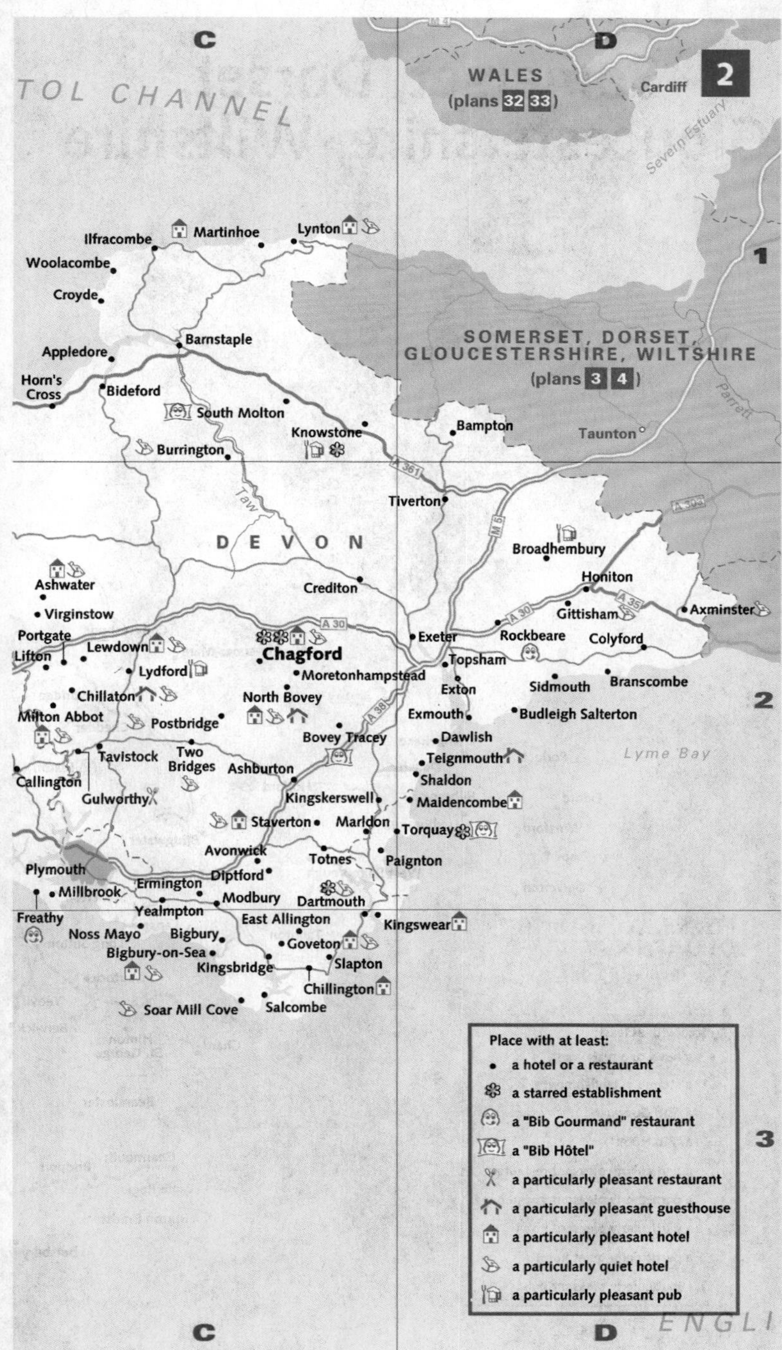
C
D
2
TOL CHANNEL
WALES
(plans 32 33)
Cardiff
Severn Estuary
1
SOMERSET, DORSET, GLOUCESTERSHIRE, WILTSHIRE
(plans 3 4)
Taunton
Parrett
Ilfracombe
Martinhoe
Lynton
Woolacombe
Croyde
Barnstaple
Appledore
Horn's Cross
Bideford
South Molton
Knowstone
Burrington
Bampton
A 361
Tiverton
Taw
DEVON
M 5
A 303
Broadhembury
Honiton
Ashwater
Crediton
Virginstow
Gittisham
Axminster
A 35
A 30
Portgate
Lifton
Lewdown
Chagford
Exeter
Rockbeare
Colyford
Topsham
Lydford
Moretonhampstead
Chillaton
North Bovey
Exton
Sidmouth
Branscombe
Milton Abbot
Postbridge
A 38
Exmouth
Budleigh Salterton
Bovey Tracey
Dawlish
Lyme Bay
Tavistock
Two Bridges
Teignmouth
Callington
Ashburton
Shaldon
Gulworthy
Kingskerswell
Maidencombe
Staverton
Marldon
Torquay
Avonwick
Totnes
Paignton
Plymouth
Diptford
Ermington
Millbrook
Modbury
Dartmouth
Freathy
Yealmpton
East Allington
Kingswear
Noss Mayo
Bigbury
Goveton
Bigbury-on-Sea
Kingsbridge
Slapton
Chillington
Soar Mill Cove
Salcombe
3
ENGLI
Place with at least:
a hotel or a restaurant
a starred establishment
a "Bib Gourmand" restaurant
a "Bib Hôtel"
a particularly pleasant restaurant
a particularly pleasant guesthouse
a particularly pleasant hotel
a particularly quiet hotel
a particularly pleasant pub

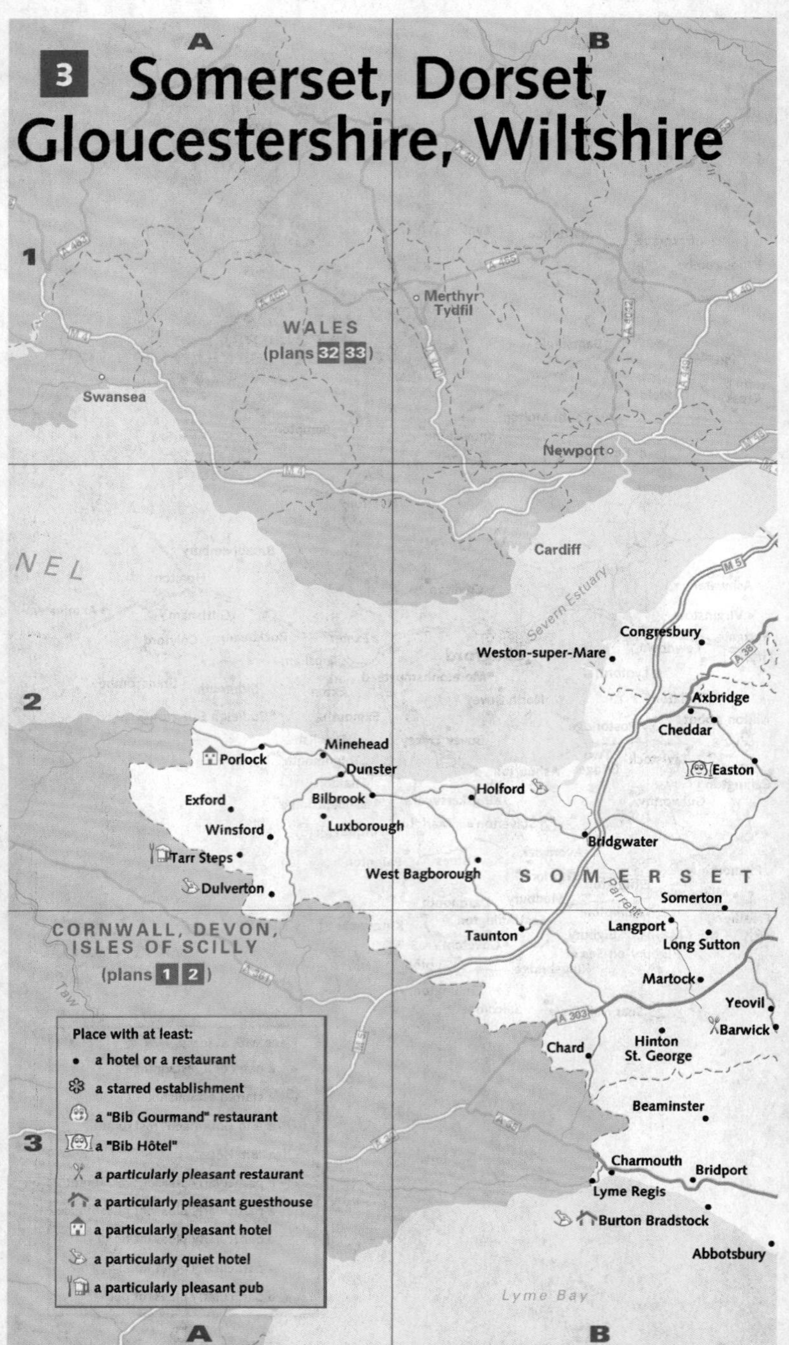
3 Somerset, Dorset, Gloucestershire, Wiltshire
A
B
1
2
3
WALES
(plans 32 33)
Merthyr Tydfil
Swansea
Newport
Cardiff
Severn Estuary
Congresbury
Weston-super-Mare
Axbridge
Cheddar
Easton
Porlock
Minehead
Dunster
Holford
Exford
Bilbrook
Luxborough
Winsford
Bridgwater
Tarr Steps
West Bagborough
Dulverton
SOMERSET
Parrett
Somerton
Langport
Long Sutton
Taunton
CORNWALL, DEVON, ISLES OF SCILLY
(plans 1 2)
Martock
Yeovil
Barwick
Chard
Hinton St. George
Beaminster
Charmouth
Bridport
Lyme Regis
Burton Bradstock
Abbotsbury
Lyme Bay
Place with at least:
a hotel or a restaurant
a starred establishment
a "Bib Gourmand" restaurant
a "Bib Hôtel"
a particularly pleasant restaurant
a particularly pleasant guesthouse
a particularly pleasant hotel
a particularly quiet hotel
a particularly pleasant pub

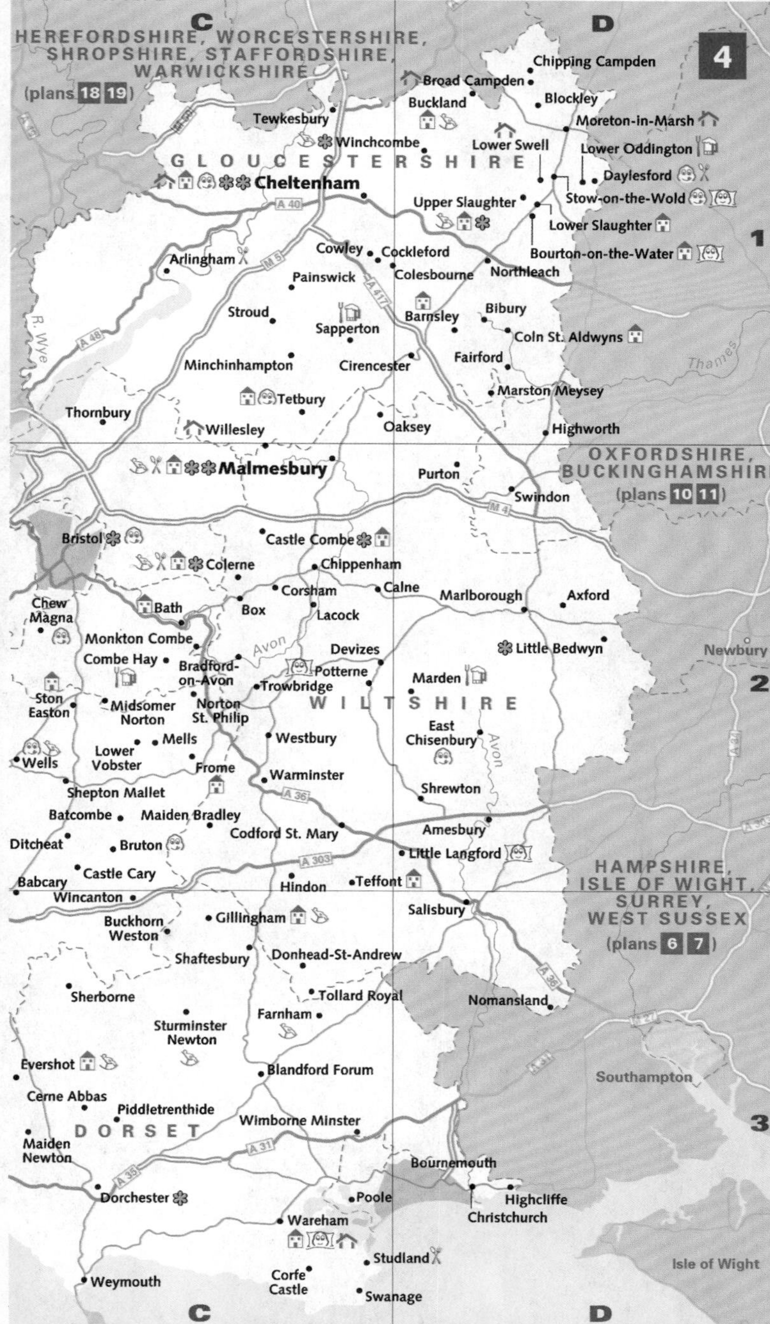
C
D
4
HEREFORDSHIRE, WORCESTERSHIRE, SHROPSHIRE, STAFFORDSHIRE, WARWICKSHIRE
(plans 18 19)
GLOUCESTERSHIRE
Chipping Campden
Broad Campden
Buckland
Blockley
Tewkesbury
Moreton-in-Marsh
Winchcombe
Lower Swell
Lower Oddington
Daylesford
Cheltenham
Stow-on-the-Wold
Upper Slaughter
Lower Slaughter
Cowley
Cockleford
Bourton-on-the-Water
Arlingham
Colesbourne
Northleach
Painswick
Stroud
Barnsley
Bibury
Sapperton
Coln St. Aldwyns
R. Wye
Minchinhampton
Cirencester
Fairford
Thames
Tetbury
Marston Meysey
Thornbury
Oaksey
Willesley
Highworth
1
OXFORDSHIRE, BUCKINGHAMSHIRE
(plans 10 11)
Malmesbury
Purton
Swindon
Bristol
Castle Combe
Colerne
Chippenham
Corsham
Calne
Marlborough
Axford
Chew Magna
Bath
Box
Lacock
Monkton Combe
Little Bedwyn
Newbury
Avon
Devizes
Combe Hay
Bradford-on-Avon
Potterne
Marden
Trowbridge
2
Ston Easton
Midsomer Norton
Norton St. Philip
WILTSHIRE
East Chisenbury
Mells
Westbury
Avon
Lower Vobster
Wells
Frome
Warminster
Shepton Mallet
Shrewton
Batcombe
Maiden Bradley
Amesbury
Codford St. Mary
Ditcheat
Bruton
Little Langford
HAMPSHIRE, ISLE OF WIGHT, SURREY, WEST SUSSEX
(plans 6 7)
Castle Cary
Babcary
Hindon
Teffont
Wincanton
Salisbury
Buckhorn Weston
Gillingham
Shaftesbury
Donhead-St-Andrew
Sherborne
Tollard Royal
Nomansland
Farnham
Sturminster Newton
Evershot
Blandford Forum
Southampton
Cerne Abbas
Piddletrenthide
Wimborne Minster
3
DORSET
Maiden Newton
Bournemouth
Dorchester
Poole
Highcliffe
Christchurch
Wareham
Studland
Isle of Wight
Corfe Castle
Weymouth
Swanage
C
D
M 5
A 40
A 417
A 48
M 4
A 36
A 303
A 31
A 35
M 50
A 34
A 27

Channel Islands 5

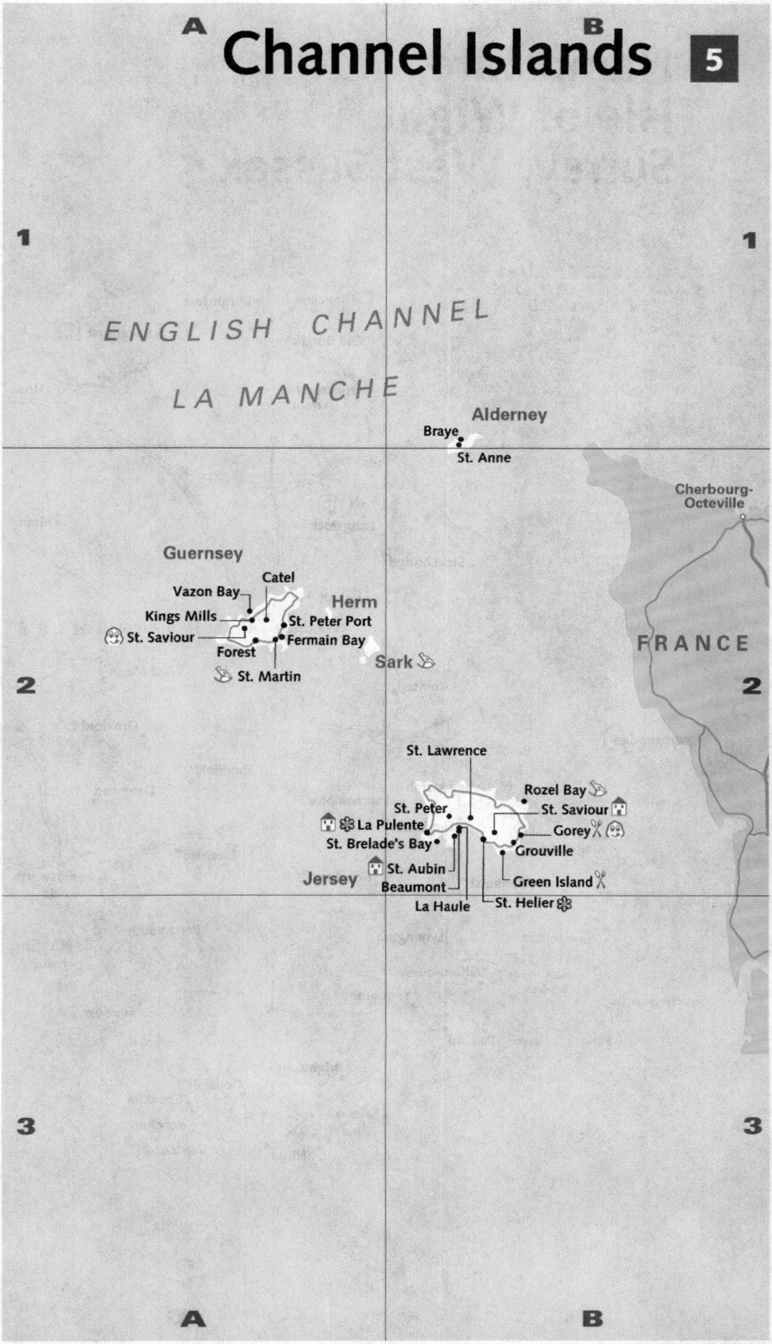

A B

1 1

ENGLISH CHANNEL

LA MANCHE

Alderney
Braye
St. Anne

Cherbourg-Octeville

Guernsey
Catel
Vazon Bay
Kings Mills
St. Saviour
Forest
St. Martin
St. Peter Port
Fermain Bay
Herm
Sark

FRANCE

2 2

St. Lawrence
Rozel Bay
St. Peter
St. Saviour
La Pulente
Gorey
St. Brelade's Bay
Grouville
St. Aubin
Jersey
Green Island
Beaumont
La Haule
St. Helier

3 3

A B

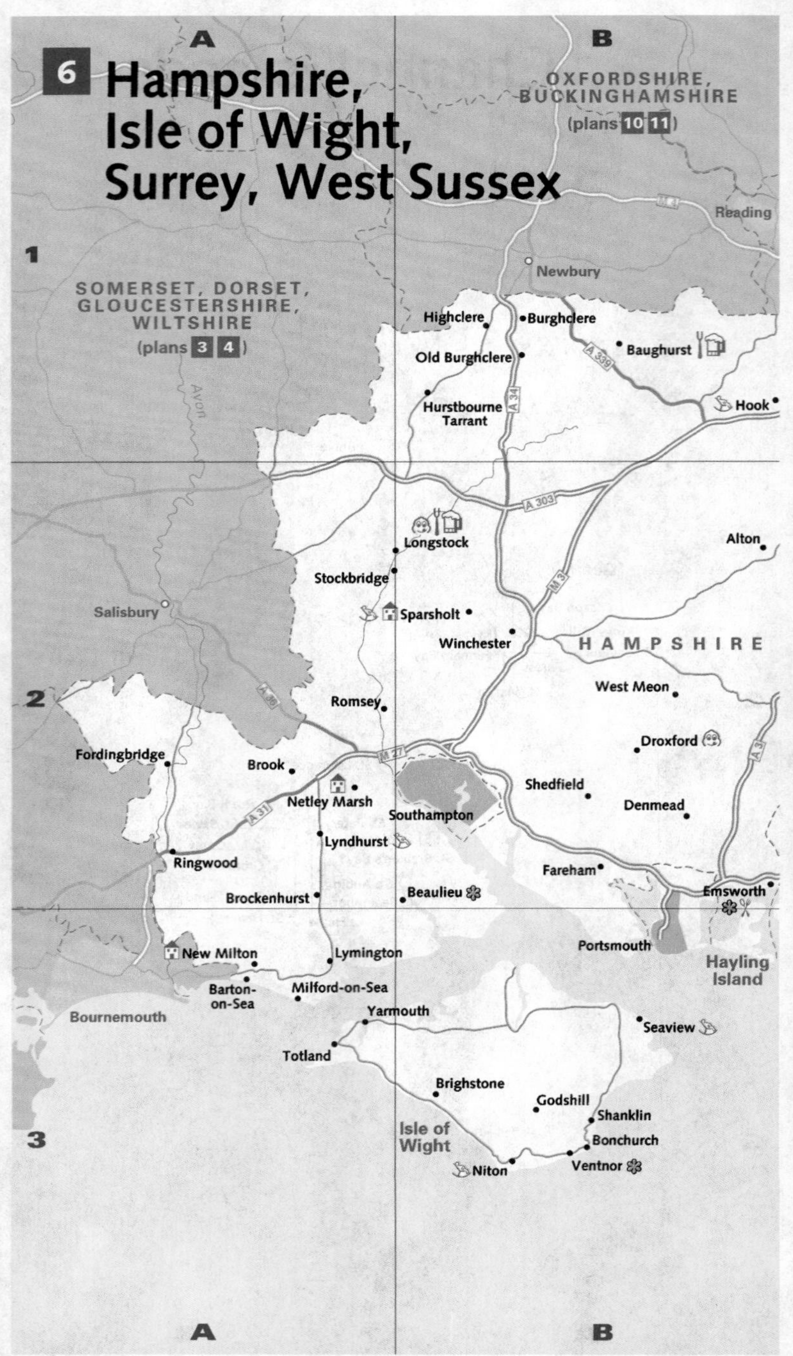

A
B
6
Hampshire, Isle of Wight, Surrey, West Sussex
OXFORDSHIRE, BUCKINGHAMSHIRE
(plans 10 11)
Reading
1
Newbury
SOMERSET, DORSET, GLOUCESTERSHIRE, WILTSHIRE
(plans 3 4)
Highclere
Burghclere
Baughurst
A 339
Old Burghclere
Avon
A 34
Hurstbourne Tarrant
Hook
A 303
Longstock
Alton
Stockbridge
M 3
Salisbury
Sparsholt
Winchester
HAMPSHIRE
2
A 36
West Meon
Romsey
Droxford
A 3
M 27
Fordingbridge
Brook
Shedfield
Netley Marsh
Denmead
Southampton
A 31
Lyndhurst
Ringwood
Fareham
Brockenhurst
Beaulieu
Emsworth
New Milton
Lymington
Portsmouth
Hayling Island
Barton-on-Sea
Milford-on-Sea
Bournemouth
Yarmouth
Seaview
Totland
Brighstone
Godshill
Shanklin
3
Isle of Wight
Bonchurch
Niton
Ventnor
A
B

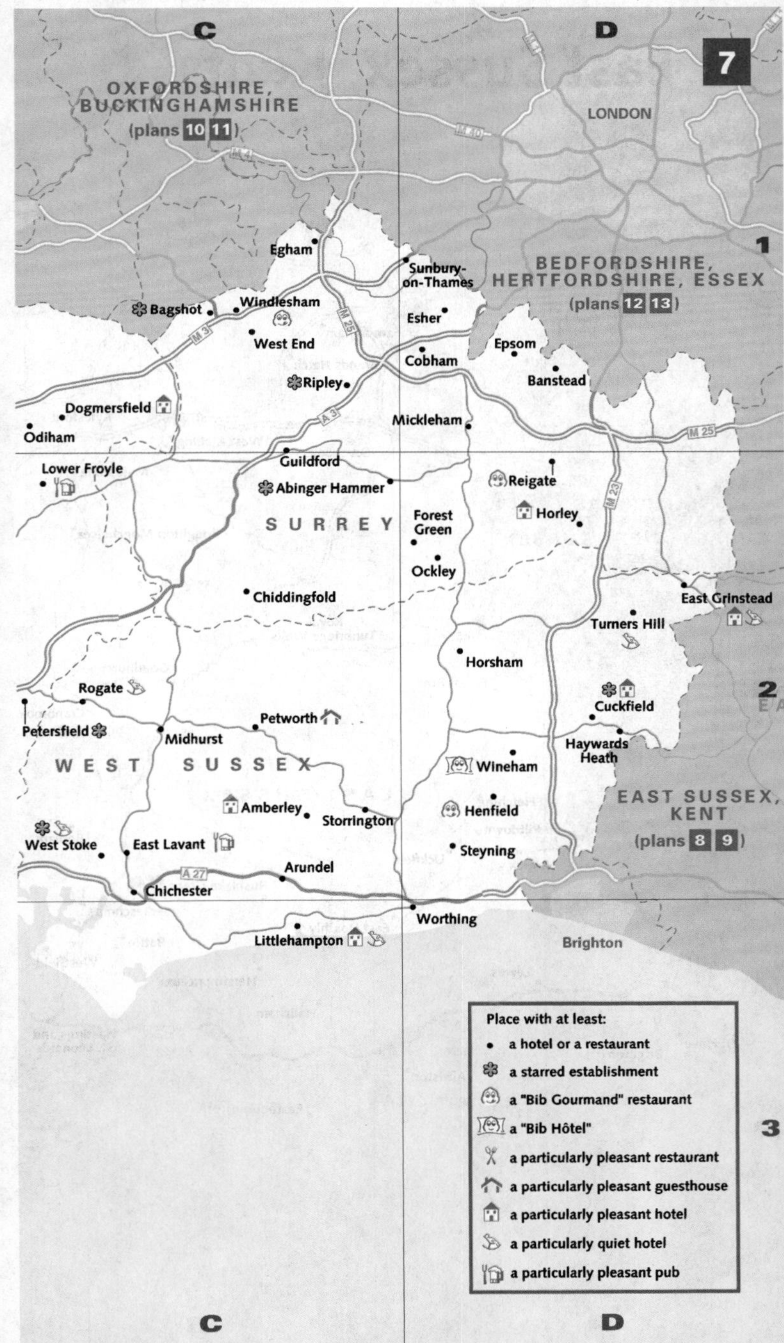
C
D
7
OXFORDSHIRE, BUCKINGHAMSHIRE
(plans 10 11)
LONDON
M 40
M 4
M 3
M 25
A 3
M 23
A 27
1
2
3
Egham
Sunbury-on-Thames
BEDFORDSHIRE, HERTFORDSHIRE, ESSEX
(plans 12 13)
Bagshot
Windlesham
Esher
West End
Epsom
Cobham
Banstead
Ripley
Dogmersfield
Mickleham
Odiham
Lower Froyle
Guildford
Reigate
Abinger Hammer
Horley
Forest Green
SURREY
Ockley
Chiddingfold
East Grinstead
Turners Hill
Horsham
Rogate
Cuckfield
Petersfield
Petworth
Midhurst
Haywards Heath
WEST SUSSEX
Wineham
EAST SUSSEX, KENT
Amberley
Henfield
Storrington
(plans 8 9)
West Stoke
East Lavant
Steyning
Arundel
Chichester
Worthing
Littlehampton
Brighton
Place with at least:
a hotel or a restaurant
a starred establishment
a "Bib Gourmand" restaurant
a "Bib Hôtel"
a particularly pleasant restaurant
a particularly pleasant guesthouse
a particularly pleasant hotel
a particularly quiet hotel
a particularly pleasant pub
C
D

8 East Sussex, Kent

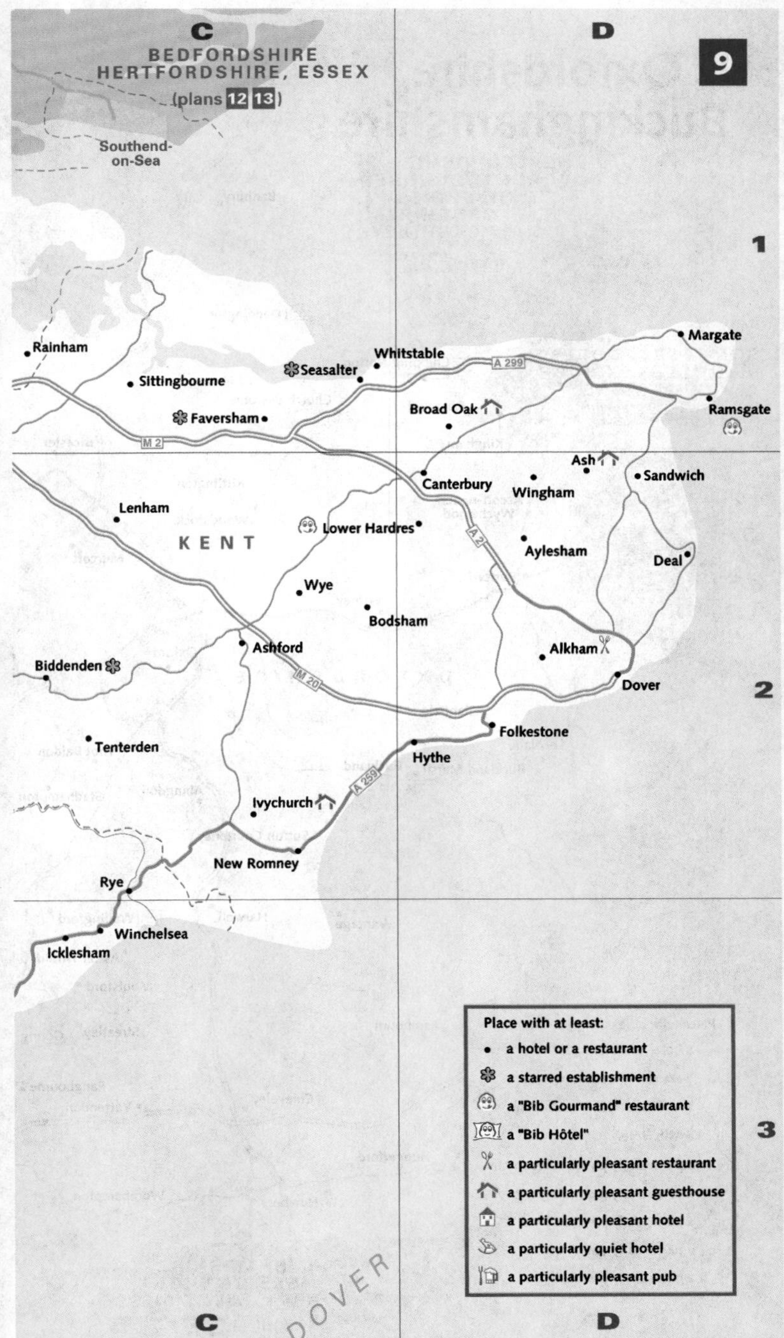

C
D
9
BEDFORDSHIRE
HERTFORDSHIRE, ESSEX
(plans 12 13)
Southend-on-Sea
1
Margate
Rainham
Whitstable
A 299
Seasalter
Sittingbourne
Ramsgate
Broad Oak
Faversham
M 2
Ash
Sandwich
Canterbury
Wingham
Lenham
Lower Hardres
KENT
A 2
Aylesham
Deal
Wye
Bodsham
Alkham
Ashford
Biddenden
M 20
Dover
2
Folkestone
Tenterden
Hythe
A 259
Ivychurch
New Romney
Rye
Winchelsea
Icklesham
Place with at least:
a hotel or a restaurant
a starred establishment
a "Bib Gourmand" restaurant
a "Bib Hôtel"
a particularly pleasant restaurant
a particularly pleasant guesthouse
a particularly pleasant hotel
a particularly quiet hotel
a particularly pleasant pub
3
C
D
DOVER

10 Oxfordshire, Buckinghamshire
A
B
1
2
3
HEREFORDSHIRE, WORCESTERSHIRE, SHROPSHIRE, STAFFORDSHIRE, WARWICKSHIRE
(plans 18 19)
SOMERSET, DORSET, GLOUCESTERSHIRE, WILTSHIRE
(plans 3 4)
HAMPSHIRE, ISLE OF WIGHT, SURREY, WEST SUSSEX
(plans 6 7)
OXFORDSHIRE
Thames
Banbury
Deddington
Chipping Norton
Church Enstone
Churchill
Kingham
Bicester
Kirtlington
Ascott-under-Wychwood
Woodstock
Murcott
Burford
Witney
Oxford
Clanfield
Lechlade
Buckland Marsh
Buckland
Toot Baldon
Abingdon
Stadhampton
Sutton Courtenay
Wantage
Harwell
Wallingford
Swindon
Aston Tirrold
Moulsford
Lambourn
Streatley
Goring
Pangbourne
Chieveley
Yattendon
Hungerford
Newbury
Woolhampton
A 40
A 34
M 40
M 4
Place with at least:
a hotel or a restaurant
a starred establishment
a "Bib Gourmand" restaurant
a "Bib Hôtel"
a particularly pleasant restaurant
a particularly pleasant guesthouse
a particularly pleasant hotel
a particularly quiet hotel
a particularly pleasant pub

11
C
D
DERBYSHIRE,
LEICESTERSHIRE,
NORTHAMPTONSHIRE,
RUTLAND, LINCOLNSHIRE,
NOTTINGHAMSHIRE
(plans 16 17)
Newport Pagnell
Milton Keynes
BEDFORDSHIRE
HERTFORDSHIRE, ESSEX
(plans 12 13)
1
Buckingham
Gt. Ouse
Newton Longville
BUCKINGHAMSHIRE
Luton
Waddesdon
Aylesbury
Cuddington
Aston Clinton
Long Crendon
Haddenham
BEDFORDSHIRE
HERTFORDSHIRE, ESSEX
(plans 12 13)
2
Great Milton
Chinnor
Great Missenden
Speen
Aston Rowant
Cuxham
Amersham
Stokenchurch
Watford
High Wycombe
Penn
Britwell Salome
Turville
Maidensgrove
Beaconsfield
Nettlebed
Marlow
Denham
Stoke Row
Cookham
Bisham
Cookham Dean
Stoke Poges
Henley-on-Thames
Hurley
Taplow
George Green
Maidenhead
BRAY-ON-THAMES
Bray Marina
Windsor
Reading
3
Ascot
Shinfield
Sunningdale
HAMPSHIRE,
ISLE OF WIGHT,
SURREY, WEST SUSSEX
(plans 6 7)
C
D
A 41
A 43
M 1
M 4
M 40
A 5

12
A
B
Huntingdon
Gt. Ouse
NORFOLK, SUFFOLK, CAMBRIDGESHIRE
(plans 14 15)
Bolnhurst
Nene
Cambridge
1
Bedford
Cam
BEDFORDSHIRE
Biggleswade
Old Warden
Shefford
Royston
Saffron Walden
Woburn
Letchworth
Anstey
Clavering
Cottered
ISHIRE
Stansted Mountfitchet
Luton
Datchworth
Bishop's Stortford
Welwyn
Welwyn Garden City
Harpenden
Hunsdon
2
Berkhamsted
St. Albans
Hemel Hempstead
HERTFORDSHIRE
Northaw
Flaunden
High Ongar
Watford
Bushey
High Wycombe
OXFORDSHIRE, BUCKINGHAMSHIRE
(plans 10 11)
LONDON
Windsor
3
HAMPSHIRE, ISLE OF WIGHT, SURREY, WEST SUSSEX
(plans 6 7)
EAST SUSSEX, KENT
(plans 8 9)
Guildford
A
B
A 6
A 45
A 428
A 10
A 5
A 1
A 41
M 1
M 11
M 25
M 40
M 4
M 3
M 26

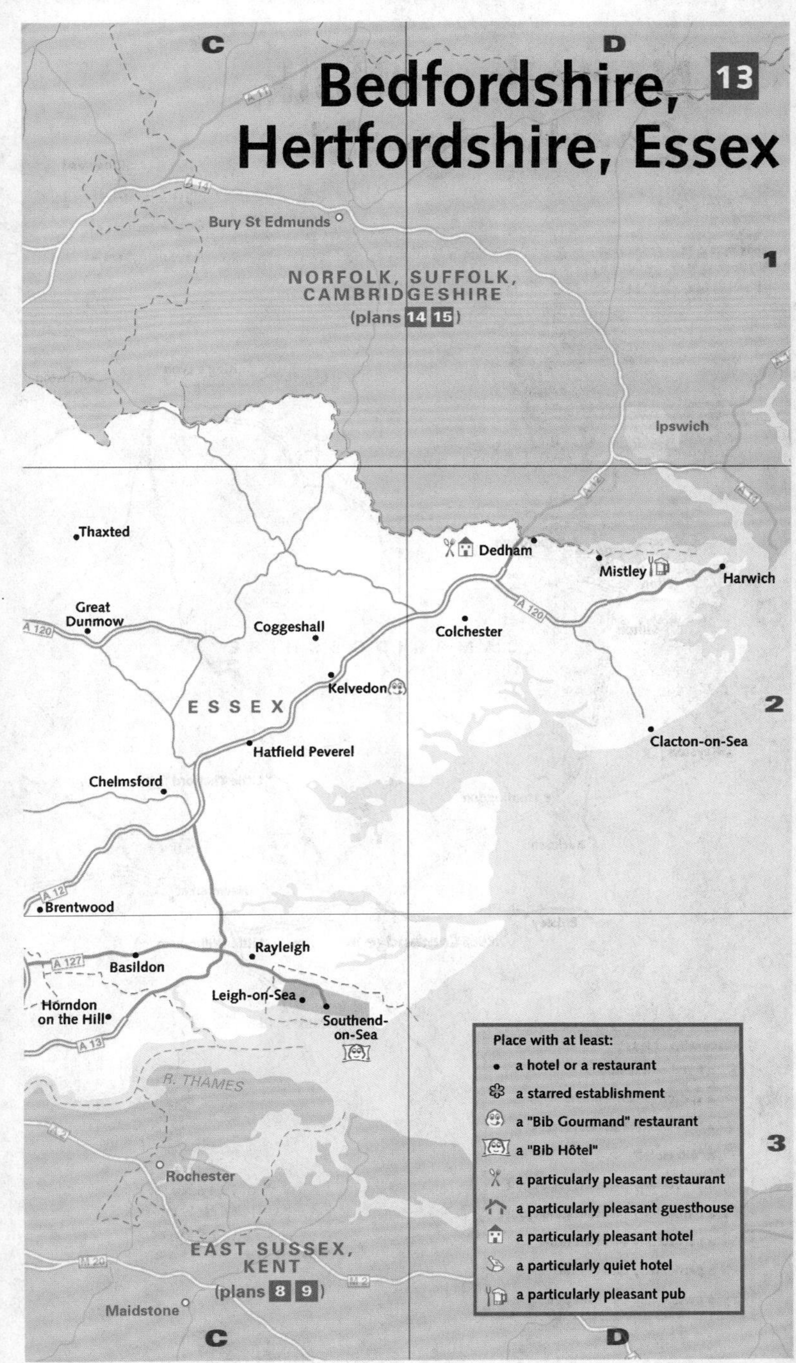
C
D
Bedfordshire, Hertfordshire, Essex
13
A 11
A 14
Bury St Edmunds
1
NORFOLK, SUFFOLK, CAMBRIDGESHIRE
(plans 14 15)
Ipswich
A 12
Thaxted
Dedham
Mistley
Harwich
A 120
Great Dunmow
A 120
Coggeshall
Colchester
Kelvedon
ESSEX
2
Clacton-on-Sea
Hatfield Peverel
Chelmsford
A 12
Brentwood
Rayleigh
A 127
Basildon
Leigh-on-Sea
Horndon on the Hill
Southend-on-Sea
A 13
R. THAMES
A 2
Rochester
3
EAST SUSSEX, KENT
(plans 8 9)
M 20
M 2
Maidstone
Place with at least:
a hotel or a restaurant
a starred establishment
a "Bib Gourmand" restaurant
a "Bib Hôtel"
a particularly pleasant restaurant
a particularly pleasant guesthouse
a particularly pleasant hotel
a particularly quiet hotel
a particularly pleasant pub

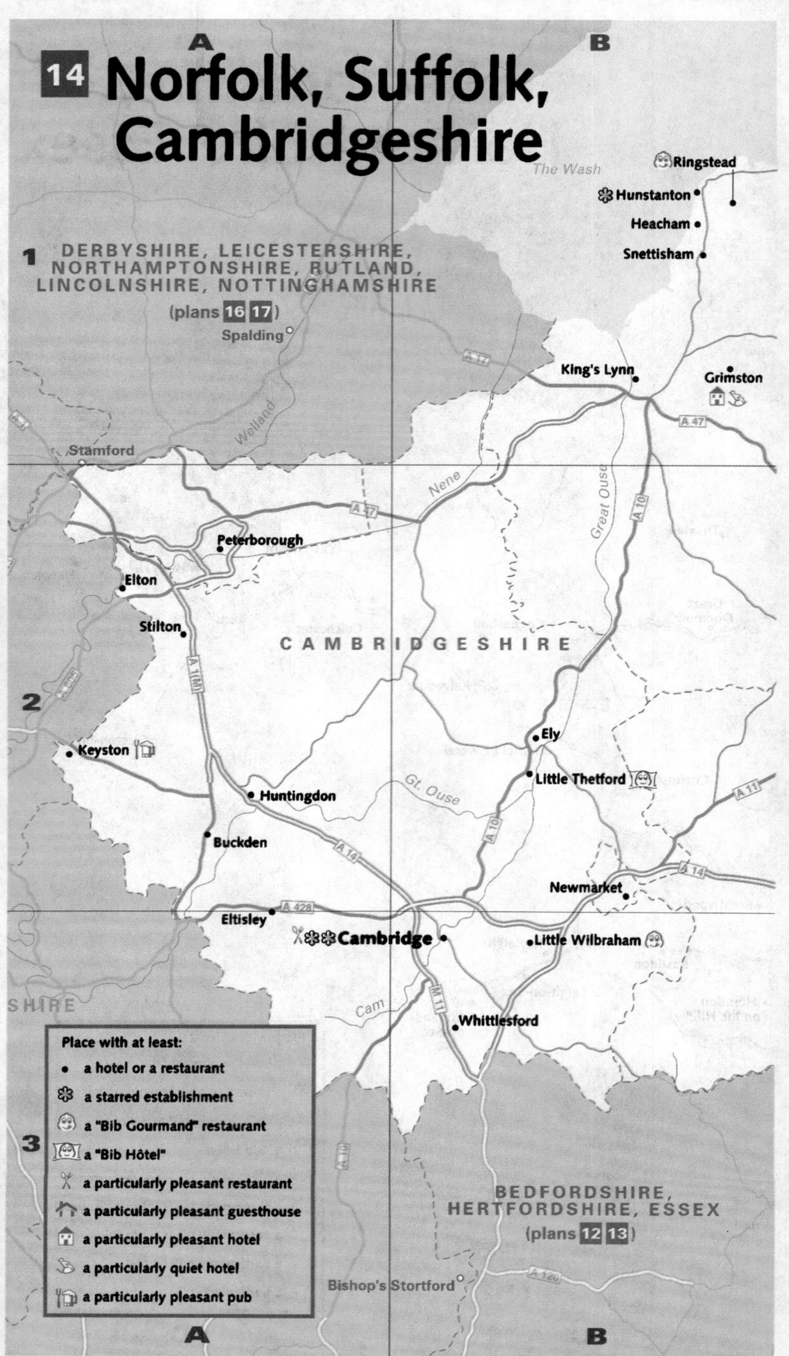
14
Norfolk, Suffolk, Cambridgeshire
A
B
1
2
3
DERBYSHIRE, LEICESTERSHIRE, NORTHAMPTONSHIRE, RUTLAND, LINCOLNSHIRE, NOTTINGHAMSHIRE
(plans 16 17)
Spalding
The Wash
Ringstead
Hunstanton
Heacham
Snettisham
King's Lynn
Grimston
A 47
Welland
Stamford
Nene
Great Ouse
A 10
Peterborough
Elton
Stilton
CAMBRIDGESHIRE
A 1(M)
Keyston
Ely
Little Thetford
Gt. Ouse
Huntingdon
A 11
Buckden
A 14
Newmarket
Eltisley
A 428
Cambridge
Little Wilbraham
Cam
M 11
Whittlesford
SHIRE
Place with at least:
a hotel or a restaurant
a starred establishment
a "Bib Gourmand" restaurant
a "Bib Hôtel"
a particularly pleasant restaurant
a particularly pleasant guesthouse
a particularly pleasant hotel
a particularly quiet hotel
a particularly pleasant pub
BEDFORDSHIRE, HERTFORDSHIRE, ESSEX
(plans 12 13)
Bishop's Stortford
A 120

C
D
15
Brancaster Staithe
Holkham
Wells-next-the-Sea
Titchwell
Burnham Market
Blakeney
Morston
Sheringham
Cromer
Holt
Aylmerton
Hindringham
Hunworth
Thursford Green
Itteringham
Erpingham
North Walsham
East Rudham
Wellingham
1
NORFOLK
Coltishall
Wroxham
East Dereham
Norwich
A 47
Bure
Brundall
Great Yarmouth
Yare
Stoke Holy Cross
Watton
A 11
Fritton
A 12
Lowestoft
Bungay
2
Pulham Market
North Lopham
Waveney
Diss
Fressingfield
Stanton
Southwold
Bramfield
Walberswick
Thornham Magna
Bury St Edmunds
Kelsale
Beyton
Framlingham
Stowmarket
Earl Stonham
Buxhall
SUFFOLK
Snape
Aldeburgh
Lavenham
Bildeston
A 12
Orford
Monks Eleigh
Woodbridge
Long Melford
Ipswich
Hadleigh
3
A 12
A 14
Stoke-by-Nayland
Levington
Harwich
A 120
Colchester
C
D

16
A
B
1
2
3
Manchester
Barnsley
Doncaster
YORKSHIRE
(plans 22 23)
Rotherham
Sheffield
Glossop
Derwent
Hope
Hathersage
CHESHIRE,
LANCASHIRE,
ISLE OF MAN
(plan 20)
Chapel-en-le-Frith
Buxton
Froggatt Edge
Baslow
Bakewell
Beeley
Rowsley
DERBYSHIRE
Hartington
Birchover
Winster
Matlock
Blyth
Retford
Workshop
Mansfield
NOTTINGHAMSHIRE
Halam
Stoke-on-Trent
Ashbourne
Belper
Hoveringham
R. Trent
Darley Abbey
Derby
Nottingham
Bingham
Langar
Colston Bassett
Stathern
HEREFORDSHIRE,
WORCESTERSHIRE,
SHROPSHIRE,
STAFFORDSHIRE,
WARWICKSHIRE
(plans 18 19)
Castle Donington
Kegworth
Loughborough
Melton Mowbray
LEICESTERSHIRE
Cropston
Leicester
Wolverhampton
Kibworth Harcourt
Kibworth Beauchamp
Medbourne
Bruntingthorpe
Birmingham
North Kilworth
Market Harborough
Coventry
NORTHAMPTONSHIRE
Daventry
Northampton
Towcester
Roade
Aynho
Gt. Ouse
LEICESTERSHIRE
A 628
A 616
A 6
A 61
A 614
A 52
A 50
A 606
A 46
A 47
A 14
A 43
A 5
A 45
A 38
A 1
M 1
M 18
M 60
M 6
M 54
M 42
M 69
Place with at least:
a hotel or a restaurant
a starred establishment
a "Bib Gourmand" restaurant
a "Bib Hôtel"
a particularly pleasant restaurant
a particularly pleasant guesthouse
a particularly pleasant hotel
a particularly quiet hotel
a particularly pleasant pub

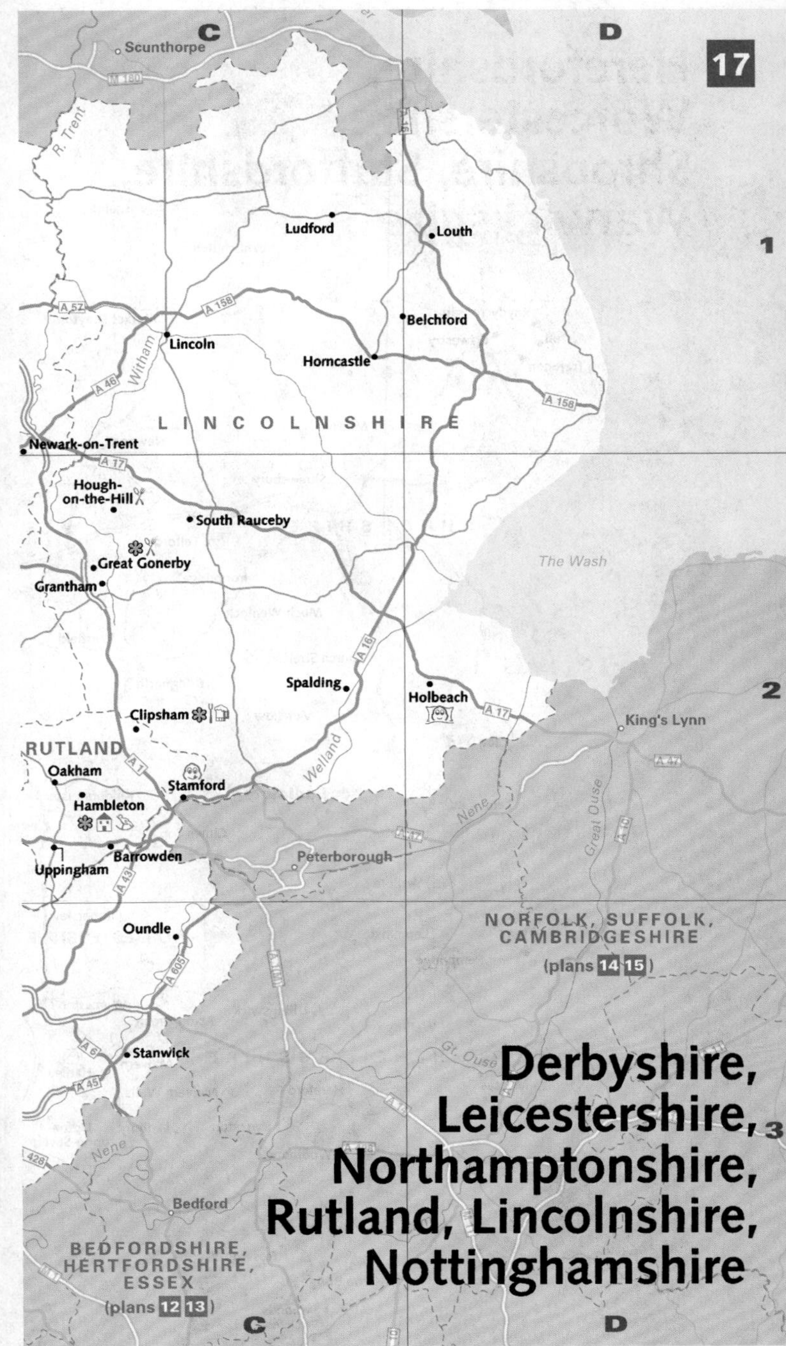

Derbyshire, Leicestershire, Northamptonshire, Rutland, Lincolnshire, Nottinghamshire

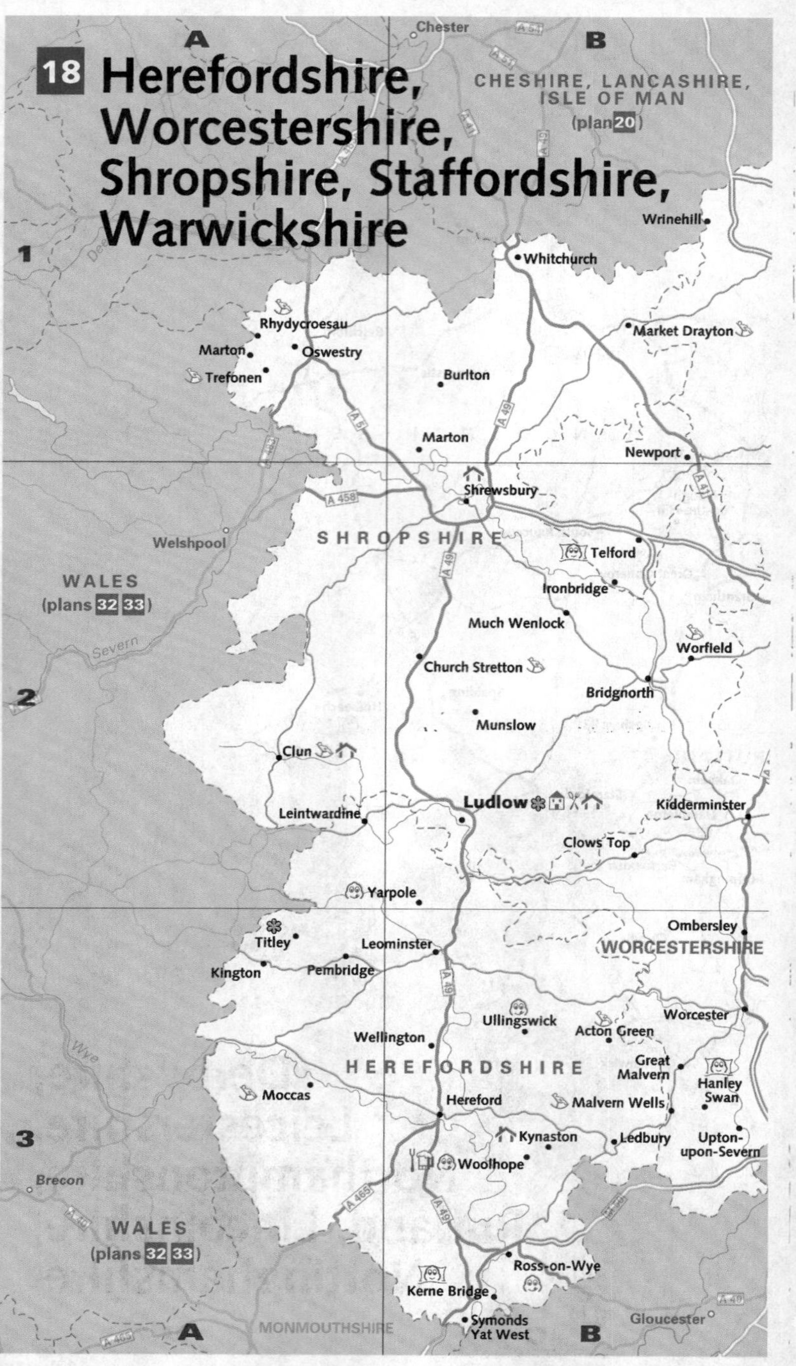
18
Herefordshire, Worcestershire, Shropshire, Staffordshire, Warwickshire
A
B
1
2
3
Chester
CHESHIRE, LANCASHIRE, ISLE OF MAN
(plan 20)
Wrinehill
Whitchurch
Rhydycroesau
Marton
Oswestry
Trefonen
Market Drayton
Burlton
Marton
Newport
Shrewsbury
A 458
A 5
A 49
A 41
Welshpool
SHROPSHIRE
Telford
WALES
(plans 32 33)
Ironbridge
Much Wenlock
Severn
Worfield
Church Stretton
Bridgnorth
Munslow
Clun
Ludlow
Kidderminster
Leintwardine
Clows Top
Yarpole
Ombersley
Titley
Leominster
WORCESTERSHIRE
Kington
Pembridge
Ullingswick
Worcester
Acton Green
Wellington
Wye
Great Malvern
HEREFORDSHIRE
Hanley Swan
Moccas
Hereford
Malvern Wells
Kynaston
Ledbury
Upton-upon-Severn
Woolhope
Brecon
A 465
WALES
(plans 32 33)
Ross-on-Wye
Kerne Bridge
Symonds Yat West
Gloucester
A 40
MONMOUTHSHIRE

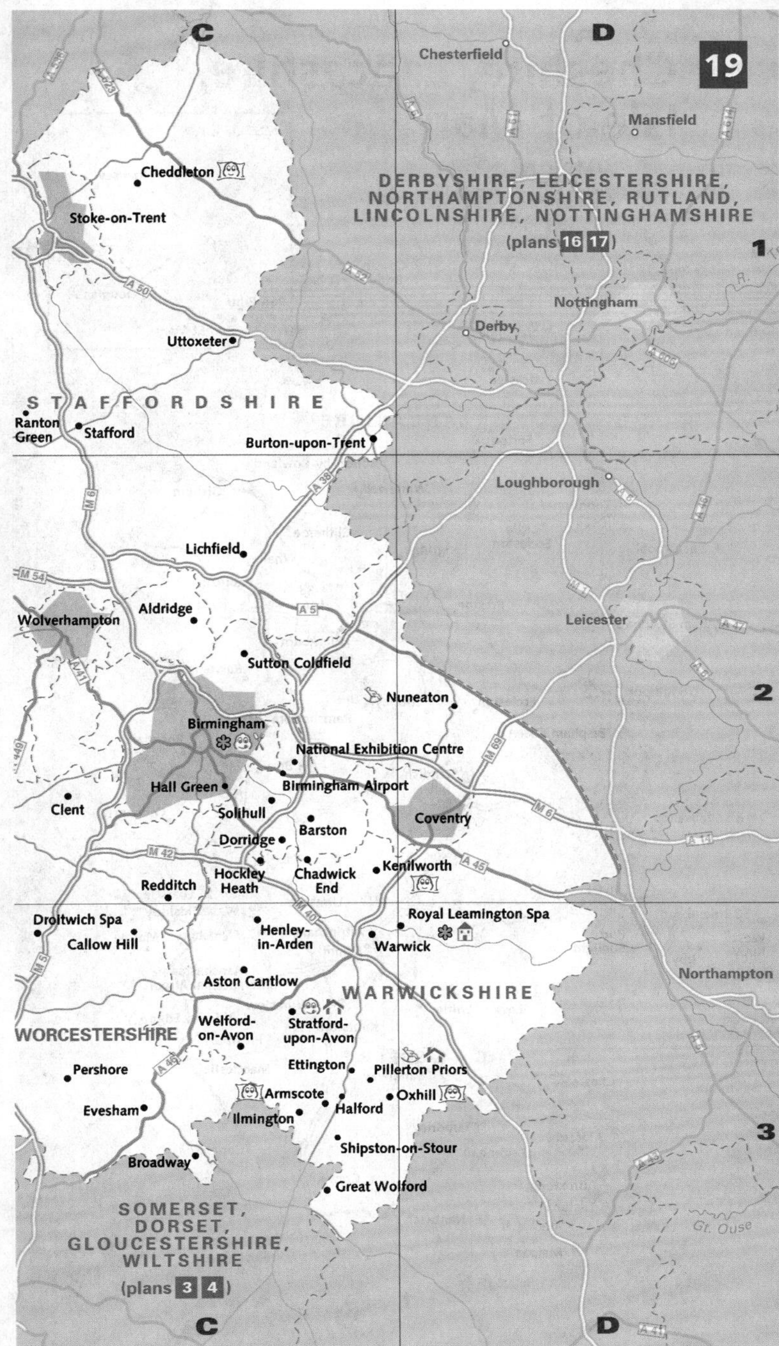
C
D
Chesterfield
Mansfield
DERBYSHIRE, LEICESTERSHIRE, NORTHAMPTONSHIRE, RUTLAND, LINCOLNSHIRE, NOTTINGHAMSHIRE
(plans 16 17)
1
Cheddleton
Stoke-on-Trent
A 50
A 52
Nottingham
Derby
Uttoxeter
STAFFORDSHIRE
Ranton Green
Stafford
Burton-upon-Trent
Loughborough
A 38
A 6
M 6
Lichfield
M 54
Aldridge
A 5
Wolverhampton
Leicester
A 47
Sutton Coldfield
A 41
Nuneaton
2
Birmingham
National Exhibition Centre
M 69
Hall Green
Birmingham Airport
Clent
Solihull
Coventry
M 6
Barston
Dorridge
A 14
M 42
Kenilworth
A 45
Hockley Heath
Chadwick End
Redditch
M 40
Royal Leamington Spa
Droitwich Spa
Callow Hill
Henley-in-Arden
Warwick
M 5
Northampton
Aston Cantlow
WARWICKSHIRE
WORCESTERSHIRE
Welford-on-Avon
Stratford-upon-Avon
A 46
Ettington
Pillerton Priors
Pershore
Armscote
Halford
Oxhill
Evesham
Ilmington
3
Shipston-on-Stour
Broadway
Great Wolford
SOMERSET, DORSET, GLOUCESTERSHIRE, WILTSHIRE
(plans 3 4)
Gt. Ouse
C
D
A 41

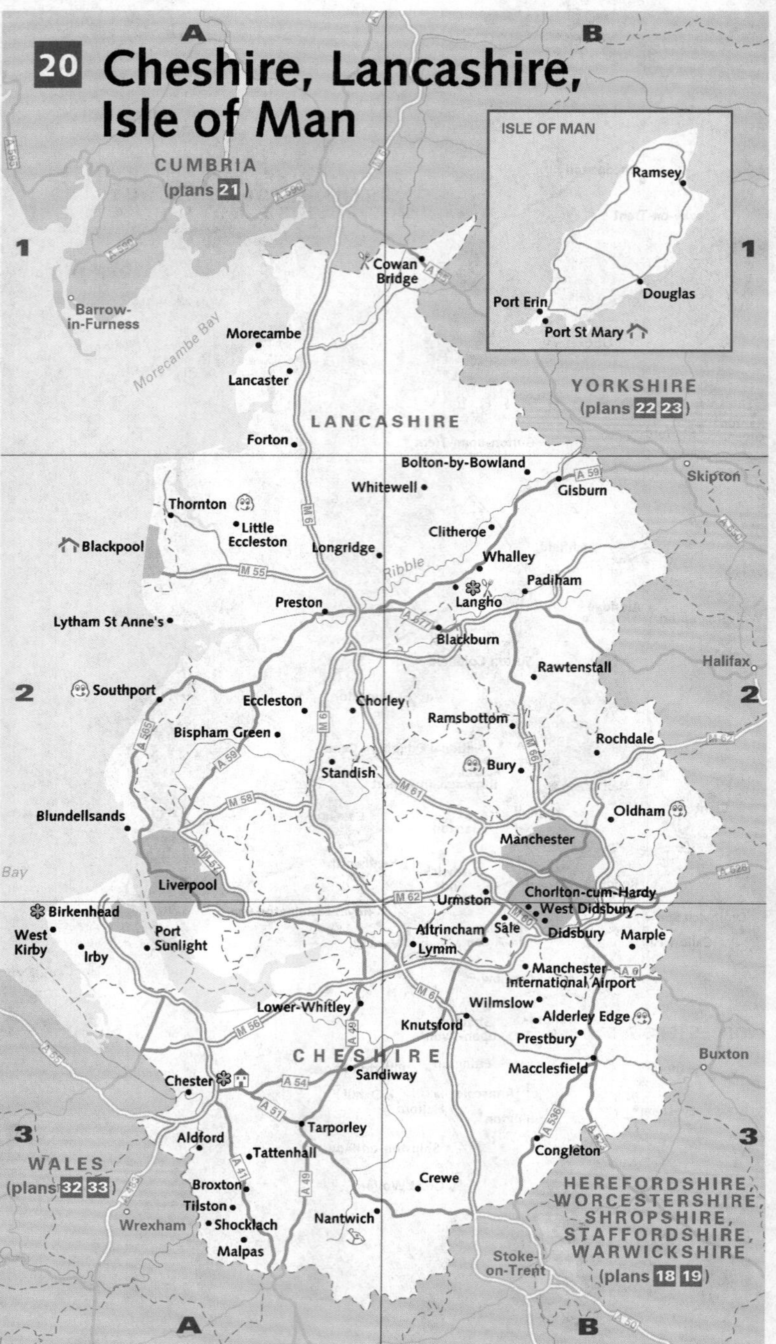
20
Cheshire, Lancashire, Isle of Man
A
B
1
2
3
CUMBRIA
(plans 21)
ISLE OF MAN
Ramsey
Douglas
Port Erin
Port St Mary
YORKSHIRE
(plans 22 23)
Barrow-in-Furness
Morecambe Bay
Morecambe
Lancaster
Cowan Bridge
LANCASHIRE
Forton
Bolton-by-Bowland
Whitewell
Gisburn
Skipton
Thornton
Little Eccleston
Blackpool
Longridge
Clitheroe
Whalley
Padiham
Ribble
Preston
Langho
Lytham St Anne's
Blackburn
Rawtenstall
Halifax
Southport
Eccleston
Chorley
Ramsbottom
Bispham Green
Rochdale
Standish
Bury
Blundellsands
Oldham
Manchester
Bay
Liverpool
Chorlton-cum-Hardy
Urmston
West Didsbury
Birkenhead
West Kirby
Irby
Port Sunlight
Altrincham
Sale
Didsbury
Marple
Lymm
Manchester International Airport
Wilmslow
Lower-Whitley
Alderley Edge
Knutsford
Prestbury
CHESHIRE
Buxton
Sandiway
Macclesfield
Chester
Tarporley
Aldford
Tattenhall
Congleton
WALES
(plans 32 33)
Broxton
Crewe
Tilston
Wrexham
Shocklach
Nantwich
Malpas
HEREFORDSHIRE, WORCESTERSHIRE, SHROPSHIRE, STAFFORDSHIRE, WARWICKSHIRE
(plans 18 19)
Stoke-on-Trent
M 6
M 55
M 58
M 57
M 61
M 62
M 66
M 60
M 56
A 59
A 565
A 677
A 590
A 595
A 65
A 650
A 628
A 6
A 49
A 54
A 51
A 41
A 55
A 483
A 536
A 523
A 50

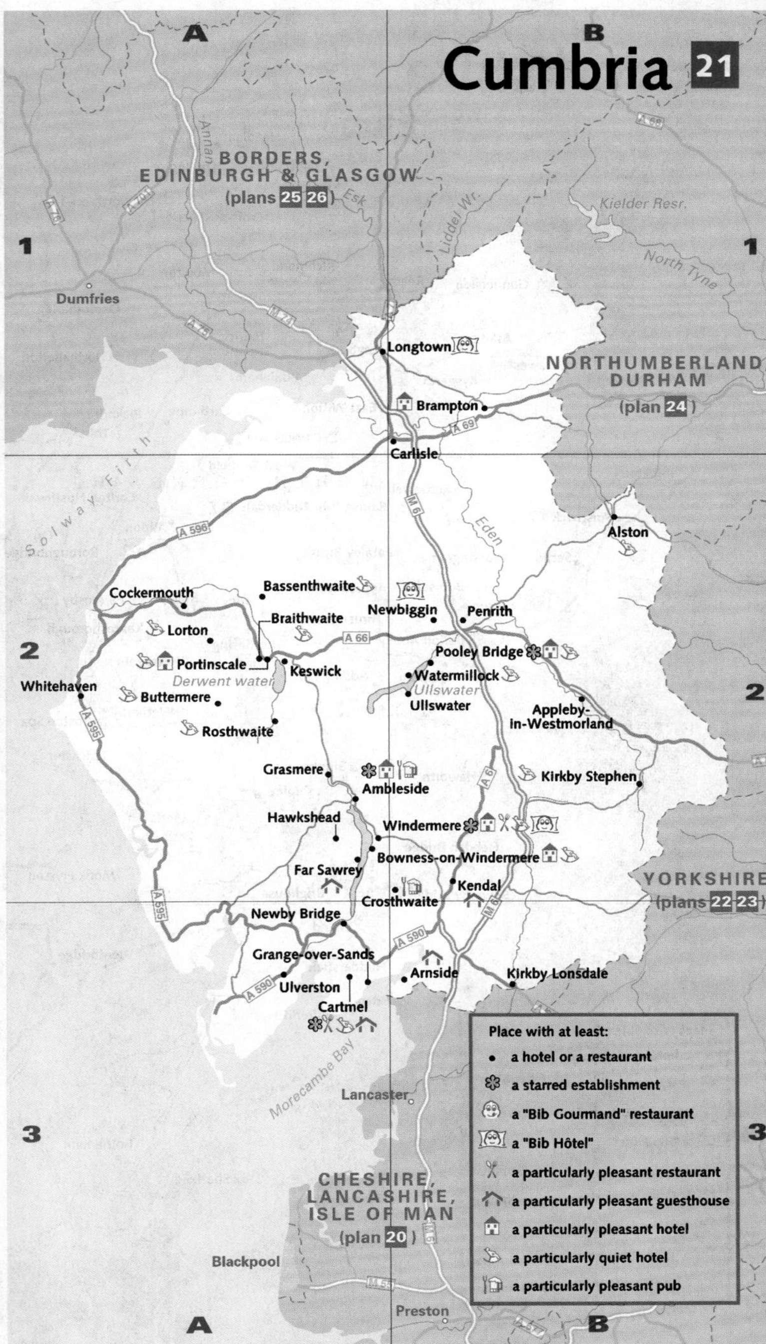
Cumbria 21
A
B
BORDERS,
EDINBURGH & GLASGOW
(plans 25 26)
NORTHUMBERLAND,
DURHAM
(plan 24)
YORKSHIRE
(plans 22-23)
CHESHIRE,
LANCASHIRE,
ISLE OF MAN
(plan 20)
1
2
3
Dumfries
Kielder Resr.
North Tyne
Annan
Esk
Liddel Wr.
Solway Firth
Eden
Derwent water
Ullswater
Morecambe Bay
Longtown
Brampton
Carlisle
Alston
Bassenthwaite
Cockermouth
Newbiggin
Penrith
Braithwaite
Lorton
Portinscale
Keswick
Pooley Bridge
Watermillock
Ullswater
Whitehaven
Buttermere
Rosthwaite
Appleby-in-Westmorland
Grasmere
Ambleside
Kirkby Stephen
Hawkshead
Windermere
Bowness-on-Windermere
Far Sawrey
Kendal
Crosthwaite
Newby Bridge
Grange-over-Sands
Ulverston
Cartmel
Arnside
Kirkby Lonsdale
Lancaster
Blackpool
Preston
A 74
A 7
A 75
M 74
A 69
A 596
A 66
M 6
A 6
A 595
A 590
M 55
Place with at least:
a hotel or a restaurant
a starred establishment
a "Bib Gourmand" restaurant
a "Bib Hôtel"
a particularly pleasant restaurant
a particularly pleasant guesthouse
a particularly pleasant hotel
a particularly quiet hotel
a particularly pleasant pub

22 Yorkshire
A
B
1
2
3
NORTHUMBERLAND, DURHAM (plan 24)
CUMBRIA (plan 21)
CHESHIRE, LANCASHIRE, ISLE OF MAN (plan 20)
NORTH YORKSHIRE
Headlam
Darlington
Hurworth-on-Tees
Croft-on-Tees
Richmond
Moulton
Gunnerside
Reeth
Osmotherley
Askrigg
Leyburn
Patrick Brompton
Northallerton
Hawes
Aysgarth
Middleham
East Witton
Carthorpe
Pickhill
Thirsk
Masham
West Tanfield
Ingleton
Kettlewell
Carlton Husthwaite
Ramsgill-in-Nidderdale
Austwick
Ripon
Settle
Grassington
Pateley Bridge
Boroughbridge
Burnsall
Appletreewick
Hetton
Darley
Ripley
Ferrensby
Thruscross
Knaresborough
Bolton Abbey
Kettlesing
Harrogate
Skipton
Addingham
Wetherby
Ilkley
Boston Spa
Tadcaster
Bingley
Haworth
Shipley
Bradford
Leeds
Hebden Bridge
Halifax
Monk Fryston
Sowerby Bridge
Brighouse
Elland
Wentbridge
Huddersfield
Marsden
Holmfirth
Rotherham
Sheffield
Blackburn
Buxton
Swale
Ure
Wharfe
Ribble
Derwent
A 66
A 65
A 59
A 650
A 64
A 1
A 19
M 1
M 62
A 638
A 616
A 628
A 57
M 6
Place with at least:
a hotel or a restaurant
a starred establishment
a "Bib Gourmand" restaurant
a "Bib Hôtel"
a particularly pleasant restaurant
a particularly pleasant guesthouse
a particularly pleasant hotel
a particularly quiet hotel
a particularly pleasant pub

C
D
23
Middlesbrough
Staithes
Runswick Bay
Whitby
Stokesley
Briggswath
1
Hawnby
Hutton-
le-Hole
Lastingham
Levisham
Kirkbymoorside
Scarborough
Helmsley
Pickering
Harome
Oldstead
Snainton
A 64
Wold Newton
Easingwold
Thwing
Whitwell-
on-the-Hill
Sutton-
on-the-Forest
A 19
York
EAST RIDING
OF
YORKSHIRE
2
A 1079
South Dalton
Brandesburton
A 19
Derwent
Beverley
Kingston
upon Hull
A 63
A 164
M 62
R. Ouse
River Humber
Winteringham
A 15
NORTH
LINCOLNSHIRE
NORTH EAST
LINCOLNSHIRE
Doncaster
M 180
M 18
R. Trent
3
A 1
DERBYSHIRE, LEICESTERSHIRE,
NORTHAMPTONSHIRE, RUTLAND,
LINCOLNSHIRE, NOTTINGHAMSHIRE
Louth
(plans 16 17)
C
D

Northumberland, Durham 24

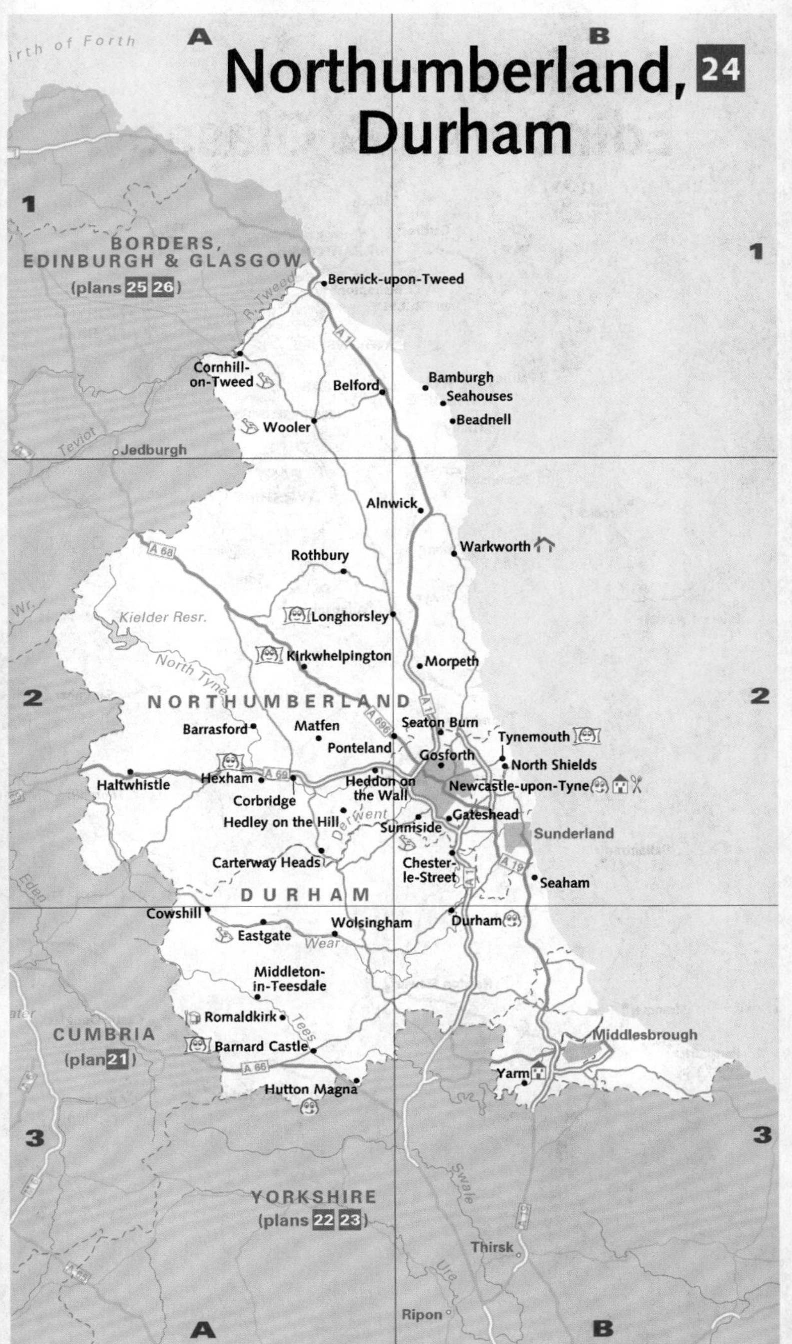

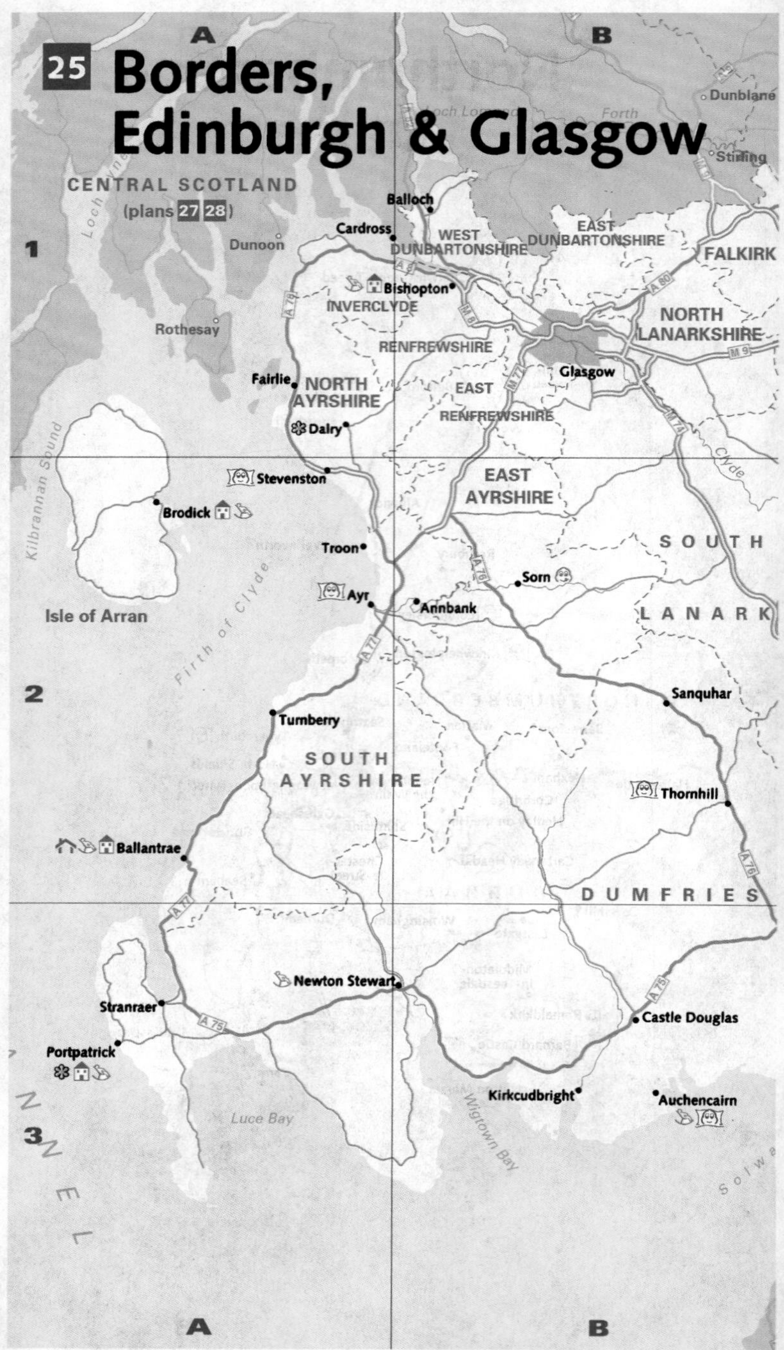
25
Borders, Edinburgh & Glasgow
CENTRAL SCOTLAND
(plans 27 28)
A
B
1
2
3
Dunblane
Forth
Stirling
Balloch
Cardross
Dunoon
WEST DUNBARTONSHIRE
EAST DUNBARTONSHIRE
FALKIRK
Bishopton
INVERCLYDE
NORTH LANARKSHIRE
Rothesay
RENFREWSHIRE
Glasgow
Fairlie
NORTH AYRSHIRE
EAST RENFREWSHIRE
Dalry
Kilbrannan Sound
Clyde
Stevenston
EAST AYRSHIRE
Brodick
Troon
SOUTH LANARK
Sorn
Ayr
Annbank
Isle of Arran
Firth of Clyde
Sanquhar
Turnberry
SOUTH AYRSHIRE
Thornhill
Ballantrae
DUMFRIES
Newton Stewart
Stranraer
Castle Douglas
Portpatrick
Kirkcudbright
Auchencairn
Luce Bay
Wigtown Bay
A 78
A 8
M 8
A 80
M 9
M 77
M 74
A 77
A 76
A 75

26
C
D
St. Andrews
CENTRAL SCOTLAND (plans 27 28)
Kirkcaldy
Dunfermline
Firth of Forth
North Berwick
Gullane
1
Leith
Linlithgow
Ingliston
Edinburgh
Kirknewton
Currie
WEST LOTHIAN
Bonnyrigg
MIDLOTHIAN
EAST LOTHIAN
Chirnside
SCOTTISH
Eddleston
Quothquan
BORDERS
Swinton
R. Tweed
Peebles
Skirling
Walkerburn
Tweed
Melrose
Ednam
Kelso
St. Boswells
Kirk Yetholm
Wooler
Teviot
Jedburgh
2
Moffat
Annan
NORTHUMBERLAND, DURHAM
(plan 24)
Kielder Resr.
Esk
Liddel Wr.
AND GALLOWAY
North Tyne
Lockerbie
Dumfries
Kirkbean
Carlisle
Eden
CUMBRIA
(plan 21)
3
Penrith
Keswick
Derwent water
Ullswater
Tees
C
D
Place with at least:
a hotel or a restaurant
a starred establishment
a "Bib Gourmand" restaurant
a "Bib Hôtel"
a particularly pleasant restaurant
a particularly pleasant guesthouse
a particularly pleasant hotel
a particularly quiet hotel
a particularly pleasant pub

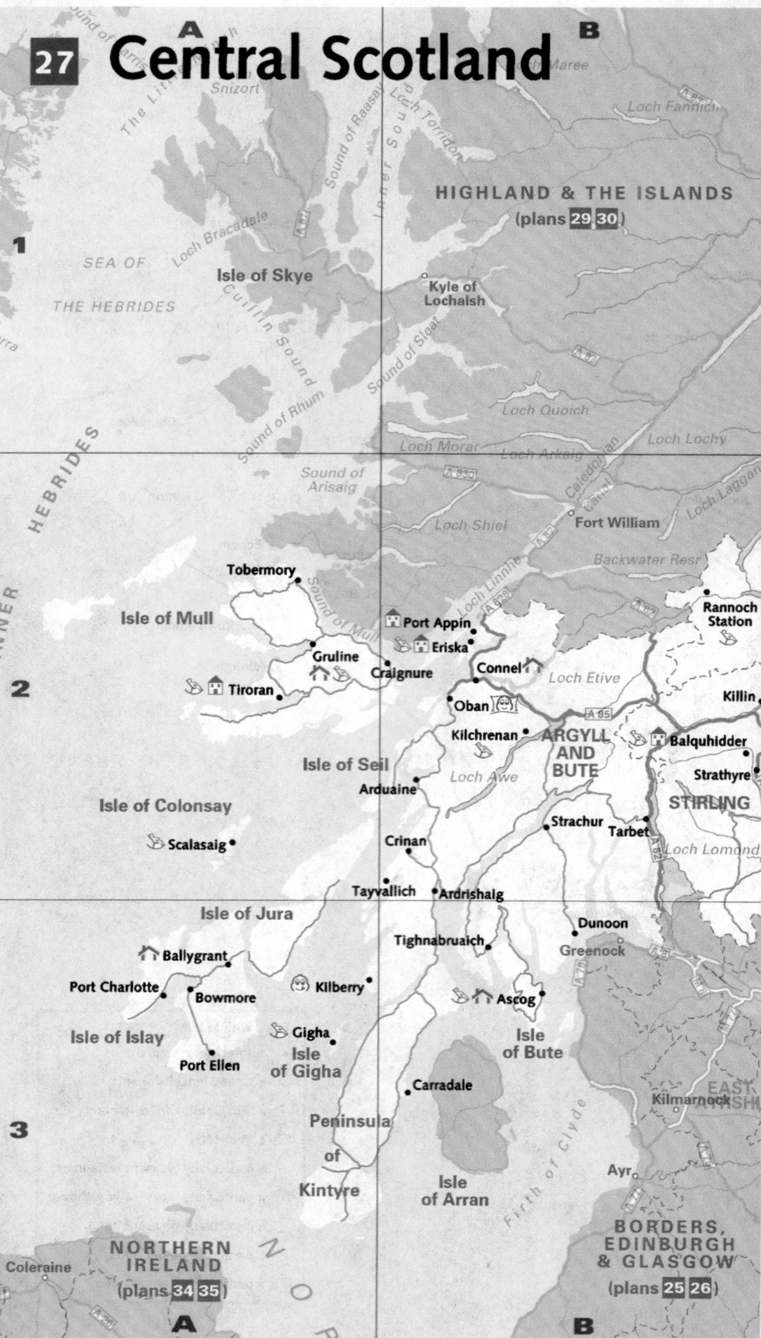
27 Central Scotland
A
B
HIGHLAND & THE ISLANDS
(plans 29 30)
1
2
3
SEA OF
THE HEBRIDES
Isle of Skye
Kyle of Lochalsh
Loch Bracadale
Cuillin Sound
Sound of Raasay
Inner Sound
Loch Torridon
Sound of Sleat
Sound of Rhum
Snizort
Loch Fannich
Loch Quoich
Loch Morar
Loch Arkaig
Loch Lochy
Caledonian Canal
Loch Laggan
Sound of Arisaig
Loch Shiel
Fort William
Backwater Resr
HEBRIDES
INNER
Tobermory
Sound of Mull
Isle of Mull
Port Appin
Eriska
Loch Linnhe
Rannoch Station
Gruline
Craignure
Connel
Loch Etive
Tiroran
Oban
Killin
Kilchrenan
ARGYLL AND BUTE
Balquhidder
Isle of Seil
Loch Awe
Strathyre
Arduaine
STIRLING
Isle of Colonsay
Strachur
Tarbet
Scalasaig
Crinan
Loch Lomond
Tayvallich
Ardrishaig
Isle of Jura
Dunoon
Tighnabruaich
Greenock
Ballygrant
Port Charlotte
Bowmore
Kilberry
Ascog
Isle of Islay
Gigha
Isle of Gigha
Isle of Bute
Port Ellen
Carradale
EAST AYRSHI
Kilmarnock
Peninsula of Kintyre
Firth of Clyde
Ayr
Isle of Arran
NORTHERN IRELAND
(plans 34 35)
Coleraine
BORDERS, EDINBURGH & GLASGOW
(plans 25 26)
A 87
A 830
A 82
A 828
A 85
A 78
A 77

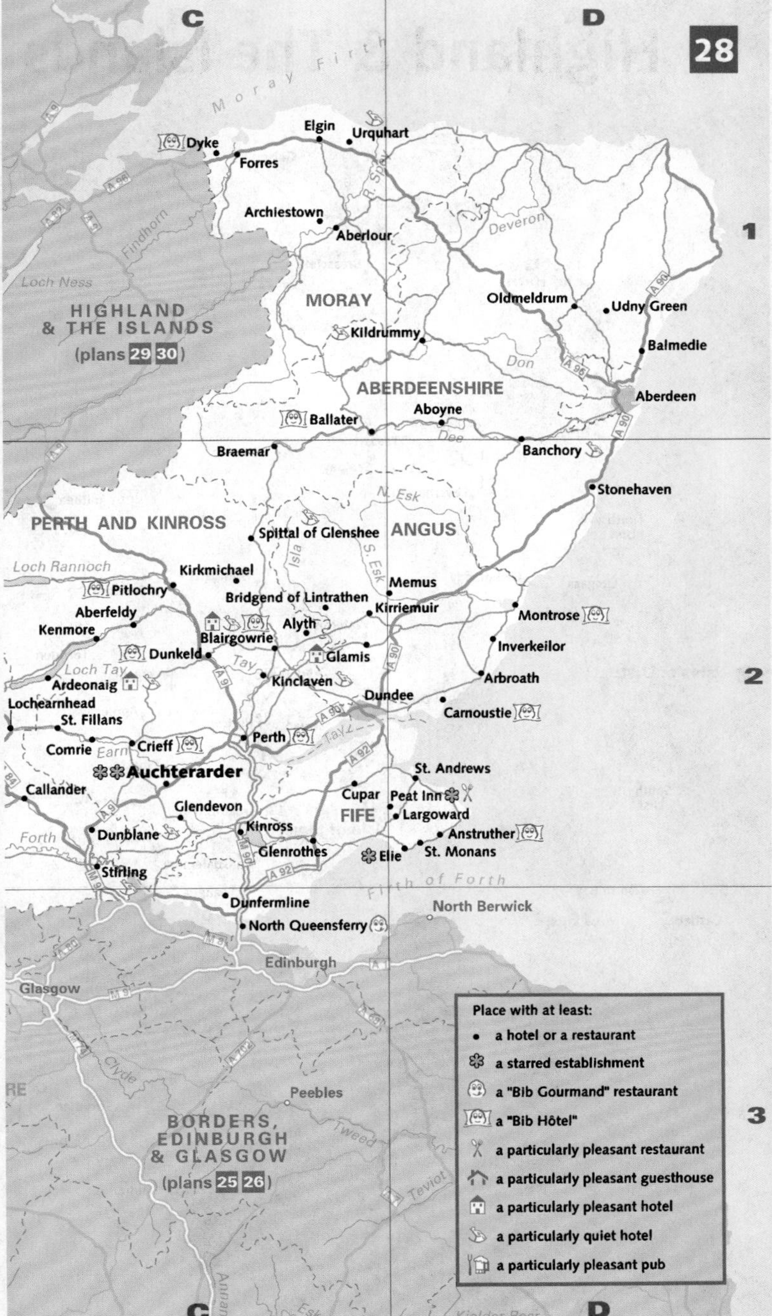
C
D
Moray Firth
Dyke
Forres
Elgin
Urquhart
Archiestown
Aberlour
Deveron
Findhorn
Loch Ness
HIGHLAND & THE ISLANDS
(plans 29 30)
MORAY
Kildrummy
Oldmeldrum
Udny Green
Balmedie
Don
ABERDEENSHIRE
Aberdeen
Aboyne
Ballater
Dee
Braemar
Banchory
Stonehaven
N. Esk
PERTH AND KINROSS
Spittal of Glenshee
ANGUS
Loch Rannoch
Kirkmichael
S. Esk
Isla
Memus
Pitlochry
Bridgend of Lintrathen
Kirriemuir
Aberfeldy
Alyth
Montrose
Kenmore
Blairgowrie
Dunkeld
Glamis
Inverkeilor
Loch Tay
Tay
Ardeonaig
Kinclaven
Arbroath
Lochearnhead
Dundee
Carnoustie
St. Fillans
Comrie
Earn
Crieff
Perth
Auchterarder
St. Andrews
Callander
Cupar
Peat Inn
Glendevon
FIFE
Largoward
Dunblane
Kinross
Anstruther
Forth
Glenrothes
St. Monans
Elie
Stirling
Firth of Forth
Dunfermline
North Berwick
North Queensferry
Edinburgh
Glasgow
Clyde
Peebles
Tweed
BORDERS, EDINBURGH & GLASGOW
(plans 25 26)
Teviot
Annan
Esk
Kielder Resr.
1
2
3
Place with at least:
a hotel or a restaurant
a starred establishment
a "Bib Gourmand" restaurant
a "Bib Hôtel"
a particularly pleasant restaurant
a particularly pleasant guesthouse
a particularly pleasant hotel
a particularly quiet hotel
a particularly pleasant pub

29 Highland & The Islands

A
B
1
2
3

Galson
Breasclete
Stornoway
Isle of Lewis and Harris
THE MINCH
OUTER HEBRIDES
West Loch Tarbert
WESTERN ISLES
Ardhasaig
Tarbert
Scarista
Scalpay
Leverburgh
Gruinard Bay
Aultbea
North Uist
Sound of Harris
The Little Minch
Loch Snizort
Langass
Lochmaddy
Flodigarry
Badachro
Loch
Sound of Monach
Carinish
Waternish
Loch Torridon
Sound of Raasay
Inner Sound
Torridon
Isles of Uist
Bernisdale
Edinbane
Shieldaig
Dunvegan
Applecross
Struan
Portree
A 87
Loch Bracadale
Plockton
South Uist
SEA OF THE HEBRIDES
Balmacara
Broadford
Isle of Skye
Sleat
Sound of Barra
Cuillin Sound
Duisdalemore
North Bay
Teangue
Sound of Sleat
Castlebay
Isle of Barra
Loch
Sound of Rhum
Loch Morar
INNER HEBRIDES
Sound of Arisaig
A 830
Loch Shiel
Onich
Strontian
Duror
A 828
Sound of Mull
Lochaline
Loch Linnhe
Isle of Mull
Firth of Lorn
Oban

A
B

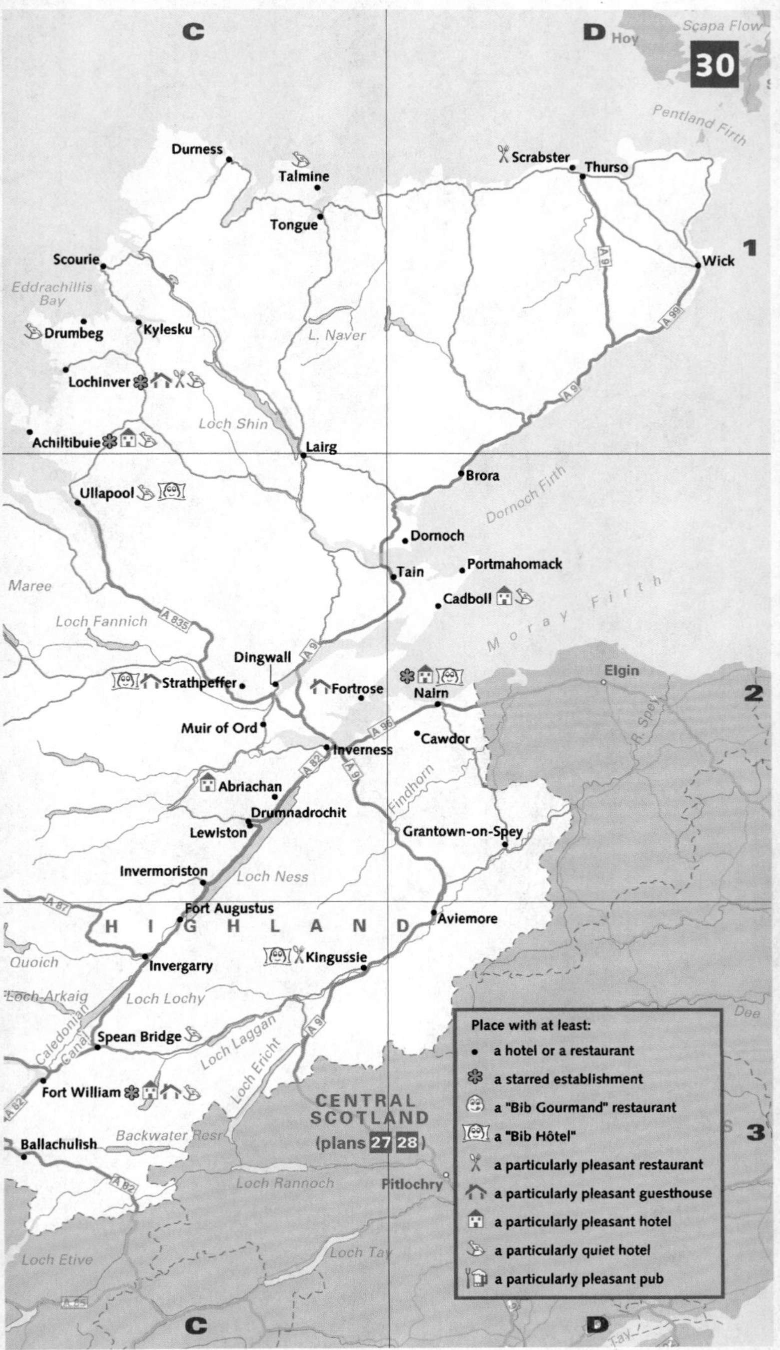

C
D
Hoy
Scapa Flow
30
Pentland Firth
Durness
Talmine
Tongue
Scrabster
Thurso
Wick
Scourie
Eddrachillis Bay
Drumbeg
Kylesku
L. Naver
Lochinver
Loch Shin
Achiltibuie
Lairg
Brora
Ullapool
Dornoch Firth
Dornoch
Tain
Portmahomack
Cadboll
Maree
Loch Fannich
Moray Firth
Dingwall
Strathpeffer
Fortrose
Nairn
Elgin
R. Spey
Muir of Ord
Inverness
Cawdor
Abriachan
Drumnadrochit
Lewiston
Findhorn
Grantown-on-Spey
Invermoriston
Loch Ness
Fort Augustus
Aviemore
HIGHLAND
Quoich
Invergarry
Kingussie
Loch Arkaig
Loch Lochy
Caledonian Canal
Spean Bridge
Loch Laggan
Loch Ericht
Fort William
CENTRAL SCOTLAND
(plans 27 28)
Ballachulish
Backwater Resr
Loch Rannoch
Pitlochry
Loch Etive
Loch Tay
Dee
Tay
1
2
3
A 9
A 99
A 835
A 96
A 82
A 87
A 62
A 85
Place with at least:
a hotel or a restaurant
a starred establishment
a "Bib Gourmand" restaurant
a "Bib Hôtel"
a particularly pleasant restaurant
a particularly pleasant guesthouse
a particularly pleasant hotel
a particularly quiet hotel
a particularly pleasant pub

Shetland & Orkney

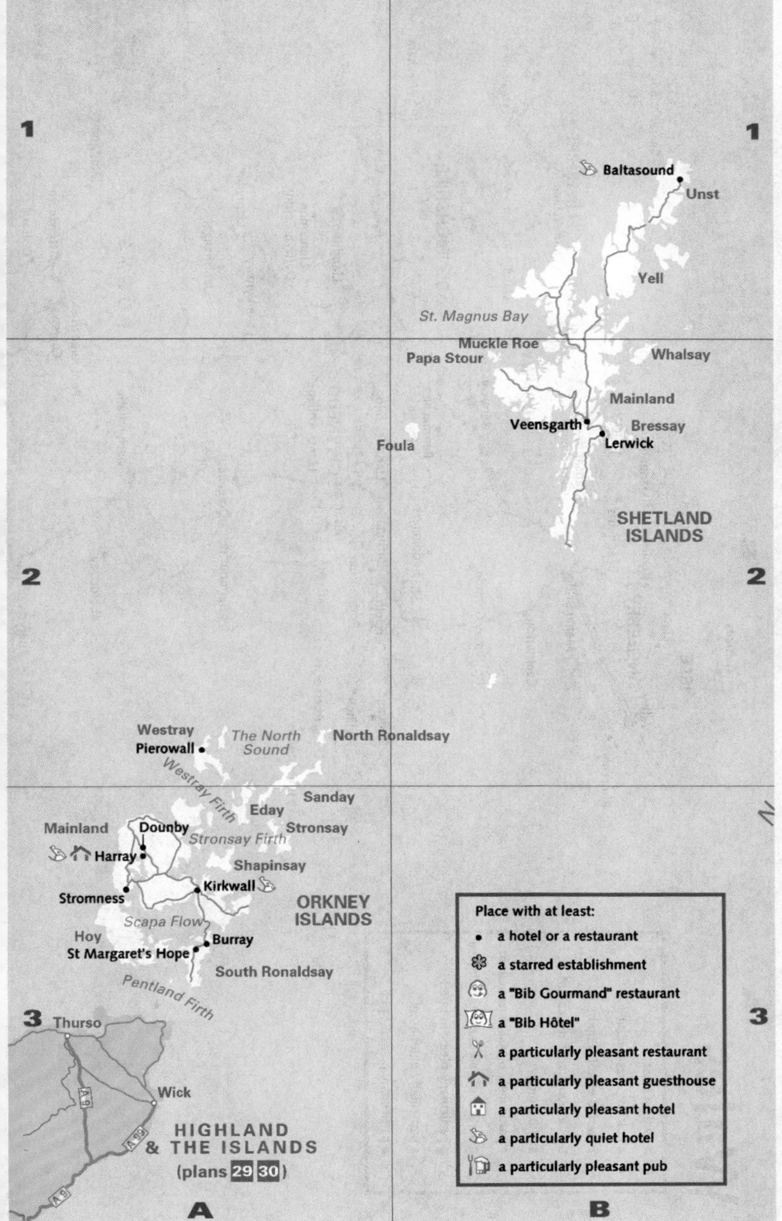

Wales

Place with at least:

- • a hotel or a restaurant
- a starred establishment
- a "Bib Gourmand" restaurant
- a "Bib Hôtel"
- a particularly pleasant restaurant
- a particularly pleasant guesthouse
- a particularly pleasant hotel
- a particularly quiet hotel
- a particularly pleasant pub

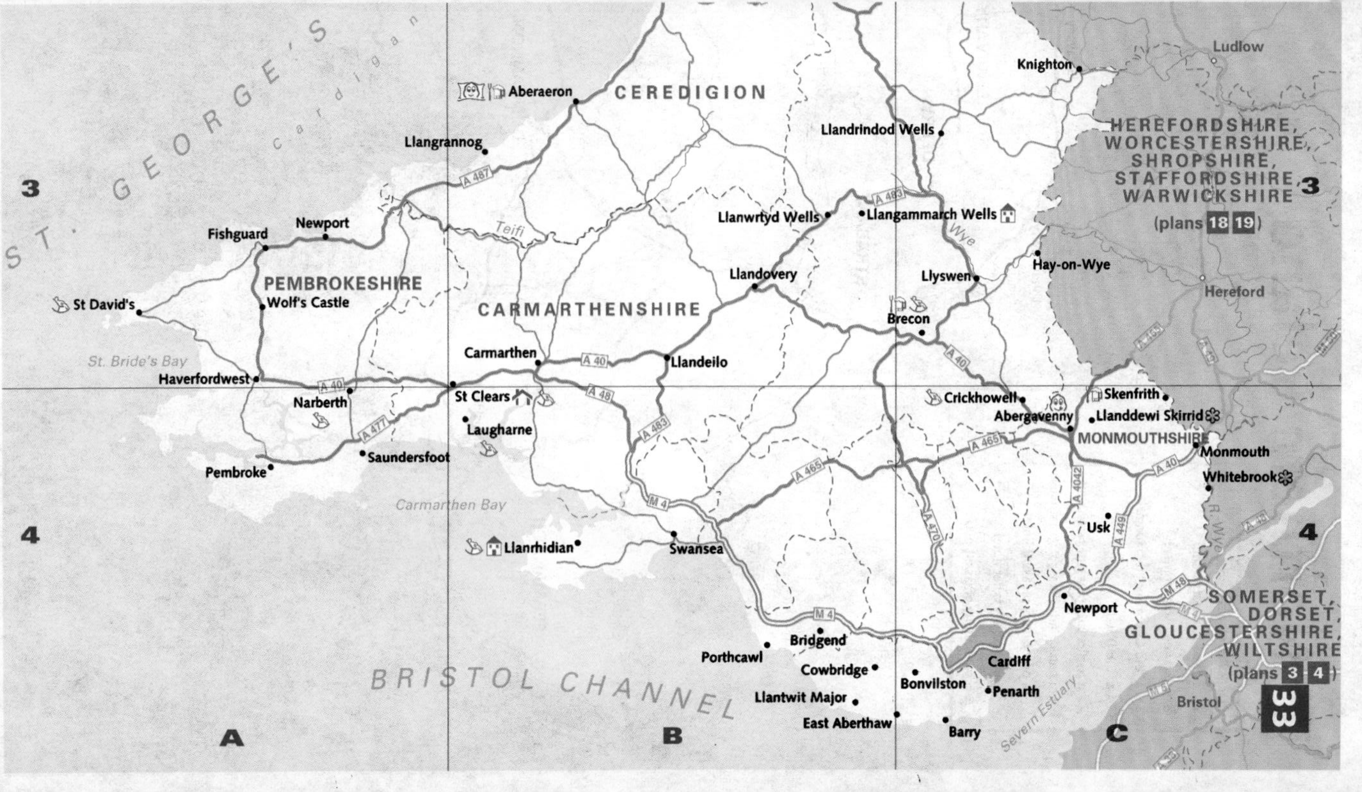
ST. GEORGE'S
Cardigan
3
CEREDIGION
Aberaeron
Llangrannog
Knighton
Ludlow
Llandrindod Wells
HEREFORDSHIRE,
WORCESTERSHIRE,
SHROPSHIRE,
STAFFORDSHIRE,
WARWICKSHIRE
(plans 18 19)
A 487
Teifi
Fishguard
Newport
Llanwrtyd Wells
Llangammarch Wells
A 483
Wye
Hay-on-Wye
Hereford
PEMBROKESHIRE
Wolf's Castle
St David's
CARMARTHENSHIRE
Llandovery
Llyswen
Brecon
St. Bride's Bay
Haverfordwest
Carmarthen
A 40
Llandeilo
A 48
Narberth
St Clears
Laugharne
A 477
A 483
Saunderfoot
Pembroke
Crickhowell
Abergavenny
Skenfrith
Llanddewi Skirrid
MONMOUTHSHIRE
Monmouth
Whitebrook
A 465
A 4042
Carmarthen Bay
M 4
A 470
Usk
A 449
4
Llanrhidian
Swansea
Newport
M 48
SOMERSET,
DORSET,
GLOUCESTERSHIRE,
WILTSHIRE
(plans 3 4)
Porthcawl
Bridgend
Cowbridge
Cardiff
Bonvilston
Penarth
Llantwit Major
East Aberthaw
Barry
Severn Estuary
BRISTOL CHANNEL
Bristol
M 5
R. Wye
A
B
C
33

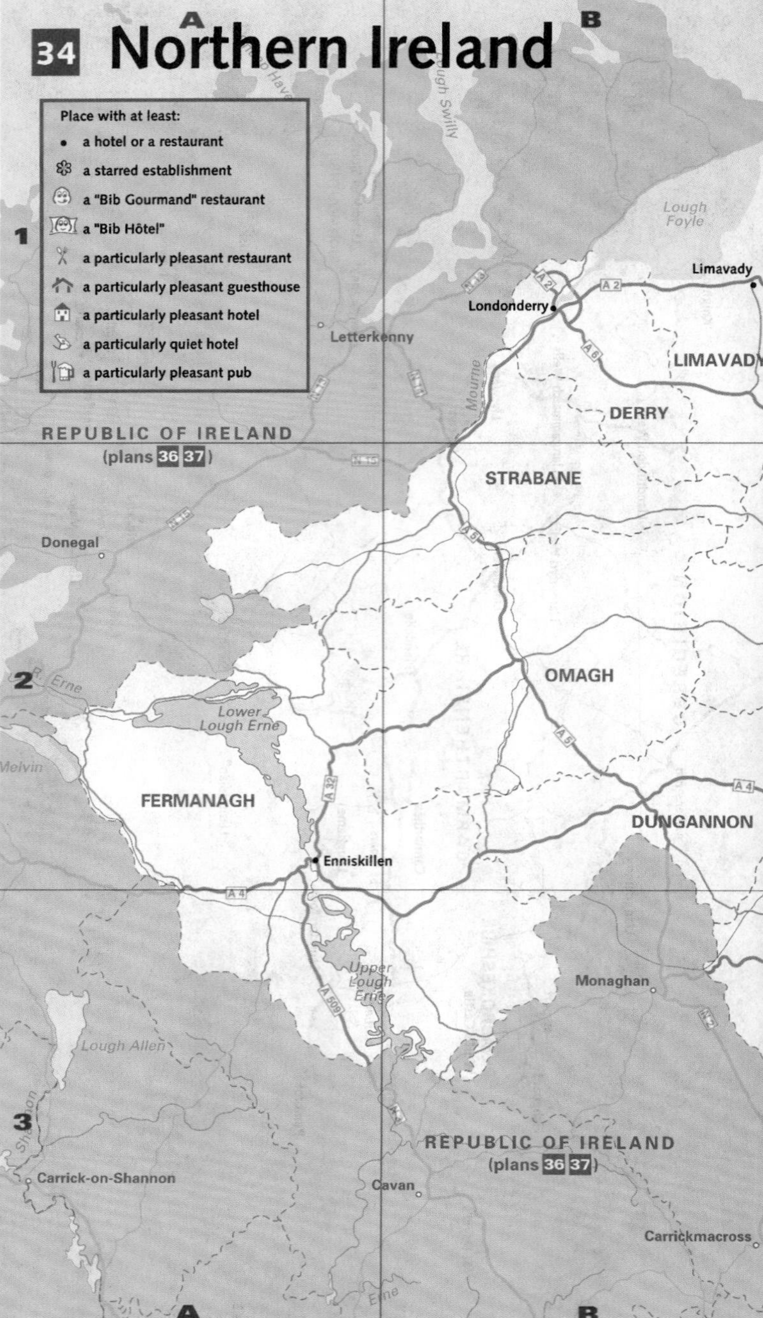
34 Northern Ireland
A
B
Place with at least:
a hotel or a restaurant
a starred establishment
a "Bib Gourmand" restaurant
a "Bib Hôtel"
a particularly pleasant restaurant
a particularly pleasant guesthouse
a particularly pleasant hotel
a particularly quiet hotel
a particularly pleasant pub
1
2
3
Lough Swilly
Lough Foyle
Limavady
Londonderry
LIMAVADY
Letterkenny
DERRY
REPUBLIC OF IRELAND
(plans 36 37)
STRABANE
Donegal
OMAGH
R. Erne
Lower Lough Erne
Melvin
FERMANAGH
DUNGANNON
Enniskillen
Upper Lough Erne
Monaghan
Lough Allen
REPUBLIC OF IRELAND
(plans 36 37)
Carrick-on-Shannon
Cavan
Carrickmacross
A 2
A 6
A 5
A 32
A 4
A 509
Erne

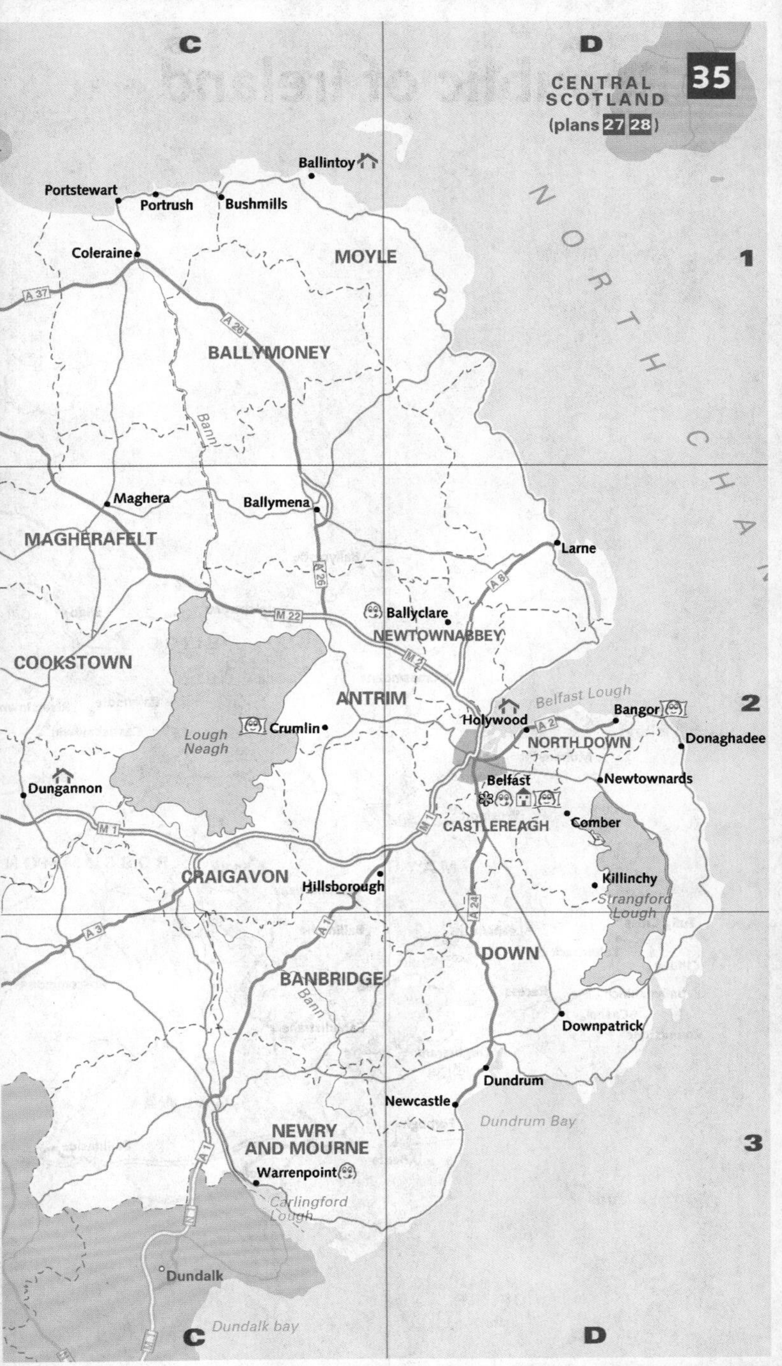
C
D
35
CENTRAL SCOTLAND
(plans 27 28)
NORTH CHANNEL
1
2
3
Ballintoy
Portstewart
Portrush
Bushmills
Coleraine
MOYLE
A 37
A 26
BALLYMONEY
Bann
Maghera
Ballymena
MAGHERAFELT
Larne
A 26
A 8
M 22
Ballyclare
NEWTOWNABBEY
COOKSTOWN
M 2
ANTRIM
Belfast Lough
Bangor
Holywood
A 2
Donaghadee
Crumlin
Lough Neagh
NORTH DOWN
Dungannon
Belfast
Newtownards
M 1
M 1
CASTLEREAGH
Comber
CRAIGAVON
Hillsborough
Killinchy
Strangford Lough
A 24
A 3
A 1
DOWN
BANBRIDGE
Bann
Downpatrick
Dundrum
Newcastle
Dundrum Bay
NEWRY AND MOURNE
A 1
Warrenpoint
Carlingford Lough
Dundalk
Dundalk bay
C
D

36 Republic of Ireland

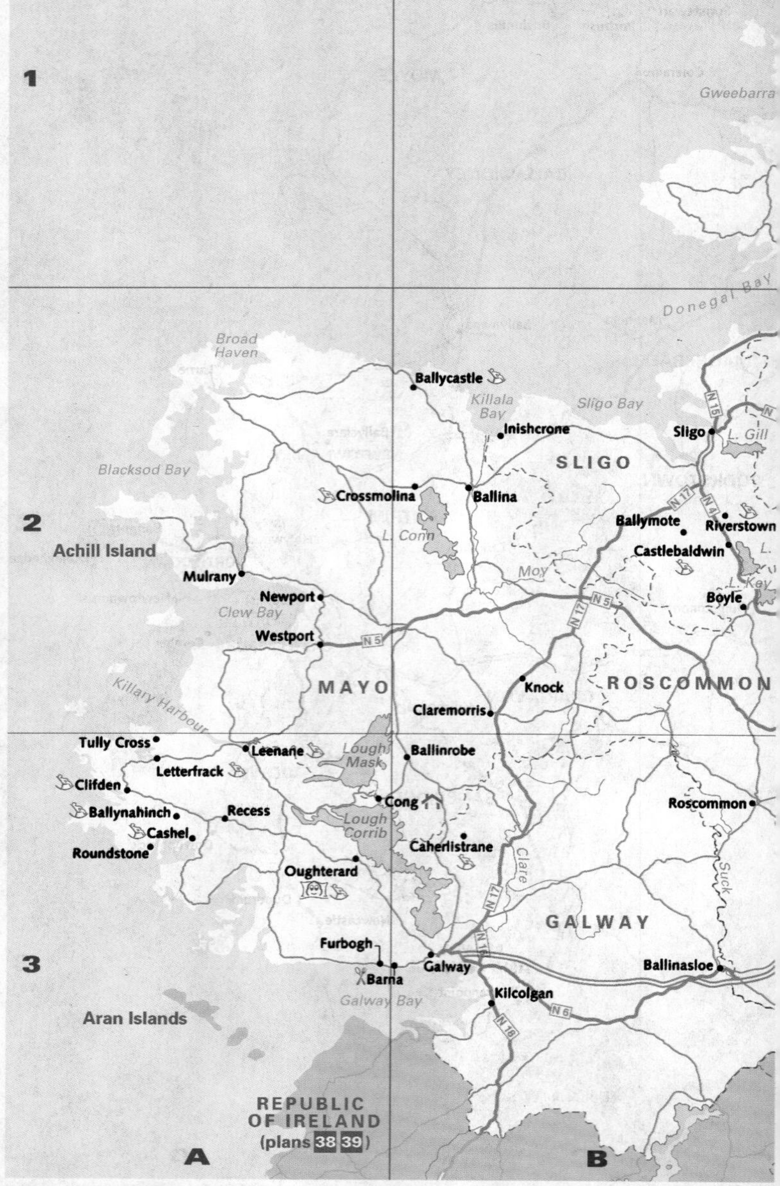

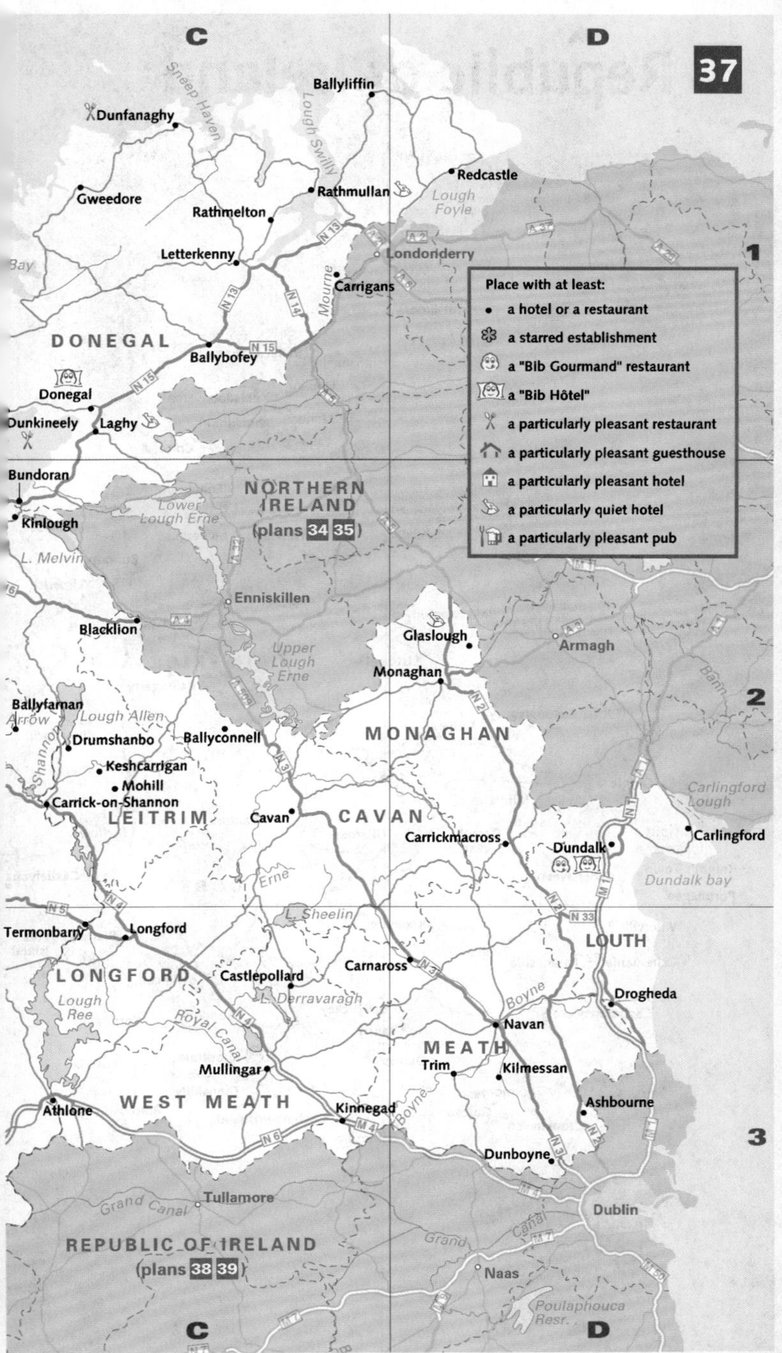

37
C
D
1
2
3
Place with at least:
a hotel or a restaurant
a starred establishment
a "Bib Gourmand" restaurant
a "Bib Hôtel"
a particularly pleasant restaurant
a particularly pleasant guesthouse
a particularly pleasant hotel
a particularly quiet hotel
a particularly pleasant pub
DONEGAL
NORTHERN IRELAND
(plans 34 35)
MONAGHAN
LEITRIM
CAVAN
LONGFORD
LOUTH
MEATH
WEST MEATH
REPUBLIC OF IRELAND
(plans 38 39)
Dunfanaghy
Sheep Haven
Ballyliffin
Lough Swilly
Gweedore
Rathmullan
Redcastle
Lough Foyle
Rathmelton
Letterkenny
Londonderry
Carrigans
Mourne
Ballybofey
Donegal
Dunkineely
Laghy
Bundoran
Kinlough
Lower Lough Erne
L. Melvin
Enniskillen
Blacklion
Upper Lough Erne
Glaslough
Armagh
Monaghan
Ballyfarnan
Arrow
Lough Allen
Shannon
Drumshanbo
Ballyconnell
Keshcarrigan
Mohill
Carrick-on-Shannon
Cavan
Carrickmacross
Dundalk
Carlingford Lough
Carlingford
Dundalk bay
Erne
L. Sheelin
Termonbarry
Longford
Lough Ree
Castlepollard
L. Derravaragh
Carnaross
Boyne
Drogheda
Navan
Royal Canal
Trim
Kilmessan
Mullingar
Athlone
Kinnegad
Ashbourne
Dunboyne
Tullamore
Grand Canal
Dublin
Naas
Poulaphouca Resr.
N 13
N 14
N 15
N 2
N 3
N 4
N 5
N 6
N 33
N 1
M 1
M 4
M 7
M 50
A 2
A 4
A 5
A 6
A 29
A 37

38 Republic of Ireland

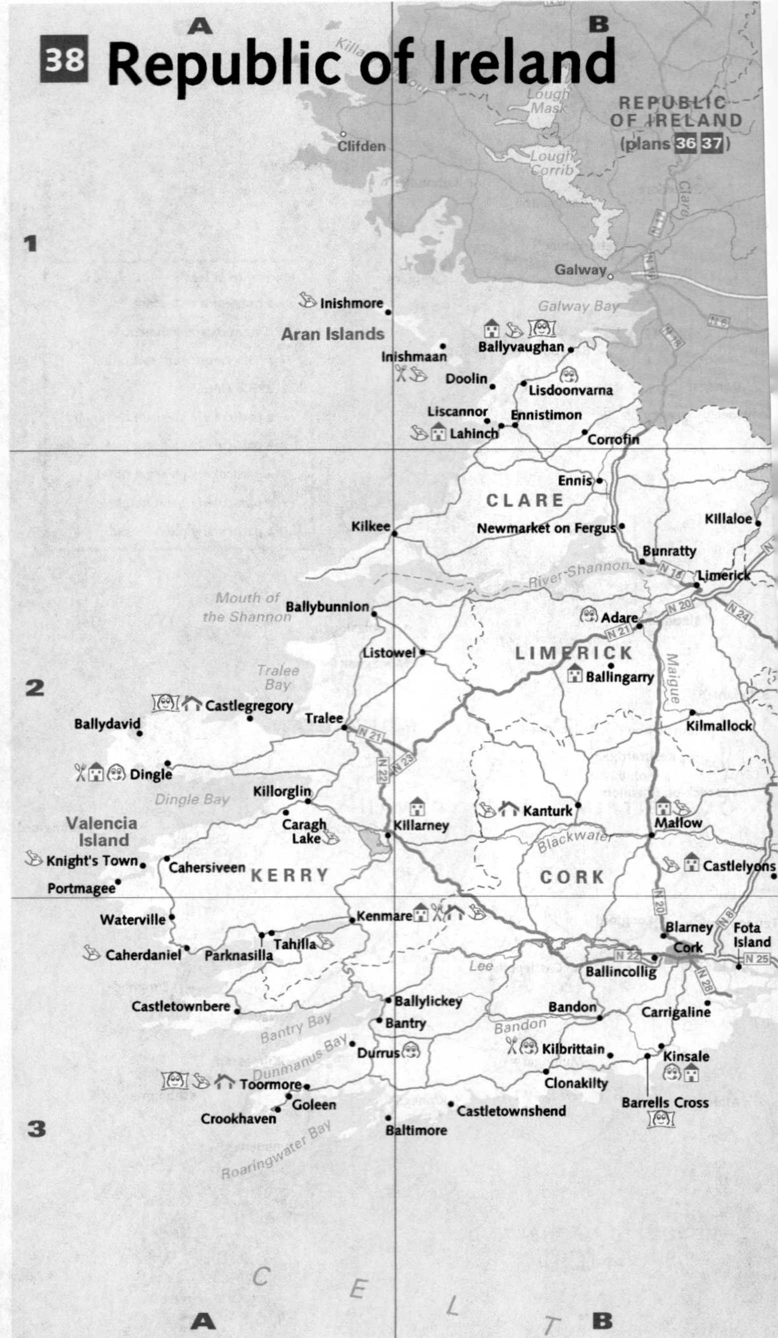

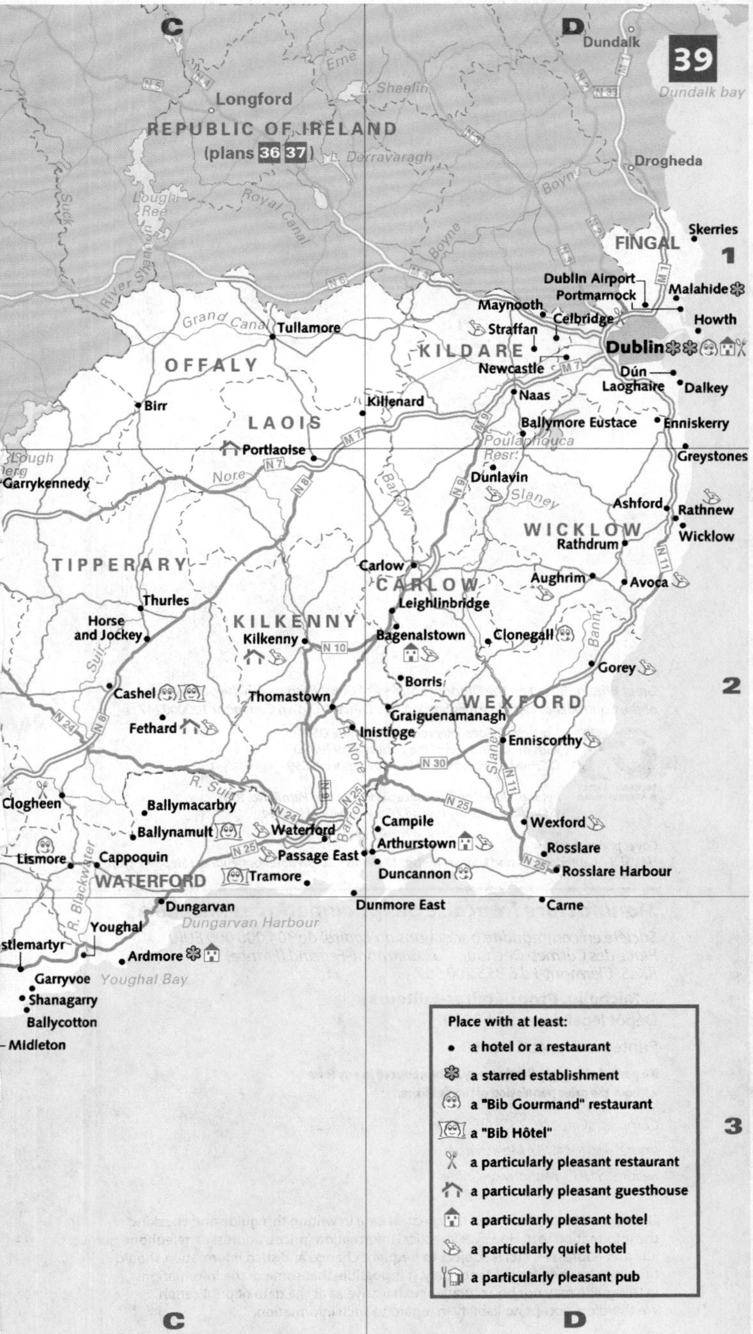

C
D
39
Dundalk
Dundalk bay
Longford
REPUBLIC OF IRELAND
(plans 36 37)
L. Sheelin
L. Derravaragh
Lough Ree
Royal Canal
River Shannon
Suck
Erne
Boyne
Drogheda
Skerries
FINGAL
1
Dublin Airport
Portmarnock
Malahide
Howth
Maynooth
Celbridge
Straffan
Dublin
KILDARE
Newcastle
Dún Laoghaire
Dalkey
Grand Canal
Tullamore
OFFALY
Birr
Naas
Killenard
LAOIS
Ballymore Eustace
Enniskerry
Poulaphouca Resr.
Portlaoise
Greystones
Lough Derg
Garrykennedy
Nore
Dunlavin
Slaney
Barrow
Ashford
Rathnew
WICKLOW
Wicklow
Rathdrum
TIPPERARY
Carlow
CARLOW
Aughrim
Avoca
Thurles
Leighlinbridge
Horse and Jockey
KILKENNY
Kilkenny
Bagenalstown
Clonegall
Bann
Gorey
Suir
Borris
2
Cashel
Thomastown
WEXFORD
Graiguenamanagh
Fethard
Inistioge
R. Nore
Enniscorthy
R. Suir
Clogheen
Ballymacarbry
Ballynamult
Waterford
Campile
Wexford
Arthurstown
Rosslare
Lismore
Cappoquin
Passage East
Duncannon
Rosslare Harbour
WATERFORD
Tramore
R. Blackwater
Dungarvan
Dunmore East
Carne
Dungarvan Harbour
Youghal
Castlemartyr
Ardmore
Garryvoe
Youghal Bay
Shanagarry
Ballycotton
Midleton
3
Place with at least:
a hotel or a restaurant
a starred establishment
a "Bib Gourmand" restaurant
a "Bib Hôtel"
a particularly pleasant restaurant
a particularly pleasant guesthouse
a particularly pleasant hotel
a particularly quiet hotel
a particularly pleasant pub
C
D

Great Britain : Based on the Ordnance Survey of Great Britain with the permission of the Controller of Her Majesty's Stationery's Office © Crown Copyright 100000247

Northern Ireland : Reproduced from the OSNI map with the permission of the Controller of HMSO © Crown Copyright 2010 Permit Number 90099

Ireland : Based on Ordnance Survey Ireland Permit No. 8591 © Ordnance Survey Ireland / Government of Ireland

Cover photographs :
HAUSER / Jupiterimages and Ludovic Maisant / Hemis / Corbis (interior designer : Stephen Ryan)

Manufacture française des pneumatiques Michelin

Société en commandite par actions au capital de 304 000 000 EUR.
Place des Carmes-Déchaux – 63 Clermont-Ferrand (France)
R.C.S. Clermont-Fd B 855 200 507

Dépôt légal décembre 2009

Printed in France 11-2009

Compogravure : MCP JOUVE, Saran

Impression : MAURY, Malesherbes

Reliure : S.I.R.C., Marigny-le-Châtel

Our editorial team has taken the greatest care in writing this guide and checking the information in it. However, practical information (prices, addresses, telephone numbers, internet addresses, etc) is subject to frequent change and such information should therefore be used for guidance only. It is possible that some of the information in this guide may not be accurate or exhaustive as at the date of publication. We therefore accept no liability in regard to such information.